D1520521

Constitutional Law

ASPEN CASEBOOK SERIES

CONSTITUTIONAL LAW:
CASES, MATERIALS, & PROBLEMS

SECOND EDITION

RUSSELL L. WEAVER

PROFESSOR OF LAW & DISTINGUISHED UNIVERSITY SCHOLAR
UNIVERSITY OF LOUISVILLE
LOUIS D. BRANDEIS SCHOOL OF LAW

STEVEN I. FRIEDLAND

PROFESSOR OF LAW AND SENIOR SCHOLAR
ELON UNIVERSITY SCHOOL OF LAW

CATHERINE HANCOCK

GEOFFREY C. BIBLE & MURRAY H. BRING
PROFESSOR OF CONSTITUTIONAL LAW
TULANE UNIVERSITY SCHOOL OF LAW

BRYAN FAIR

THOMAS E. SKINNER PROFESSOR OF LAW &
UNIVERSITY OF ALABAMA SCHOOL OF LAW

JOHN KNECHTLE

PROFESSOR OF LAW
FLORIDA COASTAL SCHOOL OF LAW

RICHARD D. ROSEN

PROFESSOR OF LAW
TEXAS TECH UNIVERSITY SCHOOL OF LAW

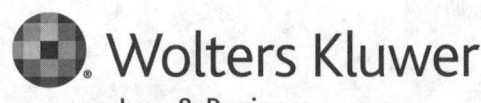

Wolters Kluwer
Law & Business

AUSTIN   BOSTON   CHICAGO   NEW YORK   THE NETHERLANDS

http://lawschool.aspenpublishers.com

Aspen Publishers
Attn: Permissions Department
76 Ninth Avenue, 7th Floor
New York, NY 10011-5201

To contact Customer Care, e-mail *customer.care@aspenpublishers.com*, call 1-800-234-1660, fax 1-800-901-9075, or mail correspondence to:

Aspen Publishers
Attn: Order Department
PO Box 990
Frederick, MD 21705

Printed in the United States of America.

1 2 3 4 5 6 7 8 9 0

ISBN 978-0-7355-0758-6

Library of Congress Cataloging-in-Publication Data

Constitutional law : cases, materials & problems / Russell L. Weaver . . . [et al.]. — 2nd ed.
  p. cm. — (Aspen casebook series)
Includes Index
ISBN-13: 978-0-7355-0758-6
ISBN-10: 0-7355-0758-9
  1. Constitutional law — United States — Cases. I. Weaver, Russell L., 1952-

KF4549.C6543 2011
342.73 — dc22   2010054025

About Wolters Kluwer Law & Business

Wolters Kluwer Law & Business is a leading provider of research information and workflow solutions in key specialty areas. The strengths of the individual brands of Aspen Publishers, CCH, Kluwer Law International, and Loislaw are aligned within Wolters Kluwer Law & Business to provide comprehensive, in-depth solutions and expert-authored content for the legal, professional, and education markets.

CCH was founded in 1913 and has served more than four generations of business professionals and their clients. The CCH products in the Wolters Kluwer Law & Business group are highly regarded electronic and print resources for legal, securities, antitrust and trade regulation, government contracting, banking, pension, payroll, employment and labor, and healthcare reimbursement and compliance professionals.

Aspen Publishers is a leading information provider for attorneys, business professionals, and law students. Written by preeminent authorities, Aspen products offer analytical and practical information in a range of specialty practice areas from securities law and intellectual property to mergers and acquisitions and pension/benefits. Aspen's trusted legal education resources provide professors and students with high-quality, up-to-date and effective resources for successful instruction and study in all areas of the law.

Kluwer Law International supplies the global business community with comprehensive English-language international legal information. Legal practitioners, corporate counsel, and business executives around the world rely on the Kluwer Law International journals, loose-leafs, books, and electronic products for authoritative information in many areas of international legal practice.

Loislaw is a premier provider of digitized legal content to small law firm practitioners of various specializations. Loislaw provides attorneys with the ability to quickly and efficiently find the necessary legal information they need, when and where they need it, by facilitating access to primary law as well as state-specific law, records, forms, and treatises.

Wolters Kluwer Law & Business, a unit of Wolters Kluwer, is headquartered in New York and Riverwoods, Illinois. Wolters Kluwer is a leading multinational publisher and information services company.

SUMMARY OF CONTENTS

TABLE OF CONTENTS

III.

THE FEDERAL
EXECUTIVE POWERS   **233**

IV.

THE RELATIONSHIP BETWEEN THE STATES
AND THE FEDERAL GOVERNMENT   **333**

XI.

FREEDOM OF SPEECH

XII.
THE RELIGION CLAUSES   1495

XIII.
THE RIGHT TO KEEP
AND BEAR ARMS   1639

PREFACE

Historically, most constitutional law casebooks have been written like mini-treatises. In addition to including the landmark constitutional law cases, most books contain detailed notes that discuss every highway and byway of the law. Most of these books have a tendency to overload rather than facilitate the learning process. Students are reluctant to read 1,500 to 1,600 pages of constitutional law, much less to pore over the details. Moreover, because most constitutional law casebooks include so many decisions (in mini-treatise fashion), authors are forced to severely edit the cases they do present.

In writing a substantially modified Second Edition of this book, our primary goal was to create an accessible and teachable book that would help students understand constitutional theory, lead students to deeper insights, generate classroom interactivity, and provide a platform for inspired learning. In addition, we were intentional about moving the spotlight from the parade of cases to effective student understanding of the subject matter, taking into account the existing literature on learning theory. One way we accomplish these objectives is through the inclusion of problems. The use of problems recognizes that students learn differently, and that working through problems can reinforce a deeper understanding of the included cases and offer active learning opportunities requiring differing skill sets and an efficient way to cover new material.

In this new edition, we have included a scaffolding for each chapter consistent with studies that find students access and absorb more information from identifiable frameworks. In each chapter, we begin with the pertinent constitutional provisions to focus student attention, and then we provide an archetypical introductory problem that precedes the cases. The introductory problems not only provide typicality for the type of issues confronted in the chapter, but also create an immediate problem-solving orientation for students. The introductory problem is threaded throughout each chapter, arising in different problem sets after cases to show students how a single problem can raise a variety of constitutional issues. In addition, each chapter offers important points to remember at its conclusion to reinforce the learning process.

Because of the complexity of the subject, we do not use a single type of problem, but instead use different models and formats in an effort to respond to a variety of student learning styles. Many problems are factual in nature and are designed to encourage students to think about constitutional doctrine in context. In some instances, these fact-based problems are premised upon actual cases, including U.S. Supreme Court cases. Other problems are theoretical in nature and are designed to help students better understand the theoretical aspects of constitutional law.

With a given problem, we are aiming to achieve any one of several objectives. We might use problems to illustrate and clarify doctrinal principles and conflicts, place students in real-life situations and ask them how they would respond, help students view constitutional law issues in modern and historical contexts, or prepare students for actual practice. Some problems probe divisions in the law, while others ask students to apply existing doctrine to new situations. Some problems place students in the position of lawyers and ask them to explain how they might argue a particular case (e.g., what facts or arguments might they use in support of their positions). In other words, the user should not expect to see a single, monolithic approach to problems.

Our ultimate objective is to encourage students to solve problems using critical thinking, developing both arguments and theory. Even though the existence of a "problem" may suggest that there is an "answer," we believe that problems can (and should) be used to promote critical thinking. In other words, we accept Realism and Critical Theory and encourage students to develop arguments and theory, rather than to treat law as simply a "deductive process." As a result, even if the Court has rendered a decision on the facts of a particular case, we might present that case as a "problem" because we want students to critically analyze the issues presented. If a student responds, "I read the decided case and the Court held . . . ," we encourage the professor to respond with questions designed to stimulate thought: "OK, fair enough. Now, do you think that the Court got it right? Did it give sufficient weight to this consideration? How could the Court possibly have reached that conclusion?" Such analysis helps students become better lawyers, judges, and law professors.

In any constitutional law casebook, trade-offs are necessary, and we have made a number of intentional trade-offs. First, although we include the landmark cases, we do not attempt to catalog every decision (even every U.S. Supreme Court decision) in each of the relevant areas. Over the past half-century, constitutional case law has multiplied to the extent that it is impossible to thoroughly discuss every decision and do justice to each one. Although this book is designed to give students a thorough grounding in constitutional law, students can always consult secondary sources if they desire more treatise-like discussions. We have chosen cases for a variety of reasons: because they are modern cases that reflect the current state of the law; because they are "landmarks" that students need to read and understand; or because, even though they might be older cases, they help students understand and evaluate the modern approach.

Because we include fewer cases overall, we are generally able to include more of the cases that we do present. In other words, we allow students to read the Court's own words and decide for themselves what the decisions mean. Other cases may be incorporated through questions, problems, or hypotheticals.

We give thanks to the many people who assisted us in the creation and revision of this book, including our research and administrative assistants. We are particularly grateful to students who helped us find and correct errors. Finally, we are thankful to our spouses, significant others, and children who supported us through the various stages of this project.

RLW, SIF, CH, BF, JK, & RDR

THE CONSTITUTION OF THE UNITED STATES

We the People of the United States, in Order to form a more perfect Union, establish justice, insure domestic Tranquility, provide for the common defence, promote the general Welfare, and secure the Blessings of Liberty to ourselves and our Posterity, do ordain and establish this Constitution for the United States of America.

ARTICLE I

Section 1. All legislative Powers herein granted shall be vested in a Congress of the United States which shall consist of a Senate and House of Representatives.

Section 2. [1] The House of Representatives shall be composed of Members chosen every second Year by the People of the several States, and the Electors in each State shall have the Qualifications requisite for Electors of the most numerous Branch of the State Legislature.

[2] No Person shall be a Representative who shall not have attained to the Age of twenty five Years, and been seven Years a Citizen of the United States, and who shall not, when elected, be an Inhabitant of that State in which he shall be chosen.

[3] Representatives and direct Taxes shall be apportioned among the several States which may be included within this Union, according to their respective Numbers, which shall be determined by adding to the whole Number of free Persons, including those bound to Service for a Term of Years, and excluding Indians not taxed, three fifths of all other Persons. The actual Enumeration shall be made within three Years after the first meeting of the Congress of the United States, and within every subsequent Term of ten Years, in such Manner as they shall by Law direct. The Number of Representatives shall not exceed one for every thirty Thousand, but each State shall have at Least One Representative; and until such enumeration shall be made, the State of New Hampshire shall be entitled to chuse three, Massachusetts eight, Rhode Island and Providence Plantations one, Connecticut five, New York six, New Jersey four, Pennsylvania eight, Delaware one, Maryland six, Virginia ten, North Carolina five, South Carolina five, and Georgia three.

[4] When vacancies happen in the Representation from any State, the Executive Authority thereof shall issue Writs of Election to fill such Vacancies.

[5] The House of Representatives shall chuse their Speaker and other Officers; and shall have the sole Power of Impeachment.

Section 3. [1] The Senate of the United States shall be composed of two Senators from each State, chosen by the Legislature thereof, for six Years; and each Senator shall have one Vote.

[2] Immediately after they shall be assembled in Consequence of the first Election, they shall be divided as equally as may be into three Classes. The Seats of the Senators of the first Class shall be vacated at the Expiration of the second Year, of the second Class at the Expiration of the fourth Year, and of the third Class at the Expiration of the sixth Year, so that one third may be chosen every second Year; and if Vacancies happen by Resignation, or otherwise, during the Recess of the Legislature of any State, the Executive thereof may make temporary Appointments until the next Meeting of the Legislature, which shall then fill such Vacancies.

[3] No Person shall be a Senator who shall not have attained to the Age of thirty Years, and been nine Years a Citizen of the United States, and who shall not, when elected, be an Inhabitant of that State for which he shall be chosen.

[4] The Vice President of the United States shall be President of the Senate, but shall have no Vote, unless they be equally divided.

[5] The Senate shall chuse their other Officers, and also a President pro tempore, in the absence of the Vice President, or when he shall exercise the Office of President of the United States.

[6] The Senate shall have the sole Power to try all Impeachments. When sitting for that Purpose, they shall be on Oath or Affirmation. When the President of the United States is tried, the Chief Justice shall preside: And no Person shall be convicted without the Concurrence of two thirds of the Members present.

[7] Judgment in Cases of Impeachment shall not extend further than to removal from Office, and disqualification to hold and enjoy any Office of honor, Trust or Profit under the United States: but the Party convicted shall nevertheless be liable and subject to Indictment, Trial, judgment and Punishment, according to Law.

Section 4. [1] The Times, Places and Manner of holding Elections for Senators and Representatives, shall be prescribed in each State by the Legislature thereof; but the Congress may at any time by law make or alter such Regulations, except as to the Places of chusing Senators.

[2] The Congress shall assemble at least once in every Year, and such Meeting shall be on the first Monday in December, unless they shall by Law appoint a different Day.

Section 5. [1] Each house shall be the Judge of the Elections, Returns and Qualifications of its own members, and a Majority of each shall constitute a Quorum to do Business; but a smaller Number may adjourn from day to day, and may be authorized to compel the Attendance of absent members, in such Manner, and under such Penalties as each House may provide.

[2] Each House may determine the Rules of its Proceedings, punish its Members for disorderly Behavior, and, with the Concurrence of two thirds, expel a Member.

[3] Each House shall keep a Journal of its Proceedings, and from time to time publish the same, excepting such Parts as may in their Judgment require Secrecy; and the Yeas and Nays of the Members of either House on any question shall, at the Desire of one fifth of those Present, be entered on the Journal.

[4] Neither House, during the Session of Congress, shall, without the Consent of the other, adjourn for more than three days, nor to any other Place than that in which the two Houses shall be sitting.

Section 6. [1] The Senators and Representatives shall receive a Compensation for their Services, to be ascertained by Law, and paid out of the Treasury of the United States. They shall in all Cases, except Treason, Felony and Breach of the Peace, be privileged from Arrest during their Attendance at the Session of their respective Houses, and in going to and returning from the same; and for any Speech or Debate in either House, they shall not be questioned in any other Place.

[2] No Senator or Representative shall, during the time for which he was elected, be appointed to any civil Office under the Authority of the United States, which shall have been created, or the Emoluments whereof shall have been encreased during such time; and no Person holding any office under the United States, shall be a Member of either House during his Continuance in Office.

Section 7. [1] All Bills for raising Revenue shall originate in the House of Representatives; but the Senate may propose or concur with Amendments as on other Bills.

[2] Every Bill which shall have passed the House of Representatives and the Senate, shall, before it becomes a Law, be presented to the President of the United States; If he approve he shall sign it, but if not he shall return it, with his Objections to the House in which it shall have originated, who shall enter the Objections at large on their Journal, and proceed to reconsider it. If after such Reconsideration two thirds of that House shall agree to pass the Bill, it shall be sent, together with the Objections, to the other House, by which it shall likewise be reconsidered, and if approved by two thirds of that House, it shall become a Law. But in all such Cases the Votes of both Houses shall be determined by Yeas and Nays, and the Names of the Persons voting for and against the Bill shall be entered on the Journal of each House respectively. If any Bill shall not be returned by the President within ten Days (Sundays excepted) after it shall have been presented to him, the Same shall be a Law, in like Manner as if he had signed it, unless the Congress by their Adjournment prevents its Return, in which Case it shall not be a Law.

[3] Every Order, Resolution, or Vote to Which the Concurrence of the Senate and House of Representatives may be necessary (except on a question of Adjournment) shall be presented to the President of the United States; and before the Same shall take Effect, shall be approved by him, or being disapproved by him, shall be repassed by two thirds of the Senate and House of Representatives, according to the Rules and Limitations prescribed in the Case of a Bill.

Section 8. [1] The Congress shall have Power To lay and collect Taxes, Duties, Imposts and Excises, to pay the Debts and provide for the common Defence and general Welfare of the United States; but all Duties, Imposts and Excises shall be uniform throughout the United States;

[2] To borrow money on the credit of the United States;

[3] To regulate Commerce with foreign Nations, and among the several States, and with the Indian Tribes;

[4] To establish an uniform Rule of Naturalization, and uniform Laws on the subject of Bankruptcies throughout the United States;

[5] To coin Money, regulate the Value thereof, and of foreign Coin, and fix the Standard of Weights and Measures;

[6] To provide the Punishment of counterfeiting the Securities and current Coin of the United States;

[7] To establish Post Offices and post Roads;

[8] To promote the Progress of Science and useful Arts, by securing for limited Times to Authors and Inventors the exclusive Right to their respective Writings and Discoveries;

[9] To constitute Tribunals inferior to the supreme Court;

[10] To define and punish Piracies and Felonies committed on the high Seas, and Offenses against the Law of Nations;

[11] To declare War, grant Letters of Marque and Reprisal, and make Rules concerning Captures on Land and Water;

[12] To raise and support Armies, but no Appropriation of Money to that Use shall be a longer Term than two Years;

[13] To provide and maintain a Navy;

[14] To make Rules for the Government and Regulation of the land and naval Forces;

[15] To provide for calling forth the Militia to execute the Laws of the Union, suppress Insurrections and repel Invasions;

[16] To provide for organizing, arming, and disciplining, the Militia, and for governing such Part of them as may be employed in the Service of the United States, reserving to the States respectively, the Appointment of the Officers, and the Authority of training the Militia according to the discipline prescribed by Congress;

[17] To exercise exclusive Legislation in all Cases whatsoever, over such District (not exceeding ten Miles square) as may, by Cession of particular States, and the Acceptance of Congress, become the Seat of the Government of the United States, and to exercise like Authority over all Places purchased by the Consent of the Legislature of the State in which the Same shall be, for the Erection of Forts, Magazines, Arsenals, dock-Yards, and other needful Buildings; — And

[18] To make all Laws which shall be necessary and proper for carrying into Execution the foregoing Powers, and all other Powers vested by this Constitution in the Government of the United States, or in any Department or Officer thereof.

Section 9. [1] The Migration or Importation of such Persons as any of the States now existing shall think proper to admit, shall not be prohibited by the Congress prior to the Year one thousand eight hundred and eight, but a Tax or duty may be imposed on such Importation, not exceeding ten dollars for each Person.

[2] The privilege of the Writ of Habeas Corpus shall not be suspended, unless when in Cases of Rebellion or Invasion the public Safety may require it.

[3] No Bill of Attainder or ex post facto Law shall be passed.

[4] No Capitation, or other direct, Tax shall be laid, unless in Proportion to the Census or Enumeration herein before directed to be taken.

[5] No Tax or Duty shall be laid on articles exported from any State.

[6] No Preference shall be given by any Regulation of Commerce or Revenue to the Ports of one State over those of another: nor shall Vessels bound to, or from, one State, be obliged to enter, clear, or pay Duties in another.

[7] No Money shall be drawn from the Treasury, but in Consequence of Appropriations made by Law; and a regular Statement and Account of the Receipts and Expenditures of all public Money shall be published from time to time.

[8] No title of Nobility shall be granted by the United States: And no Person holding any Office of Profit or Trust under them, shall, without the Consent of the Congress, accept of any present, Emolument, Office, or Title, of any kind whatever, from any King, Prince, or foreign State.

Section 10. [1] No State shall enter into any Treaty, Alliance, or Confederation; grant Letters of Marque and Reprisal; coin Money; emit Bills of Credit; make any Thing but gold and silver Coin a Tender in Payment of Debts; pass any Bill of Attainder, ex post facto Law, or Law impairing the Obligation of Contracts, or grant any title of Nobility.

[2] No State shall, without the Consent of the Congress, lay any Imposts or Duties on Imports or Exports, except what may be absolutely necessary for executing its inspection Laws: and the net Produce of all Duties and Imposts, laid by any State on Imports or Exports, shall be for the Use of the Treasury of the United States; and all such Laws be subject to the Revision and Controul of the Congress.

[3] No State shall, without the Consent of Congress, lay any Duty of Tonnage, keep Troops, or Ships of War in time of Peace, enter into any Agreement or Compact with another State, or with a foreign Power, or engage in War, unless actually invaded, or in such imminent Danger as will not admit of delay.

ARTICLE II

Section 1. [1] The executive Power shall be vested in a President of the United States of America. He shall hold his Office during the Term of four Years, and, together with the Vice President, chosen for the same Term, be elected, as follows:

[2] Each State shall appoint, in such Manner as the Legislature thereof may direct, a Number of Electors, equal to the whole Number of Senators and Representatives to which the State may be entitled in the Congress: but no Senator or Representative, or Person holding an Office of Trust or Profit under the United States, shall be appointed an Elector.

[3] The Electors shall meet in their respective States, and vote by Ballot for two Persons, of whom one at least shall not be an Inhabitant of the same State with themselves. And they shall make a List of all the Persons voted for, and of the Number of Votes for each; which List they shall sign and certify, and transmit sealed to the Seat of the Government of the United States, directed to the President of the Senate. The President of the Senate shall, in the Presence of the Senate and House of Representatives, open all the Certificates, and the Votes shall then be counted. The Person having the greatest Number of Votes shall be the President, if such Number be a Majority of the whole Number of Electors appointed; and if there be more than one who have such Majority, and have an equal Number of Votes, then the House of Representatives shall immediately chuse by Ballot one of them for President; and if no Person have a Majority, then from the five highest on the List the said House shall in like Manner chuse the President. But in chusing the President, the Votes shall be taken by States, the Representation from each State having one vote; a quorum for this Purpose shall consist of a Member or Members from two thirds of the States, and a Majority of all the States shall be necessary to a Choice. In every Case, after the Choice of the President, the Person having the Greatest Number of Votes of the Electors shall be the Vice President. But if there should remain two or more who have equal Votes, the Senate shall chuse from them by Ballot the Vice President.

[4] The Congress may determine the Time of chusing the Electors, and the Day on which they shall give their Votes; which Day shall be the same throughout the United States.

[5] No person except a natural born Citizen, or a Citizen of the United States, at the time of the Adoption of this Constitution, shall be eligible to the Office of President; neither shall any Person be eligible to that Office who shall not have attained to the Age of thirty five Years, and been fourteen Years a Resident within the United States.

[6] In case of the removal of the President from Office, or of his Death, Resignation, or Inability to discharge the Powers and Duties of the said Office, the Same shall devolve on the Vice President, and the Congress may by Law provide for the Case of Removal, Death, Resignation or Inability, both of the President and Vice President,

declaring what Officer shall then act as President, and such Officer shall act accordingly, until the Disability be removed, or a President shall be elected.

[7] The President shall, at stated Times, receive for his Services, a Compensation, which shall neither be increased nor diminished during the Period for which he shall have been elected, and he shall not receive within that Period any other Emolument from the United States, or any of them.

[8] Before he enter on the Execution of his Office, he shall take the following Oath or Affirmation: "I do solemnly swear (or affirm) that I will faithfully execute the Office of President of the United States, and will to the best of my Ability, preserve, protect and defend the Constitution of the United States."

Section 2. [1] The President shall be Commander in Chief of the Army and Navy of the United States, and of the Militia of the several States, when called into the actual Service of the United States; he may require the Opinion, in writing, of the principal Officer in each of the executive Departments, upon any subject relating to the Duties of their respective Offices, and he shall have Power to grant Reprieves and Pardons for Offenses against the United States, except in Cases of Impeachment.

[2] He shall have Power, by and with the Advice and Consent of the Senate, to make Treaties, provided two thirds of the Senators present concur; and he shall nominate, and by and with the Advice and Consent of the Senate, shall appoint Ambassadors, other public Ministers and Consuls, Judges of the supreme Court, and all other Officers of the United States, whose Appointments are not herein otherwise provided for, and which shall be established by Law: but the Congress may by Law vest the Appointment of such inferior Officers, as they think proper, in the President alone, to the Courts of Law, or in the Heads of Departments.

[3] The President shall have Power to fill up all Vacancies that may happen during the Recess of the Senate by granting Commissions which shall expire at the End of their next Session.

Section 3. He shall from time to time give to the Congress Information of the State of the Union, and recommend to their Consideration such Measures as he shall judge necessary and expedient; he may, on extraordinary Occasions, convene both Houses, or either of them, and in Case of Disagreement between them, with Respect to the time of Adjournment, he may adjourn them to such Time as he shall think proper; he shall receive Ambassadors and other public Ministers; he shall take Care that the Laws be faithfully executed, and shall Commission all the Officers of the United States.

Section 4. The President, Vice President and all civil Officers of the United States, shall be removed from Office on Impeachment for, and Conviction of, Treason, Bribery, or other high Crimes and Misdemeanors.

ARTICLE III

Section 1. The judicial Power of the United States, shall be vested in one supreme Court, and in such inferior Courts as the Congress may from time to time ordain and establish. The Judges, both of the supreme and inferior Courts, shall hold their Offices during good Behaviour, and shall, at stated Times, receive for their Services a Compensation, which shall not be diminished during their Continuance in Office.

Section 2. [1] The Judicial Power shall extend to all Cases, in Law and Equity, arising under this Constitution, the Laws of the United States, and Treaties made, or which shall be made, under their Authority; — to all Cases affecting Ambassadors, other public Ministers and Consuls; — to all Cases of admiralty and maritime Jurisdiction; — to Controversies to which the United States shall be a Party; — to Controversies between two or more States; between a State and Citizens of another State; — between Citizens of different States; — between Citizens of the same State claiming Lands under Grants of different States, and between a State, or the Citizens thereof, and foreign States, Citizens or Subjects.

[2] In all cases affecting Ambassadors, other public Ministers and Consuls, and those in which a State shall be Party, the supreme Court shall have original Jurisdiction. In all the other Cases before mentioned, the supreme Court shall have appellate Jurisdiction, both as to Law and Fact, with such Exceptions, and under such Regulations as the Congress shall make.

[3] The trial of all Crimes, except in Cases of Impeachment, shall be by Jury; and such Trial shall be held in the State where the said Crimes shall have been committed; but when not committed within any State, the Trial shall be at such Place or Places as the Congress may by Law have directed.

Section 3. [1] Treason against the United States, shall consist only in levying War against them, or in adhering to their Enemies, giving them Aid and Comfort. No person shall be convicted of Treason unless on the Testimony of two Witnesses to the same over Act, or on Confession in open Court.

[2] The Congress shall have Power to declare the Punishment of Treason, but no Attainder of Treason shall work Corruption of Blood, or Forfeiture except during the Life of the Person attainted.

ARTICLE IV

Section 1. Full Faith and Credit shall be given in each State to the public Acts, Records, and judicial Proceedings of every other State. And the Congress may by general Laws prescribe the Manner in which such Acts, Records and Proceedings shall be proved, and the Effect thereof.

Section 2. [1] The Citizens of each State shall be entitled to all Privileges and Immunities of Citizens in the several States.

[2] A Person charged in any State with Treason, Felony, or other Crime, who shall flee from Justice, and be found in another State, shall on demand of the executive Authority of the State from which he fled, be delivered up, to be removed to the State having Jurisdiction of the Crime.

[3] No Person held to Service or Labour in one State, under the Laws thereof, escaping into another, shall, in Consequence of any Law or Regulation therein, be discharged from such Service or Labour, but shall be delivered up on Claim of the Party to whom such Service or Labour may be due.

Section 3. [1] New States may be admitted by the Congress into this Union; but no new State shall be formed or erected within the Jurisdiction of any other State; nor any State be formed by the Junction of two or more States, or Parts of States, without the Consent of the Legislatures of the States concerned as well as of the Congress.

[2] The Congress shall have Power to dispose of and make all needful Rules and Regulations respecting the Territory or other Property belonging to the United

States; and nothing in this Constitution shall be so construed as to Prejudice any Claims of the United States, or of any particular State.

Section 4. The United States shall guarantee to every State in this Union a Republican Form of Government, and shall protect each of them against Invasion; and on Application of the Legislature, or of the Executive (when the Legislature cannot be convened) against domestic Violence.

ARTICLE V

The Congress, whenever two thirds of both Houses shall deem it necessary, shall propose Amendments to this Constitution, or, on the Application of the Legislatures of two thirds of the several States, shall call a Convention for proposing Amendments, which, in either Case, shall be valid to all Intents and Purposes, as part of this Constitution, when ratified by the Legislatures of three fourths of the several States, or by Conventions in three fourths thereof, as the one or the other Mode of Ratification may be proposed by the Congress; Provided that no Amendment which may be made prior to the Year One thousand eight hundred and eight shall in any Manner affect the first and fourth Clauses in the Ninth Section of the first Article; and that no State, without its Consent, shall be deprived of its equal Suffrage in the Senate.

ARTICLE VI

[1] All Debts contracted and Engagements entered into, before the Adoption of this Constitution, shall be as valid against the United States under this Constitution, as under the Confederation.

[2] This Constitution, and the Laws of the United States which shall be made in Pursuance thereof; and all Treaties made, or which shall be made, under the Authority of the United States, shall be the supreme Law of the Land; and the Judges in every State shall be bound thereby, any Thing in the Constitution or Laws of any State to the Contrary notwithstanding.

[3] The Senators and Representatives before mentioned, and the Members of the several State Legislatures, and all executive and judicial Officers, both of the United States and of the several States, shall be bound by Oath or Affirmation, to support this Constitution; but no religious Test shall ever be required as a Qualification to any Office or public Trust under the United States.

ARTICLE VII

The Ratification of the Conventions of nine States shall be sufficient for the Establishment of this Constitution between the States so ratifying the Same.

Done in Convention by the Unanimous Consent of the States present the Seventeenth Day of September in the Year of our Lord one thousand seven hundred and Eighty seven and of the Independence of the United States of America the Twelfth.

ARTICLES IN ADDITION TO, AND AMENDMENT OF, THE CONSTITUTION OF THE UNITED STATES OF AMERICA, PROPOSED BY CONGRESS, AND RATIFIED BY THE LEGISLATURES OF THE SEVERAL STATES, PURSUANT TO THE FIFTH ARTICLE OF THE ORIGINAL CONSTITUTION.

AMENDMENT I [1791]

Congress shall make no law respecting an establishment of religion, or prohibiting the free exercise thereof; or abridging the freedom of speech, or of the press; or the right of the people peaceably to assemble, and to petition the Government for a redress of grievances.

AMENDMENT II [1791]

A well regulated Militia, being necessary to the security of a free State, the right of the people to keep and bear Arms, shall not be infringed.

AMENDMENT III [1791]

No Soldier shall, in time of peace be quartered in any house, without the consent of the Owner, nor in time of war, but in a manner to be prescribed by law.

AMENDMENT IV [1791]

The right of the people to be secure in their persons, houses, papers, and effects, against unreasonable searches and seizures, shall not be violated, and no Warrants shall issue, but upon probable cause, supported by Oath or affirmation, and particularly describing the place to be searched, and the persons or things to be seized.

AMENDMENT V [1791]

No person shall be held to answer for a capital, or otherwise infamous crime, unless on a presentment or indictment of a Grand Jury, except in cases arising in the land or naval forces, or in the Militia, when in actual service in time of War or public danger; nor shall any person be subject for the same offence to be twice put in jeopardy of life or limb; nor shall be compelled in any criminal case to be a witness against himself, nor be deprived of life, liberty, or property, without due process of law; nor shall private property be taken for public use, without just compensation.

AMENDMENT VI [1791]

In all criminal prosecutions, the accused shall enjoy the right to a speedy and public trial, by an impartial jury of the State and district wherein the crime shall have been committed, which district shall have been previously ascertained by law, and to be informed of the nature and cause of the accusation; to be confronted with the witnesses against him; to have compulsory process for obtaining witnesses in his favor, and to have the Assistance of Counsel for his defence.

AMENDMENT VII [1791]

In Suits at common law, where the value in controversy shall exceed twenty dollars, the right of trial by jury shall be preserved, and no fact tried by a jury, shall be otherwise reexamined in any Court of the United States, than according to the rules of the common law.

AMENDMENT VIII [1791]

Excessive bail shall not be required, nor excessive fines imposed, nor cruel and unusual punishments inflicted.

AMENDMENT IX [1791]

The enumeration in the Constitution, of certain rights, shall not be construed to deny or disparage others retained by the people.

AMENDMENT X [1791]

The powers not delegated to the United States by the Constitution, nor prohibited by it to the States, are reserved to the States respectively, or to the people.

AMENDMENT XI [1798]

The Judicial power of the United States shall not be construed to extend to any suit in law or equity, commenced or prosecuted against one of the United States by Citizens of another State, or by Citizens or Subjects of any Foreign State.

AMENDMENT XII [1804]

The Electors shall meet in their respective states and vote by ballot for President and Vice-President, one of whom, at least, shall not be an inhabitant of the same state with themselves; they shall name in their ballots the person voted for as President, and in distinct ballots the person voted for as Vice-President, and they shall make distinct lists of all persons voted for as President, and of all persons voted for as Vice-President, and of the number of votes for each, which lists they shall sign and certify, and transmit sealed to the seat of the government of the United States, directed to the President of the Senate; — The President of the Senate shall, in the presence of the Senate and House of Representatives, open all the certificates and the votes shall then be counted; — The person having the greatest number of votes for President, shall be the President, if such number be a majority of the whole number of Electors appointed; and if no person have such majority, then from the persons having the highest numbers not exceeding three on the list of those voted for as President, the House of Representatives shall choose immediately, by ballot, the President. But in choosing the President, the votes shall be taken by states, the representation from each state having one vote; a quorum for this purpose shall consist of a member or members from two-thirds of the states, and a majority of all the states shall be necessary to a choice. And if the House of Representatives shall not choose a President whenever the right of choice shall devolve upon them, before the fourth day of March next following, then the Vice-President shall act as President, as in the case of the death or other constitutional disability of the President. — The person having the greatest number of votes as Vice-President, shall be the Vice-President, if such number be a majority of the whole number of Electors appointed, and if no person have a majority, then from the two highest numbers on the list, the Senate shall choose the Vice-President; a quorum for the purpose shall consist of two-thirds of the whole number of Senators, and a majority of the whole number shall be necessary to a choice. But no person constitutionally ineligible to the office of President shall be eligible to that of Vice-President of the United States.

AMENDMENT XIII [1865]

Section 1. Neither slavery nor involuntary servitude, except as a punishment for crime whereof the party shall have been duly convicted, shall exist within the United States, or any place subject to their jurisdiction.

Section 2. Congress shall have power to enforce this article by appropriate legislation.

AMENDMENT XIV [1868]

Section 1. All persons born or naturalized in the United States, and subject to the jurisdiction thereof, are citizens of the United States and of the State wherein they reside. No State shall make or enforce any law which shall abridge the privileges or immunities of citizens of the United States; nor shall any State deprive any person of life, liberty, or property, without due process of law; nor deny to any person within its jurisdiction the equal protection of the laws.

Section 2. Representatives shall be apportioned among the several States according to their respective numbers, counting the whole number of persons in each State, excluding Indians not taxed. But when the right to vote at any election for the choice of electors for President and Vice-President of the United States, Representatives in Congress, the Executive and Judicial officers of a State, or the members of the Legislature thereof, is denied to any of the male inhabitants of such State, being twenty-one years of age, and citizens of the United States, or in any way abridged, except for participation in rebellion, or other crime, the basis of representation therein shall be reduced in the proportion which the number of such male citizens shall bear to the whole number of male citizens twenty-one years of age in such State.

Section 3. No person shall be a Senator or Representative in Congress, or elector of President and Vice-President, or hold any office, civil or military, under the United States, or under any State, who, having previously taken an oath, as a member of Congress, or as an officer of the United States, or as a member of any State legislature, or as an executive or judicial officer of any State, to support the Constitution of the United States, shall have engaged in insurrection or rebellion against the same, or given aid or comfort to the enemies thereof. But Congress may by a vote of two-thirds of each House, remove such disability.

Section 4. The validity of the public debt of the United States, authorized by law, including debts incurred for payment of pensions and bounties for services in suppressing insurrection or rebellion, shall not be questioned. But neither the United States nor any State shall assume or pay any debt or obligation incurred in aid of insurrection or rebellion against the United States, or any claim for the loss of emancipation of any slave; but all such debts, obligations and claims shall be held illegal and void.

Section 5. The Congress shall have power to enforce, by appropriate legislation, the provisions of this article.

AMENDMENT XV [1870]

Section 1. The right of citizens of the United States to vote shall not be denied or abridged by the United States or by any State on account of race, color, or previous condition of servitude.

Section 2. The Congress shall have power to enforce this article by appropriate legislation.

AMENDMENT XVI [1913]

The Congress shall have power to lay and collect taxes on incomes, from whatever source derived, without apportionment among the several States, and without regard to any census or enumeration.

AMENDMENT XVII [1913]

[1] The Senate of the United States shall be composed of two Senators from each State, elected by the people thereof, for six years, and each Senator shall have one vote. The electors in each State shall have the qualifications requisite for electors of the most numerous branch of the State legislatures.

[2] When vacancies happen in the representation of any State in the Senate, the executive authority of such State shall issue writs of election to fill such vacancies: *Provided,* That the legislature of any State may empower the executive thereof to make temporary appointments until the people fill the vacancies by election as the legislature may direct.

[3] This amendment shall not be so construed as to affect the election or term of any Senator chosen before it becomes valid as part of the Constitution.

AMENDMENT XVIII [1919]

Section 1. After one year from the ratification of this article the manufacture, sale, or transportation of intoxicating liquors within, the importation thereof into, or the exportation thereof from the United States and all territory subject to the jurisdiction thereof for beverage purposes is hereby prohibited.

Section 2. The Congress and the several States shall have concurrent power to enforce this article by appropriate legislation.

Section 3. This article shall be inoperative unless it shall have been ratified as an amendment to the Constitution by the legislatures of the several States, as provided in the Constitution, within seven years from the date of the submission hereof to the States by the Congress.

AMENDMENT XIX [1920]

[1] The right of citizens of the United States to vote shall not be denied or abridged by the United States or by any State on account of sex.

[2] Congress shall have power to enforce this article by appropriate legislation.

AMENDMENT XX [1933]

Section 1. The terms of the President and Vice President shall end at noon on the 20th day of January, and the terms of Senators and Representatives at noon on the 3d day of January, of the years in which such terms would have ended if this article had not been ratified; and the terms of their successor shall then begin.

Section 2. The Congress shall assemble at least once in every year, and such meeting shall begin at noon on the 3d day of January, unless they shall by law appoint a different day.

Section 3. If, at the time fixed for the beginning of the term of the President, the President elect shall have died, the Vice President elect shall become President. If a President shall not have been chosen before the time fixed for the beginning of his term, or if the President elect shall have failed to qualify, then the Vice President elect shall act as President until a President shall have qualified; and the Congress may by law provide for the case wherein neither a President elect nor a Vice President elect shall have qualified, declaring who shall then act as President, or the manner in which one who is to act shall be selected, and such person shall act accordingly until a President or Vice President shall have qualified.

Section 4. The Congress may by law provide for the case of the death of any of the persons from whom the House of Representatives may choose a President whenever the right of choice shall have devolved upon them, and for the case of the death of any of the persons from whom the Senate may choose a Vice President whenever the right of choice shall have devolved upon them.

Section 5. Sections 1 and 2 shall take effect on the 15th day of October following the ratification of this article.

Section 6. This article shall be inoperative unless it shall have been ratified as an amendment to the Constitution by the legislatures of three-fourths of the several States within seven years from the date of its submission.

AMENDMENT XXI [1933]

Section 1. The eighteenth article of amendment to the Constitution of the United States is hereby repealed.

Section 2. The transportation or importation into any State, Territory, or possession of the United States for delivery or use therein of intoxicating liquors, in violation of the laws thereof, is hereby prohibited.

Section 3. This article shall be inoperative unless it shall have been ratified as an amendment to the Constitution by conventions in the several States, as provided in the Constitution, within seven years from the date of the submissions hereof to the States by the Congress.

AMENDMENT XXII [1951]

Section 1. No person shall be elected to the office of the President more than twice, and no person who has held the office of President, or acted as President, for more than two years of a term to which some other person was elected President shall be elected to the office of the President more than once. But this Article shall not apply to any person holding the office of President when this Article was proposed by the Congress, and shall not prevent any person who may be holding the office of President, or acting as President, during the term within which the Article becomes operative from holding the office of President or acting as President during the remainder of such term.

Section 2. This article shall be inoperative unless it shall have been ratified as an amendment to the Constitution by the legislatures of three-fourths of the several States within seven years from the date of its submission to the States by the Congress.

AMENDMENT XXIII [1961]

Section 1. The District constituting the seat of Government of the United States shall appoint in such manner as the Congress may direct:

A number of electors of President and Vice President equal to the whole number of Senators and Representatives in Congress to which the District would be entitled if it were a State, but in no event more than the least populous State; they shall be in addition to those appointed by the States, but they shall be considered, for the purposes of the election of President and Vice President, to be electors appointed by a State; and they shall meet in the District and perform such duties as provided by the twelfth article of amendment.

Section 2. The Congress shall have power to enforce this article by appropriate legislation.

AMENDMENT XXIV [1964]

Section 1. The right of citizens of the United States to vote in any primary or other election for President or Vice President for electors for President or Vice President, or for Senator or Representative in Congress, shall not be denied or abridged by the United States or any State by reason of failure to pay any poll tax or other tax.

Section 2. The Congress shall have power to enforce this article by appropriate legislation.

AMENDMENT XXV [1967]

Section 1. In case of the removal of the President from office or of his death or resignation, the Vice President shall become President.

Section 2. Whenever there is a vacancy in the office of the Vice President, the President shall nominate a Vice President who shall take office upon confirmation by a majority vote of both Houses of Congress.

Section 3. Whenever the President transmits to the President pro tempore of the Senate and the Speaker of the House of Representatives his written declaration that he is unable to discharge the powers and duties of his office, and until he transmits to them a written declaration to the contrary, such powers and duties shall be discharged by the Vice President as Acting President.

Section 4. Whenever the Vice President and a Majority of either the principal officers of the executive departments or of such other body as Congress may by law provide, transmit to the President pro tempore of the Senate and the Speaker of the House of Representatives their written declaration that the President is unable to discharge the powers and duties of his office, the Vice President shall immediately assume the powers and duties of the office as Acting President.

Thereafter, when the President transmits to the President pro tempore of the Senate and the Speaker of the House of Representatives his written declaration that no inability exists, he shall resume the powers and duties of his office unless the Vice President and a majority of either the principal officers of the executive department or of such other body as Congress may by law provide, transmit within four days to the President pro tempore of the Senate and the Speaker of the House of Representatives their written declaration that the President is unable to discharge the powers and duties of his office. Thereupon Congress shall decide the issue, assembling within forty-eight hours for that purpose if not in session. If the Congress, within twenty-one days after receipt of the latter written declaration, or, if Congress is not in session, within twenty-one days after Congress is required to assemble, determined by two-thirds vote of both Houses that the President is unable to discharge the powers and duties of his office, the Vice President shall continue to discharge the same as Acting President; otherwise, the President shall resume the powers and duties of his office.

AMENDMENT XXVI [1971]

Section 1. The right of citizens of the United States, who are eighteen years of age or older, to vote shall not be denied or abridged by the United States or by any State on account of age.

Section 2. The Congress shall have power to enforce this article by appropriate legislation.

AMENDMENT XXVII [1992]

Section 1. No law, varying the Compensation for the services of the Senators and Representatives, shall take effect, unless an election of Representatives shall have intervened.

Constitutional Law

1

Judicial Review

U.S. CONSTITUTION, ARTICLE III

Section 1. The judicial Power of the United States, shall be vested in one supreme Court, and in such inferior Courts as the Congress may from time to time ordain and establish. The Judges, both of the supreme and inferior Courts, shall hold their offices during good Behaviour, and shall at stated Times, receive for their Services, a Compensation, which shall not be diminished during their Continuance in Office.

Section 2. [1] The judicial Power shall extend to all Cases, in Law and Equity, arising under this Constitution, the Laws of the United States, and Treaties made, or which shall be made, under their Authority; — to all Cases affecting Ambassadors, other public Ministers and Consuls; — to all Cases of admiralty and maritime Jurisdiction; — to Controversies to which the United States shall be a Party; — to Controversies between two or more States; — between a State and Citizens of another State; — between Citizens of different States; — between Citizens of the same State claiming Lands under Grants of different States, and between a State or the Citizens thereof, and foreign States, Citizens or Subjects.

[2] In all Cases affecting Ambassadors, other public Ministers and Consuls, and those in which a State shall be Party, the supreme Court shall have original Jurisdiction. In all the other Cases before mentioned, the supreme Court shall have appellate Jurisdiction, both as to Law and Fact, with such Exceptions, and under such Regulations as the Congress shall make.

∼ PROBLEM: HEALTH CARE LEGISLATION AND ABORTION ∼

Congress recently enacted sweeping health care legislation designed to ensure that every American has affordable health care. Passage of this landmark legislation was difficult, with varied and contentious views about how the legislation should be structured (as well as about whether it should have been enacted at all). One of the most contentious issues was abortion. Pro-choice forces lobbied hard to make sure that the bill provided explicit benefits for abortion counseling and abortion-related medical services, while pro-life forces pushed hard for an explicit exclusion of such counseling and services. Assume that, at the eleventh hour, it became clear that the legislation would not have sufficient support to pass if the language advocated by the pro-choice forces was included. Assume also that a compromise was reached providing that health insurers could choose whether to provide coverage for abortion counseling and abortion-related medical services, but stipulating that no federal funds could be used to pay for, or subsidize, insurance that provided for such counseling and services.

Immediately after the new health care legislation passed, a number of lawsuits were filed challenging its constitutionality. One suit was filed by a group of abortion counselors and medical providers who claimed that the law unconstitutionally discriminates against them in violation of their right to equal protection of the laws, and further arguing that the legislation infringes the privacy rights of their patients. A second suit was filed by Citizens Favoring Choice (CFC), a pro-choice group that advocates in favor of choice and choice issues, arguing that Congress made a "bad policy" decision in excluding coverage for abortion counseling and abortion-related medical services. CFC's membership includes women both of childbearing age and beyond childbearing age, as well as men.

As we go through this chapter, you should think about whether the federal courts have the power to hear a case like this one (involving a challenge to the new health care law's exclusion of abortion-related benefits). Also consider the type of relief that the courts might be able to grant if one of the plaintiffs prevails.

A. *MARBURY* AND "THE POWER TO SAY WHAT THE LAW IS"

Constitutions inevitably address fundamental issues regarding governmental structure and the status of (and relationships between) different branches of government. In some instances, the rights and responsibilities of the various branches are clearly defined. In other instances, they are not so clearly defined and someone determines what the Constitution means. In this chapter, we examine questions relating to the U.S. Supreme Court's authority to interpret the Constitution in the face of conflicting interpretations by Congress and the Executive Branch.

Marbury v. Madison
5 U.S. (1 Cranch) 137 (1803)

Mr. Chief Justice MARSHALL delivered the opinion of the court.

[After the Federalists were defeated in the election of 1800, but before Thomas Jefferson assumed the presidency, the Federalists (who had been voted out of office) attempted to retain a measure of power by creating new federal judgeships and filling them with Federalist appointees. William Marbury was confirmed as a magistrate in the District of Columbia, and his commission was signed by President John Adams and sealed by Secretary of State James Madison. Unfortunately for Marbury, his commission was not delivered before Jefferson assumed office. Jefferson ordered that all undelivered commissions be withheld. Marbury sought a writ of mandamus to compel Madison to deliver the commission as an original action in the U.S. Supreme Court. He did so pursuant to Section 13 of the Judiciary Act of 1789, which gave the Court the "power to issue writs [of] *mandamus*, in cases warranted by the principles and usages of law, to [any] persons holding office, under the authority of the United States."]

[T]he present motion is for a mandamus. The peculiar delicacy of this case, the novelty of some of its circumstances, and the real difficulty attending the points which occur in it, require a complete exposition of the principles, on which the opinion to be given by the court, is founded. . . .

1st. Has the applicant a right to the commission he demands? [Since Marbury's] commission was signed by the President, and sealed by the secretary of state, [he] was appointed; and as the law creating the office, gave the officer a right to hold for five years, independent of the executive, the appointment was not revocable. . . . To withhold his commission [is] violative of a vested legal right. . . .

2dly. If he has a right, and that right has been violated, do the laws of this country afford him a remedy? The very essence of civil liberty certainly consists in the right of every individual to claim the protection of the laws, whenever he receives an injury. . . . The government of the United States has been emphatically termed a government of laws, and not of men. It will certainly cease to deserve this high appellation, if the laws furnish no remedy for the violation of a vested legal right.

[W]here the heads of departments are the political or confidential agents of the executive, merely to execute the will of the President, or rather to act in cases in which the executive possesses a constitutional or legal discretion, nothing can be more perfectly clear than that their acts are only politically examinable. But where a specific duty is assigned by law, and individual rights depend upon the performance of that duty, it seems equally clear that the individual who considers himself injured, has a right to resort to the laws of his country for a remedy. . . .

It remains to be inquired whether,

3dly.   He is entitled to the remedy for which he applies. This depends on,

1st.   The nature of the writ applied for, and,

2dly.   The power of this court.

1st.   The nature of the writ.

This writ, if awarded, would be directed to an officer of government, and its mandate to him would be, to use the words of Blackstone, "to do a particular thing therein specified, which appertains to his office and duty and which the court has previously determined, or at least supposes, to be consonant to right and justice." [T]o render the mandamus a proper remedy, the officer to whom it is to be directed, must be one to whom, on legal principles, such writ may be directed; and the person applying for it must be without any other specific and legal remedy.

1st. With respect to the officer to whom it would be directed. [I]t is not wonderful that [the] assertion, by an individual, of his legal claims in a court of justice; to which claims it is the duty of that court to attend; should at first view be considered by some, as an attempt to intrude into the cabinet, and to inter-meddle with the prerogatives of the executive. . . . It is scarcely necessary for the court to disclaim all pretensions to such a jurisdiction. . . . The province of the court is, solely, to decide on the rights of individuals, not to inquire how the executive, or executive officers, perform duties in which they have a discre-tion. . . . This, then, is a plain case of a mandamus, either to deliver the commis-sion, or a copy of it from the record; and it only remains to be inquired,

Whether it can issue from this court.

The act to establish the judicial courts of the United States authorizes the supreme court "to issue writs of mandamus, in cases warranted by the principles and usages of law, to any courts appointed, or persons holding office, under the authority of the United States." The secretary of state, being a person, holding an office under the authority of the United States, is precisely within the letter of the description; and if this court is not authorized to issue a writ of mandamus to such an officer, it must be because the law is unconstitutional, and therefore absolutely incapable of conferring the authority, and assigning the duties which its words purport to confer and assign.

The constitution vests the whole judicial power of the United States in one supreme court, and such inferior courts as congress shall, from time to time, ordain and establish. This power is expressly extended to all cases arising under the laws of the United States. . . . In the distribution of this power it is declared that "the supreme court shall have original jurisdiction in all cases affecting ambassadors, other public ministers and consuls, and those in which a state shall be a party. In all other cases, the supreme court shall have appellate jurisdiction."

It has been insisted [that] as the original grant of jurisdiction to the supreme and inferior courts is general, and the clause, assigning original jurisdiction to the supreme court, contains no negative or restrictive words; the power remains to the legislature to assign original jurisdiction to that court in other cases than those specified in the article which has been recited; provided those cases belong to the judicial power of the United States.

If it had been intended to leave it in the discretion of the legislature to apportion the judicial power between the supreme and inferior courts according to the will of that body, it would certainly have been useless to have proceeded further than to have defined the judicial power, and the tribunals in which it should be vested. . . . Affirmative words are often, in their operation, negative of other objects than those affirmed; and in this case, a negative or exclusive sense must be given to them or they have no operation at all. . . . It cannot be presumed that any clause in the constitution is intended to be without effect; and therefore such construction is inadmissible, unless the words require it. . . .

When an instrument organizing fundamentally a judicial system, divides it into one supreme, and so many inferior courts as the legislature may ordain and establish; then enumerates its powers, and proceeds so far to distribute them, as to define the jurisdiction of the supreme court by declaring the cases in which it shall take original jurisdiction, and that in others it shall take appellate jurisdiction, the plain import of the words seems to be, that in one class of cases its jurisdiction is original, and not appellate; in the other it is appellate, and not original. If any other construction would render the clause inoperative, that is an additional reason for rejecting such other construction, and for adhering to the obvious meaning.

To enable this court then to issue a mandamus, it must be shown to be an exercise of appellate jurisdiction, or to be necessary to enable them to exercise appellate jurisdiction. . . . It is the essential criterion of appellate jurisdiction, that it revises and corrects the proceedings in a cause already instituted, and does not create that case. Although, therefore, a mandamus may be directed to courts, yet to issue such a writ to an officer for the delivery of a paper, is in effect the same as to sustain an original action for that paper, and therefore seems not to belong to appellate, but to original jurisdiction. Neither is it necessary in such a case as this, to enable the court to exercise its appellate jurisdiction.

The authority, therefore, given to the supreme court, by the act establishing the judicial courts of the United States, to issue writs of mandamus to public officers, appears not to be warranted by the constitution; and it becomes necessary to inquire whether a jurisdiction, so conferred, can be exercised.

The question, whether an act, repugnant to the constitution, can become the law of the land, is a question deeply interesting to the United States. . . . It seems only necessary to recognize certain principles, supposed to have been long and well established, to decide it.

That the people have an original right to establish, for their future government, such principles as, in their opinion, shall most conduce to their own happiness, is the basis on which the whole American fabric has been erected. The exercise of this original right is a very great exertion; nor can it nor ought it to be frequently repeated. The principles, therefore, so established are deemed fundamental. And as the authority, from which they proceed, is supreme, and can seldom act, they are designed to be permanent.

This original and supreme will organizes the government, and assigns to different departments their respective powers. It may either stop here; or establish certain limits not to be transcended by those departments.

The government of the United States is of the latter description. The powers of the legislature are defined and limited; and that those limits may not be mistaken or forgotten, the constitution is written. . . . The distinction between a government with limited and unlimited powers is abolished, if those limits do not confine the persons on whom they are imposed, and if acts prohibited and acts allowed are of equal obligation. It is a proposition too plain to be contested, that the constitution controls any legislative act repugnant to it; or, that the legislature may alter the constitution by an ordinary act.

Between these alternatives there is no middle ground. The constitution is either a superior, paramount law, unchangeable by ordinary means, or it is on a level with ordinary legislative acts, and like other acts, is alterable when the legislature shall please to alter it.

If the former part of the alternative be true, then a legislative act contrary to the constitution is not law: if the latter part be true, then written constitutions are absurd attempts, on the part of the people, to limit a power in its own nature illimitable.

Certainly all those who have framed written constitutions contemplate them as forming the fundamental and paramount law of the nation, and consequently the theory of every such government must be, that an act of the legislature repugnant to the constitution is void.

This theory is essentially attached to a written constitution, and is consequently to be considered by this court as one of the fundamental principles of our society. . . .

If an act of the legislature, repugnant to the constitution, is void, does it, notwithstanding its invalidity, bind the courts and oblige them to give it effect? Or, in other words, though it be not law, does it constitute a rule as operative as if it was a law? This would be to overthrow in fact what was established in theory; and would seem, at first view, an absurdity too gross to be insisted on. It shall, however, receive a more attentive consideration.

It is emphatically the province and duty of the judicial department to say what the law is. Those who apply the rule to particular cases, must of necessity expound and interpret that rule. If two laws conflict with each other, the courts must decide on the operation of each.

So if a law be in opposition to the constitution: if both the law and the constitution apply to a particular case, so that the court must either decide that case conformably to the law, disregarding the constitution; or conformably to the constitution, disregarding the law: the court must determine which of these conflicting rules governs the case. This is of the very essence of judicial duty.

If then the courts are to regard the constitution; and the constitution is superior to any ordinary act of the legislature; the constitution, and not such ordinary act, must govern the case to which they both apply.

Those then who controvert the principle that the constitution is to be considered, in court, as a paramount law, are reduced to the necessity of maintaining that courts must close their eyes on the constitution, and see only the law.

This doctrine would subvert the very foundation of all written constitutions. It would declare that an act, which, according to the principles and theory of our government, is entirely void, is yet, in practice, completely obligatory. It would declare, that if the legislature shall do what is expressly forbidden, such act, notwithstanding the express prohibition, is in reality effectual. It would be giving to the legislature a practical and real omnipotence with the same breath which professes to restrict their powers within narrow limits. It is prescribing limits, and declaring that those limits may be passed at pleasure.

That it thus reduces to nothing what we have deemed the greatest improvement on political institutions — a written constitution, would of itself be sufficient, in America where written constitutions have been viewed with so much reverence, for rejecting the construction. But the peculiar expressions of the constitution of the United States furnish additional arguments in favor of its rejection.

The judicial power of the United States is extended to all cases arising under the constitution.

Could it be the intention of those who gave this power, to say that, in using it, the constitution should not be looked into? That a case arising under the constitution should be decided without examining the instrument under which it arises?

This is too extravagant to be maintained.

In some cases then, the constitution must be looked into by the judges. And if they can open it at all, what part of it are they forbidden to read, or to obey?

There are many other parts of the constitution which serve to illustrate this subject. It is declared that "no tax or duty shall be laid on articles exported from any state." Suppose a duty on the export of cotton, of tobacco, or of flour; and a suit instituted to recover it. Ought judgment to be rendered in such a case? Ought the judges to close their eyes on the constitution, and only see the law?

The constitution declares that "no bill of attainder or ex post facto law shall be passed." If, however, such a bill should be passed and a person should be prosecuted under it, must the court condemn to death those victims whom the constitution endeavors to preserve?

"No person," says the constitution, "shall be convicted of treason unless on the testimony of two witnesses to the same overt act, or on confession in open court."

Here the language of the constitution is addressed especially to the courts. It prescribes, directly for them, a rule of evidence not to be departed from. If the legislature should change that rule, and declare one witness, or a confession out of court, sufficient for conviction, must the constitutional principle yield to the legislative act?

From these and many other selections which might be made, it is apparent, that the framers of the constitution contemplated that instrument as a rule for the government of courts, as well as of the legislature.

Why otherwise does it direct the judges to take an oath to support it? This oath certainly applies, in an especial manner, to their conduct in their official character. How immoral to impose it on them, if they were to be used as the instruments, and the knowing instruments, for violating what they swear to support!

The oath of office, too, imposed by the legislature, is completely demonstrative of the legislative opinion on this subject. It is in these words: "I do solemnly swear that I will administer justice without respect to persons, and do equal right to the poor and to the rich; and that I will faithfully and impartially discharge all the duties incumbent on me as according to the best of my abilities and understanding, agreeably to the constitution and laws of the United States." . . . Why does a judge swear to discharge his duties agreeably to the constitution of the United States, if that constitution forms no rule for his government, if it is closed upon him and cannot be inspected by him.

If such be the real state of things, this is worse than solemn mockery. To prescribe, or to take this oath, becomes equally a crime.

BACKGROUND
Conflict of Interest?

Chief Justice Marshall was President Adams's secretary of state and was the official charged with delivering Marbury's commission to him. As a result, some questioned whether Marshall should have participated in the Court's resolution of the case.

[I]n declaring what shall be the supreme law of the land, the constitution itself is first mentioned; and not the laws of the United States generally, but those only which shall be made in pursuance of the constitution, have that rank. [T]he particular phraseology of the constitution of the United States confirms and strengthens the principle, supposed to be essential to all written constitutions, that a law repugnant to the constitution is void, and that courts, as well as other departments, are bound by that instrument.

The rule must be discharged.

Questions: Judicial Review

1. *Parliamentary Supremacy.* The United Kingdom functions without a written constitution, and its courts have historically refused to exercise judicial review over acts of Parliament (although they have exercised review authority vis-à-vis administrative agencies). Nevertheless, with certain exceptions (e.g., Britain is a signatory to the European Convention on Human Rights, which applies to acts of Parliament), British courts assume that a parliamentary enactment is constitutional. Is the British approach preferable to that of the United States? Is Britain regarded as any less respectful of human rights as the United States? Can we assume that Congress will act in good faith and will not enact an unconstitutional law? What would be the remedy if, for example, Congress enacts a law abridging freedom of speech? *See* Russell L. Weaver & Geoffrey J.G. Bennett, *The Northern Ireland Media Ban: Some Reflections on Judicial Review*, 22 Vand. J. Transnat'l L. 1119 (1989).

2. *Enforcement of Judicial Decrees and Practical Constraints on Judicial Authority.* In the *Marbury* case, suppose that the Court did not strike down the Judiciary Act, and instead ordered Madison to give Marbury his commission. Suppose also that Madison had refused to do so. How would the Court have enforced its decree against Madison? If we look at the matter purely from a "power perspective," the Executive Branch has control of the police and the armed forces. Does the judiciary have comparable sources of power at its disposal? If not, how does the judiciary enforce its decrees?

∽ PROBLEMS: JUDICIAL REVIEW ∽

1. *More on the Health Care Problem.* Judicial review raises fundamental questions regarding the role of the judiciary vis-à-vis other branches of government. Let's return to the health care problem described at the beginning of the chapter. Is it appropriate for the courts to dictate to Congress (in the guise of judicial review) the content of health care legislation? On the other hand, since plaintiffs are claiming that their constitutional rights (e.g., a woman's right to have an abortion) are being infringed by the new law, isn't it both necessary and appropriate for courts to decide the case and decide what the Constitution requires?

2. *Does the Constitution Really Make It "Emphatically the Province and Duty of the Judiciary to Say What the Law Is"?* Even if the courts may exercise judicial review authority, questions might be raised regarding whether other branches of government also have the power to "say what the law is." In particular, are there contexts in which Congress's or the President's interpretation of the Constitution should prevail over the Court's interpretation? President Jefferson once posed a hypothetical question about an individual who is convicted of a crime and appeals on the basis that the conviction is unconstitutional. The U.S. Supreme Court considers the case, interprets and applies the law, and decides that the conviction is constitutional. The individual, now a convict, applies to you (the President of the United States) for a pardon. As President, you are free to pardon the convict whether or not the conviction was validly obtained, but you are particularly troubled by what you regard as an invalid conviction. If you believe that the conviction was unconstitutional, notwithstanding the Supreme Court's conclusions, should you take that into account in deciding whether to pardon? Must you accept the Court's conclusions regarding the validity of the conviction?

3. *Must the Judiciary Retain the Authority to Decide All Legal Questions?* Suppose that Congress enacts the Nuclear Regulatory Act (NRA), which vests the Nuclear Regulatory Commission (NRC) with the power to oversee the development and operation of nuclear reactors in the United States. The NRA also provides the NRC with the authority to promulgate "reasonable" regulations governing the disposal of nuclear waste that are designed to serve the "public interest." Suppose that the NRC promulgates a regulation prohibiting the storage of nuclear waste "in or near" major metropolitan areas. An association of power companies seeks to challenge the regulation on the basis that it does not serve the "public interest." You are the judge assigned to hear the case. How should you go about deciding whether the regulation is "reasonable" and whether it serves the "public interest"? Must you resolve those questions independently, or is it appropriate for you to simply defer to the NRC's recommendation if it is "reasonable"? In other words, what are the role and scope of your judicial review authority? *See* Chevron v. Natural Resources Defense Council, Inc., 467 U.S. 837 (1984).

Martin v. Hunter's Lessee

14 U.S. (1 Wheat.) 304 (1816)

STORY, J., delivered the opinion of the court.

[The Court of Appeals of Virginia refused to comply with a mandate of the U.S. Supreme Court. The case came back to the Court on the issue of whether the U.S. Supreme Court could review the judgment of a Virginia court.]

The third article of the constitution [provides that] the supreme court shall have *appellate jurisdiction*, both as to law and fact, with such exceptions, and under such regulations, as the congress shall make. [T]he framers [contemplated] that cases within the judicial cognizance of the United States not only might but would arise in the state courts. [T]he sixth article declares, that "this constitution, and the laws of the United States which shall be made in pursuance thereof, and all treaties made, or which shall be made, under the authority of the United States, shall be the supreme law of the land, and the judges in every state shall be bound thereby, any thing in the constitution or laws of any state to the contrary notwithstanding." It is obvious that this obligation is imperative upon the state judges in their official, and not merely in their private, capacities. [Judges] were not to decide merely according to the laws or constitution of the state, but according to the constitution, laws and treaties of the United States — "the supreme law of the land." . . .

[T]o all these cases the judicial power, by the very terms of the constitution, is to extend. It cannot extend by original jurisdiction if that was already rightfully and exclusively attached in the state courts, which [may] occur; it must, therefore, extend by appellate jurisdiction, or not at all. . . .

It has been argued that such an appellate jurisdiction over state courts is inconsistent with the genius of our governments, and the spirit of the constitution. [The Constitution] is crowded with provisions which restrain or annul the sovereignty of the states in some of the highest branches of their prerogatives. The tenth section of the first article contains a long list of disabilities and prohibitions imposed upon the states. . . . The language of the constitution is also imperative upon the states as to the performance of many duties. It is imperative upon the state legislatures to make laws prescribing the time, places, and manner of holding elections for senators and representatives, and for electors of president and vice-president. [I]t is certainly difficult to support the argument that the appellate power over the decisions of state courts is contrary to the genius of our institutions. . . .

Nor can such a right be deemed to impair the independence of state judges. [T]hey are expressly bound to obedience by the letter of the constitution. . . . From the very nature of things, the absolute right of decision, in the last resort, must rest somewhere — wherever it may be vested it is susceptible of abuse. In all questions of jurisdiction the inferior, or appellate court, must pronounce the final judgment; and common sense, as well as legal reasoning, has conferred it upon the latter. . . .

This is not all. A motive of another kind, perfectly compatible with the most sincere respect for state tribunals, might induce the grant of appellate power over their decisions. That motive is the importance, and even necessity of *uniformity* of decisions throughout the whole United States, upon all subjects within the purview of the constitution. Judges of equal learning and integrity, in different states, might differently interpret a statute, or a treaty of the United States, or even the constitution itself: If there were no revising authority to control these jarring and discordant judgments, and harmonize them into uniformity, the laws, the treaties, and the constitution of the United States would be different in different states, and might, perhaps, never have precisely the same construction, obligation, or efficacy, in any two states. The public mischiefs that would attend such a state of things would be truly deplorable. . . .

On the whole, the court are of opinion, that the appellate power of the United States does extend to cases pending in the state courts [that] is supported by the letter and spirit of the constitution. . . . It is the opinion of the whole court, that the judgment of the court of appeals of Virginia, rendered on the mandate in this cause, be reversed, and the judgment of the district court, held at Winchester, be, and the same is, hereby affirmed.

PROBLEM: FEDERAL CONSTITUTIONS AND STATE CONSTITUTIONS

In *Martin*, the Court recognizes that the U.S. Constitution is the supreme law of the land. Many states also have their own constitutions, and some constitutional provisions give citizens more rights than are permitted under the U.S. Constitution. Suppose that you sit on a state supreme court that wishes to interpret its state constitution more expansively than the U.S. Supreme Court interprets the U.S. Constitution. For example, in California v. Greenwood, 486 U.S. 35 (1988), the Court held that there is no "search" or "seizure" under the Fourth Amendment to the U.S. Constitution when police arrange to obtain a citizen's garbage from trash collectors. In State v. Hempele, 120 N.J. 182, 576 A.2d 793 (N.J. 1990), the New Jersey Supreme Court held that similar conduct violates the New Jersey Constitution. Does New Jersey have the authority to interpret similar language in its state constitution differently than the way the U.S. Supreme Court interprets the U.S. Constitution? More important, can you choose to follow *Hempele* rather than *Greenwood* in interpreting your state constitution?

Cooper v. Aaron

358 U.S. 1 (1958)

Opinion of the Court by THE CHIEF JUSTICE, Mr. Justice BLACK, Mr. Justice FRANKFURTER, Mr. Justice DOUGLAS, Mr. Justice BURTON, Mr. Justice CLARK, Mr. Justice HARLAN, Mr. Justice BRENNAN, and Mr. Justice WHITTAKER.

[This case raises] questions of the highest importance to the maintenance of our federal system of government. [It] involves a claim by the Governor and Legislature of a State that there is no duty on state officials to obey federal court orders resting on this Court's considered interpretation of the United States Constitution. Specifically [the] Governor and Legislature of Arkansas [claim] that they are not bound by our holding in Brown v. Board of Education, 347 U.S. 483. That holding was that the Fourteenth Amendment forbids States to use their governmental powers to bar children on racial grounds from attending schools where there is state participation through any arrangement, management, funds or property. . . .

[Following the holding in *Brown*, the Little Rock, Arkansas, School Board was] going forward with its preparation for desegregating the Little Rock school system, other state authorities [were] actively pursuing a program designed to perpetuate in Arkansas the system of racial segregation [in violation of *Brown*]. First came, in November 1956, an amendment to the State Constitution flatly commanding the Arkansas General Assembly to oppose "in every Constitutional manner the Unconstitutional-constitutional desegregation decisions [of] the United States Supreme Court." [Then], a law relieving school children from compulsory attendance at racially mixed schools, [and] a law establishing a State Sovereignty Commission, [were] enacted by the General Assembly. . . .

The School Board and the Superintendent of Schools nevertheless continued with preparations to [desegregate]. Nine Negro children were scheduled for admission [to] Central High School. . . . On September 2, 1957, the day before these Negro students were to enter[,] the school authorities were met with drastic opposing action on the part of the Governor of Arkansas, who dispatched units of the Arkansas National Guard [and] placed the school "off limits" to colored students. . . . The Governor's action had not been requested by the school authorities. [As] the Negro children attempted to enter the high school[,] units of the Arkansas National Guard "acting pursuant to the Governor's order, stood shoulder to shoulder at the school grounds and thereby forcibly prevented the 9 Negro students [from] entering," as they [did] every school day during the following three weeks. . . .

[On] February 20, 1958, the School Board and the Superintendent of Schools filed a petition in the District Court seeking a postponement of their program for desegregation. Their position in essence was that because of extreme public hostility, which they stated had been engendered largely by the official attitudes and actions of the Governor and the Legislature, the maintenance of a sound educational program at Central High School, with the Negro students in attendance, would be impossible. The Board therefore proposed that the Negro students already admitted to the school be withdrawn and sent to segregated schools, and that all further steps to carry out the Board's desegregation program be postponed [for] two and one-half years. . . .

The constitutional rights of respondents are not to be sacrificed or yielded to the violence and disorder which have followed upon the actions of the Governor and Legislature. As this Court said some 41 years ago in a unanimous opinion in a case involving another aspect of racial segregation: "It is urged that this proposed segregation will promote the public peace by preventing race conflicts. Desirable as this is, and important as is the preservation of the public peace, this aim cannot be accomplished by laws or ordinances which deny rights created or protected by the federal Constitution." Buchanan v. Warley, 245 U.S. 60. Thus law and order are not here to be preserved by depriving the Negro children of their constitutional rights. [T]he constitutional rights of children not to be discriminated against in school admission on grounds of race or color [can] neither be nullified openly and directly by state legislators or state executive or judicial officers, nor nullified indirectly by them through evasive schemes for segregation. . . .

[W]e should answer the premise of the actions of the Governor and Legislature that they are not bound by our holding in the *Brown* case. It is necessary only to recall some basic constitutional propositions which are settled doctrine. . . . Article VI of the Constitution makes the Constitution the "supreme Law of the Land." In 1803, Chief Justice Marshall, speaking for a unanimous Court, referring to the Constitution as "the fundamental and paramount law of the nation," declared in the notable case of Marbury v. Madison, 1 Cranch 137 [that] "It is emphatically the province and duty of the judicial department to say what the law is." This decision declared the basic principle that the federal judiciary is supreme in the exposition of the law of the Constitution, and that principle has ever since been respected by this Court and the Country as a permanent and indispensable feature of our constitutional system. It follows that the interpretation of the Fourteenth Amendment enunciated by this Court in the *Brown* case is the supreme law of the land, and Art. VI of the Constitution makes it of binding effect on the States. . . . Every state legislator and executive and judicial officer is solemnly committed by oath taken pursuant to Art. VI, ¶3 "to support this Constitution." Chief Justice Taney, speaking for a unanimous Court in 1859, said that this requirement reflected the framers' "anxiety to preserve it [the Constitution] in full force, in all its powers, and to guard against resistance to or evasion of its authority, on the part of a State."

No state legislator or executive or judicial officer can war against the Constitution without violating his undertaking to support it. Chief Justice Marshall spoke for a unanimous Court in saying that: "If the legislatures of the several states may, at will, annul the judgments of the courts of the United States, and destroy the rights acquired under those judgments, the constitution itself becomes a solemn mockery[.]" United States v. Peters, 5 Cranch 115 [1809]. A Governor who asserts a power to nullify a federal court order is similarly restrained. If he had such power, said Chief Justice Hughes, in 1932, also for a unanimous Court, "it is manifest that the fiat of a state Governor, and not the Constitution of the United States, would be the supreme law of the land; that the restrictions of the Federal Constitution upon the exercise of state power would be but impotent phrases. . . ."

Notes: *Brown, Cooper,* and *Judicial Legitimacy*

Cases like *Cooper* suggest the importance of legitimacy to the Court's effectiveness. The Court needs public acceptance and respect for its decisions, and it needs the support of officials in the Executive Branch (at least to the extent that such officials will be called upon to enforce the Court's decisions). This need for respect limits the Court's autonomy. Although the Court often provides special protections for minority groups (also known as the Court's counter-majoritarian function), the Court is often forced to rely on the support of elected officials to enforce its judgments. If the Court becomes too far out of step with public opinion, the Court risks noncompliance or public resistance. As *Cooper* dramatically illustrates, there was widespread opposition to the Court's decision in Brown v. Board of Education mandating desegregation. Indeed, there is considerable evidence that the Court anticipated societal opposition and deliberately chose a "go slow" approach. In other words, rather than demanding an immediate end to segregation, the Court

---

BACKGROUND
The Supreme Court and Life Tenure

Proponents of judicial review often point out that federal judges are appointed for life and therefore have the independence to follow their consciences. Federal judges are unlikely to be subject to the sways and influences of the times or the prevailing political winds. But does life tenure also have disadvantages? Some justices serve for very long periods of time, spanning multiple presidential administrations. For example, Justice William O. Douglas was appointed to the Supreme Court in 1939 and served until 1972. Do justices become out of touch after such a long stint on the Court? Is it good for judges to have life tenure and never have to face the electorate? But are there political checks even on life appointees? If the Court gets too far out of step with the electorate, do the President and Congress have ways to bring them back in line? If so, what are they?

---

ordered that desegregation take place with "all deliberate speed." In fact, because of the opposition, the Court did little to enforce its mandate for many years. When the Court did move to end segregation, it still encountered significant opposition and ultimately depended on elected officials to enforce its mandate. In Little Rock, federal officials in the Executive Branch ultimately moved to force compliance.

B. RESTRAINTS ON JUDICIAL AUTHORITY

Even if we accept Justice Marshall's assertion that it is "emphatically the province and duty of the judiciary to say what the law is," there are numerous restraints on judicial authority. Some of these restraints are self-imposed, while others are imposed by the Constitution or other sources. In the remainder of this chapter, we consider the nature and impact of the various restraints.

1. Practical Limitations on Judicial Authority

There are a number of intensely practical limitations on the U.S. Supreme Court's ability to declare "what the law is." Because the Court can hear only a limited number of cases per year, the Court has always regarded its jurisdiction as discretionary rather than mandatory. As Rule 10 of the Court's rules make clear, even if the Court perceives that a lower court has erred, the Court can (and often does) decline to review the case. The Court tends to focus on important federal questions.

Rule 10. Considerations Governing Review on Certiorari

Review on a writ of certiorari is not a matter of right, but of judicial discretion. A petition for a writ of certiorari will be granted only for compelling reasons. The following, although neither controlling nor fully measuring the Court's discretion, indicate the character of the reasons the Court considers:

(a) a United States court of appeals has entered a decision in conflict with the decision of another United States court of appeals on the same important matter; has decided an important federal question in a way that conflicts with a decision by a state court of last resort; or has so far departed from the accepted and usual course of judicial proceedings, or sanctioned such a departure by a lower court, as to call for an exercise of this Court's supervisory power;

(b) a state court of last resort has decided an important federal question in a way that conflicts with the decision of another state court of last resort or of a United States court of appeals;

(c) a state court or a United States court of appeals has decided an important question of federal law that has not been, but should be, settled by this Court, or has decided an important federal question in a way that conflicts with relevant decisions of this Court.

A petition for a writ of certiorari is rarely granted when the asserted error consists of erroneous factual findings or the misapplication of a properly stated rule of law.

The discretionary nature of the Court's authority is revealed in its case statistics. Over the last two-plus centuries of the Court's existence, it has heard more and more cases For example, compared with only 51 cases on the Court's docket in 1853, the number had risen to 8,000 cases by the mid-1990s. Despite the dramatic increase, the Court is able to hear only a very small percentage of the cases presented to it. In fact, the number of cases actually heard and decided by the Court on the merits has been declining. Whereas the Court issued 145 signed opinions in 1986, the number of signed opinions had dipped to 75 by 1995. See Joan Biskupic & Elder Witt, *Guide to the U.S. Supreme Court* 494 (3d ed., Congressional Quarterly Books 1996).

2. *Congressional Control over Federal Court Jurisdiction*

An additional limitation on the Court's authority comes from the Constitution itself, and in particular Article III, which defines the Court's jurisdiction. Article III, Section 2, Clause 2 gives the Supreme Court original jurisdiction over cases involving "Ambassadors, other Public Ministers and Consuls, and those in which a State shall be a Party," and also gives the Court appellate jurisdiction "with such Exceptions, and under such Regulations as the Congress shall make." Given that most cases arrive at the Court by appeal, Congress's control over the Court's appellate jurisdiction represents a potentially significant restraint on the Court's power and prestige.

From a congressional perspective, the "with such Exceptions and under such Regulations" language gives Congress a possible avenue for reining in the U.S. Supreme Court's jurisdiction. Over the last 30 years, members of Congress have introduced bills designed to strip the Court of its jurisdiction over such controversial issues as school prayer, abortion, school busing, and the exclusionary evidence rule. During his tenure in the U.S. Senate, the late Senator Jesse Helms was distressed by the Court's decisions on school prayer (stating that state-sponsored prayer in the public schools violated the Establishment Clause of the First Amendment). In an effort to overturn those decisions, Helms proposed a constitutional amendment allowing state-sponsored prayer in public schools. When the amendment effort failed, he proposed to strip the federal courts (both the lower federal courts and the U.S. Supreme Court) of their authority to hear school prayer cases. As you read the following cases, think about the constitutionality of such a court-stripping bill.

Ex Parte McCardle

74 U.S. 506 (1868)

THE CHIEF JUSTICE delivered the opinion of the court.

[William McCardle was charged with libel and other offenses for publishing newspaper articles about the post–Civil War military government in Mississippi. He sought a writ of habeas corpus from a federal court, but the writ was denied. McCardle then appealed to the U.S. Supreme Court. While the case was pending, Congress passed an act repealing the Court's jurisdiction over the case.]

The first question necessarily is that of jurisdiction; for, if the act of March, 1868, takes away the jurisdiction defined by the act of February, 1867, it is useless, if not improper, to enter into any discussion of other questions.

It is quite true, as was argued by the counsel for the petitioner, that the appellate jurisdiction of this court is not derived from acts of Congress. It is, strictly speaking, conferred by the Constitution. But it is conferred 'with such exceptions and under such regulations as Congress shall make.'

It is unnecessary to consider whether, if Congress had made no exceptions and no regulations, this court might not have exercised general appellate jurisdiction under rules prescribed by itself. For among the earliest acts of the first Congress, at its first session, was the act of September 24th, 1789, to establish the judicial courts of the United States. That act provided for the organization of this court, and prescribed regulations for the exercise of its jurisdiction.

The source of that jurisdiction, and the limitations of it by the Constitution and by statute, have been on several occasions subjects of consideration here. In the case of Durousseau v. The United States, particularly, the whole matter was carefully examined, and the court held, that while 'the appellate powers of this court are not given by the judicial act, but are given by the Constitution,' they are, nevertheless, 'limited and regulated by that act, and by such other acts as have been passed on the subject.' The court said, further, that the judicial act was an exercise of the power given by the Constitution to Congress 'of making exceptions to the appellate jurisdiction of the Supreme Court.' 'They have described affirmatively,' said the court, 'its jurisdiction, and this affirmative description has been understood to imply a negation of the exercise of such appellate power as is not comprehended within it.' . . .

The principle that the affirmation of appellate jurisdiction implies the negation of all such jurisdiction not affirmed having been thus established, it was an almost necessary consequence that acts of Congress, providing for the exercise of jurisdiction, should come to be spoken of as acts granting jurisdiction, and not as acts making exceptions to the constitutional grant of it.

The exception to appellate jurisdiction in the case before us, however, is not an inference from the affirmation of other appellate jurisdiction. It is made in terms. The provision of the act of 1867, affirming the appellate jurisdiction of this court in cases of habeas corpus, is expressly repealed. It is hardly possible to imagine a plainer instance of positive exception.

We are not at liberty to inquire into the motives of the legislature. We can only examine into its power under the Constitution; and the power to make exceptions to the appellate jurisdiction of this court is given by express words.

What, then, is the effect of the repealing act upon the case before us? We cannot doubt as to this. Without jurisdiction the court cannot proceed at all in any cause. Jurisdiction is power to declare the law, and when it ceases to exist, the only function remaining to the court is that of announcing the fact and dismissing the cause. And this is not less clear upon authority than upon principle.

Several cases were cited by the counsel for the petitioner in support of the position that jurisdiction of this case is not affected by the repealing act. But none of them, in our judgment, afford any support to it. They are all cases of the exercise of judicial power by the legislature, or of legislative interference with courts in the exercising of continuing jurisdiction. . . .

It is quite clear, therefore, that this court cannot proceed to pronounce judgment in this case, for it has no longer jurisdiction of the appeal; and judicial duty is not less fitly performed by declining ungranted jurisdiction than in exercising firmly that which the Constitution and the laws confer.

Counsel seem to have supposed, if effect be given to the repealing act in question, that the whole appellate power of the court, in cases of habeas corpus, is denied. But this is an error. The act of 1868 does not except from that jurisdiction any cases but appeals from Circuit Courts under the act of 1867. It does not affect the jurisdiction which was previously exercised.

The appeal of the petitioner in this case must be
Dismissed for Want of Jurisdiction.

Notes: Klein *and* Plaut

1. *The* Klein *Decision.* Just three years after *McCardle*, the Court decided
United States v. Klein, 80 U.S. 128 (1871), involving a law that authorized the
government to seize abandoned or captured property from those who had aided,
countenanced, and abetted the Confederacy during the Civil War. Pursuant to
this law, the United States seized V.F. Wilson's cotton, sold it, and placed the proceeds in the U.S. Treasury. Prior to his death, Wilson took advantage of a presidential proclamation offering a "full pardon" with restoration of all rights to
those who agreed to "take and keep inviolate a prescribed oath" to support the
Constitution of the United States and the union of the states thereunder. After
Wilson's death, Klein, the administrator of Wilson's estate, sued to recover proceeds from the sale of the cotton, claiming that the pardon had restored Wilson's
rights and property.

Klein won in the Court of Claims, and the government appealed to the U.S.
Supreme Court. While the appeal was pending, Congress passed a statute declaring that a presidential pardon shall not be admissible in the Court of Claims to
support a claim for recovery. The statute also provided that, to the extent that the
Court of Claims has ruled in favor of a claimant based on a presidential pardon:
"[T]he Supreme Court, on appeal, shall have no further jurisdiction of the cause,
and shall dismiss the same for want of jurisdiction. It is further provided that
whenever any pardon, granted to any suitor in the Court of Claims, for the proceeds of captured and abandoned property, shall recite in substance that the person pardoned took part in the late rebellion, or was guilty of any act of rebellion
or disloyalty, and shall have been accepted in writing without express disclaimer
and protestation against the fact so recited, such pardon or acceptance shall be
taken as conclusive evidence in the Court of Claims, and on appeal, that the
claimant did give aid to the rebellion; and on proof of such pardon, or acceptance, which proof may be made summarily on motion or otherwise, the jurisdiction of the court shall cease, and the suit shall be forthwith dismissed." The
Supreme Court ruled the statute unconstitutional and refused to apply it:

> [T]he language of the proviso shows plainly that it does not intend to withhold appellate
> jurisdiction except as a means to an end. Its great and controlling purpose is to deny to par-
> dons granted by the President the effect which this court had adjudged them to have. The
> proviso declares that pardons shall not be considered by this court on appeal. We had already
> decided that it was our duty to consider them and give them effect, in cases like the present,
> as equivalent to proof of loyalty. . . . It seems to us that this is not an exercise of the acknowl-
> edged power of Congress to make exceptions and prescribe regulations to the appellate
> power.
>
> The court is required to ascertain the existence of certain facts and thereupon to declare
> that its jurisdiction on appeal has ceased, by dismissing the bill. What is this but to prescribe
> a rule for the decision of a cause in a particular way? In the case before us, the Court of Claims

has rendered judgment for the claimant and an appeal has been taken to this court. We are directed to dismiss the appeal, if we find that the judgment must be affirmed, because of a pardon granted to the intestate of the claimants. Can we do so without allowing one party to the controversy to decide it in its own favor? Can we do so without allowing that the legislature may prescribe rules of decision to the Judicial Department of the government in cases pending before it? We think not. . . .

We must think that Congress has inadvertently passed the limit which separates the legislative from the judicial power. . . . Congress has already provided that the Supreme Court shall have jurisdiction of the judgments of the Court of Claims on appeal. Can it prescribe a rule in conformity with which the court must deny to itself the jurisdiction thus conferred, because and only because its decision, in accordance with settled law, must be adverse to the government and favorable to the suitor? This question seems to us to answer itself.

See also Ex Parte Yerger, 75 U.S. (8 Wall.) 75 (1869).

2. *The* Plaut *Decision.* In Plaut v. Spendthrift Farm, Inc., 514 U.S. 211 (1995), petitioners brought a civil action for fraud and deceit in the sale of stock in violation of Section 10(b) of the Securities Exchange Act of 1934 and Rule 10b-5 of the Securities and Exchange Commission. In prior cases, the Court had held that Section 10(b) and Rule 10b-5 litigation must be commenced within one year after the discovery of the facts constituting the violation and within three years after such violation. These prior holdings were applied to the petitioner's suit and led to dismissal. Subsequently, Congress passed the Federal Deposit Insurance Corporation Improvement Act of 1991. Section 476 of the Act became Section 27A of the Securities Exchange Act of 1934, which provided that, when an action was commenced prior to a certain date, that "would have been timely filed under the limitation period provided by the laws applicable in the jurisdiction, including principles of retroactivity, as such laws existed on June 19, 1991." Because petitioners had filed their case prior to June 19, 1991, they moved to reinstate the action previously dismissed with prejudice. The Court held that Congress exceeded its authority by requiring the federal courts to exercise "the judicial Power of the United States" in a manner repugnant to the text, structure, and traditions of Article III: "[The Act] offends a postulate of Article III [deeply] rooted in our law. . . . Article III establishes a 'judicial department' with the 'province and duty [to] say what the law is' in particular cases and controversies. [The] Framers crafted this charter of the judicial department with an expressed understanding that it gives the Federal Judiciary the power, not merely to rule on cases, but to decide them, subject to review only by superior courts in the Article III hierarchy — [in] short, that 'a judgment conclusively resolves the case' because a 'judicial Power' is one to render dispositive judgments. [By] retroactively commanding the federal courts to reopen final judgments, Congress has violated this fundamental principle [and] effects a clear violation of the separation-of-powers principle. . . . When retroactive legislation requires its own application in a case already finally adjudicated, it does no more and no less than 'reverse a determination once made, in a particular case.'" Justice Stevens, joined by Justice Ginsburg, dissented: "A large class of investors reasonably and in good faith thought they possessed rights of action before the surprising announcement of the Lampf rule on June 20, 1991. . . . Congress' decision to extend that rule and procedure

to 10b-5 actions dismissed during the brief period between this Court's law-changing decision in *Lampf* and Congress' remedial action is not a sufficient reason to hold the statute unconstitutional."

Note: McCardle*'s Precedential Value*

Some have questioned whether *McCardle* retains vitality after *Klein*. Consider Justice Douglas's dissent in Glidden v. Zdanok, 370 U.S. 530, 605 n.11 (1962) (Douglas, J., dissenting), flatly stated that there "is serious question whether the *McCardle* case could command a majority view today." Former Yale professor, and rejected Supreme Court nominee, Robert Bork stated that "*McCardle* is a rather enigmatic precedent. If it stands for the proposition that Congress may take away any category of the Supreme Court's jurisdiction, it obviously is capable of destroying the entire institution of judicial review since Marbury v. Madison. So read, there is good reason to doubt *McCardle's* vitality as a precedent today." Robert Bork, *Constitutionality of the President's Busing Proposals* 7 (American Enterprise Institute 1972).

∽ PROBLEM: MORE ON THE HEALTH CARE LEGISLATION ∽

Now, let's think more about the health care problem described at the beginning of the chapter. Suppose that, after the plaintiffs challenge the law, Congress passes a law prohibiting the U.S. Supreme Court from exercising appellate jurisdiction over cases challenging the legislation. Would such a law be constitutional? As you think about that issue, consider the following questions.

Questions: Congressional Regulation of Judicial Power

1. *Does* McCardle *Give Congress Plenary Authority over the Supreme Court's Appellate Jurisdiction?* During the 1970s and 1980s, some members of Congress, unhappy with the Court's decisions on controversial issues like school prayer, abortion, and school busing, sought to remove the Court's appellate authority over those issues. In recent years, some have suggested that the Court should be deprived of the authority to hear appeals involving the Pledge of Allegiance (and the claim that the Pledge involves an unconstitutional establishment of religion). Suppose that Congress decides to pass a law stripping the Court of its review authority over issues like school prayer, busing, and the Ten Commandments. Would such a law be constitutional?

2. *Can Congress Take Away the Supreme Court's Original Jurisdiction?* McCardle recognizes that Congress has broad power to limit the Supreme Court's appellate jurisdiction. But what about the Supreme Court's original jurisdiction? Article III, Section 2 read in its entirety states as follows: "In all Cases affecting Ambassadors, other public Ministers and Consuls, and those in which a State shall be a

Party, the supreme Court shall have original Jurisdiction. In all the other Cases before mentioned [i.e., mentioned in §1], the supreme Court shall have appellate jurisdiction, both as to Law and Fact, with such Exceptions and under such Regulations as the Congress shall make." Section 2 clearly provides Congress leeway to make "exceptions and regulations" to the Court's appellate jurisdiction. Does it also allow Congress to strip the Court of both its original jurisdiction and its appellate authority over issues like busing and school prayer?

3. *Alternatively, Does the Supreme Court Have an "Essential Constitutional Role"?* Some commentators have argued that, even though Congress has the authority to make "exceptions" to the Supreme Court's jurisdiction, as well as to "regulate" that jurisdiction, Congress cannot "destroy the *essential role* of the Supreme Court in the constitutional plan." Henry M. Hart, *The Power of Congress to Limit the Jurisdiction of Federal Courts: An Exercise in Dialectic*, 66 Harv. L. Rev. 1362, 1365 (1953) (emphasis added). A second commentator agrees: "It is not reasonable to conclude that the Constitution gave Congress the power to destroy that role. Reasonably interpreted the clause means 'With such exceptions and under such regulations as Congress may make,' not inconsistent with the essential functions of the Supreme Court under this Constitution." Leonard G. Ratner, *Congressional Power over the Appellate Jurisdiction of the Supreme Court*, 109 U. Pa. L. Rev. 157 (1960). At least one commentator disagrees with these assessments: "[The] courts do not pass on constitutional questions because there is a special function vested in them to enforce the Constitution or police the other agencies of government. They do so rather for the reason that they must decide a litigated case that is otherwise within their jurisdiction and in doing so must give effect to the supreme law of the land." Herbert Wechsler, *The Courts and the Constitution*, 65 Colum. L. Rev. 1001, 1005-1006 (1965).

Which of these views is more consistent with *Marbury*? Does *Marbury* really make it "the province and duty of the judicial department to say what the law is," or does the judiciary share this authority with other branches? If Congress strips the Court of its review authority over controversial issues, who decides those issues? What is the ultimate effect on constitutional interpretation? Is it relevant that Congress has gradually eliminated the categories of cases in which the Court must hear an appeal, and expanded the scope of the Court's discretionary jurisdiction, to the point where the Court's appellate docket consists almost entirely of cases it has chosen to hear? Today, thousands of petitions are filed with the Court every year, asking it to hear an appeal, and the Court typically grants fewer than 100. Thus, a case that comes up through the state system will probably be heard only by state courts, even if a federal question is involved.

4. *If the Court Has an "Essential Role," What Is That Role?* Consider the statements of one commentator: "The supremacy clause of Article VI mandates one supreme federal law throughout the land, and Article III establishes the Supreme Court as the constitutional instrument for implementing that clause. [I]ts essential functions under the Constitution are: 1) ultimately to resolve inconsistent or conflicting interpretations of federal law, and particularly of the Constitution, by state and federal courts; 2) to maintain the supremacy of federal law, and particularly the Constitution, when it conflicts with state law or is challenged by state

authority." Ratner, *supra.* Do you agree with this characterization of the Court's "essential constitutional role"? Is there a preferable way to define that role?

5. *Must Some Federal Court Be Available to Hear All Federal Questions?* In *McCardle,* the habeas plaintiff could have had his case heard in the lower federal courts. Can Congress go even further and deprive all federal courts of the authority to hear particular types of federal question claims? This question is not completely hypothetical. Over the last hundred years, Congress has considered bills designed to accomplish exactly this result. In the last several decades, Congress has considered bills that would have stripped all federal courts of jurisdiction over cases involving busing and abortion. Moreover, Article III, Section 1 authorizes the creation of the lower federal courts: "The judicial Power of the United States, shall be vested in one supreme Court, and in such inferior Courts as the Congress may from time to time ordain and establish." Since Congress has the power to "ordain and establish" inferior federal courts, it also has the power to abolish them as well as to limit their jurisdiction. *See* Yakus v. United States, 321 U.S. 414 (1944); Lockerty v. Phillips, 319 U.S. 182 (1943); Sheldon v. Sill, 49 U.S. (8 How.) 441 (1850).

Despite Congress's authority, may it strip the lower federal courts of their jurisdiction over an issue (e.g., school prayer or busing) and simultaneously strip the Supreme Court of its appellate jurisdiction over that same issue? If such bills had passed, would they be constitutional? Consider the following perspectives:

A. "To remove or permit the removal from the entire federal judiciary, including the Supreme Court, of the constitutional review of state conduct would be to alter the balance of federal authority fundamentally and dangerously." Lawrence Gene Sager, *Foreword: Constitutional Limitations on Congress' Authority to Regulate the Jurisdiction of the Federal Courts,* 95 Harv. L. Rev. 17, 55 (1981).

B. The Constitution does not prohibit this sort of comprehensive stripping of jurisdiction. The Framers considered the state courts to have played a crucial role in the protection of federal constitutional rights, and thus should not be viewed as having required federal court jurisdiction over all federal question cases. See Henry M. Hart, *The Power of Congress to Limit the Jurisdiction of the Federal Courts: An Exercise in Dialectic,* 66 Harv. L. Rev. 1363 (1953).

C. Joseph Story, a Supreme Court justice in the early nineteenth century, believed not only that some federal court had to be available to hear every federal question case, but also that some federal question cases should be heard *only* by a federal court.

Which perspective is preferable? Does it matter that some state judges lack the life tenure provisions granted to federal judges? In some states, in fact, judges must stand for election. Also, does it or should it matter that most appeals to the Supreme Court stand only a very small chance of being heard?

3. The Political Question Doctrine

Even though the Court may have the authority to say what the law is, are there situations in which the Court should decline to exercise its authority? Should the Court decline out of respect for coordinate branches of government, for the individual states, or for the political process? In this section, we examine the so-called "political question" doctrine, which operates as a limitation on judicial authority.

Baker v. Carr

369 U.S. 186 (1962)

Justice BRENNAN delivered the opinion of the court.

[Tennessee's legislature apportioned legislative districts in 1901 but refused to do so again for more than 60 years. During the intervening period, Tennessee's legislative districts became so malapportioned that 37 percent of Tennessee voters elected 20 of the 33 senators and 40 percent of the voters elected 60 of the 99 House members. Plaintiffs challenged Tennessee's system for electing its state legislature, alleging that the state legislative districts were so grossly malapportioned with respect to population that the apportionment scheme denied plaintiffs' constitutional rights to equal protection. The district court dismissed the lawsuit on the ground that it presented a nonjusticiable political question.]

[We] hold that this challenge to an apportionment presents no nonjusticiable "political question." [Of] course the mere fact that the suit seeks protection of a political right does not mean it presents a political question. Such an objection "is little more than a play upon words."

[Our discussion requires] review of a number of political question cases, in order to expose the attributes of the doctrine — attributes which, in various settings, diverge, combine, appear, and disappear in seeming disorderliness. . . . It is the relationship between the judiciary and the coordinate branches of the Federal Government, and not the federal judiciary's relationship to the States, which gives rise to the "political question."

"[In] determining whether a question falls within (the political question) category, the appropriateness under our system of government of attributing finality to the action of the political departments and also the lack of satisfactory criteria for a judicial determination are dominant considerations." [The] nonjusticiability of a political question is primarily a function of the separation of powers. Much confusion results from the capacity of the "political question" label to obscure the need for case-by-case inquiry. Deciding whether a matter has in any measure been committed by the Constitution to another branch of government, or whether the action of that branch exceeds whatever authority has been committed, is itself a delicate exercise in constitutional interpretation, and is a responsibility of this Court as ultimate interpreter of the Constitution. To demonstrate this requires no less than to analyze representative cases and to infer from them the analytical threads that make up the political question doctrine. We shall then show that none of those threads catches this case.

Foreign relations: There are sweeping statements to the effect that all questions touching foreign relations are political questions. Not only does resolution of such issues frequently turn on standards that defy judicial application, or involve the exercise of a discretion demonstrably committed to the executive or legislature; but many such questions uniquely demand single-voiced statement of the Government's views. Yet it is error to suppose that every case or controversy which touches foreign relations lies beyond judicial cognizance. Our cases in this field seem invariably to show a discriminating analysis of the particular question posed, in terms of the history of its management by the political branches, of its susceptibility to judicial handling in the light of its nature and posture in the specific case, and of the possible consequences of judicial action. For example, though a court will not ordinarily inquire whether a treaty has been terminated, since on that question "governmental action [must] be regarded as of controlling importance," if there has been no conclusive "governmental action" then a court can construe a treaty and may find it provides the answer. . . . Though a court will not undertake to construe a treaty in a manner inconsistent with a subsequent federal statute, no similar hesitancy obtains if the asserted clash is with state law. . . .

While recognition of foreign governments so strongly defies judicial treatment that without executive recognition a foreign state has been called "a republic of whose existence we know nothing," and the judiciary ordinarily follows the executive as to which nation has sovereignty over disputed territory, once sovereignty over an area is politically determined and declared, courts may examine the resulting status and decide independently whether a statute applies to that area. Similarly, recognition of belligerency abroad is an executive responsibility, but if the executive proclamations fall short of an explicit answer, a court may construe them seeking, for example, to determine whether the situation is such that statutes designed to assure American neutrality have become operative.

Dates of duration of hostilities: Though it has been stated broadly that "the power which declared the necessity is the power to declare its cessation, and what the cessation requires," [here] too analysis reveals isolable reasons for the presence of political questions, underlying this Court's refusal to review the political departments' determination of when or whether a war has ended. Dominant is the need for finality in the political determination, for emergency's nature demands "A prompt and unhesitating obedience." [But] deference rests on reason, not habit. The question in a particular case may not seriously implicate considerations of finality — e.g., a public program of importance (rent control) yet not central to the emergency effort. Further, clearly definable criteria for decision may be available. In such case the political question barrier falls away: "[On] the other hand, even in private litigation which directly implicates no feature of separation of powers, lack of judicially discoverable standards and the drive for even-handed application may impel reference to the political departments' determination of dates of hostilities" beginning and ending. . . .

Validity of enactments: In Coleman v. Miller [307 U.S. 433 (1939)], this Court held that the questions of how long a proposed amendment to the Federal Constitution remained open to ratification, and what effect a prior rejection had on a subsequent ratification, were committed to congressional resolution and involved criteria of decision that necessarily escaped the judicial grasp. Similar considerations apply to the enacting process: "The respect due to coequal and independent departments," and the need for finality and certainty about the status of a statute contribute to judicial reluctance to inquire whether, as passed, it complied with all requisite formalities. . . . But it is not true that courts will never delve into a legislature's records upon such a quest: If the enrolled statute lacks an effective date, a court will not hesitate to seek it in the legislative journals in order to preserve the enactment. The political question doctrine, a tool for maintenance of governmental order, will not be so applied as to promote only disorder. . . .

We come, finally, to the ultimate inquiry whether our precedents as to what constitutes a nonjusticiable "political question" bring the case before us under the umbrella of that doctrine. A natural beginning is to note whether any of the common characteristics which we have been able to identify and label descriptively are present. We find none: The question here is the consistency of state action with the Federal Constitution. We have no question decided, or to be decided, by a political branch of government coequal with this Court. Nor do we risk embarrassment of our government abroad, or grave disturbance at home if we take issue with Tennessee as to the constitutionality of her action here challenged. Nor need the appellants, in order to succeed in this action, ask the Court to enter upon policy determinations for which judicially manageable standards are lacking. Judicial standards under the Equal Protection Clause are well developed and familiar, and it has been open to courts since the enactment of the Fourteenth Amendment to determine, if on the particular facts they must, that a discrimination reflects no policy, but simply arbitrary and capricious action. . . .

We conclude that the complaint's allegations of a denial of equal protection present a justiciable constitutional cause of action upon which appellants are entitled to a trial and a decision. The right asserted is within the reach of judicial protection under the Fourteenth Amendment.

The judgment of the District Court is reversed and the case is remanded for further proceedings consistent with this opinion.

Notes: The Political Question Doctrine

1. *The Rhode Island Constitution.* Following the American Revolution, Rhode Island continued to function under a royal charter issued by Charles II in 1663. In the 1840s, Rhode Island citizens called a constitutional convention to draft a state constitution. Although the resulting constitution was ratified by a vote of the people, and elections were held under its provisions, the charter government refused to recognize the constitution or the officials elected under it. When the charter government declared a state of martial law and used force to put down what it perceived as a "rebellion" by sending soldiers to search Martin Luther's house, the homeowner sued the soldiers for trespass. The soldiers defended on the basis that they were acting pursuant to governmental authority, thus presenting the question of whether the charter government or the constitutionally elected government constituted the legitimate authority. If the charter government was the legitimate government, then the soldiers could claim a defense in the trespass suit. In Luther v. Borden, 48 U.S. (7 How.) 1 (1849), the Court held that the case presented a nonjusticiable political question and refused to decide whether the government was legitimate: "The fourth section of the fourth article of the Constitution of the United States provides that the United States shall guarantee to every State in the Union a republican form of government. . . .

Under this article of the Constitution it rests with Congress to decide what government is the established one in a State. . . . And its decision is binding on every other department of the government, and could not be questioned in a judicial tribunal. It is true [that] Congress was not called upon to decide the controversy. Yet the right to decide is placed there, and not in the courts. . . . This tribunal [should] be the last to overstep the boundaries which limit its own jurisdiction. And while it should always be ready to meet any question confided to it by the Constitution, it is equally its duty not to pass beyond its appropriate sphere of action, and to take care not to involve itself in discussions which properly belong to other forums."

2. *Termination of the Taiwan Treaty.* In Goldwater v. Carter, 444 U.S. 996 (1979), the Court held that President Carter's decision to terminate a treaty with Taiwan, and to recognize instead the People's Republic of China, constituted a political question. The decision was challenged by members of Congress who sought declaratory and injunctive relief regarding the method by which a treaty could be terminated. Plaintiffs claimed that, since the Constitution requires Congress to ratify treaties, the Constitution implicitly requires that treaty terminations require ratification as well. President Carter argued that the Constitution's silence on the method by which a treaty could be terminated gave him unilateral authority to decide whether to continue or to terminate a treaty. A concurring Justice Powell disagreed with the Court's decision to dismiss: "[The] text of the Constitution does not unquestionably commit the power to terminate treaties to the President alone. . . . We are asked to decide whether the President may terminate a treaty under the Constitution without congressional approval. Resolution of the question may not be easy, but it only requires us to apply normal principles of interpretation to the constitutional provisions at issue. The present case involves neither review of the President's activities as Commander in Chief nor impermissible interference in the field of foreign affairs. . . . Interpretation of the Constitution does not imply lack of respect for a coordinate branch. If the President and the Congress had reached irreconcilable positions, final disposition of the question presented by this case would eliminate, rather than create, multiple constitutional interpretations. [The] suggestion that this case presents a political question is incompatible with this Court's willingness on previous occasions to decide whether one branch of our Government has impinged upon the power of another."

3. *Blocking the Elected Candidate.* In Powell v. McCormack, 395 U.S. 486 (1969), the Court rejected the argument that only the House of Representatives could decide whether to seat Adam Clayton Powell, Jr. After Powell was duly elected to the U.S. House of Representatives, the House refused to seat him because he had engaged in misconduct. The Court concluded that Article I, Section 5 of the Constitution (which provides that "[e]ach House shall be the Judge of the Elections, Returns, and Qualifications of its own Members") creates a "'textually demonstrable constitutional commitment' to the House of the 'adjudicatory power' to determine Powell's qualifications." However, the Court concluded that this textual commitment extended only to the question of "the qualifications

expressly set forth in the Constitution." The House conceded that Powell met those requirements; "[The] 'textual commitment' formulation of the political question doctrine does not bar federal courts from adjudicating petitioners' claims [that he was improperly expelled for other reasons]. Therefore, we hold that, since Adam Clayton Powell, Jr., was duly elected by the voters of the 18th Congressional District of New York and was not ineligible to serve under any provision of the Constitution, the House was without power to exclude him from its membership."

∿ PROBLEMS: SCOPE OF THE POLITICAL QUESTION DOCTRINE ∿

1. *The Scope of the Judicial Function.* Following the Court's decision in *Baker*, suppose that a federal court concludes that Tennessee's apportionment system violates the Equal Protection Clause of the U.S. Constitution. Once the court makes that declaration, what is the judicial role? The plaintiffs in *Baker* asked the Court to declare the 1901 legislation unconstitutional, and to order statewide elections for legislators without regard to counties or districts. Should a federal court enter such an order? Alternatively, does *Marbury* suggest that the federal court has the power to reapportion Tennessee's districts itself? What alternatives are available to the Court?

2. *The Health Care Legislation and the Political Question Doctrine.* Now, refer back to the health care legislation described in the opening problem. If you are the judge assigned to hear the case, should you dismiss the challenges to that legislation on the theory that the case involves a nonjusticiable political question? Why or why not?

3. *The Disputed Presidential Election.* The presidential election of 2000 hinged on the question of which candidate received the most popular votes in the State of Florida and captured that state's electoral votes. Based on the initial tally, then Governor Bush was thought to have won Florida by a margin of 1,784 votes. After much litigation in the Florida courts, which led to ballot recounts, the case was brought before the U.S. Supreme Court with Bush seeking to challenge the Florida Supreme Court's decision to order yet another ballot recount. Two questions were presented to the Court: 1) whether the Florida Supreme Court established new standards for resolving presidential election contests, thereby violating Article II, Section 1, Clause 2 of the U.S. Constitution, and failing to comply with 3 U.S.C. §5; and 2) whether the use of a standardless manual recount violates the Equal Protection and Due Process Clauses. In effect, the Court's decision in the case would (and ultimately did) determine the outcome of the presidential election. Should the U.S. Supreme Court have dismissed the challenge on the basis of the political question doctrine? In thinking about this issue, what weight do you give to the fact that the "Constitution assigns to the States the primary responsibility for determining the manner of selecting the Presidential electors."

4. *Combat Operations.* During the Vietnam War, a congresswoman and some air force officers sought to challenge the validity of combat operations being conducted in Cambodia. Article I, Section 8 of the U.S. Constitution provides that Congress shall have the power to declare war. By contrast, Article II, Section 2 provides that the President is the "Commander in Chief of the Army and Navy of the United States, and of the militia of the several States, when called into the actual service of the United States." Suppose that plaintiffs point to various congressional enactments declaring and requiring a cessation of hostilities. Defendants respond by pointing to congressional funding appropriations, which they claim authorize the war. Is it appropriate for a court to rule on whether the military action constitutes a "war" and whether congressional approval is required (or has been given)? If the court answers both of these questions in the affirmative, is it appropriate for the court to issue an order prohibiting further combat operations in Cambodia? If the courts are unwilling to intervene, how will these issues be resolved? *Compare* Holtzman v. Schlesinger, 361 F. Supp. 553 (D.C.N.Y. 1973), *with* Holtzman v. Schlesinger, 484 F.2d 1307 (2d Cir. 1973); *see also* DaCasta v. Laird, 471 F.2d 1146 (2d Cir. 1973); Sarnoff v. Connally, 457 F.2d 809 (9th Cir. 1972); Orlando v. Laird, 443 F.2d 1039 (2d Cir. 1971). Other decisions dealing with undeclared wars include Crockett v. Reagan, 720 F.2d 1355 (D.C. Cir. 1983); Campbell v. Clinton, 52 F. Supp. 2d 34 (D.D.C. 1999); Ange v. Bush, 752 F. Supp. 509 (D.D.C. 1990).

C. THE CASE OR CONTROVERSY REQUIREMENT

Article III, Section 2 of the U.S. Constitution contains perhaps the most important limitation on judicial power: the "case" and "controversy" requirement. This limitation has spawned multiple restrictions on the scope of judicial authority, including the prohibition against advisory opinions, the ripeness and mootness doctrines, and the standing requirement.

1. The Prohibition Against Advisory Opinions

The prohibition against advisory opinions is of long standing. In 1793, Secretary of State Thomas Jefferson solicited input from the U.S. Supreme Court regarding whether "it would be available in the solution of important questions of the construction of treaties, laws of nations and laws of the land, which the Secretary said were often presented under circumstances which 'do not give a cognizance of them to the tribunals of the country.'" *See* Muskrat v. United States, 219 U.S. 346 (1911). Chief Justice Jay and his associates responded that "'the lines of separation drawn by the Constitution between the three departments of government [afford] strong arguments against the propriety of extrajudicially deciding the questions alluded to, and expressing the view that the power given by the Constitution to the President, of calling on heads of departments for opinions, seems to have been purposely, as well as expressly, united to the executive departments.' *Correspondence & Public Papers of John Jay*, vol. 3, p. 486." *Id.* The justices also noted that "[b]y the express terms of the Constitution, the exercise of the judicial power is limited to 'cases' and 'controversies.' Beyond this it does not extend, and unless it is asserted in a case or controversy within the meaning of the Constitution, the power to exercise it is nowhere conferred."

What constitutes a "case" or "controversy?" In *Muskrat*, the Court suggested that the phrase "cases and controversies" refers to "the claims of litigants brought before the courts for determination by such regular proceedings as are established by law or custom for the protection or enforcement of rights, or the prevention, redress, or punishment of wrongs. Whenever the claim of a party under the Constitution, laws, or treaties of the United States takes such a form that the judicial power is capable of acting upon it, then it has become a case. The term implies

---

BACKGROUND
Declaratory Judgments

In Piedmont & Northern Ry. Co. v. United States, 280 U.S. 469 (1930), the Court held that the federal courts did not have jurisdiction to entertain a declaratory judgment action: "What plaintiffs are seeking is, therefore, in substance, a declaratory judgment. . . . Such a remedy is not within either the statutory or the equity jurisdiction of federal courts." In later decisions, the Court recognized the power of the federal courts to render declaratory judgments provided that the litigation actually presents a case or controversy.

---

the existence of present or possible adverse parties, whose contentions are submitted to the court for adjudication."

∽ PROBLEMS: DECLARATORY JUDGMENTS AND ADVISORY OPINIONS ∽

1. *The Health Care Litigation.* Let's return to the health care legislation again. If you are the judge assigned to hear the two cases, would you conclude that they present "cases" and "controversies"? Alternatively, if you hear the cases, would you be acting improperly by deciding hypothetical and speculative issues?

2. *The Protestors and the Mayor.* Suppose that a protestor demonstrates daily against the mayor on the sidewalk in front of City Hall in Louisville, Kentucky. Police officers inform the protestor that he will be arrested unless he ceases his protest and leaves the area. The protestor seeks a declaratory judgment that the police officers' actions violated his First Amendment right to freedom of speech. The protestor vows to resume his protest if he receives a favorable ruling in the

declaratory judgment action. If he does not receive a favorable ruling, he will not resume his protest for fear of arrest. Can a federal court consider the protestor's request for declaratory relief, or does the case involve an impermissible request for an advisory opinion? *See* Steffel v. Thompson, 415 U.S. 452 (1974); Samuels v. Mackell, 401 U.S. 66 (1971).

2. Ripeness

The federal courts have insisted that lawsuits be brought at the "right" time. A case that is brought too early is held to be not "ripe" for adjudication. As you read the following cases, ask yourself whether the Court's decision is based on prudential or constitutional requirements, or on a combination of both.

United Public Workers v. Mitchell
330 U.S. 75 (1947)

Mr. Justice REED delivered the opinion of the Court.

The Hatch Act, enacted in 1940, declares unlawful [certain] political activities of federal employees. Section 9 forbids officers and employees in the Executive Branch of the Federal Government, with exceptions, from taking "any active part in political management or in political campaigns." Section 15 declares that the activities [determined] by the United States Civil Service Commission to be prohibited to employees in the classified civil service of the United States by the civil service rules shall be deemed to be prohibited to federal employees covered by the Hatch Act. These sections [cover] all federal officers and employees whether in the classified civil service or not and a penalty of dismissal from employment is imposed for violation. . . .

[A]ppellants sought an injunction [against] the United States Civil Service Commission to prohibit them from enforcing against petitioners the provisions of the second sentence of §9(a) of the Hatch Act. . . . A declaratory judgment [of] unconstitutionality [was] also sought [of the section that] reads, "No officer or employee in the Executive Branch of the Federal Government [shall] take any active part in political management or in political campaigns."

Various individual employees of the federal executive civil service and the United Public Workers of America, a labor union[,] as a representative [of] its members, joined in the suit. It is alleged that the individuals desire to engage in acts of political management and in political campaigns [outside] of the hours of employment. . . . None of the appellants, except George P. Poole, has violated the provisions of the Hatch Act. They wish to act contrary to its provisions and those of §1 of the Civil Service Rules and desire a declaration of the legally permissible limits of regulation. Defendants moved to dismiss [for] lack of a justiciable case or controversy.

[W]e are called upon to decide whether the complaint states a controversy. . . . [T]he federal courts established pursuant to Article III of the Constitution do not render advisory opinions. For adjudication of constitutional issues "concrete legal issues, presented in actual cases, not abstractions" are requisite. This is as true of declaratory judgments as any other field. These appellants seem clearly to seek advisory opinions upon broad claims of rights protected by the First, Fifth, Ninth, and Tenth Amendments to the Constitution[,] but the facts of their personal interest in their civil rights, of the general threat of possible interference with those rights by the Civil Service Commission under its rules, if specified things are done by appellants, does not make a justiciable case or controversy. Appellants want to engage in "political management and political campaigns," to persuade others to follow appellants' views by discussion, speeches, articles, and other acts reasonably designed to secure the selection of appellants' political choices. Such generality of objection is really an attack on the political expediency of the Hatch Act, not the presentation of legal issues. It is beyond the competence of courts to render such a decision.

The power of courts, and ultimately of this Court, to pass upon the constitutionality of acts of Congress arises only when the interests of litigants require the use of this judicial authority for their protection against actual interference. A hypothetical threat is not enough. We can only speculate as to the kinds of political activity the appellants desire to engage in or as to the contents of their proposed public statements or the circumstances of their publication. It would not accord with judicial responsibility to adjudge, in a matter involving constitutionality, between the freedom of the individual and the requirements of public order except when definite rights appear upon the one side and definite prejudicial interferences upon the other.

[When] the courts act [within the] constitutionally imposed boundaries of their power, their ability to perform their function as a balance for the people's protection against abuse of power by other branches of government remains unimpaired. Should the courts seek to expand their power so as to bring under their jurisdiction ill defined controversies over constitutional issues, [s]uch abuse of judicial power would properly meet rebuke and restriction from other branches. [T]he determination of the trial court, that the individual appellants, other than Poole, could maintain this action, was erroneous.

The appellant Poole does present [matters] appropriate for judicial determination. . . . Poole has been charged by the Commission with political activity and a proposed order for his removal from his position adopted. . . . Because we conclude [that] the prohibition of §9 of the Hatch Act and Civil Service Rule 1 are valid, it is unnecessary to consider [whether] or not this appellant sufficiently alleges that an irreparable injury to him would result from his removal from his position. . . .

The judgment of the District Court is accordingly affirmed.

Affirmed.

Mr. Justice DOUGLAS, dissenting in part.

[What] these appellants propose to do is plain enough. If they do what they propose to do, it is clear that they will be discharged from their positions. . . . On a discharge these employees would lose their jobs, their seniority, and other civil service benefits. They could, of course, sue in the Court of Claims. But the remedy there is a money judgment, not a restoration to the office formerly held. . . . Declaratory relief is the singular remedy available here to preserve the status quo while the constitutional rights of these appellants to make these utterances and to engage in these activities are determined. The threat against them is real not fanciful, immediate not remote. The case is therefore an actual not a hypothetical one. [T]he present case [is] a good example of a situation where uncertainty, peril, and insecurity result from imminent and immediate threats to asserted rights.

Abbott Laboratories v. Gardner

387 U.S. 136 (1967)

Mr. Justice HARLAN delivered the opinion of the Court.

In 1962 Congress amended the Federal Food, Drug, and Cosmetic Act [to] require manufacturers of prescription drugs to print the "established name" of the drug "prominently and in type at least half as large as that used thereon for any proprietary name or designation for such drug," on labels and other printed material. The "established name" is one designated by the Secretary of Health, Education, and Welfare pursuant to §502(e)(2) of the Act; the "proprietary name" is usually a trade name under which a particular drug is marketed. The underlying purpose of the 1962 amendment was to bring to the attention of doctors and patients the fact that many of the drugs sold under familiar trade names are actually identical to drugs sold under their "established" or less familiar trade names at significantly lower prices. The Commissioner of Food and Drugs [published the following regulations designed to implement the statute]: "If the label or labeling of a prescription drug bears a proprietary name or designation for the drug or any ingredient thereof, the established name [corresponding] to such proprietary name or designation, shall accompany each appearance of such proprietary name or designation." . . .

The present action was brought by a group of 37 individual drug manufacturers and by the Pharmaceutical Manufacturers Association, of which [the] petitioner companies are members, and which includes manufacturers of more than 90% of the Nation's supply of prescription drugs. They challenged the regulations on the ground that the Commissioner exceeded his authority under the statute by promulgating an order requiring labels, advertisements, and other printed matter relating to prescription drugs to designate the established name of the particular drug involved every time its trade name is used anywhere in such material. . . .

[I]njunctive and declaratory judgment remedies are discretionary, and courts traditionally have been reluctant to apply them to administrative determinations unless these arise in the context of a controversy "ripe" for judicial resolution. [T]he ripeness doctrine['s] basic rationale is to prevent the courts, through avoidance of premature adjudication, from entangling themselves in abstract disagreements over administrative policies, and also to protect the agencies from judicial interference until an administrative decision has been formalized and its effects felt in a concrete way by the challenging parties. The problem is best seen in a twofold aspect, requiring us to evaluate both the fitness of the issues for judicial decision and the hardship to the parties of withholding court consideration.

[W]e believe the issues presented are appropriate for judicial resolution at this time. First, [the issue] is a purely legal one: whether the statute was properly construed by the Commissioner to require the established name of the drug to be used every time the proprietary name is employed. [B]oth sides have approached this case as one purely of congressional intent, and that the Government made no effort to justify the regulation in factual terms. . . . This is also a case in which the impact of the regulations upon the petitioners is sufficiently direct and immediate as to render the issue appropriate for judicial review at this stage. These regulations purport to give an authoritative interpretation of a statutory provision that has a direct effect on the day-to-day business of all prescription drug companies; its promulgation puts petitioners in a dilemma that it was the very purpose of the Declaratory Judgment Act to ameliorate. . . . "Either they must comply with the every time requirement and incur the costs of changing over their promotional material and labeling or they must follow their present course and risk prosecution." The regulations are clear-cut, and were made effective immediately upon publication[;] immediate compliance with their terms was expected. If petitioners wish to comply they must change all their labels, advertisements, and promotional materials; they must destroy stocks of printed matter; and they must invest heavily in new printing type and new supplies. The alternative to compliance — continued use of material which they believe in good faith meets the statutory requirements, but which clearly does not meet the regulation of the Commissioner — may be even more costly. That course would risk serious criminal and civil penalties for the unlawful distribution of "misbranded" drugs.

It is relevant [that] petitioners deal in a sensitive industry, in which public confidence in their drug products is especially important. To require them to challenge these regulations only as a defense to an action brought by the Government might harm them severely and unnecessarily. Where the legal issue presented is fit for judicial resolution, and where a regulation requires an immediate and significant change in the plaintiffs' conduct of their affairs with serious penalties attached to noncompliance, access to the courts under the Administrative Procedure Act and the Declaratory Judgment Act must be permitted, absent a statutory bar or some other unusual circumstance, neither of which appears here.

The Government does not dispute the very real dilemma in which petitioners are placed by the regulation, but contends that "mere financial expense" is not a justification for pre-enforcement judicial review. [T]here is no question in the present case that petitioners have sufficient standing as plaintiffs: the regulation is directed at them in particular; it requires them to make significant changes in their everyday business practices; if they fail to observe the Commissioner's rule they are quite clearly exposed to the imposition of strong sanctions. . . .

The Government further contends that the threat of criminal sanctions for noncompliance with a judicially untested regulation is unrealistic; the Solicitor

General has represented that if court enforcement becomes necessary, "the Department of Justice will proceed only civilly for an injunction [or] by condemnation." We cannot accept this argument as a sufficient answer to petitioners' petition. This action at its inception was properly brought and this subsequent representation of the Department of Justice should not suffice to defeat it.

Notes and Questions: Ripeness

1. *Reconciling United Public Workers and Abbott.* Are the decisions in *United Public Workers* and *Abbott Laboratories* reconcilable? If not, which decision is preferable? Why?

2. *Connecticut's Anti-Contraception Law.* Poe v. Ullman, 367 U.S. 497 (1961), decided before the Court's landmark privacy decisions in *Griswold* and *Roe*, involved a Connecticut statute that prohibited the use of contraceptive devices, and also prohibited doctors from giving medical advice regarding the use of such devices. The plaintiff wife had suffered three consecutive pregnancies that had produced infants with multiple congenital abnormalities who died shortly after birth. Doctors concluded that the infant abnormalities were genetic. Both plaintiffs (husband and wife) claimed that the possibility of an additional pregnancy placed them under great emotional stress that was damaging to their physical and mental health, and they stated that they wanted to use contraceptive devices to prevent conception. However, the wife claimed that she was unable to obtain contraceptive information because of the Connecticut law. The plaintiffs were joined by doctors who claimed that they feared prosecution for giving advice regarding the use of contraceptive devices. The Court held that the case was not justiciable. Although the plaintiffs showed that Connecticut's attorney general had stated that he intends to prosecute any offenses against Connecticut law, and even though the use of and advice concerning contraceptives would constitute offenses, the Court noted that Connecticut's law prohibiting the use of contraceptives had been in existence since 1879. "During the more than three-quarters of a century since its enactment, a prosecution for its violation seems never to have been initiated, save in State v. Nelson, 126 Conn. 412, 11 A.2d 856. The circumstances of that case, decided in 1940, only prove the abstract character of what is before us. There, a test case was brought to determine the constitutionality of the Act as applied against two doctors and a nurse who had allegedly disseminated contraceptive information. . . . The unreality of these law suits is illumined by another circumstance. We were advised by counsel for appellants that contraceptives are commonly and notoriously sold in Connecticut drug stores. . . . 'The best teaching of this Court's experience admonishes us not to entertain constitutional questions in advance of the strictest necessity.' . . . To find it necessary to pass on these statutes now, in order to protect appellants from the hazards of prosecution, would be to close our eyes to reality."

3. *The Loyalty Oath.* The Ohio legislature enacted a statute that required candidates for public office to take a loyalty oath stating in substance that the candidate's party is not engaged in an attempt to overthrow the government by force

or violence, is not associated with a group making such an attempt, and does not carry on a program of sedition or treason as defined by the criminal law. In Socialist Labor Party v. Gilligan, 406 U.S. 583 (1972), in which the Socialist Party challenged the loyalty oath requirement as unconstitutional, the Court held that the case was not justiciable: "Nothing in the record shows that appellants have suffered any injury thus far, and the law's future effect remains wholly speculative. Notwithstanding the indications that appellants have in the past executed the required affidavit without injury, it is, of course, possible that at some future time they may be able to demonstrate some injury as a result of the application of the provision challenged here. Our adjudication of the merits of such a challenge will await that time."

4. *Radioactive Waste.* New York v. United States, 505 U.S. 144 (1992), involved a congressional enactment that required the states to deal with the problem of low-level radioactive waste no later than 2016, or to assume title to the waste (which was previously owned by private individuals and companies). When individual states challenged the law as an infringement of the Tenth Amendment to the U.S. Constitution, the United States objected that the case was not ripe for review. The Court disagreed, noting that low-level radioactive waste is unlikely to disappear by 2016, and emphasizing that it takes many years to develop a new disposal site, and therefore the state must take immediate action in order to avoid the consequences.

∾ PROBLEMS: RIPENESS ∾

1. *The Health Care Legislation and Ripeness.* Is the health care litigation, described at the beginning of this chapter, ripe for judicial review? Would it matter whether a woman, presently before the court, is seeking funding for an abortion (but who cannot obtain the funding because the insurance policies do not provide it), or can the litigation be brought even though there is no pregnant woman presently before the Court?

2. *The (First) Persian Gulf War.* In the early 1990s, President George H.W. Bush deployed 230,000 U.S. troops to the Persian Gulf region in preparation for an invasion of Iraq. The President's stated objective was to provide "an adequate *offensive* military option" should that be necessary to achieve such goals as the withdrawal of Iraqi forces from Kuwait. At about the same time, Secretary of Defense Richard Cheney (later Vice President Cheney) stated that the additional military forces gave the United States the ability "to conduct *offensive* military operations." In November 1990, the plaintiffs (all members of Congress) sued, claiming that the initiation of offensive U.S. military action was imminent, that such action would be unlawful in the absence of a declaration of war by the Congress, and that a war without concurrence by the Congress would deprive the plaintiffs of the voice to which they are entitled under the Constitution. The Department of Justice claimed that the case was not ripe for review because no offensive action had been initiated. If you had been the judge assigned to hear the case, how would you have ruled? Is the case ripe for decision? If not, what

additional facts must be shown in order to make the case ripe? Must the plaintiffs wait until the President commits the troops to military action? If so, won't it be too late? *See* Dellums v. Bush, 752 F. Supp. 1141 (D.D.C. 1990).

3. *Anti-Contraception Laws.* Now, let's think a bit more about Poe v. Ullman (described above) and the additional facts that would be required to establish ripeness. Would the case be ripe if a doctor wanted to dispense contraceptive advice to his patients but was afraid to do so for fear of prosecution? Suppose that the trial court dismisses all challenges on ripeness grounds. If plaintiffs still wish to sue, how would they go about establishing ripeness?

3. Mootness

The mootness doctrine also involves timing. But, when this doctrine applies, the claim is that a case is presented too late. Even though the claim may have been ripe at one point, subsequent events have rendered it "moot."

DeFunis v. Odegaard

416 U.S. 312 (1974)

PER CURIAM.

[P]etitioner Marco DeFunis, Jr., applied for admission [at] the University of Washington Law School, a state-operated institution. . . . DeFunis was eventually [denied] admission [and sought] a mandatory injunction commanding [respondents] to admit him as a member of the first-year class[,] on the ground that the Law School admissions policy had resulted in the unconstitutional denial of his application for admission. The trial court [granted] the requested relief. DeFunis [was] admitted to the Law School and began his legal studies [in] the fall of 1971. [T]he Washington Supreme Court reversed the judgment of the trial court [when] DeFunis was in his second year at the Law School.

[DeFunis] petitioned this Court for a writ of certiorari, and [the Washington Supreme Court's judgment was stayed]. By virtue of this stay, DeFunis has remained in law school, and was in the first term of his third and final year when this Court [considered] his certiorari petition. [W]e requested the parties to brief the question of mootness. [R]espondents indicated that, if the decision of the Washington Supreme Court were permitted to stand, the petitioner could complete the term for which he was then enrolled but would have to apply to the faculty for permission to continue in the school before he could register for another term. [At] oral argument, counsel for [respondents made] clear that the Law School will not in any way seek to abrogate this registration. . . .

[The] inability of the federal judiciary "to review moot cases derives from the requirement of Art. III of the Constitution under which the exercise of judicial power depends upon the existence of a case or controversy." Liner v. Jafco, Inc., 375 U.S. 301 (1964). [U]nder Art. III "[e]ven in cases arising in the state courts, the question of mootness is a federal one which a federal court must resolve before it assumes jurisdiction." North Carolina v. Rice, *supra*, 404 U.S., at 246.

[Since DeFunis] has now registered for his final term, it is evident that he will be given an opportunity to complete all academic and other requirements for graduation, [and] will receive his diploma regardless of any decision this Court might reach on the merits of this case. . . . A determination by this Court [is] no longer necessary to compel that result, and could not serve to prevent it. DeFunis did not cast his suit as a class action, and the only remedy he requested was an injunction commanding his admission to the Law School. He was not [only] accorded that remedy, but he now [has] been irrevocably admitted to the final term of the final year of [Law School]. The controversy between the parties has thus clearly ceased to be "definite and concrete" and no longer "touch(es) the legal relations of parties having adverse legal interests." Aetna Life Ins. Co. v. Haworth, 300 U.S. 227 (1937).

It matters not that these circumstances partially stem from a policy decision on the part of the respondent Law School authorities. [I]t has been the settled practice of the Court, in contexts no less significant, [to] accept representations such as these as parameters for decision. [A] voluntary cessation of the admissions practices complained of could make this case moot only if it could be said with assurance "that there is no reasonable expectation that the wrong will be repeated." *W.T. Grant Co., supra*, 345 U.S., at 633. Otherwise, "[t]he defendant is free to return to his old ways," and [there would be a] "public interest in having the legality of the practices settled." But mootness in the present case depends [upon] the simple fact that DeFunis is now in the final quarter of the final year of his course of study, and [the] policy of the Law School to permit him to complete the term for which he is now enrolled.

It might [be] suggested that this case presents a question that is "capable of repetition, yet evading review," and is thus amenable to federal adjudication even though it might otherwise be considered moot. But DeFunis will never again be required to run the gauntlet of the Law School's admission process, and so the question is certainly not "capable of repetition" so far as he is concerned. [I]t hardly follows that the issue he raises will in the future evade review. If the admissions procedures of the Law School remain unchanged, there is no reason to suppose that a subsequent case attacking those procedures will not come with relative speed to this Court. . . .

[W]e conclude that the Court cannot, consistently with the limitations of Art. III of the Constitution, consider the substantive constitutional issues tendered by the parties. Accordingly, the judgment of the Supreme Court of Washington is vacated, and the cause is remanded for such proceedings as by that court may be deemed appropriate.

It is so ordered.

Vacated and remanded.

Justice BRENNAN, with whom Justice DOUGLAS, Justice WHITE, and Justice MARSHALL, dissenting.

[Many] weeks of the school term remain, and petitioner may not receive his degree despite respondents' assurances that petitioner will be allowed to complete this term's schooling regardless of our decision. Any number of unexpected events — illness, economic necessity, even academic failure — might prevent his graduation. . . . Were that misfortune to befall, [respondents] warn that "[DeFunis] would have [to] request continued admission for the remainder of his law school education, [and] discretionary action by the University [would] have to be taken." Thus, [petitioner] might once again have to run the gauntlet of the University's allegedly unlawful admissions policy. . . .

[B]ecause the University's position implies no concession that its admissions policy is unlawful, this controversy falls squarely within the Court's long line of decisions holding that the "[m]ere voluntary cessation of allegedly illegal conduct does not moot a case." United States v. Concentrated Phosphate Export Assn., 393 U.S. 199 (1968). [R]espondents' [have] not borne the "heavy burden" of demonstrating that there was not even a "mere possibility" that petitioner would once again be subject to the challenged admissions policy. On the contrary, respondents have positioned themselves so as to be "free to return to [their] old ways."

[While] we must be vigilant to require that litigants maintain a personal stake in the outcome of a controversy[,] there is no want of an adversary contest in this case. [T]he Court concedes that, if petitioner has lost his stake in this controversy, he did so only when he registered for the spring term. But appellant took that action only after the case had been fully litigated in the state courts, briefs had been filed in this Court, and oral argument had been heard. The case is thus ripe for decision on a fully developed factual record with sharply defined and fully canvassed legal issues.

[The] constitutional issues which are avoided today concern vast numbers of people [as] evidenced by the filing of twenty-six amicus curiae briefs. Few constitutional questions in recent history have stirred as much debate. . . . They must inevitably return to the federal courts and ultimately [to] this Court. Because avoidance of repetitious litigation serves the public interest, that inevitability counsels against mootness determinations [not] compelled by the record. [I] would find that there is an extant controversy and decide the merits of the very important constitutional questions presented.

Notes and Questions: Mootness

1. *"Capable of Repetition, Yet Evading Review."* Roe v. Wade, 410 U.S. 113 (1973), involved a Texas statute that criminalized abortion. Jane Roe, a single unmarried woman who was pregnant, claimed that she wished to terminate her pregnancy by an abortion "performed by a competent, licensed physician, under safe, clinical conditions." However, she claimed that she was unable to obtain a "legal" abortion in Texas because her life was not threatened by the pregnancy, and she claimed that she could not afford to travel to another state to obtain an abortion. By the time the U.S. Supreme Court heard the case, Roe was no longer pregnant, and the state moved to dismiss the case on mootness grounds. The Court held that the case was not moot: "[When] pregnancy is a significant fact in the litigation, the normal 266-day human gestation period is so short that the

pregnancy will come to term before the usual appellate process is complete. If that termination makes a case moot, pregnancy litigation seldom will survive much beyond the trial stage, and appellate review will be effectively denied. Our law should not be that rigid. Pregnancy often comes more than once to the same woman, and in the general population, if man is to survive, it will always be with us. Pregnancy provides a classic justification for a conclusion of nonmootness. It truly could be 'capable of repetition, yet evading review.' Southern Pacific Terminal Co. v. ICC, 219 U.S. 498 (1911). . . . We, [agree that] Jane Roe had standing to undertake this litigation, that she presented a justiciable controversy, and that the termination of her 1970 pregnancy has not rendered her case moot."

2. *Jurisdictional or Prudential?* In some instances, when the Court applies doctrines like mootness or ripeness, it dismisses because there is no "case" or "controversy" within the meaning of Article III. At other times, even though a case or controversy may exist, the Court simply decides that it is not prudent to hear the case because it is not sufficiently ripe or is nearly moot. Some complain that the Court effectively uses these doctrines to slam the courthouse door in the faces of litigants. At the end of *DeFunis*, the Court suggests that it "cannot, consistently with the limitations of Art. III of the Constitution, consider the substantive constitutional issues tendered by the parties." Is this statement true? Was the dismissal in that case really jurisdictional? What if DeFunis had become sick and was forced to postpone the conclusion of his studies for a year? Is it clear that the law school would have allowed him to complete his studies and graduate?

∽ PROBLEMS: MOOTNESS ∽

1. *Police Chokeholds.* City of Los Angeles police use chokeholds on some suspects and arrestees. The plaintiff complains that two citizens have died from the use of chokeholds, and he further alleges fear that police will use a chokehold on him in the future (as they have done before). While the case is pending, the Board of Police Commissioners imposes a six-month moratorium on the use of chokeholds except under circumstances where deadly force is authorized. Based on the moratorium, the city moves to dismiss the case as moot. The plaintiff objects, claiming that the moratorium is not permanent and may be lifted at any time. Should the case be dismissed? *See* Los Angeles v. Lyons, 461 U.S. 95 (1983).

2. *Challenging the Permit.* Laidlaw Environmental Services (Laidlaw), Inc., bought a hazardous waste incinerator facility in South Carolina that included a wastewater treatment plant. Shortly after Laidlaw acquired the facility, the South Carolina Department of Health and Environmental Control (DHEC) granted Laidlaw a permit authorizing the company to discharge treated water into a nearby river. The permit placed limits on Laidlaw's discharge of various types of pollutants, including mercury, an extremely toxic pollutant. The permit also regulated the flow, temperature, toxicity, and pH of the effluent from the facility, and imposed monitoring and reporting obligations. Repeatedly, Laidlaw's discharges exceeded the limits specified in the permit. Consequently, Friends of the Earth (FOE) and Citizens Local Environmental Action Network, Inc. (CLEAN),

filed suit. Will the suit be moot if: a) Laidlaw agrees to terminate its violations and to make "every effort" to comply with its permit obligations; and b) Laidlaw permanently closes the incinerator facility, starts dismantling it, puts the site up for sale, and ceases all discharges from the facility permanently? *See* Friends of the Earth, Inc. v. Laidlaw Environmental Services, 528 U.S. 167 (2000).

4. Standing

Standing cases focus on whether a plaintiff has "alleged such a personal stake in the outcome of the controversy as to warrant invocation of federal-court jurisdiction." As a general rule, a plaintiff must be suffering "injury in fact" that is both concrete and particularized, and the injury must be "actual and imminent" as opposed to conjectural or hypothetical, it must be fairly traceable to the defendant's challenged action, and it must be likely that a favorable judicial decision will prevent or redress the injury. Although standing is related to ripeness and mootness, because the plaintiff may lack sufficient interest when a case is not yet ripe or has become moot, standing cases do not always involve questions of timing.

The cases cited below involve suits by individuals who seek to challenge governmental action. Some base their standing claims on their status as citizens or taxpayers. Others rely on congressional authorization in the sense that there is a federal statute that authorizes those "adversely affected" by agency action to sue. Still others attempt to sue on behalf of third parties. In each of these contexts, the Court has developed special standing rules.

a. Taxpayer and Citizen Standing

Do citizens and taxpayers have the right to enforce the U.S. Constitution and, in particular, constitutional limitations on government? Some have argued that citizens and taxpayers should have an automatic right to enforce the Constitution. As you read the following cases, consider whether and to what extent this is true.

In two cases decided together in the 1920s, Frothingham v. Mellon and Massachusetts v. Mellon, 262 U.S. 447 (1923), the Court considered challenges to the Maternity Act, which appropriated money for the purpose of reducing maternal and infant mortality as well as for protecting the health of mothers and infants. The State of Massachusetts sued, claiming that its rights as a sovereign state and the rights of its citizens had been "invaded and usurped" by the Act. The Court concluded that Massachusetts's "rights" had not been invaded: "[T]he powers of the state are not invaded [since] the statute imposes no obligation but simply extends an option which the state is free to accept or reject." The Court also rejected the idea that Massachusetts could bring the suit on behalf of its citizens: "[T]he citizens of Massachusetts are also citizens of the United States. It cannot be conceded that a state, as parens patriae, may institute judicial proceedings to protect citizens of the United States from the operation of the statutes thereof. [I]t is the United States, and not the state, which represents them as parens patriae, when such representation becomes appropriate; and to the former, and not to the latter, they must look for such protective measures as flow from that status."

The Court also held that Frothingham, an individual, could not establish standing to sue based on her status as a citizen and a federal taxpayer (she had argued that her tax burden would be increased by the appropriations): "[A taxpayer's] interest in the moneys of the treasury — partly realized from taxation and partly from other sources — is shared with millions of others, is comparatively minute and indeterminable, and the effect upon future taxation, of any payment out of the funds, so remote, fluctuating and uncertain, that no basis is afforded for an appeal to the preventive powers of a court of equity. . . . The administration of any statute, likely to produce additional taxation to be imposed upon a vast number of taxpayers, the extent of whose several liability is indefinite and constantly changing, is essentially a matter of public and not of individual concern. If one taxpayer may champion and litigate such a cause, then every other taxpayer may do the same [in] respect of every other appropriation act and statute whose administration requires the outlay of public money, and whose validity may be questioned." The Court went on to note that "the functions of government under our system are apportioned. To the legislative department has been committed the duty of making laws, to the executive the duty of executing them, and to the judiciary the duty of interpreting and applying them in cases properly brought before the courts. The general rule is that neither department may invade the province of the other and neither may control, direct, or restrain the action of the other. . . . We have no power per se to review and annul acts of Congress on the ground that they are unconstitutional. That question may be considered only when the justification for some direct injury suffered or threatened, presenting a justiciable issue, is made to rest upon such an act." *Frothingham* left open the possibility that a municipal taxpayer might be able to establish standing to challenge municipal expenditures on the theory that its interest in a municipal treasury is more substantial.

DaimlerChrysler Corp. v. Cuno

547 U.S. 332 (2006)

Justice ROBERTS delivered the opinion of the Court.

Jeeps were first mass-produced in 1941 for the U.S. Army by the Willys-Overland Motor Company in Toledo, Ohio. Nearly 60 years later, the city of Toledo and State of Ohio sought to encourage the current manufacturer of Jeeps–DaimlerChrysler to expand its Jeep operation in Toledo, by offering local and state tax benefits for new investment. Taxpayers in Toledo sued, alleging that their local and state tax burdens were increased by the tax breaks for Daimler-Chrysler, tax breaks that they asserted violated the Commerce Clause. . . . We are obligated before reaching this Commerce Clause question to determine whether the taxpayers who objected to the credit have standing to press their complaint in federal court. We conclude that they do not, and we therefore can proceed no further.

Ohio levies a franchise tax "upon corporations for the privilege of doing business in the state, owning or using a part or all of its capital or property in [the] state, or holding a certificate of compliance authorizing it to do business in [the] state." Ohio Rev. Code Ann. §5733.01. A taxpayer that purchases "new manufacturing machinery and equipment" and installs it at sites in the State receives a credit against the franchise tax. Municipalities in Ohio may also offer partial property tax waivers to businesses that agree to invest in qualifying areas. With consent from local school districts, the partial property tax waiver can be increased to a complete exemption.

In 1998, DaimlerChrysler entered into a contract with the city of Toledo. Under the contract, DaimlerChrysler agreed to expand its Jeep assembly plant [in] Toledo. In exchange, the city agreed to waive the property tax for the plant, with the consent of the two school districts in which the plant is located. Because DaimlerChrysler undertook to purchase and install "new manufacturing machinery and equipment," it was also entitled to a credit against the state franchise tax.

[Most] of the plaintiffs were residents of Toledo, who paid taxes to both the city of Toledo and State of Ohio. They claimed that they were injured because the tax breaks for DaimlerChrysler diminished the funds available to the city and State, imposing a "disproportionate burden" on plaintiffs. . . . The District Court [held] that, "[a]t the bare minimum, the Plaintiffs who are taxpayers have standing to object to the property tax exemption and franchise tax credit statutes under the 'municipal taxpayer standing' rule articulated in Massachusetts v. Mellon, 262 U.S. 447 (1923)." On the merits, the District Court found that neither tax benefit violated the Commerce Clause. The Court of Appeals for the Sixth Circuit agreed [as] to the municipal property tax exemption, but held that the state franchise tax credit violated the Commerce Clause. [We] asked the parties to address whether plaintiffs have standing to challenge the franchise tax credit. . . . Friends of Earth, Inc. v. Laidlaw Environmental Services (TOC), Inc., 528 U.S. 167 (2000). . . .

Chief Justice Marshall, in Marbury v. Madison, 1 Cranch 137, 2 L.Ed. 60 (1803), grounded the Federal Judiciary's authority to exercise judicial review and interpret the Constitution on the necessity to do so in the course of carrying out the judicial function of deciding cases. As Marshall explained, "[t]hose who apply the rule to particular cases, must of necessity expound and interpret that rule." Determining that a matter before the federal courts is a proper case or controversy under Article III therefore assumes particular importance in ensuring that the Federal Judiciary respects "'the proper-and properly limited-role of the courts in a democratic society,'" Allen v. Wright, 468 U.S. 737, 750 (1984) (quoting Warth v. Seldin, 422 U.S. 490, 498 (1975)). If a dispute is not a proper case or controversy, the courts have no business deciding it, or expounding the law in the course of doing so.

This Court has recognized that the case-or-controversy limitation is crucial in maintaining the "'tripartite allocation of power'" set forth in the Constitution.

Valley Forge Christian College v. Americans United for Separation of Church and State, Inc., 454 U.S. 464, 474 (1982) (quoting Flast v. Cohen, 392 U.S. 83, 95 (1968)). . . . The "core component" of the requirement that a litigant have standing to invoke the authority of a federal court "is an essential and unchanging part of the case-or-controversy requirement of Article III." Lujan v. Defenders of Wildlife, 504 U.S. 555, 560 (1992). The requisite elements of this "core component derived directly from the Constitution" are familiar: "A plaintiff must allege personal injury fairly traceable to the defendant's allegedly unlawful conduct and likely to be redressed by the requested relief." *Allen, supra,* at 751. We have been asked to decide an important question of constitutional law concerning the Commerce Clause. But before we do so, we must find that the question is presented in a "case" or "controversy" that is, in James Madison's words, "of a Judiciary Nature." 2 *Records of the Federal Convention of 1787,* p. 430 (M. Farrand ed. 1966). That requires plaintiffs, as the parties now asserting federal jurisdiction, to carry the burden of establishing their standing under Article III.

Plaintiffs principally claim standing by virtue of their status as Ohio taxpayers, alleging that the franchise tax credit "depletes the funds of the State of Ohio to which the Plaintiffs contribute through their tax payments" and thus "diminish[es] the total funds available for lawful uses and impos[es] disproportionate burdens on" them. On several occasions, this Court has denied *federal* taxpayers standing under Article III to object to a particular expenditure of federal funds simply because they are taxpayers. Thus the alleged "deprivation of the fair and constitutional use of [a federal taxpayer's] tax dollar" cannot support a challenge to the conveyance of Government land to a private religious college, *Valley Forge, supra,* at 476, 482, and "the interest of a taxpayer in the moneys of the federal treasury furnishes no basis" to argue that a federal agency's loan practices are unconstitutional, Alabama Power Co. v. Ickes, 302 U.S. 464, 478 (1938).

The animating principle behind these cases was announced in their progenitor, Frothingham v. Mellon, decided with Massachusetts v. Mellon, 262 U.S. 447 (1923). [The logic of those decisions] is equally applicable to taxpayer challenges to expenditures that deplete the treasury, and to taxpayer challenges to so-called "tax expenditures," which reduce amounts available to the treasury by granting tax credits or exemptions. In either case, the alleged injury is based on the asserted effect of the allegedly illegal activity on public revenues, to which the taxpayer contributes.

Standing has been rejected in such cases because the alleged injury is not "concrete and particularized," but instead a grievance the taxpayer "suffers in some indefinite way in common with people generally," *Frothingham, supra,* at 488. In addition, the injury is not "actual or imminent," but instead "conjectural or hypothetical." *Defenders of Wildlife, supra,* at 560. As an initial matter, it is unclear that tax breaks of the sort at issue here do in fact deplete the treasury: The very point of the tax benefits is to spur economic activity, which in turn *increases* government revenues. In this very action, the Michigan plaintiffs claimed that they were injured because they lost out on the added revenues that would have accompanied DaimlerChrysler's decision to expand facilities in Michigan.

Plaintiffs' alleged injury is also "conjectural or hypothetical" in that it depends on how legislators respond to a reduction in revenue, if that is the consequence of the credit. Establishing injury requires speculating that elected officials will increase a taxpayer-plaintiff's tax bill to make up a deficit; establishing redressability requires speculating that abolishing the challenged credit will redound to the benefit of the taxpayer because legislators will pass along the supposed increased revenue in the form of tax reductions. Neither sort of speculation suffices to support standing. *See* ASARCO Inc. v. Kadish, 490 U.S. 605 (1989) (opinion of Kennedy, J.).

A taxpayer plaintiff has no right to insist that the government dispose of any increased revenue it might experience as a result of his suit by decreasing his tax liability or bolstering programs that benefit him. To the contrary, the decision of how to allocate any such savings is the very epitome of a policy judgment committed to the "broad and legitimate discretion" of lawmakers, which "the courts cannot presume either to control or to predict." *ASARCO, supra,* at 615 (opinion of Kennedy, J.). Under such circumstances, we have no assurance that the asserted injury is "imminent" — that it is "certainly impending." Whitmore v. Arkansas, 495 U.S. 149, 158 (1990).

The foregoing rationale for rejecting federal taxpayer standing applies with undiminished force to state taxpayers. We indicated as much in Doremus v. Board of Ed. of Hawthorne, 342 U.S. 429 (1952). In that case, we noted our earlier holdings that "the interests of a taxpayer in the moneys of the federal treasury are too indeterminable, remote, uncertain and indirect" to support standing to challenge "their manner of expenditure." We then "reiterate[d]" what we had said in rejecting a federal taxpayer challenge to a federal statute "as equally true when a state Act is assailed: 'The [taxpayer] must be able to show [that] he has sustained [some] direct injury [and] not merely that he suffers in some indefinite way in common with people generally.'"

The allegations of injury that plaintiffs make in their complaint furnish no better basis for finding standing than those made in the cases where federal taxpayer standing was denied. Plaintiffs claim that DaimlerChrysler's tax credit depletes the Ohio fisc and "impos[es] disproportionate burdens on [them]." This is no different from similar claims by federal taxpayers we have already rejected under Article III as insufficient to establish standing. . . . State policymakers, no less than their federal counterparts, retain broad discretion to make "policy decisions" concerning state spending "in different ways [depending] on their perceptions of wise state fiscal policy and myriad other circumstances." *ASARCO, supra,* at 615 (opinion of Kennedy, J.). [A] party seeking federal jurisdiction cannot rely on such "[s]peculative inferences [to] connect [his] injury to the challenged actions of [the defendant]," *Simon,* 426 U.S., at 45. Indeed, because state budgets frequently contain an array of tax and spending provisions, any number of which may be challenged on a variety of bases, affording state taxpayers standing to press such challenges simply because their tax burden gives them an interest in the state treasury would interpose the federal courts as "'virtually continuing monitors of the wisdom and soundness'" of state fiscal administration, contrary to the more modest role Article III the envisions for federal courts. *See id.*, at 760-761 (quoting Laird v. Tatum, 408 U.S. 1, 15 (1972)).

For the foregoing reasons, we hold that state taxpayers have no standing under Article III to challenge state tax or spending decisions simply by virtue of their status as taxpayers. . . .

Plaintiffs also claim that their status as *municipal* taxpayers gives them standing to challenge the *state* franchise tax credit at issue here. The *Frothingham* Court noted with approval the standing of municipal residents to enjoin the "illegal use of the moneys of a municipal corporation," relying on "the peculiar relation of the corporate taxpayer to the corporation" to distinguish such a case from the general bar on taxpayer suits. Plaintiffs here challenged the municipal property tax exemption as municipal taxpayers. . . . In plaintiffs' challenge to the state franchise tax credit, however, they identify no municipal action contributing to any claimed injury. Instead, they try to leverage the notion of municipal taxpayer standing beyond challenges to municipal action. . . . First, plaintiffs claim that because state law requires revenues from the franchise tax to be distributed to local governments, the award of a credit to DaimlerChrysler reduced such distributions and thus depleted the funds of "local governments to which Respondents pay taxes." But plaintiffs' challenge is still to the state law and state decision, not those of their municipality. . . . Any effect that enjoining DaimlerChrysler's credit will have on municipal funds, therefore, will not result from automatic operation of a statutory formula, but from a hypothesis that the state government will choose to direct the supposed revenue from the restored franchise tax to municipalities. This is precisely the sort of conjecture we may not entertain in assessing standing. . . . The second way plaintiffs seek to leverage their standing to challenge the municipal property tax exemption into a challenge to the franchise tax credit is by relying on Mine Workers v. Gibbs, 383 U.S. 715 (1966). . . . *Gibbs* held that federal-question jurisdiction over a claim may authorize a federal court to exercise jurisdiction over state-law claims that may be viewed as part of the same case because they "derive from a common nucleus of operative fact" as the federal claim. . . . Plaintiffs' reading of *Gibbs* [would] have remarkable implications. The doctrines of mootness, ripeness, and political question all originate in Article III's "case" or "controversy" language, no less than standing does. Yet if *Gibbs'* "common nucleus" formulation announced a new definition of "case" or "controversy" for all Article III purposes, a federal court would be free to entertain moot or unripe claims, or claims presenting a political question, if they "derived from" the same "operative fact[s]" as another federal claim suffering from none of these defects. Plaintiffs' reading of *Gibbs*, therefore, would amount to a significant revision of our precedent interpreting Article III. . . . Plaintiffs failed to establish Article III injury with respect to their *state* taxes, and even if they did do so with respect to their *municipal* taxes, that injury does not entitle them to seek a remedy as to the state taxes. As the Court summed up the point in *Lewis*, "standing is not dispensed in gross."

[Because] plaintiffs have no standing to challenge that credit, the lower courts erred by considering their claims against it on the merits. The judgment of the Sixth Circuit is therefore vacated in part, and the cases are remanded for dismissal of plaintiffs' challenge to the franchise tax credit.

It is so ordered.

Justice GINSBURG, concurring in part and concurring in the judgment.

Today's decision [is] solidly grounded in longstanding precedent. . . . One can accept, as I do, nonjusticiability of *Frothingham*-type federal and state taxpayer suits in federal court without endorsing as well the limitations on standing later declared in [later cases]. Noting this large reservation, I concur in the judgment, and in the balance of the Court's opinion.

BACKGROUND
Taxpayer Challenges to Bible Readings

In Doremus v. Board of Education, 342 U.S. 429 (1952), taxpayers filed an Establishment Clause challenge against the practice of Bible reading in the New Jersey public schools. The Court held that the plaintiffs could not establish standing: "There is no allegation that this activity is supported by any separate tax or paid for from any particular appropriation or that it adds any sum whatever to the cost of conducting the school. No information is given as to what kind of taxes are paid by appellants and there is no averment that the Bible reading increases any tax they do pay or that as taxpayers they are, will, or possibly can be out of pocket because of it."

Notes and Questions: Standing

1. *More on Taxpayer Status.* Taxpayers always have standing to challenge the validity of a *tax* (as opposed to an expenditure) that they are forced to pay. As a result, in Baldwin v. G.A.F. Seelig, Inc., 294 U.S. 511 (1935), milk sellers in the State of New York were held to have standing to challenge a tax on them equivalent to 5 cents per gallon sold.

2. *Leasing Public Lands.* In ASARCO, Inc. v. Kadish, 490 U.S. 605 (1989), an Arizona statute that authorized the state land department to lease minerals and school trust lands at a prescribed rate was challenged by taxpayers who claimed that the statute did not comply with congressionally imposed statutory standards for leasing or selling lands. The taxpayers were joined by a teachers' association and its members. The Court concluded that all of the plaintiffs lacked standing to bring the case: "[R]espondents [have] asserted that the Arizona statute governing mineral leases has 'deprived the school trust funds of millions of dollars thereby resulting in unnecessarily higher taxes.' Even if the first part of that assertion were correct, however, it is pure speculation whether the lawsuit would result in any actual tax relief for respondents. If they were to prevail, it is conceivable

that more money might be devoted to education; but since education in Arizona is not financed solely from the school trust fund, the State might reduce its supplement from the general funds to provide for other programs. . . . The same flaw defeats the claim that the teachers association would have had standing to bring this suit. . . . The claims raised here, moreover, are the kind of generalized grievances brought by concerned citizens that we have consistently held are not cognizable in the federal courts." Nevertheless, the Court decided that it had jurisdiction to hear the case on the theory that the case had gone to final judgment in the Arizona courts, invalidating the leases and thereby causing injury to the leaseholders: "Petitioners hold mineral leases that were granted under the state law the Arizona Supreme Court invalidated. Although no accounting of sums due under these leases remains at issue in this particular case, it is undisputed that the decision to be reviewed poses a serious and immediate threat to the continuing validity of those leases by virtue of its holding that they were granted under improper procedures and an invalid law. The state proceedings ended in a declaratory judgment adverse to petitioners, an adjudication of legal rights which constitutes the kind of injury cognizable in this Court on review from the state courts." Chief Justice Rehnquist, joined by Justice Scalia, dissented, suggesting that the original plaintiffs lacked standing and that the "subsequent proceedings in the state court have obviously not cured this defect."

∼ PROBLEMS: *FROTHINGHAM*, TAXPAYER STANDING, AND CITIZEN STANDING ∼

1. *Citizen Standing.* Should Frothingham (or Cuno, for that matter) have been able to establish standing based solely on her (his) status as a citizen of the United States? Do citizens have a sufficient interest in constitutional government that entitles them to challenge unconstitutional governmental action?

2. *Standing and the Health Care Legislation.* Can the plaintiffs who seek to challenge the health care legislation establish standing on the basis of their status as citizens of the United States? Suppose they claim that the policy of excluding abortion coverage from health care coverage represents bad public policy that will have adverse effects on society and therefore will produce a less desirable society. Are these allegations sufficient to establish standing?

3. Frothingham *and Municipal Taxpayers.* Suppose that a municipality decides to adopt a maternity program like the one at issue in *Frothingham*. A municipal taxpayer wishes to challenge the program as illegitimate and claims that expenditure under the program will increase her taxes. In light of *Frothingham* and *Cuno*, does the municipal taxpayer have standing? As you think about these issues, does it matter: a) How large the municipality is and how large the municipal budget is? b) How large the municipal taxpayer is? c) How much the taxpayer pays annually in taxes? d) How much of the municipal budget the program consumes?

4. *More on* Doremus *and Bible Readings.* In *Doremus*, the Court held that taxpayers did not have standing to challenge Bible readings in the public schools.

What would the plaintiff taxpayers have needed to allege to establish standing to challenge the Bible readings? Would it be enough to allege that the public schools spent public money purchasing copies of the Bible? Or would they have to allege something more? If so, what? Would it make a difference in *Doremus* if one of the plaintiffs had a child in the school where the Bible readings were being conducted? What would the parent have to allege in order to establish standing?

5. *Army Surveillance.* Plaintiffs claim that the Department of the Army has engaged in "surveillance of lawful and peaceful civilian political activity" and that the surveillance has a "chilling" effect on the exercise of their First Amendment rights. Suppose that plaintiffs allege that such information gathering is inappropriate to the army's role under the U.S. Constitution, that this information gathering is inherently dangerous, and that the army may at some future date misuse the information in some way that would cause direct harm to respondents. Are these allegations of injury sufficient to establish standing? Would it matter that most, if not all, of the plaintiffs and/or the organizations of which they are members have previously been the subject of army surveillance reports and their names have appeared in the army's records? *See* Laird v. Tatum, 408 U.S. 1 (1972).

Lance v. Coffman

549 U.S. 437 (2007)

Per Curiam.

The Elections Clause of the United States Constitution provides that the "Manner of holding Elections for Senators and Representatives, shall be prescribed in each State by the *Legislature* thereof; but the Congress may at any time by Law make or alter such Regulations, except as to the Places of chusing Senators." Art. I, §4, cl. 1 (emphasis added). When Colorado legislators were unable to redraw congressional districts after the 2000 census to accommodate an additional Representative, a state court did it for them. The legislature *was* able to pass a redistricting plan in 2003, which Colorado's Governor signed into law.

Colorado's attorney general [filed] an original action in the Colorado Supreme Court to enjoin Colorado's secretary of state from implementing this new plan, noting that Article V, §44, of the Colorado Constitution limits redistricting to once per census. . . . The Colorado Supreme Court granted the injunction, holding that "judicially-created districts are just as binding and permanent as districts created by the General Assembly," and that the court-drawn plan must remain in effect until the next decennial census. The court further held that this result did not offend the Elections Clause of the United States Constitution. [Afterwards, four] Colorado citizens [filed] the instant action in Federal District Court. They argued that Article V, §44, of the Colorado Constitution, as interpreted by the Colorado Supreme Court, violates their rights under the Elections Clause. . . . [The] District Court held that the citizen-plaintiffs had standing to bring their Elections Clause challenge. The court went on, however, to hold that the suit was barred by issue preclusion because the plaintiffs "stand in privity with the Secretary of State and the General Assembly," who were on the losing side in [prior] litigation. . . . Plaintiffs appeal once again.

Federal courts must determine that they have jurisdiction before proceeding to the merits. Article III of the Constitution limits the jurisdiction of federal courts to "Cases" and "Controversies." One component of the case-or-controversy requirement is standing, which requires a plaintiff to demonstrate the now-familiar elements of injury in fact, causation, and redressability. *See* Lujan v. Defenders of Wildlife, 504 U.S. 555 (1992). "We have consistently held that a plaintiff raising only a generally available grievance about government — claiming only harm to his and every citizen's interest in proper application of the Constitution and laws, and seeking relief that no more directly and tangibly benefits him than it does the public at large — does not state an Article III case or controversy." *Id.*, at 573-574.

Our refusal to serve as a forum for generalized grievances has a lengthy pedigree. In Fairchild v. Hughes, 258 U.S. 126 (1922), for example, a citizen sued the Secretary of State and the Attorney General to challenge the procedures by which the Nineteenth Amendment was ratified. We dismissed the suit because it was "not a case within the meaning [of] Article III." The plaintiff sought to assert "only the right, possessed by every citizen, to require that the Government be administered according to law and that the public moneys be not wasted." "Obviously," we held, "this general right does not entitle a private citizen to institute [a suit] in the federal courts." [A] pair of more recent cases further illustrates the point. In United States v. Richardson, 418 U.S. 166 (1974), a federal taxpayer challenged the Government's failure to disclose certain CIA expenditures as a violation of the Constitution's Accounts Clause, which requires that "a regular Statement and Account of the Receipts and Expenditures of all public Money shall be published from time to time." Art. I, §9, cl. 7. Relying on *Levitt,* this Court dismissed the claim as a "generalized grievance" that is "plainly undifferentiated and 'common to all members of the public.'" [The] same day, in Schlesinger v. Reservists Comm. to Stop the War, 418 U.S. 208 (1974), we addressed standing to bring a challenge under the Constitution's Incompatibility Clause, which provides that "no Person holding any Office under the United States, shall be a Member of either House during his Continuance in Office." Art. I, §6, cl. 2. Citizen-taxpayers brought a lawsuit contending that Members of Congress who were also members of the military Reserves violated the Incompatibility Clause. This Court dismissed for lack of standing. It "reaffirm[ed] *Levitt* in holding that standing to sue may not be predicated upon an interest of the kind alleged here which is held in common by all members of the public, because of the necessarily abstract nature of the injury all citizens share." Refusing to entertain generalized grievances ensures that "there is a real need to exercise the power of judicial review" in a particular case, and it helps guarantee that courts fashion remedies "no broader than required by the precise facts to which the court's ruling would be applied." In short, it ensures that courts exercise power that is judicial in nature.

[The] plaintiffs here are four Colorado voters. Three days after the Colorado Supreme Court issued its [redistricting decision], they filed a complaint alleging that [the decision] violated [the Elections Clause] of the U.S. Constitution by depriving the state legislature of its responsibility to draw congressional districts. "[The] only injury plaintiffs allege is that the law — specifically the Elections Clause — has not been followed. This injury is precisely the kind of undifferentiated, generalized grievance about the conduct of government that we have refused to countenance in the past. It is quite different from the sorts of injuries alleged by plaintiffs in voting rights cases where we have found standing." *See, e.g.,* Baker v. Carr, 369 U.S. 186 (1962). Because plaintiffs assert no particularized stake in the litigation, we hold that they lack standing to bring their Elections Clause claim. . . .

The judgment of the United States District Court for the District of Colorado is therefore vacated in part, and the case is remanded with instructions to dismiss the Elections Clause claim for lack of standing. We affirm the District Court's dismissal of the Petition Clause claim.

It is so ordered.

Notes: Legislator Standing

1. *Legislator Standing.* In Raines v. Byrd, 521 U.S. 811 (1997), members of Congress who had voted against the Line Item Veto Act sought to challenge that Act, which gave the President the authority to "cancel" certain spending and tax benefit measures after he had signed them into law. Members of Congress claimed that the Act adversely affected "their constitutionally prescribed lawmaking powers." The Court disagreed, noting that "the injury claimed by the Members of Congress here is not claimed in any private capacity but solely because they are Members of Congress. The claimed injury thus runs (in a sense) with the Member's seat, a seat which the Member holds (it may quite arguably be said) as trustee for his constituents, not as a prerogative of personal power." As a result, the Court held that "these individual members of Congress do not have a sufficient 'personal stake' in this dispute and have not alleged a sufficiently concrete injury to have established Article III standing."

2. *More on Legislator Standing. Raines* can be contrasted with the holding in Coleman v. Miller, 307 U.S. 433 (1939), which involved the Kansas secretary of state's decision to endorse a resolution ratifying a proposed amendment to the U.S. Constitution with the notation that it had been "passed" by the legislature. Plaintiffs, members of the Kansas Senate, sued to force the secretary of state to change his endorsement to "not passed" on the basis that the lieutenant governor had, without authority, cast the deciding vote. All 21 plaintiffs had voted against the amendment, claiming that it was not ratified within a reasonable period of time. The Court held that the legislators had standing to bring the case: "Here, the plaintiffs [include] senators, whose votes against ratification have been overridden and virtually held for naught although if they are right in their contentions their votes would have been sufficient to defeat ratification. We think that these senators have a plain, direct and adequate interest in maintaining the effectiveness of their votes. Petitioners [have] set up and claimed a right and privilege under the Constitution of the United States to have their votes given effect

and the state court has denied that right and privilege." Justice Frankfurter, joined by Justices Black and Douglas, argued that the plaintiffs lacked standing to bring the case: "What is their distinctive claim to be here, not possessed by every Kansan? [The] fact that these legislators are part of the ratifying mechanism while the ordinary citizen of Kansas is not, is wholly irrelevant to this issue. . . . We can only adjudicate an issue as to which there is a claimant before us who has a special, individualized stake in it. One who is merely the self-constituted spokesman of a constitutional point of view can not ask us to pass on it. The Kansas legislators could not bring suit explicitly on behalf of the people of the United States to determine whether Kansas could still vote for the Child Labor Amendment. They can not gain standing here by having brought such a suit in their own names. Therefore, none of the petitioners can here raise questions concerning the power of the Kansas legislature to ratify the Amendment."

∾ PROBLEM: CITIZEN STANDING TO CHALLENGE CONSTITUTIONAL AMENDMENTS ∾

Would citizens ever have standing to challenge the validity of a constitutional amendment? Suppose that an amendment is adopted prohibiting child labor. Which of the following groups could establish standing to sue: 1) all Kansas citizens on the basis that "it is the common concern of every citizen of the United States whether the Amendment is still alive, or whether Kansas could be included among the necessary 'three-fourths of the several States'"? 2) citizens of other states (if Kansas's ratification vote put the amendment "over the top" in terms of ratification)? 3) a parent who wanted his/her child to be able to work? 4) a business owner who employed children? *See* Coleman v. Miller, 307 U.S. 433 (1939).

Hein v. Freedom From Religion Foundation, Inc.

551 U.S. 587 (2007)

Justice ALITO announced the judgment of the Court and delivered an opinion in which THE CHIEF JUSTICE and Justice KENNEDY join.

This is a lawsuit in which it was claimed that conferences held as part of the President's Faith-Based and Community Initiatives program violated the Establishment Clause of the First Amendment because, among other things, President Bush and former Secretary of Education Paige gave speeches that used "religious imagery" and praised the efficacy of faith-based programs in delivering social services. The plaintiffs contend that they meet the standing requirements of Article III of the Constitution because they pay federal taxes. . . .

In 2001, the President issued an executive order creating the White House Office of Faith-Based and Community Initiatives within the Executive Office of the President. Exec. Order No. 13199, 3 CFR 752. The purpose of this new office was to ensure that "private and charitable community groups, including religious ones [have] the fullest opportunity permitted by law to compete on a level playing field, so long as they achieve valid public purposes" and adhere to "the bedrock

principles of pluralism, nondiscrimination, evenhandedness, and neutrality."
The office was specifically charged with the task of eliminating unnecessary
bureaucratic, legislative, and regulatory barriers that could impede such organizations' effectiveness and ability to compete equally for federal assistance.

By separate executive orders, the President also created Executive Department Centers for Faith-Based and Community Initiatives within several federal
agencies and departments. These centers were given the job of ensuring that
faith-based community groups would be eligible to compete for federal financial
support without impairing their independence or autonomy, as long as they did
"not use direct Federal financial assistance to support any inherently religious
activities, such as worship, religious instruction, or proselytization." Exec. Order
No. 13279, 3 CFR §2(f), p. 260. To this end, the President directed that "[n]o
organization should be discriminated against on the basis of religion or religious
belief in the administration or distribution of Federal financial assistance under
social service programs," and that "[a]ll organizations that receive Federal financial assistance under social services programs should be prohibited from discriminating against beneficiaries or potential beneficiaries of the social services
programs on the basis of religion or religious belief." Petitioners, who have been
sued in their official capacities, are the directors of the White House Office and
various Executive Department Centers.

No congressional legislation specifically authorized the creation of the White
House Office or the Executive Department Centers. Rather, they were "created
entirely within the Executive Branch [by] Presidential executive order." Nor has
Congress enacted any law specifically appropriating money for these entities'
activities. Instead, their activities are funded through general Executive Branch
appropriations. For example, the Department of Education's Center is funded
from money appropriated for the Office of the Secretary of Education, while the
Department of Housing and Urban Development's Center is funded through
that Department's salaries and expenses account.

The respondents are Freedom From Religion Foundation, Inc., a nonstock
corporation "opposed to government endorsement of religion," and three of its
members. Respondents brought suit in [federal court], alleging that petitioners
violated the Establishment Clause by organizing conferences at which faith-based
organizations allegedly "are singled out as being particularly worthy of federal
funding[,] and the belief in God is extolled as distinguishing the claimed effectiveness of faith-based social services." Respondents further alleged that the content of these conferences sent a message to religious believers "that they are
insiders and favored members of the political community" and that the conferences sent the message to nonbelievers "that they are outsiders" and "not full
members of the political community." In short, respondents alleged that the conferences were designed to promote, and had the effect of promoting, religious
community groups over secular ones.

The only asserted basis for standing was that the individual respondents are
federal taxpayers who are "opposed to the use of Congressional taxpayer appropriations to advance and promote religion." [R]espondents sought to challenge
Executive Branch expenditures for these conferences, which, they contended,

violated the Establishment Clause. . . . The District Court dismissed the claims against petitioners for lack of standing. . . . A divided panel of the United States Court of Appeals for the Seventh Circuit reversed. We granted certiorari [and] now reverse.

Article III of the Constitution limits the judicial power of the United States to the resolution of "Cases" and "Controversies," and "'Article III standing . . . enforces the Constitution's case-or-controversy requirement.'" DaimlerChrysler Corp. v. Cuno, 547 U.S. 332, 342 (2006) (quoting Elk Grove Unified School Dist. v. Newdow, 542 U.S. 1, 11 (2004)). [The] requisite elements of Article III standing are well established: "A plaintiff must allege personal injury fairly traceable to the defendant's allegedly unlawful conduct and likely to be redressed by the requested relief." Allen v. Wright, 468 U.S. 737, 751 (1984).

"[The] judicial power of the United States defined by Art. III is not an unconditioned authority to determine the constitutionality of legislative or executive acts." Valley Forge Christian College v. Americans United for Separation of Church and State, Inc., 454 U.S. 464, 471 (1982). The federal courts are not empowered to seek out and strike down any governmental act that they deem to be repugnant to the Constitution. Rather, federal courts sit "solely, to decide on the rights of individuals," Marbury v. Madison, 1 Cranch 137, 170, 2 L.Ed. 60 (1803), and must "'refrai[n] from passing upon the constitutionality of an act [unless] obliged to do so in the proper performance of our judicial function, when the question is raised by a party whose interests entitle him to raise it.'" *Valley Forge, supra,* at 474 (quoting Blair v. United States, 250 U.S. 273, 279 (1919)). . . .

As a general matter, the interest of a federal taxpayer in seeing that Treasury funds are spent in accordance with the Constitution does not give rise to the kind of redressable "personal injury" required for Article III standing. Of course, a taxpayer has standing to challenge the *collection* of a specific tax assessment as unconstitutional; being forced to pay such a tax causes a real and immediate economic injury to the individual taxpayer. *See, e.g.,* Follett v. Town of McCormick, 321 U.S. 573 (1944). But that is not the interest on which respondents assert standing here. Rather, their claim is that, having paid lawfully collected taxes into the Federal Treasury at some point, they have a continuing, legally cognizable interest in ensuring that those funds are not *used* by the Government in a way that violates the Constitution.

We have consistently held that this type of interest is too generalized and attenuated to support Article III standing. . . . In [Flast v. Cohen, 392 U.S. 83 (1968),] the Court carved out a narrow exception to the general constitutional prohibition against taxpayer standing. The taxpayer-plaintiff in that case challenged the distribution of federal funds to religious schools under the Elementary and Secondary Education Act of 1965, alleging that such aid violated the Establishment Clause. The Court set out a two-part test for determining whether a federal taxpayer has standing to challenge an allegedly unconstitutional expenditure:

First, the taxpayer must establish a logical link between that status and the type of legislative enactment attacked. Thus, a taxpayer will be a proper party to allege the unconstitutionality only of exercises of congressional power under the taxing and spending clause of Art. I, §8, of the Constitution. It will not be sufficient to allege an incidental expenditure of tax funds in the administration of an essentially regulatory statute. . . . Secondly, the taxpayer must establish a nexus between that status and the precise nature of the constitutional infringement alleged. Under this requirement, the taxpayer must show that the challenged enactment exceeds specific constitutional limitations imposed upon the exercise of the congressional taxing and spending power and not simply that the enactment is generally beyond the powers delegated to Congress by Art. I, §8. *Flast,* 392 U.S., at 102-103.

The Court held that the taxpayer-plaintiff in *Flast* had satisfied both prongs of this test: The plaintiff's "constitutional challenge [was] made to an exercise by Congress of its power under Art. I, §8, to spend for the general welfare," and she alleged a violation of the Establishment Clause, which "operates as a specific constitutional limitation upon the exercise by Congress of the taxing and spending power conferred by Art. I, §8."

Respondents argue that this case falls within the *Flast* exception, which they read to cover any "expenditure of government funds in violation of the Establishment Clause." But this broad reading fails to observe "the rigor with which the *Flast* exception to the *Frothingham* principle ought to be applied." *Valley Forge,* 454 U.S., at 481.

The expenditures at issue in *Flast* were made pursuant to an express congressional mandate and a specific congressional appropriation. The plaintiff in that case challenged disbursements made under the Elementary and Secondary Education Act of 1965. That Act expressly appropriated the sum of $100 million for fiscal year 1966, §201(b), and authorized the disbursement of those funds to local educational agencies for the education of low-income students. The Act mandated that local educational agencies receiving such funds "ma[k]e provision for including special educational services and arrangements (such as dual enrollment, educational radio and television, and mobile educational services and equipment)" in which students enrolled in private elementary and secondary schools could participate. In addition, recipient agencies were required to ensure that "library resources, textbooks, and other instructional materials" funded through the grants "be provided on an equitable basis for the use of children and teachers in private elementary and secondary schools."

The expenditures challenged in *Flast,* then, were funded by a specific congressional appropriation and were disbursed to private schools (including religiously affiliated schools) pursuant to a direct and unambiguous congressional mandate. Indeed, the *Flast* taxpayer-plaintiff's constitutional claim was premised on the contention that if the Government's actions were "'within the authority and intent of the Act, the Act is to that extent unconstitutional and void.'" And the judgment reviewed by this Court in *Flast* solely concerned the question whether "if [the challenged] expenditures are authorized by the Act the statute constitutes a 'law respecting an establishment of religion' and law 'prohibiting the free exercise thereof'" under the First Amendment.

Given that the alleged Establishment Clause violation in *Flast* was funded by a specific congressional appropriation and was undertaken pursuant to an express congressional mandate, the Court concluded that the taxpayer-plaintiffs had established the requisite "logical link between [their taxpayer] status and the type of legislative enactment attacked." In the Court's words, "[t]heir constitutional challenge [was] made to an exercise by Congress of its power under Art. I, §8, to spend for the general welfare." But as this Court later noted, *Flast* "limited taxpayer standing to challenges directed 'only [at] exercises of congressional power'" under the Taxing and Spending Clause. *Valley Forge,* 454 U.S., at 479.

The link between congressional action and constitutional violation that supported taxpayer standing in *Flast* is missing here. Respondents do not challenge any specific congressional action or appropriation; nor do they ask the Court to invalidate any congressional enactment or legislatively created program as unconstitutional. That is because the expenditures at issue here were not made pursuant to any Act of Congress. Rather, Congress provided general appropriations to the Executive Branch to fund its day-to-day activities. These appropriations did not expressly authorize, direct, or even mention the expenditures of which respondents complain. Those expenditures resulted from executive discretion, not congressional action.

We have never found taxpayer standing under such circumstances. In *Valley Forge,* we held that a taxpayer lacked standing to challenge "a decision by [the federal Department of Health, Education and Welfare] to transfer a parcel of federal property" to a religious college because this transfer was "not a congressional action." In fact, the connection to congressional action was closer in *Valley Forge* than it is here, because in that case, the "particular Executive Branch action" being challenged was at least "arguably authorized" by the Federal Property and Administrative Services Act of 1949, which permitted federal agencies to transfer surplus property to private entities. Nevertheless, we found that the plaintiffs lacked standing because *Flast* "limited taxpayer standing to challenges directed 'only [at] exercises of congressional power'" under the Taxing and Spending Clause.[1] . . .

Bowen v. Kendrick, 487 U.S. 589 (1988), on which respondents rely heavily, is not to the contrary. In that case, we held that the taxpayer-plaintiffs had standing to mount an as-applied challenge to the Adolescent Family Life Act (AFLA), which authorized federal grants to private community service groups including religious organizations. The Court found "a sufficient nexus between the taxpayer's standing as a taxpayer and the congressional exercise of taxing and spending power," notwithstanding the fact that "the funding authorized by Congress ha[d] flowed through and been administered" by an Executive Branch official.

But the key to that conclusion was the Court's recognition that AFLA was "at heart a program of disbursement of funds pursuant to Congress' taxing and spending powers," and that the plaintiffs' claims "call[ed] into question how the funds authorized by Congress [were] being disbursed *pursuant to the AFLA's statutory mandate.*" AFLA not only expressly authorized and appropriated specific funds for grant-making, it also expressly contemplated that some of those moneys might go to projects involving religious groups. Unlike this case, *Kendrick*

---

1. Valley Forge also relied on a second rationale: that the authorizing Act was an exercise of Congress' power under the Property Clause of Art. IV, §3, cl. 2, and not the Taxing and Spending Clause of Art. I, §8. But this conclusion merely provided an additional — "and perhaps redundan[t]," basis for denying a claim of standing that was already foreclosed because it was not based on any congressional action.

involved a "program of disbursement of funds pursuant to Congress' taxing and spending powers" that "Congress had created," "authorized," and "mandate[d]."

Respondents attempt to paint their lawsuit as a *Kendrick*-style as-applied challenge, but this effort is unavailing for the simple reason that they can cite no statute whose application they challenge. The best they can do is to point to unspecified, lump-sum "Congressional budget appropriations" for the general use of the Executive Branch — the allocation of which "is a[n] administrative decision traditionally regarded as committed to agency discretion." Lincoln v. Vigil, 508 U.S. 182, 192 (1993). Characterizing this case as an "as-applied challenge" to these general appropriations statutes would stretch the meaning of that term past its breaking point. It cannot be that every legal challenge to a discretionary Executive Branch action implicates the constitutionality of the underlying congressional appropriation. When a criminal defendant charges that a federal agent carried out an unreasonable search or seizure, we do not view that claim as an as-applied challenge to the constitutionality of the statute appropriating funds for the Federal Bureau of Investigation. Respondents have not established why the discretionary Executive Branch expenditures here, which are similarly funded by no-strings, lump-sum appropriations, should be viewed any differently.[2]

In short, this case falls outside the "the narrow exception" that *Flast* "created to the general rule against taxpayer standing established in *Frothingham*." *Kendrick, supra,* at 618. Because the expenditures that respondents challenge were not expressly authorized or mandated by any specific congressional enactment, respondents' lawsuit is not directed at an exercise of congressional power, and thus lacks the requisite "logical nexus" between taxpayer status "and the type of legislative enactment attacked."

Respondents argue that it is "arbitrary" to distinguish between money spent pursuant to congressional mandate and expenditures made in the course of executive discretion, because "the injury to taxpayers in both situations is the very injury targeted by the Establishment Clause and *Flast* — the expenditure for the support of religion of funds exacted from taxpayers." [But] *Flast* focused on congressional action, and we must decline this invitation to extend its holding to encompass discretionary Executive Branch expenditures. *Flast* itself distinguished the "incidental expenditure of tax funds in the administration of an essentially regulatory statute," and we have subsequently rejected the view that taxpayer standing "extends to 'the Government as a whole, regardless of which branch is at work in a particular instance,'" *Valley Forge, supra,* at 484, n.20. Moreover, we have repeatedly emphasized that the *Flast* exception has a "narrow application in our precedent," that only "slightly lowered" the bar on taxpayer standing, and that must be applied with "rigor," *Valley Forge, supra,* at 481.

---

2. Nor is it relevant that Congress may have informally "earmarked" portions of its general Executive Branch appropriations to fund the offices and centers whose expenditures are at issue here. "[W]here 'Congress merely appropriates lump-sum amounts without statutorily restricting what can be done with those funds, a clear inference arises that it does not intend to impose legally binding restrictions, and indicia in committee reports and other legislative history as to how the funds should or are expected to be spent do not establish any legal requirements on' the agency." *Lincoln,* 508 U.S., at 192.

It is significant that, in the four decades since its creation, the *Flast* exception has largely been confined to its facts. We have declined to lower the taxpayer standing bar in suits alleging violations of any constitutional provision apart from the Establishment Clause. *See* Tilton v. Richardson, 403 U.S. 672 (1971) (no taxpayer standing to sue under Free Exercise Clause of First Amendment); *Richardson*, 418 U.S., at 175 (no taxpayer standing to sue under Statement and Account Clause of Art. I); *Schlesinger*, 418 U.S., at 228 (no taxpayer standing to sue under Incompatibility Clause of Art. I); *Cuno, supra* (no taxpayer standing to sue under Commerce Clause). We have similarly refused to extend *Flast* to permit taxpayer standing for Establishment Clause challenges that do not implicate Congress' taxing and spending power. *See Valley Forge, supra,* at 479-482. In effect, we have adopted the position set forth by Justice Powell in his concurrence in *Richardson* and have "limit[ed] the expansion of federal taxpayer and citizen standing in the absence of specific statutory authorization to an outer boundary drawn by the *results* in *Flast*. . . ."

Because almost all Executive Branch activity is ultimately funded by some congressional appropriation, extending the *Flast* exception to purely executive expenditures would effectively subject every federal action — be it a conference, proclamation or speech — to Establishment Clause challenge by any taxpayer in federal court. To see the wide swathe of activity that respondents' proposed rule would cover, one need look no further than the amended complaint in this action, which focuses largely on speeches and presentations made by Executive Branch officials. Such a broad reading would ignore the first prong of *Flast*'s standing test, which requires "a logical link between [taxpayer] status and the type of legislative enactment attacked."

It would also raise serious separation-of-powers concerns. . . . By framing the standing question solely in terms of whether the dispute would be presented in an adversary context and in a form traditionally viewed as capable of judicial resolution, *Flast* "failed to recognize that this doctrine has a separation-of-powers component, which keeps courts within certain traditional bounds vis-a-vis the other branches, concrete adverseness or not." Lewis v. Casey, 518 U.S. 343, 353, n.3 (1996). Respondents' position, if adopted, would repeat and compound this mistake.

The constitutional requirements for federal-court jurisdiction — including the standing requirements and Article III — "are an essential ingredient of separation and equilibration of powers." Steel Co. v. Citizens for Better Environment, 523 U.S. 83 (1998). "Relaxation of standing requirements is directly related to the expansion of judicial power," and lowering the taxpayer standing bar to permit challenges of purely executive actions "would significantly alter the allocation of power at the national level, with a shift away from a democratic form of government." *Richardson*, 418 U.S., at 188 (Powell, J., concurring). The rule respondents propose would enlist the federal courts to superintend, at the behest of any federal taxpayer, the speeches, statements, and myriad daily activities of the President, his staff, and other Executive Branch officials. This would "be quite at odds [with] *Flast*'s own promise that it would not transform federal courts into forums for taxpayers' 'generalized grievances'" about the conduct of government, and would "open the Judiciary to an arguable charge of providing 'government by injunction,'" *Schlesinger*, 418 U.S., at 222. It would deputize federal courts as '"virtually continuing monitors of the wisdom and soundness of Executive action,'" and that, most emphatically, "is not the role of the judiciary." *Allen*, 468 U.S., at 760 (quoting Laird v. Tatum, 408 U.S. 1 (1972)).

[N]either the Court of Appeals nor respondents has identified a workable limitation. The Court of Appeals [conceded] that a taxpayer would lack standing where "the marginal or incremental cost to the taxpaying public of the alleged violation of the establishment clause" is "zero." [T]he Court of Appeals opined that a taxpayer would not have standing to challenge a President's favorable reference to religion in a State of the Union address because the costs associated with the speech "would be no greater merely because the President had mentioned Moses rather than John Stuart Mill." [I]f we take the Court of Appeals' test literally[,] taxpayers might well have standing to challenge some (and perhaps many) speeches. As Judge Easterbrook observed: "The total cost of presidential proclamations and speeches by Cabinet officers that touch on religion (Thanksgiving and several other holidays) surely exceeds $500,000 annually; it may cost that much to use Air Force One and send a Secret Service detail to a single speaking engagement." [Suppose] that it is alleged that a speech writer or other staff member spent extra time doing research for the purpose of including "religious imagery" in a speech. Suppose that a President or a Cabinet officer attends or speaks at a prayer breakfast and that the time spent was time that would have otherwise been spent on secular work.

Respondents [would] require that a challenged expenditure be "fairly traceable to the conduct alleged to violate the Establishment Clause." Applying this test, they argue, would "scree[n] out . . . challenge[s to] the content of one particular speech, for example the State of the Union address, as an Establishment Clause violation." We find little comfort in this vague and ill-defined test. As an initial matter, respondents fail to explain why the (often substantial) costs that attend, for example, a Presidential address are any less "traceable" than the expenses related to the Executive Branch statements and conferences at issue here. Indeed, respondents concede that even lawsuits involving *de minimis* amounts of taxpayer money can pass their proposed "traceability" test.

[If] the question is whether an allegedly unconstitutional executive action can somehow be traced to taxpayer funds *in general*, the answer will always be yes: Almost all Executive Branch activities are ultimately funded by *some* congressional appropriation, whether general or specific, which is in turn financed by tax receipts. If, on the other hand, the question is whether the challenged action can be traced to the contributions of a *particular* taxpayer-plaintiff, the answer will almost always be no: As we recognized in *Frothingham*, the interest of any individual taxpayer in a particular federal expenditure "is comparatively minute and indeterminable . . . and constantly changing."

Respondents set out a parade of horribles that they claim could occur if *Flast* is not extended to discretionary Executive Branch expenditures. For example, they say, a federal agency could use its discretionary funds to build a house of worship or to hire clergy of one denomination and send them out to spread their faith. Or an agency could use its funds to make bulk purchases of Stars of David, crucifixes, or depictions of the star and crescent for use in its offices or for distribution to the employees or the general public. Of course, none of these things has happened, even though *Flast* has not previously been expanded in the way that respondents urge. In the unlikely event that any of these executive actions did take place, Congress could quickly step in. And respondents make no effort to show that these improbable abuses could not be challenged in federal court by plaintiffs who would possess standing based on grounds other than taxpayer standing.

Over the years, *Flast* has been defended by some and criticized by others. But the present case does not require us to reconsider that precedent. The Court of Appeals did not apply *Flast*; it extended *Flast*. It is a necessary concomitant of the doctrine of *stare decisis* that a precedent is not always expanded to the limit of its logic. . . . We leave *Flast* as we found it. . . .

For these reasons, the judgment of the Court of Appeals for the Seventh Circuit is reversed.

It is so ordered.

Justice KENNEDY, concurring.

[*Flast*] established a "narrow exception" to the rule against taxpayer standing. . . . The Court should not authorize the constant intrusion upon the executive realm that would result from granting taxpayer standing in the instant case. . . . Government officials must make a conscious decision to obey the Constitution whether or not their acts can be challenged in a court of law and then must conform their actions to these principled determinations.

Justice SCALIA, with whom Justice THOMAS joins, concurring in the judgment.

[*Flast*] is wholly irreconcilable with the Article III restrictions on federal-court jurisdiction that this Court has repeatedly confirmed are embodied in the doctrine of standing. . . . Wallet Injury is the type of concrete and particularized injury one would expect to be asserted in a *taxpayer* suit, namely, a claim that the plaintiff's tax liability is higher than it would be, but for the allegedly unlawful government action. The stumbling block for suits challenging government expenditures based on this conventional type of injury is [that] plaintiff cannot satisfy the traceability and redressability prongs of standing. It is uncertain what the plaintiff's tax bill would have been had the allegedly forbidden expenditure not been made, and it is even more speculative whether the government will, in response to an adverse court decision, lower taxes rather than spend the funds in some other manner.

Psychic Injury, on the other hand, has nothing to do with the plaintiff's tax liability. Instead, the injury consists of the taxpayer's *mental displeasure* that money extracted from him is being spent in an unlawful manner. This shift in focus eliminates traceability and redressability problems. Psychic Injury is directly traceable to the improper *use* of taxpayer funds, and it is redressed when the improper use is enjoined, regardless of whether that injunction affects the taxpayer's purse.

Flast and the cases following its teaching have invoked a peculiarly restricted version of Psychic Injury, permitting taxpayer displeasure over unconstitutional spending to support standing *only if* the constitutional provision allegedly violated is a specific limitation on the taxing and spending power. [T]his conceptualizing of injury in fact in purely mental terms conflicts squarely with the familiar proposition that a plaintiff lacks a concrete and particularized injury when his only complaint is the generalized grievance that the law is being violated. . . .

[*Flast*] relied on Psychic Injury to support standing, describing the "injury" as the taxpayer's allegation that "his tax money is being extracted and spent in violation of specific constitutional protections against such abuses of legislative power." [The] criteria in *Flast*'s two-part test are *entirely unrelated* to the purported goal of ensuring that the plaintiff has a sufficient "stake in the outcome of the controversy." [In] reality, [there] is simply no material difference between *Flast* and *Doremus* as far as Psychic Injury is concerned: If taxpayers upset with the government's giving money to parochial schools had standing to sue, so should the taxpayers who disapproved of the government's paying public-school teachers to read the Bible. . . . Like the dissenters in *Valley Forge,* I cannot fathom why Article III standing should turn on whether the government enables a religious organization to obtain real estate by giving it a check drawn from general tax revenues or instead by buying the property itself and then transferring title. . . .

A mere six years later, *Flast* was resuscitated in *Bowen* [which] was obviously based on Psychic Injury: The taxpayers could not possibly make, and did not attempt to make, the showing required for Wallet Injury. . . . Just as *Kendrick* did not care whether the appropriated funds would have been spent anyway — given to a different, permissible recipient — so also *Doremus* should not have cared that the teachers would likely receive the same salary once their classroom activities were limited to secular conduct. *Flast* and *Kendrick*'s acceptance of Psychic Injury is fundamentally at odds with *Frothingham, Doremus,* and *Valley Forge.*

[I]n DaimlerChrysler Corp. v. Cuno, 547 U.S. [332] (2006), we concisely confirmed that *Flast* was based on Psychic Injury. . . . What *Cuno*'s conceptualization of *Flast* reveals is that there are only two logical routes available to this Court. We must initially decide whether Psychic Injury is consistent with Article III. If it is, we should apply *Flast* to *all* challenges to government expenditures in violation of constitutional provisions that specifically limit the taxing and spending power; if it is not, we should overturn *Flast*. . . .

Is a taxpayer's purely psychological displeasure that his funds are being spent in an allegedly unlawful manner ever sufficiently concrete and particularized to support Article III standing? The answer is plainly no. . . . Nor does *Flast*'s limitation on Psychic Injury — the limitation that it suffices only when the two-pronged "nexus" test is met — cure the Article III deficiency. The fact that it is the alleged violation of a specific constitutional limit on the taxing and spending power that produces the taxpayer's mental angst does not change the fundamental flaw. It remains the case that the taxpayer seeks "relief that no more directly and tangibly benefits him than it does the public at large." *Lujan, supra,* at 573-574. And it is of no conceivable relevance to this issue whether the Establishment

Clause was originally conceived of as a specific limitation on the taxing and spending power. . . .

[And] once a proper understanding of the relationship of standing to the separation of powers is brought to bear, Psychic Injury, even as limited in *Flast,* is revealed for what it is: a contradiction of the basic propositions that the function of the judicial power "is, solely, to decide on the rights of individuals," Marbury v. Madison, 1 Cranch 137, 170, 2 L.Ed. 60 (1803), and that generalized grievances affecting the public at large have their remedy in the political process. . . .

[I] can think of few cases less warranting of *stare decisis* respect. It is time — it is past time — to call an end. *Flast* should be overruled.

Justice SOUTER, with whom Justice STEVENS, Justice GINSBURG, and Justice BREYER join, dissenting.

[We] held in *Flast,* and repeated just last Term, that the "'injury' alleged in Establishment Clause challenges to federal spending" is "the very 'extract[ion] and spen[ding]' of 'tax money' in aid of religion." DaimlerChrysler Corp. v. Cuno, 547 U.S. [332] (2006) (quoting *Flast, supra,* at 106). . . . The right of conscience and the expenditure of an identifiable three pence raised by taxes for the support of a religious cause are therefore not to be split off from one another. The three pence implicates the conscience, and the injury from Government expenditures on religion is not accurately classified with the "Psychic Injury" that results whenever a congressional appropriation or executive expenditure raises hackles of disagreement with the policy supported, Justice Stewart recognized this in his concurring opinion in *Flast,* when he said that "every taxpayer can claim a personal constitutional right not to be taxed for the support of a religious institution," and thus distinguished the case from one in which a taxpayer sought only to air a generalized grievance in federal court.

Here, there is no dispute that taxpayer money in identifiable amounts is funding conferences, and these are alleged to have the purpose of promoting religion. . . . When executive agencies spend identifiable sums of tax money for religious purposes, no less than when Congress authorizes the same thing, taxpayers suffer injury. . . .

The plurality points to the separation of powers to explain its distinction between legislative and executive spending decisions, but there is no difference on that point of view between a Judicial Branch review of an executive decision and a judicial evaluation of a congressional one. We owe respect to each of the other branches, no more to the former than to the latter, and no one has suggested that the Establishment Clause lacks applicability to executive uses of money. [I]n *Bowen,* we recognized the equivalence between a challenge to a congressional spending bill and a claim that the Executive Branch was spending an appropriation, each in violation of the Establishment Clause. We held that the "claim [that] funds [were] being used improperly by individual grantees [was no] less a challenge to congressional taxing and spending power simply because the funding authorized by Congress has flowed through and been administered by the Secretary," and we added that "we have not questioned the standing of tax-payer plaintiffs to raise Establishment Clause challenges, even when their claims raised questions about the administratively made grants."

The plurality points out that the statute in *Bowen* "expressly authorized and appropriated specific funds for grantmaking" and "expressly contemplated that some of those moneys might go to projects involving religious groups." That is all true, but there is no reason to think it should matter. . . . In *Bowen* we already had found the statute valid on its face before we turned to the taxpayers' as-applied challenge so the case cannot be read to hold that taxpayers have standing only to claim that congressional action, but not its implementation, violates the Establishment Clause. . . .

In the case of economic or physical harms, of course, the "injury in fact" question is straightforward. But once one strays from these obvious cases, the enquiry can turn subtle. Are esthetic harms sufficient for Article III standing? What about being forced to compete on an uneven playing field based on race (without showing that an economic loss resulted), or living in a racially gerrymandered electoral district? These injuries are no more concrete than seeing one's tax dollars spent on religion, but we have recognized each one as enough for standing. *See* Friends of Earth, Inc. v. Laidlaw Environmental Services (TOC), Inc., 528 U.S. 167 (2000) (esthetic injury); United States v. Hays, 515 U.S. 737, 744-745 (1995). This is not to say that any sort of alleged injury will satisfy Article III, but only that intangible harms must be evaluated case by case.

Thus, *Flast* speaks for this Court's recognition (shared by a majority of the Court today) that when the Government spends money for religious purposes a taxpayer's injury is serious and concrete enough to be "judicially cognizable." The judgment of sufficient injury takes account of the Madisonian relationship of tax money and conscience, but it equally reflects the Founders' pragmatic "conviction that individual religious liberty could be achieved best under a government which was stripped of all power to tax, to support, or otherwise to assist any or all religions," Everson v. Board of Ed. of Ewing, 330 U.S. 1, 11 (1947), and the realization continuing to the modern day that favoritism for religion "'sends the . . . message to . . . nonadherents "that they are outsiders, not full members of the political community,"'" McCreary County v. American Civil Liberties Union of Ky., 545 U.S. 844, 860 (2005) (quoting Santa Fe Independent School Dist. v. Doe, 530 U.S. 290, 309-310 (2000), in turn quoting Lynch v. Donnelly, 465 U.S. 668, 688 (1984) (O'Connor, J., concurring).[3]

Because the taxpayers in this case have alleged the type of injury this Court has seen as sufficient for standing, I would affirm.

___

3. There will not always be competitors for the funds who would make better plaintiffs (and indeed there appears to be no such competitor here), so after accepting the importance of the injury there is no reason to refuse standing as a prudential matter.

Notes: Flast and the Commerce Clause

In DaimlerChrysler Corp. v. Cuno, 547 U.S. 332 (2006), the Court rejected the argument that *Flast* authorizes a special exception for Commerce Clause challenges: "[P]laintiffs' reliance on *Flast* is misguided: Whatever rights plaintiffs have under the Commerce Clause, they are fundamentally unlike the right not to "'contribute three pence . . . for the support of any one [religious] establishment.'" (quoting 2 *Writings of James Madison* 186 (G. Hunt ed. 1901)). "Indeed, plaintiffs compare the Establishment Clause to the Commerce Clause at such a high level of generality that almost any constitutional constraint on government power would 'specifically limit' a State's taxing and spending power for *Flast* purposes. And even if the two Clauses are similar in that they often implicate governments' fiscal decisions, a finding that the Commerce Clause satisfies the *Flast* test would leave no principled way of distinguishing those other constitutional provisions that we have recognized constrain governments' taxing and spending decisions. Yet such a broad application of *Flast*'s exception to the general prohibition on taxpayer standing would be quite at odds with its narrow application in our precedent and *Flast's* own promise that it would not transform federal courts into forums for taxpayers' 'generalized grievances.' . . . The *Flast* Court discerned in the history of the Establishment Clause 'the specific evils feared by [its drafters] that the taxing and spending power would be used to favor one religion over another or to support religion in general.' The Court therefore understood the 'injury' alleged in Establishment Clause challenges to federal spending to be the very 'extract[ion] and spen[ding]' of 'tax money' in aid of religion alleged by a plaintiff. And an injunction against the spending would of course redress *that* injury, regardless of whether lawmakers would dispose of the savings in a way that would benefit the taxpayer-plaintiffs personally."

∼ PROBLEMS ∼

1. *The Flast Test and Other Constitutional Provisions.* After *Hein*, can it be said that any other constitutional limitations operate as a specific limitation on Article I, Section 8 expenditures? If so, which ones? In other words, is the *Flast* decision essentially limited to its facts?

2. *Challenging Undeclared Wars.* When we examined the problem of undeclared wars, and citizen challenges to such wars, we saw that such suits are usually dismissed as involving political questions (or perhaps on ripeness grounds). Should such suits also be dismissed on standing grounds? After *Frothingham*, *Flast*, and *Valley Forge*, suppose that the President has troops massed in a foreign country in preparation for a possible invasion of a third country. Consider whether the following individuals have standing to challenge an undeclared war: a) a citizen who wants to challenge an undeclared war as illegal; b) a citizen who wants to argue that an undeclared war constitutes a violation of Congress's power to declare war; c) a soldier, about to be shipped off to the theater of operations, who claims that she is illegally being placed in harm's way; d) a member of Congress who claims that an undeclared war would constitute a violation of his/her right to

vote on whether to go to war. *See* Holtzman v. Schlesinger, 484 F.2d 1307 (2d Cir. 1973); Dellums v. Bush, 752 F. Supp. 1141 (D.D.C. 1990).

b. Causation

The Court has held that the "irreducible constitutional minimum" of standing contains three elements: 1) the plaintiff must have suffered an "injury in fact" — an invasion of a legally protected interest that is a) concrete and particularized and b) actual or imminent, not conjectural or hypothetical; 2) there must be a causal connection between the injury and the conduct complained of; and 3) it must be likely, as opposed to merely speculative, that the injury will be redressed by a favorable decision. *See* Lujan v. Defenders of Wildlife, 504 U.S. 555 (1992). The Court has also held that it will not entertain a "generalized grievance against allegedly illegal governmental conduct." *See, e.g.,* Schlesinger v. Reservists Comm. to Stop the War, 418 U.S. 208 (1974). "[I]t is the burden of the party who seeks the exercise of jurisdiction in his favor" "clearly to allege facts demonstrating that he is a proper party to invoke judicial resolution of the dispute."

Standing cases can involve both constitutional (Article III "case and controversy") and "prudential" components. By "prudential," we mean that, although the case may present enough of a case and controversy so that Article III allows a federal court to hear the case, the Court might decline to hear it for discretionary (so-called "prudential") reasons.

Lujan v. Defenders of Wildlife
504 U.S. 555 (1992)

Justice SCALIA delivered the opinion of the Court with respect to Parts I, II, III-A, and IV, and an opinion with respect to Part III-B, in which THE CHIEF JUSTICE, Justice WHITE, and Justice THOMAS join.

This case involves a challenge to a rule promulgated by the Secretary of the Interior interpreting §7 of the Endangered Species Act of 1973 (ESA), in such fashion as to render it applicable only to actions within the United States or on the high seas. The preliminary issue, and the only one we reach, is whether respondents here, plaintiffs below, have standing to seek judicial review of the rule.

I

The ESA seeks to protect species of animals against threats to their continuing existence caused by man. [The] ESA instructs the Secretary of the Interior to promulgate by regulation a list of those species which are either endangered or threatened under enumerated criteria, and to define the critical habitat of these species. Section 7(a)(2) of the Act then provides, in pertinent part:

> Each Federal agency shall, in consultation with and with the assistance of the Secretary [of the Interior], insure that any action authorized, funded, or carried out by such agency [is] not likely to jeopardize the continued existence of any endangered species or threatened species

or result in the destruction or adverse modification of habitat of such species which is determined by the Secretary, after consultation as appropriate with affected States, to be critical.

In 1978, the Fish and Wildlife Service (FWS) and the National Marine Fisheries
Service (NMFS), on behalf of the Secretary of the Interior and the Secretary of
Commerce respectively, promulgated a joint regulation stating that the obligations imposed by §7(a)(2) extend to actions taken in foreign nations. The next
year, however, the Interior Department began to reexamine its position. . . . A
revised joint regulation, reinterpreting §7(a)(2) to require consultation only for
actions taken in the United States or on the high seas, was proposed in 1983, and
promulgated in 1986.

[T]hereafter, respondents, organizations dedicated to wildlife conservation
and other environmental causes, filed this action against the Secretary of the Interior, seeking a declaratory judgment that the new regulation is in error as to the
geographic scope of §7(a)(2) and an injunction requiring the Secretary to promulgate a new regulation restoring the initial interpretation. . . .

[O]ur cases have established that the irreducible constitutional minimum of
standing contains three elements. First, the plaintiff must have suffered an
"injury in fact" — an invasion of a legally protected interest which is (a) concrete
and particularized, and (b) "actual or imminent, not 'conjectural' or 'hypothetical.'" Second, there must be a causal connection between the injury and the conduct complained of — the injury has to be "fairly [traceable] to the challenged
action of the defendant, and not [the] result [of] the independent action of some
third party not before the court." Third, it must be "likely," as opposed to merely
"speculative," that the injury will be "redressed by a favorable decision." . . .

III

We think the Court of Appeals failed to apply the foregoing principles in denying
the Secretary's motion for summary judgment. Respondents had not made the
requisite demonstration of (at least) injury and redressability.

A

Respondents' claim to injury is that the lack of consultation with respect to certain funded activities abroad "[increases] the rate of extinction of endangered
and threatened species." [Of] course, the desire to use or observe an animal species, even for purely esthetic purposes, is undeniably a cognizable interest for
purpose of standing. "But the 'injury in fact' test requires more than an injury to
a cognizable interest. It requires that the party seeking review be himself among
the injured." To survive the Secretary's summary judgment motion, respondents
had to submit affidavits or other evidence showing, through specific facts, not
only that listed species were in fact being threatened by funded activities abroad,
but also that one or more of respondents' members would thereby be "directly"
affected apart from their "'special interest' in th[e] subject."

With respect to this aspect of the case, [Ms. Joyce] Kelly stated that she traveled to Egypt in 1986 and "observed the traditional habitat of the endangered

nile crocodile there and intend[s] to do so again, and hope[s] to observe the crocodile directly," and that she "will suffer harm in fact as the result of [the] American [role] in overseeing the rehabilitation of the Aswan High Dam on the Nile [and in developing Egypt's] Master Water Plan." Ms. [Amy] Skilbred averred that she traveled to Sri Lanka in 1981 and "observed th[e] habitat" of "endangered species such as the Asian elephant and the leopard" at what is now the site of the Mahaweli project funded by the Agency for International Development (AID), although she "was unable to see any of the endangered species"; "this development project," she continued, "will seriously reduce endangered, threatened, and endemic species habitat including areas that I visited[, which] may severely shorten the future of these species"; that threat, she concluded, harmed her because she "intend[s] to return to Sri Lanka in the future and hope[s] to be more fortunate in spotting at least the endangered elephant and leopard." When Ms. Skilbred was asked at a subsequent deposition if and when she had any plans to return to Sri Lanka, she reiterated that "I intend to go back to Sri Lanka," but confessed that she had no current plans: "I don't know [when]. There is a civil war going on right now. I don't know. Not next year, I will say. In the future."

We shall assume for the sake of argument [that] certain agency-funded projects threaten listed species — though that is questionable. The [affidavits] plainly contain no facts, however, showing how damage to the species will produce "imminent" injury to Mses. Kelly and Skilbred. That the women "had visited" the areas of the projects before the projects commenced proves nothing. . . . "'Past exposure to illegal conduct does not in itself show a present case or controversy regarding injunctive relief [if] unaccompanied by any continuing, present adverse effects.'" [And] the affiants' profession of an "inten[t]" to return to the places they had visited before — where they will presumably, this time, be deprived of the opportunity to observe animals of the endangered species — is simply not enough. Such "some day" intentions — without any description of concrete plans, or indeed even any specification of when the some day will be — do not support a finding of the "actual or imminent" injury that our cases require. . . .

Besides relying upon the Kelly and Skilbred affidavits, respondents propose a series of novel standing theories. The first, inelegantly styled "ecosystem nexus," proposes that any person who uses any part of a "contiguous ecosystem" adversely affected by a funded activity has standing even if the activity is located a great distance away. This approach [is] inconsistent with our opinion in *National Wildlife Federation,* which held that a plaintiff claiming injury from environmental damage must use the area affected by the challenged activity and not an area roughly "in the vicinity" of it. 497 U.S., at 887-889. It makes no difference that the general-purpose section of the ESA states that the Act was intended in part "to provide a means whereby the ecosystems upon which endangered species and threatened species depend may be conserved," 16 U.S.C. §1531(b). To say that the Act protects ecosystems is not to say that the Act creates (if it were possible) rights of action in persons who have not been injured in fact, that is, persons who use portions of an ecosystem not perceptibly affected by the unlawful action in question.

Respondents' other theories are called [the] "animal nexus" approach, whereby anyone who has an interest in studying or seeing the endangered animals anywhere on the globe has standing; and the "vocational nexus" approach, under which anyone with a professional interest in such animals can sue. Under these theories, anyone who goes to see Asian elephants in the Bronx Zoo, and anyone who is a keeper of Asian elephants in the Bronx Zoo, has standing to sue because the Director of the Agency for International Development (AID) did not consult with the Secretary regarding the AID-funded project in Sri Lanka. This is beyond all reason. Standing is not "an ingenious academic exercise in the conceivable," [but], at the summary judgment stage, a factual showing of perceptible harm. It is clear that the person who observes or works with a particular animal threatened by a federal decision is facing perceptible harm, since the very subject of his interest will no longer exist. It is even plausible — though it goes to the outermost limit of plausibility — to think that a person who observes or works with animals of a particular species in the very area of the world where that species is threatened by a federal decision is facing such harm, since some animals that might have been the subject of his interest will no longer exist. . . . It goes beyond the limit, however, and into pure speculation and fantasy, to say that anyone who observes or works with an endangered species, anywhere in the world, is appreciably harmed by a single project affecting some portion of that species with which he has no more specific connection. . . .

B

Besides failing to show injury, respondents failed to demonstrate redressability. Instead of attacking the separate decisions to fund particular projects allegedly causing them harm, respondents chose to challenge a more generalized level of Government action (rules regarding consultation), the invalidation of which would affect all overseas projects. This programmatic approach has obvious practical advantages, but also obvious difficulties insofar as proof of causation or redressability is concerned. As we have said in another context, "suits challenging, not specifically identifiable Government violations of law, but the particular programs agencies establish to carry out their legal obligations [are], even when premised on allegations of several instances of violations of law, . . . rarely if ever appropriate for federal-court adjudication." *Allen*, 468 U.S., at 759-760.

The most obvious problem in the present case is redressability. Since the agencies funding the projects were not parties to the case, the District Court could accord relief only against the Secretary: He could be ordered to revise his regulation to require consultation for foreign projects. But this would not remedy respondents' alleged injury unless the funding agencies were bound by the Secretary's regulation, which is very much an open question. Whereas in other contexts the ESA is quite explicit as to the Secretary's controlling authority, *see, e.g.,* 16 U.S.C. §1533(a)(1) ("The Secretary shall" promulgate regulations determining endangered species); *see* §1536(a)(2) ("*Each Federal agency shall,* in consultation with and with the assistance of the Secretary, insure that any" funded action is not likely to jeopardize endangered or threatened species). When the Secretary promulgated the regulation at issue here, he thought it was binding on the agencies. The Solicitor General, however, has repudiated that position [and] the agencies themselves apparently deny the Secretary's authority.

A further impediment to redressability is the fact that the agencies generally supply only a fraction of the funding for a foreign project. AID, for example, has provided less than 10% of the funding for the Mahaweli project. Respondents have produced nothing to indicate that the projects they have named will either be suspended, or do less harm to listed species, if that fraction is eliminated. As in *Simon,* 426 U.S., at 43-44, it is entirely conjectural whether the nonagency activity that affects respondents will be altered or affected by the agency activity they seek to achieve. There is no standing. . . .

We hold that respondents lack standing to bring this action and that the Court of Appeals erred in denying the summary judgment motion filed by the United States. The opinion of the Court of Appeals is hereby reversed, and the cause is remanded for proceedings consistent with this opinion.

It is so ordered.

Justice KENNEDY, with whom Justice SOUTER joins, concurring in part and concurring in the judgment.

[As] Government programs and policies become more complex and far-reaching, we must be sensitive to the articulation of new rights of action that do not have clear analogs in our common-law tradition. Modern litigation has progressed far from the paradigm of Marbury suing Madison to get his commission, or Ogden seeking an injunction to halt Gibbons' steamboat operations. In my view, Congress has the power to define injuries and articulate chains of causation that will give rise to a case or controversy where none existed before, and I do not read the Court's opinion to suggest a contrary view. . . . In exercising this power, however, Congress must at the very least identify the injury it seeks to vindicate and relate the injury to the class of persons entitled to bring suit. The citizen-suit provision of the Endangered Species Act does not meet these minimal requirements, because while the statute purports to confer a right on "any person [to enjoin] the United States and any other governmental instrumentality or agency [who] is alleged to be in violation of any provision of this chapter," it does not of its own force establish that there is an injury in "any person" by virtue of any "violation." 16 U.S.C. §1540(g)(1)(A).

Notes and Questions: Causation

1. *Environmental Organization Standing.* In Sierra Club v. Morton, 405 U.S. 727 (1972), the Sierra Club challenged the U.S. Forest Service's (Forest Service) decision to build a 20-mile road in the Sierra Nevada Mountains in California. The area was "quasi-wilderness" with "great natural beauty," but its "relative inaccessibility and lack of development" limited the number of tourists who could visit. In order to increase usage, the Forest Service authorized the construction of a $35-million resort and a 20-mile access road. The Sierra Club, which wanted to maintain the area unchanged, sought a declaratory judgment that various aspects

of the proposed development contravened federal laws and regulations. The Sierra Club sued as an organization with "a special interest in the conservation and the sound maintenance of the national parks, game refuges and forests of the country" and invoked the judicial-review provisions of the Administrative Procedure Act, 5 U.S.C. §701 *et seq.* The Court concluded that the Sierra Club lacked standing: "[T]he complaint alleged that the development 'would destroy or otherwise adversely affect the scenery, natural and historic objects and wildlife of the park and would impair the enjoyment of the park for future generations.' We do not question that this type of harm may amount to an 'injury in fact' sufficient to lay the basis for standing under §10 of the APA. Aesthetic and environmental well-being, like economic well-being, are important ingredients of the quality of life in our society, and the fact that particular environmental interests are shared by the many rather than the few does not make them less deserving of legal protection through the judicial process. But the 'injury in fact' test requires more than an injury to a cognizable interest. It requires that the party seeking review be himself among the injured. . . . The impact of the proposed [road] will not fall indiscriminately upon every citizen. The alleged injury will be felt directly only by those who use [the park], and for whom the aesthetic and recreational values of the area will be lessened by the highway and ski resort. The Sierra Club failed to allege that it or its members would be affected in any of their activities or pastimes by the Disney development. . . . The Club apparently [believed that its] longstanding concern with and expertise in such matters were sufficient to give it standing as a 'representative of the public.' This theory reflects a misunderstanding of our cases. [I]f a 'special interest' in this subject were enough to entitle the Sierra Club to commence this litigation, there would appear to be no objective basis upon which to disallow a suit by any other bona fide 'special interest' organization however small or short-lived. And if any group with a bona fide 'special interest' could initiate such litigation, it is difficult to perceive why any individual citizen with the same bona fide special interest would not also be entitled to do so." As a result, in order to establish standing, the Sierra Club would be required to demonstrate that one of its members would actually be injured by the development. Justice Blackmun dissented: "I would permit an imaginative expansion of our traditional concepts of standing in order to enable an organization such as the Sierra Club, possessed, as it is, of pertinent, bona fide, and well-recognized attributes and purposes in the area of environment, to litigate environmental issues. This incursion upon tradition need not be very extensive. . . . It need only recognize the interest of one who has a provable, sincere, dedicated, and established status. We need not fear that Pandora's box will be opened or that there will be no limit to the number of those who desire to participate in environmental litigation. The courts will exercise appropriate restraints just as they have exercised them in the past."

2. *Do the Merits Influence the Outcome?* In *Lujan,* dissenting Justice Brennan argued that, "[w]hile the Court gives lip service to the principle [that] 'standing in no way depends on the merits of the plaintiff's contention that particular conduct is illegal,' in fact the opinion, which tosses out of court almost every conceivable kind of plaintiff who could be injured by the activity claimed to be

unconstitutional, can be explained only by an indefensible hostility to the claim on the merits." Might the Court's perspective on the merits have affected its view regarding standing issues?

3. *SCRAP and Article III's Standing Requirements.* An older decision, United States v. SCRAP, 412 U.S. 669 (1973), took a much more expansive view of causation and redressability. That case involved a challenge to the Interstate Commerce Commission's (ICC) failure to suspend a surcharge of 2.5 percent that various railroads had imposed on freight shipments because of increasing costs and inadequate resources. The suit was brought by certain environmental groups, including Students Challenging Regulatory Agency Procedures (SCRAP), an unincorporated group of five law students, and the Environmental Defense Fund (EDF), that challenged the ICC's failure to suspend the surcharge, claiming that the rate increase would lead to less recycling, as well as more litter, and therefore would cause "economic, recreational and aesthetic harm." The Court held that the plaintiffs could establish standing: "[A]ll persons who utilize the scenic resources of the country, and indeed all who breathe its air, could claim harm similar to that alleged by the environmental groups here. [But] standing is not to be denied simply because many people suffer the same injury. [The] injury alleged here [is] very different from that at issue in *Sierra Club* because here the alleged injury to the environment is far less direct and perceptible. The petitioner there complained about the construction of a specific project that would directly affect the Mineral King Valley. Here, the Court was asked to follow a far more attenuated line of causation to the eventual injury of which the appellees complained — a general rate increase would allegedly cause increased use of nonrecyclable commodities as compared to recyclable goods, thus resulting in the need to use more natural resources to produce such goods, some of which resources might be taken from the Washington area, and resulting in more refuse that might be discarded in national parks in the Washington area. The railroads protest that the appellees could never prove that a general increase in rates would have this effect. . . . Of course, pleadings must be something more than an ingenious academic exercise in the conceivable. A plaintiff must allege that he has been or will in fact be perceptibly harmed by the challenged agency action, not that he can imagine circumstances in which he could be affected by the agency's action. And it is equally clear that the allegations must be true and capable of proof at trial. But we deal here simply with the pleadings in which the appellees alleged a specific and perceptible harm that distinguished them from other citizens who had not used the natural resources that were claimed to be affected. . . . We cannot say on these pleadings that the appellees could not prove their allegations which, if proved, would place them squarely among those persons injured in fact by the Commission's action, and entitled under the clear import of Sierra Club to seek review."

SCRAP produced a number of concurrences and dissents. Justice Blackmun, joined by Justice Brennan, concurred: "I would not require that the appellees, in their individual capacities, prove that they in fact were injured. Rather, I would require only that appellees, as responsible and sincere representatives of environmental interests, show that the environment would be injured in fact and that such injury would be irreparable and substantial." Justice Douglas dissented in part: "Where a river is polluted and a person is dependent on it for drinking water, I suppose there would not be the slightest doubt that he would have standing in court to present his claim. I also suppose there is not the slightest doubt that where smog settles on a city, any person who must breathe that air or feel the sulphuric acid forming in his eyes, would have standing in court to present his claim. I think it is equally obvious that any resident of an area whose paths are strewn with litter, whose parks, or picnic grounds are defaced by it has standing to tender his complaint to the court." Justice White, joined by two other justices, dissented in part: "The majority acknowledges that these allegations reflect an 'attenuated line of causation,' but is willing to suspend its judgment in the dim hope that proof at trial will in some unexplained way flesh them out and establish the necessary nexus between these appellees and the across-the-board rate increase. . . . To me, the alleged injuries are so remote, speculative, and insubstantial in fact that they fail to confer standing. They become no more concrete, real, or substantial when it is added that materials will cost more at the marketplace and that somehow the freight rate increase will increase air pollution. Allegations such as these are no more substantial and direct and no more qualify these appellees to litigate than allegations of a taxpayer that governmental expenditures will increase his taxes and have an impact on his pocketbook, allegations that governmental decisions are offensive to reason or morals."

4. *Tax-Exempt Discriminatory Schools.* In Allen v. Wright, 468 U.S. 737 (1984), the parents of African American children sought to compel the IRS to deny tax-exempt status to racially discriminatory private schools. Plaintiffs claimed that discriminatory schools were receiving tax exemptions, and that the "deductions facilitate[d] the raising of funds to organize new schools and expand existing schools in order to accommodate white students avoiding attendance in desegregating public school districts," thereby interfering with the ability of plaintiffs' children to be educated in desegregated public schools. The Court concluded that plaintiffs did not have standing to bring the case. The Court concluded that plaintiffs were asserting "stigmatizing injury," and recognized that "this sort of noneconomic injury is one of the most serious consequences of discriminatory government action and is sufficient in some circumstances to support standing." However, "such injury accords a basis for standing only to 'those persons who are personally denied equal treatment' by the challenged discriminatory conduct." In regard to the plaintiffs' claim regarding "their children's diminished ability to receive an education in a racially integrated school," the Court concluded that the injury was "not only judicially cognizable but [is] one of the most serious injuries recognized in our legal system." However, the Court found a lack of standing because "the injury alleged is not fairly traceable to the Government conduct respondents challenge as unlawful. The illegal conduct challenged by respondents is the IRS's grant of tax exemptions to some racially discriminatory schools. The line of causation between that conduct and desegregation of respondents' schools is attenuated at best. . . . It is, first, uncertain how many racially discriminatory private schools are in fact receiving tax exemptions. Moreover, it is entirely speculative [whether] withdrawal of a tax exemption from any particular school

would lead the school to change its policies. It is just as speculative whether any given parent of a child attending such a private school would decide to transfer the child to public school [if] the private school [was] threatened with loss of tax-exempt status. It is also pure speculation whether, in a particular community, a large enough number of the numerous relevant school officials and parents would reach decisions that collectively would have a significant impact on the racial composition of the public schools. . . . The links in the chain of causation between the challenged Government conduct and the asserted injury are far too weak for the chain as a whole to sustain respondents' standing." Justice Brennan dissented: "Common sense alone would recognize that the elimination of tax-exempt status for racially discriminatory private schools would serve to lessen the impact that those institutions have in defeating efforts to desegregate the public schools." Justice Stevens, joined by Justice Blackmun, also dissented: "Without tax-exempt status, private schools will either not be competitive in terms of cost, or have to change their admissions policies, hence reducing their competitiveness for parents seeking 'a racially segregated alternative' to public schools, which is what respondents have alleged many white parents in desegregating school districts seek. . . . Considerations of tax policy, economics, and pure logic all confirm the conclusion that respondents' injury in fact is fairly traceable to the Government's allegedly wrongful conduct."

5. *Gender Discrimination.* Heckler v. Mathews, 465 U.S. 728 (1984), involved a male who brought an equal protection challenge to the Social Security Act because it contained a gender-based classification that discriminated against him. However, the law contained a severability provision that would have prevented the plaintiff from obtaining additional benefits even if he prevailed in the lawsuit. As a result, the most that he could have hoped for was to prevent women from obtaining discriminatorily high levels of benefits. The Court held that the plaintiff had standing to challenge the discrimination: "In this case, appellee claims a type of personal injury we have long recognized as judicially cognizable. He alleges that the pension offset exception subjects him to unequal treatment in the provision of his Social Security benefits solely because of his gender; specifically, as a nondependent man, he receives fewer benefits than he would if he were a similarly situated woman. . . . Although the severability clause would prevent a court from redressing this inequality by increasing the benefits payable to appellee, [a court] may either declare [the statute] a nullity and order that its benefits not extend to the class that the legislature intended to benefit, or it may extend the coverage of the statute to include those who are aggrieved by the exclusion. For that reason, we have frequently entertained attacks on discriminatory statutes or practices even when the government could deprive a successful plaintiff of any monetary relief by withdrawing the statute's benefits from both the favored and the excluded class. [T]he injury caused by the unequal treatment allegedly suffered by appellee may 'be redressed by a favorable decision,' and he therefore has standing to prosecute this action."

6. *Standing to Challenge Police Misconduct.* In City of Los Angeles v. Lyons, 461 U.S. 95 (1983), plaintiffs brought a civil rights action that sought preliminary and permanent injunctive relief barring the City of Los Angeles police from using

chokeholds. The plaintiffs alleged that the city routinely encouraged its police to use chokeholds and that numerous individuals had been injured or killed by this practice. They sought a court order prohibiting the use of chokeholds "except in situations where the proposed victim of said control reasonably appears to be threatening the immediate use of deadly force." The Court held that the plaintiffs lacked standing to sue: "That Lyons may have been illegally choked by the police, while presumably affording Lyons standing to claim damages against the individual officers and perhaps against the City, does nothing to establish a real and immediate threat that he would again be stopped for a traffic violation, or for any other offense, by an officer or officers who would illegally choke him into unconsciousness without any provocation or resistance on his part. The allegation in the complaint that the police in Los Angeles routinely apply chokeholds in situations where they are not threatened by the use of deadly force falls far short of the allegations that would be necessary to establish a case or controversy between these parties. [T]o have a case or controversy with the City[,] Lyons would have to credibly allege that he faced a realistic threat from the future application of the City's policy. [For] the injury that Lyons allegedly suffered in 1976[,] he has an adequate remedy at law. . . . Absent a sufficient likelihood that he will again be wronged in a similar way, Lyons is no more entitled to an injunction than any other citizen of Los Angeles; and a federal court may not entertain a claim by any or all citizens who no more than assert that certain practices of law enforcement officers are unconstitutional." Justice Marshall, joined by Justices Brennan, Blackmun, and Stevens, dissented: "[C]hokeholds pose a high and unpredictable risk of serious injury or death. . . . Because Lyons has a claim for damages against the City, and because he cannot prevail on that claim unless he demonstrates that the City's chokehold policy violates the Constitution, his personal stake in the outcome of the controversy adequately assures an adversary presentation of his challenge to the constitutionality of the policy. Moreover, the resolution of this challenge will be largely dispositive of his requests for declaratory and injunctive relief. . . . No doubt the requests for injunctive relief may raise additional questions. But these questions involve familiar issues relating to the appropriateness of particular forms of relief, and have never been thought to implicate a litigant's standing to sue. . . . By fragmenting the standing inquiry and imposing a separate standing hurdle with respect to each form of relief sought, the decision today departs significantly from this Court's traditional conception of the standing requirement and of the remedial powers of the federal courts."

∾ PROBLEMS: CAUSATION ∾

1. SCRAP *Reconsidered.* In the *SCRAP* decision, *supra*, the Court held that plaintiffs had established standing. However, *SCRAP* was decided in the 1970s. In light of more recent decisions, in particular *Wright* and *Lyons*, both decided in the 1980s, is *SCRAP* still good law? If *SCRAP* arose today and you were asked to argue that it is no longer good law, how would you make the argument? If hired by the other side, how would you respond to those arguments?

2. *Causation and the Health Care Legislation.* Consider the health care legisla-tion described in the problem at the beginning of the chapter. If the trial court concludes that the plaintiffs have standing, is it likely to conclude that causation exists? In other words, if the plaintiffs prevail, is the injury "redressable"? Why or why not?

3. *Racial Steering.* Plaintiffs allege that defendants engaged in "racial steer-ing" that violated Section 804 of the Fair Housing Act of 1968 at two apartment complexes in Richmond, Virginia. The complaint identified Paul Coles as a black "renter plaintiff" who attempted to rent an apartment from Havens and was falsely told that no apartments were available. The other two individual plaintiffs, Coleman and Willis, were described in the complaint as "tester plaintiffs," who were employed by an independent organization to determine whether Havens practiced racial steering. Coleman (who is black) was told more than once that no apartments were available, whereas Willis (who is white) was told that there were vacancies. The three individual plaintiffs, who at the time the complaint was filed were all residents of the City of Richmond or the adjacent county, averred that they had been injured by the discriminatory acts of petitioners. Coles, the black renter, claimed that he had been "denied the right to rent real property in Hen-rico County." He and the two tester plaintiffs alleged that Havens's practices deprived them of the "important social, professional, business and economic, political and aesthetic benefits of interracial associations that arise from living in integrated communities free from discriminatory housing practices." Coleman, the black tester, alleged that the misinformation given her by Havens had caused her "specific injury." Do both Coleman and Willis have standing to serve as plain-tiffs if they had no intention of moving into the apartment complex but were act-ing solely as testers? Does it matter that no misrepresentations were made to Willis? Would it matter that, in passing the Fair Housing Act, Congress "intended standing under §812 to extend to the full limits of Art. III" and stated that courts should not apply prudential barriers in deciding standing questions under that section? *See* Havens Realty Corp. v. Coleman, 455 U.S. 363 (1982).

4. *Challenging Apportionment Schemes.* Plaintiff voters claim that their state legislature adopted an illegal reapportionment scheme that segregated voting districts based on race. The plaintiffs rely on Shaw v. Reno, 509 U.S. 630 (1993), which held that the Equal Protection Clause of the Fourteenth Amendment is violated when a state adopts a reapportionment scheme so irrational on its face that it can be understood only as an effort to segregate voters into separate voting districts because of their race, and they also claim that there is insufficient justifica-tion for the segregation. In *Shaw,* the Court noted that segregated districts "threaten to stigmatize individuals by reason of their membership in a racial group and to incite racial hostility" and also result in "representational harms." "When a district obviously is created solely to effectuate the perceived common interests of one racial group, elected officials are more likely to believe that their primary obligation is to represent only the members of that group, rather than their constituency as a whole." Does the voters' challenge to a gerrymandered district involve a "generalized grievance" shared with all other citizens? Would it matter whether the voters lived in the district that they alleged was gerrymandered, or

could they challenge the gerrymandered district if they lived in a neighboring district? Suppose that they lived out of state? Could they still challenge the gerrymandering? *See* United States v. Hays, 515 U.S. 737 (1995).

Massachusetts v. Environmental Protection Agency
549 U.S. 497 (2007)

Justice STEVENS delivered the opinion of the Court.

[On] October 20, 1999, a group of 19 private organizations filed a rulemaking petition asking EPA to regulate "greenhouse gas emissions from new motor vehicles under §202 of the Clean Air Act." Petitioners maintained that 1998 was the "warmest year on record"; that carbon dioxide, methane, nitrous oxide, and hydrofluorocarbons are "heat trapping greenhouse gases"; that greenhouse gas emissions have significantly accelerated climate change; and that [a] 1995 report warned that "carbon dioxide remains the most important contributor to [manmade] forcing of climate change." The petition further alleged that climate change will have serious adverse effects on human health and the environment. As to EPA's statutory authority, the petition observed that the agency itself had already confirmed that it had the power to regulate carbon dioxide. . . .

Fifteen months after the petition's submission, EPA requested public comment on "all the issues raised in [the] petition," adding a "particular" request for comments on "any scientific, technical, legal, economic or other aspect of these issues that may be relevant to EPA's consideration of this petition." 66 Fed. Reg. 7486, 7487 (2001). Before the close of the comment period, the White House sought "assistance in identifying the areas in the science of climate change where there are the greatest certainties and uncertainties" from the National Research Council, asking for a response "as soon as possible." The result was a 2001 report titled Climate Change Science: An Analysis of Some Key Questions (NRC Report), which, drawing heavily on [an earlier report] concluded that "[g]reenhouse gases are accumulating in Earth's atmosphere as a result of human activities, causing surface air temperatures and subsurface ocean temperatures to rise. Temperatures are, in fact, rising."

On September 8, 2003, EPA entered an order denying the rulemaking petition. The agency gave two reasons for its decision: (1) that contrary to the opinions of its former general counsels, the Clean Air Act does not authorize EPA to issue mandatory regulations to address global climate change; and (2) that even if the agency had the authority to set greenhouse gas emission standards, it would be unwise to do so at this time. . . . The agency began by recognizing that the concentration of greenhouse gases has dramatically increased as a result of human activities, and acknowledged the attendant increase in global surface air temperatures. EPA nevertheless gave controlling importance to the NRC Report's statement that a causal link between the two "cannot be unequivocally established." Given that residual uncertainty, EPA concluded that regulating greenhouse gas emissions would be unwise. . . . The agency furthermore characterized any EPA regulation of motor-vehicle emissions as a "piecemeal approach" to climate change, and stated that such regulation would conflict with the President's "comprehensive approach" to the problem. . . . According to EPA, unilateral EPA regulation of motor-vehicle greenhouse gas emissions might also hamper the President's ability to persuade key developing countries to reduce greenhouse gas emissions.

Petitioners, [joined] by intervenor States and local governments, sought review of EPA's order in the United States Court of Appeals for the District of Columbia Circuit. [T]wo judges agreed "that the EPA Administrator properly exercised his discretion." . . .

Article III of the Constitution limits federal-court jurisdiction to "Cases" and "Controversies." Those two words confine "the business of federal courts to questions presented in an adversary context and in a form historically viewed as capable of resolution through the judicial process." Flast v. Cohen, 392 U.S. 83 (1968). [N]o justiciable "controversy" exists when parties seek adjudication of a political question, when they ask for an advisory opinion, or when the question sought to be adjudicated has been mooted by subsequent developments. This case suffers from none of these defects. . . .

EPA maintains that because greenhouse gas emissions inflict widespread harm, the doctrine of standing presents an insuperable jurisdictional obstacle. We do not agree. At bottom, "the gist of the question of standing" is whether petitioners have "such a personal stake in the outcome of the controversy as to assure that concrete adverseness which sharpens the presentation of issues upon which the court so largely depends for illumination." Baker v. Carr, 369 U.S. 186, 204 (1962). . . . To ensure the proper adversarial presentation, *Lujan* holds that a litigant must demonstrate that it has suffered a concrete and particularized injury that is either actual or imminent, that the injury is fairly traceable to the defendant, and that it is likely that a favorable decision will redress that injury. . . .

Only one of the petitioners needs to have standing to permit us to consider the petition for review. We stress here [the] special position and interest of Massachusetts. It is of considerable relevance that the party seeking review here is a sovereign State and not, as it was in *Lujan,* a private individual. . . . States are not normal litigants for the purposes of invoking federal jurisdiction. As Justice Holmes explained in Georgia v. Tennessee Copper Co., 206 U.S. 230, 237 (1907), a case in which Georgia sought to protect its citizens from air pollution originating outside its borders: "[The] State owns very little of the territory alleged to be affected, and the damage to it capable of estimate in money, possibly, at least, is small. This is a suit by a State for an injury to it in its capacity of *quasi*-sovereign. In that capacity the State has an interest independent of and behind the titles of its citizens, in all the earth and air within its domain. It has the last word as to whether its mountains shall be stripped of their forests and its inhabitants shall breathe pure air."

Just as Georgia's "independent interest [in] all the earth and air within its domain" supported federal jurisdiction[,] so too does Massachusetts' well-founded desire to preserve its sovereign territory today. That Massachusetts does in fact own a great deal of the "territory alleged to be affected" only reinforces the conclusion that its stake in the outcome of this case is sufficiently concrete to warrant the exercise of federal judicial power.

When a State enters the Union, it surrenders certain sovereign prerogatives. Massachusetts cannot invade Rhode Island to force reductions in greenhouse gas emissions, it cannot negotiate an emissions treaty with China or India, and in some circumstances the exercise of its police powers to reduce in-state motor-vehicle emissions might well be pre-empted. These sovereign prerogatives are now lodged in the Federal Government, and Congress has ordered EPA to protect Massachusetts (among others) by prescribing standards applicable to the "emission of any air pollutant from any class or classes of new motor vehicle engines, which in [the Administrator's] judgment cause, or contribute to, air pollution which may reasonably be anticipated to endanger public health or welfare." 42 U.S.C. §7521(a)(1). Congress has moreover recognized a concomitant procedural right to challenge the rejection of its rulemaking petition as arbitrary and capricious. Given that procedural right and Massachusetts' stake in protecting its quasi-sovereign interests, the Commonwealth is entitled to special solicitude in our standing analysis.

[We] held in Georgia v. Pennsylvania R. Co., 324 U.S. 439, 447 (1945), that there is a critical difference between allowing a State "to protect her citizens from the operation of federal statutes" (which is what *Mellon* prohibits) and allowing a State to assert its rights under federal law (which it has standing to do). Massachusetts does not here dispute that the Clean Air Act *applies* to its citizens; it rather seeks to assert its rights under the Act. [EPA's] steadfast refusal to regulate greenhouse gas emissions presents a risk of harm to Massachusetts that is both "actual" and "imminent." There is, moreover, a "substantial likelihood that the judicial relief requested" will prompt EPA to take steps to reduce that risk. Duke Power Co. v. Carolina Environmental Study Group, Inc., 438 U.S. 59, 79 (1978).

The Injury. The harms associated with climate change are serious and well recognized. Indeed, the NRC Report itself—which EPA regards as an "objective and independent assessment of the relevant science," identifies a number of environmental changes that have already inflicted significant harms, including "the global retreat of mountain glaciers, reduction in snow-cover extent, the earlier spring melting of ice on rivers and lakes, [and] the accelerated rate of rise of sea levels during the 20th century relative to the past few thousand years. . . ." NRC Report 16.

Petitioners allege that this only hints at the environmental damage yet to come. According to the climate scientist Michael MacCracken, "qualified scientific experts involved in climate change research" have reached a "strong consensus" that global warming threatens (among other things) a precipitate rise in sea levels by the end of the century, MacCracken Decl. ¶15, Stdg. App. 207, "severe and irreversible changes to natural ecosystems," a "significant reduction in water storage in winter snowpack in mountainous regions with direct and important economic consequences," and an increase in the spread of disease. He also observes that rising ocean temperatures may contribute to the ferocity of hurricanes.

That these climate-change risks are "widely shared" does not minimize Massachusetts' interest in the outcome of this litigation. *See* Federal Election Commn v. Akins, 524 U.S. 11, 24 (1998). According to petitioners' unchallenged affidavits, global sea levels rose somewhere between 10 and 20 centimeters over the 20th century as a result of global warming. These rising seas have already begun to swallow Massachusetts' coastal land. Because the Commonwealth "owns a substantial portion of the state's coastal property," it has alleged a particularized injury in its capacity as a landowner. . . . If sea levels continue to rise as predicted, one Massachusetts official believes that a significant fraction of coastal property will be "either permanently lost through inundation or temporarily lost through periodic storm surge and flooding events." Remediation costs alone, petitioners allege, could run well into the hundreds of millions of dollars.

Causation. EPA does not dispute the existence of a causal connection between man-made greenhouse gas emissions and global warming. At a minimum, therefore, EPA's refusal to regulate such emissions "contributes" to Massachusetts' injuries. . . . EPA nevertheless maintains that its decision not to regulate greenhouse gas emissions from new motor vehicles contributes so insignificantly to petitioners' injuries that the agency cannot be hauled into federal court to answer for them. For the same reason, EPA does not believe that any realistic possibility exists that the relief petitioners seek would mitigate global climate change and remedy their injuries. That is especially so because predicted increases in greenhouse gas emissions from developing nations, particularly China and India, are likely to offset any marginal domestic decrease.

But EPA overstates its case. Its argument rests on the erroneous assumption that a small incremental step, because it is incremental, can never be attacked in a federal judicial forum. Yet accepting that premise would doom most challenges to regulatory action. Agencies, like legislatures, do not generally resolve massive problems in one fell regulatory swoop. They instead whittle away at them over time, refining their preferred approach as circumstances change and as they develop a more-nuanced understanding of how best to proceed. *Cf.* SEC v. Chenery Corp., 332 U.S. 194, 202 (1947). That a first step might be tentative does not by itself support the notion that federal courts lack jurisdiction to determine whether that step conforms to law.

And reducing domestic automobile emissions is hardly a tentative step. Even leaving aside the other greenhouse gases, the United States transportation sector emits an enormous quantity of carbon dioxide into the atmosphere — according to the MacCracken affidavit, more than 1.7 billion metric tons in 1999 alone. That accounts for more than 6% of worldwide carbon dioxide emissions. . . . Considering just emissions from the transportation sector, which represent less than one-third of this country's total carbon dioxide emissions, the United States would still rank as the third-largest emitter of carbon dioxide in the world, outpaced only by the European Union and China. Judged by any standard, U.S. motor-vehicle emissions make a meaningful contribution to greenhouse gas concentrations and hence, according to petitioners, to global warming.

The Remedy. While it may be true that regulating motor-vehicle emissions will not by itself *reverse* global warming, it by no means follows that we lack jurisdiction to decide whether EPA has a duty to take steps to *slow* or *reduce* it. Because of the enormity of the potential consequences associated with man-made climate change, the fact that the effectiveness of a remedy might be delayed during the (relatively short) time it takes for a new motor-vehicle fleet to replace an older one is essentially irrelevant. Nor is it dispositive that developing countries such as China and India are poised to increase greenhouse gas emissions substantially over the next century: A reduction in domestic emissions would slow the pace of global emissions increases, no matter what happens elsewhere.

We moreover attach considerable significance to EPA's "agree[ment] with the President that 'we must address the issue of global climate change,'" and to EPA's ardent support for various voluntary emission-reduction programs, 68 Fed. Reg. 52932. As Judge Tatel observed in dissent below, "EPA would presumably not bother with such efforts if it thought emissions reductions would have no discernable impact on future global warming."

In sum — at least according to petitioners' uncontested affidavits — the rise in sea levels associated with global warming has already harmed and will continue to harm Massachusetts. The risk of catastrophic harm, though remote, is nevertheless real. That risk would be reduced to some extent if petitioners received the relief they seek. We therefore hold that petitioners have standing to challenge the EPA's denial of their rulemaking petition.

It is moreover quite wrong to analogize the legal claim advanced by Massachusetts and the other public and private entities who challenge EPA's parsimonious construction of the Clean Air Act to a mere "lawyer's game." . . .

The judgment of the Court of Appeals is reversed, and the case is remanded for further proceedings consistent with this opinion.

It is so ordered.

Chief Justice ROBERTS, with whom Justice SCALIA, Justice THOMAS, and Justice ALITO join, dissenting.

[I] would reject these challenges as nonjusticiable. [T]he status of Massachusetts as a State cannot compensate for petitioners' failure to demonstrate injury in fact, causation, and redressability. [The] Court [focuses] on the Commonwealth's asserted loss of coastal land as the injury in fact. . . . Global warming is a phenomenon "harmful to humanity at large," and the redress petitioners seek is focused no more on them than on the public generally — it is literally to change the atmosphere around the world. . . . If petitioners' particularized injury is loss of coastal land, it is also that injury that must be "actual or imminent, not conjectural or hypothetical," "real and immediate," and "certainly impending," [T]he Court observes that "global sea levels rose somewhere between 10 and 20 centimeters over the 20th century as a result of global warming" and that "[t]hese rising seas have already begun to swallow Massachusetts' coastal land." But none of petitioners' declarations supports that connection. . . . One of petitioners'

declarants predicts global warming will cause sea level to rise by 20 to 70 centimeters *by the year 2100*. [A]ccepting a century-long time horizon and a series of
compounded estimates renders requirements of imminence and immediacy
utterly toothless. "Allegations of possible future injury do not satisfy the requirements of Art. III. A threatened injury must be *certainly impending* to constitute
injury in fact."

Petitioners' reliance on Massachusetts's loss of coastal land as their injury in
fact for standing purposes creates insurmountable problems for them with
respect to causation and redressability. . . . The Court ignores the complexities of
global warming, and does so by now disregarding the "particularized" injury it
relied on in step one, and using the dire nature of global warming itself as a boot-
strap for finding causation and redressability. . . . Because local greenhouse gas
emissions disperse throughout the atmosphere and remain there for anywhere
from 50 to 200 years, it is global emissions data that are relevant. According to
one of petitioners' declarations, domestic motor vehicles contribute about 6 percent of global carbon dioxide emissions and 4 percent of global greenhouse gas
emissions. The amount of global emissions at issue here is smaller still; §202(a)(1)
of the Clean Air Act covers only *new* motor vehicles and *new* motor vehicle
engines, so petitioners' desired emission standards might reduce only a fraction
of 4 percent of global emissions. [As] EPA explained in its denial of petitioners'
request for rulemaking, "predicting future climate change necessarily involves a
complex web of economic and physical factors including: our ability to predict
future global anthropogenic emissions of [greenhouse gases] and aerosols; the
fate of these emissions once they enter the atmosphere (e.g., what percentage are
absorbed by vegetation or are taken up by the oceans); the impact of those emissions that remain in the atmosphere on the radiative properties of the atmosphere; changes in critically important climate feedbacks (e.g., changes in cloud
cover and ocean circulation); changes in temperature characteristics (e.g., average temperatures, shifts in daytime and evening temperatures); changes in other
climatic parameters (e.g., shifts in precipitation, storms); and ultimately the
impact of such changes on human health and welfare (e.g., increases or decreases
in agricultural productivity, human health impacts)."

Petitioners are never able to trace their alleged injuries back through this
complex web to the fractional amount of global emissions that might have been
limited with EPA standards. . . . Redressability is even more problematic. To the
tenuous link between petitioners' alleged injury and the indeterminate fractional
domestic emissions at issue here, add the fact that petitioners cannot meaningfully predict what will come of the 80 percent of global greenhouse gas emissions
that originate outside the United States. As the Court acknowledges, "developing countries such as China and India are poised to increase greenhouse gas
emissions substantially over the next century," so the domestic emissions at issue
here may become an increasingly marginal portion of global emissions, and any
decreases produced by petitioners' desired standards are likely to be overwhelmed many times over by emissions increases elsewhere in the world. . . . The
Court previously has explained that when the existence of an element of standing "depends on the unfettered choices made by independent actors not before

the courts and whose exercise of broad and legitimate discretion the courts cannot presume either to control or to predict," a party must present facts supporting an assertion that the actor will proceed in such a manner. *Defenders of Wildlife*, 504 U.S., at 562 (quoting ASARCO Inc. v. Kadish, 490 U.S. 605, 615 (1989) (opinion of Kennedy, J.). . . .

[The] limitation of the judicial power to cases and controversies "is crucial in maintaining the tripartite allocation of power set forth in the Constitution." *DaimlerChrysler*, 547 U.S., at [341]. In my view, the Court today — addressing Article III's "core component of standing," fails to take this limitation seriously. . . . Today's decision recalls the previous high-water mark of diluted standing requirements, United States v. Students Challenging Regulatory Agency Procedures (SCRAP), 412 U.S. 669 (1973). *SCRAP* involved "[p]robably the most attenuated injury conferring Art. III standing" and "surely went to the very outer limit of the law" — until today. *Whitmore*, 495 U.S., at 158-159. . . . Over time, *SCRAP* became emblematic not of the looseness of Article III standing requirements, but of how utterly manipulable they are if not taken seriously as a matter of judicial self-restraint. *SCRAP* made standing seem a lawyer's game, rather than a fundamental limitation ensuring that courts function as courts and not intrude on the politically accountable branches. Today's decision is *SCRAP* for a new generation. . . .

I respectfully dissent.

Justice Scalia, with whom The Chief Justice, Justice Thomas, and Justice Alito join, dissenting.

[T]his Court has no jurisdiction to decide this case because petitioners lack standing.

c. Congressionally Authorized Standing

Can Congress authorize plaintiffs to bring suit when standing would not otherwise exist? As previously noted, there is a constitutional aspect to the standing doctrine as well as a prudential aspect. The constitutional aspect stems from Article III's case and controversy requirement and cannot be waived by Congress. The prudential aspect is a limitation imposed by the Court on itself. In some instances, even when a case or controversy exists, the Court refuses to hear a case in deference to a coordinate branch of government. If Congress has invited the Court to hear a particular type of case, prudential restraints are minimized or disappear.

In Association of Data Processing Service Organizations, Inc. v. Camp, 397 U.S. 150 (1970), the Court discussed congressional authorization in the context of a suit brought by sellers of data-processing services challenging a ruling by the comptroller of the currency. Under the ruling, national banks were allowed to provide data-processing services to other banks and to bank customers. Petitioners alleged that they would suffer future profit losses from competition by national banks, and that at least one national bank was performing or preparing to perform such services. The suit was brought not only against the bank but also against the comptroller of the currency, who was alleged to have caused petitioners injury in fact by his ruling. In holding that plaintiffs had standing to challenge the ruling, the Court articulated a two-part test for establishing standing to sue under congressional enactments: "The first question is whether the plaintiff alleges that the challenged action has caused him injury in fact, economic or otherwise. There can be no doubt but that petitioners have satisfied this test. The petitioners not only allege that competition by national banks in the business of providing data processing services might entail some future loss of profits for the petitioners, they also allege that respondent[s] had previously agreed or negotiated to perform such services. . . . The 'legal interest' test goes to the merits. The question of standing is different. It concerns, apart from the 'case' or 'controversy' test, the question whether the interest sought to be protected by the complainant is arguably within the zone of interests to be protected or regulated by the statute or constitutional guarantee in question. Thus the Administrative Procedure Act grants standing to a person 'aggrieved by agency action within the meaning of a relevant statute.' 5 U.S.C. s 702 (1964 ed., Supp. IV). That interest, at times, may reflect 'aesthetic, conservational, and recreational' as well as economic values. . . . We mention these noneconomic values to emphasize that standing may stem from them as well as from the economic injury in which petitioners rely here."

Lujan v. Defenders of Wildlife

504 U.S. 555 (1992)

[The facts and the remainder of the Court's holding are set forth *supra*, p. 64.]

IV

The Court of Appeals found that respondents had standing for an additional reason: because they had suffered a "procedural injury." The so-called "citizen-suit" provision of the ESA provides, in pertinent part, that "any person may commence a civil suit on his own behalf (A) to enjoin any person, including the United States and any other governmental instrumentality or agency . . . who is alleged to be in violation of any provision of this chapter." The court held that, because §7(a)(2) requires interagency consultation, the citizen-suit provision creates a "procedural righ[t]" to consultation in all "persons" — so that anyone can file suit in federal court to challenge the Secretary's (or presumably any other official's) failure to follow the assertedly correct consultative procedure, notwithstanding his or her inability to allege any discrete injury flowing from that failure. To understand the remarkable nature of this holding one must be clear about what it does not rest upon: This is not a case where plaintiffs are seeking to enforce a procedural requirement the disregard of which could impair a separate concrete interest of theirs (e.g., the procedural requirement for a hearing prior to denial of their license application, or the procedural requirement for an environmental impact statement before a federal facility is constructed next door to them). Nor is it simply a case where concrete injury has been suffered by many persons, as in mass fraud or mass tort situations. Nor, finally, is it the unusual case in which Congress has created a concrete private interest in the outcome of a suit against a private party for the government's benefit, by providing a cash bounty for the victorious plaintiff. Rather, the court held that the injury-in-fact requirement had been satisfied by congressional conferral upon all persons of an abstract, self-contained, noninstrumental "right" to have the Executive observe the procedures required by law. We reject this view. . . .

We have consistently held that a plaintiff raising only a generally available grievance about government — claiming only harm to his and every citizen's interest in proper application of the Constitution and laws, and seeking relief that no more directly and tangibly benefits him than it does the public at large — does not state an Article III case or controversy. [*See* Schlesinger v. Reservists Comm. to Stop the War, 418 U.S. 208 (1974); United States v. Richardson, 418 U.S. 166 (1974).] [We reaffirm] that standing to sue may not be predicated upon an interest of th[is] kind . . . To be sure, our generalized-grievance cases have typically involved Government violation of procedures assertedly ordained by the Constitution rather than the Congress. But there is absolutely no basis for making the Article III inquiry turn on the source of the asserted right. Whether the courts were to act on their own, or at the invitation of Congress, in ignoring the concrete injury requirement described in our cases, they would be discarding a principle fundamental to the separate and distinct constitutional role of the Third Branch — one of the essential elements that identifies those "Cases" and "Controversies" that are the business of the courts rather than of the political branches. "The province of the court," as Chief Justice Marshall said in Marbury v. Madison, "is, solely, to decide on the rights of individuals." Vindicating the public interest (including the public interest in Government observance of the Constitution and laws) is the function of Congress and the Chief Executive. The question presented here is whether the public interest in proper administration of the laws (specifically, in agencies' observance of a particular, statutorily prescribed procedure) can be converted into an individual right by a statute that denominates it as such, and that permits all citizens (or, for that matter, a subclass of citizens who suffer no distinctive concrete harm) to sue. If the concrete injury requirement has the separation-of-powers significance we have always said, the answer must be obvious: To permit Congress to convert the undifferentiated public interest in executive officers' compliance with the law into an "individual right" vindicable in the courts is to permit Congress to transfer from the President to the courts the Chief Executive's most important constitutional duty, to "take Care that the Laws be faithfully executed," Art. II, §3. It would enable the courts, with the permission of Congress, "to assume a position of authority over the governmental acts of another and co-equal department." We have always rejected that vision of our role. . . .

Nothing in this contradicts the principle that "[the] injury required by Art. III may exist solely by virtue of 'statutes creating legal rights, the invasion of which creates standing.'" *Warth* (quoting Linda R. S. v. Richard D., 410 U.S. 614 (1973)). As we said in *Sierra Club*, "[Statutory] broadening [of] the categories of injury that may be alleged in support of standing is a different matter from abandoning the requirement that the party seeking review must himself have suffered an injury." Whether or not the principle set forth in *Warth* can be extended beyond that distinction, it is clear that in suits against the Government, at least, the concrete injury requirement must remain.

Notes: More on Congressional Authorization

1. *Congressional Authorization and Procedural Rights.* In Massachusetts v. Environmental Protection Agency, 549 U.S. 497 (2007), in addition to finding causation and redressability, the Court emphasized the fact of congressional authorization, noting that "authorization is of critical importance to the standing inquiry: 'Congress has the power to define injuries and articulate chains of causation that will give rise to a case or controversy where none existed before.' *Lujan,* 504 U.S., at 580 (Kennedy, J., concurring in part and concurring in judgment). 'In exercising this power, however, Congress must at the very least identify the injury it seeks to vindicate and relate the injury to the class of persons entitled to bring suit.' We will not, therefore, 'entertain citizen suits to vindicate the public's nonconcrete interest in the proper administration of the laws.'" Notwithstanding the authorization, the litigant must still "demonstrate that it has suffered a concrete and particularized injury that is either actual or imminent, that the injury is fairly traceable to the defendant, and that it is likely that a favorable decision will redress that injury." Nevertheless, "a litigant to whom Congress has 'accorded a procedural right to protect his concrete interests,'— here, the right to challenge agency action unlawfully withheld — 'can assert that right without meeting all the normal standards for redressability and immediacy.' When a litigant is vested with a procedural right, that litigant has standing if there is some possibility that the requested relief will prompt the injury-causing party to reconsider the decision that allegedly harmed the litigant."

2. *The Individuals with Disabilities Education Act (IDEA).* In Winkelman v. Parma City School District, 550 U.S. 516 (1992), the Court considered whether the IDEA gave an autistic child's parents the right to file suit to enforce a school district's obligations toward their child. In considering this issue, the Court examined the IDEA to determine Congress's intent, and concluded that the "parents enjoy enforceable rights at the administrative stage, and it would be inconsistent with the statutory scheme to bar them from continuing to assert these rights in federal court." In reaching this conclusion, the Court noted that the "Act does not *sub silentio* or by implication bar parents from seeking to vindicate the rights accorded to them once the time comes to file a civil action. Through its provisions for expansive review and extensive parental involvement, the statute leads to just the opposite result." Finally, the Court concluded that the parent had a sufficient interest in the outcome of the litigation to justify a grant of standing: "Without question a parent of a child with a disability has a particular and personal interest in fulfilling 'our national policy of ensuring equality of opportunity, full participation, independent living, and economic self-sufficiency for individuals with disabilities.'" As a result, parents could seek review on a broad range of issues, including "any matter relating to the identification, evaluation, or educational

placement of the child, or the provision of a free appropriate public education to such child."

Summers v. Earth Island Institute
129 S.Ct. 1142 (2009)

Justice SCALIA delivered the opinion of the Court.

Respondents are a group of organizations dedicated to protecting the environment [collectively "Earth Island"]. They seek to prevent the United States Forest Service from enforcing regulations that exempt small fire-rehabilitation and timber-salvage projects from the notice, comment, and appeal process used by the Forest Service for more significant land management decisions. We must determine whether respondents have standing to challenge the regulations in the absence of a live dispute over a concrete application of those regulations.

In 1992, Congress enacted the Forest Service Decisionmaking and Appeals Reform Act (Appeals Reform Act or Act), 106 Stat. 1419. Among other things, this required the Forest Service to establish a notice, comment, and appeal process for "proposed actions of the Forest Service concerning projects and activities implementing land and resource management plans developed under the Forest and Rangeland Renewable Resources Planning Act of 1974."

The Forest Service's regulations implementing the Act provided that certain of its procedures would not be applied to projects that the Service considered categorically excluded from the requirement to file an environmental impact statement (EIS) or environmental assessment (EA). Later amendments to the Forest Service's manual of implementing procedures, adopted by rule after notice and comment, provided that fire-rehabilitation activities on areas of less than 4,200 acres, and salvage-timber sales of 250 acres or less, did not cause a significant environmental impact and thus would be categorically exempt from the requirement to file an EIS or EA. 68 Fed. Reg. 33824 (2003). This had the effect of excluding these projects from the notice, comment, and appeal process.

In the summer of 2002, fire burned a significant area of the Sequoia National Forest. In September 2003, the Service issued a decision memo approving the Burnt Ridge Project, a salvage sale of timber on 238 acres damaged by that fire. Pursuant to its categorical exclusion of salvage sales of less than 250 acres, the Forest Service did not provide notice in a form consistent with the Appeals Reform Act, did not provide a period of public comment, and did not make an appeal process available.

In December 2003, respondents filed a complaint in the Eastern District of California, challenging the failure of the Forest Service to apply to the Burnt Ridge Project §215.4(a) of its regulations implementing the Appeals Reform Act (requiring prior notice and comment), and §215.12(f) of the regulations (setting forth an appeal procedure). The complaint also challenged six other Forest Service regulations implementing the Act that were not applied to the Burnt Ridge Project. They are irrelevant to this appeal.

The District Court granted a preliminary injunction against the Burnt Ridge salvage-timber sale. Soon thereafter, the parties settled their dispute over the Burnt Ridge Project and the District Court concluded that "the Burnt Ridge timber sale is not at issue in this case." The Government argued that, with the Burnt Ridge dispute settled, and with no other project before the court in which respondents were threatened with injury in fact, respondents lacked standing to challenge the regulations; and that absent a concrete dispute over a particular project a challenge to the regulations would not be ripe. The District Court proceeded, however, to adjudicate the merits of Earth Island's challenges. It invalidated five of the regulations. . . . The Ninth Circuit held that Earth Island's challenges to regulations not at issue in the Burnt Ridge Project were not ripe for adjudication because there was "not a sufficient 'case or controversy'" before the court to sustain a facial challenge. It affirmed, however, the District Court's determination that §§215.4(a) and 215.12(f), which were applicable to the Burnt Ridge Project, were contrary to law, and upheld the nationwide injunction against their application. . . . We granted certiorari.

In limiting the judicial power to "Cases" and "Controversies," Article III of the Constitution restricts it to the traditional role of Anglo-American courts, which is to redress or prevent actual or imminently threatened injury to persons caused by private or official violation of law. Except when necessary in the execution of that function, courts have no charter to review and revise legislative and executive action. *See* Lujan v. Defenders of Wildlife, 504 U.S. 555, 559-560 (1992); Los Angeles v. Lyons, 461 U.S. 95, 111-112 (1983). This limitation "is founded in concern about the proper — and properly limited — role of the courts in a democratic society." Warth v. Seldin, 422 U.S. 490 (1975).

The doctrine of standing is one of several doctrines that reflect this fundamental limitation. It requires federal courts to satisfy themselves that "the plaintiff has 'alleged such a personal stake in the outcome of the controversy' as to warrant *his* invocation of federal-court jurisdiction." 422 U.S., at 498-499. He bears the burden of showing that he has standing for each type of relief sought. To seek injunctive relief, a plaintiff must show that he is under threat of suffering "injury in fact" that is concrete and particularized; the threat must be actual and imminent, not conjectural or hypothetical; it must be fairly traceable to the challenged action of the defendant; and it must be likely that a favorable judicial decision will prevent or redress the injury. Friends of Earth, Inc. v. Laidlaw Environmental Services (TOC), Inc., 528 U.S. 167 (2000). This requirement assures that "there is a real need to exercise the power of judicial review in order to protect the interests of the complaining party," Schlesinger v. Reservists Comm. to Stop the War, 418 U.S. 208, 221 (1974). Where that need does not exist, allowing courts to oversee legislative or executive action "would significantly alter the allocation of power . . . away from a democratic form of government," *Richardson, supra,* at 188 (Powell, J., concurring).

The regulations under challenge here neither require nor forbid any action on the part of respondents. The standards and procedures that they prescribe for Forest Service appeals govern only the conduct of Forest Service officials engaged in project planning. "[W]hen the plaintiff is not himself the object of the government action or inaction he challenges, standing is not precluded, but it is ordinarily 'substantially more difficult' to establish." *Defenders of Wildlife, supra,* at 562. Here, respondents can demonstrate standing only if application of the regulations by the Government will affect *them* in the manner described above.

It is common ground that the respondent organizations can assert the standing of their members. To establish the concrete and particularized injury that standing requires, respondents point to their members' recreational interests in the National Forests. While generalized harm to the forest or the environment will not alone support standing, if that harm in fact affects the recreational or even the mere esthetic interests of the plaintiff, that will suffice. Sierra Club v. Morton, 405 U.S. 727 (1972).

Affidavits submitted to the District Court alleged that organization member Ara Marderosian had repeatedly visited the Burnt Ridge site, that he had imminent plans to do so again, and that his interests in viewing the flora and fauna of the area would be harmed if the Burnt Ridge Project went forward without incorporation of the ideas he would have suggested if the Forest Service had provided him an opportunity to comment. The Government concedes this was sufficient to establish Article III standing with respect to Burnt Ridge. Marderosian's threatened injury with regard to that project was originally one of the bases for the present suit. [H]owever, the parties settled their differences. . . . Marderosian's injury in fact with regard to that project has been remedied, and [is] "not at issue in this case." We know of no precedent for the proposition that when a plaintiff has sued to challenge the lawfulness of certain action or threatened action but has settled that suit, he retains standing to challenge the basis for that action. . . .

Respondents have identified no other application of the invalidated regulations that threatens imminent and concrete harm to the interests of their members. The only other affidavit relied on was that of Jim Bensman. He asserted [that] he had suffered injury in the past from development on Forest Service land. That does not suffice [because] it was not tied to application of the challenged regulations, because it does not identify any particular site, and because it relates to past injury rather than imminent future injury that is sought to be enjoined. . . . Bensman's affidavit further asserts that he has visited many National Forests and plans to visit several unnamed National Forests in the future. [The affidavit fails] to allege that *any* particular timber sale or other project claimed to be unlawfully subject to the regulations will impede a specific and concrete plan of Bensman's to enjoy the National Forests. The National Forests occupy more than 190 million acres, an area larger than Texas. There may be a chance, but is hardly a likelihood, that Bensman's wanderings will bring him to a parcel about to be affected by a project unlawfully subject to the regulations. Indeed, without further specification it is impossible to tell *which* projects are (in respondents' view) unlawfully subject to the regulations. . . . Here we are asked to assume not only that Bensman will stumble across a project tract unlawfully subject to the regulations, but also that the tract is about to be developed by the Forest Service in a way that harms his recreational interests, and that he would have commented on the project but for the regulation. Accepting an intention to visit the National Forests as adequate to confer standing to challenge any Government action affecting any portion of those forests would be tantamount to eliminating the requirement of concrete, particularized injury in fact.

The Bensman affidavit does refer specifically to a series of projects in the Allegheny National Forest that are subject to the challenged regulations. It does not assert, however, any firm intention to visit their locations, saying only that Bensman "'want[s] to'" go there. This vague desire to return is insufficient to satisfy the requirement of imminent injury: "Such 'some day' intentions — without any description of concrete plans, or indeed any specification of *when* the some day will be — do not support a finding of the 'actual or imminent' injury that our cases require." *Defenders of Wildlife*, 504 U.S., at 564.

Respondents argue that they have standing to bring their challenge because they have suffered procedural injury, namely that they have been denied the ability to file comments on some Forest Service actions and will continue to be so denied. But deprivation of a procedural right without some concrete interest that is affected by the deprivation — a procedural right *in vacuo* — is insufficient to create Article III standing. Only a "person who has been accorded a procedural right to protect *his concrete interests* can assert that right without meeting all the normal standards for redressability and immediacy." Respondents alleged such injury in their challenge to the Burnt Ridge Project, claiming that but for the allegedly unlawful abridged procedures they would have been able to oppose the project that threatened to impinge on their concrete plans to observe nature in that specific area. But Burnt Ridge is now off the table.

It makes no difference that the procedural right has been accorded by Congress. That can loosen the strictures of the redressability prong of our standing inquiry — so that standing existed with regard to the Burnt Ridge Project, for example, despite the possibility that Earth Island's allegedly guaranteed right to comment would not be successful in persuading the Forest Service to avoid impairment of Earth Island's concrete interests. Unlike redressability, however, the requirement of injury in fact is a hard floor of Article III jurisdiction that cannot be removed by statute. "[I]t would exceed [Article III's] limitations if, at the behest of Congress and in the absence of any showing of concrete injury, we were to entertain citizen suits to vindicate the public's nonconcrete interest in the proper administration of the laws. [T]he party bringing suit must show that the action injures him in a concrete and personal way."

The dissent proposes a hitherto unheard-of test for organizational standing: whether, accepting the organization's self-description of the activities of its members, there is a statistical probability that some of those members are threatened with concrete injury. Since, for example, the Sierra Club asserts in its pleadings that it has more than "700,000 members nationwide, including thousands of members in California" who "use and enjoy the Sequoia National Forest," it is probable (according to the dissent) that some (unidentified) members have planned to visit some (unidentified) small parcels affected by the Forest Service's procedures and will suffer (unidentified) concrete harm as a result. This novel approach to the law of organizational standing would make a mockery of our prior cases, which have required plaintiff-organizations to make specific allegations establishing that at least one identified member had suffered or would suffer harm. . . . [I]t is well established that the court has an independent obligation to assure that standing exists, regardless of whether it is challenged by any of the parties. Without individual affidavits, how is the court to assure itself that the Sierra Club, for example, has "'thousands of members'" who "'use and enjoy the Sequoia National Forest'"? . . . "Standing," we have said, "is not 'an ingenious academic exercise in the conceivable' [but] requires [a] factual showing of perceptible harm." In part because of the difficulty of verifying the facts upon which such probabilistic standing depends, the Court has required plaintiffs claiming an organizational standing to identify members who have suffered the requisite harm—surely not a difficult task here, when so many thousands are alleged to have been harmed.

The dissent would have us replace the requirement of "imminent" harm, which it acknowledges our cases establish, with the requirement of "'a *realistic* threat' that reoccurrence of the challenged activity would cause [the plaintiff] harm in the reasonably near future." [The] problem for the dissent is that the timely affidavits no more meet that requirement than they meet the usual formulation. They fail to establish that the affiants' members will *ever* visit one of the small parcels at issue. . . .

The judgment of the Court of Appeals is reversed in part and affirmed in part.

It is so ordered.

Justice KENNEDY, concurring.
[This] case would present different considerations if Congress had sought to provide redress for a concrete injury "giv[ing] rise to a case or controversy where none existed before." Nothing in the statute at issue here, however, indicates Congress intended to identify or confer some interest separate and apart from a procedural right.

Justice BREYER, with whom Justice STEVENS, Justice SOUTER, and Justice GINSBURG join, dissenting.
[To] understand the *constitutional* issue that the majority decides, it may prove helpful to imagine that Congress enacted a *statutory* provision that expressly permitted environmental groups like the respondents here to bring cases just like the present one, provided (1) that the group has members who have used salvage-timber parcels in the past and are likely to do so in the future, and (2) that the group's members have opposed Forest Service timber sales in the past (using notice, comment, and appeal procedures to do so) and will likely use those procedures to oppose salvage-timber sales in the future. The majority cannot, and does not, claim that such a statute would be unconstitutional. *See* Massachusetts v. EPA, 549 U.S. 497, 516-518 (2007). How then can it find the present case constitutionally unauthorized?

[The] majority assumes, as do I, that these unlawful Forest Service procedures will lead to substantive actions, namely the sales of salvage timber on burned lands, that might not take place if the proper procedures were followed. [The] majority holds that the plaintiff organizations, while showing that they have members who have used salvage-timber sale parcels in the past (*i.e.*, parcels that the Service does not subject to the notice, comment, and appeal procedures required by law), have failed to show that they have members likely to use such parcels in the future.

How can the majority credibly claim that salvage-timber sales, and similar projects, are unlikely to harm the asserted interests of the members of these environmental groups? [Where] the Court has directly focused upon the matter, *i.e.*, where, as here, a plaintiff has *already* been subject to the injury it wishes to challenge, the Court has asked whether there is a *realistic likelihood* that the challenged future conduct will, in fact, recur and harm the plaintiff. . . . Would courts deny *standing* to a landowner who complains that a neighbor's upstream dam constitutes a nuisance — even if the harm to his downstream property (while bound to occur) will not occur for several years? [A] threat of future harm may be realistic even where the plaintiff cannot specify precise times, dates, and GPS coordinates. Thus, we recently held that Massachusetts has *standing* to complain of a procedural failing, namely, EPA's failure properly to determine whether to restrict carbon dioxide emissions, even though that failing would create Massachusetts-based harm which (though likely to occur) might not occur for several decades. *EPA*, 549 U.S., at 522-523.

The Forest Service admits that it intends to conduct thousands of further salvage-timber sales and other projects exempted under the challenged regulations "in the reasonably near future." How then can the Court deny that the plaintiffs have shown a "realistic" threat that the Forest Service will continue to authorize (without the procedures claimed necessary) salvage-timber sales, and other Forest Service projects, that adversely affect the recreational, aesthetic, and environmental interests of the plaintiffs' members? [Respondents] allege, and the Government has conceded, that the Forest Service took wrongful actions (such as selling salvage timber) "thousands" of times in the two years prior to suit. The Complaint alleges, and no one denies, that the organizations, the Sierra Club for example, have hundreds of thousands of members who use forests regularly across the Nation for recreational, scientific, aesthetic, and environmental purposes. The Complaint further alleges, and no one denies, that these organizations (and their members), believing that actions such as salvage-timber sales harm those interests, regularly oppose salvage-timber sales (and similar actions) in proceedings before the agency. And the Complaint alleges, and no one denies, that the organizations intend to continue to express their opposition to such actions in those proceedings in the future. . . .

With respect, I dissent.

Notes: More on Congressional Authorization

1. *Standing and Federal Election Laws.* In Federal Election Commission v. Akins, 524 U.S. 11 (1998), respondents sought to challenge the Federal Election

Commission's (FEC) conclusion that the American Israel Public Affairs Committee (AIPAC) was not a "political committee" within the meaning of the Federal Election Campaign Act of 1971 (FECA or Act), and therefore did not have to make disclosures regarding its membership, contributions, and expenditures under federal election laws. In challenging the FEC's conclusion, the respondents relied on federal election laws, which provided that "[a]ny party aggrieved by an order of the Commission dismissing a complaint filed by such party [may] file a petition" in federal court seeking review of that dismissal. The Court held that the voters had standing to challenge the FEC's determination: "[P]rudential standing is satisfied when the injury asserted by a plaintiff 'arguably [falls] within the zone of interests to be protected or regulated by the statute [in] question.' [Given] the language of the statute and the nature of the injury, we conclude that Congress, intending to protect voters such as respondents from suffering the kind of injury here at issue, intended to authorize this kind of suit. . . . The 'injury in fact' that respondents have suffered consists of their inability to obtain information — lists of AIPAC donors (who are, according to AIPAC, its members), and campaign-related contributions and expenditures — that, on respondents' view of the law, the statute requires that AIPAC make public. There is no reason to doubt their claim that the information would help them (and others to whom they would communicate it) to evaluate candidates for public office, especially candidates who received assistance from AIPAC, and to evaluate the role that AIPAC's financial assistance might play in a specific election. [W]here large numbers of Americans suffer alike, the political process, rather than the judicial process, may provide the more appropriate remedy for a widely shared grievance. [T]he informational injury at issue here, directly related to voting, the most basic of political rights, is sufficiently concrete and specific such that the fact that it is widely shared does not deprive Congress of constitutional power to authorize its vindication in the federal courts." Justice Scalia, joined by Justices O'Connor and Thomas, dissented: "The interpretation that the Court gives the [statutory] provision deprives it of almost all its limiting force. *Any voter* can sue to compel the agency to require registration of an entity as a political committee, even though the 'aggrievement' consists of nothing more than the deprivation of access to information whose public availability would have been one of the consequences of registration."

2. Qui Tam *Actions*. In Vermont Agency of Natural Resources v. United States ex rel. Stevens, 529 U.S. 765 (2000), the Court interpreted a federal *qui tam* statute that provided that "[a] person may bring a civil action *for the person and for the United States Government*," and also provided that the plaintiff shall receive a bounty *out of the United States' recovery* for filing and/or prosecuting a successful action on behalf of the government. The statute gave the private citizen "the right to continue as a party to the action" even when the government itself has assumed "primary responsibility" for prosecuting the action, entitled the citizen to a hearing before the government's voluntary dismissal of the suit, and prohibited the government from settling the suit over the citizen's objection without a judicial determination of "fair[ness], adequa[cy] and reasonable-[ness]." Stevens brought a *qui tam* action against the Vermont Agency of Natural

Resources (VANR), his former employer, alleging that it had submitted false claims to the Environmental Protection Agency (EPA) in connection with various federal grant programs administered by the EPA. Specifically, he claimed that the VANR had overstated the amount of time its employees spent on the federally funded projects, thereby inducing the government to disburse more grant money than the VANR was entitled to receive. When the VANR sought to dismiss on the theory that Stevens had suffered no injury, the Court held that Stevens had standing to bring the action: "[As] to this portion of the recovery — the bounty he will receive if the suit is successful — a *qui tam* relator has a 'concrete private interest in the outcome of [the] suit.' But the same might be said of someone who has placed a wager upon the outcome. An interest unrelated to injury in fact is insufficient to give a plaintiff standing. The interest must consist of obtaining compensation for, or preventing, the violation of a legally protected right. A *qui tam* relator has suffered no such invasion — indeed, the 'right' he seeks to vindicate does not even fully materialize until the litigation is completed and the relator prevails. This is not to suggest that Congress cannot define new legal rights, which in turn will confer standing to vindicate an injury caused to the claimant. . . . We believe, however, that adequate basis for the relator's suit for his bounty is to be found in the doctrine that the assignee of a claim has standing to assert the injury in fact suffered by the assignor. The FCA can reasonably be regarded as effecting a partial assignment of the Government's damages claim. Although we have never expressly recognized 'representational standing' on the part of assignees, we have routinely entertained their suits, and also suits by subrogees, who have been described as 'equitable assign[ees].' We conclude, therefore, that the United States' injury in fact suffices to confer standing on respondent Stevens."

∾ PROBLEMS: STANDING AND CONGRESSIONAL AUTHORIZATION ∾

1. *More on the Health Care Legislation.* In regard to the health care legislation described at the beginning of the chapter, Congress did not explicitly authorize any of the plaintiffs to challenge the legislation. Indeed, to the contrary, Congress reached a political compromise adverse to their interests. How does the absence of congressional authorization affect the plaintiff's ability to file suit?

2. Lujan *Reconsidered.* What could the plaintiffs in *Lujan* have done differently that would have helped them establish standing? For example, would they have had standing if they had purchased airplane tickets to travel to Sri Lanka for three months hence and had every intention of going at that time? Would it matter that the environmental effects might not have occurred by that time? If so, would the plaintiffs be required to purchase tickets for an even later trip? Could the plaintiff organizations have substituted different individuals who had a stronger claim of injury? What types of individuals might have satisfied that requirement?

Monsanto Co. v. Geerston Seed Farms

130 S.Ct. 2743 (2010)

Justice ALITO delivered the opinion of the Court.

This case arises out of a decision by the Animal and Plant Health Inspection Service (APHIS) to deregulate a variety of genetically engineered alfalfa. The District Court held that APHIS violated the National Environmental Policy Act of 1969 (NEPA), 83 Stat. 852, 42 U.S.C. §4321 *et seq.*, by issuing its deregulation decision without first completing a detailed assessment of the environmental consequences of its proposed course of action. To remedy that violation, the District Court vacated the agency's decision completely deregulating the alfalfa variety in question; ordered APHIS not to act on the deregulation petition in whole or in part until it had completed a detailed environmental review; and enjoined almost all future planting of the genetically engineered alfalfa pending the completion of that review. The Court of Appeals affirmed the District Court's entry of permanent injunctive relief. The main issue now in dispute concerns the breadth of that relief. For the reasons set forth below, we reverse and remand for further proceedings. . . .

The Plant Protection Act (PPA), 7 U.S.C. §7701 *et seq.*, provides that the Secretary of the Department of Agriculture (USDA) may issue regulations "to prevent the introduction of plant pests into the United States or the dissemination of plant pests within the United States." The Secretary has delegated that authority to APHIS, a division of the USDA. Acting pursuant to that delegation, APHIS has promulgated regulations governing "the introduction of organisms and products altered or produced through genetic engineering that are plant pests or are believed to be plant pests." Under those regulations, certain genetically engineered plants are presumed to be "plant pests" — and thus "regulated articles" under the PPA — until APHIS determines otherwise. However, any person may petition APHIS for a determination that a regulated article does not present a plant pest risk and therefore should not be subject to the applicable regulations. APHIS may grant such a petition in whole or in part.

In deciding whether to grant nonregulated status to a genetically engineered plant variety, APHIS must comply with NEPA, which requires federal agencies "to the fullest extent possible" to prepare an environmental impact statement (EIS) for "every recommendation or report on proposals for legislation and other major Federal actio[n] significantly affecting the quality of the human environment." 42 U.S.C. §4332(2)(c). The statutory text "speaks solely in terms of *proposed* actions; it does not require an agency to consider the possible environmental impacts of less imminent actions when preparing the impact statement on proposed actions." Kleppe v. Sierra Club, 427 U.S. 390, 410, n.20 (1976).

An agency need not complete an EIS for a particular proposal if it finds, on the basis of a shorter "environmental assessment" (EA), that the proposed action will not have a significant impact on the environment. Even if a particular agency proposal requires an EIS, applicable regulations allow the agency to take at least some action in furtherance of that proposal while the EIS is being prepared. *See* §1506.1(a).

This case involves Roundup Ready Alfalfa (RRA), a kind of alfalfa crop that has been genetically engineered to be tolerant of glyphosate, the active ingredient of the herbicide Roundup. Petitioner Monsanto Company (Monsanto) owns the intellectual property rights to RRA. Monsanto licenses those rights to co-petitioner Forage Genetics International (FGI), which is the exclusive developer of RRA seed.

APHIS initially classified RRA as a regulated article, but in 2004 petitioners sought nonregulated status for two strains of RRA. In response, APHIS prepared a draft EA assessing the likely environmental impact of the requested deregulation. It then published a notice in the Federal Register advising the public of the deregulation petition and soliciting public comments on its draft EA. After considering the hundreds of public comments that it received, APHIS issued a Finding of No Significant Impact and decided to deregulate RRA unconditionally and without preparing an EIS. Prior to this decision, APHIS had authorized almost 300 field trials of RRA conducted over a period of eight years.

Approximately eight months after APHIS granted RRA nonregulated status, respondents (two conventional alfalfa seed farms and environmental groups concerned with food safety) filed this action against the Secretary of Agriculture and certain other officials in Federal District Court, challenging APHIS's decision to completely deregulate RRA. Their complaint alleged violations of NEPA, the Endangered Species Act of 1973 (ESA), 16 U.S.C. §1531 *et seq.*, and the PPA. Respondents did not seek preliminary injunctive relief pending resolution of those claims. Hence, RRA enjoyed nonregulated status for approximately two years. During that period, more than 3,000 farmers in 48 States planted an estimated 220,000 acres of RRA.

In resolving respondents' NEPA claim, the District Court accepted APHIS's determination that RRA does not have any harmful health effects on humans or livestock. Nevertheless, the District Court held that APHIS violated NEPA by deregulating RRA without first preparing an EIS. . . . The Government, Monsanto, and FGI appealed, challenging the scope of the relief granted but not disputing the existence of a NEPA violation. A divided panel of the Court of Appeals for the Ninth Circuit affirmed. . . . We granted certiorari. . . .

At the threshold, respondents contend that petitioners lack standing to seek our review of the lower court rulings at issue here. We disagree.

Standing under Article III of the Constitution requires that an injury be concrete, particularized, and actual or imminent; fairly traceable to the challenged action; and redressable by a favorable ruling. Horne v. Flores, 129 S.Ct. 2579 (2009). Petitioners here satisfy all three criteria. Petitioners are injured by their inability to sell or license RRA to prospective customers until such time as APHIS completes the required EIS. Because that injury is caused by the very remedial order that petitioners challenge on appeal, it would be redressed by a favorable ruling from this Court.

Respondents do not dispute that petitioners would have standing to contest the District Court's permanent injunction order if they had pursued a different litigation strategy. Instead, respondents argue that the injury of which petitioners complain is independently caused by a part of the District Court's order that petitioners failed to challenge, namely, the vacatur of APHIS's deregulation decision. The practical consequence of the vacatur, respondents contend, was to restore RRA to the status of a regulated article; and, subject to certain exceptions not applicable here, federal regulations ban the growth and sale of regulated articles. Because petitioners did not specifically challenge the District Court's vacatur, respondents reason, they lack standing to challenge a part of the District Court's order (*i.e.*, the injunction) that does not cause petitioners any injury not also caused by the vacatur.

Respondents' argument fails for two independent reasons. First, although petitioners did not challenge the vacatur directly, they adequately preserved their objection that the vacated deregulation decision should have been replaced by APHIS's proposed injunction. Throughout the remedial phase of this litigation, one of the main disputes between the parties has been whether the District Court was required to adopt APHIS's proposed judgment. That judgment would have replaced the vacated deregulation decision with an order expressly allowing continued planting of RRA subject to certain limited conditions. Accordingly, if the District Court had adopted the agency's suggested remedy, there would still be authority for the continued planting of RRA, because there would, in effect, be a new deregulation decision.

Second, petitioners in any case have standing to challenge the part of the District Court's order enjoining partial deregulation. Respondents focus their standing argument on the part of the judgment enjoining the planting of RRA, but the judgment also states that "[b]efore granting Monsanto's deregulation petition, *even in part,* the federal defendants shall prepare an environmental impact statement. As respondents concede, that part of the judgment goes beyond the vacatur of APHIS's deregulation decision.

At oral argument, respondents contended that the restriction on APHIS's ability to effect a partial deregulation of RRA does not cause petitioners "an actual or an imminent harm." In order for a partial deregulation to occur, respondents argued, the case would have to be remanded to the agency, and APHIS would have to prepare an EA "that may or may not come out in favor of a partial deregulation." Because petitioners cannot prove that those two events would happen, respondents contended, the asserted harm caused by the District Court's partial deregulation ban is too speculative to satisfy the actual or imminent injury requirement.

We reject this argument. If the injunction were lifted, we do not see why the District Court would have to remand the matter to the agency in order for APHIS to effect a partial deregulation. And even if a remand were required, we perceive no basis on which the District Court could decline to remand the matter to the agency so that it could determine whether to pursue a partial deregulation during the pendency of the EIS process.

Nor is any doubt as to whether APHIS would issue a new EA in favor of a partial deregulation sufficient to defeat petitioners' standing. It is undisputed that petitioners have submitted a deregulation petition and that a partial deregulation of the kind embodied in the agency's proposed judgment would afford petitioners much of the relief that they seek; it is also undisputed that, absent the

District Court's order, APHIS could attempt to effect such a partial deregulation pending its completion of the EIS. For purposes of resolving the particular standing question before us, we need not decide whether or to what extent a party challenging an injunction that bars an agency from granting certain relief must show that the agency would be likely to afford such relief if it were free to do so. In this case, as is clear from APHIS's proposed judgment and from its briefing throughout the remedial phase of this litigation, the agency takes the view that a partial deregulation reflecting its proposed limitations is in the public interest. Thus, there is more than a strong likelihood that APHIS would partially deregulate RRA were it not for the District Court's injunction. The District Court's elimination of that likelihood is plainly sufficient to establish a constitutionally cognizable injury. Moreover, as respondents essentially conceded at oral argument, that injury would be redressed by a favorable decision here, since "vacating the current injunction . . . will allow [petitioners] to go back to the agency, [to] seek a partial deregulation," even if the District Court's vacatur of APHIS's deregulation decision is left intact. We therefore hold that petitioners have standing to seek this Court's review.[4]

We next consider petitioners' contention that respondents lack standing to seek injunctive relief. *See* DaimlerChrysler Corp. v. Cuno, 547 U.S. 332, 352 (2006). Petitioners argue that respondents have failed to show that any of the named respondents is likely to suffer a constitutionally cognizable injury absent injunctive relief. We disagree.

Respondents include conventional alfalfa farmers. Emphasizing "the undisputed concentration of alfalfa seed farms," the District Court found that those farmers had "established a 'reasonable probability' that their organic and conventional alfalfa crops will be infected with the engineered gene" if RRA is completely deregulated.[5] A substantial risk of gene flow injures respondents in several ways. For example, respondents represent that, in order to continue marketing their product to consumers who wish to buy non-genetically-engineered alfalfa, respondents would have to conduct testing to find out whether and to what extent their crops have been contaminated. Respondents also allege that the risk of gene flow will cause them to take certain measures to minimize the likelihood of potential contamination and to ensure an adequate supply of non-genetically-engineered alfalfa.

Such harms, which respondents will suffer even if their crops are not actually infected with the Roundup ready gene, are sufficiently concrete to satisfy the injury-in-fact prong of the constitutional standing analysis. Those harms are readily attributable to APHIS's deregulation decision, which, as the District Court found, gives rise to a significant risk of gene flow to non-genetically-engineered varieties of alfalfa. Finally, a judicial order prohibiting the growth and

---

4. We do not rest "the primary basis for our jurisdiction on the premise that the District Court enjoined APHIS from partially deregulating RRA in any sense." Even if the District Court's order prohibiting a partial deregulation applies only to "the *particular* partial deregulation order proposed to the court by APHIS," petitioners would still have standing to challenge that aspect of the order.

5. At least one of the respondents in this case specifically alleges that he owns an alfalfa farm in a prominent seed-growing region and faces a significant risk of contamination from RRA. Other declarations in the record provide further support for the District Court's conclusion that the deregulation of RRA poses a significant risk of contamination to respondents' crops.

sale of all or some genetically engineered alfalfa would remedy respondents' injuries by eliminating or minimizing the risk of gene flow to conventional and organic alfalfa crops. We therefore conclude that respondents have constitutional standing to seek injunctive relief from the complete deregulation order at issue here.

Petitioners appear to suggest that respondents fail to satisfy the "zone of interests" test we have previously articulated as a prudential standing requirement in cases challenging agency compliance with particular statutes. That argument is unpersuasive because, as the District Court found, respondents' injury has an environmental as well as an economic component. In its ruling on the merits of respondents' NEPA claim, the District Court held that the risk that the RRA gene conferring glyphosate resistance will infect conventional and organic alfalfa is a significant environmental effect within the meaning of NEPA. Petitioners did not appeal that part of the court's ruling, and we have no occasion to revisit it here. Respondents now seek injunctive relief in order to avert the risk of gene flow to their crops—the very same effect that the District Court determined to be a significant environmental concern for purposes of NEPA. The mere fact that respondents also seek to avoid certain economic harms that are tied to the risk of gene flow does not strip them of prudential standing.

In short, respondents have standing to seek injunctive relief, and petitioners have standing to seek this Court's review of the Ninth Circuit's judgment affirming the entry of such relief. We therefore proceed to the merits of the case. . . .

The judgment of the Ninth Circuit is reversed, and the case is remanded for further proceedings consistent with this opinion.

It is so ordered.

d. *Jus Tertii* (Third-Party) Standing

To what extent do litigants have standing to raise the rights of others who are not parties to a federal court proceeding? In an older decision, Singleton v. Wulff, 428 U.S. 106 (1976), physicians brought a constitutional challenge against a Missouri statute that excluded abortions that are not "medically indicated" from the purposes for which Medicaid benefits are available to needy persons. The doctors could show that they performed nonmedically indicated abortions and that they would suffer financial injury (the loss of payment) if the statute remained in effect. However, the doctors also wanted to assert the rights of their patients. The Court began by articulating the general rule that courts should not allow individuals to assert the rights of third parties (individuals who are not parties to the case before the court): "Federal courts must hesitate before resolving a controversy, even one within their constitutional power to resolve, on the basis of the rights of third persons not parties to the litigation. . . . First, the courts should not adjudicate such rights unnecessarily, and it may be that in fact the holders of those rights either do not wish to assert them, or will be able to enjoy them regardless of whether the in-court litigant is successful or not. . . . Second, third parties themselves usually will be the best proponents of their own rights. The courts depend on effective advocacy, and therefore should prefer to construe legal rights only when the most effective advocates of those rights are before them. The holders of the rights may have a like preference, to the extent they will be bound by the courts' decisions under the doctrine of *Stare decisis*." Despite the general rule, the Court suggested that third-party standing might be appropriate in some cases: "[This] Court has looked primarily to two factual elements to determine whether the rule should apply in a particular case. The first is the relationship of the litigant to the person whose right he seeks to assert. If the enjoyment of the right is inextricably bound up with the activity the litigant wishes to pursue, the court['s] construction of the right is not unnecessary in the sense that the right's enjoyment will be unaffected by the outcome of the suit. Furthermore, the relationship between the litigant and the third party may be such that the former is fully, or very nearly, as effective a proponent of the right as the latter."

In *Singleton*, the Court relied on Griswold v. Connecticut, 381 U.S. 479 (1965), in which the Court held that a licensed physician had the ability to assert the privacy rights of married patients to receive contraceptive advice. *Singleton* concluded that the abortion providers also had standing to represent their patients: "[A] woman cannot safely secure an abortion without the aid of a physician, and an impecunious woman cannot easily secure an abortion without the physician's being paid by the State. [T]he constitutionally protected abortion decision is one in which the physician is intimately involved. Aside from the woman herself, [the] physician is uniquely qualified to litigate the constitutionality of the State's interference with, or discrimination against, that decision. . . . As to the woman's assertion of her own rights, there are several obstacles. [S]he may be chilled from such assertion by a desire to protect the very privacy of her decision from the publicity of a court suit. A second obstacle is the imminent mootness, at least in the technical sense, of any individual woman's claim. Only a few months [after] the maturing of the decision to undergo an abortion, her right thereto will have been irrevocably lost, assuming [that] unless the impecunious woman can establish Medicaid eligibility she must forgo abortion. It is true that these obstacles are not insurmountable. Suit may be brought under a pseudonym, as so frequently has been done. A woman who is no longer pregnant may nonetheless retain the right to litigate the point because it is 'capable of repetition yet evading review.' Roe v. Wade, 410 U.S., at 124-125. And it may be that a class could be assembled, whose fluid membership always included some women with live claims. But if the assertion of the right is to be 'representative' to such an extent anyway, there seems little loss in terms of effective advocacy from allowing its assertion by a physician."

In Elk Grove Unified School District v. Newdow, 542 U.S. 1 (2004), a father, an atheist, sought to challenge recitation of the Pledge of Allegiance in his daughter's school. He objected on the basis that the Pledge contains the words "under God," which he viewed as an establishment of religion. The daughter's mother, the custodial parent, intervened in opposition to the father's suit. The Court concluded that the father lacked standing to represent his daughter's interests: "The interests of the affected persons in this case are in many respects antagonistic. Of course, legal disharmony in family relations is not uncommon, and in many instances that disharmony poses no bar to federal-court adjudication of proper federal questions. What makes this case different is that Newdow's standing derives entirely from his relationship with his daughter, but he lacks the right to litigate as her next friend. In marked contrast to our case law on *jus tertii, see, e.g.,* Singleton v. Wulff, 428 U.S. 106 (1976) (plurality opinion), the interests of this parent and this child are not parallel and, indeed, are potentially in conflict."

⌒ PROBLEMS: EXCEPTIONS TO *JUS TERTII* ⌒

1. *The Health Care Legislation and* Jus Tertii. To the extent that any of the parties seeking to challenge the health care legislation (described in the problem at the beginning of the chapter) lack standing in their own right, can they assert the rights of others (e.g., patients)?

2. *Contraception Bans.* Now, let's think about *Poe* a bit more. Assume that the Court's privacy decisions have not been rendered, and that a Massachusetts statute makes it a crime to give "away [any] drug, medicine, instrument or article whatever for the prevention of conception." The statute distinguishes between married persons (who are allowed to obtain contraceptives to prevent pregnancy, but only from doctors or druggists on prescription) and single persons (who are not allowed to obtain contraceptives from anyone for the purpose of preventing pregnancy). In addition, the law prohibits both married and single persons from obtaining contraceptives for the purpose of preventing the spread of disease. William Baird was convicted of "exhibiting contraceptive articles in the course of delivering a lecture on contraception to a group of students at Boston University and for giving a young woman a package of Emko vaginal foam at the close of his address." Does Baird have standing to raise the rights of unmarried persons who are being denied access to contraceptives? Does his status as an "authorized distributor of contraceptives" allow him to assert the interests of the users of his products? *See* Eisenstadt v. Baird, 405 U.S. 438 (1972).

3. *The Murderer's Mother.* Gary Mark Gilmore was convicted of murder and sentenced to death. He waived all of his rights and agreed to submit to execution. His mother, acting as "next friend," applied for a stay of execution. Gilmore opposed the request for a stay. Does Gilmore's mother have standing to act as his "next friend" and seek an application for a stay? Should it matter that Gilmore objects to allowing his mother to serve as his "next friend"? Would it matter whether Gilmore is competent and made a knowing waiver of his rights? What if he was incompetent? *See* Gilmore v. Utah, 429 U.S. 1012 (1976).

4. *The Alleged Terrorist's Father.* Following the 9/11 attack on the World Trade Center in New York City, Yaser Easm Hamdi was detained as an enemy combatant. He was a U.S. citizen, detained on U.S. soil, but he was denied access to an attorney and therefore was effectively denied access to the courts. Hamdi's father, as "next friend," sought a writ of habeas corpus on his son's behalf. Under such circumstances, may the father assert his son's right to habeas corpus? *See* Hamdi v. Rumsfeld, 542 U.S. 507 (2004).

5. *Beer Sales.* An Oklahoma statute provides that males between the ages of 18 and 21 cannot purchase 3.2 percent beer, but that females can purchase the beer when they reach the age of 18. The plaintiff was less than 21 years old when

the suit was filed, but turned 21 before the case was decided. Does the plaintiff still have standing to bring the suit? Could the suit be maintained by anyone else (e.g., a beer distributor that sold 3.2 percent beer)? *See* Craig v. Boren, 429 U.S. 190 (1976).

6. *Challenging Restrictive Covenants.* A state statute permits restrictive covenants that prohibit covenanted property from being sold to members of specified minority groups. Everyone agrees that the specified minority groups would have standing to challenge the covenant in an appropriate case, and that members of the minority groups could not be required to pay damages for breach of the covenant. However, instead of suing the minorities, the plaintiffs seek damages from those who sell the real property in violation of the covenants. May the defendant assert the rights of the minority groups in defense of the damage action? Does the defendant have standing to challenge the covenant on the basis of his own injury? How would you argue the case for the defendant? How might the plaintiff respond? *See* Barrows v. Jackson, 346 U.S. 249 (1953).

7. *The Association.* An Alabama statute requires foreign corporations to report the names and addresses of its members to Alabama's attorney general. The National Association for the Advancement of Colored People (NAACP) refuses to comply with the reporting requirement, and the State of Alabama files suit to prohibit the NAACP from conducting further activities within the state. The NAACP responds by challenging the reporting requirements as a violation of the First Amendment's speech and assembly provisions. In particular, the NAACP claims that its members may be harassed or discriminated against if their identities are disclosed. The NAACP seeks to challenge the requirements on its own behalf as well as on behalf of its members. May the NAACP assert the constitutional rights of its members? What must it show in order to do so? Can the NAACP bring the suit in it own right? *See* NAACP v. Alabama, 357 U.S. 449 (1958).

Points to Remember

- In Marbury v. Madison, 5 U.S. (1 Cranch) 137 (1803), the Court recognized that our written constitution forms "the fundamental and paramount law of the nation, and consequently the theory of every such government must be, that an act of the legislature repugnant to the constitution is void."
- *Marbury* went on to hold that it "is emphatically the province and duty of the judicial department to say what the law is. Those who apply the rule to particular cases, must of necessity expound and interpret that rule. If two laws conflict with each other, the courts must decide on the operation of each."
- Despite *Marbury*'s sweeping language, other branches of the federal government can and do interpret the Constitution and the laws in some contexts.
- In Martin v. Hunter's Lessee, 14 U.S. (1 Wheat.) 304 (1816), the Court held that "[judges] were not to decide merely according to the laws or

constitution of the state, but according to the constitution, laws and treaties of the United States — 'the supreme law of the land.'"

- *Martin* also held that state courts are bound by the U.S. Supreme Court's interpretation of the U.S. Constitution.

- In Cooper v. Aaron, 358 U.S. 1 (1958), the Court reinforced *Martin* by holding that state courts (and state officials) are bound by federal desegregation decrees.

- Because the Court can hear only a limited number of cases per year, the Court has always regarded its jurisdiction as discretionary rather than mandatory. As Rule 10 of the Court's rules make clear, even if the Court perceives that a lower court has erred, the Court can (and often does) decline to review the case.

- Article III, Section 2, Clause 2 of the Constitution gives the Supreme Court original jurisdiction over cases involving "Ambassadors, other Public Ministers and Consuls, and those in which a State shall be a Party," and also gives the Court appellate jurisdiction "with such Exceptions, and under such Regulations as the Congress shall make."

- In Ex Parte McCardle, 74 U.S. 506 (1868), the Court upheld a federal law taking away the U.S. Supreme Court's jurisdiction over a particular class of cases.

- However, in United States v. Klein, 80 U.S. 128 (1871), the Court struck down a comparable federal law on the basis that Congress has inadvertently passed the limit that separates the legislative from the judicial power.

- There are questions about how far Congress can go in taking away the Supreme Court's "essential role."

- Even though the Court may have the authority to say what the law is, the Court frequently declines to exercise its jurisdiction. One example is when a case involves a so-called "political question."

- In Baker v. Carr, 369 U.S. 186 (1962), the Court held that in "determining whether a question falls within (the political question) category, the appropriateness under our system of government of attributing finality to the action of the political departments and also the lack of satisfactory criteria for a judicial determination are dominant considerations."

- *Baker* also said that the "fundamental issue" is whether a matter has "been committed by the Constitution to another branch of government, or whether the action of that branch exceeds whatever authority has been committed, is itself a delicate exercise in constitutional interpretation, and is a responsibility of this Court as ultimate interpreter of the Constitution."

- For example, courts are particularly inclined to apply the political question doctrine to cases involving foreign affairs (e.g., the executive's decision to recognize foreign governments).

- In Goldwater v. Carter, 444 U.S. 996 (1979), the Court held that President Carter's decision to terminate a treaty with Taiwan, and to recognize instead the People's Republic of China, constituted a political question.

- Article III, Section 2 contains perhaps the most important limitation on judicial power: the "case" and "controversy" requirement. This limitation has spawned multiple restrictions on the scope of judicial authority, including the prohibition against advisory opinions, the ripeness and mootness doctrines, and the standing requirement.
- The prohibition against advisory opinions precludes the courts from rendering advisory opinions and reserves their power for so-called "cases and controversies."
- The federal courts have insisted that lawsuits be brought at the "right" time. A case that is brought too early is held to be not "ripe" for adjudication, and therefore does not present a case or controversy.
- The mootness doctrine also involves timing. When this doctrine applies, however, the claim is that a case is presented too late. Even though the claim may have been ripe at one point, subsequent events have rendered it "moot."
- Courts sometimes hear moot cases if the issues presented by those cases are "capable of repetition but evading review." (Abortion issues meet this criterion because a pregnancy ends in nine months, but a case can rarely get to the U.S. Supreme Court in that amount of time.)
- Standing cases focus on whether the plaintiff has "alleged such a personal stake in the outcome of the controversy as to warrant invocation of federal-court jurisdiction." As a general rule, the plaintiff must suffer "injury in fact" that is both concrete and particularized. The injury must be "actual and imminent" as opposed to conjectural or hypothetical, the injury must be fairly traceable to the defendant's challenged action, and it must be likely that a favorable judicial decision will prevent or redress the injury.
- Although standing is related to ripeness and mootness, because the plaintiff may lack sufficient interest when a case is not yet ripe or has become moot, standing cases do not always involve questions of timing.
- In general, taxpayers do not have standing to challenge governmental programs despite their claims that those programs may increase their taxes. "[A taxpayer's] interest in the moneys of the treasury — partly realized from taxation and partly from other sources — is shared with millions of others, is comparatively minute and indeterminable, and the effect upon future taxation, of any payment out of the funds, so remote, fluctuating and uncertain, that no basis is afforded for an appeal to the preventive powers of a court of equity."
- Taxpayers do have standing to challenge the validity of a tax that they are required to pay.
- In Flast v. Cohen, 392 U.S. 83 (1968), the Court held that taxpayers could challenge an appropriation under the Taxing and Spending Clause provided that they could base their claim on a direct limitation on the taxing and spending power. *Flast* met that nexus by basing the claim on the Establishment Clause of the First Amendment.

- In recent years, courts have placed particular emphasis on the idea that "there must be a causal connection between the injury and the conduct complained of; . . . it must be likely, as opposed to merely speculative, that the injury will be redressed by a favorable decision."
- The constitutional aspect stems from Article III's case and controversy requirement and cannot be waived by Congress. The prudential aspect is a limitation imposed by the Court on itself. In some instances, even when a case or controversy exists, the Court refuses to hear a case in deference to a coordinate branch of government. If Congress has invited the Court to hear a particular type of case, prudential restraints are minimized or disappear.
- In Association of Data Processing Service Organizations, Inc. v. Camp, 397 U.S. 150 (1970), the Court articulated a two-part test for establishing standing to sue under congressional enactments: "whether the plaintiff alleges that the challenged action has caused him injury in fact, economic or otherwise" and whether "the interest sought to be protected by the complainant is arguably within the zone of interests to be protected or regulated by the statute or constitutional guarantee in question."
- As a general rule, individuals are expected to assert their own rights in litigation and are not allowed to assert the rights of others.
- Courts sometimes permit third-party standing in some cases despite the general rule when: "[This] Court has looked primarily to two factual elements to determine whether the rule should apply in a particular case. The first is the relationship of the litigant to the person whose right he seeks to assert. If the enjoyment of the right is inextricably bound up with the activity the litigant wishes to pursue, the court['s] construction of the right is not unnecessary in the sense that the right's enjoyment will be unaffected by the outcome of the suit. Furthermore, the relationship between the litigant and the third party may be such that the former is fully, or very nearly, as effective a proponent of the right as the latter."

2

National Legislative Power

U.S CONSTITUTION, ARTICLE I

Section 1. All legislative Powers herein granted shall be vested in a Congress of the United States, which shall consist of a Senate and House of Representatives.

Section 8. The Congress shall have Power to lay and collect Taxes, Duties, Imposts and Excises, to pay the Debts and provide for the common Defence and general Welfare of the United States, but all Duties, Imposes and Excises shall be uniform throughout the United States;

To borrow Money on the credit of the United States;

To regulate Commerce with foreign Nations, and among the several States, and with the Indian Tribes;

To establish an uniform Rule of Naturalization, and uniform Laws on the subject of Bankruptcies throughout the United States;

To coin Money; regulate the Value thereof, and of foreign Coin, and fix the Standard of Weights and Measures;

To provide for the Punishment of counterfeiting the Securities and current Coin of the United States;

To establish Post Offices and post Roads;

To promote the Progress of Science and useful Arts, by securing for limited Times to Authors and Inventors the exclusive Right to their respective Writings and Discoveries;

To constitute Tribunals inferior to the supreme Court;

To define and punish Piracies and Felonies committed on the high Seas, and Offenses against the Law of Nations;

To declare War, grants Letters of Marque and Reprisal, and make Rules concerning Captures on Land and Water;

To raise and support Armies, but no Appropriation of Money to that Use shall be for a longer Term than two years;

To provide and maintain a Navy;

To make Rules for the Government and Regulation of the land and naval Forces;

To provide for calling forth the Militia to execute the Laws of the Union, suppress Insurrections and repel Invasions;

To provide for organizing, arming, and disciplining, the Militia, and for governing such Part of them as may be employed in the Service of the United States respectively, the Appointment of the Officers, and the Authority of training the Militia according to the discipline prescribed by Congress.

To exercise exclusive Legislation in all Cases whatsoever, over such District (not exceeding ten Miles square) as may, by Cession of Particular States, and the Acceptance of Congress, become the Seat of the Government of the United States, and to exercise like Authority over all Places purchased by the Consent of the Legislature of the State in which the Same shall be, for the Erection of Forts, Magazines, Arsenals, dock-Yards and other needful Buildings; — And

To make all Laws which shall be necessary and proper for carrying into Execution the foregoing Powers, and all other Powers vested by this Constitution in the Government of the United States, or in any Department or Officer thereof.

U.S. CONSTITUTION, ARTICLE IV

Section 3. . . . . The Congress shall have Power to dispose of and make all needful Rules and Regulations respecting the Territory or other Property belonging to the United States; and nothing in this Constitution shall be so construed as to Prejudice any Claims of the United States, or of any particular State.

U.S. CONSTITUTION, FOURTEENTH AMENDMENT

[5] In the first major case to address the newly granted power of Congress to enact civil rights legislation, the Court severely limited Congress' ability to address both private and state acts of racial discrimination under the enforcement provisions of the amendments.

✌ PROBLEM: THE EDUCATION FOR A BETTER AMERICA ACT ✌

Congress, concerned about the quality of education in the United States, is considering the possibility of adopting the Education for a Better America Act. The reasons for Congress's concerns are broad and well-substantiated. For decades, American children have been falling behind their counterparts in other countries in math and science as well as other critical subjects. More troubling, some children are failing in real and critical ways. Too many children drop out of school, and the evidence shows that dropouts encounter problems such as much lower employment prospects and much higher rates of alcoholism, drug abuse, and incarceration. In addition, dropouts are more likely to be involved in domestic violence. Congress is also concerned because the nature of society is becoming more technological and more international in character. Many members of Congress believe that, in order to compete in a modern business environment, students need a better and more sophisticated education. As a result, Congress believes that education reform is vital to the health of the U.S. economy.

Evidence introduced in Congress also shows that existing schools are failing. Too many teachers are unqualified or incompetent. Schools are rife with drugs and other distracting influences. Lots of kids come from broken and dysfunctional homes. The net effect is that too many schools are not effectively educating kids.

Suppose that you are counsel to a congressional committee that is considering how to "reform" and "reshape" education. A number of suggestions have been made about how the Education for a Better America Act should be structured. Some in Congress believe that the Act should provide financial incentives to local schools that meet educational goals and objectives. Others believe that the Act should include mandates that impose requirements and obligations on local schools. As you work your way through this chapter, you will be asked to advise Congress about how it should structure the legislation, and about what types of provisions should (or should not) be included in the final legislation.

As powerful as the U.S. Supreme Court may have become over the past two centuries, primary legislative power rests with Congress. In this chapter, we focus on the parameters of national legislative power.

Under the Articles of Confederation, the federal government was given limited legislative power because the states preferred to retain that power for themselves. However, the country did not function well. The individual states erected barriers to trade (e.g., tariffs and embargos) that made interstate commerce difficult. In addition, many worried that the federal government did not have sufficient power to provide for foreign affairs and the national defense. In an effort to deal with these problems, a convention was called in the mid-1780s to amend the Articles of Confederation. That call ultimately led to the constitutional convention that produced the present U.S. Constitution.

During the constitutional convention, much debate focused on the scope of federal power. Alexander Hamilton, for one, pushed for a broad conception of federal power. He argued that Congress should be given the "power to pass all laws which [it] shall judge necessary to the common defense and general welfare of the Union." Others argued for a more limited conception of federal powers. Framing the debate was a recognition that, to the extent that the states ceded power to the federal government, their own power was diminished. Even though the states were reluctant to give too much power to the federal government, a majority of participants recognized the need to create a stronger federal government than had been created under the Articles of Confederation.

The Framers ultimately decided to create a federal government with limited powers. Instead of giving Congress the power to legislate on any matter it deems appropriate, the Framers created a government of limited, enumerated powers. Article I, Section 8 gives Congress "[a]ll legislative powers herein granted." The concept of limited powers is also reflected in the Tenth Amendment, which provides that "The powers not delegated to the United States by the Constitution, nor prohibited to it by the States, are reserved to the States respectively, or to the people."

Nevertheless, Article I, Section 8 gives Congress a variety of powers. Included in the 18 paragraphs of enumerated powers are the right to borrow money, to establish uniform rules on naturalization and bankruptcy, to coin money, to provide punishment for counterfeiting, to establish post offices and roads, to provide for the protection of scientists and artists through rules governing rights to writings and discoveries, to provide and maintain a navy, to raise and support armies, and to define and punish piracies.

Given the Constitution's plan of enumerated powers, two separate and distinct questions tend to arise in congressional power cases. First, does Congress have the power to pass a given piece of legislation? In other words, do any of the enumerated powers give it that authority? For example, does the Commerce Clause give Congress the power to pass the law in question? Second, does the law violate a limitation on that authority (e.g., free speech or equal protection)?

In this chapter, we see that the scope of congressional power has ebbed and flowed over the course of the last two centuries as the Court's interpretation of Article I has shifted. As you read the following cases, think about the broad issues in historical context. Has the federal system remained faithful to its roots, or has it morphed and expanded into a system not contemplated by the Framers of the Constitution? If the scope of federal power has expanded, was this expansion necessary and inevitable?

A. THE NECESSARY AND PROPER CLAUSE

One of the most important enumerated powers is found in Article I, Section 8, Paragraph 18, the so-called "Necessary and Proper" Clause. It provides that Congress shall have the power to "make all Laws which shall be necessary and proper for carrying into Execution the foregoing Powers, and all other Powers vested by this Constitution in the Government of the United States, or in any Department of Officer thereof."

The Necessary and Proper Clause is important because it expands the scope of the enumerated powers. For example, since Article I, Section 8 explicitly gives Congress the power to "provide and maintain a Navy," Paragraph 18 allows Congress to do those things that are "necessary and proper" to maintain a navy.

There has been much debate regarding the scope and effect of the Necessary and Proper Clause. Thomas Jefferson, who preferred a strict construction of the clause, argued that it should be interpreted to mean "absolutely necessary." In other words, in providing and maintaining a navy, Congress could only do those things that were "absolutely necessary" to the provision and maintenance of a navy. Alexander Hamilton, by contrast, preferred a "helpful" or "convenience" standard. In other words, Congress could do anything that was "helpful" or "convenient" to the provision and maintenance of a navy.

The following case arose in the early nineteenth century during a period of economic upheaval. Some believed that the Bank of the United States, far from being a passive player, had contributed to the upheaval by encouraging a speculative boom through the availability of easy credit. As a result, there was a movement (one that ultimately failed) to revoke the bank's charter. As you read *McCulloch*, think about whether Chief Justice Marshall implicitly endorses either the "absolutely necessary" or the "convenience" test, or whether he opts for some other test altogether.

McCulloch v. Maryland

17 U.S. (4 Wheat.) 316 (1819)

Chief Justice MARSHALL delivered the opinion of the Court.

[The State of Maryland enacted a statute taxing the operations of all banks that had not been charted by the state itself. The Bank of the United States, a bank chartered by Congress and owned by the federal government, refused, through James McCulloch, its cashier, to pay the tax, arguing that the state did not have the power to tax a federal government instrumentality. The Maryland Supreme Court upheld the tax, and the United States appealed.]

The first question made in the cause is — has congress power to incorporate a bank? It has been truly said, that this can scarcely be considered as an open question, entirely unprejudiced by the former proceedings of the nation respecting it. The principle now contested was introduced at a very early period of our history, has been recognized by many successive legislatures, and has been acted upon by the judicial department, in cases of peculiar delicacy, as a law of undoubted obligation. . . .

In discussing this question, the counsel for the state of Maryland have deemed it of some importance, in the construction of the constitution, to consider that instrument, not as emanating from the people, but as the act of sovereign and independent states. The powers of the general government, it has been said, are delegated by the states, who alone are truly sovereign; and must be exercised in subordination to the states, who alone possess supreme dominion. It would be difficult to sustain this proposition. The convention which framed the constitution was indeed elected by the state legislatures. But the instrument, when it came from their hands, was a mere proposal, without obligation, or pretensions to it. It was reported to the then existing congress of the United States, with a request that it might "be submitted to a convention of delegates, chosen in each state by the people thereof, under the recommendation of its legislature, for their assent and ratification." This mode of proceeding was adopted; and by the convention, by congress, and by the state legislatures, the instrument was submitted to the people. . . . It is true, they assembled in their several states — and where else should they have assembled? No political dreamer was ever wild enough to think of breaking down the lines which separate the states, and of compounding the American people into one common mass. Of consequence, when they act, they act in their states. But the measures they adopt do not, on that account, cease to be the measures of the people themselves, or become the measures of the state governments.

From these conventions, the constitution derives its whole authority. The government proceeds directly from the people; is "ordained and established," in the name of the people; . . . It required not the affirmance, and could not be negatived, by the state governments. The constitution, when thus adopted, was of complete obligation, and bound the state sovereignties. It has been said, that the people had already surrendered all their powers to the state sovereignties, and had nothing more to give. But, surely, the question whether they may resume and modify the powers granted to government, does not remain to be settled in this country. . . . [W]hen, "in order to form a more perfect union," it was deemed necessary to change this alliance into an effective government, possessing great and sovereign powers, and acting directly on the people, the necessity of referring it to the people, and of deriving its powers directly from them, was felt and acknowledged by all. The government of the Union, then (whatever may be the influence of this fact on the case), is, emphatically and truly, a government of the people. In form, and in substance, it emanates from them. Its powers are granted by them, and are to be exercised directly on them, and for their benefit. . . .

If any one proposition could command the universal assent of mankind, we might expect it would be this — that the government of the Union, though limited in its powers, is supreme within its sphere of action. This would seem to result, necessarily, from its nature. It is the government of all; its powers are delegated by all; it represents all, and acts for all. . . . But this question is not left to mere reason: the people have, in express terms, decided it, by saying, "this constitution, and the laws of the United States, which shall be made in pursuance thereof," "shall be the supreme law of the land," and by requiring that the members of the state legislatures, and the officers of the executive and judicial departments of the states, shall take the oath of fidelity to it. The government of the United States, then, though limited in its powers, is supreme; and its laws, when made in pursuance of the constitution, form the supreme law of the land, "anything in the constitution or laws of any state to the contrary notwithstanding."

Among the enumerated powers, we do not find that of establishing a bank or creating a corporation. But there is no phrase in the instrument which, like the articles of confederation, excludes incidental or implied powers; and which requires that everything granted shall be expressly and minutely described. . . . A constitution, to contain an accurate detail of all the subdivisions of which its great powers will admit, and of all the means by which they may be carried into execution, would partake of the prolixity of a legal code, and could scarcely be embraced by the human mind. It would, probably, never be understood by the public. Its nature, therefore, requires that only its great outlines should be marked, its important objects designated, and the minor ingredients which compose those objects, be deduced from the nature of the objects themselves. . . . In considering this question, then, we must never forget that it is a constitution we are expounding.

Although, among the enumerated powers of government, we do not find the word "bank" or "incorporation," we find the great powers, to lay and collect taxes; to borrow money; to regulate commerce; to declare and conduct a war; and to raise and support armies and navies. The sword and the purse, all the external relations, and no inconsiderable portion of the industry of the nation, are intrusted to its government. It can never be pretended, that these vast powers draw after them others of inferior importance, merely because they are inferior. Such an idea can never be advanced. But it may with great reason be contended, that a government, intrusted with such ample powers, on the due execution of which the happiness and prosperity of the nation so vitally depends, must also be intrusted with ample means for their execution. The power being given, it is the interest of the nation to facilitate its execution. It can never be their interest, and cannot be presumed to have been their intention, to clog and embarrass its execution, by withholding the most appropriate means. Throughout this vast republic, from the St. Croix to the Gulf of Mexico, from the Atlantic to the Pacific, revenue is to be collected and expended, armies are to be marched and supported. The exigencies of the nation may require, that the treasure raised in the north should be transported to the south, that raised in the east, conveyed to the west, or that this order should be reversed. Is that construction of the constitution to be preferred, which would render these operations difficult, hazardous and expensive? Can we adopt that construction (unless the words imperiously require it), which would impute to the framers of that instrument, when granting these powers for the public good, the intention of impeding their exercise, by withholding a choice of means? If, indeed, such be the mandate of the constitution, we have only to obey; but that instrument does not profess to enumerate the means by which the powers it confers may be executed; nor does it prohibit the creation of a corporation, if the existence of such a being be essential, to the beneficial exercise of those powers. It is, then, the subject of fair inquiry, how far such means may be employed.

[The] power of creating a corporation, though appertaining to sovereignty, is not, like the power of making war, or levying taxes or of regulating commerce, a great substantive and independent power, which cannot be implied as incidental to other powers, or used as a means of executing them. It is never the end for which other powers are exercised, but a means by which other objects are accomplished. . . . The power of creating a corporation is never used for its own sake, but for the purpose of effecting something else. No sufficient reason is, therefore, perceived, why it may not pass as incidental to those powers which are expressly given, if it be a direct mode of executing them.

But the constitution of the United States has not left the right of congress to employ the necessary means, for the execution of the powers conferred on the government, to general reasoning. To its enumeration of powers is added, that of making "all laws which shall be necessary and proper, for carrying into execution the foregoing powers, and all other powers vested by this constitution, in the government of the United States, or in any department thereof." The counsel for the state of Maryland have urged various arguments, to prove that this clause, though, in terms a grant of power, is not so, in effect; but is really restrictive of the general right, which might otherwise be implied, of selecting means for executing the enumerated powers. [T]he argument on which most reliance is placed, is drawn from that peculiar language of this clause. Congress is not empowered by it to make all laws, which may have relation to the powers conferred on the government, but such only as may be "necessary and proper" for carrying them into execution. The word "necessary" is considered as controlling the whole sentence, and as limiting the right to pass laws for the execution of the granted powers, to such as are indispensable, and without which the power would be nugatory. That it excludes the choice of means, and leaves to congress, in each case, that only which is most direct and simple. Is it true, that this is the sense in which the word "necessary" is always used? Does it always import an absolute physical necessity, so strong, that one thing to which another may be termed necessary, cannot exist without that other? We think it does not. If reference be had to its use, in the common affairs of the world, or in approved authors, we find that it frequently imports no more than that one thing is convenient, or useful, or essential to another. . . . This word, then, like others, is used in various senses; and, in its construction, the subject, the context, the intention of the person using them, are all to be taken into view.

Let this be done in the case under consideration. The subject is the execution of those great powers on which the welfare of a nation essentially depends. It must have been the intention of those who gave these powers, to insure, so far as human prudence could insure, their beneficial execution. This could not be done, by confiding the choice of means to such narrow limits as not to leave it in the power of congress to adopt any which might be appropriate, and which were conducive to the end. This provision is made in a constitution, intended to endure for ages to come, and consequently, to be adapted to the various crises of human affairs. To have prescribed the means by which government should, in all future time, execute its powers, would have been to change, entirely, the character of the instrument, and give it the properties of a legal code. It would have been an unwise attempt to provide, by immutable rules, for exigencies which, if foreseen at all, must have been seen dimly, and which can be best provided for as they occur. To have declared, that the best means shall not be used, but those alone, without which the power given would be nugatory, would have been to deprive the legislature of the capacity to avail itself of experience, to exercise its reason, and to accommodate its legislation to circumstances. . . .

We admit, as all must admit, that the powers of the government are limited, and that its limits are not to be transcended. But we think the sound construction of the constitution must allow to the national legislature that discretion, with respect to the means by which the powers it confers are to be carried into execution, which will enable that body to perform the high duties assigned to it, in the manner most beneficial to the people. Let the end be legitimate, let it be within the scope of the constitution, and all means which are appropriate, which are plainly adapted to that end, which are not prohibited, but consist with the letter and spirit of the constitution, are constitutional. . . .

Notes and Questions

1. *Reclaiming Arid Land.* In Kansas v. Colorado, 206 U.S. 46 (1907), Congress sought to divert water from the Arkansas River to reclaim arid land in Colorado. The Constitution provides Congress with the power to regulate interstate commerce, as well as the power to regulate navigation. Although the Arkansas River was navigable, however, it was not navigable in the place where the diversion occurred, and water was not being diverted for navigability purposes. The Court held that Congress had exceeded its authority under the navigability clause: "[I]f, in the present case, the national government was asserting [that] the appropriation for the purposes of irrigation of the waters of the Arkansas was affecting the navigability of the stream, it would become our duty to determine the truth of the charge. But the government makes no such contention. . . . That [raises] the question whether the reclamation of arid lands is one of the powers granted to the general government. As heretofore stated, the constant declaration of this court from the beginning is that this government is one of enumerated powers. . . . Turning to the enumeration of the powers granted to Congress by the 8th section of the 1st article of the Constitution, it is enough to say that no one of them, by any implication, refers to the reclamation of arid lands. The last paragraph of the section which authorizes Congress to make all laws which shall be necessary to proper for carrying into execution the foregoing powers, and all other powers vested by this Constitution in the government of the United States, or in any department or officer thereof, is not the delegation of a new and independent power, but simply provision for making effective the powers theretofore mentioned. . . . This natural construction of the original body of the Constitution is made absolutely certain by the 10th Amendment. This Amendment, which was seemingly adopted with prescience of just such contention as the present, disclosed the widespread fear that the national government might, under the pressure of a supposed general welfare, attempt to exercise powers which had not been granted. . . . The powers affecting the internal affairs of the states not granted to the United States by the Constitution, nor prohibited by it to the states, are reserved to the states respectively, and all powers of a national character which are not delegated to the national government by the Constitution are reserved to the people of the United States. . . . [As] our national territory has been enlarged, we have within our borders extensive tracts of arid lands which ought to be reclaimed, and it may well be that no power is adequate for their reclamation other than that of the national government. But, if no such power has been granted, none can be exercised."

2. *Is the Necessary and Proper Clause Implicit in the Constitution?* Some argue that, if Article I, Section 8 had not contained the Necessary and Proper Clause, one would have been found to exist. For example, Madison argued in *The Federalist No. 44* that: "Had the Constitution been silent on this head, there can be no doubt that all the particular powers requisite as means of executing the general powers would have resulted to the government, by unavoidable implication." Do

you agree? But, if Madison is right, should the Necessary and Proper Clause be regarded as a *limitation* on the scope of federal power rather than as an expansion?

3. *The Louisiana Purchase.* During his presidency, Thomas Jefferson made the Louisiana Purchase, which added a large section of land to the new country. Under Jefferson's construction of the Necessary and Proper Clause, can the purchase be justified? As you examine Article I, Section 8 (or, for that matter, other provisions of the Constitution), do you find any provision that explicitly authorizes the purchase? If not, how can the purchase be justified? Under his construction of the Clause, was Jefferson required to seek and obtain a constitutional amendment authorizing his actions?

4. *The Limits of Implied Powers.* If the concept of implicit powers is accepted, where does it end? Consider these comments of President Jefferson: "Congress [is] authorized to defend the nation. Ships are necessary for defense; copper is necessary for ships; mines, necessary for copper; a company necessary to work the mines; and who can doubt this reasoning who has ever played at 'This is the House that Jack Built'? Under such a process of filiation of necessities the sweeping clause makes clean work." Do you agree with Jefferson? Does his logic suggest that the Necessary and Proper Clause should be more neatly cabined? But by what standard? Is it desirable to apply an "absolutely necessary" standard?

5. *"We Must Never Forget . . ."* In deciding *McCulloch*, Chief Justice Marshall makes his now famous statement: "[In] considering this question, then, we must, never forget that it is a *Constitution* we are expounding." In the context of the case being decided, Marshall's statement argues for a broader or more liberal interpretation of the Constitution. Do you agree with Marshall? Alternatively, do you agree with: a) Justice Frankfurter, who stated that "precisely *'because* it is a *constitution* we are expounding,' we ought not to take liberties with it." National Marine Ins. Co. v. Tidewater Transfer Co., 337 U.S. 582, 647 (1949) (Frankfurter, J., dissenting); or b) Professor Kurland, who stated that "whenever a judge quotes this passage, you can be sure that the court will be throwing the constitutional text, its history, and its structure to the winds in reaching its conclusion"? Philip B. Kurland, *Curia Regis: Some Comments on the Divine Rights of Kings and Courts to Say What the Law Is*, 23 Ariz. L. Rev. 582, 591 (1981). Who is correct, and what are the implications for interpreting the Constitution?

6. *More on Kansas v. Colorado.* In the first note on this case, *supra,* pay attention to the Court's construction of the Tenth Amendment to the U.S. Constitution. As you read the remainder of this chapter, reflect on this construction and its current validity, and on whether this case would be decided the same way if it arose today.

United States v. Comstock

130 S.Ct. 1949 (2010)

Justice BREYER delivered the opinion of the Court.

A federal civil-commitment statute authorizes the Department of Justice to detain a mentally ill, sexually dangerous federal prisoner beyond the date the prisoner would otherwise be released. 18 U.S.C. §4248. We have previously examined similar statutes enacted under state law to determine whether they violate the Due Process Clause. *See* Kansas v. Crane, 534 U.S. 407 (2002). . . . Here we ask whether the Federal Government has the authority under Article I of the Constitution to enact this federal civil-commitment program or whether its doing so falls beyond the reach of a government of "enumerated powers." McCulloch v. Maryland, 4 Wheat. 316, 405 (1819). We conclude that the Constitution grants Congress the authority to enact §4248 as "necessary and proper for carrying into Execution" the powers "vested by" the "Constitution in the Government of the United States." Art. I, §8, cl. 18.

The federal statute before us allows a district court to order the civil commitment of an individual who is currently "in the custody of the [Federal] Bureau of Prisons," if that individual (1) has previously "engaged or attempted to engage in sexually violent conduct or child molestation," (2) currently "suffers from a serious mental illness, abnormality, or disorder," and (3) "as a result of" that mental illness, abnormality, or disorder is "sexually dangerous to others," in that "he would have serious difficulty in refraining from sexually violent conduct or child molestation if released." §§4247(a)(5) (6).

In order to detain such a person, the Government (acting through the Department of Justice) must certify to a federal district judge that the prisoner meets the conditions just described. . . . When such a certification is filed, the statute automatically stays the individual's release from prison, thereby giving the Government an opportunity to prove its claims at a hearing through psychiatric (or other) evidence. The statute provides that the prisoner "shall be represented by counsel" and shall have "an opportunity" at the hearing "to testify, to present evidence, to subpoena witnesses on his behalf, and to confront and crossexamine" the Government's witnesses.

If the Government proves its claims by "clear and convincing evidence," the court will order the prisoner's continued commitment in "the custody of the Attorney General," who must "make all reasonable efforts to cause" the State where that person was tried, or the State where he is domiciled, to "assume responsibility for his custody, care, and treatment." If either State is willing to assume that responsibility, the Attorney General "shall release" the individual "to the appropriate official" of that State. But if, "notwithstanding such efforts, neither such State will assume such responsibility," then "the Attorney General shall place the person for treatment in a suitable [federal] facility."

Confinement in the federal facility will last until either (1) the person's mental condition improves to the point where he is no longer dangerous (with or without appropriate ongoing treatment), in which case he will be released; or (2) a State assumes responsibility for his custody, care, and treatment, in which case he will be transferred to the custody of that State. The statute establishes a system for ongoing psychiatric and judicial review of the individual's case, including judicial hearings at the request of the confined person at six-month intervals.

[In] 2006, the Government instituted proceedings [against the] respondents in this case. Three [had] previously pleaded guilty in federal court to possession of child pornography, and the fourth [to] sexual abuse of a minor. [The] fifth respondent [had] been charged in federal court with aggravated sexual abuse of a minor, but was found mentally incompetent to stand trial. . . . Each [respondent] moved to dismiss [the] proceeding on constitutional grounds. [Among other things,] they claimed that, in enacting the statute, Congress exceeded the powers granted to it by Art. I, §8 of the Constitution, including those granted by the Commerce Clause and the Necessary and Proper Clause. . . . The District Court [granted] their motion to dismiss [and] the Court of Appeals for the Fourth Circuit upheld the dismissal. [We granted certiorari.]

The question [is] whether the Necessary and Proper Clause, Art. I, §8, cl. 18, grants Congress authority sufficient to enact the statute before us. [We] assume, but we do not decide, that other provisions of the Constitution, such as the Due Process Clause, do not prohibit civil commitment in these circumstances. [We] ask solely whether the Federal Government, exercising its enumerated powers, may enact such a statute as well. [We] conclude that the Constitution grants Congress legislative power sufficient to enact §4248. We base this conclusion on five considerations, taken together.

First, the Necessary and Proper Clause grants Congress broad authority to enact federal legislation. [The] Federal "[G]overnment is acknowledged by all to be one of enumerated powers," *McCulloch*, 4 Wheat., at 405, which means that "[e]very law enacted by Congress must be based on one or more of" those powers, United States v. Morrison, 529 U.S. 598, 607 (2000). [But] "a government, entrusted with such" powers, "must also be entrusted with ample means for their execution." *McCulloch*, 4 Wheat., at 408. [The] Necessary and Proper Clause makes clear that the Constitution's grants of specific federal legislative authority are accompanied by broad power to enact laws that are "convenient, or useful" or "conducive" to the authority's "beneficial exercise." [The] word "necessary" does not mean " 'absolutely necessary.' . . . "Let the end be legitimate, let it be within the scope of the constitution, and all means which are appropriate, which are plainly adapted to that end, which are not prohibited, but consist with the letter and spirit of the constitution, are constitutional." [I]n determining whether the Necessary and Proper Clause grants Congress the legislative authority to enact a particular federal statute, we look to see whether the statute constitutes a means that is rationally related to the implementation of a constitutionally enumerated power. Sabri v. United States, 541 U. S. 600, 605 (2004). [A]s Chief Justice Marshall stated, a federal statute, in addition to being authorized by Art. I, §8, must also "not [be] prohibited" by the Constitution. *McCulloch, supra*, at 421. . . . We have also recognized that the Constitution [leaves] the "choice of means primarily [to] the judgment of Congress. If it can be seen that the means adopted are really calculated to attain the end, the degree of their necessity, the extent to which they conduce to the end, the closeness of the relationship between the means adopted and the end to be attained, are matters for congressional determination alone." Burroughs v. United States, 290 U. S. 534, 547, 548 (1934).

[The] Constitution, which nowhere speaks explicitly about the creation of federal crimes beyond those related to "counterfeiting," "treason," or "Piracies and Felonies committed on the high Seas" or "against the Law of Nations," Art. I, §8, cls. 6, 10; Art. III, §3, nonetheless grants Congress broad authority to create such crimes. . . . And Congress routinely exercises its authority to enact criminal laws in furtherance of, for example, its enumerated powers to regulate interstate and foreign commerce, to enforce civil rights, to spend funds for the general welfare, to establish federal courts, to establish post offices, to regulate bankruptcy, to regulate naturalization, and so forth. *See, e.g., Lottery Case, supra.* . . . Similarly, Congress, in order to help ensure the enforcement of federal criminal laws enacted in furtherance of its enumerated powers, can cause a prison to be erected at any place within the jurisdiction of the United States, and direct that all persons sentenced to imprisonment under the laws of the United States shall be confined there. *Ex parte Karstendick*, 93 U.S. 396, 400 (1876). Moreover, Congress, having established a prison system, can enact laws that seek to ensure that system's safe and responsible administration by, for example, requiring prisoners to receive medical care and educational training, and can also ensure the safety of the prisoners, prison workers and visitors, and those in surrounding communities by, for example, creating further criminal laws governing entry, exit, and smuggling, and by employing prison guards to ensure discipline and security. *See, e.g.,* §1791 (prohibiting smuggling contraband). . . . Neither Congress' power to criminalize conduct, nor its power to imprison individuals who engage in that conduct, nor its power to enact laws governing prisons and prisoners, is explicitly mentioned in the Constitution. But Congress nonetheless possesses broad authority to do each of those things in the course of "carrying into Execution" the enumerated powers "vested by" the "Constitution in the Government of the United States," Art. I, §8, cl. 18 authority granted by the Necessary and Proper Clause.

Second, the civil-commitment statute before us constitutes a modest addition to a set of federal prisonrelated mental-health statutes that have existed for many decades. We recognize that even a longstanding history of related federal action does not demonstrate a statute's constitutionality. A history of involvement, however, can nonetheless be "helpful in reviewing the substance of a congressional statutory scheme," *Gonzales*, 545 U.S., at 21, and, in particular, the reasonableness of the relation between the new statute and pre-existing federal interests. . . . Here, Congress has long been involved in the delivery of mental health care to federal prisoners, and has long provided for their civil commitment. [O]ver the span of three decades, Congress created a national, federal civil-commitment program under which any person who was either charged with or convicted of any federal offense in any federal court could be confined in a federal mental institution.

These statutes did not raise the question presented here, for they all provided that commitment in a federal hospital would end upon the completion of the relevant "terms" of federal "imprisonment" as set forth in the underlying criminal sentence or statute. But in the mid-1940s that proviso was eliminated. . . .

Between 1948 and 1949[,] Congress modified the law [to provide] for the civil commitment of individuals who are, or who become, mentally incompetent at any time after their arrest and before the expiration of their federal sentence, and it set forth various procedural safeguards[,] including proof that the person if released "will probably endanger the safety of the officers, the property, or other interests of the United States. . . ."

[This] precondition [was] uniformly interpreted by the Judiciary to mean that his "release would endanger the safety of persons, property or the public interest in general—not merely the interests peculiar to the United States as such." United States v. Curry, 410 F.2d 1372, 1374 (CA4 1969). . . .

In 1984, Congress modified these basic statutes [to] conform more closely to the then-existing judicial interpretation of that language, i.e., it altered the language so as to authorize (explicitly) civil commitment if, in addition to the other conditions, the prisoner's "release would create a substantial risk of bodily injury to another person or serious damage to the property of another." §4246(d). . . .

Congress also elaborated upon the required condition "that suitable arrangements [are] not otherwise available" by directing the Attorney General to seek alternative placement in state facilities. . . .

In 2006, Congress enacted the particular statute before us. It differs from earlier statutes in that it focuses directly upon persons who, due to a mental illness, are sexually dangerous. Notably, many of these individuals were likely already subject to civil commitment under §4246, which, since 1949, has authorized the postsentence detention of federal prisoners who suffer from a mental illness and who are thereby dangerous (whether sexually or otherwise). Aside from its specific focus on sexually dangerous persons, §4248 is similar to the provisions first enacted in 1949. In that respect, it is a modest addition to a longstanding federal statutory framework, which has been in place since 1855.

Third, Congress reasonably extended its longstanding civil-commitment system to cover mentally ill and sexually dangerous persons who are already in federal custody, even if doing so detains them beyond the termination of their criminal sentence. For one thing, the Federal Government is the custodian of its prisoners. As federal custodian, it has the constitutional power to act in order to protect nearby (and other) communities from the danger federal prisoners may pose. Indeed, at common law, one "who takes charge of a third person" is "under a duty to exercise reasonable care to control" that person to prevent him from causing reasonably foreseeable "bodily harm to others." Restatement (Second) of Torts §319, p. 129 (1963, 1969). If a federal prisoner is infected with a communicable disease that threatens others, surely it would be "necessary and proper" for the Federal Government to take action, pursuant to its role as federal custodian, to refuse (at least until the threat diminishes) to release that individual among the general public, where he might infect others (even if not threatening an interstate epidemic, cf. Art. I, §8, cl. 3). And if confinement of such an individual is a "necessary and proper" thing to do, then how could it not be similarly "necessary and proper" to confine an individual whose mental illness threatens others to the same degree?

Moreover, §4248 is "reasonably adapted" to Congress' power to act as a responsible federal custodian (a power that rests, in turn, upon federal criminal statutes that legitimately seek to implement constitutionally enumerated authority). Congress could have reasonably concluded that federal inmates who suffer from a mental illness that causes them to "have serious difficulty in refraining from sexually violent conduct," would pose an especially high danger to the public if released. And Congress could also have reasonably concluded [that] a reasonable number of such individuals would likely *not* be detained by the States if released from federal custody, in part because the Federal Government itself severed their claim to "legal residence in any State" by incarcerating them in remote federal prisons. Here Congress' desire to address the specific challenges[,] taken together with its responsibilities as a federal custodian, supports the conclusion that §4248 satisfies "review for means-end rationality," i.e., that it satisfies the Constitution's insistence that a federal statute represent a rational means for implementing a constitutional grant of legislative authority.

Fourth, the statute properly accounts for state interests. Respondents and the dissent contend that §4248 violates the Tenth Amendment because it "invades the province of state sovereignty" in an area typically left to state control. . . . The powers "delegated to the United States by the Constitution" include those specifically enumerated powers listed in Article I along with the implementation authority granted by the Necessary and Proper Clause. Virtually by definition, these powers are not powers that the Constitution "reserved to the States." *See New York, supra,* at 156, 159. . . .

Nor does this statute invade state sovereignty or otherwise improperly limit the scope of "powers that remain with the States." To the contrary, it requires *accommodation* of state interests: The Attorney General must inform the State in which the federal prisoner "is domiciled or was tried" that he is detaining someone with respect to whom those States may wish to assert their authority, and he must encourage those States to assume custody of the individual. He must also immediately "release" that person "to the appropriate official of" either State "if such State will assume [such] responsibility." And either State has the right, at any time, to assert its authority over the individual, which will prompt the individual's immediate transfer to State custody. "[The] Federal Government would have no appropriate role" with respect to an individual covered by the statute once "the transfer to State responsibility and State control has occurred." . . .

Fifth, the links between §4248 and an enumerated Article I power are not too attenuated. Neither is the statutory provision too sweeping in its scope. Invoking the cautionary instruction that we may not "pile inference upon inference" in order to sustain congressional action under Article I, respondents argue that, when legislating pursuant to the Necessary and Proper Clause, Congress' authority can be no more than one step removed from a specifically enumerated power. But this argument is irreconcilable with our precedents. [As] Chief Justice Marshall recognized in *McCulloch*, "the power 'to establish post offices and post roads' [is] executed by the single act of *making* the establishment. [F]rom this has been inferred the power and duty of *carrying* the mail along the post road, from one post office to another. And, from this *implied* power, has *again* been inferred the right to *punish* those who steal letters from the post office, or rob the mail." . . .

[Our] necessary and proper jurisprudence contains multiple examples of similar reasoning. . . . Indeed even the dissent acknowledges that Congress has the implied power to criminalize any conduct that might interfere with the exercise of an enumerated power, and also the additional power to imprison people who violate those (inferentially authorized) laws, and the additional power to provide for the safe and reasonable management of those prisons, and the additional power to regulate the prisoners' behavior even after their release. Of course, each of those powers, [is] ultimately "derived from" an enumerated power. And, as the dissent agrees, that enumerated power is "the enumerated power that justifies the defendant's statute of conviction." [E]very such statute must itself be legitimately predicated on an enumerated power. And the same enumerated power that justifies the creation of a federal criminal statute, and that justifies the additional implied federal powers that the dissent considers legitimate, justifies civil commitment under §4248 as well. . . .

Nor need we fear that our holding today confers on Congress a general "police power, which the Founders denied the National Government and reposed in the States." *Morrison*, 529 U.S., at 618. . . . §4248 is narrow in scope. It has been applied to only a small fraction of federal prisoners. And its reach is limited to individuals already "in the custody of the" Federal Government. Indeed, the Solicitor General argues that "the Federal Government would not have [the] power to commit a person who [has] been released from prison and whose period of supervised release is also completed." Thus, far from a "general police power," §4248 is a reasonably adapted and narrowly tailored means of pursuing the Government's legitimate interest as a federal custodian in the responsible administration of its prison system.

To be sure, "[t]he Federal Government undertakes activities today that would have been unimaginable to the Framers in two senses; first, because the Framers would not have conceived that *any* government would conduct such activities; and second, because the Framers would not have believed that the *Federal* Government, rather than the States, would assume such responsibilities. Yet the powers conferred upon the Federal Government by the Constitution were phrased in language broad enough to allow for the expansion of the Federal Governments role." *New York*, 505 U.S., at 157. The Framers demonstrated considerable foresight in drafting a Constitution capable of such resilience through time. As Chief Justice Marshall observed nearly 200 years ago, the Necessary and Proper Clause is part of "a constitution intended to endure for ages to come, and, consequently, to be adapted to the various crises of human affairs." *McCulloch*, 4 Wheat., at 415.

[The] considerations outlined above] lead us to conclude that the statute is a "necessary and proper" means of exercising the federal authority that permits Congress to create federal criminal laws, to punish their violation, to imprison violators, to provide appropriately for those imprisoned, and to maintain the security of those who are not imprisoned but who may be affected by the federal imprisonment of others. The Constitution consequently authorizes Congress to enact the statute.

We do not reach or decide any claim that the statute or its application denies equal protection of the laws, procedural or substantive due process, or any other rights guaranteed by the Constitution. Respondents are free to pursue those claims on remand, and any others they have preserved.

The judgment of the Court of Appeals for the Fourth Circuit with respect to Congress' power to enact this statute is reversed, and the case is remanded for further proceedings consistent with this opinion.

It is so ordered.

Justice KENNEDY, concurring in the judgment.

[The] Court concludes that, when determining whether Congress has the authority to enact a specific law under the Necessary and Proper Clause, we look "to see whether the statute constitutes a means that is rationally related to the implementation of a constitutionally enumerated power."

[The] terms "rationally related" and "rational basis" must be employed with care, particularly if either is to be used as a stand-alone test. . . . The operative constitutional provision in this case is the Necessary and Proper Clause. This Court has not held that the [test under that clause is whether] "it might be thought that the particular legislative measure was a rational way to correct" an evil, is the proper test in this context. Rather, under the Necessary and Proper Clause, application of a "rational basis" test should be at least as exacting as it has been in the Commerce Clause cases, if not more so. . . . *Raich, Lopez,* and *Hodel* [require] a tangible link to commerce, not a mere conceivable rational relation. . . . The rational basis referred to in the Commerce Clause context is a demonstrated link in fact, based on empirical demonstration. While undoubtedly deferential, this may well be different from the rational-basis test [used in other cases. Congress] has acted within its powers to ensure that an abrupt end to the federal detention of prisoners does not endanger third parties. . . . Having acted within its constitutional authority to detain the person, the National Government can acknowledge a duty to ensure that an abrupt end to the detention does not prejudice the States and their citizens.

Justice ALITO, concurring in the judgment.

[The] term "necessary" [requires] an "appropriate" link between a power conferred by the Constitution and the law enacted by Congress. . . . This is not a case in which it is merely possible for a court to think of a rational basis on which Congress might have perceived an attenuated link between the powers underlying the federal criminal statutes and the challenged civil commitment provision. Here, there is a substantial link to Congress' constitutional powers.

Justice THOMAS, with whom Justice SCALIA joins in all but Part III-A-1-b, dissenting.

[No] enumerated power in Article I, §8, expressly delegates to Congress the power to enact a civil-commitment regime for sexually dangerous persons, nor does any other provision in the Constitution vest Congress or the other branches of the Federal Government with such a power. Accordingly, §4248 can be a valid exercise of congressional authority only if it is "necessary and proper for carrying into Execution" one or more of those federal powers actually enumerated in the Constitution. . . . The Government identifies no specific enumerated power or powers as a constitutional predicate for §4248, and none are readilydiscernable. . . . This Court, moreover, consistently has recognized that the power to care for the mentally ill and, where necessary, the power "to protect the community from the dangerous tendencies of some" mentally ill persons, are among the numerous powers that remain with the States. Addington v. Texas, 441 U.S. 418, 426 (1979). . . .

[I]nstead of asking the simple question of what enumerated power §4248 "carr[ies] into Execution" at *McCulloch*'s first step, the Court surveys other laws Congress has enacted and concludes that, because §4248 is related to those laws, the "links" between §4248 and an enumerated power are not "too attenuated"; hence, §4248 is a valid exercise of Congress' Necessary and Proper Clause authority. This unnecessarily confuses the analysis and, if followed to its logical extreme, would result in an unwarranted expansion of federal power. [The] Necessary and Proper Clause does not provide Congress with authority to enact any law simply because it furthers *other laws* Congress has enacted in the exercise of its incidental authority; the Clause plainly requires a showing that every federal statute "carr[ies] into Execution" one or more of the Federal Government's *enumerated* powers. [The] statute's definition of a "sexually dangerous person" [does] not require a federal court to find any connection between the reasons supporting civil commitment and the enumerated power with which that person's criminal conduct interfered. . . . §4248 allows a court to civilly commit an individual without finding that he was ever charged with or convicted of a federal crime involving sexual violence. . . . §4248 permits the term of federal civil commitment to continue beyond the date on which a convicted prisoner's sentence expires or the date on which the statute of limitations on an untried defendant's crime has run[, and] the definition of a "sexually dangerous person" [does not require] evidence that this sexually dangerous condition will manifest itself in a way that interferes with a federal law that executes an enumerated power or in a geographic location over which Congress has plenary authority. . . . Once the Federal Government's criminal jurisdiction over a prisoner ends, so does any "special relation[ship]" between the Government and the former prisoner. . . . The fact that the Federal Government has the authority to imprison a person for the purpose of punishing him for a federal crime — sex-related or otherwise — does not provide the Government with the additional power to exercise indefinite civil control over that person.

∾ PROBLEM: MORE ON THE EDUCATION FOR A BETTER AMERICA ACT ∾

Congress wants to know whether it can justify passage of the Act under the Necessary and Proper Clause, or whether the Act must be based on another clause (possibly in conjunction with the Necessary and Proper Clause). Which other clause might be used (other than the Commerce Clause, which we examine shortly)?

B. THE COMMERCE CLAUSE

Article I, Section 8, Paragraph 3 contains perhaps the most potent federal power, the Commerce Clause: "The Congress shall have Power . . . to regulate Commerce with foreign Nations, and among the several States, and with the Indian Tribes."

The U.S. Constitution differs markedly from the Articles of Confederation in regard to commerce. Under the Articles, the states reserved the commerce power to themselves and denied Congress this power. Moreover, although the Articles gave Congress some control over foreign affairs, one provision of the Articles specifically prohibited Congress from entering into treaties limiting the states' power over commerce or their right to tax imports and exports.

The Articles of Confederation did not provide the basis for a sound economy. The states used their powers to protect their own economies at the expense of neighbor states, and there "grew up a conflict of commercial regulations, destructive to the harmony of the States, and fatal to their commercial interests abroad." *Gibbons v. Ogden*, 22 U.S. (9 Wheat.) 1 (1824) (Johnson, J., concurring). Many states imposed economic sanctions, including taxes and tariffs, on trade from other states. By 1785-1786, the nation was mired in a recession caused by "a high national debt, increasing trade deficits, and economic infighting." Daniel A. Farber & Suzanna Sherry, *A History of the American Constitution* 25 (West 1990).

As the economic situation worsened, many called for a convention to amend the Articles of Confederation. The initial convention was supposed to propose amendments to the Articles that would give the federal government increased power over commerce. However, not enough states sent delegates. When the delegates finally did meet, they quickly realized that more drastic change was needed and they called for a subsequent convention to make more sweeping changes. This subsequent convention, which ultimately became known as the Constitutional Convention, produced our present Constitution and the current version of the Commerce Clause.

Under the Commerce Clause, a number of questions arise. How much power did Congress receive? Does Congress have "exclusive" power, or are the states allowed to exercise "concurrent" power? If concurrent power exists, where does federal power end and state power begin?

1. *Early Cases*

The Constitution did not define the phrase "among the several states." That task was left to the courts, and a number of cases came before the Court in the nineteenth century.

Gibbons v. Ogden

22 U.S. 1 (1824)

Mr. Chief Justice MARSHALL delivered the opinion of the Court, and, after stating the case, proceeded as follows:

[In 1803, the New York legislature granted Robert Livingston a long-term monopoly on steamship operations in New York waters. Livingston subsequently assigned to Aaron Ogden the exclusive right to run steamships between New York City and Elizabethtown, New Jersey. Thomas Gibbons, who held a federal license, began operations on a similar route. Ogden sued.]

The appellant contends that [the New York] laws which purport to give [Ogden] an exclusive privilege [are] repugnant to the constitution and laws of the United States.

They are said to be repugnant —

1st. To that clause in the constitution which authorizes Congress to regulate commerce. 2d. To that which authorizes Congress to promote the progress of science and useful arts. . . .

[R]eference has been made to the political situation of these States, anterior to its formation. It has been said, that they were sovereign, were completely independent, and were connected with each other only by a league. This is true. But, when these allied sovereigns converted their league into a government[,] empowered to enact laws[,] the whole character in which the States appear, underwent a change, the extent of which must be determined by a fair consideration of the instrument by which that change was effected.

This instrument contains an enumeration of powers expressly granted by the people to their government. It has been said, that these powers ought to be construed strictly. But why ought they to be so construed? [In] the last of the enumerated powers, that which grants, expressly, the means for carrying all others into execution, Congress is authorized "to make all laws which shall be necessary and proper" for the purpose. But this limitation on the means which may be used, is not extended to the powers which are conferred; nor is there one sentence in the constitution, which has been pointed out [that] prescribes this rule. We do not, therefore, think ourselves justified in adopting it. . . .

The words are, "Congress shall have power to regulate commerce with foreign nations, and among the several States, and with the Indian tribes." [The] subject to be regulated is commerce. [C]ounsel for the appellee would limit it to traffic, to buying and selling, or the interchange of commodities, and do not admit that it comprehends navigation. This would restrict a general term, applicable to many objects, to one of its significations. Commerce, undoubtedly, is traffic, but it is something more: it is intercourse. It describes the commercial intercourse between nations, and parts of nations, in all its branches, and is regulated by prescribing rules for carrying on that intercourse. The mind can scarcely conceive a system for regulating commerce between nations, which shall exclude all laws concerning navigation, which shall be silent on the admission of the vessels of the one nation into the ports of the other, and be confined to prescribing rules for the conduct of individuals, in the actual employment of buying and selling, or of barter.

If commerce does not include navigation, the government of the Union has no direct power over that subject, and can make no law prescribing what shall constitute American vessels, or requiring that they shall be navigated by American seamen. . . . All America understands, and has uniformly understood, the word "commerce," to comprehend navigation. It was so understood, and must have been so understood, when the constitution was framed. The power over commerce, including navigation, was one of the primary objects for which the people of America adopted their government. . . . The word used in the constitution, then, comprehends, and has been always understood to comprehend, navigation within its meaning; and a power to regulate navigation, is as expressly granted, as if that term had been added to the word "commerce."

To what commerce does this power extend? The constitution informs us, to commerce "with foreign nations, and among the several States, and with the Indian tribes." [It has been] universally admitted, that these words comprehend every species of commercial intercourse between the United States and foreign nations. No sort of trade can be carried on between this country and any other, to which this power does not extend. [C]ommerce, as the word is used in the constitution, is a unit, every part of which is indicated by the term. . . .

The subject to which the power is next applied, is to commerce "among the several States." The word "among" means intermingled with. A thing which is among others, is intermingled with them. Commerce among the States, cannot stop at the external boundary line of each State, but may be introduced into the interior. . . . It is not intended to say that these words comprehend that commerce, which is completely internal, which is carried on between man and man in a State, or between different parts of the same State, and which does not extend to or affect other States. Such a power would be inconvenient, and is certainly unnecessary.

Comprehensive as the word "among" is, it may very properly be restricted to that commerce which concerns more States than one. . . . The enumeration presupposes something not enumerated; and that something, if we regard the language or the subject of the sentence, must be the exclusively internal commerce of a State. The genius and character of the whole government seem to be, that its action is to be applied to all the external concerns of the nation, and to those internal concerns which affect the States generally; but not to those which are completely within a particular State, which do not affect other States, and with which it is not necessary to interfere, for the purpose of executing some of the general powers of the government. The completely internal commerce of a State, then, may be considered as reserved for the State itself.

But, in regulating commerce with foreign nations, the power of Congress does not stop at the jurisdictional lines of the several States. It would be a very useless power, if it could not pass those lines. . . . If Congress has the power to regulate it, that power must be exercised whenever the subject exists. If it exists within the States, if a foreign voyage may commence or terminate at a port within a State, then the power of Congress may be exercised within a State.

This principle is, if possible, still more clear, when applied to commerce "among the several States." . . . Can a trading expedition between two adjoining States, commence and terminate outside of each? And if the trading intercourse be between two States remote from each other, must it not commence in one, terminate in the other, and probably pass through a third? Commerce among the States must, of necessity, be commerce with the States. . . . The power of Congress, then, whatever it may be, must be exercised within the territorial jurisdiction of the several States. . . .

We are now arrived at the inquiry — What is this power? [It] is the power to regulate; that is, to prescribe the rule by which commerce is to be governed. This power, like all others vested in Congress, is complete in itself, may be exercised to its utmost extent, and acknowledges no limitations, other than are prescribed in the constitution. . . . The wisdom and the discretion of Congress, their identity with the people, and the influence which their constituents possess at elections, are, in this, as in many other instances, as that, for example, of declaring war, the sole restraints on which they have relied, to secure them from its abuse. They are the restraints on which the people must often [rely] solely, in all representative governments.

The power of Congress, then, comprehends navigation, within the limits of every State in the Union; so far as that navigation may be, in any manner, connected with "commerce with foreign nations, or among the several States, or with the Indian tribes." It may, of consequence, pass the jurisdictional line of New York, and act upon the very waters to which the prohibition now under consideration applies.

But it has been urged with great earnestness [that] the States may severally exercise the same power, within their respective jurisdictions. [I]t is said, that they possessed it as an inseparable attribute of sovereignty, before the formation of the constitution, and still retain it, except so far as they have surrendered it by that instrument; that this principle results from the nature of the government, and is secured by the tenth amendment; that an affirmative grant of power is not exclusive, unless in its own nature it be such that the continued exercise of it by the former possessor is inconsistent with the grant, and that this is not of that description.

[A]ppellant [contends] that full power to regulate a particular subject, implies the whole power, and leaves no residuum; that a grant of the whole is incompatible with the existence of a right in another to any part of it. . . .

The grant of the power to lay and collect taxes is, like the power to regulate commerce, made in general terms, and has never been understood to interfere with the exercise of the same power by the State; and hence has been drawn an argument which has been applied to the question under consideration. But the two grants are not, it is conceived, similar in their terms or their nature. Although many of the powers formerly exercised by the States, are transferred to the government of the Union, yet the State governments remain, and constitute a most important part of our system. The power of taxation is indispensable to their existence, and is a power which, in its own nature, is capable of residing in, and being exercised by, different authorities at the same time. . . . In imposing taxes for State purposes, they are not doing what Congress is empowered to do. Congress is not empowered to tax for those purposes which are within the exclusive province of the States. When, then, each government exercises the power of taxation, neither is exercising the power of the other. But, when a State proceeds to regulate commerce with foreign nations, or among the several States, it is exercising the very power that is granted to Congress, and is doing the very thing which Congress is authorized to do. There is no analogy, then, between the power of taxation and the power of regulating commerce.

In discussing the question, whether this power is still in the States, [we] may dismiss from it the inquiry, whether it is surrendered by the mere grant to Congress, or is retained until Congress shall exercise the power. We may dismiss that inquiry, because it has been exercised, and the regulations which Congress deemed it proper to make, are now in full operation. The sole question is, can a State regulate commerce with foreign nations and among the States, while Congress is regulating it?

[T]he inspection laws are said to be regulations of commerce, and are certainly recognised in the constitution, as being passed in the exercise of a power remaining with the States. . . . That inspection laws may have a remote and considerable influence on commerce, will not be denied; but that a power to regulate commerce is the source from which the right to pass them is derived, cannot be admitted. The object of inspection laws, is to improve the quality of articles produced by the labour of a country; to fit them for exportation; or, it may be, for domestic use. They act upon the subject before it becomes an article of foreign commerce, or of commerce among the States, and prepare it for that purpose. They form a portion of that immense mass of legislation, which embraces every thing within the territory of a State, not surrendered to the general government: all which can be most advantageously exercised by the States themselves. Inspection laws, quarantine laws, health laws of every description, as well as laws for regulating the internal commerce of a State, and those which respect turnpike roads, ferries, &c., are component parts of this mass.

No direct general power over these objects is granted to Congress; and, consequently, they remain subject to State legislation. If the legislative power of the Union can reach them, it must be for national purposes; it must be where the power is expressly given for a special purpose, or is clearly incidental to some power which is expressly given. It is obvious, that the government of the Union, in the exercise of its express powers, that, for example, of regulating commerce with foreign nations and among the States, may use means that may also be employed by a State, in the exercise of its acknowledged powers; that, for example, of regulating commerce within the State. If Congress license vessels to sail from one port to another, in the same State, the act is supposed to be, necessarily, incidental to the power expressly granted to Congress, and implies no claim of a direct power to regulate the purely internal commerce of a State, or to act directly on its system of police. So, if a State, in passing laws on subjects acknowledged to be within its control, and with a view to those subjects, shall adopt a measure of the same character with one which Congress may adopt, it does not derive its authority from the particular power which has been granted, but from some other, which remains with the State, and may be executed by the same means. All experience shows, that the same measures, or measures scarcely distinguishable from each other, may flow from distinct powers; but this does not prove that the powers themselves are identical. Although the means used in their execution may sometimes approach each other so nearly as to be confounded, there are other situations in which they are sufficiently distinct to establish their individuality. . . .

These acts were cited at the bar for the purpose of showing an opinion in Congress, that the States possess, concurrently with the Legislature of the Union, the power to regulate commerce with foreign nations and among the States. Upon reviewing them, we think they do not establish the proposition they were intended to prove. They show the opinion, that the States retain powers enabling them to pass the laws to which allusion has been made, not that those laws proceed from the particular power which has been delegated to Congress.

It has been contended [that], as the word 'to regulate' implies in its nature, full power over the thing to be regulated, it excludes, necessarily, the action of all others that would perform the same operation on the same thing. That regulation is designed for the entire result, applying to those parts which remain as they were, as well as to those which are altered. It produces a uniform whole, which is as much disturbed and deranged by changing what the regulating power designs to leave untouched, as that on which it has operated. There is great force in this argument, and the Court is not satisfied that it has been refuted. Since, however, in exercising the power of regulating their own purely internal affairs, whether of trading or police, the States may sometimes enact laws, the validity of which depends on their interfering with, and being contrary to, an act of Congress passed in pursuance of the constitution, the Court will enter upon the inquiry, whether the laws of New York, as expounded by the highest tribunal of that State, have, in their application to this case, come into collision with an act of Congress, and deprived a citizen of a right to which that act entitles him. Should this collision exist, it will be immaterial whether those laws were passed in virtue of a concurrent power 'to regulate commerce with foreign nations and among the several States,' or, in virtue of a power to regulate their domestic trade and police. In one case and the other, the acts of New York must yield to the law of Congress; and the decision sustaining the privilege they confer, against a right given by a law of the Union, must be erroneous.

This opinion has been frequently expressed in this Court, and is founded, as well on the nature of the government as on the words of the constitution. In argument, however, it has been contended, that if a law passed by a State, in the exercise of its acknowledged sovereignty, comes into conflict with a law passed by Congress in pursuance of the constitution, they affect the subject, and each other, like equal opposing powers.

But the framers of our constitution foresaw this state of things, and provided for it, by declaring the supremacy not only of itself, but of the laws made in pursuance of it. The Nullity of any act, law. The appropriate in consistent with the constitution, is produced by the declaration, that the constitution is the supreme law. The appropriate application of that part of the clause which confers the same supremacy on laws and treaties, is to such acts of the State Legislatures as do not transcend their powers, but, though enacted in the execution of acknowledged State powers, interfere with, or are contrary to the laws of Congress, made in pursuance of the constitution, or some treaty made under the authority of the United States. In every such case, the act of Congress, or the treaty, is supreme; and the law of the State, though enacted in the exercise of powers not controverted, must yield to it. . . .

Notes: The Nineteenth-Century Commerce Clause

1. Gibbons*'s Impact.* "The effects of the decision were at once felt in the waters of New York and the other States." Charles Warren, *The Supreme Court in United States History* vol. 2, 75 (Little, Brown 1922). "Shortly after the fourteenth of March, the newspapers of the North carried this item: 'Yesterday the Steamboat *United States*, [entered] New York in triumph, with streamers flying, and a large company of passengers exulting in the decision of the United States Supreme Court against the New York monopoly. She fired a salute which was loudly returned by huzzas from the wharves.'" *Id.* "A representative Southern paper spoke of 'the immense public advantages that flow from the decision. The fare in the steamboats that ply between New York and New Haven has been reduced from five to three dollars.'" *Id.* "Shortly over a year after the decision, *Niles Register* reported that the number of steamboats plying from New York had increased from six to forty-three." *Id.* "[T]he chief importance of the case in the eyes of the public of that day was its effect in shattering the great monopoly against which they had been struggling for fifteen years." *Id.* at 76.

2. *Insurance Policies as Commerce.* Despite *Gibbons*'s expansive language, the Court did not always construe the Commerce Clause broadly during the nineteenth century. Paul v. Virginia, 75 U.S. (8 Wall.) 168 (1868), involved a Virginia statute that discriminated against insurance companies incorporated in other states. The statute was challenged as repugnant to the federal commerce power. In an opinion delivered by Justice Field, the Court rejected the challenge, concluding that "[i]ssuing a policy of insurance is not a transaction of commerce" so the Commerce Clause does not reach it.

3. *Internal Commerce.* In some early decisions, the Court held that the states retained control over their internal commerce. Kidd v. Pearson, 128 U.S. 1 (1888), involved an Iowa statute that prohibited the manufacture of liquor. The statute was applied to an Iowa company that sold its entire product in other states. In an opinion by Justice Lamar, the Court upheld the law: "[Congress's power over commerce] does not comprehend the purely internal domestic commerce of a state, which is carried on between man and man within a state or between different parts of the same state. . . . [I]t does not follow that, because the products of a domestic manufacture may ultimately become the subjects of interstate commerce, at the pleasure of the manufacturer, the legislation of the state respecting such manufacture is an attempted exercise of the power to regulate commerce exclusively conferred upon congress."

4. *Interstate Steamers.* Some nineteenth-century decisions took a more expansive view of the power of the Commerce Clause. *The Daniel Ball*, 77 U.S. 557 (1870), involved a steamer that traveled routes wholly within the State of Michigan, but that carried merchandise being transported to, or from, other states. The question was whether a federal safety regulation applied to the steamer. In an opinion written by Justice Field, the Court concluded that the regulation applied: "[W]e are unable to draw any clear and distinct line between the authority of Congress to regulate an agency employed in commerce between the States, when that agency extends through two or more States, and when it is confined in its action entirely within the limits of a single State. If its authority does not extend to an agency in such commerce, when that agency is confined within the limits of a State, its entire authority over interstate commerce may be defeated. Several agencies combining, each taking up the commodity transported at the boundary line at one end of a State, and leaving it at the boundary line at the other end, the Federal jurisdiction would be entirely ousted, and the constitutional provision would become a dead letter."

∾ PROBLEM: MORE ON THE EDUCATION FOR A BETTER AMERICA ACT ∾

Under *Gibbons*'s conception of the scope of Congress's Commerce Clause power, does Congress have the power to pass the Act? Could Congress provide financial incentives to local school districts to encourage them to reform? Could it also mandate various actions (e.g., the administration of student performance tests or specific types of training for school teachers)?

2.   *Early Twentieth-Century Cases*

When the Constitution was ratified, the United States was a largely agrarian society. By the end of the nineteenth century, the economy was in a period of dramatic and rapid transition to an industrialized society. Industrialization produced profound changes in the U.S. economy. The development of railroads, and eventually cars, allowed people and goods to move freely across state borders. This movement meant that, although many commercial problems may have been local in nature at one time, they were increasingly becoming national problems. As a result, Congress began to assume a more active regulatory role, passing the Interstate Commerce Act, the Sherman Antitrust Act, and a host of other legislation.

Congress's more aggressive posture forced the Court to confront difficult questions regarding the scope of Congress's power. It did so in several cases decided early in the twentieth century. In some of these cases, the Court took an expansive view of federal power. In other cases, it took a more restrictive view.

Champion v. Ames

188 U.S. 321 (1903)

(THE LOTTERY CASE)

Mr. Justice HARLAN delivered the opinion of the court:

[The appellant, Charles Champion, was indicted for conspiring to transport lottery tickets across state lines in violation of federal law. After his arrest, Champion sought a writ of habeas corpus on the basis that the law prohibiting the transportation of lottery tickets was unconstitutional.]

The appellant insists that the carrying of lottery tickets from one state to another state by an express company engaged in carrying freight and packages from state to state, although such tickets may be contained in a box or package, does not constitute, and cannot by any act of Congress be legally made to constitute, commerce among the states within the meaning of the [Constitution]; consequently, that Congress cannot make it an offense to cause such tickets to be carried from one state to another.

[Our prior precedent] show[s] that commerce among the states embraces navigation, intercourse, communication, traffic, the transit of persons, and the transmission of messages by telegraph. They also show that the power to regulate commerce among the several states is vested in Congress as absolutely as it would be in a single government, having in its constitution the same restrictions on the exercise of the power as are found in the Constitution of the United States; that such power is plenary, complete in itself, and may be exerted by Congress to its utmost extent, subject only to such limitations as the Constitution imposes upon the exercise of the powers granted by it; and that in determining the character of the regulations to be adopted Congress has a large discretion which is not to be controlled by the courts, simply because, in their opinion, such regulations may not be the best or most effective that could be employed. . . .

It was said in argument that lottery tickets are not of any real or substantial value in themselves, and therefore are not subjects of commerce. [W]e cannot accept as accurate the broad statement that such tickets are of no value. Upon their face they showed that the lottery company offered a large capital prize, to be paid to the holder of the ticket winning the prize at the drawing. . . . We are of opinion that lottery tickets are subjects of traffic, and therefore are subjects of commerce, and the regulation of the carriage of such tickets from state to state, at least by independent carriers, is a regulation of commerce among the several states.

But it is said that the statute in question does not regulate the carrying of lottery tickets from state to state, but by punishing those who cause them to be so carried Congress in effect prohibits such carrying; that in respect of the carrying from one state to another of articles or things that are, in fact, or according to usage in business, the subjects of commerce, the authority given Congress was not to *prohibit*, but only to *regulate*. . . .

[T]he Constitution does not define what is to be deemed a legitimate regulation of interstate commerce. In Gibbons v. Ogden it was said that the power to regulate such commerce is the power to prescribe the rule by which it is to be governed. . . . While our government must be acknowledged by all to be one of enumerated powers, the Constitution does not attempt to set forth all the means by which such powers may be carried into execution. It leaves to Congress a large discretion as to the means that may be employed in executing a given power. The sound construction of the Constitution, ["]must allow to the national legislature that discretion, with respect to the means by which the powers it confers are to be carried into execution, which will enable that body to perform the high duties assigned to it, in the manner most beneficial to the people. Let the end be legitimate, let it be within the scope of the Constitution, and all means which are appropriate, which are plainly adapted to that end, which are not prohibited, but consist with the letter and spirit of the Constitution, are constitutional." 4 Wheat. 421.

We have said that the carrying from state to state of lottery tickets constitutes interstate commerce, and that the regulation of such commerce is within the power of Congress under the Constitution. Are we prepared to say that a provision which is, in effect, a *prohibition* of the carriage of such articles from state to state is not a fit or appropriate mode for the *regulation* of that particular kind of commerce? If lottery traffic, *carried on through interstate commerce*, is a matter of which Congress may take cognizance and over which its power may be exerted, can it be possible that it must tolerate the traffic, and simply regulate the manner in which it may be carried on? Or may not Congress, for the protection of the people of all the states, and under the power to regulate interstate commerce, devise such means, within the scope of the Constitution, and not prohibited by it, as will drive that traffic out of commerce among the states?

In determining whether regulation may [under] some circumstances properly take the form or have the effect of prohibition, the nature of the interstate traffic which it [sought] to suppress cannot be overlooked. . . . If a state, when considering legislation for the suppression of lotteries within its own limits, may properly take into view the evils that inhere in the raising of money, in that mode, why may not Congress, invested with the power to regulate commerce among the several states, provide that such commerce shall not be polluted by the carrying of lottery tickets from one state to another? [T]he power of Congress to regulate commerce among the states is plenary, is complete in itself, and is subject to no limitations except such as may be found in the Constitution. What provision in that instrument can be regarded as limiting the exercise of the power granted? [We] cannot think of any clause of that instrument that could possibly be invoked by those who assert their right to send lottery tickets from state to state except the one providing that no person shall be deprived of his liberty without due process of law. [S]urely it will not be said to be a part of anyone's liberty [that] he shall be allowed to introduce into commerce among the states an element that will be confessedly injurious to the public morals.

If it be said that the act of 1894 is inconsistent with the 10th Amendment, reserving to the states respectively, or to the people, the powers not delegated to the United States, the answer is that the power to regulate commerce among the states has been expressly delegated to Congress.

Besides, Congress [does] not assume to interfere with traffic or commerce in lottery tickets carried on exclusively within the limits of any state, but has in view only commerce of that kind among the several states. . . . As a state may, for the purpose of guarding the morals of its own people, forbid all sales of lottery tickets within its limits, so Congress, for the purpose of guarding the people of the United States against the "widespread pestilence of lotteries" and to protect the commerce which concerns all the states, may prohibit the carrying of lottery tickets from one state to another. . . . Congress only supplemented the action of those states [which], for the protection of the public morals, prohibit the drawing of lotteries, as well as the sale or circulation of lottery tickets, within their respective limits. . . . We should hesitate long before adjudging that an evil of such appalling character, carried on through interstate commerce, cannot be met and crushed by the only power competent to that end. We say competent to that end, because Congress alone has the power to occupy, by legislation, the whole field of interstate commerce. . . .

That regulation may sometimes appropriately assume the form of prohibition is also illustrated by the case of diseased cattle, transported from one state to another. Such cattle may have, notwithstanding their condition, a value in money for some purposes, and yet it cannot be doubted that Congress, under its power to regulate commerce, may either provide for their being inspected before transportation begins, or, in its discretion, may prohibit their being transported from one state to another. . . .

We decide nothing more in the present case than that lottery tickets are subjects of traffic among those who choose to sell or buy them; that the carriage of such tickets by independent carriers from one state to another is therefore interstate commerce; that under its power to regulate commerce among the several states Congress — subject to the limitations imposed by the Constitution upon the exercise of the powers granted — has plenary authority over such commerce, and may prohibit the carriage of such tickets from state to state; and that legislation to that end, and of that character, is not inconsistent with any limitation or restriction imposed upon the exercise of the powers granted to Congress.

The judgment is affirmed.

Mr. Chief Justice FULLER, with whom concur Mr. Justice BREWER, Mr. Justice SHIRAS, and Mr. Justice PECKHAM, dissenting:

Doubtless an act prohibiting the carriage of lottery matter would be necessary and proper to the execution of a power to suppress lotteries; but that power belongs to the states and not to Congress. To hold that Congress has general police power would be to hold that it may accomplish objects not intrusted to the general government, and to defeat the operation of the 10th Amendment, declaring that "the powers not delegated to the United States by the Constitution, nor prohibited by it to the states, are reserved to the states respectively, or to the people." . . .

Does the grant to Congress of the power to regulate interstate commerce import the absolute power to prohibit it? [The] power to prohibit the transportation of diseased animals and infected goods over railroads or on steamboats is an entirely different thing, for they would be in themselves injurious to the trans-action of interstate commerce, and, moreover, are essentially commercial in their nature. And the exclusion of diseased persons rests on different ground, for nobody would pretend that persons could be kept off the trains because they were going from one state to another to engage in the lottery business. However entic-ing that business may be, we do not understand these pieces of paper themselves can communicate bad principles by contact. . . .

I regard this decision as inconsistent with the views of the framers of the Con-stitution, and of Marshall, its great expounder. . . .

∾ PROBLEM: MORE ON THE EDUCATION FOR A BETTER AMERICA ACT ∾

Does *Champion* offer insights into whether (and how) Congress can pass the Act? Also, note the Court's conception of the Tenth Amendment. If Congress passes this legislation, does it have to worry about running afoul of the Tenth Amendment?

Houston, East & West Texas Railway Company v. United States

234 U.S. 342 (1914)

Mr. Justice HUGHES delivered the opinion of the court:
    These suits were brought in the commerce court by the Houston, East & West Texas Railway Company and the Houston & Shreveport Railroad Company, and by the Texas & Pacific Railway Company, respectively, to set aside an order of the Interstate Commerce Commission [upon] the ground that it exceeded the Com-mission's authority. . . .
    The Interstate Commerce Commission found that the interstate class rates out of Shreveport to named Texas points were unreasonable, and it established maximum class rates for this traffic. These rates [were] substantially the same as the class rates fixed by the Railroad Commission of Texas, and charged by the car-riers, for transportation for similar distances in that state. The Interstate Com-merce Commission also found that the carriers maintained "higher rates from Shreveport to points in Texas" than were in force "from cities in Texas to such points under substantially similar conditions and circumstances," and that thereby "an unlawful and undue preference and advantage" was given to the Texas cities, and a "discrimination" that was "undue and unlawful" was effected against Shreveport. In order to correct this discrimination, the carriers were directed to desist from charging higher rates for the transportation of any com-modity from Shreveport to Dallas and Houston, respectively, and intermediate than were contemporaneously charged for the carriage of such commodity from Dallas and Houston toward Shreveport for equal distances, as the Commission found that relation of rates to be reasonable.

[Appellants object] that, as the discrimination found by the Commission to be unjust arises out of the relation of intrastate rates, maintained under state authority, to interstate rates that have been upheld as reasonable, its correction was beyond the Commission's power. Manifestly the order might be complied with, and the discrimination avoided, either by reducing the interstate rates from Shreveport to the level of the competing intrastate rates, or by raising these intrastate rates to the level of the interstate rates, or by such reduction in the one case and increase in the other as would result in equality. But it is urged that, so far as the interstate rates were sustained by the Commission as reasonable, the Commission was without authority to compel their reduction in order to equalize them with the lower intrastate rates. . . .

[It] is unnecessary to repeat what has frequently [been said] with respect to the complete and paramount character of the power confided to Congress to regulate commerce among the several states. It is of the essence of this power that, where it exists, it dominates. Interstate trade was not left to be destroyed or impeded by the rivalries of local government. The purpose was to make impossible the recurrence of the evils which had overwhelmed the Confederation, and to provide the necessary basis of national unity by insuring "uniformity of regulation against conflicting and discriminating state legislation." By virtue of the comprehensive terms of the grant, the authority of Congress is at all times adequate to meet the varying exigencies that arise, and to protect the national interest by securing the freedom of interstate commercial intercourse from local control. Gibbons v. Ogden, 9 Wheat. 1.

Congress is empowered to regulate, — that is, to provide the law for the government of interstate commerce; to enact "all appropriate legislation" for its "protection and advancement," to adopt measures "to promote its growth and insure its safety," "to foster, protect, control, and restrain." Its authority, extending to these interstate carriers as instruments of interstate commerce, necessarily embraces the right to control their operations in all matters having such a close and substantial relation to interstate traffic that the control is essential or appropriate to the security of that traffic, to the efficiency of the interstate service, and to the maintenance of conditions under which interstate commerce may be conducted upon fair terms and without molestation or hindrance. As it is competent for Congress to legislate to these ends, unquestionably it may seek their attainment by requiring that the agencies of interstate commerce shall not be used in such manner as to cripple, retard, or destroy it. The fact that carriers are instruments of intrastate commerce, as well as of interstate commerce, does not derogate from the complete and paramount authority of Congress over the latter, or preclude the Federal power from being exerted to prevent the intrastate operations of such carriers from being made a means of injury to that which has been confided to Federal care. Wherever the interstate and intrastate transactions of carriers are so related that the government of the one involves the control of the other, it is Congress, and not the state, that is entitled to prescribe the final and dominant rule, for otherwise Congress would be denied the exercise of its constitutional authority, and the state, and not the nation, would be supreme within the national field. . . .

Congress, in the exercise of its paramount power, may prevent the common instrumentalities of interstate and intrastate commercial intercourse from being used in their intrastate operations to the injury of interstate commerce. This is not to say that Congress possesses the authority to regulate the internal commerce of a state, as such, but that it does possess the power to foster and protect interstate commerce, and to take all measures necessary or appropriate to that end, although intrastate transactions of interstate carriers may thereby be controlled.

This principle is applicable here. We find no reason to doubt that Congress is entitled to keep the highways of interstate communication open to interstate traffic upon fair and equal terms. That an unjust discrimination in the rates of a common carrier, by which one person or locality is unduly favored as against another under substantially similar conditions of traffic, constitutes an evil, is undeniable; and where this evil consists in the action of an interstate carrier in unreasonably discriminating against interstate traffic over its line, the authority of Congress to prevent it is equally clear. It is immaterial, so far as the protecting power of Congress is concerned, that the discrimination arises from intrastate rates as compared with interstate rates. The use of the instrument of interstate commerce in a discriminatory manner so as to inflict injury upon that commerce, or some part thereof, furnishes abundant ground for Federal intervention. Nor can the attempted exercise of state authority alter the matter, where Congress has acted, for a state may not authorize the carrier to do that which Congress is entitled to forbid and has forbidden. . . .

The decree of the Commerce Court is affirmed in each case.

Affirmed.

Note

The *Lottery Case* involved expansions of federal power. But, as the following case suggests, the trend was not uniformly expansionist.

Hammer v. Dagenhart

247 U.S. 251 (1918)

Mr. Justice DAY delivered the opinion of the Court.

[The] controlling question for decision is: Is it within the authority of Congress in regulating commerce among the states to prohibit the transportation in interstate commerce of manufactured goods, the product of a factory in which, within thirty days prior to their removal therefrom, children under the age of fourteen have been employed or permitted to work, or children between the ages of fourteen and sixteen years have been employed or permitted to work more than eight hours in any day, or more than six days in any week, or after the hour of 7 o'clock p.m., or before the hour of 6 o'clock a.m.?

The power essential to the passage of this act, the government contends, is found in the commerce clause of the Constitution which authorizes Congress to regulate commerce with foreign nations and among the states.

In Gibbons v. Ogdon, 9 Wheat. 1, Chief Justice Marshall, speaking for this court, and defining the extent and nature of the commerce power, said, "It is the power to regulate; that is, to prescribe the rule by which commerce is to be governed." In other words, the power is one to control the means by which commerce is carried on, which is directly the contrary of the assumed right to forbid commerce from moving and thus destroying it as to particular commodities. But it is insisted that adjudged cases in this court establish the doctrine that the power to regulate given to Congress incidentally includes the authority to prohibit the movement of ordinary commodities and therefore that the subject is not open for discussion. The cases demonstrate the contrary. They rest upon the character of the particular subjects dealt with and the fact that the scope of governmental authority, state or national, possessed over them is such that the authority to prohibit is as to them but the exertion of the power to regulate.

The first of these cases is Champion v. Ames, 188 U.S. 321, the so-called *Lottery Case*, in which it was held that Congress might pass a law having the effect to keep the channels of commerce free from use in the transportation of tickets used in the promotion of lottery schemes. In Hipolite Egg Co. v. United States, 220 U.S. 45, this court sustained the power of Congress to pass the Pure Food and Drug Act[, which] prohibited the introduction into the states by means of interstate commerce of impure foods and drugs. . . . In each of these instances the use of interstate transportation was necessary to the accomplishment of harmful results. In other words, although the power over interstate transportation was to regulate, that could only be accomplished by prohibiting the use of the facilities of interstate commerce to effect the evil intended.

This element is wanting in the present case. The thing intended to be accomplished by this statute is the denial of the facilities of interstate commerce to those manufacturers in the states who employ children within the prohibited ages. The act in its effect does not regulate transportation among the states, but aims to standardize the ages at which children may be employed in mining and manufacturing within the states. The goods shipped are of themselves harmless. The act permits them to be freely shipped after thirty days from the time of their removal from the factory. When offered for shipment, and before transportation begins, the labor of their production is over, and the mere fact that they were intended for interstate commerce transportation does not make their production subject to federal control under the commerce power.

Commerce "consists of intercourse and traffic [and] includes the transportation of persons and property, as well as the purchase, sale and exchange of commodities." The making of goods and the mining of coal are not commerce, nor does the fact that these things are to be afterwards shipped, or used in interstate commerce, make their production a part thereof. Delaware, Lackawanna & Western R.R. Co. v. Yurkonis, 238 U.S. 439. . . . Over interstate transportation, or its incidents, the regulatory power of Congress is ample, but the production of articles, intended for interstate commerce, is a matter of local regulation. . . . If it were otherwise, all manufacture intended for interstate shipment would be brought under federal control to the practical exclusion of the authority of the states, a result certainly not contemplated by the framers of the Constitution when they vested in Congress the authority to regulate commerce among the States. Kidd v. Pearson, 128 U.S. 1.

It is further contended that the authority of Congress may be exerted to control interstate commerce in the shipment of childmade goods because of the effect of the circulation of such goods in other states where the evil of this class of labor has been recognized by local legislation, and the right to thus employ child labor has been more rigorously restrained than in the state of production. In other words, that the unfair competition, thus engendered, may be controlled by closing the channels of interstate commerce to manufacturers in those states where the local laws do not meet what Congress deems to be the more just standard of other states.

There is no power vested in Congress to require the states to exercise their police power so as to prevent possible unfair competition. Many causes may cooperate to give one state, by reason of local laws or conditions, an economic advantage over others. The commerce clause was not intended to give to Congress a general authority to equalize such conditions. In some of the states laws have been passed fixing minimum wages for women, in others the local law regulates the hours of labor of women in various employments. Business done in such states may be at an economic disadvantage when compared with states which have no such regulations; surely, this fact does not give Congress the power to deny transportation in interstate commerce to those who carry on business where the hours of labor and the rate of compensation for women have not been fixed by a standard in use in other states and approved by Congress.

The grant of power of Congress over the subject of interstate commerce was to enable it to regulate such commerce, and not to give it authority to control the states in their exercise of the police power over local trade and manufacture.

The grant of authority over a purely federal matter was not intended to destroy the local power always existing and carefully reserved to the states in the Tenth Amendment to the Constitution.

Police regulations relating to the internal trade and affairs of the states have been uniformly recognized as within such control. "This [has] been so frequently declared by this court, results so obviously from the terms of the Constitution, and has been so fully explained and supported on former occasions, that we think it unnecessary to enter again upon the discussion." *See* Keller v. United States, 213 U.S. 138.

In the judgment which established the broad power of Congress over interstate commerce, Chief Justice Marshall said: "They [inspection laws] act upon the subject, before it becomes an article of foreign commerce, or of commerce among the states, and prepare it for that purpose. They form a portion of that immense mass of legislation, which embraces everything within the territory of a state, not surrendered to the general government; all of which can be most advantageously exercised by the states themselves. Inspection laws, quarantine laws, health laws of every description, as well as laws for regulating the internal commerce of a state, and those which respect turnpike roads, ferries, etc., are component parts of this mass." . . .

That there should be limitations upon the right to employ children in mines and factories in the interest of their own and the public welfare, all will admit. That such employment is generally deemed to require regulation is shown by the fact [that] every state in the Union has a law upon the subject, limiting the right to thus employ children. In North Carolina, the state wherein is located the factory in which the employment was had in the present case, no child under twelve years of age is permitted to work.

It may be desirable that such laws be uniform, but our federal government is one of enumerated powers; "this principle," declared Chief Justice Marshall in McCulloch v. Maryland, 4 Wheat. 316, "is universally admitted."

A statute must be judged by its natural and reasonable effect. The control by Congress over interstate commerce cannot authorize the exercise of authority not entrusted to it by the Constitution. The maintenance of the authority of the states over matters purely local is as essential to the preservation of our institutions as is the conservation of the supremacy of the federal power in all matters entrusted to the nation by the federal Constitution.

In interpreting the Constitution it must never be forgotten that the nation is made up of states to which are entrusted the powers of local government. And to them and to the people the powers not expressly delegated to the national government are reserved. The power of the states to regulate their purely internal affairs by such laws as seem wise to the local authority is inherent and has never been surrendered to the general government. Slaughter House Cases, 16 Wall. 36. To sustain this statute would not be in our judgment a recognition of the lawful exertion of congressional authority over interstate commerce, but would sanction an invasion by the federal power of the control of a matter purely local in its character, and over which no authority has been delegated to Congress in conferring the power to regulate commerce among the states.

We have neither authority nor disposition to question the motives of Congress in enacting this legislation. The purposes intended must be attained consistently with constitutional limitations and not by an invasion of the powers of the states. This court has no more important function than that which devolves upon it the obligation to preserve inviolate the constitutional limitations upon the exercise of authority federal and state to the end that each may continue to discharge, harmoniously with the other, the duties entrusted to it by the Constitution.

In our view the necessary effect of this act is, by means of a prohibition against the movement in interstate commerce of ordinary commercial commodities to regulate the hours of labor of children in factories and mines within the states, a purely state authority. Thus the act in a two-fold sense is repugnant to the Constitution. It not only transcends the authority delegated to Congress over commerce but also exerts a power as to a purely local matter to which the federal authority does not extend. The far reaching result of upholding the act cannot be more plainly indicated than by pointing out that if Congress can thus regulate matters entrusted to local authority by prohibition of the movement of commodities in interstate commerce, all freedom of commerce will be at an end, and the power of the states over local matters may be eliminated, and thus our system of government be practically destroyed.

For these reasons we hold that this law exceeds the constitutional authority of Congress. It follows that the decree of the District Court must be

Affirmed.

Mr. Justice HOLMES, dissenting.

[I]f an act is within the powers specifically conferred upon Congress, it seems to me that it is not made any less constitutional because of the indirect effects that it may have, however obvious it may be that it will have those effects, and that we are not at liberty upon such grounds to hold it void. . . . The statute confines itself to prohibiting the carriage of certain goods in interstate or foreign commerce. Congress is given power to regulate such commerce in unqualified terms. . . . Regulation means the prohibition of something, and when interstate commerce is the matter to be regulated I cannot doubt that the regulation may prohibit any part of such commerce that Congress sees fit to forbid. [I]t is established by the *Lottery Case* [that] a law is not beyond the regulative power of Congress merely because it prohibits certain transportation out and out. . . .

The Act does not meddle with anything belonging to the states. They may regulate their internal affairs and their domestic commerce as they like. But when they seek to send their products across the state line they are no longer within their rights. . . . The public policy of the United States is shaped with a view to the benefit of the nation as a whole. . . . The national welfare as understood by Congress may require a different attitude within its sphere from that of some self-seeking State. It seems to me entirely constitutional for Congress to enforce its understanding by all the means at its command.

∾ PROBLEM: MORE ON THE EDUCATION FOR A BETTER AMERICA ACT ∾

What insights does *Hammer* offer regarding whether Congress can pass the Act and how it should structure the Act? Does the Tenth Amendment explicitly limit the scope of Congress's authority and the content of the legislation?

3. *The Constitutional Crisis*

In 1929, the stock market crashed. Following the crash, the country settled into a prolonged period of economic depression. In 1932, President Franklin Delano Roosevelt (FDR) was elected on the promise of a "New Deal." The situation facing FDR and the country was grim. In 1931, the year before he was elected, more than 2,000 banks had failed. By the winter of 1932-1933, shortly before Roosevelt assumed office, "one-fourth of the nation's work force was unemployed," and the price of wheat had dropped by "nearly 90 percent." Industrial output had fallen by 60 percent. See Robert S. McElvaine, *The Great Depression: America 1929–1941* 137 (Times Books 1984).

Roosevelt took office demanding "action, and action now." One of his first acts was to call an extraordinary session of Congress to begin five days after his inauguration. During this session, the House passed 11 major bills, giving them "a total of forty hours of debate." During his first hundred days, Roosevelt managed to push through Congress a host of bills regulating financial markets, creating federal works programs, and regulating prices and wages. Congress passed the Agricultural Adjustment Act, the Bituminous Coal Act, the Farm Relief Act, the Emergency Farm Mortgage Act, the National Industrial Recovery Act, the Railway Pension Act, and the Truth-in-Securities Act. These acts were hostilely received by the federal courts.

Carter v. Carter Coal Co.

298 U.S. 238 (1936)

Mr. Justice SUTHERLAND delivered the opinion of the Court.

The purposes of the "Bituminous Coal Conservation Act of 1935," [as] declared by the title, are to stabilize the bituminous coal-mining industry and promote its interstate commerce; to provide for co-operative marketing of bituminous coal; to levy a tax on such coal and provide for a drawback under certain conditions; to declare the production, distribution, and use of such coal to be affected with a national public interest; to conserve the national resources of such coal; to provide for the general welfare, and for other purposes. The constitutional validity of the act is challenged in each of the suits. . . .

Section 1, among other things, declares that the production and distribution by producers of such coal bear upon and directly affect interstate commerce, and render regulation of production and distribution imperative for the protection of such commerce; that certain features connected with the production, distribution, and marketing have led to waste of the national coal resources, disorganization of interstate commerce in such coal, and burdening and obstructing interstate commerce therein; that practices prevailing in the production of such coal directly affect interstate commerce and require regulation for the protection of that commerce; and that the right of mine workers to organize and collectively bargain for wages, hours of labor, and conditions of employment should be guaranteed in order to prevent constant wage cutting and disparate labor costs detrimental to fair interstate competition, and in order to avoid obstructions to interstate commerce that recur in industrial disputes over labor relations at the mines. These declarations constitute not enactments of law, but legislative averments by way of inducement to the enactment which follows. . . .

Section 3 provides:

> There is hereby imposed upon the sale or other disposal of all bituminous coal produced within the United States an excise tax of 15 per centum on the sale price at the mine . . . Provided . . . That any such coal producer who has filed with the National Bituminous Coal Commission his acceptance of the code provided for in section 4 of this Act, and who acts in

compliance with the provisions of such code, shall be entitled to a drawback in the form of a credit upon the amount of such tax payable hereunder, equivalent to 90 per centum of the amount of such tax. . . .

Section 4 provides that the commission shall formulate the elaborate provisions contained therein into a working agreement to be known as the Bituminous Coal Code. . . .

Without repeating the long and involved provisions with regard to the fixing of minimum prices, it is enough to say that the act confers the power to fix the minimum price of coal at each and every coal mine in the United States. . . . The labor provisions of the code, found in part 3 of the same section, require that in order to effectuate the purposes of the act the district boards and code members shall accept specified conditions contained in the code, among which are the following:

Employees to be given the right to organize and bargain collectively. . . . Such employees to have the right of peaceable assemblage for the discussion of the principles of collective bargaining. . . .

The question involved is [whether] the labor provisions of the act can be upheld as an exercise of the power to regulate interstate commerce. . . . Since the validity of the act depends upon whether it is a regulation of interstate commerce, the nature and extent of the power conferred upon Congress by the commerce clause becomes the determinative question in this branch of the case. . . .

As used in the Constitution, the word "commerce" is the equivalent of the phrase "intercourse for the purposes of trade," and includes transportation, purchase, sale, and exchange of commodities between the citizens of the different states. And the power to regulate commerce embraces the instruments by which commerce is carried on. . . . In Adair v. United States, 208 U.S. 161[,] the phrase "Commerce among the several states" was defined as comprehending "traffic, intercourse, trade, navigation, communication, the transit of persons, and the transmission of messages by telegraph, — indeed, every species on commercial intercourse among the several states." In Veazie et al. v. Moor, 14 How. 568, this court, after saying that the phrase could never be applied to transactions wholly internal, significantly added: "Nor can it be properly concluded, that, because the products of domestic enterprise in agriculture or manufactures, or in the arts, may ultimately become the subjects of foreign commerce, that the control of the means or the encouragements by which enterprise is fostered and protected, is legitimately within the import of the phrase foreign commerce, or fairly implied in any investiture of the power to regulate such commerce. A pretension as far reaching as this, would extend to contracts between citizen and citizen of the same State, would control the pursuits of the planter, the grazier, the manufacturer, the mechanic, the immense operations of the collieries and mines and furnaces of the country; for there is not one of these avocations, the results of which may not become the subjects of foreign commerce, and be borne either by turnpikes, canals, or railroads, from point to point within the several States, towards an ultimate destination, like the one above mentioned."

The distinction between manufacture and commerce was discussed in Kidd v. Pearson, 128 U.S. 1, 20 [(1888), where] it was said:

No distinction is [more] clearly expressed in economic and political literature, than that between manufactures and commerce. Manufacture is transformation — the fashioning of raw materials into a change of form for use. The functions of commerce are different. . . . If it be held that the term includes the regulation of all such manufactures as are intended to be the subject of commercial transactions in the future, it is impossible to deny that it would also include all productive industries that contemplate the same thing. The result would be that congress would be invested, to the exclusion of the states, with the power to regulate, not only manufacture, but also agriculture, horticulture, stock-raising, domestic fisheries, mining, — in short, every branch of human industry. For is there one of them that does not contemplate, more or less clearly, an interstate or foreign market? Does not the wheat-grower of the north-west, and the cotton-planter of the south, plant, cultivate, and harvest his crop with an eye on the prices at Liverpool, New York, and Chicago? The power being vested in congress and denied to the states, it would follow as an inevitable result that the duty would devolve on congress to regulate all of these delicate, multiform, and vital interests, — interests which in their nature are, and must be, local in all the details of their successful management.

One who produces or manufactures a commodity, subsequently sold and shipped by him in interstate commerce, whether such sale and shipment were originally intended or not, has engaged in two distinct and separate activities. So far as he produces or manufactures a commodity, his business is purely local. So far as he sells and ships, or contracts to sell and ship, the commodity to customers in another state, he engages in interstate commerce. In respect of the former, he is subject only to regulation by the state; in respect of the latter, to regulation only by the federal government. . . .

We have seen that the word "commerce" is the equivalent of the phrase "intercourse for the purposes of trade." Plainly, the incidents leading up to and culminating in the mining of coal do not constitute such intercourse. The employment of men, the fixing of their wages, hours of labor, and working conditions, the bargaining in respect of these things — whether carried on separately or collectively — each and all constitute intercourse for the purposes of production, not of trade. The latter is a thing apart from the relation of employer and employee, which in all producing occupations is purely local in character. Extraction of coal from the mine is the aim and the completed result of local activities. Commerce in the coal mined is not brought into being by force of these activities, but by negotiations, agreements and circumstances entirely apart from production. Mining brings the subject-matter of commerce into existence. Commerce disposes of it. . . .

Another group of cases, of which Swift & Company v. United States [is] an example, rest upon the circumstance that the acts in question constituted direct interferences with the "flow" of commerce among the states. In the *Swift Case*, live stock was consigned and delivered to stockyards — not as a place of final destination, but [as] "a throat through which the current flows." The sales which ensued merely changed the private interest in the subject of the current without interfering with its continuity. . . . It was nowhere suggested in these cases that the interstate commerce power extended to the growth or production of the things which, after production, entered the flow. If the court had held that the raising of the cattle, which were involved in the *Swift Case*, including the wages paid to and working conditions of the herders and others employed in the business, could be regulated by Congress, that decision and decisions holding similarly would be in point; for it is that situation, and not the one with which the court actually dealt, which here concerns us. . . .

The restricted field covered by the *Swift* and kindred cases is illustrated by the *Schechter Case*. There the commodity in question, although shipped from another state, had come to rest in the state of its destination, and, as the court pointed out, was no longer in a current or flow of interstate commerce. The *Swift* doctrine was rejected as inapposite. In the *Schechter Case* the flow had ceased. Here it had not begun. The difference is not one of substance. The applicable principle is the same.

[S]ection 1 [of] the act now under review declares that all production and distribution of bituminous coal "bear upon and directly affect its interstate commerce"; and that regulation thereof is imperative for the protection of such commerce. The contention of the government is that the labor provisions of the act may be sustained in that view.

That the production of every commodity intended for interstate sale and transportation has some effect upon interstate commerce may be, if it has not already been, freely granted; and we are brought to the final and decisive inquiry, whether here that effect is direct, as the "Preamble" recites, or indirect. The distinction is not formal, but substantial in the highest degree, as we pointed out [in] *Schechter*[,] "If the commerce clause were construed," we there said, "to reach all enterprises and transactions which could be said to have an indirect effect upon interstate commerce, the federal authority would embrace practically all the activities of the people, and the authority of the state over its domestic concerns would exist only by sufferance of the federal government. . . ."

Whether the effect of a given activity or condition is direct or indirect is not always easy to determine. The word "direct" implies that the activity or condition invoked or blamed shall operate proximately — not mediately, remotely, or collaterally — to produce the effect. It connotes the absence of an efficient intervening agency or condition. And the extent of the effect bears no logical relation to its character. The distinction between a direct and an indirect effect turns, not upon the magnitude of either the cause or the effect, but entirely upon the manner in which the effect has been brought about. If the production by one man of a single ton of coal intended for interstate sale and shipment, and actually so sold and shipped, affects interstate commerce indirectly, the effect does not become direct by multiplying the tonnage, or increasing the number of men employed, or adding to the expense or complexities of the business, or by all combined. It is quite true that rules of law are sometimes qualified by considerations of degree. . . . But the matter of degree has no bearing upon the question here, since that question is not — What is the extent of the local activity or condition, or the extent of the effect produced upon interstate commerce? but — What is the relation between the activity or condition and the effect?

Much stress is put upon the evils which come from the struggle between employers and employees over the matter of wages, working conditions, the right of collective bargaining, etc., and the resulting strikes, curtailment, and irregularity of production and effect on prices; and it is insisted that interstate commerce is greatly affected thereby. But, in addition to what has just been said, the conclusive answer is that the evils are all local evils over which the federal government has no legislative control. The relation of employer and employee is a local relation. At common law, it is one of the domestic relations. The wages are paid for the doing of local work. Working conditions are obviously local conditions. The employees are not engaged in or about commerce, but exclusively in producing a commodity. And the controversies and evils, which it is the object of the act to regulate and minimize, are local controversies and evils affecting local work undertaken to accomplish that local result. Such effect as they may have upon commerce, however extensive it may be, is secondary and indirect. An increase in the greatness of the effect adds to its importance. It does not alter its character. . . .

A reading of the entire opinion makes clear, what we now declare, that the want of power on the part of the federal government is the same whether the wages, hours of service, and working conditions, and the bargaining about them, are related to production before interstate commerce has begun, or to sale and distribution after it has ended. . . .

The decrees in Nos. 636, 649, and 650 must be reversed and the causes remanded for further consideration in conformity with this opinion. The decree in No. 651 will be affirmed.

It is so ordered.

Notes: The Constitutional Crisis

1. *Other Setbacks.* *Carter* involved only one of many setbacks for FDR's "New Deal." In Panama Refining Co. v. Ryan, 293 U.S. 388 (1935), the Court struck down Section 9(c) of the National Industrial Recovery Act (NIRA) of 1933 on unlawful delegation grounds. Then, in A.L.A. Schechter Poultry Corp. v. United States, 295 U.S. 495 (1935), the Court struck down other sections of the NIRA. In all, the Court struck down four major pieces of legislation (the National Industrial Recovery Act, the Bituminous Coal Act, the Agricultural Adjustment Act, and the Railway Pension Act). In addition, the federal courts issued hundreds of injunctions against New Deal legislation.

2. *The Court Packing Plan.* Decisions like *Panama Refining* and *Schechter*, coupled with the Court's restrictive interpretation of the Commerce Clause in cases like *Carter*, angered President Roosevelt, who viewed the Court as an obstacle to his reform program. At the time, several major pieces of legislation had not been ruled on by the courts, including the National Labor Relations Act, the Social Security Act, and the Public Utility Holding Act. FDR was worried that the Court would strike them down, too.

Following his landslide reelection victory in 1936, President Roosevelt decided to move against the Court. FDR's vehicle was the now infamous "Court

Packing Plan," which would have altered the Court's membership (and, presumably, its decisions) by adding more members to the Court. The plan provided that, when a judge or justice of any federal court reached the age of 70 without availing himself of the opportunity to retire on a pension, a new member could be appointed by the President then in office. The appointment would be made in the manner prescribed by the Constitution: nomination by the President with confirmation by the Senate. See William E. Leuchtenburg, *The Origins of Franklin D. Roosevelt's "Court Packing" Plan*, 1966 Sup. Ct. Rev. 347-394. At the time, six justices were 70 or older. If the plan had passed, the Court's membership would have expanded to 15 members, giving Roosevelt a majority of members sympathetic to his position.

Despite FDR's popularity, and the popularity of his New Deal, many opposed the legislation. Everyone agreed that Congress was constitutionally authorized to control the number of Supreme Court Justices and that the number of justices had not remained static at nine. Nevertheless, many felt that it was inappropriate for FDR to manipulate the Court's membership in an effort to control the Court's decisions. Interestingly, the court packing plan never came to a vote. While the legislation was pending, the Court decided the following case.

∾ PROBLEM: MORE ON THE EDUCATION FOR A BETTER AMERICA ACT ∾

Does education have such a "direct" effect on interstate commerce that *Carter* would allow Congress to regulate it? In light of *Carter*, are you concerned about how the Tenth Amendment might affect your ability to pass or to structure the legislation?

NLRB v. Jones & Laughlin Steel Corp.

301 U.S. 1 (1937)

Mr. Chief Justice HUGHES delivered the opinion of the Court.

[The National Labor Relations Board (NLRB) concluded that Jones & Laughlin Steel Corp. had engaged in the unfair labor practice of discharging employees in order to interfere with their union organizing activities. The NLRB ordered Jones & Laughlin to cease and desist from such practices, to offer reinstatement to ten of the employees named, to make good their losses in pay, and to post notices that it would not discharge or discriminate against members or prospective members of the union. The court of appeals refused to enforce the order, holding that it lay beyond the scope of federal power.]

Contesting the ruling of the Board, the respondent [argues] that the act can have no application to the respondent's relations with its production employees because they are not subject to regulation by the federal government. [T]he Labor Board concluded that the works in Pittsburgh and Aliquippa "might be likened to the heart of a self-contained, highly integrated body. They draw in the raw materials from Michigan, Minnesota, West Virginia, Pennsylvania in part through arteries and by means controlled by the respondent; they transform the materials and then pump them out to all parts of the nation through the vast mechanism which the respondent has elaborated."

To carry on the activities of the entire steel industry, 33,000 men mine ore, 44,000 men mine coal, 4,000 men quarry limestone, 16,000 men manufacture coke, 343,000 men manufacture steel, and 83,000 men transport its product. Respondent has about 10,000 employees in its Aliquippa plant, which is located in a community of about 30,000 persons. . . .

[The] act is challenged in its entirety as an attempt to regulate all industry, thus invading the reserved powers of the States over their local concerns. It is asserted that the references in the act to interstate and foreign commerce are colorable at best; that the act is not a true regulation of such commerce or of matters which directly affect it, but on the contrary has the fundamental object of placing under the compulsory supervision of the federal government all industrial labor relations within the nation. . . .

There can be no question that the commerce thus contemplated by the act [is] interstate and foreign commerce in the constitutional sense. The act also defines the term "affecting commerce" section 2(7), 29 U.S.C.A. §152(7):

> The term "affecting commerce" means in commerce, or burdening or obstructing commerce or the free flow of commerce, or having led or tending to lead to a labor dispute burdening or obstructing commerce or the free flow of commerce.

This definition is one of exclusion as well as inclusion. The grant of authority to the Board does not purport to extend to the relationship between all industrial employees and employers. Its terms do not impose collective bargaining upon all industry regardless of effects upon interstate or foreign commerce. It purports to reach only what may be deemed to burden or obstruct that commerce and, thus qualified, it must be construed as contemplating the exercise of control within constitutional bounds. It is a familiar principle that acts which directly burden or obstruct interstate or foreign commerce, or its free flow, are within the reach of the congressional power. Acts having that effect are not rendered immune because they grow out of labor disputes. It is the effect upon commerce, not the source of the injury, which is the criterion. Whether or not particular action does affect commerce in such a close and intimate fashion as to be subject to federal control, and hence to lie within the authority conferred upon the Board, is left by the statute to be determined as individual cases arise. We are thus to inquire whether in the instant case the constitutional boundary has been passed. . . .

The congressional authority to protect interstate commerce from burdens and obstructions is not limited to transactions which can be deemed to be an essential part of a "flow" of interstate or foreign commerce. Burdens and obstructions may be due to injurious action springing from other sources. The fundamental principle is that the power to regulate commerce is the power to enact "all appropriate legislation" for its "protection or advancement"; to adopt measures "to promote its growth and insure its safety"; "to foster, protect, control, and restrain." That power is plenary and may be exerted to protect interstate commerce "no matter what the source of the dangers which threaten it." Second

Employers' Liability Cases, 223 U.S. 1, at page 51. Although activities may be intrastate in character when separately considered, if they have such a close and substantial relation to interstate commerce that their control is essential or appropriate to protect that commerce from burdens and obstructions, Congress cannot be denied the power to exercise that control. Undoubtedly the scope of this power must be considered in the light of our dual system of government and may not be extended so as to embrace effects upon interstate commerce so indirect and remote that to embrace them, in view of our complex society, would effectually obliterate the distinction between what is national and what is local and create a completely centralized government. The question is necessarily one of degree. As the Court said in Board of Trade of City of Chicago v. Olsen, 262 U.S. 1, at page 37: "Whatever amounts to more or less constant practice, and threatens to obstruct or unduly to burden the freedom of interstate commerce is within the regulatory power of Congress under the commerce clause, and it is primarily for Congress to consider and decide the fact of the danger and to meet it."

[T]he fact that the employees here concerned were engaged in production is not determinative. The question remains as to the effect upon interstate commerce of the labor practice involved. In the *Schechter Case*, we found that the effect there was so remote as to be beyond the federal power. To find "immediacy or directness" there was to find it "almost everywhere," a result inconsistent with the maintenance of our federal system. In the *Carter Case*, the Court was of the opinion that the provisions of the statute relating to production were invalid upon several grounds. . . .

[Giving] full weight to respondent's contention with respect to a break in the complete continuity of the "stream of commerce" by reason of respondent's manufacturing operations, the fact remains that the stoppage of those operations by industrial strife would have a most serious effect upon interstate commerce. In view of respondent's far-flung activities, it is idle to say that the effect would be indirect or remote. It is obvious that it would be immediate and might be catastrophic. We are asked to shut our eyes to the plainest facts of our national life and to deal with the question of direct and indirect effects in an intellectual vacuum. Because there may be but indirect and remote effects upon interstate commerce in connection with a host of local enterprises throughout the country, it does not follow that other industrial activities do not have such a close and intimate relation to interstate commerce as to make the presence of industrial strife a matter of the most urgent national concern. When industries organize themselves on a national scale, making their relation to interstate commerce the dominant factor in their activities, how can it be maintained that their industrial labor relations constitute a forbidden field into which Congress may not enter when it is necessary to protect interstate commerce from the paralyzing consequences of industrial war? We have often said that interstate commerce itself is a practical conception. It is equally true that interferences with that commerce must be appraised by a judgment that does not ignore actual experience.

Experience has abundantly demonstrated that the recognition of the right of employees to self-organization and to have representatives of their own choosing for the purpose of collective bargaining is often an essential condition of industrial peace. Refusal to confer and negotiate has been one of the most prolific causes of strife. This is such an outstanding fact in the history of labor disturbances that it is a proper subject of judicial notice and requires no citation of instances. . . .

These questions have frequently engaged the attention of Congress and have been the subject of many inquiries. The steel industry is one of the great basic industries of the United States, with ramifying activities affecting interstate commerce at every point. The Government aptly refers to the steel strike of 1919-1920 with its far-reaching consequences. The fact that there appears to have been no major disturbance in that industry in the more recent period did not dispose of the possibilities of future and like dangers to interstate commerce which Congress was entitled to foresee and to exercise its protective power to forestall. It is not necessary again to detail the facts as to respondent's enterprise. Instead of being beyond the pale, we think that it presents in a most striking way the close and intimate relation which a manufacturing industry may have to interstate commerce and we have no doubt that Congress had constitutional authority to safeguard the right of respondent's employees to self-organization and freedom in the choice of representatives for collective bargaining. . . .

Our conclusion is that the order of the Board was within its competency and that the act is valid as here applied. . . .

Reversed and remanded.

Mr. Justice McReynolds delivered the following dissenting opinion [which was joined by Justices Van Devanter, Sutherland, and Butler].

[The] Court as we think departs from well-established principles followed in *Schechter Poultry Corporation* and *Carter Coal Co.* [T]he power of Congress under the commerce clause does not extend to relations between employers and their employees engaged in manufacture, and therefore the act conferred upon the National Labor Relations Board no authority in respect of matters covered by the questioned orders. . . . Any effect on interstate commerce by the discharge of employees shown here would be indirect and remote in the highest degree. . . . The immediate effect in the factor may be to create discontent among all those employed and a strike may follow, which, in turn, may result in reducing production, which ultimately may reduce the volume of goods moving in interstate commerce. By this chain of indirect and progressively remote events we finally reach the evil with which it is said the legislation under consideration undertakes to deal. A more remote and indirect interference with interstate commerce or a more definite invasion of the powers reserved to the states is difficult, if not impossible, to imagine. . . .

Notes

1. *The "Switch That Saved Nine."* Justice Roberts, who voted to strike down federal action in *Carter Coal*, voted to sustain it in *Jones & Laughlin*.

2. *The Aftermath.* Following the *Jones & Laughlin* decision, support for the court packing plan waned. Senator Joseph Robinson developed a modified plan

that appeared to have a good chance of passage. But when he died suddenly of a heart attack, the plan was voted down. *See* William E. Leuchtenberg, *The Origins of Franklin D. Roosevelt's "Court-Packing" Plan*, 1966 Sup. Ct. Rev. 347.

∿ PROBLEM: MORE ON THE EDUCATION FOR A BETTER AMERICA ACT ∿

Does *Jones & Laughlin* alter your perspective on whether Congress can pass the legislation? Does it matter whether Congress includes spending incentives (designed to encourage school officials to act in particular ways), or whether it also includes specific mandates regarding how education reform is to be achieved? How does the Tenth Amendment come into play after this decision?

4. *Post-Switch Expansion of Federal Power: A Half Century of Deference*

Jones & Laughlin ushered in a half century during which the Court upheld essentially every assertion of federal regulatory power under the Commerce Clause. This post-1937 deferential approach is illustrated in the following cases.

United States v. Darby
312 U.S. 100 (1941)

Mr. Justice STONE delivered the opinion of the Court.

The two principal questions raised by the record in this case are, first, whether Congress has constitutional power to prohibit the shipment in interstate commerce of lumber manufactured by employees whose wages are less than a prescribed minimum or whose weekly hours of labor at that wage are greater than a prescribed maximum, and, second, whether it has power to prohibit the employment of workmen in the production of goods "for interstate commerce" at other than prescribed wages and hours. A subsidiary question is whether in connection with such prohibitions Congress can require the employer subject to them to keep records showing the hours worked each day and week by each of his employees including those engaged "in the production and manufacture of goods to wit, lumber, for 'interstate commerce.'" . . .

While manufacture is not of itself interstate commerce[,] the shipment of manufactured goods interstate is such commerce and the prohibition of such shipment by Congress is indubitably a regulation of the commerce. The power to regulate commerce is the power "to prescribe the rule by which commerce is to be governed." It extends not only to those regulations which aid, foster and protect the commerce, but embraces those which prohibit it. . . .

The power of Congress over interstate commerce "is complete in itself, may be exercised to its utmost extent, and acknowledges no limitations, other than are prescribed by the constitution." Gibbons v. Ogden. Congress, following its own conception of public policy concerning the restrictions which may appropriately be imposed on interstate commerce, is free to exclude from the commerce articles whose use in the states for which they are destined it may conceive to be injurious to the public health, morals or welfare, even though the state has not sought to regulate their use.

Such regulation is not a forbidden invasion of state power merely because either its motive or its consequence is to restrict the use of articles of commerce within the states of destination and is not prohibited unless by other Constitutional provisions. It is no objection to the assertion of the power to regulate interstate commerce that its exercise is attended by the same incidents which attend the exercise of the police power of the states.

The motive and purpose of the present regulation are plainly to make effective the Congressional conception of public policy that interstate commerce should not be made the instrument of competition in the distribution of goods produced under substandard labor conditions, which competition is injurious to the commerce and to the states from and to which the commerce flows. The motive and purpose of a regulation of interstate commerce are matters for the legislative judgment upon the exercise of which the Constitution places no restriction and over which the courts are given no control. . . .

In the more than a century which has elapsed since the decision of *Gibbons*, these principles of constitutional interpretation have been so long and repeatedly recognized by this Court as applicable to the Commerce Clause, that there would be little occasion for repeating them now were it not for the decision of this Court twenty-two years ago in Hammer v. Dagenhart, 247 U.S. 251 (1918). In that case it was held [that] Congress was without power to exclude the products of child labor from interstate commerce. . . . *Hammer* has not been followed. The distinction on which the decision was rested that Congressional power to prohibit interstate commerce is limited to articles which in themselves have some harmful or deleterious property — a distinction which was novel when made and unsupported by any provision of the Constitution — has long since been abandoned. The thesis of the opinion that the motive of the prohibition or its effect to control in some measure the use or production within the states of the article thus excluded from the commerce can operate to deprive the regulation of its constitutional authority has long since ceased to have force. . . . The conclusion is inescapable that *Hammer* was a departure from the principles which have prevailed in the interpretation of the commerce clause both before and since the decision and that such vitality, as a precedent, as it then had has long since been exhausted. It should be and now is overruled. . . .

There remains the question whether such restriction on the production of goods for commerce is a permissible exercise of the commerce power. The power of Congress over interstate commerce is not confined to the regulation of commerce among the states. It extends to those activities intrastate which so affect interstate commerce or the exercise of the power of Congress over it as to make regulation of them appropriate means to the attainment of a legitimate end, the exercise of the granted power of Congress to regulate interstate commerce. McCulloch v. Maryland.

While this Court has many times found state regulation of interstate commerce, when uniformity of its regulation is of national concern, to be incompatible with the Commerce Clause even though Congress has not legislated on the subject, the Court has never implied such restraint on state control over matters intrastate not deemed to be regulations of interstate commerce or its instrumentalities even though they affect the commerce. In the absence of Congressional legislation on the subject state laws which are not regulations of the commerce itself or its instrumentalities are not forbidden even though they affect interstate commerce.

But it does not follow that Congress may not by appropriate legislation regulate intrastate activities where they have a substantial effect on interstate commerce. *See* National Labor Relations Board v. Jones & Laughlin Steel Corp. [T]his Court ha[s] many times held that the power of Congress to regulate interstate commerce extends to the regulation through legislative action of activities intrastate which have a substantial effect on the commerce or the exercise of the Congressional power over it. . . .

The means adopted by §15(a)(2) for the protection of interstate commerce by the suppression of the production of the condemned goods for interstate commerce is so related to the commerce and so affects it as to be within the reach of the commerce power. Congress, to attain its objective in the suppression of nationwide competition in interstate commerce by goods produced under substandard labor conditions, has made no distinction as to the volume or amount of shipments in the commerce or of production for commerce by any particular shipper or producer. It recognized that in present day industry, competition by a small part may affect the whole and that the total effect of the competition of many small producers may be great. The legislation aimed at a whole embraces all its parts. . . .

Our conclusion is unaffected by the Tenth Amendment which provides: "The powers not delegated to the United States by the Constitution, nor prohibited by it to the States, are reserved to the States respectively, or to the people." The amendment states but a truism that all is retained which has not been surrendered. There is nothing in the history of its adoption to suggest that it was more than declaratory of the relationship between the national and state governments as it had been established by the Constitution before the amendment or that its purpose was other than to allay fears that the new national government might seek to exercise powers not granted, and that the states might not be able to exercise fully their reserved powers. . . .

Question

Note the dramatic shift in the Court's views on the scope of the Commerce Clause and on the Tenth Amendment as a limitation on federal power. Not only does the Court overrule *Hammer*, which treated the Tenth Amendment as an independent limitation on federal power, but the Court also flatly states that the Tenth Amendment is a "truism." What does it mean to say that the Tenth Amendment is nothing more than a "truism"?

Wickard v. Filburn
317 U.S. 111 (1942)

Mr. Justice JACKSON delivered the opinion of the Court.

[Appellee] sought to enjoin enforcement against himself of the marketing penalty imposed by [amendments] to the Agricultural Adjustment Act of 1938, upon that part of his 1941 wheat crop which was available for marketing in excess of the marketing quota established for his farm. He also sought a declaratory judgment that the wheat marketing quota provisions of the Act [were] unconstitutional because not sustainable under the Commerce Clause or consistent with the Due Process Clause of the Fifth Amendment. . . .

The general scheme of the Agricultural Adjustment Act of 1938 as related to wheat is to control the volume moving in interstate and foreign commerce in order to avoid surpluses and shortages and the consequent abnormally low or high wheat prices and obstructions to commerce. Within prescribed limits and by prescribed standards the Secretary of Agriculture is directed to ascertain and proclaim each year a national acreage allotment for the next crop of wheat, which is then apportioned to the states and their counties, and is eventually broken up into allotments for individual farms. . . .

[The appellee has owned and operated a small farm in Ohio, maintaining a herd of dairy cattle, selling milk, raising poultry, and selling poultry and eggs. It has been his practice to raise a small acreage of winter wheat, to sell a portion of the crop; to feed part to poultry and livestock on the farm, some of which is sold; to use some in making flour for home consumption; and to keep the rest for the following seeding. The appellee's 1941 wheat allotment was 11.1 acres, and he was allowed a yield of 20.1 bushels of wheat per acre. He sowed 23 acres, however, and harvested from his 11.9 acres of excess acreage 239 bushels, which, under the Act, constituted farm marketing excess, subject to a penalty of 49 cents a bushel, or $117.11 in all.]

It is urged that under the Commerce Clause of the Constitution, Article I, §8, clause 3, Congress does not possess the power it has in this instance sought to exercise. The question would merit little consideration [except] for the fact that this Act extends federal regulation to production not intended in any part for commerce but wholly for consumption on the farm. . . . Hence, marketing quotas not only embrace all that may be sold without penalty but also what may be consumed on the premises. . . . The sum of this is that the Federal Government fixes a quota including all that the farmer may harvest for sale or for his own farm needs, and declares that wheat produced on excess acreage may neither be disposed of nor used except upon payment of the penalty or except it is stored as required by the Act or delivered to the Secretary of Agriculture. . . .

Appellee says that this is a regulation of production and consumption of wheat. Such activities are, he urges, beyond the reach of Congressional power under the Commerce Clause, since they are local in character, and their effects upon interstate commerce are at most "indirect." [T]he Government argues that the statute regulates neither production nor consumption, but only marketing; and, in the alternative, that if the Act does go beyond the regulation of marketing it is sustainable as a "necessary and proper" implementation of the power of Congress over interstate commerce.

The Government's concern lest the Act be held to be a regulation of production or consumption rather than of marketing is attributable to a few dicta and decisions of this Court which might be understood to lay it down that activities such as "production," "manufacturing," and "mining" are strictly "local" and, except in special circumstances which are not present here, cannot be regulated under the commerce power because their effects upon interstate commerce are, as matter of law, only "indirect." Even today, when this power has been held to have great latitude, there is no decision of this Court that such activities may be regulated where no part of the product is intended for interstate commerce or intermingled with the subjects thereof. We believe that a review of the course of decision under the Commerce Clause will make plain, however, that questions of the power of Congress are not to be decided by reference to any formula which would give controlling force to nomenclature such as "production" and "indirect" and foreclose consideration of the actual effects of the activity in question upon interstate commerce. . . .

In the *Shreveport Rate Cases*, [this] Court held that railroad rates of an admittedly intrastate character and fixed by authority of the state might, nevertheless, be revised by the Federal Government because of the economic effects which they had upon interstate commerce. The opinion of Mr. Justice Hughes found federal intervention constitutionally authorized because of "matters having such a close and substantial relation to interstate traffic that the control is essential or appropriate to the security of that traffic, to the efficiency of the interstate service, and to the maintenance of the conditions under which interstate commerce may be conducted upon fair terms and without molestation or hindrance. . . ."

The Court's recognition of the relevance of the economic effects in the application of the Commerce Clause exemplified by this statement has made the mechanical application of legal formulas no longer feasible. Once an economic measure of the reach of the power granted to Congress in the Commerce Clause is accepted, questions of federal power cannot be decided simply by finding the activity in question to be "production" nor can consideration of its economic effects be foreclosed by calling them "indirect." [Whether] the subject of the regulation in question was "production," "consumption," or "marketing" is, therefore, not material for purposes of deciding the question of federal power before us. That an activity is of local character may help in a doubtful case to determine whether Congress intended to reach it. [But] even if appellee's activity be local and though it may not be regarded as commerce, it may still, whatever its nature, be reached by Congress if it exerts a substantial economic effect on interstate commerce and this irrespective of whether such effect is what might at some earlier time have been defined as "direct" or "indirect." . . .

Commerce among the states in wheat is large and important. Although wheat is raised in every state but one, production in most states is not equal to consumption. Sixteen states on average have had a surplus of wheat above their own requirements for feed, seed, and food. Thirty-two states and the District of Columbia, where production has been below consumption, have looked to these surplus-producing states for their supply as well as for wheat for export and carryover. [The] wheat industry has been a problem industry for some years. . . .

The effect of consumption of homegrown wheat on interstate commerce is due to the fact that it constitutes the most variable factor in the disappearance of the wheat crop. Consumption on the farm where grown appears to vary in an amount greater than 20 per cent of average production. The total amount of wheat consumed as food varies but relatively little, and use as seed is relatively constant.

The maintenance by government regulation of a price for wheat undoubtedly can be accomplished as effectively by sustaining or increasing the demand as by limiting the supply. The effect of the statute before us is to restrict the amount which may be produced for market and the extent as well to which one may forestall resort to the market by producing to meet his own needs. That appellee's own contribution to the demand for wheat may be trivial by itself is not enough to remove him from the scope of federal regulation where, as here, his contribution, taken together with that of many others similarly situated, is far from trivial.

It is well established by decisions of this Court that the power to regulate commerce includes the power to regulate the prices at which commodities in that commerce are dealt in and practices affecting such prices. One of the primary purposes of the Act in question was to increase the market price of wheat and to that end to limit the volume thereof that could affect the market. It can hardly be denied that a factor of such volume and variability as home-consumed wheat would have a substantial influence on price and market conditions. This may arise because being in marketable condition such wheat overhangs the market and if induced by rising prices tends to flow into the market and check price increases. But if we assume that it is never marketed, it supplies a need of the man who grew it which would otherwise be reflected by purchases in the open market. Home-grown wheat in this sense competes with wheat in commerce. The stimulation of commerce is a use of the regulatory function quite as definitely as prohibitions or restrictions thereon. This record leaves us in no doubt that Congress may properly have considered that wheat consumed on the farm where grown if wholly outside the scheme of regulation would have a substantial effect in defeating and obstructing its purpose to stimulate trade therein at increased prices.

It is said, however, that this Act, forcing some farmers into the market to buy what they could provide for themselves, is an unfair promotion of the markets and prices of specializing wheat growers. It is of the essence of regulation that it lays a restraining hand on the selfinterest of the regulated and that advantages from the regulation commonly fall to others. The conflicts of economic interest between the regulated and those who advantage by it are wisely left under our system to resolution by the Congress under its more flexible and responsible legislative process. Such conflicts rarely lend themselves to judicial determination.

And with the wisdom, workability, or fairness, of the plan of regulation we have nothing to do. . . .

Reversed.

Notes

1. Paul *Overturned.* Two years later, in United States v. South-Eastern Underwriters Assn, 322 U.S. 533 (1944), the Court overturned Paul v. Virginia insofar as that case had held that insurance policies do not constitute commerce within the meaning of the Commerce Clause. In *South-Eastern*, appellees were indicted for violations of the Sherman Act. Since the indictments were based on conduct involving insurance policies, the appellees argued that the Sherman Act could not be applied to them because "the business of fire insurance is not commerce." The Court disagreed: "[I]t would indeed be difficult now to hold that no activities of any insurance company can ever constitute interstate commerce so as to make it subject to such regulation; — activities which, as part of the conduct of a legitimate and useful commercial enterprise, may embrace integrated operations in many states and involve the transmission of great quantities of money, documents, and communications across dozens of state lines."

2. *Expansion of Federal Power.* In the wake of decisions like *Darby* and *Wickard*, the federal government's power over the U.S. economy increased dramatically. The federal government began to assert control over such diverse matters as consumer safety, energy, agriculture, aviation travel, civil rights, drugs, labor, commerce, securities, and banking.

∼ PROBLEM: MORE ON THE EDUCATION FOR A BETTER AMERICA ACT ∼

After *Wickard*, does it appear that Congress can enact this legislation? Can it include both incentives and mandates? Does the Tenth Amendment seem to limit the scope of Congress's authority?

Heart of Atlanta Motel, Inc., v. United States
379 U.S. 241 (1964)

Mr. Justice CLARK delivered the opinion of the Court.

This is a declaratory judgment action, attacking the constitutionality of Title II of the Civil Rights Act of 1964. . . . Appellant owns and operates the Heart of Atlanta Motel which has 216 rooms available to transient guests. The motel is located on Courtland Street, two blocks from downtown Peachtree Street. It is readily accessible to interstate highways 75 and 85 and state highways 23 and 41. Appellant solicits patronage from outside the State of Georgia through various national advertising media, including magazines of national circulation; it maintains over 50 billboards and highway signs within the State, soliciting patronage for the motel; it accepts convention trade from outside Georgia and approximately 75% of its registered guests are from out of State. Prior to passage of the Act the motel had followed a practice of refusing to rent rooms to Negroes, and it alleged that it intended to continue to do so. In an effort to perpetuate that policy this suit was filed.

The appellant contends that Congress in passing this Act exceeded its power to regulate commerce under Art. I, §8, cl. 3, of the Constitution of the United States. . . .

This Title is divided into seven sections beginning with §201(a) which provides that:

> All persons shall be entitled to the full and equal enjoyment of the goods, services, facilities, privileges, advantages, and accommodations of any place of public accommodation, as defined in this section, without discrimination or segregation on the ground of race, color, religion, or national origin.

There are listed in §201(b) four classes of business establishments, each of which "serves the public" and "is a place of public accommodation" within the meaning of §201(a) "if its operations affect commerce, or if discrimination or segregation by it is supported by State action." The covered establishments are: "(1) any inn, hotel, motel, or other establishment which provides lodging to transient guests." . . .

It is admitted that the operation of the motel brings it within the provisions of §201(a) of the Act and that appellant refused to provide lodging for transient Negroes because of their race or color and that it intends to continue that policy unless restrained.

The sole question posed is, therefore, the constitutionality of the Civil Rights Act of 1964 as applied to these facts. The legislative history of the Act indicates that Congress based the Act on §5 and the Equal Protection Clause of the Fourteenth Amendment as well as its power to regulate interstate commerce under Art. I, §8, cl. 3, of the Constitution.

The Senate Commerce Committee made it quite clear that the fundamental object of Title II was to vindicate "the deprivation of personal dignity that surely accompanies denials of equal access to public establishments." At the same time, however, it noted that such an objective has been and could be readily achieved "by congressional action based on the commerce power of the Constitution." S. Rep. No. 872, *supra*, at 16-17 . . .

While the Act as adopted carried no congressional findings[,] the record of its passage through each house is replete with evidence of the burdens that discrimination by race or color places upon interstate commerce. This testimony included the fact that our people have become increasingly mobile with millions of people of all races traveling from State to State; that Negroes in particular have been the subject of discrimination in transient accommodations, having to travel great distances to secure the same; that often they have been unable to obtain accommodations and have had to call upon friends to put them up overnight, and that these conditions had become so acute as to require the listing of available lodging for Negroes in a special guidebook which was itself "dramatic testimony to the difficulties" Negroes encounter in travel. . . .

The power of Congress to deal with these obstructions depends on the meaning of the Commerce Clause. Its meaning was first enunciated 140 years ago by the great Chief Justice John Marshall in Gibbons v. Ogden. . . . [T]he determinative test of the exercise of power by the Congress under the Commerce Clause is simply whether the activity sought to be regulated is "commerce which concerns more States than one" and has a real and substantial relation to the national interest. Let us now turn to this facet of the problem.

> That the "intercourse" of which the Chief Justice spoke included the movement of persons through more States than one was settled as early as 1849, in the Passenger Cases (Smith v. Turner), . . .

Nor does it make any difference whether the transportation is commercial in character. . . . That Congress was legislating against moral wrongs in many of these areas rendered its enactments no less valid. In framing Title II of this Act Congress was also dealing with what it considered a moral problem. But that fact does not detract from the overwhelming evidence of the disruptive effect that racial discrimination has had on commercial intercourse. It was this burden which empowered Congress to enact appropriate legislation, and, given this basis for the exercise of its power, Congress was not restricted by the fact that the particular obstruction to interstate commerce with which it was dealing was also deemed a moral and social wrong.

It is said that the operation of the motel here is of a purely local character. But, assuming this to be true, "(i)f it is interstate commerce that feels the pinch, it does not matter how local the operation which applies the squeeze." . . . As Chief Justice Stone put it in United States v. Darby:

> The power of Congress over interstate commerce is not confined to the regulation of commerce among the states. It extends to those activities intrastate which so affect interstate commerce or the exercise of the power of Congress over it as to make regulation of them appropriate means to the attainment of a legitimate end, the exercise of the granted power of Congress to regulate interstate commerce.

Thus the power of Congress to promote interstate commerce also includes the power to regulate the local incidents thereof, including local activities in both the States of origin and destination, which might have a substantial and harmful effect upon that commerce. One need only examine the evidence which we have discussed above to see that Congress may — as it has — prohibit racial discrimination by motels serving travelers, however "local" their operations may appear. . . .

We, therefore, conclude that the action of the Congress in the adoption of the Act as applied here to a motel which concededly serves interstate travelers is within the power granted it by the Commerce Clause of the Constitution, as interpreted by this Court for 140 years. It may be argued that Congress could have pursued other methods to eliminate the obstructions it found in interstate commerce caused by racial discrimination. But this is a matter of policy that rests entirely with the Congress not with the courts. How obstructions in commerce may be removed—what means are to be employed—is within the sound and exclusive discretion of the Congress. It is subject only to one caveat—that the means chosen by it must be reasonably adapted to the end permitted by the Constitution. We cannot say that its choice here was not so adapted. The Constitution requires no more.

Affirmed.

Notes

1. *Ollie's Barbecue.* Consistent with the *Heart of Atlanta* decision, in Katzenbach v. McClung, 379 U.S. 294 (1964), the Court upheld a federal law prohibiting discrimination as applied to a family-owned restaurant in Birmingham, Alabama, that specialized in barbecued meats and homemade pies and had a seating capacity of 220 customers. The restaurant catered to a family and white-collar trade and maintained only a take-out service for African Americans, although two thirds of its 36 employees were African American. In upholding the Act, the Court stated: "The record is replete with testimony of the burdens placed on interstate commerce by racial discrimination in restaurants. A comparison of per capita spending by Negroes in restaurants, theaters, and like establishments indicated less spending, after discounting income differences, in areas where discrimination is widely practiced. This condition, which was especially aggravated in the South, was attributed in the testimony of the Under Secretary of Commerce to racial segregation. This diminutive spending springing from a refusal to serve Negroes and their total loss as customers has, regardless of the absence of direct evidence, a close connection to interstate commerce. The fewer customers a restaurant enjoys the less food it sells and consequently the less it buys. . . . Moreover there was an impressive array of testimony that discrimination in restaurants had a direct and highly restrictive effect upon interstate travel by Negroes. This resulted [because] discriminatory practices prevent Negroes from buying prepared food served on the premises while on a trip, except in isolated and unkempt restaurants and under most unsatisfactory and often unpleasant conditions. [This] testimony afforded ample basis for the conclusion that established restaurants in such areas sold less interstate goods because of the discrimination, that interstate travel was obstructed directly by it, that business in general suffered and that many new businesses refrained from establishing there as a result of it. [V]iewed in isolation, the volume of food purchased by Ollie's Barbecue from sources supplied from out of state was insignificant when compared with the total foodstuffs moving in commerce. But, [the Commerce Power] 'extends to those activities intrastate which so affect interstate commerce, or the exertion of the power of Congress over it, as to make regulation of them appropriate means to the attainment of a legitimate end, the effective execution of the granted power to regulate interstate commerce." United States v. Wrightwood Dairy Co., 315 U.S. 110 (1942). [Commerce] "may still, whatever its nature, be reached by Congress if it exerts a substantial economic effect on interstate commerce."

Wickard v. Filburn, *supra*, at 125. ". . . Confronted as we are with the facts laid before Congress, we must conclude that it had a rational basis for finding that racial discrimination in restaurants had a direct and adverse effect on the free flow of interstate commerce. . . . The Civil Rights Act of 1964, as here applied, we find to be plainly appropriate in the resolution of what the Congress found to be a national commercial problem of the first magnitude."

2. *Federal Criminal Legislation.* Historically, the states have been responsible for virtually all basic criminal legislation, including murder, robbery, rape, and assault statutes. Congress has passed some criminal statutes, but most federal statutes have involved a crime against the federal government (filing a false tax return) or criminal activity that crossed state lines (e.g., *The Lottery Case*). In Perez v. United States, 402 U.S. 146 (1971), the Court upheld the Consumer Credit Protection Act, which made it illegal to engage in "extortionate credit transactions," defined as those characterized by the use or threat of the use of "violence or other criminal means" in enforcement. The law was applied to a "loan shark" (Perez) who used threats of violence as a method of collection. In upholding the Act, the Court concluded: "Extortionate credit transactions, though purely intrastate, may in the judgment of Congress affect interstate commerce. . . . In the setting of the present case there is a tie-in between local loan sharks and interstate crime. . . . The [legislation] grew out of [various reports and studies which] supplied Congress with the knowledge that the loan shark racket provides organized crime with its second most lucrative source of revenue, exacts millions from the pockets of people, coerces its victims into the commission of crimes against property, and causes the takeover by racketeers of legitimate businesses. It appears, instead, that loan sharking in its national setting is one way organized interstate crime holds its guns to the heads of the poor and the rich alike and syphons funds from numerous localities to finance its national operations." Justice Stewart dissented: "Congress surely has power under the Commerce Clause to enact criminal laws to protect the instrumentalities of interstate commerce, to prohibit the misuse of the channels or facilities of interstate commerce, and to prohibit or regulate those intrastate activities that have a demonstrably substantial effect on interstate commerce. But under the statute before us a man can be convicted without any proof of interstate movement, of the use of the facilities of interstate commerce, or of facts showing that his conduct affected interstate commerce. I think the Framers of the Constitution never intended that the National Government might define as a crime and prosecute such wholly local activity through the enactment of federal criminal laws."

3. *Environmental Regulation.* In Hodel v. Virginia Surface Mining and Reclamation Association, Inc., 452 U.S. 264 (1981), the Court upheld the Surface Mining Control and Reclamation Act, a comprehensive statute designed to "establish a nationwide program to protect society and the environment from the adverse effects of surface coal mining operations." Among other things, the Act required: restoration of land after mining to its prior condition, restoration of land to its approximate original contour, segregation and preservation of topsoil, minimization of disturbance to the hydrologic balance, construction of

coal mine waste piles used as dams and embankments, revegetation of mined areas, and spoil disposal. In upholding the Act, the Court stated: "[W]hen Congress has determined that an activity affects interstate commerce, the courts need inquire only whether the finding is rational. [The Act] recites the congressional finding that many surface mining operations result in disturbances of surface areas that burden and adversely affect commerce and the public welfare by destroying or diminishing the utility of land for commercial, industrial, residential, recreational, agricultural, and forestry purposes, by causing erosion and landslides, by contributing to floods, by polluting the water, by destroying fish and wildlife habitats, by impairing natural beauty, by damaging the property of citizens, by creating hazards dangerous to life and property, by degrading the quality of life in local communities, and by counteracting governmental programs and efforts to conserve soil, water, and other natural resources. . . . Similarly, the House Committee documented the adverse effects of surface coal mining on interstate commerce. . . . In light of the evidence available to Congress and the detailed consideration that the legislation received, we cannot say that Congress did not have a rational basis for concluding that surface coal mining has substantial effects on interstate commerce. . . . [T]he commerce power 'extends to those activities intrastate which so affect interstate commerce, or the exertion of the power of Congress over it, as to make regulation of them appropriate means to the attainment of a legitimate end, the effective execution of the granted power to regulate interstate commerce.' United States v. Wrightwood Dairy Co., 315 U.S., at 119. . . . Here, Congress rationally determined that regulation of surface coal mining is necessary to protect interstate commerce from adverse effects that may result from that activity. This congressional finding is sufficient to sustain the Act as a valid exercise of Congress' power under the Commerce Clause. . . . Moreover, the Act responds to a congressional finding that nationwide 'surface mining and reclamation standards are essential in order to insure that competition in interstate commerce among sellers of coal produced in different States will not be used to undermine the ability of the several States to improve and maintain adequate standards on coal mining operations within their borders.'"

∾ PROBLEMS ∾

1. *Comprehensive Criminal Legislation.* If Congress can reach extortionate credit transactions, is Congress free to pass comprehensive criminal legislation? Could it, for example, enact general federal crimes on such topics as murder, robbery, and rape? How would you argue that crimes like murder, robbery, and rape have a substantial impact on interstate commerce? How might you respond to these arguments?

2. *Domestic Relations.* Historically, the states have exercised power over domestic relations, including such issues as marriage and divorce. Based on decisions like *Darby, Jones & Laughlin, Wickard,* and *Heart of Atlanta,* could Congress

pass a comprehensive statute dealing with domestic relations? How could you argue that a comprehensive federal domestic relations law is constitutional?

3. *Are There Limits to the Commerce Power?* Following decisions like *Darby*, *Wickard*, and *Heart of Atlanta*, is there anything that Congress cannot reach under its Commerce Clause power? For example, take a look around your classroom. Do you see anything that Congress cannot regulate under its Commerce Clause power? The blackboard? The desks? The chairs? The computer technology?

Note: Growth of the Modern Administrative State

The constitutional crisis of the 1930s brought with it the demise of the nondelegation doctrine — the idea that congressional power could not be delegated to Executive Branch officials or agencies. Decisions like *Panama Refining* and *Schechter*, which limited Congress's power to delegate, were effectively overruled. In later cases, the Court sustained increasingly broad assertions of power. Consider the following language from INS v. Chadha, 462 U.S. 919, 985 (1983): "In practice[,] restrictions on the scope of the power that could be delegated diminished and all but disappeared. [T]he 'intelligible principle' through which agencies have attained enormous control over the economic affairs of the country was held to include such formulations as 'just and reasonable,' *'public interest,'* 'public convenience, interest, or necessity,' and 'unfair methods of competition.'"

In recent decades, Congress has delegated more and more power to administrative agencies. As the District of Columbia Circuit recently noted, "administrative agencies may well have a more far-reaching effect on the daily lives of all citizens than do the combined actions of the executive, legislative and Judicial Branches. . . ." Ballerina Pen Co. v. Kunzig, 433 F.2d 1204, 1207-1208 (D.C. Cir. 1970), *cert. denied*, 401 U.S. 950 (1971). The growth of agency power is reflected in the size of the Code of Federal Regulations, which now includes 208 volumes.

Although the growth of administrative power may have been necessary, and perhaps inevitable, that growth has not been without costs. Justice Jackson stated that "[t]he rise of administrative bodies probably has been the most significant legal trend of the last century. . . . They have become a veritable fourth branch of the Government, which has deranged our three-branch legal theories. . . ." Federal Trade Commission v. Ruberoid Co., 343 U.S. 470, 487 (1952) (Jackson, J., dissenting).

5. Revolution and Retreat?

For half a century, the Court interpreted the Commerce Clause expansively in decisions like *Wickard* and *Heart of Atlanta*. Few saw any limits to Congress's authority under the Commerce Clause, and few saw the Tenth Amendment as having any impact on Congress's authority. Then the Court decided the following case.

United States v. Lopez

514 U.S. 549 (1995)

Chief Justice REHNQUIST delivered the opinion of the Court.

In the Gun-Free School Zones Act of 1990, Congress made it a federal offense "for any individual knowingly to possess a firearm at a place that the individual knows, or has reasonable cause to believe, is a school zone." 18 U.S.C. §922(q)(1)(A). The Act neither regulates a commercial activity nor contains a requirement that the possession be connected in any way to interstate commerce. We hold that the Act exceeds the authority of Congress "[t]o regulate Commerce [among] the several States. . . ." U.S. Const., Art. I, §8, cl. 3.

[R]espondent, who was then a 12th-grade student, arrived at Edison High School in San Antonio, Texas, carrying a concealed .38 caliber handgun and five bullets. . . . He was arrested and charged [with] violating the Gun-Free School Zones Act of 1990.

[We] start with first principles. The Constitution creates a Federal Government of enumerated powers. *See* U.S. Const., Art. I, §8. As James Madison wrote, "[t]he powers delegated by the proposed Constitution to the federal government are few and defined. Those which are to remain in the State governments are numerous and indefinite." *The Federalist No. 45*, pp. 292-293 (C. Rossiter ed. 1961). . . . The Court, through Chief Justice Marshall, first defined the nature of Congress' commerce power in Gibbons v. Ogden, 9 Wheat. 1, 6 L.Ed. 23 (1824). . . . For nearly a century thereafter, the Court's Commerce Clause decisions dealt but rarely with the extent of Congress' power. . . . In 1887, Congress enacted the Interstate Commerce Act, and in 1890, Congress enacted the Sherman Antitrust Act. These laws ushered in a new era of federal regulation under the commerce power. When cases involving these laws first reached this Court, we imported from our negative Commerce Clause cases the approach that Congress could not regulate activities such as "production," "manufacturing," and "mining." *See, e.g.*, Carter v. Carter Coal Co., 298 U.S. 238 (1936). Simultaneously, however, the Court held that, where the interstate and intrastate aspects of commerce were so mingled together that full regulation of interstate commerce required incidental regulation of intrastate commerce, the Commerce Clause authorized such regulation. *See, e.g.*, Houston, E. & W.T.R. Co. v. United States, 234 U.S. 342 (1914). . . .

Jones & Laughlin Steel, Darby, and *Wickard* ushered in an era of Commerce Clause jurisprudence that greatly expanded the previously defined authority of Congress under that Clause. In part, this was a recognition of the great changes that had occurred in the way business was carried on in this country. Enterprises that had once been local or at most regional in nature had become national in scope. But the doctrinal change also reflected a view that earlier Commerce Clause cases artificially had constrained the authority of Congress to regulate interstate commerce. . . . But even these modern-era precedents [confirmed] that this power is subject to outer limits. . . .

[W]e have identified three broad categories of activity that Congress may regulate under its commerce power. First, Congress may regulate the use of the channels of interstate commerce. Second, Congress is empowered to regulate and protect the instrumentalities of interstate commerce, or persons or things in interstate commerce, even though the threat may come only from intrastate activities. *See, e.g., Shreveport Rate Cases*, 234 U.S. 342 (1914). Finally, Congress' commerce authority includes the power to regulate those activities having a substantial relation to interstate commerce, i.e., those activities that substantially affect interstate commerce. [Maryland v. Wirtz, 392 U.S. 183 (1968).] Within this final category, admittedly, our case law has not been clear whether an activity must "affect" or "substantially affect" interstate commerce in order to be within Congress' power to regulate it under the Commerce Clause. We conclude, consistent with the great weight of our case law, that the proper test requires an analysis of whether the regulated activity "substantially affects" interstate commerce.

We now turn to consider the power of Congress [to] enact §922(q). The first two categories of authority may be quickly disposed of: §922(q) is not a regulation of the use of the channels of interstate commerce, nor is it an attempt to prohibit the interstate transportation of a commodity through the channels of commerce; nor can §922(q) be justified as a regulation by which Congress has sought to protect an instrumentality of interstate commerce or a thing in interstate commerce. Thus, if §922(q) is to be sustained, it must be under the third category as a regulation of an activity that substantially affects interstate commerce.

First, we have upheld a wide variety of congressional Acts regulating intrastate economic activity where we have concluded that the activity substantially affected interstate commerce. Examples include the regulation of intrastate coal mining, intrastate extortionate credit transactions, restaurants utilizing substantial interstate supplies, and hotels catering to interstate guests, and production and consumption of home-grown wheat. . . . Where economic activity substantially affects interstate commerce, legislation regulating that activity will be sustained. . . . Even *Wickard*, which is perhaps the most far reaching example of Commerce Clause authority over intrastate activity, involved economic activity in a way that the possession of a gun in a school zone does not. . . .

Section 922(q) is a criminal statute that by its terms has nothing to do with "commerce" or any sort of economic enterprise, however broadly one might define those terms. Section 922(q) is not an essential part of a larger regulation of economic activity, in which the regulatory scheme could be undercut unless the intrastate activity were regulated. It cannot, therefore, be sustained under our cases upholding regulations of activities that arise out of or are connected with a commercial transaction, which viewed in the aggregate, substantially affects interstate commerce.

Second, §922(q) contains no jurisdictional element which would ensure, through case-by-case inquiry, that the firearm possession in question affects interstate commerce. For example, in United States v. Bass, 404 U.S. 336 (1971), the Court interpreted former 18 U.S.C. §1202(a), which made it a crime for a felon to "receiv[e], posses[s], or transpor[t] in commerce or affecting commerce [any] firearm." The Court interpreted the possession component of §1202(a) to require an additional nexus to interstate commerce both because the statute was ambiguous and because "unless Congress conveys its purpose clearly, it will not be deemed to have significantly changed the federal-state balance." [§] 922(q) has no express jurisdictional element which might limit its reach to a discrete set of firearm possessions that additionally have an explicit connection with or effect on interstate commerce.

"[N]either the statute nor its legislative history contain[s] express congressional findings regarding the effects upon interstate commerce of gun possession in a school zone." [Congress] normally is not required to make formal findings as to the substantial burdens that an activity has on interstate commerce. But to the extent that congressional findings would enable us to evaluate the legislative judgment that the activity in question substantially affected interstate commerce, even though no such substantial effect was visible to the naked eye, they are lacking here. . . . The Government argues that Congress has accumulated institutional expertise regarding the regulation of firearms through previous enactments. [I]mportation of previous findings to justify §922(q) is especially inappropriate here because the "prior federal enactments or Congressional findings [do not] speak to the subject matter of section 922(q) or its relationship to interstate commerce." . . .

[The] Government argues that possession of a firearm in a school zone may result in violent crime and that violent crime can be expected to affect the functioning of the national economy in two ways. First, the costs of violent crime are substantial, and, through the mechanism of insurance, those costs are spread throughout the population. Second, violent crime reduces the willingness of individuals to travel to areas within the country that are perceived to be unsafe. The Government also argues that the presence of guns in schools poses a substantial threat to the educational process by threatening the learning environment. A handicapped educational process, in turn, will result in a less productive citizenry. That, in turn, would have an adverse effect on the Nation's economic well-being. As a result, the Government argues that Congress could rationally have concluded that §922(q) substantially affects interstate commerce.

[The] Government admits, under its "costs of crime" reasoning, that Congress could regulate not only all violent crime, but all activities that might lead to violent crime, regardless of how tenuously they relate to interstate commerce. Similarly, under the Government's "national productivity" reasoning, Congress could regulate any activity that it found was related to the economic productivity of individual citizens: family law (including marriage, divorce, and child custody), for example. Under the theories that the Government presents in support of §922(q), it is difficult to perceive any limitation on federal power, even in areas such as criminal law enforcement or education where States historically have been sovereign. Thus, if we were to accept the Government's arguments, we are hard-pressed to posit any activity by an individual that Congress is without power to regulate.

[I]f Congress can, pursuant to its Commerce Clause power, regulate activities that adversely affect the learning environment, then, a fortiori, it also can regulate the educational process directly. Congress could determine that a school's curriculum has a "significant" effect on the extent of classroom learning. As a result, Congress could mandate a federal curriculum for local elementary and secondary schools because what is taught in local schools has a significant "effect on classroom learning," and that, in turn, has a substantial effect on interstate commerce.

[The] possession of a gun in a local school zone is in no sense an economic activity that might, through repetition elsewhere, substantially affect any sort of interstate commerce. Respondent was a local student at a local school; there is no indication that he had recently moved in interstate commerce, and there is no requirement that his possession of the firearm have any concrete tie to interstate commerce.

To uphold the Government's contentions here, we would have to pile inference upon inference in a manner that would bid fair to convert congressional authority under the Commerce Clause to a general police power of the sort retained by the States. Admittedly, some of our prior cases have taken long steps down that road, giving great deference to congressional action. The broad language in these opinions has suggested the possibility of additional expansion, but we decline here to proceed any further. To do so would require us to conclude that the Constitution's enumeration of powers does not presuppose something not enumerated and that there never will be a distinction between what is truly national and what is truly local. This we are unwilling to do.

For the foregoing reasons the judgment of the Court of Appeals is
Affirmed.

Justice KENNEDY, with whom Justice O'CONNOR joins, concurring.

The statute before us upsets the federal balance to a degree that renders it an unconstitutional assertion of the commerce power. [U]nlike the earlier cases to come before the Court here neither the actors nor their conduct have a commercial character, and neither the purposes nor the design of the statute have an evident commercial nexus. The statute makes the simple possession of a gun within 1,000 feet of the grounds of the school a criminal offense. In a sense any conduct in this interdependent world of ours has an ultimate commercial origin or consequence, but we have not yet said the commerce power may reach so far. If Congress attempts that extension, then at the least we must inquire whether the exercise of national power seeks to intrude upon an area of traditional state concern. . . . While it is doubtful that any State, or indeed any reasonable person, would argue that it is wise policy to allow students to carry guns on school premises, considerable disagreement exists about how best to accomplish that goal. In this circumstance, [the] States may perform their role as laboratories for experimentation to devise various solutions. . . . Indeed, over 40 States already have criminal laws outlawing the possession of firearms on or near school grounds. . . . The statute now before us forecloses the States from experimenting and exercising their own judgment in an area to which States lay claim by right of history and expertise, and it does so by regulating an activity beyond the realm of commerce in the ordinary and usual sense of that term. . . .

Justice THOMAS, concurring.

[O]ur case law has drifted far from the original understanding of the Commerce Clause. . . . I believe that we must further reconsider our "substantial effects" test with an eye toward constructing a standard that reflects the text and history of the Commerce Clause without totally rejecting our more recent Commerce Clause jurisprudence. . . . The aggregation principle is clever, but has no stopping point. . . .

Justice STEVENS, dissenting.

[Guns] are both articles of commerce and articles that can be used to restrain commerce. Their possession is the consequence, either directly or indirectly, of commercial activity. . . . Congress' power to regulate commerce in firearms includes the power to prohibit possession of guns at any location because of their potentially harmful use; it necessarily follows that Congress may also prohibit their possession in particular markets. The market for the possession of handguns by school-age children is, distressingly, substantial. Whether or not the national interest in eliminating that market would have justified federal legislation in 1789, it surely does today.

Justice SOUTER, dissenting.

[The] practice of deferring to rationally based legislative judgments "is a paradigm of judicial restraint." In judicial review under the Commerce Clause, it reflects our respect for the institutional competence of the Congress on a subject expressly assigned to it by the Constitution and our appreciation of the legitimacy that comes from Congress's political accountability in dealing with matters open to a wide range of possible choices. [I]t seems fair to ask whether the step taken by the Court today does anything but portend a return to the untenable jurisprudence from which the Court extricated itself almost 60 years ago. The answer is not reassuring. . . . Further glosses on rationality review [may] be in the offing. . . .

[The] suggestion is either that a connection between commerce and these subjects is remote, or that the commerce power is simply weaker when it touches subjects on which the States have historically been the primary legislators. Neither suggestion is tenable. As for remoteness, [the] commercial prospects of an illiterate State or Nation are not rosy. . . . And as for the notion that the commerce power diminishes the closer it gets to customary state concerns, that idea has been flatly rejected, and not long ago. The commerce power, we have often observed, is plenary. . . .

Justice BREYER, with whom Justice STEVENS, Justice SOUTER, and Justice GINSBURG join, dissenting.

[R]eports, hearings, and other readily available literature make clear that the problem of guns in and around schools is widespread and extremely serious. . . . And, they report that this widespread violence in schools throughout the Nation significantly interferes with the quality of education in those schools. Based on reports such as these, Congress obviously could have thought that guns and learning are mutually exclusive. And, Congress could therefore have found a substantial educational problem — teachers unable to teach, students unable to learn — and concluded that guns near schools contribute substantially to the size and scope of that problem.

Having found that guns in schools significantly undermine the quality of education in our Nation's classrooms, Congress could also have found [that] gun-related violence in and around schools is a commercial, as well as a human, problem. Education, although far more than a matter of economics, has long been inextricably intertwined with the Nation's economy. . . . Scholars estimate that nearly a quarter of America's economic growth in the early years of this century is traceable directly to increased schooling; that investment in "human capital" (through spending on education) exceeded investment in "physical capital" by a ratio of almost two to one; and that the economic returns to this investment in education exceeded the returns to conventional capital investment. . . . In recent years the link between secondary education and business has strengthened, becoming both more direct and more important. . . . Increasing global competition also has made primary and secondary education economically more important. . . . Finally, there is evidence that [many] firms base their location decisions upon the presence [of] a work force with a basic education. . . .

The third legal problem created by the Court's holding is that it threatens legal uncertainty in an area of law that, until this case, seemed reasonably well settled. Congress has enacted many statutes [including] criminal statutes, that use the words "affecting commerce" to define their scope, and other statutes that contain no jurisdictional language at all. . . .

∾ PROBLEMS ∾

1. *More on the Gun-Free School Zones Act.* In passing the Gun-Free School Zones Act, could Congress have done anything differently that would have resulted in the law being upheld? If so, what? If you had been counsel to the relevant committees, what would you have advised?

2. *More on the Education for a Better America Act.* Does *Lopez* suggest that Congress might have difficulty passing the proposed legislation? In light of *Lopez*, what might Congress be allowed to do (or precluded from doing)? How does the Tenth Amendment come into play?

United States v. Morrison

529 U.S. 598 (2000)

Chief Justice REHNQUIST delivered the opinion of the Court.

In these cases we consider the constitutionality of 42 U.S.C. §13981, which provides a federal civil remedy for the victims of gender-motivated violence. The United States Court of Appeals for the Fourth Circuit, sitting en banc, struck down §13981 because it concluded that Congress lacked constitutional authority to enact the section's civil remedy. [W]e affirm.

Petitioner Christy Brzonkala enrolled at Virginia Polytechnic Institute (Virginia Tech) in the fall of 1994. In September[,] Brzonkala met [respondents] Morrison [and] Crawford, who were both students at Virginia Tech and members of its varsity football team. Brzonkala alleges [that] Morrison and Crawford [assaulted] and repeatedly raped her. After the attack, Morrison allegedly told Brzonkala, "You better not have any . . . diseases." In the months following the rape, Morrison also allegedly announced in the dormitory's dining room that he "like[d] to get girls drunk and. . . ." The omitted portions [consist] of boasting, debased remarks about what Morrison would do to women, vulgar remarks that cannot fail to shock and offend. . . . Brzonkala alleges that this attack caused her to become severely emotionally disturbed and depressed. She sought assistance from a university psychiatrist, who prescribed antidepressant medication. Shortly after the rape Brzonkala stopped attending classes and withdrew from the university. . . . In early 1995, Brzonkala filed a complaint against respondents under Virginia Tech's Sexual Assault Policy. Morrison was found guilty of sexual assault and suspended for two semesters. The University later reopened the case and found Morrison guilty only of "using abusive language," [but this finding was set aside.] Virginia Tech did not inform Brzonkala of this decision. After learning from a newspaper that Morrison would be returning to Virginia Tech for the fall 1995 semester, she dropped out of the university.

In December 1995, Brzonkala sued Morrison, Crawford, and Virginia Tech in the United States District Court for the Western District of Virginia [alleging a violation of] §13981. . . . The District Court [dismissed] the complaint because it concluded that Congress lacked authority to enact the section under either the Commerce Clause or §5 of the Fourteenth Amendment. A divided panel of the Court of Appeals [reversed, but the] full Court of Appeals [concluded] that Congress lacked constitutional authority to enact §13981's civil remedy. [W]e granted certiorari.

Section 13981 was part of the Violence Against Women Act of 1994. It states that "[a]ll persons within the United States shall have the right to be free from crimes of violence motivated by gender." To enforce that right, subsection (c) declares:

> A person (including a person who acts under color of any statute, ordinance, regulation, custom, or usage of any State) who commits a crime of violence motivated by gender and thus deprives another of the right declared in subsection (b) of this section shall be liable to the party injured, in an action for the recovery of compensatory and punitive damages, injunctive and declaratory relief, and such other relief as a court may deem appropriate.

Section 13981 defines a "crim[e] of violence motivated by gender" as "a crime of violence committed because of gender or on the basis of gender, and due, at least in part, to an animus based on the victim's gender." §13981(d)(1). It also provides that the term "crime of violence" includes any

> (A) . . . act or series of acts that would constitute a felony against the person or that would constitute a felony against property if the conduct presents a serious risk of physical injury to another, and that would come within the meaning of State or Federal offenses described in

section 16 of Title 18, whether or not those acts have actually resulted in criminal charges, prosecution, or conviction and whether or not those acts were committed in the special maritime, territorial, or prison jurisdiction of the United States; and

(B) includes an act or series of acts that would constitute a felony described in subparagraph (A) but for the relationship between the person who takes such action and the individual against whom such action is taken.

Further clarifying the broad scope of §13981's civil remedy, subsection (e)(2) states that "[n]othing in this section requires a prior criminal complaint, prosecution, or conviction to establish the elements of cause of action under subsection (c) of this section." And subsection (e)(3) provides a §13981 litigant with choice of forums: Federal and state courts "shall have concurrent jurisdiction" over complaints brought under the section.

Although the foregoing language of §13981 covers a wide swath of criminal conduct, Congress placed some limitations on the section's federal civil remedy. Subsection (e)(1) states that "[n]othing in this section entitles a person to a cause of action under subsection (c) of this section for random acts of violence unrelated to gender or for acts that cannot be demonstrated, by a preponderance of the evidence, to be motivated by gender." Subsection (e)(4) further states that §13981 shall not be construed "to confer on the courts of the United States jurisdiction over any State law claim seeking the establishment of a divorce, alimony, equitable distribution of marital property, or child custody decree."

Every law enacted by Congress must be based on one or more of its powers enumerated in the Constitution. . . . Congress explicitly identified the sources of federal authority on which it relied in enacting §13981. It said that a "Federal civil rights cause of action" is established "[p]ursuant to the affirmative power of Congress . . . under section 5 of the Fourteenth Amendment to the Constitution, as well as under section 8 of Article I of the Constitution." We address Congress' authority to enact this remedy under each of these constitutional provisions in turn.

Due respect for the decisions of a coordinate branch of Government demands that we invalidate a congressional enactment only upon a plain showing that Congress has exceeded its constitutional bounds. *See* United States v. Lopez, 514 U.S., at 568 (Kennedy, J., concurring). . . . [As discussed] in *Lopez*, our interpretation of the Commerce Clause has changed as our Nation has developed. We need not repeat that detailed review of the Commerce Clause's history here; it suffices to say that, in the years since NLRB v. Jones & Laughlin Steel Corp., 301 U.S. 1 (1937), Congress has had considerably greater latitude in regulating conduct and transactions under the Commerce Clause than our previous case law permitted.

Lopez emphasized, however, that even under our modern, expansive interpretation of the Commerce Clause, Congress' regulatory authority is not without effective bounds. . . . As we observed in *Lopez*, modern Commerce Clause jurisprudence has "identified three broad categories of activity that Congress may regulate under its commerce power." "First, Congress may regulate the use of the channels of interstate commerce." "Second, Congress is empowered to regulate and protect the instrumentalities of interstate commerce, or persons or things in interstate commerce, even though the threat may come only from intrastate activities." "Finally, Congress' commerce authority includes the power to regulate those activities having a substantial relation to interstate commerce, . . . i.e., those activities that substantially affect interstate commerce."

Petitioners do not contend that these cases fall within either of the first two of these categories of Commerce Clause regulation. They seek to sustain §13981 as a regulation of activity that substantially affects interstate commerce. [Under *Lopez*,] the proper resolution of the present cases is clear. Gender-motivated crimes of violence are not, in any sense of the phrase, economic activity. While we need not adopt a categorical rule against aggregating the effects of any noneconomic activity in order to decide these cases, thus far in our Nation's history our cases have upheld Commerce Clause regulation of intrastate activity only where that activity is economic in nature. . . . §13981 contains no jurisdictional element establishing that the federal cause of action is in pursuance of Congress' power to regulate interstate commerce. . . . §13981 *is* supported by numerous findings regarding the serious impact that gender-motivated violence has on victims and their families. But the existence of congressional findings is not sufficient, by itself, to sustain the constitutionality of Commerce Clause legislation. As we stated in *Lopez*, . . . "[w]hether particular operations affect interstate commerce sufficiently to come under the constitutional power of Congress to regulate them is ultimately a judicial rather than a legislative question, and can be settled finally only by this Court."

In these cases, Congress' findings are substantially weakened by the fact that they rely so heavily on a method of reasoning that we have already rejected as unworkable if we are to maintain the Constitution's enumeration of powers. Congress found that gender-motivated violence affects interstate commerce "by deterring potential victims from traveling interstate, from engaging in employment in interstate business, and from transacting with business, and in places involved in interstate commerce; . . . by diminishing national productivity, increasing medical and other costs, and decreasing the supply of and the demand for interstate products." Given these findings[,] the concern that we expressed in *Lopez* that Congress might use the Commerce Clause to completely obliterate the Constitution's distinction between national and local authority seems well founded. The reasoning that petitioners advance seeks to follow the but-for causal chain from the initial occurrence of violent crime (the suppression of which has always been the prime object of the States' police power) to every attenuated effect upon interstate commerce. If accepted, petitioners' reasoning would allow Congress to regulate any crime as long as the nationwide, aggregated impact of that crime has substantial effects on employment, production, transit, or consumption. Indeed, if Congress may regulate gender-motivated violence, it would be able to regulate murder or any other type of violence since gender-motivated violence, as a subset of all violent crime, is certain to have lesser economic impacts than the larger class of which it is a part.

Petitioners' reasoning, moreover, will not limit Congress to regulating violence but may, as we suggested in *Lopez*, be applied equally as well to family law and other areas of traditional state regulation since the aggregate effect of marriage, divorce, and childrearing on the national economy is undoubtedly significant. Congress may have recognized this specter when it expressly precluded §13981 from being used in the family law context. Under our written Constitution, however, the limitation of congressional authority is not solely a matter of legislative grace.

No doubt the political branches have a role in interpreting and applying the Constitution, but ever since *Marbury* this Court has remained the ultimate expositor of the constitutional text. . . . We [reject] the argument that Congress may regulate noneconomic, violent criminal conduct based solely on that conduct's aggregate effect on interstate commerce. The Constitution requires a distinction between what is truly national and what is truly local. . . . The regulation and punishment of intrastate violence that is not directed at the instrumentalities, channels, or goods involved in interstate commerce has always been the province of the States. *See, e.g.,* Cohens v. Virginia, 6 Wheat. 264, 5 L.Ed. 257 (1821) (Marshall, C.J.). Indeed, we can think of no better example of the police power, which the Founders denied the National Government and reposed in the States, than the suppression of violent crime and vindication of its victims. *See, e.g., Lopez,* 514 U.S., at 566 ("The Constitution . . . withhold[s] from Congress a plenary police power").

[P]etitioners' [argue] that the section's civil remedy should be upheld as an exercise of Congress' remedial power under §5 of the Fourteenth Amendment. . . . Section 5 states that Congress may "'enforce' by 'appropriate legislation' the constitutional guarantee that no State shall deprive any person of 'life, liberty, or property, without due process of law,' nor deny any person 'equal protection of the laws.'" City of Boerne v. Flores, 521 U.S. 507 (1997). . . . Petitioners' §5 argument is founded on an assertion that there is pervasive bias in various state justice systems against victims of gender-motivated violence. . . . Congress concluded [that] discriminatory stereotypes often result in insufficient investigation and prosecution of gender-motivated crime, inappropriate focus on the behavior and credibility of the victims of that crime, and unacceptably lenient punishments for those who are actually convicted of gender-motivated violence. Petitioners contend that this bias denies victims of gender-motivated violence the equal protection of the laws and that Congress therefore acted appropriately in enacting a private civil remedy against the perpetrators of gender-motivated violence to both remedy the States' bias and deter future instances of discrimination in the state courts.

[It is a] time-honored principle that the Fourteenth Amendment, by its very terms, prohibits only state action. . . . Section 13981 is not aimed [at] any State or state actor, but at individuals who have committed criminal acts motivated by gender bias. . . . §13981 visits no consequence whatever on any Virginia public official involved in investigating or prosecuting Brzonkala's assault. . . . Section 13981 is also different [in] that it applies uniformly throughout the Nation. Congress' findings indicate that the problem of discrimination against the victims of gender-motivated crimes does not exist in all States, or even most States. By contrast, the §5 remedy upheld in Katzenbach v. Morgan, *supra,* was directed only to the State where the evil found by Congress existed, and in South Carolina v. Katzenbach, *supra,* the remedy was directed only to those States in which Congress found that there had been discrimination. For these reasons, we conclude that Congress' power under §5 does not extend to the enactment of §13981.

Petitioner Brzonkala's complaint alleges that she was the victim of a brutal assault. But Congress' effort in §13981 to provide a federal civil remedy can be sustained neither under the Commerce Clause nor under §5 of the Fourteenth Amendment. If the allegations here are true, no civilized system of justice could fail to provide her a remedy for the conduct of respondent Morrison. But under our federal system that remedy must be provided by the Commonwealth of Virginia, and not by the United States. The judgment of the Court of Appeals is
Affirmed.

Justice THOMAS, concurring.

[T]he very notion of a "substantial effects" test under the Commerce Clause is inconsistent with the original understanding of Congress' powers and with this Court's early Commerce Clause cases. . . . Until this Court replaces its existing Commerce Clause jurisprudence with a standard more consistent with the original understanding, we will continue to see Congress appropriating state police powers under the guise of regulating commerce.

Justice SOUTER, with whom Justice STEVENS, Justice GINSBURG, and Justice BREYER join, dissenting.

[One] obvious difference from *Lopez* is the mountain of data assembled by Congress here showing the effects of violence against women on interstate commerce. Passage of the Act in 1994 was preceded by four years of hearings, which included testimony from physicians and law professors; from survivors of rape and domestic violence; and from representatives of state law enforcement and private business. The record includes reports on gender bias from task forces in 21 States, and we have the benefit of specific factual findings in the eight separate Reports issued by Congress and its committees over the long course leading to enactment.

With respect to domestic violence, Congress received evidence for the following findings:

> Three out of four American women will be victims of violent crimes sometime during their life.
> Violence is the leading cause of injuries to women ages 15 to 44. . . .
> [A]s many as 50 percent of homeless women and children are fleeing domestic violence.
> Since 1974, the assault rate against women has outstripped the rate for men by at least twice for some age groups and far more for others.
> [B]attering "is the single largest cause of injury to women in the United States."
> An estimated 4 million American women are battered each year by their husbands or partners.
> Over 1 million women in the United States seek medical assistance each year for injuries sustained [from] their husbands or other partners.
> Between 2,000 and 4,000 women die every year from [domestic] abuse.
> [A]rrest rates may be as low as 1 for every 100 domestic assaults.

Partial estimates show that violent crime against women costs this country at least 3 billion — not million, but billion — dollars a year.

[E]stimates suggest that we spend $5 to $10 billion a year on health care, criminal justice, and other social costs of domestic violence.

The evidence as to rape was similarly extensive, supporting these conclusions:

[The incidence of] rape rose four times as fast as the total national crime rate over the past 10 years.

According to one study, close to half a million girls now in high school will be raped before they graduate.

[One hundred twenty-five thousand] college women can expect to be raped during this — or any — year.

[T]hree-quarters of women never go to the movies alone after dark because of the fear of rape and nearly 50 percent do not use public transit alone after dark for the same reason.

[Forty-one] percent of judges surveyed believed that juries give sexual assault victims less credibility than other crime victims.

Less than 1 percent of all [rape] victims have collected damages.

[A]n individual who commits rape has only about 4 chances in 100 of being arrested, prosecuted, and found guilty of any offense.

Almost one-quarter of convicted rapists never go to prison and another quarter received sentences in local jails where the average sentence is 11 months.

[A]lmost 50 percent of rape victims lose their jobs or are forced to quit because of the crime's severity.

Based on the data thus partially summarized, Congress found that

crimes of violence motivated by gender have a substantial adverse effect on interstate commerce, by deterring potential victims from traveling interstate, from engaging in employment in interstate business, and from transacting with business, and in places involved, in interstate commerce[,] by diminishing national productivity, increasing medical and other costs, and decreasing the supply of and the demand for interstate products. . . .

Congress thereby explicitly stated the predicate for the exercise of its Commerce Clause power. Is its conclusion irrational in view of the data amassed? [T]he sufficiency of the evidence [cannot] seriously be questioned.

[T]he legislative record here is far more voluminous than the record compiled by Congress and found sufficient in two prior cases upholding Title II of the Civil Rights Act of 1964 against Commerce Clause challenges. [Congress relied] on evidence of the harms caused by domestic violence and sexual assault, citing annual costs of $3 billion in 1990, and $5 to $10 billion in 1993. Equally important, though, gender-based violence in the 1990s was shown to operate in a manner similar to racial discrimination in the 1960s in reducing the mobility of employees and their production and consumption of goods shipped in interstate commerce. Like racial discrimination, "[g]ender-based violence bars its most likely targets—women—from full partic[ipation] in the national economy."

[In] *Wickard*, [the] Commerce Clause predicate was simply the effect of the production of wheat for home consumption on supply and demand in interstate commerce. Supply and demand for goods in interstate commerce will also be affected by the deaths of 2,000 to 4,000 women annually at the hands of domestic abusers, and by the reduction in the work force by the 100,000 or more rape victims who lose their jobs each year or are forced to quit. Violence against women may be found to affect interstate commerce and affect it substantially.

The Act would have passed muster at any time between *Wickard* in 1942 and *Lopez* in 1995, a period in which the law enjoyed a stable understanding that congressional power under the Commerce Clause, complemented by the authority of the Necessary and Proper Clause, extended to all activity that, when aggregated, has a substantial effect on interstate commerce. . . . The fact that the Act does not pass muster before the Court today is therefore proof, to a degree that *Lopez* was not, that the Court's nominal adherence to the substantial effects test is merely that. [S]ome congressional conclusions about obviously substantial, cumulative effects on commerce are being assigned lesser values than the once-stable doctrine would assign them. . . .

[O]ne might reasonably have doubted that Members of this Court would ever again toy with a return to the days before NLRB v. Jones & Laughlin Steel Corp., 301 U.S. 1 (1937), which brought the earlier and nearly disastrous experiment to an end. And yet today's decision can only be seen as a step toward recapturing the prior mistakes. Its revival of a distinction between commercial and noncommercial conduct is at odds with *Wickard*, which repudiated that analysis, and the enquiry into commercial purpose, first intimated by the *Lopez* concurrence is cousin to the intent-based analysis employed in *Hammer*, but rejected for Commerce Clause purposes in *Heart of Atlanta* and *Darby*.

The Court finds it relevant that the statute addresses conduct traditionally subject to state prohibition under domestic criminal law, a fact said to have some heightened significance when the violent conduct in question is not itself aimed directly at interstate commerce or its instrumentalities. Again, history seems to be recycling, for the theory of traditional state concern as grounding a limiting principle has been rejected previously, and more than once. . . .

[T]he Founders' considered judgment [was] that politics, not judicial review, should mediate between state and national interests. . . . Whereas today's majority takes a leaf from the book of the old judicial economists in saying that the Court should somehow draw the line to keep the federal relationship in a proper balance, Madison, Wilson, and Marshall understood the Constitution very differently. . . . All of this convinces me that today's ebb of the commerce power rests on error, and at the same time leads me to doubt that the majority's view will prove to be enduring law. . . .

Justice BREYER, with whom Justice STEVENS joins, and with whom Justice SOUTER and Justice GINSBURG join as to Part I-A, dissenting.

[The] "economic/noneconomic" distinction is not easy to apply. Does the local street corner mugger engage in "economic" activity or "noneconomic" activity when he mugs for money? Would evidence that desire for economic domination underlies many brutal crimes against women save the present statute? [The] Court itself would permit Congress to aggregate, hence regulate, "noneconomic" activity taking place at economic establishments. *See* Heart of Atlanta Motel, Inc. v. United States, 379 U.S. 241 (1964). And it would permit Congress to regulate where that regulation is "an essential part of a larger regulation of economic activity, in which the regulatory scheme could be undercut unless the intrastate activity were regulated." Given the former exception, can Congress simply rewrite the present law and limit its application to restaurants, hotels, perhaps universities, and other places of public accommodation? Given the latter exception, can Congress save the present law by including it, or much of it, in a broader "Safe Transport" or "Workplace Safety" act?

Notes and Questions

1. *Rewriting the Act.* At the end of his dissent, Justice Breyer asks whether Congress can "simply rewrite the present law and limit its application to restaurants, hotels, perhaps universities, and other places of public accommodation? Given the latter exception, can Congress save the present law by including it, or much of it, in a broader 'Safe Transport' or 'Workplace Safety' act?" May it?

2. *Impact on Prior Decisions.* How much do *Lopez* and *Morrison* impact the Court's Commerce Clause jurisprudence? In light of those decisions, should the Court overrule *Heart of Atlanta*, in which the Court applied the 1964 Civil Rights Act to racial discrimination by hotels? Should it overrule United States v. Darby, in which Congress prohibited the employment of workmen in the production of goods "for interstate commerce" at other than prescribed wages and hours?

3. *Has the Governing Test Changed?* At first blush, it seemed that the decision in *Heart of Atlanta* had broadly defined the term *commerce* as well as the reach of Congress's power under the Commerce Clause. "In short, the determinative test of the exercise of power by Congress under the Commerce Clause is simply whether the activity sought to be regulated is 'commerce which concerns more States than one' and has *a real and substantial relation to the national interest.*" *Heart of Atlanta,* 379 U.S. at 255. Is this still the determinative test after *Lopez* and *Morrison*?

∾ PROBLEMS ∾

1. *General Criminal Legislation.* In an earlier problem, you were asked to think about whether cases like *Darby* and *Wickard* could be construed to authorize Congress to pass a comprehensive criminal statute. After *Lopez*, do you reach the same conclusions regarding Congress's power over these issues? Similarly, do you have additional thoughts about whether Congress may pass a comprehensive law governing divorce? After reading *Lopez*, do you see Congress's power differently?

2. *More on the Education for a Better America Act.* How does *Morrison* affect your analysis of whether Congress can pass the legislation? Can Congress include specific mandates (e.g., requiring school tests and specific types of teacher training) as well as just spending incentives?

Gonzales v. Raich

125 S.Ct. 2195 (2005)

Justice STEVENS delivered the opinion of the Court.

California is one of at least nine States that authorize the use of marijuana for medicinal purposes. The question presented in this case is whether the power vested in Congress by Article I, §8, of the Constitution "[t]o make all Laws which shall be necessary and proper for carrying into Execution" its authority to "regulate Commerce with foreign Nations, and among the several States" includes the power to prohibit the local cultivation and use of marijuana in compliance with California law.

[In] 1996, California voters passed Proposition 215, now codified as the Compassionate Use Act of 1996. The proposition was designed to ensure that "seriously ill" residents of the State have access to marijuana for medical purposes, and to encourage Federal and State Governments to take steps towards ensuring the safe and affordable distribution of the drug to patients in need. The Act creates an exemption from criminal prosecution for physicians, as well as for patients and primary caregivers who possess or cultivate marijuana for medicinal purposes with the recommendation or approval of a physician. A "primary caregiver" is a person who has consistently assumed responsibility for the housing, health, or safety of the patient.

Respondents Angel Raich and Diane Monson are California residents who suffer from a variety of serious medical conditions and have sought to avail themselves of medical marijuana pursuant to the terms of the Compassionate Use Act. They are being treated by licensed, board-certified family practitioners, who have concluded, after prescribing a host of conventional medicines to treat respondents' conditions and to alleviate their associated symptoms, that marijuana is the only drug available that provides effective treatment. Both women have been using marijuana as a medication for several years pursuant to their doctors' recommendation, and both rely heavily on cannabis to function on a daily basis. Indeed, Raich's physician believes that forgoing cannabis treatments would certainly cause Raich excruciating pain and could very well prove fatal.

Respondent Monson cultivates her own marijuana, and ingests the drug in a variety of ways including smoking and using a vaporizer. Respondent Raich, by contrast, is unable to cultivate her own, and thus relies on two caregivers, litigating as "John Does," to provide her with locally grown marijuana at no charge. These caregivers also process the cannabis into hashish or keif, and Raich herself processes some of the marijuana into oils, balms, and foods for consumption.

On August 15, 2002, county deputy sheriffs and agents from the federal Drug Enforcement Administration (DEA) came to Monson's home. [T]he county officials concluded that her use of marijuana was entirely lawful as a matter of California law. Nevertheless, after a 3-hour standoff, the federal agents seized and destroyed all six of her cannabis plants.

Respondents thereafter brought this action against the Attorney General of the United States and the head of the DEA seeking injunctive and declaratory relief prohibiting the enforcement of the federal Controlled Substances Act

(CSA), 21 U.S.C. §801 *et seq.*, to the extent it prevents them from possessing, obtaining, or manufacturing cannabis for their personal medical use. . . . The District Court denied respondents' motion for a preliminary injunction. . . . A divided panel of the Court of Appeals for the Ninth Circuit reversed [placing] heavy reliance on our decisions in United States v. Lopez, 514 U.S. 549 (1995), and United States v. Morrison, 529 U.S. 598 (2000), [to] hold that this separate class of purely local activities was beyond the reach of federal power. [We] vacate the judgment of the Court of Appeals.

[In 1970,] Congress enacted the Comprehensive Drug Abuse Prevention and Control Act [CSA, which] repealed most of the earlier antidrug laws in favor of a comprehensive regime to combat the international and interstate traffic in illicit drugs. The main objectives of the CSA were to conquer drug abuse and to control the legitimate and illegitimate traffic in controlled substances. Congress was particularly concerned with the need to prevent the diversion of drugs from legitimate to illicit channels.

To effectuate these goals, Congress devised a closed regulatory system making it unlawful to manufacture, distribute, dispense, or possess any controlled substance except in a manner authorized by the CSA. The CSA categorizes all controlled substances into five schedules. The drugs are grouped together based on their accepted medical uses, the potential for abuse, and their psychological and physical effects on the body. Each schedule is associated with a distinct set of controls regarding the manufacture, distribution, and use of the substances listed therein. The CSA and its implementing regulations set forth strict requirements regarding registration, labeling and packaging, production quotas, drug security, and recordkeeping.

In enacting the CSA, Congress classified marijuana as a Schedule I drug. . . . Schedule I drugs are categorized as such because of their high potential for abuse, lack of any accepted medical use, and absence of any accepted safety for use in medically supervised treatment. . . . By classifying marijuana as a Schedule I drug, [the] manufacture, distribution, or possession of marijuana became a criminal offense, with the sole exception being use of the drug as part of a Food and Drug Administration pre-approved research study. . . . Despite considerable efforts to reschedule marijuana, it remains a Schedule I drug.

Respondents [argue] that the CSA's categorical prohibition of the manufacture and possession of marijuana as applied to the intrastate manufacture and possession of marijuana for medical purposes pursuant to California law exceeds Congress' authority under the Commerce Clause. [The] Commerce Clause emerged as the Framers' response to the central problem giving rise to the Constitution itself: the absence of any federal commerce power under the Articles of Confederation. For the first century of our history, the primary use of the Clause was to preclude the kind of discriminatory state legislation that had once been permissible. Then, in response to rapid industrial development and an increasingly interdependent national economy, Congress "ushered in a new era of federal regulation under the commerce power," beginning with the enactment of the Interstate Commerce Act in 1887 and the Sherman Antitrust Act in 1890.

Our case law firmly establishes Congress' power to regulate purely local activities that are part of an economic "class of activities" that have a substantial effect on interstate commerce. *See, e.g.*, Wickard v. Filburn, 317 U.S. 111 (1942). . . . When Congress decides that the "'total incidence'" of a practice poses a threat to a national market, it may regulate the entire class. In this vein, we have reiterated that when "a general regulatory statute bears a substantial relation to commerce, the *de minimis* character of individual instances arising under that statute is of no consequence." . . . Congress can regulate purely intrastate activity that is not itself "commercial," in that it is not produced for sale, if it concludes that failure to regulate that class of activity would undercut the regulation of the interstate market in that commodity.

The similarities between this case and *Wickard* are striking. Like the farmer in *Wickard*, respondents are cultivating, for home consumption, a fungible commodity for which there is an established, albeit illegal, interstate market. Just as the Agricultural Adjustment Act was designed "to control the volume [of wheat] moving in interstate and foreign commerce in order to avoid surpluses . . ." and consequently control the market price, a primary purpose of the CSA is to control the supply and demand of controlled substances in both lawful and unlawful drug markets. In *Wickard*, we had no difficulty concluding that Congress had a rational basis for believing that, when viewed in the aggregate, leaving home-consumed wheat outside the regulatory scheme would have a substantial influence on price and market conditions. Here too, Congress had a rational basis for concluding that leaving home-consumed marijuana outside federal control would similarly affect price and market conditions.

More concretely, one concern prompting inclusion of wheat grown for home consumption in the 1938 Act was that rising market prices could draw such wheat into the interstate market, resulting in lower market prices. The parallel concern making it appropriate to include marijuana grown for home consumption in the CSA is the likelihood that the high demand in the interstate market will draw such marijuana into that market. [T]he diversion of homegrown marijuana tends to frustrate the federal interest in eliminating commercial transactions in the interstate market in their entirety. In both cases, the regulation is squarely within Congress' commerce power because production of the commodity meant for home consumption, be it wheat or marijuana, has a substantial effect on supply and demand in the national market for that commodity.[1]

[R]espondents suggest that *Wickard* differs from this case in three respects: (1) the Agricultural Adjustment Act, unlike the CSA, exempted small farming operations; (2) *Wickard* involved a "quintessential economic activity" — a commercial farm — whereas respondents do not sell marijuana; and (3) the *Wickard* record made it clear that the aggregate production of wheat for use on farms had

---

1. To be sure, the wheat market is a lawful market that Congress sought to protect and stabilize, whereas the marijuana market is an unlawful market. . . . This difference [is] of no constitutional import. [The] power to regulate commerce includes the power to prohibit commerce in a particular commodity.

a significant impact on market prices. Those differences, though factually accurate, do not diminish the precedential force of this Court's reasoning.

The fact that Wickard's own impact on the market was "trivial by itself" was not a sufficient reason for removing him from the scope of federal regulation. [W]hile it is true that the record in the *Wickard* case itself established the causal connection between the production for local use and the national market, [f]indings in the introductory sections of the CSA explain [that the] national, and international, market for marijuana has dimensions that are fully comparable to those defining the class of activities regulated by the Secretary pursuant to the 1938 statute. . . . In assessing the scope of Congress' authority under the Commerce Clause, [we] need not determine whether respondents' activities, taken in the aggregate, substantially affect interstate commerce in fact, but only whether a "rational basis" exists for so concluding. Given the enforcement difficulties that attend distinguishing between marijuana cultivated locally and marijuana grown elsewhere, and concerns about diversion into illicit channels, we have no difficulty concluding that Congress had a rational basis for believing that failure to regulate the intrastate manufacture and possession of marijuana would leave a gaping hole in the CSA. [A]s in *Wickard*[,] Congress was acting well within its authority to "make all Laws which shall be necessary and proper" to "regulate Commerce . . . among the several States." That the regulation ensnares some purely intrastate activity is of no moment. [W]e refuse to excise individual components of that larger scheme.

[R]espondents rely heavily [on] *Lopez* and *Morrison* [and] ask us to excise individual applications of a concededly valid statutory scheme. [In] both *Lopez* and *Morrison,* the parties asserted that a particular statute or provision fell outside Congress' commerce power in its entirety. This distinction is pivotal for we have often reiterated that "[w]here the class of activities is regulated and that class is within the reach of federal power, the courts have no power 'to excise, as trivial, individual instances' of the class."

At issue in *Lopez* was the validity of the Gun-Free School Zones Act of 1990, which was a brief, single-subject statute making it a crime for an individual to possess a gun in a school zone. The Act did not regulate any economic activity and did not contain any requirement that the possession of a gun have any connection to past interstate activity or a predictable impact on future commercial activity. . . . The statutory scheme that the Government is defending in this litigation is at the opposite end of the regulatory spectrum. [T]he CSA [was] a lengthy and detailed statute creating a comprehensive framework for regulating the production, distribution, and possession of five classes of "controlled substances." Most of those substances . . . "have a useful and legitimate medical purpose and are necessary to maintain the health and general welfare of the American people." The regulatory scheme is designed to foster the beneficial use of those medications, to prevent their misuse, and to prohibit entirely the possession or use of substances listed in Schedule I, except as a part of a strictly controlled research project. [The classification of marijuana] was merely one of many "essential part[s] of a larger regulation of economic activity, in which the regulatory scheme could be undercut unless the intrastate activity were regulated." Our opinion in *Lopez* casts no doubt on the validity of such a program.

Nor does this Court's holding in *Morrison*. The Violence Against Women Act of 1994 created a federal civil remedy for the victims of gender-motivated crimes of violence. 42 U.S.C. §13981. . . . Despite congressional findings that such crimes had an adverse impact on interstate commerce, we held the statute unconstitutional because [it] did not regulate economic activity. We concluded that "the noneconomic, criminal nature of the conduct at issue was central to our decision" in *Lopez*, and that our prior cases had identified a clear pattern of analysis: "Where economic activity substantially affects interstate commerce, legislation regulating that activity will be sustained."

Unlike those at issue in *Lopez* and *Morrison,* the activities regulated by the CSA are quintessentially economic. . . . The CSA is a statute that regulates the production, distribution, and consumption of commodities for which there is an established, and lucrative, interstate market. Prohibiting the intrastate possession or manufacture of an article of commerce is a rational (and commonly utilized) means of regulating commerce in that product. . . . Because the CSA is a statute that directly regulates economic, commercial activity, our opinion in *Morrison* casts no doubt on its constitutionality.

The Court of Appeals [concluded] otherwise only by isolating a "separate and distinct" class of activities that it held to be beyond the reach of federal power, defined as "the intrastate, noncommercial cultivation, possession and use of marijuana for personal medical purposes on the advice of a physician and in accordance with state law." [We] have no difficulty concluding that Congress acted rationally in determining that none of the characteristics making up the purported class, whether viewed individually or in the aggregate, compelled an exemption from the CSA; rather, the subdivided class of activities defined by the Court of Appeals was an essential part of the larger regulatory scheme.

First, the fact that marijuana is used "for personal medical purposes on the advice of a physician" cannot itself serve as a distinguishing factor. [E]ven if respondents are correct that marijuana does have accepted medical uses and thus should be redesignated as a lesser schedule drug,[2] the CSA would still [require] manufacturers, physicians, pharmacies, and other handlers of controlled substances to comply with statutory and regulatory provisions mandating registration with the DEA, compliance with specific production quotas, security controls to guard against diversion, recordkeeping and reporting obligations, and prescription requirements. Furthermore, the dispensing of new drugs, even when doctors approve their use, must await federal approval. . . .

[If, as the] dissent contends, the personal cultivation, possession, and use of marijuana for medicinal purposes is beyond the "'outer limits' of Congress' Commerce Clause authority," it must also be true that such personal use of marijuana (or any other homegrown drug) for recreational purposes is also beyond those "outer limits," whether or not a State elects to authorize or even regulate such use. [T]the dissenters' rationale logically extends to place *any* federal regulation (including quality, prescription, or quantity controls) of *any* locally

---

2. [Evidence regarding] the effective medical uses for marijuana, if found credible[,] would cast serious doubt on [the] findings that require marijuana to be listed in Schedule I. But the possibility that the drug may be reclassified in the future has no relevance to the question whether Congress now has the power to regulate its production and distribution. . . .

cultivated and possessed controlled substance for *any* purpose beyond the "outer limits" of Congress' Commerce Clause authority. One need not have a degree in economics to understand why a nationwide exemption for the vast quantity of marijuana (or other drugs) locally cultivated for personal use (which presumably would include use by friends, neighbors, and family members) may have a substantial impact on the interstate market for this extraordinarily popular substance. The congressional judgment that an exemption for such a significant segment of the total market would undermine the orderly enforcement of the entire regulatory scheme is entitled to a strong presumption of validity. [T]hat judgment is not only rational, but "visible to the naked eye," under any commonsense appraisal of the probable consequences of such an open-ended exemption.

Second, limiting the activity to marijuana possession and cultivation "in accordance with state law" cannot serve to place respondents' activities beyond congressional reach. The Supremacy Clause unambiguously provides that if there is any conflict between federal and state law, federal law shall prevail. [The] notion that California law has surgically excised a discrete activity that is hermetically sealed off from the larger interstate marijuana market is a dubious proposition, [and] one that Congress could have rationally rejected. . . . In contrast to most prescriptions for legal drugs, which limit the dosage and duration of the usage, [the] doctor's permission to recommend marijuana use is open-ended. The authority to grant permission whenever the doctor determines that a patient is afflicted with "any other illness for which marijuana provides relief," is broad enough to allow even the most scrupulous doctor to conclude that some recreational uses would be therapeutic.[3] [O]ur cases have taught us that there are some unscrupulous physicians who overprescribe when it is sufficiently profitable to do so.

The exemption for cultivation by patients and caregivers can only increase the supply of marijuana in the California market. The likelihood that all such production will promptly terminate when patients recover or will precisely match the patients' medical needs during their convalescence seems remote; whereas the danger that excesses will satisfy some of the admittedly enormous demand for recreational use seems obvious. . . . Taking into account the fact that California is only one of at least nine States to have authorized the medical use of marijuana[,] Congress could have rationally concluded that the aggregate impact on the national market of all the transactions exempted from federal supervision is unquestionably substantial. . . .

Respondents also raise a substantive due process claim and seek to avail themselves of the medical necessity defense. [Since the Court of Appeals did not address these issues, we do not reach them. H]owever, [the] statute authorizes procedures for the reclassification of Schedule I drugs. But perhaps even more important than these legal avenues is the democratic process, in which the voices of voters allied with these respondents may one day be heard in the halls of

---

3. California's Compassionate Use Act has since been amended, limiting the catchall category to "[a]ny other chronic or persistent medical symptom that either: [s]ubstantially limits the ability of the person to conduct one or more major life activities as defined" in the Americans with Disabilities Act of 1990, or "[i]f not alleviated, may cause serious harm to the patient's safety or physical or mental health."

Congress. Under the present state of the law, [the] judgment of the Court of Appeals must be vacated. The case is remanded for further proceedings consistent with this opinion.

It is so ordered.

Justice SCALIA, concurring in the judgment.

[Congress] has undertaken to extinguish the interstate market in Schedule I controlled substances, including marijuana. . . . The power to regulate interstate commerce "extends not only to those regulations which aid, foster and protect the commerce, but embraces those which prohibit it." [That] simple possession is a noneconomic activity is immaterial to whether it can be prohibited as a necessary part of a larger regulation. . . . Congress's authority to enact all of these prohibitions of intrastate controlled-substance activities depends only upon whether they are appropriate means of achieving the legitimate end of eradicating Schedule I substances from interstate commerce. . . . By this measure, [the] regulation must be sustained. Not only is it impossible to distinguish "controlled substances manufactured and distributed intrastate" from "controlled substances manufactured and distributed interstate," but it hardly makes sense to speak in such terms. . . .

Justice O'CONNOR, with whom THE CHIEF JUSTICE and Justice THOMAS join as to all but Part III, dissenting.

We enforce the "outer limits" of [the] Commerce Clause [to] protect historic spheres of state sovereignty from excessive federal encroachment [and] to maintain the distribution of power fundamental to our federalist system of government. . . . The States' core police powers have always included authority to define criminal law and to protect the health, safety, and welfare of their citizens. Exercising those powers, California [has] come to its own conclusion about the difficult and sensitive question of whether marijuana should be available to relieve severe pain and suffering. Today the Court [extinguishes California's] experiment, without any proof that the personal cultivation, possession, and use of marijuana for medicinal purposes, if economic activity in the first place, has a substantial effect on interstate commerce and is therefore an appropriate subject of federal regulation. . . .

[T]he case before us is materially indistinguishable from *Lopez* and *Morrison*. . . . Today's decision allows Congress to regulate intrastate activity without check, so long as there is some implication by legislative design that regulating intrastate activity is essential. [T]he Court appears to reason that the placement of local activity in a comprehensive scheme confirms that it is essential to that scheme. If the Court is right, then *Lopez* stands for nothing more than a drafting guide: Congress should have described the relevant crime as "transfer or possession of a firearm anywhere in the nation" — thus including commercial and noncommercial activity, and clearly encompassing some activity with assuredly substantial effect on interstate commerce. Had it done so, the majority hints, we would have sustained its authority to regulate possession of firearms in school zones. . . . The Court's definition of economic activity is breathtaking. It defines as economic any activity involving the production, distribution, and consumption of commodities. And it appears to reason that when an interstate market for a commodity exists, regulating the intrastate manufacture or possession of that commodity is constitutional either because that intrastate activity is itself economic, or because regulating it is a rational part of regulating its market. [T]he Court's definition of economic activity for purposes of Commerce Clause jurisprudence threatens to sweep all of productive human activity into federal regulatory reach. . . .

In *Lopez* and *Morrison,* we suggested that economic activity usually relates directly to commercial activity. The homegrown cultivation and personal possession and use of marijuana for medicinal purposes has no apparent commercial character. [T]the marijuana at issue in this case was never in the stream of commerce, and neither were the supplies for growing it. [P]ossession is not itself commercial activity. And respondents have not come into possession by means of any commercial transaction; they have simply grown, in their own homes, marijuana for their own use, without acquiring, buying, selling, or bartering a thing of value. . . . Even assuming that economic activity is at issue in this case, the Government has made no showing [that] the possession and use of homegrown marijuana for medical purposes [has] a substantial effect on interstate commerce [or] is necessary to an interstate regulatory scheme. . . . I dissent.

Justice THOMAS, dissenting.

[Respondents'] local cultivation and consumption of marijuana is not "Commerce . . . among the several States." [They] neither buy nor sell the marijuana that they consume. They cultivate their cannabis entirely in the State of California — it never crosses state lines, much less as part of a commercial transaction. [N]o evidence from the founding suggests that "commerce" included the mere possession of a good or some purely personal activity that did not involve trade or exchange for value. [A] ban on the intrastate cultivation, possession and distribution of marijuana may be plainly adapted to stopping the interstate flow of marijuana. Unregulated local growers and users could swell both the supply and the demand sides of the interstate marijuana market, making the market more difficult to regulate. But [respondents] challenge the CSA [as] applied to their conduct. [R]espondents' "limited use is distinct from the broader illicit drug market," because "th[eir] medicinal marijuana [is] not intended for, nor does it enter, the stream of commerce." [When] agents from the [DEA] raided Monson's home, they seized six cannabis plants. If the Federal Government can regulate growing a half-dozen cannabis plants for personal consumption[,] then Congress' Article I powers — as expanded by the Necessary and Proper Clause — have no meaningful limits. [T]he Government's rationale — that it may regulate the production or possession of any commodity for which there is an interstate market — threatens to remove the remaining vestiges of States' traditional police powers. . . . By defining the class at a high level of generality (as the intrastate manufacture and possession of marijuana), the majority overlooks that individuals authorized by state law to manufacture and possess medical marijuana exert no demonstrable effect on the interstate drug market. [The] CSA undoubtedly regulates a great deal of interstate commerce, but that is no license to regulate conduct that is neither interstate nor commercial, however minor or incidental. . . .

Notes and Questions

1. *Reviewing* Lopez *and* Morrison. Do you agree with Justice Thomas and Justice O'Connor in their construction of the *Gonzales* opinion? In other words, if Congress had drafted the Gun-Free School Zones Act and the Violence Against Women Act differently, would the results in *Lopez* and *Morrison* have been different? How should the statutes have been modified to ensure their validity?

2. *A Return to Deference?* Does *Gonzales* signal a return to *Wickard*-era deference to congressional authority, or does the decision not go quite that far?

∿ PROBLEM: MORE ON THE EDUCATION FOR A BETTER AMERICA ACT ∿

Under *Gonzales*, is the proposed legislation sufficiently related to "commerce" so that Congress has the power to pass this broad-based educational reform legislation?

C. THE TAXING POWER

Article I, Section 8 also gives Congress the power to impose taxes: "The Congress shall have Power To lay and collect Taxes, Duties, Imposes and Excises. . . ." Most of the litigation under this clause has focused on Congress's power to regulate conduct by imposing taxes. This so-called "regulation by taxation" is generally unobjectionable if Congress seeks to tax something that it otherwise has the power to regulate (e.g., something within its Art. I, §8 power). However, what happens if Congress tries to regulate through taxation something that it does not have the power to regulate? The following cases present these issues.

Bailey v. Drexel Furniture Co.

259 U.S. 20 (1922)

(Child Labor Tax Case)

Mr. Chief Justice TAFT delivered the opinion of the Court.

This case presents the question of the constitutional validity of the Child Labor Tax Law. [Plaintiff Drexel Furniture Company] is engaged in the manufacture of furniture in the Western district of North Carolina. [I]t received a notice from [the Internal Revenue Service indicating] that it had been assessed $6,312.79 for having during the taxable year 1919 employed and permitted to work in its factory a boy under 14 years of age, thus incurring the tax of 10 per cent on its net profits for that year. The company paid the tax under protest, and, after rejection of its claim for a refund, brought this suit. On demurrer to an amended complaint, judgment was entered for the company against the collector for the full amount, with interest. . . .

The Child Labor Tax Law [is] attacked on the ground that it is a regulation of the employment of child labor in the states — an exclusively state function under the federal Constitution and within the reservations of the Tenth Amendment. [D]efendant [claims] that it is a mere excise tax levied by [Congress] under its broad power of taxation conferred by section 8, article 1, of the federal Constitution. We must construe the law and interpret the intent and meaning of Congress from the language of the act. . . . Does this law impose a tax with only that incidental restraint and regulation which a tax must inevitably involve? Or does it regulate by the use of the so-called tax as a penalty? If a tax, it is clearly an excise. If it were an excise on a commodity or other thing of value, we might not be permitted under previous decisions of this court to infer solely from its heavy burden that the act intends a prohibition instead of a tax. But this act is more. It provides a heavy exaction for a departure from a detailed and specified course of conduct in business. That course of business is that employers shall employ in mines and quarries, children of an age greater than 16 years; in mills and factories, children of an age greater than 14 years, and shall prevent children of less than 16 years in mills and factories from working more than 8 hours a day or 6 days in the week. If an employer departs from this prescribed course of business, he is to pay to the government one-tenth of his entire net income in the business for a full year. The amount is not to be proportioned in any degree to the extent or frequency of the departures, but is to be paid by the employer in full measure whether he employs 500 children for a year, or employs only one for a day. . . . In the light of these features of the act, a court must be blind not to see that the so-called tax is imposed to stop the employment of children within the age limits prescribed. Its prohibitory and regulatory effect and purpose are palpable. All others can see and understand this. How can we properly shut our minds to it?

It is the high duty and function of this court in cases regularly brought to its bar to decline to recognize or enforce seeming laws of Congress, dealing with subjects not intrusted to Congress, but left or committed by the supreme law of the land to the control of the states. We cannot avoid the duty, even though it require us to refuse to give effect to legislation designed to promote the highest good. . . .

Out of a proper respect for the acts of a co-ordinate branch of the government, this court has gone far to sustain taxing acts as such, even though there has been ground for suspecting, from the weight of the tax, it was intended to destroy its subject. But in the act before us the presumption of validity cannot prevail, because the proof of the contrary is found on the very face of its provisions. Grant the validity of this law, and all that Congress would need to do, hereafter, in seeking to take over to its control any one of the great number of subjects of public interest, jurisdiction of which the states have never parted with, and which are reserved to them by the Tenth Amendment, would be to enact a detailed measure of complete regulation of the subject and enforce it by a so-called tax upon departures from it. To give such magic to the word "tax" would be to break down all constitutional limitation of the powers of Congress and completely wipe out the sovereignty of the states.

The difference between a tax and a penalty is sometimes difficult to define, and yet the consequences of the distinction in the required method of their collection often are important. Where the sovereign enacting the law has power to impose both tax and penalty, the difference between revenue production and mere regulation may be immaterial, but not so when one sovereign can impose a tax only, and the power of regulation rests in another. Taxes are occasionally imposed in the discretion of the Legislature on proper subjects with the primary motive of obtaining revenue from them and with the incidental motive of discouraging them by making their continuance onerous. They do not lose their character as taxes because of the incidental motive. But there comes a time in the extension of the penalizing features of the so-called tax when it loses its character as such and becomes a mere penalty, with the characteristics of regulation and punishment. Such is the case in the law before us. Although Congress does not invalidate the contract of employment or expressly declare that the employment within the mentioned ages is illegal, it does exhibit its intent practically to achieve the latter result by adopting the criteria of wrongdoing and imposing its principal consequence on those who transgress its standard.

The case before us cannot be distinguished from that of Hammer v. Dagenhart, 247 U.S. 251. Congress there enacted a law to prohibit transportation in interstate commerce of goods made at a factory in which there was employment of children within the same ages and for the same number of hours a day and days in a week as are penalized by the act in this case. This court held the law in that case to be void. . . . In the case at the bar, Congress in the name of a tax which on the face of the act is penalty seeks to do the same thing, and the effort must be equally futile.

The analogy of the *Dagenhart* case is clear. The congressional power over interstate commerce is, within its proper scope, just as complete and unlimited as the congressional power to tax, and the legislative motive in its exercise is just as free from judicial suspicion and inquiry. Yet when Congress threatened to stop interstate commerce in ordinary and necessary commodities, unobjectionable as subjects of transportation, and to deny the same to the people of a state in order to coerce them into compliance with Congress' regulation of state concerns, the court said this was not in fact regulation of interstate commerce, but rather that of state concerns and was invalid. So here the so-called tax is a penalty to coerce people of a state to act as Congress wishes them to act in respect of a matter completely the business of the state government under the federal Constitution. . . .

For the reasons given, we must hold the Child Labor Tax Law invalid and the judgment of the District Court is

Affirmed.

Notes and Questions

1. *More on the Police Power.* Following the *Child Labor Tax Case*, the Court rendered a similar holding in United States v. Constantine, 296 U.S. 287 (1935). In *Constantine*, the Court struck down a law that imposed a much higher tax on liquor businesses found to be operating in violation of state law. The Court concluded that the law violated the police power of the state.

2. *Is* Dagenhart *Still Valid?* In *Bailey*, note the Court's reliance on *Dagenhart* and that decision's interpretation of the Commerce Clause and the Tenth Amendment. Does the Court still adhere to these views? If not, how have the Court's attitudes changed? How would this change affect the Court's analysis today?

United States v. Sanchez

340 U.S. 42 (1950)

Mr. Justice CLARK delivered the opinion of the Court.

This is a direct appeal from dismissal by the District Court of a suit for recovery of $8,701.65 in taxes and interest alleged to be due under §7(a)(2) of the Marihuana Tax Act, 26 U.S.C. §2590(a)(2), 26 U.S.C.A. §2590(a)(2). In their motion to dismiss, which was granted without opinion, defendants attacked the constitutionality of this subsection on the ground that it levied a penalty, not a tax. The validity of this levy is the issue here.

In enacting the Marihuana Tax Act, the Congress had two objectives: "First, the development of a plan of taxation which will raise revenue and at the same time render extremely difficult the acquisition of marihauna by persons who desire it for illicit uses and, second, the development of an adequate means of publicizing dealings in marihuana in order to tax and control the traffic effectively." S. Rep. No. 900, 75th Cong., 1st Sess., p. 3. . . .

Pursuant to these objective[s], §3230 of the Code imposes a special tax ranging from $1 to $24 on "every person who imports, manufactures, produces, compounds, sells, deals in, dispenses, prescribes, administers, or gives away marihuana." For purposes of administration, §3231 requires such persons to register at the time of the payment of the tax with the Collector of the District in which their businesses are located. The Code then makes it unlawful — with certain exceptions not pertinent here — for any person to transfer marihuana except in pursuance of a written order of the transferee on a blank form issued by the Secretary of the Treasury. Section 2590 requires the transferee at the time he applies for the order form to pay a tax on such transfer of $1 per ounce or fraction thereof if he has paid the special tax and registered, or $100 per ounce or fraction thereof if he has not paid the special tax and registered. §2590(a)(2). The transferor is also made liable for the tax so imposed, in the event the transfer is made without an order form and without the payment of the tax by the transferee. Defendants in this case are transferors.

It is obvious that §2590, by imposing a severe burden on transfers to unregistered persons, implements the congressional purpose of restricting traffic in marihuana to accepted industrial and medicinal channels. Hence the attack here rests on the regulatory character and prohibitive burden of the section as well as the penal nature of the imposition. But despite the regulatory effect and the close resemblance to a penalty, it does not follow that the levy is invalid.

First. It is beyond serious question that a tax does not cease to be valid merely because it regulates, discourages, or even definitely deters the activities taxed. Sonzinsky v. United States, (1937). The principle applies even though the revenue obtained is obviously negligible, or the revenue purpose of the tax may be secondary. Nor does a tax statute necessarily fall because it touches on activities which Congress might not otherwise regulate. As was pointed out in Magnano Co. v. Hamilton, 292 U.S. 40 (1934) 'From the beginning of our government, the courts have sustained taxes although imposed with the collateral intent of effecting ulterior ends which, considered apart, were beyond the constitutional power of the lawmakers to realize by legislation directly addressed to their accomplishment.' , , , These principles are controlling here. The tax in question is a legitimate exercise of the taxing power despite its collateral regulatory purpose and effect.

Second. The tax levied by §2590(a)(2) is not conditioned upon the commission of a crime. The tax is on the transfer of marihuana to a person who has not paid the special tax and registered. Such a transfer is not made an unlawful act under the statute. Liability for the payment of the tax rests primarily with the transferee; but if he fails to pay, then the transferor, as here, becomes liable. It is thus the failure of the transferee to pay the tax that gives rise to the liability of the transferor. Since his tax liability does not in effect rest on criminal conduct, the tax can be properly called a civil rather than a criminal sanction. The fact Congress provided civil procedure for collection indicates its intention that the tax be treated as such. Helvering v. Mitchell, 303 U.S. 391 (1938). Moreover, the Government is seeking to collect the levy by a judicial proceeding with its attendant safeguards.

Nor is the civil character of the tax imposed by §2590(a)(2) altered by its severity in relation to that assessed by §2590(a)(1). The difference has a rational foundation. Unregistered persons are not likely to procure the required order form prior to transfer or pay the required tax. Free of sanctions, dealers would be prone to accommodate such persons in their unlawful activity. The imposition of equally severe tax burdens on such transferors is reasonably adapted to secure payment of the tax by transferees or stop transfers to unregistered persons, as well as to provide an additional source from which the expense of unearthing clandestine transfers can be recovered. *Cf.* Helvering v. Mitchell, *supra*.

The judgment below must be reversed and the cause remanded for further proceedings in conformity with this opinion.

Reversed.

Constantine was decided in 1935, the Court has routinely upheld federal laws imposing taxes. *See, e.g.,* United States v. Kahriger, 345 U.S. 22 (1953) (tax on firearms); Sonzinsky v. United States, 300 U.S. 506 (1937) (tax on wagering). In part, the Court's post-1935 position has been driven by its expanded interpretation of the Commerce Clause. In other words, as Congress's Commerce Clause power expanded during the period of deference, Congress had little need to use taxes for regulatory purposes. As the Court begins to place limitations on Congress's Commerce Clause authority, in decisions like *Lopez* and *Morrison,* should the Court be less deferential to Congress's decision to regulate through taxation?

D. POWER TO SPEND FOR THE GENERAL WELFARE

Article I, Section 8, which contains the power to tax, also contains the power to spend for the general welfare: "The Congress shall have Power To lay and collect Taxes, Duties, Imposes and Excises, to pay the Debts and provide for the common Defence and general Welfare of the United States."

From cases like *Dagenhart* and *Bailey,* we know that Congress was initially unable to impose its child labor laws through either its Commerce Clause power or its taxing power. Does Congress have greater power to control or regulate conduct under its power to spend for the general welfare?

United States v. Butler

297 U.S. 1 (1935)

Mr. Justice ROBERTS delivered the opinion of the Court.

[In the Agricultural Adjustment Act of 1933, Congress concluded that an economic emergency existed because of a disparity between the prices of agricultural and other commodities. This disparity affected both farmers' purchasing power and transactions in agricultural commodities. In an effort to deal with this disparity, Congress tried to reduce farm acreage "through agreements with producers or by other voluntary methods," and to provide for rental or benefit payments to be made in exchange for the reduction. In order to finance the benefits payments, Congress levied processing taxes on various commodities. Hoosac Mills Corporation, a processor, challenged the Act's taxing and spending provisions.]

[The] government asserts that even if the respondents may question the propriety of the appropriation embodied in the statute, their attack must fail because article 1, §8 of the Constitution, authorizes the contemplated expenditure of the funds raised by the tax. . . .

[The] federal union is a government of delegated powers. It has only such as are expressly conferred upon it and such as are reasonably to be implied from those granted. [T]he government does not attempt to uphold the validity of the act on the basis of the commerce clause. . . . The clause thought to authorize the legislation, the first, confers upon the Congress power "to lay and collect Taxes, Duties, Imposts and Excises, to pay the Debts and provide for the common Defence and general Welfare of the United States. . . ." It is not contended that this provision grants power to regulate agricultural production upon the theory that such legislation would promote the general welfare. The government concedes that the phrase "to provide for the general welfare" qualifies the power "to lay and collect taxes." The view that the clause grants power to provide for the general welfare, independently of the taxing power, has never been authoritatively accepted. Mr. Justice Story points out that, if it were adopted, "it is obvious that under color of the generality of the words, to 'provide for the common defence and general welfare', the government of the United States is, in reality, a government of general and unlimited powers, notwithstanding the subsequent enumeration of specific powers." The [only] thing granted is the power to tax for the purpose of providing funds for payment of the nation's debts and making provision for the general welfare.

[T]he government asserts [that] Congress may appropriate and authorize the spending of moneys for the "general welfare"; that the phrase should be liberally construed to cover anything conducive to national welfare; that decision as to what will promote such welfare rests with Congress alone, and the courts may not review its determination; and, finally, that the appropriation under attack was in fact for the general welfare of the United States.

The Congress is expressly empowered to lay taxes to provide for the general welfare. Funds in the Treasury as a result of taxation may be expended only through appropriation. . . . The necessary implication from the terms of the grant is that the public funds may be appropriated "to provide for the general welfare of the United States." These words cannot be meaningless, else they would not have been used. The conclusion must be that they were intended to limit and define the granted power to raise and to expend money. How shall they be construed to effectuate the intent of the instrument?

Since the foundation of the nation, sharp differences of opinion have persisted as to the true interpretation of the phrase. Madison asserted it amounted to no more than a reference to the other powers enumerated in the subsequent clauses of the same section; that, as the United States is a government of limited and enumerated powers, the grant of power to tax and spend for the general national welfare must be confined to the enumerated legislative fields committed to the Congress. . . . Hamilton, on the other hand, maintained the clause confers a power separate and distinct from those later enumerated is not restricted in meaning by the grant of them, and Congress consequently has a substantive power to tax and to appropriate, limited only by the requirement that it shall be exercised to provide for the general welfare of the United States. . . . Mr. Justice Story, in his Commentaries, espouses the Hamiltonian position. [We] conclude that the reading advocated by Mr. Justice Story is the correct one. While [the] power to tax is not unlimited, its confines are set in the clause which confers it, and not in those of section 8 which bestow and define the legislative powers of the Congress. . . .

That the qualifying phrase must be given effect all advocates of broad construction admit. Hamilton [states] that the purpose must be "general, and not local." Monroe, an advocate of Hamilton's doctrine, wrote: "Have Congress a right to raise and appropriate the money to any and to every purpose according to their will and pleasure? They certainly have not." Story says that if the tax be not proposed for the common defense or general welfare, but for other objects wholly extraneous, it would be wholly indefensible upon constitutional principles. And he makes it clear that the powers of taxation and appropriation extend only to matters of national, as distinguished from local, welfare. . . .

We are not now required to ascertain the scope of the phrase "general welfare of the United States" or to determine whether an appropriation in aid of agriculture falls within it. Wholly apart from that question, another principle embedded in our Constitution prohibits the enforcement of the Agricultural Adjustment Act. The act invades the reserved rights of the states. It is a statutory plan to regulate and control agricultural production, a matter beyond the powers delegated to the federal government. The tax, the appropriation of the funds raised, and the direction for their disbursement, are but parts of the plan. They are but means to an unconstitutional end.

From the accepted doctrine that the United States is a government of delegated powers, it follows that those not expressly granted, or reasonably to be implied from such as are conferred, are reserved to the states or to the people. . . . It is an established principle that the attainment of a prohibited end may not be accomplished under the pretext of the exertion of powers which are granted. . . . The power of taxation, which is expressly granted, may, of course, be adopted as a means to carry into operation another power also expressly granted. But resort to the taxing power to effectuate an end which is not legitimate, not within the scope of the Constitution, is obviously inadmissible. . . . "It would undoubtedly be an abuse of the (taxing) power if so exercised as to impair the separate existence and independent self-government of the States, or if exercised for ends inconsistent with the limited grants of power in the Constitution." Veazie Bank v. Fenno, 8 Wall. 533, 19 L.Ed. 482.

[If] the taxing power may not be used as the instrument to enforce a regulation of matters of state concern with respect to which the Congress has no authority to interfere, may it, as in the present case, be employed to raise the money necessary to purchase a compliance which the Congress is powerless to command? The government asserts that [the plan] is constitutionally sound because the end is accomplished by voluntary co-operation. There are two sufficient answers to the contention. The regulation is not in fact voluntary. The farmer, of course, may refuse to comply, but [the] amount offered is intended to be sufficient to exert pressure on him to agree to the proposed regulation. . . . If the cotton grower elects not to accept the benefits, he will receive less for his crops; those who receive payments will be able to undersell him. The result may well be to cause financial ruin. . . . The asserted power of choice is illusory. . . .

But if the plan were one for purely voluntary co-operation it would stand no better so far as federal power is concerned. At best, it is a scheme for purchasing with federal funds submission to federal regulation of a subject reserved to the states. . . . An appropriation to be expended by the United States under contracts calling for violation of a state law clearly would offend the Constitution. Is a statute less objectionable which authorizes expenditure of federal moneys to induce action in a field in which the United States has no power to intermeddle? The Congress cannot invade state jurisdiction to compel individual action; no more can it purchase such action. . . .

We are not here concerned with a conditional appropriation of money, nor with a provision that if certain conditions are not complied with the appropriation shall no longer be available. By the Agricultural Adjustment Act the amount of the tax is appropriated to be expended only in payment under contracts whereby the parties bind themselves to regulation by the federal government. [A]n appropriation to an educational institution which by its terms is to become available only if the beneficiary enters into a contract to teach doctrines subversive of the Constitution is clearly bad. An affirmance of the authority of Congress so to condition the expenditure of an appropriation would tend to nullify all constitutional limitations upon legislative power. . . .

Congress has no power to enforce its commands on the farmer to the ends sought by the Agricultural Adjustment Act. [I]t may not indirectly accomplish those ends by taxing and spending to purchase compliance. The Constitution and the entire plan of our government negative any such use of the power to tax and to spend as the act undertakes to authorize. It does not help to declare that local conditions throughout the nation have created a situation of national concern; for this is but to say that whenever there is a widespread similarity of local conditions, Congress may ignore constitutional limitations upon its own powers and usurp those reserved to the states. If, in lieu of compulsory regulation of subjects within the states' reserved jurisdiction, which is prohibited, the Congress could invoke the taxing and spending power as a means to accomplish the same end, clause 1 of section 8 of article 1 would become the instrument for total subversion of the governmental powers reserved to the individual states.

If the act before us is a proper exercise of the federal taxing power, [the] regulation of all industry throughout the United States may be accomplished by similar exercises of the same power. It would be possible to exact money from one branch of an industry and pay it to another branch in every field of activity which lies within the province of the states. . . .

[Since] there was no power in the Congress to impose the contested exaction, it could not lawfully ratify or confirm what an executive officer had done in that regard. Consequently the Act of 1935, §30, does not affect the rights of the parties.

The judgment is affirmed.

Mr. Justice STONE (dissenting).

[The] Constitution requires that public funds shall be spent for a defined purpose, the promotion of the general welfare. Their expenditure usually involves payment on terms which will insure use by the selected recipients within the limits of the constitutional purpose. . . . It makes no difference that there is a promise to do an act which the condition is calculated to induce. Condition and promise are alike valid since both are in furtherance of the national purpose for which the money is appropriated. . . .

[The] spending power of Congress is in addition to the legislative power and not subordinate to it. This independent grant of the power of the purse, and its very nature, involving in its exercise the duty to insure expenditure within the granted power, presuppose freedom of selection among divers ends and aims, and the capacity to impose such conditions as will render the choice effective. It is a contradiction in terms to say that there is power to spend for the national welfare, while rejecting any power to impose conditions reasonably adapted to the attainment of the end which alone would justify the expenditure.

The limitation now sanctioned must lead to absurd consequences. The government may give seeds to farmers, but may not condition the gift upon their being planted in places where they are most needed or even planted at all. The government may give money to the unemployed, but may not ask that those who get it shall give labor in return, or even use it to support their families. . . . If the expenditure is for a national public purpose, that purpose will not be thwarted because payment is on condition which will advance that purpose. The action which Congress induces by payments of money to promote the general welfare, but which it does not command or coerce, is but an incident to a specifically granted power, but a permissible means to a legitimate end. [T]he power to tax and spend includes the power to relieve a nationwide economic maladjustment by conditional gifts of money.

South Dakota v. Dole

483 U.S. 203 (1987)

Chief Justice REHNQUIST delivered the opinion of the Court.

Petitioner South Dakota permits persons 19 years of age or older to purchase beer containing up to 3.2% alcohol. In 1984 Congress enacted 23 U.S.C. §158, which directs the Secretary of Transportation to withhold a percentage of federal highway funds otherwise allocable from States "in which the purchase or public possession . . . of any alcoholic beverage by a person who is less than twenty-one years of age is lawful." The State sued in United States District Court seeking a declaratory judgment that §158 violates the constitutional limitations on congressional exercise of the spending power and violates the Twenty-first Amendment to the United States Constitution. The District Court rejected the State's claims, and the Court of Appeals for the Eighth Circuit affirmed. . . .

The Constitution empowers Congress to "lay and collect Taxes, Duties, Imposts, and Excises, to pay the Debts and provide for the common Defence and general Welfare of the United States." Incident to this power, Congress may attach conditions on the receipt of federal funds, and has repeatedly employed the power "to further broad policy objectives by conditioning receipt of federal moneys upon compliance by the recipient with federal statutory and administrative directives." . . . The breadth of this power was made clear in United States v. Butler, 297 U.S. 1 (1936), where the Court, resolving a longstanding debate over the scope of the Spending Clause, determined that "the power of Congress to authorize expenditure of public moneys for public purposes is not limited by the direct grants of legislative power found in the Constitution." Thus, objectives not thought to be within Article I's "enumerated legislative fields," . . . may nevertheless be attained through the use of the spending power and the conditional grant of federal funds.

The spending power is of course not unlimited, . . . but is instead subject to several general restrictions articulated in our cases. The first of these limitations is derived from the language of the Constitution itself: the exercise of the spending power must be in pursuit of "the general welfare." . . . In considering whether a particular expenditure is intended to serve general public purposes, courts should defer substantially to the judgment of Congress. Second, we have required that if Congress desires to condition the States' receipt of federal funds, it "must do so unambiguously . . . , enabl[ing] the States to exercise their choice knowingly, cognizant of the consequences of their participation." . . . Third, our cases have suggested (without significant elaboration) that conditions on federal grants might be illegitimate if they are unrelated "to the federal interest in particular national projects or programs." . . . Finally, we have noted that other constitutional provisions may provide an independent bar to the conditional grant of federal funds. . . . We can readily conclude that the provision is designed to serve the general welfare, especially in light of the fact that "the concept of welfare or the opposite is shaped by Congress. . . ." Congress found that the differing drinking ages in the States created particular incentives for young persons to combine their desire to drink with their ability to drive, and that this interstate problem required a national solution. The means it chose to address this dangerous situation were reasonably calculated to advance the general welfare. The conditions upon which States receive the funds, moreover, could not be more clearly stated by Congress. . . . And the State itself, rather than challenging the germaneness of the condition to federal purposes, admits that it "has never contended that the congressional action was . . . unrelated to a national concern in the absence of the Twenty-first Amendment." Indeed, the condition imposed by Congress is directly related to one of the main purposes for which highway funds are expended — safe interstate travel. . . . This goal of the interstate highway system had been frustrated by varying drinking ages among the States. A Presidential commission appointed to study alcohol-related accidents and fatalities on the Nation's highways concluded that the lack of uniformity in the States' drinking ages created "an incentive to drink and drive" because "young persons commut[e] to border States where the drinking age is lower." By enacting §158, Congress conditioned the receipt of federal funds in a way reasonably calculated to address this particular impediment to a purpose for which the funds are expended.

The remaining question about the validity of §158 — and the basic point of disagreement between the parties — is whether the Twenty-first Amendment constitutes an "independent constitutional bar" to the conditional grant of federal funds. . . . Petitioner, relying on its view that the Twenty-first Amendment prohibits direct regulation of drinking ages by Congress, asserts that "Congress may not use the spending power to regulate that which it is prohibited from regulating directly under the Twenty-first Amendment." But our cases show that this "independent constitutional bar" limitation on the spending power is not of the kind petitioner suggests. United States v. Butler, . . . for example, established that the constitutional limitations on Congress when exercising its spending power are less exacting than those on its authority to regulate directly.

We have also held that a perceived Tenth Amendment limitation on congressional regulation of state affairs did not concomitantly limit the range of conditions legitimately placed on federal grants. In Oklahoma v. Civil Service Comm'n, 330 U.S. 127 (1947), the Court considered the validity of the Hatch Act insofar as it was applied to political activities of state officials whose employment was financed in whole or in part with federal funds. The State contended that an order under this provision to withhold certain federal funds unless a state official was removed invaded its sovereignty in violation of the Tenth Amendment. Though finding that "the United States is not concerned with, and has no power to regulate, local political activities as such of state officials," the Court nevertheless held that the Federal Government "does have power to fix the terms upon which its money allotments to states shall be disbursed." . . . The Court found no violation of the State's sovereignty because the State could, and did, adopt "the 'simple expedient' of not yielding to what she urges is federal coercion. . . ."

These cases establish that the "independent constitutional bar" limitation on the spending power is not, as petitioner suggests, a prohibition on the indirect achievement of objectives which Congress is not empowered to achieve directly. Instead, we think that the language in our earlier opinions stands for the unexceptionable proposition that the power may not be used to induce the States to engage in activities that would themselves be unconstitutional. Thus, for example, a grant of federal funds conditioned on invidiously discriminatory state action or the infliction of cruel and unusual punishment would be an illegitimate exercise of the Congress' broad spending power. But no such claim can be or is made here. Were South Dakota to succumb to the blandishments offered by Congress and raise its drinking age to 21, the State's action in so doing would not violate the constitutional rights of anyone.

Our decisions have recognized that in some circumstances the financial inducement offered by Congress might be so coercive as to pass the point at which "pressure turns into compulsion." . . . Here, however, Congress has directed only that a State desiring to establish a minimum drinking age lower than 21 lose a relatively small percentage of certain federal highway funds. Petitioner contends that the coercive nature of this program is evident from the degree of success it has achieved. We cannot conclude, however, that a conditional grant of federal money of this sort is unconstitutional simply by reason of its success in achieving the congressional objective.

When we consider, for a moment, that all South Dakota would lose if she adheres to her chosen course as to a suitable minimum drinking age is 5% of the funds otherwise obtainable under specified highway grant programs, the argument as to coercion is shown to be more rhetoric than fact. As we said a half century ago in Steward Machine Co. v. Davis:

> [E]very rebate from a tax when conditioned upon conduct is in some measure a temptation. But to hold that motive or temptation is equivalent to coercion is to plunge the law in endless difficulties. The outcome of such a doctrine is the acceptance of a philosophical determinism by which choice becomes impossible. Till now the law has been guided by a robust common sense which assumes the freedom of the will as a working hypothesis in the solution of its problems.

Here Congress has offered relatively mild encouragement to the States to enact higher minimum drinking ages than they would otherwise choose. But the enactment of such laws remains the prerogative of the States not merely in theory but in fact. Even if Congress might lack the power to impose a national minimum drinking age directly, we conclude that encouragement to state action found in §158 is a valid use of the spending power. Accordingly, the judgment of the Court of Appeals is
  Affirmed.

  Justice O'CONNOR, dissenting.
  [My] disagreement with the Court is relatively narrow on the spending power issue: it is a disagreement about the application of a principle rather than a disagreement on the principle itself. . . . In my view, establishment of a minimum drinking age of 21 is not sufficiently related to interstate highway construction to justify so conditioning funds appropriated for that purpose.
  [T]he Court asserts the reasonableness of the relationship between the supposed purpose of the expenditure — "safe interstate travel" — and the drinking age condition. . . . The Court reasons that Congress wishes that the roads it builds may be used safely, that drunken drivers threaten highway safety, and that young people are more likely to drive while under the influence of alcohol under existing law than would be the case if there were a uniform national drinking age of 21. It hardly needs saying, however, that if the purpose of §158 is to deter drunken driving, it is far too over and under-inclusive. It is over-inclusive because it stops teenagers from drinking even when they are not about to drive on interstate highways. It is under-inclusive because teenagers pose only a small part of the drunken driving problem in this Nation. . . .
  When Congress appropriates money to build a highway, it is entitled to insist that the highway be a safe one. But it is not entitled to insist as a condition of the use of highway funds that the State impose or change regulations in other areas of the State's social and economic life because of an attenuated or tangential relationship to highway use or safety. [I]f the rule were otherwise, the Congress could effectively regulate almost any area of a State's social, political, or economic life on the theory that use of the interstate transportation system is somehow enhanced. If, for example, the United States were to condition highway moneys upon moving the state capital, I suppose it might argue that interstate transportation is facilitated by locating local governments in places easily accessible to

interstate highways — or, conversely, that highways might become overburdened if they had to carry traffic to and from the state capital. In my mind, such a relationship is hardly more attenuated than the one which the Court finds supports §158. . . .

There is a clear place at which the Court can draw the line between permissible and impermissible conditions on federal grants. [A] condition that a State will raise its drinking age to 21 cannot fairly be said to be reasonably related to the expenditure of funds for highway construction. The only possible connection, highway safety, has nothing to do with how the funds Congress has appropriated are expended. Rather than a condition determining how federal highway money shall be expended, it is a regulation determining who shall be able to drink liquor. As such it is not justified by the spending power. . . .

Notes: Federal Funding for the Developmentally Disabled

In Pennhurst State School & Hospital v. Halderman, 451 U.S. 1 (1981), the Court upheld the Developmentally Disabled Assistance and Bill of Rights Act of 1975. In that Act, Congress provided financial assistance to states to aid them in creating programs to care for and treat the developmentally disabled. The Act was voluntary, and the states were given the choice of complying with the conditions set forth in the Act or forgoing the benefits of federal funding. However, if they chose to participate, they were subject to the Act's "bill of rights" provision, which granted mentally retarded persons a right to "appropriate treatment, services, and habilitation" in "the setting that is least restrictive of . . . personal liberty." Pennsylvania decided to accept the federal funding. Afterward, relying on the Act, a mentally retarded resident of a Pennsylvania state hospital brought suit claiming that conditions were unsanitary, inhumane, and dangerous, and asserting that the Act provided him with a right to minimally adequate habilitation in the least restrictive environment. Pennsylvania defended on the basis that Congress exceeded its power under the Spending Clause. In upholding the Act, the Court stated: "[L]egislation enacted pursuant to the spending power is much in the nature of a contract: in return for federal funds, the States agree to comply with federally imposed conditions. The legitimacy of Congress' power to legislate under the spending power thus rests on whether the State voluntarily and knowingly accepts the terms of the 'contract.' There can, of course, be no knowing acceptance if a State is unaware of the conditions or is unable to ascertain what is expected of it. Accordingly, if Congress intends to impose a condition on the grant of federal moneys, it must do so unambiguously. . . . We must carefully inquire, then, whether Congress in §6010 imposed an obligation on the States to spend state money to fund certain rights as a condition of receiving federal moneys under the Act or whether it spoke merely in precatory terms. . . . Applying those principles to these cases, we find nothing in the Act or its legislative history to suggest that Congress intended to require the States to assume the high cost of providing 'appropriate treatment' in the 'least restrictive environment' to their mentally retarded citizens. . . . In sum, the court below failed to recognize the well-settled distinction between congressional 'encouragement' of state programs and the imposition of binding obligations on the States. . . ." Justice White, joined by Justices Brennan and Marshall, dissented in part: "As an initial matter, I agree that §6010 was enacted pursuant to Congress' spending power, and not pursuant to its power under §5 of the Fourteenth Amendment. Accordingly, I agree that the Act was not intended to place duties on States independent of their participation in the program established by the Act."

∾ PROBLEMS ∾

1. Butler *Revisited*. Following *Dole*, suppose that Congress tries to reimpose the provisions of the Agricultural Adjustment Act that it tried to impose in United States v. Butler. As you may recall, in *Butler*, Congress concluded that an economic emergency existed because of a disparity between the prices of agricultural and other commodities. This disparity affected both farmers' purchasing power and transactions in agricultural commodities. In an effort to deal with this disparity, Congress tried to reduce farm acreage "through agreements with producers or by other voluntary methods," and to provide for rental or benefit payments to be made in exchange for the reduction. In order to finance the benefits payments, Congress levied processing taxes on various commodities. Would the Act be valid if enacted today?

2. Child Labor Tax Case *Revisited*. In Hammer v. Dagenhart and in the *Child Labor Tax Case*, Congress tried unsuccessfully to restrict child labor. In *Hammer*, the Court tried to achieve that objective under the Commerce Clause. In the *Child Labor Tax Case*, it tried to do so under its taxing power. Obviously, in light of the Court's subsequent interpretations of the Commerce Clause, *Hammer* has been overruled, and Congress can now regulate child labor under the Commerce Clause. After *Dole*, can it also do so under the Spending Clause through conditional grants to the states or by threatening to withhold federal funds unless the states restrict child labor?

3. *More on the Education for a Better America Act*. Can Congress impose the legislation under its spending power by offering financial incentives to local school districts that comply with the Act?

E. THE WAR POWER AND TREATY POWER

Article I also gives Congress a number of powers relating to war and foreign affairs. Included is the power to declare war and to regulate commerce with foreign states. This power is, in some respects, shared with the President, who also has substantial authority over foreign affairs. For example, under Article II, Section 2, the President is the Commander in Chief of the army and the navy, and he has the power to appoint ambassadors and consuls. In addition, as noted, he has the power to make treaties.

In Chapter 3, we examine the scope of presidential power as well as the intersection between congressional power and executive power, especially with regard to the war power. In this section, we focus primarily on congressional powers, including the war power and the treaty power. However, it is important to remember that the Constitution also gives Congress the power to "regulate foreign affairs." In Perez v. Brownell, 356 U.S. 44 (1958), the Court upheld a congressional enactment that mandated a loss of U.S. citizenship for "voting in a political election in a foreign state."

1. The War Power

The war power gives Congress the authority not only to declare war but also to pass legislation necessary to the conduct of the war. Few dispute that the war power applies to military contexts. The power is more controversial, however, when it is applied to controlling the conduct of U.S. citizens within the United States.

Woods v. Cloyd W. Miller Co.

333 U.S. 138 (1948)

Mr. Justice DOUGLAS delivered the opinion of the Court.

[Title II] of the Housing and Rent Act of 1947[, which imposed maximum rents, became] effective on July 1, 1947, and the following day the appellee demanded [increases] of 40% and 60% for rental accommodations in the Cleveland Defense-Rental Area, and admitted violation of the Act and regulations adopted pursuant thereto. Appellant thereupon instituted this proceeding under §206(b) of the Act to enjoin the violations. . . . A preliminary injunction issued. After a hearing it was dissolved and a permanent injunction denied.

The District Court was of the view that the authority of Congress to regulate rents by virtue of the war power ended with the Presidential Proclamation terminating hostilities [since] that proclamation inaugurated "peace-in-fact." . . . The District Court expressed the further view that rent control is not within the war power because "the emergency created by housing shortage came into existence long before the war." . . .

We conclude [that] the war power sustains this legislation. The Court said in Hamilton v. Kentucky Distilleries and Warehouse Co., 251 U.S. 146, that the war power includes the power "to remedy the evils which have arisen from its rise and progress" and continues for the duration of that emergency. Whatever may be the consequences when war is officially terminated, the war power does not necessarily end with the cessation of hostilities. . . . Those cases followed the reasoning of Stewart v. Kahn, 11 Wall. 493, 20 L.Ed. 176, which held that Congress had the power to toll the statute of limitations of the States during the period when the process of their courts was not available to litigants due to the conditions obtaining in the Civil War.

The constitutional validity of the present legislation follows a fortiori from those cases. The legislative history of the present Act makes abundantly clear that there has not yet been eliminated the deficit in housing which in considerable measure was caused by the heavy demobilization of veterans and by the cessation or reduction in residential construction during the period of hostilities due to the allocation of building materials to military projects. Since the war effort contributed heavily to that deficit, Congress has the power even after the cessation of hostilities to act to control the forces that a short supply of the needed article created. If that were not true, the Necessary and Proper Clause, Art. I, §8, cl. 18, would be drastically limited in its application to the several war powers. . . . It would render Congress powerless to remedy conditions the creation of which necessarily followed from the mobilization of men and materials for successful prosecution of the war. So to read the Constitution would be to make it self-defeating.

We recognize the force of the argument that the effects of war under modern conditions may be felt in the economy for years and years, and that if the war power can be used in days of peace to treat all the wounds which war inflicts on our society, it may not only swallow up all other powers of Congress but largely obliterate the Ninth and the Tenth Amendments as well. There are no such implications in today's decision. We deal here with the consequences of a housing deficit greatly intensified during the period of hostilities by the war effort. . . . And the question whether the war power has been properly employed in cases such as this is open to judicial inquiry.

The question of the constitutionality of action taken by Congress does not depend on recitals of the power which it undertakes to exercise. Here it is plain from the legislative history that Congress was invoking its war power to cope with a current condition of which the war was a direct and immediate cause. Its judgment on that score is entitled to the respect granted like legislation enacted pursuant to the police power.

Under the present Act the Housing Expediter is authorized to remove the rent controls in any defense-rental area if in his judgment the need no longer exists by reason of new construction or satisfaction of demand in other ways. . . . Nor is there here a grant of unbridled administrative discretion. The standards prescribed pass muster under our decisions.

The fact that the property regulated suffers a decrease in value is no more fatal to the exercise of the war power than it is where the police power is invoked to the same end.

Reversed.

Mr. Justice JACKSON, concurring.

[The] Government asserts no constitutional basis for this legislation other than this vague, undefined and undefinable "war power." No one will question that this power is the most dangerous one to free government in the whole catalogue of powers. It usually is invoked in haste and excitement when calm legislative consideration of constitutional limitation is difficult. It is executed in a time of patriotic fervor that makes moderation unpopular. And, worst of all, it is interpreted by the Judges under the influence of the same passions and pressures. Always, as in this case, the Government urges hasty decision to forestall some emergency or serve some purpose and pleads that paralysis will result if its claims to power are denied or their confirmation delayed.

Particularly when the war power is invoked to do things to the liberties of people, or to their property or economy that only indirectly affect conduct of the war and do not relate to the management of the war itself, the constitutional basis should be scrutinized with care.

I think we can hardly deny that the war power is as valid a ground for federal rent control now as it has been at any time. We still are technically in a state of war. I would not be willing to hold that war powers may be indefinitely prolonged merely by keeping legally alive a state of war that had in fact ended. I cannot accept the argument that war powers last as long as the effects and consequences of war for if so they are permanent — as permanent as the war debts. But I find no reason to conclude that we could find fairly that the present state of war is merely technical. We have armies abroad exercising our wa[r] power and have made no peace terms with our allies not to mention our principal enemies. I think the conclusion that the war power has been applicable during the lifetime of this legislation is unavoidable.

Note: The War Power and Domestic Regulation

During World War I, Congress passed the War-Time Prohibition Act, which authorized the President to prohibit the use of grains, cereals, fruits, or other food products in the manufacture or production of wine, beer, other intoxicating malt, or vinous liquor for beverage purposes. The legislation authorized the President to continue the prohibition until the end of the war and thereafter until the termination of demobilization. In two decisions, the Court upheld the application of the prohibition to alcoholic beverages produced after the war ended. In Ruppert v. Caffey, 251 U.S. 264 (1920), the Court stated: "Since Congress has power to increase war efficiency by prohibiting the liquor traffic, no reason appears why it should be denied the power to make its prohibition effective." Justice McReynolds, joined by two other justices, dissented: "[Our] problem concerns the power of Congress and rights of the citizen after a declaration of war, but when active hostilities have ended and demobilization has been completed. . . . I can see no reasonable relationship between the war declared in 1917, or the demobilization following (both of which in essence, if not by formal announcement, terminated before October, 1919), or restoration of peace (whose quiet had already descended upon us) and destruction of the value of complainant's beverage." Likewise, in Hamilton v. Kentucky Distilleries Co., 251 U.S. 146 (1919), the Court held: "It is conceded that the mere cessation of hostilities under the armistice did not abridge or suspend the power of Congress to resort to prohibition of the liquor traffic as a means of increasing our war efficiency, that the support and care of the army and navy during demobilization was within the war emergency, and that, hence, the act was valid when passed." The Court went on to note that demobilization was continuing at the time.

∾ PROBLEM: A PEACETIME DRAFT? ∾

Under Congress's power to wage war, Congress arguably has the authority to authorize a military draft. Such power probably also exists because of Article I, Section 8, which gives Congress the power to "raise and support Armies" and to "provide and maintain a Navy." No one doubts Congress's authority to impose a draft during periods of war. Would it also be permissible for Congress to impose a peacetime draft? Suppose Congress decided that a period of military service would help inculcate a sense of public service and commitment in youth. Is a peacetime draft permissible?

2. The Treaty Power

Although Article II, Section 2 gives the President the power to make treaties, it provides that a two-thirds vote of the Senate is required for ratification. In this section, we examine the scope of the treaty power and its impact on domestic law.

Missouri v. Holland
252 U.S. 416 (1920)

Mr. Justice HOLMES delivered the opinion of the Court.

This is a bill in equity brought by the State of Missouri to prevent a game warden of the United States from attempting to enforce the Migratory Bird Treaty Act of July 3, 1918, and the regulations made by the Secretary of Agriculture in pursuance of the same. The ground of the bill is that the statute is an unconstitutional interference with the rights reserved to the States by the Tenth Amendment, and that the acts of the defendant done and threatened under that authority invade the sovereign right of the State and contravene its will manifested in statutes. . . .

On December 8, 1916, a treaty between the United States and Great Britain was proclaimed by the President. It recited that many species of birds in their annual migrations traversed many parts of the United States and of Canada, that they were of great value as a source of food and in destroying insects injurious to vegetation, but were in danger of extermination through lack of adequate protection. It therefore provided for specified closed seasons and protection in other forms, and agreed that the two powers would take or propose to their lawmaking bodies the necessary measures for carrying the treaty out. The above mentioned act of July 3, 1918, entitled an act to give effect to the convention, prohibited the killing, capturing or selling any of the migratory birds included in the terms of the treaty except as permitted by regulations compatible with those terms, to be made by the Secretary of Agriculture. Regulations were proclaimed on July 31, and October 25, 1918. It is unnecessary to go into any details, because, as we have said, the question raised is the general one whether the treaty and statute are void as an interference with the rights reserved to the States.

To answer this question it is not enough to refer to the Tenth Amendment, reserving the powers not delegated to the United States, because by Article 2, Section 2, the power to make treaties is delegated expressly, and by Article 6 treaties made under the authority of the United States, along with the Constitution and laws of the United States made in pursuance thereof, are declared the supreme law of the land. If the treaty is valid there can be no dispute about the validity of the statute under Article 1, Section 8, as a necessary and proper means to execute the powers of the Government. The language of the Constitution as to the supremacy of treaties being general, the question before us is narrowed to an inquiry into the ground upon which the present supposed exception is placed. . . .

Acts of Congress are the supreme law of the land only when made in pursuance of the Constitution, while treaties are declared to be so when made under the authority of the United States. It is open to question whether the authority of the United States means more than the formal acts prescribed to make the convention. We do not mean to imply that there are no qualifications to the treaty-making power; but they must be ascertained in a different way. It is obvious that there may be matters of the sharpest exigency for the national well being that an act of Congress could not deal with but that a treaty followed by such an act could, and it is not lightly to be assumed that, in matters requiring national action, "a power which must belong to and somewhere reside in every civilized government" is not to be found. . . . The treaty in question does not contravene any prohibitory words to be found in the Constitution. The only question is whether it is forbidden by some invisible radiation from the general terms of the Tenth Amendment. We must consider what this country has become in deciding what that amendment has reserved. . . .

As most of the laws of the United States are carried out within the States and as many of them deal with matters which in the silence of such laws the State might regulate, such general grounds are not enough to support Missouri's claim. Valid treaties of course "are as binding within the territorial limits of the States as they are elsewhere throughout the dominion of the United States." No doubt the great body of private relations usually fall within the control of the State, but a treaty may override its power. We do not have to invoke the later developments of constitutional law for this proposition; it was recognized as early as Hopkirk v. Bell, 3 Cranch, 454, 2 L.Ed. 497, with regard to statutes of limitation, and even earlier, as to confiscation, in Ware v. Hylton, 3 Dall. 199, 1 L.Ed. 568.

Here a national interest of very nearly the first magnitude is involved. It can be protected only by national action in concert with that of another power. The subject matter is only transitorily within the State and has no permanent habitat therein. But for the treaty and the statute there soon might be no birds for any powers to deal with. We see nothing in the Constitution that compels the Government to sit by while a food supply is cut off and the protectors of our forests and our crops are destroyed. It is not sufficient to rely upon the States. The reliance is vain, and were it otherwise, the question is whether the United States is forbidden to act. We are of opinion that the treaty and statute must be upheld.

Decree affirmed.

Note: The Impact of Treaties on Local Law

In De Geofroy v. Riggs, 133 U.S. 258 (1890), a U.S. citizen died intestate but owning valuable real property. A treaty between the United States and France provided that citizens of one country can inherit property in the other country. However, local law made it illegal for foreign citizens to own property in that jurisdiction. Riggs's sister was married to a Frenchman, and her children (who claimed French citizenship) sought to inherit the property. The Court held that the treaty controlled over the local law: "That the treaty power of the United States extends to all proper subjects of negotiation between our government and the governments of other nations is clear. It is also clear that the protection which should be afforded to the citizens of one country owning property in another, and the manner in which that property may be transferred, devised, or inherited, are fitting subjects for such negotiation, and of regulation by mutual stipulations between the two countries. As commercial intercourse increases between different countries, the residence of citizens of one country within the territory of the other naturally follows; and the removal of their disability from alienage to hold, transfer, and inherit property, in such cases, tends to promote amicable relations. . . . The treaty power, as expressed in the constitution, is in terms unlimited, except by those restraints which are found in that instrument against the action of the government, or of its departments, and those arising from the nature of the government itself, and of that of the states. It would not be contended that it extends so far as to authorize what the constitution forbids, or a change in the character of the government, or in that of one of the states, or a cession of any portion of the territory of the latter, without its consent. But, with these exceptions, it is not perceived that there is any limit to the questions which can be adjusted touching any matter which is properly the subject of negotiation with a foreign country." *See also* Hauenstein v. Lynham, 100 U.S. 483 (1880); Ware v. Hylton, 3 U.S. (3 Dall.) 199 (1796).

∽ PROBLEM: RESTRICTING CITIZEN RIGHTS ∽

A country that is an influential trading partner of the United States engages in abusive labor practices and mistreats its citizens. Within the United States, human rights organizations have banded together to oppose trade with this partner and to conduct protests designed to pressure the partner. Under pressure from the trading partner, the President agrees to a treaty that restricts the right of U.S. citizens to criticize the trading partner. The treaty is ratified by the Senate. Is the treaty valid?

Whitney v. Robertson

124 U.S. 190 (1888)

FIELD, J.

The plaintiffs are merchants, doing business in the city of New York [who] imported a large quantity of "centrifugal and molasses sugars" [from] the island of San Domingo. These goods were similar in kind to sugars produced in the Hawaiian islands, which are admitted free of duty under the treaty with the king of those islands, and the act of congress passed to carry the treaty into effect. They were duly entered at the custom-house at the port of New York; the plaintiffs claiming that, by the treaty with the republic of San Domingo, the goods should be admitted on the same terms, that is, free of duty, as similar articles, the produce and manufacture of the Hawaiian islands. The defendant, who was at the time collector of the port, refused to allow this claim, treated the goods as dutiable articles under the acts of congress, and exacted duties on them to the amount of $21,936. [Plaintiffs] paid, under protest, the duties exacted, and brought the present action to recover the amount. [D]efendant demurred [and] final judgment was entered in his favor. . . .

[P]laintiffs rely for [an] exemption [upon] the ninth article of the treaty with the Dominican republic[:] "No higher or other duty shall be imposed on the importation into the United States of any article, the growth, produce, or manufacture of the Dominican republic, or of her fisheries; and no higher or other duty shall be imposed on the importation into the Dominican republic of any article, the growth, produce, or manufacture of the United States, or their fisheries, than are or shall be payable on the like articles, the growth, produce, or manufacture of any other foreign country, or its fisheries."

[The] act of congress under which the duties were collected, authorized their exaction. It is of general application, making no exception in favor of goods of any country. It was passed after the treaty with the Dominican republic, and, if there be any conflict between the stipulations of the treaty and the requirements of the law, the latter must control. A treaty is primarily a contract between two or more independent nations. . . . For the infraction of its provisions a remedy must be sought by the injured party through reclamations upon the other. When the stipulations are not self-executing, they can only be enforced pursuant to legislation to carry them into effect, and such legislation is as much subject to modification and repeal by congress as legislation upon any other subject. If the treaty contains stipulations which are self-executing, that is, require no legislation to make them operative, to that extent they have the force and effect of a legislative enactment. Congress may modify such provisions, so far as they bind the United States, or supersede them altogether. By the constitution, a treaty is placed on the same footing, and made of like obligation, with an act of legislation. Both are declared by that instrument to be the supreme law of the land, and no superior efficacy is given to either over the other. When the two relate to the same subject, the courts will always endeavor to construe them so as to give effect to both, if that can be done without violating the language of either; but, if the two are inconsistent, the one last in date will control the other: provided, always, the stipulation of the treaty on the subject is self-executing. If the country with which the treaty is made is dissatisfied with the action of the legislative department, it may present its complaint to the executive head of the government, and take such other measures as it may deem essential for the protection of its interests. The courts can afford no redress. Whether the complaining nation has just cause of complaint, or our country was justified in its legislation, are not matters for judicial cognizance. Taylor v. Morton, 2 Curt. 454, 459. . . .

[It follows that], when a law is clear in its provisions, its validity cannot be assailed before the courts for want of conformity to stipulations of a previous treaty not already executed. Considerations of that character belong to another department of the government. The duty of the courts is to construe and give effect to the latest expression of the sovereign will. . . .

Judgment affirmed.

Notes

1. More on the Scope of the Treaty Power. In Reid v. Covert, 354 U.S. 1 (1957), the Court offered further insight into the meaning of the treaty power: "[No] agreement with a foreign nation can confer power on the Congress, or on any other branch of Government, which is free from the restraints of the Constitution. Article VI, the Supremacy Clause of the Constitution, declares: 'This Constitution, and the Laws of the United States which shall be made in Pursuance thereof; and all Treaties made, or which shall be made, under the Authority of the United States, shall be the supreme Law of the Land; . . .' There is nothing in this language which intimates that treaties and laws enacted pursuant to them do not have to comply with the provisions of the Constitution. Nor is there anything in the debates which accompanied the drafting and ratification of the Constitution which even suggests such a result. These debates as well as the history that surrounds the adoption of the treaty provision in Article VI make it clear that the reason treaties were not limited to those made in 'pursuance' of the Constitution was so that agreements made by the United States under the Articles of Confederation, including the important peace treaties which concluded the Revolutionary War, would remain in effect. It would be manifestly contrary to the objectives of those who created the Constitution, as well as those who were responsible for the Bill of Rights — let alone alien to our entire constitutional history and tradition — to construe Article VI as permitting the United States to exercise power under an international agreement without observing constitutional prohibitions. In effect, such construction would permit amendment of that document in a manner not sanctioned by Article V. The prohibitions of the Constitution were designed to apply to all branches of the National Government and they cannot be nullified by the Executive or by the Executive and the Senate combined."

2. Seizure of the British Vessel. In Cook v. United States, 288 U.S. 102 (1933), the Court upheld a treaty limiting the government's ability to seize vessels. Under Section 581 of the Tariff Act, officers of the coast guard were authorized to stop and board any vessel at any place within four leagues (12 miles) of the coast of the United States "to examine the manifest and to inspect, search, and examine" the vessel and any merchandise in it. If it appeared that any violation of any law of the United States had been committed, the vessel or merchandise was subject to forfeiture. The collector of customs, acting pursuant to the Tariff Act, assessed against Frank Cook, as master of the *Mazel Tov*, a penalty for failure to include liquor in the manifest. Cook challenged the penalty, alleging that, because of a prior treaty between the United States and Great Britain, the seizure was unlawful. He argued that the four-league limit was, with respect to British vessels, modified by the treaty so as to substitute for four leagues from "our" coast, the distance that "can be traversed in one hour by the vessel suspected of endeavoring to commit the offense." In the case, the Court held that the "Treaty, being later in date than the act of 1922, superseded, so far as inconsistent with the terms of the act, the authority which had been conferred by section 581 upon officers of the Coast Guard to board, search, and seize beyond our territorial waters. Whitney v. Robertson, 124 U.S. 190. For in a strict sense the Treaty was self-executing, in that no legislation was necessary to authorize executive action pursuant to its provisions."

3. *The Rhodesian Embargo.* In Diggs v. Shultz, 470 F.2d 461 (D.C. Cir. 1972), the United Nations Security Council adopted Resolution 232, directing that all member states impose an embargo on trade with Southern Rhodesia. In compliance with this resolution, the President of the United States issued executive orders providing criminal sanctions for violation of the embargo. Later, Congress adopted the so-called "Byrd Amendment" to the Strategic and Critical Materials Stock Piling Act, 50 U.S.C. §98-98h, which provided in part: "Sec. 10. Notwithstanding any other provision of law . . . the President may not prohibit or regulate the importation into the United States of any material determined to be strategic and critical pursuant to the provisions of this Act, if such material is the product of any foreign country or area not listed as a Communist-dominated country or area . . . for so long as the importation into the United States of material of that kind which is the product of such Communist-dominated countries or areas is not prohibited by any provision of law." Since Southern Rhodesia was not a Communist-controlled country, and inasmuch as the United States imported from Communist countries substantial quantities of metallurgical chromite and other materials available from Rhodesia, the Byrd Amendment contemplated the resumption of trade between the United States and Southern Rhodesia. In the case, it was argued that the Byrd Amendment could not authorize the issuance of such a license contrary to the country's treaty obligations. The Court held: "Alleging that the Byrd Amendment did not and could not authorize issuance of such a license contrary to this country's treaty obligations, appellants sought to enjoin further importation, to require official seizure, and to restrain use, of materials already imported under the General License, and to declare the General License null and void. . . . In this court appellants do not seriously contest the first of these propositions, namely, the constitutional power of Congress to set treaty obligations at naught. . . . Under our constitutional scheme, Congress can denounce treaties if it sees fit to do so, and there is nothing the other branches of

government can do about it. We consider that this is precisely what Congress has done in this case."

∾ PROBLEMS ∾

1. *Immigration, Treaties, and Statutes.* The plaintiff sought a writ of habeas corpus to obtain release from an allegedly unlawful detention by Captain Walker, master of the steamship *Belgic*, lying within the harbor of San Francisco. The plaintiff is a Chinese laborer who had resided in San Francisco for 12 years before he traveled to China. When he left, he possessed a certificate issued by the collector of customs entitling him to return to the United States. While he was gone, Congress passed an act annulling such certificates and abrogating the right to land. The validity of the act is assailed as being in effect an expulsion from the country of Chinese laborers, in violation of existing treaties between the United States and the government of China, and of rights vested in them under the laws of Congress. Is the plaintiff entitled to the writ? *See Chae Chan Ping*, 130 U.S. 581 (1889).

2. *More on the Education for a Better America Act.* Could the President and Congress enter into a treaty on education that would allow for the imposition of educational requirements that Congress could not impose directly?

F. CONGRESSIONAL POWER TO ENFORCE CIVIL RIGHTS

U.S. CONSTITUTION, THIRTEENTH AMENDMENT (1865)

Section 1. Neither slavery nor involuntary servitude, except as punishment for crime whereof the party shall have been duly convicted, shall exist within the United States, or any place subject to their jurisdiction.
Section 2. Congress shall have power to enforce the article by appropriate legislation.

U.S. CONSTITUTION, FOURTEENTH AMENDMENT (1868)

Section 1. All persons born or naturalized in the United States and subject to the jurisdiction thereof, are citizens of the United States and of the State wherein they reside. No State shall make or enforce any law which shall abridge the privileges or immunities of citizens of the United States; nor shall any State deprive any person of life, liberty, or property, without due process of law; nor deny to any person within its jurisdiction the equal protection of the laws.
Section 2. Representatives shall be apportioned among the several States according to their respective numbers, counting the whole number of persons in each State, excluding Indians not taxed. But when the right to vote at any election for the choice of electors for President and Vice President of the United States, Representatives in Congress, the Executive and Judicial officers of a State, or the members of the Legislature thereof, is denied to any of the male inhabitants of such State, being twenty-one years of age, and citizens of the United States, or in any way abridged, except for participation in rebellion, or other crime, the basis of representation therein shall be reduced in the proportion which the number of such male citizens shall bear to the whole number of male citizens twenty-one years of age in such State.

Section 3. No person shall be a Senator or Representative in Congress, or elector of President and Vice President, or hold any office, civil or military, under the United States, or under any State, who, having previously taken an oath, as a member of Congress, or as an officer of the United States, or as a member of any State legislature, or as an executive or judicial officer of any State, to support the Constitution of the United States, shall have engaged in insurrection or rebellion against the same, or given aid or comfort to the enemies thereof. But Congress may by a vote of two-thirds of each House, remove such disability.

Section 4. The validity of the public debt of the United States, authorized by law, including debts incurred for payment of pensions and bounties for services in suppressing insurrection or rebellion, shall not be questioned. But neither the United States nor any State shall assume or pay any debt or obligation incurred in aid of insurrection or rebellion against the United States, or any claim for the loss or emancipation of any slave; but all such debts, obligations and claims shall be held illegal and void.

Section 5. The Congress shall have power to enforce, by appropriate legislation, the provisions of this article.

U.S. CONSTITUTION, FIFTEENTH AMENDMENT (1870)

Section 1. The right of citizens of the United States to vote shall not be denied or abridged by the United States or by any State on account of race, color, or previous condition of servitude.

Section 2. The Congress shall have power to enforce this article by appropriate legislation.

∾ PROBLEM: SECOND FLOOR ∾

A criminal defendant and a court reporter suffering from mobility impairments sued the State of Tennessee, claiming that the state failed to provide access to the courts for individuals with disabilities, especially to the upper floors of the local courthouses. The suit was brought under Title II of the Americans with Disabilities Act (ADA), seeking damages despite the state's position that it had sovereign immunity from suit.

∾ PROBLEM: CRITICAL CONFINEMENT ∾

Meanwhile, in nearby Georgia, a paraplegic inmate brought suit against the state, its department of corrections, and state prison officials, claiming his rights were violated under Title II of the ADA. The man, John Smith, was serving a sentence of 14 years for drug smuggling. Smith claims he is confined 23 hours a day in a 12-foot by 3-foot cell, where there is not enough room to turn his wheelchair around. Furthermore, the prison is not outfitted with facilities that permit him to use the toilet or shower without help, causing him to suffer injuries when he was forced to attempt such use on his own.

The legal questions in Smith's case include the following:

1. Can Congress, pursuant to its Section 5 power to enforce the Fourteenth Amendment, create private remedies against the states for violations of the Fourteenth Amendment?

2. Can the remedies created by Congress be prophylactic remedial legislation beyond racial discrimination?
3. Can Congress abrogate state sovereign immunity from suit to enforce the provisions of the Reconstruction Amendments?
4. Can Congress authorize prospective injunctive relief against a state pursuant to Section 5 of the Fourteenth Amendment? (*See, e.g.*, Tennessee v. Lane, 541 U.S. 509 (2004); United States v. Georgia, 546 U.S. 151 (2006).)

BACKGROUND
Famous Case Involving the Enforcement of Civil Rights

The United States charged 18 men with conspiracy for a Ku Klux Klan plot to murder three young civil rights workers, Michael Schwerner, James Chaney, and Andrew Goodman, in Philadelphia, Mississippi. It was alleged that on June 21, 1964, the three men were let out of the Neshoba County, Mississippi, jail at night. The three were allegedly picked up again by the sheriff's office in a police car later that night, transported to a remote unpaved road, and intentionally murdered to punish them for their behavior. The bodies were taken to an earthen dam under construction and buried. The conspiracy charge was not directly for the assaults and murders, but rather for the deprivation, under the color of state law, of the three men's Fourteenth Amendment due process rights to life, liberty or property of the Constitution of the United States.

Can the United States properly charge the 18 persons with these federal crimes under the Constitution? [This case led to one of the most famous criminal trials in the twentieth century, called the *Mississippi Burning* case in the popular vernacular. The defendants appealed their indictments in United States v. Price, 383 U.S. 787 (1966), which notably was argued in the Supreme Court for the United States by Solicitor General Thurgood Marshall, who later became a Supreme Court Justice. The Court observed, "we have no doubt of 'the power of Congress to enforce by appropriate criminal sanction every right guaranteed by the Due Process Clause of the Fourteenth Amendment.'" The Court held that the federal statutes in question criminalized the conduct subject to the indictment and that "under color of state law" could include private individuals acting in concert with state officials.

Seven of the 18 defendants were convicted, including Cecil Price, the chief deputy sheriff of Neshoba County. One of the defendants who was not convicted, Edgar Ray Killen, was found guilty in 2005 of three counts of manslaughter. In 1988, the trial was made into a film, *Mississippi Burning*, starring Gene Hackman and Willem Dafoe.]

Prior to the end of the Civil War, Congress proposed the Thirteenth Amendment, abolishing slavery and involuntary servitude. The vote in Congress approving the Amendment barely surpassed the two-thirds majority vote required under Article V. Many believed that the Amendment implicitly made slaves citizens, effectively overruling Dred Scott v. Sandford, 60 U.S. 393 (1857). Within a year of the Amendment's ratification, Congress enacted the Civil Rights Act of 1866, providing black citizens with "the same right in every state . . . to make and enforce contracts, to sue, be parties, . . . to inherit, purchase, sell and convey real and personal property; and to the full and equal benefit of all laws and proceedings for the security of person and property as is enjoyed by white citizens."

After the Thirteenth Amendment was ratified, the 15-member Joint Congressional Committee on Reconstruction designed and proposed the Fourteenth Amendment in December of 1865. Led by a conservative Republican senator, William Fessenden of Maine, and a radical Republican Senator, Thaddeus Stevens of Pennsylvania, the Amendment was a product not only of the Civil War but of the politics of the times as well. The Fourteenth Amendment expressly made all of the former slaves citizens and went on to offer them a variety of protections from government. The Amendment produced considerable litigation, particularly dealing with its meaning and reach.

Congress proposed the Fifteenth Amendment in 1869, and it was ratified in 1870. This Amendment gave Congress the power to ensure that voting rights were also administered fairly and equally.

These three Reconstruction Amendments, all proposed by Congress, gave Congress the power to protect the rights of blacks in America. It has been argued that Congress gave itself the power because it did not trust the Judicial Branch to do the same. In fact, after Dred Scott v. Sandford, Congress might have become leery of courts putting aside regional, popular, or cultural leanings to enforce civil rights.

Over time, the power to enforce civil rights has witnessed an ever-changing balance between the states and the federal government and between Congress and the Court. The limited power of the federal government was expanded by the Thirteenth, Fourteenth, and Fifteenth Amendments, empowering the federal government to grant and protect the citizenship of former slaves. *The Slaughterhouse Cases*, 83 U.S. (16 Wall.) 36 (1873). The legislative debates and congressional record relating to the passage and ratification of the Reconstruction Amendments were inconclusive as to the nature and scope of Congress's power to enforce the Amendment's substantive provisions. These issues were left to the courts, where early cases examined congressional efforts to remove the "badges and incidents of slavery" in public accommodations, transportation, and voting. The Civil Rights Acts of 1866, 1870, 1871, and 1875 survive in various forms today.

Modern congressional legislation protecting rights covers the spectrum of interests and includes the Civil Rights Act of 1964 and most of the Voting Rights Act of 1965. There are also acts prohibiting firearms within so many feet of a schoolyard and protecting patent rights, the rights of women, the disabled, and the expression of religious views. The following cases and notes suggest that the balance of power between the Court and Congress has been as difficult to determine as the balance of power between the states and the federal government.

1. Early Developments

Relatively few cases dealt with the meaning of the Thirteenth Amendment after its ratification. Those cases that were brought often dealt with the scope of its coverage, especially the meaning of "involuntary servitude."

∽ PROBLEM: PUBLIC SERVICE ∽

An Arizona man, Peter Mast, brought suit against a division of the State of Arizona, claiming that an Arizona law requiring all able-bodied persons between the ages of 21 and 25 to complete at least one weekend of public service appropriate to the person's skills, age, and circumstances is unconstitutional. The law has limited opt-out provisions and defines a weekend as "at most 48 hours at a time." Mast was prosecuted for refusing to comply with several requests for service and was sentenced to serve two days in jail for failing to comply with the duty requirement. Mast contends that the law requires "involuntary servitude" in violation of the Thirteenth Amendment. Who should win this lawsuit? How does Mast's claim differ from the claims in the sample enforcement of civil rights problems, *Second Floor* and *Critical Confinement*, above?

The Civil Rights Cases

109 U.S. 3 (1883)

BRADLEY, J.

[These cases involve a challenge to the constitutionality of the Civil Rights Act of 1875. Four cases appeal indictments for denying to persons of color the accommodations and privileges of an inn or a theater. The fifth case was brought by a husband and wife when a railway conductor refused to allow the wife to ride in the ladies' car because she was a person of African descent.]

The essence of the [Civil Rights Act of 1875 is to] declare that, in the enjoyment of the accommodations and privileges of inns, public conveyances, theatres, and other places of public amusement, no distinction shall be made between citizens of different race or color, or between those who have, and those who have not, been slaves. The second section makes it a penal offence in any person to deny to any citizen of any race or color, regardless of previous servitude, any of the accommodations or privileges mentioned in the first section.

Has Congress constitutional power to make such a law? Of course, no one will contend that the power to pass it was contained in the Constitution before the adoption of the last three amendments. The power is sought [in] the Fourteenth Amendment. . . . The last section of the amendment invests Congress with power to enforce it by appropriate legislation. To enforce what? To enforce the prohibition. To adopt appropriate legislation for correcting the effects of such prohibited State laws and State acts, and thus to render them effectually null, void, and innocuous. This is the legislative power conferred upon Congress, and this is the whole of it. . . . It does not authorize Congress to create a code of municipal law

for the regulation of private rights. . . . Positive rights and privileges are undoubtedly secured by the Fourteenth Amendment; but they are secured by way of prohibition against State laws and State proceedings affecting those rights and
privileges, and by power given to Congress to legislate for the purpose of carrying such prohibition into effect. . . . United States v. Cruikshank, 92 U.S. 542.

[U]ntil some State law has been passed, or some State action through its officers or agents has been taken, adverse to the rights of citizens sought to be protected by the Fourteenth Amendment, no legislation of the United States under
said amendment, nor any proceeding under such legislation, can be called into
activity: for the prohibitions of the amendment are against State laws and acts
done under State authority. [Congress] cannot properly cover the whole domain
of rights appertaining to life, liberty and property, defining them and providing
for their vindication. That would be to establish a code of municipal law regulative of all private rights between man and man in society. If this legislation is
appropriate for enforcing the prohibitions of the amendment, it is difficult to see
where it is to stop. Why may not Congress with equal show of authority enact a
code of laws for the enforcement and vindication of all rights of life, liberty, and
property? If it is supposable that the States may deprive persons of life, liberty,
and property without due process of law[,] why should not Congress proceed at
once to prescribe due process of law for the protection of every one of these fundamental [rights]?

This is not corrective legislation; it is primary and direct. . . . It supercedes
and displaces State legislation on the same subject or only allows it permissive
force. . . . It ignores such regulation and assumes that the matter is one that
belongs to the domain of national regulation. [Whether] it would not have been a
more effective protection of the rights of citizens to have clothed Congress with
plenary power over the whole subject, is not now the question. What we have to
decide is, whether such plenary power has been conferred upon Congress by the
Fourteenth Amendment; and, in our judgment, it has not. [N]o countenance of
authority for the passage of the law in question can be found in either the Thirteenth or Fourteenth Amendment of the Constitution; and no other ground of
authority for its passage being suggested, it must necessarily be declared void, at
least so far as its operation in the several States is concerned.

[T]he first and second sections of the act of congress of March 1, 1875,
entitled 'An act to protect all citizens in their civil and legal rights,' are unconstitutional and void, and that judgment should be rendered upon the several indictments in those cases accordingly. And it is so ordered.

Justice HARLAN, dissenting.
The opinion in these cases proceeds upon grounds entirely too narrow and
artificial. . . . Before considering the language and scope of these amendments it
will be proper to recall the relations subsisting, prior to their adoption, between
the national government and the institution of slavery. [Harlan then discussed
how the Court upheld Congress's power to enact the Fugitive Slave Laws pursuant to Section 2, Article 4 and direct states to act affirmatively to protect the property interest of slaveholders in fugitive slaves.] We have seen that the power of

Congress, by legislation, to enforce the master's right to have his slave delivered up on claim was implied from the recognition of that right in the national Constitution. But the power conferred by the Thirteenth Amendment does not rest upon implication or inference. Those who framed it were not ignorant of the discussion, covering many years of our country's history, as to the constitutional power of Congress to enact the Fugitive Slave Laws of 1793 and 1850. When, therefore, it was determined, by a change in the fundamental law, to uproot the institution of slavery wherever it existed in the land, and to establish universal freedom, there was a fixed purpose to place the authority of Congress in the premises beyond the possibility of a doubt. Therefore power to enforce the Thirteenth Amendment, by appropriate legislation, was expressly granted.

The assumption that this amendment consists wholly of prohibitions upon State laws and State proceedings in hostility to its provisions, is unauthorized by its language. If any right was created by that amendment, the grant of power, through appropriate legislation, to enforce its provisions, authorizes Congress, by means of legislation, operating throughout the entire Union, to guard, secure, and protect that right. If, then, exemption from discrimination, in respect of civil rights, is a new constitutional right, secured by the grant of State citizenship to colored citizens of the United States[,] why may not the nation, by means of its own legislation of a primary direct character, guard, protect and enforce that right? It is a right and privilege, which the nation conferred. This court has always given a broad and liberal construction to the Constitution, so as to enable Congress to enforce rights secured by that instrument.

∼ PROBLEM: OLLIE'S BBQ RANCH ∼

Ollie owns a roadside barbeque stand in Memphis, called Ollie's BBQ Ranch. The stand is located on Ollie's private property. The business is readily accessible to people traveling on the interstate highway going to Atlanta. By word of mouth and in-state advertising, the business has grown such that Ollie is thinking about opening another stand in northern Tennessee. On the front door, a prominently placed large sign reads, "Whites Only." After *The Civil Rights Cases*, can Congress address Ollie's practice of excluding black customers? Are the sample problems, *Second Floor* and *Critical Confinement*, above, useful? How?

2. *Modern Civil Rights Cases*

Congress did not enact any civil rights laws between 1875 and 1957. When Congress finally began to respond to growing political pressure for racial equality in the 1960s, Congress was not forced to rely solely on its authority under Section 5 of the Fourteenth Amendment, which had been severely restricted in *The Civil Rights Cases*. Instead, in passing the 1964 Civil Rights Act, it was able to rely on the now-expanded interpretation of Congress's spending and commerce powers. This avenue was not foreclosed by *The Civil Rights Cases*, which raised but did not reach the issue of whether the Commerce Clause authorized Congress to enact civil rights legislation to protect African Americans. In 1964, in Heart of Atlanta Motel v. United States, 379 U.S. 241 (1964), the Court upheld Title II of the Civil Rights Act of 1964 as applied to a motel that serves interstate passengers: "Title II is carefully limited to enterprises having a direct and substantial relation to the interstate flow of goods and people."

Two years later, in United States v. Guest, 383 U.S. 745 (1966), the Court ruled that Section 5 of the Fourteenth Amendment authorized Congress to make it a crime for white supremacists to conspire to deprive African Americans of their civil rights. While Justice Stewart's majority opinion rested on a finding of state action (defendants had acted in concert with state officials), six justices were prepared to overrule *The Civil Rights Cases*, arguing that Section 5 empowered Congress to punish all conspiracies to interfere with the exercise of rights conferred under Section 1, "whether or not state officers or others acting under the color of state law are implicated in the conspiracy."

In United States v. Morrison, 529 U.S. 598 (2000), involving the Violence Against Women Act and its federal civil remedy for the victims of gender-motivated violence, the Court finally put the question of whether Congress could reach private action under Section 5 to rest. In a five-to-four majority decision, Chief Justice Rehnquist concluded for the majority that the law could not be upheld under the Fourteenth Amendment:

> Section 5 is "a positive grant of legislative power," that includes authority to "prohibit conduct which is not itself unconstitutional and [to] intrude into 'legislative spheres of autonomy previously reserved to the States.'" Nevertheless, the majority concluded that the congressional enforcement power is not unlimited, and that several limitations inherent in §5's text and constitutional context. Petitioners' §5 argument is founded on an assertion that there is pervasive bias in various state justice systems against victims of gender-motivated violence. This assertion is supported by a voluminous congressional record. . . . Petitioners contend that this bias denies victims of gender-motivated violence the equal protection of the laws and that Congress therefore acted appropriately in enacting a private civil remedy against the perpetrators of gender-motivated violence to both remedy the States' bias and deter future instances of discrimination in the state courts. . . . As our cases have established, state-sponsored gender discrimination violates equal protection unless it serves "important governmental objectives and . . . the discriminatory means employed" are "substantially related to the achievement of those objectives." [citations omitted] However, the language and purpose of the Fourteenth Amendment place certain limitations on the manner in which Congress may attack discriminatory conduct. These limitations are necessary to prevent the Fourteenth Amendment from obliterating the Framers' carefully crafted balance of power between the States and the National Government. . . . That Amendment erects no shield against merely private conduct, however discriminatory or wrongful. [In *The Civil Rights Cases*] we held that the public accommodation provisions of the Civil Rights Act of 1875, which applied to purely private conduct, were beyond the scope of the §5 enforcement power. . . . Petitioners contend that two more recent decisions have in effect overruled this longstanding limitation on Congress' §5 authority. They rely on United States v. Guest for the proposition that the rule laid down in *The Civil Rights Cases* is no longer good law. In *Guest*, [t]hree Members of the Court, in a separate opinion by Justice Brennan, expressed the view that *The Civil Rights Cases* were wrongly decided, and that Congress could under §5 prohibit actions by private individuals. Three other Members of the Court, who joined the opinion of

the Court, joined a separate opinion by Justice Clark which in two or three sentences stated the conclusion that Congress could punish all conspiracies [that] interfere with Fourteenth Amendment rights. Though these three Justices saw fit to opine on matters not before the Court in *Guest*, the Court had no occasion to revisit *The Civil Rights Cases*. . . . To accept petitioners' argument, one must add to the three Justices joining Justice Brennan's reasoned explanation for his belief that *The Civil Rights Cases* were wrongly decided, the three Justices joining Justice Clark's opinion who gave no explanation whatever for their similar view. This is simply not the way that reasoned constitutional adjudication proceeds. We accordingly have no hesitation in saying that it would take more than the naked dicta contained in Justice Clark's opinion, when added to Justice Brennan's opinion, to cast any doubt upon the enduring vitality of *The Civil Rights Cases*. . . . For these reasons, we conclude that Congress' power under §5 does not extend to the enactment of §13981.

As previously noted, the Court also concluded that the law could not be sustained under the Commerce Clause.

In Jones v. Alfred H. Mayer Co., 392 U.S. 409 (1968), the Supreme Court rejected the view in *The Civil Rights Cases* that Congress's power under Section 2 of the Thirteenth Amendment to prohibit private discrimination is limited. Although Justice Bradley and the majority acknowledged that the Thirteenth Amendment has no state action requirement, the Court narrowly defined what constituted "the badges and incidents of slavery" to exclude discrimination by hotels, transportation companies, and other public accommodations. *Cf.* Plessy v. Ferguson. The Court in *Jones* upheld Congress's power to prohibit private and public discrimination in the sale and rental of property under 42 U.S.C. 1982, a portion of the Civil Rights Act of 1866.

∿ PROBLEMS ∿

1. *Family Medical Leave Act.* Congress decides to respond to the growing effort of state legislatures and courts to provide employment security for people forced to choose between their jobs and taking time off to recuperate from an extended illness or care for a sick family member. In 2009, Congress enacted the Family Medical Leave Act pursuant to its power under the Commerce Clause and Section 5 of the Fourteenth Amendment, providing for private injunctive relief and damages if states deprive individuals of the right to a family leave to care for family members under specific circumstances. You are the staff attorney for the congressional committee that promoted the law. You anticipate that a state will challenge the law when a new father seeks to assert his right to family leave to care for his newborn child. How should the United States defend such a claim? What should be included in the congressional record to help defend against such a claim?

2. *1866 Civil Rights Act — Take II.* As part of the Civil Rights Act of 1866, Congress provided that "all citizens within the jurisdiction of the United States have the same rights to make and enforce contracts." A group of African American parents sued a private school that denied admission to their children solely on the basis of race. Does Congress have the power to prohibit this form of discrimination pursuant to the power granted under the Thirteenth Amendment?

3. *Congressional Enforcement of the Right to Vote*

In the prior cases, the Court grappled with the line between the power of the state over "local matters" and the exercise of federal government power in these same areas under the Reconstruction Amendments and the Commerce Clause. The following cases examine the roles of Congress and the Court in declaring and responding to violations of the Constitution.

Katzenbach v. Morgan

384 U.S. 641 (1966)

Brennan, J.

These cases concern the constitutionality of §4(e) of the Voting Rights Act of 1965 [which] provides that no person who has successfully completed the sixth primary grade in a public school in, or a private school accredited by, the Commonwealth of Puerto Rico in which the language of instruction was other than English shall be denied the right to vote in any election because of his inability to read or write English. Appellees brought this suit to challenge the constitutionality of §4(e) insofar as it prohibits the enforcement of the election laws of New York requiring an ability to read and write English as a condition of voting. Under these laws many of the several hundred thousand New York City residents who have migrated there from the Commonwealth of Puerto Rico had previously been denied the right to vote, and appellees attack §4(e) insofar as it would enable many of these citizens to vote. . . . We hold that, in the application challenged in these cases, §4(e) is a proper exercise of the powers granted to Congress by § 5 of the Fourteenth Amendment and that by force of the Supremacy Clause the New York English literacy requirement cannot be enforced to the extent that it is inconsistent with §4(e).

The Attorney General of the State of New York argues that an exercise of congressional power under §5 of the Fourteenth Amendment that prohibits the enforcement of a state law can only be sustained if the Judicial Branch determines that the state law is prohibited by the provisions of the Amendment that Congress sought to enforce. More specifically, he urges that §4(e) cannot be sustained as appropriate legislation to enforce the Equal Protection Clause unless the judiciary decides — even with the guidance of a congressional judgment — that the application of the English literacy requirement prohibited by §4(e) is forbidden by the Equal Protection Clause itself. We disagree. Neither the language nor history of §5 supports such a construction. As was said with regard to §5 in *Ex parte Virginia*, "It is the power of Congress which has been enlarged. . . ."

Thus [our] task is limited to determining whether such legislation is, as required by §5, appropriate legislation to enforce the Equal Protection Clause. . . . There can be no doubt that §4(e) may be regarded as an enactment to enforce the Equal Protection Clause. Congress explicitly declared that it enacted §4(e) "to secure the rights under the fourteenth amendment of persons educated in American-flag schools in which the predominant classroom language was other than English." The persons referred to include those who have migrated from the Commonwealth of Puerto Rico to New York and who have been denied the right to vote because of their inability to read and write English, and the Fourteenth Amendment rights referred to include those emanating from the Equal Protection Clause. More specifically, §4(e) may be viewed as a measure to secure for the Puerto Rican community residing in New York nondiscriminatory treatment by government — both in the imposition of voting qualifications and the provision or administration of governmental services, such as public schools, public housing and law enforcement.

Section 4(e) may be readily seen as "plainly adapted" to furthering these aims of the Equal Protection Clause. It was for Congress [to] assess and weigh the various conflicting considerations — the risk or pervasiveness of the discrimination in governmental services, the effectiveness of eliminating the state restriction on the right to vote as a means of dealing with the evil, the adequacy or availability of alternative remedies, and the nature and significance of the state interests that would be affected by the nullification of the English literacy requirement. . . . It is not for us to review the congressional resolution of these factors. . . . We conclude that §4(e) is appropriate legislation to enforce the Equal Protection Clause and that [reverse] the judgment of the District Court.

Note

Four years after *Morgan*, five justices (Black, Douglas, Brennan, White, and Marshall) held in Oregon v. Mitchell, 400 U.S. 112 (1970), that a federal voting rights statute could lower the age for voting in federal elections to 18 from 21. Five justices (Black, Burger, Harlan, Stewart, and Blackmun) held that Congress could not interfere with the voting age set by individual states for state and local elections. Writing for those opposed to allowing Congress to set the age for state and local elections, Justice Black wrote: "[T]here are at least three limitations upon Congress' power to enforce the guarantees of the Civil War Amendments. First, Congress may not by legislation repeal other provisions of the Constitution. Second, the power granted to Congress was not intended to strip the States of their power to govern themselves or to convert our national government of enumerated powers into a central government of unrestrained authority over every inch of the whole Nation. Third, Congress may only 'enforce' the provisions of the amendments and may do so only by 'appropriate legislation.' Congress has no power under the enforcement sections to undercut the amendments' guarantees of personal equality and freedom from discrimination, or to undermine those protections of the Bill of Rights which we have held the Fourteenth Amendment made applicable to the States. . . . Of course, we have upheld congressional legislation under the Enforcement Clauses in some cases where Congress has interfered with state regulation of the local electoral process. Katzenbach v. Morgan. But division of power between state and national governments, like every provision of the Constitution, was expressly qualified by the Civil War Amendments' ban on racial discrimination. Where Congress attempts to remedy racial discrimination under its enforcement powers, its authority is enhanced by the avowed intention of the framers of the Thirteenth, Fourteenth, and Fifteenth Amendments." The Court unanimously upheld the legislative suspension of literacy testing in both state and federal elections as a qualification for voting: "In imposing a nationwide ban on literacy tests, Congress has recognized a national problem for what it is — a serious *national* dilemma that touches every corner of our land. . . . Congress has decided that the way to solve the problems of racial discrimination is to deal with nationwide discrimination with nationwide legislation." Subsequent to this decision, the Twenty-Sixth Amendment to the U.S. Constitution lowered the minimum voting age to 18 for all elections.

City of Rome v. United States

446 U.S. 156 (1980)

Mr. Justice MARSHALL delivered the opinion of the Court.

At issue in this case is the constitutionality of the Voting Rights Act of 1965 and its applicability to electoral changes and annexations made by the city of Rome, Ga.

It is clear [that] under §2 of the Fifteenth Amendment Congress may prohibit practices that in and of themselves do not violate §1 of the Amendment, so long as the prohibitions attacking racial discrimination in voting are "appropriate," as that term is defined in McCulloch v. Maryland and *Ex parte Virginia.* In the present case, we hold that the Act's ban on electoral changes that are discriminatory in effect is an appropriate method of promoting the purposes of the Fifteenth Amendment, even if it is assumed that §1 of the Amendment prohibits only intentional discrimination in voting. Congress could rationally have concluded that, because electoral changes by jurisdictions with a demonstrable history of intentional racial discrimination in voting create the risk of purposeful discrimination, it was proper to prohibit changes that have a discriminatory impact. We find no reason, then, to disturb Congress' considered judgment that banning electoral changes that have a discriminatory impact is an effective method of preventing States from "'[undoing] or [defeating] the rights recently won' by Negroes."

[The] judgment of the District Court is affirmed.

Justice REHNQUIST, with whom Justice STEWART joins, dissenting.

[The] facts of this case signal the necessity for this Court to carefully scrutinize the alleged source of congressional power to intrude so deeply in the governmental structure of the municipal corporations created by some of the 50 States. . . . There are three theories of congressional enforcement power relevant to this case. First, it is clear that if the proposed changes would violate the Constitution, Congress could certainly prohibit their implementation. It has never been seriously maintained, however, that Congress can do no more than the judiciary to enforce the Amendments' commands. Thus, if the electoral changes in issue do not violate the Constitution, as judicially interpreted, it must be determined whether Congress could nevertheless appropriately prohibit these changes under the other two theories of congressional power. Under the second theory, Congress can act remedially to enforce the judicially established substantive prohibitions of the Amendments. If not properly remedial, the exercise of this power could be sustained only if this Court accepts the premise of the third theory that Congress has the authority under its enforcement powers to determine, without more, that electoral changes with a disparate impact on race violate the Constitution, in which case Congress by a legislative Act could effectively amend the Constitution.

I think it is apparent that neither of the first two theories for sustaining the exercise of congressional power supports this application of the Voting Rights Act. . . . The result reached by the Court today can be sustained only upon the theory that Congress was empowered to determine that structural changes with a disparate impact on a minority group's ability to elect a candidate of their race violates the Fourteenth or Fifteenth Amendment. This construction of the Fourteenth Amendment was rejected in *The Civil Rights Cases*. . . . The Court today fails to heed this prior precedent. To permit congressional power to prohibit the conduct challenged in this case requires state and local governments to cede far more of their powers to the Federal Government than the Civil War Amendments ever envisioned; and it requires the judiciary to cede far more of its power to interpret and enforce the Constitution than ever envisioned. The intrusion is all the more offensive to our constitutional system when it is recognized that the only values fostered are debatable assumptions about political theory which should properly be left to the local democratic process. . . .

∾ PROBLEM: PRECLEARANCE ∾

Congress decides to extend the "preclearance" requirements of the Voting Rights Act of 1965, based on Section 2, the enforcement provision of the Fifteenth Amendment, for another 25 years. The preclearance provisions, in Section 5 of the Act, require states to obtain federal permission before election procedures can be changed in those jurisdictions that have a history of minority voter disenfranchisement. Does Congress have the power to extend Section 5 of the Act if there is currently no evidence of voter disenfranchisement or any other unconstitutional voting rights deprivations? Can Congress justify the extension if there is a credible argument that the Act will deter future violations? *See* Northwest Austin Municipal Utility District Number One v. Holder, *129 S. Ct. 2504* (2009). Do the voting rights enforcement cases parallel the enforcement of the Fourteenth Amendment cases, such as the sample problems, *Second Floor* and *Critical Confinement*, above?

4. *Religious Freedom and Congressional Fourteenth Amendment Enforcement Power*

City of Boerne v. Archbishop of San Antonio & United States

521 U.S. 507 (1997)

KENNEDY, J.

A local zoning authority's denial to a church a building permit was challenged under the Religious Freedom Restoration Act of 1993. The case calls into question the authority of Congress to enact RFRA. We conclude the statute exceeds Congress' power. . . .

Congress enacted RFRA in direct response to the Court's decision in Employment Div., Dept. of Human Resources of Ore. v. Smith. There, we considered a Free Exercise Clause claim brought by members of the Native American Church who were denied unemployment benefits when they lost their jobs because they had used peyote. . . . Many [in Congress] criticized the Court's reasoning, and this disagreement resulted in the passage of RFRA. . . .

RFRA prohibits "government" from "substantially burdening" a person's exercise of religion even if the burden results from a rule of general applicability unless the government can demonstrate the burden "(1) is in furtherance of a compelling governmental interest; and (2) is the least restrictive means of furthering that compelling governmental interest." §2000bb-1. . . .

Congress relied on its Fourteenth Amendment enforcement power in enacting the most far reaching and substantial of RFRA's provisions, those which impose its requirements on the States. . . . The parties disagree over whether RFRA is a proper exercise of Congress' §5 power "to enforce" by "appropriate legislation" the constitutional guarantee that no State shall deprive any person of "life, liberty, or property, without due process of law" nor deny any person "equal protection of the laws."

In defense of the Act respondent contends that RFRA is permissible enforcement legislation. Congress is only protecting one of the liberties guaranteed by the Fourteenth Amendment's Due Process Clause, the free exercise of religion, beyond what is necessary under *Smith*. It is said the congressional decision to dispense with proof of deliberate or overt discrimination and instead concentrate on a law's effects accords with the settled understanding that §5 includes the power to enact legislation designed to prevent as well as remedy constitutional violations. It is further contended that Congress' §5 power is not limited to remedial or preventive legislation.

It is also true, however, that "as broad as the congressional enforcement power is, it is not unlimited." Oregon v. Mitchell. In assessing the breadth of §5's enforcement power, we begin with its text. Congress has been given the power "to enforce" the "provisions of this article." We agree with respondent, of course, that Congress can enact legislation under § 5 enforcing the constitutional right to the free exercise of religion.

Congress' power under §5, however, extends only to "enforcing" the provisions of the Fourteenth Amendment. The Court has described this power as "remedial," South Carolina v. Katzenbach. The design of the Amendment and the text of §5 are inconsistent with the suggestion that Congress has the power to decree the substance of the Fourteenth Amendment's restrictions on the States. Legislation which alters the meaning of the Free Exercise Clause cannot be said to be enforcing the Clause. Congress does not enforce a constitutional right by changing what the right is. It has been given the power "to enforce," not the power to determine what constitutes a constitutional violation. Were it not so, what Congress would be enforcing would no longer be, in any meaningful sense, the "provisions of [the Fourteenth Amendment]."

While the line between measures that remedy or prevent unconstitutional actions and measures that make a substantive change in the governing law is not easy to discern, and Congress must have wide latitude in determining where it lies, the distinction exists and must be observed. There must be a congruence and proportionality between the injury to be prevented or remedied and the means adopted to that end. Lacking such a connection, legislation may become substantive in operation and effect. History and our case law support drawing the distinction, one apparent from the text of the Amendment.

The Fourteenth Amendment's history confirms the remedial, rather than substantive, nature of the Enforcement Clause. . . . The design of the Fourteenth Amendment has proved significant also in maintaining the traditional separation of powers between Congress and the Judiciary. The first eight Amendments to the Constitution set forth self-executing prohibitions on governmental action, and this Court has had primary authority to interpret those prohibitions. . . . As enacted, the Fourteenth Amendment [Section 1] confers substantive rights against the States which, like the provisions of the Bill of Rights, are self-executing. The power to interpret the Constitution in a case or controversy remains in the Judiciary.

The remedial and preventive nature of Congress' enforcement power, and the limitation inherent in the power, were confirmed in our earliest cases on the Fourteenth Amendment. *Civil Rights Cases.* . . . Although the specific holdings of these early cases might have been superseded or modified, *see, e.g.*, Heart of Atlanta Motel, Inc. v. United States; United States v. Guest, their treatment of Congress' §5 power as corrective or preventive, not definitional, has not been questioned.

Any suggestion that Congress has a substantive, non-remedial power under the Fourteenth Amendment is not supported by our case law. There is language in our opinion in Katzenbach v. Morgan, which could be interpreted as acknowledging a power in Congress to enact legislation that expands the rights contained in §1 of the Fourteenth Amendment. This is not a necessary interpretation, however, or even the best one. . . . The Court perceived a factual basis on which Congress could have concluded that New York's literacy requirement "constituted an invidious discrimination in violation of the Equal Protection Clause." As Justice Stewart explained in Oregon v. Mitchell, interpreting *Morgan* to give

Congress the power to interpret the Constitution "would require an enormous extension of that decision's rationale."

If Congress could define its own powers by altering the Fourteenth Amendment's meaning, no longer would the Constitution be "superior paramount law, unchangeable by ordinary means." It would be "on a level with ordinary legislative acts, and, like other acts, . . . alterable when the legislature shall please to alter it." Marbury v. Madison. Under this approach, it is difficult to conceive of a principle that would limit congressional power. . . . Shifting legislative majorities could change the Constitution and effectively circumvent the difficult and detailed amendment process contained in Article V.

We now turn to consider whether RFRA can be considered enforcement legislation under §5 of the Fourteenth Amendment.

Respondent contends that RFRA is a proper exercise of Congress' remedial or preventive power. . . . If Congress can prohibit laws with discriminatory effects in order to prevent racial discrimination in violation of the Equal Protection Clause, *see* Fullilove v. Klutznick, (plurality opinion); *City of Rome*, then it can do the same, respondent argues, to promote religious liberty.

While preventive rules are sometimes appropriate remedial measures, there must be a congruence between the means used and the ends to be achieved. The appropriateness of remedial measures must be considered in light of the evil presented. Strong measures appropriate to address one harm may be an unwarranted response to another, lesser one.

A comparison between RFRA and the Voting Rights Act is instructive. In contrast to the record which confronted Congress and the judiciary in the voting rights cases, RFRA's legislative record lacks examples of modern instances of generally applicable laws passed because of religious bigotry. The history of persecution in this country detailed in the hearings mentions no episodes occurring in the past 40 years. . . . It is difficult to maintain that [the evidence presented in legislative hearings] are examples of legislation enacted or enforced due to animus or hostility to the burdened religious practices or that they indicate some widespread pattern of religious discrimination in this country. . . . This lack of support in the legislative record, however, is not RFRA's most serious shortcoming. Judicial deference, in most cases, is based not on the state of the legislative record Congress compiles but "on due regard for the decision of the body constitutionally appointed to decide." Oregon v. Mitchell. As a general matter, it is for Congress to determine the method by which it will reach a decision.

Regardless of the state of the legislative record, RFRA cannot be considered remedial, preventive legislation, if those terms are to have any meaning. RFRA is so out of proportion to a supposed remedial or preventive object that it cannot be understood as responsive to, or designed to prevent, unconstitutional behavior. It appears, instead, to attempt a substantive change in constitutional protections. Preventive measures prohibiting certain types of laws may be appropriate when there is reason to believe that many of the laws affected by the congressional enactment have a significant likelihood of being unconstitutional. [citation omitted] Remedial legislation under §5 "should be adapted to the mischief and wrong which the [Fourteenth] Amendment was intended to provide against." *Civil Rights Cases.*

RFRA is not so confined. Sweeping coverage ensures its intrusion at every level of government, displacing laws and prohibiting official actions of almost every description and regardless of subject matter. RFRA's restrictions apply to every agency and official of the Federal, State, and local Governments. RFRA applies to all federal and state law, statutory or otherwise, whether adopted before or after its enactment. RFRA has no termination date or termination mechanism. Any law is subject to challenge at any time by any individual who alleges a substantial burden on his or her free exercise of religion.

The stringent test RFRA demands of state laws reflects a lack of proportionality or congruence between the means adopted and the legitimate end to be achieved. If an objector can show a substantial burden on his free exercise, the State must demonstrate a compelling governmental interest and show that the law is the least restrictive means of furthering its interest. Claims that a law substantially burdens someone's exercise of religion will often be difficult to contest. . . . Requiring a State to demonstrate a compelling interest and show that it has adopted the least restrictive means of achieving that interest is the most demanding test known to constitutional law. If "'compelling interest' really means what it says . . . many laws will not meet the test. . . . [The test] would open the prospect of constitutionally required religious exemptions from civic obligations of almost every conceivable kind." This is a considerable congressional intrusion into the States' traditional prerogatives and general authority to regulate for the health and welfare of their citizens.

The substantial costs RFRA exacts, both in practical terms of imposing a heavy litigation burden on the States and in terms of curtailing their traditional general regulatory power, far exceed any pattern or practice of unconstitutional conduct under the Free Exercise Clause as interpreted in *Smith*. Simply put, RFRA is not designed to identify and counteract state laws likely to be unconstitutional because of their treatment of religion. . . . RFRA was designed to control cases and controversies, such as the one before us; but as the provisions of the federal statute here invoked are beyond congressional authority, it is this Court's precedent, not RFRA, which must control. . . .

It is for Congress in the first instance to "determine whether and what legislation is needed to secure the guarantees of the Fourteenth Amendment," and its conclusions are entitled to much deference. Katzenbach v. Morgan. Congress' discretion is not unlimited, however, and the courts retain the power to determine if Congress has exceeded its authority under the Constitution. Broad as the power of Congress is under the Enforcement Clause of the Fourteenth Amendment, RFRA contradicts vital principles necessary to maintain separation of powers and the federal balance. The judgment of the Court of Appeals sustaining the Act's constitutionality is reversed.

It is so ordered.

∼ PROBLEMS ∼

1. *The Boerne Supremacy.* Assume Congress decides after the *City of Boerne* decision that Section 1 of the Thirteenth Amendment prohibits states from engaging in the practice of enticing unpaid interns to work at state offices with the expectation that the internship might lead to paid employment because it constitutes "involuntary servitude." If the courts disagree with Congress's position, is Congress's conclusion at all relevant to the Court's determination of what constitutes a violation of Section 1? Explain.

2. *Creating Individual Remedies.* In Fitzpatrick v. Bitzer, 427 U.S. 445 (1976), the Court held that Congress could use the power granted to it under the Fourteenth Amendment to create individual remedies against the states. Has *Fitzpatrick* been overruled?

Points to Remember

- The U.S. Constitution vests primary legislative power with Congress.
- Under the Articles of Confederation, the federal government was given limited legislative power because the states preferred to retain that power for themselves. However, the country did not function well. The individual states erected barriers to trade (e.g., tariffs, embargos) that interfered with interstate commerce.
- In an effort to deal with these problems, a convention was called in the mid-1780s to amend the Articles of Confederation. That call ultimately led to the constitutional convention that produced the present U.S. Constitution.
- During the constitutional convention, there was much debate regarding the scope of federal power. Alexander Hamilton, for one, pushed for a broad conception of federal power. He argued that Congress should be given the "power to pass all laws which [it] shall judge necessary to the common defense and general welfare of the Union." Others argued for a more limited view of federal powers.
- Framing the debate was a recognition that, to the extent that the states ceded power to the federal government, their own power was diminished. Even though the states were reluctant to grant too much power to the federal government, a majority of participants recognized the need to create a stronger federal government than had existed under the Articles of Confederation.
- The Framers ultimately decided to create a federal government with limited powers. Instead of giving Congress the power to legislate on any matter it deems appropriate, the Framers created a government of limited, enumerated, powers. Article I, Section 8 gives Congress "[a]ll legislative powers herein granted. . . ."
- The concept of limited powers is reflected in the Tenth Amendment, which provides: "The powers not delegated to the United States by the

Constitution, nor prohibited to it by the States, are reserved to the States respectively, or to the people."

- Nevertheless, Article I, Section 8 gives Congress a variety of powers. Included among the 18 paragraphs of enumerated powers are the rights to borrow money, to establish uniform rules on naturalization and bankruptcy, to coin money, to provide punishment for counterfeiting, to establish post offices and roads, to provide for the protection of scientists and artists through rules governing rights to writings and discoveries, to provide and maintain a navy, to raise and support armies, and to define and punish piracies.

- Given the Constitution's plan of enumerated powers, two separate and distinct questions tend to arise in congressional power cases. First, does Congress have the power to pass a given piece of legislation? In other words, does one of the enumerated powers give it that authority? Second, has Congress exceeded a limitation on the scope of its powers?

- The scope of congressional power has ebbed and flowed over the last two centuries as the Court's interpretation of Article I has shifted.

- One of the most important enumerated powers is found in Article I, Section 8, paragraph 18, the so-called "Necessary and Proper" Clause. It provides that Congress shall have the power to "make all Laws which shall be necessary and proper for carrying into Execution the foregoing Powers, and all other Powers vested by this Constitution in the Government of the United States, or in any Department of Officer thereof."

- The Necessary and Proper Clause is important because it expands the scope of the enumerated powers. For example, because Article I, Section 8 explicitly gives Congress the power to "provide and maintain a Navy," paragraph 18 allows Congress to do those things that are "necessary and proper" to the maintenance of a navy.

- There has been much debate regarding the scope and effect of the Necessary and Proper Clause. Thomas Jefferson, who preferred a strict construction of the clause, argued that it should be interpreted to mean "absolutely necessary." In other words, in providing and maintaining a navy, Congress could only do those things that were "absolutely necessary" to the provision and maintenance of a navy. Alexander Hamilton, by contrast, preferred a "helpful" or "convenience" standard. In other words, Congress could do anything that was "helpful" or "convenient" to the provision and maintenance of a navy.

- In McCulloch v. Maryland, 17 U.S. (4 Wheat.) 316 (1819), the Court construed the Necessary and Proper Clause relatively broadly: "Let the end be legitimate, let it be within the scope of the constitution, and all means which are appropriate, which are plainly adapted to that end, which are not prohibited, but consist with the letter and spirit of the constitution, are constitutional."

- The Commerce Clause gives Congress the power to regulate commerce among the states (as well as between the United States and foreign nations or Indian tribes). The question is how broadly this power should be construed.

- Early decisions construed the federal commerce power broadly, but assumed that there was a line of demarcation between federal power and state powers. In Gibbons v. Ogden, 22 U.S. 1 (1824), the Court stated that the Commerce Clause does not apply to those items of commerce that "are completely within a particular State, which do not affect other States, and with which it is not necessary to interfere, for the purpose of executing some of the general powers of the government. The completely internal commerce of a State, then, may be considered as reserved for the State itself."

- *Gibbons* also held that "the power of Congress does not stop at the jurisdictional lines of the several States. It would be a very useless power, if it could not pass those lines. . . . If Congress has the power to regulate it, that power must be exercised whenever the subject exists. If it exists within the States, if a foreign voyage may commence or terminate at a port within a State, then the power of Congress may be exercised within a State."

- If Congress has the power to regulate in an area and does so, then the Supremacy Clause requires invalidation of conflicting state laws.

- In Champion v. Ames (*The Lottery Case*), 188 U.S. 321 (1903), the Court held that Congress has plenary authority over interstate commerce and may prohibit the carriage of items from state to state, "and that legislation to that end, and of that character, is not inconsistent with any limitation or restriction imposed upon the exercise of the powers granted to Congress."

- In Houston, East & West Texas Railway Company v. United States, 234 U.S. 342 (1914), the Court held that Congress's power to regular interstate commerce allows it to also regulate intrastate commerce that has "such a close and substantial relation to interstate traffic that the control is essential or appropriate to the security of that traffic, to the efficiency of the interstate service, and to the maintenance of conditions under which interstate commerce may be conducted upon fair terms and without molestation or hindrance."

- Not all early decisions construed the Commerce Clause broadly. In Hammer v. Dagenhart, 247 U.S. 251 (1918), the Court struck down a federal law that purported to prohibit goods produced by child labor under certain prohibited circumstances. The Court drew a distinction between interstate "commerce" (which Congress has the right to regulate) and "production" (which is within the control of the states).

- During the early 1930s, the Court construed the Commerce Clause narrowly. In striking down a federal statute that purported to regulate working conditions in the coal industry, Carter v. Carter Coal Co., 298 U.S. 238 (1936), distinguished between things that have a "direct effect" (which Congress can regulate) and those that have an "indirect effect" (which are beyond congressional authority).

- *Carter* involved only one of many setbacks for President Franklin D. Roosevelt's (FDR) New Deal. In Panama Refining Co. v. Ryan, 293 U.S. 388 (1935), the Court struck down Section 9(c) of the National Industrial Recovery Act (NIRA) of 1933 on unlawful delegation grounds. Then, in A.L.A. Schechter Poultry Corp. v. United States, 295 U.S. 495 (1935), the Court struck down other sections of the NIRA. In all, the Court struck down four major pieces of legislation (the National Industrial Recovery Act, the Bituminous Coal Act, the Agricultural Adjustment Act, and the Railway Pension Act). In addition, the federal courts issued hundreds of injunctions against New Deal legislation.

- Decisions like *Panama Refining* and *Schechter*, coupled with the Court's restrictive interpretation of the Commerce Clause in cases like *Carter Coal Co.*, angered President Roosevelt, who viewed the Court as an obstacle to his reforms. Following his landslide reelection victory in 1936, FDR decided to move against the Court. His vehicle was the now infamous "court-packing plan," which would have altered the Court's membership (and presumably its decisions) by adding additional justices.

- Despite FDR's popularity, and the popularity of his New Deal, many opposed the legislation. Everyone agreed that Congress was constitutionally authorized to control the number of Supreme Court justices and that the number of justices had not remained static at nine. Nevertheless, many felt that it was inappropriate for FDR to manipulate the Court's membership in an effort to control its decisions. The court-packing plan never came to a vote.

- FDR's need to act was mooted by the holding in NLRB v. Jones & Laughlin Steel Corp., 301 U.S. 1 (1937). In that case, the Court construed the Commerce Clause more broadly, holding: "Although activities may be intrastate in character when separately considered, if they have such a close and substantial relation to interstate commerce that their control is essential or appropriate to protect that commerce from burdens and obstructions, Congress cannot be denied the power to exercise that control." The Court rejected prior distinctions between "production" and "commerce" and between "direct" and "indirect" effects on interstate commerce.

- In United States v. Darby, 312 U.S. 100 (1941), the Court extended *Jones & Laughlin* by holding that Congress could prohibit the shipment in interstate commerce of goods not produced in compliance with federal minimum wage laws.

- The Court broadened its interpretation of the Commerce Clause even further in Wickard v. Filburn, 317 U.S. 111 (1942). In that case, a federal law sought to restrict a farmer's production of wheat even though most of that wheat was used on his own farm and only a small amount was sold. The Court declared: "This record leaves us in no doubt that Congress may properly have considered that wheat consumed on the farm where grown if wholly outside the scheme of regulation would have a substantial effect in defeating and obstructing its purpose to stimulate trade therein at increased prices."

- In Heart of Atlanta Motel, Inc. v. United States, 379 U.S. 241 (1964), the Court held that Congress could prohibit a local hotel from engaging in discrimination. The Court concluded that discrimination has a significant effect on interstate travel.
- In Perez v. United States, 402 U.S. 146 (1971), the Court upheld a federal criminal law that prohibited extortionate lending.
- After the Court had been deferential to Congress's interpretation of the Commerce Clause for five decades, United States v. Lopez, 514 U.S. 549 (1995), struck down the Gun-Free School Zones Act of 1990, which made it a federal offense "for any individual knowingly to possess a firearm at a place that the individual knows, or has reasonable cause to believe, is a school zone." The Court found an insufficient connection between the prohibited activity and interstate commerce.
- In United States v. Morrison, 529 U.S. 598 (2000), the Court struck down a federal law that provided a civil remedy for the victims of gender-motivated violence. The Court found that the subject of the statute did not have a substantial effect on interstate commerce.
- In Gonzales v. Raich, 125 S.Ct. 2195 (2005), the Court upheld the federal Controlled Substances Act, which made it illegal (among other things) to possess, obtain, or manufacture cannabis for their personal medical use as applied to individuals who were growing cannabis for their own consumption. The Court used a *Wickard*-era analysis and concluded that when "a general regulatory statute bears a substantial relation to commerce, the *de minimis* character of individual instances arising under that statute is of no consequence."
- Article I, Section 8 also gives Congress the power to impose taxes: "The Congress shall have Power To lay and collect Taxes, Duties, Imposes and Excises. . . ."
- Most of the litigation under the taxation clause has focused on Congress's power to regulate conduct through the imposition of taxes. This so-called "regulation by taxation" is generally unobjectionable if Congress seeks to tax something that it otherwise has the power to regulate (e.g., something within its Article I, Section 8 power).
- In Bailey v. Drexel Furniture Co. (*The Child Labor Tax Case*), 259 U.S. 20 (1922), the Court struck down a tax on child labor because Congress was trying to regulate child labor and (under the Court's interpretation of the Commerce Clause at the time) it lacked the power to do so. Of course, the effect of *Bailey*'s holding was reduced by the dramatic expansion of federal power beginning in the late 1930s.
- In United States v. Sanchez, 340 U.S. 42 (1950), the Court upheld the Marihuana Tax Act against allegations that it imposed a penalty (and therefore was an attempt to regulate an activity) and was not enacted to raise money. The Court noted that "a tax does not cease to be valid merely because it regulates, discourages, or even definitely deters the

activities taxed" and even though the revenue raised is "obviously negligible."

- Article I, Section 8, which contains the power to tax, also contains the power to spend for the general welfare: "The Congress shall have Power To lay and collect Taxes, Duties, Imposes and Excises, to pay the Debts and provide for the common Defence and general Welfare of the United States."

- In United States v. Butler, 297 U.S. 1 (1935), the Court construed the Tenth Amendment as limiting the power of government to spend for the general welfare. However, the decision was rendered during the 1930s, prior to the constitutional crisis when the Court interpreted the Tenth Amendment more broadly.

- In South Dakota v. Dole, 483 U.S. 203 (1987), the Court upheld a federal law that allowed the federal government to withhold federal highway funds from states that did not limit the consumption of alcohol by individuals under 18 years old. "We can readily conclude that the provision is designed to serve the general welfare, especially in light of the fact that 'the concept of welfare or the opposite is shaped by Congress.'"

- Article I also gives Congress a number of powers relating to war and foreign affairs, including the power to declare war and to regulate commerce with foreign states.

- This power is, in some respects, shared with the President, who also has substantial authority over foreign affairs. For example, under Article II, Section 2, the President is the Commander-in-Chief of the army and the navy, and he has the power to appoint ambassadors and consuls. In addition, as noted, he has the power to make treaties.

- Although this power is shared with the President, Congress also has foreign affairs powers, including the war power and the treaty power.

- The Constitution gives Congress the power to "regulate foreign affairs."

- In Woods v. Cloyd W. Miller Co., 333 U.S. 138 (1948), the Court upheld the Housing and Rent Act of 1947, which was imposed under the war power even though World War II had ended: "the war power includes the power 'to remedy the evils which have arisen from its rise and progress' and continues for the duration of that emergency. Whatever may be the consequences when war is officially terminated, the war power does not necessarily end with the cessation of hostilities."

- In Missouri v. Holland, 252 U.S. 416 (1920), the Court upheld the Migratory Bird Treaty Act against claims that it interfered with state power to regulate such birds.

- The U.S. Constitution gives Congress power relating to the protection and enforcement of civil rights, an area that has seen an ever-changing balance of power between the states and the federal government and between Congress and the Court.

- After the Civil War, the limited power of the federal government was expanded by the Thirteenth, Fourteenth, and Fifteenth Amendments. These amendments, known collectively as the "Reconstruction

Amendments," empowered the federal government to grant citizenship to former slaves and to protect that grant.

- Modern congressional legislation runs the gamut of interests and includes the Civil Rights Act of 1964 and most of the Voting Rights Act of 1965. There are also acts prohibiting firearms within so many feet of a schoolyard and acts protecting patent rights, the rights of women and the disabled, and the expression of religious views.

- In the first major case to address the newly granted power of Congress to enact civil rights legislation, *The Civil Rights Cases*, 109 U.S. 3 (1883), the Court severely limited Congress's ability to address both private and state acts of racial discrimination under the enforcement provisions of the amendments.

- Later decisions construed the scope of federal power more broadly. In Katzenbach v. Morgan, 384 U.S. 641 (1966), the Court upheld the constitutionality of Section 4(e) of the Voting Rights Act of 1965 "[which] provides that no person who has successfully completed the sixth primary grade in a public school in, or a private school accredited by, the Commonwealth of Puerto Rico in which the language of instruction was other than English shall be denied the right to vote in any election because of his inability to read or write English." The Court concluded that it was appropriate legislation to help enforce the Equal Protection Clause.

3

The Federal Executive Powers

Section 1. The executive Power shall be vested in a President of the United States of America. He shall hold his Office during the Term of four Years, and, together with the Vice President, chosen for the same Term, be elected. . . .

Section 1, Clause 5. No person except a natural born Citizen, or a Citizen of the United States, at the time of the Adoption of this Constitution, shall be eligible to the Office of President; neither shall any person be eligible to that Office who shall not have attained to the Age of thirty five Years, and been fourteen Years a Resident within the United States.

Section 2. The President shall be Commander in Chief of the Army and Navy of the United States, and of the Militia of the several States, when called into the actual Service of the United States; he may require the Opinion, in writing, of the principal Officer in each of the executive Departments, upon any Subject relating to the Duties of their respective Offices, and he shall have Power to Grant Reprieves and Pardons for Offences against the United States, except in Cases of Impeachment. He shall have Power, by and with the Advice and Consent of the Senate, to make Treaties, provided two thirds of the Senators present concur; and he shall nominate, and by and with the Advice and Consent of the Senate, shall appoint Ambassadors, other public Ministers and Consuls, Judges of the Supreme Court, and all other Officers of the United States, whose Appointments are not herein otherwise provided for, and which shall be established by Law: but the Congress may by Law vest the Appointment of such inferior Officers, as they think proper, in the President alone, in the Courts of Law, or in the Heads of Departments. The President shall have Power to fill up all Vacancies that may happen during the Recess of the Senate, by granting Commissions which shall expire at the End of their next Session.

Section 3. He shall from time to time give to the Congress Information on the State of the Union, and recommend to their Consideration such Measures as he shall judge necessary and expedient; he may, on extraordinary Occasions, convene both Houses, or either of them, and in Case of Disagreement between them, with Respect to the Time of Adjournment, he may adjourn them to such Time as he shall think proper; he shall receive Ambassadors and other public Ministers; he shall take Care that the Laws be faithfully executed, and shall Commission all the Officers of the United States.

Section 4. The President, Vice President and all Civil Officers of the United States, shall be removed from Office on Impeachment for and Conviction of, Treason, Bribery, or other high Crimes and Misdemeanors.

U.S. CONSTITUTION, TWELFTH AMENDMENT

The person having the greatest number of votes for President, shall be the President, if such number be a majority of the whole number of electors appointed.

∼ PROBLEM: NO DRILLING OR KILLING ZONES ∼

The President decides that no oil, gas, or mineral exploration should be allowed in certain public lands and sea areas, despite a law enacted by Congress four years earlier declaring those public lands "free and open" to oil exploration and purchase by private companies. In making this decision, the President concluded that he, as the chief executive, has an obligation to act in the public interest to save the natural state of these public places. The President bases the creation of "no drilling" zones on: 1) precedent — since early in the country's history, there have been more than 200 such presidential "withdrawal" orders in the face of contrary legislation; 2) preservation of the environment — the Deepwater Horizon oil rig explosion and leak into the Gulf of Mexico off the coast of Louisiana created an emergency the country can ill afford again; and 3) national security — the President has been informed that oil drilling on these lands is particularly susceptible to a terrorist attack and has had some intelligence that drilling operations will be infiltrated by Taliban sympathizers from the Middle East. Consequently, the President prepares to issue Executive Order 4049, which has two primary parts: a) no drilling or exploration for oil, natural gas, or other minerals that would upset the ecology and environment as defined by a series of benchmarks; and b) no entry into these lands, similar to the "no-fly" list, of certain persons, including those in this country unlawfully or with expired visas, within designated, publicized areas, with "knowing" violations to be subject to deportation, if applicable, and criminal penalties.

As you go through this chapter, you will be asked to serve as White House counsel and to advise the President about whether he has the power to take such action without the express authorization of Congress, or whether he can justify his actions on other grounds. You will also be asked to think about whether the President's creation of "no drilling or killing" zones is subject to judicial review, and how it might be received by the courts.

EXECUTIVE POWERS BY THE NUMBERS

1. To become President, a majority of electors is required by the Twelfth Amendment. Given the current number of electors, 538, a person must receive the votes of at least 270 electors to become President.
2. A President can be elected twice or only once if he or she has served more than half of another President's term. See the Twenty-second Amendment.
3. A President must be at least 35 years of age, a resident of the United States for at least 14 years, and a natural born citizen.

4. The separation of powers doctrine, often used as a limit on executive action, is not mentioned anywhere in the Constitution. Instead, it is implied by the constitutional structure created by the Framers.

BACKGROUND
Who Was Our First President?

Most people are aware that the first President of the United States was George Washington, but some historians offer a footnote about John Hanson of Maryland, who was elected the first president of the Congress after the ratification of the Articles of Confederation, our first unifying Constitution. That document governed the 13 states from its ratification in 1781 through 1789, when it was replaced by the current Constitution. The Articles of Confederation were revised and essentially rewritten at the Constitutional Convention in Philadelphia in 1787, in no small measure because of the lack of an independent and fully functioning chief executive.

The chief executive of the United States, the President, might not earn as much money as other chief executives, especially those who toil in the private sector, but the President has an unparalleled job description. The President is the Commander in Chief of the U.S. armed forces, the diplomatic representative of the country, and the so-called "leader of the free world." In addition, unlike Article I of the Constitution, which vests legislative power in a bicameral Congress, the President is given the entirety of the Executive Branch's powers: "The Executive Power shall be vested in a President of the United States of America." U.S. Const., Art. II, §1.

Even though the Framers vested all executive power in a single person, it is debatable whether the Framers intended for the President to exercise far-ranging powers. After the Revolutionary War, it was logical to expect the colonists to viscerally move away from a strong central government for fear of replicating British rule. Indeed, in the years following the Declaration of Independence, the reaction of the new Americans against the strong grip of colonial British governors led to weak chief executives in most state constitutions and the national Articles of Confederation alike. *See* Daniel A. Farber and Suzanna Sherry, *A History of the American Constitution* 79-80 (West 1990). In the nascent days of America, then, the pendulum of centralized executive power had swung far in the other direction — too far, at least, for those who distrusted the Legislative Branch, a beneficiary of many of the powers stripped from the executive. With the distrust of executive governance increasingly tempered by the disarray caused by a weak centralized government, the U.S. Constitution replaced the Articles of Confederation in March 1789 and forged a more neutral balance of powers. Despite the lack of transparency of the Framers' intent regarding the scope of Executive Branch powers, it could readily be argued based on the historical context that the

Executive Branch was designed to play a forceful, if complementary, role in directing the nation.

A perspective that assists in understanding the contours of executive authority is the notion that many of the boundaries between the branches are not defined in the Constitution and have ebbed and flowed over time, particularly when the nation is at war or peace. Although the Judicial Branch has set some of the boundaries, many are unsettled or indeterminate, such as where the President's Commander in Chief power ends and Congress's power to declare war begins. These areas, though, have found their way into the mainstream culture. Some of the most prominent issues have included the appointment of federal judges; the role of the President in domestic lawmaking, foreign affairs, and war; vetoes; and the scope of executive immunity and privilege. In fact, the President is likely to be in the center of the most vexing issues of the day, from the economy, to health care, to the conflicts in Iraq and Afghanistan.

A. IMPLIED PRESIDENTIAL POWERS

A recurring theme concerning the boundaries of executive power is whether the Constitution grants the President implied powers in addition to those enumerated in Article II. Judicial analysis has raised numerous questions, including: 1) If there are implied powers, what is the scope of those powers? and 2) If the President has implied powers, are those powers derived from the express powers in the Constitution, the inherent powers lying outside of the affirmative grant of powers in the Constitution, or both?

Of particular note in the debate over implied powers is the comparative treatment of such powers in Articles I and II. Article II lacks a clause authorizing the executive to exercise implied powers that are "necessary and proper" to carrying out his express powers. By contrast, Article I, Section 8, Clause 18 supplies Congress with the power to enact those laws "necessary and proper" to carrying out its express powers. As interpreted by Chief Justice John Marshall in McCulloch v. Maryland, 17 U.S. (4 Wheat.) 316 (1819), the Necessary and Proper Clause provides an affirmative recognition of implied legislative powers. Nevertheless, the President historically has chosen to assume that he possesses implied powers as well. For example, President George Washington issued a Proclamation of Neutrality when the United States was asked to take sides during the French Revolution. He issued the proclamation despite congressional inaction and lack of constitutional authorization. *See* Youngstown Sheet & Tube Co. v. Sawyer, 343 U.S. at 683-684 (Vinson, J., dissenting). Justice Vinson, in *Youngstown Sheet & Tube Co.*, offered additional examples of implied executive actions:

> Without declaration of war, President Lincoln . . . summoned troops and paid them . . ., proclaimed a naval blockade of the Confederacy and seized ships violating the blockade [without prior Congressional approval]. Lincoln also suspended the writ of Habeas Corpus, even though the constitution creates this as an Article I, legislative power and not an Article

II, executive power. He did so even over the admonition against doing so by Supreme Court Justice Taney. Further, President John Adams issued an arrest warrant for a person to promote the execution of a treaty.

One of the earliest illustrations of judicial recognition of implied executive powers can be found in *In re Neagle*, 135 U.S. 1 (1890). There, a federal marshal was assigned by the attorney general to protect a U.S. Supreme Court Justice following threats of harm to the Justice. When the assigned marshal succeeded in stopping an attack on the Justice and killing the attacker, the marshal was arrested and charged with murder on the basis that the attorney general did not have express constitutional authority to offer such protection. It appears the California authorities who initiated the arrest reasoned that the Constitution does not contain a "bodyguard power." The U.S. Supreme Court responded to the marshal's petition for habeas corpus by holding that an express constitutional authority to appoint a bodyguard was not required. Instead, the Court recognized an inherent power of the Executive Branch to assure the safety of the government, including the Supreme Court, arising out of its "take care" enforcement powers.

Several presidents, most notably Teddy Roosevelt, have argued that the President possesses a reservoir of implied powers. These arguments were both philosophical and pragmatic, related to the fact that presidents were required to deal with pressing and immediate international problems. The arguments centered around the Constitution's text — asserting that implied powers were not formally rejected by the text of the Constitution — and, on a much broader plane, policy that the President is the necessary leader of the country. President Roosevelt stated:

> My view was that every executive officer, and above all every executive officer in high position, was a steward to the people bound actively and affirmatively to do all he could for the people, and not to content himself with the negative merit of keeping his talents undamaged in a napkin. I declined to adopt the view that what was imperatively necessary for the Nation could not be done by the President unless he could find some specific authorization to do it. My belief was that it was not only his right but his duty to do anything that the needs of the Nation demanded unless such action was forbidden by the Constitution or by the laws. Under this interpretation of executive power I did and caused to be done many things not previously done by the President and the heads of the departments. I did not usurp power, but I did greatly broaden the use of executive power. In other words, I acted for the public welfare, I acted for the common well-being of all our people, whenever and in whatever manner was necessary, unless prevented by direct constitution or legislative prohibition. [Theodore Roosevelt, *Theodore Roosevelt, An Autobiography* (vol. 20 of *The Works of Theodore Roosevelt*, national ed.), chap. 10, 347-348 (Scribner's 1926).]

∾ PROBLEMS ∾

1. *"The Little Rock 9."* After the decision in Brown v. Board of Education, 347 U.S. 483 (1954), several states decided to resist the directive to dismantle intentionally segregated schools. In Arkansas, nine African American children signed

up to attend the all-white Little Rock High School for the 1956-1957 school year. The state's strategy was to provide only half-hearted protection for the children, even in the face of angry mobs. If Congress had not authorized the use of protective force to protect the nine schoolchildren, could the President still provide protection from National Guard and Army troops in a matter concerning a single state high school? For background, *see, e.g.*, J. Williams, *Eyes on the Prize: America's Civil Rights Years, 1954–1965* (Penguin 1988).

2. *The Memorandum.* Assume that your assistant at the Office of Legal Counsel writes a memorandum titled "Inherent Powers of the Executive Branch." The memorandum states, in pertinent part, "The Executive has implied powers, independent of the positive grants provided in the Constitution, to protect its citizenry. This includes obtaining information about threats to the well-being of the polity and individuals. In this century, combating terrorism requires use of these inherent powers in several different ways, from rendition and aggressive tactics used to extract information from terrorist captives, to conducting warrantless searches in order to obtain foreign intelligence information. The Foreign Intelligence Surveillance Act (FISA) cannot interfere with this inherent constitutional power." How would you critique the accuracy of the memorandum's evaluation of the constitutional power of the President? Explain.

BACKGROUND
Are There Inherent Executive Powers?

While most scholars do not believe the executive has broad or even any inherent powers — although implied powers are a different story — there have been some adherents of this view, including scholars tapped to serve in recent administrations. The Foreign Intelligence Surveillance Court of Review, in a *per curiam* opinion, wrote, "we take for granted that the President does have [inherent authority to conduct warrantless searches to obtain foreign intelligence information] and, assuming that is so, FISA (Foreign Intelligence Surveillance Act) could not encroach on the President's constitutional power."

B. THE VOLATILE BOUNDARY BETWEEN EXECUTIVE AND LEGISLATIVE POWERS

The interface between Congress's and the President's powers is one of the more volatile boundaries in American government and has given rise to many separation of powers issues. Conflicts have arisen in both the foreign policy and domestic arenas, with the residue of these conflicts creating accepted roles and traditions.

A scoreboard of sorts has resulted, with the courts tending to favor Congress's powers in domestic disputes and the President's powers in international disputes. This oversimplification does not explain the genius of the Constitution, which involves not a complete "separation of powers" but rather a weave of interdependent powers. Much like an assembly line that requires each component to function smoothly for the overall efficiency of the line, governance of the United States requires legislative action (bicameral approval and presentment to the President) as well as executive approval (veto power) and implementation (the Take Care Clause).

Many of the following cases represent conflicts between the branches of government, in which the executive, the legislature, and even the judiciary lay claim to legitimacy in the exercise of power. A significant subtext to these claims is formalism versus functionalism: Should the President, who is vested with the entire executive power under Article II, ever be limited by the other branches in exercising that power and controlling enforcement of the federal law, particularly in national security matters? This subtext is exemplified by today's debate about the unitary presidency: How extensive and strong are a President's powers under the Constitution?

The first case, Youngstown Sheet & Tube Co. v. Sawyer, 343 U.S. 579 (1952), provides a seminal illustration of the tensions that run the length of the boundaries between the Executive and Legislative branches. In that case, the Supreme Court mediated power claims by the President and Congress, illustrating the Supreme Court's vision of a domestic boundary between the two branches and, more pragmatically, how to avoid a stand-off between the President and Congress when tackling pressing domestic problems. Often called the *Steel Seizure Case*, it could be considered the "Power Seizure Case" instead, because President Truman believed expedient Executive Branch action required him to seize domestic power during the Korean War to avoid a steel strike and maintain the continuity of military operations in Korea. Congress apparently did not share the President's view of the necessity for action, especially action by the executive.

The issues in the case focused on whether the President had implied powers to act domestically without any purported authority from the Congress. The Court was faced with a variety of possible analytical approaches — that the President's conduct was justified by the "theater of war," by a more general "pressing public importance," by the "dormancy" of Congress, or was simply not justified at all.

As in many other Supreme Court cases, the context of *Youngstown Sheet & Tube Co.* is important to the legal issues in the case. Prior to the time President Truman took control of the major steel production plants in the United States, steel was a significant ingredient in the creation of weapons supplying the war effort in Korea. In the early 1950s, defense spending increased exponentially, with much of it earmarked to fund the action in Korea. *See* Youngstown Sheet & Tube Co., 343 U.S., at 671 (Vinson, J., dissenting). Steel was a very important commodity in the defense effort. After the issues could not be resolved through negotiations, the President of the United Steelworkers called a general strike. The night before the strike was to commence, Truman gave a radio address to the

President Truman announcing the seizure of the steel mills.

country and then issued Executive Order 10340, authorizing the Secretary of Commerce, Charles Sawyer, to take possession of and operate the steel mills. The President stated in the Order that the threatened strike created "the existence of a national emergency" because "steel is an indispensable component of substantially all of such weapons and materials." Because no labor settlement had been reached, "to assure the continued availability of steel and steel products during the existing emergency, it is necessary that the United States take possession of and operate the [steel] plants." Exec. Order No. 10340, 17 Fed. Reg. 3139 (1952).

Of the seven different opinions written in the case, Justice Jackson's classic concurrence has best withstood the test of time. Jackson's concurrence resonates with both scholars and pragmatists alike in capturing the dynamic nature of the boundaries between executive and legislative powers.

Youngstown Sheet & Tube Co. v. Sawyer

343 U.S. 579 (1952)

BLACK, J.

We are asked to decide whether President [Truman] was acting within his constitutional power when he issued an order directing the Secretary of Commerce [Sawyer] to take possession of and operate most of the Nation's steel mills. The mill owners argue that the President's order amounts to lawmaking, a legislative function which the Constitution has expressly confided to the Congress and not to the President. The Government's position is that the order was made on findings of the President that his action was necessary to avert a national catastrophe which would inevitably result from a stoppage of steel production, and that in meeting this grave emergency the President was acting within the aggregate of his constitutional powers as the Nation's Chief Executive and the Commander in Chief of the Armed Forces of the United States.

The issue emerges here from the following series of events: [While the Korean War was occurring i]n the latter part of 1951, a dispute arose between the steel companies and their employees over terms and conditions that should be included in new collective bargaining agreements. Long-continued conferences failed to resolve the dispute. On December 18, 1951, the employees' representative, United Steelworkers of America, C.I.O., gave notice of an intention to strike when the existing bargaining agreements expired on December 31. On April 4, 1952, the Union gave notice of a nation-wide strike called to begin at 12:01 a.m. April 9. The indispensability of steel as a component of substantially all weapons and other war materials led the President to believe that the proposed work stoppage would immediately jeopardize our national defense and that governmental seizure of the steel mills was necessary in order to assure the continued availability of steel. Reciting these considerations for his action, the President, a few hours before the strike was to begin, issued Executive Order 10340. The order directed the Secretary of Commerce to take possession of most of the steel mills and keep them running. The Secretary immediately issued his own possessory orders, calling upon the presidents of the various seized companies to serve as operating managers for the United States. They were directed to carry on their activities in accordance with regulations and directions of the Secretary. The next morning the President sent a message to Congress reporting his action. Congress has taken no action.

Obeying the Secretary's orders under protest, the companies brought proceedings against him in the District Court. Their complaints charged that the seizure was not authorized by an act of Congress or by any constitutional provisions. The District Court was asked to declare the orders of the President and the Secretary invalid and to issue preliminary and permanent injunctions restraining their enforcement. Opposing the motion for preliminary injunction, the United States asserted that a strike disrupting steel production for even a brief period would so endanger the well-being and safety of the Nation that the President had 'inherent power' to do what he had done — power "supported by the Constitution, by historical precedent, and by court decisions."

Two crucial issues have developed: First. Should final determination of the constitutional validity of the President's order be made in this case which has proceeded no further than the preliminary injunction stage? Second. If so, is the seizure order within the constitutional power of the President?

II.

The President's power, if any, to issue the order must stem either from an act of Congress or from the Constitution itself. There is no statute that expressly authorizes the President to take possession of property as he did here. Nor is there any act of Congress to which our attention has been directed from which such a power can fairly be implied. Indeed, we do not understand the Government to rely on statutory authorization for this seizure.

Moreover, the use of the seizure technique to solve labor disputes in order to prevent work stoppages was not only unauthorized by any congressional enactment; prior to this controversy, Congress had refused to adopt that method of settling labor disputes.

The indispensability of steel as a component of substantially all weapons and other war materials led the President to believe that the proposed work stoppage would immediately jeopardize our national defense and that governmental seizure of the steel mills was necessary in order to assure the continued availability of steel. Reciting these considerations for his action, the President, a few hours before the strike was to begin, issued Executive Order 10340.

It is clear that if the President had authority to issue the order he did, it must be found in some provisions of the Constitution. And it is not claimed that express constitutional language grants this power to the President. The contention is that presidential power should be implied from the aggregate of his powers under the Constitution. Particular reliance is placed on provisions in Article II which says that "the executive Power shall be vested in a President . . ."; that "he shall take Care that the Laws be faithfully executed"; and that he "shall be Commander in Chief of the Army and Navy of the United States."

The order cannot properly be sustained as an exercise of the President's military power as Commander in Chief of the Armed Forces. The Government attempts to do so by citing a number of cases upholding broad powers in military commanders engaged in day-to-day fighting in a theater of war. Such cases need not concern us here. Even though "'theater of war" be an expanding concept, we cannot with faithfulness to our constitutional system hold that the Commander in Chief of the Armed Forces has the ultimate power as such to take possession of private property in order to keep labor disputes from stopping production. This is a job for the Nation's lawmakers, not for its military authorities.

Nor can the seizure order be sustained because of the several constitutional provisions that grant executive power to the President. In the framework of our Constitution, the President's power to see that the laws are faithfully executed refutes the idea that he is to be a lawmaker. The Constitution limits his functions in the lawmaking process to the recommending of laws he thinks wise and the vetoing of laws he thinks bad.

The President's order does not direct that a congressional policy be executed in a manner prescribed by Congress — it directs that a presidential policy be executed in a manner prescribed by the President. The power of Congress to adopt such public policies as those proclaimed by the order is beyond question. It can authorize the taking of private property for public use. It can makes laws regulating the relationships between employers and employees, prescribing rules designed to settle labor disputes, and fixing wages and working conditions in certain fields of our economy. The Constitution did not subject this law-making power of Congress to presidential or military supervision or control.

It is said that other Presidents without congressional authority have taken possession of private business enterprises in order to settle labor disputes. But even if this be true, Congress has not thereby lost its exclusive constitutional authority to make laws necessary and proper to carry out the powers vested by the Constitution "in the Government of the United States, or in any Department or Officer thereof."

Even though "theater of war" be an expanding concept, we cannot with faithfulness to our constitutional system hold that the Commander in Chief of the Armed Forces has the ultimate power as such to take possession of private property in order to keep labor disputes from stopping production. This is a job for the Nation's lawmakers, not for its military authorities. In the framework of our Constitution, the President's power to see that the laws are faithfully executed refutes the idea that he is to be a lawmaker. The Constitution limits his functions in the lawmaking process to the recommending of laws he thinks wise and the vetoing of laws he thinks bad.

The Founders of this Nation entrusted the law making power to the Congress alone in both good and bad times. It would do no good to recall the historical events, the fears of power and the hopes for freedom that lay behind their choice. Such a review would but confirm our holding that this seizure order cannot stand.

The judgment of the District Court is affirmed.

Mr. Justice Jackson, concurring in the judgment and opinion of the Court.

That comprehensive and undefined presidential powers hold both practical advantages and grave dangers for the country will impress anyone who has served as legal adviser to a President in time of transition and public anxiety.

A judge, like an executive adviser, may be surprised at the poverty of really useful and unambiguous authority applicable to concrete problems of executive power as they actually present themselves. Just what our forefathers did envision, or would have envisioned had they foreseen modern conditions, must be divined from materials almost as enigmatic as the dreams Joseph was called upon to interpret for Pharaoh. A century and a half of partisan debate and scholarly speculation yields no net result but only supplies more or less apt quotations from respected sources on each side of any question.

Presidential powers are not fixed but fluctuate, depending upon their disjunction or conjunction with those of Congress. We may well begin by a somewhat over-simplified grouping of practical situations in which a President may doubt, or others may challenge his powers, and by distinguishing roughly the legal consequences of this factor of relativity.

1. When the President acts pursuant to an express or implied authorization of Congress, his authority is at its maximum, for it includes all that he possesses in his own right plus all that Congress can delegate. In these circumstances, and in these only, may he be said (for what it may be worth), to personify the federal sovereignty. If his act is held unconstitutional under these circumstances, it usually means that the Federal Government as an undivided whole lacks power. A seizure executed by the President pursuant to an Act of Congress would be supported by the strongest of presumptions and the widest latitude of judicial interpretation, and the burden of persuasion would rest heavily upon any who might attack it.

2. When the President acts in absence of either a congressional grant or denial of authority, he can only rely upon his own independent powers, but there is a zone of twilight in which he and Congress may have concurrent authority, or in which its distribution is uncertain. Therefore, congressional inertia, indifference or quiescence may sometimes, at least as a practical matter, enable, if not invite, measures on independent presidential responsibility. In this area, any actual test of power is likely to depend on the imperatives of events and contemporary imponderables rather than on abstract theories of law.

3. When the President takes measures incompatible with the expressed or implied will of Congress, his power is at its lowest ebb, for then he can rely only upon his own constitutional powers, minus any constitutional powers of Congress over the matter. Courts can sustain exclusive Presidential control in such a case only by disabling the Congress from acting upon the subject. Presidential claim to a power at once so conclusive and preclusive must be scrutinized with caution, for what is at stake is the equilibrium established by our constitutional system.

Into which of these classifications does this executive seizure of the steel industry fit? It is eliminated from the first by admission, for it is conceded that no congressional authorization exists for this seizure. That takes away also the support of the many precedents and declarations which made in relation, and must be confined, to this category.

Can it then be defended under flexible tests available to the second category? It seems clearly eliminated from that class because Congress has not left seizure of private property an open field but has covered it by three statutory policies inconsistent with this seizure. In cases where the purpose is to supply needs of the Government itself, two courses are provided: one, seizure of a plant which fails to comply with obligatory orders placed by the Government, another, condemnation of facilities, including temporary use under the power of eminent domain. The third is applicable where it is the general economy of the country that is to be protected rather than exclusive governmental interests. None of these were invoked.

This leaves the current seizure to be justified only by the severe tests under the third grouping, where it can be supported only by any remainder of executive power after subtraction of such powers as Congress may have over the subject. In short, we can sustain the President only by holding that seizure of such strike-bound industries is within his domain and beyond control by Congress. Thus, this Court's first review of such seizures occurs under circumstances which leave Presidential power most vulnerable to attack and in the least favorable of possible constitutional postures.

The clause on which the Government next relies is that "[t]he President shall be Commander in Chief of the Army and Navy of the United States. . . ." These cryptic words have given rise to some of the most persistent controversies in our constitutional history.

Assuming that we are in a war de facto, whether it is or is not a war de jure, does that empower the Commander-in-Chief to seize industries he thinks necessary to supply our army? The Constitution expressly places in Congress power "to raise and support Armies" and "to provide and maintain a Navy." (Emphasis supplied.) This certainly lays upon Congress primary responsibility for supplying the armed forces. Congress alone controls the raising of revenues and their appropriation and may determine in what manner and by what means they shall be spent for military and naval procurement. I suppose no one would doubt that Congress can take over war supply as a Government enterprise.

But I have no illusion that any decision by this Court can keep power in the hands of Congress if it is not wise and timely in meeting its problems. A crisis that challenges the President equally, or perhaps primarily, challenges Congress. If not good law, there was worldly wisdom in the maxim attributed to Napoleon that "[t]he tools belong to the man who can use them." We may say that power to legislate for emergencies belongs in the hands of Congress, but only Congress itself can prevent power from slipping through its fingers.

Mr. Justice CLARK, concurring in the judgment of the Court.

The limits of presidential power are obscure. However, Article II, no less than Article I, is part of "a constitution intended to endure for ages to come, and, consequently, to be adapted to the various crises of human affairs." Some of our Presidents, such as Lincoln, "felt that measures otherwise unconstitutional might become lawful by becoming indispensable to the preservation of the Constitution through the preservation of the nation." Others, such as Theodore Roosevelt, thought the President to be capable, as a "steward" of the people, of exerting all power save that which is specifically prohibited by the Constitution or the Congress. In my view — taught me not only by the decision of Chief Justice Marshall in Little v. Barreme, 2 Cranch 170, 2 L.Ed. 243, but also by a score of other pronouncements of distinguished members of this bench — the Constitution does grant to the President extensive authority in times of grave and imperative national emergency. In fact, to my thinking, such a grant may well be necessary to the very existence of the Constitution itself. As Lincoln aptly said, "(is) it possible to lose the nation and yet preserve the Constitution?" In describing this authority

I care not whether one calls it "residual," "inherent," "moral," "implied," "aggregate," "emergency," or otherwise. I am of the conviction that those who have had the gratifying experience of being the President's lawyer have used one or more of these adjectives only with the utmost of sincerity and the highest of purpose.

I conclude that where Congress has laid down specific procedures to deal with the type of crisis confronting the President, he must follow those procedures in meeting the crisis; but that in the absence of such action by Congress, the President's independent power to act depends upon the gravity of the situation confronting the nation.

Mr. Chief Justice VINSON, with whom Mr. Justice REED and Mr. Justice MINTON join, dissenting.

In passing upon the question of Presidential powers in this case, we must first consider the context in which those powers were exercised.

Those who suggest that this is a case involving extraordinary powers should be mindful that these are extraordinary times. A world not yet recovered from the devastation of World War II has been forced to face the threat of another and more terrifying global conflict.

Congress also directed the President to build up our own defenses. Congress, recognizing the "grim fact [that] the United States is now engaged in a struggle for survival" and that "it is imperative that we now take those necessary steps to make our strength equal to the peril of the hour," granted authority to draft men into the armed forces. As a result, we now have over 3,500,000 men in our armed forces. One is not here called upon even to consider the possibility of executive seizure of a farm, a corner grocery store or even a single industrial plant. Such considerations arise only when one ignores the central fact of this case — that the Nation's entire basic steel production would have shut down completely if there had been no Government seizure. Even ignoring for the moment whatever confidential information the President may possess as "the Nation's organ for foreign affairs," the uncontroverted affidavits in this record amply support the finding that "a work stoppage would immediately jeopardize and imperil our national defense."

In passing upon the grave constitutional question presented in this case, we must never forget, as Chief Justice Marshall admonished, that the Constitution is "intended to endure for ages to come, and consequently, to be adapted to the various crises of human affairs," and that "(i)ts means are adequate to its ends." Cases do arise presenting questions which could not have been foreseen by the Framers. In such cases, the Constitution has been treated as a living document adaptable to new situations. In 1941, President Roosevelt acted to protect Iceland from attack by Axis powers when British forces were withdrawn by sending our forces to occupy Iceland. Congress was informed of this action on the same day that our forces reached Iceland. The occupation of Iceland was but one of 'at least 125 incidents' in our history in which Presidents, "without Congressional authorization, and in the absence of a declaration of war, (have) ordered the Armed Forces to take action or maintain positions abroad."

No basis for claims of arbitrary action, unlimited powers or dictatorial usurpation of congressional power appears from the facts of this case. On the contrary, judicial, legislative and executive precedents throughout our history demonstrate that in this case the President acted in full conformity with his duties under the Constitution. Accordingly, we would reverse the order of the District Court.

BACKGROUND
Justice Robert H. Jackson

Robert H. Jackson served as an Associate Justice on the Supreme Court from 1941 until 1954, shortly after Brown v. Board of Education was decided. He was a former attorney general and the lead prosecutor at the Nuremburg trials, taking a leave of absence from the Supreme Court to serve in this role. He also was the last Justice to be appointed to the Supreme Court without having graduated from a law school.

BACKGROUND
Justice Tom Clark

Justice Tom Clark served under President Harry Truman as his attorney general. This relationship did not interfere with Justice Clark's decision in *Youngstown Sheet & Tube Co.*, in light of the fact that Clark ruled against his former boss *See* David McCulloch, *Truman* 896-902 (Touchstone 1992).

Case Postscript

After the Supreme Court declared the President's seizure of the steel mills unconstitutional, a strike indeed occurred. Shortly thereafter, however, by July 24, 1952, a settlement was reached, quelling the fear of a significant disruption in the steel supply. In announcing the settlement, President Truman stated that, "[I was] just advised that six major steel companies and the United Steel Workers of America (CIO) have reached agreement on important basic issues. The union is calling its National Wage Policy Committee to meet in Washington for the purpose of ratifying the agreement. This should lead to a speedy resumption of steel production." Statement by President Truman on the Settlement of the Steel Strike on July 24, 1952.

∽ PROBLEMS ∽

1. *Sailin' Away.* After significant deterioration of relations with France, Congress enacted a law authorizing the President to apprehend American ships "sailing to ports of call in France." In response to this law, five ships were detained, three of which were sailing to France and two from France. The ship captains who detained the five ships were sued. Did the President comply with the legislature's directive? What are the best arguments for both sides?

2. *Tariffs.* The President enters into an executive agreement with Canada concerning tariffs associated with the importation of certain vegetables. This international agreement between the President and Canada followed a law enacted by Congress providing for higher tariffs on the importation of the same vegetables, 18 U.S.C. §2432. Can the President constitutionally lower the tariffs on the vegetables below the floor for tariffs set by Congress in its earlier law, 18 U.S.C. 2432? Explain.

3. *The President's Memorandum.* A Mexican national was convicted in Texas of gang rape and murder and given the death sentence. The petitioner appealed, claiming the state courts ignored a memorandum from the President describing his constitutional rights to include not only the *Miranda* warnings but also an opportunity to confer with the Mexican consulate based on a prior treaty. The President had issued the memorandum in question stating that pursuant to a treaty, a decision by the International Court of Justice requires state courts to first inform the defendants of their right to contact their embassy concerning their detention prior to their conviction or else the United States will provide reconsideration. The President's use of a treaty to create domestic law was not supported by an enabling statute enacted by Congress, and the treaty did not state it was "self-executing" as domestic law. Can the President, through the memorandum, unilaterally make the treaty apply domestically? Why or why not? *See* Medellin v. Texas, 552 U.S. 491 (2008).

4. *Whalers.* To combat world whaling practices, Congress enacts a law giving the President the discretionary power to refuse entry into the United States of any fish products from countries that fail to follow international whaling limits. The law was designed to protect the world's whales through an indirect sanctioning system, particularly the aggressive whaling practiced by Japanese fishermen. While whaling violations were documented after the enactment of the law, especially by Japan, the President used his discretion to do nothing, and suit was filed claiming the President did not follow the law to protect whales internationally. a) Is this challenge a question of foreign relations — specifically, Japan's whaling practices — and consequently a nonjusticiable political question? b) If the question is justiciable, did the President properly enforce the law? c) Assume Congress amended the law to remove all of the President's discretion in enforcing the law. If the President still refuses to exclude any fish products from importation, how should a court rule on this issue?

5. *No Drilling Zones.* In the introductory problem at the beginning of the chapter, if the Supreme Court upheld the President's creation of no drilling zones

under *Youngstown Sheet & Tube Co.*, what is the most likely rationale? Do you agree with that rationale? Explain.

C. ADDITIONAL SEPARATION OF POWERS ISSUES BETWEEN THE EXECUTIVE AND THE LEGISLATURE: NONDELEGATION, VETO, AND APPOINTMENT AND REMOVAL

Interactions among the legislature, the executive, and the courts often involve "separation of powers" issues. These questions concern more than the literal separation of branches and often involve either the interdependence or usurpation of powers.

Separation of powers problems can be compartmentalized either as one branch of government delegating powers to a coordinate branch of government or administrative agencies, or as one branch of government taking powers away from another branch of government. Delegation of powers questions generally arise from the doctrine prohibiting one branch of government from sharing its powers with other branches or administrative agencies. "Power grabs" by one branch from another arise in certain contexts — namely, veto, appointment, and removal situations.

While the separation of powers doctrine is universally recognized as a bedrock constitutional doctrine, it cannot be found anywhere in the text of the Constitution. Scholars and pragmatists alike infer the doctrine from the structural framework of the first three Articles, which divide the powers of government among three well-defined branches. The lack of textual recognition, however, has contributed to the doctrine's imprecise purpose and reach, with its invocation having a wide variety of meanings, often dependent on the branch that is doing the invoking and in consideration of circumstances in which the dispute arose. *See, e.g.*, Gerhard Casper, *An Essay in Separation of Powers: Some Early Versions and Practices*, 30 Wm. & Mary L. Rev. 211 (1989).

There is as much evidence of the Constitution's efforts to intertwine the powers of the three branches as there is to keep them sequestered or buffered. *See, e.g.*, Philip Kurland, *The Rise and Fall of the Doctrine of Separation of Powers*, 85 Mich. L. Rev. 592 (1986). For example, treaties require both presidential and Senate action. Legislation requires the approval of the President, unless two thirds of the Congress overrides the President's veto. In a now-famous passage from Youngstown Sheet & Tube Co. v. Sawyer, 343 U.S. 579 (1952), Justice Jackson declared: "While the Constitution diffuses power the better to secure liberty, it also contemplates that practice will integrate the dispersed powers into a workable government. It enjoins upon its branches a separateness but interdependence, autonomy but reciprocity." Thus, instead of a hermetically sealed lining between the branches, the separation of powers doctrine creates "a carefully crafted system of checked and balanced power within each Branch [to avoid tyranny in a Branch]." Mistretta v. United States, 488 U.S., at 381 (1989). The three branches are like the legs on a three-legged stool, "each leg must be approximately the same length if the stool is not to tip over." *Id.*

1.   The "Nondelegation" of Powers Doctrine

The "nondelegation" of powers doctrine is potentially applicable when one branch of government (usually Congress) attempts to delegate its powers directly to another branch or to an administrative agency in another branch. The courts have held in some instances that such delegations are unconstitutional in violation of the separation of powers doctrine. The doctrine has been strongly influenced by historical developments.

As you may recall from Chapter 2, during the 1930s the nation suffered through the Great Depression. When President Franklin Roosevelt was elected on the promise of a "New Deal," Congress enacted an array of bills designed to pull the country out of the economic malaise. The Court began to question how much power Congress could delegate to administrative agencies. Important questions were involved. At what point did Congress delegate its own lawmaking function and not just leave "the details" to agency determination or, conversely, usurp the powers vested in another branch? The answers were left to the courts and the courts' contours of the nondelegation doctrine.

The courts were faced with a dilemma, however. The framework of nondelegation was not expressly contained in the Constitution and was left to judicial interpretation through precedent, the Framers' intent, and pragmatism. While pragmatic justifications for delegation were apparent, whether the courts would uphold the doctrine against a formalistic constitutional challenge was not.

The doctrine reached its apex in 1935, when the Court struck down two statutes as unconstitutional delegations of power. The cases of A.L.A. Schecter Poultry Corp. v. United States, 295 U.S. 495 (1935), and Panama Refining Co. v. Ryan, 293 U.S. 388 (1935), stood for the proposition that delegation without sufficient standards for implementing congressional policy — without an "intelligible principle to which the person or body authorized to [exercise the delegated authority] is directed to conform," J.W. Hampton, Jr., & Co. v. United States, 276 U.S. 394 (1928) — was unconstitutional.

Since 1935, the nondelegation doctrine has retained its formal status but has lost most of its teeth. The demise of the doctrine, coupled with the Court's expanded interpretation of the Commerce Clause (which, as we know from Chapter 2, also resulted from the constitutional crisis of the 1930s), led to a dramatic expansion of the size and scope of the federal government. Because of the change in the Court's Commerce Clause jurisprudence, Congress was able to assume control over ever larger parts of the nation and the economy. Likewise, as it became possible for Congress to delegate more and more power to administrative agencies, Congress began to create large federal bureaucracies. The net effect of these developments was a significant increase in the number of federal administrative agencies, including such entities as the Federal Aviation Administration, the Internal Revenue Service, the Federal Communications

Commission, and the Environmental Protection Agency, which were charged with refining and implementing the government agenda. In addition, those agencies began to promulgate lots of regulations. Indeed, Congress began to articulate legislation in broad terms, and essentially left it to agencies to fill in the broad outlines of the regulation. As the Supreme Court observed: "In an increasingly complex society, Congress obviously could not perform its functions if it were obliged to find all the facts subsidiary to the basic conclusions which support the defined legislative policy." Opp Cotton Mills, Inc. v. Administrator, Wage and Hour Div. of Dept. of Labor, 312 U.S. 126, 145 (1941).

The complete demise of the nondelegation doctrine, however, is premature, since it still retains vitality as a limit, especially on legislative action. As noted by Justice Breyer, "The 'nondelegation' doctrine represents an added constitutional check upon Congress's authority to delegate power to the Executive Branch." Clinton v. New York, 524 U.S. 417, 484 (1998) (dissenting opinion). Many of the cases in the following sections, while labeled "appointments" or "removal" or "veto" issues, also could be viewed through the prism of nondelegation.

In Buckley v. Valeo, 424 U.S. 936 (1976), a case involving freedom of speech and separation of powers challenges to the Federal Election Campaign Act of 1971, 2 U.S.C. §431 *et seq.*, the Supreme Court struck down provisions of the Act that restructured the Federal Election Commission. The Court found that Congress had appropriated executive powers to itself by creating a commission with rule-making and enforcement powers, while at the same time reserving the appointment power for four of the eight commission members to certain officers of Congress alone. Although the Court held that the provisions violated the Appointments Clause, the violation that occurred could be viewed as the improper delegation of powers from one branch to another. The Court noted:

> Insofar as the powers confided in the Commission are essentially of an investigative and informative nature, falling in the same general category as those powers which Congress might delegate to one of its own committees, there can be no question that the Commission as presently constituted may exercise them. . . .
>
>   But when we go beyond this type of authority to the more substantial powers exercised by the Commission, we reach a different result. The commission's enforcement power, exemplified by its discretionary power to seek judicial relief, is authority that cannot possibly be regarded as merely in aid of the legislative function of Congress.

In Mistretta v. United States, 488 U.S. 361 (1989), the Supreme Court considered another nondelegation question, this time involving the constitutionality of the sentencing guidelines created by the U.S. Sentencing Commission. The commission was instituted by Congress in the Sentencing Reform Act of 1984. In upholding the creation of the commission and the guidelines against a separation of powers challenge, Justice Blackmun, for the Court, justified the porous nature of the modern doctrine by alluding to the pragmatic importance of delegation. He wrote:

> The nondelegation doctrine is rooted in the principle of separation of powers that underlies our tripartite system of Government. The Constitution provides that "[a]ll legislative Powers

herein granted shall be vested in a Congress of the United States," U.S. Const., Art. I, §1, and we long have insisted that "the integrity and maintenance of the system of government ordained by the Constitution" mandate that Congress generally cannot delegate its legislative power to another Branch. In a passage now enshrined in our jurisprudence, Chief Justice Taft, writing for the Court, explained our approach to such cooperative ventures: "In determining what [Congress] may do in seeking assistance from another branch, the extent and character of that assistance must be fixed according to common sense and the inherent necessities of the government co-ordination." J.W. Hampton, Jr., & Co. v. United States, 276 U.S. 394, 406 (1928). So long as Congress "shall lay down by legislative act an intelligible principle to which the person or body authorized to [exercise the delegated authority] is directed to conform, such legislative action is not a forbidden delegation of legislative power."

Applying this "intelligible principle" test to congressional delegations, our jurisprudence has been driven by a practical understanding that in our increasingly complex society, replete with ever changing and more technical problems, Congress simply cannot do its job absent an ability to delegate power under broad general directives.

In light of our approval of these broad delegations, we harbor no doubt that Congress's delegation of authority to the Sentencing Commission is sufficiently specific and detailed to meet constitutional requirements.

Congress provided even more detailed guidance to the Commission about categories of offenses and offender characteristics. Congress directed that guidelines require a term of confinement at or near the statutory maximum for certain crimes of violence.

Developing proportionate penalties for hundreds of different crimes by a virtually limitless array of offenders is precisely the sort of intricate, labor-intensive task for which delegation to an expert body is especially appropriate. Although Congress has delegated significant discretion to the Commission to draw judgments from its analysis of existing sentencing practice and alternative sentencing models, "Congress is not confined to that method of executing its policy which involves the least possible delegation of discretion to administrative officers." Yakus v. United States, 321 U.S., at 425-426.

∽ PROBLEMS ∽

1. *Delegation of Authority to Regulate Organic Products.* Congress enacts a law providing for the regulation of organic products in the United States, mandating different labels for distinctive methods of farming or, in the case of animal products, feeding. In part of the law, Congress directs the U.S. Department of Agriculture "to create uniform and effective standards by which to further categorize the products sold, including the nature and substance of federal seals affixed to each of the products." Does this legislation violate the nondelegation doctrine? Explain.

2. *DC National Airport Governance.* Congress seeks smoother ingress and egress to Reagan Washington National Airport, which lies just across the Potomac River and minutes away from Washington, D.C. To this end, it enacts a law, "D.C. National Airport Governance," that creates a congressional subcommittee to oversee and operate the airport. The subcommittee would consist of ten members of Congress, five from each house, who would supervise the operation of the airport, including parking, security, personnel, and most other governance decisions. Is this subcommittee constitutional? *See* Metropolitan Washington Airport Authority v. Citizens for Abatement of Aircraft Noise, Inc., 501 U.S. 252 (1991).

3. *Farm Subsidies*. Congress, after observing the increasing competition American farmers face from farmers in other countries, enacts a protectionist law. The law provides that any American farmer who goes bankrupt and has been the subject of a judgment regarding the payment of creditors can petition a special congressional committee drawn equally from each house for redress. The committee has been given the power to reduce the creditor payments and make a more favorable resolution for the bankrupt farmer. Is this law constitutional? Explain.

4. *Unreviewable Discretion*. Congress entered into the United States–China Relations Act in 2006, a wide-ranging trade agreement. Section 421 gave the President discretion to increase tariffs on Chinese imports if "market disruptions" occur. An American business that imported devices modifying the heights of wheelchairs and motorized scooters, Skootr, Inc., brought suit, claiming that the increased tariffs on scooter and wheelchair imports unilaterally imposed by the President due to an alleged market disruption were unconstitutional. How should a court rule?

2. The Veto Power

The veto power vested in the President is described in the Constitution as the "disapproval" of legislation: "Every Order, Resolution or Vote to which the Concurrence of the Senate and House of Representatives may be necessary (except on a question of Adjournment) shall be presented to the President of the United States; and before the Same shall take Effect, shall be approved by him, or being disapproved by him, shall be repassed by two thirds of the Senate and House of Representatives." Art. I, §7, cl. 3. Constitutional veto issues have arisen in two distinct contexts. One context involved the so-called "legislative veto," exercised by Congress or one of its two houses. The other involved the so-called "line item veto," exercised by the President. These veto contexts raise issues about who has the final say on legislation and whether any of the legislative powers can be held in reserve, like a rebuttal in an oral argument.

a. The Legislative Veto

Can Congress reserve a form of veto power to itself in otherwise properly enacted legislation? This is not merely an academic question. As noted by Justice Powell in his concurrence in the following case, Immigration and Naturalization Service v. Chadha, 462 U.S. 919 (1983), "Congress has included the veto in literally hundreds of statutes, dating back to the 1930s." 462 U.S., at 959-960.

BACKGROUND
A Legislative Veto That Paved the Way

One of the most significant legislative vetoes occurred in 1932, when President Herbert Hoover agreed with Congress that legislation giving the

President the power to reconfigure part of the Executive Branch could be subject to a congressional override by either the House of Representatives or the Senate. After this pragmatic arrangement was rolled out, many subsequent laws contained similar veto provisions.

Immigration and Naturalization Service v. Chadha

462 U.S. 919 (1983)

Chief Justice BURGER delivered the opinion of the Court.

We granted certiorari [to] consider the constitutionality of §244(c)(2) of the Immigration and Naturalization Act, which authorized one house of Congress to invalidate the decision of the Executive Branch.

I

Chadha is an East Indian who was born in Kenya and holds a British passport. He was lawfully admitted to the United States in 1966 on a nonimmigrant student visa. His visa expired on June 30, 1972. On October 11, 1973, the District Director of the Immigration and Naturalization Service ordered Chadha to show cause why he should not be deported for having "remained in the United States for a longer time than permitted." App. 6. Pursuant to §242(b) of the Immigration and Nationality Act (Act), 8 U.S.C. §1252(b), a deportation hearing was held before an immigration judge on January 11, 1974. Chadha conceded that he was deportable for overstaying his visa and the hearing was adjourned to enable him to file an application for suspension of deportation under §244(a)(1) of the Act, 8 U.S.C. §1254(a)(1).

The immigration judge found that Chadha met the requirements of §244(a)(1): he had resided continuously in the United States for over seven years, was of good moral character, and would suffer "extreme hardship" if deported. Pursuant to §244(c)(1) of the Act, 8 U.S.C. §1254(c)(1), the immigration judge suspended Chadha's deportation and a report of the suspension was transmitted to Congress.

On December 12, 1975, Representative Eilberg, Chairman of the Judiciary Subcommittee on Immigration, Citizenship, and International Law, introduced a resolution opposing "the granting of permanent residence in the United States to [six] aliens," including Chadha.

The resolution was passed without debate or recorded vote. Since the House action was pursuant to §244(c)(2), the resolution was not treated as an Article I legislative act; it was not submitted to the Senate or presented to the President for his action.

After the House veto of the Attorney General's decision to allow Chadha to remain in the United States, the immigration judge reopened the deportation proceedings to implement the House order deporting Chadha. Chadha moved to terminate the proceedings on the ground that §244(c)(2) is unconstitutional.

We granted certiorari [and] turn now to the question whether action of one House of Congress under §244(c)(2) violates strictures of the Constitution. We begin, of course, with the presumption that the challenged statute is valid. Its wisdom is not the concern of the courts; if a challenged action does not violate the Constitution, it must be sustained.

Justice White undertakes to make a case for the proposition that the one-House veto is a useful "political invention" and we need not challenge that assertion.

The Presentment Clauses. The records of the Constitutional Convention reveal that the requirement that all legislation be presented to the President before becoming law was uniformly accepted by the Framers.

The decision to provide the President with a limited and qualified power to nullify proposed legislation by veto was based on the profound conviction of the Framers that the powers conferred on Congress were the powers to be most carefully circumscribed.

The President's role in the lawmaking process also reflects the Framers' careful efforts to check whatever propensity a particular Congress might have to enact oppressive, improvident, or ill-considered measures.

Bicameralism. The bicameral requirement of Art. I, §1, cl. 7 was of scarcely less concern to the Framers than was the Presidential veto and indeed the two concepts are interdependent. Beginning with this presumption, we must nevertheless establish that the challenged action under §244(c)(2) is of the kind to which the procedural requirements of Art. I, §7 apply. Not every action taken by either House is subject to the bicameralism and presentment requirements of Art. I.

The legislative character of the one-House veto in this case is confirmed by the character of the Congressional action it supplants. Neither the House of Representatives nor the Senate contends that, absent the veto provision in §244(c)(2), either of them, or both of them acting together, could effectively require the Attorney General to deport an alien once the Attorney General, in the exercise of legislatively delegated authority, had determined the alien should remain in the United States.

The nature of the decision implemented by the one-House veto in this case further manifests its legislative character. After long experience with the clumsy, time consuming private bill procedure, Congress made a deliberate choice to delegate to the Executive Branch, and specifically to the Attorney General, the authority to allow deportable aliens to remain in this country in certain specified circumstances.

Finally, we see that when the Framers intended to authorize either House of Congress to act alone and outside of its prescribed bicameral legislative role, they narrowly and precisely defined the procedure for such action. There are but four provisions in the Constitution, explicit and unambiguous, by which one House may act alone with the unreviewable force of law, not subject to the President's veto: (a) The House of Representatives alone was given the power to initiate impeachments. Art. I, §2, cl. 6; (b) The Senate alone was given the power to conduct trials following impeachment on charges initiated by the House and to convict following trial. Art. I, §3, cl. 5; (c) The Senate alone was given final unreviewable power to approve or to disapprove presidential appointments. Art. II, §2, cl. 2; (d) The Senate alone was given unreviewable power to ratify treaties negotiated by the President. Art. II, §2, cl. 2. Clearly, when the Draftsmen sought to confer special powers on one House, independent of the other House, or of the President, they did so in explicit, unambiguous terms. These carefully defined exceptions from presentment and bicameralism underscore the difference between the legislative functions of Congress and other unilateral but important and binding one-House acts provided for in the Constitution.

The veto authorized by §244(c)(2) doubtless has been in many respects a convenient shortcut; the "sharing" with the Executive by Congress of its authority over aliens in this manner is, on its face, an appealing compromise.

But it is crystal clear from the records of the Convention, contemporaneous writings and debates, that the Framers ranked other values higher than efficiency. We hold that the Congressional veto provision in §244(c)(2) is severable from the Act and that it is unconstitutional. Accordingly, the judgment of the Court of Appeals is *Affirmed*.

Justice POWELL, concurring in the judgment.

The Court's decision, based on the Presentment Clauses, Art. I, §7, cls. 2 and 3, apparently will invalidate every use of the legislative veto. The breadth of this holding gives one pause. Congress has included the veto in literally hundreds of statutes, dating back to the 1930s. Congress clearly views this procedure as essential to controlling the delegation of power to administrative agencies. The history of the Immigration Act makes clear that §244(c)(2) did not alter the division of actual authority between Congress and the Executive. At all times, whether through private bills, or through affirmative concurrent resolutions, or through the present one-House veto, a permanent change in a deportable alien's status could be accomplished only with the agreement of the Attorney General, the House, and the Senate.

The central concern of the presentation and bicameralism requirements of Article I is that when a departure from the legal status quo is undertaken, it is done with the approval of the President and both Houses of Congress — or, in the event of a presidential veto, a two-thirds majority in both Houses. This interest is fully satisfied by the operation of §244(c)(2). The President's approval is found in the Attorney General's action in recommending to Congress that the deportation order for a given alien be suspended. The House and the Senate indicate their approval of the Executive's action by not passing a resolution of disapproval within the statutory period. Thus, a change in the legal status quo — the deportability of the alien — is consummated only with the approval of each of the three relevant actors. The disagreement of any one of the three maintains the alien's pre-existing status: the Executive may choose not to recommend suspension; the House and Senate may each veto the recommendation.

Thus understood, §244(c)(2) fully effectuates the purposes of the bicameralism and presentation requirements.

The Court of Appeals struck §244(c)(2) as violative of the constitutional principle of separation of powers. It is true that the purpose of separating the authority of government is to prevent unnecessary and dangerous concentration of power in one branch. But the history of the separation of powers doctrine is also a history of accommodation and practicality.

I regret that I am in disagreement with my colleagues on the fundamental questions that this case presents. But even more I regret the destructive scope of the Court's holding.

Today's decision strikes down in one fell swoop provisions in more laws enacted by Congress than the Court has cumulatively invalidated in its history. I fear it will now be more difficult "to insure that the fundamental policy decisions in our society will be made not by an appointed official but by the body immediately responsible to the people," Arizona v. California, 373 U.S. 546, 626 (1963).

∼ PROBLEMS ∼

1. *Funding for Remodeling.* Congress enacts a law requiring monies to be allocated for the remodeling of federal courthouses around the country. The law stipulates that "if the remodeling cannot be done for the amount allocated, the bookkeeper at the courthouse in question shall petition the House of Representatives for additional sums, with detailed explanations for the requests. The House of Representatives, through a special subcommittee of eight representatives from eight different geographical areas of the country (e.g., North, South, East, West, Southeast, etc.), can then decide either to grant the request or to cancel the allocation to that courthouse altogether." Is this law constitutional?

2. *Congressional Action by Majority Vote.* Congress enacted legislation providing that an independent commission, composed of three persons selected by the head of the U.S. Immigration and Customs Enforcement (ICE), shall determine whether a deportable alien can remain in the United States, subject to a veto by the entire Congress based on a majority vote. The commission approved the immigration status of an alien, Kandinsky, but that approval was vetoed by Congress. The result is that Kandinsky will soon be deported. Kandinsky brought suit, claiming the law is unconstitutional in light of the Presentment Clauses in Article I, Section 7, Clauses 2 and 3. How should a court rule on this claim?

b. The "Line Item Veto" Law

The Constitution does not expressly answer the question of whether Congress can authorize the President to veto a single "line item" of legislation. In light of the constitutional silence, arguments exist on both sides. On the one hand, if the President can veto legislation in its entirety, shouldn't the President be able to veto any of its component parts? Furthermore, if the President can fail to spend when authorized by Congress to do so, why can't the President similarly fail to execute a line item authorized by Congress? On the other hand, does the text of the Constitution and the Framers' intent confine the veto power to the entire four corners of legislation and not lesser parts of it?

On August 11, 1997, President Clinton vetoed two line items contained in legislation enacted by Congress pursuant to the Line Item Veto Act, 2 U.S.C. §691 *et seq.*, which became effective on the first day of 1997. That Act allowed the President to "cancel" certain parts or "line items" of legislation and not just the legislation in its entirety. The two canceled line items involved congressional spending. The President stated that his motive was an attempt to reduce the federal budget deficit. One line item involved a waiver of tax recoupment included in §4722(c) of the Balanced Budget Act of 1997, which could have amounted to as much as $2.6 billion in returned taxes from the State of New York. The other line item was a tax credit issued in the Taxpayer Relief Act of 1997, allowing some sellers of food processing facilities to farmers to receive preferential tax treatment.

The case elicited divergent perspectives on the separation of powers. Justice Stevens, for the majority, took a formalistic approach, concluding that the textual limits of the Constitution, requiring approval of both houses of Congress and then the President for a bill to become law, dictate the outcome of the case. The President, in performing a line item veto, had effectively changed the bill that had been approved by both houses of Congress and, consequently, was creating new legislation improperly. By contrast, Justice Breyer, in dissent, recalled Justice Marshall's words in McCulloch v. Maryland, 17 U.S. 316, 4 Wheat. 316 (1819), denying the propriety of "immutable rules," that would have marginalized the Constitution and given it "the properties of a legal code."

Clinton v. New York

524 U.S. 417 (1998)

Justice STEVENS delivered the opinion of the Court.

The Line Item Veto Act (Act), 2 U.S.C. §691 *et seq.* (1994 ed., Supp. II), was enacted in April 1996 and became effective on January 1, 1997. [R]eaching the merits, we agree that the cancellation procedures set forth in the Act violate the Presentment Clause, Art. I, §7, cl. 2, of the Constitution. . . .

The Line Item Veto Act gives the President the power to "cancel in whole" three types of provisions that have been signed into law: "(1) any dollar amount of discretionary budget authority; (2) any item of new direct spending; or (3) any limited tax benefit." 2 U.S.C. §691(a) (1994 ed., Supp. II). It is undisputed that the New York case involves an "item of new direct spending" and that the Snake River case involves a "limited tax benefit" as those terms are defined in the Act. It is also undisputed that each of those provisions had been signed into law pursuant to Article I, §7, of the Constitution before it was canceled.

The Act requires the President to adhere to precise procedures whenever he exercises his cancellation authority. In identifying items for cancellation he must consider the legislative history, the purposes, and other relevant information about the items. *See* 2 U.S.C. §691(b) (1994 ed., Supp. II).

A cancellation takes effect upon receipt by Congress of the special message from the President.

In both legal and practical effect, the President has amended two Acts of Congress by repealing a portion of each. "[R]epeal of statutes, no less than enactment, must conform with Art. I." INS v. Chadha, 462 U.S. 919, 954 (1983). There is no provision in the Constitution that authorizes the President to enact, to amend, or to repeal statutes. Moreover, after a bill has passed both Houses of Congress, but "before it become[s] a Law," it must be presented to the President. If he approves it, "he shall sign it, but if not he shall return it, with his Objections to that House in which it shall have originated, who shall enter the Objections at large on their Journal, and proceed to reconsider it." Art. I, §7, cl. 2. His "return" of a bill, which is usually described as a "veto," is subject to being overridden by a two-thirds vote in each House. There are important differences between the President's "return" of a bill pursuant to Article I, §7, and the exercise of the President's cancellation authority pursuant to the Line Item Veto Act. The constitutional return takes place before the bill becomes law; the statutory cancellation occurs after the bill becomes law. The constitutional return is of the entire bill; the statutory cancellation is of only a part. Although the Constitution expressly authorizes the President to play a role in the process of enacting statutes, it is silent on the subject of unilateral Presidential action that either repeals or amends parts of duly enacted statutes. There are powerful reasons for construing constitutional silence on this profoundly important issue as equivalent to an express prohibition. The procedures governing the enactment of statutes set forth in the text of Article I were the product of the great debates and compromises that produced the Constitution itself. Familiar historical materials provide abundant support for the conclusion that the power to enact statutes may only "be exercised in accord with a single, finely wrought and exhaustively considered, procedure." *Chadha*, 462 U.S., at 951. Our first President understood the text of the Presentment Clause as requiring that he either "approve all the parts of a Bill, or reject it in total." What has emerged in these cases from the President's exercise of his statutory cancellation powers, however, are truncated versions of two bills that passed both Houses of Congress. They are not the product of the "finely wrought" procedure that the Framers designed.

First, relying primarily on Field v. Clark, 143 U.S. 649 (1892), the Government contends that the cancellations were merely exercises of discretionary authority granted to the President by the Balanced Budget Act and the Taxpayer Relief Act read in light of the previously enacted Line Item Veto Act. Second, the Government submits that the substance of the authority to cancel tax and spending items "is, in practical effect, no more and no less than the power to "decline to spend" specified sums of money, or to "decline to implement" specified tax measures." Neither argument is persuasive.

In Field v. Clark, the Court upheld the constitutionality of the Tariff Act of 1890. Act of Oct. 1, 1890, 26 Stat. 567. That statute contained a "free list" of almost 300 specific articles that were exempted from import duties "unless otherwise specially provided for in this act." Section 3 was a special provision that directed the President to suspend that exemption for sugar, molasses, coffee, tea, and hides "whenever, and so often" as he should be satisfied that any country producing and exporting those products imposed duties on the agricultural products of the United States that he deemed to be "reciprocally unequal and unreasonable. . . ."

[There are] three critical differences between the power to suspend the exemption from import duties and the power to cancel portions of a duly enacted statute. First, the exercise of the suspension power was contingent upon a condition that did not exist when the Tariff Act was passed: the imposition of "reciprocally unequal and unreasonable" import duties by other countries. In contrast, the exercise of the cancellation power within five days after the enactment of the Balanced Budget and Tax Reform Acts necessarily was based on the same conditions that Congress evaluated when it passed those statutes. Second, under the Tariff Act, when the President determined that the contingency had arisen, he had a duty to suspend; in contrast, while it is true that the President was required by the Act to make three determinations before he canceled a provision, *see* 2 U.S.C. §691(a)(A) (1994 ed., Supp. II), those determinations did not qualify his discretion to cancel or not to cancel. Finally, whenever the President suspended an exemption under the Tariff Act, he was executing the policy that Congress had embodied in the statute. In contrast, whenever the President cancels an item of new direct spending or a limited tax benefit he is rejecting the policy judgment made by Congress and relying on his own policy judgment.

The Government's reliance upon other tariff and import statutes, discussed in *Field*, that contain provisions similar to the one challenged in *Field, is* unavailing for the same reasons. Some of those statutes authorized the President to "suspen[d] and discontinu[e]" statutory duties upon his determination that discriminatory duties imposed by other nations had been abolished. [Further, t]he cited statutes all relate to foreign trade, and this Court has recognized that in the foreign affairs arena, the President has "a degree of discretion and freedom from statutory restriction which would not be admissible were domestic affairs alone involved." United States v. Curtiss-Wright Export Corp., 299 U.S. 304, 320 (1936).

The critical difference between this statute and all of its predecessors, however, is that unlike any of them, this Act gives the President the unilateral power to change the text of duly enacted statutes. None of the Act's predecessors could even arguably have been construed to authorize such a change.

[O]ur decision rests on the narrow ground that the procedures authorized by the Line Item Veto Act are not authorized by the Constitution.

If there is to be a new procedure in which the President will play a different role in determining the final text of what may "become a law," such change must come not by legislation but through the amendment procedures set forth in Article V of the Constitution.

The judgment of the District Court is affirmed.

Justice KENNEDY, concurring.

To say the political branches have a somewhat free hand to reallocate their own authority would seem to require acceptance of two premises: first, that the public good demands it, and second, that liberty is not at risk. The former premise is inadmissible. The Constitution's structure requires a stability which transcends the convenience of the moment.

The latter premise, too, is flawed. Liberty is always at stake when one or more of the branches seek to transgress the separation of powers.

The principal object of the statute, it is true, was not to enhance the President's power to reward one group and punish another, to help one set of taxpayers and hurt another, to favor one State and ignore another. Yet these are its undeniable effects. The law establishes a new mechanism which gives the President the sole ability to hurt a group that is a visible target, in order to disfavor the group or to extract further concessions from Congress. The law is the functional equivalent of a line item veto and enhances the President's powers beyond what the Framers would have endorsed.

Justice SCALIA, with whom Justice O'CONNOR joins, and with whom Justice BREYER joins as to Part III, concurring in part and dissenting in part.

As much as the Court goes on about Art. I, §7, therefore, that provision does not demand the result the Court reaches. It no more categorically prohibits the Executive *reduction* of congressional dispositions in the course of implementing statutes that authorize such reduction, than it categorically prohibits the Executive *augmentation* of congressional dispositions in the course of implementing statutes that authorize such augmentation — generally known as substantive rulemaking.

I turn, then, to the crux of the matter: whether Congress's authorizing the President to cancel an item of spending gives him a power that our history and traditions show must reside exclusively in the Legislative Branch.

Insofar as the degree of political, "lawmaking" power conferred upon the Executive is concerned, there is not a dime's worth of difference between Congress's authorizing the President to *cancel* a spending item, and Congress's authorizing money to be spent on a particular item at the President's discretion. And the latter has been done since the founding of the Nation. From 1789-1791, the First Congress made lump-sum appropriations for the entire Government — "sum[s] not exceeding" specified amounts for broad purposes.

The short of the matter is this: had the Line Item Veto Act authorized the President to "decline to spend" any item of spending contained in the Balanced Budget Act of 1997, there is not the slightest doubt that authorization would have been constitutional. What the Line Item Veto Act does instead — authorizing the President to "cancel" an item of spending — is technically different. But the technical difference does *not* relate to the technicalities of the Presentment Clause, which have been fully complied with; and the doctrine of unconstitutional delegation, which *is* at issue here, is preeminently *not* a doctrine of technicalities. The title of the Line Item Veto Act, which was perhaps designed to simplify for public comprehension, or perhaps merely to comply with the terms of a campaign pledge, has succeeded in faking out the Supreme Court. The President's action it authorizes in fact is not a line-item veto and thus does not offend Art. I, §7; and insofar as the substance of that action is concerned, it is no different from what Congress has permitted the President to do since the formation of the Union.

For the foregoing reasons, I respectfully dissent.

Justice BREYER, with whom Justice O'CONNOR and Justice SCALIA join as to Part III, dissenting.

Chief Justice Marshall, in a well-known passage, explained, "To have prescribed the means by which government should, in all future time, execute its powers, would have been to change, entirely, the character of the instrument, and give it the properties of a legal code. It would have been an unwise attempt to provide, by immutable rules, for exigencies which, if foreseen at all, must have been seen dimly, and which can be best provided for as they occur." McCulloch v. Maryland, 4 Wheat. 316, 415, 4 L.Ed. 579 (1819).

This passage, like the cases I have just mentioned, calls attention to the genius of the Framers' pragmatic vision, which this Court has long recognized in cases that find constitutional room for necessary institutional innovation.

The Court believes that the Act violates the literal text of the Constitution. A simple syllogism captures its basic reasoning: Major Premise: The Constitution sets forth an exclusive method for enacting, repealing, or amending laws. Minor Premise: The Act authorizes the President to "repea[l] or amen[d]" laws in a different way, namely by announcing a cancellation of a portion of a previously enacted law. Conclusion: The Act is inconsistent with the Constitution.

I find this syllogism unconvincing, however, because its Minor Premise is faulty. When the President "canceled" the two appropriation measures now before us, he did not *repeal* any law nor did he *amend* any law. He simply *followed* the law, leaving the statutes, as they are literally written, intact.

Because I disagree with the Court's holding of literal violation, I must consider whether the Act nonetheless violates separation-of-powers principles — principles that arise out of the Constitution's vesting of the "executive Power" in "a President," U.S. Const., Art. II, §1, and "[a]ll legislative Powers" in "a Congress," Art. I, §1. There are three relevant separation-of-powers questions here: (1) Has Congress given the President the wrong kind of power, i.e., "non-Executive" power? (2) Has Congress given the President the power to "encroach" upon Congress's own constitutionally reserved territory? (3) Has Congress given the President too much power, violating the doctrine of "nondelegation?" These three limitations help assure "adequate control by the citizen's Representatives in Congress," upon which Justice Kennedy properly insists. And with respect to *this* Act, the answer to all these questions is "no."

Viewed conceptually, the power the Act conveys is the right kind of power. It is "executive." As explained above, an exercise of that power "executes" the Act. Conceptually speaking, it closely resembles the kind of delegated authority — to spend or not to spend appropriations, to change or not to change tariff rates — that Congress has frequently granted the President, any differences being differences in degree, not kind.

[In addition], one cannot say that the Act "encroaches" upon Congress's power, when Congress retained the power to insert, by simple majority, into any future appropriations bill, into any section of any such bill, or into any phrase of any section, a provision that says the Act will not apply. Congress also retained the power to "disapprov[e]," and thereby reinstate, any of the President's cancellations. Thus *this* Act is not the sort of delegation "without . . . sufficient check" that concerns Justice Kennedy. Indeed, the President acts only in response to, and on the terms set by, the Congress.

Consequently, with respect, I dissent.

∾ PROBLEMS ∾

1. *Legal Aid.* Congress enacts legislation providing funds for a near-Asian country in the throes of natural disasters, most recently, flooding from a monsoon. As part of the legislation, Congress states: "The funding shall be administered in three distinct subsets, going to different agencies and parts of the country. These subsets are severable and distinguishable. The President has the power under this Act to determine if funding is necessary under each of the parts and may decide not to utilize any or all of the funds in each part. If the President forgoes the use of any of the funds, however, there must be detailed and written advance notice given to Congress, describing the reasons for doing so. In the alternative, the President can simply veto any one of the three subsets prior to signing the Act into law." Is this legislation constitutional? Explain.

2. *Condition Precedent.* Congress enacts a law stating, "In the event of a health care pandemic or disaster of such significant proportions that it interferes with the normal operation of a state, the President is empowered to spend up to $50 million to ameliorate that health care problem." Can the President refuse to spend any money? Is the law constitutional? Explain.

c.   The President's Signing Statements

Presidents, from the days of George Washington onward, have used a variety of methods to strengthen and broadcast their powers. One of these methods is the signing statement, a written comment by a President as he approves a bill. The signing statement was allegedly first used by President James Monroe, and then continued by other notable presidents, such as Andrew Jackson and Ulysses S. Grant. In the past, the statements were often ceremonial, offering a rhetorical flourish to a bill's approval. In recent times, these statements have taken on a decidedly political tone, meeting a variety of goals. First, by issuing a signing statement about a law the President finds disagreeable, the President is able to voice displeasure about the law short of exercising a veto. The President also influences the shape of the law by declaring its constitutional boundaries — creating an "executive" history of sorts, similar to a legislative history. Further, a signing statement can influence how the law will operate by creating advance expectations about the law's implementation. In addition, the signing statement stakes out the President's turf and promotes the theory of a "unitary President," noting where the President finds the law constitutionally repugnant.

On one hand, signing statements do not have the force of law and reside in the shadows of the presidency. On the other hand, the statements dictate the position of the executive and can be used to diminish legislation and influence a court's review of that legislation. *See, e.g.*, Ameron Inc. v. U.S. Corps of Engineers, 787 F.2d 878 (3d Cir. 1986).

During the past several decades, presidents have favored the signing statement. Under President George W. Bush, the practice of issuing signing statements flourished, with a total of at least 150 signing statements. In 2001 alone, Bush issued 23 signing statements. The number climbed to 34 in 2002, but leveled off somewhat in 2003 to 27 and to 23 in 2004. *See* Phillip Cooper, *By Order of the President: The Use and Abuse of Direct Presidential Action* (University Press of Kansas 2002) (describing a variety of tools used by presidents to wield power, from executive orders to signing statements). The signing statements presented numerous constitutional challenges, numbering 505 according to one commentator. *Id.* Whether signing statements will take on greater significance in coming years remains to be seen. At a minimum, however, these statements provide a glimpse of the President's conceptualization of the role of the Executive Branch in implementing government policy.

Because of the significance and proliferation of signing statements, the American Bar Association convened a task force to consider the matter. After much deliberation and dialogue, the Task Force reached several conclusions. Some of these are reprinted below.

A.B.A. Taskforce on Presidential Signing Statements and the Separation of Powers – Recommendations [2006]

If our constitutional system of separation of powers is to operate as the framers intended, the President must accept the limitations imposed on his office by the Constitution itself. The use of presidential signing statements to have the last word as to which laws will be enforced and which will not is inconsistent with those limitations and poses a serious threat to the rule of law. It is this threat which the Task Force recommendations seek to address.

A.
Signing Statements Must Respect the Rule of Law and Our Constitutional System of Separation of Powers

As noted above, the first Recommendation urges that the President and those who succeed him cease the practice of using presidential signing statements to state his intention to disregard or decline to enforce a law or to interpret it in a manner inconsistent with the will of Congress. One of the most fundamental innovations of the American Constitution was to separate the executive from the legislative power. The Framers regarded this separation of powers as "essential to the preservation of liberty." James Madison, *The Federalist No. 51*.

In particular, the Framers sought to prevent in our new government the abuses that had arisen from the exercise of prerogative power by the Crown. Their device for doing so was to vest lawmaking power in the Congress and enforcement power in the President, and to provide in Article II §3 that the President "shall take Care that the Laws be faithfully executed." As the Supreme Court stated in holding that President Truman could not seize the nation's steel mills during the Korean war without congressional authorization, "In the framework of our Constitution, the President's power to see that the laws are faithfully executed refutes the idea that he is to be a lawmaker." Youngstown Sheet & Tube Co. v. Sawyer, 343 U.S. 579 (1952).

B.
Presidential Concerns Regarding Constitutionality of Pending Bills Should Be Communicated to Congress Prior to Passage

The White House and each of the 15 major executive departments maintain large and sophisticated legislative or congressional affairs offices and routinely and closely track the progress of bills introduced in the Congress. Moreover, much legislation considered by Congress each session emanates initially from the Executive Branch. For that reason, it is unlikely that important legislation would be considered and passed without the opportunity for full and fair input by the Administration.

Therefore, our second recommendation urges the President, if he believes that any provision of a bill pending before Congress would be unconstitutional if enacted, to communicate such concerns to Congress prior to passage. It is reasonable to expect the President to work cooperatively with Congress to identify and ameliorate any constitutional infirmities during the legislative process, rather than waiting until after passage of legislation to express such concerns in a signing statement.

C.
Signing Statements Should Not Be a Substitute for a Presidential Veto

The third Recommendation urges the President to confine signing statements to the meaning, purpose, or significance of bills he has signed into law, which he then must faithfully execute. For example, it is entirely appropriate for the President to praise a bill as a landmark in civil rights or environmental law and applaud its legislative sponsors, or to provide his views as to how the enactment of the law will affect the welfare of the nation.

When Congress enacted the Sarbanes-Oxley Act, President Bush wrote in his signing statement that it contained "the most far-reaching reforms of American business practices since the time of Franklin Delano Roosevelt." And when President Carter signed the Foreign Intelligence Surveillance Act of 1978, he wrote in his signing statement:

The bill requires, for the first time, a prior judicial warrant for *all* electronic surveillance for foreign intelligence or counterintelligence purposes in the United States in which communications of U.S. persons might be intercepted. It clarifies the Executive's authority to gather foreign intelligence by electronic surveillance in the United States. It will remove any doubt about the legality of those surveillances which are conducted to protect our country against espionage and international terrorism. It will assure FBI field agents and others involved in intelligence collection that their acts are authorized by statute and, if a U.S. person's communications are concerned, by a court order. And it will protect the privacy of the American people. *Id.*

Such statements contribute to public dialogue and accountability.

However, the[se] Recommendations urges the President not to use signing statements in lieu of compliance with his constitutional obligation to veto any bill that he believes violates the Constitution in whole or in part. That obligation follows from the original intent and practice of the Founding Fathers, including President George Washington.

To sign a bill and refuse to enforce some of its provisions because of constitution qualms is tantamount to exercising the line-item veto power held unconstitutional by the Supreme Court in Clinton v. New York, *supra.* By honoring his obligation to veto any bill he believes would violate the Constitution in any respect the President honors his oath to defend the Constitution. That obligation ensures that both Congress and the President will be politically accountable for their actions and that the law the President enforces will not be different from the one Congress enacted.

∾ PROBLEM: NO DRILLING ZONES II ∾

In the introductory problem on no drilling zones, would it have made a difference in the outcome of the dispute if the President had proffered a signing statement articulating the President's position that the creation of no drilling zones was constitutional under the law? What should the President have included in the statement? Explain.

D. THE PRESIDENT'S APPOINTMENT AND REMOVAL POWERS

Even though the President's appointment and removal powers are often lumped together, each is a distinct power, with its own set of rules. The President has the power to appoint and remove various government officials, some located within the Executive Branch and some in the other branches. The application of these powers is not always intuitive, particularly in light of the way the Supreme Court has carved out the Separation of Powers doctrine over the years. The powers vary, depending on whether the official is appointed or removed, designated "principal" or "inferior," or engaged in executive, judicial, or legislative types of activities.

The scope of the President's appointment and removal powers can be seen to rest as much on the conceptualization of the division of powers among the three branches as on pragmatism. Much depends on whether one believes there is elegant simplicity in placing a single person in charge of executing federal law, or whether there ought to be a less sharply defined interdependence among the branches, characterized by dynamic change over time. *See, e.g.,* Peter M. Shane, *Independent Policymaking and Presidential Power: A Constitutional Analysis,* 57 Geo. Wash. L. Rev. 596 (1989); and Peter L. Strauss, *Formal and Functional Approaches to Separation-of-Powers Questions—A Foolish Inconsistency?,* 72 Cornell L. Rev. 488 (1987). This tension often has played out on a field divided by those advancing a strong unitary theory of the executive and those opposing such a position.

These appointment and removal powers often intersect with and complement the powers of Congress. As a necessary and proper derivative of its legislative power, Congress holds the power to create offices and agencies to carry out its laws. Art. I, §8, cl. 18 (the Necessary and Proper Clause). Congress is simply precluded from creating an agency and then inserting officials to run the agency and execute the law. Such consolidated authority would belie the separation of powers principle.

Appointments Power. The Constitution states: "[The President] shall nominate, and by and with the Advice and Consent of the Senate, shall appoint Ambassadors, other public Ministers and Consuls, Judges of the Supreme Court, and all other Officers of the United States, whose Appointments are not herein otherwise provided for, and which shall be established by Law: but the Congress may by Law vest the Appointment of such inferior Officers, as they think proper, in the President alone, in the Courts of Law, or in the Heads of Departments." Art. II, §2, cl. 2. While the appointment of officers of the United States is based on a carefully described process, which officials are viewed as "Officers of the United States" and which are viewed as "inferior," as well as the meaning of "as they think proper," have been subject to judicial scrutiny and interpretation.

The Constitution effectively divides the appointment of government officials subject to constitutional limitations into two categories—those high-ranking officials considered officers of the United States, or "principal" officers, and officers considered "inferior" (although still wielding considerable power). The principal officers include the heads of departments, such as the secretary of state, other cabinet positions, ambassadors, and federal judges. Inferior officers include many remaining government officials, who often wield considerable policy power.

The process for appointing officers of the United States is prescribed by the Constitution. Art. II, §2, cl. 2. The President has the power to nominate these persons and, "by and with the advice and consent of the Senate," to appoint these individuals to their posts. *Id.* A notable example involves the appointment of a new federal judge, such as Sonia Sotomayor. She was nominated by President Obama to become an Associate Justice of the U.S. Supreme Court, sat for confirmation hearings before the Senate Judiciary Committee, and then was approved by the full Senate. The process for inferior officers is not articulated in the Constitution and has been left to judicial interpretation. A critical appointments issue often involves how much control must be ceded to the President in appointing members of the Executive Branch.

Several cases in the 1970s and 1980s developed the appointments power doctrine. Buckley v. Valeo, 424 U.S. 1 (1976), which follows, was one of several cases shaping the boundaries of the President's appointment powers (and constituted a seminal case in the landscape of campaign finance laws for many years).

Buckley v. Valeo
424 U.S. 1 (1976)

PER CURIAM

These appeals present constitutional challenges to the key provisions of the Federal Election Campaign Act of 1971 (Act), and related provisions of the Internal Revenue Code of 1954, all as amended in 1974.

The Court of Appeals, in sustaining the legislation in large part against various constitutional challenges, viewed it as "by far the most comprehensive reform legislation (ever) passed by Congress concerning the election of the President, Vice-President, and members of Congress."

The statutes at issue, summarized in broad terms, contain the following provisions: (a) individual political contributions are limited to $1,000 to any single candidate per election; independent expenditures by individuals and groups "relative to a clearly identified candidate" are limited to $1,000 a year; campaign spending by candidates for various federal offices and spending for national conventions by political parties are subject to prescribed limits; (b) contributions and expenditures above certain threshold levels must be reported and publicly disclosed; (c) a system for public funding of Presidential campaign activities is established . . . and (d) a Federal Election Commission is established to administer and enforce the legislation.

IV. THE FEDERAL ELECTION COMMISSION

The 1974 amendments to the Act create an eight-member Federal Election Commission (Commission), and vest in it primary and substantial responsibility for administering and enforcing the Act. The question that we address in this portion of the opinion is whether, in view of the manner in which a majority of its members are appointed, the Commission may under the Constitution exercise the powers conferred upon it.

Chapter 14 of Title 2 makes the Commission the principal repository of the numerous reports and statements which are required by that chapter to be filed by those engaging in the regulated political activities. Its duties under Section 438(a) with respect to these reports and statements include filing and indexing, making them available for public inspection, preservation, and auditing and field investigations.

Beyond these recordkeeping, disclosure, and investigative functions, however, the Commission is given extensive rulemaking and adjudicative powers. Its duty is "to prescribe suitable rules and regulations to carry out the provisions of . . . chapter (14)." Section 437d(a)(9) authorizes it to "formulate general policy with respect to the administration of this Act" and enumerated sections of Title 18's Criminal Code, as to all of which provisions the Commission "has primary jurisdiction with respect to (their) civil enforcement." Section 437c(b). The Commission is authorized under Section 437f(a) to render advisory opinions with respect to activities possibly violating the Act, the Title 18 sections, or the campaign funding provisions of Title 26.

The Commission's enforcement power is both direct and wide-ranging. It may institute a civil action for (i) injunctive or other relief against "any acts or practices which constitute or will constitute a violation of this Act," (ii) declaratory or injunctive relief "as may be appropriate to implement or con(s)true any provisions" governing administration of funds for Presidential election campaigns and national party conventions, and (iii) "such injunctive relief as is appropriate to implement any provision" governing the payment of matching funds for Presidential primary campaigns. In no respect do the foregoing civil actions require the concurrence of or participation by the Attorney General; conversely, the decision not to seek judicial relief in the above respects would appear to rest solely with the Commission.

The body in which this authority is reposed consists of eight members. The Secretary of the Senate and the Clerk of the House of Representatives are ex officio members of the Commission without the right to vote. Two members are appointed by the President pro tempore of the Senate "upon the recommendations of the majority leader of the Senate and the minority leader of the Senate." Two more are to be appointed by the Speaker of the House of Representatives, likewise upon the recommendations of its respective majority and minority leaders. The remaining two members are appointed by the President. Each of the six voting members of the Commission must be confirmed by the majority of both Houses of Congress, and each of the three appointing authorities is forbidden to choose both of their appointees from the same political party.

Appellants urge that since Congress has given the Commission wide-ranging rulemaking and enforcement powers with respect to the substantive provisions of the Act, Congress is precluded under the principle of separation of powers from vesting in itself the authority to appoint those who will exercise such authority. Their argument is based on the language of Art. II, §2, cl. 2, of the Constitution, which provides in pertinent part as follows:

"(The President) shall nominate, and by and with the Advice and Consent of the Senate, shall appoint . . . all other Officers of the United States, whose Appointments are not herein otherwise provided for, and which shall be established by Law: but the Congress may by Law vest the Appointment of such inferior Officers, as they think proper, in the President alone, in the Courts of Law, or in the Heads of Departments."

Appellants' argument is that this provision is the exclusive method by which those charged with executing the laws of the United States may be chosen. Congress, they assert, cannot have it both ways. If the Legislature wishes the Commission to exercise all of the conferred powers, then its members are in fact "Officers of the United States" and must be appointed under the Appointments Clause.

But if Congress insists upon retaining the power to appoint, then the members of the Commission may not discharge those many functions of the Commission which can be performed only by "Officers of the United States," as that term must be construed within the doctrine of separation of powers.

James Madison, writing in *The Federalist No. 47*, defended the work of the Framers against the charge that these three governmental powers were not entirely separate from one another in the proposed Constitution. He asserted that while there was some admixture, the Constitution was nonetheless true to Montesquieu's well-known maxim that the legislative, executive, and judicial departments ought to be separate and distinct.

Yet it is also clear from the provisions of the Constitution itself, and from the Federalist Papers, that the Constitution by no means contemplates total separation of each of these three essential branches of Government. The President is a participant in the law-making process by virtue of his authority to veto bills enacted by Congress. The Senate is a participant in the appointive process by virtue of its authority to refuse to confirm persons nominated to office by the President.

We think that the term "Officers of the United States" as used in Art. II, defined to include "all persons who can be said to hold an office under the government" in United States v. Germaine, *supra*, is a term intended to have substantive meaning. We think its fair import is that any appointee exercising significant authority pursuant to the laws of the United States is an "Officer of the United States," and must, therefore, be appointed in the manner prescribed by §2, cl. 2, of that Article.

Although two members of the Commission are initially selected by the President, his nominations are subject to confirmation not merely by the Senate, but by the House of Representatives as well. The remaining four voting members of the Commission are appointed by the President pro tempore of the Senate and by the Speaker of the House. While the second part of the Clause authorizes Congress to vest the appointment of the officers described in that part in "the Courts of Law, or in the Heads of Departments," neither the Speaker of the House nor the President pro tempore of the Senate comes within this language.

The phrase "Heads of Departments," used as it is in conjunction with the phrase "Courts of Law," suggests that the Departments referred to are themselves in the Executive Branch or at least have some connection with that branch. While the Clause expressly authorizes Congress to vest the appointment of certain officers in the "Courts of Law," the absence of similar language to include Congress must mean that neither Congress nor its officers were included within the language "Heads of Departments" in this part of cl. 2. Thus with respect to four of the six voting members of the Commission, neither the President, the head of any department, nor the Judiciary has any voice in their selection.

Insofar as the powers confided in the Commission are essentially of an investigative and informative nature, falling in the same general category as those powers which Congress might delegate to one of its own committees, there can be no question that the Commission as presently constituted may exercise them.

But when we go beyond this type of authority to the more substantial powers exercised by the Commission, we reach a different result. The Commission's enforcement power, exemplified by its discretionary power to seek judicial relief, is authority that cannot possibly be regarded as merely in aid of the legislative function of Congress. A lawsuit is the ultimate remedy for a breach of the law, and it is to the President, and not to the Congress, that the Constitution entrusts the responsibility to "take Care that the Laws be faithfully executed." Art. II, §3.

We hold that these provisions of the Act, vesting in the Commission primary responsibility for conducting civil litigation in the courts of the United States for vindicating public rights, violate Art. II, §2, cl. 2, of the Constitution. Such functions may be discharged only by persons who are "Officers of the United States" within the language of that section.

Notes

1. *Wide-Ranging*. The significant scope and sweeping nature of *Buckley* generated considerable attention in its aftermath. As one commentator noted, "Almost everyone who has commented on *Buckley* in the quarter-century since it was decided agrees with at least part of the Court's decision. There is strong disagreement, however, about which part of the decision is correct." P. Bender, *The Constitutionality of Campaign Finance Legislation: After* Buckley v. Valeo, 34 A.S.U. L. J. 1105 (2002).

2. *Mistretta v. United States*. *Mistretta*, 488 U.S. 361 (1989), further developed the understanding of the President's appointment power. In this case, the Supreme Court considered a challenge to the Sentencing Reform Act of 1984, which tasked the U.S. Sentencing Commission with creating sentencing guidelines for defendants convicted of federal crimes. A key issue was how the commission members were to be appointed under the law. The Act provided the President with the power to appoint members, subject to the advice and consent of the Senate. The persons to be appointed to the commission were to come from the Judicial Branch. Could the President control appointments involving a commission composed of judges? Justice Blackmun, writing for the Court, concluded that the President's appointment powers under the Act did not improperly interfere with the independence of the Judicial Branch. Justice Blackmun stated: "The mere fact that the President within his appointment portfolio has positions that may be attractive to federal judges does not, of itself, corrupt the integrity of the Judiciary. Were the impartiality of the Judicial Branch so easily subverted, our constitutional system of tripartite Government would have failed long ago." Justice Scalia dissented: "While the products of the Sentencing Commission's labors have been given the modest name, "Guidelines," they have the force and effect of laws, prescribing the sentences criminal defendants are to receive. A judge who disregards them will be reversed. I dissent from today's decision because I can find no place within our constitutional system for an agency created by Congress to exercise no governmental power other than the making of laws."

∽ PROBLEMS ∽

1. *Crack Cocaine Commission.* Congress enacted the Crack Cocaine Sentencing Reform Act of 1995, which created a Sentencing Commission composed of seven voting members appointed by a committee made up of the President and two federal appellate judges. The appointed members must be approved by the Senate. Does this commission, located in the Judicial Branch, violate the separation of powers requirements of the Constitution?

2. *Reprise of No Drilling Zones.* Suppose Congress permits the no drilling zones proposed by the President in the introductory problem, but decides to create a commission to oversee those zones. The commission is designed to have five members, all to be appointed by the judiciary. Is this process constitutional?

Morrison v. Olson, 487 U.S. 654 (1988), deals with several constitutional issues. One issue involved the appointment of inferior executive officers outside of the Executive Branch.

The case owed its origins to the constitutional crisis caused by the Watergate break-in and resulting cover-up, leading to President Nixon's resignation in 1974. Following that period, Congress enacted the Ethics in Government Act of 1978. The Act included a provision for the appointment of an "independent counsel" (sometimes referred to as a "special prosecutor"), imbued with the authority to investigate, report, and prosecute government conduct in violation of the law. The independent counsel was to be appointed by a special panel of three federal judges.

Morrison arose as a result of Independent Counsel Alexia Morrison's investigation of Ted Olson, who was then head of the Justice Department's Office of Legal Counsel.

Morrison v. Olson

487 U.S. 654 (1988)

Chief Justice REHNQUIST delivered the opinion of the Court.

This case presents us with a challenge to the independent counsel provisions of the Ethics in Government Act of 1978. We hold today that these provisions of the Act do not violate the Appointments Clause of the Constitution, Art. II, §2, cl. 2, or the limitations of Article III, nor do they impermissibly interfere with the President's authority under Article II in violation of the constitutional principle of separation of powers.

Briefly stated, Title VI of the Ethics in Government Act (Title VI or the Act), allows for the appointment of an "independent counsel" to investigate and, if appropriate, prosecute certain high-ranking Government officials for violations of federal criminal laws. The Act requires the Attorney General, upon receipt of information that he determines is "sufficient to constitute grounds to investigate whether any person [covered by the Act] may have violated any Federal criminal law," to conduct a preliminary investigation of the matter. When the Attorney General has completed this investigation, or 90 days has elapsed, he is required to report to a special court (the Special Division) created by the Act "for the purpose of appointing independent counsels." 28 U.S.C. §49 (1982 ed., Supp. V). If the Attorney General determines that "there are no reasonable grounds to believe that further investigation is warranted," then he must notify the Special Division of this result. In such a case, "the division of the court shall have no power to appoint an independent counsel." §592(b)(1). If, however, the Attorney General has determined that there are "reasonable grounds to believe that further investigation or prosecution is warranted," then he "shall apply to the division of the court for the appointment of an independent counsel." The Attorney General's application to the court "shall contain sufficient information to assist the [court] in selecting an independent counsel and in defining that independent counsel's prosecutorial jurisdiction." §592(d). Upon receiving this application, the Special Division "shall appoint an appropriate independent counsel and shall define that independent counsel's prosecutorial jurisdiction." §593(b).

With respect to all matters within the independent counsel's jurisdiction, the Act grants the counsel "full power and independent authority to exercise all investigative and prosecutorial functions and powers of the Department of Justice, the Attorney General, and any other officer or employee of the Department of Justice." §594(a). The functions of the independent counsel include "conducting grand jury proceedings and other investigations, participating in civil and criminal court proceedings and litigation, and appealing any decision in any case in which the counsel participates in an official capacity." §594(a)(1)-(3). Under §594(a)(9), the counsel's powers include "initiating and conducting prosecutions in any court of competent jurisdiction, framing and signing indictments, filing informations, and handling all aspects of any case, in the name of the United States." The counsel may appoint employees, §594(c), may request and obtain assistance from the Department of Justice, §594(d), and may accept referral of matters from the Attorney General if the matter falls within the counsel's jurisdiction as defined by the Special Division, §594(e). The Act also states that an independent counsel "shall, except where not possible, comply with the written or other established policies of the Department of Justice respecting enforcement of the criminal laws." §594(f). In addition, whenever a matter has been referred to an independent counsel under the Act, the Attorney General and the Justice Department are required to suspend all investigations and proceedings regarding the matter. §597(a). Two statutory provisions govern the length of an independent counsel's tenure in office. The first defines the procedure for removing an independent counsel. Section 596(a)(1) provides: "An independent counsel appointed under this chapter may be removed from office, other than by impeachment and conviction, only by the personal action of the Attorney General and only for good cause, physical disability, mental incapacity, or any other condition that substantially impairs the performance of such independent counsel's duties." The other provision governing the tenure of the independent counsel defines the procedures for "terminating" the counsel's office. Under §596(b)(1), the office of an independent counsel terminates when he or she notifies the Attorney General that he or she has completed or substantially completed any investigations or prosecutions undertaken pursuant to the Act. In addition, the Special Division, acting either on its own or on the suggestion of the Attorney General, may terminate the office of an independent counsel at any time if it finds that "the investigation of all matters within the prosecutorial jurisdiction of such independent counsel . . . have been completed or so substantially completed that it would be appropriate for the Department of Justice to complete such investigations and prosecutions." §596(b)(2).

Finally, the Act provides for congressional oversight of the activities of independent counsel. An independent counsel may from time to time send Congress statements or reports on his or her activities. §595(a)(2).

The proceedings in this case provide an example of how the Act works in practice. In 1982, two Subcommittees of the House of Representatives issued subpoenas directing the Environmental Protection Agency (EPA) to produce certain documents relating to the efforts of the EPA and the Land and Natural Resources Division of the Justice Department to enforce the "Superfund Law." . . . Acting on the advice of the Justice Department, the President ordered the Administrator of EPA to invoke executive privilege to withhold certain of the documents on the ground that they contained "enforcement sensitive information." The Administrator obeyed this order and withheld the documents. In response, the House voted to hold the Administrator in contempt, after which the Administrator and the United States together filed a lawsuit against the House. The conflict abated in March 1983, when the administration agreed to give the House Subcommittees limited access to the documents. The following year, the House Judiciary Committee began an investigation into the Justice Department's role in the controversy over the EPA documents. During this investigation, appellee Olson testified before a House Subcommittee on March 10, 1983.

After consulting with other Department officials, however, the Attorney General chose to apply to the Special Division for the appointment of an independent counsel solely with respect to appellee Olson. The Attorney General accordingly requested appointment of an independent counsel to investigate whether Olson's March 10, 1983, testimony "regarding the completeness of [OLC's] response to the Judiciary Committee's request for OLC documents, and regarding his knowledge of EPA's willingness to turn over certain disputed documents to Congress, violated 18 U.S.C. §1505, §1001, or any other provision of federal criminal law." Attorney General Report, at 2-3.

The Appointments Clause of Article II reads as follows: "[The President] shall nominate, and by and with the Advice and Consent of the Senate, shall appoint Ambassadors, other public Ministers and Consuls, Judges of the Supreme Court, and all other Officers of the United States, whose Appointments are not herein otherwise provided for, and which shall be established by Law: but the Congress may by Law vest the Appointment of such inferior Officers, as they think proper, in the President alone, in the Courts of Law, or in the Heads of Departments." U.S. Const., Art. II, §2, cl. 2. The parties do not dispute that "[t]he Constitution for purposes of appointment . . . divides all its officers into two classes." United States v. Germaine, 99 U.S. (9 Otto) 508, 509 (1879). As we stated in Buckley v. Valeo, 424 U.S. 1, 132 (1976): "[P]rincipal officers are selected by the President with the advice and consent of the Senate. Inferior officers Congress may allow to be appointed by the President alone, by the heads of departments, or by the Judiciary." The initial question is, accordingly, whether appellant is an "inferior" or a "principal" officer. If she is the latter, as the Court of Appeals concluded, then the Act is in violation of the Appointments Clause. The line between "inferior" and "principal" officers is one that is far from clear, and the Framers provided little guidance into where it should be drawn. . . . We need not attempt here to decide exactly where the line falls between the two types of officers, because in our view appellant clearly falls on the "inferior officer" side of that line. Several factors lead to this conclusion. First, appellant is subject to removal by a higher Executive Branch official . . . [that] indicates that she is to some degree "inferior" in rank and authority. Second, appellant is empowered by the Act to perform only certain, limited duties. An independent counsel's role is restricted primarily to investigation and, if appropriate, prosecution for certain federal crimes. . . .

Third, appellant's office is limited in jurisdiction. Not only is the Act itself restricted in applicability to certain federal officials suspected of certain serious federal crimes, but an independent counsel can only act within the scope of the jurisdiction that has been granted by the Special Division pursuant to a request by the Attorney General. Finally, appellant's office is limited in tenure. There is concededly no time limit on the appointment of a particular counsel. Nonetheless, the office of independent counsel is "temporary" in the sense that an independent counsel is appointed essentially to accomplish a single task, and when that task is over the office is terminated, either by the counsel herself or by action of the Special Division.

This does not, however, end our inquiry under the Appointments Clause. Appellees argue that even if appellant is an "inferior" officer, the Clause does not empower Congress to place the power to appoint such an officer outside the Executive Branch. . . . The relevant language of the Appointments Clause is worth repeating. It reads: ". . . but the Congress may by Law vest the Appointment of such inferior Officers, as they think proper, in the President alone, in the courts of Law, or in the Heads of Departments." On its face, the language of this "excepting clause" admits of no limitation on interbranch appointments. Indeed, the inclusion of "as they think proper" seems clearly to give Congress significant discretion to determine whether it is "proper" to vest the appointment of, for example, executive officials in the "courts of Law."

We also note that the history of the Clause provides no support for appellees' position. Throughout most of the process of drafting the Constitution, the Convention concentrated on the problem of who should have the authority to appoint judges.

We do not mean to say that Congress's power to provide for interbranch appointments of "inferior officers" is unlimited. In addition to separation-of-powers concerns, which would arise if such provisions for appointment had the potential to impair the constitutional functions assigned to one of the branches, *Siebold* itself suggested that Congress's decision to vest the appointment power in the courts would be improper if there was some "incongruity" between the functions normally performed by the courts and the performance of their duty to appoint. . . . In the light of the Act's provision making the judges of the Special Division ineligible to participate in any matters relating to an independent counsel they have appointed, 28 U.S.C. §49(f) (1982 ed., Supp. V) we do not think that appointment of the independent counsel by the court runs afoul of the constitutional limitation on "incongruous" interbranch appointments.

Justice SCALIA, dissenting.

It is the proud boast of our democracy that we have "a government of laws and not of men." Many Americans are familiar with that phrase; not many know its derivation. It comes from Part the First, Article XXX, of the Massachusetts Constitution of 1780, which reads in full as follows: "In the government of this Commonwealth, the legislative department shall never exercise the executive and judicial powers, or either of them: The executive shall never exercise the legislative and judicial powers, or either of them: The judicial shall never exercise the legislative and executive powers, or either of them: to the end it may be a government of laws and not of men." The Framers of the Federal Constitution similarly viewed the principle of separation of powers as the absolutely central guarantee of a just Government. In No. 47 of *The Federalist,* Madison wrote that "[n]o political truth is certainly of greater intrinsic value, or is stamped with the authority of more enlightened patrons of liberty." *The Federalist No. 47,* p. 301 (C. Rossiter ed. 1961). . . .

That is what this suit is about. Power. The allocation of power among Congress, the President, and the courts in such fashion as to preserve the equilibrium the Constitution sought to establish — so that "a gradual concentration of the several powers in the same department." *The Federalist No. 51,* p. 321 (J. Madison).

The Court concedes that "[t]here is no real dispute that the functions performed by the independent counsel are 'executive'," though it qualifies that concession by adding "in the sense that they are law enforcement functions that typically have been undertaken by officials within the Executive Branch."

As for the second question, whether the statute before us deprives the President of exclusive control over that quintessentially executive activity: The Court does not, and could not possibly, assert that it does not. That is indeed the whole object of the statute.

As I have said, however, it is ultimately irrelevant *how much* the statute reduces Presidential control. The case is over when the Court acknowledges, as it must, that "[i]t is undeniable that the Act reduces the amount of control or supervision that the Attorney General and, through him, the President exercises over the investigation and prosecution of a certain class of alleged criminal activity."

[This Court] extends into the very heart of our most significant constitutional function the "totality of the circumstances" mode of analysis that this Court has in recent years become fond of. Taking all things into account, we conclude that the power taken away from the President here is not really *too* much. . . .

BACKGROUND
Implications of the Independent Counsel Law

The independent counsel law has had a significant impact on the country's fairly recent political history. Kenneth Starr was a special prosecutor appointed under the independent counsel law to investigate the apparent suicide of Deputy White House Counsel Vince Foster and President Bill Clinton's Whitewater land investments. Starr's investigation led him to disclosures by Monica Lewinsky about an affair she had with President Clinton. Starr left the independent counsel's office to become the dean of Pepperdine Law School and then the president of Baylor University.

∽ PROBLEMS ∽

1. *The Commish.* Congress creates a new commission to oversee Major League Baseball, finding that the organization requires governmental oversight. The commission is given the power to veto team relocation, ticket price increases, and player salaries. The law states that "the Commission shall be composed of three members of Congress, two members chosen by the President, and one member chosen by the Chief Justice of the United States." Is this commission's appointment process constitutional? Explain.

2. *Newly Discovered Evidence.* Suppose a special prosecutor has been appointed to explore allegations of wrongdoing in one area of an executive officer's conduct, and the prosecutor uncovers evidence suggesting wrongdoing in another area. What are the limits of the prosecutor's pursuit of the newly discovered area, if any? Can the prosecution recommend impeachment for the wrongdoing if it was done by the President?

3. *The Special Prosecutor's Report.* If a special prosecutor intends to file a report about the President's conduct, what level of detail should be included in the report? If the report includes alleged sexual misconduct, how graphic should the report be? Can Congress impose limits on a special prosecutor's report? If so, what?

1. The President's Recess Appointment Power

A little-known but significant power of the President lies in Article II, Section 2, Clause 3. That provision states: "The President shall have the power to fill up all vacancies that may happen during the Recess of the Senate, by granting commissions which shall expire at the End of their next session."

Presidents, beginning with George Washington, have used this provision to fill hundreds of governmental vacancies, mostly federal judgeships that might not have been approved by the Senate. Presidents have sometimes appointed controversial nominees, many of whom have served for a limited time, only until the expiration of Congress's following session. Yet, for all of the nominees whose appointments expired in this way, there were many judges who used the limited term as a positive "tryout" and subsequently received full approval. Perhaps the best known of the judges in this category was Thurgood Marshall, who was a recess appointment to the Court of Appeals for the Second Circuit. Several of the other Supreme Court Justices, including Earl Warren and William Brennan, were recess appointees.

In recent years, the President's recess power has not been used quite as often as in times past, in part because of the political fallout such appointments create between a Congress on recess and a sitting President. In January 2004, for example, President George W. Bush named Charles Pickering to the Court of Appeals for the Fifth Circuit as a recess appointment. As is sometimes the case, the President pursued Pickering's approval as a nonrecess appointment, but Pickering ended the confirmation battle by retiring from the federal bench. President Bush also used his recess appointment power to name John Bolton as ambassador to the United Nations. President Obama has made multiple recess appointments as well.

Removal Powers. While it might be assumed that if the President has the power to appoint government officials, there is also an associated power to remove them, the actual rules are more complicated than that based on the conceptualization of the three branches as interdependent and not absolutely separate. Generally, Congress cannot reserve to itself the power to remove officials who are executive officers. The Court grappled with this rule in early cases such as Myers v. United States, 272 U.S. 52 (1925), where the Court struck down a law providing that some postmasters of the United States could not be removed without Congress's consent, and Humphrey's Executor v. United States, 295 U.S. 602 (1935), where the Court upheld a provision in the Federal Trade Commission (FTC) Act, permitting presidential removal of Federal Trade Commissioners, but only for certain reasons. The Court in *Humphrey's Executor* distinguished the law in *Myers,* finding that the FTC did not lie purely within the executive realm like *Myers,* because it exercised "quasi-legislative or quasi-judicial powers."

Just who is an "executive official" and what is the executive function can be difficult, if not insuperable, questions to resolve. The Supreme Court has leaned toward permitting congressional limitations on removal and even shared responsibility for the removal of officials who are considered "hybrid," in that they have some responsibilities outside of enforcement of the law, such as judicial responsibilities. These officials generally do not serve "at the pleasure of the President."

In Bowsher v. Synar, 478 U.S. 714 (1986), the Supreme Court considered whether Congress's law directing the comptroller general to help balance the federal budget, the "Gramm-Rudman-Hollings Act," was consistent with separation of powers limitations. A key issue was whether the comptroller general is an executive officer or a legislative actor who could be controlled by Congress, particularly in removal matters. The Supreme Court affirmed the lower court decision, striking down the law as a violation of the separation of powers.

The background of the case is instructive. Congress enacted the Balanced Budget and Emergency Deficit Act of 1985 to promote a balanced federal budget. To ensure that deficits did not continue to increase, the Act called for the comptroller general of the General Accounting Office, an agency under the auspices of Congress, to assist with cutting the budget in a manner prescribed by the Act. The comptroller was removable under the Act only by Congress, not by the President or any other official.

Shortly after the President approved the Act, Congressman Synar and other members of Congress filed suit. They claimed the law was unconstitutional and sought a declaratory judgment of their rights.

Bowsher v. Synar

478 U.S. 714 (1986)

Chief Justice BURGER delivered the opinion of the Court.

The question presented by these appeals is whether the assignment by Congress to the Comptroller General of the United States of certain functions under the Balanced Budget and Emergency Deficit Control Act of 1985 violates the doctrine of separation of powers.

On December 12, 1985, the President signed into law the Balanced Budget and Emergency Deficit Control Act of 1985, Pub.L. 99-177, 99 Stat. 1038, 2 U.S.C. §901 *et seq.* (1982 ed., Supp. III), popularly known as the "Gramm-Rudman-Hollings Act." The purpose of the Act is to eliminate the federal budget deficit. To that end, the Act sets a "maximum deficit amount" for federal spending for each of fiscal years 1986 through 1991. The size of that maximum deficit amount progressively reduces to zero in fiscal year 1991. [T]he Act requires across-the-board cuts in federal spending to reach the targeted deficit level, with half of the cuts made to defense programs and the other half made to nondefense programs. The Act exempts certain priority programs from these cuts. §255. These "automatic" reductions are accomplished through a rather complicated procedure, spelled out in §251, the so-called "reporting provisions" of the Act. Each year, the Directors of the Office of Management and Budget (OMB) and the Congressional Budget Office (CBO) independently estimate the amount of the federal budget deficit for the upcoming fiscal year. If that deficit exceeds the maximum targeted deficit amount for that fiscal year by more than a specified amount, the Directors of OMB and CBO independently calculate, on a program-by-program basis, the budget reductions necessary to ensure that the deficit does not exceed the maximum deficit amount. The Act then requires the Directors to report jointly their deficit estimates and budget reduction calculations to the Comptroller General. The Comptroller General, after reviewing the Directors' reports, then reports his conclusions to the President. §251(b). The President in turn must issue a "sequestration" order mandating the spending reductions specified by the Comptroller General. §252. There follows a period during which Congress may by legislation reduce spending to obviate, in whole or in part, the need for the sequestration order. If such reductions are not enacted, the sequestration order becomes effective and the spending reductions included in that order are made.

We noted recently that "[t]he Constitution sought to divide the delegated powers of the new Federal Government into three defined categories, Legislative, Executive, and Judicial." INS v. Chadha, 462 U.S. 919, 951 (1983). The declared purpose of separating and dividing the powers of government, of course, was to "diffus[e] power the better to secure liberty." Youngstown Sheet & Tube Co. v. Sawyer, 343 U.S. 579, 635 (1952) (Jackson, J., concurring). Justice Jackson's words echo the famous warning of Montesquieu, quoted by James Madison in *The Federalist No. 47*, that "'there can be no liberty where the legislative and executive powers are united in the same person, or body of magistrates'. . . ." *The Federalist No. 47*, p. 325 (J. Cooke ed. 1961).

Other, more subtle, examples of separated powers are evident as well. Unlike parliamentary systems such as that of Great Britain, no person who is an officer of the United States may serve as a Member of the Congress. Art. I, §6. Moreover, unlike parliamentary systems, the President, under Article II, is responsible not to the Congress but to the people, subject only to impeachment proceedings which are exercised by the two Houses as representatives of the people. Art. II, §4. . . .

The Constitution does not contemplate an active role for Congress in the supervision of officers charged with the execution of the laws it enacts. The President appoints "Officers of the United States" with the "Advice and Consent of the Senate. . . ." Art. II, §2. Once the appointment has been made and confirmed, however, the Constitution explicitly provides for removal of Officers of the United States by Congress only upon impeachment by the House of Representatives and conviction by the Senate. . . .

A direct congressional role in the removal of officers charged with the execution of the laws beyond this limited one is inconsistent with separation of powers. This was made clear in debate in the First Congress in 1789.

This Court first directly addressed this issue in Myers v. United States, 272 U.S. 52 (1925). At issue in *Myers* was a statute providing that certain postmasters could be removed only "by and with the advice and consent of the Senate." The President removed one such Postmaster without Senate approval, and a lawsuit ensued. Chief Justice Taft, writing for the Court, declared the statute unconstitutional on the ground that for Congress to "draw to itself, or to either branch of it, the power to remove or the right to participate in the exercise of that power . . . would be . . . to infringe the constitutional principle of the separation of governmental powers."

A decade later, in Humphrey's Executor v. United States, 295 U.S. 602 (1935), relied upon heavily by appellants, a Federal Trade Commissioner who had been removed by the President sought back pay. *Humphrey's Executor* involved an issue not presented either in the *Myers* case or in this case — i.e., the power of Congress to limit the President's powers of removal of a Federal Trade Commissioner. The relevant statute permitted removal "by the President," but only "for inefficiency, neglect of duty, or malfeasance in office." Justice Sutherland, speaking for the Court, upheld the statute, holding that "illimitable power of removal is not possessed by the President [with respect to Federal Trade Commissioners]." The Court distinguished *Myers,* reaffirming its holding that congressional participation in the removal of executive officers is unconstitutional. . . .

The Court reached a similar result in Wiener v. United States, 357 U.S. 349 (1958), concluding that, under *Humphrey's Executor,* the President did not have unrestrained removal authority over a member of the War Claims Commission. In light of these precedents, we conclude that Congress cannot reserve for itself the power of removal of an officer charged with the execution of the laws except by impeachment. . . .

Our decision in INS v. Chadha, 462 U.S. 919 (1983), supports this conclusion. In *Chadha,* we struck down a one-House "legislative veto" provision by which each House of Congress retained the power to reverse a decision Congress had expressly authorized the Attorney General to make: "Disagreement with the Attorney General's decision on Chadha's deportation — that is, Congress's decision to deport Chadha — no less than Congress's original choice to delegate to the Attorney General the authority to make that decision, involves determinations of policy that Congress can implement in only one way; bicameral passage followed by presentment to the President. Congress must abide by its delegation of authority until that delegation is legislatively altered or revoked." . . .

With these principles in mind, we turn to consideration of whether the Comptroller General is controlled by Congress.

Appellants urge that the Comptroller General performs his duties independently and is not subservient to Congress. We agree with the District Court that this contention does not bear close scrutiny. The critical factor lies in the provisions of the statute defining the Comptroller General's office relating to removability. Although the Comptroller General is nominated by the President from a list of three individuals recommended by the Speaker of the House of Representatives and the President *pro tempore* of the Senate, *see* 31 U.S.C. §703(a)(2), and confirmed by the Senate, he is removable only at the initiative of Congress. He may be removed not only by impeachment but also by joint resolution of Congress "at any time" resting on any one of the following bases: "(i) permanent disability;" "(ii) inefficiency;" "(iii) neglect of duty;" "(iv) malfeasance;" or "(v) a felony or conduct involving moral turpitude." This provision was included, as one Congressman explained in urging passage of the Act, because Congress "felt that [the Comptroller General] should be brought under the sole control of Congress, so that Congress at any moment when it found he was inefficient and was not carrying on the duties of his office as he should and as the Congress expected, could remove him without the long, tedious process of a trial by impeachment." 61 Cong. Rec. 1081 (1921). . . .

Justice White contends: "The statute does not permit anyone to remove the Comptroller at will; removal is permitted only for specified cause, with the existence of cause to be determined by Congress following a hearing. Any removal under the statute would presumably be subject to post-termination judicial review to ensure that a hearing had in fact been held and that the finding of cause for removal was not arbitrary." *Post.* That observation by the dissenter rests on at least two arguable premises: (a) that the enumeration of certain specified causes of removal excludes the possibility of removal for other causes, cf. Shurtleff v. United States, 189 U.S. 311, 315-316 (1903); and (b) that any removal would be subject to judicial review, a position that appellants were unwilling to endorse.

Glossing over these difficulties, the dissent's assessment of the statute fails to recognize the breadth of the grounds for removal. The statute permits removal for "inefficiency," "neglect of duty," or "malfeasance." These terms are very broad and, as interpreted by Congress, could sustain removal of a Comptroller General for any number of actual or perceived transgressions of the legislative will. The Constitutional Convention chose to permit impeachment of executive officers only for "Treason, Bribery, or other high Crimes and Misdemeanors." It rejected language that would have permitted impeachment for "maladministration," with Madison arguing that "[s]o vague a term will be equivalent to a tenure during pleasure of the Senate." 2 M. Farrand, *Records of the Federal Convention of 1787*, 550 (1911). . . .

The executive nature of the Comptroller General's functions under the Act is revealed in §252(a)(3) which gives the Comptroller General the ultimate authority to determine the budget cuts to be made. Indeed, the Comptroller General commands the President himself to carry out, without the slightest variation (with exceptions not relevant to the constitutional issues presented), the directive of the Comptroller General as to the budget reductions. . . . Congress of course initially determined the content of the Balanced Budget and Emergency Deficit Control Act; and undoubtedly the content of the Act determines the nature of the executive duty. However, as *Chadha* makes clear, once Congress makes its choice in enacting legislation, its participation ends. Congress can thereafter control the execution of its enactment only indirectly — by passing new legislation. *Chadha*, 462 U.S., at 958. By placing the responsibility for execution of the Balanced Budget and Emergency Deficit Control Act in the hands of an officer who is subject to removal only by itself, Congress in effect has retained control over the execution of the Act and has intruded into the executive function. The Constitution does not permit such intrusion.

We conclude that the District Court correctly held that the powers vested in the Comptroller General under Section 251 violate the command of the Constitution that the Congress play no direct role in the execution of the laws. Accordingly, the judgment and order of the District Court are affirmed.

∼ PROBLEM: THE AUDIT ∼

Congress enacts a law requiring audits of all government agency books on a rotating schedule, every four years. The law states that auditing shall occur by individuals appointed by and operating out of the General Accounting Office. These individuals shall provide detailed written reports to Congress. Removal of these officials shall occur by a committee appointed jointly by Congress and a specially appointed panel of federal judges. Is the auditing law, particularly its procedure for removing committee members, constitutional? Explain.

E. FOREIGN AFFAIRS, WAR, AND TREATY POWERS

The President has broad powers over foreign affairs. The powers extend from acting as the chief diplomat and representative of the United States, to participating in appointing ambassadors, to entering into relationships and agreements with foreign countries, and to protecting U.S. citizens as the Commander in Chief. Some of these powers are shared with Congress, which also exercises constitutional power in the international sphere. Congress's powers include regulating foreign commerce under the Commerce Clause, spending on the armed forces, and declaring war. The Senate's advice and consent also is required for treaties.

1. Foreign Affairs Powers

The President has wide-ranging powers over foreign policy and international affairs. As the chief executive, the President is by virtue of office the representative of the United States in a myriad of activities, from political visits to and from other heads of state, to a wide variety of agreements with other countries and international organizations, such as the United Nations. A significant question that arises in the foreign affairs arena is whether the President has powers as head of state that are independent of those powers derived from the Constitution.

The case of United States v. Curtiss Wright Export Corporation, 299 U.S. 304 (1936), provided a seminal opportunity for the Court to delineate the source and scope of the foreign affairs powers. In *Curtiss Wright Export Corporation*, the Court was faced with an issue asking whether there was a duality in the executive's exercise of domestic powers and foreign powers. The Court concluded that there was a distinction — and that where the President was operating indeed mattered. The Court found that the President's role in foreign affairs was both plenary and inherent, with the President serving as the representative of the entire nation.

United States v. Curtiss Wright Export Corporation
299 U.S. 304 (1936)

Mr. Justice SUTHERLAND delivered the opinion of the Court.

[On January 27, 1936, the Curtiss Wright Export Corporation was indicted for conspiring to sell military weapons to the nation of Bolivia. At the time, Bolivia was engaged in a military conflict. Curtiss Wright's action allegedly violated both a joint resolution of Congress and a proclamation issued by the President the same day. The resolution granted the President authority to prohibit the sale of arms to nations engaged in conflict in the Chaco, and President Franklin Roosevelt's proclamation prohibited such action. Then, on November 29, 1935, President Roosevelt issued a new proclamation revoking the earlier one, but leaving in place any existing violation. An issue in the case was the effect of the President's "revocation."]

Not only, as we have shown, is the federal power over external affairs in origin and essential character different from that over internal affairs, but participation in the exercise of the power is significantly limited. In this vast external realm, with its important, complicated, delicate and manifold problems, the President alone has the power to speak or listen as a representative of the nation. He makes treaties with the advice and consent of the Senate; but he alone negotiates. Into the field of negotiation the Senate cannot intrude; and Congress itself is powerless to invade it. As Marshall said in his great argument of March 7, 1800, in the House of Representatives, "The President is the sole organ of the nation in its external relations, and its sole representative with foreign nations." Annals, 6th Cong., col. 613. The Senate Committee on Foreign Relations at a very early day in our history (February 15, 1816), reported to the Senate, among other things, as follows:

> The President is the constitutional representative of the United States with regard to foreign nations. He manages our concerns with foreign nations and must necessarily be most competent to determine when, how, and upon what subjects negotiation may be urged with the greatest prospect of success. For his conduct he is responsible to the Constitution.

8 U.S. Sen. Reports Comm. on Foreign Relations, p. 24.

It is important to bear in mind that we are here dealing not alone with an authority vested in the President by an exertion of legislative power, but with such an authority plus the very delicate, plenary and exclusive power of the President as the sole organ of the federal government in the field of international relations—a power which does not require as a basis for its exercise an act of Congress, but which, of course, like every other governmental power, must be exercised in subordination to the applicable provisions of the Constitution.

> The nature of foreign negotiations requires caution, and their success must often depend on secrecy; and even when brought to a conclusion a full disclosure of all the measures, demands, or eventual concessions which may have been proposed or contemplated would be extremely impolitic; for this might have a pernicious influence on future negotiations, or produce immediate inconveniences, perhaps danger and mischief, in relation to other powers. The necessity of such caution and secrecy was one cogent reason for vesting the power of making treaties in the President, with the advice and consent of the Senate, the principle on which that body was formed confining it to a small number of members. To admit, then, a right in the House of Representatives to demand and to have as a matter of course all the papers respecting a negotiation with a foreign power would be to establish a dangerous precedent.

1 Messages and Papers of the Presidents, p. 194.

The marked difference between foreign affairs and domestic affairs in this respect is recognized by both houses of Congress in the very form of their requisitions for information from the executive departments. In the case of every department except the Department of State, the resolution directs the official to furnish the information. In the case of the State Department, dealing with foreign affairs, the President is requested to furnish the information "if not incompatible with the public interest." A statement that to furnish the information is not compatible with the public interest rarely, if ever, is questioned.

Practically every volume of the United States Statutes contains one or more acts or joint resolutions of Congress authorizing action by the President in respect of subjects affecting foreign relations, which either leave the exercise of the power to his unrestricted judgment, or provide a standard far more general than that which has always been considered requisite with regard to domestic affairs.

In Field v. Clark, 143 U.S. 649, 691, this court declared that "the practical construction of the constitution, as given by so many acts of Congress, and embracing almost the entire period of our national existence, should not be overruled, unless upon a conviction that such legislation was clearly incompatible with the supreme law of the land." The rule is one which has been stated and applied many times by this court.

The Executive proclamation recites, "I have found that the prohibition of the sale of arms and munitions of war in the United States to those countries now engaged in armed conflict in the Chaco may contribute to the reestablishment of peace between those countries, and that I have consulted with the governments of other American Republics and have been assured of the cooperation of such governments as I have deemed necessary as contemplated by the said joint resolution." This finding satisfies every requirement of the Joint Resolution. There is no suggestion that the resolution is fatally uncertain or indefinite; and a finding which follows its language, as this finding does, cannot well be challenged as insufficient.

It was not within the power of the President to repeal the Joint Resolution; and his second proclamation did not purport to do so. It "revoked" the first proclamation; and the question is, did the revocation of the proclamation have the effect of abrogating the resolution or of precluding its enforcement in so far as that involved the prosecution and punishment of offenses committed during the life of the first proclamation? We are of opinion that it did not.

∽ PROBLEMS ∽

1. *Russian Republic.* A former Soviet republic establishes its own government. The President of the United States agrees to meet with the new leader of the republic. During the meeting, the leaders agree to meet again and engage in a trade relationship, as detailed in the agreement. The agreement, generally referred to as the Litinov Agreement after the republic's leader, is challenged by the Senate as violating the treaty power requiring the Senate's consent. Was the President's action constitutional? *See* United States v. Pink, 315 U.S. 203 (1942).

2. *China.* The Executive Branch, through the Department of the Treasury, issued a travel restriction to China. The restriction stated: "No tourist or business travel to China will be permitted unless a showing of reasonable and compelling need is demonstrated." Is this travel restriction constitutional? If yes, what is the constitutional basis for the Treasury Department's actions?

2.   *War and the Commander-in-Chief Power — An Illustration of Formalism Versus Functionalism*

The Executive Branch does not have the power to declare war. That power is firmly fixed within the domain of the legislature. Art. I, §8, cl. 11 ("The Congress shall have Power . . . To declare War."). Over the past two centuries, the President has wielded an equally formidable tool, the "Commander-in-Chief" power. This power has permitted the Executive Branch to commit troops abroad and to engage in a wide variety of military actions involving weapons, ships, and airplanes. At times, the exercise of the commander's power appears to be equivalent to declaring war, and frames the tension between formalism and functionalism. Although Congress holds the formal power to declare war, the President holds the power to engage in it — and its subdivisions often labeled military actions or conflicts. The military actions in Korea in the 1950s, Vietnam from the 1950s through the 1970s, and Iraq in the 1990s and in 2003 through the present, for example, are effectively indistinguishable from a formal war. Each of these military engagements was fought with a panoply of weapons and considerable personnel, some of whom suffered injuries and death. While Congress often offered express support for military enterprises, as evidenced by the Gulf of Tonkin Resolution, Joint Resolution of Congress, H.J. Res. 1145 (Aug. 7, 1964), viewed as supporting the deployment of combat forces in Vietnam, the analytical key to these enterprises is that they still were thought to be within the Executive Branch's power to protect U.S. citizens and interests abroad.

Congress's power to declare war, when placed side by side with the executive power to commit troops abroad, underscores the tension between formal and pragmatic approaches to the Constitution. The Congress formally holds the power, but as a functional matter, the executive has wielded it most often.

∿ PROBLEMS ∿

1. *Send in the Troops.* The President decides to help protect an ally from invasion by sending in troops to protect that country. No American citizens are directly in danger. The President notifies Congress about his decision to send troops the same day the troops are sent, without seeking approval or authorization of any kind. Is the President's action constitutional? *See, e.g.,* Youngstown Sheet & Tube Co. v. Sawyer, 343 U.S. at 671 (Vinton, J., dissenting).

2. *No Nukes.* Congress enacts the following law: "Prior to initiating a preemptive strike using nuclear weapons, the President must obtain approval by the Congress, since such a strike is the equivalent of a Declaration of War." Is the law within the powers of Congress?

3. *No First Strikes.* Congress enacts the same law as in Problem 2, except that the law prohibits all first strikes with conventional weapons as well as nuclear ones, except in "self-defense" or the equivalent. Is this law constitutional?

In 1973, after an accumulation of executive military actions without an accompanying declaration of war, Congress attempted to reassert its participation in the Constitution's balance of war powers by enacting the War Powers Resolution. The Resolution was adopted over presidential veto, 50 U.S.C.A. §1541 *et seq.*, and placed various limitations on the executive's use of force abroad.

The courts have not ruled on the constitutionality of the Resolution, and its constitutional status remains in question. The Resolution permits the President, acting as Commander in Chief of the armed forces, to deploy combat troops in hostile situations, but only if there is "(1) a declaration of war, (2) specific statutory authorization, or (3) a national emergency created by attack upon the United States, its territories or possessions, or its armed forces." 50 U.S.C.A. §1541(c) (1973). The Resolution adds:

> . . . the President shall submit within 48 hours to the Speaker of the House of Representatives and to the President Pro Tempore of the Senate a report, in writing, setting forth;
> (A) the circumstances necessitating the introduction of United States Armed Forces;
> (B) the constitutional and legislative authority under which such introduction took place; and
> (C) the estimated scope and duration of the hostilities or involvement. *Id.* at §1543(a)(3)(c).
> . . . Within sixty calendar days after a report is submitted or is required to be submitted . . . the President shall terminate any use of United States Armed Forces . . . unless the Congress (1) has declared war . . . (2) has extended by law such sixty-day period . . . §1544(b).

⤴ PROBLEMS ⤴

1. *NATO.* The President of the United States, in coordination with the North Atlantic Treaty Organization (NATO), directs American troops in Croatia. Assume Congress deadlocked 213-213 on a vote to authorize the use of American troops in the NATO operation for air strikes. The President contends that the use of troops in Croatia was based on his authority as Commander in Chief and that the strikes were necessary to protect U.S. trading interests in Europe. The action in Croatia lasted 79 days, past the 60-day general limit (without congressional approval of an extension) imposed by the War Powers Resolution. The President was required by the same Resolution to submit a report to Congress within 48 hours of committing troops in actual or imminent hostilities. Assuming the President did not comply with the requirements of the War Powers Resolution, were the President's actions permissible? If the answer is no, what penalty should result? Should members of Congress be allowed to bring suit against the President to enforce the War Powers Resolution? *See* Campbell v. Clinton, 203 F.3d 19 (D.C. Cir. 2000).

2. *The Roland Amendment.* Suppose Congress enacts a law with an amendment named for its sponsor, Representative Roland. The Roland Amendment prohibits any expenditures of U.S. government funds that have the "purpose or effect" of aiding the rebel fighters in the Bolivian Mountains, known as the Bolivian Freedom Revolutionary Nation (BFRN). Representative Roland stated, "Let me

make very clear that this prohibition applies to all funds available in the coming fiscal year regardless of any accounting procedure at any agency. It clearly prohibits any expenditure, including those for salaries or all support costs." Subsequently, officials of the National Security Council, an executive agency, secretly sold some surplus supplies and arms from the air force and navy to several European nations at a profit. The National Security Council officials, led by a staff member named Ollie East, donated the profits from the sales to the BFRN. Ollie claimed that these actions were within the executive's power as Commander in Chief and the President's proper role in foreign policy. He further contended that the conduct did not violate the Roland Amendment. What arguments would you make on Ollie's behalf that his actions were in compliance with the Roland Amendment and were constitutional? What arguments would you make that his actions were in violation of the Amendment? Which arguments are more persuasive? Why?

3. *Rogues.* The dictator of a rogue state in Asia goes on the nation's television to denounce the West. At the close of his speech, he threatens to fire a nuclear missile at an "occupied North American target" if the United States does not promptly withdraw from Iraq. Can the President unilaterally attack that country without Congress's approval? Why or why not? What would be the impact if Congress passes a resolution opposing such an attack, including a vow not to fund it?

F. THE PRESIDENT'S POWER TO FIGHT TERRORISM

After the September 11, 2001, terrorist attacks on the United States, Americans attempted to create a security system to prevent future terrorist incursions. The security measures included the creation of a new cabinet-level agency, the Department of Homeland Security; the enactment of a law, called the USA PATRIOT Act;* and other significant tools, from enhanced airport security to extended border searches and antiterrorist training. One important measure was the attempt to detain indefinitely, without constitutional limitation, those persons participating in or supporting terrorist activities or groups. The detainees were considered to be "enemy combatants" by President Bush, leading to scrutiny by the courts over whether the detentions were constitutional. Although President Obama's administration no longer calls the detainees "enemy combatants," there are still people who hold a similar status.

1. The President's Powers to Detain Alleged Terrorists

One week after the September 11 attacks, Congress enacted the Authorization for Use of Military Force (AUMF), 115 Stat. 224, allowing the Executive Branch to use all "necessary and appropriate force" against the al Qaeda terrorist network,

* The name "USA PATRIOT" is an acronym for Uniting and Strengthening America by Providing Appropriate Tools Required to Intercept and Obstruct Terrorism Act of 2001, USA Patriot Act, Pub. L. No. 107-56, 115 Stat. 272 (2001).

the Taliban, other terrorists, and any nation harboring the same. Two months later, in November 2001, the President issued an order directing the military to identify and detain "enemy combatants," those persons fighting for or supporting terrorist organizations opposing the United States. Those persons were considered to be different from enemy soldiers who were part of a nation's fighting force in uniform and on the battlefield.

Numerous persons believed to be agents of terror were captured in Afghanistan and Iraq. Most of these persons were relocated to a detention facility at the U.S. Naval Base at Guantanamo Bay, Cuba, while some were detained within the United States. These detainees were thought to be foreign nationals. By June 2004, nearly 600 alleged members of the Taliban and the al Qaeda terrorist organization were detained at Guantanamo.

According to the Executive Branch, the combatants violated the law of war and thus fell outside of the requirements set forth by the Geneva Conventions for prisoners of war. By designating the detainees as enemy combatants, the President intended to create for them a distinctive and entirely military judicial process. The new model collapsed the traditional division of responsibilities in criminalizing nonmilitary conduct: definition by the Legislative Branch, prosecution by the Executive Branch, and trial by the judiciary. The President's model instead concentrated the responsibilities solely in the Executive Branch and omitted constitutional safeguards, such as the right to be charged, the right to meet with an attorney, the right not to be held indefinitely, and the right to contest the designation of enemy combatant status in court. In justifying this approach, the administration claimed the Executive Branch had inherent power to detain enemy combatants and the authorization to do so by Congress when it enacted the AUMF.

The legal issues involving the detention of enemy combatants intersect at several different levels of analysis. On one level, the cases raise a threshold question of jurisdiction: Can the civil courts, including the Supreme Court, exercise jurisdiction over a matter involving warfare on foreign soil? While courts had previously adopted a posture of deference toward the Legislative and Executive branches in times of armed conflict, *see, e.g.*, United States v. Korematsu, 323 U.S. 214 (1944), the federal courts indicated that the Judicial Branch was not ready to cede total control to the Executive Branch during pressing times of combat.

On another analytical level, bedrock separation of powers issues emerged. The detainees' claims revealed the tension between the President's Article II power as Commander in Chief and Congress's Article I power to declare war. The lack of clarity at the intersection between the two powers was strikingly evident.

Further, the cases illuminated the tension underlying the structure of checks and balances. If the power to authorize the detention of American citizens on American soil or American-held territory usually emanates from the Legislative Branch, while the prosecution of these detentions is typically within the province of the Executive Branch, when is it permissible to merge these distinctive roles?

Similarly, the cases focused attention on the uneasy coexistence between power and its limits. Even if the Executive Branch possessed the power to indefinitely detain enemy combatants, what safeguards of the Constitution apply, if any, to protect detainees from imprisonment without an endpoint — particularly if the detainee is an American citizen being detained on American soil?

Last, the fundamental societal conflict between the right to security and the right to freedom of action percolated to the surface in these cases. This basic dichotomy is particularly nettlesome in times of crisis, when the relative openness of American society receives increasing scrutiny and heightened challenges.

2. *Detention of U.S. Citizens as Alleged Terrorists*

While all of the enemy combatant detainees were assumed to have been foreign nationals, some, in fact, were American citizens. The detention of Americans as enemy combatants raised delicate and complex questions. At a minimum, are U.S. citizen detainees protected to a greater extent by the Constitution than foreign national detainees are?

As various detention cases filtered through the federal court system, the Supreme Court agreed to hear several of the cases during its 2003-2004 term. Hamdi v. Rumsfeld, 527 U.S. 506 (2004), presented the question of whether an American citizen captured in a war zone, Afghanistan, and labeled an enemy combatant could be detained indefinitely in the United States without constitutional protections, such as the right to be heard and the right to counsel. In a second case, Rumsfeld v. Padilla, 542 U.S. 426 (2004), the issue was whether the indefinite detention of an American citizen apprehended on a suspicion of terrorist activities in the United States was constitutional. The citizen, Jose Padilla, was not charged with a crime, but was instead held as an enemy combatant.

World War II provided a useful backdrop for a Supreme Court charged with deciding *Hamdi* and other enemy combatant cases. In particular, the question of whether enemy combatants deserve prisoner of war status under the Geneva Conventions was raised during World War II. *Ex parte Quirin*, 317 U.S. 1 (1942), for example, provided seminal analysis about the status and permissible treatment of enemy combatants captured on American soil. In *Quirin*, the Court ruled on the constitutionality of the President's appointment of a military commission to try German agents captured on American soil. The Court ruled that the agents, even one claiming U.S. citizenship, could be tried by a military tribunal in lieu of the civil courts and safeguards of the Constitution. The Court's decision had both theoretical and pragmatic consequences. Within days of the Court's ruling, six of the petitioners had been put to death pursuant to the military commission's sentence.

Ex Parte Quirin

317 U.S. 1 (1942)

[P]etitioners Burger, Heinck and Quirin, together with Dasch, boarded a German submarine which proceeded across the Atlantic to Amagansett Beach on Long Island, New York. The four were there landed from the submarine in the hours of darkness, on or about June 13, 1942, carrying with them a supply of explosives, fuses and incendiary and timing devices. While landing, they wore German Marine Infantry uniforms or parts of uniforms. Immediately after landing, they buried their uniforms and related articles and proceeded in civilian dress to New York City. [Other Petitioners landed, including one named Haupt, who alleged he was an American citizen.] All were taken into custody in New York or Chicago by agents of the Federal Bureau of Investigation.

The President, as President and Commander in Chief of the Army and Navy, by Order of July 2, 1942, appointed a Military Commission and directed it to try petitioners for offenses against the law of war and the Articles of War, and prescribed regulations for the procedure on the trial and for review of the record of the trial and of any judgment or sentence of the Commission. On the same day, by Proclamation, the President declared that "all persons who are subjects, citizens or residents of any nation at war with the United States or who give obedience to or act under the direction of any such nation, and who during time of war enter or attempt to enter the United States . . . through coastal or boundary defenses, and are charged with committing or attempting or preparing to commit sabotage, espionage, hostile or warlike acts, or violations of the law of war, shall be subject to the law of war and to the jurisdiction of military tribunals."

The Constitution thus invests the President as Commander in Chief with the power to wage war which Congress has declared, and to carry into effect all laws passed by Congress for the conduct of war and for the government and regulation of the Armed Forces, and all laws defining and punishing offences against the law of nations, including those which pertain to the conduct of war.

From the very beginning of its history this Court has recognized and applied the law of war as including that part of the law of nations which prescribes, for the conduct of war, the status, rights and duties of enemy nations as well as of enemy individuals. By the Articles of War, and especially Article 15, Congress has explicitly provided, so far as it may constitutionally do so, that military tribunals shall have jurisdiction to try offenders or offenses against the law of war in appropriate cases. Congress, in addition to making rules for the government of our Armed Forces, has thus exercised its authority to define and punish offenses against the law of nations by sanctioning, within constitutional limitations, the jurisdiction of military commissions to try persons for offenses which, according to the rules and precepts of the law of nations, and more particularly the law of war, are cognizable by such tribunals. And the President, as Commander in Chief, by his Proclamation in time of war his invoked that law. By his Order creating the present Commission he has undertaken to exercise the authority conferred upon him by Congress, and also such authority as the Constitution itself gives the Commander in Chief, to direct the performance of those functions which may constitutionally be performed by the military arm of the nation in time of war.

By universal agreement and practice the law of war draws a distinction between the armed forces and the peaceful populations of belligerent nations and also between those who are lawful and unlawful combatants. Lawful combatants are subject to capture and detention as prisoners of war by opposing military forces. Unlawful combatants are likewise subject to capture and detention, but in addition they are subject to trial and punishment by military tribunals for acts which render their belligerency unlawful. The spy who secretly and without uniform passes the military lines of a belligerent in time of war, seeking to gather military information and communicate it to the enemy, or an enemy combatant who without uniform comes secretly through the lines for the purpose of waging war by destruction of life or property, are familiar examples of belligerents who are generally deemed not to be entitled to the status of prisoners of war, but to be offenders against the law of war subject to trial and punishment by military tribunals. *See* Winthrop, *Military Law,* 2d Ed., pp. 1196-1197, 1219-1221; Instructions for the Government of Armies of the United States in the Field, approved by the President, General Order No. 100, April 24, 1863, §§IV and V.

Petitioners . . . stress the pronouncement of this Court in the Milligan case, 4 Wall. page 121, 18 L.Ed. 281, that the law of war "can never be applied to citizens in states which have upheld the authority of the government, and where the courts are open and their process unobstructed." Elsewhere in its opinion, the Court was at pains to point out that Milligan, a citizen twenty years resident in Indiana, who had never been a resident of any of the states in rebellion, was not an enemy belligerent either entitled to the status of a prisoner of war or subject to the penalties imposed upon unlawful belligerents. We construe the Court's statement as to the inapplicability of the law of war to Milligan's case as having particular reference to the facts before it. From them the Court concluded that Milligan, not being a part of or associated with the armed forces of the enemy, was a non-belligerent, not subject to the law of war save as — in circumstances found not there to be present and not involved here — martial law might be constitutionally established.

Affirmed.

Notes

1. *Non-Detention Act.* In 1971, Congress enacted the Non-Detention Act, 18 U.S.C. §4001(a), which limited the power of the President to detain individuals unless authorized by the Legislative Branch. This Act attempted to rein in the powers of the Executive Branch. A sponsor of the Act, Abner Mikva, noted that its purpose was to avoid the creation of internment camps for citizens, such as the camps created during World War II and described in cases such as Korematsu v. United States. *See* A. Mikva, "Dangerous Executive Power," Editorial, *The Washington Post* A21 (July 16, 2004).

2. *AUMF.* Through the AUMF, the President could "use all necessary and appropriate force against those nations, organizations, or persons he determines planned, authorized, committed, or aided the terrorist attacks," and could also use such force against any persons or groups that "harbored such organizations or persons." In addition, the President was given the power "to prevent any future acts of international terrorism against the United States by such nations, organizations or persons."

The Act did not specify whether the detention of persons was contemplated and, if it was, how the detention should be governed or the length of time permitted. The Act did not contain pertinent legislative history to help resolve such questions. Instead, case law was used to interpret the parameters of the law.

3. *Rumsfeld v. Padilla.* This case, 542 U.S. 426 (2004), involving U.S. citizen Jose Padilla, received perhaps the most attention of the detention cases because of its factual posture. After Padilla was arrested at Chicago's O'Hare Airport, it was reported that he was going to ignite a radiological or so-called "dirty" bomb on behalf of terrorists on American soil. While the facts provided fodder for publicity, the case turned out to be a lesson in jurisdictional jurisprudence — specifically, the importance of following proper procedures in habeas corpus claims. The petitioner had been detained in New York before being moved to a Navy brig located in Charleston, South Carolina. While in South Carolina, Padilla was not permitted to communicate with family, counsel, or others. Chief Justice Rehnquist, for the Court, dismissed the case prior to reaching the merits of the detention. The Court found that Padilla failed to file his habeas corpus petition in the right court. Padilla's attorney had filed the claim in the Southern District of New York, pursuant to New York's long-arm statute. The Chief Justice held that the appropriate respondent under the applicable federal statute was his custodian — the commander of the South Carolina brig. 28 U.S.C. §§2241-2243. Thus, he ruled that the federal court in New York did not have jurisdiction and dismissed the case.

Subsequently, Padilla filed a second petition for certiorari with the U.S. Supreme Court. Padilla attempted to jump over the intermediate appellate court by filing the petition prior to the Court of Appeals for the Fourth Circuit hearing the case. On June 13, 2005, the Supreme Court rejected Padilla's petition for certiorari, allowing the Fourth Circuit to move forward with oral arguments on July 19, 2005.

Hamdi v. Rumsfeld

524 U.S. 507 (2004)

O'CONNOR, J.

[Yaser Esam Hamdi, a U.S. citizen born in Louisiana, grew up in Saudi Arabia. He later traveled to Afghanistan, where he was detained by American forces and labeled an enemy combatant. After first being held at the naval base in Guantanamo Bay, Cuba, he was transferred to the continental United States, without formal charges or access to counsel. Hamdi's father filed a habeas corpus petition on his son's behalf, claiming his son was a victim of circumstance and challenging the U.S. government's ability to hold Hamdi indefinitely without charges or proceedings.]

At this difficult time in our Nation's history, we are called upon to consider the legality of the Government's detention of a United States citizen on United States soil as an "enemy combatant" and to address the process that is constitutionally owed to one who seeks to challenge his classification as such. The United States Court of Appeals for the Fourth Circuit held that petitioner's detention was legally authorized and that he was entitled to no further opportunity to challenge his enemy-combatant label. We now vacate and remand. We hold that although Congress authorized the detention of combatants in the narrow circumstances alleged here, due process demands that a citizen held in the United States as an enemy combatant be given a meaningful opportunity to contest the factual basis for that detention before a neutral decision maker.

On September 11, 2001, the al Qaeda terrorist network used hijacked commercial airliners to attack prominent targets in the United States. Approximately 3,000 people were killed in those attacks. One week later, in response to these "acts of treacherous violence," Congress passed a resolution authorizing the President to "use all necessary and appropriate force against those nations, organizations, or persons he determines planned, authorized, committed, or aided the terrorist attacks" or "harbored such organizations or persons, in order to prevent any future acts of international terrorism against the United States by such nations, organizations or persons." Authorization for Use of Military Force ("the AUMF"), 115 Stat. 224. Soon thereafter, the President ordered United States Armed Forces to Afghanistan, with a mission to subdue al Qaeda and quell the Taliban regime that was known to support it.

[Hamdi was seized as an "enemy combatant" and his father sought a writ of habeas corpus on his behalf, arguing] that, "[a]s an American citizen, Hamdi enjoys the full protections of the Constitution," and that Hamdi's detention in the United States without charges, access to an impartial tribunal, or assistance of counsel "violated and continue[s] to violate the Fifth and Fourteenth Amendments to the United States Constitution." [The] District Court [appointed] the federal public defender as counsel for the petitioners, and ordered that counsel be given access to Hamdi. The United States Court of Appeals for the Fourth Circuit reversed.

On remand, the Government filed a response and a motion to dismiss the petition. It attached to its response a declaration from one Michael Mobbs ("Mobbs Declaration"), who identified himself as Special Advisor to the Under Secretary of Defense for Policy. . . . Mobbs [set] forth what remains the sole evidentiary support that the Government has provided to the courts for Hamdi's detention. The declaration states that Hamdi "traveled to Afghanistan" in July or August 2001, and that he thereafter "affiliated with a Taliban military unit and received weapons training." It asserts that Hamdi "remained with his Taliban unit following the attacks of September 11" and that, during the time when Northern Alliance forces were "engaged in battle with the Taliban," "Hamdi's Taliban unit surrendered" to those forces, after which he "surrender[ed] his Kalishnikov assault rifle" to them. [Mobbs] also states that, because al Qaeda and the Taliban "were and are hostile forces engaged in armed conflict with the armed forces of the United States," "individuals associated with" those groups "were and continue to be enemy combatants." [The] Fourth Circuit [rejected Petitioner's claims and] denied rehearing en banc and we granted certiorari. We now vacate the judgment below and remand.

The threshold question before us is whether the Executive has the authority to detain citizens who qualify as "enemy combatants." [T]he Government has never provided any court with the full criteria that it uses in classifying individuals as such. It has made clear, however, that, [the] "enemy combatant" that it is seeking to detain [in this case] is an individual who, it alleges, was "'part of or supporting forces hostile to the United States or coalition partners'" in Afghanistan and who "'engaged in an armed conflict against the United States'" there. We therefore answer only the narrow question before us: whether the detention of citizens falling within that definition is authorized.

The Government maintains that no explicit congressional authorization is required, because the Executive possesses plenary authority to detain pursuant to Article II of the Constitution. We do not reach the question whether Article II provides such authority, however, because we agree with the Government's alternative position, that Congress has in fact authorized Hamdi's detention, through the AUMF.

[Hamdi] posits that his detention is forbidden by 18 U.S.C. §4001(a). Section 4001(a) states that "[n]o citizen shall be imprisoned or otherwise detained by the United States except pursuant to an Act of Congress." Congress passed §4001(a) in 1971 as part of a bill to repeal the Emergency Detention Act of 1950, which provided procedures for executive detention, during times of emergency, of individuals deemed likely to engage in espionage or sabotage. Congress was particularly concerned about the possibility that the Act could be used to reprise the Japanese internment camps of World War II.

[W]e conclude that the AUMF is explicit congressional authorization for the detention of individuals in the narrow category we describe (assuming, without deciding, that such authorization is required), and that the AUMF satisfied §4001(a)'s requirement that a detention be "pursuant to an Act of Congress" (assuming, without deciding, that §4001(a) applies to military detentions).

The AUMF authorizes the President to use "all necessary and appropriate force" against "nations, organizations, or persons" associated with the September 11, 2001, terrorist attacks. There can be no doubt that individuals who fought against the United States in Afghanistan as part of the Taliban, an organization known to have supported the al Qaeda terrorist network responsible for those attacks, are individuals Congress sought to target in passing the AUMF. We conclude that detention of individuals falling into the limited category we are considering, for the duration of the particular conflict in which they were captured, is so fundamental and accepted an incident to war as to be an exercise of the "necessary and appropriate force" Congress has authorized the President to use.

The capture and detention of lawful combatants and the capture, detention, and trial of unlawful combatants, by "universal agreement and practice," are "important incident[s] of war." *Ex parte Quirin*, 317 U.S., at 28. The purpose of detention is to prevent captured individuals from returning to the field of battle and taking up arms once again.

There is no bar to this Nation's holding one of its own citizens as an enemy combatant. In *Quirin*, one of the detainees, Haupt, alleged that he was a naturalized United States citizen. We held that "[c]itizens who associate themselves with the military arm of the enemy government, and with its aid, guidance and direction enter this country bent on hostile acts, are enemy belligerents within the meaning of [the] law of war." While Haupt was tried for violations of the law of war, nothing in *Quirin* suggests that his citizenship would have precluded his mere detention for the duration of the relevant hostilities. . . . A citizen, no less than an alien, can be "part of or supporting forces hostile to the United States or coalition partners" and "engaged in an armed conflict against the United States." Such a citizen, if released, would pose the same threat of returning to the front during the ongoing conflict.

[I]t is of no moment that the AUMF does not use specific language of detention. Because detention to prevent a combatant's return to the battlefield is a fundamental incident of waging war, in permitting the use of "necessary and appropriate force," Congress has clearly and unmistakably authorized detention in the narrow circumstances considered here.

Hamdi objects, nevertheless, that Congress has not authorized the *indefinite* detention to which he is now subject. . . . It is a clearly established principle of the law of war that detention may last no longer than active hostilities. *See* Article 118 of the Geneva Convention (III) Relative to the Treatment of Prisoners of War, Aug. 12, 1949 [1955]. The United States may detain, for the duration of these hostilities, individuals legitimately determined to be Taliban combatants who "engaged in an armed conflict against the United States." If the record establishes that United States troops are still involved in active combat in Afghanistan, those detentions are part of the exercise of "necessary and appropriate force," and therefore are authorized by the AUMF.

Ex parte Milligan, 4 Wall. 2, 125, 18 L.Ed. 281 (1866), does not undermine our holding. . . . Milligan was not a prisoner of war, but a resident of Indiana arrested while at home. . . . Had Milligan been captured while he was assisting Confederate soldiers by carrying a rifle against Union troops on a Confederate battlefield, [he] could have been detained under military authority for the duration of the conflict, whether or not he was a citizen. [T]he Court in *Ex parte Quirin*, 317 U.S. 1 (1942), dismissed the language of *Milligan* that the petitioners [citizenship] prevented them from being subject to military process. . . . *Quirin* was a unanimous opinion. . . .

[Justice] Scalia [argues that] *Quirin* [cannot] guide our inquiry here because "[i]n *Quirin* it was uncontested that the petitioners were members of enemy forces," while Hamdi challenges his classification as an enemy combatant. But it is unclear why [such] a concession should have any relevance. [O]ur opinion only finds legislative authority to detain under the AUMF once it is sufficiently clear that the individual is, in fact, an enemy combatant; whether that is established by concession or by some other process that verifies this fact with sufficient certainty seems beside the point.

[Justice] Scalia largely ignores the context of this case: a United States citizen captured in a *foreign* combat zone. Justice Scalia refers to only one case involving this factual scenario — a case in which a United States citizen-POW (a member of the Italian army) from World War II was seized on the battlefield in Sicily and then held in the United States. The court in that case held that the military detention of that United States citizen was lawful. *See In re Territo*, 156 F.2d, at 148. . . . Because Justice Scalia finds the fact of battlefield capture irrelevant, his distinction based on the fact that the petitioner "conceded" enemy combatant status is beside the point. . . .

Moreover, Justice Scalia presumably would come to a different result if Hamdi had been kept in Afghanistan or even Guantanamo Bay. This creates a perverse incentive. Military authorities faced with the stark choice of submitting to the full-blown criminal process or releasing a suspected enemy combatant captured on the battlefield will simply keep citizen-detainees abroad. Indeed, the Government transferred Hamdi from Guantanamo Bay to the United States naval brig only after it learned that he might be an American citizen. It is not at all clear why that should make a determinative constitutional difference.

Even in cases in which the detention of enemy combatants is legally authorized, there remains the question of what process is constitutionally due to a citizen who disputes his enemy-combatant status. All [parties] agree that, absent suspension, the writ of habeas corpus remains available to every individual detained within the United States. U.S. Const., Art. I, §9, cl. 2. Only in the rarest of circumstances has Congress seen fit to suspend the writ. At all other times, it has remained a critical check on the Executive, ensuring that it does not detain individuals except in accordance with law. *See* INS v. St. Cyr, 533 U.S. 289 (2001). All agree suspension of the writ has not occurred here. Thus, it is undisputed that Hamdi was properly before an Article III court to challenge his detention under 28 U.S.C. §2241. Section 2241 and its companion provisions provide at least a skeletal outline of the procedures to be afforded a petitioner in federal habeas review. Most notably, section 2243 provides that "the person detained may, under oath, deny any of the facts set forth in the return or allege any other material facts," and section 2246 allows the taking of evidence in habeas proceedings by deposition, affidavit, or interrogatories.

The simple outline of section 2241 makes clear both that Congress envisioned that habeas petitioners would have some opportunity to present and rebut facts and that courts in cases like this retain some ability to vary the ways in which they do so as mandated by due process. The Government recognizes the basic procedural protections required by the habeas statute, but asks us to hold that, given both the flexibility of the habeas mechanism and the circumstances presented in this case, the presentation of the Mobbs Declaration to the habeas court completed the required factual development.

[T]he "facts" that constitute the alleged concession are insufficient to support Hamdi's detention. Under the definition of enemy combatant that we accept today as falling within the scope of Congress's authorization, Hamdi would need to be "part of or supporting forces hostile to the United States or coalition partners" and "engaged in an armed conflict against the United States" to justify his detention in the United States for the duration of the relevant conflict. The habeas petition states only that "[w]hen seized by the United States Government, Mr. Hamdi resided in Afghanistan." [W]e reject any argument that Hamdi has made concessions that eliminate any right to further process.

The Government's second argument [is] that further factual exploration is unwarranted and inappropriate in light of the extraordinary constitutional interests at stake. The Government argues courts should review its determination that a citizen is an enemy combatant under a very deferential "some evidence" standard. Under this review, a court would assume the accuracy of the Government's articulated basis for Hamdi's detention, as set forth in the Mobbs Declaration, and assess only whether that articulated basis was a legitimate one. . . . Hamdi [. . .] demands that he receive a hearing in which he may challenge the Mobbs Declaration and adduce his own counter evidence.

The ordinary mechanism that we use for balancing such serious competing interests, and for determining the procedures that are necessary to ensure that a citizen is not "deprived of life, liberty, or property, without due process of law," U.S. Const., Amdt. 5, is the test that we articulated in Mathews v. Eldridge. *Mathews* dictates that the process due in any given instance is determined by weighing "the private interest that will be affected by the official action" against the Government's asserted interest, "including the function involved" and the burdens the Government would face in providing greater process. The *Mathews* calculus then contemplates a judicious balancing of these concerns, through an analysis of "the risk of an erroneous deprivation" of the private interest if the process were reduced and the "probable value, if any, of additional or substitute safeguards." We take each of these steps in turn.

"In our society liberty is the norm," and detention without trial "is the carefully limited exception." Nor is the weight on this side of the *Mathews* scale offset by the circumstances of war or the accusation of treasonous behavior, for "[i]t is clear that commitment for *any* purpose constitutes a significant deprivation of liberty that requires due process protection," and at this stage in the *Mathews* calculus, we consider the interest of the *erroneously* detained individual. Carey v. Piphus, 435 U.S. 247 (1978). Indeed, as *amicus* briefs from media and relief organizations emphasize, the risk of erroneous deprivation of a citizen's liberty in the absence of sufficient process here is very real. Moreover, as critical as the Government's interest may be in detaining those who actually pose an immediate threat to the national security of the United States during ongoing international conflict, history and common sense teach us that an unchecked system of detention carries the potential to become a means for oppression and abuse of others who do not present that sort of threat. *See Ex parte Milligan*, 4 Wall., at 125. The Founders] knew [the] nation they were founding [would] be involved in war [and] that unlimited power, wherever lodged at such a time, was especially hazardous to freemen. . . . We reaffirm today the fundamental nature of a citizen's right to be free from involuntary confinement by his own government without due process of law, and we weigh the opposing governmental interests against the curtailment of liberty that such confinement entails.

On the other side of the scale are the weighty and sensitive governmental interests in ensuring that those who have in fact fought with the enemy during a war do not return to battle against the United States. [T]he law of war and the realities of combat may render such detentions both necessary and appropriate, and our due process analysis need not blink at those realities. . . . It is during our most challenging and uncertain moments that our Nation's commitment to due process is most severely tested; and it is in those times that we must preserve our commitment at home to the principles for which we fight abroad.

We therefore hold that a citizen-detainee seeking to challenge his classification as an enemy combatant must receive notice of the factual basis for his classification, and a fair opportunity to rebut the Government's factual assertions before a neutral decision maker. . . . [T]he exigencies of the circumstances may demand that, aside from these core elements, enemy combatant proceedings may be tailored to alleviate their uncommon potential to burden the Executive at a time of ongoing military conflict. Hearsay, for example, may need to be accepted as the most reliable available evidence from the Government in such a proceeding. Likewise, the Constitution would not be offended by a presumption in favor of the Government's evidence, so long as that presumption remained a rebuttable one and fair opportunity for rebuttal were provided. Thus, once the Government puts forth credible evidence that the habeas petitioner meets the enemy-combatant criteria, the onus could shift to the petitioner to rebut that evidence with more persuasive evidence that he falls outside the criteria. A burden-shifting scheme of this sort would meet the goal of ensuring that the errant tourist, embedded journalist, or local aid worker has a chance to prove military error while giving due regard to the Executive once it has put forth meaningful support for its conclusion that the detainee is in fact an enemy combatant.

We think it unlikely that this basic process will have the dire impact on the central functions of war making that the Government forecasts. The parties agree that initial captures on the battlefield need not receive the process we have discussed here; that process is due only when the determination is made to *continue* to hold those who have been seized. The Government has made clear in its briefing that documentation regarding battlefield detainees already is kept in the ordinary course of military affairs. Any factfinding imposition created by requiring a knowledgeable affiant to summarize these records to an independent tribunal is a minimal one. . . .

In sum, while the full protections that accompany challenges to detentions in other settings may prove unworkable and inappropriate in the enemy-combatant setting, the threats to military operations posed by a basic system of independent review are not so weighty as to trump a citizen's core rights to challenge meaningfully the Government's case and to be heard by an impartial adjudicator.

We have long since made clear that a state of war is not a blank check for the President when it comes to the rights of the Nation's citizens. *Youngstown Sheet & Tube Co.*, 343 U.S., at 587. Whatever power the United States Constitution envisions for the Executive in its exchanges with other nations or with enemy organizations in times of conflict, it most assuredly envisions a role for all three branches when individual liberties are at stake. [U]nless Congress acts to suspend it, the Great Writ of habeas corpus allows the Judicial Branch to play a necessary role in maintaining this delicate balance of governance, serving as an important judicial check on the Executive's discretion in the realm of detentions. [W]hile we do not question that our due process assessment must pay keen attention to the particular burdens faced by the Executive in the context of military action, it would turn our system of checks and balances on its head to suggest that a citizen could not make his way to court with a challenge to the factual basis for his detention by his government, simply because the Executive opposes making available such a challenge.

Because we conclude that due process demands some system for a citizen detainee to refute his classification, the proposed "some evidence" standard is inadequate. Any process in which the Executive's factual assertions go wholly unchallenged or are simply presumed correct without any opportunity for the alleged combatant to demonstrate otherwise falls constitutionally short. [W]e have utilized the "some evidence" standard in the past as a standard of review, not as a standard of proof. . . . This standard therefore is ill suited to the situation in which a habeas petitioner has received no prior proceedings before any tribunal and had no prior opportunity to rebut the Executive's factual assertions before a neutral decision maker.

[Aside] from unspecified "screening" processes, and military interrogations in which the Government suggests Hamdi could have contested his classification, Hamdi has received no process. An interrogation by one's captor, however effective an intelligence-gathering tool, hardly constitutes a constitutionally adequate factfinding before a neutral decision maker. . . . That even purportedly fair adjudicators "are disqualified by their interest in the controversy to be decided is, of course, the general rule." Tumey v. Ohio, 273 U.S. 510 (1927). Plainly, the "process" Hamdi has received is not that to which he is entitled under the Due Process Clause.

There remains the possibility that the standards we have articulated could be met by an appropriately authorized and properly constituted military tribunal. Indeed, it is notable that military regulations already provide for such process in related instances, dictating that tribunals be made available to determine the status of enemy detainees who assert prisoner-of-war status under the Geneva Convention. As we have discussed, a habeas court in a case such as this may accept affidavit evidence like that contained in the Mobbs Declaration, so long as it also permits the alleged combatant to present his own factual case to rebut the Government's return. We anticipate that a District Court would proceed with the caution that we have indicated is necessary in this setting, engaging in a factfinding process that is both prudent and incremental.

[Since] our grant of certiorari in this case, Hamdi has been appointed counsel, with whom he has met for consultation purposes on several occasions, and with whom he is now being granted unmonitored meetings. He unquestionably has the right to access to counsel in connection with the proceedings on remand. No further consideration of this issue is necessary at this stage of the case.

The judgment of the United States Court of Appeals for the Fourth Circuit is vacated, and the case is remanded for further proceedings.

It is so ordered.

Justice SOUTER, with whom Justice GINSBURG joins, concurring in part, dissenting in part, and concurring in the judgment.

The plurality [accepts] the Government's position that if Hamdi's designation as an enemy combatant is correct, his detention (at least as to some period) is authorized by an Act of Congress as required by §4001(a), that is, by the Authorization for Use of Military Force. Here, I disagree and respectfully dissent. The Government has failed to demonstrate that the Force Resolution authorizes the detention complained of here. . . .

On the record in front of us, the Government has not made out a case on any theory. The [issue] is how broadly or narrowly to read the Non-Detention Act, the tone of which is severe: "No citizen shall be imprisoned or otherwise detained by the United States except pursuant to an Act of Congress." Should the severity of the Act be relieved when the Government's stated factual justification for incommunicado detention is a war on terrorism, so that the Government may be said to act "pursuant" to congressional terms that fall short of explicit authority to imprison individuals? With one possible though important qualification, the answer has to be no. For a number of reasons, the prohibition within §4001(a) has to be read broadly to accord the statute a long reach and to impose a burden of justification on the Government.

[T]he circumstances in which the Act was adopted point the way to this interpretation. . . . Congress meant to preclude another episode like the one described in Korematsu v. United States, 323 U.S. 214 (1944). The fact that Congress intended to guard against a repetition of the World War II internments when it repealed the 1950 statute and gave us §4001(a) provides a powerful reason to think that §4001(a) was meant to require clear congressional authorization before any citizen can be placed in a cell. . . . Second, when Congress passed §4001(a) it was acting in light of an interpretive regime that subjected enactments limiting liberty in wartime to the requirement of a clear statement and it presumably intended §4001(a) to be read accordingly. This need for clarity was unmistakably expressed in *Korematsu.* . . .

[E]ven if history had spared us the cautionary example of the internments in World War II, [there] would be a compelling reason to read §4001(a) to demand manifest authority to detain before detention is authorized. The defining character of American constitutional government is its constant tension between security and liberty. . . . In a government of separated powers, deciding finally on what is a reasonable degree of guaranteed liberty whether in peace or war (or some condition in between) is not well entrusted to the Executive Branch of Government, whose particular responsibility is to maintain security.

Under this principle of reading §4001(a) robustly to require a clear statement of authorization to detain, none of the Government's arguments suffices to justify Hamdi's detention.

First, there is the argument that §4001(a) does not even apply to wartime military detentions, a position resting on the placement of §4001(a) in Title 18 of the United States Code, the gathering of federal criminal law. The text of the statute does not, however, so limit its reach, and the legislative history of the provision shows its placement in Title 18 was not meant to render the statute more restricted than its terms.

Next, there is the Government's claim [that] the terms of the Force Resolution are adequate to authorize detention of an enemy combatant under the circumstances described, a claim the Government fails to support sufficiently to satisfy §4001(a) as read to require a clear statement of authority to detain. Since the Force Resolution was adopted one week after the attacks of September 11, 2001, it naturally speaks with some generality, but its focus is clear, and that is on the use of military power. It is fairly read to authorize the use of armies and weapons, whether against other armies or individual terrorists. But [it] never so much as uses the word detention, and there is no reason to think Congress might have perceived any need to augment Executive power to deal with dangerous citizens within the United States, given the well-stocked statutory arsenal of defined criminal offenses covering the gamut of actions that a citizen sympathetic to terrorists might commit.

[T]he Government here repeatedly argues that Hamdi's detention amounts to nothing more than customary detention of a captive taken on the field of battle. . . . By holding him incommunicado, however, the Government obviously has not been treating him as a prisoner of war, and in fact the Government claims that no Taliban detainee is entitled to prisoner of war status. This treatment appears to be a violation of the Geneva Convention provision that even in cases of doubt, captives are entitled to be treated as prisoners of war "until such time as their status has been determined by a competent tribunal." Art. 5, 6 U.S.T., at 3324.

[I]t is instructive to recall Justice Jackson's observation that the President is not Commander in Chief of the country, only of the military. Youngstown Sheet & Tube Co. v. Sawyer, 343 U.S. 579 (1952) (concurring opinion). . . . There may be room for one qualification to Justice Jackson's statement, however: in a moment of genuine emergency, when the Government must act with no time for deliberation, the Executive may be able to detain a citizen if there is reason to fear he is an imminent threat to the safety of the Nation and its people.

[I] find Hamdi's detention forbidden by §4001(a) and unauthorized by the Force Resolution. . . . Subject to these qualifications, I join with the plurality in a judgment of the Court vacating the Fourth Circuit's judgment and remanding the case.

Justice SCALIA, with whom Justice STEVENS joins, dissenting.

Where the Government accuses a citizen of waging war against it, our constitutional tradition has been to prosecute him in federal court for treason or some other crime. Where the exigencies of war prevent that, the Constitution's Suspension Clause, Art. I, §9, cl. 2, allows Congress to relax the usual protections temporarily. Absent suspension, however, the Executive's assertion of military exigency has not been thought sufficient to permit detention without charge. No one contends that the congressional Authorization for Use of Military Force, on which the Government relies to justify its actions here, is an implementation of the Suspension Clause. Accordingly, I would reverse the decision below.

The very core of liberty secured by our Anglo-Saxon system of separated powers has been freedom from indefinite imprisonment at the will of the Executive. . . . The gist of the Due Process Clause, as understood at the founding and since, was to force the Government to follow those common-law procedures traditionally deemed necessary before depriving a person of life, liberty, or property. When a citizen was deprived of liberty because of alleged criminal conduct, those procedures typically required committal by a magistrate followed by indictment and trial. . . . The writ of habeas corpus was preserved in the Constitution — the only common-law writ to be explicitly mentioned. See Art. I, §9, cl. 2.

The allegations here, of course, are no ordinary accusations of criminal activity. . . . Hamdi has been imprisoned because the Government believes he participated in the waging of war against the United States. The relevant question, then, is whether there is a different, special procedure for imprisonment of a citizen accused of wrongdoing *by aiding the enemy in wartime*.

Justice O'Connor, writing for a plurality of this Court, asserts that captured enemy combatants (other than those suspected of war crimes) have traditionally been detained until the cessation of hostilities and then released. That is probably an accurate description of wartime practice with respect to enemy *aliens*. The tradition with respect to American citizens, however, has been quite different. Citizens aiding the enemy have been treated as traitors subject to the criminal process. . . . There are times when military exigency renders resort to the traditional criminal process impracticable. . . . But the happiness of our constitution is, that it is not left to the executive power to determine when the danger of the state is so great, as to render this measure expedient. For the parliament only, or legislative power, whenever it sees proper, can authorize the crown, by suspending the *habeas corpus* act for a short and limited time, to imprison suspected persons without giving any reason for so doing. . . .

Our Federal Constitution contains a provision explicitly permitting suspension, but limiting the situations in which it may be invoked: "The privilege of the Writ of Habeas Corpus shall not be suspended, unless when in Cases of Rebellion or Invasion the public Safety may require it." Art. I, §9, cl. 2. Although this provision does not state that suspension must be effected by, or authorized by, a legislative act, it has been so understood, consistent with English practice and the Clause's placement in Article I. *See Ex parte Bollman*, 4 Cranch 75, 101, 2 L.Ed. 554 (1807).

Of course the extensive historical evidence of criminal convictions and habeas suspensions does not *necessarily* refute the Government's position in this case. When the writ is suspended, the Government is entirely free from judicial oversight. It does not claim such total liberation here, but argues that it need only produce what it calls "some evidence" to satisfy a habeas court that a detained individual is an enemy combatant.

The absence of military authority to imprison citizens indefinitely in wartime — whether or not a probability of treason had been established by means less than jury trial — was confirmed by three cases decided during and immediately after the War of 1812. In the first, *In re Stacy*, 10 Johns, 328 (N.Y. 1813), a citizen was taken into military custody on suspicion that he was "carrying provisions and giving information to the enemy." Stacy petitioned for a writ of habeas corpus, and, after the defendant custodian attempted to avoid complying, Chief

Justice Kent ordered attachment against him. Kent noted that the military was "without any color of authority in any military tribunal to try a citizen for that crime" and that it was "holding him in the closest confinement, and contemning the civil authority of the state."

Two other cases, later cited with approval by this Court in *Ex parte Milligan*, 4 Wall. 2, 18 L.Ed. 281 (1866), upheld verdicts for false imprisonment against military officers. In Smith v. Shaw, 12 Johns. 257 (N.Y. 1815), the court affirmed an award of damages for detention of a citizen on suspicion that he was, among other things, "an enemy's spy in time of war." Finally, in M'Connell v. Hampton, 12 Johns. 234 (N.Y. 1815), a jury awarded $9,000 for false imprisonment after a military officer confined a citizen on charges of treason.

President Lincoln, when he purported to suspend habeas corpus without congressional authorization during the Civil War, apparently did not doubt that suspension was required if the prisoner was to be held without criminal trial. . . .

Further evidence comes from this Court's decision in *Ex parte Milligan, supra*. There, the Court issued the writ to an American citizen who had been tried by military commission for offenses that included conspiring to overthrow the Government, seize munitions, and liberate prisoners of war. The Court rejected in no uncertain terms the Government's assertion that military jurisdiction was proper "under the 'laws and usages of war:'" "It can serve no useful purpose to inquire what those laws and usages are, whence they originated, where found, and on whom they operate; they can never be applied to citizens in states which have upheld the authority of the government, and where the courts are open and their process unobstructed."

The Government argues that our more recent jurisprudence ratifies its indefinite imprisonment of a citizen within the territorial jurisdiction of federal courts. It places primary reliance upon *Ex parte Quirin*, 317 U.S. 1 (1942), a World War II case upholding the trial by military commission of eight German saboteurs, one of whom, Hans Haupt, was a U.S. citizen. The case was not this Court's finest hour. The Court upheld the commission and denied relief in a brief *per curiam* issued the day after oral argument concluded, a week later the Government carried out the commission's death sentence upon six saboteurs, including Haupt. . . . Only three paragraphs of the Court's [opinion dealt with] Haupt's case. The Government argued that Haupt [could] be tried by military commission under the laws of war. In agreeing with that contention, *Quirin* purported to interpret the language of *Milligan* quoted above (the law of war "can never be applied to citizens in states which have upheld the authority of the government, and where the courts are open and their process unobstructed"). . . . *Milligan* [was] in accord with the traditional law of habeas corpus I have described: Though treason often occurred in wartime, there was, absent provision for special treatment in a congressional suspension of the writ, no exception to the right to trial by jury for citizens who could be called "belligerents" or "prisoners of war."

[In] *Quirin* it was uncontested that the petitioners were members of enemy forces. They were "*admitted* enemy invaders," and it was "undisputed" that they had landed in the United States in service of German forces. The specific holding of the Court was only that, "upon the *conceded* facts," the petitioners were "plainly within [the] boundaries" of military jurisdiction. But where those jurisdictional facts are *not* conceded—where the petitioner insists that he is *not* a belligerent—*Quirin* left the pre-existing law in place: Absent suspension of the writ, a citizen held where the courts are open is entitled either to criminal trial or to a judicial decree requiring his release.

It follows from what I have said that Hamdi is entitled to a habeas decree requiring his release unless (1) criminal proceedings are promptly brought, or (2) Congress has suspended the writ of habeas corpus. A suspension of the writ could, of course, lay down conditions for continued detention, similar to those that today's opinion prescribes under the Due Process Clause.

The plurality finds justification for Hamdi's imprisonment in the Authorization for Use of Military Force. . . . This is not remotely a congressional suspension of the writ, and no one claims that it is. . . .

Several limitations give my views in this matter a relatively narrow compass. They apply only to citizens, accused of being enemy combatants, who are detained within the territorial jurisdiction of a federal court. This is not likely to be a numerous group; currently we know of only two, Hamdi and Jose Padilla. Where the citizen is captured outside and held outside the United States, the constitutional requirements may be different.

Because the Court has proceeded to meet the current emergency in a manner the Constitution does not envision, I respectfully dissent.

Justice THOMAS, dissenting.

The Executive Branch, acting pursuant to the powers vested in the President by the Constitution and with explicit congressional approval, has determined that Yaser Hamdi is an enemy combatant and should be detained. This detention falls squarely within the Federal Government's war powers, and we lack the expertise and capacity to second-guess that decision. As such, petitioners' habeas challenge should fail, and there is no reason to remand the case.

Notes

1. *Post-Decision Actions*. After the detention rulings, the Pentagon decided to give all detainees at the Guantanamo Bay base hearings to determine whether they were indeed enemy combatants. The hearings were to be conducted by newly constituted combatant status review tribunals. *See* John Mintz, "Pentagon Sets Hearings for 595 Detainees," Section A, *The Washington Post* (July 8, 2004).

2. *Hamdi's Fate*. Less than two months after the *Hamdi* decision, it was reported that the government and the petitioner's lawyers were working out a plan to release Hamdi. *See* D. Savage, "'Enemy Combatant' May Soon Be Freed," *L.A. Times* (http://www.latimes.com) (August 14, 2004). The government agreed to release Hamdi and deport him to Saudi Arabia in October 2004. One condition of his release was that Hamdi renounce his U.S. citizenship. There also were travel restrictions, including a requirement to notify the Saudi Arabian government of plans to travel and the prohibition of travel to the United States, Israel, Gaza Strip,

Syria, Iraq, Afghanistan, and Pakistan. Hamdi also made a promise not to sue the U.S. government for a violation of his rights.

∿ PROBLEMS ∿

1. *Burden of Proof.* Suppose the military tribunal trying enemy combatants after the *Hamdi* decision places the burden of proof squarely on the defendant to prove beyond a reasonable doubt that the designation of "enemy combatant" was in error. Is this allocation of the burden of proof unconstitutional? a) Suppose the same military tribunal decides that hearsay evidence — regardless of its alleged reliability — is admissible in any hearing to determine enemy combatant status. Is the inclusion of hearsay evidence constitutional? b) Suppose the same military tribunal decides that the opportunity for refutation approved by the Supreme Court in *Hamdi* meant only that the petitioner would have two hours to argue and/or present evidence that the government erred in designating the petitioner an enemy combatant and that no discovery by the petitioner would be allowed. Permissible?

2. *The Charity Donor.* Suppose Jeffrey Morris contributed to the Human Action Front, a charity providing aid to injured and sick persons in war zones around the world. It was subsequently discovered that the charity also funneled money to the al Qaeda network. Morris, a major contributor, was arrested and held as an enemy combatant. Morris's family asks you to represent him. What would you argue on his behalf? What are his rights?

3. *The War on Drugs.* The President declares that the United States is at war against a nefarious enemy — drug lords importing illegal drugs into the country in great amounts. As part of an executive order implementing legislation cracking down on illegal drug importation, the President also declares that special military tribunals shall be instituted to try the major offenders. Are such tribunals constitutional? If the tribunals are constitutional and the detainees can be held as enemy combatants, could they be held until the "war on drugs" is officially declared over? Explain.

4. *Terrorist Pins.* The Johnson-Smith terrorist network adopts special "pins" that can be placed on jacket lapels as a uniform feature of dress. A member of the group, captured undercover in northern Indiana, Anwar Jones, was found to be wearing the special pin and openly carrying a firearm. Should Jones, a U.S. citizen raised in Afghanistan, be considered a lawful or unlawful belligerent? Explain.

The national security issues permeating the courts and society in recent years have emphasized a central dichotomy between the right to freedom of action and the right to security. These two values often conflict in the context of court intervention in executive action to fight terrorism.

The Court in Boumediene v. Bush, 553 U.S. 723 (2008), held that a provision of the Military Commissions Act of 2006 was unconstitutional insofar as it denied detainees challenging their detentions the right to bring habeas corpus claims in U.S. federal courts. The five-to-four decision effectively found that the U.S. Constitution reached the base in Guantanamo Bay, Cuba, and that the Executive Branch was overreaching in its approach to detaining people it designated as enemy combatants.

How the outcome of the case will affect the approximately 270 detainees at Guantanamo is unclear because the case left the particulars of the habeas corpus claims to the federal district courts. Nevertheless, the ruling has both legal and practical implications. On the practical side, there are countries that might not prosecute detainee nationals if such nationals end up being returned to their home countries. Also, the ruling raises questions about the future of Guantanamo as a holding camp for detainees. On the legal side, upon the retirement of Justice O'Connor and the appointment of Justice Alito, it was thought that Justice Kennedy would be entrenched firmly in the middle of the Court's close decisions. While there have been fewer close decisions than predicted in 2008, this one left Justice Kennedy centrally positioned, at least to the extent that he wrote the decision for the majority.

Boumediene v. Bush

553 U.S. 723 (2008)

KENNEDY, J.

Petitioners are aliens designated as enemy combatants and detained at the United States Naval Station at Guantanamo Bay, Cuba. There are others detained there, also aliens, who are not parties to this suit.

Petitioners present a question not resolved by our earlier cases relating to the detention of aliens at Guantanamo: whether they have the constitutional privilege of habeas corpus, a privilege not to be withdrawn except in conformance with the Suspension Clause, Art. I §9, cl. 2. We hold these petitioners do have the habeas corpus privilege. Congress has enacted a statute, the Detainee Treatment Act of 2005 (DTA), 119 Stat. 2739, that provides certain procedures for review of the detainees' status. We hold that those procedures are not an adequate and effective substitute for habeas corpus. Therefore §7 of the Military Commissions Act of 2006 (MCA), 28 U.S.C.A. §2241(e) (Supp. 2007), operates as an unconstitutional suspension of the writ. We do not address whether the President has authority to detain these petitioners nor do we hold that the writ must issue. These and other questions regarding the legality of the detention are to be resolved in the first instance by the District Court.

The Court of Appeals concluded that MCA §7 must be read to strip from it, and all federal courts, jurisdiction to consider petitioners' habeas corpus applications, *id.*, at 987; that petitioners are not entitled to the privilege of the writ or the protections of the Suspension Clause, *id.*, at 990-991; and, as a result, that it was unnecessary to consider whether Congress provided an adequate and effective substitute for habeas corpus in the DTA. We granted certiorari.

As a threshold matter, we must decide whether MCA §7 denies the federal courts jurisdiction to hear habeas corpus actions pending at the time of its enactment. We hold the statute does deny that jurisdiction, so that, if the statute is valid, petitioners' cases must be dismissed.

As amended by the terms of the MCA, 28 U.S.C.A. §2241(e)(Supp. 2007) now provides:

> (1) No court, justice, or judge shall have jurisdiction to hear or consider an application for a writ of habeas corpus filed by or on behalf of an alien detained by the United States who has been determined by the United States to have been properly detained as an enemy combatant or is awaiting such determination.
>
> (2) Except as provided in [§§1005(e)(2) and (e)(3) of the DTA] no court, justice, or judge shall have jurisdiction to hear or consider any other action against the United States or its agents relating to any aspect of the detention, transfer, treatment, trial, or conditions of confinement of an alien who is or was detained by the United States and has been determined by the United States to have been properly detained as an enemy combatant or is awaiting such determination.

Section 7(b) of the MCA provides the effective date for the amendment of §2241(e). It states:

> The amendment made by [MCA §7(a)] shall take effect on the date of the enactment of this Act, and shall apply to all cases, without exception, ending on or after the date of the enactment of this Act which relate to any aspect of the detention, transfer, treatment, trial, or conditions of detention of an alien detained by the United States since September 11, 2001.

120 Stat. 2636.

There is little doubt that the effective date provision applies to habeas corpus actions. Those actions, by definition, are cases "which relate to . . . detention." See *Black's Law Dictionary* 728 (8th ed. 2004) (defining habeas corpus as "[a] writ employed to bring a person before a court, most frequently to ensure that the party's imprisonment or detention is not illegal"). Petitioners argue, nevertheless, that MCA §7(b) is not a sufficiently clear statement of congressional intent to strip the federal courts of jurisdiction in pending cases. *See Ex parte Yerger*, 8 Wall. 85, 102-103 (1869). We disagree.

In deciding the constitutional questions now presented we must determine whether petitioners are barred from seeking the writ or invoking the protections of the Suspension Clause either because of their status, i.e., petitioners' designation by the Executive Branch as enemy combatants, or their physical location, i.e., their presence at Guantanamo Bay. The Government contends that noncitizens designated as enemy combatants and detained in territory located outside our Nation's borders have no constitutional rights and no privilege of habeas corpus. Petitioners contend they do have cognizable constitutional rights and that Congress, in seeking to eliminate recourse to habeas corpus as a means to assert those rights, acted in violation of the Suspension Clause.

The Framers viewed freedom from unlawful restraint as a fundamental precept of liberty, and they understood the writ of habeas corpus as a vital instrument to secure that freedom. Experience taught, however, that the common-law writ all too often had been insufficient to guard against the abuse of monarchial power.

That history counseled the necessity for specific language in the Constitution to secure the writ and ensure its place in our legal system.

The Court has discussed the issue of the Constitution's extraterritorial application on many occasions. These decisions undermine the Government's argument that, at least as applied to noncitizens, the Constitution necessarily stops where *de jure* sovereignty ends.

The Government's formal sovereignty-based test raises troubling separation-of-powers concerns as well. The political history of Guantanamo illustrates the deficiencies of this approach. The United States has maintained complete and uninterrupted control of the bay for over 100 years. At the close of the Spanish-American War, Spain ceded control over the entire island of Cuba to the United States and specifically "relinquished[d] all claim[s] of sovereignty . . . and title." And although it recognized, by entering into the 1903 Lease Agreement, that Cuba retained "ultimate sovereignty" over Guantanamo, the United States continued to maintain the same plenary control it had enjoyed since 1898. Yet the Government's view is that the Constitution had no effect there, at least as to noncitizens, because the United States disclaimed sovereignty in the formal sense of the term.

Our basic charter cannot be contracted away like this. The Constitution grants Congress and the President the power to acquire, dispose of, and govern territory, not the power to decide when and where its terms apply. Even when the United States acts outside its borders, its powers are not "absolute and unlimited" but are subject "to such restrictions as are expressed in the Constitution."

It is true that before today the Court has never held that noncitizens detained by our Government in territory over which another country maintains *de jure* sovereignty have any rights under our Constitution. But the cases before us lack any precise historical parallel. They involve individuals detained by executive order for the duration of a conflict that, if measured from September 11, 2001, to the present, is already among the longest wars in American history. *See Oxford Companion to American Military History* 849 (1999). The detainees, moreover, are held in a territory that, while technically not part of the United States, is under the complete and total control of our Government. Under these circumstances the lack of a precedent on point is no barrier to our holding.

We hold that Art. I, §9, cl. 2, of the Constitution has full effect at Guantanamo Bay. If the privilege of habeas corpus is to be denied to the detainees now before us, Congress must act in accordance with the requirements of the Suspension Clause. *Cf. Hamdi*, 542 U.S., at 564 (Scalia, J., dissenting) ("[I]ndefinite imprisonment on reasonable suspicion is not an available option of treatment for those accused of aiding the enemy, absent a suspension of the writ"). This Court may not impose a *de facto* suspension by abstaining from these controversies. *See Hamdan*, 548 U.S., at 585, n.16 ("[A]bstention is not appropriate in cases . . . in which the legal challenge 'turn[s] on the status of the persons as to whom the military asserted its power'" (quoting Schlesinger v. Councilman, 420 U.S. 738, 759 (1975))). The MCA does not purport to be a formal suspension of the writ; and the Government, in its submissions to us, has not argued that it is. Petitioners, therefore, are entitled to the privilege of habeas corpus to challenge the legality of their detention.

In light of this holding the question becomes whether the statute stripping jurisdiction to issue the writ avoids the Suspension Clause mandate because Congress has provided adequate substitute procedures for habeas corpus. The Government submits there has been compliance with the Suspension Clause because the DTA review process in the Court of Appeals, *see* DTA §1005(e), provides an adequate substitute. Congress has granted that court jurisdiction to consider

> (i) whether the status determination of the [CSRT] . . . was consistent with the standards and procedures specified by the Secretary of Defense . . . and (ii) to the extent the Constitution and laws of the United States are applicable, whether the use of such standards and procedures to make the determination is consistent with the Constitution and laws of the United States.

§1005(e)(2)(C), 119 Stat. 2742.

The two leading cases addressing habeas substitutes, Swain v. Pressley, 430 U.S. 372 (1977), and United States v. Hayman, 342 U.S. 205 (1952), likewise provide little guidance here. The statutes at issue were attempts to streamline habeas corpus relief, not to cut it back. Unlike in *Hayman* and *Swain*, here we confront statutes, the DTA and the MCA, that were intended to circumscribe habeas review.

We do not endeavor to offer a comprehensive summary of the requisites for an adequate substitute for habeas corpus. We do consider it uncontroversial, however, that the privilege of habeas corpus entitles the prisoner to a meaningful opportunity to demonstrate that he is being held pursuant to "the erroneous application or interpretation" of relevant law. *St. Cyr*, 533 U.S. at 302. And the habeas court must have the power to order the conditional release of an individual unlawfully detained — though release need not be the exclusive remedy and is not the appropriate one in every case in which the writ is granted.

Although we make no judgment as to whether the CSRTs [Combatant Status Review Tribunals] as currently constituted satisfy due process standards, we agree with petitioners that, even when all the parties involved in this process act with diligence and in good faith, there is considerable risk of error in the tribunal's findings of fact. This is a risk inherent in any process that, in the words of the former Chief Judge of the Court of Appeals, is "closed and accusatorial." *See Bismullah III*, 514 F.3d at 1296 (Ginsburg, C.J., concurring in denial of rehearing en banc).

Although we do not hold that an adequate substitute must duplicate [the habeas corpus statute] §2241 in all respects, it suffices that the Government has not established that the detainees' access to the statutory review provisions at issue is an adequate substitute for the writ of habeas corpus. MCA §7 thus effects an unconstitutional suspension of the writ. In view of our holding we need not discuss the reach of the writ with respect to claims of unlawful conditions of treatment or confinement.

Our opinion does not undermine the Executive's powers as Commander in Chief. On the contrary, the exercise of those powers is vindicated, not eroded, when confirmed by the Judicial Branch. Within the Constitution's separation-of-powers structure, few exercises of judicial power are as legitimate or as necessary as the responsibility to hear challenges to the authority of the Executive to imprison a person. Some of these petitioners have been in custody for six years with no definitive judicial determination as to the legality of their detention. Their access to the writ is a necessity to determine the lawfulness of their status, even if, in the end, they do not obtain the relief they seek.

It bears repeating that our opinion does not address the content of the law that governs petitioners' detention. That is a matter yet to be determined. We hold that petitioners may invoke the fundamental procedural protections of habeas corpus. The laws and Constitution are designed to survive, and remain in force, in extraordinary times. Liberty and security can be reconciled; and in our system they are reconciled within the framework of the law. The Framers decided that habeas corpus, a right of first importance, must be a part of that framework, a part of that law.

The determination by the Court of Appeals that the Suspension Clause and its protections are inapplicable to petitioners was in error. The judgment of the Court of Appeals is reversed. The cases are remanded to the Court of Appeals with instructions that it remand the cases to the District Court for proceedings consistent with this opinion.

It is so ordered.

Chief Justice ROBERTS, with whom Justice SCALIA, Justice THOMAS, and Justice ALITO join, dissenting.

Today the Court strikes down as inadequate the most generous set of procedural protections ever afforded aliens detained by this country as enemy combatants. The political branches crafted these procedures amidst an ongoing military conflict, after much careful investigation and thorough debate. The Court rejects them today out of hand, without bothering to say what due process rights the detainees possess, without explaining how the statute fails to vindicate those rights, and before a single petitioner has even attempted to avail himself of the law's operation. And to what effect? The majority merely replaces a review system designed by the people's representatives with a set of shapeless procedures to be defined by federal courts at some future date. One cannot help but think, after surveying the modest practical results of the majority's ambitious opinion, that this decision is not really about the detainees at all, but about control of federal policy regarding enemy combatants.

The majority is adamant that the Guantanamo detainees are entitled to the protections of habeas corpus — its opinion begins by deciding that question. I regard the issue as a difficult one, primarily because of the unique and unusual jurisdictional status of Guantanamo Bay. I nonetheless agree with Justice Scalia's analysis of our precedents and the pertinent history of the writ, and accordingly join his dissent. The important point for me, however, is that the Court should have resolved these cases on other grounds. Habeas is most fundamentally a procedural right, a mechanism for contesting the legality of executive detention. The critical threshold question in these cases, prior to any inquiry about the writ's scope, is whether the system the political branches designed protects whatever rights the detainees may possess. If so, there is no need for any additional process, whether called "habeas" or something else.

I believe the system the political branches constructed adequately protects any constitutional rights aliens captured abroad and detained as enemy combatants may enjoy. I therefore would dismiss these cases on that ground. With all respect for the contrary views of the majority, I must dissent.

Justice SCALIA, with whom THE CHIEF JUSTICE, Justice THOMAS, and Justice ALITO join, dissenting.

Today, for the first time in our Nation's history, the Court confers a constitutional right to habeas corpus on alien enemies detained abroad by our military forces in the course of an ongoing war. The Chief Justice's dissent, which I join, shows that the procedures prescribed by Congress in the Detainee Treatment Act provide the essential protections that habeas corpus guarantees; there has thus been no suspension of the writ, and no basis exists for judicial intervention beyond what the Act allows. My problem with today's opinion is more fundamental still: The writ of habeas corpus does not, and never has, run in favor of aliens abroad; the Suspension Clause thus has no application, and the Court's intervention in this military matter is entirely *ultra vires.*

I shall devote most of what will be a lengthy opinion to the legal errors contained in the opinion of the Court. Contrary to my usual practice, however, I think it appropriate to begin with a description of the disastrous consequences of what the Court has done today.

America is at war with radical Islamists. The enemy began by killing Americans and American allies abroad: 241 at the Marine barracks in Lebanon, 19 at the Khobar Towers in Dhahran, 224 at our embassies in Dar es Salaam and Nairobi, and 17 on the USS Cole in Yemen. *See* National Commission on Terrorist Attacks upon the United States, The 9/11 Commission Report. On September 11, 2001, the enemy brought the battle to American soil, killing 2,749 at the Twin Towers in New York City, 184 at the Pentagon in Washington, D.C., and 40 in Pennsylvania. It has threatened further attacks against our homeland; one need only walk about buttressed and barricaded Washington, or board a plane anywhere in the country, to know that the threat is a serious one. Our Armed Forces are now in the field against the enemy, in Afghanistan and Iraq. Last week, 13 of our countrymen in arms were killed.

The game of bait-and-switch that today's opinion plays upon the Nation's Commander in Chief will make the war harder on us. It will almost certainly cause more Americans to be killed. That consequence would be tolerable if necessary to preserve a time-honored legal principle vital to our constitutional Republic. But it is this Court's blatant *abandonment* of such a principle that produces the decision today.

[A]ll available historical evidence points to the conclusion that the writ would not have been available at common law for aliens captured and held outside the sovereign territory of the Crown. Despite three opening briefs, three reply briefs, and support from a legion of *amici*, petitioners have failed to identify a single case in the history of Anglo-American law that supports their claim to jurisdiction.

The Court finds it significant that there is no recorded case *denying* jurisdiction to such prisoners either. *See ante*, at 21-22. But a case standing for the remarkable proposition that the writ could issue to a foreign land would surely have been reported, whereas a case denying such a writ for lack of jurisdiction would likely not. At a minimum, the absence of a reported case either way leaves unrefuted the voluminous commentary stating that habeas was confined to the dominions of the Crown.

What history teaches is confirmed by the nature of the limitations that the Constitution places upon suspension of the common-law writ. It can be suspended only "in Cases of Rebellion or Invasion." Art. I, §9, cl. 2. The latter case (invasion) is plainly limited to the territory of the United States; and while it is conceivable that a rebellion could be mounted by American citizens abroad, surely the overwhelming majority of its occurrences would be domestic. If the extraterritorial scope of habeas turned on flexible, "functional" considerations, as the Court holds, why would the Constitution limit its suspension almost entirely to instances of domestic crisis? Surely there is an even greater justification for suspension in foreign lands where the United States might hold prisoners of war during an ongoing conflict.

In sum, because I conclude that the text and history of the Suspension Clause provide no basis for our jurisdiction, I would affirm the Court of Appeals even if *Eisentrager* did not govern these cases.

∿ PROBLEM: NO TERRORISM ZONES ∿

In addition to the no drilling zones created by the President in the introductory problem, assume the President designates several persons as "enemy combatants" after receiving a threat related to drilling operations in Alaska, near an area already considered a no drilling zone. Several of the persons so designated are captured in northern Canada preparing to enter the United States. If these persons are held at an American base in northern Canada, what rights must the detainees be accorded? Why? Does it matter whether the persons were apparently entering the United States unlawfully? Or whether they had contact with other persons on the no-entry list?

3. The War on Terror's Impact on Privacy

A particular right that is often involved in matters of national security is the right to privacy. It was revealed in the spring of 2006 that the National Security Agency (NSA) had been conducting warrantless wiretapping and mining telephone conversations and records data involving American citizens. The government mined data about international phone calls, including those originating in the United States. The resulting controversy left two polarized groups. Those opposed to the government conduct contended that the phone taps were not authorized by current laws and were anathema to constitutional protections against government overreaching, particularly the Fourth Amendment prohibition against unreasonable searches and seizures. Supporters of the executive action argued that the phone taps were consistent with and authorized by laws against terrorism and essential presidential powers to fight terrorism.

The issue remains murky, given that there has been no ruling directly on point from the Supreme Court, especially in the current post-9/11 era. In a decision in the Eastern District of Michigan more than 30 years ago, a federal judge found that wiretapping of U.S. citizens without a warrant in the interest of national security violated the constitutional requirements of the Fourth Amendment. The judge's decision was eventually upheld by the U.S. Supreme Court in United States v. United States District Court, 407 U.S. 297 (1972). That case, however, did not involve foreign terrorism issues.

The closest legislation on point, the Foreign Intelligence Surveillance Act of 1978 (FISA), requires a warrant based on probable cause for wiretapping and does not include an exception for domestic spying for terrorism prevention purposes. The question remains, however, whether the 1978 Surveillance Act was impliedly superseded by an Act passed by Congress shortly after the September 11, 2001, attacks, the Authorization of Use of Military Force (AUMF). In addition, some argue that the 1978 Surveillance Act impermissibly limits the President's Commander in Chief powers.

After the warrantless surveillance program was uncovered and then vetted in the media, a variety of lawsuits were filed, often concerning the interception of telephonic communications. The NSA was not the only defendant. For example, in In re: National Security Agency Telecommunications Records Litigation, 483 F. Supp. 2d 934 (N.D. Ca. 2007), California customers of telephone companies brought suit against those companies to enjoin them from sharing telephone calling records with the NSA. The suit was filed under state privacy law. In Hepting v. AT&T Corp., 439 F. Supp. 2d 974 (N.D. Ca. 2006), the AT&T company was sued by its own customers for violating the customers' privacy rights by participating in the warrantless surveillance program. And in A.C.L.U. v. N.S.A., 438 F. Supp. 2d 754 (E.D. Mich. 2006), the American Civil Liberties Union brought suit seeking injunctive relief against the NSA's secret program with reference to intercepted international telephone and Internet communications.

G. THE TREATY POWER

The treaty power, shared between Congress and the President, is one of the most useful tools of American foreign policy. While the Constitution prescribes how treaties are formed, the document does not delineate the relationships between treaties and domestic laws, or between laws enacted pursuant to treaties and laws based on state powers. Both separation of powers and federalism issues are implicated.

As between treaties and congressional acts, generally the last in time is considered valid. For many years, the question of whether federal treaties superseded state law remained unanswered. In Missouri v. Holland, however, the Court confronted just such an issue. Also, *Holland* opens up a proverbial "can of worms," raising a question unanswered by the text of the Constitution: Does the treaty power reside independent of the Constitution? (And if so, can the power be sustained without constitutional conformity?)

Missouri v. Holland
252 U.S. 416 (1920)

Mr. Justice HOLMES delivered the opinion of the Court.

This is a bill in equity brought by the State of Missouri to prevent a game warden of the United States from attempting to enforce the Migratory Bird Treaty Act of July 3, 1918, c. 128, 40 Stat. 755, and the regulations made by the Secretary of Agriculture in pursuance of the same. The ground of the bill is that the statute is an unconstitutional interference with the rights reserved to the States by the Tenth Amendment, and that the acts of the defendant done and threatened under that authority invade the sovereign right of the State and contravene its will manifested in statutes.

On December 8, 1916, a treaty between the United States and Great Britain was proclaimed by the President. It recited that many species of birds in their annual migrations traversed many parts of the United States and of Canada, that they were of great value as a source of food and in destroying insects injurious to vegetation, but were in danger of extermination through lack of adequate protection. It therefore provided for specified closed seasons and protection in other forms, and agreed that the two powers would take or propose to their lawmaking bodies the necessary measures for carrying the treaty out. 39 Stat. 1702.

To answer this question [of constitutionality of the treaty,] it is not enough to refer to the Tenth Amendment, reserving the powers not delegated to the United States, because by Article 2, Section 2, the power to make treaties is delegated expressly, and by Article 6 treaties made under the authority of the United States, along with the Constitution and laws of the United States made in pursuance thereof, are declared the supreme law of the land. If the treaty is valid there can be no dispute about the validity of the statute under Article 1, Section 8, as a necessary and proper means to execute the powers of the Government. The language of the Constitution as to the supremacy of treaties being general, the question before us is narrowed to an inquiry into the ground upon which the present supposed exception is placed.

It is said that a treaty cannot be valid if it infringes the Constitution, that there are limits, therefore, to the treaty-making power, and that one such limit is that what an act of Congress could not do unaided, in derogation of the powers reserved to the States, a treaty cannot do. An earlier act of Congress that attempted by itself and not in pursuance of a treaty to regulate the killing of migratory birds within the States had been held bad in the District Court. United States v. Shauver, 214 Fed. 154. United States v. McCullagh, 221 Fed. 288. Those decisions were supported by arguments that migratory birds were owned by the States in their sovereign capacity for the benefit of their people, and that under cases like Geer v. Connecticut, 161 U.S. 519, this control was one that Congress had no power to displace. The same argument is supposed to apply now with equal force.

Whether the two cases cited were decided rightly or not they cannot be accepted as a test of the treaty power. Acts of Congress are the supreme law of the land only when made in pursuance of the Constitution, while treaties are declared to be so when made under the authority of the United States. It is open to question whether the authority of the United States means more than the formal acts prescribed to make the convention. We do not mean to imply that there are no qualifications to the treaty-making power; but they must be ascertained in a different way. It is obvious that there may be matters of the sharpest exigency for the national well being that an act of Congress could not deal with but that a treaty followed by such an act could, and it is not lightly to be assumed that, in matters requiring national action, 'a power which must belong to and somewhere reside in every civilized government' is not to be found. The treaty in question does not contravene any prohibitory words to be found in the Constitution. The only question is whether it is forbidden by some invisible radiation from the general terms of the Tenth Amendment.

Here a national interest of very nearly the first magnitude is involved. It can be protected only by national action in concert with that of another power. The subject matter is only transitorily within the state and has no permanent habitat therein. But for the treaty and the statute there soon might be no birds for any powers to deal with. We see nothing in the Constitution that compels the Government to sit by while a food supply is cut off and the protectors of our forests and our crops are destroyed. It is not sufficient to rely upon the States. The reliance is vain, and were it otherwise, the question is whether the United States is forbidden to act. We are of opinion that the treaty and statute must be upheld.

Decree affirmed.

Note

1. *The Scope of Treaties.* In Medellin v. Texas, 552 U.S. 491 (2008), a Mexican national convicted of murder in Texas state court filed a habeas corpus petition seeking the protection of a treaty entered into by the United States. The Supreme Court, in an opinion written by Chief Justice Roberts, denied the petitioner relief under the treaty. The Court found that the treaty, which would have benefited the petitioner if it applied domestically, did not create binding federal law that displaced existing state law. In his opinion, Justice Roberts noted the difference between treaties that have an effect internationally and those that also extend their reach to domestic matters. Justice Roberts first laid out the general framework of analysis: that treaties can be self-executing and automatically binding domestically, or not self-executing, requiring implementation

statutes by Congress. He then analyzed the treaty in question, finding that the Vienna Convention was not automatically applicable domestically and had not been made binding to domestic law by Congress. Justice Roberts summarized the legal principle by stating, "In sum, while treaties 'may comprise international commitments . . . they are not domestic law unless Congress has either enacted implementing statutes or the treaty itself conveys an intention that it be "self-executing" and is ratified on these terms.' Igartua-De La Rosa v. United States, 417 F.3d 145, 150 (C.A.1 2005) (en banc) (Boudin, C. J.). *Id.* at 1356."

∾ PROBLEM: ALIEN INHERITANCE LAWS ∾

West Virginia enacted a law in 1982 stating that aliens could not inherit property in the state. In 1990, the United States entered into a treaty with Australia, permitting Australians to sell inherited land and recover the proceeds. In 1992, Congress passed a law permitting aliens to keep two thirds of the proceeds from land inherited in the United States and then sold. If M. Dundee, an Australian, inherits property located in Virginia worth $1 million in 1994, what are her legal rights?

H. EXECUTIVE AGREEMENTS

Executive agreements are agreements negotiated by the President with other countries. These agreements have constitutional status despite the lack of express congressional assent. The wide variety and necessity of agreements on all sorts of issues, from where heads of state will sit during meetings, to when the next meeting will take place, provide implicit support for such agreements.

Perhaps the most well-known executive agreements resulted from a dark moment in American history, the taking of American hostages by the country of Iran. On November 4, 1979, Americans were taken hostage in the U.S. Embassy by Iranian students during an uprising. President Carter was unsuccessful in negotiating the release of the hostages, and the crisis continued for 444 days. The crisis lasted until the very end of President Carter's term and the beginning of President Reagan's presidency. At that time, a deal was struck for the hostages' release. The deal involved several executive agreements, the constitutionality of which was the subject of the next case.

Dames & Moore v. Regan
453 U.S. 654 (1981)

Justice REHNQUIST delivered the opinion of the Court.

We are confined to a resolution of the dispute presented to us. That dispute involves various Executive Orders and regulations by which the President nullified attachments and liens on Iranian assets in the United States, directed that these assets be transferred to Iran, and suspended claims against Iran that may be presented to an International Claims Tribunal. This action was taken in an effort to comply with an Executive Agreement between the United States and Iran.

On November 4, 1979, the American Embassy in Tehran was seized and our diplomatic personnel were captured and held hostage. In response to that crisis, President Carter, acting pursuant to the International Emergency Economic Powers Act, 91 Stat. 1626, 50 U.S.C. §§1701-1706 (1976 ed., Supp. III) (hereinafter IEEPA), declared a national emergency on November 14, 1979, and blocked the removal or transfer of "all property and interests in property of the Government of Iran, its instrumentalities and controlled entities and the Central Bank of Iran which are or become subject to the jurisdiction of the United States . . ." Exec. Order No. 12170, 3 CFR 457 (1980). President Carter authorized the Secretary of the Treasury to promulgate regulations carrying out the blocking order. On November 15, 1979, the Treasury Department's Office of Foreign Assets Control issued a regulation providing that "[u]nless licensed or authorized . . . any attachment, judgment, decree, lien, execution, garnishment, or other judicial process is null and void with respect to any property in which on or since [November 14, 1979,] there existed an interest of Iran." 31 CFR §535.203(e) (1980). . . .

On December 19, 1979, petitioner Dames & Moore filed suit in the United States District Court for the Central District of California against the Government of Iran, the Atomic Energy Organization of Iran, and a number of Iranian banks. In its complaint, petitioner alleged that its wholly owned subsidiary, Dames & Moore International, was a party to a written contract with the Atomic Energy Organization, and that the subsidiary's entire interest in the contract had been assigned to petitioner. Under the contract, the subsidiary was to conduct site studies for a proposed nuclear power plant in Iran. As provided in the terms of the contract, the Atomic Energy Organization terminated the agreement for its own convenience on June 30, 1979. Petitioner contended, however, that it was owed $3,436,694.30 plus interest for services performed under the contract prior to the date of termination. The District Court issued orders of attachment directed against property of the defendants, and the property of certain Iranian banks was then attached to secure any judgment that might be entered against them.

On January 20, 1981, the Americans held hostage were released by Iran pursuant to an Agreement entered into the day before and embodied in two Declarations of the Democratic and Popular Republic of Algeria.

The Agreement stated that "[i]t is the purpose of [the United States and Iran] . . . to terminate all litigation as between the Government of each party and the nationals of the other, and to bring about the settlement and termination of all such claims through binding arbitration." In furtherance of this goal, the Agreement called for the establishment of an Iran-United States Claims Tribunal which would arbitrate any claims not settled within six months. Awards of the Claims Tribunal are to be "final and binding" and "enforceable . . . in the courts of any nation in accordance with its laws."

On January 19, 1981, President Carter issued a series of Executive Orders implementing the terms of the agreement. Exec. Order Nos. 12276-12285, 46 Fed. Reg. 7913-7932.

On February 24, 1981, President Reagan issued an Executive Order in which he "ratified" the January 19th Executive Orders. Exec. Order No. 12294, 46 Fed. Reg. 14111. Moreover, he "suspended" all "claims which may be presented to the . . . Tribunal" and provided that such claims "shall have no legal effect in any action now pending in any court of the United States."

The parties and the lower courts, confronted with the instant questions, have all agreed that much relevant analysis is contained in Youngstown Sheet & Tube Co. v. Sawyer, 343 U.S. 579 (1952). Justice Black's opinion for the Court in that case, involving the validity of President Truman's effort to seize the country's steel mills in the wake of a nationwide strike, recognized that "[t]he President's power, if any, to issue the order must stem either from an act of Congress or from the Constitution itself."

Although we have in the past found and do today find Justice Jackson's classification of executive actions into three general categories analytically useful, we should be mindful of Justice Holmes' admonition, quoted by Justice Frankfurter in *Youngstown, supra,* at 597 (concurring opinion), that "[t]he great ordinances of the Constitution do not establish and divide fields of black and white." Springer v. Philippine Islands, 277 U.S. 189, 209 (1928) (dissenting opinion).

In nullifying post-November 14, 1979, attachments and directing those persons holding blocked Iranian funds and securities to transfer them to the Federal Reserve Bank of New York for ultimate transfer to Iran, President Carter cited five sources of express or inherent power. The Government, however, has principally relied on §203 of the IEEPA, 91 Stat. 1626, 50 U.S.C. §1702(a)(1) (1976 ed., Supp. III), as authorization for these actions. Section 1702(a)(1) provides in part: "At the times and to the extent specified in section 1701 of this title, the President may, under such regulations as he may prescribe, by means of instructions, licenses, or otherwise — " (A) investigate, regulate, or prohibit — "(i) any transactions in foreign exchange," (ii) transfers of credit or payments between, by, through, or to any banking institution, to the extent that such transfers or payments involve any interest of any foreign country or a national thereof, "(iii) the importing or exporting of currency or securities, and" (B) investigate, regulate, direct and compel, nullify, void, prevent or prohibit, any acquisition, holding, withholding, use, transfer, withdrawal, transportation, importation or exportation of, or dealing in, or exercising any right, power, or privilege with respect to, or transactions involving, any property in which any foreign country or a national thereof has any interest; "by any person, or with respect to any property, subject to the jurisdiction of the United States." The Government contends that the acts of "nullifying" the attachments and ordering the "transfer" of the frozen assets are specifically authorized by the plain language of the above statute. The two Courts of Appeals that have considered the issue agreed with this contention. . . .

Petitioner contends that we should ignore the plain language of this statute because an examination of its legislative history as well as the history of §5(b) of the Trading With the Enemy Act (hereinafter TWEA), 40 Stat. 411, as amended,

50 U.S.C. App. §5(b) (1976 ed. and Supp. III), from which the pertinent language of §1702 is directly drawn, reveals that the statute was not intended to give the President such extensive power over the assets of a foreign state during times of national emergency.

We do not agree and refuse to read out of §1702 all meaning to the words "transfer," "compel," or "nullify." Nothing in the legislative history of either §1702 or §5(b) of the TWEA requires such a result. To the contrary, we think both the legislative history and cases interpreting the TWEA fully sustain the broad authority of the Executive when acting under this congressional grant of power. *See* Orvis v. Brownell, 345 U.S. 183 (1953).

This Court has previously recognized that the congressional purpose in authorizing blocking orders is "to put control of foreign assets in the hands of the President. . . ." Propper v. Clark, 337 U.S. 472, 493 (1949).

Because the President's action in nullifying the attachments and ordering the transfer of the assets was taken pursuant to specific congressional authorization, it is "supported by the strongest of presumptions and the widest latitude of judicial interpretation, and the burden of persuasion would rest heavily upon any who might attack it." *Youngstown*, 343 U.S., at 637 (Jackson, J., concurring). Under the circumstances of this case, we cannot say that petitioner has sustained that heavy burden.

Although we have concluded that the IEEPA constitutes specific congressional authorization to the President to nullify the attachments and order the transfer of Iranian assets, there remains the question of the President's authority to suspend claims pending in American courts. Such claims have, of course, an existence apart from the attachments which accompanied them. In terminating these claims through Executive Order No. 12294 the President purported to act under authority of both the IEEPA and 22 U.S.C. §1732, the so-called "Hostage Act." 46 Fed. Reg. 14111 (1981).

We conclude that although the IEEPA authorized the nullification of the attachments, it cannot be read to authorize the suspension of the claims.

The Hostage Act, passed in 1868, provides: "Whenever it is made known to the President that any citizen of the United States has been unjustly deprived of his liberty by or under the authority of any foreign government, it shall be the duty of the President forthwith to demand of that government the reasons of such imprisonment; and if it appears to be wrongful and in violation of the rights of American citizenship, the President shall forthwith demand the release of such citizen, and if the release so demanded is unreasonably delayed or refused, the President shall use such means, not amounting to acts of war, as he may think necessary and proper to obtain or effectuate the release; and all the facts and proceedings relative thereto shall as soon as practicable be communicated by the President to Congress."

Although the broad language of the Hostage Act suggests it may cover this case, there are several difficulties with such a view. The legislative history indicates that the Act was passed in response to a situation unlike the recent Iranian crisis. Congress in 1868 was concerned with the activity of certain countries refusing to recognize the citizenship of naturalized Americans traveling abroad, and repatriating such citizens against their will. . . . The legislative history is also somewhat ambiguous on the question whether Congress contemplated Presidential action such as that involved here or rather simply reprisals directed against the offending foreign country and *its* citizens.

Although we have declined to conclude that the IEEPA or the Hostage Act directly authorizes the President's suspension of claims for the reasons noted, we cannot ignore the general tenor of Congress's legislation in this area in trying to determine whether the President is acting alone or at least with the acceptance of Congress. . . .

Crucial to our decision today is the conclusion that Congress has implicitly approved the practice of claim settlement by executive agreement. This is best demonstrated by Congress's enactment of the International Claims Settlement Act of 1949.

Over the years Congress has frequently amended the International Claims Settlement Act to provide for particular problems arising out of settlement agreements, thus demonstrating Congress's continuing acceptance of the President's claim settlement authority.

In addition to congressional acquiescence in the President's power to settle claims, prior cases of this Court have also recognized that the President does have some measure of power to enter into executive agreements without obtaining the advice and consent of the Senate. In United States v. Pink, 315 U.S. 203 (1942), for example, the Court upheld the validity of the Litvinov Assignment, which was part of an Executive Agreement whereby the Soviet Union assigned to the United States amounts owed to it by American nationals so that outstanding claims of other American nationals could be paid.

Similarly, Judge Learned Hand recognized: The constitutional power of the President extends to the settlement of mutual claims between a foreign government and the United States, at least when it is an incident to the recognition of that government; and it would be unreasonable to circumscribe it to such controversies.

Petitioner asserts that Congress divested the President of the authority to settle claims when it enacted the Foreign Sovereign Immunities Act of 1976 (hereinafter FSIA), 28 U.S.C. §§1330, 1602 *et seq*. The FSIA granted personal and subject-matter jurisdiction in the federal district courts over commercial suits brought by claimants against those foreign states which have waived immunity. 28 U.S.C. §1330. . . . Petitioner thus insists that the President, by suspending its claims, has circumscribed the jurisdiction of the United States courts in violation of Art. III of the Constitution.

We disagree. In the first place, we do not believe that the President has attempted to divest the federal courts of jurisdiction. Executive Order No. 12294 purports only to "suspend" the claims, not divest the federal court of "jurisdiction." As we read the Executive Order, those claims not within the jurisdiction of the Claims Tribunal will "revive" and become judicially enforceable in United States courts. . . .

In light of all of the foregoing — the inferences to be drawn from the character of the legislation Congress has enacted in the area, such as the IEEPA and the Hostage Act, and from the history of acquiescence in executive claims settlement — we conclude that the President was authorized to suspend pending claims pursuant to Executive Order No. 12294.

∾ PROBLEM: NULLIFY ∾

Congress enacted a law in 2009 authorizing "the President to nullify judgments in United States courts providing for attachments of assets of foreign countries when significant foreign policy concerns require such a nullification." After North Korea took several journalists hostage in 2010 and attempts at negotiation failed, the President negotiated a window of release of the hostages, but only if the President nullified several attachments placed on North Korean–owned property and suspended several claims pending against North Korea in U.S. courts. Would the nullifications be considered constitutional?

I. EXECUTIVE PRIVILEGE AND IMMUNITY FROM SUIT

Executive privilege from disclosure of information and immunity from suit are two executive powers that can be treated as defenses against the powers of the other branches of government. These executive powers are considered necessary to promote the free and unfettered performance of the executive function, without a chilling effect caused by forced disclosure or the threat of litigation.

1. Executive Privilege

Perhaps the most noteworthy executive privilege case of its generation was precipitated by the Watergate scandal that led to the downfall of the Nixon presidency. On June 17, 1972, burglars broke into the offices of the Democratic National Committee located at the Watergate Complex in Washington, D.C. This petty burglary soon became a smoking cauldron of political intrigue. The burglary was instigated by President Nixon's Committee to Re-Elect the President (CREEP) for political reasons. Knowledge of the burglary and its cover-up was eventually traced to the President himself.

President Nixon had secretly taped all conversations in the Oval Office, including his own. These tapes were the subject of United States v. Nixon, 418 U.S. 683 (1974), the next case, in which the Court decided whether executive privilege shielded the President from forced disclosure. The tapes turned out to be significant, not only to the Watergate burglary trial but also to the survival of Nixon's presidency. They connected the President to the cover-up of the Watergate burglary.

United States v. Nixon

418 U.S. 683 (1974)

Mr. Chief Justice BURGER delivered the opinion of the Court.

This litigation presents for review the denial of a motion, filed in the District Court on behalf of the President of the United States, in the case of United States v. Mitchell et al. (D.C. Crim. No. 74-110), to quash a third-party subpoena *duces tecum* issued by the United States District Court for the District of Columbia, pursuant to Fed. Rule Crim. Proc. 17(c). The subpoena directed the President to produce certain tape recordings and documents relating to his conversations with aides and advisers. The court rejected the President's claims of absolute executive privilege, of lack of jurisdiction, and of failure to satisfy the requirements of Rule 17(c). The President appealed to the Court of Appeals. We granted both the United States' petition for certiorari before judgment (No. 73-1766), and also the President's cross-petition for certiorari before judgment (No. 73-1834), because of the public importance of the issues presented and the need for their prompt resolution.

On March 1, 1974, a grand jury of the United States District Court for the District of Columbia returned an indictment charging seven named individuals with various offenses, including conspiracy to defraud the United States and to obstruct justice. Although he was not designated as such in the indictment, the grand jury named the President, among others, as an unindicted coconspirator. On April 18, 1974, upon motion of the Special Prosecutor, *see* n.8, *infra*, a subpoena *duces tecum* was issued pursuant to Rule 17(c) to the President by the United States District Court and made returnable on May 2, 1974. This subpoena required the production, in advance of the September 9 trial date, of certain tapes, memoranda, papers, transcripts or other writings relating to certain precisely identified meetings between the President and others. The Special Prosecutor was able to fix the time, place, and persons present at these discussions because the White House daily logs and appointment records had been delivered to him. On April 30, the President publicly released edited transcripts of 43 conversations; portions of 20 conversations subject to subpoena in the present case were included. On May 1, 1974, the President's counsel, filed a 'special appearance' and a motion to quash the subpoena under Rule 17(c). This motion was accompanied by a formal claim of privilege.

The Claim of Privilege. [W]e turn to the claim that the subpoena should be quashed because it demands 'confidential conversations between a President and his close advisors that it would be inconsistent with the public interest to produce.' App. 48a. The first contention is a broad claim that the separation of powers doctrine precludes judicial review of a President's claim of privilege. The second contention is that if he does not prevail on the claim of absolute privilege, the court should hold as a matter of constitutional law that the privilege prevails over the subpoena *duces tecum*.

The Watergate Complex in Washington, D.C., where the break-in occurred.

In the performance of assigned constitutional duties each branch of the Government must initially interpret the Constitution, and the interpretation of its powers by any branch is due great respect from the others. The President's counsel, as we have noted, reads the Constitution as providing an absolute privilege of confidentiality for all Presidential communications. Many decisions of this Court, however, have unequivocally reaffirmed the holding of Marbury v. Madison, 1 Cranch, 137, 2 L.Ed. 60 (1803), that "(i)t is emphatically the province and duty of the judicial department to say what the law is."

No holding of the Court has defined the scope of judicial power specifically relating to the enforcement of a subpoena for confidential Presidential communications for use in a criminal prosecution, but other exercises of power by the Executive Branch and the Legislative Branch have been found invalid as in conflict with the Constitution.

However, neither the doctrine of separation of powers, nor the need for confidentiality of high-level communications, without more, can sustain an absolute, unqualified Presidential privilege of immunity from judicial process under all circumstances. The President's need for complete candor and objectivity from advisers calls for great deference from the courts. However, when the privilege depends solely on the broad, undifferentiated claim of public interest in the confidentiality of such conversations, a confrontation with other values arises. Absent a claim of need to protect military, diplomatic, or sensitive national security secrets, we find it difficult to accept the argument that even the very important interest in confidentiality of Presidential communications is significantly diminished by production of such material for in camera inspection with all the protection that a district court will be obliged to provide.

The impediment that an absolute, unqualified privilege would place in the way of the primary constitutional duty of the Judicial Branch to do justice in criminal prosecutions would plainly conflict with the function of the courts under Art. III. In designing the structure of our Government and dividing and allocating the sovereign power among three co-equal branches, the Framers of the Constitution sought to provide a comprehensive system, but the separate powers were not intended to operate with absolute independence.

"While the Constitution diffuses power the better to secure liberty, it also contemplates that practice will integrate the dispersed powers into a workable government. It enjoins upon its branches separateness but interdependence, autonomy but reciprocity." Youngstown Sheet & Tube Co. v. Sawyer, 343 U.S., at 635 (Jackson, J., concurring). To read the Art. II powers of the President as providing an absolute privilege as against a subpoena essential to enforcement of criminal statutes on no more than a generalized claim of the public interest in confidentiality of nonmilitary and nondiplomatic discussions would upset the constitutional balance of "a workable government" and gravely impair the role of the courts under Art. III.

Since we conclude that the legitimate needs of the judicial process may outweigh Presidential privilege, it is necessary to resolve those competing interests in a manner that preserves the essential functions of each branch. The right and indeed the duty to resolve that question does not free the Judiciary from according high respect to the representations made on behalf of the President. United States v. Burr, 25 F. Cas. pp. 187 (C.C. Va. 1807). The expectation of a President to the confidentiality of his conversations and correspondence, like the claim of confidentiality of judicial deliberations, for example, has all the values to which we accord deference for the privacy of all citizens and, added to those values, is the necessity for protection of the public interest in candid, objective, and even blunt or harsh opinions in Presidential decision making. A President and those who assist him must be free to explore alternatives in the process of shaping policies and making decisions and to do so in a way many would be unwilling to express except privately. These are the considerations justifying a presumptive privilege for Presidential communications. The privilege is fundamental to the operation of Government and inextricably rooted in the separation of powers under the Constitution. In Nixon v. Sirica, 159 U.S. App. D.C. 58, 487 F.2d 700 (1973), the Court of Appeals held that such Presidential communications are "presumptively privileged," and this position is accepted by both parties in the present litigation.

But this presumptive privilege must be considered in light of our historic commitment to the rule of law. This is nowhere more profoundly manifest than in our view that the twofold aim (of criminal justice) is that guilt shall not escape or innocence suffer.

In this case the President challenges a subpoena served on him as a third party requiring the production of materials for use in a criminal prosecution; he does so on the claim that he has a privilege against disclosure of confidential communications. He does not place his claim of privilege on the ground they are military or diplomatic secrets. As to these areas of Art. II duties the courts have traditionally shown the utmost deference to Presidential responsibilities.

In this case we must weigh the importance of the general privilege of confidentiality of Presidential communications in performance of the President's responsibilities against the inroads of such a privilege on the fair administration of criminal justice. The interest in preserving confidentiality is weighty indeed and entitled to great respect. However, we cannot conclude that advisers will be moved to temper the candor of their remarks by the infrequent occasions of disclosure because of the possibility that such conversations will be called for in the context of a criminal prosecution.

On the other hand, the allowance of the privilege to withhold evidence that is demonstrably relevant in a criminal trial would cut deeply into the guarantee of due process of law and gravely impair the basic function of the courts. A President's acknowledged need for confidentiality in the communications of his office is general in nature, whereas the constitutional need for production of relevant evidence in a criminal proceeding is specific and central to the fair adjudication of a particular criminal case in the administration of justice.

We conclude that when the ground for asserting privilege as to subpoenaed materials sought for use in a criminal trial is based only on the generalized interest in confidentiality, it cannot prevail over the fundamental demands of due process of law in the fair administration of criminal justice. The generalized assertion of privilege must yield to the demonstrated, specific need for evidence in a pending criminal trial.

Upon receiving a claim of privilege from the Chief Executive, it became the further duty of the District Court to treat the subpoenaed material as presumptively privileged and to require the Special Prosecutor to demonstrate that the Presidential material was "essential to the justice of the (pending criminal) case." United States v. Burr, 25 Fed. Cas., at 192. Here the District Court treated the material as presumptively privileged, proceeded to find that the Special Prosecutor had made a sufficient showing to rebut the presumption, and ordered an in camera examination of the subpoenaed material.

On the basis of our examination of the record we are unable to conclude that the District Court erred in ordering the inspection. Accordingly we affirm the order of the District Court that subpoenaed materials be transmitted to that court.

We have no doubt that the District Judge will at all times accord to Presidential records that high degree of deference suggested in United States v. Burr, *supra.* and will discharge his responsibility to see to it that until released to the Special Prosecutor no in camera material is revealed to anyone.

Affirmed.

Note: A Privilege for the Vice President?

Executive privilege questions that remain open include who can claim executive privilege and, when claims are permitted, under what circumstances they are allowed. In Cheney v. United States District Court, 542 U.S. 367 (2004), for example, the Supreme Court reaffirmed a partial executive privilege. This case involved a civil suit against then Vice President Cheney, seeking the disclosure of information about several meetings the vice president had with members of private industry. The Supreme Court remanded, permitting the lower court to rule on the discovery requests after balancing the interests involved.

∾ PROBLEMS ∾

1. *Leak.* During an independent counsel investigation of the disclosure of the identity of a Central Intelligence Agency secret agent, destroying the possibility of her future participation in secret operations, the President of the United States, the vice president, and several of the President's senior staff were interviewed. The reports of these interviews, conducted by the Department of Justice, were subpoenaed by a congressional committee also investigating the disclosure. a) Can the President refuse to submit the documents relating to his interview, which was led by the FBI? b) Can the President refuse to submit the documents relating to the vice president's interview by the Justice Department based on executive privilege? c) Can the President refuse to submit the documents relating to the senior staff interviews by the Justice Department based on executive privilege?

2. *More on No Drilling Zones.* In the introductory problem, the President had intelligence that al Qaeda sympathizers would infiltrate drilling operations in no drilling areas. If the President decided to engage in secret operations to detect such infiltrations, would the President have to turn over this information upon a subpoena by the courts or Congress?

2. Immunity from Suit

Executive immunity from suit has been a recurring issue stretching back to the early days of our government. The Executive Branch's amenability to suit was affirmed early in our history in the famous case of Marbury v. Madison, 5 U.S. 137 (1803), where the Court permitted a claimant, William Marbury, to sue the Secretary of State, James Madison, for failing to deliver a judicial commission. Although immunity from suit centers around official acts while the executive is in office, the Supreme Court has refused to broadly extend the immunity to conduct taking place prior to the President serving as chief executive.

In Clinton v. Jones, 520 U.S. 681 (1997), the Supreme Court allowed a civil suit against President Clinton to proceed after balancing the interests at hand. The suit was based on alleged acts occurring prior to the time Clinton became President.

Clinton v. Jones
520 U.S. 681 (1997)

Justice STEVENS delivered the opinion of the Court.

This case raises a constitutional and a prudential question concerning the Office of the President of the United States. Respondent, a private citizen, seeks to recover damages from the current occupant of that office based on actions allegedly taken before his term began. The President submits that in all but the most exceptional cases the Constitution requires federal courts to defer such litigation until his term ends and that, in any event, respect for the office warrants such a stay. Despite the force of the arguments supporting the President's submissions, we conclude that they must be rejected.

Petitioner, William Jefferson Clinton, was elected to the Presidency in 1992, and re-elected in 1996. His term of office expires on January 20, 2001. In 1991 he was the Governor of the State of Arkansas. Respondent, Paula Corbin Jones, is a resident of California. In 1991 she lived in Arkansas, and was an employee of the Arkansas Industrial Development Commission.

In response to the complaint, petitioner promptly advised the District Court that he intended to file a motion to dismiss on grounds of Presidential immunity.

The District Judge denied the motion to dismiss on immunity grounds and ruled that discovery in the case could go forward, but ordered any trial stayed until the end of petitioner's Presidency.

Both parties appealed. A divided panel of the Court of Appeals affirmed the denial of the motion to dismiss, but because it regarded the order postponing the trial until the President leaves office as the "functional equivalent" of a grant of temporary immunity, it reversed that order.

Petitioner's principal submission—that "in all but the most exceptional cases," Brief for Petitioner i, the Constitution affords the President temporary immunity from civil damages litigation arising out of events that occurred before he took office—cannot be sustained on the basis of precedent. Only three sitting Presidents have been defendants in civil litigation involving their actions prior to taking office. Complaints against Theodore Roosevelt and Harry Truman had been dismissed before they took office; the dismissals were affirmed after their respective inaugurations. Two companion cases arising out of an automobile accident were filed against John F. Kennedy in 1960 during the Presidential campaign. After taking office, he unsuccessfully argued that his status as Commander in Chief gave him a right to a stay under the Soldiers' and Sailors' Civil Relief Act of 1940. The motion for a stay was denied by the District Court, and the matter was settled out of court. Thus, none of those cases sheds any light on the constitutional issue before us.

The principal rationale for affording certain public servants immunity from suits for money damages arising out of their official acts is inapplicable to unofficial conduct. In cases involving prosecutors, legislators, and judges we have repeatedly explained that the immunity serves the public interest in enabling such officials to perform their designated functions effectively without fear that a particular decision may give rise to personal liability.

That rationale provided the principal basis for our holding that a former President of the United States was "entitled to absolute immunity from damages liability predicated on his official acts," *Fitzgerald*, 457 U.S., at 749.

Moreover, when defining the scope of an immunity for acts clearly taken *within* an official capacity, we have applied a functional approach. "Frequently our decisions have held that an official's absolute immunity should extend only to acts in performance of particular functions of his office." Hence, for example, a judge's absolute immunity does not extend to actions performed in a purely administrative capacity.

As a starting premise, petitioner contends that he occupies a unique office with powers and responsibilities so vast and important that the public interest demands that he devote his undivided time and attention to his public duties. He submits that — given the nature of the office — the doctrine of separation of powers places limits on the authority of the Federal Judiciary to interfere with the Executive Branch that would be transgressed by allowing this action to proceed.

It does not follow, however, that separation-of-powers principles would be violated by allowing this action to proceed.

As a factual matter, petitioner contends that this particular case — as well as the potential additional litigation that an affirmance of the Court of Appeals judgment might spawn — may impose an unacceptable burden on the President's time and energy, and thereby impair the effective performance of his office.

[We disagree.] As we have already noted, in the more than 200-year history of the Republic, only three sitting Presidents have been subjected to suits for their private actions. If the past is any indicator, it seems unlikely that a deluge of such litigation will ever engulf the Presidency. As for the case at hand, if properly managed by the District Court, it appears to us highly unlikely to occupy any substantial amount of petitioner's time.

[I]t is also settled that the President is subject to judicial process in appropriate circumstances. Although Thomas Jefferson apparently thought otherwise, Chief Justice Marshall, when presiding in the treason trial of Aaron Burr, ruled that a subpoena *duces tecum* could be directed to the President. United States v. Burr, 25 F. Cas. 30 (No. 14,692d) (C.C. Va. 1807). We unequivocally and emphatically endorsed Marshall's position when we held that President Nixon was obligated to comply with a subpoena commanding him to produce certain tape recordings of his conversations with his aides. United States v. Nixon, 418 U.S. 683 (1974).

In sum, "[i]t is settled law that the separation-of-powers doctrine does not bar every exercise of jurisdiction over the President of the United States."

The reasons for rejecting such a categorical rule apply as well to a rule that would require a stay "in all but the most exceptional cases." Brief for Petitioner i. Indeed, if the Framers of the Constitution had thought it necessary to protect the President from the burdens of private litigation, we think it far more likely that they would have adopted a categorical rule than a rule that required the President to litigate the question whether a specific case belonged in the "exceptional case" subcategory. In all events, the question whether a specific case should receive exceptional treatment is more appropriately the subject of the exercise of judicial discretion than an interpretation of the Constitution. Accordingly, we turn to the question whether the District Court's decision to stay the trial until after petitioner leaves office was an abuse of discretion.

We add a final comment on two matters that are discussed at length in the briefs: the risk that our decision will generate a large volume of politically motivated harassing and frivolous litigation, and the danger that national security concerns might prevent the President from explaining a legitimate need for a continuance.

We are not persuaded that either of these risks is serious. Most frivolous and vexatious litigation is terminated at the pleading stage or on summary judgment, with little if any personal involvement by the defendant. *See* Fed. Rules Civ. Proc. 12, 56. Moreover, the availability of sanctions provides a significant deterrent to litigation directed at the President in his unofficial capacity.

The Federal District Court has jurisdiction to decide this case. Like every other citizen who properly invokes that jurisdiction, respondent has a right to an orderly disposition of her claims. Accordingly, the judgment of the Court of Appeals is affirmed. *It is so ordered.*

Justice BREYER, concurring in the judgment.

I agree with the majority that the Constitution does not automatically grant the President an immunity from civil lawsuits based upon his private conduct. Nor does the "doctrine of separation of powers . . . require federal courts to stay" virtually "all private actions against the President until he leaves office."

In my view, however, once the President sets forth and explains a conflict between judicial proceeding and public duties, the matter changes. At that point, the Constitution permits a judge to schedule a trial in an ordinary civil damages action (where postponement normally is possible without overwhelming damage to a plaintiff) only within the constraints of a constitutional principle — a principle that forbids a federal judge in such a case to interfere with the President's discharge of his public duties. I have no doubt that the Constitution contains such a principle applicable to civil suits, based upon Article II's vesting of the entire "Executive Power" in a single individual, implemented through the Constitution's structural separation of powers, and revealed both by history and case precedent.

J. THE PARDON POWER

The President enjoys broad discretionary power to pardon people for their misconduct. For example, shortly after taking office, Gerald Ford, in Presidential Proclamation 4311, pardoned his predecessor. The proclamation stated: "The prospects of such a trial [of former President Richard M. Nixon] will cause prolonged and divisive debate over the propriety of exposing to further punishment and degradation a man who has already paid the unprecedented penalty of resigning the highest elective office of the United States."

Despite the breadth of presidential discretion, presidential use of the pardon power has not been without controversy. For example, President Bill Clinton ignited a firestorm when he pardoned Marc Rich, an international fugitive wanted on tax evasion, just prior to leaving office. The pardon was not warranted in the eyes of many of the President's political opponents and even some supporters were puzzled as to the President's reasoning. The pardon could not be challenged, however, because it was a political act solely committed to the President of the United States in Article II.

1. Commutation of Sentences

In United States v. I. Lewis Libby, 495 F. Supp. 2d 49 (D.D.C. 2007), the issue involved the relationship between the President's executive clemency power and federal statutory sentencing requirements. Specifically, the case presented the question of whether a President could commute the sentence of a criminal defendant while maintaining a term of supervised release in derogation of a statute that required incarceration prior to any supervised release. The district court held that the executive clemency power was bound only by the requirements of the Constitution, not the statute.

The defendant, Lewis "Scooter" Libby, was convicted of obstruction of justice and perjury and sentenced to a period of 30 months of incarceration, followed by a two-year term of supervised release. Pursuant to statute, 18 U.S.C. §3583, supervised release is intended to follow a term of incarceration. The defendant had been an aide to Vice President Dick Cheney when the underlying conduct occurred. President George W. Bush issued a Grant of Executive Clemency on July 2, 2007, for the prison term, stating that the sentence was "excessive." (Statement by the President on Executive Clemency for Lewis Libby at 1.) The two-year supervised release term, however, was not modified by the clemency.

Article II, Section 2 of the U.S. Constitution gives the executive the power to grant clemency in relation to criminal prosecutions. This pardon power is not subject to standards and is generally free from judicial review. The District Court agreed with the Government in finding that the President could "disregard established statutory requirements in commuting the sentence of a criminal defendant, so long as the conditions placed upon the commutation 'do[ ] not otherwise offend the Constitution.' Schick v. Reed, 419 U.S. 256 (1974)." *I. Lewis Libby* at 52-53. Thus, the Constitution trumps the otherwise lawful statutory requirement.

Points to Remember

- The President has no power to legislate domestically unless Congress approves or is silent about the President's actions, as per Justice Jackson's concurrence in *Youngstown Sheet & Tube Co.*
- The President often shares powers with Congress in an interdependent relationship, more so than in a formal separation of powers, such as with the presentment of a law, the veto, and the appointment power over officers of the United States.
- The view that the President has strong powers over the entire Executive Branch is somewhat controversial but extremely current, given the powers the President has utilized to fight terrorism.
- The President, as Commander in Chief, has significant power to fight terrorism, but due process rights under the Constitution still apply, even to an American base such as the one in Guantanamo Bay, Cuba.
- The executive powers of privilege and immunity from suit originate in the Constitution but are only partial safeguards.

4

The Relationship Between the States and the Federal Government

U.S. CONSTITUTION, TENTH AMENDMENT

The powers not delegated to the United States by the Constitution, nor prohibited by it to the States, are reserved to the States respectively, or to the people.

∾ PROBLEM: THE EDUCATION FOR A BETTER AMERICA (EBA) ACT, CONTINUED ∾

Congress, concerned about the quality of education in the United States, is considering the possibility of adopting the Education for a Better America (EBA) Act to promote a uniform quality education in this country, free of charge. The reasons for Congress's concerns are broad and well-substantiated. For decades, American children have been falling behind children in other countries in math and science as well as other critical subjects. More troubling, some children are failing in real and critical aspects. Too many children drop out of school, and the evidence shows that dropouts encounter such problems as much lower employment prospects and much higher rates of alcoholism, drug abuse, and incarceration. In addition, dropouts are more likely to be involved in domestic violence. Even when children stay in school, the accessibility of drugs and weapons diminishes what schools aim to accomplish. Today's society is becoming more technological and more international in character. Many members of Congress believe that, in order to compete in a modern business environment, students will need a revised and more sophisticated education.

You work for a new member of Congress, Julia St. James, who believes the states are not doing a responsible job in improving the quality of education in this country. Yet, she does not intend to enact a federal takeover of education because she was not particularly enthusiastic about the results of the No Child Left Behind Act. The congresswoman gives you the task of creating several different constitutional options related to offering states incentives and requiring mandatory directives as riders to the Education for a Better America Act. These are her three primary themes, accompanied by some specific ideas:

1. *Reward Teacher Quality.* The congresswoman has suggested that states abolish tenure for teachers and substitute a merit pay system and job security.
2. *Adopt Stay-in-School Initiatives.* The congresswoman proposes to penalize dropouts by revoking their driver's license privileges. She believes in both incentives and mandatory directives.
3. *Promote Civics and Language Arts as well as Math and Science.* The congresswoman wants to know how to best promote a fundamentally sound education.

In this chapter, you will be asked to advise the congresswoman about the permissible scope of federal government interactions with the states on a constitutional level and what specific initiatives she should propose to ameliorate these profound education problems.

The Constitution does not treat the states as subdivisions of the federal government. Instead, the Constitution creates a system of dual sovereignty that allocates some powers to the federal government and the remaining powers to state governments or to the people. Whereas Chapter 3 focused on the power of the states to regulate commerce, this chapter focuses on the on so-called "intergovernmental immunities": the right of one government (federal or state) to be free of the regulation or taxes of the other government. In earlier times, both sovereigns tested these boundaries, but in recent times, the federal government is usually alleged to be the transgressor.

A. STATE POWER TO TAX THE FEDERAL GOVERNMENT

Do the states have the power to tax entities of the federal government? The power to tax raises important and controversial issues because it is an essential element of sovereignty and can impose significant burdens on the taxed entity. Questions regarding the power of the states to tax the federal government were resolved very early in U.S. history.

> ## BACKGROUND OF MCCULLOCH
> ### *The Showdown over the Second National Bank*
>
> The 20-year run of the First National Bank was terminated in 1811 due to a lack of congressional support. A perceived need for a new bank to regulate currency prompted the creation of the Second National Bank in 1816. Many opposed the bank on policy and constitutionality grounds. The bank was challenged in Maryland by the placement of a tax on its Maryland branch. The bank refused to pay the Maryland tax and the federal–state showdown was on in McCulloch v. Maryland, 17 U.S. (4 Wheat.) 316 (1819).

> ## BACKGROUND
> ### *The Oral Argument in McCulloch*
>
> The showdown in *McCulloch* featured prominent attorneys arguing the case before the Supreme Court. One of the attorneys representing the cashier of the federal bank, James McCulloch, was Daniel Webster. Luther Martin was one of the attorneys representing Maryland. In those days, the duration of oral arguments was not limited, and the argument in this case is reputed to have lasted for six days.

McCulloch v. Maryland

17 U.S. (4 Wheat.) 316 (1819)

MARSHALL, C. J., delivered the opinion of the court.

[In 1816, Congress chartered the Second Bank of the United States, which ultimately included a Maryland branch. Maryland passed a statute taxing all banks established "without authority from the State." Banks subject to the law must pay an annual fee of $15,000 or could issue notes only on stamped paper provided by the state. The state charged differing fees for the stamped paper based on the denomination of the note. The statute was enforceable through criminal penalties as well as statutory penalties. The cashier was liable for a penalty of $500 per offense. John James, acting on his own behalf as well as on behalf of the State of Maryland, sued McCulloch, cashier of the Maryland branch, claiming that McCulloch was operating a bank without statutory authority as well as failed to comply with the Maryland law. When James won in the Maryland courts, McCulloch sought review in the U.S. Supreme Court.] [The section of the opinion that discusses the federal government's authority to establish a national bank is omitted.]

Whether the state of Maryland may, without violating the constitution, tax that branch? That the power of taxation is one of vital importance; that it is retained by the states; that it is not abridged by the grant of a similar power to the government of the Union; that it is to be concurrently exercised by the two governments — are truths which have never been denied. But such is the paramount character of the constitution, that its capacity to withdraw any subject from the action of even this power, is admitted. The states are expressly forbidden to lay any duties on imports or exports, except what may be absolutely necessary for executing their inspection laws. If the obligation of this prohibition must be conceded — if it may restrain a state from the exercise of its taxing power on imports and exports — the same paramount character would seem to restrain, as it certainly may restrain, a state from such other exercise of this power, as is in its nature incompatible with, and repugnant to, the constitutional laws of the Union. A law, absolutely repugnant to another, as entirely repeals that other as if express terms of repeal were used.

[C]ounsel for the bank place its claim to be exempted from the power of a state to tax its operations. There is no express provision for the case, but the claim has been sustained on a principle which so entirely pervades the constitution, is so intermixed with the materials which compose it, so interwoven with its web, so blended with its texture, as to be incapable of being separated from it, without rending it into shreds. This great principle is, that the constitution and the laws made in pursuance thereof are supreme; that they control the constitution and laws of the respective states, and cannot be controlled by them. From this, which may be almost termed an axiom, other propositions are deduced as corollaries, on the truth or error of which, and on their application to this case, the cause has been supposed to depend. These are, 1st. That a power to create implies a power to preserve: 2d. That a power to destroy, if wielded by a different hand, is hostile to, and incompatible with these powers to create and to preserve: 3d. That where this repugnancy exists, that authority which is supreme must control, not yield to that over which it is supreme. . . .

[T]he states have no power, by taxation or otherwise, to retard, impede, burden, or in any manner control, the operations of the constitutional laws enacted by congress to carry into execution the powers vested in the general government. This is, we think, the unavoidable consequence of that supremacy which the constitution has declared. We are unanimously of opinion, that the law passed by the legislature of Maryland, imposing a tax on the Bank of the United States, is unconstitutional and void.

∽ PROBLEMS ∽

1. *State Strategy #1: TurboTax Customers.* An attorney for the State of Maryland, Tania Tanner, went to her boss after the case and said, "After *McCulloch*, the states seem to be limited in their ability to impose taxes. But, suppose that we want to impose our state income taxes on interest received by private customers of the national bank? As I read *McCulloch*, it does not prohibit us from taxing such income." Do you agree? Why might the federal government be reluctant to allow

the states to tax this income? What state taxation might be permissible? *See* Graves v. New York, 306 U.S. 466 (1939).

2. *State Strategy #2: Neutralize.* The same Maryland attorney, Tania Tanner, thought of another creative way to impose a tax while galloping to work on her horse. She decided to propose a neutral tax on all property within the state — including the vast federal landholdings outside of Baltimore as well as the land on which the federal bank sat. Would this new law be constitutional? *See* Van Brocklin v. Anderson, 117 U.S. 151 (1886). Should it matter whether the land is owned by a private citizen and leased to the United States? What if federal land is leased to a private business? *See* United States v. County of Fresno, 429 U.S. 452 (1977). What if Tania also proposed taxing the interest on federal bonds held by Maryland residents? *See* Weston v. City Council of Charleston, 27 U.S. (2 Pet.) 449 (1829).

3. *More on the Education for a Better America Act.* Now, let's return to the problem presented at the beginning of the chapter. If the federal government raises the bar for educational goals in state public schools, as suggested in the problem, does the analysis of whether the states can tax federal entities, property, or bonds change because of the different rationale? Explain.

B. FEDERAL POWER TO TAX THE STATES

Given that states lack the power to tax the federal government, does the federal government likewise lack the power to tax the states? In several early cases, the Court held that the federal government had limited power to tax the states. For example, in Collector v. Day, 78 U.S. (11 Wall.) 113 (1871), the Court held that the salary of a state judicial officer, in that case a probate judge, was immune from federal income tax. The Court emphasized that the officer was engaged in the performance of a function that pertained to state governments at the time the Constitution was adopted. But, in the 1930s, the Court overruled *Day* and held that the salaries of state employees were subject to federal tax. *See* Helvering v. Gerhardt, 304 U.S. 405 (1938). The Court's current approach to the federal taxing power is reflected in the two cases presented next.

Massachusetts v. United States

435 U.S. 444 (1978)

Mr. Justice BRENNAN delivered the opinion of the Court.

[Congress imposed an annual registration tax on all civil aircraft that fly in the navigable airspace of the United States. The State of Massachusetts challenged the tax as applied to] a helicopter which the Commonwealth uses exclusively for patrolling highways and other police functions. [The Commonwealth claims that] the United States may not constitutionally impose a tax that directly affects the essential and traditional state function of operating a police force. . . .

[The] immunity of the Federal Government from state taxation is bottomed on the Supremacy Clause, but the States' immunity from federal taxes was judicially implied from the States' role in the constitutional scheme. Collector v. Day, [78 U.S. (11 Wall.) 113 (1871)], emphasized that the States [were] independent sovereigns when the Constitution was adopted, and that the Constitution presupposes and guarantees the continued existence of the States as governmental bodies performing traditional sovereign functions. To implement this aspect of the constitutional plan, Collector v. Day concluded that it was imperative absolutely to prohibit any federal taxation that directly affected a traditional state function, quoting Mr. Chief Justice Marshall's aphorisms that "'the power of taxing [may] be exercised so far as to destroy,'" and "'a right [to tax], in its nature, acknowledges no limits.'" The Court has more recently remarked that these maxims refer primarily to two attributes of the taxing power. First, in imposing a tax to support the services a government provides to the public at large, a legislature need not consider the value of particular benefits to a taxpayer, but may assess the tax solely on the basis of taxpayers' ability to pay. Second[,] a tax is a powerful regulatory device; a legislature can discourage or eliminate [an activity within] its regulatory jurisdiction simply by imposing a heavy tax on its exercise. Collector v. Day, [like] *McCulloch*, reflected the view that [the] taxing power required a flat and absolute prohibition against a tax implicating an essential state function because the ability of the federal courts to determine whether particular revenue measures [would] destroy such an essential function was to be doubted.

"[C]ogent reasons" were recognized for narrowly limiting the immunity of the States from federal imposts. The first is that any immunity for the protection of state sovereignty is at the expense of the sovereign power of the National Government to tax. Therefore, when the scope of the States' constitutional immunity is enlarged beyond that necessary to protect the continued ability of the States to deliver traditional governmental services, the burden of the immunity is thrown upon the National Government without any corresponding promotion of the constitutionally protected values. The second, also recognized by Mr. Chief Justice Marshall in *McCulloch*, is that the political process is uniquely adapted to accommodating the competing demands "for national revenue, on the one hand, and for reasonable scope for the independence of state action, on the other," Helvering v. Gerhardt. The Congress, composed as it is of members chosen by state constituencies, constitutes an inherent check against the possibility of abusive taxing of the States by the National Government.

[In] recognition of these considerations[,] decisions of the Court either have declined to enlarge the scope of state immunity or have in fact restricted its reach. Typical of this trend are decisions holding that the National Government may tax revenue-generating activities of the States that are of the same nature as those traditionally engaged in by private persons. It is true that some of the opinions speak of the state activity taxed as "proprietary" and thus not an immune essential governmental activity, but [New York v. United States] rejected the governmental-proprietary distinction as untenable. [T]he majority reasoned that a nondiscriminatory tax may be applied to a state business activity where [the] recognition of immunity would "accomplish a withdrawal from the taxing power of the nation a subject of taxation of a nature which has been traditionally within that power from the beginning. Its exercise [by] a nondiscriminatory tax, does not curtail the business of the state government more than it does the like business of the citizen."

Illustrative of decisions actually restricting the scope of the immunity is the line of cases that culminated in the overruling of Collector v. Day in Graves v. New York, 306 U.S. 466 (1939). *Day* [involved] a nondiscriminatory tax that was imposed not directly on the State but rather on the salary earned by a judicial officer. Neither *Day* itself nor its progeny or precursors made clear how such a taxing measure could be employed to preclude the States from performing essential functions. In any case, in the line of decisions that culminated in *Graves*, the Court demonstrated that an immunity for the salaries paid key state officials is not justifiable. Although key state officials are agents of the State, they are also citizens of the United States, so their income is a natural subject for income taxation.

More significantly, because the taxes imposed were nondiscriminatory and thus also applicable to income earned by persons in private employment, the risk was virtually nonexistent that such revenue provisions could significantly impede a State's ability to hire able persons to perform its essential functions. The only advantage conceivably to be lost by denying the States such an immunity is that essential state functions might be obtained at a lesser cost because employees exempt from taxation might be willing to work for smaller salaries. But that was regarded as an inadequate ground for sustaining the immunity and preventing the National Government from requiring these citizens to support its activities. The purpose of the implied constitutional restriction on the national taxing power is not to give an advantage to the States by enabling them to engage employees at a lower charge than those paid by private entities, but rather is solely to protect the States from undue interference with their traditional governmental functions. While a tax on the salary paid key state officers may increase the cost of government, it will no more preclude the States from performing traditional functions than it will prevent private entities from performing their missions.

These two lines of decisions illustrate the "practical construction" that the Court now gives the limitation the existence of the States constitutionally imposes on the national taxing power; "that limitation cannot be so varied or extended as seriously to impair either the taxing power of the government imposing the tax [or] the appropriate exercise of the functions of the government affected by it." Where the subject of tax is a natural and traditional source of federal revenue and where it is inconceivable that such a revenue measure could ever operate to preclude traditional state activities, the tax is valid. While the Court has by no means abandoned its doubts concerning its ability to make particularized assessments of the impact of revenue measures on essential state operations, it has recognized that some generic types of revenue measures could never seriously threaten the continued functioning of the States and hence are outside the scope of the implied tax immunity.

A nondiscriminatory taxing measure that operates to defray the cost of a federal program by recovering a fair approximation of each beneficiary's share of the cost is surely no more offensive to the constitutional scheme than is either a tax on the income earned by state employees or a tax on a State's sale of bottled water. The National Government's interest in being compensated for its expenditures is only too apparent. [S]uch revenue measures by their very nature cannot possess the attributes that led Mr. Chief Justice Marshall to proclaim that the power to tax is the power to destroy. There is no danger that such measures will not be based on benefits conferred or that they will function as regulatory devices unduly burdening essential state activities. [A] revenue provision that forces a State to pay its own way when performing an essential function will increase the cost of the state activity. But *Graves*, and its precursors teach that an economic burden on traditional state functions without more is not a sufficient basis for sustaining a claim of immunity. [S]ince the Constitution explicitly requires States to bear similar economic burdens when engaged in essential operations, it cannot be seriously contended that federal exactions from the States of their fair share of the cost of specific benefits they receive from federal programs offend the constitutional scheme.

[Our] decisions implementing these constitutional provisions have consistently recognized that the interests protected by these Clauses are not offended by revenue measures that operate only to compensate a government for benefits supplied. [A] governmental body has an obvious interest in making those who specifically benefit from its services pay the cost and, provided that the charge is structured to compensate the government for the benefit conferred, there can be no danger of the kind of interference with constitutionally valued activity that the Clauses were designed to prohibit.

[The Commonwealth argues] that §4491 should not be treated as a user fee because the amount of the tax is a flat annual fee and hence is not directly related to the degree of use of the airways. [A] State can have no constitutional objection to a revenue measure that satisfies the three-prong test of Evansville-Vanderburgh Airport Authority v. Delta Airlines, Inc[.] [So] long as the charges do not discriminate against state functions, are based on a fair approximation of use of the system, and are structured to produce revenues that will not exceed the total cost to the Federal Government of the benefits to be supplied, there can be no substantial basis for a claim that the National Government will be using its taxing powers to control, unduly interfere with, or destroy a State's ability to perform essential services. The requirement that total revenues not exceed expenditures places a natural ceiling on the total amount that such charges may generate and the further requirement that the measure be reasonable and nondiscriminatory precludes the adoption of a charge that will unduly burden state activities.

Applying these principles to this case demonstrates that the Commonwealth's claim of constitutional immunity is particularly insubstantial. First, there is no question but that the tax imposed by §4491 is nondiscriminatory. It applies not only to private users of the airways but also to civil aircraft operated by the United States — facts which minimize, if not eliminate entirely, the basis for a conclusion that §4491 might be an abusive exercise of the taxing power. Indeed, the Revenue Act discriminates in favor of the States since it retains the States' exemption from the 7-cent-per-gallon fuel tax that applies to private noncommercial general aviation — a fact that illustrates the manner in which the political process is peculiarly adapted to the protection of state interests.

Second, the tax satisfies the requirement that it be a fair approximation of the cost of the benefits civil aircraft receive from the federal activities. . . . Congress believed that four measures, taken together, would fairly reflect some of the cost of the benefits that redound to the noncommercial general aircraft that fly in the navigable airspace of the United States: a 7-cent-per-gallon fuel tax, a 5-cent-per-pound tax on aircraft tires, a 10-cent-per-pound tax on tubes and the annual aircraft registration tax. The formula contained in these four measures taken together does not [give] weight to every factor affecting appropriate compensation for airport and airway use. A probable deficiency in the formula arises because not all aircraft make equal use of the federal navigational facilities or of the airports that have been planned or constructed with federal assistance. But the present scheme nevertheless is a fair approximation of the cost of the benefits each aircraft receives. Every aircraft that flies in the navigable airspace of the United States has available to it the navigational assistance and other special services supplied by the United States. [E]ven those aircraft [that] have never received specific services from the National Government benefit from them in the sense that the services are available for their use if needed and in that [the] services makes the airways safer for all users. The four taxes, taken together, fairly reflect the benefits received, since three are geared directly to use, whereas the fourth, the aircraft registration tax, is designed to give weight to factors affecting the level of use of the navigational facilities. A more precisely calibrated formula — which would include landing fees, charges for specific services received, and less reliance on annual flat fees [would] be administratively more costly.

It follows that a State may not complain of the application of §4491 on the ground it is not a fair approximation of use. Since the fuel tax, tire and tube tax, and annual registration fee together constitute an appropriate means of recovering the amount of the federal investment, a State, being exempt from the fuel, tire, and tube taxes, can have no constitutional objection to the application of the registration fee alone.

Finally, the tax is not excessive in relation to the cost of the Government benefits supplied. When Congress enacted the Revenue Act, it contemplated that the user fees imposed on civil aircraft would not be sufficient to cover the federal expenditures on civil aviation in any one year, and the actual experience during the first years of operation was that the revenues fell far short of covering the annual civil aviation outlays. Since the Commonwealth pays far less than private noncommercial users of the airways, there therefore is no basis for a conclusion that the application of the registration tax to the States produces revenues in excess of the costs incurred by the Federal Government.

Affirmed.

A Related Case: New York v. United States

New York v. United States, 326 U.S. 572 (1946), discussed in Massachusetts v. United States, involved a tax on mineral waters that was applied to sales by a state-owned entity. The Court upheld the tax: "[When] States sought to control the liquor traffic by going into the liquor business, they were denied immunity from federal taxes upon the liquor business. . . . We certainly see no reason for putting soft drinks in a different constitutional category from hard drinks. [We] reject limitations upon the taxing power of Congress derived from such untenable criteria as 'proprietary' against 'governmental' activities of the States, or historically sanctioned activities of Government or activities conducted merely for profit, and find no restriction upon Congress to include the States in levying a tax exacted equally from private persons upon the same subject matter." Justice Douglas dissented:

> [Can] it be that a general federal tax on the issuance of securities would be constitutional if applied to the issuance of municipal securities or of state bonds or of the securities of public utility districts organized by the States? Could the States be classified with farmers, business men, industrial workers, judges and other ordinary citizens and required to pay an income tax to the federal government? It is said that a federal income tax on the tax revenues of a State would not be sustained because such a tax would interfere with a sovereign function of the State. But can it be that a federal income tax on state revenues derived not from taxes but from the sale of mineral water, liquor, lumber and the like, would be sustained?
>
> A tax is a powerful, regulatory instrument. Local government [does] not exist for itself. The fact that local government may enter the domain of private enterprise and operate a project for profit does not put it in the class of private business enterprise for tax purposes. Local government exists to provide for the welfare of its people, not for a limited group of stockholders. If the federal government can place the local governments on its tax collector's list, their capacity to serve the needs of their citizens is at once hampered or curtailed. The field of federal excise taxation alone is practically without limits. Many state activities are in marginal enterprises where private capital refuses to venture. Add to the cost of these projects a federal tax and the social program may be destroyed before it can be launched. In any case, the repercussions of such a fundamental change on the credit of the States and on their programs to take care of the needy and to build for the future would be considerable. To say the present tax will be sustained because it does not impair the State's functions of government is to conclude either that the sale by the State of its mineral water is not a function of government or that the present tax is so slight as to be no burden. The former obviously is not true. The latter overlooks the fact that the power to tax lightly is the power to tax severely. The power to tax is indeed one of the most effective forms of regulation. And no more powerful instrument for centralization of government could be devised. For with the federal government immune and the States subject to tax, the economic ability of the federal government to expand its activities at the expense of the States is at once apparent. That is the result whether the rule of State of South Carolina v. United States be perpetuated or a new rule of discrimination be adopted.

∽ PROBLEMS ∽

1. *Additional Tax Revenues.* Congress knows that education is costly, especially improved education. To raise money for its education initiatives, such as the EBA Act, Congress is interested in finding new ways to tax. Can Congress tax the following items to raise funds to pay for the EBA Act: a) operations of state-owned utilities, b) public guided tours for tourists in state parks, c) private donations to state universities, d) soda sales from machines in state office buildings?

2. *Interest on Bonds.* Suppose the federal government wishes to tax the interest received by private parties on state and local bonds. Does it have the power to do so? What are the best arguments for each side? See Willcuts v. Bunn, 282 U.S. 216 (1931). See also Group No. 1 Oil Corporation v. Bass, 283 U.S. 279 (1931); Metcalf & Eddy v. Mitchell, 269 U.S. 514 (1926); Pollock v. Farmers' Loan & Trust Co., 157 U.S. 429 (1895).

3. *Salaries of State Employees.* The states may not tax the federal government itself, but are permitted to tax the salaries of federal employees. Since many states have decided to do so, the federal government decides to reciprocate and tax the salaries of state employees. Is this tax permissible? See Helvering v. Therrell, 303 U.S. 218 (1938); McLoughlin v. Commissioner, 303 U.S. 218 (1938).

4. *A State's Income.* Most states impose an income tax on their citizens. The receipts derived from these taxes are considered revenue to the state. In light of the issue raised by Justice Douglas in his dissent in *New York,* above, can the federal government impose a tax on a state's income from its own taxes? (Rely on the majority decision in *New York* as well as the majority opinion in *Massachusetts.*)

5. *Corporate Franchises.* The federal government also wishes to impose a tax on the privilege of exercising corporate franchises granted by a state to public service companies. Would such a tax be permissible? See Flint v. Stone Tracy Co., 220 U.S. 107 (1911).

C. STATE IMMUNITY FROM FEDERAL REGULATION

Can the federal government regulate state governments? Prior to the 1930s, few commentators would have bothered to ask such a question. At that time, the Court regarded the Tenth Amendment as a significant independent limitation on congressional power. In addition, prior to the 1930s, the Court construed the scope of federal power, particularly the power of the Commerce Clause, more restrictively. As we have seen, in decisions like Hammer v. Dagenhart, 247 U.S. 251 (1918), the Court struck down restrictions on child labor. During this period, it was highly doubtful whether Congress could regulate in such areas as the wages and hours of private-sector workers, much less the wages and hours of state workers.

In the post-1937 period, as the Court gave great deference to Congress in the use of its Commerce Clause power, federal assertions of authority expanded dramatically. In United States v. Darby, 312 U.S. 100 (1941), the Court upheld wage and hour restrictions on employees. Emboldened by these favorable decisions, Congress began to impose more and more restrictions on wages and hours. In the cases that follow, Congress has gone beyond trying to regulate the wages and hours of private employees and is directly regulating the wages and hours of state employees.

BACKGROUND
The National League of Cities

The National League of Cities (NLC) was founded in 1924 and has more than 1,600 cities, municipalities, towns, and villages as members. With headquarters in Washington, D.C., the organization works in conjunction with 49 equivalent state "league of cities" organizations. The NLC sometimes engages in litigation on behalf of its members, as the following case illustrates.

National League of Cities v. Usery
426 U.S. 833 (1976)

Mr. Justice REHNQUIST delivered the opinion of the Court.

Nearly 40 years ago Congress enacted the Fair Labor Standards Act, and required employers covered by the Act to pay their employees a minimum hourly wage and to pay them at one and one-half times their regular rate of pay for hours worked in excess of 40 during a work week. [C]overed employers were required to keep [records] to aid in the enforcement of the Act, and to comply with specified child labor standards. This Court unanimously upheld the Act as a valid exercise of congressional authority under the commerce [power].

The original Fair Labor Standards Act [specifically] excluded the States and their political subdivisions from its coverage. In 1974[,] Congress [extended] the minimum wage and maximum hour provisions to almost all public employees employed by the States and by their various political subdivisions. [The Act did make some provision for public employment relationships that are without counterpart in the private sector, such as those presented by fire protection and law enforcement personnel. Appellants] include individual cities and States, the National League of Cities[, who challenge] the validity of the 1974 amendments. . . . Their contention [is] that when Congress seeks to regulate directly the activities of States as public employers, it transgresses an affirmative limitation on the exercise of its power. . . .

[In] Lane County v. Oregon, 7 Wall. 71 (1869), [Chief Justice Chase] said: "[I]n many articles of the Constitution the necessary existence of the States, and, within their proper spheres, the independent authority of the States, is distinctly recognized." [Appellee] Secretary argues that the cases in which this Court has upheld sweeping exercises of authority by Congress [have] already curtailed the sovereignty of the States quite as much as the 1974 amendments. . . . We do not agree. It is one thing to recognize the authority of Congress to enact laws regulating individual businesses. . . . It is quite another to uphold a similar exercise of congressional authority directed [to] the States as States. [T]here are attributes of sovereignty attaching to every state government which may not be impaired by Congress, not because Congress may lack an affirmative grant of legislative authority to reach the matter, but because the Constitution prohibits it from exercising the authority in that manner. In Coyle v. Oklahoma, 221 U.S. 559 (1911), the Court gave this example of such an attribute: "The power to locate its own seat of government, and to determine when and how it shall be changed from one place to another, and to appropriate its own public funds for that purpose, are essentially and peculiarly state powers. That one of the original thirteen states could now be shorn of such powers by an act of Congress would not be for a moment entertained."

One undoubted attribute of state sovereignty is the States' power to determine the wages which shall be paid to those whom they employ in order to carry out their governmental functions, what hours those persons will work, and what compensation will be provided where these employees may be called upon to work overtime. The question we must resolve here, then, is whether these determinations are "'functions essential to separate and independent existence,'" so that Congress may not abrogate the States' otherwise plenary authority to make them.

[A]ppellants advanced estimates of substantial costs which will be imposed upon them by the 1974 amendments. . . . The Metropolitan Government of Nashville and Davidson County, Tenn., for example, asserted that the Act will increase its costs of providing essential police and fire protection, without any increase in service or in current salary levels, by $938,000 per year. Cape Girardeau, Mo., estimated that its annual budget for fire protection may have to be increased by anywhere from $250,000 to $400,000 over the current figure of $350,000. . . . California asserted that it could not comply with the overtime costs ($750,000 per year) which the Act required to be paid to California Highway Patrol cadets during their academy training program. California reported that it had thus been forced to reduce its academy training program from 2,080 hours to only 960 hours, a compromise undoubtedly of substantial importance to those whose safety and welfare may depend upon the preparedness of the California Highway Patrol. . . .

[T]he Act displaces state policies regarding the manner in which they will structure delivery of those governmental services which their citizens require. The Act, speaking directly to the States qua States, requires that they shall pay all but an extremely limited minority of their employees the minimum wage rates currently chosen by Congress. It may well be that as a matter of economic policy it would be desirable that States [comply] with these minimum wage requirements. But [the] federal requirement directly supplants the considered policy choices of the States' elected officials and administrators as to how they wish to structure pay scales in state employment. The State might wish to employ persons with little or no training, or those who wish to work on a casual basis, or those who for some other reason do not possess minimum employment requirements, and pay them less than the federally prescribed minimum wage. It may wish to offer part-time or summer employment to teenagers at a figure less than the minimum wage, and if unable to do so may decline to offer such employment at all. But the Act would forbid such choices by the States. The only "discretion" left to them under the Act is either to attempt to increase their revenue to meet the additional financial burden imposed upon them by paying congressionally prescribed wages to their existing complement of employees, or to reduce that complement to a number which can be paid the federal minimum wage without increasing revenue.

This dilemma presented by the minimum wage restrictions may seem not immediately different from that faced by private employers. . . . The difference, however, is that a State is not merely a factor in the "shifting economic arrangements" of the private sector of the economy, but is itself a coordinate element in the system established by the Framers for governing our Federal Union. . . . This congressionally imposed displacement of state decisions may substantially restructure traditional ways in which the local governments have arranged their affairs. . . . The requirement imposing premium rates upon any employment in excess of what Congress has decided is appropriate for [a] workweek [appears likely to coerce] the States to structure work periods in some employment areas, such as police and fire protection, in a manner substantially different from practices which have long been commonly accepted among local governments. . . . [The Act also requires] that the premium compensation for overtime worked must be paid in cash, rather than with compensatory time off, unless such compensatory time is taken in the same pay period. This, too, appears likely to be highly disruptive of accepted employment practices in many governmental areas where the demand for a number of employees to perform important jobs for extended periods on short notice can be both unpredictable and critical. Another example of congressional choices displacing those of the States in the area of what are without doubt essential governmental decisions may be found in the practice of using volunteer firemen, a source of manpower crucial to many of our smaller towns' existence. [P]rovisions such as these contemplate a significant reduction of traditional volunteer assistance which has been in the past drawn on to complement the operation of many local governmental functions.

Our examination of the effect of the 1974 amendments [satisfies] us that both the minimum wage and the maximum hour provisions will impermissibly interfere with the integral governmental functions of these bodies. [T]heir application [will] significantly alter or displace the States' abilities to structure employer-employee relationships in such areas as fire prevention, police protection, sanitation, public health, and parks and recreation. These activities are typical of those performed by state and local governments in discharging their dual functions of administering the public law and furnishing public services. Indeed, it is functions such as these which governments are created to provide, services such as these which the States have traditionally afforded their citizens. If Congress may withdraw from the States the authority to make those fundamental employment decisions upon which their systems for performance of these functions must rest, we think there would be little left of the States' "'separate and independent existence.'" [The] dispositive factor is that Congress has attempted to exercise its Commerce Clause authority to prescribe minimum wages and maximum hours to be paid by the States in their capacities as sovereign governments. In so doing, Congress has sought to wield its power in a fashion that would impair the States' "ability to function effectively in a federal system." This exercise of congressional authority does not comport with the federal system of government embodied in the Constitution. We hold that insofar as the challenged amendments operate to directly displace the States' freedom to structure integral operations in areas of traditional governmental functions, they are not within the authority granted Congress by Art. I, §8, cl. 3.

[T]he States as States stand on a quite different footing from an individual or a corporation when challenging the exercise of Congress' power to regulate commerce. . . . Congress may not exercise [its] power so as to force directly upon the States its choices as to how essential decisions regarding the conduct of integral governmental functions are to be made. [S]uch assertions of power if unchecked, would[,] as Mr. Justice Douglas cautioned[,] allow "the National Government [to] devour the essentials of state sovereignty," and would therefore transgress the bounds of the authority granted Congress under the Commerce Clause. . . .

The judgment of the District Court is accordingly reversed, and the cases are remanded for further proceedings consistent with this opinion.

So ordered.

Mr. Justice BRENNAN, with whom Mr. Justice WHITE and Mr. Justice MARSHALL join, dissenting.

[One hundred fifty-two] years ago Mr. Chief Justice Marshall enunciated that principle to which, until today, his successors on this Court have been faithful. "[T]he power over commerce [is] vested in Congress as absolutely as it would be in a single government, having in its constitution the same restrictions on the exercise of the power as are found in the constitution of the United States. The wisdom and the discretion of Congress, their identity with the people, and the influence which their constituents possess at elections, are [the] sole restraints on which they have relied, to secure them from its abuse. They are the restraints on which the people must often rely solely, in all representative governments." Gibbons v. Ogden, 9 Wheat. 1, 197 (1824) (emphasis added). . . . Congress is constituted of representatives in both the Senate and House Elected from the States. Decisions upon the extent of federal intervention under the Commerce Clause into the affairs of the States are in that sense decisions of the States themselves. . . .

Garcia v. San Antonio Metropolitan Transit Authority

469 U.S. 528 (1985)

Justice BLACKMUN delivered the opinion of the Court.

We revisit in these cases an issue raised in National League of Cities v. Usery. In that litigation, this Court, by a sharply divided vote, ruled that the Commerce Clause does not empower Congress to enforce the minimum-wage and overtime provisions of the Fair Labor Standards Act (FLSA) against the States "in areas of traditional governmental functions." Although *National League of Cities* supplied some examples of "traditional governmental functions," it did not offer a general explanation of how a "traditional" function is to be distinguished from a "nontraditional" one. Since then, federal and state courts have struggled with the task [of] identifying a traditional function for purposes of state immunity under the Commerce Clause. . . . In the present cases, a [lower federal court held] that municipal ownership and operation of a mass-transit system is a traditional governmental function and thus [is] exempt from [FLSA]. [Other lower courts] reached the opposite conclusion. . . . Our examination of this "function" standard applied in these and other cases over the last eight years [persuades] us that the attempt to draw the boundaries of state regulatory immunity in terms of "traditional governmental function" is not only unworkable but is also inconsistent with established principles of federalism and [with] those very federalism principles on which *National League of Cities* purported to rest. That case, accordingly, is overruled.

I

The history of public transportation in San Antonio, Tex., is characteristic of the history of local mass transit in the United States generally. Passenger transportation for hire [was] originally [provided] on a private basis [subject to governmental regulation.] [In 1959, the city] purchased [a private transit company] and replaced it with a public authority [that eventually became known as the] San Antonio Metropolitan Transit Authority (SAMTA), a public mass-transit authority organized on a countywide basis. . . .

[Under] *National League of Cities*[,] four conditions must be satisfied before a state activity may be deemed immune from a particular federal regulation under the Commerce Clause. First, [the] federal statute [must] regulate "the 'States as States.'" Second, the statute must "address matters that are indisputably 'attribute[s] of state sovereignty.'" Third, state compliance with the federal obligation must "directly impair [the States'] ability 'to structure integral operations in areas of traditional governmental functions.'" Finally, the relation of state and federal interests must not be such that "the nature of the federal interest [justifies] state submission."

The controversy in the present cases has focused on the [third] requirement — that the challenged federal statute trench on "traditional governmental functions." The District Court voiced a common concern: "Despite the abundance of adjectives, identifying which particular state functions are immune remains difficult." Just how troublesome the task has been is revealed by the results reached in other federal cases. [C]ourts have held that regulating ambulance services, licensing automobile drivers, operating a municipal airport, performing solid waste disposal, and operating a highway authority, are functions protected under *National League of Cities*. At the same time, courts have held that issuance of industrial development bonds, regulation of intrastate natural gas sales, regulation of traffic on public roads, regulation of air transportation, operation of a telephone system, leasing and sale of natural gas, operation of a mental health facility, and provision of in-house domestic services for the aged and handicapped, are not entitled to immunity. We find it difficult, if not impossible, to identify an organizing principle that places each of the cases in the first group on one side of a line and each of the cases in the second group on the other side. The constitutional distinction [is] elusive. . . .

[T]his Court itself has made little headway in defining the scope of the governmental functions deemed protected under *National League of Cities*. [That case] set forth examples of protected and unprotected functions, but provided no explanation of how those examples were identified. [It] might be fair to [assume] that case-by-case development would lead to a workable standard for [resolving this issue. A] cautionary note is sounded, however, by the Court's experience in the related field of state immunity from federal taxation. In South Carolina v. United States, 199 U.S. 437 (1905), the Court held [that] the state tax immunity [extended] only to the "ordinary" and "strictly governmental" instrumentalities of state governments and not to instrumentalities "used by the State in the carrying on of an ordinary private business." While the Court applied [this distinction] for the following 40 years, at no time [did] the Court develop a consistent formulation of the kinds of governmental functions that were entitled to immunity. [T]hese tax-immunity [attempted] to distinguish between "governmental" and "proprietary" functions. To say that the distinction [proved] to be stable [would be] an overstatement. In 1911, [the] Court declared that [a] municipal water supply "is no part of the essential governmental functions of a State." [Later, the Court] decided that the provision of a municipal water supply was immune from federal taxation as an essential governmental function, even though municipal water-works long had been operated for profit by private industry. . . . It was this uncertainty and instability that led the Court[,] in New York v. United States, 326 U.S. 572 (1946), [to] conclude that the distinction between "governmental" and "proprietary" functions was "untenable" and must be abandoned. . . .

The distinction the Court discarded as unworkable in the field of tax immunity has proved no more fruitful in the field of regulatory immunity under the Commerce Clause. Neither do any of the alternative standards [appear] manageable. We rejected the possibility of making immunity turn on [a] standard of "tradition[."] The most obvious defect of a historical approach [is] that it prevents a court from accommodating changes in the historical functions of States, changes that have resulted in a number of once-private functions like education being assumed by the States. [T]he only apparent virtue of a rigorous historical standard, namely, its promise of a reasonably objective measure for state immunity, is illusory. Reliance on history as an organizing principle results in line-drawing of the most arbitrary sort; the genesis of state governmental functions stretches over a historical continuum from before the Revolution to the present, and courts would have to decide [how] longstanding a pattern of state involvement had to be for federal regulatory authority to be defeated.

A nonhistorical standard for selecting immune governmental functions is likely to be just as unworkable. . . . The goal of identifying "uniquely" governmental functions, for example, has been rejected by the Court in the field of governmental tort liability in part because the notion of a "uniquely" governmental function is unmanageable. Another possibility would be to confine immunity to "necessary" governmental services, that is, services that would be provided inadequately or not at all unless the government provided them. The set of services that fits into this category, however, may well be negligible. The fact that an unregulated market produces less of some service than a State deems desirable does not mean that the State itself must provide the service; in most if not all cases, the State can "contract out" by hiring private firms to provide the service or simply by providing subsidies to existing suppliers. It also is open to question how well equipped courts are to make this kind of determination about the workings of economic markets.

[T]here is a more fundamental problem [that] explains why the Court was never able to provide a basis for the governmental-proprietary distinction [and] why an attempt to draw [such] distinctions [is] unlikely to succeed. . . . The problem is that neither the governmental-proprietary distinction nor any other that purports to separate out important governmental functions can be faithful to the role of federalism in a democratic society. The essence of our federal system is that within the realm of authority left open to them under the Constitution, the States must be equally free to engage in any activity that their citizens choose for the common weal, no matter how unorthodox or unnecessary anyone else [deems] state involvement to be. Any rule [that] looks to the "traditional," "integral," or "necessary" nature of governmental functions inevitably invites an unelected federal judiciary to make decisions about which state policies it favors and which ones it dislikes. "The science of government [is] the science of experiment," and the States cannot serve as laboratories for social and economic experiment, if they must pay an added price when they [meet] changing needs [by] taking up functions that an earlier day and a different society left in private hands. In the words of Justice Black: "There is not, and there cannot be, any unchanging line of demarcation between essential and non-essential governmental functions. Many governmental functions of today have at some time in the past been non-governmental. The genius of our government provides that, within the sphere of constitutional action, the people — acting not through the courts but through their elected legislative representatives — have the power to determine as conditions demand, what services and functions the public welfare requires." Helvering v. Gerhardt, 304 U.S., at 427 (concurring opinion).

We therefore now reject, as unsound in principle and unworkable in practice, a rule of state immunity from federal regulation that turns on a judicial appraisal of whether a particular governmental function is "integral" or "traditional." Any such rule leads to inconsistent results at the same time that it disserves principles of democratic self-governance, and it breeds inconsistency precisely because it is divorced from those principles. If there are to be limits on the Federal Government's power to interfere with state functions[,] we must look elsewhere to find them. . . . The central theme of *National League of Cities* was that the States occupy a special position in our constitutional system and that the scope of Congress' authority under the Commerce Clause must reflect that position. . . . *National League of Cities* reflected the general conviction that the Constitution precludes "the National Government [from] devour[ing] the essentials of state sovereignty." In order to be faithful to the underlying federal premises of the Constitution, courts must look for the "postulates which limit and control."

What has proved problematic is not the perception that the Constitution's federal structure imposes limitations on the Commerce Clause, but rather the nature and content of those limitations. One approach to defining the limits on Congress' authority to regulate the States under the Commerce Clause is to identify certain underlying elements of political sovereignty that are deemed essential to the States' "separate and independent existence." This approach obviously underlay the Court's use of the "traditional governmental function" concept. . . . It also has led to the separate requirement that the challenged federal statute "address matters that are indisputably 'attribute[s] of state sovereignty.'" In *National League of Cities* itself, for example, the Court concluded that decisions by a State concerning the wages and hours of its employees are an "undoubted attribute of state sovereignty." The opinion did not explain what aspects of such decisions made them such an "undoubted attribute," and the Court since then has remarked on the uncertain scope of the concept. . . .

We doubt that courts ultimately can identify principled constitutional limitations on the scope of Congress' Commerce Clause powers over the States merely by relying on a priori definitions of state sovereignty. In part, this is because of the elusiveness of objective criteria for "fundamental" elements of state sovereignty, a problem we have witnessed in the search for "traditional governmental functions." There is, however, a more fundamental reason: the sovereignty of the States is limited by the Constitution itself. A variety of sovereign powers, for example, are withdrawn from the States by Article I, §10. Section 8 of the same Article works an equally sharp contraction of state sovereignty by authorizing Congress to exercise a wide range of legislative powers and (in conjunction with the Supremacy Clause of Article VI) to displace contrary state legislation. By providing for final review of questions of federal law in this Court, Article III curtails the sovereign power of the States' judiciaries to make authoritative determinations of law. Finally, the developed application, through the Fourteenth Amendment, of the greater part of the Bill of Rights to the States limits the sovereign authority that States otherwise would possess to legislate with respect to their citizens and to conduct their own affairs.

The States unquestionably do "retai[n] a significant measure of sovereign authority." They do so, however, only to the extent that the Constitution has not divested them of their original powers and transferred those powers to the Federal Government. [T]o say that the Constitution assumes the continued role of the States is to say little about the nature of that role. . . . With rare exceptions, like the guarantee, in Article IV, §3, of state territorial integrity, the Constitution does not carve out express elements of state sovereignty that Congress may not employ its delegated powers to displace. [The] fact that the States remain sovereign as to all powers not vested in Congress or denied them by the Constitution offers no guidance about where the frontier between state and federal power lies. . . .

When we look for the States' "residuary and inviolable sovereignty," in the shape of the constitutional scheme[,] a different measure of state sovereignty emerges. Apart from the limitation on federal authority inherent in the delegated nature of Congress' Article I powers, the principal means chosen by the Framers to ensure the role of the States in the federal system lies in the structure of the Federal Government itself. [T]he Federal Government was designed in large part to protect the States from overreaching by Congress. The Framers thus gave the States a role in the selection both of the Executive and the Legislative Branches of the Federal Government. The States were vested with indirect influence over the House of Representatives and the Presidency by their control of electoral qualifications and their role in Presidential elections. They were given more direct influence in the Senate, where each State received equal representation and each Senator was to be selected by the legislature of his State. The significance attached to the States' equal representation in the Senate is underscored by the prohibition of any constitutional amendment divesting a State of equal representation without the State's consent. . . . James Madison explained that the Federal Government "will partake sufficiently of the spirit [of the States], to be disinclined to invade the rights of the individual States, or the prerogatives of their governments." . . .

The effectiveness of the federal political process in preserving the States' interests is apparent even today in the course of federal legislation. [T]he States have been able to direct a substantial proportion of federal revenues into their own treasuries in the form of general and program-specific grants in aid. . . . In the past quarter-century[,] federal grants to States and localities have grown from $7 billion to $96 billion. . . . The States have obtained federal funding for such services as police and fire protection, education, public health and hospitals, parks and recreation, and sanitation. Moreover, at the same time[,] the States have [been] able to exempt themselves from a wide variety of obligations imposed by Congress under the Commerce Clause. For example, the Federal Power Act, the National Labor Relations Act, the Labor-Management Reporting and Disclosure Act, the Occupational Safety and Health Act, the Employee Retirement Income Security Act, and the Sherman Act all contain express or implied exemptions for States and their subdivisions. [A]gainst this background, we are convinced that the fundamental limitation that the constitutional scheme imposes on the Commerce Clause to protect the "States as States" is one of process rather than one of result. Any substantive restraint on the exercise of Commerce Clause powers must find its justification in the procedural nature of this basic limitation, and it must be tailored to compensate for possible failings in the national political process rather than to dictate a "sacred province of state autonomy."

Insofar as the present cases are concerned, [we] need go no further than to state that we perceive nothing in the overtime and minimum-wage requirements of the FLSA [that] is destructive of state sovereignty or violative of any constitutional provision. [T]he status of public mass transit simply underscores the extent to which the structural protections of the Constitution insulate the States from federally imposed burdens. When Congress first subjected state mass-transit systems to FLSA obligations[,] and when it expanded those obligations[,] it simultaneously provided extensive funding for state and local mass transit through UMTA. . . . Congress has not simply placed a financial burden on the shoulders of States and localities that operate mass-transit systems, but has provided substantial countervailing financial assistance [that] may leave individual mass-transit systems better off than they would have been had Congress never intervened [in] the area. Congress's treatment of public mass transit reinforces our conviction that the national political process systematically protects States from the risk of having their functions in that area handicapped by Commerce Clause regulation. [I]n affording SAMTA employees the protections of the wage and hour provisions of the FLSA contravened no affirmative limit on Congress's power under the Commerce Clause. . . .

[W]e continue to recognize that the States occupy a special and specific position in our constitutional system and that the scope of Congress' authority under the Commerce Clause must reflect that position. But the principal and basic limit on the federal commerce power is that inherent in all congressional action — the built-in restraints that our system provides through state participation in federal governmental action. The political process ensures that laws that unduly burden the States will not be promulgated. In [these] cases the internal safeguards of the political process have performed as intended. . . .

We do not lightly overrule recent precedent. We have not hesitated, however, when it has become apparent that a prior decision has departed from a proper understanding of congressional power under the Commerce Clause. Due respect for the reach of congressional power within the federal system mandates that we do so now. . . . National League of Cities v. Usery is overruled. The judgment of the District Court is reversed, and these cases are remanded to that court for further proceedings consistent with this opinion.

It is so ordered.

Justice POWELL, with whom THE CHIEF JUSTICE, Justice REHNQUIST, and Justice O'CONNOR join, dissenting.

[T]oday's decision effectively reduces the Tenth Amendment to meaningless rhetoric when Congress acts pursuant to the Commerce Clause. [Today's] opinion does not explain how the States' role in the electoral process guarantees that particular exercises of the Commerce Clause power will not infringe on residual state sovereignty. Members of Congress are elected from the various States, but once in office they are Members of the Federal Government. Although the States participate in the Electoral College, this is hardly a reason to view the President as a representative of the States' interest against federal encroachment. . . . The Court apparently thinks that the State's success at obtaining federal funds for various projects and exemptions from the obligations of some federal statutes is indicative of the "effectiveness of the federal political process in preserving the

States' [interests]." [The] fact that Congress generally does not transgress constitutional limits on its power to reach state activities does not make judicial review
any less necessary. . . . The States' role in our system of government is a matter of
constitutional law, not of legislative grace. . . .

More troubling than the logical infirmities in the Court's reasoning is the
result of its holding, i.e., that federal political officials, invoking the Commerce
Clause, are the sole judges of the limits of their own power. This result is inconsistent with the fundamental principles of our constitutional system. At least since
Marbury, it has been the settled province of the federal judiciary "to say what the
law is" with respect to the constitutionality of Acts of Congress. . . .

[Much] of the initial opposition to the Constitution was rooted in the fear
that the National Government would be too powerful and eventually would eliminate the States as viable political entities. This concern was voiced repeatedly
until proponents of the Constitution made assurances that a Bill of Rights,
including a provision explicitly reserving powers in the States, would be among
the first business of the new Congress. . . . So strong was the concern that the proposed Constitution was seriously defective without a specific bill of rights, including a provision reserving powers to the States, that in order to secure the votes for
ratification, the Federalists eventually conceded that such provisions were necessary. [The] Bill of Rights were proposed and adopted early in the first session of
the First Congress.

[The] Framers believed that the separate sphere of sovereignty reserved to
the States would ensure that the States would serve as an effective "counterpoise"
to the power of the Federal Government. [T]the harm to the States that results
from federal overreaching under the Commerce Clause is not simply a matter of
dollars and cents. [B]y usurping functions traditionally performed by the States,
federal overreaching under the Commerce Clause undermines the constitutionally mandated balance of power between the States and the Federal Government,
a balance designed to protect our fundamental liberties. . . .

[T]he Court today propounds a view of federalism that pays only lipservice
to the role of the States. Although it says that the States "unquestionably do
'retai[n] a significant measure of sovereign authority,'" it fails to recognize the
broad, yet specific areas of sovereignty that the Framers intended the States to
retain. [T]he Court barely acknowledges that the Tenth Amendment exists[and
recasts it] to say that the States retain their sovereign powers "only to the extent
that the Constitution has not divested them of their original powers and transferred those powers to the Federal Government." This rephrasing [reflects] the
Court's unprecedented view that Congress is free under the Commerce Clause to
assume a State's traditional sovereign power, and to do so without judicial review
of its action. [T]he Court's view of federalism appears to relegate the States to
precisely the trivial role that opponents of the Constitution feared. . . .

In *National League of Cities*, we spoke of fire prevention, police protection,
sanitation, and public health as "typical of [the services] performed by state and
local governments in discharging their dual functions of administering the public law and furnishing public services." Not only are these activities remote from

any normal concept of interstate commerce, they are also activities that epitomize the concerns of local, democratic self-government. In emphasizing the need to protect traditional governmental functions, we identified the kinds of activities engaged in by state and local governments that affect the everyday lives of citizens. These are services that people are in a position to understand and evaluate, and in a democracy, have the right to oversee. We recognized that "it is functions such as these which governments are created to [provide]" and that the States and local governments are better able than the National Government to perform them.

The Court maintains that the standard approved in *National League of Cities* "disserves principles of democratic self-governance." In reaching this conclusion, the Court looks myopically only to persons elected to positions in the Federal Government. It disregards entirely the far more effective role of democratic self-government at the state and local levels. . . . The administration and enforcement of federal laws and regulations necessarily are largely in the hands of staff and civil service employees. [M]embers of the immense federal bureaucracy are not elected, know less about the services traditionally rendered by States and localities, and are inevitably less responsive to recipients of such services, than are state legislatures, city councils, boards of supervisors, and state and local commissions, boards, and agencies. It is at these state and local levels — not in Washington[—]that "democratic self-government" is best exemplified.

[In] overruling *National League of Cities*, today's opinion apparently authorizes federal control [over] the terms and conditions of employment of all state and local employees. . . . The Court's action reflects a serious misunderstanding, if not an outright rejection, of the history of our country and the intention of the Framers of the Constitution. [Although] the Court's opinion purports to recognize that the States retain some sovereign power, it does not identify even a single aspect of state authority that would remain when the Commerce Clause is invoked to justify federal regulation. . . . As I view the Court's decision today as rejecting the basic precepts of our federal system and limiting the constitutional role of judicial review, I dissent.

Justice O'CONNOR, with whom Justice POWELL and Justice REHNQUIST join, dissenting.

[The] true "essence" of federalism is that the States as States have legitimate interests which the National Government is bound to respect even though its laws are supreme. If federalism [is] to remain meaningful, this Court cannot abdicate its constitutional responsibility to oversee the Federal Government's compliance with its duty to respect the legitimate interests of the States.

[T]he Framers of our Constitution intended Congress to have sufficient power to address national problems. [They] also envisioned a republic whose vitality was assured by the diffusion of power not only among the branches of the Federal Government, but also between the Federal Government and the States. In the 18th century these intentions did not conflict because technology had not yet converted every local problem into a national one. A conflict has now emerged, and the Court today retreats rather than reconcile the Constitution's dual concerns for federalism and an effective commerce power.

[The] Framers perceived the interstate commerce power to be important but limited, and expected that it would be used primarily if not exclusively to remove interstate tariffs and to regulate maritime affairs and large-scale mercantile enterprise. This perception [suggests why] the Framers could believe the Constitution assured significant state authority even as it bestowed a range of powers, including the commerce power, on the Congress. In an era when interstate commerce represented a tiny fraction of economic activity and most goods and services were produced and consumed close to home, the interstate commerce power left a broad range of activities beyond the reach of Congress.

In the decades since ratification of the Constitution, interstate economic activity has steadily expanded. Industrialization, coupled with advances in transportation and communications, has created a national economy in which virtually every activity occurring within the borders of a State plays a part. . . . This Court has been increasingly generous in its interpretation of the commerce power of Congress, primarily to assure that the National Government would be able to deal with national economic problems. . . . Because virtually every state activity, like virtually every activity of a private individual, arguably "affects" interstate commerce, [t]here is now a real risk that Congress will gradually erase the diffusion of power between State and Nation on which the Framers based their faith in the efficiency and vitality of our Republic. . . .

[The] spirit of the Tenth Amendment [is] that the States [retain] their integrity in a system in which the laws of the United States are nevertheless supreme. . . . It is not enough that the "end be legitimate"; the means to that end chosen by Congress must not contravene the spirit of the Constitution. . . . For example, Congress might rationally conclude that the location a State chooses for its capital may affect interstate commerce, but [Congress] would nevertheless be barred from dictating that location because such an exercise of a delegated power would undermine the state sovereignty inherent in the Tenth Amendment. . . . Similarly, Congress in the exercise of its taxing and spending powers can protect federal savings and loan associations, but if it chooses to do so [by] converting quasi-public state savings and loan associations into federal associations, [it] contravenes the reserved powers of the States because the conversion is not a reasonably necessary exercise of power to reach the desired end. [S]tate autonomy is a relevant factor in assessing the means by which Congress exercises its powers.

This principle requires the Court to enforce affirmative limits on federal regulation of the States to complement the judicially crafted expansion of the interstate commerce power. *National League of Cities* represented an attempt to define such limits. The Court today [washes] its hands of all efforts to protect the States. In the process, the Court opines that unwarranted federal encroachments on state authority [will] remain "horrible possibilities that never happen in the real world." There is ample reason to believe to the contrary. . . . The last two decades have seen an unprecedented growth of federal regulatory activity.

[R]ecently the Federal Government has, with this Court's blessing, undertaken to tell the States the age at which they can retire their law enforcement officers, and the regulatory standards, procedures, and even the agenda which their utilities commissions must consider and follow. The political process has not protected against these encroachments on state activities, even though they directly impinge on a State's ability to make and enforce its laws. With the abandonment of *National League of Cities*, all that stands between the remaining essentials of state sovereignty and Congress is the latter's underdeveloped capacity for self-restraint.

[A] proper resolution [lies] in weighing state autonomy as a factor in the balance when interpreting the means by which Congress can exercise its authority on the States as States. It is insufficient [to] ask only whether the same regulation would be valid if enforced against a private party. That reasoning [is] inconsistent with the spirit of our Constitution. It remains relevant that a State is being regulated. [T]he autonomy of a State is an essential component of federalism. . . .

It has been difficult for this Court to craft bright lines defining the scope of the state autonomy. . . . Such difficulty is to be expected whenever constitutional concerns as important as federalism and the effectiveness of the commerce power come into conflict. Regardless of the difficulty, it [remains] the duty of this Court to reconcile these concerns in the final instance. [I] would not shirk the duty. . . .

I respectfully dissent.

◇ PROBLEMS ◇

1. *All In.* Congress enacts a law after *Garcia* that includes the following provision: "All state or local employees are subject to the FLSA, including fire protection personnel, police employees, state legislators, and judges." The law notes Justice Powell's dissent, particularly where he stated, "today's opinion apparently authorizes federal control [over] the terms and conditions of employment of all state and local employees." Is the law constitutional?

2. *Capital Relocation Program.* Suppose that Congress decides that the location a state has chosen for its state capital negatively affects interstate commerce (by affecting how far people have to drive). Can Congress dictate a change in the state capital's location? Would the political process solve this problem?

3. *Mandatory Retirement Age.* After *Garcia*, Congress imposes a mandatory retirement age for all law enforcement officers, including those employed by states and their subdivisions. Is this law constitutional?

4. *Teacher Pay.* To ensure that the teaching profession attracts highly qualified applicants, Congress considers adding a rider to the Education for a Better America Act, requiring all public school teachers in the United States to be paid equal to or more than a special wage scale correlated to the highest paying professions, accounting for experience, educational advancement, and success of students on standardized tests. Would such a requirement be constitutional? Would the requirement be good policy? Explain your conclusions.

D. FEDERAL COMMANDEERING OF STATE RESOURCES

Since Congress has broad regulatory power, including the power to regulate the states, can it tell the states which laws to enact? Consider the following case.

New York v. United States
505 U.S. 144 (1992)

Justice O'CONNOR delivered the opinion of the Court.

[W]e address the constitutionality of three provisions of the Low-Level Radioactive Waste Policy Amendments Act of 1985. The constitutional question [consists] of discerning the proper division of authority between the Federal Government and the States. We conclude that while Congress has substantial power under the Constitution to encourage the States to provide for the disposal of the radioactive waste generated within their borders, the Constitution does not confer upon Congress the ability simply to compel the States to do so. We therefore find that only two of the Act's three provisions at issue are consistent with the Constitution's allocation of power to the Federal Government.

I

We live in a world full of low level radioactive waste. Radioactive material is present in luminous watch dials, smoke alarms, measurement devices, medical fluids, research materials, and the protective gear and construction materials used by workers at nuclear power plants. Low level radioactive waste is generated by the Government, by hospitals, by research institutions, and by various industries. The waste must be isolated from humans for long periods of time, often for hundreds of years. Millions of cubic feet of low level radioactive waste must be disposed of each year.

[Although there were five sites for disposal of low-level radioactive waste in the early 1970s, only three remained in existence by 1979. The problem reached crisis proportions when two of those sites shut down temporarily and then announced plans to close permanently, and the state with the only remaining site (South Carolina) announced a 50 percent reduction in the quantity of waste that would be accepted.] Faced with the possibility that the Nation would be left with no disposal sites[,] Congress [enacted] the Low-Level Radioactive Waste Policy Act. . . . Congress declared a federal policy of holding each State "responsible for providing for the availability of capacity either within or outside the State for the disposal of low-level radioactive waste generated within its borders," and found that such waste could be disposed of "most safely and efficiently [on] a regional basis." The 1980 Act authorized States to enter into regional compacts that, once ratified by Congress, would have the authority beginning [to] restrict the use of their disposal facilities to waste generated within member States. [There were] no penalties for States that failed to participate in this plan.

By 1985, only three approved regional compacts had operational disposal facilities. . . . The following year, the 1980 Act would have given these three compacts the ability to exclude waste from nonmembers, and the remaining 31 States would have had no assured outlet for their low level radioactive waste. With this prospect looming, Congress [passed] the Low-Level Radioactive Waste Policy Amendments Act of 1985 [which embodied] a compromise. . . . The sited States agreed to extend for seven years the period in which they would accept low level radioactive waste from other States. In exchange, the unsited States agreed to end their reliance on the sited States by 1992.

[The] Act directs: "Each State shall be responsible for providing, either by itself or in cooperation with other States, for the disposal [of] low-level radioactive waste generated within the State," with the exception of certain waste generated by the Federal Government. The Act authorizes States to "enter into such [interstate] compacts as may be necessary to provide for the establishment and operation of regional disposal facilities for low-level radioactive waste." For an additional seven years beyond the period contemplated by the 1980 Act, from the beginning of 1986 through the end of 1992, the three existing disposal sites "shall make disposal capacity available for low-level radioactive waste generated by any source," with certain exceptions not relevant here. But the three States in which the disposal sites are located are permitted to exact a graduated surcharge for waste arriving from outside the regional compact. After the 7-year transition period expires, approved regional compacts may exclude radioactive waste generated outside the region.

The Act provides three types of incentives to encourage the States to comply with their statutory obligation to provide for the disposal of waste generated within their borders.

1. *Monetary incentives.* One quarter of the surcharges collected by the sited States must be transferred to an escrow account held by the Secretary of Energy. The Secretary then makes payments from this account to each State that has complied with a series of deadlines. By July 1, 1986, each State was to have ratified legislation either joining a regional compact or indicating an intent to develop a disposal facility within the State. By January 1, 1988, each unsited compact was to have identified the State in which its facility would be located, and each compact or stand-alone State was to have developed a siting plan and taken other identified steps. By January 1, 1990, each State or compact was to have filed a complete application for a license to operate a disposal facility, or the Governor of any State that had not filed an application was to have certified that the State would be capable of disposing of all waste generated in the State after 1992. The rest of the account is to be paid out to those States or compacts able to dispose of all low level radioactive waste generated within their borders by January 1, 1993. Each State that has not met the 1993 deadline must either take title to the waste generated within its borders or forfeit to the waste generators the incentive payments it has received.

2. *Access incentives.* The second type of incentive involves the denial of access to disposal sites. States that fail to meet the July 1986 deadline may be charged twice the ordinary surcharge for the remainder of 1986 and may be denied access to disposal facilities thereafter. States that fail to meet the 1988 deadline may be charged double surcharges for the first half of 1988 and quadruple surcharges for

the second half of 1988, and may be denied access thereafter. States that fail to meet the 1990 deadline may be denied access. Finally, States that have not filed complete applications by January 1, 1992, for a license to operate a disposal facility, or States belonging to compacts that have not filed such applications, may be charged triple surcharges.

3. *The take title provision.* The third type of incentive is the most severe. The Act provides:

> If a State (or, where applicable, a compact region) in which low-level radioactive waste is generated is unable to provide for the disposal of all such waste generated within such State or compact region by January 1, 1996, each State in which such waste is generated, upon the request of the generator or owner of the waste, shall take title to the waste, be obligated to take possession of the waste, and shall be liable for all damages directly or indirectly incurred by such generator or owner as a consequence of the failure of the State to take possession of the waste as soon after January 1, 1996, as the generator or owner notifies the State that the waste is available for shipment.

These three incentives are the focus of petitioners' constitutional challenge.

In the seven years since the Act took effect, Congress has approved nine regional compacts, encompassing 42 of the States. . . . New York, a State whose residents generate a relatively large share of the Nation's low level radioactive waste, did not join a regional compact. [New York] complied with the Act's requirements by enacting legislation providing for the siting and financing of a disposal facility in New York, [and it identified five potential sites, but never developed them]. Instead, the State of New York and the two counties filed this suit. . . . Petitioners [claim] that the Act is inconsistent with the Tenth Amendment and the Guarantee Clause.

II

[T]he constitutional line between federal and state power has given rise to many of the Court's most difficult [cases]. In some cases the Court has inquired whether an Act of Congress is authorized by one of the powers delegated to Congress in Article I of the Constitution. In other cases the Court has sought to determine whether an Act of Congress invades the province of state sovereignty reserved by the Tenth Amendment. In a case like these, [the] two inquiries are mirror images of each other. If a power is delegated to Congress in the Constitution, the Tenth Amendment expressly disclaims any reservation of that power to the States; if a power is an attribute of state sovereignty reserved by the Tenth Amendment, it is necessarily a power the Constitution has not conferred on Congress. . . . It is in this sense that the Tenth Amendment "states but a truism that all is retained which has not been surrendered." United States v. Darby, 312 U.S. 100 (1941). . . . Congress exercises its conferred powers subject to the limitations contained in the Constitution. . . .

Petitioners do not contend that Congress lacks the power to regulate the disposal of low level radioactive waste. Space in radioactive waste disposal sites is frequently sold by residents of one State to residents of another. Regulation of the resulting interstate market in waste disposal is therefore well within Congress' authority under the Commerce Clause. *Cf.* Philadelphia v. New Jersey, 437 U.S. 617 (1978). Petitioners likewise do not dispute that under the Supremacy Clause Congress could, if it wished, pre-empt state radioactive waste regulation. Petitioners contend only that the Tenth Amendment limits the power of Congress to [direct] the States to regulate in this field.

Most of our recent cases interpreting the Tenth Amendment have concerned the authority of Congress to subject state governments to generally applicable laws. . . . This litigation instead concerns [whether] Congress may direct or otherwise motivate the States to regulate in a particular field or a particular way. . . . As an initial matter, Congress may not simply "commandee[r] the legislative processes of the States by directly compelling them to enact and enforce a federal regulatory program." Hodel v. Virginia Surface Mining & Reclamation Assn., Inc., 452 U.S. 264 (1981). . . . While Congress has substantial powers to govern the Nation directly, [the] Constitution has never been understood to confer upon Congress the ability to require the States to govern according to Congress's instructions. . . . Texas v. White, 7 Wall. 700, 19 L.Ed. 227 (1869). . . .

This is not to say that Congress lacks the ability to encourage a State to regulate in a particular way, or that Congress may not hold out incentives to the States as a method of influencing a State's policy choices. Our cases have identified a variety of methods, short of outright coercion, by which Congress may urge a State to adopt a legislative program consistent with federal interests. . . . First, under Congress' spending power, "Congress may attach conditions on the receipt of federal funds." South Dakota v. Dole, 483 U.S., at 206. [The] conditions attached to the funds by Congress may influence a State's legislative choices. . . . Second, where Congress has the authority to regulate private activity under the Commerce Clause, we have recognized Congress' power to offer States the choice of regulating that activity according to federal standards or having state law pre-empted by federal regulation. Hodel v. Virginia Surface Mining & Reclamation Assn., Inc., *supra*. [This "program] of cooperative federalism," is replicated in numerous federal statutory schemes [including] the Clean Water Act, [and] the Occupational Safety and Health Act of 1970.

By either of these methods, [the] residents of the State retain the ultimate decision as to whether or not the State will comply. If a State's citizens view federal policy as sufficiently contrary to local interests, they may elect to decline a federal grant. If state residents would prefer their government to devote its attention and resources to problems other than those deemed important by Congress, they may choose to have the Federal Government rather than the State bear the expense of a federally mandated regulatory program, and they may continue to supplement that program to the extent state law is not pre-empted. Where Congress encourages state regulation rather than compelling it, state governments remain responsive to the local electorate's preferences; state officials remain accountable to the people.

By contrast, where the Federal Government compels States to regulate, the accountability of both state and federal officials is diminished. If the citizens of New York, for example, do not consider that making provision for the disposal of radioactive waste is in their best interest, they may elect state officials who share their view. That view can always be pre-empted under the Supremacy Clause if it is contrary to the national view, but in such a case it is the Federal Government that makes the decision in full view of the public, and it will be federal officials that suffer the consequences if the decision turns out to be detrimental or unpopular. But where the Federal Government directs the States to regulate, it may be state officials who will bear the brunt of public disapproval, while the federal officials who devised the regulatory program may remain insulated from the electoral ramifications of their decision. Accountability is thus diminished when, due to federal coercion, elected state officials cannot regulate in accordance with the views of the local electorate in matters not pre-empted by federal regulation. . . .

III

[We] decline petitioners' invitation to construe §2021c(a)(1)(A), alone and in isolation, as a command to the States independent of the remainder of the Act. Construed as a whole, the Act comprises three sets of "incentives" for the States to provide for the disposal of low level radioactive waste generated within their borders. We consider each in turn.

The first set of incentives works in three steps. First, Congress has authorized States with disposal sites to impose a surcharge on radioactive waste received from other States. Second, the Secretary of Energy collects a portion of this surcharge and places the money in an escrow account. Third, States achieving a series of milestones receive portions of this fund.

The first of these steps is an unexceptionable exercise of Congress' power to authorize the States to burden interstate commerce. While the Commerce Clause has long been understood to limit the States' ability to discriminate against interstate commerce, that limit may be lifted, as it has been here, by an expression of the "unambiguous intent" of Congress. . . . The second step, the Secretary's collection of a percentage of the surcharge, is no more than a federal tax on interstate commerce, which petitioners do not claim to be an invalid exercise of either Congress' commerce or taxing power. *Cf.* Steward Machine Co. v. Davis, 301 U.S. 548 (1937). . . . The third step is a conditional exercise of Congress' authority under the Spending Clause: Congress has placed conditions — the achievement of the milestones — on the receipt of federal funds. Petitioners do not contend that Congress has exceeded its authority in any of the four respects our cases have identified. *See generally* South Dakota v. Dole, 483 U.S., at 207-208. . . .

Petitioners contend nevertheless that the *form* of these expenditures removes them from the scope of Congress' spending power. . . . Petitioners argue that because the money collected and redisbursed to the States is kept in an account separate from the general treasury, because the Secretary holds the funds only as a trustee, and because the States themselves are largely able to control whether they will pay into the escrow account or receive a share, the Act "in no manner calls for the spending of federal funds." [A] great deal of federal spending comes from segregated trust funds collected and spent for a particular purpose. *See, e.g.,* 23 U.S.C. §118 (Highway Trust Fund). The Spending Clause has never been construed to deprive Congress of the power to structure federal spending in this manner. . . . The Act's first set of incentives, in which Congress has conditioned grants to the States upon the States' attainment of a series of milestones, is thus well within the authority of Congress under the Commerce and Spending Clauses. Because the first set of incentives is supported by affirmative constitutional grants of power to Congress, it is not inconsistent with the Tenth Amendment.

In the second set of incentives, Congress has authorized States and regional compacts with disposal sites gradually to increase the cost of access to the sites, and then to deny access altogether, to radioactive waste generated in States that do not meet federal deadlines. [T]his provision would be within the power of Congress to authorize the States to discriminate against interstate commerce. Where federal regulation of private activity is within the scope of the Commerce Clause, we have recognized the ability of Congress to offer States the choice of regulating that activity according to federal standards or having state law pre-empted by federal regulation. *See* Hodel v. Virginia Surface Mining & Reclamation Assn., Inc., 452 U.S., at 288. . . . The affected States are not compelled by Congress to regulate, because any burden caused by a State's refusal to regulate will fall on those who generate waste and find no outlet for its disposal, rather than on the State as a sovereign. A State whose citizens do not wish it to attain the Act's milestones may devote its attention and its resources to issues its citizens deem more worthy; the choice remains at all times with the residents of the State, not with Congress. [T]he State may continue to regulate the generation and disposal of radioactive waste in any manner its citizens see fit. . . . The Act's second set of incentives thus represents a conditional exercise of Congress' commerce power, along the lines of those we have held to be within Congress' authority. As a result, the second set of incentives does not intrude on the sovereignty reserved to the States by the Tenth Amendment.

The take title provision is of a different character. . . . In this provision, Congress has crossed the line distinguishing encouragement from coercion. . . . The take title provision offers state governments a "choice" of either accepting ownership of waste or regulating according to the instructions of Congress. [T]he Constitution would not permit Congress simply to transfer radioactive waste from generators to state governments. . . . The same is true of the provision requiring the States to become liable for the generators' damages. . . . Either type of federal action would "commandeer" state governments into the service of federal regulatory purposes, and would for this reason be inconsistent with the Constitution's division of authority between federal and state governments. On the other hand, the second alternative held out to state governments—regulating pursuant to Congress' direction—would, standing alone, present a simple command to state governments to implement legislation enacted by Congress. [T]he Constitution does not empower Congress to subject state governments to this type of instruction. [I]t follows that Congress lacks the power to offer the States a choice between the two. . . . A choice between two unconstitutionally coercive regulatory techniques is no choice at all. Either way, "the Act commandeers the legislative processes of the States by directly compelling them to enact and enforce a federal regulatory program," an outcome that has never been understood to lie within the authority conferred upon Congress by the Constitution. . . . Whether one views the take title provision as lying outside Congress' enumerated powers, or as infringing upon the core of state sovereignty reserved by the Tenth Amendment, the provision is inconsistent with the federal structure of our Government established by the Constitution.

IV

[The] United States proposes three alternative views of the constitutional line separating state and federal authority. . . . First, the United States argues that the Constitution's prohibition of congressional directives to state governments can be overcome where the federal interest is sufficiently important to justify state submission. . . . No matter how powerful the federal interest involved, the Constitution simply does not give Congress the authority to require the States to regulate. . . . Where a federal interest is sufficiently strong to cause Congress to legislate, it must do so directly; it may not conscript state governments as its agents.

Second, the United States argues that the Constitution does, in some circumstances, permit federal directives to state governments. . . . *See* Testa v. Katt, 330 U.S. 386 (1947). . . . Federal statutes enforceable in state courts do, in a sense, direct state judges to enforce them, but this sort of federal "direction" of state judges is mandated by the text of the Supremacy Clause. . . . [T]he cases relied upon by the United States hold only that federal law is enforceable in state courts and that federal courts may in proper circumstances order state officials to comply with federal law, propositions that by no means imply any authority on the part of Congress to mandate state regulation.

Third, the United States [argues] that the Constitution envisions a role for Congress as an arbiter of interstate disputes. [T]he Framers did *not* intend that Congress should exercise that power through the mechanism of mandating state regulation. [When] Congress exceeds its authority relative to the States, [the] departure from the constitutional plan cannot be ratified by the "consent" of state officials. . . .

[T]he facts of these cases raise the possibility that powerful incentives might lead both federal and state officials to view departures from the federal structure to be in their personal interests. Most citizens recognize the need for radioactive waste disposal sites, but few want sites near their homes. As a result, while it would be well within the authority of either federal or state officials to choose where the disposal sites will be, it is likely to be in the political interest of each individual official to avoid being held accountable to the voters for the choice of location. If a federal official is faced with the alternatives of choosing a location or directing the States to do it, the official may well prefer the latter, as a means of shifting responsibility for the eventual decision. If a state official is faced with the same set of alternatives — choosing a location or having Congress direct the choice of a location — the state official may also prefer the latter, as it may permit the avoidance of personal responsibility. The interests of public officials thus may not coincide with the Constitution's intergovernmental allocation of authority. Where state officials purport to submit to the direction of Congress in this manner, federalism is hardly being advanced. . . .

V

Petitioners also contend that the Act is inconsistent with the Constitution's Guarantee Clause, which directs the United States to "guarantee to every State in this Union a Republican Form of Government." U.S. Const., Art. IV, §4. Because we have found the take title provision [irreconcilable with] the Tenth Amendment's reservation to the States of those powers not delegated to the Federal Government, we need only address the applicability of the Guarantee Clause to the Act's other two challenged provisions. . . . Even if we assume that petitioners' claim is justiciable, neither the monetary incentives provided by the Act nor the possibility that a State's waste producers may find themselves excluded from the disposal sites of another State can reasonably be said to deny any State a republican form of government. . . . Under each, Congress offers the States a legitimate choice rather than issuing an unavoidable command. The States thereby retain the ability to set their legislative agendas; state government officials remain accountable to the local electorate. . . . [The Court went on to hold that the take title provision could be severed from the remainder of the Act].

VII

[States] are not mere political subdivisions of the United States. State governments are neither regional offices nor administrative agencies of the Federal Government. . . . The Constitution instead "leaves to the several States a residuary and inviolable sovereignty," *The Federalist No. 39*, p. 245 (C. Rossiter ed., 1961), reserved explicitly to the States by the Tenth Amendment.

Whatever the outer limits of that sovereignty may be, one thing is clear: The Federal Government may not compel the States to enact or administer a federal regulatory program. The Constitution permits both the Federal Government and the States to enact legislation regarding the disposal of low level radioactive waste. The Constitution enables the Federal Government to pre-empt state regulation contrary to federal interests, and it permits the Federal Government to hold out incentives to the States as a means of encouraging them to adopt suggested regulatory schemes. It does not, however, authorize Congress simply to direct the States to provide for the disposal of the radioactive waste generated within their borders. While there may be many constitutional methods of achieving regional self-sufficiency in radioactive waste disposal, the method Congress has chosen is not one of them. The judgment of the Court of Appeals is accordingly

Affirmed in part and reversed in part.

Justice WHITE, with whom Justice BLACKMUN and Justice STEVENS join, concurring in part and dissenting in part.

[Congress] could have pre-empted the field by directly regulating the disposal of this waste[,] but [the] States wished to take the lead in achieving a solution to this problem and agreed among themselves to the various incentives and penalties implemented by Congress to ensure adherence to the various deadlines and goals. . . . New York's actions subsequent to enactment of the 1980 and 1985 Acts fairly indicate its approval of the interstate agreement process embodied in those laws within the meaning of Art. I, §10, cl. 3, of the Constitution [relating to agreements or compacts between states]. First, the States — including New York — [petitioned] Congress for the 1980 and 1985 Acts. . . . Second, New York acted in compliance with the requisites of both statutes in key respects [by entering] into compact negotiations with several other northeastern States before withdrawing [to] "go it alone." [By] 1988, New York had identified five potential sites[,] but public opposition [caused] the State to reconsider where to locate its waste disposal facility. New York continued to take full advantage of the import concession [by] exporting its low-level radioactive waste for the full 7-year extension period provided in the 1985 Act. By gaining these benefits and complying with [the] Act's deadlines, therefore, New York fairly evidenced its acceptance of the federal-state arrangement — including the take title provision. . . . The State should be estopped from asserting the unconstitutionality of [the] provision. . . .

[S]een as a term of an agreement entered into between the several States, this measure proves to be less constitutionally odious. . . . The Court's refusal to force New York to accept responsibility for its own problem inevitably means that some other States' sovereignty will be impinged by it being forced, for public health reasons, to accept New York's low-level radioactive waste. I do not understand the principle of federalism to impede the National Government from acting as referee among the States to prohibit one from bullying another. . . .

[T]o say [that] the incursion on state sovereignty "cannot be ratified by the 'consent' of state officials," is flatly wrong. [T]he Court's holding [essentially] misunderstands that the 1985 take title provision was part of a complex interstate agreement about which New York should not now be permitted to complain. . . .

The Court's distinction between a federal statute's regulation of States and private parties for general purposes, as opposed to a regulation solely on the activities of States, is unsupported by our recent Tenth Amendment cases. [In] *Garcia,* [we] stated the proper inquiry: "[W]e are convinced that the fundamental limitation that the constitutional scheme imposes on the Commerce Clause to protect the 'States as States' is one of process rather than one of result. Any substantive restraint [must] be tailored to compensate for possible failings in the national political process rather than to dictate a 'sacred province of state autonomy.'" . . .

[O]ur precedents leave open the possibility that Congress may create federal rights of action in the generators of low-level radioactive waste against persons acting under color of state law for their failure to meet certain functions designated in federal-state programs. . . . In addition to compensating injured parties for the State's failure to act, the exposure to liability established by such suits also potentially serves as an inducement to compliance with the program mandate.

[The] irony of the decision today is that in its formalistically rigid obeisance to "federalism," the Court gives Congress fewer incentives to defer to the wishes of state officials in achieving local solutions to local problems. This legislation was a classic example of Congress acting as arbiter among the States in their attempts to accept responsibility for managing a problem of grave import. . . . By invalidating the measure[,] the Court upsets the delicate compromise achieved among the

States and forces Congress to erect several additional formalistic hurdles to clear before achieving exactly the same objective. . . .

Justice STEVENS, concurring in part and dissenting in part.

[The] notion that Congress does not have the power to issue "a simple command to state governments to implement legislation enacted by Congress," is incorrect and unsound. [T]he Federal Government directs state governments in many realms. The Government regulates state-operated railroads, state school systems, state prisons, state elections, and a host of other state functions. Similarly, there can be no doubt that, in time of war, Congress could either draft soldiers itself or command the States to supply their quotas of troops. I see no reason why Congress may not also command the States to enforce federal water and air quality standards or federal standards for the disposition of low-level radioactive wastes. [I]f litigation should develop between States that have joined a compact, we would surely have the power to grant relief in the form of specific enforcement of the take title provision. [E]ven if the statute had never been passed, if one State's radioactive waste created a nuisance that harmed its neighbors, it seems clear that we would have had the power to command the offending State to take remedial action. If this Court has such authority, surely Congress has similar authority.

[I] respectfully dissent.

∼ PROBLEM: THE EDUCATION FOR A BETTER AMERICA ACT REPRISED — THERE'S GOT TO BE A BETTER WAY ∼

Suppose Congresswoman St. James says that federal resources are now so tight that the best way to improve education is for Congress to direct the states in doing so, and she would like you to advise her about what measures Congress might impose on the states. How would you advise her? In other words, what options are available after New York v. United States? How would you prioritize these options?

BACKGROUND
The "Brady Bill"

The "Brady Bill," more formally known as the Handgun Violence Prevention Act, took its name as a result of the handgun violence that occurred in Washington, D.C., on March 30, 1981. John Hinckley, a drifter who wanted to impress the actress Jodie Foster by assassinating President Ronald Reagan, shot Reagan and three others, including James Brady, President Reagan's press secretary. Brady, who was the most severely injured and remains paralyzed on his left side, became an active gun control advocate. Hinckley was prosecuted in Washington, D.C., and the jury found him not guilty by reason of insanity. Except for short court-approved releases, Hinckley remains confined to St. Elizabeth's Hospital in Washington.

Printz v. United States

521 U.S. 898 (1997)

Justice SCALIA delivered the opinion of the Court.

The question presented in these cases is whether certain interim provisions of the Brady Handgun Violence Prevention Act commanding state and local law enforcement officers to conduct background checks on prospective handgun purchasers and to perform certain related tasks, violate the Constitution.

I

The Gun Control Act of 1968 (GCA) establishes a detailed federal scheme governing the distribution of firearms. It prohibits firearms dealers from transferring handguns to any person under 21, not resident in the dealer's State, or prohibited by state or local law from purchasing or possessing firearms. It also forbids possession of a firearm by, and transfer of a firearm to, convicted felons, fugitives from justice, unlawful users of controlled substances, persons adjudicated as mentally defective or committed to mental institutions, aliens unlawfully present in the United States, persons dishonorably discharged from the Armed Forces, persons who have renounced their citizenship, and persons who have been subjected to certain restraining orders or been convicted of a misdemeanor offense involving domestic violence.

In 1993, Congress amended the GCA by enacting the Brady Act. The Act requires the Attorney General to establish a national instant background check system by November 30, 1998, and immediately puts in place certain interim provisions until that system becomes operative. Under the interim provisions, a firearms dealer who proposes to transfer a handgun must first: (1) receive from the transferee a statement (the Brady Form), containing the name, address and date of birth of the proposed transferee along with a sworn statement that the transferee is not among any of the classes of prohibited purchasers; (2) verify the identity of the transferee by examining an identification document; and (3) provide the "chief law enforcement officer" (CLEO) of the transferee's residence with notice of the contents (and a copy) of the Brady Form. With some exceptions, the dealer must then wait five business days before consummating the sale, unless the CLEO earlier notifies the dealer that he has no reason to believe the transfer would be illegal.

[When] a CLEO receives the required notice of a proposed transfer from the firearms dealer, the CLEO must "make a reasonable effort to ascertain within 5 business days whether receipt or possession would be in violation of the law, including research in whatever State and local recordkeeping systems are available and in a national system designated by the Attorney General." The Act does not require the CLEO to take any particular action if he determines that a pending transaction would be unlawful; he may notify the firearms dealer to that effect, but is not required to do so. If, however, the CLEO notifies a gun dealer that a prospective purchaser is ineligible to receive a handgun, he must, upon request, provide the would-be purchaser with a written statement of the reasons for that determination. Moreover, if the CLEO does not discover any basis for objecting to the sale, he must destroy any records in his possession relating to the transfer, including his copy of the Brady Form. Under a separate provision of the GCA, any person who "knowingly violates [the section of the GCA amended by the Brady Act] shall be fined under this title, imprisoned for no more than 1 year, or both."

Petitioners Jay Printz and Richard Mack, the CLEOs for Ravalli County, Montana, and Graham County, Arizona, respectively, filed separate actions challenging the constitutionality of the Brady Act's interim provisions. . . .

II

[T]he Brady Act purports to direct state law enforcement officers to participate, albeit only temporarily, in the administration of a federally enacted regulatory scheme. Regulated firearms dealers are required to forward Brady Forms not to a federal officer or employee, but to the CLEOs, whose obligation to accept those forms is implicit in the duty imposed upon them to make "reasonable efforts" within five days to determine whether the sales reflected in the forms are lawful. While the CLEOs are subjected to no federal requirement that they prevent the sales determined to be unlawful (it is perhaps assumed that their state-law duties will require prevention or apprehension), they are empowered to grant, in effect, waivers of the federally prescribed 5-day waiting period for handgun purchases by notifying the gun dealers that they have no reason to believe the transactions would be illegal.

The petitioners here object to being pressed into federal service, and contend that congressional action compelling state officers to execute federal laws is unconstitutional. [The] Government observes that statutes enacted by the first Congresses required state courts to record applications for citizenship, to transmit abstracts of citizenship applications and other naturalization records to the Secretary of State, and to register aliens seeking naturalization and issue certificates of registry. It may well be, however, that these requirements applied only in States that authorized their courts to conduct naturalization proceedings. [W]e do not think the early statutes [imply] a power of Congress to impress the state executive into its service. Indeed, it can be argued that the numerousness of these statutes, contrasted with the utter lack of statutes imposing obligations on the States' executive (notwithstanding the attractiveness of that course to Congress), suggests an assumed absence of such power. The only early federal law the Government has brought to our attention that imposed duties on state executive officers is the Extradition Act of 1793, which required the "executive authority" of a State to cause the arrest and delivery of a fugitive from justice upon the request of the executive authority of the State from which the fugitive had fled. That was in direct implementation, however, of the Extradition Clause of the Constitution itself.

To complete the historical record, we must note that there is not only an absence of executive-commandeering statutes in the early Congresses, but there is an absence of them in our later history as well, at least until very recent years. . . .

III

[We] turn next to consideration of the structure of the Constitution, to see if we can discern among its "essential postulate[s]" a principle that controls the present cases. [T]he Constitution established a system of "dual sovereignty." Although the States surrendered many of their powers to the new Federal Government, they retained "a residuary and inviolable sovereignty." [The] Framers' experience under the Articles of Confederation had persuaded them that using the States as the instruments of federal governance was both ineffectual and provocative of federal-state conflict. [T]he Framers rejected the concept of a central government that would act upon and through the States, and instead designed a system in which the state and federal governments would exercise concurrent authority over the people — who were, in Hamilton's words, "the only proper objects of government." [The] Constitution thus contemplates that a State's government will represent and remain accountable to its own citizens. . . .

This separation of the two spheres is one of the Constitution's structural protections of liberty. "Just as the separation and independence of the coordinate branches of the Federal Government serve to prevent the accumulation of excessive power in any one branch, a healthy balance of power between the States and the Federal Government will reduce the risk of tyranny and abuse from either front." [The] power of the Federal Government would be augmented immeasurably if it were able to impress into its service — and at no cost to itself-the police officers of the 50 States.

[The] Constitution does not leave to speculation who is to administer the laws enacted by Congress; the President, it says, "shall take Care that the Laws be faithfully executed," personally and through officers whom he appoints (save for such inferior officers as Congress may authorize to be appointed by the "Courts of Law" or by "the Heads of Departments" who are themselves presidential appointees). The Brady Act effectively transfers this responsibility to thousands of CLEOs in the 50 States, who are left to implement the program without meaningful Presidential control (if indeed meaningful Presidential control is possible without the power to appoint and remove). The insistence of the Framers upon unity in the Federal Executive — to insure both vigor and accountability — is well known. That unity would be shattered, and the power of the President would be subject to reduction, if Congress could act as effectively without the President as with him, by simply requiring state officers to execute its laws.

The dissent of course resorts to the last, best hope of those who defend ultra vires congressional action, the Necessary and Proper Clause. [What] destroys the dissent's Necessary and Proper Clause argument, however, is not the Tenth Amendment but the Necessary and Proper Clause itself. When a "La[w] for carrying into Execution" the Commerce Clause violates the principle of state sovereignty reflected in the various constitutional provisions we mentioned earlier, it is not a "La[w] proper for carrying into Execution the Commerce Clause," and is thus, in the words of *The Federalist*, "merely [an] ac[t] of usurpation" which "deserve[s] to be treated as such." . . .

IV

[Federal] commandeering of state governments is such a novel phenomenon that this Court's first experience with it did not occur until the 1970's, when the Environmental Protection Agency promulgated regulations requiring States to prescribe auto emissions testing, monitoring and retrofit programs, and to designate preferential bus and carpool lanes. [After] we granted certiorari to review the statutory and constitutional validity of the regulations, the Government declined even to defend them, and instead rescinded some and conceded the invalidity of those that remained. [L]ater opinions of ours have made clear that the Federal Government may not compel the States to implement, by legislation or executive action, federal regulatory programs. In Hodel v. Virginia Surface Mining & Reclamation Assn., Inc., 452 U.S. 264 (1981), and FERC v. Mississippi, 456 U.S. 742 (1982), we sustained statutes against constitutional challenge only after assuring ourselves that they did not require the States to enforce federal law. . . .

[At] issue in New York v. United States, 505 U.S. 144 (1992), were the so-called "take title" provisions of the Low-Level Radioactive Waste Policy Amendments Act of 1985, which required States either to enact legislation providing for the disposal of radioactive waste generated within their borders, or to take title to, and possession of the waste — effectively requiring the States either to legislate pursuant to Congress's directions, or to implement an administrative solution. We concluded that Congress could constitutionally require the States to do neither. "The Federal Government," we held, "may not compel the States to enact or administer a federal regulatory program."

The Government contends that *New York* is distinguishable [in that] the background-check provision of the Brady Act does not require state legislative or executive officials to make policy, but instead issues a final directive to state CLEOs. . . . The Government's distinction between "making" law and merely "enforcing" it, between "policymaking" and mere "implementation," is an interesting one. It is perhaps not meant to be the same as, but it is surely reminiscent of, the line that separates proper congressional conferral of Executive power from unconstitutional delegation of legislative authority for federal separation-of-powers purposes. This Court has not been notably successful in describing the latter line; indeed, some think we have abandoned the effort to do so. We are doubtful that the new line the Government proposes would be any more distinct. Executive action that has utterly no policymaking component is rare, particularly at an executive level as high as a jurisdiction's chief law-enforcement officer. Is it really true that there is no policymaking involved in deciding, for example, what "reasonable efforts" shall be expended to conduct a background check? . . .

Even assuming [that] the Brady Act leaves no "policymaking" discretion with the States, we fail to see how that improves rather than worsens the intrusion upon state sovereignty. Preservation of the States as independent and autonomous political entities is arguably less undermined by requiring them to make policy in certain fields [than] by "reduc[ing][them] to puppets of a ventriloquist Congress." It is an essential attribute of the States' retained sovereignty that they remain independent and autonomous within their proper sphere of authority. It is no more compatible with this independence and autonomy that their officers be "dragooned" into administering federal law, than it would be compatible with the independence and autonomy of the United States that its officers be impressed into service for the execution of state laws.

[The] Government also maintains that requiring state officers to perform discrete, ministerial tasks specified by Congress does not violate the principle of *New York* because it does not diminish the accountability of state or federal officials. This argument fails even on its own terms. By forcing state governments to absorb the financial burden of implementing a federal regulatory program, Members of Congress can take credit for "solving" problems without having to ask their constituents to pay for the solutions with higher federal taxes. [E]ven when the States are not forced to absorb the costs of implementing a federal program, they are still put in the position of taking the blame for its burdensomeness and for its defects. Under the present law, for example, it will be the CLEO and not some federal official who stands between the gun purchaser and immediate possession of his gun. And it will likely be the CLEO, not some federal official, who will be blamed for any error (even one in the designated federal database) that causes a purchaser to be mistakenly rejected.

[The] Brady Act, the dissent asserts, is different from the "take title" provisions invalidated in *New York* because the former is addressed to individuals — namely CLEOs — while the latter were directed to the State itself. "A suit against a state official in his or her official capacity is not a suit against the official but rather is a suit against the official's office. . . . As such, it is no different from a suit against the State itself." And the same must be said of a directive to an official in his or her official capacity. To say that the Federal Government cannot control the State, but can control all of its officers, is to say nothing of significance. . . .

Finally, the Government puts forward a cluster of arguments[:] "The Brady Act serves very important purposes, is most efficiently administered by CLEOs during the interim period, and places a minimal and only temporary burden upon state officers." [W]here, as here, it is the whole object of the law to direct the functioning of the state executive, and hence to compromise the structural framework of dual sovereignty, such a "balancing" analysis is inappropriate. . . .

V

[We] held in *New York* that Congress cannot compel the States to enact or enforce a federal regulatory program. Today we hold that Congress cannot circumvent that prohibition by conscripting the States' officers directly. The Federal Government may neither issue directives requiring the States to address particular problems, nor command the States' officers, or those of their political subdivisions, to administer or enforce a federal regulatory program. It matters not whether policymaking is involved, and no case-by-case weighing of the burdens or benefits is necessary; such commands are fundamentally incompatible with our constitutional system of dual sovereignty. Accordingly, the judgment of the Court of Appeals for the Ninth Circuit is reversed.

It is so ordered.

Justice O'CONNOR, concurring.

[Our] holding [does] not spell the end of [the] Brady Act. States and chief law enforcement officers may voluntarily continue to participate in the federal program. [Congress] is also free to amend the interim program to provide for its continuance on a contractual basis with the States if it wishes, as it does with a number of other federal programs. . . .

Justice THOMAS, concurring.

[T]he Brady Act violates the Tenth Amendment in that it compels state law enforcement officers to "administer or enforce a federal regulatory program." . . .

Justice STEVENS, with whom Justice SOUTER, Justice GINSBURG, and Justice BREYER join, dissenting.

[Article I, §8 supports] the regulation of commerce in handguns effected by the Brady Act. [The Necessary and Proper Clause] is surely adequate to support the temporary enlistment of local police officers in the process of identifying persons who should not be entrusted with the possession of handguns. [T]he Tenth Amendment imposes no restriction on the exercise of delegated powers. . . . [H]istorical materials strongly suggest that the Founders intended to enhance the capacity of the federal government by empowering it — as a part of the new authority to make demands directly on individual citizens — to act through local officials. . . . For example, statutes of the early Congresses required in mandatory terms that state judges and their clerks perform various executive duties with respect to applications for citizenship. . . .

The fact that the Framers intended to preserve the sovereignty of the several States simply does not speak to the question whether individual state employees may be required to perform federal obligations, such as registering young adults for the draft, creating state emergency response commissions designed to manage the release of hazardous substances, collecting and reporting data on underground storage tanks that may pose an environmental hazard, and reporting traffic fatalities, and missing children to a federal agency. . . . As we explained in *Garcia*: "[T]he principal means chosen by the Framers to ensure the role of the States in the federal system lies in the structure of the Federal Government itself. . . ." Given the fact that the Members of Congress are elected by the people of the several States, with each State receiving an equivalent number of Senators in order to ensure that even the smallest States have a powerful voice in the legislature, it is quite unrealistic to assume that they will ignore the sovereignty concerns of their constituents. It is far more reasonable to presume that their decisions to impose modest burdens on state officials from time to time reflect a considered judgment that the people in each of the States will benefit. . . .

[The] majority expresses special concern that were its rule not adopted the Federal Government would be able to avail itself of the services of state government officials "at no cost to itself." [T]he majority's rule seems more likely to damage than to preserve the safeguards against tyranny provided by the existence of vital state governments. By limiting the ability of the Federal Government to enlist state officials in the implementation of its programs, the Court creates incentives for the National Government to aggrandize itself. In the name of State's rights, the majority would have the Federal Government create vast national bureaucracies to implement its policies. This is exactly the sort of thing that the early Federalists promised would not occur, in part as a result of the National Government's ability to rely on the magistracy of the states.

[New York v. United States] squarely approved of cooperative federalism programs, designed at the national level but implemented principally by state governments. *New York* disapproved of a particular method of putting such programs into place. [N]othing in the majority's holding calls into question the three mechanisms for constructing such programs that *New York* expressly approved. Congress may require the States to implement its programs as a condition of federal spending, in order to avoid the threat of unilateral federal action in the area, or as a part of a program that affects States and private parties alike. . . .

[T]his case [merely] involves the imposition of modest duties on individual officers. The Court seems to accept the fact that Congress could require private persons, such as hospital executives or school administrators, to provide arms merchants with relevant information about a prospective purchaser's fitness to own a weapon; indeed, the Court does not disturb the conclusion [that] the burden on police officers would be permissible if a similar burden were also imposed on private parties with access to relevant data. [The] provision of the Brady Act that crosses the Court's newly defined constitutional threshold is more comparable to a statute requiring local police officers to report the identity of missing children to the Crime Control Center of the Department of Justice than to an offensive federal command to a sovereign state. If Congress believes that such a statute will benefit the people of the Nation, and serve the interests of cooperative federalism better than an enlarged federal bureaucracy, we should respect both its policy judgment and its appraisal of its constitutional power. . . .

Justice SOUTER, dissenting.

[In *The Federalist,* Hamilton] says that the state governmental machinery "will be incorporated" into the Nation's operation. [T]heir auxiliary functions will be the products of their obligations thus undertaken to support federal law, not of their own, or the States', unfettered choices. . . .

Justice BREYER, with whom Justice STEVENS joins, dissenting.

[T]here is no need [to] read the Brady Act as permitting the Federal Government to overwhelm a state civil service. The statute uses the words "reasonable effort" — words that easily can encompass the considerations of, say, time or cost, necessary to avoid any such result. . . .

∾ PROBLEMS ∾

1. *Mandatory Continuing Teacher Education.* In considering whether to vote for the EBA Act, a Senator states, "I will vote for it with this addition: "States

must provide a minimum of 12 hours of teaching training for the improvement of pedagogy, methodology, and student learning every year for all teachers." Would such an addition be constitutional under *Printz*?

2. *Civics.* Congresswoman St. James, and others in Congress, have become worried that the focus on math and science diminishes the attention paid to other subjects in American schools, particularly civics. She proposes a law requiring all public schools to teach a progression of three civics courses through sixth, seventh, and eighth grades. Would this law be constitutional under *Printz*?

3. *Driver's Privacy Protection Act.* The Driver's Privacy Protection Act of 1994 (DPPA) limits the ability of state departments of motor vehicles (DMVs) to disclose or resell personal information. The law was passed because state DMVs typically require drivers and automobile owners to provide personal information, including name, address, telephone number, vehicle description, Social Security number, medical information, and a photograph, as a condition of obtaining a driver's license or registering an automobile. Historically, many states have sold this personal information to individuals and businesses. Under the DPPA, the states may not disclose a driver's personal information without the driver's consent. The DPPA imposes civil and criminal penalties for violations.

Contrary to the DPPA, Kentucky law provides that information contained in the state's DMV records is available to any person or entity that fills out a form listing the requester's name and address and stating that the information will not be used for telephone solicitation. State law allows the Kentucky DMV to charge a fee for releasing personal information, and it allows drivers to prohibit disclosure of their personal information by filling out a form.

Does the DPPA violate the Tenth Amendment to the U.S. Constitution? In evaluating the constitutionality, which of the following arguments do you find more persuasive:

a) The personal, identifying information that the DPPA regulates is an item of interstate commerce, and the sale or release of that information in interstate commerce is therefore a proper subject of congressional regulation;

b) The DPPA violates the Tenth Amendment because it "thrusts upon the states all of the day-to-day responsibility for administering its complex provisions," and thereby makes "state officials the unwilling implementers of federal policy";

c) The DPPA requires the state's employees to learn and apply the Act's substantive restrictions, and consumes the employees' time and thus the state's resources;

d) The DPPA does not require the states in their sovereign capacity to regulate their own citizens; or

e) The DPPA does not require the Kentucky legislature to enact any laws or regulations, and it does not require state officials to assist in the enforcement of federal statutes regulating private individuals, but simply regulates Kentucky's DMV.

See Reno v. Condon, 528 U.S. 141 (2000).

∾ REVIEW PROBLEMS ∾

1. *King of the World*. After *Garcia*, one member of Congress text-messaged another: "Armed with the Commerce Clause, we are now unstoppable!" How would you reply? How does *Lopez*, a Commerce Clause decision, affect the Court's view of intergovernmental immunity issues?

2. *Prison or Jail—Take Your Pick*. Congress directs states to hold prisoners in jails, which usually hold persons awaiting trial, for no more than one year, unless documented "extraordinary circumstances" exist. Is this law constitutional?

3. *Tax Equity and Fiscal Responsibility Act*. In the past several years, Congress has become increasingly concerned about documentation showing noncompliance with federal tax laws. The evidence revealed that unreported income had grown from $31.1 billion in 1973 to $97 billion in 1981, and that unregistered bonds were a factor in unreported income. Bonds can be issued as either registered bonds or bearer bonds; the two types of bonds differ in the way ownership and payments are made. Registered bonds are recorded on a central list, and a transfer of record ownership gets a notation on the list. The record owner is automatically sent interest payments. A bearer bond's ownership is presumed from possession, and transfer is made by physically delivering the bond. The bond owner presents the bond coupons to a bank, which presents the coupons to the issuer's paying agent.

To address this problem, Congress passed Section 310(b)(1) of the Tax Equity and Fiscal Responsibility Act of 1982 (TEFRA), which denied federal tax-exempt status to interest earned on publicly offered long-term bonds issued by state and local governments unless they are issued in registered form. Kentucky challenges Section 310. Which of the following arguments for and against the law are the most persuasive regarding its constitutionality? a) Section 310 forces states to increase the interest paid on state bonds by 28 to 35 percent. b) Even though almost all state bonds were issued in bearer form before Section 310 became effective, since then no state has issued a bearer bond. c) Because of its practical effects, for purposes of the Tenth Amendment, we must treat Section 310 as if it simply banned bearer bonds altogether without giving states the option to issue nonexempt bearer bonds. d) A blanket prohibition by Congress on the issuance of bearer bonds can apply to states without violating the Tenth Amendment. e) Kentucky has not alleged that it was deprived of any right to participate in the national political process or that it was singled out in a way that left it politically isolated and powerless. f) The political process failed here because Section 310(b)(1) was "imposed by the vote of an uninformed Congress relying upon incomplete information." g) Section 310 is invalid because it commandeers the state legislative and administrative process by coercing states into enacting legislation authorizing bond registration and into administering the registration scheme. h) Section 310 does not abolish the tax exemption for state bond interest entirely but rather taxes the interest on state bonds only if the bonds are not issued in the form Congress requires. Should the law be upheld? *See* South Carolina v. Baker, 485 U.S. 505 (1988).

Points to Remember

- State power to tax the federal government is circumscribed. It is important to identify the nature of the tax, such as whether it is a tax on federal agencies or property or federal employee salaries, and whether it is neutral and nondiscriminatory.
- A key prefatory issue in considering the use of federal power to tax state governments is whether the tax is direct or indirect.
- Most claims of state immunity from regulation will fail after *Garcia.*
- Congress cannot cross the "no coercion" line by ordering states to regulate or act. Instead, Congress can encourage states to act through incentives and inducements.

5

State Power to Regulate Commerce

U.S. CONSTITUTION, ARTICLE I

Section 8, Clause 3. The Congress shall have Power . . . To regulate Commerce with foreign Nations, and among the several States, and with the Indian Tribes; . . .

Section 10. No State shall enter into any Treaty, Alliance, or Confederation; grant Letters of Marque and Reprisal; coin Money; emit Bills of Credit; make any Thing but gold and silver Coin a Tender in Payment of Debts; pass any Bill of Attainder, ex post facto Law, or Law impairing the Obligation of Contracts, or grant any Title of Nobility.

No State shall, without the Consent of the Congress, lay any Imposts or Duties on Imports or Exports, except what may be absolutely necessary for executing its inspection Laws; and the net Produce of all Duties and Imposts, laid by any State on Imports or Exports, shall be for the Use of the Treasury of the United States; and all such Laws shall be subject to the Revision and Control of the Congress.

No State shall, without the Consent of Congress, lay any Duty of Tonnage, keep Troops, or Ships of War in time of Peace, enter into any Agreement or Compact with another State, or with a foreign Power, or engage in War, unless actually invaded, or in such imminent Danger as well not admit of delay.

U.S. CONSTITUTION, ARTICLE VI

Clause 3. This Constitution, and the laws of the United States which shall be made in Pursuance thereof; and all Treaties made, or which shall be made, under the Authority of the United States, shall be the supreme Law of the Land; and the Judges in every State shall be bound thereby, any Thing in the Constitution or Laws of any State to the contrary notwithstanding.

U.S. CONSTITUTION, ARTICLE IV

Section 2. The Citizens of each State shall be entitled to all Privileges and Immunities of Citizens in the several States. . . .

U.S. CONSTITUTION, TENTH AMENDMENT

The powers not delegated to the United States by the Constitution, nor prohibited to it by the States, are reserved to the States respectively, or the people.

∾ PROBLEM: KENTUCKY'S PROHIBITION AGAINST INTERNET GAMBLING ∾

The Commonwealth of Kentucky has a large horse racing industry that contributes much to the state economy. In recent years, the racing industry has been in a state of decline due to a variety of factors. First, the population of horse racing enthusiasts is rapidly growing older and dying, and is not being replaced by younger enthusiasts. Second, the neighboring State of Indiana has legalized casino gambling and has authorized the creation of several casinos near the Kentucky border (prompting Kentucky's gambling interests to call for government help designed to place them on an equal footing with Indiana). Finally, the horse racing industry is facing competition from other entertainment industries (e.g., cable and satellite television and the Internet) that make horse racing and horse gambling less attractive to the population as a whole.

The decline of Kentucky's horse racing industry is amply illustrated in economic data. Betting "handles" and horse racing purses have declined in value. In addition, as other states have begun to provide incentives to their horse racing industries, Kentucky's breeders and trainers have moved their breeding and racing operations out of state. Kentucky's business and political leaders regard the situation as an "economic crisis."

Kentucky's governor, Wilbur Wonkley, was elected on a platform of legalizing additional gambling at Kentucky racetracks. Following his election, Wonkley floated proposals for video slots, as well as for casino-style gambling, at racetracks. Despite Wonkley's persistent advocacy for the additional gambling, his proposals were never enacted because of strong legislative opposition.

Recently, Governor Wonkley became aware of Internet gambling in the state. These "Internet casinos" are operated outside of the Commonwealth as well as outside the borders of the United States. Wonkley has expressed alarm about what he has termed this new "scourge" on the citizens of Kentucky. He fears that the citizens of Kentucky are being (and will be) lured into betting their "hard-earned money" at these new Internet casinos, and that this new "gambling scourge" will have a devastating impact on Kentucky's families (who will be unable to buy bread and other necessities for their children because of gambling losses). As a result, Wonkley has urged the Kentucky legislature to immediately pass legislation protecting the state against what he has referred to as the "Internet casino menace."

Kentucky is a diverse state that includes some major cities (Louisville, Lexington, Covington, and Paducah) as well as a large rural population and a large group of folks who live in the Appalachian Mountains on the eastern side of the state. In general, the population is fairly conservative (having voted decisively for John McCain over Barack Obama in the 2008 presidential election), and that is a significant part of the reason Wonkley's proposals for expanded gambling died in the state legislature. However, the evidence shows that Kentucky's horse racing interests enthusiastically support the Internet casino legislation. Some believe that they seek the new anti-Internet gambling legislation as a protectionist measure.

The anti-Internet casino gambling legislation (the Internet Casino Prohibition Act) passed quickly and overwhelmingly through the Kentucky legislature. It contained the following language:

> All Internet-based gambling (whether conducted by Kentuckians or by out-of-staters) is hereby prohibited within the borders of the Commonwealth. Any business or person that offers Internet gambling within the borders of the state is subject to imprisonment for up to 10 years, as well as fines of $10,000 per violation. The phrase "offers Internet gambling within the borders of the state" is defined to mean that a company or individual makes its gambling service available to Kentuckians over the Internet. However, sanctions apply only when, and if, a Kentuckian actually accesses the website. However, each access by a Kentuckian constitutes a violation under this law, and constitutes a separate violation of the Act. Kentucky's Attorney General is hereby authorized to seize the Internet domain names of any Internet gambling site that operates within the Commonwealth.

In hearings leading up to the Act's passage, evidenced was adduced suggesting that Internet gambling is a greater threat, and poses greater social evils, than other types of gambling. In particular, the evidence shows that Internet gambling is more "available" to the average citizen than other forms of gambling because citizens can play at home at any time of the day or night. In other words, there are no "closing hours" for Internet gambling. In addition, because Internet gambling can be done in secret, it is more difficult for society to intervene in the sense of trying to protect citizens who have become addicted to gambling and who might be wreaking havoc on their families.

As you work your way through this chapter, consider whether the Internet Casino Prohibition Act is valid.

As we saw in Chapter 2, during the first third of the twentieth century, although Congress had the power to regulate commerce "among" the states, the Court construed the Tenth Amendment as giving the states a reserved power over "purely local" commerce. Thus, most Commerce Clause cases involved claims that the federal government was violating the states' reserved power, and many Commerce Clause cases focused on state power.

Following the constitutional crisis of the 1930s, the distinction between "local" commerce and commerce "among" the states began to disappear. Under decisions like *Wickard* and *Perez*, the federal government assumed much broader authority over both interstate and local commerce. Moreover, the Court began to treat the Tenth Amendment as a truism, thereby depriving states of their reserved power over commerce. Even though recent decisions (e.g., *Lopez* and *Morrison*) have pared back the scope of federal power, the federal commerce power remains broad.

Since the 1930s, the federal courts have faced quite different questions regarding the scope of state power. Some cases involve questions about whether federal law preempts state law. In other words, does the existence of federal regulation preclude state regulation? Most of the remaining cases involve so-called "dormant" power situations — situations in which the federal government has the power to regulate a subject, but has not done so or has done so incompletely. In these dormant power situations, the question is whether the Commerce Clause contains negative implications that limit or preclude state regulation. In other words, is the federal commerce power "exclusive," so that the states are precluded from regulating an area within federal authority even in the absence of federal regulation? Or do the states have "concurrent" jurisdiction so that they are also free to regulate? If concurrent power exists, what limits apply to state power? A few cases focus on the Privileges and Immunities Clause, which protects citizens against discrimination in one state because of their status as citizens of another state.

The Constitution provides little guidance on these issues. Article I, Section 8 explicitly gives Congress the power to regulate commerce "among" the several states but does not say whether the states can also regulate commerce. That issue was left to the courts.

A. EARLY CASES

A number of early cases focused on whether the federal government's authority over commerce was exclusive, or whether the states also had concurrent power.

Gibbons v. Ogden
22 U.S. (9 Wheat.) 1 (1824)

Mr. Chief Justice MARSHALL delivered the opinion of the Court, and, after stating the case, proceeded as follows:

[By the terms of a New York statute, Robert Livingston and Robert Fulton had the exclusive right to navigate steamboats in certain state waters. They assigned the route between New York and New Jersey to Aaron Ogden. When Thomas Gibbons sought to operate ships on the same route, under a license granted by an Act of Congress, Ogden sought injunctive relief on the basis that the federal license was invalid. After finding that the federal license was valid, the Court struck down New York's exclusive license on Supremacy Clause grounds. The Court did not resolve the question of whether, in the absence of a conflict between the state and federal license, the state was free to regulate and license navigation. The Court did make the following statements in dicta.]

[I]t has been urged with great earnestness, that, although the power of Congress to regulate commerce with foreign nations, and among the several States, be co-extensive with the subject itself, and have no other limits than are prescribed in the constitution, yet the States may severally exercise the same power, within their respective jurisdictions. In support of this argument, it is said, that they possessed it as an inseparable attribute of sovereignty, before the formation of the constitution, and still retain it, except so far as they have surrendered it by that instrument; that this principle results from the nature of the government, and is secured by the tenth amendment; that an affirmative grant of power is not exclusive, unless in its own nature it be such that the continued exercise of it by the former possessor is inconsistent with the grant, and that this is not of that description. . . .

The grant of the power to lay and collect taxes is, like the power to regulate commerce, made in general terms, and has never been understood to interfere with the exercise of the same power by the State; and hence has been drawn an argument which has been applied to the question under consideration. But the two grants are not, it is conceived, similar in their terms or their nature. Although many of the powers formerly exercised by the States, are transferred to the government of the Union, yet the State governments remain, and constitute a most important part of our system. The power of taxation is indispensable to their existence, and is a power which, in its own nature, is capable of residing in, and being exercised by, different authorities at the same time. . . .

[I]nspection laws are said to be regulations of commerce, and are certainly recognized in the constitution, as being passed in the exercise of a power remaining with the States. That inspection laws may have a remote and considerable influence on commerce, will not be denied; but that a power to regulate commerce is the source from which the right to pass them is derived, cannot be admitted. The object of inspection laws, is to improve the quality of articles produced by the labour of a country; to fit them for exportation; or, it may be, for domestic use. They act upon the subject before it becomes an article of foreign commerce, or of commerce among the States, and prepare it for that purpose. They form a portion of that immense mass of legislation, which embraces every thing within the territory of a State, not surrendered to the general government: all which can be most advantageously exercised by the States themselves. Inspection laws, quarantine laws, health laws of every description, as well as laws for regulating the internal commerce of a State, and those which respect turnpike roads, ferries, &c., are component parts of this mass.

No direct general power over these objects is granted to Congress; and, consequently, they remain subject to State legislation. If the legislative power of the Union can reach them, it must be for national purposes; it must be where the power is expressly given for a special purpose, or is clearly incidental to some power which is expressly given. . . .

It has been contended by the counsel for the appellant, that, as the word "to regulate" implies in its nature, full power over the thing to be regulated, it excludes, necessarily, the action of all others that would perform the same operation on the same thing. That regulation is designed for the entire result, applying to those parts which remain as they were, as well as to those which are altered. It produces a uniform whole, which is as much disturbed and deranged by changing what the regulating power designs to leave untouched, as that on which it has operated.

There is great force in this argument, and the Court is not satisfied that it has been refuted.

Notes and Questions

1. Plumley v. Commonwealth of Massachusetts, 155 U.S. 461 (1894), reinforced the notion that the states retain control over certain internal matters. Plumley was convicted of violating a Massachusetts law prohibiting the sale of adulterated oleomargarine. Following his incarceration, Plumley sought a writ of habeas corpus, which was denied on the theory that the Massachusetts law did not violate Congress's power under the Commerce Clause: "If there be any subject over which it would seem the states ought to have plenary control, and the power to legislate in respect to which, it ought not to be supposed, was intended to be surrendered to the general government, it is the protection of the people against fraud and deception in the sale of food products."

2. *Chief Justice Marshall's Conception of Federal Power.* Note how broadly Chief Justice Marshall interprets the federal government's authority to regulate commerce in *Gibbons*: "the word 'to regulate' implies in its nature, full power over the thing to be regulated, it excludes, necessarily, the action of all others that would perform the same operation on the same thing." If the courts give this language full effect, following holdings like *Wickard* and *Perez* (which, of course, were restricted somewhat by later holdings like *Lopez*), how much power would the states have to regulate commerce today? Indeed, would states have the power to pass the inspection laws that Marshall suggested were within the scope of their authority?

3. *Inspection Laws.* Justice Marshall characterizes inspection laws as acting "upon the subject before it becomes an article of foreign commerce, or of commerce among the States, and prepare it for that purpose." As a result, he deems "[i]nspection laws, quarantine laws, health laws of every description, as well as laws for regulating the internal commerce of a State" to be within the scope of state authority. "No direct general power over these objects is granted to Congress." Is the latter statement true? Do you agree that Congress lacks the power to enact inspection laws relating to interstate commerce?

∼ PROBLEM: MORE ON THE INTERNET CASINO PROHIBITION ACT ∼

Under Justice Marshall's conception of federal powers and state powers, would Kentucky's Internet Casino Prohibition Act be valid?

Cooley v. Board of Wardens
53 U.S. (12 How.) 299 (1851)

Mr. Justice CURTIS delivered the opinion of the court.

[A Pennsylvania law required all ships either to use local pilots when they navigated in the Delaware River or to pay a penalty. The plaintiff paid the penalty and sued for restitution, claiming that the Pilot Law violated Congress's power to regulate commerce. Pennsylvania defended based on a 1789 federal law that gave states authority to enact local pilot laws.]

[W]e are brought directly and unavoidably to [the] question, whether the grant of the commercial power to Congress, did per se deprive the states of all power to regulate pilots. . . . The grant of commercial power to Congress does not contain any terms which expressly exclude the states from exercising an authority over its subject-matter. If they are excluded it must be because the nature of the power, thus granted to Congress, requires that a similar authority should not exist in the states. . . .

[T]he power to regulate commerce, embraces a vast field, containing not only many, but exceedingly various subjects, quite unlike in their nature; some imperatively demanding a single uniform rule, operating equally on the commerce of the United States in every port; and some, like the subject now in question, as imperatively demanding that diversity, which alone can meet the local necessities of navigation.

Either absolutely to affirm, or deny that the nature of this power requires exclusive legislation by Congress, is to lose sight of the nature of the subjects of this power. . . . Whatever subjects of this power are in their nature national, or admit only of one uniform system, or plan of regulation, may justly be said to be of such a nature as to require exclusive legislation by Congress. That this cannot be affirmed of laws for the regulation of pilots and pilotage is plain. The act of 1789 contains a clear and authoritative declaration by the first Congress, that the nature of this subject is such, that until Congress should find it necessary to exert its power, it should be left to the legislation of the states; that it is local and not national; that it is likely to be the best provided for, not by one system, or plan of regulations, but by as many as the legislative discretion of the several states should deem applicable to the local peculiarities of the ports within their limits.

Viewed in this light, so much of this act of 1789 as declares that pilots shall continue to be regulated "by such laws as the states may respectively hereafter enact for that purpose," instead of being held to be inoperative, as an attempt to confer on the states a power to legislate, of which the Constitution had deprived them, is allowed an appropriate and important signification. It manifests the understanding of Congress [that] the nature of this subject is not such as to require its exclusive legislation. The practice of the states, and of the national government, has been in conformity with this declaration, from the origin of the national government to this time; and the nature of the subject when examined, is such as to leave no doubt of the superior fitness and propriety, not to say the absolute necessity, of different systems of regulation, drawn from local knowledge and experience, and conformed to local wants. How then can we say, that by the mere grant of power to regulate commerce, the states are deprived of all the power to legislate on this subject, because from the nature of the power the legislation of Congress must be exclusive. . . .

It is the opinion of a majority of the court that the mere grant to Congress of the power to regulate commerce, did not deprive the states of power to regulate pilots, and that although Congress has legislated on this subject, its legislation manifests an intention, with a single exception, not to regulate this subject, but to leave its regulation to the several states. [This opinion] does not extend to the question what other subjects, under the commercial power, are within the exclusive control of Congress, or may be regulated by the states in the absence of all congressional legislation; nor to the general question how far any regulation of a subject by Congress, may be deemed to operate as an exclusion of all legislation by the states upon the same subject. . . .

For more than sixty years this subject has been acted on by the states, and the systems of some of them created and of others essentially modified during that period. To hold that pilotage fees and penalties demanded and received during that time, have been illegally exacted, under color of void laws, would work an amount of mischief which a clear conviction of constitutional duty, if entertained, must force us to occasion, but which could be viewed by no just mind without deep regret. Nor would the mischief be limited to the past. If Congress were now to pass a law adopting the existing state laws, if enacted without authority, and in violation of the Constitution, it would seem to us to be a new and questionable mode of legislation.

If the grant of commercial power in the Constitution has deprived the states of all power to legislate for the regulation of pilots, if their laws on this subject are mere usurpations upon the exclusive power of the general government, and utterly void, it may be doubted whether Congress could, with propriety, recognize them as laws, and adopt them as its own acts; and how are the legislatures of the states to proceed in future, to watch over and amend these laws, as the progressive wants of a growing commerce will require, when the members of those legislatures are made aware that they cannot legislate on this subject without violating the oaths they have taken to support the Constitution of the United States?

We are of opinion that this state law was enacted by virtue of a power, residing in the state to legislate; that it is not in conflict with any law of Congress; that it does not interfere with any system which Congress has established by making regulations, or by intentionally leaving individuals to their own unrestricted action; that this law is therefore valid, and the judgment of the Supreme Court of Pennsylvania in each case must be affirmed.

Mr. Justice MCLEAN.

[If] the states had not the power to enact pilot laws, as connected with foreign commerce, in 1789, when did they get it? [Congress] may adopt the laws of a state, but it cannot enable a state to legislate. In other words, it cannot transfer to a state legislative powers. [The majority concludes that state regulation is appropriate] because the subject [of this legislation] is more appropriate for state than federal action; and consequently, it must be presumed the Constitution cannot have intended to inhibit state action. This is not a rule by which the Constitution is to be construed. It can receive but little support from the discussions which took place on the adoption of the Constitution, and none at all from the earlier decisions of this court. . . .

Notes and Questions

1. *Cooley and Gibbons.* *Cooley* rejects the exclusivity approach articulated in *Gibbons*. Is *Cooley*'s approach better than *Gibbons*'s approach? How does a court know whether a matter is national or local in character?

2. *Congressional Authorization.* Can Congress authorize the states to exercise regulatory authority that they would not have in the absence of congressional authorization? In Leisy v. Hardin, 135 U.S. 100 (1890), the Court held that "as the grant of the power to regulate commerce among the states, so far as one system is required, is exclusive, the states cannot exercise that power without the assent of congress." Likewise, in Prudential Ins. Co. v. Benjamin, 328 U.S. 408 (1946), the Court upheld a South Carolina tax imposed on foreign insurance companies as a condition of doing business in the state. The Court concluded that a federal law authorized the tax: "[Congress] has expressly stated its intent and policy in the Act. [We] think that the declaration's effect is clearly to sustain the exaction and that this can be done without violating any constitutional provision. . . . Congress's purpose was [to remove] obstructions which might be thought to flow from its own power, whether dormant or exercised, except as otherwise expressly provided in the Act itself or in future legislation. The other was by declaring expressly and affirmatively that continued state regulation and taxation of this business is in the public interest and that the business and all who engage in it 'shall be subject to' the laws of the several states in these respects." Should congressional authorization matter?

∼ PROBLEM: MORE ON THE INTERNET CASINO PROHIBITION ACT ∼

How would you assess the validity of the Internet Casino Prohibition Act under the *Cooley* approach to state power?

B. DISCRIMINATION AGAINST INTERSTATE COMMERCE

The Court has always scrutinized state and local legislation more closely when it involves discrimination against interstate commerce. Statutes that discriminate against or directly regulate interstate commerce are presumptively unconstitutional and survive only if there are no less–commerce-restrictive methods of achieving the statute's goals. This approach reflects the fact that the Framers gave Congress the power to regulate interstate commerce in order to prevent trade wars between the states. Thus, the Interstate Commerce Clause embodies a substantive policy of free trade among the states, a policy that a state can countermand only for the most compelling reasons.

A number of questions are presented. First, why are discriminatory state statutes objectionable? Second, how does the Court go about determining whether a state law is discriminatory or non-discriminatory? Third, how does the Court apply these tests once it determines into which category the statute falls? Finally, does the doctrine make any sense? If it doesn't, what alternatives are available to guard against the Framers' fear of state-to-state trade wars? Consider the following cases.

1. Facial Discrimination

In some instances, state legislation explicitly and facially discriminates against out-of-state interests. The following cases illustrate the idea.

Granholm v. Heald

544 U.S. 460 (2005)

Justice KENNEDY delivered the opinion of the Court.

[Like] many other States, Michigan and New York regulate the sale and importation of alcoholic beverages, including wine, through a three-tier distribution system. Separate licenses are required for producers, wholesalers, and retailers. The three-tier scheme is preserved by a complex set of overlapping state and federal regulations. For example, both state and federal laws limit vertical integration between tiers. We have held previously that States can mandate a three-tier distribution scheme in the exercise of their authority under the Twenty-first Amendment. [The] three-tier system is, in broad terms and with refinements to be discussed, mandated by Michigan and New York only for sales from out-of-state wineries. In-state wineries, by contrast, can obtain a license for direct sales to consumers. The differential treatment between in-state and out-of-state wineries constitutes explicit discrimination against interstate commerce.

This discrimination substantially limits the direct sale of wine to consumers, an otherwise emerging and significant business. From 1994 to 1999, consumer spending on direct wine shipments doubled, reaching $500 million per year. . . . The expansion has been influenced by several related trends. First, the number of small wineries in the United States has significantly increased. . . . At the same time, the wholesale market has consolidated. Between 1984 and 2002, the number of licensed wholesalers dropped from 1,600 to 600. The increasing winery-to-wholesaler ratio means that many small wineries do not produce enough wine or have sufficient consumer demand for their wine to make it economical for wholesalers to carry their products. This has led many small wineries to rely on direct shipping to reach new markets. Technological improvements, in particular the ability of wineries to sell wine over the Internet, have helped make direct shipments an attractive sales channel.

Approximately 26 States allow some direct shipping of wine, with various restrictions. Thirteen of these States have reciprocity laws, which allow direct shipment from wineries outside the State, provided the State of origin affords similar nondiscriminatory treatment. In many parts of the country, however, state laws that prohibit or severely restrict direct shipments deprive consumers of access to the direct market. . . .

The wine producers in the cases before us are small wineries that rely on direct consumer sales as an important part of their businesses. Domaine Alfred, [a plaintiff] in the Michigan suit, is a small winery located in San Luis Obispo, California. . . . Domaine Alfred has received requests for its wine from Michigan consumers but cannot fill the orders because of the State's direct-shipment ban. Even if the winery could find a Michigan wholesaler to distribute its wine, the wholesaler's markup would render shipment through the three-tier system economically infeasible. . . . Similarly, Juanita Swedenburg and David Lucas, two of the plaintiffs in the New York suit, operate small wineries in Virginia (the Swedenburg Estate Vineyard) and California (the Lucas Winery). Some of their customers are tourists, from other States, who purchase wine while visiting the wineries. If these customers wish to obtain Swedenburg or Lucas wines after they return home, they will be unable to do so if they reside in a State with restrictive direct-shipment laws. [They] are unable to fill orders from New York, the Nation's second-largest wine market, because of the limits that State imposes on direct wine shipments.

[Most] alcoholic beverages in Michigan are distributed through the State's three-tier system. Producers or distillers of alcoholic beverages, whether located in state or out of state, generally may sell only to licensed in-state wholesalers. Wholesalers, in turn, may sell only to in-state retailers. Licensed retailers are the final link in the chain, selling alcoholic beverages to consumers at retail locations and, subject to certain restrictions, through home delivery. . . . There is, however, an exception for Michigan's approximately 40 in-state wineries, which are eligible for wine maker licenses that allow direct shipment to in-state consumers. . . . For a small winery, the license is $25. Out-of-state wineries can apply for a $300 outside seller of wine license, but this license only allows them to sell to in-state wholesalers. [The] District Court sustained the Michigan scheme. The Court of Appeals for the Sixth Circuit reversed. Relying on Bacchus Imports, Ltd. v. Dias, 468 U.S. 263 (1984), the court rejected the argument that the Twenty-first Amendment immunizes all state liquor laws from the strictures of the Commerce Clause. . . .

New York's licensing scheme [channels] most wine sales through the three-tier system, but it too makes exceptions for in-state wineries. [The] result is to allow local wineries to make direct sales to consumers in New York on terms not available to out-of-state wineries. Wineries that produce wine only from New York grapes can apply for a license that allows direct shipment to in-state consumers. These licensees are authorized to deliver the wines of other wineries as well, but only if the wine is made from grapes at least seventy-five percent the volume of which were grown in New York state. An out-of-state winery may ship directly to New York consumers only if it becomes a licensed New York winery, which requires the establishment of a branch factory, office or storeroom within the state of New York. [The] District Court granted summary judgment to the plaintiffs [and the] Court of Appeals for the Second Circuit reversed. . . .

Time and again this Court has held that, in all but the narrowest circumstances, state laws violate the Commerce Clause if they mandate differential treatment of in-state and out-of-state economic interests that benefits the former and burdens the latter. Oregon Waste Systems, Inc. v. Department of Environmental Quality of Ore., 511 U.S. 93, 99 (1994). This rule is essential to the foundations of the Union. The mere fact of nonresidence should not foreclose a producer in one State from access to markets in other States. H.P. Hood & Sons, Inc. v. Du Mond, 336 U.S. 525 (1949). States may not enact laws that burden out-of-state producers or shippers simply to give a competitive advantage to in-state businesses. This mandate reflect[s] a central concern of the Framers that was an immediate reason for calling the Constitutional Convention: the conviction that in order to succeed, the new Union would have to avoid the tendencies toward economic Balkanization that had plagued relations among the Colonies and later among the States under the Articles of Confederation. Hughes v. Oklahoma, 441 U.S. 322, 325-326 (1979).

The rule prohibiting state discrimination against interstate commerce follows also from the principle that States should not be compelled to negotiate with each other regarding favored or disfavored status for their own citizens. States do not need, and may not attempt, to negotiate with other States regarding their mutual economic interests. Cf. U.S. Const., Art. I, §10, cl. 3. Rivalries among the States are thus kept to a minimum, and a proliferation of trade zones is prevented. See C & A Carbone, Inc. v. Clarkstown, 511 U.S. 383 (1994).

Laws of the type at issue in the instant cases contradict these principles. They deprive citizens of their right to have access to the markets of other States on equal terms. The perceived necessity for reciprocal sale privileges risks generating the trade rivalries and animosities, the alliances and exclusivity, that the Constitution and, in particular, the Commerce Clause were designed to avoid. State laws that protect local wineries have led to the enactment of statutes under which some States condition the right of out-of-state wineries to make direct wine sales to in-state consumers on a reciprocal right in the shipping State. California, for example, passed a reciprocity law in 1986, retreating from the State's previous regime that allowed unfettered direct shipments from out-of-state wineries. . . . The obvious aim of the California statute was to open the interstate direct-shipping market for the State's many wineries. The current patchwork of laws — with some States banning direct shipments altogether, others doing so only for out-of-state wines, and still others requiring reciprocity — is essentially the product of an ongoing, low-level trade war. Allowing States to discriminate against out-of-state wine invite[s] a multiplication of preferential trade areas destructive of the very purpose of the Commerce Clause. Dean Milk Co. v. Madison, 340 U.S. 349, 356 (1951).

The discriminatory character of the Michigan system is obvious. Michigan allows in-state wineries to ship directly to consumers, subject only to a licensing requirement. Out-of-state wineries, whether licensed or not, face a complete ban on direct shipment. The differential treatment requires all out-of-state wine, but not all in-state wine, to pass through an in-state wholesaler and retailer before reaching consumers. These two extra layers of overhead increase the cost of out-of-state wines to Michigan consumers. The cost differential, and in some cases the inability to secure a wholesaler for small shipments, can effectively bar small wineries from the Michigan market.

The New York regulatory scheme differs from Michigan's in that it does not ban direct shipments altogether. Out-of-state wineries are instead required to establish a distribution operation in New York in order to gain the privilege of direct shipment. . . . The New York scheme grants in-state wineries access to the State's consumers on preferential terms. . . . In-state producers, with the applicable licenses, can ship directly to consumers from their wineries. Out-of-state wineries must open a branch office and warehouse in New York. . . . For most wineries, the expense of establishing a bricks-and-mortar distribution operation in 1 State, let alone all 50, is prohibitive. It comes as no surprise that not a single out-of-state winery has availed itself of New York's direct-shipping privilege. We have viewed with particular suspicion state statutes requiring business operations to be performed in the home State that could more efficiently be performed elsewhere. Pike v. Bruce Church, Inc., 397 U.S. 137, 145 (1970). New York's in-state presence requirement runs contrary to our admonition that States cannot require an out-of-state firm to become a resident in order to compete on equal terms. Halliburton Oil Well Cementing Co. v. Reily, 373 U.S. 64, 72 (1963). . . . New York discriminates against out-of-state wineries in other ways. Out-of-state wineries that establish the requisite branch office and warehouse in New York are still ineligible for a farm winery license, the license that provides the most direct means of shipping to New York consumers. Out-of-state wineries may apply only for a commercial winery license. Unlike farm wineries, however, commercial wineries must obtain a separate certificate from the state liquor authority authorizing direct shipments to consumers; and, of course, for out-of-state wineries there is the additional requirement of maintaining a distribution operation in New York. New York law also allows in-state wineries without direct-shipping licenses to distribute their wine through other wineries that have the applicable licenses. This is another privilege not afforded out-of-state wineries. . . . We have no difficulty concluding that New York, like Michigan, discriminates against interstate commerce through its direct-shipping laws.

[Michigan and New York] contend their statutes are saved by §2 of the Twenty-first Amendment, which provides: "The transportation or importation into any State, Territory, or possession of the United States for delivery or use therein of intoxicating liquors, in violation of the laws thereof, is hereby prohibited. [The] aim of the Twenty-first Amendment was to allow States to maintain an effective and uniform system for controlling liquor by regulating its transportation, importation, and use. The Amendment did not give States the authority to pass nonuniform laws in order to discriminate against out-of-state goods, a privilege they had not enjoyed at any earlier time." . . . The modern §2 cases fall into three categories. First, the Court has held that state laws that violate other provisions of the Constitution are not saved by the Twenty-first Amendment. The Court has applied this rule in the context of the First Amendment, the Establishment Clause, the Equal Protection Clause, and the Import-Export Clause. Second, the Court has held that §2 does not abrogate Congress' Commerce Clause powers with regard to liquor. . . . Finally, and most relevant to the issue at hand, the Court has held that state regulation of alcohol is limited by the nondiscrimination principle of the Commerce Clause. *Bacchus*, 468 U.S., at 276; Brown-Forman Distillers Corp. v. New York State Liquor Authority, 476 U.S. 573 (1986). When a state statute directly regulates or discriminates against interstate commerce, or when its effect is to favor in-state economic interests over out-of-state interests, we have generally struck down the statute without further inquiry. *Brown-Forman, supra,* at 579.

[A] State which chooses to ban the sale and consumption of alcohol altogether could bar its importation. . . . States may also assume direct control of liquor distribution through state-run outlets or funnel sales through the three-tier system. . . . State policies are protected under the Twenty-first Amendment when they treat liquor produced out of state the same as its domestic equivalent. The instant cases, in contrast, involve straightforward attempts to discriminate in favor of local producers. The discrimination is contrary to the Commerce Clause and is not saved by the Twenty-first Amendment.

[We] still must consider whether either state regime advances a legitimate local purpose that cannot be adequately served by reasonable nondiscriminatory alternatives. *New Energy Co. of Ind.*, 486 U.S., at 278. The States [claim] that allowing direct shipment from out-of-state wineries undermines their ability to police underage drinking. Minors, the States argue, have easy access to credit cards and the Internet and are likely to take advantage of direct wine shipments as a means of obtaining alcohol illegally. . . . A recent study [found] that the 26 States currently allowing direct shipments report no problems with minors' increased access to wine. FTC Report 34. This is not surprising. . . . First, minors are less likely to consume wine, as opposed to beer, wine coolers, and hard liquor. Second, minors who decide to disobey the law have more direct means of doing so. Third, direct shipping is an imperfect avenue of obtaining alcohol for minors [who] want instant gratification. [Our] precedents [require] the clearest showing to justify discriminatory state regulation, *C & A Carbone, Inc.*, 511 U.S., at 393. . . .

Even were we to credit the States' largely unsupported claim that direct shipping of wine increases the risk of underage drinking, this would not justify regulations limiting only out-of-state direct shipments. [M]inors are just as likely to order wine from in-state producers as from out-of-state ones. . . . Michigan counters that it has greater regulatory control over in-state producers than over out-of-state wineries. This does not justify Michigan's discriminatory ban on direct shipping. Out-of-state wineries face the loss of state and federal licenses if they fail to comply with state law. This provides strong incentives not to sell alcohol to minors. In addition, the States can take less restrictive steps to minimize the risk that minors will order wine by mail. For example, the Model Direct Shipping Bill developed by the National Conference of State Legislatures requires an adult signature on delivery and a label so instructing on each package.

The States' tax-collection justification is also insufficient. Increased direct shipping, whether originating in state or out of state, brings with it the potential for tax evasion. . . . Michigan, unlike many other States, does not rely on wholesalers to collect taxes on wines imported from out of state. Instead, Michigan collects taxes directly from out-of-state wineries on all wine shipped to in-state wholesalers. If licensing and self-reporting provide adequate safeguards for wine distributed through the three-tier system, there is no reason to believe they will not suffice for direct shipments. . . . New York could protect itself against lost tax revenue by requiring a permit as a condition of direct shipping. This is the approach taken by New York for in-state wineries. The State offers no reason to believe the system would prove ineffective for out-of-state wineries. Licensees could be required to submit regular sales reports and to remit taxes. Indeed, various States use this approach for taxing direct interstate wine shipments, and report no problems with tax collection. See FTC Report 38-40. This is also the procedure sanctioned by the National Conference of State Legislatures in their Model Direct Shipping Bill.

Michigan and New York benefit, furthermore, from provisions of federal law that supply incentives for wineries to comply with state regulations. The Tax and Trade Bureau (formerly the Bureau of Alcohol, Tobacco and Firearms) has authority to revoke a winery's federal license if it violates state law. Without a federal license, a winery cannot operate in any State. *See* 27 U.S.C. §204. In addition the Twenty-first Amendment Enforcement Act gives state attorneys general the power to sue wineries in federal court to enjoin violations of state law. . . . These federal remedies, when combined with state licensing regimes, adequately protect States from lost tax revenue. The States have not shown that tax evasion from out-of-state wineries poses such a unique threat that it justifies their discriminatory regimes.

Michigan and New York offer a handful of other rationales, such as facilitating orderly market conditions, protecting public health and safety, and ensuring regulatory accountability. These objectives can also be achieved through the alternative of an evenhanded licensing requirement. Finally, it should be noted that improvements in technology have eased the burden of monitoring out-of-state wineries. Background checks can be done electronically. Financial records and sales data can be mailed, faxed, or submitted via e-mail.

In summary, the States provide little concrete evidence for the sweeping assertion that they cannot police direct shipments by out-of-state wineries. Our Commerce Clause cases demand more than mere speculation to support discrimination against out-of-state goods. The burden is on the State to show that the *discrimination* is 'demonstrably justified,' Chemical Waste Management, Inc. v. Hunt, 504 U.S. 334, 344 (1992). The Court has upheld state regulations that discriminate against interstate commerce only after finding, based on concrete record evidence, that a State's nondiscriminatory alternatives will prove unworkable. *See, e.g.*, Maine v. Taylor, 477 U.S. 131 (1986). Michigan and New York have not satisfied this exacting standard. [If] a State chooses to allow direct shipment of wine, it must do so on evenhanded terms. Without demonstrating the need for discrimination, New York and Michigan have enacted regulations that disadvantage out-of-state wine producers. Under our Commerce Clause jurisprudence, these regulations cannot stand.

We affirm the judgment of the Court of Appeals for the Sixth Circuit; and we reverse the judgment of the Court of Appeals for the Second Circuit and remand the case for further proceedings consistent with our opinion.

It is so ordered.

Justice STEVENS, with whom Justice O'CONNOR joins, dissenting.

[Because] the New York and Michigan laws regulate the transportation or importation of intoxicating liquors for delivery or use therein, they are exempt from dormant Commerce Clause scrutiny. . . .

Justice THOMAS, with whom THE CHIEF JUSTICE, Justice STEVENS, and Justice O'CONNOR join, dissenting.

[The] Twenty-first Amendment [freed] the States from negative Commerce Clause restraints on discriminatory regulation. . . .

Notes

1. *The Baldwin Decision.* One of the most famous discrimination decisions was rendered in Baldwin v. G.A.F. Seelig, Inc., 294 U.S. 511 (1935). In that case, a milk dealer who purchased Vermont milk sought to challenge the New York Milk Control Act, which established "minimum prices" to be paid by dealers to milk producers. The producer was able to purchase the Vermont milk at prices below the minimum price, but New York refused to license his business unless he complied with the Act. In striking down the Act, the Court stated:

> New York has no power to project its legislation into Vermont by regulating the price to be paid in that state for milk acquired there. . . . New York is equally without power to prohibit the introduction within her territory of milk of wholesome quality acquired in Vermont, whether at high prices or at low ones. . . . New York asserts her power to outlaw milk so introduced by prohibiting its sale thereafter if the price that has been paid for it to the farmers of Vermont is less than would be owing in like circumstances to farmers in New York. The importer in that view may keep his milk or drink it, but sell it he may not. . . . Such a power, if exerted, will set a barrier to traffic between one state and another as effective as if customs duties, equal to the price differential, had been laid upon the thing transported. Imposts or duties upon commerce with other countries are placed, by an express prohibition of the Constitution, beyond the power of a state, "except what may be absolutely necessary for executing its inspection Laws." U.S. Const., art. 1, §10, cl. 2. Imposts and duties upon interstate

commerce are placed beyond the power of a state, without the mention of an exception, by the provision committing commerce of that order to the power of the Congress. U.S. Const., art. 1, §8, cl. 3. [A] chief occasion of the commerce clauses was "the mutual jealousies and aggressions of the States, taking form in customs barriers and other economic retaliation." Farrand, *Records of the Federal Convention*, vol. II, p. 308; vol. III, pp. 478, 547, 548; *The Federalist No. XLII*. If New York, in order to promote the economic welfare of her farmers, may guard them against competition with the cheaper prices of Vermont, the door has been opened to rivalries and reprisals that were meant to be averted by subjecting commerce between the states to the power of the nation.

The Court also rejected New York's argument that the law could be sustained on the basis that it was designed to ensure New Yorkers "a regular and adequate supply of pure and wholesome milk; the supply being put in jeopardy when the farmers of the state are unable to earn a living income." The Court disagreed: "Economic welfare is always related to health, for there can be no health if men are starving. Let such an exception be admitted, and all that a state will have to do in times of stress and strain is to say that its farmers and merchants and workmen must be protected against competition from without, lest they go upon the poor relief lists or perish altogether. To give entrance to that excuse would be to invite a speedy end of our national solidarity. The Constitution was framed under the dominion of a political philosophy [that] the peoples of the several states must sink or swim together, and that in the long run prosperity and salvation are in union and not division." The Court concluded that New York could deal with the problem of unsanitary milk in other, nonsanitary, ways: "[The] evils springing from uncared for cattle must be remedied by measures of repression more direct and certain than the creation of a parity of prices between New York and other states. Appropriate certificates may be exacted from farmers in Vermont and elsewhere; milk may be excluded if necessary safeguards have been omitted; but commerce between the states is burdened unduly when one state regulates by indirection the prices to be paid to producers in another, in the faith that augmentation of prices will lift up the level of economic welfare, and that this will stimulate the observance of sanitary requirements in the preparation of the product. The next step would be to condition importation upon proof of a satisfactory wage scale in factory or shop, or even upon proof of the profits of the business." The Court nonetheless recognized that "a state may regulate the importation of unhealthy swine or cattle or decayed or noxious foods," but noted that there was no evidence of problems with Vermont milk. The Court concluded: "[O]ne state in its dealings with another may not place itself in a position of economic isolation. Formulas and catchwords are subordinate to this overmastering requirement. Neither the power to tax nor the police power may be used by the state of destination with the aim and effect of establishing an economic barrier against competition with the products of another state or the labor of its residents. Restrictions so contrived are an unreasonable clog upon the mobility of commerce. They set up what is equivalent to a rampart of customs duties designed to neutralize advantages belonging to the place of origin. They are thus hostile in conception as well as burdensome in result."

2. *Licensing Requirements*. May a state impose different licensing requirements on out-of-state individuals and businesses than it imposes on in-state individuals and businesses? Welton v. Missouri, 91 U.S. (1 Otto) 275 (1876), involved a Missouri law that provided that peddlers who sold products that were not the growth, produce, or manufacture of Missouri must first obtain a license, but those who sold products grown, produced, or manufactured in Missouri were not required to obtain one. The law was challenged by a sewing machine dealer who was convicted for selling sewing machines manufactured outside of Missouri without a license. The Court struck down the law: "[The] question presented is, whether legislation thus discriminating against the products of other States in the conditions of their sale by a certain class of dealers is valid under the Constitution of the United States. . . . [The Constitution protects] property which is transported as an article of commerce from hostile or interfering legislation, until it has mingled with and become a part of the general property of the country, and subjected like it to similar protection, and to no greater burdens. . . . It is sufficient to hold now that the commercial power continues until the commodity has ceased to be the subject of discriminating legislation by reason of its foreign character. That power protects it, even after it has entered the State, from any burdens imposed by reason of its foreign origin. The act of Missouri encroaches upon this power in this respect, and is therefore, in our judgment, unconstitutional and void."

3. *Protecting Local Needs and Interests*. Can a state prohibit exportation of products produced within the state? Pennsylvania v. West Virginia, 262 U.S. 553 (1923), involved a West Virginia law that prohibited the interstate shipment of natural gas unless and until the state's own need for natural gas had been met. The law was passed following a winter in which gas supplies ran short and West Virginia consumer needs were unmet. The Court struck down the law on the basis that it involved discrimination against interstate commerce: "[I]n the matter of interstate commerce we are a single nation — one and the same people. All the states have assented to it, all are alike bound by it, and all are equally protected by it. . . . Natural gas is a lawful article of commerce, and its transmission from one state to another for sale and consumption in the latter is interstate commerce. A state law, whether of the state where the gas is produced or that where it is to be sold, which by its necessary operation prevents, obstructs or burdens such transmission is a regulation of interstate commerce — a prohibited interference. . . . [West Virginia argued] that the gas is a natural product of the state and has become a necessity therein, that the supply is waning and no longer sufficient to satisfy local needs and be used abroad, and that the act is therefore a legitimate measure of conservation in the interest of the people of the state. . . . If the situation be as stated, it affords no ground for the assumption by the state of power to regulate interstate commerce. . . . 'If the states have such power a singular situation might result. Pennsylvania might keep its coal, the Northwest its timber, the mining states their minerals. . . . [E]mbargo may be retaliated by embargo, and commerce will be halted at state lines. [We] have said that 'in matters of foreign and interstate commerce there are no state lines.'" Justice Holmes dissented: "[The] Constitution does not prohibit a State from securing a reasonable

preference for its own inhabitants in the enjoyment of its products even when the effect of its law is to keep property within its boundaries that otherwise would have passed outside."

In Hughes v. Oklahoma, 441 U.S. 322 (1979), the Court rendered a similar decision in a case involving an Oklahoma law that provided that "[n]o person may transport or ship minnows for sale outside the state which were seined or procured within the waters of this state." The Court held: "At a minimum such facial discrimination invokes the strictest scrutiny of any purported legitimate local purpose and of the absence of nondiscriminatory alternatives. . . . The State's interest in maintaining the ecological balance in state waters by avoiding the removal of inordinate numbers of minnows may well qualify as a legitimate local purpose. . . . But [the] fiction of state ownership may no longer be used to force those outside the State to bear the full costs of 'conserving' the wild animals within its borders when equally effective nondiscriminatory conservation measures are available. . . . Far from choosing the least discriminatory alternative, Oklahoma has chosen to 'conserve' its minnows in the way that most overtly discriminates against interstate commerce. The State places no limits on the numbers of minnows that can be taken by licensed minnow dealers; nor does it limit in any way how these minnows may be disposed of within the State. Yet it forbids the transportation of any commercially significant number of natural minnows out of the State for sale." Justice Rehnquist, joined by Chief Justice Burger, dissented: "The Oklahoma law [serves] the special interest of the State, as representative of its citizens, in preserving and regulating exploitation of free-swimming minnows found within its waters. . . . This is not a case where a State's regulation permits residents to export naturally seined minnows but prohibits nonresidents from so doing. No person is allowed to export natural minnows for sale outside of Oklahoma. . . . The State has not used its power to protect its own citizens from outside competition. . . . Appellant, or anyone else, may freely export as many minnows as he wishes, so long as the minnows so transported are hatchery minnows and not naturally seined minnows."

4. *Assessing Neutrality.* How does a court decide whether a facially neutral state law involves discrimination? Kassel v. Consolidated Freightways Corp., 450 U.S. 662 (1981), involved an Iowa statute that prohibited most uses of 65-foot trucks on Iowa highways. In striking down the law, the Court found that it imposed a substantial burden on interstate commerce. Although the law generally banned large double trucks, it contained "several exemptions that secure to Iowans many of the benefits of large trucks while shunting to neighboring States many of the costs associated with their use. . . . First, singles hauling livestock or farm vehicles were permitted to be as long as 60 feet. . . . Second cities abutting other States were permitted to enact local ordinances adopting the larger length limitation of the neighboring State. . . . The origin of the 'border cities exemption' also suggests that Iowa's statute may not have been designed to ban dangerous trucks, but rather to discourage interstate truck traffic. . . . Iowa seems to have hoped to limit the use of its highways by deflecting some through traffic. . . ." Justice Rehnquist, joined by Chief Justice Burger and Justice Stewart,

dissented, claiming that the law was reasonable: "Iowa adduced evidence supporting the relation between vehicle length and highway safety. [L]onger vehicles
take greater time to be passed, thereby increasing the risks of accidents, particularly during the inclement weather not uncommon in Iowa. The 65-foot vehicle
exposes a passing driver to visibility-impairing splash and spray during bad
weather for a longer period than do the shorter trucks permitted in Iowa. Longer
trucks are more likely to clog intersections. [T]rucks involved in accidents often
must be unloaded at the scene, which would take longer the bigger the load. . . .
In sum, there was sufficient evidence [to] support the legislative determination
that length is related to safety, and nothing in Consolidated's evidence undermines this conclusion. . . ." In addition, the dissenters rejected the idea that the
legislation was protectionist.

∾ PROBLEM: MORE ON THE INTERNET
CASINO PROHIBITION ACT ∾

Is Kentucky's Internet Casino Prohibition Act facially discriminatory against
interstate commerce? Would a court be inclined, given the facts set forth in the
problem described at the beginning of the chapter, to conclude that Kentucky
intended to discriminate against interstate commerce? What weight do you
attach to the fact that Governor Wonkley, ordinarily a strong supporter of gambling and gambling interests, strongly opposed Internet gambling and decried
the adverse effects of Internet gambling on society and on Kentucky families? Was
he concerned about those issues when he proposed expanded gambling at Kentucky's racetracks? Should that matter in assessing the validity of the Act? To what
extent should the demographics of Kentucky and the defeat of the idea of
expanded gambling at racetracks enter into your analysis?

City of Philadelphia v. New Jersey et al.
437 U.S. 617 (1978)

Mr. Justice STEWART delivered the opinion of the Court.
A New Jersey law prohibits the importation of most "solid or liquid waste
which originated or was collected outside the territorial limits of the State . . ." In
this case we are required to decide whether this statutory prohibition violates the
Commerce Clause of the United States Constitution . . .
Immediately affected by [this law] were the operators of private landfills in
New Jersey, and several cities in other States that had agreements with these
operators for waste disposal. They brought suit against New Jersey and its
Department of Environmental Protection in state court, attacking the statute and
regulations on a number of state and federal grounds.
[W]e reject the state court's suggestion that the banning of "valueless" out-
of-state wastes by ch. 363 implicates no constitutional protection. Just as Congress has power to regulate the interstate movement of these wastes, States are
not free from constitutional scrutiny when they restrict that movement. . . . The

crucial inquiry [must] be directed to determining whether ch. 363 is basically a protectionist measure, or whether it can fairly be viewed as a law directed to legitimate local concerns, with effects upon interstate commerce that are only incidental.

The purpose of ch. 363 is set out in the statute itself as follows: "The Legislature finds and determines [that] the volume of solid and liquid waste continues to rapidly increase, that the treatment and disposal of these wastes continues to pose an even greater threat to the quality of the environment of New Jersey, that the available and appropriate landfill sites within the State are being diminished, that the environment continues to be threatened by the treatment and disposal of waste which originated or was collected outside the State, and that the public health, safety and welfare require that the treatment and disposal within this State of all wastes generated outside of the State be prohibited."

The New Jersey Supreme Court accepted this statement of the state legislature's purpose. The state court additionally found that New Jersey's existing landfill sites will be exhausted within a few years; that to go on using these sites or to develop new ones will take a heavy environmental toll, both from pollution and from loss of scarce open lands; that new techniques to divert waste from landfills to other methods of disposal and resource recovery processes are under development, but that these changes will require time; and finally, that "the extension of the lifespan of existing landfills, resulting from the exclusion of out-of-state waste, may be of crucial importance in preventing further virgin wetlands or other undeveloped lands from being devoted to landfill purposes." Based on these findings, the court concluded that ch. 363 was designed to protect, not the State's economy, but its environment, and that its substantial benefits outweigh its "slight" burden on interstate commerce.

The appellants strenuously contend that ch. 363, "while outwardly cloaked 'in the currently fashionable garb of environmental protection,' . . . is actually no more than a legislative effort to suppress competition and stabilize the cost of solid waste disposal for New Jersey residents. . . ." They cite passages of legislative history suggesting that the problem addressed by ch. 363 is primarily financial: Stemming the flow of out-of-state waste into certain landfill sites will extend their lives, thus delaying the day when New Jersey cities must transport their waste to more distant and expensive sites.

[Appellees] deny that ch. 363 was motivated by financial concerns or economic protectionism. In the words of their brief, "[n]o New Jersey commercial interests stand to gain advantage over competitors from outside the state as a result of the ban on dumping out-of-state waste." Noting that New Jersey landfill operators are among the plaintiffs, the appellee's brief argues that "[t]he complaint is not that New Jersey has forged an economic preference for its own commercial interests, but rather that it has denied a small group of its entrepreneurs an economic opportunity to traffic in waste in order to protect the health, safety and welfare of the citizenry at large."

This dispute about ultimate legislative purpose need not be resolved, because its resolution would not be relevant to the constitutional issue to be decided in this case. [T]he evil of protectionism can reside in legislative means as well as legislative ends. Thus, it does not matter whether the ultimate aim of ch. 363 is to reduce the waste disposal costs of New Jersey residents or to save remaining open lands from pollution, for we assume New Jersey has every right to protect its residents' pocketbooks as well as their environment. And it may be assumed as well that New Jersey may pursue those ends by slowing the flow of all waste into the State's remaining landfills, even though interstate commerce may incidentally be affected. But whatever New Jersey's ultimate purpose, it may not be accomplished by discriminating against articles of commerce coming from outside the State unless there is some reason, apart from their origin, to treat them differently. Both on its face and in its plain effect, ch. 363 violates this principle of nondiscrimination.

The Court has consistently found parochial legislation of this kind to be constitutionally invalid, whether the ultimate aim of the legislation was to assure a steady supply of milk by erecting barriers to allegedly ruinous outside competition, or to create jobs by keeping industry within the State, or to preserve the State's financial resources from depletion by fencing out indigent immigrants. In each of these cases, a presumably legitimate goal was sought to be achieved by the illegitimate means of isolating the State from the national economy.

Also relevant here are the Court's decisions holding that a State may not accord its own inhabitants a preferred right of access over consumers in other States to natural resources located within its borders. West, Attorney General of Oklahoma v. Kansas Natural Gas Co., 221 U.S. 229; Pennsylvania v. West Virginia, 262 U.S. 553. These cases stand for the basic principle that a "State is without power to prevent privately owned articles of trade from being shipped and sold in interstate commerce on the ground that they are required to satisfy local demands or because they are needed by the people of the State." Foster-Fountain Packing Co. v. Haydel, *supra*, 278 U.S., at 10.

The New Jersey law at issue in this case falls squarely within the area that the Commerce Clause puts off limits to state regulation. On its face, it imposes on out-of-state commercial interests the full burden of conserving the State's remaining landfill space. It is true that in our previous cases the scarce natural resource was itself the article of commerce, whereas here the scarce resource and the article of commerce are distinct. But that difference is without consequence. In both instances, the State has overtly moved to slow or freeze the flow of commerce for protectionist reasons. It does not matter that the State has shut the article of commerce inside the State in one case and outside the State in the other. What is crucial is the attempt by one State to isolate itself from a problem common to many by erecting a barrier against the movement of interstate trade.

The appellees argue that not all laws which facially discriminate against out-of-state commerce are forbidden protectionist regulations. In particular, they point to quarantine laws, which this Court has repeatedly upheld even though they appear to single out interstate commerce for special treatment. In the appellees' view, ch. 363 is analogous to such health-protective measures, since it reduces the exposure of New Jersey residents to the allegedly harmful effects of landfill sites.

It is true that certain quarantine laws have not been considered forbidden protectionist measures, even though they were directed against out-of-state commerce. *See* Asbell v. Kansas, 209 U.S. 251. But those quarantine laws banned the importation of articles such as diseased livestock that required destruction as soon as possible because their very movement risked contagion and other evils. Those laws thus did not discriminate against interstate commerce as such, but simply prevented traffic in noxious articles, whatever their origin.

The New Jersey statute is not such a quarantine law. There has been no claim here that the very movement of waste into or through New Jersey endangers health, or that waste must be disposed of as soon and as close to its point of generation as possible. The harms caused by waste are said to arise after its disposal in landfill sites, and at that point [there] is no basis to distinguish out-of-state waste from domestic waste. If one is inherently harmful, so is the other. Yet New Jersey has banned the former while leaving its landfill sites open to the latter. The New Jersey law blocks the importation of waste in an obvious effort to saddle those outside the State with the entire burden of slowing the flow of refuse into New Jersey's remaining landfill sites. That legislative effort is clearly impermissible under the Commerce Clause of the Constitution.

Today, cities in Pennsylvania and New York find it expedient or necessary to send their waste into New Jersey for disposal, and New Jersey claims the right to close its borders to such traffic. Tomorrow, cities in New Jersey may find it expedient or necessary to send their waste into Pennsylvania or New York for disposal, and those States might then claim the right to close their borders. The Commerce Clause will protect New Jersey in the future, just as it protects her neighbors now, from efforts by one State to isolate itself in the stream of interstate commerce from a problem shared by all. The judgment is

Reversed.

Mr. Justice REHNQUIST, with whom THE CHIEF JUSTICE joins, dissenting.

[The] Court recognizes that States can prohibit the importation of items "which, on account of their existing condition, would bring in and spread disease, pestilence, and death, such as rags or other substances infected with the germs of yellow fever or the virus of small-pox, or cattle or meat or other provisions that are diseased or decayed or otherwise, from their condition and quality, unfit for human use or consumption." As the Court points out, such "quarantine laws have not been considered forbidden protectionist measures, even though they were directed against out-of-state commerce."

In my opinion, these cases are dispositive of the present one. Under them, New Jersey may require germ-infected rags or diseased meat to be disposed of as best as possible within the State, but at the same time prohibit the importation of such items for disposal at the facilities that are set up within New Jersey for disposal of such material generated within the State. The physical fact of life that New Jersey must somehow dispose of its own noxious items does not mean that it must serve as a depository for those of every other State. Similarly, New Jersey should be free under our past precedents to prohibit the importation of solid waste because of the health and safety problems that such waste poses to its citizens. The fact that New Jersey continues to, and indeed must continue to, dispose of its own solid waste does not mean that New Jersey may not prohibit the importation of even more solid waste into the State. I simply see no way to distinguish solid waste, on the record of this case, from germ-infected rags, diseased meat, and other noxious items.

The Court's effort to distinguish these prior cases is unconvincing. It first asserts that the quarantine laws which have previously been upheld "banned the importation of articles such as diseased livestock that required destruction as soon as possible because their very movement risked contagion and other evils." Solid waste which is a health hazard when it reaches its destination may in all likelihood be an equally great health hazard in transit. . . . [T]he Court implies that the challenged laws must be invalidated because New Jersey has left its landfills open to domestic waste. But, as the Court notes, this Court has repeatedly upheld quarantine laws "even though they appear to single out interstate commerce for special treatment." . . .

The Supreme Court of New Jersey expressly found that ch. 363 was passed "to preserve the health of New Jersey residents by keeping their exposure to solid waste and landfill areas to a minimum." The Court points to absolutely no evidence that would contradict this finding by the New Jersey Supreme Court. . . .

Note: State Quarantine Laws

The Supreme Court has upheld state quarantine laws (e.g., laws prohibiting the importation of diseased livestock), despite the effects those laws have on interstate commerce. *See, e.g.,* Mintz v. Baldwin, 289 U.S. 346 (1933); Asbell v. Kansas, 209 U.S. 251 (1908). In quarantine cases, the Court characterized the statutes as police measures designed to protect the citizenry's health and safety. By contrast, in Railroad Co. v. Husen, 95 U.S. 465 (1877), the Court struck down a Missouri statute banning the importation of Texas, Mexican, or Indian cattle between March 1 and November 1. The Court declined to characterize the law as a valid quarantine measure due to its categorical nature (i.e., not banning the importation of just diseased cattle, but of all cattle from a certain origin).

Question: Distinguishing Baldwin

Baldwin indicates that states may quarantine out-of-state diseased cattle in order to protect the health, welfare, and safety of their citizens. Does the *Philadelphia* Court adequately distinguish *Baldwin*? Is it really true, as the Court claims, that there "has been no claim [in the *Philadelphia* case] that the very movement of waste into or through New Jersey endangers health, or that waste must be disposed of as soon and as close to its point of generation as possible"?

∼ PROBLEM: OTHER WAYS TO SKIN THE CAT? ∼

If New Jersey does not have the power to ban out-of-state waste, does that mean that New Jersey is powerless to protect its citizens? What regulatory laws might it impose? Could New Jersey place the following regulations on the dumps themselves without discriminating against interstate commerce? a) A requirement that all New Jersey trash dumps be licensed; b) a requirement that all New Jersey trash dumps are subject to health and safety restrictions regarding the handling of certain types of toxic chemicals; c) a requirement that all New Jersey dumps be periodically inspected to make sure that they are being operated in compliance with local health and safety laws; d) a per-truckload fee ($100) on each truckload of refuse deposited in a New Jersey dump; e) a limit on the total amount of refuse that can be deposited in a given dump; f) an "environmental fee" imposed on each truckload of refuse deposited in a New Jersey dump, designed to help New Jersey combat and clean up the ill effects of refuse in New Jersey dumps. Does the amount of the fee (e.g., $500 or $5,000) matter? As we shall see in the next section, such restrictions will also be subject to review under the Court's dormant Commerce Clause analysis.

2. Facially Neutral Statutes with Discriminatory Purposes or Effects

Rarely does a legislature announce its intention to discriminate against interstate commerce. In *Baldwin*, for example, the State of New York proclaimed an allegedly nondiscriminatory purpose: "The end to be served is the maintenance of a regular and adequate supply of pure and wholesome milk; the supply being put in jeopardy when the farmers of the state are unable to earn a living income." However, the Court pierced through the state's analysis and concluded that its real goal was economic isolation. Suppose that a state has a valid nondiscriminatory purpose that cannot be served by other means. Can it then impose a restriction on interstate commerce? If the state has a bona fide alternative purpose, can the state argue that it has no intent to discriminate?

Dean Milk Co. v. City of Madison
340 U.S. 349 (1951)

Mr. Justice CLARK delivered the opinion of the Court.

This appeal challenges the constitutional validity of two sections of an ordinance of the City of Madison, Wisconsin, regulating the sale of milk and milk products within the municipality's jurisdiction. One section [makes] it unlawful to sell any milk as pasteurized unless it has been processed and bottled at an approved pasteurization plant within a radius of five miles from the central square of Madison. Another section, which prohibits the sale of milk, or the importation, receipt or storage of milk for sale, in Madison unless from a source of supply possessing a permit issued after inspection by Madison officials, is attacked insofar as it expressly relieves municipal authorities from any duty to inspect farms located beyond twenty-five miles from the center of the city.

Appellant is an Illinois corporation engaged in distributing milk and milk products in Illinois and Wisconsin. It [contends] that both the five-mile limit on pasteurization plants and the twenty-five-mile limit on sources of milk violate the Commerce Clause. . . .

Appellant purchases and gathers milk from approximately 950 farms in northern Illinois and southern Wisconsin, none being within twenty-five miles of Madison. Its pasteurization plants [are in] Illinois, about 65 and 85 miles respectively from Madison. Appellant was denied a license to sell its products within Madison solely because its pasteurization plants were more than five miles away.

It is conceded that the milk which appellant seeks to sell in Madison is supplied from farms and processed in plants licensed and inspected by public health authorities of Chicago, and is labeled "Grade A" under the Chicago ordinance which adopts the rating standards recommended by the United States Public Health Service. Both the Chicago and Madison ordinances [are] largely patterned after the Model Milk Ordinance of the Public Health Service. However, Madison contends and we assume that in some particulars its ordinance is more rigorous than that of Chicago.

[W]e agree with appellant that the ordinance imposes an undue burden on interstate commerce. [In] erecting an economic barrier protecting a major local industry against competition from without the State, Madison plainly discriminates against interstate commerce. This it cannot do, even in the exercise of its unquestioned power to protect the health and safety of its people, if reasonable nondiscriminatory alternatives, adequate to conserve legitimate local interests, are available. A different view, that the ordinance is valid simply because it professes to be a health measure, would mean that the Commerce Clause of itself imposes no limitations on state action other than those laid down by the Due Process Clause, save for the rare instance where a state artlessly discloses an avowed purpose to discriminate against interstate goods. Our issue then is whether the discrimination inherent in the Madison ordinance can be justified in view of the character of the local interests and the available methods of protecting them. . . .

It appears that reasonable and adequate alternatives are available. If the City of Madison prefers to rely upon its own officials for inspection of distant milk sources, such inspection is readily open to it without hardship for it could charge the actual and reasonable cost of such inspection to the importing producers and processors. . . . Moreover, appellee Health Commissioner of Madison testified that as proponent of the local milk ordinance he had submitted the provisions here in controversy and an alternative proposal based on §11 of the Model Milk Ordinance recommended by the United States Public Health Service. . . . The Commissioner testified that Madison consumers "would be safeguarded adequately" under either proposal and that he had expressed no preference. The milk sanitarian of the Wisconsin State Board of Health testified that the State Health Department recommends the adoption of a provision based on the Model Ordinance. Both officials agreed that a local health officer would be justified in relying upon the evaluation by the Public Health Service of enforcement conditions in remote producing areas. . . .

To permit Madison to adopt a regulation not essential for the protection of local health interests and placing a discriminatory burden on interstate commerce would invite a multiplication of preferential trade areas destructive of the very purpose of the Commerce Clause. Under the circumstances here presented, the regulation must yield to the principle that 'one state in its dealings with another may not place itself in a position of economic isolation.' . . .

For these reasons we conclude that the judgment below sustaining the five-mile provision as to pasteurization must be reversed.

The Supreme Court of Wisconsin thought it unnecessary to pass upon the validity of the twenty-five-mile limitation, apparently in part for the reason that this issue was made academic by its decision upholding the five-mile section. In view of our conclusion as to the latter provision, a determination of appellant's contention as to the other section is now necessary. As to this issue, therefore, we vacate the judgment below and remand for further proceedings not inconsistent with the principles announced in this opinion. It is so ordered.

Judgment vacated and cause remanded. . . .

Note: Live Baitfish

In Maine v. Taylor, 477 U.S. 131 (1986), the Court upheld a Maine statute banning the importation of live baitfish. The statute discriminated against interstate commerce by imposing an embargo against imports of baitfish. The Court held that the statute satisfied strict scrutiny because the state's purpose (protection of Maine's "unique and ecologically fragile" fisheries) could not be protected by a less burdensome method. The Court concluded that inspection methods, which tested imported baitfish for parasites, could not reliably produce disease-free shipments.

⟿ PROBLEM: MORE ON THE INTERNET
CASINO PROHIBITION ACT ⟿

Even if the Internet Casino Prohibition Act is facially neutral, can it be argued that the Act has a discriminatory purpose or effect? If so, how can you make that argument? How might the state refute the notion of a discriminatory purpose or effect?

Exxon Corporation v. Maryland

437 U.S. 117 (1978)

Mr. Justice STEVENS delivered the opinion of the Court.

A Maryland statute provides that a producer or refiner of petroleum products [may] not operate any retail service station within the State. . . . The questions presented are whether the statute violates [the Commerce Clause] of the Constitution of the United States. . . .

The Maryland statute is an outgrowth of the 1973 shortage of petroleum. In response to complaints about inequitable distribution of gasoline among retail stations, the Governor of Maryland directed the State Comptroller to conduct a market survey. The results of that survey indicated that gasoline stations operated by producers or refiners had received preferential treatment during the period of short supply. The Comptroller therefore proposed legislation which [was] "designed to correct the inequities in the distribution and pricing of gasoline reflected by the survey." After legislative hearings and a "special veto hearing" before the Governor, the bill was enacted and signed into law. . . . Shortly before the effective date of the Act, Exxon Corp. filed a declaratory judgment action challenging the statute. . . . After trial, the Circuit Court held the entire statute invalid. . . . The Maryland Court of Appeals reversed. . . .

III

Appellants argue that the divestiture provisions of the Maryland statute violate the Commerce Clause in three ways: (1) by discriminating against interstate commerce; (2) by unduly burdening interstate commerce; and (3) by imposing controls on a commercial activity of such an essentially interstate character that it is not amenable to state regulation.

Plainly, the Maryland statute does not discriminate against interstate goods, nor does it favor local producers and refiners. Since Maryland's entire gasoline supply flows in interstate commerce and since there are no local producers or refiners, such claims of disparate treatment between interstate and local commerce would be meritless. Appellants, however, focus on the retail market arguing that the effect of the statute is to protect in-state independent dealers from out-of-state competition. They contend that the divestiture provisions "create a protected enclave for Maryland independent dealers. . . ." [T]hey rely on the fact that the burden of the divestiture requirements falls solely on interstate companies. But this fact does not lead, either logically or as a practical matter, to a conclusion that the State is discriminating against interstate commerce at the retail level.

As the record shows, there are several major interstate marketers of petroleum that own and operate their own retail gasoline stations. These interstate dealers, who compete directly with the Maryland independent dealers, are not affected by the Act because they do not refine or produce gasoline. In fact, the Act creates no barriers whatsoever against interstate independent dealers; it does not prohibit the flow of interstate goods, place added costs upon them, or distinguish between in-state and out-of-state companies in the retail market. The absence of any of these factors fully distinguishes this case from those in which a State has been found to have discriminated against interstate commerce. *See, e.g.* Hunt v. Washington Apple Advertising Comm'n., 432 U.S. 333 [(1977)]. [These other cases involved statutes that] raised the cost of doing business for out-of-state dealers, and, in various other ways, favored the in-state dealer in the local market. No comparable claim can be made here. While the refiners will no longer enjoy their same status in the Maryland market, in-state independent dealers will have no competitive advantage over out-of-state dealers. The fact that the burden of a state regulation falls on some interstate companies does not, by itself, establish a claim of discrimination against interstate commerce.

Appellants argue [that] this fact does show that the Maryland statute impermissibly burdens interstate commerce. They point to evidence [which] indicates that, because of the divestiture requirements, at least three refiners will stop selling in Maryland, and which also [shows] that the elimination of company-operated stations will deprive the consumer of certain special services. [Neither assertion] warrants a finding that the statute impermissibly burdens interstate commerce.

Some refiners may choose to withdraw entirely from the Maryland market, but there is no reason to assume that their share of the entire supply will not be promptly replaced by other interstate refiners. The source of the consumers' supply may switch from company-operated stations to independent dealers, but interstate commerce is not subjected to an impermissible burden simply because an otherwise valid regulation causes some business to shift from one interstate supplier to another.

[Appellants claim that], regardless of whether the State has interfered with the movement of goods in interstate commerce, it has interfered "with the natural functioning of the interstate market either through prohibition or through burdensome regulation." Appellants then claim that the statute "will surely change the market structure by weakening the independent refiners. . . ." We cannot, however, accept appellants' underlying notion that the Commerce Clause protects the particular structure or methods of operation in a retail market. [T]he [dormant Commerce] Clause protects the interstate market, not particular interstate firms, from prohibitive or burdensome regulations. It may be true that the consuming public will be injured by the loss of the high-volume, low-priced stations operated by the independent refiners, but [that] argument relates to the wisdom of the statute, not to its burden on commerce.

[W]e cannot adopt appellants' novel suggestion that because the economic market for petroleum products is nationwide, no State has the power to regulate the retail marketing of gas. Appellants point out that many state legislatures have either enacted or considered proposals similar to Maryland's, and that the cumulative effect of this sort of legislation may have serious implications for their national marketing operations. While this concern is a significant one, we do not find that the Commerce Clause, by its own force, pre-empts the field of retail gas marketing. [T]his Court has only rarely held that the Commerce Clause [pre-empts] an entire field from state regulation, and then only when a lack of national uniformity would impede the flow of interstate goods. . . . In the absence of a relevant congressional declaration of policy, or a showing of a specific discrimination against, or burdening of, interstate commerce, we cannot conclude that the States are without power to regulate in this area. . . .

The judgment is affirmed.

So ordered.

Mr. Justice BLACKMUN, concurring in part and dissenting in part.

[The] divestiture provisions preclude out-of-state competitors from retailing gasoline within Maryland. The effect is to protect in-state retail service station dealers from the competition of the out-of-state businesses. This protectionist discrimination is not justified by any legitimate state interest that cannot be vindicated by more evenhanded regulation. . . .

[In] 1974, of the 3,780 gasoline service stations in the State, 3,547 were operated by nonintegrated local retail dealers. Of the 233 company-operated stations, 197 belonged to out-of-state integrated producers or refiners. Thirty-four were operated by nonintegrated companies that would not have been affected immediately by the Maryland statute. The only in-state integrated petroleum firm, Crown Central Petroleum, Inc., operated just two service stations. Of the class of stations statutorily insulated from the competition of the out-of-state integrated firms, then, more than 99% were operated by local business interests. Of the class of enterprises excluded entirely from participation in the retail gasoline market, 95% were out-of-state firms, operating 98% of the stations in the class.

The discrimination suffered by the out-of-state integrated producers and refiners is significant. Five of the excluded enterprises, market nonbranded gasoline through price competition rather than through brand recognition. Of the 98 stations marketing gasoline in this manner, all but 6 are company operated. The company operations result from the dominant fact of price competition marketing. [S]uch nonbranded stations can compete successfully only if they have day-to-day control of the retail price of their products, the hours of operation of their stations, and related business details. Only with such control can sufficient sales volume be achieved to produce satisfactory profits at prices two to three cents a gallon below those of the major branded stations. . . . Therefore, because §§(b) and (c) forbid company operations, these out-of-state competitors will have to abandon the Maryland retail market altogether. For the same reason 32 other out-of-state national nonbranded integrated marketers, who operate their own stations without dealers, will be precluded from entering the Maryland retail gasoline market.

[T]he discrimination will burden the operations of major branded companies, such as appellants Exxon, Phillips, Shell, and Gulf, all of which are out-of-state firms. [T]he divestiture provisions, which will require the appellant majors to cease operation of property valued at more than $10 million, will inflict significant economic hardship on Maryland's major brand companies, all of which are out-of-state firms.

Similar hardship is not imposed upon the local service station dealers by the divestiture provisions. Indeed, rather than restricting their ability to compete, the Maryland Act effectively and perhaps intentionally improves their competitive position by insulating them from competition by out-of-state integrated producers and refiners. In its answers to the various complaints in this case, the State repeatedly conceded that the Act was intended to protect "the retail dealer as an independent businessman [by] reducing the control and dominance of the vertically integrated petroleum producer and refiner in the retail market." In short, the foundation of the discrimination in this case is that the local dealers may continue to enter retail transactions and to compete for retail profits while the statute will deny similar opportunities to the class composed almost entirely of out-of-state businesses. . . .

[T]he Court says that the discrimination against the class of out-of-state producers and refiners does not violate the Commerce Clause because the State has not imposed similar discrimination against other out-of-state retailers. . . . To accept the argument of the Court, that is, that discrimination must be universal to offend the Commerce Clause, naively will foster protectionist discrimination against interstate commerce. In the future, States will be able to insulate in-state interests from competition by identifying the most potent segments of out-of-state business, banning them, and permitting less effective out-of-state actors to remain. . . .

[T]he Court asserts [that] "The fact that the burden of a state regulation falls on some interstate companies does not, by itself, establish a claim of discrimination against interstate commerce." [W]hen the burden is significant, when it falls on the most numerous and effective group of out-of-state competitors, when a similar burden does not fall on the class of protected in-state businessmen, and when the State cannot justify the resulting disparity by showing that its legislative interests cannot be vindicated by more evenhanded regulation, unconstitutional discrimination exists. The facts of this litigation demonstrate such discrimination, and the Court does not argue persuasively to the contrary.

[T]he Court of Appeals reasoned that §§(b) and (c) did not discriminate against the class of out-of-state refiners and producers because the wholesale flow of petroleum products into the State was not restricted. This supposedly distinguished the present facts from those of Dean Milk Co. v. Madison, which involved unconstitutional discrimination against interstate commerce. To begin with, however, the distinction drawn by the Court of Appeals is basically irrelevant. The Maryland statute has not effected discrimination with regard to the wholesaling or interstate transport of petroleum. The discrimination exists with regard to retailing. The fact that gasoline will continue to flow into the State does not permit the State to deny out-of-state firms the opportunity to retail it once it arrives. . . .

[T]he State argues that discrimination against interstate commerce has not occurred because "[n]o nexus between interstate as opposed to local interests inheres in the production or refining of petroleum." Although this statement might be correct in the abstract, it is incorrect in reality, given the structure of the Maryland petroleum market. Due to geological formation as so far known, no petroleum is produced in Maryland; due to the economics of production and refining, as well as to the geology, no petroleum is refined in Maryland. As a matter of actual fact, then, an inherent nexus does exist between the out-of-state status of producers and refiners and the distribution and retailing of gasoline in Maryland. The Commerce Clause does not forbid only legislation that discriminates under all factual circumstances. It forbids discrimination in effect against interstate commerce on the specific facts of each case. If production or refining of gasoline occurred in Maryland, §§(b) and (c) might not be unconstitutional. Under those different circumstances, however, the producers and refiners would have a fair opportunity to influence their local legislators and thereby to prevent the enactment of economically disruptive legislation. Under those circumstances, the economic disruption would be felt directly in Maryland, which would tend to make the local political processes responsive to the problems thereby created. Under those circumstances, §§(b) and (c) might never have been passed. In this case however, the economic disruption of the sections is visited upon out-of-state economic interests and not upon in-state businesses. One of the basic assumptions of the Commerce Clause is that local political systems will tend to be unresponsive to problems not felt by local constituents; instead, local political units are expected to act in their constituents' interests. One of the basic purposes of the Clause, therefore, is to prevent the vindication of such self-interest from unfairly burdening out-of-state concerns and thereby disrupting the national economy.

[I] would reverse the judgment of the Maryland Court of Appeals.

Notes

1. *May a Legislature Determine That All of a Particular Type of Item Is Bad?* In Bowman v. Chicago & N.W. Ry. Co., 125 U.S. 465 (1888), the Court struck down an Iowa statute prohibiting common carriers (i.e., railroads) from bringing alcohol into the state without first being furnished with a certificate stating that the recipient is licensed by the state. The Court suggested that it would disapprove of state laws banning all importation of a particular good, even if the law was motivated by a state policy against use of such a product.

2. *Fuel Sales-Tax Credits.* In New Energy Co. of Indiana v. Limbach, 486 U.S. 289 (1988), the Court struck down an Ohio law that awarded a tax credit against the Ohio motor vehicle fuel sales tax for each gallon of ethanol sold (as a component of gasohol) by fuel dealers, but only if the ethanol was produced in Ohio or in a state that granted similar tax advantages to those for ethanol produced in Ohio. The evidence showed that ethanol is made from corn and was originally promoted as a means of achieving energy independence while providing a market for surplus corn. Ethanol has environmental advantages as a replacement for lead in enhancing fuel octane, but it is more expensive than gasoline. The Court struck down the law: "[The] 'negative' aspect of the Commerce Clause prohibits economic protectionism — that is, regulatory measures designed to benefit in-state economic interests by burdening out-of-state competitors. . . . The Ohio provision at issue here explicitly deprives certain products of generally available beneficial tax treatment because they are made in certain other States. [The] present law [imposes] an economic disadvantage upon out-of-state sellers; and the promise to remove that if reciprocity is accepted no more justifies disparity of treatment than it would justify categorical exclusion." The Court rejected the idea that the law could be justified under the "market-participant" doctrine: "The Ohio action [is] neither its purchase nor its sale of ethanol, but its assessment and computation of taxes — a primeval governmental activity. To be sure, the tax credit scheme has the purpose and effect of subsidizing a particular industry, as

do many dispositions of the tax laws. That does not transform it into a form of state participation in the free market." Finally, the Court rejected the argument that Ohio could validate the law "by showing that it advances a legitimate local purpose that cannot be adequately served by reasonable nondiscriminatory alternatives": "Appellees advance two justifications[:] health and commerce. As to the first, they argue that the provision encourages use of ethanol (in replacement of lead as a gasoline octane-enhancer) to reduce harmful exhaust emissions. . . . Certainly the protection of health is a legitimate state goal, and we assume for purposes of this argument that use of ethanol generally furthers it. [But] there is no reason to suppose that ethanol produced in a State that does not offer tax advantages to ethanol produced in Ohio is less healthy, and thus should have its importation into Ohio suppressed by denial of the otherwise standard tax credit. [The] same reasoning also responds to [the] justification [that] the reciprocity requirement is designed to increase commerce in ethanol by encouraging other States to enact ethanol subsidies. What is encouraged is not ethanol subsidies in general, but only favorable treatment for Ohio-produced ethanol."

C. NONDISCRIMINATORY BURDENS ON INTERSTATE COMMERCE

Even when a state law does not discriminate against interstate commerce, the law may still affect interstate commerce and is still subject to judicial review. In general, when statutes regulate local and out-of-state interests evenhandedly and have only an indirect effect on interstate commerce, they are examined to determine whether the burden on interstate commerce clearly exceeds the local benefits. *See, e.g.,* Brown-Forman Distillers Corp. v. New York State Liquor Authority, 476 U.S. 573, 578 (1986).

1. The Scope of Judicial Review

Some argue that the federal courts should be deferential to state legislation and that Congress is free to override state laws with which it disagrees. Others argue that the courts should actively review state laws, and should strike down laws that burden interstate commerce. Which approach is preferable? Consider the following two cases, which reflect divergent approaches.

South Carolina State Highway Department v. Barnwell Bros.

303 U.S. 177 (1938)

Mr. Justice STONE delivered the opinion of the Court.

Act No. 259 of the General Assembly of South Carolina, of April 28, 1933, prohibits use on the state highways of motor trucks and "semi-trailer motor trucks" whose width exceeds 90 inches, and whose weight including load exceeds 20,000 pounds. . . . The principal question for decision is whether these prohibitions impose an unconstitutional burden upon interstate commerce. . . .

[Congress] has not undertaken to regulate the weight and size of motor vehicles in interstate motor traffic and has left undisturbed whatever authority in that regard the states have retained under the Constitution.

While the constitutional grant to Congress of power to regulate interstate commerce has been held to operate of its own force to curtail state power in some measure, [there] are matters of local concern, the regulation of which unavoidably involves some regulation of interstate commerce but which, because of their local character and their number and diversity, may never be fully dealt with by Congress. Notwithstanding the commerce clause, such regulation in the absence of congressional action has for the most part been left to the states by the decisions of this Court, subject to the other applicable constitutional restraints. . . .

[T]he present case affords no occasion for saying that the bare possession of power by Congress to regulate the interstate traffic forces the states to conform to standards which Congress might, but has not adopted, or curtails their power to take measures to insure the safety and conservation of their highways which may be applied to like traffic moving intrastate. Few subjects of state regulation are so peculiarly of local concern as is the use of state highways. There are few, local regulation of which is so inseparable from a substantial effect on interstate commerce. Unlike the railroads, local highways are built, owned, and maintained by the state or its municipal subdivisions. The state has a primary and immediate concern in their safe and economical administration. The present regulations, or any others of like purpose, if they are to accomplish their end, must be applied alike to interstate and intrastate traffic both moving in large volume over the highways. The fact that they affect alike shippers in interstate and intrastate commerce in large number within as well as without the state is a safeguard against their abuse.

[The states] may not, under the guise of regulation, discriminate against interstate commerce. But, "In the absence of national legislation especially covering the subject of interstate commerce, the state may rightly prescribe uniform regulations adapted to promote safety upon its highways and the conservation of their use, applicable alike to vehicles moving in interstate commerce and those of its own citizens." Morris v. Duby, 274 U.S. 135, 143. . . . This Court has often sustained the exercise of that power, although it has burdened or impeded interstate commerce. It has upheld weight limitations lower than those presently imposed, applied alike to motor traffic moving interstate and intrastate. Restrictions favoring passenger traffic over the carriage of interstate merchandise by truck have been similarly sustained, as has the exaction of a reasonable fee for the use of the highways. . . .

Congress, in the exercise of its plenary power to regulate interstate commerce, may determine whether the burdens imposed on it by state regulation, otherwise permissible, are too great, and may, by legislation designed to secure uniformity or in other respects to protect the national interest in the commerce, curtail to some extent the state's regulatory power. But that is a legislative, not a judicial, function, to be performed in the light of the congressional judgment of what is appropriate regulation of interstate commerce, and the extent to which, in that field, state power and local interests should be required to yield to the national authority and interest. In the absence of such legislation the judicial function, under the commerce clause, Const. art. 1, §8, cl. 3, as well as the Fourteenth Amendment, stops with the inquiry whether the state Legislature in adopting regulations such as the present has acted within its province, and whether the means of regulation chosen are reasonably adapted to the end sought.

Here the first inquiry has already been resolved by our decisions that a state may impose nondiscriminatory restrictions with respect to the character of motor vehicles moving in interstate commerce as a safety measure and as a means of securing the economical use of its highways. In resolving the second, courts do not sit as Legislatures, either state or national. They cannot act as Congress does when, after weighing all the conflicting interests, state and national, it determines when and how much the state regulatory power shall yield to the larger interests of a national commerce. And in reviewing a state highway regulation where Congress has not acted, a court is not called upon, as are state Legislatures, to determine what, in its judgment, is the most suitable restriction to be applied of those that are possible, or to choose that one which in its opinion is best adapted to all the diverse interests affected. When the action of a Legislature is within the scope of its power, fairly debatable questions as to its reasonableness, wisdom, and propriety are not for the determination of courts, but for the legislative body, on which rests the duty and responsibility of decision. This is equally the case when the legislative power is one which may legitimately place an incidental burden on interstate commerce. It is not any the less a legislative power committed to the states because it affects interstate commerce, and courts are not any the more entitled, because interstate commerce is affected, to substitute their own for the legislative judgment.

Since the adoption of one weight or width regulation, rather than another, is a legislative, not a judicial, choice, its constitutionality is not to be determined by weighing in the judicial scales the merits of the legislative choice and rejecting it if the weight of evidence presented in court appears to favor a different standard. Being a legislative judgment it is presumed to be supported by facts known to the Legislature unless facts judicially known or proved preclude that possibility. Hence, in reviewing the present determination, we examine the record, not to see whether the findings of the court below are supported by evidence, but to ascertain upon the whole record whether it is possible to say that the legislative choice is without rational basis. Not only does the record fail to exclude that possibility but it shows affirmatively that there is adequate support for the legislative judgment. . . .

The regulatory measures taken by South Carolina are within its legislative power. They do not infringe the Fourteenth Amendment, and the resulting burden on interstate commerce is not forbidden.

Reversed.

∼ PROBLEM: MORE ON THE INTERNET
CASINO PROHIBITION ACT ∼

Under the *Barnwell* holding, is the Internet Casino Prohibition Act likely to pass constitutional muster? If so, why (or why not)?

Southern Pac. Co. v. Arizona
325 U.S. 761 (1945)

Mr. Chief Justice STONE delivered the opinion of the Court.

The Arizona Train Limit Law of May 16, 1912 makes it unlawful for any person or corporation to operate within the state a railroad train of more than fourteen passenger or seventy freight cars. . . .

For a hundred years it has been accepted constitutional doctrine that the commerce clause, without the aid of Congressional legislation, thus affords some protection from state legislation inimical to the national commerce, and that [where] Congress has not acted, this Court, and not the state legislature, is under the commerce clause the final arbiter of the competing demands of state and national interests. Cooley v. Board of Wardens, *supra.*

[There] has thus been left to the states wide scope for the regulation of matters of local state concern, even though it in some measure affects the commerce, provided it does not materially restrict the free flow of commerce across state lines, or interfere with it in matters with respect to which uniformity of regulation is of predominant national concern.

Hence the matters for ultimate determination here are the nature and extent of the burden which the state regulation of interstate trains, adopted as a safety measure, imposes on interstate commerce, and whether the relative weights of the state and national interests involved are such as to make inapplicable the rule, generally observed, that the free flow of interstate commerce and its freedom from local restraints in matters requiring uniformity of regulation are interests safeguarded by the commerce clause from state interference. . . .

The findings show that the operation of long trains, that is trains of more than fourteen passenger and more than seventy freight cars, is standard practice over the main lines of the railroads of the United States, and that, if the length of trains is to be regulated at all, national uniformity in the regulation adopted, such as only Congress can prescribe, is practically indispensable to the operation of an efficient and economical national railway system. On many railroads passenger trains of more than fourteen cars and freight trains of more than seventy cars are operated, and on some systems freight trains are run ranging from one hundred and twenty-five to one hundred and sixty cars in length. Outside of Arizona, where the length of trains is not restricted, appellant runs a substantial proportion of long trains. In 1939 on its comparable route for through traffic through Utah and Nevada from 66 to 85% of its freight trains were over 70 cars in length and over 43% of its passenger trains included more than fourteen passenger cars. . . . In Arizona, approximately 93% of the freight traffic and 95% of the passenger traffic is interstate. Because of the Train Limit Law appellant is required to haul over 30% more trains in Arizona than would otherwise have been necessary. . . .

The unchallenged findings leave no doubt that the Arizona Train Limit Law imposes a serious burden [on] interstate commerce. . . . It materially impedes the movement of appellant's interstate trains through that state and interposes a substantial obstruction to the national policy proclaimed by Congress, to promote adequate, economical and efficient railway transportation service. Enforcement of the law in Arizona, while train lengths remain unregulated or are regulated by varying standards in other states, must inevitably result in an impairment of uniformity of efficient railroad operation because the railroads are subjected to regulation which is not uniform in its application. Compliance with a state statute limiting train lengths requires interstate trains of a length lawful in other states to be broken up and reconstituted as they enter each state according as it may impose varying limitations upon train lengths. The alternative is for the carrier to conform to the lowest train limit restriction of any of the states through which its trains pass, whose laws thus control the carriers' operations both within and without the regulating state.

[At] present the seventy freight car laws are enforced only in Arizona and Oklahoma, with a fourteen car passenger car limit in Arizona. The record [shows] that [the] Arizona statute results in freight trains being broken up and reformed at the California border and in New Mexico, some distance from the Arizona line. Frequently it is not feasible to operate a newly assembled train from the New Mexico yard nearest to Arizona, with the result that the Arizona limitation governs the flow of traffic as far east as El Paso, Texas. For similar reasons the Arizona law often controls the length of passenger trains all the way from Los Angeles to El Paso.

If one state may regulate train lengths, so may all the others, and they need not prescribe the same maximum limitation. The practical effect of such regulation is to control train operations beyond the boundaries of the state exacting it because of the necessity of breaking up and reassembling long trains at the nearest terminal points before entering and after leaving the regulating state. The serious impediment to the free flow of commerce by the local regulation of train lengths and the practical necessity that such regulation, if any, must be prescribed by a single body having a nation-wide authority are apparent.

The trial court found that the Arizona law had no reasonable relation to safety, and made train operation more dangerous. [T]his conclusion [facts] which indicate that such increased danger of accident and personal injury as may result from the greater length of trains is more than offset by the increase in the number of accidents resulting from the larger number of trains when train lengths are reduced. In considering the effect of the statute as a safety measure, therefore, the factor of controlling significance for present purposes is not whether there is basis for the conclusion of the Arizona Supreme Court that the increase in length of trains beyond the statutory maximum has an adverse effect upon safety of operation. The decisive question is whether in the circumstances the total effect of the law as a safety measure in reducing accidents and casualties is so slight or problematical as not to outweigh the national interest in keeping interstate commerce free from interferences which seriously impede it and subject it to local regulation which does not have a uniform effect on the interstate train journey which it interrupts.

The principal source of danger of accident from increased length of trains is the resulting increase of "slack action" of the train. Slack action is the amount of free movement of one car before it transmits its motion to an adjoining coupled car. This free movement results from the fact that in railroad practice cars are loosely coupled, and the coupling is often combined with a stock-absorbing device, a "draft gear" which, under stress, substantially increases the free movement as the train is started or stopped. Loose coupling is necessary to enable the train to proceed freely around curves and is an aid in starting heavy trains, since the application of the locomotive power to the train operates on each car in the train successively, and the power is thus utilized to start only one car at a time.

The slack action between cars due to loose couplings varies from seven-eighths of an inch to one and one-eighth inches and, with the added free movement due to the use of draft gears, may be as high as six or seven inches between cars. The length of the train increases the slack since the slack action of a train is the total of the free movement between its several cars. The amount of slack action has some effect on the severity of the shock of train movements, and on freight trains sometimes results in injuries to operatives, which most frequently occur to occupants of the caboose. The amount and severity of slack action, however, are not wholly dependent upon the length of train, as they may be affected by the mode and conditions of operation as to grades, speed, and load. And accidents due to slack action also occur in the operation of short trains. On comparison of the number of slack action accidents in Arizona with those in Nevada, where the length of trains is now unregulated, the trial court found that with substantially the same amount of traffic in each state the number of accidents was relatively the same in long as in short train operations. While accidents from slack action do occur in the operation of passenger trains, it does not appear that they are more frequent or the resulting shocks more severe on long than on short passenger trains. Nor does it appear that slack action accidents occurring on passenger trains, whatever their length, are of sufficient severity to cause serious injury or damage. . . .

Upon an examination of the whole case the trial court found that "if short-train operation may or should result in any decrease in the number or severity of the 'slack' or 'slack-surge' type of accidents or casualties, such decrease is substantially more than offset by the increased number of accidents and casualties from other causes that follow the arbitrary limitation of freight trains to 70 cars [and] passenger trains to 14 cars."

We think [that] the Arizona Train Limit Law, viewed as a safety measure, affords at most slight and dubious advantage, if any, over unregulated train lengths, because it results in an increase in the number of trains and train operations and the consequent increase in train accidents of a character generally more severe than those due to slack action. Its undoubted effect on the commerce is the regulation, without securing uniformity, of the length of trains operated in interstate commerce, which lack is itself a primary cause of preventing the free flow of commerce by delaying it and by substantially increasing its cost and impairing its efficiency. In these respects the case differs from those where a state, by regulatory measures affecting the commerce, has removed or reduced safety hazards without substantial interference with the interstate movement of trains. . . .

Here we conclude that the state does go too far. Its regulation of train lengths, admittedly obstructive to interstate train operation, and having a seriously adverse effect on transportation efficiency and economy, passes beyond what is plainly essential for safety since it does not appear that it will lessen rather than increase the danger of accident. Its attempted regulation of the operation of interstate trains cannot establish nation-wide control such as is essential to the maintenance of an efficient transportation system, which Congress alone can prescribe. The state interest cannot be preserved at the expense of the national interest by an enactment which regulates interstate train lengths without securing such control, which is a matter of national concern. To this the interest of the state here asserted is subordinate. . . .

Reversed.

Mr. Justice BLACK, dissenting.

[The] state trial judge [heard] evidence over a period of 5 months which appears in about 3000 pages of the printed record before us. It then adopted findings of fact [which] cover 148 printed pages, and conclusions of law which cover 5 pages. . . . This new pattern of trial procedure makes it necessary for a judge to hear all the evidence offered as to why a legislature passed a law and to make findings of fact as to the validity of those reasons. If [a] court does make findings, as to a danger contrary to the findings of the legislature, and the evidence heard "lends support" to those findings, a court can then invalidate the law. In this respect, the Arizona County Court acted, and this Court today is acting, as a "super-legislature."

Even if this method of invalidating legislative acts is a correct one, I still think that the "findings" of the state court do not authorize today's decision. That court did not find that there is no unusual danger from slack movements in long trains. It did decide on disputed evidence that the long train "slack movement" dangers were more than offset by prospective dangers as a result of running a larger number of short trains, since many people might be hurt at grade crossings. There was undoubtedly some evidence before the state court from which it could have reached such a conclusion. There was undoubtedly as much evidence before it which would have justified a different conclusion.

Under those circumstances, the determination of whether it is in the interest of society for the length of trains to be governmentally regulated is a matter of public policy. Someone must fix that policy — either the Congress, or the state, or the courts. A century and a half of constitutional history and government admonishes this Court to leave that choice to the elected legislative representatives of the people themselves, where it properly belongs both on democratic principles and the requirements of efficient government. . . .

There have been many sharp divisions of this Court concerning its authority, in the absence of congressional enactment, to invalidate state laws as violating the

Commerce Clause. [E]ven the broadest exponents of judicial power in this field have not heretofore expressed doubt as to a state's power, absent a paramount congressional declaration, to regulate interstate trains in the interest of safety. . . .

When we finally get down to the gist of what the Court today actually decides, it is this: Even though more railroad employees will be injured by "slack action" movements on long trains than on short trains, there must be no regulation of this danger in the absence of "uniform regulations." That means that no one can legislate against this danger except the Congress; and even though the Congress is perfectly content to leave the matter to the different state legislatures, this Court, on the ground of "lack of uniformity", will require it to make an express avowal of that fact before it will permit a state to guard against that admitted danger. . . .

Mr. Justice DOUGLAS, dissenting.

[C]ourts should intervene only where the state legislation discriminated against interstate commerce or was out of harmony with laws which Congress had enacted. . . .

Notes and Questions

1. *Distinguishing* Barnwell *and* S. Pacific. Note how differently the Court perceives its role in the *Barnwell* and *S. Pacific* cases. Which approach is better? In the absence of congressional action, should the courts be deferential to state legislation? After all, if the states decide to regulate and Congress does not like what the states have done, Congress can pass a law overriding the state law. Moreover, if a state law unreasonably burdens commerce (e.g., the Arizona law), shouldn't we assume that those adversely affected by the law (in this case, the national railroad companies) will urge Congress to pass overriding legislation? If Congress decides not to pass such legislation, why should the courts intervene? On the other hand, is judicial intervention justified on the assumption that Congress does not have time to individually legislate on all of the burdens that states may place on commerce?

2. *The Black Dissent.* Justice Black's *Southern Pacific* dissent notes that the trial court heard five months of testimony and compiled a 3,000-page record before ruling on the validity of Arizona's law. Is it appropriate for a trial court to engage in such an intensive review process? If it does, is the trial court assuming more of a legislative role?

3. *Can a State Require Interstate Truckers to Install Contoured Mud Flaps?* Bibb v. Navajo Freight Lines, Inc., 359 U.S. 520 (1959), involved an Illinois statute that required the use of contoured rear fender mudguards on trucks and trailers. This mud flap differed from the conventional or straight mud flap permitted in 45 states and required in Arkansas. In *Bibb*, the Court struck the law down, emphasizing that contour mudguards have no advantages over conventional mudguards and indeed create safety hazards (they tend to cause heat to accumulate in the brake drum, thus decreasing their effectiveness and potentially causing them to fall off on the highway). The Court also found that the Illinois law "seriously

interferes with the 'interline' operations of motor carriers — [the] interchanging of trailers between an originating carrier and another carrier. . . . These 'interline' operations provide a speedy through-service for the shipper[, but] contemplates the physical transfer of the entire trailer [with] no unloading and reloading of the cargo. The interlining process is particularly vital in connection with shipment of perishables, [or] with the movement of explosives carried under seal. [If] an interchanged trailer of that carrier were hauled to or through Illinois, the statute would require that it contain contour guards. Since carriers which operate in and through Illinois cannot compel the originating carriers to equip their trailers with contour guards, they may be forced to cease interlining with those who do not meet the Illinois requirements. Over 60 percent of the business of 5 of the 6 plaintiffs is interline traffic." In addition, the Court found that it is extremely difficult to change mudguards at the state line, thereby "causing a significant delay [in] prompt movement may be of the essence. [F]rom two to four hours of labor are required to install or remove a contour mudguard. Moreover, the contour guard is attached [by] welding and if the trailer is conveying a cargo of explosives [it] would be exceedingly dangerous [to] weld on a contour mudguard without unloading the trailer." As a result, the Court concluded that the case involved one of those instances "few in number — where local safety measures that are nondiscriminatory place an unconstitutional burden on interstate commerce."

4. *Regulating Truck Length.* There has been much litigation about the extent to which the states can regulate truck lengths. For example, in Raymond Motor Transportation, Inc. v. Rice, 434 U.S. 429 (1978), a Wisconsin statute prohibited trucks from pulling double trailers and also prohibited truck rigs longer than 55 feet in length, absent a special permit. Even though the Court emphasized its reluctance to invalidate "'state legislation in the field of safety where the propriety of local regulation has long been recognized," and suggested that it usually gives great deference to state safety regulations and applies a "strong presumption of [their] validity," the Court struck the Wisconsin law down, noting that the state's asserted safety justification (65-foot doubles take longer to pass or be passed than 55-foot singles) did not hold up as applied to trucks "on limited access, four-lane divided highways." In addition, the Court found that the law imposed a substantial burden on the interstate movement of goods: "The regulations substantially increase the cost of such movement [and] slow the movement of goods in interstate commerce by forcing appellants to haul doubles across the State separately, to haul doubles around the State altogether, or to incur the delays caused by using singles instead of doubles to pick up and deliver goods. Finally, the regulations prevent appellants from accepting interline transfers of 65-foot doubles for movement through Wisconsin from carriers that operate only in the 33 States where the doubles are legal." Finally, when the Court analyzed the law's exceptions, it found that at "least one of these exceptions discriminates on its face in favor of Wisconsin industries and against the industries of other States, and there are indications in the record that a number of the other exceptions, although neutral on their face, were enacted at the instance of, and primarily benefit, important Wisconsin industries." As a result, the Court concluded that

"the challenged regulations violate the Commerce Clause because they place a substantial burden on interstate commerce and they cannot be said to make more than the most speculative contribution to highway safety."

∾ PROBLEMS ∾

1. *State Regulation and New Technologies.* At this point, let's think a bit more about the *Bibb* decision, but let's alter the facts. In the actual case, the Court noted that Arkansas required a conventional mudguard and that the overwhelming majority of states permitted it. In addition, the Court found that the contoured mudguard possessed no safety advantages vis-à-vis the conventional mudguard and that it could even be dangerous. Suppose that a new type of mudguard is developed — the modified contoured mudguard ("modified mudguard") — and the scientific evidence demonstrates that this new mudguard possesses significant safety advantages over conventional mudguards. However, at this point, no other state has required the use of the modified mudguard, and three states require the use of the conventional mudguard. Could Illinois mandate use of the modified mudguard despite the possible impact on interline operations? Could Illinois argue that the contradictory state laws should, instead, be invalidated?

2. *More on the Internet Casino Prohibition Act.* Under the *Southern Pacific* balancing test, is the Internet Casino Prohibition Act likely to be upheld? If you were hired to represent the casinos, how might you argue that the Act places an undue burden on interstate commerce? Now, suppose that you represent the Commonwealth of Kentucky. How might you respond to these arguments?

2.   Modern Applications of the S. Pacific Test

Modern cases have used the *S. Pacific* balancing test rather than the *Barnwell* test. The following cases illustrate modern applications of the test.

Minnesota v. Clover Leaf Creamery Company

449 U.S. 456 (1981)

Justice BRENNAN delivered the opinion of the Court.

In 1977, the Minnesota Legislature enacted a statute banning the retail sale of milk in plastic nonreturnable, nonrefillable containers, but permitting such sale in other nonreturnable, nonrefillable containers, such as paperboard milk cartons. . . . The purpose of the Minnesota statute is set out as §1:

> The legislature finds that the use of nonreturnable, nonrefillable containers for the packaging of milk and other milk products presents a solid waste management problem for the state, promotes energy waste, and depletes natural resources. The legislature therefore [determines] that the use of nonreturnable, nonrefillable containers for packaging milk and other milk products should be discouraged and that the use of returnable and reusable packaging for these products is preferred and should be encouraged.

Section 2 of the Act forbids the retail sale of milk and fluid milk products, other than sour cream, cottage cheese, and yogurt, in nonreturnable, nonrefillable rigid or semi-rigid containers composed at least 50% of plastic.

The Act was introduced with the support of the state Pollution Control Agency, Department of Natural Resources, Department of Agriculture, Consumer Services Division, and Energy Agency, and debated vigorously [in] the state legislature. Proponents of the legislation argued that it would promote resource conservation, ease solid waste disposal problems, and conserve energy. Relying on the results of studies[,] they stressed the need to stop introduction of the plastic nonreturnable container before it became entrenched in the market. Opponents of the Act, also presenting empirical evidence, argued that the Act would not promote the goals asserted by the proponents, but would merely increase costs of retail milk products and prolong the use of ecologically undesirable paperboard milk cartons.

After the Act was passed, respondents filed suit in [state court] to enjoin its enforcement. The [trial court held that the [statute] unconstitutional under the Commerce Clause because it imposes an unreasonable burden on interstate commerce. The Supreme Court of Minnesota affirmed.] We [conclude] that the ban on plastic nonreturnable milk containers bears a rational relation to the State's objectives, and must be sustained. . . .

[If] a state law purporting to promote environmental purposes is in reality "simple economic protectionism," we have applied a "virtually per se rule of invalidity." Philadelphia v. New Jersey. Even if a statute regulates "evenhandedly," and imposes only "incidental" burdens on interstate commerce, the courts must nevertheless strike it down if "the burden imposed on such commerce is clearly excessive in relation to the putative local benefits." Moreover, "the extent of the burden that will be tolerated will of course depend on the nature of the local interest involved, and on whether it could be promoted as well with a lesser impact on interstate activities."

Minnesota's statute does not effect "simple protectionism," but "regulates evenhandedly" by prohibiting all milk retailers from selling their products in plastic, nonreturnable milk containers, without regard to whether the milk, the containers, or the sellers are from outside the State. This statute is therefore unlike statutes discriminating against interstate commerce, which we have consistently struck down. E.g., Philadelphia v. New Jersey, supra. Since the statute does not discriminate between interstate and intrastate commerce, the controlling question is whether the incidental burden imposed on interstate commerce by the Minnesota Act is "clearly excessive in relation to the putative local benefits."

The burden imposed on interstate commerce by the statute is relatively minor. Milk products may continue to move freely across the Minnesota border, and since most dairies package their products in more than one type of containers, the inconvenience of having to conform to different packaging requirements in Minnesota and the surrounding States should be slight. Within Minnesota, business will presumably shift from manufacturers of plastic nonreturnable containers to producers of paperboard cartons, refillable bottles, and plastic pouches, but there is no reason to suspect that the gainers will be Minnesota firms, or the losers out-of-state firms. Indeed, two of the three dairies, the sole milk retailer, and the sole milk container producer challenging the statute in this litigation are Minnesota firms.

Pulpwood producers are the only Minnesota industry likely to benefit significantly from the Act at the expense of out-of-state firms. [P]lastic resin, the raw material used for making plastic nonreturnable milk jugs, is produced entirely by non-Minnesota firms, while pulpwood, used for making paperboard, is a major Minnesota product. Nevertheless, it is clear that respondents exaggerate the degree of burden on out-of-state interests, both because plastics will continue to be used in the production of plastic pouches, plastic returnable bottles, and paperboard itself, and because out-of-state pulpwood producers will presumably absorb some of the business generated by the Act.

Even granting that the out-of-state plastics industry is burdened relatively more heavily than the Minnesota pulpwood industry, we find that this burden is not "clearly excessive" in light of the substantial state interest in promoting conservation of energy and other natural resources and easing solid waste disposal problems. . . . We find these local benefits ample to support Minnesota's decision under the Commerce Clause. Moreover, we find that no approach with "a lesser impact on interstate activities" is available. [Suggested] alternatives are either more burdensome on commerce than the Act (as, for example, banning all nonreturnables) or less likely to be effective (as, for example, providing incentives for recycling).

[A] nondiscriminatory regulation serving substantial state purposes is not invalid simply because it causes some business to shift from a predominantly out-of-state industry to a predominantly in-state industry. Only if the burden on interstate commerce clearly outweighs the State's legitimate purposes does such a regulation violate the Commerce Clause.

The judgment of the Minnesota Supreme Court is
Reversed.

West Lynn Creamery, Inc. v. Healy

512 U.S. 186 (1994)

Justice STEVENS delivered the opinion of the Court.

A Massachusetts pricing order imposes an assessment on all fluid milk sold by dealers to Massachusetts retailers. About two-thirds of that milk is produced out of State. The entire assessment, however, is distributed to Massachusetts dairy farmers. The question presented is whether the pricing order unconstitutionally discriminates against interstate commerce. We hold that it does.

Petitioner West Lynn Creamery, Inc., is a milk dealer licensed to do business in Massachusetts. It purchases raw milk, which it processes, packages, and sells to wholesalers, retailers, and other milk dealers. About 97% of the raw milk it purchases is produced by out-of-state farmers. Petitioner LeComte's Dairy, Inc., is also a licensed Massachusetts milk dealer. It purchases all of its milk from West Lynn and distributes it to retail outlets in Massachusetts.

In the 1980's and early 1990's, Massachusetts dairy farmers began to lose market share to lower cost producers in neighboring States. In response, the Governor of Massachusetts appointed a Special Commission to study the dairy industry. The Commission found that many producers had sold their dairy farms during the past decade and that if prices paid to farmers for their milk were not significantly increased, a majority of the remaining farmers in Massachusetts would be "forced out of business within the year." [R]elying on the Commission's Report, the Commissioner of the Massachusetts Department of Food and Agriculture (respondent) declared a State of Emergency. . . . Promptly after his declaration of emergency, respondent issued the pricing order that is challenged in this proceeding.

The order requires every "dealer" in Massachusetts to make a monthly "premium payment" into the "Massachusetts Dairy Equalization Fund." The amount of those payments is computed in two steps. First, the monthly "order premium" is determined. . . . Second, the premium is multiplied by the amount (in pounds) of the dealer's [milk] sales in Massachusetts. Each month the fund is distributed to Massachusetts producers. Each Massachusetts producer receives a share of the total fund equal to his proportionate contribution to the State's total production of raw milk.

[P]etitioners refused to make the premium payments, and respondent commenced license revocation proceedings. Petitioners then filed [suit] seeking an injunction against enforcement of the order on the ground that it violated the Commerce Clause of the Federal Constitution. The state court denied relief. . . . We granted certiorari and now reverse.

[The] paradigmatic example of a law discriminating against interstate commerce is the protective tariff or customs duty, which taxes goods imported from other States, but does not tax similar products produced in State. A tariff is an attractive measure because it simultaneously raises revenue and benefits local producers by burdening their out-of-state competitors. Nevertheless, it violates the principle of the unitary national market by handicapping out-of-state competitors, thus artificially encouraging in-state production even when the same goods could be produced at lower cost in other States.

Because of their distorting effects on the geography of production, tariffs have long been recognized as violative of the Commerce Clause. [*See*] Baldwin v. G.A.F. Seelig, Inc., 294 U.S. 511 (1935). . . . Under these cases, Massachusetts' pricing order is clearly unconstitutional. Its avowed purpose and its undisputed effect are to enable higher cost Massachusetts dairy farmers to compete with lower cost dairy farmers in other States. The "premium payments" are effectively a tax which makes milk produced out of State more expensive. Although the tax also applies to milk produced in Massachusetts, its effect on Massachusetts producers is entirely (indeed more than) offset by the subsidy provided exclusively to Massachusetts dairy farmers. Like an ordinary tariff, the tax is thus effectively imposed only on out-of-state products. The pricing order thus allows Massachusetts dairy farmers who produce at higher cost to sell at or below the price charged by lower cost out-of-state producers. . . .

[Respondent] argues that the payments to Massachusetts dairy farmers from the Dairy Equalization Fund are valid, because subsidies are constitutional exercises of state power, and that the order premium which provides money for the Fund is valid, because it is a nondiscriminatory tax. Therefore the pricing order is constitutional, because it is merely the combination of two independently lawful regulations. In effect, [if] the State may impose a valid tax on dealers, it is free to use the proceeds of the tax as it chooses; and if it may independently subsidize its farmers, it is free to finance the subsidy by means of any legitimate tax.

Even granting respondent's assertion that both components of the pricing order would be constitutional standing alone, the pricing order nevertheless must fall. A pure subsidy funded out of general revenue ordinarily imposes no burden on interstate commerce, but merely assists local business. The pricing order in this case [is] funded principally from taxes on the sale of milk produced in other States. By so funding the subsidy, respondent not only assists local farmers, but burdens interstate commerce. The pricing order thus violates the cardinal principle that a State may not "benefit in-state economic interests by burdening out-of-state competitors." New Energy Co. of Indiana v. Limbach.

More fundamentally, respondent errs in assuming that the constitutionality of the pricing order follows logically from the constitutionality of its component parts. By conjoining a tax and a subsidy, Massachusetts has created a program more dangerous to interstate commerce than either part alone. Nondiscriminatory measures, like the evenhanded tax at issue here, are generally upheld, in spite of any adverse effects on interstate commerce, in part because "[t]he existence of major in-state interests adversely affected [is] a powerful safeguard against legislative abuse." Minnesota v. Clover Leaf Creamery Co. However, when a nondiscriminatory tax is coupled with a subsidy to one of the groups hurt by the tax, a state's political processes can no longer be relied upon to prevent legislative abuse, because one of the in-state interests which would otherwise lobby against the tax has been mollified by the subsidy. [O]ne would ordinarily have expected at least three groups to lobby against the order premium, which, as a tax, raises the price (and hence lowers demand) for milk: dairy farmers, milk dealers, and consumers. But because the tax was coupled with a subsidy, one of the most powerful of these groups, Massachusetts dairy farmers, instead of exerting their influence against the tax, were in fact its primary supporters.

Respondent's argument would require us to analyze separately two parts of an integrated regulation, but we cannot divorce the premium payments from the use to which the payments are put. It is the entire program — not just the contributions to the fund or the distributions from that fund — that simultaneously burdens interstate commerce and discriminates in favor of local producers. The choice of constitutional means — nondiscriminatory tax and local subsidy — cannot guarantee the constitutionality of the program as a whole. . . .

Respondent also argues that since the Massachusetts milk dealers who pay the order premiums are not competitors of the Massachusetts farmers, the pricing order imposes no discriminatory burden on commerce. This argument cannot withstand scrutiny. . . . For over 150 years, our cases have rightly concluded that the imposition of a differential burden on any part of the stream of commerce—from wholesaler to retailer to consumer—is invalid, because a burden placed at any point will result in a disadvantage to the out-of-state producer. . . .

Respondent also argues that "the operation of the Order disproves any claim of protectionism," because "only in-state consumers feel the effect of any retail price increase [and the] dealers themselves [have] a substantial in-state presence." This argument [would] undermine almost every discriminatory tax case. State taxes are ordinarily paid by in-state businesses and consumers, yet if they discriminate against out-of-state products, they are unconstitutional. [The] cost of a tariff is also borne primarily by local consumers, yet a tariff is the paradigmatic Commerce Clause violation. . . .

Finally, respondent argues that any incidental burden on interstate commerce "is outweighed by the 'local benefits' of preserving the Massachusetts dairy industry." [Respondent also] urges that "the purpose of the order, to save an industry from collapse, is not protectionist." If we were to accept these arguments, we would make a virtue of the vice that the rule against discrimination condemns. Preservation of local industry by protecting it from the rigors of interstate competition is the hallmark of the economic protectionism that the Commerce Clause prohibits. . . .

The judgment of the Supreme Judicial Court of Massachusetts is reversed.

It is so ordered.

Justice SCALIA, with whom Justice THOMAS joins, concurring in judgment.

In my view the challenged Massachusetts pricing order is invalid under our negative Commerce-Clause jurisprudence. . . . I concur only in the judgment of the Court.

The purpose of the negative Commerce Clause [is] to create a national market. It does not follow from that, however, and we have never held, that every state law which obstructs a national market violates the Commerce Clause. Yet that is what the Court says today. . . .

[T]his expansive view of the Commerce Clause calls into question a wide variety of state laws that have hitherto been thought permissible. [A] State subsidy would clearly be invalid under any formulation of the Court's guiding principle identified above. The Court guardedly asserts that a "pure subsidy funded out of general revenue ordinarily imposes no burden on interstate commerce, but merely assists local business," but under its analysis that must be taken to be true only because most local businesses (e.g., the local hardware store) are not competing with businesses out of State. The Court notes that, in funding this subsidy, Massachusetts has taxed milk produced in other States, and thus "not only assists local farmers, but burdens interstate commerce." But the same could be said of almost all subsidies funded from general state revenues, which almost invariably include monies from use taxes on out-of-state products. And even where the funding does not come in any part from taxes on out-of-state goods, "merely assist[ing]" in-state businesses, unquestionably neutralizes advantages possessed by out-of-state enterprises. Such subsidies, particularly where they are in the form of cash or (what comes to the same thing) tax forgiveness, are often admitted to have as their purpose—indeed, are nationally advertised as having as their purpose—making it more profitable to conduct business in-state than elsewhere, i.e., distorting normal market incentives.

The Court's guiding principle also appears to call into question many garden-variety state laws heretofore permissible under the negative Commerce Clause. A state law, for example, which requires, contrary to the industry practice, the use of recyclable packaging materials, favors local non-exporting producers, who do not have to establish an additional, separate packaging operation for in-state sales. If the Court's analysis is to be believed, such a law would be unconstitutional without regard to whether disruption of the "national market" is the real purpose of the restriction, and without the need to "balance" the importance of the state interests thereby pursued. These results would greatly extend the negative Commerce Clause beyond its current scope. If the Court does not intend these consequences, and does not want to foster needless litigation concerning them, it should not have adopted its expansive rationale. Another basis for deciding the case is available, which I proceed to discuss.

"The historical record provides no grounds for reading the Commerce Clause to be other than what it says—an authorization for Congress to regulate commerce." Nonetheless, we formally adopted the doctrine of the negative Commerce Clause 121 years ago, *see Case of the State Freight Tax*, 15 Wall. 232 (1873), and since then have decided a vast number of negative-Commerce-Clause cases, engendering considerable reliance interests. [I] will, on stare decisis grounds, enforce a self-executing "negative" Commerce Clause in two situations: (1) against a state law that facially discriminates against interstate commerce, and (2) against a state law that is indistinguishable from a type of law previously held unconstitutional by this Court. . . .

There are at least four possible devices that would enable a State to produce the economic effect that Massachusetts has produced here: (1) a discriminatory tax upon the industry, imposing a higher liability on out-of-state members than on their in-state competitors; (2) a tax upon the industry that is nondiscriminatory in its assessment, but that has an "exemption" or "credit" for in-state members; (3) a nondiscriminatory tax upon the industry, the revenues from which are placed into a segregated fund, which fund is disbursed as "rebates" or "subsidies" to in-state members of the industry (the situation at issue in this case); and (4) with or without nondiscriminatory taxation of the industry, a subsidy for the in-state members of the industry, funded from the State's general revenues. It is long settled that the first of these methodologies is unconstitutional under the negative Commerce Clause. . . .

The issue before us in the present case is whether the third of these methodologies must fall. Although the question is close, I conclude it would not be a principled point at which to disembark from the negative-Commerce-Clause train. The only difference between methodology (2) (discriminatory "exemption" from nondiscriminatory tax) and methodology (3) (discriminatory refund of nondiscriminatory tax) is that the money is taken and returned rather than simply left with the favored in-state taxpayer in the first place. The difference between

(3) and (4), on the other hand, is the difference between assisting in-state industry through discriminatory taxation, and assisting in-state industry by other means.

I would therefore allow a State to subsidize its domestic industry so long as it does so from nondiscriminatory taxes that go into the State's general revenue fund. Perhaps [that] line comports with an important economic reality: a State is less likely to maintain a subsidy when its citizens perceive that the money (in the general fund) is available for any number of competing, non-protectionist, purposes. That is not, however, the basis for my position, for as the Chief Justice explains, "[a]nalysis of interest group participation in the political process may serve many useful purposes, but serving as a basis for interpreting the dormant Commerce Clause is not one of them." Instead, I draw the line where I do because it is a clear, rational line at the limits of our extant negative-Commerce-Clause jurisprudence.

Chief Justice REHNQUIST, with whom Justice BLACKMUN joins, dissenting. . . .

[T]he Court strikes down this method of state subsidization because [of] its view that the method of imposing the tax and subsidy distorts the State's political process: the dairy farmers, who would otherwise lobby against the tax, have been mollified by the subsidy. But [there] there are still at least two strong interest groups opposed to the milk order — consumers and milk dealers. . . . Analysis of interest group participation in the political process may serve many useful purposes, but serving as a basis for interpreting the dormant Commerce Clause is not one of them. . . . The wisdom of a messianic insistence on a grim sink-or-swim policy of laissez-faire economics would be debatable had Congress chosen to enact it; but Congress has done nothing of the kind. It is the Court which has imposed the policy under the dormant Commerce Clause, a policy which bodes ill for the values of federalism which have long animated our constitutional jurisprudence.

Note: Tolling Statutes

In Bendix Autolite Corp. v. Midwesco Enterprises, Inc., 486 U.S. 888 (1998), the Court struck down an Ohio statute that tolled the four-year statute of limitations in actions for breach of contract or fraud for any period that a person or corporation is not "present" in the state. To be present in Ohio, a foreign corporation must appoint an agent for service of process, which operates as consent to the general jurisdiction of the Ohio courts. Although the Court could have struck the law down as involving discrimination against interstate commerce, the Court concluded that the law imposed an unreasonable burden on interstate commerce. The Court concluded that the law imposed a significant burden because it required foreign corporations to appoint an agent for service of process in all cases, and to defend themselves "with reference to all transactions, including those in which it did not have the minimum contacts necessary for supporting personal jurisdiction." The Court rejected Ohio's assertion that the law should be sustained as a means of protecting Ohio residents from corporations "who become liable for acts done within the State but later withdraw from the jurisdiction." The Court noted that Midwesco was subject to service under Ohio's long-arm statute throughout the limitations period. Justice Scalia concurred, arguing that he would "abandon the 'balancing' approach to these negative Commerce Clause cases, [and hold that] a state statute is invalid under the Commerce Clause if, and only if, it accords discriminatory treatment to interstate commerce in a respect not required to achieve a lawful state purpose. When such a validating purpose exists, it is for Congress and not us to determine it is not significant enough to justify the burden on commerce."

Questions and Problems

1. *Reconsidering* Bendix Autolite. Do you agree with Justice Scalia, dissenting in *Bendix Autolite*, that the Courts should abandon the balancing test and invalidate only legislation that involves discrimination against interstate commerce? Are courts competent to assess and evaluate claims relating to the burdensomeness of regulation?

2. *Subsidies to Dairy Farmers.* After this decision, could Massachusetts pass a law providing financial subsidies to its dairy farmers? Could it withhold the benefits of those subsidies from farmers in surrounding states?

3. *Funding the Subsidies.* In the preceding problem, could Massachusetts fund the subsidy by a retail tax on the price of milk? Would it matter whether the tax was directly linked to the subsidy? What if the tax was passed a year later with no reference to the subsidy whatsoever?

American Trucking Associations, Inc. v. Michigan Public Service Commission

545 U.S. 429 (2005)

Justice BREYER delivered the opinion of the Court.

In this case, we consider whether a flat $100 fee that Michigan charges trucks engaging in intrastate commercial hauling violates the dormant Commerce Clause. We hold that it does not.

A subsection of Michigan's Motor Carrier Act imposes upon each motor carrier for the administration of this act, an annual fee of $100.00 for each self-propelled motor vehicle operated by or on behalf of the motor carrier. Mich. Comp. Laws Ann. §478.2 (1) (West 2002). The provision assesses the fee upon, and only upon, vehicles that engage in intrastate commercial operations — that is, on trucks that undertake point-to-point hauls between Michigan cities. Petitioners, USF Holland, Inc., a trucking company with trucks that engage in both interstate and intrastate hauling, and the American Trucking Associations, Inc. (ATA), asked the Michigan courts to invalidate the provision. Both petitioners told those courts that trucks that carry *both* interstate *and* intrastate loads engage in intrastate business less than trucks that confine their operations to the Great Lakes State. Hence, because Michigan's fee is flat, it discriminates against interstate carriers and imposes an unconstitutional burden upon interstate trade.

The Michigan Court of Claims rejected the carriers' claim [and the] Michigan Court of Appeals affirmed. . . . The Michigan Supreme Court denied petitioners leave to appeal. We granted their petition for certiorari and consolidated the case with a[nother] case in which interstate truckers sought review of a separate state motor carrier fee. We now affirm the Michigan court's judgment sustaining §478.2 (1).

Our Constitution was framed upon the theory that the peoples of the several states must sink or swim together. Baldwin v. G.A.F. Seelig, Inc., 294 U.S. 511, 523 (1935). Thus, this Court has consistently held that the Constitution's express grant to Congress of the power to regulate Commerce . . . among the several States, Art. I, contains a further, negative command, known as the dormant Commerce Clause, that create[s] an area of trade free from interference by the States, Boston Stock Exchange v. State Tax Comm'n., 429 U.S. 318 (1977). This negative command prevents a State from jeopardizing the welfare of the Nation as a whole by plac[ing] burdens on the flow of commerce across its borders that commerce wholly within those borders would not bear.

Thus, we have found unconstitutional state regulations that unjustifiably discriminate on their face against out-of-state entities, or that impose burdens on interstate trade that are clearly excessive in relation to the putative local benefits, Pike v. Bruce Church, Inc., 397 U.S. 137, 142 (1970). We have held that States may not impose taxes that facially discriminate against interstate business and offer commercial advantage to local enterprises, that improperly apportion state assessments on transactions with out-of-state components, or that have the inevitable effect [of] threaten[ing] the free movement of commerce by placing a financial barrier around the State, American Trucking Assns., Inc. v. Scheiner, 483 U.S. 266, 284 (1987).

Applying these principles and precedents, we find nothing in §478.2 (1) that offends the Commerce Clause. To begin with, Michigan imposes the flat $100 fee only upon intrastate transactions — that is, upon activities taking place exclusively within the State's borders. Section 478.2 (1) does not facially discriminate against interstate or out-of-state activities or enterprises. The statute applies evenhandedly to all carriers that make domestic journeys. It does not reflect an effort to tax activity that takes place, in whole or in part, outside the State. Nothing in our case law suggests that such a neutral, locally focused fee or tax is inconsistent with the dormant Commerce Clause. . . . States impose numerous flat fees upon local businesses and service providers, including, for example, upon insurers, auctioneers, ambulance operators, and hosts of others. Although we have long since rejected any suggestion that a state tax . . . affecting interstate commerce is immune from Commerce Clause scrutiny because it attaches only to a local or intrastate activity, we have also made clear that the Constitution neither displaces States' authority to shelter [their] people from menaces to their health or safety, nor unduly curtail[s] States' power to lay taxes for the support of state government, McGoldrick v. Berwind-White Coal Mining Co., 309 U.S. 33, 48 (1940).

The record, moreover, shows no special circumstance suggesting that Michigan's fee operates in practice as anything other than an unobjectionable exercise of the State's police power. To the contrary, [the] record contains little, if any, evidence that the $100 fee imposes any significant practical burden upon interstate trade. The record does show, for example, that some interstate trucks top off some interstate hauls with intrastate pickups and deliveries. But it does not tell us the answers to such questions as: How often does topping off occur across the industry? Does the $100 charge make a difference by significantly discouraging interstate carriers from engaging in topping off? Does the possibility of obtaining a 72-hour intrastate permit for $10 alleviate the alleged problem? If the fees ($100 and $10) discourage topping off, does that *local* commercial effect make a significant *interstate* difference? Would a variable fee (of the kind the truckers advocate) eliminate such difference? The minimal facts in the record tell us little about these matters. And at oral argument, ATA conceded the absence of record facts that empirically could show that the $100 fee significantly deters interstate trade.

Neither does the record show that the flat assessment unfairly discriminates against interstate truckers. The fee seeks to defray costs such as those of regulating vehicular size and weight, of administering insurance requirements, and of applying safety standards. The bulk of such costs would seem more likely to vary per truck or per carrier than to vary per mile traveled. And that fact means that a per-truck, rather than a per-mile, assessment is likely fair. . . .

Nor would an effort to switch the manner of fee assessment—from lump sum to, for example, miles traveled—be burden free. [To] obtain the same revenue (about $3.5 million) through a per-mile fee would require the State to create a data accumulation system capable of separating out intrastate hauls and determining their length, and to develop related liability, billing, and auditing mechanisms. [The] game is unlikely to be worth the candle. [Petitioners] do not provide the details of their preferred alternative administrative system nor point to record evidence showing its practicality.

Petitioners insist that they do not need empirically to demonstrate the existence of a burdensome or discriminatory impact upon interstate trucking, or (presumably) the unfairness of the assessment in relation to defrayed costs, or (presumably) the administrative practicality of the alternatives. They say that our earlier case, American Trucking Assns., Inc. v. Scheiner, 483 U.S. 266 (1987), requires invalidation of the $100 flat fee, even in the absence of such proof. We disagree. . . .

Petitioners add that Michigan's fee fails the internal consistency test—a test that we have typically used where taxation of interstate transactions is at issue. Generally speaking, that test asks, What would happen if all States did the same? *See, e.g.,* Goldberg v. Sweet, 488 U.S. 252, 261 (1989). [If] all States did the same, an interstate truck would have to pay fees totaling several hundred dollars, or even several thousand dollars, were it to top off its business by carrying local loads in many (or even all) other States. But it would have to do so only because it engages in *local* business in all those States. An interstate firm with local outlets normally expects to pay local fees that are uniformly assessed upon all those who engage in local business, interstate and domestic firms alike. A motor carrier is not special in this respect.

In sum, petitioners have failed to show that Michigan's fee, which does not seek to tax a share of interstate transactions, which focuses upon local activity, and which is assessed evenhandedly, either burdens or discriminates against interstate commerce, or violates the Commerce Clause in any other relevant way. *See* Complete Auto Transit, Inc. v. Brady, 430 U.S. 274 (1977).

For these reasons, the judgment of the Michigan Court of Appeals is affirmed.

It is so ordered.

Justice SCALIA, concurring in the judgment.

[I] agree [that] this fee does not violate the negative Commerce Clause. Unlike the Court, [I] ask whether the fee facially discriminates against interstate commerce and whether it is indistinguishable from a type of law previously held unconstitutional by this Court. . . . Michigan's fee [does] not facially discriminate against interstate commerce, and it is distinguishable from [other cases].

Justice THOMAS, concurring in the judgment.

I would affirm [because] " '[t]he negative Commerce Clause has no basis in the text of the Constitution, makes little sense, and has proved virtually unworkable in application,' and, consequently, cannot serve as a basis for striking down a state statute."

PROBLEM: MORE ON THE INTERNET CASINO PROHIBITION ACT

As you read the modern decisions, did your views regarding the possible validity or invalidity of the Internet Casino Prohibition Act change? If so, what factors led you to that conclusion? Do the more recent cases provide other ways to argue that the Act is valid (or, for that matter, invalid)?

D. THE STATE AS A MARKET PARTICIPANT

In some instances, instead of trying to regulate interstate commerce, the states intervene in commercial markets and become "market participants." Do different rules apply when a state acts as a market participant rather then as a market regulator?

Reeves, Inc. v. Stake

447 U.S. 429 (1980)

Mr. Justice BLACKMUN delivered the opinion of the Court.

The issue in this case is whether, consistent with the Commerce Clause, the State of South Dakota, in a time of shortage, may confine the sale of the cement it produces solely to its residents.

In 1919, South Dakota [built] a cement plant [in] response to recent regional cement shortages that "interfered with and delayed both public and private enterprises," and that were "threatening the people of this state." The plant [soon] produced more cement than South Dakotans could use. Over the years, buyers in no less than nine nearby States purchased cement from the State's plant. Between 1970 and 1977, some 40% of the plant's output went outside the State.

[Reeves, Inc.] is a ready-mix concrete distributor organized under Wyoming law. . . . From the beginning of its operations [and] until 1978, Reeves purchased about 95% of its cement from the South Dakota plant. In 1977, its purchases were $1,172,000. In turn, Reeves has supplied three northwestern Wyoming counties with more than half their ready-mix concrete needs. For 20 years the relationship between Reeves and the South Dakota cement plant was amicable, uninterrupted, and mutually profitable.

As the 1978 construction season approached, difficulties at the plant slowed production. Meanwhile, a booming construction industry spurred demand for cement both regionally and nationally. The plant found itself unable to meet all orders. Faced with the same type of "serious cement shortage" that inspired the plant's construction, the Commission "reaffirmed its policy of supplying all South Dakota customers first and to honor all contract commitments, with the remaining volume allocated on a first come, first served basis." [Reeves,] which had no pre-existing long-term supply contract, was hit hard and quickly by this development. . . . Unable to find another supplier, Reeves was forced to cut production by 76% in mid-July. . . .

[T]he Commerce Clause responds principally to state taxes and regulatory measures impeding free private trade in the national marketplace. There is no indication of a constitutional plan to limit the ability of the States themselves to operate freely in the free market. . . .

Restraint in this area is also counseled by considerations of state sovereignty, the role of each State "'as guardian and trustee for its people,'" and "the long recognized right of trader or manufacturer, engaged in an entirely private business, freely to exercise his own independent discretion as to parties with whom he will deal." United States v. Colgate & Co., 250 U.S. 300 (1919). Moreover, state proprietary activities may be, and often are, burdened with the same restrictions imposed on private market participants. Evenhandedness suggests that, when acting as proprietors, States should similarly share existing freedoms from federal constraints, including the inherent limits of the Commerce Clause. [T]he competing considerations in cases involving state proprietary action often will be subtle, complex, politically charged, and difficult to assess under traditional

Commerce Clause analysis. [As] a rule, the adjustment of interests in this context is a task better suited for Congress than this Court. . . . South Dakota, as a seller of cement, unquestionably fits the "market participant" label. . . . Thus, the general rule of [Hughes v. Alexandria Scrap Corp., 426 U.S. 794 (1976),] plainly applies here. . . .

In finding a Commerce Clause violation, the District Court [found that,] [h]aving long exploited the interstate market, South Dakota should not be permitted to withdraw from it when a shortage arises. . . . It is somewhat self-serving to say that South Dakota has "exploited" the interstate market. An equally fair characterization is that neighboring States long have benefitted from South Dakota's foresight and industry. . . .

[P]etitioner protests that South Dakota's preference for its residents responds solely to the "non-governmental objectiv[e]" of protectionism. Therefore, petitioner argues, the policy is per se invalid. *See* Philadelphia v. New Jersey, 437 U.S. 617 (1978). . . . We find the label "protectionism" of little help in this context. The State's refusal to sell to buyers other than South Dakotans is "protectionist" only in the sense that it limits benefits generated by a state program to those who fund the state treasury and whom the State was created to serve. Petitioner's argument apparently also would characterize as "protectionist" rules restricting to state residents the enjoyment of state educational institutions, energy generated by a state-run plant, police and fire protection, and agricultural improvement and business development programs. Such policies, while perhaps "protectionist" in a loose sense, reflect the essential and patently unobjectionable purpose of state government — to serve the citizens of the State.

[Petitioner argues that,] "If a state in this union, were allowed to hoard its commodities or resources for the use of their own residents only, a drastic situation might evolve. For example, Pennsylvania or Wyoming might keep their coal, the northwest its timber, and the mining states their minerals. The result being that embargo may be retaliated by embargo and commerce would be halted at state lines." *See, e.g.,* Baldwin v. Montana Fish & Game Comm'n., 436 U.S. 371 (1978). This argument, although rooted in the core purpose of the Commerce Clause, does not fit the present facts. Cement is not a natural resource, like coal, timber, wild game, or minerals. *Cf.* Hughes v. Oklahoma, 441 U.S. 322 (1979) (minnows); Philadelphia v. New Jersey, *supra* (landfill sites); Pennsylvania v. West Virginia, 262 U.S. 553 (1923) (natural gas). It is the end product of a complex process whereby a costly physical plant and human labor act on raw materials. South Dakota has not sought to limit access to the State's limestone or other materials used to make cement. Nor has it restricted the ability of private firms or sister States to set up plants within its borders. Moreover, petitioner has not suggested that South Dakota possesses unique access to the materials needed to produce cement. Whatever limits might exist on a State's ability to invoke the *Alexandria Scrap* exemption to hoard resources which by happenstance are found there, those limits do not apply here.

[I]t is suggested that the South Dakota program is infirm because it places South Dakota suppliers of ready-mix concrete at a competitive advantage in the out-of-state market; Wyoming suppliers [have] little chance against South Dakota suppliers who can purchase cement from the State's plant and freely sell beyond South Dakota's borders. . . . The force of this argument is seriously diminished, if not eliminated by several considerations. The argument necessarily implies that the South Dakota scheme would be unobjectionable if sales in other States were totally barred. It therefore proves too much, for it would tolerate even a greater measure of protectionism and stifling of interstate commerce than the challenge system allows. Nor is it to be forgotten that *Alexandria Scrap* approved a state program that "not [only] effectively protect[ed] scrap processors with existing plants in Maryland from the pressures of competitors with nearby out-of-state plants, but [that] implicitly offer[ed] to extend similar protection to any competitor [willing] to erect a scrap processing facility within Maryland's boundaries." Finally, the competitive plight of out-of-state ready-mix suppliers cannot be laid solely at the feet of South Dakota. It is attributable as well to their own States' not providing or attracting alternative sources of supply and to the suppliers' own failure to guard against shortages by executing long-term supply contracts with the South Dakota plant.

In its last argument, petitioner urges that, had South Dakota not acted, free market forces would have generated an appropriate level of supply at free market prices for all buyers in the region. Having replaced free market forces, South Dakota should be forced to replicate how the free market would have operated under prevailing conditions. . . . This argument [is] simplistic and speculative. The very reason South Dakota built its plant was because the free market had failed adequately to supply the region with cement. [I]t is quite possible that petitioner would never have existed—far less operated successfully for 20 years—had it not been for South Dakota cement.

We conclude, then, that the arguments for invalidating South Dakota's resident-preference program are weak at best. . . . Reversal would discourage similar state projects, even though this project demonstrably has served the needs of state residents and has helped the entire region for more than a half century. Reversal also would rob South Dakota of the intended benefit of its foresight, risk, and industry. Under these circumstances, there is no reason to depart from the general rule of *Alexandria Scrap*.

The judgment of the United States Court of Appeals is affirmed.

It is so ordered.

Mr. Justice POWELL, with whom Mr. Justice BRENNAN, Mr. Justice WHITE, and Mr. Justice STEVENS join, dissenting.

[South Dakota's] policy represents precisely the kind of economic protectionism that the Commerce Clause was intended to prevent. . . . I cannot agree that South Dakota may withhold its cement from interstate commerce in order to benefit private citizens and businesses within the State. . . . The Commerce Clause has proved an effective weapon against protectionism. The Court has used it to strike down limitations on access to local goods, be they animal, vegetable, or mineral. . . .

[The] application of the Commerce Clause [should] turn on the nature of the governmental activity involved. If a public enterprise undertakes an "integral operatio[n] in areas of traditional governmental functions," National League of Cities v. Usery, 426 U.S. 833 (1976), the Commerce Clause is not directly relevant. If, however, the State enters the private market and operates a commercial enterprise for the advantage of its private citizens, it may not evade the constitutional policy against economic Balkanization.

This distinction derives from the power of governments to supply their own needs, and from the purpose of the Commerce Clause itself, which is designed to protect "the natural functioning of the interstate market." In procuring goods and services for the operation of government, a State may act without regard to the private marketplace and remove itself from the reach of the Commerce Clause. But when a State itself becomes a participant in the private market for other purposes, the Constitution forbids actions that would impede the flow of interstate commerce. . . . The threshold issue is whether South Dakota has undertaken integral government operations in an area of traditional governmental functions, or whether it has participated in the marketplace as a private firm. If the latter characterization applies, we also must determine whether the State Commission's marketing policy burdens the flow of interstate trade. . . .

[T]he marketing policy of the South Dakota Cement Commission has cut off interstate trade. The State can raise such a bar when it enters the market to supply its own needs. In order to ensure an adequate supply of cement for public uses, the State can withhold from interstate commerce the cement needed for public projects. . . . The State, however, has no parallel justification for favoring private, in-state customers over out-of-state customers. In response to political concerns that likely would be inconsequential to a private cement producer, South Dakota has shut off its cement sales to customers beyond its borders. . . . The effect on interstate trade is the same as if the state legislature had imposed the policy on private cement producers. . . . The creation of a free national economy was a major goal of the States when they resolved to unite under the Federal Constitution. The decision today cannot be reconciled with that purpose.

Note: Fuel Taxes and Market Participation

Recall New Energy Co. of Indiana v. Limbach, 486 U.S. 269 (1988), which we described earlier. As you may recall, that case involved an Ohio statute that awarded a tax credit against the Ohio motor vehicle fuel sales tax for each gallon of ethanol sold (as a component of gasohol) by fuel dealers, but only if the ethanol was produced in Ohio or in a state that grants similar tax advantages to ethanol produced in Ohio. In *Limbach*, the Court also rejected the idea that the law could be upheld on a market-participant theory: "The market-participant doctrine has no application here. The Ohio action ultimately at issue is neither its purchase nor its sale of ethanol, but its assessment and computation of taxes — a primeval governmental activity. To be sure, the tax credit scheme has the purpose and effect of subsidizing a particular industry, as do many dispositions of the tax laws. That does not transform it into a form of state participation in the free market. Our opinion in [Hughes v. Alexandria Scrap Corp., 426 U.S. 794 (1976),] does not remotely establish such a proposition. There we [upheld] against Commerce Clause attack on the basis of the market-participant doctrine, a Maryland cash subsidy program that discriminated in favor of in-state auto-hulk processors. The purpose of the program was to achieve the removal of unsightly abandoned autos from the State, and the Court characterized it as proprietary rather than regulatory activity, based on the analogy of the State to a private purchaser of the auto hulks. We have subsequently observed that subsidy programs unlike that of *Alexandria Scrap* might not be characterized as proprietary. *See Reeves, Inc., supra,* 447 U.S., at 440. We think it clear that Ohio's assessment and computation of its fuel sales tax, regardless of whether it produces a subsidy, cannot plausibly be analogized to the activity of a private purchaser."

South-Central Timber Development, Inc. v. Wunnicke

467 U.S. 82 (1984)

Justice WHITE delivered the opinion of the Court with respect to Parts I and II, and delivered an opinion with respect to Parts III and IV, in which Justice BRENNAN, Justice BLACKMUN, and Justice STEVENS joined.

We granted certiorari in this case to review a decision of the Court of Appeals for the Ninth Circuit that held that Alaska's requirement that timber taken from state lands be processed within the State prior to export was "implicitly authorized" by Congress and therefore does not violate the Commerce Clause. We hold that it was not authorized and reverse the judgment of the Court of Appeals. . . .

Our cases make clear that if a State is acting as a market participant, rather than as a market regulator, the dormant Commerce Clause places no limitation on its activities. The precise contours of the market-participant doctrine have yet to be established, however, the doctrine having been applied in only three cases of this Court to date.

The most recent of this Court's cases developing the market-participant doctrine is White v. Massachusetts Council of Construction Employers, Inc., [460 U.S. 204 (1983),] in which the Court rejected against a Commerce Clause to an executive order of the Mayor of Boston that required all construction projects funded in whole or in part by city funds or city-administered funds to be performed by a work force of at least 50% city residents. The Court rejected the argument that the city was not entitled to the protection of the doctrine because the order had the effect of regulating employment contracts between public contractors and their employees. Recognizing that "there are some limits on a state or local government's ability to impose restrictions that reach beyond the immediate parties with which the government transacts business," the Court found it unnecessary to define those limits because "[e]veryone affected by the order [was], in a substantial if informal sense, 'working for the city.'" The fact that the employees were "working for the city" was "crucial" to the market-participant analysis in *White*.

The State of Alaska contends that its primary-manufacture requirement fits squarely within the market-participant doctrine, arguing that "Alaska's entry into the market may be viewed as precisely the same type of subsidy to local interests that the Court found unobjectionable in *Alexandria Scrap*." However, when Maryland became involved in the scrap market it was as a purchaser of scrap; Alaska, on the other hand, participates in the timber market, but imposes conditions downstream in the timber-processing market. Alaska is not merely subsidizing local timber processing in an amount "roughly equal to the difference between the price the timber would fetch in the absence of such a requirement and the amount the state actually receives." If the State directly subsidized the timber-processing industry by such an amount, the purchaser would retain the option of taking advantage of the subsidy by processing timber in the State or forgoing the benefits of the subsidy and exporting unprocessed timber. Under the Alaska requirement, however, the choice is made for him: if he buys timber from the State he is not free to take the timber out of state prior to processing.

The State also would have us find *Reeves* controlling. It states that "*Reeves* made it clear that the Commerce Clause imposes no limitation on Alaska's power to choose the terms on which it will sell its timber." [Although] *Reeves* did strongly endorse the right of a State to deal with whomever it chooses when it participates in the market, it did [not] sanction the imposition of any terms that the State might desire. [T]he Court expressly noted in *Reeves* that "Commerce Clause scrutiny may well be more rigorous when a restraint on foreign commerce is alleged"; that a natural resource "like coal, timber, wild game, or minerals," was not involved, but instead the cement was "the end product of a complex process whereby a costly physical plant and human labor act on raw materials," and that South Dakota did not bar resale of South Dakota cement to out-of-state purchasers. In this case, all three of the elements that were not present in *Reeves* — foreign commerce, a natural resource, and restrictions on resale — are present.

Finally, Alaska argues that [the] primary-manufacture requirement is permissible, because the State is not regulating contracts for resale of timber or regulating the buying and selling of timber, but is instead "a seller of timber, pure and simple." Yet it is clear that the State is more than merely a seller of timber. In the commercial context, the seller usually has no say over, and no interest in, how the product is to be used after sale; in this case, however, payment for the timber does not end the obligations of the purchaser, for, despite the fact that the purchaser has taken delivery of the timber and has paid for it, he cannot do with it as he pleases. Instead, he is obligated to deal with a stranger to the contract after completion of the sale.

That privity of contract is not always the outer boundary of permissible state activity does not necessarily mean that the Commerce Clause has no application within the boundary of formal privity. The market-participant doctrine permits a State to influence "a discrete, identifiable class of economic activity in which [it] is a major participant." White v. Massachusetts Council of Construction Workers, Inc., 103 S.Ct., at 1046, n.7. Contrary to the State's contention, the doctrine is not carte blanche to impose any conditions that the State has the economic power to dictate, and does not validate any requirement merely because the State imposes it upon someone with whom it is in contractual privity.

The limit of the market-participant doctrine must be that it allows a State to impose burdens on commerce within the market in which it is a participant, but allows it to go no further. The State may not impose conditions, whether by statute, regulation, or contract, that have a substantial regulatory effect outside of that particular market. Unless the "market" is relatively narrowly defined, the doctrine has the potential of swallowing up the rule that States may not impose substantial burdens on interstate commerce even if they act with the permissible state purpose of fostering local industry.

[There] are sound reasons for distinguishing between a State's preferring its own residents in the initial disposition of goods when it is a market participant and a State's attachment of restrictions on dispositions subsequent to the goods coming to rest in private hands. First, [a] State market participant has a greater interest as a "private trader" in the immediate transaction than it has in what its purchaser does with the goods after the State no longer has an interest in them. The common law recognized such a notion in the doctrine of restraints on alienation. . . . We reject the contention that a State's action as a market regulator may be upheld against Commerce Clause challenge on the ground that the State could achieve the same end as a market participant. We therefore find it unimportant for present purposes that the State could support its processing industry by selling only to Alaska processors, by vertical integration, or by direct subsidy.

Second, downstream restrictions have a greater regulatory effect than do limitations on the immediate transaction. Instead of merely choosing its own trading partners, the State is attempting to govern the private, separate economic relationships of its trading partners; that is, it restricts the post-purchase activity of the purchaser, rather than merely the purchasing activity. [T]his restriction on private economic activity takes place after the completion of the parties' direct commercial obligations, rather than during the course of an ongoing commercial relationship in which the city retained a continuing proprietary interest in the subject of the contract. In sum, the State may not avail itself of the market-participant doctrine to immunize its downstream regulation of the timber-processing market in which it is not a participant. . . .

The judgment of the Court of Appeals is reversed and the case is remanded for proceedings consistent with the opinion of this Court.

It is so ordered.

Justice REHNQUIST, with whom Justice O'CONNOR joins, dissenting.

[Alaska] is merely paying the buyer of the timber indirectly, by means of a reduced price, to hire Alaska residents to process the timber. Under existing precedent, the State could accomplish that same result in any number of ways. For example, the State could choose to sell its timber only to those companies that maintain active primary-processing plants in Alaska. Reeves, Inc. v. Stake, 447 U.S. 429 (1980). Or the State could directly subsidize the primary-processing industry within the State. Hughes v. Alexandria Scrap Corp., 426 U.S. 794 (1976). The State could even pay to have the logs processed and then enter the market only to sell processed logs. It seems to me unduly formalistic to conclude that the one path chosen by the State as best suited to promote its concerns is the path forbidden it by the Commerce Clause.

∾ PROBLEM: MORE ON THE INTERNET CASINO PROHIBITION ACT ∾

Suppose that, in addition to regulating gambling interests in the state, Kentucky owns and operates a state lottery. Funds from the lottery are used to pay education-related expenses. Could Kentucky justify the Internet Casino Prohibition Act under the "market participation" doctrine?

E. INTERSTATE PRIVILEGES AND IMMUNITIES CLAUSE

Article IV, Section 2 contains the Interstate Privileges and Immunities Clause: "The Citizens of each State shall be entitled to all Privileges and Immunities of Citizens in the several States." This clause was designed to ensure that states would not discriminate against the citizens of other states because of their citizenship in those states. Like most constitutional rights, the Privileges and Immunities Clause does not require states to treat nonresidents in exactly the same way that they treat their own citizens, and it does not impose an absolute ban on discrimination by one state against the citizens of another. States can treat the citizens of other states differently in some instances.

Baldwin v. Fish and Game Commission of Montana
436 U.S. 371 (1978)

Mr. Justice BLACKMUN delivered the opinion of the Court.

This case presents issues, under the Privileges and Immunities Clause of the Constitution's Art. IV, §2, and the Equal Protection Clause of the Fourteenth Amendment, as to the constitutional validity of disparities, as between residents and nonresidents, in a State's hunting license system.

Appellant Lester Baldwin is a Montana resident. He also is an outfitter holding a state license as a hunting guide. The majority of his customers are nonresidents who come to Montana to hunt elk and other big game. Appellants Carlson, Huseby, Lee and Moris are residents of Minnesota. They have hunted big game, particularly elk, in Montana in past years and wish to continue to do so. . . .

[For] the 1975 hunting season, a Montana resident could purchase a license solely for elk for $4. The nonresident, however, in order to hunt elk, was required to purchase a combination license at a cost of $151; this entitled him to take one elk and two deer. . . . For the 1976 season, the Montana resident could purchase a license solely for elk for $9. The nonresident, in order to hunt elk was required to purchase a combination license at a cost of $225; this entitled him to take one elk, one deer, one black bear, and game birds, and to fish with hook and line. A resident was not required to buy any combination of licenses, but if he did, the cost to him of all the privileges granted by the nonresident combination license was $30. The nonresident thus paid 7½ times as much as the resident, and if the nonresident wished to hunt only elk, he paid 25 times as much as the resident. . . .

Montana maintains significant populations of big game, including elk, deer, and antelope. Its elk population is one of the largest in the United States. Elk are prized by big-game hunters who come from near and far to pursue the animals for sport. [F]rom 1960 to 1970 licenses issued by Montana increased by approximately 67% for residents and by approximately 530% for nonresidents. . . . Owing to its successful management programs for elk, the State has not been compelled to limit the overall number of hunters by means of drawings or lotteries as have other States with harvestable elk populations. Elk are not hunted commercially in Montana. Nonresident hunters seek the animal for its trophy value; the trophy is the distinctive set of antlers. The interest of resident hunters more often may be in the meat. Elk are now found in the mountainous regions of western Montana. . . . During the summer the animals move to higher elevations and lands that are largely federally owned. In the late fall they move down to lower privately owned lands that provide the winter habitat necessary to their survival. During the critical midwinter period elk are often supported by ranchers. . . . Elk management is expensive. In regions of the State with significant elk population, more personnel time of the Fish and Game Commission is spent on elk than on any other species of big game. . . .

Privileges and immunities. Appellants strongly urge here that the Montana licensing scheme for the hunting of elk violates the Privileges and Immunities Clause of Art. IV, §2, of our Constitution. [T]he Privileges and Immunities Clause [has] been interpreted to prevent a State from imposing unreasonable burdens on citizens of other States in their pursuit of common callings within the State, Ward v. Maryland, 12 Wall. 418 (1871); in the ownership and disposition of privately held property within the State, Blake v. McClung, 172 U.S. 239 (1898); and in access to the courts of the State, Canadian Northern Ry. Co. v. Eggen, 252 U.S. 553 (1920).

It has not been suggested, however, that state citizenship or residency may never be used by a State to distinguish among persons. . . . No one would suggest that the Privileges and Immunities Clause requires a State to open its polls to a person who declines to assert that the State is the only one where he claims a right to vote. The same is true as to qualification for an elective office of the State. Kanapaux v. Ellisor, 419 U.S. 891 (1974). Nor must a State always apply all its laws or all its services equally to anyone, resident or nonresident, who may request it so to do. Some distinctions between residents and nonresidents merely reflect the fact that this is a Nation composed of individual States, and are permitted; other distinctions are prohibited because they hinder the formation, the purpose, or the development of a single Union of those States. Only with respect to those "privileges" and "immunities" bearing upon the vitality of the Nation as a single entity must the State treat all citizens, resident and nonresident, equally. Here we must decide into which category falls a distinction with respect to access to recreational big-game hunting.

Many [early] cases embrace the concept that the States had complete ownership over wildlife within their boundaries, [and] the power to preserve this bounty for their citizens alone. [A]lthough the States were obligated to treat all those within their territory equally in most respects, they were not obliged to share those things they held in trust for their own people. In Corfield [v. Coryell, 6 Fed. Cas. 546, although] recognizing that the States may not interfere with the "right of a citizen of one state to pass through, or to reside in any other state, for purposes of trade, agriculture, professional pursuits, or otherwise; to claim the benefit of the writ of habeas corpus; to institute and maintain actions of any kind in the courts of the state; to take, hold and dispose of property, either real or personal," nonetheless concluded that access to oyster beds determined to be owned by New Jersey could be limited to New Jersey residents. . . .

In more recent years, however, the Court has recognized that the States' interest in regulating and controlling those things they claim to "own," including wildlife, is by no means absolute. States may not compel the confinement of the benefits of their resources, even their wildlife, to their own people whenever such hoarding and confinement impedes interstate commerce. Nor does a State's control over its resources preclude the proper exercise of federal power. And a State's interest in its wildlife and other resources must yield when, without reason, it interferes with a nonresident's right to pursue a livelihood in a State other than his own, a right that is protected by the Privileges and Immunities Clause. Toomer v. Witsell, 334 U.S. 385 (1948). . . .

Does the distinction made by Montana between residents and nonresidents in establishing access to elk hunting threaten a basic right in a way that offends the Privileges and Immunities Clause? [Elk] hunting by nonresidents in Montana is a recreation and a sport. [I]t is costly and obviously available only to the wealthy nonresident or to the one so taken with the sport that he sacrifices other values in order to indulge in it and to enjoy what it offers. It is not a means to the nonresident's livelihood. The mastery of the animal and the trophy are the ends that are sought; appellants are not totally excluded from these. The elk supply, which has been entrusted to the care of the State by the people of Montana, is finite and must be carefully tended in order to be preserved.

Appellants' interest in sharing this limited resource on more equal terms with Montana residents simply does not fall within the purview of the Privileges and Immunities Clause. Equality in access to Montana elk is not basic to the maintenance or well-being of the Union. Appellants do not — and cannot — contend that they are deprived of a means of a livelihood by the system or of access to any part of the State to which they may seek to travel. . . . Whatever rights or activities may be "fundamental" under the Privileges and Immunities Clause, we are persuaded, and hold, that elk hunting by nonresidents in Montana is not one of them. . . .

The judgment of the District Court is affirmed.
It is so ordered.

Mr. Justice BRENNAN, with whom Mr. Justice WHITE and Mr. Justice MARSHALL join, dissenting.

[A]n inquiry into whether a given right is "fundamental" has no place in our analysis of whether a State's discrimination against nonresidents — who "are not represented in the [discriminating] State's legislative halls" — violates the Clause. [O]ur primary concern is the State's justification for its discrimination. [A] State's discrimination against nonresidents is permissible where (1) the presence or activity of nonresidents is the source or cause of the problem or effect with which the State seeks to deal, and (2) the discrimination practiced against nonresidents bears a substantial relation to the problem they present. [A] State['s] mere assertion that the discrimination practiced against nonresidents is justified by the peculiar problem nonresidents present will not prevail in the face of a prima facie showing that the discrimination is not supportable on the asserted grounds. This requirement that a State's unequal treatment of nonresidents be reasoned and suitably tailored furthers the federal interest in ensuring that "a norm of comity," prevails throughout the Nation while simultaneously guaranteeing to the States the needed leeway to draw viable distinctions between their citizens and those of other States.

It is clear that under a proper privileges and immunities analysis Montana's discriminatory treatment of nonresident big-game hunters in this case must fail. [T]here are three possible justifications for charging nonresident elk hunters an amount at least 7.5 times the fee imposed on resident big-game hunters. The first is conservation. The State did not attempt to assert this as a justification for its discriminatory licensing scheme [and] it is difficult to see how it could [do so]. First, there is nothing in the record to indicate that the influx of nonresident hunters created a special danger to Montana's elk or to any of its other wildlife species. . . . Nonresidents [constituted] only 13% of all hunters pursuing their sport in the State. . . . Second, if Montana's discriminatorily high big-game license fee is an outgrowth of general conservation policy to discourage elk hunting[,] Montana makes no effort similarly to inhibit its own residents. As we said in Douglas v. Seacoast Products, Inc., 431 U.S. 265 (1977), "[a] statute that leaves a State's residents free to destroy a natural resource while excluding aliens or nonresidents is not a conservation law at all." [The] second possible justification for the fee differential [is] a cost justification. [The Clause allows] additional charges to be made on nonresidents based on both the added enforcement costs the presence of nonresident hunters imposes on Montana and the State's conservation expenditures supported by resident-borne taxes. [However, Montana's higher fee for nonresident elk hunters does not reflect an attempt to recoup state expenditures.] Montana's attempt to cost-justify its discriminatory licensing practices thus fails under the second prong of a correct privileges and immunities analysis — that which requires the discrimination a State visits upon nonresidents to bear a substantial relation to the problem or burden they pose. . . .

Note: **Toomer** *and Shrimp Fishing*

Toomer v. Witsell, 334 U.S. 385 (1948), involved a South Carolina law that regulated commercial shrimp fishing in the three-mile maritime belt off the coast of that state. Among other things, the law imposed a $2,500-per-boat fee on non-residents while imposing a $25 fee on residents. Georgia shrimpers challenged the law as a violation of the Interstate Privileges and Immunities Clause. The Court struck down the law, noting that nothing "indicates that non-residents use larger boats or different fishing methods than residents, that the cost of enforcing the laws against them is appreciably greater, or that any substantial amount of the state's general funds is devoted to shrimp conservation." The Court did note that the state is not "without power [to] restrict the type of equipment used in its fisheries, to graduate license fees according to the size of the boats, or even to charge non-residents a differential which would merely compensate the State for any added enforcement burden they may impose or for any conservation expenditures from taxes which only residents pay." The Court specifically rejected the "whole ownership theory," which suggests that states have the "power to preserve and regulate the exploitation of an important resource."

Hicklin v. Orbeck

437 U.S. 518 (1978)

Mr. Justice BRENNAN delivered the opinion of the Court.

In 1972, professedly for the purpose of reducing unemployment in the State, the Alaska Legislature passed an Act entitled "Local Hire Under State Leases." Alaska Stat. Ann. §§38.40.010 to 38.40.090 (1977). The key provision of "Alaska Hire," as the Act has come to be known, is the requirement that "all oil and gas leases, easements or right-of-way permits for oil or gas pipeline purposes, unitization agreements, or any renegotiation of any of the preceding to which the state is a party" contain a provision "requiring the employment of qualified Alaska residents" in preference to nonresidents. This employment preference is administered by providing persons meeting the statutory requirements for Alaskan residency with certificates of residence — "resident cards" — that can be presented to an employer covered by the Act as proof of residency. Appellants [were] desirous of securing jobs covered by the Act but unable to qualify for the necessary resident cards. . . .

Appellants' principal challenge to Alaska Hire is made under the Privileges and Immunities Clause of Art. IV, §2. [Appellants'] appeal to the protection of the Clause is strongly supported by this Court's decisions holding violative of the Clause state discrimination against nonresidents seeking to ply their trade, practice their occupation, or pursue a common calling within the State. For example, in Ward v. Maryland, 12 Wall. 418 (1871), a Maryland statute regulating the sale of most goods in the city of Baltimore fell to the privileges and immunities challenge of a New Jersey resident against whom the law discriminated. The statute discriminated against nonresidents of Maryland in several ways: It required nonresident merchants to obtain licenses in order to practice their trade without requiring the same of certain similarly situated Maryland merchants; it charged nonresidents a higher license fee than those Maryland residents who were required to secure licenses; and it prohibited both resident and nonresident merchants from using nonresident salesmen, other than their regular employees, to sell their goods in the city. In holding that the statute violated the Privileges and Immunities Clause, the Court observed that "the clause plainly and unmistakably secures and protects the right of a citizen of one State to pass into any other State of the Union for the purpose of engaging in lawful commerce, trade, or business without molestation." *Ward* thus recognized that a resident of one State is constitutionally entitled to travel to another State for purposes of employment free from discriminatory restrictions in favor of state residents imposed by the other State.

[E]ven where the presence or activity of nonresidents causes or exacerbates the problem the State seeks to remedy, there must be a "reasonable relationship between the danger represented by non-citizens, as a class, and [the] discrimination practiced upon them." *Toomer*'s analytical framework was confirmed in Mullaney v. Anderson, 342 U.S. 415 (1952), where it was applied to invalidate a scheme used by the Territory of Alaska for the licensing of commercial fishermen in territorial waters; under that scheme residents paid a license fee of only $5 while nonresidents were charged $50.

Even assuming that a State may validly attempt to alleviate its unemployment problem by requiring private employers within the State to discriminate against nonresidents[,] it is clear that under the *Toomer* analysis reaffirmed in *Mullaney*, Alaska Hire's discrimination against nonresidents cannot withstand scrutiny under the Privileges and Immunities Clause. For although the statute may not violate the Clause if the State shows "something to indicate that noncitizens constitute a peculiar source of the evil at which the statute is aimed." And, beyond this, the State "has no burden to prove that its laws are not violative of [the] Clause," Baldwin v. Montana Fish and Game Commn., 436 U.S., at 402 (Brennan, J., dissenting), certainly no showing was made on this record that nonresidents were "a peculiar source of the evil" Alaska Hire was enacted to remedy, namely, Alaska's "uniquely high unemployment." Alaska Stat. Ann. §38.40.020 (1977). [The record] indicates that the major cause of Alaska's high unemployment was not the influx of nonresidents seeking employment, but rather the fact that a substantial number of Alaska's jobless residents — especially the unemployed Eskimo and Indian residents — were unable to secure employment either because of their lack of education and job training or because of their geographical remoteness from job opportunities; and that the employment of nonresidents threatened to deny jobs to Alaska residents only to the extent that jobs for which untrained residents were being prepared might be filled by nonresidents before the residents' training was completed.

[E]ven if the State's showing is accepted as sufficient to indicate that nonresidents were "a peculiar source of evil," *Toomer* and *Mullaney* compel the conclusion that Alaska Hire nevertheless fails to pass constitutional muster. For the discrimination the Act works against nonresidents does not bear a substantial relationship to the particular "evil" they are said to present. Alaska Hire simply grants all Alaskans, regardless of their employment status, education, or training, a flat employment preference for all jobs covered by the Act. A highly skilled and educated resident who has never been unemployed is entitled to precisely the same preferential treatment as the unskilled, habitually unemployed Arctic Eskimo enrolled in a job-training program. If Alaska is to attempt to ease its unemployment problem by forcing employers within the State to discriminate against nonresidents — again, a policy which may present serious constitutional questions — the means by which it does so must be more closely tailored to aid the unemployed the Act is intended to benefit. . . .

Relying on McCready v. Virginia, 94 U.S. 391 (1877)[,] Alaska contends that because the oil and gas that are the subject of Alaska Hire are owned by the State, this ownership, of itself, is sufficient justification for the Act's discrimination against nonresidents, and takes the Act totally without the scope of the Privileges and Immunities Clause. As the State sees it "the privileges and immunities clause [does] not apply [to] decisions by the states as to how they would permit [the] use and distribution of the natural resources which they own. . . ." We do not agree. . . . "[I]n more recent years[,] the Court has recognized that the States' interest in regulating and controlling those things they claim to 'own' [is] by no means absolute." Baldwin v. Montana Fish and Game Comm'n., 436 U.S., at 385. [A] State's ownership of the property with which the statute is concerned is a factor — although often the crucial factor — to be considered in evaluating whether the statute's discrimination against noncitizens violates the Clause. Dispositive though this factor may be[,] it is not dispositive here.

[But] Alaska Hire extends to employers who have no connection whatsoever with the State's oil and gas, perform no work on state land, have no contractual relationship with the State, and receive no payment from the State. . . . Moreover, the Act's coverage is not limited to activities connected with the extraction of Alaska's oil and gas. It [encompasses] "employment opportunities at refineries and in distribution systems utilizing oil and gas obtained under Alaska leases." [In] sum, the Act is an attempt to force virtually all businesses that benefit in some way from the economic ripple effect of Alaska's decision to develop its oil and gas resources to bias their employment practices in favor of the State's residents. We believe that Alaska's ownership of the oil and gas that is the subject matter of Alaska Hire simply constitutes insufficient justification for the pervasive discrimination against nonresidents that the Act mandates. . . .

[Prior precedent establishes] that the Commerce Clause circumscribes a State's ability to prefer its own citizens in the utilization of natural resources found within its borders, but destined for interstate commerce. . . . Alaska's oil and gas here are bound for out-of-state consumption. . . . Although the fact that a state-owned resource is destined for interstate commerce does not, of itself, disable the State from preferring its own citizens in the utilization of that resource, it does inform analysis under the Privileges and Immunities Clause as to the permissibility of the discrimination the State visits upon nonresidents based on its ownership of the resource. Here, the oil and gas upon which Alaska hinges its discrimination against nonresidents are of profound national importance. [T]he breadth of the discrimination mandated by Alaska Hire goes far beyond the degree of resident bias Alaska's ownership of the oil and gas can justifiably support. The confluence of these realities points to but one conclusion: Alaska Hire cannot withstand constitutional scrutiny. As Mr. Justice Cardozo observed in Baldwin v. G.A.F. Seelig, Inc., 294 U.S. 511, 523 (1935), the Constitution "was framed upon the theory that the peoples of the several states must sink or swim together, and that in the long run prosperity and salvation are in union and not division."

Reversed.

Notes

1. *May a City Favor Its Residents on Public Works Contracts?* In United Building and Construction Trades Council of Camden County v. City of Camden, 465 U.S. 208 (1984), the City of Camden, New Jersey, adopted an ordinance that required that at least 40 percent of the employees of contractors and subcontractors working on city construction projects be Camden residents. A resident was defined as anyone who lives in the City of Camden without regard to the length of residency. The Court concluded that the Privileges and Immunities Clause was applicable, and it remanded for further hearings: "Given the Camden ordinance, an out-of-state citizen who ventures into New Jersey will not enjoy the same privileges as the New Jersey citizen residing in Camden. It is true that New Jersey citizens not residing in Camden will be affected by the ordinance as well as out-of-state citizens. And it is true that the disadvantaged New Jersey residents have no claim under the Privileges and Immunities Clause. But New Jersey residents at least have a chance to remedy at the polls any discrimination against them. . . . We conclude that Camden's ordinance is not immune from constitutional review at the behest of out-of-state residents merely because some in-state residents are similarly disadvantaged." The Court went on to note that the "fact that Camden is expending its own funds or funds it administers in accordance with the terms of a grant is certainly a factor — perhaps the crucial factor — to be considered in evaluating whether the statute's discrimination violates the Privileges and Immunities Clause. But it does not remove the Camden ordinance completely from the purview of the Clause." Therefore, the Court remanded for consideration of whether Camden could offer a "substantial reason" for treating nonresidents differently as a remedy for the "peculiar source of the evil at which the statute is aimed." Justice Blackmun dissented, arguing that the Article VI Privileges and Immunities Clause was intended only to prohibit a state from discriminating between its own residents and residents of other states on the basis of state citizenship. In his view, it was not intended to prohibit discrimination "*among* state residents on the basis of *municipal* residence."

2. *The Practice of Law.* Does the Privileges and Immunities Clause protect the right to practice law in another state? Supreme Court of New Hampshire v. Piper, 470 U.S. 274 (1985), involved a New Hampshire law that allowed only New Hampshire residents to become attorneys as challenged by a Vermont resident

who lived only 400 yards from the New Hampshire border. She had passed the New Hampshire bar examination, had been found to be of good moral character, and had met all other requirements for admission. In striking down the law, the Court emphasized that the clause was designed to ensure noncitizens the right to do business "on terms of substantial equality with the citizens" of the state. The Court concluded that this right extended to the practice of law because "out-of-state lawyers may — and often do — represent persons who raise unpopular federal claims. In some cases, representation by nonresident counsel may be the only means available for the vindication of federal rights." The Court rejected the idea that the clause should not apply because lawyers exercised "state power." The Court then evaluated and rejected the state's alleged justifications for the law, which included allegations that nonresident lawyers "would be less likely (i) to become, and remain, familiar with local rules and procedures; (ii) to behave ethically; (iii) to be available for court proceedings; and (iv) to do *pro bono* and other volunteer work in the State." The Court concluded: "[We may not] assume that a nonresident lawyer — any more than a resident — would disserve his clients by failing to familiarize himself with the rules. . . . The nonresident lawyer's professional duty and interest in his reputation should provide the same incentive to maintain high ethical standards as they do for resident lawyers. . . . One may assume that a high percentage of nonresident lawyers willing to take the state bar examination and pay the annual dues will reside in places reasonably convenient to New Hampshire. Furthermore, [the] State can protect its interests through less restrictive means [by requiring] any lawyer who resides at a great distance to retain a local attorney who will be available for unscheduled meetings and hearings. . . . The final reason advanced by appellant is that nonresident members of the state bar would be disinclined to do their share of *pro bono* and volunteer work. [I]t is reasonable to believe, however, that most lawyers who become members of a state bar will endeavor to perform their share of these services. . . . Furthermore, a nonresident bar member, like the resident member, could be required to represent indigents and perhaps to participate in formal legal-aid work."

Justice Rehnquist dissented: "[The] practice of law is — almost by definition — fundamentally different [from] other occupations that are practiced across state lines. [The] State has a substantial interest in creating its own set of laws responsive to its own local interests[, and] may decide that it has an interest in maximizing the number of resident lawyers, so as to increase the quality of the pool from which its lawmakers can be drawn. [E]ach out-of-state lawyer who is allowed to practice necessarily takes legal work that could support an in-state lawyer. . . . And the State likewise might conclude that those citizens trained in the law are likely to bring their useful expertise to other important functions that benefit from such expertise [such] as trusteeships, or directorships of corporations or charitable organizations, or school board positions, or merely the role of the interested citizen at a town meeting. [The] uncertainties of managing a trial docket are such that lawyers rarely are given a single date on which a trial will begin; they may be required to 'stand by' [for] days at a time, and then be expected to be ready in a matter of hours, with witnesses, when the case in front of them suddenly settles. A State reasonably can decide that a trial court should not have added to its present scheduling difficulties the uncertainties and added delays fostered by counsel who might reside 1,000 miles from New Hampshire. . . . Surely the State has a substantial interest in taking steps to minimize this problem."

❧ PROBLEMS ❧

1. *More on the* Camden *Case.* In the *City of Camden* case, the city argued that it enacted the ordinance to counteract "grave economic and social ills," including "spiraling unemployment, a sharp decline in population, and a dramatic reduction in the number of businesses located in the city have eroded property values and depleted the city's tax base." The plan was designed "to increase the number of employed persons living in Camden and to arrest the 'middle class flight' currently plaguing the city." The city argues that all non-Camden residents employed on city public works projects essentially "live off" Camden without "living in" Camden. Finally, Camden argued that its municipal residency requirement was "carefully tailored to alleviate this evil without unreasonably harming nonresidents, who still have access to 60% of the available positions." Under this analysis, can Camden justify discrimination against nonresidents notwithstanding the Privileges and Immunities Clause?

2. *More on the Internet Casino Prohibition Act.* If you were asked to represent companies that wish to challenge the Internet Casino Prohibition Act, how would you argue that it runs afoul of the Interstate Privileges and Immunities Clause? How might the state respond? Does the clause come into play at all in a situation like this?

F. PREEMPTION

Preemption occurs when the federal government has exercised its power to regulate commerce and there is a conflict or a potential conflict between the federal law and the state law. *Gibbons* holds that, if the federal government has regulated a subject within the scope of its authority, and a state law conflicts, then the state law is invalid by virtue of the Supremacy Clause. In other words, the federal law preempts the state law.

Preemption can be either express or implied. In some instances, Congress makes a conscious decision to "preempt" a field and preclude state regulation. Assuming that the federal law is valid, state law must give way. *See* Cipollone v. Liggett Group, Inc., 505 U.S. 504 (1992). In most instances, Congress does not clearly state its intention regarding preemption, and a reviewing court must decide whether Congress intended to preempt a field. The following cases focus on how the courts decide whether preemption exists.

Pacific Gas and Electric Co. v. State Energy Resources Conservation & Development Commission

461 U.S. 190 (1983)

Justice WHITE delivered the opinion of the Court.

The turning of swords into plowshares has symbolized the transformation of atomic power into a source of energy in American society. To facilitate this development the federal government relaxed its monopoly over fissionable materials and nuclear technology, and in its place, erected a complex scheme to promote the civilian development of nuclear energy, while seeking to safeguard the public and the environment from the unpredictable risks of a new technology. Early on, it was decided that the states would continue their traditional role in the regulation of electricity production. The interrelationship of federal and state authority in the nuclear energy field has not been simple; the federal regulatory structure has been frequently amended to optimize the partnership.

This case emerges from the intersection of the federal government's efforts to ensure that nuclear power is safe with the exercise of the historic state authority over the generation and sale of electricity. At issue is whether provisions in the 1976 amendments to California's Warren-Alquist Act, which condition the construction of nuclear plants on findings by the State Energy Resources Conservation and Development Commission that adequate storage facilities and means of disposal are available for nuclear waste, are preempted by the Atomic Energy Act of 1954.

I

A nuclear reactor must be periodically refueled and the "spent fuel" removed. This spent fuel is intensely radioactive and must be carefully stored. The general practice is to store the fuel in a water-filled pool at the reactor site. For many years, it was assumed that this fuel would be reprocessed; accordingly, the storage pools were designed as short-term holding facilities with limited storage capacities. As expectations for reprocessing remained unfulfilled, the spent fuel accumulated in the storage pools, creating the risk that nuclear reactors would have to be shut down. This could occur if there were insufficient room in the pool to store spent fuel and also if there were not enough space to hold the entire fuel core when certain inspections or emergencies required unloading of the reactor. In recent years, the problem has taken on special urgency. Some 8,000 metric tons of spent nuclear fuel have already accumulated, and it is projected that by the year 2000 there will be some 72,000 metric tons of spent fuel. Government studies indicate that a number of reactors could be forced to shut down in the near future due to the inability to store spent fuel.

There is a second dimension to the problem. Even with water-pools adequate to store safely all the spent fuel produced during the working lifetime of the reactor, permanent disposal is needed because the wastes will remain radioactive for thousands of years. A number of long-term nuclear waste management strategies have been extensively examined. These range from sinking the wastes in stable deep seabeds, to placing the wastes beneath ice sheets in Greenland and

Antarctica, to ejecting the wastes into space by rocket. The greatest attention has been focused on disposing of the wastes in subsurface geologic repositories such as salt deposits. Problems of how and where to store nuclear wastes has engendered considerable scientific, political, and public debate. There are both safety and economic aspects to the nuclear waste issue: first, if not properly stored, nuclear wastes might leak and endanger both the environment and human health; second, the lack of a long-term disposal option increases the risk that the insufficiency of interim storage space for spent fuel will lead to reactor-shutdowns, rendering nuclear energy an unpredictable and uneconomical adventure.

The California laws at issue here are responses to these concerns. In 1974, California adopted the Warren-Alquist State Energy Resources Conservation and Development Act. The Act requires that a utility seeking to build in California any electric power generating plant, including a nuclear power plant, must apply for certification to the State Energy Resources and Conservation Commission (Energy Commission). The Warren-Alquist Act was amended in 1976 to provide additional state regulation of new nuclear power plant construction.

Two sections of these amendments are before us. Section 25524.1(b) provides that before additional nuclear plants may be built, the Energy Commission must determine on a case-by-case basis that there will be "adequate capacity" for storage of a plant's spent fuel rods "at the time such nuclear facility requires [such] storage." The law also requires that each utility provide continuous, on-site, "full core reserve storage capacity" in order to permit storage of the entire reactor core if it must be removed to permit repairs of the reactor. In short, §25524.1(b) addresses the interim storage of spent fuel.

Section 25524.2 deals with the long-term solution to nuclear wastes. This section imposes a moratorium on the certification of new nuclear plants until the Energy Commission "finds that there has been developed and that the United States through its authorized agency has approved and there exists a demonstrated technology or means for the disposal of high-level nuclear waste." "Disposal" is defined as a "method for the permanent and terminal disposition of high-level nuclear waste. . . ." Cal. Pub. Res. Code §25524.2(a), (c). Such a finding must be reported to the state legislature, which may nullify it. . . .

It is well-established that within Constitutional limits Congress may preempt state authority by so stating in express terms. Absent explicit preemptive language, Congress' intent to supersede state law altogether may be found from a "scheme of federal regulation so pervasive as to make reasonable the inference that Congress left no room to supplement it," "because the Act of Congress may touch a field in which the federal interest is so dominant that the federal system will be assumed to preclude enforcement of state laws on the same subject," or because "the object sought to be obtained by the federal law and the character of obligations imposed by it may reveal the same purpose." Fidelity Federal Savings & Loan Assn. v. de la Cuesta, 102 S.Ct. 3014 (1982). Even where Congress has not entirely displaced state regulation in a specific area, state law is preempted to the extent that it actually conflicts with federal law. Such a conflict arises when "compliance with both federal and state regulations is a physical impossibility," or where state law "stands as an obstacle to the accomplishment and execution of the full purposes and objectives of Congress." Hines v. Davidowitz, 312 U.S. 52, 67 (1941). . . .

Even a brief perusal of the Atomic Energy Act reveals that, despite its comprehensiveness, it does not at any point expressly require the States to construct or authorize nuclear power plants or prohibit the States from deciding, as an absolute or conditional matter, not to permit the construction of any further reactors. Instead, petitioners argue that the Act is intended to preserve the federal government as the sole regulator of all matters nuclear, and that §25524.2 falls within the scope of this impliedly preempted field. But as we view the issue, Congress, in passing the 1954 Act and in subsequently amending it, intended that the federal government should regulate the radiological safety aspects involved in the construction and operation of a nuclear plant, but that the States retain their traditional responsibility in the field of regulating electrical utilities for determining questions of need, reliability, cost and other related state concerns.

Need for new power facilities, their economic feasibility, and rates and services, are areas that have been characteristically governed by the States. . . . "Congress legislated here in a field which the States have traditionally occupied . . . so we start with the assumption that the historic police powers of the States were not to be superseded by the Federal Act unless that was the clear and manifest purpose of Congress." Rice v. Santa Fe Elevator Corp., *supra*, 331 U.S., at 230.

The Atomic Energy Act must be read, however, against another background. . . . The Atomic Energy Act of 1954, 42 U.S.C. §§2011-2281 (1976), grew out of Congress' determination that the national interest would be best served if the Government encouraged the private sector to become involved in the development of atomic energy for peaceful purposes under a program of federal regulation and licensing. The Act implemented this policy decision by providing for licensing of private construction, ownership, and operation of commercial nuclear power reactors. Duke Power Co. v. Carolina Environmental Study Group, Inc., 438 U.S., at 63. The AEC, however, was given exclusive jurisdiction to license the transfer, delivery, receipt, acquisition, possession and use of nuclear materials. 42 U.S.C. §§2014(e), (z), (aa), 2061-2064, 2071-2078, 2091-2099, 2111-2114 (1976 and Supp. IV 1980). Upon these subjects, no role was left for the states.

The Commission, however, was not given authority over the generation of electricity itself, or over the economic question whether a particular plant should be built. We observed in *Vermont Yankee, supra*, 435 U.S., at 550, that "The Commission's prime area of concern in the licensing context, . . . is national security, public health, and safety." The Nuclear Regulatory Commission (NRC), which now exercises the AEC's regulatory authority, does not purport to exercise its authority based on economic considerations, and has recently repealed its regulations concerning the financial qualifications and capabilities of a utility proposing to construct and operate a nuclear power plant. 47 Fed. Reg. 13751. In its notice of rule repeal, the NRC stated that utility financial qualifications are only of concern to the NRC if related to the public health and safety. It is almost inconceivable that Congress would have left a regulatory vacuum; the only reasonable inference is that Congress intended the states to continue to make these judgments. Any doubt that ratemaking and plant-need questions were to remain in state hands was removed by §271 which provided: "Nothing in this chapter shall be construed to affect the authority or regulations of any Federal, State or local agency with respect to the generation, sale, or transmission of electric power produced through the use of nuclear facilities licensed by the Commission. . . ." . . .

This account indicates that from the passage of the Atomic Energy Act in 1954, through several revisions, and to the present day, Congress has preserved the dual regulation of nuclear-powered electricity generation: the federal government maintains complete control of the safety and "nuclear" aspects of energy generation; the states exercise their traditional authority over the need for additional generating capacity, the type of generating facilities to be licensed, land use, ratemaking, and the like.

The above is not particularly controversial. But deciding how §25524.2 is to be construed and classified is a more difficult proposition. [T]he statute does not seek to regulate the construction or operation of a nuclear powerplant. It would clearly be impermissible for California to attempt to do so, for such regulation, even if enacted out of non-safety concerns, would nevertheless directly conflict with the NRC's exclusive authority over plant construction and operation. Respondents appear to concede as much. Respondents do broadly argue, however, that although safety regulation of nuclear plants by states is forbidden, a state may completely prohibit new construction until its safety concerns are satisfied by the federal government. We reject this line of reasoning. State safety regulation is not preempted only when it conflicts with federal law. Rather, the federal government has occupied the entire field of nuclear safety concerns, except the limited powers expressly ceded to the states. When the federal government completely occupies a given field or an identifiable portion of it, as it has done here, the test of preemption is whether "the matter on which the state asserts the right to act is in any way regulated by the federal government." A state moratorium on nuclear construction grounded in safety concerns falls squarely within the prohibited field. Moreover, a state judgment that nuclear power is not safe enough to be further developed would conflict directly with the countervailing judgment of the NRC, that nuclear construction may proceed notwithstanding extant uncertainties as to waste disposal. A state prohibition on nuclear construction for safety reasons would also be in the teeth of the Atomic Energy Act's objective to insure that nuclear technology be safe enough for widespread development and use—and would be preempted for that reason.

That being the case, it is necessary to determine whether there is a non-safety rationale for §25524.2. California has maintained [that] §25524.2 was aimed at economic problems, not radiation hazards. The California Assembly Committee on Resources, Land Use, and Energy, which proposed a package of bills including §25524.2, reported that the waste disposal problem was "largely economic or the result of poor planning, not safety related." The Committee explained that the lack of a federally approved method of waste disposal created a "clog" in the nuclear fuel cycle. Storage space was limited while more nuclear wastes were continuously produced. Without a permanent means of disposal, the nuclear waste problem could become critical leading to unpredictably high costs to contain the problem or, worse, shutdowns in reactors. "Waste disposal safety," the Reassessment Report notes, "is not directly addressed by the bills, which ask only that a method [of waste disposal] be chosen and accepted by the federal government." [W]e accept California's avowed economic purpose as the rationale for enacting §25524.2. Accordingly, the statute lies outside the occupied field of nuclear safety regulation.

Petitioners' second major argument concerns federal regulation aimed at the nuclear waste disposal problem itself. It is contended that §25524.2 conflicts with federal regulation of nuclear waste disposal, with the NRC's decision that it is permissible to continue to license reactors, notwithstanding uncertainty surrounding the waste disposal problem, and with Congress' recent passage of legislation directed at that problem.

[The] NRC's imprimatur, however, indicates only that it is safe to proceed with such plants, not that it is economically wise to do so. Because the NRC order does not and could not compel a utility to develop a nuclear plant, compliance with both it and §25524.2 are possible. Moreover, because the NRC's regulations are aimed at insuring that plants are safe, not necessarily that they are economical, §25524.2 does not interfere with the objective of the federal regulation.

Nor has California sought through §25524.2 to impose its own standards on nuclear waste disposal. The statute accepts that it is the federal responsibility to develop and license such technology. As there is no attempt on California's part to enter this field, one which is occupied by the federal government, we do not find §25524.2 preempted any more by the NRC's obligations in the waste disposal field than by its licensing power over the plants themselves. . . .

Finally, it is strongly contended that §25524.2 frustrates the Atomic Energy Act's purpose to develop the commercial use of nuclear power. It is well established that state law is preempted if it "stands as an obstacle to the accomplishment of the full purposes and objectives of Congress." Hines v. Davidowitz, 312 U.S. 52, 67 (1941).

There is little doubt that a primary purpose of the Atomic Energy Act was, and continues to be, the promotion of nuclear power. The Act itself states that it is a program "to encourage widespread participation in the development and utilization of atomic energy for peaceful purposes to the maximum extent consistent with the common defense and security and with the health and safety of the public." 42 U.S.C. §2013(b). . . .

The Court of Appeals is right, however, that the promotion of nuclear power is not to be accomplished "at all costs." The elaborate licensing and safety provisions and the continued preservation of state regulation in traditional areas belie that. Moreover, Congress has allowed the States to determine — as a matter of economics — whether a nuclear plant vis-a-vis a fossil fuel plant should be built. The decision of California to exercise that authority does not, in itself, constitute a basis for preemption. . . .

The judgment of the Court of Appeals is
Affirmed.

Notes

1. *State Alien Registration Laws.* In Hines v. Davidowitz, 312 U.S. 52 (1941), Pennsylvania adopted a registration law that required all aliens 18 years of age or over to register with the state, pay a $1 annual registration fee, and carry an alien identification card. Subsequently, Congress enacted the federal Alien Registration Act, which required a single registration of aliens 14 years of age and older and submission of detailed information, but which did not require aliens to carry a registration card and did not indicate whether the states could impose their own registration systems. The Court struck down the Pennsylvania law, stating: "[The] supremacy of the national power in the general field of foreign affairs, including power over immigration, naturalization and deportation, is made clear by the Constitution [and has] been given continuous recognition by this Court. When the national government by treaty or statute has established rules and regulations touching the rights, privileges, obligations or burdens of aliens as such, the treaty or statute is the supreme law of the land. [T]he power to restrict, limit, regulate, and register aliens as a distinct group is not an equal and continuously existing concurrent power of state and nation, [but] whatever power a state may have is subordinate to supreme national law. [The] legislative history of the [Act] indicates that Congress was trying to steer a middle path, realizing that any registration requirement was a departure from our traditional policy of not treating aliens as a thing apart, but also feeling that the Nation was in need of the type of information to be secured. [Congress] provided a standard for alien registration in a single integrated and all-embracing system. [In doing so, Congress] plainly manifested a purpose [to] protect the personal liberties of law-abiding aliens through one uniform national registration system, and to leave them free from the possibility of inquisitorial practices and police surveillance that might not only affect our international relations but might also generate the very disloyalty which the law has intended guarding against. Under these circumstances, the Pennsylvania Act cannot be enforced." Justice Stone dissented: "[A]fter entry, an alien resident within a state, like a citizen, is subject to the police powers of the state and, in the exercise of that power, state legislatures may pass laws applicable exclusively to aliens so long as the distinction taken between aliens and citizens is not shown to be without rational basis. [Nothing indicates] that Congress intended to withdraw from the state any part of their constitutional power over aliens within their borders. . . . Congress was not unaware that some nineteen states have statutes or ordinances requiring some form of registration for aliens, seven of them dating from the last war. . . . Here compliance with the state law does not preclude or even interfere with compliance with the act of Congress."

2. *Sedition Laws.* Congress passed the Smith Act, which prohibited the knowing advocacy of the overthrow of the government of the United States by force and violence. A few years later, Pennsylvania adopted a law that prohibited advocacy of either the overthrow of the U.S. government or the Commonwealth of Pennsylvania's government. In Pennsylvania v. Nelson, 350 U.S. 497 (1956), the Court held that the Smith Act preempted the Pennsylvania law: "Looking [at these laws] in the aggregate, the conclusion is inescapable that Congress

[intended] to occupy the field of sedition. . . . Therefore, a state sedition statute is superseded regardless of whether it purports to supplement the federal law. [T]he federal statutes 'touch a field in which the federal interest is so dominant that the federal system (must) be assumed to preclude enforcement of state laws on the same subject.' Rice v. Santa Fe Elevator Corp., 331 U.S., at 230. Congress has devised an all-embracing program for resistance to the various forms of totalitarian aggression." Justice Reed, joined by two other justices, dissented: "Congress has [not] specifically barred the exercise of state power to punish the same Acts. [A]bsent federal legislation, there is no constitutional bar to punishment of sedition against the United States by both a State and the Nation. [The] federal sedition laws are distinct criminal statutes that punish willful advocacy of the use of force against 'the government of the United States or the government of any State.' These criminal laws proscribe certain local activity without creating any statutory or administrative regulation. There is, consequently, no question as to whether some general congressional regulatory scheme might be upset by a coinciding state plan. In these circumstances the conflict should be clear and direct before this Court reads a congressional intent to void state legislation into the federal sedition acts. [S]ince 1940 Congress has been keenly aware of the magnitude of existing state legislation proscribing sedition."

Gade v. National Solid Wastes Management Association
505 U.S. 88 (1992)

Justice O'CONNOR announced the judgment of the Court and delivered the opinion of the Court with respect to Parts I, III, and IV, and an opinion with respect to Part II in which THE CHIEF JUSTICE, Justice WHITE, and Justice SCALIA join.

In 1988, the Illinois General Assembly enacted the Hazardous Waste Crane and Hoisting Equipment Operators Licensing Act and the Hazardous Waste Laborers Licensing Act. The stated purpose of the licensing acts is both "to promote job safety" and "to protect life, limb and property." In this case, we consider whether these "dual impact" statutes, which protect both workers and the general public, are pre-empted by the federal Occupational Safety and Health Act of 1970, 29 U.S.C. §651 *et seq.* (OSH Act), and the standards promulgated thereunder by the Occupational Safety and Health Administration (OSHA).

The OSH Act authorizes the Secretary of Labor to promulgate federal occupational safety and health standards. In the Superfund Amendments and Reauthorization Act of 1986 (SARA), Congress directed the Secretary of Labor to "promulgate standards for the health and safety protection of employees engaged in hazardous waste operations" pursuant to her authority under the OSH Act. . . . In response to this congressional directive, [OSHA] promulgated regulations on "Hazardous Waste Operations and Emergency Response," including detailed regulations on worker training requirements. [W]hile OSHA's interim hazardous waste regulations were in effect, the State of Illinois enacted the licensing acts at issue here. The laws are designated as acts "in relation to environmental protection," and their stated aim is to protect both employees and the general public by licensing hazardous waste equipment operators and laborers working at certain facilities. . . .

[Respondent] National Solid Wastes Management Association (Association) [brought] a declaratory judgment action [to] enjoin [the Illinois Environmental Protection Agency] from enforcing the Illinois licensing acts. . . . The District Court held that [federal law did not preempt Illinois law.] [T]he United States Court of Appeals for the Seventh Circuit affirmed in part and reversed in part. We granted certiorari. . . .

"[T]he question whether a certain state action is pre-empted by federal law is one of congressional intent. . . ." In the OSH Act, Congress endeavored "to assure so far as possible every working man and woman in the Nation safe and healthful working conditions." To that end, Congress authorized the Secretary of Labor to set mandatory occupational safety and health standards applicable to all businesses affecting interstate commerce, and thereby brought the Federal Government into a field that traditionally had been occupied by the States. Federal regulation of the workplace was not intended to be all encompassing, however. First, Congress expressly saved two areas from federal pre-emption. Section 4(b)(4) of the OSH Act states that the Act does not "supersede or in any manner affect any workmen's compensation law [or] enlarge or diminish or affect in any other manner the common law or statutory rights, duties, or liabilities of employers and employees under any law with respect to injuries, diseases, or death of employees arising out of, or in the course of, employment." [Second,] Section 18(a) provides that the Act does not "prevent any State agency or court from asserting jurisdiction under State law over any occupational safety or health issue with respect to which no [federal] standard is in effect." 29 U.S.C. §667(a).

Congress not only reserved certain areas to state regulation, but it also, in §18(b) of the Act, gave the States the option of pre-empting federal regulation entirely. That section provides:

Submission of State plan for development and enforcement of State standards to preempt applicable Federal standards

Any State which, at any time, desires to assume responsibility for development and enforcement therein of occupational safety and health standards relating to any occupational safety or health issue with respect to which a Federal standard has been promulgated [by the Secretary under the OSH Act] shall submit a State plan for the development of such standards and their enforcement. 29 U.S.C. §667(b).

About half the States have received the Secretary's approval for their own state plans as described in this provision. . . . Illinois is not among them. . . .

Pre-emption may be either expressed or implied, and "is compelled whether Congress' command is explicitly stated in the statute's language or implicitly contained in its structure and purpose." [Absent] explicit pre-emptive language, we have recognized at least two types of implied pre-emption: field pre-emption, where the scheme of federal regulation is "so pervasive as to make reasonable the inference that Congress left no room for the States to supplement it," and conflict pre-emption, where "compliance with both federal and state regulations is a physical impossibility," or where state law "stands as an obstacle to the accomplishment and execution of the full purposes and objectives of Congress,". . .

Our ultimate task in any pre-emption case is to determine whether state regulation is consistent with the structure and purpose of the statute as a whole. Looking to "the provisions of the whole law, and to its object and policy," we hold that nonapproved state regulation of occupational safety and health issues for which a federal standard is in effect is impliedly pre-empted as in conflict with the full purposes and objectives of the OSH Act. The design of the statute persuades us that Congress intended to subject employers and employees to only one set of regulations, be it federal or state, and that the only way a State may regulate an OSHA-regulated occupational safety and health issue is pursuant to an approved state plan that displaces the federal standards.

The principal indication that Congress intended to pre-empt state law is §18(b)'s statement that a State "shall" submit a plan if it wishes to "assume responsibility" for "development and enforcement [of] occupational safety and health standards relating to any occupational safety or health issue with respect to which a Federal standard has been promulgated." The unavoidable implication of this provision is that a State may not enforce its own occupational safety and health standards without obtaining the Secretary's approval. . . . Petitioner contends, however, that an approved plan is necessary only if the State wishes completely to replace the federal regulations, not merely to supplement them. . . . [The] OSH Act as a whole evidences Congress' intent to avoid subjecting workers and employers to duplicative regulation; a State may develop an occupational safety and health program tailored to its own needs, but only if it is willing completely to displace the applicable federal regulations. [§18(a)] saves from pre-emption any state law regulating an occupational safety and health issue with respect to which no federal standard is in effect. Although this is a saving clause, not a pre-emption clause, the natural implication of this provision is that state laws regulating the same issue as federal laws are not saved, even if they merely supplement the federal standard. . . .

Our understanding of the implications of §18(b) [is] bolstered by §18(c) of the Act. . . . State standards that affect interstate commerce will be approved only if they "are required by compelling local conditions" and "do not unduly burden interstate commerce." If a State could supplement federal regulations without undergoing the §18(b) approval process, then the protections that §18(c) offers to interstate commerce would easily be undercut. It would make little sense to impose such a condition on state programs intended to supplant federal regulation and not those that merely supplement it. . . .

Section 18(f) also confirms our view that States are not permitted to assume an enforcement role without the Secretary's approval, unless no federal standard is in effect. That provision gives the Secretary the authority to withdraw her approval of a state plan. . . . §18(f) assumes that the State loses the power to enforce all of its occupational safety and health standards once approval is withdrawn. . . .

Looking at the provisions of §18 as a whole, we conclude that the OSH Act precludes any state regulation of an occupational safety or health issue with respect to which a federal standard has been established, unless a state plan has been submitted and approved pursuant to §18(b). . . . Congress sought to promote occupational safety and health while at the same time avoiding duplicative, and possibly counterproductive, regulation. It thus established a system of uniform federal occupational health and safety standards, but gave States the option of pre-empting federal regulations by developing their own occupational safety and health programs. In addition, Congress offered the States substantial federal grant moneys to assist them in developing their own programs. . . . To allow a State selectively to "supplement" certain federal regulations with ostensibly nonconflicting standards would be inconsistent with this federal scheme of establishing uniform federal standards, on the one hand, and encouraging States to assume full responsibility for development and enforcement of their own OSH programs, on the other.

We cannot accept petitioner's argument that the OSH Act does not pre-empt nonconflicting state laws because those laws, like the Act, are designed to promote worker safety. In determining whether state law "stands as an obstacle" to the full implementation of a federal law "[it] is not enough to say that the ultimate goal of both federal and state law" is the same. . . . "A state law also is pre-empted if it interferes with the methods by which the federal statute was designed to reach th[at] goal." . . .

Petitioner next argues that, even if Congress intended to pre-empt all non-approved state occupational safety and health regulations whenever a federal standard is in effect, the OSH Act's pre-emptive effect should not be extended to state laws that address public safety as well as occupational safety concerns. [A] dual impact state regulation cannot avoid OSH Act pre-emption simply because the regulation serves several objectives rather than one. [Whatever] the purpose or purposes of the state law, pre-emption analysis cannot ignore the effect of the challenged state action on the pre-empted field. The key question is thus at what point the state regulation sufficiently interferes with federal regulation that it should be deemed pre-empted under the Act. [S]tate laws of general applicability (such as laws regarding traffic safety or fire safety) that do not conflict with OSHA standards and that regulate the conduct of workers and nonworkers alike would generally not be pre-empted. Although some laws of general applicability may have a "direct and substantial" effect on worker safety, they cannot fairly be characterized as "occupational" standards, because they regulate workers simply as members of the general public. [A] law directed at workplace safety is not saved from pre-emption simply because the State can demonstrate some additional effect outside of the workplace. . . . That such a law may also have a nonoccupational impact does not render it any less of an occupational standard for purposes of pre-emption analysis. If the State wishes to enact a dual impact law that regulates an occupational safety or health issue for which a federal standard is in effect, §18 of the Act requires that the State submit a plan for the approval of the Secretary.

[The] judgment of the Court of Appeals is hereby
Affirmed.

Justice SOUTER, with whom Justice BLACKMUN, Justice STEVENS, and Justice THOMAS join, dissenting.

"Where [the] field which Congress is said to have pre-empted has been traditionally occupied by the States[,] 'we start with the assumption that the historic police powers of the States were not to be superseded by the Federal Act unless that was the clear and manifest purpose of Congress.'" [This] assumption provides assurance that the 'federal-state balance' [will] not be disturbed unintentionally by Congress or unnecessarily by the courts. . . . Subject to this principle, the enquiry into the possibly pre-emptive effect of federal legislation is an exercise of statutory construction. If the statute's terms can be read sensibly not to have a pre-emptive effect, the presumption controls and no pre-emption may be inferred.

[Respondent argues that] the only way that a state rule on a particular occupational safety and health issue may be enforced once a federal standard on the issue is also in place is by incorporating the state rule in a plan approved by the Secretary. [T]hat is not the necessary implication. [§18(b)] does [not] provide that absent such state pre-emption of federal rules, the State may [not] supplement the federal standards with consistent regulations of its own. . . . The provision [makes] perfect sense [if] a dual regulatory scheme is permissible but subject to state pre-emption if the State wishes to shoulder enough of the federal mandate to gain approval of a plan. . . . Nor does the provision setting out conditions for the Secretary's approval of a plan indicate that a state regulation on an issue federally addressed is never enforceable unless incorporated in a plan so approved.

[I]n the absence of any clear expression of congressional intent to pre-empt, I can only conclude that, as long as compliance with federally promulgated standards does not render obedience to Illinois' regulations impossible, the enforcement of the state law is not prohibited by the Supremacy Clause. I respectfully dissent.

Notes

1. *The Scope of Federal Power and Preemption.* As we have seen, even after *Lopez*, the Commerce Clause provides Congress with a great deal of power to regulate economic activity. This power, when combined with the Supremacy Clause, means that if Congress decides to regulate in a given area, conflicting state regulations must give way. Preemption principles help courts determine whether there is a conflict.

2. *Strict Liability for Oil Spills.* In Askew v. American Waterways Operators, Inc., 411 U.S. 325 (1973), the Court considered a Florida law that imposed strict liability for any damage incurred by the state or private persons as a result of an oil spill in the state's territorial waters. Liability was imposed on spills from any waterfront facility used for drilling for oil or handling the transfer or storage of oil (terminal facility) and from any ship destined for or leaving such facility. Each owner or operator of a terminal facility or ship subject to the Act was required to show evidence of financial responsibility by insurance or a surety bond. The Act

also required the state's Department of Natural Resources to regulate containment gear and other equipment that must be maintained by ships and terminal facilities for the prevention of oil spills. Several months prior to the enactment of the Act, Congress enacted the Water Quality Improvement Act of 1970, which subjected shipowners and terminal facilities to liability without fault up to $14,000,000 and $8,000,000, respectively, for cleanup costs incurred by the federal government as a result of oil spills. It also authorized the President to promulgate regulations requiring ships and terminal facilities to maintain equipment for the prevention of oil spills. In upholding the Florida law against a preemption challenge, the Court stated: "We find no constitutional or statutory impediment to permitting Florida, in the present setting of this case, to establish any 'requirement or liability' concerning the impact of oil spillages on Florida's interests or concerns. . . . It is clear at the outset that the Federal Act does not preclude, but in fact allows, state regulation. . . . The reason for the provision in §1161(o)(2), stating that nothing in §1161 pre-empts any State 'from imposing any requirement or liability with respect to the discharge of oil into any waters within such State,' is that the scheme of the Act is one which allows — though it does not require — co-operation of the federal regime with a state regime."

3. *Arizona's Anti-Illegal Immigration Law.* Amidst a national dialogue on how to deal with persons crossing the borders into the United States unlawfully, Arizona's governor signed S.B. 1070, set to become effective 90 days following her signing, on July 29, 2010.

These undocumented persons, called aliens in many statutes and the earlier vernacular, often cross into the United States through the southern border with Mexico. Arizona's law was designed to prosecute and/or deport persons who are in the United States illegally. At least two of the law's components sparked controversy: the requirement that police check immigration status upon a reasonable suspicion for those persons who are arrested and those persons who are lawfully detained, and other regulation of the immigration of persons.

Arguments in favor of the law revolved around a need to take strong action to stem unlawful immigration. Arguments against the law focused on whether the law unconstitutionally exceeded federalism boundaries between federal and state laws and encouraged racial and ethnic profiling.

Shortly after it was signed into law, the United States challenged the law in federal court in Arizona, seeking an injunction. Federal District Court Judge Susan Bolton enjoined enforcement of the law, *inter alia*, on the ground that federal law preempted the Arizona law. See United States v. Arizona, 703 F. Supp.2d 980 (D. Ariz. 2010). Undoubtedly, there will be additional litigation over the issue.

∾ PROBLEMS ∾

1. *Local Noise Control.* A local ordinance makes it unlawful for aircraft to take off from the local airport during night hours (defined as between 11 P.M. and 7 A.M.). The ordinance is passed as a noise control measure. Two federal laws — the

Federal Aviation Act of 1958 and the Noise Control Act of 1972 — also pertain to aircrafts and aircraft noise. In deciding whether the federal law preempts the local ordinance, which of these factors are relevant? a) Noise control has traditionally been a matter reserved to the states; b) federal control over airplanes is relatively intensive in that planes move only by federal permission, subject to federal inspection, in the hands of federally certified personnel.

2. *More on the Internet Casino Prohibition Act.* Is the Internet Casino Prohibition Act preempted by federal law? Does it matter whether the U.S. Congress has, or has not, enacted legislation regulating (or, for that matter, outlawing) Internet-based casino gambling? Should it matter that almost all Internet casino gambling operations are located outside the United States?

Points to Remember

- During the first third of the twentieth century, although Congress had the power to regulate commerce "among" the states, the Court construed the Tenth Amendment as giving the states a reserved power over "purely local" commerce.
- Following the constitutional crisis of the 1930s, the distinction between "local" commerce and commerce "among" the states began to disappear. Under decisions like *Wickard* and *Perez*, the federal government assumed much broader authority over both interstate and local commerce.
- Moreover, the Court began to treat the Tenth Amendment as a truism, thereby depriving states of their reserved power over commerce. Even though recent decisions (e.g., *Lopez* and *Morrison*) have pared down the scope of federal power, federal power under the Commerce Clause remains broad.
- Since the 1930s, the federal courts have faced varying questions regarding the scope of state power. Some cases involve questions about whether federal law preempts state law. In other words, does the existence of federal regulation preclude state regulation?
- Most of the remaining cases involve so-called "dormant" power situations — situations in which the federal government has the power to regulate a subject, but has not done so or has done so incompletely. In these dormant power situations, the question is whether the Commerce Clause contains negative implications that limit or preclude state regulation.
- In other words, is federal power under the Commerce Clause "exclusive," so that the states are precluded from regulating an area under federal authority even in the absence of federal regulation? Or do the states have "concurrent" jurisdiction so that they are also free to regulate? If concurrent power exists, what limits apply to state power? A few cases focus on the Privileges and Immunities Clause, which protects citizens against discrimination in one state because of their status as citizens of another state.

- A number of early cases focused on whether the federal government's authority over commerce was exclusive, or whether the states had concurrent power.
- In Gibbons v. Ogden, 22 U.S. (9 Wheat.) 1 (1824), the Court held that, although "many of the powers formerly exercised by the States, are transferred to the government of the Union, yet the State governments remain, and constitute a most important part of our system."
- Some powers can reside in both the federal government and the state governments (e.g., the power to tax). Other types of power remain with the states (e.g., inspection laws, quarantine laws, health laws of every description, as well as laws that regulate the internal commerce of a state and those with respect to turnpike roads, ferries, etc.). Still other powers reside exclusively in the federal government.
- The U.S. Supreme Court has always scrutinized state and local legislation more closely when it involves discrimination against interstate commerce. Statutes that discriminate against or directly regulate interstate commerce are presumptively unconstitutional. They survive only if there are no methods of achieving the statute's goals that are less restrictive.
- The prohibition against discrimination by the states reflects the fact that the Framers gave Congress the power to regulate interstate commerce in order to prevent trade wars between the states. Thus, the Interstate Commerce Clause embodies a substantive policy of free trade among the states, a policy that a state can countermand only for the most compelling of reasons.
- In some instances, state legislation explicitly and facially discriminates against out-of-state interests. State laws that discriminate deprive citizens of their right to have access to the markets of other states on equal terms. In general, such laws will be struck down unless they advance a legitimate local purpose that cannot be adequately served by reasonable nondiscriminatory alternatives.
- One of the most famous discrimination decisions was rendered in Baldwin v. G.A.F. Seelig, Inc., 294 U.S. 511 (1935), which struck down the New York Milk Control Act that established "minimum prices" to be paid by dealers to milk producers. The Court held that New York adopted the law in order to insulate New York producers from out-of-state competition.
- In City of Philadelphia v. New Jersey, 437 U.S. 617 (1978), the Court struck down a New Jersey law that prohibited the importation of out-of-state garbage into New York.
- The Court has upheld state quarantine laws (e.g., laws prohibiting the importation of diseased livestock) despite the effects those laws have on interstate commerce. See, e.g., Mintz v. Baldwin, 289 U.S. 346 (1933); Asbell v. Kansas, 209 U.S. 251 (1908). In quarantine cases, the Court characterized the statutes as police measures designed to protect the citizenry's health and safety.

- Rarely does a legislature announce its intention to discriminate against interstate commerce. More commonly, a state law is facially neutral but has discriminatory effects.
- In Dean Milk Co. v. City of Madison, 340 U.S. 349 (1951), the Court struck down a city milk inspection law. Although the law served health objectives (to ensure the safety of milk), the Court struck it down because the city had other adequate means at its disposal for addressing health and safety concerns.
- In Maine v. Taylor, 477 U.S. 131 (1986), the Court upheld a Maine statute banning the importation of live baitfish. The statute discriminated against interstate commerce by imposing an embargo on imports of baitfish. The Court held that the statute satisfied strict scrutiny because the state's purpose (protection of Maine's "unique and ecologically fragile" fisheries) could not be protected by a less burdensome method. The Court concluded that inspection methods, which tested imported baitfish for parasites, could not reliably produce disease-free shipments.
- Even when a state law does not discriminate against interstate commerce, the law may still affect interstate commerce and will still be subject to judicial review. In general, when statutes regulate local and out-of-state interests evenhandedly and have only an indirect effect on interstate commerce, they are examined to determine whether the burden on interstate commerce clearly exceeds the local benefits. *See, e.g.,* Brown-Forman Distillers Corp. v. New York State Liquor Authority, 476 U.S. 573, 578 (1986).
- In South Carolina State Highway Department v. Barnwell Bros., 303 U.S. 177 (1938), the Court held that a state law that imposed a burden on interstate commerce should be deferentially reviewed to determine whether there is a rational basis for the law.
- However, in Southern Pacific Co. v. Arizona, 325 U.S. 761 (1945), the Court endorsed a more active level of review that was less deferential to legislative judgment. The Court made its own determination regarding the reasonableness of state legislation.
- In some instances, instead of trying to regulate interstate commerce, the states intervene in commercial markets and become "market participants."
- In Reeves, Inc. v. Stake, 447 U.S. 429 (1980), the Court held that a state that acted as a market participant could discriminate in favor of its own citizens.
- Article IV, Section 2 contains the Interstate Privileges and Immunities Clause: "The Citizens of each State shall be entitled to all Privileges and Immunities of Citizens in the several States."
- This interstate Privileges and Immunities Clause was designed to ensure that states would not discriminate against the citizens of other states because of their citizenship in those states.

- Like most constitutional rights, the Privileges and Immunities Clause does not require states to treat nonresidents in exactly the same way that they treat their own citizens, and it does not impose an absolute ban on discrimination by one state against the citizens of another state. States can treat the citizens of other states differently in some instances.
- In Baldwin v. Fish and Game Commission of Montana, 436 U.S. 371 (1978), the Court held that the Privileges and Immunities Clause is implicated only as to those "privileges" and "immunities" bearing on the vitality of the nation as a single entity must the state treat all citizens, resident and nonresident, equally.
- The Court went on to hold that a state's control over its resources precludes the proper exercise of federal power. And a state's interest in its wildlife and other resources must yield when, without reason, it interferes with a nonresident's right to pursue a livelihood in a state other than his or her own, a right that is protected by the Privileges and Immunities Clause. *See* Toomer v. Witsell, 334 U.S. 385 (1948).
- In Toomer v. Witsell, the Court used the Privileges and Immunities Clause to strike down a South Carolina law that imposed different fees on out-of-state and in-state shrimp boats.
- In Hicklin v. Orbeck, 437 U.S. 518 (1978), the Court struck down an Alaska law that required those who held state contracts to extract oil and gas to hire only Alaskans. The Court held "that a resident of one State is constitutionally entitled to travel to another State for purposes of employment free from discriminatory restrictions in favor of state residents imposed by the other State."
- Preemption occurs when the federal government has exercised its power to regulate commerce and there is a conflict or a potential conflict between the federal law and the state law. *Gibbons* holds that, if the federal government has regulated a subject within the scope of its authority, and a state law conflicts, then the state law is invalid by virtue of the Supremacy Clause. In other words, the federal law preempts the state law.
- Preemption can be either expressed or implied. In some instances, Congress makes a conscious decision to "preempt" a field and preclude state regulation. Assuming that the federal law is valid, then state law must give way. *See* Cipollone v. Liggett Group, Inc., 505 U.S. 504 (1992).
- In most instances, Congress does not clearly state its intention regarding preemption, and a reviewing court must decide whether Congress intended to preempt a field.

6

State Action

U.S. CONSTITUTION, FIRST AMENDMENT

Congress shall make no law respecting an establishment of religion, or prohibiting the free exercise thereof; or abridging the freedom of speech, or of the press, or the right of the people peaceably to assemble, and to petition the Government for a redress of grievances.

U.S. CONSTITUTION, FOURTEENTH AMENDMENT

No State shall make or enforce any law which shall abridge the privileges or immunities of citizens of the United States; nor shall any State deprive any person of life, liberty, or property, without due process of law; nor deny to any person within its jurisdiction the equal protection of the laws.

∾ PROBLEM: THE TOWN, THE PRIVATE UTILITY, AND THE CLUB ∾

Town Orange, which has 35,000 residents, is located in the sunny state of Florida. The community holds concerts and other public events in the Downtown District, where many popular restaurants are located as well as the town's only movie theater and park. The district covers almost the entire downtown and accounts for a third of the town's land area.

Power House, Inc., is a private utility corporation that provides electric and water services for the town. Power House is certified by the state and bound by state regulatory requirements. Power House owns the Downtown District. When citizens of Town Orange wish to hold events in the park, sidewalks, or streets of the Downtown District, they are required to submit a permit application to Power House. Under Town Orange's rules and regulations, Power House "has sole discretion to approve events it considers appropriate."

Power House recently purchased land and the larger of the two public swimming pools from Town Orange in order to develop an exclusive country club,

Palm Valley Country Club. One day Mr. and Mrs. Johnson, two well-off African American citizens who reside on the west side of Town Orange, attended the club's cocktail hour and applied for membership. Their experience was not pleasant, however, as the club's management refused to believe the 50-year-old citizens were over 21, the minimum age to legally drink alcohol. Furthermore, three days later the Johnsons received a letter from the club stating that their membership applications were denied because the club does not admit "African Americans, Hispanics, Asians, Jews, Muslims, women, and homosexuals" as members.

As a result of the pool closing and membership restrictions at the new country club, there has been a large influx of citizens wanting to use the only remaining Town Orange community pool. However, after several members of the community filed complaints with the town about "overcrowding, noise, and undesirable elements" at the community pool, Town Orange decided to close the pool. Five members of the community applied to Power House for a permit to hold a rally in the Downtown District's park to protest the town's recent decisions. Power House denied their permit application, stating "this type of protest is inappropriate." Then, without prior notice, Power House shut off power and water to the homes of those five members of the community who had applied for the permit because they were late with their utility payments.

As we go through this chapter, we will ask you to place yourself in the role of attorneys representing the various parties in the dispute. You will need to argue on behalf of those parties as to whether Power House's actions constitute state action.

Most provisions of the Bill of Rights, as well as the Fourteenth and Fifteenth Amendments, are designed to protect individuals against action by federal, state, or local governments, but not action by private persons or entities. They protect only against "state action," with the word *state* meaning *governmental*. An exception to this state action requirement is the Thirteenth Amendment's prohibition of slavery, which applies to private persons as well as the state.

Although private conduct may be actionable under civil law (e.g., tort or contract law) or criminal law, the general rule is that only state actors can violate your constitutional rights because it is only against the state that one has constitutional rights.

A. REQUIRING STATE ACTION

The Thirteenth Amendment ("Neither slavery nor involuntary servitude . . . shall exist within the United States . . .") applies to both the state and private individuals. It was coauthored and sponsored by Representatives James Mitchell Ashley (Republican, Ohio) and James F. Wilson (Republican, Iowa) and Senator

John B. Henderson (Democrat, Missouri). President Abraham Lincoln took an active role in pushing its passage through the House by ensuring that the amendment was added to the Republican Party platform for the upcoming presidential election. Adopted in 1865, the Thirteenth Amendment formally abolished slavery, thus fulfilling the Emancipation Proclamation issued by President Lincoln in 1863.

State action became an issue after the Civil War Amendments were enacted under the authority of the Thirteenth, Fourteenth, and Fifteenth Amendments, which grant Congress the power to protect civil rights and to enforce them "by appropriate legislation." Pursuant to those Amendments, Congress adopted the Civil Rights Acts of 1866, 1870, 1871, and 1875 to address pervasive racial discrimination in the public and private sectors. In *The Civil Rights Cases*, indictments were brought against individuals and railroads that had excluded black persons from railroads, hotels, and theaters because of race in contravention of the Acts. The defendants appealed, arguing that Congress exceeded its constitutional authority in enacting the Acts because it attempted to regulate private action. The decision in those cases established the requirement of state action.

The Civil Rights Cases

109 U.S. 3 (1883)

BRADLEY, J.

[The Civil Rights Act of 1875 declares] that, in the enjoyment of the accommodations and privileges of inns, public conveyances, theaters, and other places of public amusement, no distinction shall be made between citizens of different race or color, or between those who have, and those who have not, been slaves. Its effect is to declare [that] colored citizens [shall] have the same accommodations and privileges [as] are enjoyed by white citizens; and vice versa. . . .

Has congress constitutional power to make such a law? [It] is state action [that] is prohibited. Individual invasion of individual rights is not the subject-matter of the [fourteenth amendment]. It nullifies and makes void all state legislation, and state action of every kind, which impairs the privileges and immunities of citizens of the United States, or which injures them in life, liberty, or property without due process of law, or which denies to any of them the equal protection of the laws. [T]he last section of the amendment invests congress with power to enforce it by appropriate legislation. To enforce what? [To] adopt appropriate legislation for correcting the effects of such prohibited state law and state acts, and thus to render them effectually null, void, and innocuous. . . . It does not authorize congress to create a code of municipal law for the regulation of private rights. . . .

[The Civil Rights Act] makes no reference whatever to any supposed or apprehended violation of the fourteenth amendment on the part of the states. . . . It [declares] that certain acts committed by individuals shall be deemed offenses, and shall be prosecuted and punished by proceedings in the courts of the United States. . . . It applies equally to cases arising in states which have the justest laws respecting the personal rights of citizens, and whose authorities are ever ready to enforce such laws as to those which arise in states that may have violated the prohibition of the amendment. In other words, [it] lays down rules for the conduct of individuals in society towards each other, and imposes sanctions for the enforcement of those rules, without referring in any manner to any supposed action of the state or its authorities.

If this legislation is appropriate for enforcing the prohibitions of the amendment, it is difficult to see where it is to stop. Why may not congress, with equal show of authority, enact a code of laws for the enforcement and vindication of all rights of life, liberty, and property? [The assumption is made] that if the states are forbidden to legislate or act in a particular way on a particular subject, and power is conferred upon congress to enforce the prohibition, this gives congress power to legislate generally upon that subject, and not merely power to provide modes of redress against such state legislation or action. The assumption [is] repugnant to the tenth amendment of the constitution, which declares that powers not delegated to the United States by the constitution, nor prohibited by it to the states, are reserved to the states respectively or to the people. . . .

Civil rights, such as are guarantied by the constitution against state aggression, cannot be impaired by the wrongful acts of individuals, unsupported by state authority in the shape of laws, customs, or judicial or executive proceedings. The wrongful act of an individual, unsupported by any such authority, is simply a private wrong, or a crime of that individual; an invasion of the rights of the injured party, it is true, whether they affect his person, his property, or his reputation; but if not sanctioned in some way by the state, or not done under state authority, his rights remain in full force, and may presumably be vindicated by resort to the laws of the state for redress. . . .

Of course, these remarks do not apply [when] congress is clothed with direct and plenary powers of legislation over the whole subject, accompanied with an express or implied denial of such power to the states, as in the regulation of commerce with foreign nations, among the several states, and with the Indian tribes, the coining of money, the establishment of post-offices and post-roads, the declaring of war, etc. In these cases congress has power to pass laws for regulating the subjects specified, [and] the conduct and transactions of individuals respect thereof. But where a subject is not submitted to the general legislative power of congress, but is only submitted [for] the purpose of rendering effective some prohibition against particular state legislation or state action in reference to that subject, the power given is limited by its object, and any legislation by congress in the matter must necessarily be corrective in its character, adapted to counteract and redress the operation of such prohibited state laws or proceedings of state officers.

If the principles of interpretation which we have laid down are correct[, the] law in question cannot be sustained by any grant of legislative power made to congress by the fourteenth amendment. . . .

[T]he power of congress to adopt direct and primary, as distinguished from corrective, legislation on the subject [is] sought, in the second place, from the thirteenth amendment, which abolishes slavery. [I]t is assumed that the power vested in congress to enforce the [Thirteenth Amendment] by appropriate legislation, clothes congress with power to pass all laws necessary and proper for abolishing all badges and incidents of slavery in the United States; and upon this assumption it is claimed that this is sufficient authority for declaring by law that all persons shall have equal accommodations and privileges in all inns, public conveyances, and places of public amusement; the argument being that the denial of such equal accommodations and privileges is in itself a subjection to a species of servitude within the meaning of the amendment. [A]n act of refusal has nothing to do with slavery or involuntary servitude. [I]f it is violative of any right of the party, his redress [is] under the laws of the state; or, if those laws are adverse to his rights and do not protect him, his remedy will be found in the corrective legislation which congress has adopted, or may adopt, for counteracting the effect of state laws, or state action, prohibited by the fourteenth amendment. It would be running the slavery argument into the ground to make it apply to every act of discrimination. . . .

[T]he law in question [must] necessarily be declared void, at least so far as its operation in the several states is concerned.

So ordered.

HARLAN, J., dissenting.

[If] any right was created by [the Fourteenth Amendment], the grant of power, through appropriate legislation, to enforce its provisions authorizes congress, by means of legislation operating throughout the entire Union, to guard, secure, and protect that right. . . .

This restrictive reading of the state action requirement in *The Civil Rights Cases* permitted racial discrimination to flourish in the South. For example, the Supreme Court upheld the "white primary," a device used to circumvent the Fifteenth Amendment, in Grovey v. Townsend, 295 U.S. 45, 55 S.Ct. 622, 79 L.Ed. 1292 (1935). The Court reasoned that because political parties were private organizations, their primary elections did not constitute state action.

The Supreme Court began to move away from a strict state action requirement in the 1940s. In Smith v. Allwright, 321 U.S. 649, 64 S.Ct. 757, 88 L.Ed. 987 (1944), the Court struck down the white primary as violating the Fifteenth Amendment, thus overruling *Grovey*. The Court now found that primary elections played an important part in the democratic process and must be considered as officially sanctioned by the state.

Notes and Questions

1. *Sufficient Governmental Involvement?* In most instances, when plaintiffs assert a violation of the Bill of Rights or the Fourteenth Amendment, state involvement will be obvious. In other words, Congress or a state legislature will have passed a law, or a governmental agency or government official will have

taken action against the citizen. More difficult questions arise when the violation seems to be the result of private action but the government is involved or implicated in the private action in some way. As we shall see, government is involved in virtually all private conduct in one way or another (for example, because it either passed a law authorizing the conduct or failed to pass a law prohibiting the conduct). Thus, the real question is whether the government is sufficiently involved so that the ostensibly private action effectively becomes "state action." Questions about state action present difficult issues for the courts.

2. *Modern Civil Rights Statutes.* Many modern civil rights statutes are based on Congress's Commerce Clause power rather than on the Fourteenth Amendment. Of course, as we saw in Chapter 2, in order for such legislation to be sustained, there must be a sufficient relationship between the prohibited activity and interstate commerce.

❧ PROBLEM: REWRITING THE CIVIL RIGHTS ACT ❧

In *The Civil Rights Cases*, the Court finds that Congress was trying to limit and control private action. However, the Court suggests that there are circumstances in which the actions of private individuals might be attributed to the state. What is the Court referring to? What governmental actions might make state and local governments responsible for private discrimination? Would it have been possible to rewrite the Civil Rights Act so that it is constitutional and encompasses only such actions?

B. GOVERNMENT FUNCTION

One situation in which the Court has found state action is when a private entity performs a traditional governmental function. There are a number of "governmental function" cases.

1. Company Towns

So-called "company towns," as found to exist in the following case, provide a classic example of state action.

Marsh v. Alabama

326 U.S. 501 (1946)

Mr. Justice BLACK delivered the opinion of the Court.

[W]e are asked to decide whether a State, consistently with the First and Fourteenth Amendments, can impose criminal punishment on a person who undertakes to distribute religious literature on the premises of a company-owned town contrary to the wishes of the town's management. The town, a suburb of Mobile, Alabama, known as Chickasaw, is owned by the Gulf Shipbuilding Corporation. [I]t has all the characteristics of any other American town. The property consists of residential buildings, streets, a system of sewers, a sewage disposal plant and a "business block" on which business places are situated. A deputy of the Mobile County Sheriff, paid by the company, serves as the town's policeman. Merchants and service establishments have rented the stores and business places on the business block and the United States uses one of the places as a post office from which six carriers deliver mail to the [town] and the adjacent area. The town [cannot be distinguished from] the surrounding neighborhood [by] anyone not familiar with the property lines, [and] the residents use the business block as their regular shopping center. To do so, [they] make use of a company-owned paved street and sidewalk [in] order to enter and leave the stores and the post office. Intersecting company-owned roads at each end of the business block lead into a four-lane public highway which runs parallel to the business block at a distance of thirty feet. There is nothing to stop highway traffic from coming onto the business block and upon arrival a traveler may make free use of the facilities available there. In short the town and its shopping district are accessible to and freely used by the public in general and there is nothing to distinguish them from any other town and shopping center except the fact that the title to the property belongs to a private corporation.

Appellant, a Jehovah's Witness, came onto the sidewalk [and] undertook to distribute religious literature. [T]he corporation had posted a notice which read as follows: "This Is Private Property, and Without Written Permission, No Street, or House Vendor, Agent or Solicitation of Any Kind Will Be Permitted." Appellant was warned that she could not distribute the literature without a permit and told that no permit would be issued to her. [She was asked to leave, but refused.] The deputy sheriff arrested her and she was charged in the state court with [remaining] on the premises of another after having been warned not to do so. [Appellant argued that the statute abridged her First and Fourteenth Amendment rights to freedom of the press and freedom of religion]. [S]he was convicted. . . .

Had the title to Chickasaw belonged not to a private but to a municipal corporation[,] it would have been clear that appellant's conviction must be reversed. [Under] Lovell v. Griffin, 303 U.S. 444[,] neither a state nor a municipality can completely bar the distribution of literature containing religious or political ideas on its streets, sidewalks and public places or make the right to distribute dependent on a flat license tax or permit to be issued by an official who could deny it at will. [The State argues] that the corporation's right to control the inhabitants of Chickasaw is coextensive with the right of a homeowner to regulate the conduct of his guests. We can not accept that contention. . . . The more an owner, for his advantage, opens up his property for use by the public[,] the more [his] rights become circumscribed by the statutory and constitutional rights of those who use it. . . .

[It makes no] significant constitutional difference as to the relationship between the rights of the owner and those of the public [that] the State [allowed] the corporation [to] use its property as a town. . . . Whether a corporation or a municipality owns or possesses the town the public [has an interest] that the channels of communication remain free. [T]he town of Chickasaw does not function differently from any other town. The "business block" serves as the community shopping center and is freely accessible and open to the people in the area and those passing through. The managers [of] the corporation cannot curtail the liberty of press and religion [in violation of] the Constitutional guarantees, and a state statute [which criminally punishes] those who attempt to distribute religious literature [violates] the First and Fourteenth Amendments to the Constitution. . . .

When we balance the Constitutional rights of owners of property against those of the people to enjoy freedom of press and religion, [the] latter occupy a preferred position. [T]he right to exercise the liberties safeguarded by the First Amendment "lies at the foundation of free government by free men." [Schneider v. State, 308 U.S. 147]. [T]he circumstance that the property rights to the premises where the deprivation of liberty [took] place, were held by others than the public, is not sufficient to justify the State's permitting a corporation to govern a community of citizens so as to restrict their fundamental liberties and the enforcement of such restraint by the application of a State statute. Insofar as the State has attempted to impose criminal punishment on appellant for undertaking to distribute religious literature in a company town, its action cannot stand. . . .

Reversed and remanded.

Mr. Justice REED, dissenting.

[T]his is the first case to extend by law the privilege of religious exercises beyond public places or to private places without the assent of the owner. [W]e find nothing in the principles of the First Amendment, adopted now into the Fourteenth, which justifies their application to the facts of this case. . . .

Notes and Questions

1. *Are Shopping Malls the Modern Equivalent of "Company Towns"?* As city life has gravitated from downtown to the suburbs, have suburban shopping malls become the functional equivalent of company towns? If so, should individuals have the right to engage in First Amendment activities (e.g., give speeches and distribute fliers and circulars) on shopping mall premises? In Amalgamated Food Employees Union v. Logan Valley Plaza, Inc., 391 U.S. 308 (1968), union members peacefully picketed a business located in a private shopping center. When the owners of the center sought to enjoin the picketing as a trespass, the picketers defended on First Amendment grounds. The Court held that the shopping center's actions constituted state action so that the First Amendment applied: "The similarities between the business block in *Marsh* and the shopping center in the present case are striking. The perimeter of Logan Valley Mall is a little less than 1.1 miles. Inside the mall were [two] substantial commercial enterprises. . . . Immediately adjacent to the mall are two roads, one of which is a heavily traveled state

highway and from both of which lead entrances directly into the mall. Adjoining the buildings in the middle of the mall are sidewalks for the use of pedestrians going to and from their cars and from building to building. In the parking areas [are] roadways for the use of vehicular traffic entering and leaving the mall. . . . The general public has unrestricted access to the mall property. The shopping center here is clearly the functional equivalent of the business district of Chickasaw involved in *Marsh*. . . ." Do you agree?

2. *More on Shopping Centers: Take Two.* Lloyd Corp., Ltd. v. Tanner, 407 U.S. 551 (1972), involved a shopping center that covered nearly 50 acres of ground. All stores were located within a single large, multilevel building complex that contained interior promenades with large sidewalks. The center was generally open to the public, and various civic groups were allowed to hold events on the premises. The center was "policed" by private security guards hired by the center. Litigation arose when the center's security guards told several individuals, who were distributing handbills in the shopping center, to leave or they would be arrested. The handbills stated opposition to the Vietnam War and the draft. The individuals distributing handbills left, but then sought declaratory relief and injunctive relief on First Amendment grounds. The Supreme Court concluded that the center's conduct constituted private action, distinguishing *Marsh* and *Logan Valley*: "[*Logan Valley*] was carefully phrased to limit its holding to the picketing involved, where the picketing was 'directly related in its purpose to the use to which the shopping center property was being put,' and where the store was located in the center of a large private enclave with the consequence that no other reasonable opportunities for the pickets to convey their message to their intended audience were available. . . . Neither of these elements is present in the case now before the Court."

3. *More on Shopping Centers: Take Three.* In Hudgens v. NLRB, 424 U.S. 507 (1976), the Court overruled *Logan Valley*. *Hudgens* involved union members who engaged in peaceful protesting inside a privately owned shopping center. When the protesters were threatened with arrest by an agent of the owner, they sought declaratory and injunctive relief. The question was whether the threat constituted an unfair labor practice within the meaning of the National Labor Relations Act. The National Labor Relations Board (NLRB) issued a cease-and-desist order concluding that the picketers had a First Amendment right to picket Hudgens's mall. The Court disagreed: "the constitutional guarantee of free expression has no part to play in a case such as this." Are the holdings in *Lloyd Corp.* and *Hudgens* preferable to the holding in *Logan Valley*?

∿ PROBLEM: MORE ON THE TOWN, THE PRIVATE UTILITY, AND THE CLUB ∿

Let's return to the problem at the beginning of the chapter. Based on your reading of *Marsh* and the cases mentioned in this section, does Power House's control over the Downtown District in Town Orange amount to the performance of a traditional government function? How would you argue the case for the plaintiffs? How might the utility respond? In formulating your arguments, consider whether you can draw an analogy between the Downtown District and a company town or a shopping mall. Does it matter that the Downtown District includes streets, sidewalks, and the only park in Town Orange? Is the size of the Downtown District relevant?

2. Party Primaries

The party primaries cases arose from the Texas Democratic Party's efforts to preclude blacks from participating in party primaries. Since political parties are generally treated as voluntary associations of private individuals, defendants argued that their conduct should be treated as private action. However, in a series of cases decided between 1927 and 1953, the Court concluded otherwise.

Nixon v. Herndon, 273 U.S. 536 (1927), involved a Texas statute that explicitly prohibited blacks from voting in the Democratic primary. The Court struck down the law, concluding that its mandated discrimination constituted state action. Following *Nixon*, after the Texas legislature passed a new law giving the Democratic Party's executive committee the right to decide who could vote in its party primaries, the party passed a resolution providing that only white Democrats would be allowed to vote. In Nixon v. Condon, 286 U.S. 73 (1932), the Court struck this law down, too. The Court found "state action" on the basis that the "Committee operated as representative of the State in the discharge of the State's authority."

Condon left open the question of a party's inherent power "to determine its own membership." That issue was presented in Smith v. Allwright, 321 U.S. 649 (1944). After the prior laws were struck down, the Texas Democratic Party passed a resolution limiting party membership to white citizens of the State of Texas. Because only party members could vote in the Democratic primary, this resolution effectively precluded blacks from participating. The resolution was adopted by the party on its own without statutory authorization. Although the Court initially upheld a similar restriction in Grovey v. Townsend, the Court reversed in Smith v. Allwright and held that state action existed: The "statutory system for the selection of party nominees for inclusion on the general election ballot makes the party which is required to follow these legislative directions an agency of the state in so far as it determines the participants in a primary election." "The privilege of membership in a party may [be] no concern of a state. But when, as here, that privilege is also the essential qualification for voting in a primary to select nominees for a general election, the state makes the action of the party the action of the [state]."

Following *Smith,* the following case came before the Court.

Terry v. Adams

345 U.S. 461 (1953)

Mr. Justice BLACK announced the judgment of the Court and an opinion in which Mr. Justice DOUGLAS and Mr. Justice BURTON join.

[This] case raises questions concerning the constitutional power of a Texas county political organization called the Jaybird Democratic Association or Jaybird Party to exclude Negroes from its primaries on racial grounds. The Jaybirds deny that their racial exclusions violate the Fifteenth Amendment. They contend that the Amendment applies only to elections or primaries held under state regulation, that their association is not regulated by the state at all, and that it is not a political party but a self-governing voluntary club. . . .

[The] Jaybird Association or Party was organized in 1889. Its membership [has always] been limited to white people; they are automatically members if their names appear on the official list of county voters. It [is] run like other political parties with an executive committee. . . . Expenses of the party are paid by the assessment of candidates for office in its primaries. Candidates for county offices submit their names to the Jaybird Committee. . . . Advertisements and posters proclaim that these candidates are running subject to the action of the Jaybird primary. While there is no legal compulsion on successful Jaybird candidates to enter Democratic primaries they have nearly always done so and with few exceptions [have] won without opposition in [the] primaries and the general elections. . . . Thus the party has been the dominant political group in the county since organization, having endorsed every county-wide official elected since 1889.

[P]recisely the same qualifications [to] vote at county-operated primaries are adopted as the sole qualifications entitling electors to vote at the county-wide Jaybird primaries with a single proviso — Negroes are excluded. Everyone concedes that such a proviso in the county-operated primaries would be unconstitutional. The Jaybird Party thus brings into being and holds precisely the kind of election that the Fifteenth Amendment seeks to prevent. When it produces the equivalent of the prohibited election, the damage has been done.

[The] use of the county-operated primary to ratify the result of the prohibited election merely compounds the offense. It violates the Fifteenth Amendment for a state, by such circumvention, to permit within its borders the use of any device that produces an equivalent of the prohibited election. . . . The only election that has counted in this Texas county for more than fifty years has been that held by the Jaybirds from which Negroes were excluded. . . . It is immaterial that the state does not control that part of this elective process which it leaves for the Jaybirds to manage. The Jaybird primary has become an integral part, indeed the only effective part, of the elective process that determines who shall rule and govern in the county. The effect of the whole procedure, Jaybird primary plus Democratic primary plus general election, is to do precisely that which the Fifteenth Amendment forbids — strip Negroes of every vestige of influence in selecting the officials who control the local county matters that intimately touch the daily lives of citizens. [T]he combined Jaybird-Democratic-general election machinery has deprived these petitioners of their right to vote on account of their race and color. . . .

Reversed and remanded.

Mr. Justice FRANKFURTER.

[T]hose charged by State law with the duty of assuring all eligible voters an opportunity to participate in the selection of candidates [participate] in the Jaybird primary. They join the white voting community in [a] wholly successful effort to withdraw significance from the State-prescribed primary, to subvert the operation of what is formally the law of the State for primaries in this county.

Mr. Justice CLARK, with whom THE CHIEF JUSTICE, Mr. Justice REED, and Mr. Justice JACKSON join, concurring.

[B]ecause the Jaybird-indorsed nominee meets no opposition in the Democratic primary, the Negro minority's vote is nullified at the sole stage of the local political process where the bargaining and interplay of rival political forces would make it count.

Mr. Justice MINTON, dissenting.

I am not concerned in the least as to what happens to the Jaybirds or their unworthy scheme. [T]his Court has power to redress a wrong under that [Fifteenth] Amendment only if the wrong is done by the State. . . . That Amendment erects no shield against merely private conduct, however discriminatory or wrongful. . . . Mr. Justice Frankfurter [thinks] it is enough to constitute state action if a state official participates in the Jaybird primary. [E]verything done by a person who is an official is not done officially and as a representative of the State. [I] find nothing [that] shows the state or county officials participating in the Jaybird primary.

[There is not] one iota of state action sufficient to support [an] inference that the Jaybird Association [is] associated with [or] cooperates in any manner with the Democratic Party [or] with the State. It calls itself the Jaybird Democratic Association because its interest is only in the candidates of the Democratic Party in the county. . . . Even if it be said to be a political organization, the Jaybird Association avails itself of no state law open to political organizations. . . .

[The Association's activities are] not forbidden by the law of the State of Texas. Does such failure of the State to act to prevent individuals from doing what they have the right as individuals to do amount to state action? [I]t does not. . . . Surely white or colored members of any political faith or economic belief may hold caucuses. It is only when the State by action of its legislative bodies or action of some of its officials in their official capacity cooperates with such political party or gives it direction in its activities that the Federal Constitution may come into play. A political organization not using state machinery or depending upon state law to authorize what it does could not be within the ban of the Fifteenth Amendment. [T]he Jaybird Association did not attempt to conform or in any way [comply] with the statutes of Texas covering primaries. No action of any legislative or quasi-legislative body or of any state official or agency ever [denied] the vote to

Negroes, even in the Jaybird primaries. [So] there is no state action, and the Jaybird Democratic Association is in no sense a part of the Democratic Party. . . .

I do not understand that concerted action of individuals which is successful somehow becomes state action. [T]he candidates endorsed by the Jaybird Association have several times been defeated in primaries and elections [and the] Jaybird Association's activities [are] confined to one County where a group of citizens have appointed themselves the censors of those who would run for public offices. Apparently so far they have succeeded in convincing the voters of this County in most instances that their supported candidates should win. . . . In other localities, candidates are carefully selected [to] give proper weight to Jew, Protestant and Catholic, and certain posts are considered the sole possession of certain ethnic groups. The propriety of these practices is something the courts sensibly have left to the good or bad judgment of the electorate. It must be recognized that elections and other public business are influenced by all sorts of pressures [including] pressure from labor unions, from the National Association of Manufacturers, [from] the National Association for the Advancement of Colored People, from the Ku Klux Klan and others. . . . The courts do not normally pass upon these pressure groups, whether their causes are good or bad, highly successful [or unsuccessful]. It is difficult [to] see how this Jaybird Association is anything but such a pressure group. . . .

Notes and Questions

1. *"Careful Selection" of Candidates.* Justice Minton refers to places where candidates are "carefully selected" to give proper weight to Jewish, Protestant, or Catholic interests. After this decision, does such selection constitute private action or state action? Does it matter who does the selection?

2. *Committee for a Feminist Majority.* The Committee for a Feminist Majority (COFM) was organized to help elect women to public office in Louisville, Kentucky. In addition to its efforts to encourage and recruit female candidates, COFM holds a pre-primary designed to pick a "preferred" candidate behind whom COFM members can unite. Since women comprise a clear majority of the Louisville population, and women (and some men) tend to rally behind the COFM-endorsed candidate, COFM candidates almost always win. COFM precludes men from membership as well as from voting in its pre-primary. Under *Terry*, does COFM's pre-primary constitute state action?

3. *African American Jaybirds?* Would there be a state action if blacks organized a pre-primary in a city that has a majority black population? Would your analysis be affected by the fact that the black candidate always wins?

3. Utility Service

Marsh, Herndon, and *Condon* were decided during the first half of the twentieth century. During the latter part of the century, the Court's analysis of state action cases began to change. The following case illustrates the Court's modern precedent.

Jackson v. Metropolitan Edison Company

419 U.S. 345 (1974)

Mr. Justice REHNQUIST delivered the opinion of the Court.

Respondent Metropolitan Edison Co. is a privately owned and operated Pennsylvania corporation which holds a certificate of public convenience issued by the Pennsylvania Public Utility Commission empowering it to deliver electricity to [an] area which includes the city of York, Pa. As a condition of holding its certificate, it is subject to extensive regulation by the Commission. Under a provision of its general tariff filed with the Commission, it has the right to discontinue service to any customer on reasonable notice of nonpayment of bills.

Petitioner Catherine Jackson is a resident of York. [When petitioner failed to pay her bills, Metropolitan terminated her service. Petitioner filed] suit against Metropolitan [under] the Civil Rights Act of 1871, 42 U.S.C. §1983, seeking damages for the termination and an injunction requiring [continued] service to her residence. . . . She urged that under state law she had an entitlement to reasonably continuous electrical service [and] that Metropolitan's termination of her service for alleged nonpayment, action allowed by a provision of its general tariff filed with the Commission, constituted "state action" depriving her of property in violation of the Fourteenth Amendment's guarantee of due process of law. . . .

[While] the principle that private action is immune from the restrictions of the Fourteenth Amendment is well established and easily stated, the question whether particular conduct is "private," on the one hand, or "state action," [frequently] admits of no easy answer. . . . Here the action complained of was taken by a utility company which is privately owned and operated, but which in many particulars of its business is subject to extensive state regulation. The mere fact that a business is subject to state regulation does not by itself convert its action into that of the State for purposes of the Fourteenth Amendment. Nor does the fact that the regulation is extensive and detailed. . . . It may well be that acts of a heavily regulated utility with at least something of a governmentally protected monopoly will more readily be found to be "state" acts than will the acts of an entity lacking these characteristics. But [there must be] a sufficiently close nexus between the State and the challenged action of the regulated entity so that the action of the latter may be fairly treated as that of the State itself. . . .

Petitioner [argues] that "state action" is present because of the monopoly status allegedly conferred upon Metropolitan by the State of Pennsylvania. [A]ssuming that [Metroplitan] had [been granted a monopoly], this fact is not determinative. . . .

Petitioner next urges that state action is present because respondent provides an essential public service required to be supplied on a reasonably continuous basis by Pa. Stat. Ann., Tit. 66, §1171 (1959), and hence performs a "public function." We have [found] state action present in the exercise by a private entity of powers traditionally exclusively reserved to the State. If we were dealing with the exercise by Metropolitan of some power delegated to it by the State which is traditionally associated with sovereignty, such as eminent domain, [the] case would be quite [different]. But while the Pennsylvania statute imposes an obligation to furnish service on regulated utilities, it imposes no such obligation on the State. [Pennsylvania] courts have rejected the contention that the furnishing of utility services is either a state function or a municipal duty.

[P]etitioner invites [adoption of] a broad principle that all businesses "affected with the public interest" are state actors in all their actions. . . . We decline the invitation for reasons stated long ago in Nebbia v. New York, 291 U.S. 502 (1934). . . . "It is clear that there is no closed class or category of businesses affected with a public interest. . . ." Doctors, optometrists, lawyers, Metropolitan, and Nebbia's [milk sales] are all in regulated businesses, providing arguably essential goods and services, "affected with a public interest." We do not believe that such a status converts their every action, absent more, into that of the State.

We also reject the notion that Metropolitan's termination is state action because the State "has specifically authorized and approved" the termination practice. . . . Metropolitan filed with the Public Utility Commission a general tariff—a provision of which states [the] right to terminate service for nonpayment. This provision has appeared in Metropolitan's previously filed tariffs for many years and has never been the subject [of] scrutiny by the Commission. Although the Commission did hold hearings [on] Metropolitan's [rate] increase, it [never] considered [this] provision[.] The provision became effective [when] not disapproved. . . .

Metropolitan is a privately owned corporation, and it does not lease its facilities from the [state]. It alone is responsible for the provision of power to its customers. In common with all corporations of the State it pays taxes to the State, and it is subject to a form of extensive regulation by the State in a way that most other business enterprises are not. But this was likewise true of the appellant club in Moose Lodge No. 107 v. Irvis, where we said: "However detailed this type of regulation may be in some particulars, it cannot be said [to] make the State in any realistic sense a partner or even a joint venturer in the club's enterprise."

All of petitioner's arguments taken together show no more than that Metropolitan was a heavily regulated, privately owned utility, enjoying at least a partial monopoly in the providing of electrical service within its territory, and that it elected to terminate service to petitioner in a manner which the Pennsylvania Public Utility Commission found permissible under state law. [T]his is not sufficient to connect the State of Pennsylvania with respondent's action so as to make the latter's conduct attributable to the State for purposes of the Fourteenth Amendment. . . . The judgment of the Court of Appeals for the Third Circuit is therefore

Affirmed.

Mr. Justice DOUGLAS, dissenting.

[This case depicts] a monopolist providing essential public services as a licensee of the State [within] a framework of extensive state supervision and control.

The particular regulations[, promulgated] by the monopolist, were authorized by state law and [were] enforceable by the weight and authority of the State. [T]he State retains the power of oversight to review and amend the regulations if the public interest so requires. Respondent's actions are sufficiently intertwined with those of the State, and its termination-of-service provisions are sufficiently buttressed by state law to warrant a holding that respondent's actions in terminating this householder's service were "state action" for the purpose of giving federal jurisdiction over respondent under 42 U.S.C. §1983. . . .

Mr. Justice MARSHALL, dissenting.

[Metropolitan] Edison Co. provides an essential public service [and] is the only entity public or private, that is authorized to [do so in] most of the community. [T]he State imposes extensive regulations [and] cooperates with the company in myriad ways. [T]he State has granted its approval to the company's mode of service termination. [I] have no difficulty finding state action. [T]he State has sufficiently "insinuated itself into a position of interdependence with (the company) that it must be recognized as a joint participant in the challenged activity." . . .

∽ PROBLEM: MORE ON THE TOWN, THE PRIVATE UTILITY, AND THE CLUB ∽

Returning to the problem at the beginning of the chapter, suppose that you are hired to represent the five members of the community whose permit application was denied and whose power was turned off. How would you argue that Power House's status as a public utility implicates state action? Now, assuming that you are hired instead to represent Power House, how would you respond to these arguments? Has the Court's attitude regarding state action and the governmental function exception changed from *Marsh*?

4. Schools and School Associations

When, and under what circumstances, may the actions of private schools and private school associations be regarded as performing a government function? Consider the following cases.

Rendell-Baker v. Kohn
457 U.S. 830 (1982)

Chief Justice BURGER delivered the opinion of the Court.

We granted certiorari to decide whether a private school, whose income is derived primarily from public sources and which is regulated by public authorities, acted under color of state law when it discharged certain employees. . . .

Respondent Kohn is the director of the New Perspectives School, a nonprofit institution located on privately owned property in Brookline, Massachusetts. The school was founded as a private institution and is operated by a board of directors, none of whom are public officials or are chosen by public officials. The school specializes in dealing with students who have experienced difficulty completing public high schools; many have drug, alcohol, or behavioral problems, or other special needs. In recent years, nearly all of the students at the school have been referred to it by the Brookline or Boston School Committees, or by the Drug Rehabilitation Division of the Massachusetts Department of Mental Health. The school issues high school diplomas certified by the Brookline School Committee.

When students are referred to the school by Brookline or Boston under Chapter 766 of the Massachusetts Acts of 1972, the School Committees in those cities pay for the students' education. The school also receives funds from a number of other state and federal agencies. In recent years, public funds have accounted for at least 90%, and in one year 99%, of respondent school's operating budget. There were approximately 50 students at the school in those years and none paid tuition.

To be eligible for tuition funding under Chapter 766, the school must comply with a variety of regulations, many of which are common to all schools. The State has issued detailed regulations concerning matters ranging from record-keeping to student-teacher ratios. Concerning personnel policies, the Chapter 766 regulations require the school to maintain written job descriptions and written statements describing personnel standards and procedures, but they impose few specific requirements.

The school is also regulated by Boston and Brookline as a result of its Chapter 766 funding. By its contract with the Boston School Committee, which refers to the school as a "contractor," the school must agree to carry out the individualized plan developed for each student referred to the school by the Committee. The contract specifies that school employees are not city employees.

The school also has a contract with the State Drug Rehabilitation Division. Like the contract with the Boston School Committee, that agreement refers to the school as a "contractor." It provides for reimbursement for services provided for students referred to the school by the Drug Rehabilitation Division, and includes requirements concerning the services to be provided. Except for general requirements, such as an equal employment opportunity requirement, the agreement does not cover personnel policies.

[P]etitioner Rendell-Baker was a vocational counselor hired under a grant from the federal Law Enforcement Assistance Administration, whose funds are distributed in Massachusetts through the State Committee on Criminal Justice. As a condition of the grant, the Committee on Criminal Justice must approve the school's initial hiring decisions. The purpose of this requirement is to insure that the school hires vocational counselors who meet the qualifications described in the school's grant proposal to the Committee; the Committee does not interview applicants for counselor positions.

[Rendell-Baker] was discharged by the school in January 1977, and the five other petitioners were discharged in June 1978. . . . A dispute arose when some students presented a petition to the school's board of directors [seeking] greater responsibilities for the student-staff council. Director Kohn opposed the proposal, but Rendell-Baker supported it and so advised the board. On December 13, Kohn notified the State Committee on Criminal Justice, which funded Rendell-Baker's position, that she intended to dismiss Rendell-Baker and employ someone else. [Rendell-Baker then] filed this suit [under] 42 U.S.C. §1983, alleging that she had been discharged in violation of her rights under the First, Fifth, and Fourteenth Amendments. [When other teachers protested the dismissal and indiciated that they were going to form a union,] Kohn discharged the teachers. . . . They [sued seeking relief] under §1983, alleging that their rights under the First, Fifth, and Fourteenth Amendments had been violated.

[The] issue presented in this case [is] whether the school's action in discharging [petitioners] can fairly be seen as state action. [In] Blum v. Yaretsky, 457 U.S. 991, the Court [considered] whether certain nursing homes were state actors for the purpose of determining whether decisions regarding transfers of patients could be fairly attributed to the State, and hence be subjected to Fourteenth Amendment due process requirements. The challenged transfers primarily involved decisions, made by physicians and nursing home administrators, to move patients from "skilled nursing facilities" to less expensive "health related facilities." [Like] the New Perspectives School, the nursing homes were privately owned and operated. [This] Court held that, "a State normally can be held responsible for a private decision only when it has exercised coercive power or has provided such significant encouragement, either overt or covert, that the choice must in law be deemed to be that of the State." In determining that the transfer decisions were not actions of the State, the Court considered each of the factors alleged by petitioners here to make the discharge decisions of the New Perspectives School fairly attributable to the State.

First, the nursing homes, like the school, depended on the State for funds; the State subsidized the operating and capital costs of the nursing homes, and paid the medical expenses of more than 90% of the patients. [W]e held that [the] dependence of the nursing homes did not make the acts of the physicians and nursing home administrators acts of the State, and we conclude that the school's receipt of public funds does not make the discharge decisions acts of the State. . . . Acts of such private contractors do not become acts of the government by reason of their significant or even total engagement in performing public contracts. . . .

A second factor considered in Blum was the extensive regulation of the nursing homes by the State. There the State was indirectly involved in the transfer decisions [because] a primary goal of the State in regulating nursing homes was to keep costs down by transferring patients from intensive treatment centers to less expensive facilities when possible. Both state and federal regulations encouraged the nursing homes to transfer patients to less expensive facilities when appropriate. . . . The Court relied on Jackson, where we held that state regulation, even if "extensive and detailed" did not make a utility's actions state action. . . . Here the decisions to discharge the petitioners were not compelled or even influenced by any state regulation. Indeed, [the] various regulators showed relatively little interest in the school's personnel matters. [The] Committee on Criminal

Justice had the power to approve persons hired as vocational counselors. Such a regulation is not sufficient to make a decision to discharge, made by private management, state action.

The third factor asserted to show that the school is a state actor is that it performs a "public function." [T]he question is whether the function performed has been "traditionally the exclusive prerogative of the State." There can be no doubt that the education of maladjusted high school students is a public function. . . . Chapter 766 of the Massachusetts Acts of 1972 demonstrates that the State intends to provide services for such students at public expense. That legislative policy choice in no way makes these services the exclusive province of the State. Indeed[,] until recently the State had not undertaken to provide education for students who could not be served by traditional public schools. That a private entity performs a function which serves the public does not make its acts state action.

Fourth, petitioners argue that there is a "symbiotic relationship" between the school and the State similar to the relationship involved in Burton v. Wilmington Parking Authority, 365 U.S. 715 (1961). [T]he school's fiscal relationship with the State is not different from that of many contractors performing services for the government. No symbiotic relationship such as existed in *Burton* exists here.

We hold that petitioners have not stated a claim for relief under 42 U.S.C. §1983; accordingly, the judgment of the Court of Appeals for the First Circuit is
Affirmed.

Justice WHITE, concurring in the judgments.
[T]he critical factor is the absence of any allegation that the employment decision was itself based upon some rule of conduct or policy put forth by the State. . . . The employment decision remains [a] private decision not fairly attributable to the State.

Justice MARSHALL, with whom Justice BRENNAN joins, dissenting.
[W]here there is a symbiotic relationship between the State and a privately owned enterprise, so that [they] are participants in a joint venture, the actions of the private enterprise may be attributable to the State. . . . Here, an examination of the facts and circumstances leads inexorably to the conclusion that the actions of the New Perspectives School should be attributed to the State; it is difficult to imagine a closer relationship between a government and a private enterprise. . . . The New Perspectives School receives virtually all of its funds from state sources. . . . The school's very survival depends on the State. If the State chooses, it may exercise complete control over the school's operations simply by threatening to withdraw financial support if the school takes action that it considers objectionable. . . . The school is heavily regulated and closely supervised by the State. . . . Almost every decision the school makes is substantially affected in some way by the State's regulations. . . . The fact that the school is providing a substitute for public education is also an important indicium of state action. The provision of education is one of the most important tasks performed by government: it ranks at the very apex of the function of a State. [T]he fact that a private entity

is performing a vital public function, when coupled with other factors demonstrating a close connection with the State, may justify a finding of state action. . . . Clearly, if the State had decided to provide the service itself, its conduct would be measured against constitutional standards. The State should not be permitted to avoid constitutional requirements simply by delegating its statutory duty to a private entity. . . .

Brentwood Academy v. Tennessee Secondary
School Athletic Association

531 U.S. 288 (2001)

Justice SOUTER delivered the opinion of the Court.

The issue is whether a statewide association incorporated to regulate interscholastic athletic competition among public and private secondary schools may be regarded as engaging in state action when it enforces a rule against a member school. . . . We hold that the association's regulatory activity may and should be treated as state action owing to the pervasive entwinement of state school officials in the structure of the association, there being no offsetting reason to see the association's acts in any other way.

Respondent Tennessee Secondary School Athletic Association (Association) is a not-for-profit membership corporation organized to regulate interscholastic sport among the public and private high schools in Tennessee. . . . No school is forced to join, but [TSSAA] enjoys the memberships of almost all the State's public high schools (290 or 84% of the Association's voting membership), far outnumbering the 55 private schools that belong. A member school's team may play or scrimmage only against the team of another member, absent a dispensation.

The Association's rulemaking arm is its legislative council, while its board of control tends to administration. The voting membership of each of these nine-person committees is limited under the Association's bylaws to high school principals, assistant principals, and superintendents elected by the member schools. . . . Although the Association's staff members are not paid by the State, they are eligible to join the State's public retirement system for its employees. Member schools pay dues to the Association, though the bulk of its revenue is gate receipts at member teams' football and basketball tournaments, many of them held in public arenas rented by the Association.

The constitution, bylaws, and rules of the Association set standards of school membership and the eligibility of students to play in interscholastic games. Each school [is] regulated in awarding financial aid, most coaches must have a Tennessee state teaching license, and players must meet minimum academic standards and hew to limits on student employment. Under the bylaws, "in all matters pertaining to the athletic relations of his school," the principal is responsible to the Association, which has the power "to suspend, to fine, or otherwise penalize any member school for the violation of any of the rules of the Association or for other just cause."

[S]ince the Association was incorporated in 1925, Tennessee's State Board of Education (State Board) has acknowledged the corporation's functions "in providing standards, rules and regulations for interscholastic competition in the public schools of Tennessee." [I]n 1972, it went so far as to adopt a rule expressly "designat[ing]" the Association as "the organization to supervise and regulate the athletic activities in which the public junior and senior high schools in Tennessee participate on an interscholastic basis." The Rule [instructed] the State Board's chairman to "designate a person or persons to serve in an ex-officio capacity on the [Association's governing bodies]." That same year, the State Board specifically approved the Association's rules and regulations, while reserving the right to review future changes. [O]n several occasions over the next 20 years, the State Board reviewed, approved, or reaffirmed its approval of the recruiting Rule at issue in this case. In 1996, [the] State Board dropped the original [rule] expressly designating the Association as regulator [and] substituted a statement "recogniz-[ing] the value of participation in interscholastic athletics and the role of [the Association] in coordinating interscholastic athletic competition," while "authoriz[ing] the public schools of the state to voluntarily maintain membership in [the Association]."

[This action involves a] regulatory enforcement proceeding brought against petitioner, Brentwood Academy, a private parochial high school member of the Association. [The] board of control found that Brentwood violated a rule prohibiting "undue influence" in recruiting athletes, when it wrote to incoming students and their parents about spring football practice. The Association [placed] Brentwood's athletic program on probation for four years, declared its football and boys' basketball teams ineligible to compete in playoffs for two years, and imposed a $3,000 fine. When these penalties were imposed, all the voting members of the board of control and legislative council were public school administrators. . . . Brentwood sued the Association and its executive director [under] 42 U.S.C. §1983, claiming that enforcement of the Rule was state action and a violation of the First and Fourteenth Amendments. The District Court [found] the Association to be a state actor. . . . The United States Court of Appeals for the Sixth Circuit reversed [applying] criteria derived from Blum v. Yaretsky, 457 U.S. 991 (1982), Lugar v. Edmondson Oil Co., 457 U.S. 922 (1982), and Rendell-Baker v. Kohn, 457 U.S. 830 (1982). . . . We granted certiorari [and] now reverse.

Our cases try to plot a line between state action subject to Fourteenth Amendment scrutiny and private conduct [that] is not. The judicial obligation is not only to "'preserv[e] an area of individual freedom by limiting the reach of federal law' and avoi[d] the imposition of responsibility on a State for conduct it could not control," but also to assure that constitutional standards are invoked "when it can be said that the State is *responsible* for the specific conduct of which the plaintiff complains." If the Fourteenth Amendment is not to be displaced, [the] deed of an ostensibly private organization or individual is to be treated sometimes as if a State had caused it to be performed. [S]tate action may be found if, though only if, there is such a "close nexus between the State and the challenged action" that seemingly private behavior "may be fairly treated as that of the State itself."

[What] is fairly attributable is a matter of normative judgment, and the criteria lack rigid simplicity.

[N]o one fact can function as a necessary condition across the board for finding state action; nor is any set of circumstances absolutely sufficient, for there may be some countervailing reason against attributing activity to the government. . . . Our cases have identified a host of facts that can bear on the fairness of such an attribution. We have [held] that a challenged activity may be state action when it results from the State's exercise of "coercive power," when the State provides "significant encouragement, either overt or covert," or when a private actor operates as a "willful participant in joint activity with the State or its agents." We have treated a nominally private entity as a state actor when it is controlled by an "agency of the State," when it has been delegated a public function by the State, when it is "entwined with governmental policies," or when government is "entwined in [its] management or control," Evans v. Newton, 382 U.S. 296 (1966).

[T]he character of a legal entity is determined neither by its expressly private characterization in statutory law, nor by the failure of the law to acknowledge the entity's inseparability from recognized government officials or agencies. Lebron v. National Railroad Passenger Corporation, 513 U.S. 374 (1995), held that Amtrak was the Government for constitutional purposes, regardless of its congressional designation as private; it was organized under federal law to attain governmental objectives and was directed and controlled by federal appointees. Pennsylvania v. Board of Directors of City Trusts of Philadelphia held the privately endowed Girard College to be a state actor and enforcement of its private founder's limitation of admission to whites attributable to the State, because [the] college's board of directors was a state agency established by state law. [The converse] occurred in Evans v. Newton which held that private trustees to whom a city had transferred a park were nonetheless state actors [since] the park served the public purpose [and] "the municipality remain[ed] entwined in [its] management [and] control."

[The] nominally private character of the Association is overborne by the pervasive entwinement of public institutions and public officials in its composition and workings, and there is no substantial reason to claim unfairness in applying constitutional standards to it. . . . The Association is not an organization of natural persons acting on their own, but of schools, and of public schools to the extent of 84% of the total. Under the Association's bylaws, each member school is represented by its principal or a faculty member, who has a vote in selecting members of the governing legislative council and board of control from eligible principals, assistant principals, and superintendents.

[P]ublic school officials act within the scope of their duties when they represent their institutions. . . . Interscholastic athletics obviously play an integral part in the public education of Tennessee, where nearly every public high school spends money on competitions among schools. [T]hese public teams need some mechanism to produce rules and regulate competition. The mechanism is an organization overwhelmingly composed of public school officials who select representatives (all of them public officials at the time in question here), who in turn adopt and enforce the rules that make the system work. [B]y giving these jobs to the Association, the 290 public schools of Tennessee [can] sensibly be seen as exercising their own authority to meet their own responsibilities. [H]alf the council or board meetings [were] held during official school hours, and [public] schools have largely provided for the Association's financial support. A small portion of the Association's revenue comes from membership dues paid by the schools, and the principal part from gate receipts at tournaments among the member schools. [T]he schools here obtain membership in the service organization and give up sources of their own income to their collective association. The Association thus exercises the authority of the predominantly public schools to charge for admission to their games [and] enjoys the schools' moneymaking capacity as its own.

In sum, to the extent of 84% of its membership, the Association is an organization of public schools represented by their officials acting in their official capacity to provide an integral element of secondary public schooling. There would be no recognizable Association, legal or tangible, without the public school officials, who do not merely control but overwhelmingly perform all but the purely ministerial acts by which the Association exists and functions in practical terms. Only the 16% minority of private school memberships prevents this entwinement of the Association and the public school system from being total and their identities totally indistinguishable. . . . State Board members are assigned *ex officio* to serve as members of the board of control and legislative council, and the Association's ministerial employees are treated as state employees to the extent of being eligible for membership in the state retirement system.

[T]he terms of the State Board's Rule expressly designating the Association as regulator of interscholastic athletics in public schools were deleted in 1996, the year after a [court] held that the Association was a state actor. . . . But the removal of the designation language [affected] nothing but words. Today the State Board's member-designees continue to sit on the Association's committees as nonvoting members, and the State continues to welcome Association employees in its retirement scheme. The close relationship is confirmed by the Association's enforcement of the same preamendment rules and regulations reviewed and approved by the State Board [and] by the State Board's continued willingness to allow students to satisfy its physical education requirement by taking part in interscholastic athletics sponsored by the Association. [T]he State Board once freely acknowledged the Association's official character but now does it by winks and nods. . . .

Entwinement will support a conclusion that an ostensibly private organization ought to be charged with a public character and judged by constitutional standards; entwinement to the degree shown here requires it. [I]t avails the Association nothing to stress that the State neither coerced nor encouraged the actions complained of. "Coercion" and "encouragement" are like "entwinement" in referring to kinds of facts that can justify characterizing an ostensibly private action as public. . . . Facts that address any of these criteria are significant, but no one criterion must necessarily be applied. When [the] relevant facts show pervasive entwinement to the point of largely overlapping identity, the implication of state action is not affected by pointing out that the facts might not loom large under a different test.

[Even] facts that suffice to show public action [may] be outweighed in the name of some value at odds with finding public accountability in the circumstances. In *Polk County*, 454 U.S., at 322, a defense lawyer's actions were deemed private even though she was employed by the county and was acting within the scope of her duty as a public defender. Full-time public employment would be conclusive of state action for some purposes, but not when the employee is doing a defense lawyer's primary job; then, the public defender does "not ac[t] on behalf of the State; he is the State's adversary." The state-action doctrine does not convert opponents into virtual agents.

[Every other] Court of Appeals to consider a statewide athletic association [has] found it a state actor. . . . No one, however, has pointed to any explosion of §1983 cases against interscholastic athletic associations in the affected jurisdictions. . . .

The judgment of the Court of Appeals for the Sixth Circuit is reversed, and the case is remanded for further proceedings consistent with this opinion.

It is so ordered.

Justice THOMAS, with whom THE CHIEF JUSTICE, Justice SCALIA, and Justice KENNEDY join, dissenting.

We have never found state action based upon mere "entwinement." Until today, we have found a private organization's acts to constitute state action only when the organization performed a public function; was created, coerced, or encouraged by the government; or acted in a symbiotic relationship with the government. The majority's holding [not] only extends state-action doctrine beyond its permissible limits but also encroaches upon the realm of individual freedom that the doctrine was meant to protect. . . .

[C]ommon sense dictates that the TSSAA's actions [cannot] constitute state action. . . . The State of Tennessee did not create the TSSAA. The State does not fund the TSSAA and does not pay its employees. In fact, only 4% of the TSSAA's revenue comes from the dues paid by member schools; the bulk of its operating budget is derived from gate receipts at tournaments it sponsors. The State does not permit the TSSAA to use state-owned facilities for a discounted fee, and it does not exempt the TSSAA from state taxation. No Tennessee law authorizes the State to coordinate interscholastic athletics or empowers another entity to organize interscholastic athletics on behalf of the State. The only state pronouncement acknowledging the TSSAA's existence is a rule providing that the State Board of Education permits public schools to maintain membership in the TSSAA. . . .

Moreover, the State of Tennessee has never had any involvement in the particular action taken by the TSSAA in this case. [T]he TSSAA's authority to enforce its recruiting rule arises solely from the voluntary membership contract that each member school signs, agreeing to conduct its athletics in accordance with the rules and decisions of the TSSAA.

[The] TSSAA has not performed a function that has been "traditionally exclusively reserved to the State." The organization of interscholastic sports is neither a traditional nor an exclusive public function of the States. [I]n Tennessee, the State did [not] show an interest in interscholastic athletics until 47 years after the TSSAA had been in existence. . . . Even then, the State Board of Education merely acquiesced in the TSSAA's actions and did not assume the role of regulating interscholastic athletics. The TSSAA no doubt serves the public, particularly the public schools, but the mere provision of a service to the public does not render such provision a traditional and exclusive public function.

It is also obvious that the TSSAA is not an entity created and controlled by the government for the purpose of fulfilling a government objective. [The] State of Tennessee played [no] role in the creation of the TSSAA as a private corporation. [A]lthough the board of control currently is composed of public school officials, [and] public schools currently account for the majority of the TSSAA's membership, this is not required by the TSSAA's constitution.

In addition, the State of Tennessee has not "exercised coercive power [or] provided such significant encouragement [to the TSSAA], either overt or covert," that the TSSAA's regulatory activities must in law be deemed to be those of the State. The State has not promulgated any regulations of interscholastic sports, and [has not] encouraged or coerced the TSSAA in enforcing its recruiting rule. [P]ublic schools do provide a small portion of the TSSAA's funding through their membership dues, but no one argues that these dues are somehow conditioned on the TSSAA's enactment and enforcement of recruiting rules. [E]ven if the TSSAA were dependent on state funding[, mere] financial dependence on the State does not convert the TSSAA's actions into acts of the State. [T]here is no evidence of "joint participation" between the State and the TSSAA in the TSSAA's enforcement of its recruiting rule. The TSSAA's board of control enforces its recruiting rule solely in accordance with the authority granted to it under the contract that each member signs.

[T]here is no "symbiotic relationship" between the State and the TSSAA. [T]he TSSAA's "fiscal relationship with the State is not different from that of many contractors performing services for the government." The TSSAA provides a service — the organization of athletic tournaments — in exchange for membership dues and gate fees, just as a vendor could contract with public schools to sell refreshments at school events. . . .

[T]he majority holds that the combination of factors it identifies evidences "entwinement" of the State with the TSSAA, and that such entwinement converts private action into state action. [This] new "entwinement" theory [lacks] any support in our state-action jurisprudence. . . . Because the majority never defines "entwinement," the scope of its holding is unclear. [T]he majority's new entwinement test [could] affect many organizations that foster activities, enforce rules, and sponsor extracurricular competition among high schools — not just in athletics, but in such diverse areas as agriculture, mathematics, music, marching bands, forensics, and cheerleading. . . . The state-action doctrine was developed to reach only those actions that are truly attributable to the State, not to subject private citizens to the control of federal courts hearing §1983 actions. . . . I respectfully dissent.

Notes and Questions

1. *Private Prisons.* The Commonwealth of Kentucky contracts with a private corrections corporation (Ajax Prison Corporation) to house and rehabilitate prison inmates. An Ajax employee subjects a state prisoner to cruel and inhumane treatment (the employee beat the inmate and led him around on a dog leash). Under such circumstances, does Ajax qualify as a state actor? Does the decision hinge on whether the housing of prisoners is a traditional governmental function?

2. *Is the National Collegiate Athletic Association a "State Actor"?* Jerry Tarkanian, the head basketball coach of the University of Nevada–Las Vegas (UNLV) earned the title "winningest active basketball coach" based on his team's incredible streak of wins. He became a national celebrity when he transformed a mediocre team to the third-place finisher in the National Collegiate Athletic Association (NCAA) final basketball tournament, sometimes referred to as March Madness. After the championship games, the NCAA put the basketball team on probation and threatened additional penalties unless the university severed its ties with the coach. The university informed Tarkanian that he was fired based on 38 violations reported by the NCAA — 10 of which involved the coach. The NCAA is a 960-member unincorporated association, which includes private and state colleges. The coach filed suit against the NCAA, claiming that UNLV delegated its own functions to the NCAA, clothing the association with authority both to adopt rules governing UNLV's athletic programs and to enforce those rules on behalf of UNLV. Is the NCAA a state actor? In National Collegiate Athletic Assn. v. Tarkanian, 488 U.S. 170 (1988), the majority relied on the fact that the NCAA did not have any power to take action directly against Tarkanian as indicating that the NCAA was not a state actor.

C. STATE INVOLVEMENT OR ENCOURAGEMENT

State action may also be found to exist when the government is involved with, or encourages, private action. But what level of government support or encouragement is sufficient? Consider the following cases.

1. Government Regulation

Burton v. Wilmington Parking Authority

365 U.S. 715 (1961)

Mr. Justice CLARK delivered the opinion of the Court.

[T]he Eagle Coffee Shoppe, Inc., a restaurant located within an off-street automobile parking building in Wilmington, Delaware, [refused] to serve appellant food or drink solely because he is a Negro. The parking building is owned and operated by the Wilmington Parking Authority, an agency of the State of Delaware, and the restaurant is the Authority's lessee. Appellant claims that such refusal abridges his rights under the Equal Protection Clause of the Fourteenth Amendment to the United States Constitution. The Supreme Court of Delaware [held] that Eagle was acting in "a purely private capacity" under its lease; that its action was not that of the Authority and was not, therefore, state action within the contemplation of the prohibitions contained in that Amendment. [We conclude] that the exclusion of appellant under the circumstances [present] here was discriminatory state action in violation of the Equal Protection Clause of the Fourteenth Amendment.

The Authority was created by the City of Wilmington pursuant to 22 Del. Code, §§501-515. It is "a public body [exercising] public powers of the State as an agency thereof." Its statutory purpose is to provide adequate parking facilities for the convenience of the public. . . . To secure additional capital[,] and thereby to make bond financing practicable, the Authority decided [to] enter long-term leases [for] commercial use of some of the space available in the projected "garage building." [A] lease [was] made with Eagle Coffee Shoppe, Inc., for [operation of] a "restaurant, dining room, banquet hall, cocktail lounge and bar. . . . " [Eagle's space], although "within the exterior walls of the structure, has no marked public entrance leading from the parking [facility] into the restaurant. . . . " [T]he Authority [agreed to complete] "the decorative finishing of the leased premises and utilities [without] cost to [Eagle]." Eagle [then spent] $220,000 to make the space suitable for its operation. . . . The Authority retained the right to [place] directional signs on the exterior to the let space which would not interfere with or obscure Eagle's display signs. [At] an annual rental of $28,700, Eagle covenanted to "occupy and use the leased premises in accordance with all applicable laws, statutes, ordinances and rules and regulations of any federal, state or municipal authority." Its lease, however, contains no requirement that its restaurant services be made available to the general public on a nondiscriminatory basis, in spite of the fact that the Authority has power to adopt rules and regulations respecting the use of its facilities except any as would impair the security of its bondholders. [T]he Authority [placed signs on the building] indicating the public character of the building, [and flew] state and national flags [on the roof].

[Only] by sifting facts and weighing circumstances can the [involvement] of the State in private conduct be attributed its true significance. . . . The land and building were publicly owned. As an entity, the building was dedicated to "public uses" in performance of the Authority's "essential governmental functions." The costs of land acquisition, construction, and maintenance are defrayed entirely from donations by the City of Wilmington, from loans and revenue bonds and from the proceeds of rentals and parking services out of which the loans and bonds were payable. [T]he commercially leased areas were not surplus state property, but constituted a physically and financially integral and, indeed, indispensable part of the State's plan to operate its project as a self-sustaining unit. Upkeep and maintenance of the building, including necessary repairs, were responsibilities of the Authority and were payable out of public funds. It cannot be doubted that the peculiar relationship of the restaurant to the parking facility in which it is located confers on each an incidental variety of mutual benefits. Guests of the restaurant are afforded a convenient place to park their automobiles, even if they cannot enter the restaurant directly from the parking area. Similarly, its convenience for diners may well provide additional demand for the Authority's parking facilities. Should any improvements effected in the leasehold by Eagle become part of the realty, there is no possibility of increased taxes being passed on to it since the fee is held by a tax-exempt government agency. Neither can it be ignored, especially in view of Eagle's affirmative allegation that for it to serve Negroes would injure its business, that profits earned by discrimination not only contribute to, but also are indispensable elements in, the financial success of a governmental agency.

Addition of all these activities, obligations and responsibilities of the Authority, the benefits mutually conferred, together with the obvious fact that the restaurant is operated as an integral part of a public building devoted to a public parking service, indicates that degree of state participation and involvement in discriminatory action which it was the design of the Fourteenth Amendment to condemn. It is irony amounting to grave injustice that in one part of a single building, erected and maintained with public funds by an agency of the State to serve a public purpose, all persons have equal rights, while in another portion, also serving the public, a Negro is a second-class citizen, offensive because of his race, without rights and unentitled to service. [T]he Authority could have affirmatively required Eagle to discharge the responsibilities under the Fourteenth Amendment imposed upon the private enterprise as a consequence of state participation. But no State may effectively abdicate its responsibilities by either ignoring them or by merely failing to discharge them whatever the motive may be. It is of no consolation to an individual denied the equal protection of the laws that it was done in good faith. . . . By its inaction, the Authority, and through it the State, has not only made itself a party to the refusal of service, but has elected to place its power, property and prestige behind the admitted discrimination. The State has so far insinuated itself into a position of interdependence with Eagle that it must be recognized as a joint participant in the challenged activity, which, on that account, cannot be considered to have been so "purely private" as to fall without the scope of the Fourteenth Amendment.

[W]e hold today [that] when a State leases public property in the manner and for the purpose shown to have been the case here, the proscriptions of the

Fourteenth Amendment must be complied with by the lessee as certainly as though they were binding covenants written into the agreement itself.

The judgment of the Supreme Court of Delaware is reversed and the cause remanded for further proceedings consistent with this opinion.

Reversed and remanded.

Mr. Justice STEWART, concurring.

[The] highest court of Delaware [has] construed this legislative enactment as authorizing discriminatory classification based exclusively on color. Such a law seems to me clearly violative of the Fourteenth Amendment. . . .

Notes and Questions

1. *Racially Segregated Parks.* Gilmore v. City of Montgomery, 417 U.S. 556 (1974), involved the City of Montgomery, Alabama's decision to allow racially segregated schools, and other nonschool groups that allegedly discriminate on the basis of race, to use public park recreational facilities. Petitioners claimed that Montgomery officials were under an affirmative duty to bring about and to maintain a desegregated public school system, and argued that the City's decision to allow the schools and groups to use the parks involved the state in the private discrimination. The Court concluded that, while private schools could use the park, they could not be given exclusive use. Justice Frankfurter dissented: "[T]he city's actions significantly enhanced the attractiveness of segregated private schools, formed in reaction against the federal court school order, by enabling them to offer complete athletic programs. [T]his assistance significantly tended to undermine the federal court order mandating the establishment and maintenance of a unitary school system in Montgomery. It therefore was wholly proper for the city to be enjoined from permitting exclusive access to public recreational facilities by segregated private schools and by groups affiliated with such schools." Justice White concurred: "I [would also] bar the use of city-owned recreation facilities by students from segregated schools for events or occasions that are part of the school curriculum or organized and arranged by the school as part of its own program. I see no difference of substance between this type of use and the exclusive use that the majority agrees may not be permitted consistent with the Equal Protection Clause."

2. *The Segregation Ordinance.* In Peterson v. City of Greenville, 373 U.S. 244 (1963), petitioners were convicted of trespassing for refusing to leave a lunch counter when asked to do so "because integrated service was 'contrary to local customs of segregation at lunch counters' as well as in violation of a Greenville City ordinance requiring separation of the races in restaurants." Petitioners argued that South Carolina had deprived them of equal protection under the Fourteenth Amendment. The Court agreed, finding that the restaurant's action constituted state action: "[T]hese convictions cannot stand, even assuming [that] the manager would have acted as he did independently of the existence of the ordinance. . . . When a state agency passes a law compelling persons to discriminate against other persons because of race, and the State's criminal processes are

employed in a way which enforces the discrimination mandated by that law, such a palpable violation of the Fourteenth Amendment cannot be saved by attempting to separate the mental urges of the discriminators."

3. *The Textbook Loans.* In Norwood v. Harrison, 413 U.S. 455 (1973), the State of Mississippi provided textbooks to private schools that discriminated on the basis of race. The Court held that the state thereby implicated itself in the private discrimination: "An inescapable educational cost . . . is the expense of providing all necessary learning materials. When, as here, that necessary expense is borne by the State, the economic consequence is to give aid to the enterprise; if the school engages in discriminatory practices the State by tangible aid in the form of textbooks thereby gives support to such discrimination. Racial discrimination in state-operated schools is barred by the Constitution and it is also axiomatic that a state may not induce, encourage or promote private persons to accomplish what it is constitutionally forbidden to accomplish."

Moose Lodge v. Irvis
407 U.S. 163 (1972)

Mr. Justice REHNQUIST delivered the opinion of the Court.

Appellee Irvis, a Negro, was refused service by appellant Moose Lodge, a local branch of the national fraternal organization located in Harrisburg, Pennsylvania[, and] then brought this action under 42 U.S.C. §1983. [W]hile conceding the right of private clubs to choose members upon a discriminatory basis, [appellee] asserts that the licensing of Moose Lodge to serve liquor by the Pennsylvania Liquor Control Board amounts to such state involvement with the club's activities as to make its discriminatory practices forbidden by the Equal Protection Clause of the Fourteenth Amendment. The relief sought [was] an injunction forbidding the licensing by the liquor authority of Moose Lodge until it ceased its discriminatory practices. We conclude that Moose Lodge's refusal to serve food and beverages to a guest by reason of the fact that he was a Negro does not, under the circumstances here presented, violate the Fourteenth Amendment. . . .

The Court has never held [that] discrimination by an otherwise private entity would be violative of the Equal Protection Clause if the private entity receives any sort of benefit or service at all from the State, or if it is subject to state regulation in any degree whatever. Since state-furnished services include such necessities of life as electricity, water, and police and fire protection, such a holding would utterly emasculate the distinction between private as distinguished from state conduct set forth in *The Civil Rights Cases*. . . . Our holdings indicate that where the impetus for the discrimination is private, the State must have "significantly involved itself with invidious discriminations," Reitman v. Mulkey, 387 U.S. 369, 380 (1967), in order for the discriminatory action to fall within the ambit of the constitutional prohibition.

Our prior decisions dealing with discriminatory refusal of service in public eating places are significantly different factually from the case now before us.

Peterson v. City of Greenville, 373 U.S. 244 (1963), dealt with the trespass prosecution of persons who "sat in" at a restaurant to protest its refusal of service to Negroes. There the Court held that although the ostensible initiative for the trespass prosecution came from the proprietor, the existence of a local ordinance requiring segregation of races in such places was tantamount to the State having "commanded a particular result." [T]here is no suggestion in this record that the Pennsylvania statutes and regulations governing the sale of liquor are intended either overtly or covertly to encourage discrimination. . . .

Here there is nothing approaching the symbiotic relationship between lessor and lessee that was present in *Burton*. [T]he Moose Lodge [is] on land owned by it, not by any public authority. Far [from] holding itself out as a place of public accommodation, Moose Lodge [ostentatiously] proclaims the fact that it is not open to the public. . . . Nor is it located and operated [in] surroundings that although private in name, it discharges a function or performs a service that would otherwise [be] performed by the State. [W]hile Eagle was a public restaurant in a public building, Moose Lodge is a private social club in a private building.

[T]he Pennsylvania Liquor Control Board plays absolutely no part in establishing or enforcing the membership or guest policies of the club that it licenses to serve liquor. There is no suggestion [that] Pennsylvania law, either as written or as applied, discriminates against minority groups [in] their right to apply for club licenses [or] in their right to purchase and be served liquor in places of public accommodation. The only effect that the state [license] to serve liquor can be said to have on the right of any other Pennsylvanian to buy or be served liquor [is that] club licenses are counted in the maximum number of licenses that may be issued in a given municipality. . . .

The District Court [pointed out] what it considered to be the "pervasive" nature of the regulation of private clubs by the Pennsylvania Liquor Control Board. [A]n applicant for a club license must make such physical alterations in its premises as the board may require, must file a list of the names and addresses of its members and employees, and must keep extensive financial records. The board is granted the right to inspect the licensed premises at any time when patrons, guests, or members are present.

However detailed this type of regulation may be in some particulars, it cannot be said [to] foster or encourage racial discrimination. Nor can it be said to make the State [a] partner or even a joint venturer in the club's enterprise. The limited effect of the prohibition against obtaining additional club licenses when the maximum number of retail licenses allotted to a municipality has been issued, when considered together with the availability of liquor from hotel, restaurant, and retail licensees, falls far short of conferring upon club licensees a monopoly in the dispensing of liquor in any given municipality or in the State as a whole. We therefore hold that, with the exception hereafter noted, the operation of the regulatory scheme enforced by the Pennsylvania Liquor Control Board does not sufficiently implicate the State in the discriminatory guest policies of Moose Lodge to make the latter "state action" within the ambit of the Equal Protection Clause of the Fourteenth Amendment.

[T]he regulations of the Liquor Control Board adopted pursuant to statute affirmatively require that "[e]very club licensee shall adhere to all of the provisions of its Constitution and By-Laws." [Even] though the Liquor Control Board regulation in question is neutral in its terms, the result of its application in a case where the constitution and bylaws of a club required racial discrimination would be to invoke the sanctions of the State to enforce a concededly discriminatory private rule. . . . Shelley v. Kraemer, 334 U.S. 1 (1948), makes it clear that the application of state sanctions to enforce such a rule would violate the Fourteenth Amendment. . . . Appellee was entitled to a decree enjoining the enforcement of §113.09 of the regulations promulgated [insofar] as that regulation requires compliance by Moose Lodge [with] provisions of its constitution and bylaws containing racially discriminatory provisions. . . . The judgment of the District Court is reversed, and the cause remanded with instructions to enter a decree in conformity with this opinion.

Reversed and remanded.

Mr. Justice DOUGLAS, with whom Mr. Justice MARSHALL joins, dissenting.

[Liquor] licenses in Pennsylvania, unlike driver's licenses, or marriage licenses, are not freely available to those who meet racially neutral qualifications. There is a complex quota system [and] the quota for Harrisburg [has] been full for many years. . . . This state-enforced scarcity of licenses restricts the ability of blacks to obtain liquor, for liquor is commercially available only at private clubs for a significant portion of each week. [W]ithout a liquor license a fraternal organization would be hard pressed to survive. . . . Thus, the State of Pennsylvania is putting the weight of its liquor license, concededly a valued and important adjunct to a private club, behind racial discrimination. . . .

Mr. Justice BRENNAN, with whom Mr. Justice MARSHALL joins, dissenting.

When Moose Lodge obtained its liquor license, the State of Pennsylvania became an active participant in the operation of the Lodge bar. Liquor licensing laws [are] primarily pervasive regulatory schemes under which the State dictates and continually supervises virtually every detail of the operation of the licensee's business. . . .

Note and Question: Broadcasters and Advertising

In CBS, Inc. v. Democratic National Committee, 412 U.S. 94 (1973), the Democratic National Committee (DNC) and the Business Executives' Move for Vietnam Peace (BEM), a national organization of businessmen opposed to U.S. involvement in the Vietnam conflict, filed a complaint with the Federal Communications Commission (FCC) against radio station WTOP in Washington, D.C. BEM charged that WTOP refused to sell it time to broadcast a series of one-minute spot announcements expressing BEM views on Vietnam. WTOP, in common with many, but not all, broadcasters, followed a policy of refusing to sell time for spot announcements to individuals and groups who wished to expound their views on controversial issues. WTOP took the position that since it presented full and fair coverage of important public questions, including the Vietnam conflict, it was justified in refusing to accept editorial advertisements. WTOP submitted evidence showing that the station had aired the views of critics of the Vietnam policy on numerous occasions. BEM challenged the fairness of WTOP's coverage. BEM challenged WTOP's action on First Amendment grounds. Is WTOP a "state actor"?

CBS argued that because the nation has a limited number of broadcast frequencies, and the government chooses those on whom licenses are bestowed, state action is implicated. FCC rules and regulations do not require, or prohibit, licensees from broadcasting ads like BEM's. The FCC does regard licensees as "public trustees" who are obligated to broadcast with fairness, balance, and objectivity, but otherwise it grants licensees discretion about what to air. The Court held that a broadcast licensee's refusal to accept a paid editorial advertisement does not constitute "governmental action" for First Amendment purposes. The Court explained that the Government is neither a "partner" to the action complained of nor engaged in a "symbiotic relationship" with the licensee. Under the Communications Act a broadcast licensee is vested with substantial journalistic discretion in deciding how to meet its statutory obligations as a "public trustee." The licensee's policy against accepting editorial advertising is compatible with the Communications Act and with the broadcaster's obligation to provide a balanced treatment of controversial questions. It was a matter within the area of journalistic discretion.

PROBLEM: MORE ON THE TOWN, THE PRIVATE UTILITY, AND THE CLUB

Suppose that Mr. and Mrs. Johnson come to you for legal advice. They would like to bring an equal protection claim against Palm Valley Country Club. How would you advise them? Can they establish state action based on the close relationships among the club, Power House, and Town Orange? Does the club's legal requirement to comply with state liquor license regulations help them?

Reitman v. Mulkey

387 U.S. 369 (1967)

Mr. Justice WHITE delivered the opinion of the Court.

The question here is whether Art. I, §26, of the California Constitution denies "to any person [the] equal protection of the laws" within the meaning of the Fourteenth Amendment of the Constitution of the United States. Section 26 of Art. I, an initiated measure submitted to the people as Proposition 14 in a statewide ballot in 1964, provides in part as follows: "Neither the State nor any subdivision or agency thereof shall deny, limit or abridge, directly or indirectly, the right of any person, who is willing or desires to sell, lease or rent any part or all of his real property, to decline to sell, lease or rent such property to such person or persons as he, in his absolute discretion, chooses." The real property covered by

§26 is limited to residential property and contains an exception for state-owned real estate.

[In *Reitman*,] the Mulkeys who are husband and wife[,] sued under §51 and §52 of the California Civil Code alleging that petitioners had refused to rent them an apartment solely on account of their race. . . . Petitioners moved for summary judgment on the ground that §§51 and 52 [had] been rendered null and void [by] Proposition 14. [In *Prendergast*], respondents [filed] suit [to] enjoin eviction from their apartment [alleging] that the eviction was motivated by racial prejudice. [Petitioner sought a] declaration that he was entitled to terminate the month-to-month tenancy even if his action was based on racial considerations. [T]he California Supreme Court [held in both cases] that Art. I, §26, was invalid as denying the equal protection of the laws guaranteed by the Fourteenth Amendment. . . . We granted certiorari [and] affirm. . . .

[The California Legislature has attempted to prohibit discrimination in various contexts.] It was against this background that Proposition 14 was enacted. Its immediate design and intent [were] "to overturn state laws that bore on the right of private sellers and lessors to discriminate," [and] "to forestall future state action that might circumscribe this right." This aim was successfully achieved: the adoption of Proposition 14 "generally nullifies both [the] Acts as they apply to the housing market," and establishes "a purported constitutional right to privately discriminate on grounds which admittedly would be unavailable under the Fourteenth Amendment should state action be involved."

[Petitioners] contend that the California court [misconstrued] the Fourteenth Amendment [in holding that] the repeal of [a] statute prohibiting racial discrimination, which is constitutionally permissible, may be said to "authorize" and "encourage" discrimination because it makes legally permissible that which was formerly proscribed. [A]s we understand the California court, it did not posit a constitutional violation on the mere repeal of the [California] Acts. . . . What the court [did was to] reject the notion that the State was required to have a statute prohibiting racial discriminations in housing. Second, it held the intent of §26 was to authorize private racial discriminations in the housing market, to repeal [existing] Acts and to create a constitutional right to discriminate on racial grounds in the sale and leasing of real property. Hence, the court dealt with §26 as though it expressly authorized and constitutionalized the private right to discriminate. Third, the court [concluded] that the section would encourage and significantly involve the State in private racial discrimination contrary to the Fourteenth Amendment.

The California court could very reasonably conclude that §26 would and did have wider impact than a mere repeal of existing statutes. Section 26 mentioned [no statute] in so many words. Instead, it announced the constitutional right of any person to decline to sell or lease his real property to anyone to whom he did not desire to sell or lease. [Existing statutes] were thereby *pro tanto* repealed. But the section struck more deeply and more widely. Private discriminations in housing were now not only free from [existing statutes] but they also enjoyed a far different status than was true before the passage of those statutes. The right to discriminate, including the right to discriminate on racial grounds, was now embodied in the State's basic charter, immune from legislative, executive, or judicial regulation at any level of the state government. Those practicing racial discriminations need no longer rely solely on their personal choice. They could now invoke express constitutional authority, free from censure or interference of any kind from official sources. All individuals, partnerships, corporations and other legal entities, as well as their agents and representatives, could now discriminate with respect to their residential real property, which is defined as any interest in real property of any kind or quality, "irrespective of how obtained or financed," and seemingly irrespective of the relationship of the State to such interests in real property. Only the State is excluded with respect to property owned by it.

This Court has never attempted the "impossible task" of formulating an infallible test for determining whether the State "in any of its manifestations" has become significantly involved in private discriminations. . . . Here the California court, armed as it was with the knowledge of the facts and circumstances concerning the passage and potential impact of §26, and familiar with the milieu in which that provision would operate, has determined that the provision would involve the State in private racial discriminations to an unconstitutional degree. We accept this holding. . . .

The assessment of §26 by the California court is similar to what this Court has done in appraising state statutes or other official actions in other contexts. In McCabe v. Atchison, Topeka & Santa Fe Ry. Co., 235 U.S. 151, the Court dealt with a statute [which] authorized carriers to provide cars for white persons but not for Negroes. [T]he Court [held that the] statute was invalid under the Fourteenth Amendment because a carrier refusing equal service to Negroes would be "acting in the matter under the authority of a state law." . . . Nixon v. Condon, 286 U.S. 73, [involved] a statute empowering the executive committee of a political party to prescribe the qualifications of its members for voting or for other participation, but containing no directions with respect to the exercise of that power. . . . Reposing this power in the executive committee was said to insinuate the State into the self-regulatory, decision-making scheme of the voluntary association; the exercise of the power was viewed as an expression of state authority contrary to the Fourteenth Amendment. . . .

None of these cases squarely controls the case we now have before us. But they do illustrate the range of situations in which discriminatory state action has been identified. They do exemplify the necessity for a court to assess the potential impact of official action in determining whether the State has significantly involved itself with invidious discriminations. Here we are dealing with a provision which does not just repeal an existing law forbidding private racial discriminations. Section 26 was intended to authorize, and does authorize, racial discrimination in the housing market. The right to discriminate is now one of the basic policies of the State. The California Supreme Court believes that the section will significantly encourage and involve the State in private discriminations. We have been presented with no persuasive considerations indicating that these judgments should be overturned.

Affirmed.

Mr. Justice DOUGLAS, concurring.

[Proposition 14] is a form of sophisticated discrimination whereby the people of California harness the energies of private groups to do indirectly what they cannot under our decisions allow their government to do. . . .

Mr. Justice HARLAN, whom Mr. Justice BLACK, Mr. Justice CLARK, and Mr. Justice STEWART join, dissenting.

[California,] acting through the initiative and referendum, has decided to remain "neutral" in the realm of private discrimination affecting the sale or rental of private residential property; in such transactions private owners are now free to act in a discriminatory manner previously forbidden to them. [A]ll that has happened is that California has effected a pro tanto repeal of its prior statutes forbidding private discrimination. This runs no more afoul of the Fourteenth Amendment than would have California's failure to pass any such antidiscrimination statutes in the first instance. The fact that such repeal was also accompanied by a constitutional prohibition against future enactment of such laws by the California Legislature cannot well be thought to affect [the] validity of what California has done. The Fourteenth Amendment does not reach such state constitutional action any more than it does a simple legislative repeal of legislation forbidding private discrimination. . . .

∾ PROBLEM: CONSTITUTIONAL AMENDMENTS PERMITTING DISCRIMINATION ∾

After *Reitman*, would it have been possible for California citizens to pass a constitutional amendment permitting private discrimination? If so, how should the amendment have been phrased?

2. *Judicial Involvement*

May the courts enforce private rights without transforming private discrimination into state action? Or does judicial involvement necessarily implicate state action?

Shelley v. Kreamer
334 U.S. 1 (1948)

Mr. Chief Justice VINSON delivered the opinion of the Court.

These cases present [questions] relating to the validity of court enforcement of private agreements, generally described as restrictive covenants, which have as their purpose the exclusion of persons of designated race or color.

[On] February 16, 1911, thirty [of] thirty-nine [property owners signed] an agreement, which was subsequently recorded, providing in part:

[the] said property is hereby restricted to the use and occupancy for the term of Fifty (50) years from this date, so that it shall be a condition [whether] recited and referred to as (sic) not in subsequent conveyances and shall attach to the land, as a condition precedent to the sale of the same, that [no] part of said property or any portion thereof shall [be] occupied by any person not of the Caucasian race, it being intended hereby to restrict the use of said property [against] the occupancy as owners or tenants of any portion of said property for resident or other purpose by people of the Negro or Mongolian Race.

[The] agreement included fifty-seven parcels of land [including the] parcel involved in this case. [F]ive of the parcels in the district were owned by Negroes. . . .

On August 11, 1945, pursuant to [contract], petitioners Shelley, who are Negroes, for valuable consideration received from one Fitzgerald a warranty deed to the parcel in question. The trial court found that petitioners had no actual knowledge of the restrictive agreement at the time of the purchase.

[R]espondents, as owners of other property subject to the terms of the restrictive covenant, brought suit in [state court] praying that petitioners Shelley be restrained from taking possession of the property and that judgment be entered divesting title out of petitioners Shelley and reverting title in the immediate grantor or in such other person as the court should direct. The trial court denied the requested relief. . . .

Petitioners [argue] that judicial enforcement of the restrictive agreements in these cases has violated rights guaranteed to petitioners by the Fourteenth Amendment of the Federal Constitution. . . . Specifically, petitioners urge that they have been denied the equal protection of the laws, deprived of property without due process of law, and have been denied privileges and immunities of citizens of the United States. . . .

[Not] only does the restriction seek to proscribe use and occupancy of the affected properties by members of the excluded class, but [the] agreement requires that title of any person who uses his property in violation of the restriction shall be divested. [The] excluded class is defined wholly in terms of race or color. . . .

[Here] the particular patterns of discrimination [are] determined [by] the terms of agreements among private individuals. [We] conclude [that] the restrictive agreements standing alone cannot be regarded as a violation of any rights guaranteed to petitioners by the Fourteenth Amendment. So long as the purposes of those agreements are effectuated by voluntary adherence to their terms, it would appear clear that there has been no action by the State and the provisions of the Amendment have not been violated.

But [these] are cases in which the purposes of the agreements were secured only by judicial enforcement by state courts of the restrictive terms of the agreements. [R]espondents urge that judicial enforcement of private agreements does not amount to state action; or, in any event, the participation of the State is so attenuated in character as not to amount to state action within the meaning of the Fourteenth Amendment. . . . That the action of state courts and of judicial officers in their official capacities is to be regarded as action of the State within the meaning of the Fourteenth Amendment, is a proposition which has long been established by decisions of this Court. *Ex parte Commonwealth of Virginia,* 1880, 100 U.S. 339. [I]n Strauder v. West Virginia, 1880, 100 U.S. 303, this Court declared invalid a state statute restricting jury service to white persons as amounting to a denial of the equal protection of the laws to the colored defendant in that case. . . . The action of state courts in imposing penalties or depriving parties of other substantive rights without providing adequate notice and opportunity to defend, has, of course, long been regarded as a denial of the due process of law guaranteed by the Fourteenth Amendment. [Moore v. Dempsey, 1923, 261 U.S. 86.]

But the examples of state judicial action which have been held by this Court to violate the Amendment's commands are not restricted to situations in which the judicial proceedings were found in some manner to be procedurally unfair. It has been recognized that the action of state courts in enforcing a substantive common-law rule formulated by those courts, may result in the denial of rights guaranteed by the Fourteenth Amendment, even though the judicial proceedings in such cases may have been in [accord with] procedural due process. [In] Cantwell v. Connecticut, 1940, 310 U.S. 296, a conviction in a state court of the common-law crime of breach of the peace [was] found to be a violation of the Amendment's commands relating to freedom of religion. [F]rom the time of the adoption of the Fourteenth Amendment until the present, it has been the consistent ruling of this Court that the action of the States to which the Amendment has reference, includes action of state courts and state judicial officials. . . .

Against this background of judicial construction, extending over a period of some three-quarters of a century, we are called upon to consider whether enforcement by state courts of the restrictive agreements in these cases may be deemed to be the acts of those States; and, if so, whether that action has denied these petitioners the equal protection of the laws which the Amendment was intended to insure.

We have no doubt that there has been state action in these cases in the full and complete sense of the phrase. The undisputed facts disclose that petitioners were willing purchasers of properties upon which they desired to establish homes. The owners of the properties were willing sellers; and contracts of sale were accordingly consummated. It is clear that but for the active intervention of the state courts, supported by the full panoply of state power, petitioners would have been free to occupy the properties in question without restraint.

These are not cases [in] which the States have merely abstained from action, leaving private individuals free to impose such discriminations as they see fit. Rather, these are cases in which the States have made available to such individuals the full coercive power of government to deny to petitioners, on the grounds of race or color, the enjoyment of property rights in premises which petitioners are willing and financially able to acquire and which the grantors are willing to sell. The difference between judicial enforcement and nonenforcement of the restrictive covenants is the difference to petitioners between being denied rights of property available to other members of the community and being accorded full enjoyment of those rights on an equal footing.

The enforcement of the restrictive agreements by the state courts in these cases was directed pursuant to the common-law policy of the states as formulated by those courts in earlier decisions. In the Missouri case, enforcement of the covenant was directed [by] the highest court of the State after the trial court had determined the agreement to be invalid for want of the requisite number of signatures. . . . The judicial action in each case bears the clear and unmistakable imprimatur of the State. [P]revious decisions of this Court have established the proposition that judicial action is not immunized from the operation of the Fourteenth Amendment simply because it is taken pursuant to the state's common-law policy. Nor is the Amendment ineffective simply because the particular pattern of discrimination, which the State has enforced, was defined initially by the terms of a private agreement. State action [refers] to exertions of state power in all forms. And when the effect of that action is to deny rights subject to the protection of the Fourteenth Amendment, it is the obligation of this Court to enforce the constitutional commands.

We hold that in granting judicial enforcement of the restrictive agreements in these cases, the States have denied petitioners the equal protection of the laws and that, therefore, the action of the state courts cannot stand. [T]he judgment of the Supreme Court of Missouri and the judgment of the Supreme Court of Michigan must be reversed.

Reversed.

Notes and Questions

1. *The Segregated Park.* In Evans v. Newton, 382 U.S. 296 (1966), a U.S. Senator devised land in his will to the City of Macon on condition that the land be reserved as a park for Caucasians. The will stated that, while the Senator had only the kindest feeling for blacks, he believed that the two races should be kept separate. The city kept the park segregated for years, but then began to integrate the park, contending that it was constitutionally impermissible to segregate a public facility. At that point, the trustees of the will sued to remove the city as trustee and to appoint private trustees. The Court concluded that the park could not be segregated whether or not it was in private hands: "[W]here the tradition of municipal control had become firmly established, we cannot take judicial notice that the mere substitution of trustees instantly transferred this park from the public to the private sector. [T]he predominant character and purpose of this park are municipal [and] requires that it be treated as a public institution subject to the command of the Fourteenth Amendment, regardless of who now has title under state law." Justice Harlan, joined by Justice Stewart, dissented: "I do not think that the Fourteenth Amendment permits this Court [to] frustrate the terms of [the] will, now that the [city] is no longer connected [with] the administration of [the park]. The Equal Protection Clause reaches only discriminations that are the product of capricious state action; it does not touch discriminations whose origins and effectuation arise solely out of individual predilections, prejudices, and acts. . . ."

2. *Reclaiming the Park*. Following the decision in *Newton* (see the preceding note), suppose that the Senator's heirs sue to reclaim the park. They claim that, since the Senator's intention to provide a park for whites only cannot be fulfilled, the trust fails and the park reverts by law to the heirs. The petitioners challenge the termination as a violation of equal protection. Does judicial enforcement of the reversion provision constitute discriminatory state action? *See* Evans v. Abney, 396 U.S. 435 (1970).

3. *Damages for Covenant Violations*. Despite *Shelley*'s holding, would it be possible to seek damages for violation of a racially restrictive covenant without there being state action? *See* Barrows v. Jackson, 346 U.S. 249 (1953).

4. *Examining* Shelley. Do you agree with the holding in *Shelley*? Indisputably, the actions of judicial officials in their official capacities constitute governmental action. But, if judicial enforcement of private rights constitutes state action, is it possible to maintain a meaningful distinction between private action and state action? After all, private rights come from the state in the sense that the law (be it constitutional, statutory, or common law) either grants the right or fails to forbid it. Moreover, the essence of a "right" is enforceability in state courts; otherwise, a "right" is not a "right." So, if private individuals have the right to discriminate, should they also have the power to enforce that right in court?

5. Shelley's *Limits*. How far can *Shelley*'s reasoning be pushed? Suppose that a racist couple issues invitations to a dinner party on a racially discriminatory basis. Someone of a different race, who was not invited to the dinner party, decides to crash it. The racists call the police and seek to press charges against the trespassers. Does judicial enforcement of state trespass laws, which under *Shelley* is viewed as involving state support for the discrimination, transform the private discrimination into state-sanctioned discrimination?

◦ PROBLEM: MORE ON THE TOWN, THE PRIVATE UTILITY, AND THE CLUB ◦

If a citizen of Town Orange believes that the town's decision to turn one community pool into a private club and close the other pool involved illegal racial discrimination, would the state action doctrine bar the citizen from suing Town Orange or Power House, Inc.?

Flagg Brothers, Inc. v. Brooks

436 U.S. 149 (1978)

Mr. Justice REHNQUIST delivered the opinion of the Court.

The question presented by this litigation is whether a warehouseman's proposed sale of goods entrusted to him for storage, as permitted by New York Uniform Commercial Code §7-210 (McKinney 1964), is an action properly attributable to the State of New York. . . .

[R]espondent Shirley Brooks and her family were evicted from their apartment in Mount Vernon, N.Y. The city marshal arranged for Brooks' possessions to be stored by petitioner Flagg Brothers, Inc., in its warehouse. Brooks was informed of the cost of moving and storage, and she instructed the workmen to proceed, although she found the price too high. [A]fter a series of disputes over the validity of the charges being claimed[,] Brooks received a letter demanding that her account be brought up to date within 10 days "or your furniture will be sold." [When Brooks was unable to resolve the dispute, she] initiated this class action [under] 42 U.S.C. §1983, seeking damages, an injunction against the threatened sale of her belongings, and the declaration that [a] sale pursuant to §7-210 would violate the Due Process and Equal Protection Clauses of the Fourteenth Amendment. . . . We granted certiorari [to decide] the meaning of "state action" as that term is associated with the Fourteenth Amendment.

[Some] rights established [by] the Constitution or by federal law are protected from both governmental and private deprivation. Although a private person may cause a deprivation of such a right, he may be subjected to liability under §1983 only when he does so under color of law. [M]ost rights secured by the Constitution are protected only against infringement by governments. [R]espondents allege that Flagg Brothers has deprived them of [their] Fourteenth Amendment [right] to be free from state deprivations of property without due process of law. [T]hey must establish not only that Flagg Brothers acted under color of the challenged statute, but also that its actions are properly attributable to the State of New York.

[R]espondents have named no public officials [in] this action. The City Marshal, who supervised their evictions, was dismissed from the case by the consent of all the parties. This total absence of overt official involvement plainly distinguishes this case from earlier decisions imposing procedural restrictions on creditors' remedies such as North Georgia Finishing, Inc. v. Di-Chem, Inc., 419 U.S. 601 (1975); Fuentes v. Shevin, 407 U.S. 67 (1972); Sniadach v. Family Finance Corp., 395 U.S. 337 (1969). In those cases, the Court was careful to point out that the dictates of the Due Process Clause "attac[h] only to the deprivation of an interest encompassed within the Fourteenth Amendment's protection." [T]he only issue presented by this case is whether Flagg Brothers' action may fairly be attributed to the State of New York. We conclude that it may not.

Respondents' primary contention is that New York has delegated to Flagg Brothers a power "traditionally exclusively reserved to the State." They argue that the resolution of private disputes is a traditional function of civil government, and that the State in §7-210 has delegated this function to Flagg Brothers. Respondents [read] too much into [our] previous cases. While many functions have been traditionally performed by governments, very few have been "exclusively reserved to the State."

One such area has been elections. . . . A second line of cases under the public-function doctrine originated with Marsh v. Alabama, 326 U.S. 501 (1946) [involving company towns.] These two branches of the public-function doctrine have in common the feature of exclusivity. Although the elections held by the Democratic Party and its affiliates were the only meaningful elections in Texas, and the streets owned by the Gulf Shipbuilding Corp. were the only streets in Chickasaw, the proposed sale by Flagg Brothers under §7-210 is not the only means of resolving this purely private dispute. Respondent Brooks has never alleged that state law barred her from seeking a waiver of Flagg Brothers' right to sell her goods at the time she authorized their storage. . . . The challenged statute itself provides a damages remedy against the warehouseman for violations of its provisions. This system of rights and remedies, recognizing the traditional place of private arrangements in ordering relationships in the commercial world, can hardly be said to have delegated to Flagg Brothers an exclusive prerogative of the sovereign.

Whatever the particular remedies available under New York law, we do not consider a more detailed description of them necessary to our conclusion that the settlement of disputes between debtors and creditors is not traditionally an exclusive public function. Creditors and debtors have had available to them historically a far wider number of choices than has one who would be an elected public official, or a member of Jehovah's Witnesses who wished to distribute literature in [*Marsh*]. [T]his entire field of activity is outside the scope of *Terry* and *Marsh*. This is true whether these commercial rights and remedies are created by statute or decisional law. . . .

Respondents further urge that Flagg Brothers' proposed action is properly attributable to the State because the State has authorized and encouraged it in enacting §7-210. . . . This Court [has] never held that a State's mere acquiescence in a private action converts that action into that of the State. . . . It is quite immaterial that the State has embodied its decision not to act in statutory form. If New York had no commercial statutes at all, its courts would still be faced with the decision whether to prohibit or to permit the sort of sale threatened here the first time an aggrieved bailor came before them for relief. A judicial decision to deny relief would be no less an "authorization" or "encouragement" of that sale than the legislature's decision embodied in this statute. . . . If the mere denial of judicial relief is considered sufficient encouragement to make the State responsible for those private acts, all private deprivations of property would be converted into public acts whenever the State [denies] relief sought by the putative property owner. [T]he State of New York is in no way responsible for Flagg Brothers' decision, a decision which the State in §7-210 permits but does not compel, to threaten to sell these respondents' belongings. . . .

We conclude that the allegations of these complaints do not establish a violation of these respondents' Fourteenth Amendment rights by either petitioner Flagg Brothers or the State of New York. The District Court properly concluded that their complaints failed to state a claim for relief under 42 U.S.C. §1983. The judgment of the Court of Appeals holding otherwise is

Reversed.

Mr. Justice MARSHALL, dissenting.

[T]he Court approaches the question before us as if it can be decided without reference to the role that the State has always played in lien execution by forced sale. In so doing, the Court treats the State as if it [were] "a monolithic, abstract concept hovering in the legal stratosphere." . . .

Mr. Justice STEVENS, with whom Mr. Justice WHITE and Mr. Justice MARSHALL join, dissenting.

[W]hatever power of sale the warehouseman [has] derives solely from the State, and specifically from §7-210 of the New York Uniform Commercial Code. [T]he Court reasons that the warehouseman's proposed sale is solely private action because the state statute "permits but does not compel" the sale, and because the warehouseman has not been delegated a power "exclusively reserved to the State." Under this approach a State could enact laws authorizing private citizens to use self-help in countless situations. . . . A state statute could [authorize] finance companies to enter private homes to repossess merchandise; [or] could authorize "any person with sufficient physical power," to acquire and sell the property of his weaker neighbor. . . . The Court's rationale would characterize action pursuant to such a statute as purely private action, which the State permits but does not compel, in an area not exclusively reserved to the State.

[T]he distinctions between "permission" and "compulsion" on the one hand, and "exclusive" and "nonexclusive," on the other, cannot be determinative factors in state-action analysis. [T]he State of New York, by enacting §7-210 of the Uniform Commercial Code, has acted in the most effective and unambiguous way a State can act. This section specifically authorizes petitioner Flagg Brothers to sell respondents' possessions; it details the procedures that petitioner must follow; and it grants petitioner the power to convey good title to goods that are now owned by respondents to a third party.

[New York] has authorized the warehouseman to perform what is clearly a state function. The test of what is a state function [is most frequently] presented in terms of whether the State has delegated a function traditionally and historically associated with sovereignty. [T]he Court reasons that state action cannot be found because the State has not delegated to the warehouseman an exclusive sovereign function. This distinction, however, is not consistent with our prior decisions on state action [and] is inconsistent with the line of cases beginning with Sniadach v. Family Finance Corp., 395 U.S. 337.

Since *Sniadach* this Court has scrutinized various state statutes regulating the debtor-creditor relationship for compliance with the Due Process Clause. *See also North Georgia Finishing*, Mitchell v. W. T. Grant Co., [and] *Shevin*. . . . The Court today seeks to explain these findings on the ground [that] there was some element of "overt official involvement." [T]his explanation is baffling. In *North Georgia Finishing*, the official involvement [consisted] of a court clerk who issued a writ of garnishment based solely on the affidavit of the creditor. The clerk's actions were purely ministerial. [*North Georgia Finishing*] must be viewed as reflecting [the] significance of the State's role in defining and controlling the debtor-creditor relationship. . . . In *Shevin* the Court stressed that the statutes in question "abdicate[d] effective state control over state power." [O]f concern [was] the private use of state power to achieve a nonconsensual resolution of a commercial dispute. . . . This same point was made [in] *Mitchell* and *North Georgia Finishing*. Yet the very defect that made the statutes in *Shevin* and *North Georgia Finishing* unconstitutional—lack of state control—is, under today's decision, the factor that precludes constitutional review. . . . If it is unconstitutional for a State to allow a private party to exercise a traditional state power because the state supervision of that power is purely mechanical, the State surely cannot immunize its actions from constitutional scrutiny by removing even the mechanical supervision.

Not only has the State [removed nominal supervision, it has] authorized a private party to exercise a governmental power that is equally, if not more, significant than the power exercised in *Shevin* or *North Georgia Finishing*. In *Shevin,* the Florida statute allowed the debtor's property to be seized and held pending the outcome of the creditor's action for repossession. [I]n *North Georgia Finishing,* the state statute provided for a garnishment procedure which deprived the debtor of the use of property in the garnishee's hands pending the outcome of litigation. The warehouseman's power under §7-210 is far broader. . . . The warehouseman, unquestionably an interested party, [is] authorized by law to resolve any disputes over storage charges finally and unilaterally. [Whether] termed "traditional," "exclusive," or "significant," the state power to order binding, nonconsensual resolution of a conflict between debtor and creditor is exactly the sort of power with which the Due Process Clause is concerned. [T]he State's delegation of that power to a private party is, accordingly, subject to due process scrutiny. . . . [T]his conclusion does not even remotely suggest that "all private deprivations of property [will] be converted into public acts. . . ." The focus is not on the private deprivation but on the state authorization. . . . The State's conduct in this case takes the concrete form of a statutory enactment, and it is that statute that may be challenged. . . .

[T]he overwhelming majority of disputes in our society are resolved in the private sphere. But it is no longer possible, if it ever was, to believe that a sharp line can be drawn between private and public actions. [W]e expect government "to provide a reasonable and fair framework of rules which facilitate commercial transactions. . . ." [The] power to order legally binding surrenders of property and the constitutional restrictions on that power are necessary correlatives in our system. [T]oday's decision allows the State to divorce these two elements by the simple expedient of transferring the implementation of its policy to private parties. . . . I respectfully dissent.

Lugar v. Edmonson Oil Co.
457 U.S. 922 (1982)

Justice WHITE delivered the opinion of the Court.

In 1977, petitioner, a lessee-operator of a truckstop in Virginia, was indebted to his supplier, Edmondson Oil Co., Inc. Edmondson sued on the debt in Virginia state court. Ancillary to that action and pursuant to state law, Edmondson sought prejudgment attachment of certain of petitioner's property. The prejudgment attachment procedure required only that Edmondson allege, in an *ex parte* petition, a belief that petitioner was disposing of or might dispose of his property in order to defeat his creditors. Acting upon that petition, a Clerk of the state court issued a writ of attachment, which was then executed by the County Sheriff. This effectively sequestered petitioner's property, although it was left in his possession. Pursuant to the statute, a hearing on the propriety of the attachment and levy was later conducted. Thirty-four days after the levy, a state trial judge ordered the attachment dismissed because Edmondson had failed to establish the statutory grounds for attachment alleged in the petition.

Petitioner subsequently brought this action under against Edmondson and its president. His complaint alleged that in attaching his property respondents had acted jointly with the State to deprive him of his property without due process of law.

Although the Court of Appeals correctly perceived the importance of *Flagg Brothers* to a proper resolution of this case, it misread that case. It also failed to give sufficient weight to that line of cases, beginning with Sniadach v. Family Finance Corp., 395 U.S. 337 (1969), in which the Court considered constitutional due process requirements in the context of garnishment actions and prejudgment attachments. *See* North Georgia Finishing, Inc. v. Di-Chem, Inc., 419 U.S. 601 (1975); Mitchell v. W. T. Grant Co., 416 U.S. 600 (1974); Fuentes v. Shevin, 407 U.S. 67 (1972). Each of these cases involved a finding of state action as an implicit predicate of the application of due process standards. *Flagg Brothers* distinguished them on the ground that in each there was overt, official involvement in the property deprivation; there was no such overt action by a state officer in *Flagg Brothers.*

As a matter of substantive constitutional law the state-action requirement reflects judicial recognition of the fact that "most rights secured by the Constitution are protected only against infringement by governments."

Careful adherence to the "state action" requirement preserves an area of individual freedom by limiting the reach of federal law and federal judicial power. It also avoids imposing on the State, its agencies or officials, responsibility for conduct for which they cannot fairly be blamed. A major consequence is to require the courts to respect the limits of their own power as directed against state governments and private interests. Whether this is good or bad policy, it is a fundamental fact of our political order.

Our cases have accordingly insisted that the conduct allegedly causing the deprivation of a federal right be fairly attributable to the State. These cases reflect a two-part approach to this question of "fair attribution." First, the deprivation must be caused by the exercise of some right or privilege created by the State or by a rule of conduct imposed by the state or by a person for whom the State is responsible. In *Sniadach, Fuentes, W. T. Grant,* and *North Georgia,* for example, a state statute provided the right to garnish or to obtain prejudgment attachment, as well as the procedure by which the rights could be exercised. Second, the party charged with the deprivation must be a person who may fairly be said to be a state actor. This may be because he is a state official, because he has acted together with or has obtained significant aid from state officials, or because his conduct is otherwise chargeable to the State. Without a limit such as this, private parties could face constitutional litigation whenever they seek to rely on some state rule governing their interactions with the community surrounding them.

Turning to this case, the first question is whether the claimed deprivation has resulted from the exercise of a right or privilege having its source in state authority. The second question is whether, under the facts of this case, respondents, who are private parties, may be appropriately characterized as "state actors."

While private misuse of a state statute does not describe conduct that can be attributed to the State, the procedural scheme created by the statute obviously is the product of state action. This is subject to constitutional restraints and properly may be addressed in a §1983 action, if the second element of the state-action requirement is met as well.

We have consistently held that a private party's joint participation with state officials in the seizure of disputed property is sufficient to characterize that party as a "state actor" for purposes of the Fourteenth Amendment.

The Court of Appeals erred in holding that in this context "joint participation" required something more than invoking the aid of state officials to take advantage of state-created attachment procedures. That holding is contrary to the conclusions we have reached as to the applicability of due process standards to such procedures. Whatever may be true in other contexts, this is sufficient when the State has created a system whereby state officials will attach property on the *ex parte* application of one party to a private dispute.

Chief Justice Burger, dissenting.

Whether we are dealing with suits under §1983 or suits brought pursuant to the Fourteenth Amendment, in my view the inquiry is the same: is the claimed infringement of a federal right fairly attributable to the State. Applying this standard, it cannot be said that the actions of the named respondents are fairly attributable to the State. Respondents did no more than invoke a presumptively valid state prejudgment attachment procedure available to all. Relying on a dubious "but for" analysis, the Court erroneously concludes that the subsequent procedural steps taken by the State in attaching a putative debtor's property in some way transforms respondents' acts into actions of the State. This case is no different from the situation in which a private party commences a lawsuit and secures injunctive relief which, even if temporary, may cause significant injury to the defendant. Invoking a judicial process, of course, implicates the State and its officers but does not transform essentially private conduct into actions of the State.

Notes and Questions

1. *Distinguishing* Lugar *from* Flagg Brothers. Is the primary difference between *Lugar* and *Flagg Brothers* the direct involvement of the sheriff in *Lugar* whereas *Flagg Brothers* involved self-help?

2. *State Workers' Compensation Schemes.* In American Manufacturers Mutual Insurance Company v. Sullivan, 526 U.S. 40 (1999), the Court evaluated whether the decisions of private insurers to defer workers' compensation payments as well as its review process, constituted state action. Prior to the enactment of workers'

compensation laws, employees who suffered work-related injuries or occupational disease could recover compensation from their employers only through common-law tort remedies. Recovery was often difficult because employees were forced to prove negligence and damages. In the early twentieth century, most states created compulsory insurance systems that required employers to compensate employees for work-related injuries without regard to fault. Pennsylvania's Workers' Compensation Act [PWCA] created such a system by forcing employers to obtain insurance or to request permission to self-insure. In an attempt to control costs, the PWCA created a "utilization review" procedure under which the reasonableness and necessity of an employee's past, ongoing, or prospective medical treatment could be reviewed before a medical bill must be paid. If an insurer "disputes the reasonableness or necessity of the treatment provided," it may request a utilization review and withhold the payment. A "utilization review organization" (URO), a private organization consisting of health care providers who are "licensed in the same profession and having the same or similar specialty," then reviews the care and decides whether treatment was reasonable or necessary.

Do the decisions of private insurers to defer payment, and the URO review process, constitute state action? Consider the following arguments: 1) action taken by private entities with the mere approval or acquiescence of the state is not state action; 2) the state authorizes, but does not require, insurers to withhold payments for disputed medical treatment; 3) while the decision of a URO, like that of any judicial official, may properly be considered state action, a private party's mere use of the state's dispute resolution machinery, without the "overt, significant assistance of state officials," cannot; 4) the state has delegated to insurers the traditionally exclusive governmental function of deciding whether to suspend payment for disputed medical treatment; 5) the PWCA "inextricably entangles the insurance companies in a partnership with the Commonwealth such that they become an integral part of the state in administering the statutory scheme"; 6) the relevant state actors, rather than the particular parties to the payment disputes, are the state-appointed decision makers who implement the exclusive procedure that the state has created to protect respondents' rights. The court concluded that an insurer's decision to withhold payment and seek utilization review of the reasonableness and necessity of particular medical treatment was not fairly attributable to the state.

3. *The Welfare Agency and the Abused Boy.* A boy who was being beaten by his father was removed from the home by state-employed social workers but was later returned to the father's care. Subsequently, the boy was beaten again by his father and suffered permanent injuries, including retardation. The petitioner sued the social workers and other local officials, claiming that their failure to remove the boy from a dangerous situation deprived him of his liberty in violation of the Due Process Clause of the Fourteenth Amendment to the U.S. Constitution. Was there sufficient state action to hold the government accountable for the injuries caused by the father? In DeShaney v. Winnebago County, 489 U.S. 189 (1989), the Court found no state action, holding that "nothing in the language of the Due

Process Clause itself requires the State to protect the life, liberty, and property of its citizens against invasion by private actors."

4. *Disguised Merits Decisions.* Doctrines like standing and ripeness (and other justiciability doctrines) have frequently been regarded as "disguised decisions on the merits." In other words, if the Court is disinclined to rule in favor of the plaintiff on the merits, the Court rejects the case on threshold grounds (e.g., standing or ripeness). Does the state action doctrine serve that same function?

Edmonson v. Leesville Concrete Company, Inc.

500 U.S. 614 (1991)

Justice KENNEDY delivered the opinion of the Court.

[Thaddeus Edmonson,] a construction worker, was injured [and] sued Leesville Concrete Company for negligence. . . . During *voir dire*, Leesville used [two] peremptory challenges [to] remove black persons from the prospective jury. [Relying on] Batson v. Kentucky, 476 U.S. 79 (1986), Edmonson, who [is] black, requested that the [court] require Leesville to articulate a race-neutral explanation for striking [the] jurors. The [trial court] denied the request on the ground that *Batson* does not apply in civil proceedings. [A divided court of appeals affirmed.] We granted certiorari and now reverse.

In Powers v. Ohio, 499 U.S. 400 (1991), we held that a criminal defendant, regardless of his or her race, may object to a prosecutor's race-based exclusion of persons from the petit jury. [D]iscrimination on the basis of race in selecting a jury in a civil proceeding harms the excluded juror no less than discrimination in a criminal trial. In either case, race is the sole reason for denying the excluded venireperson the [privilege] of participating in our system of justice.

[The] Constitution's protections of individual liberty and equal protection apply in general only to action by the government. Racial discrimination, though invidious[,] violates the Constitution only when it may be attributed to state action. Thus, the legality of the exclusion [here] turns on the extent to which a litigant in a civil case may be subject to the Constitution's restrictions. . . .

[In prior cases, we asked] first whether the claimed constitutional deprivation resulted from the exercise of a right or privilege having its source in state authority, and second, whether the private party charged with the deprivation could be described in all fairness as a state actor. [T]he first part of [the test] is satisfied here. By their very nature, peremptory challenges have no significance outside a court of law. Their sole purpose is to permit litigants to assist the government in the selection of an impartial trier of fact. [T]here is no constitutional obligation to allow [peremptory challenges which] are permitted [when] the government, by statute or decisional law, [decides] to allow parties to exclude a given number of persons who otherwise would satisfy the requirements for [jury service]. In the case before us, the challenges were exercised under a federal statute. . . . Without this authorization, granted by an Act of Congress[,] Leesville would not have been able to engage in the alleged discriminatory acts.

[The second part of the test focuses on] whether a private litigant in all fairness must be deemed a government actor in the use of peremptory challenges. [I]n determining whether a particular action [is] governmental in character, it is relevant to examine [the] extent to which the actor relies on governmental assistance and benefits, whether the actor is performing a traditional governmental function, and whether the injury caused is aggravated in a unique way by the incidents of governmental authority. Based on [these] principles[,] we hold that the exercise of peremptory challenges [involves] state action.

[O]ur cases have found state action when private parties make extensive use of state procedures with "the overt, significant assistance of state officials." [Without such participation], the peremptory challenge system [could] not exist. . . . In the federal system, Congress has established the qualifications for jury service, and has outlined the procedures by which jurors are selected [including] policies of random juror selection from a fair cross section of the community, and non-exclusion on account of race, color, religion, sex, national origin, or economic status. Statutes prescribe many of the details of the jury plan, defining the jury wheel, voter lists, and jury commissions. A statute also authorizes [procedures] for assignment to grand and petit juries, and for lawful excuse from jury service.

At the outset of the selection process, prospective jurors must complete jury qualification forms. [C]ounsel [rely on these forms] when exercising their peremptory strikes. The clerk of the [court], a federal official, summons potential jurors [who] are required to travel to a United States courthouse, where they must report [at] the direction of the court and its officers. [S]ummoned jurors receive a per diem [for] their service. . . . The trial judge exercises substantial control over *voir dire* in the federal system. The judge determines the range of information that may be discovered about a prospective juror. [J]udges may even conduct [the] *voir dire* [themselves and they] oversee the exclusion of jurors for cause. . . . In cases involving multiple parties, the trial judge decides how peremptory challenges shall be allocated. . . . When a lawyer exercises a peremptory challenge, the judge advises the juror he or she has been excused.

[A] private party could not exercise its peremptory challenges absent the overt, significant assistance of the court. The government summons jurors, constrains their freedom of movement, and subjects them to public scrutiny and examination. The party who exercises a challenge invokes the formal authority of the court, which must discharge the prospective juror, thus effecting the "final and practical denial" of the excluded individual's opportunity to serve on the petit jury. Without the direct and indispensable participation of the judge, who beyond all question is a state actor, the peremptory challenge system would serve no purpose. By enforcing a discriminatory peremptory challenge, the court "has not only made itself a party to the [biased act], but has elected to place its power, property and prestige behind the [alleged] discrimination." In so doing, the government has "create[d] the legal framework governing the [challenged] conduct," and in a significant way has involved itself with invidious discrimination.

[A] traditional function of government is evident here. . . . The jury exercises the power of the court and of the government. [T]he jury [performs] the critical governmental functions of guarding the rights of litigants and "ensur[ing] continued acceptance of the laws by all of the people." In the federal system, the Constitution [commits] the trial of facts in a civil cause to the jury [which] becomes the principal factfinder, charged with weighing the evidence, judging the credibility of witnesses, and reaching a verdict. The jury's factual determinations as a general rule are final. [I]n all jurisdictions a true verdict will be incorporated in a judgment enforceable by the court. These are traditional functions of government, not of a select, private group beyond the reach of the Constitution.

If a government confers on a private body the power to choose the government's employees or officials, the private body will be bound by the constitutional mandate of race neutrality. [Terry v. Adams, 345 U.S. 461 (1953). This applies] with even greater force in the context of jury selection through the use of peremptory challenges. . . . The fact that the government delegates some portion of this power to private litigants does not change the governmental character of the power exercised. The delegation of authority [occurs] here through explicit statutory authorization. . . . The selection of jurors represents a unique governmental function delegated to private litigants by the government and attributable to the government for purposes of invoking constitutional protections against discrimination. . . .

[I]n most civil cases, the initial decision whether to sue at all, the selection of counsel, and any number of ensuing tactical choices in the course of discovery and trial may be without the requisite governmental character to be deemed state action. That cannot be said of the exercise of peremptory challenges, however; when private litigants participate in the selection of jurors, they serve an important function within the government and act with its substantial assistance. If peremptory challenges based on race were permitted, persons could be required by summons to be put at risk of open and public discrimination as a condition of their participation in the justice system. The injury to excluded jurors would be the direct result of governmental delegation and participation. [T]he injury caused by the discrimination is made more severe because the government permits it to occur within the courthouse itself. . . . Within the courtroom, the government invokes its laws to determine the rights of those who stand before it. . . . Race discrimination within the courtroom raises serious questions as to the fairness of the proceedings conducted there. Racial bias mars the integrity of the judicial system and prevents the idea of democratic government from becoming a reality. . . . To permit racial exclusion in this official forum compounds the racial insult inherent in judging a citizen by the color of his or her skin. . . .

The judgment is reversed, and the case is remanded for further proceedings consistent with our opinion.

It is so ordered.

Justice O'CONNOR, with whom THE CHIEF JUSTICE and Justice SCALIA join, dissenting.

[Not] everything that happens in a courtroom is state action. [A] civil trial is by design largely a stage on which private parties may act; it is a forum through which they can resolve their disputes in a peaceful and ordered manner. The government erects the platform; it does not thereby become responsible for all that occurs upon it. As much as we would like to eliminate [from] the courtroom the specter of racial discrimination, the Constitution does not sweep that broadly. Because I believe that a peremptory strike by a private litigant is fundamentally a matter of private choice and not state action, I dissent.

[The] peremptory challenge [allows] *private* parties, to exclude potential jurors [and] is left wholly within the discretion of the litigant. . . . The peremptory is, by design, an enclave of private action in a government-managed proceeding. [T]his evidence is irrelevant. . . . The bulk of the practices the Court describes — the establishment of qualifications for jury service, the location and summoning of prospective jurors, the jury wheel, the voter lists, the jury qualification forms, the per diem for jury service — are independent of the statutory entitlement to peremptory strikes. [T]he Government would do these things even if there were no peremptory challenges. . . .

[The] judge does not "encourage" the use of a peremptory challenge at all. The decision to strike a juror is entirely up to the litigant, and the reasons for doing so are of no consequence to the judge. . . . The judge does little more than acquiesce in this decision by excusing the juror. . . . The [action] here is a far cry [from] Shelley v. Kraemer, 334 U.S. 1 (1948). . . . The state courts in *Shelley* used coercive force to impose conformance on parties who did not wish to discriminate. "Enforcement" of peremptory challenges [does] not compel anyone to discriminate; the discrimination is wholly a matter of private choice. Judicial acquiescence does not convert private choice into that of the State. . . .

[In] Polk County v. Dodson, 454 U.S. 312 (1981)[, we] held that a public defender [does] not act under color of state law when representing a defendant in a criminal trial. [G]overnment employment is not sufficient to create state action. . . . Attorneys for private litigants do not act on behalf of the government, or even the public as a whole; attorneys represent their clients. [A] peremptory strike is a traditional adversarial act; parties use these strikes to further their own perceived interests, not as an aid to the government's process of jury selection. . . . The government does not encourage or approve these strikes, or direct that they be used in any particular way, or even that they be used at all. The government is simply not "responsible" for the use of peremptory strikes by private litigants. . . .

Racism is a terrible thing[,] particularly [in] a courtroom. . . . But [the] Fifth Amendment's Due Process Clause prohibits only actions for which the Government can be held responsible. . . . The Government is not responsible for a peremptory challenge by a private litigant. . . .

Justice SCALIA, dissenting.

[The] Court's newly discovered constitutional rule [will] not necessarily [help] minority litigants [obtain] racially diverse juries. [A] minority defendant can no longer seek to prevent an all-white jury, or to seat as many jurors of his own race as possible. [P]eremptory challenges [are] sometimes used to *assure* rather than to *prevent* a racially diverse jury. . . .

Note and Question: Physician Contracted to Provide Care for Prison Inmates

A private physician contracts with a state prison to provide medical care for the inmates. The physician is not on the state payroll, but instead is paid on a contract basis. However, inmates are allowed to use only this physician. Does the doctor's care constitute "state action" if he exhibits "deliberate indifference" to the medical needs of inmates? In West v. Atkins, 487 U.S. 42 (1988), the court held that "the dispositive issue concerns the relationship among the State, the physician, and the prisoner. Contracting out prison medical care does not relieve the State of its constitutional duty to provide adequate medical treatment to those in its custody, and it does not deprive the State's prisoners of the means to vindicate their Eighth Amendment rights. The State bore an affirmative obligation to provide adequate medical care to West; the State delegated that function to respondent Atkins; and respondent voluntarily assumed that obligation by contract. . . . Doctor Atkins must be considered to be a state actor."

3. Government Funding

Blum v. Yaretsky
457 U.S. 991 (1982)

Justice REHNQUIST delivered the opinion of the Court.

Respondents represent a class of Medicaid patients challenging decisions by the nursing homes in which they reside to discharge or transfer patients without notice or an opportunity for a hearing. The question is whether the State may be held responsible for those decisions so as to subject them to the strictures of the Fourteenth Amendment. Congress established the Medicaid program in 1965 as Title XIX of the Social Security Act, 42 U.S.C. §1396, to provide federal financial assistance to states that choose to reimburse certain medical costs incurred by the poor. As a participating state, New York provides Medicaid assistance to eligible persons who receive care in private nursing homes, which are designated as either "skilled nursing facilities" (SNF's) or "health related facilities" (HRF's). The latter provide less extensive, and generally less expensive, medical care than the former. Nursing homes chosen by Medicaid patients are directly reimbursed by the State for the reasonable cost of health care services.

An individual must meet two conditions to obtain Medicaid assistance. He must satisfy eligibility standards defined in terms of income or resources and he must seek medically necessary services. To assure that the latter condition is satisfied, federal regulations require each nursing home to establish a utilization review committee (URC) of physicians whose functions include periodically assessing whether each patient is receiving the appropriate level of care, and thus whether the patient's continued stay in the facility is justified. If the URC determines that the patient should be discharged or transferred to a different level of care, either more or less intensive, it must notify the state agency responsible for administering Medicaid assistance.

[Respondents were Medicaid] patients in the American Nursing Home, an SNF located in New York City. [T]he nursing home's URC decided that respondents did not need the care they were receiving and should be transferred to a lower level of care in an HRF. New York City officials, [responsible] for administering the Medicaid program[,] were notified of this decision and prepared to reduce or terminate payments to the nursing home for respondents' care. Following administrative hearings, state social service officials affirmed the decision. . . . Respondents then commenced this suit, [individually and as a class, alleging that] the defendants had not afforded them adequate notice either of URC decisions and the reasons supporting them or of their right to an administrative hearing to challenge those decisions. Respondents [alleged a violation of the] Due Process Clause of the Fourteenth Amendment [and] sought injunctive relief and damages. [The District Court issued various orders and court of appeals affirmed]. We granted certiorari to consider the Court of Appeals' conclusions about the nature of state action. . . .

[R]espondents are not challenging particular state regulations or procedures, and their arguments concede that the decision to discharge or transfer a patient originates not with state officials, but with nursing homes that are privately owned and operated. Their lawsuit, therefore, seeks to hold state officials liable for the actions of private parties, and the injunctive relief they have obtained requires the State to adopt regulations that will prohibit the private conduct of which they complain.

This case is obviously different from those cases in which the defendant is a private party and the question is whether his conduct has sufficiently received the imprimatur of the State so as to make it "state" action for purposes of the Fourteenth Amendment. It also differs from other "state action" cases in which the challenged conduct consists of enforcement of state laws or regulations by state officials who are themselves parties in the lawsuit; in such cases the question typically is whether the private motives which triggered the enforcement of those laws can fairly be attributed to the State. . . .

"[T]he mere fact that a business is subject to state regulation does not by itself convert its action into that of the State for purposes of the Fourteenth Amendment." Jackson v. Metropolitan Edison Co., 419 U.S., at 350. The complaining party must also show that "there is a sufficiently close nexus between the State and the challenged action of the regulated entity so that the action of the latter may be fairly treated as that of the State itself." The purpose of this requirement is to assure that constitutional standards are invoked only when it can be said that the State is *responsible* for the specific conduct of which the plaintiff complains. [A] State normally can be held responsible for a private decision only when it has exercised coercive power or has provided such significant encouragement, either overt or covert, that the choice must in law be deemed to be that of the State. Mere approval of or acquiescence in the initiatives of a private party is not sufficient to justify holding the State responsible for those initiatives under the terms of the Fourteenth Amendment. [The] required nexus may be present if the private entity has exercised powers that are "traditionally the exclusive prerogative of the State."

[The] finding of state action cannot stand. The court reasoned that state action was present in the discharge or transfer decisions [because] the State responded to those decisions by adjusting the patient's Medicaid benefits. Respondents, however, do not challenge the adjustment of benefits, but the discharge or transfer of patients to lower levels of care without adequate notice or hearings. That the State responds to such actions by adjusting benefits does not render it *responsible* for those actions. The decisions [are] made by physicians and nursing home administrators, all of whom are concededly private parties. There is no suggestion that those decisions were influenced in any degree by the State's obligation to adjust benefits in conformity with changes in the cost of medically necessary care.

Respondents [argue] that the State "affirmatively commands" the summary discharge or transfer of Medicaid patients who are thought to be inappropriately placed in their nursing facilities. . . . The regulations [require] SNF's and HRF's "to make all efforts possible to transfer patients to the appropriate level of care or home as indicated by the patient's medical condition or needs." The nursing homes are required to complete patient care assessment forms designed by the State and "provide the receiving facility or provider with a current copy of same at the time of discharge to an alternate level of care facility or home." [The] regulations do not require the nursing homes to rely on the forms in making discharge or transfer decisions, nor do they demonstrate that the State is responsible for the decision to discharge or transfer particular patients. Those decisions ultimately turn on medical judgments made by private parties according to professional standards that are not established by the State. . . .

Respondents [point] to regulations which, they say, impose a range of penalties on nursing homes that fail to discharge or transfer patients whose continued stay is inappropriate. [T]hose regulations themselves do not dictate the decision to discharge or transfer in a particular case. Consequently, penalties imposed for violating the regulations add nothing to respondents' claim of state action.

[R]espondents argue that even if the State does not command the transfers at issue, it reviews and either approves or rejects them on the merits. [N]othing in the regulations authorizes the officials to approve or disapprove decisions either to retain or discharge particular patients, and petitioners specifically disclaim any such responsibility. . . .

Finally, respondents [argue] that such a relationship exists between the State and the nursing homes it regulates that the State may be considered a joint participant in the homes' discharge and transfer of Medicaid patients. . . . Respondents argue that state subsidization of the operating and capital costs of the facilities, payment of the medical expenses of more than 90% of the patients in the facilities, and the licensing of the facilities by the State, taken together convert the action of the homes into "state" action. [We are] unable to agree. [P]rivately owned enterprises providing services that the State would not necessarily provide, even though they are extensively regulated, do not fall within the ambit of *Burton*. That programs undertaken by the State result in substantial funding of the activities of a private entity is no more persuasive than the fact of regulation of such an entity in demonstrating that the State is responsible for decisions made by the entity in the course of its business.

We are also unable to conclude that the nursing homes perform a function that has been "traditionally the exclusive prerogative of the State." Respondents [argue] that both the Medicaid statute and the New York Constitution make the State responsible for providing every Medicaid patient with nursing home services. . . . Even if respondents' characterization of the State's duties were correct, [it] would not follow that decisions made in the day-to-day administration of a nursing home are the kind of decisions traditionally and exclusively made by the sovereign for and on behalf of the public. . . .

We conclude that respondents have failed to establish "state action" in the nursing homes' decisions to discharge or transfer Medicaid patients to lower levels of care. . . . The contrary judgment of the Court of Appeals is accordingly
 Reversed.

Justice BRENNAN, with whom Justice MARSHALL joins, dissenting.

[T]he level-of-care decisions at issue in this case, even when characterized as the "independent" decision of the nursing home, have far less to do with the exercise of independent professional judgment than they do with the *State's* desire to save money. To be sure, standards for implementing the level-of-care scheme established by the Medicaid program are framed with reference to the underlying purpose of that program — to provide needed medical services. [N]ot surprisingly, the State relies on doctors to implement this aspect of its Medicaid program. But [the] two levels of long-term institutionalized care enshrined in the Medicaid scheme are legislative constructs, designed to serve governmental cost-containment policies. . . . The vigor with which these reviews are performed in the nursing home context is extraordinarily *un* medical in character. From a purely medical standpoint, the idea of shifting nursing home residents from a "higher level of care" to a "lower level of care," which almost invariably involves transfer from one facility to another, rarely makes sense. [T]he proportion of SNF and ICF beds varied enormously from State to State. [T]he answer to this disparity lies not in medical considerations or judgments, but rather in the varying fiscal policies, and the vigor of enforcement, in the participating States. . . .

[T]he State established the system of treatment levels and utilization review in order to further its own fiscal goals, [but] the state (and Federal Government) have created, and administer, the level system as a cost-saving tool of the Medicaid program. The impetus for this active program of review imposed upon the nursing home operator is primarily this fiscal concern. The State has set forth precisely the standards upon which the level-of-care determinations are to be made, and has delegated administration of the program to the nursing home operators, rather than assume the burden of administering the program itself. "[T]hese requirements [make] the State responsible for actual decisions to discharge or transfer particular patients." Where [a] private party acts on behalf of the State to implement state policy, his action is state action.

[The] private nursing homes of the Nation exist, and profit, at the sufferance of state and federal Medicaid and Medicare agencies. . . . The State subsidizes practically all of the operating and capital costs of the facility, and pays the medical expenses of more than 90% of its residents. And, in setting reimbursement rates, the State generally affords the nursing homes a profit as well. [T]he residents of those homes [are] utterly dependent on the State for their support and their placement. For many, the totality of their social network is the nursing home community. Within that environment, the nursing home operator is the immediate authority, the provider of food, clothing, shelter, and health care, and, in every significant respect, the functional equivalent of a State. [W]e must be especially alert to those situations in which the State "has elected to place its power, property and prestige behind" the actions of the nursing home owner.

[T]he State has not simply left nursing home patients to the care of nursing home operators. [N]ursing homes are "pervasively regulated" by State and Federal Governments; virtually every action by the operator is subject to state oversight. . . . We are confronted with the question *preliminary* to any Fourteenth Amendment challenge: whether the State has brought its force to bear against the plaintiffs through the office [of] private parties. [W]hen the State chooses to [perform] governmental undertakings through private institutions, and with the aid of private parties, not every action of those private parties is state action. [W]hen the State directs, supports, and encourages those private parties to take specific action, that is state action. . . .

4. Quasi-Governmental Corporations

Should the actions of a quasi-governmental corporation be regarded as the actions of the government (e.g., state action) or the actions of a private corporation? Consider the following case.

Lebron v. National Railroad Passenger Corporation
115 S.Ct. 961 (1995).

Justice SCALIA delivered the opinion of the Court.

In this case we consider whether actions of the National Railroad Passenger Corporation, commonly known as Amtrak, are subject to the constraints of the Constitution.

Petitioner, Michael A. Lebron, creates billboard displays that involve commentary on public issues. [In] 1991, he contacted Transportation Displays, Incorporated (TDI), which manages the leasing of the billboards in Amtrak's Pennsylvania Station in New York City, seeking to display an advertisement on a billboard of colossal proportions, known to New Yorkers as "the Spectacular." The Spectacular is a curved, illuminated billboard, approximately 103 feet long and 10 feet high, which dominates the main entrance to Penn Station's waiting room and ticket area.

[Lebron] signed a contract with TDI to display an advertisement on the Spectacular for two months beginning in January 1993. The contract provided that "[a]ll advertising copy is subject to approval of TDI and [Amtrak] as to character, text, illustration, design and operation." Lebron declined to disclose the specific content of his advertisement throughout his negotiations with TDI, although he did explain to TDI that it was generally political. [H]e submitted to TDI (and TDI later forwarded to Amtrak) [the following advertisement]: "The work is a photomontage, accompanied [by] text. Taking off on a widely circulated Coors beer advertisement which proclaims Coors to be the 'Right Beer,' Lebron's piece is captioned 'Is it the Right's Beer Now?' It includes photographic images of convivial drinkers of Coors beer, juxtaposed with a Nicaraguan village scene in which peasants are menaced by a can of Coors that hurtles towards them, leaving behind a trail of fire, as if it were a missile. [The] text, appearing on either end of the montage, criticizes the Coors family for its support of right-wing causes, particularly the contras in Nicaragua. Again taking off on Coors' advertising which uses the slogan of 'Silver Bullet' for its beer cans, the text proclaims that Coors is 'The Silver Bullet that aims The Far Right's political agenda at the heart of America.'" Amtrak's vice president disapproved the advertisement, invoking Amtrak's policy, inherited from its predecessor as landlord of Penn Station, the Pennsylvania Railroad Company, "that it will not allow political advertising on the [S]pectacular advertising sign." Lebron then filed suit against Amtrak and TDI, claiming, *inter alia*, that the refusal to place his advertisement on the Spectacular had violated his First and Fifth Amendment rights. . . .

[A]ctions of private entities can sometimes be regarded as governmental action for constitutional purposes. [Congress] established Amtrak in order to avert the threatened extinction of passenger trains in the United States. The statute that created it begins with the congressional finding [that] "the public convenience and necessity require the continuance and improvement" of railroad passenger service. Rail Passenger Service Act of 1970 (RPSA). . . . Amtrak is incorporated under the District of Columbia Business Corporation Act, but is subject to the provisions of that Act only insofar as the RPSA does not provide to the contrary. It does provide to the contrary with respect to many matters of structure and power, including the manner of selecting the company's board of directors. The RPSA provides for a board of nine members, six of whom are appointed directly by the President of the United States. The Secretary of Transportation, or his designee, sits *ex officio*. The President appoints three more directors with the advice and consent of the Senate, selecting one from a list of individuals recommended by the Railway Labor Executives Association, one "from among the Governors of States with an interest in rail transportation," and one as a "representative of business with an interest in rail transportation." [The] President appoints two additional directors without the involvement of the Senate, choosing them from a list of names submitted by various commuter rail authorities. . . . The holders of Amtrak's preferred stock select two more directors. . . . Since the United States presently holds all of Amtrak's preferred stock, which it received [in] exchange for its subsidization of Amtrak's perennial losses, the Secretary of Transportation selects these two directors. The ninth member of the board is Amtrak's president, who serves as the chairman of the board, is selected by the other eight directors, and serves at their pleasure. Amtrak's four private shareholders have not been entitled to vote in selecting the board of directors since 1981. . . . Amtrak is required to submit three different annual reports to the President and Congress. One of these, a "report on the effectiveness of this chapter in meeting the requirements for a balanced national transportation system, together with any legislative recommendations," is made part of the Department of Transportation's annual report to Congress. . . .

Amtrak claims that, whatever its relationship with the Federal Government, its charter's disclaimer of agency status prevents it from being considered a Government entity. . . . Section 541 is assuredly dispositive of Amtrak's status as a Government entity for purposes of matters [within] Congress' control — for example, whether it is subject to statutes that impose obligations or confer powers upon Government entities, such as the Administrative Procedure Act, the Federal Advisory Committee Act, and the laws governing Government procurement. [E]ven beyond that, [the] statutory disavowal of Amtrak's agency status deprives Amtrak of sovereign immunity from suit, and of the ordinarily presumed power of Government agencies authorized to incur obligations to pledge the credit of the United States. But it is not for Congress to make the final determination of Amtrak's status as a government entity for purposes of determining the constitutional rights of citizens affected by its actions. [W]e conclude that it is an agency or instrumentality of the United States for the purpose of individual rights guaranteed against the Government by the Constitution.

This conclusion seems to us in accord with public and judicial understanding of the nature of Government-created and -controlled corporations over the years. A remarkable feature of the heyday of those corporations, in the 1930's and 1940's, was that, even while they were praised for their status "as agencies separate and distinct, administratively and financially and legally, from the government itself, [which] has facilitated their adoption of commercial methods of accounting and financing, avoidance of political controls, and utilization of regular procedures of business management," it was fully acknowledged that they were a "device" of "government," and constituted "federal corporate agencies" apart from "regular government departments." [This] Court has shared that view. For example, in Reconstruction Finance Corp. v. J.G. Menihan Corp., 312 U.S. 81 (1941), Chief Justice Hughes, writing for the Court, described the RFC, whose organic statute did not state it to be a Government instrumentality, as, nonetheless, "a corporate agency of the government," and said that "it acts as a governmental agency in performing its functions." [Even] Congress itself appeared to acknowledge [that] Government-created and -controlled corporations were part of the Government. . . . From the 1930's onward, many of the statutes creating Government-controlled corporations said explicitly that they were agencies or instrumentalities of the United States. . . . That Government-created and -controlled corporations are (for many purposes at least) part of the Government itself has a strong basis, not merely in past practice and understanding, but in reason itself. It surely cannot be that government, state or federal, is able to evade the most solemn obligations imposed in the Constitution by simply resorting to the corporate form. On that thesis, Plessy v. Ferguson, 163 U.S. 537 (1896), can be resurrected by the simple device of having the State of Louisiana operate segregated trains through a state-owned Amtrak. . . .

Amtrak was created by a special statute, explicitly for the furtherance of federal governmental goals. [S]ix of the corporation's eight externally named directors (the ninth is named by a majority of the board itself) are appointed directly by the President of the United States — four of them (including the Secretary of Transportation) with the advice and consent of the Senate. Although the statute restricts most of the President's choices to persons suggested by certain organizations or persons having certain qualifications, those restrictions have been tailor-made by Congress for this entity alone. They do not in our view establish an absence of control by the Government as a whole, but rather constitute a restriction imposed by one of the political branches upon the other. Moreover, Amtrak is not merely in the temporary control of the Government (as a private corporation whose stock comes into federal ownership might be); it is established and organized under federal law for the very purpose of pursuing federal governmental objectives, under the direction and control of federal governmental appointees. It is in that respect no different from the so-called independent regulatory agencies such as the Federal Communications Commission or the Securities Exchange Commission, which are run by Presidential appointees with fixed terms. It is true that the directors of Amtrak, unlike commissioners of independent regulatory agencies, are not, by the explicit terms of the statute, removable by the President for cause, and are not impeachable by Congress. But any reduction in the immediacy of accountability for Amtrak directors vis-a-vis regulatory commissioners seems to us of minor consequence for present purposes — especially since, by the very terms of the chartering Act, Congress's "right to repeal, alter, or amend this chapter at any time is expressly reserved."

[W]here, as here, the Government creates a corporation by special law, for the furtherance of governmental objectives, and retains for itself permanent authority to appoint a majority of the directors of that corporation, the corporation is part of the Government for purposes of the First Amendment. We express no opinion as to whether Amtrak's refusal to display Lebron's advertisement violated that Amendment. . . . The judgment of the Court of Appeals is reversed, and the case is remanded for further proceedings consistent with this opinion.

It is so ordered.

Justice O'CONNOR, dissenting.

[I] see no basis to impute to the Government Amtrak's decision to disapprove Lebron's advertisement. Although a number of factors indicate the Government's pervasive influence in Amtrak's management and operation, none suggest that the Government had any effect on Amtrak's decision to turn down Lebron's proposal. The advertising policy that allegedly violates the First Amendment originated with a predecessor to Amtrak, the wholly private Pennsylvania Railroad Company. . . . Amtrak simply continued this policy after it took over. The specific decision to disapprove Lebron's advertising was made by

Amtrak's Vice President of Real Estate and Operations Development, who, as a corporate officer, was neither appointed by the President nor directed by the President-appointed board to disapprove Lebron's proposal. [The] particular lease which permitted Amtrak to disallow Lebron's billboard was neither reviewed nor approved directly by the board. . . . In short, nothing in this case suggests that the Government controlled, coerced, or even influenced Amtrak's decision, made pursuant to corporate policy and private business judgment, to disapprove the advertisement proposed by Lebron. [T]he Court of Appeals properly [did] not impute Amtrak's decision to the Government. . . .

Notes and Questions

1. *U.S. Olympic Committee.* Should the U.S. Olympic Committee (USOC), another quasi-governmental corporation, be regarded as a "state actor" when it engages in discrimination on the basis of sexual orientation? The facts reveal that Congress has authorized the USOC to assume responsibility for coordinating amateur athletics (something not previously coordinated by the government), granted the USOC a corporate charter, and provided for some USOC funding through exclusive use of the Olympic words and symbols, and through direct grants. However, the USOC functions independently of the government, which played no role in the decision to discriminate (other than acquiescence). In evaluating the USOC's status, should it matter that the USOC is the nation's "exclusive representative to the International Olympic Committee (IOC)," that membership in the IOC is "structured according to nations," that athletes are viewed as representing their nations (e.g., athletes never say that they want to win "for the USOC" but instead say that they want to win "for the United States"), or that "Olympic participation is inescapably nationalist"? Also, should it matter that the Olympic pageant is nation focused — with athletes wearing national costumes, the raising of national flags and the playing of national anthems at the medal ceremony, and an official tally of medals won by each national team reinforcing the national significance of Olympic participation? Is the USOC acting "privately," or is it more like the company town in *Marsh*? Or is it more like the NCAA in *NCAA v. Tarkanian*?

In San Francisco Arts & Athletics, Inc. v. United States Olympic Committee, 483 U.S. 522 (1987), the Court found that the USOC was not a state actor. The Court stated that government "normally can be held responsible for a private decision only when it has exercised coercive power or has provided such significant encouragement, either overt or covert, that the choice must in law be deemed to be that of the [government]." The Court reasoned that the "USOC's choice of how to enforce its exclusive right to use the word 'Olympic' simply is not a governmental decision. There is no evidence that the Federal Government coerced or encouraged the USOC in the exercise of its right. At most, the Federal Government, by failing to supervise the USOC's use of its rights, can be said to exercise '[m]ere approval of or acquiescence in the initiatives' of the USOC. This is not enough to make the USOC's actions those of the Government."

2. *Reconsidering Prior Decisions After* Brentwood. Would the Court's "entwinement" test in *Brentwood* require a different result in previously decided cases? Consider the following cases: a) Moose Lodge v. Irvis, in which the state granted a liquor license to a racially exclusive club. The evidence revealed that only a limited number of licenses were available, and the allotment had been exhausted. Moose Lodge conceded that it would be extremely difficult for a club to survive without a liquor license; b) *Jackson*, in which a utility service terminated service to a delinquent customer; c) *Rendall-Kohn*, in which a teacher was fired from a private school. The overwhelming majority of the school's students were referred to the school, and their tuition was paid for, by the government. In addition, the teacher was hired using government funds; d) Blum v. Yaretsky, in which a nursing home patient was reclassified and reassigned to a different facility.

3. *Restructuring Amtrak?* Could the government have structured Amtrak in such a way as to prevent its actions from being labeled as "state action"? If so, how?

∿ PROBLEM: MORE ON THE TOWN, THE PRIVATE UTILITY, AND THE CLUB ∿

Based on your reading of *Blum* and *Lebron*, if Town Orange initiated the creation of Power House and holds a 50 percent interest in the company, is Power House now a state actor? What if Town Orange appoints a percentage of the board of directors?

Points to Remember

- As a general rule, under the U.S. Constitution, only state actors can be held responsible for the violation of constitutional rights.
- There are four categories of exceptions for which the courts have held that there is state action and thus that the Constitution applies to private conduct:
  (1) the Thirteenth Amendment (this is the one clear exception, which applies to the state and individuals alike);
  (2) private actors performing public or *government functions*;
  (3) the *authorization,* encouragement, or enforcement of private action by the state; and
  (4) the *entanglement* or joint participation of state and private actors.
- The narrow, modern view of state action is that the courts will find state action only when:
  - the private organization is performing *a traditional and exclusive state function*;
  - the level of entanglement has risen to the level of a *symbiotic relationship*; or

- there is not only passive regulation but also active authorization, encouragement, and enforcement, to the point of almost requiring commandment.
- In 1982, the Court articulated two similar, but distinctive, modern tests for the fourth exception — namely, the *Lugar* and *Blum* tests.
  (1) In *Lugar*, the Court stated that:
    - "the deprivation must be caused by the exercise of some right or privilege created by the state or by a person for whom the state is responsible" and
    - "the party charged with the deprivation must be a person who may fairly be said to be a state actor."
  (2) In *Blum*, the Court held that the state will be responsible for private conduct if:
    - the state "has provided such significant encouragement . . . that the choice must in law be deemed that of the state" or
    - the state's coercive power backed the private action.
- Recently, the Supreme Court created a hybrid category, *entwinement*. The Court used this idea in a case that would not satisfy the narrow, modern test's three prongs individually but that had aspects of all three (state function, entanglement, and authorization) to such a degree that there was "such a close nexus between the State and the challenged action that seemingly private behavior [could] be fairly treated as that of the State itself."

7

Procedural Due Process

U.S. CONSTITUTION, FIFTH AMENDMENT

No person shall be . . . deprived of life, liberty, or property, without due process of law. . . .

U.S. CONSTITUTION, FOURTEENTH AMENDMENT

. . . nor shall any State deprive any person of life, liberty, or property, without due process of law. . . .

∾ PROBLEM: THE PROFESSOR AND THE AMSTERDAM TRIP ∾

A sociology professor routinely teaches a course about public mores and social attitudes toward sex. As part of the course, he takes a group of students to Amsterdam, Netherlands, so that they can view the red-light district and observe the free use of marijuana. While in Amsterdam, the professor holds discussions with his students about what they have seen. One student, on condition of anonymity, reports to the university that the professor made sexually suggestive comments to her.

The university's Office of Discrimination investigated the complaint and decided that there was no sexual harassment in the strict sense. However, the investigating official concluded (based on discussions with the complaining student) that the professor really should have been a bit more discreet in how he talked with students about the controversial issues raised in his course. The investigating official did not discuss the student's allegations with the professor. No other student made a similar complaint.

The dean of the college has indicated his intention to remove the professor from the class and to prohibit the professor from going on overnight trips with his students. From the professor's perspective, these proposed actions would have substantial professional repercussions. In addition to precluding the professor from taking students on the Amsterdam trip, he could not take research trips with his students or go with them to academic conferences (to support them when they are making presentations). Because of the potential impact on his career, the professor demands a full-scale adversary hearing at which he would be entitled to "confront the witnesses against him." The university is reluctant to provide the professor with such a hearing because it doubts that the complaining student would be willing to testify.

As you work your way through this chapter, consider whether the professor is entitled to a due process hearing. If you decide that he is, think about the type of hearing to which he might be entitled.

A. LEGISLATIVE DETERMINATIONS

For procedural due process purposes, a distinction is made between so-called "legislative" determinations and "adjudicative" determinations. Consider the following two cases.

Bi-Metallic Investment Co. v. State Board of Equalization
239 U.S. 441 (1915)

Mr. Justice HOLMES delivered the opinion of the Court.

This is a suit to enjoin the State Board of Equalization and the Colorado Tax Commission from putting in force and the defendant Pitcher, as assessor of Denver, from obeying, an order of the boards, increasing the valuation of all taxable property in Denver 40 per cent. The order was sustained and the suit directed to be dismissed by the supreme court of the state. The plaintiff is the owner of real estate in Denver and [contends] that it was given no opportunity to be heard, and that therefore its property will be taken without due process of law, contrary to the 14th Amendment of the Constitution of the United States. . . .

[W]e assume that the constitutional question is presented in the baldest way, — that neither the plaintiff nor the assessor of Denver, who presents a brief on the plaintiff's side, nor any representative of the city and county, was given an opportunity to be heard, other than such as they may have had by reason of the fact that the time of meeting of the boards is fixed by law. On this assumption it is obvious that injustice may be suffered if some property in the county already has been valued at its full worth. But if certain property has been valued at a rate different from that generally prevailing in the county, the owner has had his opportunity to protest and appeal as usual in our system of taxation, so that it must be assumed that the property owners in the county all stand alike. The question, then, is whether all individuals have a constitutional right to be heard before a matter can be decided in which all are equally concerned, — here, for instance, before a superior board decides that the local taxing officers have adopted a system of undervaluation throughout a county, as notoriously often has been the case. The answer of this court in the *State R. Tax Cases*, 92 U.S. 575, 23 L.Ed. 663, at least, as to any further notice, was that it was hard to believe that the proposition was seriously made.

Where a rule of conduct applies to more than a few people, it is impracticable that everyone should have a direct voice in its adoption. The Constitution does not require all public acts to be done in town meeting or an assembly of the whole. General statutes within the state power are passed that affect the person or property of individuals, sometimes to the point of ruin, without giving them a chance to be heard. Their rights are protected in the only way that they can be in a complex society, by their power, immediate or remote, over those who make the rule. If the result in this case had been reached, as it might have been by the state's doubling the rate of taxation, no one would suggest that the 14th Amendment was violated unless every person affected had been allowed an opportunity to raise his voice against it before the body intrusted by the state Constitution with the power. In considering this case in this court we must assume that the proper state machinery has been used, and the question is whether, if the state Constitution had declared that Denver had been undervalued as compared with the rest of the state, and had decreed that for the current year the valuation should be 40 per cent higher, the objection now urged could prevail. It appears to us that to put the question is to answer it. There must be a limit to individual argument in such matters if government is to go on. [*See*] Londoner v. Denver, 210 U.S. 373.

Judgment affirmed.

Londoner v. City of Denver

210 U.S. 373 (1908)

Mr. Justice MOODY delivered the opinion of the Court.

The plaintiffs in error [challenge a tax assessment] for the cost of paving a street upon which the lands abutted. The [Colorado Supreme Court] held that the tax was assessed in conformity with the Constitution and laws of the state, and its decision of that question is conclusive. . . .

The tax [was] assessed under [the] charter of the city of Denver, which confers upon the city the power to make local improvements and to assess the cost upon property specially benefitted. . . . The board of public works, upon the petition of a majority of the owners of the frontage to be assessed, may order the paving of a street. The board [must] recommend to the city council a form of ordinance authorizing it, and establishing an assessment district, which is not amendable by the council. The council may then, in its discretion, pass or refuse to pass the ordinance. If the ordinance is passed, the contract for the work is made by the mayor. [The Board then assesses] the cost upon the landowners after due notice and opportunity for hearing.

[T]he board took the first step by transmitting to the council the resolution to do the work and the form of an ordinance authorizing it. . . . That ordinance, after reciting a compliance by the board with the charter in other respects, and that "certain petitions for said improvements were first presented to the said board, subscribed by the owners of a majority of the frontage to be assessed for said improvements, as by the city charter required," enacted "That, upon consideration of the premises, by city council doth find that, in their action and proceedings in relation to said Eighth avenue paving district Number 1, the said board of public works has fully complied with the requirements of the city charter relating thereto." The state supreme court held that the determination of the city council was conclusive that a proper petition was filed, and that decision must be accepted by us as the law of the state. The only question for this court is whether the charter provision authorizing such a finding, without notice to the landowners, denies to them due process of law. We think it does not. The proceedings, from the beginning up to and including the passage of the ordinance authorizing the work, did not include any assessment or necessitate any assessment, although they laid the foundation for an assessment, which might or might not subsequently be made. [A]ll this might validly be done without hearing to the landowners, provided a hearing upon the assessment itself is afforded. Voigt v. Detroit, 184 U.S. 115. The legislature might have authorized the making of improvements by the city council without any petition. . . .

The fifth assignment [raises] the question whether the assessment was made without notice and opportunity for hearing to those affected by it, thereby denying to them due process of law. . . . After the improvement was completed, the board of public works, in compliance with §29 of the charter, certified to the city clerk a statement of the cost, and an apportionment of it to the lots of land to be assessed. Thereupon the city clerk . . . published a notice, stating, *inter alia,* that the written complaints or objections of the owners, if filed within thirty days, would be "heard and determined by the city council before the passage of any ordinance assessing the cost." Those interested, therefore, were informed that if they reduced their complaints and objections to writing, and filed them within thirty days, those complaints and objections would be heard, and would be heard before any assessment was made. [T]he notice purported only to fix the time for filing the complaints and objections, and to inform those who should file them that they would be heard before action. . . .

In the assessment, apportionment, and collection of taxes upon property within their jurisdiction, the Constitution of the United States imposes few restrictions upon the states. In the enforcement of such restrictions as the Constitution does impose, this court has regarded substance, and not form. [W]here the legislature of a state, instead of fixing the tax itself, commits to some subordinate body the duty of determining whether, in what amount, and upon whom it shall be levied, and of making its assessment and apportionment, due process of law requires that, at some stage of the proceedings, before the tax becomes irrevocably fixed, the taxpayer shall have an opportunity to be heard, of which he must have notice, either personal, by publication, or by a law fixing the time and place of the hearing. Hagar v. Reclamation Dist. No. 108, 111 U.S. 701. . . .

If it is enough that, under such circumstances, an opportunity is given to submit in writing all objections to and complaints of the tax to the board, then there was a hearing afforded in the case at bar. But we think that something more than that, even in proceedings for taxation, is required by due process of law. Many requirements essential in strictly judicial proceedings may be dispensed with in proceedings of this nature. But even here a hearing, in its very essence, demands that he who is entitled to it shall have the right to support his allegations by argument, however brief: and, if need be, by proof, however informal. Pittsburgh, C.C. & St. L. R. Co. v. Backus, 154 U.S. 421.

It is apparent that such a hearing was denied to the plaintiffs in error. The denial was by the city council, which, while acting as a board of equalization, represents the state. The assessment was therefore void, and the plaintiffs in error were entitled to a decree discharging their lands from a lien on account of it. It is not now necessary to consider the tenth assignment of error.

Judgment reversed.

∾ PROBLEMS ∾

1. *The State Income Tax.* Your state legislature decides to enact a statute providing for a state income tax (or, if your state already has a state income tax, it decides to increase the tax by 1 percent). Taxpayers claim a due process right to a hearing before the legislature regarding the wisdom and desirability of enacting the tax (or the tax increase, as the case may be). Under *Londoner* and *Bi-Metallic,* do taxpayers have a right to notice and an opportunity to be heard before the tax is imposed?

2. *An Individual Taxpayer's Bill.* In the preceding problem, after the tax (or tax increase) is adopted and goes into effect, the state assesses a taxpayer $10,000 for taxes. Does the individual taxpayer have the right to notice and an opportunity to be heard regarding the amount of his taxes?

3. Londoner *Assessments.* In *Londoner,* once the assessments are made, does the taxpayer have a due process right to challenge the amount of tax levied on his property?

B. ADJUDICATIVE DETERMINATIONS

Londoner and *Bi-Metallic* suggest that legislative determinations are generally not subject to due process protections. What about individual adjudicative-type determinations? Are they subject to procedural due process protections?

1. Foundational Principles

BACKGROUND
Privilege Cases?

Under the Court's pre-*Goldberg* jurisprudence, a distinction was made between the deprivation of so-called "privileges" and the deprivation of life, liberty, or property. As a general rule, there was no right to a hearing when the deprivation of a privilege was involved.

Under both the Fifth Amendment and the Fourteenth Amendment, however, there is a constitutional right to be heard prior to the deprivation of "life, liberty, or property." This right applies when the state seeks to deprive someone of liberty (e.g., through imprisonment), property (e.g., through fines), or life (e.g., through capital punishment). The difficulty is that, in the modern welfare society, many "rights" or "benefits" that citizens possess do not necessarily qualify as "property." The question is whether individuals have the right to a hearing before being deprived of these benefits.

Goldberg v. Kelly

397 U.S. 254 (1970)

Mr. Justice BRENNAN delivered the opinion of the Court.

[This] action was brought [by] residents of New York City receiving financial aid under the federally assisted program of Aid to Families with Dependent Children (AFDC) or under New York State's general Home Relief program. Their complaint alleged that the New York State and New York City officials administering these programs terminated, or were about to terminate, such aid without prior notice and hearing, thereby denying them due process of law. At the time the suits were filed there was no requirement of prior notice or hearing of any kind before termination of financial aid. However, the State and city adopted procedures for notice and hearing after the suits were brought, and the [appellees challenged] the constitutional adequacy of those procedures.

The State Commissioner of Social Services amended the State Department of Social Services' Official Regulations to require that local social services officials proposing to discontinue or suspend a recipient's financial aid do so according to a procedure that conforms to either subdivision (a) or subdivision (b) of §351.26 of the regulations as amended. The City of New York elected to promulgate a local procedure according to subdivision (b). . . .

Pursuant to subdivision (b), the New York City Department of Social Services promulgated Procedure No. 68-18. A caseworker who has doubts about the recipient's continued eligibility must first discuss them with the recipient. If the caseworker concludes that the recipient is no longer eligible, he recommends termination of aid to a unit supervisor. If the latter concurs, he sends the recipient a letter stating the reasons for proposing to terminate aid and notifying him that within seven days he may request that a higher official review the record, and may support the request with a written statement prepared personally or with the aid of an attorney or other person. If the reviewing official affirms the determination of ineligibility, aid is stopped immediately and the recipient is informed by letter of the reasons for the action. 'Appellees' challenge to this procedure emphasizes the absence of any provisions for the personal appearance of the recipient before the reviewing official, for oral presentation of evidence, and for confrontation and cross-examination of adverse witnesses. [T]he letter does inform the recipient that he may request a post-termination "fair hearing." This is a proceeding before an independent state hearing officer at which the recipient may appear personally, offer oral evidence, confront and cross-examine the witnesses against him, and have a record made of the hearing. If the recipient prevails at the "fair hearing" he is paid all funds erroneously withheld. A recipient whose aid is not restored by a "fair hearing" decision may have judicial review. The recipient is so notified.

The constitutional issue to be decided [is] the narrow one whether the Due Process Clause requires that the recipient be afforded an evidentiary hearing before the termination of benefits. The District Court held that only a pretermination evidentiary hearing would satisfy the [Constitution], and rejected the argument [that] the combination of the post-termination "fair hearing" with the informal pre-termination review disposed of all due process claims. . . .

Appellant does not contend that procedural due process is not applicable to the termination of welfare benefits. Such benefits are a matter of statutory entitlement for persons qualified to receive them.[1] Their termination involves state action that adjudicates important rights. The constitutional challenge cannot be answered by an argument that public assistance benefits are "a 'privilege' and not a 'right.'" Relevant constitutional restraints apply as much to the withdrawal of public assistance benefits as to disqualification for unemployment compensation, or to denial of a tax exemption, or to discharge from public employment. The extent to which procedural due process must be afforded the recipient is influenced by the extent to which he may be "condemned to suffer grievous loss," and depends upon whether the recipient's interest in avoiding that loss outweighs the governmental interest in summary adjudication. Accordingly, as we said in Cafeteria & Restaurant Workers Union v. McElroy, 367 U.S. 886 (1961), "consideration of what procedures due process may require under any given set of circumstances must begin with a determination of the precise nature of the government function involved as well as of the private interest that has been affected by governmental action."

---

1. It may be realistic today to regard welfare entitlements as more like 'property' than a 'gratuity.' Much of the existing wealth in this country takes the form of rights that do not fall within traditional common-law concepts of property. . . . Many of the most important of these entitlements now flow from government: subsidies to farmers and businessmen, routes for airlines and channels for television stations; long term contracts for defense, space, and education; social security pensions for individuals. Such sources of security, whether private or public, are no longer regarded as luxuries or gratuities; to the recipients they are essentials, fully deserved, and in no sense a form of charity. It is only the poor whose entitlements, although recognized by public policy, have not been effectively enforced." Reich, *Individual Rights and Social Welfare: The Emerging Legal Issues*, 74 Yale L.J. 1245, 1225 (1965).

It is true, of course, that some governmental benefits may be administratively terminated without affording the recipient a pre-termination evidentiary hearing. But [when] welfare is discontinued, only a pre-termination evidentiary hearing provides the recipient with procedural due process. For qualified recipients, welfare provides the means to obtain essential food, clothing, housing, and medical care. Thus the crucial factor in this context — a factor not present in the case of the blacklisted government contractor, the discharged government employee, the taxpayer denied a tax exemption, or virtually anyone else whose governmental entitlements are ended — is that termination of aid pending resolution of a controversy over eligibility may deprive an eligible recipient of the very means by which to live while he waits. Since he lacks independent resources, his situation becomes immediately desperate. His need to concentrate upon finding the means for daily subsistence, in turn, adversely affects his ability to seek redress from the welfare bureaucracy.

Moreover, important governmental interests are promoted by affording recipients a pre-termination evidentiary hearing. From its founding the Nation's basic commitment has been to foster the dignity and well-being of all persons within its borders. We have come to recognize that forces not within the control of the poor contribute to their poverty. This perception, against the background of our traditions, has significantly influenced the development of the contemporary public assistance system. Welfare, by meeting the basic demands of subsistence, can help bring within the reach of the poor the same opportunities that are available to others to participate meaningfully in the life of the community. At the same time, welfare guards against the societal malaise that may flow from a widespread sense of unjustified frustration and insecurity. Public assistance, then, is not mere charity, but a means to "promote the general Welfare, and secure the Blessings of Liberty to ourselves and our Posterity." The same governmental interests that counsel the provision of welfare, counsel as well its uninterrupted provision to those eligible to receive it; pre-termination evidentiary hearings are indispensable to that end.

Appellant does not challenge the force of these considerations but argues that they are outweighed by countervailing governmental interests in conserving fiscal and administrative resources. These interests, the argument goes, justify the delay of any evidentiary hearing until after discontinuance of the grants. Summary adjudication protects the public fisc by stopping payments promptly upon discovery of reason to believe that a recipient is no longer eligible. Since most terminations are accepted without challenge, summary adjudication also conserves both the fisc and administrative time and energy by reducing the number of evidentiary hearings actually held.

[T]hese governmental interests are not overriding in the welfare context. The requirement of a prior hearing doubtless involves some greater expense, and the benefits paid to ineligible recipients pending decision at the hearing probably cannot be recouped, since these recipients are likely to be judgment-proof. But the State is not without weapons to minimize these increased costs. Much of the drain on fiscal and administrative resources can be reduced by developing procedures for prompt pre-termination hearings and by skillful use of personnel and facilities. Indeed, the very provision for a post-termination evidentiary hearing in New York's Home Relief program is itself cogent evidence that the State recognizes the primacy of the public interest in correct eligibility determinations and therefore in the provision of procedural safeguards. Thus, the interest of the eligible recipient in uninterrupted receipt of public assistance, coupled with the State's interest that his payments not be erroneously terminated, clearly outweighs the State's competing concern to prevent any increase in its fiscal and administrative burdens. As the District Court correctly concluded, "[t]he stakes are simply too high for the welfare recipient, and the possibility for honest error or irritable misjudgment too great, to allow termination of aid without giving the recipient a chance, if he so desires, to be fully informed of the case against him so that he may contest its basis and produce evidence in rebuttal." . . .

Affirmed.

Mr. Justice BLACK, dissenting.

In the last half century the United States, along with many [other] nations of the world, has moved far toward becoming a welfare state, that is, a nation that for one reason or another taxes its most affluent people to help support, feed, clothe, and shelter its less fortunate citizens. The result is that today more than nine million men, women, and children in the United States receive some kind of state or federally financed public assistance in the form of allowances or gratuities, generally paid them periodically, usually by the week, month, or quarter. Since these gratuities are paid on the basis of need, the list of recipients is not static, and some people go off the lists and others are added from time to time. These ever-changing lists put a constant administrative burden on government and it certainly could not have reasonably anticipated that this burden would include the additional procedural expense imposed by the Court today.

[The] more than a million names on the relief rolls in New York, and the more than nine million names on the rolls of all the 50 States were not put there at random. The names are there because state welfare officials believed that those people were eligible for assistance. Probably[,] many names were put there erroneously in order to alleviate immediate suffering, and undoubtedly some people are drawing relief who are not entitled under the law to do so. Doubtless some draw relief checks from time to time who know they are not eligible. . . . Many of those who thus draw undeserved gratuities are without sufficient property to enable the government to collect back from them any money they wrongfully receive. But the Court today holds that it would violate the Due Process Clause of the Fourteenth Amendment to stop paying those people weekly or monthly allowances unless the government first affords them a full "evidentiary hearing" even though welfare officials are persuaded that the recipients are not rightfully entitled to receive a penny under the law. [A]lthough some recipients might be on the lists [because] of deliberate fraud on their part, [the] government is helpless and must continue, until after an evidentiary hearing, to pay money that it does not owe, never has owed, and never could owe. I do not believe there is any provision in our Constitution that should thus paralyze the government's efforts to protect itself against making payments to people who are not entitled to them.

[The] Court [relies] upon the Fourteenth Amendment and in effect says that failure of the government to pay a promised charitable instalment to an individual deprives that individual of his own property, in violation of the Due Process Clause of the Fourteenth Amendment. It somewhat strains credulity to say that the government's promise of charity to an individual is property belonging to that individual when the government denies that the individual is honestly entitled to receive such a payment. [T]oday's result doesn't depend on the language of the Constitution itself or the principles of other decisions, but solely on the collective judgment of the majority as to what would be a fair and humane procedure in this case.

[I] know of no situation in our legal system in which the person alleged to owe money to another is required by law to continue making payments to a judgment-proof claimant without the benefit of any security or bond to insure that these payments can be recovered if he wins his legal argument. . . .

Notes

1. *Due Process for Contract Professors*. *Goldberg* dramatically expanded the potential application of the Due Process Clause, and subsequent cases were required to determine the scope of the due process guarantee. For example, in Board of Regents v. Roth, 408 U.S. 564 (1972), an assistant professor was hired by state university for a fixed term of one academic year. When he was informed that he would not be rehired for the next academic year, the Court held that he was not entitled to a hearing before the decision not to renew was made: "to determine whether due process requirements apply in the first place, we must look not to the 'weight' but to the nature of the interest at stake. We must look to see if the interest is within the Fourteenth Amendment's protection of liberty and property. [T]he Court has fully and finally rejected the wooden distinction between 'rights' and 'privileges' that once seemed to govern the applicability of procedural due process rights. The Court has also made clear that the property interests protected by procedural due process extend well beyond actual ownership of real estate, chattels, or money. . . . 'While this court has not attempted to define with exactness the liberty [guaranteed] (by the Fourteenth Amendment), the term [denotes] not merely freedom from bodily restraint but also the right of the individual to contract, to engage in any of the common occupations of life, to acquire useful knowledge, to marry, establish a home and bring up children, to worship God according to the dictates of his own conscience, and generally to enjoy those privileges long recognized [as] essential to the orderly pursuit of happiness by free men.' In a Constitution for a free people, there can be no doubt that the meaning of 'liberty' must be broad indeed. . . . There might be cases in which a State refused to re-employ a person under such circumstances that interests in liberty would be implicated. But this is not such a case. The State, in declining to rehire the respondent, did not make any charge against him that might seriously damage his standing and associations in his community. . . . Similarly, there is no suggestion that the State [imposed] on him a stigma or other disability that foreclosed his

freedom to take advantage of other employment opportunities. . . . To be sure, the respondent has alleged that the nonrenewal of his contract was based on his exercise of his right to freedom of speech. But this allegation is not now before us. [O]n the record before us, all that clearly appears is that the respondent was not rehired for one year at one university. It stretches the concept too far to suggest that a person is deprived of 'liberty' when he simply is not rehired in one job but remains as free as before to seek another. . . . The Fourteenth Amendment's procedural protection of property is a safeguard of the security of interests that a person has already acquired in specific benefits. . . . To have a property interest in a benefit, a person clearly must have more than an abstract need or desire for it. He must have more than a unilateral expectation of it. He must, instead, have a legitimate claim of entitlement to it. . . . Just as the welfare recipients' 'property' interest in welfare payments was created and defined by statutory terms, so the respondent's 'property' interest in employment at Wisconsin State University–Oshkosh was created and defined by the terms of his appointment. Those terms . . . specifically provided that the respondent's employment was to terminate on June 30. They did not provide for contract renewal absent 'sufficient cause.' Indeed, they made no provision for renewal whatsoever. . . . Thus, the terms of the respondent's appointment secured absolutely no interest in re-employment for the next year. They supported absolutely no possible claim of entitlement to re-employment. . . . In these circumstances, the respondent surely had an abstract concern in being rehired, but he did not have a property interest sufficient to require the University authorities to give him a hearing when they declined to renew his contract of employment." Justice Douglas dissented, arguing that Roth was entitled to a hearing because of a suspected infringement of his First Amendment rights.

2. *The Bitter with the Sweet? Roth* seemed to suggest that an individual's right to a hearing should be determined by the law creating that right. In Arnett v. Kennedy, 416 U.S. 134 (1974), a plurality of the Court affirmed that idea when it suggested that the legislature could limit and condition an individual's right to a hearing: "[W]here the grant of a substantive right is inextricably intertwined with the limitations on the procedures which are to be employed in determining that right, a litigant in the position of appellee must take the bitter with the sweet." However, in Cleveland Board of Education v. Loudermill, 470 U.S. 532 (1985), the Court reversed itself and rejected the "bitter with the sweet" approach because it "misconceives the constitutional guarantee. [T]he Due Process Clause provides that certain substantive rights — life, liberty, and property — cannot be deprived except pursuant to constitutionally adequate procedures. . . . The right to due process 'is conferred, not by legislative grace, but by constitutional guarantee. While the legislature may elect not to confer a property interest in [public] employment, it may not constitutionally authorize the deprivation of such an interest, once conferred, without appropriate procedural safeguards.' Arnett v. Kennedy, *supra*, 416 U.S., at 167 (Powell, J., concurring). . . . In short, once it is determined that the Due Process Clause applies, 'the question remains what process is due.' The answer to that question is not to be found in the Ohio statute."

Justice Rehnquist dissented: "[The Court] ignores our duty under *Roth* to rely on state law as the source of property interests for purposes of applying the Due Process Clause of the Fourteenth Amendment."

Paul v. Davis
424 U.S. 693 (1976)

Mr. Justice REHNQUIST delivered the opinion of the Court.

[Petitioner Edgar] Paul is the Chief of Police of the Louisville, Ky., Division of Police, while petitioner McDaniel occupies the same position in the Jefferson County, Ky., Division of Police. In late 1972 they agreed to combine their efforts for the purpose of alerting local area merchants to possible shoplifters who might be operating during the Christmas season. In early December petitioners distributed to approximately 800 merchants in the Louisville metropolitan area a "flyer," which began as follows: "TO: BUSINESS MEN IN THE METROPOLITAN AREA The Chiefs of The Jefferson County and City of Louisville Police Departments, in an effort to keep their officers advised on shoplifting activity, have approved the attached alphabetically arranged flyer of subjects known to be active in this criminal field. This flyer is being distributed to you, the business man, so that you may inform your security personnel to watch for these subjects. These persons have been arrested during 1971 and 1972 or have been active in various criminal fields in high density shopping areas. Only the photograph and name of the subject is shown on this flyer, if additional information is desired, please forward a request in [writing]." The flyer consisted of five pages of "mug shot" photos, arranged alphabetically. [In] approximately the center of page 2 there appeared photos and the name of the respondent, Edward Charles Davis III.

Respondent appeared on the flyer because on June 14, 1971, he had been arrested in Louisville on a charge of shoplifting. He had been arraigned on this charge in September 1971, and, upon his plea of not guilty, the charge had been "filed away with leave (to reinstate)," a disposition which left the charge outstanding. Thus, at the time petitioners caused the flyer to be prepared and circulated respondent had been charged with shoplifting but his guilt or innocence of that offense had never been resolved. Shortly after circulation of the flyer the charge against respondent was finally dismissed by a judge of the Louisville Police Court.

At the time the flyer was circulated respondent was employed as a photographer by the Louisville Courier-Journal and Times. The flyer, and respondent's inclusion therein, soon came to the attention of respondent's supervisor, the executive director of photography for the two newspapers. This individual called respondent in to hear his version of the events leading to his appearing in the flyer. Following this discussion, the supervisor informed respondent that although he would not be fired, he "had best not find himself in a similar situation" in the future.

Respondent thereupon brought this §1983 action in the District Court for the Western District of Kentucky, seeking redress for the alleged violation of rights guaranteed to him by the Constitution of the United States. . . .

Respondent's due process claim is grounded upon his assertion that the flyer, and in particular the phrase "Active Shoplifters" appearing at the head of the page upon which his name and photograph appear, impermissibly deprived him of some "liberty" protected by the Fourteenth Amendment. His complaint asserted that the "active shoplifter" designation would inhibit him from entering business establishments for fear of being suspected of shoplifting and possibly apprehended, and would seriously impair his future employment opportunities. . . .

[The] words "liberty" and "property" as used in the Fourteenth Amendment do not in terms single out reputation as a candidate for special protection over and above other interests that may be protected by state law. While we have in a number of our prior cases pointed out the frequently drastic effect of the "stigma" which may result from defamation by the government in a variety of contexts, this line of cases does not establish the proposition that reputation alone, apart from some more tangible interests such as employment, is either "liberty" or "property" by itself sufficient to invoke the procedural protection of the Due Process Clause. [While] not uniform in their treatment of the subject, we think that the weight of our decisions establishes no constitutional doctrine converting every defamation by a public official into a deprivation of liberty within the meaning of the Due Process Clause of the Fifth or Fourteenth Amendment.

[It] is apparent from our decisions that there exists a variety of interests which are difficult of definition but are nevertheless comprehended within the meaning of either "liberty" or "property" as meant in the Due Process Clause. These interests attain this constitutional status by virtue of the fact that they have been initially recognized and protected by state law, and we have repeatedly ruled that the procedural guarantees of the Fourteenth Amendment apply whenever the State seeks to remove or significantly alter that protected status. In Bell v. Burson, 402 U.S. 535 (1971), for example, the State by issuing drivers' licenses recognized in its citizens a right to operate a vehicle on the highways of the State. The Court held that the State could not withdraw this right without giving petitioner due process. In Morrissey v. Brewer, 408 U.S. 471 (1972), the State afforded parolees the right to remain at liberty as long as the conditions of their parole were not violated. Before the State could alter the status of a parolee because of alleged violations of these conditions, we held that the Fourteenth Amendment's guarantee of due process of law required certain procedural safeguards.

[The] interest in reputation alone which respondent seeks to vindicate in this action in federal court is quite different from the "liberty" or "property" recognized in those decisions. Kentucky law does not extend to respondent any legal guarantee of present enjoyment of reputation which has been altered as a result of petitioners' actions. Rather his interest in reputation is simply one of a number which the State may protect against injury by virtue of its tort law, providing a forum for vindication of those interests by means of damages actions. And any harm or injury to that interest, even where as here inflicted by an officer of the State, does not result in a deprivation of any "liberty" or "property" recognized by state or federal law, nor has it worked any change of respondent's status as theretofore recognized under the State's laws. For these reasons we hold that the interest in reputation asserted in this case is neither "liberty" nor "property" guaranteed against state deprivation without due process of law.

Respondent in this case cannot assert denial of any right vouchsafed to him by the State and thereby protected under the Fourteenth Amendment. That being the case, petitioners' defamatory publications, however seriously they may have harmed respondent's reputation, did not deprive him of any "liberty" or "property" interests protected by the Due Process Clause. . . .

Reversed.

Mr. Justice BRENNAN, with whom Mr. Justice MARSHALL concurs and Mr. Justice WHITE concurs in part, dissenting.

[The] stark fact is that the police here have officially imposed on respondent the stigmatizing label "criminal" without the salutary and constitutionally mandated safeguards of a criminal trial. [Our prior decisions] are cogent authority that a person's interest in his good name and reputation falls within the broad term "liberty" and clearly require that the government afford procedural protections before infringing that name and reputation by branding a person as a criminal. The Court is reduced to discrediting the clear thrust of [these decisions] by excluding the interest in reputation from all constitutional protection "if there is any other possible interpretation" by which to deny their force as precedent according constitutional protection for the interest in reputation. . . .

Moreover, the analysis has a hollow ring in light of the Court's acceptance of the truth of the allegation that the "active shoplifter" label would "seriously impair (respondent's) future employment opportunities." This is clear recognition that an official "badge of infamy" affects tangible interests of the defamed individual and not merely an abstract interest in how people view him; for the "badge of infamy" has serious consequences in its impact on no less than the opportunities open to him to enjoy life, liberty, and the pursuit of happiness. It is inexplicable how the Court can say that a person's status is "altered" when the State suspends him from school, revokes his driver's license, fires him from a job, or denies him the right to purchase a drink of alcohol, but is in no way "altered" when it officially pins upon him the brand of a criminal, particularly since the Court recognizes how deleterious will be the consequences that inevitably flow from its official act. Our precedents clearly mandate that a person's interest in his good name and reputation is cognizable as a "liberty" interest within the meaning of the Due Process Clause, and the Court has simply failed to distinguish those precedents in any rational manner in holding that no invasion of a "liberty" interest was effected in the official stigmatizing of respondent as a criminal without any "process" whatsoever.

I have always thought that one of this Court's most important roles is to provide a formidable bulwark against governmental violation of the constitutional safeguards securing in our free society the legitimate expectations of every person to innate human dignity and sense of worth. It is a regrettable abdication of that role and a saddening denigration of our majestic Bill of Rights when the Court tolerates arbitrary and capricious official conduct branding an individual as a criminal without compliance with constitutional procedures designed to ensure the fair and impartial ascertainment of criminal culpability. Today's decision must surely be a short-lived aberration.

∾ PROBLEMS ∾

1. *More on the Contract Professor.* Let's think about the *Roth* case a bit more. Would the result have been different (in the sense that Roth would have been entitled to a due process hearing) if Roth: a) was fired for "moral turpitude" prior to the expiration of his contract; or b) did not have his contract renewed because the university concluded (and stated) that he was incompetent and dishonest? Do *Roth* and *Paul* suggest that Roth would be entitled to a hearing regarding his renewal under those two circumstances?

2. *The Tenured Professor.* The terms of tenure at a state university provide for continued employment absent "incompetence" or "immoral" behavior. The university wants to fire a tenured professor for incompetence. You are the university counsel. Does the professor have a constitutional right to a hearing prior to dismissal?

3. *The Psychiatric Commitment.* Eddie was found not guilty of murder by reason of insanity under Alabama law and was committed indefinitely to a psychiatric hospital even though he was admittedly no longer mentally ill (the insanity was caused by a tumor on his brain, which was subsequently removed). Under state law, the hospital is allowed to release Eddie only if he "is no longer dangerous to himself or others." Eddie, who desperately wants to be released, claims that he is entitled to a hearing on whether he is dangerous. Does procedural due process apply? Explain.

4. *More on the Professor and the Amsterdam Trip.* Consider the problem at the beginning of the chapter. You represent the dean of the college, who is deciding how to proceed (if at all) against the professor. Based on your reading of *Goldberg* and *Paul*, and the other cases mentioned in this section, is the professor entitled to a due process hearing? Why or why not?

2. Procedural Requirements

Goldberg v. Kelly opened a Pandora's box for the Court. If due process requires notice and an opportunity to be heard, what type of hearing is required? Does the hearing requirement vary from one type of case to another?

In *Goldberg*, the Court concluded that welfare recipients were not entitled to a formal proceeding, in the sense of including a "complete record and a comprehensive opinion," but rather were entitled to only a "fair hearing." In reaching this conclusion, the Court emphasized that both the state and the recipients have an "interest in relatively speedy resolution of questions of eligibility," both are "used to dealing with one another informally," and "some welfare departments have very burdensome caseloads." As a result, the Court required only "minimum procedural safeguards, adapted to the particular characteristics of welfare recipients, and to the limited nature of the controversies to be resolved." In the Court's view, welfare recipients were entitled to an "opportunity to be heard" at a "meaningful time and in a meaningful manner." This included a requirement that the agency provide the recipient with "timely and adequate notice detailing the reasons for a proposed termination, and an effective opportunity to defend by confronting any adverse witnesses and by presenting his own arguments and evidence orally." Absent extraordinary circumstances, the agency need not provide the recipient with the opportunity to file a written brief, especially given that many welfare recipients may "lack the educational attainment necessary to write effectively and . . . cannot obtain professional assistance." However, welfare recipients must be allowed to state their positions orally using informal procedures, and recipients must be allowed "to confront and cross-examine adverse witnesses." In addition, to the extent that the agency engages in fact finding, "the evidence used to prove the government's case must be disclosed to the individual so that he has an opportunity to show that it is untrue." Although the agency need not provide a recipient with an attorney, "the recipient must be allowed to retain an attorney if he so desires." "Finally, the decisionmaker's conclusion as to a recipient's eligibility must rest solely on the legal rules and evidence adduced at the hearing [and] the decision maker should state the reasons for his determination and indicate the evidence he relied on, though his statement need not amount to a full opinion or even formal findings of fact and conclusions of law. And, of course, an impartial decision maker is essential."

After *Goldberg*, questions arose about whether a "fair hearing" would be required in other contexts, and whether this hearing must be provided before termination. The following cases address that issue.

Mathews v. Eldridge

424 U.S. 319 (1976)

Mr. Justice POWELL delivered the opinion of the Court.

[Cash] benefits are provided to workers during periods in which they are completely disabled under the disability insurance benefits program created by the 1956 amendments to Title II of the Social Security Act. Respondent Eldridge was first awarded benefits [in] 1968. [In] 1972, he received a questionnaire from the state agency charged with monitoring his medical condition. Eldridge completed the questionnaire, indicating that his condition had not improved and identifying the medical sources, including physicians, from whom he had received treatment recently. The state agency then obtained reports from his physician and a psychiatric consultant. After considering these reports and other information in his file the agency informed Eldridge by letter that it had made a tentative determination that his disability had ceased in May 1972. The letter included a statement of reasons for the proposed termination of benefits, and advised Eldridge that he might request reasonable time in which to obtain and submit additional information pertaining to his condition.

In his written response, Eldridge disputed one characterization of his medical condition and indicated that the agency already had enough evidence to establish his disability. The state agency then made its final determination that he had ceased to be disabled in May 1972. This determination was accepted by the Social Security Administration (SSA), which notified Eldridge in July that his benefits would terminate after that month. The notification also advised him of his right to seek reconsideration by the state agency of this initial determination within six months.

Instead of requesting reconsideration Eldridge commenced this action challenging the constitutional validity of the administrative procedures established by the Secretary of Health, Education, and Welfare for assessing whether there exists a continuing disability. He sought an immediate reinstatement of benefits pending a hearing on the issue of his disability. The Secretary moved to dismiss on the grounds that Eldridge's benefits had been terminated in accordance with valid administrative regulations and procedures and that he had failed to exhaust available remedies. In support of his contention that due process requires a pretermination hearing, Eldridge relied exclusively upon this Court's decision in Goldberg v. Kelly which established a right to an "evidentiary hearing" prior to termination of welfare benefits. . . .

[This] Court consistently has held that some form of hearing is required before an individual is finally deprived of a property interest. The "right to be heard before being condemned to suffer grievous loss of any kind, even though it may not involve the stigma and hardships of a criminal conviction, is a principle basic to our society." The fundamental requirement of due process is the opportunity to be heard "at a meaningful time and in a meaningful manner." Eldridge agrees that the review procedures available to a claimant before the initial determination of ineligibility becomes final would be adequate if disability benefits were not terminated until after the evidentiary hearing stage of the administrative process. The dispute centers upon what process is due prior to the initial termination of benefits, pending review.

In recent years this Court increasingly has had occasion to consider the extent to which due process requires an evidentiary hearing prior to the deprivation of some type of property interest even if such a hearing is provided thereafter. In only one case, Goldberg v. Kelly, has the Court held that a hearing closely approximating a judicial trial is necessary. In other cases requiring some type of pretermination hearing as a matter of constitutional right the Court has spoken sparingly about the requisite procedures. . . .

These decisions underscore the truism that "'[d]ue process,' unlike some legal rules, is not a technical conception with a fixed content unrelated to time, place and circumstances." "[D]ue process is flexible and calls for such procedural protections as the particular situation demands." Accordingly, resolution of the issue whether the administrative procedures provided here are constitutionally sufficient requires analysis of the governmental and private interests that are affected. More precisely, our prior decisions indicate that identification of the specific dictates of due process generally requires consideration of three distinct factors: First, the private interest that will be affected by the official action; second, the risk of an erroneous deprivation of such interest through the procedures used, and the probable value, if any, of additional or substitute procedural safeguards; and finally, the Government's interest, including the function involved and the fiscal and administrative burdens that the additional or substitute procedural requirement would entail.

We turn first to a description of the procedures for the termination of Social Security disability benefits and thereafter consider the factors bearing upon the constitutional adequacy of these procedures. . . . The disability insurance program is administered jointly by state and federal agencies. State agencies make the initial determination whether a disability exists, when it began, and when it ceased. The standards applied and the procedures followed are prescribed by the Secretary who has delegated his responsibilities and powers under the Act to the SSA. [The] principal reasons for benefits terminations are that the worker is no longer disabled or has returned to work. As Eldridge's benefits were terminated because he was determined to be no longer disabled, we consider only the sufficiency of the procedures involved in such cases.

The continuing-eligibility investigation is made by a state agency acting through a "team" consisting of a physician and a nonmedical person trained in disability evaluation. The agency periodically communicates with the disabled worker, usually by mail in which case he is sent a detailed questionnaire or by telephone, and requests information concerning his present condition, including current medical restrictions and sources of treatment, and any additional information that he considers relevant to his continued entitlement to benefits.

Information regarding the recipient's current condition is also obtained from his sources of medical treatment. If there is a conflict between the information provided by the beneficiary and that obtained from medical sources such as his physician, or between two sources of treatment, the agency may arrange for an examination by an independent consulting physician. Whenever the agency's tentative assessment of the beneficiary's condition differs from his own assessment, the beneficiary is informed that benefits may be terminated, provided a summary of the evidence upon which the proposed determination to terminate is based, and afforded an opportunity to review the medical reports and other evidence in his case file. He also may respond in writing and submit additional evidence.

The state agency then makes its final determination, which is reviewed by an examiner in the SSA Bureau of Disability Insurance. [If] the SSA accepts the agency determination it notifies the recipient in writing, informing him of the reasons for the decision, and of his right to seek de novo reconsideration by the state agency. Upon acceptance by the SSA, benefits are terminated effective two months after the month in which medical recovery is found to have occurred.

If the recipient seeks reconsideration by the state agency and the determination is adverse, the SSA reviews the reconsideration determination and notifies the recipient of the decision. He then has a right to an evidentiary hearing before an SSA administrative law judge. The hearing is nonadversary, and the SSA is not represented by counsel. As at all prior and subsequent stages of the administrative process, however, the claimant may be represented by counsel or other spokesmen. If this hearing results in an adverse decision, the claimant is entitled to request discretionary review by the SSA Appeals Council.

Should it be determined at any point after termination of benefits, that the claimant's disability extended beyond the date of cessation initially established, the worker is entitled to retroactive payments. If, on the other hand, a beneficiary receives any payments to which he is later determined not to be entitled, the statute authorizes the Secretary to attempt to recoup these funds in specified circumstances.

Despite the elaborate character of the administrative procedures provided by the Secretary, the courts below held them to be constitutionally inadequate, concluding that due process requires an evidentiary hearing prior to termination. In light of the private and governmental interests at stake here and the nature of the existing procedures, we think this was error. . . . Since a recipient whose benefits are terminated is awarded full retroactive relief if he ultimately prevails, his sole interest is in the uninterrupted receipt of this source of income pending final administrative decision on his claim. His potential injury is thus similar in nature to that of the welfare recipient in *Goldberg*. . . .

Only in *Goldberg* has the Court held that due process requires an evidentiary hearing prior to a temporary deprivation. It was emphasized there that welfare assistance is given to persons on the very margin of subsistence: "The crucial factor in this context a factor not present in the case [of] virtually anyone else whose governmental entitlements are ended is that termination of aid pending resolution of a controversy over eligibility may deprive an eligible recipient of the very means by which to live while he waits." Eligibility for disability benefits, in contrast, is not based upon financial need. Indeed, it is wholly unrelated to the worker's income or support from many other sources, such as earnings of other family members, workmen's compensation awards, tort claims awards, savings, private insurance, public or private pensions, veterans' benefits, food stamps, public assistance, or the "many other important programs, both public and private, which contain provisions for disability payments affecting a substantial portion of the work [force]." Richardson v. Belcher, 404 U.S., at 85-87 (Douglas, J., dissenting).

As *Goldberg* illustrates, the degree of potential deprivation that may be created by a particular decision is a factor to be considered in assessing the validity of any administrative decisionmaking process. The potential deprivation here is generally likely to be less than in *Goldberg*, although the degree of difference can be overstated. [T]o remain eligible for benefits a recipient must be "unable to engage in substantial gainful activity." Thus, in contrast to the discharged federal employee in *Arnett*, there is little possibility that the terminated recipient will be able to find even temporary employment to ameliorate the interim loss.

[The] Secretary concedes that the delay between a request for a hearing before an administrative law judge and a decision on the claim is currently between 10 and 11 months. Since a terminated recipient must first obtain a reconsideration decision as a prerequisite to invoking his right to an evidentiary hearing, the delay between the actual cutoff of benefits and final decision after a hearing exceeds one year.

In view of the torpidity of this administrative review process, and the typically modest resources of the family unit of the physically disabled worker, the hardship imposed upon the erroneously terminated disability recipient may be significant. Still, the disabled worker's need is likely to be less than that of a welfare recipient. In addition to the possibility of access to private resources, other forms of government assistance will become available where the termination of disability benefits places a worker or his family below the subsistence level. In view of these potential sources of temporary income, there is less reason here than in *Goldberg* to depart from the ordinary principle, established by our decisions, that something less than an evidentiary hearing is sufficient prior to adverse administrative action.

An additional factor to be considered here is the fairness and reliability of the existing pretermination procedures, and the probable value, if any, of additional procedural safeguards. Central to the evaluation of any administrative process is the nature of the relevant inquiry. In order to remain eligible for benefits the disabled worker must demonstrate by means of "medically acceptable clinical and laboratory diagnostic techniques," that he is unable "to engage in any substantial gainful activity by reason of any medically determinable physical or mental [impairment]." In short, a medical assessment of the worker's physical or mental condition is required. This is a more sharply focused and easily documented decision than the typical determination of welfare entitlement. In the latter case, a wide variety of information may be deemed relevant, and issues of witness credibility and veracity often are critical to the decisionmaking process. *Goldberg* noted that in such circumstances "written submissions are a wholly unsatisfactory basis for decision."

By contrast, the decision whether to discontinue disability benefits will turn, in most cases, upon "routine, standard, and unbiased medical reports by physician specialists," concerning a subject whom they have personally examined. In *Richardson* the Court recognized the "reliability and probative worth of written medical reports," emphasizing that while there may be "professional disagreement with the medical conclusions" the "specter of questionable credibility and veracity is not present." To be sure, credibility and veracity may be a factor in the ultimate disability assessment in some cases. But procedural due process rules are shaped by the risk of error inherent in the truthfinding process as applied to the generality of cases, not the rare exceptions. The potential value of an evidentiary hearing, or even oral presentation to the decisionmaker, is substantially less in this context than in *Goldberg*.

The decision in *Goldberg* also was based on the Court's conclusion that written submissions were an inadequate substitute for oral presentation because they did not provide an effective means for the recipient to communicate his case to the decisionmaker. Written submissions were viewed as an unrealistic option, for most recipients lacked the "educational attainment necessary to write effectively" and could not afford professional assistance. In addition, such submissions would not provide the "flexibility of oral presentations" or "permit the recipient to mold his argument to the issues the decision maker appears to regard as important." In the context of the disability-benefits-entitlement assessment the administrative procedures under review here fully answer these objections.

The detailed questionnaire which the state agency periodically sends the recipient identifies with particularity the information relevant to the entitlement decision, and the recipient is invited to obtain assistance from the local SSA office in completing the questionnaire. More important, the information critical to the entitlement decision usually is derived from medical sources, such as the treating physician. Such sources are likely to be able to communicate more effectively through written documents than are welfare recipients or the lay witnesses supporting their cause. The conclusions of physicians often are supported by X-rays and the results of clinical or laboratory tests, information typically more amenable to written than to oral presentation.

A further safeguard against mistake is the policy of allowing the disability recipient's representative full access to all information relied upon by the state agency. In addition, prior to the cutoff of benefits the agency informs the recipient of its tentative assessment, the reasons therefor, and provides a summary of the evidence that it considers most relevant. Opportunity is then afforded the recipient to submit additional evidence or arguments, enabling him to challenge directly the accuracy of information in his file as well as the correctness of the agency's tentative conclusions. These procedures, again as contrasted with those before the Court in *Goldberg*, enable the recipient to "mold" his argument to respond to the precise issues which the decisionmaker regards as crucial.

[Amici] point to the significant reversal rate for appealed cases as clear evidence that the current process is inadequate. Depending upon the base selected and the line of analysis followed, the relevant reversal rates urged by the contending parties vary from a high of 58.6% for appealed reconsideration decisions to an overall reversal rate of only 3.3%. Bare statistics rarely provide a satisfactory measure of the fairness of a decisionmaking process. Their adequacy is especially suspect here since the administrative review system is operated on an open-file basis. . . .

In striking the appropriate due process balance the final factor to be assessed is the public interest. This includes the administrative burden and other societal costs that would be associated with requiring, as a matter of constitutional right, an evidentiary hearing upon demand in all cases prior to the termination of disability benefits. The most visible burden would be the incremental cost resulting from the increased number of hearings and the expense of providing benefits to ineligible recipients pending decision. No one can predict the extent of the increase, but the fact that full benefits would continue until after such hearings would assure the exhaustion in most cases of this attractive option. Nor would the theoretical right of the Secretary to recover undeserved benefits result, as a practical matter, in any substantial offset to the added outlay of public funds. The parties submit widely varying estimates of the probable additional financial cost.

We only need say that experience with the constitutionalizing of government procedures suggests that the ultimate additional cost in terms of money and administrative burden would not be insubstantial.

Financial cost alone is not a controlling weight in determining whether due process requires a particular procedural safeguard prior to some administrative decision. But the Government's interest, and hence that of the public, in conserving scarce fiscal and administrative resources is a factor that must be weighed. At some point the benefit of an additional safeguard to the individual affected by the administrative action and to society in terms of increased assurance that the action is just, may be outweighed by the cost. Significantly, the cost of protecting those whom the preliminary administrative process has identified as likely to be found undeserving may in the end come out of the pockets of the deserving since resources available for any particular program of social welfare are not unlimited.

But more is implicated in cases of this type than *ad hoc* weighing of fiscal and administrative burdens against the interests of a particular category of claimants. The ultimate balance involves a determination as to when, under our constitutional system, judicial-type procedures must be imposed upon administrative action to assure fairness. [The] judicial model of an evidentiary hearing is neither a required, nor even the most effective, method of decisionmaking in all circumstances. The essence of due process is the requirement that "a person in jeopardy of serious loss [be given] notice of the case against him and opportunity to meet it." [All] that is necessary is that the procedures be tailored, in light of the decision to be made, to "the capacities and circumstances of those who are to be heard," Goldberg v. Kelly, 397 U.S., at 268-269, to insure that they are given a meaningful opportunity to present their case. In assessing what process is due in this case, substantial weight must be given to the good-faith judgments of the individuals charged by Congress with the administration of social welfare programs that the procedures they have provided assure fair consideration of the entitlement claims of individuals. This is especially so where, as here, the prescribed procedures not only provide the claimant with an effective process for asserting his claim prior to any administrative action, but also assure a right to an evidentiary hearing, as well as to subsequent judicial review, before the denial of his claim becomes final.

We conclude that an evidentiary hearing is not required prior to the termination of disability benefits and that the present administrative procedures fully comport with due process.

The judgment of the Court of Appeals is
Reversed.

∽ PROBLEMS ∽

1. *The Tenured Professor*. Recall the tenured professor at a state university who was fired for incompetence. What, if any, procedural protections apply to a hearing regarding the professor's dismissal?

2. *The Grievance Against the Tenured Professor*. Suppose that a grievance is brought against a tenured professor, claiming that he intentionally and willfully

misrepresented an applicant's employment history (the applicant was a visiting faculty member at the professor's university when his application was rejected). The university's grievance procedures do not provide for (or, for that matter, prohibit) discovery by participants in grievance proceedings. However, since the professor is being charged with moral turpitude, and because the grievant is seeking severe sanctions (up to and including dismissal), the professor seeks discovery from the applicant. The professor believes that the applicant misrepresented his employment history during the employment process, believes that he will continue to do so during the grievance process, and claims that he cannot fairly and adequately defend himself without discovery. Does the Due Process Clause require the grievance committee to provide the professor with discovery regarding the grievant's employment history?

Goss v. Lopez

419 U.S. 565 (1975)

Mr. Justice WHITE delivered the opinion of the Court.

[Ohio] law empowers the principal of an Ohio public school to suspend a pupil for misconduct for up to 10 days or to expel him. In either case, he must notify the student's parents within 24 hours and state the reasons for his action. A pupil who is expelled, or his parents, may appeal the decision to the Board of Education and in connection therewith shall be permitted to be heard at the board meeting. The Board may reinstate the pupil following the hearing. No similar procedure is provided in §3313.66 or any other provision of state law for a suspended student. Aside from a regulation tracking the statute, at the time of the imposition of the suspensions in this case the CPSS [Cleveland Public School System] itself had not issued any written procedure applicable to suspensions. Nor, so far as the record reflects, had any of the individual high schools involved in this case. Each, however, had formally or informally described the conduct for which suspension could be imposed.

The nine named appellees, each of whom [had] been suspended from public high school in Columbus for up to 10 days without a hearing pursuant to §3313.66, filed an action under 42 U.S.C. §1983 against the Columbus Board of Education and various administrators of the CPSS. The complaint sought a declaration that §3313.66 was unconstitutional in that it permitted public school administrators to deprive plaintiffs of their rights to an education without a hearing of any kind, in violation of the procedural due process component of the Fourteenth Amendment. It also sought to enjoin the public school officials from issuing future suspensions pursuant to §3313.66 and to require them to remove references to the past suspensions from the records of the students in question.

[The] suspensions arose out of a period of widespread student unrest in the CPSS during February and March 1971. Six of the named plaintiffs [were] students at the Marion-Franklin High School and were each suspended for 10 days on account of disruptive or disobedient conduct committed in the presence of the school administrator who ordered the suspension. One of these, Tyrone

Washington, was among a group of students demonstrating in the school auditorium while a class was being conducted there. He was ordered by the school principal to leave, refused to do so, and was suspended. Rudolph Sutton, in the presence of the principal, physically attacked a police officer who was attempting to remove Tyrone Washington from the auditorium. He was immediately suspended. The other four [students] were suspended for similar conduct. None was given a hearing to determine the operative facts underlying the suspension, but each, together with his or her parents, was offered the opportunity to attend a conference, subsequent to the effective date of the suspension, to discuss the student's future. . . .

Two named plaintiffs [were] students at the Central High School and McGuffey Junior High School, respectively. [One] was suspended in connection with a disturbance in the lunchroom which involved some physical damage to school property. Lopez [another of the students] testified that at least 75 other students were suspended from his school on the same day. He also testified [that] he was not a party to the destructive conduct but was instead an innocent bystander. Because no one from the school testified with regard to this incident, there is no evidence in the record indicating the official basis for concluding otherwise. Lopez never had a hearing. . . . Betty Crome [a third student] was present at a demonstration at a high school other than the one she was attending. There she was arrested together with others, taken to the police station, and released without being formally charged. Before she went to school on the following day, she was notified that she had been suspended for a 10-day period. Because no one from the school testified with respect to this incident, the record does not disclose how the McGuffey Junior High School principal went about making the decision to suspend Crome, nor does it disclose on what information the decision was based. It is clear from the record that no hearing was ever held. . . . There was no testimony with respect to the suspension of the ninth named plaintiff, Carl Smith. The school files were also silent as to his suspension, although as to some, but not all, of the other named plaintiffs the files contained either direct references to their suspensions or copies of letters sent to their parents advising them of the suspension.

[A]ppellants contend that because there is no constitutional right to an education at public expense, the Due Process Clause does not protect against expulsions from the public school system. . . . The Fourteenth Amendment forbids the State to deprive any person of life, liberty, or property without due process of law. Protected interests in property are normally "not created by the Constitution. Rather, they are created and their dimensions are defined" by an independent source such as state statutes or rules entitling the citizen to certain benefits. [A]ppellees plainly had legitimate claims of entitlement to a public education. Ohio Rev. Code Ann. §§3313.48 and 3313.64 direct local authorities to provide a free education to all residents between five and 21 years of age, and a compulsory-attendance law requires attendance for a school year of not less than 32 weeks. . . . Having chosen to extend the right to an education to people of appellees' class generally, Ohio may not withdraw that right on grounds of misconduct absent, fundamentally fair procedures to determine whether the misconduct has occurred. . . . The authority possessed by the State to prescribe and enforce standards of conduct in its schools, although concededly very broad, must be exercised consistently with constitutional safeguards. Among other things, the State is constrained to recognize a student's legitimate entitlement to a public education as a property interest which is protected by the Due Process Clause and which may not be taken away for misconduct without adherence to the minimum procedures required by that Clause.

[Appellants argue that the] loss of 10 days [is] neither severe nor grievous and the Due Process Clause is therefore of no relevance. [I]n determining "whether due process requirements apply in the first place, we must look not to the 'weight' but to the nature of the interest at stake." Appellees were excluded from school only temporarily, it is true, but the length and consequent severity of a deprivation, while another factor to weigh in determining the appropriate form of hearing, "is not decisive of the basic right" to a hearing of some kind. The Court's view has been that as long as a property deprivation is not *de minimis*, its gravity is irrelevant to the question whether account must be taken of the Due Process Clause. A 10-day suspension from school is not *de minimis* in our view and may not be imposed in complete disregard of the Due Process Clause.

A short suspension is, of course, a far milder deprivation than expulsion. But, "education is perhaps the most important function of state and local governments," and the total exclusion from the educational process for more than a trivial period, and certainly if the suspension is for 10 days, is a serious event in the life of the suspended child. Neither the property interest in educational benefits temporarily denied nor the liberty interest in reputation, which is also implicated, is so insubstantial that suspensions may constitutionally be imposed by any procedure the school chooses, no matter how arbitrary.

"Once it is determined that due process applies, the question remains what process is due." We turn to that question, fully realizing as our cases regularly do that the interpretation and application of the Due Process Clause are intensely practical matters and that "[t]he very nature of due process negates any concept of inflexible procedures universally applicable to every imaginable situation." [At] the very minimum, therefore, students facing suspension and the consequent interference with a protected property interest must be given some kind of notice and afforded some kind of hearing. . . .

It also appears from our cases that the timing and content of the notice and the nature of the hearing will depend on appropriate accommodation of the competing interests involved. The student's interest is to avoid unfair or mistaken exclusion from the educational process, with all of its unfortunate consequences. The Due Process Clause will not shield him from suspensions properly imposed, but it disserves both his interest and the interest of the State if his suspension is in fact unwarranted. The concern would be mostly academic if the disciplinary process were a totally accurate, unerring process, never mistaken and never unfair. Unfortunately, that is not the case, and no one suggests that it is. Disciplinarians, although proceeding in utmost good faith, frequently act on the reports and advice of others; and the controlling facts and the nature of the conduct under challenge are often disputed. The risk of error is not at all trivial, and it should be guarded against if that may be done without prohibitive cost or interference with the educational process.

The difficulty is that our schools are vast and complex. Some modicum of discipline and order is essential if the educational function is to be performed. Events calling for discipline are frequent occurrences and sometimes require immediate, effective action. Suspension is considered not only to be a necessary tool to maintain order but a valuable educational device. The prospect of imposing elaborate hearing requirements in every suspension case is viewed with great concern, and many school authorities may well prefer the untrammeled power to act unilaterally, unhampered by rules about notice and hearing. But it would be a strange disciplinary system in an educational institution if no communication was sought by the disciplinarian with the student in an effort to inform him of his dereliction and to let him tell his side of the story in order to make sure that an injustice is not done. . . .

We do not believe that school authorities must be totally free from notice and hearing requirements if their schools are to operate with acceptable efficiency. Students facing temporary suspension have interests qualifying for protection of the Due Process Clause, and due process requires, in connection with a suspension of 10 days or less, that the student be given oral or written notice of the charges against him and, if he denies them, an explanation of the evidence the authorities have and an opportunity to present his side of the story. The Clause requires at least these rudimentary precautions against unfair or mistaken findings of misconduct and arbitrary exclusion from school.

There need be no delay between the time "notice" is given and the time of the hearing. In the great majority of cases the disciplinarian may informally discuss the alleged misconduct with the student minutes after it has occurred. We hold only that, in being given an opportunity to explain his version of the facts at this discussion, the student first be told what he is accused of doing and what the basis of the accusation is. . . . Since the hearing may occur almost immediately following the misconduct, it follows that as a general rule notice and hearing should precede removal of the student from school. [T]here are recurring situations in which prior notice and hearing cannot be insisted upon. Students whose presence poses a continuing danger to persons or property or an ongoing threat of disrupting the academic process may be immediately removed from school. In such cases, the necessary notice and rudimentary hearing should follow as soon as practicable. . . .

[W]e do not believe that we have imposed procedures on school disciplinarians which are inappropriate in a classroom setting. Instead we have imposed requirements which are, if anything, less than a fair-minded school principal would impose upon himself in order to avoid unfair suspensions. . . . We stop short of construing the Due Process Clause to require, countrywide, that hearings in connection with short suspensions must afford the student the opportunity to secure counsel, to confront and cross-examine witnesses supporting the charge, or to call his own witnesses to verify his version of the incident.

Brief disciplinary suspensions are almost countless. To impose in each such case even truncated trial-type procedures might well overwhelm administrative facilities in many places and, by diverting resources, cost more than it would save in educational effectiveness. Moreover, further formalizing the suspension process and escalating its formality and adversary nature may not only make it too costly as a regular disciplinary tool but also destroy its effectiveness as part of the teaching process.

On the other hand, requiring effective notice and informal hearing permitting the student to give his version of the events will provide a meaningful hedge against erroneous action. At least the disciplinarian will be alerted to the existence of disputes about facts and arguments about cause and effect. He may then determine himself to summon the accuser, permit cross-examination, and allow the student to present his own witnesses. In more difficult cases, he may permit counsel. In any event, his discretion will be more informed and we think the risk of error substantially reduced.

Requiring that there be at least an informal give-and-take between student and disciplinarian, preferably prior to the suspension, will add little to the fact-finding function where the disciplinarian himself has witnessed the conduct forming the basis for the charge. But things are not always as they seem to be, and the student will at least have the opportunity to characterize his conduct and put it in what he deems the proper context.

[We] have addressed ourselves solely to the short suspension, not exceeding 10 days. Longer suspensions or expulsions for the remainder of the school term, or permanently, may require more formal procedures. Nor do we put aside the possibility that in unusual situations, although involving only a short suspension, something more than the rudimentary procedures will be required. [The] District Court found each of the suspensions involved here to have occurred without a hearing, either before or after the suspension, and that each suspension was therefore invalid and the statute unconstitutional insofar as it permits such suspensions without notice or hearing. Accordingly, the judgment is

Affirmed.

Mr. Justice POWELL, with whom THE CHIEF JUSTICE, Mr. Justice BLACKMUN, and Mr. Justice REHNQUIST join, dissenting.

[I] would conclude that a deprivation of not more than 10 days' suspension from school, imposed as a routine disciplinary measure, does not assume constitutional dimensions. . . . Absences of such limited duration will rarely affect a pupil's opportunity to learn or his scholastic performance. Indeed, the record in this case reflects no educational injury to appellees. Each completed the semester in which the suspension occurred and performed at least as well as he or she had in previous years. [T]his Court has explicitly recognized that school authorities must have broad discretionary authority in the daily operation of public schools. This includes wide latitude with respect to maintaining discipline and good order. . . . Such an approach properly recognizes the unique nature of public education and the correspondingly limited role of the judiciary in its supervision. . . .

[The] State's generalized interest in maintaining an orderly school system is not incompatible with the individual interest of the student. Education in any meaningful sense includes the inculcation of an understanding in each pupil of the necessity of rules and obedience thereto. [In] assessing in constitutional terms the need to protect pupils from unfair minor discipline by school authorities, the Court ignores the commonality of interest of the State and pupils in the public school system. Rather, it thinks in traditional judicial terms of an adversary situation. To be sure, there will be the occasional pupil innocent of any rule infringement who is mistakenly suspended or whose infraction is too minor to justify suspension. But, while there is no evidence indicating the frequency of unjust suspensions, common sense suggests that they will not be numerous in relation to the total number, and that mistakes or injustices will usually be righted by informal means.

One of the more disturbing aspects of today's decision is its indiscriminate reliance upon the judiciary, and the adversary process, as the means of resolving many of the most routine problems arising in the classroom. In mandating due process procedures the Court misapprehends the reality of the normal teacher-pupil relationship. There is an ongoing relationship, one in which the teacher must occupy many roles — educator, adviser, friend, and, at times, parent-substitute. It is rarely adversary in nature except with respect to the chronically disruptive or insubordinate pupil whom the teacher must be free to discipline without frustrating formalities. [If,] as seems apparent, the Court will now require due process procedures whenever such routine school decisions are challenged, the impact upon public education will be serious indeed. The discretion and judgment of federal courts [will] be substituted for that of the 50-state legislatures, the 14,000 school boards, and the 2,000,000 teachers who heretofore have been responsible for the administration of the American public school system. . . .

∾ PROBLEMS ∾

1. *Suspended.* Pursuant to Arizona law, "All suspensions from public schools of ten days or longer require the provision of oral or written notice after the suspension has commenced." Chante is suspended for smoking cigarettes on the grounds of her public high school in Phoenix. Because she feels that there is a stigma attached to a suspension, and because she believes that her absence from school will adversely affect her grades and class rank, Chante demands a presuspension hearing. Is she entitled to one? Why or why not?

2. *The Lawyer's Basketball League.* The City of Louisville maintains a variety of basketball leagues including the "Lawyer's Basketball League," in which all participants must be licensed lawyers or work for a local law firm. One team, upset by a referee's call that cost them the game, demands the write to "file briefs and have oral argument" regarding the validity of the call. The team is seeking to have the call invalidated and the game replayed (the complaining team lost by a point).

You are the city's lawyer. Must you grant the request for a hearing, or can you treat the referee's call as "final"?

Board of Curators of the University of Missouri v. Horowitz

435 U.S. 78 (1978)

Mr. Justice REHNQUIST delivered the opinion of the Court.

Respondent, a student at the University of Missouri–Kansas City Medical School, was dismissed by petitioner officials of the school during her final year of study for failure to meet academic standards. Respondent sued [alleging] that petitioners had not accorded her procedural due process prior to her dismissal. [We] granted certiorari to consider what procedures must be accorded to a student at a state educational institution whose dismissal may constitute a deprivation of "liberty" or "property" within the meaning of the Fourteenth Amendment. . . .

I

Respondent was admitted with advanced standing to the Medical School in the fall of 1971. During the final years of a student's education at the school, the student is required to pursue in "rotational units" academic and clinical studies pertaining to various medical disciplines such as obstetrics-gynecology, pediatrics, and surgery. Each student's academic performance at the school is evaluated on a periodic basis by the Council on Evaluation, a body composed of both faculty and students, which can recommend various actions including probation and dismissal. The recommendations of the Council are reviewed by the Coordinating Committee, a body composed solely of faculty members, and must ultimately be approved by the Dean. Students are not typically allowed to appear before either the Council or the Coordinating Committee on the occasion of their review of the student's academic performance.

In the spring of respondent's first year of study, several faculty members expressed dissatisfaction with her clinical performance during a pediatrics rotation. The faculty members noted that respondent's "performance was below that of her peers in all clinical patient-oriented settings," that she was erratic in her attendance at clinical sessions, and that she lacked a critical concern for personal hygiene. Upon the recommendation of the Council on Evaluation, respondent was advanced to her second and final year on a probationary basis.

Faculty dissatisfaction with respondent's clinical performance continued during the following year. For example, respondent's docent, or faculty adviser, rated her clinical skills as "unsatisfactory." In the middle of the year, the Council again reviewed respondent's academic progress and concluded that respondent should not be considered for graduation in June of that year; [the] Council recommended that, absent "radical improvement," respondent be dropped from the school.

Respondent was permitted to take a set of oral and practical examinations as an "appeal" of the decision not to permit her to graduate. Pursuant to this "appeal," respondent spent a substantial portion of time with seven practicing physicians in the area who enjoyed a good reputation among their peers. The physicians were asked to recommend whether respondent should be allowed to graduate on schedule and, if not, whether she should be dropped immediately or allowed to remain on probation. Only two of the doctors recommended that respondent be graduated on schedule. Of the other five, two recommended that she be immediately dropped from the school. The remaining three recommended that she not be allowed to graduate in June and be continued on probation pending further reports on her clinical progress. Upon receipt of these recommendations, the Council on Evaluation reaffirmed its prior position.

The Council met again in mid-May to consider whether respondent should be allowed to remain in school beyond June of that year. Noting that the report on respondent's recent surgery rotation rated her performance as "low-satisfactory," the Council unanimously recommended that "barring receipt of any reports that Miss Horowitz has improved radically, [she] not be allowed to re-enroll in [the] School of Medicine." The Council delayed making its recommendation official until receiving reports on other rotations; when a report on respondent's emergency rotation also turned out to be negative, the Council unanimously reaffirmed its recommendation that respondent be dropped from the school. The Coordinating Committee and the Dean approved the recommendation and notified respondent, who appealed the decision in writing to the University's Provost for Health Sciences. The Provost sustained the school's actions after reviewing the record compiled during the earlier proceedings.

To be entitled to the procedural protections of the Fourteenth Amendment, respondent must in a case such as this demonstrate that her dismissal from the school deprived her of either a "liberty" or a "property" interest. Respondent has never alleged that she was deprived of a property interest [recognized] by Missouri state law. Instead, respondent argued that her dismissal deprived her of "liberty" by substantially impairing her opportunities to continue her medical education or to return to employment in a medically related field.

[We] have recently had an opportunity to elaborate upon the circumstances under which an employment termination might infringe a protected liberty interest. In Bishop v. Wood, 426 U.S. 341 (1976), we upheld the dismissal of a policeman without a hearing; we rejected the theory that the mere fact of dismissal, absent some publicizing of the reasons for the action, could amount to a stigma infringing one's liberty: In Board of Regents v. Roth, 408 U.S. 564, we recognized that the nonretention of an untenured college teacher might make him somewhat less attractive to other employers, but nevertheless concluded that it would stretch the concept too far "to suggest that a person is deprived of 'liberty' when he simply is not rehired in one position but remains as free as before to seek another." This same conclusion applies to the discharge of a public employee whose position is terminable at the will of the employer when there is no public disclosure of the reasons for the discharge. . . .

We need not decide [whether] respondent's dismissal deprived her of a liberty interest in pursuing a medical career. Nor need we decide whether respondent's dismissal infringed any other interest constitutionally protected against deprivation without procedural due process. Assuming the existence of a liberty or property interest, respondent has been awarded at least as much due process as the Fourteenth Amendment requires. The school fully informed respondent of the faculty's dissatisfaction with her clinical progress and the danger that this posed to timely graduation and continued enrollment. The ultimate decision to dismiss respondent was careful and deliberate. These procedures were sufficient under the Due Process Clause of the Fourteenth Amendment. [R]espondent "was afforded full procedural due process by the [school]." In fact, "[the] school went beyond [constitutionally required] procedural due process by affording [respondent] the opportunity to be examined by seven independent physicians in order to be absolutely certain that their grading of the [respondent] in her medical skills was correct."

In Goss v. Lopez, 419 U.S. 565 (1975), we held that due process requires, in connection with the suspension of a student from public school for disciplinary reasons, "that the student be given oral or written notice of the charges against him and, if he denies them, an explanation of the evidence the authorities have and an opportunity to present his side of the story." The Court of Appeals apparently read Goss as requiring some type of formal hearing at which respondent could defend her academic ability and performance. All that Goss required was an "informal give-and-take" between the student and the administrative body dismissing him that would, at least, give the student "the opportunity to characterize his conduct and put it in what he deems the proper context." But we have frequently emphasized that "[t]he very nature of due process negates any concept of inflexible procedures universally applicable to every imaginable situation." The need for flexibility is well illustrated by the significant difference between the failure of a student to meet academic standards and the violation by a student of valid rules of conduct. This difference calls for far less stringent procedural requirements in the case of an academic dismissal.

Since the issue first arose 50 years ago, state and lower federal courts have recognized that there are distinct differences between decisions to suspend or dismiss a student for disciplinary purposes and similar actions taken for academic reasons which may call for hearings in connection with the former but not the latter. [Reason] clearly supports the perception of these decisions. A school is an academic institution, not a courtroom or administrative hearing room. In Goss, this Court felt that suspensions of students for disciplinary reasons have a sufficient resemblance to traditional judicial and administrative factfinding to call for a "hearing" before the relevant school authority. While recognizing that school authorities must be afforded the necessary tools to maintain discipline, the Court concluded: "[I]t would be a strange disciplinary system in an educational institution if no communication was sought by the disciplinarian with the student in an effort to inform him of his dereliction and to let him tell his side of the story in order to make sure that an injustice is not [done]."

"[R]equiring effective notice and informal hearing permitting the student to give his version of the events will provide a meaningful hedge against erroneous action. At least the disciplinarian will be alerted to the existence of disputes about facts and arguments about cause and effect." Even in the context of a school disciplinary proceeding, however, the Court stopped short of requiring a formal hearing since "further formalizing the suspension process and escalating its formality and adversary nature may not only make it too costly as a regular disciplinary tool but also destroy its effectiveness as a part of the teaching process."

Academic evaluations of a student, in contrast to disciplinary determinations, bear little resemblance to the judicial and administrative fact-finding proceedings to which we have traditionally attached a full-hearing requirement. In *Goss,* the school's decision to suspend the students rested on factual conclusions that the individual students had participated in demonstrations that had disrupted classes, attacked a police officer, or caused physical damage to school property. The requirement of a hearing, where the student could present his side of the factual issue, could under such circumstances "provide a meaningful hedge against erroneous action." The decision to dismiss respondent, by comparison, rested on the academic judgment of school officials that she did not have the necessary clinical ability to perform adequately as a medical doctor and was making insufficient progress toward that goal. Such a judgment is by its nature more subjective and evaluative than the typical factual questions presented in the average disciplinary decision. Like the decision of an individual professor as to the proper grade for a student in his course, the determination whether to dismiss a student for academic reasons requires an expert evaluation of cumulative information and is not readily adapted to the procedural tools of judicial or administrative decisionmaking.

Under such circumstances, we decline to ignore the historic judgment of educators and thereby formalize the academic dismissal process by requiring a hearing. The educational process is not by nature adversary; instead it centers around a continuing relationship between faculty and students, "one in which the teacher must occupy many roles — educator, adviser, friend, and, at times, parent-substitute." Goss v. Lopez, 419 U.S., at 594 (Powell, J., dissenting). This is especially true as one advances through the varying regimes of the educational system, and the instruction becomes both more individualized and more specialized. In *Goss,* this Court concluded that the value of some form of hearing in a disciplinary context outweighs any resulting harm to the academic environment. Influencing this conclusion was clearly the belief that disciplinary proceedings, in which the teacher must decide whether to punish a student for disruptive or insubordinate behavior, may automatically bring an adversary flavor to the normal student-teacher relationship. The same conclusion does not follow in the academic context. We decline to further enlarge the judicial presence in the academic community and thereby risk deterioration of many beneficial aspects of the faculty-student relationship. We recognize, as did the Massachusetts Supreme Judicial Court over 60 years ago, that a hearing may be "useless or harmful in finding out the truth as to scholarship." . . . "Judicial interposition in the operation of the public school system of the Nation raises problems requiring care and restraint." . . .

[W]e agree with the District Court that no showing of arbitrariness or capriciousness has been made in this case. Courts are particularly ill-equipped to evaluate academic performance. The factors discussed in Part II with respect to procedural due process speak a fortiori here and warn against any such judicial intrusion into academic decisionmaking.

The judgment of the Court of Appeals is therefore

Reversed.

Mr. Justice MARSHALL, concurring in part and dissenting in part.

[R]esolution of this case under our traditional approach does not turn on whether the dismissal of respondent is characterized as one for "academic" or "disciplinary" reasons. [A] talismanic reliance on labels should not be a substitute for sensitive consideration of the procedures required by due process. When the facts disputed are of a type susceptible of determination by third parties, as the allegations about respondent plainly were, there is no more reason to deny all procedural protection to one who will suffer a serious loss than there was in *Goss*, and indeed there may be good reason to provide even more protection. A court's characterization of the reasons for a student's dismissal adds nothing to the effort to find procedures that are fair to the student and the school, and that promote the elusive goal of determining the truth in a manner consistent with both individual dignity and society's limited resources. . . .

∽ PROBLEMS ∾

1. *More on the Professor and the Amsterdam Trip.* Let's return to the problem at the beginning of the chapter. Assume that you represent the dean who must decide what action to take against the professor (if any). Is the professor entitled to a hearing before you impose the contemplated sanctions (e.g., barring him from taking the Amsterdam trip as well as from going on overnight trips with students, because of his prior inappropriate behavior)? If so, how must the hearing be structured, and what rights does the professor have (right to counsel, right to cross-examination, etc.)? If you were asked to represent the professor, what arguments would you make on his behalf for expanded hearing rights?

2. *The Plagiarizing Student.* Professor Royster, who teaches at a state law school, believes that a student (John O'Reilly) engaged in plagiarism on a take-home writing project. The professor reached his conclusion based on statements made by other students (who purportedly overheard O'Reilly bragging that he plagiarized) as well as on an Internet search through law-school-papers.com (a website that provides research papers for law students). The Internet search revealed that the identical paper was available for purchase online. Royster took the information about O'Reilly to the law school dean. You are the university

counsel, and the dean has come to you for advice about how to proceed. You have checked the law school's rules and regulations and found that the university does not have an established disciplinary procedure for students. The dean has asked you for advice about what procedures must be accorded to O'Reilly as a necessary predicate to disciplinary action. What advice would you give about how to proceed?

3. *The Failing Grade.* A student receives a failing grade. The student has met with the professor, who adamantly defends the grade. In his view, the student was "off track" and missed the critical issue. Just as adamantly, the student disagrees and believes that the grade was unfair. He believes that the professor undervalued the issue that the student actually discussed. Does the student have a due process right to a review of the professor's grade? If so, what must the student allege? If a hearing is granted, what procedures must be accorded to the student?

Points to Remember

- For procedural due process purposes, a distinction is made between so-called "legislative" determinations and "adjudicative" determinations.
- In general, while individuals may have the right to a hearing before an adjudicative determination is rendered against them, they have no right to a hearing before a legislative determination is made.
- As a result, although individuals may not be entitled to a hearing before the state raises income tax rates, they may be entitled to a hearing regarding the application of those rates to their individual situation.
- Under both the Fifth Amendment and the Fourteenth Amendment, there is a constitutional right to be heard prior to the deprivation of "life, liberty, or property," such as depriving someone of liberty (e.g., through imprisonment), property (e.g., through fines), or life (e.g., through capital punishment).
- For many years, many things not regarded as "life, liberty, or property" were dismissed as "privileges," and the state could take away privileges without providing due process.
- Goldberg v. Kelly, 397 U.S. 254 (1970), extended the Due Process Clause broadly enough to include the state's decision to deprive a woman of welfare benefits on the basis that such "benefits are a matter of statutory entitlement for persons qualified to receive them."
- The Court refused to focus on whether public assistance benefits are "a 'privilege' and not a 'right,'" and instead focused on whether the recipient would be "condemned to suffer grievous loss" (if the assistance were withdrawn), and "depends upon whether the recipient's interest in avoiding that loss outweighs the governmental interest in summary adjudication."
- The Court held that Goldberg was entitled to a pretermination hearing.
- In post-*Goldberg* cases, the Court struggled to determine what other types of governmental benefits or contracts should be entitled to due process.

- In Board of Regents v. Roth, 408 U.S. 564 (1972), for example, the Court held that an assistant professor who was hired for a fixed term of one academic year was not entitled to a due process hearing when his contract was not renewed.
- The Court focused on whether the interest is within the Fourteenth Amendment's protection of liberty and property, and concluded that it was not because it "stretches the concept too far to suggest that a person is deprived of 'liberty' when he simply is not rehired in one job but remains as free as before to seek another." The "terms of the respondent's appointment secured absolutely no interest in re-employment for the next year."
- In Arnett v. Kennedy, 416 U.S. 134 (1974), a plurality of the Court affirmed the idea that the legislature could limit and condition an individual's right to a hearing because "a litigant in the position of appellee must take the bitter with the sweet."
- However, in Cleveland Board of Education v. Loudermill, 470 U.S. 532 (1985), the Court reversed itself and rejected the "bitter with the sweet" approach because the "Due Process Clause provides that certain substantive rights — life, liberty, and property — cannot be deprived except pursuant to constitutionally adequate procedures. . . . The right to due process 'is conferred, not by legislative grace, but by constitutional guarantee.'"
- In Paul v. Davis, 424 U.S. 693 (1976), the Court held that an individual did not have a "liberty interest" in not being identified by the police as a possible shoplifter.
- Goldberg v. Kelly opened a Pandora's box for the Court. If due process requires notice and an opportunity to be heard, what type of hearing is required? Does the hearing requirement vary from one type of case to another?
- In *Goldberg*, the Court concluded that welfare recipients were not entitled to a formal proceeding, in the sense of including a "complete record and a comprehensive opinion," but rather were entitled to only a "fair hearing" in the sense of "minimum procedural safeguards, adapted to the particular characteristics of welfare recipients, and to the limited nature of the controversies to be resolved."
- In the Court's view, welfare recipients were entitled to an "opportunity to be heard" at a "meaningful time and in a meaningful manner." This included a requirement that the agency provide the recipient with "timely and adequate notice detailing the reasons for a proposed termination, and an effective opportunity to defend by confronting any adverse witnesses and by presenting his own arguments and evidence orally." "Although the agency need not provide a recipient with an attorney, 'the recipient must be allowed to retain an attorney if he so desires.' 'Finally, the decisionmaker's conclusion as to a recipient's eligibility must rest solely on the legal rules and evidence adduced at the hearing [and] the decision maker should state the reasons for his determination and

indicate the evidence he relied on, though his statement need not amount to a full opinion or even formal findings of fact and conclusions of law. And, of course, an impartial decision maker is essential.'"

- In Mathews v. Eldridge, 424 U.S. 319 (1976), the Court articulated the concept of "flexible due process," which suggests that "[D]ue process is flexible and calls for such procedural protections as the particular situation demands."

- In a given case, in deciding the level of process required, a court must consider "the private interest that will be affected by the official action, the risk of an erroneous deprivation of such interest through the procedures used, and the probable value, if any, of additional or substitute procedural safeguards," and "the Government's interest, including the function involved and the fiscal and administrative burdens that the additional or substitute procedural requirement would entail."

8

Substantive Protection of Economic Rights

∽ PROBLEM: SAVE THE BEACH ∽

The City of Pensacola, Florida, has become increasingly concerned about issues involving beach erosion, storms, and especially oil spills, given the relatively close Deepwater Horizon oil leak. That leak occurred after an April 20, 2010, explosion on the rig, killing 11 people. The oil spilled out at a rate of up to several hundred thousand barrels a day, meaning that it equaled the Exxon Valdez spill in Alaska in a little over a week.

Pensacola decided it needs to make significant changes to its current relaxed approach to property preservation. The basis for its concern derived from studies that show some beach areas on the Gulf of Mexico are eroding at a rate of 5 to 10 feet per year. Other studies show that the force of hurricanes is greater without the coastal wetlands to act as buffers.

Since Pensacola does not have the resources to finance environmentally sound development, it is determined to find inexpensive ways to implement its preservation proposals. The city council is considering adopting a variety of different proposals. One proposal is tentatively titled "Save Our Beaches." After asserting that each of the provisions is severable upon a finding of invalidity, the law states in part:

(a) *Seawalls.* All private property owners whose property is located directly on the beach must build seawalls or implement acceptable alternative wave dispersal technology, such as breakwaters, or dredge sand off the beach.

(b) *Accretions and Avulsions.* Accretions are sand, sediment, and other similar deposits that create additional dry land. Accretions usually occur slowly over time. Unlike the common law and prior Florida law, in Pensacola the city shall from this day forward have title to any accretions that occur. Avulsions are areas of dry land created from land once covered by water and are usually uncovered based on sudden events. Regardless of how they are uncovered, the state shall continue to hold title to such land in trust for the people. Thus, while the technical property boundary of littoral land owners might change, the right to access to the water shall be preserved as will other common law riparian rights, unless changed by valid state law.

(c) *Contracts.* Any contractual agreements changed by this law shall be based only on substantial justification of preserving the beach and its central role in Pensacola culture.

(d) *Natural State.* All property owners within one-half mile of the beach must leave at least 50 percent of that property in its natural state or with some form of wetland vegetation, if feasible, after neutral study. (This section applies prospectively only, with no change to existing structures.)

(e) *Clean-up.* All beach-front landowners must clean-up any oil, oil products, or related waste on their property within seven (7) days of its deposit on the property.

(f) *Building Moratorium.* There shall be no more building on beach-front property for a minimum of six months to assess and determine the impact of the Deepwater Horizon oil leak.

(g) *Colors.* To promote Pensacola, all buildings within a mile of the beach must comply with the city color scheme, with yellow and blue predominating, unless a variance is permitted.

The city council is thinking about imposing fines of up to $10,000 a month for each violation and seeking injunctive relief and possibly criminal penalties.

As you work your way through this chapter, you will be asked to put yourself in various roles—for example, an attorney who is advising the city council or an attorney who represents affected landowners—and to consider the validity of this legislation under various factual scenarios.

———

Economic rights have assumed increasing significance in recent years, especially in light of the serious financial difficulties experienced by the United States. Terms such as *collateralized debt obligations* and *credit swap derivatives* have surfaced in the American vernacular, and the consequences of those financial instruments have led to a call for greater regulation of financial markets. Some politicians and observers have framed the issue as a clash between the interests of Wall Street and Main Street.

The question whether economic interests warrant protection, as a matter of constitutional right or liberty, highlights a long-persisting controversy over the role of the judiciary and its relationship to the elected branches of government. Early interpretations of the Contract Clause reflected a judicial interest in prohibiting state laws that retroactively impaired private contractual rights and expectations. Indeed, until the late Nineteenth Century, the Contract Clause represented the primary constitutional basis for protecting private property interests against government action.

By contrast, judicial interpretations of the Takings Clause suggest that it applies when government acquires private property through eminent domain or regulates land in a manner that impairs its use. However, over the years, the Takings Clause has tended to be an inconsistent and uncertain source of protection for private property rights. The Commerce Clause, sometimes in conjunction with preemption principles, has been another significant tool for managing the boundaries of economic freedom. Interpretation of the Commerce Clause, depending upon prevailing doctrine, has expanded or restricted a state's power to regulate economic activity.

Although largely consigned to history, utilization of the substantive due process clauses to define and protect economic rights and liberties has been a focal point of the debate over constitutional interpretation and the role of the judiciary. The emergence of substantive due process, to develop and account for economic rights and liberties, was previewed in Dred Scott v. Sandford, 60 U.S. 393 (1857), when the Court attempted to resolve the slavery issue on constitutional grounds. As Chief Justice Roger B. Taney put it, "the right of property in a slave is distinctly and expressly affirmed in the Constitution. And, federal legislation depriving a citizen of "his property in a particular Territory . . . could hardly be dignified with the name due process of law." Id. at 451.

Notwithstanding the eventual repudiation of *Dred Scott* by war, constitutional amendment, and later judicial review, economic rights theory gained increasing currency as the latter half of the nineteenth century progressed. In *The Slaughterhouse Cases*, 83 U.S. 36 (1873), the Court's seminal interpretation of the Fourteenth Amendment, Justice Stephen Field urged an understanding that would include "the right to acquire and possess property of every kind" as a matter that "of right belong[s] to the citizens of all free governments." Justice Field's argument, echoed by three other dissenting justices, pertained to the Privileges and Immunities Clause of the Fourteenth Amendment. His broad interpretation of the incidents of federal citizenship did not command a majority of the *Slaughterhouse* Court, and the Privileges and Immunities Clause largely has been of limited consequence since.

Economic rights theory, which the Court repudiated in the privileges and immunities context, broke though slightly as an animating source for the Due Process Clause more than two decades later. In Allgeyer v. Louisiana, 165 U.S. 578 (1896), the Court embraced the Due Process Clause as the basis for "the right of the citizen to be free in the enjoyment of all his faculties; to be free to use them in all lawful ways; to live and work where he will; to earn his livelihood by any lawful calling; to pursue any livelihood or avocation; and for that purpose to enter into all contracts which may be proper, necessary and essential to his carrying out to a successful conclusion the purposes above mentioned." Id. at 589.

The *Allgeyer* decision heralded an era of judicially identified and developed rights and liberties that engendered controversy with respect to not only the Court's outputs but also to its standards of review and role in the context of representative governance. Debate over the Court's performance and function has persisted long after the economic rights doctrine was abandoned in the late 1930s. Among other things, it is a reference point for modern dialogue regarding the Due Process Clause as a source of fundamental albeit unenumerated rights and liberties.

This chapter focuses on the substantive Due Process Clauses of the Fifth and Fourteenth Amendments, the Takings Clause, and the Contracts Clause as constitutional means of accounting for economic rights and liberties.

A. SUBSTANTIVE DUE PROCESS: FROM *ALLGEYER* TO *LOCHNER* TO *NEBBIA*

The concept of "substantive due process" has emerged as a limit on government powers. The idea of a "substantive" limit distinguishes the "process" orientation of the Due Process Clause and tends to protect particular values, such as economic freedom or personal privacy.

The need for substantive due process presupposes an otherwise valid exercise of government power. It is well established that states possess "police powers" that predated the Constitution and were acknowledged in it. The federal government also may enact laws that indirectly provide for the health, welfare, safety, and morals of society through the Commerce Clause and other powers. These "police power" regulations (also known as "health and welfare regulations") can take many different forms. For example, a legislature might limit the number of hours that employees can work or mandate minimum compensation. Alternatively, a legislature might place conditions on the ability of out-of-state companies to do business within the state, or choose to prohibit certain types of businesses (e.g., brothels).

Health, welfare, and safety regulations might be challenged and curtailed on any number of constitutional grounds, including the Contract Clause, the protection of "liberty" contained in the Fourteenth Amendment, the Equal Protection Clause, and sometimes the Privileges and Immunities Clause. The conceptualization of economic substantive due process emerged from the interpretation of the word *liberty* in the Fourteenth Amendment. For example, in Allgeyer v. Louisiana, 165 U.S. 578 (1897), a state law prohibited foreign insurance companies from doing business within the state without a license and an agent authorized to conduct business on its behalf. The Court struck down the law:

> [W]e think the statute is a violation of the fourteenth amendment of the federal constitution, in that it deprives the defendants of their liberty without due process of law. . . . The 'liberty' mentioned in that amendment means, not only the right of the citizen to be free from the mere physical restraint of his person, as by incarceration, but the term is deemed to embrace the right of the citizen to be free in the enjoyment of all his faculties; to be free to use them in all lawful ways; to live and work where he will; to earn his livelihood by any lawful calling; to pursue any livelihood or avocation; and for that purpose to enter into all contracts which may be proper, necessary, and essential to his carrying out to a successful conclusion the purposes above mentioned

See also Holden v. Hardy, 169 U.S. 366 (1898) (the Court sustained a Utah law regulating the hours of employment in underground mines and in smelters and ore reduction works).

Resolution of these controversies implicates competing theories of judicial review, and judicial outcomes hinge in large part on whether the Court embraces a model that defers to or independently evaluates legislative outputs and premises. Early substantive due process review, which focused largely on economic rights and liberties, proceeded on the premise that the judiciary should evaluate both legislative means and ends. This practice was challenged by critics then and now who viewed it as "antidemocratic" in the sense that it transformed the Court into a super-legislature. The following case illuminates the methodology of constitutionally managed economic rights through the Due Process Clause. It also is the source of shorthand terminology (*Lochnerism*) that detractors use in criticizing the judiciary's development of rights that the Constitution does not specifically enumerate.

A "sweatshop" in Chicago, Illinois, 1903

Lochner v. New York

198 U.S. 45 (1905)

Mr. Justice PECKHAM [delivered] the opinion of the Court.

[Joseph Lochner was indicted on a charge that he "wrongfully and unlawfully required and permitted an employee working for him in his biscuit, bread, and cake bakery and confectionery establishment, at the city of Utica, [to] work more than sixty hours in one week." The plaintiff [was] convicted and ordered to pay a fine of $50.]

[There] is no pretense [that] the statute was intended to meet a case of involuntary labor in any form. . . . The mandate of the statute [provides] that 'no employee shall contract or agree to work,' more than ten hours per day. . . . The employee may desire to earn the extra money which would arise from his working more than the prescribed time, but this statute forbids the employer from permitting the employee to earn it.

The statute necessarily interferes with the right of contract between the employer and employees. . . . The general right to make a contract in relation to his business is part of the liberty of the individual protected by the 14th Amendment of the Federal Constitution. Allgeyer v. Louisiana, 165 U.S. 578. [N]o state can deprive any person of life, liberty, or property without due process of law. The right to purchase or to sell labor is part of the liberty protected by this amendment, unless there are circumstances which exclude the right. There are, however, [powers] existing in the sovereignty of each state in the Union, somewhat vaguely termed police powers [that] relate to the safety, health, morals, and general welfare of the public. Both property and liberty are held on such reasonable conditions as may be imposed by the governing power of the state in the exercise of those powers, and with such conditions the 14th Amendment was not designed to interfere.

The state [has] power to prevent the individual from making certain kinds of contracts. [W]hen the state, by its legislature, in the assumed exercise of its police powers, has passed an act which seriously limits the right to labor or the right of contract in regard to their means of livelihood between [employer and employee], it becomes of great importance to determine which shall prevail, — the right of the individual to labor for such time as he may choose, or the right of the state to prevent the individual from laboring, or from entering into any contract to labor, beyond a certain time prescribed by the state. . . .

It must, of course, be conceded that there is a limit to the valid exercise of the police power by the state. . . . Otherwise the 14th Amendment would have no efficacy and the legislatures of the states would have unbounded power, and it would be enough to say that any piece of legislation was enacted to conserve the morals, the health, or the safety of the people. . . . In every case [where] legislation of this character is concerned, [the] question necessarily arises: Is this a fair, reasonable, and appropriate exercise of the police power of the state, or is it an unreasonable, unnecessary, and arbitrary interference with the right of the individual to his personal liberty, or to enter into those contracts in relation to labor which may seem to him appropriate or necessary for the support of himself and his family? Of course the liberty of contract relating to labor includes both parties. . . . The one has as much right to purchase as the other to sell labor. . . .

This is not a question of substituting the judgment of the court for that of the legislature. If the act be within the power of the state it is valid, although the judgment of the court might be totally opposed to the enactment of such a law. But the question would still remain: Is it within the police power of the state? and that question must be answered by the court.

The question whether this act is valid as a labor law, pure and simple, may be dismissed in a few words. There is no reasonable ground for interfering with the liberty of person or the right of free contract, by determining the hours of labor, in the occupation of a baker. There is no contention that bakers as a class are not equal in intelligence and capacity to men in other trades or manual occupations, or that they are not able to assert their rights and care for themselves without the protecting arm of the state, interfering with their independence of judgment and of action. They are in no sense wards of the state. [This law] involves neither the safety, the morals, nor the welfare, of the public, and that the interest of the public is not in the slightest degree affected by such an act. The law must be upheld, if at all, as a law pertaining to the health of the individual engaged in the occupation of a baker. It does not affect any other portion of the public. . . . Clean and wholesome bread does not depend upon whether the baker works but ten hours per day or only sixty hours a week. . . .

[The] mere assertion that the subject relates, though but in a remote degree, to the public health, does not necessarily render the enactment valid. The act must have a more direct relation, as a means to an end, and the end itself must be appropriate and legitimate, before an act can be held to be valid which interferes with the general right of an individual to be free in his person and in his power to contract in relation to his own labor. . . .

We think the limit of the police power has been reached and passed in this case. There is, in our judgment, no reasonable foundation for holding this to be necessary or appropriate as a health law to safeguard the public health, or the health of the individuals who are following the trade of a baker. If this statute be valid, and if [a] proper case is made out in which to deny the right of an individual[,] as employer or employee, to make contracts for the labor of the latter under the protection of the provisions of the Federal Constitution, there would seem to be no length to which legislation of this nature might not go. . . .

[T]here can be no fair doubt that the trade of a baker, in and of itself, is not an unhealthy one to that degree which would authorize the legislature to interfere with the right to labor, and with the right of free contract on the part of the individual, either as employer or employee. . . . There must be more than the mere fact of the possible existence of some small amount of unhealthiness to warrant legislative interference with liberty. [L]abor, [in] any department, may possibly carry with it the seeds of unhealthiness. But are we all, on that account, at the mercy of legislative majorities? A printer, a tinsmith, a locksmith, a carpenter, a cabinetmaker, a dry goods clerk, a bank's, a lawyer's, or a physician's clerk, or a clerk in almost any kind of business, would all come under the power of the legislature, on this assumption. No trade, no occupation, no mode of earning one's living, could escape this all-pervading power, and the acts of the legislature in limiting the hours of labor in all employments would be valid, although such limitation might seriously cripple the ability of the laborer to support himself and his family. . . .

[It is urged that] it is to the interest of the state that its population should be strong and robust, and therefore any legislation which may be said to tend to make people healthy must be valid as health laws, enacted under the police power. [Any law] might find shelter under such assumptions, and conduct [as] well as contract, would come under the restrictive sway of the legislature. Not only the hours of employees, but the hours of employers, could be regulated, and doctors, lawyers, scientists, all professional men, as well as athletes and artisans, could be forbidden to fatigue their brains and bodies by prolonged hours of exercise, lest the fighting strength of the state be impaired. [W]e think that such a law as this, although passed in the assumed exercise of the police power, and as relating to the public health, or the health of the employees named, is not within that power, and is invalid. The act is not, within any fair meaning of the term, a health law, but is an illegal interference with the rights of individuals, both employers and employees, to make contracts regarding labor upon such terms as they may think best, or which they may agree upon with the other parties to such contracts. Statutes of th[is] nature[,] limiting the hours in which grown and intelligent men may labor to earn their living, are mere meddlesome interferences with the rights of the individual, and they are not saved from condemnation by the claim that they are passed in the exercise of the police power and upon the subject of the health of the individual whose rights are interfered with, unless there be some fair ground, reasonable in and of itself, to say that there is material danger to the public health, or to the health of the employees, if the hours of labor are not curtailed. [A] prohibition to enter into any contract of labor in a bakery for more than a certain number of hours a week is, in our judgment, so wholly beside the matter of a proper, reasonable, and fair provision as to run counter to that liberty of person and of free contract provided for in the Federal Constitution.

It was further urged on the argument that restricting the hours of labor in the case of bakers was valid because it tended to cleanliness on the part of the workers, as a man was more apt to be cleanly when not overworked, and if cleanly then his 'output' was also more likely to be so. What has already been said applies with equal force to this contention. . . .

[From] the character of the law and the subject upon which it legislates, it is apparent that the public health or welfare bears but the most remote relation to the law. . . . It seems to us that the real object and purpose were simply to regulate the hours of labor between the master and his employees [in] a private business, not dangerous in any degree to morals, or in any real and substantial degree to the health of the employees. . . .

The judgment [must] be reversed and the case remanded to the County Court for further proceedings not inconsistent with this opinion.

Reversed.

Mr. Justice HOLMES dissenting:

[If] it were a question whether I agreed with [the legislature's economic] theory, I should desire to study it further [before] making up my mind. But I do not conceive that to be my duty, because [my] agreement or disagreement has nothing to do with the right of a majority to embody their opinions in law. It is settled by various decisions of this court that state constitutions and state laws may regulate life in many ways which we [might] think as injudicious, [or] tyrannical, [and which interfere] with the liberty to contract. . . . Some of these laws embody convictions or prejudices which judges are likely to share. Some may not. But a Constitution is not intended to embody a particular economic theory. [T]he word 'liberty,' in the 14th Amendment, is perverted when it is held to prevent the natural outcome of a dominant opinion, unless it can be said that a rational and fair man necessarily would admit that the statute proposed would infringe fundamental principles as they have been understood by the traditions of our people and our law. [N]o such sweeping condemnation can be passed upon the statute before us. A reasonable man might think it a proper measure on the score of health. . . .

Mr. Justice HARLAN (with whom Mr. Justice WHITE and Mr. Justice DAY concurred) dissenting:

[The police] power extends at least to the protection of the lives, the health, and the safety of the public against the injurious exercise by any citizen of his own rights. [T]he state, in the exercise of its powers, may not unduly interfere with the right of the citizen to enter into contracts that may be necessary and essential in the enjoyment of the inherent rights belonging to everyone, among which rights is the right 'to be free in the enjoyment of all his faculties, to be free to use them in all lawful ways, to live and work where he will, to earn his livelihood by any lawful calling, to pursue any livelihood or avocation.' [*See*] Allgeyer v. Louisiana, 165 U.S. 578. 'But [the] liberty of contract may, within certain limits, be subjected to regulations designed and calculated to promote the general welfare, or to guard the public health, the public morals, or the public safety. . . .' Jacobson v. Massachusetts, 197 U.S. 11.

[A] legislative enactment, Federal or state, is never to be disregarded or held invalid unless it [be] plainly and palpably in excess of legislative power. . . . If there be doubt[,] that doubt must [be] resolved in favor of its validity, and the courts must keep their hands off, leaving the legislature to meet the responsibility for unwise legislation. If the end which the legislature seeks to accomplish be one to which its power extends, and if the means employed to that end, although not the wisest or best, are yet not plainly and palpably unauthorized by law, then the court cannot interfere. [T]he burden of proof, so to speak, is upon those who assert it to be unconstitutional.

[It] is plain that this statute was enacted in order to protect the physical well-being of those who work in bakery and confectionery establishments. It may be that the statute had its origin [in] the belief that employers and employees in such establishments were not upon an equal footing, and that the necessities of the latter often compelled them to submit to such exactions as unduly taxed their strength. Be this as it may, the statute must be taken as expressing the belief of the people of New York that, [in] the case of the average man, labor in excess of sixty hours during a week in such establishments may endanger the health of those who thus labor. Whether or not this be wise legislation it is not the province of the court to inquire. Under our systems of government the courts are not concerned with the wisdom or policy of legislation. [I]n determining the question of power to interfere with liberty of contract, the court may inquire whether the means devised by the state are germane to an end which may be lawfully accomplished and have a real or substantial relation to the protection of health, as involved in the daily work of the persons, male and female, engaged in bakery and confectionery establishments. [I] find it impossible, in view of common experience, to say that there is here no real or substantial relation between the means employed by the state and the end sought to be accomplished by its legislation. Nor can I say that the statute has no appropriate or direct connection with that protection to health which each state owes to her citizens or that it is not promotive of the health of the employees in question or that the regulation prescribed by the state is utterly unreasonable and extravagant or wholly arbitrary. Still less can I say that the statute is, beyond question, a plain, palpable invasion of rights secured by the fundamental law. Therefore I submit that this court will transcend its functions if it assumes to annul the statute of New York. It must be remembered that this statute does not apply to all kinds of business. It applies only to work in bakery and confectionery establishments, in which, as all know, the air constantly breathed by workmen is not as pure and healthful as that to be found in some other establishments or out of doors. . . .

We [know] that the question of the number of hours during which a workman should continuously labor has been, for a long period, and is yet, a subject of serious consideration among civilized peoples, and by those having special knowledge of the laws of health. Suppose the statute prohibited labor in bakery and confectionery establishments in excess of eighteen hours each day. No one, I take it, could dispute the power of the state to enact such a statute. [T]he statute before us does not embrace extreme or exceptional cases. [T]he number of hours that should constitute a day's labor in particular occupations involving the physical strength and safety of workmen has been the subject of enactments by Congress and by nearly all of the states. Many, if not most, of those enactments fix eight hours as the proper basis of a day's labor.

I do not stop to consider whether any particular view of this economic question presents the sounder theory. . . . It is enough for the determination of this case [that] there is room for debate and for an honest difference of opinion. There are many reasons of a weighty, substantial character, based upon the experience of mankind, in support of the theory that, all things considered, more than ten hours' steady work each day, from week to week, in a bakery or confectionery establishment, may endanger the health and shorten the lives of the workmen, thereby diminishing their physical and mental capacity to serve the state and to provide for those dependent upon them.

If such reasons exist that ought to be the end of this case, for the state is not amenable to the judiciary, in respect of its legislative enactments, unless such enactments are plainly, palpably, beyond all question, inconsistent with the Constitution of the United States. . . . Our duty [is] to sustain the statute as not being in conflict with the Federal Constitution, [it] is not shown to be plainly and palpably inconsistent with that instrument. Let the state alone in the management of its purely domestic affairs, so long as it does not appear beyond all question that it has violated the Federal Constitution. This view necessarily results from the principle that the health and safety of the people of a state are primarily for the state to guard and protect. . . .

The judgment, in my opinion, should be affirmed.

Notes

1. Lochner's *Aftermath*. The Court used the *Lochner* decision to strike down legislation in several other cases. *See, e.g.,* Coppage v. Kansas, 236 U.S. 1 (1915) (striking down state law that made it illegal for an employer to require employees not to join a union); Adair v. United States, 208 U.S. 161 (1908).

2. *Means-Ends Analysis.* Note how both the majority and dissenting opinions invoke "means-ends" analysis. Under such analysis, a reviewing court examines the "end" that the legislature is seeking to accomplish as well as the "means" by which the legislature seeks to accomplish it. Means-ends analysis remains important today, and its application is examined in various contexts in this and succeeding chapters.

∾ PROBLEMS ∾

1. *Save the Beach, Continued.* Do the private property owners' "liberty interests" in the City of Pensacola preclude the city from imposing significant restrictions on their ownership rights to deter waterfront erosion and deterioration? Would *Lochner* provide the property owners with a winning argument in the early 1900s? Justice Scalia, in Stop the Beach Renourishment v. Florida Dept. of Environmental Protection, 560 U.S. __ (2010), *infra*, criticized Justice Kennedy for using substantive due process relating to a matter involving economic rights: "The second problem is that we have held for many years (logically or not) that the 'liberties' protected by Substantive Due Process do not include economic liberties. *See, e.g.,* Lincoln Fed. Labor Union v. Northwestern Iron & Metal Co., 335 U.S. 525 (1949). Justice Kennedy's language ('If a judicial decision . . . eliminates an established property right, the judgment could be set aside as a deprivation of property without due process of law') propels us back to what is referred to (usually deprecatingly) as 'the *Lochner* era.' Lochner v. New York, 198 U.S. 45 (1905). Would Justice Scalia endorse a constrained return to a *Lochner*-type analysis?

2. *Cigarettes and Twinkies.* Suppose that a New York Columbia Hospital study conclusively demonstrates that cigarette smoking in the workplace is unhealthy for the workers. It also proves that it is unhealthy for workers to eat foods such as Twinkies. In response, New York enacts a new law prohibiting both of these

activities in the workplace. Suppose you are a federal judge assigned to hear the case. Using the majority opinion in *Lochner*, should you uphold the law? What if you rely on the reasoning in Justice Holmes's dissent? Which result is preferable? Why?

3. *Cigarettes and Twinkies II.* Suppose the court agrees with the study with respect to cigarettes but not Twinkies. Will the outcome of the two opinions be affected by whether the court agrees or disagrees with the legislature? What is the appropriate judicial role?

Nebbia v. New York

291 U.S. 502 (1934)

Mr. Justice ROBERTS delivered the opinion of the Court.

[In 1932, New York milk prices were below the cost of production. The plight of dairy producers became so desperate that the New York legislature appointed a committee to study the causes of the decline and the effect of low prices on the dairy industry. Based on the study, the legislature established] a Milk Control Board with power, among other things to 'fix minimum and maximum [retail] prices to be charged [by] stores to consumers for consumption off the premises where sold.' The board fixed nine cents as the price to be charged by a store for a quart of milk. Nebbia, the proprietor of a grocery store in Rochester, sold two quarts and a 5-cent loaf of bread for 18 cents; and was convicted for violating the board's order. . . . The question [is] whether the Federal Constitution prohibits a state from so fixing the selling price of milk. . . .

Under our form of government the use of property and the making of contracts are normally matters of private and not of public concern. The general rule is that both shall be free of governmental interference. But neither property rights nor contract rights are absolute; for government cannot exist if the citizen may at will use his property to the detriment of his fellows, or exercise his freedom of contract to work them harm. Equally fundamental with the private right is that of the public to regulate it in the common interest. . . . The Fifth Amendment [and] the Fourteenth [do] not prohibit governmental regulation for the public welfare. They merely condition the exertion of the admitted power, by securing that the end shall be accomplished by methods consistent with due process. And the guaranty of due process [demands] only that the law shall not be unreasonable, arbitrary, or capricious, and that the means selected shall have a real and substantial relation to the object sought to be attained. It results that a regulation valid for one sort of business, or in given circumstances, may be invalid for another sort, or for the same business under other circumstances, because the reasonableness of each regulation depends upon the relevant facts. . . .

The court has repeatedly sustained curtailment of enjoyment of private property in the public interest. . . . Laws passed for the suppression of immorality, in the interest of health, to secure fair trade practices, and to safeguard the interests of depositors in banks, have been found consistent with due process.

These measures not only affected the use of private property, but also interfered with the right of private contract. Other instances are numerous where valid regulation has restricted the right of contract, while less directly affecting property rights. . . . The Constitution does not guarantee the unrestricted privilege to engage in a business or to conduct it as one pleases. . . .

The milk industry in New York has been the subject of long-standing and drastic regulation in the public interest. The legislative investigation of 1932 [showed that] unrestricted competition aggravated existing evils and [that] the normal law of supply and demand was insufficient to correct maladjustments detrimental to the community. The inquiry disclosed destructive and demoralizing competitive conditions and unfair trade practices which resulted in retail price cutting and reduced the income of the farmer below the cost of production. [T]he legislature [believed] conditions could be improved by preventing destructive price-cutting by stores which, due to the flood of surplus milk, were able to buy at much lower prices than the larger distributors and to sell without incurring the delivery costs of the latter. [T]he Milk Control Board fixed a price of 10 cents per quart for sales by a distributor to a consumer, and 9 cents by a store to a consumer, thus recognizing the lower costs of the store, and endeavoring to establish a differential which would be just to both. In the light of the facts the order appears not to be unreasonable or arbitrary, or without relation to the purpose to prevent ruthless competition from destroying the wholesale price structure on which the farmer depends for his livelihood, and the community for an assured supply of milk.

[A]ppellant urges that direct fixation of prices is a type of regulation absolutely forbidden. . . . The argument runs that the public control of rates or prices is per se unreasonable and unconstitutional, save as applied to businesses affected with a public interest [such as a] public utility. [If the] dairy industry [is] subject to regulation in the public interest, what constitutional principle bars the state from correcting existing maladjustments by legislation touching prices? We think there is no such principle. The due process clause makes no mention of sales or of prices any more than it speaks of business or contracts or buildings or other incidents of property. . . . It is clear that there is no closed class or category of businesses affected with a public interest, and the function of courts in the application of the Fifth and Fourteenth Amendments is to determine in each case whether circumstances vindicate the challenged regulation as a reasonable exertion of governmental authority or condemn it as arbitrary or discriminatory. The phrase "affected with a public interest" can [mean] no more than that an industry, for adequate reason, is subject to control for the public good. [T]here can be no doubt that upon proper occasion and by appropriate measures the state may regulate a business in any of its aspects, including the prices to be charged for the products or commodities it sells.

So far as the requirement of due process is concerned, and in the absence of other constitutional restriction, a state is free to adopt whatever economic policy may reasonably be deemed to promote public welfare, and to enforce that policy by legislation adapted to its purpose. The courts are without authority either to declare such policy, or, when it is declared by the legislature, to override it. If the laws passed are seen to have a reasonable relation to a proper legislative purpose, and are neither arbitrary nor discriminatory, the requirements of due process are satisfied. [I]f the legislative policy be to curb unrestrained and harmful competition by measures which are not arbitrary or discriminatory it does not lie with the courts to determine that the rule is unwise. With the wisdom of the policy adopted, with the adequacy or practicability of the law enacted to forward it, the courts are both incompetent and unauthorized to deal. The course of decision in this court exhibits a firm adherence to these principles. [T]he Legislature is primarily the judge of the necessity of such an enactment, [every] possible presumption is in favor of its validity, [and] though the court may hold views inconsistent with the wisdom of the law, it may not be annulled unless palpably in excess of legislative power. . . .

Tested by these considerations we find no basis in the due process clause of the Fourteenth Amendment for condemning the provisions of the Agriculture and Markets Law here drawn into question.

The judgment is affirmed.

Mr. Justice McReynolds, joined by Justices Butler, Sutherland, and Van Devanter, dissented.

[T]his Court must have regard to the wisdom of the enactment. At least, we must inquire concerning its purpose and decide whether the means proposed have reasonable relation to something within legislative power—whether the end is legitimate, and the means appropriate. If a statute to prevent conflagrations, should require householders to pour oil on their roofs as a means of curbing the spread of fire when discovered in the neighborhood, we could hardly uphold it. Here, we find direct interference with guaranteed rights defended upon the ground that the purpose was to promote the public welfare by increasing milk prices at the farm. Unless we can affirm that the end proposed is proper and the means adopted have reasonable relation to it, this action is unjustifiable.

The court below has not [indicated] how higher charges at stores to impoverished customers [can] possibly increase receipts at the farm. The Legislative Committee pointed out as the obvious cause of decreased consumption, notwithstanding low prices, the consumers' reduced buying power. Higher store prices will not enlarge this power; nor will they decrease production. . . . Not only does the statute interfere arbitrarily with the rights of the little grocer to conduct his business [but] it takes away the liberty of 12,000,000 consumers to buy a necessity of life in an open market. . . . To [those] with less than 9 cents it says: You cannot procure a quart of milk from the grocer although he is anxious to accept what you can pay and the demands of your household are urgent! A superabundance; but no child can purchase from a willing storekeeper below the figure appointed by three men at headquarters! And this is true although the storekeeper himself may have bought from a willing producer at half that rate and must sell quickly or lose his stock through deterioration. . . .

[The] Legislature cannot lawfully destroy guaranteed rights of one man with the prime purpose of enriching another, even if for the moment, this may seem advantageous to the public. . . . Grave concern for embarrassed farmers is everywhere; but this should neither obscure the rights of others nor obstruct judicial appraisement of measures proposed for relief. The ultimate welfare of the producer, like that of every other class, requires dominance of the Constitution. And zealously to uphold this in all its parts is the highest duty entrusted to the courts. . . .

Notes and Questions

1. *Aftermath.* By the 1930s, following the constitutional crisis (see the discussion of President Roosevelt's so-called Court Packing Plan in Chapter 2, *supra*, at 145-146), *Lochnerian* approaches to economic rights disappeared along with the Court's more restrictive interpretation of the Commerce Clause. In addition to *Nebbia*, the Court decided West Coast Hotel Co. v. Parrish, 300 U.S. 379 (1937), which involved a constitutional challenge to a State of Washington law stipulating minimum wages for women and minors. In an opinion by Justice Hughes, the Court upheld the law:

> [The] constitutional provision invoked is the due process clause of the Fourteenth Amendment. . . . In each case the violation alleged by those attacking minimum wage regulations for women is deprivation of freedom of contract. What is this freedom? The Constitution does not speak of freedom of contract. It speaks of liberty and prohibits the deprivation of liberty without due process of law. In prohibiting that deprivation, the Constitution does not recognize an absolute and uncontrollable liberty. . . . Liberty under the Constitution is thus necessarily subject to the restraints of due process, and regulation which is reasonable in relation to its subject and is adopted in the interests of the community is due process. . . . The point that has been strongly stressed that adult employees should be deemed competent to make their own contracts was decisively met nearly forty years ago. [The] exploitation of a class of workers who are in an unequal position with respect to bargaining power and are thus relatively defenseless against the denial of a living wage is not only detrimental to their health and well being, but casts a direct burden for their support upon the community. What these workers lose in wages the taxpayers are called upon to pay. The bare cost of living must be met. We may take judicial notice of the unparalleled demands for relief which arose during the recent period of depression and still continue to an alarming extent despite the degree of economic recovery which has been achieved. It is unnecessary to cite official statistics to establish what is of common knowledge through the length and breadth of the land. . . .

2. *More on* Lochner's *Aftermath.* In Williamson v. Lee Optical, 348 U.S. 483 (1955), an Oklahoma law made it illegal for anyone except a licensed optometrist or ophthalmologist to fit lenses to a face or to duplicate or replace into frames lenses or other optical appliances, except upon written prescriptive authority of an Oklahoma-licensed ophthalmologist or optometrist. Effectively, the law precluded an optician from fitting old glasses into new frames or supplying a lens, whether it be a new lens or one to duplicate a lost or broken lens, without a prescription. In an opinion by Justice Douglas, the Court upheld the law:

> The Oklahoma law may exact a needless, wasteful requirement in many cases. But it is for the legislature, not the courts, to balance the advantages and disadvantages of the new requirement. . . . The day is gone when this Court uses the Due Process Clause of the Fourteenth

Amendment to strike down state laws, regulatory of business and industrial conditions, because they may be unwise, improvident, or out of harmony with a particular school of thought. We emphasize again what Chief Justice Waite said in Munn v. State of Illinois, 94 U.S. 113, 'For protection against abuses by legislatures the people must resort to the polls, not to the courts.'

3. Carolene Products *Footnote 4*. The now-famous footnote 4 from the *Carolene Products* case offered a new approach to constitutional analysis: "There may be narrower scope for operation of the presumption of constitutionality when legislation appears on its face to be within a specific prohibition of the Constitution, such as those of the first ten Amendments, which are deemed equally specific when held to be embraced within the Fourteenth. *See* Stromberg v. California, 283 U.S. 359; Lovell v. Griffin, 303 U.S. 444. It is unnecessary to consider now whether legislation which restricts those political processes which can ordinarily be expected to bring about repeal of undesirable legislation, is to be subjected to more exacting judicial scrutiny under the general prohibitions of the Fourteenth Amendment than are most other types of legislation. On restrictions upon the right to vote, *see* Nixon v. Herndon, 273 U.S. 536; on restraints upon the dissemination of information, *see* Near v. Minnesota, 283 U.S. 697; *Lovell v. Griffin, supra*; on interferences with political organizations, *see* Stromberg v. California, *supra*, 283 U.S. 359; as to prohibition of peaceable assembly, *see* De Jonge v. Oregon, 299 U.S. 353. Nor need we enquire whether similar considerations enter into the review of statutes directed at particular religious, Pierce v. Society of Sisters, 268 U.S. 510, or national, Meyer v. Nebraska, 262 U.S. 390, or racial minorities. Nixon v. Herndon, *supra;* Nixon v. Condon, *supra*; whether prejudice against discrete and insular minorities may be a special condition, which tends seriously to curtail the operation of those political processes ordinarily to be relied upon to protect minorities, and which may call for a correspondingly more searching judicial inquiry. *Compare* McCulloch v. Maryland, 4 Wheat. 316, 428, 4 L.Ed. 579."

∾ PROBLEMS ∾

1. Lochner's *Reprise*. After *Nebbia* was decided, suppose that the New York legislature immediately reimposes the law that was struck down in *Lochner*. After *Nebbia*, would the Court uphold the law, or would it still strike it down? Explain.

2. *Legal Grounds*. Wilkes-Barre, Pennsylvania, enacts a statute "protecting the right to contract and to sell one's economic labor as a fundamental right of individuals in society." The statute is premised on the proposition that "economic interests go to the heart of an individual's ability to support him or herself and are essential to the individual's well-being." It goes on to state: "Under the Contract Clause, the Takings Clause, and the original constitutional imperative of forming a viable economic union, economic freedom should be viewed as an implied fundamental right, no different than voting or travel." a) Do you agree with the premise of the statute? Do constitutional rights have to be enumerated?

Why or why not? Are there logical indications of a union or constitutional governance, such as a right to travel or the right to vote, that do not require enumeration? Answers to questions like these are critical to the ability to frame and develop a theory of judicial review. b) Would such a statute be upheld after *Nebbia*?

B. THE TAKINGS CLAUSE

The Fifth Amendment Takings Clause, sometimes referred to as the "Eminent Domain" Clause, prohibits the government from taking private property for public purpose without providing "just compensation." A taking for purposes of this clause either involves an actual taking (in the sense that government assumes title to the property) or results from the government's regulation of land that significantly restricts its use. Two major issues arise under this clause. First, some litigants question whether their property is being taken for a "public purpose" (as opposed to a private purpose) and therefore argue that the taking is impermissible. Second, at times, there are disputes about whether there is a "taking" at all.

As the following case illustrates, the first question, whether a taking is for a public purpose, has generally been resolved in favor of the government.

Kelo v. City of New London

125 S.Ct. 2655 (2005)

Justice STEVENS delivered the opinion of the Court.

[T]he city of New London approved a development plan that, in the words of the Supreme Court of Connecticut, was "projected to create in excess of 1,000 jobs, to increase tax and other revenues, and to revitalize an economically distressed city, including its downtown and waterfront areas." [T]he city's development agent [seeks] to use the power of eminent domain to acquire [property from those unwilling to sell]. The question presented is whether the city's proposed disposition of this property qualifies as a "public use" within the meaning of the Takings Clause of the Fifth Amendment to the Constitution.[11]

I

[Decades] of economic decline led a state agency in 1990 to designate the City [of New London] a "distressed municipality." In 1996, the Federal Government closed the Naval Undersea Warfare Center, which [had] employed over 1,500 people. In 1998, the City's unemployment rate was nearly double that of the State. . . . These conditions prompted state and local officials to target New

---

11. "[N]or shall private property be taken for public use, without just compensation." U.S. Const., Amdt. 5. That Clause is made applicable to the States by the Fourteenth Amendment.

London, and particularly its Fort Trumbull area, for economic revitalization. To this end, respondent New London Development Corporation (NLDC), a private nonprofit entity established some years earlier to assist the City in planning economic development, was reactivated. In January 1998, the State authorized a $5.35 million bond issue to support the NLDC's planning activities and a $10 million bond issue toward the creation of a Fort Trumbull State Park. In February, the pharmaceutical company Pfizer Inc. announced that it would build a $300 million research facility on a site immediately adjacent to Fort Trumbull; local planners hoped that Pfizer would draw new business to the area, thereby serving as a catalyst to the area's rejuvenation. [After] a series of neighborhood meetings[,] the city council authorized the NLDC to formally submit its plans to the relevant state agencies for review. Upon obtaining state-level approval, the NLDC finalized an integrated development plan focused on 90 acres of the Fort Trumbull area.

The Fort Trumbull area is situated on a peninsula that juts into the Thames River. The area comprises approximately 115 privately owned properties, as well as the 32 acres of land formerly occupied by the naval facility (Trumbull State Park now occupies 18 of those 32 acres). The development plan encompasses seven parcels. Parcel 1 is designated for a waterfront conference hotel at the center of a "small urban village" that will include restaurants and shopping. This parcel will also have marinas for both recreational and commercial uses. A pedestrian "riverwalk" will originate here and continue down the coast, connecting the waterfront areas of the development. Parcel 2 will be the site of approximately 80 new residences organized into an urban neighborhood and linked by public walkway to the remainder of the development, including the state park. This parcel also includes space reserved for a new U.S. Coast Guard Museum. Parcel 3, which is located immediately north of the Pfizer facility, will contain at least 90,000 square feet of research and development office space. Parcel 4A is a 2.4-acre site that will be used either to support the adjacent state park, by providing parking or retail services for visitors, or to support the nearby marina. Parcel 4B will include a renovated marina, as well as the final stretch of the riverwalk. Parcels 5, 6, and 7 will provide land for office and retail space, parking, and water-dependent commercial uses.

The NLDC intended the development plan to capitalize on the arrival of the Pfizer facility and the new commerce it was expected to attract. In addition to creating jobs, generating tax revenue, and helping to "build momentum for the revitalization of downtown New London," the plan was also designed to make the City more attractive and to create leisure and recreational opportunities on the waterfront and in the park.

The city council approved the plan in January 2000, and designated the NLDC as its development agent in charge of implementation. The city council also authorized the NLDC to purchase property or to acquire property by exercising eminent domain in the City's name. The NLDC successfully negotiated the purchase of most of the real estate in the 90-acre area, but its negotiations with petitioners failed. As a consequence, [the] NLDC initiated the condemnation proceedings that gave rise to this case.

II

Petitioner Susette Kelo has lived in the Fort Trumbull area since 1997. She has made extensive improvements to her house, which she prizes for its water view. Petitioner Wilhelmina Dery was born in her Fort Trumbull house in 1918 and has lived there her entire life. Her husband Charles (also a petitioner) has lived in the house since they married some 60 years ago. In all, the nine petitioners own 15 properties in Fort Trumbull — 4 in parcel 3 [and] 11 in parcel 4A. Ten of the parcels are occupied by the owner or a family member; the other five are held as investment properties. There is no allegation that any of these properties is blighted or otherwise in poor condition; [they] were condemned only because they happen to be located in the development area.

In December 2000, petitioners brought this action in the New London Superior Court. They claimed, among other things, that the taking of their properties would violate the "public use" restriction in the Fifth Amendment. [T]he Superior Court granted a permanent restraining order prohibiting the taking of the properties located in parcel 4A (park or marina support). It, however, denied petitioners relief as to the properties located in parcel 3 (office space).[12] [T]he Supreme Court of Connecticut [held] that all of the City's proposed takings were valid. . . . [R]elying on cases such as Hawaii Housing Authority v. Midkiff, 467 U.S. 229 (1984), and Berman v. Parker, 348 U.S. 26 (1954), the court held that such economic development qualified as a valid public use under both the Federal and State Constitutions. . . . We granted certiorari to determine whether a city's decision to take property for the purpose of economic development satisfies the "public use" requirement of the Fifth Amendment.

III

[I]t has long been accepted that the sovereign may not take the property of *A* for the sole purpose of transferring it to another private party *B*, even though *A* is paid just compensation. On the other hand, it is equally clear that a State may transfer property from one private party to another if future "use by the public" is the purpose of the taking; the condemnation of land for a railroad with common-carrier duties is a familiar example. . . .

[T]he City would no doubt be forbidden from taking petitioners' land for the purpose of conferring a private benefit on a particular private party. See *Midkiff*, 467 U.S., at 245. Nor would the City be allowed to take property under the mere pretext of a public purpose, when its actual purpose was to bestow a private benefit. The takings before us, however, would be executed pursuant to a "carefully considered" development plan. The trial judge [and] the Supreme Court of Connecticut agreed that there was no evidence of an illegitimate purpose. . . . Therefore, as was true [in] *Midkiff*, the City's development plan was not adopted "to benefit a particular class of identifiable individuals."

On the other hand, this is not a case in which the City is planning to open the condemned land — at least not in its entirety — to use by the general public.

12. While this litigation was pending[,] the NLDC announced that it would lease some of the parcels to private developers [for development] according to the [plan].

Nor will the private lessees of the land in any sense be required to operate like common carriers, making their services available to all comers. [W]hile many state courts in the mid-19th century endorsed "use by the public" as the proper definition of public use, that narrow view steadily eroded over time. Not only was the "use by the public" test difficult to administer (e.g., what proportion of the public need have access to the property? at what price?), but it proved to be impractical given the diverse and always evolving needs of society. Accordingly, when this Court began applying the Fifth Amendment to the States at the close of the 19th century, it embraced the broader and more natural interpretation of public use as "public purpose." *See, e.g.,* Fallbrook Irrigation Dist. v. Bradley, 164 U.S. 112 (1896). . . .

The disposition of this case therefore turns on the question whether the City's development plan serves a "public purpose." [O]ur cases have defined that concept broadly, reflecting our longstanding policy of deference to legislative judgments in this field. . . . In *Berman,* this Court upheld a redevelopment plan targeting a blighted area of Washington, D.C., in which most of the housing for the area's 5,000 inhabitants was beyond repair. Under the plan, the area would be condemned and part of it utilized for the construction of streets, schools, and other public facilities. The remainder of the land would be leased or sold to private parties for the purpose of redevelopment, including the construction of low-cost housing. . . . The owner of a department store located in the area challenged the condemnation, pointing out that his store was not itself blighted and arguing that the creation of a "better balanced, more attractive community" was not a valid public use. Writing for a unanimous Court, Justice Douglas refused to evaluate this claim in isolation, deferring instead to the legislative and agency judgment that the area "must be planned as a whole" for the plan to be successful. The Court explained that "community redevelopment programs need not, by force of the Constitution, be on a piecemeal basis — lot by lot, building by building." The public use underlying the taking was unequivocally affirmed:

> We do not sit to determine whether a particular housing project is or is not desirable. The concept of the public welfare is broad and inclusive. . . . The values it represents are spiritual as well as physical, aesthetic as well as monetary. It is within the power of the legislature to determine that the community should be beautiful as well as healthy, spacious as well as clean, well-balanced as well as carefully patrolled. In the present case, the Congress and its authorized agencies have made determinations that take into account a wide variety of values. It is not for us to reappraise them. If those who govern the District of Columbia decide that the Nation's Capital should be beautiful as well as sanitary, there is nothing in the Fifth Amendment that stands in the way.

In *Hawaii Housing Authority* the Court considered a Hawaii statute whereby fee title was taken from lessors and transferred to lessees (for just compensation) in order to reduce the concentration of land ownership. We unanimously upheld the statute and rejected the Ninth Circuit's view that it was "a naked attempt on the part of the state of Hawaii to take the property of *A* and transfer it to *B* solely for *B*'s private use and benefit." Reaffirming *Berman's* deferential approach to legislative judgments in this field, we concluded that the State's purpose of eliminating the "social and economic evils of a land oligopoly" qualified as a valid public use. Our opinion also rejected the contention that the mere fact that the State immediately transferred the properties to private individuals upon condemnation somehow diminished the public character of the taking. "[I]t is only the taking's purpose, and not its mechanics," we explained, that matters in determining public use.

In that same Term we decided another public use case that arose in a purely economic context. In Ruckelshaus v. Monsanto, Co., 467 U.S. 986 (1984), the Court dealt with provisions of the Federal Insecticide, Fungicide, and Rodenticide Act under which the Environmental Protection Agency could consider the data (including trade secrets) submitted by a prior pesticide applicant in evaluating a subsequent application, so long as the second applicant paid just compensation for the data. We acknowledged that the "most direct beneficiaries" of these provisions were the subsequent applicants, but we nevertheless upheld the statute under *Berman* and *Midkiff*. We found sufficient Congress' belief that sparing applicants the cost of time-consuming research eliminated a significant barrier to entry in the pesticide market and thereby enhanced competition.

[O]ur jurisprudence has recognized that the needs of society have varied between different parts of the Nation, just as they have evolved over time in response to changed circumstances. Our earliest cases [embodied] a strong theme of federalism, emphasizing the "great respect" that we owe to state legislatures and state courts in discerning local public needs. For more than a century, our public use jurisprudence has wisely eschewed rigid formulas and intrusive scrutiny in favor of affording legislatures broad latitude in determining what public needs justify the use of the takings power.

IV

Those who govern the City were not confronted with the need to remove blight in the Fort Trumbull area, but their determination that the area was sufficiently distressed to justify a program of economic rejuvenation is entitled to our deference. The City has carefully formulated an economic development plan that it believes will provide appreciable benefits to the community, including — but by no means limited to — new jobs and increased tax revenue. As with other exercises in urban planning and development, the City is endeavoring to coordinate a variety of commercial, residential, and recreational uses of land, with the hope that they will form a whole greater than the sum of its parts. To effectuate this plan, the City has invoked a state statute that specifically authorizes the use of eminent domain to promote economic development. Given the comprehensive character of the plan, the thorough deliberation that preceded its adoption, and the limited scope of our review, it is appropriate for us, as it was in *Berman*, to resolve the challenges of the individual owners, not on a piecemeal basis, but rather in light of the entire plan. Because that plan unquestionably serves a public purpose, the takings challenged here satisfy the public use requirement of the Fifth Amendment.

[P]etitioners urge us to adopt a new bright-line rule that economic development does not qualify as a public use. . . . Promoting economic development is a traditional and long accepted function of government. There is, moreover, no principled way of distinguishing economic development from the other public purposes that we have recognized. In our cases upholding takings that facilitated agriculture and mining, for example, we emphasized the importance of those industries to the welfare of the States in question; in *Berman*, we endorsed the purpose of transforming a blighted area into a "well-balanced" community through redevelopment,[13] in *Midkiff*, we upheld the interest in breaking up a land oligopoly that "created artificial deterrents to the normal functioning of the State's residential land market," and in *Monsanto*, we accepted Congress' purpose of eliminating a "significant barrier to entry in the pesticide market." It would be incongruous to hold that the City's interest in the economic benefits to be derived from the development of the Fort Trumbull area has less of a public character than any of those other interests. [T]here is no basis for exempting economic development from our traditionally broad understanding of public purpose.

[T]he government's pursuit of a public purpose will often benefit individual private parties. [I]n *Midkiff*, the forced transfer of property conferred a direct and significant benefit on those lessees who were previously unable to purchase their homes. In *Monsanto*, [the] "most direct beneficiaries" of the data-sharing provisions were the subsequent pesticide applicants, but benefiting them [was] necessary to promoting competition in the pesticide market. The owner of the department store in *Berman* objected to "taking from one businessman for the benefit of another businessman," referring to the fact that under the redevelopment plan land would be leased or sold to private developers for redevelopment. . . .

It is further argued that without a bright-line rule nothing would stop a city from transferring citizen *A*'s property to citizen *B* for the sole reason that citizen *B* will put the property to a more productive use and thus pay more taxes. [T]he hypothetical cases posited by petitioners can be confronted if and when they arise. . . .

[P]etitioners maintain that for takings of this kind we should require a "reasonable certainty" that the expected public benefits will actually accrue. . . . "When the legislature's purpose is legitimate and its means are not irrational, our cases make clear that empirical debates over the wisdom of takings [are] not to be carried out in the federal courts." *Midkiff*, 467 U.S., at 242. . . . A constitutional rule that required postponement of the judicial approval of every condemnation until the likelihood of success of the plan had been assured would unquestionably impose a significant impediment to the successful consummation of many such plans.

[W]e also decline to second-guess the City's determinations as to what lands it needs to acquire in order to effectuate the project. "[Once] the question of the

---

13. It is a misreading of *Berman* to suggest that the only public use upheld in that case was the initial removal of blight. The public use [in] *Berman* extended beyond that to encompass the purpose of *developing* that area to create conditions that would prevent a reversion to blight in the future. Had the public use in *Berman* been defined more narrowly, it would have been difficult to justify the taking of the plaintiff's nonblighted department store.

public purpose has been decided, the amount and character of land to be taken for the project and the need for a particular tract to complete the integrated plan rests in the discretion of the legislative branch." *Berman,* 348 U.S., at 35-36.

[W]e do not minimize the hardship that condemnations may entail, notwithstanding the payment of just compensation. [Nothing] precludes any State from placing further restrictions on its exercise of the takings power. Indeed, many States already impose "public use" requirements that are stricter than the federal baseline. Some of these requirements have been established as a matter of state constitutional law. [T]he necessity and wisdom of using eminent domain to promote economic development are certainly matters of legitimate public debate. This Court's authority, however, extends only to determining whether the City's proposed condemnations are for a "public use" within the meaning of the Fifth Amendment to the Federal Constitution. Because over a century of our case law interpreting that provision dictates an affirmative answer to that question, we may not grant petitioners the relief that they seek.

The judgment of the Supreme Court of Connecticut is affirmed.

It is so ordered.

Justice KENNEDY, concurring.

[Even] the dissenting justices on the Connecticut Supreme Court agreed that respondents' development plan was intended to revitalize the local economy, not to serve the interests of Pfizer, Corcoran Jennison, or any other private party. This case, then, survives the meaningful rational basis review that in my view is required under the Public Use Clause. . . . My agreement with the Court [does] not foreclose the possibility that [there] may be private transfers in which the risk of undetected impermissible favoritism of private parties is so acute that a presumption (rebuttable or otherwise) of invalidity is warranted under the Public Use Clause. . . .

This taking occurred in the context of a comprehensive development plan meant to address a serious city-wide depression, and the projected economic benefits of the project cannot be characterized as *de minimus.* The identity of most of the private beneficiaries were unknown at the time the city formulated its plans. . . . In sum, while there may be categories of cases in which the transfers are so suspicious, or the procedures employed so prone to abuse, or the purported benefits are so trivial or implausible, that courts should presume an impermissible private purpose, no such circumstances are present in this case. . . .

Justice O'CONNOR, with whom THE CHIEF JUSTICE, Justice SCALIA, and Justice THOMAS join, dissenting.

[I]in *Berman* and *Midkiff*[,] precondemnation use of the targeted property inflicted affirmative harm on society — in *Berman* through blight resulting from extreme poverty and in *Midkiff* through oligopoly resulting from extreme wealth. And in both cases, the relevant legislative body had found that eliminating the existing property use was necessary to remedy the harm. Thus a public purpose was realized when the harmful use was eliminated. Because each taking *directly* achieved a public benefit, it did not matter that the property was turned over to private use. Here, in contrast, New London does not claim that Susette Kelo's and Wilhelmina Dery's well-maintained homes are the source of any social harm. . . . In moving away from our decisions sanctioning the condemnation of harmful property use, the Court today significantly expands the meaning of public use. It holds that the sovereign may take private property currently put to ordinary private use, and give it over for new, ordinary private use, so long as the new use is predicted to generate some secondary benefit for the public — such as increased tax revenue, more jobs, maybe even aesthetic pleasure. But nearly any lawful use of real private property can be said to generate some incidental benefit to the public. Thus, if predicted . . . positive side-effects are enough to render transfer from one private party to another constitutional, then the words "for public use" do not realistically exclude *any* takings, and thus do not exert any constraint on the eminent domain power. . . . The beneficiaries are likely to be those citizens with disproportionate influence and power in the political process, including large corporations and development firms. . . . The Founders cannot have intended this perverse result. . . . I would hold that the takings in both Parcel 3 and Parcel 4A are unconstitutional. . . .

Justice THOMAS, dissenting.

[When] the government takes property and gives it to a private individual, and the public has no right to use the property, it strains language to say that the public is "employing" the property, regardless of the incidental benefits that might accrue to the public from the private use. [It is] implausible that the Framers intended to defer to legislatures as to what satisfies the Public Use Clause. . . . Yet today the Court tells us that we are not to "second-guess the City's considered judgments," when the issue [is] whether the government may take the infinitely more intrusive step of tearing down petitioners' homes. . . . Though citizens are safe from the government in their homes, the homes themselves are not. . . .

[I] would [return] to the original meaning of the Public Use Clause: that the government may take property only if it actually uses or gives the public a legal right to use the property. . . . So-called "urban renewal" programs provide some compensation for the properties they take, but no compensation is possible for the subjective value of these lands to the individuals displaced and the indignity inflicted by uprooting them from their homes. [E]xtending the concept of public purpose to encompass any economically beneficial goal guarantees that these losses will fall disproportionately on poor communities. Those communities are not only systematically less likely to put their lands to the highest and best social use, but are also the least politically powerful. . . . The deferential standard this Court has adopted [encourages] "those citizens with disproportionate influence and power in the political process, including large corporations and development firms" to victimize the weak. . . .

Note: The **Kelo** *Property*

The City of New London condemned Susette Kelo's home and the homes of her neighbors. The city and state then spent millions of dollars to get the property ready for luxury condominiums. Pfizer, Inc., instead of pursuing further development, stated that it would close its headquarters in New London.

BACKGROUND
The **Kelo** *Backlash*

After *Kelo*, many citizens, members of the media, businesspersons, and politicians decried the result. In the backlash that followed, state legislatures enacted laws limiting the purposes for which land could be taken. Some businesses announced they would not lend money to developers who planned to build on condemned land. George Will, the columnist, wrote in *Newsweek* that the Kelo decision was "the best thing that has happened since the New Deal to the movement to strengthen property rights." ("Legal Theft In Norwood," April 24, 2006). Many states enacted laws limiting their own use of the eminent domain power. One example was Ohio, which made eminent domain much more challenging for public entities with respect to any property not within a blighted area if the primary purpose of the condemnation was to transfer the property to another private party. Congress also included language in the Federal Appropriations Act of 2006 prohibiting the use of funds for eminent domain outside of traditional governmental purposes.

∾ PROBLEMS ∾

1. *Berwick*. You are the Mayor of Berwick, a small town in Pennsylvania. You are asked to propose legislation to placate angry landowners about the possibility of condemning their land for use by corporate and other private entities. What legislation would you propose?

2. *Berwick II*. Before you can propose legislation, a Dell computer company representative approaches you with a proposition. The representative informs you that if a large house and its 20 acres on the edge of town are taken by eminent domain and given to a subsidiary of Dell, then a Dell equipment quality control operation will operate out of the house, creating seven new jobs. The house and surrounding land are worth $250,000. The jobs are worth $150,000 in salaries. Having Dell present in the community is worth at least $50,000. Could the property be properly taken under *Kelo*?

BACKGROUND
Remaining Takings Issues

In addition to the question whether a taking has been effected for a public purpose, the second dominant issue in the field relates to whether government action typically in the form of land use regulation constitutes a taking. This issue has generated the highest volume of litigation under the Takings Clause and yielded disparate outcomes. These results are consistent with persisting differences in perspective on the Takings Clause's meaning. It is a provision that clearly applies when government condemns a person's property and assumes title to it. Government may acquire private property, but it must pay "just compensation." Many Takings Clause cases do not involve a literal "taking" in the sense of an acquisition, however, but instead concern land use control for an articulated public good. Such regulation can assume many different forms, including zoning restrictions. In these cases, the question is whether government may regulate without paying the property owner for the diminished value of the property.

Penn Central Transportation Company v. City of New York

438 U.S. 104 (1978)

Mr. Justice BRENNAN delivered the opinion of the Court.

[New York City] adopted its Landmarks Preservation Law in 1965 [because] "the standing of [New York City] as a world-wide tourist center and world capital of business, culture and government" would be threatened if legislation were not enacted to protect historic landmarks and neighborhoods from precipitate decisions to destroy or fundamentally alter their character. The city believed that comprehensive measures to safeguard desirable features of the existing urban fabric would benefit its citizens in a variety of ways: e.g., fostering "civic pride in the beauty and noble accomplishments of the past"; protecting and enhancing "the city's attractions to tourists and visitors"; "support[ing] and stimul[ating] business and industry"; "strengthen[ing] the economy of the city"; and promoting "the use of historic districts, landmarks, interior landmarks and scenic landmarks for the education, pleasure and welfare of the people of the city."

The New York City law is typical of many urban landmark laws in that its primary method of achieving its goals is not by acquisitions of historic properties, but rather by involving public entities in land-use decisions affecting these properties and providing services, standards, controls, and incentives that will encourage preservation by private owners and users. While the law does place special restrictions on landmark properties as a necessary feature to the attainment of its larger objectives, the major theme of the law is to ensure the owners of any such properties both a "reasonable return" on their investments and maximum latitude to use their parcels for purposes not inconsistent with the preservation goals. . . .

Final designation as a landmark results in restrictions upon the property owner's options concerning use of the landmark site. [T]he law imposes a duty upon the owner to keep the exterior features of the building "in good repair" to assure that the law's objectives not be defeated by the landmark's falling into a state of irremediable disrepair. [T]he Commission must approve in advance any proposal to alter the exterior architectural features of the landmark or to construct any exterior improvement on the landmark site, thus ensuring that decisions concerning construction on the landmark site are made with due consideration of both the public interest in the maintenance of the structure and the landowner's interest in use of the property. . . .

Although the designation of a landmark and landmark site restricts the owner's control over the parcel, designation also enhances the economic position of the landmark owner in one significant respect. Under New York City's zoning laws, owners of real property who have not developed their property to the full extent permitted by the applicable zoning laws are allowed to transfer development rights to contiguous parcels on the same city block. A 1968 ordinance gave the owners of landmark sites additional opportunities to transfer development rights to other parcels. . . . 1969 amendment permits, in highly commercialized areas like midtown Manhattan, the transfer of all unused development rights to a single parcel.

[Grand Central Terminal (Terminal) is] owned by the Penn Central Transportation Co. [and] is one of New York City's most famous buildings. Opened in 1913, it is regarded not only as providing an ingenious engineering solution to the problems presented by urban railroad stations, but also as a magnificent example of the French beaux-arts style. . . . The Terminal is located in midtown Manhattan [near] 42d Street [and] Park Avenue. . . . The Terminal itself is an eight-story structure which Penn Central uses as a railroad station and in which it rents space not needed for railroad purposes. . . . Penn Central [entered into a] 50-year lease [with] appellant UGP Properties, Inc. (UGP). . . . UGP was to construct a multistory office building above the Terminal [and] to pay Penn Central $1 million annually during construction and at least $3 million annually thereafter. . . . UGP and Penn Central then applied to the Commission for permission to construct an office building atop the Terminal. [T]he Commission denied [the] application. . . . Appellants filed suit [claiming that] application of the Landmarks Preservation Law had "taken" their property without just compensation in violation of the Fifth and Fourteenth Amendments. . . . We noted probable jurisdiction. We affirm [lower court decisions rejecting this contention].

II

[While] this Court has recognized that the "Fifth Amendment's guarantee [is] designed to bar Government from forcing some people alone to bear public burdens which, in all fairness and justice, should be borne by the public as a whole," this Court [has] been unable to develop any "set formula" for determining when "justice and fairness" require that economic injuries caused by public action be compensated by the government, rather than remain disproportionately concentrated on a few persons. [This] Court's decisions [identify] several factors that have particular significance. The economic impact of the regulation on the claimant and, particularly, the extent to which the regulation has interfered with distinct investment-backed expectations [are] relevant considerations. *See* Goldblatt v. Hempstead [369 U.S. 590 (1962)]. So, too, is the character of the governmental action. A "taking" may more readily be found when the interference with property can be characterized as a physical invasion by government, than when interference arises from some public program adjusting the benefits and burdens of economic life to promote the common good. "Government hardly could go on if to some extent values incident to property could not be diminished without paying for every such change in the general law," Pennsylvania Coal Co. v. Mahon, 260 U.S. 393 (1922), and this Court [has] recognized, in a wide variety of contexts, that government may execute laws or programs that adversely affect recognized economic values. [T]his Court has dismissed "taking" challenges on the ground that, while the challenged government action caused economic harm, it did not interfere with interests that were sufficiently bound up with the reasonable expectations of the claimant to constitute "property" for Fifth Amendment purposes. *See, e.g.,* United States v. Willow River Power Co., 324 U.S. 499 (1945).

[I]n instances in which a state tribunal reasonably concluded that "the health, safety, morals, or general welfare" would be promoted by prohibiting particular contemplated uses of land, this Court has upheld land-use regulations that destroyed or adversely affected recognized real property interests. Zoning laws are, of course, the classic example which has been viewed as permissible governmental action even when prohibiting the most beneficial use of the property. *See* Goldblatt v. Hempstead, *supra,* 369 U.S., at 592-593.

Zoning laws generally do not affect existing uses of real property, but "taking" challenges have also been held to be without merit in a wide variety of situations when the challenged governmental actions prohibited a beneficial use to which individual parcels had previously been devoted and thus caused substantial individualized harm. . . . Goldblatt v. Hempstead [involved a] city safety ordinance [that] banned any excavations below the water table and effectively prohibited the claimant from continuing a sand and gravel mining business that had been [in operation] since 1927. [T]he ordinance did not prevent the owner's reasonable use of the property since the owner made no showing of an adverse effect on the value of the land. Because the restriction served a substantial public purpose, the Court [held] no taking had occurred. It is, of course, implicit in *Goldblatt* that a use restriction on real property may constitute a "taking" if not reasonably necessary to the effectuation of a substantial public purpose or perhaps if it has an unduly harsh impact upon the owner's use of the property.

Pennsylvania Coal Co. v. Mahon, 260 U.S. 393 (1922), is the leading case for the proposition that a state statute that substantially furthers important public policies may so frustrate distinct investment-backed expectations as to amount to a "taking." There the claimant had sold the surface rights to particular parcels of property, but expressly reserved the right to remove the coal thereunder. A Pennsylvania statute, enacted after the transactions, forbade any mining of coal that caused the subsidence of any house, unless the house was the property of the owner of the underlying coal and was more than 150 feet from the improved property of another. Because the statute made it commercially impracticable to mine the coal, and thus had nearly the same effect as the complete destruction of rights claimant had reserved from the owners of the surface land, the Court held that the statute was invalid as effecting a "taking" without just compensation.

Finally, government actions that may be characterized as acquisitions of resources to permit or facilitate uniquely public functions have often been held to constitute "takings." United States v. Causby, 328 U.S. 256 (1946), is illustrative. In holding that direct overflights above the claimant's land, that destroyed the present use of the land as a chicken farm, constituted a "taking," *Causby* emphasized that Government had not "merely destroyed property [but was] using a part of it for the flight of its planes." . . .

In contending that the New York City law has "taken" their property in violation of the Fifth and Fourteenth Amendments, [appellants] urge that the Landmarks Law has deprived them of any gainful use of their "air rights" above the Terminal and that, irrespective of the value of the remainder of their parcel, the city has "taken" their right to this superadjacent airspace, thus entitling them to "just compensation. . . ." [The argument] that appellants may establish a "taking" simply by showing that they have been denied the ability to exploit a property interest that they heretofore had believed was available for development [is] untenable. . . . "Taking" jurisprudence does not divide a single parcel into discrete segments and attempt to determine whether rights in a particular segment have been entirely abrogated. In deciding whether a particular governmental action has effected a taking, this Court focuses rather both on the character of the action and on the nature and extent of the interference with rights in the parcel as a whole — here, the city tax block designated as the "landmark site."

[A]ppellants, focusing on the character and impact of [the] law, argue that it effects a "taking" because its operation has significantly diminished the value of the Terminal site. Appellants concede that the decisions sustaining other land-use regulations . . . uniformly reject the proposition that diminution in property value, standing alone, can establish a "taking," *see* Euclid v. Ambler Realty Co., 272 U.S. 365 (1926) (75% diminution in value caused by zoning law), and that the "taking" issue in these contexts is resolved by focusing on the uses the regulations permit. Appellants [also] do not dispute that a showing of diminution in property value would not establish a taking if the restriction had been imposed as a result of historic-district legislation, but appellants argue that New York City's regulation of individual landmarks is fundamentally different from zoning or from historic-district legislation because the controls imposed by New York City's law apply only to individuals who own selected properties.

[A]ppellants' position appears to be that the only means of ensuring that selected owners are not singled out to endure financial hardship for no reason is to hold that any restriction imposed on individual landmarks pursuant to the New York City scheme is a "taking" requiring the payment of "just compensation." Agreement with this argument would, of course, invalidate [all] comparable landmark legislation in the Nation. We find no merit in it.

It is true [that] both historic-district legislation and zoning laws regulate all properties within given physical communities whereas landmark laws apply only to selected parcels. [But], landmark laws are not like discriminatory, or "reverse spot," zoning: that is, a land-use decision which arbitrarily singles out a particular parcel for different, less favorable treatment than the neighboring ones. In contrast to discriminatory zoning, [the] New York City law embodies a comprehensive plan to preserve structures of historic or aesthetic interest wherever they might be found in the city, [and] over 400 landmarks and 31 historic districts have been designated pursuant to this plan.

Equally without merit is [the] argument that the decision to designate a structure as a landmark "is inevitably arbitrary or at least subjective, because it is basically a matter of taste," thus unavoidably singling out individual landowners for disparate and unfair treatment. The argument has [a] hollow ring. . . . [A]ppellants not only did not seek judicial review of either the designation[,] but do not even now suggest that the Commission's decisions concerning the Terminal were in any sense arbitrary or unprincipled. . . .

[A]ppellants observe that New York City's law differs from zoning laws and historic-district ordinances in that the Landmarks Law does not impose identical or similar restrictions on all structures located in particular physical communities. It follows, they argue, that New York City's law is inherently incapable of producing the fair and equitable distribution of benefits and burdens of governmental action which is characteristic of zoning laws and historic-district legislation and which they maintain is a constitutional requirement if "just compensation" is not to be afforded. It [is] true that the Landmarks Law has a more severe impact on some landowners than on others, but that in itself does not mean that the law affects a "taking." Legislation designed to promote the general welfare commonly burdens some more than others. The owners of the brickyard in *Hadacheck*, of the cedar trees in Miller v. Schoene, and of the gravel and sand mine in *Goldblatt*, were uniquely burdened by the legislation sustained in those cases. Similarly, zoning laws often affect some property owners more severely than others but have not been held to be invalid on that account. For example, the property owner in *Euclid* who wished to use its property for industrial purposes was affected far more severely by the ordinance than its neighbors who wished to use their land for residences.

In any event, appellants' repeated suggestions that they are solely burdened and unbenefited are factually inaccurate. This contention overlooks the fact that the New York City law applies to vast numbers of structures in the city in addition to the Terminal — all the structures contained in the 31 historic districts and over 400 individual landmarks, many of which are close to the Terminal. Unless we are to reject the judgment of the New York City Council that the preservation of landmarks benefits all New York citizens and all structures, both economically and by improving the quality of life in the city as a whole — which we are unwilling to do — we cannot conclude that the owners of the Terminal have in no sense been benefited by the Landmarks Law. . . .

Appellants' final broad-based attack would have us treat the law as an instance [in] which government, acting in an enterprise capacity, has appropriated part of their property for some strictly governmental purpose. [T]he Landmarks Law neither exploits appellants' parcel for city purposes nor facilitates nor arises from any entrepreneurial operations of the city. The situation is not remotely like that in *Causby* where the airspace above the property was in the flight pattern for military aircraft. The Landmarks Law's effect is simply to prohibit appellants or anyone else from occupying portions of the airspace above the Terminal, while permitting appellants to use the remainder of the parcel in a gainful fashion. This is no more an appropriation of property by government for its own uses than is a zoning law prohibiting, for "aesthetic" reasons, two or more adult theaters within a specified area or a safety regulation prohibiting excavations below a certain level.

[We still] must consider whether the interference with appellants' property is of such a magnitude that "there must be an exercise of eminent domain and compensation to sustain [it]." Pennsylvania Coal Co. v. Mahon, 260 U.S., at 413. That inquiry may be narrowed to the question of the severity of the impact of the law on appellants' parcel, and its resolution in turn requires a careful assessment of the impact of the regulation on the Terminal site.

Unlike the governmental acts in *Goldblatt, Miller, Causby, Griggs*, and *Hadacheck*, the New York City law does not interfere in any way with the present uses of the Terminal. Its designation as a landmark not only permits but contemplates that appellants may continue to use the property precisely as it has been used for the past 65 years: as a railroad terminal containing office space and concessions. So the law does not interfere with what must be regarded as Penn Central's primary expectation concerning the use of the parcel. More importantly, [we regard] the New York City law as permitting Penn Central not only to profit from the Terminal but also to obtain a "reasonable return" on its investment.

[Appellants] exaggerate the effect of the law on their ability to make use of the air rights above the Terminal in two respects. First, it simply cannot be maintained [that] appellants have been prohibited from occupying *any* portion of the airspace above the Terminal. [T]he Commission's report emphasized that whether any construction would be allowed depended upon whether the proposed addition "would harmonize in scale, material and character with [the Terminal]." Since appellants have not sought approval for the construction of a smaller structure, we do not know that appellants will be denied any use of any portion of the airspace above the Terminal.

Second, to the extent appellants have been denied the right to build above the Terminal, it is not literally accurate to say that they have been denied *all* use of even those pre-existing air rights. Their ability to use these rights has not been abrogated; they are made transferable to at least eight parcels in the vicinity of the Terminal, one or two of which have been found suitable for the construction of new office buildings. . . . While these rights may well not have constituted "just compensation" if a "taking" had occurred, the rights nevertheless undoubtedly mitigate whatever financial burdens the law has imposed on appellants [and] are to be taken into account in considering the impact of regulation.

[W]e conclude that the application of New York City's Landmarks Law has not affected a "taking" of appellants' property. The restrictions imposed are substantially related to the promotion of the general welfare and not only permit reasonable beneficial use of the landmark site but also afford appellants opportunities further to enhance not only the Terminal site proper but also other properties.

Affirmed.

Mr. Justice REHNQUIST, with whom THE CHIEF JUSTICE and Mr. Justice STEVENS join, dissenting.

[Typical] zoning restrictions [may] so limit the prospective uses of a piece of property as to diminish the value of that property in the abstract because it may not be used for the forbidden purposes. But any such abstract decrease in value will more than likely be at least partially offset by an increase in value which flows from similar restrictions as to use on neighboring properties. . . . Where a relatively few individual buildings, all separated from one another, are singled out and treated differently from surrounding buildings, no such reciprocity exists. The cost to the property owner which results from the imposition of restrictions applicable only to his property and not that of his neighbors may be substantial — in this case, several million dollars — with no comparable reciprocal benefits. And the cost associated with landmark legislation is likely to be of a completely different order of magnitude than that which results from the imposition of normal zoning restrictions. . . . Under the historic-landmark preservation scheme adopted by New York, the property owner is under an affirmative duty to *preserve* his property *as a landmark* at his own expense. . . .

[Before] the city of New York declared Grand Central Terminal to be a landmark, Penn Central could have used its "air rights" over the Terminal to build a multistory office building, at an apparent value of several million dollars per year. Today, the Terminal cannot be modified in *any* form, including the erection of additional stories, without the permission of the Landmark Preservation Commission, a permission which appellants, despite good-faith attempts, have so far been unable to obtain. . . . While neighboring landowners are free to use their land and "air rights" in any way consistent with the broad boundaries of New York zoning, Penn Central, absent the permission of appellees, must forever maintain its property in its present state. The property has been thus subjected to a nonconsensual servitude not borne by any neighboring or similar properties. . . . Appellees have thus destroyed — in a literal sense, "taken" — substantial property rights of Penn Central. . . .

As early as 1887, the Court recognized that the government can prevent a property owner from using his property to injure others without having to compensate the owner for the value of the forbidden use. [But the] proposed addition to the Grand Central Terminal would be in full compliance with zoning, height limitations, and other health and safety requirements. [A]ppellees are seeking to preserve what they believe to be an outstanding example of beaux-arts architecture. Penn Central is prevented from further developing its property basically because *too good* a job was done in designing and building it. [New York], because of its unadorned admiration for the design, has decided that the owners of the building must preserve it unchanged for the benefit of sightseeing New Yorkers and tourists.

[A]ppellees' actions do not merely *prohibit* Penn Central from using its property in a narrow set of noxious ways. Instead, appellees have placed an *affirmative* duty on Penn Central to maintain the Terminal in its present state and in "good repair." [While] Penn Central may continue to use the Terminal as it is presently designed, appellees otherwise "exercise complete dominion and control over the surface of the land," and must compensate the owner for his loss. Property is taken in the constitutional sense when inroads are made upon an owner's use of it to an extent that, as between private parties, a servitude has been acquired." United States v. Dickinson, 331 U.S. 745 (1947).

Even where the government prohibits a noninjurious use, the Court has ruled that a taking does not take place if the prohibition applies over a broad cross section of land and thereby "secure[s] an average reciprocity of advantage." Pennsylvania Coal Co. v. Mahon, 260 U.S., at 415. . . . Here, [a] multimillion dollar loss has been imposed on appellants; it is uniquely felt and is not offset by any benefits flowing from the preservation of some 400 other "landmarks" in New York City. Appellees have imposed a substantial cost on less than one one-tenth of one percent of the buildings in New York City for the general benefit of all its people. It is exactly this imposition of general costs on a few individuals at which the "taking" protection is directed. The Fifth Amendment "prevents the public from loading upon one individual more than his just share of the burdens of government, and says that when he surrenders to the public something more and different from that which is exacted from other members of the public, a full and just equivalent shall be returned to him." Monongahela Navigation Co. v. United States, 148 U.S. 312 (1893). [T]he "Fifth Amendment's guarantee that private property shall not be taken for a public use without just compensation was designed to bar Government from forcing some people alone to bear public burdens which, in all fairness and justice, should be borne by the public as a whole." Armstrong v. United States, 364 U.S., at 49.

[The] benefits that appellees believe will flow from preservation of the Grand Central Terminal will accrue to all the citizens of New York City. There is no reason to believe that appellants will enjoy a substantially greater share of these benefits. If the cost of preserving Grand Central Terminal were spread evenly across the entire population of the city of New York, the burden per person would be in cents per year. [H]owever, appellees [impose] the entire cost of several million dollars per year on Penn Central. [I]t is precisely this sort of discrimination that the Fifth Amendment prohibits.

Appellees [argue] that a taking only occurs where a property owner is denied *all* reasonable value of his property. The Court has frequently held that, even where a destruction of property rights would not *otherwise* constitute a taking, the inability of the owner to make a reasonable return on his property requires compensation under the Fifth Amendment. But the converse is not true. A taking does not become a noncompensable exercise of police power simply because the government in its grace allows the owner to make some "reasonable" use of his property. "[I]t is the character of the invasion, not the amount of damage resulting from it, so long as the damage is substantial, that determines the question whether it is a taking." United States v. Cress, 243 U.S. 316 (1917); United States v. Causby, 328 U.S., at 266.

Appellees [allow a] property owner [to] "transfer" his previous right to develop the landmark property to adjacent properties [under] his control. Appellees [call] this system "Transfer Development Rights," or TDR's. . . . The Fifth Amendment does not allow [approximate] compensation but requires "a full and perfect equivalent for the property taken." Monongahela Navigation Co. v. United States, 148 U.S., at 326. [I] would remand [for] a determination of whether TDR's constitute a "full and perfect equivalent for the property taken." . . .

Notes

1. *What Constitutes Property?* In United States v. General Motors Corp., 323 U.S. 373 (1945), the Court held that the concept of "property" should be broadly defined: Property refers to the entire "group of rights inhering in the citizen's relation to the physical thing, as the right to possess, use and dispose of it. . . . The constitutional provision is addressed to every sort of interest the citizen may possess." Id. at 378.

2. *Lawyers Trust Accounts.* In Phillips v. Washington Legal Foundation, 524 U.S. 156 (1998), the Court was confronted by a challenge to the District of Columbia's Interest on Lawyers Trust Account (IOLTA) program. Under this program, the interest generated on client funds held by attorneys in connection with their practices are paid into foundations that finance legal services for low-income individuals. The Court held that the interest was the client's.

3. *Mandatory Easements.* In Nollan v. California Coastal Commission, 483 U.S. 825 (1987), the Nollans applied for permission to demolish a small old oceanfront home and build a new one in its place. The California Coastal Commission approved the project on condition that the Nollans create a public easement across their oceanfront property. The commission found that the new home would block the ocean views, thus contributing to the development of "a 'wall' of residential structures" that would prevent the public "psychologically [from] realizing a stretch of coastline exists nearby that they have every right to visit." The new house would also increase private use of the shorefront. These effects of the new construction, along with other area development, would cumulatively "burden the public's ability to traverse to and along the shorefront." Therefore the commission concluded that it could properly require the Nollans to offset that burden by providing additional lateral access to the public beaches in the form of an easement across their property. The Court concluded that the easement requirement constituted a taking without just compensation:

Had California simply required the Nollans to make an easement across their beachfront available to the public on a permanent basis in order to increase public access to the beach, rather than conditioning their permit to rebuild their house on their agreeing to do so, we have no doubt there would have been a taking. . . . [T]he question becomes whether requiring it to be conveyed as a condition for issuing a land-use permit alters the outcome. We have long recognized that land-use regulation does not affect a taking if it "substantially advance[s] legitimate state interests" and does not "den[y] an owner economically viable use of his land," Agins v. Tiburon, 447 U.S. 255 (1980). . . . The Commission argues that among these permissible purposes are protecting the public's ability to see the beach, assisting the public in overcoming the "psychological barrier" to using the beach created by a developed shorefront, and preventing congestion on the public beaches. We assume, without deciding, that this is so — in which case the Commission unquestionably would be able to deny the Nollans their permit outright if their new house (alone, or by reason of the cumulative impact produced in conjunction with other construction) would substantially impede these purposes. . . .

The Commission argues that a permit condition that serves the same legitimate police-power purpose as a refusal to issue the permit should not be found to be a taking if the refusal to issue the permit would not constitute a taking. We agree. Thus, if the Commission attached to the permit some condition that would have protected the public's ability to see the beach notwithstanding construction of the new house — for example, a height limitation, a width restriction, or a ban on fences — so long as the Commission could have exercised its police power (as we have assumed it could) to forbid construction of the house altogether, imposition of the condition would also be constitutional. Moreover (and here we come closer to the facts of the present case), the condition would be constitutional even if it consisted of the requirement that the Nollans provide a viewing spot on their property for passersby with whose sighting of the ocean their new house would interfere. [T]he Commission's assumed power to forbid construction of the house in order to protect the public's view of the beach must surely include the power to condition construction upon some concession by the owner, even a concession of property rights, that serves the same end. . . .

The evident constitutional propriety disappears, however, if the condition substituted for the prohibition utterly fails to further the end advanced as the justification for the prohibition. [H]ere, the lack of nexus between the condition and the original purpose of the building restriction converts that purpose to something other than what it was. The purpose then becomes, quite simply, the obtaining of an easement to serve some valid governmental purpose, but without payment of compensation. Whatever may be the outer limits of "legitimate state interests" in the takings and land-use context, this is not one of them. In short, unless the permit condition serves the same governmental purpose as the development ban, the building restriction is not a valid regulation of land use but "an out-and-out plan of extortion."

[It] is quite impossible to understand how a requirement that people already on the public beaches be able to walk across the Nollans' property reduces any obstacles to viewing the beach created by the new house. It is also impossible to understand how it lowers any "psychological barrier" to using the public beaches, or how it helps to remedy any additional congestion on them " 'caused by construction of the Nollans' new house. We therefore find that the Commission's imposition of the permit condition cannot be treated as an exercise of its land-use power for any of these purposes.' Id. at 838-839.

(Justices Brennan, Marshall, Blackburn, and Stevens dissented.)

4. *Unconstitutional Conditions.* In Dolan v. City of Tigard, 512 U.S. 374 (1994), Dolan sought a permit allowing her to double the size of her store and pave her gravel parking lot. Under the city's land development plan, property that

bordered Fanno Creek was to be used only as "greenways" to minimize flooding. The city granted Dolan's request on condition that she dedicate portions of her property for a public greenway. Dolan claimed that conditioning the permit in exchange for the dedication was an unconstitutional condition. Dolan claimed the condition was unconstitutional because it did not have the required "essential nexus" between the state's interest and the permit condition as required in *Nollan, supra*. The Court found that the city did not meet the nexus requirement here, without some quantification of some of its findings about how a greenway would offset traffic congestion.

∾ PROBLEMS ∾

1. *Setback Requirements*. The city of Glenview Hills, worried about crowding, establishes setback requirements that prohibit the building of homes within five (5) feet of a property line. The city first imposes the requirement on all property within the city, even in the northeast section called Virginia-Lowlands, which has many houses comfortably located within five (5) feet of the property boundaries. Two years later, the city council, led by Dana, modifies the law to permit a street-by-street vote of the property owners. A nonconsenting property owner, Dana's brother Damon, who lives on a fiercely divided street, claims a taking. Should he win? *See* Eubank v. Richmond, 226 U.S. 137 (1912).

2. *Save the Beach, Continued*. Did Pensacola's law, which changed existing statutory and common law property rights, constitute a taking? Does it matter if the rights were changed minimally? If only one of the rights, accretion of land, was changed by the law, and all of the other "bundle of rights" were left in place, would it be a taking? Explain.

3. *Rent Control*. Congress passed a law in 1919 establishing a commission in the District of Columbia to ensure that rents are "fair and reasonable," after many complaints in the growing federal enclave, and allowing tenants to hold over after the expiration of their lease in many circumstances. The law was enacted due to deplorable conditions in rental properties as an outgrowth of World War I and the need to maintain standards in the nation's capitol. Is the rent control law constitutional? *See* Block v. Hirsh, 256 U.S. 135 (1921) (Holmes, J.). (Does the rent control law also raise an impairment of contracts issue under the Contract Clause?)

4. *The Public Park*. Greensboro, North Carolina, eyed a portion of town it wanted to turn into a public park. It bought some of the land in question, but realized it did not have the money to buy all of it without straining its finances. Rather than giving up on its goal, Greensboro devised a plan to secure the park. It passed a law stating that for the transfer of parcels privately owned in that part of town, any conveyance, *inter vivos* or by will, requires the city of Greensboro to have the right of first refusal. Is this law constitutional? *See* Hodel v. Irving, 481 U.S. 704 (1987).

Lucas v. South Carolina Coastal Council

505 U.S. 1103 (1992)

Justice SCALIA delivered the opinion of the Court.

In 1986, petitioner David H. Lucas paid $975,000 for two residential lots on the Isle of Palms in Charleston County, South Carolina, on which he intended to build single-family homes. In 1988, however, the South Carolina Legislature enacted the Beachfront Management Act, S.C. Code Ann. §48-39-250 *et seq.*, which had the direct effect of barring petitioner from erecting any permanent habitable structures on his two parcels. A state trial court found that this prohibition rendered Lucas's parcels "valueless." This case requires us to decide whether the Act's dramatic effect on the economic value of Lucas's lots accomplished a taking of private property under the Fifth and Fourteenth Amendments requiring the payment of "just compensation." U.S. Const., Amdt. 5.

I

[I]n the aftermath of Congress's passage of the federal Coastal Zone Management Act of 1972, the [South Carolina] legislature enacted [its own law]. [T]he South Carolina Act required owners of coastal zone land that qualified as a "critical area" (defined in the legislation to include beaches and immediately adjacent sand dunes) to obtain a permit from the newly created South Carolina Coastal Council (Council) prior to committing the land to a "use other than the use the critical area was devoted to on [September 28, 1977]."

In the late 1970's, Lucas and others began extensive residential development of the Isle of Palms, a barrier island situated eastward of the city of Charleston. [I]n 1986[, Lucas] purchased the two lots at issue in this litigation. . . . No portion of the lots, which were located approximately 300 feet from the beach, qualified as a "critical area" under the 1977 Act; accordingly, at the time Lucas acquired these parcels, he was not legally obliged to obtain a permit from the Council in advance of any development activity. His intention with respect to the lots was to do what the owners of the immediately adjacent parcels had already done: erect single-family residences. He commissioned architectural drawings for this purpose.

The Beachfront Management Act brought Lucas's plans to an abrupt end. Under that 1988 legislation, the Council was directed to establish a "baseline" connecting the landward-most "point[s] of erosion [during] the past forty years" in the region of the Isle of Palms. [T]he Council fixed this baseline landward of Lucas's parcels. [U]nder the Act construction of occupiable improvements was flatly prohibited seaward of a line drawn 20 feet landward of, and parallel to, the baseline. The Act provided no exceptions.

Lucas promptly filed suit [contending] that the Beachfront Management Act's construction bar effected a taking of his property without just compensation. [The trial] court agreed [concluding] Lucas's properties had been "taken" [and] it ordered respondent to pay "just compensation" in the amount of

$1,232,387.50. . . . The Supreme Court of South Carolina reversed [holding] that when a regulation respecting the use of property is designed "to prevent serious public harm," no compensation is owing under the Takings Clause regardless of the regulation's effect on the property's value. . . . We granted certiorari. . . .

III

Prior to Justice Holmes's exposition in Pennsylvania Coal Co. v. Mahon, 260 U.S. 393 (1922), it was generally thought that the Takings Clause reached only a "direct appropriation" of property, or the functional equivalent of a "practical ouster of [the owner's] possession," Transportation Co. v. Chicago, 99 U.S. 635 (1879). Justice Holmes recognized in *Mahon* [that] if the protection against physical appropriations of private property was to be meaningfully enforced, the government's power to redefine the range of interests included in the ownership of property was necessarily constrained by constitutional limits. If, instead, the uses of private property were subject to unbridled, uncompensated qualification under the police power, "the natural tendency of human nature [would be] to extend the qualification more and more until at last private property disappear[ed]." These considerations gave birth in that case to the oft-cited maxim that, "while property may be regulated to a certain extent, if regulation goes too far it will be recognized as a taking."

[*Mahon*] offered little insight into when, and under what circumstances, a given regulation would be seen as going "too far" for purposes of the Fifth Amendment. [W]e have generally eschewed any "'set formula'" for determining how far is too far, preferring to "engag[e in] essentially ad hoc, factual inquiries." Penn Central Transportation Co. v. New York City, 438 U.S. 104 (1978). We have, however, described at least two discrete categories of regulatory action as compensable without case-specific inquiry into the public interest advanced in support of the restraint. The first encompasses regulations that compel the property owner to suffer a physical "invasion" of his property. In general (at least with regard to permanent invasions), no matter how minute the intrusion, and no matter how weighty the public purpose behind it, we have required compensation. For example, [we] determined that New York's law requiring landlords to allow television cable companies to emplace cable facilities in their apartment buildings constituted a taking even though the facilities occupied at most only 1½ cubic feet of the landlords' property.

The second situation in which we have found categorical treatment appropriate is where regulation denies all economically beneficial or productive use of land. [We] have never set forth the justification for this rule. Perhaps it is simply, as Justice Brennan suggested, that total deprivation of beneficial use is, from the landowner's point of view, the equivalent of a physical appropriation. *See* San Diego Gas & Electric Co. v. San Diego, 450 U.S., at 652 (dissenting opinion). [I]n the extraordinary circumstance when *no* productive or economically beneficial use of land is permitted, it is less realistic to indulge our usual assumption that the legislature is simply "adjusting the benefits and burdens of economic life," in a manner that secures an "average reciprocity of advantage" to everyone concerned. And the *functional* basis for permitting the government, by regulation, to affect property values without compensation — that "Government hardly could go on if to some extent values incident to property could not be diminished without paying for every such change in the general law," — does not apply to the relatively rare situations where the government has deprived a landowner of all economically beneficial uses.

[R]egulations that leave the owner of land without economically beneficial or productive options for its use [carry] with them a heightened risk that private property is being pressed into some form of public service under the guise of mitigating serious public harm. . . . The many statutes on the books [that] provide for the use of eminent domain to impose servitudes on private scenic lands preventing developmental uses, or to acquire such lands altogether, suggest the practical equivalence in this setting of negative regulation and appropriation. [I]n short, that there are good reasons for our frequently expressed belief that when the owner of real property has been called upon to sacrifice *all* economically beneficial uses in the name of the common good, that is, to leave his property economically idle, he has suffered a taking.

The trial court found Lucas's two beachfront lots to have been rendered valueless by respondent's enforcement of the coastal-zone construction ban. [P]etitioner "concede[d] that the beach/dune area of South Carolina's shores is an extremely valuable public resource; that the erection of new construction, *inter alia,* contributes to the erosion and destruction of this public resource; and that discouraging new construction in close proximity to the beach/dune area is necessary to prevent a great public harm." In the [trial] court's view, these concessions brought petitioner's challenge within a long line of this Court's cases sustaining against Due Process and Takings Clause challenges the State's use of its "police powers" to enjoin a property owner from activities akin to public nuisances. *See* Mugler v. Kansas, 123 U.S. 623 (1887) (law prohibiting manufacture of alcoholic beverages). . . . It is correct that many of our prior opinions have suggested that "harmful or noxious uses" of property may be proscribed by government regulation without the requirement of compensation. [H]owever, we think the South Carolina Supreme Court was too quick to conclude that that principle decides the present case. The "harmful or noxious uses" principle was the Court's early attempt to describe in theoretical terms why government may, consistent with the Takings Clause, affect property values by regulation without incurring an obligation to compensate — a reality we nowadays acknowledge explicitly with respect to the full scope of the State's police power. *See, e.g., Penn Central Transportation Co.,* 438 U.S., at 125. . . . "Harmful or noxious use" analysis was, in other words, simply the progenitor of our more contemporary statements that "land-use regulation does not effect a taking if it 'substantially advance[s] legitimate state interests.' . . ."

The transition from our early focus on control of "noxious" uses to our contemporary understanding of the broad realm within which government may regulate without compensation was an easy one, since the distinction between "harm-preventing" and "benefit-conferring" regulation is often in the eye of the beholder. It is quite possible, for example, to describe in *either* fashion the ecological, economic, and esthetic concerns that inspired the South Carolina Legislature in the present case. One could say that imposing a servitude on Lucas's land is necessary in order to prevent his use of it from "harming" South Carolina's ecological resources; or, instead, in order to achieve the "benefits" of an ecological preserve.... Whether Lucas's construction of single-family residences on his parcels should be described as bringing "harm" to South Carolina's adjacent ecological resources thus depends principally upon whether the describer believes that the State's use interest in nurturing those resources is so important that *any* competing adjacent use must yield.... *A fortiori* the legislature's recitation of a noxious-use justification cannot be the basis for departing from our categorical rule that total regulatory takings must be compensated. If it were, departure would virtually always be allowed....

Where the State seeks to sustain regulation that deprives land of all economically beneficial use, we think it may resist compensation only if the logically antecedent inquiry into the nature of the owner's estate shows that the proscribed use interests were not part of his title to begin with. This accords, we think, with our "takings" jurisprudence, which has traditionally been guided by the understandings of our citizens regarding the content of, and the State's power over, the "bundle of rights" that they acquire when they obtain title to property. It seems to us that the property owner necessarily expects the uses of his property to be restricted, from time to time, by various measures newly enacted by the State in legitimate exercise of its police powers.... And in the case of personal property, by reason of the State's traditionally high degree of control over commercial dealings, he ought to be aware of the possibility that new regulation might even render his property economically worthless (at least if the property's only economically productive use is sale or manufacture for sale). [T]he notion [that] title is somehow held subject to the "implied limitation" that the State may subsequently eliminate all economically valuable use is inconsistent with the historical compact recorded in the Takings Clause that has become part of our constitutional culture.

Where "permanent physical occupation" of land is concerned, we have refused to allow the government to decree it anew (without compensation), no matter how weighty the asserted "public interests" involved—though we assuredly *would* permit the government to assert a permanent easement that was a pre-existing limitation upon the landowner's title. We believe similar treatment must be accorded confiscatory regulations, i.e., regulations that prohibit all economically beneficial use of land: Any limitation so severe cannot be newly legislated or decreed (without compensation), but must inhere in the title itself, in the restrictions that background principles of the State's law of property and nuisance already place upon land ownership. A law or decree with such an effect must, in other words, do no more than duplicate the result that could have been achieved in the courts—by adjacent landowners (or other uniquely affected persons) under the State's law of private nuisance, or by the State under its complementary power to abate nuisances that affect the public generally, or otherwise.

On this analysis, the owner of a lake-bed, for example, would not be entitled to compensation when he is denied the requisite permit to engage in a landfilling operation that would have the effect of flooding others' land. Nor the corporate owner of a nuclear generating plant, when it is directed to remove all improvements from its land upon discovery that the plant sits astride an earthquake fault. Such regulatory action may well have the effect of eliminating the land's only economically productive use, but it does not proscribe a productive use that was previously permissible under relevant property and nuisance principles. [T]his recognition that the Takings Clause does not require compensation when an owner is barred from putting land to a use that is proscribed by those "existing rules or understandings" is surely unexceptional. When, however, a regulation that declares "off-limits" all economically productive or beneficial uses of land goes beyond what the relevant background principles would dictate, compensation must be paid to sustain it.[14]

The "total taking" inquiry we require today will ordinarily entail [analysis] of, among other things, the degree of harm to public lands and resources, or adjacent private property, posed by the claimant's proposed activities, the social value of the claimant's activities and their suitability to the locality in question, and the relative ease with which the alleged harm can be avoided through measures taken by the claimant and the government (or adjacent private landowners) alike. The fact that a particular use has long been engaged in by similarly situated owners ordinarily imports a lack of any common-law prohibition (though changed circumstances or new knowledge may make what was previously permissible no longer so). So also does the fact that other landowners, similarly situated, are permitted to continue the use denied to the claimant.

It seems unlikely that common-law principles would have prevented the erection of any habitable or productive improvements on petitioner's land; they rarely support prohibition of the "essential use" of land. The question, however, is one of state law to be dealt with on remand. [T]o win its case South Carolina must do more than proffer the legislature's declaration that the uses Lucas desires are inconsistent with the public interest, or the conclusory assertion that they violate a common-law maxim. . . . Instead, as it would be required to do if it sought to restrain Lucas in a common-law action for public nuisance, South Carolina must identify background principles of nuisance and property law that prohibit the uses he now intends in the circumstances in which the property is presently found. Only on this showing can the State fairly claim that, in proscribing all such beneficial uses, the Beachfront Management Act is taking nothing.

The judgment is reversed, and the case is remanded for proceedings not inconsistent with this opinion.

So ordered.

---

14. Of course, the State may elect to rescind its regulation and thereby avoid having to pay compensation for a permanent deprivation. But "where the [regulation has] already worked a taking of all use of property, no subsequent action by the government can relieve it of the duty to provide compensation for the period during which the taking was effective."

Justice KENNEDY, concurring in the judgment.

[The] finding of no value must be considered under the Takings Clause by reference to the owner's reasonable, investment-backed expectations. The Takings Clause, while conferring substantial protection on property owners, does not eliminate the police power of the State to enact limitations on the use of their property. Mugler v. Kansas, 123 U.S. 623 (1887). The rights conferred by the Takings Clause and the police power of the State may coexist without conflict. Property is bought and sold, investments are made, subject to the State's power to regulate. Where a taking is alleged from regulations which deprive the property of all value, the test must be whether the deprivation is contrary to reasonable, investment-backed expectations. . . .

In my view, reasonable expectations must be understood in light of the whole of our legal tradition. The common law of nuisance is too narrow a confine for the exercise of regulatory power in a complex and interdependent society. Goldblatt v. Hempstead, 369 U.S. 590 (1962). The State should not be prevented from enacting new regulatory initiatives in response to changing conditions, and courts must consider all reasonable expectations whatever their source. The Takings Clause does not require a static body of state property law; it protects private expectations to ensure private investment. . . . The promotion of tourism, for instance, ought not to suffice to deprive specific property of all value without a corresponding duty to compensate. Furthermore, the means, as well as the ends, of regulation must accord with the owner's reasonable expectations. Here, the State did not act until after the property had been zoned for individual lot development and most other parcels had been improved, throwing the whole burden of the regulation on the remaining lots. This too must be measured in the balance. . . .

Justice BLACKMUN, dissenting.

Today the Court launches a missile to kill a mouse. . . . Petitioner Lucas is a contractor, manager, and part owner of the Wild Dune development on the Isle of Palms. He has lived there since 1978. In December 1986, he purchased two of the last four pieces of vacant property in the development. The area is notoriously unstable. In roughly half of the last 40 years, all or part of petitioner's property was part of the beach or flooded twice daily by the ebb and flow of the tide. . . . Between 1963 and 1973 the shoreline was 100 to 150 feet onto petitioner's property. The first line of stable vegetation was about halfway through the property. Between 1981 and 1983, the Isle of Palms issued 12 emergency orders for sandbagging to protect property in the Wild Dune development. Determining that local habitable structures were in imminent danger of collapse, the Council issued permits for two rock revetments to protect condominium developments near petitioner's property from erosion; one of the revetments extends more than halfway onto one of his lots.

The South Carolina Supreme Court found that the Beachfront Management Act did not take petitioner's property without compensation. The decision rested on two premises that until today were unassailable — that the State has the power to prevent any use of property it finds to be harmful to its citizens, and that a state statute is entitled to a presumption of constitutionality. . . .

The Beachfront Management Act includes a finding by the South Carolina General Assembly that the beach/dune system serves the purpose of "protect[ing] life and property by serving as a storm barrier which dissipates wave energy and contributes to shoreline stability in an economical and effective manner." The General Assembly also found that "development unwisely has been sited too close to the [beach/dune] system. This type of development has jeopardized the stability of the beach/dune system, accelerated erosion, and endangered adjacent property."

If the state legislature is correct that the prohibition on building in front of the setback line prevents serious harm, then, under this Court's prior cases, the Act is constitutional. "Long ago it was recognized that all property in this country is held under the implied obligation that the owner's use of it shall not be injurious to the community. . . ." Keystone Bituminous Coal Assn. v. DeBenedictis, 480 U.S. 470 (1987). The Court consistently has upheld regulations imposed to arrest a significant threat to the common welfare, whatever their economic effect on the owner. See, e.g., Goldblatt v. Hempstead, 369 U.S. 590 (1962).

. . . "[T]he existence of facts supporting the legislative judgment is to be presumed." United States v. Carolene Products Co., 304 U.S. 144 (1938). . . . [T]his Court always has required plaintiffs challenging the constitutionality of an ordinance to provide "some factual foundation of record" that contravenes the legislative findings. O'Gorman & Young, 282 U.S., at 258. In the absence of such proof, "the presumption of constitutionality must prevail." [Rather] than invoking these traditional rules, the Court decides the State has the burden to convince the courts that its legislative judgments are correct. . . .

The Court [takes] the opportunity to create a new scheme for regulations that eliminate all economic value. From now on, there is a categorical rule finding these regulations to be a taking unless the use they prohibit is a background common-law nuisance or property principle.

I first question the Court's rationale in creating a category that obviates a "case-specific inquiry into the public interest advanced," if all economic value has been lost. . . . When the government regulation prevents the owner from any economically valuable use of his property, the private interest is unquestionably substantial, but we have never before held that no public interest can outweigh it. [T]he Court's prior decisions "uniformly reject the proposition that diminution in property value, standing alone, can establish a 'taking.'" Penn Central Transp. Co. v. New York City, 438 U.S. 104 (1978).

This Court repeatedly has recognized the ability of government, in certain circumstances, to regulate property without compensation no matter how adverse the financial effect on the owner may be. More than a century ago, the Court explicitly upheld the right of States to prohibit uses of property injurious to public health, safety, or welfare without paying compensation. . . . Mugler v. Kansas, 123 U.S., at 668-669. . . . The Court [seeks] to reconcile [our prior decisions] with its categorical rule by claiming that the Court never has upheld a regulation when the owner alleged the loss of all economic value. Even if the Court's factual premise were correct, its understanding of the Court's cases is distorted. In none of the cases did the Court suggest that the right of a State to prohibit certain activities without paying compensation turned on the availability of some residual valuable use. Instead, the cases depended on whether the government interest was sufficient to prohibit the activity, given the significant private cost. . . . [T]he State has full power to prohibit an owner's use of property if it is harmful to the public. . . .

[T]he Court decides that it will permit a State to regulate all economic value only if the State prohibits uses that would not be permitted under "background principles of nuisance and property law." [Until] today, the Court explicitly had rejected the contention that the government's power to act without paying compensation turns on whether the prohibited activity is a common-law nuisance. . . . The threshold inquiry for imposition of the Court's new rule, "deprivation of all economically valuable use," itself cannot be determined objectively. As the Court admits, whether the owner has been deprived of all economic value of his property will depend on how "property" is defined. [T]here is no "objective" way to define what that denominator should be. . . .

Even more perplexing, however, is the Court's reliance on common-law principles of nuisance in its quest for a value-free takings jurisprudence. In determining what is a nuisance at common law, state courts make exactly the decision that the Court finds so troubling when made by the South Carolina General Assembly today: They determine whether the use is harmful. Common-law public and private nuisance law is simply a determination whether a particular use causes harm. . . . There simply is no reason to believe that new interpretations of the hoary common-law nuisance doctrine will be particularly "objective" or "value free." [O]ne searches in vain, I think, for anything resembling a principle in the common law of nuisance. . . .

Nor does history indicate any common-law limit on the State's power to regulate harmful uses even to the point of destroying all economic value. Nothing in the discussions in Congress concerning the Takings Clause indicates that the Clause was limited by the common-law nuisance doctrine. Common-law courts themselves rejected such an understanding. . . . *Tewksbury*, 11 Metc., at 57. . . . In short, I find no clear and accepted "historical compact" or "understanding of our citizens" justifying the Court's new takings doctrine. . . .

The Court makes sweeping and, in my view, misguided and unsupported changes in our takings doctrine. While it limits these changes to the most narrow subset of government regulation — those that eliminate all economic value from land — these changes go far beyond what is necessary to secure petitioner Lucas' private benefit. . . . I dissent.

Justice STEVENS, dissenting.

[Although] in dicta we have sometimes recited that a law "effects a taking if [it] . . . denies an owner economically viable use of his land," our *rulings* have rejected such an absolute position. . . . *See, e.g.,* First English Evangelical Lutheran Church of Glendale v. County of Los Angeles, 482 U.S. 304 (1987),

"'Although a comparison of values before and after' a regulatory action 'is relevant, [it] is by no means conclusive.'"

In addition to lacking support in past decisions, the Court's new rule is wholly arbitrary. A landowner whose property is diminished in value 95% recovers nothing, while an owner whose property is diminished 100% recovers the land's full value. . . .

Moreover, because of the elastic nature of property rights, the Court's new rule will also prove unsound in practice. . . . [D]evelopers and investors may market specialized estates to take advantage of the Court's new rule. The smaller the estate, the more likely that a regulatory change will effect a total taking. Thus, an investor may, for example, purchase the right to build a multifamily home on a specific lot, with the result that a zoning regulation that allows only single-family homes would render the investor's property interest "valueless." In short, the categorical rule will likely have one of two effects: Either courts will alter the definition of the "denominator" in the takings "fraction," rendering the Court's categorical rule meaningless, or investors will manipulate the relevant property interests, giving the Court's rule sweeping effect. To my mind, neither of these results is desirable or appropriate, and both are distortions of our takings jurisprudence. . . .

The Court's holding today effectively freezes the State's common law, denying the legislature much of its traditional power to revise the law governing the rights and uses of property. . . . New appreciation of the significance of endangered species, the importance of wetlands, and the vulnerability of coastal lands, shapes our evolving understandings of property rights. . . . The Court's categorical approach rule will, I fear, greatly hamper the efforts of local officials and planners who must deal with increasingly complex problems in land-use and environmental regulation. . . .

Viewed more broadly, the Court's new rule and exception conflict with the very character of our takings jurisprudence. We have frequently and consistently recognized that the definition of a taking cannot be reduced to a "set formula" and that determining whether a regulation is a taking is "essentially [an] ad hoc, factual inquir[y]." Penn Central Transportation Co. v. New York City, 438 U.S. 104 (1978). This is unavoidable, for the determination whether a law effects a taking is ultimately a matter of "fairness and justice," and "necessarily requires a weighing of private and public interests." The rigid rules fixed by the Court today clash with this enterprise: "fairness and justice" are often disserved by categorical rules. . . .

The Just Compensation Clause "was designed to bar Government from forcing some people alone to bear public burdens which, in all fairness and justice, should be borne by the public as a whole." [A] diminution in value caused by a zoning regulation is far less likely to constitute a taking if it is part of a general and comprehensive land-use plan conversely, "spot zoning" is far more likely to constitute a taking, *see Penn Central,* 438 U.S., at 132, and n.28.

The presumption that a permanent physical occupation, no matter how slight, effects a taking is wholly consistent with this principle. A physical taking entails a certain amount of "singling out." [C]ourts have long recognized the difference between a regulation that targets one or two parcels of land and a regulation that enforces a statewide policy. [T]he generality of the Beachfront Management Act is significant. The Act does not target particular landowners, but rather regulates the use of the coastline of the entire State. Indeed, South Carolina's Act is best understood as part of a national effort to protect the coastline. . . . Moreover, the Act did not single out owners of undeveloped land. The Act also prohibited owners of developed land from rebuilding if their structures were destroyed, and what is equally significant, from repairing erosion control devices, such as seawalls. . . . In short, the South Carolina Act imposed substantial burdens on owners of developed and undeveloped land alike. This generality indicates that the Act is not an effort to expropriate owners of undeveloped land.

Admittedly, the economic impact of this regulation is dramatic and petitioner's investment-backed expectations are substantial. Yet, if anything, the costs to and expectations of the owners of developed land are even greater: I doubt, however, that the cost to owners of developed land of renourishing the beach and allowing their seawalls to deteriorate effects a taking. The costs imposed on the owners of undeveloped land, such as petitioner, differ from these costs only in degree, not in kind. . . .

In view of all of these factors, even assuming that petitioner's property was rendered valueless, the risk inherent in investments of the sort made by petitioner, the generality of the Act, and the compelling purpose motivating the South Carolina Legislature persuade me that the Act did not effect a taking of petitioner's property. . . . I respectfully dissent.

∾ PROBLEMS ∾

1. *The Woodpecker.* Oklahoma City enacts an ordinance related to undeveloped land after recent sightings of the red-cockaded woodpecker. While this bird is considered to be somewhat of a pest because it pokes small holes in cavities in the bark of pine trees in order to create its home, the city wants to save the bird's habitat. The ordinance permits "recreational use of the properties, such as hunting, fishing and camping," but no development. Is this ordinance constitutional after *Lucas*?

2. *Louisville Lights Out.* The City of Louisville believes that the Shelbyville Road corridor (on the east side of Louisville) is becoming too commercial. Accordingly, the city bans all further commercial development in that corridor, the dimensions of which are specified in the law. For an owner of undeveloped property who would like to develop it, does the ban constitute a taking under *Lucas*?

3. *Required Maintenance.* Suppose that, after *Lucas* is decided, the State of South Carolina decides not to pay him, but instead to let Lucas build on the property. However, the State imposes building conditions requiring owners who wish to erect new structures to take steps to prevent beach erosion. a) South Carolina restricts the costs of the erosion-prevention structures to 1 percent of the cost of the property, with the State paying the rest. Is this provision constitutional? b)

What if the costs are not restricted and vary from year to year? For example, during especially windy and stormy years, the costs of sand replenishment, maintenance of sea walls, and more could triple, all to be paid by the landowner. Is this provision constitutional?

Tahoe-Sierra Preservation Council v. Tahoe Regional Planning Agency
535 U.S. 302 (2002)

Justice STEVENS delivered the opinion of the Court.

[Lake Tahoe] is "uniquely beautiful. . . ." President Clinton [called] it a "'national treasure that must be protected and preserved,'" [and] Mark Twain aptly described the clarity of its waters as "'not *merely* transparent, but dazzlingly, brilliantly so.'" . . . Lake Tahoe's exceptional clarity is attributed to the absence of algae that obscures the waters of most other lakes. Historically, the lack of nitrogen and phosphorous, which nourish the growth of algae, has ensured the transparency of its waters. Unfortunately, the lake's pristine state has deteriorated rapidly over the past 40 years; increased land development in the Lake Tahoe Basin (Basin) has threatened the "'noble sheet of blue water'" beloved by Twain and countless others. "[D]ramatic decreases in clarity first began to be noted in the late 1950's/early 1960's, shortly after development at the lake began in earnest." The lake's unsurpassed beauty, it seems, is the wellspring of its undoing. . . . The upsurge of development in the area has caused "increased nutrient loading of the lake largely because of the increase in impervious coverage of land in the Basin resulting from that development." "Impervious coverage — such as asphalt, concrete, buildings, and even packed dirt — prevents precipitation from being absorbed by the soil. Instead, the water is gathered and concentrated by such coverage. Larger amounts of water flowing off a driveway or a roof have more erosive force than scattered raindrops falling over a dispersed area — especially one covered with indigenous vegetation, which softens the impact of the raindrops themselves." [T]he District Court predicted that "unless the process is stopped, the lake will lose its clarity and its trademark blue color, becoming green and opaque for eternity. . . ."

In the 1960's, when the problems associated with the burgeoning development began to receive significant attention, jurisdiction over the Basin, which occupies 501 square miles, was shared by the States of California and Nevada, five counties, several municipalities, and the Forest Service of the Federal Government. In 1968, the legislatures of the two States adopted the Tahoe Regional Planning Compact. . . . The compact set goals for the protection and preservation of the lake and created TRPA as the agency assigned "to coordinate and regulate development in the Basin and to conserve its natural resources." . . . [In order to give itself time to develop an adequate plan, TRPA imposed an eight month moratorium on development [and followed it with] a 32 month moratorium. . . . [It is argued that moratoria constitute a taking.]

III

Petitioners [contend] that the mere enactment of a temporary regulation that, while in effect, denies a property owner all viable economic use of her property gives rise to an unqualified constitutional obligation to compensate her for the value of its use during that period. . . . Under their proposed rule, there is no need to evaluate the landowners' investment-backed expectations, the actual impact of the regulation on any individual, the importance of the public interest served by the regulation, or the reasons for imposing the temporary restriction. For petitioners, it is enough that a regulation imposes a temporary deprivation — no matter how brief — of all economically viable use to trigger a *per se* rule that a taking has occurred. [In] our view the answer to the abstract question whether a temporary moratorium effects a taking is neither "yes, always" nor "no, never"; the answer depends upon the particular circumstances of the case. [T]he circumstances in this case are best analyzed within the *Penn Central* framework.

The text of the Fifth Amendment itself provides a basis for drawing a distinction between physical takings and regulatory takings. Its plain language requires the payment of compensation whenever the government acquires private property for a public purpose, whether the acquisition is the result of a condemnation proceeding or a physical appropriation. But the Constitution contains no comparable reference to regulations that prohibit a property owner from making certain uses of her private property. . . .

When the government physically takes possession of an interest in property for some public purpose, it has a categorical duty to compensate the former owner regardless of whether the interest that is taken constitutes an entire parcel or merely a part thereof. Thus, compensation is mandated when a leasehold is taken and the government occupies the property for its own purposes, even though that use is temporary. United States v. General Motors Corp., 323 U.S. 373 (1945). Similarly, when the government appropriates part of a rooftop in order to provide cable TV access for apartment tenants, or when its planes use private airspace to approach a government airport, it is required to pay for that share no matter how small. But a government regulation that merely prohibits landlords from evicting tenants unwilling to pay a higher rent, Block v. Hirsh, 256 U.S. 135 (1921); that bans certain private uses of a portion of an owner's property, or that forbids the private use of certain airspace, does not constitute a categorical taking. "The first category of cases requires courts to apply a clear rule; the second necessarily entails complex factual assessments of the purposes and economic effects of government actions." Yee v. Escondido, 503 U.S. 519 (1992).

This longstanding distinction between acquisitions of property for public use, on the one hand, and regulations prohibiting private uses, on the other, makes it inappropriate to treat cases involving physical takings as controlling precedents for the evaluation of a claim that there has been a "regulatory taking," and vice versa. For the same reason that we do not ask whether a physical appropriation advances a substantial government interest or whether it deprives the owner of all economically valuable use, we do not apply our precedent from the physical takings context to regulatory takings claims. Land-use regulations are ubiquitous and most of them impact property values in some tangential way — often in completely unanticipated ways. Treating them all as *per se* takings would transform government regulation into a luxury few governments could afford. By contrast, physical appropriations are relatively rare, easily identified, and usually represent a greater affront to individual property rights. . . .

[Petitioners] rely principally on our decision in Lucas v. South Carolina Coastal Council, 505 U.S. 1003 (1992) — a regulatory takings case that, nevertheless, applied a categorical rule — to argue that the *Penn Central* framework is inapplicable here. . . . Pennsylvania Coal Co. v. Mahon, 260 U.S. 393 (1922), [gave] birth to our regulatory takings jurisprudence. In subsequent opinions we have repeatedly and consistently endorsed Holmes' observation that "if regulation goes too far it will be recognized as a taking." [After] *Mahon*, neither a physical appropriation nor a public use has ever been a necessary component of a "regulatory taking."

In the decades following that decision, we have "generally eschewed" any set formula for determining how far is too far, choosing instead to engage in "'essentially ad hoc, factual inquiries.'" Indeed, we still resist the temptation to adopt *per se* rules [in] cases involving partial regulatory takings, preferring to examine "a number of factors" rather than a simple "mathematically precise" formula. [E]ven though multiple factors are relevant in the analysis of regulatory takings claims, in such cases we must focus on "the parcel as a whole" [including] the character of the action [and] the nature and extent of the interference with rights in the parcel as a whole — here, the city tax block designated as the "landmark site."

This requirement that "the aggregate must be viewed in its entirety" explains why [restrictions] on the use of only limited portions of the parcel, such as setback ordinances, or a requirement that coal pillars be left in place to prevent mine subsidence, were not considered regulatory takings. In each of these cases, we affirmed that "where an owner possesses a full 'bundle' of property rights, the destruction of one 'strand' of the bundle is not a taking."

First English, 482 U.S., at 315[, identified] two reasons why a regulation temporarily denying an owner all use of her property might not constitute a taking. First, we recognized that "the county might avoid the conclusion that a compensable taking had occurred by establishing that the denial of all use was insulated as a part of the State's authority to enact safety regulations." Second, we limited our holding "to the facts presented" and recognized "the quite different questions that would arise in the case of normal delays in obtaining building permits, changes in zoning ordinances, variances, and the like which [were] not before us." Thus, our decision in *First English* surely did not approve, and implicitly rejected, the categorical submission that petitioners are now advocating.

Similarly, our decision in *Lucas* is not dispositive. . . . The categorical rule that we applied in *Lucas* states that compensation is required when a regulation deprives an owner of "*all* economically beneficial uses" of his land. . . . But our holding was limited to "the extraordinary circumstance when *no* productive or economically beneficial use of land is permitted." The emphasis on the word "no" in the text of the opinion was, in effect, reiterated in a footnote explaining that the categorical rule would not apply if the diminution in value were 95% instead of 100%. Anything less than a "complete elimination of value," or a "total loss," the Court acknowledged, would require the kind of analysis applied in *Penn Central*.

Certainly, our holding that the permanent "obliteration of the value" of a fee simple estate constitutes a categorical taking does not answer the question whether a regulation prohibiting any economic use of land for a 32-month period has the same legal effect. Petitioners seek to bring this case under the rule announced in *Lucas* by arguing that we can effectively sever a 32-month segment from the remainder of each landowner's fee simple estate, and then ask whether that segment has been taken in its entirety by the moratoria. Of course, defining the property interest taken in terms of the very regulation being challenged is circular. With property so divided, every delay would become a total ban; the moratorium and the normal permit process alike would constitute categorical takings. Petitioners' "conceptual severance" argument is unavailing because it ignores *Penn Central*'s admonition that in regulatory takings cases we must focus on "the parcel as a whole." [The] starting point for the court's analysis should have been to ask whether there was a total taking of the entire parcel; if not, then *Penn Central* was the proper framework.

An interest in real property is defined by the metes and bounds that describe its geographic dimensions and the term of years that describes the temporal aspect of the owner's interest. Both dimensions must be considered if the interest is to be viewed in its entirety. Hence, a permanent deprivation of the owner's use of the entire area is a taking of "the parcel as a whole," whereas a temporary restriction that merely causes a diminution in value is not. Logically, a fee simple estate cannot be rendered valueless by a temporary prohibition on economic use, because the property will recover value as soon as the prohibition is lifted.

Neither *Lucas*, nor *First English*, nor any of our other regulatory takings cases compels us to accept petitioners' categorical submission. In fact, these cases make clear that the categorical rule in *Lucas* was carved out for the "extraordinary case" in which a regulation permanently deprives property of all value; the default rule remains that, in the regulatory taking context, we require a more fact specific inquiry. Nevertheless, we will consider whether the interest in protecting individual property owners from bearing public burdens "which, in all fairness and justice, should be borne by the public as a whole," justifies creating a new rule for these circumstances. . . .

[Petitioners' argument] would apply to numerous "normal delays in obtaining building permits, changes in zoning ordinances, variances, and the like," as well as to orders temporarily prohibiting access to crime scenes, businesses that violate health codes, fire-damaged buildings, or other areas that we cannot now foresee. Such a rule would undoubtedly require changes in numerous practices that have long been considered permissible exercises of the police power. . . . A rule that required compensation for every delay in the use of property would render routine government processes prohibitively expensive or encourage hasty decision-making. Such an important change in the law should be the product of legislative rulemaking rather than adjudication.

[W]e are persuaded that the better approach to claims that a regulation has effected a temporary taking requires careful examination and weighing of all the relevant circumstances. [The] concepts of 'fairness and justice' that underlie the Takings Clause, of course, are less than fully determinate. Accordingly, we have eschewed "any 'set formula' for determining when 'justice and fairness' require that economic injuries caused by public action be compensated by the government, rather than remain disproportionately concentrated on a few persons. The outcome instead depends largely upon the particular circumstances [in that] case."

In rejecting petitioners' *per se* rule, we do not hold that the temporary nature of a land-use restriction precludes finding that it effects a taking; we simply recognize that it should not be given exclusive significance one way or the other. . . . A narrower rule that excluded the normal delays associated with processing permits, or that covered only delays of more than a year, would certainly have a less severe impact on prevailing practices, but it would still impose serious financial constraints on the planning process. Unlike the "extraordinary circumstance" in which the government deprives a property owner of all economic use, moratoria like Ordinance 81-5 and Resolution 83-21 are used widely among land-use planners to preserve the status quo while formulating a more permanent development strategy. In fact, the consensus in the planning community appears to be that moratoria, or "interim development controls" as they are often called, are an essential tool of successful development. Yet even the weak version of petitioners' categorical rule would treat these interim measures as takings regardless of the good faith of the planners, the reasonable expectations of the landowners, or the actual impact of the moratorium on property values.

The interest in facilitating informed decision-making by regulatory agencies counsels against adopting a *per se* rule that would impose such severe costs on their deliberations. Otherwise, the financial constraints of compensating property owners during a moratorium may force officials to rush through the planning process or to abandon the practice altogether. To the extent that communities are forced to abandon using moratoria, landowners will have incentives to develop their property quickly before a comprehensive plan can be enacted, thereby fostering inefficient and ill-conceived growth. . . . Indeed, the interest in protecting the decisional process is even stronger when an agency is developing a regional plan than when it is considering a permit for a single parcel. In the proceedings involving the Lake Tahoe Basin, for example, the moratoria enabled TRPA to obtain the benefit of comments and criticisms from interested parties [during] its deliberations. . . . Moreover, with a temporary ban on development there is a lesser risk that individual landowners will be "singled out" to bear a special burden that should be shared by the public as a whole. At least with a moratorium there is a clear "reciprocity of advantage," because it protects the interests of all affected landowners against immediate construction that might be inconsistent with the provisions of the plan that is ultimately adopted. "While each of us is burdened somewhat by such restrictions, we, in turn, benefit greatly from the restrictions that are placed on others." In fact, there is reason to believe property values often will continue to increase despite a moratorium.

Such an increase makes sense in this context because property values throughout the Basin can be expected to reflect the added assurance that Lake Tahoe will remain in its pristine state. Since in some cases a 1-year moratorium may not impose a burden at all, we should not adopt a rule that assumes moratoria always force individuals to bear a special burden that should be shared by the public as a whole.

It may well be true that any moratorium that lasts for more than one year should be viewed with special skepticism. But given the fact that the District Court found that the 32 months required by TRPA to formulate the 1984 Regional Plan was not unreasonable, we could [not] conclude that every delay of over one year is constitutionally unacceptable. [T]he duration of the restriction is one of the important factors that a court must consider in the appraisal of a regulatory takings claim, but [the] "temptation to adopt what amount to *per se* rules in either direction must be resisted." [P]etitioners' proposed rule is simply "too blunt an instrument" for identifying those cases. We conclude, therefore, that the interest in "fairness and justice" will be best served by relying on the familiar *Penn Central* approach when deciding cases like this, rather than by attempting to craft a new categorical rule.

Accordingly, the judgment of the Court of Appeals is affirmed.

It is so ordered.

Chief Justice REHNQUIST, with whom Justice SCALIA and Justice THOMAS join, dissenting.

For over half a decade petitioners were prohibited from building homes, or any other structures, on their land. Because the Takings Clause requires the government to pay compensation when it deprives owners of all economically viable use of their land [and] because a ban on all development lasting almost six years does not resemble any traditional land-use planning device, I dissent. . . .

[A] distinction between "temporary" and "permanent" prohibitions is tenuous. The "temporary" prohibition in this case that the Court finds is not a taking lasted almost six years. The "permanent" prohibition that the Court held to be a taking in *Lucas* lasted less than two years [because] the law, as it often does, changed. The South Carolina Legislature in 1990 decided to amend the 1988 Beachfront Management Act to allow the issuance of "'special permits' for the construction or reconstruction of habitable structures seaward of the baseline." Land-use regulations are not irrevocable. And the government can even abandon condemned land. Under the Court's decision today, the takings question turns entirely on the initial label given a regulation, a label that is often without much meaning. There is every incentive for government to simply label any prohibition on development "temporary," or to fix a set number of years. As in this case, this initial designation does not preclude the government from repeatedly extending the "temporary" prohibition into a long-term ban on all development. The Court now holds that such a designation by the government is conclusive even though in fact the moratorium greatly exceeds the time initially specified. Apparently, the Court would not view even a 10-year moratorium as a taking under *Lucas* because the moratorium is not "permanent." . . .

[E]ven if a practical distinction between temporary and permanent deprivations were plausible, to treat the two differently in terms of takings law would be
at odds with the justification for the *Lucas* rule. The *Lucas* rule is derived from the
fact that a "total deprivation of beneficial use is, from the landowner's point of
view, the equivalent of a physical appropriation." The regulation in *Lucas* was the
"practical equivalence" of a long-term physical appropriation, i.e., a condemnation, so the Fifth Amendment required compensation. The "practical equivalence," from the landowner's point of view, of a "temporary" ban on all economic
use is a forced leasehold. . . .

[T]he Court analogizes to other areas of takings law in which we have distinguished between regulations and physical appropriations. But whatever basis
there is for such distinctions in those contexts does not apply when a regulation
deprives a landowner of all economically beneficial use of his land. . . . In "the
extraordinary circumstance when *no* productive or economically beneficial use of
land is permitted," it is less likely that "the legislature is simply 'adjusting the benefits and burdens of economic life' . . . in a manner that secures an 'average reciprocity of advantage' to everyone concerned," and more likely that the property
"is being pressed into some form of public service under the guise of mitigating
serious public harm."

[The] Court worries that applying *Lucas* here compels finding that an array
of traditional, short-term, land-use planning devices are takings. . . . When a
regulation merely delays a final land-use decision, we have recognized that there
are other background principles of state property law that prevent the delay from
being deemed a taking. We thus noted in *First English* that our discussion of temporary takings did not apply "in the case of normal delays in obtaining building
permits, changes in zoning ordinances, variances, and the like." [T]he short-term
delays attendant to zoning and permit regimes are a longstanding feature of
state property law and part of a landowner's reasonable investment-backed
expectations.

But a moratorium prohibiting all economic use for a period of six years is not
one of the longstanding, implied limitations of state property law. . . . Typical
moratoria thus prohibit only certain categories of development, such as fast-food
restaurants, or adult businesses, or all commercial development. Such moratoria
do not implicate *Lucas* because they do not deprive landowners of all economically beneficial use of their land. As for moratoria that prohibit all development,
these do not have the lineage of permit and zoning requirements and thus it is
less certain that property is acquired under the "implied limitation" of a moratorium prohibiting all development. Moreover, unlike a permit system in which it
is expected that a project will be approved so long as certain conditions are satisfied, a moratorium that prohibits all uses is by definition contemplating a new
land-use plan that would prohibit all uses.

[T]he duration of this "moratorium" far exceeds that of ordinary
moratoria. . . . California, where much of the land at issue in this case is located,
provides that a moratorium "shall be of no further force and effect 45 days from its
date of adoption," and caps extension of the moratorium so that the total duration
cannot exceed two years. Others limit moratoria to six months without any

possibility of an extension. . . . Resolution 83-21 reflected this understanding of the limited duration of moratoria in initially limiting the moratorium in this case to 90 days. But what resulted — a "moratorium" lasting nearly six years — bears no resemblance to the short-term nature of traditional moratoria as understood from these background examples of state property law. . . . Because the prohibition on development of nearly six years in this case cannot be said to resemble any "implied limitation" of state property law, it is a taking that requires compensation. . . .

Justice THOMAS, with whom Justice SCALIA joins, dissenting.

[I] would hold that regulations prohibiting all productive uses of property are subject to *Lucas' per se* rule, regardless of whether the property so burdened retains theoretical useful life and value if, and when, the "temporary" moratorium is lifted. [S]uch potential future value bears on the amount of compensation due and has nothing to do with [whether] there was a taking in the first place. . . .

∾ PROBLEMS ∾

1. *Remodeling TBA*. Suppose a federal financial reform law places a number of limitations on firms receiving federal T.A.R.P. money. The law contains a provision that prohibited remodeling or upgrading of property owned by persons subject to bonus restrictions for eight months from the date of the law's enactment. Would this provision be constitutional? *See* First English Evangelical Lutheran Church v. County of Los Angeles, 482 U.S. 304 (1987).

2. *Jackpot*. Suppose in Reno, Nevada, the city council imposed a six-month moratorium on development in the most congested area of town. A local casino, Calico Jack's, which did not intend to expand and actually had no resources with which to do so, brought suit, challenging the constitutionality of the law because it "took a valued and essential right of property ownership, that of developing property." Should Calico Jack's prevail? Suppose Reno condemns land owned by Calico Jack's that lies in a sump-hole and has been used for garbage dumping for many years. Calico Jack's had tried to sell the land, but it was unsuitable for any development. If fixed up at a cost of $1 million, the land would be worth $50,000. (Reno wanted to fix up the property because it bordered a beautiful public recreational area, the value of which was reduced by estimates of up to $2 million since it was next to such a messy piece of property.) What should Reno pay Calico Jack's for the land, if anything? *See* Brown v. Legal Foundation of Washington, 538 U.S. 216 (2003).

3. *Save the Beach, Continued*. Was the moratorium on beach development in the Pensacola law presented in the introductory problem at the beginning of the chapter justified after *Tahoe-Sierra Preservation Council*? How would you argue both sides of the issue?

In the following case, Stop the Beach Renourishment, Inc. v. Florida Dept. of Environmental Protection, 130 S.Ct. 2592 (2010), Justice Scalia opined that a judicial taking should be recognized. This idea did not have the support of a majority of the Court.

Stop the Beach Renourishment, Inc. v. Florida Department of Environmental Protection et al.

130 S.Ct. 2592 (2010)

SCALIA, J., for the Court with respect to Parts I, IV, and V, and an opinion with respect to Parts II and III, joined by ROBERTS, C.J., THOMAS, J., and ALITO, J.

We consider a claim that the decision of a State's court of last resort took property without just compensation in violation of the Takings Clause of the Fifth Amendment, as applied against the States through the Fourteenth.

I

A

Generally speaking, state law defines property interests, including property rights in navigable waters and the lands underneath them. In Florida, the State owns in trust for the public the land permanently submerged beneath navigable waters and the foreshore (the land between the low-tide line and the mean high-water line). Thus, the mean high-water line (the average reach of high tide over the preceding 19 years) is the ordinary boundary between private beachfront, or littoral property, and state-owned land.

Littoral owners have, in addition to the rights of the public, certain "special rights" with regard to the water and the foreshore, rights which Florida considers to be property, generally akin to easements. These include the right of access to the water, the right to use the water for certain purposes, the right to an unobstructed view of the water, and the right to receive accretions and relictions to the littoral property. This is generally in accord with well-established common law, although the precise property rights vary among jurisdictions.

At the center of this case is the right to accretions and relictions. Accretions are additions of alluvion (sand, sediment, or other deposits) to waterfront land; relictions are lands once covered by water that become dry when the water recedes. (For simplicity's sake, we shall refer to accretions and relictions collectively as accretions, and the process whereby they occur as accretion.) In order for an addition to dry land to qualify as an accretion, it must have occurred gradually and imperceptibly — that is, so slowly that one could not see the change occurring, though over time the difference became apparent. When, on the other hand, there is a "sudden or perceptible loss of or addition to land by the action of the water or a sudden change in the bed of a lake or the course of a stream," the change is called an avulsion.

In Florida, as at common law, the littoral owner automatically takes title to dry land added to his property by accretion; but formerly submerged land that has become dry land by avulsion continues to belong to the owner of the seabed (usually the State). Maloney §126.6, at 392; 2 W. Blackstone, Commentaries on the Laws of England 261-262 (1766) (hereinafter Blackstone). Thus, regardless of whether an avulsive event exposes land previously submerged or submerges land previously exposed, the boundary between littoral property and sovereign land does not change; it remains (ordinarily) what was the mean high-water line before the event. It follows from this that, when a new strip of land has been added to the shore by avulsion, the littoral owner has no right to subsequent accretions. Those accretions no longer add to *his* property, since the property abutting the water belongs not to him but to the State.

B

In 1961, Florida's Legislature passed the Beach and Shore Preservation Act. The Act establishes procedures for "beach restoration and nourishment projects," designed to deposit sand on eroded beaches (restoration) and to maintain the deposited sand (nourishment). §§161.021(3), (4). A local government may apply to the Department of Environmental Protection for the funds and the necessary permits to restore a beach, *see* §§161.101(1), 161.041(1). When the project involves placing fill on the State's submerged lands, authorization is required from the Board of Trustees of the Internal Improvement Trust Fund, which holds title to those lands, §253.12(1).

Once a beach restoration "is determined to be undertaken," the Board sets what is called "an erosion control line." It must be set by reference to the existing mean high-water line, though in theory it can be located seaward or landward of that. Much of the project work occurs seaward of the erosion-control line, as sand is dumped on what was once submerged land. The fixed erosion-control line replaces the fluctuating mean high-water line as the boundary between privately owned littoral property and state property. Once the erosion-control line is recorded, the common law ceases to increase upland property by accretion (or decrease it by erosion). §161.191(2). Thus, when accretion to the shore moves the mean high-water line seaward, the property of beachfront landowners is not extended to that line (as the prior law provided), but remains bounded by the permanent erosion-control line. Those landowners "continue to be entitled," however, "to all common-law riparian rights" other than the right to accretions. §161.201. If the beach erodes back landward of the erosion-control line over a substantial portion of the shoreline covered by the project, the Board may, on its own initiative, or must, if asked by the owners or lessees of a majority of the property affected, direct the agency responsible for maintaining the beach to return the beach to the condition contemplated by the project. If that is not done within a year, the project is canceled and the erosion-control line is null and void. §161.211(2), (3). Finally, by regulation, if the use of submerged land would "unreasonably infringe on riparian rights," the project cannot proceed unless the local governments show that they own or have a property interest in the upland property adjacent to the project site. Fla. Admin. Code Rule 18-21.004(3)(b) (2009).

C

In 2003, the city of Destin and Walton County applied for the necessary permits to restore 6.9 miles of beach within their jurisdictions that had been eroded by several hurricanes. The project envisioned depositing along that shore sand dredged from further out. *See* Walton Cty. v. Stop the Beach Renourishment, Inc., 998 So.2d 1102, 1106 (Fla. 2008). It would add about 75 feet of dry sand seaward of the mean high-water line (to be denominated the erosion-control line). The Department issued a notice of intent to award the permits, App. 27-41, and the Board approved the erosion-control line, *Id.*, at 49-50.

The petitioner here, Stop the Beach Renourishment, Inc., is a nonprofit corporation formed by people who own beachfront property bordering the project area (we shall refer to them as the Members). It brought an administrative challenge to the proposed project, see *Id.*, at 10-26, which was unsuccessful; the Department approved the permits. Petitioner then challenged that action in state court under the Florida Administrative Procedure Act. The District Court of Appeal for the First District concluded that, contrary to the Act's preservation of "all common-law riparian rights," the order had eliminated two of the Members' littoral rights: (1) the right to receive accretions to their property; and (2) the right to have the contact of their property with the water remain intact. Save Our Beaches, Inc. v. Florida Dept. of Environmental Protection, 27 So.3d 48, 57 (2006). This, it believed, would be an unconstitutional taking, which would "unreasonably infringe on riparian rights," and therefore require the showing under Fla. Admin. Code Rule 18-21.004(3)(b) that the local governments owned or had a property interest in the upland property. It set aside the Department's final order approving the permits and remanded for that showing to be made. It also certified to the Florida Supreme Court the following question (as rephrased by the latter court): "On its face, does the Beach and Shore Preservation Act unconstitutionally deprive upland owners of littoral rights without just compensation?"

The Florida Supreme Court answered the certified question in the negative, and quashed the First District's remand. It faulted the Court of Appeal for not considering the doctrine of avulsion, which it concluded permitted the State to reclaim the restored beach on behalf of the public. It described the right to accretions as a future contingent interest, not a vested property right, and held that there is no littoral right to contact with the water independent of the littoral right of access, which the Act does not infringe. Petitioner sought rehearing on the ground that the Florida Supreme Court's decision itself effected a taking of the Members' littoral rights contrary to the Fifth and Fourteenth Amendments to the Federal Constitution. The request for rehearing was denied. We granted certiorari.

II

A

Before coming to the parties' arguments in the present case, we discuss some general principles of our takings jurisprudence. The Takings Clause — "nor shall private property be taken for public use, without just compensation," U.S. Const., Amdt. 5 — applies as fully to the taking of a landowner's riparian rights as it does to the taking of an estate in land. *See* Yates v. Milwaukee, 10 Wall. 497, 504, 19 L.Ed. 984 (1871). Moreover, though the classic taking is a transfer of property to the State or to another private party by eminent domain, the Takings Clause applies to other state actions that achieve the same thing. Thus, when the government uses its own property in such a way that it destroys private property, it has taken that property. *See* United States v. Causby, 328 U.S. 256, 261-262 (1946). Similarly, our doctrine of regulatory takings "aims to identify regulatory actions that are functionally equivalent to the classic taking." Lingle v. Chevron U.S.A. Inc., 544 U.S. 528, 539 (2005). Thus, it is a taking when a state regulation forces a property owner to submit to a permanent physical occupation, Loretto v. Teleprompter Manhattan CATV Corp., 458 U.S. 419, 425-426 (1982), or deprives him of all economically beneficial use of his property, Lucas v. South Carolina Coastal Council, 505 U.S. 1003, 1019 (1992). Finally (and here we approach the situation before us), States effect a taking if they recharacterize as public property what was previously private property. *See* Webb's Fabulous Pharmacies, Inc. v. Beckwith, 449 U.S. 155, 163-165 (1980).

The Takings Clause (unlike, for instance, the Ex Post Facto Clauses, see Art. I, §9, cl. 3; §10, cl. 1) is not addressed to the action of a specific branch or branches. It is concerned simply with the act, and not with the governmental actor ("nor shall private property *be taken*" (emphasis added)). There is no textual justification for saying that the existence or the scope of a State's power to expropriate private property without just compensation varies according to the branch of government effecting the expropriation. Nor does common sense recommend such a principle. It would be absurd to allow a State to do by judicial decree what the Takings Clause forbids it to do by legislative fiat.

Our precedents provide no support for the proposition that takings effected by the judicial branch are entitled to special treatment, and in fact suggest the contrary. PruneYard Shopping Center v. Robins, 447 U.S. 74 (1980).

Webb's Fabulous Pharmacies, supra, is even closer in point. There the purchaser of an insolvent corporation had interpleaded the corporation's creditors, placing the purchase price in an interest-bearing account in the registry of the Circuit Court of Seminole County, to be distributed in satisfaction of claims approved by a receiver. The Florida Supreme Court construed an applicable statute to mean that the interest on the account belonged to the county, because the account was "considered 'public money,'" Beckwith v. Webb's Fabulous Pharmacies, 374 So.2d 951, 952-953 (1979) (*per curiam*). We held this to be a taking. We noted that "[t]he usual and general rule is that any interest on an interpleaded and deposited fund follows the principal and is to be allocated to those who are ultimately to be the owners of that principal." "Neither the Florida Legislature by statute, nor the Florida courts by judicial decree," we said, "may accomplish the result the county seeks simply by recharacterizing the principal as 'public money.'"

In sum, the Takings Clause bars *the State* from taking private property without paying for it, no matter which branch is the instrument of the taking. To be sure, the manner of state action may matter: Condemnation by eminent domain, for example, is always a taking, while a legislative, executive, or judicial restriction of property use may or may not be, depending on its nature and extent. But the particular state *actor* is irrelevant. If a legislature *or a court* declares that what was once an established right of private property no longer exists, it has taken that property, no less than if the State had physically appropriated it or destroyed its value by regulation. "[A] State, by *ipse dixit,* may not transform private property into public property without compensation."

B

It is not true that deciding the constitutional question in this case contradicts our settled practice. To the contrary, we have often recognized the existence of a constitutional right, or established the test for violation of such a right (or both), and then gone on to find that the claim at issue fails. *See, e.g.,* New Jersey v. T.L.O., 469 U.S. 325 (1985); Village of Euclid v. Ambler Realty Co., 272 U.S. 365 (1926).

Justice Breyer cannot decide that petitioner's claim fails without first deciding what a valid claim would consist of. His agreement with Part IV of our opinion necessarily implies agreement with the test for a judicial taking (elaborated in Part II-A) which Part IV applies: whether the state court has "declare[d] that what was once an established right of private property no longer exists." Justice Breyer must either agree with that standard or craft one of his own. And agreeing to or crafting a *hypothetical* standard for a *hypothetical* constitutional right is sufficiently unappealing (we have eschewed that course many times in the past) that Justice Breyer might as well acknowledge the right as well. Or he could avoid the need to agree with or craft a hypothetical standard by *denying* the right. But embracing a standard while being coy about the right is, well, odd; and deciding this case while addressing *neither* the standard *nor* the right is quite impossible.

Justice Breyer responds that he simply advocates resolving this case without establishing "*the precise* standard under which a party wins or loses." (emphasis added) But he relies upon no standard at all, precise or imprecise. He simply pronounces that this is not a judicial taking if there is such a thing as a judicial taking. The cases he cites to support this Queen-of-Hearts approach provide no precedent. In each of them the existence of the right in question was settled, and we faced a choice between *competing* standards that had been applied by the courts. We simply held that the right in question had not been infringed under *any* of them. There is no established right here, and no competing standards.

C

Like Justice Breyer's concurrence, Justice Kennedy's concludes that the Florida Supreme Court's action here does not meet the standard for a judicial taking, while purporting not to determine what is the standard for a judicial taking, or indeed whether such a thing as a judicial taking even exists. That approach is invalid for the reasons we have discussed.

Justice Kennedy says that we need not take what he considers the bold and risky step of holding that the Takings Clause applies to judicial action, because the Due Process Clause "would likely prevent a State from doing by judicial decree what the Takings Clause forbids it to do by legislative fiat." He invokes the Due Process Clause "in both its substantive and procedural aspects," not specifying which of his arguments relates to which.

The first respect in which Justice Kennedy thinks the Due Process Clause can do the job seems to sound in Procedural Due Process. Because, he says, "[c]ourts, unlike the executive or legislature, are not designed to make policy decisions" about expropriation, "[t]he Court would be on strong footing in ruling that a judicial decision that eliminates or substantially changes established property rights" violates the Due Process Clause. Let us be clear what is being proposed here. This Court has held that the separation-of-powers principles that the Constitution imposes upon the Federal Government do not apply against the States. *See* Dreyer v. Illinois, 187 U.S. 71, 83-84 (1902). But in order to avoid the bold and risky step of saying that the Takings Clause applies to *all* government takings, Justice Kennedy would have us use Procedural Due Process to impose judicially crafted separation-of-powers limitations upon the States: courts cannot be used to perform the governmental function of expropriation. The asserted reasons for the due-process limitation are that the legislative and executive branches "are accountable in their political capacity" for takings, and "[c]ourts . . . are not designed to make policy decisions" about takings. These reasons may have a lot to do with sound separation-of-powers principles that ought to govern a democratic society, but they have nothing whatever to do with the protection of individual rights that is the object of the Due Process Clause.

Of course even taking those reasons at face value, it is strange to proclaim a democracy deficit and lack of special competence for the judicial taking of an individual property right, when this Court has had no trouble deciding matters of much greater moment, contrary to congressional desire or the legislated desires of most of the States, with no special competence except the authority we possess to enforce the Constitution. In any case, our opinion does *not* trust judges with the relatively small power Justice Kennedy now objects to. It is we who propose setting aside judicial decisions that take private property; it is he who insists that judges cannot be so limited. Under his regime, the citizen whose property has been judicially redefined to belong to the State would presumably be given the Orwellian explanation: "The court did not take your property. Because it is neither politically accountable nor competent to make such a decision, it cannot take property."

Justice Kennedy's injection of separation-of-powers principles into the Due Process Clause would also have the ironic effect of preventing the assignment of the expropriation function to the branch of government whose procedures are, by far, the *most* protective of individual rights. So perhaps even this first respect in which Justice Kennedy would have the Due Process Clause do the work of the Takings Clause pertains to Substantive, rather than Procedural, Due Process.

The first problem with using Substantive Due Process to do the work of the Takings Clause is that we have held it cannot be done. "Where a particular Amendment 'provides an explicit textual source of constitutional protection' against a particular sort of government behavior, 'that Amendment, not the more generalized notion of "substantive due process," must be the guide for analyzing these claims.'" Albright v. Oliver, 510 U.S. 266, 273 (1994) (four-Justice plurality opinion) (quoting Graham v. Connor, 490 U.S. 386, 395 (1989)). The second problem is that we have held for many years (logically or not) that the "liberties" protected by Substantive Due Process do not include economic liberties. *See, e.g.,* Lincoln Fed. Labor Union v. Northwestern Iron & Metal Co., 335 U.S. 525, 536 (1949). Justice Kennedy's language ("If a judicial decision . . . eliminates an established property right, the judgment could be set aside as a deprivation of property without due process of law,") propels us back to what is referred to (usually deprecatingly) as "the *Lochner* era." *See* Lochner v. New York, 198 U.S. 45, 56-58 (1905). That is a step of much greater novelty, and much more unpredictable effect, than merely applying the Takings Clause to judicial action. And the third and last problem with using Substantive Due Process is that either (1) it will not do all that the Takings Clause does, or (2) if it does all that the Takings Clause does, it will encounter the same supposed difficulties that Justice Kennedy finds troublesome.

Moreover, and more importantly, Justice Kennedy places no constraints whatever upon *this* Court. Not only does his concurrence only *think about* applying Substantive Due Process; but because Substantive Due Process is such a wonderfully malleable concept, *see, e.g.,* Lawrence v. Texas, 539 U.S. 558, 562 (2003) (referring to "liberty of the person both in its spatial and in its more transcendent dimensions"), even a firm commitment to apply it would be a firm commitment to nothing in particular. The great attraction of Substantive Due Process as a substitute for more specific constitutional guarantees is that it *never* means never — because it never means anything precise.

III

Respondents put forward a number of arguments which contradict, to a greater or lesser degree, the principle discussed above, that the existence of a taking does not depend upon the branch of government that effects it. First, in a case claiming a judicial taking they would add to our normal takings inquiry a requirement that the court's decision have no "fair and substantial basis." This is taken from our jurisprudence dealing with the question whether a state-court decision rests upon adequate and independent state grounds, placing it beyond our jurisdiction to review. *See* E. Gressman, K. Geller, S. Shapiro, T. Bishop, & E. Hartnett,

Supreme Court Practice, ch. 3.26, p. 222 (9th ed. 2007). A test designed to determine whether there has been an evasion is not obviously appropriate for determining whether there has been a taking of property. But if it is to be extended there it must mean (in the present context) that there is a "fair and substantial basis" for believing that petitioner's Members did not have a property right to future accretions which the Act would take away. This is no different, we think, from our requirement that petitioners' Members must prove the elimination of an established property right.

Next, respondents argue that federal courts lack the knowledge of state law required to decide whether a judicial decision that purports merely to clarify property rights has instead taken them. But federal courts must often decide what state property rights exist in nontakings contexts, *see, e.g.,* Board of Regents of State Colleges v. Roth, 408 U.S. 564, 577-578 (1972) (Due Process Clause).

For its part, petitioner proposes an unpredictability test. Quoting Justice Stewart's concurrence in Hughes v. Washington, 389 U.S. 290, 296 (1967), petitioner argues that a judicial taking consists of a decision that "constitutes a sudden change in state law, unpredictable in terms of relevant precedents." The focus of petitioner's test is misdirected. What counts is not whether there is precedent for the allegedly confiscatory decision, but whether the property right allegedly taken was established. If, for example, a state court held in one case, to which the complaining property owner was not a party, that it had the power to limit the acreage of privately owned real estate to 100 acres, and then, in a second case, applied that principle to declare the complainant's 101st acre to be public property, the State would have taken an acre from the complainant even though the decision was predictable.

IV

Petitioner argues that the Florida Supreme Court took two of the property rights of the Members by declaring that those rights did not exist: the right to accretions, and the right to have littoral property touch the water (which petitioner distinguishes from the mere right of access to the water). Under petitioner's theory, because no prior Florida decision had said that the State's filling of submerged tidal lands could have the effect of depriving a littoral owner of contact with the water and denying him future accretions, the Florida Supreme Court's judgment in the present case abolished those two easements to which littoral property owners had been entitled. This puts the burden on the wrong party. There is no taking unless petitioner can show that, before the Florida Supreme Court's decision, littoral-property owners had rights to future accretions and contact with the water superior to the State's right to fill in its submerged land. Though some may think the question close, in our view the showing cannot be made.

Two core principles of Florida property law intersect in this case. First, the State as owner of the submerged land adjacent to littoral property has the right to fill that land, so long as it does not interfere with the rights of the public and the rights of littoral landowners. Second, as we described, if an avulsion exposes land seaward of littoral property that had previously been submerged, that land belongs to the State even if it interrupts the littoral owner's contact with the water. *See Bryant,* 238 So.2d, at 837, 838-839. The issue here is whether there is an exception to this rule when the State is the cause of the avulsion. Prior law suggests there is not. In Martin v. Busch, 93 Fla. 535, 112 So. 274 (1927), the Florida Supreme Court held that when the State drained water from a lakebed belonging to the State, causing land that was formerly below the mean high-water line to become dry land, that land continued to belong to the State. *Id.,* at 574, 112 So., at 287. "The riparian rights doctrine of accretion and reliction," the Florida Supreme Court later explained, "does not apply to such lands." *Bryant, supra,* at 839 (quoting *Martin, supra,* at 578, 112 So., at 288 (Brown, J., concurring)). This is not surprising, as there can be no accretions to land that no longer abuts the water.

Thus, Florida law as it stood before the decision below allowed the State to fill in its own seabed, and the resulting sudden exposure of previously submerged land was treated like an avulsion for purposes of ownership. The right to accretions was therefore subordinate to the State's right to fill.

The Florida Supreme Court decision before us is consistent with these background principles of state property law. It did not abolish the Members' right to future accretions, but merely held that the right was not implicated by the beach-restoration project, because the doctrine of avulsion applied. The Florida Supreme Court's opinion describes beach restoration as the reclamation by the State of the public's land, just as *Martin* had described the lake drainage in that case. Although the opinion does not cite *Martin* and is not always clear on this point, it suffices that its characterization of the littoral right to accretion is consistent with *Martin* and the other relevant principles of Florida law we have discussed.

What we have said shows that the rule of *Sand Key,* which petitioner repeatedly invokes, is inapposite. There the Florida Supreme Court held that an artificial accretion does not change the right of a littoral-property owner to claim the accreted land as his own (as long as the owner did not cause the accretion himself). The reason *Martin* did not apply, *Sand Key* explained, is that the drainage that had occurred in *Martin*n did not lower the water level by "'imperceptible degrees,'" and so did not qualify as an accretion.

The result under Florida law may seem counter-intuitive. After all, the Members' property has been deprived of its character (and value) as oceanfront property by the State's artificial creation of an avulsion. Perhaps state-created avulsions ought to be treated differently from other avulsions insofar as the property right to accretion is concerned. But nothing in prior Florida law makes such a distinction, and *Martin* suggests, if it does not indeed hold, the contrary. Even if there might be different interpretations of *Martin* and other Florida property-law cases that would prevent this arguably odd result, we are not free to adopt them. The Takings Clause only protects property rights as they are established under state law, not as they might have been established or ought to have been established. We cannot say that the Florida Supreme Court's decision eliminated a right of accretion established under Florida law.

Petitioner also contends that the State took the Members' littoral right to have their property continually maintain contact with the water. To be clear, petitioner does not allege that the State relocated the property line, as would have happened if the erosion-control line were *landward* of the old mean high-water line (instead of identical to it). Petitioner argues instead that the Members have a separate right for the boundary of their property to be always the mean high-water line. Petitioner points to dicta in *Sand Key* that refers to "the right to have the property's contact with the water remain intact." Even there, the right was included in the definition of the right to access, which is consistent with the Florida Supreme Court's later description that "there is no independent right of contact with the water" but it "exists to preserve the upland owner's core littoral right of access to the water." Petitioner's expansive interpretation of the dictum in *Sand Key* would cause it to contradict the clear Florida law governing avulsion. One cannot say that the Florida Supreme Court contravened established property law by rejecting it.

V

Because the Florida Supreme Court's decision did not contravene the established property rights of petitioner's Members, Florida has not violated the Fifth and Fourteenth Amendments.

The judgment of the Florida Supreme Court is therefore affirmed.

It is so ordered.

Justice STEVENS took no part in the decision of this case.

KENNEDY, J., joined by SOTOMAYOR, J., concurring in part and concurring in the judgment.

The Court's analysis of the principles that control ownership of the land in question, and of the rights of petitioner's members as adjacent owners, is correct in my view, leading to my joining Parts I, IV, and V of the Court's opinion. As Justice Breyer observes, however, this case does not require the Court to determine whether, or when, a judicial decision determining the rights of property owners can violate the Takings Clause of the Fifth Amendment of the United States Constitution. This separate opinion notes certain difficulties that should be considered before accepting the theory that a judicial decision that eliminates an "established property right," constitutes a violation of the Takings Clause.

The Takings Clause is an essential part of the constitutional structure, for it protects private property from expropriation without just compensation. The right to retain property without the fact or even the threat of that sort of expropriation is, of course, applicable to the States under the Due Process Clause of the Fourteenth Amendment.

The right of the property owner is subject, however, to the rule that the government does have power to take property for a public use, provided that it pays just compensation. This is a vast governmental power. And typically, legislative bodies grant substantial discretion to executive officers to decide what property can be taken for authorized projects and uses. As a result, if an authorized executive agency or official decides that Blackacre is the right place for a fire station or

Greenacre is the best spot for a freeway interchange, then the weight and authority of the State are used to take the property, even against the wishes of the owner, who must be satisfied with just compensation.

[A]s a matter of custom and practice, [the important responsibility of selecting what property to condemn and associated judgments] are matters for the political branches — the legislature and the executive — not the courts. *See First English, supra,* at 321.

If a judicial decision, as opposed to an act of the executive or the legislature, eliminates an established property right, the judgment could be set aside as a deprivation of property without due process of law. The Due Process Clause, in both its substantive and procedural aspects, is a central limitation upon the exercise of judicial power. And this Court has long recognized that property regulations can be invalidated under the Due Process Clause (*see also* Pennsylvania Coal Co. v. Mahon, 260 U.S. 393, 413 (1922)). It is thus natural to read the Due Process Clause as limiting the power of courts to eliminate or change established property rights.

The Takings Clause also protects property rights, and it "operates as a conditional limitation, permitting the government to do what it wants so long as it pays the charge." Eastern Enterprises v. Apfel, 524 U.S. 498, 545 (1998) (Kennedy, J., concurring in judgment and dissenting in part). Unlike the Due Process Clause, therefore, the Takings Clause implicitly recognizes a governmental power while placing limits upon that power. Thus, if the Court were to hold that a judicial taking exists, it would presuppose that a judicial decision eliminating established property rights is "otherwise constitutional" so long as the State compensates the aggrieved property owners. There is no clear authority for this proposition.

When courts act without direction from the executive or legislature, they may not have the power to eliminate established property rights by judicial decision. "Given that the constitutionality" of a judicial decision altering property rights "appears to turn on the legitimacy" of whether the court's judgment eliminates or changes established property rights "rather than on the availability of compensation, . . . the more appropriate constitutional analysis arises under general due process principles rather than under the Takings Clause." *Ibid.* Courts, unlike the executive or legislature, are not designed to make policy decisions about "the need for, and likely effectiveness of, regulatory actions." *Lingle, supra,* at 545. State courts generally operate under a common-law tradition that allows for incremental modifications to property law, but "this tradition cannot justify a *carte blanch* judicial authority to change property definitions wholly free of constitutional limitations." Walston, *The Constitution and Property: Due Process, Regulatory Takings, and Judicial Takings,* 2001 Utah L. Rev. 379, 435.

The Court would be on strong footing in ruling that a judicial decision that eliminates or substantially changes established property rights, which are a legitimate expectation of the owner, is "arbitrary or irrational" under the Due Process Clause. *Lingle,* 544 U.S., at 542. Thus, without a judicial takings doctrine, the Due Process Clause would likely prevent a State from doing "by judicial decree what the Takings Clause forbids it to do by legislative fiat." The objection that a due process claim might involve close questions concerning whether a judicial decree extends beyond what owners might have expected is not a sound argument; for the same close questions would arise with respect to whether a judicial decision is a taking.

To announce that courts too can effect a taking when they decide cases involving property rights would raise certain difficult questions. Since this case does not require those questions to be addressed, in my respectful view, the Court should not reach beyond the necessities of the case to announce a sweeping rule that court decisions can be takings, as that phrase is used in the Takings Clause.

The Framers most likely viewed this [Takings] Clause as applying only to physical appropriation pursuant to the power of eminent domain. *See* Lucas v. South Carolina Coastal Council, 505 U.S. 1003, 1028, n.15 (1992). And it appears these physical appropriations were traditionally made by legislatures. *See* 3 J. Story, Commentaries on the Constitution of the United States §1784, p. 661 (1833). Courts, on the other hand, lacked the power of eminent domain. *See* 1 W. Blackstone, Commentaries 135 (W. Lewis ed. 1897). The Court's Takings Clause jurisprudence has expanded beyond the Framers' understanding, as it now applies to certain regulations that are not physical appropriations. *See Lucas, supra,* at 1014.

There are two additional practical considerations that the Court would need to address before recognizing judicial takings. First, it may be unclear in certain situations how a party should properly raise a judicial takings claim.

Second, it is unclear what remedy a reviewing court could enter after finding a judicial taking. It appears under our precedents that a party who suffers a taking is only entitled to damages, not equitable relief. It makes perfect sense that the remedy for a Takings Clause violation is only damages, as the Clause "does not proscribe the taking of property; it proscribes taking without just compensation." Williamson County Regional Planning Commn. v. Hamilton Bank of Johnson City, 473 U.S. 172, 194 (1985).

It is thus questionable whether reviewing courts could invalidate judicial decisions deemed to be judicial takings; they may only be able to order just compensation. In the posture discussed above where Case A changes the law and Case B addresses whether that change is a taking, it is not clear how the Court, in Case B, could invalidate the holding of Case A.

These difficult issues are some of the reasons why the Court should not reach beyond the necessities of the case to recognize a judicial takings doctrine. If and when future cases show that the usual principles, including constitutional principles that constrain the judiciary like due process, are somehow inadequate to protect property owners, then the question whether a judicial decision can effect a taking would be properly presented. In the meantime, it seems appropriate to recognize that the substantial power to decide whose property to take and when to take it should be conceived of as a power vested in the political branches and subject to political control.

BREYER, J., with GINSBURG, J. joining, concurring in part and concurring in the judgment.

I agree that no unconstitutional taking of property occurred in this case, and I therefore join Parts I, IV, and V of today's opinion. I cannot join Parts II and III, however, for in those Parts the plurality unnecessarily addresses questions of constitutional law that are better left for another day.

In Part II of its opinion, the plurality concludes that courts, including federal courts, may review the private property law decisions of state courts to determine whether the decisions unconstitutionally take "private property" for "public use without just compensation." U.S. Const., Amdt. 5. And in doing so it finds "irrelevant" that the "particular state *actor*" that takes private property (or unconstitutionally redefines state property law) is the judicial branch, rather than the executive or legislative branch. *Cf.* Hughes v. Washington, 389 U.S. 290, 296-298 (1967) (Stewart, J., concurring).

In Part III, the plurality determines that it is "not obviously appropriate" to apply this Court's "'fair and substantial basis'" test, familiar from our adequate and independent state ground jurisprudence, when evaluating whether a state-court property decision enacts an unconstitutional taking. The plurality further concludes that a state-court decision violates the Takings Clause not when the decision is "unpredictab[le]" on the basis of prior law, but rather when the decision takes private property rights that are "established." And finally, it concludes that all those affected by a state-court property law decision can raise a takings claim in federal court, *but for* the losing party in the initial state-court proceeding, who can only raise her claim (possibly for the first time) in a petition for a writ of certiorari here.

I do not claim that all of these conclusions are unsound. I do not know. But I do know that, if we were to express our views on these questions, we would invite a host of federal takings claims without the mature consideration of potential procedural or substantive legal principles that might limit federal interference in matters that are primarily the subject of state law. Property owners litigate many thousands of cases involving state property law in state courts each year. Each state-court property decision may further affect numerous nonparty property owners as well. Losing parties in many state-court cases may well believe that erroneous judicial decisions have deprived them of property rights they previously held and may consequently bring federal takings claims. And a glance at Part IV makes clear that such cases can involve state property law issues of considerable complexity. Hence, the approach the plurality would take today threatens to open the federal court doors to constitutional review of many, perhaps large numbers of, state-law cases in an area of law familiar to state, but not federal, judges. And the failure of that approach to set forth procedural limitations or canons of deference would create the distinct possibility that federal judges would play a major role in the shaping of a matter of significant state interest-state property law.

The plurality criticizes me for my cautious approach, and states that I "cannot decide that petitioner's claim fails without first deciding what a valid claim would consist of." But, of course, courts frequently find it possible to resolve cases — even those raising constitutional questions — without specifying the precise standard under which a party wins or loses. *See, e.g.,* Smith v. Spisak, 130 S.Ct. 676, 688 (2010); Quilloin v. Walcott, 434 U.S. 246, 256 (1978).

In the past, Members of this Court have warned us that, when faced with difficult constitutional questions, we should "confine ourselves to deciding only what is necessary to the disposition of the immediate case." Whitehouse v. Illinois Central R. Co., 349 U.S. 366, 373 (1955); I heed this advice here. There is no need now to decide more than what the Court decides in Parts IV and V, namely, that the Florida Supreme Court's decision in this case did not amount to a "judicial taking."

∼ PROBLEM: SAVE THE BEACH, CONTINUED ∼

Assume the Pensacola law in the introductory problem, which changed existing statutory and common law property rights, was challenged in the Florida courts. Assume the trial court found that no taking occurred, and on appeal the First District Court of Appeals affirmed, as did the Florida Supreme Court. More than two years after the litigation was initiated, the case was reviewed by the U.S. Supreme Court on a writ of certiorari, and the decision was reversed. Should the Court find that a judicial taking has occurred? If so, what should be the "just compensation"?

C. THE CONTRACT CLAUSE

As noted at the beginning of this chapter, contractual interests and expectations inform more than one constitutional provision. The emergence of liberty of contract, as a fundamental right driven by judicial construction rather than textual specificity, was a defining aspect of the *Lochner* era's substantive due process review. Prior to this controversial and eventually abandoned application of the Fourteenth Amendment, constitutional protection of contractual interests was grounded in the Contract Clause. As set forth by Article I, Section 10, this clause prohibits the state from enacting any "Law impairing the Obligation of Contracts." This provision specifically applies to existing contracts.

Early use of the Contract Clause yielded results that were consistent with the Marshall Court's vision and the facilitation of nation building. In Fletcher v. Peck, 10 U.S. (6 Cranch) 87 (1810), the Court reviewed the Georgia legislature's rescission of a land grant that had been tainted by bribery and fraud. The law was challenged by persons who acquired land in the aftermarket and claimed they were purchasers in due course. The Court, in an ambiguous decision referencing the Contract Clause and principles of natural law, overturned the rescission. *See also* Dartmouth College v. Woodward, 17 U.S. (4 Wheat.) 518 (1819) (striking down New Hampshire's attempt to alter the college's charter, in an effort to change the composition of the board, violating the existing charter, which gave the board the right to fill vacancies). Modern interpretation of the Contract Clause is less expansive and ambitious, but not without potential force particularly with respect to a state's power to modify public contracts and private expectations.

Home Building & Loan Assn. v. Blaisdell
290 U.S. 398 (1934)

Mr. Chief Justice HUGHES delivered the opinion of the Court.

Appellant contests the validity [of] the Minnesota Mortgage Moratorium Law as being repugnant to the contract clause (Art. 1, §10). . . . The act provides that, during the emergency declared to exist, relief may be had through authorized judicial proceedings with respect to foreclosures of mortgages, and execution sales, of real estate; that sales may be postponed and periods of redemption may be extended. . . . The act is to remain in effect 'only during the continuance of the emergency and in no event beyond May 1, 1935.' No extension of the period for redemption and no postponement of sale is to be allowed which would have the effect of extending the period of redemption beyond that date.

[This case concerns] the provisions of part 1, §4, authorizing the district court of the county to extend the period of redemption from foreclosure sales 'for such additional time as the court may deem just and equitable,' subject to the above-described limitation. The extension is to be made upon application to the court, on notice, for an order determining the reasonable value of the income on the property involved in the sale, or, if it has no income, then the reasonable rental value of the property, and directing the mortgagor 'to pay all or a reasonable part of such income or rental value, in or toward the payment of taxes, insurance, interest, [mortgage] indebtedness at such times and in such manner' as shall be determined by the court. [The] time for redemption from foreclosure sales[,] which otherwise would expire less than thirty days after the approval of the act, shall be extended to a date thirty days after its approval, and application may be made to the court within that time for a further extension as provided in the section. [N]o action, prior to May 1, 1935, may be maintained for a deficiency judgment until the period of redemption as allowed by existing law or as extended under the provisions of the act has expired. Prior to the expiration of the extended period of redemption, the court may revise or alter the terms of the extension as changed circumstances may require.

Invoking [the] statute, appellees applied [for] an order extending the period of redemption from a foreclosure sale. Their petition stated that they owned a lot in Minneapolis which they had mortgaged to appellant; that the mortgage contained a valid power of sale by advertisement, and that by reason of their default the mortgage had been foreclosed and sold to appellant[;] that appellant was the holder of the sheriff's certificate of sale; that, because of the economic depression, appellees had been unable to obtain a new loan or to redeem, and that, unless the period of redemption were extended, the property would be irretrievably lost; and that the reasonable value of the property greatly exceeded the amount due on the mortgage, including all liens, costs, and expenses.

[A]ppellant objected [that] the statute was invalid under the federal and state Constitutions. . . . The motion was granted. . . . [T]he Supreme Court of the state reversed the decision of the district court. . . .

We [assume] that the mortgage contained a valid power of sale to be exercised in case of default; that this power was validly exercised; that under the law then applicable the period of redemption from the sale was one year, and that it has been extended by the judgment of the court over the opposition of the mortgagee-purchaser; and that, during the period thus extended, and unless the order for extension is modified, the mortgagee-purchaser will be unable to obtain possession, or to obtain or convey title in fee, as he would have been able to do had the statute not been enacted. The statute does not impair the integrity of the mortgage indebtedness. The obligation for interest remains. The statute does not affect the validity of the sale or the right of a mortgagee-purchaser to title in fee, or his right to obtain a deficiency judgment, if the mortgagor fails to redeem within the prescribed period. Aside from the extension of time, the other conditions of redemption are unaltered. While the mortgagor remains in possession, he must pay the rental value as that value has been determined, upon notice and hearing, by the court. The rental value so paid is devoted to the carrying of the property by the application of the required payments to taxes, insurance, and interest on the mortgage indebtedness. While the mortgagee-purchaser is debarred from actual possession, he has, so far as rental value is concerned, the equivalent of possession during the extended period. . . .

While emergency does not create power, emergency may furnish the occasion for the exercise of power. [T]he reasons which led to the adoption of that clause, and of the other prohibitions of section 10 of article 1, are not left in doubt. . . . The widespread distress following the revolutionary period and the plight of debtors had called forth in the States an ignoble array of legislative schemes for the defeat of creditors and the invasion of contractual obligations. Legislative interferences had been so numerous and extreme that the confidence essential to prosperous trade had been undermined and the utter destruction of credit was threatened. 'The sober people of America' were convinced that some 'thorough reform' was needed which would 'inspire a general prudence and industry, and give a regular course to the business of society.' *The Federalist No. 44*. . . .

[The contract clause] is not an absolute and is not to be read with literal exactness like a mathematical formula. . . . This Court has said that 'the laws which subsist at the time and place of the making of a contract, and where it is to be performed, enter into and form a part of it, as if they were expressly referred to or incorporated in its terms. [Nothing] can be more material to the obligation than the means of enforcement. . . . But [w]ithout impairing the obligation of the contract, the remedy may certainly be modified as the wisdom of the nation shall direct.' [The] policy of protecting contracts against impairment presupposes the maintenance of a government by virtue of which contractual relations are worthwhile, — a government which retains adequate authority to secure the peace and good order of society. This principle of harmonizing the constitutional prohibition with the necessary residuum of state power has had progressive recognition in the decisions of this Court. . . .

The economic interests of the state may justify the exercise of its continuing and dominant protective power notwithstanding interference with contracts. . . . The question is not whether the legislative action affects contracts incidentally, or directly or indirectly, but whether the legislation is addressed to a legitimate end and the measures taken are reasonable and appropriate to that end. [T]he state power may be addressed directly to the prevention of the enforcement of contracts only when these are of a sort which the Legislature in its discretion may denounce as being in themselves hostile to public morals, or public health, safety, or welfare, or where the prohibition is merely of injurious practices; that interference with the enforcement of other and valid contracts according to appropriate legal procedure, although the interference is temporary and for a public purpose, is not permissible. This is but to contend that in the latter case the end is not legitimate in the view that it cannot be reconciled with a fair interpretation of the constitutional provision.

Undoubtedly, whatever is reserved of state power must be consistent with the fair intent of the constitutional limitation of that power. . . . This principle precludes a construction which would permit the state to adopt as its policy the repudiation of debts or the destruction of contracts or the denial of means to enforce them. But it does not follow that conditions may not arise in which a temporary restraint of enforcement may be consistent with the spirit and purpose of the constitutional provision and thus be found to be within the range of the reserved power of the state to protect the vital interests of the community. . . . [I]f state power exists to give temporary relief from the enforcement of contracts in the presence of disasters due to physical causes such as fire, flood, or earthquake, that power cannot be said to be nonexistent when the urgent public need demanding such relief is produced by other and economic causes.

[T]here has been a growing appreciation of public needs and of the necessity of finding ground for a rational compromise between individual rights and public welfare. . . . It is no answer to say that this public need was not apprehended a century ago, or to insist that what the provision of the Constitution meant to the vision of that day it must mean to the vision of our time. If by the statement that what the Constitution meant at the time of its adoption it means to-day, it is intended to say that the great clauses of the Constitution must be confined to the interpretation which the framers, with the conditions and outlook of their time, would have placed upon them, the statement carries its own refutation. . . . Chief Justice Marshall uttered the memorable warning: 'We must never forget, that it is a constitution we are expounding' (McCulloch v. Maryland, 4 Wheat. 316, 407, 4 L.Ed. 579); 'a constitution intended to endure for ages to come, and, consequently, to be adapted to the various crises of human affairs.' When we are dealing with the words of the Constitution, said this Court in Missouri v. Holland, 252 U.S. 416, 'we must realize that they have called into life a being the development of which could not have been foreseen completely by the most gifted of its begetters. [The] case before us must be considered in the light of our whole experience and not merely in that of what was said a hundred years ago.'

Nor is it helpful to attempt to draw a fine distinction between the intended meaning of the words of the Constitution and their intended application. . . . With a growing recognition of public needs and the relation of individual right to public security, the court has sought to prevent the perversion of the clause through its use as an instrument to throttle the capacity of the states to protect their fundamental interests. . . . Applying the criteria established by our decisions, we conclude:

1. An emergency existed in Minnesota which furnished a proper occasion for the exercise of the reserved power of the state to protect the vital interests of the community. . . .

2. The legislation was addressed to a legitimate end; that is, the legislation was not for the mere advantage of particular individuals but for the protection of a basic interest of society.

3. In view of the nature of the contracts in question — mortgages of unquestionable validity — the relief afforded and justified by the emergency, in order not to contravene the constitutional provision, could only be of a character appropriate to that emergency, and could be granted only upon reasonable conditions.

4. The conditions upon which the period of redemption is extended do not appear to be unreasonable. The initial extension of the time of redemption for thirty days from the approval of the act was obviously to give a reasonable opportunity for the authorized application to the court. [T]he integrity of the mortgage indebtedness is not impaired; interest continues to run; the validity of the sale and the right of a mortgagee-purchaser to title or to obtain a deficiency judgment, if the mortgagor fails to redeem within the extended period, are maintained; and the conditions of redemption, if redemption there be, stand as they were under the prior law. The mortgagor during the extended period is not ousted from possession, but he must pay the rental value of the premises as ascertained in judicial proceedings and this amount is applied to the carrying of the property and to interest upon the indebtedness. The mortgagee-purchaser during the time that he cannot obtain possession thus is not left without compensation for the withholding of possession. Also important is the fact that mortgagees, as is shown by official reports of which we may take notice, are predominantly corporations, such as insurance companies, banks, and investment and mortgage companies. These, and such individual mortgagees as are small investors, are not seeking homes or the opportunity to engage in farming. Their chief concern is the reasonable protection of their investment security. It does not matter that there are, or may be, individual cases of another aspect. The Legislature was entitled to deal with the general or typical situation. The relief afforded by the statute has regard to the interest of mortgagees as well as to the interest of mortgagors. The legislation seeks to prevent the impending ruin of both by a considerate measure of relief.

In the absence of legislation, courts of equity have exercised jurisdiction in suits for the foreclosure of mortgages to fix the time and terms of sale and to refuse to confirm sales upon equitable grounds where they were found to be unfair or inadequacy of price was so gross as to shock the conscience. . . . Although the courts would have no authority to alter a statutory period of redemption, the legislation in question permits the courts to extend that period, within limits and upon equitable terms, thus providing a procedure and relief which are cognate to the historic exercise of the equitable jurisdiction. If it be determined, as it must be, that the contract clause is not an absolute and utterly unqualified restriction of the state's protective power, this legislation is clearly so reasonable as to be within the legislative competency.

5. The legislation is temporary in operation. It is limited to the exigency which called it forth. While the postponement of the period of redemption from the foreclosure sale is to May 1, 1935, that period may be reduced by the order of the court under the statute, in case of a change in circumstances, and the operation of the statute itself could not validly outlast the emergency or be so extended as virtually to destroy the contracts.

We are of the opinion that the Minnesota statute as here applied does not violate the contract clause of the Federal Constitution. Whether the legislation is wise or unwise as a matter of policy is a question with which we are not concerned.

The judgment of the Supreme Court of Minnesota is affirmed.

Judgment affirmed.

Mr. Justice SUTHERLAND, dissenting.

'[The] Constitution of the United States is a law for rulers and people, equally in war and in peace, and covers with the shield of its protection all classes of men, at all times, and under all circumstances. No doctrine, involving more pernicious consequences, was ever invented by the wit of man than that any of its provisions can be suspended during any of the great exigencies of government. Such a doctrine leads directly to anarchy or despotism. . . .' [T]he contract impairment clause denies to the several states the power to mitigate hard consequences resulting to debtors from financial or economic exigencies by an impairment of the obligation of contracts of indebtedness. . . . The present exigency is nothing new. From the beginning of our existence as a nation, periods of depression, of industrial failure, of financial distress, of unpaid and unpayable indebtedness, have alternated with years of plenty. . . . The defense of the Minnesota law is made upon grounds which were discountenanced by the makers of the Constitution and have many times been rejected by this Court. . . . A statute which materially delays enforcement of the mortgagee's contractual right of ownership and possession does not modify the remedy merely; it destroys, for the period of delay, all remedy so far as the enforcement of that right is concerned.

∾ PROBLEMS ∾

1. Blaisdell *Revisited*. Arizona enacts a new law, the Mortgage Modification Act of 2009, requiring lenders and borrowers of problem loans, as defined in the statute, to go to mediation to come up with an alternative payment plan, if feasible, prior to pursuing foreclosure proceedings. Would this law violate the Contract Clause under *Blaisdell*?

2. *Tolls*. In order to ensure that toll revenue would be available to pay bondholders, New Jersey and New York passed laws providing that toll revenue from

the Port Authority of New Jersey and New York could not be used to subsidize rail-road passenger service (but instead would be devoted to bond payments). The statutory provisions were incorporated into the bonds. In the early 1970s, during an energy crisis, both states passed laws authorizing the use of toll revenues to subsidize railroad passenger service.

a) Does the statutory repeal impair the obligation of contracts under *Blaisdell*?

b) What if the Court adopts rules that treat the impairment of government contracts—in which the government is a party—differently than the impair-ment of contracts between private parties? Should the courts be more deferential to state impairment of private contracts or contracts in which the government is a party? *See* United States Trust Co. v. New Jersey, 431 U.S. 1 (1997).

3. *The New York Financial Reform Law.* After the collapse of the mortgage mar-ket and the failure of many banks, which caused a severe recession, the State of New York is considering the possibility of enacting a law prohibiting "excessive bonuses in the finance industry." *Excessive* would be defined as any bonus that exceeds 10 percent of the employee's ordinary salary, adjusted by the percentage of profit of the company over the preceding five years. Under the proposed law, excessive bonuses would be considered unlawful, would subject the company that gives the bonus to a $500,000 fine, and would subject the receiver of the bonus to a fine of up to $100,000 and imprisonment for a period of up to one year, if the excess bonus is not returned within one month. You are counsel to the legislative committee that is considering the law. If it is enacted, would the law be constitu-tional?

4. *Save the Beach, Continued.* Suppose Pensacola in the introductory problem contemplated modifying its contractual obligations through the enactment of the Pensacola "save our beaches" law for the specific purpose of saving its beaches from oil spills, hurricanes, and general erosion. Would such modifications run afoul of the Contract Clause? Why or why not?

Allied Structural Steel Company v. Spannaus
438 U.S. 234 (1978)

Mr. Justice STEWART delivered the opinion of the Court.

The issue in this case is whether the application of Minnesota's Private Pen-sion Benefits Protection Act to the appellant violates the Contract Clause of the United States Constitution. . . .

[In 1963,] Allied Structural Steel Co. (company) [adopted] a single-employer [pension] plan under [the] Internal Revenue Code, 26 U.S.C. §401 (1976 ed.), [for] salaried employees. . . . The company was the sole contributor to the pension trust fund, and each year it made contributions to the fund. . . . Although those contributions [were] irrevocable, [the] plan neither required the company to make specific contributions nor imposed any sanction on it for fail-ing to contribute adequately to the fund. . . . The company not only retained a virtually unrestricted right to amend the plan[,] but was also free to terminate the plan and distribute the trust assets at any time and for any reason. . . . In sum, an employee who did not die, did not quit, and was not discharged before meeting [the] requirements of the plan would receive a fixed pension at age 65 if the company remained in business and elected to continue the pension plan in essentially its existing form.

[In] 1974, Minnesota enacted [the] Private Pension Benefits Protection Act [which provided that] a private employer of 100 employees or more — at least one of whom was a Minnesota resident — who provided pension benefits under a plan meeting the qualifications of §401 of the Internal Revenue Code, was subject to a "pension funding charge" if he either terminated the plan or closed a Minnesota office. The charge was assessed if the pension funds were not sufficient to cover full pensions for all employees who had worked at least 10 years. The Act required the employer to satisfy the deficiency by purchasing deferred annuities, payable to the employees at their normal retirement age. [When] the company began closing its Minnesota office [in 1974, it] discharged 11 of its 30 Minnesota employees. [N]ine of the discharged employees did not have any vested pension rights under the company's plan, but had worked for the company for 10 years or more and thus qualified as pension obligees [under Minnesota law]. [T]he State notified the company that it owed a pension funding charge of [$185,000 under the] Act. . . . The company brought suit [claiming] that the Act unconstitutionally impaired its contractual obligations to its employees under its pension agreement. . . . We noted probable jurisdiction.

[Although the contract clause] was perhaps the strongest single constitutional check on state legislation during our early years as a Nation, the Contract Clause receded into comparative desuetude with the adoption of the Fourteenth Amendment, and particularly with the development of the large body of jurisprudence under the Due Process Clause of that Amendment. . . . Nonetheless, the Contract Clause [is] not a dead letter. . . .

[T]he Contract Clause does [not] obliterate the police power of the States. . . . This power, which [is] an exercise of the sovereign right of the Government to protect the lives, health, morals, comfort and general welfare of the people, and is paramount to any rights under contracts between individuals." Manigault v. Springs, 199 U.S. 473. . . . If the Contract Clause is to retain any meaning at all, however, it must be understood to impose *some* limits upon the power of a State to abridge existing contractual relationships, even in the exercise of its otherwise legitimate police power. The existence and nature of those limits were clearly indicated in a series of cases in this Court arising from the efforts of the States to deal with the unprecedented emergencies brought on by the severe economic depression of the early 1930's. . . . In Home Building & Loan Assn. v. Blaisdell, 290 U.S. 398, the Court upheld against a Contract Clause attack a mortgage moratorium law that Minnesota had enacted to provide relief for homeowners threatened with foreclosure. Although the legislation conflicted directly with lenders' contractual foreclosure rights, the Court [acknowledged] that, despite the Contract Clause, the States retain residual authority to enact laws "to safeguard the vital interests of [their] people." In upholding the state mortgage moratorium law, the Court found five factors significant. First, the state legislature had declared in the Act itself that an emergency need for the protection of homeowners existed. Second, the state law was enacted to protect a basic societal interest, not a favored group. Third, the relief was appropriately tailored to the emergency that it was designed to meet. Fourth, the imposed conditions were reasonable. And, finally, the legislation was limited to the duration of the emergency. . . .

The most recent Contract Clause case in this Court was United States Trust Co. v. New Jersey, 431 U.S. 1. In that case the Court again recognized that [the] absolute language of the Clause must leave room for "the 'essential attributes of sovereign power,' [necessarily] reserved by the States to safeguard the welfare of their citizens," that power has limits when its exercise effects substantial modifications of private contracts. Despite the customary deference courts give to state laws directed to social and economic problems, "[l]egislation adjusting the rights and responsibilities of contracting parties must be upon reasonable conditions and of a character appropriate to the public purpose justifying its adoption." Evaluating with particular scrutiny a modification of a contract to which the State itself was a party, the Court [held] that legislative alteration of the rights and remedies of Port Authority bondholders violated the Contract Clause because the legislation was neither necessary nor reasonable.

In applying these principles to the present case, the first inquiry must be whether the state law [has] operated as a substantial impairment of a contractual relationship. The severity of the impairment measures the height of the hurdle the state legislation must clear. Minimal alteration of contractual obligations may end the inquiry at its first stage. Severe impairment, on the other hand, will push the inquiry to a careful examination of the nature and purpose of the state legislation. . . . The severity of an impairment of contractual obligations can be measured by the factors that reflect the high value the Framers placed on the protection of private contracts. Contracts enable individuals to order their personal and business affairs according to their particular needs and interests. Once arranged, those rights and obligations are binding under the law, and the parties are entitled to rely on them.

Here, the company's contracts of employment with its employees included as a fringe benefit or additional form of compensation, the pension plan. The company's maximum obligation was to set aside each year an amount based on the plan's requirements for vesting. The plan satisfied the current federal income tax code and was subject to no other legislative requirements. And, of course, the company was free to amend or terminate the pension plan at any time. The company thus had no reason to anticipate that its employees' pension rights could become vested except in accordance with the terms of the plan. It relied heavily, and reasonably, on this legitimate contractual expectation in calculating its annual contributions to the pension fund.

The effect of Minnesota's Private Pension Benefits Protection Act on this contractual obligation was severe. The company was required in 1974 to have made its contributions throughout the pre-1974 life of its plan as if employees' pension rights had vested after 10 years, instead of vesting in accord with the terms of the plan. Thus a basic term of the pension contract — one on which the company had relied for 10 years — was substantially modified. The result was that, although the company's past contributions were adequate when made, they were not adequate when computed under the 10-year statutory vesting requirement. The Act thus forced a current recalculation of the past 10 years' contributions based on the new, unanticipated 10-year vesting requirement.

Not only did the state law thus retroactively modify the compensation that the company had agreed to pay its employees from 1963 to 1974, but also it did so by changing the company's obligations in an area where the element of reliance was vital — the funding of a pension plan. . . . Moreover, the retroactive state-imposed vesting requirement was applied only to those employers who terminated their pension plans or [who] closed their Minnesota offices. The company was thus forced to make all the retroactive changes in its contractual obligations at one time. By simply proceeding to close its office in Minnesota, a move that had been planned before the passage of the Act, the company was assessed an immediate pension funding charge of approximately $185,000.

Thus, the statute in question here nullifies express terms of the company's contractual obligations and imposes a completely unexpected liability in potentially disabling amounts. There is not even any provision for gradual applicability or grace periods. Yet there is no showing in the record before us that this severe disruption of contractual expectations was necessary to meet an important general social problem. The presumption favoring "legislative judgment as to the necessity and reasonableness of a particular measure," simply cannot stand in this case. . . . "It seems clear that the problem of plant closure and pension plan termination was brought to the attention of the Minnesota legislature when the Minneapolis-Moline Division of White Motor Corporation closed one of its Minnesota plants and attempted to terminate its pension plan." [W]hether or not the legislation was aimed largely at a single employer, it clearly has an extremely narrow focus. It applies only to private employers who have at least 100 employees, at least one of whom works in Minnesota, and who have established voluntary private pension plans, qualified under §401 of the Internal Revenue Code. And it applies only when such an employer closes his Minnesota office or terminates his pension plan. Thus, this law can hardly be characterized, like the law at issue in the *Blaisdell* case, as one enacted to protect a broad societal interest rather than a narrow class.

Moreover, in at least one other important respect the Act does not resemble the mortgage moratorium legislation whose constitutionality was upheld in the *Blaisdell* case. This legislation, imposing a sudden, totally unanticipated, and substantial retroactive obligation upon the company to its employees, was not enacted to deal with a situation remotely approaching the broad and desperate emergency economic conditions of the early 1930's. . . .

Entering a field it had never before sought to regulate, the Minnesota Legislature grossly distorted the company's existing contractual relationships with its employees by superimposing retroactive obligations upon the company substantially beyond the terms of its employment contracts. And that burden was imposed upon the company only because it closed its office in the State.

This Minnesota law simply does not possess the attributes of those state laws that in the past have survived challenge under the Contract Clause of the Constitution. The law was not even purportedly enacted to deal with a broad, generalized economic or social problem. It did not operate in an area already subject to state regulation at the time the company's contractual obligations were originally undertaken, but invaded an area never before subject to regulation by the State. It did not effect simply a temporary alteration of the contractual relationships of those within its coverage, but worked a severe, permanent, and immediate change in those relationships — irrevocably and retroactively. And its narrow aim was leveled, not at every Minnesota employer, not even at every Minnesota employer who left the State, but only at those who had in the past been sufficiently enlightened as voluntarily to agree to establish pension plans for their employees.

[I]f the Contract Clause means anything at all, it means that Minnesota could not constitutionally do what it tried to do to the company in this case.

The judgment of the District Court is reversed.

It is so ordered.

Mr. Justice BRENNAN, with whom Mr. Justice WHITE and Mr. Justice MARSHALL join, dissenting.

Today's decision greatly expands the reach of the [Contract] Clause. The Minnesota Private Pension Benefits Protection Act (Act) does not abrogate or dilute any obligation due a party to a private contract; rather, like all positive social legislation, the Act imposes new, additional obligations on a particular class of persons. In my view, any constitutional infirmity in the law must therefore derive, not from the Contract Clause, but from the Due Process Clause of the Fourteenth Amendment. I perceive nothing in the Act that works a denial of due process and therefore I dissent.

[Minnesota adopted] the Act to remedy, *inter alia*, what was viewed as a related serious social problem: the frustration of expectation interests that can occur when an employer closes a single plant and terminates the employees who work there. [H]ere and as will generally be true, the possibility of a plant's closing was not relied upon by actuaries in calculating the amount of the employer's contributions to the plan, an adequate pension plan fund would include contributions on behalf of terminated employees of 10 or more years' service whose rights had not vested. Indeed, without the Act, the closing of the plant would create a windfall for the employer, because, due to the resulting surplus in the fund, his future contributions would be reduced. In denying the windfall, the Act requires that the employer use the money he will save in the future to purchase annuities for the terminated employees. Of course, the consequence for the employer may be a slightly higher pension expense [because] the past contributions to the plan would have reflected the actuarial possibility that some of the employees who had served 10 years might not ultimately satisfy the plan's vesting requirement. . . .

It is [an] abuse [to] interpret [the] term "impairing" as including laws which create new duties. While such laws may be conceptualized as "enlarging" the obligation of a contract when they add to the burdens that had previously been imposed by a private agreement, such laws cannot be prohibited by the Clause because they do not dilute or nullify a duty a person had previously obligated himself to perform. . . .

More fundamentally, the Court's distortion of the meaning of the Contract Clause creates anomalies of its own and threatens to undermine the jurisprudence of property rights developed over the last 40 years. The Contract Clause [is] but one of several clauses in the Constitution that protect existing economic values from governmental interference. . . . Decisions over the past 50 years have developed a coherent, unified interpretation of all the constitutional provisions that may protect economic expectations and these decisions have recognized a broad latitude in States to effect even severe interference with existing economic values when reasonably necessary to promote the general welfare. *See* Penn Central Transp. Co. v. New York City, 438 U.S. 104. [T]he prohibition of the Contract Clause, consistently with its wording and historic purposes, has been limited in application to state laws that diluted, with utter indifference to the legitimate interests of the beneficiary of a contract duty, the existing contract obligation.

Today's conversion of the Contract Clause into a limitation on the power of States to enact laws that impose duties additional to obligations assumed under private contracts must inevitably produce results difficult to square with any rational conception of a constitutional order. . . . To permit this level of scrutiny of laws that interfere with contract-based expectations is an anomaly. . . . Laws that interfere with settled expectations created by state property law (and which impose severe economic burdens) are uniformly held constitutional where reasonably related to the promotion of the general welfare. . . .

∽ PROBLEMS ∽

1. *Severance Tax Passthroughs.* Oil and gas producers entered into contracts for the sale of their product. These contracts allowed them to pass along any severance taxes paid on the product. A subsequent Alabama law increased the severance tax and made it illegal for oil and gas producers to pass the tax on (directly or indirectly) to consumers. Does the Alabama law violate the Contract Clause? Should it matter that the new law was broadly applicable to all producers and was not aimed at the appellant producers? *See* Exxon Corp. v. Eagerton, 462 U.S. 176 (1983).

2. *Increased Exemptions.* A debtor entered into an agreement with a creditor. During a period of economic distress, although the State of North Carolina did not remove the creditor's right to sue on the debt, it did increase the number of exemptions available to a debtor in bankruptcy. Does an increase in bankruptcy exemptions amount to an impairment of the obligation of contract under the Contract Clause? *See* Edwards v. Kearzey, 96 U.S. 595 (1878).

3. *Moratorium on Rental Contracts.* A landlord entered into a number of rental contracts that provided for the surrender of possession in the event of default. The contracts were all valid under New York law in existence at the time of contracting. Subsequently, during a period of economic distress, New York placed a

temporary moratorium on forced surrenders. However, tenants remaining on the premises were required to pay a reasonable rent for their use and occupation. Does the New York law impair the obligation of contract under the Contract Clause? *See* Block v. Hirsh, 256 U.S. 135 (1921).

The Contract Clause represented a seminal constitutional restraint on state police power. Although states may not bargain away their police power, the Contract Clause has imposed a reasonableness requirement on its exercise. Case law has varied with respect to the intensity of reasonableness as a standard of review. With the Fourteenth Amendment as a primary incident of Reconstruction, the growing significance of the Commerce Clause power over the course of the twentieth century, and preemption principles under the Supremacy Clause, the Court acquired more powerful tools for evaluating the constitutionality of action pursuant to state police power. Varied as these constitutional reference points may be, each in its own way implicates and engenders an ongoing debate over whether the judiciary should play a larger or smaller role in reviewing outputs of the political branches of government.

Points to Remember

- The rise and fall of substantive economic due process travels a twisted path from *Allgeyer,* to *Lochner* to *Nebbia,* a path that is generally in disrepute today. Remnants and fallout remain, though. When constitutional interpretation is believed to have improperly implied substantive rights in the Constitution, the allegation often is that the Court is *Lochnerizing*.
- The Takings Clause prohibits the taking of private property for a public use, either by design or through regulation, without just compensation. The term "public use" has a much broader definition after *Kelo* than in the past. Regulatory takings can be temporary or permanent and can result from regulations that go too far, such as those that deprive the property owner of any economically beneficial use. Even minor government intrusions can qualify as a taking.
- The Contract Clause prohibits the state government impairment of contracts, but the Court has parsed the analysis into two categories: government impairment of state contracts; and government impairment of private contracts. The Court gives greater deference to governments impairing private contracts than to the impairment of contracts to which the government is a party.

9

Substantive Due Process: Modern Fundamental Rights

U.S. CONSTITUTION, FIFTH AMENDMENT

No person shall . . . be deprived of life, liberty, or property, without due process of law.

U.S. CONSTITUTION, NINTH AMENDMENT

The enumeration in the Constitution, of certain rights, shall not be construed to deny or disparage others retained by the people.

U.S. CONSTITUTION, FOURTEENTH AMENDMENT

Section 1. . . . nor shall any State deprive any person of life, liberty, or property, without due process of law. . . .

∾ PROBLEM: CHILD CUSTODY, TRANSSEXUALS, AND SAME-SEX RELATIONSHIPS ∾

Suppose that a state legislature, in a state that has amended its state constitution to prohibit same-sex marriage, is considering the possibility of passing a statute that discriminates against gays both in child custody in family law disputes and in child adoption. The proposed statute, which has already been introduced in the legislature, contains this provision:

In any custody dispute between a heterosexual individual and a homosexual individual, the Family Courts of this state shall presume that the heterosexual individual is the more fit and appropriate parent to assume custody, and that awarding custody to the heterosexual parent is in the child's best interest. Custody may not be awarded to the homosexual parent unless the Court finds, as a matter of law, that the heterosexual parent is "unfit."

The proposed statute would also contain a presumption that transsexuals are unfit parents.

Suppose that you are working as a legal advisor to a legislative committee that is about to hold hearings on this bill. The committee has asked you for your opinion about whether the proposed law is constitutional. As you work your way through this chapter, you will be asked to give your thoughts on that issue. You can ignore the equal protection issues (which will be examined in the next chapter) and focus on issues related to privacy and liberty.

Modern substantive due process review generates much the same debate that was triggered by the judiciary's identification, development, and protection of economic rights during the first third of the twentieth century. Critics of this judicial function view it essentially as neo-*Lochnerian* and an antidemocratic exercise. Exponents maintain that there are fundamental values that are not textually expressed or rights and liberties, but are no less basic. From their perspective, it is better to have them defined and fathomed by an institution that is buffered from rather than driven by political pressures.

The generally discredited legacy of economic rights jurisprudence has left a significant mark on the Court's approach to substantive due process review. Cases establishing or expanding the right to privacy, for instance, include disclaimers to the effect that the Court is not replicating its stigmatized past. Consistent with this interest in separating modern substantive due process review from its relatively standardless antecedent, the Court has introduced criteria to guide its discernment of fundamental rights that are not explicated by the Constitution itself. The primary focal points for this purpose are whether an interest is "implicit in the concept of ordered liberty," "rooted in the Nation's traditions and history," or "fundamental to the American scheme of justice." To the extent the Court finds that an interest can be so described, the Court is prepared to recognize it as fundamental and thus of constitutional stature. Debate persists as to whether these imprecise standards sufficiently cabin the judiciary in its relationship to the political process.

The Due Process Clauses of the Fifth and Fourteenth Amendments are multidimensional with respect to their function. They are a source of procedural fairness, when state deprivation of life, liberty, and property is a possibility. The liberty component of the Due Process Clauses also has emerged, through the process of judicial review, as a platform for establishing fundamental rights that operate against the state and federal governments. It also has served as the vehicle through which provisions of the Bill of Rights have been applied to the states.

A. INCORPORATION

The Bill of Rights, as originally framed and ratified, charted basic rights and liberties for individuals only in their relationship with the federal government. The push to extend the scope of operation of the Bill of Rights was initially prevented by the Court in Barron v. City Council of Baltimore, 32 U.S. 242 (1833). In that case, it was argued that the Fifth Amendment prohibition against taking property without just compensation applied not only to the federal government but also to state governments. In an opinion by Chief Justice Marshall, the Court found that the question was "of great importance, but not of much difficulty," and that the proposition should be rejected: "[T]he Constitution was ordained and established by the people of the United States [for] their own government, and not for the government of the individual [states]. Each state established a constitution for itself, and in that constitution, provided such limitations and restrictions on the powers of its particular government, as its judgment dictated. [T]he Fifth Amendment to the Constitution, declaring that private property shall not be taken for public use, without just compensation, is intended solely as a limitation on the exercise of the power by the government of the United States, and is not applicable to the legislation of the states."

Reconstruction of the Union following the Civil War reordered the relationship between national citizenship and state citizenship, insofar as it made the latter a derivative of the former, and established the incidents of federal citizenship. Although it did not represent a consensual point of view, significant sentiment supported the notion that these incidents included the Bill of Rights. The original vessel touted for their incorporation was the Privileges and Immunities Clause. This proposed structure crashed, however, when the *Slaughterhouse Cases*, 83 U.S. 36 (1873), defined the privileges and immunities of national citizenship in narrow terms that pointedly excluded the Bill of Rights. This ruling reverted the Privileges and Immunities Clause to a functionally dormant status.

With the Privileges and Immunities Clause foreclosed as a predicate, the incorporation agenda pushed toward other platforms. Early incorporations of provisions of the Bill of Rights were effected through substantive due process review. By amplifying the meaning of *liberty* as set forth in the Due Process Clause, the Court developed a set of fundamental rights applicable to the states. Some of these guarantees paralleled those set forth in the Bill of Rights, and others like liberty of contract were judicially constructed. The liberty provision of the Due Process Clause itself, rather than the Bill of Rights, was the springboard for rights implementation. Although the effect may have been the same, the process at this stage thus was direct application rather than incorporation.

With the foreclosure of the *Lochner* model of substantive due process, the Court announced in United States v. Carolene Products Co., 304 U.S. 144, 154 n.4 (1938), that it would reserve heightened review to instances "when legislation appears to be within a specific provision of the Constitution, such as the first ten amendments, which are deemed equally specific when held to be embraced within the Fourteenth." The Court thus established that the Fourteenth Amendment was not an incubator of rights independently but a structure through which provisions of the Bill of Rights itself would be incorporated. This understanding, however, prefaced a significant debate that shaped the incorporation process. The issue, which generated sharp debate within the Court over the subsequent decades, was whether provisions of the Bill of Rights should be incorporated on a selective or wholesale basis. In Palko v. Connecticut, the Court considered arguments that the Double Jeopardy Clause was incorporated through the Due Process Clause of the Fourteenth Amendment. Justice Cardozo authored an opinion for the Court that rejected this proposition and subscribed to the theory of selective incorporation.

Palko v. Connecticut

302 U.S. 319 (1937)

Mr. Justice CARDOZO delivered the opinion of the Court.

[Appellant] was indicted in Fairfield County, Conn., for the crime of murder in the first degree. A jury found him guilty of murder in the second degree, and he was sentenced to confinement in the state prison for life. Thereafter the State of Connecticut, with the permission of the judge presiding at the trial, gave notice of appeal to the Supreme Court of Errors.

[Pursuant] to the mandate of the Supreme Court of Errors, defendant was brought to trial again. Before a jury was impaneled, and also at later stages of the case, he made the objection that the effect of the new trial was to place him twice in jeopardy for the same offense, and in so doing to violate the Fourteenth Amendment of the Constitution of the United States. Upon the overruling of the objection the trial proceeded. The jury returned a verdict of murder in the first degree, and the court sentenced the defendant to the punishment of death. The Supreme Court of Errors affirmed the judgment of conviction.

[The] argument for appellant is that whatever is forbidden by the Fifth Amendment is forbidden by the Fourteenth also. The Fifth Amendment, which is not directed to the States, but solely to the federal government, creates immunity from double jeopardy. No person shall be "subject for the same offense to be twice put in jeopardy of life or limb." The Fourteenth Amendment ordains, "nor shall any State deprive any person of life, liberty, or property, without due process of law." To retry a defendant, though under one indictment and only one, subjects him, it is said, to double jeopardy in violation of the Fifth Amendment, if the prosecution is one on behalf of the United States. From this the consequence is said to follow that there is a denial of life or liberty without due process of law, if the prosecution is one on behalf of the people of a state.

[Appellant's] thesis is [that w]hatever would be a violation of the original bill of rights (Amendments 1 to 8) if done by the federal government is now equally unlawful by force of the Fourteenth Amendment if done by a state. There is no such general rule.

The Fifth Amendment provides, among other things, that no person shall be held to answer for a capital or otherwise infamous crime unless on presentment or indictment of a grand jury. This court has held that, in prosecutions by a state, presentment or indictment by a grand jury may give way to informations at the instance of a public officer. The Fifth Amendment provides also that no person shall be compelled in any criminal case to be a witness against himself. This court has said that, in prosecutions by a state, the exemption will fail if the state elects to end it. . . . [On] the other hand, the due process clause of the Fourteenth Amendment may make it unlawful for a state to abridge by its statutes the freedom of speech which the First Amendment safeguards against encroachment by the Congress, or the like freedom of the press, or the free exercise of religion (or the right of peaceable assembly, without which speech would be unduly trammeled), or the right of one accused of crime to the benefit of counsel. In these and other situations immunities that are valid as against the federal government by force of the specific pledges of particular amendments have been found to be implicit in the concept of ordered liberty, and thus, through the Fourteenth Amendment, become valid as against the states.

The line of division may seem to be wavering and broken if there is a hasty catalogue of the cases on the one side and the other. Reflection and analysis will induce a different view. There emerges the perception of a rationalizing principle which gives to discrete instances a proper order and coherence. The right to trial by jury and the immunity from prosecution except as the result of an indictment may have value and importance. Even so, they are not of the very essence of a scheme of ordered liberty. To abolish them is not to violate a "principle of justice so rooted in the traditions and conscience of our people as to be ranked as fundamental." Few would be so narrow or provincial as to maintain that a fair and enlightened system of justice would be impossible without them. What is true of jury trials and indictments is true also [of] the immunity from compulsory self-incrimination. This too might be lost, and justice still be done. . . . No doubt there would remain the need to give protection against torture, physical or mental. Justice, however, would not perish if the accused were subject to a duty to respond to orderly inquiry. The exclusion of these immunities and privileges from the privileges and immunities protected against the action of the States has not been arbitrary or casual. It has been dictated by a study and appreciation of the meaning, the essential implications, of liberty itself.

We reach a different plane of social and moral values when we pass to the privileges and immunities that have been taken over from the earlier articles of the Federal Bill of Rights and brought within the Fourteenth Amendment by a process of absorption. These in their origin were effective against the federal government alone. If the Fourteenth Amendment has absorbed them, the process of absorption has had its source in the belief that neither liberty nor justice would exist if they were sacrificed. This is true, for illustration, of freedom of thought and speech. Of that freedom one may say that it is the matrix, the indispensable condition, of nearly every other form of freedom. With rare aberrations a pervasive recognition of that truth can be traced in our history, political and legal. So it has come about that the domain of liberty, withdrawn by the Fourteenth Amendment from encroachment by the states, has been enlarged by latter-day judgments to include liberty of the mind as well as liberty of action. The extension became, indeed, a logical imperative when once it was recognized, as long ago it was, that liberty is something more than exemption from physical restraint, and that even in the field of substantive rights and duties the legislative judgment, if oppressive and arbitrary, may be overridden by the courts.

[Our] survey of the cases serves, we think, to justify the statement that the dividing line between them, if not unfaltering throughout its course, has been true for the most part to a unifying principle. On which side of the line the case made out by the appellant has appropriate location must be the next inquiry and the final one. Is that kind of double jeopardy to which the statute has subjected him a hardship so acute and shocking that our policy will not endure it? Does it violate those "fundamental principles of liberty and justice which lie at the base of all our civil and political institutions?" The answer surely must be "no." What the answer would have to be if the state were permitted after a trial free from error to try the accused over again or to bring another case against him, we have no occasion to consider. We deal with the statute before us and no other. The state is not attempting to wear the accused out by a multitude of cases with accumulated trials. It asks no more than this, that the case against him shall go on until there shall be a trial free from the corrosion of substantial legal error. This is not cruelty at all, nor even vexation in any immoderate degree. If the trial had been infected with error adverse to the accused, there might have been review at his instance, and as often as necessary to purge the vicious taint. A reciprocal privilege, subject at all times to the discretion of the presiding judge has now been granted to the state. There is here no seismic innovation. The edifice of justice stands, its symmetry, to many, greater than before. . . .

Notes and Questions

1. *Total versus Selective Incorporation.* The Court eventually incorporated the Double Jeopardy Clause into the Fourteenth Amendment, but not without significant debate concerning the method for achieving this result. Benton v. Maryland, 395 U.S. 784 (1969). The absorption of federal rights and liberties was possible on either a wholesale or discrete basis. The theory of total incorporation advocated applying the entire Bill of Rights to the states. Selective incorporation proposed that each guarantee should be assessed for purposes of determining whether it was essential to liberty and justice. In Adamson v. California, the competing viewpoints on selective and total incorporation were illuminated by Justice Frankfurter and Justice Black, respectively.

2. *Is It Appropriate to Construe the Fourteenth Amendment as Containing Substantive Protections?* The Fourteenth Amendment, Section 1 (the Fourteenth Amendment Due Process Clause) seems to be phrased in procedural terms ("[N]or shall any State deprive any person of life, liberty, or property, without due process of

law"). How is the clause construed as containing substantive protections for "liberty"?

3. *Necessity for Substantive Protections?* Are substantive protections both inevitable and necessary in a free society?

∽ PROBLEMS ∽

1. *Life Shall End at Age 75.* Suppose that, as the baby boom generation moves into its retirement years, the Social Security system falls into bankruptcy. As the crisis worsens, Congress passes a law decreeing "Life shall end at age 75." Under this law, no one shall be allowed to draw social security benefits, or for that matter to live, beyond the age of 75. We all know that it is extremely unlikely that Congress would pass such a law. After all, many members of Congress are of advanced age (or will be someday), and many more have senior parents and other older relatives. In addition, it is extremely unlikely that the people would accept such a law. But, if the Fourteenth Amendment is not construed as containing a substantive component, is there any other constitutional provision that would render the law unconstitutional? If the courts apply the Due Process Clause literally, does that mean that the courts are allowed to inquire only whether Congress duly passed the law and whether it provided affected citizens with a "full and fair hearing" on the issue of whether they have reached age 75? If they answer those questions in the affirmative, are they required to uphold the law?

2. *One Child per Family.* Suppose that, as the U.S. population continues to grow, Congress decides to take measures to limit the rate of future growth. To this end, Congress passes a law providing that no family can have more than one child and mandating sterilization of all persons who have a living child. Is there any provision in the Constitution that specifically prohibits Congress from enacting such a law?

3. *Bans on Interracial Marriage.* At one point in history, various states prohibited interracial marriage. Is there any constitutional provision that guarantees people the right to marry? Is there any provision that prohibits interracial marriage? Can the Fourteenth Amendment be construed as including a prohibition that relates to racial discrimination?

4. *The Ninth Amendment.* As you think about the preceding problems, consider the text of the Ninth Amendment: "The enumeration in the Constitution, of certain rights, shall not be construed to deny or disparage others retained by the people." If "other" rights exist, how does the judiciary find or declare them without simply imposing its own wishes and desires?

Adamson v. California

332 U.S. 46 (1947)

Mr. Justice REED delivered the opinion of the Court.

Appellant [contends] that if the privilege against self-incrimination is not a right protected by the Privileges and Immunities Clause of the Fourteenth

Amendment against state action, this privilege, to its full scope under the Fifth Amendment, inheres in the right to a fair trial. A right to a fair trial is a right admittedly protected by the due process clause of the Fourteenth Amendment. Therefore, appellant argues, the due process clause of the Fourteenth Amendment protects his privilege against self-incrimination. The due process clause of the Fourteenth Amendment, however, does not draw all the rights of the federal Bill of Rights under its protection. That contention was made and rejected in Palko v. Connecticut. It was rejected with citation of the cases excluding several of the rights, protected by the Bill of Rights, against infringement by the National Government. Nothing has been called to our attention that either the framers of the Fourteenth Amendment or the states that adopted intended its due process clause to draw within its scope the earlier amendments to the Constitution. *Palko* held that such provisions of the Bill of Rights as were "implicit in the concept of ordered liberty," became secure from state interference by the clause. But it held nothing more. . . .

Mr. Justice FRANKFURTER (concurring).

[Between] the incorporation of the Fourteenth Amendment into the Constitution and the beginning of the present membership of the Court — a period of 70 years — the scope of that Amendment was passed upon by 43 judges. Of all these judges, only one, who may respectfully be called an eccentric exception, ever indicated [that] due process incorporated those eight Amendments as restrictions upon the powers of the States. [T]hey were [judges] mindful of the relation of our federal system to a progressively democratic society and therefore duly regardful of the scope of authority that was left to the States even after the Civil War. And so they did not find that the Fourteenth Amendment, concerned as it was with matters fundamental to the pursuit of justice, fastened upon the States procedural arrangements which, in the language of Mr. Justice Cardozo, only those who are "narrow or provincial" would deem essential to "a fair and enlightened system of justice." . . .

The short answer to the suggestion that the provision of the Fourteenth Amendment, which ordains "nor shall any State deprive any person of life, liberty, or property, without due process of law," was a way of saying that every State must thereafter initiate prosecutions through indictment by a grand jury, must have a trial by a jury of 12 in criminal cases, and must have trial by such a jury in common law suits where the amount in controversy exceeds $20, is that it is a strange way of saying it. It would be extraordinarily strange for a Constitution to convey such specific commands in such a roundabout and inexplicit way. [A]t the time of the ratification of the Fourteenth Amendment the constitutions of nearly half of the ratifying States did not have the rigorous requirements of the Fifth Amendment for instituting criminal proceedings through a grand jury. It could hardly have occurred to these States that by ratifying the Amendment they uprooted their established methods for prosecuting crime and fastened upon themselves a new prosecutorial system. . . .

[A] construction which gives to due process no independent function but turns it into a summary of the specific provisions of the Bill of Rights [would] tear up by the roots much of the fabric of law in the several States, and would deprive the States of opportunity for reforms in legal process designed for extending the area of freedom. It would assume that no other abuses would reveal themselves in the course of time than those which had become manifest in 1791. Such a view not only disregards the historic meaning of "due process." It leads inevitably to a warped construction of specific provisions of the Bill of Rights to bring within their scope conduct clearly condemned by due process but not easily fitting into the pigeon-holes of the specific provisions. . . .

[When] a conviction in a State court is here for review under a claim that a right protected by the Due Process Clause of the Fourteenth Amendment has been denied, [the] relevant question is whether the criminal proceedings which resulted in conviction deprived the accused of the due process of law to which the United States Constitution entitled him. Judicial review of that guaranty of the Fourteenth Amendment inescapably imposes upon this Court an exercise of judgment upon the whole course of the proceedings in order to ascertain whether they offend those canons of decency and fairness which express the notions of justice of English-speaking peoples even toward those charged with the most heinous offenses. These standards of justice are not authoritatively formulated anywhere as though they were prescriptions in a pharmacopoeia. But neither does the application of the Due Process Clause imply that judges are wholly at large. The judicial judgment in applying the Due Process Clause must move within the limits of accepted notions of justice and is not to be based upon the idiosyncrasies of a merely personal judgment. The fact that judges among themselves may differ whether in a particular case a trial offends accepted notions of justice is not disproof that general rather than idiosyncratic standards are applied. An important safeguard against such merely individual judgment is an alert deference to the judgment of the State court under review. . . .

Mr. Justice BLACK, dissenting.

[Prior decisions have suggested that the] Court is endowed by the Constitution with boundless power under "natural law" periodically to expand and contract constitutional standards to conform to the Court's conception of what at a particular time constitutes "civilized decency" and "fundamental principles of liberty and justice." [I] think that [the] "natural law" theory of the Constitution [degrades] the constitutional safeguards of the Bill of Rights and simultaneously appropriates for this Court a broad power which we are not authorized by the Constitution to exercise.

[The] first 10 amendments were proposed and adopted largely because of fear that Government might unduly interfere with prized individual liberties. [My] study of the historical events that culminated in the Fourteenth Amendment, and the expressions of those who sponsored and favored, as well as those who opposed its submission and passage, persuades me that one of the chief objects that the provisions of the Amendment's first section, separately, and as a whole, were intended to accomplish was to make the Bill of Rights, applicable to the states. . . . This historical purpose has never received full consideration or exposition in any opinion of this Court interpreting the Amendment. . . .

[I fear the] consequences of the Court's practice of substituting its own concepts of decency and fundamental justice for the language of the Bill of Rights as its point of departure in interpreting and enforcing that Bill of Rights. If the choice must be between the selective process of the *Palko* decision applying some of the Bill of Rights to the States, or the *Twining* rule applying none of them, I would choose the *Palko* selective process. But rather than accept either of these choices. I would follow what I believe was the original purpose of the Fourteenth Amendment — to extend to all the people of the nation the complete protection of the Bill of Rights. . . . I would therefore hold in this case that the full protection of the Fifth Amendment's proscription against compelled testimony must be afforded by California. . . .

It is an illusory apprehension that literal application of some or all of the provisions of the Bill of Rights to the States would unwisely increase the sum total of the powers of this Court to invalidate state legislation. . . . Since Marbury v. Madison was decided, the practice has been firmly established for better or worse, that courts can strike down legislative enactments which violate the Constitution. This process, of course, involves interpretation, and since words can have many meanings, interpretation obviously may result in contraction or extension of the original purpose of a constitutional provision thereby affecting policy. But to pass upon the constitutionality of statutes by looking to the particular standards enumerated in the Bill of Rights and other parts of the Constitution is one thing; to invalidate statutes because of application of "natural law" deemed to be above and undefined by the Constitution is another. "In the one instance, courts proceeding within clearly marked constitutional boundaries seek to execute policies written into the Constitution; in the other they roam at will in the limitless area of their own beliefs as to reasonableness and actually select policies, a responsibility which the Constitution entrusts to the legislative representatives of the people."

[Mr. Justice DOUGLAS joins in this opinion.]

Note: More on Incorporation

The primary formulas for selective incorporation have focused on whether a provision of the Bill of Rights is so fundamental as to be "implicit in the concept of ordered liberty" or "so rooted in the traditions and conscience of our people as to be fundamental." Palko v. Connecticut, 302 U.S. 319, 325 (1937). In the context of reviewing constitutional guarantees relating to the criminal justice process, the Court has pondered whether the procedure is "necessary to an Anglo-American regime of ordered liberty." Duncan v. Louisiana, 391 U.S. 145, 148-149 (1968). The incorporation process for practical purposes has achieved over the course of time what total incorporation would have achieved in a single exercise. The only provisions of the Bill of Rights that have failed the incorporation test are the grand jury clause of the Fifth Amendment and the Seventh Amendment guarantee of a jury trial in civil cases.

Although the incorporation process largely has become a historical concern, there is a corollary debate that survived the incorporation controversy. The issue is whether incorporation passed through not only a given right or liberty but also the case law associated with it. In Malloy v. Hogan, 378 U.S. 1 (1964), the second Justice Harlan argued that failure to factor the entire body of law was unsettling to principles of federalism. As he put it, in *Malloy:*

> [The argument is made] that continuing reexamination of the constitutional conception of Fourteenth Amendment "due process" of law is required, and that development of the community's sense of justice may in time lead to expansion of the protection, which due process affords. . . . I do not understand, however, how this process of re-examination, which must refer always to the guiding standard of due process of law, including, of course, reference to the particular guarantees of the Bill of Rights, can be short-circuited by the simple device of incorporating into due process, without critical examination, the whole body of law which surrounds a specific prohibition directed against the Federal Government. The consequence of such an approach to due process as it pertains to the States is inevitably disregard of all relevant differences which may exist between state and federal criminal law and its enforcement. The ultimate result is compelled uniformity, which is inconsistent with the purpose of our federal system and which is achieved either by encroachment of the States' sovereign powers or by dilution in federal law enforcement of specific protections found in the Bill of Rights. [It] is apparent that Mr. Justice Cardozo's metaphor of "absorption" was not intended to suggest the transplantation of case law surrounding the specifics of the first eight Amendments to the very different soil of the Fourteenth Amendment's Due Process Clause. [A]s he made perfectly plain, what the Fourteenth Amendment requires of the States does not basically depend on what the first eight Amendments require of the Federal Government.

Justice Harlan's perspective correlates to earlier usage of the Due Process Clause as the actual platform for rights and liberties applicable to the states rather than an incorporating device for prohibitions set forth in the Bill of Rights. Writing for the majority in Malloy v. Hogan, Justice Brennan maintained that incorporation transplanted not only the basic principle but also its interpretive incidents. As he put it, incorporated rights and liberties were to be "enforced against the States under the Fourteenth Amendment according to the same standards that protect those personal rights against federal encroachment. . . . The Court thus has rejected the notion that the Fourteenth Amendment applies to the States only a 'watered-down, subjective version of the individual guarantees of the Bill of Rights.'"

The debate with respect to the details of incorporation resurfaced in the context of the right to a jury trial. In Duncan v. Louisiana, Justice Fortas advanced the notion that jury trials concerned not just a right but systems of administration such as jury size and the nature of a verdict. He thus argued that these aspects or traditions, such as a 12-person jury or unanimous verdict, might not be fundamental and thus apt for incorporation. In Williams v. Florida, 399 U.S. 78 (1970), the Court upheld a state's provision for six-person juries. This determination reflected the Court's sense that the traditional 12-person jury was a historical accident and not specifically mandated by the Sixth Amendment. Justice Harlan, in a concurring opinion, expressed concern that the space being afforded to the states had the potential for reverse incorporation and a consequent dilution of federal guarantees. In Apodaca v. Oregon, 406 U.S. 404 (1972), the Court split on whether the requirement of a unanimous verdict was implicit in the right to a jury trial. In a separate opinion, which determined the result, Justice Powell maintained that the Sixth Amendment required unanimity in the federal system but that this incident did not carry through to the states through the Fourteenth Amendment. Despite the outcome, and the difference over whether a unanimous verdict was required at the federal level, near unanimity was reached on the proposition that the rights and liberties incorporated through the Fourteenth Amendment apply with equal force to both federal and state governments.

Question: Privileges and Immunities

The Fourteenth Amendment contains several key clauses that were significant in the reconstruction of the Union after the Civil War. The citizenship clause inverted prior understandings by making state citizenship derivative of federal citizenship. The Due Process Clause replicated a similar Fifth Amendment provision that operates against the federal government and traditionally had accounted for procedural fairness. The Equal Protection Clause accounted for inequalities under the law that postdated slavery. The Privileges and Immunities Clause was rejected by the Court as an agent for extending the Bill of Rights to the states. Based on the arguments presented in *Adamson,* and historical experience with the Due Process Clause, would the Privileges and Immunities Clause be a more logical and less distorting basis for incorporation and for generating rights that are not constitutionally enumerated?

B. THE RIGHT OF PRIVACY

Does the concept of ordered liberty include a right of privacy against governmental intrusion?

1. Seminal Developments

The Constitution speaks to privacy interests in discrete contexts such as the First, Third, and Fourth Amendments. A general right of privacy in the constitutional sense, however, is a function of judicial construction. The origin of this guarantee was recognized in late-nineteenth-century legal scholarship. Samuel D. Warren and Louis D. Brandeis, in a pioneering law review article, described the interest as "the right to be let alone." Samuel D. Warren & Louis D. Brandeis, *The Right to Privacy,* 4 Harv. L. Rev. 193 (1890). This concept initially was introduced as, and became the basis for, tort-based laws that developed protection against various types of invasion of privacy. Over the course of the twentieth century, it acquired dimension.

The first significant constitutional statement on privacy was made during a period of peak activity in the Court's development of liberty as a substantive incident of due process. In Meyer v. Nebraska, 262 U.S. 390 (1923), the Court invalidated a state law that prohibited teaching in any language other than English in public and private schools. The majority opinion stated that the liberty protected by the Due Process Clause included "not merely freedom from bodily restraint but also the right of the individual to contract, to engage in any of the common occupations of life, to acquire useful knowledge, to marry, establish a home and bring up children, to worship God according to the dictates of his own conscience, and generally to enjoy those privileges long recognized at common law as essential to the orderly pursuit of happiness by free men."

The *Meyer* decision was reinforced by the Court's ruling in Pierce v. Society of Sisters, 268 U.S. 510 (1925), which struck down a state law requiring parents to send their children to public schools. Taken together, these decisions established a predicate for expanding privacy beyond notions of place and experience to concepts of personal and family autonomy. These understandings survived the Court's abandonment of economic due process in United States v. Carolene Products Co., 304 U.S. 144 (1938). Although the Court indicated in *Carolene Products* that searching review would be reserved for instances when enumerated rights and liberties or discrete and insular minorities were burdened, it became apparent a few years later that this characterization was an overstatement. In Skinner v. Oklahoma, 316 U.S. 535 (1942), the Court reviewed a state law that mandated sterilization for habitual felons. Although it had determined in Buck v. Bell, 274 U.S. 200 (1927), that compulsory sterilization was not a constitutional concern, the Court invalidated the measure on the grounds that it implicated fundamental interests in marriage and procreation.

Skinner v. Oklahoma

316 U.S. 535 (1942)

Mr. Justice Douglas delivered the opinion of the Court.

This case touches a sensitive and important area of human rights. Oklahoma deprives certain individuals of a right which is basic to the perpetuation of a race — the right to have offspring. Oklahoma has decreed the enforcement of its law against petitioner, overruling his claim that it violated the Fourteenth Amendment. Because that decision raised grave and substantial constitutional questions, we granted the petition for certiorari.

The statute involved is Oklahoma's Habitual Criminal Sterilization Act. That Act defines an "habitual criminal" as a person who, having been convicted two or more times for crimes "amounting to felonies involving moral turpitude" either in an Oklahoma court or in a court of any other State, is thereafter convicted of such a felony in Oklahoma and is sentenced to a term of imprisonment in an Oklahoma penal institution. Machinery is provided for the institution by the Attorney General of a proceeding against such a person in the Oklahoma courts for a judgment that such person shall be rendered sexually sterile.

[There] is a feature of the Act which clearly condemns it. That is its failure to meet the requirements of the equal protection clause of the Fourteenth Amendment. . . . We do not stop to point out all of the inequalities in this Act. A few examples will suffice. [A] person who enters a chicken coop and steals chickens commits a felony; and he may be sterilized if he is thrice convicted. If, however, he is a bailee of the property and fraudulently appropriates it, he is an embezzler. Hence no matter how habitual his proclivities for embezzlement are and no matter how often his conviction, he may not be sterilized. Thus the nature of the two crimes is intrinsically the same and they are punishable in the same manner.

It was stated in Buck v. Bell that the claim that state legislation violates the equal protection clause of the Fourteenth Amendment is "the usual last resort of constitutional arguments." [But] the instant legislation runs afoul of the equal protection clause, though we give Oklahoma that large deference which the rule of the foregoing cases requires. We are dealing here with legislation which involves one of the basic civil rights of man. Marriage and procreation are fundamental to the very existence and survival of the race. The power to sterilize, if exercised, may have subtle, far-reaching and devastating effects. In evil or reckless hands it can cause races or types which are inimical to the dominant group to wither and disappear. There is no redemption for the individual whom the law touches. Any experiment which the State conducts is to his irreparable injury. He is forever deprived of a basic liberty. We mention these matters not to reexamine the scope of the police power of the States. We advert to them merely in emphasis of our view that strict scrutiny of the classification which a State makes in a sterilization law is essential, lest unwittingly or otherwise invidious discriminations are made against groups or types of individuals in violation of the constitutional guaranty of just and equal laws. The guaranty of "equal protection of the laws is a pledge of the protection of equal laws." When the law lays an unequal hand on those who have committed intrinsically the same quality of offense and sterilizes one and not the other, it has made as an invidious a discrimination as if it had selected a particular race or nationality for oppressive treatment. Sterilization of those who have thrice committed grand larceny with immunity for those who are embezzlers is a clear, pointed, unmistakable discrimination.

Mr. Chief Justice STONE concurring.

I concur in the result, but I am not persuaded that we are aided in reaching it by recourse to the equal protection clause. . . . If Oklahoma may resort generally to the sterilization of criminals on the assumption that their propensities are transmissible to future generations by inheritance, I seriously doubt that the equal protection clause requires it to apply the measure to all criminals in the first instance, or to none. . . .

There are limits to the extent to which the presumption of constitutionality can be pressed, especially where the liberty of the person is concerned and where the presumption is resorted to only to dispense with a procedure which the ordinary dictates of prudence would seem to demand for the protection of the individual from arbitrary action. Although petitioner here was given a hearing to ascertain whether sterilization would be detrimental to his health, he was given none to discover whether his criminal tendencies are of an inheritable type. Undoubtedly a state may, after appropriate inquiry, constitutionally interfere with the personal liberty of the individual to prevent the transmission by inheritance of his socially injurious tendencies. But until now we have not been called upon to say that it may do so without giving him a hearing and opportunity to challenge the existence as to him of the only facts which could justify so drastic a measure. . . . A law which condemns, without hearing, all the individuals of a class to so harsh a measure as the present because some or even many merit condemnation, is lacking in the first principles of due process. . . .

Mr. Justice JACKSON, concurring.

I join the Chief Justice in holding that the hearings provided are too limited [to] afford due process of law. I also agree [with] Justice Douglas that the scheme of classification set forth in the Act denies equal protection of the law. I disagree with [each opinion] insofar as it rejects or minimizes the grounds taken by the other. . . . I also think the present plan [presents] other constitutional questions of gravity. [There] are limits to the extent to which a legislatively represented majority may conduct biological experiments at the expense of the dignity and personality and natural powers of a minority — even those who have been guilty of what the majority define as crimes. . . .

Note: "Fundamental" Rights

The *Skinner* Court, sensitive to the recently disavowed legacy of *Lochner*-style review, grounded its decision in the Equal Protection Clause and avoided any reference to due process. Identification of rights as fundamental, when not enumerated by the Constitution, required a theory of review that was demonstrably and understandably principled. Toward this end, and mindful still of the discredited nature of substantive due process review, the Court explored other possibilities for anchorage. These alternatives included penumbras, which had a mixed history. In Dred Scott v. Sandford, 60 U.S. 393 (1857), the Court referenced several constitutional provisions relating to slavery as an indication of a general right to own slaves. A century later, in NAACP v. Alabama ex rel. Patterson, 357 U.S. 449 (1958), the Court constructed the right of association as an implication of freedom of speech. Drawing upon this model, the Court in Griswold v. Connecticut announced a right to privacy and used it as the basis for striking down a state law prohibiting the distribution and use of contraceptives.

Question: Alternative Theories

The *Skinner* decision was announced five years after the Court abandoned substantive due process review in United States v. Carolene Products Co. Establishing marriage and procreation as fundamental rights, and protecting them through the Equal Protection Clause, do not avoid the controversy triggered by the judiciary's identification and development of rights that are not constitutionally enumerated. Is there a principled way of recognizing and accounting for these interests through privileges and immunities or due process review? Is there an advantage to using the Equal Protection Clause in this context?

Griswold v. Connecticut
381 U.S. 479 (1965)

Mr. Justice DOUGLAS delivered the opinion of the Court.

[The executive director of the Planned Parenthood League of Connecticut and the medical director for the league at its New Haven Center were arrested and convicted for giving information, instruction, and medical advice on birth control to married persons. State law prohibited the use of anticonception devices and imposed liability upon anyone who assisted, abetted, or counseled a violation.]

Coming to the merits, we are met with a wide range of questions that implicate the Due Process Clause of the Fourteenth Amendment. Overtones of some arguments suggest that Lochner v. New York should be our guide. [W]e decline that invitation. We do not sit as a super-legislature to determine the wisdom, need, and propriety of laws that touch economic problems, business affairs, or social conditions. This law, however, operates directly on an intimate relation of husband and wife and their physician's role in one aspect of that relation.

The association of people is not mentioned in the Constitution nor in the Bill of Rights. The right to educate a child in a school of the parents' choice—whether public or private or parochial—is also not mentioned. Nor is the right to study any particular subject or any foreign language. Yet the First Amendment has been construed to include certain of those rights.

By Pierce v. Society of Sisters, the right to educate one's children as one chooses is made applicable to the States by the force of the First and Fourteenth Amendments. By Meyer v. State of Nebraska, the same dignity is given the right to study the German language in a private school. In other words, the State may not, consistently with the spirit of the First Amendment, contract the spectrum of available knowledge. The right of freedom of speech and press includes not only the right to utter or to print, but the right to distribute, the right to receive, the right to read and freedom of inquiry, freedom of thought, and freedom to teach—indeed the freedom of the entire university community. Without those peripheral rights the specific rights would be less secure. And so we reaffirm the principle of the *Pierce* and the *Meyer* cases.

In NAACP v. Alabama, we protected the "freedom to associate and privacy in one's associations," noting that freedom of association was a peripheral First Amendment right. Disclosure of membership lists of a constitutionally valid association, we held, was invalid "as entailing the likelihood of a substantial restraint upon the exercise by petitioner's members of their right to freedom of association." In other words, the First Amendment has a penumbra where privacy is protected from governmental intrusion. In like context, we have protected forms of "association" that are not political in the customary sense but pertain to the social, legal, and economic benefit of the members. [Those] cases involved more than the "right of assembly" — a right that extends to all irrespective of their race or ideology. The right of "association," like the right of belief is more than the right to attend a meeting; it includes the right to express one's attitudes or philosophies by membership in a group or by affiliation with it or by other lawful means. Association in that context is a form of expression of opinion; and while it is not expressly included in the First Amendment its existence is necessary in making the express guarantees fully meaningful.

The foregoing cases suggest that specific guarantees in the Bill of Rights have penumbras, formed by emanations from those guarantees that help give them life and substance. Various guarantees create zones of privacy. The right of association contained in the penumbra of the First Amendment is one. . . . The Third Amendment in its prohibition against the quartering of soldiers "in any house" in time of peace without the consent of the owner is another facet of that privacy. The Fourth Amendment explicitly affirms the "right of the people to be secure in their persons, houses, papers, and effects, against unreasonable searches and seizures." The Fifth Amendment in its Self-Incrimination Clause enables the citizen to create a zone of privacy which government may not force him to surrender to his detriment. The Ninth Amendment provides: "The enumeration in the Constitution, of certain rights, shall not be construed to deny or disparage others retained by the people."

The Fourth and Fifth Amendments [have been] described as protection against all governmental invasions "of the sanctity of a man's home and the privacies of life." We recently referred to the Fourth Amendment as creating a "right to privacy, no less important than any other right carefully and particularly reserved to the people."

We have had many controversies over these penumbral rights of "privacy and repose." These cases bear witness that the right of privacy which presses for recognition here is a legitimate one.

The present case, then, concerns a relationship lying within the zone of privacy created by several fundamental constitutional guarantees. And it concerns a law which, in forbidding the use of contraceptives rather than regulating their manufacture or sale, seeks to achieve its goals by means having a maximum destructive impact upon that relationship. Such a law cannot stand in light of the familiar principle, so often applied by this Court, that a "governmental purpose to control or prevent activities constitutionally subject to state regulation may not be achieved by means which sweep unnecessarily broadly and thereby invade the area of protected freedoms." Would we allow the police to search the sacred precincts of marital bedrooms for telltale signs of the use of contraceptives? The very idea is repulsive to the notions of privacy surrounding the marriage relationship.

We deal with a right of privacy older than the Bill of Rights — older than our political parties, older than our school system. Marriage is a coming together for better or for worse, hopefully enduring, and intimate to the degree of being sacred. It is an association that promotes a way of life, not causes; a harmony in living, not political faiths; a bilateral loyalty, not commercial or social projects. Yet it is an association for as noble a purpose as any involved in our prior decisions.

Reversed.

Mr. Justice GOLDBERG, whom THE CHIEF JUSTICE and Mr. Justice BRENNAN join, concurring.

I agree with the Court that Connecticut's birth-control law unconstitutionally intrudes upon the right of marital privacy. . . . Although I have not accepted the view that "due process" as used in the Fourteenth Amendment includes all of the first eight Amendments, I do agree that the concept of liberty protects those personal rights that are fundamental, and is not confined to the specific terms of the Bill of Rights. [T]he concept of liberty [embraces] the right of marital privacy though that right is not mentioned explicitly in the Constitution is supported both by numerous decisions of this Court, referred to in the Court's opinion, and by the language and history of the Ninth Amendment. . . .

The Court stated many years ago that the Due Process Clause protects those liberties that are "so rooted in the traditions and conscience of our people as to be ranked as fundamental." [This] Court [has] held that the Fourteenth Amendment absorbs and applies to the States those specifics of the first eight amendments which express fundamental personal rights. The language and history of the Ninth Amendment reveal that the Framers of the Constitution believed that there are additional fundamental rights, protected from governmental infringement, which exist alongside those fundamental rights specifically mentioned in the first eight constitutional amendments.

The Ninth Amendment reads, "The enumeration in the Constitution, of certain rights, shall not be construed to deny or disparage others retained by the people." The Amendment [was] proffered to quiet expressed fears that a bill of specifically enumerated rights could not be sufficiently broad to cover all essential rights and that the specific mention of certain rights would be interpreted as a denial that others were protected. . . .

[In] determining which rights are fundamental, judges are not left at large to decide cases in light of their personal and private notions. Rather, they must look to the "traditions and (collective) conscience of our people" to determine whether a principle is "so rooted [there as] to be ranked as fundamental." The inquiry is whether a right involved is of such a character that it cannot be denied without violating those "fundamental principles of liberty and justice which lie at the base of all our civil and political institutions." "Liberty" also "gains content from the emanations [of] specific [constitutional] guarantees" and "from experience with the requirements of a free society."

[The] entire fabric of the Constitution and the purposes that clearly underlie its specific guarantees demonstrate that the rights to marital privacy and to marry and raise a family are of similar order and magnitude as the fundamental rights specifically protected. . . . The fact that no particular provision of the Constitution explicitly forbids the State from disrupting the traditional relation of the family — a relation as old and as fundamental as our entire civilization — surely does not show that the Government was meant to have the power to do so. Rather, as the Ninth Amendment expressly recognizes, there are fundamental personal rights such as this one, which are protected from abridgment by the Government though not specifically mentioned in the Constitution.

[The] logic of the dissents would sanction federal or state legislation that seems to me even more plainly unconstitutional than the statute before us. Surely the Government, absent a showing of a compelling subordinating state interest, could not decree that all husbands and wives must be sterilized after two children have been born to them. Yet by their reasoning such an invasion of marital privacy would not be subject to constitutional challenge because, while it might be "silly," no provision of the Constitution specifically prevents the Government from curtailing the marital right to bear children and raise a family. While it may shock some of my Brethren that the Court today holds that the Constitution protects the right of marital privacy, in my view it is far more shocking to believe that the personal liberty guaranteed by the Constitution does not include protection against such totalitarian limitation of family size, which is at complete variance with our constitutional concepts. Yet, if upon a showing of a slender basis of rationality, a law outlawing voluntary birth control by married persons is valid, then, by the same reasoning, a law requiring compulsory birth control also would seem to be valid. In my view, however, both types of law would unjustifiably intrude upon rights of marital privacy which are constitutionally protected.

[I] believe that the right of privacy in the marital relation is fundamental and basic — a personal right "retained by the people" within the meaning of the Ninth Amendment. Connecticut cannot constitutionally abridge this fundamental right, which is protected by the Fourteenth Amendment from infringement by the States.

Mr. Justice HARLAN, concurring in the judgment.

[T]he proper constitutional inquiry [is] whether this Connecticut statute infringes the Due Process Clause of the Fourteenth Amendment because the enactment violates basic values "implicit in the concept of ordered liberty." [I] believe that it does. While [the] inquiry may be aided by resort to one or more of the provisions of the Bill of Rights, it is not dependent on them or any of their radiations. The Due Process Clause of the Fourteenth Amendment stands [on] its own bottom.

Mr. Justice WHITE, concurring in the judgment.

[T]his Connecticut law as applied to married couples deprives them of "liberty" without due process of law, as that concept is used in the Fourteenth Amendment. [T]his is not the first time this Court has had occasion to articulate that the liberty entitled to protection under the Fourteenth Amendment includes the right "to marry, establish a home and bring up children." [Our] decisions affirm that there is a "realm of family life which the state cannot enter" without substantial justification. Surely the right invoked in this case, to be free of regulation of the intimacies of the marriage relationship, "come[s] to this Court with a momentum for respect lacking when appeal is made to liberties which derive merely from shifting economic arrangements."

Mr. Justice BLACK, with whom Mr. Justice STEWART joins, dissenting.

[The] Court talks about a constitutional "right of privacy" as though there is some constitutional provision or provisions forbidding any law ever to be passed which might abridge the "privacy" of individuals. But there is not. There are, of course, guarantees in certain specific constitutional provisions which are designed in part to protect privacy at certain times and places with respect to certain activities. Such, for example, is the Fourth Amendment's guarantee against "unreasonable searches and seizures." But I think it belittles that Amendment to talk about it as though it protects nothing but "privacy." . . .

[The] due process argument which my Brothers Harlan and White adopt here is based [on] the premise that this Court is vested with power to invalidate all state laws that it consider to be arbitrary, capricious, unreasonable, or oppressive, or this Court's belief that a particular state law under scrutiny has no "rational or justifying" purpose, or is offensive to a "sense of fairness and justice." If these formulas based on "natural justice," or others which mean the same thing, are to prevail, they require judges to determine what is or is not constitutional on the basis of their own appraisal of what laws are unwise or unnecessary. The power to make such decisions is of course that of a legislative body. Surely it has to be admitted that no provision of the Constitution specifically gives such blanket power to courts to exercise such a supervisory veto over the wisdom and value of legislative policies and to hold unconstitutional those laws which they believe unwise or dangerous. I readily admit that no legislative body, state or national, should pass laws that can justly be given any of the invidious labels invoked as constitutional excuses to strike down state laws. But perhaps it is not too much to say that no legislative body ever does pass laws without believing that they will accomplish a sane, rational, wise and justifiable purpose. While I completely subscribe to the holding of *Marbury*, [I] do not believe that we are granted power by the Due Process Clause or any other constitutional provision [to] measure constitutionality by our belief that legislation is arbitrary, capricious or unreasonable, or accomplishes no justifiable purpose, or is offensive to our own notions of "civilized standards of conduct." Such an appraisal of the wisdom of legislation is an attribute of the power to make laws, not of the power to interpret them. The use by federal courts of such a formula or doctrine [to] veto federal or state laws simply takes away from Congress and States the power to make laws based on their own judgment of fairness and wisdom and transfers that power to this Court for ultimate determination—a power which was specifically denied to federal courts by the convention that framed the Constitution.

Of the cases on which my Brothers White and Goldberg rely so heavily, undoubtedly the reasoning of two of them supports their result here—as would that of a number of others which they do not bother to name, e.g., Lochner v. State of New York. . . .

My Brother Goldberg [suggests] that the Ninth Amendment as well as the Due Process Clause can be used by this Court as authority to strike down all state legislation which this Court thinks violates "fundamental principles of liberty and justice," or is contrary to the "traditions and (collective) conscience of our people." He also states [that] in making decisions on this basis judges will not consider "their personal and private notions." One may ask how they can avoid considering them. Our Court certainly has no machinery with which to take a Gallup Poll. And the scientific miracles of this age have not yet produced a gadget which the Court can use to determine what traditions are rooted in the "[collective] conscience of our people." Moreover, one would certainly have to look far beyond the language of the Ninth Amendment to find that the Framers vested in this Court any such awesome veto powers over lawmaking. . . . Nor does anything in the history of the Amendment offer any support for such a shocking doctrine. The whole history of the adoption of the Constitution and Bill of Rights points the other way, and the very material quoted by my Brother Goldberg shows that the Ninth Amendment [was] passed, not to broaden the powers of this Court or any other department of "the General Government," but [to] assure the people that the Constitution in all its provisions was intended to limit the Federal Government to the powers granted expressly or by necessary implication. If any broad, unlimited power to hold laws unconstitutional because they offend what this Court conceives to be the "[collective] conscience of our people" is vested in this Court by the Ninth Amendment, the Fourteenth Amendment, or any other provision of the Constitution, it was not given by the Framers, but rather has been bestowed on the Court by the Court. This fact is perhaps responsible for the peculiar phenomenon that for a period of a century and a half no serious suggestion was ever made that the Ninth Amendment, enacted to protect state powers against federal invasion, could be used as a weapon of federal power to prevent state legislatures from passing laws they consider appropriate to govern local affairs. Use of any such broad, unbounded judicial authority would make of this Court's members a day-to-day constitutional convention.

[T]his Court does have power, which it should exercise, to hold laws unconstitutional where they are forbidden by the Federal Constitution. My point is that there is no provision of the Constitution which either expressly or impliedly vests power in this Court to sit as a supervisory agency over acts of duly constituted legislative bodies and set aside their laws because of the Court's belief that the legislative policies adopted are unreasonable, unwise, arbitrary, capricious or irrational. The adoption of such a loose, flexible, uncontrolled standard for holding laws unconstitutional, if ever it is finally achieved, will amount to a great unconstitutional shift of power to the courts which [will] be bad for the courts and worse for the country. Subjecting federal and state laws to such an unrestrained and unrestrainable judicial control as to the wisdom of legislative enactments would, I fear, jeopardize the separation of governmental powers that the Framers set up and at the same time threaten to take away much of the power of States to govern themselves which the Constitution plainly intended them to have.

I realize that many good and able men have eloquently spoken and written, sometimes in rhapsodical strains, about the duty of this Court to keep the Constitution in tune with the times. The idea is that the Constitution must be changed from time to time and that this Court is charged with a duty to make those changes. [I] must with all deference reject that philosophy. The Constitution makers knew the need for change and provided for it. Amendments suggested by the people's elected representatives can be submitted to the people or their selected agents for ratification. . . . The Due Process Clause with an "arbitrary and capricious" or "shocking to the conscience" formula was liberally used by this Court to strike down economic legislation in the early decades of this century, threatening, many people thought, the tranquility and stability of the Nation. That formula, based on subjective considerations of "natural justice," is no less dangerous when used to enforce this Court's views about personal rights than those about economic rights. I had thought that we had laid that formula, as a means for striking down state legislation, to rest once and for all. . . .

So far as I am concerned, Connecticut's law as applied here is not forbidden by any provision of the Federal Constitution as that Constitution was written, and I would therefore affirm.

Mr. Justice STEWART, whom Mr. Justice BLACK joins, dissenting.

Since 1879 Connecticut has had on its books a law which forbids the use of contraceptives by anyone. I think this is an uncommonly silly law. . . . I believe the use of contraceptives in the relationship of marriage should be left to personal and private choice, based upon each individual's moral, ethical, and religious beliefs. As a matter of social policy, I think professional counsel about methods of birth control should be available to all, so that each individual's choice can be meaningfully made. But we are not asked in this case to say whether we think this law is unwise, or even asinine. We are asked to hold that it violates the United States Constitution. And that I cannot do.

In the course of its opinion the Court refers to no less than six Amendments to the Constitution: the First, the Third, the Fourth, the Fifth, the Ninth, and the Fourteenth. But the Court does not say which of these Amendments, if any, it thinks is infringed by this Connecticut law.

[There] is no claim that this law, duly enacted by the Connecticut Legislature, is unconstitutionally vague. There is no claim that the appellants were denied any of the elements of procedural due process at their trial, so as to make their convictions constitutionally invalid. And, as the Court says, the day has long passed since the Due Process Clause was regarded as a proper instrument for determining 'the wisdom, need, and propriety' of state laws.

[As] to the First, Third, Fourth, and Fifth Amendments, I can find nothing in any of them to invalidate this Connecticut law, even assuming that all those Amendments are fully applicable against the States. . . . The Court also quotes the Ninth Amendment. . . . But to say that the Ninth Amendment has anything to do with this case is to turn somersaults with history. The Ninth Amendment, like its companion the Tenth, which this Court held "states but a truism that all is retained which has not been surrendered," was framed by James Madison and adopted by the States simply to make clear that the adoption of the Bill of Rights did not alter the plan that the Federal Government was to be a government of express and limited powers, and that all rights and powers not delegated to it were retained by the people and the individual States. Until today no member of this Court has ever suggested that the Ninth Amendment meant anything else, and the idea that a federal court could ever use the Ninth Amendment to annul a law passed by the elected representatives of the people of the State of Connecticut would have caused James Madison no little wonder.

What provision of the Constitution, then, does make this state law invalid? The Court says it is the right of privacy "created by several fundamental constitutional guarantees." With all deference, I can find no such general right of privacy in the Bill of Rights, in any other part of the Constitution, or in any case ever before decided by this Court.

[We] are here to decide cases "agreeably to the Constitution and laws of the United States." It is the essence of judicial duty to subordinate our own personal views, our own ideas of what legislation is wise and what is not. If [the] law before us does not reflect the standards of the people of Connecticut, the people of Connecticut can freely exercise their true Ninth and Tenth Amendment rights to persuade their elected representatives to repeal it. That is the constitutional way to take this law off the books. . . .

Notes and Questions

1. *Griswold's Logic.* Does *Griswold*'s logic hold together? Consider the following: Justice Douglas's argument seems to go something like this: Since the Constitution, in various "specifics of the Bill of Rights and in their penumbra, protects rights which partake of privacy, it protects other aspects of privacy as well, indeed it recognizes a general, complete right of privacy. And since the right emanates from specific fundamental rights, it too is 'fundamental,' its infringement is suspect and calls for strict scrutiny, and it can be justified only by a high level of public good. A logician, I suppose, might have trouble with that argument. A legal draftsman, indeed, might suggest the opposite: when the Constitution sought to protect private rights it specified them; that it explicitly protects some elements of privacy, but not others, suggests that it did not mean to protect those not mentioned." *See* Louis Henkin, *Privacy and Autonomy,* 74 Colum. L. Rev. 1410, 1421-22 (1974).

2. *The Ninth Amendment.* Does the Ninth Amendment (which provides that "the enumeration in the Constitution, of certain rights, shall not be construed to deny or disparage others retained by the people") provide a basis for disagreeing with the views expressed in the prior paragraph? But, if other rights are to be found under the Ninth Amendment, where are they to come from? Are there neutral principles for ascertaining and articulating them?

∽ PROBLEMS ∽

1. *Are There Limits to the Individual Interest in Liberty and Privacy?* As we see in *Griswold,* the Fourteenth Amendment has been interpreted as protecting the individual interest in "liberty" and "privacy." But are those individual interests

absolute? During a time of war, may the government draft young men and women and force them to serve in the armed forces? As part of this armed service, may the government send draftees (against their will) into harm's way and force them to risk life and limb? If the individual interest must give way to the societal interest in some cases, where is the dividing line?

2. *More on the Proposed Child Custody Statute*. Consider the problem that introduces this chapter. Does the proposed statute implicate privacy interests? Does it also implicate interests protected by the Ninth Amendment or by "liberty" interests?

In Poe v. Ullman, 367 U.S. 497 (1961), the Court dismissed a challenge to a Connecticut contraception law on grounds that a real threat of enforcement was lacking and thus no case or controversy existed. In a dissenting opinion, Justice Harlan laid significant groundwork for further development of the right of privacy.

Poe v. Ullman

367 U.S. 497 (1961)

Mr. Justice HARLAN, dissenting.

I consider that this Connecticut legislation, as construed to apply to these appellants, violates the Fourteenth Amendment. I believe that a statute making it a criminal offense for married couples to use contraceptives is an intolerable and unjustifiable invasion of privacy in the conduct of the most intimate concerns of an individual's personal life. [Since] the contention [draws its] basis from no explicit language of the Constitution, and ha[s] yet to find expression in any decision of this Court, I feel it desirable at the outset to state the framework of Constitutional principles in which I think the issue must be judged.

Were due process merely a procedural safeguard it would fail to reach those situations where the deprivation of life, liberty or property was accomplished by legislation which by operating in the future could, given even the fairest possible procedure in application to individuals, nevertheless destroy the enjoyment of all three. Thus the guaranties of due process, though having their roots in Magna Carta's *"per legem terrae"* and considered as procedural safeguards "against executive usurpation and tyranny," have in this country "become bulwarks also against arbitrary legislation."

However it is not the particular enumeration of rights in the first eight Amendments which spells out the reach of Fourteenth Amendment due process, but rather, as was suggested in another context long before the adoption of that Amendment, those concepts which are considered to embrace those rights "which are . . . fundamental; *which belong . . . to the citizens of all free governments, for "the purposes [of securing] which men enter into society."* Again and again this Court has resisted the notion that the Fourteenth Amendment is no more than a shorthand reference to what is explicitly set out elsewhere in the Bill of Rights. Indeed the fact that an identical provision limiting federal action is found among the first eight Amendments, applying to the Federal Government, suggests that due process is a discrete concept which subsists as an independent guaranty of liberty and procedural fairness, more general and inclusive than the specific prohibitions.

Due process has not been reduced to any formula; its content cannot be determined by reference to any code. The best that can be said is that through the course of this Court's decisions it has represented the balance which our Nation, built upon postulates of respect for the liberty of the individual, has struck between that liberty and the demands of organized society. If the supplying of content to this Constitutional concept has of necessity been a rational process, it certainly has not been one where judges have felt free to roam where unguided speculation might take them. The balance of which I speak is the balance struck by this country, having regard to what history teaches are the traditions from which it developed as well as the traditions from which it broke. That tradition is a living thing. A decision of this Court which radically departs from it could not long survive, while a decision which builds on what has survived is likely to be sound. No formula could serve as a substitute, in this area, for judgment and restraint.

It is this outlook which has led the Court continuingly to perceive distinctions in the imperative character of Constitutional provisions, since that character must be discerned from a particular provision's larger context. And inasmuch as this context is one not of words, but of history and purposes, the full scope of the liberty guaranteed by the Due Process Clause cannot be found in or limited by the precise terms of the specific guarantees elsewhere provided in the Constitution. This "liberty" is not a series of isolated points pricked out in terms of the taking of property; the freedom of speech, press, and religion; the right to keep and bear arms; the freedom from unreasonable searches and seizures; and so on. It is a rational continuum which, broadly speaking, includes a freedom from all substantial arbitrary impositions and purposeless restraints, and which also recognizes, what a reasonable and sensitive judgment must, that certain interests require particularly careful scrutiny of the state needs asserted to justify their abridgment.

[Each] new claim to Constitutional protection must be considered against a background of Constitutional purposes, as they have been rationally perceived and historically developed. Though we exercise limited and sharply restrained judgment, yet there is no "mechanical yardstick," no "mechanical answer." The decision of an apparently novel claim must depend on grounds which follow closely on well-accepted principles and criteria. The new decision must take "its place in relation to what went before and further [cut] a channel for what is to come." The matter was well put in Rochin v. California:

> The vague contours of the Due Process Clause do not leave judges at large. We may not draw on our merely personal and private notions and disregard the limits that bind judges in their judicial function. Even though the concept of due process of law is not final and fixed, these limits are derived from considerations that are fused in the whole nature of our judicial process. . . . These are considerations deeply rooted in reason and in the compelling traditions of the legal profession.

Notes and Questions

1. *Post*-Griswold *Decisions.* The *Griswold* decision established the right of privacy, albeit not without significant dissent and uncertainty with respect to its anchorage. The right was expanded in Eisenstadt v. Baird, 405 U.S. 438 (1972), when the Court struck down a state law restricting the availability of contraceptives to unmarried persons. Relying upon equal protection principles, the Court determined that "[i]f the right [of] privacy means anything, it is the right of the individual, married or single, to be free from unwanted intrusion into matters so fundamentally affecting a person as the decision whether to bear or beget a child." In Carey v. Population Services International, 431 U.S. 678 (1977), the Court struck down a state law authorizing only pharmacists to sell nonprescription contraceptives and prohibiting their sale to persons under the age of 16. The Court referenced *Eisenstadt* for the proposition that "the teaching of *Griswold* is that the Constitution protects individual decisions in matters of childbearing from unjustified intrusion by the State." This observation reflects the passage from a concept that protected choice with respect to contraceptive usage to one that secured reproductive autonomy.

2. *Thinking About Penumbras.* How apt or unprincipled is the penumbral model as a basis for identifying and developing fundamental rights? Does it avoid the concerns of *Lochnerian* substantive due process review? Does it follow logically that freedom of association is an extension of and thus within the penumbra of freedom of speech? Does it follow logically that a right to own slaves is an extension of and thus within the various constitutional provisions that accounted for or accommodated slavery?

∾ PROBLEM: *BUCK* AND PRIVACY ∾

Justice Black expressed an appreciation of privacy but no tolerance for it as a constitutional right. In Buck v. Bell, 274 U.S. 200 (1927), the Court upheld a state law that mandated sterilization for "mentally defective" or "feebleminded" persons. This decision is memorable, among other things, for Justice Holmes's seemingly gratuitous observation that "three generations of imbeciles is enough." How would Justice Black respond to this enactment? If he was unwilling to budge, how would this hard line affect your assessment of his position? Would it make any difference that the criteria for mental deficiency under the law were calibrated so that half of the nation's adult male population might be candidates for surgery? *See* Laurence H. Tribe, *God Save This Honorable Court* (Random House 1988).

2. Abortion

Clarity with respect to the basis of the right of privacy was provided in Roe v. Wade, when the Court established that a woman's liberty to elect an abortion was grounded in the Due Process Clause of the Fourteenth Amendment.

Roe v. Wade
410 U.S. 113 (1973)

Mr. Justice BLACKMUN delivered the opinion of the Court.

This Texas federal appeal and its Georgia companion present constitutional challenges to state criminal abortion legislation.

[We] acknowledge [the] sensitive and emotional nature of the abortion controversy, of the vigorous opposing views, even among physicians, and of the deep and seemingly absolute convictions that the subject inspires. One's philosophy, one's experiences, one's exposure to the raw edges of human existence, one's religious training, one's attitudes toward life and family and their values, and the moral standards one establishes and seeks to observe, are all likely to influence and to color one's thinking and conclusions about abortion. . . . In addition, population growth, pollution, poverty, and racial overtones tend to complicate and not to simplify the problem.

Our task, of course, is to resolve the issue by constitutional measurement, free of emotion and of predilection. We seek earnestly to do this, and, because we do, we have inquired into, and in this opinion place some emphasis upon, medical and medical-legal history and what that history reveals about man's attitudes toward the abortion procedure over the centuries. We bear in mind, too, Mr. Justice Holmes' admonition in his now-vindicated dissent in Lochner v. New York:

> [The Constitution] is made for people of fundamentally differing views, and the accident of our finding certain opinions natural and familiar, or novel, and even shocking, ought not to conclude our judgment upon the question whether statutes embodying them conflict with the Constitution of the United States.

The Texas statutes that concern us here [make] it a crime to "procure an abortion," as therein defined, or to attempt one, except with respect to "an abortion procured or attempted by medical advice for the purpose of saving the life of the mother." Similar statutes are in existence in a majority of the States.

Jane Roe, a single woman [residing in] Texas instituted this federal action [seeking] a declaratory judgment that the Texas criminal abortion statutes were unconstitutional on their face, and an injunction restraining the defendant from enforcing the statutes.

Roe alleged that she was unmarried and pregnant; that she wished to terminate her pregnancy by an abortion "performed by a competent, licensed physician, under safe, clinical conditions"; that she was unable to get a "legal" abortion in Texas because her life did not appear to be threatened by the continuation of her pregnancy; and that she could not afford to travel to another jurisdiction in order to secure a legal abortion under safe conditions. She claimed that the Texas statutes were unconstitutionally vague and that they abridged her right of personal privacy, protected by the First, Fourth, Fifth, Ninth, and Fourteenth Amendments. By an amendment to her complaint Roe purported to sue "on behalf of herself and all other women" similarly situated.

The principal thrust of appellant's attack on the Texas statutes is that they improperly invade a right, said to be possessed by the pregnant woman, to choose to terminate her pregnancy. Appellant would discover this right in the concept of personal "liberty" embodied in the Fourteenth Amendment's Due Process Clause; or in personal marital, familial, and sexual privacy said to be protected by the Bill of Rights or its penumbras.

[*The*] *American law.* In this country, the law in effect in all but a few States until mid-19th century was the pre-existing English common law. Connecticut, the first State to enact abortion legislation, adopted in 1821 that part of Lord Ellenborough's Act that related to a woman "quick with child." The death penalty was not imposed. Abortion before quickening was made a crime in that State only in 1860. In 1828, New York enacted legislation that [was] to serve as a model for early anti-abortion statutes. First, while barring destruction of an unquickend fetus as well as a quick fetus, it made the former only a misdemeanor, but the latter second-degree manslaughter. Second, it incorporated a concept of therapeutic abortion by providing that an abortion was excused if it "shall have been necessary to preserve the life of such mother, or shall have been advised by two physicians to be necessary for such purpose." By 1840, when Texas [received] the common law, only eight American States had statutes dealing with abortion. It was not until after the War Between the States that legislation began generally to replace the common law. Most of these initial statutes dealt severely with abortion after quickening but were lenient with it before quickening. Most punished attempts equally with completed abortions. While many statutes included [exception] for an abortion thought by one or more physicians to be necessary to save the mother's life, that provision soon disappeared and the typical law required that the procedure actually be necessary for that purpose.

Gradually, in the middle and late 19th century the quickening distinction disappeared from the statutory law of most States and the degree of the offense and the penalties were increased. By the end of the 1950s a large majority of the jurisdictions banned abortion, however and whenever performed, unless done to save or preserve the life of the mother. The exceptions, Alabama and the District of Columbia, permitted abortion to preserve the mother's health. Three States permitted abortions that were not "unlawfully" performed or that were not "without lawful justification," leaving interpretation of those standards to the courts. In the past several years, however, a trend toward liberalization of abortion statutes has resulted in adoption, by about one-third of the States, of less stringent laws, most of them patterned after the ALI Model Penal Code.

It is thus apparent that at common law, at the time of the adoption of our Constitution, and throughout the major portion of the 19th century, abortion was viewed with less disfavor than under most American statutes currently in effect. Phrasing it another way, a woman enjoyed a substantially broader right to terminate a pregnancy than she does in most States today. At least with respect to the early stage of pregnancy, and very possibly without such a limitation, the opportunity to make this choice was present in this country well into the 19th century. Even later, the law continued for some time to treat less punitively an abortion procured in early pregnancy.

Three reasons have been advanced to explain historically the enactment of criminal abortion laws in the 19th century and to justify their continued existence.

It has been argued occasionally that these laws were the product of a Victorian social concern to discourage illicit sexual conduct. Texas, however, does not advance this justification in the present case, and it appears that no court or commentator has taken the argument seriously. . . . A second reason is concerned with abortion as a medical procedure. When most criminal abortion laws were first enacted, the procedure was a hazardous one for the woman. Abortion mortality was high. Even after 1900, and perhaps until as late as the development of antibiotics in the 1940s, standard modern techniques such as dilation and curettage were not nearly so safe as they are today. Thus, it has been argued that a State's real concern in enacting a criminal abortion law was to protect the pregnant woman, that is, to restrain her from submitting to a procedure that placed her life in serious jeopardy.

Modern medical techniques have altered this situation. Appellants [refer] to medical data indicating that abortion in early pregnancy, that is, prior to the end of the first trimester, although not without its risk, is now relatively safe. Mortality rates for women undergoing early abortions, where the procedure is legal, appear to be as low as or lower than the rates for normal childbirth. Consequently, any interest of the State in protecting the woman from an inherently hazardous procedure, except when it would be equally dangerous for her to forgo it, has largely disappeared. Of course, important state interests in the areas of health and medical standards do remain.

[The] third reason is the State's interest — some phrase it in terms of duty — in protecting prenatal life. Some of the argument for this justification rests on the theory that a new human life is present from the moment of conception. The State's interest and general obligation to protect life then extends, it is argued, to prenatal life. Only when the life of the pregnant mother herself is at stake, balanced against the life she carries within her, should the interest of the embryo or fetus not prevail. Logically, of course, a legitimate state interest in this area need not stand or fall on acceptance of the belief that life begins at conception or at some other point prior to life birth. In assessing the State's interest, recognition may be given to the less rigid claim that as long as at least potential life is involved, the State may assert interests beyond the protection of the pregnant woman alone. . . . Parties challenging state abortion laws have sharply disputed [that] a purpose of these laws [was] to protect prenatal life. [T]hey claim that most state laws were designed solely to protect the woman. Because medical advances have lessened this concern, at least with respect to abortion in early pregnancy, they argue that with respect to such abortions the laws can no longer be justified by any state interest. . . .

The Constitution does not explicitly mention any right of privacy. [T]he Court has recognized that a right of personal privacy, or a guarantee of certain areas or zones of privacy, does exist under the Constitution. These decisions make it clear that only personal rights that can be deemed "fundamental" or "implicit in the concept of ordered liberty," are included in this guarantee of personal privacy. They also make it clear that the right has some extension to activities relating to marriage; procreation; contraception; family relationships; and child rearing and education.

This right of privacy, whether it be founded in the Fourteenth Amendment's concept of personal liberty and restrictions upon state action, as we feel it is, or, as the District Court determined, in the Ninth Amendment's reservation of rights to the people, is broad enough to encompass a woman's decision whether or not to terminate her pregnancy. The detriment that the State would impose upon the pregnant woman by denying this choice altogether is apparent. Specific and direct harm medically diagnosable even in early pregnancy may be involved. Maternity, or additional offspring, may force upon the woman a distressful life and future. Psychological harm may be imminent. Mental and physical health may be taxed by child care. There is also the distress, for all concerned, associated with the unwanted child, and there is the problem of bringing a child into a family already unable, psychologically and otherwise, to care for it. In other cases, as in this one, the additional difficulties and continuing stigma of unwed motherhood may be involved. All these are factors the woman and her responsible physician necessarily will consider in consultation.

On the basis of elements such as these, appellant and some amici argue that the woman's right is absolute and that she is entitled to terminate her pregnancy at whatever time, in whatever way, and for whatever reason she alone chooses. With this we do not agree. Appellant's arguments that Texas either has no valid interest at all in regulating the abortion decision, or no interest strong enough to support any limitation upon the woman's sole determination, are unpersuasive. The Court's decisions recognizing a right of privacy also acknowledge that some state regulation in areas protected by that right is appropriate. [A] State may properly assert important interests in safeguarding health, in maintaining medical standards, and in protecting potential life. At some point in pregnancy, these respective interests become sufficiently compelling to sustain regulation of the factors that govern the abortion decision. The privacy right involved, therefore, cannot be said to be absolute. In fact, it is not clear to us that the claim asserted by some amici that one has an unlimited right to do with one's body as one pleases bears a close relationship to the right of privacy previously articulated in the Court's decisions. The Court has refused to recognize an unlimited right of this kind in the past.

We, therefore, conclude that the right of personal privacy includes the abortion decision, but that this right is not unqualified and must be considered against important state interests in regulation. [Where] certain "fundamental rights" are involved, the Court has held that regulation limiting these rights may be justified only by a "compelling state interest." [The] District Court held that the appellee failed to meet his burden of demonstrating that the Texas statute's infringement upon Roe's rights was necessary to support a compelling state interest, and that, although the appellee presented "several compelling justifications for state presence in the area of abortions," the statutes outstripped these justifications and swept "far beyond any areas of compelling state interest." . . .

The appellee and certain amici argue that the fetus is a "person" within the language and meaning of the Fourteenth Amendment. In support of this, they outline at length and in detail the well-known facts of fetal development. If this suggestion of personhood is established, the appellant's case [collapses] for the fetus' right to life would then be guaranteed specifically by the Amendment. . . . On the other hand, [no] case could be cited that holds that a fetus is a person within the meaning of the Fourteenth Amendment. . . . The Constitution does not define "person" in so many words. [Although the term is used throughout the document,] in nearly all these instances, the use of the word is such that it has application only postnatally. None indicates, with any assurance, that it has any possible prenatal application. . . . All this, together with our observation, that throughout the major portion of the 19th century prevailing legal abortion practices were far freer than they are today, persuades us that the word "person," as used in the Fourteenth Amendment, does not include the unborn. This is in accord with the results reached in those few cases where the issue has been squarely presented.

[The] pregnant woman [carries] an embryo and, later, a fetus, if one accepts the medical definitions of the developing young in the human uterus. The situation therefore is inherently different from marital intimacy, or bedroom possession of obscene material, or marriage, or procreation, or education, with which [prior cases were] concerned. [I]t is reasonable and appropriate for a State to decide that at some point in time another interest, that of health of the mother or that of potential human life, becomes significantly involved. The woman's privacy is no longer sole and any right of privacy she possesses must be measured accordingly.

Texas urges that, apart from the Fourteenth Amendment, life begins at conception and is present throughout pregnancy, and that, therefore, the State has a compelling interest in protecting that life from and after conception. We need not resolve the difficult question of when life begins. When those trained in the respective disciplines of medicine, philosophy, and theology are unable to arrive at any consensus, the judiciary, at this point in the development of man's knowledge, is not in a position to speculate as to the answer.

It should be sufficient to note briefly the wide divergence of thinking on this most sensitive and difficult question. There has always been strong support for the view that life does not begin until live birth. . . . It appears to be the predominant [attitude] of the Jewish faith. [A] large segment of the Protestant community [has] generally regarded abortion as a matter for the conscience of the individual and her family. . . . Physicians and their scientific colleagues [have] tended to focus either upon conception, upon live birth, or upon the interim point at which the fetus becomes "viable," that is, potentially able to live outside the mother's womb, albeit with artificial aid. Viability is usually placed at about seven months (28 weeks) but may occur earlier, even at 24 weeks. The Aristotelian theory of "mediate animation," that held sway throughout the Middle Ages and the Renaissance in Europe, continued to be official Roman Catholic dogma until the 19th century, despite opposition to this "ensoulment" theory from those in the Church who would recognize the existence of life from the moment of conception. The latter is now, of course, the official belief of the Catholic Church. [T]his is a view strongly held by many non-Catholics as well, and by many physicians. Substantial problems for precise definition of this view are posed, however, by new embryological data that purport to indicate that conception is a "process" over time, rather than an event, and by new medical techniques such as menstrual extraction, the "morning-after" pill, implantation of embryos, artificial insemination, and even artificial wombs. . . . In areas other than criminal abortion, the law has been reluctant to endorse any theory that life, as we recognize it, begins before life birth or to accord legal rights to the unborn except in narrowly defined situations and except when the rights are contingent upon life birth.

[In] view of all this, we do not agree that, by adopting one theory of life, Texas may override the rights of the pregnant woman that are at stake. [T]he State does have an important and legitimate interest in preserving and protecting the health of the pregnant woman, whether she be a resident of the State or a non-resident who seeks medical consultation and treatment there, and that it has still another important and legitimate interest in protecting the potentiality of human life. These interests are separate and distinct. Each grows in substantiality as the woman approaches term and, at a point during pregnancy, each becomes "compelling."

With respect to the State's important and legitimate interest in the health of the mother, the "compelling" point, in the light of present medical knowledge, is at approximately the end of the first trimester. This is so because of the now-established medical fact [that] until the end of the first trimester mortality in abortion may be less than mortality in normal childbirth. It follows that, from and after this point, a State may regulate the abortion procedure to the extent that the regulation reasonably relates to the preservation and protection of maternal health. Examples of permissible state regulation in this area are requirements as to the qualifications of the person who is to perform the abortion; as to the licensure of that person; as to the facility in which the procedure is to be performed, that is, whether it must be a hospital or may be a clinic or some other place of less-than-hospital status; as to the licensing of the facility; and the like.

This means [that], for the period of pregnancy prior to this "compelling" point, the attending physician, in consultation with his patient, is free to determine, without regulation by the State, that, in his medical judgment, the patient's pregnancy should be terminated. If that decision is reached, the judgment may be effectuated by an abortion free of interference by the State.

With respect to the State's important and legitimate interest in potential life, the "compelling" point is at viability. This is so because the fetus then presumably has the capability of meaningful life outside the mother's womb. State regulation protective of fetal life after viability thus has both logical and biological justifications. If the State is interested in protecting fetal life after viability, it may go so far as to proscribe abortion during that period, except when it is necessary to preserve the life or health of the mother.

Measured against these standards, the Texas law, in restricting legal abortions to those "procured or attempted by medical advice for the purpose of saving the life of the mother," sweeps too broadly. The statute makes no distinction between abortions performed early in pregnancy and those performed later, and it limits to a single reason, "saving" the mother's life, the legal justification for the procedure. The statute, therefore, cannot survive the constitutional attack made upon it here.

To summarize and to repeat: A state criminal abortion statute of the current Texas type, that excepts from criminality only a life-saving procedure on behalf of the mother, without regard to pregnancy stage and without recognition of the other interests involved, is violative of the Due Process Clause of the Fourteenth Amendment.

(a) For the stage prior to approximately the end of the first trimester, the abortion decision and its effectuation must be left to the medical judgment of the pregnant woman's attending physician.

(b) For the stage subsequent to approximately the end of the first trimester, the State, in promoting its interest in the health of the mother, may, if it chooses, regulate the abortion procedure in ways that are reasonably related to maternal health.

(c) For the stage subsequent to viability, the State in promoting its interest in the potentiality of human life may, if it chooses, regulate, and even proscribe, abortion except where it is necessary, in appropriate medical judgment, for the preservation of the life or health of the mother.

This holding [is] consistent with the relative weights of the respective interests involved, with the lessons and examples of medical and legal history, with the lenity of the common law, and with the demands of the profound problems of the present day. The decision leaves the State free to place increasing restrictions on abortion as the period of pregnancy lengthens, so long as those restrictions are tailored to the recognized state interests. The decision vindicates the right of the physician to administer medical treatment according to his professional judgment up to the points where important state interests provide compelling justifications for intervention. Up to those points, the abortion decision in all its aspects is inherently, and primarily, a medical decision, and basic responsibility for it must rest with the physician. If an individual practitioner abuses the privilege of exercising proper medical judgment, the usual remedies, judicial and intra-professional, are available.

Affirmed in part and reversed in part.

Mr. Justice STEWART, concurring.

[Several] decisions of this Court make clear that freedom of personal choice in matters of marriage and family life is one of the liberties protected by the Due Process Clause of the Fourteenth Amendment. [That] right necessarily includes the right of a woman to decide whether or not to terminate her pregnancy. Certainly the interests of a woman in giving of her physical and emotional self during pregnancy and the interests that will be affected throughout her life by the birth and raising of a child are of a far greater degree of significance and personal intimacy than the right to send a child to private school [or] the right to teach a foreign language. . . . Clearly, therefore, the Court today is correct in holding that the right asserted by Jane Roe is embraced within the personal liberty protected by the Due Process Clause of the Fourteenth Amendment.

Mr. Justice REHNQUIST, dissenting.

[While] the Court's opinion quotes from the dissent of Mr. Justice Holmes in Lochner v. New York, the result it reaches is more closely attuned to the majority opinion [in] that case. As in *Lochner* and similar cases applying substantive due process standards to economic and social welfare legislation, the adoption of the compelling state interest standard will inevitably require this Court to examine the legislative policies and pass on the wisdom of these policies in the very process of deciding whether a particular state interest put forward may or may not be "compelling." The decision here to break pregnancy into three distinct terms and to outline the permissible restrictions the State may impose in each one, for example, partakes more of judicial legislation than it does of a determination of the intent of the drafters of the Fourteenth Amendment.

The fact that a majority of the States reflecting [have] had restrictions on abortions for at least a century is a strong indication [that] the asserted right to an abortion is not "so rooted in the traditions and conscience of our people as to be ranked as fundamental." [W]hen society's views on abortion are changing, the very existence of the debate is evidence that the "right" to an abortion is [not] universally accepted. . . .

To reach its result, the Court necessarily has had to find within the Scope of the Fourteenth Amendment a right that was apparently completely unknown to the drafters of the Amendment. As early as 1821, the first state law dealing directly with abortion was enacted by the Connecticut Legislature. By the time of the adoption of the Fourteenth Amendment in 1868, there were at least 36 laws enacted by state or territorial legislatures limiting abortion. While many States have amended or updated their laws, 21 of the laws on the books in 1868 remain in effect today. Indeed, the Texas statute struck down today was, as the majority notes, first enacted in 1857 and "has remained substantially unchanged to the present time." There apparently was no question concerning the validity of this provision or of any of the other state statutes when the Fourteenth Amendment was adopted. The only conclusion possible from this history is that the drafters did not intend to have the Fourteenth Amendment withdraw from the States the power to legislate with respect to this matter.

BACKGROUND
Roe's Impact

The *Roe* decision undid abortion laws in nearly half of the union. Two decades earlier, when the Court struck down segregation in the South, resistance to the Court in most affected states was intense. A similar response was engendered by the abortion decision. Unlike the united front that the Court presented throughout the 1960s on the desegregation front, it was divided on abortion from the outset. Despite these internal divisions and an abundance of challenges, the Court was generally consistent through the late 1980s in striking down laws perceived as a significant burden upon a woman's liberty to elect an abortion.

Notes

1. *Criticism of* Roe. The *Roe* decision was a lightning rod for criticism that the Court had overreached its function and reverted to the antidemocratic model of the *Lochner* era. A particularly strong critic of the decision, Judge Robert Bork, characterized it as "an exercise in moral and political philosophy" and an "assumption of illegitimate power and a usurpation of the democratic authority of the American people." Robert Bork, *The Tempting of America* (Touchstone 1990). Exponents of modern substantive due process review distinguish outputs like *Roe* on grounds that the Court's review is not unbounded. Consistent with Justice Harlan's concurrence in *Griswold,* the Court, pursuant to self-imposed standards, must probe whether an interest is "implicit in the concept of ordered liberty" or "rooted in the Nation's history and tradition." Interpretivists are not impressed with what some have dismissed as "pretty vaporous stuff" and what they contrast with the greater clarity and framing of a textually enumerated right or liberty.

2. *Restrictions on Abortion.* In Doe v. Bolton, 410 U.S. 179 (1973), the Court invalidated provisions of a state law that required abortions to be performed in a hospital approved by a specific accrediting agency, to be authorized by a hospital committee, and to be done only after examination by two other physicians. Critical to the Court's analysis was the fact that these restrictions applied to no other surgical procedure but abortion. The Court, in Planned Parenthood v. Danforth, 428 U.S. 52 (1976), struck down state provisions for spousal and parental consent for unmarried women under the age of 18. The basis for this holding was that the state could not delegate to a person power it did not have during the first trimester. The Court emphasized that the woman, as the child bearer, "is the more directly and immediately affected by the pregnancy, the balance weighs in her favor." Because of age and maturity factors, it also noted that some minor children might not be able to provide effective consent.

Following up on this point, the Court in Planned Parenthood v. Ashcroft, 462 U.S. 476 (1983), upheld a parental consent or notification requirement provided that the minor could bypass it through a judicial procedure. The responsibility of the court, in this circumstance, is to find either that the minor was sufficiently mature to make the decision herself or that an abortion was in her best interest.

3. *Further Abortion Issues.* The Court continued to strike down regulations that constituted significant roadblocks to a woman's ability to exercise her liberty. In Akron v. Akron Center for Reproductive Health, 462 U.S. 416 (1983), it struck down a state law requiring physicians to provide specific information concerning the medical risks and morality of abortion, impose a 24-hour waiting period, and require all post–first-trimester abortions to be performed in hospitals. The Court found that these restrictions constituted "a heavy and unnecessary burden" upon a woman's liberty interest.

Another set of restrictions, requiring disclosure of the names of referring and performing physicians and the woman seeking an abortion and mandating that post-viability abortions be conducted in a way that maximizes the chances for fetal survival, was struck down in Thornburgh v. American College of Obstetricians and

Gynecologists, 476 U.S. 747 (1986). These restrictions were perceived as imposing too high a risk of deterring the exercise of the liberty. Through the *Thornburgh* decision, the Court rather consistently had struck down laws that limited a woman's freedom to choose an abortion. It also had etched a line between burdens that restricted the liberty and public funding decisions that imposed no obligation upon government to subsidize the right.

Questions

1. *Are There Significant Differences Between* Lochner *and* Roe? *Lochner* is now widely repudiated on the basis that the federal courts should not sit as "super-legislatures" that pass on the wisdom of legislation. How does *Griswold* review differ from *Lochner* review? Are the values, the results, or the model of review more principled in *Griswold*? How helpful is it to focus on the "implications of ordered liberty" or "the nation's traditions and history" as a basis for separating the two models of substantive due process review? Does it matter that a majority of the states at the time of *Roe* had imposed restrictions on abortion for more than a century? Is the better analogy for *Roe* not *Lochner* but Brown v. Board of Education, the decision that struck down official segregation in public schools? If *Brown* is the better reference point, does this relationship cut in favor of *Roe* or against *Brown*?

2. Roe *and Judicial Legitimacy.* Justice Rehnquist, in his dissent, notes that "a majority of the States [have] had restrictions on abortions for at least a century. . . ." If Justice Rehnquist is correct, how does that fact affect (if at all) *Roe*'s legitimacy? Do you agree with Justice Rehnquist that this fact shows "the asserted right to an abortion is not 'so rooted in the traditions and conscience of our people as to be ranked as fundamental'"?

3. *Defining Privacy Rights. Roe* makes clear that the right to an abortion constitutes a "fundamental" right that is "implicit in the concept of ordered liberty." In earlier cases, the Court had indicated that it is not "at large" in defining the Fourteenth Amendment, and that it is not free to substitute its own views for that of the legislature. But are there neutral principles that dictate recognition of a right to privacy that includes the right to have an abortion? How might the State of Texas argue that abortion falls outside the right?

4. *Status of the Fetus.* In *Roe,* the Court refused to decide whether a fetus is a "person" within the meaning of the Constitution. Some churches (e.g., the Catholic Church) and others believe that life begins at conception. Had the Court accepted that view, how would it have affected the outcome of the case? If life prior to viability is a potentiality, does subordination of a fetus to actual personhood and the real life incident to it become sensible? *See* Catherine MacKinnon, *Reflections on Sex Equality Under Law,* 100 Yale L.J. 1281, 1315 (1991); John Noonan, *The Root and Branch of Roe v. Wade,* 63 Neb. L. Rev. 668 (1984).

5. *Establishment Clause Concerns.* Does the argument that life, real or potential, is valuable to the point that it overrides a right to obtain an abortion represent an essentially religious viewpoint? Are restrictions on abortion thus

susceptible to review on grounds that they violate the Establishment Clause? *See* Harris v. McRae, 448 U.S. 297 (1980); Ronald Dworkin, *Unenumerated Rights: Whether and How* Roe *Should Be Overruled,* 59 U. Chi. L. Rev. 381 (1992).

6. *More on Griswold's Limits.* The *Griswold* decision established a right of privacy that accounts for personal choice that was denied by prohibitions on using birth control devices. Under the right of privacy, is there a logical connection between protecting choice in the context of contraception and accounting for it in the purview of child bearing? *See* Charles Fried, *Order and Law* 77 (Simon & Schuster 1991).

∾ PROBLEMS ∾

1. Roe *and the Shifting State of Medical Technology.* When *Roe* was decided, a fetus was not sustainable outside the womb until the third trimester. As medical technology advances, suppose that it becomes possible to sustain a fetus outside the womb as early as the tenth week of pregnancy, and that medical procedures advance to the point that it is possible to remove the fetus (without aborting) with no greater risk to the mother than in an abortion. a) Under such circumstances, would the pregnant woman still have an absolute right to abort the fetus? b) Under the *Roe* line of cases, the Court has held that the woman may choose to abort notwithstanding the objections of the father. Under the circumstances listed above, would the father's wishes assume greater significance? Why or why not? c) Does the Court have to periodically update the *Roe* decision in light of current technology? If so, how? What should the Court hold? Does the idea of "periodic updating" in light of technology suggest that the judiciary has exceeded its function?

2. *The Divorcing Couple and the Embryos.* A married couple is having difficulty conceiving and resorts to in vitro fertilization. As a result of this process, eight eggs are fertilized and three are implanted in the wife. The pregnancy does not take. Following the unsuccessful implantation, the couple divorce. In the divorce proceeding, the mother seeks "custody" of the eggs on the theory that she is (otherwise) unlikely to be able to conceive. She claims a "liberty" and "privacy" interest in being able to choose whether to have children. The father opposes the mother's request because he does not wish to be a father, especially with his soon-to-be ex-wife, and he bases his argument on "liberty" and "privacy" concerns. Does the wife have a constitutional liberty or privacy right that entitles her to the eggs?

Webster and Doctrinal Turmoil

In Webster v. Reproductive Health Systems, Inc., 492 U.S. 490 (1989), the Court signaled that it might be backing away from *Roe* in some respects. The Missouri statute in question contained a preamble that stated that "[t]he life of each human being begins at conception," and that "[u]nborn children have protectable interests in life, health, and well-being." It also mandated that state laws be interpreted to provide unborn children with "all the rights, privileges, and immunities available to other persons, citizens, and residents of this state," subject to the Constitution and prior precedent. A plurality of the Court upheld the preamble, noting that it "does not by its terms regulate abortion or any other aspect of appellees' medical practice" and can be regarded as nothing more than the state's value judgment.

The statute also provided that "[i]t shall be unlawful for any public employee within the scope of his employment to perform or assist an abortion, not necessary to save the life of the mother," and also made it "unlawful for any public facility to be used for the purpose of performing or assisting an abortion not necessary to save the life of the mother." The plurality also upheld these provisions. "[O]ur cases have recognized that the Due Process Clauses generally confer no affirmative right to governmental aid, even where such aid may be necessary to secure life, liberty, or property interests of which the government itself may not deprive the individual."

Finally, the Missouri statute imposed a viability testing requirement that applied when a physician has reason to believe that a woman is "carrying an unborn child of twenty or more weeks of gestational age." The Court explained that the statute creates what is essentially a presumption of viability at 20 weeks, which the physician must rebut with tests indicating that the fetus is not viable prior to performing an abortion. It also directs the physician's determination as to viability by specifying consideration, if feasible, of gestational age, fetal weight, and lung capacity. The plurality upheld the provision: "[The] Missouri testing requirement here is reasonably designed to ensure that abortions are not performed where the fetus is viable — an end which all concede is legitimate — and that is sufficient to sustain its constitutionality."

While *Webster*'s holding on the merits was significant, the decision was doctrinally important because it signaled that a number of justices had reservations about *Roe* and its trimester analysis. The plurality stated:

> [We] think that the doubt cast upon the Missouri statute by these cases is not so much a flaw in the statute as it is a reflection of the fact that the rigid trimester analysis of the course of a pregnancy enunciated in *Roe* has [made] this area a virtual Procrustean bed.
>
> [*Stare decisis*] is a cornerstone of our legal system, but it has less power in constitutional cases, where, save for constitutional amendments, this Court is the only body able to make needed changes. We have not refrained from reconsideration of a prior construction of the Constitution that has proved "unsound in principle and unworkable in practice." We think the *Roe* trimester framework falls into that category.
>
> In the first place, the rigid *Roe* framework is hardly consistent with the notion of a Constitution cast in general terms, as ours is, and usually speaking in general principles, as ours does. The key elements of the *Roe* framework — trimesters and viability — are not found in the text of the Constitution or in any place else one would expect to find a constitutional principle. Since the bounds of the inquiry are essentially indeterminate, the result has been a web of legal rules that have become increasingly intricate, resembling a code of regulations rather

than a body of constitutional doctrine. As Justice White has put it, the trimester framework has left this Court to serve as the country's "ex officio medical board with powers to approve or disapprove medical and operative practices and standards throughout the United States."

In the second place, we do not see why the State's interest in protecting potential human life should come into existence only at the point of viability, and that there should therefore be a rigid line allowing state regulation after viability but prohibiting it before viability. The dissenters in *Thornburgh* [would] have recognized this fact by positing against the "fundamental right" recognized in *Roe* the State's "compelling interest" in protecting potential human life throughout pregnancy. "[T]he State's interest, if compelling after viability, is equally compelling before viability."

Nevertheless, the plurality rejected the request of some appellants and amici to flatly overrule *Roe*. Justice Scalia, concurring, suggested outright that he "would overrule Roe v. Wade." Justice Blackmun, who also concurred, suggested that "Today, Roe v. Wade, and the fundamental constitutional right of women to decide whether to terminate a pregnancy, survive but are not secure."

The *Webster* decision was widely cited as an indication that the *Roe* ruling was in a terminal condition. Doctrinal turmoil was evidenced further in Hodgson v. Minnesota, when the Court invalidated a two-parent notice requirement for minors 48 hours prior to undergoing an abortion but upheld it when coupled with a judicial bypass requirement. These outcomes were reached pursuant to five-to-four votes, with Justice O'Connor being the pivotal figure with respect to both outcome and rationale. From her perspective, the two-parent constitutional requirement imposed an "undue burden" particularly to the extent that only half of the state's minors lived with both biological parents. For a majority of the judges, the question was whether the notification requirement "reasonably" promoted a legitimate state interest. This terminology, reminiscent of rational basis analysis, compounded the uncertainty with respect to the standard of review governing abortion regulations. In Planned Parenthood of Southeastern Pennsylvania v. Casey, the Court reviewed statutory provisions for informed consent, a 24-hour waiting period, parental consent with a judicial bypass option, spousal notification, and reporting requirements for abortion providers. Although affirming that a woman's liberty to elect an abortion is fundamental, the Court effectively previewed the dismantling of *Roe*'s trimester regime.

∾ PROBLEMS ∾

1. *Must the State Pay for Abortions for Indigent Women?* *Roe* makes clear that the "right of personal privacy includes the abortion decision" and that such "fundamental rights" can only be overridden by a "compelling state interest." If a woman is too poor to pay for her own abortion, does her "fundamental right" include the right to state funding for an abortion? Should it matter that the state discriminates between abortion and childbirth by paying for the costs of childbirth but not the costs of abortion? Consider the following arguments regarding the validity of the state denial:

A. The stark reality for too many indigent pregnant women is that indigency makes access to competent licensed physicians not merely "difficult" but "impossible." The State's denial of funding, therefore, operates to coerce indigent pregnant women to bear children they would not otherwise choose to have, and this coercion can only operate upon the poor, who are uniquely the victims of this form of financial pressure.

B. Roe v. Wade and cases following it hold that an area of privacy invulnerable to the State's intrusion surrounds the decision of a pregnant woman whether or not to carry her pregnancy to term. The Connecticut scheme clearly infringes upon that area of privacy by bringing financial pressures on indigent women that force them to bear children they would not otherwise have.

C. An indigent woman who desires an abortion suffers no disadvantage as a consequence of Connecticut's decision to fund childbirth; she continues as before to be dependent on private sources for the service she desires. The State may have made childbirth a more attractive alternative, thereby influencing the woman's decision, but it has imposed no restriction on access to abortions that was not already there. The indigency that may make it difficult and in some cases, perhaps, impossible for some women to have abortions is neither created nor in any way affected by the Connecticut regulation.

D. There is a basic difference between direct state interference with a protected activity and state encouragement of an alternative activity consonant with legislative policy. Constitutional concerns are greatest when the State attempts to impose its will by force of law; the State's power to encourage actions deemed to be in the public interest is necessarily far broader.

E. The State unquestionably has a "strong and legitimate interest in encouraging normal childbirth," an interest honored over the centuries. Nor can there be any question that the Connecticut regulation rationally furthers that interest. The medical costs associated with childbirth are substantial, and have increased significantly in recent years. [S]uch costs are significantly greater than those normally associated with elective abortions during the first trimester. The subsidizing of costs incident to childbirth is a rational means of encouraging childbirth.

F. We certainly are not unsympathetic to the plight of an indigent woman who desires an abortion, but "the Constitution does not provide judicial remedies for every social and economic ill." Our cases uniformly have accorded the States a wider latitude in choosing among competing demands for limited public funds.

Which arguments are more persuasive? *See* Maher v. Roe, 432 U.S. 464 (1977).

2. *Denying Abortion Funding.* Instead of a state law that denies funding for abortions, suppose that a federal statute precludes the medical program for indigents (Medicaid) from providing coverage for abortions. Is it permissible for the federal government to provide a general program of medical care for indigents, but to deny coverage even for medically necessary abortions? Does protection of the woman's health, coupled with the woman's constitutional right to have an abortion, justify forcing the state to pay for a medically necessary abortion? Is it enough to say that the denial of Medicaid coverage leaves an indigent woman with at least the same range of choice in deciding whether to obtain a medically necessary abortion as she would have had if Congress had chosen to subsidize no health care costs at all? Which arguments hold greater sway? *See* Harris v. McRae, 448 U.S. 297 (1980).

3. *Moral Objections.* In evaluating the preceding problem, what weight (if any) would you attach to the fact that the chief sponsor of the federal legislation flatly

stated that a motivating consideration behind the law was the fact that he regarded abortion as a means for killing innocent pre-born children. Is moral objectionability a basis for restricting abortion funding? How should the government lawyer respond to arguments that the amendment is fatally flawed?

Planned Parenthood of Southeastern Pennsylvania v. Casey

410 U.S. 113 (1993)

Justice O'CONNOR, Justice KENNEDY, and Justice SOUTER announced the judgment of the Court and delivered the opinion of the Court with respect to Parts I, II, III, V-A, V-C, and VI, an opinion with respect to Part V-E, in which Justice STEVENS joins, and an opinion with respect to Parts IV, V-B, and V-D.

I

[19] years after our holding that the Constitution protects a woman's right to terminate her pregnancy in its early stages, Roe v. Wade, that definition of liberty is still questioned. [T]he United States, as it has done in five other cases in the last decade, again asks us to overrule *Roe*.

At issue in these cases are five provisions of the Pennsylvania Abortion Control Act of 1982, as amended in 1988 and 1989. [We] acknowledge that our decisions after *Roe* cast doubt upon the meaning and reach of its holding. Further, the Chief Justice admits that he would overrule the central holding of *Roe* and adopt the rational relationship test as the sole criterion of constitutionality. State and federal courts as well as legislatures throughout the Union must have guidance as they seek to address this subject in conformance with the Constitution. Given these premises, we find it imperative to review once more the principles that define the rights of the woman and the legitimate authority of the State respecting the termination of pregnancies by abortion procedures.

After considering the fundamental constitutional questions resolved by *Roe*, principles of institutional integrity, and the rule of *stare decisis,* we are led to conclude this: the essential holding of Roe v. Wade should be retained and once again reaffirmed. [*Roe*'s] essential holding [has] three parts. First is a recognition of the right of the woman to choose to have an abortion before viability and to obtain it without undue interference from the State. Before viability, the State's interests are not strong enough to support a prohibition of abortion or the imposition of a substantial obstacle to the woman's effective right to elect the procedure. Second is a confirmation of the State's power to restrict abortions after fetal viability, if the law contains exceptions for pregnancies which endanger the woman's life or health. And third is the principle that the State has legitimate interests from the outset of the pregnancy in protecting the health of the woman and the life of the fetus that may become a child. These principles do not contradict one another; and we adhere to each.

II

Constitutional protection of the woman's decision to terminate her pregnancy derives from the Due Process Clause of the Fourteenth Amendment. It declares that no State shall "deprive any person of life, liberty, or property, without due process of law." The controlling word in the cases before us is "liberty." Although a literal reading of the Clause might suggest that it governs only the procedures by which a State may deprive persons of liberty, for at least 105 years, the Clause has been understood to contain a substantive component as well, one "barring certain government actions regardless of the fairness of the procedures used to implement them." ["Thus] all fundamental rights comprised within the term liberty are protected by the Federal Constitution from invasion by the States."

[The] most familiar of the substantive liberties protected by the Fourteenth Amendment are those recognized by the Bill of Rights. We have held that the Due Process Clause of the Fourteenth Amendment incorporates most of the Bill of Rights against the States. It is tempting, as a means of curbing the discretion of federal judges, to suppose that liberty encompasses no more than those rights already guaranteed to the individual against federal interference by the express provisions of the first eight Amendments to the Constitution. But of course this Court has never accepted that view.

It is also tempting [to] suppose that the Due Process Clause protects only those practices, defined at the most specific level, that were protected against government interference by other rules of law when the Fourteenth Amendment was ratified. But such a view would be inconsistent with our law. It is a promise of the Constitution that there is a realm of personal liberty which the government may not enter. Neither the Bill of Rights nor the specific practices of States at the time of the adoption of the Fourteenth Amendment marks the outer limits of the substantive sphere of liberty which the Fourteenth Amendment protects.

[The] inescapable fact is that adjudication of substantive due process claims may call upon the Court in interpreting the Constitution to exercise that same capacity which by tradition courts always have exercised: reasoned judgment. Its boundaries are not susceptible of expression as a simple rule. That does not mean we are free to invalidate state policy choices with which we disagree; yet neither does it permit us to shrink from the duties of our office.

Men and women of good conscience can disagree, and we suppose some always shall disagree, about the profound moral and spiritual implications of terminating a pregnancy, even in its earliest stage. Some of us as individuals find abortion offensive to our most basic principles of morality, but that cannot control our decision. Our obligation is to define the liberty of all, not to mandate our own moral code. The underlying constitutional issue is whether the State can resolve these philosophic questions in such a definitive way that a woman lacks all choice in the matter, except perhaps in those rare circumstances in which the pregnancy is itself a danger to her own life or health, or is the result of rape or incest.

Our law affords constitutional protection to personal decisions relating to marriage, procreation, contraception, family relationships, child rearing, and education. . . . These matters, involving the most intimate and personal choices a person may make in a lifetime, choices central to personal dignity and autonomy, are central to the liberty protected by the Fourteenth Amendment. At the heart of liberty is the right to define one's own concept of existence, of meaning, of the universe, and of the mystery of human life. Beliefs about these matters could not define the attributes of personhood were they formed under compulsion of the State.

These considerations begin our analysis of the woman's interest in terminating her pregnancy but cannot end it, for this reason: though the abortion decision may originate within the zone of conscience and belief, it is more than a philosophic exercise. Abortion is a unique act. It is an act fraught with consequences for others: for the woman who must live with the implications of her decision; for the persons who perform and assist in the procedure; for the spouse, family, and society which must confront the knowledge that these procedures exist, procedures some deem nothing short of an act of violence against innocent human life; and, depending on one's beliefs, for the life or potential life that is aborted. Though abortion is conduct, it does not follow that the State is entitled to proscribe it in all instances. That is because the liberty of the woman is at stake in a sense unique to the human condition and so unique to the law. The mother who carries a child to full term is subject to anxieties, to physical constraints, to pain that only she must bear. That these sacrifices have from the beginning of the human race been endured by woman with a pride that ennobles her in the eyes of others and gives to the infant a bond of love cannot alone be grounds for the State to insist she make the sacrifice. Her suffering is too intimate and personal for the State to insist, without more, upon its own vision of the woman's role, however dominant that vision has been in the course of our history and our culture. The destiny of the woman must be shaped to a large extent on her own conception of her spiritual imperatives and her place in society.

[T]he reservations any of us may have in reaffirming the central holding of *Roe* are outweighed by the explication of individual liberty [combined with] *stare decisis*. . . .

III

[For] two decades of economic and social developments, people have organized intimate relationships and made choices that define their views of themselves and their places in society, in reliance on the availability of abortion in the event that contraception should fail. The ability of women to participate equally in the economic and social life of the Nation has been facilitated by their ability to control their reproductive lives. The Constitution serves human values, and while the effect of reliance on *Roe* cannot be exactly measured, neither can the certain cost of overruling *Roe* for people who have ordered their thinking and living around that case be dismissed. . . .

We have seen how time has overtaken some of *Roe*'s factual assumptions: advances in maternal health care allow for abortions safe to the mother later in pregnancy than was true in 1973, and advances in neonatal care have advanced viability to a point somewhat earlier. But these facts [have] no bearing on the validity of *Roe*'s central holding, that viability marks the earliest point at which the State's interest in fetal life is constitutionally adequate to justify a legislative ban on nontherapeutic abortions. The soundness or unsoundness of that constitutional judgment in no sense turns on whether viability occurs at approximately 28 weeks, as was usual at the time of *Roe,* at 23 to 24 weeks, as it sometimes does today, or at some moment even slightly earlier in pregnancy, as it may if fetal respiratory capacity can somehow be enhanced in the future. Whenever it may occur, the attainment of viability may continue to serve as the critical fact, just as it has done since *Roe* was decided; which is to say that no change in *Roe*'s factual underpinning has left its central holding obsolete, and none supports an argument for overruling it. . . .

An entire generation has come of age free to assume *Roe*'s concept of liberty in defining the capacity of women to act in society, and to make reproductive decisions; no erosion of principle going to liberty or personal autonomy has left *Roe*'s central holding a doctrinal remnant. . . . [The] stronger argument is for affirming *Roe*'s central holding[,] not for overruling it.

[The] Court's power lies [in] its legitimacy, a product of substance and perception that shows itself in the people's acceptance of the Judiciary as fit to determine what the Nation's law means and to declare what it demands. . . . The underlying substance of this legitimacy is of course the warrant for the Court's decisions in the Constitution and the lesser sources of legal principle on which the Court draws. [A] decision without principled justification would be no judicial act at all. [E]ven when justification is furnished[,] something more is required. . . . The Court must take care to speak and act in ways that allow people to accept its decisions on the terms the Court claims for them, as grounded truly in principle, not as compromises with social and political pressures having, as such, no bearing on the principled choices that the Court is obliged to make. Thus, the Court's legitimacy depends on making legally principled decisions under circumstances in which their principled character is sufficiently plausible to be accepted by the Nation.

[Where], in the performance of its judicial duties, the Court decides a case in such a way as to resolve the sort of intensely divisive controversy reflected in *Roe*[,] only the most convincing justification under accepted standards of precedent could suffice to demonstrate that a later decision overruling the first was anything but a surrender to political pressure, and an unjustified repudiation of the principle on which the Court staked its authority in the first instance. [P]ressure to overrule [*Roe*], like pressure to retain it, has grown [more] intense. A decision to overrule *Roe*'s essential holding under the existing circumstances would address error, if error there was, at the cost of both profound and unnecessary damage to the Court's legitimacy, and to the Nation's commitment to the rule of law. It is therefore imperative to adhere to the essence of *Roe*'s original decision, and we do so today.

IV

[M]uch criticism has been directed at *Roe,* a criticism that always inheres when the Court draws a specific rule from what in the Constitution is but a general standard. We conclude, however, that the urgent claims of the woman to retain the ultimate control over her destiny and her body, claims implicit in the meaning of liberty, require us to perform that function. Liberty must not be extinguished for want of a line that is clear. And it falls to us to give some real substance to the woman's liberty to determine whether to carry her pregnancy to full term.

We conclude the line should be drawn at viability, so that before that time the woman has a right to choose to terminate her pregnancy. We adhere to this principle for two reasons. First, as we have said, is the doctrine of *stare decisis.* Any judicial act of line-drawing may seem somewhat arbitrary, but *Roe* was a reasoned statement, elaborated with great care. [The] second reason is that the concept of viability, as we noted in *Roe,* is the time at which there is a realistic possibility of maintaining and nourishing a life outside the womb, so that the independent existence of the second life can in reason and all fairness be the object of state protection that now overrides the rights of the woman. [The] woman's right to terminate her pregnancy before viability is the most central principle of *Roe.* It is a rule of law and a component of liberty we cannot renounce.

[On] the other side of the equation is the interest of the State in the protection of potential life. [*Roe*] recognized the State's "important and legitimate interest in protecting the potentiality of human life." [S]ubsequent cases [decided] that any regulation touching upon the abortion decision must survive strict scrutiny, to be sustained only if drawn in narrow terms to further a compelling state interest. Not all of the[se] cases [can] be reconciled with the holding in *Roe* itself. . . . In resolving this tension, we choose to rely upon *Roe,* as against the later cases.

We reject the trimester framework, which we do not consider to be part of the essential holding of *Roe.* Measures aimed at ensuring that a woman's choice contemplates the consequences for the fetus do not necessarily interfere with the right recognized in *Roe,* although those measures have been found to be inconsistent with the rigid trimester framework announced in that case. A logical reading of the central holding in *Roe* itself, and a necessary reconciliation of the liberty of the woman and the interest of the State in promoting prenatal life, require [that] we abandon the trimester framework as a rigid prohibition on all previability regulation aimed at the protection of fetal life. The trimester framework suffers from these basic flaws: in its formulation it misconceives the nature of the pregnant woman's interest; and in practice it undervalues the State's interest in potential life, as recognized in *Roe.*

[N]ot every law which makes a right more difficult to exercise is, *ipso facto,* an infringement of that right. . . . Numerous forms of state regulation might have the incidental effect of increasing the cost or decreasing the availability of medical care, whether for abortion or any other medical procedure. . . . Only where state regulation imposes an undue burden on a woman's ability to make this decision does the power of the State reach into the heart of the liberty protected by the Due Process Clause.

[Not] all governmental intrusion is of necessity unwarranted; and that brings us to the other basic flaw in the trimester framework: even in *Roe*'s terms, in practice it undervalues the State's interest in the potential life within the woman. . . . *Roe* was express in its recognition of the State's "important and legitimate interests in preserving and protecting the health of the pregnant woman [and] in protecting the potentiality of human life." The trimester framework, however, does not fulfill *Roe*'s own promise that the State has an interest in protecting fetal life or potential life. [T]he undue burden standard is the appropriate means of reconciling the State's interest with the woman's constitutionally protected liberty. [A] statute which, while furthering the interest in potential life or some other valid state interest, has the effect of placing a substantial obstacle in the path of a woman's choice cannot be considered a permissible means of serving its legitimate ends. In our considered judgment, an undue burden is an unconstitutional burden. . . .

. . . We give this summary:

(a) To protect the central right recognized by Roe v. Wade while at the same time accommodating the State's profound interest in potential life, we will employ the undue burden analysis. . . . An undue burden exists, and therefore a provision of law is invalid, if its purpose or effect is to place a substantial obstacle in the path of a woman seeking an abortion before the fetus attains viability.

(b) We reject the rigid trimester framework of *Roe*. To promote the State's profound interest in potential life, throughout pregnancy the State may take measures to ensure that the woman's choice is informed, and measures designed to advance this interest will not be invalidated as long as their purpose is to persuade the woman to choose childbirth over abortion. These measures must not be an undue burden on the right.

(c) As with any medical procedure, the State may enact regulations to further the health or safety of a woman seeking an abortion. Unnecessary health regulations that have the purpose or effect of presenting a substantial obstacle to a woman seeking an abortion impose an undue burden on the right.

(d) [T]he undue burden analysis does not disturb the central holding of *Roe*, and we reaffirm that holding. [A] State may not prohibit any woman from making the ultimate decision to terminate her pregnancy before viability.

(e) We also reaffirm *Roe*'s holding that "subsequent to viability, the State in promoting its interest in the potentiality of human life may, if it chooses, regulate, and even proscribe, abortion except where it is necessary, in appropriate medical judgment, for the preservation of the life or health of the mother."

These principles control our assessment of the Pennsylvania statute. . . .

V

A

[W]e begin with the statute's definition of medical emergency. [A] medical emergency is that condition which, on the basis of the physician's good faith clinical judgment, so complicates the medical condition of a pregnant woman as to necessitate the immediate abortion of her pregnancy to avert her death or for which a delay will create serious risk of substantial and irreversible impairment of a major bodily function.

Petitioners argue that the definition [forecloses] the possibility of an immediate abortion despite some significant health risks. [While] the definition could be interpreted in an unconstitutional manner, the Court of Appeals construed the phrase "serious risk" [to] assure that compliance with its abortion regulations would not in any way "pose a significant threat to the life or health of a woman." [We] conclude that, as construed[,] the medical emergency definition imposes no undue burden on a woman's abortion right.

B

We next consider the informed consent requirement. Except in a medical emergency, the statute requires that at least 24 hours before performing an abortion a physician inform the woman of the nature of the procedure, the health risks of the abortion and of childbirth, and the "probable gestational age of the unborn child." The physician or a qualified nonphysician must inform the woman of the availability of printed materials published by the State describing the fetus and providing information about medical assistance for childbirth, information about child support from the father, and a list of agencies which provide adoption and other services as alternatives to abortion. An abortion may not be performed unless the woman certifies in writing that she has been informed of the availability of these printed materials and has been provided them if she chooses to view them.

[The] idea that important decisions will be more informed and deliberate if they follow some period of reflection does not strike us as unreasonable, particularly where the statute directs that important information become part of the background of the decision. The statute [permits] avoidance of the waiting period in the event of a medical emergency and the record [shows] that in the vast majority of cases, a 24-hour delay does not create any appreciable health risk. In theory, at least, the waiting period is a reasonable measure to implement the State's interest in protecting the life of the unborn, a measure that does not amount to an undue burden.

Whether the mandatory 24-hour waiting period [is] nonetheless invalid because [it] is a substantial obstacle to a woman's choice to terminate her pregnancy is a closer question. [The District Court found] that because of the distances many women must travel to reach an abortion provider, the practical effect will often be a delay of much more than a day because the waiting period requires that a woman seeking an abortion make at least two visits to the doctor. The District Court also found that in many instances this will increase the exposure of women seeking abortions to "the harassment and hostility of antiabortion protestors demonstrating outside a clinic." As a result, the District Court found that for those women who have the fewest financial resources, those who must travel long distances, and those who have difficulty explaining their whereabouts to husbands, employers, or others, the 24-hour waiting period will be "particularly burdensome." . . . These findings are troubling[,] but they do not demonstrate that the waiting period constitutes an undue burden. We do not doubt that [the] waiting period has the effect of "increasing the cost and risk of delay of abortions," but the District Court did not conclude that the increased costs and potential delays amount to substantial obstacles.

C

[The state] abortion law provides, except in cases of medical emergency, that no physician shall perform an abortion on a married woman without receiving a signed statement from the woman that she has notified her spouse that she is about to undergo an abortion. The woman has the option of providing an alternative signed statement certifying that her husband is not the man who impregnated her; that her husband could not be located; that the pregnancy is the result of spousal sexual assault which she has reported; or that the woman believes that notifying her husband will cause him or someone else to inflict bodily injury upon her. A physician who performs an abortion on a married woman without receiving the appropriate signed statement will have his or her license revoked, and is liable to the husband for damages.

   In well-functioning marriages, spouses discuss important intimate decisions such as whether to bear a child. But there are millions of women in this country who are the victims of regular physical and psychological abuse at the hands of their husbands. Should these women become pregnant, they [are] not exempt from [the] notification requirement. Many may fear devastating forms of psychological abuse from their husbands, including verbal harassment, threats of future violence, the destruction of possessions, physical confinement to the home, the withdrawal of financial support, or the disclosure of the abortion to family and friends. These methods of psychological abuse may act as even more of a deterrent to notification than the possibility of physical violence, but women who are the victims of the abuse are not exempt from [the] notification requirement. And many women who are pregnant as a result of sexual assaults by their husbands will be unable to avail themselves of the exception for spousal sexual assault, because the exception requires that the woman have notified law enforcement authorities within 90 days of the assault, and her husband will be notified of her report once an investigation begins. . . . The spousal notification requirement is thus likely to prevent a significant number of women from obtaining an abortion. . . . It is an undue burden, and therefore invalid. . . . Whether the prospect of notification itself deters such women from seeking abortions, or whether the husband, through physical force or psychological pressure or economic coercion, prevents his wife from obtaining an abortion until it is too late, the notice requirement will often be tantamount to the veto found unconstitutional in *Danforth*. . . .

D

[We] next consider the parental consent provision. Except in a medical emergency, an unemancipated young woman under 18 may not obtain an abortion unless she and one of her parents (or guardian) provides informed consent as defined above. If neither a parent nor a guardian provides consent, a court may authorize the performance of an abortion upon a determination that the young woman is mature and capable of giving informed consent and has in fact given her informed consent, or that an abortion would be in her best interests. . . . Our cases establish, and we reaffirm today, that a State may require a minor seeking an abortion to obtain the consent of a parent or guardian, provided that there is an adequate judicial bypass procedure.

E

Under the recordkeeping and reporting requirements of the statute, every facility which performs abortions is required to file a report stating its name and address as well as the name and address of any related entity, such as a controlling or subsidiary organization. In the case of state-funded institutions, the information becomes public.

For each abortion performed, a report must be filed identifying: the physician (and the second physician where required); the facility; the referring physician or agency; the woman's age; the number of prior pregnancies and prior abortions she has had; gestational age; the type of abortion procedure; the date of the abortion; whether there were any pre-existing medical conditions which would complicate pregnancy; medical complications with the abortion; where applicable, the basis for the determination that the abortion was medically necessary; the weight of the aborted fetus; and whether the woman was married, and if so, whether notice was provided or the basis for the failure to give notice. Every abortion facility must also file quarterly reports showing the number of abortions performed broken down by trimester. In all events, the identity of each woman who has had an abortion remains confidential.

[We have held] that record keeping and reporting provisions "that are reasonably directed to the preservation of maternal health and that properly respect a patient's confidentiality and privacy are permissible." [A]ll the provisions at issue here, except that relating to spousal notice, are constitutional. . . . The collection of information with respect to actual patients is a vital element of medical research. . . . Nor do we find that the requirements impose a substantial obstacle to a woman's choice. At most they might increase the cost of some abortions by a slight amount. [There is no showing that the increased cost has] become a substantial obstacle. . . .

VI

Our Constitution is a covenant running from the first generation of Americans to us and then to future generations. . . . We accept our responsibility not to retreat from interpreting the full meaning of the covenant in light of all of our precedents. We invoke it once again to define the freedom guaranteed by the Constitution's own promise, the promise of liberty.

Affirmed in part and reversed in part.

Justice STEVENS, concurring in part and dissenting in part.

[*Roe*] has been a "part of our law" for almost two decades. The societal costs of overruling *Roe* at this late date would be enormous. *Roe* is an integral part of a correct understanding of both the concept of liberty and the basic equality of men and women.

[The statute includes] sections requir[ing] a physician or counselor to provide the woman with a range of materials clearly designed to persuade her to choose not to undergo the abortion. While the Commonwealth is free to produce and disseminate such material, the Commonwealth may not inject such information into the woman's deliberations just as she is weighing such an important choice.

[Provisions] which require the physician to inform a woman of the nature and risks of the abortion procedure and the medical risks of carrying to term, are neutral requirements comparable to those imposed in other medical procedures. Those sections indicate no effort by the Commonwealth to influence the woman's choice in any way. If anything, such requirements enhance, rather than skew, the woman's decision-making. . . .

The 24-hour waiting period [raises] serious concerns. Such a requirement arguably furthers the Commonwealth's interests in two ways, neither of which is constitutionally permissible. . . . First, it may be argued that the 24-hour delay [is] likely to reduce the number of abortions, thus furthering the Commonwealth's interest in potential life. . . . The Commonwealth cannot further its interests by simply wearing down the ability of the pregnant woman to exercise her constitutional right. Second, [the] 24-hour delay furthers the Commonwealth's interest in ensuring that the woman's decision is informed and thoughtful. But there is no evidence that the mandated delay benefits women or that it is necessary to enable the physician to convey any relevant information to the patient. The mandatory delay thus appears to rest on outmoded and unacceptable assumptions about the decisionmaking capacity of women. . . .

[T]he delay requirement may be premised on the belief that the decision to terminate a pregnancy is presumptively wrong. . . . A woman who has, in the privacy of her thoughts and conscience, weighed the options and made her decision cannot be forced to reconsider all, simply because the State believes she has come to the wrong conclusion. . . . A woman who decides to terminate her pregnancy is entitled to the same respect as a woman who decides to carry the fetus to term. The mandatory waiting period denies women that equal respect.

[A] correct application of the "undue burden" standard leads to the same conclusion concerning the constitutionality of these requirements. . . . The

24-hour delay requirement fails both parts of this test. [T]he 24-hour delay [requirement] imposes [a severe burden] on many pregnant women [and] there is no evidence that such a delay serves a useful and legitimate purpose. [The] counseling provisions are similarly infirm. Whenever government commands private citizens to speak or to listen, careful review of the justification for that command is particularly appropriate. In these cases, the Pennsylvania statute directs that counselors provide women seeking abortions with information concerning alternatives to abortion, the availability of medical assistance benefits, and the possibility of child-support payments. . . . I conclude that the information requirements do not serve a useful purpose and thus constitute an unnecessary — and therefore undue — burden on the woman's constitutional liberty to decide to terminate her pregnancy. . . .

Justice BLACKMUN, concurring in part, concurring in the judgment in part, and dissenting in part.

I join Parts I, II, III, V-A, V-C, and VI of the joint opinion of Justices O'Connor, Kennedy, and Souter.

Three years ago, in *Webster,* four Members of this Court appeared poised to "cast into darkness the hopes and visions of every woman in this country" who had come to believe that the Constitution guaranteed her the right to reproductive choice. . . . But now, just when so many expected the darkness to fall, the flame has grown bright. [I] remain steadfast in my belief that the right to reproductive choice is entitled to the full protection afforded by this Court before *Webster*. And I fear for the darkness as four Justices anxiously await the single vote necessary to extinguish the light.

[T]he Constitution and decisions of this Court require that a State's abortion restrictions be subjected to the strictest judicial scrutiny. . . . Under this standard, the Pennsylvania statute's provisions requiring content-based counseling, a 24-hour delay, informed parental consent, and reporting of abortion-related information must be invalidated. [While] a State has "legitimate interests from the outset of the pregnancy in protecting the health of the woman and the life of the fetus that may become a child," legitimate interests are not enough. [T]he interests must be compelling. . . . *Roe*'s requirement of strict scrutiny as implemented through a trimester framework should not be disturbed. . . .

The 24-hour waiting period [could] lead to delays in excess of 24 hours, thus increasing health risks [and] would require two visits to the abortion provider, thereby increasing travel time, exposure to further harassment, and financial cost. [The] mandatory delay rests either on outmoded or unacceptable assumptions about the decision-making capacity of women or the belief that the decision to terminate the pregnancy is presumptively wrong. . . .

While the State has an interest in encouraging parental involvement in the minor's abortion decision, [the state law] is not narrowly drawn to serve that interest.

[T]he Pennsylvania statute requires every facility performing abortions to report its activities to the Commonwealth [including] the identities and medical judgment of physicians involved in abortions. [M]any physicians, particularly those who have previously discontinued performing abortions because of harassment, would refuse to refer patients to abortion clinics if their names were to appear on these reports. [T]he confidential reporting requirements are unconstitutional insofar as they require the name of the referring physician. . . .

The Chief Justice's criticism of *Roe* follows from his stunted conception of individual liberty. . . . In the Chief Justice's world, a woman considering whether to terminate a pregnancy is entitled to no more protection than adulterers, murderers, and so-called sexual deviates. Given The Chief Justice's exclusive reliance on tradition, people using contraceptives seem the next likely candidate for his list of outcasts.

Even more shocking than The Chief Justice's cramped notion of individual liberty is his complete omission of any discussion of the effects that compelled childbirth and motherhood have on women's lives. . . . The Chief Justice's view of the State's compelling interest in maternal health has less to do with health than it does with compelling women to be maternal.

The Chief Justice's narrow conception of individual liberty and *stare decisis* leads him to propose the same standard of review proposed by the plurality in *Webster*. "States may regulate abortion procedures in ways rationally related to a legitimate state interest." The Chief Justice then further weakens the test by providing an insurmountable requirement for facial challenges: Petitioners must "'show that no set of circumstances exists under which the [provision] would be valid.'" [W]e are reassured there is always the protection of the democratic process. While there is much to be praised about our democracy, our country since its founding has recognized that there are certain fundamental liberties that are not to be left to the whims of an election. A woman's right to reproductive choice is one of those fundamental liberties. [T]hat liberty need not seek refuge at the ballot box. . . .

I am 83 years old. I cannot remain on this Court forever, and when I do step down, the confirmation process for my successor well may focus on the issue before us today. That, I regret, may be exactly where the choice between the two worlds will be made.

Chief Justice REHNQUIST, with whom Justice WHITE, Justice SCALIA, and Justice THOMAS join, concurring in the judgment in part and dissenting in part.

[We] believe that *Roe* was wrongly decided, and that it can and should be overruled. . . . Although they reject the trimester framework that formed the underpinning of *Roe*, [the joint opinion adopts] a revised undue burden standard to analyze the challenged regulations. [S]uch an outcome is an unjustified constitutional compromise. . . .

Unlike marriage, procreation, and contraception, abortion "involves the purposeful termination of a potential life." The abortion decision must therefore "be recognized as *sui generis*, different in kind from the others that the Court has protected under the rubric of personal or family privacy and autonomy." [T]he decision to abort necessarily involves the destruction of a fetus.

Nor do the historical traditions of the American people support the view that the right to terminate one's pregnancy is "fundamental." The common law which we inherited from England made abortion after "quickening" an offense. At the time of the adoption of the Fourteenth Amendment, statutory prohibitions or restrictions on abortion were commonplace; in 1868, at least 28 of the then-37 States and 8 Territories had statutes banning or limiting abortion. By the turn of the century virtually every State had a law prohibiting or restricting abortion on its books. By the middle of the present century, a liberalization trend had set in. But 21 of the restrictive abortion laws in effect in 1868 were still in effect in 1973 when *Roe* was decided, and an overwhelming majority of the States prohibited abortion unless necessary to preserve the life or health of the mother. On this record, it can scarcely be said that any deeply rooted tradition of relatively unrestricted abortion in our history supported the classification of the right to abortion as "fundamental" under the Due Process Clause of the Fourteenth Amendment.

[B]oth in view of this history and of our decided cases dealing with substantive liberty under the Due Process Clause, [the] Court was mistaken in *Roe* when it classified a woman's decision to terminate her pregnancy as a "fundamental right" that could be abridged only in a manner which withstood "strict scrutiny." [The] Court in *Roe* reached too far when it analogized the right to abort a fetus to the rights involved in *Pierce, Meyer, Loving,* and *Griswold,* and thereby deemed the right to abortion fundamental. . . .

Instead of claiming that *Roe* was correct as a matter of original constitutional interpretation, the [joint opinion] contains an elaborate discussion of *stare decisis*. . . . *Roe* decided that a woman had a fundamental right to an abortion. The joint opinion rejects that view. *Roe* decided that abortion regulations were to be subjected to "strict scrutiny" and could be justified only in the light of "compelling state interests." The joint opinion rejects that view. *Roe* analyzed abortion regulation under a rigid trimester framework, a framework which has guided this Court's decisionmaking for 19 years. The joint opinion rejects that framework. . . . While purporting to adhere to precedent, the joint opinion instead revises it. *Roe* continues to exist, but only in the way a storefront on a western movie set exists: a mere facade to give the illusion of reality.

[A]uthentic principles of *stare decisis* do not require that any portion of the reasoning in *Roe* be kept intact. . . . It [is] our duty to reconsider constitutional interpretations that "depart from a proper understanding" of the Constitution. [T]he correct analysis is that set forth by the plurality opinion in *Webster*. A woman's interest in having an abortion is a form of liberty protected by the Due Process Clause, but States may regulate abortion procedures in ways rationally related to a legitimate state interest. [Each provision of the state law was found to be rationally related to a legitimate state interest.]

Justice SCALIA, with whom THE CHIEF JUSTICE, Justice WHITE, and Justice THOMAS join, concurring in the judgment in part and dissenting in part.

My views on this matter are unchanged from those I set forth [in] *Webster*. . . . The permissibility of abortion, and the limitations upon it, are to be resolved like most important questions in our democracy: by citizens trying to persuade one another and then voting. . . . A State's choice between two positions on which reasonable people can disagree is constitutional even when [it] intrudes upon a "liberty" in the absolute sense. [The issue is not] whether it is a liberty of great importance to many women. . . . The issue is whether it is a liberty protected by the Constitution of the United States. I am sure it is not. . . .

The ultimately standardless nature of the "undue burden" inquiry is a reflection of the underlying fact that the concept has no principled or coherent legal basis. . . .

Roe's mandate for abortion on demand destroyed the compromises of the past, rendered compromise impossible for the future, and required the entire issue to be resolved uniformly, at the national level. . . . *Roe* fanned into life an issue that has inflamed our national politics in general, and has obscured with its smoke the selection of Justices to this Court in particular, ever since. And by keeping us in the abortion-umpiring business, it is the perpetuation of that disruption, rather than of any *Pax Roeana,* that the Court's new majority decrees. . . .

[It] is particularly difficult [to] sit still for the Court's lengthy lecture upon the virtues of "constancy," of "remaining steadfast," and adhering to "principle." Among the five Justices who purportedly adhere to *Roe,* at most three agree upon the principle that constitutes adherence (the joint opinion's "undue burden" standard)—and that principle is inconsistent with *Roe.* To make matters worse, two of the three, in order thus to remain steadfast, had to abandon previously stated positions. It is beyond me how the Court expects these accommodations to be accepted "as grounded truly in principle, not as compromises with social and political pressures having, as such, no bearing on the principled choices that the Court is obliged to make." The only principle the Court "adheres" to, it seems to me, is the principle that the Court must be seen as standing by *Roe.* That is not a principle of law (which is what I thought the Court was talking about), but a principle of Realpolitik—and a wrong one at that.

[W]hether it would "subvert the Court's legitimacy" or not, the notion that we would decide a case differently from the way we otherwise would have in order to show that we can stand firm against public disapproval is frightening. It is a bad enough idea, even in the head of someone like me, who believes that the text of the Constitution, and our traditions, say what they say and there is no fiddling with them. But when it is in the mind of a Court that believes the Constitution has an evolving meaning, that the Ninth Amendment's reference to "other" rights is not a disclaimer, but a charter for action, and that the function of this Court is to "speak before all others for [the people's] constitutional ideals" unrestrained by meaningful text or tradition—then the notion that the Court must adhere to a decision for as long as the decision faces "great opposition" and the Court is "under fire" acquires a character of almost czarist arrogance. We are offended by these marchers who descend upon us, every year on the anniversary of *Roe,* to protest our saying that the Constitution requires what our society has never thought the Constitution requires. These people who refuse to be "tested by following" must be taught a lesson. We have no Cossacks, but at least we can stubbornly refuse to abandon an erroneous opinion that we might otherwise change—to show how little they intimidate us.

[I] am as distressed as the Court is [about] the "political pressure" directed to the Court: the marches, the mail, the protests aimed at inducing us to change our opinions. How upsetting it is, that so many of our citizens (good people, not law-less ones, on both sides of this abortion issue, and on various sides of other issues as well) think that we Justices should properly take into account their views, as though we were engaged not in ascertaining an objective law but in determining some kind of social consensus. The Court would profit, I think, from giving less attention to the fact of this distressing phenomenon, and more attention to the cause of it. That cause permeates today's opinion: a new mode of constitutional adjudication that relies not upon text and traditional practice to determine the law, but upon what the Court calls "reasoned judgment," which turns out to be nothing but philosophical predilection and moral intuition. All manner of "lib-erties," the Court tells us, inhere in the Constitution and are enforceable by this Court — not just those mentioned in the text or established in the traditions of our society. Why even the Ninth Amendment — which says only that "the enu-meration in the Constitution, of certain rights, shall not be construed to deny or disparage others retained by the people" — is, despite our contrary understand-ing for almost 200 years, a literally boundless source of additional, unnamed, unhinted-at "rights," definable and enforceable by us, through "reasoned judgment."

[As] long as this Court thought (and the people thought) that we Justices were doing essentially lawyers' work up here — reading text and discerning our society's traditional understanding of that text — the public pretty much left us alone. Texts and traditions are facts to study, not convictions to demonstrate about. But if [our] pronouncement of constitutional law rests primarily on value judgments, then a free and intelligent people's attitude towards us can be expected to be (ought to be) quite different. The people know that their value judgments are quite as good as those taught in any law school — maybe better. If, indeed, the "liberties" protected by the Constitution are, as the Court says, unde-fined and unbounded, then the people should demonstrate, to protest that we do not implement their values instead of ours. Not only that, but confirmation hear-ings for new Justices should deteriorate into question-and-answer sessions in which Senators go through a list of their constituents' most favored and most dis-favored alleged constitutional rights, and seek the nominee's commitment to support or oppose them. Value judgments, after all, should be voted on, not dic-tated; and if our Constitution has somehow accidently committed them to the Supreme Court, at least we can have a sort of plebiscite each time a new nominee to that body is put forward. Justice Blackmun not only regards this prospect with equanimity, he solicits it. . . .

[B]y foreclosing all democratic outlet for the deep passions this issue arouses, by banishing the issue from the political forum that gives all participants, even the losers, the satisfaction of a fair hearing and an honest fight, by continuing the imposition of a rigid national rule instead of allowing for regional differences, the Court merely prolongs and intensifies the anguish. . . . We should get out of this area, where we have no right to be, and where we do neither ourselves nor the country any good by remaining.

Note: Undue Burdens

Although propounded by three justices in *Casey,* the undue burden test has gained traction with a majority of the Court. In Mazurek v. Armstrong, 520 U.S. 968 (1997), the Court reviewed a state law limiting the performance of abortions to licensed physicians. The law was upheld on grounds that it did not impose a substantial obstacle to obtaining an abortion. Criticism of the undue burden standard focuses largely on its ad hoc nature, which critics believe reduces it to an exercise in value selection and judgment. From their perspective, the undue burden test replicates the evils of *Lochnerism* and correlates outputs to the unpredictable perspectives of individual justices. Although differences were evident with respect to what constituted an undue burden, a majority of the Court in Stenberg v. Carhart determined that a state law prohibiting partial birth abortions created substantial obstacles to a woman's freedom to obtain an abortion.

∾ PROBLEM: THE ABORTION FORM ∾

Congress passed a law, 21 U.S.C. §1802, that states: "(A) all individuals obtaining an abortion must sign a form indicating they 1) recognize the importance of such a decision and 2) are having the abortion only because it is reasonably necessary and beyond mere convenience." Is this law constitutional?

Stenberg v. Carhart
530 U.S. 914 (2000)

Justice BREYER delivered the opinion of the Court.

We again consider the right to an abortion. We understand the controversial nature of the problem. Millions of Americans believe that life begins at conception and consequently that an abortion is akin to causing the death of an innocent child; they recoil at the thought of a law that would permit it. Other millions fear that a law that forbids abortion would condemn many American women to lives that lack dignity, depriving them of equal liberty and leading those with least resources to undergo illegal abortions with the attendant risks of death and suffering. Taking account of these virtually irreconcilable points of view, aware that constitutional law must govern a society whose different members sincerely hold directly opposing views, and considering the matter in light of the Constitution's guarantees of fundamental individual liberty, this Court, in the course of a generation, has determined and then redetermined that the Constitution offers basic protection to the woman's right to choose. We shall not revisit those legal principles. Rather, we apply them to the circumstances of this case.

Three established principles determine the issue before us. . . . First, before "viability [the] woman has a right to choose to terminate her pregnancy." . . . Second, "a law designed to further the State's interest in fetal life which imposes an undue burden on the woman's decision before fetal viability" is unconstitutional. An "undue burden [is] shorthand for the conclusion that a state regulation has the purpose or effect of placing a substantial obstacle in the path of a woman seeking an abortion of a nonviable fetus." . . . Third, "'subsequent to viability, the State in promoting its interest in the potentiality of human life may, if it chooses, regulate, and even proscribe, abortion except where it is necessary, in appropriate medical judgment, for the preservation of the life or health of the mother.'"

We apply these principles to a Nebraska law banning "partial birth abortion." The statute reads as follows:

> No partial birth abortion shall be performed in this state, unless such procedure is necessary to save the life of the mother whose life is endangered by a physical disorder, physical illness, or physical injury, including a life-endangering physical condition caused by or arising from the pregnancy itself.

The statute defines "partial birth abortion" as "an abortion procedure in which the person performing the abortion partially delivers vaginally a living unborn child before killing the unborn child and completing the delivery."

[The Nebraska statute,] making criminal the performance of a "partial birth abortion," violates the Federal Constitution [for] at least two independent reasons. First, the law lacks any exception "'for the preservation of [the] health of the mother.'" Second, it "imposes an undue burden on a woman's ability" to choose a D&E abortion, thereby unduly burdening the right to choose abortion itself.

The *Casey* joint opinion reiterated what the Court held in *Roe;* that "subsequent to viability, the State in promoting its interest in the potentiality of human life may, if it chooses, regulate, and even proscribe, abortion except where it is necessary, in appropriate medical judgment, for the preservation of the life or health of the mother."

The fact that Nebraska's law applies both pre- and postviability aggravates the constitutional problem presented. The State's interest in regulating abortion previability is considerably weaker than postviability. Since the law requires a health exception in order to validate even a postviability abortion regulation, it at a minimum requires the same in respect to previability regulation.

The quoted standard also depends on the state regulations "promoting [the State's] interest in the potentiality of human life." The Nebraska law, of course, does not directly further an interest "in the potentiality of human life" by saving the fetus in question from destruction, as it regulates only a method of performing abortion. Nebraska describes its interests differently. It says the law "'shows concern for the life of the unborn,'" "prevents cruelty to partially born children," and "preserves the integrity of the medical profession." But we cannot see how the interest-related differences could make any difference to the question at hand, namely, the application of the "health" requirement.

Consequently, the governing standard requires an exception "where it is necessary, in appropriate medical judgment for the preservation of the life or health of the mother," for this Court has made clear that a State may promote but not endanger a woman's health when it regulates the methods of abortion.

Justice Thomas says that the cases just cited limit this principle to situations where the pregnancy itself creates a threat to health. He is wrong. The cited cases, reaffirmed in *Casey*, recognize that a State cannot subject women's health to significant risks both in that context, and also where state regulations force women to use riskier methods of abortion. Our cases have repeatedly invalidated statutes that in the process of regulating the methods of abortion, imposed significant health risks. They make clear that a risk to a women's health is the same whether it happens to arise from regulating a particular method of abortion, or from barring abortion entirely. Our holding does not go beyond those cases, as ratified in *Casey*. . . .

Our earlier discussion of the D&E procedure shows that it falls within the statutory prohibition. The statute forbids "deliberately and intentionally delivering into the vagina a living unborn child, or a substantial portion thereof, for the purpose of performing a procedure that the person performing such procedure knows will kill the unborn child." We do not understand how one could distinguish, using this language, between D&E (where a foot or arm is drawn through the cervix) and D&X (where the body up to the head is drawn through the cervix). Evidence before the trial court makes clear that D&E will often involve a physician pulling a "substantial portion" of a still living fetus, say, an arm or leg, into the vagina prior to the death of the fetus. Indeed D&E involves dismemberment that commonly occurs only when the fetus meets resistance that restricts the motion of the fetus: "The dismemberment occurs between the traction of [the] instrument and the counter-traction of the internal os of the cervix." And these events often do not occur until after a portion of a living fetus has been pulled into the vagina.

Even if the statute's basic aim is to ban D&X, its language makes clear that it also covers a much broader category of procedures. The language does not track the medical differences between D&E and D&X — though it would have been a simple matter, for example, to provide an exception for the performance of D&E and other abortion procedures. Nor does the statute anywhere suggest that its application turns on whether a portion of the fetus' body is drawn into the vagina as part of a process to extract an intact fetus after collapsing the head as opposed to a process that would dismember the fetus. Thus, the dissenters' argument that the law was generally intended to bar D&X can be both correct and irrelevant. The relevant question is not whether the legislature wanted to ban D&X; it is whether the law was intended to apply only to D&X. The plain language covers both procedures.

[The] Nebraska State Attorney General argues that the statute does differentiate between the two procedures. He says that the statutory words "substantial portion" mean "the child up to the head." He consequently denies the statute's application where the physician introduces into the birth canal a fetal arm or leg or anything less than the entire fetal body. [O]ur precedent warns against accepting as "authoritative" an Attorney General's interpretation of state law when "the Attorney General does not bind the state courts or local law enforcement authorities." [S]ome present prosecutors and future Attorneys General may choose to pursue physicians who use D&E procedures, the most commonly used method for performing previability second trimester abortions. All those who perform abortion procedures using that method must fear prosecution, conviction, and imprisonment. The result is an undue burden upon a woman's right to make an abortion decision. We must consequently find the statute unconstitutional.

Justice STEVENS, with whom Justice GINSBURG joins, concurring.

Although much ink is spilled today describing the gruesome nature of late-term abortion procedures, that rhetoric does not provide me a reason to believe that the procedure Nebraska here claims it seeks to ban is more brutal, more gruesome, or less respectful of "potential life" than the equally gruesome procedure Nebraska claims it still allows. . . . [T]he notion that either of these two equally gruesome procedures performed at this late stage of gestation is more akin to infanticide than the other, or that the State furthers any legitimate interest by banning one but not the other, is simply irrational.

Justice O'CONNOR, concurring.

[I] agree that Nebraska's statute cannot be reconciled with our decision in *Casey,* and is therefore unconstitutional. [T]he Nebraska statute [lacks] an exception for those instances when the banned procedure is necessary to preserve the health of the mother [and] imposes an undue burden on a woman's right to choose to terminate her pregnancy before viability. Nebraska's ban [also] covers [the] dilation and evacuation (D&E) procedure. . . . [A] ban on partial-birth abortion that only proscribed the D&X method of abortion and that included an exception to preserve the life and health of the mother would be constitutional in my view.

Justice GINSBURG, with whom Justice STEVENS joins, concurring.

[A] state regulation that "has the purpose or effect of placing a substantial obstacle in the path of a woman seeking an abortion of a nonviable fetus" violates the Constitution. Such an obstacle exists if the State stops a woman from choosing the procedure her doctor "reasonably believes will best protect the woman in [the] exercise of [her] constitutional liberty." . . .

Chief Justice REHNQUIST, dissenting.

I did not join the joint opinion in *Casey* and continue to believe that case is wrongly decided. Despite my disagreement with the opinion, [I] believe Justice Kennedy and Justice Thomas have correctly applied *Casey's* principles and join their dissenting opinions.

Justice SCALIA, dissenting.

I am optimistic enough to believe that, one day, Stenberg v. Carhart will be assigned its rightful place in the history of this Court's jurisprudence beside *Korematsu* and *Dred Scott.* The method of killing a human child — one cannot even accurately say an entirely unborn human child — proscribed by this statute is so horrible that the most clinical description of it evokes a shudder of revulsion. And the Court must know (as most state legislatures banning this procedure have concluded) that demanding a "health exception" — which requires the abortionist to assure himself that, in his expert medical judgment, this method is, in the case at

702 9. Substantive Due Process: Modern Fundamental Rights

hand, marginally safer than others (how can one prove the contrary beyond a reasonable doubt?) — is to give live-birth abortion free rein. The notion that the Constitution of the United States, designed, among other things, "to establish Justice, insure domestic Tranquility, . . . and secure the Blessings of Liberty to ourselves and our Posterity," prohibits the States from simply banning this visibly brutal means of eliminating our half-born posterity is quite simply absurd. . . .

[T]he Court [invalidates] this humane [law because] it fails to allow an exception for the situation in which the abortionist believes that this live-birth method of destroying the child might be safer for the woman. [T]oday's decision is an "unprecedented expansion" of our prior cases, "is not mandated" by *Casey's* "undue burden" test, and can even be called (though this pushes me to the limit of my belief) "obviously irreconcilable with *Casey's* explication of what its undue-burden standard requires." But I never put much stock in *Casey's* explication of the inexplicable. In the last analysis, my judgment that *Casey* does not support today's tragic result can be traced to the fact that what I consider to be an "undue burden" is different from what the majority considers to be an "undue burden" — a conclusion that can not be demonstrated true or false by factual inquiry or legal reasoning. It is a value judgment, dependent upon how much one respects (or believes society ought to respect) the life of a partially delivered fetus, and how much one respects (or believes society ought to respect) the freedom of the woman who gave it life to kill it. Evidently, the five Justices in today's majority value the former less, or the latter more, (or both), than the four of us in dissent. Case closed. There is no cause for anyone who believes in *Casey* to feel betrayed by this outcome. It has been arrived at by precisely the process *Casey* promised — a democratic vote by nine lawyers, not on the question whether the text of the Constitution has anything to say about this subject (it obviously does not); nor even on the question (also appropriate for lawyers) whether the legal traditions of the American people would have sustained such a limitation upon abortion (they obviously would); but upon the pure policy question whether this limitation upon abortion is "undue" — i.e., goes too far.

[T]he "undue burden" test [created] a standard that was "as doubtful in application as it is unprincipled in origin," "hopelessly unworkable in practice," [and] "ultimately standardless." Today's decision is the proof. [I]t is really quite impossible for us dissenters to contend that the majority is wrong on the law. . . . The most that we can honestly say is that we disagree with the majority on their policy-judgment-couched-as-law. And those who believe that a 5-to-4 vote on a policy matter by unelected lawyers should not overcome the judgment of 30 state legislatures have a problem, not with the application of *Casey*, but with its existence. *Casey* must be overruled.

. . . Today's decision, that the Constitution of the United States prevents the prohibition of a horrible mode of abortion, will be greeted by a firestorm of criticism — as well it should. I cannot understand why those who acknowledge that, in the opening words of Justice O'Connor's concurrence, "the issue of abortion is one of the most contentious and controversial in contemporary American society," persist in the belief that this Court, armed with neither constitutional text nor accepted tradition, can resolve that contention and controversy rather than be consumed by it. If only for the sake of its own preservation, the Court should return this matter to the people — where the Constitution, by its silence on the subject, left it — and let them decide, State by State, whether this practice should be allowed. *Casey* must be overruled.

Justice KENNEDY, with whom THE CHIEF JUSTICE joins, dissenting.

[When] the Court reaffirmed the essential holding of *Roe,* a central premise was that the States retain a critical and legitimate role in legislating on the subject of abortion, as limited by the woman's right the Court restated and again guaranteed. The political processes of the State are not to be foreclosed from enacting laws to promote the life of the unborn and to ensure respect for all human life and its potential. The State's constitutional authority is a vital means for citizens to address these grave and serious issues, as they must if we are to progress in knowledge and understanding and in the attainment of some degree of consensus.

The Court's decision today, in my submission, repudiates this understanding by invalidating a statute advancing critical state interests, even though the law denies no woman the right to choose an abortion and places no undue burden upon the right. The legislation is well within the State's competence to enact. . . . States may take sides in the abortion debate and come down on the side of life, even life in the unborn. . . . States also have an interest in forbidding medical procedures which, in the State's reasonable determination, might cause the medical profession or society as a whole to become insensitive, even disdainful, to life, including life in the human fetus. . . . A State may take measures to ensure the medical profession and its members are viewed as healers, sustained by a compassionate and rigorous ethic and cognizant of the dignity and value of human life, even life which cannot survive without the assistance of others.

[Some argue that] the D&E method, which Nebraska claims to be beyond its intent to regulate, can still be used to abort a fetus and is no less dehumanizing than the D&X method. . . . The issue is not whether members of the judiciary can see a difference between the two procedures. It is whether Nebraska can. The Court's refusal to recognize Nebraska's right to declare a moral difference between the procedure is a dispiriting disclosure of the illogic and illegitimacy of the Court's approach to the entire case.

Nebraska was entitled to find the existence of a consequential moral difference between the procedures. . . . The Court is without authority to second-guess this conclusion. . . . [It] ill-serves the Court, its institutional position, and the constitutional sources it seeks to invoke to refuse to issue a forthright affirmation of Nebraska's right to declare that critical moral differences exist between the two procedures. . . .

Demonstrating a further and basic misunderstanding of *Casey,* the Court holds the ban on the D&X procedure fails because it does not include an exception permitting an abortionist to perform a D&X whenever he believes it will best preserve the health of the woman. Casting aside the views of distinguished physicians and the statements of leading medical organizations, the Court awards each physician a veto power over the State's judgment that the procedures should not be performed. [No] studies support the contention that the D&X abortion method is safer than other abortion methods. . . . *Casey* recognized [that] the physician's ability to practice medicine was "subject to reasonable . . . regulation by the State" and would receive the "same solicitude it receives in other contexts." In other contexts, the State is entitled to make judgments where high medical authority is in disagreement.

Ignoring substantial medical and ethical opinion, the Court substitutes its own judgment for the judgment of Nebraska and some 30 other States and sweeps the law away. . . . The decision nullifies a law expressing the will of the people of Nebraska that medical procedures must be governed by moral principles having their foundation in the intrinsic value of human life, including life of the unborn. . . .

From the decision, the reasoning, and the judgment, I dissent.

Justice THOMAS, with whom THE CHIEF JUSTICE and Justice SCALIA join, dissenting.

[The *Roe*] decision was grievously wrong. . . . Nothing in our Federal Constitution deprives the people of this country of the right to determine whether the consequences of abortion to the fetus and to society outweigh the burden of an unwanted pregnancy on the mother. Although a State may permit abortion, nothing in the Constitution dictates that a State must do so.

[S]o long as state regulation of abortion furthers legitimate interests—that is, interests not designed to strike at the right itself—the regulation is invalid only if it imposes an undue burden on a woman's ability to obtain an abortion, meaning that it places a substantial obstacle in the woman's path. . . . Today's decision is so obviously irreconcilable with *Casey*'s explication of what its undue-burden standard requires, let alone the Constitution, that it should be seen for what it is, a reinstitution of the pre-*Webster* abortion-on-demand era in which the mere invocation of "abortion rights" trumps any contrary societal interest. . . .

[From] reading the majority's sanitized description, one would think that this case involves state regulation of a widely accepted routine medical procedure. Nothing could be further from the truth. The most widely used method of abortion during this stage of pregnancy is so gruesome that its use can be traumatic even for the physicians and medical staff who perform it. [T]he particular procedure at issue in this case, "partial birth abortion," so closely borders on infanticide that 30 States have attempted to ban it.

Nebraska, along with 29 other States, has attempted to ban the partial birth abortion procedure. Although the Nebraska statute purports to prohibit only "partial birth abortion," a phrase which is commonly used [to] refer to the breech extraction version of intact D&E, the majority concludes that this statute could also be read in some future case to prohibit ordinary D&E. . . . According to the majority, such an application would pose a substantial obstacle to some women seeking abortions and, therefore, the statute is unconstitutional. The majority errs with its very first step. [T]he Nebraska statute does not prohibit the D&E procedure. [T]he Nebraska statute, by its own terms, applies only to "partial birth abortion." . . .

There is no question that the State of Nebraska has a valid interest — one not designed to strike at the right itself — in prohibiting partial birth abortion. *Casey* itself noted that States may "express profound respect for the life of the unborn." States may, without a doubt, express this profound respect by prohibiting a procedure that approaches infanticide, and thereby dehumanizes the fetus and trivializes human life. . . . [The] "partial birth" gives the fetus an autonomy which separates it from the right of the woman to choose treatments for her own body. Thirty States have concurred with this view. . . .

[We] were reassured repeatedly in *Casey* that not all regulations of abortion are unwarranted and that the States may express profound respect for fetal life. Under *Casey*, the regulation before us today should easily pass constitutional muster. But the Court's abortion jurisprudence is a particularly virulent strain of constitutional exegesis. And so today we are told that 30 States are prohibited from banning one rarely used form of abortion that they believe to border on infanticide. It is clear that the Constitution does not compel this result. . . .

∼ PROBLEM: SPOUSAL NOTIFICATION AND MEDIATION ∼

Consider a state law that gives a woman the final decision about terminating her pregnancy but requires her to notify her spouse and give him an opportunity, when there is no risk of abuse, to negotiate on behalf of the child's birth. Would it be permissible to mandate an accelerated mediation process, subsidized by the state, provided that the woman's ultimate autonomy was preserved?

3. *Family Liberty*

Well-established case law suggests that there is a constitutional right to personal choice with respect to family life. In Meyer v. Nebraska, 262 U.S. 390 (1923), the Court referenced a liberty interest in "establish[ing] a home and bring[ing] up children." This characterization preceded the formal recognition of privacy as a fundamental right several decades later. In Village of Belle Terre v. Boraas, 416 U.S. 1 (1974), the Court marked an outer limit of this liberty when it upheld a local ordinance restricting occupancy in single-family dwellings to persons related by blood. A few years later, in Moore v. City of East Cleveland, a plurality of the Court struck down a law that prohibited extended families from living together in the same home.

Moore v. City of East Cleveland
431 U.S. 494 (1977)

Mr. Justice POWELL announced the judgment of the Court, and delivered an opinion in which Mr. Justice BRENNAN, Mr. Justice MARSHALL, and Mr. Justice BLACKMUN joined.

East Cleveland's housing ordinance, like many throughout the country, limits occupancy of a dwelling unit to members of a single family. But the ordinance contains an unusual and complicated definitional section that recognizes as a "family" only a few categories of related individuals. Because her family, living together in her home, fits none of those categories, appellant stands convicted of a criminal offense. The question in this case is whether the ordinance violates the Due Process Clause of the Fourteenth Amendment.

The city argues that our decision in Village of Belle Terre v. Boraas requires us to sustain the ordinance attacked here. [But] one overriding factor sets this case apart from *Belle Terre*. The ordinance there affected only unrelated individuals. It expressly allowed all who were related by "blood, adoption, or marriage" to live together, and in sustaining the ordinance we were careful to note that it promoted "family needs" and "family values." East Cleveland, in contrast, has chosen to regulate the occupancy of its housing by slicing deeply into the family itself. This is no mere incidental result of the ordinance. On its face it selects certain categories of relatives who may live together and declares that others may not. In particular, it makes a crime of a grandmother's choice to live with her grandson in circumstances like those presented here.

When a city undertakes such intrusive regulation of the family, [*Belle Terre*] does not govern]; the usual judicial deference to the legislature is inappropriate. "This Court has long recognized that freedom of personal choice in matters of marriage and family life is one of the liberties protected by the Due Process Clause of the Fourteenth Amendment." A host of cases, tracing their lineage to Meyer v. Nebraska and Pierce v. Society of Sisters, have consistently acknowledged a "private realm of family life which the state cannot enter." Of course, the family is not beyond regulation. But when the government intrudes on choices concerning family living arrangements, this Court must examine carefully the importance of the governmental interests advanced and the extent to which they are served by the challenged regulation.

When thus examined, this ordinance cannot survive. The city seeks to justify it as a means of preventing overcrowding, minimizing traffic and parking congestion, and avoiding an undue financial burden on East Cleveland's school system. Although these are legitimate goals, the ordinance before us serves them marginally, at best. For example, the ordinance permits any family consisting only of husband, wife, and unmarried children to live together, even if the family contains a half dozen licensed drivers, each with his or her own car. At the same time it forbids an adult brother and sister to share a household, even if both faithfully use public transportation. The ordinance would permit a grandmother to live with a single dependent son and children, even if his school-age children number a dozen, yet it forces Mrs. Moore to find another dwelling for her grandson John, simply because of the presence of his uncle and cousin in the same household. We need not labor the point. [The ordinance] has but a tenuous relation to alleviation of the conditions mentioned by the city.

The city would distinguish the cases based on *Meyer* and *Pierce*. It points out that none of them "gives grandmothers any fundamental rights with respect to grandsons," and suggests that any constitutional right to live together as a family extends only to the nuclear family essentially a couple and their dependent children. . . . To be sure, these cases did not expressly consider the family relationship presented here. [But] unless we close our eyes to the basic reasons why certain rights associated with the family have been accorded shelter under the Fourteenth Amendment's Due Process Clause, we cannot avoid applying the force and rationale of these precedents to the family choice involved in this case.

Substantive due process has at times been a treacherous field for this Court. There are risks when the judicial branch gives enhanced protection to certain substantive liberties without the guidance of the more specific provisions of the Bill of Rights. As the history of the *Lochner* era demonstrates, there is reason for concern lest the only limits to such judicial intervention become the predilections of those who happen at the time to be Members of this Court. That history counsels caution and restraint. But it does not counsel abandonment, nor does it require what the city urges here: cutting off any protection of family rights at the first convenient, if arbitrary boundary the boundary of the nuclear family.

Appropriate limits on substantive due process come not from drawing arbitrary lines but rather from careful "respect for the teachings of history (and), solid recognition of the basic values that underlie our society." Our decisions establish that the Constitution protects the sanctity of the family precisely because the institution of the family is deeply rooted in this Nation's history and tradition. It is through the family that we inculcate and pass down many of our most cherished values, moral and cultural.

Ours is by no means a tradition limited to respect for the bonds uniting the members of the nuclear family. The tradition of uncles, aunts, cousins, and especially grandparents sharing a household along with parents and children has roots equally venerable and equally deserving of constitutional recognition. Over the years millions of our citizens have grown up in just such an environment, and most, surely, have profited from it. Even if conditions of modern society have brought about a decline in extended family households, they have not erased the accumulated wisdom of civilization, gained over the centuries and honored throughout our history, that supports a larger conception of the family. Out of choice, necessity, or a sense of family responsibility, it has been common for close relatives to draw together and participate in the duties and the satisfactions of a common home. Decisions concerning child rearing [long] have been shared with grandparents or other relatives who occupy the same household indeed who may take on major responsibility for the rearing of the children. Especially in times of adversity, such as the death of a spouse or economic need, the broader family has tended to come together for mutual sustenance and to maintain or rebuild a secure home life. This is apparently what happened here.

Whether or not such a household is established because of personal tragedy, the choice of relatives in this degree of kinship to live together may not lightly be denied by the State. [T]he Constitution prevents East Cleveland from standardizing its children and its adults by forcing all to live in certain narrowly defined family patterns.

Reversed.

Mr. Justice BRENNAN, with whom Mr. Justice MARSHALL joins, concurring.

[The] "extended family" that provided generations of early Americans with social services and economic and emotional support in times of hardship, and was the beachhead for successive waves of immigrants who populated our cities, remains not merely still a pervasive living pattern, but under the goad of brutal economic necessity, a prominent pattern virtually a means of survival for large numbers of the poor and deprived minorities of our society. . . . The "extended" form is especially familiar among black families. . . . I do not wish to be understood as implying that East Cleveland's enforcement of its ordinance is motivated by a racially discriminatory purpose. . . . It suffices that in prohibiting this pattern of family living as a means of achieving its objectives, appellee city has chosen a device that deeply intrudes into family associational rights that historically have been central, and today remain central, to a large proportion of our population.

Mr. Justice STEVENS, concurring in the judgment.

[T]here appears to be no precedent for an ordinance which excludes any of an owner's relatives from the group of persons who may occupy his residence on a permanent basis. Nor does there appear to be any justification for such a restriction on an owner's use of his property. . . . Since this ordinance has not been shown to have any "substantial relation to the public health, safety, morals, or general welfare" of the city of East Cleveland, and since it cuts so deeply into a fundamental right normally associated with the ownership of residential property that of an owner to decide who may reside on his or her property it must fall. . . . East Cleveland's unprecedented ordinance constitutes a taking of property without due process and without just compensation.

Mr. Chief Justice BURGER, dissenting.

It is unnecessary for me to reach the difficult constitutional issue this case presents. Appellant's deliberate refusal to use a plainly adequate administrative remedy [a variance proceeding] provided by the city should foreclose her from pressing in this Court any constitutional objections to the city's zoning ordinance.

Mr. Justice STEWART, with whom Mr. Justice REHNQUIST joins, dissenting.

[When] the Court has found that the Fourteenth Amendment placed a substantive limitation on a State's power to regulate, it has been in those rare cases in which the personal interests at issue have been deemed "'implicit in the concept of ordered liberty.'" The interest that the appellant may have in permanently sharing a single kitchen and a suite of contiguous rooms with some of her relatives simply does not rise to that level. To equate this interest with the fundamental decisions to marry and to bear and raise children is to extend the limited substantive contours of the Due Process Clause beyond recognition.

Mr. Justice WHITE, dissenting.

[I would] underline Mr. Justice Black's constant reminder to his colleagues that the Court has no license to invalidate legislation which it thinks merely arbitrary or unreasonable. And no one was more sensitive than Mr. Justice Harlan to any suggestion that his approach to the Due Process Clause would lead to judges "roaming at large in the constitutional field." . . .

[That] the Court has ample precedent for the creation of new constitutional rights should not lead it to repeat the process at will. The Judiciary, including this Court is the most vulnerable and comes nearest to illegitimacy when it deals with judge-made constitutional law having little or no cognizable roots in the language or even the design of the Constitution. [T]he Court should be extremely reluctant to breathe still further substantive content into the Due Process Clause so as to strike down legislation adopted by a State or city to promote its welfare. Whenever the Judiciary does so, it unavoidably pre-empts for itself another part of the governance of the country without express constitutional authority.

There are various "liberties" [which] require that infringing legislation be given closer judicial scrutiny, not only with respect to existence of a purpose and the means employed, but also with respect to the importance of the purpose itself relative to the invaded interest. Some interest would appear almost impregnable to invasion, such as the freedoms of speech, press, and religion, and the freedom from cruel and unusual punishments. Other interests, for example, the right of association, the right to vote, and various claims sometimes referred to under the general rubric of the right to privacy, also weigh very heavily against state claims of authority to regulate. It is this category of interests which, as I understand it, Mr. Justice Stewart refers to as "'implicit in the concept of ordered liberty.'" . . .

Given his premise, he is surely correct. Under our cases, the Due Process Clause extends substantial protection to various phases of family life, but none requires that the claim made here be sustained. I cannot believe that the interest in residing with more than one set of grandchildren is one that calls for any kind of heightened protection under the Due Process Clause. To say that one has a personal right to live with all, rather than some, of one's grandchildren and that this right is implicit in ordered liberty is, as my Brother Stewart says, "to extend the limited substantive contours of the Due Process Clause beyond recognition." The present claim is hardly one of which it could be said that "neither liberty nor justice would exist if (it) were sacrificed." . . .

Mr. Justice Powell would apparently construe the Due Process Clause to protect from all but quite important state regulatory interests any right or privilege that in his estimate is deeply rooted in the country's traditions. For me, this suggests a far too expansive charter for this Court. . . . What the deeply rooted traditions of the country are is arguable; which of them deserve the protection of the Due Process Clause is even more debatable. The suggested view would [have the courts] substantively weighing and very likely invalidating a wide range of measures that Congress and state legislatures think appropriate to respond to a changing economic and social order.

Notes and Questions

1. *The* Moore *Standard.* The family living restrictions struck down in *Moore* implicated a concern that, at least from the Powell plurality's perspective, was

fundamental. The Court's factoring of whether the state had an "important" interest indicated a standard of review that was heightened but not strict. The elevated standard of review nonetheless was triggered by a sense that the interest was grounded in the nation's history and traditions. Critics have noted that this criterion, which is supposed to be a limiting principle for otherwise unbounded judicial review, has rather limitless potential for purposes of developing fundamental rights and liberties. This concern was manifest in the dissenting opinions in *Moore*, which indicate a growing interest in how precisely the tradition should be defined.

2. *Cultural Myopia?* Justices Brennan and Marshall express concern that the East Cleveland ordinance reflects a sense of "cultural myopia" by prioritizing the nuclear family model "found in much of white suburbia" over the extended family structure that they characterized as a "means of survival" for many poor African American families. To what extent should it matter that the burden in this instance was imposed in a community that was predominantly African American and where political leadership reflected this makeup?

∼ PROBLEMS ∼

1. *Defining "Family."* Suppose a community enacts an ordinance that restricts housing occupancy to single families, but defines a family unit in a way that excludes cousins beyond the first order. Would this restriction be analyzed more appropriately pursuant to *Boraas* or *Moore*?

2. *Natural Fathers.* Consider a state law providing that a mother's consent is sufficient for adoption if the natural but unwed father has not legitimized the child. Would the natural father have a right to protest and preclude the adoption? *See* Quilloin v. Walcott, 434 U.S. 246 (1978). Would it make any difference whether the adoption was by the mother's husband or into an entirely different family unit?

3. *More on the Proposed Child Custody Statute.* If the proposed statute described in the introductory problem is enacted, what standard of review should apply? What would you guess is the state's asserted interest in passing such a law? Is it legitimate? Is the interest sufficient to overcome the parents' privacy interests in being involved in the raising of their children?

4. The Right to Marry

Marriage is a relationship with a well-established tradition and history that the Court has protected through due process review. In Meyer v. Nebraska, 262 U.S. 290 (1923), the right was referenced explicitly as a constitutionally protected liberty interest. In Loving v. Virginia, 388 U.S. 1 (1967), the right to marry also was identified as a basis for striking down antimiscegenation laws. In the following case, the Court reviewed a state law that prohibited marriage by residents who were in arrears in their child support obligations and could not demonstrate that their offspring were unlikely to become "public charges."

Zablocki v. Redhail
434 U.S. 374 (1978)

Mr. Justice MARSHALL delivered the opinion of the Court.

At issue in this case is the constitutionality of a Wisconsin statute restricting marriage by a "resident having minor children not in his custody and which he is under obligation to support by any court order or judgment." For such individuals a marriage license may be granted only upon proof of compliance with the child support obligation and that the children "are not then and are not likely thereafter to become public charges. . . ."

The leading decision of this Court on the right to marry is Loving v. Virginia. In that case, an interracial couple who had been convicted of violating Virginia's miscegenation laws challenged the statutory scheme on both equal protection and due process grounds. The Court's opinion could have rested solely on the ground that the statutes discriminated on the basis of race in violation of the Equal Protection Clause. But the Court went on to hold that the laws arbitrarily deprived the couple of a fundamental liberty protected by the Due Process Clause, the freedom to marry. The Court's language on the latter point bears repeating:

> The freedom to marry has long been recognized as one of the vital personal rights essential to the orderly pursuit of happiness by free men.
> Marriage is one of the "basic civil rights of man," fundamental to our very existence and survival.

Although *Loving* arose in the context of racial discrimination, prior and subsequent decisions of this Court confirm that the right to marry is of fundamental importance for all individuals. Long ago, the Court characterized marriage as "the most important relation in life," and as "the foundation of the family and of society, without which there would be neither civilization nor progress."

[More] recent decisions have established that the right to marry is part of the fundamental "right of privacy" implicit in the Fourteenth Amendment's Due Process Clause. [It] is not surprising that the decision to marry has been placed on the same level of importance as decisions relating to procreation, childbirth, child rearing, and family relationships. As the facts of this case illustrate, it would make little sense to recognize a right of privacy with respect to other matters of family life and not with respect to the decision to enter the relationship that is the foundation of the family in our society.

By reaffirming the fundamental character of the right to marry, we do not mean to suggest that every state regulation which relates in any way to the incidents of or prerequisites for marriage must be subjected to rigorous scrutiny. To the contrary, reasonable regulations that do not significantly interfere with decisions to enter into the marital relationship may legitimately be imposed. The statutory classification at issue here, however, clearly does interfere directly and substantially with the right to marry.

Under the challenged statute, no Wisconsin resident in the affected class may marry in Wisconsin or elsewhere without a court order, and marriages contracted in violation of the statute are both void and punishable as criminal offenses. Some of those in the affected class, like appellee, will never be able to obtain the necessary court order, because they either lack the financial means to meet their support obligations or cannot prove that their children will not become public charges. These persons are absolutely prevented from getting married. Many others, able in theory to satisfy the statute's requirements, will be sufficiently burdened by having to do so that they will in effect be coerced into forgoing their right to marry. And even those who can be persuaded to meet the statute's requirements suffer a serious intrusion into their freedom of choice in an area in which we have held such freedom to be fundamental.

When a statutory classification significantly interferes with the exercise of a fundamental right, it cannot be upheld unless it is supported by sufficiently important state interests and is closely tailored to effectuate only those interests. Appellant asserts that two interests are served by the challenged statute: the permission-to-marry proceeding furnishes an opportunity to counsel the applicant as to the necessity of fulfilling his prior support obligations; and the welfare of the out-of-custody children is protected. We may accept for present purposes that these are legitimate and substantial interests, but, since the means selected by the State for achieving these interests unnecessarily impinge on the right to marry, the statute cannot be sustained.

[With] regard to safeguarding the welfare of the out-of-custody children, appellant's brief does not make clear the connection between the State's interest and the statute's requirements. At argument, appellant's counsel suggested that, since permission to marry cannot be granted unless the applicant shows that he has satisfied his court-determined support obligations to the prior children and that those children will not become public charges, the statute provides incentive for the applicant to make support payments to his children. This "collection device" rationale cannot justify the statute's broad infringement on the right to marry.

First, with respect to individuals who are unable to meet the statutory requirements, the statute merely prevents the applicant from getting married, without delivering any money at all into the hands of the applicant's prior children. More importantly, regardless of the applicant's ability or willingness to meet the statutory requirements, the State already has numerous other means for exacting compliance with support obligations, means that are at least as effective as the instant statute's and yet do not impinge upon the right to marry. Under Wisconsin law, whether the children are from a prior marriage or were born out of wedlock, court-determined support obligations may be enforced directly via wage assignments, civil contempt proceedings, and criminal penalties. And, if the State believes that parents of children out of their custody should be responsible for ensuring that those children do not become public charges, this interest can be achieved by adjusting the criteria used for determining the amounts to be paid under their support orders.

There is also some suggestion that [the law] protects the ability of marriage applicants to meet support obligations to prior children by preventing the applicants from incurring new support obligations. But the challenged provisions are grossly underinclusive with respect to this purpose, since they do not limit in any way new financial commitments by the applicant other than those arising out of the contemplated marriage. The statutory classification is substantially overinclusive as well: Given the possibility that the new spouse will actually better the applicant's financial situation, by contributing income from a job or otherwise, the statute in many cases may prevent affected individuals from improving their ability to satisfy their prior support obligations. And, although it is true that the applicant will incur support obligations to any children born during the contemplated marriage, preventing the marriage may only result in the children being born out of wedlock, as in fact occurred in appellee's case. Since the support obligation is the same whether the child is born in or out of wedlock, the net result of preventing the marriage is simply more illegitimate children.

The statutory classification created by [this law] thus cannot be justified by the interests advanced in support of it.

Mr. Justice STEWART, concurring in the judgment.

The Constitution does not specifically mention freedom to marry, but it is settled that the "liberty" protected by the Due Process Clause of the Fourteenth Amendment embraces more than those freedoms expressly enumerated in the Bill of Rights. And the decisions of this Court have made clear that freedom of personal choice in matters of marriage and family life is one of the liberties so protected.

Mr. Justice REHNQUIST, dissenting.

[I] would view this legislative judgment in the light of the traditional presumption of validity. I think that under the Equal Protection Clause the statute need pass only the "rational basis test," and that under the Due Process Clause it need only be shown that it bears a rational relation to a constitutionally permissible objective. The statute so viewed is a permissible exercise of the State's power to regulate family life and to assure the support of minor children, despite its possible imprecision in the extreme cases envisioned in the concurring opinions.

Notes

1. Zablocki *and Substantive Due Process Review.* The *Zablocki* decision reaffirmed an established principle, but recast it to the extent that the right to marry was brought within the right of privacy. Utilization of the Equal Protection Clause may have reflected the Court's general uneasiness with substantive due process review and the discredited legacy of which it evoked memories. As with the use of penumbras in *Griswold*, reliance on the Equal Protection Clause did not obscure a model of review that fundamentally is indistinguishable from substantive due process review.

2. *Same-Sex Marriage and Substantive Due Process.* A number of state supreme courts, applying state constitutional provisions, have invalidated state laws that do not permit same-sex couples to marry. At the time of this writing, a challenge based on the U.S. Constitution is working its way through the federal courts, and the plaintiffs (who are seeking to challenge a state law on federal constitutional grounds) have prevailed in the trial court. Undoubtedly, litigation over this issue will continue for some years to come.

⚭ PROBLEMS ⚭

1. *Remarriage and Support Orders.* What if the state adopts a law that presumes that remarriage will have a detrimental effect on children of a previous marriage who are the subject of a support order? So long as there was an opportunity to rebut this presumption, or demonstrate good reason for not being able to comply with the support order, would there be a due process problem?

2. *Same-Sex Marriage.* Later in this chapter, we examine whether gay and homosexual individuals have a constitutional right of privacy. But, if the concepts of "liberty" and "privacy" mean anything, must they include the right of same-sex couples to marry?

3. *Polygamy.* Some religions believe in polygamy. Does the fundamental right to marry include the right to engage in polygamy? *See* Reynolds v. United States, 98 U.S. (8 Otto) 145, 25 L.Ed. 244 (1878) (upholding a federal law prohibiting polygamy, as applied to a Mormon whose religion required him to engage in that practice, drawing a distinction between "belief" and "conduct," and concluding that the government has broad authority to prohibit religious conduct); Davis v. Beason, 133 U.S. 333 (1890) (reaffirming *Reynolds*).

4. *Transsexual Marriage.* Joel Behr, at the age of 18, underwent a successful operation to change his sex. Ten years later, Joel, now named Noel and a successful internist at a local South Dakota hospital, wishes to marry Arthur Rhodes, a Stanford University graduate and an accountant with a Fortune 500 company. The Rapid City Department of Marriage Licenses refuses to grant them a marriage license, stating that South Dakota law does not recognize same-sex marriages. Noel Behr and Arthur Rhodes file suit, claiming that their constitutional right to marry has been violated. The trial court hears evidence from both parties and concludes: "In light of the totality of the evidence, I must conclude that Noel Behr is not a woman. Consequently, the State of South Dakota can not legally recognize a marriage between Noel Behr and Arthur Rhodes. The State's refusal to sanction their marriage was lawfully within the State's police powers." The South Dakota Supreme Court affirms the trial court's decision, and Noel Behr and Arthur Rhodes petition the U.S. Supreme Court for a writ of certiorari. The petition is granted and oral argument has been held. How should the Supreme Court rule on this question? Explain.

5. Parental Rights

The nature and scope of parental liberty have been factored in a series of contexts. In Wisconsin v. Yoder, 406 U.S. 205 (1972), the Court found that a mandatory school attendance law was at odds with the free exercise of religion when applied to members of the Amish religion. It also noted that compulsory education in this circumstance implicated "traditional concepts of parental control over the religious upbringing and education of their minor children." Parental rights have been balanced against a minor child's liberty to obtain an abortion, insofar as the Court has upheld parental consent requirements but insisted on a judicial bypass option. *E.g.*, Hodgson v. Minnesota, 497 U.S. 417 (1990).

The relationship between parent and child, though implicating fundamental interests, is not constitutionally sacrosanct. In Quilloin v. Walcott, the Court upheld a state law that allowed the mother to adopt her child in a new family unit if the natural father did not object. As the Court saw it, a contrary outcome would have undermined a result sought by everyone except the natural father, who was not himself seeking custody. In Michael H. v. Gerald D., the Court reviewed a natural father's claim of a filial relationship and visitation rights with his daughter. The child's birth as a result of an extramarital affair led a plurality of the Court to conclude that the father had no liberty interest protected under the Fourteenth Amendment.

Michael H. v. Gerald D.

491 U.S. 110 (1989)

Justice SCALIA announced the judgment of the Court and delivered an opinion, in which THE CHIEF JUSTICE joins, and in all but footnote 6 of which Justice O'CONNOR and Justice KENNEDY join.

Under California law, a child born to a married woman living with her husband is presumed to be a child of the marriage. The presumption of legitimacy may be rebutted only by the husband or wife, and then only in limited circumstances. The instant appeal presents the claim that this presumption infringes upon the due process rights of a man who wishes to establish his paternity of a child born to the wife of another man, and the claim that it infringes upon the constitutional right of the child to maintain a relationship with her natural father.

The facts of this case are, we must hope, extraordinary. [In 1976], Carole D., an international model, and Gerald D., a top executive in a French oil company, were married. The couple established a home [in] California in which they resided as husband and wife when one or the other was not out of the country on business. [In] 1978, Carole became involved in an adulterous affair with a neighbor, Michael H. In September 1980, she conceived a child, Victoria D., who was born [in] 1981. Gerald was listed as father on the birth certificate and has always held Victoria out to the world as his daughter. Soon after delivery of the child, however, Carole informed Michael that she believed he might be the father. [For her first three years, the child and mother lived at times with Michael, who held out that the child was his. The mother and child also resided at times with Gerald and another man. Gerald was listed on the birth certificate as the father and has claimed her accordingly, but blood tests showed a 98.07 percent probability that the child is Michael's. California law presumes that a child born to a mother living with her husband is of the marriage. Pursuant to this presumption, the state courts denied Michael paternity and visitation rights.]

[Michael] contends as a matter of substantive due process that, because he has established a parental relationship with Victoria, protection of Gerald's and Carole's marital union is an insufficient state interest to support termination of that relationship. This argument [is] predicated on the assertion that Michael has a constitutionally protected liberty interest in his relationship with Victoria.

In an attempt to limit and guide interpretation of the Clause, we have insisted not merely that the interest denominated as a "liberty" be "fundamental" (a concept that, in isolation, is hard to objectify), but also that it be an interest traditionally protected by our society. As we have put it, the Due Process Clause affords only those protections "so rooted in the traditions and conscience of our people as to be ranked as fundamental."

This insistence that the asserted liberty interest be rooted in history and tradition is evident, as elsewhere, in our cases according constitutional protection to certain parental rights. Michael [maintains] that a liberty interest is created by biological fatherhood plus an established parental relationship—factors that exist in the present case. . . . We think that distorts the rationale of [prior] cases. As we view them, they rest not upon such isolated factors but upon the historic respect—indeed, sanctity would not be too strong a term—traditionally accorded to the relationships that develop within the unitary family.

[T]he legal issue in the present case reduces to whether the relationship between persons in the situation of Michael and Victoria has been treated as a protected family unit under the historic practices of our society, or whether on any other basis it has been accorded special protection. We think it impossible to find that it has. In fact, quite to the contrary, our traditions have protected the marital family (Gerald, Carole, and the child they acknowledge to be theirs) against the sort of claim Michael asserts.

We have found nothing in the older sources, nor in the older cases, addressing specifically the power of the natural father to assert parental rights over a child born into a woman's existing marriage with another man. Since it is Michael's burden to establish that such a power (at least where the natural father has established a relationship with the child) is so deeply embedded within our traditions as to be a fundamental right, the lack of evidence alone might defeat his case. But the evidence shows that even in modern times—when, as we have noted, the rigid protection of the marital family has in other respects been relaxed—the ability of a person in Michael's position to claim paternity has not been generally acknowledged. . . .

Moreover, even if it were clear that one in Michael's position generally possesses, and has generally always possessed, standing to challenge the marital child's legitimacy, that would still not establish Michael's case. As noted earlier, what is at issue here is not entitlement to a state pronouncement that Victoria was begotten by Michael. It is no conceivable denial of constitutional right for a State to decline to declare facts unless some legal consequence hinges upon the requested declaration. What Michael asserts here is a right to have himself declared the natural father and thereby to obtain parental prerogatives. What he must establish, therefore, is not that our society has traditionally allowed a natural father in his circumstances to establish paternity, but that it has traditionally accorded such a father parental rights, or at least has not traditionally denied them. Even if the law in all States had always been that the entire world could challenge the marital presumption and obtain a declaration as to who was the natural father, that would not advance Michael's claim.

Thus, it is ultimately irrelevant, even for purposes of determining current social attitudes towards the alleged substantive right Michael asserts, that the present law in a number of States appears to allow the natural father — including the natural father who has not established a relationship with the child — the theoretical power to rebut the marital presumption. What counts is whether the States in fact award substantive parental rights to the natural father of a child conceived within, and born into, an extant marital union that wishes to embrace the child. We are not aware of a single case, old or new, that has done so. This is not the stuff of which fundamental rights qualifying as liberty interests are made.[6]

We do not accept Justice Brennan's criticism that this result "squashes" the liberty that consists of "the freedom not to conform." It seems to us that reflects the erroneous view that there is only one side to this controversy — that one disposition can expand a "liberty" of sorts without contracting an equivalent "liberty" on the other side. . . . Here, to provide protection to an adulterous natural father is to deny protection to a marital father, and vice versa. If Michael has a "freedom not to conform" (whatever that means), Gerald must equivalently have a "freedom to conform." One of them will pay a price for asserting that "freedom" — Michael by being unable to act as father of the child he has adulterously begotten, or Gerald by being unable to preserve the integrity of the traditional family unit he and Victoria have established. Our disposition does not choose between these two "freedoms," but leaves that to the people of California. Justice Brennan's approach chooses one of them as the constitutional imperative, on no apparent basis except that the unconventional is to be preferred.

The judgment of the California Court of Appeal is
Affirmed.

Justice O'CONNNOR, with whom Justice KENNEDY joins, concurring in part.
I concur in all but footnote 6 of Justice Scalia's opinion. This footnote sketches a mode of historical analysis to be used when identifying liberty interests

6. Justice Brennan criticizes our methodology in using historical traditions specifically relating to the rights of an adulterous natural father, rather than inquiring more generally "whether parenthood is an interest that historically has received our attention and protection." There seems to us no basis for the contention that this methodology is "nove[l]." [We] refer to the most specific level at which a relevant tradition protecting, or denying protection to, the asserted right can be identified. If, for example, there were no societal tradition, either way, regarding the rights of the natural father of a child adulterously conceived, we would have to consult, and (if possible) reason from, the traditions regarding natural fathers in general. But there is such a more specific tradition, and it unqualifiedly denies protection to such a parent. . . .

protected by the Due Process Clause of the Fourteenth Amendment that may be somewhat inconsistent with our past decisions in this area. On occasion the Court has characterized relevant traditions protecting asserted rights at levels of generality that might not be "the most specific level" available. I would not foreclose the unanticipated by the prior imposition of a single mode of historical analysis.

Justice STEVENS, concurring in the judgment.

[Justice Scalia] seems to reject the possibility that a natural father might ever have a constitutionally protected interest in his relationship with a child whose mother was married to, and cohabiting with, another man at the time of the child's conception and birth. [Prior] cases demonstrate that enduring "family" relationships may develop in unconventional settings. I therefore would not foreclose the possibility that a constitutionally protected relationship between a natural father and his child might exist in a case like this. Indeed, I am willing to assume for the purpose of deciding this case that Michael's relationship with Victoria is strong enough to give him a constitutional right to try to convince a trial judge that Victoria's best interest would be served by granting him visitation rights. I am satisfied, however, that the California statute, as applied in this case, gave him that opportunity.

Justice BRENNAN, with whom Justice MARSHALL and Justice BLACKMUN join, dissenting.

It is ironic that an approach so utterly dependent on tradition is so indifferent to our precedents. [T]he plurality acts as though English legal treatises and the American Law Reports always have provided the sole source for our constitutional principles. They have not. . . . "'[L]iberty' and 'property' are broad and majestic terms. They are among the '[g]reat [constitutional] concepts . . . purposely left to gather meaning from experience. . . . [T]hey relate to the whole domain of social and economic fact, and the statesmen who founded this Nation knew too well that only a stagnant society remains unchanged.'"

[The plurality] does not ask whether parenthood is an interest that historically has received our attention and protection; the answer to that question is too clear for dispute. Instead, the plurality asks whether the specific variety of parenthood under consideration — a natural father's relationship with a child whose mother is married to another man — has enjoyed such protection. . . . If we had looked to tradition with such specificity in past cases, many a decision would have reached a different result. Surely the use of contraceptives by unmarried couples, or even by married couples, [were] not "interest[s] traditionally protected by our society," at the time of their consideration by this Court. . . . That we did not ask this question in those cases highlights the novelty of the interpretive method that the plurality opinion employs today.

[In] the plurality's constitutional universe, we may not take notice of the fact that the original reasons for the conclusive presumption of paternity are out of place in a world in which blood tests can prove virtually beyond a shadow of a doubt who sired a particular child and in which the fact of illegitimacy no longer plays the burdensome and stigmatizing role it once did. [B]y describing the decisive question as whether Michael's and Victoria's interest is one that has been "traditionally protected by our society," rather than one that society traditionally has thought important (with or without protecting it), and by suggesting that our sole function is to "discern the society's views," the plurality acts as if the only purpose of the Due Process Clause is to confirm the importance of interests already protected by a majority of the States. . . .

The document that the plurality construes today is unfamiliar to me. It is not the living charter that I have taken to be our Constitution; it is instead a stagnant, archaic, hidebound document steeped in the prejudices and superstitions of a time long past. This Constitution does not recognize that times change, does not see that sometimes a practice or rule outlives its foundations. I cannot accept an interpretive method that does such violence to the charter that I am bound by oath to uphold. . . .

Justice WHITE, with whom Justice BRENNAN joins, dissenting.

[Prior cases have] recognized the liberty interest of a father in his relationship with his child. In none of these cases did we indicate that the father's rights were dependent on the marital status of the mother or biological father. The basic principle enunciated in the Court's unwed father cases is that an unwed father who has demonstrated a sufficient commitment to his paternity by way of personal, financial, or custodial responsibilities has a protected liberty interest in a relationship with his child.

"The emphasis of the Due Process Clause is on 'process.'" [I] fail to see how Michael was granted any meaningful opportunity to be heard when he was precluded at the very outset from introducing evidence which would support his assertion of paternity. Michael has never been afforded an opportunity to present his case in any meaningful manner.

As the Court has said: "The significance of the biological connection is that it offers the natural father an opportunity that no other male possesses to develop a relationship with his offspring. If he grasps that opportunity and accepts some measure of responsibility for the child's future, he may enjoy the blessings of the parent-child relationship and make uniquely valuable contributions to the child's development." . . . Michael eagerly grasped the opportunity to have a relationship with his daughter (he lived with her; he declared her to be his child; he provided financial support for her) and still, with today's opinion, his opportunity has vanished. He has been rendered a stranger to his child.

Because [the state law] as applied, should be held unconstitutional under the Due Process Clause of the Fourteenth Amendment, I respectfully dissent.

Note: Defining "Liberty"

A particularly notable aspect of Justice Scalia's opinion was his argument (in footnote 6) that the inquiry into whether a right or liberty is fundamental should "refer to the most specific level at which a relevant tradition . . . can be identified." Defining the liberty interest at a high level of specificity correspondingly diminishes the likelihood that the interest will be denominated fundamental. Although the general concept of parental rights thus might be understood as rooted in the nation's traditions, societal support predictably would diminish for this proposition when extended to parents of children who were conceived in an adulterous relationship. Definition of the liberty interest with specificity thus represents a method of review that limits the judiciary's role in identifying and developing rights and liberties that are not enumerated by the Constitution.

∾ PROBLEMS ∾

1. *Reference Points.* Consider the implications of tradition depending on whether the concept is defined with specificity or as an abstraction. Would specificity or abstraction be a friendlier inquiry for purposes of determining whether, prior to Reconstruction, there was a fundamental right to own slaves? Which of these reference points would be more supportive of segregation as a system that reflects the different property interest of racial identity? Since traditions evolve, at what point would concepts like desegregation become a factor in defining racial liberties and equalities?

2. *More on the Proposed Child Custody Statute.* Let's go back to the problem at the beginning of the chapter. In light of the Court's decisions on parental rights, what standard of review would you expect courts to apply to the proposed statute if it is enacted? What result? Why?

6.   *Sexual Orientation*

The understanding of the liberty interest at stake and thus how it is defined have an outcome-determinative bearing on fundamental rights analysis. This predictability factor was evidenced in Bowers v. Hardwick, 478 U.S. 186 (1986), when the Court examined a law that made sodomy a crime. The law was applied to an individual who was found engaged in homosexual conduct in the privacy of his home. In upholding the law, the Court concluded that the U.S. Constitution does not confer a fundamental right on homosexuals to engage in sodomy. The Court distinguished sodomy from other privacy cases such as Meyer v. Nebraska (dealing with child rearing and education), Prince v. Massachusetts (family relationships), Skinner v. Oklahoma (procreation), Loving v. Virginia (marriage), Griswold v. Connecticut and Eisenstadt v. Baird (contraception), and Roe v. Wade (abortion), on the following basis:

> [N]one of the rights announced in those cases bears any resemblance to the claimed constitutional right of homosexuals to engage in acts of sodomy that is asserted in this case. No connection between family, marriage, or procreation on the one hand and homosexual activity on the other has been demonstrated. . . . Moreover, any claim that these cases nevertheless stand for the proposition that any kind of private sexual conduct between consenting adults is constitutionally insulated from state proscription is unsupportable. Indeed, the Court's opinion in *Carey* twice asserted that the privacy right, which the *Griswold* line of cases found to be one of the protections provided by the Due Process Clause, did not reach so far. . . .
>
>   It is obvious to us that neither of these formulations would extend a fundamental right to homosexuals to engage in acts of consensual sodomy. Proscriptions against that conduct

have ancient roots. Sodomy was a criminal offense at common law and was forbidden by the laws of the original thirteen States when they ratified the Bill of Rights. In 1868, when the Fourteenth Amendment was ratified, all but 5 of the 37 States in the Union had criminal sodomy laws. In fact, until 1961, all 50 States outlawed sodomy, and today, 24 States and the District of Columbia continue to provide criminal penalties for sodomy performed in private and between consenting adults. Against this background, to claim that a right to engage in such conduct is "deeply rooted in this Nation's history and tradition" or "implicit in the concept of ordered liberty" is, at best, facetious.

Nor are we inclined to take a more expansive view of our authority to discover new fundamental rights imbedded in the Due Process Clause. The Court is most vulnerable and comes nearest to illegitimacy when it deals with judge-made constitutional law having little or no cognizable roots in the language or design of the Constitution. That this is so was painfully demonstrated by the face-off between the Executive and the Court in the 1930's, which resulted in the repudiation of much of the substantive gloss that the Court had placed on the Due Process Clauses of the Fifth and Fourteenth Amendments. There should be, therefore, great resistance to expand the substantive reach of those Clauses, particularly if it requires redefining the category of rights deemed to be fundamental. Otherwise, the Judiciary necessarily takes to itself further authority to govern the country without express constitutional authority. The claimed right pressed on us today falls far short of overcoming this resistance.

Although the Court repudiated any basis for sexual orientation being a concern of the Due Process Clause, it has been responsive to government action that singles out homosexuals for disadvantaged treatment under the law. In Roemer v. Evans, the Court invalidated a state constitutional amendment that prohibited government action that would protect homosexuals from discrimination. This result was achieved without reference to a fundamental right, and thus the Court's orientation in *Hardwick* was unaltered. It is noteworthy, moreover, that the result was based on the Equal Protection Clause pursuant to a rational basis standard of review. In a dissenting opinion, Justice Scalia found no basis for distinguishing the power to criminalize homosexuality from the restrictions reviewed in *Evans*. In both instances, homosexuality was targeted. In neither instance was sexual orientation identified as a fundamental liberty interest.

Lawrence v. Texas

539 U.S. 558 (2003)

Justice KENNEDY delivered the opinion of the Court.

Liberty protects the person from unwarranted government intrusions into a dwelling or other private places. In our tradition the State is not omnipresent in the home. And there are other spheres of our lives and existence, outside the home, where the State should not be a dominant presence. Freedom extends beyond spatial bounds. Liberty presumes an autonomy of self that includes freedom of thought, belief, expression, and certain intimate conduct. The instant case involves liberty of the person both in its spatial and more transcendent dimensions.

The question before the Court is the validity of a Texas statute making it a crime for two persons of the same sex to engage in certain intimate sexual conduct.

In Houston, Texas, officers of the Harris County Police Department were dispatched to a private residence in response to a reported weapons disturbance. They entered an apartment where one of the petitioners, John Geddes Lawrence, resided. The right of the police to enter does not seem to have been questioned. The officers observed Lawrence and another man, Tyron Garner, engaging in a sexual act. The two petitioners were arrested, held in custody over night, and charged and convicted before a Justice of the Peace. The complaints described their crime as "deviate sexual intercourse, namely anal sex, with a member of the same sex (man)."

We granted certiorari to consider three questions:

"1. Whether Petitioners' criminal convictions under the Texas "Homosexual Conduct" law — which criminalizes sexual intimacy by same-sex couples, but not identical behavior by different-sex couples — violate the Fourteenth Amendment guarantee of equal protection of laws?

"2. Whether Petitioners' criminal convictions for adult consensual sexual intimacy in the home violate their vital interests in liberty and privacy protected by the Due Process Clause of the Fourteenth Amendment?

"3. Whether Bowers v. Hardwick should be overruled?"

The petitioners were adults at the time of the alleged offense. Their conduct was in private and consensual.

We conclude the case should be resolved by determining whether the petitioners were free as adults to engage in the private conduct in the exercise of their liberty under the Due Process Clause of the Fourteenth Amendment to the Constitution. For this inquiry we deem it necessary to reconsider the Court's holding in *Bowers*.

There are broad statements of the substantive reach of liberty under the Due Process Clause in earlier cases, including Pierce v. Society of Sisters and Meyer v. Nebraska; but the most pertinent beginning point is our decision in Griswold v. Connecticut. [*Griswold*] invalidated a state law prohibiting the use of drugs or devices of contraception and counseling or aiding and abetting the use of contraceptives. The Court described the protected interest as a right to privacy and placed emphasis on the marriage relation and the protected space of the marital bedroom.

The opinions in *Griswold* and *Eisenstadt* were part of the background for the decision in Roe v. Wade. *Roe* recognized the right of a woman to make certain fundamental decisions affecting her destiny and confirmed once more that the protection of liberty under the Due Process Clause has a substantive dimension of fundamental significance in defining the rights of the person.

The Court began its substantive discussion in *Bowers* as follows: "The issue presented is whether the Federal Constitution confers a fundamental right upon homosexuals to engage in sodomy and hence invalidates the laws of the many States that still make such conduct illegal and have done so for a very long time." That statement, we now conclude, discloses the Court's own failure to appreciate the extent of the liberty at stake. To say that the issue in *Bowers* was simply the right to engage in certain sexual conduct demeans the claim the individual put forward, just as it would demean a married couple were it to be said marriage is simply about the right to have sexual intercourse. The laws involved in *Bowers* and here are, to be sure, statutes that purport to do no more than prohibit a particular sexual act. Their penalties and purposes, though, have more far-reaching consequences, touching upon the most private human conduct, sexual behavior, and in the most private of places, the home. The statutes do seek to control a personal relationship that, whether or not entitled to formal recognition in the law, is within the liberty of persons to choose without being punished as criminals.

This, as a general rule, should counsel against attempts by the State, or a court, to define the meaning of the relationship or to set its boundaries absent injury to a person or abuse of an institution the law protects. It suffices for us to acknowledge that adults may choose to enter upon this relationship in the confines of their homes and their own private lives and still retain their dignity as free persons. When sexuality finds overt expression in intimate conduct with another person, the conduct can be but one element in a personal bond that is more enduring. The liberty protected by the Constitution allows homosexual persons the right to make this choice.

Having misapprehended the claim of liberty there presented to it, and thus stating the claim to be whether there is a fundamental right to engage in consensual sodomy, the *Bowers* Court said: "Proscriptions against that conduct have ancient roots." [I]t should be noted that there is no longstanding history in this country of laws directed at homosexual conduct as a distinct matter. . . . [It] was not until the 1970's that any State singled out same-sex relations for criminal prosecution, and only nine States have done so. Post-*Bowers* even some of these States did not adhere to the policy of suppressing homosexual conduct. Over the course of the last decades, States with same-sex prohibitions have moved toward abolishing them. In summary, the historical grounds relied upon in *Bowers* are more complex than the majority opinion and the concurring opinion by Chief Justice Burger indicate. Their historical premises are not without doubt and, at the very least, are overstated.

It must be acknowledged, of course, that the Court in *Bowers* was making the broader point that for centuries there have been powerful voices to condemn homosexual conduct as immoral. The condemnation has been shaped by religious beliefs, conceptions of right and acceptable behavior, and respect for the traditional family. For many persons these are not trivial concerns but profound and deep convictions accepted as ethical and moral principles to which they aspire and which thus determine the course of their lives. These considerations do not answer the question before us, however. The issue is whether the majority may use the power of the State to enforce these views on the whole society through operation of the criminal law.

Chief Justice Burger joined the opinion for the Court in *Bowers* and further explained his views as follows: "Decisions of individuals relating to homosexual conduct have been subject to state intervention throughout the history of Western civilization. Condemnation of those practices is firmly rooted in Judeo-Christian moral and ethical standards." As with Justice White's assumptions about history, scholarship casts some doubt on the sweeping nature of the statement by Chief Justice Burger as it pertains to private homosexual conduct between consenting adults. In all events we think that our laws and traditions in the past half century are of most relevance here. These references show an emerging awareness that liberty gives substantial protection to adult persons in deciding how to conduct their private lives in matters pertaining to sex. "History and tradition are the starting point but not in all cases the ending point of the substantive due process inquiry."

This emerging recognition should have been apparent when *Bowers* was decided. In 1955 the American Law Institute promulgated the Model Penal Code and made clear that it did not recommend or provide for "criminal penalties for consensual sexual relations conducted in private." It justified its decision on three grounds: (1) The prohibitions undermined respect for the law by penalizing conduct many people engaged in; (2) the statutes regulated private conduct not harmful to others; and (3) the laws were arbitrarily enforced and thus invited the danger of blackmail.

In *Bowers* the Court referred to the fact that before 1961 all 50 States had outlawed sodomy, and that at the time of the Court's decision 24 States and the District of Columbia had sodomy laws. Justice Powell pointed out that these prohibitions often were being ignored, however. Georgia, for instance, had not sought to enforce its law for decades. . . . [The] sweeping references by Chief Justice Burger to the history of Western civilization and to Judeo-Christian moral and ethical standards did not take account of other authorities pointing in an opposite direction. A committee advising the British Parliament recommended in 1957 repeal of laws punishing homosexual conduct. [Of] even more importance, almost five years before *Bowers* was decided the European Court of Human Rights considered a case with parallels to *Bowers* and to today's case. . . . The court held that the laws proscribing the conduct were invalid under the European Convention on Human Rights. Authoritative in all countries that are members of the Council of Europe (21 nations then, 45 nations now), the decision is at odds with the premise in *Bowers* that the claim put forward was insubstantial in our Western civilization.

In our own constitutional system the deficiencies in Bowers became even more apparent in the years following its announcement. The 25 States with laws prohibiting the relevant conduct referenced in the *Bowers* decision are reduced now to 13, of which 4 enforce their laws only against homosexual conduct. In those States where sodomy is still proscribed, whether for same-sex or heterosexual conduct, there is a pattern of nonenforcement with respect to consenting adults acting in private. The State of Texas admitted in 1994 that as of that date it had not prosecuted anyone under those circumstances.

Two principal cases decided after *Bowers* cast its holding into even more doubt. In Planned Parenthood of Southeastern Pa. v. Casey, the Court reaffirmed the substantive force of the liberty protected by the Due Process Clause. The *Casey* decision again confirmed that our laws and tradition afford constitutional protection to personal decisions relating to marriage, procreation, contraception, family relationships, child rearing, and education. In explaining the respect the

B. The Right of Privacy

Constitution demands for the autonomy of the person in making these choices, we stated as follows:

> These matters, involving the most intimate and personal choices a person may make in a lifetime, choices central to personal dignity and autonomy, are central to the liberty protected by the Fourteenth Amendment. At the heart of liberty is the right to define one's own concept of existence, of meaning, of the universe, and of the mystery of human life. Beliefs about these matters could not define the attributes of personhood were they formed under compulsion of the State.

Persons in a homosexual relationship may seek autonomy for these purposes, just as heterosexual persons do. The decision in *Bowers* would deny them this right.

The second post-*Bowers* case of principal relevance is Romer v. Evans. There the Court struck down class-based legislation directed at homosexuals as a violation of the Equal Protection Clause. *Romer* invalidated an amendment to Colorado's constitution which named as a solitary class persons who were homosexuals, lesbians, or bisexual either by "orientation, conduct, practices or relationships," and deprived them of protection under state antidiscrimination laws. We concluded that the provision was "born of animosity toward the class of persons affected" and further that it had no rational relation to a legitimate governmental purpose.

As an alternative argument in this case, counsel for the petitioners and some amici contend that *Romer* provides the basis for declaring the Texas statute invalid under the Equal Protection Clause. That is a tenable argument, but we conclude the instant case requires us to address whether *Bowers* itself has continuing validity. Were we to hold the statute invalid under the Equal Protection Clause some might question whether a prohibition would be valid if drawn differently, say, to prohibit the conduct both between same-sex and different-sex participants.

Equality of treatment and the due process right to demand respect for conduct protected by the substantive guarantee of liberty are linked in important respects, and a decision on the latter point advances both interests. If protected conduct is made criminal and the law which does so remains unexamined for its substantive validity, its stigma might remain even if it were not enforceable as drawn for equal protection reasons. When homosexual conduct is made criminal by the law of the State, that declaration in and of itself is an invitation to subject homosexual persons to discrimination both in the public and in the private spheres. The central holding of *Bowers* has been brought in question by this case, and it should be addressed. Its continuance as precedent demeans the lives of homosexual persons.

The stigma this criminal statute imposes, moreover, is not trivial. The offense, to be sure, is but [a] minor offense in the Texas legal system. Still, it remains a criminal offense with all that imports for the dignity of the persons charged. The petitioners will bear on their record the history of their criminal convictions. . . . We are advised that if Texas convicted an adult for private, consensual homosexual conduct under the statute here in question the convicted

9. Substantive Due Process: Modern Fundamental Rights

person would come within the registration laws of a least four States were he or she to be subject to their jurisdiction. This underscores the consequential nature of the punishment and the state-sponsored condemnation attendant to the criminal prohibition. Furthermore, the Texas criminal conviction carries with it the other collateral consequences always following a conviction, such as notations on job application forms, to mention but one example.

The foundations of *Bowers* have sustained serious erosion from our recent decisions in *Casey* and *Romer*. When our precedent has been thus weakened, criticism from other sources is of greater significance. In the United States criticism of *Bowers* has been substantial and continuing, disapproving of its reasoning in all respects, not just as to its historical assumptions. The courts of five different States have declined to follow it in interpreting provisions in their own state constitutions parallel to the Due Process Clause of the Fourteenth Amendment.

To the extent *Bowers* relied on values we share with a wider civilization, it should be noted that the reasoning and holding in *Bowers* have been rejected elsewhere. The European Court of Human Rights has followed not *Bowers* but its own decision in Dudgeon v. United Kingdom. Other nations, too, have taken action consistent with an affirmation of the protected right of homosexual adults to engage in intimate, consensual conduct. The right the petitioners seek in this case has been accepted as an integral part of human freedom in many other countries. There has been no showing that in this country the governmental interest in circumscribing personal choice is somehow more legitimate or urgent. *Bowers* itself causes uncertainty, for the precedents before and after its issuance contradict its central holding.

The rationale of *Bowers* does not withstand careful analysis. In his dissenting opinion in *Bowers* Justice Stevens came to these conclusions:

> Our prior cases make two propositions abundantly clear. First, the fact that the governing majority in a State has traditionally viewed a particular practice as immoral is not a sufficient reason for upholding a law prohibiting the practice; neither history nor tradition could save a law prohibiting miscegenation from constitutional attack. Second, individual decisions by married persons, concerning the intimacies of their physical relationship, even when not intended to produce offspring, are a form of "liberty" protected by the Due Process Clause of the Fourteenth Amendment. Moreover, this protection extends to intimate choices by unmarried as well as married persons.

Justice Stevens' analysis, in our view, should have been controlling in *Bowers* and should control here.

Bowers was not correct when it was decided, and it is not correct today. It ought not to remain binding precedent. Bowers v. Hardwick should be and now is overruled.

The present case does not involve minors. It does not involve persons who might be injured or coerced or who are situated in relationships where consent might not easily be refused. It does not involve public conduct or prostitution. It does not involve whether the government must give formal recognition to any relationship that homosexual persons seek to enter. The case does involve two adults who, with full and mutual consent from each other, engaged in sexual practices common to a homosexual lifestyle. The petitioners are entitled to respect for their private lives.

The State cannot demean their existence or control their destiny by making their private sexual conduct a crime. Their right to liberty under the Due Process Clause gives them the full right to engage in their conduct without intervention of the government. "It is a promise of the Constitution that there is a realm of personal liberty which the government may not enter."

The Texas statute furthers no legitimate state interest which can justify its intrusion into the personal and private life of the individual.

Had those who drew and ratified the Due Process Clauses of the Fifth Amendment or the Fourteenth Amendment known the components of liberty in its manifold possibilities, they might have been more specific. They did not presume to have this insight. They knew times can blind us to certain truths and later generations can see that laws once thought necessary and proper in fact serve only to oppress. As the Constitution endures, persons in every generation can invoke its principles in their own search for greater freedom.

The judgment of the Court of Appeals for the Texas Fourteenth District is reversed, and the case is remanded for further proceedings not inconsistent with this opinion.

It is so ordered.

Justice O'CONNOR, concurring in the judgment.

The Court today overrules Bowers v. Hardwick. I joined *Bowers*, and do not join the Court in overruling it. Nevertheless, I agree with the Court that Texas' statute banning same-sex sodomy is unconstitutional. Rather than relying on the substantive component of the Fourteenth Amendment's Due Process Clause, as the Court does, I base my conclusion on the Fourteenth Amendment's Equal Protection Clause.

The statute at issue here makes sodomy a crime only if a person "engages in deviate sexual intercourse with another individual of the same sex." Sodomy between opposite-sex partners, however, is not a crime in Texas. That is, Texas treats the same conduct differently based solely on the participants. Those harmed by this law are people who have a same-sex sexual orientation and thus are more likely to engage in behavior prohibited by [the state law].

[The] Texas statute makes homosexuals unequal in the eyes of the law by making particular conduct — and only that conduct — subject to criminal sanction. It appears that prosecutions under Texas' sodomy law are rare. This case shows, however, that prosecutions under [the state law] do occur. And while the penalty imposed on petitioners in this case was relatively minor, the consequences of conviction are not.

[Texas] attempts to justify its law, and the effects of the law, by arguing that the statute satisfies rational basis review because it furthers the legitimate governmental interest of the promotion of morality. [W]e have never held that moral disapproval, without any other asserted state interest, is a sufficient rationale under the Equal Protection Clause to justify a law that discriminates among groups of persons.

[That] this law as applied to private, consensual conduct is unconstitutional under the Equal Protection Clause does not mean that other laws distinguishing between heterosexuals and homosexuals would similarly fail under rational basis review. . . . Unlike the moral disapproval of same-sex relations — the asserted state interest in this case — other reasons exist to promote the institution of marriage beyond mere moral disapproval of an excluded group.

Justice SCALIA, with whom THE CHIEF JUSTICE and Justice THOMAS join, dissenting.

[Though] there is discussion of "fundamental propositions" and "fundamental decisions," nowhere does the Court's opinion declare that homosexual sodomy is a "fundamental right" under the Due Process Clause; nor does it subject the Texas law to the standard of review that would be appropriate (strict scrutiny) if homosexual sodomy were a "fundamental right." . . .

[The Texas statute] undoubtedly imposes constraints on liberty. So do laws prohibiting prostitution, recreational use of heroin, and, for that matter, working more than 60 hours per week in a bakery. . . . Our opinions applying the doctrine known as "substantive due process" hold that the Due Process Clause prohibits States from infringing fundamental liberty interests, unless the infringement is narrowly tailored to serve a compelling state interest. We have held repeatedly, in cases the Court today does not overrule, that only fundamental rights qualify for this so-called "heightened scrutiny" protection — that is, rights which are "'deeply rooted in this Nation's history and tradition.'" All other liberty interests may be abridged or abrogated pursuant to a validly enacted state law if that law is rationally related to a legitimate state interest.

Bowers held, first, that criminal prohibitions of homosexual sodomy are not subject to heightened scrutiny because they do not implicate a "fundamental right" under the Due Process Clause. Noting that "proscriptions against that conduct have ancient roots," that "sodomy was a criminal offense at common law and was forbidden by the laws of the original 13 States when they ratified the Bill of Rights," and that many States had retained their bans on sodomy, *Bowers* concluded that a right to engage in homosexual sodomy was not "'deeply rooted in this Nation's history and tradition.'"

The Court today does not overrule this holding. Not once does it describe homosexual sodomy as a "fundamental right" or a "fundamental liberty interest," nor does it subject the Texas statute to strict scrutiny. Instead, having failed to establish that the right to homosexual sodomy is "'deeply rooted in this Nation's history and tradition,'" the Court concludes that the application of Texas's statute to petitioners' conduct fails the rational-basis test, and overrules *Bowers*' holding to the contrary. "The Texas statute furthers no legitimate state interest which can justify its intrusion into the personal and private life of the individual."

The Court makes the claim [that] "laws prohibiting sodomy do not seem to have been enforced against consenting adults acting in private." The key qualifier here is "acting in private" — since the Court admits that sodomy laws were enforced against consenting adults (although the Court contends that prosecutions were "infrequent"). . . . Surely that lack of evidence would not sustain the proposition that consensual sodomy on private premises with the doors closed and windows covered was regarded as a "fundamental right," even though all other consensual sodomy was criminalized. . . . Realizing that fact, the Court instead says: "We think that our laws and traditions in the past half century are of most relevance here. These references show an emerging awareness that liberty gives substantial protection to adult persons in deciding how to conduct their private lives in matters pertaining to sex." Apart from the fact that such an "emerging awareness" does not establish a "fundamental right," the statement is factually false. States continue to prosecute all sorts of crimes by adults "in matters pertaining to sex."

I turn now to the ground on which the Court squarely rests its holding: the contention that there is no rational basis for the law here under attack. This proposition is so out of accord with our jurisprudence — indeed, with the jurisprudence of any society we know — that it requires little discussion. . . . The Texas statute undeniably seeks to further the belief of its citizens that certain forms of sexual behavior are "immoral and unacceptable," the same interest furthered by criminal laws against fornication, bigamy, adultery, adult incest, bestiality, and obscenity. *Bowers* held that this was a legitimate state interest. The Court today reaches the opposite conclusion. The Texas statute, it says, "furthers no legitimate state interest which can justify its intrusion into the personal and private life of the individual." The Court embraces instead Justice Stevens' declaration in his *Bowers* dissent, that "the fact that the governing majority in a State has traditionally viewed a particular practice as immoral is not a sufficient reason for upholding a law prohibiting the practice." This effectively decrees the end of all morals legislation. If, as the Court asserts, the promotion of majoritarian sexual morality is not even a legitimate state interest, none of the above-mentioned laws can survive rational-basis review.

[Today's] opinion is the product of a Court, which is the product of a law-profession culture, that has largely signed on to the so-called homosexual agenda, by which I mean the agenda promoted by some homosexual activists directed at eliminating the moral opprobrium that has traditionally attached to homosexual conduct. I noted in an earlier opinion the fact that the American Association of Law Schools (to which any reputable law school must seek to belong) excludes from membership any school that refuses to ban from its job-interview facilities a law firm (no matter how small) that does not wish to hire as a prospective partner a person who openly engages in homosexual conduct.

One of the most revealing statements in today's opinion is the Court's grim warning that the criminalization of homosexual conduct is "an invitation to subject homosexual persons to discrimination both in the public and in the private spheres." It is clear from this that the Court has taken sides in the culture war, departing from its role of assuring, as neutral observer, that the democratic rules of engagement are observed. Many Americans do not want persons who openly engage in homosexual conduct as partners in their business, as scoutmasters for their children, as teachers in their children's schools, or as boarders in their home. They view this as protecting themselves and their families from a lifestyle that they believe to be immoral and destructive. The Court views it as "discrimination" which it is the function of our judgments to deter. So imbued is the Court with the law profession's anti-anti-homosexual culture, that it is seemingly unaware that the attitudes of that culture are not obviously "mainstream"; that in most States what the Court calls "discrimination" against those who engage in homosexual acts is perfectly legal; that proposals to ban such "discrimination" under Title VII have repeatedly been rejected by Congress; that in some cases such "discrimination" is mandated by federal statute; and that in some cases such "discrimination" is a constitutional right.

Let me be clear that I have nothing against homosexuals, or any other group, promoting their agenda through normal democratic means. Social perceptions of sexual and other morality change over time, and every group has the right to persuade its fellow citizens that its view of such matters is the best. That homosexuals have achieved some success in that enterprise is attested to by the fact that Texas is one of the few remaining States that criminalize private, consensual homosexual acts. But persuading one's fellow citizens is one thing, and imposing one's views in absence of democratic majority will is something else. I would no more require a State to criminalize homosexual acts — or, for that matter, display any moral disapprobation of them — than I would forbid it to do so. What Texas has chosen to do is well within the range of traditional democratic action, and its hand should not be stayed through the invention of a brand-new "constitutional right" by a Court that is impatient of democratic change. It is indeed true that "later generations can see that laws once thought necessary and proper in fact serve only to oppress," and when that happens, later generations can repeal those laws. But it is the premise of our system that those judgments are to be made by the people, and not imposed by a governing caste that knows best.

One of the benefits of leaving regulation of this matter to the people rather than to the courts is that the people, unlike judges, need not carry things to their logical conclusion. The people may feel that their disapprobation of homosexual conduct is strong enough to disallow homosexual marriage, but not strong enough to criminalize private homosexual acts — and may legislate accordingly. The Court today pretends that it possesses a similar freedom of action, so that that we need not fear judicial imposition of homosexual marriage, as has recently occurred in Canada (in a decision that the Canadian Government has chosen not to appeal). At the end of its opinion — after having laid waste the foundations of our rational-basis jurisprudence — the Court says that the present case "does not involve whether the government must give formal recognition to any relationship that homosexual persons seek to enter." Do not believe it. More illuminating than this bald, unreasoned disclaimer is the progression of thought displayed by an earlier passage in the Court's opinion, which notes the constitutional protections afforded to "personal decisions relating to marriage, procreation, contraception, family relationships, child rearing, and education," and then declares that "persons in a homosexual relationship may seek autonomy for these purposes, just as heterosexual persons do." Today's opinion dismantles the structure of constitutional law that has permitted a distinction to be made between heterosexual and homosexual unions, insofar as formal recognition in marriage is concerned. If moral disapprobation of homosexual conduct is "no legitimate state interest" for purposes of proscribing that conduct, and if, as the Court coos (casting aside all pretense of neutrality), "when sexuality finds overt expression in intimate conduct with another person, the conduct can be but one element in a personal bond that is more enduring;" what justification could there possibly be for denying the benefits of marriage to homosexual couples exercising "the liberty protected by the Constitution"? Surely not the encouragement of procreation, since the sterile and the elderly are allowed to marry. This case "does not involve" the issue of homosexual marriage only if one entertains the belief that principle and logic have nothing to do with the decisions of this Court. Many will hope that, as the Court comfortingly assures us, this is so.

Justice THOMAS, dissenting.

[A]s a member of this Court I am not empowered to help petitioners and others similarly situated. My duty, rather, is to "decide cases 'agreeably to the Constitution and laws of the United States.'" And, just like Justice Stewart, I "can find [neither in the Bill of Rights nor any other part of the Constitution a] general right of privacy," or as the Court terms it today, the "liberty of the person both in its spatial and more transcendent dimensions."

∾ PROBLEMS ∾

1. *How Would You Have Voted?* Assume that you were to cast the deciding votes in *Bowers* and *Lawrence*. Would your inclination be to define the proposed liberty interest as the right of privacy generally or the right to engage in sodomy or homosexual sodomy? What would be the basis for your choice?

2. *Defining Privacy After* Bowers. How would you describe the right of privacy in light of the Court's decision in *Bowers*? Don't the boundaries of this right extend beyond family, procreation, and marriage? Is it logical to separate sex from this equation? How would you define the right of privacy after *Lawrence*?

3. *Grooming Restrictions.* Consider a police department regulation that imposes grooming restrictions on officers. Does this restriction implicate a constitutionally protected privacy interest? *See* Kelley v. Johnson, 425 U.S. 238 (1976).

4. *More on Same-Sex Marriage.* Jan and Joy are a lesbian couple who have lived together as a same-sex couple for nearly 20 years. During that time, the two have made a "commitment" to each other; they have produced two children and adopted three more. The group functions and regards itself as a family. However, Jan and Joy have always been disturbed by the fact that Kentucky laws prevent same-sex couples from marrying. Following *Lawrence*, Jan and Joy file suit against the commonwealth seeking injunctive relief allowing them to marry. Jan and Joy

claim that the constitutional right of privacy includes a right of intimate association that extends to same-sex couples and includes the right to marry. How would you argue the case for Jan and Joy? How might the commonwealth respond? Who should win?

5. *More on the Proposed Child Custody Statute.* Consider the problem presented at the beginning of the chapter. In light of *Lawrence*, have you altered your conclusions regarding the constitutionality of the proposed statute? Why? Explain.

7. Right to Die

Termination of life other than by natural causes presents questions of a profound moral nature. Issues of this type have intersected with the debate over capital punishment and abortion, insofar as fundamental values have vied to shape the law and the judiciary's role in developing principles that affect the understanding, potential, and duration of life. Case law concerning a right to die reflects a cautious attitude toward the concept and operation of this liberty interest. In Cruzan v. Director, Missouri Department of Health, the Court announced the right's existence but found that it does not trump a state's interest in determining by clear and convincing evidence a person's desire to discontinue medical treatment.

Cruzan v. Director, Missouri Department of Health
497 U.S. 261 (1990)

Chief Justice REHNQUIST delivered the opinion of the Court.

Petitioner Nancy Beth Cruzan was rendered incompetent as a result of severe injuries sustained during an automobile accident. Co-petitioners Lester and Joyce Cruzan, Nancy's parents and coguardians, sought a court order directing the withdrawal of their daughter's artificial feeding and hydration equipment after it became apparent that she had virtually no chance of recovering her cognitive faculties. The Supreme Court of Missouri held that because there was no clear and convincing evidence of Nancy's desire to have life-sustaining treatment withdrawn under such circumstances, her parents lacked authority to effectuate such a request. We granted certiorari and now affirm.

The Fourteenth Amendment provides that no State shall "deprive any person of life, liberty, or property, without due process of law." The principle that a competent person has a constitutionally protected liberty interest in refusing unwanted medical treatment may be inferred from our prior decisions.

[But] determining that a person has a "liberty interest" under the Due Process Clause does not end the inquiry; "whether respondent's constitutional rights have been violated must be determined by balancing his liberty interests against the relevant state interests."

Petitioners insist that under the general holdings of our cases, the forced administration of life-sustaining medical treatment, and even of artificially delivered food and water essential to life, would implicate a competent person's liberty interest. Although we think the logic of the cases discussed above would embrace such a liberty interest, the dramatic consequences involved in refusal of such treatment would inform the inquiry as to whether the deprivation of that interest is constitutionally permissible. But for purposes of this case, we assume that the United States Constitution would grant a competent person a constitutionally protected right to refuse lifesaving hydration and nutrition.

Petitioners go on to assert that an incompetent person should possess the same right in this respect as is possessed by a competent person. [T]he difficulty with petitioners' claim is that in a sense it begs the question: An incompetent person is not able to make an informed and voluntary choice to exercise a hypothetical right to refuse treatment or any other right. Such a "right" must be exercised for her, if at all, by some sort of surrogate. Here, Missouri has in effect recognized that under certain circumstances a surrogate may act for the patient in electing to have hydration and nutrition withdrawn in such a way as to cause death, but it has established a procedural safeguard to assure that the action of the surrogate conforms as best it may to the wishes expressed by the patient while competent. Missouri requires that evidence of the incompetent's wishes as to the withdrawal of treatment be proved by clear and convincing evidence. The question, then, is whether the United States Constitution forbids the establishment of this procedural requirement by the State. We hold that it does not.

Whether or not Missouri's clear and convincing evidence requirement comports with the United States Constitution depends in part on what interests the State may properly seek to protect in this situation. Missouri relies on its interest in the protection and preservation of human life, and there can be no gainsaying this interest. As a general matter, the States — indeed, all civilized nations — demonstrate their commitment to life by treating homicide as a serious crime. Moreover, the majority of States in this country have laws imposing criminal penalties on one who assists another to commit suicide. We do not think a State is required to remain neutral in the face of an informed and voluntary decision by a physically able adult to starve to death.

But in the context presented here, a State has more particular interests at stake. The choice between life and death is a deeply personal decision of obvious and overwhelming finality. We believe Missouri may legitimately seek to safeguard the personal element of this choice through the imposition of heightened evidentiary requirements. It cannot be disputed that the Due Process Clause protects an interest in life as well as an interest in refusing life-sustaining medical treatment. Not all incompetent patients will have loved ones available to serve as surrogate decision-makers. And even where family members are present, "[t]here will, of course, be some unfortunate situations in which family members will not act to protect a patient." A State is entitled to guard against potential abuses in such situations. Similarly, a State is entitled to consider that a judicial proceeding to make a determination regarding an incompetent's wishes may very well not be an adversarial one, with the added guarantee of accurate factfinding that the adversary process brings with it. Finally, we think a State may properly decline to make judgments about the "quality" of life that a particular individual may enjoy, and simply assert an unqualified interest in the preservation of human life to be weighed against the constitutionally protected interests of the individual.

In our view, Missouri has permissibly sought to advance these interests through the adoption of a "clear and convincing" standard of proof to govern such proceedings. "The function of a standard of proof, as that concept is embodied in the Due Process Clause and in the realm of factfinding, is to 'instruct the factfinder concerning the degree of confidence our society thinks he should have in the correctness of factual conclusions for a particular type of adjudication.'"

[We] think it self-evident that the interests at stake in the instant proceedings are more substantial, both on an individual and societal level, than those involved in a run-of-the-mine civil dispute. But not only does the standard of proof reflect the importance of a particular adjudication, it also serves as "a societal judgment about how the risk of error should be distributed between the litigants." The more stringent the burden of proof a party must bear, the more that party bears the risk of an erroneous decision. We believe that Missouri may permissibly place an increased risk of an erroneous decision on those seeking to terminate an incompetent individual's life-sustaining treatment. An erroneous decision not to terminate results in a maintenance of the status quo; the possibility of subsequent developments such as advancements in medical science, the discovery of new evidence regarding the patient's intent, changes in the law, or simply the unexpected death of the patient despite the administration of life-sustaining treatment at least create the potential that a wrong decision will eventually be corrected or its impact mitigated. An erroneous decision to withdraw life-sustaining treatment, however, is not susceptible of correction.

[In] sum, we conclude that a State may apply a clear and convincing evidence standard in proceedings where a guardian seeks to discontinue nutrition and hydration of a person diagnosed to be in a persistent vegetative state. We note that many courts which have adopted some sort of substituted judgment procedure in situations like this, whether they limit consideration of evidence to the prior expressed wishes of the incompetent individual, or whether they allow more general proof of what the individual's decision would have been, require a clear and convincing standard of proof for such evidence.

Petitioners alternatively contend that Missouri must accept the "substituted judgment" of close family members even in the absence of substantial proof that their views reflect the views of the patient. [But] we do not think these cases support their claim. [Here] again petitioners would seek to turn a decision which allowed a State to rely on family decisionmaking into a constitutional requirement that the State recognize such decisionmaking. But constitutional law does not work that way.

No doubt is engendered by anything in this record but that Nancy Cruzan's mother and father are loving and caring parents. If the State were required by the United States Constitution to repose a right of "substituted judgment" with anyone, the Cruzans would surely qualify. But we do not think the Due Process Clause requires the State to repose judgment on these matters with anyone but the patient herself. Close family members may have a strong feeling — a feeling not at all ignoble or unworthy, but not entirely disinterested, either — that they do not wish to witness the continuation of the life of a loved one which they regard as hopeless, meaningless, and even degrading. But there is no automatic assurance that the view of close family members will necessarily be the same as the patient's would have been had she been confronted with the prospect of her situation while competent. All of the reasons previously discussed for allowing Missouri to require clear and convincing evidence of the patient's wishes lead us to conclude that the State may choose to defer only to those wishes, rather than confide the decision to close family members.

The judgment of the Supreme Court of Missouri is
Affirmed.

Justice O'CONNOR, concurring.

I agree that a protected liberty interest in refusing unwanted medical treatment may be inferred from our prior decisions, and that the refusal of artificially delivered food and water is encompassed within that liberty interest. I write separately to clarify why I believe this to be so.

[T]he liberty interest in refusing medical treatment flows from decisions involving the State's invasions into the body. Because our notions of liberty are inextricably entwined with our idea of physical freedom and self-determination, the Court has often deemed state incursions into the body repugnant to the interests protected by the Due Process Clause. Our Fourth Amendment jurisprudence has echoed this same concern. The State's imposition of medical treatment on an unwilling competent adult necessarily involves some form of restraint and intrusion. A seriously ill or dying patient whose wishes are not honored may feel a captive of the machinery required for life-sustaining measures or other medical interventions. Such forced treatment may burden that individual's liberty interests as much as any state coercion.

The State's artificial provision of nutrition and hydration implicates identical concerns. Artificial feeding cannot readily be distinguished from other forms of medical treatment. Whether or not the techniques used to pass food and water into the patient's alimentary tract are termed "medical treatment," it is clear they all involve some degree of intrusion and restraint. Feeding a patient by means of a nasogastric tube requires a physician to pass a long flexible tube through the patient's nose, throat, and esophagus and into the stomach. Because of the discomfort such a tube causes, "[m]any patients need to be restrained forcibly and their hands put into large mittens to prevent them from removing the tube." [A] gastrostomy tube (as was used to provide food and water to Nancy Cruzan) or jejunostomy tube must be surgically implanted into the stomach or small intestine. Requiring a competent adult to endure such procedures against her will burdens the patient's liberty, dignity, and freedom to determine the course of her own treatment. Accordingly, the liberty guaranteed by the Due Process Clause must protect, if it protects anything, an individual's deeply personal decision to reject medical treatment, including the artificial delivery of food and water.

[T]he Court does not today decide the issue whether a State must also give effect to the decisions of a surrogate decision-maker. In my view, such a duty may well be constitutionally required to protect the patient's liberty interest in refusing medical treatment. Few individuals provide explicit oral or written instructions regarding their intent to refuse medical treatment should they become incompetent. States which decline to consider any evidence other than such instructions may frequently fail to honor a patient's intent. Such failures might be avoided if the State considered an equally probative source of evidence: the patient's appointment of a proxy to make health care decisions on her behalf. [These] procedures for surrogate decisionmaking, which appear to be rapidly gaining in acceptance, may be a valuable additional safeguard of the patient's interest in directing his medical care. Moreover, as patients are likely to select a family member as a surrogate giving effect to a proxy's decisions may also protect the "freedom of personal choice in matters of . . . family life."

Today's decision, holding only that the Constitution permits a State to require clear and convincing evidence of Nancy Cruzan's desire to have artificial hydration and nutrition withdrawn, does not preclude a future determination that the Constitution requires the States to implement the decisions of a patient's duly appointed surrogate. Nor does it prevent States from developing other approaches for protecting an incompetent individual's liberty interest in refusing medical treatment. As is evident from the Court's survey of state court decisions, no national consensus has yet emerged on the best solution for this difficult and sensitive problem. Today we decide only that one State's practice does not violate the Constitution. . . .

Justice SCALIA, concurring.
The various opinions in this case portray quite clearly the difficult, indeed agonizing, questions that are presented by the constantly increasing power of science to keep the human body alive for longer than any reasonable person would want to inhabit it. . . . While I agree with the Court's analysis today[, I] would have preferred that we announce [that] the federal courts have no business in this field[, and] hence, that even when it is demonstrated by clear and convincing evidence that a patient no longer wishes certain measures to be taken to preserve his or her life, it is up to the citizens of Missouri to decide, through their elected representatives, whether that wish will be honored. . . .

The text of the Due Process Clause does not protect individuals against deprivations of liberty simpliciter. It protects them against deprivations of liberty "without due process of law." To determine that such a deprivation would not occur if Nancy Cruzan were forced to take nourishment against her will, it is unnecessary to reopen the historically recurrent debate over whether "due process" includes substantive restrictions. It is at least true that no "substantive due process" claim can be maintained unless the claimant demonstrates that the State has deprived him of a right historically and traditionally protected against state interference. That cannot possibly be established here.

The dissents of Justices Brennan and Stevens make a plausible case for our intervention here only by embracing [a] political principle that the States are free to adopt, but that is demonstrably not imposed by the Constitution. "[T]he State," says Justice Brennan, "has no legitimate general interest in someone's life, completely abstracted from the interest of the person living that life, that could outweigh the person's choice to avoid medical treatment." . . . Justice Brennan's position ultimately rests upon the proposition that it is none of the State's business if a person wants to commit suicide. Justice Stevens is explicit on the point: "Choices about death touch the core of liberty. . . . [N]ot much may be said with confidence about death unless it is said from faith, and that alone is reason enough to protect the freedom to conform choices about death to individual conscience." This is a view that some societies have held, and that our States are free to adopt if they wish. But it is not a view imposed by our constitutional traditions, in which the power of the State to prohibit suicide is unquestionable. . . .

Our salvation is the Equal Protection Clause, which requires the democratic majority to accept for themselves and their loved ones what they impose on you and me. This Court need not, and has no authority to, inject itself into every field of human activity where irrationality and oppression may theoretically occur, and if it tries to do so it will destroy itself.

Justice BRENNAN, with whom Justice MARSHALL and Justice BLACKMUN join, dissenting.

[Because] I believe that Nancy Cruzan has a fundamental right to be free of unwanted artificial nutrition and hydration, which right is not outweighed by any interests of the State, and because I find that the improperly biased procedural obstacles imposed by the Missouri Supreme Court impermissibly burden that right, I respectfully dissent. Nancy Cruzan is entitled to choose to die with dignity. . . .

The question before this Court is a relatively narrow one: whether the Due Process Clause allows Missouri to require a now-incompetent patient in an irreversible persistent vegetative state to remain on life support absent rigorously clear and convincing evidence that avoiding the treatment represents the patient's prior, express choice.

[T]he Court concedes that our prior decisions "support the recognition of a general liberty interest in refusing medical treatment." [But] if a competent person has a liberty interest to be free of unwanted medical treatment, [it] must be fundamental. "We are dealing here with [a decision] which involves one of the basic civil rights of man." Whatever other liberties protected by the Due Process Clause are fundamental, "those liberties that are 'deeply rooted in this Nation's history and tradition'" are among them. "Such a tradition commands respect in part because the Constitution carries the gloss of history." [No] material distinction can be drawn between the treatment to which Nancy Cruzan continues to be subject — artificial nutrition and hydration — and any other medical treatment. The artificial delivery of nutrition and hydration is undoubtedly medical treatment.

Nor does the fact that Nancy Cruzan is now incompetent deprive her of her fundamental rights. [As] the majority recognizes, the question is not whether an incompetent has constitutional rights, but how such rights may be exercised. . . .

There are also affirmative reasons why someone like Nancy might choose to forgo artificial nutrition and hydration under these circumstances. Dying is personal. And it is profound. For many, the thought of an ignoble end, steeped in decay, is abhorrent. A quiet, proud death, bodily integrity intact, is a matter of extreme consequence.

Although the right to be free of unwanted medical intervention, like other constitutionally protected interests, may not be absolute, no state interest could outweigh the rights of an individual in Nancy Cruzan's position. Whatever a State's possible interests in mandating life-support treatment under other circumstances, there is no good to be obtained here by Missouri's insistence that Nancy Cruzan remain on life-support systems if it is indeed her wish not to do so. Missouri does not claim, nor could it, that society as a whole will be benefited by Nancy's receiving medical treatment. No third party's situation will be improved and no harm to others will be averted.

The only state interest asserted here is a general interest in the preservation of life. But the State has no legitimate general interest in someone's life, completely abstracted from the interest of the person living that life, that could outweigh the person's choice to avoid medical treatment. . . . This is not to say that the State has no legitimate interests to assert here. As the majority recognizes, Missouri has a parens patriae interest in providing Nancy Cruzan, now incompetent, with as accurate as possible a determination of how she would exercise her rights under these circumstances. Second, if and when it is determined that Nancy Cruzan would want to continue treatment, the State may legitimately assert an interest in providing that treatment. But until Nancy's wishes have been determined, the only state interest that may be asserted is an interest in safe-guarding the accuracy of that determination. . . .

The majority claims that the allocation of the risk of error is justified because it is more important not to terminate life support for someone who would wish it continued than to honor the wishes of someone who would not. An erroneous decision to terminate life support is irrevocable, says the majority, while an erro- neous decision not to terminate "results in a maintenance of the status quo." But, from the point of view of the patient, an erroneous decision in either direction is irrevocable. An erroneous decision to terminate artificial nutrition and hydra- tion, to be sure, will lead to failure of that last remnant of physiological life, the brain stem, and result in complete brain death. An erroneous decision not to ter- minate life support, however, robs a patient of the very qualities protected by the right to avoid unwanted medical treatment. His own degraded existence is per- petuated; his family's suffering is protracted; the memory he leaves behind becomes more and more distorted.

[Finally], I cannot agree with the majority that where it is not possible to determine what choice an incompetent patient would make, a State's role as parens patriae permits the State automatically to make that choice itself. . . . A State may ensure that the person who makes the decision on the patient's behalf is the one whom the patient himself would have selected to make that choice for him. And a State may exclude from consideration anyone having improper motives. But a State generally must either repose the choice with the person whom the patient himself would most likely have chosen as proxy or leave the decision to the patient's family.

Justice STEVENS, dissenting.

[T]he Constitution requires the State to care for Nancy Cruzan's life in a way that gives appropriate respect to her own best interests. . . . Medical advances have altered the physiological conditions of death in ways that may be alarming: Highly invasive treatment may perpetuate human existence through a merger of body and machine that some might reasonably regard as an insult to life rather than as its continuation. But those same advances, and the reorganization of medical care accompanying the new science and technology, have also transformed the political and social conditions of death: People are less likely to die at home, and more likely to die in relatively public places, such as hospitals or nursing homes.

Ultimate questions that might once have been dealt with in intimacy by a family and its physician have now become the concern of institutions. When the institution is a state hospital, as it is in this case, the government itself becomes involved. Dying nonetheless remains a part of "the life which characteristically has its place in the home." The "integrity of that life is something so fundamental that it has been found to draw to its protection the principles of more than one explicitly granted Constitutional right," and our decisions have demarcated a "private realm of family life which the state cannot enter." The physical boundaries of the home, of course, remain crucial guarantors of the life within it. Nevertheless, this Court has long recognized that the liberty to make the decisions and choices constitutive of private life is so fundamental to our "concept of ordered liberty," that those choices must occasionally be afforded more direct protection.

[It] is against this background of decisional law, and the constitutional tradition which it illuminates, that the right to be free from unwanted life-sustaining medical treatment must be understood. . . . Choices about death touch the core of liberty. Our duty, and the concomitant freedom, to come to terms with the conditions of our own mortality are undoubtedly "so rooted in the traditions and conscience of our people as to be ranked as fundamental," and indeed are essential incidents of the unalienable rights to life and liberty endowed us by our Creator. . . .

[To] be constitutionally permissible, Missouri's intrusion upon these fundamental liberties must, at a minimum, bear a reasonable relationship to a legitimate state end. Missouri asserts that its policy is related to a state interest in the protection of life. In my view, however, it is an effort to define life, rather than to protect it, that is the heart of Missouri's policy. Missouri insists, without regard to Nancy Cruzan's own interests, upon equating her life with the biological persistence of her bodily functions. Nancy Cruzan, it must be remembered, is not now simply incompetent. She is in a persistent vegetative state and has been so for seven years. The trial court found, and no party contested, that Nancy has no possibility of recovery and no consciousness.

My disagreement with the Court is thus unrelated to its endorsement of the clear and convincing standard of proof for cases of this kind. Indeed, I agree that the controlling facts must be established with unmistakable clarity. . . . The failure of Missouri's policy to heed the interests of a dying individual with respect to matters so private is ample evidence of the policy's illegitimacy. . . . A State that seeks to demonstrate its commitment to life may do so by aiding those who are actively struggling for life and health. In this endeavor, unfortunately, no State can lack for opportunities: There can be no need to make an example of tragic cases like that of Nancy Cruzan.

Notes and Questions

1. Cruzan's *Underpinnings.* The *Cruzan* decision grounded the right to refuse medical treatment in the Due Process Clause. The majority opinion's authorship by Chief Justice Rehnquist was noteworthy insofar as he generally had been a forceful exponent of the notion that modern substantive due process review essentially constituted a neo-*Lochnerian* exercise. In Washington v. Glucksberg, the Court considered a due process challenge to a state law making it a felony knowingly to assist in an individual's suicide. Referencing traditional prohibitions against suicide, and pursuant to a careful description of the proposed liberty interest, the Court found no protected right.

2. *More on Defining "Liberty."* Is the liberty interest at stake in *Cruzan* defined with a high level of specificity or a high level of abstraction? How could a description of it be drafted with more specificity? What difference would that make?

∿ PROBLEMS ∿

1. *The Schiavo Case.* In 2005, right-to-die issues resurfaced in the Terri Schiavo case. Schiavo, who was in a persistent vegetative state, was the subject of a bitter dispute between her husband (who claimed that she had expressed a desire not to remain alive in a vegetative state) and her parents (who wanted to keep her alive). After lengthy judicial proceedings, and an attempt by Congress to intervene, the husband was allowed to exercise a decision to let Terri die. How should the courts resolve such disputes between spouses and parents?

2. *Terminally Ill Patients and Refusal of Treatment.* Consider Justice Scalia's arguments against recognizing the right to refuse unwanted medical treatment as fundamental. Minus this right, would a terminal cancer patient be compelled to take drugs that prolong life even though they diminish the quality of life?

3. *Required Immunizations.* Consider state laws or school district rules that require children to be immunized against certain diseases. May a child, or parent or guardian, refuse immunization on grounds it constitutes unwanted medical treatment?

Washington v. Glucksberg

521 U.S. 702 (1997)

Chief Justice REHNQUIST delivered the opinion of the Court.

The question presented in this case is whether Washington's prohibition against "caus[ing]" or "aid[ing]" a suicide offends the Fourteenth Amendment to the United States Constitution. We hold that it does not.

It has always been a crime to assist a suicide in the State of Washington. . . . At the same time, Washington's Natural Death Act, enacted in 1979, states that the "withholding or withdrawal of life-sustaining treatment" at a patient's direction "shall not, for any purpose, constitute a suicide."

[Respondents] . . . are physicians who practice in Washington. These doctors occasionally treat terminally ill, suffering patients, and declare that they would assist these patients in ending their lives if not for Washington's assisted-suicide ban. [They are] seeking a declaration that is, on its face, unconstitutional.

We begin, as we do in all due process cases, by examining our Nation's history, legal traditions, and practices. In almost every State — indeed, in almost every western democracy — it is a crime to assist a suicide. The States' assisted-suicide bans are not innovations. Rather, they are longstanding expressions of the States' commitment to the protection and preservation of all human life. Indeed, opposition to and condemnation of suicide — and, therefore, of assisting suicide — are consistent and enduring themes of our philosophical, legal, and cultural heritages. . . . More specifically, for over 700 years, the Anglo-American common-law tradition has punished or otherwise disapproved of both suicide and assisting suicide.

The Due Process Clause guarantees more than fair process, and the "liberty" it protects includes more than the absence of physical restraint. The Clause also provides heightened protection against government interference with certain fundamental rights and liberty interests. In a long line of cases, we have held that, in addition to the specific freedoms protected by the Bill of Rights, the "liberty" specially protected by the Due Process Clause includes the rights to marry; to have children; to direct the education and upbringing of one's children; to marital privacy; to use contraception; to bodily integrity; and to abortion. We have also assumed, and strongly suggested, that the Due Process Clause protects the traditional right to refuse unwanted lifesaving medical treatment.

But we "ha[ve] always been reluctant to expand the concept of substantive due process because guideposts for responsible decision-making in this unchartered area are scarce and open-ended." By extending constitutional protection to an asserted right or liberty interest, we, to a great extent, place the matter outside the arena of public debate and legislative action. We must therefore "exercise the utmost care whenever we are asked to break new ground in this field," lest the liberty protected by the Due Process Clause be subtly transformed into the policy preferences of the Members of this Court.

Our established method of substantive-due-process analysis has two primary features: First, we have regularly observed that the Due Process Clause specially protects those fundamental rights and liberties which are, objectively, "deeply rooted in this Nation's history and tradition," and "implicit in the concept of ordered liberty," such that "neither liberty nor justice would exist if they were sacrificed." Second, we have required in substantive-due-process cases a "careful description" of the asserted fundamental liberty interest. Our Nation's history, legal traditions, and practices thus provide the crucial "guideposts for responsible decision-making, that direct and restrain our exposition of the Due Process Clause."

As we stated recently in *Flores,* the Fourteenth Amendment "forbids the government to infringe . . . 'fundamental' liberty interests at all, no matter what process is provided, unless the infringement is narrowly tailored to serve a compelling state interest."

Justice Souter, relying on Justice Harlan's dissenting opinion in Poe v. Ullman, would largely abandon this restrained methodology, and instead ask "whether [Washington's] statute sets up one of those 'arbitrary impositions' or 'purposeless restraints' at odds with the Due Process Clause of the Fourteenth Amendment." In our view, however, the development of this Court's substantive-due-process jurisprudence has been a process whereby the outlines of the "liberty" specially protected by the Fourteenth Amendment — never fully clarified, to be sure, and perhaps not capable of being fully clarified — have at least been carefully refined by concrete examples involving fundamental rights found to be deeply rooted in our legal tradition. This approach tends to rein in the subjective elements that are necessarily present in due-process judicial review. In addition, by establishing a threshold requirement — that a challenged state action implicate a fundamental right — before requiring more than a reasonable relation to a legitimate state interest to justify the action, it avoids the need for complex balancing of competing interests in every case.

[A]s noted above, we have a tradition of carefully formulating the interest at stake in substantive-due-process cases. For example, although *Cruzan* is often described as a "right to die" case, we were, in fact, more precise: We assumed that the Constitution granted competent persons a "constitutionally protected right to refuse lifesaving hydration and nutrition." The Washington statute at issue in this case prohibits "aid[ing] another person to attempt suicide," and, thus, the question before us is whether the "liberty" specially protected by the Due Process Clause includes a right to commit suicide which itself includes a right to assistance in doing so.

We now inquire whether this asserted right has any place in our Nation's traditions. Here, we are confronted with a consistent and almost universal tradition that has long rejected the asserted right, and continues explicitly to reject it today, even for terminally ill, mentally competent adults. To hold for respondents, we would have to reverse centuries of legal doctrine and practice, and strike down the considered policy choice of almost every State.

[T]he right assumed in *Cruzan* was not simply deduced from abstract concepts of personal autonomy. Given the common-law rule that forced medication was a battery, and the long legal tradition protecting the decision to refuse unwanted medical treatment, our assumption was entirely consistent with this Nation's history and constitutional traditions. The decision to commit suicide with the assistance of another may be just as personal and profound as the decision to refuse unwanted medical treatment, but it has never enjoyed similar legal protection. Indeed, the two acts are widely and reasonably regarded as quite distinct. In *Cruzan* itself, we recognized that most States outlawed assisted suicide — and even more do today — and we certainly gave no intimation that the right to refuse unwanted medical treatment could be somehow transmuted into a right to assistance in committing suicide.

[T]he history of the law's treatment of assisted suicide in this country has been and continues to be one of the rejection of nearly all efforts to permit it. That being the case, our decisions lead us to conclude that the asserted "right" to assistance in committing suicide is not a fundamental liberty interest protected by the Due Process Clause. The Constitution also requires, however, that Washington's assisted-suicide ban be rationally related to legitimate government interests. This requirement is unquestionably met here.

First, Washington has an "unqualified interest in the preservation of human life." The State's prohibition on assisted suicide, like all homicide laws, both reflects and advances its commitment to this interest. This interest is symbolic and aspirational as well as practical.

[Washington] . . . has rejected this sliding-scale approach and, through its assisted-suicide ban, insists that all persons' lives, from beginning to end, regardless of physical or mental condition, are under the full protection of the law. As we have previously affirmed, the States "may properly decline to make judgments about the 'quality' of life that a particular individual may enjoy." This remains true, as *Cruzan* makes clear, even for those who are near death.

Relatedly, all admit that suicide is a serious public-health problem, especially among persons in otherwise vulnerable groups. The State has an interest in preventing suicide, and in studying, identifying, and treating its causes.

Those who attempt suicide — terminally ill or not — often suffer from depression or other mental disorders. Research indicates, however, that many people who request physician-assisted suicide withdraw that request if their depression and pain are treated. Thus, legal physician-assisted suicide could make it more difficult for the State to protect depressed or mentally ill persons, or those who are suffering from untreated pain, from suicidal impulses.

The State also has an interest in protecting the integrity and ethics of the medical profession. [The] American Medical Association, like many other medical and physicians' groups, has concluded that "[p]hysician-assisted suicide is fundamentally incompatible with the physician's role as healer."

Next, the State has an interest in protecting vulnerable groups — including the poor, the elderly, and disabled persons — from abuse, neglect, and mistakes. [If] physician-assisted suicide were permitted, many might resort to it to spare their families the substantial financial burden of end-of-life health-care costs.

The State's interest here goes beyond protecting the vulnerable from coercion; it extends to protecting disabled and terminally ill people from prejudice, negative and inaccurate stereotypes, and "societal indifference." The State's assisted-suicide ban reflects and reinforces its policy that the lives of terminally ill, disabled, and elderly people must be no less valued than the lives of the young and healthy, and that a seriously disabled person's suicidal impulses should be interpreted and treated the same way as anyone else's.

Finally, the State may fear that permitting assisted suicide will start it down the path to voluntary and perhaps even involuntary euthanasia. [If] suicide is protected as a matter of constitutional right, it is argued, "every man and woman in the United States must enjoy it." [Thus], it turns out that what is couched as a limited right to "physician-assisted suicide" is likely, in effect, a much broader license, which could prove extremely difficult to police and contain. Washington's ban on assisting suicide prevents such erosion.

[We] need not weigh exactly the relative strengths of these various interests. They are unquestionably important and legitimate, and Washington's ban on assisted suicide is at least reasonably related to their promotion and protection. We therefore hold that [the state law] does not violate the Fourteenth Amendment, either on its face or "as applied to competent, terminally ill adults who wish to hasten their deaths by obtaining medication prescribed by their doctors."

Throughout the Nation, Americans are engaged in an earnest and profound debate about the morality, legality, and practicality of physician-assisted suicide. Our holding permits this debate to continue, as it should in a democratic society. The decision of the en banc Court of Appeals is reversed, and the case is remanded for further proceedings consistent with this opinion.

Justice SOUTER, concurring in the judgment.

[We] are dealing with a claim to one of those rights sometimes described as rights of substantive due process and sometimes as unenumerated rights, in view of the breadth and indeterminacy of the "due process" serving as the claim's textual basis. The doctors accordingly arouse the skepticism of those who find the Due Process Clause an unduly vague or oxymoronic warrant for judicial review of substantive state law, just as they also invoke two centuries of American constitutional practice in recognizing unenumerated, substantive limits on governmental action. Although this practice has neither rested on any single textual basis nor expressed a consistent theory (or, before Poe v. Ullman, a much articulated one), a brief overview of its history is instructive on two counts. The persistence of substantive due process in our cases points to the legitimacy of the modern justification for such judicial review found in Justice Harlan's dissent in *Poe*, on which I will dwell further on, while the acknowledged failures of some of these cases point with caution to the difficulty raised by the present claim.

[The *Poe*] dissent is important for three things that point to our responsibilities today. The first is Justice Harlan's respect for the tradition of substantive due process review itself, and his acknowledgment of the Judiciary's obligation to carry it on. For two centuries American courts, and for much of that time this Court, have thought it necessary to provide some degree of review over the substantive content of legislation under constitutional standards of textual breadth. . . . This enduring tradition of American constitutional practice is, in

Justice Harlan's view, nothing more than what is required by the judicial author-ity and obligation to construe constitutional text and review legislation for con-formity to that text. Like many judges who preceded him and many who followed, he found it impossible to construe the text of due process without recognizing substantive, and not merely procedural, limitations. "Were due process merely a procedural safeguard it would fail to reach those situations where the deprivation of life, liberty or property was accomplished by legislation which by operating in the future could, given even the fairest possible procedure in application to indi-viduals, nevertheless destroy the enjoyment of all three." The text of the Due Process Clause thus imposes nothing less than an obligation to give substantive content to the words "liberty" and "due process of law."

Following the first point of the *Poe* dissent, on the necessity to engage in the sort of examination we conduct today, the dissent's second and third implicitly address those cases, already noted, that are now condemned with virtual unanim-ity as disastrous mistakes of substantive due process review. The second of the dissent's lessons is a reminder that the business of such review is not the identi-fication of extratextual absolutes but scrutiny of a legislative resolution (perhaps unconscious) of clashing principles, each quite possibly worthy in and of itself, but each to be weighed within the history of our values as a people. It is a com-parison of the relative strengths of opposing claims that informs the judicial task, not a deduction from some first premise. Thus informed, judicial review still has no warrant to substitute one reasonable resolution of the contending positions for another, but authority to supplant the balance already struck between the con-tenders only when it falls outside the realm of the reasonable. Part III, below, deals with this second point, and also with the dissent's third, which takes the form of an object lesson in the explicit attention to detail that is no less essential to the intellectual discipline of substantive due process review than an under-standing of the basic need to account for the two sides in the controversy and to respect legislation within the zone of reasonableness.

My understanding of unenumerated rights in the wake of the *Poe* dissent and subsequent cases avoids the absolutist failing of many older cases without embrac-ing the opposite pole of equating reasonableness with past practice described at a very specific level.

"Due Process has not been reduced to any formula; its content cannot be determined by reference to any code. The best that can be said is that through the course of this Court's decisions it has represented the balance which our Nation, built upon postulates of respect for the liberty of the individual, has struck between that liberty and the demands of organized society. If the supplying of content to this Constitutional concept has of necessity been a rational process, it certainly has not been one where judges have felt free to roam where unguided speculation might take them. The balance of which I speak is the balance struck by this country, having regard to what history teaches are the traditions from which it developed as well as the traditions from which it broke. That tradition is a living thing. A decision of this Court which radically departs from it could not long survive, while a decision which builds on what has survived is likely to be sound. No formula could serve as a substitute, in this area, for judgment and restraint."

After the *Poe* dissent, as before it, this enforceable concept of liberty would bar statutory impositions even at relatively trivial levels when governmental restraints are undeniably irrational as unsupported by any imaginable rationale. . . .

This approach calls for a court to assess the relative "weights" or dignities of the contending interests, and to this extent the judicial method is familiar to the common law. Common-law method is subject, however, to two important constraints in the hands of a court engaged in substantive due process review. First, such a court is bound to confine the values that it recognizes to those truly deserving constitutional stature, either to those expressed in constitutional text, or those exemplified by "the traditions from which [the Nation] developed," or revealed by contrast with "the traditions from which it broke." "We may not draw on our merely personal and private notions and disregard the limits . . . derived from considerations that are fused in the whole nature of our judicial process . . . 'considerations deeply rooted in reason and in the compelling traditions of the legal profession.'"

The second constraint, again, simply reflects the fact that constitutional review, not judicial lawmaking, is a court's business here. The weighing or valuing of contending interests in this sphere is only the first step, forming the basis for determining whether the statute in question falls inside or outside the zone of what is reasonable in the way it resolves the conflict between the interests of state and individual. It is no justification for judicial intervention merely to identify a reasonable resolution of contending values that differs from the terms of the legislation under review. It is only when the legislation's justifying principle, critically valued, is so far from being commensurate with the individual interest as to be arbitrarily or pointlessly applied that the statute must give way. Only if this standard points against the statute can the individual claimant be said to have a constitutional right. Precision in terminology, however, favors reserving the label "right" for instances in which the individual's liberty interest actually trumps the government's countervailing interests; only then does the individual have anything legally enforceable as against the state's attempt at regulation.

The *Poe* dissent thus reminds us of the nature of review for reasonableness or arbitrariness and the limitations entailed by it. But the opinion cautions against the repetition of past error in another way as well, more by its example than by any particular statement of constitutional method: it reminds us that the process of substantive review by reasoned judgment is one of close criticism going to the details of the opposing interests and to their relationships with the historically recognized principles that lend them weight or value.

[The] *Poe* dissent disclaims the possibility of a general formula for due process analysis (beyond the basic analytic structure just described). [When] identifying and assessing the competing interests of liberty and authority, for example, the breadth of expression that a litigant or a judge selects in stating the competing principles will have much to do with the outcome and may be dispositive. As in any process of rational argumentation, we recognize that when a generally accepted principle is challenged, the broader the attack the less likely it is to succeed. The principle's defenders will, indeed, often try to characterize any challenge as just such a broadside, perhaps by couching the defense as if a broadside attack had occurred. So the Court in *Dred Scott* treated prohibition of slavery in the Territories as nothing less than a general assault on the concept of property.

Just as results in substantive due process cases are tied to the selections of statements of the competing interests, the acceptability of the results is a function of the good reasons for the selections made. It is here that the value of common-law method becomes apparent, for the usual thinking of the common law is suspicious of the all-or-nothing analysis that tends to produce legal petrification instead of an evolving boundary between the domains of old principles. Common-law method tends to pay respect instead to detail, seeking to understand old principles afresh by new examples and new counterexamples. The "tradition is a living thing," albeit one that moves by moderate steps carefully taken. "The decision of an apparently novel claim must depend on grounds which follow closely on well-accepted principles and criteria. The new decision must take its place in relation to what went before and further [cut] a channel for what is to come." Exact analysis and characterization of any due process claim are critical to the method and to the result.

[The] argument supporting respondents' position thus progresses through three steps of increasing forcefulness. First, it emphasizes the decriminalization of suicide. Reliance on this fact is sanctioned under the standard that looks not only to the tradition retained, but to society's occasional choices to reject traditions of the legal past. While the common law prohibited both suicide and aiding a suicide, with the prohibition on aiding largely justified by the primary prohibition on self-inflicted death itself, the State's rejection of the traditional treatment of the one leaves the criminality of the other open to questioning that previously would not have been appropriate. The second step in the argument is to emphasize that the State's own act of decriminalization gives a freedom of choice much like the individual's option in recognized instances of bodily autonomy. One of these, abortion, is a legal right to choose in spite of the interest a State may legitimately invoke in discouraging the practice, just as suicide is now subject to choice, despite a state interest in discouraging it. The third step is to emphasize that respondents claim a right to assistance not on the basis of some broad principle that would be subject to exceptions if that continuing interest of the State's in discouraging suicide were to be recognized at all. Respondents base their claim on the traditional right to medical care and counsel, subject to the limiting conditions of informed, responsible choice when death is imminent, conditions that support a strong analogy to rights of care in other situations in which medical counsel and assistance have been available as a matter of course. There can be no stronger claim to a physician's assistance than at the time when death is imminent, a moral judgment implied by the State's own recognition of the legitimacy of medical procedures necessarily hastening the moment of impending death.

In my judgment, the importance of the individual interest here, as within that class of "certain interests" demanding careful scrutiny of the State's contrary claim, cannot be gainsaid. Whether that interest might in some circumstances, or at some time, be seen as "fundamental" to the degree entitled to prevail is not, however, a conclusion that I need draw here, for I am satisfied that the State's interests described in the following section are sufficiently serious to defeat the present claim that its law is arbitrary or purposeless.

The State has put forward several interests to justify the Washington law as applied to physicians treating terminally ill patients, even those competent to make responsible choices: protecting life generally, and protecting terminally ill patients from involuntary suicide and euthanasia, both voluntary and nonvoluntary.

It is not necessary to discuss the exact strengths of the first two claims of justification in the present circumstances, for the third is dispositive for me. That third justification is different from the first two, for it addresses specific features of respondents' claim, and it opposes that claim not with a moral judgment contrary to respondents', but with a recognized state interest in the protection of nonresponsible individuals and those who do not stand in relation either to death or to their physicians as do the patients whom respondents describe. The State claims interests in protecting patients from mistakenly and involuntarily deciding to end their lives, and in guarding against both voluntary and involuntary euthanasia. Leaving aside any difficulties in coming to a clear concept of imminent death, mistaken decisions may result from inadequate palliative care or a terminal prognosis that turns out to be error; coercion and abuse may stem from the large medical bills that family members cannot bear or unreimbursed hospitals decline to shoulder. Voluntary and involuntary euthanasia may result once doctors are authorized to prescribe lethal medication in the first instance, for they might find it pointless to distinguish between patients who administer their own fatal drugs and those who wish not to, and their compassion for those who suffer may obscure the distinction between those who ask for death and those who may be unable to request it. The argument is that a progression would occur, obscuring the line between the ill and the dying, and between the responsible and the unduly influenced, until ultimately doctors and perhaps others would abuse a limited freedom to aid suicides by yielding to the impulse to end another's suffering under conditions going beyond the narrow limits the respondents propose. The State thus argues, essentially, that respondents' claim is not as narrow as it sounds, simply because no recognition of the interest they assert could be limited to vindicating those interests and affecting no others. The State says that the claim, in practical effect, would entail consequences that the State could, without doubt, legitimately act to prevent.

Respondents propose an answer to all this, the answer of state regulation with teeth. Legislation proposed in several States, for example, would authorize physician-assisted suicide but require two qualified physicians to confirm the patient's diagnosis, prognosis, and competence; and would mandate that the patient make repeated requests witnessed by at least two others over a specified timespan; and would impose reporting requirements and criminal penalties for various acts of coercion.

But at least at this moment there are reasons for caution in predicting the effectiveness of the teeth proposed. Respondents' proposals, as it turns out, sound much like the guidelines now in place in the Netherlands, the only place where experience with physician-assisted suicide and euthanasia has yielded empirical evidence about how such regulations might affect actual practice. Dutch physicians must engage in consultation before proceeding, and must decide whether the patient's decision is voluntary, well considered, and stable, whether the request to die is enduring and made more than once, and whether the patient's future will involve unacceptable suffering. There is, however, a substantial dispute today about what the Dutch experience shows. Some commentators marshall evidence that the Dutch guidelines have in practice failed to protect patients from involuntary euthanasia and have been violated with impunity. This evidence is contested. The day may come when we can say with some assurance which side is right, but for now it is the substantiality of the factual disagreement, and the alternatives for resolving it, that matter. They are, for me, dispositive of the due process claim at this time.

I take it that the basic concept of judicial review with its possible displacement of legislative judgment bars any finding that a legislature has acted arbitrarily when the following conditions are met: there is a serious factual controversy over the feasibility of recognizing the claimed right without at the same time making it impossible for the State to engage in an undoubtedly legitimate exercise of power; facts necessary to resolve the controversy are not readily ascertainable through the judicial process; but they are more readily subject to discovery through legislative factfinding and experimentation. It is assumed in this case, and must be, that a State's interest in protecting those unable to make responsible decisions and those who make no decisions at all entitles the State to bar aid to any but a knowing and responsible person intending suicide, and to prohibit euthanasia. How, and how far, a State should act in that interest are judgments for the State, but the legitimacy of its action to deny a physician the option to aid any but the knowing and responsible is beyond question.

Legislatures . . . have superior opportunities to obtain the facts necessary for a judgment about the present controversy. Not only do they have more flexible mechanisms for factfinding than the Judiciary, but their mechanisms include the power to experiment, moving forward and pulling back as facts emerge within their own jurisdictions. There is, indeed, good reason to suppose that in the absence of a judgment for respondents here, just such experimentation will be attempted in some of the States.

[Sometimes] a court may be bound to act regardless of the institutional preferability of the political branches as forums for addressing constitutional claims. Now, it is enough to say that our examination of legislative reasonableness should consider the fact that the Legislature of the State of Washington is no more obviously at fault than this Court is in being uncertain about what would happen if respondents prevailed today. We therefore have a clear question about which institution, a legislature or a court, is relatively more competent to deal with an emerging issue as to which facts currently unknown could be dispositive. The answer has to be, for the reasons already stated, that the legislative process is to be preferred. There is a closely related further reason as well.

One must bear in mind that the nature of the right claimed, if recognized as one constitutionally required, would differ in no essential way from other constitutional rights guaranteed by enumeration or derived from some more definite textual source than "due process." An unenumerated right should not therefore be recognized, with the effect of displacing the legislative ordering of things, without the assurance that its recognition would prove as durable as the recognition of those other rights differently derived. To recognize a right of lesser promise would simply create a constitutional regime too uncertain to bring with it the expectation of finality that is one of this Court's central obligations in making constitutional decisions.

Legislatures, however, are not so constrained. The experimentation that should be out of the question in constitutional adjudication displacing legislative judgments is entirely proper, as well as highly desirable, when the legislative power addresses an emerging issue like assisted suicide. The Court should accordingly stay its hand to allow reasonable legislative consideration. While I do not decide for all time that respondents' claim should not be recognized, I acknowledge the legislative institutional competence as the better one to deal with that claim at this time.

Note

In Vacco v. Quill, 521 U.S. 793 (1997), the Court rejected an equal protection challenge to a state law prohibiting physician-assisted suicide.

∽ PROBLEMS ∽

1. *Constructing Arguments.* In constructing an argument for physician-assisted suicide as a fundamental liberty interest, how would counsel best use Roe v. Wade in support of his or her position? What case law would provide the best counterpoint?

2. *Describing the Right of Privacy.* Based on how the right of privacy has evolved over the past several decades, how might counsel describe it in a way that makes sense to a client?

Points to Remember

- Proponents of modern due process review argue that there are fundamental values that are not textually expressed or rights and liberties, but are no less basic.
- The discredited legacy of economic rights jurisprudence has left a significant mark on the Court's approach to substantive due process review in that judicial pronouncements expanding the right to privacy generally contain disclaimers to the effect that the Court is not replicating its stigmatized past.

- Generally, modern due process review focuses on the question of whether a particular interest is "implicit in the concept of ordered liberty," "rooted in the Nation's traditions and history," or "fundamental to the American scheme of justice."
- Debate continues regarding whether these imprecise standards sufficiently limit the judiciary in its relationship to the political process.
- Although the Due Process Clauses of the Fifth and Fourteenth Amendments contain explicit protections requiring procedural fairness for deprivations of life, liberty, or property, those clauses have also been used as a basis for establishing fundamental substantive rights that apply against the state and federal governments.
- The Due Process Clauses have also served as the vehicle through which provisions of the Bill of Rights have been applied to the states.
- The Bill of Rights, as originally framed and ratified, charted basic rights and liberties for individuals only in their relationship with the federal government.
- In United States v. Carolene Products Co., 304 U.S. 144 (1938), the Court announced that it would reserve heightened review to instances "when legislation appears to be within a specific provision of the Constitution, such as the first ten amendments, which are deemed equally specific when held to be embraced within the Fourteenth."
- However, through the Due Process Clauses, most provisions of the Bill of Rights now apply against the states.
- Under Palko v. Connecticut, 302 U.S. 319 (1937), portions of the Bill of Rights have been selectively incorporated into the Fourteenth Amendment and applied to the states rather than incorporated and applied in total.
- Under Adamson v. California, 332 U.S. 46 (1947), in determining whether a right is incorporated, the question is whether the particular provision in question is "implicit in the concept of ordered liberty." If it is, then the particular provision is deemed incorporated. Courts have also required whether a particular provision is "so rooted in the traditions and conscience of our people as to be fundamental."
- Under this approach, the only provisions of the Bill of Rights that have failed the incorporation test are the grand jury clause of the Fifth Amendment and the Seventh Amendment guarantee of a jury trial in civil cases.
- The Constitution protects privacy interests in discrete contexts such as the First, Third, and Fourth Amendments, but does not explicitly protect a general right of privacy.
- In Meyer v. Nebraska, 262 U.S. 390 (1923), the Court invalidated a state law that prohibited teaching in any language other than English in public and private schools. The Court held that the Due Process Clause included "not merely freedom from bodily restraint but also the right of the individual to contract, to engage in any of the common occupations of life, to acquire useful knowledge, to marry, establish a home and bring up children, to worship God according to the dictates of his own

conscience, and generally to enjoy those privileges long recognized at common law as essential to the orderly pursuit of happiness by free men."

- In Pierce v. Society of Sisters, 268 U.S. 510 (1925), the Court struck down a state law requiring parents to send their children to public schools.
- In Skinner v. Oklahoma, 316 U.S. 535 (1942), the Court struck down a state law that mandated sterilization for habitual felons. The Court held that the legislation dealt with "one of the basic civil rights of man" because "[m]arriage and procreation are fundamental to the very existence and survival of the race."
- However, the *Skinner* Court, sensitive to the recently disavowed legacy of *Lochner*-style review, grounded its decision in the Equal Protection Clause and avoided any reference to due process.
- In Griswold v. Connecticut, 381 U.S. 479 (1965), the Court struck down a state law that prohibited the distribution of information on birth control to married persons. In doing so, the Court suggested that various provisions of the Bill of Rights contain "penumbras" that create zones of privacy. The Court used those penumbras to articulate a generalized right of privacy.
- In Roe v. Wade, 410 U.S. 113 (1973), the Court struck down a state statute that made it a crime for a woman to have an abortion on the basis of the Due Process Clause of the Fourteenth Amendment.
- In Doe v. Bolton, 410 U.S. 179 (1973), the Court invalidated provisions of a state law that required abortions to be performed in a hospital approved by a specific accrediting agency, to be authorized by a hospital committee, and to be done only after examination by two other physicians.
- In Planned Parenthood v. Danforth, 428 U.S. 52 (1976), the Court struck down state provisions for spousal and parental consent for unmarried women under the age of 18.
- In Planned Parenthood v. Ashcroft, 462 U.S. 476 (1983), the Court upheld a parental consent or notification requirement provided that the minor could bypass it through a judicial procedure. The responsibility of the Court, in this circumstance, is to find either that the minor was sufficiently mature to make the decision herself or that an abortion was in her best interest.
- In Akron v. Akron Center for Reproductive Health, 462 U.S. 416 (1983), the Court struck down a state law requiring physicians to provide specific information concerning the medical risks and morality of abortion, impose a 24-hour waiting period, and require all post–first-trimester abortions to be performed in hospitals because they constituted "a heavy and unnecessary burden" upon a woman's liberty interest.
- In Thornburgh v. American College of Obstetricians and Gynecologists, 476 U.S. 747 (1986), the Court struck down a statute mandating that post-viability abortions be conducted in a way that maximizes the chances for fetal survival.

- In Webster v. Reproductive Health Systems, Inc., 492 U.S. 490 (1989), the Court signaled that it might be backing away from *Roe* in some respects. Indeed, a number of justices expressed concern regarding *Roe*'s trimester analysis.
- However, in Planned Parenthood of Southeastern Pennsylvania v. Casey, 410 U.S. 113 (1993), the Court reaffirmed *Roe* in important respects, but suggested that, although women retain the right to choose to have an abortion before viability, and to obtain it without undue interference from the state, the state's interests are not strong enough to support a prohibition of abortion or the imposition of a substantial obstacle to the woman's effective right to elect the procedure. However, the Court affirmed the state's power to restrict abortions after fetal viability, if the law contains exceptions for pregnancies that endanger the woman's life or health. Finally, the state has legitimate interests from the outset of the pregnancy in protecting the health of the woman and the life of the fetus that may become a child.
- Although the *Planned Parenthood* Court refused to apply strict scrutiny, or require proof of a compelling governmental interest, and it rejected *Roe*'s trimester analysis, the Court nonetheless held that restrictions on the right to have an abortion would be subject to an "undue burden" analysis. The Court held that an "informed consent" provision, coupled with a 24-hour waiting period, did not impose an undue burden. Finally, the Court upheld a parental consent provision for a minor to obtain an abortion provided that there is an adequate judicial bypass procedure as well as record keeping and reporting procedures regarding all abortions performed at each facility.
- In Stenberg v. Carhart, 530 U.S. 914 (2000), the Court struck down a state statute that prohibited "partial birth abortion" because it imposed an undue burden on the right to have an abortion.
- The Court has also held that there is a constitutional right to personal choice with respect to family life. In Meyer v. Nebraska, the Court referenced a liberty interest in "establish[ing] a home and bring[ing] up children." This characterization preceded the formal recognition of privacy as a fundamental right several decades later.
- In Moore v. City of East Cleveland, 431 U.S. 494 (1977), a plurality of the Court struck down a law that prohibited extended families from living together in the same home.
- Marriage is also a relationship with a well-established tradition and history that the Court has protected through due process review. In Meyer v. Nebraska, the right was referenced explicitly as a constitutionally protected liberty interest.
- In Loving v. Virginia, 388 U.S. 1 (1967), the right to marry was identified as a basis for striking down antimiscegenation laws. The Court reviewed a state law that prohibited marriage by residents who were in arrears in their child support obligations and could not demonstrate that their offspring were unlikely to become "public charges."

- In Zablocki v. Redhail, 434 U.S. 374 (1978), the Court struck down a Wisconsin statute restricting marriage by a "resident having minor children not in his custody and which he is under obligation to support by any court order or judgment." Under the law, marriage would be allowed only upon proof of compliance with the child support obligation and that the children "are not then and are not likely thereafter to become public charges."
- The Court has recognized parental rights in child raising in a number of different contexts.
- In Wisconsin v. Yoder, 406 U.S. 205 (1972), the Court found that a mandatory school attendance law was at odds with the free exercise of religion when applied to members of the Amish religion. It also noted that compulsory education in this circumstance implicated "traditional concepts of parental control over the religious upbringing and education of their minor children."
- The relationship between parent and child, though implicating fundamental interests, is not constitutionally sacrosanct. In Quilloin v. Walcott, 434 U.S. 246 (1978), the Court upheld a state law that allowed the mother to adopt her child in a new family unit if the natural father did not object.
- In Michael H. v. Gerald D., 491 U.S. 110 (1989), the Court reviewed a natural father's claim of a filial relationship and visitation rights with his daughter. The child's birth as a result of an extramarital affair led a plurality of the Court to conclude that the father had no liberty interest protected under the Fourteenth Amendment.
- In Bowers v. Hardwick, 478 U.S. 186 (1986), the Court upheld a law that made sodomy a crime as applied to an individual who was found engaged in homosexual conduct in the privacy of his home. The Court concluded that the U.S. Constitution does not confer a fundamental right upon homosexuals to engage in sodomy on the basis that "no connection between family, marriage, or procreation on the one hand and homosexual activity on the other has been demonstrated."
- In Lawrence v. Texas, 539 U.S. 558 (2003), the Court reversed Bowers in striking down Texas's "Homosexual Conduct" law, noting that there is "an emerging awareness that liberty gives substantial protection to adult persons in deciding how to conduct their private lives in matters pertaining to sex," and that this is a form of "liberty" protected by the Due Process Clause of the Fourteenth Amendment.
- In Cruzan v. Director, Missouri Department of Health, 497 U.S. 261 (1990), the Court recognized that individuals have a liberty interest that lets them choose whether to die, but found that this individual interest did not trump a state's interest in determining by clearly and convincing evidence a person's desire to discontinue medical treatment (at least, as to a woman in a coma). The Court applied a requirement that the state restriction must bear a reasonable relationship to a legitimate state end.

- In Washington v. Glucksberg, 521 U.S. 702 (1997), the Court upheld a state statute that prohibited anyone (including doctors and medical personnel) from "caus[ing]" or "aid[ing]" a suicide as applied to physicians who occasionally treat terminally ill, suffering patients and who declared that they would assist these patients in ending their lives if not for Washington's assisted-suicide ban.

10

Equal Protection

U.S. CONSTITUTION, FOURTEENTH AMENDMENT

Section 1. All persons born or naturalized in the United States, and subject to the jurisdiction thereof, are citizens of the United States and of the State wherein they reside. No State shall make or enforce any law which shall abridge the privileges or immunities of citizens of the United States; nor shall any State deprive any person of life, liberty, or property, without due process of law; nor deny to any person within its jurisdiction equal protection of the laws.

Section 5. The Congress shall have power to enforce, by appropriate legislation, the provisions of this article.

∾ PROBLEM: THE DIVERSITY INITIATIVE ∾

New World University (NWU) is a state institution that seeks to prepare its students to thrive in an increasingly diverse, twenty-first-century world. To that end, NWU is considering the adoption of a new mission statement that will help it better educate and prepare its students. In particular, NWU is thinking about a statement that adopts the goal of "preparing students for a multicultural and diverse world, while ensuring that they do not lose pride in their racial or ethnic identity." NWU is also thinking about revising its admissions and financial aid policies to gain a more diverse student body. It thinks broad educational diversity is attainable when students come from different backgrounds, including differences based on race, gender, socioeconomic class, sexual orientation, nationality, geography, and other factors. You have recently been appointed university counsel at NWU, and its board of regents has asked for your advice about whether it can adopt the proposed mission statement, as well as whether it can adjust its admissions and financial aid policies to take various diversity factors into account. If you believe such changes are possible, the Board would like your advice about how to frame the mission statement and the diversity plans. As we progress through this chapter, we will examine these issues, and we will ask you to advise NWU's board of regents.

Equality under the law, as understood today, was not a significant factor or concern in the original constitutional framing process. Although the Declaration of Independence flatly declares that "all men [are] created equal," the idea of equality did not animate the new Union. Indeed, at the time of the Republic's founding, slavery was well established and many states, in both the North and South, denied persons of African descent the right to sue in court, contract, or acquire, own, or sell property. *See* Don E. Fehrenbacher, *The Dred Scott Case* 349-350 (Oxford 1978).

The Fourteenth Amendment's provision that no state shall "deny to any person within its jurisdiction the equal protection of the laws" is a constitutional guarantee of mixed signals. In its initial reading of the Fourteenth Amendment, the Court observed in the *Slaughterhouse Cases*, 83 U.S. 36, 81 (1873), that "[t]he existence of laws in the States where the newly emancipated negroes resided, which discriminated with gross injustice and hardship against them as a class, was the evil to be remedied by" the Equal Protection Clause.

The laws, which the Court referenced, were the Black Codes that many states in the former Confederacy adopted in response to the Thirteenth Amendment (which abolished slavery). These codes defined racial status, prohibited intermarriage, established dual systems of criminal justice, and imposed restrictions on employment, travel, residence, and assembly. The codes diminished the force of the Thirteenth Amendment's abolishment of badges and incidents of slavery, and consequently inspired the Reconstruction Congress to pass the Civil Rights Act of 1866. As the nation's first civil rights law, the 1866 Act prohibited "discrimination in civil rights or immunities" and extended to persons of every race "the same rights to make and enforce contracts, to sue, be parties, and give evidence, to inherit, purchase, lease, sell, hold and convey real and personal property, and to full and equal benefit of all laws and proceedings for the security of persons and property, [and] be subject to like punishment." *Cong. Globe*, 39th Cong., 1st Sess. 474 (1866).

Although members of the Reconstruction Congress varied in their sense of the Fourteenth Amendment's scope, it was generally agreed that it at least was "designed to embody or incorporate the Civil Rights Act." Howard J. Graham, *Everyman's Constitution* 291 n.73 (State Historical Society of Wisconsin 1968). The equal protection guarantee in particular responded to the "gross injustice and hardship" of the Black Codes, which were the Civil Rights Act of 1866's primary concern. Charles Fairman, VII *History of the Supreme Court of the United States, Reconstruction and Reunion,* pt. 1, at 134 (MacMillan 1987). Consistent with this understanding, the *Slaughterhouse* Court doubted whether "any action of a State not directed by way of discrimination against the negroes as a class, or on account of their race, will ever be held to come within the purview of this provision." *Slaughterhouse Cases*, 83 U.S., at 81.

This race-specific vision of equal protection was reaffirmed in Bradwell v. Illinois, 83 U.S. 130 (1873), when the Court upheld a state law that denied women the opportunity to practice law. Hesitation to expand the contours of equal protection set a pattern that has persisted for much of the provision's history. Restrained use of the guarantee initially reflected resistance toward or caution with respect to the implications of Reconstruction. Even as the Due Process Clause became a basis for expansive judicial review during the early twentieth century, equal protection's currency remained limited. Justice Holmes thus dismissed the provision as "the usual last resort of constitutional arguments." Buck v. Bell, 274 U.S. 200, 208 (1927).

The equal protection guarantee eventually emerged as a powerful tool for undoing official segregation. Outside a few well-defined contexts, however, the Court has used the Equal Protection Clause sparingly and with deference to the legislative process. As the Court stated in Lindsley v. Natural Carbonic Gas Co., 220 U.S. 61, 78 (1911), "if any state of facts reasonably can be conceived that would sustain the classification, the existence of that state of facts at the time the law was enacted must be assumed." The Court went on to hold that classifications that have a reasonable basis do not violate equal protection "merely because [they] are not made with mathematical nicety or because in practice [they] result in some inequality." This deference to the legislative process reflects the judicial concern that, because laws by their nature classify, an untethered equal protection guarantee might "invalidate, a whole range of tax, welfare, public service, regulatory, and licensing statutes." Washington v. Davis, 426 U.S. 229, 248 (1976).

From the beginning, the Supreme Court has struggled to define the exact contours of the Equal Protection Clause of the Fourteenth Amendment. Initially, the Court announced the doctrine of reasonable government classifications, applying rational basis scrutiny to government policies. By the mid-twentieth century, the Court had established strict scrutiny for government classifications based on race, national origin, and alienage. The Court also applied heightened, intermediate scrutiny to gender and illegitimacy classifications. As you read each line of equal protection cases, try to identify and master the level of scrutiny applied by the Court to difficult types of classifications.

An equality principle once established is difficult to confine and, as noted by a constitutional scholar, has a tendency to spread and eventually "to lift all to the level of the most favored." Fairman, *Reconstruction and Reunion*, at 134. Indeed, once the Court used the equal protection guarantee to undo racial segregation, it was predictable that other groups would seek to invoke it to advance their causes. For purposes of judicial review, the challenge has been to determine which classifications or discriminations merit close attention. Historically, factors such as historical disadvantage, exclusion from the political process, and immutable physical characteristics have been regarded by the courts as relevant considerations. *See* United States v. Carolene Products Co., 304 U.S. 144, n.4 (1938). Indeed, the Court has identified four types of classification — race, gender, alienage, and illegitimacy — that warrant a heightened level of review. It also has determined that selective denial of a fundamental right or liberty, regardless of the group affected, merits a more robust standard of review.

For purposes of equal protection, the standards of review are strict scrutiny, intermediate scrutiny, and rational basis scrutiny. Rational basis scrutiny applies to most legislative classifications. Strict scrutiny is used for all racial and most alienage classifications, as well as selective denials of or burdens on fundamental rights. Intermediate scrutiny governs gender and illegitimacy classifications. The elements of these tests are set forth in ascending order in the following table.

Standard of review	Quality of government interest	Relationship between classification and goal
Rational basis scrutiny	Rational basis	Reasonably related
Intermediate scrutiny	Important	Substantially related
Strict scrutiny	Compelling	Narrowly tailored

The goals of this chapter are to provide an understanding of 1) the history behind and evolution of the Equal Protection Clause, 2) the practical usage and application of the Equal Protection Clause, and 3) competing theories with respect to the scope and intensity of judicial review.

As we proceed, we will examine three recurring questions. First, *does the law classify?* After reading a few cases, you should recognize that laws that create classifications are indeed common. Legislatures "classify" in tax codes, welfare guidelines, and many other laws. For equal protection purposes, the terms *classification* and *discrimination* are interchangeable. Second, *what is the nature of the classification?* The starting point for equal protection review is to determine the nature of the classification. Most classifications are not constitutionally significant and do not invoke heightened judicial scrutiny. To the extent that classifications are based on race, gender, alienage, or illegitimacy, or they burden or deny someone a "fundamental right," courts are more likely to apply a heightened standard of review. Third, when a classification is challenged, *which standard of review should a court apply?* In general, courts apply rational basis scrutiny to economic and social classifications. All classifications based on race and, in some instances, alienage are subject to strict scrutiny. Gender classifications are subject to intermediate scrutiny. As you read the cases, try to identify the standard of review applied by the Court.

A. STATE ECONOMIC REGULATIONS (AND OTHER CLASSIFICATIONS OF MINIMAL CONSTITUTIONAL CONCERN)

For most government classifications, the Court applies rational basis review. The government policy is presumed valid and the person challenging the policy must allege and prove that it is arbitrary or irrational. Under rational basis scrutiny, the government almost always prevails.

Equal protection standards of review are informed by many of the same concerns that operate in the due process context. In United States v. Carolene Products Co., 304 U.S. 144, n.4 (1938), the Court announced that it would reserve searching review for instances when a specific provision of the Bill of Rights was implicated or a burden was imposed on a group that was excluded formally from the political process. Rational basis review thus became the primary model for evaluating economic or social legislation, whether it was challenged as a violation of due process or equal protection. The rational basis test typically reflects the utmost in judicial deference. Its accommodating nature is reflected in the following case, which is widely regarded as a benchmark for the review of general economic or social classifications.

Railway Express Agency v. New York

336 U.S. 106 (1949)

Mr. Justice Douglas delivered the opinion of the Court.

[A city ordinance provides that no person may operate a vehicle that displays advertising, except for business delivery vehicles engaged in their usual business or the owner's regular work.]

[The] question of equal protection of the laws is pressed more strenuously on us. It is pointed out that the regulation draws the line between advertisements of products sold by the owner of the truck and general advertisements. It is argued that unequal treatment on the basis of such a distinction is not justified by the aim and purpose of the regulation. It is said, for example, that one of appellant's trucks carrying the advertisement of a commercial house would not cause any greater distraction of pedestrians and vehicle drivers than if the commercial house carried the same advertisement on its own truck. Yet the regulation allows the latter to do what the former is forbidden from doing. It is therefore contended that the classification which the regulation makes has no relation to the traffic problem since a violation turns not on what kind of advertisements are carried on trucks but on whose trucks they are carried.

That, however, is a superficial way of analyzing the problem, even if we assume that it is premised on the correct construction of the regulation. The local authorities may well have concluded that those who advertised their own wares on their trucks do not present the same traffic problem in view of the nature or extent of the advertising which they use. It would take a degree of omniscience which we lack to say that such is not the case. If that judgment is correct, the advertising displays that are exempt have less impact on traffic than those of appellants.

We cannot say that that judgment is not an allowable one. Yet if it is, the classification has relation to the purpose for which it is made and does not contain the kind of discrimination against which the Equal Protection Clause affords protection. It is by such practical considerations based on experience rather than by theoretical inconsistencies that the question of equal protection is to be answered.

And the fact that New York City sees fit to eliminate from traffic this kind of distraction but does not touch what may be even greater ones in a different category, such as the vivid displays on Times Square, is immaterial. It is no requirement of equal protection that all evils of the same genus be eradicated or none at all.

Mr. Justice JACKSON, concurring.

[Invocation] of the equal protection clause, [as opposed to the due process clause], does not disable any governmental body from dealing with the subject at hand. It merely means that the prohibition or regulation must have a broader impact. I regard it as a salutary doctrine that cities, states and the Federal Government must exercise their powers so as not to discriminate between their inhabitants except upon some reasonable differentiation fairly related to the object of regulation. This equality is not merely abstract justice. The framers of the Constitution knew, and we should not forget today, that there is no more effective practical guaranty against arbitrary and unreasonable government than to require that the principles of law which officials would impose upon a minority must be imposed generally. Conversely, nothing opens the door to arbitrary action so effectively as to allow those officials to pick and choose only a few to whom they will apply legislation and thus to escape the political retribution that might be visited upon them if larger numbers were affected. Courts can take no better measure to assure that laws will be just than to require that laws be equal in operation. . . .

Notes and Questions

1. *Standards of Review.* One of the key questions in equal protection cases is the appropriate standard of review to be applied. In general, as noted, economic classifications are subjected to a low standard of review (typically, rational basis scrutiny). Why is that so?

2. *"Rigorous" Rational Basis Review.* The rational basis test generally is renowned for its deference to the political process. There are instances, however, when the Court employs a higher intensity version of rational basis review. Although a classification may not be "facially invidious," it nonetheless may reflect a "recurring constitutional difficult[y]." The Court thus may insist that the "classification reflects a reasoned judgment" and advances "substantial interests of the State. Plyler v. Doe, 457 U.S. 202 (1982). This enhanced version of rational basis review has been evidenced in decisions invalidating laws that discriminated against persons on the basis of mental retardation, Cleburne v. Cleburne Living Center, 473 U.S. 432 (1985); sexual orientation, Romer v. Evans, 517 U.S. 620 (1996); and children of undocumented aliens, Plyler v. Doe.

3. *First Amendment Considerations.* The outcome in *Railway Express Agency* was achieved before the Court determined, nearly 30 years later, that the First Amendment protected commercial speech. Fundamental rights, whether denied selectively or on a wholesale basis, are usually subject to more rigorous scrutiny.

The advertising regulation, if challenged today, thus would likely be subjected to a higher level of review.

4. *Underinclusiveness.* The *Railway Express Agency* Court's allowance of piece-meal legislative efforts (a partial ban on display advertising) to respond to a larger problem (distractions to motorists) illustrates the concept of underinclusiveness. A particularly good example of underinclusiveness (and overinclusiveness) is a statute that the Court invalidated a quarter of a century later as an impermissible gender classification. This statute, reviewed in Craig v. Boren, 429 U.S. 190 (1976), prohibited the sale of 3.2 percent beer to males under the age of 21 and females under the age of 18. The law's burden was underinclusive (and the law's benefit overinclusive) to the extent it did not reach women who would be a source of such risk. The burden was overinclusive (and the benefit underinclusive) inso-far as many between the ages of 18 and 21 would not present the risk of an alcohol-related driving offense. The tolerance level for overinclusiveness and underinclusiveness depends on the standard of review, which is a function of whether the classification counts for equal protection purposes.

∾ PROBLEMS ∾

1. *Is Discrimination Necessarily "Bad"?* Many assume that the term *discrimina-tion* has only negative connotations, and to say that someone is a *discriminator* is usually regarded as a pejorative statement. But does the word *discrimination* also have positive connotations? For example, a person might be described as a "dis-criminating shopper" — meaning, of course, that he or she exercises good judg-ment. Of course, the astute student may suggest that there is a substantial difference between governmental discrimination and shopper discrimination. But is there really a difference? Suppose that a city decides to provide reduced bus fares to senior citizens and to students. Such a scheme necessarily involves dis-crimination (between seniors and students on the one hand, and everyone else on the other hand), but is the discrimination constitutionally impermissible? In fact, are there sound and desirable reasons for providing seniors and students with reduced fares? Should government have discretion to provide seniors and students with that benefit?

2. *Are There Sound Reasons for Providing Less Protection to Economic Classifica-tions Than to Racial Classifications?* If some discrimination is desirable and other discrimination is objectionable, how do courts distinguish between permissible and impermissible discrimination? That issue is the overriding concern of this chapter. As the preceding problem reveals, one role of government is to make decisions, and those decisions frequently involve classifications that discriminate. In some cases (e.g., reduced bus fares for senior citizens and students), those clas-sifications may be permissible. In other instances (e.g., invidious race discrimina-tion), those classifications are impermissible. How and why do courts decide which classifications are permissible and which are impermissible?

Federal Communications Commission v. Beach Communications, Inc.

508 U.S. 307 (1993)

Justice THOMAS delivered the opinion of the Court.

This case arises out of an FCC proceeding clarifying the agency's interpretation of the term cable system as it is used in the Cable Act. In this proceeding, the Commission addressed the application of the exemption codified in §602(7)(B) to satellite master antenna television (SMATV) facilities. Unlike a traditional cable television system, which delivers video programming to a large community of subscribers through coaxial cables laid under city streets or along utility lines, an SMATV system typically receives a signal from a satellite through a small satellite dish located on a rooftop and then retransmits the signal by wire to units within a building or complex of buildings. The Commission ruled that an SMATV system that serves multiple buildings via a network of interconnected physical transmission lines is a cable system, unless it falls within the §602(7)(B) exemption. Consistent with the plain terms of the statutory exemption, the Commission concluded that such an SMATV system is subject to the franchise requirement if its transmission lines interconnect separately owned and managed buildings or if its lines use or cross any public right of way.

Respondents Beach Communications, Inc., et al., — SMATV operators that would be subject to franchising under the Cable Act as construed by the Commission — petitioned the Court of Appeals for review. The Court of Appeals rejected respondents' statutory challenge to the Commission's interpretation, but a majority of the court found merit in the claim that §602(7) violates the implied equal protection guarantee of the Due Process Clause. In the absence of what it termed the predominant rationale for local franchising (use of public rights of way), the court saw no rational basis [o]n the record, and was unable to imagine any conceivable basis, for distinguishing between those facilities exempted by the statute and those SMATV cable systems that link separately owned and managed buildings. The court remanded the record and directed the FCC to provide additional legislative facts to justify the distinction.

A report subsequently filed by the Commission failed to satisfy the Court of Appeals. Because the Court of Appeals held an Act of Congress unconstitutional, we granted certiorari. . . . We now reverse.

Whether embodied in the Fourteenth Amendment or inferred from the Fifth, equal protection is not a license for courts to judge the wisdom, fairness, or logic of legislative choices. In areas of social and economic policy, a statutory classification that neither proceeds along suspect lines nor infringes fundamental constitutional rights must be upheld against equal protection challenge if there is any reasonably conceivable state of facts that could provide a rational basis for the classification. Where there are plausible reasons for Congress' action, our inquiry is at an end. This standard of review is a paradigm of judicial restraint. The Constitution presumes that, absent some reason to infer antipathy, even improvident decisions will eventually be rectified by the democratic process and that judicial intervention is generally unwarranted no matter how unwisely we may think a political branch has acted.

On rational basis review, a classification in a statute such as the Cable Act comes to us bearing a strong presumption of validity, and those attacking the rationality of the legislative classification have the burden to negative every conceivable basis which might support it. Moreover, because we never require a legislature to articulate its reasons for enacting a statute, it is entirely irrelevant for constitutional purposes whether the conceived reason for the challenged distinction actually motivated the legislature.

Applying these principles, we conclude that the common ownership distinction is constitutional. There are at least two possible bases for the distinction; either one suffices. First, Congress borrowed §602(7)(B) from pre-Cable Act regulations, and although the existence of a prior administrative scheme is certainly not necessary to the rationality of the statute, it is plausible that Congress also adopted the FCC's earlier rationale. Under that rationale, common ownership was thought to be indicative of those systems for which the costs of regulation would outweigh the benefits to consumers. Because the number of subscribers was a similar indicator, the Commission also exempted cable facilities that served fewer than 50 subscribers. *See* 47 C.F.R. §76.5(a) (1984). There is a second conceivable basis for the statutory distinction. Suppose competing SMATV operators wish to sell video programming to subscribers in a group of contiguous buildings, such as a single city block, which can be interconnected by wire without crossing a public right of way. If all the buildings belong to one owner or are commonly managed, that owner or manager could freely negotiate a deal for all subscribers on a competitive basis. But if the buildings are separately owned and managed, the first SMATV operator who gains a foothold by signing a contract and installing a satellite dish and associated transmission equipment on one of the buildings would enjoy a powerful cost advantage in competing for the remaining subscribers: he could connect additional buildings for the cost of a few feet of cable, whereas any competitor would have to recover the cost of his own satellite headend facility. Thus, the first operator could charge rates well above his cost and still undercut the competition. This potential for effective monopoly power might theoretically justify regulating the latter class of SMATV systems and not the former.

The Court of Appeals quite evidently believed that the crossing or use of a public right of way is the only conceivable basis upon which Congress could rationally require local franchising of SMATV systems. Delete all cites to lower court opinions from the same case. As we have indicated, however, there are plausible rationales unrelated to the use of public rights of way for regulating cable facilities serving separately owned and managed buildings. The assumptions underlying these rationales may be erroneous, but the very fact that they are arguable is sufficient, on rational basis review, to immuniz[e] the congressional choice from constitutional challenge.

The judgment of the Court of Appeals is reversed, and the case is remanded for further proceedings consistent with this opinion.

∾ PROBLEMS ∾

1. *More on the Diversity Initiative.* Suppose that the board of regents in the introductory problem is thinking about basing all scholarships at NWU on need, and wants your advice about whether it would be permissible to do so. What standard of review would apply?

2. *The Diversity Initiative and Preferential Admissions.* Suppose that the board of regents is also thinking about giving preferential admission (especially to the law and medical schools) based on economic need. In other words, the university will preferentially admit students who come from poor backgrounds. Is such an admissions policy permissible? What standard of review should be applied?

3. *Age and Driving Restrictions.* The City of Restraint has enacted an ordinance that prohibits persons under the age of 21 and over the age of 70 from driving on public highways. In enacting the ordinance, the city stated that younger persons have a tendency to drive recklessly and that older drivers have poorer vision because of their age. Suppose that Bart (an 18-year-old college freshman and campus president of Mothers Against Drunk Driving) and Homer (a 71-year-old CEO of a Fortune 500 company who pilots his own plane) seek your counsel on whether to file discrimination lawsuits. What would your advice be with respect to whether they could bring viable equal protection claims? *See* Massachusetts Board of Retirement v. Murgia, 427 U.S. 307 (1976). Would your counsel be influenced by the fact that neither Bart nor Homer is as reckless as many drivers in the licensed driver group?

B. RACIAL CLASSIFICATIONS

The Constitutional Convention was inspired largely by the political and economic dysfunction experienced under the Articles of Confederation. Trade wars among the new states resulted in a nation whose sum was less than its parts. Despite a common objective of creating a viable political and economic union, some significant divisions among the Framers had to be overcome. Political representation in the national government, for instance, pitted larger states against smaller states. This dispute was resolved by the creation of a bicameral legislature.

One of the most problematic issues confronting the Framers was slavery. James Madison observed that "sectional friction was attributable partly to climate but principally [to] the effects of [states] having or not having slaves. These two causes concur in forming the great division of interests in the United States. It did not lie between the large [and] small states; it lay, between the Northern [and] Southern states." 1 M. Farrand, *The Records of the Federal Convention of 1787* 486 (Yale 1937).

The premise that slave and nonslave states could coexist within a single union ultimately foundered upon the realities of territorial expansion and fugitive slave controversies. With the creation of each new territory and state, the question of slavery's expansion was renewed. Congress attempted to resolve the problem through processes of compromise. Lasting solutions broke down as westward expansion increased and each side feared that the other would gain the upper hand and define the Union according to its will. The abolitionist movement in the 1830s campaigned for revising the Constitution, through either interpretation or amendment, to eliminate slavery. This development reflected an intensifying constitutional competition. The southern counterpoint was that slave owner rights were protected by the Due Process Clause of the Fifth Amendment. The federal government was an agent of the states, and it thus was obligated to support their policies.

As slave owners traveled to and from nonslave states and territories, questions arose regarding the legal status of the slaves. The southern position was the dominant influence on case law concerning sojourning or fugitive status. Northern case law with respect to sojourning slaves generally applied the law of the relevant slave state to questions of whether their presence in a free jurisdiction was sufficient grounds for emancipating them. Many northern states, however, adopted laws that prevented slave owners from recapturing a runaway slave without judicial process. In Prigg v. Pennsylvania, 41 U.S. 539 (1842), the Court invalidated an antikidnapping law on grounds it conflicted with federal law allowing slave owners to recapture runaway slaves. This outcome had significant consequences for both the North and the South. While northerners were sensitized to their complicity in slavery, southerners became aware that the federal interest that cut in its favor eventually could turn the other way.

By the 1850s, the political process had become gridlocked on the various issues relating to slavery. Within this context, the political branches themselves welcomed the Supreme Court's engagement. As the Court soon discovered, it could choose sides but ultimately not impose its will.

Dred Scott v. Sandford
60 U.S. 393 (1857)

Mr. Chief Justice TANEY delivered the opinion of the Court.

[The] question is simply this: Can a negro, whose ancestors were imported into this country, and sold as slaves, become a member of the political community formed and brought into existence by the Constitution of the United States, and as such become entitled to all the rights, and privileges, and immunities, guaranteed by that instrument to the citizen? One of which rights is the privilege of suing in a court of the United States in the cases specified in the Constitution. . . .

[The] words "people of the United States" and "citizens" are synonymous terms. . . . They both describe the political body who, according to our republican institutions, form the sovereignty, and who hold the power and conduct the Government through their representatives. They are what we familiarly call the "sovereign people," and every citizen is one of this people, and a constituent member of this sovereignty. The question before us is, whether the class of persons described in the [plea] compose a portion of this people, and are constituent members of this sovereignty? We think they are not, and that they are not included, and were not intended to be included, under the word "citizens" in the Constitution, and can therefore claim none of the rights and privileges which that instrument provides for and secures to citizens of the United States. On the contrary, they were at that time considered as a subordinate and inferior class of beings, who had been subjugated by the dominant race, and, whether emancipated or not, yet remained subject to their authority, and had no rights or privileges but such as those who held the power and the Government might choose to grant them. . . .

The question [arises] whether the provisions of the Constitution, in relation to the personal rights and privileges to which the citizen of a State should be entitled, embraced the negro African race, at that time in this country, or who might afterwards be imported, who had then or should afterwards be made free in any State; and to put it in the power of a single State to make him a citizen of the United States, and endue him with the full rights of citizenship in every other State without their consent? Does the Constitution of the United States act upon him whenever he shall be made free under the laws of a State, and raised there to the rank of a citizen, and immediately cloth him with all the privileges of a citizen in every other State, and in its own courts?

The court thinks the affirmative of these propositions cannot be maintained. And if it cannot, the plaintiff in error could not be a citizen of the State of Missouri, within the meaning of the Constitution of the United States, and, consequently, was not entitled to sue in its courts. . . .

It is true, every person, and every class and description of persons, who were at the time of the adoption of the Constitution recognized as citizens in the several States, became also citizens of this new political body; but none other; it was formed by them, and for them and their posterity, but for no one else. And the personal rights and privileges guarantied to citizens of this new sovereignty were intended to embrace those only who were then members of the several State communities, or who should afterwards by birthright or otherwise become members, according to the provisions of the Constitution and the principles on which it was founded. . . .

It becomes necessary, therefore, to determine who were citizens of the several States when the Constitution was adopted. [We] must inquire who, at that time, were recognized as the people or citizens of a State, whose rights and liberties had been outraged by the English Government; and who declared their independence, and assumed the powers of Government to defend their rights by force of arms. [T]he legislation and histories of the times, and the language used in the Declaration of Independence, show, that neither the class of persons who had been imported as slaves, nor their descendants, whether they had become free or not, were then acknowledged as a part of the people, nor intended to be included in the general words used in that memorable instrument. . . . They had for more than a century before been regarded as beings of an inferior order, and altogether unfit to associate with the white race, either in social or political relations; and so far inferior, that they had no rights which the white man was bound to respect; and that the negro might justly and lawfully be reduced to slavery for his benefit. He was bought and sold, and treated as an ordinary article of merchandise and traffic, whenever a profit could be made by it. This opinion was at that time fixed and universal in the civilized portion of the white race.

[T]he rights of property are united with the rights of person, and placed on the same ground by the fifth amendment to the Constitution, which provides that no person shall be deprived of life, liberty, and property, without due process of law. And an act of Congress which deprives a citizen of the United States of his liberty or property, merely because he came himself or brought his property into a particular Territory of the United States, and who had committed no offence against the laws, could hardly be dignified with the name of due process of law. . . .

[T]he right of property in a slave is distinctly and expressly affirmed in the Constitution. The right to traffic in it, like an ordinary article of merchandise and property, was guarantied to the citizens of the United States, in every State that might desire it, for twenty years. And the Government in express terms is pledged to protect it in all future time, if the slave escapes from his owner. This is done in plain words. . . . And no word can be found in the Constitution which gives Congress a greater power over slave property, or which entitles property of that kind to less protection than property of any other description. The only power conferred is the power coupled with the duty of guarding and protecting the owner in his rights.

Upon these considerations, it is the opinion of the court that the act of Congress which prohibited a citizen from holding and owning property of this kind in the territory of the United States north of the line therein mentioned, is not warranted by the Constitution, and is therefore void; and that neither Dred Scott himself, nor any of his family, were made free by being carried into this territory; even if they had been carried there by the owner, with the intention of becoming a permanent resident. [Although there were many separate opinions, only two justices dissented from the holding.]

Notes and Questions

1. *The Black Codes.* The constitutional end of slavery gave rise to a new model of racial control in the form of the Black Codes. These enactments, adopted by former slave states, "forbade blacks from pursuing certain occupations or professions, [forbade] owning firearms or weapons; controlled the movement of blacks by systems of passes; required proof of residence; prohibited the congregation of groups of blacks; restricted blacks from residing in certain areas; [specified] an etiquette of deference to whites[,] forbade racial intermarriage and provided the death penalty for blacks raping white women [and] excluded blacks from jury duty, public office, and voting." Harold Hyman & William Wiecek, *Equal Justice Under Law* 319 (Harper & Row 1982).

2. *The Civil Rights Act of 1866.* Congress responded to the Black Codes by enacting the Civil Rights Act of 1866, which prohibited discrimination on the basis of race with respect to civil rights and immunities and provided that the "inhabitants of every race [shall] have the same rights to make and enforce contracts, to sue, be parties, and give evidence, to inherit, purchase, lease, sell, hold and convey real and personal property, and to full and equal benefit of all laws and proceedings for the security of persons and property, and shall be subject to like punishment." *Cong. Globe,* 39th Cong., 1st Sess. 474 (1866).

3. *The Fourteenth Amendment.* To ensure the act's long-term vitality, and acting from concern that the Thirteenth Amendment was an inadequate predicate for civil rights legislation, the Reconstruction Congress framed the Fourteenth Amendment.

There is a general consensus among historians that the Fourteenth Amendment was fashioned to incorporate and fortify the Civil Rights Act of 1866. If correct, the guarantee as it has evolved is much more and much less. The amendment has become the basis for prohibiting classifications on the basis of not only race but also other grounds such as gender, alienage, and illegitimacy. It also has become a predicate for securing fundamental rights, such as privacy, travel, and voting, that are not textually enumerated. Although it expanded into contexts beyond what the Framers anticipated, as a function of judicial review, the Fourteenth Amendment for most of its history has been interpreted in ways that have accommodated rather than prohibited racial discrimination.

Notably missing from the Fourteenth Amendment's ambit of concern, as initially framed, was the right to vote. This omission reflected the reality that the constitutional impact would touch not only the South, but also the North. Reluctance to protect this political right broke down, however, as the nation factored in southern intransigence and the burdens and costs of reconstruction. As the right to vote became viewed as a means of speeding reconstruction toward its end, the Fifteenth Amendment was framed and ratified. Its exponents anticipated that the right to vote would provide the ultimate protection against hostile legislation.

4. *The* Slaughterhouse Cases. The Court's first exposure to the Fourteenth Amendment arose in a context unrelated to race. In the *Slaughterhouse Cases,* 83 U.S. 36 (1873), the Court spurned arguments that the Fourteenth Amendment represented a redistribution of authority over civil rights from states to the federal government. It thus defined the incidents of national citizenship, under the Privileges and Immunities Clause, in profoundly narrow terms. At the same time, the Court stressed that the equal protection guarantee was concerned exclusively with racial discrimination. It observed that:

> [i]n the light of the history of these amendments, and the pervading purpose of them, which we have already discussed, it is not difficult to give a meaning to this clause. The existence of laws in the States where the newly emancipated negroes resided, which discriminated with gross injustice and hardship against them as a class, was the evil to be remedied by this clause, and by it such laws are forbidden.
>
> If, however, the States did not conform their laws to its requirements, then by the fifth section of the article of amendment Congress was authorized to enforce it by suitable

legislation. We doubt very much whether any action of a State not directed by way of discrimination against the negroes as a class, or on account of their race, will ever be held to come
within the purview of this provision. It is so clearly a provision for that race and that emergency, that a strong case would be necessary for its application to any other. But as it is a State
that is to be dealt with, and not alone the validity of its laws, we may safely leave that matter
until Congress shall have exercised its power, or some case of State oppression, by denial of
equal justice in its courts, shall have claimed a decision at our hands. We find no such case in
the one before us, and do not deem it necessary to go over the argument again, as it may have
relation to this particular clause of the amendment. 83 U.S., at 81.

5. *Discrimination Implying Inferiority*. In striking down the Civil Rights Act of
1875, which prohibited discrimination in public accommodations, the Court in
The Civil Rights Cases, 109 U.S. 3, 24-25 (1883), indicated that these "mere discriminations" were constitutionally insignificant. It also noted that "[w]hen a man
has emerged from slavery, and by the aid of beneficent legislation has shaken off
the inseparable concomitants of that state, there must be some stage in the
progress of his elevation when he takes the rank of mere citizen, and ceases to be
the special favorite of the laws. . . . "

1. Separate but Equal

The letter and spirit of *The Civil Rights Cases* heralded an accommodating constitutional environment for the ideology of racial supremacy. Beginning in the late
1880s, southern states implemented laws designed to maintain racial separation,
protect racial integrity, preserve white supremacy, and minimize cross-racial min-
gling. This system of racial management actually had its prototype in the North,
where public education was often segregated and economic opportunity was
racially determined. *E.g.*, State v. McCann, 21 Ohio St. 198 (1872); Roberts v. City
of Boston, 59 Mass. 198 (1850). The Court referenced this history when, in Plessy
v. Ferguson, it determined that official segregation was the extension of a natural
societal order.

Plessy v. Ferguson

163 U.S. 537 (1896)

Mr. Justice BROWN [delivered] the opinion of the Court.

This case turns upon the constitutionality of an act of the general assembly
of the state of Louisiana, passed in 1890, providing for separate railway carriages
for the white and colored races. . . .

[The] constitutionality of this act is attacked upon the ground that it conflicts
both with the thirteenth amendment of the constitution, abolishing slavery, and
the fourteenth amendment, which prohibits certain restrictive legislation on the
part of the states. . . . The object of the [fourteenth] amendment was undoubtedly to enforce the absolute equality of the two races before the law, but, in the
nature of things, it could not have been intended to abolish distinctions based

upon color, or to enforce social, as distinguished from political, equality, or a commingling of the two races upon terms unsatisfactory to either. Laws permitting, and even requiring, their separation, in places where they are liable to be brought into contact, do not necessarily imply the inferiority of either race to the other, and have been generally, if not universally, recognized as within the competency of the state legislatures in the exercise of their police power. The most common instance of this is connected with the establishment of separate schools for white and colored children, which have been held to be a valid exercise of the legislative power even by courts of states where the political rights of the colored race have been longest and most earnestly enforced. . . . Laws forbidding the intermarriage of the two races may be said in a technical sense to interfere with the freedom of contract, and yet have been universally recognized as within the police power of the state. . . . The distinction between laws interfering with the political equality of the negro and those requiring the separation of the two races in schools, theaters, and railway carriages has been frequently drawn by this court. . . .

It is claimed by the plaintiff in error that, in any mixed community, the reputation of belonging to the dominant race, in this instance the white race, is "property," in the same sense that a right of action or of inheritance is property. [W]e are unable to see how this statute deprives him of, or in any way affects his right to, such property. If he be a white man, and assigned to a colored coach, he may have his action for damages against the company for being deprived of his so-called "property." Upon the other hand, if he be a colored man, and be so assigned, he has been deprived of no property, since he is not lawfully entitled to the reputation of being a white man.

[So] far, then, as a conflict with the fourteenth amendment is concerned, the case reduces itself to the question whether the statute of Louisiana is a reasonable regulation, and with respect to this there must necessarily be a large discretion on the part of the legislature. In determining the question of reasonableness, it is at liberty to act with reference to the established usages, customs, and traditions of the people, and with a view to the promotion of their comfort, and the preservation of the public peace and good order. Gauged by this standard, we cannot say that a law which authorizes or even requires the separation of the two races in public conveyances is unreasonable, or more obnoxious to the fourteenth amendment than the acts of congress requiring separate schools for colored children in the District of Columbia, the constitutionality of which does not seem to have been questioned, or the corresponding acts of state legislatures.

We consider the underlying fallacy of the plaintiff's argument to consist in the assumption that the enforced separation of the two races stamps the colored race with a badge of inferiority. If this be so, it is not by reason of anything found in the act, but solely because the colored race chooses to put that construction upon it. The argument necessarily assumes that if, [the] colored race should become the dominant power in the state legislature, and should enact a law in precisely similar terms, it would thereby relegate the white race to an inferior position. We imagine that the white race, at least, would not acquiesce in this assumption. The argument also assumes that social prejudices may be overcome by legislation, and that equal rights cannot be secured to the negro except by an enforced commingling of the two races. . . . If the two races are to meet upon terms of social equality, it must be the result of natural affinities, a mutual appreciation of each other's merits, and a voluntary consent of individuals. . . . When the government, therefore, has secured to each of its citizens equal rights before the law, and equal opportunities for improvement and progress, it "has accomplished the end for which it was organized, and performed all of the functions respecting social advantages with which it is endowed." Legislation is powerless to eradicate racial instincts, or to abolish distinctions based upon physical differences, and the attempt to do so can only result in accentuating the difficulties of the present situation. If the civil and political rights of both races be equal, one cannot be inferior to the other civilly or politically. If one race be inferior to the other socially, the constitution of the United States cannot put them upon the same plane.

The judgment of the court below is therefore *affirmed*.

Mr. Justice HARLAN dissenting.

[It] was said in argument that the statute of Louisiana does not discriminate against either race, but prescribes a rule applicable alike to white and colored citizens. . . . Everyone knows that the statute in question had its origin in the purpose [to] exclude colored people from coaches occupied by or assigned to white persons. . . . The thing to accomplish was, under the guise of giving equal accommodation for whites and blacks, to compel the latter to keep to themselves while traveling in railroad passenger coaches. . . . The fundamental objection, therefore, to the statute, is that it interferes with the personal freedom of citizens. . . . If a white man and a black man choose to occupy the same public conveyance on a public highway, it is their right to do so; and no government, proceeding alone on grounds of race, can prevent it without infringing the personal liberty of each.

[The] white race deems itself to be the dominant race in this country. And so it is, in prestige, in achievements, in education, in wealth, and in power. . . . But in view of the constitution, in the eye of the law, there is in this country no superior, dominant, ruling class of citizens. . . . Our constitution is color-blind, and neither knows nor tolerates classes among citizens. [A]ll citizens are equal before the law. . . . It is therefore to be regretted that this high tribunal, the final expositor of the fundamental law of the land, has reached the conclusion that it is competent for a state to regulate the enjoyment by citizens of their civil rights solely upon the basis of race.

[T]he judgment this day rendered will, in time, prove to be quite as pernicious as the decision made by this tribunal in the *Dred Scott* case. . . . The recent amendments of the constitution, it was supposed, had eradicated [that decision and its] principles from our institutions. But it seems that we have yet, in some of the states, a dominant race, — a superior class of citizens, — which assumes to regulate the enjoyment of civil rights, common to all citizens, upon the basis of race. The present decision [will] encourage the belief that it is possible [to] defeat the beneficent purposes [of] the recent amendments of the constitution, by one of which the blacks of this country were made citizens of the United States and of the states in which they respectively reside, and whose privileges and immunities, as citizens, the states are forbidden to abridge. . . . What can more certainly arouse race hate, what more certainly create and perpetuate a feeling of distrust between these races, than state enactments which, in fact, proceed on the ground that colored citizens are so inferior and degraded that they cannot be allowed to sit in public coaches occupied by white citizens? That [is] the real meaning of such legislation as was enacted in Louisiana. . . .

For the reasons stated, I am constrained to withhold my assent from the opinion and judgment of the majority.

Notes and Questions

1. *"Equality" Under "Separate but Equal."* Notwithstanding its facial symmetry, the separate but equal doctrine provided much more "separateness" than "equality." In Cumming v. Richmond County Board of Education, 175 U.S. 528 (1899), the Court upheld the closure of an all-black high school. The school board justified the closure on grounds that its financial resources were limited. The Court refused to order the closure of the all-white school, noting that it would burden one set of students without benefiting the other. This outcome evidenced that equality was a secondary concern. Segregation in public schools was revisited in Gong Lum v. Rice, 275 U.S. 78, 86-87 (1927). The plaintiff was the father of a nine-year-old girl who argued that she had been misclassified as "colored" and thus denied the opportunity to attend a public school reserved for whites. The Court concluded that the same claim had been rejected numerous times in cases brought by black children who were excluded from attending schools for whites. The Court found no basis for differentiating the outcome where the issue is between white pupils and pupils of Asian races.

BACKGROUND

For race and most alienage classifications, the Court applies strict scrutiny to government action. Here, the government action is presumed invalid and the government must justify its classification by showing that there is a compelling government interest and that the classification is narrowly tailored to achieve the compelling interest. Under strict scrutiny, the government action usually is invalidated, either because the government interest is not sufficiently compelling or, most often, because the regulation is not narrowly tailored.

---

2. *The NAACP's Role.* A key factor in the eventual dismantling of official segregation was the National Association for the Advancement of Colored People's (NAACP) emergence as a litigation force. The NAACP, in the 1930s, launched a desegregation strategy that successfully attacked the overt inequalities in education. Its early successes included a ruling, in Missouri ex rel. Gaines v. Canada,

305 U.S. 337 (1938), that a state must create a law school for nonwhites or else admit them to its only public law school.

3. *The* Carolene *Decision.* Another significant step toward segregation's deconstruction was the Court's indication, in United States v. Carolene Products Co., 304 U.S. 144, 154 n.4 (1938), that "prejudice against discrete and insular minorities may be a special condition, which tends seriously to curtail the operation of th[e] political processes ordinarily relied upon to protect minorities, and which may call for a correspondingly more searching inquiry." The Court thus indicated that it might use a higher standard of review when a group was excluded from and could not represent itself in the political process. In Korematsu v. United States, 323 U.S. 214 (1944), the Court introduced "strict scrutiny" as the standard of review for racial classifications.

Korematsu v. United States

323 U.S. 214 (1944)

Mr. Justice BLACK delivered the opinion of the Court.

The petitioner, an American citizen of Japanese descent, was convicted in a federal district court for remaining in San Leandro, California, a 'Military Area', contrary to Civilian Exclusion Order No. 34 of the Commanding General of the Western Command, U.S. Army, which directed that after May 9, 1942, all persons of Japanese ancestry should be excluded from that area. No question was raised as to petitioner's loyalty to the United States. . . .

[A]ll legal restrictions which curtail the civil rights of a single racial group are immediately suspect. That is not to say that all such restrictions are unconstitutional. It is to say that courts must subject them to the most rigid scrutiny. Pressing public necessity may sometimes justify the existence of such restrictions; racial antagonism never can. . . .

It is said that we are dealing here with the case of imprisonment of a citizen in a concentration camp solely because of his ancestry, without evidence or inquiry concerning his loyalty and good disposition towards the United States. Our task would be simple, our duty clear, were this a case involving the imprisonment of a loyal citizen in a concentration camp because of racial prejudice. Regardless of the true nature of the assembly and relocation centers — and we deem it unjustifiable to call them concentration camps with all the ugly connotations that term implies — we are dealing specifically with nothing but an exclusion order. To cast this case into outlines of racial prejudice, without reference to the real military dangers which were presented, merely confuses the issue. Korematsu was not excluded from the Military Area because of hostility to him or his race. He was excluded because we are at war with the Japanese Empire, because the properly constituted military authorities feared an invasion of our West Coast and felt constrained to take proper security measures, because they decided that the military urgency of the situation demanded that all citizens of Japanese ancestry be segregated from the West Coast temporarily, and finally, because Congress, reposing its confidence in this time of war in our military leaders — as inevitably it must — determined that they should have the power to do just this. There was evidence of disloyalty on the part of some, the military authorities considered that the need for action was great, and time was short. We cannot — by availing ourselves of the calm perspective of hindsight — now say that at that time these actions were unjustified.

Affirmed.

Mr. Justice MURPHY, dissenting.

This exclusion of 'all persons of Japanese ancestry, both alien and non-alien,' from the Pacific Coast area on a plea of military necessity in the absence of martial law ought not to be approved. Such exclusion goes over 'the very brink of constitutional power' and falls into the ugly abyss of racism.

[Justification] for the exclusion is sought [mainly] upon questionable racial and sociological grounds not ordinarily within the realm of expert military judgment, supplemented by certain semi-military conclusions drawn from an unwarranted use of circumstantial evidence. Individuals of Japanese ancestry are condemned because they are said to be 'a large, unassimilated, tightly knit racial group, bound to an enemy nation by strong ties of race, culture, custom and religion.' They are claimed to be given to 'emperor worshipping ceremonies' and to 'dual citizenship.' Japanese language schools and allegedly pro-Japanese organizations are cited as evidence of possible group disloyalty, together with facts as to certain persons being educated and residing at length in Japan. It is intimated that many of these individuals deliberately resided 'adjacent to strategic points,' thus enabling them 'to carry into execution a tremendous program of sabotage on a mass scale should any considerable number of them have been inclined to do so.' The need for protective custody is also asserted. The report refers without identity to 'numerous incidents of violence' as well as to other admittedly unverified or cumulative incidents. From this, plus certain other events not shown to have been connected with the Japanese Americans, it is concluded that the 'situation was fraught with danger to the Japanese population itself' and that the general public 'was ready to take matters into its own hands.' Finally, it is intimated, though not directly charged or proved, that persons of Japanese ancestry were responsible for three minor isolated shellings and bombings of the Pacific Coast area, as well as for unidentified radio transmissions and night signaling.

The main reasons relied upon by those responsible for the forced evacuation, therefore, do not prove a reasonable relation between the group characteristics of Japanese Americans and the dangers of invasion, sabotage and espionage. The reasons appear, instead, to be largely an accumulation of much of the misinformation, half-truths and insinuations that for years have been directed against Japanese Americans by people with racial and economic prejudices — the same people who have been among the foremost advocates of the evacuation. A military judgment based upon such racial and sociological considerations is not entitled to the great weight ordinarily given the judgments based upon strictly military considerations. Especially is this so when every charge relative to race, religion, culture, geographical location, and legal and economic status has been substantially discredited by independent studies made by experts in these matters. . . .

I dissent, therefore, from this legalization of racism. Racial discrimination in any form and in any degree has no justifiable part whatever in our democratic way of life. It is unattractive in any setting but it is utterly revolting among a free people who have embraced the principles set forth in the Constitution of the United States. All residents of this nation are kin in some way by blood or culture to a foreign land. Yet they are primarily and necessarily a part of the new and distinct civilization of the United States. They must accordingly be treated at all times as the heirs of the American experiment and as entitled to all the rights and freedoms guaranteed by the Constitution.

Mr. Justice JACKSON, dissenting.

Korematsu was born on our soil, of parents born in Japan. The Constitution makes him a citizen of the United States by nativity and a citizen of California by residence. No claim is made that he is not loyal to this country. There is no suggestion that apart from the matter involved here he is not law-abiding and well disposed. Korematsu, however, has been convicted of an act not commonly a crime. It consists merely of being present in the state whereof he is a citizen, near the place where he was born, and where all his life he has lived. . . .

[Much] is said of the danger to liberty from the Army program for deporting and detaining these citizens of Japanese extraction. But a judicial construction of the due process clause that will sustain this order is a far more subtle blow to liberty than the promulgation of the order itself. A military order, however unconstitutional, is not apt to last longer than the military emergency. . . . But once a judicial opinion rationalizes such an order to show that it conforms to the Constitution, or rather rationalizes the Constitution to show that the Constitution sanctions such an order, the Court for all time has validated the principle of racial discrimination in criminal procedure and of transplanting American citizens. The principle then lies about like a loaded weapon ready for the hand of any authority that can bring forward a plausible claim of an urgent need. . . . Nothing better illustrates this danger than does the Court's opinion in this case.

Notes

1. *Applying Strict Scrutiny.* The strict scrutiny standard of review eventually became a key tool for dismantling official segregation. Another decade would pass, however, before the separate but equal doctrine was laid to rest. During this time, the NAACP shifted its strategy from a focus on funding equality to the premise that segregation inherently was unequal. Its initial efforts in this regard were unproductive. Upon being ordered to desegregate its public law school or create a parallel institution for nonwhites, Oklahoma cordoned off a section of the state capitol building and declared it a separate but equal facility. The difficulty of maintaining a system of segregation increased when the Court determined that equalization of professional education was not reducible to tangible

factors alone. In Sweatt v. Painter, 339 U.S. 629 (1950), it noted that factors such as faculty reputation, alumni influence, institutional prestige, and networking potential could not be equalized by dollars. The Court in McLaurin v. Oklahoma State Board of Regents, 339 U.S. 637 (1950), found that racially based restrictions on classroom seating and access to the library and cafeteria undermined an effective education. It thus ordered the university to desegregate its program.

2. *The* Brown *Decision.* The outcomes described in the preceding note did not eliminate the separate but equal doctrine but significantly weakened its foundation. Movement beyond this increment of change was dependent on a change in the Court's leadership. A new Chief Justice, Earl Warren, was appointed to the Court one year after Brown v. Board of Education first was argued. *Brown* was the lead case in a group of five lower court decisions in Kansas, Delaware, Virginia, South Carolina, and the District of Columbia that addressed the separate but equal doctrine's continuing vitality.

2. Desegregation

Brown v. Board of Education
347 U.S. 483 (1954)

Mr. Chief Justice WARREN delivered the opinion of the Court.

These cases come to us from the States of Kansas, South Carolina, Virginia, and Delaware. They are premised on different facts and different local conditions, but a common legal question justifies their consideration together in this consolidated opinion.

In each of the cases, minors of the Negro race, through their legal representatives, seek the aid of the courts in obtaining admission to the public schools of their community on a nonsegregated basis. In each instance, they have been denied admission to schools attended by white children under laws requiring or permitting segregation according to race. This segregation was alleged to deprive the plaintiffs of the equal protection of the laws under the Fourteenth Amendment. . . .

The plaintiffs contend that segregated public schools are not 'equal' and cannot be made 'equal,' and that hence they are deprived of the equal protection of the laws. Because of the obvious importance of the question presented, the Court took jurisdiction. Argument was heard in the 1952 Term, and reargument was heard this Term on certain questions propounded by the Court.

Reargument was largely devoted to the circumstances surrounding the adoption of the Fourteenth Amendment in 1868. It covered exhaustively consideration of the Amendment in Congress, ratification by the states, then existing practices in racial segregation, and the views of proponents and opponents of the Amendment. This discussion and our own investigation convince us that, although these sources cast some light, it is not enough to resolve the problem with which we are faced. At best, they are inconclusive. . . .

An additional reason for the inconclusive nature of the Amendment's history, with respect to segregated schools, is the status of public education at that time. In the South, the movement toward free common schools, supported by general taxation, had not yet taken hold. Education of white children was largely in the hands of private groups. Education of Negroes was almost nonexistent, and practically all of the race were illiterate. In fact, any education of Negroes was forbidden by law in some states. Today, in contrast, many Negroes have achieved outstanding success in the arts and sciences as well as in the business and professional world. It is true that public school education at the time of the Amendment had advanced further in the North, but the effect of the Amendment on Northern States was generally ignored in the congressional debates. Even in the North, the conditions of public education did not approximate those existing today. The curriculum was usually rudimentary; ungraded schools were common in rural areas; the school term was but three months a year in many states; and compulsory school attendance was virtually unknown. As a consequence, it is not surprising that there should be so little in the history of the Fourteenth Amendment relating to its intended effect on public education.

[In] approaching this problem, we cannot turn the clock back to 1868 when the Amendment was adopted, or even to 1896 when Plessy v. Ferguson was written. We must consider public education in the light of its full development and its present place in American life throughout the Nation. Only in this way can it be determined if segregation in public schools deprives these plaintiffs of the equal protection of the laws.

Today, education is perhaps the most important function of state and local governments. Compulsory school attendance laws and the great expenditures for education both demonstrate our recognition of the importance of education to our democratic society. It is required in the performance of our most basic public responsibilities, even service in the armed forces. It is the very foundation of good citizenship. Today it is a principal instrument in awakening the child to cultural values, in preparing him for later professional training, and in helping him to adjust normally to his environment. In these days, it is doubtful that any child may reasonably be expected to succeed in life if he is denied the opportunity of an education. Such an opportunity, where the state has undertaken to provide it, is a right which must be made available to all on equal terms.

We come then to the question presented: Does segregation of children in public schools solely on the basis of race, even though the physical facilities and other 'tangible' factors may be equal, deprive the children of the minority group of equal educational opportunities? We believe that it does. . . . Such considerations apply with added force to children in grade and high schools. To separate them from others of similar age and qualifications solely because of their race generates a feeling of inferiority as to their status in the community that may affect their hearts and minds in a way unlikely ever to be undone.

[Whatever] may have been the extent of psychological knowledge at the time of Plessy v. Ferguson, this finding is amply supported by modern authority. Any language in Plessy v. Ferguson contrary to this finding is rejected. . . .

We conclude that in the field of public education the doctrine of 'separate but equal' has no place. Separate educational facilities are inherently unequal. Therefore, we hold that the plaintiffs and others similarly situated for whom the actions have been brought are, by reason of the segregation complained of, deprived of the equal protection of the laws guaranteed by the Fourteenth Amendment. This disposition makes unnecessary any discussion whether such segregation also violates the Due Process Clause of the Fourteenth Amendment.

Because these are class actions, because of the wide applicability of this decision, and because of the great variety of local conditions, the formulation of decrees in these cases presents problems of considerable complexity. On reargument, the consideration of appropriate relief was necessarily subordinated to the primary question — the constitutionality of segregation in public education. We have now announced that such segregation is a denial of the equal protection of the laws. In order that we may have the full assistance of the parties in formulating decrees, the cases will be restored to the docket, and the parties are requested to present further argument [pertaining to remediation].

It is so ordered.

Notes and Questions

1. *Scrutiny of Racial Classifications.* Earlier, we saw that economic classifications are subjected to a lower level of scrutiny, typically rational basis review. After *Brown*, is it apparent that racial classifications should be subjected to heightened scrutiny? Does the *Brown* decision explain clearly why that should be the case? What factors might lead you to conclude that racial classifications should be treated differently than, say, economic classifications, and that they should be subject to a higher standard of review?

2. *Desegregation.* As the NAACP continued to chip away at the foundation of the separate but equal doctrine, states began to pay more attention to the second half of the doctrine. Dramatic increases in funding of minority schools were a hallmark of segregation's final years. Last-minute efforts to shore up the separate but equal doctrine failed, however, when the Court heard rearguments in *Brown*. The Vinson Court had asked lawyers for both sides to research the history of the Fourteenth Amendment and present their findings. Under the leadership of Chief Justice Warren, the Court determined that it could "not turn the clock back to 1868 when the [Fourteenth] was adopted, or even to 1896 when Plessy v. Ferguson was written." It thus abandoned the separate but equal doctrine altogether in the field of public education.

3. *District of Columbia Segregation.* Segregation in the District of Columbia presented a technical challenge, insofar as the Fifth Amendment does not include an Equal Protection Clause. The Court, in Bolling v. Sharpe, 347 U.S. 497 (1954), found that the narrower guarantee of equal protection is implicit in the more generalized Fifth Amendment Due Process Clause.

∾ PROBLEMS ∾

1. *A Competing African American Perspective.* Desegregation of public education was challenged within the African American community by those who believed it

would cause more harm than good. Among its detractors was W.E.B. DuBois, who cofounded the NAACP but split from the organization once it embarked upon its desegregation strategy. DuBois maintained that "[o]ther things being equal, the [racially] mixed school is the broader, more natural basis for the education of all youth, [but] things seldom are equal, and in that case sympathy, knowledge, and the truth outweigh all the mixed school can offer." As an attorney making the state's case for segregation, and in particular having to dispute evidence of psychological damage to minority children, how might DuBois's premise help support the state's case?

2. *The Historical Record.* After the initial hearing in Brown v. Board of Education, the Court asked each side to examine the original purpose of the Fourteenth Amendment. Both sides conducted extensive historical research. Assume that you are a historian who has been retained by the NAACP. What evidence might you muster in support of desegregation? How would you respond to the reality that, at the time the Fourteenth Amendment was framed and ratified, Congress provided for segregation of public schools in the District of Columbia and some northern states did likewise?

Viewed as an abstraction, the desegregation principle had the potential for societal restructuring that ranged from formalistic to profound. The mildest action might have been for the Court to declare segregation unconstitutional but require no affirmative action to undo it. Pursuant to this option, segregation probably would have persisted in function following tradition and personal choice (at least unless and until the political process insisted otherwise). The Court chose a remedial course that required the actual dismantling of official segregation in public schools and the creation of racially unitary schools. The remedial process was set forth in Brown v. Board of Education II, which set out the standard of desegregation "with all deliberate speed." In framing this process, the Court referenced traditional equitable powers and the need for flexibility in reckoning with problems that might vary from one district to another.

Brown v. Board of Education

349 U.S. 294 (1955)

Mr. Chief Justice WARREN delivered the opinion of the Court.

[Because] these cases arose under different local conditions and their disposition will involve a variety of local problems, we requested further argument on the question of relief. In view of the nationwide importance of the decision, we invited the Attorney General of the United States and the Attorneys General of all states requiring or permitting racial discrimination in public education to present their views on that question. . . .

Full implementation of these constitutional principles may require solution of varied local school problems. School authorities have the primary responsibility for elucidating, assessing, and solving these problems; courts will have to consider whether the action of school authorities constitutes good faith implementation of the governing constitutional principles. Because of their proximity to local conditions and the possible need for further hearings, the courts which originally heard these cases can best perform this judicial appraisal. Accordingly, we believe it appropriate to remand the cases to those courts. In fashioning and effectuating the decrees, the courts will be guided by equitable principles. Traditionally, equity has been characterized by a practical flexibility in shaping its remedies and by a facility for adjusting and reconciling public and private needs. These cases call for the exercise of these traditional attributes of equity power. At stake is the personal interest of the plaintiffs in admission to public schools as soon as practicable on a nondiscriminatory basis. To effectuate this interest may call for elimination of a variety of obstacles in making the transition to school systems operated in accordance with the constitutional principles set forth in our May 17, 1954, decision. Courts of equity may properly take into account the public interest in the elimination of such obstacles in a systematic and effective manner. But it should go without saying that the vitality of these constitutional principles cannot be allowed to yield simply because of disagreement with them.

While giving weight to these public and private considerations, the courts will require that the defendants make a prompt and reasonable start toward full compliance with our . . . ruling. Once such a start has been made, the courts may find that additional time is necessary to carry out the ruling in an effective manner. The burden rests upon the defendants to establish that such time is necessary in the public interest and is consistent with good faith compliance at the earliest practicable date. To that end, the courts may consider problems related to administration, arising from the physical condition of the school plant, the school transportation system, personnel, revision of school districts and attendance areas into compact units to achieve a system of determining admission to the public schools on a nonracial basis, and revision of local laws and regulations which may be necessary in solving the foregoing problems. They will also consider the adequacy of any plans the defendants may propose to meet these problems and to effectuate a transition to a racially nondiscriminatory school system. During this period of transition, the courts will retain jurisdiction of these cases.

Notes

1. *"All Deliberate Speed" and Resistance.* The "all deliberate speed" standard was framed pursuant to input that the Court had invited from the parties and those states that would be most affected by the desegregation mandate. This engagement, however, did not defuse resistance to their effective implementation. Lower courts generally interpreted *Brown* in undemanding ways. Typifying this performance was the district court's opinion in the South Carolina case. In

Briggs v. Elliott, 132 F. Supp. 776, 77 (E.D.S.C. 1955), the district court in a per curiam opinion concluded that "[t]he Constitution [does] not require integration. It merely forbids discrimination. It does not forbid such segregation as occurs as the result of voluntary action. It merely forbids the use of governmental power to enforce segregation." As the South Carolina court saw it, constitutional requirements were satisfied merely by dispelling the legal force of segregation.

2. *Hostility to the NAACP.* Official reaction to the desegregation mandate, in those states ordered to comply with it, was characterized generally by efforts to avoid or delay its impact. In some instances, the response was more belligerent. The Arkansas legislature denounced the desegregation decision as unconstitutional and maintained that no remedy could be imposed without its approval. Some states resorted to preemptive tactics in an effort to deter litigation aimed at compelling desegregation. As the primary organizer of desegregation lawsuits in the decade after the *Brown* ruling, the NAACP was a target of legislation aimed at disabling its viability. The Alabama legislature, for instance, passed a law requiring the organization to make its membership list public. NAACP ex. rel. Alabama v. Patterson, 357 U.S. 449 (1958). Virginia used an antisolicitation rule against the NAACP to deter its litigative activities. NAACP v. Button, 371 U.S. 415 (1963). Although the Court struck down both laws, the states' actions reflected the generally hostile environment in which the desegregation mandate operated.

Donald E. Lively, *The Constitution and Race* 114-117 (Praeger 1992)

Reaction to the desegregation mandate was electric [and] decidedly negative. . . . Typical desegregation plans were shams, subterfuges, or inactions that effectively maintained segregation as a function of custom rather than official dictate. Some states passed laws intended to preclude actual desegregation or at least ripple the process. [Deferring] to local idiosyncrasies, sensing the need for grass-roots support, and aiming to minimize the divisive potential of its decision, the Court originally structured desegregation with an eye to enhancing its accountability. Reality, however, quickly defeated anticipation.

The first major test of the *Brown* principle presented itself in Little Rock, Arkansas. Although local authorities had devised a desegregation plan, the state legislature [enacted] a law purporting to relieve students from compulsory attendance at racially mixed schools. When the governor summoned the National Guard to prevent black students from entering the city's all-white high school, President Eisenhower responded by dispatching federal troops to enforce desegregation. The intensity of public reaction to the events prompted the school board to move for a delay in the implementation of its plan. In support of postponement, the board cited impairment of the educational process attributable to demonstrable tension and conflict. Although acknowledging that the educational process might suffer, and without doubting the board's good faith, the Court in Cooper v. Aaron denied the requested delay.

The *Cooper* case was an extension of the persisting debate over federal and state interests reckoned with in *Brown* but for practical purposes still unresolved.

Commencing with the premise that the Constitution is supreme and the judiciary has the power to "say what the law is," the Court characterized the desegregation mandate as "the supreme law of the land and binding on the states." The decision in *Cooper* was prompted by the sense that "the constitutional rights of respondents are not to be sacrificed or yielded to the violence and disorder which have followed upon the actions of the Governor and Legislature." Given the linkage between official action and public antagonism in Little Rock, the Court determined that "law and order are not here to be preserved by depriving the Negro children of their constitutional rights." It also warned that the desegregation mandate was not to be compromised either directly by legislative, executive, or judicial officers or indirectly by official evasion.

BACKGROUND

De jure segregation in public schools is unconstitutional. School districts operating a de jure segregated schools have an affirmative duty to establish unitary school systems in which students are not segregated by race. De facto segregation in public schools is not unconstitutional unless it is the result of intentional segregative acts by school officials. Where de facto segregation results from private economic choices or changing demographics school officials have no duty to maintain racial balance.

By the end of the 1960s, the changes contemplated by *Brown* had bypassed an entire generation of public school students. [C]onditions in the region most affected by the desegregation principle for practical purposes had remained largely unchanged. One of the districts subject to the original desegregation order in *Brown* remained "totally segregated" a decade later. Given such unvaried circumstances, the Court in [Green v. County School Board of New Kent County, Virginia] asserted that "[t]he time for mere 'deliberate speed' has run out." It accordingly demanded that school boards come forward with a desegregation "plan that promises realistically to work, and promises realistically to work *now*." [The *Green* Court also announced "an affirmative duty to take whatever steps might be necessary to convert to a unitary system in which racial discrimination would be eliminated root and branch."]

Movement from a standard of "all deliberate speed" to one of immediate relief fortified the Court's role in the desegregation process. The Griffin v. County School Board decision had suggested that equitable powers might be used prohibitively and affirmatively to halt public funding of private schools and to reopen and operate public schools. In Swann v. Charlotte-Mecklenburg Board of Education, the Court elaborated on the subject of remedial authority and defined the possibilities for relief expansively.

Swann v. Charlotte-Mecklenburg Board of Education
402 U.S. 1 (1971)

Mr. Chief Justice BURGER delivered the opinion of the Court.

[These] cases present us with the problem of defining in more precise terms than heretofore the scope of the duty of school authorities and district courts in implementing *Brown I* and the mandate to eliminate dual systems and establish unitary systems at once.

[If] school authorities fail in their affirmative obligations under these holdings, judicial authority may be invoked. Once a right and a violation have been shown, the scope of a district court's equitable powers to remedy past wrongs is broad, for breadth and flexibility are inherent in equitable remedies. . . .

[In] seeking to define even in broad and general terms how far this remedial power extends it is important to remember that judicial powers may be exercised only on the basis of a constitutional violation. Remedial judicial authority does not put judges automatically in the shoes of school authorities whose powers are plenary. Judicial authority enters only when local authority defaults.

School authorities are traditionally charged with broad power to formulate and implement educational policy and might well conclude, for example, that in order to prepare students to live in a pluralistic society each school should have a prescribed ratio of Negro to white students reflecting the proportion for the district as a whole. To do this as an educational policy is within the broad discretionary powers of school authorities; absent a finding of a constitutional violation, however, that would not be within the authority of a federal court. As with any equity case, the nature of the violation determines the scope of the remedy. In default by the school authorities of their obligation to proffer acceptable remedies, a district court has broad power to fashion a remedy that will assure a unitary school system.

[The] central issue in this case is that of student assignment, and there are essentially four problem areas: (1) to what extent racial balance or racial quotas may be used as an implement in a remedial order to correct a previously segregated system; (2) whether every all-Negro and all-white school must be eliminated as an indispensable part of a remedial process of desegregation; (3) what the limits are, if any, on the rearrangement of school districts and attendance zones, as a remedial measure; and (4) what the limits are, if any, on the use of transportation facilities to correct state-enforced racial school segregation.

(1) Racial Balances or Racial Quotas. The constant theme and thrust of every holding from *Brown I* to date is that state-enforced separation of races in public schools is discrimination that violates the Equal Protection Clause. The remedy commanded was to dismantle dual school systems.

[Our] objective in dealing with the issues presented by these cases is to see that school authorities exclude no pupil of a racial minority from any school, directly or indirectly, on account of race. . . . In this case it is urged that the District Court has imposed a racial balance requirement of 71%-29% on individual schools. . . . The constitutional command to desegregate schools does not mean that every school in every community must always reflect the racial composition of the school system as a whole.

[T]he use made of mathematical ratios was no more than a starting point in the process of shaping a remedy, rather than an inflexible requirement. From that starting point the District Court proceeded to frame a decree that was within its discretionary powers, as an equitable remedy for the particular circumstances. [A] school authority's remedial plan or a district court's remedial decree is to be judged by its effectiveness. Awareness of the racial composition of the whole school system is likely to be a useful starting point in shaping a remedy to correct past constitutional violations. In sum, the very limited use made of mathematical ratios was within the equitable remedial discretion of the District Court.

(2) One-Race Schools. [T]he existence of some small number of one-race, or virtually one-race, schools within a district is not in and of itself the mark of a system that still practices segregation by law. The district judge or school authorities should make every effort to achieve the greatest possible degree of actual desegregation and will thus necessarily be concerned with the elimination of one-race schools. No per se rule can adequately embrace all the difficulties of reconciling the competing interests involved; but in a system with a history of segregation the need for remedial criteria of sufficient specificity to assure a school authority's compliance with its constitutional duty warrants a presumption against schools that are substantially disproportionate in their racial composition. . . .

(3) Remedial Altering of Attendance Zones. [Absent] a constitutional violation there would be no basis for judicially ordering assignment of students on a racial basis. All things being equal, with no history of discrimination, it might well be desirable to assign pupils to schools nearest their homes. But all things are not equal in a system that has been deliberately constructed and maintained to enforce racial segregation. The remedy for such segregation may be administratively awkward, inconvenient, and even bizarre in some situations and may impose burdens on some; but all awkwardness and inconvenience cannot be avoided in the interim period when remedial adjustments are being made to eliminate the dual school systems. . . .

(4) Transportation of Students. The scope of permissible transportation of students as an implement of a remedial decree has never been defined by this Court. . . . No rigid guidelines as to student transportation can be given for application to the infinite variety of problems presented in thousands of situations. Bus transportation has been an integral part of the public education system for years, and was perhaps the single most important factor in the transition from the one-room schoolhouse to the consolidated school. Eighteen million of the Nation's public school children, approximately 39%, were transported to their schools by bus in 1969-1970 in all parts of the country.

The importance of bus transportation as a normal and accepted tool of educational policy is readily discernible. . . . The decree provided that the buses used to implement the plan would operate on direct routes. Students would be picked up at schools near their homes and transported to the schools they were to attend. The trips for elementary school pupils average about seven miles and the District Court found that they would take 'not over 35 minutes at the most.' This system compares favorably with the transportation plan previously operated in Charlotte under which each day 26,600 students on all grade levels were transported an average of 15 miles one way for an average trip requiring over an hour. In these circumstances, we find no basis for holding that the local school authorities may not be required to employ bus transportation as one tool of school desegregation. Desegregation plans cannot be limited to the walk-in school.

An objection to transportation of students may have validity when the time or distance of travel is so great as to either risk the health of the children or significantly impinge on the educational process.

[At] some point, these school authorities and others like them should have achieved full compliance with this Court's decision in *Brown I*. The systems would then be 'unitary.' . . .

It does not follow that the communities served by such systems will remain demographically stable, for in a growing, mobile society, few will do so. Neither school authorities nor district courts are constitutionally required to make year-by-year adjustments of the racial composition of student bodies once the affirmative duty to desegregate has been accomplished and racial discrimination through official action is eliminated from the system. This does not mean that federal courts are without power to deal with future problems; but in the absence of a showing that either the school authorities or some other agency of the State has deliberately attempted to fix or alter demographic patterns to affect the racial composition of the schools, further intervention by a district court should not be necessary. . . .

Note: Political Realities and Desegregation

Case law of the late 1960s and early 1970s represented the high-water mark of the desegregation mandate. The overarching remedial benchmark, as stated by the Court in Green v. County School Board, was elimination of "the vestiges of racial discrimination root and branch." Achievement of this goal, however, required change that extended beyond those places where segregation was formal and highly visible. Particularly as busing came to be understood as the primary methodology for effecting unitary schools, the political process began to hedge its support for the desegregation process. Personnel turnover on the Court was a critical factor in making the *Brown* decision possible. The same phenomenon influenced the desegregation mandate's eventual reach.

∾ PROBLEMS ∾

1. *Segregative Intent.* Assume that the school board decides to locate a high school in a neighborhood that is 95 percent African American. Because students attend neighborhood schools, it can be anticipated that enrollments will reflect residential demographics. You have been retained as counsel for a parents' group that opposes the school board's decision. Would the foreseeability of the outcome

give you a basis for establishing segregative intent? *See* Columbus Board of Education v. Penick, 443 U.S. 449 (1979).

2. *Passage of Time.* Assume that you were counsel for a school board in a midwestern community where a de jure system of segregation was maintained. No action ever was taken after Brown v. Board of Education was decided to dismantle the dual school system. Your advice to the school board, 25 years later, was that there was no constitutional obligation to desegregate the school system. How would that advice stand up in the context of litigation? See Dayton Board of Education v. Brinkman, 443 U.S. 406 (1977).

3. *White Flight.* Assume that you represent a parents' group in a community that, to avoid the possibility of having to desegregate, white families have exited. If you were to prove de jure segregation, and absent any responsibility on the part of other communities, what remedy would be available? Is there a difference between desegregation and integration? If so, does it reduce desegregation to formalism? If so, would desegregation differ from what was achievable under the separate but equal doctrine? *See* Milliken v. Bradley II, 433 U.S. 267 (1977).

4. *"Normal Pattern of Human Migration."* Assume you are a legal historian who is researching the history of segregation. Would you equate or differentiate Justice Rehnquist's reference to a "quite normal pattern of human migration" and the characterization of racial segregation (in Plessy v. Ferguson) as "in the nature of things"?

Case law in the 1970s increasingly accommodated circumstances that made desegregation in many metropolitan settings an exercise in form rather than function. Insistence on effective remedies became displaced by concern that the courts were not the appropriate authority for achieving durable results. Second thoughts about the judiciary's role were expressed by Justice Powell, who noted that "in city after city" desegregation merely was a prelude to "resegregation, stimulated by resentment against judicial coercion." Columbus Board of Education v. Penick, 443 U.S. 449, 483 (1979) (Powell, J., dissenting). He also adverted to "familiar segregated housing patterns . . . caused by social, economic, and demographic forces for which no school board is responsible." Consistent with this spirit, Justice Rehnquist observed that "[e]ven if the Constitution required it, and it were possible for federal courts to do it, no equitable decree can fashion an 'Emerald City' where all races, ethnic groups, and persons of various income levels live side by side." Cleveland Board of Education v. Reed, 445 U.S. 935, 938 (1980) (Rehnquist, J., dissenting from denial of certiorari). These sentiments reflected a growing sense of judicial restraint coupled with an interest in restoring full control over education to school boards. By the 1990s, the desegregation mandate had been recalibrated accordingly. Insistence upon erasing the vestiges of segregation "root and branch" thus was reduced, in Board of Education of Oklahoma City Schools v. Dowell, to a requirement that they be eliminated "to the extent practicable."

Board of Education of Oklahoma City Schools v. Dowell

498 U.S. 237 (1991)

Chief Justice REHNQUIST delivered the opinion of the Court.

[This] school desegregation litigation began almost 30 years ago. In 1961, respondents, black students and their parents, sued petitioners, the Board of Education of Oklahoma City (Board), to end de jure segregation in the public schools. In 1963, the District Court found that Oklahoma City had intentionally segregated both schools and housing in the past, and that Oklahoma City was operating a "dual" school system — one that was intentionally segregated by race. In 1965, the District Court found that the School Board's attempt to desegregate by using neighborhood zoning failed to remedy past segregation because residential segregation resulted in one-race schools. Residential segregation had once been state imposed, and it lingered due to discrimination by some realtors and financial institutions. The District Court found that school segregation had caused some housing segregation. In 1972, finding that previous efforts had not been successful at eliminating state imposed segregation, the District Court ordered the Board to adopt the "Finger Plan," under which kindergartners would be assigned to neighborhood schools unless their parents opted otherwise; children in grades 1-4 would attend formerly all white schools, and thus black children would be bused to those schools; children in grade five would attend formerly all black schools, and thus white children would be bused to those schools; students in the upper grades would be bused to various areas in order to maintain integrated schools; and in integrated neighborhoods there would be stand-alone schools for all grades.

In 1977, after complying with the desegregation decree for five years, the Board made a "Motion to Close Case." The District Court held in its "Order Terminating Case": "The Court has concluded that [the Finger Plan] worked and that substantial compliance with the constitutional requirements has been achieved. . . .

In 1984, the School Board faced demographic changes that led to greater burdens on young black children. As more and more neighborhoods became integrated, more stand-alone schools were established, and young black students had to be bused further from their inner-city homes to outlying white areas. In an effort to alleviate this burden and to increase parental involvement, the Board adopted the Student Reassignment Plan (SRP), which relied on neighborhood assignments for students in grades K-4 beginning in the 1985-1986 school year. Busing continued for students in grades 5-12. Any student could transfer from a school where he or she was in the majority to a school where he or she would be in the minority. Faculty and staff integration was retained, and an "equity officer" was appointed.

In 1985, respondents filed a "Motion to Reopen the Case," contending that the School District had not achieved "unitary" status and that the SRP was a return to segregation. Under the SRP, 11 of 64 elementary schools would be greater than 90% black, 22 would be greater than 90% white plus other minorities, and 31 would be racially mixed. . . .

[T]he District Court found that demographic changes made the Finger Plan unworkable, that the Board had done nothing for 25 years to promote residential segregation, and that the school district had bused students for more than a decade in good-faith compliance with the court's orders. The District Court found that present residential segregation was the result of private decisionmaking and economics, and that it was too attenuated to be a vestige of former school segregation. It also found that the district had maintained its unitary status, and that the neighborhood assignment plan was not designed with discriminatory intent. The court concluded that the previous injunctive decree should be vacated and the school district returned to local control. The Court of Appeals [reversed].

[In] Milliken v. Bradley (*Milliken II*), 433 U.S. 267 (1977), we said: "[F]ederal-court decrees must directly address and relate to the constitutional violation itself. Because of this inherent limitation upon federal judicial authority, federal-court decrees exceed appropriate limits if they are aimed at eliminating a condition that does not violate the Constitution or does not flow from such a [violation]." From the very first, federal supervision of local school systems was intended as a temporary measure to remedy past discrimination. *Brown* considered the "complexities arising from the transition to a system of public education freed of racial discrimination" in holding that the implementation of desegregation was to proceed "with all deliberate speed." *Green* also spoke of the "transition to a unitary, nonracial system of public education."

[Local] control over the education of children allows citizens to participate in decision-making, and allows innovation so that school programs can fit local needs. The legal justification for displacement of local authority by an injunctive decree in a school desegregation case is a violation of the Constitution by the local authorities. Dissolving a desegregation decree after the local authorities have operated in compliance with it for a reasonable period of time properly recognizes that "necessary concern for the important values of local control of public school systems dictates that a federal court's regulatory control of such systems not extend beyond the time required to remedy the effects of past intentional discrimination.

[A] district court need not accept at face value the profession of a school board which has intentionally discriminated that it will cease to do so in the future. But in deciding whether to modify or dissolve a desegregation decree, a school board's compliance with previous court orders is obviously relevant. In this case the original finding of de jure segregation was entered in 1961, the injunctive decree from which the Board seeks relief was entered in 1972, and the Board complied with the decree in good faith until 1985.

Justice MARSHALL, with whom Justice BLACKMUN and Justice STEVENS join, dissenting.

[The] practical question now before us is whether, 13 years after th[e] injunction was imposed, the same School Board should have been allowed to return many of its elementary schools to their former one-race status. The majority today suggests that 13 years of desegregation was enough. The Court remands the case for further evaluation of whether the purposes of the injunctive decree were achieved sufficient to justify the decree's dissolution. However, the inquiry it commends to the District Court fails to recognize explicitly the threatened reemergence of one-race schools as a relevant "vestige" of de jure segregation.

In my view, the standard for dissolution of a school desegregation decree must reflect the central aim of our school desegregation precedents. In Brown v. Board of Education, a unanimous Court declared that racially "[s]eparate educational facilities are inherently unequal." This holding rested on the Court's recognition that state-sponsored segregation conveys a message of "inferiority as to th[e] status [of Afro–American school children] in the community that may affect their hearts and minds in a way unlikely ever to be undone." Remedying this evil and preventing its recurrence were the motivations animating our requirement that formerly de jure segregated school districts take all feasible steps to eliminate racially identifiable schools.

I believe a desegregation decree cannot be lifted so long as conditions likely to inflict the stigmatic injury condemned in *Brown I* persist and there remain feasible methods of eliminating such conditions. Because the record here shows, and the Court of Appeals found, that feasible steps could be taken to avoid one-race schools, it is clear that the purposes of the decree have not yet been achieved and the Court of Appeals' reinstatement of the decree should be affirmed. I therefore dissent. . . .

Notes

1. *Partial Relinquishment of Control.* Insofar as local authorities comply with particular aspects of a desegregation order, a court may downsize its supervision incrementally. This proposition was set forth in Freeman v. Pitts, 503 U.S. 467, 489-490 (1992). The case concerned the DeKalb County School System (DCCS) in Georgia, which, until placed under judicial supervision in 1969, had maintained a racially segregated school system. On determining that the DCCS had achieved unitary status in some but not all categories, the district court relinquished control over those elements but retained supervision in those areas where full compliance had not been achieved. The Court determined that partial withdrawal of judicial supervision was permissible and desirable. It thus noted:

> [Partial] relinquishment of judicial control, where justified by the facts of the case, can be an important and significant step in fulfilling the district court's duty to return the operations and control of schools to local authorities. In *Dowell*, we emphasized that federal judicial supervision of local school systems was intended as a "temporary measure." Although this temporary measure has lasted decades, the ultimate objective has not changed — to return school districts to the control of local authorities.
>
> [Just] as a court has the obligation at the outset of a desegregation decree to structure a plan so that all available resources of the court are directed to comprehensive supervision of its decree, so too must a court provide an orderly means for withdrawing from control when it is shown that the school district has attained the requisite degree of compliance. A transition phase in which control is relinquished in a gradual way is an appropriate means to this end.

2. *Resegregation and Contemporary Constitutional Realities*. Although courts have a broad arsenal of devices for remedying segregation, these tools are usable only in instances of de jure segregation and may not exceed the scope of the violation. Modern segregation has been attributable primarily to demographic realignments, as findings of intentional segregation have become increasingly rare. The reemergence of racially identifiable schools, that are constitutionally inconsequential, has prompted efforts through judicial and political processes to increase or maintain diversity. Although diversity has been recognized as a compelling interest in higher education (as discussed later), the Court has rejected diversity initiatives in primary and secondary public school settings.

Missouri v. Jenkins

515 U.S. 70 (1995)

Chief Justice REHNQUIST delivered the opinion of the Court.

[In 1977,] the KCMSD, the school board, and the children of two school board members brought suit against the State and other defendants. Plaintiffs alleged that the State, the surrounding suburban school districts (SSD's), and various federal agencies had caused and perpetuated a system of racial segregation in the schools of the Kansas City metropolitan area. [T]he District Court dismissed the case against the federal defendants and the SSD's, but determined that the State and the KCMSD were liable for an intradistrict violation, i.e., they had operated a segregated school system within the KCMSD. The District Court determined that prior to 1954 "Missouri mandated segregated schools for black and white children." Furthermore, the KCMSD and the State had failed in their affirmative obligations to eliminate the vestiges of the State's dual school system within the KCMSD.

[The] District Court, pursuant to plans submitted by the KCMSD and the State, ordered a wide range of quality education programs for all students attending the KCMSD. . . . The total cost for these quality education programs has exceeded $220 million.

The District Court also set out to desegregate the KCMSD but believed that "[t]o accomplish desegregation within the boundary lines of a school district whose enrollment remains 68.3% black is a difficult task." Because it had found no interdistrict violation, the District Court could not order mandatory interdistrict redistribution of students between the KCMSD and the surrounding SSD's.

In November 1986, the District Court approved a comprehensive magnet school and capital improvements plan and held the State and the KCMSD jointly and severally liable for its funding. Under the District Court's plan, every senior high school, every middle school, and one-half of the elementary schools were converted into magnet schools. The District Court adopted the magnet-school program to "provide a greater educational opportunity to all KCMSD students," and because it believed "that the proposed magnet plan [was] so attractive that it would draw non-minority students from the private schools who have abandoned or avoided the KCMSD, and draw in additional non-minority students from the suburbs." The District Court felt that "[t]he long-term benefit of all KCMSD students of a greater educational opportunity in an integrated environment is worthy of such an investment." Since its inception, the magnet school program has operated at a cost, including magnet transportation, in excess of $448 million. . . .

[The District Court also adopted a long-range capital improvement plan costing more than $187 million and teacher salary increases exceeding $200 million.]

The District Court's desegregation plan has been described as the most ambitious and expensive remedial program in the history of school desegregation. The annual cost per pupil at the KCMSD far exceeds that of the neighboring SSD's or of any school district in Missouri. Nevertheless, the KCMSD, which has pursued a "friendly adversary" relationship with the plaintiffs, has continued to propose ever more expensive programs. As a result, the desegregation costs have escalated and now are approaching an annual cost of $200 million. These massive expenditures have financed

> high schools in which every classroom will have air conditioning, an alarm system, and 15 microcomputers; a 2,000-square-foot planetarium; green houses and vivariums; a 25-acre farm with an air-conditioned meeting room for 104 people; a Model United Nations wired for language translation; broadcast capable radio and television studios with an editing and animation lab; a temperature controlled art gallery; movie editing and screening rooms; a 3,500-square-foot dust-free diesel mechanics room; 1,875-square-foot elementary school animal rooms for use in a zoo project; swimming pools; and numerous other facilities.

Not surprisingly, the cost of this remedial plan has "far exceeded KCMSD's budget, or for that matter, its authority to tax." The State, through the operation of joint-and-several liability, has borne the brunt of these costs.

[The] proper response by the District Court should have been to eliminate to the extent practicable the vestiges of prior de jure segregation within the KCMSD: a system-wide reduction in student achievement and the existence of 25 racially identifiable schools with a population of over 90% black students. . . . The District Court and Court of Appeals, however, have felt that because the KCMSD's enrollment remained 68.3% black, a purely intradistrict remedy would be insufficient. . . . Instead of seeking to remove the racial identity of the various schools within the KCMSD, the District Court has set out on a program to create a school district that was equal to or superior to the surrounding SSD's. Its remedy has focused on "desegregative attractiveness," coupled with "suburban comparability."

[The] purpose of desegregative attractiveness has been not only to remedy the system-wide reduction in student achievement, but also to attract nonminority students not presently enrolled in the KCMSD. This remedy has included an elaborate program of capital improvements, course enrichment, and extracurricular enhancement not simply in the formerly identifiable black schools, but in schools throughout the district. The District Court's remedial orders have converted every senior high school, every middle school, and one-half of the elementary schools in the KCMSD into "magnet" schools. The District Court's remedial order has all but made the KCMSD itself into a magnet district.

We previously have approved of intradistrict desegregation remedies involving magnet schools. Magnet schools have the advantage of encouraging voluntary movement of students within a school district in a pattern that aids desegregation on a voluntary basis, without requiring extensive busing and redrawing of district boundary lines. . . . The District Court's remedial plan in this case, however, is not designed solely to redistribute the students within the KCMSD in order to eliminate racially identifiable schools within the KCMSD. Instead, its purpose is to attract nonminority students from outside the KCMSD schools. But this interdistrict goal is beyond the scope of the intradistrict violation identified by the District Court. In effect, the District Court has devised a remedy to accomplish indirectly what it admittedly lacks the remedial authority to mandate directly: the interdistrict transfer of students. . . .

[Respondents] argue that the District Court's reliance upon desegregative attractiveness is justified in light of the District Court's statement that segregation has "led to white flight from the KCMSD to suburban districts." [In] *Freeman*, we stated that "[t]he vestiges of segregation that are the concern of the law in a school case may be subtle and intangible but nonetheless they must be so real that they have a causal link to the de jure violation being remedied." The record here does not support the District Court's reliance on "white flight" as a justification for a permissible expansion of its intradistrict remedial authority through its pursuit of desegregative attractiveness.

[Nor] are there limits to the duration of the District Court's involvement. The expenditures per pupil in the KCMSD currently far exceed those in the neighboring SSD's. Sixteen years after this litigation began, the District Court recognized that the KCMSD has yet to offer a viable method of financing the "wonderful school system being built." . . . But our cases recognize that local autonomy of school districts is a vital national tradition, and that a district court must strive to restore state and local authorities to the control of a school system operating in compliance with the Constitution.

[T]he District Court's order requiring the State to continue to fund the quality education programs because student achievement levels were still "at or below national norms at many grade levels" cannot be sustained. The State [challenges] the requirement of indefinite funding of a quality education program until national norms are met, based on the assumption that while a mandate for significant educational improvement, both in teaching and in facilities, may have been justified originally, its indefinite extension is not. . . .

[The] basic task of the District Court is to decide whether the reduction in achievement by minority students attributable to prior de jure segregation has been remedied to the extent practicable. [The District Court] never has identified the incremental effect that segregation has had on minority student achievement or the specific goals of the quality education programs. . . .

In reconsidering this order, the District Court should apply our three-part test from Freeman v. Pitts. . . .

[On] remand, the District Court must bear in mind that its end purpose is not only "to remedy the violation" to the extent practicable, but also "to restore state and local authorities to the control of a school system that is operating in compliance with the Constitution." The judgment of the Court of Appeals is reversed.

Justice O'CONNOR, concurring.

[Remedying] desegregative attractiveness [is] within the District Court's authority only if it is "directly caused by the constitutional violation." [The District Court admitted that] the segregative effects of KCMSD's constitutional violation did not transcend its geographical boundaries. In light of that finding, the District Court cannot order remedies seeking to rectify regional demographic trends that go beyond the nature and scope of the constitutional violation. . . . The necessary restrictions on our jurisdiction and authority contained in Article III of the Constitution limit the judiciary's institutional capacity to prescribe palliatives for societal ills. The unfortunate fact of racial imbalance and bias in our society, however pervasive or invidious, does not admit of judicial intervention absent a constitutional violation. . . .

Justice THOMAS, concurring.

[T]he District Court here sought to convert the [KCMSD] into a "magnet district" that would reverse the "white flight" caused by desegregation. [Courts] must not confuse the consequences of de jure segregation with the results of larger social forces or of private decisions. . . . When a district court holds the State liable for discrimination almost 30 years after the last official state action, it must do more than show that there are schools with high black populations or low test scores. . . . Without a basis in any real finding of intentional government action, the District Court's imposition of liability upon the State of Missouri improperly rests upon a theory that racial imbalances are unconstitutional. [This] position appears to rest upon the idea that any school that is black is inferior, and that blacks cannot succeed without the benefit of the company of whites.

Justice SOUTER, with whom Justice STEVENS, Justice GINSBURG, and Justice BREYER join, dissenting.

[In] 1984, 30 years [after] *Brown*, [the] State of Missouri [had] failed to reform the segregated scheme of public school education in the KCMSD, previously mandated by the State. [B]efore a district court may grant a school district [partial] release from a desegregation decree, it must first consider "whether there has been full and satisfactory compliance with the decree in those aspects of the system where supervision is to be [withdrawn]." [B]efore the District Court's remedial plan was placed into effect the schools in the unreformed segregated system were physically a shambles. [The] cost of turning this shambles into habitable schools was enormous. . . . Property tax-paying parents of white children, seeing the handwriting on the wall in 1985, could well have decided that the inevitable cost of clean-up would produce an intolerable tax rate and could have moved to escape it. . . . Was the white flight caused by segregation or desegregation? The distinction has no significance. . . .

a. Discriminatory Purpose Requirement

The desegregation principle, as announced in *Brown*, was quickly extended to public contexts beyond education. To the extent that laws were a function of segregative or discriminatory intent, they consistently were invalidated. This result was achieved even when racial sensitivity and selectivity arguably were factors that connected with other legitimate purposes. The use of peremptory challenges of prospective jurors, for instance, traditionally has included an appreciation that racial bias may be a factor in how evidence is processed. In a series of cases beginning with Batson v. Kentucky, 476 U.S. 79 (1986), the Court determined that peremptory challenges could not be correlated to race. Given the demands of the discriminatory purpose standard, and human ability to cover actual motive, proving wrongful intent has remained a challenge.

The reconstruction of constitutional principle to defeat prescriptive segregation nonetheless recaptured the promise of Strauder v. West Virginia, which had interpreted the Fourteenth Amendment as a barrier to legislation reflecting racial animus. In Loving v. Virginia, the Court examined an antimiscegenation law that the state justified on grounds it applied evenhandedly. Despite this neutrality argument, the Court concluded that the enactment was an extension of racist ideology and thus invidious.

∼ PROBLEM: RACE IN PRISONS ∼

The separate but equal doctrine was grounded, at least in part, on the need to preserve "public peace and good order." Assume that you have been asked to provide counsel to a state prison warden who is concerned with racial tensions among inmates and the potential for violence. Would you recommend racial segregation of the prison population as a policy option? *See* Johnson v. California, 543 U.S. 499 (2005).

Loving v. Virginia

388 U.S. 1 (1968)

Mr. Chief Justice WARREN delivered the opinion of the Court.

This case presents a constitutional question never addressed by this Court: whether a statutory scheme adopted by the State of Virginia to prevent marriages between persons solely on the basis of racial classifications violates the Equal Protection and Due Process Clauses of the Fourteenth Amendment. . . .

In June 1958, two residents of Virginia, Mildred Jeter, a Negro woman, and Richard Loving, a white man, were married in the District of Columbia pursuant to its laws. Shortly after their marriage, the Lovings returned to Virginia and established their marital abode in Caroline County. [A] grand jury issued an indictment charging the Lovings with violating Virginia's ban on interracial marriages. [T]he Lovings pleaded guilty to the charge and were sentenced to one year in jail; however, the trial judge suspended the sentence for a period of 25 years on the condition that the Lovings leave the State and not return. . . . He stated in an opinion that: 'Almighty God created the races white, black, yellow, malay and red, and he placed them on separate continents. And but for the interference with his arrangement there would be no cause for such marriages. The fact that he separated the races shows that he did not intend for the races to mix.' . . . [T]he Supreme Court of Appeals of Virginia upheld the constitutionality of the anti-miscegenation statutes and, after modifying the sentence, affirmed the convictions. . . .

Virginia is now one of 16 States which prohibit and punish marriages on the basis of racial classifications. Penalties for miscegenation arose as an incident to slavery and have been common in Virginia since the colonial period. The present statutory scheme dates from the adoption of the Racial Integrity Act of 1924, passed during the period of extreme nativism which followed the end of the First World War. The central features of this Act [are] the absolute prohibition of a 'white person' marrying other than another 'white person,' a prohibition against issuing marriage licenses until the issuing official is satisfied that the applicants' statements as to their race are correct, certificates of 'racial composition' to be kept by both local and state registrars, and the carrying forward of earlier prohibitions against racial intermarriage. . . .

[T]he State contends that, because its miscegenation statutes punish equally both the white and the Negro participants in an interracial marriage, these statutes, despite their reliance on racial classifications do not constitute an invidious discrimination based upon race. . . . Because we reject the notion that the mere 'equal application' of a statute containing racial classifications is enough to remove the classifications from the Fourteenth Amendment's proscription of all invidious racial discriminations, we do not accept the State's contention that these statutes should be upheld if there is any possible basis for concluding that they serve a rational purpose. . . . [We] deal with statutes containing racial classifications, and the fact of equal application does not immunize the statute from the very heavy burden of justification which the Fourteenth Amendment has traditionally required of state statutes drawn according to race. . . .

There can be no question but that Virginia's miscegenation statutes rest solely upon distinctions drawn according to race. The statutes proscribe generally accepted conduct if engaged in by members of different races. [T]his Court has consistently repudiated '[d]istinctions between citizens solely because of their ancestry' as being 'odious to a free people whose institutions are founded upon the doctrine of equality.' At the very least, the Equal Protection Clause demands that racial classifications, especially suspect in criminal statutes, be subjected to the 'most rigid scrutiny,' and, if they are ever to be upheld, they must be shown to be necessary to the accomplishment of some permissible state objective, independent of the racial discrimination which it was the object of the Fourteenth Amendment to eliminate. . . .

There is patently no legitimate overriding purpose independent of invidious racial discrimination which justifies this classification. The fact that Virginia prohibits only interracial marriages involving white persons demonstrates that the racial classifications must stand on their own justification, as measures designed to maintain White Supremacy. We have consistently denied the constitutionality of measures which restrict the rights of citizens on account of race. There can be no doubt that restricting the freedom to marry solely because of racial classifications violates the central meaning of the Equal Protection Clause.

These statutes also deprive the Lovings of liberty without due process of law in violation of the Due Process Clause of the Fourteenth Amendment. The freedom to marry has long been recognized as one of the vital personal rights essential to the orderly pursuit of happiness by free men. . . . The Fourteenth Amendment requires that the freedom of choice to marry not be restricted by invidious racial discriminations. . . . These convictions must be reversed.

Mr. Justice STEWART, concurring.

'[I]t is simply not possible for a state law to be valid under our Constitution which makes the criminality of an act depend upon the race of the actor.' [I] concur. . . .

Note: Discriminatory Purpose and Disproportionate Impact

The *Loving* decision reflected an instance in which discriminatory purpose was overt. Once declared illegal, discrimination increasingly morphed from visible and easily discernible to subtle and difficult to detect. Given the nation's well-documented history of racial discrimination, one school of thought argued that showings of disproportionate impact should be sufficient to establish an equal protection claim. In Palmer v. Thompson, 403 U.S. 217 (1971), the Court declined to review legislative motive as a basis for determining whether closure of city pools constituted an equal protection violation. Because the ruling was premised on the ground that the city had no obligation to operate public pools, it did not help either the discriminatory purpose requirement or the discriminatory effect standard to gain traction.

The Court's decision in Keyes v. School District No. 1, 413 U.S. 189 (1973), established intentional segregation as the basis for relief in the public school context. In Washington v. Davis, the Court confirmed that purposeful discrimination was a threshold requirement for a viable equal protection claim.

Washington v. Davis

426 U.S. 229 (1976)

Mr. Justice WHITE delivered the opinion of the Court.

This case involves the validity of a qualifying test administered to applicants for positions as police officers in the District of Columbia Metropolitan Police Department. [T]o be accepted by the Department and to enter an intensive

17-week training program, the police recruit was required to satisfy certain physical and character standards, to be a high school graduate or its equivalent, and to receive a grade of at least 40 out of 80 on "Test 21," which is "an examination that is used generally throughout the federal service," which "was developed by the Civil Service Commission, not the Police Department," and which was "designed to test verbal ability, vocabulary, reading and comprehension."

The validity of Test 21 was the sole issue before the court on the motions for summary judgment. The [District Court denied the motion for summary judgment, but the Court of Appeals reversed holding that] Test 21 invidiously discriminated against Negroes and hence denied them due process of law contrary to the commands of the Fifth Amendment. . . . We reverse its judgment in respondents' favor. . . .

The central purpose of the Equal Protection Clause of the Fourteenth Amendment is the prevention of official conduct discriminating on the basis of race. It is also true that the Due Process Clause of the Fifth Amendment contains an equal protection component prohibiting the United States from invidiously discriminating between individuals or groups. But our cases have not embraced the proposition that a law or other official act, without regard to whether it reflects a racially discriminatory purpose, is unconstitutional solely because it has a racially disproportionate impact.

Almost 100 years ago, Strauder v. West Virginia, 100 U.S. 303 (1879), established that the exclusion of Negroes from grand and petit juries in criminal proceedings violated the Equal Protection Clause, but the fact that a particular jury or a series of juries does not statistically reflect the racial composition of the community does not in itself make out an invidious discrimination forbidden by the Clause. "A purpose to discriminate must be present which may be proven by systematic exclusion of eligible jurymen of the proscribed race or by unequal application of the law to such an extent as to show intentional discrimination." . . .

The school desegregation cases have also adhered to the basic equal protection principle that the invidious quality of a law claimed to be racially discriminatory must ultimately be traced to a racially discriminatory purpose. That there are both predominantly black and predominantly white schools in a community is not alone violative of the Equal Protection Clause. The essential element of de jure segregation is "a current condition of segregation resulting from intentional state action. The differentiating factor between de jure segregation and so-called de facto segregation [is the] purpose or intent to segregate." . . .

This is not to say that the necessary discriminatory racial purpose must be express or appear on the face of the statute, or that a law's disproportionate impact is irrelevant in cases involving Constitution-based claims of racial discrimination. A statute, otherwise neutral on its face, must not be applied so as invidiously to discriminate on the basis of race. [When] a prima facie case made out, "the burden of proof shifts to the State to rebut the presumption of unconstitutional action by showing that permissible racially neutral selection criteria and procedures have produced the monochromatic result.

[A]n invidious discriminatory purpose may often be inferred from the totality of the relevant facts, including the fact, if it is true, that the law bears more heavily on one race than another. [This may be true where there is] the total or seriously disproportionate exclusion of Negroes [that] is very difficult to explain on nonracial grounds. Nevertheless, we have not held that a law, neutral on its face and serving ends otherwise within the power of government to pursue, is invalid under the Equal Protection Clause simply because it may affect a greater proportion of one race than of another. Disproportionate impact is not irrelevant, but it is not the sole touchstone of an invidious racial discrimination forbidden by the Constitution. Standing alone, it does not trigger the rule, that racial classifications are to be subjected to the strictest scrutiny and are justifiable only by the weightiest of considerations.

[Test 21], which is administered generally to prospective Government employees, concededly seeks to ascertain whether those who take it have acquired a particular level of verbal skill; and it is untenable that the Constitution prevents the Government from seeking modestly to upgrade the communicative abilities of its employees rather than to be satisfied with some lower level of competence, particularly where the job requires special ability to communicate orally and in writing. Respondents, as Negroes, could no more successfully claim that the test denied them equal protection than could white applicants who also failed. The conclusion would not be different in the face of proof that more Negroes than whites had been disqualified by Test 21. That other Negroes also failed to score well would, alone, not demonstrate that respondents individually were being denied equal protection of the laws by the application of an otherwise valid qualifying test being administered to prospective police recruits.

Nor on the facts of the case before us would the disproportionate impact of Test 21 warrant the conclusion that it is a purposeful device to discriminate against Negroes and hence an infringement of the constitutional rights of respondents as well as other black applicants. [T]he test is neutral on its face and rationally may be said to serve a purpose the Government is constitutionally empowered to pursue. [T]he affirmative efforts of the Metropolitan Police Department to recruit black officers, the changing racial composition of the recruit classes and of the force in general, and the relationship of the test to the training program negated any inference that the Department discriminated on the basis of race or that "a police officer qualifies on the color of his skin rather than ability."

[A] rule that a statute designed to serve neutral ends is nevertheless invalid, absent compelling justification, if in practice it benefits or burdens one race more than another would be far-reaching and would raise serious questions about, and perhaps invalidate, a whole range of tax, welfare, public service, regulatory, and licensing statutes that may be more burdensome to the poor and to the average black than to the more affluent white. [I]n our view, extension of the rule beyond those areas where it is already applicable by reason of statute, such as in the field of public employment, should await legislative prescription. . . .

The judgment of the Court of Appeals accordingly is *reversed*.

Mr. Justice STEVENS, concurring.

[Frequently] the most probative evidence of intent will be objective evidence of what actually happened rather than evidence describing the subjective state of mind of the actor. For normally the actor is presumed to have intended the natural consequences of his deeds. This is particularly true in the case of governmental action which is frequently the product of compromise, of collective decision-making, and of mixed motivation. It is unrealistic, on the one hand, to require the victim of alleged discrimination to uncover the actual subjective intent of the decision-maker or, conversely, to invalidate otherwise legitimate action simply because an improper motive affected the deliberation of a participant in the decisional process. A law conscripting clerics should not be invalidated because an atheist voted for it.

My point in making this observation is to suggest that the line between discriminatory purpose and discriminatory impact is not nearly as bright, and perhaps not quite as critical, as the reader of the Court's opinion might assume. I agree, of course, that a constitutional issue does not arise every time some disproportionate impact is shown. On the other hand, when the disproportion is as dramatic, it really does not matter whether the standard is phrased in terms of purpose or effect. . . .

Mr. Justice BRENNAN, with whom Mr. Justice MARSHALL joins, dissenting.

The Court holds that the job qualification examination (Test 21) given by the District of Columbia Metropolitan Police Department does not unlawfully discriminate on the basis of race under either constitutional or statutory standards.

Initially, it seems to me that the Court should not pass on the statutory questions, because they are not presented by this case. The Court says that respondents' summary judgment motion "rested on purely constitutional grounds," and that "the Court of Appeals erroneously applied the legal standards applicable to Title VII cases in resolving the constitutional issue before it." There is a suggestion, however, that petitioners are entitled to prevail because they met the burden of proof imposed by 5 U.S.C. §3304. As I understand the opinion, the Court therefore holds that Test 21 is job related under §3304, but not necessarily under Title VII. But that provision, by the Court's own analysis, is no more in the case than Title VII; respondents' "complaint asserted no claim under §3304." If it was "plain error" for the Court of Appeals to apply a statutory standard to this case, as the Court asserts, then it is unfortunate that the Court does not recognize that it is also plain error to address the statutory issues in Part III of its opinion.

Nevertheless, although it appears unnecessary to reach the statutory questions, I will accept the Court's conclusion that respondents were entitled to summary judgment if they were correct in their statutory arguments, and I would affirm the Court of Appeals because petitioners have failed to prove that Test 21 satisfies the applicable statutory standards. All parties' arguments and both lower court decisions were based on Title VII standards. In this context, I think it wrong to focus on §3304 to the exclusion of the Title VII standards, particularly because the Civil Service Commission views the job-relatedness standards of Title VII and §3304 as identical.

In applying a Title VII test, both the District Court and the Court of Appeals held that respondents had offered sufficient evidence of discriminatory impact to shift to petitioners the burden of proving job-relatedness. The Court does not question these rulings, and the only issue before us is what petitioners were required to show and whether they carried their burden. The Court agrees with the District Court's conclusion that Test 21 was validated by a positive relationship between Test 21 scores and performance in police training courses. This result is based upon the Court's reading of the record, its interpretation of instructions governing testing practices issued by the Civil Service Commission (CSC), and "the current views of the Civil Service Commissioners who were parties to the case." We are also assured that today's result is not foreclosed by Griggs v. Duke Power Co., 401 U.S. 424 (1971), and Albemarle Paper Co. v. Moody, 422 U.S. 405 (1975). Finally, the Court asserts that its conclusion is "the much more sensible construction of the job-relatedness requirement."

But the CSC instructions cited by the Court do not support the District Court's conclusion. More importantly, the brief filed in this Court by the CSC takes the position that petitioners did not satisfy the burden of proof imposed by the CSC guidelines. It also appears that longstanding regulations of the Equal Employment Opportunity Commission (EEOC) — previously endorsed by this Court — require a result contrary to that reached by the Court. Furthermore, the Court's conclusion is inconsistent with my understanding of the interpretation of Title VII in *Griggs* and *Albemarle*. I do not find this conclusion "much more sensible," and with all respect I suggest that today's decision has the potential of significantly weakening statutory safeguards against discrimination in employment.

Village of Arlington Heights v. Metropolitan Housing Development Corp.

429 U.S. 252 (1977)

Mr. Justice POWELL delivered the opinion of the Court.

[This case concerns a village's refusal to rezone land from single-family usage to accommodate multiple family dwellings and thus enable the respondent to construct racially integrated housing.]

Our decision last Term in Washington v. Davis made it clear that official action will not be held unconstitutional solely because it results in a "racially disproportionate impact." Disproportionate impact is not irrelevant, but it is not the sole touchstone of an invidious racial discrimination. Proof of racially discriminatory intent or purpose is required to show a violation of the Equal Protection Clause. Although some contrary indications may be drawn from some of our cases, the holding in *Davis* reaffirmed a principle well established in a variety of contexts.

Davis does not require a plaintiff to prove that the challenged action rested solely on racially discriminatory purposes. Rarely can it be said that a legislature or administrative body operating under a broad mandate made a decision motivated solely by a single concern, or even that a particular purpose was the "dominant" or "primary" one. In fact, it is because legislators and administrators are properly concerned with balancing numerous competing considerations that courts refrain from reviewing the merits of their decisions, absent a showing of arbitrariness or irrationality. But racial discrimination is not just another competing consideration. When there is a proof that a discriminatory purpose has been a motivating factor in the decision, this judicial deference is no longer justified.

Determining whether invidious discriminatory purpose was a motivating factor demands a sensitive inquiry into such circumstantial and direct evidence of intent as may be available. The impact of the official action whether it "bears more heavily on one race than another," may provide an important starting point. Sometimes a clear pattern, unexplainable on grounds other than race, emerges from the effect of the state action even when the governing legislation appears neutral on its face. The evidentiary inquiry is then relatively easy. But such cases are rare. Absent a pattern as stark as that in *Gomillion* or *Yick Wo*, impact alone is not determinative, and the Court must look to other evidence.

The historical background of the decision is one evidentiary source, particularly if it reveals a series of official actions taken for invidious purposes. The specific sequence of events leading up the challenged decision also may shed some light on the decision-maker's purposes. For example, if the property involved here always had been zoned R-5 but suddenly was changed to R-3 when the town learned of MHDC's plans to erect integrated housing, we would have a far different case. Departures from the normal procedural sequence also might afford evidence that improper purposes are playing a role. Substantive departures too may be relevant, particularly if the factors usually considered important by the decision-maker strongly favor a decision contrary to the one reached. The legislative or administrative history may be highly relevant, especially where there are contemporary statements by members of the decision-making body, minutes of its meetings, or reports.

[The] foregoing summary identifies, without purporting to be exhaustive, subjects of proper inquiry in determining whether racially discriminatory intent existed. With these in mind, we now address the case before us.

[We] have reviewed the evidence. The impact of the Village's decision does arguably bear more heavily on racial minorities. Minorities constitute 18% of the Chicago area population, and 40% of the income groups said to be eligible for Lincoln Green. But there is little about the sequence of events leading up to the decision that would spark suspicion. The area around the Viatorian property has been zoned R-3 since 1959, the year when Arlington Heights first adopted a zoning map. Single-family homes surround the 80-acre site, and the Village is undeniably committed to single-family homes as its dominant residential land use. The rezoning request progressed according to the usual procedures. The Planning Commission even scheduled two additional hearings, at least in part to accommodate MHDC and permit it to supplement its presentation with answers to questions generated at the first hearing.

The statements by the Plan Commission and Village Board members, as reflected in the official minutes, focused almost exclusively on the zoning aspects of the MHDC petition, and the zoning factors on which they relied are not novel criteria in the Village's rezoning decisions. There is no reason to doubt that there has been reliance by some neighboring property owners on the maintenance of single-family zoning in the vicinity. The Village originally adopted its buffer policy long before MHDC entered the picture and has applied the policy too consistently for us to infer discriminatory purpose from its application in this case. Finally, MHDC called one member of the Village Board to the stand at trial. Nothing in her testimony supports an inference of invidious purpose.

In sum, the evidence does not warrant overturning the concurrent findings of both courts below. Respondents simply failed to carry their burden of proving that discriminatory purpose was a motivating factor in the Village's decision. . . .

Note: Applying the Discriminatory Motive Requirement

The discriminatory motive requirement represented a critical milestone in the evolution of equal protection jurisprudence. Review hinged on discernment of official intent has the capacity to detect discrimination only if it is prescriptive or overt. In this vein, the Court in Hunter v. Underwood, 471 U.S. 222 (1981), struck down a law that denied voting rights to persons who had been convicted of a crime involving "moral turpitude." Tracing the law to its early-twentieth-century origin, the Court was able to glean "beyond peradventure" an intent to discriminate. Case law also demonstrates that the Court will strike down laws that it finds, through a process of elimination, have no basis for existence other than a purpose to discriminate. Legislative redistricting that attempted to increase minority representation, by configuring districts with highly irregular contours, exemplifies this type of outcome. In Shaw v. Reno, 509 U.S. 630, 642 (1993), the Court determined that a North Carolina congressional redistricting plan constituted one of "those 'rare' statutes that, although race neutral, are, on their face unexplainable on grounds other than race." The Court, in Miller v. Johnson, 515 U.S. 900 (1995), noted that that a plaintiff must "show, either through circumstantial evidence or a district's shape and demographics or more direct evidence going to legislative purpose, that race was the predominant factor motivating the legislature's decision to place a significant number of voters within or without a particular district." Strict scrutiny, which was fatal to the districting plan in Miller v. Johnson, thus may be triggered when race is the "predominant factor" in decision making. Despite the identification of some racially neutral considerations in North Carolina, the Court in Shaw v. Hunt, 517 U.S. 899 (1996), found that the irregularly shaped congressional district was predominantly a function of race. The predominant factor test also was used, in Bush v. Vera, 517 U.S. 952 (1996), to strike down a majority-minority redistricting plan.

In Ashcroft v. Iqbal, 129 S.Ct. 1937 (2009), a case concerning claims of discrimination against a detained Pakistani Muslim, the Court determined that government officials were not liable for the alleged wrongful acts of prison officials. The plaintiff, who had been charged with fraud in the use of a social security card, claimed federal officials (including the director of the FBI and the attorney general) condoned the discrimination. He maintained that his race, religion, and national origin had been the basis for characterizing him as a person "of high Interest" in the wake of terrorist attacks in New York on September 11, 2001. The plaintiff maintained that, while in detention, prison guards physically attacked him, impeded his right to pray, and committed other violations. A Justice Department investigation confirmed that he had been abused by prison guards.

The Court determined that the government officials could not be held liable for their subordinates' alleged unconstitutional conduct. It noted that, to prevail on a discrimination claim under either the First or Fifth Amendment, the plaintiff must plead and prove discriminatory purpose. Minus a facially adequate basis for inferring liability, the Court concluded that the claim could not survive a motion to dismiss. It observed that, to the extent terrorist attacks had been perpetrated by Arab Muslims, it was not unexpected that there would be a disparate impact on this group. From the Court's perspective there were no facts stated from which discrimination reasonably could be inferred. It thus remanded the case for a determination of whether the plaintiff should be allowed to amend his claim. Four justices dissented.

∽ PROBLEM: MORE ON THE DIVERSITY INITIATIVE ∽

Let's return to the problem described at the beginning of the chapter. Suppose that NWU is thinking about giving preferential admission to law and medical school applicants who come from economically disadvantaged backgrounds. The board of regents does not appear to have any intent to discriminate in favor of any particular racial or ethnic group. However, the evidence shows that a disproportionate number of poor and economically disadvantaged students in the applicant pool are of African American or Hispanic heritage. As a result, while the policy of favoring economically disadvantaged applicants will benefit students of all races who come from economically disadvantaged backgrounds, it will disproportionately benefit African American and Hispanic applicants. Under these circumstances, what would you tell the board about whether the proposed admissions policy creates a racial classification? If the policy is challenged in court, what standard of review would you expect a reviewing court to apply?

b. Affirmative Action

The desegregation experience established a model of remediation that aimed to redress the wrongs committed by official discrimination. In the context of public education, not only did official segregation have to be undone, but also schools that were racially identifiable had to become racially unitary. This result was achieved by a process of affirmative action that included racial quotas and goals.

The term *affirmative action* typically refers to programs or policies that establish preferences on the basis of group status. The separate but equal doctrine, upheld in Plessy v. Ferguson, exemplified an affirmative action model that allocated burdens and benefits consistent with the interests of the dominant racial group. Affirmative action for contemporary purposes initially was designed to help minorities who had been the victims of racial discrimination. The Court has restricted remedial classifications to discrete instances where intentional discrimination has been established. It also has recognized diversity in postsecondary education as a compelling justification for taking race into account on a limited basis.

Much of the constitutional debate over affirmative action has focused on whether it can be used to remedy the consequences of racial discrimination. The Court has acknowledged the "nation's sorry legacy of private and public discrimination." City of Richmond v. J.A. Croson Co., 488 U.S. 469 (1989). This understanding, however, did not lead to a conclusion that remedial classifications are permissible. Whether racial classifications designed to remedy the vestiges of discrimination should be strictly scrutinized (like those that burdened minorities) was the subject of extended and intense debate.

Over the course of the 1980s, the Court's decisions yielded mixed and uncertain results. In Fullilove v. Klutznick, 448 U.S. 448 (1980), it upheld a federal set-aside program for minority contractors in public works projects. A three-justice plurality, in an opinion authored by Chief Justice Burger, referenced Congress's power to enforce the Fourteenth Amendment as a determinative factor. Three justices, maintaining that remedial classifications that benefited minorities were less objectionable than classifications that burdened them, advocated an intermediate standard of review that required careful but not strict scrutiny. Two justices expressed opposition to any racial classifications, and another objected to them under most circumstances.

Movement toward a majority position was evident in Wygant v. Jackson Board of Education, 476 U.S. 267 (1986). This case concerned a collectively bargained layoff plan that protected more recently hired minorities in the event of job cutbacks. The *Wygant* case focused on whether remediation of societal discrimination was an adequate basis for race-conscious remedies. Justice Powell, writing for a plurality of four justices, maintained that societal discrimination by itself was "too amorphous a basis for imposing a racially classified remedy." From the plurality's perspective, a racially based remedy was permissible only upon "some showing of prior discrimination by the governmental unit involved." The plurality dismissed the interest in minority role models as an adequate basis for remedial classifications. It also identified strict scrutiny as the appropriate standard of review. Justice Stevens dissented and proposed a forward-looking perspective that stressed the value of diversity as it relates to the educational process.

Consistent with the plurality's premise in *Wygant*, the Court in United States v. Paradise, 480 U.S. 149 (1987), provided race-conscious relief that addressed an identifiable instance of discrimination by a government unit. At issue was a court-ordered plan that set aside, for qualified black state troopers in Alabama, at least 50 percent of the promotions to the rank of corporal. This order was made pursuant to well-documented findings of discrimination and a record of remedial inaction. Justice Brennan, in a plurality opinion, maintained that the plan would survive even strict scrutiny. Agreeing with the result in a separate opinion, Justice Powell referenced a persistent violation of constitutional rights and disregard of court orders. In an opinion joined by Justices Rehnquist and Scalia, Justice O'Connor maintained that the remedial classifications were not narrowly tailored and thus did not survive strict scrutiny. She noted the availability of alternative remedies, such as appointment of a trustee to establish promotion procedures and penalties for violation of court orders.

Adarand Constructors, Inc. v. Pena

515 U.S. 200 (1995)

Justice O'CONNOR announced the judgment of the Court and delivered an opinion with respect to Parts I, II, III-A, III-B, III-D, and IV, which is for the Court except insofar as it might be inconsistent with the views expressed in Justice SCALIA'S concurrence, and an opinion with respect to Part III-C in which Justice KENNEDY joins.

Petitioner Adarand Constructors, Inc., claims that the Federal Government's practice of giving general contractors on Government projects a financial incentive to hire subcontractors controlled by "socially and economically disadvantaged individuals," [and] the Government's use of race-based presumptions in identifying such individuals, violates the equal protection component of the Fifth Amendment's Due Process Clause. The Court of Appeals rejected Adarand's claim. [We vacate and] remand the case for further proceedings.

III

A

[Through] the 1940's, this Court had routinely taken the view in non-race-related cases that, "[u]nlike the Fourteenth Amendment, the Fifth contains no equal protection clause and it provides no guaranty against discriminatory legislation by Congress." [In] Bolling v. Sharpe, 347 U.S. 497 (1954), the Court [explicitly] questioned the existence of any difference between the obligations of the Federal Government and the States to avoid racial classifications. [The] Court's observations that "[d]istinctions between citizens solely because of their ancestry are by their very nature odious," and that "all legal restrictions which curtail the civil rights of a single racial group are immediately suspect," carry no less force in the context of federal action than in the context of action by the States.

B

[In] City of Richmond v. J.A. Croson Co., 488 U.S. 469 (1989), the Court finally agreed that the Fourteenth Amendment requires strict scrutiny of all race-based action by state and local governments. But *Croson* of course had no occasion to declare what standard of review the Fifth Amendment requires for such action taken by the Federal Government.

[A] year later, [the] Court took a surprising turn. Metro Broadcasting, Inc. v. FCC, 497 U.S. 547 (1990), involved a Fifth Amendment challenge to two race-based policies of the Federal Communications Commission (FCC). In *Metro Broadcasting*, the Court repudiated the long-held notion that "it would be unthinkable that the same Constitution would impose a lesser duty on the Federal Government" than it does on a State to afford equal protection of the laws.

[We] adhere to [*Croson's*] view today, despite the surface appeal of holding "benign" racial classifications to a lower standard, because "it may not always be clear that a so-called preference is in fact benign," "[M]ore than good motives should be required when government seeks to allocate its resources by way of an explicit racial classification system."

[The] Fifth and Fourteenth Amendments to the Constitution protect *persons*, not *groups*. It follows from that principle that all governmental action based on race — a *group* classification long recognized as "in most circumstances irrelevant and therefore prohibited" — should be subjected to detailed judicial inquiry to ensure that the *personal* right to equal protection of the laws has not been infringed. These ideas have long been central to this Court's understanding of equal protection, and holding "benign" state and federal racial classifications to different standards does not square with them. "[A] free people whose institutions are founded upon the doctrine of equality," should tolerate no retreat from the principle that government may treat people differently because of their race only for the most compelling reasons. Accordingly, we hold today that all racial classifications, imposed by whatever federal, state, or local governmental actor, must be analyzed by a reviewing court under strict scrutiny. [S]uch classifications are constitutional only if they are narrowly tailored measures that further compelling governmental interests. To the extent that *Metro Broadcasting* is inconsistent with that holding, it is overruled.

[Justice] Stevens chides us for our "supposed inability to differentiate between 'invidious' and 'benign' discrimination," because it is in his view sufficient that "people understand the difference between good intentions and bad." But [the] point of strict scrutiny is to "differentiate between" permissible and impermissible governmental use of race. And Justice Stevens himself has already explained in his dissent in *Fullilove* why "good intentions" alone are not enough to sustain a supposedly "benign" racial classification: "[A] statute of this kind inevitably is perceived by many as resting on an assumption that those who are granted this special preference are less qualified in some respect that is identified purely by their race. Because that perception — *especially when fostered by the Congress of the United States* — can only exacerbate rather than reduce racial prejudice, it will delay the time when race will become a truly irrelevant, or at least insignificant, factor." [The] application of strict scrutiny [determines] whether a compelling governmental interest justifies the infliction of that injury.

D

[Federal] racial classifications, like those of a State, must serve a compelling governmental interest, and must be narrowly tailored to further that interest. [T]o the extent [that] *Fullilove* held federal racial classifications to be subject to a less rigorous standard, it is no longer controlling. [W]e agree with Justice Stevens that, "[b]ecause racial characteristics so seldom provide a relevant basis for disparate treatment, and because classifications based on race are potentially so harmful to the entire body politic, it is especially important that the reasons for any such classification be clearly identified and unquestionably legitimate," and that "[r]acial classifications are simply too pernicious to permit any but the most exact connection between justification and classification." [R]equiring strict scrutiny is the best way to ensure that courts will consistently give racial classifications that kind of detailed examination, both as to ends and as to means. . . .

Finally, we wish to dispel the notion that strict scrutiny is "strict in theory, but fatal in fact." The unhappy persistence of both the practice and the lingering effects of racial discrimination against minority groups in this country is an unfortunate reality, and government is not disqualified from acting in response to it. As recently as 1987, for example, every Justice of this Court agreed that the Alabama Department of Public Safety's "pervasive, systematic, and obstinate discriminatory conduct" justified a narrowly tailored race-based remedy. [United States v. Paradise]. When race-based action is necessary to further a compelling interest, such action is within constitutional constraints if it satisfies the "narrow tailoring" test this Court has set out in previous cases.

IV

[T]he question whether any of the ways in which the Government uses subcontractor compensation clauses can survive strict scrutiny, and any relevance distinctions such as these may have to that question, should be addressed in the first instance by the lower courts.

Accordingly, the judgment of the Court of Appeals is vacated, and the case is remanded for further proceedings consistent with this opinion.

Justice SCALIA, concurring in part and concurring in the judgment.

[G]overnment can never have a "compelling interest" in discriminating on the basis of race in order to "make up" for past racial discrimination in the opposite direction. Individuals who have been wronged by unlawful racial discrimination should be made whole; but under our Constitution there can be no such thing as either a creditor or a debtor race. That concept is alien to the Constitution's focus upon the individual, and its rejection of dispositions based on race, or based on blood. To pursue the concept of racial entitlement — even for the most admirable and benign of purposes — is to reinforce and preserve for future mischief the way of thinking that produced race slavery, race privilege and race hatred. In the eyes of government, we are just one race here. It is American. [It] is unlikely, if not impossible, that the challenged program would survive under this understanding of strict scrutiny.

Justice THOMAS, concurring in part and concurring in the judgment.

[S]trict scrutiny applies to *all* government classifications based on race. . . . [T]here is a "moral [and] constitutional equivalence," between laws designed to subjugate a race and those that distribute benefits on the basis of race in order to foster some current notion of equality. Government cannot make us equal; it can only recognize, respect, and protect us as equal before the law. [That] these programs may have been motivated, in part, by good intentions cannot provide refuge from the principle that under our Constitution, the government may not make distinctions on the basis of race. [T]he paternalism that appears to lie at the heart of this program is at war with the principle of inherent equality that underlies and infuses our Constitution.

[These] programs [undermine] the moral basis of the equal protection principle. [S]uch classifications ultimately have a destructive impact on the individual and our society. [R]acial paternalism and its unintended consequences can be as poisonous and pernicious as any other form of discrimination. So-called "benign" discrimination teaches many [that] minorities cannot compete with them without their patronizing indulgence. Inevitably, such programs engender attitudes of superiority or, alternatively, provoke resentment among those who believe that they have been wronged by the government's use of race. These programs stamp minorities with a badge of inferiority and may cause them to develop dependencies or to adopt an attitude that they are "entitled" to preferences. [G]overnment-sponsored racial discrimination based on benign prejudice is just as noxious as discrimination inspired by malicious prejudice. In each instance, it is racial discrimination, plain and simple.

Justice STEVENS, with whom Justice GINSBURG joins, dissenting.

[A] court should be wary of a governmental decision that relies upon a racial classification. "Because racial characteristics so seldom provide a relevant basis for disparate treatment, and because classifications based on race are potentially so harmful to the entire body politic," a reviewing court must satisfy itself that the reasons for any such classification are "clearly identified and unquestionably legitimate."

[There] is no moral or constitutional equivalence between a policy that is designed to perpetuate a caste system and one that seeks to eradicate racial subordination. Invidious discrimination is an engine of oppression, subjugating a disfavored group to enhance or maintain the power of the majority. Remedial race-based preferences reflect the opposite impulse: a desire to foster equality in society. [P]eople understand the difference between good intentions and bad. [Nothing] is inherently wrong with applying a single standard to fundamentally different situations, as long as that standard takes relevant differences into account. [But] a single standard that purports to equate remedial preferences with invidious discrimination cannot be defended in the name of "equal protection." [As] a matter of constitutional and democratic principle, a decision by representatives of the majority to discriminate against the members of a minority race is fundamentally different from those same representatives' decision to impose incidental costs on the majority of their constituents in order to provide a benefit to a disadvantaged minority. [T]he former is virtually always repugnant to the principles of a free and democratic society, whereas the latter is, in some circumstances, entirely consistent with the ideal of equality.

[The] Court's concept of "congruence" assumes that there is no significant difference between a decision by the Congress of the United States to adopt an affirmative-action program and such a decision by a State or a municipality. In my opinion that assumption is untenable. [I] would affirm the judgment of the Court of Appeals.

Justice SOUTER, with whom Justice GINSBURG and Justice BREYER join, dissenting.

[The Court's] recognition today that strict scrutiny can be compatible with the survival of a classification [demonstrates] that our concepts of equal protection enjoy a greater elasticity than the standard categories might suggest.

Justice GINSBURG, with whom Justice BREYER joins, dissenting.

[The] divisions in this difficult case should not obscure the Court's recognition of the persistence of racial inequality and a majority's acknowledgment of Congress' authority to act affirmatively, not only to end discrimination, but also to counteract discrimination's lingering effects. Those effects, reflective of a system of racial caste only recently ended, are evident in our workplaces, markets, and neighborhoods. Job applicants with identical resumes, qualifications, and interview styles still experience different receptions, depending on their race. White and African-American consumers still encounter different deals. People of color looking for housing still face discriminatory treatment by landlords, real estate agents, and mortgage lenders. Minority entrepreneurs sometimes fail to gain contracts though they are the low bidders, and they are sometimes refused work even after winning contracts. [Given] this history and its practical consequences, Congress surely can conclude that a carefully designed affirmative action program may help to realize, finally, the "equal protection of the laws."

[T]he strict standard announced is indeed "fatal" for classifications burdening groups that have suffered discrimination in our society. [For] a classification made to hasten the day when "we are just one race," however, the lead opinion has dispelled the notion that "strict scrutiny" is "'fatal in fact.'" Properly, a majority of the Court calls for review that is searching, in order to ferret out classifications in reality malign, but masquerading as benign.

∾ PROBLEM: THE DIVERSITY INITIATIVE AND RACE-BASED ADMISSIONS POLICIES ∾

In the introductory problem, suppose that NWU is also thinking about giving preferential admission to members of certain specified minority groups (e.g., African Americans, Hispanics, and Asian Americans). NWU's board of regents has asked you for advice about whether it may do so. Based on what you have read to this point, how would you advise the board? What must the university show in order to adopt such a policy? Can it adopt the policy for all "minority" racial groups? Continue to think about these issues as you review the following cases and notes.

The Court's initial exposure to affirmative action was in DeFunis v. Odegaard, 416 U.S. 412 (1974). This case concerned a state university's admission policy that gave preference to members of groups that traditionally had experienced discrimination. Because the student was nearing graduation, the Court determined that the parties would be unaffected by any relief and thus dismissed the case as moot.

Four years later, in Regents of the University of California v. Bakke, 438 U.S. 265 (1978), the Court examined a preferential admissions program at a state university medical school. The policy was challenged by a white male who maintained that he had been denied admission on the basis of his race. In striking down the admissions program, the Court treated the race-based program as a suspect classification. The opinion noted that if "petitioner's purpose is to assure within its student body some specified percentage of a particular group merely because of its race or ethnic origin, such a preferential purpose must be rejected not as insubstantial but as facially invalid. Preferring members of any one group for no reason other than race or ethnic origin is discrimination for its own sake. This the Constitution forbids." The Court acknowledged that the State "certainly has a legitimate and substantial interest in ameliorating, or eliminating where feasible, the disabling effects of identified discrimination." Nevertheless, the Court noted that it had "never approved a classification that aids persons perceived as members of relatively victimized groups at the expense of other innocent individuals in the absence of judicial, legislative, or administrative findings of constitutional or statutory violations. After such findings have been made, the governmental interest in preferring members of the injured groups at the expense of others is substantial, since the legal rights of the victims must be vindicated."

The Court also addressed the medical school's assertion that it had a legitimate interest in attaining a "diverse student body." It noted that:

> Ethnic diversity, however, is only one element in a range of factors a university properly may consider in attaining the goal of a heterogeneous student body. Although a university must have wide discretion in making the sensitive judgments as to who should be admitted, constitutional limitations protecting individual rights may not be disregarded. . . . It may be assumed that the reservation of a specified number of seats in each class for individuals from the preferred ethnic groups would contribute to the attainment of considerable ethnic diversity in the student body. But petitioner's argument that this is the only effective means of serving the interest of diversity is seriously flawed. In a most fundamental sense the argument misconceives the nature of the state interest that would justify consideration of race or ethnic background. It is not an interest in simple ethnic diversity, in which a specified percentage of the student body is in effect guaranteed to be members of selected ethnic groups, with the remaining percentage an undifferentiated aggregation of students. The diversity that furthers a compelling state interest encompasses a far broader array of qualifications and characteristics of which racial or ethnic origin is but a single though important element.

Petitioner's special admissions program, focused *solely* on ethnic diversity, would hinder rather than further attainment of genuine diversity.

Nor would the state interest in genuine diversity be served by expanding petitioner's two-track system into a multitrack program with a prescribed number of seats set aside for each identifiable category of applicants. . . . The experience of other university admissions programs, which take race into account in achieving the educational diversity valued by the First Amendment, demonstrates that the assignment of a fixed number of places to a minority group is not a necessary means toward that end. . . .

[R]ace or ethnic background may be deemed a "plus" in a particular applicant's file, yet it does not insulate the individual from comparison with all other candidates for the available seats. The file of a particular black applicant may be examined for his potential contribution to diversity without the factor of race being decisive when compared, for example, with that of an applicant identified as an Italian-American if the latter is thought to exhibit qualities more likely to promote beneficial educational pluralism. Such qualities could include exceptional personal talents, unique work or service experience, leadership potential, maturity, demonstrated compassion, a history of overcoming disadvantage, ability to communicate with the poor, or other qualifications deemed important. In short, an admissions program operated in this way is flexible enough to consider all pertinent elements of diversity in light of the particular qualifications of each applicant, and to place them on the same footing for consideration, although not necessarily according them the same weight. Indeed, the weight attributed to a particular quality may vary from year to year depending upon the "mix" both of the student body and the applicants for the incoming class.

Justice Powell's opinion, though standing alone, was a strong influence on the Court's eventual adoption of a strict scrutiny standard and determination that race could be a nonexclusive factor in the university admission process.

Grutter v. Bollinger

539 U.S. 306 (2003)

Justice O'CONNOR delivered the opinion of the Court.

This case requires us to decide whether the use of race as a factor in student admissions by the University of Michigan Law School (Law School) is unlawful.

The Law School ranks among the Nation's top law schools. It receives more than 3,500 applications each year for a class of around 350 students. Seeking to "admit a group of students who individually and collectively are among the most capable," the Law School looks for individuals with "substantial promise for success in law school" and "a strong likelihood of succeeding in the practice of law and contributing in diverse ways to the well-being of others." More broadly, the Law School seeks "a mix of students with varying backgrounds and experiences who will respect and learn from each other."

The hallmark of [the school's admissions] policy is its focus on academic ability coupled with a flexible assessment of applicants' talents, experiences, and potential "to contribute to the learning of those around them." The policy requires admissions officials to evaluate each applicant based on all the information available in the file, including a personal statement, letters of recommendation, and an essay describing the ways in which the applicant will contribute to the life and diversity of the Law School. In reviewing an applicant's file, admissions officials must consider the applicant's undergraduate grade point average (GPA) and Law School Admissions Test (LSAT) score because they are important (if imperfect) predictors of academic success in law school. The policy stresses that "no applicant should be admitted unless we expect that applicant to do well enough to graduate with no serious academic problems." The policy makes clear, however, that even the highest possible score does not guarantee admission to the Law School. Nor does a low score automatically disqualify an applicant. Rather, the policy requires admissions officials to look beyond grades and test scores to other criteria that are important to the Law School's educational objectives. So-called "'soft' variables" such as "the enthusiasm of recommenders, the quality of the undergraduate institution, the quality of the applicant's essay, and the areas and difficulty of undergraduate course selection" are all brought to bear in assessing an "applicant's likely contributions to the intellectual and social life of the institution."

The policy aspires to "achieve that diversity which has the potential to enrich everyone's education and thus make a law school class stronger than the sum of its parts." The policy does not restrict the types of diversity contributions eligible for "substantial weight" in the admissions process, but instead recognizes "many possible bases for diversity admissions." The policy does, however, reaffirm the Law School's longstanding commitment to "one particular type of diversity," that is, "racial and ethnic diversity with special reference to the inclusion of students from groups which have been historically discriminated against, like African-Americans, Hispanics and Native Americans, who without this commitment might not be represented in our student body in meaningful numbers." By enrolling a "'critical mass' of [underrepresented] minority students," the Law School seeks to "ensur[e] their ability to make unique contributions to the character of the Law School."

The policy does not define diversity "solely in terms of racial and ethnic status." Nor is the policy "insensitive to the competition among all students for admission to the [L]aw [S]chool." Rather, the policy seeks to guide admissions officers in "producing classes both diverse and academically outstanding, classes made up of students who promise to continue the tradition of outstanding contribution by Michigan Graduates to the legal profession."

Petitioner Barbara Grutter is a white Michigan resident who applied to the Law School in 1996 with a 3.8 grade point average and 161 LSAT score. The Law School initially placed petitioner on a waiting list, but subsequently rejected her application. [She sued, alleging] that respondents discriminated against her on the basis of race in violation of the Fourteenth Amendment. Petitioner also alleged that respondents "had no compelling interest to justify their use of race in the admissions process."

[Since] *Bakke*, Justice Powell's opinion [has] served as the touchstone for constitutional analysis of race-conscious admissions policies. Public and private universities across the Nation have modeled their own admissions programs on Justice Powell's views on permissible race-conscious policies. [W]e endorse Justice Powell's view that student body diversity is a compelling state interest that can justify the use of race in university admissions.

[We] apply strict scrutiny to all racial classifications to "'smoke out' illegitimate uses of race by assuring that [the government] is pursuing a goal important enough to warrant use of a highly suspect tool." Strict scrutiny is not "strict in theory, but fatal in fact." [Not] all governmental uses of race [are] invalidated by it. . . . When race-based action is necessary to further a compelling governmental interest, such action does not violate the constitutional guarantee of equal protection so long as the narrow-tailoring requirement is also satisfied. . . .

[R]espondents assert only one justification for their use of race in the admissions process: obtaining "the educational benefits that flow from a diverse student body." [T]he Law School asks us to recognize, in the context of higher education, a compelling state interest in student body diversity. [W]e have never held that the only governmental use of race that can survive strict scrutiny is remedying past discrimination. . . . Today, we hold that the Law School has a compelling interest in attaining a diverse student body. . . . The Law School's educational judgment that such diversity is essential to its educational mission is one to which we defer. . . . Our holding today is in keeping with our tradition of giving a degree of deference to a university's academic decisions, within constitutionally prescribed limits.

[G]iven the important purpose of public education and the expansive freedoms of speech and thought associated with the university environment, universities occupy a special niche in our constitutional tradition. In announcing the principle of student body diversity as a compelling state interest, Justice Powell invoked our cases recognizing a constitutional dimension, grounded in the First Amendment, of educational autonomy: "The freedom of a university to make its own judgments as to education includes the selection of its student body." [B]y claiming "the right to select those students who will contribute the most to the 'robust exchange of ideas,'" a university "seek[s] to achieve a goal that is of paramount importance in the fulfillment of its mission." Our conclusion that the Law School has a compelling interest in a diverse student body is informed by our view that attaining a diverse student body is at the heart of the Law School's proper institutional mission, and that "good faith" on the part of a university is "presumed" absent "a showing to the contrary."

As part of its goal of "assembling a class that is both exceptionally academically qualified and broadly diverse," the Law School seeks to "enroll a 'critical mass' of minority students." The Law School's interest is not simply "to assure within its student body some specified percentage of a particular group merely because of its race or ethnic origin." That would amount to outright racial balancing, which is patently unconstitutional. Rather, the Law School's concept of critical mass is defined by reference to the educational benefits that diversity is designed to produce. . . . These benefits are substantial. [T]he Law School's admissions policy promotes "cross-racial understanding," helps to break down racial stereotypes, and "enables [students] to better understand persons of different races." These benefits are "important and laudable," because "classroom discussion is livelier, more spirited, and simply more enlightening and interesting" when the students have "the greatest possible variety of backgrounds."

These benefits are not theoretical but real, as major American businesses have made clear that the skills needed in today's increasingly global marketplace can only be developed through exposure to widely diverse people, cultures, ideas, and viewpoints. [H]igh-ranking retired officers and civilian leaders of the United States military assert that [a] "highly qualified, racially diverse officer corps [is] essential to the military's ability to fulfill its principle mission to provide national security." "[T]he military cannot achieve an officer corps that is both highly qualified and racially diverse [without using] limited race-conscious recruiting and admissions policies." . . .

We have repeatedly acknowledged the overriding importance of preparing students for work and citizenship, describing education as pivotal to "sustaining our political and cultural heritage" with a fundamental role in maintaining the fabric of society. [T]he diffusion of knowledge and opportunity through public institutions of higher education must be accessible to all individuals regardless of race or ethnicity. The United States [affirms] that "[e]nsuring that public institutions are open and available to all segments of American society, including people of all races and ethnicities, represents a paramount government objective." "[N]owhere is the importance of such openness more acute than in the context of higher education." Effective participation by members of all racial and ethnic groups in the civic life of our Nation is essential if the dream of one Nation, indivisible, is to be realized.

Even in the limited circumstance when drawing racial distinctions is permissible to further a compelling state interest, [the] means chosen to accomplish the [government's] asserted purpose must be specifically and narrowly framed to accomplish that purpose." . . .

[We] find that the Law School's admissions program bears the hallmarks of a narrowly tailored plan. [U]niversities cannot establish quotas for members of certain racial groups or put members of those groups on separate admissions tracks. Nor can universities insulate applicants who belong to certain racial or ethnic groups from the competition for admission. Universities can, however, consider race or ethnicity more flexibly as a "plus" factor in the context of individualized consideration of each and every applicant. [The] Law School's goal of attaining a critical mass of underrepresented minority students does not transform its program into a quota. . . . Here, the Law School engages in a highly individualized, holistic review of each applicant's file, giving serious consideration to all the ways an applicant might contribute to a diverse educational environment. The Law School affords this individualized consideration to applicants of all races. There is no policy, either de jure or de facto, of automatic acceptance or rejection based on any single "soft" variable.

[Petitioner] and the United States argue that the Law School's plan is not narrowly tailored because race-neutral means exist to obtain the educational benefits of student body diversity that the Law School seeks. We disagree. Narrow tailoring does not require exhaustion of every conceivable race-neutral alternative. Nor does it require a university to choose between maintaining a reputation for excellence or fulfilling a commitment to provide educational opportunities to members of all racial groups.

[We] acknowledge that "there are serious problems of justice connected with the idea of preference itself." Narrow tailoring, therefore, requires that a race-conscious admissions program not unduly harm members of any racial group. . . . [We] are satisfied that the Law School's admissions program does not. Because the Law School considers "all pertinent elements of diversity," it can (and does) select nonminority applicants who have greater potential to enhance student body diversity over underrepresented minority applicants. As Justice Powell recognized in *Bakke*, so long as a race-conscious admissions program uses race as a "plus" factor in the context of individualized consideration, a rejected applicant "will not have been foreclosed from all consideration for that seat simply because he was not the right color or had the wrong surname. . . .

[The] Law School [concedes] that all "race-conscious programs must have reasonable durational limits." [It] has been 25 years since Justice Powell first approved the use of race to further an interest in student body diversity in the context of public higher education [and] the number of minority applicants with high grades and test scores has indeed increased. We expect that 25 years from now, the use of racial preferences will no longer be necessary to further the interest approved today.

In summary, the Equal Protection Clause does not prohibit the Law School's narrowly tailored use of race in admissions decisions to further a compelling interest in obtaining the educational benefits that flow from a diverse student body.

Justice GINSBURG, with whom Justice BREYER joins, concurring.

[C]onscious and unconscious race bias, even rank discrimination based on race, remain alive in our land, impeding realization of our highest values and ideals. [M]any minority students encounter markedly inadequate and unequal educational opportunities. [O]ne may hope, but not firmly forecast, that over the next generation's span, progress toward nondiscrimination and genuinely equal opportunity will make it safe to sunset affirmative action.

Chief Justice REHNQUIST, with whom Justice SCALIA, Justice KENNEDY, and Justice THOMAS join, dissenting.

[Stripped] of its "critical mass" veil, the Law School's program is revealed as a naked effort to achieve racial balancing. [Before today's decision], we consistently applied the same strict scrutiny analysis regardless of the government's purported reason for using race and regardless of the setting in which race was being used. [Although] the Court recites the language of our strict scrutiny analysis, its application of that review is unprecedented in its deference. . . .

[Only] when the "critical mass" label is discarded does a likely explanation for these numbers emerge. [From] 1995 through 2000 the percentage of admitted applicants who were members of these minority groups closely tracked the percentage of individuals in the school's applicant pool who were from the same groups. [The] Law School [has] managed its admissions program, not to achieve a "critical mass," but to extend offers of admission to members of selected minority groups in proportion to their statistical representation in the applicant pool.

[T]his is precisely the type of racial balancing that the Court itself calls "patently unconstitutional."

[T]he Law School's program fails strict scrutiny because it is devoid of any reasonably precise time limit on the Law School's use of race in admissions. [The] Court suggests a possible 25-year limitation. . . . In truth, they permit the Law School's use of racial preferences on a seemingly permanent basis. Thus, an important component of strict scrutiny — that a program be limited in time — is casually subverted. . . .

Note and Question: The Gratz Decisions

Gratz v. Bollinger, 539 U.S. 244 (2003), was decided on the same day as *Grutter*, but it struck down an undergraduate affirmative action plan at the University of Michigan. In that case, the plaintiffs filed a class action lawsuit challenging the undergraduate admission policies, which gave an undergraduate applicant 20 points based solely on his or her membership in an underrepresented racial or ethnic group. An applicant needed approximately 100 points for presumptive admission. The plaintiffs alleged that the allocation of a fixed number of points based on race violated their constitutional and statutory rights. The Supreme Court agreed, holding that the manner in which Michigan considered the race of the applicant in undergraduate admissions was not narrowly tailored to achieve a compelling state interest and therefore violated the equal protection guarantee of the Fourteenth Amendment as well as Title VI of the 1964 Civil Rights Act. Three justices filed dissenting opinions.

∼ PROBLEM: MORE ON THE DIVERSITY INITIATIVE ∼

Think back to the introductory problem. Suppose that NWU's board of regents is thinking about adopting a policy designed to bring greater diversity to NWU's faculty and student body. The evidence shows that both the faculty and students are overwhelmingly white, and overwhelmingly from middle- and upper-class backgrounds. The board wants you to advise it about how to construct a constitutionally permissible policy. What advice would you give? Try to construct an appropriate plan.

3. Diversity

BACKGROUND

School officials cannot assign students to schools based on crude racial categories to maintain racial balance. School officials may consider the racial makeup of schools and adopt general policies to encourage a diverse student body. They are also free to devise race-conscious measures to advance the goal of equal opportunity, so long as school officials do not treat each student differently solely on the basis of a systematic, individual typing by race. School boards may seek diverse educational environments by employing strategic site selection, drawing attendance zones, using targeted recruitment of students and faculty, and tracking enrollments, performance, and other statistics by race.

As demographic trends continued to erode many of the diversity gains incident to desegregation, and consistent with a sense that student diversity has inherent value, some school systems adopted plans to achieve or maintain racially balanced student bodies. The Court, in Parents Involved in Community Schools v. Seattle School District No. 1, assessed two of these plans (in Seattle and Louisville, respectively). The result was a decision that narrowly circumscribed the use of race as a factor in determining where students attend school. The case split the Court into two factions (four justices each): one that advocated absolute color-blindness and the second that viewed this position as compromising the "promise" of *Brown*.

Parents Involved in Community Schools v. Seattle School District No.1

551 U.S. 701 (2007)

Chief Justice ROBERTS announced the judgment of the Court, and delivered the opinion of the Court with respect to Parts I, II, III-A, and III-C, and an opinion with respect to Parts III-B and IV, in which Justices SCALIA, THOMAS, and ALITO join.

The school districts in these cases voluntarily adopted student assignment plans that rely upon race to determine which public schools certain children may attend. The Seattle school district classifies children as white or nonwhite; the Jefferson County school district as black or "other." In Seattle, this racial classification is used to allocate slots in oversubscribed high schools. In Jefferson County, it is used to make certain elementary school assignments and to rule on transfer requests. In each case, the school district relies upon an individual student's race in assigning that student to a particular school, so that the racial balance at the school falls within a predetermined range based on the racial composition of the school district as a whole. Parents of students denied assignment to particular schools under these plans solely because of their race brought suit, contending that allocating children to different public schools on the basis of race violated the Fourteenth Amendment guarantee of equal protection. The Courts of Appeals below upheld the plans. We granted certiorari, and now reverse.

I

Both cases present the same underlying legal question — whether a public school that had not operated legally segregated schools or has been found to be unitary may choose to classify students by race and rely upon that classification in making school assignments. Although we examine the plans under the same legal framework, the specifics of the two plans, and the circumstances surrounding their adoption, are in some respects quite different. . . .

III

A

It is well established that when the government distributes burdens or benefits on the basis of individual racial classifications, that action is reviewed under strict scrutiny. As the Court recently reaffirmed, "'racial classifications are simply too pernicious to permit any but the most exact connection between justification and classification.'" Gratz v. Bollinger, 539 U.S. 244, 270 (2003). In order to satisfy this searching standard of review, the school districts must demonstrate that the use of individual racial classifications in the assignment plans here under review is "narrowly tailored" to achieve a "compelling" government interest.

Without attempting in these cases to set forth all the interests a school district might assert, it suffices to note that our prior cases, in evaluating the use of racial classifications in the school context, have recognized two interests that qualify as compelling. The first is the compelling interest of remedying the effects of past intentional discrimination. See Freeman v. Pitts, 503 U.S. 467, 494 (1992). Yet the Seattle public schools have not shown that they were ever segregated by law, and were not subject to court-ordered desegregation decrees. The Jefferson County public schools were previously segregated by law and were subject to a desegregation decree entered in 1975. In 2000, the District Court that entered that decree dissolved it, finding that Jefferson County had "eliminated the vestiges associated with the former policy of segregation and its pernicious effects," and thus had achieved "unitary" status. Hampton, 102 F. Supp. 2d, at 360. Jefferson County accordingly does not rely upon an interest in remedying the effects of past intentional discrimination in defending its present use of race in assigning students. Nor could it. We have emphasized that the harm being remedied by mandatory desegregation plans is the harm that is traceable to segregation, and that "the Constitution is not violated by racial imbalance in the schools, without more." Milliken v. Bradley, 433 U.S. 267, 280, n.14 (1977). Once Jefferson County achieved unitary status, it had remedied the constitutional wrong that allowed race-based assignments. Any continued use of race must be justified on some other basis.

The second government interest we have recognized as compelling for purposes of strict scrutiny is the interest in diversity in higher education upheld in Grutter, 539 U.S., at 328. The specific interest found compelling in Grutter was student body diversity "in the context of higher education." The diversity interest was not focused on race alone but encompassed "all factors that may contribute to student body diversity." We described the various types of diversity that the law school sought:

[The law school's] policy makes clear there are many possible bases for diversity admissions, and provides examples of admittees who have lived or traveled widely abroad, are fluent in several languages, have overcome personal adversity and family hardship, have exceptional records of extensive community service, and have had successful careers in other fields.

The Court quoted the articulation of diversity from Justice Powell's opinion in Regents of the University of California v. Bakke, 438 U.S. 265 (1978), noting that "it is not an interest in simple ethnic diversity, in which a specified percentage of the student body is in effect guaranteed to be members of selected ethnic groups, that can justify the use of race." Instead, what was upheld in *Grutter* was consideration of "a far broader array of qualifications and characteristics of which racial or ethnic origin is but a single though important element."

The entire gist of the analysis in *Grutter* was that the admissions program at issue there focused on each applicant as an individual, and not simply as a member of a particular racial group. The classification of applicants by race upheld in *Grutter* was only as part of a "highly individualized, holistic review," As the Court explained, "[t]he importance of this individualized consideration in the context of a race-conscious admissions program is paramount." The point of the narrow tailoring analysis in which the *Grutter* Court engaged was to ensure that the use of racial classifications was indeed part of a broader assessment of diversity, and not simply an effort to achieve racial balance, which the Court explained would be "patently unconstitutional."

In the present cases, by contrast, race is not considered as part of a broader effort to achieve "exposure to widely diverse people, cultures, ideas, and viewpoints," race, for some students, is determinative standing alone. The districts argue that other factors, such as student preferences, affect assignment decisions under their plans, but under each plan when race comes into play, it is decisive by itself. It is not simply one factor weighed with others in reaching a decision, as in *Grutter*; it is *the* factor. Like the University of Michigan undergraduate plan struck down in *Gratz*, 539 U.S., at 275, the plans here "do not provide for a meaningful individualized review of applicants" but instead rely on racial classifications in a "nonindividualized, mechanical" way.

Even when it comes to race, the plans here employ only a limited notion of diversity, viewing race exclusively in white/nonwhite terms in Seattle and black/"other" terms in Jefferson County.

In upholding the admissions plan in *Grutter*, though, this Court relied upon considerations unique to institutions of higher education, noting that in light of "the expansive freedoms of speech and thought associated with the university environment, universities occupy a special niche in our constitutional tradition." The Court explained that "[c]ontext matters" in applying strict scrutiny, and repeatedly noted that it was addressing the use of race "in the context of higher education." The Court in *Grutter* expressly articulated key limitations on its holding — defining a specific type of broad-based diversity and noting the unique context of higher education — but these limitations were largely disregarded by the lower courts in extending *Grutter* to uphold race-based assignments in elementary and secondary schools. The present cases are not governed by *Grutter*.

B

Perhaps recognizing that reliance on *Grutter* cannot sustain their plans, both school districts assert additional interests, distinct from the interest upheld in *Grutter*, to justify their race-based assignments. In briefing and argument before this Court, Seattle contends that its use of race helps to reduce racial concentration in schools and to ensure that racially concentrated housing patterns do not prevent nonwhite students from having access to the most desirable schools. Jefferson County has articulated a similar goal, phrasing its interest in terms of educating its students "in a racially integrated environment." Each school district argues that educational and broader socialization benefits flow from a racially diverse learning environment, and each contends that because the diversity they seek is racial diversity — not the broader diversity at issue in *Grutter* — it makes sense to promote that interest directly by relying on race alone.

The parties and their *amici* dispute whether racial diversity in schools in fact has a marked impact on test scores and other objective yardsticks or achieves intangible socialization benefits. The debate is not one we need to resolve, however, because it is clear that the racial classifications employed by the districts are not narrowly tailored to the goal of achieving the educational and social benefits asserted to flow from racial diversity. In design and operation, the plans are directed only to racial balance, pure and simple, an objective this Court has repeatedly condemned as illegitimate.

In *Grutter*, the number of minority students the school sought to admit was an undefined "meaningful number" necessary to achieve a genuinely diverse student body. Although the matter was the subject of disagreement on the Court, the majority concluded that the law school did not count back from its applicant pool to arrive at the "meaningful number" it regarded as necessary to diversify its student body. Here the racial balance the districts seek is a defined range set solely by reference to the demographics of the respective school districts.

This working backward to achieve a particular type of racial balance, rather than working forward from some demonstration of the level of diversity that provides the purported benefits, is a fatal flaw under our existing precedent. We have many times over reaffirmed that "[r]acial balance is not to be achieved for its own sake." *Grutter* itself reiterated that "outright racial balancing" is "patently unconstitutional."

Accepting racial balancing as a compelling state interest would justify the imposition of racial proportionality throughout American society, contrary to our repeated recognition that "[a]t the heart of the Constitution's guarantee of equal protection lies the simple command that the Government must treat citizens as individuals, not as simply components of a racial, religious, sexual or national class." Allowing racial balancing as a compelling end in itself would "effectively assur[e] that race will always be relevant in American life, and that the 'ultimate goal' of 'eliminating entirely from governmental decisionmaking such irrelevant factors as a human being's race' will never be achieved." An interest "linked to nothing other than proportional representation of various races . . . would support indefinite use of racial classifications, employed first to obtain the appropriate mixture of racial views and then to ensure that the [program] continues to reflect that mixture."

The principle that racial balancing is not permitted is one of substance, not semantics. Racial balancing is not transformed from "patently unconstitutional" to a compelling state interest simply by relabeling it "racial diversity." While the school districts use various verbal formulations to describe the interest they seek to promote—racial diversity, avoidance of racial isolation, racial integration—they offer no definition of the interest that suggests it differs from racial balance.

Jefferson County phrases its interest as "racial integration," but integration certainly does not require the sort of racial proportionality reflected in its plan. Even in the context of mandatory desegregation, we have stressed that racial proportionality is not required, Swann v. Charlotte-Mecklenburg Bd. of Ed., 402 U.S. 1, 24 (1971) ("The constitutional command to desegregate schools does not mean that every school in every community must always reflect the racial composition of the school system as a whole"), and here Jefferson County has already been found to have eliminated the vestiges of its prior segregated school system.

The en banc Ninth Circuit declared that "when a racially diverse school system is the goal (or racial concentration or isolation is the problem), there is no more effective means than a consideration of race to achieve the solution." For the foregoing reasons, this conclusory argument cannot sustain the plans. However closely related race-based assignments may be to achieving racial balance, that itself cannot be the goal, whether labeled "racial diversity" or anything else. To the extent the objective is sufficient diversity so that students see fellow students as individuals rather than solely as members of a racial group, using means that treat students solely as members of a racial group is fundamentally at cross-purposes with that end.

The districts have also failed to show that they considered methods other than explicit racial classifications to achieve their stated goals. Narrow tailoring requires "serious, good faith consideration of workable race-neutral alternatives," Grutter, supra, at 339, and yet in Seattle several alternative assignment plans—many of which would not have used express racial classifications—were rejected with little or no consideration. Jefferson County has failed to present any evidence that it considered alternatives, even though the district already claims that its goals are achieved primarily through means other than the racial classifications.

IV

Justice Breyer's dissent takes a different approach to these cases, one that fails to ground the result it would reach in law. Instead, it selectively relies on inapplicable precedent and even dicta while dismissing contrary holdings, alters and misapplies our well-established legal framework for assessing equal protection challenges to express racial classifications, and greatly exaggerates the consequences of today's decision. . . .

If the need for the racial classifications embraced by the school districts is unclear, even on the districts' own terms, the costs are undeniable. "[D]istinctions between citizens solely because of their ancestry are by their very nature odious to a free people whose institutions are founded upon the doctrine of equality." Government action dividing us by race is inherently suspect because such classifications promote "notions of racial inferiority and lead to a politics of racial hostility, reinforce the belief, held by too many for too much of our history, that individuals should be judged by the color of their skin," and "endorse race-based reasoning and the conception of a Nation divided into racial blocs, thus contributing to an escalation of racial hostility and conflict." As the Court explained in Rice v. Cayetano, 528 U.S. 495, 517 (2000), "[o]ne of the principal reasons race is treated as a forbidden classification is that it demeans the dignity and worth of a person to be judged by ancestry instead of by his or her own merit and essential qualities."

All this is true enough in the contexts in which these statements were made—government contracting, voting districts, allocation of broadcast licenses, and electing state officers—but when it comes to using race to assign children to schools, history will be heard. In Brown v. Board of Education, 347 U.S. 483 (1954) (*Brown I*), we held that segregation deprived black children of equal educational opportunities regardless of whether school facilities and other tangible factors were equal, because government classification and separation on grounds of race themselves denoted inferiority. It was not the inequality of the facilities but the fact of legally separating children on the basis of race on which the Court relied to find a constitutional violation in 1954. The next Term, we accordingly stated that "full compliance" with *Brown I* required school districts "to achieve a system of determining admission to the public schools *on a nonracial basis*."

The parties and their *amici* debate which side is more faithful to the heritage of *Brown*, but the position of the plaintiffs in *Brown* was spelled out in their brief and could not have been clearer: "[T]he Fourteenth Amendment prevents states from according differential treatment to American children on the basis of their color or race." What do the racial classifications at issue here do, if not accord differential treatment on the basis of race? As counsel who appeared before this Court for the plaintiffs in *Brown* put it: "We have one fundamental contention which we will seek to develop in the course of this argument, and that contention is that no State has any authority under the equal-protection clause of the Fourteenth Amendment to use race as a factor in affording educational opportunities among its citizens." There is no ambiguity in that statement. And it was that position that prevailed in this Court, which emphasized in its remedial opinion that what was "[a]t stake is the personal interest of the plaintiffs in admission to public schools as soon as practicable *on a nondiscriminatory basis*," and what was required was "determining admission to the public schools *on a nonracial basis*." What do the racial classifications do in these cases, if not determine admission to a public school on a racial basis? Before *Brown*, schoolchildren were told where they could and could not go to school based on the color of their skin. The school districts in these cases have not carried the heavy burden of demonstrating that we should allow this once again—even for very different reasons. For schools that never segregated on the basis of race, such as Seattle, or that have removed the vestiges of past segregation, such as Jefferson County, the way "to achieve a system of determining admission to the public schools on a nonracial basis," is to stop assigning students on a racial basis. The way to stop discrimination on the basis of race is to stop discriminating on the basis of race.

The judgments of the Courts of Appeals for the Sixth and Ninth Circuits are reversed, and the cases are remanded for further proceedings. It is so ordered.

Justice KENNEDY, concurring in part and concurring in the judgment.

The Nation's schools strive to teach that our strength comes from people of different races, creeds, and cultures uniting in commitment to the freedom of all. In these cases two school districts in different parts of the country seek to teach that principle by having classrooms that reflect the racial makeup of the surrounding community. That the school districts consider these plans to be necessary should remind us our highest aspirations are yet unfulfilled. But the solutions mandated by these school districts must themselves be lawful. To make race matter now so that it might not matter later may entrench the very prejudices we seek to overcome. In my view the state-mandated racial classifications at issue, official labels proclaiming the race of all persons in a broad class of citizens—elementary school students in one case, high school students in another—are unconstitutional as the cases now come to us.

I agree with the Chief Justice that we have jurisdiction to decide the cases before us and join Parts I and II of the Court's opinion. I also join Parts III-A and III-C for reasons provided below. My views do not allow me to join the balance of the opinion by the Chief Justice, which seems to me to be inconsistent in both its approach and its implications with the history, meaning, and reach of the Equal Protection Clause. Justice Breyer's dissenting opinion, on the other hand, rests on what in my respectful submission is a misuse and mistaken interpretation of our precedents. This leads it to advance propositions that, in my view, are both erroneous and in fundamental conflict with basic equal protection principles. As a consequence, this separate opinion is necessary to set forth my conclusions in the two cases before the Court.

The opinion of the Court and Justice Breyer's dissenting opinion (hereinafter dissent) describe in detail the history of integration efforts in Louisville and Seattle. These plans classify individuals by race and allocate benefits and burdens on that basis; and as a result, they are to be subjected to strict scrutiny. The dissent finds that the school districts have identified a compelling interest in increasing diversity, including for the purpose of avoiding racial isolation. The plurality, by contrast, does not acknowledge that the school districts have identified a compelling interest here. For this reason, among others, I do not join Parts III-B and IV. Diversity, depending on its meaning and definition, is a compelling educational goal a school district may pursue.

It is well established that when a governmental policy is subjected to strict scrutiny, "the government has the burden of proving that racial classifications 'are narrowly tailored measures that further compelling governmental interests.'"

"Absent searching judicial inquiry into the justification for such race-based measures, there is simply no way of determining what classifications are 'benign' or 'remedial' and what classifications are in fact motivated by illegitimate notions of racial inferiority or simple racial politics." And the inquiry into less restrictive alternatives demanded by the narrow tailoring analysis requires in many cases a thorough understanding of how a plan works. The government bears the burden of justifying its use of individual racial classifications. As part of that burden it must establish, in detail, how decisions based on an individual student's race are made in a challenged governmental program.

II

Our Nation from the inception has sought to preserve and expand the promise of liberty and equality on which it was founded. Today we enjoy a society that is remarkable in its openness and opportunity. Yet our tradition is to go beyond present achievements, however significant, and to recognize and confront the flaws and injustices that remain. This is especially true when we seek assurance that opportunity is not denied on account of race. The enduring hope is that race should not matter; the reality is that too often it does.

This is by way of preface to my respectful submission that parts of the opinion by the Chief Justice imply an all-too-unyielding insistence that race cannot be a factor in instances when, in my view, it may be taken into account. The plurality opinion is too dismissive of the legitimate interest government has in ensuring all people have equal opportunity regardless of their race. The plurality's postulate that "[t]he way to stop discrimination on the basis of race is to stop discriminating on the basis of race," is not sufficient to decide these cases. Fifty years of experience since Brown v. Board of Education should teach us that the problem before us defies so easy a solution. School districts can seek to reach Brown's objective of equal educational opportunity. The plurality opinion is at least open to the interpretation that the Constitution requires school districts to ignore the problem of de facto resegregation in schooling. I cannot endorse that conclusion. To the extent the plurality opinion suggests the Constitution mandates that state and local school authorities must accept the status quo of racial isolation in schools, it is, in my view, profoundly mistaken.

The statement by Justice Harlan that "[o]ur Constitution is color-blind" was most certainly justified in the context of his dissent in Plessy v. Ferguson. The Court's decision in that case was a grievous error it took far too long to overrule. Plessy, of course, concerned official classification by race applicable to all persons who sought to use railway carriages. And, as an aspiration, Justice Harlan's axiom must command our assent. In the real world, it is regrettable to say, it cannot be a universal constitutional principle.

In the administration of public schools by the state and local authorities it is permissible to consider the racial makeup of schools and to adopt general policies to encourage a diverse student body, one aspect of which is its racial composition. If school authorities are concerned that the student-body compositions of certain schools interfere with the objective of offering an equal educational opportunity to all of their students, they are free to devise race-conscious measures to address the problem in a general way and without treating each student in different fashion solely on the basis of a systematic, individual typing by race.

School boards may pursue the goal of bringing together students of diverse backgrounds and races through other means, including strategic site selection of new schools; drawing attendance zones with general recognition of the demographics of neighborhoods; allocating resources for special programs; recruiting students and faculty in a targeted fashion; and tracking enrollments, performance, and other statistics by race. These mechanisms are race conscious but do not lead to different treatment based on a classification that tells each student he or she is to be defined by race, so it is unlikely any of them would demand strict scrutiny to be found permissible.

C

The idea that if race is the problem, race is the instrument with which to solve it cannot be accepted as an analytical leap forward. And if this is a frustrating duality of the Equal Protection Clause it simply reflects the duality of our history and our attempts to promote freedom in a world that sometimes seems set against it. Under our Constitution the individual, child or adult, can find his own identity, can define her own persona, without state intervention that classifies on the basis of his race or the color of her skin. . . .

This Nation has a moral and ethical obligation to fulfill its historic commitment to creating an integrated society that ensures equal opportunity for all of its children. A compelling interest exists in avoiding racial isolation, an interest that a school district, in its discretion and expertise, may choose to pursue. Likewise, a district may consider it a compelling interest to achieve a diverse student population. Race may be one component of that diversity, but other demographic factors, plus special talents and needs, should also be considered. What the government is not permitted to do, absent a showing of necessity not made here, is to classify every student on the basis of race and to assign each of them to schools based on that classification. Crude measures of this sort threaten to reduce children to racial chits valued and traded according to one school's supply and another's demand.

That statement, to be sure, invites this response: A sense of stigma may already become the fate of those separated out by circumstances beyond their immediate control. But to this the replication must be: Even so, measures other than differential treatment based on racial typing of individuals first must be exhausted.

The decision today should not prevent school districts from continuing the important work of bringing together students of different racial, ethnic, and economic backgrounds. Due to a variety of factors — some influenced by government, some not — neighborhoods in our communities do not reflect the diversity of our Nation as a whole. Those entrusted with directing our public schools can bring to bear the creativity of experts, parents, administrators, and other concerned citizens to find a way to achieve the compelling interests they face without resorting to widespread governmental allocation of benefits and burdens on the basis of racial classifications.

With this explanation I concur in the judgment of the Court.

Justice BREYER, with whom Justice STEVENS, Justice SOUTER, and Justice GINSBURG join, dissenting.

These cases consider the longstanding efforts of two local school boards to integrate their public schools. The school board plans before us resemble many others adopted in the last 50 years by primary and secondary schools throughout the Nation. All of those plans represent local efforts to bring about the kind of racially integrated education that Brown v. Board of Education, long ago promised — efforts that this Court has repeatedly required, permitted, and encouraged local authorities to undertake. This Court has recognized that the public interests at stake in such cases are "compelling." We have approved of "narrowly tailored" plans that are no less race-conscious than the plans before us. And we have understood that the Constitution *permits* local communities to adopt desegregation plans even where it does not *require* them to do so.

The plans in both Louisville and Seattle grow out of these earlier remedial efforts. Both districts faced problems that reflected initial periods of severe racial segregation, followed by such remedial efforts as busing, followed by evidence of resegregation, followed by a need to end busing and encourage the return of suburban students through increased student choice. When formulating the plans under review, both districts drew upon their considerable experience with earlier plans, having revised their policies periodically in light of that experience. Both districts rethought their methods over time and explored a wide range of other means, including non-race-conscious policies. Both districts also considered elaborate studies and consulted widely within their communities.

II

The Legal Standard. A longstanding and unbroken line of legal authority tells us that the Equal Protection Clause permits local school boards to use race-conscious criteria to achieve positive race-related goals, even when the Constitution does not compel it. Because of its importance, I shall repeat what this Court said about the matter in *Swann*. Chief Justice Burger, on behalf of a unanimous Court in a case of exceptional importance, wrote:

> School authorities are traditionally charged with broad power to formulate and implement educational policy and might well conclude, for example, that in order to prepare students to live in a pluralistic society each school should have a prescribed ratio of Negro to white students reflecting the proportion for the district as a whole. To do this as an educational policy is within the broad discretionary powers of school authorities.

The statement was not a technical holding in the case. But the Court set forth in *Swann* a basic principle of constitutional law — a principle of law that has found "wide acceptance in the legal culture."

Thus, in North Carolina Bd. of Ed. v. Swann, 402 U.S. 43, 45 (1971), this Court, citing *Swann*, restated the point. "[S]chool authorities," the Court said, "have wide discretion in formulating school policy, and . . . as a matter of educational policy school authorities may well conclude that some kind of racial balance in the schools is desirable quite apart from any constitutional requirements." Then-Justice Rehnquist echoed this view in Bustop, Inc. v. Los Angeles Bd. of Ed., 439 U.S. 1380, 1383 (1978), making clear that he too believed that *Swann*'s statement reflected settled law: "While I have the gravest doubts that [a state supreme court] was *required* by the United States Constitution to take the [desegregation] action that it has taken in this case, I have very little doubt that it was *permitted* by that Constitution to take such action."

These statements nowhere suggest that this freedom is limited to school districts where court-ordered desegregation measures are also in effect. Indeed, in *McDaniel*, a case decided the same day as *Swann*, a group of parents challenged a race-conscious student assignment plan that the Clarke County School Board had *voluntarily* adopted as a remedy without a court order (though under federal agency pressure — pressure Seattle also encountered). The plan required that each elementary school in the district maintain 20% to 40% enrollment of African-American students, corresponding to the racial composition of the district. This Court upheld the plan, rejecting the parents' argument that "a person may not be *included* or *excluded* solely because he is a Negro or because he is white."

This Court has also held that school districts may be required by federal statute to undertake race-conscious desegregation efforts even when there is no likelihood that *de jure* segregation can be shown. In Board of Ed. of City School Dist. of New York v. Harris, 444 U.S. 130, 148-149 (1979), the Court concluded that a federal statute required school districts receiving certain federal funds to remedy faculty segregation, even though in this Court's view the racial disparities in the affected schools were purely *de facto* and would not have been actionable under the Equal Protection Clause. Not even the dissenters thought the race-conscious remedial program posed a *constitutional* problem. Lower state and federal courts had considered the matter settled and uncontroversial even before this Court decided *Swann*. Indeed, in 1968, the Illinois Supreme Court rejected an equal protection challenge to a race-conscious state law seeking to undo *de facto* segregation:

> To support [their] claim, the defendants heavily rely on three Federal cases, each of which held, no State law being involved, that a local school board does not have an affirmative constitutional duty to act to alleviate racial imbalance in the schools that it did not cause." However, the question as to whether the constitution requires a local school board, or a State, to act to undo *de facto* school segregation is simply not here concerned. The issue here is whether the constitution permits, rather than prohibits, voluntary State action aimed toward reducing and eventually eliminating *de facto* school segregation.
>
> "State laws or administrative policies, directed toward the reduction and eventual elimination of *de facto* segregation of children in the schools and racial imbalance, have been approved by every high State court which has considered the issue. Similarly, the Federal courts which have considered the issue . . . have recognized that voluntary programs of local school authorities designed to alleviate *de facto* segregation and racial imbalance in the schools are not constitutionally forbidden.

That *Swann*'s legal statement should find such broad acceptance is not surprising. For *Swann* is predicated upon a well-established legal view of the Fourteenth Amendment. That view understands the basic objective of those who wrote the Equal Protection Clause as forbidding practices that lead to racial exclusion. The Amendment sought to bring into American society as full members those whom the Nation had previously held in slavery.

There is reason to believe that those who drafted an Amendment with this basic purpose in mind would have understood the legal and practical difference between the use of race-conscious criteria in defiance of that purpose, namely to keep the races apart, and the use of race-conscious criteria to further that purpose, namely to bring the races together.

Several of these cases were significantly more restrictive than *Swann* in respect to the degree of leniency the Fourteenth Amendment grants to programs designed to *include* people of all races. *See, e.g., Adarand, supra; Gratz, supra; Grutter, supra*. But that legal circumstance cannot make a critical difference here for two separate reasons.

First, no case — not *Adarand, Gratz, Grutter*, or any other — has ever held that the test of "strict scrutiny" means that all racial classifications — no matter whether they seek to include or exclude — must in practice be treated the same. The Court did not say in *Adarand* or in *Johnson* or in *Grutter* that it was overturning *Swann* or its central constitutional principle.

Indeed, in its more recent opinions, the Court recognized that the "fundamental purpose" of strict scrutiny review is to "take relevant differences" between "fundamentally different situations . . . into account." The Court made clear that "[s]trict scrutiny does not trea[t] dissimilar race-based decisions as though they were equally objectionable." It added that the fact that a law "treats [a person] unequally because of his or her race . . . says nothing about the ultimate validity of any particular law." And the Court, using the very phrase that Justice Marshall had used to describe strict scrutiny's application to any *exclusionary* use of racial criteria, sought to "*dispel the notion* that strict scrutiny" is as likely to condemn *inclusive* uses of "race-conscious" criteria as it is to invalidate *exclusionary* uses. That is, it is *not* in all circumstances "'strict in theory, but fatal in fact.'"

The Court in *Grutter* elaborated: "Strict scrutiny is not 'strict in theory, but fatal in fact.' . . . Although all governmental uses of race are subject to strict scrutiny, not all are invalidated by it. . . . " "Context matters when reviewing race-based governmental action under the Equal Protection Clause. Not every decision influenced by race is equally objectionable, and strict scrutiny is designed to provide a framework for carefully examining the importance and the sincerity of the reasons advanced by the governmental decisionmaker for the use of race in that particular context." The Court's holding in *Grutter* demonstrates that the Court meant what it said, for the Court upheld an elite law school's race-conscious admissions program.

The cases to which the plurality refers, though all applying strict scrutiny, do not treat exclusive and inclusive uses the same. Rather, they apply the strict scrutiny test in a manner that is "fatal in fact" only to racial classifications that harmfully *exclude;* they apply the test in a manner that is *not* fatal in fact to racial classifications that seek to *include*.

The plurality cannot avoid this simple fact. Today's opinion reveals that the plurality would rewrite this Court's prior jurisprudence, at least in practical application, transforming the "strict scrutiny" test into a rule that is fatal in fact across the board. In doing so, the plurality parts company from this Court's prior cases, and it takes from local government the longstanding legal right to use race-conscious criteria for inclusive purposes in limited ways.

Second, as *Grutter* specified, "[c]ontext matters when reviewing race-based governmental action under the Equal Protection Clause." And contexts differ dramatically one from the other. Governmental use of race-based criteria can arise in the context of, for example, census forms, research expenditures for diseases, assignments of police officers patrolling predominantly minority-race neighborhoods, efforts to desegregate racially segregated schools, policies that favor minorities when distributing goods or services in short supply, actions that create majority-minority electoral districts, peremptory strikes that remove potential jurors on the basis of race, and others. Given the significant differences among these contexts, it would be surprising if the law required an identically strict legal test for evaluating the constitutionality of race-based criteria as to each of them.

Here, the context is one in which school districts seek to advance or to maintain racial integration in primary and secondary schools. It is a context, as *Swann* makes clear, where history has required special administrative remedies. And it is a context in which the school boards' plans simply set race-conscious limits at the outer boundaries of a broad range.

This context is *not* a context that involves the use of race to decide who will receive goods or services that are normally distributed on the basis of merit and which are in short supply. It is not one in which race-conscious limits stigmatize or exclude; the limits at issue do not pit the races against each other or otherwise significantly exacerbate racial tensions. They do not impose burdens unfairly upon members of one race alone but instead seek benefits for members of all races alike. The context here is one of racial limits that seek, not to keep the races apart, but to bring them together.

If one examines the context more specifically, one finds that the districts' plans reflect efforts to overcome a history of segregation, embody the results of broad experience and community consultation, seek to expand student choice while reducing the need for mandatory busing, and use race-conscious criteria in highly limited ways that diminish the use of race compared to preceding integration efforts. They do not seek to award a scarce commodity on the basis of merit, for they are not magnet schools; rather, by design and in practice, they offer substantially equivalent academic programs and electives. Although some parents or children prefer some schools over others, school popularity has varied significantly over the years. In a word, the school plans under review do not involve the kind of race-based harm that has led this Court, in other contexts, to find the use of race-conscious criteria unconstitutional.

In my view, this contextual approach to scrutiny is altogether fitting. I believe that the law requires application here of a standard of review that is not "strict" in the traditional sense of that word, although it does require the careful review I have just described. Apparently Justice Kennedy also agrees that strict scrutiny would not apply in respect to certain "race-conscious" school board policies.

Nonetheless, in light of *Grutter* and other precedents, I shall adopt the first alternative. I shall apply the version of strict scrutiny that those cases embody. I shall consequently ask whether the school boards in Seattle and Louisville adopted these plans to serve a "compelling governmental interest" and, if so, whether the plans are "narrowly tailored" to achieve that interest. If the plans survive this strict review, they would survive less exacting review *a fortiori*. Hence, I conclude that the plans before us pass both parts of the strict scrutiny test. Consequently I must conclude that the plans here are permitted under the Constitution.

Until today, this Court understood the Constitution as affording the people, acting through their elected representatives, freedom to select the use of "race-conscious" criteria from among their available options. Today, however, the Court restricts (and some Members would eliminate) that leeway. I fear the consequences of doing so for the law, for the schools, for the democratic process, and for America's efforts to create, out of its diversity, one Nation.

VI

To show that the school assignment plans here meet the requirements of the Constitution, I have written at exceptional length. But that length is necessary. I cannot refer to the history of the plans in these cases to justify the use of race-conscious criteria without describing that history in full. I cannot rely upon *Swann*'s statement that the use of race-conscious limits is permissible without showing, rather than simply asserting, that the statement represents a constitutional principle firmly rooted in federal and state law. Nor can I explain my disagreement with the Court's holding and the plurality's opinion, without offering a detailed account of the arguments they propound and the consequences they risk.

Thus, the opinion's reasoning is long. But its conclusion is short: The plans before us satisfy the requirements of the Equal Protection Clause. And it is the plurality's opinion, not this dissent that "fails to ground the result it would reach in law." . . .

Finally, what of the hope and promise of *Brown*? For much of this Nation's history, the races remained divided. It was not long ago that people of different races drank from separate fountains, rode on separate buses, and studied in separate schools. In this Court's finest hour, Brown v. Board of Education challenged this history and helped to change it. For *Brown* held out a promise. It was a promise embodied in three Amendments designed to make citizens of slaves. It was the promise of true racial equality — not as a matter of fine words on paper, but as a matter of everyday life in the Nation's cities and schools. It was about the nature of a democracy that must work for all Americans. It sought one law, one Nation, one people, not simply as a matter of legal principle but in terms of how we actually live.

The last half-century has witnessed great strides toward racial equality, but we have not yet realized the promise of *Brown*. To invalidate the plans under review is to threaten the promise of *Brown*. The plurality's position, I fear, would break that promise. This is a decision that the Court and the Nation will come to regret.

I must dissent.

Note and Question: Grutter's Vitality

Does the *Parents Involved* decision affect *Grutter*'s continuing vitality? Based on *Grutter*, would you have expected the *Parents Involved* case to have been decided differently? If so, how do you explain the result in the *Parents Involved* decision?

C. GENDER

Does the Constitution require that gender classifications receive heightened review like classifications that involve race? Among gender classifications, should it matter whether a classification disadvantages women as opposed to men? As we shall see, the Court's approach to gender-based classifications has changed considerably over the years.

1. Early Gender Jurisprudence

For more than a century, until the 1970s, the Court applied minimal scrutiny to gender classifications. In the process, the Court routinely upheld sex-based stereotypes that were used to justify treating women differently than men (and, in some instances, to disadvantage men). In many instances, these stereotypes resulted in protective legislation that hampered women's ability to work or manage their affairs, and conversely gave men much greater control over their affairs.

Bradwell v. Illinois, 16 Wall. 130 (1873), reflects the early stereotype-based jurisprudence. That decision held that the federal Privileges and Immunities Clause did not apply to women. Rejecting a woman's claimed right to practice law, the Court used the woman-as-homemaker stereotype to justify the exclusion of women from the workplace and from full participation in civil society. In a concurring opinion, Justice Bradley explained why women had no claim to the privileges and immunities of men "to engage in any lawful employment" under either common law or the Constitution:

> It certainly cannot be affirmed, as an historical fact, [that the right of females to pursue any lawful employment] has ever been established as one of the fundamental privileges and

immunities of the sex. . . . On the contrary, the civil law, as well as nature herself, has always recognized a wide difference in the respective spheres and destinies of man and woman. Man is, or should be, woman's protector and defender. The natural and proper timidity and delicacy which belongs to the female sex evidently unfits it for many of the occupations of civil life. The constitution of the family organization, which is founded in the divine ordinance, as well as in the nature of things, indicates the domestic sphere as that which properly belongs to the domain and functions of womanhood. The harmony, not to say identity, of interest and views which belong, or should belong, to the family institution is repugnant to the idea of a woman adopting a distinct and independent career from that of her husband. So firmly fixed was this sentiment in the founders of the common law that it became a maxim of that system of jurisprudence that a woman had no legal existence separate from her husband, who was regarded as her head and representative in the social state; and, notwithstanding some recent modifications of this civil status, many of the special rules of law flowing from and dependent upon this cardinal principle still exist in full force in most States. . . . It is true that many women are unmarried and not affected by any of the duties, complications, and incapacities arising out of the married state, but these are exceptions to the general rule. The paramount destiny and mission of woman are to fulfill the noble and benign offices of wife and mother. This is the law of the Creator. And the rules of civil society must be adapted to the general constitution of things, and cannot be based upon exceptional cases. . . . The humane movements of modern society, which have for their object the multiplication of avenues for woman's advancement, and of occupations adapted to her condition and sex, have my heartiest concurrence. But I am not prepared to say that it is one of her fundamental rights and privileges to be admitted into every office and position, including those which require highly special qualifications and demanding special responsibilities.

Two terms later, in Minor v. Happersett, 88 U.S. 162 (1875), the Court upheld a state law denying women the right to vote.

Despite the Court-imposed limits on women's federal constitutional rights under the Privileges and Immunities Clause, the statutory law of some states began to recognize men and women as equal even in the institution of marriage. Lawyers seeking equality for women relied on the developing substantive due process analysis associated with *Lochner.* Recognizing this trend, the Court, in Muller v. Oregon, 208 U.S. 41 (1908), stated: "The current runs steadily and strongly in the direction of the emancipation of the wife, and the policy [in this state] is to place her upon the same footing as if she were a femme sole, not only with respect to her separate property, but as it affects her right to make binding contracts; and [the] remedies for the enforcement of liabilities. . . . " In *Muller,* an employer was convicted for violating a state statute that prohibited women from working more than 10 hours per day in laundry facilities. The law was challenged on the ground that it abridged women's individual liberty right of contract under *Lochner*. Social progressives were fighting for more state and federal legislative protection of workers and the eventual reversal of *Lochner*. Ironically, *Lochner* provided the primary basis for gaining protective legislation for women in the workplace.

Yet even cases like *Muller,* brought to protect women from harsh working conditions, employed the weaker-sex paradigm to justify excluding women from more lucrative employment in the same workplace. The Court cited extensively from the legal realist "Brandeis' brief," progressive in its day, but based on the prevailing natural law view of women as married, child-bearing, and in the home. The Court noted that the brief contained extracts from more than 90 government reports from this country and Europe to the effect that "long hours of labor are dangerous for women, primarily because of their special physical organization, [their] maternal functions, the rearing and education of the children, the maintenance of the home—all so important and so far reaching that the need for such reduction need hardly be discussed." The Court took "judicial cognizance of all matters of general knowledge," noting:

> That woman's physical structure and the performance of maternal functions place her at a disadvantage in the struggle for subsistence is obvious. This is especially true when the burdens of motherhood are upon her. Even when they are not, [healthy] mothers are essential to vigorous offspring [and] the physical well-being of woman becomes an object of public interest and care in order to preserve the strength and vigor of the race. [H]istory discloses [that] woman has always been dependent upon man. [W]hile now the doors of the school room are opened and her opportunities for acquiring knowledge are great, [it] is still true that in the struggle for subsistence she is not an equal competitor with her brother. Though limitations upon personal and contractual rights may be removed by legislation, there is that in her disposition and habits of life which will operate against a full assertion of those rights. She will still be where some legislation to protect her seems necessary to secure a real equality of right. . . . The limitations which this statute places upon her contractual powers, upon her right to agree with her employer as to the time she shall labor, are not imposed solely for her benefit, but also largely for the benefit of all. . . . The two sexes differ [and] this difference justifies a difference in legislation and upholds that which is designed to compensate for some of the burdens which rest upon her.

The Court also rejected women's claims under the Equal Protection Clause. Quong Wing v. Kirkendall, 223 U.S. 59 (1912), dealt with a Montana statute that imposed a higher tax on hand laundry shops than on steam laundry shops. The statute was challenged on the grounds that it discriminated against men in favor of women (Chinese men operated the majority of hand laundries). Justice Holmes, writing for the majority, said, "[T]he Fourteenth Amendment does not [create] a fictitious equality where there is real difference." The "real difference" according to Justice Holmes was between men and women, and these differences justified the different tax scheme.

BACKGROUND
Older Gender Cases

In Dominion Hotel v. Arizona, 249 U.S. 265 (1919), Justice Holmes upheld a law restricting the number of hours women could work. Likewise, in Holt v. Florida, 368 U.S. 57 (1961), the Court upheld a state statute that exempted women from jury duty. The Court characterized women as the "center of home and family life" and reasoned that women should be allowed to decide whether their "special responsibilities" were consistent with such duty.

❦ PROBLEM: PRECIPITATING SOCIAL CHANGE ❦

During the *Bradwell, Muller,* and *Holt* era, suppose that you were working with a group (composed of both men and women) that wanted to bring about social change, in particular to establish and recognize women as equal citizens with equal rights in the workplace. Given the prevailing judicial climate, how would you have gone about achieving your objectives? Would you have been better off proceeding through the judicial arena, the legislative arena, or some other arena?

2. *Doctrinal Turmoil and Evolution*

In the 1960s and 1970s, attitudes and approaches toward gender issues began to change. As the historical stereotypes started to break down, they gave way to remedial legislation such as the Equal Pay Act and Title VII and Title IX of the Civil Rights Act. In the 1970s, Congress passed the Equal Rights Amendment (ERA), which provided that "equality of rights under the law shall not be denied or abridged by the United States or by any State on account of sex" and authorized Congress to enact implementing legislation. Although the deadline for ratification was extended to 1982, and although 35 states ultimately ratified the Amendment, the ERA failed to gain ratification from the 38 states needed for it to become law.

Beginning in the 1970s, while the ERA was pending, the Court's gender-based equal protection analysis began to undergo a significant shift toward what has come to be called "gender-neutral equality."

Reed v. Reed

404 U.S. 71 (1971)

Mr. Chief Justice BURGER delivered the opinion of the Court.

[A separated husband and wife both seek to be appointed as administrator of their deceased son's estate. By law, when competing applications for letters of administration have been filed by both male and female members of the same entitlement class, the male must be chosen. The state justified the presumption in favor of males on the basis that it would reduce the court's workload.]

§15-314 provides that different treatment be accorded to the applicants on the basis of their sex; it thus establishes a classification subject to scrutiny under the Equal Protection Clause. . . . In applying that clause, this Court has consistently recognized that the Fourteenth Amendment does not deny to States the power to treat different classes of persons in different ways. Railway Express Agency v. New York, 336 U.S. 106 (1949). . . . A classification 'must be reasonable, not arbitrary, and must rest upon some ground of difference having a fair and substantial relation to the object of the legislation, so that all persons similarly circumstanced shall be treated alike.' The question presented by this case [is] whether a difference in the sex of competing applicants for letters of administration bears a rational relationship to a state objective that is sought to be advanced. [T]he objective of reducing the workload on probate courts by eliminating one class of contests is not without some legitimacy. . . . To give a mandatory preference to members of either sex over members of the other, merely to accomplish the elimination of hearings on the merits, is to make the very kind of arbitrary legislative choice forbidden by the Equal Protection Clause of the Fourteenth Amendment; and whatever may be said as to the positive values of avoiding intrafamily controversy, the choice in this context may not lawfully be mandated solely on the basis of sex. . . . By providing dissimilar treatment for men and women who are thus similarly situated, the challenged section violates the Equal Protection Clause.

The judgment of the Idaho Supreme Court is reversed and the case remanded for further proceedings not inconsistent with this opinion.

Frontiero v. Richardson

411 U.S. 677 (1973)

Mr. Justice BRENNAN announced the judgment of the Court in an opinion in which Mr. Justice DOUGLAS, Mr. Justice WHITE, and Mr. Justice MARSHALL join.

[Appellant] Sharon Frontiero, a lieutenant in the United States Air Force, sought increased quarters allowances, and housing and medical benefits for her husband on the ground that he was her 'dependent.' Although such benefits would automatically have been granted with respect to the wife of a male member of the uniformed services, appellant's application was denied because she failed to demonstrate that her husband was dependent on her for more than one-half of his support. . . . In essence, appellants asserted that the discriminatory impact of the statutes is twofold: first, as a procedural matter, a female member is required to demonstrate her spouse's dependency, while no such burden is imposed upon male members; and, second, as a substantive matter, a male member who does not provide more than one-half of his wife's support receives benefits, while a similarly situated female member is denied such benefits.

[The District Court] surmised that Congress might reasonably have concluded that, since the husband in our society is generally the 'breadwinner' in the family — and the wife typically the 'dependent' partner — 'it would be more economical to require married female members claiming husbands to prove actual dependency than to extend the presumption of dependency to such members. Indeed, given the fact that approximately 99% of all members of the uniformed services are male, the District Court speculated that such differential treatment might conceivably lead to a 'considerable saving of administrative expense and manpower.'

[A]ppellants contend that classifications based upon sex, like classifications based upon race, alienage, and national origin, are inherently suspect and must therefore be subjected to close judicial scrutiny. We agree and, indeed, find at least implicit support for such an approach in our unanimous decision only last

Term in Reed v. Reed. 'There can be no doubt that our Nation has had a long and unfortunate history of sex discrimination,' Bradwell v. State of Illinois, 16 Wall. 130 (1873) (Bradley, J., concurring). [It] is true that the position of women in America has improved markedly in recent decades. Nevertheless, it can hardly be doubted [that] women still face pervasive, although [more] subtle, discrimination in our educational institutions, in the job market and, perhaps most conspicuously, in the political arena. It is true, of course, that when viewed in the abstract, women do not constitute a small and powerless minority. Nevertheless, in part because of past discrimination, women are vastly underrepresented in this Nation's decisionmaking councils.

Moreover, since sex, like race and national origin, is an immutable characteristic determined solely by the accident of birth, the imposition of special disabilities upon the members of a particular sex because of their sex would seem to violate 'the basic concept of our system that legal burdens should bear some relationship to individual responsibility. . . .' And what differentiates sex from such non-suspect statuses as intelligence or physical disability, and aligns it with the recognized suspect criteria, is that the sex characteristic frequently bears no relation to ability to perform or contribute to society. As a result, statutory distinctions between the sexes often have the effect of invidiously relegating the entire class of females to inferior legal status without regard to the actual capabilities of its individual members.

With these considerations in mind, we can only conclude that classifications based upon sex, like classifications based upon race, alienage, or national origin, are inherently suspect, and must therefore be subjected to strict judicial scrutiny. Applying the analysis mandated by that stricter standard of review, it is clear that the statutory scheme now before us is constitutionally invalid. . . .

Reversed.

Mr. Justice POWELL, with whom THE CHIEF JUSTICE and Mr. Justice BLACKMUN join, concurring in the judgment.

[T]he challenged statutes constitute an unconstitutional discrimination against servicewomen in violation of the Due Process Clause of the Fifth Amendment, but I cannot [agree] that classifications based upon sex, 'like classifications based upon race, alienage, and national origin,' are 'inherently suspect and must therefore be subjected to close judicial scrutiny.' [We should] decide this case on the authority of *Reed* and reserve for the future any expansion of its rationale.

Notes and Questions

1. *Charting a New Course.* Following *Reed* and *Frontiero,* it was clear that the Court was prepared to chart a new course with regard to gender classifications, but the new course was far from clear. Obviously, *Reed*'s approach differed significantly from the approach applied by the *Frontiero* plurality. In some instances, the Court invoked non-equal protection principles to invalidate gender classifications. *See, e.g.,* Stanley v. Illinois, 405 U.S. 645 (1972) (holding that a gender classification that created a "conclusive presumption" violated due process).

2. *Gender Scrutiny.* Do you agree with the *Frontiero* plurality that classifications based on gender should be subjected to strict scrutiny? In the conclusion that race is a suspect class, what criteria did the Court rely on? Does it make sense to apply strict scrutiny to gender classifications? Have women suffered from a history of discrimination? But do women constitute a discrete and insular minority? Is the characteristic immutable? What significance do you attach to the fact that women constitute a majority, rather than a minority, in this country?

Craig v. Boren

429 U.S. 190 (1976)

Mr. Justice BRENNAN delivered the opinion of the Court.

The interaction of two sections of an Oklahoma statute prohibits the sale of "nonintoxicating" 3.2% beer to males under the age of 21 and to females under the age of 18. The question to be decided is whether such a gender-based differential constitutes a denial to males 18–20 years of age of the equal protection of the laws in violation of the Fourteenth Amendment. . . . To withstand constitutional challenge, previous cases establish that classifications by gender must serve important governmental objectives and must be substantially related to achievement of those objectives. We turn then to the question whether, under *Reed,* the difference between males and females with respect to the purchase of 3.2% beer warrants the differential in age drawn by the Oklahoma statute. We conclude that it does not. . . .

[Statutes justified on grounds of administrative convenience, the use of gender as an inaccurate proxy for "archaic and overbroad generalizations" about the financial position of women, and increasingly outdated misconceptions concerning the role of females in the home rather than in the "marketplace and world of ideas" have been rejected as loose-fitting characterizations incapable of supporting state statutory schemes that were premised upon their accuracy.]

We accept for purposes of discussion the District Court's identification of the [legislative] objective [as] the enhancement of traffic safety. Clearly, the protection of public health and safety represents an important function of state and local governments. However, appellees' statistics [cannot] support the conclusion that the gender-based distinction closely serves to achieve that objective and therefore the distinction cannot under *Reed* withstand equal protection challenge.

Even were statistical evidence accepted as accurate, it nevertheless offers only a weak answer to the equal protection question presented here. [I]f maleness is to serve as a proxy for drinking and driving, a correlation of 2% must be considered an unduly tenuous "fit." [P]rior cases have consistently rejected the use of sex as a decisionmaking factor even [when] the statutes in question [rested] on far more predictive empirical relationships than this. [M]any of the studies, while graphically documenting the unfortunate increase in driving while under the influence of alcohol, make no effort to relate their findings to age-sex differentials. [T]he only survey that explicitly centered its attention upon young drivers and their use of beer albeit apparently not of the diluted 3.2% variety reached results that hardly can be viewed as impressive in justifying either a gender or age classification. [T]he showing offered [by] appellees does not satisfy us that sex represents a legitimate, accurate proxy for the regulation of drinking and driving. In fact, when it is further recognized that Oklahoma's statute prohibits only the selling of 3.2% beer to young males and not their drinking the beverage once acquired (even after purchase by their 18–20-year-old female companions), the relationship between gender and traffic safety becomes far too tenuous to satisfy *Reed*'s requirement that the gender-based difference be substantially related to achievement of the statutory objective.

We hold [that] Oklahoma's 3.2% beer statute invidiously discriminates against males 18–20 years of age. [The statute] constitutes a denial of the equal protection of the laws to males aged 18–20. [Judgement reversed.]

Mr. Justice POWELL, concurring.

[I] find it unnecessary [to] read [*Reed*] as broadly as some of the Court's language may imply. [T]he Court has had difficulty in agreeing upon a standard of equal protection analysis that can be applied consistently to the wide variety of legislative classifications. There are valid reasons for dissatisfaction with the "two-tier" approach that has been prominent in the Court's decisions in the past decade. Although viewed by many as a result-oriented substitute for more critical analysis, that approach with its narrowly limited "upper-tier" now has substantial precedential support. [O]ur decision today will be viewed by some as a "middle-tier" approach. While I would not endorse that characterization and would not welcome a further subdividing of equal protection analysis, candor compels the recognition that the relatively deferential "rational basis" standard of review normally applied takes on a sharper focus when we address a gender-based classification. So much is clear from our recent cases.

Mr. Justice STEVENS, concurring.

There is only one Equal Protection Clause. It requires every State to govern impartially. It does not direct the courts to apply one standard of review in some cases and a different standard in other cases. [W]hat has become known as the two-tiered analysis of equal protection claims does not describe a completely logical method of deciding cases, but rather is a method the Court has employed to explain decisions that actually apply a single standard in a reasonably consistent fashion. [A] careful explanation of the reasons motivating particular decisions may contribute more to an identification of that standard than an attempt to articulate it in all-encompassing terms. . . .

Mr. Justice REHNQUIST, dissenting.

The Court's disposition of this case is objectionable on two grounds. First is its conclusion that men challenging a gender-based statute which treats them less favorably than women may invoke a more stringent standard of judicial review than pertains to most other types of classifications. Second is the Court's enunciation of this standard [as] being that "classifications by gender must serve important governmental objectives and must be substantially related to achievement of those objectives." The only redeeming feature of the Court's opinion [is] that it apparently signals a retreat [from] *Frontiero*['s] view that sex is a "suspect" classification for purposes of equal protection analysis. [T]he Oklahoma statute challenged here need pass only the "rational basis" equal protection analysis [and] is constitutional under that analysis. . . .

[B]efore today, no decision of this Court has applied an elevated level of scrutiny to invalidate a statutory discrimination harmful to males, except where the statute impaired an important personal interest protected by the Constitution. There being no such interest here, and there being no plausible argument that this is a discrimination against females, the Court's reliance on our previous sex-discrimination cases is ill-founded. . . . The Court's conclusion that a law which treats males less favorably than females "must serve important governmental objectives and must be substantially related to achievement of those objectives" apparently comes out of thin air. The Equal Protection Clause contains no such language. . . . How is this Court to divine what objectives are important? How is it to determine whether a particular law is "substantially" related to the achievement of such objective, rather than related in some other way to its achievement? Both of the phrases used are so diaphanous and elastic as to invite subjective judicial preferences. . . .

This is not a case where the classification can only be justified on grounds of administrative convenience. . . . Since males drink and drive at a higher rate than the age group as a whole, I fail to see how a statutory bar with regard only to them can create any due process problem. . . . There being no violation of either equal protection or due process, the statute should accordingly be upheld.

Notes and Questions

1. *Administrative Convenience.* In *Reed, Frontiero,* and *Craig,* the Court rejected the government's claim of "administrative convenience" to justify the differential treatment accorded men and women. In *Frontiero,* there was no concrete evidence to establish that the government saved money by requiring women, but not men, to prove that their spouse was a dependent. The Court in *Craig* noted that "[d]ecisions following *Reed* rejected administrative ease and convenience as sufficiently important objectives to justify gender-based classifications."

2. *Analyzing Craig.* Do you agree with the *Craig* majority that gender classifications should be subjected to intermediate scrutiny rather than strict scrutiny? Why or why not?

3. Recognition of Differences

In recent years, the Court has moved away from the doctrine of gender equality toward a recognition that there are legitimate biological differences between males and females. In such cases, the task for the courts is to differentiate legitimate gender differences from unjustified stereotypes. Consider the following case.

United States v. Virginia

518 U.S. 515 (1996)

Justice Ginsburg delivered the opinion of the Court.

Virginia's public institutions of higher learning include an incomparable military college, Virginia Military Institute (VMI). The United States maintains that the Constitution's equal protection guarantee precludes Virginia from reserving exclusively to men the unique educational opportunities VMI affords. We agree.

Founded in 1839, VMI is today the sole single-sex school among Virginia's 15 public institutions of higher learning. VMI's distinctive mission is to produce "citizen-soldiers," men prepared for leadership in civilian life and in military service. . . . Assigning prime place to character development, VMI uses an "adversative method" modeled on English public schools and once characteristic of military instruction. VMI constantly endeavors to instill physical and mental discipline in its cadets and impart to them a strong moral code. The school's graduates leave VMI with heightened comprehension of their capacity to deal with duress and stress, and a large sense of accomplishment for completing the hazardous course. . . . VMI has notably succeeded in its mission to produce leaders; among its alumni are military generals, Members of Congress, and business executives. The school's alumni overwhelmingly perceive that their VMI training helped them to realize their personal goals. VMI's endowment reflects the loyalty of its graduates. . . . [T]he school's impressive record in producing leaders has made admission desirable to some women. Nevertheless, Virginia has elected to preserve exclusively for men the advantages and opportunities a VMI education affords.

[VMI is] financially supported by Virginia and "subject to the control of the [Virginia] General Assembly." [In] contrast to the federal service academies, institutions maintained "to prepare cadets for career service in the armed forces," VMI's program "is directed at preparation for both military and civilian life"; "[o]nly about 15% of VMI cadets enter career military service."

VMI produces its "citizen-soldiers" through "an adversative, or doubting, model of education" which features "[p]hysical rigor, mental stress, absolute equality of treatment, absence of privacy, minute regulation of behavior, and indoctrination in desirable values." [T]he adversative method "'dissects the young student,'" and makes him aware of his "'limits and capabilities,'" so that he knows "'how far he can go with his anger[,] how much he can take under stress[,] exactly what he can do when he is physically exhausted.'"

VMI cadets live in spartan barracks where surveillance is constant and privacy nonexistent; they wear uniforms, eat together in the mess hall, and regularly participate in drills. Entering students are incessantly exposed to the rat line, "an extreme form of the adversative model," comparable in intensity to Marine Corps boot camp. Tormenting and punishing, the rat line bonds new cadets to their fellow sufferers and, when they have completed the 7-month experience, to their former tormentors. . . . "[W]omen have no opportunity anywhere to gain the benefits of [the system of education at VMI]."

In 1990, [the] United States sued the Commonwealth of Virginia and VMI, alleging that VMI's exclusively male admission policy violated the Equal Protection Clause of the Fourteenth Amendment. . . . The District Court ruled in favor of VMI. [The] Court of Appeals for the Fourth Circuit [vacated] the District Court's judgment. . . . In response to the Fourth Circuit's ruling, Virginia proposed a parallel program for women: Virginia Women's Institute for Leadership (VWIL). The 4-year, state-sponsored undergraduate program would be located at Mary Baldwin College, a private liberal arts school for women, and would be open, initially, to about 25 to 30 students. Although VWIL would share VMI's mission — to produce "citizen-soldiers" — the VWIL program would differ [from] VMI in academic offerings, methods of education, and financial resources. . . . The average combined SAT score of entrants at Mary Baldwin is about 100 points lower than the score for VMI freshmen. Mary Baldwin's faculty holds "significantly fewer Ph.D.'s than the faculty at VMI," and receives significantly lower salaries. While VMI offers degrees in liberal arts, the sciences, and engineering, Mary Baldwin, at the time of trial, offered only bachelor of arts degrees. A VWIL student seeking to earn an engineering degree could gain one, without public support, by attending Washington University in St. Louis, Missouri, for two years, paying the required private tuition.

Experts in educating women at the college level composed the Task Force charged with designing the VWIL program. . . . VWIL students would participate in ROTC programs and a newly established, "largely ceremonial" Virginia Corps of Cadets, but the VWIL House would not have a military format, and VWIL would not require its students to eat meals together or to wear uniforms during the schoolday. [T]he VWIL Task Force favored "a cooperative method which reinforces self-esteem." In addition to the standard bachelor of arts program[,] VWIL students would take courses in leadership, complete an off-campus leadership externship, participate in community service projects, and assist in arranging a speaker series.

Virginia represented that it will provide equal financial support for in-state VWIL students and VMI cadets, and the VMI Foundation agreed to supply a $5.4625 million endowment for the VWIL program. . . . The VMI Alumni Association has developed a network of employers interested in hiring VMI graduates. The Association has agreed to open its network to VWIL graduates. . . .

Virginia returned to the District Court seeking approval of its proposed remedial plan, and the court decided the plan met the requirements of the Equal Protection Clause. . . . A divided Court of Appeals affirmed. . . .

The [suit] presents two ultimate issues. First, does Virginia's exclusion of women from the educational opportunities provided by VMI [deny] to women "capable of all of the individual activities required of VMI cadets," the equal protection of the laws guaranteed by the Fourteenth Amendment? Second, if VMI's "unique" situation [offends] the Constitution's equal protection principle, what is the remedial requirement?

[Under] J.E.B. v. Alabama ex rel. T. B., 511 U.S. 127 (1994), and *Mississippi Univ. for Women*, 458 U.S., at 724[, parties] who seek to defend gender-based government action must demonstrate an "exceedingly persuasive justification" for that action. . . . Without equating gender classifications [to] classifications based on race or national origin, the Court, in post-*Reed* decisions, has carefully inspected official action that closes a door or denies opportunity to women (or to men). . . . [T]he reviewing court must determine whether the proffered justification is "exceedingly persuasive." [The] State must show "at least that the [challenged] classification serves 'important governmental objectives and that the discriminatory means employed' are 'substantially related to the achievement of those objectives.'" The justification must be genuine, not hypothesized or invented *post hoc* in response to litigation. And it must not rely on overbroad generalizations about the different talents, capacities, or preferences of males and females.

The heightened review standard our precedent establishes does not make sex a proscribed classification. Supposed "inherent differences" are no longer accepted as a ground for race or national origin classifications. . . . "Inherent differences" between men and women [remain] cause for celebration, but not for denigration of the members of either sex or for artificial constraints on an individual's opportunity. Sex classifications may be used to compensate women "for particular economic disabilities [they have] suffered," to "promot[e] equal employment opportunity," to advance full development of the talent and capacities of our Nation's people. But such classifications may not be used, as they once were, to create or perpetuate the legal, social, and economic inferiority of women.

[W]e conclude that Virginia has shown no "exceedingly persuasive justification" for excluding all women from the citizen-soldier training afforded by VMI. . . . Because the remedy proffered by Virginia — the Mary Baldwin VWIL program — does not cure the constitutional violation, i.e., it does not provide equal opportunity, we reverse the Fourth Circuit's final judgment in this case.

[Virginia asserts] two justifications in defense of VMI's exclusion of women. First, the Commonwealth contends, "single-sex education provides important educational benefits," and the option of single-sex education contributes to "diversity in educational approaches." Second, [the] "unique VMI method of character development and leadership training," the school's adversative approach, would have to be modified were VMI to admit women. . . .

Single-sex education affords pedagogical benefits to at least some students [and] it is not disputed that diversity among public educational institutions can serve the public good. But Virginia has not shown that VMI was established, or has been maintained, with a view to diversifying, by its categorical exclusion of women, educational opportunities within the Commonwealth. . . . No such policy [can] be discerned from the movement of all other public colleges and universities in Virginia away from single-sex education. . . . A purpose genuinely to advance an array of educational options [is] not served by VMI's historic and constant plan [to] "affor[d] a unique educational benefit only to males." However "liberally" this plan serves the Commonwealth's sons, it makes no provision whatever for her daughters. That is not *equal* protection.

Virginia next argues that VMI's adversative method of training provides educational benefits that cannot be made available [to] women. Alterations to accommodate women would necessarily be "radical," so "drastic," Virginia asserts, as to transform, indeed "destroy," VMI's program. . . . Men would be deprived of the unique opportunity currently available to them; women would not gain that opportunity because their participation would "eliminat[e] the very aspects of [the] program that distinguish [VMI from] other institutions of higher education in Virginia." [The] District Court forecast [that] coeducation would materially affect "at least these three aspects of VMI's program — physical training, the absence of privacy, and the adversative approach."

[I]t is uncontested that women's admission would require accommodations, primarily in arranging housing assignments and physical training programs for female cadets. It is also undisputed [that] "the VMI methodology could be used to educate women" [and] that some women may prefer it to the methodology a women's college might pursue. . . . The parties [agree] that "*some* women can meet the physical standards. . . . " In sum[,] "neither the goal of producing citizen soldiers," VMI's *raison d'etre,* "nor VMI's implementing methodology is inherently unsuitable to women."

[T]he District Court made "findings" on "gender-based developmental differences." These "findings" restate the opinions of Virginia's expert witnesses [about] typically male or typically female "tendencies." For example, "[m]ales tend to need an atmosphere of adversativeness," while "[f]emales tend to thrive in a cooperative atmosphere." . . . State actors controlling gates to opportunity [may] not exclude qualified individuals based on "fixed notions concerning the roles and abilities of males and females." *Mississippi Univ. for Women,* 458 U.S., at 725. . . . It may be assumed [that] most women would not choose VMI's adversative method. [The] issue [is] whether the Commonwealth can constitutionally deny to women who have the will and capacity, the training and attendant opportunities that VMI uniquely affords.

The notion that admission of women would downgrade VMI's stature, destroy the adversative system and, with it, even the school, is a judgment [hardly] different from other "self-fulfilling prophec[ies]," once routinely used to deny rights or opportunities. . . . Women's successful entry into the federal military academies, and their participation in the Nation's military forces, indicate that Virginia's fears for the future of VMI may not be solidly grounded. The Commonwealth's justification for excluding all women from "citizen-soldier" training for which some are qualified [cannot] rank as "exceedingly persuasive. . . . " [VMI's] mission [is] to produce "citizen-soldiers," individuals. . . . Surely that goal is great enough to accommodate women. . . . Just as surely, the Commonwealth's great goal is not substantially advanced by women's categorical exclusion, in total disregard of their individual merit, from the Commonwealth's premier "citizen-soldier" corps. Virginia, in sum, "has fallen far short of establishing the 'exceedingly persuasive justification'" [that] must be the solid base for any gender-defined classification.

[A] remedial decree [must] closely fit the constitutional violation; it must be shaped to place persons unconstitutionally denied an opportunity or advantage in "the position they would have occupied in the absence of [discrimination]." *See* Milliken v. Bradley, 433 U.S. 267 (1977). . . . Virginia chose not to eliminate, but to leave untouched, VMI's exclusionary policy [and] proposed a separate program, different in kind from VMI and unequal in tangible and intangible facilities. . . . Virginia was obliged to show that its remedial proposal "directly address[ed] and relate[d] to" the violation, the equal protection denied to women ready, willing, and able to benefit from educational opportunities of the kind VMI offers. . . .

VWIL affords women no opportunity to experience the rigorous military training for which VMI is famed. Instead, the VWIL program "deemphasize[s]" military education, and uses a "cooperative method" of education "which reinforces self-esteem." [Virginia] maintains that these methodological differences are "justified pedagogically," based on "important differences between men and women in learning and developmental needs," "psychological and sociological differences" Virginia describes as "real" and "not stereotypes." [G]eneralizations about "the way women are," estimates of what is appropriate for *most women,* no longer justify denying opportunity to women whose talent and capacity place them outside the average description. [VMI] offers an educational opportunity no other Virginia institution provides, and the school's "prestige" — associated with its success in developing "citizen-soldiers" — is unequaled. Virginia has closed this facility to its daughters and, instead, has devised for them a "parallel program," with a faculty less impressively credentialed and less well paid, more limited course offerings, fewer opportunities for military training and for scientific specialization. VMI, beyond question, "possesses to a far greater degree" than the VWIL program "those qualities which are incapable of objective measurement but which make for greatness in [a] school," including "position and influence of the alumni, standing in the community, traditions and prestige." Women seeking and fit for a VMI-quality education cannot be offered anything less, under the Commonwealth's obligation to afford them genuinely equal protection. . . . A prime part of the history of our Constitution [is] the story of the extension of constitutional rights and protections to people once ignored or excluded. . . .

For the reasons stated, the initial judgment of the Court of Appeals is affirmed, the final judgment of the Court of Appeals is reversed, and the case is remanded for further proceedings consistent with this opinion.

It is so ordered.

Chief Justice REHNQUIST, concurring in the judgment.

[I]n Craig v. Boren, 429 U.S. 190 (1976), we announced that "[t]o withstand constitutional challenge[,] classifications by gender must serve important governmental objectives and must be substantially related to achievement of those objectives." [T]he majority [says] that the Commonwealth must demonstrate an "exceedingly persuasive justification" to support a gender-based classification. It is unfortunate that the Court thereby introduces an element of uncertainty respecting the appropriate test. . . .

[Had] Virginia made a genuine effort to devote comparable public resources to a facility for women, and followed through on such a plan, it might well have avoided an equal protection violation. . . . [But] neither the governing board of VMI nor the Commonwealth took any action after 1982. . . . If diversity in the form of single-sex, as well as coeducational, institutions of higher learning were to be available to Virginians, that diversity had to be available to women as well as to men. . . .

[A] State does not have substantial interest in the adversative methodology unless it is pedagogically beneficial. [There is no evidence] that an adversative method is pedagogically beneficial or is any more likely to produce character traits than other methodologies. . . . In the end, the women's institution Virginia proposes, VWIL, fails as a remedy, because it is distinctly inferior to the existing men's institution and will continue to be for the foreseeable future. . . . I therefore ultimately agree with the Court that Virginia has not provided an adequate remedy.

Justice SCALIA, dissenting.

[The Court] explicitly rejects the finding that there exist "gender-based developmental differences" supporting Virginia's restriction of the "adversative" method to only a men's institution, and the finding that the all-male composition of the Virginia Military Institute (VMI) is essential to that institution's character. "[W]hen a practice not expressly prohibited by the text of the Bill of Rights bears the endorsement of a long tradition of open, widespread, and unchallenged use that dates back to the beginning of the Republic, we have no proper basis for striking it down." Rutan v. Republican Party of Ill., 497 U.S. 62 (1990) (Scalia, J., dissenting). [T]he same applies, more broadly, to single-sex education in general. . . . Government-run *non*military educational institutions for the two sexes have until very recently also been part of our national tradition. . . .

[W]e evaluate a statutory classification based [on gender using] "intermediate scrutiny" and under it have inquired whether the statutory classification is "substantially related to an important governmental objective." Heckler v. Mathews, 465 U.S. 728 (1984). [T]he Court instead prefers the phrase "exceedingly persuasive justification" from *Hogan*. . . . Only the amorphous "exceedingly persuasive justification" phrase, and not the standard elaboration of intermediate scrutiny, can be made to yield this conclusion that VMI's single-sex composition is unconstitutional because there exist several women (or, one would have to conclude under the Court's reasoning, a single woman) willing and able to undertake VMI's program. Intermediate scrutiny has never required a least-restrictive-means analysis, but only a "substantial relation" between the classification and the state interests that it serves. [I]f the question of the applicable standard of review for sex-based classifications were to be regarded as an appropriate subject for reconsideration, the stronger argument would be not for elevating the standard to strict scrutiny, but for reducing it to rational-basis review. The latter certainly has a firmer foundation in our past jurisprudence. . . . It is hard to consider women a "discrete and insular minorit[y]" unable to employ the "political processes ordinarily to be relied upon," when they constitute a majority of the electorate. And the suggestion that they are incapable of exerting that political power smacks of the same paternalism that the Court so roundly condemns. Moreover, a long list of legislation proves the proposition false. *See, e.g.,* Equal Pay Act of

1963, 29 U.S.C. §206(d); Title VII of the Civil Rights Act of 1964, 42 U.S.C. §2000e-2; Title IX of the Education Amendments of 1972, 20 U.S.C. §1681; Women's Business Ownership Act of 1988, 102 Stat. 2689; Violence Against Women Act of 1994, 108 Stat. 1902. . . .

[Virginia] has an important state interest in providing effective college education for its citizens. That single-sex instruction is an approach substantially related to that interest should be evident [from] the long and continuing history in this country of men's and women's colleges. . . . Virginia demonstrated at trial that "[a] substantial body of contemporary scholarship and research supports the proposition that, although males and females have significant areas of developmental overlap, they also have differing developmental needs that are deep-seated." . . .

[VMI] employs a "distinctive educational method," sometimes referred to as the "adversative, or doubting, model of education." [A] State's decision to maintain [one] school that provides the adversative method is "substantially related" to its goal of good education. [I]t was uncontested that "if the state were to establish a women's VMI-type [i.e., adversative] program, the program would attract an insufficient number of participants to make the program work," and [if] Virginia were to include women in VMI, the school "[would] find it necessary to drop the adversative system altogether." Thus, Virginia's options were an adversative method that excludes women or no adversative method at all. . . . There can be no serious dispute [that] single-sex education and a distinctive educational method "represent legitimate contributions to diversity in the Virginia higher education system." . . .

The Court argues that VMI would not have to change very much if it were to admit women. . . . Changes that the District Court's detailed analysis found would be required include new allowances for personal privacy in the barracks, such as locked doors and coverings on windows, which would detract from VMI's approach of regulating minute details of student behavior, "contradict the principle that everyone is constantly subject to scrutiny by everyone else," and impair VMI's "total egalitarian approach" under which every student must be "treated alike"; changes in the physical training program, which would reduce "[t]he intensity and aggressiveness of the current program"; and various modifications in other respects of the adversative training program that permeates student life. . . .

[VWIL] is, under our established test, irrelevant, so long as VMI's all-male character is "substantially related" to an important state goal. . . . VWIL was carefully designed by professional educators who have long experience in educating young women. . . . [T]he Court simply declares, with no basis in the evidence, that these professionals acted on "'overbroad' generalizations."

Notes

1. *Jurisprudence of Difference.* The Court has rejected the original jurisprudence of difference, but it has yet to fully embrace the modern view. Commentators question both the original equality of difference represented in

Mueller v. Oregon and the modern liberal neutrality principle governing gender claims of inequality since Craig v. Boren, the ultimate statement of gender-neutral equality. In cases rejecting single-sex schools and upholding sex-based affirmative action plans, the "similarly situated" concept employed under gender-neutral interpretations of the Fourteenth Amendment Equal Protection Clause is reconceived as a barrier to equality for women. Moreover, although the terms *sex* and *gender* were used interchangeably in earlier eras, courts and academics question not only the distinction between but also the meaning of gender and sex equality. *See* Katherine Franke, *The Central Mistake of Sex Discrimination Law: The Disaggregation of Sex from Gender,* 144 U. Pa. L. Rev. 1 (1995). Finally, just as the levels of heightened scrutiny appear to shift in racial equality cases, the meaning of intermediate scrutiny has also shifted from its first iteration in *Frontiero* to more recent pronouncements in *Casey* and United States v. Virginia.

2. *The Formal Equality Model.* Geduldig v. Aiello, 417 U.S. 484 (1974), triggered a rethinking of the formal equality model, which had succeeded in getting the courts and lawmakers to identify where men and women are similarly situated. The issue was whether women were entitled to disability benefits for pregnancy and delivery: "[We] cannot agree that the exclusion of this disability from coverage amounts to invidious discrimination under the Equal Protection Clause. . . . The classification challenged [relates] to the asserted underinclusiveness of the set of risks that the State has selected to insure. Although California has created a program to insure most risks of employment disability, it has not chosen to insure all such risks, and this decision is reflected in the level of annual contributions exacted from participating employees. This Court has held that, consistently with the Equal Protection Clause, a State 'may take one step at a time, addressing itself to the phase of the problem which seems most acute to the legislative mind. . . . The legislature may select one phase of one field and apply a remedy there, neglecting the others. . . . Particularly with respect to social welfare programs, so long as the line drawn by the State is rationally supportable, the courts will not interpose their judgment as to the appropriate stopping point. . . . The District Court suggested that moderate alterations in what it regarded as 'variables' of the disability insurance program could be made to accommodate the substantial expense required to include normal pregnancy within the program's protection. The same can be said, however, with respect to the other expensive class of disabilities that are excluded from coverage — short-term disabilities. If the Equal Protection Clause were thought to compel disability payments for normal pregnancy, it is hard to perceive why it would not also compel payments for short-term disabilities suffered by participating employees."

Justice Brennan, joined by two other justices, dissented: "Because I believe that *Reed* and *Frontiero* mandate a stricter standard of scrutiny which the State's classification fails to satisfy, I respectfully dissent. . . . The essence of the State's justification for excluding disabilities caused by a normal pregnancy from its disability compensation scheme is that covering such disabilities would be too costly. To be sure[, t]he present level of benefits for insured disabilities could not be maintained without increasing the employee contribution rate, raising or lifting the yearly contribution ceiling, or securing state subsidies. But whatever role such monetary considerations may play in traditional equal protection analysis, the State's interest in preserving the fiscal integrity of its disability insurance program simply cannot render the State's use of a suspect classification constitutional. [W]hile 'a State has a valid interest in preserving the fiscal integrity of its programs[,] a State may not accomplish such a purpose by invidious distinctions between classes of its citizens. [W]hen a statutory classification is subject to strict judicial scrutiny, the State 'must do more than show that denying (benefits to the excluded class) saves money.'"

∽ PROBLEMS ∽

1. *Analyzing* Virginia's *Holding.* Does the *Virginia* holding make sense? The Court requires VMI to admit women but allows it to hold them to the male-based system used at VMI. While that approach might give some women (those who are interested in, and capable of, performing in VMI's system) what they desire, where does that leave women who might prefer a cooperative approach to education? Would women, as a group, have been better off if the Court had required the Commonwealth of Virginia to devote more resources to VWIL rather than requiring it to integrate VMI?

2. *"Real" versus "Stereotypical" Gender Differences.* The Court seems to suggest that there are "real" as opposed to "stereotypical" differences between men and women. Obviously, there are physical and chemical differences between the sexes. There are also perceived behavioral differences. However, for years a debate has raged about whether these behavioral differences are rooted in "nature" or "nurture." In other words, are behavioral differences attributable to socialization, or are they attributable to real differences between the sexes? How does a court determine whether differences are based on stereotypes or on physical differences?

3. *Formal Equality or Relevant Differences?* Consider the following excerpts from United States v. Virginia in regard to the question of whether social and biological differences have relevance for Fourteenth Amendment equal protection jurisprudence: a) Physical differences between men and women, however, are enduring: "[T]he two sexes are not fungible; a community made up exclusively of one [sex] is different from a community composed of both." Ballard v. United States, 329 U.S. 187 (1946). b) "Inherent differences" between men and women, we have come to appreciate, remain cause for celebration, but not for denigration of the members of either sex or for artificial constraints on an individual's opportunity. Sex classifications may be used to compensate women "for particular economic disabilities [they have] suffered," Califano v. Webster, 430 U.S. 313 (1977) (per curiam); to "promot[e] equal employment opportunity," *see* California Federal Savings & Loan Assn. v. Guerra, 479 U.S. 272 (1987); or to advance full development of the talents and capacities of our Nation's people. But such classifications may not be used, as they once were, *see Goesaert,* 335 U.S., at 467, to create or perpetuate the legal, social, and economic inferiority of women. c) Single-sex education affords pedagogical benefits to at least some students,

Virginia emphasizes, and that reality is uncontested in this litigation. Similarly, it is not disputed that diversity among public educational institutions can serve the public good. . . . In cases of this genre, our precedent instructs that "benign" justifications proffered in defense of categorical exclusions will not be accepted automatically; a tenable justification must describe actual state purposes, not rationalizations for actions in fact differently grounded.

4. *Reconsidering Hypotheticals.* The following hypotheticals are based on cases decided by the Supreme Court during the three periods of constitutional jurisprudence on sex and gender. As you understand the law of each era, determine how the outcome in each problem would differ during each of the three eras.

   a. As part of a state's system for controlling the sale of liquor, bartenders are required to be licensed in all cities that have a population of 50,000 or more, but no female may be licensed unless she is the wife or the daughter of the male owner of a licensed liquor establishment. The effect of the statute is that a male owner, although he himself is always absent from his bar, may employ his wife and daughter as barmaids. A female owner may neither work as a barmaid herself nor employ her daughter in that position, even if a man is always present in the establishment to keep order. The state contends that the statute is motivated by the judgment that bartending by women gives rise to moral and social problems against which it may devise preventive measures. The opponents contend that the statute arbitrarily discriminates between male and female owners of liquor establishments.

   b. A minor dies intestate. Her divorced parents file separate petitions in probate court to be appointed as the administrator of the daughter's estate. The state statute requires that "of several persons claiming an equal entitlement to administer, males must be preferred to females."

   c. A state statute requires that children born out of wedlock can stay with their mother if the father dies, but they cannot stay with their father if the mother dies.

5. *Hockey Scholarships.* The State of Maine enacts a law "providing for ice hockey scholarships to special ice hockey camps that will convene every December." The scholarships, a $700 value each, were given to 21 males and 2 females in 2002. Nine out of every ten ice hockey players in Maine are male. The bill's sponsor stated in arguing for its passage: "Our young lads need the extra work if they are to compete against the neighboring states. The boys are losing out to the big-spending ways of Massachusetts and New Hampshire." If this law is challenged, what level of scrutiny will apply?

6. *More on the Diversity Initiative.* Consider again the problem described at the beginning of the chapter. Suppose that NWU decides to include women as part of its diversity initiative. As a result, NWU is considering giving women preferences in admissions and financial aid as well as in faculty hiring. NWU is contemplating this approach on the theory that women have suffered from discrimination and stereotypes, and therefore deserve a "boost" in terms of admissions and aid. Under the gender precedent that you have examined thus far,

would it be permissible to provide such preferences? How would you advise NWU? What would the university have to show in order to justify the preferences?

4. Discrimination Against Men

The theory of formal equality rejects gender-based classifications. Justice Brennan was the major proponent of this view in gender discrimination cases, although he advocated against the application of formal equality in race discrimination cases. According to Justice Brennan and others on the Court, men are as entitled as women to challenge gender-based classifications. Pay close attention to Justice Rehnquist's critique of this logic.

Michael M. v. Superior Court of Sonoma County

450 U.S. 464 (1981)

Justice REHNQUIST announced the judgment of the Court and delivered an opinion, in which THE CHIEF JUSTICE, Justice STEWART, and Justice POWELL joined.

The question presented in this case is whether California's "statutory rape" law violates the Equal Protection Clause of the Fourteenth Amendment. . . . The statute makes men alone criminally liable for the act of sexual intercourse.

[T]he Court has had some difficulty in agreeing upon the proper approach and analysis in cases involving challenges to gender-based classifications. . . . [W]e have not held that gender-based classifications are "inherently suspect" and thus we do not apply so-called "strict scrutiny" to those classifications. Our cases have held, however, that the traditional minimum rationality test takes on a somewhat "sharper focus" when gender-based classifications are challenged.

Underlying our decisions is the principle that a legislature may not "make overbroad generalizations based on sex which are entirely unrelated to any differences between men and women or which demean the ability or social status of the affected class." But because the Equal Protection Clause does not "demand that a statute necessarily apply equally to all persons" or require "'things which are different in fact [to] be treated in law as though they were the same,'" this Court has consistently upheld statutes where the gender classification is not invidious, but rather realistically reflects the fact that the sexes are not similarly situated in certain circumstances. As the Court has stated, a legislature may "provide for the special problems of women." Weinberger v. Wiesenfeld, 420 U.S. 636 (1975).

The justification for the statute offered by the State [is] that the legislature sought to prevent illegitimate teenage pregnancies. That finding, of course, is entitled to great deference. . . . We are satisfied not only that the prevention of illegitimate pregnancy is at least one of the "purposes" of the statute, but also that the State has a strong interest in preventing such pregnancy. [T]eenage pregnancies, which have increased dramatically over the last two decades, have significant social, medical, and economic consequences for both the mother and her child, and the State. [H]alf of all teenage pregnancies end in abortion. And of those children who are born, their illegitimacy makes them likely candidates to become wards of the State. . . . We need not be medical doctors to discern that young men and young women are not similarly situated with respect to the problems and the risks of sexual intercourse. Only women may become pregnant, and they suffer disproportionately the profound physical, emotional and psychological consequences of sexual activity. The statute at issue here protects women from sexual intercourse at an age when those consequences are particularly severe.

The question thus boils down to whether a State may attack the problem of sexual intercourse and teenage pregnancy directly by prohibiting a male from having sexual intercourse with a minor female. We hold that such a statute is sufficiently related to the State's objectives to pass constitutional muster. . . . Because virtually all of the significant harmful and inescapably identifiable consequences of teenage pregnancy fall on the young female, a legislature acts well within its authority when it elects to punish only the participant who, by nature, suffers few of the consequences of his conduct. It is hardly unreasonable for a legislature acting to protect minor females to exclude them from punishment. Moreover, the risk of pregnancy itself constitutes a substantial deterrence to young females. No similar natural sanctions deter males. A criminal sanction imposed solely on males thus serves to roughly "equalize" the deterrents on the sexes.

[T]his is not a case where a statute is being challenged on the grounds that it "invidiously discriminates" against females. To the contrary, the statute places a burden on males which is not shared by females. But we find nothing to suggest that men, because of past discrimination or peculiar disadvantages, are in need of the special solicitude of the courts. Nor is this a case where the gender classification is made "solely [for] administrative convenience," as in or rests on "the baggage of sexual stereotypes." [T]he statute instead reasonably reflects the fact that the consequences of sexual intercourse and pregnancy fall more heavily on the female than on the male. Accordingly, the judgment of the California Supreme Court is

Affirmed.

Justice STEWART, concurring.

The Constitution is violated when government, state or federal, invidiously classifies similarly situated people on the basis of the immutable characteristics with which they were born. [D]etrimental racial classifications by government always violate the Constitution, for the simple reason that, so far as the Constitution is concerned, people of different races are always similarly situated. [W]hile detrimental gender classifications by government often violate the Constitution, they do not always do so, for the reason that there are differences between males and females that the Constitution necessarily recognizes. In this case we deal with the most basic of these differences: females can become pregnant as the result of sexual intercourse; males cannot. [T]he Equal Protection Clause does not mean that the physiological differences between men and women must be disregarded. While those differences must never be permitted to become a pretext for invidious discrimination, no such discrimination is presented by this case. The Constitution surely does not require a State to pretend that demonstrable differences between men and women do not really exist.

Justice BRENNAN, with whom Justices WHITE and MARSHALL join, dissenting.

[The issue is:] Whether the admittedly gender-based classification in [the statutory rape law] bears a sufficient relationship to the State's asserted goal of preventing teenage pregnancies to survive the "mid-level" constitutional scrutiny mandated by Craig v. Boren. Applying the analytical framework provided by our precedents, [the] classification must be declared unconstitutional. [T]he plurality opinion [places] too much emphasis on the desirability of achieving the State's asserted statutory goal — prevention of teenage pregnancy — and not enough emphasis on the fundamental question of whether the sex-based discrimination in the California statute is *substantially* related to the achievement of that goal. . . . [T]the State has not shown that [this statute] is any more effective than a gender-neutral law would be in deterring minor females from engaging in sexual intercourse. It has therefore not met its burden of proving that the statutory classification is substantially related to the achievement of its asserted goal. . . .

Justice STEVENS, dissenting.

[T]he only acceptable justification for a general rule requiring disparate treatment of the two participants in a joint act must be a legislative judgment that one is more guilty than the other. The risk-creating conduct that this statute is designed to prevent requires the participation of two persons — one male and one female. In many situations it is probably true that one is the aggressor and the other is either an unwilling, or at least a less willing, participant in the joint act. If a statute authorized punishment of only one participant and required the prosecutor to prove that that participant had been the aggressor, [the] discrimination would be valid. . . . I also assume [that] it would be permissible to punish only the male participant, if one element of the offense were proof that he had been the aggressor, or at least in some respects the more responsible participant in the joint act. The statute at issue in this case, however, requires no such proof. . . .

Notes

1. *Parental Rights of Unmarried Fathers.* In a series of family law cases, the Court extended protection to the parental rights of unmarried fathers. In Stanley v. Illinois, 405 U.S. 645 (1972), the Court held that a father of illegitimate children was entitled to a hearing on his fitness as a parent before the children could be taken from him by the State of Illinois. The interests that the Court found controlling in *Stanley* were the integrity of the family against state interference and the freedom of a father to raise his own children. Quilloin v. Walcott, 434 U.S. 246 (1978), involved the constitutionality of a Georgia statute that authorized the adoption, over the objection of the natural father, of a child born out of wedlock. The father in that case had never legitimated the child. It was only after the mother had remarried and her new husband had filed an adoption petition that the natural father sought visitation rights and filed a petition for legitimation. The trial court found adoption by the new husband to be in the child's best interests, and unanimously held that action to be consistent with the Due Process Clause.

2. *Property Tax Exemptions.* In Kahn v. Shevin, 415 U.S. 351 (1974), the Court upheld a Florida law that provided a $500-per-year property tax exemption for widows but not for widowers. The Court held that the legislation involved an effort to reduce "the disparity between the economic capabilities of men and women," noting that there could "be no dispute that the financial difficulties confronting the lone woman in Florida or in any other State exceed those facing the man. Whether from overt discrimination or from the socialization process of a male-dominated culture, the job market is inhospitable to the woman seeking any but the lowest paid jobs."

3. *Peremptory Challenges.* In JEB v. Alabama, 511 U.S. 127 (1994), the State of Alabama filed a complaint seeking to establish paternity and imposing child support obligations against a man. The trial involved a panel of 36 potential jurors, 12 males and 24 females, of which the judge excused three jurors for cause. Only 10 of the remaining 33 jurors were male. The State then used nine of its ten peremptory strikes to remove male jurors, and the petitioner used all but one of his strikes to remove female jurors. As a result, all the selected jurors were female. The jury found that the petitioner was the father of the child, and entered an order directing him to pay child support. Relying on Batson v. Kentucky, 476 U.S. 79 (1986), in which the Court held that peremptory challenges could not be used to exclude blacks from a jury, the Court held that the state's gender-based peremptory strikes violated equal protection. The State had argued that its decision "may reasonably have been based upon the perception, supported by history, that men otherwise totally qualified to serve upon a jury in any case might be more sympathetic and receptive to the arguments of a man alleged in a paternity action to be the father of an out-of-wedlock child, while women equally qualified to serve upon a jury might be more sympathetic and receptive to the arguments of the complaining witness who bore the child." The Court found a violation of equal protection: "Respondent offers virtually no support for the conclusion that gender alone is an accurate predictor of juror's attitudes; yet it urges this Court to condone the same stereotypes that justified the wholesale exclusion of women from juries and the ballot box. Respondent seems to assume that gross generalizations that would be deemed impermissible if made on the basis of race are somehow permissible when made on the basis of gender. Discrimination in jury selection, whether based on race or on gender, causes harm to the litigants, the community, and the individual jurors who are wrongfully excluded from participation in the judicial process. The litigants are harmed by the risk that the prejudice that motivated the discriminatory selection of the jury will infect the entire proceedings. The community is harmed by the State's participation in the perpetuation of invidious group stereotypes and the inevitable loss of confidence in our judicial system that state-sanctioned discrimination in the courtroom engenders."

4. *Citizenship Requirements.* U.S. law provides different proof requirements for a child born out of wedlock abroad to establish citizenship depending on whether the father or the mother is a citizen. If the mother is a citizen and the father is an alien, the status of the child as a U.S. citizenship is considered confirmed at birth. If the father is a citizen and the mother is an alien, the law required the father to

take steps to confirm the relationship, and also required that those steps be taken before the child's 18th birthday. The differential requirements were challenged by the illegitimate daughter of an American father in Miller v. Albright, 523 U.S. 420 (1998). In that case, the Court upheld the differential requirements as constitutionally permissible: "There is no doubt that ensuring reliable proof of a biological relationship between the potential citizen and its citizen parent is an important governmental objective. Nor can it be denied that the male and female parents are differently situated in this respect. The blood relationship to the birth mother is immediately obvious and is typically established by hospital records and birth certificates; the relationship to the unmarried father may often be undisclosed and unrecorded in any contemporary public record. Thus, the requirement that the father make a timely written acknowledgment under oath, or that the child obtain a court adjudication of paternity, produces the rough equivalent of the documentation that is already available to evidence the blood relationship between the mother and the child. . . . Surely the fact that the statute allows 18 years in which to provide evidence that is comparable to what the mother provides immediately after birth cannot be viewed as discriminating against the father or his child."

5. *Adoption and Parental Rights.* In Caban v. Mohammed, 441 U.S. 380 (1979), the Court considered a case involving a man and woman who produced two illegitimate children together and maintained joint custody of the children from the time of their birth until the children were two and four years old. After the mother left the father and remarried, the father maintained close contact with the children. Nevertheless, the mother sought to have her new husband adopt the children. Under New York's Domestic Relations Law, an unwed mother can block the adoption of her children simply by withholding consent, but an unwed father has far fewer rights. The Court struck down the law: "Gender-based distinctions 'must serve important governmental objectives and must be substantially related to achievement of those objectives' in order to withstand judicial scrutiny under the Equal Protection Clause." In *Caban*, although the state argued that it had an important interest in making sure that illegitimate children obtained fathers, the Court concluded that this interest was insufficient, stating that the law "is another example of 'overbroad generalizations' in gender-based classifications. The effect of New York's classification is to discriminate against unwed fathers even when their identity is known and they have manifested a significant paternal interest in the child. . . . Section 111 both excludes some loving fathers from full participation in the decision whether their children will be adopted and, at the same time, enables some alienated mothers arbitrarily to cut off the paternal rights of fathers. We conclude that this undifferentiated distinction between unwed mothers and unwed fathers, . . . does not bear a substantial relationship to the State's asserted interests." By contrast, the Court upheld a state law cutting off a father's rights in Lehr v. Robertson, 463 U.S. 248 (1983). In that case, the Court emphasized that the father had never established a substantial relationship with his child, and therefore that the failure to give him notice of pending adoption proceedings did not deprive him of equal protection. The Court noted

that the father could have protected his rights by sending a postcard to the putative father registry.

6. *Wrongful Death Actions.* In Parham v. Hughes, 441 U.S. 347 (1979), the Court dealt with a Georgia law that allowed the mother of an illegitimate child to sue for the wrongful death of that child, but precluded a father from doing so unless he has previously legitimated the child. In upholding the law, the Court stated: "[The] Georgia statute does not invidiously discriminate against the appellant simply because he is of the male sex. The fact is that mothers and fathers of illegitimate children are not similarly situated. Under Georgia law, only a father can by voluntary unilateral action make an illegitimate child legitimate. Unlike the mother of an illegitimate child whose identity will rarely be in doubt, the identity of the father will frequently be unknown. By coming forward[,] a father can both establish his identity and make his illegitimate child legitimate. Thus, the conferral of the right of a natural father to sue for the wrongful death of his child only if he has previously acted to identify himself, undertake his paternal responsibilities, and make his child legitimate, does not reflect any overbroad generalizations about men as a class, but rather the reality that in Georgia only a father can by unilateral action legitimate an illegitimate child. Since fathers who do legitimate their children can sue for wrongful death in precisely the same circumstances as married fathers whose children were legitimate *ab initio*, the statutory classification does not discriminate against fathers as a class but instead distinguishes between fathers who have legitimated their children and those who have not."

∾ PROBLEMS ∾

1. *Is It Appropriate to Apply the Same Standard of Review to Classifications Involving Men?* Do historical decisions like *Bradwell* suggest that men historically held a privileged position, indeed a dominant position, vis-à-vis women? If so, should they receive less protection under the Equal Protection Clause? However, consider Leo Kanowitz, *"Benign" Sex Discrimination: Its Troubles and Their Cure*, 31 Hastings L.J. 1379, 1394 (1980): "[A] casual glance at the treatment males have received at the hands of the law solely because they are males suggests that they have paid an awesome price for other advantages they have presumably enjoyed over females in our society. Whether one talks of the male's unique obligation of compulsory military service, his primary duty for spousal and child support, his lack of the same kinds of protective labor legislation that have traditionally been enjoyed by women, or the statutory or judicial preference in child custody disputes that has long been accorded to mothers vis-à-vis fathers of minor children, sex discrimination against males in statutes and judicial decisions has been widespread and severe."

2. *Alimony Discrimination.* A state statute provides that husbands may be required to pay alimony to their ex-wives, but it contains no comparable provision for women. Jane James, a high-level corporate official in a Fortune 500 company, files for divorce against her husband, John James, an unemployed construction

worker. John's request for post-divorce alimony is rejected on the basis that state law does not provide for an alimony award in favor of a man. The state seeks to justify the law on grounds of administrative convenience. In the state's view, few men need alimony compared to women. Does this state law violate the Equal Protection Clause? Why or why not? *See* Orr v. Orr, 440 U.S. 268 (1979).

3. *Even More on the Diversity Initiative.* In regard to the introductory problem, suppose that, instead of adopting a preference in favor of women, NWU decides that women and men should be represented equally in the student body and on the faculty in proportion to their percentages in the overall population. In other words, in a given year, if women are underrepresented in the student body or on the faculty, then preferences in terms of hiring, admissions, and financial aid will be extended to women. By contrast, if men are underrepresented, then they will receive the preferences. Under the gender precedent that you have examined thus far, would these proposals be constitutional? How would you advise NWU? What would the university have to show to justify such policies?

Nguyen v. INS

533 U.S. 53 (2001)

Justice KENNEDY delivered the opinion of the Court.

This case presents a question not resolved by a majority of the Court in a case before us three Terms ago [in Miller v. Albright]. Title 8 U.S.C. §1409 governs the acquisition of United States citizenship by persons born to one United States citizen parent and one noncitizen parent when the parents are unmarried and the child is born outside of the United States or its possessions. The statute imposes different requirements for the child's acquisition of citizenship depending upon whether the citizen parent is the mother or the father. The question before us is whether the statutory distinction is consistent with the equal protection guarantee embedded in the Due Process Clause of the Fifth Amendment.

Petitioner Tuan Anh Nguyen was born in Saigon, Vietnam, [in] 1969, to copetitioner Joseph Boulais and a Vietnamese citizen. Boulais and Nguyen's mother were not married. . . . In June 1975, Nguyen, then almost six years of age, came to the United States. He became a lawful permanent resident and was raised in Texas by Boulais. . . . In 1992, Nguyen pleaded guilty in a Texas state court to two counts of sexual assault on a child. He was sentenced to eight years in prison on each count. Three years later, the United States Immigration and Naturalization Service (INS) initiated deportation proceedings against Nguyen as a convicted alien. Though later he would change his position and argue he was a United States citizen, Nguyen testified at his deportation hearing that he was a citizen of Vietnam. The Immigration Judge found him deportable.

The constitutionality of the distinction between unwed fathers and mothers was argued in *Miller,* but a majority of the Court did not resolve the issue. . . . Since *Miller,* the Courts of Appeal have divided over the constitutionality of §1409. The father is before the Court in this case; [and] we now resolve it. We hold that §1409(a) is consistent with the constitutional guarantee of equal protection. . . .

For a gender-based classification to withstand equal protection scrutiny, it must be established "at least that the [challenged] classification serves 'important governmental objectives and that the discriminatory means employed' are 'substantially related to the achievement of those objectives.'" [W]e conclude the statute satisfies this standard. . . .

[The] first governmental interest to be served is the importance of assuring that a biological parent-child relationship exists. In the case of the mother, the relation is verifiable from the birth itself. The mother's status is documented in most instances by the birth certificate or hospital records and the witnesses who attest to her having given birth. . . . Given the proof of motherhood that is inherent in birth itself, it is unremarkable that Congress did not require the same affirmative steps of mothers.

[T]o require Congress to speak without reference to the gender of the parent with regard to its objective of ensuring a blood tie between parent and child would be to insist on a hollow neutrality. . . . Congress could have required both mothers and fathers to prove parenthood within 30 days or, for that matter, 18 years, of the child's birth. Given that the mother is always present at birth, but that the father need not be, the facially neutral rule would sometimes require fathers to take additional affirmative steps which would not be required of mothers, whose names will appear on the birth certificate as a result of their presence at the birth, and who will have the benefit of witnesses to the birth to call upon. The issue is not the use of gender specific terms instead of neutral ones. Just as neutral terms can mask discrimination that is unlawful, gender specific terms can mark a permissible distinction. The equal protection question is whether the distinction is lawful. Here, the use of gender specific terms takes into account a biological difference between the parents. The differential treatment is inherent in a sensible statutory scheme, given the unique relationship of the mother to the event of birth. . . .

Having concluded that facilitation of a relationship between parent and child is an important governmental interest, the question remains whether the means Congress chose to further its objective — the imposition of certain additional requirements upon an unwed father — substantially relate to that end. Under this test, the means Congress adopted must be sustained. . . . In this difficult context of conferring citizenship on vast numbers of persons, the means adopted by Congress are in substantial furtherance of important governmental objectives. The fit between the means and the important end is "exceedingly persuasive." *See Virginia, supra.* . . . The statutory scheme's satisfaction of the equal protection scrutiny we apply to gender-based classifications constitutes a sufficient basis for upholding it.

To fail to acknowledge even our most basic biological differences — such as the fact that a mother must be present at birth but the father need not be — risks making the guarantee of equal protection superficial, and so disserving it. Mechanistic classification of all our differences as stereotypes would operate to obscure those misconceptions and prejudices that are real. The distinction embodied in the statutory scheme here at issue is not marked by misconception and prejudice, nor does it show disrespect for either class. The difference between men and women in relation to the birth process is a real one, and the principle of equal protection does not forbid Congress to address the problem at hand in a manner specific to each gender. The judgment of the Court of Appeals is

Affirmed.

Justice O'CONNOR, with whom Justice SOUTER, Justice GINSBURG, and Justice BREYER join, dissenting.

In a long line of cases spanning nearly three decades, this Court has applied heightened scrutiny to legislative classifications based on sex. The Court today confronts another statute that classifies individuals on the basis of their sex. While the Court invokes heightened scrutiny, the manner in which it explains and applies this standard is a stranger to our precedents. Because the Immigration and Naturalization Service (INS) has not shown an exceedingly persuasive justification for the sex-based classification embodied in 8 U.S.C. §1409(a)(4) — i.e., because it has failed to establish at least that the classification substantially relates to the achievement of important governmental objectives — I would reverse the judgment of the Court of Appeals.

∽ PROBLEMS ∽

1. *The Self-Defense Course.* Jacksonville State University (JSU), a public university with approximately 5,000 undergraduate and 1,000 graduate students, decided to boost safety on its Jacksonville, Florida, campus in July 2002. With a budget of more than $1 million, the school added security personnel, closed-circuit cameras, and an advertising campaign to promote public safety awareness. In addition, the school created a noncredit self-defense course, paid for entirely by the school, taught in a side room in the school gym. The course was designed to teach women the art of self-defense and consequently was restricted to women only. The course was taught by renowned judo and karate experts for both beginners and advanced students and consisted of one class per week for nine weeks of intensive training, including discussions about sexual assault and how to fight off an attacker. A psychologist also lectured on the psychology of female protection and instructed the students in the art of psychological self-defense. The course was filled to capacity — 25 students — and a second section was added with the same number of students. The second section also was filled to capacity, with at least 20 women turned away from the program.

Chad Bailey, a 5-foot 8-inch, 140-pound male sophomore engineering student at JSU, was very interested in self-defense classes but could not find any corresponding class for males on campus. He did find several self-defense courses just off campus, at a fee of $20 per course. These courses had seven classes total, were comparable to the JSU course in content, and were co-ed. The instructors were just as renowned as those who taught the JSU classes. There was no psychology component to the off-campus courses, however. In addition, Chad had to walk for 10 minutes to reach the off-campus courses, whereas the on-campus JSU course required only a 5-minute walk. Chad brought suit against JSU in federal court, seeking to attend the self-defense class offered by the university. The district court ruled in Chad's favor and the circuit court of appeals reversed in favor of the university. The U.S. Supreme Court granted Chad's certiorari petition. What is the most likely ruling by the current Supreme Court? Why?

2. *Field Hockey.* Mark loves to play field hockey. At his public high school, he states his desire to play. Unfortunately, there is no men's/boys' field hockey team, only a girls' team. Mark files suit, claiming that his equal protection rights have been violated. How would you argue the case for Mark? How might the school respond?

5. Gender Classifications in Context

Over the last 30-plus years, the Court has applied gender review standards in a variety of contexts.

a. Single-Sex Schools

One issue that has generated much litigation is the fact that some states provide single-sex schools. As United States v. Virginia illustrates, the courts have generally focused on whether such discrimination is based on stereotypes or on real differences in ability. For example, in Mississippi University for Women v. Hogan, 458 U.S. 718 (1982), men sought admission to an all-women's nursing school. The state-asserted justification for excluding men was that it was engaging in "educational affirmative action" by "compensat[ing] for discrimination against women." Undertaking a "searching analysis," the Court found no close resemblance between "the alleged objective" and "the actual purpose underlying the discriminatory classification."

～ PROBLEMS ～

1. *Does United States v. Virginia Doom the Possibility of Single-Sex Schools?* Suppose that you are the attorney for a school district that is thinking about establishing single-sex schools for girls. The school points to sociological studies demonstrating that many girls thrive in such schools because they can more readily free themselves from sexual stereotypes and they feel less pressure about their clothes and looks. The school has asked you to advise them whether they can establish girls-only single-sex schools. Can they? What would the district need to be able to show in order to do so? What does United States v. Virginia require? What weight, if any, would you give to Justice Scalia's dissent in United States v. Virginia, which states that "educational experts in recent years have increasingly come to 'suppor[t] [the] view that substantial educational benefits flow from a single-gender environment, be it male or female, *that cannot be replicated in a coeducational setting.*'"

2. *More on Single-Sex Schools.* In the preceding problem, assume that the district decides to establish the single-sex schools. After the schools have been in operation for several years, the evidence reveals that girls are performing far better than they performed in co-ed schools. They are also performing better than boys. As a result, most girls opt to attend all-girl schools. At that point, a boy, claiming that he is being deprived of an equal education, seeks to challenge the single-sex school system. Is it a defense to argue that the co-ed schools are "separate but equal"? How else might the all-girl, single-sex schools be defended?

3. *Single-Sex Schools for Boys.* Suppose that sociological studies also demonstrate that African American (and other minority) boys thrive better in single-sex schools. Would it be permissible for the states to establish single-sex schools either for boys or for African American boys? Do the same rules apply to single-sex schools for boys that would apply to single-sex schools for girls? Would United States v. Virginia allow local school districts to establish boys-only schools?

4. *Single-Sex Bathrooms.* Are there ways in which society should or must distinguish between men and women? For example, is it necessary or desirable to maintain single-sex bathrooms? In some countries (e.g., Belgium) unisex bathrooms have been established (although they have individual stalls so that persons have some privacy when performing excretory functions). Suppose that women in Louisville, Kentucky, seek to challenge a local ordinance mandating single-sex bathrooms. They claim that the law is discriminatory because, for some unknown reason (biology?), there are always long lines at the women's bathroom at public events (e.g., at the Kentucky Center for the Arts or at University of Louisville football and basketball games). One woman, frustrated with the long lines, decides to use the male bathroom (where there was no line) and is charged under the ordinance. Should the ordinance be struck down?

5. *More on the Diversity Initiative.* In the introductory problem, suppose that NWU believes that single-sex classes would be beneficial for both men and women. May it create segregated classes in traditional subjects (e.g., English literature) on the theory that women will learn better in such classes? May it create such classes if it thinks that *both* men and women will learn better under such conditions?

b. Public Benefits

In the 1970s, the Court reviewed a series of cases brought by both men and women challenging the differential treatment of men and women in establishing eligibility for public benefits under Social Security and in the military. In general, these laws favored women. One issue raised in these cases was whether laws favoring women disfavored men and, if so, whether the continued favored treatment of women was necessary to compensate for societal and workplace discrimination. Another issue was whether the different treatment of women was based on "archaic and overbroad generalizations."

In Weinberger v. Wiesenfeld, 420 U.S. 636 (1975), a man who had been left to care for his infant son upon the death of his wife applied for Social Security Act survivors' benefits for himself and his son. His wife had been a teacher whose earnings had been the couple's principal source of support during their marriage and from whose earnings social security contributions had been deducted. Although he obtained benefits for the son, the widower was denied benefits for himself on the ground that survivors' benefits were allowable only to women. In an opinion by Justice Brennan, joined by six other justices, the Court held that the statute's sex-based distinction, which meant that the efforts of women workers required to make social security contributions produced less protection for their families than was produced by the efforts of men, violated the right to equal protection under the Due Process Clause of the Fifth Amendment. The Court found that the distinction could not be justified on the basis of the "noncontractual" character of social security benefits, or the ground that the sex-based classification was one really designed to compensate women beneficiaries as a group for the economic difficulties confronting women who sought to support themselves and their families. A series of cases challenging the gender-based distinctions in the Social Security statutes followed.

Califano v. Goldfarb

430 U.S. 199 (1977)

Mr. Justice BRENNAN announced the judgment of the Court and delivered an opinion in which Mr. Justice WHITE, Mr. Justice MARSHALL, and Mr. Justice POWELL joined.

[Leon Goldfarb, a widower, applied for social security survivors' benefits upon the death of his wife Hannah. During the 25 years of her employment in the New York City public school system, she paid all required social security taxes in full. The application was denied.]

Under the Federal Old-Age, Survivors, and Disability Insurance Benefits (OASDI) program, survivors' benefits based on the earnings of a deceased husband covered by the Act are payable to his widow. Such benefits on the basis of the earnings of a deceased wife covered by the Act are payable to the widower, however, only if he 'was receiving at least one-half of his support' from his deceased wife. The question in this case is whether this gender-based distinction violates the Due Process Clause of the Fifth Amendment.

A three-judge [court] held that the different treatment of men and women mandated by [the statute] constituted invidious discrimination against female wage earners by affording them less protection for their surviving spouses than is provided to male employees. We affirm.

[The] gender-based distinction drawn by [the statute] burdening a widower but not a widow with the task of proving dependency upon the deceased spouse presents an equal protection question indistinguishable from that decided in Weinberger v. Wiesenfeld, *supra*. That decision and the decision in *Frontiero* plainly require affirmance of the judgment. . . . *Wiesenfeld* [inescapably] compels the conclusion [that] the gender-based differentiation [that] results in the efforts of female workers required to pay social-security taxes producing less protection for their spouses than is produced by the efforts of men is forbidden by the

Constitution, at least when supported by no more substantial justification than 'archaic and overbroad' generalizations such as 'assumptions as to dependency.' [These generalizations] are more consistent with 'the role-typing society has long imposed,' than with contemporary reality. [B]y providing dissimilar treatment for men and women who [are] similarly situated[, the statute violates the (Fifth Amendment)].'

Appellant [would] focus equal protection analysis, not upon the discrimination against the covered wage earning female, but rather upon whether her surviving widower was unconstitutionally discriminated against by burdening him but not a surviving widow with proof of dependency. The gist of the argument is [that] 'the denial of benefits reflected the congressional judgment that aged widowers as a class were sufficiently likely not to be dependent upon their wives that it was appropriate to deny them benefits unless they were in fact dependent.'

But *Wiesenfeld* rejected the virtually identical argument when appellant's predecessor argued that the statutory classification there attacked should be regarded from the perspective of the prospective beneficiary and not from that of the covered wage earner. . . . The disadvantage to the woman wage earner is even more pronounced in the case of old-age benefits, to which a similarly unequal dependency requirement applies. [W]here the insured herself is still living, she is denied not only 'the dignity of knowing (during her working career) that her social security tax would contribute to their joint welfare when the couple or one of them retired and to her husband's welfare should she predecease him,' but also the more tangible benefit of an increase in the income of the family unit of which she remains a part. . . .

Finally, the legislative history of [the Act] refutes appellant's contention. . . . There is every indication [that] "the framers of the Act legislated on the 'then generally accepted presumption that a man is responsible for the support of his wife and children.'"

We conclude, therefore, that the differential treatment of nondependent widows and widowers results not from a deliberate congressional intention to remedy the arguably greater needs of the former, but rather from an intention to aid the dependent spouses of deceased wage earners, coupled with a presumption that wives are usually dependent. This presents precisely the situation faced in *Frontiero* and *Wiesenfeld*. The only conceivable justification for writing the presumption of wives' dependency into the statute is the assumption, not verified by the Government in *Frontiero,* or here, but based simply on 'archaic and overbroad' generalizations that it would save the Government time, money, and effort simply to pay benefits to all widows, rather than to require proof of dependency of both sexes. [S]uch assumptions do not suffice to justify a gender-based discrimination in the distribution of employment-related benefits.

Affirmed.

Mr. Justice REHNQUIST, with whom THE CHIEF JUSTICE, Mr. Justice STEWART, and Mr. Justice BLACKMUN join, dissenting.

[T]he effect of the statutory scheme is to make it easier for widows to obtain benefits than it is for widowers, since the former qualify automatically while the latter must show proof of need. Such a requirement in no way perpetuates or exacerbates the economic disadvantage which has led the Court to conclude that gender-based discrimination must meet a different test from other types of classifications. It is, like the property tax exemption to widows in *Kahn,* a differing treatment which "rest(s) upon some ground of difference having a fair and substantial relation to the object of the legislation." . . .

The very most that can be squeezed out of the facts of this case in the way of cognizable 'discrimination' is a classification which favors aged widows. [T]his is scarcely an invidious discrimination. . . . A waiver of the dependency prerequisite for benefits, in the case of this same class of aged widows, under a program explicitly aimed at the assistance of needy groups, appears to be well within the holding of the *Kahn* case, which upheld a flat $500 exemption to widows, without any consideration of need.

Note: Review Standards in Benefits Cases

In the benefits cases, the Court split on these issues: the applicable level of scrutiny; when administrative convenience was a legitimate reason for gender-based classification; and who was actually being discriminated against, women or men. Who is actually being discriminated against?

∽ PROBLEMS ∾

1. *Workers' Compensation.* Missouri's workers' compensation law provides that, when a man dies, his widow is automatically entitled to benefits. By contrast, when a woman dies, benefits are payable to her spouse only if he is mentally or physically incapacitated or was to some extent dependent upon her. In evaluating the law, is it appropriate to view the law as involving a classification affecting only men (the widower), only women (the deceased female's spouse), or both?

2. *More on Workers' Compensation.* Under the statute referred to in the preceding problem, suppose that, when a man's wife dies, he challenges the law as discrimination against her (her work is devalued because her surviving husband must prove incapacity or dependency in order to recover). Does the law involve invalid gender discrimination? Consider the following arguments: a) The substantive difference in the economic standing of working men and women justifies the advantage that the statute administratively gives to a widow. b) Surely the needs of surviving widows and widowers would be completely served either by paying benefits to all members of both classes or by paying benefits only to those members of either class who can demonstrate their need. c) The substantive difference in the economic standing of working men and women justifies the advantage that the law administratively gives to a widow. d) Why pay all surviving widows without requiring proof of dependency? e) It is more efficient to presume dependency in the case of women than to engage in case-to-case determination because individualized inquiries in the postulated few cases in which men might be

dependent are not prohibitively costly. *See* Wengler v. Druggist, 446 U.S. 142 (1980).

c. The Military

Historically, women were restricted from certain jobs in the U.S. military. Are sexual classifications relating to military service now subject to heightened review?

Rostker v. Goldberg

453 U.S. 57 (1981)

REHNQUIST, J., delivered the opinion of the Court.

The question presented is whether the Military Selective Service Act violates the Fifth Amendment to the United States Constitution in authorizing the President to require the registration of males and not females.

Congress is given the power under the Constitution "To raise and support Armies," "To provide and maintain a Navy," and "To make Rules for the Government and Regulation of the land and naval Forces." Art. I, §8, cls. 12-14. . . . Congress is a coequal branch of government whose Members take the same oath we do to uphold the Constitution of the United States. [W]e must have "due regard to the fact that this Court is not exercising a primary judgment but is sitting in judgment upon those who also have taken the oath to observe the Constitution and who have the responsibility for carrying on government." The customary deference accorded the judgments of Congress is certainly appropriate when, as here, Congress specifically considered the question of the Act's constitutionality. . . . This is not, however, merely a case involving the customary deference accorded congressional decisions. The case arises in the context of Congress' authority over national defense and military affairs, and perhaps in no other area has the Court accorded Congress greater deference. In rejecting the registration of women, Congress explicitly relied upon its constitutional powers under Art. I, §8, cls. 12-14. . . . This Court has consistently recognized Congress' "broad constitutional power" to raise and regulate armies and navies.

Not only is the scope of Congress' constitutional power in this area broad, but the lack of competence on the part of the courts is marked. "[It] is difficult to conceive of an area of governmental activity in which the courts have less competence. . . . " The operation of a healthy deference to legislative and executive judgments in the area of military affairs is evident in several recent decisions of this Court. . . . None of this is to say that Congress is free to disregard the Constitution when it acts in the area of military affairs. . . . Congress remains subject to the limitations of the Due Process Clause but the tests and limitations to be applied may differ because of the military context. We [do] not abdicate [our] responsibility to decide the constitutional question, but simply recognize that the Constitution itself [requires] deference to congressional choice. [W]e must be particularly careful not to substitute our judgment of what is desirable for that of

Congress, or our own evaluation of evidence for a reasonable evaluation by the Legislative Branch.

[This] case is quite different from several of the gender-based discrimination cases we have considered in that Congress did not act "unthinkingly" or "reflexively and not for any considered reason." . . . The principle that women should not intentionally and routinely engage in combat is fundamental, and enjoys wide support among our people. It is universally supported by military leaders who have testified before the Committee. . . . Current law and policy exclude women from being assigned to combat in our military forces, and the Committee reaffirms this policy. [The] existence of the combat restrictions clearly indicates the basis for Congress' decision to exempt women from registration. The purpose of registration was to prepare for a draft of combat troops. Since women are excluded from combat, Congress concluded that they would not be needed in the event of a draft, and therefore decided not to register them.

Congress' decision to authorize the registration of only men [does] not violate the Due Process Clause. The exemption of women from registration is not only sufficiently but also closely related to Congress' purpose in authorizing registration. . . . The Constitution requires that Congress treat similarly situated persons similarly, not that it engage in gestures of superficial equality. . . . In light of the foregoing, we conclude that Congress acted well within its constitutional authority when it authorized the registration of men, and not women, under the Military Selective Service Act. The decision of the District Court holding otherwise is accordingly,

Reversed.

Justice WHITE, with whom Justice BRENNAN joins, dissenting.

I assume what has not been challenged in this case — that excluding women from combat positions does not offend the Constitution. [I]f during mobilization for war, all noncombat military positions must be filled by combat-qualified personnel available to be moved into combat positions, there would be no occasion whatsoever to have any women in the Army, whether as volunteers or inductees. The Court appears to say, that Congress concluded as much and that we should accept that judgment. . . . The Court's position in this regard is most unpersuasive. [There is little indication] that Congress itself concluded that every position in the military, no matter how far removed from combat, must be filled with combat-ready men. Common sense and experience in recent wars, where women volunteers were employed in substantial numbers, belie this view. . . . I discern no adequate justification for this kind of discrimination between men and women. . . . I dissent.

Justice MARSHALL, with whom Justice BRENNAN joins, dissenting.

The Court today places its imprimatur on one of the most potent remaining public expressions of "ancient canards about the proper role of women." It upholds a statute that requires males but not females to register for the draft, and which thereby categorically excludes women from a fundamental civic obligation.

Because I believe the Court's decision is inconsistent with the Constitution's guarantee of equal protection of the laws, I dissent.

[Statutes] which discriminate on the basis of gender, must be examined under "heightened" scrutiny. . . . The Government does not defend the exclusion of women from registration on the ground that preventing women from serving in the military is substantially related to the effectiveness of the Armed Forces. . . . "Legislative classifications which distribute benefits and burdens on the basis of gender *carry the inherent risk of [reinforcing] sexual stereotypes about the 'proper place' of women and their need for special protection.*" [N]either the Senate Report itself nor the testimony presented at the congressional hearings provides any support for the conclusion [that] drafting a limited number of women [would] burden training and administrative facilities. . . . In concluding that the Government has carried its burden in this case, the Court adopts "an appropriately deferential examination of *Congress'* evaluation of [the] evidence." (emphasis in original). . . . Congressional enactments in the area of military affairs must, like all other laws, be *judged* by the standards of the Constitution. "[When] it appears that an Act of Congress conflicts with [a constitutional] [provision], we have no choice but to enforce the paramount commands of the Constitution. . . . I would affirm the judgment. . . . "

Notes: Gender Ambiguity

1. *Gender Ambiguity*. The discussion about sex discrimination assumes that the sex of a human can be easily determined. Yet, the more research that is done, the less this assumption holds up. The old chromosome tests, in which scientists looked at whether the individual had XX or XY chromosomes, do not suffice. Some people are intersex, meaning they have characteristics of both sexes. "The problem, said Dr. Joe Leigh Simpson, a pediatric geneticist at Florida International University, is that genetic or hormonal abnormalities can affect any organ system, including the gonads and external genitalia. When such anomalies occur, 'it can produce confusion' because hormone levels and other aspects of physiology may not match appearance. Moreover, there is 'no single process' for determining sex because every case is different, he said." Thomas Maugh II, "Row over South African Athlete Highlights Ambiguities of Gender," *Los Angeles Times*, Sports (Aug. 21, 2009).

2. *Sports, Gender, and an Equal Playing Field*. Sports is one area of particular concern involving the equal protection notion of an even playing field. This issue becomes readily evident in the Olympics, when gender testing occurs with publicized frequency, and, in particular, with the controversy surrounding the South African 800-meter runner, Caster Semenya, who won the 2009 World Championship. The problems for the testers are considerable.

Genes are only a blueprint, and sometimes nature doesn't follow the blueprint precisely. Take the examples of XY athletes who appear to be women. At least five enzymes are required to synthesize testosterone, the hormone that produces most male characteristics. Occasionally one of those enzymes is defective. When that happens, the genitals are typically male, but tiny, the person doesn't have much body hair and is generally feminized. Such people are normally eligible to compete as women. In other genetic males, the receptor that the testosterone binds to is defective and it doesn't matter how much testosterone is present. That male is classified as androgen insensitive, but the results are the same: feminization. Genitalia are typically female. Often, such people grow up as females and don't find out they have male genes until they don't get menstrual periods. They are often tall, slender and attractive. Neither anomaly gives the person strength or endurance beyond that of a normal woman and subjects are allowed to compete as women. The condition of being genetically female, or XX, but appearing male can often be traced to congenital adrenal hyperplasia, in which the adrenal glands produce excess testosterone. The woman may look like a boy with tiny male genitals, but once a month will pass blood. If the condition is caught early in life, doctors usually recommend surgery to create female genitalia. But many persons with the condition live normal lives as men.

Thomas Maugh II, "Row over South African Athlete Highlights Ambiguities of Gender," *Los Angeles Times,* Sports (Aug. 21, 2009). One expert further highlighted why rigid sex categories do not work: "Eric Vilain, a professor of human genetics and pediatrics at U.C.L.A., specializes in sex development, so he knows that looking at genes will not tell you simply how a body is functioning. And what we care about is function. 'The best biological marker, if you want a level playing field, would probably be functional testosterone,' Vilain said. 'There is a good correlation between functional testosterone and muscle mass.'" Alice Dreger, "The Sex of Athletes: One Issue, Many Variables," *New York Times,* New York Ed. SP 8 (Oct. 24, 2009).

∾ PROBLEMS ∾

1. Rostker *Today.* If *Rostker* arose today, would it be decided the same way? During the past 25 years, women have assumed a much larger role in the military and have even been assigned to combat roles (from which they were previously excluded). Do these facts require a difference in result? How does the holding in United States v. Virginia affect the analysis?

2. *The Draft.* You are a law clerk to a federal judge who is hearing the case of United States v. Sprague. In this case, a law enacted by Congress is at the heart of the dispute. It provides: "There shall be a special draft for combat purposes of both men and women between the ages of eighteen and twenty. Those persons from this special draft who can demonstrate (a) a certain level of physical fitness, to be measured by cardiovascular, endurance and strength tests such as running, jumping and the lifting of weights, and (b) psychological suitability, shall be considered for elite combat units. The men and women chosen for these units shall be strictly separated based on gender — one unit of twenty spots shall be reserved for women and one unit of twenty spots will be reserved for men. If more men and women qualify, additional separate units shall be created. This separation is justified by gender differences in biology and physiology as well as affirmative action goals." Advise the judge. Is the law constitutional?

3. *Armed Services Tenure.* Congress has placed a limit on the navy's enlisted personnel and a correlative limit on the number of active line officers as a percentage of the personnel figure. Congress has also established the ratio of the

distribution of line officers in the several grades above lieutenant in fixed proportions to the total number of line officers. Because the navy has a pyramidal organizational structure, fewer officers are needed at each higher rank than are needed in the rank below. In the absence of some mandatory attrition of naval officers, the result would be stagnation of promotion of younger officers and disincentive to naval service. Accordingly, Congress has provided that male lieutenants who have been twice passed over for promotion will be mandatorily discharged. Women are entitled to a 13-year tenure of commissioned service before they face mandatory discharge regardless of whether they have been passed over twice. Consider the following arguments in favor of and against the statute: a) Male and female line officers in the navy are not similarly situated with respect to opportunities for professional service because of restrictions on women officers' participation in combat and in most sea duty. Congress may thus quite rationally have believed that women line officers had less opportunity for promotion than did their male counterparts, and that a longer period of tenure for women officers would, therefore, be consistent with the goal to provide women officers with "fair and equitable career advancement programs." b) A legislative classification that is premised solely on gender must be subjected to close judicial scrutiny, and the State's asserted interest is insufficient to satisfy that standard. Schlesinger v. Ballard, 419 U.S. 498 (1975).

D. THE RIGHTS OF ALIENS

Are aliens deserving of special protection, or should classifications involving them be subjected to rational basis review? The Court has used different standards of scrutiny for government classifications that affect legal resident aliens. In its early decisions, the Court gave little protection to persons in this class. Even though aliens were held to be "persons" entitled to the protection of the Equal Protection Clause, see Yick Wo v. Hopkins, 118 U.S. 356 (1886), this protection was limited for more than 60 years. The Court permitted discrimination against aliens when they were justified by a "special public interest," and that doctrine was used to uphold statutes that prohibited aliens from using natural resources, from entering various occupations, and from owning land. The Court's precedents upholding laws limiting the rights of aliens served as de facto recognition of racial classifications, since Chinese and Japanese persons were not eligible for citizenship during the era when their "alienage" was a permanent status.

The turning point for the new era of modern doctrine came in Takahashi v. Fish & Game Commission, 334 U.S. 410 (1948), where the Court rejected the "special public interest" as a justification for denying a resident Japanese alien the right to make a living in commercial fishing activity in state coastal waters. The Court revived the use of the equal protection doctrine as a source of legal rights for aliens, thus laying the foundation for the constitutional challenges that aliens would bring to the Court in the 1970s and thereafter.

In the early 1970s, the Court invalidated state laws that denied aliens the right to receive social welfare benefits, to practice law and other professions, and to seek employment in civil service positions. In these cases, the Court established the principle that discrimination against aliens required strict scrutiny. But in the late 1970s, the Court developed a "political function" exception to strict scrutiny of alienage classifications, and used a rational basis standard to uphold regulations that fell under this exception. The Court's modern cases involving challenges to federal laws also exhibit greater deference to alienage classifications than cases involving challenges to state laws, because of the federal government's constitutional authority in matters relating to immigration and the regulation of resident aliens.

∾ PROBLEM: STANDARDS OF REVIEW ∾

What standard of review should be applied to classifications that affect aliens? Are aliens a "distinct and insular" minority? In terms of political clout, aliens are distinct minorities, since they do not have the right to vote. Historically, have aliens been subject to discrimination? Is the status of alienage immutable? If not, does that fact alone justify treating aliens differently than classifications involving race?

1. The Right to Receive Social Welfare Benefits, to Practice Law, and to Seek Employment in the Civil Service

Do the states have a special interest in limiting the right of aliens to receive social welfare benefits, to practice law, or to seek employment in the civil service?

Graham v. Richardson

403 U.S. 365 (1971)

Mr. Justice BLACKMUN delivered the opinion of the Court.

[The issue] is whether the Equal Protection Clause [prevents] a State from conditioning welfare benefits either (a) upon the beneficiary's possession of United States citizenship, or (b) if the beneficiary is an alien, upon his having resided in this country for a specified number of years. [In the Arizona case, a legal alien became permanently and totally disabled after 13 years of residency, but he was ineligible for benefits because the state law required 15 years of residency for an alien to receive such benefits. In the Pennsylvania case, a legal alien gave up her employment because of illness after four years of residency and was denied public assistance benefits because of her alien status.]

[It] has long been settled [that] the term "person" [encompasses] lawfully admitted resident aliens as well as citizens of the United States and entitles both citizens and aliens to the equal protection of the laws of the State in which they reside. Yick Wo v. Hopkins, 118 U.S. 356 (1886). [C]lassifications based on alienage, like those based on nationality or race, are inherently suspect and subject to close judicial scrutiny. Aliens as a class are a prime example of a "discrete and insular" minority for whom such heightened judicial solicitude is appropriate.

Arizona and Pennsylvania seek to justify their restrictions on the eligibility of aliens for public assistance solely on the basis of a State's "special public interest" in favoring its own citizens over aliens in the distribution of limited resources such as welfare benefits. It is true that this Court on occasion has upheld state statutes that treat citizens and noncitizens differently [on this basis]. Takahashi v. Fish & Game Commn., 334 U.S. 410 (1948), [cast] doubt on the continuing validity of the special public-interest doctrine in all contexts. There the Court held that California's purported ownership of fish in the ocean off its shores was not such a special public interest as would justify prohibiting aliens from making a living by fishing in those waters while permitting all others to do so. [We] conclude that a State's desire to preserve limited welfare benefits for its own citizens is inadequate to justify Pennsylvania's making noncitizens ineligible for public assistance and Arizona's restricting benefits to citizens and longtime resident aliens.

[The justification] of limiting expenses is particularly inappropriate and unreasonable when the discriminated class consists of aliens. Aliens like citizens pay taxes and may be called into the armed forces. [Aliens] may live within a state for many years, work in the state and contribute to the economic growth of the [state]. There can be no "special public interest" in tax revenues to which aliens have contributed on an equal basis with the residents of the State.

Accordingly, we hold that [the Arizona and Pennsylvania statutes] violate the Equal Protection Clause. Also, these statutes conflict with "overriding national policies in an area constitutionally entrusted to the Federal Government." This is because these statutes "impose auxiliary burdens upon the entrance or residence of aliens who [suffer] economic dependency," and thereby operate "to discourage entry into or continued residency in the State." Thus, these statutes [equate with the assertion of a right [to] deny entrance and abode [to aliens], which encroaches upon exclusive federal power in a way that is "constitutionally impermissible."]

Notes

1. *The Right to Work as a Civil Service Employee.* In Sugarman v. Dougall, 413 U.S. 634 (1973), the Court invalidated a state law that allowed only citizens to hold jobs as career civil service employees in a state or public agency. The plaintiffs were employed by a nonprofit organization, and when their jobs were absorbed by a part of the Human Resources Administration of New York City, they were discharged because they were aliens. The jobs held by the plaintiffs included administrative assistant, human resources technician, and clerk-typist. The strict scrutiny standard of *Graham* was employed, and although the state's interest was found to be substantial, its statute was found to be drawn with insufficient precision. The substantial state interest in "limiting participation in state government to those who are within" the "political community" was not confined

properly to "the person who directly participates in the formulation and execution of important state policy." Instead, the statute swept "indiscriminately" by excluding aliens from jobs as office workers or even sanitation workers.

As in *Graham*, the *Dougall* Court rejected the pre-*Graham* "special public interest" doctrine. The argument that aliens were less likely than citizens to remain long-term employees was dismissed by the Court for lack of evidence. However, in dicta, the *Dougall* Court announced a "political function" concept that would become a blueprint in later cases for upholding alienage restrictions on state employees and for departing from the strict scrutiny standard, reasoning as follows: "[We do not] hold that a State may not, in an appropriately defined class of positions, require citizenship as a qualification for office. [Such] power inheres in the State by virtue of its obligation [to] preserve the basic conception of a political community. [This] power and responsibility of the State applies, not only to the qualifications of voters, but also to persons holding state elective or important nonelective executive, legislative, and judicial positions, for officers who participate directly in the formulation, execution or review of broad public policy, perform functions that go to the heart of representative [government. Our] scrutiny will not be so demanding where we deal with matters resting firmly within a State's constitutional prerogatives. This is no more than a recognition of a State's historical power to exclude aliens from participation in its democratic political institutions, and a recognition of a State's constitutional responsibility for the establishment and operation of its own government, as well as the qualifications of an appropriately designated class of public office holders. [A] restriction on the employment of noncitizens, narrowly confined, could have particular relevance to this important state responsibility, for alienage itself is a factor that reasonably could be employed in defining 'political community.'"

2. *Aliens and the Practice of Law. In re Griffiths*, 413 U.S. 717 (1973), struck down a Connecticut law that prohibited aliens from practicing law in the state. The plaintiff was an immigrant, was married to a U.S. citizen, was eligible to become a naturalized citizen but had chosen not to do so, and had graduated from law school and sought to take the bar exam. The Court reaffirmed the general principle that aliens have the right to work for a living, which "is of the very essence of the personal freedom and opportunity that it was the purpose of the (Fourteenth) Amendment to secure," and reaffirmed the idea that restrictions on that right are subject to strict scrutiny. Although the Court agreed that states have an interest in ensuring that applicants for the bar possess "the character and general fitness requisite for an attorney and counselor-at-law," the Court concluded that the states did not have an interest in limiting the practice of law to citizens: "It is no way denigrates a lawyer's high responsibilities to observe that the powers 'to sign writs and subpoenas, take recognizances, (and) administer oaths' hardly involve matters of state policy or acts of such unique responsibility as to entrust them only to citizens. Nor do we think that the practice of law offers meaningful opportunities adversely to affect the interest of the United States. Certainly the Committee has failed to show the relevance of citizenship to any likelihood that a lawyer will fail to protect faithfully the interest of his clients."

∾ PROBLEMS ∾

1. *Reconsidering* Graham. Would the result in *Graham* have been different if the federal government, rather than a state government, had decided to disfavor aliens in their ability to receive social welfare benefits? Suppose that Congress amends the federal welfare law and inserts a provision that ties federal welfare aid to a state's willingness to enact provisions similar to the Arizona law. Is the federal law valid? What about the result in *Griffiths*?

2. *Congressional Authorization.* May Congress authorize the states to discriminate against aliens in the administration of their social welfare laws? Suppose that federal law was neutral on the question of whether aliens should be entitled to receive benefits. However, in enacting the federal welfare law and providing welfare block grants to the states, Congress inserted the following provision: "In spending federal money, states shall be free to decide whether to include or exclude aliens from their programs." To the extent that Arizona was spending federal money under its statute, would the statute be valid? What if Arizona also spent state funds in support of its program, but the funds were "matching funds" required by the federal welfare law as a condition of participation in the program?

3. *Alien Psychologists.* Congress passes a law that "prohibits all lawful aliens admitted to this country from engaging in the practice of elementary school psychologist." What level of scrutiny will the court apply? Why?

4. *More on the Diversity Initiative.* Consider the problem described at the beginning of the chapter. Suppose that NWU decides to include immigrants in its diversity initiative on the theory that they bring unique socioeconomic perspectives, and other cultural and life perspectives, to the educational process. As a result, NWU has decided to give immigrants preferences in admissions and financial aid. What standard of review would apply to such a program? Is it constitutional to include immigrants in the initiative? Would the Court review the program any differently if it applied to illegal immigrants as well as legal immigrants and was challenged by a U.S. citizen who was denied similar assistance and similar financial aid?

2.   Restrictions Based on the "Political Function" Doctrine

Sugarman's "political function" doctrine has generated considerable litigation in recent years. Consider the following case.

Bernal v. Fainter

467 U.S. 216 (1984)

Justice MARSHALL delivered the opinion of the Court.

The question [is] whether a [Texas] statute violates the Equal Protection Clause [by] denying aliens the opportunity to become notaries public. [Bernal is a Mexican citizen who has lived in Texas as a resident alien for more than 20 years. As a paralegal for Texas Rural Legal Aid, he helps migrant farm workers on employment and civil rights matters, and he wishes to administer oaths to these workers and notarize their statements for use in civil litigation.] Under Texas law, notaries public authenticate written instruments, administer oaths, and take out-of-court depositions. The Texas Secretary of State denied [Bernal's] application because [he was not] a citizen of the United States.

[We have] developed a narrow exception to the rule that discrimination based on alienage triggers strict scrutiny. This exception has been labeled the "political function" exception and applies to laws that exclude aliens from positions intimately related to the process of democratic self-government. [*See*] Foley v. Connellie, 435 U.S. 291 (1978). [In] Cabell v. Chavez-Salido, 454 U.S. 432 (1982), we held that a State may bar aliens from positions as probation officers because they, like [the police in *Foley*], routinely exercise discretionary power, involving a basic governmental function, that places them in a position of direct authority over other individuals.

The rationale behind the political-function exception is that within broad boundaries a State may establish its own form of government and limit the right to govern to those who are full-fledged members of the political community. Some public positions are so closely bound up with the formulation and implementation of self-government that the State is permitted to exclude from those positions persons outside the political community, hence persons who have not become part of the process of democratic self-determination.

We have therefore lowered our standard of review when evaluating the validity of exclusions that entrust only to citizens important elective and nonelective positions whose operations "go to the heart of representative government." Sugarman v. Dougall, 413 U.S. [634 (1973)]. [To] determine whether a restriction based on alienage fits within the narrow political-function exception, we devised in *Cabell* a two-part test.

> First, the specificity of the classification will be examined: a classification that is substantially overinclusive or underinclusive tends to undercut the governmental claim that the classification serves legitimate political ends. [Second,] even if the classification is sufficiently tailored, it may be applied in the particular case only to 'persons holding state elective or important nonelective executive, legislative, and judicial positions,' those officers who 'participate directly in the formulation, execution, or review of broad public policy' and hence 'perform functions that go to the heart of representative government.'

[Unlike] the statute invalidated in *Sugarman*, [the Texas statute] does not indiscriminately sweep within its ambit a wide range of offices and occupations but specifies only one particular post with respect to which the State has a right to exclude aliens. Clearly, then, the statute is not overinclusive; it applies narrowly to only one category of persons: those wishing to obtain appointments as notaries. Less clear is whether the [statute] is fatally underinclusive. Texas does not require court reporters to be United States citizens even though they perform some of the same services as notaries. Nor does Texas require that its Secretary of State be a citizen, even though he holds the highest appointive position in the State and performs many important functions, including supervision of the licensing of all notaries public. We need not decide this issue, however, because of our decision with respect to the second prong of the *Cabell* test.

[Texas] maintains that [the] designation [of notaries as public officers by the Texas Constitution] indicates that the State views notaries as important officials occupying posts central to the State's definition of itself as a political community. This Court, however, has never deemed the source of a position [as] the dispositive factor in determining whether a State may entrust the position only to citizens. Rather, this Court has always looked to the actual function of the position as the dispositive factor.

[The] State maintains that [the] duties of Texas notaries entail the performance of functions sufficiently consequential to be deemed "political." [We] recognize the critical need for a notary's duties to be carried out correctly and with integrity. But a notary's duties, important as they are, [are] essentially clerical and ministerial. [To] be sure, considerable damage could result from the negligent or dishonest performance of a notary's duties. But the same could be said for the duties performed by cashiers, building inspectors, the janitors who clean up the offices of public officials, and numerous other categories of [personnel]. What distinguishes such personnel from those to whom the political-function exception is properly applied is that the latter are invested either with policymaking responsibility or broad discretion in the execution of public policy that requires the routine exercise of authority over individuals. Neither of these characteristics pertains to the functions performed by Texas notaries.

The inappropriateness of applying the political-function exception to Texas notaries is further underlined by our decision in *In re Griffiths*, 413 U.S. 634 (1973). [If] it is improper to apply the political-function exception to a citizenship requirement governing eligibility for membership in a state bar, it would be anomalous to apply the exception to the citizenship requirement that governs eligibility to become a Texas notary. We conclude, then, that the "political function" exception is inapplicable to the [Texas statute] and that the statute is therefore subject to strict judicial scrutiny.

To satisfy strict scrutiny, the State must show that [the statute] furthers a compelling state interest by the least restrictive means practically available. [The State] maintains that [the statute] serves its "legitimate concern that notaries be reasonably familiar with state law and institutions" and "that notaries may be called upon years later to testify to acts they have performed." However, both of these asserted justifications utterly fail to meet the stringent requirements of strict scrutiny. There is nothing in the record that indicates that resident aliens, as a class, are so incapable of familiarizing themselves with Texas law as to justify the State's absolute and classwide exclusion. [If] the State's concern [were] truly "compelling," one would expect the State to give some sort of test actually measuring a person's familiarity with the law. [But there is] no such test. [Similarly] inadequate is the State's purported interest in insuring the later availability of notaries' testimony. [The] State fails to advance a factual showing that the unavailability of notaries' testimony presents a real, as opposed to a merely speculative, problem to the State. Without a factual underpinning, the State's asserted interest lacks the weight we have required of interests properly denominated as compelling.

We conclude that [the Texas statute] violates the Fourteenth Amendment of the United States Constitution. Accordingly the judgment of the Court of Appeals is reversed, and the case is remanded. . . .

It is so ordered.

∾ PROBLEMS ∾

1. *Aliens and In-State Tuition at Public Universities.* May a state deny lawful resident aliens and their dependents eligibility for in-state status relating to admission to the state university and tuition fees? Does a state have valid reasons for denying preferential admission and in-state tuition to aliens? Should it matter whether the aliens are long-time residents who pay taxes in the state?

2. *Preemption.* Does Congress's power over immigration, and the special status accorded to diplomats, affect the analysis? Suppose that the plaintiffs were dependents of "nonimmigrant aliens" holding a "G-4" visa, issued to officers and employees of certain international organizations and members of their immediate families. Because of the University of Maryland's proximity to Washington, D.C., significant numbers of such dependents sought to enroll in the university. Should it matter that, under the federal Immigration and Nationality Act of 1952, "G-4 aliens" are not barred from acquiring a domicile in the United States? Can it be argued that Maryland's law creates a burden on such aliens that conflicts with the federal policies exemplified in various federal tax statutes, treaties, and international agreements? *See* Toll v. Moreno, 458 U.S. 1 (1982).

Foley v. Connelie
435 U.S. 291 (1978)

Mr. Chief Justice BURGER delivered the opinion of the Court.

[Edmund Foley] is an alien eligible in due course to become a naturalized citizen, who is lawfully in this country as a permanent resident. He applied for appointment as a New York State trooper, a position which is filled on the basis of competitive examinations. Pursuant to [state law], state authorities refused to allow Foley to take the examination. [The statute provides that "No person shall be appointed to the New York state police force unless he shall be a citizen of the United States." It was enacted in 1927. Foley "is not currently eligible for American citizenship due to waiting periods imposed by congressional enactment," and the statute effectively prevents some aliens from ever becoming state troopers because only those between the ages of 21 and 29 are eligible for these positions.]

[Following Graham v. Richardson, 403 U.S. 365 (1971)], a series of decisions has resulted requiring state action to meet close scrutiny to exclude aliens as a class from educational benefits, eligibility for a broad range of public employment, or the practice of licensed professions. These exclusions struck at the noncitizens' ability to exist in the community, a position seemingly inconsistent with the congressional determination to admit the alien to permanent residence. [It] would be inappropriate, however, to require every statutory exclusion of aliens to clear the high hurdle of "strict scrutiny" [and] we have recognized "a State's historical power to exclude aliens from participation in its democratic political institutions," as part of the sovereign's obligation "to preserve the basic conception of a political community." [Sugarman v. Dougall, 413 U.S. 634 (1973). The] essence of our holdings to date is that although we extend to aliens the right to education and public welfare, along with the ability to earn a livelihood and engage in licensed professions, the right to govern is reserved to citizens.

[A] discussion of the police function is essentially a description of one of the basic functions of government, especially in a complex modern society where police presence is pervasive. The police function fulfills a most fundamental obligation of government to its constituency. Police officers in the ranks do not formulate policy, *per se*, but they are clothed with authority to exercise an almost infinite variety of discretionary powers. The execution of the broad powers vested in them affects members of the public significantly and often in the most sensitive areas of daily life.

[Clearly] the exercise of police authority calls for a very high degree of judgment and discretion, the abuse or misuse of which can have serious impact on individuals. [A] policeman vested with the plenary discretionary powers we have described is not to be equated with a private person engaged in routine public employment or other "common occupations of the community" who exercises no broad power over people generally. [In] short, it would be as anomalous to conclude that citizens may be subjected to the broad discretionary powers of noncitizen police officers as it would be to say that judicial officers and jurors with power to judge citizens can be aliens. It is not surprising, therefore, that most States expressly confine the employment of police officers to citizens, whom the State may reasonably presume to be more familiar with and sympathetic to American traditions. Police officers very clearly fall within the category of "important nonelective [officers] who participate directly in the [execution of] broad public policy." *Dougall*, 413 U.S., at 647. In the enforcement and execution of the laws the police function is one where citizenship bears a rational relationship to the special demands of the particular position. A State may, therefore, consonant with the Constitution, confine the performance of this important public responsibility to citizens of the United States.

Note: The Foley Dissent

Justice Marshall wrote for three dissenters in *Foley*, arguing that the *Foley* majority misinterpreted the *Sugarman* dicta concerning the permissibility of denying aliens employment in positions involving the "execution of broad public policy." Justice Marshall reasoned as follows: "In one sense[,] state troopers participate in the execution of public policy. Just as firefighters execute the public policy that fires should be extinguished, and sanitation workers execute the public policy that streets should be kept clean, state troopers execute the public policy that persons believed to have committed crimes should be arrested. But this fact simply demonstrates that the *Sugarman* exception, if read without regard to its context, [would] swallow the rule. Although every state employee is charged with the 'execution' of public policy, *Sugarman* unambiguously holds that a blanket exclusion of aliens from state jobs is unconstitutional. [T]he phrase 'execution of broad public policy' [cannot] be read to mean simply the carrying out of government programs, but rather must be interpreted to include responsibility for actually setting government policy pursuant to a delegation of substantial authority from the legislature. The head of an executive agency for example, charged with promulgating complex regulations under a statute, executes broad public policy in a sense that file clerks in the agency clearly do not. [There] is a vast difference between the formulation and execution of broad public policy and the application of that policy to specific factual settings. [The] judgments required [of state troopers] are factual in nature; the policy judgments that govern an officer's conduct are contained in [c]onstitutions, statutes and regulations. The officer responding to a particular situation is only applying the basic policy choices — which he has no role in shaping — to the facts as he perceives them. . . . Since no other rational reason has been advanced in support of the statute here, [the] statute's exclusion of aliens from state trooper positions violates the Equal Protection Clause. . . ."

∼ PROBLEM: THE TEACHING CERTIFICATE ∼

Norwick is a lawful resident alien who is married to a U.S. citizen. She meets all of New York's educational requirements for certification as a public school teacher, but her application for a teaching certificate covering nursery school through sixth grade was denied because she is not a U.S. citizen. Norwick is eligible to become a citizen but does not wish to do so. The state argues that this exclusion of aliens is justified under a rational basis standard according to the "political function" doctrine of *Foley* and Sugarman v. Dougall. What arguments may be made on both sides of this argument? *See* Ambach v. Norwick, 441 U.S. 68 (1979).

3. *Federal Regulation of Aliens*

In Hampton v. Mow Sun Wong, 426 U.S. 88 (1976), the Court reviewed a challenge brought by lawful resident aliens to a federal civil service regulation that excluded all persons except citizens and natives of Samoa from most federal civil service jobs. Each of the plaintiffs was qualified for an available job, including a job at the post office, a janitor at the General Services Administration, a file clerk with the Federal Records Center, and an evaluator of educational programs in the Department of Health, Education, and Welfare. The Court recognized that *Sugarman* did not control because "overriding national interests may provide a justification for a citizenship requirement in the federal service even though an identical requirement may not be enforced by a State." However, the Court rejected the government's argument that "federal power over aliens is so plenary that any agent of the National Government may arbitrarily subject all resident aliens to different substantive rules from those applied to citizens." In response to the plaintiffs' equal protection challenge, the Court noted that "it is not necessary to resolve respondents' substantive claim, if a narrower inquiry discloses that essential procedures have not been followed." The Court then assumed, without deciding, that various national interests would permit Congress or the President "to exclude all noncitizens from the federal service," but the Court held as follows: "Since these residents were admitted as a result of decisions made by the Congress and the President, implemented by the Immigration and Naturalization Service acting under the Attorney General of the United States, due process requires that the decision to impose that deprivation of an important liberty be made either at a comparable level of government or, if it is to be permitted to be made by the Civil Service Commission, that it be justified by reasons which are properly the concern of that agency. [In the absence of those justifications, the Court held] that the [regulation] has deprived [the aliens] of liberty without due process of law and is invalid."

∾ PROBLEMS ∾

1. *Aliens and Medicaid.* Plaintiffs are legal resident aliens in New York State, and all suffer from potentially life-threatening illnesses. They are "permanently residing in the United States under color of law (PRUCOLS), but not lawfully admitted permanent residents (that is, green-card holders)." PRUCOL is a designation used to classify aliens of whom the INS is aware but has no plans to deport. But for their exclusion under state law, they would qualify for Medicaid benefits funded solely by the state. The New York legislature established the state Medicaid system in 1966, soon after Congress created the federally funded program. The federal and state governments share the cost of providing Medicaid to needy individuals, including the disabled, the blind, the elderly, children, pregnant women, and single-parent families. If a state wants to extend Medicaid benefits to others, it may do so at its own expense. New York has done so by providing non-federally subsidized benefits to New York residents between the ages of 21 and 65 whose incomes fall below a statutory "standard of need" criterion (and who are not eligible for federally subsidized Medicaid). Until 1996, New York law did not distinguish between aliens and citizens when funding needy recipients of state-funded Medicaid. But after Congress enacted the Personal Responsibility and Work Opportunity Reconciliation Act of 1996 (PRWORA), New York altered its law. The legislative history of the Act reveals that one goal was to "discourage aliens from immigrating here just to avail themselves of welfare or other public resources." The Act divides aliens into two groups in terms of federal Medicaid eligibility. One group includes green-card holders, those granted asylum, designated refugees, Cuban and Haitian entrants, and victims of battering by a spouse or family member. All other aliens, including PRUCOLs like the plaintiffs, are "not qualified." The federal Act makes PRUCOLs ineligible for state Medicaid

(the shared program between state and federal governments) but authorizes states to provide state Medicaid to PRUCOLs (even to illegal aliens) by enacting a new statute that expressly provides for such aid. In response to PRWORA, New York enacted a law terminating Medicaid for PRUCOLS and other "nonqualified" aliens under federal law. This is the law that is challenged by the PRUCOLS in their suit against the state defendant, the New York Commissioner of Health. The plaintiffs argue that strict scrutiny should apply to the law and it should be held unconstitutional; the defendant argues that the law should be upheld under a rational basis standard. Explain how this debate should be resolved in light of *Graham, In re Griffiths, Hampton,* and *Mathews. See* In re Aliessa v. Novello, 754 N.E.2d 1085 (N.Y. 2001); *compare* Lewis v. Thompson, 252 F.2d 567 (2d Cir. 2001).

2. *College Tuition.* In Toll v. Moreno, the Court concluded that the State of Maryland could not discriminate against aliens with regard to admissions and tuition at the University of Maryland. Could Congress authorize the State of Maryland to discriminate on this basis?

3. *Supplemental Medical Insurance.* A Social Security Act provision limits the eligibility of aliens for supplemental medical insurance. The statute provides that only resident citizens who are 65 or older who have resided continuously in the United States for at least five years and have been admitted for permanent residence are eligible. Does *Graham* suggest that the federal law is invalid? Does the fact that the federal government, rather than a state, passed the law make a difference? Is it appropriate for such a law to distinguish between categories of aliens? Is it permissible for Congress to make an alien's eligibility depend on both the character and the duration of his or her residence? Is a five-year minimum residency requirement constitutional? *See* Mathews v. Diaz, 426 U.S. 67 (1976).

E. THE RIGHTS OF UNMARRIED PARENTS AND THEIR CHILDREN

Are the children of unmarried parents entitled to heightened review in regard to classifications that discriminate against them? During the 1960s, the evolution of the equal protection doctrine led to the invalidation of arbitrary legislative classifications based on the "illegitimate" status of children born out of wedlock and their parents. Modern judicial review of such classifications may be characterized as intermediate scrutiny, which falls between rational basis and strict scrutiny standards. Intermediate scrutiny requires that the classification must be substantially related to an important government interest. Most of the Court's holdings between 1968 and 1988 may be interpreted as being consistent with this standard, and in the post-1988 era, the Court has explicitly embraced the standard. In the fields of inheritance rights and the rights to sue for wrongful death benefits and parental support, the Court has invalidated government regulations in most of its decisions. The Court has also invalidated regulations in the fields of welfare and workers' compensation benefits. Although the Court has strongly supported parents' rights to notice and consent in the context of adoption of their children, federal immigration preferences that exclude some children of U.S. unmarried citizens have been held to be constitutional.

1. Inheritance Rights

Trimble v. Gordon
430 U.S. 762 (1977)

Mr. Justice POWELL delivered the opinion of the Court.

At issue in this case is the constitutionality of [§]12 of the Illinois Probate Act which allows illegitimate children to inherit by intestate succession only from their mothers. Under Illinois law, legitimate children are allowed to inherit by intestate succession from both their mothers and their fathers. [Jessie Trimble and Sherman Gordon lived with their illegitimate daughter for four years until Gordon died intestate. The father openly acknowledged his daughter as his child and supported her under a paternity order. When the child's mother filed a petition for a determination of heirship in probate court, the child was excluded as an heir because of her illegitimate status; if she had been a legitimate child, she would have inherited her father's entire estate, which consisted of an automobile worth $2,500. The Illinois statute required not only the father's acknowledgment of the paternity of an illegitimate child, but also the legitimation of a child through the "intermarriage" of his or her parents after the child's birth, as absolute preconditions to inheritance through intestate succession from the child's father.] [We] conclude that the statutory discrimination against illegitimate children is unconstitutional. . . .

[In upholding Section 3, the] Illinois Supreme Court relied [on] the State's purported interest in "the promotion of (legitimate) family relationships." [Section] 12 bears only the most attenuated relationship to the asserted goal. [The] Equal Protection Clause requires more than the mere incantation of a proper state purpose. [In our precedents], we have expressly considered and rejected the argument that a State may attempt to influence the actions of men and women by imposing sanctions on the children born of their illegitimate relationships. [While] parents have the ability to conform their conduct to societal norms, [their] illegitimate children can affect neither their parents' conduct nor their own status.

[The] Illinois Supreme Court relied on [a] more substantial justification: the State's interest in "establish(ing) a method of property disposition." [Focusing] on the difficulty of proving paternity and the related danger of spurious claims, the court concluded that this interest explained and justified the asymmetrical statutory discrimination against the illegitimate children of intestate men. The more favorable treatment of illegitimate children claiming from their mothers' estates was justified because "proof of a lineal relationship is more readily ascertainable when dealing with maternal ancestors." Alluding to the possibilities of abuse, the court rejected a case-by-case approach to claims based on alleged paternity.

[We think] that the [state] court failed to consider the possibility of a middle ground between the extremes of complete exclusion and case-by-case determination of paternity. For at least some significant categories of illegitimate children of intestate men, inheritance rights can be recognized without jeopardizing the orderly settlement of estates or the dependability of titles to property passing under intestacy laws. Because it excludes those categories of illegitimate children unnecessarily, [§]12 is constitutionally flawed. [We conclude that section 12 is not] "carefully tuned to alternative considerations[.]" [Difficulties] of proving paternity in some situations do not justify the total statutory disinheritance of illegitimate children whose fathers die intestate. The facts of this case graphically illustrate the constitutional defect of [§]12. [The state court's finding of paternity and support order] should be equally sufficient to establish [Gordon's daughter's] right to claim a child's share of Gordon's estate, for the State's interest in the accurate and efficient disposition of property at death would not be compromised in any way by allowing her claim in these circumstances. The reach of the statute extends well beyond the asserted purposes.

[We] conclude that [§]12 of the Illinois Probate Act cannot be squared with the command of the Equal Protection Clause of the Fourteenth Amendment.

Accordingly, we reverse the judgment of the Illinois Supreme Court and remand the case for further proceedings not inconsistent with this opinion.

Notes

1. *Pre-*Trimble *Precedent.* The Illinois Supreme Court had upheld the succession statute in *Trimble* on the authority of Labine v. Vincent, 401 U.S. 532 (1971). The child in *Labine* had been formally "acknowledged" as the "natural child" of her father in a notarized document signed by both parents, which served as a recognition of "paternity." But the father had not taken the extra step of "legitimating" his daughter by "stating his desire to legitimate" her in the acknowledgement document. A Louisiana statute barred such a child from receiving a share of the father's intestate succession in the same way as children born to married parents. The *Labine* Court affirmed the constitutional validity of this statute, and the *Trimble* Court did not overrule this holding. Instead, the Court distinguished *Labine,* by emphasizing that the *Labine* statute allowed a child of unmarried parents to inherit either through a simple "legitimation" document or through postbirth marriage to the child's mother, whereas the *Trimble* statute completely barred a child of unmarried parents from inheriting from her father in the absence of such a marriage. Justice Rehnquist wrote for the four dissenters in *Trimble* who would have upheld the Illinois statute, reasoning that the *Trimble* majority's decision "requires a conscious second-guessing of legislative judgment in an area where this Court has no special expertise."

2. *Post-*Trimble *Developments.* In Reed v. Campbell, 476 U.S. 852 (1986), the Court held that the *Trimble* doctrine applied to a child of unmarried parents in Texas whose father had died before *Trimble* was decided, but whose father's estate was in progress on the date of that decision. The Court noted that "[a]fter an estate has been finally distributed, the interest in finality may provide [a] valid justification for barring the belated assertion of claims, even though they may be meritorious"; however, in *Reed,* the post-*Trimble* assertion of the *Trimble* equal protection right by a child of unmarried parents "should [have] been given controlling effect." *Reed* did not hold that *Trimble* should be retroactively applied in all cases, however.

∽ PROBLEMS ∽

1. *Suspect Classification?* Given the other equal protection categories that have been held to be "suspect" classifications, are there reasons for treating classifications relating to "nonmarital" children as suspect as well? Is the condition immutable? Have those in this classification historically been subject to discrimination? Are there valid reasons, related to the status, for treating them differently?

2. *Intestate Succession.* A New York statute requires children of unmarried parents to provide a particular form of proof of paternity (an "order of filiation") in order to inherit from their fathers by intestate succession. Children born to married parents are not subject to the same requirement. Robert claims to be the son of Mario, who died intestate. Robert's mother, Rosa, died five years before his father's death and never was married to his father. Neither of Robert's parents obtained for him a court "order of filiation," declaring the paternity of Mario either during Rosa's pregnancy or within two years from the date of Robert's birth. Yet the New York statute provides that such an order is required in order for a child of unmarried parents to inherit from a father by intestate succession, and that "the existence of an agreement obligating the father to support the [child] does not qualify such child to inherit from the father in the absence of an order of filiation." Robert challenges the New York law as a violation of the Equal Protection Clause. How would you argue the case on Robert's behalf? How might the state respond? Who should win? *See* Lalli v. Lalli, 439 U.S. 259 (1978).

2. Rights to Sue and to Receive Government Benefits

a.   Suits for Wrongful Death or Parental Support

In two of the Supreme Court's earliest decisions involving the rights of nonmarital children and their parents, statutory bars to tort suits for wrongful death were invalidated in cases where such persons were prohibited from exercising the right to bring such suits. These decisions were followed by others that invalidated time limits on suits by nonmarital children who sought to establish the right to parental support through paternity actions.

Levy v. Louisiana

391 U.S. 68 (1968)

Mr. Justice DOUGLAS delivered the opinion of the Court.

[Five children sought to recover wrongful-death damages for the loss of their mother as well as damages based on a cause of action for pain and suffering that their mother had at the time of her death. The defendants were the doctor who treated their mother and an insurance company. The children lived with their mother, who worked as a domestic servant to support them and to pay for their education. The tort action was dismissed, and the state courts ruled that the right to bring such a suit was limited to children born to married parents, "based on morals and the general welfare because it discourages bringing children into the world out of wedlock." By contrast, state law allowed a dependent child of unmarried parents to recover worker's compensation benefits for the death of a parent; state law also imposed a duty on parents to support all their children, including those born when the parents are not married.]

[The] rights asserted here involve the intimate, familial relationship between a child and his own mother. When the child's claim of damage for loss of his mother is in issue, why, in terms of "equal protection," should the tortfeasors go free merely because the child is illegitimate? Why should the illegitimate child be denied rights merely because of his birth out of wedlock? He certainly is subject to all the responsibilities of a citizen, including the payment of taxes and conscription under the Selective Service Act. How under our constitutional regime can he be denied correlative rights which other citizens enjoy?

Legitimacy or illegitimacy of birth has no relation to the nature of the wrong allegedly inflicted on the mother. . . . These children, though illegitimate, were dependent on her; she cared for them and nurtured them; they were indeed hers in the biological and in the spiritual sense; in her death they suffered wrong in the sense that any dependent would.

We conclude that it is invidious to discriminate against them when no action, conduct, or demeanor of theirs is possibly relevant to the harm that was done the mother.

Reversed.

Note: Wrongful Death Actions

In Glona v. American Guarantee & Liability Insurance Co., 391 U.S. 73 (1968), a case decided the same day as *Levy*, the Court upheld the right of a mother to bring suit for the wrongful death of her child, who had been killed in a car accident. The mother was not married to the father of the child. The Louisiana courts interpreted the state wrongful death statute to require that a decedent must be "legitimate" in order for a parent or sibling to bring an action. The *Glona* Court invalidated this interpretation, holding that the mother's right to equal protection had been violated by the bar to her wrongful death suit, reasoning as follows: "[W]e see no possible rational basis for assuming that if the natural mother is allowed recovery for the wrongful death of her illegitimate child, the cause of illegitimacy will be served. It would, indeed, be farfetched to assume that women have illegitimate children so that they can be compensated in damages for their death. A law which creates an open season on illegitimates in the area of automobile accidents gives a windfall to tortfeasors. But it hardly has a causal connection with the 'sin,' which is, we are told, the historic reason for the creation of the disability. To say that the test of equal protection should be the 'legal' rather than the biological relationship is to avoid the issue. For the Equal Protection Clause necessarily limits the authority of a State to draw such 'legal' lines as it chooses. . . . Opening the courts to suits of this kind may conceivably be a temptation to some to assert motherhood fraudulently. That problem, however, concerns burden of proof. Where the claimant is plainly the mother, the State denies equal protection of the laws to withhold relief merely because the child, wrongfully killed, was born to her out of wedlock."

∼ PROBLEMS ∼

1. *Formalization?* Justice Harlan wrote for three justices who dissented in *Levy* and *Glona,* arguing that when a state bases the right to recover for wrongful death strictly on family relationships, the state should be able to demand "that those relationships be formalized." Justice Harlan reasoned: "One important reason why recovery for wrongful death had everywhere to await statutory delineation is that the interest one person has in the life of another is inherently intractable. Rather than hear offers of proof of love and affection and economic dependence from every person who might think or claim that the bell had tolled for him, the courts stayed their hands pending legislative action. Legislatures, responding to the same diffuseness of interests, generally defined classes of proper plaintiffs by highly arbitrary lines based on family relationships, excluding issues concerning the actual effect of the death on the plaintiff. Louisiana has chosen [to] define these classes of proper plaintiffs in terms of their legal rather than their biological relation to the deceased. [The majority] rules that the State must base its arbitrary definition of the plaintiff class on biological rather than legal relationships. Exactly how this makes the Louisiana scheme even marginally more 'rational' is not clear, for neither a biological relationship nor legal acknowledgment is indicative of the love or economic dependence that may exist between two persons. [If] the State has power to provide that people who choose to live together should go through the formalities of marriage and, in default, that people who bear children should acknowledge them, it is logical to enforce these requirements by declaring that the general class of rights that are dependent upon family relationships shall be accorded only when the formalities as well as the biology of those relationships are present. Moreover, [a] State may choose to simplify a particular proceeding by reliance on formal papers rather than a contest of proof. That suits for wrongful death [must] as a constitutional matter deal with every claim of biological paternity or maternity on its merits is an exceedingly odd proposition." Do you agree with the majority or with Justice Harlan?

2. *Wrongful Death.* Curtis is the biological father of Lemuel. Lemuel and his mother are killed in an auto accident. Curtis and Lemuel's mother were never married, and Curtis never "legitimated" Lemuel under Georgia law by court order. Curtis did sign Lemuel's birth certificate and contribute to his support. Lemuel took Curtis's name and Curtis visited him regularly. However, when Curtis sought to file a wrongful death action against the driver of the car that caused Lemuel's death, his suit was dismissed because a Georgia statute prohibits a father who has not "legitimated" a child by court order from pursuing a wrongful death action. By contrast, an unmarried mother of a child can sue for the wrongful death of that child, and a father who has legitimated a child by court order can sue for the wrongful death of the child if "there is no mother." When Curtis challenges the dismissal of his action on equal protection grounds, this challenge is rejected by the trial and appellate courts, which find that three state interests justify the statutory bar to suit by Curtis: a) the interest in avoiding difficult problems of proving paternity in wrongful death actions, b) the interest in promoting a "legitimate" family unit, and c) the interest in setting a standard of morality by not according to the father of a nonmarital child the statutory right to sue for the child's death. What arguments will Curtis make to attack the statute in the Supreme Court? What counter-arguments may be made to justify the statutory bar to Curtis's suit? *See* Parham v. Hughes, 441 U.S. 347 (1979).

Clark v. Jeter

486 U.S. 456 (1988)

Justice O'CONNOR delivered the opinion of the Court.

Under Pennsylvania law, an illegitimate child must prove paternity before seeking support from his or her father, and a suit to establish paternity ordinarily must be brought within six years of an illegitimate child's birth. By contrast, a legitimate child may seek support from his or her parents at any time. [Ten years after the birth out of wedlock of her daughter, the mother, Cherlyn Clark, filed a support complaint on behalf of her child, naming Gene Jeter as the father. The court ordered blood tests, which showed a 99.3 percent probability that Jeter was the father. Jeter moved to dismiss on the ground that the suit on behalf of his daughter was barred by the six-year statute of limitations for paternity actions. Clark's response challenged this statute on equal protection grounds.]

[This] Court has developed a particular framework for evaluating equal protection challenges to statutes of limitations that apply to suits to establish paternity, and thereby limit the ability of illegitimate children to obtain support.

> First, the period for obtaining support . . . must be sufficiently long in duration to present a reasonable opportunity for those with an interest in such children to assert claims on their behalf. Second, any time limitations placed on that opportunity must be substantially related to the State's interest in avoiding the litigation of stale or fraudulent claims.

Mills v. Habluetzel, 456 U.S. 91 (1982) [holding that the Texas one-year statute of limitations failed both criteria].

[We] conclude that Pennsylvania's 6-year statute of limitations violates the Equal Protection Clause. Even six years does not necessarily provide a reasonable opportunity to assert a claim on behalf of an illegitimate child. "The unwillingness of the mother to file a paternity action on behalf of her child, which could stem from her relationship with the natural father [or] from the emotional strain of having an illegitimate child, or even from the desire to avoid community and family disapproval, may continue years after the child is [born.] *Mills, supra,* at 105, n.4 (O'Connor, J., concurring). Not all of these difficulties are likely to abate in six years. A mother might realize only belatedly "a loss of income attributable to the need to care for the child." *Pickett* [v. Brown], 462 U.S. [1, 12 (1983) (holding that the two-year Tennessee statute of limitations failed both *Mills* criteria)]. Furthermore, financial difficulties are likely to increase as the child matures and incurs expenses for clothing, school, and medical care. Thus, it is questionable whether a State acts reasonably when it requires most paternity and support actions to be brought within six years of an illegitimate child's birth.

[Moreover,] we are confident that the 6-year statute of limitations is not substantially related to Pennsylvania's interest in avoiding the litigation of stale or fraudulent claims. In a number of circumstances, Pennsylvania permits the issue of paternity to be litigated more than six years after the birth of an illegitimate child. The statute itself permits a suit to be brought more than six years after the child's birth if it is brought within two years of a support payment made by the father. And in other types of suits, Pennsylvania places no limits on when the issue of paternity may be [litigated].

A more recent indication that Pennsylvania does not consider proof problems insurmountable is the enactment by the Pennsylvania Legislature in 1985 of an 18-year statute of limitations for paternity and support actions. To be sure the legislature did not act spontaneously, but rather under the threat of losing some federal funds. [The federal Child Support Enforcement Amendments of 1984 required all States participating in the federal child support program to have procedures to establish the paternity of a child who is less than 18 years old.] Nevertheless, the new statute is a tacit concession that proof problems are not overwhelming. The legislative history of the [Amendments] explains why Congress thought such statutes of limitations are reasonable. Congress adverted to the problem of stale and fraudulent claims, but recognized that increasingly sophisticated tests for genetic markers permit the exclusion of over 99% of those who might be accused of paternity, regardless of the age of the child. This scientific evidence is available throughout the child's minority, and it is an additional reason to doubt that Pennsylvania had a substantial reason for limiting the time within which paternity and support actions could be brought.

We conclude that the Pennsylvania statute does not withstand heightened scrutiny under the Equal Protection Clause. [The] judgment of the Superior Court is reversed, and the case is remanded for further proceedings not inconsistent with this opinion.

Note: Judicially Enforceable Rights and Unmarried Parents

In Gomez v. Perez, 409 U.S. 535 (1973), the Court established the foundation for the decisions in *Mills, Pickett,* and *Clark,* by holding that a state cannot create a judicially enforceable right for children of married parents to seek needed support from their natural fathers and then deny this right to children of unmarried parents. After a hearing on a child's petition for support from Perez, a court found that Perez was the biological father of the child (whose mother was Gomez) and that the child needed the support and maintenance of her father. However, the court dismissed the child's petition because she was born to unmarried parents. The Supreme Court held that this dismissal violated equal protection, relying on *Levy*'s holding that "a State may not create a right of action in favor of children for the wrongful death of a parent and exclude illegitimate children from the benefit of such a right." The more general principle endorsed by *Gomez* was that "a State may not invidiously discriminate against illegitimate children by denying them substantial benefits accorded children generally." The *Gomez* Court acknowledged that it was important to "recognize the lurking problems with respect to proof of paternity" in the context of claims for support by children of unmarried parents. Yet it concluded that while "[t]hose problems are not to be lightly brushed aside, [neither] can they be made into an impenetrable barrier that works to shield otherwise invidious discrimination."

∾ PROBLEM: ADVISING ON LEGISLATION ∾

Assume that after the *Clark* decision is announced, you are asked to provide a legal opinion concerning the constitutionality of new legislation in Pennsylvania that creates a time limit for suits like the one in *Clark*. What time limit do you think is likely to pass constitutional muster? Why?

b. **Workers' Compensation, Welfare, and Social Security Survivors' Benefits**

Weber v. Aetna Casualty & Surety Co.
406 U.S. 164 (1972)

Mr. Justice POWELL delivered the opinion of the Court.

The question before us [concerns] the right of dependent unacknowledged, illegitimate children to recover under Louisiana workmen's compensation laws benefits for the death of their natural father on an equal footing with his dependent legitimate children. We hold that Louisiana's denial of equal recovery rights to dependent unacknowledged illegitimates violates the Equal Protection Clause of the Fourteenth Amendment. [Two children sought to recover compensation benefits when their father, Stokes, died of injuries received during the course of his employment. Stokes and Weber (the mother) had never married. They lived with their children and with four other children born of a marriage between Stokes and another woman who was committed to a mental hospital. Stokes never divorced his wife. The Louisiana workmen's compensation statute defined children to include "only legitimate children, stepchildren, posthumous children, adopted children, and illegitimate children acknowledged under [civil code requirements]." Unacknowledged children of unmarried parents were relegated to the lesser status of "other dependents" who could recover benefits only if the benefits were not exhausted by the surviving dependents in the classification of "children." The children of Stokes and Weber were not eligible for legal "acknowledgement" as their parents "were incapable of contract marriage at the time of conception" because Stokes was already married.]

[Both] the statute in *Levy* [v. Louisiana, 391 U.S. 68 (1968),] and the present case involve state-created compensation schemes, designed to provide close relatives and dependents of a deceased a means of recovery for his often abrupt and accidental death. Both wrongful-death statutes and workmen's compensation codes represent outgrowths and modifications of our basic tort law. The former alleviated the harsh common-law rule under which 'no person could inherit the personal right of another to recover for tortuous injuries to his body'; the latter removed difficult obstacles to recovery in work-related injuries by offering a more certain, though generally less remunerative, compensation. In the instant case, the recovery sought under the workmen's compensation statute was in lieu of an action under the identical death statute which was at issue in *Levy*. Given the similarities in the origins and purposes of these two statutes, and the similarity of Louisiana's pattern of discrimination in recovery rights, it would require a disregard of precedent and the principles of *stare decisis* to hold that *Levy* did not control the facts of the case before us. It makes no difference that illegitimates are not so absolutely or broadly barred here as in *Levy;* the discrimination remains apparent.

[The] Louisiana Supreme Court emphasized strongly the State's interest in protecting "legitimate family relationships," and the regulation and protection of the family unit have indeed been a venerable state concern. We do not question the importance of that interest; what we do question is how the challenged statute will promote it. [It cannot be thought] here that persons will shun illicit relations because the offspring may not one day reap the benefits of workmen's compensation.

It may perhaps be said that statutory distinctions between the legitimate and illegitimate reflect closers family relationships in that the illegitimate is more often not under care in the home of the father nor even supported by him. The illegitimate, so this argument runs, may thus be made less eligible for the statutory recoveries and inheritances reserved for those more likely to be within the ambit of familial care and affection. [This contention] is not compelling in a statutory compensation scheme where dependency on the deceased is a prerequisite to anyone's recovery, and where the acknowledgment so necessary to equal recovery rights may be unlikely to occur or legally impossible to effectuate even where the illegitimate child may be nourished and loved.

[By] limiting recovery to dependents of the deceased, Louisiana substantially lessens the possible problems of locating illegitimate children and of determining uncertain claims of parenthood. Our decision [will] not expand claimants for workmen's compensation beyond those in a direct blood and dependency relationship with the [deceased]. [The] state interest in legitimate family relationships is not served by the statute; the state interest in minimizing problems of proof is not significantly disturbed by our decision. The inferior classification of dependent unacknowledged illegitimates bears, in this instance, no significant relationship to those recognized purposes of recovery which workmen's compensation statutes commendably serve.

[Reversed] and remanded.

Notes

1. *The Rehnquist Dissent.* Justice Rehnquist dissented in *Weber,* noting his support for Justice Harlan's objections to the results in *Levy* and *Glona:* "In [this] case I cannot condemn as irrational Louisiana's distinction between legitimate and illegitimate children. In a statutory compensation scheme such as this, the State must inevitably draw rather fine and arbitrary lines. For example, Louisiana declares that parents will have priority in this scheme over first cousins, regardless of the degree of dependency or affection in any given case. Surely, no one would condemn this classification as violative of the Fourteenth Amendment, since it is likely to reflect fairly the unarticulated intent of the decedent. Similarly, the State might rationally presume that the decedent would have preferred the compensation to go to his legitimate children, rather than those illegitimates whom he has not acknowledged."

2. *Welfare Benefits.* In New Jersey Welfare Rights Organization v. Cahill, 411 U.S. 619 (1973), the Court invalidated a state welfare program rule that limited benefits to families of married adults who have at least one child of both parents, or the "natural" child of one adopted by the other, or a child adopted by both. The trial court had recognized that the classification "operates almost invariably to deny benefits to illegitimate children while granting benefits to those children who are legitimate," but upheld the rule on the ground that its purpose was "to preserve and strengthen traditional family life." The Supreme Court rejected this justification for the state welfare law, relying on the holdings and rationales of *Levy, Weber,* and *Gomez* to hold that welfare benefits "are as indispensable to the health and well-being of illegitimate children as to those who are legitimate." The state interest was viewed as identical to the interest rejected in prior precedents — namely, the condemnation of extramarital relations through the imposition of disabilities on children of unmarried parents. Justice Rehnquist dissented on the grounds that a rational basis for the law could be found, based on the idea that the state was trying to protect certain family units "from dissolution due to the economic vicissitudes of modern life." Justice Rehnquist would have upheld the limit on welfare benefits.

3. *Disability Benefits.* In Jiminez v. Weinberger, 417 U.S. 628 (1974), the Court invalidated a statutory classification relating to the eligibility of children of unmarried parents for disability benefits under the Social Security Act. One group of children was eligible for benefits, even if they were born after the onset of the parent's disability; this group included these subgroups: a) "legitimate" children, b) children capable of inheriting personal property under state intestacy law, and c) children who were "illegitimate" solely because of a "nonobvious defect" in their parents' marriage. Another group of "afterborn" children were not eligible for benefits — namely, all other children of unmarried parents. They were denied benefits, regardless of any showing of dependency. The finding of a violation of the Equal Protection Clause because of the discrimination against the "afterborn" children of unmarried parents was based on the Court's rejection of the government's claim that the classification system was based on the need for trustworthy proof of dependency.

∾ PROBLEM: SURVIVORSHIP BENEFITS ∾

Robert lived with Belmira for 18 years; they had two children but never married. Then they separated and Robert died two years later. Robert never acknowledged in writing his paternity of either child, and his paternity was never determined in a judicial proceeding during his lifetime. Belmira filed an application for "surviving children's benefits" under the federal Social Security Act, on behalf of the two children. Robert did die "insured" under the Act. The Act requires that a survivor's benefit will be provided to a child who is under 18 and "dependent" on an insured parent at the time of the parent's death. A child qualifies as "dependent," in fact, if the child can prove that the insured father was living with or contributing to the child's support at the time of death. Some children are entitled to a presumption of dependency, including the following groups: a) "legitimate" children; b) children who would be entitled to inherit personal property from the insured parent's estate under state intestacy law; and c) children whose decedent parent (i) went through a marriage ceremony with the other parent that would have been valid, or (ii) in writing acknowledged the child to be his child, or (iii) had been decreed by a court to be the child's father, or (iv) had been ordered by a court to support the child because the child was his. After a hearing on Belmira's application, the social security examiner found that Robert was the children's father but that the children were unable to prove that they were "dependents" under the statute. Robert was not living with the children or contributing to their support at the time of his death, and the children did not fit any of the six statutory classifications that created a presumption of dependency. The denial of "surviving children's benefits" was challenged as a violation of equal protection because other children, including all "legitimate" children, are statutorily entitled to survivorship benefits regardless of actual dependency, whereas the children of Robert were not. What arguments can be made on both sides of the constitutional issue? *See* Mathews v. Lucas, 427 U.S. 495 (1976).

3. *Rights of Unmarried Parents to Retain Custody of Their Children*

In Stanley v. Illinois, 405 U.S. 645 (1972), the Supreme Court struck down a law that caused the children of unwed fathers to be declared wards of the state upon the death of their mother. This declaration did not require a hearing on the parental fitness of the father or proof of any neglect of the children by the father. The effect of the declaration was to place the children with court-appointed guardians, and thus to cause the father to lose custody of the children. By contrast, the children of married parents, divorced parents, and unmarried mothers could not legally be separated from their parents or mothers without a hearing on parental fitness and proof of neglect. The *Stanley* Court found that the denial of a "fitness" hearing to an unmarried father was a form of discrimination that violated equal protection. Chief Justice Burger authored a dissent for two justices, arguing that the state could distinguish constitutionally between unwed fathers and mothers because unwed mothers are more readily identifiable and locatable, and because a mother is a more dependable protector. In a decision that is consistent with *Stanley*'s concern with the rights of unwed fathers, the Court invalidated a New York law that treated unwed mothers and unwed fathers differently with respect to their right to block an adoption of their children in Caban v. Mohammed, 441 U.S. 380 (1979). The law allowed an unwed mother to block the adoption of her child simply by withholding consent, but gave an unwed father no such right; instead, an unwed father was required to show that the adoption of his child was not in the child's best interest. In *Caban*, a mother succeeded in gaining the adoption of her child (whose father she had not married) by her husband (whom she married after the breakup of her relationship with the child's father), over the father's objection. The *Caban* Court invalidated the law because the classification that discriminated against unwed fathers "does not bear a substantial relation" to the state's interest in providing adoptive homes for children of unmarried parents. Four justices dissented, arguing that the different treatment of the unwed father in *Caban* was not as harsh as the law in *Stanley* that treated unwed fathers as unfit parents as a matter of law. Because the dissenters endorsed the assumption that the mother "will be the more, and often the only, responsible parent" in the context of adoption proceedings for children of unmarried parents, a state should be allowed to reject a paternal consent requirement in order to facilitate that process.

4. *Immigration Preferences*

In Fiallo v. Bell, 430 U.S. 787 (1977), the Court upheld provisions of the federal Immigration and Nationality Act that distinguished between children of married parents and children of unmarried parents for purposes of the immigration status of "aliens." Under the Act, one group of children (or parents of such children) is allowed entry into the United States without regard to numerical quotas or labor certification requirements, while another group is not. The favored group includes these subgroups: 1) "legitimate" or "legitimated" children, 2) stepchildren, 3) adopted children, and 4) children of unmarried parents who seek an immigration preference by virtue of their relationship with their natural mothers. The disfavored group includes illegitimate children seeking preference by virtue of their relationship with their natural fathers. The *Fiallo* Court emphasized the "limited scope of judicial inquiry into immigration legislation," and noted that Congress presumably had determined that "preferential status is not warranted" for the disfavored group "because of a perceived absence in most cases of close family ties as well as a concern with the serious problems of proof that usually lurk in paternity determinations." *See also* Miller v. Albright, 523 U.S. 420 (1998) (no denial of equal protection based on sex of citizen parent where a "legitimate" child born outside the United States is entitled to citizenship if one citizen is a parent, and where a child of unmarried parents born outside the United States is entitled to citizenship if mother is a citizen, but a child of unmarried parents born outside the United States to a foreign-national mother and father-citizen is entitled to citizenship only if father acknowledges child before age 18).

F. THE RIGHTS OF PERSONS WITH MENTAL DISABILITIES

Should people with mental disabilities be treated differently, for equal protection purposes, than people without disabilities? The Court considered a government classification relating to mentally ill persons in Schweiker v. Wilson, 450 U.S. 221 (1981), which involved the question of whether Congress had the power to deny small monthly cash stipends to "inmates" in public mental institutions, while providing such stipends to inmates of institutions that received Medicaid funds (including public medical hospitals and private mental institutions). The stipends were Supplementary Security Income (SSI) benefits, called a "comfort allowance," and were provided for the purpose of meeting personal needs other than maintenance or medical care. The *Schweiker* plaintiffs argued that a classification based on mental illness required "special justification" because mental illness "greatly resembles other characteristics [found to be] inherently suspect as a means of legislative classification." The Court declined to address that argument, finding that the statute did not "classify directly on the basis of mental health" because some mentally ill individuals received benefits along with non-mentally ill individuals. The Court applied the rational basis standard of equal protection analysis, and upheld the classification. The Court recognized the validity of the asserted government purpose "to avoid spending federal resources on behalf of individuals whose care and treatment" are deemed to be a state responsibility.

The *Schweiker* Court expressly reserved the question as to "what standard of review applies to legislation expressly classifying the mentally ill as a discrete group." Only a few years later, the Court decided to resolve that issue and to retain the rational basis standard for such a classification.

City of Cleburne v. Cleburne Living Center

473 U.S. 432 (1985)

Justice WHITE delivered the opinion of the Court.

A Texas city denied a special use permit for the operation of a group home for the mentally retarded, acting pursuant to a municipal zoning ordinance requiring permits for such homes. The Court of Appeals for the Fifth Circuit held that mental retardation is a "quasi-suspect" classification and that the ordinance violated the Equal Protection Clause because it did not substantially further an important governmental purpose. We hold that a lesser standard of scrutiny is appropriate, but conclude that under [that] the ordinance is invalid as applied. . . .

The Equal Protection Clause of the Fourteenth Amendment commands that no State shall "deny to any person within its jurisdiction the equal protection of the laws," which is essentially a direction that all persons similarly situated should be treated alike. [L]egislation is presumed to be valid and will be sustained if the classification drawn by the statute is rationally related to a legitimate state interest. When social or economic legislation is at issue, the Equal Protection Clause allows the States wide latitude, and the Constitution presumes that even improvident decisions will eventually be rectified by the democratic processes.

The general rule gives way, however, when a statute classifies by race, alienage, or national origin. These factors are so seldom relevant to the achievement of any legitimate state interest that laws grounded in such considerations are deemed to reflect prejudice and antipathy — a view that those in the burdened class are not as worthy or deserving as others. [T]hese laws are subjected to strict scrutiny and will be sustained only if they are suitably tailored to serve a compelling state interest.

[Where] individuals in the group affected by a law have distinguishing characteristics relevant to interests the State has the authority to implement, the courts have been very reluctant, as they should be in our federal system and with our respect for the separation of powers, to closely scrutinize legislative choices as to whether, how, and to what extent those interests should be pursued. In such cases, the Equal Protection Clause requires only a rational means to serve a legitimate end.

[T]he Court of Appeals erred in holding mental retardation a quasi-suspect classification calling for a more exacting standard of judicial review than is normally accorded economic and social legislation. First, it is undeniable [that] those who are mentally retarded have a reduced ability to cope with and function in the everyday world. [T]hey range from those whose disability is not immediately evident to those who must be constantly cared for. They are thus different, immutably so, in relevant respects, and the States' interest in dealing with and providing for them is plainly a legitimate one. How this large and diversified group is to be treated [is] very much a task for legislators guided by qualified professionals and not by the perhaps ill-informed opinions of the judiciary. Heightened scrutiny inevitably involves substantive judgments about legislative decisions, and we doubt that the predicate for such judicial oversight is present where the classification deals with mental retardation. Second, the distinctive legislative response, both national and state, to the plight of those who are mentally retarded demonstrates not only that they have unique problems, but also [that] lawmakers have [addressed] their difficulties in a manner that belies a continuing antipathy or prejudice. . . . [T]he Federal Government has not only outlawed discrimination against the mentally retarded in federally funded programs, but it has also provided the retarded with the right to receive "appropriate treatment, services, and habilitation" in a setting that is "least restrictive of [their] personal liberty." In addition, the Government has conditioned federal education funds on a State's assurance that retarded children will enjoy an education that, "to the maximum extent appropriate," is integrated with that of nonmentally retarded children. The Government has also facilitated the hiring of the mentally retarded into the federal civil service by exempting them from the requirement of competitive examination. The State of Texas has similarly enacted legislation that acknowledges the special status of the mentally retarded by conferring certain rights upon them, such as "the right to live in the least restrictive setting appropriate to [their] individual needs and abilities," including "the right to live [in] a group home." [Such] legislation thus singling out the retarded for special treatment reflects the real and undeniable differences between the retarded and others. . . . It may be [that] legislation designed to benefit, rather than disadvantage, the retarded would generally withstand examination under a test of heightened scrutiny. . . . Third, the legislative response, which could hardly have occurred and survived without public support, negates any claim that the mentally retarded are politically powerless in the sense that they have no ability to attract the attention of the lawmakers. . . . Fourth, if the large and amorphous class of the mentally retarded were deemed quasi-suspect[,] it would be difficult to find a principled way to distinguish a variety of other groups who have perhaps immutable disabilities setting them off from others. . . . One need mention in this respect only the aging, the disabled, the mentally ill, and the infirm. We are reluctant to set out on that course, and we decline to do so.

Doubtless, there have been and there will continue to be instances of discrimination against the retarded that are in fact invidious, and that are properly subject to judicial correction under constitutional norms. But the appropriate method of reaching such instances is not to create a new quasi-suspect classification and subject all governmental action based on that classification to more searching evaluation. Rather, we should look to the likelihood that governmental action premised on a particular classification is valid as a general matter, not merely to the specifics of the case before us. Because mental retardation is a characteristic that the government may legitimately take into account in a wide range of decisions, and because both State and Federal Governments have recently committed themselves to assisting the retarded, we will not presume that any given legislative action, even one that disadvantages retarded individuals, is rooted in considerations that the Constitution will not tolerate.

Our refusal to recognize the retarded as a quasi-suspect class does not leave them entirely unprotected from invidious discrimination. To withstand equal protection review, legislation that distinguishes between the mentally retarded and others must be rationally related to a legitimate governmental purpose. This standard [affords] government the latitude necessary both to pursue policies designed to assist the retarded in realizing their full potential, and to freely and efficiently engage in activities that burden the retarded in what is essentially an incidental manner. The State may not rely on a classification whose relationship to an asserted goal is so attenuated as to render the distinction arbitrary or irrational. Furthermore, some objectives such as "a bare [desire] to harm a politically unpopular group," are not legitimate state interests. Beyond that, the mentally retarded, like others, have and retain their substantive constitutional rights in addition to the right to be treated equally by the law.

[The] city does not require a special use permit in an R-3 zone for apartment houses, multiple-dwellings, boarding and lodging houses, fraternity or sorority houses, dormitories, apartment hotels, hospitals, sanitariums, nursing homes for convalescents or the aged (other than for the insane or feebleminded or alcoholics or drug addicts), private clubs or fraternal orders, and other specified uses. It does, however, insist on a special permit for [a] facility for the mentally retarded. May the city require the permit for this facility when other care and multiple-dwelling facilities are freely permitted? [T]he record does not reveal any rational basis for believing that [the] home would pose any special threat to the city's legitimate interests. [W]e affirm the judgment below insofar as it holds the ordinance invalid as applied in this case.

[The] City Council's insistence on the permit rested on several factors. First, the Council was concerned with the negative attitude of the majority of property owners [as] well as with the fears of elderly residents. . . . But mere negative attitudes, or fear, unsubstantiated by factors which are properly cognizable in a zoning proceeding, are not permissible bases for treating a home for the mentally retarded differently from apartment houses, multiple dwellings, and the like. [T]he electorate as a whole, whether by referendum or otherwise, could not order city action violative of the Equal Protection Clause, and the city may not avoid the strictures of that Clause by deferring to the wishes or objections of some fraction of the body politic. "Private biases may be outside the reach of the law, but the law cannot, directly or indirectly, give them effect."

Second, the Council had two objections to the location of the facility. It was concerned that the facility was across the street from a junior high school, and it feared that the students might harass the occupants of [the] home. But the school itself is attended by about 30 mentally retarded students, and denying a permit based on such vague, undifferentiated fears is again permitting some portion of the community to validate what would otherwise be an equal protection violation.

The other objection to the home's location was that it was located on "a five hundred year flood plain." This concern with the possibility of a flood, however, can hardly be based on a distinction between [this] home and, for example, nursing homes, homes for convalescents or the aged, or sanitariums or hospitals, any of which could be located on [the] site without obtaining a special use permit. The same may be said of another concern of the Council — doubts about the legal responsibility for actions which the mentally retarded might take. If there is no concern about legal responsibility with respect to other uses that would be permitted in the area, such as boarding and fraternity houses, it is difficult to believe that the groups of mildly or moderately mentally retarded individuals [would] present any different or special hazard.

Fourth, the Council was concerned with the size of the home and the number of people that would occupy it. [But] there would be no restrictions on the number of people who could occupy this home as a boarding house, nursing home, family dwelling, fraternity house, or dormitory. [R]equiring the permit in this case appears to us to rest on an irrational prejudice against the mentally retarded, including those who would occupy [the] facility and who would live under the closely supervised and highly regulated conditions expressly provided for by state and federal law.

The judgment of the Court of Appeals is affirmed insofar as it invalidates the zoning ordinance as applied to the Featherston home. The judgment is otherwise vacated, and the case is remanded.

It is so ordered.

Justice STEVENS, with whom THE CHIEF JUSTICE joins, concurring.

[O]ur cases reflect a continuum of judgmental responses to differing classifications [ranging] from "strict scrutiny" at one extreme to "rational basis" at the other. I have never been persuaded that these so-called "standards" adequately explain the decisional process. . . . [The] term "rational," of course, includes a requirement that an impartial lawmaker could logically believe that the classification would serve a legitimate public purpose that transcends the harm to the members of the disadvantaged class. . . . The rational-basis test [adequately] explains why a law that deprives a person of the right to vote because his skin has a different pigmentation than that of other voters violates the Equal Protection Clause. . . . None of these attributes has any bearing at all on the citizen's willingness or ability to exercise that civil right. We do not need to apply a special standard, or to apply "strict scrutiny," or even "heightened scrutiny," to decide such cases. . . .

Every law that places the mentally retarded in a special class is not presumptively irrational. The differences between mentally retarded persons and those with greater mental capacity are obviously relevant to certain legislative decisions. An impartial lawmaker [could] rationally vote in favor of a law providing funds for special education and special treatment for the mentally retarded. A mentally retarded person could also recognize that he is a member of a class that might need special supervision in some situations, both to protect himself and to protect others. Restrictions on his right to drive cars or to operate hazardous equipment might well seem rational even though they deprived him of employment opportunities and the kind of freedom of travel enjoyed by other citizens.

Justice MARSHALL, with whom Justice BRENNAN and Justice BLACKMUN join, concurring in the judgment in part and dissenting in part.

[M]ental retardation per se cannot be a proxy for depriving retarded people of their rights and interests without regard to variations in individual ability. . . .

The Equal Protection Clause requires attention to the capacities and needs of retarded people as individuals. . . . [The] Court holds the ordinance invalid on rational-basis grounds and disclaims that anything special, in the form of heightened scrutiny, is taking place. Yet Cleburne's ordinance surely would be valid under the traditional rational-basis test applicable to economic and commercial regulation. [I] dissent from [the] Court's disclaimer that no "more exacting standard" than ordinary rational-basis review is being applied. . . .

[T]he level of scrutiny employed in an equal protection case should vary with "the constitutional and societal importance of the interest adversely affected and the recognized invidiousness of the basis upon which the particular classification is drawn." When a zoning ordinance works to exclude the retarded from all residential districts in a community, these two considerations require that the ordinance be convincingly justified as substantially furthering legitimate and important purposes. . . . First, the interest of the retarded in establishing group homes is substantial. . . . Excluding group homes deprives the retarded of much of what makes for human freedom and fulfillment—the ability to form bonds and take part in the life of a community. . . . Second, the mentally retarded have been subject to a "lengthy and tragic history" of segregation and discrimination that can only be called grotesque. . . .

In light of the importance of the interest at stake and the history of discrimination the retarded have suffered, the Equal Protection Clause requires us to do more than review the distinctions drawn by Cleburne's zoning ordinance as if they appeared in a taxing statute or in economic or commercial legislation. . . . For the retarded[,] much has changed in recent years, but much remains the same; outdated statutes are still on the books, and irrational fears or ignorance, traceable to the prolonged social and cultural isolation of the retarded, continue to stymie recognition of the dignity and individuality of retarded people. Heightened judicial scrutiny of action appearing to impose unnecessary barriers to the retarded is required in light of increasing recognition that such barriers are inconsistent with evolving principles of equality embedded in the Fourteenth Amendment.

Notes

1. *The Classification of Mentally Retarded Persons.* As the *City of Cleburne* Court noted, mentally retarded individuals fall into four "distinct" categories. Eighty-nine percent are "mildly" retarded with IQs between 50 and 70, 6 percent are "moderately" retarded with IQs between 35 and 50, and 5 percent are either severely or profoundly retarded with IQs between 20 and 35 or below 20. However, as *Cleburne* noted, "Mental retardation is not defined by reference to intelligence or IQ alone, however. The American Association on Mental Deficiency (AAMD) has defined mental retardation as 'significantly subaverage general intellectual functioning existing concurrently with deficits in adaptive behavior and manifested during the developmental period.' Mental retardation is caused by a variety of factors, some genetic, some environmental, and some unknown."

2. *The Rehabilitation Act.* In recent years, legislation has been passed that shows sensitivity to the needs of mentally retarded persons, including the Rehabilitation Act of 1973 (outlawing discrimination against the mentally retarded in federally funded programs); the Developmental Disabilities Assistance and Bill of Rights Act (guaranteeing "treatment, services and habilitation" in a setting that is "least restrictive of [their] personal liberty"); the Education of the Handicapped Act (states receive federal education funds on the condition that retarded children enjoy an education that is integrated with that of non-mentally retarded children "to the maximum extent appropriate"); and legislation that facilitates "the hiring of the mentally retarded into the federal civil service by exempting them from the requirement of competitive examination."

3. *The As-Applied Remedy in City of Cleburne.* Justice Marshall's dissent in *City of Cleburne* objected to the Court's use of a "novel and truncated" remedy that was to invalidate the ordinance only as it applied to the plaintiff group home, instead of invalidating the ordinance on its face. By contrast, the *City of Cleburne* majority preferred an as-applied inquiry that required a constitutional invalidation of the statute. The Court described this approach as "the preferred course of adjudication since it enables courts to avoid making unnecessarily broad constitutional judgments."

∾ PROBLEMS ∾

1. *Should Mental Disability Classifications Be Regarded as Suspect?* When we examined racial classifications, we saw that the Court has historically treated them as suspect for a variety of reasons, including the fact that race is immutable, it generally bears no rational relationship to one's ability (or lack of ability), and there has been a long history of discrimination (both de jure and de facto) on the basis of race. Do these factors provide insight into the question of whether classifications based on mental disability should be subjected to strict scrutiny? Are there other factors that should be considered? Do these factors suggest that classifications based on mental disability should be subjected to rational basis review or to a higher standard? If a higher standard, which one?

2. *Advising the City.* You have been asked by the city council of Cleburne for advice on the types of future applications of the zoning ordinance that might be upheld under the Equal Protection Clause. Do any examples come to mind? If so, describe them. What are the benefits of redrafting the ordinance to achieve narrower objectives instead of leaving the ordinance on the books and applying it to future applicants?

3. *Commitment to Mental Institutions.* A state law provides that mentally ill persons may be involuntarily committed to an institution based on a higher burden of proof than what applies to mentally retarded persons. Mentally ill persons may be institutionalized against their will pursuant to the beyond a reasonable doubt standard.. The standard that governs involuntary commitment of mentally retarded persons is clear and convincing evidence. What version of rational basis review should govern an equal protection challenge to the criteria governing

involuntary commitment of mentally ill persons? How should this issue be resolved? *See* Heller v. Doe, 509 U.S. 312 (1993).

G. SEXUAL ORIENTATION/SEXUAL PREFERENCE

What standard of review should apply to distinctions based on sexual orientation? For some time, the most contentious issues in sexual orientation cases have involved the protection of sexual intimacy against criminal sodomy laws and same-sex marriage. Bowers v. Hardwick, 476 U.S. 186 (1986), upheld criminal sodomy laws and rejected claims of due process violations based on sexual orientation. However, *Bowers* did not close the door to constitutional challenges to classifications intended to require different treatment based on sexual orientation. In Romer v. Evans, 517 U.S. 620 (1996), the majority of the Supreme Court, applying rational basis scrutiny, held that legislation discriminating against homosexuals violates the Equal Protection Clause. Finally, in Texas v. Lawrence, the Court overturned *Bowers* and extended constitutional protections to homosexual activities.

At the moment, there is considerable litigation regarding the rights of same-sex partners to marry. For example, the Supreme Court of Massachusetts upheld a lower court ruling that struck down the state's marriage licensing laws because they allowed for only marriage between a man and a woman, and did not permit marriage between couples of the same sex. *See* Goodridge v. Department of Public Health, 440 Mass. 309 (2003). Earlier decisions in Hawaii and Vermont also struck down marriage laws that defined marriage as between a man and a woman as violating state equal protection norms. Baker v. State, 744 A.2d 864 (Vt. 1999); Baehr v. Lewin, 74 Haw. 530, 852 P.2d 44 (1993). In *Goodridge*, the Massachusetts court held that barring an individual from marrying someone of the same sex violated the state constitution. The state has failed to identify any constitutionally adequate reason for denying civil marriage to same-sex couples and penalizes their children by denying them benefits because of the sexual orientation of their parents. The sine qua non of marriage is the exclusive and permanent commitment to another individual, not procreation, the optimal setting for child rearing, and the preservation of scarce state and private financial resources. *Marriage* should be defined as "the voluntary union of two persons as spouses." Massachusetts interpreted the scope of protection afforded by *Lawrence* much more broadly than did the Arizona court a month earlier. *See also* Halpern v. Attorney General, *http://www.Ontariocourts.on.ca/decisions/2003/june/halpernC39172.htm.* Likewise, in Varnum v. Brien, 763 N.W.2d 862 (Iowa, 2009), the Iowa Supreme Court issued an opinion that was broadly supportive of same-sex marriage. The Court held that same-sex couples were similarly situated as opposite-sex couples with respect to the subject and purposes of the state's marriage laws; that sexual orientation was a quasi-suspect classification requiring the application of heightened scrutiny; that society could not show that protection of traditional marriage between a man and a woman was an important governmental objective; that the existing law (limiting marriage to a man and a woman) was not "substantially related" to the government objective of ensuring that children are raised in an optimal environment; that the statute was not "substantially related" to the government goals of promoting procreation, promoting the stability of opposite-sex relationships, and conserving state resources; that religious opposition to same-sex marriage could not be regarded as a government interest supporting the statute; and therefore that the statutory language limiting civil marriage to a man and a woman was invalid.

On the other hand, 36 states have enacted laws declaring that same-sex marriages are void and that same-sex marriage licenses from other states are not recognized as valid. In November 2004, 11 states gave overwhelming approval to constitutional amendments banning same-sex marriage; some banned all cohabiting couples from receiving domestic partner benefits. For various views on the issue of same-sex marriage and whether the courts, the legislature, or the voters should decide its fate, see Stephen A. Newman, *The Use and Abuse of Social Science in the Same-Sex Marriage Debate*, 2004, *http://ssrn.com/abstract=569302;* David D. Meyer, *Domesticating Lawrence*, 2004, *http://ssrn.com/abstract=593902;* Cass Sunstein, *Sexual Orientation and the Constitution: A Note on the Relationship Between Due Process and Equal Protection*, 55 U. Chi. L. Rev. 1161 (1988).

Congress has passed the Defense of Marriage Act, which authorizes states to deny full faith and credit to same-sex marriages. Likewise, in Standhardt v. Superior Court Maricopa County, 206 Ariz. 276, 77 P.3d 451 (Ariz. Ct. App. 2003), an Arizona court reasoned that *Lawrence* did not recognize a fundamental right to enter a same-sex marriage. The state court found the Arizona ban on same-sex marriage rationally related to the state's legitimate interest in promoting procreation and child rearing within marriage, and concluded that there is no fundamental right to same-sex marriage "deeply rooted in the state constitutional protection of fundamental liberty interest." Fundamental rights are those that are firmly rooted in the state's history and tradition and implicit in the concept of ordered liberty that may, or may not, be shared with the rest of the country. The majority applied rational basis review (with a bite) and struck down the ban on same-sex marriage. The court also converged its due process and equal protection analyses.

In Commonwealth of Massachusetts v. U.S. Dept. of Health and Human Services, C.A. No. 1:09-11156-JLT (July 8, 2010), Judge Joseph Tauro of the federal district court granted summary judgment to the plaintiff commonwealth and struck down Section 3 of the federal Defense of Marriage Act, 1 U.S.C. §7. The law stated, in pertinent part:

> In determining the meaning of any Act of Congress, or of any ruling, regulation, or interpretation of the various administrative bureaus and agencies of the United States, the word "marriage" means only a legal union between one man and one woman as husband and wife, and the word "spouse" refers only to a person of the opposite sex who is a husband or a wife.

Consequently, any same-sex partners who were legally married under Massachusetts law would not be considered married under the federal law. The court considered Tenth Amendment and Spending Clause challenges to conclude:

> That the Supreme Court, over the past century, has repeatedly offered family law as an example of a quintessential area of state concern, also persuades this court that marital status determinations are an attribute of state sovereignty. For instance, in [U.S. v.] *Morrison*, the Supreme Court noted that an overly expansive view of the Commerce Clause could lead to federal legislation of "family law and other areas of traditional state regulation since the aggregate effect of marriage, divorce, and childrearing on the national economy is undoubtedly significant." Similarly, in Elk Grove Unified Sch. Dist. v. Newdow, the Supreme Court observed "that '[t]he whole subject of the domestic relations of husband and wife, parent and child, belongs to the laws of the States and not to the laws of the United States.'"

Moreover, state and lower court decisions have not been uniform in their recognition of the right to same-sex marriage.

Undoubtedly, the same-sex marriage issue will be resolved in the next few years because of events in California. In 2000, California voters adopted Proposition 22, entitled the California Defense of Marriage Act, which amended the state's Family Code by adding this language: "Only marriage between a man and a woman is valid or recognized in California." Cal. Fam. Code §308.5. Passage of the initiative was followed in 2004 by the mayor of San Francisco's decision to instruct county officials to issue marriage licenses to same-sex couples. The following month, the California Supreme Court ordered San Francisco to stop issuing such licenses and later nullified the marriage licenses that same-sex couples had received. *See* Lockyer v. City & County of San Francisco, 33 Cal. 4th 1055, 17 Cal. Rptr. 3d 225, 95 P.3d 459 (2004). Shortly thereafter, San Francisco and various other parties filed state court actions challenging or defending California's exclusion of same-sex couples from marriage under the state constitution, and the California Supreme Court invalidated Proposition 22, holding that all California counties were required to issue marriage licenses to same-sex couples. *See In re Marriage Cases*, 76 Cal. Rptr. 3d 683, 183 P.3d 384. From June 17, 2008, until the passage of Proposition 8 in November of that year, San Francisco and other California counties issued approximately 18,000 marriage licenses to same-sex couples. At that time, California adopted Proposition 8, which provides: "Only marriage between a man and a woman is valid or recognized in California." Proposition 8 was challenged by Kristin Perry and Sandra Stier, who reside in Berkeley, California, and raise four children together, and by Jeffrey Zarrillo and Paul Katami, who reside in Burbank, California. Plaintiffs who seek to marry their partners and have been denied marriage licenses by their respective county authorities on the basis of Proposition 8 claimed that Proposition 8 violates their federal constitutional rights. In Perry v. Schwarzenegger, [704 F. Supp. 2d 921] (N.D. Cal. 2010), a federal trial court struck down Proposition 8 as a violation of the Due Process Clause of the Fourteenth Amendment. Undoubtedly, this case will eventually make its way to the U.S. Supreme Court.

∼ PROBLEMS ∼

1. *Higher Review for Gay and Lesbian Classifications?* Throughout this chapter, we have focused on factors that suggest that a particular equal protection classification should be subject to a higher level of scrutiny. What factors suggest that classifications affecting gays and lesbians should be subjected to a higher level of review? For example, is homosexual behavior immutable? Have gays been subject to a history of discrimination? Does homosexual behavior have any correlation with ability or performance? How might you argue that classifications affecting homosexuals should not be subject to heightened scrutiny? How would you argue for the contrary proposition?

2. *The Defense of Marriage Act.* Under the Defense of Marriage Act (DOMA), Congress authorized the states to deny full faith and credit to same-sex marriages. John Romer and Sam Johnson were married in Massachusetts following the *Goodridge* decision. Shortly thereafter, Romer accepted a job in Kentucky, and the couple moved to Louisville. Romer and Johnson are disturbed by the fact that Kentucky does not recognize their marriage or treat them as married individuals. Relying on the Equal Protection Clause of the U.S. Constitution, Romer and Johnson file suit challenging DOMA. Should they prevail? If you represented Romer and Johnson, how would you argue the case on their behalf? How might the state respond? *See* Comment, *Litigating the Defense of Marriage Act: The Next Battleground for Same Sex Marriage,* 117 Harv. L. Rev. 2684 (2004).

3. *Framing Arguments.* Following the holdings in *Lawrence* and *Goodridge,* and fearing that their own state supreme courts might render similar decisions, a number of politicians sponsored state constitutional amendments prohibiting same-sex marriage. In the 2004 elections, some of these constitutional amendments passed. Do these constitutional amendments prevent the courts from imposing same-sex marriage in the affected states? Now, suppose that you represent a group that wants to challenge the constitutional amendments as a violation of the U.S. Constitution. How would you frame your arguments?

4. *Congress's Power to Define Marriage.* Under the Constitution, does Congress retain the power to legislatively define marriage? Does it matter that various federal laws (e.g., income tax laws, social security laws, military laws) define marriage for federal purposes? Should, therefore, Congress have the right to define the subject? In this respect, consider the language from *Goodridge:* "The genius of our federal system is that each State's Constitution has vitality specific to its own traditions and that, subject to the minimum requirements of the Fourteenth Amendment, each state is free to address difficult issues of individual liberty in the manner its own constitution demands."

5. *A Constitutional Amendment?* During the 2004 presidential election, President George W. Bush repeatedly called for a constitutional amendment that would preclude the federal courts from recognizing same-sex marriage as a constitutional right. Suppose that you represent a fundamentalist religious group that opposes same-sex marriage. Would you advise the group that the amendment is necessary (because, otherwise, the "imperial" courts might impose their views regarding same-sex marriage in the guise of constitutional interpretation)?

If, instead of representing the fundamentalist group, you instead represented a gay and lesbian group, how would you argue that a constitutional amendment should be defeated?

6. *More on the Diversity Initiative.* Let's return to the problem described at the beginning of the chapter. Suppose that NWU decides to offer preferential admissions and financial aid to gay, lesbian, and transgender students. NWU believes that such students bring diverse perspectives to the classroom, that such students have suffered from social disadvantage and stigma, and that therefore they deserve preferences. What standard of review would the courts apply to these preferences? Are the preferences likely to be upheld or struck down?

H. THE FUNDAMENTAL RIGHTS STRAND OF EQUAL PROTECTION

Equal protection interests are implicated when government classifies for purposes of distributing burdens or benefits. A heightened standard of review may be triggered when discrimination is a function of group status. It also may be generated when a fundamental right has been denied on a selective basis. In this instance, the nature of the group is irrelevant. What counts, for purposes of elevating the standard of review, is the discriminatory deprivation of a fundamental right.

Fundamental rights analysis in the equal protection context parallels the standards of review and controversies that arise in the due process context. Insofar as a textually enumerated right or liberty is selectively denied, such as freedom of speech, the standard of review for the alleged equal protection and First Amendment violation will be coextensive. Protection of rights and liberties not set forth by the Constitution itself engenders the same debate encountered in the due process setting. In either instance, the judiciary's power to identify and develop fundamental rights minus textual enumeration is a central issue. Competing perspectives have vied in the context of economic liberty and its contours in the early twentieth century and the right of privacy and its incidents over the past several decades. The debate generally has not extended to the right to vote and the right to travel. The right to vote, though not specifically provided by the Constitution, generally is understood to be implicit in a system of representative governance. Likewise, the right to travel can be viewed as a logical extension of a viable union. The Privileges and Immunities Clause of Article IV, Section II provides an additional predicate for this guarantee.

In determining whether due process or equal protection analysis governs the deprivation of a fundamental right or liberty, it is important to focus on the impact of the violation. Government action that operates in a broad-spectrum manner and thus denies a right or liberty to all persons is reviewable under the Due Process Clause. Equal protection interests are implicated only when the deprivation is directed at a particular subset of persons. The right of privacy, which includes the choice to have an abortion, the right to marry and procreate, family structure interests, and the right to refuse unwanted medical treatment, is discussed from a due process perspective in Chapter 7. The equal protection dimensions are not discussed in this chapter, which focuses on actual and proposed rights and liberties that are not grounded in the Due Process Clause itself.

1. Freedom of Speech

Equal protection interests intersect First Amendment concerns when government discriminates on the basis of content or viewpoint. The significance of this convergence was noted in Police Department of Chicago v. Mosley, 408 U.S. 92, 95 (1972), where the Court observed:

> [u]nder the Equal Protection Clause, not to mention the First Amendment itself, government may not grant the use of a forum to people whose views it finds acceptable, but deny use to those wishing to express less favored or more controversial views. And it may not select which issues are worth discussing or debating in public facilities. There is an "equality of status in the field of ideas," and government must afford all points of view an equal opportunity to be heard.

This sense of equal opportunity in the marketplace of ideas is a fundamental predicate for First Amendment jurisprudence relating to public forum management. The basic principle is that when a forum is opened to assembly or speaking, individuals may not be excluded on the basis of content or viewpoint.

2. Access to the Justice System: The Right to Counsel

Case law relating to an individual's access to the justice system, or the rights therein, implicates both equal protection and procedural due process issues. It also comprehends specific constitutional guarantees and other incidents of fairness.

The Sixth Amendment gives the accused "[i]n all criminal prosecutions . . . the Assistance of Counsel for his defense." U.S. Const., Amend. VI. In Gideon v. Wainwright, 372 U.S. 335 (1963), the Court determined that this guarantee was incorporated through the Fourteenth Amendment. Indigent defendants thus were entitled to state-appointed counsel in the event they could not afford their representation.

The equal protection guarantee has been the basis for extending the right to counsel to the appellate process. In Douglas v. California, 368 U.S. 815 (1963), the Court determined that the state must appoint counsel to indigent appellants when pursuing a first appeal as a matter of right. Consistent with this marking, the Court declined to extend the right to the circumstances of a discretionary appeal. Ross v. Moffitt, 417 U.S. 600 (1974). As the Douglas Court saw it, the state had etched "an unconstitutional line between rich and poor" that it was obligated to erase. This result cuts against the general current of constitutional law insofar as government typically is not required to subsidize the exercise of a right or liberty. *E.g.,* Harris v. McRae, 448 U.S. 297 (1980) (no government duty to subsidize a woman's abortion).

Case law concerning subsidized access to counsel and other support systems in the criminal justice process has referenced both equal protection and due process concerns. As the Court noted in Bearden v. Georgia, different inquiries are required pursuant to each guarantee. Due process analysis focuses on the fairness of the relationship between the defendant and the criminal justice process, whereas equal protection inquiry centers on whether the defendant invidiously has been denied an important benefit afforded other classes of defendants.

Bearden v. Georgia
461 U.S. 660 (1983)

Justice O'CONNOR delivered the opinion of the Court.

[This] Court has long been sensitive to the treatment of indigents in our criminal justice system. Over a quarter-century ago, Justice Black declared that "[there] can be no equal justice where the kind of trial a man gets depends on the amount of money he has." Griffin v. Illinois, 351 U.S. 12 (1956). *Griffin's* principle of "equal justice," which the Court applied there to strike down a state practice of granting appellate review only to persons able to afford a trial transcript, has been applied in numerous other contexts. *See, e.g.,* Douglas v. California (indigent entitled to counsel on first direct appeal); Roberts v. LaVallee (indigent entitled to free transcript of preliminary hearing for use at trial); Mayer v. Chicago, 404 U.S. 189 (1971) (indigent cannot be denied an adequate record to appeal a conviction under a fine-only statute). Most relevant to the issue here is the holding in Williams v. Illinois, 339 U.S. 235 (1970), that a State cannot subject a certain class of convicted defendants to a period of imprisonment beyond the statutory maximum solely because they are too poor to pay the fine. *Williams* was followed and extended in Tate v. Short, 401 U.S. 395 (1971), which held that a State cannot convert a fine imposed under a fine-only statute into a jail term solely because the defendant is indigent and cannot immediately pay the fine in full. But the Court has also recognized limits on the principle of protecting indigents in the criminal justice system. For example, in Ross v. Moffitt, 417 U.S. 600 (1974), we held that indigents had no constitutional right to appointed counsel for a discretionary appeal. In United States v. MacCollum, 426 U.S. 317 (1976), we rejected an equal protection challenge to a federal statute which permits a district court to provide an indigent with a free trial transcript only if the court certifies that the challenge to his conviction is not frivolous and the transcript is necessary to prepare his petition.

Due process and equal protection principles converge [in] these cases. [We] generally analyze the fairness of relations between the criminal defendant and the State under the Due Process Clause, while we approach the question whether the State has invidiously denied one class of defendants a substantial benefit available to another class of defendants under the Equal Protection Clause.

The question presented here is whether a sentencing court can revoke a defendant's probation for failure to pay the imposed fine and restitution, absent evidence and findings that the defendant was somehow responsible for the failure or that alternative forms of punishment were inadequate. . . . There is no doubt that the State has treated the petitioner differently from a person who did not fail to pay the imposed fine and therefore did not violate probation. To determine whether this differential treatment violates the Equal Protection Clause, one must determine whether, and under what circumstances, a defendant's indigent status may be considered in the decision whether to revoke probation. This is substantially similar to asking directly the due process question of whether and when it is fundamentally unfair or arbitrary for the State to revoke probation when an indigent is unable to pay the fine. Whether analyzed in terms of equal protection or due process, the issue [requires] a careful inquiry into such factors as "the nature of the individual interest affected, the extent to which it is affected, the rationality of the connection between legislative means and purpose, [and] the existence of alternative means for effectuating the purpose." . . .

The rule of *Williams* and *Tate* [is] that the State cannot "'[impose] a fine as a sentence and then automatically [convert] it into a jail term solely because the defendant is indigent and cannot forthwith pay the fine in full.'" [A] distinction, based on the reasons for nonpayment, is of critical importance here. If the probationer has willfully refused to pay the fine or restitution when he has the means to pay, the State is perfectly justified in using imprisonment as a sanction to enforce collection. Similarly, a probationer's failure to make sufficient bona fide efforts to seek employment or borrow money in order to pay the fine or restitution may reflect an insufficient concern for paying the debt he owes to society for his crime. In such a situation, the State is likewise justified in revoking probation and using imprisonment as an appropriate penalty for the offense. But if the probationer has made all reasonable efforts to pay the fine or restitution, and yet cannot do so through no fault of his own, it is fundamentally unfair to revoke probation automatically without considering whether adequate alternative methods of punishing the defendant are available. This lack of fault provides a "substantial [reason] which [justifies] or [mitigates] the violation and [makes] revocation inappropriate." [The] State, of course, has a fundamental interest in appropriately punishing persons—rich and poor—who violate its criminal laws. A defendant's poverty in no way immunizes him from punishment. Thus, when determining initially whether the State's penological interests require imposition of a term of imprisonment, the sentencing court can consider the entire background of the defendant, including his employment history and financial resources.

The decision to place the defendant on probation, however, reflects a determination by the sentencing court that the State's penological interests do not require imprisonment. A probationer's failure to make reasonable efforts to repay his debt to society may indicate that this original determination needs reevaluation, and imprisonment may now be required to satisfy the State's interests. But a probationer who has made sufficient bona fide efforts to pay his fine and restitution, and who has complied with the other conditions of probation, has demonstrated a willingness to pay his debt to society and an ability to conform his conduct to social norms. The State nevertheless asserts three reasons why imprisonment is required to further its penal goals.

[We] hold, therefore, that in revocation proceedings for failure to pay a fine or restitution, a sentencing court must inquire into the reasons for the failure to pay. If the probationer willfully refused to pay or failed to make sufficient bona fide efforts legally to acquire the resources to pay, the court may revoke probation and sentence the defendant to imprisonment within the authorized range of its sentencing authority. If the probationer could not pay despite sufficient bona fide efforts to acquire the resources to do so, the court must consider alternative measures of punishment other than imprisonment. Only if alternative measures are not adequate to meet the State's interests in punishment and deterrence may the court imprison a probationer who has made sufficient bona fide efforts to pay. To do otherwise would deprive the probationer of his conditional freedom simply because, through no fault of his own, he cannot pay the fine. Such a deprivation would be contrary to the fundamental fairness required by the Fourteenth Amendment.

[At] the probation revocation hearing, the petitioner and his wife testified about their lack of income and assets and of his repeated efforts to obtain work. [T]he sentencing court [made] no finding that the petitioner had not made sufficient bona fide efforts to find work, and the record as it presently stands would not justify such a finding. . . . The focus of the court's concern, then, was that the petitioner had disobeyed a prior court order to pay the fine, and for that reason must be imprisoned. . . . By sentencing petitioner to imprisonment simply because he could not pay the fine, without considering the reasons for the inability to pay or the propriety of reducing the fine or extending the time for payments or making alternative orders, the court automatically turned a fine into a prison sentence.

If, upon remand, the Georgia courts determine that petitioner did not make sufficient bona fide efforts to pay his fine, or determine that alternative punishment is not adequate to meet the State's interests in punishment and deterrence, imprisonment would be a permissible sentence. Unless such determinations are made, however, fundamental fairness requires that the petitioner remain on probation.

The judgment is reversed, and the case remanded for further proceedings not inconsistent with this opinion.

It is so ordered.

Justice WHITE, with whom THE CHIEF JUSTICE, Justice POWELL, and Justice REHNQUIST join, concurring in the judgment.

[When] probation is revoked for failure to pay a fine, I find nothing in the Constitution to prevent the trial court from revoking probation and imposing a term of imprisonment if revocation does not automatically result in the imposition of a long jail term and if the sentencing court makes a good-faith effort to impose a jail sentence that in terms of the State's sentencing objectives will be roughly equivalent to the fine and restitution that the defendant failed to pay.

Note

Although similar results are achievable pursuant to due process and equal protection review, the focal points of these analytical models are different. Justice Harlan, in Griffin v. Douglas, criticized the Court's "blend of the Equal Protection and Due Process Clauses." He noted that the equal protection guarantee prohibited states from formally discriminating between rich and poor in developing and applying the law. Justice Harlan maintained, however, that the guarantee did not bar states from enacting laws of general applicability that disproportionately affect the poor more severely. As he put it: "[e]very financial exaction which the State imposes on a uniform basis is more easily satisfied by the well-to-do than by the indigent. Yet I take it that no one would dispute the constitutional power of the State to levy a uniform sales tax, to charge tuition at a state university, to fix rates for the purchase of water from a municipal corporation, to impose a standard fine for criminal violations, or to establish minimum bail for certain categories of offenses. Nor could it be contended that the State may not classify as crimes acts which the poor are more likely to commit than are the rich. And surely, there would be no basis for attacking a state law which provided benefits for the needy simply because those benefits fell short of the goods or services that others could purchase for themselves. Laws such as these do not deny equal protection to the less fortunate for one essential reason: the Equal Protection Clause does not impose on the States 'an affirmative duty to lift the handicaps flowing from differences in economic circumstances.'

"To so construe it would read into the Constitution a philosophy of leveling that would be foreign to many of our basic concepts of the proper relations between government and society." Douglas v. California, 372 U.S. 353 (1963) (Harlan, J., dissenting).

∾ PROBLEMS ∾

1. *Imprisoning for Failure to Pay.* A statute converts fines into prison terms for persons unable to make payment. The statute was applied to all offenses, including traffic violations and even offenses that were punishable only by fine in the absence of inability to pay. Does the statute violate the Equal Protection Clause? *See* Tate v. Short, 401 U.S. 395 (1971).

2. *Counsel in Postconviction Proceedings.* Based on the factors that are balanced and accounted for in *Griffin* and its progeny, should counsel be provided to indigent parties in the context of postconviction proceedings? What about claims that the death penalty violates the Eighth Amendment prohibition against cruel and unusual punishment? *See* Murray v. Giarratano, 492 U.S. 1 (1989). What about garden-variety habeas corpus claims?

3. *Bankruptcy Filing Fee.* A majority of the Court in *Boddie* determined that the $60 filing fee denied due process, although two justices would have found an equal protection violation. The Court, in United States v. Kras, 409 U.S. 434 (1973), concluded that a $50 filing fee for voluntary bankruptcy contravened neither the due process nor the equal protection guarantee. With respect to the

equal protection claim in particular, the Court determined that bankruptcy is not as fundamental a concern as marriage. In reviewing whether an indigent plaintiff had to pay a $25 court filing fee to contest the reduction of his welfare benefits, should a court be guided by *Boddie* or *Kras*? *See* Ortwein v. Schwab, 410 U.S. 656 (1973).

4. *Explaining the Vacillation.* Why has the Court vacillated between reference to the due process and the equal protection guarantees in these cases? What, if any, difference does the choice of provision make?

3. The Right to Travel

The Constitution, as previously noted, does not indicate specifically a right to interstate travel. Discerning its fundamental nature may be facilitated by attempting to comprehend a viable political and economic union without a right to travel freely across state lines. Consistent with this reality, the Court evolved the right to travel initially without any grounding in a particular constitutional provision. It thus has been regarded historically as a logical incident of the nation's structure.

As the Court recognized in Saenz v. Roe, 526 U.S. 489 (1999), the right to travel has three separate and distinct components: "It protects the right of a citizen of one State to enter and to leave another State, the right to be treated as a welcome visitor rather than an unfriendly alien when temporarily present in the second State, and for those travelers who elect to become permanent residents, the right to be treated like other citizens of that State. . . ."

For equal protection purposes, the right to travel has been examined most often in connection with residence-based eligibility requirements for public benefits. These cases do not turn upon the state's legitimate interest in establishing bona fide residence. A state law conditioning free education on a student's attendance in the relevant school district, Martinez v. Bynum, 461 U.S. 321 (1983), for instance, reflects this type of law. Although it classifies on the basis of in-state and out-of-state residence, the Court reviews such differentiations pursuant to a rational basis standard. Equal protection issues may rise to a higher level, however, when eligibility for a benefit or right hinges on residence for a designated length of time. Depending on the nature of the benefit, a prolonged delay in qualifying for it may be construed as a burden on the right to interstate travel.

Shapiro v. Thompson

394 U.S. 618 (1969)

Mr. Justice BRENNAN delivered the opinion of the Court.

[This case concerns a challenge to state laws that condition eligibility for welfare benefits on a one-year residence requirement. The] effect of the waiting-period requirement in each case is to create two classes of needy resident families indistinguishable from each other except that one is composed of residents who have resided a year or more, and the second of residents who have resided less than a year, in the jurisdiction. On the basis of this sole difference the first class is granted and the second class is denied welfare aid upon which may depend the ability of the families to obtain the very means to subsist — food, shelter, and other necessities of life. [A]ppellees met the test for residence in their jurisdictions, as well as all other eligibility requirements except the requirement of residence for a full year prior to their applications. . . . Appellees' central contention is that the statutory prohibition of benefits to residents of less than a year creates a classification which constitutes an invidious discrimination denying them equal protection of the laws. We agree. . . .

[A]ppellants justify the waiting-period requirement as a protective device to preserve the fiscal integrity of state public assistance programs. It is asserted that people who require welfare assistance during their first year of residence in a State are likely to become continuing burdens on state welfare programs. Therefore, the argument runs, if such people can be deterred from entering the jurisdiction by denying them welfare benefits during the first year, state programs to assist long-time residents will not be impaired by a substantial influx of indigent newcomers. [We] do not doubt that the one-year waiting period device is well suited to discourage the influx of poor families in need of assistance. An indigent who desires to migrate, resettle, find a new job, and start a new life will doubtless hesitate if he knows that he must risk making the move without the possibility of falling back on state welfare assistance during his first year of residence, when his need may be most acute. But the purpose of inhibiting migration by needy persons into the State is constitutionally impermissible.

This Court long ago recognized that the nature of our Federal Union and our constitutional concepts of personal liberty unite to require that all citizens be free to travel throughout the length and breadth of our land uninhibited by statutes, rules, or regulations which unreasonably burden or restrict this movement. [The] right finds no explicit mention in the Constitution. The reason, it has been suggested, is that a right so elementary was conceived from the beginning to be a necessary concomitant of the stronger Union the Constitution created. In any event, freedom to travel throughout the United States has long been recognized as a basic right under the Constitution. . . . Thus, the purpose of deterring the in-migration of indigents cannot serve as justification for the classification created by the one-year waiting period, since that purpose is constitutionally impermissible. "If a law has no other purpose [than] to chill the assertion of constitutional rights by penalizing those who choose to exercise them, then it (is) patently unconstitutional."

[A]ppellants argue that even if it is impermissible for a State to attempt to deter the entry of all indigents, the challenged classification may be justified as a permissible state attempt to discourage those indigents who would enter the State solely to obtain larger benefits. [N]one of the statutes before us is tailored to serve that objective. Rather, the class of barred newcomers is all-inclusive, lumping the great majority who come to the State for other purposes with those who come for the sole purpose of collecting higher benefits. [More] fundamentally, a

State may no more try to fence out those indigents who seek higher welfare benefits than it may try to fence out indigents generally. Implicit in any such distinction is the notion that indigents who enter a State with the hope of securing higher welfare benefits are somehow less deserving than indigents who do not take this consideration into account. But we do not perceive why a mother who is seeking to make a new life for herself and her children should be regarded as less deserving because she considers, among others factors, the level of a State's public assistance. . . .

Appellants argue [that] the challenged classification may be sustained as an attempt to distinguish between new and old residents on the basis of the contribution they have made to the community through the payment of taxes. We have difficulty seeing how long-term residents who qualify for welfare are making a greater present contribution to the State in taxes than indigent residents who have recently arrived. [Appellants'] reasoning would logically permit the State to bar new residents from schools, parks, and libraries or deprive them of police and fire protection. Indeed it would permit the State to apportion all benefits and services according to the past tax contributions of its citizens. The Equal Protection Clause prohibits such an apportionment of state services.

We recognize that a State has a valid interest in preserving the fiscal integrity of its programs. It may legitimately attempt to limit its expenditures, whether for public assistance, public education, or any other program. But a State may not accomplish such a purpose by invidious distinctions between classes of its citizens. It could not, for example, reduce expenditures for education by barring indigent children from its schools. [I]n the cases before us, appellants must do more than show that denying welfare benefits to new residents saves money. The saving of welfare costs cannot justify an otherwise invidious classification.

In sum, neither deterrence of indigents from migrating to the State nor limitation of welfare benefits to those regarded as contributing to the State is a constitutionally permissible state objective.

Appellants next advance as justification certain administrative and related governmental objectives allegedly served by the waiting-period requirement. They argue that the requirement (1) facilitates the planning of the welfare budget; (2) provides an objective test of residency; (3) minimizes the opportunity for recipients fraudulently to receive payments from more than one jurisdiction; and (4) encourages early entry of new residents into the labor force. [W]e reject appellants' argument. . . . [I]n moving from State to State or to the District of Columbia appellees were exercising a constitutional right, and any classification which serves to penalize the exercise of that right, unless shown to be necessary to promote a compelling governmental interest, is unconstitutional. . . . Under this standard, the waiting-period requirement clearly violates the Equal Protection Clause.

Mr. Justice STEWART, concurring.

[The constitutional right to travel] is a virtually unconditional personal right, guaranteed by the Constitution to us all.

Mr. Justice HARLAN, dissenting.

[I] disagree both with the Court's result and with its reasoning. [A] legislature might rationally find that the imposition of a welfare residence requirement would aid in the accomplishment of at least four valid governmental objectives. It might also find that residence requirements have advantages not shared by other methods of achieving the same goals. In light of this undeniable relation of residence requirements to valid legislative aims, it cannot be said that the requirements are "arbitrary" or "lacking in rational justification." [I] can find no objection to these residence requirements under the Equal Protection Clause of the Fourteenth Amendment or under the analogous standard embodied in the Due Process Clause of the Fifth Amendment.

The [issue] is whether a one-year welfare residence requirement amounts to an undue burden upon the right of interstate travel. . . . In my view, a number of considerations militate in favor of constitutionality. [T]he requirements upon the freedom of individuals to travel interstate is indirect [and] insubstantial. [T]hese are not cases in which a State or States, acting alone, have attempted to interfere with the right of citizens to travel. . . . [T]he governmental purposes served by the requirements are legitimate and real, and the residence requirements are clearly suited to their accomplishment. . . . Residence requirements have advantages, such as administrative simplicity and relative certainty, which are not shared by the alternative solutions proposed by the appellees. [I] cannot find that the burden imposed by residence requirements upon ability to travel outweighs the governmental interests in their continued employment. Nor do I believe that the period of residence required to these cases — one year — is so excessively long as to justify a finding of unconstitutionality on that score. [For] anyone who, like myself, believes that it is an essential function of this Court to maintain the constitutional divisions between state and federal authority and among the three branches of the Federal Government, today's decision is a step in the wrong direction.

Notes

1. *Welfare Benefits and Waiting Periods.* In Saenz v. Roe, 526 U.S. 489 (1999), the Court struck down a California law that limited welfare benefits under the state's Temporary Assistance for Needy Families (TANF) program during an individual's first year of residence in the state. Such individuals could not receive more than the amount they received in their prior state of residence even if California pays higher benefits to its own residents. The Court held that an individual's right to travel is explicitly protected under the Constitution, and guarantees individuals who elect to become a citizen of another state "the right to be treated like other citizens of that State." The Court concluded that the California law burdened that right, noting that California's asserted interest (saving money) "would logically permit the State to bar new residents from schools, parks, and libraries or deprive them of police and fire protection. Indeed it would permit the State to apportion all benefits and services according to the past tax contributions

of its citizens." In short, the Court held that the state's interest in saving money provides "no justification for its decision to discriminate among equally eligible citizens."

2. *Medical Care.* In Memorial Hospital v. Maricopa County, 415 U.S. 250 (1974), the Court struck down a state law that limited subsidized nonemergency medical care to individuals who had lived in the state for one year. Once again, because the law interfered with the right to travel, the Court applied strict scrutiny. The Court held that it is "clear that medical care is as much 'a basic necessity of life' to an indigent as welfare assistance. And, governmental privileges or benefits necessary to basic sustenance have often been viewed as being of greater constitutional significance than less essential forms of governmental entitlements. of residence." The Court rejected the state's claim that the limitation was needed to preserve the public fisc, noting that "a State may not protect the public fisc by drawing an invidious distinction between classes of its citizens."

3. *The Right to Divorce.* In Sosna v. Iowa, 419 U.S. 393 (1975), the Court upheld an Iowa law that imposed a one-year residency requirement on the right to obtain a divorce. The Court held that the restriction was justified by the state's interest in requiring those seeking a divorce from its courts to be genuinely attached to the state, as well as by the state's desire to insulate its divorce decrees from the likelihood of successful collateral attack.

4. *Interstate Travel and the Right to Vote.* Dunn v. Blumstein, 405 U.S. 330 (1972), struck down Tennessee's requirement of one-year of residency in the state and one year of residency in the county as conditions for voting in state elections. Tennessee had asserted that the requirements were needed to "insure the purity of the ballot box" against fraud (and to insure that those who attempted to vote were actually entitled to do so), as well as by the state interest in having "knowledgeable voters." The Court concluded that the interests were not compelling and could be adequately protected by other means. "Durational residence laws penalize those persons who have traveled from one place to another to establish a new residence during the qualifying period. By denying some citizens the right to vote, such laws deprive them of 'a fundamental political right, . . . preservative of all rights.' Reynolds v. Sims, 377 U.S. 533, 562 (1964)." The Court noted that the state's interest could be adequately protected by voter registration schemes as well as by "a variety of criminal laws that are more than adequate to detect and deter whatever fraud may be feared."

∾ PROBLEMS ∾

1. *More on Limiting Welfare Benefits.* After *Shapiro*, we know that a state may not limit welfare benefits to those who have lived in the state for at least a year. Suppose that the State of California passes a law that omits the one-year residency requirement, but instead provides that the amount of welfare benefits new residents may receive is limited to the amount they would have received in the state of their prior residence. Would such a limitation violate the fundamental right to travel? Does it matter that the state sought to justify the limitation as a financial

measure that would save it more than $10 million per year? *See* Saenz v. Roe, 526 U.S. 489 (1999).

2. *Residency Requirement for City Employees.* The City of Louisville adopts a law requiring all municipal employees to be residents of the city. The city believes that taxpayer resources should be expended only on residents and not on nonresidents. Would this condition be a bona fide residency requirement or an equal protection problem? *See* McCarthy v. Philadelphia Civil Service Commission, 424 U.S. 645 (1976).

3. *Penalty Enhancement.* Can a state enhance the penalty for abandonment of a child if the parent leaves the state? Does this constitute disparate treatment of the type encountered in *Shapiro* and its progeny? *See* Jones v. Helms, 452 U.S. 412 (1981).

Zobel v. Williams

457 U.S. 55 (1982)

Chief Justice BURGER delivered the opinion of the Court.

The question presented on this appeal is whether a statutory scheme by which a State distributes income derived from its natural resources to the adult citizens of the State in varying amounts, based on the length of each citizen's residence, violates the equal protection rights of newer state citizens.

I

The 1967 discovery of large oil reserves on state-owned land in the Prudhoe Bay area of Alaska resulted in a windfall to the State. The State, which had a total budget of $124 million in 1969, before the oil revenues began to flow into the state coffers, received $3.7 billion in petroleum revenues during the 1981 fiscal year. This income will continue, and most likely grow for some years in the future. Recognizing that its mineral reserves, although large, are finite and that the resulting income will not continue in perpetuity, the State took steps to assure that its current good fortune will bring long-range benefits. To accomplish this, Alaska in 1976 adopted a constitutional amendment establishing the Permanent Fund into which the State must deposit at least 25% of its mineral income each year. The amendment prohibits the legislature from appropriating any of the principal of the Fund but permits use of the Fund's earnings for general governmental purposes.

In 1980, the legislature enacted a dividend program to distribute annually a portion of the Fund's earnings directly to the State's adult residents. Under the plan, each citizen 18 years of age or older receives one dividend unit for each year of residency subsequent to 1959, the first year of statehood. The statute fixed the value of each dividend unit at $50 for the 1979 fiscal year; a one-year resident thus would receive one unit, or $50, while a resident of Alaska since it became a State in 1959 would receive 21 units, or $1,050. The value of a dividend unit will vary each year depending on the income of the Permanent Fund and the amount of that income the State allocates for other purposes. The State now estimates that the 1985 fiscal year dividend will be nearly four times as large as that for 1979.

The Alaska dividend distribution law is quite unlike the durational residency requirements we examined in Shapiro v. Thompson, [which] required new residents to reside in the State a fixed minimum period to be eligible for [welfare] benefits available on an equal basis to all other residents. . . . The Alaska statute does not impose any threshold waiting period on those seeking dividend benefits; persons with less than a full year of residency are entitled to share in the distribution. Nor does the statute purport to establish a test of the bona fides of state residence. Instead, the dividend statute creates fixed, permanent distinctions between an ever-increasing number of perpetual classes of concededly bona fide residents, based on how long they have been in the State.

Appellants established residence in Alaska two years before the dividend law was passed. The distinction they complain of is not one which the State makes between those who arrived in Alaska after the enactment of the dividend distribution law and those who were residents prior to its enactment. Appellants instead challenge the distinctions made within the class of persons who were residents when the dividend scheme was enacted in 1980. The distinctions appellants attack include the preference given to persons who were residents when Alaska became a State in 1959 over all those who have arrived since then, as well as the distinctions made between all bona fide residents who settled in Alaska at different times during the 1959 to 1980 period.

The Alaska statute does not simply make distinctions between native-born Alaskans and those who migrate to Alaska from other states; it does not discriminate only against those who have recently exercised the right to travel, as did the statute involved in *Shapiro*. The Alaska statute also discriminates among long-time residents and even native-born residents. For example, a person born in Alaska in 1962 would have received $100 less than someone who was born in the State in 1960. Of course the native Alaskan born in 1962 would also receive $100 less than the person who moved to the State in 1960. The statute does not involve the kind of discrimination which the Privileges and Immunities Clause of Art. IV was designed to prevent. That Clause "was designed to insure to a citizen of State A who ventures into State B the same privileges which the citizens of State B enjoy." The Clause is thus not applicable to this case.

When a state distributes benefits unequally, the distinctions it makes are subject to scrutiny under the Equal Protection Clause of the Fourteenth Amendment. Generally, a law will survive that scrutiny if the distinction it makes rationally furthers a legitimate state purpose. Some particularly invidious distinctions are subject to more rigorous scrutiny. . . .

The State advanced and the Alaska Supreme Court accepted three purposes justifying the distinctions made by the dividend program: (a) creation of a financial incentive for individuals to establish and maintain residence in Alaska; (b) encouragement of prudent management of the Permanent Fund; and (c) apportionment of benefits in recognition of undefined "contributions of various kinds, both tangible and intangible, which residents have made during their years of residency."

[The] first two state objectives — creating a financial incentive for individuals to establish and maintain Alaska residence, and assuring prudent management of the Permanent Fund and the State's natural and mineral resources — are not rationally related to the distinctions Alaska seeks to make between newer residents and those who have been in the State since 1959. Assuming, *arguendo*, that granting increased dividend benefits for each year of continued Alaska residence might give some residents an incentive to stay in the State in order to reap increased dividend benefits in the future, the State's interest is not in any way served by granting greater dividends to persons for their residency during the 21 years prior to the enactment. Nor does the State's purpose of furthering the prudent management of the Permanent Fund and the State's resources support retrospective application of its plan to the date of statehood. On this score the State's contention is straightforward.

[The] State similarly argues that equal per capita distribution would encourage rapacious development of natural resources. Even if we assume that the state interest is served by increasing the dividend for each year of residency beginning with the date of enactment, is it rationally served by granting greater dividends in varying amounts to those who resided in Alaska during the 21 years prior to enactment? We think not.

The last of the State's objectives — to reward citizens for past contributions — alone was relied upon by the Alaska Supreme Court to support the retrospective application of the law to 1959. However, that objective is not a legitimate state purpose. [If] the states can make the amount of a cash dividend depend on length of residence, what would preclude varying university tuition on a sliding scale based on years of residence — or even limiting access to finite public facilities, eligibility for student loans, for civil service jobs, or for government contracts by length of domicile? Could states impose different taxes based on length of residence? Alaska's reasoning could open the door to state apportionment of other rights, benefits, and services according to length of residency. It would permit the states to divide citizens into expanding numbers of permanent classes. Such a result would be clearly impermissible.

The only apparent justification for the retrospective aspect of the program, "favoring established residents over new residents," is constitutionally unacceptable. In our view Alaska has shown no valid state interests which are rationally served by the distinction it makes between citizens who established residence before 1959 and those who have become residents since then.

We hold that the Alaska dividend distribution plan violates the guarantees of the Equal Protection Clause of the Fourteenth Amendment. Accordingly, the judgment of the Alaska Supreme Court is reversed, and the case is remanded for further proceedings not inconsistent with this opinion.

Justice BRENNAN with whom Justice MARSHALL, Justice BLACKMUN, and Justice POWELL join, concurring.

[T]he retrospective aspects of Alaska's dividend-distribution law are not rationally related to a legitimate state purpose. [The] Fourteenth Amendment guarantees the equal protection of the law to anyone who may be within the territorial jurisdiction of a State. That Amendment does not suggest [that] equal treatment might be denied a person depending upon how long that person *has been* within the jurisdiction of the State. . . . Equality of citizenship is of the essence in our Republic. . . . States may not "divide citizens into expanding numbers of permanent classes."

[T]he Constitution does not bar the States from making reasoned distinctions between citizens [if] those distinctions are rationally related [to] legitimate ends. . . . But we have never suggested that duration of residence *vel non* provides a valid justification for discrimination. . . . To be sure, allegiance and attachment may be rationally measured by length of residence. . . . But those instances in which length of residence could provide a legitimate basis for distinguishing one citizen from another are rare. [T]o a limited extent, recognition and reward of past public service have independent utility for the State, for such recognition may encourage other people to engage in comparably meritorious service. But even the idea of rewarding past public service offers scarce support for [the] durational-residence classifications since length of residence has only the most tenuous relation to the *actual* service of individuals to the State. [I]t is difficult to escape from the recognition that underlying any scheme of classification on the basis of duration of residence, we shall almost invariably find the unstated premise that "some citizens are more equal than others." We rejected that premise and, I believe, implicitly rejected most forms of discrimination based upon length of residence, when we adopted the Equal Protection Clause.

Justice O'CONNOR, concurring in the judgment.

[Alaska's] desire "to reward citizens for past contributions . . ." is neither inherently invidious nor irrational. . . . Even a generalized desire to reward citizens for past endurance, particularly in a State where years of hardship only recently have produced prosperity, is not innately improper. The difficulty is that plans enacted to further this objective necessarily treat new residents of a State less favorably than the longer term residents who have past contributions to "reward." This inequality [conflicts] with the constitutional purpose of maintaining a Union rather than a mere "league of States." [T]he right infringed in this case is "fundamental." . . . Alaska has not shown that its new residents are the "peculiar source" of any evil addressed by its disbursement scheme [and] has not chosen a cure that bears a "substantial relationship" to the malady. . . . The dividends awarded to new residents may be too small to encourage them to stay in Alaska [and gives them] only a weak interest in prudent management of the State's resources. As a reward for prior contributions[,] Alaska's scheme is quite ill-suited. [P]ersons who have migrated to Alaska may have contributed significantly more to the State, both before and after their arrival, than have some natives. . . . Alaska's disbursement scheme violates Art. IV's Privileges and Immunities Clause. . . .

Justice REHNQUIST, dissenting.

Alaska's dividend distribution scheme represents one State's effort to apportion unique economic benefits among its citizens. . . . The distribution scheme being in the nature of economic regulation, I am at a loss to see the rationality behind the Court's invalidation of it as a denial of equal protection. This Court has long held that state economic regulations are presumptively valid, and violate the Fourteenth Amendment only in the rarest of circumstances. [The] distribution scheme at issue in this case impedes no person's right to travel to and settle in Alaska; if anything, the prospect of receiving annual cash dividends would encourage immigration to Alaska. [T]he state legislature acted rationally when it concluded that dividends retroactive to the year of statehood would "recognize the 'contributions of various kinds, both tangible and intangible,' which residents have made during their years of state residency." . . . Alaska, perhaps more than any other State in the Union, has good reason for recognizing such contributions. . . .

Note

The *Zobel* decision was notable for disclosing a compounding lack of consensus on a theory for the right to travel. In his concurring opinion, Justice Brennan cited the Citizenship Clause of the Fourteenth Amendment as a basis for limiting state power to discriminate on the basis of length of residence. Justice O'Connor, in her concurrence, advocated reinvigoration of the Article IV, Section II Privileges and Immunities Clause as the predicate for the right to travel. The influence of her thinking in this regard was evidenced in Saenz v. Roe, which, as previously noted, cited this Privileges and Immunities Clause as a basis for the right to travel. Justice Rehnquist argued in dissent that, because no Alaska citizen was denied benefits under the plan, the right to travel was not burdened.

∼ PROBLEMS ∼

1. *Shifting the Focus?* The Court has evaluated burdens on the right to travel in terms of whether they penalize interstate travel. Should the focus instead be on whether residence requirements deter interstate travel? Would it make a difference with respect to the outcomes in *Shapiro* and *Memorial Hospital,* cases in which no proof was presented of any person actually being deterred?

2. *College Education as a Basic Necessity.* Public universities typically establish separate tuition schedules for in-state and out-of-state residents. Does a university or college education represent a basic necessity, particularly in an increasingly competitive environment? Are these differentials at odds with the equal protection guarantee? *See* Vlandis v. Kline, 412 U.S. 441 (1973).

3. *Preferential Hiring for Kentucky Veterans.* The Commonwealth of Kentucky creates a preferential hiring policy that favors veterans who were residents when they entered military service. The commonwealth justifies the preference on the basis that resident veterans who take time away from their careers to serve their country are entitled to help as they try to restart or develop their civilian careers. Kentucky does not prefer out-of-state veterans because it believes that they

should receive help from their home states. Is the preference constitutional? *See* Attorney General v. Soto-Lopez, 476 U.S. 898 (1986).

4. *Voting*

The Constitution does not establish a general right to vote. Consistent with this premise, the Court has found that "the right to vote in federal elections is conferred by Art. I, §2, of the Constitution, but the right to vote in state elections is nowhere expressly mentioned." Harper v. Virginia Board of Elections, 383 U.S. 663, 665 (1966). Notwithstanding this differentiation in grounding, and within the context of state political processes, the franchise has been described as "a fundamental matter in a free and democratic society, [e]specially since the right to exercise the franchise in a free and unimpaired manner is preservative of other basic civil and political rights." The importance of the franchise is further evidenced by the volume of constitutional amendments concerned with protecting it. The Fifteenth Amendment prohibits denial of the right to vote "on account of race, color, or previous condition of servitude." U.S. Const., Amend. XV. The Nineteenth Amendment prohibits abridgment of the right to vote "on account of sex." *Id.*, Amend. XIX. The Twenty-fourth Amendment prohibits poll taxes. *Id.*, Amend. XXIV. The Twenty-sixth Amendment extends the right to vote to citizens who are 18 or older. *Id.*, Amend. XXVI.

The concept of voting as a fundamental right was introduced in the context of equal protection review. In Baker v. Carr, 369 U.S. 186 (1962), the Court struck down a state's legislative apportionment scheme on grounds it violated the premise of "one man, one vote." An equality principle thus was established as a primary basis for challenging laws that denied or diluted the right to vote.

a.   Denial of the Right to Vote

Although the states have authority to establish the basic terms of voting, conditions that burden the franchise through qualifications unrelated to age, citizenship, or residence typically will "be carefully and meticulously scrutinized." Harper v. Virginia State Board of Elections, 383 U.S. 663 (1966). This higher level of review may extend to residence requirements, as evidenced by the Court's invalidation of a one-year state and three-month county waiting period for local, state, and congressional elections. Dunn v. Blumstein, 405 U.S. 330 (1972).

Equal protection activity with respect to denial of the right to vote has centered primarily on poll taxes and voter eligibility requirements for special-purpose government districts. Poll taxes historically were part of the system of racial management that denied meaningful participation in the political process. They were prohibited by the Twenty-fourth Amendment. The Court's output with respect to voter requirements for special-purpose district elections has been mixed with respect to both standards of review and results.

(1)   Poll Taxes

A classic example of an impermissible denial of the right to vote is a poll tax. In Harper v. Virginia State Board of Elections, 383 U.S. 663 (1966), the Court found no basis for making wealth a qualification for voting. As Justice Douglas put it for the Court: "[W]ealth, like race, creed, or color, is not germane to the power to participate intelligently in the electoral process. Lines drawn on the basis of wealth or property, like those of race, are traditionally disfavored. To introduce wealth or payment of a fee as a measure of a voter's qualifications is to introduce a capricious or irrelevant factor. The degree of the discrimination is irrelevant. In this context — that is, as a condition of obtaining a ballot — the requirement of fee paying causes an 'invidious' discrimination."

∾ PROBLEM: ENSURING AN INFORMED AND LITERATE ELECTORATE ∾

Like poll taxes, literacy tests have a history of being used to discriminate against persons on the basis of race. Assume that a state wants to ensure that its voters can read and are conversant with candidates and issues before they cast their ballot. Assume further that it can be demonstrated that the state's only concern is that voting reflect the informed judgment of the electorate. Is a test designed to ensure competency in this regard inappropriate as a means for establishing voter qualifications?

(2)   Land Ownership

Special restrictions on eligibility for school board elections also have been the basis for "a close and exacting examination." In Kramer v. Union Free School District, 395 U.S. 621 (1969), the Court reviewed a state law that narrowed eligibility for voting in school board elections to otherwise qualified voters who owned or leased property in the district or whose children were enrolled in the district's schools. The eligibility requirements were designed to limit electoral participation to resident citizens "'primarily interested' in school affairs." The Court determined that this objective was not promoted with "satisfactory precision." To the contrary, it excluded some who had a distinct and direct interest in school affairs and included others who had a remote and indirect concern with them.

For districts that have a special purpose, eligibility requirements may be a function of how narrow the scope of governmental authority is. Case law suggests that districts with a narrower purpose may have the ability to establish more detailed voter eligibility standards. In Salyer Land Co. v. Tulare Lake Basin Water Storage District, 410 U.S. 719 (1973), the Court upheld a law limiting participation in water storage district elections to landowners. Absentee landowners thus could vote, but district residents who did not own land were excluded. The result reflected the Court's sense that the water storage district was not a "'normal government' authority" and "its actions disproportionately affect landowners." It also was achieved pursuant to rational basis review rather than the strict scrutiny standard used in *Kramer*. The different standards of review appear to correlate with a sense that, as a district's ambit of concern narrows, more room is needed to establish requirements that ensure an "interested" electorate. Barring a special-interest election, as the Court noted in Hill v. Stone, 421 U.S. 289 (1975), classifications restricting the right to vote "cannot stand unless the district or State can demonstrate that the classification serves a compelling state interest."

∼ PROBLEMS ∼

1. *Landownership Requirements.* Would landownership be a valid requirement for voting in an election to select members of a board of freeholders? Would this condition be justified by the need for an informed electorate? *See* Quinn v. Millsap, 491 U.S. 95 (1989). Would a system that correlated voting strength with the amount of land owned, in a district that managed water and sold electricity, violate the equal protection guarantee? *See* Ball v. James, 451 U.S. 355 (1981).

2. *Bonds and Property Interests.* Consider a city bond issue that limited the right to vote based on whether property owners had listed or rendered their property for taxation in the election district. This requirement varied from state law, which established listing alone as the basis for eligibility. Is the election one of general or special interest? Does the provision for rendering constitute an equal protection problem? *See* Hill v. Stone, 421 U.S. 289 (1975).

b. Dilution of the Right to Vote

The right to vote may be abridged by means of not only deprivation but also dilution. Methodologies of dilution include apportionment schemes that weight votes differently, restrictions on ballot access that may narrow the range of voter options, and processes for recording and counting votes. Districting processes for political representation generally are governed by the principle of one person, one vote. Allowable deviations from the norm and standards of review vary depending on whether federal, state, or local representation is implicated. With respect to ballot access, the focus is on the degree of burden imposed by the restriction.

(1) Apportionment

The basis for determining representation in the political process has been a source of contention since the nation's founding. Next to slavery, the determining factors for representation in the national government probably were the most divisive issue at the Constitutional Convention. The compromise effected by the founders was a bicameral legislature that correlated representation in the House with state population and gave every state the same number of senators. Most states also have adopted a bicameral model. The dual sovereign relationship between the federal and state governments, however, is not replicated at the state level. Counties and districts are subsets or units of state government, rather than independent sovereigns. Minus a true parallel to the federal system, the Court has concluded that representation in state legislatures must follow a rule of proportionality that translates generally into one person, one vote.

Reynolds v. Sims
377 U.S. 533 (1964)

Mr. Chief Justice WARREN delivered the opinion of the Court.

[The Alabama legislature failed to reapportion legislative districts after 1901. By 1960, the state's legislative districts were lopsided so that 25 percent of the population was able to elect a majority of the state Senate, and 25 percent could elect a majority of the House of Representatives. Lower courts struck down the existing districts] under the Equal Protection Clause of the Federal Constitution, [and also struck down two proposed apportionment plans. In addition, they put] into effect a temporary reapportionment plan comprised of parts of the proposed but judicially disapproved measures.

[T]he Constitution of the United States protects the right of all qualified citizens to vote, in state as well as in federal elections, [and] to have their votes counted. [*See* United States v. Mosley, 238 U.S. 383 (1915).] Racially based gerrymandering and the conducting of white primaries, both of which result in denying to some citizens their right to vote, have been held to be constitutionally impermissible. And history has seen a continuing expansion of the scope of the right of suffrage in this country. The right to vote freely for the candidate of one's choice is of the essence of a democratic society, and any restrictions on that right strike at the heart of representative government. . . .

A predominant consideration in determining whether a State's legislative apportionment scheme constitutes an invidious discrimination violative of rights asserted under the Equal Protection Clause is that the rights allegedly impaired are individual and personal in nature. . . . While [a] court decision in a state legislative apportionment controversy [restructured] the geographical distribution of seats in a state legislature, the judicial focus must be concentrated upon ascertaining whether there has [been] discrimination [against] citizens which constitutes an impermissible impairment of their constitutionally protected right to vote. . . . [T]he right of suffrage is a fundamental matter in a free and democratic society. Especially since the right to exercise the franchise in a free and unimpaired manner is preservative of other basic civil and political rights, any alleged infringement of the right of citizens to vote must be carefully and meticulously scrutinized. . . .

Legislators represent people, not trees or acres. Legislators are elected by voters, not farms or cities or economic interests. As long as ours is a representative form of government, and our legislatures are those instruments of government elected directly by and directly representative of the people, the right to elect legislators in a free and unimpaired fashion is a bedrock of our political system. It could hardly be gainsaid that a constitutional claim had been asserted by an allegation that certain otherwise qualified voters had been entirely prohibited from voting for members of their state legislature. And, if a State should provide that the votes of citizens in one part of the State should be given two times, or five times, or 10 times the weight of votes of citizens in another part of the State, it could hardly be contended that the right to vote of those residing in the disfavored areas had not been effectively diluted. [T]he effect of state legislative districting schemes which give the same number of representatives to unequal numbers of constituents is identical. . . .

We are told that the matter of apportioning representation in a state legislature is a complex and many-faceted one [and] that States can rationally consider factors other than population in apportioning legislative representation. We are admonished not to restrict the power of the States to impose differing views as to political philosophy on their citizens. We are cautioned about the dangers of entering into political thickets and mathematical quagmires. Our answer is this: a denial of constitutionally protected rights demands judicial protection; our oath and our office require no less of us. [T]he basic principle of representative government remains, and must remain, unchanged — the weight of a citizen's vote cannot be made to depend on where he lives. Population is, of necessity, the starting point for consideration and the controlling criterion for judgment in legislative apportionment controversies. A citizen, a qualified voter, is no more nor no less so because he lives in the city or on the farm. . . . This is an essential part of the concept of a government of laws and not men. . . . The Equal Protection Clause demands no less than substantially equal state legislative representation for all citizens, of all places as well as of all races. . . . Since, under neither the existing apportionment provisions nor either of the proposed plans was either of the houses of the Alabama Legislature apportioned on a population basis, [all] three of these schemes were constitutionally invalid.

[The] system of representation in the two Houses of the Federal Congress is one ingrained in our Constitution. . . . Arising from unique historical circumstances, it is based on the consideration that in establishing our type of federalism a group of formerly independent States bound themselves together under one national government. [A]t the time of the inception of the system of representation in the Federal Congress, a compromise between the larger and smaller States on this matter averted a deadlock in the Constitutional Convention which had threatened to abort the birth of our Nation. . . . Political subdivisions of States — counties, cities, or whatever — never were and never have been considered as sovereign entities. Rather, they have been traditionally regarded as subordinate governmental instrumentalities created by the State to assist in the carrying out of state governmental functions. . . . The relationship of the States to the Federal Government could hardly be less analogous.

[We hold] that the Equal Protection Clause requires both houses of a state legislature to be apportioned on a population basis. The right of a citizen to equal representation and to have his vote weighted equally with those of all other citizens in the election of members of one house of a bicameral state legislature would amount to little if States could effectively submerge the equal-population principle in the apportionment of seats in the other house. If such a scheme were permissible, an individual citizen's ability to exercise an effective voice in the only instrument of state government directly representative of the people might be almost as effectively thwarted as if neither house were apportioned on a population basis. Deadlock between the two bodies might result in compromise and concession on some issues. [I]n all too many cases the more probable result would be frustration of the majority will through minority veto in the house not apportioned on a population basis, stemming directly from the failure to accord adequate overall legislative representation to all of the State's citizens on a nondiscriminatory basis. [W]e can perceive no constitutional difference, with respect to the geographical distribution of state legislative representation, between the two houses of a bicameral state legislature.

We do not believe that the concept of bicameralism is rendered anachronistic and meaningless when the predominant basis of representation in the two state legislative bodies is required to be the same — population. A prime reason for bicameralism, modernly considered, is to insure mature and deliberate consideration of, and to prevent precipitate action on, proposed legislative measures. Simply because the controlling criterion for apportioning representation is required to be the same in both houses does not mean that there will be no differences in the composition and complexion of the two bodies. . . . One body could be composed of single-member districts while the other could have at least some multimember districts. The length of terms of the legislators in the separate bodies could differ. The numerical size of the two bodies could be made to differ, even significantly, and the geographical size of districts from which legislators are elected could also be made to differ. And apportionment in one house could be arranged so as to balance off minor inequities in the representation of certain areas in the other house. [T]hese and other factors could be, and are presently in many States, utilized to engender differing complexions and collective attitudes in the two bodies of a state legislature, although both are apportioned substantially on a population basis.

[T]he Equal Protection Clause requires that a State make an honest and good faith effort to construct districts, in both houses of its legislature, as nearly of equal population as is practicable. We realize that it is a practical impossibility to arrange legislative districts so that each one has an identical number of residents, or citizens, or voters. [S]ome distinctions may well be made between congressional and state legislative representation. Since, almost invariably, there is a significantly larger number of seats in state legislative bodies to be distributed within a State than congressional seats, it may be feasible to use political subdivision lines to a greater extent in establishing state legislative districts than in congressional districting while still affording adequate representation to all parts of the State. To do so would be constitutionally valid, so long as the resulting apportionment was one based substantially on population and the equal-population principle was not diluted in any significant way. . . . [W]e deem it expedient not to attempt to spell out any precise constitutional tests. What is marginally permissible in one State may be unsatisfactory in another, depending on the particular circumstances of the case. . . .

History indicates, however, that many States have deviated, to a greater or lesser degree, from the equal-population principle in the apportionment of seats in at least one house of their legislatures. So long as the divergences from a strict population standard are based on legitimate considerations incident to the effectuation of a rational state policy, some deviations from the equal-population principle are constitutionally permissible with respect to the apportionment of seats in either or both of the two houses of a bicameral state legislature. But neither history alone, nor economic or other sorts of group interests, are permissible factors in attempting to justify disparities from population-based representation. Citizens [cast] votes. Considerations of area alone provide an insufficient justification for deviations from the equal-population principle. . . . Modern developments and improvements in transportation and communications make rather hollow, in the mid-1960's, most claims that deviations from population-based representation can validly be based solely on geographical considerations. Arguments for allowing such deviations in order to insure effective representation for sparsely settled areas and to prevent legislative districts from becoming so large that the availability of access of citizens to their representatives is impaired are today, for the most part, unconvincing.

A consideration that appears to be of more substance in justifying some deviations from population-based representation in state legislatures is that of insuring some voice to political subdivisions, as political subdivisions. [A] State can rationally consider according political subdivisions some independent representation in at least one body of the state legislature, as long as the basic standard of equality of population among districts is maintained. Local governmental entities are frequently charged with various responsibilities incident to the operation of state government. In many States much of the legislature's activity involves the enactment of so-called local legislation, directed only to the concerns of particular political subdivisions. And a State may legitimately desire to construct districts along political subdivision lines to deter the possibilities of gerrymandering. However, permitting deviations from population-based representation does not mean that each local governmental unit or political subdivision can be given separate representation, regardless of population. . . . But if, even as a result of a clearly rational state policy of according some legislative representation to political subdivisions, population is submerged as the controlling consideration in the apportionment of seats in the particular legislative body, then the right of all of the State's citizens to cast an effective and adequately weighted vote would be unconstitutionally impaired.

That the Equal Protection Clause requires that both houses of a state legislature be apportioned on a population basis does not mean that States cannot adopt some reasonable plan for periodic revision of their apportionment schemes. [Limitations] on the frequency of reapportionment are justified by the need for stability and continuity in the organization of the legislative system, although undoubtedly reapportioning no more frequently than every 10 years leads to some imbalance in the population of districts toward the end of the decennial period and also to the development of resistance to change on the part of some incumbent legislators. [W]e do not regard the Equal Protection Clause as requiring daily, monthly, annual or biennial reapportionment, so long as a State has a reasonably conceived plan for periodic readjustment of legislative representation. [D]ecennial reapportionment [would] clearly meet the minimal requirements for maintaining a reasonably current scheme of legislative representation. . . . But if reapportionment were accomplished with less frequency, it would assuredly be constitutionally suspect.

We find, therefore, that the action taken by the District Court in this case, in ordering into effect a reapportionment of both houses of the Alabama Legislature for purposes of the 1962 primary and general elections, by using the best parts of the two proposed plans which it had found, as a whole, to be invalid, was an appropriate and well-considered exercise of judicial power. . . .

Affirmed and remanded.

Mr. Justice CLARK, concurring in the affirmance.

The Court goes much beyond the necessities of this case in laying down a new 'equal population' principle for state legislative apportionment. [All] that the Court need say [is] that each plan considered by the trial court is 'a crazy quilt,' clearly revealing invidious discrimination in each house of the Legislature and therefore violative of the Equal Protection Clause.

Mr. Justice HARLAN, dissenting.

[T]he Equal Protection Clause was never intended to inhibit the States in choosing any democratic method they pleased for the apportionment of their legislatures. . . . The consequence of today's decision is that [the] local [courts] are given blanket authority and the constitutional duty to supervise apportionment of the State Legislatures. It is difficult to imagine a more intolerable and inappropriate interference by the judiciary with the independent legislatures of the States. [No] set of standards can guide a court which has to decide how many legislative districts a State shall have, or what the shape of the districts shall be, or where to draw a particular district line. No judicially manageable standard can determine whether a State should have single-member districts or multimember districts or some combination of both. No such standard can control the balance between keeping up with population shifts and having stable districts. In all these respects, the courts will be called upon to make particular decisions with respect to which a principle of equally populated districts will be of no assistance whatsoever. [T]here are limitless possibilities for districting consistent with such a principle. . . . [The Court's] opinion nevertheless fully demonstrates how far removed these problems are from fields of judicial competence. . . .

I know of no principle of logic or practical or theoretical politics, still less any constitutional principle, which [supports this decision. The Court] says only that 'legislators represent people, not trees or acres,' that 'citizens, not history or economic interests, cast votes,' that 'people, not land or trees or pastures, vote.' [I]t is surely equally obvious, and, in the context of elections, more meaningful to note that people are not ciphers and that legislators can represent their electors only by speaking for their interests — economic, social, political — many of which do reflect the place where the electors live. The Court does not establish [that] conflicting interests within a State can only be adjusted by disregarding them when voters are grouped for purposes of representation.

[J]udicial entry into this realm is profoundly ill-advised and constitutionally impermissible. [T]he vitality of our political system, on which in the last analysis all else depends, is weakened by reliance on the judiciary for political reform; in time a complacent body politic may result. . . . These decisions also cut deeply into the fabric of our federalism. [T]he aftermath of these cases [will] have been achieved at the cost of a radical alteration in the relationship between the States and the Federal Government, more particularly the Federal Judiciary. [These] decisions give support to a current mistaken view [that] every major social ill in this country can find its cure in some constitutional "principle," and that this Court should "take the lead" in promoting reform when other branches of government fail to act. . . . The Constitution is an instrument of government, fundamental to which is the premise that in a diffusion of governmental authority lies the greatest promise that this Nation will realize liberty for all its citizens. This Court [does] not serve its high purpose when it exceeds its authority, even to satisfy justified impatience with the slow workings of the political process. [W]hen, in the name of constitutional interpretation, the Court adds something to the Constitution that was deliberately excluded from it, the Court in reality substitutes its view of what should be so for the amending process. . . .

Note: Local Elections

In Hadley v. Junior College District of Metropolitan Kansas City, 397 U.S. 50 (1970), the Court extended *Reynolds* to local government elections and nonlegislative officials: "[W]henever a state or local government decides to select persons by popular election to perform governmental functions, the Equal Protection Clause of the Fourteenth Amendment requires that each qualified voter must be given an equal opportunity to participate in that election, and when members of an elected body are chosen from separate districts, each district must be established on a basis that will insure, as far as is practicable, that equal numbers of voters can vote for proportionally equal numbers of officials."

∾ PROBLEMS ∾

1. *Fashioning Court Orders.* A court concludes that the State of Alabama's congressional districts are malapportioned. How should the court reapportion? Should the court undertake the reapportionment itself? Or, should it "remand" the matter to the state legislature, ordering it to constitutionally apportion districts? What is the proper relationship between the courts and the state legislature?

2. *Advising the Legislature.* Suppose that you are the counsel to a state legislative committee, and the committee is thinking about amending the state constitution. The amendment would provide for a bicameral legislature, with the house apportioned on the basis of population but the senate apportioned by taking into account various factors including population, which is not regarded as "controlling." Other relevant factors are "geography, compactness and contiguity of

territory, accessibility, observance of natural boundaries, [and] conformity to historical divisions such as county lines and prior representation districts. . . ." After *Reynolds,* how would you advise the committee regarding the constitutionality of this proposed provision? *See* Lucas v. Forty-Fourth General Assembly of Colorado, 377 U.S. 713 (1964).

3. *At-Large Representation.* A county government's charter provides that county commissioners must live in specified districts, but that commissioners are elected by the population of the entire county and are expected to represent the entire county. Under such circumstances, must legislative districts be equal? *See* Dallas County v. Reese, 421 U.S. 477 (1975).

4. *Permissible-Impermissible Deviations.* How much deviation from "one person, one vote" is permissible? Again, suppose that you are the counsel to a legislative committee that is undertaking redistricting. The committee proposes a redistricting plan that contemplates 46,685 persons per delegate. However, the district population totals vary from 6.8 percent above the 46,685 figure to 9.6 percent below the figure. How would you advise the committee? Is the proposed plan constitutional? Can the deviation be justified by the committee's desire to maintain district lines consistent with county and city boundaries? *See* Mahan v. Howell, 410 U.S. 315 (1973).

5. *One Person, One Vote, and Supermajorities.* Suppose that a state apportions its legislative districts in accordance with *Reynolds*. However, the state constitution prohibits the state from increasing taxes without the vote of a supermajority of legislators. Is the supermajority requirement constitutional under *Reynolds* given that a minority can thwart the majority's will? *See* Gordon v. Lance, 403 U.S. 1 (1971); Lockport v. Citizens for Community Action, 430 U.S. 259 (1977).

6. *Proportional Representation.* Is there a constitutional right to proportional representation? Although a city is divided into legislative districts, and commissioners must reside in the districts they represent, all commissioners are elected on an "at large" basis. In other words, the entire county is allowed to vote in each commissioner's election. Minority voters challenge the at-large elections on the basis that the county has a Caucasian majority and the system helps ensure that all elected representatives are Caucasian. Do minority voters (who make up 20 percent of the population) have the right to proportional representation? Do they have a "right" to have only voters from their own district (which is dominated by minorities) vote for their commissioner? *See* City of Mobile v. Bolden, 446 U.S. 55 (1980).

7. *More on Proportional Representation.* In the preceding problem, suppose that minority voters file suit alleging that the at-large system is designed to prevent them from electing a minority commissioner. What must the minority voters show to establish the at-large system as a racial classification that is subject to strict scrutiny?

(2) Political Gerrymandering

The principle of one person, one vote has had a significant impact on how state legislative districts are drawn. The *Reynolds* decision itself responded to apportionment models that largely had become outdated, but entrenched, as a function of demographic evolution from rural to urban. Equal weighting of votes may be difficult to achieve with mathematical precision. The one person, one vote principle also operates in conjunction with other legitimate apportionment factors, including, as the Court noted in Karcher v. Daggett, "making districts compact, respecting municipal boundaries, preserving the cores of private districts, and avoiding contests between incumbent Representatives." Karcher v. Daggett, 462 U.S. 725 (1983). Against this backdrop, greater deviation is permitted in legislative districting for state purposes. State apportionment may factor in traditional political boundaries, but it must reflect a good-faith effort to achieve equality of representation. Because congressional districts do not correlate with traditional state subdivisions, deviation from the equality principle is minimal. A 0.7 percent deviation thus was found impermissible in *Karcher*.

For state legislative districting processes, which may consider traditional political boundaries, there is more tolerance for deviation. A 16.4 percent deviation thus was allowed in Virginia and an 89 percent underrepresentation factor was permitted in Wyoming. *See* Mahan v. Howell, 410 U.S. 315 (1973). The allowable deviation in the first instance was coupled with the observation that there are no "specialized calipers" that enable courts or legislatures to determine "what range of percentage deviations are permissible, and what are not." In the Wyoming scenario, deviation largely was a function of a legislative seat being assigned to the state's least-populated county. It is unlikely that such an extreme departure would be justified on a broader-spectrum basis.

Multimember districts may represent a subtle mechanism for diluting the right to vote. Systems of at-large representation on city councils, for instance, historically have operated to diminish the influence of minority voters. At-large voting schemes that discriminate on the basis of race, as noted in Rogers v. Lodge, 458 U.S. 613 (1982), violate the equal protection guarantee. To establish a classification on the basis of race, as with any other equal protection claim correlated with group status, it is necessary to prove discriminatory purpose. City of Mobile v. Bolden, 446 U.S. 55 (1980).

Inherent in a political process driven by competing self-interests is the motivation to tilt the playing field for partisan purposes. The opportunity to achieve this result is presented by processes of reapportionment based on population changes reflected in decennial census reports. The mere lack of proportional representation owing to gerrymandering, as the Court noted in Davis v. Bandemer, does not violate the equal protection guarantee. Constitutional interests are implicated only when a group is the target of intentional discrimination and the effects are more than minimal.

Davis v. Bandemer

478 U.S. 109 (1986)

Justice WHITE announced the judgment of the Court and delivered the opinion of the Court as to Part II and an opinion as to Parts I, III, and IV, in which Justice BRENNAN, Justice MARSHALL, and Justice BLACKMUN join.

In this case, we review a judgment from a three-judge District Court, which sustained an equal protection challenge to Indiana's 1981 state apportionment [adopted by a Republican legislature and governor] on the basis that the law unconstitutionally diluted the votes of Indiana Democrats. [W]e conclude that the District Court applied an insufficiently demanding standard in finding unconstitutional vote dilution. Consequently, we reverse.

II

We address first the question whether this case presents a justiciable controversy or a nonjusticiable political question. [We] have consistently adjudicated equal protection claims in the legislative districting context regarding inequalities in population between districts. [Prior] decisions support a conclusion that this case is justiciable.

III

[Appellees] claim that the 1981 apportionment discriminates against Democrats on a statewide basis. [In] order to succeed[, they] were required to prove both intentional discrimination against an identifiable political group and an actual discriminatory effect on that group. . . . As long as redistricting is done by a legislature, it should not be very difficult to prove that the likely political consequences of the reapportionment were intended.

[Our cases] foreclose any claim that the Constitution requires proportional representation or that legislatures in reapportioning must draw district lines to come as near as possible to allocating seats to the contending parties in proportion to what their anticipated statewide vote will be. . . . The typical election for legislative seats in the United States is conducted in described geographical districts, with the candidate receiving the most votes in each district winning the seat allocated to that district. If all or most of the districts are competitive — [districts] in which the anticipated split in the party vote is within the range of 45% to 55% — even a narrow statewide preference for either party would produce an overwhelming majority for the winning party in the state legislature. This consequence, however, is inherent in winner-take-all, district-based elections, and we cannot hold that such a reapportionment law would violate the Equal Protection Clause because the voters in the losing party do not have representation in the legislature in proportion to the statewide vote received by their party candidates. . . . This is true of a racial as well as a political group. It is also true of a statewide claim as well as an individual district claim.

To draw district lines to maximize the representation of each major party would require creating as many safe seats for each party as the demographic and predicted political characteristics of the State would permit. This in turn would leave the minority in each safe district without a representative of its choice. We [have] upheld this "political fairness" approach, despite its tendency to deny safe district minorities any realistic chance to elect their own representatives.

In cases involving individual multimember districts, we have required a substantially greater showing of adverse effects than a mere lack of proportional representation to support a finding of unconstitutional vote dilution. Only where there is evidence that excluded groups have "less opportunity to participate in the political processes and to elect candidates of their choice" have we refused to approve the use of multimember districts. In these cases, we have also noted the lack of responsiveness by those elected to the concerns of the relevant groups. [T]he mere fact that a particular apportionment scheme makes it more difficult for a particular group in a particular district to elect the representatives of its choice does not render that scheme constitutionally infirm. [T]he power to influence the political process is not limited to winning elections. An individual or a group of individuals who votes for a losing candidate is usually deemed to be adequately represented by the winning candidate and to have as much opportunity to influence that candidate as other voters in the district. We cannot presume[,] without actual proof to the contrary, that the candidate elected will entirely ignore the interests of those voters. This is true even in a safe district where the losing group loses election after election. . . .

[W]here unconstitutional vote dilution is alleged in the form of statewide political gerrymandering, the mere lack of proportional representation will not be sufficient to prove unconstitutional discrimination. [W]ithout specific supporting evidence, a court cannot presume in such a case that those who are elected will disregard the disproportionately underrepresented group. [U]nconstitutional discrimination occurs only when the electoral system is arranged in a manner that will consistently degrade a voter's or a group of voters' influence on the political process as a whole. . . . In a challenge to an individual district, this inquiry focuses on the opportunity of members of the group to participate in party deliberations in the slating and nomination of candidates, their opportunity to register and vote, and hence their chance to directly influence the election returns and to secure the attention of the winning candidate. Statewide, however, the inquiry centers on the voters' direct or indirect influence on the elections of the state legislature as a whole. [An] equal protection violation may be found only where the electoral system substantially disadvantages certain voters in their opportunity to influence the political process effectively. [S]uch a finding [must] be supported by evidence of continued frustration of the will of a majority of the voters or effective denial to a minority of voters of a fair chance to influence the political process.

[We] reject the District Court's [holding] that *any* interference with an opportunity to elect a representative of one's choice would be sufficient to allege or make out an equal protection violation, unless justified by some acceptable state interest. . . . District-based elections hardly ever produce a perfect fit between votes and representation. . . . Inviting attack on minor departures from some supposed norm would too much embroil the judiciary in second-guessing what has consistently been referred to as a political task for the legislature, a task that should not be monitored too closely unless the express or tacit goal is to effect its removal from legislative halls. . . .

[It is] appropriate to require allegations and proof that the challenged legislative plan has had or will have effects that are sufficiently serious to require intervention by the federal courts in state reapportionment decisions. . . . The District Court's findings do not satisfy this threshold condition to stating and proving a cause of action. [T]he District Court relied primarily on the results of the 1982 elections: Democratic candidates for the State House of Representatives had received 51.9% of the votes cast statewide and Republican candidates 48.1%; yet, out of the 100 seats to be filled, Republican candidates won 57 and Democrats 43. In the Senate, 53.1% of the votes were cast for Democratic candidates and 46.9% for Republicans; of the 25 Senate seats to be filled, Republicans won 12 and Democrats 13. . . . Relying on a single election to prove unconstitutional discrimination is unsatisfactory. . . . Indiana is a swing State. Voters sometimes prefer Democratic candidates, and sometimes Republican. [There was no] finding that the 1981 reapportionment would consign the Democrats to a minority status in the Assembly throughout the 1980's or that the Democrats would have no hope of doing any better in the reapportionment that would occur after the 1990 census. Without findings of this nature, the District Court erred in concluding that the 1981 Act violated the Equal Protection Clause.

The District Court's discussion of the multimember districts created by the 1981 Act does not undermine this conclusion. [T]hese districts appear indistinguishable from safe Republican and safe Democratic single-member districts. . . . Simply showing that there are multimember districts in the State and that those districts are constructed so as to be safely Republican or Democratic in no way bolsters the contention that there has been *statewide* discrimination against Democratic voters. It could be [that] multimember districts could be demonstrated to be suspect on the ground that they [attain] impermissibly discriminatory ends; at this stage of the inquiry, however, the multimember district evidence does not materially aid the appellees' case.

[W]e have rejected the view that "any group with distinctive interests must be represented in legislative halls if it is numerous enough to command at least one seat and represents a minority living in an area sufficiently compact to constitute a single-member district." Rather, we have required that there be proof that the complaining minority "had less opportunity [to] participate in the political processes and to elect legislators of their choice." [For] constitutional purposes, the Democratic claim in this case, insofar as it challenges *vel non* the legality of the multimember districts in certain counties, is like that of the Negroes [who] failed to prove a racial gerrymander, for it boils down to a complaint that they failed to attract a majority of the voters in the challenged multimember districts.

[Justice] Powell suggests [that] courts should look at a number of factors in considering these claims: the nature of the legislative procedures by which the challenged redistricting was accomplished and the intent behind the redistricting; the shapes of the districts and their conformity with political subdivision boundaries; and "evidence concerning population disparities and statistics tending to show vote dilution." [T]he crux of Justice Powell's analysis seems to be that [the] intentional drawing of district boundaries for partisan ends and for no other reason violates the Equal Protection Clause in and of itself. We disagree. [E]ven if a state legislature redistricts with the specific intention of disadvantaging one political party's election prospects, we do not believe that there has been an unconstitutional discrimination against members of that party unless the redistricting does in fact disadvantage it at the polls. . . . Justice Powell's view would allow a constitutional violation to be found where the only proven effect on a political party's electoral power was disproportionate results in one (or possibly two) elections. . . . In rejecting Justice Powell's approach, we do not mean to intimate that the factors he considers are entirely irrelevant. The election results obviously are relevant to a showing of the effects required to prove a political gerrymandering claim under our view. And the district configurations may be combined with vote projections to predict future election results, which are also relevant to the effects showing. [E]vidence of exclusive legislative process and deliberate drawing of district lines in accordance with accepted gerrymandering principles would be relevant to intent, and evidence of valid and invalid configuration would be relevant to whether the districting plan met legitimate state interests. [But, in] our view, [Justice Powell's] approach departs from our past cases and invites judicial interference in legislative districting whenever a political party suffers at the polls. . . . Determining when an electoral system has been "arranged in a manner that will consistently degrade a voter's or a group of voters' influence on the political process as a whole," is of necessity a difficult inquiry. . . .

In sum, we hold that political gerrymandering cases are properly justiciable under the Equal Protection Clause. We also conclude, however, that a threshold showing of discriminatory vote dilution is required for a prima facie case of an equal protection violation. In this case, the findings made by the District Court of an adverse effect on the appellees do not surmount the threshold requirement.

[We conclude] that a threshold showing of discriminatory vote dilution is required for a prima facie case of an equal protection violation. In this case, the findings made by the District Court of an adverse effect on the appellees do not surmount the threshold requirement. Consequently, the judgment of the District Court is

Reversed.

Chief Justice BURGER, concurring in the judgment.

[I question] the Court's urge to craft a judicial remedy for this perceived "injustice." [T]he Framers of the Constitution [placed] responsibility for correction of such flaws in the people, relying on them to influence their elected representatives.

Justice O'CONNOR, with whom THE CHIEF JUSTICE and Justice REHNQUIST join, concurring in the judgment.

[I] would hold that the partisan gerrymandering claims of major political parties raise a nonjusticiable political question that the judiciary should leave to the legislative branch as the Framers of the Constitution unquestionably intended. . . . To turn these matters over to the federal judiciary is to inject the courts into the most heated partisan issues. . . .

[If] members of the major political parties are protected by the Equal Protection Clause from dilution of their voting strength, then members of every identifiable group that possesses distinctive interests and tends to vote on the basis of those interests should be able to bring similar claims. Federal courts will have no alternative but to attempt to recreate the complex process of legislative apportionment in the context of adversary litigation in order to reconcile the competing claims of political, religious, ethnic, racial, occupational, and socio-economic groups. . . . There is simply no clear stopping point to prevent the gradual evolution of a requirement of roughly proportional representation for every cohesive political group. [The] Equal Protection Clause does not supply judicially manageable standards for resolving purely political gerrymandering claims, and no group right to an equal share of political power was ever intended by the Framers of the Fourteenth Amendment. . . .

Clearly, members of the Democratic and Republican Parties cannot claim that they are a discrete and insular group vulnerable to exclusion from the political process by some dominant group: these political parties *are* the dominant groups, and the Court has offered no reason to believe that they are incapable of fending for themselves through the political process. Indeed, there is good reason to think that political gerrymandering is a self-limiting enterprise. In order to gerrymander, the legislative majority must weaken some of its safe seats, thus exposing its own incumbents to greater risks of defeat — risks they may refuse to accept past a certain point. Similarly, an overambitious gerrymander can lead to disaster for the legislative majority: because it has created more seats in which it hopes to win relatively narrow victories, the same swing in overall voting strength will tend to cost the legislative majority more and more seats as the gerrymander becomes more ambitious. . . .

[Furthermore], the Court fails to explain why a bipartisan gerrymander [affects] individuals any differently than a partisan gerrymander, which the Court makes vulnerable to constitutional challenge today. . . . In each instance, groups of individuals are assigned to districts with an eye towards promoting the ends of a political party and its incumbent legislators. Some groups within each party will lose any chance to elect a representative who belongs to their party, because they have been assigned to a district in which the opposing party holds an overwhelming advantage. Independent voters may lose any chance to influence the outcome of elections in their district, if one party has a sufficiently strong majority. . . .

Vote dilution analysis is far less manageable when extended to major political parties than if confined to racial minority groups. . . . Designing an apportionment plan that does not impair or degrade the voting strength of several groups is more difficult than designing a plan that does not have such an effect on one group for the simple reason that, as the number of criteria the plan must meet increases, the number of solutions that will satisfy those criteria will decrease. [T]he predictable result will be greater judicial intrusion into the apportionment process.

[W]hile membership in a racial group is an immutable characteristic, voters can — and often do — move from one party to the other or support candidates from both parties. Consequently, the difficulty of measuring voting strength is heightened in the case of a major political party. [A]ny such intervention is likely to move in the direction of proportional representation for political parties. . . . To be sure, the plurality has qualified its use of a *standard* of proportional representation in a variety of ways so as to avoid a *requirement* of proportional representation. The question is whether these qualifications are likely to be enduring in the face of the tremendous political pressures that courts will confront when called on to decide political gerrymandering claims. . . .

I would avoid the difficulties generated by the plurality's efforts to confine the effects of a generalized group right to equal representation by not recognizing such a right in the first instance. . . . Racial gerrymandering should remain justiciable, for the harms it engenders run counter to the central thrust of the Fourteenth Amendment. But no such justification can be given for judicial intervention on behalf of mainstream political parties, and the risks such intervention poses to our political institutions are unacceptable. . . .

Justice POWELL, with whom Justice STEVENS joins, concurring in part and dissenting in part.

[T]he plurality expresses the view, with which I agree, that a partisan political gerrymander violates the Equal Protection Clause only on proof of "both intentional discrimination against an identifiable political group and an actual discriminatory effect on that group." The plurality acknowledges that [the] challenged redistricting plan was adopted for the purpose of discriminating against Democratic voters. The plurality argues, however, that appellees failed to establish that their voting strength was diluted statewide despite uncontradicted proof that certain key districts were grotesquely gerrymandered to enhance the election prospects of Republican candidates.

[The] most basic flaw in the plurality's opinion is its failure to enunciate any standard that affords guidance to legislatures and courts. Legislators and judges are left to wonder whether compliance with "one person, one vote" completely insulates a partisan gerrymander from constitutional scrutiny, or whether a fairer but as yet undefined standard applies. The failure to articulate clear doctrine in this area places the plurality in the curious position of inviting further litigation even as it appears to signal the "constitutional green light" to would-be gerrymanderers.

[A] court should look first to the legislative process by which the challenged plan was adopted. [The] procedures used in redistricting Indiana were carefully designed to exclude Democrats from participating in the legislative process. [T]he mapmakers carved up counties, cities, and even townships in their effort to draw lines beneficial to the majority party. Many districts meander through several counties, picking up a number of townships from each. . . . The redistricting dissects counties into strange shapes lacking in common interests, on one occasion even placing the seat of one county in a voting district composed of townships from other counties. Under these conditions, [the] "potential for voter disillusion and nonparticipation is great," as voters are forced to focus their political activities in artificial electoral units. . . .

[There was] substantial evidence that appellants were motivated solely by partisan considerations. . . . Appellees further demonstrated through a statistical showing that the House plan debased the effectiveness of their votes. In 1982, all 100 House seats were up for election. Democratic candidates received about 51.9

percent of the vote, and Republican candidates received about 48.1 percent. Forty-three Democratic representatives were elected; 57 Republicans were elected. [I]n Marion and Allen Counties[,] Democratic candidates earned 46.3 percent of the vote, but won only 3 of 21 House seats. As the District Court observed, "such a disparity speaks for itself."

Note

The focus on effect in *Bandemer* reflects the limited utility of discriminatory purpose inquiry in the gerrymandering setting. Almost by definition, gerrymandering represents an effort to achieve partisan advantage. Notwithstanding the heightened importance of effect, a significant deviation between party voting percentages and representation was permitted. In this context, therefore, effects inquiry represents a limiting principle that has the profundity of discriminatory purpose criteria in other equal protection settings.

∾ PROBLEMS ∾

1. *Discriminatory Purpose.* The Court has insisted on establishing discriminatory purpose in other equal protection settings. Why would it not be satisfied with a showing of discriminatory intent in the gerrymandering context? Isn't it a discriminatory motive that makes discrimination invidious in many instances? *See* Washington v. Davis, 426 U.S. 229 (1976). Is it the nature of the discrimination that is critical for determining the model of review?

2. *Advising the Political Party.* Suppose that you are general counsel to the Democratic Party in Indiana. After Davis, what kind of proof will you need to amass to establish a cognizable claim to relief?

(3) Racial Gerrymandering

The political gerrymandering cases establish that a mere failure of proportionality in representation does not establish an equal protection violation. Rather, there must be purposeful discrimination and a demonstrable discriminatory effect on the targeted group. Considerations such as compactness, contiguity, and respect for political subdivisions and communities with common interests have been recognized bases for deviation from otherwise strict proportionality. Bloc voting on the basis of race is a common phenomenon in elections that reflects a perceived shared interest on the basis of group identity. Districting plans that overtly accounted for this factor presented an analytical choice for the Court. They could be assessed pursuant to the political gerrymandering decisions, in which case race would be simply another factor among many competing interests. Or, race-conscious policies could be analyzed as a form of affirmative action that merited strict scrutiny. Beginning in Shaw v. Reno, the Court opted for the latter model of review.

Shaw v. Reno

509 U.S. 630 (1993)

Justice O'CONNOR delivered the opinion of the Court.

This case involves two of the most complex and sensitive issues this Court has faced in recent years: the meaning of the constitutional "right" to vote, and the propriety of race-based state legislation designed to benefit members of historically disadvantaged racial minority groups. As a result of the 1990 census, North Carolina became entitled to a 12th seat in the United States House of Representatives. The General Assembly enacted a reapportionment plan that included one majority-black congressional district. After the Attorney General of the United States objected to the plan pursuant [to] the Voting Rights Act of 1965, the General Assembly passed new legislation creating a second majority-black district. Appellants allege that the revised plan, which contains district boundary lines of dramatically irregular shape, constitutes an unconstitutional racial gerrymander. The question before us is whether appellants have stated a cognizable claim.

The voting age population of North Carolina is approximately 78% white, 20% black, and 1% Native American; the remaining 1% is predominantly Asian. The black population is relatively dispersed; blacks constitute a majority of the general population in only 5 of the State's 100 counties. Geographically, the State divides into three regions: the eastern Coastal Plain, the central Piedmont Plateau, and the western mountains. The largest concentrations of black citizens live in the Coastal Plain, primarily in the northern part. The General Assembly's first redistricting plan contained one majority-black district centered in that area of the State.

[The] first of the two majority-black districts contained in the revised plan, District 1, is somewhat hook shaped. Centered in the northeast portion of the State, it moves southward until it tapers to a narrow band; then, with finger-like extensions, it reaches far into the southern-most part of the State near the South Carolina border. District 1 has been compared to a "Rorschach inkblot test," and a "bug splattered on a windshield."

The second majority-black district, District 12, is even more unusually shaped. It is approximately 160 miles long and, for much of its length, no wider than the I-85 corridor. It winds in snake like fashion through tobacco country, financial centers, and manufacturing areas "until it gobbles in enough enclaves of black neighborhoods." Northbound and southbound drivers on I-85 sometimes find themselves in separate districts in one county, only to "trade" districts when they enter the next county. Of the 10 counties through which District 12 passes, 5 are cut into 3 different districts; even towns are divided. At one point, the district remains contiguous only because it intersects at a single point with two other districts before crossing over them. One state legislator has remarked that "'[i]f you drove down the interstate with both car doors open, you'd kill most of the people in the district.'" The district even has inspired poetry: "Ask not for whom the line is drawn; it is drawn to avoid thee."

[A]ppellants appear to concede that race-conscious redistricting is not always unconstitutional. . . . What appellants object to is redistricting legislation that is so extremely irregular on its face that it rationally can be viewed only as an effort to segregate the races for purposes of voting, without regard for traditional districting principles and without sufficiently compelling justification. For the reasons that follow, we conclude that appellants have stated a claim upon which relief can be granted under the Equal Protection Clause.

The Equal Protection Clause provides that "[n]o State shall . . . deny to any person within its jurisdiction the equal protection of the laws." U.S. Const., Amdt. 14, 1. Its central purpose is to prevent the States from purposefully discriminating between individuals on the basis of race. Laws that explicitly distinguish between individuals on racial grounds fall within the core of that prohibition.

No inquiry into legislative purpose is necessary when the racial classification appears on the face of the statute. Express racial classifications are immediately suspect because, "[a]bsent searching judicial inquiry[,] there is simply no way of determining what classifications are 'benign' or 'remedial' and what classifications are in fact motivated by illegitimate notions of racial inferiority or simple racial politics." [These] principles [also] apply [to] those "rare" statutes that, although race neutral, are, on their face, "unexplainable on grounds other than race." [Appellants] contend that redistricting legislation that is so bizarre on its face that it is "unexplainable on grounds other than race," demands the same close scrutiny that we give other state laws that classify citizens by race. Our voting rights precedents support that conclusion.

[A] reapportionment statute typically does not classify persons at all; it classifies tracts of land, or addresses. Moreover, redistricting differs from other kinds of state decisionmaking in that the legislature always is aware of race when it draws district lines, just as it is aware of age, economic status, religious and political persuasion, and a variety of other demographic factors. That sort of race consciousness does not lead inevitably to impermissible race discrimination. [W]hen members of a racial group live together in one community, a reapportionment plan that concentrates members of the group in one district and excludes them from others may reflect wholly legitimate purposes. The district lines may be drawn, for example, to provide for compact districts of contiguous territory, or to maintain the integrity of political subdivisions.

The difficulty of proof, of course, does not mean that a racial gerrymander, once established, should receive less scrutiny under the Equal Protection Clause than other state legislation classifying citizens by race. Moreover, it seems clear to us that proof sometimes will not be difficult at all. In some exceptional cases, a reapportionment plan may be so highly irregular that, on its face, it rationally cannot be understood as anything other than an effort to "segregat[e] voters" on the basis of race. [A good example involves] a tortured municipal boundary line [that] was drawn to exclude black voters. So, too, would be a case in which a State concentrated a dispersed minority population in a single district by disregarding traditional districting principles such as compactness, contiguity, and respect for political subdivisions. [T]hese criteria are important not because they are constitutionally required[,] but because they are objective factors that may serve to defeat a claim that a district has been gerrymandered on racial lines.

[A] reapportionment plan that includes in one district individuals who belong to the same race, but who are otherwise widely separated by geographical and political boundaries, and who may have little in common with one another but the color of their skin, bears an uncomfortable resemblance to political apartheid. It reinforces the perception that members of the same racial group — regardless of their age, education, economic status, or the community in which they live — think alike, share the same political interests, and will prefer the same candidates at the polls. We have rejected such perceptions elsewhere as impermissible racial stereotypes. By perpetuating such notions, a racial gerrymander may exacerbate the very patterns of racial bloc voting that majority-minority districting is sometimes said to counteract.

The message that such districting sends to elected representatives is equally pernicious. When a district obviously is created solely to effectuate the perceived common interests of one racial group, elected officials are more likely to believe that their primary obligation is to represent only the members of that group, rather than their constituency as a whole. This is altogether antithetical to our system of representative democracy.

For these reasons, we conclude that a plaintiff challenging a reapportionment statute under the Equal Protection Clause may state a claim by alleging that the legislation, though race neutral on its face, rationally cannot be understood as anything other than an effort to separate voters into different districts on the basis of race, and that the separation lacks sufficient justification. It is unnecessary for us to decide whether or how a reapportionment plan that, on its face, can be explained in nonracial terms successfully could be challenged. Thus, we express no view as to whether "the intentional creation of majority-minority districts, without more," always gives rise to an equal protection claim. We hold only that, on the facts of this case, appellants have stated a claim sufficient to defeat the state appellees' motion to dismiss.

The dissenters consider the circumstances of this case "functionally indistinguishable" from multimember districting and at-large voting systems, which are loosely described as "other varieties of gerrymandering." We have considered the constitutionality of these practices in other Fourteenth Amendment cases, and have required plaintiffs to demonstrate that the challenged practice has the purpose and effect of diluting a racial group's voting strength. At-large and multimember schemes, however, do not classify voters on the basis of race. Classifying citizens by race, as we have said, threatens special harms that are not present in our vote-dilution cases. It therefore warrants different analysis.

Justice Souter apparently believes that racial gerrymandering is harmless unless it dilutes a racial group's voting strength. [R]eapportionment legislation that cannot be understood as anything other than an effort to classify and separate voters by race injures voters in other ways. It reinforces racial stereotypes and threatens to undermine our system of representative democracy by signaling to elected officials that they represent a particular racial group, rather than their constituency as a whole. Justice Souter does not adequately explain why these harms are not cognizable under the Fourteenth Amendment.

Racial classifications of any sort pose the risk of lasting harm to our society. They reinforce the belief, held by too many for too much of our history, that individuals should be judged by the color of their skin. Racial classifications with respect to voting carry particular dangers. Racial gerrymandering, even for remedial purposes, may balkanize us into competing racial factions; it threatens to carry us further from the goal of a political system in which race no longer matters — a goal that the Fourteenth and Fifteenth Amendments embody, and to which the Nation continues to aspire. It is for these reasons that race-based districting by our state legislatures demands close judicial scrutiny.

[We] hold only that appellants have stated a claim under the Equal Protection Clause by alleging that the North Carolina General Assembly adopted a reapportionment scheme so irrational on its face that it can be understood only as an effort to segregate voters into separate voting districts because of their race, and that the separation lacks sufficient justification. If the allegation of racial gerrymandering remains uncontradicted, the District Court further must determine whether the North Carolina plan is narrowly tailored to further a compelling governmental interest. Accordingly, we reverse the judgment of the District Court and remand the case for further proceedings consistent with this opinion.

It is so ordered.

Justice WHITE, with whom Justice BLACKMUN and Justice STEVENS join, dissenting.

[The] notion that North Carolina's plan, under which whites remain a voting majority in a disproportionate number of congressional districts, and pursuant to which the State has sent its first black representatives since Reconstruction to the United States Congress, might have violated appellants' constitutional rights is both a fiction and a departure from settled equal protection principles. . . . I dissent.

[A]ppellants have not presented a cognizable claim, because they have not alleged a cognizable injury. [A]n equal protection violation may be found only where the electoral system "substantially disadvantages certain voters in their opportunity to influence the political process effectively." [T]he issue is whether the classification based on race discriminates against anyone by denying equal access to the political process. [I]t strains credulity to suggest that North Carolina's purpose in creating a second majority-minority district was to discriminate against members of the majority group by "impair[ing] or burden[ing their] opportunity [to] participate in the political process." The State has made no mystery of its intent, which was to respond to the Attorney General's objections, by improving the minority group's prospects of electing a candidate of its choice. I doubt that this constitutes a discriminatory purpose as defined in the Court's equal protection cases. . . . But even assuming that it does, there is no question that appellants have not alleged the requisite discriminatory effects. Whites constitute roughly 76% of the total population and 79% of the voting age population in North Carolina. [U]nder the State's plan, they still constitute a voting majority in 10 (or 83%) of the 12 congressional districts. Though they might be dissatisfied at the prospect of casting a vote for a losing candidate — a lot shared by many, including a disproportionate number of minority voters — surely they cannot complain of discriminatory treatment. . . .

Racial gerrymanders come in various shades: at-large voting schemes; the fragmentation of a minority group among various districts "so that it is a majority in none," otherwise known as "cracking," the "stacking" of "a large minority population concentration [with] a larger white population," and, finally, the "concentration of [minority voters] into districts where constitute an excessive majority," also called "packing." In each instance, race is consciously utilized by the legislature for electoral purposes; in each instance, we have put the plaintiff challenging the district lines to the burden of demonstrating that the plan was meant to, and did in fact, exclude an identifiable racial group from participation in the political process.

Not so, apparently, when the districting "segregates" by drawing odd-shaped lines. In that case, we are told, such proof no longer is needed. Instead, it is the State that must rebut the allegation that race was taken into account, a fact that, together with the legislators' consideration of ethnic, religious, and other group characteristics, I had thought we practically took for granted. . . . A plan that "segregates" being functionally indistinguishable from any of the other varieties of gerrymandering, we should be consistent in what we require from a claimant: proof of discriminatory purpose and effect.

The other part of the majority's explanation of its holding is related to its simultaneous discomfort and fascination with irregularly shaped districts. . . . Disregard for geographic divisions and compactness often goes hand in hand with partisan gerrymandering. [W]hile district irregularities may provide strong indicia of a potential gerrymander, [they] have no bearing on whether the plan ultimately is found to violate the Constitution. . . . By focusing on looks, rather than impact, the majority "immediately casts attention in the wrong direction — toward superficialities of shape and size, rather than toward the political realities of district composition."

[T]he Court's approach nonetheless will unnecessarily hinder to some extent a State's voluntary effort to ensure a modicum of minority representation. This will be true in areas where the minority population is geographically dispersed. It also will be true where the minority population is not scattered, but, for reasons unrelated to race [the] State would rather not create the majority-minority district in its most "obvious" location. When, as is the case here, the creation of a majority-minority district does not unfairly minimize the voting power of any other group, the Constitution does not justify, much less mandate, such obstruction.

[I] have no doubt that a State's compliance with the Voting Rights Act clearly constitutes a compelling interest. [The] Court, while seemingly agreeing with this position, warns that the State's redistricting effort must be "narrowly tailored" to further its interest in complying with the law. [W]hat North Carolina did was precisely tailored to meet the objection of the Attorney General to its prior plan. Hence, I see no need for a remand at all. . . . To the extent that no other racial group is injured, remedying a Voting Rights Act violation does not involve preferential treatment. It involves, instead, an attempt to equalize treatment, and to provide minority voters with an effective voice in the political process. The Equal Protection Clause of the Constitution, surely, does not stand in the way.

Justice BLACKMUN, dissenting.

[T]he conscious use of race in redistricting does not violate the Equal Protection Clause unless the effect of the redistricting plan is to deny a particular group equal access to the political process or to minimize its voting strength unduly. It is particularly ironic that the case in which today's majority chooses to abandon settled law [is] a challenge by white voters to the plan under which North Carolina has sent black representatives to Congress for the first time since Reconstruction. I dissent.

Justice STEVENS, dissenting.

[T]wo critical facts in this case are undisputed: First, the shape of District 12 is so bizarre that it must have been drawn for the purpose of either advantaging or disadvantaging a cognizable group of voters; and, second, regardless of that shape, it was drawn for the purpose of facilitating the election of a second black representative from North Carolina.

[There] is no independent constitutional requirement of compactness or contiguity. . . . The existence of bizarre and uncouth district boundaries is powerful evidence of an ulterior purpose behind the shaping of those boundaries. . . . In this case, however, we know [the] legislators' [drew] District 12 to include a majority of African-American voters. . . .

[T]he Equal Protection Clause is violated when the State creates the kind of uncouth district boundaries seen [in] this case, for the sole purpose of making it more difficult for members of a minority group to win an election. . . . That duty, however, is not violated when the majority acts to facilitate the election of a member of a group that lacks such power because it remains underrepresented in the state legislature — whether that group is defined by political affiliation, by common economic interests, or by religious, ethnic, or racial characteristics. [If] it is permissible to draw boundaries to provide adequate representation for rural voters, for union members, for Hasidic Jews, for Polish Americans, or for Republicans, it necessarily follows that it is permissible to do the same thing for members of the very minority group whose history in the United States gave birth to the Equal Protection Clause. A contrary conclusion could only be described as perverse.

Accordingly, I respectfully dissent.

Justice SOUTER, dissenting.

[E]lectoral districting calls for decisions that nearly always require some consideration of race for legitimate reasons where there is a racially mixed population. . . . One need look no further than the Voting Rights Act to understand that this may be required, and we have held that race may constitutionally be taken into account in order to comply with that Act. [Unlike] most other governmental decisions in which race has figured[, electoral districting] decisions using racial criteria characteristically occur in circumstances in which the use of race to the advantage of one person is necessarily at the obvious expense of a member of a different race.

[In] districting, [the] mere placement of an individual in one district instead of another denies no one a right or benefit provided to others. All citizens may register, vote, and be represented. [O]ne's constitutional rights are not violated merely because the candidate one supports loses the election or because a group (including a racial group) to which one belongs winds up with a representative from outside that group. It is true, of course, that one's vote may be more or less effective depending on the interests of the other individuals who are in one's district, and our cases recognize the reality that members of the same race often have shared interests. "Dilution" thus refers to the effects of districting decisions not on an individual's political power viewed in isolation, but on the political power of a group. This is the reason that the placement of given voters in a given district, even on the basis of race, does not, without more, diminish the effectiveness of the individual as a voter.

Our different approaches to equal protection in electoral districting and nondistricting cases reflect these differences. . . . Presumably because the legitimate consideration of race in a districting decision is usually inevitable under the Voting Rights Act when communities are racially mixed, however, and because, without more, it does not result in diminished political effectiveness for anyone, we have not taken the approach of applying the usual standard of such heightened "scrutiny" to race-based districting decisions. [I]n order to obtain relief under the Fourteenth Amendment, the purpose and effect of the districting must be to devalue the effectiveness of a voter compared to what, as a group member, he would otherwise be able to enjoy.

[A] consequence of this categorical approach is the absence of any need for further searching "scrutiny" once it has been shown that a given districting decision has a purpose and effect falling within one of those categories. If a cognizable harm like dilution or the abridgment of the right to participate in the electoral process is shown, the districting plan violates the Fourteenth Amendment. If not, it does not. Under this approach, in the absence of an allegation of such cognizable harm, there is no need for further scrutiny because a gerrymandering claim cannot be proven without the element of harm. Nor if dilution is proven is there any need for further constitutional scrutiny; there has never been a suggestion that such use of race could be justified under any type of scrutiny, since the dilution of the right to vote can not be said to serve any legitimate governmental purpose. . . .

The Court offers no adequate justification for treating the narrow category of bizarrely shaped district claims differently from other districting claims. The only justification I can imagine would be the preservation of "sound districting principles," such as compactness and contiguity. But [we] have held that such principles are not constitutionally required. . . . Since there is no justification for the departure here from the principles that continue to govern electoral districting cases generally[,] I would not respond to the seeming egregiousness of the redistricting now before us by untethering the concept of racial gerrymander in such a case from the concept of harm exemplified by dilution. In the absence of an allegation of such harm, I would affirm the judgment of the District Court. I respectfully dissent.

Note

Upon remand, the Court in Shaw v. Hunt, 517 U.S. 899 (1996), determined that race was the predominant factor in configuring the congressional district and that the plan could not withstand strict scrutiny. Because it was not designed to remedy past discrimination, the plan was not supported by a compelling state interest. Although compliance with the Voting Rights Act might rise to the level of a compelling state interest, the Court found that the plan exceeded this enactment's mandate and thus was not narrowly tailored. In Hunt v. Cromartie, 526 U.S. 541 (1999), the Court reversed a summary judgment award on a claim alleging that subsequent drawing of the congressional district still was motivated by racial factors. Noting competing evidence of political motivations, the Court concluded that summary judgment was inappropriate. It also stressed "the sensitive nature of redistricting" and the need to presume that legislation is enacted in "good faith."

The *Hunt* ruling tracked the Court's thinking a year earlier in a Georgia case concerning three majority-minority congressional districts. The Court's concern in Shaw v. Reno seemed to be driven by the district's bizarre shape, a configuration that was found to leave no inference but race as a motivating factor. In Miller v. Johnson, 515 U.S. 900 (1995), the Court correlated review more closely with the premises underlying its affirmative action jurisprudence. When race is a predominant factor in districting, therefore, it is necessary to show a compelling interest in remedying past discrimination. Although compliance with the Voting Rights Act may be an imperative, the Court indicated that it will strike down plans that reflect or facilitate racial stereotyping.

Miller v. Johnson
515 U.S. 900 (1995)

Justice KENNEDY delivered the opinion of the Court.

[The] question [is] whether Georgia's new Eleventh District gives rise to a valid equal protection claim under the principles announced in *Shaw*, and, if so, whether it can be sustained nonetheless as narrowly tailored to serve a compelling governmental interest.

"The dense population centers of the approved Eleventh District were all majority-black, all at the periphery of the district, and in the case of Atlanta, Augusta and Savannah, all tied to a sparsely populated rural core by even less populated land bridges. Extending from Atlanta to the Atlantic, the Eleventh covered 6,784.2 square miles, splitting eight counties and five municipalities along the way." . . . Georgia's plan included three majority-black districts, though, and received Justice Department preclearance. [Elections] were held under the new congressional redistricting plan, [and] black candidates were elected to Congress from all three majority-black districts. [Five] white voters from the Eleventh District, filed this action against various state officials.

"Racial classifications with respect to voting carry particular dangers. Racial gerrymandering, even for remedial purposes, may balkanize us into competing racial factions; it threatens to carry us further from the goal of a political system in which race no longer matters—a goal that the Fourteenth and Fifteenth Amendments embody, and to which the Nation continues to aspire. It is for these reasons that race-based districting by our state legislatures demands close judicial scrutiny."

Our observation in *Shaw* of the consequences of racial stereotyping was not meant to suggest that a district must be bizarre on its face before there is a constitutional violation. Nor was our conclusion [that] in certain instances a district's appearance (or, to be more precise, its appearance in combination with certain demographic evidence) can give rise to an equal protection claim, a holding that bizarreness was a threshold showing, as appellants believe it to be. . . . *Shaw* did not erect an artificial rule barring accepted equal protection analysis in other redistricting cases. Shape is relevant not because bizarreness is a necessary element of the constitutional wrong or a threshold requirement of proof, but because it may be persuasive circumstantial evidence that race for its own sake, and not other districting principles, was the legislature's dominant and controlling rationale in drawing its district lines. [P]arties may rely on evidence other than bizarreness to establish race-based districting.

Federal court review of districting legislation represents a serious intrusion on the most vital of local functions. It is well settled that "reapportionment is primarily the duty and responsibility of the State." [Although] race-based decision-making is inherently suspect, until a claimant makes a showing sufficient to support that allegation the good faith of a state legislature must be presumed. The courts, in assessing the sufficiency of a challenge to a districting plan, must be sensitive to the complex interplay of forces that enter a legislature's redistricting calculus. Redistricting legislatures will, for example, almost always be aware of racial demographics; but it does not follow that race predominates in the redistricting process. . . . The plaintiff's burden is to show, either through circumstantial evidence of a district's shape and demographics or more direct evidence going to legislative purpose, that race was the predominant factor motivating the legislature's decision to place a significant number of voters within or without a particular district. To make this showing, a plaintiff must prove that the legislature subordinated traditional race-neutral districting principles, including but not limited to compactness, contiguity, respect for political subdivisions or communities defined by actual shared interests, to racial considerations. Where these or other race-neutral considerations are the basis for redistricting legislation, and are not subordinated to race, a state can "defeat a claim that a district has been gerrymandered on racial lines."

To satisfy strict scrutiny, the State must demonstrate that its districting legislation is narrowly tailored to achieve a compelling interest. There is a "significant state interest in eradicating the effects of past racial discrimination."

The State does not argue [that] it created the Eleventh District to remedy past discrimination. . . . [T]here is little doubt that the State's true interest in designing the Eleventh District was creating a third majority-black district to satisfy the Justice Department's preclearance demands. . . . [We] do not accept the contention that the State has a compelling interest in complying with whatever preclearance mandates the Justice Department issues. When a state governmental entity seeks to justify race-based remedies to cure the effects of past discrimination, we do not accept the government's mere assertion that the remedial action is required. [W]e insist on a strong basis in evidence of the harm being remedied. . . . Our presumptive skepticism of all racial classifications prohibits us [from] accepting on its face the Justice Department's conclusion that racial districting is necessary under the Voting Rights Act. [T]he judiciary retains an independent obligation in adjudicating consequent equal protection challenges to ensure that the State's actions are narrowly tailored to achieve a compelling interest. . . .

[Georgia's] drawing of the Eleventh District was not required under the Act because there was no reasonable basis to believe that Georgia's earlier enacted plans violated [the law]. Georgia's first and second proposed plans increased the number of majority-black districts from 1 out of 10 (10%) to 2 out of 11 (18.18%). These plans were "ameliorative. . . ." [T]he United States now relies on the fact that the Justice Department may object to a state proposal either on the ground that it has a prohibited purpose or a prohibited effect. The Government justifies its preclearance objections on the ground that the submitted plans violated [the Act's] purpose element. The key to the Government's position, which is plain from its objection letters if not from its briefs to this Court, is and always has been that Georgia failed to proffer a nondiscriminatory purpose for its refusal in the first two submissions to take the steps necessary to create a third majority-minority district.

The Government's position is insupportable. "[A]meliorative changes, even if they fall short of what might be accomplished in terms of increasing minority representation, cannot be found to violate section 5 unless they so discriminate on the basis of race or color as to violate the Constitution." [The] State's policy of adhering to other districting principles instead of creating as many majority-minority districts as possible does not support an inference that the plan "so discriminates on the basis of race or color as to violate the Constitution," and thus cannot provide any basis under 5 for the Justice Department's objection.

Instead of grounding its objections on evidence of a discriminatory purpose, it would appear the Government was driven by its policy of maximizing majority-black districts. [T]he Justice Department's implicit command that States engage in presumptively unconstitutional race-based districting brings the Voting Rights Act, once upheld as a proper exercise of Congress' authority under 2 of the Fifteenth Amendment, into tension with the Fourteenth Amendment. . . . Congress' exercise of its Fifteenth Amendment authority even when otherwise proper still must "consist with the letter and spirit of the constitution." [There] is no indication Congress intended such a far-reaching application of 5, so we reject the Justice Department's interpretation of the statute and avoid the constitutional problems that interpretation raises.

The Voting Rights Act, and its grant of authority to the federal courts to uncover official efforts to abridge minorities' right to vote, has been of vital importance in eradicating invidious discrimination from the electoral process and enhancing the legitimacy of our political institutions. Only if our political system and our society cleanse themselves of that discrimination will all members of the polity share an equal opportunity to gain public office regardless of race. . . . The end is neither assured nor well served, however, by carving electorates into racial blocs. . . . It takes a shortsighted and unauthorized view of the Voting Rights Act to invoke that statute, which has played a decisive role in redressing some of our worst forms of discrimination, to demand the very racial stereotyping the Fourteenth Amendment forbids.

Justice O'CONNOR, concurring.

[To] invoke strict scrutiny, a plaintiff must show that the State has relied on race in substantial disregard of customary and traditional districting practices. . . . Application of the Court's standard does not throw into doubt the vast majority of the Nation's 435 congressional districts, where presumably the States have drawn the boundaries in accordance with their customary districting principles. That is so even though race may well have been considered in the redistricting process. But application of the Court's standard helps achieve *Shaw*'s basic objective of making extreme instances of gerrymandering subject to meaningful judicial review.

Justice STEVENS, dissenting.

[T]he Court's equation of traditional gerrymanders, designed to maintain or enhance a dominant group's power, with a dominant group's decision to share its power with a previously underrepresented group [is distressing]. [I] do not see how a districting plan that favors a politically weak group can violate equal protection. [The] Constitution [certainly] permits a State to adopt a policy that promotes fair representation of different groups. . . . [R]acial minorities should not be less eligible than other groups to benefit from districting plans the majority designs to aid them.

Justice GINSBURG, with whom Justices STEVENS and BREYER join, and with whom Justice SOUTER joins except as to Part III-B, dissenting.

Legislative districting is highly political business. This Court has generally respected the competence of state legislatures to attend to the task. When race is the issue, however, we have recognized the need for judicial intervention to prevent dilution of minority voting strength. Generations of rank discrimination against African-Americans, as citizens and voters, account for that surveillance. [Although] the Georgia General Assembly prominently considered race in shaping the Eleventh District, race did not crowd out all other factors. . . . In contrast to the snake-like North Carolina district inspected in *Shaw*, Georgia's Eleventh District is hardly "bizarre," "extremely irregular," or "irrational on its face." Instead, the Eleventh District's design reflects significant consideration of "traditional districting factors (such as keeping political subdivisions intact) and the usual political process of compromise and trades for a variety of nonracial reasons." The District covers a core area in central and eastern Georgia, and its total land area of 6,780 square miles is about average for the State. [Nor] does the Eleventh District disrespect the boundaries of political subdivisions. [T]he District [is] not among those on a statistically calculated list of the 28 most bizarre districts in the United States. . . .

[Along] with attention to size, shape, and political subdivisions, the Court recognizes as an appropriate districting principle, "respect [for] communities defined by actual shared interests." The Court finds no community here, however, because a report in the record showed "fractured political, social, and economic interests within the Eleventh District's black population." [But] ethnicity itself can tie people together [even] people with divergent economic interests. For this reason, ethnicity is a significant force in political life. . . . Our Nation's cities are full of districts identified by their ethnic character — Chinese, Irish, Italian, Jewish, Polish, Russian, for example. The creation of ethnic districts reflecting felt identity is not ordinarily viewed as offensive or demeaning to those included in the delineation.

To separate permissible and impermissible use of race in legislative apportionment, the Court orders strict scrutiny for districting plans "predominantly motivated" by race. [A] federal case can be mounted whenever plaintiffs plausibly allege that other factors carried less weight than race. This invitation to litigate against the State seems to me neither necessary nor proper. . . . Apportionment schemes, by their very nature, assemble people in groups. [L]egislators classify voters in groups — by economic, geographical, political, or social characteristics — and then "reconcile the competing claims of [these] groups." [That] ethnicity defines some of these groups is a political reality. . . . Until now, no constitutional infirmity has been seen in districting Irish or Italian voters together, for example, so long as the delineation does not abandon familiar apportionment practices. . . .

Under the Court's approach, judicial review of the same intensity, i.e., strict scrutiny, is in order once it is determined that an apportionment is predominantly motivated by race. It matters not at all, in this new regime, whether the apportionment dilutes or enhances minority voting strength. . . . Special circumstances justify vigilant judicial inspection to protect minority voters — circumstances that do not apply to majority voters. A history of exclusion from state politics left racial minorities without clout to extract provisions for fair representation in the lawmaking forum. . . . White voters in Georgia do not lack means to exert strong pressure on their state legislators. The force of their numbers is itself a powerful determiner of what the legislature will do that does not coincide with perceived majority interests. . . .

Note

When legislative efforts to construct a new districting plan broke down, a federal court devised a scheme that included one majority-minority district. This plan was found to be consistent with traditional districting principles and was upheld in *Abrams v. Johnson*, 521 U.S. 74 (1997). Insofar as race is a consideration in redistricting, strict scrutiny depends on whether it is a predominant factor. This point was reaffirmed in *Bush v. Vera*, 517 U.S. 292 (1996), when the Court struck down a congressional districting plan that had three majority-minority districts. Although race was not the exclusive factor, it was the predominant consideration and thus the plan was subject to strict scrutiny. For such a redistricting plan to survive, it must be a narrowly tailored remedy that responds to specific instances of discrimination. Compliance with the Voting Rights Act may constitute a compelling interest, but legislators must be careful not to exceed the scope of the enactment's requirements.

∽ PROBLEMS ∽

1. *Relevant Factors.* What factors should a court consider in determining whether a district has been racially gerrymandered in violation of the Equal Protection Clause? What factors were important in *Shaw* and *Miller*?

2. *Advising the Legislature.* Following the decisions in *Shaw* and *Miller,* and after the 2000 census, the Commonwealth of Kentucky decides to redraw its congressional district lines. The legislature is approached by the U.S. Department of Justice (DOJ), which expresses concern about the fact that, although Kentucky has large African American populations in some cities, it has no African American representatives in Congress. Relying on the Voting Rights Act, DOJ demands that Kentucky draw its district lines to create a majority African American district. You serve as counsel to the legislative committee that is drawing the redistricting plan. Although it is possible to create a majority African American district, it will be extremely difficult to do so without creating a very strangely configured district. How would you advise the legislature to respond to DOJ?

(4) Vote Recording and Counting

Voter understanding of equipment operation is a factor that typically is accounted for by officials who provide instructions for recording preferences on the ballot. The quality of this education may vary from one district or state to another. Variances also exist with respect to processes for counting votes, which may affect their relative weighting.

Bush v. Gore

531 U.S. 98 (2000)

PER CURIAM

On December 8, 2000, the Supreme Court of Florida ordered that the Circuit Court of Leon County tabulate by hand 9,000 ballots in Miami-Dade County. It also ordered the inclusion in the certified vote totals of 215 votes identified in Palm Beach County and 168 votes identified in Miami-Dade County for Vice

President Albert Gore, Jr., and Senator Joseph Lieberman, Democratic candidates for President and Vice President. The State Supreme Court noted that petitioner, George W. Bush, asserted that the net gain for Vice President Gore in Palm Beach County was 176 votes, and directed the Circuit Court to resolve that dispute on remand. The court further held that relief would require manual recounts in all Florida counties where so-called "undervotes" had not been subject to manual tabulation. The court ordered all manual recounts to begin at once. Governor Bush and Richard Cheney, Republican candidates for President and Vice President, filed an emergency application for a stay of this mandate.

[The] day following the Presidential election, the Florida Division of Elections reported that petitioner Bush had received 2,909,135 votes, and respondent Gore had received 2,907,351 votes, a margin of 1,784 for Governor Bush. Because Governor Bush's margin of victory was less than "one-half of a percent . . . of the votes cast," an automatic machine recount was conducted, the results of which showed Governor Bush still winning the race but by a diminished margin. Vice President Gore then sought manual recounts in [several counties], pursuant to Florida's election protest provisions. A dispute arose concerning the deadline for local county canvassing boards to submit their returns to the Secretary of State (Secretary). The Secretary declined to waive [the] deadline imposed by statute. The Florida Supreme Court, however, set [a new] deadline. We granted certiorari and vacated the Florida Supreme Court's decision, finding considerable uncertainty as to the grounds on which it was based. [The] Florida Supreme Court [then] issued a decision on remand reinstating that date.

On November 26, the Florida Elections Canvassing Commission certified the results of the election and declared Governor Bush the winner of Florida's 25 electoral votes. [Vice President Gore], pursuant to Florida's contest provisions, filed a complaint in Leon County Circuit Court contesting the certification. The Circuit Court denied relief, stating that Vice President Gore failed to meet his burden of proof.

The Supreme Court held that Vice President Gore had satisfied his burden of proof with respect to his challenge to Miami-Dade County's failure to tabulate, by manual count, 9,000 ballots on which the machines had failed to detect a vote for President ("undervotes"). Noting the closeness of the election, the court explained that "[o]n this record, there can be no question that there are legal votes within the 9,000 uncounted votes sufficient to place the results of this election in doubt." A "legal vote," as determined by the Supreme Court, is "one in which there is a 'clear indication of the intent of the voter.'" The court therefore ordered a hand recount of the 9,000 ballots in Miami-Dade County. Observing that the contest provisions vest broad discretion in the circuit judge to "provide any relief appropriate under such circumstances," the Supreme Court further held that the Circuit Court could order "the Supervisor of Elections and the Canvassing Boards, as well as the necessary public officials, in all counties that have not conducted a manual recount or tabulation of the undervotes [to] do so forthwith, said tabulation to take place in the individual counties where the ballots are located."

The Supreme Court [explained that the recount] deadline was not intended to exclude votes identified after that date through ongoing manual recounts. As to Miami-Dade County, the court concluded that although the 168 votes identified were the result of a partial recount, they were "legal votes [that] could change the outcome of the election." The Supreme Court therefore directed the Circuit Court to include those totals in the certified results, subject to resolution of the actual vote total from the Miami-Dade partial recount.

The petition presents the following question[]: whether [the] use of standardless manual recounts violates the Equal Protection and Due Process Clauses. With respect to the equal protection question, we find a violation of the Equal Protection Clause.

II

The closeness of this election, and the multitude of legal challenges which have followed in its wake, have brought into sharp focus a common, if heretofore unnoticed, phenomenon. Nationwide statistics reveal that an estimated 2% of ballots cast do not register a vote for President for whatever reason, including deliberately choosing no candidate at all or some voter error, such as voting for two candidates or insufficiently marking a ballot. [This] case has shown that punchcard balloting machines can produce an unfortunate number of ballots which are not punched in a clean, complete way by the voter. . . .

The individual citizen has no federal constitutional right to vote for electors for the President of the United States unless and until the state legislature chooses a statewide election as the means to implement its power to appoint members of the Electoral College. U.S. Const., Art. II, §1. . . . When the state legislature vests the right to vote for President in its people, the right to vote as the legislature has prescribed is fundamental; and one source of its fundamental nature lies in the equal weight accorded to each vote and the equal dignity owed to each voter. . . . The right to vote is protected in more than the initial allocation of the franchise. Equal protection applies as well to the manner of its exercise. Having once granted the right to vote on equal terms, the State may not, by later arbitrary and disparate treatment, value one person's vote over that of another. "[T]he right of suffrage can be denied by a debasement or dilution of the weight of a citizen's vote just as effectively as by wholly prohibiting the free exercise of the franchise."

[The] question before us [is] whether the recount procedures the Florida Supreme Court has adopted are consistent with its obligation to avoid arbitrary and disparate treatment of the members of its electorate. . . . Much of the controversy seems to revolve around ballot cards designed to be perforated by a stylus but which, either through error or deliberate omission, have not been perforated with sufficient precision for a machine to register the perforations. In some cases a piece of the card — a chad — is hanging, say, by two corners. In other cases there is no separation at all, just an indentation.

The Florida Supreme Court has ordered that the intent of the voter be discerned from such ballots. [I]t is not necessary to decide whether the Florida Supreme Court had the authority under the legislative scheme for resolving election disputes to define what a legal vote is and to mandate a manual recount implementing that definition. The recount mechanisms implemented in response to the decisions of the Florida Supreme Court do not satisfy the minimum requirement for nonarbitrary treatment of voters necessary to secure the fundamental right. Florida's basic command for the count of legally cast votes is to consider the "intent of the voter." This is unobjectionable as an abstract proposition and a starting principle. The problem inheres in the absence of specific standards to ensure its equal application. The formulation of uniform rules to determine intent based on these recurring circumstances is practicable and, we conclude, necessary.

The law does not refrain from searching for the intent of the actor in a multitude of circumstances; and in some cases the general command to ascertain intent is not susceptible to much further refinement. In this instance, however, the question is not whether to believe a witness but how to interpret the marks or holes or scratches on an inanimate object, a piece of cardboard or paper which, it is said, might not have registered as a vote during the machine count. The factfinder confronts a thing, not a person. The search for intent can be confined by specific rules designed to ensure uniform treatment.

The want of those rules here has led to unequal evaluation of ballots in various respects. [T]he standards for accepting or rejecting contested ballots might vary not only from county to county but indeed within a single county from one recount team to another.

An early case in our one-person, one-vote jurisprudence arose when a State accorded arbitrary and disparate treatment to voters in its different counties. The Court found a constitutional violation. "[The] idea that one group can be granted greater voting strength than another is hostile to the one man, one vote basis of our representative government."

The State Supreme Court ratified this uneven treatment. It mandated that the recount totals from two counties, Miami-Dade and Palm Beach, be included in the certified total. The court also appeared to hold *sub silentio* that the recount totals from Broward County, which were not completed until after the [original] certification by the Secretary, were to be considered part of the new certified vote totals even though the county certification was not contested by Vice President Gore. Yet each of the counties used varying standards to determine what was a legal vote. Broward County used a more forgiving standard than Palm Beach County, and uncovered almost three times as many new votes, a result markedly disproportionate to the difference in population between the counties.

In addition, the recounts in these three counties were not limited to so-called undervotes but extended to all of the ballots. The distinction has real consequences. A manual recount of all ballots identifies not only those ballots which show no vote but also those which contain more than one, the so-called overvotes. Neither category will be counted by the machine. This is not a trivial concern. [R]espondents estimated there are as many as 110,000 overvotes statewide.

As a result, the citizen whose ballot was not read by a machine because he failed to vote for a candidate in a way readable by a machine may still have his vote counted in a manual recount; on the other hand, the citizen who marks two candidates in a way discernible by the machine will not have the same opportunity to have his vote count, even if a manual examination of the ballot would reveal the requisite indicia of intent. Furthermore, the citizen who marks two candidates, only one of which is discernible by the machine, will have his vote counted even though it should have been read as an invalid ballot. The State Supreme Court's inclusion of vote counts based on these variant standards exemplifies concerns with the remedial processes that were under way.

That brings the analysis to yet a further equal protection problem. The votes certified by the court included a partial total from one county. The Florida Supreme Court's decision thus gives no assurance that the recounts included in a final certification must be complete. Indeed, [respondents contend] that it would be consistent with the rules of the recount procedures to include whatever partial counts are done by the time of final certification, and we interpret the Florida Supreme Court's decision to permit this. [The] press of time does not diminish the constitutional concern. A desire for speed is not a general excuse for ignoring equal protection guarantees.

[The] question before the Court is not whether local entities, in the exercise of their expertise, may develop different systems for implementing elections. Instead, we are presented with a situation where a state court with the power to assure uniformity has ordered a statewide recount with minimal procedural safeguards. When a court orders a statewide remedy, there must be at least some assurance that the rudimentary requirements of equal treatment and fundamental fairness are satisfied.

[Upon] due consideration of the difficulties identified to this point, it is obvious that the recount cannot be conducted in compliance with the requirements of equal protection and due process without substantial additional work. It would require not only the adoption (after opportunity for argument) of adequate statewide standards for determining what is a legal vote, and practicable procedures to implement them, but also orderly judicial review of any disputed matters that might arise. In addition, the Secretary has advised that the recount of only a portion of the ballots requires that the vote tabulation equipment be used to screen out undervotes, a function for which the machines were not designed. If a recount of overvotes were also required, perhaps even a second screening would be necessary. Use of the equipment for this purpose, and any new software developed for it, would have to be evaluated for accuracy by the Secretary, as required by [state law].

The Supreme Court of Florida has said that the legislature intended the State's electors to "participat[e] fully in the federal electoral process." That statute, in turn, requires that any controversy or contest that is designed to lead to a conclusive selection of electors be completed by December 12. That date is upon us, and there is no recount procedure in place under the State Supreme Court's order that comports with minimal constitutional standards. Because it is evident that any recount seeking to meet the December 12 date will be unconstitutional for the reasons we have discussed, we reverse the judgment of the Supreme Court of Florida ordering a recount to proceed.

None are more conscious of the vital limits on judicial authority than are the Members of this Court, and none stand more in admiration of the Constitution's design to leave the selection of the President to the people, through their legislatures, and to the political sphere. When contending parties invoke the process of the courts, however, it becomes our unsought responsibility to resolve the federal and constitutional issues the judicial system has been forced to confront.

The judgment of the Supreme Court of Florida is reversed, and the case is remanded for further proceedings not inconsistent with this opinion.

Chief Justice REHNQUIST, with whom Justice SCALIA and Justice THOMAS join, concurring.

We join the *per curiam* opinion. We write separately because we believe there are additional grounds that require us to reverse the Florida Supreme Court's decision. [In] most cases, comity and respect for federalism compel us to defer to the decisions of state courts on issues of state law. That practice reflects our understanding that the decisions of state courts are definitive pronouncements of the will of the States as sovereigns. Of course, in ordinary cases, the distribution of powers among the branches of a State's government raises no questions of federal constitutional law, subject to the requirement that the government be republican in character. [But] Article II, §1, cl. 2, provides that "[e]ach State shall appoint, in such Manner as the *Legislature* thereof may direct," electors for President and Vice President. Thus, the text of the election law itself, and not just its interpretation by the courts of the States, takes on independent significance. . . . [W]ith respect to a Presidential election, the court must be both mindful of the legislature's role under Article II in choosing the manner of appointing electors and deferential to those bodies expressly empowered by the legislature to carry out its constitutional mandate.

In order to determine whether a state court has infringed upon the legislature's authority, we necessarily must examine the law of the State as it existed prior to the action of the court. Though we generally defer to state courts on the interpretation of state law, there are of course areas in which the Constitution requires this Court to undertake an independent, if still deferential, analysis of state law. [This] inquiry does not imply a disrespect for state *courts* but rather a respect for the constitutionally prescribed role of state *legislatures*. . . .

Justice STEVENS, with whom Justice GINSBURG and Justice BREYER join, dissenting.

The Constitution assigns to the States the primary responsibility for determining the manner of selecting the Presidential electors. See Art. II, §1, cl. 2. When questions arise about the meaning of state laws, including election laws, it is our settled practice to accept the opinions of the highest courts of the States as providing the final answers. On rare occasions, however, either federal statutes or the Federal Constitution may require federal judicial intervention in state elections. This is not such an occasion. [Admittedly], the use of differing substandards for determining voter intent in different counties employing similar voting systems may raise serious concerns. Those concerns are alleviated — if not eliminated — by the fact that a single impartial magistrate will ultimately adjudicate all objections arising from the recount process. . . .

Even assuming that aspects of the remedial scheme might ultimately be found to violate the Equal Protection Clause, I could not subscribe to the majority's disposition of the case. [O]nce a state legislature determines to select electors through a popular vote, the right to have one's vote counted is of constitutional stature. . . . Florida law holds that all ballots that reveal the intent of the voter constitute valid votes. Recognizing these principles, the majority nonetheless orders the termination of the contest proceeding before all such votes have been tabulated. Under their own reasoning, the appropriate course of action would be to remand to allow more specific procedures for implementing the legislature's uniform general standard to be established.

In the interest of finality, however, the majority effectively orders the disenfranchisement of an unknown number of voters whose ballots reveal their intent — and are therefore legal votes under state law — but were for some reason rejected by ballot-counting machines. It does so on the basis of the deadlines set forth in Title 3 of the United States Code. [T]hose provisions merely provide rules of decision for Congress to follow when selecting among conflicting slates of electors. They do not prohibit a State from counting what the majority concedes to be legal votes until a bona fide winner is determined. [As] the majority notes, "[a] desire for speed is not a general excuse for ignoring equal protection guarantees."

[T]he Florida Supreme Court['s] decisions were rooted in long-established precedent and were consistent with the relevant statutory provisions, taken as a whole. It did what courts do — it decided the case before it in light of the legislature's intent to leave no legally cast vote uncounted. In so doing, it relied on the sufficiency of the general "intent of the voter" standard articulated by the state legislature, coupled with a procedure for ultimate review by an impartial judge, to resolve the concern about disparate evaluations of contested ballots. If we assume — as I do — that the members of that court and the judges who would have carried out its mandate are impartial, its decision does not even raise a colorable federal question. . . .

Justice SOUTER, with whom Justice BREYER joins, and with whom Justice STEVENS and Justice GINSBURG join a[s] to all but Part III, dissenting.

The Court should not have reviewed [this] case, and should not have stopped Florida's attempt to recount all undervote ballots by issuing a stay of the Florida Supreme Court's orders during the period of this review. . . . [The] interpretations by the Florida court raise no substantial question under Article II. That court engaged in permissible construction in determining that Gore had instituted a contest authorized by the state statute, and it proceeded to direct the trial judge to deal with that contest in the exercise of the discretionary powers generously conferred by [state law]. [O]ur customary respect for state interpretations of state law counsels against rejection of the Florida court's determinations in this case. . . .

Petitioners have raised an equal protection claim (or, alternatively, a due process claim) in the charge that unjustifiably disparate standards are applied in different electoral jurisdictions to otherwise identical facts. It is true that the Equal Protection Clause does not forbid the use of a variety of voting mechanisms within a jurisdiction, even though different mechanisms will have different levels of effectiveness in recording voters' intentions; local variety can be justified by concerns about cost, the potential value of innovation, and so on. But evidence in the record here suggests that a different order of disparity obtains under rules for determining a voter's intent that have been applied (and could continue to be applied) to identical types of ballots used in identical brands of machines and exhibiting identical physical characteristics (such as "hanging" or "dimpled" chads). I can conceive of no legitimate state interest served by these differing treatments of the expressions of voters' fundamental rights. The differences appear wholly arbitrary.

In deciding what to do about this, we should take account of the fact that electoral votes are due to be cast in six days. I would therefore remand the case to the courts of Florida with instructions to establish uniform standards for evaluating the several types of ballots that have prompted differing treatments, to be applied within and among counties when passing on such identical ballots in any further recounting (or successive recounting) that the courts might order. . . . I see no warrant for this Court to assume that Florida could not possibly comply with this requirement before the date set for the meeting of electors, December 18. Although one of the dissenting justices of the State Supreme Court estimated that disparate standards potentially affected 170,000 votes, the number at issue is significantly smaller. [To] recount these manually would be a tall order, but before this Court stayed the effort to do that the courts of Florida were ready to do their best to get that job done. There is no justification for denying the State the opportunity to try to count all disputed ballots now.

Justice GINSBURG, with whom Justice STEVENS joins, and with whom Justice SOUTER and Justice BREYER join as to Part I, dissenting.

[The] extraordinary setting of this case has obscured the ordinary principle that dictates its proper resolution: Federal courts defer to state high courts' interpretations of their state's own law. This principle reflects the core of federalism, on which all agree. [Were] the other Members of this Court as mindful as they generally are of our system of dual sovereignty, they would affirm the judgment of the Florida Supreme Court.

I agree with Justice Stevens that petitioners have not presented a substantial equal protection claim. Ideally, perfection would be the appropriate standard for judging the recount. But we live in an imperfect world, one in which thousands of votes have not been counted. I cannot agree that the recount adopted by the Florida court, flawed as it may be, would yield a result any less fair or precise than the certification that preceded that recount.

[The] Court assumes that time will not permit "orderly judicial review of any disputed matters that might arise." But no one has doubted the good faith and diligence with which Florida election officials, attorneys for all sides of this controversy, and the courts of law have performed their duties. Notably, the Florida Supreme Court has produced two substantial opinions within 29 hours of oral argument. In sum, the Court's conclusion that a constitutionally adequate recount is impractical is a prophecy the Court's own judgment will not allow to be tested. Such an untested prophecy should not decide the Presidency of the United States.

Justice BREYER, with whom Justice STEVENS and Justice GINSBURG join except as to Part I-A-1, and with whom Justice SOUTER joins as to Part I, dissenting.

The Court was wrong to take this case. It was wrong to grant a stay. It should now vacate that stay and permit the Florida Supreme Court to decide whether the recount should resume. . . . The political implications of this case for the country are momentous. But the federal legal questions presented, with one exception, are insubstantial. The majority raises three equal protection problems with the Florida Supreme Court's recount order: first, the failure to include overvotes in the manual recount; second, the fact that *all* ballots, rather than simply the undervotes, were recounted in some, but not all, counties; and third, the absence of a uniform, specific standard to guide the recounts. As far as the first issue is concerned, petitioners presented no evidence, to this Court or to any Florida court, that a manual recount of overvotes would identify additional legal votes. The same is true of the second, and, in addition, the majority's reasoning would seem to invalidate any state provision for a manual recount of individual counties in a statewide election.

[T]here is no justification for the majority's remedy, which is simply to reverse the lower court and halt the recount entirely. An appropriate remedy would be, instead, to remand this case with instructions that, even at this late date, would permit the Florida Supreme Court to require recounting *all* undercounted votes in Florida[,] whether or not previously recounted prior to the end of the protest period, and to do so in accordance with a single uniform standard. [By] halting the manual recount, and thus ensuring that the uncounted legal votes will not be counted under any standard, this Court crafts a remedy out of proportion to the asserted harm. And that remedy harms the very fairness interests the Court is attempting to protect. The manual recount would itself redress a problem of unequal treatment of ballots. . . . Nor do I understand why the Florida Supreme Court's recount order, which helps to redress this inequity, must be entirely prohibited based on a deficiency that could easily be remedied.

∾ PROBLEMS ∾

1. *Tolerance Levels.* States and jurisdictions within states use varying technologies to record and count votes. Implicit in these differences are variances with respect to reliability. What tolerance level should there be for deviations not just in the recounting process but in the counting process itself?

2. *Standing and Political Question Issues.* Should Bush v. Gore have been dismissed on standing or political question grounds? Did then-Governor Bush have standing to challenge the recount methods in Florida? Third-party standing?

3. *Halting the Recount.* Do you agree with the Court that the recount should be halted? What about the argument, in more than one dissent, that the case should have been remanded to the Florida Supreme Court for the development of standards that would satisfy the Equal Protection Clause?

c. Access to the Ballot

Standards of review for determining access to the ballot depend on the degree of burden. Regulations that seriously impede access to the ballot will be evaluated more carefully than those perceived as imposing minimal burdens. In American Party of Texas v. White, the Court upheld a provision requiring parties that received less than 2 percent of the gubernatorial vote in the prior election to obtain signatures of at least 1 percent of those who voted. This prescription, from the Court's perspective, was not excessively burdensome. A law that requires candidates to pay a filing fee, totaling 2 percent of the annual salary of the office sought, was found to violate the Equal Protection Clause. In Lubin v. Panish, the Court found that the regulation unduly burdened the ability of indigent candidates to secure a position on the ballot. In addition to being a method of diluting the right to vote, restrictions on access to the ballot may implicate the right of association.

5. Education

An understanding that education is a fundamental right goes back to the early twentieth century. In Pierce v. Society of Sisters, 268 U.S. 510 (1925), the Court struck down a state law requiring parents to send their children to public schools. The holding was accompanied by the observation that the statute "unreasonably interferes with the liberty of parents and guardians to direct the upbringing and education of their children." The importance of education, from both individual and societal perspectives, was noted in case law that undid official segregation. In Brown v. Board of Education, the Court described education as "perhaps the most important function of state and local government, . . . the very foundation of good citizenship, [and] . . . a principal instrument in awakening the child to cultural values, in preparing him for later professional training, and in helping him to adjust normally to his environment." The *Brown* Court further observed that when the state provides for public education, it is "a right that must be made available to all on equal terms." In Bolling v. Sharpe, 347 U.S. 497 (1954), the Court found that segregated public education effected a "deprivation of . . . liberty under the Due Process Clause." Equalization of educational opportunity implicates not only desegregation but also social, philosophical, and economic policy.

San Antonio Independent School District v. Rodriguez

411 U.S. 1 (1973)

Mr. Justice POWELL delivered the opinion of the Court.

This suit attacking the Texas system of financing public education was initiated by Mexican-American parents whose children attend the elementary and secondary schools in the Edgewood Independent School District, an urban school district in San Antonio, Texas. They brought a class action on behalf of schoolchildren throughout the State who are members of minority groups or who are poor and reside in school districts having a low property tax base.

[Texas] was a predominantly rural State and its population and property wealth were spread relatively evenly across the State. Sizable differences in the value of assessable property between local school districts became increasingly evident as the State became more industrialized and as rural-to-urban population shifts became more pronounced. . . . These growing disparities in population and taxable property between districts were responsible in part for increasingly notable differences in levels of local expenditure for education.

[Recognizing] the need for increased state funding to help offset disparities in local spending and to meet Texas' changing educational requirements, the state legislature in the late 1940's undertook a thorough evaluation of public education with an eye toward major reform. [It enacted the "Foundation Program," which provided] for state and local contributions to a fund earmarked specifically for teacher salaries, operating expenses, and transportation costs. The State, supplying funds from its general revenues, finances approximately 80% of the Program, and the school districts are responsible—as a unit—for providing the remaining 20%. The districts' share, known as the Local Fund Assignment, is apportioned among the school districts under a formula designed to reflect each district's relative taxpaying ability. . . . The district [finances] its share of the Assignment out of revenues from local property taxation.

The design of this complex system was twofold. First, it was an attempt to assure that the Foundation Program would have an equalizing influence on expenditure levels between school districts by placing the heaviest burden on the school districts most capable of paying. Second, the Program's architects sought to establish a Local Fund Assignment that would force every school district to contribute to the education of its children but that would not by itself exhaust any district's resources. Today every school district does impose a property tax from which it derives locally expendable funds in excess of the amount necessary to satisfy its Local Fund Assignment under the Foundation Program.

The school district in which appellees reside, the Edgewood Independent School District, has been compared throughout this litigation with the Alamo Heights Independent School District. This comparison between the least and most affluent districts in the San Antonio area serves to illustrate the manner in which the dual system of finance operates and to indicate the extent to which substantial disparities exist despite the State's impressive progress in recent years. Edgewood is one of seven public school districts in the metropolitan area. . . . The district [has] 25 elementary [schools] situated in the core-city sector of San

Antonio in a residential neighborhood that has little commercial or industrial property. The residents are predominantly of Mexican-American descent: approximately 90% of the student population is Mexican-American and over 6% is Negro. The average assessed property value per pupil is $5,960 — the lowest in the metropolitan area — and the median family income ($4,686) is also the lowest. At an equalized tax rate of $1.05 per $100 of assessed property — the highest in the metropolitan area — the district contributed $26 to the education of each child for the 1967-1968 school year above its Local Fund Assignment for the Minimum Foundation Program. The Foundation Program contributed $222 per pupil for a state-local total of $248. Federal funds added another $108 for a total of $356 per pupil.

Alamo Heights is the most affluent school district in San Antonio. Its six schools hous[e] approximately 5,000 students. . . . The school population is predominantly 'Anglo,' having only 18% Mexican-Americans and less than 1% Negroes. The assessed property value per pupil exceeds $49,000, and the median family income is $8,001. In 1967-1968 the local tax rate of $.85 per $100 of valuation yielded $333 per pupil over and above its contribution to the Foundation Program. Coupled with the $225 provided from that Program, the district was able to supply $558 per student. Supplemented by a $36 per-pupil grant from federal sources, Alamo Heights spent $594 per pupil.

[I]t was these disparities, largely attributable to differences in the amounts of money collected through local property taxation, that led the District Court to conclude that Texas' dual system of public school financing violated the Equal Protection Clause. The District Court held that the Texas system discriminates on the basis of wealth in the manner in which education is provided for its people. Finding that wealth is a 'suspect' classification and that education is a 'fundamental' interest, the District Court held that the Texas system could be sustained only if the State could show that it was premised upon some compelling state interest. [The court found no compelling or even reasonable basis for the classifications.]

Texas virtually concedes that its historically rooted dual system of financing education could not withstand the strict judicial scrutiny that this Court has found appropriate in reviewing legislative judgments that interfere with fundamental constitutional rights or that involve suspect classifications. . . .

[We] must decide, first, whether the Texas system of financing public education operates to the disadvantage of some suspect class or impinges upon a fundamental right explicitly or implicitly protected by the Constitution, thereby requiring strict judicial scrutiny. If so, the judgment of the District Court should be affirmed. If not, the Texas scheme must still be examined to determine whether it rationally furthers some legitimate, articulated state purpose and therefore does not constitute an invidious discrimination in violation of the Equal Protection Clause of the Fourteenth Amendment.

[In] concluding that strict judicial scrutiny was required, [the District Court] relied on decisions dealing with the rights of indigents to equal treatment in the criminal trial and appellate processes, and on cases disapproving wealth restrictions on the right to vote. . . . It then reasoned [that] there is a fundamental right to education and that, absent some compelling state justification, the Texas system could not stand. [W]e find neither the suspect-classification nor the fundamental-interest analysis persuasive.

The wealth discrimination [is] quite unlike any of the forms of wealth discrimination heretofore reviewed by this Court. . . . The courts [assumed that] since, under the traditional systems of financing public schools, some poorer people receive less expensive educations than other more affluent people, these systems discriminate on the basis of wealth. . . . However described, [appellees'] suit asks this Court to extend its most exacting scrutiny to review a system that allegedly discriminates against a large, diverse, and amorphous class, unified only by the common factor of residence in districts that happen to have less taxable wealth than other districts. The system of alleged discrimination and the class it defines have none of the traditional indicia of suspectness: the class is not saddled with such disabilities, or subjected to such a history of purposeful unequal treatment, or relegated to such a position of political powerlessness as to command extraordinary protection from the majoritarian political process. . . . We thus conclude that the Texas system does not operate to the peculiar disadvantage of any suspect class. [T]his Court has never heretofore held that wealth discrimination alone provides an adequate basis for invoking strict scrutiny. . . .

[Appellees] also assert that the State's system impermissibly interferes with the exercise of a 'fundamental' right. . . . It is this question — whether education is a fundamental right, in the sense that it is among the rights and liberties protected by the Constitution — which has so consumed the attention of courts and commentators in recent years. . . . In Brown v. Board of Education, a unanimous Court recognized that 'education is perhaps the most important function of state and local governments.' What was said there in the context of racial discrimination has lost none of its vitality with the passage of time:

> Compulsory school attendance laws and the great expenditures for education both demonstrate our recognition of the importance of education to our democratic society. It is required in the performance of our most basic public responsibilities, even service in the armed forces. It is the very foundation of good citizenship. Today it is a principal instrument in awakening the child to cultural values, in preparing him for later professional training, and in helping him to adjust normally to his environment. In these days, it is doubtful that any child may reasonably be expected to succeed in life if he is denied the opportunity of an education. Such an opportunity, where the state has undertaken to provide it, is a right which must be made available to all on equal terms.

This theme, expressing an abiding respect for the vital role of education in a free society, may be found in numerous opinions of Justices of this Court writing both before and after *Brown* was decided. [We] are in complete agreement [that] 'the grave significance of education both to the individual and to our society' cannot be doubted.

But the importance of a service performed by the State does not determine whether it must be regarded as fundamental for purposes of examination under the Equal Protection Clause. [In] Dandridge v. Williams, the Court's explicit recognition of the fact that the 'administration of public welfare assistance [involves] the most basic economic needs of impoverished human beings,' provided no basis for departing from the settled mode of constitutional analysis of legislative classifications involving questions of economic and social policy. As in the case of housing, the central importance of welfare benefits to the poor was not an adequate foundation for requiring the State to justify its law by showing some compelling state interest. . . . The lesson of these cases [is] plain. It is not the province of this Court to create substantive constitutional rights in the name of guaranteeing equal protection of the laws. [T]he key to discovering whether education is 'fundamental' is not to be found in comparisons of the relative societal significance of education as opposed to subsistence or housing. Nor is it to be found by weighing whether education is as important as the right to travel. Rather, the answer lies in assessing whether there is a right to education explicitly or implicitly guaranteed by the Constitution.

Education, of course, is not among the rights afforded explicit protection under our Federal Constitution. Nor do we find any basis for saying it is implicitly so protected. [Appellees contend], however, that education is distinguishable from other services and benefits provided by the State because it bears a peculiarly close relationship to other rights and liberties accorded protection under the Constitution. Specifically, they insist that education is itself a fundamental personal right because it is essential to the effective exercise of First Amendment freedoms and to intelligent utilization of the right to vote. In asserting a nexus between speech and education, appellees urge that the right to speak is meaningless unless the speaker is capable of articulating his thoughts intelligently and persuasively. The 'marketplace of ideas' is an empty forum for those lacking basic communicative tools. Likewise, they argue that the corollary right to receive information becomes little more than a hollow privilege when the recipient has not been taught to read, assimilate, and utilize available knowledge.

A similar line of reasoning is pursued with respect to the right to vote. Exercise of the franchise, it is contended, cannot be divorced from the educational foundation of the voter. The electoral process, if reality is to conform to the democratic ideal, depends on an informed electorate: a voter cannot cast his ballot intelligently unless his reading skills and thought processes have been adequately developed.

We need not dispute any of these propositions. The Court has long afforded zealous protection against unjustifiable governmental interference with the individual's rights to speak and to vote. Yet we have never presumed to possess either the ability or the authority to guarantee to the citizenry the most effective speech or the most informed electoral choice. . . . Even if it were conceded that some identifiable quantum of education is a constitutionally protected prerequisite to the meaningful exercise of either right, we have no indication that the present levels of educational expenditures in Texas provide an education that falls short. . . . Furthermore, the logical limitations on appellees' nexus theory are difficult to perceive. How, for instance, is education to be distinguished from the significant personal interests in the basics of decent food and shelter? [T]he ill-fed, ill-clothed, and ill-housed are among the most ineffective participants in the political process, [and] they derive the least enjoyment from the benefits of the First Amendment.

We have carefully considered each of the arguments supportive of the District Court's finding that education is a fundamental right or liberty and have found those arguments unpersuasive. . . . The present case, in another basic sense, is significantly different from any of the cases in which the Court has applied strict scrutiny to state or federal legislation touching upon constitutionally protected rights. Each of our prior cases involved legislation which 'deprived,' 'infringed,' or 'interfered' with the free exercise of some such fundamental personal right or liberty.

It should be clear [that] this is not a case in which the challenged state action must be subjected to the searching judicial scrutiny reserved for laws that create suspect classifications or impinge upon constitutionally protected rights. [A]pplication of the traditional standard of review [requires] only that the State's system be shown to bear some rational relationship to legitimate state purposes. . . . We have here nothing less than a direct attack on the way in which Texas has chosen to raise and disburse state and local tax revenues. We are asked to condemn the State's judgment in conferring on political subdivisions the power to tax local property to supply revenues for local interests. In so doing, appellees would have the Court intrude in an area in which it has traditionally deferred to state legislatures. This Court has often admonished against such interferences with the State's fiscal policies under the Equal Protection Clause.

[W]e stand on familiar grounds when we continue to acknowledge that the Justices of this Court lack both the expertise and the familiarity with local problems so necessary to the making of wise decisions with respect to the raising and disposition of public revenues. Yet, we are urged to direct the States either to alter drastically the present system or to throw out the property tax altogether in favor of some other form of taxation. No scheme of taxation, whether the tax is imposed on property, income, or purchases of goods and services, has yet been devised which is free of all discriminatory impact. In such a complex arena in which no perfect alternatives exist, the Court does well not to impose too rigorous a standard of scrutiny lest all local fiscal schemes become subjects of criticism under the Equal Protection Clause.

In addition to matters of fiscal policy, this case also involves the most persistent and difficult questions of educational policy, another area in which this Court's lack of specialized knowledge and experience counsels against premature interference with the informed judgments made at the state and local levels. . . . The very complexity of the problems of financing and managing a statewide public school system suggests that 'there will be more than one constitutionally permissible method of solving them,' and that, within the limits of rationality, 'the legislature's efforts to tackle the problems' should be entitled to respect. [T]he judiciary is well advised to refrain from imposing on the States inflexible constitutional restraints that could circumscribe or handicap the continued research and experimentation so vital to finding even partial solutions to educational problems and to keeping abreast of ever-changing conditions.

It must be remembered, also, that every claim arising under the Equal Protection Clause has implications for the relationship between national and state power under our federal system. [I]t would be difficult to imagine a case having a greater potential impact on our federal system than the one now before us, in which we are urged to abrogate systems of financing public education presently in existence in virtually every State.

The foregoing considerations buttress our conclusion that Texas' system of public school finance is an inappropriate candidate for strict judicial scrutiny. These same considerations are relevant to the determination whether that system, with its conceded imperfections, nevertheless bears some rational relationship to a legitimate state purpose. It is to this question that we next turn our attention.

[T]o the extent that the Texas system of school financing results in unequal expenditures between children who happen to reside in different districts, we cannot say that such disparities are the product of a system that is so irrational as to be invidiously discriminatory. . . . The Texas plan is not [the] product of purposeful discrimination against any group or class. [I]t is rooted in decades of experience in Texas and elsewhere, and in major part is the product of responsible studies by qualified people. [T]he system here challenged is not peculiar to Texas or to any other State. In its essential characteristics, the Texas plan for financing public education reflects what many educators for a half century have thought was an enlightened approach to a problem for which there is no perfect solution. We are unwilling to assume for ourselves a level of wisdom superior to that of legislators, scholars, and educational authorities in 50 States, especially where the alternatives proposed are only recently conceived and nowhere yet tested. The constitutional standard under the Equal Protection Clause is whether the challenged state action rationally furthers a legitimate state purpose or interest. We hold that the Texas plan abundantly satisfies this standard. [T]he ultimate solutions must come from the lawmakers and from the democratic pressures of those who elect them.

Mr. Justice STEWART, concurring.

[I join the judgment because] I am convinced that any other course would mark an extraordinary departure from principled adjudication under the Equal Protection Clause of the Fourteenth Amendment. . . . Unlike other provisions of the Constitution, the Equal Protection Clause confers no substantive rights and creates no substantive liberties. The function of the Equal Protection Clause [is] simply to measure the validity of classifications created by state laws. There is hardly a law on the books that does not affect some people differently from others. [I]it has long been settled that the Equal Protection Clause is offended only by laws that are invidiously discriminatory — only by classifications that are wholly arbitrary or capricious. [T]he Texas system has hardly created the kind of objectively identifiable classes that are cognizable under the Equal Protection Clause. [E]ven assuming the existence of such discernible categories, the classifications are in no sense based upon constitutionally 'suspect' criteria. [T]he Texas system does not rest 'on grounds wholly irrelevant to the achievement of the State's objective.' Finally, the Texas system impinges upon no substantive constitutional rights or liberties.

Mr. Justice BRENNAN, dissenting.

[I disagree] with the Court's rather distressing assertion that a right may be deemed 'fundamental' for the purposes of equal protection analysis only if it is 'explicitly or implicitly guaranteed by the Constitution.' [O]ur prior cases stand for the proposition that 'fundamentality' is, in large measure, a function of the right's importance in terms of the effectuation of those rights which are in fact constitutionally guaranteed. [T]here can be no doubt that education is inextricably linked to the right to participate in the electoral process and to the rights of free speech and association guaranteed by the First Amendment. This being so, any classification affecting education must be subjected to strict judicial scrutiny, and since even the State concedes that the statutory scheme now before us cannot pass constitutional muster under this stricter standard of review, I can only conclude that the Texas school-financing scheme is constitutionally invalid.

Mr. Justice WHITE, with whom Mr. Justice DOUGLAS and Mr. Justice BRENNAN join, dissenting.

[The] Equal Protection Clause permits discriminations between classes but requires that the classification bear some rational relationship to a permissible object sought to be attained by the statute [and that] the means chosen by the State must also be rationally related to the end sought to be achieved. . . . If the State aims at maximizing local initiative and local choice, by permitting school districts to resort to the real property tax if they choose to do so, it utterly fails in achieving its purpose in districts with property tax bases so low that there is little if any opportunity for interested parents, rich or poor, to augment school district revenues. Requiring the State to establish only that unequal treatment is in furtherance of a permissible goal, without also requiring the State to show that the means chosen to effectuate that goal are rationally related to its achievement, makes equal protection analysis no more than an empty gesture. [T]he parents and children in Edgewood, and in like districts, suffer from an invidious discrimination violative of the Equal Protection Clause.

Mr. Justice MARSHALL, with whom Mr. Justice DOUGLAS concurs, dissenting.

[T]he right of every American to an equal start in life, so far as the provision of a state service as important as education is concerned, is far too vital to permit state discrimination on grounds as tenuous as those presented by this record. Nor can I accept the notion that it is sufficient to remit these appellees to the vagaries of the political process. . . .

[E]ven before this Court recognized its duty to tear down the barriers of state-enforced racial segregation in public education, it acknowledged that inequality in the educational facilities provided to students may be discriminatory state action as contemplated by the Equal Protection Clause. [A] difference in the funds available to districts results in a difference in educational inputs available for a child's public education in Texas. [T]his situation, which is directly attributable to the Texas financing scheme, raises a grave question of state-created discrimination in the provision of public education. [T]he burden of proving that these disparities do not in fact affect the quality of children's education must fall upon the appellants. Yet appellants made no effort [to] demonstrate that educational quality is not affected by variations in funding and in resulting inputs. . . .

[I]t is inequality — not some notion of gross inadequacy — of educational opportunity that raises a question of denial of equal protection of the laws. [A]ppellees have made a substantial showing of wide variations in educational funding and the resulting educational opportunity afforded to the schoolchildren of Texas. This discrimination is, in large measure, attributable to significant disparities in the taxable wealth of local Texas school districts. This is a sufficient showing to raise a substantial question of discriminatory state action in violation of the Equal Protection Clause.

[This] Court has repeatedly held that state discrimination which either adversely affects a 'fundamental interest' or is based on a distinction of a suspect character must be carefully scrutinized to ensure that the scheme is necessary to promote a substantial, legitimate state interest. [I] cannot accept the majority's labored efforts to demonstrate that fundamental interests, which call for strict scrutiny of the challenged classification, encompass only established rights which we are somehow bound to recognize from the text of the Constitution itself. [T]he fundamental importance of education is amply indicated by the prior decisions of this Court, by the unique status accorded public education by our society, and by the close relationship between education and some of our most basic constitutional values.

[D]iscrimination on the basis of group wealth in this case likewise calls for careful judicial scrutiny. [L]ocal district wealth [bears] no relationship whatsoever to the interest of Texas schoolchildren in the educational opportunity afforded them by the State of Texas. [I]nsofar as group wealth discrimination involves wealth over which the disadvantaged individual has no significant control, it represents in fact a more serious basis of discrimination than does personal wealth. [S]uch discrimination is no reflection of the individual's characteristics or his abilities. And thus — particularly in the context of a disadvantaged class composed of children — we have previously treated discrimination on a basis which the individual cannot control as constitutionally disfavored.

Nor can we ignore the extent to which [the] State is responsible for the wealth discrimination in this instance. . . . The means for financing public education in Texas are selected and specified by the State. [T]he invidious characteristics of the group wealth classification present in this case merely serve to emphasize the need for careful judicial scrutiny of the State's justifications for the resulting interdistrict discrimination in the educational opportunity afforded to the schoolchildren of Texas.

Note

The *Rodriguez* decision illuminated the Court's general reticence to use the Equal Protection Clause as a means for redistributing wealth. The majority opinion, authored by Justice Powell, nonetheless left open the possibility of a different result in the event that the state "occasioned an absolute denial of educational opportunities." This reservation prefaced the Court's determination, in Plyler v. Doe, that denial of public education to the children of illegal aliens violated the Equal Protection Clause.

∾ PROBLEMS ∾

1. *"Rooted in the Nation's Traditions"*? The Court in Brown v. Board of Education characterized education as "perhaps the most important function of state and local governments" and as "the very foundation of good citizenship." Given the significance of education for purposes of developing individual opportunity and an informed electorate, has it become "rooted in the nation's traditions"?

2. *Judicial Review.* How should a state law distributing monies unevenly among state school districts be reviewed when there is no local real estate tax factored into the equation?

Plyler v. Doe

457 U.S. 202 (1982)

Justice BRENNAN delivered the opinion of the Court.

The question presented by these cases is whether, consistent with the Equal Protection Clause of the Fourteenth Amendment, Texas may deny to undocumented school-age children the free public education that it provides to children who are citizens of the United States or legally admitted aliens.

Since the late 19th century, the United States has restricted immigration into this country. [Despite] legal restrictions, a substantial number of persons have succeeded in unlawfully entering the United States, and now live within various States. [In] 1975, the Texas Legislature revised its education laws to withhold from local school districts any state funds for the education of children who were not "legally admitted" into the United States. [The law] also authorized local school districts to deny enrollment [to] children not "legally admitted" to the country.

[Appellants] argue [that] undocumented aliens, because of their immigration status, are not "persons within the jurisdiction" of the State of Texas, and that they therefore have no right to the equal protection of Texas law. We reject this argument. Whatever his status under the immigration laws, an alien is surely a "person" in any ordinary sense of that term. . . . The Equal Protection Clause was intended to work nothing less than the abolition of all caste-based and invidious class-based legislation. That objective is fundamentally at odds with the power the State asserts here to classify persons subject to its laws as nonetheless excepted from its protection.

[The] more difficult question is whether the Equal Protection Clause has been violated by the refusal of the State of Texas to reimburse local school boards for the education of children who cannot demonstrate that their presence within the United States is lawful, or by the imposition by those school boards of the burden of tuition on those children. . . . The Equal Protection Clause directs that "all persons similarly circumstanced shall be treated alike." But so too, "[t]he Constitution does not require things which are different in fact or opinion to be treated in law as though they were the same." The initial discretion to determine what is "different" and what is "the same" resides in the legislatures of the States. A legislature must have substantial latitude to establish classifications that roughly approximate the nature of the problem perceived, that accommodate competing concerns both public and private, and that account for limitations on the practical ability of the State to remedy every ill. In applying the Equal Protection Clause to most forms of state action, we thus seek only the assurance that the classification at issue bears some fair relationship to a legitimate public purpose.

But we would not be faithful to our obligations under the Fourteenth Amendment if we applied so deferential a standard to every classification. The Equal Protection Clause was intended as a restriction on state legislative action inconsistent with elemental constitutional premises. Thus we have treated as presumptively invidious those classifications that disadvantage a "suspect class," or that impinge upon the exercise of a "fundamental right." With respect to such classifications, it is appropriate to enforce the mandate of equal protection by requiring the State to demonstrate that its classification has been precisely tailored to serve a compelling governmental interest. In addition, we have recognized that certain forms of legislative classification, while not facially invidious, nonetheless give rise to recurring constitutional difficulties; in these limited circumstances we have sought the assurance that the classification reflects a reasoned judgment consistent with the ideal of equal protection by inquiring whether it may fairly be viewed as furthering a substantial interest of the State. . . .

Sheer incapability or lax enforcement of the laws barring entry into this country, coupled with the failure to establish an effective bar to the employment of undocumented aliens, has resulted in the creation of a substantial "shadow population" of illegal migrants — numbering in the millions — within our borders. This situation raises the specter of a permanent caste of undocumented resident aliens, encouraged by some to remain here as a source of cheap labor, but nevertheless denied the benefits that our society makes available to citizens and lawful residents. The existence of such an underclass presents most difficult problems for a Nation that prides itself on adherence to principles of equality under law.

The children who are plaintiffs in these cases are special members of this underclass. [A] State may withhold its beneficence from those whose very presence within the United States is the product of their own unlawful conduct. . . . But the children of those illegal entrants are not comparably situated [and] "can affect neither their parents' conduct nor their own status." Of course, undocumented status is not irrelevant to any proper legislative goal. Nor is undocumented status an absolutely immutable characteristic since it is the product of conscious, indeed unlawful, action. But [the state law] is directed against children, and imposes its discriminatory burden on the basis of a legal characteristic over which children can have little control. It [is] difficult to conceive of a rational justification for penalizing these children for their presence within the United States. . . .

Public education is not a "right" granted to individuals by the Constitution. But neither is it merely some governmental "benefit" indistinguishable from other forms of social welfare legislation. Both the importance of education in maintaining our basic institutions, and the lasting impact of its deprivation on the life of the child, mark the distinction. [E]ducation has a fundamental role in maintaining the fabric of our society. We cannot ignore the significant social costs borne by our Nation when select groups are denied the means to absorb the values and skills upon which our social order rests.

In addition to the pivotal role of education in sustaining our political and cultural heritage, denial of education to some isolated group of children poses an affront to one of the goals of the Equal Protection Clause: the abolition of governmental barriers presenting unreasonable obstacles to advancement on the basis of individual merit. [B]y depriving the children of any disfavored group of an education, we foreclose the means by which that group might raise the level of esteem in which it is held by the majority. But more directly, "education prepares individuals to be self-reliant and self-sufficient participants in society." Illiteracy is an enduring disability. . . . The inestimable toll of that deprivation on the social, economic, intellectual, and psychological well-being of the individual, and the obstacle it poses to individual achievement, make it most difficult to reconcile the cost or the principle of a status-based denial of basic education with the framework of equality embodied in the Equal Protection Clause.

These well-settled principles allow us to determine the proper level of deference to be afforded [the state law]. Undocumented aliens cannot be treated as a suspect class because their presence in this country in violation of federal law is not a "constitutional irrelevancy." Nor is education a fundamental right; a State need not justify by compelling necessity every variation in the manner in which education is provided to its population. But [the state law] imposes a lifetime hardship on a discrete class of children not accountable for their disabling status. The stigma of illiteracy will mark them for the rest of their lives. By denying these children a basic education, we deny them the ability to live within the structure of our civic institutions, and foreclose any realistic possibility that they will contribute in even the smallest way to the progress of our Nation. In determining the [state law's] rationality[,] we may appropriately take into account its costs to the Nation and to the innocent children who are its victims. In light of these countervailing costs, the discrimination contained in [the state law] can hardly be considered rational unless it furthers some substantial goal of the State.

[The State argues] that the undocumented status of these children *vel non* establishes a sufficient rational basis for denying them benefits that a State might choose to afford other residents. The State notes that while other aliens are admitted "on an equality of legal privileges with all citizens under non-discriminatory laws," the asserted right of these children to an education can claim no implicit congressional imprimatur. [I]n the State's view, Congress' apparent disapproval of the presence of these children within the United States, and the evasion of the federal regulatory program that is the mark of undocumented status, provides authority for its decision to impose upon them special disabilities. . . . But we are unable to find in the congressional immigration scheme any statement of policy that might weigh significantly in arriving at an equal protection balance concerning the State's authority to deprive these children of an education. [L]ike all persons who have entered the United States unlawfully, these children are subject to deportation. But there is no assurance that a child subject to deportation will ever be deported. . . . We are reluctant to impute to Congress the intention to withhold from these children, for so long as they are present in this country through no fault of their own, access to a basic education. . . .

Appellants argue that the classification at issue furthers an interest in the "preservation of the state's limited resources for the education of its lawful residents." Of course, a concern for the preservation of resources standing alone can hardly justify the classification used in allocating those resources. The State must do more than justify its classification with a concise expression of an intention to discriminate. . . .

[W]e discern three colorable state interests that might support [the law]. First, appellants [suggest] that the State may seek to protect itself from an influx of illegal immigrants. [F]ew if any illegal immigrants come to this country [in] order to avail themselves of a free education. "[C]harging tuition to undocumented children constitutes a ludicrously ineffectual attempt to stem the tide of illegal immigration," at least when compared with the alternative of prohibiting the employment of illegal aliens. . . . Second, [appellants] suggest that undocumented children are appropriately singled out for exclusion because of the special burdens they impose on the State's ability to provide high-quality public education. [I]n terms of educational cost and need[,] undocumented children are "basically indistinguishable" from legally resident alien children. . . . Finally, appellants suggest that undocumented children are appropriately singled out because their unlawful presence within the United States renders them less likely than other children to remain within the boundaries of the State, and to put their education to productive social or political use within the State. [The] record is clear that many of the undocumented children disabled by this classification will remain in this country indefinitely, and that some will become lawful residents or citizens of the United States. It is difficult to understand precisely what the State hopes to achieve by promoting the creation and perpetuation of a subclass of illiterates within our boundaries, surely adding to the problems and costs of unemployment, welfare, and crime. [W]hatever savings might be achieved by denying these children an education, they are wholly insubstantial in light of the costs involved to these children, the State, and the Nation.

If the State is to deny a discrete group of innocent children the free public education that it offers to other children residing within its borders, that denial must be justified by a showing that it furthers some substantial state interest. No such showing was made here. Accordingly, the judgment of the Court of Appeals in each of these cases is affirmed.

Justice MARSHALL, concurring.

[A]n individual's interest in education is fundamental. [A] class-based denial of public education is utterly incompatible with the Equal Protection Clause of the Fourteenth Amendment.

Justice BLACKMUN, concurring.

[T]he children involved in this litigation "should not be left on the streets uneducated." [W]hen the State provides an education to some and denies it to others, it immediately and inevitably creates class distinctions of a type fundamentally inconsistent with [the] purposes [of] the Equal Protection Clause. Children denied an education are placed at a permanent and insurmountable competitive disadvantage [and] will have been converted into a discrete underclass. . . .

Justice POWELL, concurring.

[T]he State's denial of education to these children bears no substantial relation to any substantial state interest. [A]n uncertain but significant percentage of illegal alien children will remain in Texas as residents and many eventually will become citizens. [T]he exclusion of appellees' class of children from state-provided education is a type of punitive discrimination based on status that is impermissible under the Equal Protection Clause.

Chief Justice BURGER, with whom Justice WHITE, Justice REHNQUIST, and Justice O'CONNOR join, dissenting.

Were it our business to set the Nation's social policy, I would agree without hesitation that it is senseless for an enlightened society to deprive any children — including illegal aliens — of an elementary education. . . . However, the Constitution does [not] vest in this Court the authority to strike down laws because they do not meet our standards of desirable social policy, "wisdom," or "common sense." [The] Court employs, and in my view abuses, the Fourteenth Amendment in an effort to become an omnipotent and omniscient problem solver. That the motives for doing so are noble and compassionate does not alter the fact that the Court distorts our constitutional function. . . .

Once it is conceded — as the Court does — that illegal aliens are not a suspect class, and that education is not a fundamental right, our inquiry should focus on and be limited to whether the legislative classification at issue bears a rational relationship to a legitimate state purpose. . . . The State contends [that the state law prevents] undue depletion of its limited revenues available for education, and [preserves] the fiscal integrity of the State's school-financing system against an ever-increasing flood of illegal aliens. . . . Of course such fiscal concerns alone could not justify discrimination against a suspect class or an arbitrary and irrational denial of benefits to a particular group of persons. Yet I assume no Member of this Court would argue that prudent conservation of finite state revenues is *per se* an illegitimate goal. . . .

[I]t simply is not "irrational" for a state to conclude that it does not have the same responsibility to provide benefits for persons whose very presence in the state and this country is illegal as it does to provide for persons lawfully present.

[I]llegal aliens have no right whatever to be here, and the state may reasonably, and constitutionally, elect not to provide them with governmental services at the expense of those who are lawfully in the state. . . . [T]he fact that there are sound *policy* arguments against the Texas Legislature's choice does not render that choice an unconstitutional one. . . . Today's cases [present] yet another example of unwarranted judicial action which in the long run tends to contribute to the weakening of our political processes.

Note

The *Plyler* decision was an anomaly in two regards. First, it departed from the Court's reluctance to use the Equal Protection Clause to effect redistribution of wealth or opportunity. Second, though applying rational basis scrutiny in form, the Court independently reviewed the logic and utility of the state's methods. This functional application of heightened scrutiny was consistent with the Court's sense that education, while not a fundamental right, is not "merely some governmental 'benefit' indistinguishable from other forms of social welfare legislation."

The possibility that the *Plyler* decision might elevate the importance of education for equal protection purposes, or establish the basis for more analytical flexibility, was diminished by subsequent case law. In Kadrmas v. Dickinson Public Schools, 487 U.S. 450 (1988), the Court upheld a state law that allowed school districts to charge a school bus transportation fee. Although indigent children could not afford the cost, the Court restated that education was not a fundamental right and employed the traditionally deferential rational basis standard of review. For practical purposes the *Plyler* decision was limited to its facts.

∼ PROBLEMS ∼

1. *Denial of Public Education.* Consider a state law that denies free public education to a student who lives in a district, apart from his or her parent or guardian, for the primary purpose of attending on a tuition-free basis. This law is applied to an eight-year-old child who is a citizen of the United States, but whose parents live in Mexico, where they are citizens. Should this provision be analyzed pursuant to *Rodriguez* or *Plyler*? Does it burden the right to travel?

2. *A Constitutional Right to Food?* In discussions of matters fundamental to personhood and livelihood, food is almost always taken for granted. In light of the current significant recession and the growing number of Americans receiving food stamps and other assistance for necessities, should there be a constitutional right to food? This question is being addressed in other countries. India, which has some supportive aspirational language in its constitution, was considering this question in July 2010. The party in power, the Indian National Congress Party, has been divided over whether to support such a right. *See* Jim Yardley, "India Asks, Should Food Be a Right for the Poor?" *New York Times,* Asia Pacific

(Aug. 8, 2010). Would it be appropriate for the U.S. Supreme Court to hold that people have a constitutional right to food?

Points to Remember

- The Fourteenth Amendment's provision that no state shall "deny to any person within its jurisdiction the equal protection of the laws" is a constitutional guarantee with mixed signals because it was framed and ratified at a time when laws in both the North and South discriminated against persons of African descent.
- For purposes of equal protection, the three standards of review are strict scrutiny, intermediate scrutiny, and rational basis scrutiny. Rational basis scrutiny applies to most legislative classifications. Strict scrutiny is used for all racial and most alienage classifications, as well as selective denials of or burdens on fundamental rights. Intermediate scrutiny governs gender and illegitimacy classifications.
- Equal protection cases generally involve three questions: 1) Does the law classify? 2) What is the nature of the classification? 3) When a classification is challenged, which standard of review applies?
- For most government classifications, the U.S. Supreme Court applies rational basis review. The government policy is presumed valid and the person challenging the policy must allege and prove that it is arbitrary or irrational. Under rational basis scrutiny, the government almost always prevails.
- In United States v. Carolene Products Co., 304 U.S. 144, n.4 (1938), the Court announced that it would reserve searching review for instances when a specific provision of the Bill of Rights was implicated or a burden was imposed on a group that was excluded formally from the political process.
- Rational basis review thus became the primary standard for evaluating economic or social legislation, whether it was challenged as a violation of the Due Process Clause or the Equal Protection Clause. The rational basis scrutiny typically reflects the utmost in judicial deference.
- Early decisions did not impose a high standard of review on racial classifications. The Court upheld segregation provided that, even though the races were "separate," they were treated equally. In most states, there was more separation than "equality."
- In modern jurisprudence, the Court has applied strict scrutiny to racial classifications. Race is immutable and bears no reasonable relationship to competence.
- Under strict scrutiny, the government action is presumed to be invalid and the government must justify its classification by showing that there is a compelling government interest and that the classification is narrowly tailored to achieve the compelling interest. The government action usually is invalidated, either because the government interest is not

sufficiently compelling or, most often, because the regulation is not narrowly tailored.

- In Brown v. Board of Education, 347 U.S. 483 (1954), the Court used the Equal Protection Clause to overturn segregation in public schools. However, the Court held that segregation must be eliminated only with "all deliberate speed." Even then, desegregation was met with hostility in many parts of the country. It was not until the 1960s and 1970s that desegregation began in earnest.

- In Washington v. Davis, 426 U.S. 229 (1976), the Court held that a racial classification could not be found to exist unless there was evidence of discriminatory purpose. This purpose can be found either on the face of the law or because of the way in which the law is applied.

- Affirmative action, in the sense of providing special treatment based on race, has been used as a remedy for racial discrimination.

- In Adarand Constructors, Inc. v. Pena, 515 U.S. 200 (1995), the Court made clear that strict scrutiny would apply to discrimination against all racial groups, both minority and nonminority.

- In Grutter v. Bollinger, 539 U.S. 306 (2003), the Court suggested that diversity could be a compelling governmental interest that could justify taking race into account and using it as a "plus" factor in law school admissions.

- In Gratz v. Bollinger, 539 U.S. 244 (2003), the Court struck down a university admissions program that provided minority racial groups with a 20-point preference in the admissions process that effectively determined the outcome.

- In Parents Involved in Community Schools v. Seattle School District No.1, 551 U.S. 701 (2007), the Court held that school boards could not assign students to public schools on the basis of race. Although considerations of race could be justified when school assignments are designed to remedy the effects of segregation, but could not be based on "diversity" when only race is considered in the diversity equation.

- For more than a century, until the 1970s, the Court applied minimal scrutiny to gender classifications. In the process, the Court routinely upheld sex-based stereotypes that were used to justify treating women differently than men (and, in some instances, to disadvantage men). In many instances, these stereotypes resulted in protective legislation that hampered women's ability to work or manage their affairs, and conversely gave men much greater control over their affairs.

- In the 1960s and 1970s, attitudes and approaches toward gender issues began to change. As the historical stereotypes began to break down, they gave way to remedial legislation such as the Equal Pay Act and Title VII and Title IX of the Civil Rights Act. In the 1970s, Congress passed the Equal Rights Amendment (ERA), which provided that "equality of rights under the law shall not be denied or abridged by the United States or by any State on account of sex" and authorized Congress to enact implementing legislation. Although the deadline for ratification was extended to 1982, and although 35 states ultimately ratified the Amendment, the ERA failed to gain ratification from the 38 states needed for it to become law.

- In Frontiero v. Richardson, 411 U.S. 677 (1973), in a plurality opinion, the Court noted that "sex, like race and national origin, is an immutable characteristic determined solely by the accident of birth," and therefore "the imposition of special disabilities upon the members of a particular sex because of their sex would seem to violate 'the basic concept of our system that legal burdens should bear some relationship to individual responsibility. . . . '" The Court suggested that "sex, like classifications based upon race, alienage, or national origin, are inherently suspect, and must therefore be subjected to strict judicial scrutiny."

- In Craig v. Boren, 429 U.S. 190 (1976), the Court held that gender classifications "must serve important governmental objectives and must be substantially related to achievement of those objectives."

- In recent years, the Court has moved away from the doctrine of gender equality toward a doctrine recognizing that there are legitimate biological differences between males and females. The task for the courts is to separate legitimate gender differences from unjustified stereotypes.

- In United States v. Virginia, 518 U.S. 515 (1996), the Court suggested that it "has carefully inspected official action that closes a door or denies opportunity to women (or to men). . . . [T]he reviewing court must determine whether the proffered justification is "exceedingly persuasive." [The] State must show "at least that the [challenged] classification serves 'important governmental objectives and that the discriminatory means employed' are 'substantially related to the achievement of those objectives.'" The justification must be genuine, not hypothesized or invented post hoc in response to litigation. And it must not "rely on overbroad generalizations about the different talents, capacities, or preferences of males and females."

- The Court has used different standards of scrutiny for government classifications that affect legal resident aliens. In its early decisions, the Court gave little protection to persons in this class. The Court permitted discrimination against aliens when they were justified by a "special public interest," and that doctrine was used to uphold statutes that prohibited aliens from using natural resources, from entering various occupations, and from owning land.

- The new era of modern doctrine began with Takahashi v. Fish & Game Commission, 334 U.S. 410 (1948), where the Court rejected the "special public interest" as a justification for denying a resident Japanese alien the right to make a living in commercial fishing activity in state coastal waters. The Court revived the use of the equal protection doctrine to support legal rights for aliens, thus laying the foundation for the constitutional challenges that aliens would bring to the Court in the 1970s and later.

- In the early 1970s, the Court invalidated state laws that denied aliens the right to receive social welfare benefits, to practice law and other professions, and to seek employment in civil service positions. In these cases, the Court established the principle that discrimination against aliens required strict scrutiny. But in the late 1970s, the Court developed a "political function" exception to strict scrutiny of alienage classifications, and used a rational basis standard to uphold regulations that fell under this exception. The Court's modern cases involving challenges to federal laws also exhibit greater deference to alienage classifications than cases involving challenges to state laws, because of the federal government's constitutional authority in matters relating to immigration and the regulation of resident aliens.

- In City of Cleburne v. Cleburne Living Center, 473 U.S. 432 (1985), the Court held that classifications based on mental disabilities should not be regarded as a suspect or quasi-suspect class. The Equal Protection Clause requires only that a rational means serves a legitimate end.

- Even though the Court explicitly purports to apply only rational basis review to classifications involving mental disabilities, the review is heightened in many cases involving that classification.

- For some time, the most contentious issues in sexual orientation cases have involved the protection of sexual intimacy against criminal sodomy and same-sex marriage laws. In Texas v. Lawrence, 539 U.S. 558 (2003), the Court extended constitutional protections to homosexual activities.

- In recent years, there has been much litigation regarding the constitutionality of bans on same-sex marriage as well as the U.S. military's "don't ask, don't tell" policy. Proponents of same-sex marriage and opponents of the military policy have won significant victories in the lower courts. These cases are making their way to the U.S. Supreme Court.

- Equal protection interests are implicated when government classifies for purposes of distributing burdens or benefits. A heightened standard of review may be applied when a fundamental right has been denied on a selective basis. In that case, the nature of the group is irrelevant. What counts, for purposes of elevating the standard of review, is the discriminatory deprivation of a fundamental right.

- Insofar as a textually enumerated right or liberty is selectively denied, such as freedom of speech, the standards of review for the alleged violations of the Equal Protection Clause and the First Amendment will be coextensive.

- Case law relating to an individual's access to the justice system, or the rights therein, implicates both equal protection and procedural due process issues. It also implicates specific constitutional guarantees and other incidents of fairness.

- The Equal Protection Clause has been the basis for extending the right to counsel to the appellate process. In Douglas v. California, 368 U.S. 815 (1963), the Court determined that the state must appoint counsel to indigent appellants pursuing a first appeal as a matter of right. Consistent with this marking, the Court declined to extend the right to the circumstances of a discretionary appeal. Ross v. Moffitt, 417 U.S. 600 (1974).

- Case law concerning subsidized access to counsel and other support systems in the criminal justice process has referenced both equal protection and due process concerns. As the Court noted in Bearden v. Georgia, 461 U.S. 660 (1983), different inquiries are required pursuant to each guarantee. Due process analysis focuses on the fairness of the relationship between the defendant and the criminal justice process, whereas equal protection inquiry centers on whether the defendant invidiously has been denied an important benefit afforded to other classes of defendants.

- The Constitution does not specifically articulate a right to interstate travel, but one has been applied in an effort to create a viable political and economic union that requires that individuals be allowed to travel freely across state lines.

- As the Court recognized in Saenz v. Roe, 526 U.S. 489 (1999), the right to travel has three separate and distinct components: "[The] 'right to travel' [embraces] at least three different components. It protects the right of a citizen of one State to enter and to leave another State, the right to be treated as a welcome visitor rather than an unfriendly alien when temporarily present in the second State, and for those travelers who elect to become permanent residents, the right to be treated like other citizens of that State. . . ."

- For equal protection purposes, the right to travel has been examined most often in connection with residence-based eligibility requirements for public benefits. In Saenz v. Roe, the Court struck down a California law that limited welfare benefits under the state's Temporary Assistance for Needy Families (TANF) program during an individual's first year of residency in the state.

- The Constitution does not establish a general right to vote. Consistent with this premise, the Court has found that "the right to vote in federal elections is conferred by Art. I, §2, of the Constitution, but the right to vote in state elections is nowhere expressly mentioned." Harper v. Virginia Board of Elections, 383 U.S. 663, 665 (1966). Notwithstanding this differentiation in grounding, and within the context of state political processes, the franchise has been described as "a fundamental matter in a free and democratic society, [e]specially since the right to exercise the franchise in a free and unimpaired manner is preservative of other basic civil and political rights."

- The importance of the franchise is further evidenced by the number of constitutional amendments concerned with protecting it. The Fifteenth Amendment prohibits denial of the right to vote "on account of race, color, or previous condition of servitude." The Nineteenth Amendment prohibits abridgment of the right to vote "on account of sex." The

Twenty-fourth Amendment prohibits poll taxes. The Twenty-sixth Amendment extends the right to vote to citizens who are 18 or older.

- The concept of voting as a fundamental right was introduced in the context of equal protection review. In Baker v. Carr, 369 U.S. 186 (1962), the Court struck down a state's legislative apportionment scheme on grounds it violated the premise of "one man, one vote." An equality principle thus was established as a primary basis for challenging laws that denied or diluted the right to vote.

- Although the states have the authority to establish the basic terms of voting, conditions that burden the franchise through qualifications unrelated to age, citizenship, or residence typically will "be carefully and meticulously scrutinized." Harper v. Virginia State Board of Elections, 383 U.S. 663 (1966). This higher level of review may extend to residence requirements, as evidenced by the Court's invalidation of a one-year state and three-month county waiting period for local, state, and congressional elections. Dunn v. Blumstein, 405 U.S. 330 (1972).

- Equal protection activity with respect to denial of the right to vote has centered primarily on poll taxes and voter eligibility requirements for special-purpose government districts. A classic example of an impermissible denial of the right to vote is a poll tax. In Harper v. Virginia State Board of Elections, 383 U.S. 663 (1966), the Court found no basis for making wealth a qualification for voting.

- Special restrictions on eligibility for voting in school board elections also have been the basis for "a close and exacting examination."

- The right to vote may be abridged not only by deprivation but also by dilution. Methods of dilution include apportionment schemes that weight votes differently, restrictions on ballot access that may narrow the range of voter options, and differential processes for recording and counting votes. Districting processes for political representation generally are governed by the principle of one person, one vote. Allowable deviations from the norm and standards of review vary depending on whether federal, state, or local representation is implicated. With respect to ballot access, the focus is on the degree of burden imposed by the restriction.

- Political gerrymandering cases establish that a mere failure of proportionality in representation does not establish a violation of the Equal Protection Clause. Rather, there must be purposeful discrimination and a demonstrable discriminatory effect on the targeted group. Considerations such as compactness, contiguity, and respect for political subdivisions and communities with common interests have been recognized bases for deviation from otherwise strict proportionality.

- In Shaw v. Hunt, 517 U.S. 899 (1996), the Court determined that race was the predominant factor in configuring a congressional district and held that the plan could not withstand strict scrutiny. Because it was not designed to remedy past discrimination, the plan was not supported by a compelling state interest.

- In Miller v. Johnson, 515 U.S. 900 (1995), the Court correlated review more closely with the premises underlying its affirmative action jurisprudence. When race is a predominant factor in districting, therefore, it is necessary to show a compelling interest in remedying past discrimination. Although compliance with the Voting Rights Act may be an imperative, the Court indicated that it will strike down plans that reflect or facilitate racial stereotyping.
- In Bush v. Gore, 531 U.S. 98 (2000), the Court's application of equal protection principles decided the presidential contest between George W. Bush and Albert Gore.
- Regulations that seriously impede access to the ballot will be evaluated more carefully than those perceived as imposing minimal burdens.
- In American Party of Texas v. White, 415 U.S. 767 (1974), the Court upheld a provision requiring parties that received less than 2 percent of the gubernatorial vote in the preceding election to obtain the signatures of at least 1 percent of those who voted. This prescription, from the Court's perspective, was not excessively burdensome. A law requiring candidates to pay a filing fee equal to 2 percent of the annual salary of the office sought was found to violate the Equal Protection Clause.
- In Lubin v. Panish, 415 U.S. 709 (1974), the Court found that the regulation unduly burdened the ability of indigent candidates to secure a position on the ballot. In addition to being a way to dilute the right to vote, restrictions on ballot access may implicate the right of association.
- Equal protection principles have also been applied to the right to obtain an education. In Brown v. Board of Education, 347 U.S. 483 (1954), the Court described education as "perhaps the most important function of state and local government, . . . the very foundation of good citizenship, [and] . . . a principal instrument in awakening the child to cultural values, in preparing him for later professional training, and in helping him to adjust normally to his environment."
- In San Antonio Independent School District v. Rodriguez, 411 U.S. 1 (1973), the Court struck down Texas's system for financing public education on equal protection grounds.
- In Plyler v. Doe, 457 U.S. 202 (1982), the Court extended equal protection guarantees to hold that Texas may not deny undocumented school-age children the free public education that it provides to children who are citizens of the United States or legally admitted aliens.

11

Freedom of Speech

∾ PROBLEM: AN INTERNATIONAL TREATY REGULATING THE INTERNET ∾

During the last 20 years, the Internet has developed as a major method of communication. It is an inherently democratic medium in the sense that anyone can easily and readily gain access, and therefore Internet communication is accessible by individuals at all levels of society. As a result, many have hailed the Internet as a way to enhance knowledge, improve political processes, and generally facilitate communication. However, the Internet also has a dark underside. Unscrupulous individuals have tried to use the Internet to perpetrate financial scams and various types of swindles. In addition, the Internet is routinely used by purveyors of hate as well as peddlers of pornography and child pornography.

Because of concerns about harmful material on the Internet, an international conference has been called to address questions related to regulation of the Internet. Representatives from various nations will attend the conference, and they all have very different concerns about the types of speech that should be regulated and how they should be regulated. Governments in some countries (e.g., China and Iran) think that any treaty that results from the talks should address issues related to defamatory political speech and sedition, and should also promote intergovernmental cooperation to curb "subversive" speech. Governments in other countries (e.g., Germany and France) believe that the treaty should prohibit such things as Holocaust denial, race-based speech, and other types of speech that degrade human dignity. Some countries believe that all pornography should be prohibited both because of its adverse effects on society and because it is degrading to women. Most societies agree that child pornography should be prohibited in order to protect children.

Suppose that you have been designated the U.S. representative to the talks. As your work your way through this chapter, think about the type of treaty that the United States might be able to enter into (or, for that matter, might be precluded from entering into). As you do, recall the discussion of treaties in Chapters 2 and 3.

A. HISTORICAL INTENTIONS AND UNDERLYING VALUES

The First Amendment is phrased in unqualified terms: "Congress shall make no law . . . abridging the freedom of speech, or of the press." Justice Black argued that the language should be taken literally: "[The] unequivocal command that there shall be no abridgment of the rights of free speech and assembly shows that [those] who drafted our Bill of Rights did all the 'balancing' that was to be done in this field. [The] very object of adopting the First Amendment [was] to put the freedoms protected there completely out of the area of any congressional control that may be attempted through the exercise of precisely those powers that are now being used to 'balance' the Bill of Rights out of existence." Konigsberg v. State Bar of California, 366 U.S. 36, 60-61 (1961). But the U.S. Supreme Court ultimately rejected Justice Black's position in favor of a less "absolutist" view of the First Amendment. As Justice Holmes argued, "[t]he most stringent protection of free speech would not protect a man in falsely shouting fire in a theatre and causing a panic." Schenck v. United States, 249 U.S. 47 (1919). But if First Amendment protections are not absolute and must give way at times to "other interests," what are those "other interests"?

1. Framers' Intent

The Framers of the U.S. Constitution omitted speech protections from the original Constitution because they believed that such protections were unnecessary. They viewed the federal government's powers as limited and enumerated, and argued that there was no need to enumerate specific rights. Indeed, some Framers believed that it would be undesirable to list specific rights because the mere fact of enumeration might imply that other rights were not constitutionally protected. However, when the Constitution was sent to the states for ratification, it became clear that the Constitution would not be ratified without some protection for speech. Because this sentiment was so pronounced, there was little debate in Congress or the states about why the First Amendment was needed or how it should be applied.

We do know something about historical conditions in the colonies that might have led the colonists to demand speech protections. In addition to licensing restrictions (which required a publisher to have approval from authorities in the form of a license to publish), the colonists were subjected to seditious libel prosecutions. "Seditious libel" developed in England in the case of *de Libellis Famosis*, 77 Eng. Rep. 250 (Star Chamber 1606), a case involving defendants who had ridiculed clergy of high station. Over time, government officials used the crime to stifle criticism. See William T. Mayton, *Seditious Libel and the Lost Guarantee of a Freedom of Expression*, 84 Colum. L. Rev. 91 (1984). The crime was particularly objectionable because truth was no defense: "Since maintaining a proper regard for government was the goal . . . , it followed that truth was just as reprehensible as falsehood [and] was eliminated as a defense." *Id.* Seditious libel also existed in the colonies. *See* Lawrence W. Crispo, Jill M. Slansky & Geanene M. Yriarte, *Jury Nullification: Law Versus Anarchy*, 31 Loy. L.A. L. Rev. 1, 7 (1997). As in England, truth was not a defense.

Zechariah Chafee has argued that the Framers intended to "wipe out the common law of sedition and make further prosecutions for criticism of the government, without any incitement to law-breaking, forever impossible." Zechariah Chafee, *Free Speech in the United States* (Harvard University 1941). However, others have disagreed. *See, e.g.*, Leonard W. Levy, *The Legacy Reexamined*, 37 Stan. L. Rev. 767 (1985). Notwithstanding the existence of the First Amendment, Congress enacted the Alien and Sedition Act of 1798, which made it illegal to publish "false, scandalous, and malicious writing [against] the Government of the United States [with] intent to defame, or to bring [them] into contempt or disrepute, or to excite against them hatred of the good people of the United States, or to stir up sedition within the United States." In addition, just prior to the Civil War, some states enacted laws prohibiting speech that advocated the abolition of slavery.

2. Underlying Values

Given that the drafters and ratifiers of the First Amendment did not leave clear evidence regarding their intent, the meaning of the First Amendment has been a subject of debate. As part of that debate, various scholars have offered theories about the function of the First Amendment and its application.

Thomas I. Emerson, *Toward a General Theory of the First Amendment*

72 Yale L.J. 877 (1963)[1]

The right of the individual to freedom of expression [is] an integral part of the great intellectual and social movement beginning with the Renaissance which

---

1. Reprinted by permission of The Yale Law Journal Company and William S. Hein Company from The Yale Law Journal, Vol. 72, pages 877-956.

transformed the Western world from a feudal and authoritarian society to one whose faith rested upon the dignity, the reason and the freedom of the individual. . . . The values sought by society in protecting the right to freedom of expression may be grouped into four broad categories. . . .

A. INDIVIDUAL SELF-FULFILLMENT

The right to freedom of expression is justified first of all . . . from the widely accepted premise of Western thought that the proper end of man is the realization of his character and potentialities as a human being. . . . The achievement of self-realization commences with development of the mind. But the process of conscious thought . . . can have no limits. . . . It is an individual process. . . . Every [person] — in the development of [his/or her] own personality — has the right to form his own beliefs and opinions [and] the right to express these beliefs and opinions. . . . For expression is an integral part of the development of ideas, of mental exploration and of the affirmation of self. . . . [T]here follows the right of the individual to access to knowledge; to shape his own views; to communicate his needs, preferences and judgments; in short, to participate in formulating the aims and achievements of his society and his state. To cut off his search for truth, or his expression of it, is thus to elevate society and the state to a despotic command and to reduce the individual to the arbitrary control of others. . . . [F]reedom of expression, while not the sole or sufficient end of society, is a good in itself, or at least an essential element in a good society. . . . [A] society or the state is entitled to exercise control over action — whether by prohibiting or compelling it — on an entirely different and vastly more extensive basis. But expression occupies a specially protected position. . . .

B. ATTAINMENT OF TRUTH

[F]reedom of expression is not only an individual but also a social good. It is, to begin with, the best process for advancing knowledge and discovering truth. . . . [The] soundest and most rational judgment is arrived at by considering all facts and arguments, which can be put forth on behalf of or against any proposition. . . . [S]uppression of information, discussion, or the clash of opinion prevents one from reaching the most rational judgment, blocks the generation of new ideas, and tends to perpetuate error. . . . The theory demands that discussion must be kept open no matter how certainly true an accepted opinion may seem to be. Many of the most widely acknowledged truths have turned out to be erroneous. Many of the most significant advances in human knowledge — from Copernicus to Einstein — have resulted from challenging hitherto unquestioned assumptions. . . . The process also applies regardless of how false or pernicious the new opinion appears to be. For . . . there is no way of suppressing the false without suppressing the true. Furthermore, even if the new opinion is wholly false, its presentation and open discussion serves a vital social purpose. It compels a rethinking and retesting of the accepted opinion. It results in a deeper understanding of the reasons for holding the opinion and a fuller appreciation of its meaning. . . . The only justification for suppressing an opinion is that those who seek to suppress it are infallible in their judgment of the truth. But no individual or group can be infallible, particularly in a constantly changing world. . . . Through the acquisition of new knowledge, the toleration of new ideas, the testing of opinion in open competition, the discipline of rethinking its assumptions, a society will be better able to reach common decisions that will meet the needs and aspirations of its members.

C. PARTICIPATION IN DECISIONMAKING

. . . Every government must have some process for feeding back to it information concerning the attitudes, needs and wishes of its citizens. . . . The crucial point [is] not that freedom of expression is politically useful, but that it is indispensable to the operation of a democratic form of government. Once one accepts the premise of the Declaration of Independence — that governments derive "their just powers from the consent of the governed" — it follows that the governed must, in order to exercise their right of consent, have full freedom of expression both in forming individual judgments and in forming the common judgment. . . . [O]nce a society was committed to democratic procedures, or rather in the process of committing itself, it necessarily embraced the principle of open political discussion.

D. BALANCE BETWEEN STABILITY AND CHANGE

. . . Suppression of discussion makes a rational judgment impossible. In effect it substitutes force for logic. Moreover, coercion of expression is likely to be ineffective. While it may prevent social change, at least for a time, it cannot eradicate thought or belief; nor can it promote loyalty or unity. . . . [S]uppression of expression conceals the real problems confronting a society and diverts public attention from the critical issues. It is likely to result in neglect of the grievances which are the actual basis of the unrest, and thus prevent their correction. . . . Further, suppression drives opposition underground, leaving those suppressed either apathetic or desperate. It thus saps the vitality of the society or makes resort to force more likely. And finally it weakens and debilitates the majority whose support for the common decision is necessary. For it hinders an intelligent understanding of the reasons for adopting the decision. . . . In short, suppression of opposition may well mean that when change is finally forced on the community it will come in more violent and radical form. . . . [A]llowing dissidents to expound their views enables them "to let off steam." . . . This results in a release of energy, a lessening of frustration, and a channeling of resistance into courses consistent with law and order. It operates, in short, as a catharsis throughout the body politic. . . . The principle of political legitimation . . . asserts that persons who have had full freedom to state their position and to persuade others to adopt it will, when the decision goes against them, be more ready to accept the common judgment. They will recognize that they have been treated fairly, in accordance with rational rules for social living. . . . Only a government which consistently fails to relieve valid grievances need fear the outbreak of violent opposition. . . .

C. Edwin Baker, *Scope of the First Amendment*
Freedom of Speech

25 UCLA L. Rev. 964 (1978)[2]

[The] classic marketplace of ideas model argues that truth (or the best perspectives or solutions) can be discovered through robust debate, free from governmental interference. Defending this theory in *On Liberty*, John Stuart Mill argued that three situations are possible: 1) if heretical opinion contains the truth, and if we silence it, we lose the chance of exchanging truth for error; 2) if received and contesting opinions each hold part of the truth, their clash in open discussion provides the best means to discover the truth in each; 3) even if the heretical view is wholly false and the orthodoxy contains the whole truth, the received truth, unless debated and challenged, will be held in the manner of prejudice or dead dogma, its meaning may be forgotten or enfeebled, and it will be inefficacious for good. Moreover, without free speech, totally false heretical opinions which could not survive open discussion will not disappear; instead, driven underground, these opinions will smolder, their fallacies protected from exposure and opposition. In this model, the value of free speech lies not in the liberty interests of individual speakers but in the societal benefits derived from unimpeded discussion. This social gain is so great, and any loss from allowing speech is so small, that society should tolerate no restraint on the verbal search for truth. . . .

The assumptions on which the classic marketplace of ideas theory rests are almost universally rejected today. [T]he hope that the marketplace leads to truth, or even to the best or most desirable decision, becomes implausible. First, truth is not objective. . . . [K]nowledge depends on how people's interests, needs, and experiences lead them to slice and categorize an expanding mass of sense data. . . . And even if "rational" debate can play some role in advancing understanding within a given paradigm, discussion appears insufficient by itself to evaluate different paradigms. . . . Protecting free speech insures that the individual will have more information and, thus, be able to make a more informed choice. The problem with this defense is that the individual is as likely to find needed information in experiences as in free speech. . . .

[I]f truth or understanding are created or chosen, an evaluation of the marketplace must consider whether the values of different people or groups are furthered by the choice or creation of the same truth or understanding. . . . [I]f groups have divergent interests concerning the choice of perspectives, one can presume that the marketplace of ideas (and other activities which might be protected) leads to the "best" or "proper" or "progressive" understanding only if the marketplace favors those groups who should be favored or "properly" distributes influence among various people or groups such that optimal compromises are reached. For example, Herbert Marcuse concluded that in the present historical circumstances the marketplace of ideas would work properly only if the rich and powerful were completely excluded and access were limited to progressive, leftist elements; others argue for more or less equal access for all groups in the market place. . . .

The classic model also requires that people be able to use their rational capacities to eliminate distortion caused by the form and frequency of message presentation and to find the core of relevant information or argument. . . . Emotional or "irrational" appeals have great impact; "subconscious" repressions, phobias, or desires influence people's assimilation of messages; and, most obviously, stimulus-response mechanisms and selective attention and retention processes influence understanding or perspectives. . . . Since interests vary with social position, the perspectives that are reinforced will also vary. . . . [P]eople maintain perspectives which promote one's interest even when presented with contrary information or alterative perspectives. . . . These psychological insights, extensively relied upon in practice by advertisers and propagandists, eviscerate the faith in the ability of the marketplace of ideas to lead to the "best" truths or understandings. Even if one assumes that some understandings are best, one has no reason to expect these to be discovered in the marketplace of ideas. . . . Furthermore, . . . the theory cannot be defended on the grounds that it provides a "fair" or otherwise justifiable process for regulating the struggle between opposing groups. The incredible inequalities of opportunity to use the marketplace cause a fairness defense to fail. . . .

My thesis is that the first amendment protects a broad realm of nonviolent, noncoercive activity. . . . Professor Emerson . . . finds first amendment freedom essential for four values. . . . However, it is informative to see that the first value, self-fulfillment, and the third, participation in change, are key values. . . . To justify legal obligation, the community must respect individuals as equal, rational and autonomous moral beings. [R]especting people's autonomy as well as people's equal worth requires that people be allowed an equal right to participate in the process of group decision making—which is precisely Emerson's other key value, participation in collective decision making. . . . Either all people have a right to participate in the individual and social processes of *self*-determination or a "better" individual and collective expression of humanity results from this social process because of the increased opportunity of each to freely participate. Either ground justifies protecting people's liberty to engage in substantively valued conduct. . . .

Robert H. Bork, *Neutral Principles and Some First Amendment Problems*

47 Ind. L.J. 1 (1971)[3]

[Constitutional] protection should be accorded only to speech that is explicitly political. There is no basis for judicial intervention to protect any other form of expression, be it scientific, literary or that variety of expression we call obscene or pornographic. Moreover, within that category of speech we ordinarily call political, there should be no constitutional obstruction to laws making criminal any speech that advocates forcible overthrow of the government or the violation of any law. . . . [T]he men who adopted the first amendment did not display a strong libertarian stance with respect to speech. . . . In colonial times and during and after the Revolution they displayed a determination to punish speech thought dangerous to government, much of it expression that we should think harmless and well within the bounds of legitimate discourse. . . .

. . . The first amendment indicates that there is something special about speech. [T]he entire structure of the Constitution creates a representative democracy, a form of government that would be meaningless without freedom to discuss government and its policies. Freedom for political speech could and should be inferred even if there were no first amendment. . . .

The first two [proffered] benefits [of speech]—development of individual faculties and the achievement of pleasure—are . . . found, for both speaker and hearer, in all varieties of speech, from political discourse to shop talk or salacious literature. [T]hese benefits do not distinguish speech from any other human activity. An individual may develop [his or her] faculties or derive pleasure from trading on the stock market, . . . working as a barmaid, engaging in sexual activity, playing tennis, [or] in any of thousands of endeavors. Speech with only the first two benefits can be preferred to other activities only by ranking forms of personal gratification. These functions or benefits of speech are, therefore, to the principled judge, indistinguishable from the functions or benefits of all other human activity. [A judge] cannot, on neutral grounds, choose to protect speech that has only these functions more than [he or she] protects any other claimed freedom. . . . The third benefit of speech [the safety valve function] raises only issues of expediency or prudence, and, therefore, raises issues to be determined solely by the legislature or, in some cases, by the executive. The legislature may decide not to repress speech advocating the forcible overthrow of the government . . . because it thinks repression would cause more trouble than it would prevent. . . . The category of protected speech should consist of speech concerned with governmental behavior, policy or personnel, whether the government unit involved is executive, legislative, judicial or administrative. . . . The line drawn must . . . lie between the explicitly political and all else. . . .

Alexander Meiklejohn, *The First Amendment as an Absolute*
1961 Sup. Ct. Rev. 245[4]

[The] First Amendment does not protect a "freedom to speak." It protects the freedom of these activities of thought and communication by which we "govern." It is concerned, not with a private right, but with a public power, a governmental responsibility. [But] voting is merely the external expression of a wide and diverse number of activities by means of which citizens attempt to meet the responsibilities of making judgments, which that freedom to govern lays upon them. That freedom implies and requires what we call "the dignity of the individual."

4. Reprinted by permission.

Self-government can exist only insofar as the voters acquire the intelligence, integrity, sensitivity, and generous devotion to the general welfare that, in theory, casting a ballot is assumed to express.

. . . [T]here are many forms of thought and expression within the range of human communications from which the voter derives the knowledge, intelligence, sensitivity to human values; the capacity for sane and objective judgment which, so far as possible, a ballot should express. . . . I list four of them below.

1.   Education . . . is the attempt to so inform and cultivate the mind and will of a citizen that [each person] shall have the wisdom, the independence, and, therefore, the dignity of a governing citizen. Freedom of education is, thus, as we all recognize, a basic postulate in the planning of a free society.

2.   The achievements of philosophy and the sciences in creating knowledge and understanding of [ourselves] and [our] world must be made available, without abridgement, to every citizen.

3.   Literature and the arts must be protected by the First Amendment. They lead the way toward sensitive and informed appreciation and response to the values out of which the riches of the general welfare are created.

4.   Public discussions of public issues, together with the spreading of information and opinion bearing on those issues, must have a freedom unabridged by our agents. . . . Over our governing, they have no power. Over their governing we have sovereign power. . . .

[L]iterature and the arts are protected because they have a "social importance" which I have called a "governing" importance. [T]he novel [is] a powerful determinative of our views of what human beings are, how they can be influenced, in which directions they should be influenced by many forces, including, especially, their own judgments and appreciations. . . . Shall the government establish a censorship to distinguish between "good" novels and "bad" ones? . . . The First Amendment seems to answer that question with an unequivocal "no." [T]he authority of citizens to decide what they shall write, and, more fundamental, what they shall read and see, has not been delegated to any of the subordinate branches of government. It is "reserved to the people," each deciding to whom [each] will listen, whom [each] will read, what portrayal of the human scene [each] finds worthy of his attention. . . .

Questions

1. *Evaluating the Justifications for Protecting Speech.* Do you accept the four justifications for protecting speech (marketplace of ideas, safety valve, self-fulfillment, and democratic process)? For example, if one accepts the idea of self-fulfillment as a justification for protecting speech, is there *any* speech that does not deserve protection? Under that justification, does speech protection become subjective and individualistic in that any speech that an individual deems to be "self-fulfilling" is necessarily worthy of protection?

2. *Weighing and Balancing the Justifications.* Are some of the justifications for protecting speech more compelling than others? For example, should we ascribe more importance to speech related to the democratic process than to speech that promotes self-fulfillment?

∽ PROBLEMS: MORE ON THE INTERNATIONAL TREATY REGULATING THE INTERNET ∽

1. *Can There Be Agreement Regarding the Justifications for Protecting Speech?* Should the new treaty reflect one of the justifications for protecting speech presented in the articles above? A multitude of countries will be in attendance at the conference, and it is likely that they will have very different governmental systems (e.g., some democratic, some not). In addition, they are likely to hold very different views regarding the value of speech and its place in society. Are there certain fundamental ideas about the importance of speech, and the justifications for protecting speech, that all countries might be able to agree on? If so, what are they?

2. *The Justifications for and Shape of the Treaty.* As you prepare to attend the convention, think about which underlying values help shape your views regarding whether particular types of speech should (or should not) be protected. For example, with regard to sexual speech (some of which may be obscene and some not obscene), which justifications make you more or less likely to argue that it deserves protection (e.g., self-fulfillment, safety valve, marketplace of ideas, or democratic process theory)? Could hard-core sexual speech contain political ideas?

B. CATEGORIES OF SPEECH

The U.S. Supreme Court has never regarded the right to freedom of expression as absolute. In Chaplinsky v. New Hampshire, 315 U.S. 568 (1942), a unanimous Supreme Court flatly stated that there are "certain well-defined and narrowly limited *classes* of speech, the prevention and punishment of which have never been thought to raise any Constitutional problem." *Chaplinsky* included within these classes "the lewd and obscene, the profane, the libelous, and the insulting or 'fighting' words. . . ." In this section, we examine the Court's handling of various "excluded" categories of speech.

1. *Advocacy of Illegal Action*

In applying the First Amendment, there has been much debate about whether the First Amendment protects those who advocate illegal action. Indubitably, certain types of speech (e.g., solicitation to commit murder) can and should be criminalized. However, in many instances, advocacy of illegal action cases involve nothing more than criticism of government, and therefore criminalization raises the specter of seditious libel.

a. Early Cases

Early seditious libel cases arose during World War I. There was significant opposition to U.S. entry into the war, including calls to resist or obstruct recruitment and enlistment in the U.S. armed forces. The situation was aggravated by the collapse of the Russian monarchy and the emergence of the Bolshevik regime. These events led to a "Red Scare" — a fear that Communism would sweep the world.

Schenck v. United States
249 U.S. 47 (1919)

Mr. Justice HOLMES delivered the opinion of the Court.

This is an indictment in three counts. The first charges a conspiracy to violate the Espionage Act of June 15, 1917, §3, by causing and attempting to cause insubordination, &c., in the military and naval forces of the United States, and to obstruct the recruiting and enlistment service of the United States, when the United States was at war with the German Empire, to-wit, that the defendant wilfully conspired to have printed and circulated to men who had been called and accepted for military service under the Act of May 18, 1917, a document set forth and alleged to be calculated to cause such insubordination and obstruction. The count alleges overt acts in pursuance of the conspiracy, ending in the distribution of the document. [Defendants were also charged with using the U.S. mail to transmit the documents.] The defendants were found guilty on all the counts. They set up the First Amendment to the Constitution forbidding Congress to make any law abridging the freedom of speech, or of the press [as a defense].

The document in question upon its first printed side recited the first section of the Thirteenth Amendment, said that the idea embodied in it was violated by the Conscription Act and that a conscript is little better than a convict. In impassioned language it intimated that conscription was despotism in its worst form and a monstrous wrong against humanity in the interest of Wall Street's chosen few. It said, "Do not submit to intimidation," but in form at least confined itself to peaceful measures such as a petition for the repeal of the act. The [other] side of the sheet was headed "Assert Your Rights." It stated reasons for alleging that any one violated the Constitution when he refused to recognize "your right to assert your opposition to the draft," and went on "If you do not assert and support your rights, you are helping to deny or disparage rights which it is the solemn duty of all citizens and residents of the United States to retain." It described the arguments on the other side as coming from cunning politicians and a mercenary capitalist press, and even silent consent to the conscription law as helping to support an infamous conspiracy. It denied the power to send our citizens away to foreign shores to shoot up the people of other lands, and added that words could not express the condemnation such cold-blooded ruthlessness deserves, [and] winding up, "You must do your share to maintain, support and uphold the rights of the people of this country." Of course the document would not have been sent unless it had been intended to have some effect, and we do not see what effect it could be expected to have upon persons subject to the draft except to influence them to obstruct the carrying of it out. The defendants do not deny that the jury might find against them on this point.

But it is said [that the circular] is protected by the First Amendment to the Constitution. . . . We admit that in many places and in ordinary times the defendants in saying all that was said in the circular would have been within their constitutional rights. But the character of every act depends upon the circumstances in which it is done. The most stringent protection of free speech would not protect a man in falsely shouting fire in a theatre and causing a panic. . . . The question in every case is whether the words used are used in such circumstances and are of such a nature as to create a clear and present danger that they will bring about the substantive evils that Congress has a right to prevent. It is a question of proximity and degree. When a nation is at war many things that might be said in time of peace are such a hindrance to its effort that their utterance will not be endured so long as men fight and that no Court could regard them as protected by any constitutional right. [I]f an actual obstruction of the recruiting service were proved, liability for words that produced that effect might be enforced. The statute of 1917 [punishes] conspiracies to obstruct as well as actual obstruction. If the act, (speaking, or circulating a paper,) its tendency and the intent with which it is done are the same, we perceive no ground for saying that success alone warrants making the act a crime. Indeed that case might be said to dispose of the present contention. . . . But as the right to free speech was not referred to specially, we have thought fit to add a few words. . . .

Judgments affirmed.

Notes and Questions

1. *The "Fire in a Crowded Theatre" Analogy.* Implicitly, Justice Holmes appeared to compare Schenck to a man in a theatre who maliciously urges a crowd to flee from a nonexistent fire and thereby creates a terrible danger of death and serious injury to the people in that crowd. Justice Holmes also noted that while no actual obstruction of the draft was proved in *Schenck*, the "tendency" of the flyer and the "intent" behind its circulation were the same as they would be in a case where speech led to the completed crime of obstruction. Implicitly, Justice Holmes appeared to reason that the facts in *Schenck* brought about a clear enough and present enough danger of obstruction to justify conviction. Is he correct? What other purposes does the crowded theatre analogy serve?

2. Frohwerk *and Pro-Germany Editorials.* In Frohwerk v. United States, 249 U.S. 204 (1919), Justice Holmes found that publication of a newspaper that was critical of the war against Germany in 1917 justified a conspiracy conviction for obstruction of the draft under the Espionage Act and a ten-year sentence. The

defendants, Frohwerk and his employer, Gleeser, "prepared and published the *Missouri Staats Zeitung*." The newspaper published articles condemning the illegal use of troops in support of Britain, praising the "unconquerable spirit and undiminished strength of the German nation," blaming the war on Wall Street, and giving "a picture [of] the sufferings of a drafted man, of his then recognizing that his country is not in danger and that he is being sent to a foreign land to fight in a cause that neither he nor any one else knows anything of, and reaching the conviction that this is but a war to protect some rich men's money." That man is praised for following the impulse of self-preservation by resisting the draft. The text argues that "we are led and ruled by England, [that] our sons, our taxes and our sacrifices are only in the interest of England," and that "the Central powers are carrying on a defensive war." Justice Holmes reasoned as follows in affirming the conviction:

> [T]he First Amendment while prohibiting legislation against free speech [cannot] have been, and obviously was not, intended to give immunity for every possible use of language. We venture to believe that neither Hamilton nor Madison [ever] supposed that to make criminal the counseling of a murder within the jurisdiction of Congress would be an unconstitutional interference with free speech. . . . We do not lose our right to condemn either measures or men because the country is at war. It does not appear that there was any special effort to reach men who were subject to the draft; and if the evidence should show that the defendant was a poor man, turning out copy for Gleeser, his employer, at less than a day laborer's pay, for Gleeser to use or reject as he saw fit, in a newspaper of small circulation, there would be a natural inclination to test every question of law [very] thoroughly before upholding the very severe penalty imposed. [But, on the record,] it is impossible to say that it might not have been found that the circulation of the paper was in quarters where a little breath would be enough to kindle a flame and that the fact was known and relied upon by those who sent the paper out. Small compensation would not exonerate the defendant if it were found that he expected the result, even if pay were his chief desire.

3. *The Presidential Campaign Speech.* Debs v. United States, 249 U.S. 211 (1919), involved a U.S. presidential candidate, Eugene Debs, who was charged with violating the Espionage Act by attempting to obstruct the draft and incite insubordination in the military forces. The charges were based on a speech that Debs gave in Canton, Ohio, in 1918 (during World War I), as part of his campaign for the presidency as the Socialist Party candidate. The speech discussed Socialism, its growth, and a prophecy of its ultimate success. During the speech, Debs claimed that he had visited "loyal comrades" who had been convicted of aiding and abetting another person in failing to register for the draft, that the men were "paying the penalty for standing erect and for seeking to pave the way to better conditions for all mankind," and that the master class "has always declared the war and the subject class has always fought the battles — that the subject class has had nothing to gain and all to lose, including their lives; that the working class, who furnish the corpses, have never yet had a voice in declaring war and never yet had a voice in declaring peace." He also referred to the conviction of a woman for attempting to cause insubordination and refusal of duty in the military forces, and stated that "she went out to render her service to the cause in this day of crises, and they sent her to the penitentiary for ten years." He then forecast the success of the international Socialist crusade and stated "You need to know that you

are fit for something better than slavery and cannon fodder," and "Don't worry about the charge of treason to your masters; but be concerned about the treason that involves yourselves." In reference to a charge that he had obstructed the war, he said, "I have been accused of obstructing the war. I admit it. Gentlemen, I abhor war. I would oppose the war if I stood alone." Justice Holmes noted that about an hour before his speech, Debs had stated that he approved "in spirit and substance" of the Socialist Party platform (entitled the "Anti-War Proclamation and Program"), which declared: "We brand the declaration of war by our Governments as a crime against the people of the United States and against the nations of the world. In all modern history there has been no war more unjustifiable than the war in which we are about to engage." Its first recommendation was, "continuous, active, and public opposition to the war, through demonstrations, mass petitions, and all other means within our power." In upholding Debs's conviction, Justice Holmes writing for the Court stated:

> The [jury was warranted in finding] that one purpose of the [campaign] speech, whether incidental or not does not matter, was to oppose not only war in general but this war, and that the opposition was so expressed that its natural and intended effect would be to obstruct recruiting. If that was intended and if, in all the circumstances, that would be its probable effect, it would not be protected by reason of its being part of a general program and expressions of a general and conscientious belief. Evidence that the defendant accepted [the view expressed in the Party platform] at the time that he made his speech is evidence that if in that speech he used words tending to obstruct the recruiting service he meant that they should have that effect. [We] should add that the jury were most carefully instructed that they could not find the defendant guilty for advocacy of any of his opinions unless the words used had as their natural tendency and reasonably probable effect to obstruct the recruiting service, [and] unless the defendant had the specific intent to do so in his mind.

Holmes derived the "tendency and intent" test set forth in *Schenck* from criminal law conspiracy concepts in a traditional criminal law context removed from factual situations involving the expression of political protest.

∽ PROBLEMS ∽

1. *Schenck, Debs, and the Justifications for Protecting Speech.* Now, consider the *Schenck* and *Debs* decisions in light of the justifications for according special status to speech. Which, if any, of the four justifications (self-fulfillment, safety valve, democratic process, marketplace of ideas) did Schenck's and Debs's speech serve? Can you make an argument that their speech deserves constitutional protection?

2. *Incitement to Illegal Action.* How would *Schenck* apply if the crime charged in examples a, b, c, and e is conspiracy to obstruct the draft and the crime in example d is "advocacy of the violent overthrow of government"?

   a. A group of college students opposed to World War I holds a "peace vigil" at which they "rally for peace" as well as against the war and the draft.

b.   A professor discusses the "moral imperative" that requires every "good and moral citizen" to oppose the war and the draft. Would it matter whether students actually resisted the draft?

c.   A student wears a jacket bearing the message "Fuck the Draft" to express his opposition to the war.

d.   On a remote piece of property, Ku Klux Klan members hold a rally at which they burn a cross, denounce public officials, and discuss the need to take "revengeance" against members of certain minority groups as well as against government officials.

e.   *The Courier-Journal*, a large daily newspaper in Louisville, Kentucky, publishes editorials and articles that are critical of the war and the draft and that discuss the "moral imperative" of all citizens to resist the draft.

3. *Expressing Opposition.* Under *Schenck*, *Frohwerk*, and *Debs*, how could a newspaper publisher, journalist, or politician have expressed opposition during wartime to the participation of the United States in World War I without risking conviction under the Espionage Act for conspiracy to obstruct the draft? What language would have been safe to use, expressed in what manner, and under what circumstances?

4. *More on the International Treaty Regulating the Internet.* Suppose that the European delegates to the convention would like to add language to the treaty that tracks the European Convention on Human Rights, and in particular Article 10, Section 2, of that convention, which provides:

> The exercise of these freedoms, since it carries with it duties and responsibilities, may be subject to such formalities, conditions, restrictions or penalties as are prescribed by law and are necessary in a democratic society, in the interests of national security, territorial integrity or public safety, for the prevention of disorder or crime, for the protection of health or morals, for the protection of the reputation or the rights of others, for preventing the disclosure of information received in confidence, or for maintaining the authority and impartiality of the judiciary. . . . "

In light of the cases that you have read thus far, could you agree to such language consistent with the First Amendment?

b.   Justice Holmes's *Abrams* Dissent

Justice Holmes challenged the Court's approach to subversive advocacy in Abrams v. United States, 250 U.S. 616 (1919), when he dissented from the affirmance of convictions of a group of self-described Russian-born "anarchists" and "socialists" who distributed 5,000 circulars. Some of the circulars were thrown from the window of a building, while others were distributed secretly in New York. The Espionage Act amendments of 1918 made it a crime to conspire, during the war with Germany, to publish "disloyal, scurrilous and abusive language about the form of government," or language "intended to bring the form of government" into "contempt, scorn, contumely and disrepute," or language "intended to incite, provoke and encourage resistance" to the United States in the war. The fourth crime encompassed those who would "urge, incite and advocate curtailment of production of things," like ordnance and ammunition, "necessary and essential to the prosecution of the war."

The defendants were charged with all four crimes based on two circulars. The first circular was entitled "The Hypocrisy of the United States and Her Allies." After denouncing President Wilson as "a hypocrite and a coward," it went on to state: "His [the President's] shameful, cowardly silence about the intervention in Russia reveals the hypocrisy of the plutocratic gang in Washington and vicinity. He [the President] is too much of a coward to come out openly and say: We capitalistic nations cannot afford to have a proletarian republic in Russia. The Russian Revolution cries: Workers of the World!; Awake!; Rise!; Put down your enemy and mine!; Yes friends, there is only one enemy of the workers of the world and that is CAPITALISM." The circular concluded, "Awake!; Awake, you Workers of the World!; REVOLUTIONISTS."

The second circular was entitled "Workers—Wake Up." After referring to "his Majesty, Mr. Wilson, and the rest of the gang, dogs of all colors!;" it continued: "Workers, Russian emigrants, you who had the least belief in the honesty of *our* government must now throw away all confidence, must spit in the face of the false, hypocritic, military propaganda which has fooled you so relentlessly, calling forth your sympathy, your help, to the prosecution of the war. With the money which you have loaned, or are going to loan them, they will make bullets not only for the Germans, but also for the Workers Soviets of Russia. *Workers in the ammunition factories, you are producing bullets, bayonets, cannon, to murder not only the Germans, but also your dearest, best, who are in Russia and are fighting for freedom*. America and her Allies have betrayed [the Workers]. Their robberish aims are clear to all men. The destruction of the Russian Revolution, that is the politics of the march to Russia. *Workers, our reply to the barbaric intervention has to be a general strike!; An open challenge* only will let the government know that not only the Russian Worker fights for freedom, but also *here in America lives the spirit of Revolution*. Do not let the government scare you with their wild punishment in prisons, hanging and shooting. We must not and will not betray the splendid fighters of Russia. *Workers, up to fight*. Woe unto those who will be in the way of progress. Let solidarity live!;" It was signed "The Rebels."

The majority opinion interpreted the language of the circular as appealing to workers to put down the government of the United States by force, and as seeking to persuade its readers "to cease to render [assistance] to the government" in the war effort. "Even if their primary purpose [was] to aid the cause of the Russian Revolution, [their] plan of action [necessarily] involved [defeat] of the war program of the United States." The "obvious effect" of this appeal would be to persuade people "not to aid government loans and not to work in ammunition factories." Furthermore, the purpose was to defeat the war plans "by bringing upon the country the paralysis of a general [strike]," "to throw the country into a state of revolution, [and] to thereby frustrate" the war effort. Justice Holmes responded with the following dissent.

Abrams v. United States

250 U.S. 616 (1919)

Mr. Justice HOLMES, dissenting.

This indictment is founded wholly upon the publication of two leaflets. . . . The third count alleges a conspiracy to encourage resistance to the United States in the [war against Germany] and to attempt to effectuate the purpose by publishing the same leaflets. The fourth count lays a conspiracy to incite curtailment of production of things necessary to the prosecution of the war and to attempt to accomplish it by publishing the second leaflet. . . .

[Focusing on the fourth count,] it seems too plain to be denied that the suggestion to workers in the ammunition factories that they are producing bullets to murder their dearest, and the further advocacy of a general strike, both in the second leaflet, do urge curtailment of production of things necessary to the prosecution of the war within the meaning of the [Act]. But to make the conduct criminal that statute requires that it should be "with intent by such curtailment to cripple or hinder the United States in the prosecution of the war." It seems to me that no such intent is proved. [A] deed is not done with intent to produce a consequence unless that consequence is the aim of the deed. . . .

[T]his statute must be taken to use its words in a strict and accurate sense. . . . A patriot might think that we were wasting money on aeroplanes, or making more cannon of a certain kind than we needed, and might advocate curtailment with success, yet even if it turned out that the curtailment hindered and was thought by other minds to have been obviously likely to hinder the United States in the prosecution of the war, no one would hold such conduct a crime. . . .

I never have seen any reason to doubt that the questions of law that [were] before this Court in the cases of *Schenck*, *Frohwerk*, and *Debs*, were rightly decided. [T]he United States constitutionally may punish speech that produces or is intended to produce a clear and imminent danger that it will bring about forthwith certain substantive evils that the United States constitutionally may seek to prevent. The power undoubtedly is greater in time of war than in time of peace because war opens dangers that do not exist at other times.

But as against dangers peculiar to war, [it] is only the present danger of immediate evil or an intent to bring it about that warrants Congress in setting a limit to the expression of opinion where private rights are not concerned. Congress certainly cannot forbid all effort to change the mind of the country. [N]obody can suppose that the surreptitious publishing of a silly leaflet by an unknown man, without more, would present any immediate danger that its opinions would hinder the success of the government arms or have any appreciable tendency to do so. Publishing those opinions for the very purpose of obstructing, however, might indicate a greater danger and at any rate would have the quality of an attempt. So I assume that the second leaflet if published for the purposes alleged in the fourth count might be punishable. . . .

I do not see how anyone can find the intent required by the statute in any of the defendant's words. The second leaflet is the only one that affords even a foundation for the charge. [W]ithout invoking the hatred of German militarism expressed in the former one, it is evident from the beginning to the end that the only object of the paper is to help Russia and stop American intervention there against the popular government — not to impede the United States in the war that it was carrying on. . . .

In this case sentences of twenty years imprisonment have been imposed for the publishing of two leaflets that I believe the defendants had as much right to publish as the Government has to publish the Constitution of the United States now vainly invoked by them. Even if I am technically wrong[,] the most nominal punishment seems to me all that possibly could be inflicted, unless the defendants are to be made to suffer [for] the creed that they avow. . . .

Persecution for the expression of opinions seems to me perfectly logical. If you have no doubt of your premises or your power and want a certain result with all your heart you naturally express your wishes in law and sweep away all opposition. To allow opposition by speech seems to indicate that you think the speech impotent, as when a man says that he has squared the circle, or that you do not care whole-heartedly for the result, or that you doubt either your power or your premises. But when men have realized that time has upset many fighting faiths, they may come to believe even more than they believe the very foundations of their own conduct that the ultimate good desired is better reached by free trade in ideas — that the best test of truth is the power of the thought to get itself accepted in the competition of the market, and that truth is the only ground upon which their wishes safely can be carried out. That at any rate is the theory of our Constitution. It is an experiment, as all life is an experiment. Every year if not every day we have to wager our salvation upon some prophecy based upon imperfect knowledge. [W]e should be eternally vigilant against attempts to check the expression of opinions that we loathe [unless] they so imminently threaten immediate interference with the lawful and pressing purposes of the law that an immediate check is required to save the country. I wholly disagree with the argument [that] the First Amendment left the common law as to seditious libel in force. History seems to me against the notion. . . . Only the emergency that makes it immediately dangerous to leave the correction of evil counsels to time warrants making any exception to the sweeping command, "Congress shall make no law . . . abridging the freedom of speech." Of course I am speaking only of expressions of opinion and exhortations, which were all that were uttered here, but I regret that I cannot put into more impressive words my belief that in their conviction upon this indictment the defendants were deprived of their rights under the Constitution of the United States. . . .

Notes and Questions

1. *"Acts" versus "Utterances."* The original Espionage Act of 1917 purportedly punished only "acts" such as "obstruction" or "causing insubordination," rather than the utterance of certain language or the advocacy of certain ideas. By

contrast, the amendments to the 1917 Act created various "speech" crimes for which the *Abrams* defendants were convicted. In the *Schenck* era, the "clear and present danger" test was applied to both conduct crimes and speech crimes, and it was used to express the Court's confidence in the inherent power of the legislature to punish speech that caused harm. Justice Holmes assumed that the role of the courts in cases where defendants asserted a "First Amendment defense" was to engage in the traditional oversight function allowed in criminal cases — namely, to examine the record to ascertain whether sufficient evidence of the elements of the crime had been produced at trial. That role entitled courts to create "sufficiency of the evidence" formulas that could be either demanding or deferential, depending on the crime and on a court's judgment about the need for controlling prosecutorial discretion and providing guidance for juries. Thus, the "clear and present danger" test began as such a formula, and it possessed the inherent flexibility to be used for either affirming convictions based on ready assumptions about an antiwar speaker's dangerousness or for creating safeguards for such speakers in the form of stringent proof requirements concerning the "clarity" (or great likelihood) and "presentness" (or great imminence) of a dangerous act of lawlessness. Once the test was launched in the Espionage Act cases, the Court continued to rely on it in cases involving state criminal syndicalism statutes and federal Smith Act prosecutions, both of which primarily involved criminalization of Communist or Socialist Party advocacy. After *Abrams*, Justices Holmes and Brandeis continued to dissent from the Court's applications of the "clear and present danger" test, and to articulate the policy reasons for creating broad First Amendment defenses to criminal prosecutions of antigovernment speakers and writers.

2. *The* Holmes *Dissent and Prior Precedent.* Can you reconcile Justice Holmes's *Abrams* dissent with his willingness to uphold convictions in *Schenck*, *Frohwerk*, and *Debs*?

3. *Incitement Reprise.* How would Justice Holmes's *Abrams* dissent apply to the scenarios in Problem 2 following the *Schenck* opinion?

∽ PROBLEMS ∽

1. *Newspaper Reprise.* Explain how a newspaper publisher, journalist, or politician could have expressed opposition during wartime to the participation of the United States in World War I without risking conviction under the Espionage Act for conspiracy to obstruct the draft under Justice Holmes's *Abrams* dissent. What language would have been safe to use, expressed in what manner, and under what circumstances?

2. *More on the International Treaty Regulating the Internet.* If Justice Holmes's *Abrams* dissent were treated as "law" (in the sense that the Court adopted it as the prevailing test), what would be your position on whether the United States can accept the European request to include the proposed language from the European Convention on Human Rights in the treaty on the Internet?

c.   The Criminal Syndicalism Cases of the 1920s

Gitlow and *Whitney* are the most famous decisions from the "Red Scare" era, and *Gitlow* is especially noteworthy because the Court announced that "we may and do assume that freedom of speech and of the press — which are protected by the First Amendment from abridgment by Congress — are among the fundamental personal rights and 'liberties' protected by the due process clause of the Fourteenth Amendment from impairment by the States."

Gitlow v. New York

268 U.S. 652 (1925)

Mr. Justice SANFORD delivered the opinion of the Court.

[Benjamin Gitlow was convicted of criminal anarchy.] The contention here is that the statute [is] repugnant to the due process clause of the Fourteenth Amendment. Its material provisions are:

> §160. *Criminal anarchy defined.* Criminal anarchy is the doctrine that organized government should be overthrown by force or violence, or by assassination of the executive head or of any of the executive officials of government, or by any unlawful means. The advocacy of such doctrine either by word of mouth or writing is a felony.
>
> §161. *Advocacy of criminal anarchy.* Any person who:
>
> 1. By word of mouth or writing advocates, advises or teaches the duty, necessity or propriety of overthrowing or overturning organized government by force or violence, or by assassination of the executive head or of any of the executive officials of government, or by any unlawful means; or,
>
> 2. Prints, publishes, edits, issues or knowingly circulates, sells, distributes or publicly displays any book, paper, document, or written or printed matter in any form, containing or advocating, advising or teaching the doctrine that organized government should be overthrown by force, violence or any unlawful means 'Is guilty of a felony and punishable' by imprisonment or fine, or both.

The indictment was in two counts. The first charged that the defendant had advocated, advised and taught the duty, necessity and propriety of overthrowing and overturning organized government by force, violence and unlawful means, by certain writings therein set forth entitled "The Left Wing Manifesto"; the second that he had printed, published and knowingly circulated and distributed a certain paper called "The Revolutionary Age," containing the writings set forth in the first count. . . .

[The] statute does not penalize the utterance or publication of abstract "doctrine" or academic discussion having no quality of incitement to any concrete action. It is not aimed against mere historical or philosophical essays. It does not restrain the advocacy of changes in the form of government by constitutional and lawful means. What it prohibits is language advocating, advising or teaching the overthrow of organized government by unlawful means. These words imply urging to action. . . . It is not the abstract "doctrine" of overthrowing organized government by unlawful means which is denounced by the statute, but the advocacy of action for the accomplishment of that purpose. . . .

The Manifesto, plainly, is neither the statement of abstract doctrine [nor] mere prediction that industrial disturbances and revolutionary mass strikes will result spontaneously in an inevitable process of evolution in the economic system. It advocates and urges in fervent language mass action which shall progressively foment industrial disturbances and through political mass strikes and revolutionary mass action overthrow and destroy organized parliamentary government. It concludes with a call to action in these words: "The proletariat revolution and the Communist reconstruction of society — *the struggle for these* — is now indispensable. . . . The Communist International calls the proletariat of the world to the final struggle!;" This is not the expression of philosophical abstraction, the mere prediction of future events; it is the language of direct incitement.

The means advocated for bringing about the destruction of organized parliamentary government, namely, mass industrial revolts usurping the functions of municipal government, political mass strikes directed against the parliamentary state, and revolutionary mass action for its final destruction, necessarily imply the use of force and violence, and in their essential nature are inherently unlawful in a constitutional government of law and order. That the jury were warranted in finding that the Manifesto advocated not merely the abstract doctrine of overthrowing organized government by force, violence and unlawful means, but action to that end, is clear.

[We] assume that freedom of speech and of the press — which are protected by the First Amendment from abridgment by Congress — are among the fundamental personal rights and "liberties" protected by the due process clause of the Fourteenth Amendment from impairment by the States. . . . By enacting the present statute the State has determined, through its legislative body, that utterances advocating the overthrow of organized government by force, violence and unlawful means, are so inimical to the general welfare and involve such danger of substantive evil that they may be penalized in the exercise of its police power. That determination must be given great weight. . . . Such utterances, by their very nature, involve danger to the public peace and to the security of the State. They threaten breaches of the peace and ultimate revolution. And the immediate danger is none the less real and substantial, because the effect of a given utterance cannot be accurately foreseen. . . . A single revolutionary spark may kindle a fire that, smouldering for a time, may burst into a sweeping and destructive conflagration. [The State] cannot reasonably be required to defer the adoption of measures for its own peace and safety until the revolutionary utterances lead to actual disturbances of the public peace or imminent and immediate danger of its own destruction; but it may, in the exercise of its judgment, suppress the threatened danger in its incipiency. . . .

We cannot hold that the present statute is an arbitrary or unreasonable exercise of the police power of the State unwarrantably infringing the freedom of speech or press. . . . This being so it may be applied to every utterance — not too trivial to be beneath the notice of the law — which is of such a character and used with such intent and purpose as to bring it within the prohibition of the statute. . . . In other words, when the legislative body has determined generally, in the constitutional exercise of its discretion, that utterances of a certain kind involve such danger of substantive evil that they may be punished, the question whether any specific utterance coming within the prohibited class is likely, in and of itself, to bring about the substantive evil, is not open to consideration. It is sufficient that the statute itself be constitutional and that the use of the language comes within its prohibition.

[T]he general provisions of the statute may be constitutionally applied to the specific utterance of the defendant if its natural tendency and probable effect was to bring about the substantive evil which the legislative body might prevent. And the general statement in the *Schenck* case that the "question in every case is whether the words used are used in such circumstances and are of such a nature as to create a clear and present danger that they will bring about the substantive evils" — upon which great reliance is placed in the defendant's argument — was manifestly intended, as shown by the context, to apply only in cases of this class, and has no application to those like the present, where the legislative body itself has previously determined the danger of substantive evil arising from utterances of a specified character.

[None of these convictions] involved any invasion of the constitutional rights of the defendant. It was not necessary, within the meaning of the statute, that the defendant should have advocated "some definite or immediate act or acts" of force, violence or unlawfulness. It was sufficient if such acts were advocated in general terms; and it was not essential that their immediate execution should have been advocated. Nor was it necessary that the language should have been "reasonably and ordinarily calculated to incite certain persons" to acts of force, violence or unlawfulness. The advocacy need not be addressed to specific persons. . . .

Affirmed.

Mr. Justice HOLMES, dissenting.

Mr. Justice Brandeis and I are of opinion that this judgment should be reversed. The general principle of free speech [is] included in the Fourteenth Amendment. . . . [The] criterion sanctioned by the full Court in *Schenck* applies. . . . It is said that this manifesto was more than a theory, that it was an incitement. Every idea is an incitement. It offers itself for belief and if believed it is acted on unless some other belief outweighs it or some failure of energy stifles the movement at its birth. The only difference between the expression of an opinion and an incitement in the narrower sense is the speaker's enthusiasm for the result. Eloquence may set fire to reason. But whatever may be thought of the redundant discourse before us it had no chance of starting a present conflagration. If in the long run the beliefs expressed in proletarian dictatorship are destined to be accepted by the dominant forces of the community, the only meaning of free speech is that they should be given their chance and have their way. . . . If the publication of this document had been laid as an attempt to induce an uprising against government at once and not at some indefinite time in the future it would have presented a different question. The object would have been one with which the law might deal, subject to the doubt whether there was any danger that the publication could produce any result, or in other words, whether it was not futile and too remote from possible consequences. But the indictment alleges the publication and nothing more.

Whitney v. California
274 U.S. 357 (1927)

Mr. Justice SANFORD delivered the opinion of the Court.

[A California statute defined *criminal syndicalism* as "any doctrine or precept advocating, teaching or aiding and abetting the commission of crime, sabotage (which is hereby defined as willful and malicious physical damage or injury to physical property), or unlawful acts of force and violence or unlawful methods of terrorism as a means of accomplishing a change in industrial ownership or control or effecting any political change." Anita Whitney was convicted based on proof that she "did organize and assist in organizing, and was, is, and knowingly became a member of an organization, society, group and assemblage of persons organized and assembled to advocate, teach, aid and abet criminal syndicalism."]

The defendant [had] been a member of the Local Oakland branch of the Socialist Party. This Local sent delegates to the national convention of the Socialist Party held in Chicago in 1919, which resulted in a split between the "radical" group and the old-wing Socialists. The "radicals" — to whom the Oakland delegates adhered — being ejected, went to another hall, and formed the Communist Labor Party of America. . . . In its "Platform and Program" the Party declared [that] its purpose was "to create a unified revolutionary working class movement in America," organizing the workers as a class, in a revolutionary class struggle to conquer the capitalist state, for the overthrow of capitalist rule, the conquest of political power and the establishment of a working class government, the Dictatorship of the Proletariat. . . . Shortly thereafter the Local Oakland withdrew from the Socialist Party, and sent accredited delegates, including the defendant, to a convention held in Oakland in November 1919, for the purpose of organizing a California branch of the Communist Labor Party. [D]efendant, after taking out a temporary membership in the Communist Labor Party, attended this convention as a delegate and took an active part in its proceedings. . . .

While it is not denied that the evidence warranted the jury in finding that the defendant became a member of and assisted in organizing the Communist Labor Party of California, and that this was organized to advocate, teach, aid or abet criminal syndicalism as defined by the Act, it is urged that the Act, as here construed and applied, deprived the defendant of her liberty without due process of law in that it has made her action in attending the Oakland convention unlawful by reason of "a subsequent event brought about against her will, by the agency of others," with no showing of a specific intent on her part to join in the forbidden purpose of the association, and merely because, by reason of a lack of "prophetic" understanding, she failed to foresee the quality that others would give to the convention. . . . This contention [is] in effect nothing more than an effort to review the weight of the evidence. . . . This question [is] foreclosed by the verdict of the jury[,] involving as it does no constitutional question whatever. . . .

Nor is the Syndicalism Act as applied in this case repugnant to the due process clause as a restraint of the rights of free speech, assembly, and association. . . . By enacting [the] Syndicalism Act the State has declared, through its legislative body, that to knowingly be or become a member of or assist in organizing an association to advocate, teach or aid and abet the commission of crimes or unlawful acts of force, violence or terrorism as a means of accomplishing industrial or political changes, involves such danger to the public peace and the security of the State, that these acts should be penalized in the exercise of its police power. That determination must be given great weight. [The statute] may not be declared unconstitutional unless it is an arbitrary or unreasonable attempt to exercise the authority vested in the State in the public interest.

The essence of the offense denounced by the Act is the combining with others in an association for the accomplishment of the desired ends through the advocacy and use of criminal and unlawful methods. It partakes of the nature of a criminal conspiracy. That such united and joint action involves even greater danger to the public peace and security than the isolated utterances and acts of individuals, is clear. We cannot hold that [the] Act is an unreasonable or arbitrary exercise of the police power of the State, unwarrantably infringing any right of free speech, assembly or association, or that those persons are protected from punishment by the due process clause who abuse such rights by joining and furthering an organization thus menacing the peace and welfare of the State. . . .

Affirmed.

Mr. Justice BRANDEIS, concurring.

[A]lthough the rights of free speech and assembly are fundamental, they are not in their nature absolute. Their exercise is subject to restriction, if the particular restriction proposed is required in order to protect the state from destruction or from serious injury, political, economic or moral. That the necessity which is essential to a valid restriction does not exist unless speech would produce, or is intended to produce, a clear and imminent danger of some substantive evil which the State constitutionally may seek to prevent has been settled.

Those who won our independence believed that [in] its government the deliberative forces should prevail over the arbitrary. . . . Believing in the power of reason as applied through public discussion, they eschewed silence coerced by law — the argument of force in its worst form. Recognizing the occasional tyrannies of governing majorities, they amended the Constitution so that free speech and assembly should be guaranteed.

Fear of serious injury cannot alone justify suppression of free speech and assembly. . . . It is the function of speech to free men from the bondage of irrational fears. To justify suppression of free speech there must be reasonable ground to fear that serious evil will result if free speech is practiced. There must be reasonable ground to believe that the danger apprehended is imminent. There must be reasonable ground to believe that the evil to be prevented is a serious one. Every denunciation of existing law tends in some measure to increase the probability that there will be violation of it. . . . Propagation of the criminal state of mind by teaching syndicalism increases it. Advocacy of law-breaking heightens it still further. But even advocacy of violation, however reprehensible morally, is not a justification for denying free speech where the advocacy falls short of incitement and there is nothing to indicate that the advocacy would be immediately acted on. . . .

Those who won our independence by revolution [did] not fear political change. They did not exalt order at the cost of liberty. [E]ven imminent danger cannot justify resort to prohibition of these functions essential to effective democracy, unless the evil apprehended is relatively serious. Prohibition of free speech and assembly is a measure so stringent that it would be inappropriate as the means for averting a relatively trivial harm to society. . . . The fact that speech is likely to result in some violence or in destruction of property is not enough to justify its suppression. There must be the probability of serious injury to the State. Among free men, the deterrents ordinarily to be applied to prevent crime are education and punishment for violations of the law, not abridgment of the rights of free speech and assembly. . . .

[The Syndicalism Act] satisfies the requirement of the constitution of the State concerning emergency legislation. But [it] must remain open to a defendant to present the issue whether there actually did exist at the time a clear danger; whether the danger, if any, was imminent; and whether the evil apprehended was one so substantial as to justify the stringent restriction interposed by the legislature. The legislative declaration [creates] merely a rebuttable presumption that these conditions have been satisfied. [I] am unable to assent to the suggestion in the opinion of the Court that assembling with a political party, formed to advocate the desirability of a proletarian revolution by mass action at some date necessarily far in the future, is not a right within the protection of the Fourteenth Amendment. In the present case, however, there was other testimony which tended to establish the existence of a conspiracy, on the part of members of the International Workers of the World, to commit present serious crimes; and likewise to show that such a conspiracy would be furthered by the activity of the society of which Miss Whitney was a member. Under these circumstances the judgment of the state court cannot be disturbed. . . .

Question: Reconciling **Whitney, Abrams,** *and* **Gitlow**

How do the policy ideas in the Brandeis concurrence in *Whitney* compare to the ideas in the dissents of Justice Holmes in *Abrams* and *Gitlow*?

∽ PROBLEMS ∽

1. *Applying* Whitney *and* Gitlow. How would *Whitney* and *Gitlow* apply to the following situations if the crime charged is advocacy of criminal syndicalism?

   a.   A group of Marxist college students holds a rally on campus calling for a radical restructuring of the government and economy of the United States.

b. In a philosophy class, a professor discusses Marxist theory, presents criticisms of the U.S. system, and concludes that the U.S. governmental and economic system is immoral.

c. A student wears a jacket with the message "Communism Now" that contains Communist symbols, including an upraised fist, as a way of expressing his concerns about the U.S. governmental and economic system.

d. On a remote piece of property, Ku Klux Klan members hold a rally at which they burn a cross, denounce public officials, and discuss the need to take "revengeance" against members of certain minority groups.

e. The *Glenview-Journal*, a large daily newspaper in Glenview Hills, Kentucky, publishes editorials and articles that are critical of the U.S. governmental and economic system and suggest a "moral imperative" to move toward a Marxist system.

2. *Applying* Whitney *and* Gitlow *to the International Treaty Regulating the Internet.* Do *Whitney* and *Gitlow* affect your conclusions about whether you can accept European demands to include language from the European Convention on Human Rights in the treaty regulating the Internet?

d. "Clear and Present Danger" Cases from the McCarthy Era

Subversive advocacy cases reappeared before the Court in the 1950s in the so-called "Smith Act prosecutions."

Dennis v. United States
341 U.S. 494 (1951)

Mr. Chief Justice VINSON announced the judgment of the Court and an opinion in which Mr. Justice REED, Mr. Justice BURTON, and Mr. Justice MINTON join.

Petitioners were indicted in July, 1948, for violation of the conspiracy provisions of the Smith Act, during the period of April, 1945, to July, 1948 [and found guilty.] The Court of Appeals affirmed the convictions. We granted certiorari. . . .

Sections 2 and 3 of the Smith Act provide as follows:

Sec. 2. (a) It shall be unlawful for any person —

(1) to knowingly or willfully advocate, abet, advise, or teach the duty, necessity, desirability, or propriety of overthrowing or destroying any government in the United States by force or violence, or by the assassination of any officer of any such government;

(2) with intent to cause the overthrow or destruction of any government in the United States, to print, publish, edit, issue, circulate, sell, distribute, or publicly display any written or printed matter advocating, advising, or teaching the duty, necessity, desirability, or propriety of overthrowing or destroying any government in the United States by force or violence;

(3) to organize or help to organize any society, group, or assembly of persons who teach, advocate, or encourage the overthrow or destruction of any government in the United States by force or violence; or to be or become a member of, or affiliate with, any such society, group, or assembly of persons, knowing the purposes thereof. . . .

Sec. 3. It shall be unlawful for any person to attempt to commit, or to conspire to commit, any of the acts prohibited by the provisions of . . . this title.

The indictment charged the petitioners with wilfully and knowingly conspiring (1) to organize as the Communist Party of the United States of America a society, group and assembly of persons who teach and advocate the overthrow and destruction of the Government of the United States by force and violence, and (2) knowingly and wilfully to advocate and teach the duty and necessity of overthrowing and destroying the Government of the United States by force and violence. The indictment further alleged that §2 of the Smith Act proscribes these acts and that any conspiracy to take such action is a violation of §3 of the Act.

The trial of the case extended over nine months, six of which were devoted to the taking of evidence, resulting in a record of 16,000 pages. [The Court of Appeals found] that the Communist Party is a highly disciplined organization, adept at infiltration into strategic positions, use of aliases, and double-meaning language; that the Party is rigidly controlled; that Communists, unlike other political parties, tolerate no dissension from the policy laid down by the guiding forces, but that the approved program is slavishly followed by the members of the Party; that the literature of the Party and the statements and activities of its leaders, petitioners here, advocate, and the general goal of the Party was, during the period in question, to achieve a successful overthrow of the existing order by force and violence. . . .

The obvious purpose of the [Smith Act] is to protect existing Government, not from change by peaceable, lawful and constitutional means, but from change by violence, revolution and terrorism. That it is within the *power* of the Congress to protect the Government of the United States from armed rebellion is a proposition which requires little discussion. . . . The question with which we are concerned here is not whether Congress has such *power*, but whether the *means* which it has employed conflict with the First and Fifth Amendments to the Constitution. . . .

[*Gitlow*] made no distinction between a federal statute which made certain acts unlawful, the evidence to support the conviction being speech, and a statute which made speech itself the crime. [*Whitney*] repeated that even though the legislature had designated certain speech as criminal, this could not prevent the defendant from showing that there was no danger that the substantive evil would be brought about. . . . Although no case subsequent to *Whitney* and *Gitlow* has expressly overruled the majority opinions in those cases, there is little doubt that subsequent opinions have inclined toward the Holmes-Brandeis rationale. . . .

In this case we are squarely presented with the application of the "clear and present danger" test, and must decide what that phrase imports. [M]any of the cases in which this Court has reversed convictions [have] been based on the fact that the interest which the State was attempting to protect was itself too insubstantial to warrant restriction of speech. . . . Overthrow of the Government by force and violence is certainly a substantial enough interest for the Government to limit speech. . . . If, then, this interest may be protected, the literal problem which is presented is what has been meant by the use of the phrase "clear and present danger" of the utterances bringing about the evil within the power of Congress to punish.

Obviously, the words cannot mean that before the Government may act, it must wait until the *putsch* is about to be executed, the plans have been laid and the signal is awaited. If Government is aware that a group aiming at its overthrow is attempting to indoctrinate its members and to commit them to a course whereby they will strike when the leaders feel the circumstances permit, action by the Government is required. . . . Certainly an attempt to overthrow the Government by force, even though doomed from the outset because of inadequate numbers or power of the revolutionists, is a sufficient evil for Congress to prevent. The damage which such attempts create both physically and politically to a nation makes it impossible to measure the validity in terms of the probability of success, or the immediacy of a successful attempt. In the instant case the trial judge charged the jury that they could not convict unless they found that petitioners intended to overthrow the Government "as speedily as circumstances would permit." This does not mean [that] they would not strike until there was certainty of success. What was meant was that the revolutionists would strike when they thought the time was ripe. We must therefore reject the contention that success or probability of success is the criterion.

The situation with which Justices Holmes and Brandeis were concerned in *Gitlow* was a comparatively isolated event, bearing little relation in their minds to any substantial threat to the safety of the community. [The Court was] not confronted with [a] situation comparable to the instant one — the development of an apparatus designed and dedicated to the overthrow of the Government, in the context of world crisis after crisis.

Chief Judge Learned Hand, writing for the majority below, interpreted the phrase as follows: "In each case [courts] must ask whether the gravity of the 'evil,' discounted by its improbability, justifies such invasion of free speech as is necessary to avoid the danger." We adopt this statement of the rule. . . . It takes into consideration those factors which we deem relevant. . . .

[T]he requisite danger existed. The mere fact that from the period 1945 to 1948 petitioners' activities did not result in an attempt to overthrow the Government by force and violence is of course no answer to the fact that there was a group that was ready to make the attempt. The formation by petitioners of such a highly organized conspiracy, with rigidly disciplined members subject to call when the leaders [felt] that the time had come for action, coupled with the inflammable nature of world conditions, similar uprisings in other countries, and the touch-and-go nature of our relations with countries with whom petitioners were in the very least ideologically attuned, convince us that their convictions were justified. . . . And this analysis disposes of the contention that a conspiracy to advocate, as distinguished from the advocacy itself, cannot be constitutionally restrained, because it comprises only the preparation. It is the existence of the conspiracy which creates the danger. If the ingredients of the reaction are present, we cannot bind the Government to wait until the catalyst is added.

[Defendants argue] that a jury must decide a question of the application of the First Amendment. We do not agree. . . . The doctrine that there must be a clear and present danger of a substantive evil that Congress has a right to prevent is a judicial rule to be applied as a matter of law by the courts. . . .

We hold that §§2(a)(1), 2(a)(3) and 3 of the Smith Act do not inherently, or as construed or applied in the instant case, violate the First Amendment and other provisions of the Bill of Rights. . . . Petitioners intended to overthrow the Government of the United States as speedily as the circumstances would permit. Their conspiracy to organize the Communist Party and to teach and advocate the overthrow of the Government of the United States by force and violence created a "clear and present danger" of an attempt to overthrow the Government by force and violence. They were properly and constitutionally convicted for violation of the Smith Act.

The judgments of conviction are *affirmed*.

Mr. Justice FRANKFURTER, concurring in affirmance of the judgment.

[Free-speech] cases are not an exception to the principle that we are not legislators, that direct policy-making is not our province. . . . The defendants have been convicted of conspiring to organize a party of persons who advocate the overthrow of the Government by force and violence. The jury has found that the object of the conspiracy is advocacy as "a rule or principle of action," "by language reasonably and ordinarily calculated to incite persons to such action," and with the intent to cause the overthrow "as speedily as circumstances would permit." On any scale of values which we have hitherto recognized, speech of this sort ranks low.

Throughout our decisions there has recurred a distinction between the statement of an idea which may prompt its hearers to take unlawful action, and advocacy that such action be taken. . . . Exposition of ideas readily merges into advocacy. . . . That such a distinction could be used unreasonably by those in power against hostile or unorthodox views does not negate the fact that it may be used reasonably against an organization wielding the power of the centrally controlled international Communist movement. The object of the conspiracy before us is so clear that the chance of error in saying that the defendants conspired to advocate rather than to express ideas is slight. [T]he conspiracy before us is not a conspiracy to overthrow the Government. But it would be equally wrong to treat it as a seminar in political theory.

[On] the one hand is the interest in security. The Communist Party [rejects] the basic premise of our political system — that change is to be brought about by nonviolent constitutional process. [The evidence] would amply justify a legislature in concluding that recruitment of additional members for the Party would create a substantial danger to national security. . . . On the other hand is the interest in free speech. The right to exert all governmental powers in aid of maintaining our institutions and resisting their physical overthrow does not include intolerance of opinions and speech that cannot do harm although opposed and perhaps alien to dominant, traditional opinion. . . . It is better for those who have almost unlimited power of government in their hands to err on the side of freedom. We have enjoyed so much freedom for so long that we are perhaps in danger of forgetting how much blood it cost to establish the Bill of Rights.

[A] public interest is not wanting in granting freedom to speak their minds even to those who advocate the overthrow of the Government by force. For [coupled] with such advocacy is criticism of defects in our society. . . . No matter how clear we may be that the defendants now before us are preparing to over-throw our Government at the propitious moment, it is self-delusion to think that we can punish them for their advocacy without adding to the risks run by loyal citizens who honestly believe in some of the reforms these defendants advance. . . .

[Congress] has determined that the danger created by advocacy of overthrow justifies the ensuing restriction on freedom of speech. The determination was made after due deliberation. . . . To make validity of legislation depend on judi-cial reading of events still in the womb of time — a forecast, that is, of the outcome of forces at best appreciated only with knowledge of the topmost secrets of nations — is to charge the judiciary with duties beyond its equipment. . . . In find-ing that Congress has acted within its power, a judge does not remotely imply that he favors the implications that lie beneath the legal issues. . . .

Mr. Justice JACKSON, concurring.

The Communist Party [is] a relatively small party whose strength is in selected, dedicated, indoctrinated, and rigidly disciplined members. . . . It seeks members that are, or may be, secreted in strategic posts in transportation, com-munications, industry [and government]. Through these placements in positions of power it seeks a leverage over society that will make up in power of coercion what it lacks in power of persuasion. . . . Communist technique in the overturn of a free government was disclosed by the *coup d'etat* in which they seized power in Czechoslovakia. . . . A virtually bloodless abdication . . . whereupon they insti-tuted a reign of oppression and terror, and ruthlessly denied to all others the free-doms which had sheltered their conspiracy. . . .

[When] the issue is criminality of a hot-headed speech on a street corner, or circulation of a few incendiary pamphlets, or parading by some zealots behind a red flag, or refusal of a handful of school children to salute our flag, it is not beyond the capacity of the judicial process to gather, comprehend, and weigh the necessary materials for decision whether it is a clear and present danger of sub-stantive evil or a harmless letting off of steam. [But if] we must decide that this Act and its application are constitutional only if we are convinced that petition-er's conduct creates a "clear and present danger" of violent overthrow, [we] would have to foresee and predict the effectiveness of Communist propaganda, oppor-tunities for infiltration, whether, and when, a time will come that they consider propitious for action, and whether and how fast our existing government will deteriorate. . . . The authors of the clear and present danger test never applied it to a case like this. [I]t means that the Communist plotting is protected during its period of incubation; its preliminary stages of organization and preparation are immune from the law; the Government can move only after imminent action is manifest, when it would, of course, be too late. [D]irect incitement [to violent overthrow] by speech or writing can be made a crime, and I think there can be a conviction [without] proving that the odds favored its success by 99 to 1. . . . [If] it is not forbidden to put down force or violence, it is not forbidden to punish its teaching or advocacy, and the end being punishable, there is no doubt of the power to punish conspiracy for the purpose. . . .

Mr. Justice BLACK, dissenting.

[T]he only way to affirm these convictions is to repudiate directly or indirectly the established "clear and present danger" rule. . . . I cannot agree that the First Amendment permits us to sustain laws suppressing freedom of speech and press on the basis of Congress' or our own notions of mere "reasonableness." . . .

Mr. Justice DOUGLAS, dissenting.

If this were a case where those who claimed protection under the First Amendment were teaching the techniques of sabotage, the assassination of the President, the filching of documents from public files, the planting of bombs, the art of street warfare, and the like, I would have no doubts. . . . But [no] such evidence was introduced at the trial. [W]hat petitioners did was to organize people to teach and themselves teach the Marxist-Leninist doctrine contained chiefly in four books: Stalin, *Foundations of Leninism* (1924); Marx and Engels, *The Communist Manifesto* (1848); Lenin, *The State and Revolution* (1917) (1939). The opinion of the Court does not outlaw these texts nor condemn them to the fire, as the Communists do literature offensive to their creed. But if the books themselves are not outlawed, if they can lawfully remain on library shelves, by what reasoning does their use in a classroom become a crime? [The] Act, as construed, requires the element of intent — that those who teach the creed believe in it. The crime then depends not on what is taught but on who the teacher is. That is to make freedom of speech turn not on *what is said*, but on the *intent* with which it is said. . . .

There comes a time when even speech loses its constitutional immunity. . . . When conditions are so critical that there will be no time to avoid the evil that the speech threatens, it is time to call a halt. . . . This record, however, contains no evidence whatsoever showing that the acts charged *viz.*, the teaching of the Soviet theory of revolution with the hope that it will be realized, have created any clear and present danger to the Nation. [A]s a political party they are of little consequence. . . . Communism has been so thoroughly exposed in this country that it has been crippled as a political force. Free speech has destroyed it as an effective political party. . . . How it can be said that there is a clear and present danger that this advocacy will succeed is, therefore, a mystery. Some nations less resilient than the United States, where illiteracy is high and where democratic traditions are only budding, might have to take drastic steps and jail these men for merely speaking their creed. But in America they are miserable merchants of unwanted ideas; their wares remain unsold. . . .

The political impotence of the Communists in this country does not, of course, dispose of the problem. Their numbers; their positions in industry and government; the extent to which they have in fact infiltrated the police, the armed services, transportation, stevedoring, power plants, munitions works, and other critical places — these facts all bear on the likelihood that their advocacy of the Soviet theory of revolution will endanger the Republic. But the record is silent on these facts. . . . On this record no one can say that petitioners and their converts are in such a strategic position as to have even the slightest chance of achieving their aims. . . .

Notes

1. *An "Advocacy of Action" Requirement.* In Yates v. United States, 354 U.S. 298 (1957), the Court interpreted *Dennis* to require the sort of "advocacy to action" requirement that Justices Douglas and Black had urged upon the Court in their dissenting opinions in *Dennis*. Fourteen Communist Party leaders were charged with an 11-year conspiracy and sentenced to five years in prison. Based on defects at the trial court level, Justice Harlan's opinion for the Court reversed the convictions of all defendants, entered judgments of acquittal for five of them, and remanded for the retrial of nine defendants under proper instructions. He explained that the legislative history of the Smith Act revealed that it was aimed at the "advocacy and teaching of concrete action for the forcible overthrow of the Government, and not of principles divorced from action." Most important, he took pains to elaborate on the meaning of *Dennis*:

> The essence of the *Dennis* holding was that indoctrination of a group in preparation for future violent action, as well as exhortation to immediate action, by advocacy found to be directed to "action for the accomplishment" of forcible overthrow, to violence as "a rule or principle of action," and employing "language of incitement," is not constitutionally protected when the group is of sufficient size and cohesiveness, is sufficiently oriented towards action, and other circumstances are such as reasonably to justify apprehension that action will occur. This is quite a different thing from the view [that] mere doctrinal justification of forcible overthrow, if engaged in with the intent to accomplish overthrow, is punishable per se under the Smith Act. That sort of advocacy, even though uttered with the hope that it may ultimately lead to violent revolution, is too remote from concrete action to be regarded as the kind of indoctrination preparatory to action which was condemned in *Dennis*. [*Dennis*] was thus concerned [with] a conspiracy to advocate presently the taking of forcible action in the future. It was action, not advocacy, that was to be postponed until "circumstances" would "permit."

Justice Clark dissented, as he would have affirmed all the convictions, while Justices Black and Douglas would have reversed all the convictions, according to the views expressed in their dissents in *Dennis*.

2. *Membership Convictions Under the Smith Act.* Four years after *Yates*, in two companion cases, the Court applied its *Yates* standard reinterpreting *Dennis* to the "membership" provision of the Smith Act. In Noto v. United States, 367 U.S. 203

(1961), Justice Harlan explained the Court's judgment that the evidence was insufficient to show "some substantial direct or circumstantial evidence of a call to violence now or in the future which is both sufficiently strong and sufficiently pervasive to lend color to the otherwise ambiguous theoretical material regarding Communist Party teaching, and to justify the inference that such a call to violence may fairly be imputed to the Party as a whole, and not merely to some narrow segment of it." When "there is no evidence that [acts] of sabotage were presently advocated," there is insufficient evidence of "present advocacy" of "action," which is a required element of the crime under the membership clause. A second element requires "clear proof that a defendant 'specifically intend(s) to accomplish (the aims of the organization) by resort to violence.'" In Scales v. United States, 367 U.S. 203 (1961), the Court approved a jury instruction that required proof that the defendant Party member was "an 'active' member of the Party, and not merely 'a nominal, passive, inactive or purely technical' member, with knowledge of the Party's illegal advocacy and a specific intent to bring about violent overthrow 'as speedily as circumstances would permit.'" Justice Harlan also summarized the types of evidence that could be used to prove "present advocacy" of "action": "(a) the teaching of forceful overthrow, accompanied by directions as to the type of illegal action which must be taken when the time for the revolution is reached; and (b) the teaching of forceful overthrow, accompanied by a contemporary, though legal, course of conduct clearly undertaken for the specific purpose of rendering effective the later illegal activity which is advocated." The *Scales* Court upheld the convictions in a five-to-four decision, with Chief Justice Warren and Justices Black, Douglas, and Brennan dissenting.

3. *Movement Away from* Dennis. The Court's movement away from *Dennis* can be seen not only in other post-*Dennis* Smith Act cases but also in a variety of precedents in fields outside of "subversive advocacy" speech laws. One dramatic doctrinal evolution in the civil rights era occurred in the field of "hostile audience" law, where the Court expanded the rights of antisegregation protestors to march and demonstrate without being convicted of "disorderly conduct" when crowds of antipathetic onlookers threatened violence. In the field of "fighting words," the Court narrowed the definition of unprotected speech of this sort and thereby expanded speech protections for soapbox orators whose commentary offended their audiences and possessed the potential for provoking disorder. The definition of "unprotected speech" shrank as obscenity definitions narrowed, and as greater protections were afforded to critics of government officials through new tort law immunities from libel suits. The Court also protected antiwar speech on some occasions during the Vietnam War under circumstances that would have led to convictions under the Espionage Act of 1917. The Court's protection of Vietnam War protestors signaled another step in its readiness to reverse speech convictions when a majority of the Court concluded that the record lacked concrete proof of imminent harm — and another step toward *Brandenburg* and away from all the old "clear and present danger" formulas.

～ PROBLEM: APPLYING *DENNIS* ～

How would *Dennis* apply to the five scenarios in Problem 1 following the *Gitlow* and *Whitney* opinions, if the crime charged is conspiracy to advocate criminal syndicalism?

e.   Modern Cases

Brandenburg v. Ohio

395 U.S. 444 (1969)

PER CURIAM.

The appellant, a leader of a Ku Klux Klan group, was convicted under the Ohio Criminal Syndicalism statute for "advocat[ing] the duty, necessity, or propriety of crime, sabotage, violence, or unlawful methods of terrorism as a means of accomplishing industrial or political reform" and for "voluntarily assembl[ing] with any society, group, or assemblage of persons formed to teach or advocate the doctrines of criminal syndicalism." Ohio Rev. Code Ann. §2923.13. He was fined $1,000 and sentenced to one to 10 years' imprisonment. The appellant challenged the constitutionality of the criminal syndicalism statute under the First and Fourteenth Amendments to the United States Constitution, but the [Ohio court of appeals and Supreme Court affirmed]. Appeal was taken to this Court, and [we] reverse.

The record shows that [appellant] telephoned an announcer-reporter on the staff of a Cincinnati television station and invited him to come to a Ku Klux Klan "rally" to be held at a farm in Hamilton County. With the cooperation of the organizers, the reporter and a cameraman attended the meeting and filmed the events. Portions of the films were later broadcast on the local station and on a national network.

The prosecution's case rested on the films and on testimony identifying the appellant as the person who communicated with the reporter and who spoke at the rally. The State also introduced into evidence several articles appearing in the film, including a pistol, a rifle, a shotgun, ammunition, a Bible, and a red hood worn by the speaker in the films.

One film showed 12 hooded figures, some of whom carried firearms. They were gathered around a large wooden cross, which they burned. No one was present other than the participants and the newsmen who made the film. Most of the words uttered during the scene were incomprehensible when the film was projected, but scattered phrases could be understood that were derogatory of Negroes and, in one instance, of Jews. Another scene on the same film showed the appellant, in Klan regalia, making a speech. The speech, in full, was as follows:

> This is an organizers' meeting. We have had quite a few members here today which are — we have hundreds, hundreds of members throughout the State of Ohio. I can quote from a newspaper clipping from the Columbus, Ohio Dispatch, five weeks ago Sunday morning. The

Klan has more members in the State of Ohio than does any other organization. We're not a revengeant organization, but if our President, our Congress, our Supreme Court, continues to suppress the white, Caucasian race, it's possible that there might have to be some revengeance taken.

We are marching on Congress July the Fourth, four hundred thousand strong. From there we are dividing into two groups, one group to march on St. Augustine, Florida, the other group to march into Mississippi. Thank you.

[The] second film showed six hooded figures one of whom, later identified as the appellant, repeated a speech very similar to that recorded on the first film. The reference to the possibility of 'revengeance' was omitted, and one sentence was added: 'Personally, I believe the nigger should be returned to Africa, the Jew returned to Israel.' Though some of the figures in the films carried weapons, the speaker did not.

The Ohio Criminal Syndicalism Statute was enacted in 1919. From 1917 to 1920, identical or quite similar laws were adopted by 20 States and two territories. E. Dowell, *A History of Criminal Syndicalism Legislation in the United States* 21 (Johns Hopkins University 1939). In 1927, this Court sustained the constitutionality of California's Criminal Syndicalism Act, the text of which is quite similar to that of the laws of Ohio. Whitney v. California, 274 U.S. 37 (1927). The Court upheld the statute on the ground that, without more, "advocating" violent means to effect political and economic change involves such danger to the security of the State that the State may outlaw it. But *Whitney* has been thoroughly discredited by later decisions. *See* Dennis v. United States, 341 U.S. 494 (1951). These later decisions have fashioned the principle that the constitutional guarantees of free speech and free press do not permit a State to forbid or proscribe advocacy of the use of force or of law violation except where such advocacy is directed to inciting or producing imminent lawless action and is likely to incite or produce such action. As we said in Noto v. United States, 367 U.S. 290 (1961), "the mere abstract teaching [of] the moral propriety or even moral necessity for a resort to force and violence, is not the same as preparing a group for violent action and steeling it to such action." A statute which fails to draw this distinction impermissibly intrudes upon the freedoms guaranteed by the First and Fourteenth Amendments. It sweeps within its condemnation speech which our Constitution has immunized from governmental control. *Cf.* Yates v. United States, 354 U.S. 298 (1957).

Measured by this test, Ohio's Criminal Syndicalism Act cannot be sustained. The Act punishes persons who "advocate or teach the duty, necessity, or propriety" of violence "as a means of accomplishing industrial or political reform"; or who publish or circulate or display any book or paper containing such advocacy; or who "justify" the commission of violent acts "with intent to exemplify, spread or advocate the propriety of the doctrines of criminal syndicalism"; or who "voluntarily assemble" with a group formed "to teach or advocate the doctrines of criminal syndicalism." Neither the indictment nor the trial judge's instructions to the jury in any way refined the statute's bald definition of the crime in terms of mere advocacy not distinguished from incitement to imminent lawless action.

Accordingly, we are here confronted with a statute which, by its own words and as applied, purports to punish mere advocacy and to forbid, on pain of criminal punishment, assembly with others merely to advocate the described type of action. Such a statute falls within the condemnation of the First and Fourteenth Amendments. The contrary teaching of Whitney v. California cannot be supported, and that decision is therefore overruled.

Mr. Justice BLACK, concurring.

I agree [with] Mr. Justice Douglas [that] the "clear and present danger" doctrine should have no place in the interpretation of the First Amendment. . . .

Mr. Justice DOUGLAS, concurring.

While I join the opinion of the Court, I desire to enter a caveat. [The] dissents in *Abrams*, *Schaefer*, and *Pierce* show how easily "clear and present danger" is manipulated to crush what Brandeis called "[t]he fundamental right of free men to strive for better conditions through new legislation and new institutions" by argument and discourse even in time of war. Though I doubt if the "clear and present danger" test is congenial to the First Amendment in time of a declared war, I am certain it is not reconcilable with the First Amendment in days of peace. . . . The Court quite properly overrules Whitney v. California, 274 U.S. 357, which involved advocacy of ideas which the majority of the Court deemed unsound and dangerous.

Mr. Justice Holmes, though never formally abandoning the 'clear and present danger' test, moved closer to the First Amendment ideal when he said in dissent in *Gitlow*:

> Every idea is an incitement. It offers itself for belief and if believed it is acted on unless some other belief outweighs it or some failure of energy stifles the movement at its birth. The only difference between the expression of an opinion and an incitement in the narrower sense is the speaker's enthusiasm for the result. Eloquence may set fire to reason. But whatever may be thought of the redundant discourse before us it had no chance of starting a present conflagration. If in the long run the beliefs expressed in proletarian dictatorship are destined to be accepted by the dominant forces of the community, the only meaning of free speech is that they should be given their chance and have their way.

We have never been faithful to the philosophy of that dissent.

The Court in Herndon v. Lowry, 301 U.S. 242, overturned a conviction for exercising First Amendment rights to incite insurrection because of lack of evidence of incitement. [In] Dennis v. United States, 341 U.S. 494, we opened wide the door, distorting the 'clear and present danger' test beyond recognition. . . . In that case the prosecution dubbed an agreement to teach the Marxist creed a "conspiracy." . . . The Court sustained convictions under the charge, construing it to mean a determination of "whether the gravity of the 'evil,' discounted by its improbability, justifies such invasion of free speech as is necessary to avoid the danger."

Out of the "clear and present danger" test came other offspring. Advocacy and teaching of forcible overthrow of government as an abstract principle is immune from prosecution. Yates v. United States, 354 U.S. 298. But an "active" member, who has a guilty knowledge and intent of the aim to overthrow the Government by violence, may be prosecuted. Scales v. United States, 367 U.S. 203. Judge Learned Hand, who wrote for the Court of Appeals in affirming the judgment in *Dennis*, coined the "not improbable" test which this Court adopted and which Judge Hand preferred over the "clear and present danger" test. . . .

[I] see no place in the regime of the First Amendment for any "clear and present danger" test, whether strict and tight as some would make it, or freewheeling as the Court in *Dennis* rephrased it. . . . When one reads the opinions closely and sees when and how the "clear and present danger" test has been applied, great misgivings are aroused. First, the threats were often loud but always puny and made serious only by judges so wedded to the status quo that critical analysis made them nervous. Second, the test was so twisted and perverted in *Dennis* as to make the trial of those teachers of Marxism an all-out political trial which was part and parcel of the cold war that has eroded substantial parts of the First Amendment.

Action is often a method of expression and within the protection of the First Amendment. . . . One's beliefs have long been thought to be sanctuaries which government could not invade. . . . The lines drawn by the Court between the criminal act of being an "active" Communist and the innocent act of being a nominal or inactive Communist mark the difference only between deep and abiding belief and casual or uncertain belief. But I think that all matters of belief are beyond the reach of subpoenas or the probings of investigators. That is why the invasions of privacy made by investigating committees were notoriously unconstitutional. That is the deep-seated fault in the infamous loyalty-security hearings which, since 1947 when President Truman launched them, have processed 20,000,000 men and women. Those hearings were primarily concerned with one's thoughts, ideas, beliefs, and convictions. They were the most blatant violations of the First Amendment we have ever known.

The line between what is permissible and not subject to control and what may be made impermissible and subject to regulation is the line between ideas and overt acts. . . . The example usually given by those who would punish speech is the case of one who falsely shouts fire in a crowded theatre. . . . This is, however, a classic case where speech is brigaded with action. They are indeed inseparable and a prosecution can be launched for the overt acts actually caused. Apart from rare instances of that kind, speech is, I think, immune from prosecution. [T]here is no constitutional line between advocacy of abstract ideas as in *Yates* and advocacy of political action as in *Scales*. The quality of advocacy turns on the depth of the conviction; and government has no power to invade that sanctuary of belief and conscience.

Notes and Questions

1. **Brandenburg's *Ambiguities*.** The *Brandenburg* Court clearly repudiates one decision of the 1920s (*Whitney*), but it is entirely silent concerning the earlier decisions of the World War I era (*Schenck*, *Frohwerk*, *Debs*), while citing the decisions of

the McCarthy era cases with approval (*Dennis*, *Yates*, *Noto*). Justice Douglas provides a brief overview of all these decisions, and argues that in *Brandenburg* the Court should have repudiated explicitly both the "clear and present danger" test and the *Dennis* decision's reliance upon it. Thus, several mysteries are presented initially by the different portraits of the past provided by the *Brandenburg* opinions. First, why is the "clear and present danger" test so controversial? The per curiam opinion scrupulously avoids any reference to this test, and instead endorses the formula for which *Brandenburg* is now famous. A second mystery concerns the effect of *Brandenburg* on the various precedents from the three earlier doctrinal eras. Besides *Whitney*, it is unclear which opinions are now a "dead letter" and which remain operative. The third mystery concerns whether a narrowly drafted indictment and jury instruction incorporating the new "imminent lawless action" test would permit a conviction on the facts of *Brandenburg*.

2. *The* Hess *Decision.* Hess v. Indiana, 414 U.S. 105 (1973), involved an anti-war demonstration at Indiana University at which 100 to 150 demonstrators blocked a public street. When the demonstrators refused directions to "clear the street," the police began forcibly moving demonstrators to the curb. After being moved to the side of the road, Gregory Hess yelled, "We'll take the fucking street later," or "We'll take the fucking street again." Hess did not appear to be exhorting the crowd to return into the streets. Even though he was facing the crowd when he uttered the statement, his statement did not appear to be addressed to any particular person or group, and his tone, though loud, was no louder than that of the other people in the area. In overturning Hess's conviction, the Court concluded that the statements did not satisfy the requirements for conviction under *Brandenburg*: "At best, [the] statement could be taken as counsel for present moderation; at worst, it amounted to nothing more than advocacy of illegal action at some indefinite future time." Moreover, the Court noted that since "uncontroverted evidence showed that Hess's statement was not directed to, any person or group of persons," the Court held that "it cannot be said that he was advocating in the normal sense, any action." The "import of the language" used by the defendant provided neither "evidence" nor a "rational inference" that his words "were intended to produce, and likely to produce, imminent disorder." The *Hess* dissenters found that the defendant's statement was "susceptible of characterization as an exhortation, particularly when uttered in a loud voice while facing a crowd." The dissenters also disagreed with the Court's emphasis on the word *later* in the defendant's statement, and found that "there are surely possible constructions of the statement which would encompass more or less immediate and continuing action against the harrassed police."

3. Schenck *and* Brandenburg. How would *Schenck* be decided under the *Brandenburg* test?

4. *Return to the Justifications for Protecting Speech.* At the beginning of this chapter, we noted four justifications for protecting free speech: the marketplace of ideas, self-fulfillment, safety valve, and democratic process. Which decision, *Schenck* or *Brandenburg*, better illustrates these justifications?

∾ PROBLEMS ∾

1. *The New Ohio Statute.* The Ohio legislature enacts a statute that incorporates the *Brandenburg* definition of criminal syndicalism. Following passage, if the *Brandenburg* defendant commits the same acts, is there sufficient evidence to convict? How will the state argue that sufficient evidence exists? How might defendant respond?

2. *Reconsideration of Earlier Problems.* How would *Brandenberg* apply to the situations listed earlier in the chapter?

   a. A group of college students opposed to World War I holds a "peace vigil" at which they "rally for peace" as well as against the war and the draft.
   b. A professor discusses the "moral imperative" that requires every "good and moral citizen" to oppose the war and the draft. Would it matter whether students actually resisted the draft?
   c. A student wears a jacket with the message "Fuck the Draft" to express his opposition to the war.
   d. On a remote piece of property, Ku Klux Klan members hold a rally at which they burn a cross, denounce public officials, and discuss the need to take "revengeance" against members of certain minority groups as well as against governmental officials.
   e. *The Courier-Journal*, a large daily newspaper in Louisville, Kentucky, publishes editorials and articles that are critical of the war and the draft and that discuss the "moral imperative" of all citizens to resist the draft.

3. *More on Newspapers and Expressing Opposition.* Recall the earlier problem that dealt with a newspaper publisher, journalist, or politician who wanted to express opposition during wartime to the participation of the United States in a war without risking conviction under the Espionage Act for conspiracy to obstruct the draft. Suppose that you were asked to give legal advice on how to construct an article so as to avoid conviction under *Brandenburg*'s standards. What would your advice be?

4. *The Sociology Professor's Comments.* During a sociology class discussion of President George W. Bush, a sociology professor at the University of Louisville purportedly made the statement: "It was the religious zealots who say they are voting on morals. I think we should all buy AK-47s and shoot them all!; That's what I would suggest, if it were allowed." *See* Mark Pitsch, "U of L Gets 1,600 E-Mails Over Instructor's Remark: It Involved Violence Against Bush Voters," *The Courier-Journal*, B-2, c. 1-6 (Oct. 10, 2004). The professor is subsequently charged with incitement to murder. Can he be convicted consistent with the First Amendment? Suppose that the professor contends that the statement was made sarcastically and that the students understood the comment in that vein.

5. *More on the Sociology Professor's Comments.* In the preceding problem, even if the professor cannot be criminally prosecuted for his comments, consistent with the First Amendment, might the university take disciplinary action against the professor for his comments?

6. *The Abdel Rahman Case.* A federal statute, 18 U.S.C. §2384, punishes the crime of "seditious conspiracy." It provides: "If two or more persons in any State or Territory, or in any place subject to the jurisdiction of the United States, conspire to overthrow, put down, or destroy by force the Government of the United States, or to levy war against them, or to oppose by force the authority thereof . . . they shall be imprisoned not more than twenty years." Abdel Rahman, a scholar and cleric, was alleged to be the leader of a seditious conspiracy. The government claims that, by urging his coconspirators to "do jihad with the sword, with the cannon, with the grenades and with the missile against God's enemies," and by advising the conspirators concerning the best strategies for violent attacks on persons and property, Rahman supported the violent conduct of the defendants, which included the bombing of the World Trade Center and attempts to bomb the United Nations and the Lincoln and Holland Tunnels in New York. Rahman told his followers that the formation of a jihad army was necessary in order to defeat the oppressors of Islam, including the United States. In effect, the government accused Rahman and his followers of being members of a conspiracy to wage a war of urban terrorism against the United States and forcibly oppose its authority. Under the language of the statute, the government contends that speech is punished only when it constitutes a "conspiracy" — that is, an agreement to use force against the United States. On appeal Rahman's counsel argues that Section 2384 is facially invalid under the First Amendment because it criminalizes protected expression. You are a law clerk to a judge on the Court of Appeals for the Second Circuit who has been assigned to write the opinion in Rahman's appeal. The judge tells you that the panel has voted unanimously to reject the First Amendment attack on the statute. Draft the opinion for the judge rejecting the First Amendment challenge.

7. *More on the International Treaty Regulating the Internet.* In light of the *Brandenburg* decision, what would be your position at the convention on whether the United States can accept the European request to include the following language from the European Convention on Human Rights in the treaty regulating the Internet? "The exercise of these freedoms, since it carries with it duties and responsibilities, may be subject to such formalities, conditions, restrictions or penalties as are prescribed by law and are necessary in a democratic society, in the interests of national security, territorial integrity or public safety, for the prevention of disorder or crime, for the protection of health or morals, for the protection of the reputation or the rights of others, for preventing the disclosure of information received in confidence, or for maintaining the authority and impartiality of the judiciary." What language might you be able to propose to the other delegates? Do you anticipate that your alternative language will be acceptable to them?

2. *Fighting Words and Hostile Audiences*

During the World War II era, the Court created two First Amendment doctrines in an attempt to balance the needs of the police to maintain public order with the rights of individuals to exercise their freedom of speech in public appearances, whether in demonstrations or in a variety of "street corner" activities related to speech rights. The "fighting words" doctrine established the power of the police to arrest an individual for using insulting speech that might provoke another individual to fight. Although a person who actually fights could be arrested for assault or battery, the Court recognized the police power to treat the provoking speaker as a guilty participant in the ensuing or potentially ensuing "breach of the peace." However, the judicial recognition of the criminality of "fighting words" created a new imperative to define such words (and the circumstances in which their utterance could lead to prosecution) in a sufficiently narrow way to protect the exercise of First Amendment "dissenters" whose provocatively unpopular ideas could not be punished. The concept of the "hostile audience" doctrine does not similarly describe a category of "unprotected speech" like fighting words, but rather identifies a situation where an individual speaker is using "protected speech" that provokes his or her audience to violent action or that may provoke such action.

Cantwell v. Connecticut
310 U.S. 296 (1940)

Mr. Justice ROBERTS, delivered the opinion of the Court.

Newton Cantwell and his two sons, Jesse and Russell, members of [the] Jehovah's witnesses, and claiming to be ordained ministers, were [going] singly from house to house [in] New Haven [in April 1938], [equipped] with [books] and pamphlets on religious subjects, a portable phonograph and a set of records. . . . Cassius Street is in a thickly populated neighborhood, where about ninety per cent of the residents are Roman Catholics. [Jesse Cantwell] stopped two men in the street, asked, and received, permission to play a phonograph record, and played the record "Enemies," which attacked the religion and church of the two men, who were Catholics. Both were incensed by the contents of the record and were tempted to strike Cantwell unless he went away. On being told to be on his way he left their presence. There was no evidence that he was personally offensive or entered into any argument with those he interviewed. [The record played by Cantwell "single[d out the Roman Catholic Church for strictures couched in terms which naturally would offend not only persons of that persuasion, but all others who respect the honestly held religious faith of their fellows. The hearers were in fact highly offended. One of them said he felt like hitting Cantwell and the other that he was tempted to throw Cantwell off the street."] The [lower] court held that the charge was not assault or breach of the peace or threats on Cantwell's part, but [the common law offense of] invoking or inciting others to breach of the peace, and that the facts supported the conviction of that offense.

We hold that [the] conviction of Jesse Cantwell [must] be set aside. [The] state of Connecticut has an obvious interest in the preservation and protection of peace and good order within her borders. [But Cantwell's] conviction was not pursuant to a statute evincing a legislative judgment [that] the playing of a phonograph on the streets should in the interest of comfort or privacy be limited or prevented. [T]he judgment is based on a common law concept of the most general and undefined nature. . . . The offense known as breach of the peace embraces a great variety of conduct destroying or menacing public order and tranquility. It includes not only violent acts but acts and words likely to produce violence in others. No one would have the hardihood to suggest that the principle of freedom of speech sanctions incitement to riot or that religious liberty connotes the privilege to exhort others to physical attack upon those belonging to another sect. When clear and present danger of riot, disorder, interference with traffic upon the public streets, or other immediate threat to public safety, peace, or order, appears, the power of the state to prevent or punish is obvious. Equally obvious is that a state may not unduly suppress free communication of views, religious or other, under the guise of conserving desirable conditions. Here we have a situation analogous to a conviction under a statute sweeping in a great variety of conduct under a general and indefinite characterization, and leaving to the executive and judicial branches too wide a discretion in its application.

[One may] be guilty of the offense if he commit acts or make statements likely to provoke violence and disturbance of good order, even though no such eventuality be intended. [I]n practically all [decisions], the provocative language which was held to amount to a breach of the peace consisted of profane, indecent, or abusive remarks directed to the person of the hearer. Resort to epithets or personal abuse is not in any proper sense communication of information or opinion safeguarded by the Constitution, and its punishment as a criminal act would raise no question under that instrument.

We find in the instant case no assault or threatening of bodily harm, no truculent bearing, no intentional discourtesy, no personal abuse. On the contrary, we find only an effort to persuade a willing listener to buy a book or to contribute money in the interest of what Cantwell, however misguided others may think him, conceived to be true religion. . . . In the realm of religious faith, and in that of political belief, sharp differences arise. In both fields the tenets of one man may seem the rankest error to his neighbor. To persuade others to his own point of view, the pleader[,] at times, resorts to exaggeration, to vilification of men who have been, or are, prominent in church or state, and even to false statement. But the people of this nation have ordained in the light of history, that, in spite of the probability of excesses and abuses, these liberties are, in the long view, essential to enlightened opinion and right conduct on the part of the citizens of a democracy.

The essential characteristic of these liberties is, that under their shield many types of life, character, opinion and belief can develop unmolested and unobstructed. Nowhere is this shield more necessary than in our own country for a people composed of many races and of many creeds. There are limits to the exercise of these liberties. The danger in these times from the coercive activities of those who in the delusion of racial or religious conceit would incite violence and breaches of the peace in order to deprive others of their equal right to the exercise of their liberties, is emphasized by events familiar to all. These and other transgressions of those limits the states appropriately may punish.

Although the contents of the record not unnaturally aroused animosity, we think that, in the absence of a statute narrowly drawn to define and punish specific conduct as constituting a clear and present danger to a substantial interest of the State, [Cantwell's] communication, considered in the light of the constitutional guarantees, raised no such clear and present menace to public peace and order as to render him liable to conviction of the common law offense in question.

The judgment affirming the [conviction is] reversed and the cause is remanded for further proceedings not inconsistent with this opinion. So ordered.

∽ PROBLEM: THE ANTIABORTION CAMPAIGN ∽

The Center for Bio-Ethical Reform promotes "prenatal justice" through a variety of means, including graphic displays of aborted first-term fetuses on the sides of trucks. The center typically targets middle and high school students in an effort to discourage abortions, and a member frequently drives one of the center's trucks around the perimeters of school grounds. A local ordinance makes it illegal to enter school grounds, or to drive on adjacent streets, without lawful business there, when "one's presence or acts interfere with the peaceful conduct of the activities of the school or disrupt the school or its pupils or school activities." When some teachers complained, the center was asked to remove its truck from the vicinity of a high school. The evidence showed that several female students cried after seeing the truck, that some boys threw rocks, and that some teachers strongly objected to the antiabortion message. Can the center be forced to discontinue its speech and be successfully prosecuted if it fails to do so? How does the presence of the school affect the analysis? *See* Center for Bio-Ethical Reform Inc. v. Los Angeles County Sheriff Department, 533 F.3d 780 (9th Cir. 2008).

Chaplinsky v. New Hampshire

315 U.S. 568 (1942)

Mr. Justice MURPHY delivered the opinion of the Court.

[Walter Chaplinsky,] a member of the sect known as Jehovah's Witnesses[,] was convicted [for violating the following New Hampshire statute]: "No person shall address any offensive, derisive or annoying word to any other person who is lawfully in any street or other public place, nor call him by any offensive or derisive name, nor make any noise or exclamation in his presence and hearing with intent to deride, offend or annoy him, or to prevent him from pursuing his lawful business or occupation." [Chaplinsky was charged only with addressing "offensive, derisive and annoying words and names" to another.]

[Chaplinsky] was distributing the literature of his sect on the streets of Rochester on a busy Saturday afternoon. Members of the local citizenry complained to the City Marshal, Bowering, that Chaplinsky was denouncing all religion as a 'racket.' Bowering told them that Chaplinsky was lawfully engaged, and then warned Chaplinsky that the crowd was getting restless. Some time later a disturbance occurred and the traffic officer on duty at the busy intersection started with

Chaplinsky for the police station, but did not inform him that he was under arrest or that he was going to be arrested. On the way they encountered Marshal Bowering who had been advised that a riot was under way and was therefore hurrying to the scene. Bowering repeated his earlier warning to Chaplinsky who then addressed to Bowering [these words: "You are a God damned racketeer" and "a damned Fascist and the whole government of Rochester are Fascists or agents of Fascists"]. Chaplinsky [testified] that when he met Bowering, he asked him to arrest the ones responsible for the disturbance. In reply Bowering cursed him. [Chaplinsky] admitted that he said the words charged in the complaint with the exception of the name of the Deity.

Over [Chaplinsky's] objection the trial court excluded as immaterial testimony relating to [his] treatment at the hands of the crowd, and the alleged neglect of duty on the part of the police. This action was approved by the court below which held that neither provocation nor the truth of the utterance would constitute a defense to the charge. [Chaplinsky argues that the statute violated the Fourteenth Amendment in that it placed an unreasonable restraint on freedom of speech, and because it was vague and indefinite.]

[Allowing] the broadest scope to the language and purpose of the Fourteenth Amendment, it is well understood that the right of free speech is not absolute at all times and under all circumstances. There are certain well-defined and narrowly limited classes of speech, the prevention and punishment of which has never been thought to raise any Constitutional problem. These include the lewd and obscene, the profane, the libelous, and the insulting or 'fighting' words — those which by their very utterance inflict injury or tend to incite an immediate breach of the peace. [Chafee, *Free Speech in the United States* 149 (1941).] It has been well observed that such utterances are no essential part of any exposition of ideas, and are of such slight social value as a step to truth that any benefit that may be derived from them is clearly outweighed by the social interest in order and morality. "Resort to epithets or personal abuse is not in any proper sense communication of information or opinion safeguarded by the Constitution, and its punishment as a criminal act would raise no question under that instrument." Cantwell v. Connecticut, 310 U.S. 296 [1940].

The state statute here challenged comes to us authoritatively construed by the highest court of New Hampshire. [T]he state court declared that the statute's purpose was to preserve the public peace, no words being "forbidden except such as have a direct tendency to cause acts of violence by the person to whom, individually, the remark is addressed." It was further said [by that court]:

> [The] word "offensive" is not to be defined in terms of what a particular addressee thinks. [The] test is what men of common intelligence would understand would be words likely to cause an average addressee to fight. [The] English language has a number of words [that] are expressions which by general consent are "fighting words" when said without a disarming smile. [Such] words, as ordinary men know, are likely to cause a fight. So are threatening, profane or obscene revilings. Derisive and annoying words can be taken as coming within the purview of the statute as heretofore interpreted only when they have this characteristic of plainly tending to excite the addressee to a breach of the peace. [The] statute, as construed, does no more than prohibit the face-to-face words plainly likely to cause a breach of the

peace by the addressee, words whose speaking constitute a breach of the peace by the speaker — including "classical fighting words," words in current use less "classical" but equally likely to cause violence, and other disorderly words, including profanity, obscenity and threats.

We are unable to say that the limited scope of the statute as thus construed contravenes the constitutional right of free expression. It is a statute narrowly drawn and limited to define and punish specific conduct lying within the domain of state power, the use in a public place of words likely to cause a breach of the peace. [Thus] the statute is [not] so vague and indefinite as to render a conviction [a] violation of due process.

[Nor] can we say that the application of the statute to the facts disclosed by the record substantially or unreasonably impinges upon the privilege of free speech. Argument is unnecessary to demonstrate that the appellations 'damn racketeer' and 'damn Fascist' are epithets likely to provoke the average person to retaliation, and thereby cause a breach of the peace. The refusal of the state court to admit evidence of provocation and evidence bearing on the truth or falsity of the utterances is open to no Constitutional objection. Whether the facts sought to be proved by such evidence constitute a defense to the charge or may be shown in mitigation are questions for the state court to determine. Our function is fulfilled by a determination that the challenged statute, on its face and as applied, does not contravene the Fourteenth Amendment.

Affirmed.

Notes and Questions

1. Cantwell *and the Justifications for Protecting Speech.* Do "fighting words," as reflected in *Chaplinsky* and *Cantwell*, meet any of the justifications for protecting speech presented at the beginning of this chapter? In other words, do they provide a safety valve, do they promote self-fulfillment or the marketplace of ideas, or are they related to the democratic process? If so, what type of showing should be required to allow the prosecution of statements like those made in *Chaplinsky* and *Cantwell*? Given the justifications, was *Cantwell* correctly decided?

2. *Early Perspective on "Incitement."* The *Cantwell* Court's reliance on the "clear and present danger" standard reflects the pre-*Brandenburg* approach to assessing the likelihood of violence or lawless action in response to an "incitement." At the time of *Cantwell*, the deferential approach of Gitlow v. New York was still good law. Precedents in 1940 permitted the Court to observe that convictions may be based on proof that acts or statements are "likely to provoke violence and disturbance of good order, even though no such eventuality be intended."

3. *Overbreadth and Vagueness.* The *Cantwell* Court's concern with "overbreadth" foreshadows a speech-protective doctrine that was to arrive with even greater force two decades later. In later years, the Court's scrutiny of potentially vague language in fighting words statutes would become more rigorous.

4. *The Narrow Scope of the "Fighting Words" Doctrine.* In the decades after *Cantwell* and *Chaplinsky*, the Court relied on specific language from these cases to

emphasize that the scope of the "fighting words" definition was limited to "face-to-face words," "directed to the person of the hearer," and with an inflammatory content that was likely to provoke "the average person to retaliation, and thereby cause a breach of the peace." *See* Street v. New York, 394 U.S. 576 (1969).

∽ PROBLEMS ∽

1. *Unprotected Words?* Under the *Chaplinsky* "fighting words" doctrine, which of the following situations contain statements that qualify as unprotected "fighting words"?

   a.   A man, upset by a second man's religious and political views, approaches him on the street and loudly and angrily denounces the man's views.
   b.   In the preceding situation, the first man prefaces his statements by referring to the other man as a "dirty, rotten SOB."
   c.   At a protest against the Iraq War, observed by both supporters and opponents of the war, a man burns an American flag while stating, "We don't need no damned flag."
   d.   During the Vietnam War, when the government is drafting young men to serve in the Army, a man wears a jacket emblazoned with a profane expression ("Fuck the Draft") into a courthouse.
   e.   At a protest demonstration, a man burns an American flag.
   f.   A speaker delivers an anti-Semitic speech to a crowd of 800 people while 1,000 people gather outside in a hostile audience. The crowd gets increasingly restless and upset.

2. *Fighting Words Directed at Public Officials.* Should it matter whether fighting words are directed at public officials rather than at private individuals? The *Chaplinsky* Court does not deem it relevant that the defendant's "fighting words" were uttered in the context of criticism of public officials, explicitly directed at the city marshal. But consider the comments of Justice Powell in referring to a case involving fighting words: "If these words had been addressed by one citizen to another, face to face and in a hostile manner, I would have no doubt that they would be 'fighting words.' But the situation may be different where such words are addressed to a police officer trained to exercise a higher degree of restraint than the average citizen." Lewis v. City of New Orleans, 408 U.S. 913 (1972) (Powell, J., concurring). *See also* New York Times v. Sullivan, 376 U.S. 254 (1964). Which approach is preferable?

3. *More on the International Treaty Regulating the Internet.* Does the *Chaplinsky* decision alter your position on whether the United States can accept the European request to include language from the European Convention on Human Rights (in particular the language authorizing government to limit speech as necessary to the "public safety" as well as for "the prevention of disorder or crime") as part of the treaty regulating the Internet? If you cannot accept the convention's language, what language might you be able to agree to accept? What language would you propose to the other delegates?

Gooding v. Wilson

405 U.S. 518 (1972)

Mr. Justice BRENNAN delivered the opinion of the Court.

[Johnny Wilson] was convicted on two counts of using opprobrious words and abusive language in violation of [the] Georgia Code which provides: "Any person who shall, without provocation, use to or of another, and in his presence . . . opprobrious words or abusive language, tending to cause a breach of the peace [shall] be guilty of a misdemeanor." [T]he Supreme Court of Georgia [rejected his contention that the statute was] vague and overbroad. The Georgia Supreme Court [sustained] the conviction. [Wilson then sought and obtained federal habeas corpus relief. The Court of Appeals affirmed.] We affirm.

[With others, Wilson] picketed the building in which the 12th Corps Headquarters of the United States Army was located, carrying signs opposing the war in Viet Nam. When the inductees arrived at the building, these persons began to block the door so that the inductees could not enter. They were requested by police officers to move from the door, but refused to do so. The officers attempted to remove them from the door, and a scuffle ensued. [Wilson also] committed assault and battery on the two police officers named in the indictment. [T]he indictment alleged that [Wilson] "did [use] to and of M. G. Redding [the] following [language]: 'White son of a bitch, I'll kill you.' 'You son of a bitch, I'll choke you to death,' [and] that [Gooding] did [use] to and of T. L. Raborn [the] following [language]: 'You son of a bitch, if you ever put your hands on me again, I'll cut you all to pieces.'"

[The state] argues that the Georgia appellate courts have by construction limited the proscription of [opprobrious words or abusive language, tending to cause a breach of the peace] to "fighting" words [as defined in *Chaplinsky*]. [Our] examination brings us to the conclusion, in agreement with the courts below, that the Georgia appellate decisions have not construed [the statute] to be limited[,] as in *Chaplinsky*, to words that "have a direct tendency to cause acts of violence by the person to whom, individually, the remark is addressed."

The dictionary definitions of "opprobrious" and "abusive" give them greater reach than "fighting" words. Webster's *Third New International Dictionary* (1961) defined "opprobrious" as "conveying or intended to convey disgrace," and "abusive" as including "harsh insulting language." Georgia appellate decisions have construed [the statute] to apply to utterances that, although within these definitions, are not "fighting" words as *Chaplinsky* defines them. [The statute] is not limited [to] words that "naturally tend to provoke violent resentment." [We] conclude that "(t)he separation of legitimate from illegitimate speech calls for more sensitive tools than (Georgia) has supplied." Speiser v. Randall, 357 U.S. [513 (1958)]. Because earlier appellate decisions applied [the statute] to utterances where there was no likelihood that the person addressed would make an immediate violent response, it is clear that the standard allowing juries to determine guilt "measured by common understanding and practice" does not limit the application of [the statute] to "fighting" words defined by *Chaplinsky*. Rather, that broad standard effectively "licenses the jury to create its own standard in each case."

Accordingly, we agree with the conclusion of the District Court, "[t]he fault of the statute is that it leaves wide open the standard of responsibility, so that it is easily susceptible to improper application." Unlike the construction of the New Hampshire statute by the New Hampshire Supreme Court [in *Chaplinsky*], the Georgia appellate courts have not construed [the statute] "so as to avoid all constitutional difficulties."

Affirmed.

Note: The Gooding *Dissents*

Chief Justice Burger dissented in *Gooding*, arguing that even if all the Georgia precedents cited by the *Gooding* majority "had been decided yesterday, they do nothing to demonstrate that the narrow language of the Georgia statute has any significant potential for sweeping application to suppress or deter important protected speech." Justice Blackmun also dissented and argued that "[the] words of Georgia Code [statute] are clear. They are also concise. They are not, in my view, overbroad or incapable of being understood. Except perhaps for the 'big' word 'opprobrious,' [any] Georgia schoolboy would expect that this defendant's fighting and provocative words to the officers were covered by [the statute]."

∽ PROBLEMS ∽

1. *Fighting Words in Context.* After *Chaplinsky* and *Gooding*, which of the following statements constitute prohibitable fighting words?

   a. A mother, upset about her son's arrest, referred to police officers as you "G — d — m — — — f — — — police" and is prosecuted under a statute that provides that "[i]t shall be unlawful and a breach of the peace for any person wantonly to curse or revile or to use obscene or opprobrious language toward or with reference to any member of the city police while in the actual performance of his duty." *See* Lewis v. New Orleans, 408 U.S. 913 (1972).
   b. In Lyons v. State, 94 Ga. App. 570, 95 S.E.2d 478 (1956), a man was charged for awakening ten women scout leaders on a campout by shouting, "Boys, this is where we are going to spend the night." "Get the G — d — bed rolls out . . . let's see how close we can come to the G — d — tents."
   c. In Fish v. State, 124 Ga. 416, 52 S.E. 737 (1905), a man was charged for stating to another man: "You swore a lie."
   d. In Jackson v. State, 14 Ga. App. 19, 80 S.E. 20 (1913), a motorist was charged for saying to another motorist: "God damn you, why don't you get out of the road?"

2. *Construing* Gooding. Assume that in the aftermath of *Gooding*, the Supreme Court of Georgia decides that it is necessary to construe the *Gooding* statute in a manner that will permit convictions to be affirmed on a "fighting words" theory. Describe the interpretation that will be necessary to satisfy the U.S. Supreme Court based on the reasoning of *Gooding, Chaplinsky,* and *Cantwell.*

3. *Deciding* Chaplinsky *Today.* Consider how *Chaplinsky* would be decided in the post-*Gooding* era. Identify the arguments that the defendant would make relying on the reasoning of *Gooding,* and explain how the government lawyer would attempt to distinguish the *Chaplinsky* facts, statutory language, and state court interpretation of that language from the same elements of *Gooding,* and thereby defend against a modern vagueness challenge in *Chaplinsky.*

4. *Remarks to Police Officers.* Police officers, believing that two teenage girls have stolen some bicycles, decide to question the girls. When the questioning is over, as the girls are walking away, they turn and yell in unison, "Fuck you, pigs." The officers pursue the girls down an alley and arrest them for disorderly conduct under a statute that reads: "Whoever in a public or private place, having reasonable grounds to know that the conduct of engaging in offensive, obscene or abusive language will tend to alarm, anger or disturb others or provoke an assault or breach of peace, is guilty of disorderly conduct." One of the officers testified at trial: "I was mad. I was upset. They didn't have a right to say that to me." The officer admitted during cross-examination that he had received some sensitivity training on how to respond to name calling, and that he did not react violently in this case or even consider such behavior because of the speakers' age, sex, and relative size. Assume that the girls are convicted and that on appeal in state court they bring an overbreadth and vagueness challenge. How must the state supreme court construe the disorderly conduct statute in order to satisfy *Gooding* and uphold the statute against the overbreadth and vagueness challenge? Assuming that the statute is construed narrowly in compliance with *Gooding,* is there sufficient evidence to uphold the conviction? *See Matter of Welfare of S.L.J.,* 263 N.W.2d 412 (Minn. 1978).

5. *The Danish Cartoons as "Fighting Words"?* A Danish newspaper published caricatures of the Prophet Mohammed to criticize Muslim violence and suicide bombing. Many Muslims were furious about the publication because Muslim law prohibits the publication of pictures of the Prophet and because the Prophet was portrayed as a terrorist. The publication produced widespread protests, some peaceful, but others very violent with property damage and deaths. Does the "fighting words" doctrine apply to the cartoons so that the government may prohibit them or prosecute their publication under an appropriately worded law? Does the doctrine apply to publication as opposed to spoken words?

The "hostile audience" doctrine is traditionally traced to Feiner v. New York, which was decided in 1951, the same year as Dennis v. United States.

Feiner v. New York

340 U.S. 315 (1951)

Mr. Chief Justice VINSON delivered the opinion of the Court.

[On] the evening of March 8, 1949, petitioner Irving Feiner was addressing an open-air meeting [in] the City of Syracuse. [T]he police received a telephone complaint concerning the meeting, and two officers were detailed to investigate. . . . They found a crowd of about seventy-five or eighty people, both Negro and white, filling the sidewalk and spreading out into the street. Feiner, standing on a large wooden box on the sidewalk, was addressing the crowd through a loudspeaker system attached to an automobile. Although the purpose of his speech was to urge his listeners to attend a meeting to be held that night in the Syracuse Hotel, in its course he was making derogatory remarks concerning President Truman, the American Legion, the Mayor of Syracuse, and other local political officials.

The police officers made no effort to interfere with petitioner's speech, but [were] concerned with the effect of the crowd on both pedestrian and vehicular traffic. [S]ome pedestrians were forced to walk in the street to avoid the crowd. Since traffic was passing[,] the officers attempted to get the people [back] on the sidewalk. The crowd was restless and there was some pushing, shoving and milling around. One [officer] telephoned the police station. . . . At this time, [Feiner] was speaking in a "loud, high-pitched voice." He gave the impression that he was endeavoring to arouse the Negro people against the whites, urging that they rise up in arms and fight for equal rights. The statements before such a mixed audience "stirred up a little excitement." Some of the onlookers made remarks to the police about their inability to handle the crowd and at least one threatened violence if the police did not act. There were others who appeared to be favoring [Feiner's] arguments. Because of the feeling that existed in the crowd both for and against the speaker, the officers finally "stepped in to prevent it from resulting in a fight." One of the officers approached [Feiner], not for the purpose of arresting him, but to get him to break up the crowd. He asked [Feiner] to get down off the box, but [Feiner] refused to accede to his request and continued talking. The officer waited for a minute and then demanded that he cease talking. Although the officer had thus twice requested [Feiner] to stop over the course of several minutes, [Feiner] not only ignored him but continued talking. During all this time, the crowd was pressing closer. . . . Finally, the officer told [Feiner] he was under arrest and ordered him to get down from the box, reaching up to grab him. [Feiner] stepped down, announcing over the microphone that "the law has arrived, and I suppose they will take over now." In all, the officer had asked petitioner to get down off the box three times over a space of four or five minutes. [Feiner] had been speaking for over a half hour.

[Feiner was] charged [with] "ignoring and refusing to heed and obey reasonable police orders issued at the time and place mentioned in the Information to regulate and control said crowd and to prevent a breach or breaches of the peace and to prevent injury to pedestrians attempting to use said walk, and being forced into the highway adjacent to the place in question, and prevent injury to the public generally." [The statute defined disorderly conduct as follows: "Any person who with intent to provoke a breach of the peace, or whereby a breach of the peace may be occasioned, commits any of the following acts shall be deemed to have committed the offense of disorderly conduct: '1. Uses offensive, disorderly, threatening, abusive or insulting language, conduct or behavior; 2. Acts in such a manner as to annoy, disturb, interfere with, obstruct, or be offensive to others; 3. Congregates with others on a public street and refuses to move on when ordered by the police.'" Feiner was convicted of the offense of disorderly conduct, and was sentenced to thirty days in the county penitentiary. The conviction was affirmed by the state courts.]

[The] language of Cantwell v. State of Connecticut, 310 U.S. 296 (1940), is appropriate here. "The offense known as breach of the peace embraces a great variety of conduct destroying or menacing public order and tranquility. It includes not only violent acts but acts and words likely to produce violence in others. [When] clear and present danger of riot, disorder, interference with traffic upon the public streets, or other immediate threat to public safety, peace, or order, appears, the power of the State to prevent or punish is obvious." The findings of the New York courts as to the condition of the crowd and [Feiner's] refusal to obey the police requests [are] persuasive that [Feiner's conviction] for violation of public peace, order and authority does not exceed the bounds of proper state police action. This Court respects, as it must, the interest of the community in maintaining peace and order on its streets.

We are well aware that the ordinary murmurings and objections of a hostile audience cannot be allowed to silence a speaker, and are also mindful of the possible danger of giving overzealous police officials complete discretion to break up otherwise lawful public meetings. [As *Cantwell* determined,] "[a] State may not unduly suppress free communication of views, religious or other, under the guise of conserving desirable conditions." But [it] is one thing to say that the police cannot be used as an instrument for the suppression of unpopular views, and another to say that, when [the] speaker passes the bounds of argument or persuasion and undertakes incitement to riot, they are powerless to prevent a breach of the peace. . . . The findings of the state courts as to the existing situation and the imminence of greater disorder coupled with [Feiner's] deliberate defiance of the police officers convince us that we should not reverse this conviction in the name of free speech.

Affirmed.

Mr. Justice BLACK, dissenting.

[Feiner], a young college student, has been sentenced to the penitentiary for the unpopular views he expressed on matters of public interest while lawfully making a street-corner speech. . . . The end result [approves] a simple and readily available technique by which cities and states [can] subject all speeches [to] the supervision and censorship of the local police. [T]his [is] a long step toward totalitarian authority. . . .

[I]t seems farfetched to suggest that the "facts" show any imminent threat of riot or uncontrollable disorder. It is neither unusual nor unexpected that some people at public street meetings mutter, mill about, push, shove, or disagree, even violently, with the speaker. Indeed, it is rare where controversial topics are discussed that an outdoor crowd does not do some or all of these things. Nor does one isolated threat to assault the speaker forebode disorder. Especially should the danger be discounted where, as here, the person threatening was a man whose wife and two small children accompanied him and who [was] never close enough to petitioner to carry out the threat. [A]ssuming that the "facts" did indicate a critical situation, I reject the implication [that] the police had no obligation to protect [Feiner's] constitutional right to talk. [I]f, in the name of preserving order, they ever can interfere with a lawful public speaker, they first must make all reasonable efforts to protect him. Here the policemen did not even [try] to protect petitioner [or arrest] the man who threatened to interfere. Instead, they shirked that duty and acted only to suppress the right to speak.

[I] cannot agree [that Feiner's] disregard of the policeman's unexplained request amounted to such "deliberate defiance" as would justify an arrest or conviction for disorderly conduct. [The] policeman's action was a 'deliberate defiance' of ordinary official duty as well as of the constitutional right of free speech. [Feiner] was 'asked' then 'told' then 'commanded' to stop speaking, but a man making a lawful address [is] not required to be silent merely because an officer directs it. [Feiner] was entitled to know why he should cease doing a lawful act. [P]eople in authoritarian countries must obey arbitrary orders. I had hoped that there was no such duty in the United States. . . . In my judgment, today's holding means that as a practical matter, minority speakers can be silenced in any city. [D]espite the First and Fourteenth Amendments, the policeman's club can take heavy toll of a current administration's public critics. Criticism of public officials will be too dangerous for all but the most courageous.

[I] would reverse the conviction. . . .

Notes and Questions

1. *The* Feiner *Trial Record.* Justice Douglas dissented in *Feiner*, in an opinion joined by Justice Minton, and noted that the record revealed only six "excerpts" of Feiner's speech: "Mayor Costello (of Syracuse) is a champagne-sipping bum; he does not speak for the negro people; The 15th Ward is run by corrupt politicians, and there are horse rooms operating there; President Truman is a bum; Mayor O'Dwyer is a bum; The American Legion is a Nazi Gestapo; The negroes don't have equal rights; they should rise up in arms and fight for their rights."

2. *The Heckler's Veto.* In the "hostile audience" situation, the police order the speaker to cease talking and may eventually arrest if there is noncompliance. The arrest usually is for the offense of disobeying a police order, disorderly conduct, or breach of the peace. The constitutional imperative in this scenario is to create a doctrine that will protect the provocatively unpopular speaker from "the heckler's veto." As one scholar explains the "hostile audience" problem, "[b]y giving

the police wide discretion to stop the speaker because of audience hostility, the state [in] effect transfers the power of censorship to the crowd. Moreover, the police are likely to share the views of the angry audience; hence, their perception of the unrest may be colored by their assessment of the speaker's message. [T]he end result is the censorship of wholly permissible content." Harry Kalven, Jr., *A Worthy Tradition: Freedom of Speech in America* 90 (Harper & Row 1988). Kalven's insight may be applicable to the "fighting words" doctrine as well, because this concept reflects an assumption that police require the discretion to make judgments about whether a "provoking" speaker should be arrested, and thereby to act as censors of a message that police view as inimical to public order. The police power of censorship is masked in both the "fighting words" and "hostile audience" contexts by the neutral nature of the conduct crimes for which the speaker typically is arrested.

3. *The Level of Danger.* The Court notes in *Feiner* that "[when] clear and present danger of riot, disorder, interference with traffic upon the public streets, or other immediate threat to public safety, peace, or order, appears, the power of the State to prevent or punish is obvious." Although the "clear and present danger" test is largely of historical significance today, do you agree that the facts reveal a clear and present danger of riot, disorder, and interference with traffic in this case? Or do the facts suggest that the police were trying to repress Feiner's ideas?

4. *The Nazi March.* In Village of Skokie v. National Socialist Party of America, 69 Ill. 2d 605, 373 N.E.2d 21 (Ill. 1978), members of the National Socialist Party of America wanted to hold a march in Skokie, Illinois, a predominantly Jewish village with a significant number of Holocaust survivors, and the marchers planned to wear Nazi uniforms and swastikas. Jewish groups threatened a violent response to the march. The Illinois Supreme Court held that the Nazis had a right to march, noting that "the heavy presumption against the constitutional validity of a prior restraint" could not be overcome. The court cited 1960s precedents like *Gregory* for the proposition that "a hostile audience is not a basis for restraining otherwise legal First Amendment activity," and noted that "courts have consistently refused to ban speech because of the possibility of unlawful conduct by those opposed to the speaker's philosophy." In a different phase of the Skokie litigation, the village conceded that it did not rely on a fear of responsive violence as an argument for stopping the Nazi march, and also promised to "make every effort to protect the demonstrators" from "responsive violence" if required by a court order to permit the march to take place. Ultimately, the Nazis decided to hold the march elsewhere.

❧ PROBLEMS ❧

1. *The Police Duty.* In *Feiner*, the Court concludes that the police may stop Feiner's speech in order to protect the public against riot or disorder. Suppose that Feiner is allowed to continue to speak and others begin to threaten him unless he stops. What is the proper police response? Should the police be

required to protect Feiner against the hostile crowd and to arrest those who threaten a breach of the peace?

2. *Eventual Suppression?* In the preceding problem, assume that the police do try to protect Feiner and suppose that the crowd becomes increasingly disorderly. Is there a point at which First Amendment rights should give way in favor of the public interest in maintaining the peace? With regard to Feiner's speech, when would he reach that point?

3. *Future Similar Speeches.* Finally, assume that you have been asked to advise Feiner after he lost his case in the U.S. Supreme Court. He would like to avoid arrest for disorderly conduct, but he would like to make a similar sort of speech on the same street corner. Describe the specific advice that you would provide. Then explain what advice you could give Feiner as to how he may preserve his ability to make First Amendment arguments at trial, assuming that he is arrested.

3. Offensive Speech

Is "offensive speech" entitled to special constitutional protection? Prior decisions, like *Chaplinsky* and *Cantwell*, pointed in different directions. *Chaplinsky* seemed to punish the defendant for uttering "offensive words," and his conviction was upheld because the crime was construed as requiring the use of fighting words that had a "'direct tendency to cause acts of violence'" by the person to whom they were addressed. Yet *Cantwell* established that "offensive words," involving criticism of the religion of the listener, were protected speech. As a result, "offensive words" did not fall into the fighting words category when the "offensive words" were not "epithets" or "abuse" directed at the listener. Even if the listener was offended personally by such criticism and even if any reasonable listener would be similarly offended, the critical speech did not lose its protection. In the absence of evidence of intent to incite, the religious criticism could not be punished by the common law crime of "inciting" the listener to a breach of the peace. In 1971, the Court used the following case to construct an edifice of policy judgments about the governmental interests in regulating offensive speech.

Cohen v. California

403 U.S. 15 (1971)

Mr. Justice HARLAN delivered the opinion of the Court.

[On] April 26, 1968, the defendant was observed in the Los Angeles County Courthouse in the corridor outside of division 20 of the municipal court wearing a jacket bearing the words "Fuck the Draft" which were plainly visible. There were women and children present in the corridor. [The] defendant testified that he wore the jacket knowing that the words were on the jacket as a means of informing the public of the depth of his feelings against the Vietnam War and the draft. The defendant did not engage in, nor threaten to engage in, nor did anyone as the result of his conduct in fact commit or threaten to commit any act of violence.

The defendant did not make any loud or unusual noise, nor was there any evidence that he uttered any sound prior to his [arrest]. When Cohen entered a courtroom in the building, "he removed his jacket and stood with it folded over his arm"; then "a policeman sent the presiding judge a note suggesting that Cohen be held in contempt of court," but "the judge declined to do so and Cohen was arrested by the officer only after he emerged from the courtroom." [Cohen was convicted and given 30 days in prison for the crime of "maliciously and willfully disturb[ing] the peace or quiet of any neighborhood or person [by] offensive conduct."] The California Supreme Court declined review. . . . We now reverse.

I

[The] conviction quite clearly rests upon the asserted offensiveness of the words Cohen used to convey his message to the public. The only "conduct" which the State sought to punish is the fact of communication. Thus, we deal here with a conviction resting solely upon "speech," not upon any separately identifiable conduct which allegedly was intended by Cohen to be perceived by others as expressive of particular views but which, on its face, does not necessarily convey any message and hence arguably could be regulated without effectively repressing Cohen's ability to express himself. *Cf.* United States v. O'Brien, 391 U.S. 367 (1968). Further, the State certainly lacks power to punish Cohen for the underlying content of the message the inscription conveyed. At least so long as there is no showing of an intent to incite disobedience to or disruption of the draft, Cohen could not, consistently with the First and Fourteenth Amendments, be punished for asserting the evident position on the inutility or immorality of the draft his jacket reflected. Yates v. United States, 354 U.S. 298 (1957).

[Cohen's] conviction, then, rests squarely upon his exercise of the "freedom of speech" protected from arbitrary governmental interference by the Constitution and can be justified, if at all, only as a valid regulation of the manner in which he exercised that freedom, not as a permissible prohibition on the substantive message it conveys. [T]he First and Fourteenth Amendments have never been thought to give absolute protection to every individual to speak whenever or wherever he pleases or to use any form of address in any circumstances that he chooses. . . .

[Any] attempt to support this conviction on the ground that the statute seeks to preserve an appropriately decorous atmosphere in the courthouse where Cohen was arrested must fail in the absence of any language in the statute that would have put appellant on notice that certain kinds of otherwise permissible speech or conduct would nevertheless, under California law, not be tolerated in certain places. No fair reading of the phrase "offensive conduct" can be said sufficiently to inform the ordinary person that distinctions between certain locations are thereby created.

[T]his case cannot be said to fall within those relatively few categories of instances where prior decisions have established the power of government to deal [with] certain forms of individual expression simply upon a showing that such a form was employed. This is not, for example, an obscenity case. [S]uch expression must be, in some significant way, erotic. Roth v. United States, 354 U.S. 476

(1957). It cannot plausibly be maintained that this vulgar allusion to the Selective Service System would conjure up such psychic stimulation in anyone likely to be confronted with Cohen's crudely defaced jacket. [T]he States are free to ban the simple use, without a demonstration of additional justifying circumstances, of so-called "fighting words. . . ." Chaplinsky v. New Hampshire, 315 U.S. 568 (1942). While the four-letter word displayed by Cohen in relation to the draft is not uncommonly employed in a personally provocative fashion, in this instance it was clearly not "directed to the person of the hearer." No individual actually or likely to be present could reasonably have regarded the words on appellant's jacket as a direct personal insult. Nor do we have here an instance of the exercise of the State's police power to prevent a speaker from intentionally provoking a given group to hostile reaction. Cf. Feiner v. New York, 340 U.S. 315 (1951). There is [no] showing that anyone who saw Cohen was in fact violently aroused or that appellant intended such a result.

[M]uch has been made of the claim that Cohen's distasteful mode of expression was thrust upon unwilling or unsuspecting viewers, and that the State might therefore legitimately act as it did in order to protect the sensitive from otherwise unavoidable exposure to appellant's crude form of protest. Of course, the mere presumed presence of unwitting listeners or viewers does not serve automatically to justify curtailing all speech capable of giving offense. While this Court has recognized that government may properly act in many situations to prohibit intrusion into the privacy of the home of unwelcome views and ideas which cannot be totally banned from the public dialogue, we [have] consistently stressed that "we are often 'captives' outside the sanctuary of the home and subject to objectionable speech." [Rowan v. United States Post Office Dept., 397 U.S. 728 (1970).] The ability of government, consonant with the Constitution, to shut off discourse solely to protect others from hearing it [is] dependent upon a showing that substantial privacy interests are being invaded in an essentially intolerable manner. Any broader view of this authority would effectively empower a majority to silence dissidents simply as a matter of personal predilections.

[P]ersons confronted with Cohen's jacket were in a quite different posture than, say, those subjected to the raucous emissions of sound trucks blaring outside their residences. Those in the Los Angeles courthouse could effectively avoid further bombardment of their sensibilities simply by averting their eyes. And, while it may be that one has a more substantial claim to a recognizable privacy interest when walking through a courthouse corridor than, for example, strolling through Central Park, surely it is nothing like the interest in being free from unwanted expression in the confines of one's own home. Given the subtlety and complexity of the factors involved, if Cohen's "speech" was otherwise entitled to constitutional protection, we do not think the fact that some unwilling "listeners" in a public building may have been briefly exposed to it can serve to justify this breach of the peace conviction where, as here, there was no evidence that persons powerless to avoid appellant's conduct did in fact object to it, and where that portion of the statute upon which Cohen's conviction rests evinces no concern, either on its face or as construed by the California courts, with the special plight of the captive auditor, but, instead, indiscriminately sweeps within its prohibitions all "offensive conduct" that disturbs "any neighborhood or person."

Against this background, the issue [is] whether California can excise, as "offensive conduct," one particular scurrilous epithet from the public discourse, either upon the theory of the court below that its use is inherently likely to cause violent reaction or upon a more general assertion that the States, acting as guardians of public morality, may properly remove this offensive word from the public vocabulary.

The rationale of the California court is plainly untenable. At most it reflects an "undifferentiated fear or apprehension of disturbance [which] is not enough to overcome the right to freedom of expression." Tinker v. Des Moines Indep. Community School Dist., 393 U.S. 503 (1969). We have been shown no evidence that substantial numbers of citizens are standing ready to strike out physically at whoever may assault their sensibilities with execrations like that uttered by Cohen. There may be some persons about with such lawless and violent proclivities, but that is an insufficient base upon which to erect, consistently with constitutional values, a governmental power to force persons who wish to ventilate their dissident views into avoiding particular forms of expression. The argument amounts to little more than the self-defeating proposition that to avoid physical censorship of one who has not sought to provoke such a response by a hypothetical coterie of the violent and lawless, the States may more appropriately effectuate that censorship themselves.

Admittedly, it is not so obvious that the First and Fourteenth Amendments must be taken to disable the States from punishing public utterance of this unseemly expletive in order to maintain what they regard as a suitable level of discourse within the body politic. We think, however, that examination and reflection will reveal the shortcomings of a contrary viewpoint.

[M]ost situations where the State has a justifiable interest in regulating speech will fall within one or more of the various established exceptions [to] the usual rule that governmental bodies may not prescribe the form or content of individual expression. . . . The constitutional right of free expression is powerful medicine in a society as diverse and populous as ours. It is designed and intended to remove governmental restraints from the arena of public discussion, putting the decision as to what views shall be voiced largely into the hands of each of us, in the hope that use of such freedom will ultimately produce a more capable citizenry and more perfect polity and in the belief that no other approach would comport with the premise of individual dignity and choice upon which our political system rests. . . . To many, the immediate consequence of this freedom may often appear to be only verbal tumult, discord, and even offensive utterance. These are, however, within established limits, in truth necessary side effects of the broader enduring values which the process of open debate permits us to achieve. That the air may at times seem filled with verbal cacophony is, in this sense not a sign of weakness but of strength. We cannot lose sight of the fact that, in what otherwise might seem a trifling and annoying instance of individual distasteful abuse of a privilege, these fundamental societal values are truly [implicated].

Against this perception of the constitutional policies involved, we discern certain more particularized considerations that peculiarly call for reversal of this conviction. First, the principle contended for by the State seems inherently boundless. How is one to distinguish this from any other offensive word? Surely the State has no right to cleanse public debate to the point where it is grammatically palatable to the most squeamish among us. Yet no readily ascertainable general principle exists for stopping short of that result were we to affirm the judgment below. For, while the particular four-letter word being litigated here is perhaps more distasteful than most others of its genre, it is nevertheless often true that one man's vulgarity is another's lyric. Indeed, we think it is largely because governmental officials cannot make principled distinctions in this area that the Constitution leaves matters of taste and style so largely to the individual.

[W]e cannot overlook the fact, because it is well illustrated by the episode involved here, that much linguistic expression serves a dual communicative function: it conveys not only ideas capable of relatively precise, detached explication, but otherwise inexpressible emotions as well. In fact, words are often chosen as much for their emotive as their cognitive force. We cannot sanction the view that the Constitution, while solicitous of the cognitive content of individual speech has little or no regard for that emotive function which practically speaking, may often be the more important element of the overall message sought to be [communicated].

[I]n the same vein, we cannot indulge the facile assumption that one can forbid particular words without also running a substantial risk of suppressing ideas in the process. Indeed, governments might soon seize upon the censorship of particular words as a convenient guise for banning the expression of unpopular views. We have been able [to] discern little social benefit that might result from running the risk of opening the door to such grave results. . . . It is, in sum, our judgment that, absent a more particularized and compelling reason for its actions, the State may not, consistently with the First and Fourteenth Amendments, make the simple public display here involved of this single four-letter expletive a criminal offense. . . .

> *Reversed.*

Mr. Justice BLACKMUN, with whom THE CHIEF JUSTICE and Mr. Justice BLACK join.

[I dissent.] Cohen's absurd and immature antic [was] mainly conduct and little speech. [T]he case appears [to] be well within the sphere of Chaplinsky v. New Hampshire, 315 U.S. 568 (1942). . . . As a consequence, this Court's agonizing over First Amendment values seem[s] misplaced and unnecessary.

Notes and Questions

1. Cohen's *Catalogue of "Inapplicable Theories" About First Amendment Values.* Once the *Cohen* majority establishes a preliminary endorsement for a narrow definition of "fighting words," its subsequent rejection of the first government theory to support the statute (that Cohen's message might cause others to "rise

up to commit a violent act") seems foreordained. The staying power of *Cohen's* narrow definition of fighting words is illustrated in Texas v. Johnson, 491 U.S. 397 (1989) (striking down a statute that punished flag desecration). The *Cohen* Court's subsequent analysis of the theory that the "state should be the moral guardian of speech" led to a discussion of First Amendment values that has been influential in subsequent case law, especially the notion of the "emotive value of speech" and the reminder about the difficulty of making "principled distinctions" in a field of offensive speech when one person's "vulgarity" is another's "lyric."

2. Cohen *and* Chaplinsky. *Cohen* contradicts the "slight social value" rationale for the unprotected status of "fighting words" endorsed in *Chaplinsky*, given *Cohen's* emphasis that "fundamental societal values are truly implicated" even in the "trifling and annoying instance of individual distasteful abuse of a privilege" represented by Cohen's message on his jacket. However, *Cohen* did not explicitly repudiate the "slight social value" theory, but ignored it.

3. Cohen *and the Justifications for Protecting Speech.* Did Cohen's speech meet any of the justifications for protecting speech presented at the beginning of this chapter? In other words, did it provide a safety valve, did it promote self-fulfillment or the marketplace of ideas, or was it related to the democratic process? If so, what type of showing should be required to allow the prosecution of statements like those made by Cohen?

4. *Little Eichmanns.* In April 2009, a jury held that Professor Ward Churchill was wrongfully dismissed from his post at the University of Colorado. Churchill was a tenured ethnic studies professor who referred to some victims of the 9/11 terrorist attacks as "little Eichmanns." The jury concluded that Churchill's views were a substantial or motivating factor in his dismissal, and that he otherwise would not have been dismissed (despite claims of plagiarism and falsification of research). Although the jury awarded Churchill only $1 in damages (because damages were not requested), the court is deliberating whether to order reinstatement. *See* Kirk Johnson & Katharine Q. Seelye, "Jury Says Professor Was Wrongly Fired," *New York Times* (Apr. 2, 2009); *see also http://www.nytimes.com/2009/ 04/03/us/03churchill.html?_r=1&scp=3&sq=ward%20churchill&st=cse.*

∾ PROBLEMS ∾

1. Cohen's *Implications.* Under *Cohen*, which of these situations can be prohibited under the First Amendment?

   a.   At a public school board meeting, the defendant "used the adjective 'm———f———' on four different occasions" with nouns that included "teachers, the community, the school system, the school board, the country, the county, and the town." He is prosecuted under a statute that provides that "[a]ny person who utters loud and offensive or profane or indecent language in any public street or other public place, public conveyance, or place to which the public is invited . . . is a disorderly person." *See* Rosenfield v. New Jersey, 408 U.S. 901 (1972).

b. At a political meeting at which the defendant was invited to present the "Black Panther viewpoint," he refers to some police officers as "m———f———fascist pig cops." He is prosecuted under a statute that prohibits "any obscene or lascivious language or word in any public place, or in the presence of females." *See* Brown v. Oklahoma, 408 U.S. 914 (1972).

2. *More on the International Treaty Regulating the Internet.* At the convention, a number of European representatives are keen to ban both Nazi symbols and denial that the Holocaust actually occurred, and they think that it is very important for the United States to support them in this effort. Under the First Amendment, can you agree to a treaty that allows governments to ban all Nazi symbols from the Internet, or that allows a prohibition against Holocaust denial?

3. *The Nursing Student's MySpace Comments.* A nursing student at the University of Louisville, whose overall performance had consistently been rated satisfactory, was expelled after posting offensive comments on her MySpace page. On the page, the student defended the right to bear arms and made profane observations regarding race, sex, and religion, including statements about Christians and blacks. In dismissing the student, the university claimed that she had violated the School of Nursing Honor Code, which provides as follows: "As a representative of the School of Nursing, I pledge to adhere to the highest standards of honesty, integrity, accountability, confidentiality, and professionalism, in all my written work, spoken words, actions and interactions with patients, families, peers and faculty." Although the student did not reveal any confidential information about her patients, the MySpace posting did state that the area surrounding the School of Nursing is "inhabited by humanoids who have an IQ of 10 and whose needs and actions are basically instinctive. As in, all they do is ——, eat, —— and kill each other." In another entry, she refers to the birth of a child (in which she does not name the patient), stating: "Out came a wrinkly bluish creature, all Picasso-like and weird, ugly as hell . . . screeching and waving its tentacles in the air. Fifteen minutes later, it turned into a pink, itty bitty baby girl." Did the university violate the First Amendment in expelling the student? *See* Andrew Wolfson, "U of L Dismisses Student Over Blog Posts: Woman Files Lawsuit to Gain Restatement," *The Courier-Journal*, B-1, c. 1-5 (Mar. 14, 2009).

4. *The Skokie Ordinance.* In response to the American Nazi Party's decision to hold a march in Skokie, Illinois, suppose that the Skokie Village Council drafts an ordinance that provides as follows: "[T]he dissemination of any materials within the Village of Skokie which promotes and incites hatred against persons by reason of their race, national origin, or religion, and is intended to do so, is prohibited. Dissemination of materials includes publication or display or distribution of posters, signs, handbills, or writings and public display of markings and clothing of symbolic significance. Public demonstrations by members of political parties while wearing 'military-style' uniforms is also prohibited. [The penalty is a fine of up to $500 and imprisonment up to six months.]" If you are asked to represent the Nazi Party, how would you argue that the law is unconstitutional? Now, assume

that you represent the Village Council. How would you argue that the ordinance is constitutional?

4. Defamatory Statements

The Court's attitude toward defamation has shifted over time. As previously noted, *Chaplinsky* held that defamatory statements are not protected under the First Amendment. *Chaplinsky* was reinforced by the holding in Beauharnais v. Illinois, 343 U.S. 250 (1952), where the Court rejected a due process challenge to a criminal law prohibiting libels based on race, color, creed, or religion. The Court emphasized that such utterances are unprotected speech, and that courts need not evaluate the efficacy of such laws." As a result, the states were free to define the tort of defamation and to determine the scope of the remedy. Most states readily imposed liability for defamatory statements.

a. The Constitutionalization of Defamation

New York Times Co. v. Sullivan
376 U.S. 254 (1964)

Mr. Justice BRENNAN delivered the opinion of the Court.

We are required in this case to determine [the] extent to which the constitutional protections for speech and press limit a State's power to award damages in a libel action brought by a public official against critics of his official conduct.

Respondent L.B. Sullivan is one [of] three elected Commissioners of the City of Montgomery, Alabama. [His duties involve] "supervision of the Police Department, Fire Department, Department of Cemetery and Department of Scales." He brought this civil libel action against [petitioners], who are Negroes and Alabama clergymen, [and] the New York Times Company, a New York corporation which publishes the New York Times, a daily newspaper. [An Alabama jury] awarded him $500,000 [against] all the petitioners, and the Supreme Court of Alabama affirmed.

[Respondent alleges that he was] libeled by statements in a full-page advertisement [in] the New York Times. . . . Entitled "Heed Their Rising Voices," the advertisement began by stating that "As the whole world knows[,] thousands of Southern Negro students are engaged in widespread non-violent demonstrations in positive affirmation of the right to live in human dignity as guaranteed by the U.S. Constitution and the Bill of Rights." It went on to charge that "in their efforts to uphold these guarantees, they are being met by an unprecedented wave of terror by those who would deny and negate that document which the whole world looks upon as setting the pattern for modern [freedom]." Succeeding paragraphs [illustrate] the "wave of terror" by describing [alleged] events. The text concluded with an appeal for funds for three purposes: support of the student movement, "the struggle for the right-to-vote," and the legal defense of Dr. Martin Luther

King, Jr., leader of the movement, against a perjury indictment. . . . The text appeared over the names of 64 persons, many widely known for their activities in public affairs, religion, trade unions, and the performing arts. Below these names, and under a line reading "We in the south who are struggling daily for dignity and freedom warmly endorse this appeal," appeared the names of the four individual petitioners and of 16 other persons, all but two of whom were identified as clergymen in various Southern cities. The advertisement was signed at the bottom of the page by the "Committee to Defend Martin Luther King and the Struggle for Freedom in the South," and the officers of the Committee were listed.

[T]he third [paragraph] and a portion of the sixth were the basis of respondent's claim of libel. They read as follows: Third paragraph: "In Montgomery, Alabama, after students sang 'My Country, 'Tis of Thee' on the State Capitol steps, their leaders were expelled from school, and truckloads of police armed with shotguns and tear-gas ringed the Alabama State College Campus. When the entire student body protested to state authorities by refusing to re-register, their dining hall was padlocked in an attempt to starve them into submission." Sixth paragraph: "Again and again the Southern violators have answered Dr. King's peaceful protests with intimidation and violence. They have bombed his home almost killing his wife and child. They have assaulted his person. They have arrested him seven times — for 'speeding,' 'loitering' and similar 'offenses.' And now they have charged him with 'perjury' — a felony under which they could imprison him for ten [years]."

Although neither of these statements mentions respondent by name, he contended that the word "police" in the third paragraph referred to him as the Montgomery Commissioner who supervised the Police Department, so that he was being accused of "ringing" the campus with police. He further claimed that the paragraph would be read as imputing to the police, and hence to him, the padlocking of the dining hall in order to starve the students into submission. As to the sixth paragraph, he contended that since arrests are ordinarily made by the police, the statement "They have arrested [Dr. King] seven times" would be read as referring to him; he further contended that the "They" who did the arresting would be equated with the "They" who committed the other described acts and with the "Southern violators." Thus, he argued, the paragraph would be read as accusing the Montgomery police, and hence him, of answering Dr. King's protests with "intimidation and violence," bombing his home, assaulting his person, and charging him with perjury. Respondent and six other Montgomery residents testified that they read some or all of the statements as referring to him in his capacity as Commissioner.

It is uncontroverted that some of the statements contained in the two paragraphs were not accurate descriptions of events which occurred in Montgomery. Although Negro students staged a demonstration on the State Capital steps, they sang the National Anthem and not "My Country, 'Tis of Thee." Although nine students were expelled[,] this was not for leading the demonstration at the Capitol, but for demanding service at a lunch counter in the Montgomery County Courthouse on another day. Not the entire student body, but most of it, had protested the expulsion, not by refusing to register, but by boycotting classes on a single day; virtually all the students did register for the ensuing semester. The campus dining hall was not padlocked on any occasion, and the only students who may have been barred from eating there were the few who had neither signed a preregistration application nor requested temporary meal tickets. Although the police were deployed near the campus in large numbers on three occasions, they did [not] "ring" the campus, and they were not called to the campus in connection with the demonstration on the State Capitol steps[.] Dr. King had not been arrested seven times, but only four; and although he claimed to have been assaulted some years earlier in connection with his arrest for loitering outside a courtroom, one of the officers who made the arrest denied that there was such an assault.

On the premise that the charges in the sixth paragraph could be read as referring to him, respondent was allowed to prove that he had not participated in the events described. Although Dr. King's home had in fact been bombed twice when his wife and child were there, both of these occasions antedated respondent's tenure as Commissioner, and the police were not only not implicated in the bombings, but had made every effort to apprehend those who were. Three of Dr. King's four arrests took place before respondent became Commissioner. Although Dr. King had in fact been indicted (he was subsequently acquitted) on two counts of perjury, each of which carried a possible five-year sentence, respondent had nothing to do with procuring the indictment.

Respondent made no effort to prove that he suffered actual pecuniary loss as a result of the alleged libel.[5] One of his witnesses, a former employer, testified that if he had believed the statements, he doubted whether he "would want to be associated with anybody who would be a party to such things that are stated in that ad," and that he would not re-employ respondent if he believed "that he allowed the Police Department to do the things that the paper say he did." But neither this witness nor any [other] testified that [he] actually believed the statements in their supposed reference to respondent.

The cost of the advertisement was approximately $4800, and it was published by the Times upon an order from a New York advertising agency acting for the signatory Committee. The agency submitted the advertisement with a letter [certifying] that the persons whose names appeared on the advertisement had given their [permission]. The manager of the Advertising [Department] testified that he had approved the advertisement [because] he knew nothing to cause him to believe that anything in it was false, and because it bore the endorsement of "a number of people who are well known and whose reputation" he "had no reason to question." Neither he nor anyone else at the Times made an effort to confirm the accuracy of the advertisement, either by checking it against recent Times news stories [or] by any other means.

5. Approximately 394 copies of the edition of the *Times* containing the advertisement were circulated in Alabama. Of these, about 35 copies were distributed in Montgomery County. The total circulation of the *Times* for that day was approximately 650,000 copies.

[Because] of the importance of the constitutional issues involved, we granted [certiorari]. We reverse the judgment. . . .

II

Under Alabama law[, o]nce "libel per se" has been established, the defendant has no defense as to stated facts unless he can persuade the jury that they were true in all their particulars. His privilege of "fair comment" for expressions of opinion depends on the truth of the facts upon which the comment is based. Unless he can discharge the burden of proving truth, general damages are presumed, and may be awarded without proof of pecuniary injury. A showing of actual malice is apparently a prerequisite to recovery of punitive damages, [and] defendant may [forestall] a punitive award by a retraction meeting the statutory requirements. Good motives and belief in truth do not negate an inference of malice, but are relevant only in mitigation of punitive damages[.]

The question before us is whether this rule of liability, as applied to an action brought by a public official against critics of his official conduct, abridges the freedom of speech and of the press that is guaranteed by the First and Fourteenth Amendments. . . . Respondent relies heavily [on] statements of this Court to the effect that the Constitution does not protect libelous publications. Those statements do not foreclose our inquiry here. . . . The general proposition that freedom of expression upon public questions is secured by the First Amendment has long been settled by our decisions. The constitutional [safeguard] "was fashioned to assure unfettered interchange of ideas for the bringing about of political and social changes desired by the people." "The maintenance of the opportunity for free political discussion to the end that government may be responsive to the will of the people and that changes may be obtained by lawful means, an opportunity essential to the security of the Republic, is a fundamental principle of our constitutional system." Stromberg v. California, 283 U.S. 359. . . .

Thus we consider this case against the background of a profound national commitment to the principle that debate on public issues should be uninhibited, robust, and wide-open, and that it may well include vehement, caustic, and sometimes unpleasantly sharp attacks on government and public officials. The present advertisement, as an expression of grievance and protest on one of the major public issues of our time, would seem clearly to qualify for the constitutional protection. The question is whether it forfeits that protection by the falsity of some of its factual statements and by its alleged defamation of respondent.

Authoritative interpretations of the First Amendment guarantees have consistently refused to recognize an exception for any test of truth — whether administered by judges, juries, or administrative officials — and especially one that puts the burden of proving truth on the speaker. The constitutional protection does not turn upon "the truth, popularity, or social utility of the ideas and beliefs which are offered." [E]rroneous statement is inevitable in free debate, and [it] must be protected if the freedoms of expression are to have the "breathing space" that they "need [to] survive," N.A.A.C.P. v. Button, 371 U.S. 415. . . .

Injury to official reputation [affords] no more warrant for repressing speech that would otherwise be free than does factual error. Where judicial officers are involved, this Court has held that concern for the dignity and reputation of the courts does not justify the punishment as criminal contempt of criticism of the judge or his decision. This is true even though the utterance contains "half-truths" and "misinformation." Such repression can be justified, if at all, only by a clear and present danger of the obstruction of justice. If judges are to be treated as "men of fortitude, able to thrive in a hardy climate," surely the same must be true of other government officials, such as elected city commissioners. Criticism of their official conduct does not lose its constitutional protection merely because it is effective criticism and hence diminishes their official reputations.

If neither factual error nor defamatory content suffices to remove the constitutional shield from criticism of official conduct, the combination of the two elements is no less inadequate. . . . What a State may not constitutionally bring about by means of a criminal statute is likewise beyond the reach of its civil law of libel. The fear of damage awards under a rule such as that invoked by the Alabama courts here may be markedly more inhibiting than the fear of prosecution under a criminal statute. [The] judgment awarded in this case — without the need for any proof of actual pecuniary loss — was one thousand times greater than the maximum fine provided by the Alabama criminal [libel] statute, and one hundred times greater than that provided by the Sedition Act. And since there is no double-jeopardy limitation applicable to civil lawsuits, this is not the only judgment that may be awarded against petitioners for the same publication.[6] Whether or not a newspaper can survive a succession of such judgments, the pall of fear and timidity imposed upon those who would give voice to public criticism is an atmosphere in which the First Amendment freedoms cannot survive. Plainly the Alabama law of civil libel is "a form of regulation that creates hazards to protected freedoms markedly greater than those that attend reliance upon the criminal law."

The state rule of law is not saved by its allowance of the defense of truth. [A] rule compelling the critic of official conduct to guarantee the truth of all his factual assertions — and to do so on pain of libel judgments virtually unlimited in amount — leads to a comparable "self-censorship." Allowance of the defense of truth, with the burden of proving it on the defendant, does not mean that only false speech will be deterred. Even courts accepting this defense as an adequate safeguard have recognized the difficulties of adducing legal proofs that the alleged libel was true in all its factual particulars. Under such a rule, would-be critics of official conduct may be deterred from voicing their criticism, even though it is believed to be true and even though it is in fact true, because of doubt whether it can be proved in court or fear of the expense of having to do so. They tend to make only statements which "steer far wider of the unlawful zone." The rule thus dampens the vigor and limits the variety of public debate. It is inconsistent with the First and Fourteenth Amendments.

---

6. The *Times* states that four other libel suits based on the advertisement have been filed against it by others who have served as Montgomery City Commissioners and by the Governor of Alabama; that another $500,000 verdict has been awarded in the only one of these cases that has yet gone to trial; and that the damages sought in the other three total $2,000,000.

The constitutional guarantees require, we think, a federal rule that prohibits a public official from recovering damages for a defamatory falsehood relating to his official conduct unless he proves that the statement was made with "actual malice" — that is, with knowledge that it was false or with reckless disregard of whether it was false or not. . . .

Such a privilege for criticism of official conduct is appropriately analogous to the protection accorded a public official when he is sued for libel by a private citizen. In Barr v. Matteo, 360 U.S. 564, this Court held the utterance of a federal official to be absolutely privileged if made "within the outer perimeter" of his duties. [The] threat of damage suits would otherwise "inhibit the fearless, vigorous, and effective administration of policies of government" and "dampen the ardor of all but the most resolute, or the most irresponsible, in the unflinching discharge of their duties." Analogous considerations support the privilege for the citizen-critic of government. [It] would give public servants an unjustified preference over the public they serve, if critics of official conduct did not have a fair equivalent of the immunity granted to the officials themselves. [We] conclude that such a privilege is required by the First and Fourteenth Amendments. [While] Alabama law apparently requires proof of actual malice for an award of punitive damages, where general damages are concerned malice is "presumed." Such a presumption is inconsistent with the federal rule. . . .

Since respondent may seek a new trial, [considerations] of effective judicial administration require us to review the evidence in the present record to determine whether it could constitutionally support a judgment for [respondent]. We must "make an independent examination of the whole record," so as to assure ourselves that the judgment does not constitute a forbidden intrusion on the field of free expression. [W]e consider that the proof presented to show actual malice lacks the convincing clarity which the constitutional standard demands, and hence [would] not constitutionally sustain the judgment for respondent under the proper rule of law. [Even] assuming that [the individual respondents authorized] the use of their names on the advertisement, there was no evidence [that] they were aware of any erroneous statements or were in any way reckless in that regard. The judgment against them is thus without constitutional support.

As to the Times, we similarly conclude that the facts do not support a finding of actual malice. The statement by the Times' Secretary [that] he thought the advertisement was "substantially correct," affords no [warrant] for the Alabama Supreme Court's conclusion "[of bad faith and maliciousness]." The statement does not indicate malice at the time of the publication [and] there was no evidence to impeach the witness' good faith in holding it. The Times' failure to retract upon respondent's demand [is] likewise not adequate evidence of malice. . . . Whether or not a failure to retract may ever constitute such evidence, there are two reasons why it does not here. First, the letter written by the Times reflected a reasonable doubt on its part as to whether the advertisement could reasonably be taken to refer to respondent at all. Second, it was not a final refusal, since it asked for [an] explanation — a request that respondent chose to ignore. . . .

[T]here is evidence that the Times published the advertisement without checking its accuracy against the news stories in the Times' own files. The mere presence of the stories in the files does not, of course, establish that the Times "knew" the advertisement was false, since the state of mind required for actual malice [involves] the persons [having] responsibility [for] publication of the advertisement. With respect to the failure of those persons to make the check, the record shows that they relied upon their knowledge of the good reputation of many of those whose names were listed as sponsors of the advertisement, and upon the letter from A. Philip Randolph, known to them as a responsible individual, certifying that the use of the names was authorized. There was testimony that the persons handling the advertisement saw nothing in it that would render it unacceptable under the Times' policy of rejecting advertisements containing "attacks of a personal character"; their failure to reject it on this ground was not unreasonable. We think the evidence against the Times supports at most a finding of negligence in failing to discover the misstatements, and is constitutionally insufficient to show the recklessness that is required for a finding of actual malice.

[The] judgment of the Supreme Court of Alabama is reversed and the case is remanded to that court for further proceedings not inconsistent with this opinion.

Reversed and remanded.

Mr. Justice BLACK, with whom Mr. Justice DOUGLAS joins (concurring).

[T]he Federal Constitution has dealt with this deadly danger to the press in the only way possible without leaving the free press open to destruction—by granting the press an absolute immunity for criticism of the way public officials do their public duty. Stopgap measures like those the Court adopts are in my judgment not enough. [S]ince the adoption of the Fourteenth Amendment a State has no more power than the Federal Government to use a civil libel law or any other law to impose damages for merely discussing public affairs and criticizing public officials. The power of the United States to do that [is] precisely nil. . . .

[Elected] officials are responsible to the people for the way they perform their [duties]. To punish the exercise of this right to discuss public affairs or to penalize it through libel judgments is to abridge or shut off discussion of the very kind most needed. This Nation, I suspect, can live in peace without libel suits based on public discussions of public affairs and public officials. But I doubt that a country can live in freedom where its people can be made to suffer physically or financially for criticizing their government, its actions, or its officials. [An] unconditional right to say what one pleases about public affairs is what I consider to be the minimum guarantee of the First Amendment. . . . I regret that the Court has stopped short of this holding indispensable to preserve our free press from destruction.

Mr. Justice GOLDBERG, with whom Mr. Justice DOUGLAS joins (concurring in the result).

[In] a democratic society, one who assumes to act for the citizens in an executive, legislative, or judicial capacity must expect that his official acts will be commented upon and criticized. Such criticism cannot, in my opinion, be muzzled or deterred by the courts at the instance of public officials under the label of libel. . . . It may be urged that deliberately and maliciously false statements have no conceivable value as free speech. That argument, however, is not responsive to the [issue of] whether that freedom of speech which all agree is constitutionally protected can be effectively safeguarded by a rule allowing the imposition of liability upon a jury's evaluation of the speaker's state of mind. If individual citizens may be held liable in damages for strong words, which a jury finds false and maliciously motivated, there can be little doubt that public debate and advocacy will be constrained. And if newspapers, publishing advertisments dealing with public issues, thereby risk liability, there can also be little doubt that the ability of minority groups to secure publication of their views on public affairs and to seek support for their causes will be greatly diminished. [The] conclusion that the Constitution affords the citizen and the press an absolute privilege for criticism of official conduct does not leave the public official without defenses against unsubstantiated opinions or deliberate misstatements. "Under our system of government, counterargument and education are the weapons available to expose these matters, not abridgment [of free speech]." Wood v. Georgia, 370 U.S. 375, 389. . . .

Notes and Questions

1. Sullivan *and the Justifications for Protecting Speech.* Did the speech involved in *Sullivan* meet any of the justifications for protecting speech presented at the beginning of this chapter? In other words, did the ad provide a safety valve, did it promote self-fulfillment or the marketplace of ideas, or was the ad related to the democratic process?

2. *Public Figures.* A few years after the Court decided *Sullivan*, it extended the actual malice standard to defamatory statements made about public figures. Curtis Publishing Co. v. Butts, 388 U.S. 130 (1967), involved a *Saturday Evening Post* article that alleged that Wallace Butts, the former football coach and then-athletic director at the University of Georgia, had conspired to fix a football game. The jury returned a verdict for $60,000 in general damages and for $3 million in punitive damages, reduced to $460,000 on appeal. Associated Press v. Walker, 388 U.S. 130 (1967), involved a press release stating that Edwin Walker, a retired major general and candidate for Texas governor, led a violent crowd against federal marshals during the riot in response to James Meredith's enrollment at Ole Miss. The Court concluded that Butts and Walker were public figures, and Justice Hanan's plurality advocated a gross negligence standard for their cases:

> [T]he public interest in the circulation of the materials here involved, and the publisher's interest in circulating them, is not less than that involved in *New York Times*. [B]oth Butts and Walker commanded a substantial amount of independent public interest at the time of the publications; both, in our opinion, would have been labeled "public figures" under ordinary tort rules. Butts may have attained that status by position alone and Walker by his purposeful activity amounting to a thrusting of his personality into the "vortex" of an important public controversy, but both commanded sufficient continuing public interest and had sufficient

access to the means of counterargument to be able "to expose through discussion the false-hood and fallacies" of the defamatory statements.

These similarities and differences between libel actions involving persons who are pub-lic officials and libel actions involving those circumstanced as were Butts and Walker, viewed in light of the principles of liability which are of general applicability in our society, lead us to the conclusion that libel actions of the present kind cannot be left entirely to state libel laws, unlimited by any overriding constitutional safeguard, but that the rigorous federal require-ments of *New York Times* are not the only appropriate accommodation of the conflicting inter-ests at stake. We [hold] that a "public figure" who is not a public official may also recover damages for a defamatory falsehood whose substance makes substantial danger to reputation apparent, on a showing of highly unreasonable conduct constituting an extreme departure from the standards of investigation and reporting ordinarily adhered to by responsible pub-lishers.

But the *Sullivan* rule prevailed and Chief Justice Warren's plurality opinion rea-soned:

[A]lthough they are not subject to the restraints of the political process, "public figures," like "public officials," often play an influential role in ordering society. And surely as a class these "public figures" have as ready access as "public officials" to mass media of communication, both to influence policy and to counter criticism of their views and activities. Our citizenry has a legitimate and substantial interest in the conduct of such persons, and freedom of the press to engage in uninhibited debate about their involvement in public issues and events is as crucial as it is in the case of "public officials." The fact that they are not amenable to the restraints of the political process only underscores the legitimate and substantial nature of the interest, since it means that public opinion may be the only instrument by which society can attempt to influence their conduct.

3. *Injunctive Relief and Prior Restraints.* Prior to the *Sullivan* decision, the Court applied its general prohibition against prior restraints to defamatory state-ments. In Near v. Minnesota, 283 U.S. 697 (1931), public officials sought and obtained an injunction against what they described as a "malicious, scandalous and defamatory newspaper." The U.S. Supreme Court reversed, establishing a broad rule against prior restraints: "Public officers, whose character and conduct remain open to debate and free discussion in the press, find their remedies for false accusations in actions under libel laws providing for redress and punish-ment, and not in proceedings to restrain the publication of newspapers and periodicals."

4. *Confidentiality of Sources.* In *Sullivan*'s aftermath, one issue that arose was whether a journalist could protect his or her sources against disclosure. In Desai v. Hersh, 954 F.2d 1408 (7th Cir. 1992), the court rejected a journalist's claimed right to protect the confidentiality of his sources in a defamation action: "[I]n defamation actions in which a plaintiff must establish 'malice' on the part of a defendant, [the] reporters privilege must give way to disclosure."

5. *Does the "Actual Malice" Standard Provide Too Little Protection to the Media?* In Herbert v. Lando, 441 U.S. 153 (1979), in an effort to prove that an article was published with "actual malice," plaintiff sought extensive discovery regarding the editorial processes that led to publication of an article. In *Lando*, the deposition continued for more than a year and involved 3,000 pages and 240 exhibits. In *Dun & Bradstreet*, *infra*, Justice White offered these thoughts about *Lando*: "[T]he

burden that plaintiffs must meet invites long and complicated discovery involving detailed investigation of the workings of the press, how a news story is developed, and the state of mind of the reporter and publisher. That kind of litigation is very expensive. I suspect that the press would be no worse off financially if the common-law rules were to apply and if the judiciary was careful to insist that damages awards be kept within bounds. . . ." Similarly, in the 1980s, a Libel Defense Resource Center Press Release showed "a dramatic increase in the already-high average of damage awards against media defendants in libel (and related) cases. Compared to the prior two-year period, the average award increased ten-fold, from almost half-a-million in 1987-88 to just under $4.5 million in 1989-90." These statistics prompted Professor Richard Epstein to observe that "the onslaught of defamation actions is greater in number and severity than it was in the 'bad old days' of common law libel [notwithstanding] *New York Times*." Richard A. Epstein, *Was New York Times v. Sullivan Wrong*, 53 U. Chi. L. Rev. 782, 783 (1986). Do these facts suggest that the Court should provide even greater protection to newspapers and broadcasters including, possibly, a ban on libel suits by public officials? *See* Martin Garbus, *25 Years After "Times v. Sullivan": What Remains to Be Done*, 201 N.Y. L.J. 2-3 (1989).

6. *Empirical Evidence*. The Libel Resource Defense Center's data are contradicted by empirical research conducted by Professors Russell L. Weaver and Geoffrey J.G. Bennett during the 1990s. Weaver and Bennett found that the U.S. media are generally unconcerned about the threat of defamation liability:

> [The] reason U.S. newspapers and broadcasters are less concerned about defamation is because they are threatened with suit, and actually sued, far less frequently than their British [counterparts]. . . . Editors and producers in the United States are not so relaxed that they ignore the possibility of defamation liability. But, because the threat of suit is much lower, they often tend to be more worried about other matters (e.g., journalistic accuracy and integrity) than they are about the threat of liability. . . .
>
> [These] attitudes are reflected in the day-to-day functioning of U.S. newspapers and broadcasters. Unlike the British, U.S. newspapers and broadcasters do not have teams of lawyers that comb through copy searching for material that may be defamatory. Most papers and broadcasters allow editors and producers to decide for themselves whether material is potentially defamatory and whether to involve counsel. If an editor or producer feels comfortable with a piece, he may publish or air it without any input from counsel.
>
> Thus, the possibility of defamation suits has some impact on reporting. But most interviewees indicated that the impact was minimal. Few editors or producers reported that they had ever killed a story for fear of defamation liability. Moreover, few indicated that they were unable to make a statement for fear of liability. They were often reluctant to rely entirely on confidential sources. In addition, if they had inadequate support for a piece, they might seek additional support. Alternatively, they might soften a statement or attempt to present it in a more balanced way. But there was a very good chance that the allegation would still be made.

Russell L. Weaver & Geoffrey J.G. Bennett, *Is the* New York Times *"Actual Malice" Standard Really Necessary? A Comparative Perspective*, 53 La. L. Rev. 1153 (1993).

7. *Is a "Public Interest" Standard Preferable to a "Public Figure" Standard?* The *Sullivan* decision focused not on whether the communication involved matters of "public interest" (although notions of public interest seemed to impact the

analysis), but on whether the plaintiff was a public official. In Rosenbloom v. Metromedia, Inc., 403 U.S. 29 (1971), a plurality suggested that the *Sullivan* standard derives "from the question whether the allegedly defamatory publication concerns a matter of public or general interest." But, in the Court's later decision in Gertz v. Robert Welch, Inc., *infra*, the Court ultimately rejected a "public interest" standard. Should the focus be on the individual or the issue? England has adopted press protections based on a public interest standard. *See* Reynolds v. Times Newspapers, [2001] 2 AC 127 (HL).

8. *Declarations of Truth and Falsity.* In *Dun & Bradstreet, infra,* Justice White, concurring, suggested that even if damages are not permitted, juries should be able to declare whether statements are true or false. "I [can] discern nothing in the Constitution which forbids a plaintiff to obtain a judicial decree that a statement is false — a decree he can then use in the community to clear his name and to prevent further damage from a defamation already published." Would it be desirable to allow officials to obtain a declaration of truth or falsity?

9. *Enforcement of Foreign Speech Judgments.* Foreign judgments awarding damages that implicate speech interests are not enforceable in U.S. courts unless they were rendered under standards consistent with the First Amendment to the U.S. Constitution. *See* Sarl Louis Feraud International v. Viewfinder, Inc., 406 F. Supp. 2d 274 (S.D.N.Y. 2005).

∼ PROBLEMS ∼

1. *The Offended Mayor.* The *Louisville Times* publishes an exposé about corruption in city government that makes extensive allegations regarding mayoral corruption. The mayor, incensed by the allegations, which he regards as viciously untrue, comes to you for legal advice. The mayor seeks a remedy against the *Times*. How would you advise the mayor to proceed? Would it be advisable for the mayor to a) seek injunctive relief against the *Times* to prevent publication of further articles on the subject, or b) bring a damage action against the *Times* to recover for defamatory injury? If you are unwilling to recommend either action, how would you advise the mayor to proceed? What remedies are open to him? Is there any remedy that will be effective under these circumstances?

2. *Proving "Actual Malice."* Assume that the mayor in the preceding problem decides to bring a damage action against the *Times*. Under the *Sullivan* decision, you know that the mayor will be required to prove that the *Times* acted with "actual malice" in publishing the stories. As an attorney, how will you go about satisfying that standard? In discovery, whom might you depose? What types of questions will you ask in the deposition?

3. *Defamation on Contingency?* Many U.S. lawyers take various types of tort cases (e.g., personal injury cases) on a contingency fee basis. Given the requirements of the actual malice standard and the nature of appellate review in defamation cases, would you be inclined to take the mayor's case on a contingency fee basis? Or would you insist on an hourly rate?

4. *More on the International Treaty Regulating the Internet.* The German Basic Law (effectively, the German Constitution) provides specific protections for "human dignity." Accordingly, the German delegates to the convention demand that the treaty contain specific protections against defamatory speech. What kind of language can you agree to in the treaty that is consistent with the U.S. Constitution? Is such language likely to satisfy the German delegates?

b.   Application of the "Actual Malice" Standard

Post-*Sullivan* decisions reveal how the actual malice standard has been applied.

St. Amant v. Thompson

390 U.S. 727 (1968)

Mr. Justice WHITE delivered the opinion of the Court.

[P]etitioner St. Amant, a candidate for public office, made a televised speech in Baton Rouge, Louisiana. In the course of this speech, St. Amant read a series of questions which he had put to J.D. Albin, a member of a Teamsters Union local, and Albin's answers to those questions. The exchange concerned the allegedly nefarious activities of E.G. Partin, the president of the local, and the alleged relationship between Partin and St. Amant's political opponent. One of Albin's answers concerned his efforts to prevent Partin from secreting union records; in this answer Albin referred to Herman A. Thompson, an East Baton Rouge Parish deputy sheriff and respondent here:

> Now, we knew that this safe was gonna be moved that night, but imagine our predicament, knowing of Ed's connections with the Sheriff's office through Herman Thompson, who made recent visits to the Hall to see Ed. We also knew of money that had passed hands between Ed and Herman Thompson. . . . We also knew of his connections with State Trooper Lieutenant Joe Green. We knew we couldn't get any help from there and we didn't know how far that he was involved in the Sheriff's office or the State Police office through that, and it was out of the jurisdiction of the City Police.

Thompson promptly brought suit for defamation, claiming that the publication had "impute[d] gross misconduct" and "infer[red] conduct of the most nefarious nature." The case was tried prior to the decision in *New York Times*. The trial judge ruled in Thompson's favor and awarded $5,000 in damages. . . .

[We] accept the determinations of the Louisiana courts that the material published by St. Amant charged Thompson with criminal conduct, that the charge was false, and that Thompson was a public official and so had the burden of proving that the false statements about Thompson were made with actual malice. . . . We cannot, however, agree [that] Thompson sustained this burden.

[T]he Louisiana Supreme Court ruled that St. Amant had broadcast false information about Thompson recklessly, though not knowingly. Several reasons were given for this conclusion. St. Amant had no personal knowledge of Thompson's activities; he relied solely on Albin's affidavit although the record was silent as to Albin's reputation for veracity; he failed to verify the information with those in the union office who might have known the facts; he gave no consideration to whether or not the statements defamed Thompson and went ahead heedless of the consequences; and he mistakenly believed he had no responsibility for the broadcast because he was merely quoting Albin's words.

These considerations fall short of proving St. Amant's reckless disregard for the accuracy of his statements about Thompson. "Reckless disregard" [cannot] be fully encompassed in one infallible definition. Inevitably its outer limits will be marked [through] case-by-case adjudication. . . . Our cases, however, have furnished meaningful guidance for the further definition of a reckless publication. In *New York Times*, the plaintiff did not satisfy his burden because the record failed to show that the publisher was aware of the likelihood that he was circulating false information. In Garrison v. State of Louisiana, 379 U.S. 64 (1964), [the] opinion emphasized the necessity for a showing that a false publication was made with a "high degree of awareness of [probable] falsity." Mr. Justice Harlan's opinion in Curtis Publishing Co. v. Butts, 388 U.S. 130 (1967), stated that evidence of either deliberate falsification or reckless publication "despite the publisher's awareness of probable falsity" was essential to recovery by public officials in defamation actions. These cases are clear that reckless conduct is not measured by whether a reasonably prudent man would have published, or would have investigated before publishing. There must be sufficient evidence to permit the conclusion that the defendant in fact entertained serious doubts as to the truth of his publication. Publishing with such doubts shows reckless disregard for truth or falsity and demonstrates actual malice.

It may be said that such a test puts a premium on ignorance, encourages the irresponsible publisher not to inquire, and permits the issue to be determined by the defendant's testimony that he published the statement in good faith and unaware of its probable falsity. Concededly the reckless disregard standard may permit recovery in fewer situations than would a rule that publishers must satisfy the standard of the reasonable man or the prudent publisher. But *New York Times* [emphasized] that the stake of the people in public business and the conduct of public officials is so great that neither the defense of truth nor the standard of ordinary care would protect against self-censorship and thus adequately implement First Amendment policies. Neither lies nor false communications serve the ends of the First Amendment, and no one suggests their desirability or further proliferation. But to insure the ascertainment and publication of the truth about public affairs, it is essential that the First Amendment protect some erroneous publications as well as true ones. . . .

The defendant in a defamation action brought by a public official cannot, however, automatically insure a favorable verdict by testifying that he published with a belief that the statements were true. The finder of fact must determine whether the publication was indeed made in good faith. Professions of good faith will be unlikely to prove persuasive, for example, where a story is fabricated by the defendant, is the product of his imagination, or is based wholly on an unverified anonymous telephone call. Nor will they be likely to prevail when the publisher's allegations are so inherently improbable that only a reckless man would have put them in circulation. Likewise, recklessness may be found where there are obvious reasons to doubt the veracity of the informant or the accuracy of his reports.

By no proper test of reckless disregard was St. Amant's broadcast a reckless publication about a public officer. Nothing [indicates] an awareness by St. Amant of the probable falsity of Albin's statement about Thompson. Failure to investigate does not in itself establish bad faith. St. Amant's mistake about his probable legal liability does not evidence a doubtful mind on his part. That he failed to realize the import of what he broadcast — and was thus "heedless" of the consequences for Thompson — is similarly colorless. Closer to the mark are considerations of Albin's reliability. However, the most the state court could say was that there was no evidence in the record of Albin's reputation for veracity, and this fact merely underlines the failure of Thompson's evidence to demonstrate a low community assessment of Albin's trustworthiness or unsatisfactory experience with him by St. Amant.

Other facts in this record support our view. St. Amant made his broadcast in June 1962. He had known Albin since October 1961, when he first met with members of the dissident Teamsters faction. St. Amant testified that he had verified other aspects of Albin's information and that he had affidavits from others. Moreover Albin swore to his answers, first in writing and later in the presence of newsmen. According to Albin, he was prepared to substantiate his charges. St. Amant knew that Albin was engaged in an internal struggle in the union; Albin seemed to St. Amant to be placing himself in personal danger by publicly airing the details of the dispute.

Because the state court misunderstood and misapplied the actual malice standard which must be observed in a public official's defamation action, the judgment is reversed and the case remanded for further proceedings not inconsistent with this opinion.

Reversed and remanded.

Mr. Justice FORTAS, dissenting.

I do not believe that petitioner satisfied the minimal standards of care specified by *New York Times*. The affidavit that petitioner broadcast contained a seriously libelous statement directed against respondent. [Petitioner's] casual, careless, callous use of the libel cannot be rationalized as resulting from the heat of a campaign. Under *New York Times*, this libel was broadcast by petitioner with "actual malice." [The] First Amendment is not a shelter for the character assassinator, whether his action is heedless and reckless or deliberate. [The] occupation of public officeholder does not forfeit one's membership in the human race. The public official should be subject to severe scrutiny and to free and open criticism. But if he is needlessly, heedlessly, falsely accused of crime, he should have a remedy in law. *New York Times* does not preclude this minimal standard of civilized living. . . . Petitioner had a duty here to check the reliability of the libelous statement about respondent. If he had made a good-faith check, [he] should be protected even if the statement were false, because the interest of public officials in their reputation must endure this degree of assault. But since he made no check, [*New York Times*] does not prohibit recovery. . . . I would affirm.

Notes and Questions

1. *Irresponsible Journalism?* Does the actual malice standard encourage the media to act irresponsibly? Does it provide too little protection to public officials and thereby discourage quality individuals from running for office? Consider the remarks of Honorable Abner J. Mikva, *In My Opinion, Those Are Not Facts*, 11 Ga. St. U. L. Rev. 291 (1995): "a feeling is abroad among some judges that the Supreme Court has gone too far in protecting the media from defamation actions resulting [from] irresponsible [journalism]."

2. *Should the "Actual Malice" Standard Apply to Low-Level Officials?* Does *New York Times* justify subjecting low-level governmental officials (an assistant deputy sheriff or a desk worker in the department of motor vehicles) to the "actual malice" standard? In your analysis, should it matter whether a low-level official has a realistic opportunity to invoke the press and use it to rebut allegations as prominent? Does it matter whether the allegations relate to a matter of "public interest"? *See* Coughlin v. Westinghouse Broadcasting and Cable, Inc., 780 F.2d 340 (3d Cir. 1985).

3. *Officials Who Have Left Office.* After the mayor of a large city leaves public office, suppose that the local newspaper continues to report incessantly regarding her activities. After leaving office, is the mayor still subject to the actual malice standard? Should it matter whether the reporting relates to the mayor's administration or to her private life? *See* Zerangue v. TSP Newspapers, Inc., 814 F.2d 1066 (5th Cir. 1987).

4. *Actual Malice and Quotations.* Masson v. New Yorker Magazine, Inc., 501 U.S. 496 (1991), involved a reporter for the *New Yorker* magazine who published an interview with a prominent individual that contained a number of statements in quotation marks. The interviewee sued, claiming that he did not make some of the statements, and alleging that the reporter falsely placed them in quotation marks to suggest that they were the interviewee's remarks. The Court concluded that the mere fact that a reporter fabricated a quotation was not sufficient to satisfy the actual malice standard. Indeed, the Court indicated that it might be permissible for a reporter, who is interviewing a prominent athlete, to change statements to make them grammatical. The Court ultimately concluded that liability should turn on whether the alteration results in a material change in the meaning conveyed by the statement or is merely a trivial change.

∼ PROBLEM: PROVING ACTUAL MALICE ∼

In a prior problem, we focused on the mayor of a city who was allegedly defamed by the local newspaper, which alleged corruption and extramarital affairs. Notwithstanding the fact that the mayor will have to satisfy the "actual malice" standard, the mayor has decided to sue the newspaper. You know that the allegations are untrue. How will you go about proving that the newspaper acted with "actual malice"?

c.   Private Plaintiffs

After the Court rendered the *Sullivan* and *Butts* decisions, it struggled to determine whether a different and lesser liability standard should be applied when the plaintiff is a private individual rather than a public figure.

Gertz v. Robert Welch, Inc.

418 U.S. 323 (1974)

Mr. Justice POWELL delivered the opinion of the Court.

[In] 1968 a Chicago policeman named Nuccio shot and killed a youth named Nelson. [S]tate authorities prosecuted Nuccio for the homicide and ultimately obtained a conviction for murder in the second degree. The Nelson family retained petitioner Elmer Gertz, a reputable attorney, to represent them in civil litigation against Nuccio.

Respondent publishes *American Opinion,* a monthly outlet for the views of the John Birch Society. [I]n the 1960's the magazine began to warn of a nationwide conspiracy to discredit local law enforcement agencies and create [a] national police force capable of supporting a Communist dictatorship. [In an] effort to alert the public to this assumed danger, [the] *American Opinion* commissioned an article on the murder trial of Officer Nuccio. [In] 1969 respondent published the resulting article under the title "FRAME-UP: Richard Nuccio And The War On Police." The article purports to demonstrate that the testimony against Nuccio at his criminal trial was false and that his prosecution was part of the Communist campaign against the police.

[A]s counsel for the Nelson family in the civil litigation, petitioner attended the coroner's inquest into the boy's death and initiated actions for damages, but he neither discussed Officer Nuccio with the press nor played any part in the criminal proceeding. Notwithstanding petitioner's remote connection with the prosecution of Nuccio, respondent's magazine portrayed him as an architect of the "frame-up." According to the article, the police file on petitioner took "a big, Irish cop to lift." The article stated that petitioner had been an official of the "Marxist League for Industrial Democracy, originally known as the Intercollegiate Socialist Society, which has advocated the violent seizure of our government." It labeled Gertz a "Leninist" and a "Communist-fronter." It also stated that Gertz had been an officer of the National Lawyers Guild, described as a Communist organization that "probably did more than any other outfit to plan the Communist attack on the Chicago police during the 1968 Democratic Convention."

[The article] contained serious inaccuracies. The implication that petitioner had a criminal record was false. Petitioner had been a member and officer of the National Lawyers Guild some 15 years earlier, but there was no evidence that he or that organization had taken any part in planning the 1968 demonstrations in Chicago. There was also no basis for the charge that petitioner was a "Leninist" or a "Communist-fronter." And he had never been a member of the "Marxist League for Industrial Democracy" or the "Intercollegiate Socialist Society."

The managing editor of *American Opinion* made no effort to verify or substantiate the charges against petitioner. Instead, he appended [an] introduction stating that the author had "conducted extensive research into [the] Nuccio Case." And he included in the article a photograph of petitioner and wrote the caption that appeared under it: "Elmer Gertz of Red Guild harasses Nuccio." Respondent placed the [issue] containing the article on sale at newsstands throughout the country and distributed reprints of the article on the streets of Chicago. [T]he District Court [entered] judgment for respondent. . . .

The principal issue [is] whether a newspaper or broadcaster that publishes defamatory falsehoods about an individual who is neither a public official nor a public figure may claim a constitutional privilege against liability for the injury inflicted by those statements. The Court considered this question on the rather different set of facts presented in Rosenbloom v. Metromedia, Inc., 403 U.S. 29 (1971). Rosenbloom, a distributor of nudist magazines, was arrested for selling allegedly obscene material while making a delivery to a retail dealer. [Afterward, he sued a radio station for defamation related to its report on the arrest and obtained a judgment. In *Rosenbloom*, this] Court affirmed the decision below, but no majority could agree on a controlling rationale. The eight Justices [announced] their views in five separate opinions. [The] several statements [reflect] divergent traditions of thought about the general problem of reconciling the law of defamation with the First Amendment. One approach has been to extend the *New York Times* test to an expanding variety of situations. Another has been to vary the level of constitutional privilege for defamatory falsehood with the status of the person defamed. And a third view would grant to the press and broadcast media absolute immunity from liability for defamation. . . . In his opinion for the plurality[,] Mr. Justice Brennan [concluded] that [the actual malice standard] should extend to defamatory falsehoods relating to private persons if the statements concerned matters of general or public interest. . . .

[Our] decisions recognize that a rule of strict liability that compels a publisher or broadcaster to guarantee the accuracy of his factual assertions may lead to intolerable self-censorship. [The] need to avoid self-censorship by the news media is, however, not the only societal value at issue. If it were, this Court would have embraced [the] view that publishers and broadcasters enjoy an unconditional and indefeasible immunity from liability for defamation. [The] legitimate state interest underlying the law of libel is the compensation of individuals for the harm inflicted on them by defamatory falsehood. We would not lightly require the State to abandon this purpose, for, as Mr. Justice Stewart has reminded us, the individual's right to the protection of his own good name "reflects no more than our basic concept of the essential dignity and worth of every human being—a concept at the root of any decent system of ordered liberty." Rosenblatt v. Baer, 383 U.S. 75 (1966) (concurring opinion).

Some tension necessarily exists between the need for a vigorous and uninhibited press and the legitimate interest in redressing wrongful injury. [In] our continuing effort to define the proper accommodation between these competing concerns, we have been especially anxious to assure to the freedoms of speech and press that "breathing space" essential to their fruitful exercise. To that end this Court has extended a measure of strategic protection to defamatory false-hood. . . .

The *New York Times* standard defines the level of constitutional protection appropriate to the context of defamation of a public person. Those who, by reason of the notoriety of their achievements or the vigor and success with which they seek the public's attention, are properly classed as public figures and those who hold governmental office. . . . This standard [exacts a] high price from the victims of defamatory falsehood. [M]any deserving plaintiffs, including some intentionally subjected to injury, will be unable to surmount the barrier of the *New York Times* test. [We] think that these decisions are correct, but [we] believe that the *New York Times* rule states an accommodation between this concern and the limited state interest present in the context of libel actions brought by public persons. [T]he state interest in compensating injury to the reputation of private individuals requires that a different rule should obtain with respect to them.

[W]e have no difficulty in distinguishing among defamation plaintiffs. The first remedy of any victim of defamation is self-help — using available opportu-nities to contradict the lie or correct the error and thereby to minimize its adverse impact on reputation. Public officials and public figures usually enjoy signifi-cantly greater access to the channels of effective communication and hence have a more realistic opportunity to counteract false statements then private individu-als normally enjoy.[7] Private individuals are therefore more vulnerable to injury, and the state interest in protecting them is correspondingly greater. . . .

More important[,] there is a compelling normative consideration underly-ing the distinction between public and private defamation plaintiffs. An indi-vidual who decides to seek governmental office must accept certain necessary consequences of that involvement in public affairs. He runs the risk of closer pub-lic scrutiny than might otherwise be the case. And society's interest in the officers of government is not strictly limited to the formal discharge of official duties. [T]he public's interest extends to "anything which might touch on an official's fit-ness for [office]. Few personal attributes are more germane to fitness for office than dishonesty, malfeasance, or improper motivation, even though these char-acteristics may also affect the official's private character." . . . Those classed as public figures stand in a similar position. Hypothetically, it may be possible for someone to become a public figure through no purposeful action of his own, but the instances of truly involuntary public figures must be exceedingly rare. For the most part those who attain this status have assumed roles of especial prominence in the affairs of society. Some occupy positions of such persuasive power and influence that they are deemed public figures for all purposes. More commonly, those classed as public figures have thrust themselves to the forefront of particu-lar public controversies in order to influence the resolution of the issues involved. In either event, they invite attention and comment.

---

7. Of course, an opportunity for rebuttal seldom suffices to undo harm of defamatory falsehood. Indeed, the law of defamation is rooted in our experience that the truth rarely catches up with a lie. But the fact that the self-help remedy of rebuttal, standing alone, is inadequate to its task does not mean that it is irrelevant to our inquiry.

Even if the foregoing generalities do not obtain in every instance, the communications media are entitled to act on the assumption that public officials and public figures have voluntarily exposed themselves to increased risk of injury from defamatory falsehood concerning them. No such assumption is justified with respect to a private individual. He has not accepted public office or assumed an "influential role in ordering society." He has relinquished no part of his interest in the protection of his own good name, and consequently he has a more compelling call on the courts for redress of injury inflicted by defamatory falsehood. Thus, private individuals are not only more vulnerable to injury than public officials and public figures; they are also more deserving of recovery.

For these reasons we conclude that the States should retain substantial latitude in their efforts to enforce a legal remedy for defamatory falsehood injurious to the reputation of a private individual. The extension of the *New York Times* test proposed by the *Rosenbloom* plurality would abridge this legitimate state interest to a degree that we find unacceptable. And it would occasion [the] difficulty of forcing [judges] to decide [which] publications address issues of "general or public interest" and which do not. . . . We doubt the wisdom of committing this task to the conscience of judges. [The] "public or general interest" test for determining the applicability of the *New York Times* standard to private defamation actions inadequately serves both of the competing values at stake. . . .

We hold that, so long as they do not impose liability without fault, the States may define for themselves the appropriate standard of liability for a publisher or broadcaster of defamatory falsehood injurious to a private individual. This approach provides a more equitable boundary between the competing concerns involved here. It recognizes the strength of the legitimate state interest in compensating private individuals for wrongful injury to reputation, yet shields the press and broadcast media from the rigors of strict liability for defamation. [The] strong and legitimate state interest in compensating private individuals for injury to reputation [extends] no further than compensation for actual injury. [W]e hold that the States may not permit recovery of presumed or punitive damages, at least when liability is not based on a showing of knowledge of falsity or reckless disregard for the truth.

The common law of defamation is an oddity of tort law, for it allows recovery of purportedly compensatory damages without evidence of actual loss. Under the traditional rules pertaining to actions for libel, the existence of injury is presumed from the fact of publication. Juries may award substantial sums as compensation for supposed damage to reputation without any proof that such harm actually occurred. The largely uncontrolled discretion of juries to award damages where there is no loss unnecessarily compounds the potential of any system of liability for defamatory falsehood to inhibit the vigorous exercise of First Amendment freedoms. Additionally, the doctrine of presumed damages invites juries to punish unpopular opinion rather than to compensate individuals for injury sustained by the publication of a false fact. [T]he States have no substantial interest in securing for plaintiffs such as this petitioner gratuitous awards of money damages far in excess of any actual injury.

[H]ere we are attempting to reconcile state law with a competing interest grounded in the constitutional command of the First Amendment. It is therefore appropriate to require that state remedies for defamatory falsehood reach no farther than is necessary to protect the legitimate interest involved. It is necessary to restrict defamation plaintiffs who do not prove knowledge of falsity or reckless disregard for the truth to compensation for actual injury [which] is not limited to out-of-pocket loss. [T]he more customary types of actual harm inflicted by defamatory falsehood include impairment of reputation and standing in the community, personal humiliation, and mental anguish and suffering. Of course, juries must be limited by appropriate instructions, and all awards must be supported by competent evidence concerning the injury, although there need be no evidence which assigns an actual dollar value to the injury.

We also find no justification for allowing awards of punitive damages against publishers and broadcasters. [J]uries assess punitive damages in wholly unpredictable amounts bearing no necessary relation to the actual harm caused. And they remain free to use their discretion selectively to punish expressions of unpopular views. Like the doctrine of presumed damages, jury discretion to award punitive damages [exacerbates] the danger of media self-censorship, [but] punitive damages are wholly irrelevant to the state interest that justifies a negligence standard for private defamation actions. They are not compensation for injury. Instead, they are private fines levied by civil juries to punish reprehensible conduct and to deter its future occurrence. In short, the private defamation plaintiff who establishes liability under a less demanding standard than that stated by *New York Times* may recover only such damages as are sufficient to compensate him for actual injury.

[R]espondent contends that we should affirm [on] the ground that petitioner is either a public official or a public figure. There is little basis for the former assertion. Several years prior to the present incident, petitioner [served] briefly on housing committees appointed by the mayor of Chicago, but [he] never held any remunerative governmental position. Respondent [argues] that petitioner's appearance at the coroner's inquest rendered him a "de facto public official." Our cases recognized no such concept. Respondent's suggestion would sweep all lawyers under the *New York Times* rule as officers of the court and distort the plain meaning of the "public official" category beyond all recognition. We decline to follow it.

Respondent's characterization of petitioner as a public figure raises a different question. That designation may rest on either of two alternative bases. In some instances an individual may achieve such pervasive fame or notoriety that he becomes a public figure for all purposes and in all contexts. More commonly, an individual voluntarily injects himself or is drawn into a particular public controversy and thereby becomes a public figure for a limited range of issues. In either case such persons assume special prominence in the resolution of public questions.

Petitioner has long been active in community and professional affairs. He has served as an officer of local civic groups and of various professional organizations, and he has published several books and articles on legal subjects. Although petitioner was consequently well known in some circles, he had achieved no general fame or notoriety in the community. [We] would not lightly assume that a citizen's participation in community and professional affairs rendered him a public figure for all purposes. Absent clear evidence of general fame or notoriety in the community, and pervasive involvement in the affairs of society, an individual should not be deemed a public personality for all aspects of his life. . . . In this context it is plain that petitioner was not a public figure. He played a minimal role at the coroner's inquest, and his participation related solely to his representation of a private client. He took no part in the criminal prosecution of Officer Nuccio. Moreover, he never discussed either the criminal or civil litigation with the press and was never quoted as having done so. He plainly did not thrust himself into the vortex of this public issue, nor did he engage the public's attention in an attempt to influence its outcome. We are persuaded that the trial court did not err in refusing to characterize petitioner as a public figure for the purpose of this litigation.

We therefore conclude that the *New York Times* standard is inapplicable to this case and that the trial court erred in entering judgment for respondent. Because the jury was allowed to impose liability without fault and was permitted to presume damages without proof of injury, a new trial is necessary. We reverse and remand for further proceedings in accord with this opinion.

It is ordered.

Reversed and remanded.

Mr. Chief Justice BURGER, dissenting.

[The] important public policy which underlies [the] right to counsel [would] be gravely jeopardized if every lawyer who takes an "unpopular" case, civil or criminal, would automatically become fair game for irresponsible reporters and editors who might, for example, describe the lawyer as a "mob mouthpiece" for representing a client with a serious prior criminal record. . . .

Mr. Justice DOUGLAS, dissenting.

[The] vehicle for publication in this case was the *American Opinion,* a most controversial periodical which disseminates the views of the John Birch Society, an organization which many deem to be quite offensive. The subject matter involved "Communist plots," "conspiracies against law enforcement agencies," and the killing of a private citizen by the police. With any such amalgam of controversial elements[,] a jury determination, unpredictable in the most neutral circumstances, becomes [a] virtual roll of the dice separating them from liability for often massive claims of damage. [It] is only the hardy publisher who will engage in discussion in the face of such risk, and the Court's preoccupation with proliferating standards [increases] the risks. [T]he First and Fourteenth Amendments prohibit the imposition of damages [for] this discussion of public affairs. . . .

Mr. Justice BRENNAN, dissenting.

[Matters] of public or general interest do not "suddenly become less so merely because a private individual is involved, or because in some sense the individual did not 'voluntarily' choose to become involved." [The] Court's broad-ranging examples of "actual injury," including impairment of reputation and standing in the community, as well as personal humiliation, and mental anguish and suffering, inevitably allow a jury bent on punishing expression of unpopular views a formidable weapon for doing so. Finally, even a limitation of recovery to "actual injury" [will] not provide the necessary elbowroom for First Amendment expression. . . . "The very possibility of having to engage in litigation, an expensive and protracted process, is threat enough to cause discussion and debate to 'steer far wider of the unlawful zone' thereby keeping protected discussion from public [cognizance]. . . ."

Notes and Questions

1. *Private Individuals and Matters of Purely Private Concern.* In Dun & Bradstreet, Inc. v. Greenmoss Builders, Inc., 472 U.S. 749 (1985), the Court confronted the question whether a lower defamation liability standard should apply in cases involving "private plaintiffs" in matters of "purely private concern." The case involved a credit reporting agency that inaccurately reported that the plaintiff's business was in bankruptcy:

> [It] is speech on "matters of public concern" that is "at the heart of the First Amendment's protection." [S]peech on matters of purely private concern is of less First Amendment concern. [T]he role of the Constitution in regulating state libel law is far more limited when the concerns that activated *New York Times* and *Gertz* are absent. In such a case, "[t]here is no threat to the free and robust debate of public issues; there is no potential interference with a meaningful dialogue of ideas concerning self-government; and there is no threat of liability causing a reaction of self-censorship by the press. . . . [C]ourts for centuries have allowed juries to presume that some damage occurred from many defamatory utterances and publications. This rule furthers the state interest in providing remedies for defamation by ensuring that those remedies are effective. In light of the reduced constitutional value of speech involving no matters of public concern, we hold that the state interest adequately supports awards of presumed and punitive damages — even absent a showing of 'actual malice.'"
>
> "[W]hether [speech] addresses a matter of public concern must be determined by [the expression's] content, form, and context [as] revealed by the whole record." These factors indicate that petitioner's credit report concerns no public issue. It was speech solely in the individual interest of the speaker and its specific business audience. [S]ince the credit report was made available to only five subscribers, who [could] not disseminate it further, it cannot be said that the report involves any "strong interest in the free flow of commercial information." There is simply no credible argument that this type of credit reporting requires special protection to ensure that "debate on public issues [will] be uninhibited, robust, and wideopen." [We] conclude that permitting recovery of presumed and punitive damages in defamation cases absent a showing of "actual malice" does not violate the First Amendment when the defamatory statements do not involve matters of public concern. . . .

Justice Brennan dissented: "Speech about commercial or economic matters [is] an important part [of] public discourse. . . . [It] is difficult to suggest that a bankruptcy is not a subject matter of public concern when federal law requires invocation of judicial mechanisms to effectuate it and makes the fact of the bankruptcy a matter of public record. . . ."

2. *Burden of Proof.* At common law, in a defamation case, the defendant bore the burden of proving that the allegedly defamatory statements were true. In Philadelphia Newspapers, Inc. v. Hepps, 475 U.S. 767 (1986), the Court reversed

that presumption and held that, when a newspaper publishes matters of public concern, a private-figure plaintiff cannot recover damages without proving that the statements are false. Justice Stevens dissented: "[T]he overriding concern for reliable protection of truthful statements must make room for '[t]he legitimate state interest in [compensating] individuals for the harm inflicted on them by defamatory falsehood.'"

3. *Does* Gertz *Make Sense?* Given that Gertz was a lawyer, had served on various community committees, and was involved (albeit peripherally) in a case of great public interest, should the story have been treated as allied with the public interest and the *Sullivan* rule applied?

4. *The* Firestone *Case.* In Time, Inc. v. Firestone, 424 U.S. 448 (1976), the Court rejected public-figure status for a petitioner in a divorce proceeding:

> Dissolution of a marriage through judicial proceedings is not the sort of "public controversy" referred to in *Gertz*, even though the marital difficulties of extremely wealthy individuals may be of interest to some portion of the reading public. Nor did respondent freely choose to publicize issues as to the propriety of her married life. She was compelled to go to court by the State in order to obtain legal release from the bonds of matrimony. [Her] actions, both in instituting the litigation and in its conduct, were quite different from those of General Walker in *Curtis Publishing Co.* She assumed no "special prominence in the resolution of public questions." We hold respondent was not a "public figure." . . .

Consider Justice Marshall's dissent in *Firestone*:

> [Mrs.] Firestone [was] "prominent among the '400' of Palm Beach society," and an "active (member) of the sporting set," whose activities predictably attracted the attention of a sizable portion of the public. [Mrs.] Firestone's appearances in the press were [frequent] enough to warrant her subscribing to a press-clipping service. . . . Mr. and Mrs. Firestone's "marital difficulties [were] well-known," and the lawsuit became "a veritable cause celebre in social circles across the country." The 17-month trial and related events attracted national news coverage, and elicited no fewer than [88] articles in [three local newspapers]. Far from shunning the publicity, Mrs. Firestone held several press conferences in the course of the proceedings. [These] facts [warrant] the conclusion that Mary Alice Firestone was a "public figure" for purposes of reports on the judicial proceedings she initiated. . . . If these actions [fail] to establish [that she] "voluntarily exposed (herself) to increased risk of injury from defamatory falsehood," surely they are sufficient to entitle the press to act on the assumption that she did. . . .

Do you agree with the majority or with Justice Marshall?

5. *Public Figures — Private Lives.* There has been much debate about whether a different and lower standard should apply to allegations regarding the private life of a public official or public figure. Suppose, for example, a newspaper alleges that a politician has engaged in an adulterous affair. Should the *Sullivan* actual malice standard apply to the allegation, or should some lower standard (the *Gertz* or *Dun & Bradstreet* standard) apply? *See* Monitor Patriot Co. v. Roy, 401 U.S. 265 (1971).

6. *The Internet and Defamatory Speech.* As the Internet has spawned new forms of communication, defamation principles are being applied in new contexts involving non-media professionals. For example, in a number of instances, individual bloggers have been sued for defamation. *See* Caryn Rousseau, "Bloggers

Learn to Deal with Media Pitfalls: Citizen Journalists Get Training," *The Courier-Journal*, A-6, c. 1-3 (June 15, 2008). While some bloggers are journalists who work for traditional newspapers, others are individuals who choose to comment on social, political, or economic issues. *See id.* Similar issues have arisen regarding websites. *See* David L. Hudson, Jr., *Taming the Gossip Mongers: Websites That Dish Dirt May Seen Get Their Publishers' Hands Muddy*, ABA J. 19 (July 2008).

∼ PROBLEMS ∼

1. *Bloggers and the International Treaty Regulating the Internet*. Should bloggers, as the new "press," receive special protections under the treaty that you are negotiating? Indeed, in light of the *New York Times* "actual malice" standard, would U.S. courts draw a distinction between traditional media (e.g., newspapers, radio, and television) and Internet publications (e.g., blogs)?

2. *More on the International Treaty Regulating the Internet*. Let's think a bit more about the German delegates' demands that the treaty provide specific protections for "human dignity." Do the holdings in *Gertz* and *Dun & Bradstreet* give you more freedom to craft language that, while not totally acceptable to the German delegates, at least gives a nod toward their concerns? Can you agree to include language in the treaty that would leave the German government free to handle defamatory speech in a manner consistent with the German Constitution?

d. Fact versus Opinion

Should a distinction be made between statements of "fact" and statements of "opinion"? Consider the next case.

Milkovich v. Lorain Journal Co.

497 U.S. 1 (1990)

Chief Justice REHNQUIST delivered the opinion of the Court.

Respondent J. Theodore Diadiun authored [a newspaper article that implied] that petitioner Michael Milkovich, [a] high school wrestling coach, lied under oath in a judicial proceeding about an incident involving [his] team which occurred at a wrestling match. Petitioner sued Diadiun and the newspaper for libel. . . .

[Respondents] would have us [recognize First Amendment protection] for defamatory statements which are categorized as "opinion" as opposed to "fact." For this proposition they rely principally on the following dictum from our opinion in *Gertz*: "Under the First Amendment there is no such thing as a false idea. However pernicious an opinion may seem, we depend for its correction not on the conscience of judges and juries but on the competition of other ideas. But there is no constitutional value in false statements of fact."

[W]e do not think this passage [was] intended to create a wholesale [exemption] for anything that might be labeled "opinion." Not only would such an interpretation be contrary to the tenor and context of the passage, but it would also ignore the fact that expressions of "opinion" may often imply an assertion of objective fact. [If] a speaker says, "In my opinion John Jones is a liar," he implies a knowledge of facts which lead to the conclusion that Jones told an untruth. . . .

[W]e think the "'breathing space'" which "'[f]reedoms of expression require in order to survive'" is adequately secured by existing constitutional doctrine without the creation of an artificial dichotomy between "opinion" and fact. [A] statement on matters of public concern must be provable as false before there can be liability under state defamation law, at least [where] a media defendant is involved. Next, [our] cases provide protection for statements that cannot "reasonably [be] interpreted as stating actual facts" about an individual. This provides assurance that public debate will not suffer for lack of "imaginative expression" or the "rhetorical hyperbole" which has traditionally added much to the discourse of our Nation.

[W]here a statement of "opinion" on a matter of public concern reasonably implies false and defamatory facts regarding public figures or officials, those individuals must show that such statements were made with knowledge of their false implications or with reckless disregard of their truth. Similarly, where [a] statement involves a private figure on a matter of public concern, a plaintiff must show that the false connotations were made with some level of fault as required by *Gertz*. [Enhanced] appellate review [provides] assurance that the foregoing determinations will be made [so] as not to "constitute a forbidden intrusion [into] free expression."

[T]he connotation that petitioner committed perjury is sufficiently factual to be susceptible of being proved true or false. A determination whether petitioner lied [can] be made on a core of objective evidence by comparing, inter alia, petitioner's testimony before the OHSAA board with his subsequent testimony before the trial court. . . .

[The] judgment of the Ohio Court of Appeals is reversed, and the case is remanded for further proceedings not inconsistent with this opinion.

Reversed.

Justice BRENNAN, with whom Justice MARSHALL joins, dissenting.

[No] reasonable reader could understand Diadiun to be impliedly asserting — as fact — that Milkovich had perjured himself. Nor could such a reader infer that Diadiun had further information about Milkovich's court testimony on which his belief was based. It is plain from the column that Diadiun did not attend the court hearing. Diadiun also clearly had no detailed second-hand information about what Milkovich had said in court. Instead, what suffices for "detail" and "color" are quotations from the OHSAA hearing — old news compared to the court decision which prompted the column — and a vague quotation from an OHSAA commissioner. Readers could see that Diadiun was focused on the court's reversal of the OHSAA's decision and was angrily supposing what must have led to it.

Even the insinuation that Milkovich had repeated, in court, a more plausible version of the misrepresentations he had made at the OHSAA hearing is preceded by the cautionary term "apparently" — an unmistakable sign that Diadiun did not know what Milkovich had actually said in court. "[C]autionary language or interrogatories of this type put the reader on notice that what is being read is opinion and thus weaken any inference that the author possesses knowledge of damaging, undisclosed [facts]. In a word, when the reasonable reader encounters cautionary language, he tends to 'discount that which follows.'" . . .

Furthermore, the tone and format of the piece notify readers to expect speculation and personal judgment. The tone is pointed, exaggerated, and heavily laden with emotional rhetoric and moral outrage. Diadiun never says [that] Milkovich committed perjury. He says that "[a]nyone who attended the meet [knows] in his heart" that Milkovich lied — obvious hyperbole as Diadiun does not purport to have researched what everyone who attended the meet knows in his heart. [Punishing] such conjecture protects reputation only at the cost of expunging a genuinely useful mechanism for public debate. "In a society which takes seriously the principle that government rests upon the consent of the governed, freedom of the press must be the most cherished tenet."

Note: "Statements of Fact" and "Hyperbole"

Within the defamation continuum, there has been considerable litigation regarding whether certain labels can be regarded as defamatory, in the sense that they involve false assertions of fact, or whether (perhaps) they involve just "hyperbole." In Buckley v. Littell, 539 F.2d 882, 895 (2d Cir. 1976), *cert. denied*, 429 U.S. 1062 (1977), the court held that the use of the term *fascist* could not "be regarded as [a] statement of fact [because] of the tremendous imprecision of the meaning and usage of [this] term." In Henderson v. Times Mirror Co., 669 F. Supp. 356 (D. Colo. 1987), in a statement to newspaper reporters, the defendant referred to the plaintiff as a "sleaze-bag agent" who "slimed up from the bayou." The plaintiff, an agent for professional football players, sued, naming as defendants a news editor and two newspaper companies whose papers published the defendant's remarks. The Court held that the statements constituted just hyperbole.

∼ PROBLEM: ALLEGATIONS OF "BLACKMAIL" ∼

Is it defamatory to suggest that someone engaged in "blackmail"? The plaintiff, a developer, negotiated with the Greenbelt City Council to obtain zoning variances that would allow him to construct high-density housing on his land. At the same time, the city was seeking to acquire another one of the plaintiff's tracts of land in order to construct a new high school. Extensive litigation concerning the acquisition of the school site seemed imminent, and the negotiations provided both parties considerable bargaining leverage. The negotiations created much controversy at tumultuous city council meetings. The meetings were reported in a local newspaper, which stated that some people at the public meetings had characterized the plaintiff's negotiating position as "blackmail." The word appeared several times, both with and without quotation marks, and was used once as a subheading within a news story. Were the remarks defamatory? How might the defendant argue that they were not defamatory? *See* Greenbelt Cooperative Publishing Assn., Inc. v. Bresler, 398 U.S. 6 (1970).

5. *Privacy*

The tort of invasion of privacy was influenced by the landmark article, *The Right of Privacy*, 4 Harv. L. Rev. 193 (1890). In that article, Justice Louis Brandeis and Samuel Warren described the right of "privacy," which they also referred to as "the right to be let alone" and "the right most valued by civilized men." The common law tort of privacy included four separate and distinct actions: 1) appropriation of the plaintiff's name or likeness in commercial advertising; 2) intrusion on the plaintiff's solitude or seclusion or on the plaintiff's private affairs in a way that would be highly offensive to a reasonable person; 3) publication of private facts about the plaintiff's life when disclosure would be highly offensive to a reasonable person and is not a matter of public concern; and 4) a showing of the plaintiff in a false light.

In some instances, the tort action directly conflicts with the right of free speech. For example, Florida Star v. B.J.F., 491 U.S. 524 (1989), involved a Florida statute that made it unlawful to "print, publish, or broadcast [in] any instrument of mass communication" the name of the victim of a sexual offense. Under the statute, the *Florida Star* was held civilly liable for publishing the name of a rape victim, which it had obtained from a publicly released police report. The Court struck down the law as unconstitutional: "[I]f a newspaper lawfully obtains truthful information about a matter of public significance then state officials may not constitutionally punish publication of the information, absent a need to further a state interest of the highest order." The Court concluded that the interest in shielding the rape victim (which the Court suggested might be an interest of the "highest order") was insufficient given that the name was already in the public domain.

Time, Inc. v. Hill

385 U.S. 374 (1967)

Mr. Justice BRENNAN delivered the opinion of the Court.

The question [is] whether appellant, publisher of *Life* magazine, was denied constitutional protections of speech and press by [an award of] damages on allegations that *Life* falsely reported that a new play portrayed an experience suffered by appellee and his family.

The article appeared in *Life* in February 1955. It was entitled "'True Crime Inspires Tense Play,' with the subtitle, 'The ordeal of a family trapped by convicts gives Broadway a new thriller, *The Desperate Hours*.'" The text of the article reads as follows:

> "Three years ago Americans all over the country read about the desperate ordeal of the James Hill family, who were held prisoners in their home outside Philadelphia by three escaped convicts. Later they read about it in Joseph Hayes's novel, *The Desperate Hours*, inspired by the family's experience. Now they can see the story re-enacted in Hayes's Broadway play based on the book, and next year will see it in his movie, which has been filmed but is being held up until the play has a chance to pay off.
>
> "The play, directed by Robert Montgomery and expertly acted, is a heart-stopping account of how a family rose to heroism in a crisis. LIFE photographed the play during its Philadelphia tryout, transported some of the actors to the actual house where the Hills were besieged. On the next page scenes from the play are re-enacted on the site of the crime."
>
> The pictures on the ensuing two pages included an enactment of the son being "roughed up" by one of the convicts, entitled "brutish convict," a picture of the daughter biting the hand of a convict to make him drop a gun, entitled "daring daughter," and one of the father throwing his gun through the door after a "brave try" to save his family is foiled.

The James Hill referred to in the article [is] appellee. He and his wife and five children involuntarily became the subjects of a front-page news story after being held hostage by three escaped convicts in their suburban, Whitemarsh, Pennsylvania, home for 19 hours. . . . The family was released unharmed. In an interview with newsmen after the convicts departed, appellee stressed that the convicts had treated the family courteously, had not molested them, and had not been at all violent. The convicts were thereafter apprehended in a widely publicized encounter with the police which resulted in the killing of two of the convicts. Shortly thereafter the family moved to Connecticut. The appellee discouraged all efforts to keep them in the public spotlight through magazine articles or appearances on television.

[A year later,] Joseph Hayes' novel, *The Desperate Hours*, was published. The story depicted the experience of a family of four held hostage by three escaped convicts in the family's suburban home. But, unlike Hill's experience, the family of the story suffer violence at the hands of the convicts; the father and son are beaten and the daughter subjected to a verbal sexual insult. . . . The book was made into a play [and] it is *Life*'s article about the play which is the subject of appellee's action. The complaint sought damages under [state law] on allegations that the *Life* article was intended to, and did, give the impression that the play mirrored the Hill family's experience, which, to the knowledge of defendant "[was] false and untrue." Appellant's defense was that the article was "a subject of legitimate news interest," "a subject of general interest and of value and concern to the public" at the time of publication, and that it was "published in good faith without any malice whatsoever. . . ."

The jury awarded appellee $50,000 compensatory and $25,000 punitive damages. On appeal the Appellate Division of the Supreme Court ordered a new trial as to damages but sustained the jury verdict of liability. The court said as to liability: "Although the play was fictionalized, *Life*'s article portrayed it as a reenactment of the Hills' experience. It is an inescapable conclusion that this was done to advertise and attract further attention to the play, and to increase present and future magazine circulation as well. It is evident that the article cannot be characterized as a mere dissemination of news, nor even an effort to supply legitimate newsworthy information in which the public had, or might have a proper interest." At the new trial on damages, a jury was waived and the court awarded $30,000 compensatory damages without punitive damages.

[The] guarantees for speech and press are not the preserve of political expression or comment upon public affairs, essential as those are to healthy government. One need only pick up any newspaper or magazine to comprehend the vast range of published matter which exposes persons to public view, both private citizens and public officials. Exposure of the self to others in varying degrees is a concomitant of life in a civilized community. The risk of this exposure is an essential incident of life in a society which places a primary value on freedom of speech and of press. "Freedom of discussion, if it would fulfill its historic function in this nation, must embrace all issues about which information is needed or appropriate to enable the members of society to cope with the exigencies of their period." [W]e have no doubt that the subject of the *Life* article, the opening of a new play linked to an actual incident, is a matter of public interest. [Erroneous] statement is no less inevitable in such a case than in the case of comment upon public affairs, and in both, if innocent or merely negligent, [it] must be protected if [the] "freedoms of expression are to have the 'breathing space' that they 'need [to] survive.'" [We] create a grave risk of serious impairment of the indispensable service of a free press in a free society if we saddle the press with the impossible burden of verifying to a certainty the facts associated in news articles with a person's name, picture or portrait, particularly as related to nondefamatory matter. Even negligence would be a most elusive standard, especially when the content of the speech itself affords no warning of prospective harm to another through falsity. A negligence test would place on the press the intolerable burden of guessing how a jury might assess the reasonableness of steps taken by it to verify the accuracy of every reference to a name, picture or portrait.

In this context, sanctions against either innocent or negligent misstatement would present a grave hazard of discouraging the press from exercising the constitutional guarantees. Those guarantees are not for the benefit of the press so much as for the benefit of all of us. A broadly defined freedom of the press assures the maintenance of our political system and an open society. Fear of large verdicts in damage suits for innocent or merely negligent misstatement, even fear of the expense involved in their defense, must inevitably cause publishers to "steer . . . wider of the unlawful zone," and thus "create the danger that the legitimate utterance will be penalized." But the constitutional guarantees can tolerate sanctions against calculated falsehood without significant impairment of their essential function. We held in *New York Times* that calculated falsehood enjoyed no immunity in the case of alleged defamation of a public official concerning his official conduct. Similarly, calculated falsehood should enjoy no immunity in the situation here presented [us].

[We] find applicable here the standard of knowing or reckless falsehood. . . . This is neither a libel action by a private individual nor a statutory action by a public official. Therefore, although the First Amendment principles pronounced in *New York Times* guide our conclusion, we reach that conclusion only by applying these principles in this discrete context. . . . Were this a libel action, the distinction which has been suggested between the relative opportunities of the public official and the private individual to rebut defamatory charges might be germane. And the additional state interest in the protection of the individual against damage to his reputation would be involved. Moreover, a different test might be required in a statutory action by a public official, as opposed to a libel action by a public official or a statutory action by a private individual. Different considerations might arise concerning the degree of "waiver" of the protection the State might afford. But the question whether the same standard should be applicable both to persons voluntarily and involuntarily thrust into the public limelight is not here before us.

Turning to the facts of the present case, the proofs reasonably would support either a jury finding of innocent or merely negligent misstatement by *Life,* or a finding that *Life* portrayed the play as a reenactment of the Hill family's experience reckless of the truth or with actual knowledge that the portrayal was [false]. We do not think, however, that the instructions confined the jury to a verdict of liability based on a finding that the statements in the article were made with knowledge of their falsity or in reckless disregard of the [truth].

[The] judgment of the Court of Appeals is set aside and the case is remanded for further proceedings not inconsistent with this opinion.

It is so ordered.

Notes and Questions

1. *The Rape Victim.* In Cox Broadcasting Corporation v. Cohn, 420 U.S. 469 (1975), the plaintiff sought damages on privacy grounds for a broadcast that revealed the name of his daughter (identifying her as a dead rape victim) during the news coverage of the trial of the alleged perpetrators of the crime. The television reporter obtained the daughter's name from official court documents, which were open to public inspection. The Court held that the First Amendment barred recovery against the broadcaster under such circumstances, but left open the question whether tort liability could be allowed if a name were obtained from other unofficial sources.

2. *Can an Injunction Issue Against an Extremely Aggressive Paparazzi?* Galella v. Onassis, 353 F. Supp. 196 (S.D.N.Y. 1972), involved former First Lady Jacqueline Onassis's suit against a freelance "paparazzi" photographer (Donald Galella) for, among other things, invasion of privacy. In an effort to produce interesting pictures of Onassis and her children, Galella engaged in conduct that was extremely aggressive in that he "tried to frighten" ("jumping," "lunging," "leaping," "rushing out," "bumping," "scuffling," "blocking" Onassis and her children); made "offensive mouthings" (making "grunts," "yells," "strange sounds," and calls to Onassis); created "bogus events" (hiring a costumed Santa to try to force himself close to the defendant); engaged in "self-aggrandizement" (conniving to have himself photographed with Onassis and claiming an intimate knowledge of her

every move); sought a "payoff" in exchange for suppressing his story; and engaged in "incessant surveillance" (threatening that he would follow her hour after hour wherever she goes) and "secret agent" tactics (hiding behind restaurant coat racks, sneaking into beauty parlors, donning "disguises," hiding in bushes and theater boxes, intruding into school buildings, bribing doormen, and romancing maids). The *Gallela* court held that the photographer's conduct was not protected by the First Amendment and held that Onassis had a valid claim for privacy tort liability as well as for the torts of infliction of emotional distress, assault, battery, and harassment. In addition, the court granted injunctive relief to Onassis. While acknowledging that she and her children were "the object of legitimate public interest," the court emphasized that the suit did not relate to the actions of a news photographer, a news reporter, or a photojournalist who endeavors to obtain information to do a story about them. The court accepted the photographer's characterization of himself as the world's only "American paparazzi," and concluded that his actions were "unnerving and frightening" and that his tactics caused severe emotional distress for Onassis and her children, especially since their experience with assassinations gave them a "very special fear of startling movements, violent activity, crowds and other hostile behavior." When the photographer argued that there are no limits to First Amendment protection of "newsgathering activity," the court rejected this position, relying on decisions that limit press access to courthouses and trials. The court analogized the plaintiff's suit to the actionable invasion of privacy in another case caused by *Life* magazine photographers who secretly took photographs and recorded conversations inside a person's house with a hidden camera and radio transmitter.

3. *Private Individuals.* In Gertz v. Robert Welch, Inc., 418 U.S. 323 (1974), the Court distinguished between public officials and public figures, on the one hand, and private individuals, on the other, and held that lesser liability standards should apply in *defamation* cases involving private individuals. Does *Gertz* affect *Hill*'s holding so that a lower standard (than the actual malice standard) applies in privacy cases involving private individuals? If a distinction is made between private individuals and public officials or public figures, how should the Hills be treated? Did they become "involuntary public figures" by the extensive news reporting about their ordeal?

4. *Stealing the Show.* A performer's act involved him serving a "human cannonball." Although the plaintiff conceded that the press could report his appearance at the fair where he was performing his act, and could both describe his act and comment on it, he sued when a television station filmed his entire act in a 15-second film clip and displayed it on the nightly news. He claimed that this involved an "appropriation of his professional property" that was protected by the state tort law right of publicity, and he sought compensatory damages. In Zacchini v. Scripps-Howard Broadcasting Co., 433 U.S. 562 (1977), the Court sided with the entertainer. The Court emphasized that the state interest in creating a publicity action for a performer like Zacchini is to "protect the proprietary interest of an individual in his art," in order to encourage the production of entertainment. The Court noted that performers who bring publicity suits usually have no objection to publicity as long as they receive

commercial benefit from their performances. The Court held that the First Amendment did not permit the broadcast without compensation of "a performer's entire act without his consent," because such publicity is no different from the impermissible broadcast of "a copyrighted dramatic work without liability to the copyright owner."

∽ PROBLEMS ∽

1. *The Disc Jockey and the Anchor.* A radio talk show host dates a female anchor of a morning television show. After the two break up, the talk show host talks about the female anchor on his show. In particular, he mentions that the anchor has had breast implants and gives some really personal details (e.g., how she grooms her pubic hair). Because the allegations are true, the anchor cannot recover for defamation. Does she have a claim for invasion of privacy? Of the common law theories, which apply? How should the First Amendment apply to that theory or theories?

2. *The* Galella *Injunction.* After the court concluded that Onassis was entitled to injunctive relief against Galella, how should the injunction have been framed? For example, would it have been appropriate for the judge to prohibit Galella from reporting on Onassis as well as from taking her picture? Or was a more limited injunction more appropriate?

3. *Dealing with Aggressive Paparazzi.* Suppose that you are the legal adviser to the Los Angeles City Council. In recent years, there have been a number of incidents between famous personalities and aggressive paparazzi (journalists who follow personalities around hoping to snap interesting pictures). Concerns have been raised regarding the fact that paparazzi travel in packs, run red lights, and make unsafe U-turns. In addition, because of their aggressiveness and their willingness to place themselves in the way of personalities who are trying to avoid them, paparazzi have sometimes suffered broken toes when cars run over them. A good deal of police work is devoted to dealing with the paparazzi. *See* Jennifer Steinhauer, "Los Angeles Proposes Restraints on Paparazzi," *New York Times*, A-12, c. 1-6 (Aug. 1, 2008). So, the city counsel has asked you for advice about how it might limit or control the paparazzi. Some have proposed that the paparazzi be licensed. Others have suggested the creation of "comfort zones" around personalities in which the paparazzi may not intrude. Is either of these suggestions constitutional? What other steps might the city counsel take?

4. *Privacy Interests and the International Treaty Regulating the Internet.* Many European governments provide a much higher level of protection for privacy interests and are willing to proscribe speech (to a greater or lesser extent) in pursuit of those interests. In some instances, they impose privacy protections under their general protections for "human dignity." Suppose that some European delegates push for the treaty to contain very specific protections designed to protect individual privacy as part of human dignity. Can you agree to such provisions? What language might you be able to agree to in the proposed treaty?

5. *Copyright Interests and the International Treaty Regulating the Internet.* Suppose that artists and performers are clamoring for protections against what they regard as "Internet piracy" (the practice of some individuals to steal the art and performances of others). They are seeking protections under the new treaty regulating the Internet. Although these copyright protections can be easily enforced in the United States, there are many countries where copyright enforcement is lax or nonexistent. You have been asked whether it is possible to incorporate language in the treaty protecting copyright interests on the Internet and giving copyright holders the ability to enforce those interests in foreign countries. Can you accommodate this interest? What language would you use?

6. *Paparazzi and the International Treaty Regulating the Internet.* A number of famous people have approached you about whether it might be possible to use the treaty to constrain the actions of paparazzi by prohibiting or limiting (in some fashion) their publication of pictures or information on the Internet. European delegates, who are concerned about the more aggressive paparazzi found in Europe, are particularly desirous of including a provision of this type. Various suggestions have been made to you about how this might be done. For example, some have suggested that (as a condition of using the Internet) paparazzi should be forced to "register" and to "certify" that they are using "nonaggressive methods" and that they are giving due deference to "privacy interests." In addition, a proposal has been made to allow governments to ban extremely aggressive paparazzi from publishing on the Internet. Can you agree to either of these proposals? If not, what other language might be acceptable?

6. Emotional Distress

Should the tort of intentional infliction of mental and emotional distress be treated differently, from a constitutional free speech perspective, than the torts of defamation or privacy? Consider the following case.

Hustler Magazine v. Falwell

485 U.S. 46 (1988)

Chief Justice REHNQUIST delivered the opinion of the Court.

Respondent Jerry Falwell [is] a nationally known minister who has been active as a commentator on politics and public affairs. . . . The inside front cover of the November 1983 issue of *Hustler* magazine featured a "parody" of an advertisement for Campari Liqueur that contained the name and picture of respondent and was entitled "Jerry Falwell talks about his first time." This parody was modeled after actual Campari ads that included interviews with various celebrities about their "first times." Although it was apparent by the end of each interview that this meant the first time they sampled Campari, the ads clearly played on the sexual double entendre of the general subject of "first times." Copying the form and layout of these Campari ads, *Hustler*'s editors chose respondent as the featured celebrity and drafted an alleged "interview" with him in which he states that his "first time" was during a drunken incestuous rendezvous with his mother in an outhouse. The *Hustler* parody portrays respondent and his mother as drunk and immoral, and suggests that respondent is a hypocrite who preaches only when he is drunk. In small print at the bottom of the page, the ad contains the disclaimer, "ad parody — not to be taken seriously." The magazine's table of contents also lists the ad as "Fiction; Ad and Personality Parody."

[Falwell brought suit for intentional infliction of mental distress, and a jury awarded him] $100,000 in compensatory damages, as well as $50,000 each in punitive damages from petitioners. . . . [The verdict was affirmed on appeal. W]e granted certiorari.

[We] must decide whether a public figure may recover damages for emotional harm caused by the publication of an ad parody offensive to him, and doubtless gross and repugnant in the eyes of most. Respondent would have us find that a State's interest in protecting public figures from emotional distress is sufficient to deny First Amendment protection to speech that is patently offensive and is intended to inflict emotional injury, even when that speech could not reasonably have been interpreted as stating actual facts about the public figure involved. This we decline to do.

At the heart of the First Amendment is the recognition of the fundamental importance of the free flow of ideas and opinions on matters of public interest and concern. . . . The sort of robust political debate encouraged by the First Amendment is bound to produce speech that is critical of those who hold public office or those public figures who are "intimately involved in the resolution of important public questions or, by reason of their fame, shape events in areas of concern to society at large." . . .

Of course, this does not mean that any speech about a public figure is immune from sanction in the form of damages. Since New York Times Co. v. Sullivan, 376 U.S. 254 (1964), we have consistently ruled that a public figure may hold a speaker liable for [a] defamatory falsehood [if] the statement was made "with knowledge that it was false or with reckless disregard of whether it was false or not." [Respondent argues] that a different standard should apply in this case because here the State seeks to prevent [the] severe emotional distress suffered by the person who is the subject of an offensive publication. In respondent's view, [so] long as the utterance was intended to inflict emotional distress, was outrageous, and did in fact inflict serious emotional distress, it is of no constitutional import whether the statement was a fact or an opinion, or whether it was true or false. It is the intent to cause injury that is the gravamen of the tort, and the State's interest in preventing emotional harm simply outweighs whatever interest a speaker may have in speech of this type.

Generally speaking the law does not regard the intent to inflict emotional distress as one which should receive much solicitude, [and] most if not all jurisdictions have chosen to make it civilly culpable where the conduct in question is sufficiently "outrageous." But in the world of debate about public affairs, many things done with motives that are less than admirable are protected by the First Amendment. In Garrison v. Louisiana, 379 U.S. 64 (1964), we held that even when a speaker or writer is motivated by hatred or ill-will his expression was protected by the First Amendment: "Debate on public issues will not be uninhibited if the speaker must run the risk that it will be proved in court that he spoke out of hatred; even if he did speak out of hatred, utterances honestly believed contribute to the free interchange of ideas and the ascertainment of truth." Thus while such a bad motive may be deemed controlling for purposes of tort liability in other areas of the law, we think the First Amendment prohibits such a result in the area of public debate about public figures.

Were we to hold otherwise, there can be little doubt that political cartoonists and satirists would be subjected to damages awards without any showing that their work falsely defamed its subject. . . . The appeal of the political cartoon or caricature is often based on exploitation of unfortunate physical traits or politically embarrassing events—an exploitation often calculated to injure the feelings of the subject of the portrayal. The art of the cartoonist is often not reasoned or evenhanded, but slashing and one-sided. One cartoonist expressed the nature of the art in these words: "The political cartoon is a weapon of attack, of scorn and ridicule and satire; it is least effective when it tries to pat some politician on the back. It is usually as welcome as a bee sting and is always controversial in some quarters." Long, "The Political Cartoon: Journalism's Strongest Weapon," *The Quill* 56, 57 (Nov. 1962). Several famous examples of this type of intentionally injurious speech were drawn by Thomas Nast, probably the greatest American cartoonist to date, who was associated for many years during the post-Civil War era with *Harper's Weekly*. In the pages of that publication Nast conducted a graphic vendetta against William M. "Boss" Tweed and his corrupt associates in New York City's "Tweed Ring." It has been described by one historian of the subject as "a sustained attack which in its passion and effectiveness stands alone in the history of American graphic art." Morton Keller, *The Art and Politics of Thomas Nast* 177 (Oxford 1968). . . .

Despite their sometimes caustic nature, from the early cartoon portraying George Washington as an ass down to the present day, graphic depictions and satirical cartoons have played a prominent role in public and political debate. Nast's castigation of the Tweed Ring, Walt McDougall's characterization of Presidential candidate James G. Blaine's banquet with the millionaires at Delmonico's as "The Royal Feast of Belshazzar," and numerous other efforts have undoubtedly had an effect on the course and outcome of contemporaneous debate. . . . [O]ur political discourse would have been considerably poorer without them.

Respondent contends [that] the caricature in question here was so "outrageous" as to distinguish it from more traditional political cartoons. There is no doubt that the caricature of respondent and his mother published in *Hustler* is at best a distant cousin of the political cartoons described above, and a rather poor relation at that. If it were possible by laying down a principled standard to separate the one from the other, public discourse would probably suffer little or no harm. But we doubt that there is any such standard, and we are quite sure that the pejorative description "outrageous" does not supply one. "Outrageousness" in the area of political and social discourse has an inherent subjectiveness about it which would allow a jury to impose liability on the basis of the jurors' tastes or views, or perhaps on the basis of their dislike of a particular expression. An "outrageousness" standard thus runs afoul of our longstanding refusal to allow damages to be awarded because the speech in question may have an adverse emotional impact on the audience. . . .

Admittedly, these oft-repeated First Amendment principles, like other principles, are subject to limitations. We recognized in FCC v. Pacifica Foundation that speech that is vulgar, offensive, and shocking is not entitled to absolute constitutional protection under all circumstances. In *Chaplinsky*, we held that a State could lawfully punish an individual for the use of insulting fighting words — those which by their very utterance inflict injury or tend to incite an immediate breach of the peace. These limitations are but recognition [that] this Court has long recognized that not all speech is of equal First Amendment importance. But the sort of expression involved in this case does not seem to us to be governed by any exception to the general First Amendment principles stated above.

We conclude that public figures and public officials may not recover for the tort of intentional infliction of emotional distress by reason of publications such as the one here [without] showing [that] the publication contains a false statement of fact which was made with "actual malice," i.e., with knowledge that the statement was false or with reckless disregard as to whether or not it was true. This is not merely a "blind application" of the *New York Times* standard, it reflects our considered judgment that such a standard is necessary to give adequate "breathing space" to the freedoms protected by the First Amendment.

[It is clear that] Falwell is a "public figure."[8] The jury found against respondent on his libel claim [because the] ad parody could not "reasonably be understood as describing actual facts. . . ." [F]or reasons heretofore stated this claim cannot, consistently with the First Amendment, form a basis for the award of damages when the conduct in question is the publication of a caricature such as the ad parody involved here. The judgment of the Court of Appeals is accordingly

Reversed.

∾ PROBLEMS ∾

1. Falwell *and the Justifications for Protecting Speech.* Did the speech involved in *Falwell* meet any of the justifications for protecting speech presented earlier in the chapter? In other words, did it provide a safety valve, did it promote self-fulfillment or the marketplace of ideas, or was it related to the democratic process?

2. *Public Figures versus Private Individuals.* As previously noted, in the Court's defamation decisions, particularly *Gertz* and *Dun & Bradstreet*, the Court has drawn a distinction between public officials and public figures, on the one hand,

---

8. [He] is the host of a nationally syndicated television show and was the founder and president of a political organization formerly known as the Moral Majority. He is also the founder of Liberty University in Lynchburg, Virginia, and is the author of several books and publications.

and private individuals, on the other. The states are free to provide fewer protections to those who defame private individuals. Should a similar distinction apply to the tort of intentional infliction of mental and emotional distress? If such a distinction is to be made, how would it apply? In the *Falwell* case, suppose that the suit had been brought by Falwell's mother rather than Falwell, and also suppose that she is very private and shuns the spotlight. Should she be able to recover?

3. *Should First Amendment Protections Apply to Only "High-Minded Discourse"?* Suppose that *Falwell* had asserted a dividing line, between constitutionally protected and unprotected speech, that focuses on whether the defendant's action involves "high-minded" discourse. Do you agree? Should it matter that *Hustler* parodies Falwell in a lewd and disgusting manner as opposed to a "high-minded" manner? *See* Dworkin v. Hustler Magazine, Inc., 867 F.2d 1188 (9th Cir. 1988).

4. *More on the International Treaty Regulating the Internet.* The German Basic Law provides very specific protections for "personal dignity," and French law provides very specific prohibitions against "degrading human dignity." Suppose that the German and French delegates to the convention push hard for language that bans "outrageous speech" designed to damage personal dignity or degrade human dignity. Can you accept such language? Is there language that you might be able to accept that would be acceptable to both the German and French delegates?

7. Obscenity

Chaplinsky named "obscenity" as one of those categories of speech the prohibition of which had "never been thought to raise any Constitutional problem." Although later cases affirmed the "unprotected" status of "obscene" speech, the Court struggled to define the term *obscenity* and to distinguish it from other sex-related speech.

a. Defining Obscenity

Roth v. United States   Alberts v. California
354 U.S. 476 (1957)

Mr. Justice BRENNAN delivered the opinion of the Court.

[Samuel Roth, a publisher of] books, photographs and magazines [was] convicted of mailing obscene circulars and advertising, and an obscene book. [David Alberts] conducted a mail-order business from Los Angeles [and] was convicted [of] keeping for sale obscene and indecent books, and with writing, composing and publishing an obscene advertisement of [them].

[T]his Court has always assumed that obscenity is not protected by the freedoms of speech and press. . . . 10 of the 14 States which by 1792 had ratified the Constitution [gave] no absolute protection for every utterance. . . . As early as 1712, Massachusetts made it criminal to publish "any filthy, obscene, or profane song, pamphlet, libel or mock sermon" in imitation or mimicking of religious services. . . . In light of this history, it is apparent that the unconditional phrasing of the First Amendment was not intended to protect every utterance. . . . The protection given speech and press was fashioned to assure unfettered interchange of ideas for the bringing about of political and social changes desired by the people. [All] ideas having even the slightest redeeming social importance — unorthodox ideas, controversial ideas, even ideas hateful to the prevailing climate of opinion — have the full protection of the guaranties, unless excludable because they encroach upon the limited area of more important interests. But implicit in the history of the First Amendment is the rejection of obscenity as utterly without redeeming social importance. This rejection [is] mirrored in the universal judgment that obscenity should be restrained, reflected in the international agreement of over 50 nations, in the obscenity laws of all of the 48 States, and in the 20 obscenity laws enacted by the Congress from 1842 to 1956. [I]n Chaplinsky v. New Hampshire, 315 U.S. 568[, we recognized that] obscene speech is "no essential part of any exposition of ideas, and are of such slight social value as a step to truth that any benefit that may be derived from them is clearly outweighed by the social interest in order and morality."] We hold that obscenity is not within the area of constitutionally protected speech or press.

It [is] insisted that the constitutional guaranties are violated because convictions may be had without proof either that obscene material will perceptibly create a clear and present danger of antisocial conduct, or will probably induce its recipients to such conduct. [I]n light of our holding that obscenity is not protected speech, [it] is unnecessary [to] consider the issues behind the phrase "clear and present [danger]."

However, sex and obscenity are not synonymous. Obscene material is material which deals with sex in a manner appealing to prurient interest. [The A.L.I. *Model Penal Code* §207.10(2) (Tent. Draft No. 6, 1957) defines obscenity in the following way: "[A] thing is obscene if, considered as a whole, its predominant appeal is to prurient interest, i.e., a shameful or morbid interest in nudity, sex or excretion, and if it goes substantially beyond customary limits of candor in description or representation of such [matters]."] The portrayal of sex, e.g., in art, literature and scientific works, is not itself sufficient reason to deny material the constitutional protection of freedom of speech and press. Sex, a great and mysterious motive force in human life, has indisputably been a subject of absorbing interest to mankind through the ages; it is one of the vital problems of human interest and public concern.

[The] fundamental freedoms of speech and press have contributed greatly to the development and well-being of our free society and are indispensable to its continued growth. Ceaseless vigilance is the watchword to prevent their erosion by Congress or by the States. . . . It is therefore vital that the standards for judging obscenity safeguard the protection of freedom of speech and press for material which does not treat sex in a manner appealing to prurient interest.

The early leading standard of obscenity allowed material to be judged merely by the effect of an isolated excerpt upon particularly susceptible persons. Regina v. Hicklin, (1868) L.R. 3 Q.B. 360. Some American courts adopted this standard but later decisions have rejected it and [asked] whether to the average person, applying contemporary community standards, the dominant theme of the material taken as a whole appeals to prurient interest. The *Hicklin* test, judging obscenity by the effect of isolated passages upon the most susceptible persons, might well encompass material legitimately treating with sex, and so it must be rejected as unconstitutionally restrictive of the freedoms of speech and press. On the other hand, the substituted standard provides safeguards adequate to withstand the charge of constitutional infirmity.

[It] is argued that the statutes do not provide reasonably ascertainable standards of guilt and therefore violate the constitutional requirements of due process. The federal obscenity statute makes punishable the mailing of material that is "obscene, lewd, lascivious, or filthy [or] other publication of an indecent character." The California statute makes punishable, *inter alia*, the keeping for sale or advertising material that is "obscene or indecent." [Many] decisions have recognized that these terms of obscenity statutes are not precise. This Court, however, has consistently held that lack of precision is not itself offensive to the requirements of due process. [T]he Constitution does not require impossible standards; all that is required is that the language "conveys sufficiently definite warning as to the proscribed conduct when measured by common understanding and practices." United States v. Petrillo, 332 U.S. 1. These words [give] adequate warning of the conduct proscribed and mark "boundaries sufficiently distinct for judges and juries fairly to administer the [law]. That there may be marginal cases in which it is difficult to determine the side of the line on which a particular fact situation falls is no sufficient reason to hold the language too ambiguous to define a criminal [offense]."

In summary, then, we hold that these statutes, applied according to the proper standard for judging obscenity, do not offend constitutional safeguards against convictions based upon protected material, or fail to give mean in acting adequate notice of what is prohibited.

[The] judgments are affirmed.

Mr. Chief Justice WARREN, concurring in the result.

[The] line dividing the salacious or pornographic from literature or science is not straight and unwavering. [T]he same object may have a different impact, varying according to the part of the community it reached. [The] conduct of the defendant is the central issue. . . . The nature of the materials is, of course, relevant as an attribute of the defendant's conduct, but the materials are thus placed in context from which they draw color and character. A wholly different result might be reached in a different setting.

[Under] the California law, the prohibited activity must be done "wilfully and lewdly." The federal statute limits the crime to acts done "knowingly." In his charge to the jury, the district judge stated that the matter must be "calculated" to corrupt or debauch. The defendants in both these cases were engaged in the business of purveying textual or graphic matter openly advertised to appeal to the erotic interest of their customers. They were plainly engaged in the commercial exploitation of the morbid and shameful craving for materials with prurient effect. [T]he State and Federal Governments can constitutionally punish such conduct. . . .

Mr. Justice Harlan, concurring in the result in [*Alberts*], and dissenting in [*Roth*].

[Many] juries might find that Joyce's "Ulysses" or Bocaccio's "Decameron" was obscene, and yet the conviction of a defendant for selling either book would raise [the] gravest constitutional problems, for no such verdict could convince me, without more, that these books are "utterly without redeeming social importance." . . .

[I] concur in the judgment [in *Alberts*]. [We can] inquire only whether the state action so subverts the fundamental liberties implicit in the Due Process Clause that it cannot be sustained as a rational exercise of power. [T]he state legislature has made the judgment that printed words can "deprave or corrupt" the reader — that words can incite to anti-social or immoral action. [There] is a large school of thought, particularly in the scientific community, which denies any causal connection between the reading of pornography and immorality, crime, or delinquency. [I]t is not our function to decide this question. That function belongs to the state legislature. . . . The State can reasonably draw the inference that over a long period of time the indiscriminate dissemination of materials, the essential character of which is to degrade sex, will have an eroding effect on moral standards. And the State has a legitimate interest in protecting the privacy of the home against invasion of unsolicited obscenity. [T]his Court should be slow to interfere with state legislation calculated to protect that morality. [A]ppellant's conviction must be affirmed.

[I] dissent [in] *Roth*. . . . The same book which is freely read in one State might be classed as obscene in another. [Justice Harlan noted that Edmund Wilson's "Memoirs of Hecate County" was found obscene in New York, *see* Doubleday v. New York, 354 U.S. 476 (1957); but a bookseller indicted for selling the same book was acquitted in California. "God's Little Acre" was held to be obscene in Massachusetts, not obscene in New York and Pennsylvania.] [N]o overwhelming danger to our freedom to experiment and to gratify our tastes in literature is likely to result from the suppression of a borderline book in one of the States, so long [as] other States are free to experiment with the same or bolder books. . . . Quite a different situation is presented, however, where the Federal Government imposes the ban. . . . The fact that [no] person in the United States should be allowed to do so seems to me to be intolerable, and violative of both the letter and spirit of the First Amendment.

[Roth] was convicted under a statute which [makes] it criminal to sell books which "tend to stir sexual impulses and lead to sexually impure thoughts." [M]uch of the great literature of the world could lead to conviction under such a view of the statute. . . . The Federal Government has no business [to] bar the sale of books because they might lead to any kind of "thoughts." [It] is no answer to say [that] obscenity is not protected speech. [T]his statute [defines] obscenity so widely that it encompasses matters which might very well be protected speech. I do not think that the federal statute can be constitutionally construed to reach other [than] "hard-core" pornography. Nor do I think the statute can fairly be read as directed only at persons who are engaged in the business of catering to the prurient minded, even though their wares fall short of hard-core pornography. [S]ince [the] material here involved cannot be said to be hard-core pornography, I would reverse this case with instructions to dismiss the indictment.

Mr. Justice DOUGLAS, with whom Mr. Justice BLACK concurs, dissenting.

[Even] the ill-starred *Dennis* case conceded that speech to be punishable must have some relation to action which could be penalized by government. Dennis v. United States, 341 U.S. 494. This issue cannot be avoided by saying that obscenity is not protected by the First Amendment. . . . The question remains, what is the constitutional test of obscenity? [The] tests by which these convictions were obtained require only the arousing of sexual thoughts. Yet the arousing of sexual thoughts and desires happens every day in normal life in dozens of ways. . . . To allow the State to step in and punish mere speech or publication that the judge or the jury thinks has an undesirable impact on thoughts but that is not shown to be a part of unlawful action is drastically to curtail the First Amendment. [If] we were certain that impurity of sexual thoughts impelled to action, we would be on less dangerous ground in punishing the distributors of this sex literature. But it is by no means clear that obscene literature [is] a significant factor in influencing substantial deviations from the community standards. [The] absence of dependable information [should] put us on the side of protecting society's interest in literature, except and unless it can be said that the particular publication has an impact on action that the government can control. . . . I have the same confidence in the ability of our people to reject noxious literature as I have in their capacity to sort out the true from the false in theology, economics, politics, or any other field.

Notes and Questions

1. *"Patently Offensive" and "Redeeming Social Value."* In the post-*Roth* era, the Court added two new elements to the "prurient interest" test for obscenity: the requirements of "patent offensiveness" and "utterly without redeeming social importance." Jacobellis v. Ohio, 378 U.S. 184 (1964); Manual Enterprises v. Day, 370 U.S. 478 (1962). The latter element was restated as "utterly without redeeming social value" in the famous three-part *Memoirs* test, which captured the votes of only a plurality of the Court: "(a) the dominant theme of the material taken as a whole appeals to a prurient interest in sex; (b) the material is patently offensive because it affronts contemporary community standards relating to the description or representation of sexual matters; and (c) the material is utterly without redeeming social value." *See* Memoirs v. Massachusetts, 383 U.S. 413 (1966). "[In] the absence of a majority view, [the] Court was compelled to embark on the practice of summarily reversing convictions for the dissemination of materials that at least five members of the Court, applying their separate tests, found to be protected by the First Amendment. Redrup v. New York, 386 U.S. 767 (1967). . . . The *Redrup* procedure [cast] us in the role of an unreviewable board of censorship for the 50 States, subjectively judging each piece of material brought before us."

Miller v. California, 413 U.S. 15, 23 n.3 (1973). During the post-*Memoirs* era, Justices Black and Douglas remained committed to their positions in *Roth* and *Alberts* that obscenity is not unprotected. Justices White and Clark objected to the third element of *Memoirs* concerning the utter lack of redeeming social value. Justice Stewart maintained his view that "hard-core pornography" should be unprotected speech, but he could not define it: "I shall not [attempt] further to describe the kinds of material [included] within that shorthand description. [But] I know it when I see [it.]" Jacobellis v. Ohio, U.S. 184, 197 (1964) (Stewart, J., concurring).

2. *Obscenity and the Justifications for Protecting Speech.* Does obscene speech meet any of the justifications for protecting speech presented earlier in this chapter? In other words, does it provide a safety valve, does it promote self-fulfillment or the marketplace of ideas, or is it related to the democratic process? Does the answer to this question depend on the content and purpose of the obscene speech?

3. *More on Defining Obscenity.* After reading *Roth* and the above note discussing *Memoirs*, are you clear about what constitutes "obscenity"? For example, do magazines like *Playboy* and *Penthouse* (which display nude pictures but also include articles about art, literature, and famous people) qualify as "obscene"? If not, what must be shown to establish obscenity?

4. *National or Local Standards?* In *Roth* and *Alberts*, the Court did not explicitly address the issue of whether a national or a state-by-state standard (or other "local" standard) should be used when applying the prurient interest test. Justice Harlan argued for a state-by-state standard, but in Jacobellis v. Ohio, 378 U.S. 184 (1964), the Court endorsed a national standard, declaring that such a standard was implicit in *Roth*, and also endorsed the principle that de novo review of the fact-finding on the legal issue of obscenity would be available in reviewing courts. Does it make sense to use a national versus a local standard? How will the use of one of these standards, as opposed to the other, affect the outcome of a case?

5. *Fanny Hill.* In 1967, a state trial court found that John Cleland's book, *Fanny Hill*, written in around 1750, was obscene. The evidence at trial consisted solely of expert evidence from literature professors and book reviews. One expert concluded that "the book is without literary merit and is obscene, impure, hard core pornography, and is patently offensive." Other critical commentary on the book provides the following observations:

> [Fanny Hill is] nothing but a harlot — a sensualist — exploiting her sexual attractions which she sold for fun, for money, for lodging and keep, for an inheritance, and finally for a husband. If she was curious about life, her curiosity extended only to the pursuit of sexual delight wherever she found it. The book describes nothing in the 'external world' except bawdy houses and debaucheries. As an empiricist, Fanny confines her observations and 'experiments' to sex, with primary attention to depraved, lewd, and deviant practices. [However,] several experts testify that the book [has] merit. For example, one expert testifies that the book represents "social history of interest to anyone who is interested in fiction as a way of understanding society in the past." Another expert's testimony is summarized by the trial court as follows: "[A]lthough many scenes, if translated into the present day language of 'the realistic, naturalistic novel, could be quite offensive' these scenes are not described in such

language. The book contains no dirty words and its language 'functions [to] create a distance, even when the sexual experiences are portrayed.' The response, therefore, is a literary response. The descriptions of depravity are not obscene because 'they are subordinate to an interest which is primarily literary'; Fanny's reaction to the scenes of depravity was 'anger,' 'disgust, horror, (and) indignation.' The book 'belongs to the history of English literature rather than the history of smut.'"

The conviction is affirmed by the state supreme court. What arguments will each side make in the U.S. Supreme Court about whether the judgment as to obscenity should be affirmed?

Miller v. United States

413 U.S. 15 (1973)

Mr. Chief Justice BURGER delivered the opinion of the Court.

[Marvin Miller] conducted a mass mailing campaign to advertise the sale of illustrated books, euphemistically called 'adult' material. Appellant's conviction was specifically based on his conduct in causing five unsolicited advertising brochures to be sent through the mail [to] California. The envelope was opened by [the addressee] and his mother. They had not requested the brochures; they complained to the police. [The Court described the brochures as advertisements for four books "entitled 'Intercourse,' 'Man-Woman,' 'Sex Orgies Illustrated,' and 'An Illustrated History of Pornography'" and a film "entitled 'Marital Intercourse.'" The brochures "primarily consist of pictures and drawings very explicitly depicting men and women in groups of two or more engaging in a variety of sexual activities, with genitals often prominently displayed."]

This case involves the application of a State's criminal obscenity statute to a situation in which sexually explicit materials have been thrust by aggressive sales action upon unwilling recipients who had in no way indicated any desire to receive such materials. [W]e are called on to define the standards which must be used to identify obscene material that a State may regulate without infringing on the First Amendment as applicable to the States through the Fourteenth Amendment. [The Court noted that "the material we are discussing in this case is more accurately defined [in lay terms] as 'pornography' or 'pornographic material,'" and that "[p]ornographic material which is obscene forms a subgroup of all 'obscene' expression," which has "a specific judicial meaning which derives from the *Roth* case." The California statute was amended after *Alberts* to incorporate the MPC definition of prurient interest and the three-part *Memoirs* test; it covered a long list of written materials, and punished the acts of knowingly sending or bringing obscene material into the state for sale or distribution, or knowingly preparing, publishing, printing, exhibiting, or distributing such material.]

[We] acknowledge [the] inherent dangers of undertaking to regulate any form of expression. State statutes designed to regulate obscene materials must be carefully limited. As a result, we now confine the permissible scope of such regulation to works which depict or describe sexual conduct. That conduct must be specifically defined by the applicable state law, as written or authoritatively construed. [The Court noted with approval that the Oregon and Hawaii obscenity statutes are "directed at depiction of defined physical conduct, as opposed to expression," and that other statutory formulations "could be equally valid in this respect."] A state offense must also be limited to works which, taken as a whole, appeal to the prurient interest in sex, which portray sexual conduct in a patently offensive way, and which, taken as a whole, do not have serious literary, artistic, political, or scientific value.

The basic guidelines for the trier of fact must be: (a) whether "the average person, applying contemporary community standards" would find that the work, taken as a whole, appeals to the prurient interest; (b) whether the work depicts or describes, in a patently offensive way, sexual conduct specifically defined by the applicable state law; and (c) whether the work, taken as a whole, lacks serious literary, artistic, political, or scientific value. We do not adopt as a constitutional standard the "utterly without redeeming social value" test [of *Memoirs*]; that concept has never commanded the adherence of more than three Justices at one time. If a state law that regulates obscene material is thus limited, as written or construed, the First Amendment values applicable to the States through the Fourteenth Amendment are adequately protected by the ultimate power of appellate courts to conduct an independent review of constitutional claims when necessary.

We emphasize that it is not our function to propose regulatory schemes for the States. That must await their concrete legislative efforts. It is possible, however, to give a few plain examples of what a state statute could define for regulation under part (b) of the standard announced in this opinion [that is, sexual conduct specifically defined].

(a) Patently offensive representations or descriptions of ultimate sexual acts, normal or perverted, actual or simulated.

(b) Patently offensive representation or descriptions of masturbation, excretory functions, and lewd exhibition of the genitals.

[Sex] and nudity may not be exploited without limit by films or pictures exhibited or sold in places of public accommodation any more than live sex and nudity can be exhibited or sold without limit in such public places. At a minimum, prurient, patently offensive depiction or description of sexual conduct must have serious literary, artistic, political, or scientific value to merit First Amendment protection. For example, medical books for the education of physicians and related personnel necessarily use graphic illustrations and descriptions of human anatomy. In resolving the inevitably sensitive questions of fact and law, we must continue to rely on the jury system, accompanied by the safeguards that judges, rules of evidence, presumption of innocence, and other protective features provide, as we do with rape, murder, and a host of other offenses against society and its individual members.

[Under] the holdings announced today, no one will be subject to prosecution for the sale or exposure of obscene materials unless these materials depict or describe patently offensive 'hard core' sexual conduct specifically defined by the regulating state law, as written or construed. We are satisfied that these specific prerequisites will provide fair notice to a dealer in such materials that his public and commercial activities may bring prosecution. If the inability to define regulated materials with ultimate, god-like precision altogether removes the power of the States or the Congress to regulate, then "hard core" pornography may be exposed without limit to the juvenile, the passerby, and the consenting adult [alike]. [T]oday, for the first time since *Roth* was decided in 1957, a majority of this Court has agreed on concrete guidelines to isolate "hard core" pornography from expression protected by the First Amendment. Now we may [attempt] to provide positive guidance to federal and state courts alike.

[Under] a National Constitution, fundamental First Amendment limitations on the powers of the States do not vary from community to community, but this does not mean that there are, or should or can be, fixed, uniform national standards of precisely what appeals to the "prurient interest" or is "patently offensive." These are essentially questions of fact, and our Nation is simply too big and too diverse for this Court to reasonably expect that such standards could be articulated for all 50 States in a single formulation, even assuming the prerequisite consensus exists. When triers of fact are asked to decide whether "the average person, applying contemporary community standards" would consider certain materials "prurient," it would be unrealistic to require that the answer be based on some abstract formulation. The adversary system, with lay jurors as the usual ultimate factfinders in criminal prosecutions, has historically permitted triers of fact to draw on the standards of their community, guided always by limiting instructions on the law. To require a State to structure obscenity proceedings around evidence of a national "community standard" would be an exercise in futility.

[During] the trial, both the prosecution and the defense assumed that the relevant "community standards" in making the factual determination of obscenity were those of the State of California, not some hypothetical standard of the entire United States of America. Defense counsel at trial never objected to the testimony of the State's expert on community standards or to the instructions of the trial judge on "statewide" standards. On appeal [to the state appellate court] appellant for the first time contended that application of state, rather than national, standards violated the First and Fourteenth Amendments.

We conclude that neither the State's alleged failure to offer evidence of "national standards," nor the trial court's charge that the jury consider state community standards, were constitutional errors. Nothing in the First Amendment requires that a jury must consider hypothetical and unascertainable "national standards" when attempting to determine whether certain materials are obscene as a matter of fact. [It] is neither realistic nor constitutionally sound to read the First Amendment as requiring that the people of Maine or Mississippi accept public depiction of conduct found tolerable in Las Vegas, or New York City. People in different States vary in their tastes and attitudes, and this diversity is not to be strangled by the absolutism of imposed uniformity. As the Court [has] made clear[,] the primary concern with requiring a jury to apply the standard of "the average person, applying contemporary community standards" is to be certain that, so far as material is not aimed at a deviant group, it will be judged by its impact on an average person, rather than a particularly susceptible or sensitive person — or indeed a totally insensitive one. We hold that the requirement that the jury evaluate the materials with reference to "contemporary standards of the State of California" serves this protective purpose and is constitutionally adequate.

[T]o equate the free and robust exchange of ideas and political debate with commercial exploitation of obscene material demeans the grand conception of the First Amendment and its high purposes in the historic struggle for freedom. . . . The First Amendment protects works which, taken as a whole, have serious literary, artistic, political, or scientific value, regardless of whether the government or a majority of the people approve of the ideas these works represent. "The protection given speech and press was fashioned to assure unfettered interchange of ideas for the bringing about of political and social changes desired by the people[.]" But the public portrayal of hard-core sexual conduct for its own sake, and for the ensuing commercial gain, is a different matter.

There is no evidence, empirical or historical, that the stern 19th century American censorship of public distribution and display of material relating to sex in any way limited or affected expression of serious literary, artistic, political, or scientific ideas. On the contrary, it is beyond any question that the era following Thomas Jefferson to Theodore Roosevelt was an "extraordinarily vigorous period," not just in economics and politics, but in belles lettres and in "the outlying fields of social and political philosophies." We do not see the harsh hand of censorship of ideas — good or bad, sound or unsound — and "repression" of political liberty lurking in every state regulation of commercial exploitation of human interest in sex.

In sum, we (a) reaffirm the *Roth* holding that obscene material is not protected by the First Amendment; (b) hold that such material can be regulated by the States, subject to the specific safeguards enunciated above, without a showing that the material is "utterly without redeeming social value"; and (c) hold that obscenity is to be determined by applying "contemporary community standards," not "national standards." The judgment [is] vacated and the case remanded to that court for further proceedings not inconsistent with the First Amendment standards established by this opinion.

Vacated and remanded.

Mr. Justice DOUGLAS, dissenting.

[Today] the Court retreats from the earlier formulations of the constitutional test and undertakes to make new definitions. This effort, like the earlier ones, is earnest and well intentioned. The difficulty is that we do not deal with constitutional terms, since "obscenity" is not mentioned in the Constitution or Bill of Rights. [T]here are no constitutional guidelines for deciding what is and what is not "obscene." The Court is at large because we deal with tastes and standards of literature. What shocks me may be sustenance for my neighbor. What causes one person to boil up in rage over one pamphlet or movie may reflect only his neurosis, not shared by others. We deal here with a regime of censorship which, if adopted, should be done by constitutional amendment after full debate by the people.

[We] deal with highly emotional, not rational, questions. To many the Song of Solomon is obscene. I do not think we, the judges, were ever given the constitutional power to make definitions of obscenity. If it is to be defined, let the people debate and decide by a constitutional amendment what they want to ban as obscene and what standards they want the legislatures and the courts to apply. Perhaps the people will decide that the path towards a mature, integrated society requires that all ideas competing for acceptance must have no censor. Perhaps they will decide otherwise. Whatever the choice, the courts will have some guidelines. Now we have none except our own predilections.

Mr. Justice BRENNAN, with whom Mr. Justice STEWART and Mr. Justice MARSHALL join, dissenting.

[In] the case before us, appellant was convicted of distributing obscene matter in violation of [state law] on the basis of evidence that he had caused to be mailed unsolicited brochures advertising various books and a movie. I need not now decide whether a statute might be drawn to impose, within the requirements of the First Amendment, criminal penalties for the precise conduct at issue here. For it is clear that [the] statute under which the prosecution was brought is unconstitutionally overbroad, and therefore invalid on its face. "[T]he transcendent value to all society of constitutionally protected expression is deemed to justify allowing 'attacks on overly broad statutes with no requirement that the person making the attack demonstrate that his own conduct could not be regulated by a statute drawn with the requisite narrow specificity.'" Gooding v. Wilson, 405 U.S. 518 (1972). [Justice Brennan would reverse the judgment and remand the case for proceedings not inconsistent with his dissent in Paris Adult Theatre I v. Slaton, 413 U.S. 49 (1973), *infra.*]

Notes

1. *Serious Value and National Standards.* In Pope v. Illinois, 481 U.S. 497 (1987), the Court decided that *Miller* implicitly required that the element of "lack of serious literary, artistic, political, or scientific value" should be judged by national standards, reasoning as follows: "Just as the ideas a work represents need not obtain majority approval to merit protection, neither, insofar as the First Amendment is concerned, does the value of the work vary from community to community based on the degree of local acceptance it has won. The proper inquiry is not whether an ordinary member of any given community would find serious literary, artistic, political, or scientific value in allegedly obscene material, but whether a reasonable person would find such value in the material, taken as a whole." *See also* Smith v. United States, 431 U.S. 291 (1977).

2. *Jury Instructions.* In decisions after *Miller*, the Court took a flexible approach to resolving specific challenges to jury instructions that defined the key elements of *Miller*'s obscenity definitions. *See, e.g.,* Hamling v. United States, 418 U.S. 87 (1974) ("a juror is entitled to draw on his own knowledge of the views of the average person in the community or vicinage from which he comes for

making the required determination," and precise "statewide standard" is not required in instructions); Jenkins v. Georgia, 418 U.S. 153 (1974) (approving instructions to "apply community standards" without specifying what "community").

∼ PROBLEMS ∼

1. *More on Defining Obscenity.* After *Miller* and *Pope,* are you more clear about what constitutes "obscenity" and whether (or why) magazines like *Playboy* and *Penthouse* fit within the definition? If they do not fit, what more is required to render a publication "obscene"?

2. *Carnal Knowledge.* Now consider the movie *Carnal Knowledge.* The plot involves two college-age men, roommates and lifelong friends, who are obsessed with their sex lives. While the two first met as virgins, one (Jack Nicholson) is more attractive and is described as a "burgeoning bastard." The other man (Art Garfunkel) is a nice but troubled guy who falls in love with the lovely Susan (Candice Bergen) and unknowingly shares her with his college buddy. Since the Garfunkel character is the "safer" one of the two, Susan selects him for marriage. Later scenes show the two men, now in their 30s, pursuing successful careers in New York. Nicholson dates about a dozen women a year but has never managed to meet the "right one" (defined as a woman with a full bosom, good legs, and properly rounded bottom) until he comes across Ann-Margret, an aging bachelorette with substantial cleavage and something of a past. She accepts Nicholson's invitation to "shack up," and a "horrendous relationship ensues" complicated "by her paranoidal desire to marry." By this time, the thrill has gone out of Garfunkel's marriage. The movie contains occasional scenes of nudity and scenes in which sexual conduct, including "ultimate sexual acts," is understood to be taking place, even though the camera does not focus on the bodies or genitals of the actors at such times. Is the movie "obscene" under *Miller*? *See* Jenkins v. Georgia, 436 U.S. 293 (1978).

3. *Nasty as We Wanna Be.* A county sheriff seizes copies of the music CD by 2 Live Crew entitled *Nasty as We Wanna Be* (*Nasty*). The band has made another version of *Nasty* with the same music but different lyrics (without the use of profanities), entitled *Clean as We Wanna Be.* The sheriff commences an obscenity prosecution against the music CD *Nasty,* seeking an injunction to ban its distribution in the county. At the obscenity trial, one of the members of 2 Live Crew testifies that no social message of any importance was intended by the band when they created the CD as their musical work. One expert testifies that the work has value because the music and lyrics represent a variety of musical traditions. How will the lawyer for the band argue that the music CD is not obscene under *Miller*?

4. *More on the International Treaty Regulating the Internet.* Some delegates to the convention believe that the treaty should contain tight restrictions on sexually oriented material on the Internet. They view such speech as "damaging to society" and believe that it should be prohibited. Others, particularly the Danish, Swedish, and French delegates, believe that the American attitude toward sexual

speech is a bit "prudish." They argue that the sexual urge is one of the most basic and instinctual urges, and contend that the right to distribute and view sexual materials should be regarded as a "fundamental right in a free society." As a result, the Danish, Swedish, and French delegates believe that sexual speech should be limited and controlled only to the extent that it protects children from exposure to the material or protects children from exploitation. What kind of language should you agree to in the treaty regarding the regulation of sexual material? Can you strike a balance between these very different perspectives on sexual speech? What type of language do you think the final treaty should contain?

b. "Consenting Adults" and "Adult Possession"

Do adults have special rights to purchase, view, or possess obscenity? Consider the following cases.

Paris Adult Theatre I v. Slaton
413 U.S. 49 (1973)

Mr. Chief Justice BURGER delivered the opinion of the Court.

Petitioners are two Atlanta, Georgia, movie theaters and their owners and managers, operating in the style of "adult" theaters. [Civil complaints were filed against the petitioners alleging that they were exhibiting two obscene films, and an injunction was sought against the exhibition of the films.] The two films in question, "Magic Mirror" and "It All Comes Out in the End," depict sexual conduct characterized by the Georgia Supreme Court as "hard core pornography" leaving "little to the imagination."

[The two films were exhibited at trial along with pictures of the theater entrance, which showed] a conventional, inoffensive theater entrance, without any pictures, but with signs indicating that the theaters exhibit "Atlanta's Finest Mature Feature Films." On the door itself is a sign saying: "Adult Theatre — You must be 21 and able to prove it. If viewing the nude body offends you, Please Do Not Enter." [Criminal investigators testified] that they [saw] nothing on the outside of the theater [which] indicated [that] the films depicted — as they did — scenes of simulated fellatio, cunnilingus, and group sex intercourse. There was no evidence [that] minors had ever entered the theater. Nor was there evidence presented that petitioners had a systematic policy of barring minors, apart from posting signs at the entrance. [T]he trial judge dismissed [the] complaints, [assuming] "that obscenity is established," but holding "that the display of these films in a commercial theatre, when surrounded by requisite notice to the public of their nature and by reasonable protection against the exposure of these films to minors, is constitutionally permissible." [T]he Georgia Supreme Court unanimously reversed [holding] that the films were without protection under the First Amendment. . . .

[We] categorically disapprove the theory [that] obscene, pornographic films acquire constitutional immunity from state regulation simply because they are exhibited for consenting adults only. . . . Although we have [often] recognized the high importance of the state interest in regulating the exposure of obscene materials to juveniles and unconsenting adults, this Court has never declared these to be the only legitimate state interests permitting regulation of obscene material. The States have a long-recognized legitimate interest in regulating the use of obscene material in local commerce and in all places of public accommodation. . . . These include the interest of the public in the quality of life and the total community environment, the tone of commerce in the great city centers, and, possibly, the public safety itself. The Hill-Link Minority Report of the Commission on Obscenity and Pornography indicates that there is at least an arguable correlation between obscene material and crime. Quite apart from sex crimes, however, there remains one problem of large proportions aptly described by Professor Bickel:

> It concerns the tone of the society, the mode, or to use terms that have perhaps greater currency, the style and quality of life, now and in the future. A man may be entitled to read an obscene book in his room, or expose himself indecently there. . . . We should protect his privacy. But if he demands a right to obtain the books and pictures he wants in the market, and to foregather in public places — discreet, if you will, but accessible to all — with others who share his tastes, then to grant him his right is to affect the world about the rest of us, and to impinge on other privacies. [W]hat is commonly read and seen and heard and done intrudes upon us all, want it or not.

22 *The Public Interest* 25-26 (Winter 1971).

[Although] there is no conclusive proof of a connection between antisocial behavior and obscene material, the legislature of Georgia could quite reasonably determine that such a connection does or might exist. In deciding *Roth*, this Court implicitly accepted that a legislature could legitimately act on such a conclusion to protect "the social interest in order and morality." [If] we accept the unprovable assumption that a complete education requires the reading of certain books, and the well nigh universal belief that good books, plays, and art lift the spirit, improve the mind, enrich the human personality, and develop character, can we then say that a state legislature may not act on the corollary assumption that commerce in obscene books, or public exhibitions focused on obscene conduct, have a tendency to exert a corrupting and debasing impact leading to antisocial behavior? [The] sum of experience [affords] an ample basis for legislatures to conclude that a sensitive, key relationship of human existence, central to family life, community welfare, and the development of human personality, can be debased and distorted by crass commercial exploitation of sex. Nothing in the Constitution prohibits a State from reaching such a conclusion and acting on it legislatively simply because there is no conclusive evidence or empirical data.

[Our] prior decisions [recognizing] a right to privacy guaranteed by the Fourteenth Amendment included only personal rights that can be deemed "fundamental" or "implicit in the concept of ordered liberty." Roe v. Wade, 410 U.S. 113 (1973). This privacy right encompasses and protects the personal intimacies of the home, the family, marriage, motherhood, procreation, and child rearing.

Nothing, however, in this Court's decisions intimates that there is any "fundamental" privacy right "implicit in the concept of ordered liberty" to watch obscene movies in places of public accommodation. [F]or us to say that our Constitution incorporates the proposition that conduct involving consenting adults only is always beyond state regulation, is a step we are unable to take. [W]e hold that the States have a legitimate interest in regulating commerce in obscene material and in regulating exhibition of obscene material in places of public accommodation, including so-called "adult" theaters from which minors are excluded. [N]othing precludes the State of Georgia from the regulation of the allegedly obscene material exhibited in Paris Adult Theatre I or II, provided that the applicable Georgia law, as written or authoritatively interpreted by the Georgia courts, meets the First Amendment standards set forth in [Miller v. California]. The judgment is vacated and the case remanded to the Georgia Supreme Court for further proceedings not inconsistent with this [opinion].

Vacated and remanded.

Mr. Justice BRENNAN, with whom Mr. Justice STEWART and Mr. Justice MARSHALL join, dissenting.

[A]fter 16 years of experimentation and debate I am reluctantly forced to the conclusion that none of the available formulas [can] reduce the vagueness to a tolerable level while at the same time striking an acceptable balance between the protections of the First and Fourteenth Amendments [and] the asserted state interest in regulating the dissemination of certain sexually oriented materials. Any effort to draw a constitutionally acceptable boundary on state power must resort to such indefinite concepts as "prurient interest," "patent offensiveness," "serious literary value," and the like. The meaning of these concepts necessarily varies with the experience, outlook, and even idiosyncrasies of the person defining them. Although we have assumed that obscenity does exist and that we "know it when (we) see it," we are manifestly unable to describe it in advance except by reference to concepts so elusive that they fail to distinguish clearly between protected and unprotected speech.

The vagueness of the standards in the obscenity area produces a number of separate problems. . . . First, a vague statute fails to provide adequate notice to persons who are engaged in the type of conduct that the statute could be thought to proscribe. [E]ven the most painstaking efforts to determine in advance whether certain sexually oriented expression is obscene must inevitably prove unavailing. [T]he insufficiency of the notice compels persons to guess not only whether their conduct is covered by a criminal statute, but also whether their conduct falls within the constitutionally permissible reach of the [statute. As] a result[,] [o]ne cannot say with certainty that material is obscene until at least five members of this Court, applying inevitably obscure standards, have pronounced it so. . . .

[Our] experience since *Roth* requires us not only to abandon the effort to pick out obscene material on a case-by-case basis, but also to reconsider a fundamental postulate of *Roth*: that there exists a definable class of sexually oriented expression that may be totally suppressed by the Federal and State Governments. [T]he concept of "obscenity" cannot be defined with sufficient specificity and clarity to provide fair notice to persons who create and distribute sexually oriented materials, to prevent substantial erosion of protected speech as a byproduct of the attempt to suppress unprotected speech, and to avoid very costly institutional harms. [If,] as the Court today assumes, "a state legislature may [act] on [the] assumption that commerce in obscene books, or public exhibitions focused on obscene conduct, have a tendency to exert a corrupting and debasing impact leading to antisocial behavior," then it is hard to see how state-ordered regimentation of our minds can ever be forestalled. . . .

[W]hile I cannot say that the interests of the State — apart from the question of juveniles and unconsenting adults — are trivial or nonexistent, I am compelled to conclude that these interests cannot justify the substantial damage to constitutional rights [that] inevitably results from state efforts to bar the distribution even of unprotected material to consenting adults. I would hold, therefore, that at least in the absence of distribution to juveniles or obtrusive exposure to unconsenting adults, the First and Fourteenth Amendments prohibit the State and Federal Governments from attempting wholly to suppress sexually oriented materials on the basis of their allegedly "obscene" contents. Nothing in this approach precludes those governments from taking action to serve what may be strong and legitimate interests through regulation of the manner of distribution of sexually oriented material.

Stanley v. Georgia
394 U.S. 557 (1969)

Mr. Justice MARSHALL delivered the opinion of the Court.

[While executing a search warrant for Robert Stanley's home to look for evidence of bookmaking, officers found three reels of eight-millimeter film in a bedroom, and viewed them by using a projector found in the living room. The officers seized the reels after concluding that the films were obscene. Stanley was convicted by a jury under a statute that prohibited "knowingly" having possession of any obscene matter.] [Stanley argues] that the Georgia obscenity statute, insofar as it punishes mere private possession of obscene matter, violates the First Amendment, [and] we agree that the mere private possession of obscene matter cannot constitutionally be made a crime. [The Court noted that it assumed that the seized films were obscene.]

[Georgia] concedes that the present case appears to be one of "first impression" [but] contends that since "obscenity is not within the area of constitutionally protected speech or press" [under Roth v. United States,] the States are free, subject to the limits of other provisions of the Constitution, to deal with it any way deemed necessary, just as they may deal with possession of other things thought to be detrimental to the welfare of their citizens. If the State can protect the body of a citizen, may it not, argues Georgia, protect his mind?

[*Roth*] and the cases following it discerned such an "important interest" in the regulation of commercial distribution of obscene material. That holding cannot foreclose an examination of the constitutional implications of a statute forbidding mere private possession of such material. It is now well established that the Constitution protects the right to receive information and ideas. "This freedom (of speech and press) [necessarily] protects the right to receive. . . ." Martin v. City of Struthers, 319 U.S. 141 (1943). This right to receive information and ideas, regardless of their social worth, is fundamental to our free society. Moreover, in the context of this case — a prosecution for mere possession of printed or filmed matter in the privacy of a person's own home — that right takes on an added dimension. For also fundamental is the right to be free, except in very limited circumstances, from unwanted governmental intrusions into one's privacy.

These are the rights that appellant is asserting in the case before us. He is asserting the right to read or observe what he pleases — the right to satisfy his intellectual and emotional needs in the privacy of his own home. He is asserting the right to be free from state inquiry into the contents of his library. Georgia contends that appellant does not have these rights, that there are certain types of materials that the individual may not read or even possess. Georgia justifies this assertion by arguing that the films in the present case are obscene. But we think that mere categorization of these films as "obscene" is insufficient justification for such a drastic invasion of personal liberties guaranteed by the First and Fourteenth Amendments. Whatever may be the justifications for other statutes regulating obscenity, we do not think they reach into the privacy of one's own home. If the First Amendment means anything, it means that a State has no business telling a man, sitting alone in his own house, what books he may read or what films he may watch. Our whole constitutional heritage rebels at the thought of giving government the power to control men's minds.

And yet, in the face of these traditional notions of individual liberty, Georgia asserts the right to protect the individual's mind from the effects of obscenity. We are not certain that this argument amounts to anything more than the assertion that the State has the right to control the moral content of a person's thoughts. To some, this may be a noble purpose, but it is wholly inconsistent with the philosophy of the First Amendment. As the Court said in Kingsley International Pictures Corp. v. Regents, 360 U.S. 684 (1959), "[the Constitution's] guarantee is not confined to the expression of ideas that are conventional or shared by a majority. [And] in the realm of ideas it protects expression which is eloquent no less than that which is unconvincing." Nor is it relevant that obscene materials in general, or the particular films before the Court, are arguably devoid of any ideological content. The line between the transmission of ideas and mere entertainment is much too elusive for this Court to draw, if indeed such a line can be drawn at all. Whatever the power of the state to control public dissemination of ideas inimical to the public morality, it cannot constitutionally premise legislation on the desirability of controlling a person's private thoughts.

Perhaps recognizing this, Georgia asserts that exposure to obscene materials may lead to deviant sexual behavior or crimes of sexual violence. There appears to be little empirical basis for that assertion. But more important, if the State is only concerned about printed or filmed materials inducing antisocial conduct, we believe that in the context of private consumption of ideas and information we should adhere to the view that "(a)mong free men, the deterrents ordinarily to be applied to prevent crime are education and punishment for violations of the [law]." Whitney v. California, 274 U.S. 357 (1927) (Brandeis, J., concurring). Given the present state of knowledge, the State may no more prohibit mere possession of obscene matter on the ground that it may lead to antisocial conduct than it may prohibit possession of chemistry books on the ground that they may lead to the manufacture of homemade spirits.

It is true that in *Roth* this Court rejected the necessity of proving that exposure to obscene material would create a clear and present danger of antisocial conduct or would probably induce its recipients to such conduct. But that case dealt with public distribution of obscene materials and such distribution is subject to different objections. For example, there is always the danger that obscene material might fall into the hands of children, or that it might intrude upon the sensibilities or privacy of the general public. No such dangers are present in this case. [The Court also noted that "the Model Penal Code provisions dealing with obscene materials are limited to cases of commercial dissemination."]

Finally, we are faced with the argument that prohibition of possession of obscene materials is a necessary incident to statutory schemes prohibiting distribution. That argument is based on alleged difficulties of proving an intent to distribute or in producing evidence of actual distribution. We are not convinced that such difficulties exist, but even if they did we do not think that they would justify infringement of the individual's right to read or observe what he pleases. Because that right is so fundamental to our scheme of individual liberty, its restriction may not be justified by the need to ease the administration of otherwise valid criminal laws. We hold that the First and Fourteenth Amendments prohibit making mere private possession of obscene material a crime. *Roth* and the cases following that decision are not impaired by today's holding. As we have said, the States retain broad power to regulate obscenity; that power simply does not extend to mere possession by the individual in the privacy of his own home. Accordingly, the judgment of the court below is reversed and the case is remanded for proceedings not inconsistent with this opinion.

It is so ordered.

Judgment reversed and case remanded.

Note: Stanley's Limits and Impact

Although *Stanley* was unanimous in its judgment, three justices concurred on Fourth Amendment grounds. The reluctance of some members of the Court to endorse *Stanley*'s First Amendment holding was later reflected in a pre-*Miller* case that limited *Stanley*'s impact. In United States v. Reidel, 402 U.S. 351 (1971), the Court held that even though a person has the right to possess obscene material under *Stanley*, no one else has the right to sell or deliver it to that person. As a result, the Court upheld a federal statute that prohibited the knowing use of the mails for the delivery of obscene matter, and held that *Roth* precluded the invalidation of the statute as applied to willing adult recipients of such matter. In

Osborne v. Ohio, 495 U.S. 103 (1990), the Court distinguished *Stanley* in holding that possession of child pornography could be prohibited.

c. Special Rules for Minors?

Are their special rules for sexual material that is obscene or harmful for minors?

Ginsberg v. New York

390 U.S. 629 (1968)

Mr. Justice BRENNAN delivered the opinion of the Court.

[Ginsberg] and his wife operate "Sam's Stationery and Luncheonette" in Bellmore, Long Island. They have a lunch counter, and, among other things, also sell magazines including some so-called "girlie" magazines. [Ginsberg] was [charged with and convicted of] selling a 16-year-old boy two "girlie" magazines. [The statute made it a crime knowingly to sell to a minor under 17 (a) any picture [which] depicts nudity [and] which is harmful to minors, and (b) [any] magazine [which] contains [such pictures] and which, taken as a whole, is harmful to minors.] The judge found (1) that the magazines contained pictures which depicted female "nudity" in a manner defined in [the statute,] that is "the showing of [female] buttocks with less than a full opaque covering, or the showing of the female breast with less than a fully opaque covering of any portion thereof below the top of the nipple" [and also found] (2) that the pictures were "harmful to minors" in that they had [that] "quality [of] representation [of] nudity [which] (i) predominantly appeals to the prurient, shameful or morbid interest of minors, and (ii) is patently offensive to prevailing standards in the adult community as a whole with respect to what is suitable material for minors, and (iii) is utterly without redeeming social importance for minors." [We] affirm.

[The] "girlie" picture magazines involved in the sales here are not obscene for adults, [and the statute] does not bar the appellant from stocking the magazines and selling them to persons 17 years of age or [older]. Ginsberg's primary attack upon [the statute] is leveled at the power of the State to adapt [the] *Memoirs* formulation to define the material's obscenity on the basis of its appeal to minors, and thus exclude material so defined from the area of protected expression. He makes no argument that the magazines are not "harmful to minors. . . ." [Ginsberg's] contention is the broad proposition that the scope of the constitutional freedom of expression secured to a citizen to read or see material concerned with sex cannot be made to depend upon whether the citizen is an adult or a minor. He [insists] that the denial to minors under 17 of access to material condemned by [the statute], insofar as that material is not obscene for persons 17 years of age or older, constitutes an unconstitutional deprivation of protected liberty.

[We] do not regard New York's regulation in defining obscenity on the basis of its appeal to minors under 17 as involving an invasion of such minors' constitutionally protected freedoms. Rather [the statute] simply adjusts the definition of obscenity "to social realities by permitting the appeal of this type of material to be assessed in term of the sexual [interests]" of such minors. That the State has power to make that adjustment seems clear, for we have recognized that even where there is an invasion of protected freedoms "the power of the state to control the conduct of children reaches beyond the scope of its authority over [adults]." Prince v. Commonwealth of Massachusetts, 321 U.S. 158.

[The] well-being of its children is of course a subject within the State's constitutional power to regulate, and, in our view, two interests justify the limitations in [the statute] upon the availability of sex material to minors under 17, at least if it was rational for the legislature to find that the minors' exposure to such material might be harmful. First of all, constitutional interpretation has consistently recognized that the parents' claim to authority in their own household to direct the rearing of their children is basic in the structure of our society. [The] legislature could properly conclude that parents and [teachers] who have this primary responsibility for children's well-being are entitled to the support of laws designed to aid discharge of that responsibility. Indeed, [the statute] expressly recognizes the parental role in assessing sex-related material harmful to minors according "to prevailing standards in the adult community as a whole with respect to what is suitable material for minors." Moreover, the prohibition against sales to minors does not bar parents who so desire from purchasing the magazines for their children. [The] State also has an independent interest in the well-being of its youth.

[To] sustain state power to exclude material defined as obscenity by [the statute] requires only that we be able to say that it was not irrational for the legislature to find that exposure to material condemned by the statute is harmful to minors. [To] be sure, there is no lack of "studies" which purport to demonstrate that obscenity is or is not "a basic factor in impairing the ethical and moral development [of] youth and a clear and present danger to the people of the state." But the growing consensus of commentators is that "[a] causal link has not been disproved either." [We] therefore cannot say that [the statute,] in defining the obscenity of material on the basis of its appeal to minors under 17, has no rational relation to the objective of safeguarding such minors from harm.

[Ginsberg argues] that the definition of obscenity "harmful to minors" is so vague that an honest distributor of publications cannot know when he might be held to have violated [the statute]. But the New York Court of Appeals construed this definition to be "virtually identical to the Supreme Court's most recent statement of the elements of obscenity." The definition therefore gives "men in acting adequate notice of what is prohibited" and does not offend the requirements of due process.

Affirmed.

Mr. Justice FORTAS, dissenting.

[T]he Court cannot properly avoid its fundamental duty to define "obscenity" for purposes of censorship of material sold to [youths]. The Court certainly cannot mean that the States and cities and counties and villages have unlimited power to withhold anything and everything that is written or pictorial from younger people. But it here justifies the conviction of [Ginsberg] because the impact of the Constitution, it says, is variable, and what is not obscene for an adult may be obscene for a child. This it calls "variable obscenity." [To] assess the principle — certainly to apply it — the Court must define it. We must know the extent to which literature or pictures may be less offensive than *Roth* requires in order to be "obscene" for purposes of a statute confined to youth. . . . This decision does not merely protect children from activities which all sensible parents would condemn. Rather, its undefined and unlimited approval of state censorship in this area denies to children free access to books and works of art to which many parents may wish their children to have uninhibited access. For denial of access to these magazines, without any standard or definition of their allegedly distinguishing characteristics, is also denial of access to great works of art and literature. If this statute were confined to the punishment of pushers or panderers of vulgar literature I would not be so concerned by the Court's failure to circumscribe state power by defining its limits in terms of the meaning of "obscenity" in this field. . . . I would therefore reverse the [conviction.]

Notes

1. *Software Filters in Libraries to Prevent Juvenile Access to Pornography.* In United States v. American Library Association, Inc., 123 S.Ct. 2297 (2003), the Court upheld the constitutionality of the Children's Internet Protection Act provision that conditioned federal funds for Internet services at public libraries on the installation of software to block minors from obtaining access to "obscenity," "child pornography," and "visual depictions" that are "harmful to minors." The Court relied on the fact that library staff have the ability to unblock any erroneously blocked site, and that a "legislature's decision not to subsidize the exercise of a fundamental right does not infringe that right." Rust v. Sullivan, 500 U.S. 173 (1991).

2. *Transmitting, Sending, or Displaying Indecent Messages to Juveniles.* In 1996, Congress enacted the Communications Decency Act (CDA) to regulate the Internet transmission of "indecent," "patently offensive," or "obscene" messages to juveniles. The obscenity ban was not challenged, but the other provisions were held to be overbroad and vague in Reno v. American Civil Liberties Union, 521 U.S. 844 (1997). After *Reno,* Congress enacted the Child Online Protection Act (COPA) in 1998, in an effort to respond to the *Reno* Court's criticisms of the CDA and to come closer to the standards of Ginsberg v. New York and Miller v. California. In Ashcroft v. American Civil Liberties Union [*Ashcroft I*], 535 U.S. 564 (2002), the courts partially upheld COPA. However, the Court later struck COPA down. American Civil Liberties Union v. Mukasey, 534 F.3d 181 (3d Cir. 2008), *cert. denied*, 129 S.Ct. 1032 (2009). These cases are discussed more fully later in this chapter.

~ PROBLEMS ~

1. *Appeal to "Lust."* What arguments could be made after *Ginsberg* to challenge a statute that prohibits the sale to minors "of any magazine" that "would appeal to the lust of persons under the age of eighteen years or to their curiosity as to sex or to anatomical differences between the sexes?" *See* Rabeck v. New York, 391 U.S. 462 (1968).

2. *Movie Classifications.* What arguments could be made after *Ginsberg* to challenge a statute that classifies movies as either suitable or unsuitable for minors, and makes it a crime to admit a minor to a movie classified as unsuitable, when one definition of *unsuitable* is: the portrayal "of sexual promiscuity or extramarital sexual relations in such a manner as to encourage sexual promiscuity on the part of young persons"? *See* Interstate Circuit, Inc. v. Dallas, 390 U.S. 676 (1968).

3. *"Harmful Matter" in Vending Machines.* Assume that a California statute bans the sale of "harmful matter" in unsupervised sidewalk vending machines. Harmful matter is defined as: "matter, taken as a whole, which to the average person, applying contemporary community standards, appeals to the prurient interest, and which, taken as a whole, depicts or describes in a patently offensive way sexual conduct, and which, taken as a whole, lacks literary, artistic, political or scientific value for minors." The California legislature did not make any specific findings concerning the purpose of the statute. Publishers and vendors of adult-oriented publications file suit to enjoin the enforcement of the statute on First Amendment grounds. You represent the State of California. What arguments do you expect the plaintiffs to make to attack the statute on First Amendment grounds (aside from overbreadth and vagueness)? What arguments will you make in response to defend the statute?

4. *More on the International Treaty Regulating the Internet.* At the convention, there is much discussion about the extent to which the treaty should protect minors against sexually explicit material. In light of *Ginsburg* and other U.S. precedents, what type of restrictions can you agree to in the treaty? What language would you suggest to the other delegates?

8. Child Pornography

Between the 1950s and the 1970s, *Chaplinsky*'s catalogue of unprotected speech categories continued to shrink. By the 1980s, however, the Court had adopted a new starting point for the analysis of speech regulations that are "content based," while allowing the various doctrines created for speech in the *Chaplinsky* catalogue to retain validity as *sui generis*, historic exceptions to the new "content based" model. For content regulations of speech in other contexts, however, government litigants faced the burden of satisfying the Court's "strict scrutiny" and of demonstrating that regulations were narrowly tailored and necessary to achieve a compelling governmental interest. This burden also might include the need to prove that the regulation was the least restrictive alternative in terms of its impact on protected speech. Perhaps not surprisingly, some government litigants sought to expand the *Chaplinsky* catalogue in order to escape the burden of strict scrutiny. Yet the doctrinal demands to be met for the creation of a new unprotected speech category were necessarily different in the 1980s. In the 1940s, *Chaplinsky* simply announced the catalogue as reflecting the consensus of history, according to the Court's own jurisprudence and the views of state courts. By the 1980s, the overbreadth and vagueness doctrines had become significant limitations on content regulations of speech. Moreover, the speech-protective values of the strict scrutiny model implicitly required that a category of unprotected speech should be created in a way that satisfied those values. Ultimately, the most notable such category created in this era was "child pornography" speech.

Ferber v. New York

458 U.S. 747 (1982)

Justice WHITE delivered the opinion of the Court.

At issue in this case is the constitutionality of a New York criminal statute which prohibits persons from knowingly promoting sexual performances by children under the age of 16 by distributing material which depicts such performances.

In recent years, the exploitive use of children in the production of pornography has become a serious national problem. The Federal Government and 47 States have sought to combat the problem with statutes specifically directed at the production of child pornography. At least half of such statutes do not require that the materials produced be legally obscene. Thirty-five States and the United States Congress have also passed legislation prohibiting the distribution of such materials; 20 States prohibit the distribution of material depicting children engaged in sexual conduct without requiring that the material be legally obscene.

New York is one of the 20. In 1977, the New York Legislature enacted [a child pornography statutes, which provides:] "A person is guilty of promoting a sexual performance by a child when, knowing the character and content thereof, he produces, directs or promotes any performance which includes sexual conduct by a child less than sixteen years of age." To "promote" is also defined: "'Promote' means to procure, manufacture, issue, sell, give, provide, lend, mail, deliver, transfer, transmute, publish, distribute, circulate, disseminate, present, exhibit or advertise, or to offer or agree to do the same." [A "[s]exual performance" is defined as "any performance or part thereof which includes sexual conduct by a child less than sixteen years of age." "Sexual conduct" is in turn defined [as] "actual or simulated sexual intercourse, deviate sexual intercourse, sexual bestiality, masturbation, sado-masochistic abuse, or lewd exhibition of the genitals." A "performance" is defined as "any play, motion picture, photograph or dance" or "any other visual representation exhibited before an audience."]

This case arose when Paul Ferber, the proprietor of a Manhattan bookstore specializing in sexually oriented products, sold two films to an undercover police

officer. The films are devoted almost exclusively to depicting young boys masturbating. Ferber was [charged with violating the child pornography statute and convicted, [but] his convictions were reversed by the] New York Court of Appeals.
[We] granted the State's petition for [certiorari].

This case [constitutes] our first examination of a statute directed at and limited to depictions of sexual activity involving children. We believe our inquiry
should begin with the question of whether a State has somewhat more freedom in
proscribing works which portray sexual acts or lewd exhibitions of genitalia by
children.

[In] Miller v. California, [413 U.S. 15 (1973),] a majority of the Court agreed
that a "state offense must also be limited to works which, taken as a whole, appeal
to the prurient interest in sex, which portray sexual conduct in a patently offensive way, and which, taken as a whole, do not have serious literary, artistic, political, or scientific value." Over the past decade, we have adhered to the guidelines
expressed in *Miller* which [was] an accommodation between the State's interests
in protecting the "sensibilities of unwilling recipients" from exposure to pornographic material and the dangers of censorship inherent in unabashedly content-
based laws. Like obscenity statutes, laws directed at the dissemination of child
pornography run the risk of suppressing protected expression by allowing the
hand of the censor to become unduly heavy. For the following reasons, however,
we are persuaded that the States are entitled to greater leeway in the regulation
of pornographic depictions of children.

First. It is evident [that] a State's interest in "safeguarding the physical and
psychological well-being of a minor" is "compelling." Globe Newspaper Co. v.
Superior Court, 457 U.S. 596 (1982). "A democratic society rests, for its
continuance, upon the healthy, well-rounded growth of young people into full
maturity as citizens." Prince v. Massachusetts, 321 U.S. 158 (1944). Accordingly,
we have sustained legislation aimed at protecting the physical and emotional
well-being of youth even when the laws have operated in the sensitive area of
constitutionally protected rights. [In] Ginsberg v. New York, [390 U.S. 629
(1968),] we sustained a New York law protecting children from exposure to
nonobscene literature. Most recently, we held that the Government's interest in
the "well-being of its youth" justified special treatment of indecent broadcasting
received by adults as well as children. FCC v. Pacifica Foundation, 438 U.S. 726
(1978).

The prevention of sexual exploitation and abuse of children constitutes a
government objective of surpassing importance. The legislative findings accompanying passage of the New York laws reflect this concern: "[T]here has been a
proliferation of exploitation of children as subjects in sexual performances. The
care of children is a sacred trust and should not be abused by those who seek to
profit through a commercial network based upon the exploitation of children.
The public policy of the state demands the protection of children from exploitation through sexual performances. 1977 N.Y. Laws, ch. 910, §1." We shall not
second-guess this legislative judgment. [V]irtually all of the States and the United
States have passed legislation proscribing the production of or otherwise combating "child pornography." The legislative judgment, as well as the judgment

found in the relevant literature, is that the use of children as subjects of pornographic materials is harmful to the physiological, emotional, and mental health of the child. That judgment, we think, easily passes muster under the First Amendment. [Research shows] "that sexually exploited children are unable to develop healthy affectionate relationships in later life, have sexual dysfunctions, and have a tendency to become sexual abusers as adults," that "sexually exploited children predisposed to self-destructive behavior such as drug and alcohol abuse or prostitution," and that "sexual molestation by adults is often involved in the production of child sexual performances."

Second. The distribution of photographs and films depicting sexual activity by juveniles is intrinsically related to the sexual abuse of children in at least two ways. First, the materials produced are a permanent record of the children's participation and the harm to the child is exacerbated by their circulation. Second, the distribution network for child pornography must be closed if the production of material which requires the sexual exploitation of children is to be effectively controlled. Indeed, there is no serious contention that the legislature was unjustified in believing that it is difficult, if not impossible, to halt the exploitation of children by pursuing only those who produce the photographs and movies. While the production of pornographic materials is a low-profile, clandestine industry, the need to market the resulting products requires a visible apparatus of distribution. The most expeditious if not the only practical method of law enforcement may be to dry up the market for this material by imposing severe criminal penalties on persons selling, advertising, or otherwise promoting the product. Thirty-five States and Congress have concluded that restraints on the distribution of pornographic materials are required in order to effectively combat the problem, and there is a body of literature and testimony to support these legislative conclusions.

[Ferber] does not contend that the State is unjustified in pursuing those who distribute child pornography. Rather, he argues that it is enough for the State to prohibit the distribution of materials that are legally obscene under the *Miller* test. . . . The *Miller* standard, like all general definitions of what may be banned as obscene, does not reflect the State's particular and more compelling interest in prosecuting those who promote the sexual exploitation of children. [T]he question under the *Miller* test of whether a work, taken as a whole, appeals to the prurient interest of the average person bears no connection to the issue of whether a child has been physically or psychologically harmed in the production of the work. Similarly, a sexually explicit depiction need not be "patently offensive" in order to have required the sexual exploitation of a child for its production. In addition, a work which, taken on the whole, contains serious literary, artistic, political, or scientific value may nevertheless embody the hardest core of child pornography. "It is irrelevant to the child [who has been abused] whether or not the material [has] a literary, artistic, political or social value." Memorandum of Assemblyman Lasher. . . . We therefore cannot conclude that the *Miller* standard is a satisfactory solution to the child pornography problem. [L]egal obscenity under *Miller* is a function of "contemporary community standards," [and] "[i]t would be equally unrealistic to equate a community's toleration for sexually oriented material with the permissible scope of legislation aimed at protecting children from sexual exploitation."

Third. The advertising and selling of child pornography provide an economic motive for and are thus an integral part of the production of such materials, an activity illegal throughout the Nation. . . .

Fourth. The value of permitting live performances and photographic reproductions of children engaged in lewd sexual conduct is exceedingly modest, if not *de minimis.* We consider it unlikely that visual depictions of children performing sexual acts or lewdly exhibiting their genitals would often constitute an important and necessary part of a literary performance or scientific or educational work. [I]f it were necessary for literary or artistic value, a person over the statutory age who perhaps looked younger could be utilized. Simulation outside of the prohibition of the statute could provide another alternative. Nor is there any question here of censoring a particular literary theme or portrayal of sexual activity. The First Amendment interest is limited to that of rendering the portrayal somewhat more "realistic" by utilizing or photographing children.

Fifth. Recognizing and classifying child pornography as a category of material outside the protection of the First Amendment is not incompatible with our earlier decisions. [I]t is not rare that a content-based classification of speech has been accepted because it may be appropriately generalized that within the confines of the given classification, the evil to be restricted so overwhelmingly outweighs the expressive interests, if any, at stake, that no process of case-by-case adjudication is required. When a definable class of material, such as that covered by [the statute here], bears so heavily and pervasively on the welfare of children engaged in its production, we think the balance of competing interests is clearly struck and that it is permissible to consider these materials as without the protection of the First Amendment.

There are, of course, limits on the category of child pornography which, like obscenity, is unprotected by the First Amendment. As with all legislation in this sensitive area, the conduct to be prohibited must be adequately defined by the applicable state law, as written or authoritatively construed. Here the nature of the harm to be combated requires that the state offense be limited to works that *visually* depict sexual conduct by children below a specified age. The category of "sexual conduct" proscribed must also be suitably limited and described.

The test for child pornography is separate from the obscenity standard enunciated in *Miller,* but may be compared to it for the purpose of clarity. The *Miller* formulation is adjusted in the following respects: A trier of fact need not find that the material appeals to the prurient interest of the average person; it is not required that sexual conduct portrayed be done so in a patently offensive manner; and the material at issue need not be considered as a whole. We note that the distribution of descriptions or other depictions of sexual conduct, not otherwise obscene, which do not involve live performance or photographic or other visual reproduction of live performances, retains First Amendment protection. As with obscenity laws, criminal responsibility may not be imposed without some element of scienter on the part of the defendant.

[The New York statute's] prohibition incorporates a definition of sexual conduct that comports with the above-stated principles. The forbidden acts to be depicted are listed with sufficient precision and represent the kind of conduct that, if it were the theme of a work, could render it legally obscene: "actual or simulated sexual intercourse, deviate sexual intercourse, sexual bestiality, masturbation, sado-masochistic abuse, or lewd exhibition of the genitals." The term "lewd exhibition of the genitals" is not unknown in this area and, indeed, was given in *Miller* as an example of a permissible regulation. A performance is defined only to include live or visual depictions: "any play, motion picture, photograph or dance [or] other visual representation exhibited before an audience." §263.00(4). [The statute] expressly includes a scienter requirement.

We hold that [the New York statute] sufficiently describes a category of material the production and distribution of which is not entitled to First Amendment protection. It is therefore clear that there is nothing unconstitutionally "under-inclusive" about a statute that singles out this category of material for proscription. It also follows that the State is not barred by the First Amendment from prohibiting the distribution of unprotected materials produced outside the State.

It remains to address the claim that the New York statute is unconstitutionally overbroad because it would forbid the distribution of material with serious literary, scientific, or educational value or material which does not threaten the harms sought to be combated by the State. [We] consider this the paradigmatic case of a state statute whose legitimate reach dwarfs its arguably impermissible applications. New York [may] constitutionally prohibit dissemination of material specified in [the statute]. While the reach of the statute is directed at the hard core of child pornography, the Court of Appeals [was] concerned that some protected expression, ranging from medical textbooks to pictorials in the *National Geographic* would fall prey to the statute. How often, if ever, it may be necessary to employ children to engage in conduct clearly within the reach of [the statute] in order to produce educational, medical, or artistic works cannot be known with certainty. Yet we seriously doubt [that] these arguably impermissible applications of the statute amount to more than a tiny fraction of the materials within the statute's reach. Nor will we assume that the New York courts will widen the possibly invalid reach of the statute by giving an expansive construction to the proscription on "lewd exhibition[s] of the genitals." Under these circumstances, [the statute] is "not substantially overbroad [and] whatever overbreadth may exist should be cured through case-by-case analysis of the fact situations to which its sanctions, assertedly, may not be applied." Broadrick v. Oklahoma, 413 U.S., at 615-616.

Because [the statute] is not substantially overbroad, it is unnecessary to consider its application to material that does not depict sexual conduct of a type that New York may restrict consistent with the First Amendment. As applied to Paul Ferber and to others who distribute similar material, the statute does not violate the First Amendment as applied to the States through the Fourteenth. . . . The judgment of the New York Court of Appeals is reversed, and the case is remanded to that court for further proceedings not inconsistent with this opinion.

So ordered.

Justice O'CONNOR, concurring.

[T]he Court does not hold that New York must except "material with serious literary, scientific, or educational value," from its statute. The Court merely holds that, even if the First Amendment shelters such material, New York's current statute is not sufficiently overbroad to support respondent's facial attack. The compelling interests identified in today's opinion, suggest that the Constitution might in fact permit New York to ban knowing distribution of works depicting minors engaged in explicit sexual conduct, regardless of the social value. [Or it] is quite possible that New York's statute is overbroad because it bans depictions that do not actually threaten the harms identified by the Court. For example, clinical pictures of adolescent sexuality, such as those that might appear in medical textbooks, might not involve the type of sexual exploitation and abuse targeted by New York's statute. Nor might such depictions feed the poisonous "kiddie porn" market that New York and other States have attempted to regulate. Similarly, pictures of children engaged in rites widely approved by their cultures, such as those that might appear in issues of the *National Geographic*, might not trigger the compelling interests identified by the Court. It is not necessary to address these possibilities further today, however, because this potential overbreadth is not sufficiently substantial to warrant facial invalidation of New York's statute.

Justice BRENNAN, with whom Justice MARSHALL joins, concurring in the judgment.

[The] special and compelling interest, and the particular vulnerability of children, afford the State the leeway to regulate pornographic material, the promotion of which is harmful to children, even though the State does not have such leeway when it seeks only to protect consenting adults from exposure to such material. I also agree with the Court that the "tiny fraction," of material of serious artistic, scientific, or educational value that could conceivably fall within the reach of the statute is insufficient to justify striking the statute on the grounds of overbreadth. [I]n my view application of [the statute] or any similar statute to depictions of children that in themselves do have serious literary, artistic, scientific, or medical value, would violate the First Amendment. [T]he limited classes of speech, the suppression of which does not raise serious First Amendment concerns, have two attributes. They are of exceedingly "slight social value," and the State has a compelling interest in their regulation. The First Amendment value of depictions of children that are in themselves serious contributions to art, literature, or science, is, by definition, simply not "*de minimis.*" At the same time, the State's interest in suppression of such materials is likely to be far less compelling. [The] production of materials of serious value is not the "low-profile, clandestine industry" that according to the Court produces purely pornographic materials. In short, it is inconceivable how a depiction of a child that is itself a serious contribution to the world of art or literature or science can be deemed "material outside the protection of the First Amendment." [With] this understanding, I concur in the Court's judgment in this case.

Notes and Questions

1. Ferber*'s Scope.* The *Ferber* opinion could be read narrowly as defining the speech category of child pornography under the parameters of the New York statute, requiring elements of sexual performance, sexual conduct, and visual images of real minors under 16. But the opinion could also be read more broadly, so that not all of its many justifications supporting its holding would have to be satisfied in order to uphold a more broadly phrased child pornography statute. The Court's assessment of this speech as having "*de minimis*" value, as well as its refusal to impose a requirement that material of "literary, artistic, political and social value" should be exempted from the *Ferber* ban, implied that the Court might find other types of bans to be constitutional. Once the Court broke from the *Miller* model in *Ferber* because of *Miller*'s inapposite policy goals, it was evident that the Court might similarly break from the *Miller* commitment to requiring a single "approved" statutory definition of obscenity, and approve instead a variety of statutory definitions of child pornography. Finally, the role of the overbreadth and vagueness doctrines in the context of a *Ferber* type of speech regulation remained unclear after *Ferber*. Initially, the Court continued to interpret *Ferber* speech as a distinctly different category from *Miller* speech, and validated the consensus judgment of the lower courts that rejected the *Stanley* doctrine as applied to possession prosecutions for child pornography. Later, as we shall see, as legislatures enacted a wide range of "juvenile protection" statutes involving speech on the Internet, the Court retreated from an expansive interpretation of *Ferber*.

2. *Child Pornography and the Justifications Protecting Speech.* Does "child pornography" meet any of the justifications for protecting speech presented at the beginning of this chapter? In other words, does it provide a safety valve, does it promote self-fulfillment or the marketplace of ideas, or is it related to the democratic process? Does the answer to this question depend on the content of the pornography?

3. Miller *and* Ferber *Approaches.* The *Miller* and *Ferber* opinions recognize and define "unprotected" categories of speech, yet each opinion reflects a different approach to several common elements of First Amendment doctrine: a) the articulation of a government interest, b) the examination of the evidence supporting the legislative concern for the interest, c) the adoption of a definition of speech that will serve the governmental interest, and d) the creation or endorsement of doctrinal safeguards against the chilling effect on protected speech that may be caused by criminal prosecution of the unprotected speech category. Identify the approaches in the *Ferber* opinion to each of these four elements, and compare each of them with the approaches used in *Miller*.

4. *Blocking Child Pornography.* In July 2008, the largest cable operators in the United States agreed to block child pornography websites identified by the National Center for Missing and Exploited Children. Since most cable operators also provide broadband service, the agreement provides some protection against child pornography sites.

5. *Sexting.* In recent years, some prosecutors have charged teens who send text messages that show nude photos of themselves or other minors with child pornography. *See* Chana Joffe-Walt, *"Sexting": A Disturbing New Teen Trend?*, National Public Radio (Mar. 12, 2009). Prosecutors have also charged minors who received the text message photos and did not delete them from their phones. Students have a variety of motivations for sending these text images. In some instances, when they send text message photos of themselves, they are engaging in a high-tech method of flirting. In other instances, students send text message photos of others to harass or embarrass them (e.g., after a high school boy and girl break up, one sends nude pictures of the other to friends out of spite). Are child pornography charges appropriate under an appropriately drafted statute? Can or should the problem be dealt with through charges or in other ways?

6. *Possession of Child Pornography.* Osborne v. Ohio, 495 U.S. 103 (1990), involved an Ohio law that made it illegal to possess child pornography, and the Court was forced to determine whether the holding in Stanley v. Georgia, 394 U.S. 557 (1969) (individuals have a right to possess obscenity in the privacy of their own homes), extended to and protected the possession of child pornography in one's own home. In *Osborne,* the Court held that a criminal statute that prohibited the possession of child pornography in one's home did not violate the Constitution. In reaching that conclusion, the Court relied on several considerations, including the following: The Court observed that the value of unprotected *Ferber* materials is *de minimis,* and that the compelling government interests in restricting child pornography "far exceed the interests" that justified the *Stanley* statute. The Court viewed the *Stanley* statute as a "paternalistic" attempt to exercise thought control over people, whereas the Ohio law was designed to protect victims of child sexual abuse who have been used as models for pornography. The Court also found that the criminalization of possession of child pornography would likely decrease its production, and that the criminalization of possession was even more important since the child pornography industry had been "driven underground" by the *Ferber* decision, causing 17 states to enact possession statutes in an attempt to "dry up the market." In addition, the Court found that the law might encourage consumers to destroy child pornography "which might not only dry up the market but also remove materials from the hands of pedophiles who might use it for luring children into sexual activity."

Ashcroft v. Free Speech Coalition
122 U.S. 1389 (2002)

Justice KENNEDY delivered the opinion of the Court.

We consider in this case whether the Child Pornography Prevention Act of 1996 (CPPA) abridges the freedom of speech. The CPPA extends the federal prohibition against child pornography to sexually explicit images that appear to depict minors but were produced without using any real children. The statute prohibits, in specific circumstances, possessing or distributing these images, which may be created by using adults who look like minors or by using computer imaging. The new technology [makes] it possible to create realistic images of children who do not exist. By prohibiting child pornography that does not depict an actual child, the statute goes beyond New York v. Ferber, 458 U.S. 747 (1982), which distinguished child pornography from other sexually explicit speech because of the State's interest in protecting the children exploited by the production process. As a general rule, pornography can be banned only if obscene, but under *Ferber,* pornography showing minors can be proscribed whether or not the images are obscene under the definition set forth in Miller v. California, 413 U.S. 15 (1973). *Ferber* recognized that "[t]he *Miller* standard, like all general definitions of what may be banned as obscene, does not reflect the State's particular and more compelling interest in prosecuting those who promote the sexual exploitation of children."

[W]e may assume that the apparent age of persons engaged in sexual conduct is relevant to whether a depiction offends community standards. Pictures of young children engaged in certain acts might be obscene where similar depictions of adults, or perhaps even older adolescents, would not. The CPPA, however, is not directed at speech that is obscene. [T]he CPPA seeks to reach beyond obscenity, and it makes no attempt to conform to the *Miller* standard. For instance, the statute would reach visual depictions, such as movies, even if they have redeeming social value. . . .

I

Before 1996, Congress defined child pornography as the type of depictions at issue in *Ferber,* images made using actual minors. The CPPA retains that prohibition [and] and adds three other prohibited categories of speech. . . . Section 2256(8)(B) prohibits "any visual depiction, including any photograph, film, video, picture, or computer or computer-generated image or picture," that "is, or appears to be, of a minor engaging in sexually explicit conduct." The prohibition on "any visual depiction" does not depend at all on how the image is produced. The section captures a range of depictions, sometimes called "virtual child pornography," which include computer-generated images, as well as images produced by more traditional means. For instance, the literal terms of the statute embrace a Renaissance painting depicting a scene from classical mythology, a "picture" that "appears to be, of a minor engaging in sexually explicit conduct." The statute also prohibits Hollywood movies, filmed without any child actors, if a jury believes an actor "appears to be" a minor engaging in "actual or simulated . . . sexual intercourse." §2256(2).

These images do not involve, let alone harm, any children in the production process; but Congress decided the materials threaten children in other, less direct, ways. Pedophiles might use the materials to encourage children to participate in sexual activity. . . . Congressional Finding (3). Furthermore, pedophiles might "whet their own sexual appetites" with the pornographic images, "thereby increasing the creation and distribution of child pornography and the sexual abuse and exploitation of actual children." Findings (4). Under these rationales, harm flows from the content of the images, not from the means of their production. In addition, Congress identified another problem created by computer-generated images: Their existence can make it harder to prosecute pornographers who do use real minors. Finding (6)(A). As imaging technology improves, Congress found, it becomes more difficult to prove that a particular picture was produced using actual children. To ensure that defendants possessing child pornography using real minors cannot evade prosecution, Congress extended the ban to virtual child pornography.

Section 2256(8)(C) prohibits a more common and lower tech means of creating virtual images, known as computer morphing. Rather than creating original images, pornographers can alter innocent pictures of real children so that the children appear to be engaged in sexual activity. Although morphed images may fall within the definition of virtual child pornography, they implicate the interests of real children and are in that sense closer to the images in *Ferber*. Respondents do not challenge this provision, and we do not consider it.

Respondents do challenge §2256(8)(D). . . . Section 2256(8)(D) defines child pornography to include any sexually explicit image that was "advertised, promoted, presented, described, or distributed in such a manner that conveys the impression" it depicts "a minor engaging in sexually explicit conduct." One Committee Report identified the provision as directed at sexually explicit images pandered as child pornography. The statute is not so limited in its reach [as] it punishes even those possessors who took no part in pandering. Once a work has been described as child pornography, the taint remains on the speech in the hands of subsequent possessors, making possession unlawful even though the content otherwise would not be objectionable.

[R]espondent Free Speech Coalition and others challenged the statute in [federal court]. The Coalition, a California trade association for the adult-entertainment industry, alleged that its members did not use minors in their sexually explicit works, but they believed some of these materials might fall within the CPPA's expanded definition of child pornography. The other respondents are Bold Type, Inc., the publisher of a book advocating the nudist lifestyle; Jim Gingerich, a painter of nudes; and Ron Raffaelli, a photographer specializing in erotic images. Respondents alleged that the "appears to be" and "conveys the impression" provisions are overbroad and vague, chilling them from producing works protected by the First Amendment. The District Court disagreed and granted summary judgment to the Government. [The] Court of Appeals for the Ninth Circuit reversed. [Four other Courts of Appeals sustained the CPPA.]

II

[A] law imposing criminal penalties on protected speech is a stark example of speech suppression. The CPPA's penalties are indeed severe. A first offender may be imprisoned for 15 years. A repeat offender faces a prison sentence of not less than 5 years and not more than 30 years in prison. [With] these severe penalties in force, few legitimate movie producers or book publishers, or few other speakers in any capacity, would risk distributing images in or near the uncertain reach of this law. The Constitution gives significant protection from overbroad laws that chill speech within the First Amendment's vast and privileged sphere. Under this principle, the CPPA is unconstitutional on its face if it prohibits a substantial amount of protected expression. *See* Broadrick v. Oklahoma, 413 U.S. 601 (1973).

The sexual abuse of a child is a most serious crime and an act repugnant to the moral instincts of a decent people. In its legislative findings, Congress recognized that there are subcultures of persons who harbor illicit desires for children and commit criminal acts to gratify the impulses. Congress also found that surrounding the serious offenders are those who flirt with these impulses and trade pictures and written accounts of sexual activity with young children.

Congress may pass valid laws to protect children from abuse, and it has. The prospect of crime, however, by itself does not justify laws suppressing protected speech. It [is] well established that speech may not be prohibited because it concerns subjects offending our sensibilities. *See* FCC v. Pacifica Foundation, 438 U.S. 726 (1978). As a general principle, the First Amendment bars the government from dictating what we see or read or speak or hear. The freedom of speech has its limits; it does not embrace certain categories of speech, including defamation, incitement, obscenity, and pornography produced with real children. While these categories may be prohibited without violating the First Amendment, none of them includes the speech prohibited by the CPPA. . . .

[T]he CPPA is much more than a supplement to the existing federal prohibition on obscenity. . . . The CPPA [extends] to images that appear to depict a minor engaging in sexually explicit activity without regard to the *Miller* requirements. The materials need not appeal to the prurient interest. Any depiction of sexually explicit activity, no matter how it is presented, is proscribed. The CPPA applies to a picture in a psychology manual, as well as a movie depicting the horrors of sexual abuse. It is not necessary, moreover, that the image be patently offensive. Pictures of what appear to be 17-year-olds engaging in sexually explicit activity do not in every case contravene community standards. The CPPA prohibits speech despite its serious literary, artistic, political, or scientific value. The statute proscribes the visual depiction of an idea — that of teenagers engaging in sexual activity — that is a fact of modern society and has been a theme in art and literature throughout the ages. Under the CPPA, images are prohibited so long as the persons appear to be under 18 years of age. This is higher than the legal age for marriage in many States, as well as the age at which persons may consent to sexual relations. It is, of course, undeniable that some youths engage in sexual activity before the legal age, either on their own inclination or because they are victims of sexual abuse.

Both themes — teenage sexual activity and the sexual abuse of children — have inspired countless literary works. William Shakespeare created the most famous pair of teenage lovers, one of whom is just 13 years of age. *See Romeo and Juliet*, act I, sc. 2, l. 9. In the drama, Shakespeare portrays the relationship as something splendid and innocent, but not juvenile. The work has inspired no less than 40 motion pictures, some of which suggest that the teenagers consummated their relationship. Shakespeare may not have written sexually explicit scenes for the Elizabethan audience, but were modern directors to adopt a less conventional approach, that fact alone would not compel the conclusion that the work was obscene. Contemporary movies pursue similar themes. Last year's Academy Awards featured the movie, *Traffic*, which was nominated for Best Picture. The film portrays a teenager, identified as a 16-year-old, who becomes addicted to drugs. The viewer sees the degradation of her addiction, which in the end leads her to a filthy room to trade sex for drugs. The year before, *American Beauty* won the Academy Award for Best Picture. In the course of the movie, a teenage girl engages in sexual relations with her teenage boyfriend, and another yields herself to the gratification of a middle-aged man. The film also contains a scene where, although [the] audience understands the act is not taking place, one character believes he is watching a teenage boy performing a sexual act on an older man.

Our society, like other cultures, has empathy and enduring fascination with the lives and destinies of the young. Art and literature express the vital interest we all have in the formative years we ourselves once knew, when wounds can be so grievous, disappointment so profound, and mistaken choices so tragic, but when moral acts and self-fulfillment are still in reach. Whether or not the films we mention violate the CPPA, they explore themes within the wide sweep of the statute's prohibitions. If these films, or hundreds of others [that] explore those subjects, contain a single graphic depiction of sexual activity within the statutory definition, the possessor of the film would be subject to severe punishment without inquiry into the work's redeeming value. This is inconsistent with an essential First Amendment rule: The artistic merit of a work does not depend on the presence of a single explicit scene. Under *Miller*, the First Amendment requires that redeeming value be judged by considering the work as a whole. Where the scene is part of the narrative, the work itself does not for this reason become obscene, even though the scene in isolation might be offensive. For this reason, [the] CPPA cannot be read to prohibit obscenity, because it lacks the required link between its prohibitions and the affront to community standards prohibited by the definition of obscenity. . . .

Ferber upheld a prohibition on the distribution and sale of child pornography, as well as its production, because these acts were "intrinsically related" to the sexual abuse of children in two ways. First, as a permanent record of a child's abuse, the continued circulation itself would harm the child who had participated. [E]ach new publication of the speech would cause new injury to the child's reputation and emotional well-being. Second, because the traffic in child pornography was an economic motive for its production, the State had an interest in closing the distribution network. "The most expeditious if not the only practical method of law enforcement may be to dry up the market for this material by imposing severe criminal penalties on persons selling, advertising, or otherwise promoting the product." Under either rationale, the speech had what the Court in effect held was a proximate link to the crime from which it came. . . . Later, in Osborne v. Ohio, 495 U.S. 103 (1990), the Court ruled that these same interests justified a ban on the possession of pornography produced by using children. . . .

In contrast to the speech in *Ferber*, speech that itself is the record of sexual abuse, the CPPA prohibits speech that records no crime and creates no victims by its production. Virtual child pornography is not "intrinsically related" to the sexual abuse of children. . . . While the Government asserts that the images can lead to actual instances of child abuse, the causal link is contingent and indirect. The harm does not necessarily follow from the speech, but depends upon some unquantified potential for subsequent criminal acts. . . . The Government says these indirect harms are sufficient [because] child pornography rarely can be valuable speech. This argument [suffers] from two flaws. First, *Ferber*'s judgment about child pornography was based upon how it was made, not on what it communicated. The case reaffirmed that where the speech is neither obscene nor the product of sexual abuse, it does not fall outside the protection of the First Amendment. . . . The second flaw in the Government's position is that *Ferber* did not hold that child pornography is by definition without value. [T]he Court recognized some works in this category might have significant value, but relied on virtual images — the very images prohibited by the CPPA — as an alternative and permissible means of expression. . . .

III

[The] Government [argues] that the CPPA is necessary because pedophiles may use virtual child pornography to seduce children. There are many things innocent in themselves, however, such as cartoons, video games, and candy, that might be used for immoral purposes, yet we would not expect those to be prohibited because they can be misused. The Government, of course, may punish adults who provide unsuitable materials to children, *see* Ginsberg v. New York, 390 U.S. 629 (1968), and it may enforce criminal penalties for unlawful solicitation. The precedents establish, however, that speech within the rights of adults to hear may not be silenced completely in an attempt to shield children from it. In Butler v. Michigan, 352 U.S. 380 (1957), the Court invalidated a statute prohibiting distribution of an indecent publication because of its tendency to "'incite minors to violent or depraved or immoral acts.'" A unanimous Court agreed [that] the State could not "reduce the adult population [to] reading only what is fit for children." We have reaffirmed this holding.

Here, the Government wants to keep speech from children not to protect them from its content but to protect them from those who would commit other crimes. [However, the] Government cannot ban speech fit for adults simply because it may fall into the hands of children. The evil in question depends upon the actor's unlawful conduct, conduct defined as criminal quite apart from any link to the speech in question. This establishes that the speech ban is not narrowly drawn. The objective is to prohibit illegal conduct, but this restriction goes well beyond that interest by restricting the speech available to law-abiding adults.

The Government submits further that virtual child pornography whets the appetites of pedophiles and encourages them to engage in illegal conduct. . . . The mere tendency of speech to encourage unlawful acts is not a sufficient reason for banning it. The government "cannot constitutionally premise legislation on the desirability of controlling a person's private thoughts." Stanley v. Georgia, 394 U.S. 557 (1969). First Amendment freedoms are most in danger when the government seeks to control thought or to justify its laws for that impermissible end. The right to think is the beginning of freedom, and speech must be protected from the government because speech is the beginning of thought.

[T]he Court's First Amendment cases draw vital distinctions between words and deeds, between ideas and conduct. The government may not prohibit speech because it increases the chance an unlawful act will be committed "at some indefinite future time." The government may suppress speech for advocating the use of force or a violation of law only if "such advocacy is directed to inciting or producing imminent lawless action and is likely to incite or produce such action." Brandenburg v. Ohio, 395 U.S. 444 (1969) (per curiam). There is here no attempt, incitement, solicitation, or conspiracy. The Government has shown no more than a remote connection between speech that might encourage thoughts or impulses and any resulting child abuse. Without a significantly stronger, more direct connection, the Government may not prohibit speech on the ground that it may encourage pedophiles to engage in illegal conduct.

The Government next argues that its objective of eliminating the market for pornography produced using real children necessitates a prohibition on virtual images as well. Virtual images, the Government contends, are indistinguishable from real ones; they are part of the same market and are often exchanged. In this way, it is said, virtual images promote the trafficking in works produced through the exploitation of real children. The hypothesis is somewhat implausible. If virtual images were identical to illegal child pornography, the illegal images would be driven from the market by the indistinguishable substitutes. Few pornographers would risk prosecution by abusing real children if fictional, computerized images would suffice.

In the case of the material covered by *Ferber*, the creation of the speech is itself the crime of child abuse; the prohibition deters the crime by removing the profit motive. Even where there is an underlying crime, however, the Court has not allowed the suppression of speech in all cases. We need not consider where to strike the balance in this case, because here, there is no underlying crime at all. Even if the Government's market deterrence theory were persuasive in some contexts, it would not justify this statute.

Finally, the Government says that the possibility of producing images by using computer imaging makes it very difficult for it to prosecute those who produce pornography by using real children. Experts, we are told, may have difficulty in saying whether the pictures were made by using real children or by using computer imaging. The necessary solution, the argument runs, is to prohibit both kinds of images. . . . The Government may not suppress lawful speech as the means to suppress unlawful speech. . . . The overbreadth doctrine prohibits the Government from banning unprotected speech if a substantial amount of protected speech is prohibited or chilled in the process.

[T]he Government would have us read the CPPA not as a measure suppressing speech but as a law shifting the burden to the accused to prove the speech is lawful. [T]he Government relies on an affirmative defense [which] allows a defendant to avoid conviction for nonpossession offenses by showing that the materials were produced using only adults and were not otherwise distributed in a manner conveying the impression that they depicted real children. *See* 18 U.S.C.

§2252A(C). The Government raises serious constitutional difficulties by seeking to impose on the defendant the burden of proving his speech is not unlawful. An affirmative defense applies only after prosecution has begun, and the speaker must himself prove, on pain of a felony conviction, that his conduct falls within the affirmative defense. . . . Where the defendant is not the producer of the work, he may have no way of establishing the identity, or even the existence, of the actors. . . . The statute, moreover, applies to work created before 1996, and the producers themselves may not have preserved the records necessary to meet the burden of proof. Failure to establish the defense can lead to a felony conviction.

We need not decide [whether] the Government could impose this burden on a speaker. [T]he defense is incomplete and insufficient. . . . It allows persons to be convicted in some instances where they can prove children were not exploited in the production. A defendant charged with possessing, as opposed to distributing, proscribed works may not defend on the ground that the film depicts only adult actors. So while the affirmative defense may protect a movie producer from prosecution for the act of distribution, that same producer, and all other persons in the subsequent distribution chain, could be liable for possessing the prohibited work. Furthermore, the affirmative defense provides no protection to persons who produce speech by using computer imaging, or through other means that do not involve the use of adult actors who appear to be minors. In these cases, the defendant can demonstrate no children were harmed in producing the images, yet the affirmative defense would not bar the prosecution. [T]he affirmative defense cannot save the statute, for it leaves unprotected a substantial amount of speech not tied to the Government's interest in distinguishing images produced using real children from virtual ones.

In sum, §2256(8)(B) covers materials beyond the categories recognized in *Ferber* and *Miller,* and the reasons the Government offers in support of limiting the freedom of speech have no justification in our precedents or in the law of the First Amendment. The provision abridges the freedom to engage in a substantial amount of lawful speech. For this reason, it is overbroad and unconstitutional.

IV

Respondents challenge §2256(8)(D) as well. This provision bans depictions of sexually explicit conduct that are "advertised, promoted, presented, described, or distributed in such a manner that conveys the impression that the material is or contains a visual depiction of a minor engaging in sexually explicit conduct." The parties treat the section as nearly identical to the provision prohibiting materials that appear to be child pornography. In the Government's view, the difference between the two is that "the 'conveys the impression' provision requires the jury to assess the material at issue in light of the manner in which it is promoted." The Government's assumption, however, is that the determination would still depend principally upon the content of the prohibited work.

We disagree with this view. The CPPA prohibits sexually explicit materials that "conve[y] the impression" they depict minors. While that phrase may sound like the "appears to be" prohibition[,] it requires little judgment about the content of the image. . . . Even if a film contains no sexually explicit scenes involving minors, it could be treated as child pornography if the title and trailers convey the impression that the scenes would be found in the movie. The determination turns on how the speech is presented, not on what is depicted. While the legislative findings address at length the problems posed by materials that look like child pornography, they are silent on the evils posed by images simply pandered that way.

The Government does not offer a serious defense of this provision. . . . The Court has recognized that pandering may be relevant, as an evidentiary matter, to the question whether particular materials are obscene. *See* Ginzburg v. United States, 383 U.S. 463 (1966). . . . Section 2256(8)(D), however, prohibits a substantial amount of speech that falls outside *Ginzburg*'s rationale. Materials falling within the proscription are tainted and unlawful in the hands of all who receive it, though they bear no responsibility for how it was marketed, sold, or described. The statute, furthermore, does not require that the context be part of an effort at "commercial exploitation." As a consequence, the CPPA does more than prohibit pandering. It prohibits possession of material described, or pandered, as child pornography by someone earlier in the distribution chain. The provision prohibits a sexually explicit film containing no youthful actors, just because it is placed in a box suggesting a prohibited movie. Possession is a crime even when the possessor knows the movie was mislabeled. The First Amendment requires a more precise restriction. . . . §2256(8)(D) is substantially overbroad and in violation of the First Amendment.

V

For the reasons we have set forth, the prohibitions of §§2256(8)(B) and 2256(8)(D) are overbroad and unconstitutional. Having reached this conclusion, we need not address respondents' further contention that the provisions are unconstitutional because of vague statutory language.

The judgment of the Court of Appeals is affirmed.

It is so ordered.

Justice O'CONNOR, with whom THE CHIEF JUSTICE and Justice SCALIA join as to Part II, concurring in the judgment in part and dissenting in part.

[The] Court has long recognized that the Government has a compelling interest in protecting our Nation's children. . . . These efforts [are] supported by the CPPA's ban on virtual child pornography. Such images whet the appetites of child molesters who may use the images to seduce young children. Of even more serious concern is the prospect that defendants indicted for the production, distribution, or possession of actual child pornography may evade liability by claiming that the images attributed to them are in fact computer-generated. [G]iven the rapid pace of advances in computer-graphics technology, the Government's concern is reasonable. [Our] cases do not require Congress to wait for harm to occur before it can legislate against it. . . .

The Court concludes that the CPPA's ban on virtual child pornography is overbroad. [Overbreadth litigants] bear the heavy burden of demonstrating that the regulation forbids a substantial amount of valuable or harmless speech.

Respondents have not made such a demonstration. Respondents provide no examples of films or other materials that are wholly computer generated and contain images that "appea[r] to be [of] minors" engaging in indecent conduct, but that have serious value or do not facilitate child abuse. Their overbreadth challenge therefore fails. . . . I would strike down the CPPA's ban on material that "conveys the impression" that it contains actual child pornography, but uphold the ban on pornographic depictions that "appea[r] to be" of minors so long as it is not applied to youthful adult pornography.

Chief Justice REHNQUIST, with whom Justice SCALIA joins in part, dissenting.

[Congress] has a compelling interest in ensuring the ability to enforce prohibitions of actual child pornography, and we should defer to its findings that rapidly advancing technology soon will make it all but impossible to do so. . . . I also agree with Justice O'Connor that serious First Amendment concerns would arise were the Government ever to prosecute someone for simple distribution or possession of a film with literary or artistic value, such as *Traffic* or *American Beauty*. [The CPPA] need not be construed to reach such materials. . . . [Read as a whole, the Act] reaches only the sort of "hard core of child pornography" that we found without protection in *Ferber*. So construed, the CPPA bans visual depictions of youthful looking adult actors engaged in *actual* sexual activity; mere *suggestions* of sexual activity, such as youthful looking adult actors squirming under a blanket, are more akin to written descriptions than visual depictions, and thus fall outside the purview of the statute. [The] inclusion of "simulated" conduct, alongside "actual" conduct, does not change the "hard core" nature of the image banned. . . . Neither actual conduct nor simulated conduct, however, is properly construed to reach depictions such as those in a film portrayal of *Romeo and Juliet*. . . . Indeed, we should be loath to construe a statute as banning film portrayals of Shakespearian tragedies, without some indication — from text or legislative history — that such a result was intended. In fact, Congress explicitly instructed that such a reading of the CPPA would be wholly [unwarranted].

[H]ad "sexually explicit conduct" been thought to reach the sort of material the Court says it does, then films such as *Traffic* and *American Beauty* would not have been made the way they were. . . . To the extent the CPPA prohibits possession or distribution of materials that "convey the impression" of a child engaged in sexually explicit conduct, that prohibition can and should be limited to reach "the sordid business of pandering" which lies outside the bounds of First Amendment protection. Ginzburg v. United States, 383 U.S. 463 (1966). . . . The First Amendment may protect the video shopowner or film distributor who promotes material as "entertaining" or "acclaimed" regardless of whether the material contains depictions of youthful looking adult actors engaged in nonobscene but sexually suggestive conduct. The First Amendment does not, however, protect the panderer. . . . The Court says that "conveys the impression" goes well beyond *Ginzburg* to "prohibi[t] [the] possession of material described, or pandered, as child pornography by someone earlier in the distribution chain." [C]onsistent with the narrow class of images the CPPA is intended to prohibit, the CPPA can be construed to prohibit only the knowing possession of [such] materials. . . . The mere possession of materials containing only suggestive depictions of youthful looking adult actors need not be so included.

[The] aim of ensuring the enforceability of our Nation's child pornography laws is a compelling one. The CPPA is targeted to this aim by extending the definition of child pornography to reach computer-generated images that are virtually indistinguishable from real children engaged in sexually explicit conduct. The statute need not be read to do any more than precisely this, which is not offensive to the First Amendment. . . . I would construe the CPPA in a manner consistent with the First Amendment, reverse the Court of Appeals' judgment, and uphold the statute in its entirety.

Note: **Ginsberg** *and* **Ashcroft**

Like the 1968 *Ginsberg* decision regarding the government interest in the protection of minors from nonobscene sex-related materials, the 1966 *Ginzburg* decision involving "pandering" as a basis for an obscenity prosecution has retained vitality in the modern era, providing a source of government arguments for regulating speech outside the obscenity context. For a view favoring further expansion of the scope of unprotected speech in the context of sex-related materials, see Ashcroft v. American Civil Liberties Union [*Ashcroft II*], 542 U.S. 656 (2004) (Scalia, J., dissenting) ("commercial entities which engage in 'the sordid business of pandering' by 'deliberately emphasiz[ing] the sexually provocative aspects of [their nonobscene] products], in order to catch the salaciously disposed,' engage in constitutionally unprotected behavior").

∽ PROBLEMS ∽

1. *Advancing Technology.* Suppose that computer technology advances to the point that it becomes virtually (no pun intended) impossible to distinguish between actual child pornography and virtual child pornography. Would or should the Court shift its position on Congress's ability to prohibit virtual child pornography? Would it matter whether there was proof that pornographers continued to use actual children in the production of their images?

2. *Pandering Material as Child Pornography.* After the decision in Ashcroft v. Free Speech Coalition, 535 U.S. 234 (2002), invalidated the "pandering" provision of the Child Pornography Prevention Act, Congress enacted a "pandering" provision in the 2003 Prosecutorial Remedies and Other Tools to End the Exploitation of Children Today Act (PROTECT Act). This provision makes it a crime to "knowingly advertise or promote in interstate or foreign commerce any material in a manner that reflects the belief, or that is intended to cause another to believe, that the material is or contains either a) an obscene visual depiction of a minor engaging in sexually explicit conduct, or b) a visual depiction of an actual minor engaging in sexually explicit conduct." The term *sexually explicit conduct* is defined to include "the lascivious exhibition of the genitals or pubic area of any person." There is no community standard required for determining whether an image of

a nude child is "lascivious." In its defense of the statute, the government relies on Ginzburg v. United States, 383 U.S. 463 (1966). When the statute is challenged on the grounds that it cannot survive strict scrutiny, how should the court rule? Explain. *See* United States v. Williams, 444 F.3d 1286 (11th Cir. 2006).

3. *More on the International Treaty Regulating the Internet.* Most countries agree that child pornography should be prohibited. Of course, part of the problem is that some web posters use so-called "anonymous re-mailers" to distribute child pornography. The re-mailer receives child pornography from one source, strips all identifying information from the e-mail message (thereby rendering it anonymous), and then e-mails the child pornography to others. When such re-mailers are used, it can be very difficult to determine the original source of the child pornography. For example, in one case, when governmental officials seized the computers of an anonymous re-mailer in Europe (in an attempt to determine the source of child pornography), the government learned that the child pornography had been sent by another anonymous re-mailer in Asia. In an effort to stop child pornography, what language might you be able to agree to for inclusion in the treaty that would help control the spread of child pornography on the Internet? Would you suggest any special provisions that would assist governments in tracking down the source of these anonymous postings?

9. Pornography That Degrades Women

After *Ferber* revealed that the Court was willing to expand the definition of unprotected speech, a movement began to enact ordinances that would define pornography as being harmful to women, and to impose civil penalties on specific types of such pornography, including violent pornography. When these ordinances were adopted by some cities, they were challenged on First Amendment grounds.

American Booksellers Association, Inc. v. Hudnut

771 F.2d 323 (7th Cir. 1985)

EASTERBROOK, Circuit Judge

Indianapolis enacted an ordinance defining "pornography" as a practice that discriminates against women. "Pornography" is to be redressed through the administrative and judicial methods used for other discrimination. The City's definition of "pornography" is considerably different from "obscenity," which the Supreme Court has held is not protected by the First Amendment.

To be "obscene" under Miller v. California, 413 U.S. 15 (1973), "a publication must, taken as a whole, appeal to the prurient interest, must contain patently offensive depictions or descriptions of specified sexual conduct, and on the whole have no serious literary, artistic, political, or scientific value." Offensiveness must be assessed under the standards of the community. Both offensiveness and an appeal to something other than "normal, healthy sexual desires" are essential elements of "obscenity."

"Pornography" under the ordinance is "the graphic sexually explicit subordination of women, whether in pictures or in words, that also includes one or more of the following:

(1)   Women are presented as sexual objects who enjoy pain or humiliation; or
(2)   Women are presented as sexual objects who experience sexual pleasure in being raped; or
(3)   Women are presented as sexual objects tied up or cut up or mutilated or bruised or physically hurt, or as dismembered or truncated or fragmented or severed into body parts; or
(4)   Women are presented as being penetrated by objects or animals; or
(5)   Women are presented in scenarios of degradation, injury, abasement, torture, shown as filthy or inferior, bleeding, bruised, or hurt in a context that makes these conditions sexual; or
(6)   Women are presented as sexual objects for domination, conquest, violation, exploitation, possession, or use, or through postures or positions of servility or submission or display."

Indianapolis Code §16-3(q). The statute provides that the "use of men, children, or transsexuals in the place of women in paragraphs (1) through (6) above shall also constitute pornography under this section."

The Indianapolis ordinance does not refer to the prurient interest, to offensiveness, or to the standards of the community. It demands attention to particular depictions, not to the work judged as a whole. It is irrelevant under the ordinance whether the work has literary, artistic, political, or scientific value. The City and many amici point to these omissions as virtues. They maintain that pornography influences attitudes, and the statute is a way to alter the socialization of men and women rather than to vindicate community standards of offensiveness. And as one of the principal drafters of the ordinance has asserted, "if a woman is subjected, why should it matter that the work has other value?" Catharine A. MacKinnon, *Pornography, Civil Rights, and Speech*, 20 Harv. C.R.-C.L. L. Rev. 1, 21 (1985).

[Those] supporting the ordinance say that it will play [a] role in reducing the tendency of men to view women as sexual objects, a tendency that leads to both unacceptable attitudes and discrimination in the workplace and violence away from it. Those opposing the ordinance point out that much radical feminist literature is explicit and depicts women in ways forbidden by the ordinance. . . . It is unclear how Indianapolis would treat works from James Joyce's *Ulysses* to Homer's *Iliad*; both depict women as submissive objects for conquest and domination.

We do not try to balance the arguments for and against an ordinance such as this. The ordinance discriminates on the ground of the content of the speech. Speech treating women in the approved way — in sexual encounters "premised on equality" — is lawful no matter how sexually explicit. Speech treating women in the disapproved way — as submissive in matters sexual or as enjoying humiliation — is unlawful no matter how significant the literary, artistic, or political qualities of the work taken as a whole. The state may not ordain preferred viewpoints in this way. The Constitution forbids the state to declare one perspective right and silence opponents.

I

The ordinance contains four prohibitions. People may not "traffic" in pornography, "coerce" others into performing in pornographic works, or "force" pornography on anyone. Anyone injured by someone who has seen or read pornography has a right of action against the maker or seller. . . . Trafficking is defined in §16-3(g)(4) as the "production, sale, exhibition, or distribution of pornography." The offense excludes exhibition in a public or educational library, but a "special display" in a library may be sex discrimination. Section 16-3(g)(4)(C) provides that the trafficking paragraph "shall not be construed to make isolated passages or isolated parts actionable."

"Coercion into pornographic performance" is defined in §16-3(g)(5) as "[c]oercing, intimidating or fraudulently inducing any person [into] performing for pornography. . . ." The ordinance specifies that proof of any of the following "shall not constitute a defense: I. That the person is a woman[;] VI. That the person has previously posed for sexually explicit pictures [with anyone;] VIII. That the person actually consented to a use of the performance that is changed into pornography[;] IX. That the person knew that the purpose of the acts or events in question was to make pornography[;] XI. That the person signed a contract, or made statements affirming a willingness to cooperate in the production of pornography; XII. That no physical force, threats, or weapons were used in the making of the pornography; or XIII. That the person was paid or otherwise compensated."

"Forcing pornography on a person," according to §16-3(g)(5), is the "forcing of pornography on any woman, man, child, or transsexual in any place of employment, in education, in a home, or in any public place." The statute does not define forcing, but one of its authors states that the definition reaches pornography shown to medical students as part of their education or given to language students for translation. *MacKinnon, supra,* at 40-41.

Section 16-3(g)(7) defines as a prohibited practice the "assault, physical attack, or injury of any woman, man, child, or transsexual in a way that is directly caused by specific pornography."

For purposes of all four offenses, it is generally "not [a] defense that the respondent did not know or intend that the materials were pornography. . . ." Section 16-3(g)(8). But the ordinance provides that damages are unavailable in trafficking cases unless the complainant proves "that the respondent knew or had reason to know that the materials were pornography." It is a complete defense to a trafficking case that all of the materials in question were pornography only by virtue of category (6) of the definition of pornography. In cases of assault caused by pornography, those who seek damages from "a seller, exhibitor or distributor" must show that the defendant knew or had reason to know of the material's status as pornography. By implication, those who seek damages from an author need not show this.

A woman aggrieved by trafficking in pornography may file a complaint "as a woman acting against the subordination of women" with the office of equal opportunity. A man, child, or transsexual also may protest trafficking "but must prove injury in the same way that a woman is injured. . . ." Subsection (a) also provides, however, that "any person claiming to be aggrieved" by trafficking, coercion, forcing, or assault may complain against the "perpetrators." [The office] may make findings and enter orders, including both orders to cease and desist and orders "to take further affirmative action [including] but not limited to the power to restore complainant's losses. . . ." . . . The district court held the ordinance unconstitutional. . . .

III

"If there is any fixed star in our constitutional constellation, it is that no official, high or petty, can prescribe what shall be orthodox in politics, nationalism, religion, or other matters of opinion or force citizens to confess by word or act their faith therein." West Virginia State Board of Education v. Barnette, 319 U.S. 624 (1943). Under the First Amendment the government must leave to the people the evaluation of ideas. Bald or subtle, an idea is as powerful as the audience allows it to be. A belief may be pernicious — the beliefs of Nazis led to the death of millions, those of the Klan to the repression of millions. A pernicious belief may prevail. Totalitarian governments today rule much of the planet, practicing suppression of billions and spreading dogma that may enslave others. One of the things that separates our society from theirs is our absolute right to propagate opinions that the government finds wrong or even hateful.

[Under] the ordinance graphic sexually explicit speech is "pornography" or not depending on the perspective the author adopts. Speech that "subordinates" women and also, for example, presents women as enjoying pain, humiliation, or rape, or even simply presents women in "positions of servility or submission or display" is forbidden, no matter how great the literary or political value of the work taken as a whole. Speech that portrays women in positions of equality is lawful, no matter how graphic the sexual content. This is thought control. It establishes an "approved" view of women, of how they may react to sexual encounters, of how the sexes may relate to each other. Those who espouse the approved view may use sexual images; those who do not, may not.

Indianapolis justifies the ordinance on the ground that pornography affects thoughts. Men who see women depicted as subordinate are more likely to treat them so. Pornography is an aspect of dominance. It does not persuade people so much as change them. It works by socializing, by establishing the expected and the permissible. In this view pornography is not an idea; pornography is the injury.

There is much to this perspective. Beliefs are also facts. People often act in accordance with the images and patterns they find around them. People raised in a religion tend to accept the tenets of that religion, often without independent examination. People taught from birth that black people are fit only for slavery rarely rebelled against that creed; beliefs coupled with the self-interest of the masters established a social structure that inflicted great harm while enduring for centuries. Words and images act at the level of the subconscious before they persuade at the level of the conscious. Even the truth has little chance unless a statement fits within the framework of beliefs that may never have been subjected to rational study.

Therefore we accept the premises of this legislation. Depictions of subordination tend to perpetuate subordination. The subordinate status of women in turn leads to affront and lower pay at work, insult and injury at home, battery and rape on the streets. In the language of the legislature, "[p]ornography is central in creating and maintaining sex as a basis of discrimination. Pornography is a systematic practice of exploitation and subordination based on sex which differentially harms women. The bigotry and contempt it produces, with the acts of aggression it fosters, harm women's opportunities for equality and rights [of all kinds]." Indianapolis Code §16-1(a)(2).

Yet this simply demonstrates the power of pornography as speech. All of these unhappy effects depend on mental intermediation. Pornography affects how people see the world, their fellows, and social relations. If pornography is what pornography does, so is other speech. . . . Racial bigotry, anti-semitism, violence on television, reporters' biases — these and many more influence the culture and shape our socialization. None is directly answerable by more speech, unless that speech too finds its place in the popular culture. Yet all is protected as speech, however insidious. Any other answer leaves the government in control of all of the institutions of culture, the great censor and director of which thoughts are good for us.

Sexual responses often are unthinking responses, and the association of sexual arousal with the subordination of women therefore may have a substantial effect. But almost all cultural stimuli provoke unconscious responses. Religious ceremonies condition their participants. . . . Television scripts contain unarticulated assumptions. People may be conditioned in subtle ways. If the fact that speech plays a role in a process of conditioning were enough to permit governmental regulation, that would be the end of freedom of speech.

[Indianapolis] emphasizes the injury that models in pornographic films and pictures may suffer. The record contains materials depicting sexual torture, penetration of women by red-hot irons and the like. [T]he image of pain is not necessarily pain. In *Body Double,* a suspense film[,] a woman who has disrobed and presented a sexually explicit display is murdered by an intruder with a drill. . . . The film is sexually explicit and a murder occurs — yet no one believes that the actress suffered pain or died. . . . In *Carnal Knowledge* a woman grovels to please the sexual whims of a character played by Jack Nicholson; no one believes that there was a real sexual submission. . . . Depictions may affect slavery, war, or sexual roles, but a book about slavery is not itself slavery, or a book about death by poison a murder.

Much of Indianapolis's argument rests on the belief that when speech is "unanswerable," and the metaphor that there is a "marketplace of ideas" does not apply, the First Amendment does not apply either. The metaphor is honored [on] the ground that the truth will prevail. . . . The Framers undoubtedly believed it. As a general matter it is true. But the Constitution does not make the dominance of truth a necessary condition of freedom of speech. To say that it does would be to confuse an outcome of free speech with a necessary condition for the application of the amendment.

A power to limit speech on the ground that truth has not yet prevailed and is not likely to prevail implies the power to declare truth. . . . Under the First Amendment, however, there is no such thing as a false idea so the government may not restrict speech on the ground that in a free exchange truth is not yet dominant. . . . Supporters of minority candidates may be forever "excluded" from the political process because their candidates never win, because few people believe their positions. This does not mean that freedom of speech has failed. . . .

We come, finally, to the argument that pornography is "low value" speech, that it is enough like obscenity that Indianapolis may prohibit it. Some cases hold that speech far removed from politics and other subjects at the core of the Framers' concerns may be subjected to special regulation. *E.g.,* FCC v. Pacifica Foundation, 438 U.S. 726 (1978). These cases do not sustain statutes that select among viewpoints, however. . . . At all events, "pornography" is not low value speech within the meaning of these cases. Indianapolis seeks to prohibit certain speech because it believes this speech influences social relations and politics on a grand scale, that it controls attitudes at home and in the legislature. This precludes a characterization of the speech as low value. True, pornography and obscenity have sex in common. But Indianapolis left out of its definition any reference to literary, artistic, political, or scientific value. The ordinance applies to graphic sexually explicit subordination in works great and small. The Court sometimes balances the value of speech against the costs of its restriction, but it does this by category of speech and not by the content of particular works. Indianapolis has created an approved point of view and so loses the support of these cases.

Any rationale we could imagine in support of this ordinance could not be limited to sex discrimination. Free speech has been on balance an ally of those seeking change. Governments that want stasis start by restricting speech. Culture is a powerful force of continuity; Indianapolis paints pornography as part of the culture of power. Change in any complex system ultimately depends on the ability of outsiders to challenge accepted views and the reigning institutions. Without a strong guarantee of freedom of speech, there is no effective right to challenge what is.

The definition of "pornography" is unconstitutional. No construction or excision of particular terms could save it. . . . Without question a state may prohibit fraud, trickery, or the use of force to induce people to perform — in pornographic films or in any other films. Such a statute may be written without regard to the viewpoint depicted in the work. . . . But the Indianapolis ordinance [is] not neutral with respect to viewpoint. The ban on distribution of works containing coerced performances is limited to pornography; coercion is irrelevant if the work is not "pornography," and we have held the definition of "pornography" to be defective root and branch. . . .

The offense of forcing pornography on unwilling recipients is harder to assess. Many kinds of forcing [may] themselves be protected speech. Rowan v. Post Office, 397 U.S. 728 (1970), shows that a state may permit people to insulate themselves from categories of speech — in *Rowan* sexual mail — but that the government must leave the decision about what items are forbidden in the hands of the potentially offended recipients. Exposure to sex is not something the government may prevent. We therefore could not save the offense of "forcing" by redefining "pornography" as all sexually-offensive speech or some related category. The statute needs a definition of "forcing" that removes the government from the role of censor.

The section creating remedies for injuries and assaults attributable to pornography also is salvageable in principle. . . . The First Amendment does not prohibit redress of all injuries caused by speech. . . . Cases such as Brandenburg v. Ohio and NAACP v. Claiborne Hardware hold that a state may not penalize speech that does not cause immediate injury. But we do not doubt that if, immediately after the Klan's rally in *Brandenburg,* a mob had burned to the ground the house of a nearby black person, that person could have recovered damages from the speaker who whipped the crowd into a frenzy. . . . Certainly no damages could be awarded unless the harm flowed directly from the speech and there was an element of intent on the part of the speaker. . . .

Much speech is dangerous. Chemists whose work might help someone build a bomb, political theorists whose papers might start political movements that lead to riots, speakers whose ideas attract violent protesters, all these and more leave loss in their wake. Unless the remedy is very closely confined, it could be more dangerous to speech than all the libel judgments in history. The constitutional requirements for a valid recovery for assault caused by speech might turn out to be too rigorous for any plaintiff to meet. But the Indianapolis ordinance requires the complainant to show that the attack was "directly caused by specific pornography," and it is not beyond the realm of possibility that a state court could construe this limitation in a way that would make the statute constitutional. We are not authorized to prevent the state from trying.

[No] amount of struggle with particular words and phrases in this ordinance can leave anything in effect. The district court came to the same conclusion. Its judgment is therefore

Affirmed.

Note and Question: A "Feminist Critique"

In evaluating the Indianapolis ordinance, consider Nadine Strossen, *A Feminist Critique of "the" Feminist Critique of Pornography,* 79 Va. L. Rev. 1099 (1993). Strossen argues that, given "the pervasive presence of sexist, violent imagery in mainstream American culture, most such imagery would remain intact, even if 'pornography' could be effectively suppressed." Moreover, she questions the assumptions on which the ordinance is based: The "conclusion that the costs of 'pornography' censorship outweigh its putative benefits, in terms of women's rights, is reinforced by the lack of evidence to substantiate the alleged casual link between exposure to 'pornography' and misogynistic discrimination or violence." Finally, she argues that the "speculative, attenuated benefits of censoring 'pornography,' in terms of reducing violence and discrimination against women, are far outweighed by the substantial, demonstrable costs of such a censorship regime in terms of women's rights." She notes that "[t]hroughout history, . . . censorial power has consistently been used to stifle women's sexuality, women's expression, and women's full and equal participation in our society." As a result, she concludes that "[as] is true for all relatively disempowered groups, women have a special stake in preserving our system of free expression. For those women who find certain 'pornographic' imagery troubling, their most effective weapon is to raise their voices and say so." Do you agree?

∼ PROBLEMS ∼

1. *Redrafting the Ordinance.* Assume that the Indianapolis City Council wants to try to redraft some parts of the ordinance in a way that may survive constitutional challenge. You are the city attorney. How would you redraft the ordinance?

2. *More on the International Treaty Regulating the Internet.* Again, as part of their general effort to protect individuals against degradation of their human dignity, European delegates demand that the treaty contain explicit language prohibiting the "degradation of women." In light of the First Amendment, can you agree to such language? What language might you agree to that could (potentially) be acceptable to (or, at least, would make a good faith effort to satisfy) the European delegates?

10. Near Obscene

After the boundaries of "obscene" speech were settled in *Miller,* the question remained whether content regulations of nonobscene materials related to sex should be treated in the same manner as other content regulations. Varying answers to this question have been given, and although all nonobscene sex-related speech is theoretically treated as "protected speech," there are contexts in which the "low value" of that speech may be used to justify deviation from the strict scrutiny model. For example, some regulations of nonobscene speech that is close to the obscenity boundary, and hence "near obscene," have provoked controversial uses of a variety of "content-neutral" doctrines, including the "time, place, manner" test, the "secondary effects" analysis, and the *O'Brien* test. Sharp divisions on the Court have produced opinions where only a plurality consensus can be reached, sometimes to yield to a majority produced after years of debate. However, some "near-obscene" speech regulations remain subject to strict scrutiny analysis. The "near-obscene" category of speech, not envisioned before *Miller,* is not a category that is characterized by uniform standards of review, and since the 1980s it has become one of the most rapidly evolving fields of speech doctrine.

Erznoznik v. City of Jacksonville

422 U.S. 205 (1975)

Mr. Justice POWELL delivered the opinion of the Court.

This case presents a challenge to the facial validity of a Jacksonville, Fla., ordinance that prohibits showing films containing nudity by a drive-in movie theater when its screen is visible from a public street or place.

Appellant, Richard Erznoznik, is the manager of the University Drive-In Theatre in Jacksonville. On March 13, 1972, [when the theatre was showing *Class of '74*, a movie rated R] he was charged with the crime of exhibiting a motion picture, visible from public streets, in which "female buttocks and bare breasts were shown." The ordinance [provides]:

> It shall be unlawful and it is hereby declared a public nuisance for any ticket seller, ticket taker, usher, motion picture projection machine operator, manager, owner, or any other person connected with or employed by any drive-in theater in the City to exhibit, or aid or assist in exhibiting, any motion picture, slide, or other exhibit in which the human male or female bare buttocks, human female bare breasts, or human bare pubic areas are shown, if such motion picture, slide, or other exhibit is visible from any public street or public place.

[Appellant] successfully stay[ed the] prosecution so that the validity of the ordinance could be tested. [The city] introduced evidence showing that [appellant's] screen [is] visible from two adjacent public streets and a nearby church parking lot [and] people had been observed watching films while sitting outside the theater in parked cars and in the [grass].

[The City] concedes that its ordinance sweeps far beyond the permissible restraints on obscenity, and thus applies to films that are protected by the First Amendment. Nevertheless, it maintains that any movie containing nudity which is visible from a public place may be suppressed as a nuisance [and that] it may protect its citizens against unwilling exposure to materials that may be offensive. Jacksonville's ordinance, however, does not protect citizens from all movies that might offend; rather it singles out films containing nudity, presumably because the lawmakers considered them especially offensive to passersby.

This Court has considered analogous issues — pitting the First Amendment rights of speakers against the privacy rights of those who may be unwilling viewers or auditors — in a variety of contexts. [S]ome general principles have emerged. A State or municipality may protect individual privacy by enacting reasonable time, place, and manner regulations applicable to all speech irrespective of content. But when the government, acting as censor, undertakes selectively to shield the public from some kinds of speech on the ground that they are more offensive than others, the First Amendment strictly limits its power. Such selective restrictions have been upheld only when the speaker intrudes on the privacy of the home, or the degree of captivity makes it impractical for the unwilling viewer or auditor to avoid exposure. As Mr. Justice Harlan cautioned: "The ability of government, consonant with the Constitution, to shut off discourse solely to protect others from hearing it [is] dependent upon a showing that substantial privacy interests are being invaded in an essentially intolerable manner. Any broader view of this authority would effectively empower a majority to silence dissidents simply as a matter of personal predilections." Cohen v. California, 403 U.S., at 21.

The plain, if at times disquieting, truth is that in our pluralistic society, constantly proliferating new and ingenious forms of expression, "we are inescapably captive audiences for many purposes." Much that we encounter offends our esthetic, if not our political and moral, sensibilities. Nevertheless, the Constitution does not permit government to decide which types of otherwise protected speech are sufficiently offensive to require protection for the unwilling listener or viewer. Rather, absent the narrow circumstances described above, the burden normally falls upon the viewer to "avoid further bombardment of (his) sensibilities simply by averting (his) eyes." Cohen v. California, *supra,* 403 U.S., at 21.

The Jacksonville ordinance discriminates among movies solely on the basis of content. Its effect is to deter drive-in theaters from showing movies containing any nudity, however innocent or even educational. This discrimination cannot be justified as a means of preventing significant intrusions on privacy. The ordinance seeks only to keep these films from being seen from public streets and places where the offended viewer readily can avert his eyes. In short, the screen of a drive-in theater is not "so obtrusive as to make it impossible for an unwilling individual to avoid exposure to it." Thus, we conclude that the limited privacy interest of persons on the public streets cannot justify this censorship of otherwise protected speech on the basis of its content.

[The City also] maintains that even though it cannot prohibit the display of films containing nudity to adults, the present ordinance is a reasonable means of protecting minors from this type of visual influence. . . . It is well settled that a State or municipality can adopt more stringent controls on communicative materials available to youths than on those available to adults. *See, e.g.,* Ginsberg v. New York, 390 U.S. 629 (1968). Nevertheless, minors are entitled to a significant measure of First Amendment protection, and only in relatively narrow and well-defined circumstances may government bar public dissemination of protected materials to them. . . . In this case, assuming the ordinance is aimed at prohibiting youths from viewing the films, the restriction is broader than permissible. The ordinance is not directed against sexually explicit nudity, nor is it otherwise limited. Rather, it sweepingly forbids display of all films containing any uncovered buttocks or breasts, irrespective of context or pervasiveness. Thus it would bar a film containing a picture of a baby's buttocks, the nude body of a war victim, or scenes from a culture in which nudity is indigenous. The ordinance also might prohibit newsreel scenes of the opening of an art exhibit as well as shots of bathers on a beach. Clearly all nudity cannot be deemed obscene even as to minors. Nor can such a broad restriction be justified by any other governmental interest pertaining to minors. Speech that is neither obscene as to youths nor subject to some other legitimate proscription cannot be suppressed solely to protect the young from ideas or images that a legislative body thinks unsuitable for them. In most circumstances, the values protected by the First Amendment are no less applicable when government seeks to control the flow of information to minors.

Thus, if Jacksonville's ordinance is intended to regulate expression accessible to minors it is overbroad in its proscription.

At oral argument [the City], for the first time, sought to justify its ordinance as a traffic regulation. It claimed that nudity on a drive-in movie screen distracts passing motorists, thus slowing the flow of traffic and increasing the likelihood of accidents. . . . Nothing in the record or in the text of the ordinance suggests that it is aimed at traffic regulation. . . . But even if this were the purpose of the ordinance, it nonetheless would be invalid. By singling out movies containing even the most fleeting and innocent glimpses of nudity the legislative classification is strikingly underinclusive. There is no reason to think that a wide variety of other scenes in the customary screen diet, ranging from soap opera to violence, would be any less distracting to the passing motorist. . . . This Court frequently has upheld underinclusive classifications on the sound theory that a legislature may deal with one part of a problem without addressing all of it. This presumption of statutory validity, however, has less force when a classification turns on the subject matter of expression. . . . [Even] a traffic regulation cannot discriminate on the basis of content unless there are clear reasons for the distinctions. . . .

[T]he Court has held that a state statute should not be deemed facially invalid unless it is not readily subject to a narrowing construction by the state courts, and its deterrent effect on legitimate expression is both real and substantial. *See* Broadrick v. Oklahoma, 413 U.S. 601 (1973). [The] ordinance by its plain terms is not easily susceptible of a narrowing construction. . . . Moreover, the deterrent effect of this ordinance is both real and substantial. Since it applies specifically to all persons employed by or connected with drive-in theaters, the owners and operators of these theaters are faced with an unwelcome choice: to avoid prosecution of themselves and their employees they must either restrict their movie offerings or construct adequate protective fencing which may be extremely expensive or even physically impracticable.

[Where] First Amendment freedoms are at stake we have repeatedly emphasized that precision of drafting and clarity of purpose are essential. These prerequisites are absent here. Accordingly the judgment below is reversed.

Reversed.

Mr. Chief Justice Burger, with whom Mr. Justice Rehnquist, joins, dissenting.

[Whatever] validity the notion that passersby may protect their sensibilities by averting their eyes may have when applied to words printed on an individual's jacket, it distorts reality to apply that notion to the outsize screen of a drive-in movie theater [that] is a unique type of eye-catching display that can be highly intrusive and distracting. Public authorities have a legitimate interest in regulating such displays under the police power. . . . I think it not unreasonable for lawmakers to believe that public nudity on a giant screen, visible at night to hundreds of drivers of automobiles, may have a tendency to divert attention from their task and cause accidents.

[T]he owner of a drive-in movie theater is not prevented from exhibiting nonobscene films involving nudity so long as he effectively shields the screen from public view. Thus, [the] ordinance [is] not a restriction of any "message."

The First Amendment interests involved in this case are trivial at best. [Assuming] that there could be a play performed in a theater by nude actors involving genuine communication of ideas, the same conduct in a public park or street could be prosecuted under an ordinance prohibiting indecent exposure. This is so because the police power has long been interpreted to authorize the regulation of nudity in areas to which all members of the public have access, regardless of any incidental effect upon communication. . . . Whether such regulation is justified as necessary to protect public mores or simply to insure the undistracted enjoyment of open areas by the greatest number of people — or for traffic safety — its rationale applies a fortiori to giant displays which through technology are capable of revealing and emphasizing the most intimate details of human anatomy. . . .

∾ PROBLEMS ∾

1. *Ordinance Drafting.* Assume that you are asked to help the city council draft an ordinance regulating drive-in movie theaters that is addressed to the government interest in traffic safety. Can such an ordinance be drafted without overbreadth problems?

2. *More on Drafting.* In order to avoid strict scrutiny of content-based regulations of drive-in movie theaters as exemplified in *Erznoznik*, the city council asks you to draft an ordinance that may be deemed to be "content neutral" and that will also solve a variety of problems the city has with drive-in movie theaters. First, think of all the possible problems that the city may have with such theaters. Then explain what sorts of suggested ordinances you can offer.

Young v. American Mini Theatres, Inc.
427 U.S. 50 (1976)

Mr. Justice STEVENS delivered the opinion of the Court. [Part III of this opinion is joined by only THE CHIEF JUSTICE, Mr. Justice WHITE, and Mr. Justice REHNQUIST.]

[Detroit adopted ordinances requiring that] "adult" theaters [be] dispersed. Specifically, an adult theater may not be located within 1,000 feet of any two other "regulated uses" or within 500 feet of a residential area. The term "regulated uses" includes 10 different kinds of establishments in addition to adult theaters [including adult bookstores; cabarets; establishments for the sale of beer or intoxicating liquor for consumption on the premises; hotels or motels; pawnshops; pool or billiard halls; public lodging houses; secondhand stores; shoeshine parlors; and taxi dance halls.]

The classification of a theater as "adult" is expressly predicated on the character of the motion pictures which it exhibits. If the theater is used to present "material distinguished or characterized by an emphasis on matter depicting, describing or relating to 'Specified Sexual Activities' or 'Specified Anatomical Areas,'" it is an adult establishment. ["Specified Sexual Activities" is defined as: 1) Human genitals in a state of sexual stimulation or arousal; 2) Acts of human masturbation, sexual intercourse, or sodomy; 3) Fondling or other erotic touching of human genitals, pubic region, buttock, or female breast. And "Specified Anatomical Areas" is defined as: 1) Less than completely and opaquely covered: a) human genitals, pubic region, b) buttock, and c) female breast below a point immediately above the top of the areola; and 2) Human male genitals in a discernibly turgid state, even if completely and opaquely covered.]

The [ordinance involved] amendments to an "Anti-Skid Row Ordinance" which had been adopted 10 years earlier. At that time the Detroit Common Council made a finding that some uses of property are especially injurious to a neighborhood when they are concentrated in limited areas. The decision to add adult motion picture theaters and adult book stores to the list [was], in part, a response to the significant growth in the number of such establishments. In the opinion of urban planners and real estate experts[,] the location of several such businesses in the same neighborhood tends to attract an undesirable quantity and quality of transients, adversely affects property values, causes an increase in crime, especially prostitution, and encourages residents and businesses to move elsewhere. . . .

I

We find it unnecessary to consider the validity of [the vagueness] arguments. [I]f the statute's deterrent effect on legitimate expression is not "both real and substantial," and if the statute is "readily subject to a narrowing construction by the state courts," *see* Erznoznik v. City of Jacksonville, 422 U.S. 205, the litigant is not permitted to assert the rights of third parties. . . . We are not persuaded that the Detroit zoning ordinances will have a significant deterrent effect on the exhibition of films protected by the First Amendment. [Since] there is surely a less vital interest in the uninhibited exhibition of material that is on the borderline between pornography and artistic expression than in the free dissemination of ideas of social and political significance, and since the limited amount of uncertainty in the ordinances is easily susceptible of a narrowing construction, we think this is an inappropriate case in which to adjudicate the hypothetical claims of persons not before the [Court].

II

[Respondents argue that the ordinances are invalid prior restraints on free speech.] The ordinances [do not] impose a limit on the total number of adult theaters which may operate in the city of Detroit. There is no claim that distributors or exhibitors of adult films are denied access to the market or, conversely, that the viewing public is unable to satisfy its appetite for sexually explicit fare. [W]e have no doubt that the municipality may control the location of theaters as well as the location of other commercial establishments, either by confining them to certain specified commercial zones or by requiring that they be dispersed throughout the city. [We are] persuaded that the 1,000-foot restriction does not, in itself, create an impermissible restraint on protected communication. The city's interest in planning and regulating the use of property for commercial purposes is clearly adequate to support that kind of restriction applicable to all theaters within the city limits. . . .

III

[As] we said in *Mosley:* "[Above] all else, the First Amendment means that government has no power to restrict expression because of its message, its ideas, its subject matter, or its content." [Police Dept. of Chicago v. Mosley, 408 U.S. 92 (1972).] [But the] question whether speech is, or is not, protected by the First Amendment often depends on the content of the speech. [E]ven though we recognize that the First Amendment will not tolerate the total suppression of erotic materials that have some arguably artistic value, it is manifest that society's interest in protecting this type of expression is of a wholly different, and lesser, magnitude than the interest in untrammeled political debate. [T]he State may legitimately use the content of these materials as the basis for placing them in a different classification from other motion pictures.

The remaining question is whether the line drawn by these ordinances is justified by the city's interest in preserving the character of its neighborhoods. . . . It is not our function to appraise the wisdom of its decision to require adult theaters to be separated rather than concentrated in the same areas. In either event, the city's interest in attempting to preserve the quality of urban life is one that must be accorded high respect. Moreover, the city must be allowed a reasonable opportunity to experiment with solutions to admittedly serious problems.

Since what is ultimately at stake is nothing more than a limitation on the place where adult films may be exhibited, even though the determination of whether a particular film fits that characterization turns on the nature of its content, we conclude that the city's interest in the present and future character of its neighborhoods adequately supports its classification of motion pictures. We hold that the zoning ordinances requiring that adult motion picture theaters not be located within 1,000 feet of two other regulated uses does not violate the [constitution].

The judgment of the Court of Appeals is
Reversed.

Mr. Justice POWELL, concurring in the judgment and portions of the opinion.
[T]here is no indication that the application of the Anti-Skid Row Ordinance to adult theaters has the effect of suppressing production of or, to any significant degree, restricting access to adult movies. . . . At most the impact of the ordinance on [First Amendment] interests is incidental and minimal. Detroit has silenced no message, has invoked no censorship, and has imposed no limitation upon those who wish to view them. The ordinance is addressed only to the places at which this type of expression may be presented, a restriction that does not interfere with content. Nor is there any significant overall curtailment of adult movie presentations, or the opportunity for a message to reach an [audience]. In these circumstances, it is appropriate to analyze the permissibility of Detroit's

action under the four-part test of United States v. O'Brien, 391 U.S. 367 (1968). Under that test, a governmental regulation is sufficiently justified, despite its incidental impact upon First Amendment interests, "if it is within the constitutional power of the Government; if it furthers an important or substantial governmental interest; if the governmental interest is unrelated to the suppression of free expression; and if the incidental restriction on . . . First Amendment freedoms is no greater than is essential to the furtherance of that interest." [Under the *O'Brien* analysis, Justice Powell would uphold the ordinance.]

Mr. Justice STEWART, with whom Mr. Justice BRENNAN, Mr. Justice MARSHALL, and Mr. Justice BLACKMUN join, dissenting.

[T]his case [involves] the constitutional permissibility of selective interference with protected speech whose content is thought to produce distasteful effects. [T]he Court has not shied from its responsibility to protect "offensive" speech from governmental interference. . . . Erznoznik v. City of Jacksonville [is] almost on "all fours" with this case. . . . Much speech that seems to be of little or no value will enter the market place of ideas, threatening the quality of our social discourse and, more generally, the serenity of our lives. But that is the price to be paid for constitutional freedom.

Question: Time, Place, and Manner Analysis

Does the *Young* case pose a public forum issue in the same way that *Erznoznik* does? If not, then why and how is the "time, place, manner" doctrine being used in the *Young* plurality opinion?

~ PROBLEM: MORE ON ZONING ~

A city adopts a zoning ordinance that prohibits adult motion picture theaters from locating within 1,000 feet of any residential zone, single- or multiple-family dwelling, church, park, or school. The term *adult motion picture theater* was defined as "[a]n enclosed building used for presenting motion picture films, video cassettes, cable television, or any other such visual media, distinguished or characteri[zed] by an emphasis on matter depicting, describing or relating to 'specified sexual activities' or 'specified anatomical areas' . . . for observation by patrons therein." Under the precedent established in *Young*, is this ordinance valid? Suppose that the city argues that the ordinance is directed at the "secondary effects" of adult theaters, including crime prevention, protection of the city's retail trade, the maintenance of property values, and a general desire to "protec[t] and preserv[e] the quality of [the city's] neighborhoods, commercial districts, and the quality of urban life." Is there a "substantial government interest" that supports the regulation? Does the city leave open "reasonable alternative avenues of communication"? *See* Renton v. Playtime Theatres, Inc., 475 U.S. 41 (1986).

Schad v. Borough of Mount Ephraim

452 U.S. 61 (1981)

Justice WHITE delivered the opinion of the Court.

[Appellants, who operate an adult bookstore, were convicted of offering coin-operated live dancing that could be viewed behind a glass panel.] As the Mount Ephraim Code has been construed[,] "live entertainment," including nude dancing, is "not a permitted use in any establishment" in the Borough of Mount Ephraim. By excluding live entertainment throughout the Borough, [the] ordinance prohibits a wide range of expression that has long been held to be within the protections of the First and Fourteenth Amendments. Entertainment, as well as political and ideological speech, [falls] within the First Amendment guarantee. Nor may an entertainment program be prohibited solely because it displays the nude human figure. "[N]udity alone" does not place otherwise protected material outside the mantle of the First Amendment. . . .

[T]he Mount Ephraim ordinance prohibits all live entertainment in the Borough: no property in the Borough may be principally used for the commercial production of plays, concerts, musicals, dance, or any other form of live entertainment. [The Borough's counsel conceded that noncommercial live entertainment such as a high school play would be allowed if the school did not charge admission.] "Because overbroad laws, like vague ones, deter privileged activit[ies], our cases firmly establish appellant's standing to raise an overbreadth challenge." Grayned v. City of Rockford, 408 U.S. 104 (1972).

[T]his case is not controlled by Young v. American Mini Theatres, Inc., [427 U.S. 50 (1976)]. Although the Court there stated that a zoning ordinance is not invalid merely because it regulates activity protected under the First Amendment, it emphasized that the challenged restriction on the location of adult movie theaters imposed a minimal burden on protected speech. The restriction did not affect the number of adult movie theaters that could operate in the city; it merely dispersed them. The Court did not imply that a municipality could ban all adult theaters — much less all live entertainment or all nude dancing — from its commercial districts citywide. Moreover, [the] evidence [indicated] that the concentration of adult movie theaters in limited areas led to deterioration of surrounding neighborhoods, and it was concluded that the city had justified the incidental burden on First Amendment interests resulting from merely dispersing, but not excluding, adult theaters.

[Mount Ephraim] has not adequately justified its substantial restriction of protected activity. . . . First, the Borough contends that permitting live entertainment would conflict with its plan to create a commercial area that caters only to the "immediate needs" of its residents and that would enable them to purchase at local stores the few items they occasionally forgot to buy outside the Borough. [But the Borough permits m]otels, hardware stores, lumber stores, banks, offices, and car showrooms [in its] commercial zones. . . . Virtually the only item or service that may not be sold in a commercial zone [is] live entertainment. The Borough's first justification is patently insufficient. . . . Second, Mount Ephraim contends that it may selectively exclude commercial live entertainment from the broad range of commercial uses permitted in the Borough [to] avoid the problems that may be associated with live entertainment, such as parking, trash, police protection, and medical facilities. [It] may be that some forms of live entertainment would create problems that are not associated with the commercial uses presently permitted in Mount Ephraim. Yet this ordinance is not narrowly drawn to respond to what might be the distinctive problems arising from certain types of live [entertainment]. The Borough has not established that its interests could not be met by restrictions that are less intrusive on protected forms of expression.

The Borough also suggests that [the zoning ordinance] is a reasonable "time, place, and manner" restriction. . . . To be reasonable, time, place, and manner restrictions not only must serve significant state interests but also must leave open adequate alternative channels of communication. Here, the Borough totally excludes all live entertainment, including nonobscene nude dancing that is otherwise protected by the First Amendment. [The] Borough nevertheless contends that live entertainment in general and nude dancing in particular are amply available in close-by areas outside the limits of the Borough. . . . "[O]ne is not to have the exercise of his liberty of expression in appropriate places abridged on the plea that it may be exercised in some other place." Schneider v. State, 308 U.S. [147] [(1939)].

Accordingly, the convictions of these appellants are infirm, and the judgment of the Appellate Division of the Superior Court of New Jersey is reversed and the case is remanded for further proceedings not inconsistent with this opinion.

So ordered.

Justice STEVENS, concurring in the judgment.

[T]he Borough must shoulder the burden of demonstrating that appellants' introduction of live entertainment had an identifiable adverse impact on the neighborhood or on the Borough as a whole. It might be appropriate to presume that such an adverse impact would occur if the zoning plan itself were narrowly drawn to create categories of commercial uses that unambiguously differentiated this entertainment from permitted uses. However, this open-ended ordinance affords no basis for any such [presumption].

Chief Justice BURGER, with whom Justice REHNQUIST joins, dissenting.

[Even] assuming that the "expression" manifested in the nude dancing that is involved here is somehow protected speech under the First Amendment, the Borough of Mount Ephraim is entitled to regulate it. [Here], as in [*Young*], the zoning ordinance imposes a minimal intrusion on genuine rights of expression. . . . Mount Ephraim is a small community on the periphery of two major urban centers where this kind of entertainment may be found acceptable. The fact that nude dancing has been totally banned in this community is irrelevant. . . . Citizens should be free to choose to shape their community so that it embodies their conception of the "decent life." This will sometimes mean deciding that certain forms of activity—factories, gas stations, sports stadia, bookstores, and surely live nude shows—will not be allowed. That a community is willing to tolerate such a commercial use as a convenience store, a gas station, a pharmacy, or a delicatessen does not compel it also to tolerate every other "commercial use," including pornography peddlers and live nude shows.

∽ PROBLEMS ∽

1. *Additional Facts.* If you were the attorney for the Borough of Mount Ephraim, could you have won the case if you had presented various other kinds of evidence at trial in defense of the ordinance? Consider what sort of evidence you would have used to attempt to satisfy the requirements of the *Schad* majority, in light of these additional details about the borough community (as set forth in the *Schad* dissent): The Borough of Mount Ephraim is a small borough in Camden County, N.J. It is located on the Black Horse Turnpike, the main artery connecting Atlantic City with two major cities, Camden and Philadelphia. Mount Ephraim is about 17 miles from Camden and about the same distance from the river that separates New Jersey from the State of Pennsylvania. For 250 feet on either side of the turnpike, the borough has established a commercial zone. The rest of the community is zoned for residential use, with either single- or multiple-family units permitted. Most of the inhabitants of Mount Ephraim commute to either Camden or Philadelphia for work. This small enclave is a placid, "bedroom" community of a few thousand people.

2. *Ordinance Drafting.* Assume that you are the attorney for the Borough of Mount Ephraim, and you have been assigned to redraft the ordinance to limit "live nude dancing" as much as possible. What changes would you propose to make in the ordinance to avoid the problems of the *Schad* ordinance and take advantage of *Young*?

3. *Couch Dancing.* A Nashville ordinance provides: "No entertainer, employee or customer, in any adult cabaret providing live entertainment involving any nudity, shall be permitted to have any physical contact with any other entertainer, employee or customer on the premises during any live performance, and all live performances shall only occur upon a stage removed at least six feet from the nearest entertainer, employee or customer." The Zoom Lens (ZL), a nightclub where erotic topless dancing takes place, presents "couch dancing" between entertainers and customers in an area separated from the main stage. This activity involves an entertainer sitting in the lap of a clothed customer and "dancing." ZL also presents "interactive" dances during which customers take spoons and scrape various substances (e.g., Cool Whip) off the bodies of dancers. The local prosecutor sues, seeking to close down ZL because of these violations. You represent the City of Nashville. What arguments do you expect the club's lawyer to make to attack the ordinance on First Amendment grounds? What arguments will you make to defend the statute in response? Explain how you will use *Erznoznik*, *Young*, *Schad*, and *City of Renton* in making arguments for both sides.

Erie v. Pap's A. M.

529 U.S. 277 (2000)

Justice O'CONNOR announced the judgment of the Court and delivered the opinion of the Court with respect to Parts I and II, and an opinion with respect to Parts III and IV, in which THE CHIEF JUSTICE, Justice KENNEDY, and Justice BREYER join.

[T]he city council for the city of Erie, Pennsylvania, enacted [a public indecency ordinance] that makes it a summary offense to knowingly or intentionally appear in public in a "state of nudity." [The ordinance provides that *nudity* means "the showing of the human male or female genital [*sic*], pubic area or buttocks with less than a fully opaque covering; the showing of the female breast with less than a fully opaque covering of any part of the nipple; the exposure of any device, costume, or covering which gives the appearance of or simulates the genitals, pubic hair, natal cleft, perineum anal region or pubic hair region; or the exposure of any device worn as a cover over the nipples and/or areola of the female breast, which device simulates and gives the realistic appearance of nipples and/or areola." The ordinance defines *public place* as including "all outdoor places owned by or open to the general public, and all buildings and enclosed places owned by or open to the general public, including such places of entertainment, taverns, restaurants, clubs, theaters, dance halls, banquet halls, party rooms or halls limited to specific members, restricted to adults or to patrons invited to attend, whether or not an admission charge is levied."] Respondent Pap's [operated] an establishment in Erie known as "Kandyland" that featured totally nude erotic dancing performed by women. To comply with the ordinance, these dancers must wear, at a minimum, "pasties" and a "G-string." [Two] days after the ordinance went into effect, Pap's filed a [suit] seeking declaratory relief and a permanent injunction against the enforcement of the [ordinance].

III

[In Barnes v. Glen Theater, Inc., 501 U.S. 560 (1991),] we analyzed an almost identical statute, holding that Indiana's public nudity ban did not violate the First Amendment, although no five Members of the Court agreed on a single rationale for that conclusion. We now clarify that government restrictions on public nudity such as the ordinance at issue here should be evaluated under the framework set forth in *O'Brien* for content-neutral restrictions on symbolic speech.

The city of Erie argues that the ordinance is a content-neutral restriction that is reviewable under [United States v. O'Brien, 391 U.S. 367 (1968)], because the ordinance bans conduct, not speech; specifically, public nudity. Respondent counters that the ordinance targets nude dancing and, as such, is aimed specifically at suppressing expression, making the ordinance a content-based restriction that must be subjected to strict scrutiny. . . . The ordinance here, like the statute in *Barnes*, is on its face a general prohibition on public nudity. By its terms, the ordinance regulates conduct alone. It does not target nudity that contains an erotic message; rather, it bans all public nudity, regardless of whether that nudity is accompanied by expressive activity. And like the statute in *Barnes* the Erie ordinance replaces and updates provisions of an "Indecency and Immorality" ordinance that has been on the books since 1866, predating the prevalence of nude dancing establishments such as Kandyland.

Respondent [contends] nonetheless that the ordinance is related to the suppression of expression because [the] ordinance's preamble suggests that its actual purpose is to prohibit erotic dancing of the type performed at Kandyland. . . . In the preamble[,] the city council stated that it was adopting the regulation "'for the purpose of limiting a recent increase in nude live entertainment within the City, which activity adversely impacts and threatens to impact on the public health, safety and welfare by providing an atmosphere conducive to violence, sexual harassment, public intoxication, prostitution, the spread of sexually transmitted diseases and other deleterious effects.'" The Pennsylvania Supreme Court construed this language to mean that one purpose of the ordinance was "to combat negative secondary effects."

As Justice Souter noted in *Barnes*, "on its face, the governmental interest in combating prostitution and other criminal activity is not at all inherently related to expression." In that sense, this case is similar to *O'Brien*. [In that case,] the Government regulation prohibiting the destruction of draft cards was aimed at maintaining the integrity of the Selective Service System and not at suppressing the message of draft resistance that O'Brien sought to convey by burning his draft card. So too here, the ordinance prohibiting public nudity is aimed at combating crime and other negative secondary effects caused by the presence of adult entertainment establishments like Kandyland and not at suppressing the erotic message conveyed by this type of nude dancing. Put another way, the ordinance does not attempt to regulate the primary effects of the expression, i.e., the effect on the audience of watching nude erotic dancing, but rather the secondary effects, such as the impacts on public health, safety, and welfare, which we have previously recognized are "caused by the presence of even one such" establishment. Renton v. Playtime Theatres, Inc., 475 U.S. 41 (1986).

[Respondent's] argument that the ordinance is "aimed" at suppressing expression through a ban on nude dancing [is] really an argument that the city council also had an illicit motive in enacting the ordinance. [T]his Court will not strike down an otherwise constitutional statute on the basis of an alleged illicit motive. *O'Brien, supra,* at 382-383. In light of the Pennsylvania court's determination that one purpose of the ordinance is to combat harmful secondary effects, the ban on public nudity here is no different from the ban on burning draft registration cards in *O'Brien*. . . . The State's interest in preventing harmful secondary effects is not related to the suppression of expression. In trying to control the secondary effects of nude dancing, the ordinance seeks to deter crime and the other deleterious effects caused by the presence of such an establishment in the neighborhood. [E]ven if Erie's public nudity ban has some minimal effect on the erotic message by muting that portion of the expression that occurs when the last stitch is dropped, the dancers at Kandyland and other such establishments are free to perform wearing pasties and G-strings. Any effect on the overall expression is *de minimis*. [If] States are to be able to regulate secondary effects, then *de minimis* intrusions on expression such as those at issue here cannot be sufficient to render the ordinance content based.

While the doctrinal theories behind "incidental burdens" and "secondary effects" are, of course, not identical, there is nothing objectionable about a city passing a general ordinance to ban public nudity (even though such a ban may place incidental burdens on some protected speech) and at the same time recognizing that one specific occurrence of public nudity — nude erotic dancing — is particularly problematic because it produces harmful secondary effects.

[We] conclude that Erie's asserted interest in combating the negative secondary effects associated with adult entertainment establishments like Kandyland is unrelated to the suppression of the erotic message conveyed by nude dancing. The ordinance prohibiting public nudity is therefore valid if it satisfies the four-factor test from *O'Brien* for evaluating restrictions on symbolic speech.

IV

[W]e conclude that Erie's ordinance is justified under *O'Brien*. The first factor of the *O'Brien* test is whether the government regulation is within the constitutional power of the government to enact. Here, Erie's efforts to protect public health and safety are clearly within the city's police powers. The second factor is whether the regulation furthers an important or substantial government interest. The asserted interests of regulating conduct through a public nudity ban and of combating the harmful secondary effects associated with nude dancing are undeniably important. And in terms of demonstrating that such secondary effects pose a threat, the city need not "conduct new studies or produce evidence independent of that already generated by other cities" to demonstrate the problem of secondary effects, "so long as whatever evidence the city relies upon is reasonably believed to be relevant to the problem that the city addresses." Because the nude dancing at Kandyland is of the same character as the adult entertainment at issue in *Renton,* it was reasonable for Erie to conclude that such nude dancing was likely to produce the same secondary effects. And Erie could reasonably rely on the evidentiary foundation set forth in *Renton* and *American Mini Theatres* to the effect that secondary effects are caused by the presence of even one adult entertainment establishment in a given neighborhood. In fact, Erie expressly relied on *Barnes* and its discussion of secondary effects, including its reference to *Renton* and *American Mini Theatres*. [The] evidentiary standard described in *Renton* controls here, and Erie meets that [standard]. [The] ordinance also satisfies *O'Brien*'s third factor, that the government interest is unrelated to the suppression of free [expression]. The fourth and final *O'Brien* factor — that the restriction is no greater than is essential to the furtherance of the government interest — is satisfied as well. The ordinance regulates conduct, and any incidental impact on the expressive element of nude dancing is *de minimis*. The requirement that dancers wear pasties and G-strings is a minimal restriction in furtherance of the asserted government interests, and the restriction leaves ample capacity to convey the dancer's erotic [message].

We hold, therefore, that Erie's ordinance is a content-neutral regulation that is valid under *O'Brien*. Accordingly, the judgment of the Pennsylvania Supreme Court is reversed, and the case is remanded for further proceedings.

It is so ordered.

Justice SCALIA, with whom Justice THOMAS joins, concurring in the judgment.

[E]ven if one hypothesizes that the city's object was to suppress only nude dancing, that would not establish an intent to suppress what (if anything) nude dancing communicates. I do not feel the need, as the Court does, to identify some "secondary effects" associated with nude dancing that the city could properly seek to eliminate. (I [am] skeptical [that] addition of pasties and G-strings will at all reduce the tendency of establishments such as Kandyland to attract crime and prostitution, and hence to foster sexually transmitted disease.) The traditional power of government to foster good morals, and the acceptability of the traditional judgment that nude public dancing *itself* is immoral, have not been repealed by the First Amendment.

Justice SOUTER, concurring in part and dissenting in part.

[Erie's] stated interest in combating the secondary effects associated with nude dancing establishments is an interest unrelated to the suppression of expression under *O'Brien*. . . . I do not believe [that] the city has made a sufficient evidentiary showing to sustain its regulation. [The] record before us today is deficient in its failure to reveal any evidence on which Erie may have relied, either for the seriousness of the threatened harm or for the efficacy of its chosen remedy. . . .

Justice STEVENS, with whom Justice GINSBURG joins, dissenting.

[In] both *Renton* and *American Mini Theatres*, the zoning ordinances were analyzed as mere "time, place, and manner" regulations. Because time, place, and manner regulations must "leave open ample alternative channels for communication of the information," a total ban would necessarily fail that test. [W]e so held in Schad v. Mount Ephraim, 452 U.S. 61 (1981). . . . The Court's use of the secondary effects rationale to permit a total ban has grave implications for basic free speech principles. . . . Under today's opinion, a State may totally ban speech based on its secondary effects — which are defined as those effects that "happen to be associated" with speech; yet the regulation is not presumptively invalid. [T]oday's holding has the effect of swallowing whole a most fundamental principle of First Amendment jurisprudence.

[T]he plurality concedes that "requiring dancers to wear pasties and G-strings may not greatly reduce these secondary effects." To believe that the mandatory addition of pasties and a G-string will have *any* kind of noticeable impact on secondary effects requires nothing short of a titanic surrender to the implausible. [T]here is no reason to believe that such a requirement "will at all reduce the tendency of establishments such as Kandyland to attract crime and prostitution, and hence to foster sexually transmitted disease." . . .

The plurality is also mistaken in equating our secondary effects cases with the "incidental burdens" doctrine applied in cases such as *O'Brien*. . . . The incidental burdens doctrine applies when "'speech' and 'nonspeech' elements are combined in the same course of conduct," and the government's interest in regulating the latter justifies incidental burdens on the former. Secondary effects, on the other hand, are indirect consequences of protected speech and may justify regulation of the places where that speech may occur. When a State enacts a regulation, it might focus on the secondary effects of speech as its aim, or it might concentrate on nonspeech related concerns, having no thoughts at all with respect to how its regulation will affect speech — and only later, when the regulation is found to burden speech, justify the imposition as an unintended incidental consequence. But those interests are not the same, and the plurality cannot ignore their differences and insist that both aims are equally unrelated to speech simply because Erie might have "recogniz[ed]" that it could possibly have had either aim in mind. One can think of an apple and an orange at the same time; that does not turn them into the same fruit.

[I]f Erie's concern with the effects of the message were unrelated to the message itself, it is strange that the only means used to combat those effects is the suppression of the message. . . .

Question: Reappraisal of the Justifications for Protecting Speech

Does the "speech" involved in *Erie* meet any of the justifications for protecting speech presented at the beginning of this chapter? In other words, does it provide a safety valve, does it promote self-fulfillment or the marketplace of ideas, or is it related to the democratic process?

∾ PROBLEMS ∾

1. *Drafting Issues.* Now that city attorneys, city council members, and prosecutors know what evidence is required to obtain a majority vote for a "secondary-effects-*O'Brien*" analysis (at least, they did while Justice Souter was still on the Court), how will such evidence be obtained? As the city attorney for Erie, what advice would you give regarding the legislative history that must be created to support a "secondary effects" government interest in a future case, in order to obtain Justice Souter's vote?

2. *The Full Monty.* Suppose that a city prosecutor wants to enforce the Erie ordinance against a theater that is planning to produce a musical in which nudity occurs, such as *The Full Monty*. What arguments will the prosecutor and the theater owner make about the constitutionality of this action under all the "near-obscene" precedents?

3. *Cocoa Beach Ordinance.* The City of Cocoa Beach, Fla., passes an ordinance regulating adult entertainment establishments. The city is 6 miles long and 1 mile wide, with 2,000 acres, of which 150 are zoned for general commercial use.

The ordinance defines an adult entertainment establishment as one in which the dancers dance for tips or in close proximity to the patrons (no matter how much skin the dancers expose). This ordinance also contains a total ban on total nudity on the part of the employees of such establishments, defining *nudity* as the exposure of specified anatomical areas including genitalia, buttocks, and female breasts, so that G-strings and pasties are sufficient to avoid violation of the ordinance. However, the ordinance does not prohibit nudity anywhere else in the city of Cocoa Beach. Sass, an adult night club that has not yet opened, attacks this ordinance on First Amendment grounds, arguing that the ordinance should be struck down so that Sass dancers will be able to dance nude. Should Sass prevail?

4. *Second Cocoa Beach Ordinance.* Suppose that Cocoa Beach also adopts an ordinance regulating the location of adult entertainment establishments. The ordinance sets aside only three sites for such businesses, which happen to correspond exactly to the sites of three other adult businesses that have been open for 30 years. Sass, which has not yet opened, argues that its proposed site is excluded and that there is no site at which it can locate under this zoning ordinance. As a result, Sass claims a violation of the First Amendment. Should Sass prevail?

11. *"Hate" Speech*

The term *hate speech* is difficult to define, but it is often used to refer to expression that targets individuals or groups by reason of their race, ethnicity, sex, or sexual preference. In an early decision, Beauharnais v. Illinois, 343 U.S. 250 (1952), the Court upheld a conviction under an Illinois statute that made it unlawful to portray "depravity, criminality, unchastity, or lack of virtue of a class of citizens, of any race, color, creed or religion which said publication or exhibition exposes the citizens of any race, color, creed or religion to contempt, derision, or obloquy or which is productive of breach of the peace or riots." The Court stated that the "precise question before us, then, is whether the protection of 'liberty' in the Due Process Clause of the Fourteenth Amendment prevents a State from punishing such libels — as criminal libel has been defined, limited and constitutionally recognized time out of mind — directed at designated collectivities and flagrantly disseminated." The Court concluded that it could not "deny to a State power to punish the same utterance directed at a defined group." However, in subsequent decisions, the Court cast doubt on *Beauharnais*'s validity, as well as on the power of the state to impose punishment for criminal libel.

R.A.V. v. City of St. Paul
505 U.S. 377 (1992)

Justice SCALIA delivered the opinion of the Court.

In the predawn hours of June 21, 1990, petitioner and several other teenagers allegedly assembled a crudely made cross by taping together broken chair legs. They then allegedly burned the cross inside the fenced yard of a black family that lived across the street from the house where petitioner was staying.

Although this conduct could have been punished under any of a number of laws,[9] one of the two provisions under which respondent city of St. Paul chose to charge petitioner (then a juvenile) was the St. Paul Bias-Motivated Crime Ordinance which provides:

> Whoever places on public or private property a symbol, object, appellation, characterization or graffiti, including, but not limited to, a burning cross or Nazi swastika, which one knows or has reasonable grounds to know arouses anger, alarm or resentment in others on the basis of race, color, creed, religion or gender commits disorderly conduct and shall be guilty of a misdemeanor.

Petitioner moved to dismiss this count on [First Amendment grounds]. . . . The trial court granted this motion, but the Minnesota Supreme Court reversed. . . .

I

[W]e accept the Minnesota Supreme Court's authoritative statement that the ordinance reaches only those expressions that constitute "fighting words" within the meaning of *Chaplinsky* [v. New Hampshire, 315 U.S. 568 (1942)]. Assuming, arguendo, that all of the expression reached by the ordinance is proscribable under the "fighting words" doctrine, we nonetheless conclude that the ordinance is facially unconstitutional in that it prohibits otherwise permitted speech solely on the basis of the subjects the speech addresses.

The First Amendment generally prevents government from proscribing speech, or even expressive conduct, because of disapproval of the ideas expressed. Content-based regulations are presumptively invalid. From 1791 to the present, [our] society [has] permitted restrictions upon the content of speech in a few limited areas, which are "of such slight social value as a step to truth that any benefit that may be derived from them is clearly outweighed by the social interest in order and morality." *Chaplinsky*, 315 U.S., at 572. . . . Our decisions since the 1960's have narrowed the scope of the traditional categorical exceptions for defamation, and for obscenity, but a limited categorical approach has remained an important part of our First Amendment jurisprudence.

We have sometimes said that these categories of expression are "not within the area of constitutionally protected speech," or that the "protection of the First Amendment does not extend" to them. Such statements must be taken in context, however, and are no more literally true than is the occasionally repeated shorthand characterizing obscenity "as not being speech at all." What they mean is that these areas of speech can, consistently with the First Amendment, be regulated *because of their constitutionally proscribable content* (obscenity, defamation, etc.) — not that they are categories of speech entirely invisible to the Constitution, so that they may be made the vehicles for content discrimination unrelated to their distinctively proscribable content. Thus, the government may proscribe

---

9. *See, e.g.*, Minn. Stat. §609.713(1) (1987) (providing for up to five years in prison for terroristic threats); §609.563 (arson) (providing for up to five years and a $10,000 fine, depending on the value of the property intended to be damaged); §609.595 (Supp. 1992) (criminal damage to property) (providing for up to one year and a $3,000 fine, depending upon the extent [of damage].

libel; but it may not make the further content discrimination of proscribing *only* libel critical of the government. . . .

Our cases surely do not establish the proposition that the First Amendment imposes no obstacle whatsoever to regulation of particular instances of such proscribable expression, so that the government "may regulate [them] freely." That would mean that a city council could enact an ordinance prohibiting only those legally obscene works that contain criticism of the city government or, indeed, that do not include endorsement of the city government. Such a simplistic, all-or-nothing-at-all approach to First Amendment protection is at odds with common sense and with our jurisprudence as well. It is not true that "fighting words" have at most a "*de minimis*" expressive content, or that their content is *in all respects* "worthless and undeserving of constitutional protection"; sometimes they are quite expressive indeed. We have not said that they constitute "*no* part of the expression of ideas," but only that they constitute "no *essential* part of any exposition of ideas."

The proposition that a particular instance of speech can be proscribable on the basis of one feature (e.g., obscenity) but not on the basis of another (e.g., opposition to the city government) [has] found application in many contexts. We have long held, for example, that nonverbal expressive activity can be banned because of the action it entails, but not because of the ideas it expresses — so that burning a flag in violation of an ordinance against outdoor fires could be punishable, whereas burning a flag in violation of an ordinance against dishonoring the flag is not. Similarly, we have upheld reasonable "time, place, or manner" restrictions, but only if they are "*justified* without reference to the content of the regulated speech." And just as the power to proscribe particular speech on the basis of a noncontent element (e.g., noise) does not entail the power to proscribe the same speech on the basis of a content element; so also, the power to proscribe it on the basis of *one* content element (e.g., obscenity) does not entail the power to proscribe it on the basis of *other* content elements.

In other words, the exclusion of "fighting words" from the scope of the First Amendment simply means that, for purposes of that Amendment, the unprotected features of the words are, despite their verbal character, essentially a "nonspeech" element of communication. Fighting words are thus analogous to a noisy sound truck: Each is, as Justice Frankfurter recognized, a "mode of speech"; both can be used to convey an idea; but neither has, in and of itself, a claim upon the First Amendment. As with the sound truck, however, so also with fighting words: The government may not regulate use based on hostility — or favoritism — towards the underlying message expressed.

The concurrences describe us as setting forth a new First Amendment principle that prohibition of constitutionally proscribable speech cannot be "underinclusiv[e]" — a First Amendment "absolutism" whereby "[w]ithin a particular 'proscribable' category of expression, [a] government must either proscribe *all* speech or no speech at all." [In] our view, the First Amendment imposes not an "underinclusiveness" limitation but a "content discrimination" limitation upon a State's prohibition of proscribable speech. There is no problem whatever, for example, with a State's prohibiting obscenity (and other forms of proscribable expression) only in certain media or markets, for although that prohibition would be "underinclusive," it would not discriminate on the basis of content.

Even the prohibition against content discrimination [is] not absolute. It applies differently in the context of proscribable speech than in the area of fully protected speech. The rationale of the general prohibition, after all, is that content discrimination "raises the specter that the Government may effectively drive certain ideas or viewpoints from the marketplace." But content discrimination among various instances of a class of proscribable speech often does not pose this threat. . . . When the basis for the content discrimination consists entirely of the very reason the entire class of speech at issue is proscribable, no significant danger of idea or viewpoint discrimination exists. Such a reason, having been adjudged neutral enough to support exclusion of the entire class of speech from First Amendment protection, is also neutral enough to form the basis of distinction within the class. [A] State might choose to prohibit only that obscenity which is the most patently offensive *in its prurience* — i.e., that which involves the most lascivious displays of sexual activity. But it may not prohibit, for example, only that obscenity which includes offensive *political* messages. . . .

Another valid basis for according differential treatment to even a content-defined subclass of proscribable speech is that the subclass happens to be associated with particular "secondary effects" of the speech, so that the regulation is "*justified* without reference to the content of [the] speech." A State could, for example, permit all obscene live performances except those involving minors. Moreover, since words can in some circumstances violate laws directed not against speech but against conduct (a law against treason, for example, is violated by telling the enemy the Nation's defense secrets), a particular content-based subcategory of a proscribable class of speech can be swept up incidentally within the reach of a statute directed at conduct rather than speech. Thus, for example, sexually derogatory "fighting words," among other words, may produce a violation of Title VII's general prohibition against sexual discrimination in employment practices. Where the government does not target conduct on the basis of its expressive content, acts are not shielded from regulation merely because they express a discriminatory idea or philosophy.

These bases for distinction refute the proposition that the selectivity of the restriction is "even arguably 'conditioned upon the sovereign's agreement with what a speaker may intend to say.'" There may be other such bases as well. Indeed, to validate such selectivity (where totally proscribable speech is at issue) it may not even be necessary to identify any particular "neutral" basis, so long as the nature of the content discrimination is such that there is no realistic possibility that official suppression of ideas is afoot. (We cannot think of any First Amendment interest that would stand in the way of a State's prohibiting only those obscene motion pictures with blue-eyed actresses.) Save for that limitation, the regulation of "fighting words," like the regulation of noisy speech, may address some offensive instances and leave other, equally offensive, instances alone.

II

Applying these principles to the St. Paul ordinance, we conclude that, even as narrowly construed by the Minnesota Supreme Court, the ordinance is facially unconstitutional. Although the phrase in the ordinance, "arouses anger, alarm or resentment in others," has been limited by the Minnesota Supreme Court's construction to reach only those symbols or displays that amount to "fighting words," [the] ordinance applies only to "fighting words" that insult, or provoke violence, "on the basis of race, color, creed, religion or gender." Displays containing abusive invective, no matter how vicious or severe, are permissible unless they are addressed to one of the specified disfavored topics. Those who wish to use "fighting words" in connection with other ideas — to express hostility, for example, on the basis of political affiliation, union membership, or homosexuality — are not covered. The First Amendment does not permit St. Paul to impose special prohibitions on those speakers who express views on disfavored subjects.

In its practical operation, moreover, the ordinance goes even beyond mere content discrimination, to actual viewpoint discrimination. Displays containing some words — odious racial epithets, for example — would be prohibited to proponents of all views. But "fighting words" that do not themselves invoke race, color, creed, religion, or gender — aspersions upon a person's mother, for example — would seemingly be usable *ad libitum* in the placards of those arguing *in favor* of racial, color, etc., tolerance and equality, but could not be used by those speakers' opponents. One could hold up a sign saying, for example, that all "anti-Catholic bigots" are misbegotten; but not that all "papists" are, for that would insult and provoke violence "on the basis of religion." St. Paul has no such authority to license one side of a debate to fight freestyle, while requiring the other to follow Marquis of Queensberry rules.

What we have here [is] not a prohibition of fighting words that are directed at certain persons or groups (which would be *facially* valid if it met the requirements of the Equal Protection Clause); but rather, a prohibition of fighting words that [contain] messages of "bias-motivated" hatred and in particular, as applied to this case, messages "based on virulent notions of racial supremacy." One must [agree] with the Minnesota Supreme Court that "[i]t is the responsibility, even the obligation, of diverse communities to confront such notions in whatever form they appear," but the manner of that confrontation cannot consist of selective limitations upon speech. [St. Paul] asserts that a general "fighting words" law would not meet the city's needs because only a content-specific measure can communicate to minority groups that the "group hatred" aspect of such speech "is not condoned by the majority." The point of the First Amendment is that majority preferences must be expressed in some fashion other than silencing speech on the basis of its content.

Despite the fact that the Minnesota Supreme Court and St. Paul acknowledge that the ordinance is directed at expression of group hatred, Justice Stevens suggests that [it is directed] not to speech of a particular content, but to particular "injur[ies]" that are "qualitatively different" from other injuries. This is wordplay. What makes the anger, fear, sense of dishonor, etc., produced by violation of this ordinance distinct from the anger, fear, sense of dishonor, etc., produced by other fighting words is nothing other than the fact that it is caused by a distinctive idea, conveyed by a distinctive message. The First Amendment cannot be evaded that easily. It is obvious that the symbols which will arouse "anger, alarm or resentment in others on the basis of race, color, creed, religion or gender" are those symbols that communicate a message of hostility based on one of these characteristics. St. Paul concedes [that] the ordinance applies only to "racial, religious, or gender-specific symbols" such as "a burning cross, Nazi swastika or other instrumentality of like import." Indeed, St. Paul [argued] that "[t]he burning of a cross does express a message and it [is] the content of that message which the St. Paul Ordinance attempts to legislate."

The content-based discrimination reflected in the St. Paul ordinance [does] not fall within the exception for content discrimination based on the very reasons why the particular class of speech at issue (here, fighting words) is proscribable. [T]he reason why fighting words are categorically excluded from the protection of the First Amendment is not that their content communicates any particular idea, but that their content embodies a particularly intolerable (and socially unnecessary) *mode* of expressing *whatever* idea the speaker wishes to convey. St. Paul has not singled out an especially offensive mode of expression — it has not, for example, selected for prohibition only those fighting words that communicate ideas in a threatening (as opposed to a merely obnoxious) manner. Rather, it has proscribed fighting words of whatever manner that communicate messages of racial, gender, or religious intolerance. Selectivity of this sort creates the possibility that the city is seeking to handicap the expression of particular ideas. That possibility would alone be enough to render the ordinance presumptively invalid, but St. Paul's comments and concessions in this case elevate the possibility to a certainty.

St. Paul argues that the ordinance comes within another of the specific exceptions we mentioned, the one that allows content discrimination aimed only at the "secondary effects" of the speech. According to St. Paul, the ordinance is intended, "not to impact on [*sic*] the right of free expression of the accused," but rather to "protect against the victimization of a person or persons who are particularly vulnerable because of their membership in a group that historically has been discriminated against." [I]t is clear that the St. Paul ordinance is not directed to secondary effects within the meaning of *Renton*. As we said in Boos v. Barry, 485 U.S. 312 (1988), "Listeners' reactions to speech are not the type of 'secondary effects' we referred to in *Renton*." "The emotive impact of speech on its audience is not a 'secondary effect.'"[10]

It hardly needs discussion that the ordinance does not fall within some more general exception permitting all selectivity that for any reason is beyond the

---

10. St. Paul has not argued in this case that the ordinance merely regulates that subclass of fighting words which is most likely to provoke a violent response. But even if one assumes [that] the categories selected may be so described, that would not justify selective regulation under a "secondary effects" theory. [I]t is clear that the St. Paul ordinance regulates on the basis of the "primary" effect of the speech — i.e., its persuasive (or repellant) force.

suspicion of official suppression of ideas. The statements of St. Paul in this very case afford ample basis for, if not full confirmation of, that suspicion.

Finally, St. Paul [argues] that, even if the ordinance regulates expression based on hostility towards its protected ideological content, this discrimination is nonetheless justified because it is narrowly tailored to serve compelling state interests. Specifically, they assert that the ordinance helps to ensure the basic human rights of members of groups that have historically been subjected to discrimination, including the right of such group members to live in peace where they wish. We do not doubt that these interests are compelling, and that the ordinance can be said to promote them. But the "danger of censorship" presented by a facially content-based statute requires that that weapon be employed only where it is *necessary* to serve the asserted [compelling] interest." [The] dispositive question in this case [is] whether content discrimination is reasonably necessary to achieve St. Paul's compelling interests; it plainly is not. An ordinance not limited to the favored topics [would] have precisely the same beneficial effect. In fact the only interest distinctively served by the content limitation is that of displaying the city council's special hostility towards the particular biases thus singled out. That is precisely what the First Amendment forbids. The politicians of St. Paul are entitled to express that hostility — but not through the means of imposing unique limitations upon speakers [who] disagree.

Let there be no mistake about our belief that burning a cross in someone's front yard is reprehensible. But St. Paul has sufficient means at its disposal to prevent such behavior without adding the First Amendment to the fire.

The judgment of the Minnesota Supreme Court is reversed, and the case is remanded for proceedings not inconsistent with this opinion.

It is so ordered.

Justice WHITE, with whom Justice BLACKMUN and Justice O'CONNOR join, and with whom Justice STEVENS joins except as to Part I-A, concurring in the judgment.

[This] Court's decisions have plainly stated that expression falling within certain limited categories so lacks the values the First Amendment was designed to protect that the Constitution affords no protection to that expression. . . . [The] present Court submits that such clear statements "must be taken in context" and are not "literally true." [To] the contrary, [t]he categorical approach is a firmly entrenched part of our First Amendment jurisprudence. . . .

[Fighting] words are not a means of exchanging views, rallying supporters, or registering a protest; they are directed against individuals to provoke violence or to inflict injury. Therefore, a ban on all fighting words or on a subset of the fighting words category would restrict only the social evil of hate speech, without creating the danger of driving viewpoints from the marketplace.

[Any] contribution of this holding to First Amendment jurisprudence is surely a negative one, since it necessarily signals that expressions of violence, such as the message of intimidation and racial hatred conveyed by burning a cross on someone's lawn, are of sufficient value to outweigh the social interest in order and morality that has traditionally placed such fighting words outside the First

Amendment.[11] Indeed, by characterizing fighting words as a form of "debate," the majority legitimates hate speech as a form of public discussion.

Furthermore, the Court obscures the line between speech that could be regulated freely on the basis of content (i.e., the narrow categories of expression falling outside the First Amendment) and that which could be regulated on the basis of content only upon a showing of a compelling state interest (i.e., all remaining expression). By placing fighting words, which the Court has long held to be valueless, on at least equal constitutional footing with political discourse and other forms of speech that we have deemed to have the greatest social value, the majority devalues the latter category.

[Assuming,] *arguendo,* that the St. Paul ordinance is a content-based regulation of protected expression, it nevertheless would pass First Amendment review under settled law upon a showing that the regulation "'is necessary to serve a compelling state interest and is narrowly drawn to achieve that end.'" St. Paul has urged that its ordinance, in the words of the majority, "helps to ensure the basic human rights of members of groups that have historically been subjected to discrimination. . . ." [T]he majority has engrafted the following exception onto its newly announced First Amendment rule: Content-based distinctions may be drawn within an unprotected category of speech if the basis for the distinctions is "the very reason the entire class of speech at issue is proscribable." [The] exception swallows the majority's rule. Certainly, it should apply to the St. Paul ordinance, since "the reasons why [fighting words] are outside the First Amendment [have] special force when applied to [groups that have historically been subjected to discrimination]."

[T]he Court suggests that fighting words are simply a mode of communication, rather than a content-based category, and that the St. Paul ordinance has not singled out a particularly objectionable mode of communication. . . . A prohibition on fighting words is not a time, place, or manner restriction; it is a ban on a class of speech that conveys an overriding message of personal injury and imminent violence, a message that is at its ugliest when directed against groups that have long been the targets of discrimination. Accordingly, the ordinance falls within the first exception to the majority's theory.

[T]he St. Paul ordinance is unconstitutional. However, I would decide the case on overbreadth grounds. [T]he Minnesota court [has] ruled that St. Paul may constitutionally prohibit expression that "by its very utterance" causes "anger, alarm or resentment." [Our] fighting words cases have made clear, however, that such generalized reactions are not sufficient to strip expression of its constitutional protection. The mere fact that expressive activity causes hurt feelings, offense, or resentment does not render the expression unprotected. . . .

Justice BLACKMUN, concurring in the judgment.

[I] see no First Amendment values that are compromised by a law that prohibits hoodlums from driving minorities out of their homes by burning crosses on

---

11. This does not suggest, of course, that cross burning is always unprotected. Burning a cross at a political rally would almost certainly be protected expression. But in such a context, the cross burning could not be characterized as a "direct personal insult or an invitation to exchange fisticuffs," to which the fighting words doctrine applies.

their lawns, but I see great harm in preventing the people of Saint Paul from specifically punishing the race-based fighting words that so prejudice their community. [I] concur [because] this particular ordinance reaches beyond fighting words to speech protected by the First Amendment.

Justice STEVENS, with whom Justice WHITE and Justice BLACKMUN join as to Part I, concurring in the judgment.

[I] agree that the St. Paul ordinance is unconstitutionally overbroad. . . . [I am troubled by the Court's suggestion that content based distinctions are not permissible.] [O]ur entire First Amendment jurisprudence creates a regime based on the content of speech. . . . Whether a magazine is obscene, a gesture a fighting word, or a photograph child pornography is determined, in part, by its content. . . .

[A] selective, subject-matter regulation on proscribable speech is constitutional. . . . [T]wo things are clear. First, by hypothesis the ordinance bars only low-value speech, namely, fighting words. . . . Second, the ordinance regulates "expressive conduct [rather] than [the] written or spoken word." [It is] significant that the ordinance (by hypothesis) regulates *only* fighting words. [T]he St. Paul ordinance restricts speech in confrontational and potentially violent situations. The case at hand is illustrative. The cross burning in this case — directed as it was to a single African-American family trapped in their home — was nothing more than a crude form of physical intimidation. That this cross burning sends a message of racial hostility does not automatically endow it with complete constitutional protection.

Significantly, the St. Paul ordinance regulates speech not on the basis of its subject matter or the viewpoint expressed, but rather on the basis of the *harm* the speech causes. [T]he ordinance regulates only a subcategory of expression that causes *injuries based on* "race, color, creed, religion or gender," not a subcategory that involves *discussions* that concern those characteristics. The ordinance [criminalizes] expression that "one knows [by its very utterance inflicts injury on] others on the basis of race, color, creed, religion or gender." In this regard, the ordinance resembles the child pornography law at issue in *Ferber*, which in effect singled out child pornography because those publications caused far greater harms than pornography involving adults.

[The] St. Paul ordinance is evenhanded. In a battle between advocates of tolerance and advocates of intolerance, the ordinance does not prevent either side from hurling fighting words at the other on the basis of their conflicting ideas, but it does bar both sides from hurling such words on the basis of the target's "race, color, creed, religion or gender." To extend the Court's pugilistic metaphor, the St. Paul ordinance simply bans punches "below the belt" — by either party. It does not, therefore, favor one side of any debate.

Finally, it is noteworthy that the St. Paul ordinance [is] quite narrow. The St. Paul ordinance does not ban all "hate speech," nor does it ban, say, all cross burnings or all swastika displays. Rather it only bans a subcategory of the already narrow category of fighting words. Such a limited ordinance leaves open and protected a vast range of expression on the subjects of racial, religious, and gender equality. [T]he ordinance certainly does not "'rais[e] the specter that the

Government may effectively drive certain ideas or viewpoints from the market-place.'" Petitioner is free to burn a cross to announce a rally or to express his views about racial supremacy, he may do so on private property or public land, at day or at night, so long as the burning is not so threatening and so directed at an individual as to "by its very [execution] inflict injury." Such a limited proscription scarcely offends the First Amendment.

In sum, the St. Paul ordinance [regulates] expressive activity that is wholly proscribable and does so not on the basis of viewpoint, but rather in recognition of the different harms caused by such activity. . . .

Notes and Questions

1. *Sentencing and Associational Evidence.* Dawson v. Delaware, 503 U.S. 159 (1992), involved testimony in a capital sentencing proceeding to the effect that the defendant was a member of the Aryan Brotherhood, a white supremacist group. The trial court admitted the evidence. The jury concluded that the aggravating evidence outweighed the mitigating evidence and recommended that Dawson be sentenced to death. The trial court imposed the death penalty. The U.S. Supreme Court reversed: "[T]he First Amendment protects an individual's right to join groups and associate with others holding similar beliefs. [Even] if the Delaware group to which Dawson allegedly belongs is racist, those beliefs [had] no relevance to the sentencing proceeding in this case. [T]he murder victim was white, as is Dawson; elements of racial hatred were therefore not involved in the killing. [A]ssociational evidence might serve a legitimate purpose in showing that a defendant represents a future danger to society. . . . Other evidence concerning a defendant's associations might be relevant in proving other aggravating circumstances. [O]ne is left with the feeling that the Aryan Brotherhood evidence was employed simply because the jury would find these beliefs morally reprehensible. Because Delaware failed to do more, we cannot find the evidence was properly admitted as relevant character evidence." Justice Thomas dissented: "[Under] Delaware law, after a jury finds a statutory aggravating factor, it may consider 'all relevant evidence in aggravation or mitigation' relating to either the crime or the 'character and propensities' of the defendant. Under this provision, Dawson's character became an issue in determining whether he should receive the death penalty. [A] jury reasonably could infer that its members in one way or another act upon their racial prejudice. [T]he Aryan Brotherhood does not exist merely to facilitate formulation of abstract racist thoughts, but to 'respon[d]' to gangs of racial minorities. The evidence thus tends to establish that Dawson has not been 'a well-behaved and well-adjusted prisoner' which itself is an indication of future dangerousness."

2. *Sentence Enhancement.* In Wisconsin v. Mitchell, 508 U.S. 476 (1993), Mitchell's sentence for aggravated battery was enhanced because he intentionally selected his victim on account of the victim's race. The Court upheld the enhancement, rejecting arguments that "the only reason for the enhancement is the defendant's discriminatory motive for selecting his victim" and therefore that

"the statute violates the First Amendment by punishing offenders' bigoted beliefs." The Court noted:

> Traditionally, sentencing judges have considered a wide variety of factors in addition to evidence bearing on guilt in determining what sentence to impose on a convicted defendant. The defendant's motive for committing the offense is one important factor. Thus, in many States the commission of a murder, or other capital offense, for pecuniary gain is a separate aggravating circumstance under the capital sentencing statute. . . . But [a] defendant's abstract beliefs, however obnoxious to most people, may not be taken into consideration by a sentencing judge. . . . But motive plays the same role under the Wisconsin statute as it does under federal and state antidiscrimination laws, which we have previously upheld against constitutional challenge. . . . Nothing [in] *R.A.V.* compels a different result. [W]hereas the ordinance struck down in *R.A.V.* was explicitly directed at expression (i.e., "speech" or "messages"), the statute in this case is aimed at conduct unprotected by the First Amendment. . . . Moreover, the Wisconsin statute singles out for enhancement bias-inspired conduct because this conduct is thought to inflict greater individual and societal harm. [B]ias-motivated crimes are more likely to provoke retaliatory crimes, inflict distinct emotional harms on their victims, and incite community unrest. The State's desire to redress these perceived harms provides an adequate explanation for its penalty-enhancement provision over and above mere disagreement with offenders' beliefs or biases. . . .

3. *Campus Speech Codes.* In recent years, many colleges and universities have enacted speech codes designed to prohibit so-called "hate speech." In general, these codes have been struck down on vagueness or overbreadth grounds. *See* UMW Post, Inc. v. Board of Regents of University of Wisconsin, 774 F. Supp. 1162 (E.D. Wis. 1991) (striking down the University of Wisconsin's prohibition against discriminatory epithets); Doe v. University of Michigan, 721 F. Supp. 852 (E.D. Mich. 1989) (striking down the University of Michigan's antiharassment code as vague and overbroad).

4. *Hate Speech and the Justifications for Protecting Speech.* Did the speech involved in *R.A.V.* meet any of the justifications for protecting speech presented at the beginning of this chapter? In other words, did it provide a safety valve, did it promote self-fulfillment or the marketplace of ideas, or was it related to the democratic process?

5. *The Lawrence Argument.* Professor Charles R. Lawrence III, in *If He Hollers Let Him Go: Regulating Racist Speech on Campus*, 1990 Duke L.J. 431 (1990), contends that minorities and women often find "themselves speechless in the face of discriminatory verbal attacks." Why? In his view, the words "denote one's subhuman status and untouchability," and "there is little (if anything) that can be said to redress either the emotional or reputational injury." He questions whether minorities and women should be required to bear this "burden for the good of society — to pay the price for the societal benefit of creating more room for speech." He goes on to note that "we assign this burden to them without seeking their advice, or consent. This amounts to white domination, pure and simple. It is taxation without representation." Is Lawrence right? Should the right of free speech give way in this context?

∽ PROBLEMS ∽

1. *Ordinance Drafting.* After *R.A.V.*, is it possible for the City of St. Paul to draft a valid ordinance designed to deal with the problem of "hate speech"? Can the ordinance avoid the problems of content-based and viewpoint-based discrimination against speech as well as vagueness and overbreadth? If so, how should the ordinance be drafted?

2. *More on the International Treaty Regulating the Internet.* At the convention, suppose that the German and French delegates demand protections against hate speech on the grounds that it "degrades human dignity" and that it is likely to cause breaches of the peace. In light of the holding in *R.A.V.*, what restrictions can you agree to impose on hate speech?

3. *Messages of Inferiority.* The University of Louisville promulgates a regulation that prohibits any student from engaging in speech that conveys a "message of inferiority" to any racial group, or makes that group feel "excluded." In promulgating the regulation, the university emphasizes that Louisville (and Kentucky) have a history of slavery and segregation, and that black students have historically felt "excluded" at the university. Is the regulation valid?

4. *Regulatory Applications.* Suppose that, after the regulation referred to in the preceding problem is promulgated, the following events occur:

   a. At a Halloween party, a number of students perform skits. One student dresses up in Ku Klux Klan robes and poses as a Klansman. At the end of the skit, he pulls off his Klan robes (thereby revealing his identity) and burns them.
   b. Suppose the student is African American (as was true in an actual case at the University of Louisville). Does that change the result?
   c. At the same Halloween party, a white student wears "black face" and imitates a black rapper. The lyrics used are not racist, but instead are the lyrics from one of the rapper's songs. After *R.A.V.* and *Black*, can the student be punished by the university under the regulation?

5. *The KKK and the Adopt-a-Highway Program.* Suppose that the Commonwealth of Kentucky creates an "adopt-a-highway" program. Under this program, groups can agree to "adopt" highway sections in the sense that they agree to regularly pick up litter in those sections. Suppose that you work for the Kentucky Department of Transportation office when the Ku Klux Klan applies to adopt a section of a state highway. Can you reject the application on the theory that the KKK is an extremist group and its participation in the program would be morally offensive to many Kentuckians? Suppose that the state decides to grant the application. Is there anything that prevents the state from granting the KKK's request, but then renaming that section of the highway "The Martin Luther King, Jr., Highway"?

Virginia v. Black

538 U.S. 343 (2003)

Justice O'CONNOR announced the judgment of the Court and delivered the opinion of the Court with respect to Parts I, II, and III, and an opinion with respect to Parts IV and V, in which THE CHIEF JUSTICE, Justice STEVENS, and Justice BREYER join.

In this case we consider whether the Commonwealth of Virginia's statute banning cross burning with "an intent to intimidate a person or group of persons" violates the First Amendment. We conclude that while a State, consistent with the First Amendment, may ban cross burning carried out with the intent to intimidate, the provision in the Virginia statute treating any cross burning as prima facie evidence of intent to intimidate renders the statute unconstitutional in its current form.

I

Respondents Barry Black, Richard Elliott, and Jonathan O'Mara were convicted separately of violating Virginia's cross-burning statute, §18.2-423. That statute provides:

> It shall be unlawful for any person or persons, with the intent of intimidating any person or group of persons, to burn, or cause to be burned, a cross on the property of another, a highway or other public place. Any person who shall violate any provision of this section shall be guilty of a Class 6 felony.
>
> Any such burning of a cross shall be prima facie evidence of an intent to intimidate a person or group of persons.

On August 22, 1998, Barry Black led a Ku Klux Klan rally [in] Virginia. Twenty-five to thirty people attended this gathering, which occurred on private property with the permission of the owner. . . . The property was located on an open field just off [a state highway]. When the sheriff [learned] that a Klan rally was occurring in his county, he went to observe it from the side of the road. During the approximately one hour that the sheriff was present, about 40 to 50 cars passed the site, a "few" of which stopped to ask the sheriff what was happening. . . . Eight to ten houses were located in the vicinity of the rally. Rebecca Sechrist . . . "sat and watched to see wha[t][was] going on" from the lawn of her in-laws' house. . . . During the rally, Sechrist heard Klan members speak about "what they were" and "what they believed in." The speakers "talked real bad about the blacks and the Mexicans." One speaker told the assembled gathering that "he would love to take a .30/.30 and just random[ly] shoot the blacks." The speakers also talked about "President Clinton and Hillary Clinton," and about how their tax money "goes [to] the black people." Sechrist testified that this language made her "[very] scared." [At] the conclusion of the rally, the crowd circled around a 25- to 30-foot cross. The cross was between 300 and 350 yards away from the road. [T]he cross "then all of a sudden [went] up in a flame." As the cross burned, the Klan played *Amazing Grace* over the loudspeakers. Sechrist stated that the cross burning made her feel "awful" and "terrible." [The] sheriff then [arrested Black for] burning a cross with the intent of intimidating a person or group of persons, in violation of §18.2-423. At his trial, the jury was instructed that "intent to intimidate means the motivation to intentionally put a person or a group of persons in fear of bodily harm. Such fear must arise from the willful conduct of the accused rather than from some mere temperamental timidity of the victim." The trial court also instructed the jury that "the burning of a cross by itself is sufficient evidence from which you may infer the required intent." [The] jury found Black guilty, and fined him $2,500. The Court of Appeals of Virginia affirmed Black's conviction.

On May 2, 1998, respondents Richard Elliott and Jonathan O'Mara, as well as a third individual, attempted to burn a cross on the yard of James Jubilee. Jubilee, an African-American, was Elliott's next-door neighbor [in] Virginia. . . . Before the cross burning, Jubilee spoke to Elliott's mother to inquire about shots being fired from behind the Elliott home. . . . The next morning, as Jubilee was pulling his car out of the driveway, he noticed the partially burned cross approximately 20 feet from his house. After seeing the cross, Jubilee was "very nervous" because he "didn't know what would be the next phase," and because "a cross burned in your yard . . . tells you that it's just the first round." [Elliott] and O'Mara were charged with attempted cross burning and conspiracy to commit cross burning. O'Mara pleaded guilty to both counts [and was sentenced to] 90 days in jail and [fined $2,500, but the judge] suspended 45 days of the sentence and $1,000 of the fine. . . . At Elliott's trial, [the] jury found Elliott guilty of attempted cross burning and acquitted him of conspiracy to commit cross burning. It sentenced Elliott to 90 days in jail and a $2,500 fine. The Court of Appeals of Virginia affirmed[, but the Supreme Court of Virginia struck the law down, relying on R.A.V. v. St. Paul, 505 U.S. 377 (1992)].

II

Cross burning originated in the 14th century as a means for Scottish tribes to signal each other. Sir Walter Scott used cross burnings for dramatic effect in *The Lady of the Lake*, where the burning cross signified both a summons and a call to arms. *See* W. Scott, *The Lady of the Lake*, canto third. Cross burning in this country, however, long ago became unmoored from its Scottish ancestry. Burning a cross in the United States is inextricably intertwined with the history of the Ku Klux Klan.

The first Ku Klux Klan began [in] 1866. . . . The Klan fought Reconstruction and the corresponding drive to allow freed blacks to participate in the political process. [T]he Klan imposed "a veritable reign of terror" throughout the South. The Klan employed tactics such as whipping, threatening to burn people at the stake, and murder. The Klan's victims included blacks, southern whites who disagreed with the Klan, and "carpetbagger" northern whites. . . . [In response,] Congress passed what is now known as the Ku Klux Klan Act. 42 U.S.C. §§1983, 1985, and 1986. President Grant used these new powers to suppress the Klan. . . . By the end of Reconstruction in 1877, the first Klan no longer existed.

The genesis of the second Klan began in 1905, with the publication of Thomas Dixon's *The Clansmen: An Historical Romance of the Ku Klux Klan*. Dixon's book was a sympathetic portrait of the first Klan, depicting the Klan as a group of heroes "saving" the South from blacks and the "horrors" of Reconstruction. Although the first Klan never actually practiced cross burning, Dixon's book depicted the Klan burning crosses to celebrate the execution of former slaves. . . . When D.W. Griffith turned Dixon's book into the movie *The Birth of a Nation* in 1915, the association between cross burning and the Klan became indelible. In addition to the cross burnings in the movie, a poster advertising the film displayed a hooded Klansman riding a hooded horse, with his left hand holding the reins of the horse and his right hand holding a burning cross above his head. . . .

From the inception of the second Klan, cross burnings have been used to communicate both threats of violence and messages of shared ideology. . . . The new Klan's ideology did not differ much from that of the first Klan. As one Klan publication emphasized, "We avow the distinction between [the] races, [and] we shall ever be true to the faithful maintenance of White Supremacy and will strenuously oppose any compromise thereof in any and all things." Violence was also an elemental part of this new Klan. By September 1921, the *New York World* newspaper documented 152 acts of Klan violence, including 4 murders, 41 floggings, and 27 tar-and-featherings. . . . Often, the Klan used cross burnings as a tool of intimidation and a threat of impending violence. . . . After one cross burning at a synagogue, a Klan member noted that if the cross burning did not "shut the Jews up, we'll cut a few throats and see what happens." In Miami in 1941, the Klan burned four crosses in front of a proposed housing project, declaring, "We are here to keep niggers out of your town. . . . When the law fails you, call on us." [These] cross burnings embodied threats to people whom the Klan deemed antithetical to its goals. And these threats had special force given the long history of Klan violence.

The Klan continued to use cross burnings to intimidate after World War II. In one incident, an African-American "school teacher who recently moved his family into a block formerly occupied only by whites asked the protection of city police [after] the burning of a cross in his front yard." [These] incidents of cross burning, among others, helped prompt Virginia to enact its first version of the cross-burning statute in 1950.

The decision of this Court in Brown v. Board of Education, 347 U.S. 483 (1954), along with the civil rights movement of the 1950's and 1960's, sparked another outbreak of Klan violence. These acts of violence included bombings, beatings, shootings, stabbings, and mutilations. Members of the Klan burned crosses on the lawns of those associated with the civil rights movement, assaulted the Freedom Riders, bombed churches, and murdered blacks as well as whites whom the Klan viewed as sympathetic toward the civil rights movement.

Throughout the history of the Klan, cross burnings have also remained potent symbols of shared group identity and ideology. The burning cross became a symbol of the Klan itself and a central feature of Klan gatherings. According to the Klan constitution (called the kloran), the "fiery cross" was the "emblem of that sincere, unselfish devotedness of all klansmen to the sacred purpose and principles we have espoused." And the Klan has often published its newsletters and magazines under the name The Fiery Cross. . . . At Klan gatherings[,] cross burning became the climax of the rally or the initiation.

Posters advertising an upcoming Klan rally often featured a Klan member holding a cross. . . . Throughout the Klan's history, the Klan continued to use the burning cross in their ritual ceremonies. . . . [In] 1960, the Klan engaged in rallies and cross burnings throughout the South in an attempt to recruit 10 million members. . . . [C]ross burnings featured prominently in Klan rallies when the Klan attempted to move toward more nonviolent tactics to stop integration. In short, a burning cross has remained a symbol of Klan ideology and of Klan unity.

[R]egardless of whether the message is a political one or whether the message is also meant to intimidate, the burning of a cross is a "symbol of hate." And while cross burning sometimes carries no intimidating message, at other times the intimidating message is the *only* message conveyed. [W]hen a cross burning is directed at a particular person not affiliated with the Klan, the burning cross often serves as a message of intimidation, designed to inspire in the victim a fear of bodily harm. Moreover, the history of violence associated with the Klan shows that the possibility of injury or death is not just hypothetical. The person who burns a cross directed at a particular person often is making a serious threat, meant to coerce the victim to comply with the Klan's wishes unless the victim is willing to risk the wrath of the Klan. [A]s the cases of respondents Elliott and O'Mara indicate, individuals without Klan affiliation who wish to threaten or menace another person sometimes use cross burning because of this association between a burning cross and violence. . . . In sum, while a burning cross does not inevitably convey a message of intimidation, often the cross burner intends that the recipients of the message fear for their lives. And when a cross burning is used to intimidate, few if any messages are more powerful.

III

The First Amendment, applicable to the States through the Fourteenth Amendment, provides that "Congress shall make no law . . . abridging the freedom of speech." The hallmark of the protection of free speech is to allow "free trade in ideas" — even ideas that the overwhelming majority of people might find distasteful or discomforting. . . . The First Amendment affords protection to symbolic or expressive conduct as well as to actual speech.

The protections afforded by the First Amendment, however, are not absolute, and we have long recognized that the government may regulate certain categories of expression consistent with the Constitution. . . . Thus, for example, a State may punish those words "which by their very utterance inflict injury or tend to incite an immediate breach of the peace." We have consequently held that fighting words — "those personally abusive epithets which, when addressed to the ordinary citizen, are, as a matter of common knowledge, inherently likely to provoke violent reaction" — are generally proscribable under the First Amendment. Furthermore, "the constitutional guarantees of free speech and free press do not permit a State to forbid or proscribe advocacy of the use of force or of law violation except where such advocacy is directed to inciting or producing imminent lawless action and is likely to incite or produce such action." Brandenburg v. Ohio, 395 U.S. 444 (1969) (per curiam). And the First Amendment also permits a State to ban a "true threat." Watts v. United States, 394 U.S. 705 (1969) (per curiam).

"True threats" encompass those statements where the speaker means to communicate a serious expression of an intent to commit an act of unlawful violence to a particular individual or group of individuals. The speaker need not actually intend to carry out the threat. Rather, a prohibition on true threats "protect[s] individuals from the fear of violence" and "from the disruption that fear engenders," in addition to protecting people "from the possibility that the threatened violence will occur." Intimidation in the constitutionally proscribable sense of the word is a type of true threat, where a speaker directs a threat to a person or group of persons with the intent of placing the victim in fear of bodily harm or death. Respondents do not contest that some cross burnings fit within this meaning of intimidating speech, and rightly so. [T]he history of cross burning in this country shows that cross burning is often intimidating, intended to create a pervasive fear in victims that they are a target of violence.

The Supreme Court of Virginia ruled that in light of *R.A.V.,* even if it is constitutional to ban cross burning in a content-neutral manner, the Virginia cross-burning statute is unconstitutional because it discriminates on the basis of content and viewpoint. It is true [that] the burning of a cross is symbolic expression. The reason why the Klan burns a cross at its rallies, or individuals place a burning cross on someone else's lawn, is that the burning cross represents the message that the speaker wishes to communicate. Individuals burn crosses as opposed to other means of communication because cross burning carries a message in an effective and dramatic manner. . . . The fact that cross burning is symbolic expression, however, does not resolve the constitutional question. . . .

In *R.A.V.,* we held that a local ordinance that banned certain symbolic conduct, including cross burning, [was] unconstitutional. We held that the ordinance did not pass constitutional muster because it discriminated on the basis of content by targeting only those individuals who "provoke violence" on a basis specified in the law. . . . This content-based discrimination was unconstitutional because it allowed the city "to impose special prohibitions on those speakers who express views on disfavored subjects." [We] did not hold in *R.A.V.* that the First Amendment prohibits *all* forms of content-based discrimination within a proscribable area of speech. Rather, we specifically stated that some types of content discrimination did not violate the First Amendment:

> When the basis for the content discrimination consists entirely of the very reason the entire class of speech at issue is proscribable, no significant danger of idea or viewpoint discrimination exists. Such a reason, having been adjudged neutral enough to support exclusion of the entire class of speech from First Amendment protection, is also neutral enough to form the basis of distinction within the class.

Indeed, we noted that it would be constitutional to ban only a particular type of threat: "[T]he Federal Government can criminalize only those threats of violence that are directed against the President [since] the reasons why threats of violence are outside the First Amendment [have] special force when applied to the person of the President." And a State may "choose to prohibit only that obscenity which is the most patently offensive *in its prurience* — i.e., that which involves the most lascivious displays of sexual activity." Consequently, [while] *R.A.V.* does not permit a State to ban only obscenity based on "offensive *political* messages," or "only those threats against the President that mention his policy on aid to inner cities," the First Amendment permits content discrimination "based on the very reasons why the particular class of speech at issue [is] proscribable."

Similarly, Virginia's statute does not run afoul of the First Amendment insofar as it bans cross burning with intent to intimidate. [T]he Virginia statute does not single out for opprobrium only that speech directed toward "one of the specified disfavored topics." It does not matter whether an individual burns a cross with intent to intimidate because of the victim's race, gender, or religion, or because of the victim's "political affiliation, union membership, or homosexuality." [I]t is not true that cross burners direct their intimidating conduct solely to racial or religious minorities. *See, e.g.,* State v. Miller, 6 Kan. App. 2d 432, 629 P.2d 748 (1981) (describing the case of a defendant who burned a cross in the yard of the lawyer who had previously represented him and who was currently prosecuting him). Indeed, in the case of Elliott and O'Mara, it is at least unclear whether the respondents burned a cross due to racial animus.

The First Amendment permits Virginia to outlaw cross burnings done with the intent to intimidate because burning a cross is a particularly virulent form of intimidation. Instead of prohibiting all intimidating messages, Virginia may choose to regulate this subset of intimidating messages in light of cross burning's long and pernicious history as a signal of impending violence. Thus, just as a State may regulate only that obscenity which is the most obscene due to its prurient content, so too may a State choose to prohibit only those forms of intimidation that are most likely to inspire fear of bodily harm. A ban on cross burning carried out with the intent to intimidate is fully consistent with our holding in *R.A.V.* and is proscribable under the First Amendment.

IV

The Supreme Court of Virginia ruled [that] Virginia's cross-burning statute was unconstitutionally overbroad due to its provision stating that "[a]ny such burning of a cross shall be prima facie evidence of an intent to intimidate a person or group of persons." Va. Code Ann. §18.2-423 (1996). [T]he prima facie provision strips away the very reason why a State may ban cross burning with the intent to intimidate. The prima facie evidence provision permits a jury to convict in every cross-burning case in which defendants exercise their constitutional right not to put on a defense. And even where a defendant like Black presents a defense, the prima facie evidence provision makes it more likely that the jury will find an intent to intimidate regardless of the particular facts of the case. The provision permits the Commonwealth to arrest, prosecute, and convict a person based solely on the fact of cross burning itself.

[T]he provision as so interpreted "would create an unacceptable risk of the suppression of ideas." The act of burning a cross may mean that a person is engaging in constitutionally proscribable intimidation. But that same act may mean only that the person is engaged in core political speech. The prima facie evidence [chills] constitutionally protected political speech because of the possibility that a State will prosecute — and potentially convict — somebody engaging only in lawful political speech at the core of what the First Amendment is designed to protect.

[A] burning cross is not always intended to intimidate. [S]ometimes the cross burning is a statement of ideology, a symbol of group solidarity. It is a ritual used at Klan gatherings, and it is used to represent the Klan itself. "[B]urning a cross at a political rally would almost certainly be protected expression." Indeed, occasionally a person who burns a cross does not intend to express either a statement of ideology or intimidation. Cross burnings have appeared in movies such as *Mississippi Burning,* and in plays such as the stage adaptation of Sir Walter Scott's *The Lady of the Lake.*

The prima facie provision makes no effort to distinguish among these different types of cross burnings. It does not distinguish between a cross burning done with the purpose of creating anger or resentment and a cross burning done with the purpose of threatening or intimidating a victim. It does not distinguish between a cross burning at a public rally or a cross burning on a neighbor's lawn. It does not treat the cross burning directed at an individual differently from the cross burning directed at a group of like-minded believers. It allows a jury to treat a cross burning on the property of another with the owner's acquiescence in the same manner as a cross burning on the property of another without the owner's permission. [T]he prima facie evidence provision can "skew jury deliberations toward conviction in cases where the evidence of intent to intimidate is relatively weak and arguably consistent with a solely ideological reason for burning."

It may be true that a cross burning, even at a political rally, arouses a sense of anger or hatred among the vast majority of citizens who see a burning cross. But this sense of anger or hatred is not sufficient to ban all cross burnings. . . . The prima facie evidence provision in this case ignores all of the contextual factors that are necessary to decide whether a particular cross burning is intended to intimidate. The First Amendment does not permit such a shortcut.

For these reasons, the prima facie evidence provision, as interpreted through the jury instruction and as applied in Barry Black's case, is unconstitutional on its face. [W]e refuse to speculate on whether *any* interpretation of the prima facie evidence provision would satisfy the First Amendment. [We] recognize the theoretical possibility that the court, on remand, could interpret the provision in a manner different from that so far set forth in order to avoid the constitutional objections we have described. . . . We also leave open the possibility that the provision is severable. . . .

V

With respect to Barry Black, we agree with the Supreme Court of Virginia that his conviction cannot stand, and we affirm the judgment of the Supreme Court of Virginia. With respect to Elliott and O'Mara, we vacate the judgment of the Supreme Court of Virginia, and remand the case for further proceedings.

It is so ordered.

Justice STEVENS, concurring.

Cross burning with "an intent to intimidate" unquestionably qualifies as the kind of threat that is unprotected by the First Amendment. . . .

Justice SCALIA, with whom Justice THOMAS joins as to Parts I and II, concurring in part, concurring in the judgment in part, and dissenting in part.

[Under] *R.A.V.*, a State may, without infringing the First Amendment, prohibit cross burning carried out with the intent to intimidate. Accordingly, I join Parts I-III of the Court's opinion. I also agree that we should vacate and remand the judgment of the Virginia Supreme Court so that that Court can have an opportunity authoritatively to construe the prima-facie-evidence provision. [T]he Virginia Supreme Court did not suggest [that] a jury may [ignore] any rebuttal evidence that has been presented and, solely on the basis of a showing that the defendant burned a cross, find that he intended to intimidate. [The] effect of the prima-facie-evidence provision is far more limited. It suffices to "insulate the Commonwealth from a motion to strike the evidence *at the end of its case-in-chief*," but it does nothing more. [O]ur overbreadth jurisprudence has consistently focused on whether *the prohibitory terms* of a particular statute extend to protected conduct; that is, we have inquired whether individuals who engage in protected conduct can be *convicted* under a statute, not whether they might be subject to arrest and prosecution. *E.g.*, Houston v. Hill, 482 U.S. 451. . . .

Justice SOUTER, with whom Justice KENNEDY and Justice GINSBURG join, concurring in the judgment in part and dissenting in part.

I agree [that] the Virginia statute makes a content-based distinction within the category of punishable intimidating or threatening expression, the very type of distinction we considered in *R.A.V.* I disagree that any exception should save Virginia's law from unconstitutionality under the holding in *R.A.V.* or any acceptable variation of it.

[T]he specific prohibition of cross burning with intent to intimidate selects a symbol with particular content from the field of all proscribable expression meant to intimidate. [E]ven when the symbolic act is meant to terrify, a burning cross may carry a further, ideological message of white Protestant supremacy. The ideological message not only accompanies many threatening uses of the symbol, but is also expressed when a burning cross is not used to threaten but merely to symbolize the supremacist ideology and the solidarity of those who espouse it. [T]he burning cross can broadcast threat and ideology together, ideology alone, or threat alone, as was [the] choice of respondents Elliott and O'Mara.

[Because] of the burning cross's extraordinary force as a method of intimidation, the *R.A.V.* exception most likely to cover the statute is [an] exception for content discrimination on a basis that "consists entirely of the very reason the entire class of speech at issue is proscribable." [I] do not think that the Virginia statute qualifies for this virulence exception. . . . The first example of permissible distinction is for a prohibition of obscenity unusually offensive "in its prurience." [D]istinguishing obscene publications on this basis does not suggest discrimination on the basis of the message conveyed. The opposite is true, however, when a general prohibition of intimidation is rejected in favor of a distinct proscription of intimidation by cross burning. The cross may have been selected because of its special power to threaten, but it may also have been singled out because of disapproval of its message of white supremacy, either because a legislature thought white supremacy was a pernicious doctrine or because it found that dramatic, public espousal of it was a civic embarrassment. . . . Nor does this case present any analogy to the statute prohibiting threats against the President. [T]hreats against the President are not generally identified by reference to the content of any message that may accompany the threat, let alone any viewpoint, and there is no obvious correlation in fact between victim and message. . . .

[R.A.V.'s] third exception [allows] content-based discrimination within a proscribable category when its "nature" is such "that there is no realistic possibility that official suppression of ideas is afoot." I believe the prima facie evidence provision stands in the way of any [such] finding. . . . To the extent the prima facie evidence provision skews prosecutions, then, it skews the statute toward suppressing ideas. . . .

[I] would therefore affirm the judgment of the Supreme Court of Virginia vacating the respondents' convictions and dismissing the indictments. . . .

Justice THOMAS, dissenting.

[Although] I agree [that] it is constitutionally permissible to "ban [cross] burning carried out with intent to intimidate," [the] majority errs in imputing an expressive component to [this] activity. [The Klan is] a terrorist organization, which, in its endeavor to intimidate, or even eliminate those its dislikes, uses the most brutal of methods. . . . For those not easily frightened, cross burning has been followed by more extreme measures, such as beatings and murder. . . . In our culture, cross burning has almost invariably meant lawlessness and understandably instills in its victims well-grounded fear of physical violence. . . . It is simply beyond belief that [the] Virginia legislature was concerned with anything but penalizing conduct it must have viewed as particularly vicious. [J]ust as one cannot burn down someone's house to make a political point and then seek refuge in the First Amendment, those who hate cannot terrorize and intimidate to make their point. [Since the statute] addresses only conduct, there is no need to analyze it under any of our First Amendment tests. [The] fact that the statute permits a jury to draw an inference of intent to intimidate from the cross burning itself presents no constitutional problems. . . . Virginia law still requires the jury to find the existence of each element, including intent to intimidate, beyond a reasonable doubt. . . .

Notes and Questions

1. *True Threats Against the President.* Watts v. United States, 394 U.S. 705 (1969), involved a federal statute that prohibited anyone from "knowingly and willfully threatening to take the life of or to inflict bodily harm upon the President of the United States." During a public rally on the Washington Monument

grounds, participants divided into small groups to discuss police brutality. Robert Watts, who was 18 years old, was upset by one group member who disparaged young people, and stated (as transcribed by a member of the Army Counter Intelligence Corps): "I have received my draft classification as 1-A and I have to report for my physical this Monday coming. If they ever make me carry a rifle, the first man I want to get in my sights is the President. They are not going to make me kill my black brothers." The Court held that Watts could not be convicted: "[Defendant's statement] was made during a political debate, [and] expressly made conditional upon an event—induction into the Armed Forces—which [the defendant] vowed would never occur, [and both the defendant] and the crowd laughed after the statement was made. [A]ctually what happened here in all this was a kind of very crude offensive method of stating a political opposition to the President. What he was saying [was], I don't want to shoot black people because I don't consider them my enemy, and if they put a rifle in my hand it is the people that put the rifle in my hand, as symbolized by the President, who are my real enemy." The Court recognized that the statute was constitutional on its face because of the overwhelming interest in protecting the safety of the President. However, the Court reasoned that "what is a threat must be distinguished from what is constitutionally protected speech." The Court then concluded that "the statute initially requires the Government to prove a 'true threat,'" and that the defendant's language was political hyperbole that does not fit that concept. In doing so, the Court emphasized that the case was being decided "against the background of a profound national commitment to the principle that debate on public issues should be uninhibited, robust, and wide open, and that it may well include vehement, caustic, and sometimes unpleasantly sharp attacks on government and public officials." New York Times Co. v. Sullivan, 376 U.S. 254, 270 (1964).

2. Black *and* Brandenburg. Does Virginia v. Black cast doubt on the holding in Brandenburg v. Ohio? Note that the Court quotes *Brandenburg* with approval. If *Brandenburg* arose today, involving as it does a burning cross, would the result be different? Does the fact that *Brandenburg* invited a reporter to the rally and allowed him to film the proceedings affect the analysis?

3. *California Cross-Burning Statute.* Would a California cross-burning statute necessarily be treated (for constitutional purposes) like the Virginia statute? Does California have the same history of cross burning as Virginia does? Is a Los Angeles resident as likely to perceive a burning cross as a "true threat" and as "intimidation" as a Virginia resident is? In other words, does cultural and historical context affect the Court's view of cross burning?

4. *The Abortion "Wanted" Posters.* In Planned Parenthood of Columbia/ Willamette, Inc. v. American Coalition of Life Activists, 422 F.3d 949 (9th Cir. 2005), the Court applied the "true threat" doctrine to abortion protestors who sought to intimidate abortion providers. The case involved a civil suit by four physicians and two health clinics that provided abortions against the American Coalition of Life Activists (ACLA), which produced posters that made threats, including the Deadly Dozen "GUILTY" poster (which set forth the names of various abortion providers), the Crist "GUILTY" poster (which contained a

physician's name, address, and photograph), and the "Nuremberg Files" (which involved a list of names of abortion providers whom the ACLA believed or hoped might be put on trial for crimes against humanity one day). The posters were regarded as "true threats" because they were circulated following the circulation of other similar posters that had identified abortion providers who were subsequently murdered. The suit was brought under the Freedom of Access to Clinic Entrances (FACE) Act and the Racketeer Influenced and Corrupt Organizations (RICO) Act, 18 U.S.C. §§1961-1968. The plaintiffs were awarded both compensatory damages and punitive damages. However, the initial award of $108.5 million in punitive damages was remitted to $45,000 to $75,000 per defendant.

∽ PROBLEMS ∽

1. *Other Comparable Symbols?* Are there any other symbols that carry the message of intimidation conveyed by a burning cross, or is the cross *sui generis*? Suppose that a Los Angeles gang has a symbol (a coiled snake) that it marks on the door of those whom it intends to hurt, maim, or kill. Might this symbol be treated like the burning cross for constitutional purposes?

2. *Kentucky Cross Burning.* Assume that Kentucky has a cross-burning statute that is identical to the Virginia statute. On Halloween night, a student at the University of Louisville dresses up like a Klansman and burns a cross as part of a skit. When the police charge the student under the statute, he defends on the basis that it was Halloween night and he was just "having fun." In other words, there was no intent to intimidate. At the student's trial, black students testify that they were "intimidated" by the cross burning, which they viewed as racist and designed to place them in a subservient status. The jury convicts the defendant. After *Black*, can the conviction stand?

3. *Open Fires Regulation.* Suppose that the burning in the preceding problem takes place on the oval in front of the University of Louisville's administration building. The university has a regulation that prohibits "open fires" on campus. The student is charged with violating the regulation. After *Black*, is it permissible to punish the student for violating the open fires regulation? Would it matter why the regulation was promulgated? Suppose that the university adopted the rule to limit the potential for fire hazards on campus. On the other hand, suppose that the university adopted the policy to prevent the KKK from burning crosses on campus.

4. *More on True Threats Against the President.* Suppose that a member of a white supremacist group writes a poem about the murder of a black President and posts it on the Internet.[12] The poem, which describes in graphic detail how the murder is committed, has been posted on the Internet for some time when federal agents arrest the author (and poster) for making a threat against the life of the President.

12. The poem read as follows:

THE SNIPER
   As the tyrant enters his cross hairs the breath he takes is deep His focus is square on the target as he begins to release A patriot for his people he knows this shot will cost his life But for his race and their existence it is a small sacrifice.

Is the speech protected under the precedent established in *Brandenburg, Black,* and *Watts*?

5. *Hanging Barack Obama in Effigy.* Before the 2008 presidential election, a number of incidents occurred during which then-candidate Barack Obama was hung in effigy. For example, in Clarksville, Ind., a man hung an effigy of Obama from a tree in his front yard. *See* Harold J. Adams, "Indiana Man Hung Obama Doll from Tree," *The Courier-Journal*, B. 3, c. 2-4 (Oct. 30, 2008). The man explained that he was opposed to having Obama become President because he would then become the Commander-in-Chief, and the man was fearful because he has relatives fighting in the Middle East. *Id.* In a like incident, a student hung an Obama effigy from a tree on the University of Kentucky campus. *See* Nancy S. Rodriguez, "Obama Effigy Sparks Anger: Dummy Was Hung from Tree at UK," *The Courier-Journal*, B-1, c. 2-5 (Oct. 30, 2008). Can the two men be prosecuted for threatening then-candidate Obama? Does the fact that Obama is black make a difference? Does the history of violence against blacks in the South by the KKK make a difference?

6. *The University of Louisville Response.* In response to the Obama incident at the University of Kentucky (referred to in the prior problem), the University of Louisville issued this statement:

> The University of Louisville strives to foster and sustain an environment of inclusiveness that empowers us all to achieve our highest potential without fear of prejudice or bias.
>
> We commit ourselves to building an exemplary educational community that offers a nurturing and challenging intellectual climate, a respect for the spectrum of human diversity, and a genuine understanding of the many differences — including race, ethnicity, gender identity/expression, sexual orientation, age, socioeconomic status, disability, religion, national origin or military status — that enrich a vibrant metropolitan reserarch university.
>
> We expect every member of our academic family to embrace the underyling values of this vision and to demonstrate a strong commitment to attracting, retaining and supporting students, faculty and staff who reflect the diversity of our larger society.

Should the university's policy be regarded as mandatory or as aspirational? If mandatory, in the sense that those who do not join or comply can be sanctioned, is it constitutionally valid?

7. *The Sexual Harassment Policy.* Glen View Hills University adopts a sexual harassment policy that prohibits "expressive, visual or physical conduct of a sexual or gender-motivated nature that has the purpose or effect of unreasonably interfering with another individual's work, educational performance or status, or that has the effect of creating a hostile, intimidating or offensive environment." The university seeks to justify the policy as necessary to create a welcoming and

---

The bullet that he has chambered is one of the purest pride And the inspiration on the casing reads DIE negro DIE He breathes out as he pulls the trigger releasing all his hate And a smile appears upon his face as he seals that monkey's fate.

The bullet screams toward its mark bringing with it death And where there was once a face there is nothing left Two blood covered agents star[sic] in horror and dismay Looking down toward the where ground their president now lay.

Now the screams of one old negro broad pierces through the air Setting off panic from every eyewitness that was there And among all the confusion the hero calmly slips away Laughing for he knows there will be another negro holiday.

tolerant environment for women, as well as a way to implement federal antidiscrimination laws. The policy is challenged by a graduate history student who
claims that the policy inhibits him from expressing his opinions in class regarding women in combat and women in the military, as well as from expressing his
broader social, cultural, religious, and political views. Is the policy constitutional?
How might the student argue that the policy is unconstitutional? *See* DeJohn v.
Temple University, 537 F.3d 301 (3d Cir. 2008).

   8. *More on the Danish Cartoons.* In the "Fighting Words" section earlier in this
chapter, there is a discussion of the Danish cartoons. You should re-read it. Under
Black, or the Court's other hate speech precedent, may the government prohibit
publication of the cartoons?

   9. *More on the International Treaty Regulating the Internet.* At the convention,
suppose that the German and French delegates again demand that all Nazi symbols be banned from the Internet. Based on the holding in *Black*, can you agree
to their demands? Would *Black* allow you to ban any other symbols (besides swastikas and other Nazi symbols) from the Internet?

12.   Crush Videos

Should the Court find that other categories of speech do not deserve constitutional protection? In the following case, the Court considered whether to except
so-called "crush videos" from First Amendment protection.

United States v. Stevens

130 S.Ct. 1577 (2010)

Chief Justice ROBERTS delivered the opinion of the Court.

   [Section 48] establishes a criminal penalty of up to five years in prison for
anyone who knowingly "creates, sells, or possesses a depiction of animal cruelty,"
if done "for commercial gain" in interstate or foreign commerce. [18 U.S.C.]
§48(a). A depiction of "animal cruelty" is defined as one "in which a living animal
is intentionally maimed, mutilated, tortured, wounded, or killed," if that conduct
violates federal or state law where "the creation, sale, or possession takes place."
§48(c)(1). In what is referred to as the "exceptions clause," the law exempts from
prohibition any depiction "that has serious religious, political, scientific, educational, journalistic, historical, or artistic value." §48(b).

   The legislative background of §48 focused primarily on the interstate market for "crush videos." According to the House Committee Report on the bill,
such videos feature the intentional torture and killing of helpless animals, including cats, dogs, monkeys, mice, and hamsters. Crush videos often depict women
slowly crushing animals to death "with their bare feet or while wearing high
heeled shoes," sometimes while "talking to the animals in a kind of dominatrix
patter" over "[t]he cries and squeals of the animals, obviously in great pain."
Apparently these depictions "appeal to persons with a very specific sexual fetish
who find them sexually arousing or otherwise exciting." The acts depicted in

crush videos are typically prohibited by the animal cruelty laws enacted by all 50 States and the District of Columbia. But crush videos rarely disclose the participants' identities, inhibiting prosecution of the underlying conduct.

This case, however, involves an application of §48 to depictions of animal fighting. Dogfighting, for example, is unlawful in all 50 States and the District of Columbia, and has been restricted by federal law since 1976. Respondent Robert J. Stevens ran a business, "Dogs of Velvet and Steel," and an associated Web site, through which he sold videos of pit bulls engaging in dogfights and attacking other animals. Among these videos were Japan Pit Fights and Pick-A-Winna: A Pit Bull Documentary, which include contemporary footage of dogfights in Japan (where such conduct is allegedly legal) as well as footage of American dogfights from the 1960's and 1970's. A third video, Catch Dogs and Country Living, depicts the use of pit bulls to hunt wild boar, as well as a "gruesome" scene of a pit bull attacking a domestic farm pig. On the basis of these videos, Stevens was indicted on three counts of violating §48.

Stevens moved to dismiss the indictment, arguing that §48 is facially invalid under the First Amendment. The District Court [held] that the depictions subject to §48, like obscenity or child pornography, are categorically unprotected by the First Amendment. . . . The en banc Third Circuit [declared] §48 facially unconstitutional [and] declined to recognize a new category of unprotected speech for depictions of animal cruelty. . . . We granted certiorari.

The Government's primary submission is that §48 necessarily complies with the Constitution because the banned depictions of animal cruelty, as a class, are categorically unprotected by the First Amendment. We disagree.

The First Amendment provides that "Congress shall make no law . . . abridging the freedom of speech." "[A]s a general matter, the First Amendment means that government has no power to restrict expression because of its message, its ideas, its subject matter, or its content." Ashcroft v. American Civil Liberties Union, 535 U.S. 564, 573 (2002). Section 48 explicitly regulates expression based on content: The statute restricts "visual [and] auditory depiction[s]," such as photographs, videos, or sound recordings, depending on whether they depict conduct in which a living animal is intentionally harmed. As such, §48 is "'presumptively invalid,' and the Government bears the burden to rebut that presumption." United States v. Playboy Entertainment Group, Inc., 529 U.S. 803, 817 (2000) (quoting R.A.V. v. St. Paul, 505 U.S. 377, 382 (1992)).

"From 1791 to the present," however, the First Amendment has "permitted restrictions upon the content of speech in a few limited areas," and has never "include[d] a freedom to disregard these traditional limitations." Id., at 382-383. These "historic and traditional categories long familiar to the bar," including obscenity, defamation, fraud, incitement, and speech integral to criminal conduct—are "well-defined and narrowly limited classes of speech, the prevention and punishment of which have never been thought to raise any Constitutional problem." Chaplinsky v. New Hampshire, 315 U.S. 568, 571-572 (1942).

The Government argues that "depictions of animal cruelty" should be added to the list. It contends that depictions of "illegal acts of animal cruelty" that are "made, sold, or possessed for commercial gain" necessarily "lack expressive value," and may accordingly "be regulated as *unprotected* speech." The claim is not just that Congress may regulate depictions of animal cruelty subject to the First Amendment, but that these depictions are outside the reach of that Amendment altogether — that they fall into a "First Amendment Free Zone." Board of Airport Commrs. of Los Angeles v. Jews for Jesus, Inc., 482 U.S. 569, 574 (1987).

As the Government notes, the prohibition of animal cruelty itself has a long history in American law, starting with the early settlement of the Colonies. But we are unaware of any similar tradition excluding *depictions* of animal cruelty from "the freedom of speech" codified in the First Amendment, and the Government points us to none.

The Government contends that "historical evidence" about the reach of the First Amendment is not "a necessary prerequisite for regulation today," and that categories of speech may be exempted from the First Amendment's protection without any long-settled tradition of subjecting that speech to regulation. Instead, the Government points to Congress's "legislative judgment that depictions of animals being intentionally tortured and killed [are] of such minimal redeeming value as to render [them] unworthy of First Amendment protection," and asks the Court to uphold the ban on the same basis. The Government thus proposes that a claim of categorical exclusion should be considered under a simple balancing test: "Whether a given category of speech enjoys First Amendment protection depends upon a categorical balancing of the value of the speech against its societal costs."

As a free-floating test for First Amendment coverage, that sentence is startling and dangerous. The First Amendment's guarantee of free speech does not extend only to categories of speech that survive an ad hoc balancing of relative social costs and benefits. The First Amendment itself reflects a judgment by the American people that the benefits of its restrictions on the Government outweigh the costs. Our Constitution forecloses any attempt to revise that judgment simply on the basis that some speech is not worth it. The Constitution is not a document "prescribing limits, and declaring that those limits may be passed at pleasure." Marbury v. Madison, 1 Cranch 137, 178, 2 L.Ed. 60 (1803).

To be fair to the Government, its view did not emerge from a vacuum. As the Government correctly notes, this Court has often *described* historically unprotected categories of speech as being " 'of such slight social value as a step to truth that any benefit that may be derived from them is clearly outweighed by the social interest in order and morality.' " *R.A.V., supra,* at 383 (quoting *Chaplinsky, supra,* at 572). In New York v. Ferber, 458 U.S. 747 (1982), we noted that within these categories of unprotected speech, "the evil to be restricted so overwhelmingly outweighs the expressive interests, if any, at stake, that no process of case-by-case adjudication is required," because "the balance of competing interests is clearly struck." The Government derives its proposed test from these descriptions in our precedents.

But such descriptions are just that — descriptive. They do not set forth a test that may be applied as a general matter to permit the Government to imprison any speaker so long as his speech is deemed valueless or unnecessary, or so long as an ad hoc calculus of costs and benefits tilts in a statute's favor.

When we have identified categories of speech as fully outside the protection of the First Amendment, it has not been on the basis of a simple cost-benefit analysis. In *Ferber*, for example, we classified child pornography as such a category. We noted that the State of New York had a compelling interest in protecting children from abuse, and that the value of using children in these works (as opposed to simulated conduct or adult actors) was *de minimis*. But our decision did not rest on this "balance of competing interests" alone. We made clear that *Ferber* presented a special case: The market for child pornography was "intrinsically related" to the underlying abuse, and was therefore "an integral part of the production of such materials, an activity illegal throughout the Nation." As we noted, "'[i]t rarely has been suggested that the constitutional freedom for speech and press extends its immunity to speech or writing used as an integral part of conduct in violation of a valid criminal statute.'" *Ferber* thus grounded its analysis in a previously recognized, long-established category of unprotected speech, and our subsequent decisions have shared this understanding. *See* Osborne v. Ohio, 495 U.S. 103, 110 (1990); Ashcroft v. Free Speech Coalition, 535 U.S. 234, 249-250 (2002).

Our decisions in *Ferber* and other cases cannot be taken as establishing a free-wheeling authority to declare new categories of speech outside the scope of the First Amendment. Maybe there are some categories of speech that have been historically unprotected, but have not yet been specifically identified or discussed as such in our case law. But if so, there is no evidence that "depictions of animal cruelty" is among them. We need not foreclose the future recognition of such additional categories to reject the Government's highly manipulable balancing test as a means of identifying them.

[In addition, the law suffers from overbreadth.] However "growing" and "lucrative" the markets for crush videos and dogfighting depictions might be, they are dwarfed by the market for other depictions, such as hunting magazines and videos, that we have determined to be within the scope of §48. We therefore need not and do not decide whether a statute limited to crush videos or other depictions of extreme animal cruelty would be constitutional. We hold only that §48 is not so limited but is instead substantially overbroad, and therefore invalid under the First Amendment.

The judgment of the United States Court of Appeals for the Third Circuit is affirmed.

It is so ordered.

Justice ALITO, dissenting.

The Court strikes down in its entirety a valuable statute that was enacted not to suppress speech, but to prevent horrific acts of animal cruelty — in particular, the creation and commercial exploitation of "crush videos," a form of depraved entertainment that has no social value. The Court's approach, which has the practical effect of legalizing the sale of such videos and is thus likely to spur a resumption of their production, is unwarranted.

As the Court of Appeals recognized, "the primary conduct that Congress sought to address through its passage [of §48] was the creation, sale, or possession of 'crush videos.'" [It] is undisputed that the *conduct* depicted in crush videos may constitutionally be prohibited. All 50 States and the District of Columbia have enacted statutes prohibiting animal cruelty. But before the enactment of §48, the underlying conduct depicted in crush videos was nearly impossible to prosecute. These videos, which "often appeal to persons with a very specific sexual fetish," were made in secret, generally without a live audience, and "the faces of the women inflicting the torture in the material often were not shown, nor could the location of the place where the cruelty was being inflicted or the date of the activity be ascertained from the depiction." Thus, law enforcement authorities often were not able to identify the parties responsible for the torture. In the rare instances in which it was possible to identify and find the perpetrators, they "often were able to successfully assert as a defense that the State could not prove its jurisdiction over the place where the act occurred or that the actions depicted took place within the time specified in the State statute of limitations." H.R. Rep., at 3.

In light of the practical problems thwarting the prosecution of the creators of crush videos under state animal cruelty laws, Congress concluded that the only effective way of stopping the underlying criminal conduct was to prohibit the commercial exploitation of the videos of that conduct. And Congress' strategy appears to have been vindicated. We are told that "[b]y 2007, sponsors of §48 declared the crush video industry dead. Even overseas Websites shut down in the wake of §48. Now, after the Third Circuit's decision [facially invalidating the statute], crush videos are already back online."

The First Amendment protects freedom of speech, but it most certainly does not protect violent criminal conduct, even if engaged in for expressive purposes. Crush videos present a highly unusual free speech issue because they are so closely linked with violent criminal conduct. The videos record the commission of violent criminal acts, and it appears that these crimes are committed for the sole purpose of creating the videos. In addition, as noted above, Congress was presented with compelling evidence that the only way of preventing these crimes was to target the sale of the videos. Under these circumstances, I cannot believe that the First Amendment commands Congress to step aside and allow the underlying crimes to continue.

The most relevant of our prior decisions is *Ferber*, which concerned child pornography. The Court there held that child pornography is not protected speech, and I believe that *Ferber*'s reasoning dictates a similar conclusion here. In *Ferber*, an important factor — I would say the most important factor — was that child pornography involves the commission of a crime that inflicts severe personal injury to the "children who are made to engage in sexual conduct for commercial purposes." Second, *Ferber* emphasized the fact that these underlying crimes could not be effectively combated without targeting the distribution of child pornography. . . . Third, the *Ferber* Court noted that the value of child pornography "is exceedingly modest, if not *de minimis*," and that any such value was "overwhelmingly outweigh[ed]" by "the evil to be restricted."

All three of these characteristics are shared by §48, as applied to crush videos. First, the conduct depicted in crush videos is criminal in every State and the District of Columbia. Thus, any crush video made in this country records the actual commission of a criminal act that inflicts severe physical injury and excruciating pain and ultimately results in death. Those who record the underlying criminal acts are likely to be criminally culpable, either as aiders and abettors or conspirators. And in the tight and secretive market for these videos, some who sell the videos or possess them with the intent to make a profit may be similarly culpable. (For example, in some cases, crush videos were commissioned by purchasers who specified the details of the acts that they wanted to see performed.) To the extent that §48 reaches such persons, it surely does not violate the First Amendment. Second, the criminal acts shown in crush videos cannot be prevented without targeting the conduct prohibited by §48 — the creation, sale, and possession for sale of depictions of animal torture with the intention of realizing a commercial profit. . . . Finally, the harm caused by the underlying crimes vastly outweighs any minimal value that the depictions might conceivably be thought to possess. [U]nlike the child pornography statute in *Ferber* or its federal counterpart, 18 U.S.C. §2252, §48(b) provides an exception for depictions having any "serious religious, political, scientific, educational, journalistic, historical, or artistic value."

It must be acknowledged that §48 differs from a child pornography law in an important respect: preventing the abuse of children is certainly much more important than preventing the torture of the animals used in crush videos. . . . The animals used in crush videos are living creatures that experience excruciating pain. Our society has long banned such cruelty, which is illegal throughout the country. . . . Section 48's ban on trafficking in crush videos also helps to enforce the criminal laws and to ensure that criminals do not profit from their crimes. We have already judged that taking the profit out of crime is a compelling interest. *See* Simon & Schuster, Inc. v. Members of N.Y. State Crime Victims Bd., 502 U.S. 105, 119 (1991). . . . Applying the principles set forth in *Ferber*, I would hold that crush videos are not protected by the First Amendment.

Application of the *Ferber* framework also supports the constitutionality of §48 as applied to depictions of brutal animal fights. (For convenience, I will focus on videos of dogfights, which appear to be the most common type of animal fight videos.) First, such depictions, like crush videos, record the actual commission of a crime involving deadly violence. Dogfights are illegal in every State and the District of Columbia, and under federal law constitute a felony punishable by imprisonment for up to five years. Second, Congress had an ample basis for concluding that the crimes depicted in these videos cannot be effectively controlled without targeting the videos. . . . The commercial trade in videos of dogfights is "an integral part of the production of such materials." [S]ome dogfighting videos are made "solely for the purpose of selling the video (and not for a live audience)." . . . In short, because videos depicting live dogfights are essential to the success of the criminal dogfighting subculture, the commercial sale of such videos helps to fuel the market for, and thus to perpetuate the perpetration of, the criminal conduct depicted in them.

Third, depictions of dogfights that fall within §48's reach have by definition no appreciable social value. . . . Finally, the harm caused by the underlying criminal acts greatly outweighs any trifling value that the depictions might be thought to possess. As the Humane Society explains:

> The abused dogs used in fights endure physical torture and emotional manipulation throughout their lives to predispose them to violence; common tactics include feeding the animals hot peppers and gunpowder, prodding them with sticks, and electrocution. Dogs are conditioned never to give up a fight, even if they will be gravely hurt or killed. As a result, dogfights inflict horrific injuries on the participating animals, including lacerations, ripped ears, puncture wounds and broken bones. Losing dogs are routinely refused treatment, beaten further as 'punishment' for the loss, and executed by drowning, hanging, or incineration.

For these dogs, unlike the animals killed in crush videos, the suffering lasts for years rather than minutes. As with crush videos, moreover, the statutory ban on commerce in dogfighting videos is also supported by compelling governmental interests in effectively enforcing the Nation's criminal laws and preventing criminals from profiting from their illegal activities.

13. Commercial Speech

In Virginia State Board of Pharmacy v. Virginia Citizens Consumer Council, 425 U.S. 748 (1976), the Court extended to commercial speech special protection under the First Amendment. The Court referred to commercial speech as speech that does "no more than propose a commercial transaction." However, not all advertisements are commercial speech; some advertisements may be treated as traditional noncommercial "political speech." *See* New York Times v. Sullivan, 376 U.S. 254 (1964). In addition, the reference to a specific product or the economic motivation of the speaker does not automatically demonstrate that speech qualifies as "commercial speech." *See* Bolger v. Youngs Drug Products Corp., 463 U.S. 60 (1963). In *Bolger*, a drug company mailed information brochures about birth control devices; these advertisements were held to be commercial speech, and the Court declared that the fact that advertising of a product is linked "to a current public debate" is not sufficient per se to qualify the advertising as non-commercial speech.

Even though commercial speech may not be accorded the same status as political speech, *Virginia State Board of Pharmacy* recognized that society (advertisers, consumers, and society at large) needs commercial speech information related to advertisements (about prescription drug prices, in this case):

> [We] may assume that the advertiser's interest is a purely economic one. That hardly disqualifies him from protection under the First Amendment. . . . As to the particular consumer's interest in the free flow of commercial information, that interest may be as keen, if not keener by far, than his interest in the day's most urgent political debate. . . . Those whom the suppression of prescription drug price information hits the hardest are the poor, the sick, and particularly the aged. A disproportionate amount of their income tends to be spent on

prescription drugs; yet they are the least able to learn, by shopping from pharmacist to pharmacist, where their scarce dollars are best spent. When drug prices vary as strikingly as they do, information as to who is charging what becomes more than a convenience. It could mean the alleviation of physical pain or the enjoyment of basic necessities.

Generalizing, society also may have a strong interest in the free flow of commercial information. Even an individual advertisement, though entirely "commercial," may be of general public interest. The facts of decided cases furnish illustrations: advertisements stating that referral services for legal abortions are available, that a manufacturer of artificial furs promotes his product as an alternative to the extinction by his competitors of fur-bearing mammals, and that a domestic producer advertises his product as an alternative to imports that tend to deprive American residents of their jobs. Obviously, not all commercial messages contain the same or even a very great public interest element. There are few to which such an element, however, could not be added. Our pharmacist, for example, could cast himself as a commentator on store-to-store disparities in drug prices, giving his own and those of a competitor as proof. We see little point in requiring him to do so, and little difference if he does not.

Moreover, there is another consideration that suggests that no line between publicly "interesting" or "important" commercial advertising and the opposite kind could ever be drawn. Advertising, however tasteless and excessive it sometimes may seem, is nonetheless dissemination of information as to who is producing and selling what product, for what reason, and at what price. So long as we preserve a predominantly free enterprise economy, the allocation of our resources in large measure will be made through numerous private economic decisions. It is a matter of public interest that those decisions, in the aggregate, be intelligent and well informed. To this end, the free flow of commercial information is indispensable. And if it is indispensable to the proper allocation of resources in a free enterprise system, it is also indispensable to the formation of intelligent opinions as to how that system ought to be regulated or altered. Therefore, even if the First Amendment were thought to be primarily an instrument to enlighten public decisionmaking in a democracy, we could not say that the free flow of information does not serve that goal.

Lorillard Tobacco Co. v. Reilly

533 U.S. 525 (2001)

Justice O'Connor delivered the opinion of the Court.

In January 1999[,] Massachusetts promulgated comprehensive regulations governing the advertising and sale of cigarettes, smokeless tobacco, and cigars. Petitioners, a group of cigarette, smokeless tobacco, and cigar manufacturers and retailers, [sued claiming] that the regulations violate [the] United States Constitution.

I

[The] purpose of the cigarette and smokeless tobacco regulations is "to eliminate deception and unfairness in the way cigarettes and smokeless tobacco products are marketed, sold and distributed in Massachusetts in order to address the incidence of cigarette smoking and smokeless tobacco use by children under legal age [and] in order to prevent access to such products by underage consumers." The similar purpose of the cigar regulations is "to eliminate deception and unfairness in the way cigars and little cigars are packaged, marketed, sold and distributed in Massachusetts [so that] consumers may be adequately informed about the health risks associated with cigar smoking, its addictive properties, and the false perception that cigars are a safe alternative to cigarettes [and so that] the incidence of cigar use by children under legal age is addressed [in] order to prevent access to such products by underage consumers." [The] regulations place a variety of restrictions on outdoor advertising, point-of-sale advertising, retail sales transactions, transactions by mail, promotions, sampling of products, and labels for cigars.

The cigarette and smokeless tobacco regulations being challenged before this Court provide:

> (2) Retail Outlet Sales Practices. [Except as otherwise provided], it shall be an unfair or deceptive act or practice for any person who sells or distributes cigarettes or smokeless tobacco products through a retail outlet located within Massachusetts to engage in any of the following retail outlet sales practices:
>
>> (c) Using self-service displays of cigarettes or smokeless tobacco products;
>>
>> (d) Failing to place cigarettes and smokeless tobacco products out of the reach of all consumers, and in a location accessible only to outlet personnel.
>
> (5) Advertising Restrictions. [Except as otherwise provided], it shall be an unfair or deceptive act or practice for any manufacturer, distributor or retailer to engage in any of the following practices:
>
>> (a) Outdoor advertising, including advertising in enclosed stadiums and advertising from within a retail establishment that is directed toward or visible from the outside of the establishment, in any location that is within a 1,000 foot radius of any public playground, playground area in a public park, elementary school or secondary school;
>>
>> (b) Point-of-sale advertising of cigarettes or smokeless tobacco products any portion of which is placed lower than five feet from the floor of any retail establishment which is located within a one thousand foot radius of any public playground, playground area in a public park, elementary school or secondary school, and which is not an adult-only retail establishment.

The cigar regulations that are still at issue provide:

> (1) Retail Sales Practices. [Except as otherwise provided] it shall be an unfair or deceptive act or practice for any person who sells or distributes cigars or little cigars directly to consumers within Massachusetts to engage in any of the following practices:
>
>> (a) Sampling of cigars or little cigars or promotional give-aways of cigars or little cigars.
>
> (2) Retail Outlet Sales Practices. [Parallel provisions to those relating to cigarettes were cited.]

[W]e must analyze the cigarette as well as the smokeless tobacco and cigar petitioners' claim that certain sales practices regulations for tobacco products violate the First Amendment.

For over 25 years, the Court has recognized that commercial speech does not fall outside the purview of the First Amendment. In recognition of the "distinction between speech proposing a commercial transaction, which occurs in an area traditionally subject to government regulation, and other varieties of speech," we developed a framework for analyzing regulations of commercial speech that is "substantially similar" to the test for time, place, and manner [restrictions]. The analysis contains four elements:

> At the outset, we must determine whether the expression is protected by the First Amendment. For commercial speech to come within that provision, it at least must concern lawful activity and not be misleading. Next, we ask whether the asserted governmental interest is substantial. If both inquiries yield positive answers, we must determine whether the regulation directly advances the governmental interest asserted, and whether it is not more extensive than is necessary to serve that interest." *Central Hudson* [Gas & Electric Corp. v. Public Service Commission of New York, 447 U.S. 557 1980].

Petitioners urge us to reject the *Central Hudson* analysis and apply strict scrutiny. They are not the first litigants to do so. [But] here [we] see [no] need to break new ground. *Central Hudson,* as applied in our more recent commercial speech cases, provides an adequate basis for [decision].

Only the last two steps of *Central Hudson*'s four-part analysis are at issue here. The Attorney General has assumed for purposes of summary judgment that petitioners' speech is entitled to First Amendment protection. With respect to the second step, none of the petitioners contests the importance of the State's interest in preventing the use of tobacco products by minors.

The third step of *Central Hudson* concerns the relationship between the harm that underlies the State's interest and the means identified by the State to advance that interest. It requires that

> the speech restriction directly and materially advanc[es] the asserted governmental interest. "This burden is not satisfied by mere speculation or conjecture; rather, a governmental body seeking to sustain a restriction on commercial speech must demonstrate that the harms it recites are real and that its restriction will in fact alleviate them to a material degree."

Greater New Orleans [Broadcasting Assn., Inc. v. United States, 527 U.S. 173 (1999)]. We do not, however, require that "empirical data [come] accompanied by a surfeit of background information [and we] have permitted litigants to justify speech restrictions by reference to studies and anecdotes pertaining to different locales altogether, or even, in a case applying strict scrutiny, to justify restrictions based solely on history, consensus, and 'simple common sense.'"

The last step of the *Central Hudson* analysis "complements" the third step, "asking whether the speech restriction is not more extensive than necessary to serve the interests that support it." *Greater New Orleans, supra,* at 188. We have made it clear that "the least restrictive means" is not the standard; instead, the case law requires a reasonable "'fit between the legislature's ends and the means chosen to accomplish those ends, [a] means narrowly tailored to achieve the desired objective.'" Board of Trustees of State Univ. of N.Y. v. Fox [492 U.S. 469 (1989)]. Focusing on the third and fourth steps of the *Central Hudson* analysis, we first address the outdoor advertising and point-of-sale advertising regulations for smokeless tobacco and cigars. We then address the sales practices regulations for all tobacco products.

The outdoor advertising regulations prohibit smokeless tobacco or cigar advertising within a 1,000-foot radius of a school or [playground]. The smokeless tobacco and cigar petitioners contend that the Attorney General's regulations do not satisfy *Central Hudson*'s third step. They maintain that although the Attorney General may have identified a problem with underage cigarette smoking, he has not identified an equally severe problem with respect to underage use of smokeless tobacco or cigars. The smokeless tobacco petitioner emphasizes the "lack of parity" between cigarettes and smokeless tobacco. The cigar petitioners catalog a list of differences between cigars and other tobacco products, including the characteristics of the products and marketing strategies. The petitioners finally contend that the Attorney General cannot prove that advertising has a causal link to tobacco use such that limiting advertising will materially alleviate any problem of underage use of their products.

In previous cases, we have acknowledged the theory that product advertising stimulates demand for products, while suppressed advertising may have the opposite effect. *See* United States v. Edge Broadcasting Co., 509 U.S. 418 (1993). The Attorney General cites numerous studies to support this theory in the case of tobacco [products].

Our review of the record reveals that the Attorney General has provided ample documentation of the problem with underage use of smokeless tobacco and cigars. In addition, we disagree with petitioners' claim that there is no evidence that preventing targeted campaigns and limiting youth exposure to advertising will decrease underage use of smokeless tobacco and cigars. On this record and in the posture of summary judgment, we are unable to conclude that the Attorney General's decision to regulate advertising of smokeless tobacco and cigars in an effort to combat the use of tobacco products by minors was based on mere "speculation [and] conjecture." Edenfield v. Fane [507 U.S. 761 (1993)].

[W]e conclude that the regulations do not satisfy the fourth step of the *Central Hudson* analysis. The final step of the *Central Hudson* analysis, the "critical inquiry in this case," requires a reasonable fit between the means and ends of the regulatory scheme. The Attorney General's regulations do not meet this standard. The broad sweep of the regulations indicates that the Attorney General did not "carefully calculat[e] the costs and benefits associated with the burden on speech imposed" by the regulations. The outdoor advertising regulations prohibit any smokeless tobacco or cigar advertising within 1,000 feet of schools or playgrounds. In the District Court, petitioners maintained that this prohibition would prevent advertising in 87% to 91% of Boston, Worcester, and Springfield, Massachusetts. The 87% to 91% figure appears to include not only the effect of the regulations, but also the limitations imposed by other generally applicable zoning restrictions. . . . The substantial geographical reach of the Attorney General's outdoor advertising regulations is compounded by other factors. "Outdoor" advertising includes not only advertising located outside an establishment, but also advertising inside a store if that advertising is visible from outside the store. The regulations restrict advertisements of any size and the term advertisement also includes oral statements.

In some geographical areas, these regulations would constitute nearly a complete ban on the communication of truthful information about smokeless tobacco and cigars to adult consumers. The breadth and scope of the regulations, and the process by which the Attorney General adopted the regulations, do not demonstrate a careful calculation of the speech interests involved.

First, the Attorney General did not seem to consider the impact of the 1,000-foot restriction on commercial speech in major metropolitan areas. The Attorney General apparently selected the 1,000-foot distance based on the FDA's decision to impose an identical 1,000-foot restriction when it attempted to regulate cigarette and smokeless tobacco advertising. But the FDA's 1,000-foot regulation was not an adequate basis for the Attorney General to tailor the Massachusetts regulations. The degree to which speech is suppressed — or alternative avenues for speech remain available — under a particular regulatory scheme tends to be case specific. . . . The FDA's regulations would have had widely disparate effects nationwide. Even in Massachusetts, the effect of the Attorney General's speech regulations will vary based on whether a locale is rural, suburban, or urban. The uniformly broad sweep of the geographical limitation demonstrates a lack of tailoring.

In addition, the range of communications restricted seems unduly broad. For instance, it is not clear from the regulatory scheme why a ban on oral communications is necessary to further the State's interest. Apparently that restriction means that a retailer is unable to answer inquiries about its tobacco products if that communication occurs outdoors. . . . To the extent that studies have identified particular advertising and promotion practices that appeal to youth, tailoring would involve targeting those practices while permitting others. As crafted, the regulations make no distinction among practices on this basis.

[The] State's interest in preventing underage tobacco use is substantial, and even compelling, but it is no less true that the sale and use of tobacco products by adults is a legal activity. We must consider that tobacco retailers and manufacturers have an interest in conveying truthful information about their products to adults, and adults have a corresponding interest in receiving truthful information about tobacco products. [As] the State protects children from tobacco advertisements, tobacco manufacturers and retailers and their adult consumers still have a protected interest in communication.

In some instances, Massachusetts' outdoor advertising regulations would impose particularly onerous burdens on speech. For example, we disagree with the Court of Appeals' conclusion that because cigar manufacturers and retailers conduct a limited amount of advertising in comparison to other tobacco products, "the relative lack of cigar advertising also means that the burden imposed on cigar advertisers is correspondingly small." If some retailers have relatively small advertising budgets, and use few avenues of communication, then the Attorney General's outdoor advertising regulations potentially place a greater, not lesser, burden on those retailers' speech. Furthermore, to the extent that cigar products and cigar advertising differ from that of other tobacco products, that difference should inform the inquiry into what speech restrictions are necessary.

In addition, a retailer in Massachusetts may have no means of communicating to passersby on the street that it sells tobacco products because alternative forms of advertisement, like newspapers, do not allow that retailer to propose an instant transaction in the way that onsite advertising does. The ban on any indoor advertising that is visible from the outside also presents problems in establishments like convenience stores, which have unique security concerns that counsel in favor of full visibility of the store from the outside. It is these sorts of considerations that the Attorney General failed to incorporate into the regulatory scheme.

A careful calculation of the costs of a speech regulation does not mean that a State must demonstrate that there is no incursion on legitimate speech interests, but a speech regulation cannot unduly impinge on the speaker's ability to propose a commercial transaction and the adult listener's opportunity to obtain information about products. After reviewing the outdoor advertising regulations, we find the calculation in these cases insufficient for purposes of the First Amendment.

Massachusetts has also restricted indoor, point-of-sale advertising for smokeless tobacco and cigars. Advertising cannot be "placed lower than five feet from the floor of any retail establishment which is located within a one thousand foot radius of" any school or playground. The District Court invalidated these provisions, concluding that the Attorney General had not provided a sufficient basis for regulating indoor advertising. [We] conclude that the point-of-sale advertising regulations fail both the third and fourth steps of the *Central Hudson* analysis. A regulation cannot be sustained if it "'provides only ineffective or remote support for the government's purpose,'" or if there is "little chance" that the restriction will advance the State's goal, *Greater New Orleans, supra,* at 193. As outlined above, the State's goal is to prevent minors from using tobacco products and to curb demand for that activity by limiting youth exposure to advertising. The 5-foot rule does not seem to advance that goal. Not all children are less than 5 feet tall, and those who are certainly have the ability to look up and take in their surroundings. . . . Massachusetts may wish to target tobacco advertisements and displays that entice children, much like floor-level candy displays in a convenience store, but the blanket height restriction does not constitute a reasonable fit with that goal. [We] conclude that the restriction on the height of indoor advertising is invalid under *Central Hudson*'s third and fourth prongs.

The Attorney General also promulgated a number of regulations that restrict sales practices by cigarette, smokeless tobacco, and cigar manufacturers and retailers. [T]he regulations [require] tobacco retailers to place tobacco products behind counters and require customers to have contact with a salesperson before they are able to handle a tobacco product. [Assuming] that petitioners have a cognizable speech interest in a particular means of displaying their products, these regulations withstand First Amendment scrutiny. We conclude that the State has demonstrated a substantial interest in preventing access to tobacco products by minors and has adopted an appropriately narrow means of advancing that interest.

Unattended displays of tobacco products present an opportunity for access without the proper age verification required by law. Thus, the State prohibits self-service and other displays that would allow an individual to obtain tobacco products without direct contact with a salesperson. It is clear that the regulations leave open ample channels of communication. The regulations do not significantly impede adult access to tobacco products. Moreover, retailers have other means of exercising any cognizable speech interest in the presentation of their products. We presume that vendors may place empty tobacco packaging on open display, and display actual tobacco products so long as that display is only accessible to sales personnel. As for cigars, there is no indication in the regulations that a customer is unable to examine a cigar prior to purchase, so long as that examination takes place through a salesperson.

[We] conclude that the sales practices regulations withstand First Amendment scrutiny. The means chosen by the State are narrowly tailored to prevent access to tobacco products by minors, are unrelated to expression, and leave open alternative avenues for vendors to convey information about products and for would-be customers to inspect products before purchase.

We have observed that "tobacco use, particularly among children and adolescents, poses perhaps the single most significant threat to public health in the United States." From a policy perspective, it is understandable for the States to attempt to prevent minors from using tobacco products before they reach an age where they are capable of weighing for themselves the risks and potential benefits of tobacco use, and other adult activities. [The] First Amendment, [however,] constrains state efforts to limit advertising of tobacco products, because so long as the sale and use of tobacco is lawful for adults, the tobacco industry has a protected interest in communicating information about its products and adult customers have an interest in receiving that information.

To the extent that federal law and the First Amendment do not prohibit state action, States and localities remain free to combat the problem of underage tobacco use by appropriate means. The judgment of the United States Court of Appeals for the First Circuit is therefore affirmed in part and reversed in part, and the cases are remanded for further proceedings consistent with this opinion.

It is so ordered.

Justice THOMAS, concurring in part and concurring in the judgment.

[W]hen the government seeks to restrict truthful speech in order to suppress the ideas it conveys, strict scrutiny is appropriate, whether or not the speech in question may be characterized as "commercial." I would [hold that] all of the advertising restrictions [violate] the First Amendment. [Underlying] many of the arguments of respondents and their *amici* is the idea that tobacco is in some sense *sui generis* [and that] application of normal First Amendment principles should be suspended. Smoking poses serious health risks, and advertising may induce children (who lack the judgment to make an intelligent decision about whether to smoke) to begin smoking, which can lead to addiction. The State's assessment of the urgency of the problem posed by tobacco is a policy judgment, and it is not this Court's place to second-guess it. Nevertheless, [to] uphold the Massachusetts tobacco regulations would be to accept a line of reasoning that would permit restrictions on advertising for a host of other products. . . .

Although every State prohibits the sale of alcohol to those under age 21, much alcohol advertising is viewed by children. Not surprisingly, there is considerable evidence that exposure to alcohol advertising is associated with underage drinking. Like underage tobacco use, underage drinking has effects that cannot be undone later in life. Those who begin drinking early are much more likely to become dependent on alcohol. . . . Respondents have identified no principle of law or logic that would preclude the imposition of restrictions on fast food and alcohol advertising similar to those they seek to impose on tobacco advertising. In effect, they seek a "vice" exception to the First Amendment. No such exception exists. If it did, it would have almost no limit, for "any product that poses some threat to public health or public morals might reasonably be characterized by a state legislature as relating to 'vice activity.'" . . .

No legislature has ever sought to restrict speech about an activity it regarded as harmless and inoffensive. Calls for limits on expression always are made when the specter of some threatened harm is looming. . . . It is therefore no answer for the State to say that the makers of cigarettes are doing harm: perhaps they are. But in that respect they are no different from the purveyors of other harmful products, or the advocates of harmful ideas. When the State seeks to silence them, they are all entitled to the protection of the First Amendment.

Notes and Questions

1. *The* Lorillard *Consensus.* In 44 Liquormart, Inc. v. Rhode Island, 517 U.S. 484 (1996), a plurality, led by Justice O'Connor, advocated reliance on *Central Hudson* for all commercial speech problems; another plurality, led by Justice Stevens, advocated a two-track system of scrutiny. Specifically, the *Central Hudson* test (deemed to require less than strict scrutiny) would be used when a regulation seeks to protect consumers from misleading, deceptive, or aggressive sales practices or to require the disclosure of beneficial consumer information. However, a tougher form of scrutiny, labeled "special care" review, was advocated for cases where a state entirely prohibits the dissemination of truthful, nonmisleading commercial messages for reasons unrelated to the preservation of a fair bargaining process. In *Lorillard*, the debate between these two pluralities dropped from sight. However, four justices dissented "in part" and would have remanded for trial on the validity of the "1,000-foot rule," on the grounds that the record did not contain enough information to evaluate the existence of "alternate avenues of communication." Justice Stevens also led a plurality of the Court in arguing that the sales practices and indoor advertising restrictions should be upheld as conduct regulations under *O'Brien*.

2. *The Regulation of Professionals.* The Court's decisions relating to advertisements by lawyers, accountants, and other professionals both recognize the right to advertise and the state's interest in regulating advertisements. *See, e.g.,* Florida Bar v. Went For It., Inc., 515 U.S. 618 (1995) (personal injury attorneys may not use targeted direct-mail solicitations for 30 days after an accident); Ibanez v. Florida Department of Business and Professional Regulation, Board of Accountancy, 512 U.S. 136 (1994) (lawyer may refer to CPA and certification as financial planner in stationery, business cards, and advertising); Edenfield v. Fane, 507 U.S. 761 (1993) (accountants may solicit business clients in person); Peel v.

Attorney Registration and Disciplinary Commission of Illinois, 496 U.S. 91 (1990) (lawyer may advertise certification as trial specialist); Shapero v. Kentucky Bar Association, 486 U.S. 466 (1988) (lawyer may solicit legal business by sending letters to potential clients known to face particular legal problems); *In re R.M.J.*, 455 U.S. 191 (1982) (lawyer may not be disciplined for identifying the jurisdiction where licensed to practice, or for mailing cards to friends, relatives, and clients about opening a new office); *In re Primus*, 436 U.S. 412 (1978) (ACLU "cooperating lawyer" may not be disciplined for soliciting a prospective litigant by mail after meeting litigant at a gathering related to particular issue); Ohralik v. Ohio State Bar Association, 436 U.S. 447 (1978) (lawyer may be disciplined for contacting accident victims in hospital room); Bates v. State Bar of Arizona, 433 U.S. 350 (1977) (lawyers may advertise legal services and fees in newspaper).

3. *Geographic Limitations on Commercial Speech.* Some of the Court's commercial speech cases have established limits on the power of the state to regulate particular locations, including the public forum. *See, e.g.,* City of Cincinnati v. Discovery Network, 507 U.S. 410 (1993) (city may not refuse to allow commercial speech advertisements to be placed in newsracks on sidewalks throughout the city when noncommercial speech is allowed in newsracks); Metromedia, Inc. v. San Diego, 453 U.S. 490 (1981) (allowing city to ban outdoor advertising billboards when "offsite" but not to ban "onsite" advertising signs); Linmark Associates, Inc. v. Township of Willingboro, 431 U.S. 85 (1977) (town may not ban "For Sale" and "Sold" signs from residential property).

4. *Broadcasting and Commercial Speech.* The Court's decisions involving advertising bans on broadcasting have relied on *Central Hudson* and have reached different results in different contexts. Compare Greater New Orleans Broadcasting Association v. United States, 527 U.S. 173 (1999) (federal ban on broadcasting advertisements of private casino gambling information violated the right of radio and television stations in a state where gambling is legal to broadcast such advertisements), with United States v. Edge Broadcasting Co., 509 U.S. 418 (1993) (same federal ban is constitutional as applied to broadcast advertising by radio station in a state where such gambling is not authorized).

5. *Commercial Speech and the Justifications for Protecting Speech.* Does commercial speech, as reflected in *Lorillard*, serve any of the justifications for protecting speech presented at the beginning of this chapter? In other words, does it provide a safety valve, does it promote self-fulfillment or the marketplace of ideas, or is it related to the democratic process?

6. *Liquor Advertising.* A Rhode Island law prohibited liquor vendors licensed in the state (as well as out-of-state manufacturers, wholesalers, and shippers) from "advertising in any manner whatsoever" the price of any alcoholic beverage offered for sale in the state. The only exception permitted under the law was for price tags or signs displayed with the merchandise inside licensed premises and not visible from the street. The law also prohibited the news media from publishing or broadcasting any advertisements, even those referring to liquor being sold in other states, that "make reference to the price of any alcoholic beverage." In 44 Liquormart, Inc. v. Rhode Island, 517 U.S. 484 (1996), a plurality concluded that

the law was unconstitutional: "It is perfectly obvious that alternative forms of regulation that would not involve any restriction on speech would be more likely to achieve the State's goal of promoting temperance. As the State's own expert conceded, higher prices can be maintained either by direct regulation or by increased taxation. 829 F. Supp., at 549. Per capita purchases could be limited as is the case with prescription drugs. Even educational campaigns focused on the problems of excessive, or even moderate, drinking might prove to be more effective. The alcohol ad ban statutes are even more extensive than the tobacco regulations that were invalidated in *Lorillard*, including the outdoor 1,000 foot regulation and indoor five-feet-from-the-floor regulation. So the alcohol ad ban statutes must be invalidated under *Central Hudson*."

7. *Craigslist and Prostitution Advertisements.* Since prostitution is illegal in most jurisdictions, the state has the power to prohibit commercial advertising by prostitutes. In recent years, some prostitutes have tried to advertise their wares on craigslist. Recently, an Illinois sheriff sued craigslist to require it to monitor sex advertisements or to shut the list down. *See Illinois Sheriff Sues Craigslist over Advertisement*, National Public Radio broadcast (Mar. 9, 2009). Craigslist ultimately agreed not to carry such advertisements.

8. *Fraudulent Calls.* Under the *Central Hudson* test, federal and state governments retain the power to prohibit unlawful and misleading advertisements. In Federal Trade Commission v. Helping Hands of Hope, Inc. (D. Ariz. 2010), the court upheld a prohibition against telemarketing that was falsely suggesting it was selling overpriced products in order to benefit the elderly and the disabled.

∾ PROBLEMS ∾

1. *Gun Sale Advertising.* In San Mateo County, California, there is a fairgrounds that is leased by the county government for various events throughout the year. Between 1990 and 1997, gun shows were held at the fairgrounds. But in 1998, a new clause is added to the lease that says that any tenant "shall not permit any gun shows" at the fairgrounds. The San Mateo County Board of Supervisors offered three purposes for the ban: "to avoid sending the wrong message to the community relative to support of gun usage, to improve the Fairgrounds' image, and to reduce the fiscal impact of criminal justice activities in response to gun-related violence." GunsAmerica (GA) has previously conducted gun shows at the fairgrounds, and the lawyer for GA tries to negotiate with the county in order to remove the new clause from the lease for an event sponsored by GA. During negotiations, the county sends a letter informing GA that this new clause is "intended to prohibit gun sales or offers to sell guns later, but not to prohibit the exchange of information or ideas about guns, gun safety, or the display of guns for historical or educational purposes." After receiving the letter, GA files suit in federal district court, seeking a declaratory judgment that the new clause violates the First Amendment. The trial judge rejects GA's First Amendment claims, and GA appeals. You represent GA on appeal. What arguments will you make to persuade

the Court of Appeals for the Ninth Circuit to reverse the trial judge's First Amendment decision? What counterarguments do you expect the county's lawyer to make in response? (Do not argue vagueness or overbreadth.)

2. *Telemarketing.* The FTC's Telemarketing Sales Rule creates a national do-not-call list, which is a registry of the telephone numbers of consumers who have indicated that they do not wish to receive unsolicited telephone calls from commercial telemarketers, and prohibits those telemarketers from making sales calls to consumers on the list. Commercial telemarketers are exempt from the FTC's do-not-call prohibitions if they have received express written consent from the consumers they call, or if they call consumers with whom they have an established business relationship. The FTC's list also specifically excludes calls from charitable organizations.

In formulating the Sales Rule, the FTC examined Congress's adoption of the Telephone Consumer Protection Act of 1991, which empowered a different agency, the Federal Communications Commission (FCC), to take action on telemarketing issues. That Act authorized the FCC (*not* the FTC) to establish a national database of residential subscribers who object to receiving telephone solicitations, defined as a telephone call or message "for the purpose of encouraging the purchase or rental of, or investment in, property, goods, or services," excluding calls from a tax-exempt nonprofit organization and charitable telemarketers. The legislative history of this 1991 statute cited statistical data reporting that consumer complaints were directed mostly at commercial sales calls.

A few years later, when Congress enacted the Telemarketing and Consumer Fraud and Abuse Prevention Act (a different statute), it directed the FTC to prescribe rules prohibiting deceptive and abusive telemarketing acts and practice, including calls that a reasonable consumer would consider coercive or abusive of such consumer's right to privacy. Congress found that consumers lose an estimated $40 billion each year owing to telemarketing fraud. So the FTC in 1995 promulgated its first Sales Rule, and in 2003 amended that Rule. The first FTC Sales Rule did not apply to a charitable organization that was not organized "to carry on business for its own profit or that of its members," echoing the earlier FCC interpretation of the Telephone Consumer Protection Act of 1991. However, the FTC's first Sales Rule prohibited telemarketers only from making sales calls to persons *who had previously stated their desire not to receive such calls from that solicitor*. By 2003, the FTC decided that the first Sales Rule was inadequate to prevent the type of abusive commercial sales calls it was intended to prohibit because telemarketers ignored consumers' repeated requests to be placed on company-specific do-not-call lists. So the amended 2003 Sales Rule allows individuals to block all commercial sales calls, while exempting calls on behalf of charitable organizations. The FTC's 2003 Sales Rule is the subject of the federal lawsuit in which the Court of Appeals for the Tenth Circuit reversed the federal district court's decision, described earlier.

You represent the telemarketers who have challenged the constitutionality of the 2003 Sales Rule under the First Amendment. What arguments will you make to support the federal district court's decision to strike down the Rule on First

Amendment grounds? What counterarguments do you expect the FTC to make to support the Tenth Circuit's decision to uphold the rule? (Do not argue vagueness or overbreadth.)

3. *Calorie Posting.* New York City's health code requires all chain restaurants that have 15 or more establishments nationally to reveal the calorie counts of their food. The information must be displayed on menus and menu boards in a specific formulation that is clear and conspicuous and that is adjacent or close to each menu item. A restaurant association challenges the code provisions, claiming an infringement of its members' right to free speech. Consistent with the First Amendment, can New York impose the health code requirements? *See* New York State Restaurant Assn. v. New York City Board of Health, 556 F.3d 114 (2d Cir. 2009).

4. *More on the International Treaty Regulating the Internet.* Various delegates to the convention want to place restrictions on commercial speech. Some want to ban commercial speech that is "fraudulent." Others want to ban speech that infringes on commercial interests in their own countries. For example, in France, it is impermissible to use the word *champagne* to refer to "sparkling wine" unless the grapes were grown in the Champagne region of France. France would like to see similar restrictions placed on Internet advertising of sparkling wine. What restrictions on commercial speech can you agree to? Can you accede to the French demands? American sparkling wine producers prefer to use the label *champagne* for their product (rather than the term *sparkling wine*) because they believe that it has greater commercial appeal.

5. *Regulating Bulk E-Mail (Spam) Transmissions.* In an effort to control the dissemination of "spam" (unsolicited bulk e-mail messages), the Virginia Computer Crimes Act (VCCA) makes it illegal to use a computer or computer network with the intent to falsify or forge electronic mail transmission information or other routing information in any manner in connection with the transmission of unsolicited bulk electronic mail through or into the computer network of an electronic mail service provider or its subscribers. However, unlike some other statutes that prohibit only commercial e-mail messages, the VCCA applies to all e-mail messages, including those that contain religious or political messages. The VCCA makes it a felony to transmit more than 10,000 e-mail messages to attempted recipients in any 24-hour time period, to 100,000 attempted recipients in any 30-day time period, or to 1 million attempted recipients in any 1-year time period. The defendant sent 10,000 messages to subscribers of America Online (AOL). Although the defendant tried to hide his identity, investigators were able to track him down. Would the VCCA be valid as applied to e-mail messages proposing a commercial transaction? Does the state have an interest in controlling unsolicited bulk commercial e-mail messages (based either on the annoyance to e-mail recipients or on the increased costs to Internet service providers)? Does the state also have an interest in ensuring that the senders of such e-mail messages identify themselves? *See* Jaynes v. Commonwealth, 666 S.E.2d 303 (Va. 2008).

6. *More on Spam E-Mail Transmissions.* Would the VCCA be valid as applied to all e-mail messages, including those with religious or political subjects? Could Virginia also prohibit anonymous e-mail messages? What standard of review would apply? What result? *See id.; see also* McIntyre v. Ohio Elections Commn., 514 U.S. 334, 342 (1995).

C. SYMBOLIC SPEECH

The civil rights era required the Court to confront First Amendment issues arising in the context of public demonstrations, and initially the Court was divided as to how to distinguish "speech" from "conduct." Ultimately, however, the Court developed a consensus that "conduct" may be "sufficiently imbued with elements of communication" to deserve constitutional protection, as long as the speaker has "an intent to convey a particularized message" under circumstances where "the likelihood was great that the message would be understood by those who viewed it." Spence v. Washington, 418 U.S. 405, 409 (1974). In 1989, the Court enumerated the cases where "communicative conduct" or "symbolic speech" was protected:

> [We] have recognized the expressive nature of students' wearing of black armbands to protest American military involvement in Vietnam, Tinker v. Des Moines Independent Community School Dist., 393 U.S. [503] (1969); of a sit-in by blacks in a "whites only" area to protest segregation, Brown v. Louisiana, 383 U.S. [131] (1966); of the wearing of American military uniforms in a dramatic presentation criticizing American involvement in Vietnam, Schacht v. United States, 398 U.S. [58] (1970); and of picketing about a wide variety of causes, *see, e.g.,* United States v. Grace, 461 U.S. [171] (1983) [picketing on the sidewalk across from the Court]. Attaching a peace sign to the flag, *Spence* [v. Washington, 418 U.S. 405 (1974)]; refusing to salute the flag, [West Virginia Board of Education v.] *Barnette,* 319 U.S. [624 (1943)]; and displaying a red flag, Stromberg v. California, 283 U.S. [359] (1931), we have held, all may find shelter under the First Amendment.

Texas v. Johnson, 491 U.S. 397, 404-405 (1989) (holding that burning a flag during a public demonstration was protected speech).

The more difficult issue in "symbolic speech" cases is how to treat the government interest. During the almost 50 years between the *Barnette* flag salute case and the *Johnson* flag-burning case, the Court evolved a strict scrutiny test for content-based regulations of speech. Yet in a "symbolic speech" case, the government interest expressed a statutory regulation of "conduct" that might not resemble the typical censorship-oriented interest advanced to support a "content" regulation of a particular kind of speech. Therefore, the question arising in many "symbolic speech" regulation cases is whether the government's interest might be characterized as "content neutral," and if so, what sort of scrutiny might be appropriate for such a non-censorship-oriented interest and what sort of government burden of "tailoring" the regulation might require.

United States v. O'Brien

391 U.S. 367 (1968)

Mr. Chief Justice WARREN delivered the opinion of the Court.

[On] March 31, 1966, David Paul O'Brien and three companions burned their Selective Service registration certificates on the steps of the South Boston Courthouse. A sizable crowd, including several agents of the Federal Bureau of Investigation, witnessed the event. Immediately after the burning, members of the crowd began attacking O'Brien and his companions. . . . For this act, O'Brien was indicted, tried, convicted, and sentenced [under a federal law prohibiting the destruction of draft cards]. [O'Brien] did not contest the fact that he had burned the certificate. He stated [that] he burned the certificate publicly to influence others to adopt his antiwar beliefs[,] "so that other people would reevaluate their positions with Selective Service, with the armed forces, and reevaluate their place in the culture of today. . . ."

When a male reaches the age of 18, he is required by the Universal Military Training and Service Act to register with a local draft board. He is assigned a Selective Service number, and within five days he is issued a registration certificate. Subsequently, and based on a questionnaire completed by the registrant, he is assigned a classification denoting his eligibility for induction, and '[a]s soon as practicable' thereafter he is issued a Notice of Classification. This initial classification is not necessarily permanent, and if in the interim before induction the registrant's status changes in some relevant way, he may be reclassified. After such a reclassification, the local board 'as soon as practicable' issues to the registrant a new Notice of Classification.

[The] registration [certificate is a] small white [card], approximately 2 by 3 inches. The registration certificate specifies the name of the registrant, the date of registration, and the number and address of the local board with which he is registered. Also inscribed upon it are the date and place of the registrant's birth, his residence at registration, his physical description, his signature, and his Selective Service number. The Selective Service number itself indicates his State of registration, his local board, his year of birth, and his chronological position in the local board's classification record. [The] registration [certificate bears] notices that the registrant must notify his local board in writing of every change in address, physical condition, and occupational, marital, family, dependency, and military status, and of any other fact which might change his classification. [It also contains] a notice that the registrant's Selective Service number should appear on all communications to his local board.

Congress demonstrated its concern that certificates issued by the Selective Service System might be abused well before the 1965 Amendment here challenged. The 1948 Act itself prohibited many different abuses involving "any registration certificate" [including alteration or forgery]. [In] addition, regulations of the Selective Service System required registrants to keep both their registration and classification certificates in their personal possession at all times. And the Act made knowing violation of any provision of the Act or rules and regulations [a] felony.

By the 1965 Amendment, Congress added [the] provision here at issue, subjecting to criminal liability not only one who "forges, alters, or in any manner changes" but also one who "knowingly destroys (or) knowingly mutilates" a certificate. We note at the outset that the 1965 Amendment plainly does not abridge free speech on its face, and we do not understand O'Brien to argue otherwise. [The amendment] deals with conduct having no connection with speech. It prohibits the knowing destruction of certificates issued by the Selective Service System. . . . The Amendment does not distinguish between public and private destruction, and it does not punish only destruction engaged in for the purpose of expressing views. A law prohibiting destruction of Selective Service certificates no more abridges free speech on its face than a motor vehicle law prohibiting the destruction of drivers' licenses, or a tax law prohibiting the destruction of books and records. . . . O'Brien nonetheless argues that the 1965 Amendment is unconstitutional in its application to him, and is unconstitutional as enacted because what he calls the "purpose" of Congress was "to suppress freedom of speech." We consider these arguments separately.

O'Brien first argues that the 1965 Amendment is unconstitutional as applied to him because his act of burning his registration certificate was protected "symbolic speech" within the First Amendment. His argument is that the freedom of expression [includes] all modes of "communication of ideas by conduct," and that his conduct is within this definition because he did it in "demonstration against the war and against the draft." [On] the assumption that the alleged communicative element in O'Brien's conduct is sufficient to bring into play the First Amendment, it does not necessarily follow that the destruction of a registration certificate is constitutionally protected activity. [When] "speech" and "nonspeech" elements are combined in the same course of conduct, a sufficiently important governmental interest in regulating the nonspeech element can justify incidental limitations on First Amendment freedoms. [W]e think it clear that a government regulation is sufficiently justified if it is within the constitutional power of the Government; if it furthers an important or substantial governmental interest; if the governmental interest is unrelated to the suppression of free expression; and if the incidental restriction on alleged First Amendment freedoms is no greater than is essential to the furtherance of that interest. We find that the 1965 Amendment [meets] all of these requirements, and consequently that O'Brien can be constitutionally convicted for violating it.

The constitutional power of Congress to raise and support armies and to make all laws necessary and proper to that end is broad and sweeping. The power of Congress to classify and conscript manpower for military service is "beyond question." Pursuant to this power, Congress may establish a system of registration for individuals liable for training and service, and may require such individuals within reason to cooperate in the registration system. The issuance of certificates indicating the registration and eligibility classification of individuals is a legitimate and substantial administrative aid in the functioning of this system. And legislation to insure the continuing availability of issued certificates serves a legitimate and substantial purpose in the system's administration.

O'Brien's argument to the contrary is necessarily premised upon his unrealistic characterization of Selective Service certificates. He essentially adopts the position that such certificates are so many pieces of paper designed to notify registrants of their registration or classification, to be retained or tossed in the wastebasket according to the convenience or taste of the registrant. Once the registrant has received notification, according to this view, there is no reason for him to retain the certificates. O'Brien notes that most of the information on a registration certificate serves no notification purpose at all; the registrant hardly needs to be told his address and physical characteristics. We agree that the registration certificate contains much information of which the registrant needs no notification. This circumstance, however, does not lead to the conclusion that the certificate serves no purpose, but that, like the classification certificate, it serves purposes in addition to initial notification. Many of these purposes would be defeated by the certificates' destruction or mutilation. Among these are:

1. The registration certificate serves as proof that the individual described thereon has registered for the draft. . . . Voluntarily displaying the two certificates is an easy and painless way for a young man to dispel a question as to whether he might be delinquent in his Selective Service obligations. Correspondingly, the availability of the certificates for such display relieves the Selective Service System of the administrative burden it would otherwise have in verifying the registration and classification of all suspected delinquents. [I]t is in the interest of the just and efficient administration of the system that they be continually available. [I]n a time of national crisis, reasonable availability to each registrant of the two small cards assures a rapid and uncomplicated means for determining his fitness for immediate induction, no matter how distant in our mobile society he may be from his local board.

2. The information supplied on the certificates facilitates communication between registrants and local boards, simplifying the system and benefiting all concerned. [E]ach certificate bears the address of the registrant's local board. . . . Further, each card bears the registrant's Selective Service number, and a registrant [can] make simpler the board's task in locating his file. Finally, a registrant's inquiry [concerning] his eligibility status is frequently answerable simply on the basis of his classification certificate. . . .

3. Both certificates carry continual reminders that the registrant must notify his local board of any change of address, and other specified changes in his status. [T]he destruction of certificates deprives the system of a potentially useful notice device.

4. The regulatory scheme involving Selective Service certificates includes clearly valid prohibitions against the alteration, forgery, or similar deceptive misuse of certificates. The destruction or mutilation of certificates obviously increases the difficulty of detecting and tracing

abuses. . . . Further, a mutilated certificate might itself be used for deceptive purposes.

The many functions performed by Selective Service certificates establish beyond doubt that Congress has a legitimate and substantial interest in preventing their wanton and unrestrained destruction and assuring their continuing availability by punishing people who knowingly and wilfully destroy or mutilate them. And we are unpersuaded that the pre-existence of the nonpossession regulations in any way negates this interest.

[A] comparison of the regulations with the 1965 Amendment indicates that they protect overlapping but not identical governmental interests, and that they reach somewhat different classes of wrongdoers. The gravamen of the offense defined by the statute is the deliberate rendering of certificates unavailable for the various purposes which they may serve. Whether registrants keep their certificates in their personal possession at all times, as required by the regulations, is of no particular concern under the 1965 Amendment, as long as they do not mutilate or destroy the certificates so as to render them unavailable. [Finally], the 1965 Amendment, like [the statutory provision] which it amended, is concerned with abuses involving any issued Selective Service certificates, not only with the registrant's own certificates. The knowing destruction or mutilation of someone else's certificates would therefore violate the statute but not the nonpossession regulations.

We think it apparent that the continuing availability to each registrant of his Selective Service certificates substantially furthers the smooth and proper functioning of the system that Congress has established to raise armies. We think it also apparent that the Nation has a vital interest in having a system for raising armies that functions with maximum efficiency and is capable of easily and quickly responding to continually changing circumstances. For these reasons, the Government has a substantial interest in assuring the continuing availability of issued Selective Service certificates.

It is equally clear that the 1965 Amendment specifically protects this substantial governmental interest. We perceive no alternative means that would more precisely and narrowly assure the continuing availability of issued Selective Service certificates than a law which prohibits their wilful mutilation or destruction. The 1965 Amendment prohibits such conduct and does nothing more. In other words, both the governmental interest and the operation of the 1965 Amendment are limited to the noncommunicative aspect of O'Brien's conduct. The governmental interest and the scope of the 1965 Amendment are limited to preventing harm to the smooth and efficient functioning of the Selective Service System. When O'Brien deliberately rendered unavailable his registration certificate, he wilfully frustrated this governmental interest. For this noncommunicative impact of his conduct, and for nothing else, he was convicted. The case at bar is therefore unlike one where the alleged governmental interest in regulating conduct arises in some measure because the communication allegedly integral to the conduct is itself thought to be [harmful].

In conclusion, we find that because of the Government's substantial interest in assuring the continuing availability of issued Selective Service certificates, because amended §462(b) is an appropriately narrow means of protecting this interest and condemns only the independent noncommunicative impact of conduct within its reach, and because the noncommunicative impact of O'Brien's act of burning his registration certificate frustrated the Government's interest, a sufficient governmental interest has been shown to justify O'Brien's conviction.

O'Brien finally argues that the 1965 Amendment is unconstitutional as enacted because what he calls the "purpose" of Congress was "to suppress freedom of speech." We reject this argument because under settled principles the purpose of Congress, as O'Brien uses that term, is not a basis for declaring this legislation unconstitutional. . . . Inquiries into congressional motives or purposes are a hazardous matter. When the issue is simply the interpretation of legislation, the Court will look to statements by legislators for guidance as to the purpose of the legislature, because the benefit to sound decision-making in this circumstance is thought sufficient to risk the possibility of misreading Congress' purpose. It is entirely a different matter when we are asked to void a statute that is, under well-settled criteria, constitutional on its face, on the basis of what fewer than a handful of Congressmen said about it. What motivates one legislator to make a speech about a statute is not necessarily what motivates scores of others to enact it, and the stakes are sufficiently high for us to eschew guesswork. We decline to void essentially on the ground that it is unwise legislation which Congress had the undoubted power to enact and which could be reenacted in its exact form if the same or another legislator made a 'wiser' speech about it.

[We] think it not amiss, in passing, to comment upon O'Brien's legislative-purpose argument. There was little floor debate on this legislation in either House. Only Senator Thurmond commented on its substantive features. . . . After his brief statement, and without any additional substantive comments, the bill [passed] the Senate. In the House debate only two Congressmen addressed themselves to the Amendment. . . . The bill was passed after their statements without any further debate by a vote of 393 to 1. It is principally on the basis of the statements [by] three Congressmen that O'Brien makes his congressional-"purpose" argument. We note that if we were to examine legislative purpose in the instant case, we would be obliged to consider not only these statements but also the more authoritative reports of the Senate and House Armed Services Committees. [While] both reports make clear a concern with the "defiant" destruction of so-called "draft cards" and with "open" encouragement to others to destroy their cards, both reports also indicate that this concern stemmed from an apprehension that unrestrained destruction of cards would disrupt the smooth functioning of the Selective Service System.

Since the 1965 Amendment [is] constitutional as enacted and as applied, the Court of Appeals should have affirmed the judgment of conviction entered by the District Court. Accordingly, we vacate the judgment of the Court of Appeals, and reinstate the judgment and sentence of the District [Court].

It is so ordered.

Note: The O'Brien Test

The *O'Brien* four-part test has been applied to a range of First Amendment problems. Typically, the triggers for the use of the *O'Brien* test are the existence of a regulation that might be a labeled a "conduct" regulation, a government inter-est that might be labeled as being "unrelated to the suppression of expression," the existence of a claim for the protection of "symbolic speech" or "communica-tive conduct," or some combination of these elements. The *O'Brien* opinion did not describe the analysis that might be appropriate when a government regula-tion is aimed at conduct that occurs in a public forum, thus implicating both the four-part *O'Brien* test and the "time, place, manner" test of the "public forum" doctrine. When the occasion arose for the Court to deal with such a two-dimensional problem, its solution was to require the government to satisfy the requirements of each test separately. The apparent similarity of the two tests was revealed by their simultaneous use in Clark v. Community for Creative Non-Violence in 1984. Yet despite the similarities between them, each test is used most commonly in its own doctrinal sphere. The *O'Brien* test's usage in the context of symbolic speech has taken on particular importance in the field of "near obscene" speech regulation. (See the discussion earlier in this chapter.) Further examina-tion of the "time, place, manner" test for the "public forum" doctrine is provided in the section below on "Access to Government Property." The *Clark* opinion that follows provides further insight into the application of *O'Brien*, and also serves as an introduction to the elements of "time, place, manner" analysis.

∾ PROBLEMS ∾

1. *The Hypothetical Dissent.* You are the law clerk for one of the justices in *O'Brien* who wants to file a dissent on the merits. What arguments can be made to rebut the *O'Brien* Court's arguments on each of the elements of the four-part test?

2. *More on the International Treaty Regulating the Internet.* At the convention, suppose that the German and French delegates again demand a prohibition against Nazi symbols. Does the *O'Brien* decision alter (or cause you to rethink) your position regarding those demands?

Clark v. Community for Creative Non-Violence

468 U.S. 288 (1984)

Justice WHITE delivered the opinion of the Court.

The issue in this case is whether a National Park Service regulation prohib-iting camping in certain parks violates the First Amendment when applied to pro-hibit demonstrators from sleeping in Lafayette Park and the Mall in connection with a demonstration intended to call attention to the plight of the homeless. We hold that it does [not].

The Interior Department, through the National Park Service, is charged with responsibility for the management and maintenance of the National Parks and is authorized to promulgate rules and regulations for the use of the parks in accordance with the purposes for which they were established. The network of National Parks includes the National Memorial-core parks, Lafayette Park and the Mall, which are set in the heart of Washington, D.C. . . . Lafayette Park is a roughly 7-acre square located across Pennsylvania Avenue from the White House. Although originally part of the White House grounds, President Jefferson set it aside as a park for the use of residents and visitors. It is a "garden park with [a] formal landscaping of flowers and trees, with fountains, walks and benches." The Mall is a stretch of land running westward from the Capitol to the Lincoln Memorial some two miles away. It includes the Washington Monument, a series of reflecting pools, trees, lawns, and other greenery. It is bordered by, *inter alia,* the Smithsonian Institution and the National Gallery of Art. Both the Park and the Mall were included in Major Pierre L'Enfant's original plan for the Capital. Both are visited by vast numbers of visitors from around the country, as well as by large numbers of residents of the Washington [area].

Under the regulations[,] camping in National Parks is permitted only in campgrounds designated for that purpose. No such campgrounds have ever been designated in Lafayette Park or the Mall. . . . Demonstrations for the airing of views or grievances are permitted in the Memorial-core parks, but for the most part only by Park Service permits. Temporary structures may be erected for demonstration purposes but may not be used for camping. In 1982, the Park Service issued a renewable permit to respondent Community for Creative Non-Violence (CCNV) to conduct a wintertime demonstration in Lafayette Park and the Mall for the purpose of demonstrating the plight of the homeless. The permit authorized the erection of two symbolic tent cities: 20 tents in Lafayette Park that would accommodate 50 people and 40 tents in the Mall with a capacity of up to 100. The Park Service, however, relying on the above regulations, specifically denied CCNV's request that demonstrators be permitted to sleep in the symbolic tents. . . . CCNV and several individuals then filed an action to prevent the application of the no-camping regulations to the proposed demonstration. . . . The District Court granted summary judgment in favor of the Park Service. The Court of Appeals [reversed]. [We] reverse.

[We assume that] overnight sleeping in connection with the demonstration is expressive conduct protected to some extent by the First Amendment. [But] this assumption only begins the inquiry. Expression, whether oral or written or symbolized by conduct, is subject to reasonable time, place, or manner restrictions. We have often noted that restrictions of this kind are valid provided that they are justified without reference to the content of the regulated speech, that they are narrowly tailored to serve a significant governmental interest, and that they leave open ample alternative channels for communication of the information.

It is also true that a message may be delivered by conduct that is intended to be communicative and that, in context, would reasonably be understood by the viewer to be communicative. Symbolic expression of this kind may be forbidden or regulated if the conduct itself may constitutionally be regulated, if the regulation is narrowly drawn to further a substantial governmental interest, and if the interest is unrelated to the suppression of free speech.

Petitioners submit [that] the regulation forbidding sleeping is defensible either as a time, place, or manner restriction or as a regulation of symbolic conduct. We agree with that assessment. The permit that was issued authorized the demonstration but required compliance with [the regulation] which prohibits "camping" on park lands, that is, the use of park lands for living accommodations, such as sleeping, storing personal belongings, making fires, digging, or cooking. These provisions, including the ban on sleeping, are clearly limitations on the manner in which the demonstration could be carried out. That sleeping, like the symbolic tents themselves, may be expressive and part of the message delivered by the demonstration does not make the ban any less a limitation on the manner of demonstrating, for reasonable time, place, or manner regulations normally have the purpose and direct effect of limiting expression but are nevertheless valid. Neither does the fact that sleeping, *arguendo*, may be expressive conduct, rather than oral or written expression, render the sleeping prohibition any less a time, place, or manner regulation. To the contrary, the Park Service neither attempts to ban sleeping generally nor to ban it everywhere in the parks. It has established areas for camping and forbids it elsewhere, including Lafayette Park and the Mall. Considered as such, we have very little trouble concluding that the Park Service may prohibit overnight sleeping in the parks involved here.

The requirement that the regulation be content-neutral is clearly satisfied. [I]t is not disputed [that] the prohibition on camping, and on sleeping specifically, is content-neutral and is not being applied because of disagreement with the message presented. Neither was the regulation faulted [on] the ground that without overnight sleeping the plight of the homeless could not be communicated in other ways. The regulation otherwise left the demonstration intact, with its symbolic city, signs, and the presence of those who were willing to take their turns in a day-and-night vigil. Respondents do not suggest that there was, or is, any barrier to delivering to the media, or to the public by other means, the intended message concerning the plight of the homeless.

[T]he regulation narrowly focuses on the Government's substantial interest in maintaining the parks in the heart of our Capital in an attractive and intact condition, readily available to the millions of people who wish to see and enjoy them by their presence. To permit camping—using these areas as living accommodations—would be totally inimical to these purposes, as would be readily understood by those who have frequented the National Parks across the country and observed the unfortunate consequences of the activities of those who refuse to confine their camping to designated areas.

[Respondents argue that] if the symbolic city of tents was to be permitted and if the demonstrators did not intend to cook, dig, or engage in aspects of camping other than sleeping, the incremental benefit to the parks could not justify the ban on sleeping, which was here an expressive activity said to enhance the message concerning the plight of the poor and homeless. We cannot agree. In the first place, we seriously doubt that the First Amendment requires the Park Service to permit a demonstration in Lafayette Park and the Mall involving a 24-hour vigil and the erection of tents to accommodate 150 people. Furthermore, although we have assumed for present purposes that the sleeping banned in this case would have an expressive element, it is evident that its major value to this demonstration would be facilitative. Without a permit to sleep, it would be difficult to get the poor and homeless to participate or to be present at all. . . . The sleeping ban, if enforced, would thus effectively limit the nature, extent, and duration of the demonstration and to that extent ease the pressure on the parks.

Beyond this, however, it is evident from our cases that the validity of this regulation need not be judged solely by reference to the demonstration at hand. Absent the prohibition on sleeping, there would be other groups who would demand permission to deliver an asserted message by camping in Lafayette Park. Some of them would surely have as credible a claim [as] does CCNV, and the denial of permits to still others would present difficult problems for the Park Service. With the prohibition, however[,] at least some around-the-clock demonstrations lasting for days on end will not materialize, others will be limited in size and duration, and the purposes of the regulation will thus be materially served. Perhaps these purposes would be more effectively and not so clumsily achieved by preventing tents and 24-hour vigils entirely in the core areas. But the Park Service's decision to permit nonsleeping demonstrations does not, in our view, impugn the camping prohibition as a valuable, but perhaps imperfect, protection to the parks. If the Government has a legitimate interest in ensuring that the National Parks are adequately protected[,] and if the parks would be more exposed to harm without the sleeping prohibition than with it, the ban is safe from invalidation under the First Amendment as a reasonable regulation of the manner in which a demonstration may be carried [out].

We have difficulty, therefore, in understanding why the prohibition against camping, with its ban on sleeping overnight, is not a reasonable time, place, or manner regulation that withstands constitutional scrutiny. . . . None of its provisions appears unrelated to the ends that it was designed to serve. Nor is it any less valid when applied to prevent camping in Memorial-core parks by those who wish to demonstrate and deliver a message to the public and the central Government. Damage to the parks as well as their partial inaccessibility to other members of the public can as easily result from camping by demonstrators as by nondemonstrators. In neither case must the Government tolerate it. All those who would resort to the parks must abide by otherwise valid rules for their use, just as they must observe the traffic laws, sanitation regulations, and laws to preserve the public peace. This is no more than a reaffirmation that reasonable time, place, or manner restrictions on expression are constitutionally acceptable.

[The] foregoing analysis demonstrates that the Park Service regulation is sustainable under the four-factor standard of United States v. O'Brien, 391 U.S. 367 (1968), for validating a regulation of expressive conduct, which [is] little, if any, different from the standard applied to time, place, or manner restrictions. No one contends that aside from its impact on speech a rule against camping or overnight sleeping in public parks is beyond the constitutional power of the Government to enforce. [And] there is a substantial Government interest in conserving park property, an interest that is plainly served by, and requires for its implementation, measures such as the proscription of sleeping that are designed to limit the wear and tear on park properties. That interest is unrelated to suppression of expression.

We are unmoved by the [view] that the challenged regulation is unnecessary, and hence invalid, because there are less speech-restrictive alternatives that could have satisfied the Government interest in preserving park lands. . . . The [suggestions] that the Park Service minimize the possible injury by reducing the size, duration, or frequency of demonstrations would still curtail the total allowable expression in which demonstrators could engage [and] these suggestions represent no more than a disagreement with the Park Service over how much protection the core parks require or how an acceptable level of preservation is to be attained. We do not believe, however, that either *O'Brien* or the time, place, or manner decisions assign to the judiciary the authority to replace the Park Service as the manager of the Nation's parks or endow the judiciary with the competence to judge how much protection of park lands is wise and how that level of conservation is to be attained.

Accordingly, the judgment of the Court of Appeals is
Reversed.

Justice MARSHALL, with whom Justice BRENNAN joins, dissenting.

[The] activity in which respondents seek to engage — sleeping in a highly public place, outside, in the winter for the purpose of protesting homelessness — is symbolic speech protected by the First Amendment. [Missing] from the majority's description is any inkling that Lafayette Park and the Mall have served as the sites for some of the most rousing political demonstrations in the Nation's history. "[O]n any given day there will be an average of three or so demonstrations going on" in the Mall-Lafayette Park area. . . .

In a long line of cases, this Court has afforded First Amendment protection [to] symbolic speech. [Here] respondents clearly intended to protest the reality of homelessness by sleeping outdoors in the winter in the near vicinity of the magisterial residence of the President of the United States. . . . Nor can there be any doubt that in the surrounding circumstances the likelihood was great that the political significance of sleeping in the parks would be understood by those who viewed it. Certainly the news media understood the significance of respondents' proposed activity. . . . Ordinary citizens, too, would likely understand the political message intended by respondents. This likelihood stems from the remarkably apt fit between the activity in which respondents seek to engage and the social problem they seek to [highlight].

[The] Government contends that a forseeable difficulty of administration counsels against recognizing sleep as a mode of expression protected by the First Amendment. The predicament the Government envisions can be termed "the imposter problem": the problem of distinguishing bona fide protesters from imposters whose requests for permission to sleep in Lafayette Park or the Mall on First Amendment grounds would mask ulterior designs — the simple desire, for example, to avoid the expense of hotel lodgings. [The] administrative difficulty the Government envisions is now nothing more than a vague apprehension. . . .

[I] agree with the standard enunciated by the majority. . . . I conclude, however, that the regulations at issue in this case, as applied to respondents, fail to satisfy this standard. . . . [T]he significant Government interest advanced by denying respondents' request to engage in sleep-speech is the interest in "maintaining the parks in the heart of our capital in an attractive and intact condition, readily available to the millions of people who wish to see and enjoy them by their presence." That interest is indeed significant. However, neither the Government nor the majority adequately explains how prohibiting respondents' planned activity will substantially further that interest. . . . The majority fails to offer any evidence indicating that the absence of an absolute ban on sleeping would present administrative problems to the Park Service that are substantially more difficult than those it ordinarily confronts. A mere apprehension of difficulties should not be enough to overcome the right to free expression. Moreover, if the Government's interest in avoiding administrative difficulties were truly "substantial," one would expect the agency most involved in administering the parks at least to allude to such an interest. Here, however, the perceived difficulty of administering requests from other demonstrators seeking to convey messages through sleeping was not among the reasons underlying the Park Service regulations. Nor was it mentioned by the Park Service in its rejection of respondents' particular request. [The] majority cites no evidence indicating that sleeping engaged in as symbolic speech will cause substantial wear and tear on park property. . . . Here, [the] tailoring requirement is virtually forsaken inasmuch as the Government offers no justification for applying its absolute ban on sleeping yet is willing to allow respondents to engage in activities — such as feigned sleeping — that is no less burdensome. . . . In short, there are no substantial Government interests advanced by the Government's regulations as applied to respondents. . . . [The] Court evidently assumes that the balance struck by officials is deserving of deference so long as it does not appear to be tainted by content discrimination. What the Court fails to recognize is that public officials have strong incentives to overregulate even in the absence of an intent to censor particular views. [The evidence] in this case [should] have impelled the Court to subject the Government's restrictive policy to something more than minimal scrutiny. . . . I respectfully dissent.

Note: The "Gateway" Element

In later years, the third part of the *O'Brien* test emerged as the "gateway" element. That is, once the government litigant persuades a court that "the governmental interest is unrelated to the suppression of free expression," the remaining parts of the four-part test control the analysis. Thus, a vital element for a court's use of the *O'Brien* test is the identification of a government interest that can be labeled as "unrelated" to the suppression of speech. In subsequent cases, the Court established a dichotomy between a government interest that may be characterized as being related only to the "secondary effects" of speech and an interest that is related to the effect that speech may have on an audience. The former type of interest typically qualifies as being "unrelated" to the suppression of speech, whereas the latter type of interest is usually treated as being aimed at the suppression of speech. Thus, the failure of the government litigant to satisfy the third part of the *O'Brien* test must lead to a determination that a government interest is related to the suppression of expression, which in turn may lead to the requirement that the strict scrutiny test must be satisfied.

∾ PROBLEM: SYMBOLIC SPEECH ANALYSIS ∾

Consider how the analysis or result in *Clark* might have been different if "symbolic speech" had not been involved in the case, so that *O'Brien* would have been irrelevant to the decision. For example, suppose that the regulation at issue in *Clark* was a speech regulation that limited the use of the park, for example, to small groups of demonstrators (no more than ten people in a group and only one demonstration a day) in order to protect the park grounds. How would the "time, place, manner" arguments by the demonstrators and the Park Service in that hypothetical case differ from the arguments made in *Clark* on the "time, place, manner" issue?

Texas v. Johnson
491 U.S. 397 (1989)

Justice BRENNAN delivered the opinion of the Court.

After publicly burning an American flag as a means of political protest, Gregory Lee Johnson was convicted of desecrating a flag in violation of Texas law. This case presents the question whether his conviction is consistent with the First Amendment. We hold that it is not.

While the Republican National Convention was taking place in Dallas in 1984, respondent Johnson participated in a political demonstration dubbed the "Republican War Chest Tour." As explained in literature distributed by the demonstrators and in speeches made by them, the purpose of this event was to protest the policies of the Reagan administration and of certain Dallas-based corporations. The demonstrators marched through the Dallas streets, chanting political slogans and stopping at several corporate locations to stage "die-ins" intended to dramatize the consequences of nuclear war. On several occasions they spray-painted the walls of buildings and overturned potted plants, but Johnson himself took no part in such activities. He did, however, accept an American flag handed to him by a fellow protestor who had taken it from a flag-pole outside one of the targeted buildings. . . . The demonstration ended in front of Dallas City Hall, where Johnson unfurled the American flag, doused it with kerosene, and set it on fire. While the flag burned, the protestors chanted: "America, the red, white, and blue, we spit on you." [No] one was physically injured or threatened with injury, though several witnesses testified that they had been seriously offended by the flag burning.

[Johnson was charged with] desecration of a venerated object [in violation of a state statute that provides: A person commits an offense if he intentionally or knowingly desecrates [a] state or national flag; "desecrate" means deface, damage, or otherwise physically mistreat in a way that the actor knows will seriously offend one or more persons likely to observe or discover his action.] After a trial, he was convicted, sentenced to one year in prison, and fined [$2,000].

[We] must first determine whether Johnson's burning of the flag constituted expressive conduct, permitting him to invoke the First Amendment in challenging his conviction. *See, e.g.,* Spence v. Washington, 418 U.S. 405 (1974). If his conduct was expressive, we next decide whether the State's regulation is related to the suppression of free expression. *See, e.g.,* United States v. O'Brien, 391 U.S. 367 (1968). If the State's regulation is not related to expression, then the less stringent standard we announced [in] *O'Brien* for regulations of noncommunicative conduct controls. If it is, then we are outside of *O'Brien*'s test, and we must ask whether this interest justifies Johnson's conviction under a more demanding standard. A third possibility is that the State's asserted interest is simply not implicated on these facts, and in that event the interest drops out of the picture.

The First Amendment literally forbids the abridgment only of "speech," but we have long recognized that its protection does not end at the spoken or written word. While we have rejected "the view that an apparently limitless variety of conduct can be labeled 'speech' whenever the person engaging in the conduct intends thereby to express an idea," we have acknowledged that conduct may be "sufficiently imbued with elements of communication to fall within the scope of the First and Fourteenth Amendments." In deciding whether particular conduct possesses sufficient communicative elements to bring the First Amendment into play, we have asked whether "[a]n intent to convey a particularized message was present, and [whether] the likelihood was great that the message would be understood by those who viewed it." *Spence, supra,* at 409.

[We] have not automatically concluded [that] any action taken with respect to our flag is expressive. . . . In *Spence,* [we] emphasized that Spence's taping of a peace sign to his flag was "roughly simultaneous with and concededly triggered by the Cambodian incursion and the Kent State tragedy." [We concluded] that Spence's conduct was a form of communication. . . . The State of Texas conceded [that] Johnson's conduct was expressive conduct. . . . Johnson burned an American flag as part — indeed, as the culmination — of a political demonstration that coincided with the convening of the Republican Party and its renomination of Ronald Reagan for President. The expressive, overtly political nature of this conduct was both intentional and overwhelmingly apparent. . . . In these circumstances, Johnson's burning of the flag was conduct "sufficiently imbued with elements of communication," to implicate the First Amendment.

The government generally has a freer hand in restricting expressive conduct than it has in restricting the written or spoken word. It may not, however, proscribe particular conduct *because* it has expressive elements. [It] is, in short, not simply the verbal or nonverbal nature of the expression, but the governmental interest at stake, that helps to determine whether a restriction on that expression is valid.

[A]lthough we have recognized that where "'speech' and 'nonspeech' elements are combined in the same course of conduct, a sufficiently important governmental interest in regulating the non-speech element can justify incidental limitations on First Amendment freedoms," we have limited the applicability of *O'Brien*'s relatively lenient standard to those cases in which "the governmental interest is unrelated to the suppression of free expression."

[In] order to decide whether *O'Brien*'s test applies here, therefore, we must decide whether Texas has asserted an interest in support of Johnson's conviction that is unrelated to the suppression of expression. . . . The State offers two separate interests to justify this conviction: preventing breaches of the peace and preserving the flag as a symbol of nationhood and national unity. We hold that the first interest is not implicated on this record and that the second is related to the suppression of expression.

Texas claims that its interest in preventing breaches of the peace justifies Johnson's conviction for flag desecration. However, no disturbance of the peace actually occurred or threatened to occur because of Johnson's burning of the flag. . . . The only evidence offered by the State at trial to show the reaction to Johnson's actions was the testimony of several persons who had been seriously offended by the flag burning. . . . The State's position, therefore, amounts to a claim that an audience that takes serious offense at particular expression is necessarily likely to disturb the peace and that the expression may be prohibited on this basis. Our precedents do not countenance such a presumption. On the contrary, they recognize that a principal "function of free speech under our system of government is to invite dispute. It may indeed best serve its high purpose when it induces a condition of unrest, creates dissatisfaction with conditions as they are, or even stirs people to anger." [W]e have not permitted the government to assume that every expression of a provocative idea will incite a riot, but have instead required careful consideration of the actual circumstances surrounding such expression, asking whether the expression "is directed to inciting or producing imminent lawless action and is likely to incite or produce such action." Brandenburg v. Ohio, 395 U.S. 444 (1969). To accept Texas' arguments that it need only demonstrate "the potential for a breach of the peace," and that every flag burning necessarily possesses that potential, would be to eviscerate our holding in *Brandenburg*. . . . Nor does Johnson's expressive conduct fall within that small class of "fighting words" that are "likely to provoke the average person to retaliation, and thereby cause a breach of the peace." Chaplinsky v. New Hampshire, 315 U.S. 568 (1942). No reasonable onlooker would have regarded Johnson's generalized expression of dissatisfaction with the policies of the Federal Government as a direct personal insult or an invitation to exchange fisticuffs. . . . We thus conclude that the State's interest in maintaining order is not implicated on these facts. . . . Texas already has a statute specifically prohibiting breaches of the peace, which tends to confirm that Texas need not punish this flag desecration in order to keep the peace.

The State also asserts an interest in preserving the flag as a symbol of nationhood and national unity. In *Spence,* we acknowledged that the government's interest in preserving the flag's special symbolic value "is directly related to expression in the context of activity" such as affixing a peace symbol to a flag. We are equally persuaded that this interest is related to expression in the case of Johnson's burning of the flag. The State, apparently, is concerned that such conduct will lead people to believe either that the flag does not stand for nationhood and national unity, but instead reflects other, less positive concepts, or that the concepts reflected in the flag do not in fact exist, that is, that we do not enjoy unity as a Nation. These concerns blossom only when a person's treatment of the flag communicates some message, and thus are related "to the suppression of free expression" within the meaning of *O'Brien*. We are thus outside of *O'Brien*'s test altogether.

It remains to consider whether the State's interest in preserving the flag as a symbol of nationhood and national unity justifies Johnson's conviction. . . . Johnson was [not] prosecuted for the expression of just any idea; he was prosecuted for his expression of dissatisfaction with the policies of this country, expression situated at the core of our First Amendment values. . . . Moreover, Johnson was prosecuted because he knew that his politically charged expression would cause "serious offense." If he had burned the flag as a means of disposing of it because it was dirty or torn, he would not have been convicted of flag desecration under this Texas law. . . . The Texas law [is] designed [to] protect it only against impairments that would cause serious offense to others. . . .

Whether Johnson's treatment of the flag violated Texas law thus depended on the likely communicative impact of his expressive conduct. Our decision in Boos v. Barry [485 U.S. 312 (1988)] tells us that "[t]he emotive impact of speech on its audience is not a 'secondary effect'" unrelated to the content of the expression itself. According to the principles announced in *Boos*, Johnson's political expression was restricted because of the content of the message he conveyed. We must therefore subject the State's asserted interest in preserving the special symbolic character of the flag to "the most exacting scrutiny." . . . Texas argues that its interest in preserving the flag as a symbol of nationhood and national unity survives this close analysis. Quoting extensively from the writings of this Court chronicling the flag's historic and symbolic role in our society, the State emphasizes the "special place" reserved for the flag in our Nation. The State's argument [is] that it has an interest in preserving the flag as a symbol of *nationhood* and *national unity,* a symbol with a determinate range of meanings. According to Texas, if one physically treats the flag in a way that would tend to cast doubt on either the idea that nationhood and national unity are the flag's referents or that national unity actually exists, the message conveyed thereby is a harmful one and therefore may be prohibited.

If there is a bedrock principle underlying the First Amendment, it is that the government may not prohibit the expression of an idea simply because society finds the idea itself offensive or disagreeable. We have not recognized an exception to this principle even where our flag has been involved. In Street v. New York, 394 U.S. 576 (1969), we held that a State may not criminally punish a person for uttering words critical of the flag. . . . Nor may the government, we have held [in West Virginia Board of Education v. Barnette, 319 U.S. 624 (1943)], compel conduct that would evince respect for the flag. . . . In *Spence*, we held that the same interest asserted by Texas here was insufficient to support a criminal conviction under a flag-misuse statute for the taping of a peace sign to an American flag. . . . We never before have held that the Government may ensure that a symbol be used to express only one view of that symbol or its referents. . . . Could the government [prohibit] the burning of state flags? Of copies of the Presidential seal? Of the Constitution? In evaluating these choices under the First Amendment, how would we decide which symbols were sufficiently special to warrant this unique status? To do so, we would be forced to consult our own political preferences, and impose them on the citizenry, in the very way that the First Amendment forbids us to do.

There is, moreover, no indication — either in the text of the Constitution or in our cases interpreting it — that a separate juridical category exists for the American flag alone. . . . The First Amendment does not guarantee that other concepts virtually sacred to our Nation as a whole — such as the principle that discrimination on the basis of race is odious and destructive — will go unquestioned in the marketplace of ideas. We decline, therefore, to create for the flag an exception to the joust of principles protected by the First Amendment.

It is not the State's ends, but its means, to which we object. [T]here is a special place reserved for the flag in this Nation, and thus we do not doubt that the government has a legitimate interest in making efforts to "preserv[e] the national flag as an unalloyed symbol of our country." *Spence*, 418 U.S., at 412. . . . To say that the government has an interest in encouraging proper treatment of the flag, however, is not to say that it may criminally punish a person for burning a flag as a means of political protest. . . . [We] are tempted to say [that] the flag's deservedly cherished place in our community will be strengthened, not weakened, by our holding today. Our decision is a reaffirmation of the principles of freedom and inclusiveness that the flag best reflects, and of the conviction that our toleration of criticism such as Johnson's is a sign and source of our strength. Indeed, one of the proudest images of our flag, the one immortalized in our own national anthem, is of the bombardment it survived at Fort McHenry. It is the Nation's resilience, not its rigidity, that Texas sees reflected in the flag — and it is that resilience that we reassert today.

The way to preserve the flag's special role is not to punish those who feel differently about these matters. It is to persuade them that they are wrong. [And,] precisely because it is our flag that is involved, one's response to the flag burner may exploit the uniquely persuasive power of the flag itself. We can imagine no more appropriate response to burning a flag than waving one's own, no better way to counter a flag burner's message than by saluting the flag that burns, no surer means of preserving the dignity even of the flag that burned than by — as one witness here did — according its remains a respectful burial. We do not consecrate the flag by punishing its desecration, for in doing so we dilute the freedom that this cherished emblem represents.

Johnson was convicted for engaging in expressive conduct. The State's interest in preventing breaches of the peace does not support his conviction because Johnson's conduct did not threaten to disturb the peace. Nor does the State's interest in preserving the flag as a symbol of nationhood and national unity justify his criminal conviction for engaging in political expression. The judgment of the Texas Court of Criminal Appeals is therefore

Affirmed.

Justice KENNEDY, concurring.

[S]ometimes we must make decisions we do not like. We make them because they are right, right in the sense that the law and the Constitution, as we see them, compel the result. . . . This is one of those rare cases. . . . I agree that the flag holds a lonely place of honor in an age when absolutes are distrusted and simple truths are burdened by unneeded apologetics. . . . It is poignant but fundamental that the flag protects those who hold it in contempt. [T]he fact remains that [Johnson's] acts were speech. . . . So I agree with the Court that he must go free.

Chief Justice REHNQUIST, with whom Justice WHITE and Justice O'CONNOR join, dissenting.

[For] more than 200 years, the American flag has occupied a unique position as the symbol of our Nation, a uniqueness that justifies a governmental prohibition against flag burning in the way respondent Johnson did here. [The] flag symbolizes the Nation in peace as well as in war. It signifies our national presence on battleships, airplanes, military installations, and public buildings from the United States Capitol to the thousands of county courthouses and city halls throughout the country. Two flags are prominently placed in our courtroom. Countless flags are placed by the graves of loved ones each year on what was first called Decoration Day, and is now called Memorial Day. The flag is traditionally placed on the casket of deceased members of the Armed Forces, and it is later given to the deceased's family. Congress has provided that the flag be flown at half-staff upon the death of the President, Vice President, and other government officials "as a mark of respect to their memory."

[No] other American symbol has been as universally honored as the flag. In 1931, Congress declared "The Star-Spangled Banner" to be our national anthem. In 1949, Congress declared June 14th to be Flag Day. In 1987, John Philip Sousa's "The Stars and Stripes Forever" was designated as the national march. Congress has also established "The Pledge of Allegiance to the Flag" and the manner of its deliverance. The flag has appeared as the principal symbol on approximately 33 United States postal stamps and in the design of at least 43 more. . . .

Both Congress and the States have enacted numerous laws regulating misuse of the American flag. Until 1967, Congress left the regulation of misuse of the flag up to the States. Now, however, 18 U.S.C. §700(a) provides that: "Whoever knowingly casts contempt upon any flag of the United States by publicly mutilating, defacing, defiling, burning, or trampling upon it shall be fined not more than $1,000 or imprisoned for not more than one year, or both." [With] the exception of Alaska and Wyoming, all of the States now have statutes prohibiting the burning of the flag. . . . Most were passed by the States at about the time of World War I.

The American flag, then, throughout more than 200 years of our history, has come to be the visible symbol embodying our Nation. . . . The flag is not simply another "idea" or "point of view" competing for recognition in the marketplace of ideas. Millions and millions of Americans regard it with an almost mystical reverence regardless of what sort of social, political, or philosophical beliefs they may have. I cannot agree that the First Amendment invalidates the Act of Congress, and the laws of 48 of the 50 States, which make criminal the public burning of the flag. . . .

[F]reedom of expression [is] not absolute. [As] with "fighting words," so with flag burning, for purposes of the First Amendment: It is "no essential part of any exposition of ideas, and [is] of such slight social value as a step to truth that any benefit that may be derived from [it] is clearly outweighed" by the public interest in avoiding a probable breach of the peace. The highest courts of several States have upheld state statutes prohibiting the public burning of the flag on the grounds that it is so inherently inflammatory that it may cause a breach of public order.

[Far] from being a case of "one picture being worth a thousand words," flag burning is the equivalent of an inarticulate grunt or roar that, it seems fair to say, is most likely to be indulged in not to express any particular idea, but to antagonize others. [The] Texas statute deprived Johnson of [one] rather inarticulate symbolic form of protest — a form of protest that was profoundly offensive to many — and left him with a full panoply of other symbols and every conceivable form of verbal expression to express his deep disapproval of national policy. Thus, in no way can it be said that Texas is punishing him because his hearers — or any other group of people — were profoundly opposed to the message that he sought to convey. . . . It was Johnson's use of this particular symbol, and not the idea that he sought to convey by it or by his many other expressions, for which he was punished. . . . Surely one of the high purposes of a democratic society is to legislate against conduct that is regarded as evil and profoundly offensive to the majority of people — whether it be murder, embezzlement, pollution, or flag burning. . . . I would uphold the Texas statute as applied in this case.

Justice STEVENS, dissenting.
[A] country's flag is a symbol of more than "nationhood and national unity." It also signifies the ideas that characterize the society that has chosen that emblem as well as the special history that has animated the growth and power of those ideas. [It] is more than a proud symbol of the courage, the determination, and the gifts of nature that transformed 13 fledgling Colonies into a world power. It is a symbol of freedom, of equal opportunity, of religious tolerance, and of good will for other peoples who share our aspirations. The symbol carries its message to dissidents both at home and abroad who may have no interest at all in our national unity or survival.

[The] value of the flag as a symbol cannot be measured. [T]he interest in preserving that value for the future is both significant and legitimate. Conceivably that value will be enhanced by the Court's conclusion that our national commitment to free expression is so strong that even the United States as ultimate guarantor of that freedom is without power to prohibit the desecration of its unique symbol. [I]n my considered judgment, sanctioning the public desecration of the flag will tarnish its value. . . . That tarnish is not justified by the trivial burden on free expression occasioned by requiring that an available, alternative mode of expression — including uttering words critical of the [flag].

[The] Court [is] quite wrong in blandly asserting that respondent "was prosecuted for his expression of dissatisfaction with the policies of this country, expression situated at the core of our First Amendment values." Respondent was prosecuted because of the method he chose to express his dissatisfaction with those policies. Had he chosen to spray-paint [his] message of dissatisfaction on the facade of the Lincoln Memorial, there would be no question about the power of the Government to prohibit his means of expression. The prohibition would be supported by the legitimate interest in preserving the quality of an important national asset. Though the asset at stake in this case is intangible, given its unique value, the same interest supports a prohibition on the desecration of the American flag. . . . I respectfully dissent.

Christian Legal Society Chapter of the University of California v. Martinez

130 S.Ct. 2791 (2010)

Justice GINSBURG delivered the opinion of the Court.

[May] a public law school condition its official recognition of a student group — and the attendant use of school funds and facilities — on the organization's agreement to open eligibility for membership and leadership to all students?

[Like] many institutions of higher education, Hastings encourages students to form extracurricular associations that "contribute to the Hastings community and experience." These groups offer students "opportunities to pursue academic and social interests outside of the classroom [to] further their education" and to help them "develo[p] leadership skills."

Through its "Registered Student Organization" (RSO) program, Hastings extends official recognition to student groups. Several benefits attend this school-approved status. RSOs are eligible to seek financial assistance from the Law School, which subsidizes their events using funds from a mandatory student-activity fee imposed on all students. RSOs may also use Law-School channels to communicate with students: They may place announcements in a weekly Office-of-Student-Services [newsletter; advertise events on designated bulletin boards; send e-mails using a Hastings-organization address; participate in an annual Student Organizations Fair designed to advance recruitment efforts; apply for permission to use the Law School's facilities for meetings and office space; and use the Hastings] name and logo.

In exchange for these benefits, RSOs must abide by certain conditions. Only a "non-commercial organization whose membership is limited to Hastings students may become [an RSO]." A prospective RSO must submit its bylaws to Hastings for approval, and if it intends to use the Law School's name or logo, it must sign a license agreement. Critical here, all RSOs must undertake to comply with Hastings' "Policies and Regulations Applying to College Activities, Organizations and Students."

The Law School's Policy on Nondiscrimination (Nondiscrimination Policy), which binds RSOs, states: "[Hastings] is committed to a policy against legally impermissible, arbitrary or unreasonable discriminatory practices. All groups, including administration, faculty, student governments, [Hastings]-owned student residence facilities and programs sponsored by [Hastings], are governed by this policy of nondiscrimination. [Hasting's] policy on nondiscrimination is to comply fully with applicable law. [Hastings] shall not discriminate unlawfully on the basis of race, color, religion, national origin, ancestry, disability, age, sex or sexual orientation. This nondiscrimination policy covers admission, access and treatment in Hastings-sponsored programs and activities."

Hastings interprets the Nondiscrimination Policy, as it relates to the RSO program, to mandate acceptance of all comers: School-approved groups must "allow any student to participate, become a member, or seek leadership positions in the organization, regardless of [her] status or beliefs."[13] Other law schools have adopted similar all-comers policies. . . .

In 2004, [Christian Legal Society (CLS)] became the first student group to [seek an exemption from the policy]. Christian Legal Society (CLS-National)[,] an association of Christian lawyers and law students, charters student chapters at law schools throughout the country. CLS chapters must adopt bylaws that, *inter alia*, require members and officers to sign a "Statement of Faith" and to conduct their lives in accord with prescribed principles. Among those tenets is the belief that sexual activity should not occur outside of marriage between a man and a woman; CLS thus interprets its bylaws to exclude from affiliation anyone who engages in "unrepentant homosexual conduct." CLS also excludes students who hold religious convictions different from those in the Statement of Faith.

[CLS] submitted to Hastings an application for RSO status. . . . Several days later, the Law School rejected the application; CLS's bylaws, Hastings explained, did not comply with the Nondiscrimination Policy because CLS barred students based on religion and sexual orientation.

CLS formally requested an exemption from the Nondiscrimination Policy, but Hastings declined to grant one. . . . If CLS [chose] to operate outside the RSO program, [the] school "would be pleased to provide [CLS] the use of Hastings facilities for its meetings and activities." CLS would also have access to chalkboards and generally available campus bulletin boards to announce its events. In other words, Hastings would do nothing to suppress CLS's endeavors, but neither would it lend RSO-level support for them.

---

13. "Th[is] policy," Hastings clarifies, "does not foreclose neutral and generally applicable membership requirements unrelated to 'status or beliefs.'" So long as all students have the *opportunity* to participate on equal terms, RSOs may require them, *inter alia*, to pay dues, maintain good attendance, refrain from gross misconduct, or pass a skill-based test, such as the writing competitions administered by law journals. . . .

Refusing to alter its bylaws, CLS did not obtain RSO status. It did, however, operate independently during the 2004-2005 academic year. CLS held weekly Bible-study meetings and invited Hastings students to Good Friday and Easter Sunday church services. It also hosted a beach barbeque, Thanksgiving dinner, campus lecture on the Christian faith and the legal practice, several fellowship dinners, an end-of-year banquet, and other informal social activities.

[CLS] filed suit against various Hastings officers and administrators under 42 U.S.C. §1983. Its complaint alleged that Hastings' refusal to grant the organization RSO status violated CLS's First and Fourteenth Amendment rights to free speech, expressive association, and free exercise of religion. The suit sought injunctive and declaratory relief. On cross-motions for summary judgment, the U.S. District Court [ruled] in favor of Hastings [and] the Ninth Circuit affirmed. We granted certiorari and now affirm. . . .

In support of the argument that Hastings' all-comers policy treads on its First Amendment rights to free speech and expressive association, CLS draws on two lines of decisions. First, [this] Court has employed forum analysis to determine when a governmental entity, in regulating property in its charge, may place limitations on speech. [The] Court has permitted restrictions on access to a limited public forum, like the RSO program here, with this key caveat: Any access barrier must be reasonable and viewpoint neutral, *e.g.*, *Rosenberger* [v. Rector and Visitors of Univ. of Va.], 515 U.S. [819], 829 [(1995)].

Second, [this] Court has rigorously reviewed laws and regulations that constrain associational freedom. In the context of public accommodations, we have subjected restrictions on that freedom to close scrutiny; such restrictions are permitted only if they serve "compelling state interests" that are "unrelated to the suppression of ideas"—interests that cannot be advanced "through . . . significantly less restrictive [means]." Roberts v. United States Jaycees, 468 U.S. 609, 623 (1984). "Freedom of association," we have recognized, "plainly presupposes a freedom not to associate." *Roberts*, 468 U.S., at 623. Insisting that an organization embrace unwelcome members, we have therefore concluded, "directly and immediately affects associational rights." [Boy Scouts of America v.] *Dale*, 530 U.S. [640], 659 [(2000)].

CLS would have us engage each line of cases independently, but its expressive-association and free-speech arguments merge: *Who* speaks on its behalf, CLS reasons, colors *what* concept is conveyed. It therefore makes little sense to treat CLS's speech and association claims as discrete. Instead, three observations lead us to conclude that our limited-public-forum precedents supply the appropriate framework for assessing both CLS's speech and association rights. . . . First, the same considerations that have led us to apply a less restrictive level of scrutiny to speech in limited public forums as compared to other environments, apply with equal force to expressive association occurring in limited public forums. [S]peech and expressive-association rights are closely linked. . . . Second, [the] strict scrutiny we have applied in some settings to laws that burden expressive association would, in practical effect, invalidate a defining characteristic of limited public forums—the State may "reserv[e] [them] for certain groups." *Rosenberger*, 515 U.S., at 829. . . . Schools, including Hastings, ordinarily, and without controversy, limit official student-group recognition to organizations comprising only students — even if those groups wish to associate with nonstudents. The same ground rules must govern both speech and association challenges in the limited-public-forum context, lest strict scrutiny trump a public university's ability to "confin[e] a [speech] forum to the limited and legitimate purposes for which it was created." *Rosenberger,* 515 U.S., at 829. . . . Third, this case fits comfortably within the limited-public-forum category, for CLS, in seeking what is effectively a state subsidy, faces only indirect pressure to modify its membership policies; CLS may exclude any person for any reason if it forgoes the benefits of official recognition. The expressive-association precedents on which CLS relies, in contrast, involved regulations that *compelled* a group to include unwanted members, with no choice to opt out. [Our] decisions have distinguished between policies that require action and those that withhold benefits. Application of the less-restrictive limited-public-forum analysis better accounts for the fact that Hastings, through its RSO program, is dangling the carrot of subsidy, not wielding the stick of prohibition. . . . In sum, we are persuaded that our limited-public-forum precedents adequately respect both CLS's speech and expressive-association rights, and fairly balance those rights against Hastings' interests as property owner and educational institution. . . .

[We] have three times before considered clashes between public universities and student groups seeking official recognition or its attendant benefits. First, in *Healy* [v. James, 408 U.S. 169, 170 (1972)], a state college denied school affiliation to a student group that wished to form a local chapter of Students for a Democratic Society (SDS). [A] public educational institution exceeds constitutional bounds, we held, when it "restrict[s] speech or association simply because it finds the views expressed by [a] group to be abhorrent." [In] *Widmar* [v. Vincent, 454 U.S. 263, 270 (1981),] a public university [had] closed its facilities to a registered student group that sought to use university space for religious worship and discussion. [B]ecause the university singled out religious organizations for disadvantageous treatment, we [found that the schools interest] "in maintaining strict separation of church and State [was not] sufficiently compelling to justify [viewpoint] discrimination [against] religious speech." [In] *Rosenberger*, we reiterated that [by] "select[ing] for disfavored treatment those student journalistic efforts with religious editorial viewpoints," [the] university had engaged in "viewpoint discrimination, which is presumed impermissible when directed against speech otherwise within the forum's limitations." In all three cases, we ruled that student groups had been unconstitutionally singled out because of their points of view. "Once it has opened a limited [public] forum," we emphasized, "the State must respect the lawful boundaries it has itself set[,] [and] may not exclude speech where its distinction is not reasonable in light of the purpose served by the forum, . . . nor may it discriminate against speech on the basis of . . . viewpoint."

We first consider whether Hastings' policy is reasonable taking into account the RSO forum's function and "all the surrounding circumstances." [Our] inquiry is shaped by the educational context in which it arises. . . . This Court is the final arbiter of the question whether a public university has exceeded constitutional constraints, and we owe no deference to universities when we consider that question. Cognizant that judges lack the on-the-ground expertise and experience of school administrators, however, we have cautioned courts in various contexts to resist "substitut[ing] their own notions of sound educational policy for those of the school authorities which they review." Board of Ed. of Hendrick Hudson Central School Dist., Westchester Cty. v. Rowley, 458 U.S. 176, 206 (1982).

A college's commission—and its concomitant license to choose among pedagogical approaches—is not confined to the classroom, for extracurricular programs are, today, essential parts of the educational process. Schools [enjoy] "a significant measure of authority over the type of officially recognized activities in which their students participate." Board of Ed. of Westside Community Schools (Dist. 66) v. Mergens, 496 U.S. 226, 240 (1990). We therefore "approach our task with special caution," mindful that Hastings' decisions about the character of its student-group program are due decent respect.

[The] justifications Hastings offers in defense of its all-comers requirement. First, the open-access policy "ensures that the leadership, educational, and social opportunities afforded by [RSOs] are available to all students." Just as "Hastings does not allow its professors to host classes open only to those students with a certain status or belief," so the Law School may decide, reasonably in our view, "that [the] educational experience is best promoted when all participants in the forum must provide equal access to all students." RSOs, we count it significant, are eligible for financial assistance drawn from mandatory student-activity fees; the all-comers policy ensures that no Hastings student is forced to fund a group that would reject her as a member.

[The] all-comers requirement helps Hastings police the written terms of its Nondiscrimination Policy without inquiring into an RSO's motivation for membership restrictions. To bring the RSO program within CLs's view of the Constitution's limits, CLS proposes that Hastings permit exclusion because of *belief* but forbid discrimination due to *status*. But that proposal would impose on Hastings a daunting labor. How should the Law School go about determining whether a student organization cloaked prohibited status exclusion in belief-based garb? If a hypothetical Male-Superiority Club barred a female student from running for its presidency, for example, how could the Law School tell whether the group rejected her bid because of her sex or because, by seeking to lead the club, she manifested a lack of belief in its fundamental philosophy? . . . This case itself is instructive in this regard. CLS contends that it does not exclude individuals because of sexual orientation, but rather "on the basis of a conjunction of conduct and the belief that the conduct is not wrong." Our decisions have declined to distinguish between status and conduct in this context. *See* Lawrence v. Texas, 539 U.S. 558, 575 (2003).

[The] Law School reasonably adheres to the view that an all-comers policy, to the extent it brings together individuals with diverse backgrounds and beliefs, "encourages tolerance, cooperation, and learning among students." And if the policy sometimes produces discord, Hastings can rationally rank among RSO-program goals development of conflict-resolution skills, toleration, and readiness to find common ground.

[Hastings'] policy, which incorporates — in fact, subsumes — state-law proscriptions on discrimination, conveys the Law School's decision "to decline to subsidize with public monies and benefits conduct of which the people of California disapprove." State law, of course, may not *command* that public universities take action impermissible under the First Amendment. But so long as a public university does not contravene constitutional limits, its choice to advance state-law goals through the school's educational endeavors stands on firm footing.

In sum, the several justifications Hastings asserts in support of its all-comers requirement are surely reasonable in light of the RSO forum's purposes.

The Law School's policy is all the more creditworthy in view of the "substantial alternative channels that remain open for [CLS-student] communication to take place." *Perry Ed. Assn.*, 460 U.S., at 53. If restrictions on access to a limited public forum are viewpoint discriminatory, the ability of a group to exist outside the forum would not cure the constitutional shortcoming. But when access barriers are viewpoint neutral, our decisions have counted it significant that other available avenues for the group to exercise its First Amendment rights lessen the burden created by those barriers.

In this case, Hastings offered CLS access to school facilities to conduct meetings and the use of chalkboards and generally available bulletin boards to advertise events. Although CLS could not take advantage of RSO-specific methods of communication, the advent of electronic media and social-networking sites reduces the importance of those channels. . . . Based on the record before us, CLS [hosted] a variety of activities the year after Hastings denied it recognition, and the number of students attending those meetings and events doubled. . . . It is beyond dissenter's license . . . constantly to maintain that nonrecognition of a student organization is equivalent to prohibiting its members from speaking.

CLS nevertheless deems Hastings' all-comers policy "frankly absurd." "There can be no diversity of viewpoints in a forum," it asserts, "if groups are not permitted to form around viewpoints." This catchphrase confuses CLS's preferred policy with constitutional limitation — the *advisability* of Hastings' policy does not control its *permissibility*. [W]e have repeatedly stressed that a State's restriction on access to a limited public forum "need not be the most reasonable or the only reasonable limitation." *Cornelius*, 473 U.S., at 808.

CLS also assails the reasonableness of the all-comers policy in light of the RSO forum's function by forecasting that the policy will facilitate hostile takeovers; . . . saboteurs will infiltrate groups to subvert their mission and message. This supposition strikes us as more hypothetical than real. CLS points to no history or prospect of RSO-hijackings at Hastings. Students tend to self-sort and presumably will not endeavor en masse to join — let alone seek leadership positions in — groups pursuing missions wholly at odds with their personal beliefs. And if a rogue student intent on sabotaging an organization's objectives nevertheless attempted a takeover, the members of that group would not likely elect her as an officer.

RSOs, moreover, in harmony with the all-comers policy, may condition eligibility for membership and leadership on attendance, the payment of dues, or other neutral requirements designed to ensure that students join because of their commitment to a group's vitality, not its demise. Several RSOs at Hastings limit their membership rolls and officer slates in just this way.

Hastings, furthermore, could reasonably expect more from its law students than the disruptive behavior CLS hypothesizes — and to build this expectation into its educational approach. A reasonable policy need not anticipate and pre-emptively close off every opportunity for avoidance or manipulation. If students begin to exploit an all-comers policy by hijacking organizations to distort or destroy their missions, Hastings presumably would revisit and revise its policy. . . . Hastings, caught in the crossfire between a group's desire to exclude and students' demand for equal access, may reasonably draw a line in the sand permitting *all* organizations to express what they wish but *no* group to discrimi-nate in membership.

We next consider whether Hastings' all-comers policy is viewpoint neutral. [It is] hard to imagine a more viewpoint-neutral policy than one requiring *all* stu-dent groups to accept *all* comers. In contrast to *Healy, Widmar,* and *Rosenberger,* in which universities singled out organizations for disfavored treatment because of their points of view, Hastings' all-comers requirement draws no distinction between groups based on their message or perspective. An all-comers condition on access to RSO status, in short, is textbook viewpoint neutral.

Conceding that Hastings' all-comers policy is "nominally neutral," CLS attacks the regulation by pointing to its effect: The policy is vulnerable to consti-tutional assault, CLS contends, because "it systematically and predictably bur-dens most heavily those groups whose viewpoints are out of favor with the campus mainstream." This argument stumbles from its first step because "[a] regulation that serves purposes unrelated to the content of expression is deemed neutral, even if it has an incidental effect on some speakers or messages but not others." Ward v. Rock Against Racism, 491 U.S. 781, 791 (1989).

Even if a regulation has a differential impact on groups wishing to enforce exclusionary membership policies, "[w]here the [State] does not target conduct on the basis of its expressive content, acts are not shielded from regulation merely because they express a discriminatory idea or philosophy." R.A.V. v. St. Paul, 505 U.S. 377, 390 (1992).

Hastings' requirement that student groups accept all comers, we are satis-fied, "is justified without reference to the content [or viewpoint] of the regulated speech." *Ward,* 491 U.S., at 791. The Law School's policy aims at the *act* of reject-ing would-be group members without reference to the reasons motivating that behavior: Hastings' "desire to redress th[e] perceived harms" of exclusionary membership policies "provides an adequate explanation for its [all-comers con-dition] over and above mere disagreement with [any student group's] beliefs or biases." Wisconsin v. Mitchell, 508 U.S. 476, 488 (1993). CLS's conduct — not its Christian perspective — is, from Hastings' vantage point, what stands between the group and RSO status. "In the end," as Hastings observes, "CLS is simply confusing its *own* viewpoint-based objections to . . . nondiscrimination laws (which it is entitled to have and [to] voice) with viewpoint *discrimination*."

Finding Hastings' open-access condition on RSO status reasonable and view-point neutral, we reject CLS' free-speech and expressive-association claims. . . .

For the foregoing reasons, we affirm the Court of Appeals' ruling that the all-comers policy is constitutional and remand the case for further proceedings consistent with this opinion.

It is so ordered.

Justice STEVENS, concurring.

[The] Nondiscrimination Policy is content and viewpoint neutral. It does not reflect a judgment by school officials about the substance of any student group's speech. Nor does it exclude any would-be groups on the basis of their convictions. Indeed, it does not regulate expression or belief at all. The policy is "directed at the organization's activities rather than its philosophy," Healy v. James, 408 U.S. 169 (1972). Those who hold religious beliefs are not "singled out," those who engage in discriminatory *conduct* based on someone else's religious status and belief are singled out. Regardless of whether they are the product of secular or spiritual feeling, hateful or benign motives, all acts of religious discrimination are equally covered. The discriminator's beliefs are simply irrelevant. There is, moreover, no evidence that the policy was adopted because of any reason related to the particular views that religious individuals or groups might have, much less because of a desire to suppress or distort those views. The policy's religion clause was plainly meant to promote, not to undermine, religious freedom. . . .

[An] RSO program is a *limited* forum — the boundaries of which may be *delimited* by the proprietor. When a religious association, or a secular association, operates in a wholly public setting, it must be allowed broad freedom to control its membership and its message, even if its decisions cause offense to outsiders. Profound constitutional problems would arise if the State of California tried to "demand that all Christian groups admit members who believe that Jesus was merely human." But the CLS chapter that brought this lawsuit does not want to be just a Christian group; it aspires to be a recognized student organization. The Hastings College of Law is not a legislature. And no state actor has demanded that anyone do anything outside the confines of a discrete, voluntary academic program. . . .

The campus is, in fact, a world apart from the public square in numerous respects, and religious organizations, as well as all other organizations, must abide by certain norms of conduct when they enter an academic community. Public universities serve a distinctive role in a modern democratic society. Like all specialized government entities, they must make countless decisions about how to allocate resources in pursuit of their role. Some of those decisions will be controversial; many will have differential effects across populations; virtually all will entail value judgments of some kind. As a general matter, courts should respect universities' judgments and let them manage their own affairs.

The RSO forum is no different. It is not an open commons that Hastings happens to maintain. It is a mechanism through which Hastings confers certain benefits and pursues certain aspects of its educational mission. Having exercised its discretion to establish an RSO program, a university must treat all participants evenhandedly. But the university need not remain neutral — indeed it could not remain neutral — in determining which goals the program will serve and which rules are best suited to facilitate those goals. These are not legal questions but policy questions; they are not for the Court but for the university to make. When any given group refuses to comply with the rules, the RSO sponsor need not admit that group at the cost of undermining the program and the values reflected therein. On many levels, a university administrator has a "greater interest in the content of student activities than the police chief has in the content of a soapbox oration." Widmar v. Vincent, 454 U.S. 263, 280 (1981) (Stevens, J., concurring in judgment).

[P]etitioner excludes students who will not sign its Statement of Faith or who engage in "unrepentant homosexual conduct." The expressive association argument it presses, however, is hardly limited to these facts. Other groups may exclude or mistreat Jews, blacks, and women — or those who do not share their contempt for Jews, blacks, and women. A free society must tolerate such groups. It need not subsidize them, give them its official imprimatur, or grant them equal access to law school facilities.

Justice KENNEDY, concurring.

To be effective, a limited forum often will exclude some speakers based on their affiliation (e.g., student versus nonstudent) or based on the content of their speech, interests, and expertise (e.g., art professor not chosen as speaker for conference on public transit). When the government does exclude from a limited forum, however, other content-based judgments may be impermissible. For instance, an otherwise qualified and relevant speaker may not be excluded because of hostility to his or her views or beliefs. See Healy v. James, 408 U.S. 169, 187-188 (1972). . . . Rosenberger is distinguishable from the instant case in various respects. Not least is that here the school policy in question is not content based either in its formulation or evident purpose. . . . Here, the policy applies equally to all groups and views. And, given the stipulation of the parties, there is no basis for an allegation that the design or purpose of the rule was, by subterfuge, to discriminate based on viewpoint.

An objection might be that the all-comers policy, even if not so designed or intended, in fact makes it difficult for certain groups to express their views in a manner essential to their message. A group that can limit membership to those who agree in full with its aims and purposes may be more effective in delivering its message or furthering its expressive objectives; and the Court has recognized that this interest can be protected against governmental interference or regulation. See Boy Scouts of America v. Dale, 530 U.S. 640 (2000). By allowing like-minded students to form groups around shared identities, a school creates room for self-expression and personal development. See Board of Regents of Univ. of Wis. System v. Southworth, 529 U.S. 217, 229 (2000). . . .

The school's objectives thus might not be well served if, as a condition to membership or participation in a group, students were required to avow particular personal beliefs or to disclose private, off-campus behavior. Students whose views are in the minority at the school would likely fare worse in that regime.

Indeed, were those sorts of requirements to become prevalent, it might undermine the principle that in a university community — and in a law school community specifically — speech is deemed persuasive based on its substance, not the identity of the speaker. The era of loyalty oaths is behind us. A school quite properly may conclude that allowing an oath or belief-affirming requirement, or an outside conduct requirement, could be divisive for student relations and inconsistent with the basic concept that a view's validity should be tested through free and open discussion. The school's policy therefore represents a permissible effort to preserve the value of its forum.

[P]etitioner also would have a substantial case on the merits if it were shown that the all-comers policy was either designed or used to infiltrate the group or challenge its leadership in order to stifle its views. But that has not been shown to be so likely or self-evident as a matter of group dynamics in this setting that the Court can declare the school policy void without more facts. . . .

Justice ALITO, with whom THE CHIEF JUSTICE, Justice SCALIA, and Justice THOMAS join, dissenting.

[Once] a public university opens a limited public forum, [it] "must maintain strict viewpoint neutrality. Board of Regents of Univ. of Wis. System v. Southworth, 529 U.S. 217, 234 (2000); *Rosenberger, supra,* at 829. [We] have made it perfectly clear that "[r]eligion is [a] viewpoint from which ideas are conveyed." Good News Club v. Milford Central School, 533 U.S. 98, 112, and n.4 (2001).

[W]hen Hastings refused to register CLS, it claimed that the CLS bylaws impermissibly discriminated on the basis of religion and sexual orientation. [B]oth of these grounds constituted impermissible viewpoint discrimination. [The] policy singled out one category of expressive associations for disfavored treatment: groups formed to express a religious message. Only religious groups were required to admit students who did not share their views. An environmentalist group was not required to admit students who rejected global warming. An animal rights group was not obligated to accept students who supported the use of animals to test cosmetics. But CLS was required to admit avowed atheists. This was patent viewpoint discrimination. "By the very terms of the [Nondiscrimination Policy], the University . . . select[ed] for disfavored treatment those student [groups] with religious . . . viewpoints." *Rosenberger,* 515 U.S., at 831. It is no wonder that the Court makes no attempt to defend the constitutionality of the Nondiscrimination Policy. . . .

[The] Nondiscrimination Policy permitted membership requirements that expressed a secular viewpoint. But religious groups were not permitted to express a religious viewpoint by limiting membership to students who shared their religious viewpoints. Under established precedent, this was viewpoint discrimination. [T]he Hastings Nondiscrimination Policy [also] discriminated on the basis of viewpoint regarding sexual morality. CLS has a particular viewpoint on this subject, namely, that sexual conduct outside marriage between a man and a woman is wrongful. Hastings would not allow CLS to express this viewpoint by limiting membership to persons willing to express a sincere agreement with CLS's views. By contrast, nothing in the Nondiscrimination Policy prohibited a group from expressing a contrary viewpoint by limiting membership to persons willing to endorse that group's beliefs. A Free Love Club could require members to affirm that they reject the traditional view of sexual morality to which CLS adheres. It is hard to see how this can be viewed as anything other than viewpoint discrimination. . . .

Once a state university opens a limited forum, it "must respect the lawful boundaries it has itself set." *Rosenberger,* 515 U.S., at 829. . . . Taken as a whole, the regulations plainly contemplate the creation of a forum within which Hastings students are free to form and obtain registration of essentially the same broad range of private groups that nonstudents may form off campus. [The] accept-all-comers policy is antithetical to the design of the RSO forum for the same reason that a state-imposed accept-all-comers policy would violate the First Amendment rights of private groups if applied off campus. [A] group's First Amendment right of expressive association is burdened by the "forced inclusion" of members whose presence would "affec[t] in a significant way the group's ability to advocate public or private viewpoints." *Dale,* 530 U.S., at 648. The Court has therefore held that the government may not compel a group that engages in "expressive association" to admit such a member unless the government has a compelling interest, "'unrelated to the suppression of ideas, that cannot be achieved through means significantly less restrictive of associational freedoms.'" . . .

There can be no dispute that this standard would not permit a generally applicable law mandating that private religious groups admit members who do not share the groups' beliefs. [The] State of California surely could not demand that all Christian groups admit members who believe that Jesus was merely human. Jewish groups could not be required to admit anti-Semites and Holocaust deniers. [The] Court now holds that Hastings, a state institution, may impose these very same requirements on students who wish to participate in a forum that is designed to foster the expression of diverse viewpoints. [We] must conclude that the justifications offered by Hastings and accepted by the Court are insufficient. [Here], CLS has made a strong showing that Hastings' sudden adoption and selective application of its accept-all-comers policy was a pretext for the law school's unlawful denial of CLs's registration application under the Nondiscrimination Policy. . . .

[During] a recent year, CLS had seven members. Suppose that 10 students who are members of denominations that disagree with CLS decided that CLS was misrepresenting true Christian doctrine. Suppose that these students joined CLS, elected officers who shared their views, ended the group's affiliation with the national organization, and changed the group's message. [A] true accept-all-comers policy permits small unpopular groups to be taken over by students who wish to change the views that the group expresses. Rules requiring that members attend meetings, pay dues, and behave politely, would not eliminate this threat. . . .

Notes

1. *Flag Desecration.* In United States v. Eichman, 496 U.S. 310 (1990), the Court invalidated a federal statute that was enacted by Congress as a response to the decision in Texas v. Johnson. The relevant provision of the Flag Protection Act of 1989 punished the knowing mutilation, defacement, burning, maintaining on the floor or ground, or trampling upon any flag of the United States. The government interest was the protection of the physical flag, including privately owned flags. The Court found this interest to be related to the suppression of free expression: "[T]he Government's desire to preserve the flag as a symbol for certain national ideals is implicated 'only when a person's treatment of the flag communicates [a] message' to others that is inconsistent with those ideals." The dissenting justices argued that the government's interest in protecting the flag's symbolic value outweighed the interest of a speaker in expressing a message through the conduct of flag burning.

2. *A Constitutional Amendment?* Following the decisions in *Johnson* and *Eichman*, there have been numerous attempts to amend the Constitution to permit punishment of flag desecration. All of these attempts have failed.

∾ PROBLEMS ∾

1. *More on Flag Burning.* A local newspaper reports that a constitutional amendment to ban flag burning is only a few votes shy of passage in the House of Representatives. Jane and friends, upset by the proposed amendment, decide to protest by marching to the town center. Jane takes her U.S. flag with her. Although the friends march, no one takes any notice. Eventually, one of Jane's fellow marchers says, "Maybe we should burn the flag. People aren't paying enough attention." So Jane borrows some matches and sets the flag on fire. Sandy shouts, "Save the First Amendment." The flag doesn't burn very well, but the event begins to attract attention. "Hey," someone shouts, "they're burning a flag!;" The crowd quickly swells to 40, including two police officers, and one of the officers says, "We think you should put out the fire and go home, or we'll take you in." At that moment, a man steps forward and yells at Jane: "This is disgusting!; You don't belong in America!;" He throws a punch at Jane but misses. The police blow their whistles and order Jane's group to disperse. When they do not leave, Jane is arrested and the fire is put out. You are Jane's lawyer at trial. Consider what arguments you will make when Jane is charged with each of these five state crimes: a) arson (defined as creating or maintaining an open fire in public); b) burning the U.S. flag ("it is a crime to burn the United States flag"); c) using fighting words ("it is a crime to cause a breach of the peace by the use of words that are, or actions that constitute, personally abusive epithets which are inherently likely to provoke a violent reaction when directed to the person of an ordinary citizen"); d) disorderly conduct ("it is a crime to engage in conduct which causes an imminent, unlawful threat of public riot or breach of the peace"); and e) unlawful burning ("it is a crime to burn any material in a public place without a permit"). What First

Amendment arguments will you make against each of these charges? (Do not argue overbreadth or vagueness.) What counterarguments do you expect the prosecutor to make in reply? Explain how you would use the *O'Brien* and *Johnson* opinions in your arguments.

2. *Save Our Wildlife.* Harry is a member of Save Our Wildlife, an organization devoted to publicizing the plight of hunted animals and advocating government bans on hunting. Sally is a hunter and she has traveled to Oakdale, Indiana, to hunt deer. Harry approaches Sally as she stands on public land with her rifle aimed at a nearby deer. Harry takes Sally's photograph with his camera and puts a leaflet with antihunting messages at her feet. Sally reports Harry to the Oakdale police, and he is arrested and charged under the Indiana Hunter Interference Prohibition Act, which makes it a crime to: "Disturb another person who is engaged in the lawful taking of a wild animal, with intent to dissuade or otherwise prevent the taking." The statute defines *wild animal* as "any wild creature whose capture or killing is authorized by state fish and game laws," and this category includes deer. The statute defines *taking* as "the capture or killing of a wild animal." Harry is convicted and appeals. On appeal, Harry's lawyer concedes that the elements of the crime were proved by the facts introduced at trial, but maintains that the statute violates the First Amendment. You are the prosecutor defending the conviction on appeal. What arguments do you expect Harry to make? Are there any arguments you can make successfully in response? (Do not argue vagueness or overbreadth.)

3. *The Stolen Valor Act of 2005.* Congress enacted the Stolen Valor Act of 2005, which makes it a crime for an individual to falsely assert that he or she has received any of certain military service medals, including the Congressional Medal of Honor. The law was enacted to recognize the great sacrifice of those who won these medals, and to preclude dilution of the honor accorded to these medal winners by allowing others to falsely assert that they had obtained the medals. Suppose that a man makes this false assertion at a public meeting: "I'm a retired Marine of 25 years. Back in 1987, I was awarded the Congressional Medal of Honor. I got wounded many times by the same guy. I'm still around." Suppose that the man is charged with violating the Act, and you have agreed to represent him. What challenges might you raise regarding the validity of the Act? Now, assume that you have instead been asked to represent the government. How might you respond to those arguments?

4. *The Sagging Pants Ordinance.* Holly Beach, Florida, recently enacted the following "Sagging Pants" (SP) ordinance: "It is a crime to knowingly wear pants below the waistline, in a public place, in a manner that exposes the person's underwear or bare buttocks. For purposes of this ordinance, underwear is any clothing worn between the skin and outer layer of clothing, including but not limited to boxer shorts and thongs. The first offense is punishable by a $150 fine or twenty-five hours of community service. A second offense is punishable by a $300 fine or fifty hours of community service." The ordinance was enacted with support from more than 75 percent of voters. During the hearings leading up to passage, the mayor stated that "Cities should have the right to maintain social standards of decency." Since its enactment, two dozen young men have been charged with violating the ordinance, most of them African Americans. Several

of them seek to challenge the ordinance. At the hearing, the plaintiffs presented an expert witness who is a former New York fashion designer who testified that the "low slung pants look" started off "as an expressive concept" and has "gone mainstream" in recent years. The plaintiffs testified concerning their experiences during their arrests for violating the SP ordinance. When each plaintiff asked the arresting officer why he was being singled out for arrest, the answers of the officers varied. One replied, "We have to consider the fact that weapons can be hidden in overly large pants, and your sagging pants fit that description." Another officer responded, "I just enforce the law, and for me, when I can see some part of the waistband of your underwear, and that waistband is below your belly button, then that's against the law." You are the judge's law clerk, and she asks for your help in evaluating the ordinance and in deciding whether it should be upheld or invalidated. How would you advise her? What arguments would you give?

5. *More on the International Treaty Regulating the Internet.* At the convention, a number of countries wish to include language that precludes depictions of their flags that involve desecration. What, if anything, can you agree to regarding the content of such a prohibition?

D. OVERBREADTH AND VAGUENESS

The vagueness doctrine is designed to ensure that a statute's meaning is clear enough to provide fair notice of its prohibitions to people who wish to engage in protected speech activities, and to ensure that the statute will not be subject to arbitrary enforcement. By contrast, the overbreadth doctrine is designed to ensure that a statute sweeps in only speech that the government has the power to regulate (either a core of unprotected speech or a core of speech subject to legitimate regulation) and does not sweep in activities that the government does not have the power to regulate. A statute that sweeps in both is "overbroad." Both the vagueness and overbreadth doctrines reflect a concern that statutes "chill" individuals in their exercise of First Amendment rights.

Board of Airport Commissioners of the City of Los Angeles v. Jews for Jesus, Inc.

482 U.S. 569 (1987)

Justice O'CONNOR delivered the opinion of the Court.

The issue presented in this case is whether a resolution banning all "First Amendment activities" at Los Angeles International Airport (LAX) violates the First Amendment. [On] July 13, 1983, the Board of Airport Commissioners (Board) adopted Resolution No. 13787, which provides in pertinent part:

NOW, THEREFORE, BE IT RESOLVED by the Board of Airport Commissioners that the Central Terminal Area at Los Angeles International Airport is not open for First Amendment activities by any individual and/or entity; [and]

BE IT FURTHER RESOLVED that after the effective date of this Resolution, if any individual and/or entity seeks to engage in First Amendment activities within the Central Terminal Area at Los Angeles International Airport, said individual and/or entity shall be deemed to be acting in contravention of the stated policy of the Board of Airport Commissioners in reference to the uses permitted within the Central Terminal Area at Los Angeles International Airport; and

BE IT FURTHER RESOLVED that if any individual or entity engages in First Amendment activities within the Central Terminal Area at Los Angeles International Airport, the City Attorney of the City of Los Angeles is directed to institute appropriate litigation against such individual and/or entity to ensure compliance with this Policy statement of the Board of Airport Commissioner[s].

Respondent Jews for Jesus, Inc., is a nonprofit religious corporation. . . . Alan Snyder, a minister of the Gospel for Jews for Jesus, was stopped by a Department of Airports peace officer while distributing free religious literature on a pedestrian walkway in the Central Terminal Area at LAX. The officer showed Snyder a copy of the resolution, explained that Snyder's activities violated the resolution, and requested that Snyder leave LAX. The officer warned Snyder that the city would take legal action against him if he refused to leave as requested. Snyder stopped distributing the leaflets and left the airport terminal. . . . Jews for Jesus and Snyder then filed this action [challenging] the constitutionality of the resolution. [Both the federal district court and the Ninth Circuit Court of Appeals] held that the [resolution is] facially unconstitutional. [We] granted certiorari [and] affirm. . . .

[Under] the First Amendment overbreadth doctrine, an individual whose own speech or conduct may be prohibited is permitted to challenge a statute on its face "because it also threatens others not before the court — those who desire to engage in legally protected expression but who may refrain from doing so rather than risk prosecution or undertake to have the law declared partially invalid." Brockett v. Spokane Arcades, Inc., 472 U.S. 491 (1985). A statute may be invalidated on its face, however, only if the overbreadth is "substantial." Broadrick v. Oklahoma, 413 U.S. 601 (1973). The requirement that the overbreadth be substantial arose from our recognition that application of the overbreadth doctrine is "manifestly, strong medicine," and that "there must be a realistic danger that the statute itself will significantly compromise recognized First Amendment protections of parties not before the Court for it to be facially challenged on overbreadth grounds." City Council of Los Angeles v. Taxpayers for Vincent, 466 U.S. 789 (1984).

On its face, the resolution at issue in this case reaches the universe of expressive activity, and, by prohibiting *all* protected expression, purports to create a virtual "First Amendment Free Zone" at LAX. The resolution does not merely regulate expressive activity in the Central Terminal Area that might create problems such as congestion or the disruption of the activities of those who use LAX. Instead, the resolution expansively states that LAX "is not open for First Amendment activities by any individual and/or entity," and that "any individual and/or entity [who] seeks to engage in First Amendment activities within the Central Terminal Area [shall] be deemed to be acting in contravention of the stated policy of the Board of Airport Commissioners." The resolution therefore does not merely reach the activity of respondents at LAX; it prohibits even talking and reading, or the wearing of campaign buttons or symbolic clothing. Under such a sweeping ban, virtually every individual who enters LAX may be found to violate the resolution by engaging in some "First Amendment activit[y]." We think it obvious that such a ban cannot be justified even if LAX were a nonpublic forum because no conceivable governmental interest would justify such an absolute prohibition of speech.

Additionally, we find no apparent saving construction of the resolution. The resolution expressly applies to all "First Amendment activities," and the words of the resolution simply leave no room for a narrowing construction. In the past the Court sometimes has used either abstention or certification when, as here, the state courts have not had the opportunity to give the statute under challenge a definite construction. Neither option, however, is appropriate in this case because California has no certification procedure, and the resolution is not "fairly subject to an interpretation which will render unnecessary or substantially modify the federal constitutional question." [This Court has invalidated a law on overbreadth grounds when it] was not "open to one or a few interpretations, but to an indefinite number," and concluded that "[i]t is fictional to believe that anything less than extensive adjudications, under the impact of a variety of factual situations, would bring the [law] within the bounds of permissible constitutional certainty." [Baggett v. Bullitt, 377 U.S. 360 (1964).] Here too, it is difficult to imagine that the resolution could be limited by anything less than a series of adjudications, and the chilling effect of the resolution on protected speech in the meantime would make such a case-by-case adjudication intolerable.

The petitioners suggest that the resolution is not substantially overbroad because it is intended to reach only expressive activity unrelated to airport-related purposes. Such a limiting construction, however, is of little assistance in substantially reducing the overbreadth of the resolution. Much nondisruptive speech—such as the wearing of a T-shirt or button that contains a political message—may not be "airport related," but is still protected speech even in a nonpublic forum. Moreover, the vagueness of this suggested construction itself presents serious constitutional difficulty. The line between airport-related speech and nonairport-related speech is, at best, murky. The petitioners [suggest] that an individual who reads a newspaper or converses with a neighbor at LAX is engaged in permitted "airport-related" activity because reading or conversing permits the traveling public to "pass the time." We presume, however, that petitioners would not so categorize the activities of a member of a religious or political organization who decides to "pass the time" by distributing leaflets to fellow travelers. In essence, the result of this vague limiting construction would be to give LAX officials alone the power to decide in the first instance whether a given activity is airport related. Such a law that "confers on police a virtually unrestrained power to arrest and charge persons with a violation" of the resolution is unconstitutional because "[t]he opportunity for abuse, especially where a statute has received a virtually open-ended interpretation, is self-evident." Lewis v. City of New Orleans, 425 U.S. 130 (1974) (Powell, J., concurring).

We conclude that the resolution is substantially overbroad, and is not fairly subject to a limiting construction. Accordingly, we hold that the resolution violates the First Amendment. The judgment of the Court of Appeals is

   Affirmed.

Note: Distinguishing Vagueness and Overbreadth

The plaintiff in *Board of Airport Commissioners* argued that the resolution was "vague" as well as "overbroad," and such a pairing of these theories is common in First Amendment litigation. Laws are sometimes characterized as vague when no reasonable person can ascertain the meaning of their language. In Papachristou v. City of Jacksonville, 405 U.S. 156 (1972), the Court stated: "[This] ordinance is void for vagueness, both in the sense that it fails to give a person of ordinary intelligence fair notice that his contemplated conduct is forbidden by the statute, and because it encourages arbitrary and erratic arrests and convictions. Living under a rule of law entails various suppositions, one of which is that (all persons) are entitled to be informed as to what the State commands or forbids." It is possible that a statute may be vague but not substantially overbroad, or arguably overbroad but not particularly vague. However, it is also true that a high degree of vagueness in a statute is likely to create a potential overbreadth problem, and that an extremely overbroad statute may be vague in its contours. Thus, the two statutory "vices" may coexist in a statute.

∾ PROBLEMS ∾

1. *Tools for Analyzing Vagueness.* Any law may have a degree of overbreadth, and the Court's task in an overbreadth case is to perform the difficult subjective assessment of measuring that degree to determine whether it is "substantial" or in effect "too overbroad." What analytical tools does Justice O'Connor use in the reasoning of *Board of Airport Commissioners* to perform this measurement?

2. *The Identification Statute.* A California criminal statute provides: "Every person who commits any of the following acts is guilty of disorderly conduct, a misdemeanor: (e) Who loiters or wanders upon the streets or from place to place without apparent reason or business and who refuses to identify himself and to account for his presence when requested by any peace officer to do so, if the surrounding circumstances are such as to indicate to a reasonable man that the public safety demands such identification." A state court has interpreted the identification requirement as necessitating the production of "credible and reliable" identification, meaning that the identification "carries a reasonable assurance that the identification is authentic and providing means for later getting in touch with the person who has identified himself." Is the statute unduly vague because it fails to define the term *identification* (e.g., does it vest arbitrary and potentially discriminatory power in the police to arrest)? Does the clarification of

credible and reliable provide adequate qualification? Could the California statute constitutionally be applied to 1) a man who is caught jogging on a city street late at night; 2) a homeless person found "loitering" on city streets? *See* Kolender v. Lawson, 461 U.S. 352 (1983).

3. *The Student Demonstration.* Suppose that an ordinance makes it a crime "for three or more persons to assemble, except at a public meeting of citizens, on any of the sidewalks, street corners, vacant lots, or mouths of alleys, and there conduct themselves in a manner annoying to persons passing by, or occupants of adjacent buildings." Assume that a student who is involved in a political street demonstration is arrested and convicted under this ordinance. As the lawyer for the student, how will you argue that the ordinance is overbroad and vague, and how will your overbreadth and vagueness arguments differ? *See* Coates v. City of Cincinnati, 402 U.S. 611 (1971).

4. *Rogues and Vagabonds.* Suppose that you are hired to challenge the following ordinance. What arguments might you raise? "Rogues and vagabonds, or dissolute persons who go about begging, common gamblers, persons who use juggling or unlawful games or plays, common drunkards, common night walkers, thieves, pilferers or pickpockets, traders in stolen property, lewd, wanton and lascivious persons, keepers of gambling places, common railers and brawlers, persons wandering or strolling around from place to place without any lawful purpose or object, habitual loafers, disorderly persons, persons neglecting all lawful business and habitually spending their time by frequenting houses of ill fame, gaming houses, or places where alcoholic beverages are sold or served, persons able to work but habitually living upon the earnings of their wives or minor children shall be deemed vagrants and, upon conviction in the Municipal Court shall be punished as provided for Class D offenses [up to 90 days imprisonment, up to a $500 fine, or both]." *See* Papachristou v. City of Jacksonville, 405 U.S. 156 (1972).

5. *Flag Desecration.* Assume that a man wears a small cloth version of the U.S. flag sewn to the seat of his pants. The flag is approximately 4 by 6 inches and is displayed on the left rear pocket of his jeans. A police officer sees the man and arrests him under the following statute: "Whoever publicly mutilates, tramples upon, defaces or treats contemptuously the flag of the United States, whether such flag is public or private property, shall be punished by a fine of not less than ten nor more than one hundred dollars or by imprisonment for not more than one year or both." Construct arguments to challenge the ordinance on the grounds of vagueness. How might the state respond? *See* Smith v. Goguen, 415 U.S. 566 (1974).

6. *The Noise Ordinance.* This statute is challenged on vagueness and overbreadth grounds: "[N]o person, while on public or private grounds adjacent to any building in which a school or any class thereof is in session, shall willfully make or assist in the making of any noise or diversion which disturbs or tends to disturb the peace or good order of such school session or class thereof." Explain how the defense to the vagueness challenge differs from the defense to the overbreadth challenge. *See* Grayned v. Rockford, 408 U.S. 104 (1972).

City of Houston, Texas v. Hill

482 U.S. 451 (1987)

Justice BRENNAN delivered the opinion of the Court.

[Appellee] Raymond Wayne Hill is a lifelong resident of Houston, Texas[, who] worked as a paralegal and as executive director of the Houston Human Rights League. [O]n February 14, 1982. Hill observed a friend, Charles Hill, intentionally stopping traffic on a busy street, evidently to enable a vehicle to enter traffic. Two Houston police officers, one of whom was named Kelley, approached Charles and began speaking with him. "[S]hortly thereafter" Hill began shouting at the officers "in an admitted attempt to divert Kelley's attention from Charles Hill." [Hill] testified that his "motivation was to stop [the officers] from hitting Charles." He also explained: "I would rather that I get arrested than those whose careers can be damaged [or] whose families wouldn't understand [or] couldn't spend a long time in jail. I am prepared to respond in any legal, nonaggressive or nonviolent way, to any illegal police activity, at any time, under any circumstances." Hill first shouted: "Why don't you pick on somebody your own size?" After Officer Kelley responded: "[A]re you interrupting me in my official capacity as a Houston police officer?" Hill then shouted: "Yes, why don't you pick on somebody my size?" Hill was arrested under Houston Code of Ordinances §34-11(a), for "wilfully or intentionally interrupt[ing] a city policeman [by] verbal challenge during an investigation." Charles Hill was not arrested. Hill was then acquitted after a nonjury trial in Municipal Court.

Code of Ordinances, City of Houston, Texas, §34-11(a) (1984), reads:

> Sec. 34-11. Assaulting or interfering with policemen.
> (a) It shall be unlawful for any person to assault, strike or in any manner oppose, molest, abuse or interrupt any policeman in the execution of his duty, or any person summoned to aid in making an arrest.

[A conviction for this misdemeanor is punishable by a fine of not more than $200.] Following his acquittal[,] Hill brought [suit] seeking [declaratory and injunctive relief, as well as damages and attorney's fees] under 42 U.S.C. §§1983 and 1988 [arguing that the ordinance violated the First Amendment on its face and as applied, and that it was both vague and overbroad].

The District Court [rejected] Hill's contention that the ordinance was unconstitutionally vague or overbroad on its face. [The] Court of Appeals reversed. [We] affirm.

The elements of First Amendment overbreadth analysis are familiar. Only a statute that is substantially overbroad may be invalidated on its face. "In a facial challenge to the overbreadth and vagueness of a law, a court's first task is to determine whether the enactment reaches a substantial amount of constitutionally protected conduct." Kolender v. Lawson, 461 U.S. 352 (1983). Criminal statutes must be scrutinized with particular care [and] those that make unlawful a substantial amount of constitutionally protected conduct may be held facially invalid even if they also have legitimate application.

The city's principal argument is that the ordinance does not inhibit the exposition of ideas, and that it bans "core criminal conduct" not protected by the First Amendment. . . . We disagree with the city's characterization for several reasons. First, the enforceable portion of the ordinance deals not with core criminal conduct, but with speech. [T]he language in the ordinance making it unlawful for any person to "assault" or "strike" a police officer is pre-empted by the Texas Penal Code. . . . Accordingly, the enforceable portion of the ordinance makes it "unlawful for any person to [in] any manner oppose, molest, abuse or interrupt any policeman in the execution of his duty," and thereby prohibits verbal interruptions of police officers. . . . Second, [the] First Amendment protects a significant amount of verbal criticism and challenge directed at police officers. "Speech is often provocative and challenging. [But it] is nevertheless protected against censorship or punishment, unless shown likely to produce a clear and present danger of a serious substantive evil that rises far above public inconvenience, annoyance, or unrest." Terminiello v. Chicago, 337 U.S. 1 (1949). In Lewis v. City of New Orleans, 415 U.S. 130 (1974)[,] appellant was found to have yelled obscenities and threats at an officer who had asked appellant's husband to produce his driver's license. . . . We vacated the conviction and invalidated the ordinance as facially overbroad [because] the ordinance "punishe[d] only spoken words" and was not limited in scope to fighting words that "by their very utterance inflict injury or tend to incite an immediate breach of the peace."

The Houston ordinance is much more sweeping than the municipal ordinance struck down in Lewis. It is not limited to fighting words nor even to obscene or opprobrious language, but prohibits speech that "in any manner [interrupts]" an officer. The Constitution does not allow such speech to be made a crime. The freedom of individuals verbally to oppose or challenge police action without thereby risking arrest is one of the principal characteristics by which we distinguish a free nation from a police state. . . . The city argues [that] even if the ordinance encompasses some protected speech, its sweeping nature is both inevitable and essential to maintain public order. [Although] we appreciate the difficulties of drafting precise laws, we have repeatedly invalidated laws that provide the police with unfettered discretion to arrest individuals for words or conduct that annoy or offend them. [In] Lewis, [we stated that,] "Many arrests are made in 'one-on-one' situations where the only witnesses are the arresting officer and the person charged. All that is required for conviction is that the court accept the testimony of the officer that obscene or opprobrious language had been used toward him while in the performance of his duties." [I]t is unlikely that limiting the ordinance's application to genuine 'fighting words' would be incompatible with the full and adequate performance of an officer's duties. . . . The present type of ordinance tends to be invoked only where there is no other valid basis for arresting an objectionable or suspicious person. The opportunity for abuse, especially where a statute has received a virtually open-ended interpretation, is self-evident.

Houston's ordinance criminalizes a substantial amount of constitutionally protected speech, and accords the police unconstitutional discretion in enforcement. The ordinance's plain language is admittedly violated scores of times daily, yet only some individuals—those chosen by the police in their unguided discretion—are arrested. Far from providing the "breathing space" that "First Amendment freedoms need [to] survive," the ordinance is susceptible of regular application to protected expression. We conclude that the ordinance is substantially overbroad, and that the Court of Appeals did not err in holding it facially invalid.

The city has also urged us not to reach the merits of Hill's constitutional challenge, but rather to abstain [and thereby require the plaintiff to file the same suit in state court because] there are certain limiting constructions readily available to the state courts that would eliminate the ordinance's overbreadth. [Even] if this case did not involve a facial challenge under the First Amendment, we would find abstention inappropriate. [This] ordinance is not susceptible to a limiting construction because [its] language is plain and its meaning unambiguous. Its constitutionality cannot "turn upon a choice between one or several alternative meanings." Baggett v. Bullitt, 377 U.S. 360 (1964). Nor can the ordinance be limited by severing discrete unconstitutional subsections from the rest. For example, it cannot be limited to "core criminal conduct" such as physical assaults or fighting words because those applications are pre-empted by state law. The enforceable portion of this ordinance is a general prohibition of speech that "simply has no core" of constitutionally unprotected expression to which it might be limited. The city's proposed constructions are insufficient and it is doubtful that even "a remarkable job of plastic surgery upon the face of the ordinance" could save it. In sum, "[s]ince 'the naked question, uncomplicated by [ambiguous language], is whether the Act on its face is unconstitutional, abstention [is not] required.'"

The city relies heavily on its claim that the state courts have not had an opportunity to construe the statute. [W]hen a statute is not ambiguous, there is no need to abstain even if state courts have never interpreted the statute. But [it] is undisputed that Houston's Municipal Courts [have] had numerous opportunities to narrow the scope of the ordinance. There is no evidence that they have done so. . . .

[I]n the face of verbal challenges to police action, officers and municipalities must respond with restraint. We are mindful that the preservation of liberty depends in part upon the maintenance of social order. But the First Amendment recognizes, wisely we think, that a certain amount of expressive disorder not only is inevitable in a society committed to individual freedom, but must itself be protected if that freedom would survive. We therefore affirm the judgment of the Court of Appeals.

It is so ordered.

Justice Powell, with whom Justice O'Connor joins, and with whom The Chief Justice joins as to Parts I and II, and Justice Scalia joins as to Parts II and III, concurring in the judgment in part and dissenting in part.

[The] terms of the ordinance—"oppose, molest, abuse or interrupt any policeman in the execution of his duty"—include general words that can apply as fully to conduct as to speech. . . . For example, the ordinance evidently would punish individuals who—without saying a single word—obstructed an officer's access to the scene of an ongoing public disturbance, or indeed the scene of a crime. . . . [I] agree that the ordinance can be applied to speech in some cases. And I also agree that the First Amendment protects a good deal of speech that may be directed at police officers. [B]ut I question the implication [that] the First Amendment generally protects verbal "challenge[s] directed at police officers." A "challenge" often takes the form of opposition or interruption of performance of duty. In many situations, speech of this type directed at police officers will be functionally indistinguishable from conduct that the First Amendment clearly does not protect. For example, [a] municipality constitutionally may punish an individual who chooses to stand near a police officer and persistently attempt to engage the officer in conversation while the officer is directing traffic at a busy intersection. Similarly, an individual, by contentious and abusive speech, could interrupt an officer's investigation of possible criminal conduct. A person observing an officer pursuing a person suspected of a felony could run beside him in a public street shouting at the officer. Similar tactics could interrupt a policeman lawfully attempting to interrogate persons believed to be witnesses to a crime.

[T]he Court's opinion appears to reflect a failure to apprehend that this ordinance [is] intended primarily to further the public's interest in law enforcement. [I] nevertheless agree that the ambiguous terms of this ordinance "confe[r] on police a virtually unrestrained power to arrest and charge persons with a violation. . . . The opportunity for abuse, especially where a statute has received a virtually open-ended interpretation, is self-evident." . . . People have been charged with such crimes as "Failure to remain silent and stationary," "Remaining," "Refusing to remain silent," and "Talking." Although some of these incidents may have involved unprotected conduct, the vagueness of these charges suggests [that] Houston officials have not been acting with proper sensitivity to the constitutional rights of their citizens. When government protects society's interests in a manner that restricts some speech the law must be framed more precisely than the ordinance before us. . . .

[In] view of the difficulty of drafting precise language that never restrains speech and yet serves the public interest, the attempts of States and municipalities to draft laws of this type should be accorded some leeway. I am convinced, however, that the Houston ordinance is too vague to comport with the First and Fourteenth Amendments. [I]t should be possible for the present ordinance to be reframed in a way that would limit the present broad discretion of officers and at the same time protect substantially the city's legitimate interests. For example, the ordinance could make clear that it applies to speech only if the purpose of the speech were to interfere with the performance by a police officer of his lawful duties.

Chief Justice REHNQUIST, dissenting.
[I] do not agree [that] the Houston ordinance, in the absence of an authoritative construction by the Texas courts, is unconstitutional. . . .

Notes and Questions

1. *Analytical Tools.* The opinions in City of Houston v. Hill reveal that over-breadth analysis can be more complex in some cases than the analysis in *Board of Airport Commissioners*. Describe the analytical tools that Justice Brennan uses in the reasoning in his opinion in *City of Houston*. Then identify which tools were used also in *Board of Airport Commissioners* and which tools are new.

2. *Merits versus Overbreadth Challenges.* From plaintiff Hill's point of view, what were the benefits of bringing an overbreadth challenge against the Houston ordinance compared to a challenge to the ordinance "on the merits"? From the Supreme Court's point of view, describe the costs and benefits of grounding a First Amendment holding in the overbreadth doctrine instead of ruling on the merits of a First Amendment claim.

∾ PROBLEMS ∾

1. *The Beggar's Signs.* An Arizona criminal statute provides six months' imprisonment for "persons wandering abroad and begging, or who go about from door to door or in public or private ways, areas to which the general public is invited, or in other places for the purpose of begging or receiving alms." Sara Bounds challenges the statute on First Amendment grounds, claiming that she is homeless and subsists on the money she receives from begging. During the day, she sits in various Phoenix parks holding signs that request help and refer to love, peace, and food. She also holds a cup into which people may deposit money. Sometimes, if a passerby is willing, Sara talks about the messages on her signs and about her homelessness. Sara does not approach anyone and she does not block any sidewalk or store entrance. Sara has been arrested several times for violating the antibegging statute. What arguments can be made by Sara and by the attorney general of Arizona to attack and defend the statute on both overbreadth and vagueness grounds?

2. *The Code of Judicial Conduct.* Assume that a public official who wishes to sue a defendant for libel must prove that the defendant either knew or acted with reckless disregard as to whether a statement about the plaintiff was false and defamatory. In effect, a defendant may act negligently in criticizing a public official by making a false and defamatory statement. However, Canon 7 of the Code of Judicial Conduct in Georgia provides that candidates for any judicial office that is filled by public election between competing candidates "[shall] not use or participate in the use of any form of public communication which the candidate knows or reasonably should know is false, fraudulent, misleading, deceptive, or which contains a material misrepresentation of fact or law or omits a fact necessary to make the communication considered as a whole not materially misleading or which is likely to create an unjustified expectation about results the candidate can achieve." Assume that a candidate for judicial office is sanctioned under Canon 7 for statements about a public official (a sitting judge) who is her opponent in a race for the judicial office. The sanctioned candidate files suit to have

Canon 7 declared unconstitutional on both overbreadth and vagueness grounds. Construct arguments on both issues for the candidate, and explain the differences between the arguments on each issue. *See* Weaver v. Bonner, 309 F.3d 1312 (2002); *see also* Republican Party of Minnesota v. White, 536 U.S. 765 (2002).

United States v. Stevens

130 S.Ct. 1577 (2010)

Chief Justice ROBERTS delivered the opinion of the Court.

[Section 48] establishes a criminal penalty of up to five years in prison for anyone who knowingly "creates, sells, or possesses a depiction of animal cruelty," if done "for commercial gain" in interstate or foreign commerce. [18 U.S.C.] §48(a). A depiction of "animal cruelty" is defined as one "in which a living animal is intentionally maimed, mutilated, tortured, wounded, or killed," if that conduct violates federal or state law where "the creation, sale, or possession takes place." §48(c)(1). In what is referred to as the "exceptions clause," the law exempts from prohibition any depiction "that has serious religious, political, scientific, educational, journalistic, historical, or artistic value." §48(b).

The legislative background of §48 focused primarily on the interstate market for "crush videos." According to the House Committee Report on the bill, such videos feature the intentional torture and killing of helpless animals, including cats, dogs, monkeys, mice, and hamsters. Crush videos often depict women slowly crushing animals to death "with their bare feet or while wearing high heeled shoes," sometimes while "talking to the animals in a kind of dominatrix patter" over "[t]he cries and squeals of the animals, obviously in great pain." Apparently these depictions "appeal to persons with a very specific sexual fetish who find them sexually arousing or otherwise exciting." The acts depicted in crush videos are typically prohibited by the animal cruelty laws enacted by all 50 States and the District of Columbia. But crush videos rarely disclose the participants' identities, inhibiting prosecution of the underlying conduct.

This case, however, involves an application of §48 to depictions of animal fighting. Dogfighting, for example, is unlawful in all 50 States and the District of Columbia, and has been restricted by federal law since 1976. Respondent Robert J. Stevens ran a business, "Dogs of Velvet and Steel," and an associated Web site, through which he sold videos of pit bulls engaging in dogfights and attacking other animals. Among these videos were Japan Pit Fights and Pick-A-Winna: A Pit Bull Documentary, which include contemporary footage of dogfights in Japan (where such conduct is allegedly legal) as well as footage of American dogfights from the 1960's and 1970's. A third video, Catch Dogs and Country Living, depicts the use of pit bulls to hunt wild boar, as well as a "gruesome" scene of a pit bull attacking a domestic farm pig. On the basis of these videos, Stevens was indicted on three counts of violating §48.

Stevens moved to dismiss the indictment, arguing that §48 is facially invalid under the First Amendment. The District Court [held] that the depictions subject to §48, like obscenity or child pornography, are categorically unprotected by the

First Amendment. . . . The en banc Third Circuit [declared] §48 facially unconstitutional [and] declined to recognize a new category of unprotected speech for
depictions of animal cruelty. . . . We granted certiorari.

The Government's primary submission is that §48 necessarily complies with
the Constitution because the banned depictions of animal cruelty, as a class, are
categorically unprotected by the First Amendment. We disagree. . . . Because we
decline to carve out from the First Amendment any novel exception for §48, we
review Stevens's First Amendment challenge under our existing doctrine.

Stevens challenged §48 on its face, arguing that any conviction secured
under the statute would be unconstitutional. . . . To succeed in a typical facial
attack, Stevens would have to establish "that no set of circumstances exists under
which [§48] would be valid," or that the statute lacks any "plainly legitimate
sweep," Washington v. Glucksberg, 521 U.S. 702, 740, n.7 (1997) (Stevens, J., concurring in judgments). Which standard applies in a typical case is a matter of dispute that we need not and do not address. . . . Here the Government asserts that
Stevens cannot prevail because §48 is plainly legitimate as applied to crush videos and animal fighting depictions. Deciding this case through a traditional facial
analysis would require us to resolve whether these applications of §48 are in fact
consistent with the Constitution.

In the First Amendment context, however, this Court recognizes "a second
type of facial challenge," whereby a law may be invalidated as overbroad if "a substantial number of its applications are unconstitutional, judged in relation to the
statute's plainly legitimate sweep." Washington State Grange v. Washington State
Republican Party, 552 U.S. 442, 449, n.6 (2008). Stevens argues that §48 applies
to common depictions of ordinary and lawful activities, and that these depictions
constitute the vast majority of materials subject to the statute. The Government
makes no effort to defend such a broad ban as constitutional. Instead, the Government's entire defense of §48 rests on interpreting the statute as narrowly limited to specific types of "extreme" material. [T]herefore, the constitutionality of
§48 hinges on how broadly it is construed. . . .

As we explained two Terms ago, "[t]he first step in overbreadth analysis is to
construe the challenged statute; it is impossible to determine whether a statute
reaches too far without first knowing what the statute covers." United States v.
Williams, 553 U.S. 285, 293 (2008). Because §48 is a federal statute, there is no
need to defer to a state court's authority to interpret its own law. We read §48 to
create a criminal prohibition of alarming breadth. To begin with, the text of the
statute's ban on a "depiction of animal cruelty" nowhere requires that the
depicted conduct be cruel. That text applies to "any . . . depiction" in which "a
living animal is intentionally maimed, mutilated, tortured, wounded, or killed."
§48(c)(1). "[M]aimed, mutilated, [and] tortured" convey cruelty, but "wounded"
or "killed" do not suggest any such limitation.

The Government contends that the terms in the definition should be read to
require the additional element of "accompanying acts of cruelty." (The dissent
hinges on the same assumption.) The Government bases this argument on the
definiendum, "depiction of animal cruelty," and on "'the commonsense canon of
noscitur a sociis.'" As that canon recognizes, an ambiguous term may be "given

more precise content by the neighboring words with which it is associated." Likewise, an unclear definitional phrase may take meaning from the term to be defined.

But the phrase "wounded . . . or killed" at issue here contains little ambiguity. The Government's opening brief properly applies the ordinary meaning of these words, stating for example that to "kill is 'to deprive of life.'" We agree that "wounded" and "killed" should be read according to their ordinary meaning. Nothing about that meaning requires cruelty.

While not requiring cruelty, §48 does require that the depicted conduct be "illegal." But this requirement does not limit §48 along the lines the Government suggests. There are myriad federal and state laws concerning the proper treatment of animals, but many of them are not designed to guard against animal cruelty. Protections of endangered species, for example, restrict even the humane "wound[ing] or kill[ing]" of "living animal[s]." §48(c)(1). Livestock regulations are often designed to protect the health of human beings, and hunting and fishing rules (seasons, licensure, bag limits, weight requirements) can be designed to raise revenue, preserve animal populations, or prevent accidents. The text of §48(c) draws no distinction based on the reason the intentional killing of an animal is made illegal, and includes, for example, the humane slaughter of a stolen cow.

What is more, the application of §48 to depictions of illegal conduct extends to conduct that is illegal in only a single jurisdiction. Under subsection (c)(1), the depicted conduct need only be illegal in "the State in which the creation, sale, or possession takes place, regardless of whether the [wounding] or killing took place in [that] State." A depiction of entirely lawful conduct runs afoul of the ban if that depiction later finds its way into another State where the same conduct is unlawful. This provision greatly expands the scope of §48, because although there may be "a broad societal consensus" against cruelty to animals, there is substantial disagreement on what types of conduct are properly regarded as cruel. Both views about cruelty to animals and regulations having no connection to cruelty vary widely from place to place.

In the District of Columbia, for example, all hunting is unlawful. D.C. Mun. Regs., tit. 19, §1560 (2009). Other jurisdictions permit or encourage hunting, and there is an enormous national market for hunting-related depictions in which a living animal is intentionally killed. Hunting periodicals have circulations in the hundreds of thousands or millions, and hunting television programs, videos, and Web sites are equally popular. The demand for hunting depictions exceeds the estimated demand for crush videos or animal fighting depictions by several orders of magnitude. Nonetheless, because the statute allows each jurisdiction to export its laws to the rest of the country, §48(a) extends to *any* magazine or video depicting lawful hunting, so long as that depiction is sold within the Nation's Capital.

Those seeking to comply with the law thus face a bewildering maze of regulations from at least 56 separate jurisdictions. Some States permit hunting with crossbows, while others forbid it, or restrict it only to the disabled. Missouri allows the "canned" hunting of ungulates held in captivity, but Montana restricts such hunting to certain bird species. The sharp-tailed grouse may be hunted in Idaho, but not in Washington.

The disagreements among the States — and the "commonwealth[s], territor[ies], or possession[s] of the United States," 18 U.S.C. §48(c)(2) — extend well beyond hunting. State agricultural regulations permit different methods of live-stock slaughter in different places or as applied to different animals. California has recently banned cutting or "docking" the tails of dairy cattle, which other States permit. Even cockfighting, long considered immoral in much of America, is legal in Puerto Rico, and was legal in Louisiana until 2008. An otherwise-lawful image of any of these practices, if sold or possessed for commercial gain within a State that happens to forbid the practice, falls within the prohibition of §48(a).

The only thing standing between defendants who sell such depictions and five years in federal prison — other than the mercy of a prosecutor — is the statute's exceptions clause. Subsection (b) exempts from prohibition "any depiction that has serious religious, political, scientific, educational, journalistic, historical, or artistic value." The Government argues that this clause substantially narrows the statute's reach: News reports about animal cruelty have "journalistic" value; pictures of bullfights in Spain have "historical" value; and instructional hunting videos have "educational" value. Thus, the Government argues, §48 reaches only crush videos, depictions of animal fighting (other than Spanish bullfighting), and perhaps other depictions of "extreme acts of animal cruelty."

The Government's attempt to narrow the statutory ban, however, requires an unrealistically broad reading of the exceptions clause. As the Government reads the clause, any material with "redeeming societal value," "at least some minimal value," or anything more than "scant social value," is excluded under §48(b). But the text says "serious" value, and "serious" should be taken seriously. We decline the Government's invitation [to] regard as "serious" anything that is not "scant." (Or, as the dissent puts it, "trifling.") As the Government recognized below, "serious" ordinarily means a good bit more. The District Court's jury instructions required value that is "significant and of great import," and the Government defended these instructions as properly relying on "a commonly accepted meaning of the word 'serious.'"

Quite apart from the requirement of "serious" value in §48(b), the excepted speech must also fall within one of the enumerated categories. Much speech does not. Most hunting videos, for example, are not obviously instructional in nature, except in the sense that all life is a lesson. According to Safari Club International and the Congressional Sportsmen's Foundation, many popular videos "have primarily entertainment value" and are designed to "entertai[n] the viewer, marke[t] hunting equipment, or increas[e] the hunting community." The National Rifle Association agrees that "much of the content of hunting media [is] merely *recreational* in nature." The Government offers no principled explanation why these depictions of hunting or depictions of Spanish bullfights would be *inherently* valuable while those of Japanese dogfights are not. The dissent contends that hunting depictions must have serious value because hunting has serious value, in a way that dogfights presumably do not. But §48(b) addresses the value of the *depictions*, not of the underlying activity. There is simply no adequate reading of the exceptions clause that results in the statute's banning only the depictions the Government would like to ban.

The Government explains that the language of §48(b) was largely drawn from our opinion in Miller v. California, 413 U.S. 15 (1973), which excepted from its definition of obscenity any material with "serious literary, artistic, political, or scientific value." According to the Government, this incorporation of the *Miller* standard into §48 is therefore surely enough to answer any First Amendment objection.

In *Miller* we held that "serious" value shields depictions of sex from regulation as obscenity. Limiting *Miller*'s exception to "serious" value ensured that "'[a] quotation from Voltaire in the flyleaf of a book [would] not constitutionally redeem an otherwise obscene publication.'" We did not, however, determine that serious value could be used as a general precondition to protecting *other* types of speech in the first place. *Most* of what we say to one another lacks "religious, political, scientific, educational, journalistic, historical, or artistic value" (let alone serious value), but it is still sheltered from government regulation. Even "'[w]holly neutral futilities [come] under the protection of free speech as fully as do Keats' poems or Donne's sermons.'" Cohen v. California, 403 U.S. 15, 25 (1971) (quoting Winters v. New York, 333 U.S. 507, 528 (1948) (Frankfurter, J., dissenting)).

Thus, the protection of the First Amendment presumptively extends to many forms of speech that do not qualify for the serious-value exception of §48(b), but nonetheless fall within the broad reach of §48(C).

Not to worry, the Government says: The Executive Branch construes §48 to reach only "extreme" cruelty, and it "neither has brought nor will bring a prosecution for anything less." The Government hits this theme hard, invoking its prosecutorial discretion several times. But the First Amendment protects against the Government; it does not leave us at the mercy of *noblesse oblige*. We would not uphold an unconstitutional statute merely because the Government promised to use it responsibly.

This prosecution is itself evidence of the danger in putting faith in government representations of prosecutorial restraint. When this legislation was enacted, the Executive Branch announced that it would interpret §48 as covering only depictions "of wanton cruelty to animals designed to appeal to a prurient interest in sex." *See* Statement by President William J. Clinton upon Signing H.R. 1887, 34 Weekly Comp. Pres. Doc. 2557 (Dec. 9, 1999). No one suggests that the videos in this case fit that description. The Government's assurance that it will apply §48 far more restrictively than its language provides is pertinent only as an implicit acknowledgment of the potential constitutional problems with a more natural reading.

Nor can we rely upon the canon of construction that "ambiguous statutory language [should] be construed to avoid serious constitutional doubts." FCC v. Fox Television Stations, Inc., 129 S.Ct. 1800, 1811 (2009). "[T]his Court may impose a limiting construction on a statute only if it is 'readily susceptible' to such a construction." Reno v. American Civil Liberties Union, 521 U.S. 844, 884

(1997). We "'will not rewrite a . . . law to conform it to constitutional require-ments,'" for doing so would constitute a "serious invasion of the legislative domain," and sharply diminish Congress's "incentive to draft a narrowly tailored law in the first place," *Osborne*, 495 U.S., at 121. To read §48 as the Government desires requires rewriting, not just reinterpretation.

Our construction of §48 decides the constitutional question; the Govern-ment makes no effort to defend the constitutionality of §48 as applied beyond crush videos and depictions of animal fighting. It argues that those particular depictions are intrinsically related to criminal conduct or are analogous to obscenity (if not themselves obscene), and that the ban on such speech is narrowly tailored to reinforce restrictions on the underlying conduct, prevent additional crime arising from the depictions, or safeguard public mores. But the Govern-ment nowhere attempts to extend these arguments to depictions of any other activities — depictions that are presumptively protected by the First Amendment but that remain subject to the criminal sanctions of §48.

Nor does the Government seriously contest that the presumptively imper-missible applications of §48 (properly construed) far outnumber any permissible ones. However "growing" and "lucrative" the markets for crush videos and dog-fighting depictions might be, they are dwarfed by the market for other depic-tions, such as hunting magazines and videos, that we have determined to be within the scope of §48. We therefore need not and do not decide whether a stat-ute limited to crush videos or other depictions of extreme animal cruelty would be constitutional. We hold only that §48 is not so limited but is instead substan-tially overbroad, and therefore invalid under the First Amendment.

The judgment of the United States Court of Appeals for the Third Circuit is affirmed.

It is so ordered.

Justice ALITO, dissenting.

[Today's] decision [strikes] down §48 using what has been aptly termed the "strong medicine" of the overbreadth doctrine, United States v. Williams, 553 U.S. 285, 293 (2008), a potion that generally should be administered only as "a last resort." Los Angeles Police Dept. v. United Reporting Publishing Corp., 528 U.S. 32 (1999). . . .

A party seeking to challenge the constitutionality of a statute generally must show that the statute violates the party's own rights. New York v. Ferber, 458 U.S. 747, 767 (1982). The First Amendment overbreadth doctrine carves out a narrow exception to that general rule. Because an overly broad law may deter constitu-tionally protected speech, the overbreadth doctrine allows a party to whom the law may constitutionally be applied to challenge the statute on the ground that it violates the First Amendment rights of others. See, e.g., Board of Trustees of State Univ. of N.Y. v. Fox, 492 U.S. 469, 483 (1989).

The "strong medicine" of overbreadth invalidation need not and generally should not be administered when the statute under attack is unconstitutional as applied to the challenger before the court. . . . I see no reason to depart here from the generally preferred procedure of considering the question of overbreadth only as a last resort. Because the Court has addressed the overbreadth question, however, I will explain why I do not think that the record supports the conclusion that §48, when properly interpreted, is overly broad.

The overbreadth doctrine "strike[s] a balance between competing social costs." Specifically, the doctrine seeks to balance the "harmful effects" of "invalidating a law that in some of its applications is perfectly constitutional" against the possibility that "the threat of enforcement of an overbroad law [will] dete[r] people from engaging in constitutionally protected speech." "In order to maintain an appropriate balance, we have vigorously enforced the requirement that a statute's overbreadth be *substantial,* not only in an absolute sense, but also relative to the statute's plainly legitimate sweep."

In determining whether a statute's overbreadth is substantial, we consider a statute's application to real-world conduct, not fanciful hypotheticals. Accordingly, we have repeatedly emphasized that an overbreadth claimant bears the burden of demonstrating, "from the text of [the law] *and from actual fact,*" that substantial overbreadth exists. Similarly, "there must be a *realistic danger* that the statute itself will significantly compromise recognized First Amendment protections of parties not before the Court for it to be facially challenged on overbreadth grounds." Members of City Council of Los Angeles v. Taxpayers for Vincent, 466 U.S. 789, 801 (1984).

In holding that §48 violates the overbreadth rule, the Court declines to decide whether, as the Government maintains, §48 is constitutional as applied to two broad categories of depictions that exist in the real world: crush videos and depictions of deadly animal fights. Instead, the Court tacitly assumes for the sake of argument that §48 is valid as applied to these depictions, but the Court concludes that §48 reaches too much protected speech to survive. The Court relies primarily on depictions of hunters killing or wounding game and depictions of animals being slaughtered for food. . . .

I turn first to depictions of hunting. As the Court notes, photographs and videos of hunters shooting game are common. But hunting is legal in all 50 States, and §48 applies only to a depiction of conduct that is illegal in the jurisdiction in which the depiction is created, sold, or possessed. Therefore, in all 50 States, the creation, sale, or possession for sale of the vast majority of hunting depictions indisputably falls outside §48's reach.

Straining to find overbreadth, the Court suggests that §48 prohibits the sale or possession in the District of Columbia of any depiction of hunting because the District — undoubtedly because of its urban character — does not permit hunting within its boundaries. The Court also suggests that, because some States prohibit a particular type of hunting (e.g., hunting with a crossbow or "canned" hunting) or the hunting of a particular animal (e.g., the "sharp-tailed grouse"), §48 makes it illegal for persons in such States to sell or possess for sale a depiction of hunting that was perfectly legal in the State in which the hunting took place.

The Court's interpretation is seriously flawed. "When a federal court is dealing with a federal statute challenged as overbroad, it should, of course, construe the statute to avoid constitutional problems, if the statute is subject to such a limiting construction." *Ferber,* 458 U.S., at 769, n.24. Applying this canon, I would hold that §48 does not apply to depictions of hunting. First, because §48 targets depictions of "animal cruelty," I would interpret that term to apply only to depictions involving acts of animal cruelty as defined by applicable state or federal law, not to depictions of acts that happen to be illegal for reasons having nothing to do with the prevention of animal cruelty. Virtually all state laws prohibiting animal cruelty either expressly define the term "animal" to exclude wildlife or else specifically exempt lawful hunting activities, so the statutory prohibition set forth in §48(a) may reasonably be interpreted not to reach most if not all hunting depictions.

Second, even if the hunting of wild animals were otherwise covered by §48(a), I would hold that hunting depictions fall within the exception in §48(b) for depictions that have "serious" (i.e., not "trifling") "scientific," "educational," or "historical" value. While there are certainly those who find hunting objectionable, the predominant view in this country has long been that hunting serves many important values, and it is clear that Congress shares that view. Since 1972, when Congress called upon the President to designate a National Hunting and Fishing Day, Presidents have regularly issued proclamations extolling the values served by hunting. Thus, it is widely thought that hunting has "scientific" value in that it promotes conservation, "historical" value in that it provides a link to past times when hunting played a critical role in daily life, and "educational" value in that it furthers the understanding and appreciation of nature and our country's past and instills valuable character traits. And if hunting itself is widely thought to serve these values, then it takes but a small additional step to conclude that depictions of hunting make a non-trivial contribution to the exchange of ideas. Accordingly, I would hold that hunting depictions fall comfortably within the exception set out in §48(b).

I do not have the slightest doubt that Congress, in enacting §48, had no intention of restricting the creation, sale, or possession of depictions of hunting. Proponents of the law made this point clearly. . . . But even if §48 did impermissibly reach the sale or possession of depictions of hunting in a few unusual situations[,] those isolated applications would hardly show that §48 bans a substantial amount of protected speech.

Although the Court's overbreadth analysis rests primarily on the proposition that §48 substantially restricts the sale and possession of hunting depictions, the Court cites a few additional examples, including depictions of methods of slaughter and the docking of the tails of dairy cows. . . . Such examples do not show that the statute is substantially overbroad, for two reasons. First[,] §48 can reasonably be construed to apply only to depictions involving acts of animal cruelty as defined by applicable state or federal law, and anti-cruelty laws do not ban the sorts of acts depicted in the Court's hypotheticals. Second, nothing in the record suggests that any one has ever created, sold, or possessed for sale a depiction of the slaughter of food animals or of the docking of the tails of dairy cows that would not easily qualify under the exception set out in §48(b). Depictions created to show proper methods of slaughter or tail-docking would presumably have serious "educational" value, and depictions created to focus attention on methods thought to be inhumane or otherwise objectionable would presumably have either serious "educational" or "journalistic" value or both. . . .

The Court notes, finally, that cockfighting, which is illegal in all States, is still legal in Puerto Rico, and I take the Court's point to be that it would be impermissible to ban the creation, sale, or possession in Puerto Rico of a depiction of a cockfight that was legally staged in Puerto Rico. But assuming for the sake of argument that this is correct, this veritable sliver of unconstitutionality would not be enough to justify striking down §48 *in toto*.

In sum, we have a duty to interpret §48 so as to avoid serious constitutional concerns, and §48 may reasonably be construed not to reach almost all, if not all, of the depictions that the Court finds constitutionally protected. Thus, §48 does not appear to have a large number of unconstitutional applications. Invalidation for overbreadth is appropriate only if the challenged statute suffers from *substantial* overbreadth — judged not just in absolute terms, but in relation to the statute's "plainly legitimate sweep." As I explain in the following Part, §48 has a substantial core of constitutionally permissible applications.

As the Court of Appeals recognized, "the primary conduct that Congress sought to address through its passage [of §48] was the creation, sale, or possession of 'crush videos.'" [It] is undisputed that the *conduct* depicted in crush videos may constitutionally be prohibited. All 50 States and the District of Columbia have enacted statutes prohibiting animal cruelty. But before the enactment of §48, the underlying conduct depicted in crush videos was nearly impossible to prosecute. These videos, which "often appeal to persons with a very specific sexual fetish," were made in secret, generally without a live audience, and "the faces of the women inflicting the torture in the material often were not shown, nor could the location of the place where the cruelty was being inflicted or the date of the activity be ascertained from the depiction." Thus, law enforcement authorities often were not able to identify the parties responsible for the torture. In the rare instances in which it was possible to identify and find the perpetrators, they "often were able to successfully assert as a defense that the State could not prove its jurisdiction over the place where the act occurred or that the actions depicted took place within the time specified in the State statute of limitations." H.R. Rep., at 3. . . .

The First Amendment protects freedom of speech, but it most certainly does not protect violent criminal conduct, even if engaged in for expressive purposes. Crush videos present a highly unusual free speech issue because they are so closely linked with violent criminal conduct. The videos record the commission of violent criminal acts, and it appears that these crimes are committed for the sole purpose of creating the videos. In addition, as noted above, Congress was presented with compelling evidence that the only way of preventing these crimes was to target the sale of the videos. Under these circumstances, I cannot believe that the First Amendment commands Congress to step aside and allow the underlying crimes to continue. . . .

In sum, §48 may validly be applied to at least two broad real-world categories of expression covered by the statute: crush videos and dogfighting videos. Thus, the statute has a substantial core of constitutionally permissible applications. Moreover, [the] record does not show that §48, properly interpreted, bans a substantial amount of protected speech in absolute terms. *A fortiori,* respondent has not met his burden of demonstrating that any impermissible applications of the statute are "substantial" in relation to its "plainly legitimate sweep." Accordingly, I would reject respondent's claim that §48 is facially unconstitutional under the overbreadth doctrine. . . .

E. PRIOR RESTRAINTS

A "prior restraint" is a restriction on speech that is imposed prior to publication or dissemination. In common law England, prior restraints were common and took many different forms. In this country, there has been a general presumption against the validity of prior restraints. As the Court stated in Bantam Books, Inc. v. Sullivan, 372 U.S. 58, 70 (1962): "Any system of prior restraints of expression comes to this Court bearing a heavy presumption against its constitutional validity." Prior restraints are undesirable because they prevent ideas from reaching the marketplace of ideas.

1. Licensing

The invention of the printing press brought about a major technological shift that made it possible for people to communicate among themselves much more easily and effectively. Prior to that invention, people were forced to communicate orally or by handwritten documents, methods that were slow and inefficient. Because the printing press enabled mass communication, many governments regarded it as dangerous. The English Crown responded by imposed licensing restrictions that required the press to obtain the approval of censors prior to publication. If governmental ministers found that the proposed publication contained objectionable ideas, they could deny the license or grant it on condition that objectionable information be modified or deleted.

Lovell v. City of Griffin

303 U.S. 444 (1938)

Mr. Chief Justice Hughes delivered the opinion of the Court.

Appellant, Alma Lovell, was convicted in the recorder's court of the City of Griffin, Ga., of the violation of a city ordinance and was sentenced to imprisonment for fifty days in default of the payment of a fine of $50. [The] case comes here on appeal.

The ordinance in question is as follows:

Section 1. That the practice of distributing, either by hand or otherwise, circulars, hand-books, advertising, or literature of any kind, whether said articles are being delivered free, or whether same are being sold, within the limits of the City of Griffin, without first obtaining written permission from the City Manager of the City of Griffin, such practice shall be deemed a nuisance, and punishable as an offense against the City of Griffin.

[The] violation, which is not denied, consisted of the distribution without the required permission of a pamphlet and magazine in the nature of religious tracts, setting forth the gospel of the "Kingdom of Jehovah." Appellant did not apply for a permit, as she regarded herself as sent "by Jehovah to do His work" and that such an application would have been "an act of disobedience to His commandment."

[The] ordinance in its broad sweep prohibits the distribution of "circulars, handbooks, advertising, or literature of any kind." It manifestly applies to pamphlets, magazines, and periodicals. The evidence against appellant was that she distributed a certain pamphlet and a magazine called the "Golden Age." Whether in actual administration the ordinance is applied, as apparently it could be, to newspapers does not appear. . . . The ordinance is not limited to "literature" that is obscene or offensive to public morals or that advocates unlawful conduct. There is no suggestion that the pamphlet and magazine distributed in the instant case were of that character. The ordinance embraces "literature" in the widest sense.

The ordinance is comprehensive with respect to the method of distribution. It covers every sort of circulation "either by hand or otherwise." There is thus no restriction in its application with respect to time or place. It is not limited to ways which might be regarded as inconsistent with the maintenance of public order, or as involving disorderly conduct, the molestation of the inhabitants, or the misuse or littering of the streets. The ordinance prohibits the distribution of literature of any kind at any time, at any place, and in any manner without a permit from the city manager.

We think that the ordinance is invalid on its face. Whatever the motive which induced its adoption, its character is such that it strikes at the very foundation of the freedom of the press by subjecting it to license and censorship. The struggle for the freedom of the press was primarily directed against the power of the licensor. It was against that power that John Milton directed his assault by his "Appeal for the Liberty of Unlicensed Printing." And the liberty of the press became initially a right to publish "without a license what formerly could be published only with one." While this freedom from previous restraint upon publication cannot be regarded as exhausting the guaranty of liberty, the prevention of that restraint was a leading purpose in the adoption of the constitutional provision. Legislation of the type of the ordinance in question would restore the system of license and censorship in its baldest form.

The liberty of the press is not confined to newspapers and periodicals. It necessarily embraces pamphlets and leaflets. These indeed have been historic weapons in the defense of liberty, as the pamphlets of Thomas Paine and others in our own history abundantly attest. The press in its connotation comprehends every sort of publication which affords a vehicle of information and opinion. What we have had recent occasion to say with respect to the vital importance of protecting this essential liberty from every sort of infringement need not be repeated.

The ordinance cannot be saved because it relates to distribution and not to publication. "Liberty of circulating is as essential to that freedom as liberty of publishing; indeed, without the circulation, the publication would be of little value." *Ex parte Jackson*, 96 U.S. 727. . . .

As the ordinance is void on its face, it was not necessary for appellant to seek a permit under it. She was entitled to contest its validity in answer to the charge against her.

The judgment is reversed and the cause is remanded for further proceedings not inconsistent with this opinion.

It is so ordered.

Notes

1. *Content-Neutral Time, Place, and Manner Restrictions.* Even though the Court routinely strikes down prior restraints, it has upheld content-neutral time, place, and manner restrictions (including permit requirements) on events like public parades. *See* Cox v. New Hampshire, 312 U.S. 569 (1941). Permit requirements are regarded as essential in this context because they "prevent confusion by overlapping parades or processions, to secure convenient use of the streets by other travelers, and to minimize the risk of disorder."

2. *Licenses for Professional Fundraisers.* Riley v. National Federation of the Blind, 487 U.S. 781 (1988), involved a North Carolina act that required licenses for professional fundraisers. In striking down the law, the Court stated that "[a] speaker is no less a speaker because he or she is paid to speak. Generally, speakers need not obtain a license to speak." Chief Justice Rehnquist, joined by Justice O'Connor, dissented: "[T]he requirement [does] not put any burden on the charities' ability to speak. [T]he effect of the statute is to require only that the fundraiser the charity hires is a fundraiser who has been licensed by the State."

∿ PROBLEM: MORE ON THE INTERNATIONAL TREATY REGULATING THE INTERNET ∿

At the convention, China and other countries argue that "seditious" and "subversive" speech, as well as "defamatory" speech, has been posted on the Internet, and they suggest the creation of an international licensing board for Internet communications. Under the proposed scheme, before any information can be posted on the Internet, it must be submitted to the review board and must be licensed. Can you agree to such a proposal in any form?

Freedman v. Maryland

380 U.S. 51 (1965)

Mr. Justice BRENNAN delivered the opinion of the Court.

Appellant sought to challenge the constitutionality of the Maryland motion picture censorship statute, Md. Ann. Code, 1957, Art. 66A, and exhibited the film "Revenge at Daybreak" at his Baltimore theatre without first submitting the picture to the State Board of Censors as required by §2 thereof. The State concedes that the picture does not violate the statutory standards and would have received a license if properly submitted, but the appellant was convicted of a §2 violation despite his contention that the statute in its entirety unconstitutionally impaired freedom of expression. The Court of Appeals of Maryland affirmed, and we noted probable jurisdiction. We reverse.

I

In Times Film Corp. v. City of Chicago, 365 U.S. 43 (1961), we considered and upheld a requirement of submission of motion pictures in advance of exhibition. [The] question tendered for decision in that case was "whether a prior restraint was necessarily unconstitutional *under all circumstances*." The [exhibitor contended] that the "constitutional protection includes complete and absolute freedom to exhibit, at least once, any and every kind of motion picture [even] if this film contains the basest type of pornography, or incitement to riot, or forceful overthrow of orderly [government]." The Court held that [the] argument stated the principle against prior restraints too broadly. . . .

Unlike the petitioner in *Times Film*, appellant does not argue that §2 is unconstitutional simply because it may prevent even the first showing of a film whose exhibiting may legitimately be the subject of an obscenity prosecution. He [argues] that §2 constitutes an invalid prior restraint because [it] presents a danger of unduly suppressing protected expression. He focuses particularly on the procedure for an initial decision by the censorship board, which, without any judicial participation, effectively bars exhibition of any disapproved film, unless and until the exhibitor undertakes a time-consuming appeal to the Maryland courts and succeeds in having the Board's decision reversed. Under the statute, the exhibitor is required to submit the film to the Board for examination, but no time limit is imposed for completion of Board action. . . .

Thus there is no statutory provision for judicial participation in the procedure which bars a film, nor even assurance of prompt judicial review. Risk of delay is built into the Maryland procedure, as is borne out by experience; in the only reported case indicating the length of time required to complete an appeal, the initial judicial determination has taken four months and final vindication of the film on appellate review, six months. . . .

In the area of freedom of expression it is well established that one has standing to challenge a statute on the ground that it delegates overly broad licensing discretion to an administrative office, whether or not his conduct could be proscribed by a properly drawn statute, and whether or not he applied for a license. . . . Standing is recognized in such cases because of [the] "danger of tolerating, in the area of First Amendment freedoms, the existence of a penal statute susceptible of sweeping and improper application." NAACP v. Button, 371 U.S. 145, 433. Although we have no occasion to decide whether the vice of overbroadness infects the Maryland statute, we think that appellant's assertion of a similar danger in the Maryland apparatus of censorship — one always fraught with danger and viewed with suspicion — gives him standing to make that challenge. In substance his argument is that, because the apparatus operates in a statutory context in which judicial review may be too little and too late, the Maryland statute lacks sufficient safeguards for confining the censor's action to judicially determined constitutional limits, and therefore contains the same vice as a statute delegating excessive administrative discretion.

Although the Court has said that motion pictures are not "necessarily subject to the precise rules governing any other particular method of expression," it is as true [that] "[a]ny system of prior restraints of expression comes to this Court bearing a heavy presumption against its constitutional validity." *Bantam Books.* . . . The administration of a censorship system for motion pictures presents peculiar dangers to constitutionally protected speech. Unlike a prosecution for obscenity, a censorship proceeding puts the initial burden on the exhibitor or distributor. Because the censor's business is to censor, there inheres the danger that he may well be less responsive than a court — part of an independent branch of government — to the constitutionally protected interests in free expression. And if it is made unduly onerous, by reason of delay or otherwise, to seek judicial review, the censor's determination may in practice be final.

[W]e hold that a noncriminal process which requires the prior submission of a film to a censor avoids constitutional infirmity only if it takes place under procedural safeguards designed to obviate the dangers of a censorship system. First, the burden of proving that the film is unprotected expression must rest on the censor. . . . Second, while the State may require advance submission of all films, in order to proceed effectively to bar all showings of unprotected films, the requirement cannot be administered in a manner which would lend an effect of finality to the censor's determination whether a film constitutes protected expression. The teaching of our cases is that, because only a judicial determination in an adversary proceeding ensures the necessary sensitivity to freedom of expression, only a procedure requiring a judicial determination suffices to impose a valid final restraint. To this end, the exhibitor must be assured, by statute or authoritative judicial construction, that the censor will, within a specified brief period, either issue a license or go to court to restrain showing the film. Any restraint imposed in advance of a final judicial determination on the merits must similarly be limited to preservation of the status quo for the shortest fixed period compatible with sound judicial resolution. Moreover, we are well aware that, even after expiration of a temporary restraint, an administrative refusal to license, signifying the censor's view that the film is unprotected, may have a discouraging effect on the exhibitor. Therefore, the procedure must also assure a prompt final judicial decision, to minimize the deterrent effect of an interim and possibly erroneous denial of a license.

Without these safeguards, it may prove too burdensome to seek review of the censor's determination. Particularly in the case of motion pictures, it may take very little to deter exhibition in a given locality. The exhibitor's stake in any one picture may be insufficient to warrant a protracted and onerous course of litigation. The distributor, on the other hand, may be equally unwilling to accept the burdens and delays of litigation in a particular area when, without such difficulties, he can freely exhibit his film in most of the rest of the country; for we are told that only four States and a handful of municipalities have active censorship laws.

It is readily apparent that the Maryland procedural scheme does not satisfy these criteria. First, once the censor disapproves the film, the exhibitor must assume the burden of instituting judicial proceedings and of persuading the courts that the film is protected expression. Second, once the Board has acted against a film, exhibition is prohibited pending judicial review, however protracted. Under the statute, appellant could have been convicted if he had shown the film after unsuccessfully seeking a license, even though no court had ever ruled on the obscenity of the film. Third, it is abundantly clear that the Maryland statute provides no assurance of prompt judicial determination. We hold, therefore, that appellant's conviction must be reversed. The Maryland scheme fails to provide adequate safeguards against undue inhibition of protected expression, and this renders the §2 requirement of prior submission of films to the Board an invalid previous restraint.

How or whether Maryland is to incorporate the required procedural safeguards in the statutory scheme is, of course, for the State to decide. But a model is not lacking: In Kingsley Books, Inc. v. Brown, 354 U.S. 436, we upheld a New York injunctive procedure designed to prevent the sale of obscene books. That procedure postpones any restraint against sale until a judicial determination of obscenity following notice and an adversary hearing. The statute provides for a hearing one day after joinder of issue; the judge must hand down his decision within two days after termination of the hearing. The New York procedure operates without prior submission to a censor, but the chilling effect of a censorship order, even one which requires judicial action for its enforcement, suggests all the more reason for expeditious determination of the question whether a particular film is constitutionally protected.

The requirement of prior submission to a censor sustained in *Times Film* is consistent with our recognition that films differ from other forms of expression. Similarly, we think that the nature of the motion picture industry may suggest different time limits for a judicial determination. It is common knowledge that films are scheduled well before actual exhibition, and the requirement of advance submission in §2 recognizes this. . . . We do not mean to lay down rigid time limits or procedures, but to suggest considerations in drafting legislation to accord with local exhibition practices, and in doing so to avoid the potentially chilling effect of the Maryland statute on protected expression.

Reversed.

Notes and Questions

1. *Film Licensing.* Kingsley International Pictures Corp. v. Regents, 354 U.S. 436 (1957), involved a New York statute that allowed censors to refuse to license any film that contained material that was "obscene, indecent, immoral, inhuman, sacrilegious, or [was] of such a character that its exhibition would tend to corrupt morals or incite to [crime]." The appellant's application for a license to distribute *Lady Chatterley's Lover* was denied on the basis that the film was immoral because it presented "adultery as a desirable, acceptable and proper pattern of behavior." The Court held that the licensing authority had acted improperly: "What New York has done [is] to prevent the exhibition of a motion picture because that picture advocates an idea — that adultery under certain circumstances may be proper behavior. [T]he First Amendment's basic guarantee is of freedom to advocate ideas. . . ." Mr. Justice Douglas concurred: "I can find in the First Amendment no room for any censor whether he is scanning an editorial, reading a news broadcast, editing a novel or a play, or previewing a movie. . . ."

2. *Licensing of Sexually Oriented Businesses.* In FW/PBS, Inc. v. Dallas, 493 U.S. 215 (1990), the Court applied the *Freedman* standards to a municipal ordinance requiring a license for the operation of a sexually oriented business. The Court held that the Dallas licensing scheme did not provide sufficient procedural safeguards. Although there was no majority opinion, a majority agreed that "the first two [*Freedman*] safeguards are essential: the licensor must make the decision whether to issue the license within a specified and reasonable time period during which the status quo is maintained, and there must be the possibility of prompt judicial review in the event that the license is erroneously denied."

3. *Prompt Judicial Review.* Does the term *prompt judicial review* mean that the unsuccessful applicant for an adult business license must be assured a prompt judicial *determination* on the merits of the permit denial, or does it mean only that prompt *access* to judicial review is required? If a statute provides for "prompt review" but the court fails to promptly review, is that sufficient? In City News & Novelty, Inc. v. City of Waukesha, 531 U.S. 278 (2001), although the Court failed to reach the issue on mootness grounds, it suggested that a defendant could not suffer adverse action until judicial action was complete.

4. *Commission to Encourage Morality.* Rhode Island created the Rhode Island Commission to Encourage Morality in Youth and charged it with "[the duty] to educate the public concerning any book, picture, pamphlet, ballad, printed paper or other thing containing obscene, indecent or impure language, or manifestly tending to the corruption of the [youth], and to investigate and recommend the prosecution of all violations of said [sections]." The commission exercised its authority by issuing notices to distributors on official commission stationery, stating that certain designated books or magazines distributed by them had been reviewed by the commission and had been declared by a majority of its members to be objectionable for sale, distribution, or display to youths under 18 years of age. The notice reminded distributors of the commission's obligation to recommend to the attorney general the prosecution of purveyors of obscenity. In

Bantam Books, Inc. v. Sullivan, 372 U.S. 58 (1963), the Court held that the commission's actions were unconstitutional and that a system of informal censorship of this nature was not permitted under the First Amendment.

5. *Newspaper Racks.* A city ordinance permitted newspapers to place coin-operated newspaper-dispensing devices on city sidewalks, but only with the consent of the mayor, who has broad discretion to deny applications (on any "terms and conditions deemed reasonable and necessary by the mayor") but is required to "stat[e] the reasons for such denial." Dispensing device licenses had to be renewed every year. In City of Lakewood v. Plain Dealer Publishing Co., 486 U.S. 750 (1988), the Court struck down the ordinance because it vested too much discretionary licensing authority in governmental officials.

↜ PROBLEM: MORE ON THE INTERNATIONAL TREATY REGULATING THE INTERNET ↝

Does the holding in *Freedman*, and other precedent cited in the Notes above, change your thoughts about whether the treaty can provide for a review board and licensing restrictions on speech? As presently constituted, the Internet contains many movies and other videos (on YouTube, for example). Some of these movies and other videos are arguably "indecent" (e.g., George Carlin's monologue "The Seven Filthy Words") or blasphemous (e.g., George Carlin's monologue "Religion Is Bullshit"). In light of *Freedman*, and other precedent interpreting and applying the First Amendment, can you agree to create such a licensing board? If you can, what kind of content may the board license, and what type of content must be free of licensorial control? Can you accede to the Chinese demands regarding the scope of the board's authority? Could you, perhaps, agree that each country (to the extent that its law permits) can establish its own licensing board and apply whatever rules its domestic law permits? Should you agree to such a provision?

2. *Injunctions*

We have examined prior restraints imposed by statute (or ordinance) and administered by Executive Branch bureaucrats. Prior restraints can also take the form of injunctions. Are injunctions, which are imposed by courts rather than by administrative officials, less objectionable (or more objectionable)?

Near v. State of Minnesota

283 U.S. 697 (1931)

Mr. Chief Justice HUGHES delivered the opinion of the Court.

Chapter 285 of the Session Laws of Minnesota for the year 1925 provides for the abatement, as a public nuisance, of a "malicious, scandalous and defamatory newspaper, magazine or other periodical."

[Under] this statute (section 1, clause (b)), the county attorney of Hennepin County brought this action to enjoin the publication of what was described as a "malicious, scandalous and defamatory newspaper, magazine or other periodical," known as *The Saturday Press*, published by the defendants in the city of Minneapolis. The complaint alleged that the defendants, on September 24, 1927, and on eight subsequent dates in October and November, 1927, published and circulated editions of that periodical which were "largely devoted to malicious, scandalous and defamatory articles." . . .

[T]he articles charged, in substance, that a Jewish gangster was in control of gambling, bootlegging, and racketeering in Minneapolis, and that law enforcing officers and agencies were not energetically performing their duties. Most of the charges were directed against the chief of police; he was charged with gross neglect of duty, illicit relations with gangsters, and with participation in graft. The county attorney was charged with knowing the existing conditions and with failure to take adequate measures to remedy them. The mayor was accused of inefficiency and dereliction. One member of the grand jury was stated to be in sympathy with the gangsters. A special grand jury and a special prosecutor were demanded to deal with the situation in general, and, in particular, to investigate an attempt to assassinate one Guilford, one of the original defendants, who, it appears from the articles, was shot by gangsters after the first issue of the periodical had been published. There is no question but that the articles made serious accusations against the public officers named and others in connection with the prevalence of crimes and the failure to expose and punish them. [The trial court continued the injunction, and the Minnesota courts affirmed.]

[T]he operation and effect of the statute [is] that public authorities may bring the owner or publisher of a newspaper or periodical before a judge upon a charge of conducting a business of publishing scandalous and defamatory matter — in particular that the matter consists of charges against public officers of official dereliction — and, unless the owner or publisher is able and disposed to bring competent evidence to satisfy the judge that the charges are true and are published with good motives and for justifiable ends, his newspaper or periodical is suppressed and further publication is made punishable as a contempt. This is of the essence of censorship.

The question is whether a statute authorizing such proceedings in restraint of publication is consistent with the conception of the liberty of the press as historically conceived and guaranteed. [I]t has been generally, if not universally, considered that it is the chief purpose of the guaranty to prevent previous restraints upon publication. The struggle in England, directed against the legislative power of the licenser, resulted in renunciation of the censorship of the press. The liberty deemed to be established was thus described by Blackstone: "The liberty of the press is indeed essential to the nature of a free state; but this consists in laying no previous restraints upon publications, and not in freedom from censure for criminal matter when published. Every freeman has an undoubted right to lay what sentiments he pleases before the public; to forbid this, is to destroy the freedom of the press; but if he publishes what is improper, mischievous or illegal, he must take the consequence of his own temerity." 4 William Blackstone, Commentaries 151, 152. [A]s Madison said, "[security] of the freedom of the press requires that it should be exempt not only from previous restraint by the Executive, as in Great Britain, but from legislative restraint also." Report on the Virginia Resolutions, *Madison's Works,* vol. IV, p. 543. [For] whatever wrong the appellant has committed or may commit, by his publications, the state appropriately affords both public and private redress by its libel laws. [T]he statute in question does not deal with punishments[,] except in case of contempt for violation of the court's order, but for suppression and injunction — that is, for restraint upon publication.

[T]he protection even as to previous restraint is not absolutely unlimited. But the limitation has been recognized only in exceptional cases. "When a nation is at war many things that might be said in time of peace are such a hindrance to its effort that their utterance will not be endured so long as men fight and that no Court could regard them as protected by any constitutional right." Schenck v. United States, 249 U.S. 47, 52. No one would question but that a government might prevent actual obstruction to its recruiting service or the publication of the sailing dates of transports or the number and location of troops. On similar grounds, the primary requirements of decency may be enforced against obscene publications. The security of the community life may be protected against incitements to acts of violence and the overthrow by force of orderly government. The constitutional guaranty of free speech does not "protect a man from an injunction against uttering words that may have all the effect of force." Schenck v. United States. These limitations are not applicable here. Nor are we now concerned with questions as to the extent of authority to prevent publications in order to protect private rights according to the principles governing the exercise of the jurisdiction of courts of equity.

The exceptional nature of its limitations places in a strong light the general conception that liberty of the press, historically considered and taken up by the Federal Constitution, has meant, principally although not exclusively, immunity from previous restraints or censorship. The conception of the liberty of the press in this country had broadened with the exigencies of the colonial period and with the efforts to secure freedom from oppressive administration. That liberty was especially cherished for the immunity it afforded from previous restraint of the publication of censure of public officers and charges of official misconduct. . . .

"Some degree of abuse is inseparable from the proper use of everything, and in no instance is this more true than in that of the press. It has accordingly been decided by the practice of the States, that it is better to leave a few of its noxious branches to their luxuriant growth, than, by pruning them away, to injure the vigour of those yielding the proper fruits. And can the wisdom of this policy be doubted by any who reflect that to the press alone, chequered as it is with abuses, the world is indebted for all the triumphs which have been gained by reason and humanity over error and oppression; who reflect that to the same beneficent source the United States owe much of the lights which conducted them to the ranks of a free and independent nation, and which have improved their political system into a shape so auspicious to their happiness? Had 'Sedition Acts,' forbidding every publication that might bring the constituted agents into contempt or disrepute, or that might excite the hatred of the people against the authors of unjust or pernicious measures, been uniformly enforced against the press, might not the United States have been languishing at this day under the infirmities of a sickly Confederation? Might they not, possibly, be miserable colonies, graning under a foreign yoke?"

The fact that for approximately one hundred and fifty years there has been almost an entire absence of attempts to impose previous restraints upon publications relating to the malfeasance of public officers is significant of the deep-seated conviction that such restraints would violate constitutional right. Public officers, whose character and conduct remain open to debate and free discussion in the press, find their remedies for false accusations in actions under libel laws providing for redress and punishment, and not in proceedings to restrain the publication of newspapers and periodicals. The general principle that the constitutional guaranty of the liberty of the press gives immunity from previous restraints has been approved in many decisions under the provisions of state constitutions.

The importance of this immunity has not lessened. While reckless assaults upon public men, and efforts to bring obloquy upon those whom are endeavoring faithfully to discharge official duties, exert a baleful influence and deserve the severest condemnation in public opinion, it cannot be said that this abuse is greater, and it is believed to be less, than that which characterized the period in which our institutions took shape. Meanwhile, the administration of government has become more complex, the opportunities for malfeasance and corruption have multiplied, crime has grown to most serious proportions, and the danger of its protection by unfaithful officials and of the impairment of the fundamental security of life and property by criminal alliances and official neglect, emphasizes the primary need of a vigilant and courageous press, especially in great cities. The fact that the liberty of the press may be abused by miscreant purveyors of scandal does not make any the less necessary the immunity of the press from previous restraint in dealing with official misconduct. Subsequent punishment for such abuses as may exist is the appropriate remedy, consistent with constitutional privilege.

In attempted justification of the statute, it is said that it deals not with publication per se, but with the "business" of publishing defamation. If, however, the publisher has a constitutional right to publish, without previous restraint, an edition of his newspaper charging official derelictions, it cannot be denied that he may publish subsequent editions for the same purpose. He does not lose his right by exercising it. If his right exists, it may be exercised in publishing nine editions, as in this case, as well as in one edition. If previous restraint is permissible, it may be imposed at once; indeed, the wrong may be as serious in one publication as in several. Characterizing the publication as a business, and the business as a nuisance, does not permit an invasion of the constitutional immunity against restraint. Similarly, it does not matter that the newspaper or periodical is found to be "largely" or "chiefly" devoted to the publication of such derelictions. If the publisher has a right, without previous restraint, to publish them, his right cannot be deemed to be dependent upon his publishing something else, more or less, with the matter to which objection is made.

Nor can it be said that the constitutional freedom from previous restraint is lost because charges are made of derelictions which constitute crimes. With the multiplying provisions of penal codes, and of municipal charters and ordinances carrying penal sanctions, the conduct of public officers is very largely within the purview of criminal statutes. The freedom of the press from previous restraint has never been regarded as limited to such animadversions as lay outside the range of renal enactments. Historically, there is no such limitation; it is inconsistent with the reason which underlies the privilege, as the privilege so limited would be of slight value for the purposes for which it came to be established.

The statute in question cannot be justified by reason of the fact that the publisher is permitted to show, before injunction issues, that the matter published is true and is published with good motives and for justifiable ends. If such a statute, authorizing suppression and injunction on such a basis, is constitutionally valid, it would be equally permissible for the Legislature to provide that at any time the publisher of any newspaper could be brought before a court, or even an administrative officer (as the constitutional protection may not be regarded as resting on mere procedural details), and required to produce proof of the truth of his publication, or of what he intended to publish and of his motives, or stand enjoined. If this can be done, the Legislature may provide machinery for determining in the complete exercise of its discretion what are justifiable ends and restrain publication accordingly. And it would be but a step to a complete system of censorship. The recognition of authority to impose previous restraint upon publication in order to protect the community against the circulation of charges of misconduct, and especially of official misconduct, necessarily would carry with it the admission of the authority of the censor against which the constitutional barrier was erected. The preliminary freedom, by virtue of the very reason for its existence, does not depend, as this court has said, on proof of truth.

Equally unavailing is the insistence that the statute is designed to prevent the circulation of scandal which tends to disturb the public peace and to provoke assaults and the commission of crime. Charges of reprehensible conduct, and in particular of official malfeasance, unquestionably create a public scandal, but the theory of the constitutional guaranty is that even a more serious public evil would be caused by authority to prevent publication. "To prohibit the intent to excite those unfavorable sentiments against those who administer the Government, is equivalent to a prohibition of the actual excitement of them; and to prohibit the actual excitement of them is equivalent to a prohibition of discussions having that tendency and effect; which, again, is equivalent to a protection of those who administer the Government, if they should at any time deserve the contempt or hatred of the people, against being exposed to it by free animadversions on their characters and conduct." There is nothing new in the fact that charges of reprehensible conduct may create resentment and the disposition to resort to violent means of redress, but this well-understood tendency did not alter the determination to protect the press against censorship and restrain upon publication. As was said in New Yorker Staats-Zeitung v. Nolan, 89 N.J. Eq. 387, 388, 105 A. 72: "If the township may prevent the circulation of a newspaper for no reason other than that some of its inhabitants may violently disagree with it, and resent it circulation by resorting to physical violence, there is no limit to what may be prohibited." The danger of violent reactions becomes greater with effective organization of defiant groups resenting exposure, and, if this consideration warranted legislative interference with the initial freedom of publication, the constitutional protection would be reduced to a mere form of words.

For these reasons we hold the statute, so far as it authorized the proceedings in this action under clause (b) of section 1, to be an infringement of the liberty of the press guaranteed by the Fourteenth Amendment. We should add that this decision rests upon the operation and effect of the statute, without regard to the question of the truth of the charges contained in the particular periodical. The fact that the public officers named in this case, and those associated with the charges of official dereliction, may be deemed to be impeccable, cannot affect the conclusion that the statute imposes an unconstitutional restraint upon publication.

Judgment reversed.

Mr. Justice BUTLER (dissenting).

[D]efendants' regular business was the publication of malicious, scandalous, and defamatory articles concerning the principal public officers, leading newspapers of the city, many private persons, and the Jewish race. It [was their intent] to continue to carry on the business. In every edition slanderous and defamatory matter predominates to the practical exclusion of all else. Many of the statements are so highly improbable as to compel a finding that they are false. The articles themselves show malice.

It is of the greatest importance that the states shall be untrammeled and free to employ all just and appropriate measures to prevent abuses of the liberty of the press.

"[T]he language of [the First] amendment imports no more than that every man shall have a right to speak, write, and print his opinions upon any subject whatsoever, without any prior restraint, so always that he does not injure any other person in his rights, person, property, or reputation; and so always that he does not thereby disturb the public peace, or attempt to subvert the government. It is neither more nor less than an expansion of the great doctrine recently brought into operation in the law of libel, that every man shall be at liberty to publish what is true, with good motives and for justifiable ends. And with this reasonable limitation it is not only right in itself, but it is an inestimable privilege in a free government. Without such a limitation, it might become the scourge of the republic, first denouncing the principles of liberty, and then, by rendering the most virtuous patriots odious through the terrors of the press, introducing despotism in its worst form."

[The] Minnesota statute does not operate as a previous restraint on publication within the proper meaning of that phrase. It does not authorize administrative control in advance such as was formerly exercised by the licensers and censors, but prescribes a remedy to be enforced by a suit in equity. In this case there was previous publication made in the course of the business of regularly producing malicious, scandalous, and defamatory periodicals. The business and publications unquestionably constitute an abuse of the right of free press. The statute denounces the things done as a nuisance on the ground, as stated by the state Supreme Court, that they threaten morals, peace, and good order. There is no question of the power of the state to denounce such transgressions. The restraint authorized is only in respect of continuing to do what has been duly adjudged to constitute a nuisance. . . .

It is well known, as found by the state Supreme Court, that existing libel laws are inadequate effectively to suppress evils resulting from the kind of business and publications that are shown in this case. The doctrine that measures such as the one before us are invalid because they operate as previous restraints to infringe freedom of press exposes the peace and good order of every community and the business and private affairs of every individual to the constant and protracted false and malicious assaults of any insolvent publisher who may have purpose and sufficient capacity to contrive and put into effect a scheme or program for oppression, blackmail or extortion.

The judgment should be affirmed.

Notes and Questions

1. *Help Wanted Advertising.* In Pittsburgh Press Co. v. Pittsburgh Commission on Human Relations, 413 U.S. 376 (1973), the Court upheld an ordinance that prohibited newspapers from carrying "help wanted" advertisements in sex-designated columns except where the employer or advertiser was free to make hiring or employment referral decisions on the basis of sex. The Court concluded that the ads constituted commercial speech and upheld the ordinance.

2. *Remedies for Public Officials?* What remedies (if any) are available to plaintiffs like those in *Near?* How do defamed public officials vindicate their reputations? What happened to the notion that equity will act when a plaintiff's legal remedies are inadequate?

3. *Defamation of Public Figures.* In Tory v. Cochran, 125 S.Ct. 2108 (2005), a former client, Ulysses Tory, made numerous allegations of dishonesty and lack of professionalism against famous lawyer (now deceased) Johnnie Cochran. Cochran gained notoriety as one of O.J. Simpson's defense attorneys in his murder trial. At trial, the evidence shows that Tory claims that Cochran owes him money and that he has written Cochran threatening letters demanding $10 million, has picketed Cochran's office with signs containing insults and obscenities, and has pursued Cochran while chanting similar threats and insults. If the trial court concludes that Tory's claims are without basis (as it did), may it enjoin Tory from engaging in further such conduct? Is injunctive relief consistent with the holding in *Near?* Is your analysis affected by the news of Cochran's death (which, of course, means that Cochran is no longer practicing law)?

∽ PROBLEM: MORE ON THE INTERNATIONAL TREATY REGULATING THE INTERNET ∽

At the convention, some countries (e.g., China) demand the right to seek injunctive relief against "defamatory," "seditious," and "subversive" speech, and they demand that the treaty contain provisions authorizing the courts of each country to grant injunctive relief and providing that the courts of other countries shall give "full faith and credit" to such injunctions. You are concerned because you know that a number of Chinese dissidents live in the United States, and you know that they use the Internet to air their criticisms of the Chinese government (as ex-patriots from other countries air their critiques of their own countries). In addition, you are aware that Google and other U.S. companies do business in China, and therefore are subject to the jurisdiction of Chinese courts. In light of *Near*, what treaty provisions can or should you agree to regarding injunctive relief and the enforceability of injunctions in the United States?

New York Times Company v. United States

403 U.S. 713 (1971)

(The "Pentagon Papers" Case)

PER CURIAM.

[The "Pentagon Papers" case was a consolidation of two separate proceedings. In each, the United States sought to enjoin a newspaper from publishing classified documents involving U.S. participation in the Vietnam War. In both cases the district courts refused to issue injunctions. On appeal, the government prevailed in the Court of Appeals for the Second Circuit (the *New York Times* case) but lost in the District of Columbia (the *Washington Post* case). The cases then went to the U.S. Supreme Court. In his dissent, *infra*, Justice Harlan describes the "frenzied train of events" leading to the Court's decision.]

We granted certiorari in these cases in which the United States seeks to enjoin the *New York Times* and the *Washington Post* from publishing the contents of a classified study entitled "History of U.S. Decision-Making Process on Viet Nam Policy."

"Any system of prior restraints of expression comes to this Court bearing a heavy presumption against its constitutional validity." Bantam Books, Inc. v. Sullivan, 372 U.S. 58, 70 (1963). The Government "thus carries a heavy burden of showing justification for the imposition of such a restraint." The District Court for the Southern District of New York in the *New York Times* case, and the District Court for the District of Columbia and the Court of Appeals for the District of Columbia Circuit in the *Washington Post* case held that the Government had not met that burden. We agree.

The judgment of the Court of Appeals for the District of Columbia Circuit is therefore affirmed. The order of the Court of Appeals for the Second Circuit is reversed, and the case is remanded with directions to enter a judgment affirming the judgment of the District Court for the Southern District of New York. The stays entered June 25, 1971, by the Court are vacated. The judgments shall issue forthwith.

So ordered.

Mr. Justice BLACK, with whom Mr. Justice DOUGLAS joins, concurring.

[T]he Government's case against the *Washington Post* should have been dismissed [and] the injunction [vacated] without oral argument. [E]very moment's continuance of the injunctions against these newspapers amounts to a flagrant, indefensible, and continuing violation of the First Amendment. [I]t is unfortunate that some of my Brethren are apparently willing to hold that the publication of news may sometimes be enjoined. . . . Both the history and language of the First Amendment support the view that the press must be left free to publish news, whatever the source, without censorship, injunctions, or prior restraints. [P]aramount among the responsibilities of a free press is the duty to prevent any part of the government from deceiving the people and sending them off to distant lands to die of foreign fevers and foreign shot and shell. In my view, far from deserving condemnation for their courageous reporting, the *New York Times,* the *Washington Post,* and other newspapers should be commended for serving the purpose that the Founding Fathers saw so clearly. In revealing the workings of government that led to the Vietnam war, the newspapers nobly did precisely that which the Founders hoped and trusted they would do.

[W]e are asked to hold that despite the First Amendment's emphatic command, the Executive Branch, the Congress, and the Judiciary can make laws enjoining publication of current news and abridging freedom of the press in the name of "national security." [The] word "security" is a broad, vague generality whose contours should not be invoked to abrogate the fundamental law embodied in the First Amendment. The guarding of military and diplomatic secrets at the expense of informed representative government provides no real security for our Republic. . . .

Mr. Justice DOUGLAS, with whom Mr. Justice BLACK joins, concurring.

[T]he First Amendment [leaves] no room for governmental restraint on the press. . . . These disclosures may have a serious impact. But that is no basis for sanctioning a previous restraint on the press. . . . The Government says that it has inherent powers to go into court and obtain an injunction to protect the national interest, which in this case is alleged to be national security. . . . Near v. Minnesota repudiated that expansive doctrine in no uncertain terms. . . . It is common knowledge that the First Amendment was adopted against the widespread use of the common law of seditious libel to punish the dissemination of material that is embarrassing to the powers-that-be. . . . A debate of large proportions goes on in the Nation over our posture in Vietnam. That debate antedated the disclosure of the contents of the present documents. The latter are highly relevant to the debate in progress. . . . Secrecy in government is fundamentally anti-democratic, perpetuating bureaucratic errors. Open debate and discussion of public issues are vital to our national health. On public questions there should be "uninhibited, robust, and wide-open" debate. New York Times Co. v. Sullivan, 376 U.S. 254.

I would affirm the judgment of the Court of Appeals in the *Post* case, vacate the stay of the Court of Appeals in the *Times* case and direct that it affirm the District Court. . . . The stays in these cases that have been in effect for more than a week constitute a flouting of the principles of the First Amendment as interpreted in *Near*.

Mr. Justice BRENNAN, concurring.

[T]he First Amendment stands as an absolute bar to the imposition of judicial restraints in circumstances of the kind presented by these cases. . . . The error that has pervaded these cases from the outset was the granting of any injunctive relief whatsoever, interim or otherwise. The entire thrust of the Government's claim throughout these cases has been that publication of the material sought to be enjoined "could," or "might," or "may" prejudice the national interest in various ways. But the First Amendment tolerates absolutely no prior judicial restraints of the press predicated upon surmise or conjecture that untoward consequences may result. Our cases [have] indicated that there is a single, extremely narrow class of cases in which the First Amendment's ban on prior judicial restraint may be overridden. [S]uch cases may arise only when the Nation "is at war," during which times "[n]o one would question but that a government might prevent actual obstruction to its recruiting service or the publication of the sailing dates of transports or the number and location of troops." Even if the present world situation were assumed to be tantamount to a time of war, or if the power of presently available armaments would justify even in peacetime the suppression of information that would set in motion a nuclear holocaust, in neither of these actions has the Government presented or even alleged that publication of items from or based upon the material at issue would cause the happening of an event of that nature. [O]nly governmental allegation and proof that publication must inevitably, directly, and immediately cause the occurrence of an event kindred to imperiling the safety of a transport already at sea can support even the issuance of an interim restraining order. . . . Unless and until the Government has clearly made out its case, the First Amendment commands that no injunction may issue.

Mr. Justice STEWART, with whom Mr. Justice WHITE joins, concurring.

[T]he only effective restraint upon executive policy and power in the areas of national defense and international affairs may lie in an enlightened citizenry — in an informed and critical public opinion which alone can here protect the values of democratic government. For this reason, it is perhaps here that a press that is alert, aware, and free most vitally serves the basic purpose of the First Amendment. . . . Yet it is elementary that the successful conduct of international diplomacy and the maintenance of an effective national defense require both confidentiality and secrecy. Other nations can hardly deal with this Nation in an atmosphere of mutual trust unless they can be assured that their confidences will be kept. And within our own executive departments, the development of considered and intelligent international policies would be impossible if those charged with their formulation could not communicate with each other freely, frankly, and in confidence. . . .

[If] the Constitution gives the Executive a large degree of unshared power in the conduct of foreign affairs and the maintenance of our national defense, then under the Constitution the Executive must have the largely unshared duty to determine and preserve the degree of internal security necessary to exercise that power successfully. . . . This is not to say that Congress and the courts have no role to play. Undoubtedly Congress has the power to enact specific and appropriate criminal laws to protect government property and preserve government secrets. Congress has passed such laws. [I]f a criminal prosecution is instituted, it will be the responsibility of the courts to decide the applicability of the criminal law under which the charge is brought. . . .

But in the cases before us we are asked neither to construe specific regulations nor to apply specific laws. We are asked, instead, to perform a function that the Constitution gave to the Executive, not the Judiciary. We are asked, quite simply, to prevent the publication by two newspapers of material that the Executive Branch insists should not, in the national interest, be published. I am convinced that the Executive is correct with respect to some of the documents involved. But I cannot say that disclosure of any of them will surely result in direct, immediate, and irreparable damage to our Nation or its people. That being so, there can under the First Amendment be but one judicial resolution of the issues before us. I join the judgments of the Court.

Mr. Justice WHITE, with whom Mr. Justice STEWART joins, concurring.

I concur in today's judgments [only] because of the concededly extraordinary protection against prior restraints enjoyed by the press under our constitutional system. [T]he United States has not satisfied the very heavy burden that it must meet to warrant an injunction against publication in these cases, at least in the absence of express and appropriately limited congressional authorization for prior restraints in circumstances such as these.

[I]n the absence of legislation by Congress[,] I am quite unable to agree that the inherent powers of the Executive and the courts reach so far as to authorize remedies having such sweeping potential for inhibiting publications by the press. Much of the difficulty inheres in the "grave and irreparable danger" standard suggested by the United States. If the United States were to have judgment under such a standard in these cases, our decision would be of little guidance to other courts in other cases, for the material at issue here would not be available from the Court's opinion or from public records, nor would it be published by the press. . . .

[Congress] has addressed itself to the problems of protecting the security of the country and the national defense from unauthorized disclosure of potentially damaging information. It has not, however, authorized the injunctive remedy against threatened publication. . . . I am not, of course, saying that either of these newspapers has yet committed a crime or that either would commit a crime if it published all the material now in its possession. That matter must await resolution in the context of a criminal proceeding if one is instituted. . . .

Mr. Justice MARSHALL, concurring.

[It] is a traditional axiom of equity that a court of equity will not do a useless thing just as it is a traditional axiom that equity will not enjoin the commission of a crime. Here there has been no attempt to make such a showing. The Solicitor General does not even mention in his brief whether the Government considers that there is probable cause to believe a crime has been committed or whether there is a conspiracy to commit future crimes. . . .

Mr. Chief Justice BURGER, dissenting.

[T]he Times has had unauthorized possession of the documents for three to four months, during which it has had its expert analysts studying them, presumably digesting them and preparing the material for publication. During all of this time, the Times, presumably in its capacity as trustee of the public's "right to know," has held up publication for purposes it considered proper and thus public knowledge was delayed. . . . After these months of deferral, the alleged "right to know" has somehow and suddenly become a right that must be vindicated instanter. . . . The consequence of all this melancholy series of events is that we literally do not know what we are acting on. [W]e have been forced to deal with litigation concerning rights of great magnitude without an adequate record, and surely without time for adequate treatment. . . . I agree generally with Mr. Justice Harlan and Mr. Justice Blackmun but I am not prepared to reach the merits. . . . We all crave speedier judicial processes but when judges are pressured as in these cases the result is a parody of the judicial function.

Mr. Justice HARLAN, with whom THE CHIEF JUSTICE and Mr. Justice BLACKMUN join, dissenting.

Both the Court of Appeals for the Second Circuit and the Court of Appeals for the District of Columbia Circuit rendered judgment on June 23. The New York Times' petition for certiorari, its motion for accelerated consideration thereof, and its application for interim relief were filed in this Court on June 24 at about 11 a.m. The application of the United States for interim relief in the Post case was also filed here on June 24 at about 7:15 p.m. This Court's order setting a hearing before us on June 26 at 11 a.m., a course which I joined only to avoid the possibility of even more peremptory action by the Court, was issued less than 24 hours before. The record in the *Post* case was filed with the Clerk shortly before 1 p.m. on June 25; the record in the *Times* case did not arrive until 7 or 8 o'clock that same night. The briefs of the parties were received less than two hours before argument on June 26.

This frenzied train of events took place in the name of the presumption against prior restraints created by the First Amendment. Due regard for the extraordinarily important and difficult questions involved in these litigations should have led the Court to shun such a precipitate timetable. . . .

Forced as I am to reach the merits of these cases, I dissent. . . . I agree that, in performance of its duty to protect the values of the First Amendment against political pressures, the judiciary must review the initial Executive determination to the point of satisfying itself that the subject matter of the dispute does lie within the proper compass of the President's foreign relations power. . . . Moreover, the judiciary may properly insist that the determination that disclosure of the subject matter would irreparably impair the national security be made by the head of the Executive Department concerned [after] actual personal consideration by that officer. . . . But in my judgment the judiciary may not properly go beyond these two inquiries and redetermine for itself the probable impact of disclosure on the national security. . . . Accordingly, I would vacate the judgment of the Court of Appeals for the District of Columbia Circuit on this ground and remand the case for further proceedings in the District Court. . . .

Mr. Justice BLACKMUN, dissenting.

The First Amendment [is] only one part of an entire Constitution. Article II of the great document vests in the Executive Branch primary power over the conduct of foreign affairs and places in that branch the responsibility for the Nation's safety. Each provision of the Constitution is important, and I cannot subscribe to a doctrine of unlimited absolutism for the First Amendment at the cost of downgrading other provisions. . . . What is needed here is a weighing, upon properly developed standards, of the broad right of the press to print and of the very narrow right of the Government to prevent. Such standards are not yet developed. [E]ven the newspapers concede that there are situations where restraint is in order and is constitutional. Mr. Justice Holmes gave us a suggestion when he said in *Schenck*, "It is a question of proximity and degree. When a nation is at war many things that might be said in time of peace are such a hindrance to its effort that their utterance will not be endured so long as men fight and that no Court could regard them as protected by any constitutional right." [I] would remand these cases to be developed expeditiously, of course, but on a schedule permitting the orderly presentation of evidence from both sides, with the use of discovery, if necessary[,] and with the preparation of briefs, oral argument, and court opinions of a quality better than has been seen to this point. [T]hese cases and the issues involved and the courts, including this one, deserve better than has been produced thus far.

Note: The Progressive *Case and the H-Bomb Secret*

United States v. The Progressive, Inc., 467 F. Supp. 990 (W.D. Wis. 1979), involved a federal law, 42 U.S.C. §§2274(b) and 2280, that authorized the government to seek relief against anyone who attempted to disclose restricted data "with reason to believe such data will be utilized to injure the United States or to secure an advantage to any foreign [nation]." *The Progressive* magazine wanted to publish an article on how to build an H-bomb. When the U.S. government sought injunctive relief to prevent publication, the magazine defended on the basis that its goal was to demonstrate laxness in the government's security system. It would do so by showing that it compiled the article based on publicly available information. The government nonetheless sought to prevent disclosure, asserting that the public would be harmed because others (including medium-sized nations) might not have the capability to build thermonuclear weapons without reading the article. In the case, although the trial court initially entered the injunction, it lifted the injunction when it became clear that another magazine had published similar information.

∾ PROBLEMS ∾

1. *More on* The Progressive *Case.* As noted, in United States v. The Progressive, the trial court lifted its injunction when another magazine published similar information. Did the court act properly in issuing the injunction in the first place? Are the facts of this case sufficiently distinguishable from the "Pentagon Papers" case as to make injunctive relief appropriate? Why or why not?

2. *NSL Gag Orders.* Under federal law, the Federal Bureau of Investigation (FBI) can issue "national security letters" (NSLs) to Internet service providers (ISPs) seeking information about customers' Internet usage. *See* 18 U.S.C. §§2709 and 3511. The law also contains a provision allowing the government to impose a "gag order" that prohibits the ISP from disclosing the existence of the NSL. Such gag orders can be imposed only when a senior FBI official certifies that, absent the gag order, "there may result a danger to the national security of the United States, interference with a criminal, counterterrorism, or counterintelligence investigation, interference with diplomatic relations, or danger to the physical safety of any person." An ISP, against which a gag order has been obtained, wishes to disclose to its customers the fact that the FBI has obtained access to customer information. Are the gag orders permissible prior restraints? Should any sort of judicial review or intervention be mandated as a condition for sustaining a gag order? *See* John Doe, Inc. v. Mukasey, 549 F.3d 861 (2d Cir. 2008).

3. *More on the International Treaty Regulating the Internet.* After reading the "Pentagon Papers" case, have your views on the inclusion of language regarding injunctions, and the enforceability of foreign injunctions, changed? What language would you be inclined to agree to regarding those issues?

Madsen v. Women's Health Center, Inc.
512 U.S. 753 (1994)

Chief Justice Rehnquist delivered the opinion of the Court.

Petitioners challenge the constitutionality of an injunction entered by a Florida state court which prohibits antiabortion protestors from demonstrating in certain places and in various ways outside of a health clinic that performs abortions. We hold that the establishment of a 36-foot buffer zone on a public street from which demonstrators are excluded passes muster under the First Amendment, but that several other provisions of the injunction do not.

I

Respondents operate abortion clinics throughout central Florida. Petitioners and other groups and individuals are engaged in activities near the site of one such clinic in Melbourne, Florida. They picketed and demonstrated where the public street gives access to the clinic. In September 1992, a Florida state court permanently enjoined petitioners from blocking or interfering with public access to the clinic, and from physically abusing persons entering or leaving the clinic. Six months later, respondents sought to broaden the injunction, complaining that access to the clinic was still impeded by petitioners' activities and that such activities had also discouraged some potential patients from entering the clinic, and had deleterious physical effects on others. The trial court thereupon issued a broader injunction, which is challenged here. . . .

II

We begin by addressing petitioners' contention that the state court's order, because it is an injunction that restricts only the speech of antiabortion protesters, is necessarily content or viewpoint based. Accordingly, they argue, we should examine the entire injunction under the strictest standard of scrutiny. We disagree. To accept petitioners' claim would be to classify virtually every injunction as content or viewpoint based. An injunction, by its very nature, applies only to a particular group (or individuals) and regulates the activities, and perhaps the speech, of that group. It does so, however, because of the group's past actions in the context of a specific dispute between real parties. The parties seeking the injunction assert a violation of their rights; the court hearing the action is charged with fashioning a remedy for a specific deprivation, not with the drafting of a statute addressed to the general public.

The fact that the injunction in the present case did not prohibit activities of those demonstrating in favor of abortion is justly attributable to the lack of any similar demonstrations by those in favor of abortion, and of any consequent request that their demonstrations be regulated by injunction. There is no suggestion in this record that Florida law would not equally restrain similar conduct directed at a target having nothing to do with abortion; none of the restrictions imposed by the court were directed at the contents of petitioner's message.

Our principal inquiry in determining content neutrality is whether the government has adopted a regulation of speech "without reference to the content of the regulated speech." Ward v. Rock Against Racism, 491 U.S. 781, 791 (1989); R.A.V. v. St. Paul, 505 U.S. 377, 386 (1992) ("The government may not regulate [speech] based on hostility — or favoritism — towards the underlying message expressed"). We thus look to the government's purpose as the threshold consideration. Here, the state court imposed restrictions on petitioners incidental to their antiabortion message because they repeatedly violated the court's original order. That petitioners all share the same viewpoint regarding abortion does not in itself demonstrate that some invidious content- or viewpoint-based purpose motivated the issuance of the order. It suggests only that those in the group whose conduct violated the court's order happen to share the same opinion regarding abortions being performed at the clinic. In short, the fact that the injunction covered people with a particular viewpoint does not itself render the injunction content or viewpoint based. Accordingly, the injunction issued in this case does not demand [a] level of heightened [scrutiny].

III

If this were a content-neutral, generally applicable statute, instead of an injunctive order, its constitutionality would be assessed under the standard set forth in Ward v. Rock Against Racism, *supra*, 491 U.S., at 791, and similar cases. Given that the forum around the clinic is a traditional public forum, we would determine whether the time, place, and manner regulations were "narrowly tailored to serve a significant governmental interest." *Ward, supra*, 491 U.S., at 791.

There are obvious differences, however, between an injunction and a generally applicable ordinance. Ordinances represent a legislative choice regarding the promotion of particular societal interests. Injunctions, by contrast, are remedies imposed for violations (or threatened violations) of a legislative or judicial decree. Injunctions also carry greater risks of censorship and discriminatory application than do general ordinances. . . .

We believe that these differences require a somewhat more stringent application of general First Amendment principles in this context. In past cases evaluating injunctions restricting speech, we have relied upon such general principles while also seeking to ensure that the injunction was no broader than necessary to achieve its desired goals. Our close attention to the fit between the objectives of an injunction and the restrictions it imposes on speech is consistent with the general rule, quite apart from First Amendment considerations, "that injunctive relief should be no more burdensome to the defendants than necessary to provide complete relief to the plaintiffs." Califano v. Yamasaki, 442 U.S. 682 (1979). Accordingly, when evaluating a content-neutral injunction, we think that our standard time, place, and manner analysis is not sufficiently rigorous. We must ask instead whether the challenged provisions of the injunction burden no more speech than necessary to serve a significant government interest. . . .

A

We begin with the 36-foot buffer zone. The state court prohibited petitioners from "congregating, picketing, patrolling, demonstrating or entering" any portion of the public right-of-way or private property within 36 feet of the property line of the clinic as a way of ensuring access to the clinic. This speech-free buffer zone requires that petitioners move to the other side of Dixie Way and away from the driveway of the clinic, where the state court found that they repeatedly had interfered with the free access of patients and staff. The buffer zone also applies to private property to the north and west of the clinic property. We examine each portion of the buffer zone separately.

We have noted a distinction between the type of focused picketing banned from the buffer zone and the type of generally disseminated communication that cannot be completely banned in public places, such as handbilling and solicitation. Here the picketing is directed primarily at patients and staff of the clinic.

The 36-foot buffer zone protecting the entrances to the clinic and the parking lot is a means of protecting unfettered ingress to and egress from the clinic, and ensuring that petitioners do not block traffic on Dixie Way. The state court seems to have had few other options to protect access given the narrow confines around the clinic. . . . Dixie Way is only 21 feet wide in the area of the clinic. [A]llowing the petitioners to remain on the clinic's sidewalk and driveway was not a viable option in view of the failure of the first injunction to protect access. And allowing the petitioners to stand in the middle of Dixie Way would obviously block vehicular traffic.

The need for a complete buffer zone near the clinic entrances and driveway may be debatable, but some deference must be given to the state court's familiarity with the facts and the background of the dispute between the parties even under our heightened review. Moreover, one of petitioners' witnesses during the evidentiary hearing before the state court conceded that the buffer zone was narrow enough to place petitioners at a distance of no greater than 10 to 12 feet from cars approaching and leaving the clinic. Protesters standing across the narrow street from the clinic can still be seen and heard from the clinic parking lots. We also bear in mind the fact that the state court originally issued a much narrower injunction, providing no buffer zone, and that this order did not succeed in protecting access to the clinic. The failure of the first order to accomplish its purpose may be taken into consideration in evaluating the constitutionality of the broader order. On balance, we hold that the 36-foot buffer zone around the clinic entrances and driveway burdens no more speech than necessary to accomplish the governmental interest at stake. . . .

The inclusion of private property on the back and side of the clinic in the 36-foot buffer zone raises different concerns. The accepted purpose of the buffer zone is to protect access to the clinic and to facilitate the orderly flow of traffic on Dixie Way. Patients and staff wishing to reach the clinic do not have to cross the private property abutting the clinic property on the north and west, and nothing in the record indicates that petitioners' activities on the private property have obstructed access to the clinic. Nor was evidence presented that protestors located on the private property blocked vehicular traffic on Dixie Way. Absent evidence that petitioners standing on the private property have obstructed access to the clinic, blocked vehicular traffic, or otherwise unlawfully interfered with the clinic's operation, this portion of the buffer zone fails to serve the significant government interests relied on by the Florida Supreme Court. We hold that on the record before us the 36-foot buffer zone as applied to the private property to the north and west of the clinic burdens more speech than necessary to protect access to the clinic.

B

In response to high noise levels outside the clinic, the state court restrained the petitioners from "singing, chanting, whistling, shouting, yelling, use of bullhorns, auto horns, sound amplification equipment or other sounds or images observable to or within earshot of the patients inside the [c]linic" during the hours of 7:30 a.m. through noon on Mondays through Saturdays. We must, of course, take account of the place to which the regulations apply in determining whether these restrictions burden more speech than necessary. We have upheld similar noise restrictions in the past, and as we noted in upholding a local noise ordinance around public schools, "the nature of a place, 'the pattern of its normal activities, dictate the kinds of regulations [that] are reasonable.'" Grayned v. City of Rockford, 408 U.S. 104, 116 (1972). Noise control is particularly important around hospitals and medical facilities during surgery and recovery periods. We hold that the limited noise restrictions imposed by the state court order burden no more speech than necessary to ensure the health and well-being of the patients at the clinic. The First Amendment does not demand that patients at a medical facility undertake Herculean efforts to escape the cacophony of political protests. . . .

C

The same, however, cannot be said for the "images observable" provision of the state court's order. Clearly, threats to patients or their families, however communicated, are proscribable under the First Amendment. But rather than prohibiting the display of signs that could be interpreted as threats or veiled threats, the state court issued a blanket ban on all "images observable." This broad prohibition on all "images observable" burdens more speech than necessary to achieve the purpose of limiting threats to clinic patients or their families. Similarly, if the blanket ban on "images observable" was intended to reduce the level of anxiety and hypertension suffered by the patients inside the clinic, it would still fail. The only plausible reason a patient would be bothered by "images observable" inside the clinic would be if the patient found the expression contained in such images disagreeable. But it is much easier for the clinic to pull its curtains than for a patient to stop up her ears, and no more is required to avoid seeing placards through the windows of the clinic. This provision of the injunction violates the First Amendment.

D

The state court ordered that petitioners refrain from physically approaching any person seeking services of the clinic "unless such person indicates a desire to communicate" in an area within 300 feet of the clinic. The state court was attempting to prevent clinic patients and staff from being "stalked" or "shadowed" by the petitioners as they approached the clinic. . . . But it is difficult, indeed, to justify a prohibition on all uninvited approaches of persons seeking the services of the clinic, regardless of how peaceful the contact may be, without burdening more speech than necessary to prevent intimidation and to ensure access to the clinic. Absent evidence that the protesters' speech is independently proscribable (i.e., "fighting words" or threats), or is so infused with violence as to be indistinguishable from a threat of physical harm, this provision cannot stand. "As a general matter, [in] public debate our own citizens must tolerate insulting, and even outrageous, speech in order to provide adequate breathing space to the freedoms protected by the First Amendment." Boos v. Barry, 485 U.S., at 322. The "consent" requirement alone invalidates this provision; it burdens more speech than is necessary to prevent intimidation and to ensure access to the clinic.

E

The final substantive regulation challenged by petitioners relates to a prohibition against picketing, demonstrating, or using sound amplification equipment within 300 feet of the residences of clinic staff. The prohibition also covers impeding access to streets that provide the sole access to streets on which those residences are located. The same analysis applies to the use of sound amplification equipment here as that discussed above: the government may simply demand that petitioners turn down the volume if the protests overwhelm the neighborhood.

As for the picketing, our prior decision upholding a law banning targeted residential picketing remarked on the unique nature of the home, as "'the last citadel of the tired, the weary, and the sick.'" *Frisby*, 487 U.S., at 484. "'[T]he State's interest in protecting the well-being, tranquility, and privacy of the home is certainly of the highest order in a free and civilized society.'"

But the 300-foot zone around the residences in this case is much larger than the zone provided for in the ordinance which we approved in *Frisby*. The ordinance at issue there made it "unlawful for any person to engage in picketing before or about the residence or dwelling of any individual." The prohibition was limited to "focused picketing taking place solely in front of a particular residence." By contrast, the 300-foot zone would ban "[g]eneral marching through residential neighborhoods, or even walking a route in front of an entire block of houses." The record before us does not contain sufficient justification for this broad a ban on picketing; it appears that a limitation on the time, duration of picketing, and number of pickets outside a smaller zone could have accomplished the desired result. . . .

V

In sum, we uphold the noise restrictions and the 36-foot buffer zone around the clinic entrances and driveway because they burden no more speech than necessary to eliminate the unlawful conduct targeted by the state court's injunction. We strike down as unconstitutional the 36-foot buffer zone as applied to the private property to the north and west of the clinic, the "images observable" provision, the 300-foot no-approach zone around the clinic, and the 300-foot buffer zone around the residences, because these provisions sweep more broadly than necessary to accomplish the permissible goals of the injunction. Accordingly, the judgment of the Florida Supreme Court is

Affirmed in part, and reversed in part.

Justice STEVENS, concurring in part and dissenting in part.

[I]njunctive relief should be judged by a more lenient standard than legislation. As the Court notes, legislation is imposed on an entire community, regardless of individual culpability. By contrast, injunctions apply solely to an individual or a limited group of individuals who, by engaging in illegal conduct, have been judicially deprived of some liberty — the normal consequence of illegal activity. Given this distinction, a statute prohibiting demonstrations within 36 feet of an abortion clinic would probably violate the First Amendment, but an injunction directed at a limited group of persons who have engaged in unlawful conduct in a similar zone might well be constitutional.

The standard governing injunctions has two obvious dimensions. On the one hand, the injunction should be no more burdensome than necessary to provide complete relief. In a First Amendment context, as in any other, the propriety of the remedy depends almost entirely on the character of the violation and the likelihood of its recurrence. . . . On the other hand, even when an injunction impinges on constitutional rights, more than "a simple proscription against the precise conduct previously pursued" may be required; the remedy must include appropriate restraints on "future activities both to avoid a recurrence of the violation and to eliminate its consequences." "[T]he judicial remedy for a proven violation of law will often include commands that the law does not impose on the community at large." Teachers v. Hudson, 475 U.S. 292, 309-310, n.22 (1986). [R]epeated violations may justify sanctions that might be invalid if applied to a first offender or if enacted by the legislature. . . . In this case, the trial judge heard three days of testimony and found that petitioners not only had engaged in tortious conduct, but also had repeatedly violated an earlier injunction. The injunction is thus twice removed from a legislative proscription applicable to the general public and should be judged by a standard that gives appropriate deference to the judge's unique familiarity with the facts. . . .

Justice SCALIA, with whom Justice KENNEDY and Justice THOMAS join, concurring in the judgment in part and dissenting in part.

[A] restriction upon speech imposed by injunction (whether nominally content based or nominally content neutral) is at least as deserving of strict scrutiny as a statutory, content-based restriction. . . . That is so for several reasons: The danger of content-based statutory restrictions upon speech is that they may be designed and used precisely to suppress the ideas in question rather than to achieve any other proper governmental aim. But that same danger exists with injunctions. [A] speech-restricting injunction [lends] itself just as readily to the targeted suppression of particular ideas. [T]argeting of one or the other side of an ideological dispute cannot readily be achieved in speech-restricting general legislation except by making content the basis of the restriction; it is achieved in speech-restricting injunctions almost invariably. [The injunction in this case] was sought against a single-issue advocacy group by persons and organizations with a business or social interest in suppressing that group's point of view.

The second reason speech-restricting injunctions are at least as deserving of strict scrutiny is obvious enough: they are the product of individual judges rather than of legislatures — and often of judges who have been chagrined by prior disobedience of their orders. The right to free speech should not lightly be placed within the control of a single man or woman. And the third reason is that the injunction is a much more powerful weapon than a statute, and so should be subjected to greater safeguards. [W]hen injunctions are enforced through contempt proceedings, only the defense of factual innocence is available. The collateral bar rule . . . eliminates the defense that the injunction itself was unconstitutional. Thus, persons subject to a speech-restricting injunction who have not the money or not the time to lodge an immediate appeal face a Hobson's choice: they must remain silent, since if they speak their First Amendment rights are no defense in subsequent contempt proceedings. This is good reason to require the strictest standard for issuance of such orders. . . .

Finally, [the] injunction in the present case was content based (indeed, viewpoint based) to boot. The Court claims that it was directed, not at those who spoke certain things (anti-abortion sentiments), but at those who did certain things (violated the earlier injunction). If that were true, then the injunction's residual coverage of "all persons acting in concert or participation with [the named individuals and organizations], or on their behalf" would not include those who merely entertained the same beliefs and wished to express the same views as the named defendants. [A]ll those who wish to express the same views as the named defendants are deemed to be "acting in concert or participation." . . .

[A]n injunction against speech is the very prototype of the greatest threat to First Amendment values, the prior restraint. [We] have said that a "prior restraint on expression comes to this Court with a 'heavy presumption' against its constitutional validity," and have repeatedly struck down speech-restricting injunctions. . . .

∾ PROBLEM: PROTESTS AT MILITARY FUNERALS ∾

Would it make a difference if the *Madsen* ban had been imposed by statute rather than by injunction? The Reverend Fred Phelps and members of the Westboro Baptist Church of Topeka, Kansas, believe that the deaths of military soldiers in Iraq are a "sign" of God's wrath for America's tolerance of homosexuality. As a result, Phelps and members of his church have been traveling around the country protesting at military funerals. In response to protests in the state, the Kentucky legislature enacts the following statute on interference with funerals:

A person is guilty of interference with a funeral when he or she at any time on any day:
    1. Blocks, impedes, inhibits, or in any other manner obstructs or interferes with access into or from any building or parking lot of a building in which a funeral, wake, memorial service, or burial is being conducted, or any burial plot or the parking lot of the cemetery in which a funeral, wake, memorial service, or burial is being conducted;
    2. Congregates, pickets, patrols, demonstrates, or enters on that portion of a public right-of-way or private property that is within three hundred (300) feet of an event specified in paragraph (1 of this subsection); or
    3. Without authorization from the family of the deceased or person conducting the service, during a funeral, wake, memorial service, or burial:

A. Sings, chants, whistles, shouts, yells, or uses a bullhorn, auto horn, sound amplification equipment, or other sounds or images observable to or within earshot of participants in the funeral, wake, memorial service, or burial; or
B. Distributes literature or any other item.
Interference with a funeral is a Class B misdemeanor.

In support of the legislation, Kentucky legislators made statements to the effect
that "people should be allowed to attend funerals without outside stress from protesters" and "virtually every civilized society today holds sacred the right to peacefully bury their dead." Is this statute (or parts thereof) any more constitutional
than the injunctive ban imposed in *Madsen*?

F. THE PRESS

In England before the modern era, the government tried to control the press by
imposing licensing restrictions and by using seditious libel to criminally prosecute those who criticized the government. In the American colonies, although
licensing schemes were rare, there were prosecutions for seditious libel. *See*
Leonard W. Levy, *Legacy of Suppression* 8-17 (Belknap 1960). The Framers
were aware of this history when they included press protections in the First
Amendment.
    Despite the First Amendment, press suppression was commonplace in the
postcolonial era. Early in the twentieth century, those who expressed opposition
to American participation in World War I or advocated Communism were routinely prosecuted under federal espionage and state sedition laws. This was possible because the press clause was not incorporated into the Fourteenth
Amendment and imposed on the states until 1931.

1. Does the Constitution Grant the Press a Privileged Position?

Some have argued that the press clause provides the press with special privileges
different from those granted to the general public under the free speech clause.
Justice Powell stated in a concurring opinion in Branzburg v. Hayes, 408 U.S. 665
(1972): "The press has a preferred position in our constitutional scheme, not to
enable it to make money, not to set newsmen apart as a favored class, but to bring
fulfillment to the public's right to know. The right to know is crucial to the governing powers of the people. . . . Knowledge is essential to informed decisions."
Justice Stewart agreed: "[T]he Free Press Clause extends protection to an institution. The publishing business is, in short, the only organized private business that
is given explicit constitutional protection. . . . If the Free Press guarantee meant
no more than freedom of expression, it would be a constitutional redundancy."
Potter Stewart, *Or of the Press,* 26 Hastings L.J. 631 (1975).
    Others believe that the press receives no special protection under the press
clause. In First National Bank of Boston v. Bellotti, 435 U.S. 765 (1978), Chief

Justice Burger stated: "[The] history of the [Press] Clause does not suggest that the authors contemplated a "special" or "institutional" privilege. . . . The Speech Clause standing alone [makes] no fundamental distinction between expression and dissemination. The liberty encompassed by the Press Clause, although complementary to and a natural extension of Speech Clause liberty, merited special mention simply because it had been more often the object of official restraints. Soon after the invention of the printing press, English and continental monarchs, fearful of the power implicit in its use and the threat to Establishment thought and order — political and religious — devised restraints, such as licensing, censors, [lists of] of prohibited books, and prosecutions for seditious libel, which generally were unknown in the pre-printing press era. . . ."

Note and Question: Is It Possible to Define "the Press"?

In recent years, new types of media have emerged, including (but not limited to) blogs and listserves. In addition, entirely online newspapers have emerged in certain locales. Indeed, because of economic challenges, some traditional newspapers (e.g., the *Seattle Post-Intelligencer*) have shifted from being produced as print media to being produced as digital media. Do these new forms of publication require us to alter our definition of "the press"? For example, should someone who publishes a blog on political and social issues be regarded as a member of the press? For that matter, should online newspapers be treated similarly to newspapers that are published in print form?

2. Does the Press Have Special Immunities?

Some have argued that the press is entitled to special immunities, including the right to shield their sources and their notes from disclosure in criminal proceedings.

Branzburg v. Hayes
408 U.S. 665 (1972)

Opinion of the Court by Mr. Justice WHITE, announced by THE CHIEF JUSTICE.

[The] issue before us is the obligation of reporters to respond to grand jury subpoenas as other citizens do and to answer questions relevant to an investigation into the commission of crime. Citizens generally are not constitutionally immune from grand jury subpoenas; and neither the First Amendment nor any other constitutional provision protects the average citizen from disclosing to a grand jury information that he has received in confidence. The claim is, however, that reporters are exempt from these obligations because if forced to respond to subpoenas and identify their sources or disclose other confidences, their informants will refuse to be reluctant to furnish newsworthy information in the future. This asserted burden on news gathering is said to make compelled testimony from newsmen constitutionally suspect and to require a privileged position for them. . . .

Until now the only testimonial privilege for unofficial witnesses that is rooted in the Federal Constitution is the Fifth Amendment privilege against compelled self-incrimination. We are asked to create another by interpreting the First Amendment to grant newsmen a testimonial privilege that other citizens do not enjoy. This we decline to do. Fair and effective law enforcement aimed at providing security for the person and property of the individual is a fundamental function of government, and the grand jury plays an important, constitutionally mandated role in this process. [We perceive] no basis for holding that the public interest in law enforcement and in ensuring effective grand jury proceedings is insufficient to override the consequential, but uncertain, burden on news gathering that is said to result from insisting that reporters, like other citizens, respond to relevant questions put to them in the course of a valid grand jury investigation or criminal trial.

This conclusion itself involves no restraint on what newspapers may publish or on the type or quality of information reporters may seek to acquire, nor does it threaten the vast bulk of confidential relationships between reporters and their sources. . . . Only where news sources themselves are implicated in crime or possess information relevant to the grand jury's task need they or the reporter be concerned about grand jury subpoenas. Nothing before us indicates that a [large] percentage of *all* confidential news sources falls into either category and would in any way be deterred by our holding that the Constitution does [not] exempt the newsman from performing the citizen's normal duty of appearing and furnishing information relevant to the grand jury's task.

[W]e cannot seriously entertain the notion that the First Amendment protects a newsman's agreement to conceal the criminal conduct of his source, or evidence thereof, on the theory that it is better to write about crime than to do something about it. . . . The crimes of news sources are no less reprehensible and threatening to the public interest when witnessed by a reporter than when they are not.

There remain those situations where a source is not engaged in criminal conduct but has information suggesting illegal conduct by others. Newsmen frequently receive information from such sources pursuant to a tacit or express agreement to withhold the source's name and suppress any information that the source wishes not published. Such informants presumably desire anonymity in order to avoid being entangled as a witness in a criminal trial or grand jury investigation. They may fear that disclosure will threaten their job security or personal safety or that it will simply result in dishonor or embarrassment.

The argument that the flow of news will be diminished by compelling reporters to aid the grand jury in a criminal investigation is not irrational. . . . But we remain unclear how often and to what extent informers are actually deterred from furnishing information when newsmen are forced to testify before a grand jury. The available data indicate that some newsmen rely a great deal on confidential sources and that some informants are particularly sensitive to the threat of exposure and may be silenced if it is held by this Court that, ordinarily, news-men must testify pursuant to subpoenas, but the evidence fails to demonstrate that there would be a significant constriction of the flow of news to the public if this Court reaffirms the prior common-law and constitutional rule regarding the testimonial obligations of newsmen. . . . Reliance by the press on confidential informants does not mean that all such sources will in fact dry up because of the later possible appearance of the newsman before a grand jury. The reporter may never be called and if he objects to testifying, the prosecution may not insist. Also, the relationship of many informants to the press is a symbiotic one which is unlikely to be greatly inhibited by the threat of subpoena: quite often, such infor-mants are members of a minority political or cultural group that relies heavily on the media to propagate its views, publicize its aims, and magnify its exposure to the public. Moreover, grand juries characteristically conduct secret proceedings, and law enforcement officers are themselves experienced in dealing with inform-ers, and have their own methods for protecting them without interference with the effective administration of justice. There is little before us indicating that informants whose interest in avoiding exposure is that it may threaten job secu-rity, personal safety, or peace of mind, would in fact be in a worse position, or would think they would be, if they risked placing their trust in public officials as well as reporters. We doubt if the informer who prefers anonymity but is sincerely interested in furnishing evidence of crime will always or very often be deterred by the prospect of dealing with these public authorities characteristically charged with the duty to protect the public interest as well as his.

Accepting the fact, however, that an undetermined number of informants not themselves implicated in crime will nevertheless, for whatever reason, refuse to talk to newsmen if they fear identification by a reporter in an official investigation, we cannot accept the argument that the public interest in possible future news about crime from undisclosed, unverified sources must take precedence over the public interest in pursuing and prosecuting those crimes reported to the press by informants and in thus deterring the commission of such crimes in the future. . . .

We are admonished that refusal to provide a First Amendment reporter's privilege will undermine the freedom of the press to collect and disseminate news. But this is not the lesson history teaches us. . . . From the beginning of our country the press has operated without constitutional protection for press infor-mants, and the press has flourished. The existing constitutional rules have not been a serious obstacle to either the development or retention of confidential news sources by the press.

[Congress and the states have] freedom to determine whether a statutory newsman's privilege is necessary and desirable and to fashion standards and rules as narrow or broad as deemed necessary to deal with the evil discerned and, equally important, to refashion those rules as experience from time to time may dictate. . . . Furthermore, if what the newsmen urged in these cases is true — that law enforcement cannot hope to gain and may suffer from subpoenaing newsmen before grand juries — prosecutors will be loath to risk so much for so little. . . . Official harassment of the press undertaken not for purposes of law enforcement but to disrupt a reporter's relationship with his news sources would have no justification. Grand juries are subject to judicial control and subpoenas to motions to quash. . . .

Mr. Justice POWELL, concurring.

[The] Court does not hold that newsmen, subpoenaed to testify before a grand jury, are without constitutional rights with respect to the gathering of news or in safeguarding their sources. [If] the newsman is called upon to give information bearing only a remote and tenuous relationship to the subject of the investigation, or if he has some other reason to believe that his testimony implicates confidential source relationship without a legitimate need of law enforcement, he will have access to the court on a motion to quash and an appropriate protective order may be entered. The asserted claim to privilege should be judged on its facts by the striking of a proper balance between freedom of the press and the obligation of all citizens to give relevant testimony with respect to criminal conduct. . . . In short, the courts will be available to newsmen under circumstances where legitimate First Amendment interests require protection.

Mr. Justice DOUGLAS, dissenting.

Today's decision will impede the wide-open and robust dissemination of ideas and counter-thought which a free press both fosters and protects and which is essential to the success of intelligent self-government. Forcing a reporter before a grand jury will have two retarding effects upon the ear and the pen of the press. Fear of exposure will cause dissidents to communicate less openly to trusted reporters. And, fear of accountability will cause editors and critics to write with more restrained pens. [The] press has a preferred position in our constitutional scheme. . . . A reporter is not better than his source of information. . . . If he can be summoned to testify in secret before a grand jury, his sources will dry up and the attempted exposure, the effort to enlighten the public, will be ended. If what the Court sanctions today becomes settled law, then the reporter's main function in American society will be to pass on to the public the press releases which the various departments of government issue. . . .

Mr. Justice STEWART, with whom Mr. Justice BRENNAN and Mr. Justice MARSHALL join, dissenting.

The Court's crabbed view of the First Amendment reflects a disturbing insensitivity to the critical role of an independent press in our society. . . . A corollary to the right to publish must be the right to gather news. . . . The right to gather news implies, in turn, a right to a confidential relationship between a reporter and his source. This proposition follows as a matter of simple logic once three factual predicates are recognized: (1) newsmen require informants to gather news; (2) confidentiality [is] essential to the creation and maintenance of a news-gathering relationship with informants; and (3) an unbridled subpoena power — the absence of a constitutional right protecting, in *any* way, a confidential relationship from compulsory process — will either deter sources from divulging information or deter reporters from gathering and publishing information. . . .

Notes

1. *The* Cooper and Miller *Case. Branzburg* was followed by a case that arose out of the Court of Appeals for the District of Columbia. *See In Re Grand Jury Subpoena, Judith Miller*, 397 F.3d 964 (D.C. Cir. 2005). That case involved a special counsel investigation relating to leaks that outed a CIA operative. Grand jury subpoenas were issued to the *New York Times* and two of its reporters, Matthew Cooper and Judith Miller, requiring them to divulge their sources. Both refused to comply with the subpoenas. Miller was ultimately sent to jail for her refusal. Cooper escaped imprisonment when, at the eleventh hour, his source authorized disclosure.

2. *Reporter Protections.* Despite *Branzburg*, some courts have used the First Amendment to protect reporters from compelled disclosure of sources. *See, e.g.,* Silkwood v. Kerr-McGee Corp., 563 F.2d 433, 437 (10th Cir. 1977). In addition, federal and state laws protect reporters legislatively. *See* 42 U.S.C. §2000aa:

§2000aa. Searches and Seizures By Government Officers and Employees in Connection with Investigation or Prosecution of Criminal Offenses

(a) Work product materials

Notwithstanding any other law, it shall be unlawful for a government officer or employee, in connection with the investigation or prosecution of a criminal offense, to search for or seize any work product materials possessed by a person reasonably believed to have a purpose to disseminate to the public a newspaper, book, broadcast, or other similar form of public communication, in or affecting interstate or foreign commerce; but this provision shall not impair or affect the ability of any government officer or employee, pursuant to otherwise applicable law, to search for or seize such materials, if —

(1) there is probable cause to believe that the person possessing such materials has committed or is committing the criminal offense to which the materials relate[;] or

(2) there is reason to believe that the immediate seizure of such materials is necessary to prevent the death of, or serious bodily injury to, a human being.

The Act contains another provision regarding "documentary materials, other than work product materials, possessed by a person in connection with a purpose to disseminate to the public a newspaper, book, broadcast, or other similar form of public communication, in or affecting interstate or foreign commerce. . . ." The Act also creates a civil action on behalf of those whose rights under the Act are violated.

3. *Search Warrants.* In Zurcher v. Stanford Daily, 436 U.S. 547 (1978), following a demonstration at Stanford University during which police officers were attacked, the *Stanford Daily* published articles and photographs about the incident. Afterward, the police sought and obtained a warrant authorizing them to search the *Daily*'s offices for negatives, film, and pictures showing the events and occurrences. The ensuring search extended to the *Daily*'s photographic laboratories, filing cabinets, desks, and wastepaper baskets. The officers read notes and correspondence during the search. The *Daily*, and various members of its staff, sought declaratory and injunctive relief against further such invasions. The Court held that injunctive relief was inappropriate:

[T]he Framers took the enormously important step of subjecting searches to the test of reasonableness and to the general rule requiring search warrants issued by neutral magistrates. They nevertheless did not forbid warrants where the press was involved, did not require special showings that subpoenas would be impractical, and did not insist that the owner of the place to be searched, if connected with the press, must be shown to be implicated in the offense being investigated. [Our] cases do no more than insist that the courts apply the warrant requirements with particular exactitude when First Amendment interests would be endangered by the search. . . . Properly administered, the preconditions for a warrant — probable cause, specificity with respect to the place to be searched and the things to be seized, and overall reasonableness — should afford sufficient protection against the harms that are assertedly threatened by warrants for searching newspaper offices.

Justice Stewart dissented: "[P]olice searches of newspaper offices burden the freedom of the press. The most immediate and obvious First Amendment injury caused by such a visitation by the police is physical disruption of the operation of the newspaper. . . . But there is another and more serious burden on a free press imposed by an unannounced police search of a newspaper office: the possibility of disclosure of information received from confidential sources, or of the identity of the sources themselves. . . . A search warrant allows police officers to ransack the files of a newspaper, reading each and every document until they have found the one named in the warrant. . . . The knowledge that police officers can make an unannounced raid on a newsroom is thus bound to have a deterrent effect on the availability of confidential news sources. The end result [will] be a diminishing flow of potentially important information to the public."

4. *Disseminating Discovery.* Seattle Times Co. v. Rhinehart, 467 U.S. 20 (1984), involved the question whether parties to civil litigation have a First Amendment right to disseminate information gained through the pretrial discovery process. The Court answered the question in the negative even though the information pertained to a public figure: "A litigant has no First Amendment right of access to information made available only for purposes of trying his suit. [C]ontinued court control over the discovered information does not raise the same specter of government censorship that such control might suggest in other situations. [R]estraints placed on discovered, but not yet admitted, information are not a restriction on a traditionally public source of information. [Rule] 26(c) furthers a substantial governmental interest unrelated to the suppression of expression."

5. *Breach of Confidentiality Suits.* In Cohen v. Cowles Media Co., 501 U.S. 663 (1991), a newspaper reporter promised a source confidentiality in exchange for information, but subsequently breached that promise and revealed the name of the source. When the source sued, seeking damages for promissory estoppel, the reporter asserted the First Amendment as a shield against liability (on the theory that he had truthfully reported on matters of public interest). In *Cohen*, the Court held that the reporter could be held liable, noting that the action for promissory estoppel is applicable to all of society, and there is no exemption for reporters.

～ PROBLEM: MORE ON THE INTERNATIONAL TREATY REGULATING THE INTERNET ～

At the convention, questions arise regarding whether reporters should be allowed to shield their sources from disclosure. Under the First Amendment, can you agree to shield them against disclosure? Should you? What impact would a treaty provision (shielding reporters' sources from disclosure) have in a state or federal court criminal proceeding where disclosure of sources is sought?

3. Access to Judicial Proceedings

The Court has rendered a number of decisions on press access. In Gannett, Inc. v. DePasquale, 443 U.S. 363 (1979), the Court upheld a district court order closing pretrial proceedings on the basis that the Sixth Amendment right to a public trial is personal to the defendant and may not be asserted by anyone else. In Richmond Newspapers, Inc. v. Virginia, 448 U.S. 555 (1980), the Court held that open trials provide an important check on official misconduct, and access to the judicial process is necessary if the public is to be informed and educated. Finally, in Waller v. Georgia, 467 U.S. 39 (1984), the Court held that a trial court could not close a hearing over the defendant's objections. On the contrary, closure is appropriate only when there is an overriding interest, a narrowly tailored order, and an exhaustion of less burdensome alternatives.

Globe Newspaper Co. v. Superior Court
457 U.S. 596 (1982)

Justice BRENNAN delivered the opinion of the Court.

Section 16A of Chapter 278 of the Massachusetts General Laws, as construed by the Massachusetts Supreme Judicial Court, requires trial judges, at trials for specific sexual offenses involving a victim under the age of 18, to exclude the press and general public from the courtroom during the testimony of that victim. The question presented is whether the statute thus construed violates the First Amendment as applied to the States through the Fourteenth Amendment.

The Court's recent decision in Richmond Newspapers, Inc. v. Virginia, 448 U.S. 555 (1980), firmly established for the first time that the press and general public have a constitutional right of access to criminal trials. [This right of access is] not explicitly mentioned in terms in the First Amendment. But we have long eschewed any "narrow, literal conception" of the Amendment's terms, for the Framers were concerned with broad principles, and wrote against a background of shared values and practices. The First Amendment is thus broad enough to encompass those rights that, while not unambiguously enumerated in the very terms of the Amendment, are nonetheless necessary to the enjoyment of other First Amendment rights. . . . To the extent that the First Amendment embraces a right of access to criminal trials, it is to ensure that this constitutionally protected "discussion of governmental affairs" is an informed one.

Two features of the criminal justice system, emphasized in the various opinions in *Richmond Newspapers*, together serve to explain why a right of access [is] properly afforded protection by the First Amendment. First, the criminal trial historically has been open to the press and general public. "[A]t the time when our organic laws were adopted, criminal trials both here and in England had long been presumptively open." Richmond Newspapers, Inc. v. Virginia, 448 U.S. 555 (1980) (plurality opinion). And since that time, the presumption of openness has remained secure. Indeed, at the time of this Court's decision *In re Oliver*, 333 U.S. 257 (1948), the presumption was so solidly grounded that the Court was "unable to find a single instance of a criminal trial conducted in camera in any federal, state, or municipal court during the history of this country." This uniform rule of openness has been viewed as significant in constitutional terms not only "because the Constitution carries the gloss of history," but also because "a tradition of accessibility implies the favorable judgment of experience."

Second, the right of access to criminal trials plays a particularly significant role in the functioning of the judicial process and the government as a whole. Public scrutiny of a criminal trial enhances the quality and safeguards the integrity of the factfinding process, with benefits to both the defendant and to society as a whole. Moreover, public access to the criminal trial fosters an appearance of fairness, thereby heightening public respect for the judicial process. And in the broadest terms, public access to criminal trials permits the public to participate in and serve as a check upon the judicial process — an essential component in our structure of self-government. In sum, the institutional value of the open criminal trial is recognized in both logic and experience.

Although the right of access to criminal trials is of constitutional stature, it is not absolute. But the circumstances under which the press and public can be barred from a criminal trail are limited; the State's justification in denying access must be a weighty one. Where [the] State attempts to deny the right of access in order to inhibit the disclosure of sensitive information, it must be shown that the denial is necessitated by a compelling governmental interest, and is narrowly tailored to serve that interest. . . .

The state interests asserted to support §16A, though articulated in various ways, are reducible to two: the protection of minor victims of sex crimes from further trauma and embarrassment; and the encouragement of such victims to come forward and testify in a truthful and credible manner. We consider these interests in turn.

We agree with appellee that the first interest — safeguarding the physical and psychological well-being of a minor — is a compelling one. But as compelling as that interest is, it does not justify a mandatory closure rule, for it is clear that the circumstances of the particular case may affect the significance of the interest. A trial court can determine on a case-by-case basis whether closure is necessary to protect the welfare of a minor victim. Among the factors to be weighed are the minor victim's age, psychological maturity and understanding, the nature of the crime, the desires of the victim, and the interests of parents and relatives.

Section 16A, in contrast, requires closure even if the victim does not seek the exclusion of the press and general public and would not suffer injury by their presence. . . .

Nor can §16A be justified on the basis of the Commonwealth's second asserted interest — the encouragement of minor victims of sex crimes to come forward and provide accurate testimony. The Commonwealth has offered no empirical support for the claim that the rule of automatic closure contained in §16A bars the press and general public from the courtroom during the testimony of minor sex victims, the press is not denied access to the transcript, court personnel, or another possible source that could provide an account of the minor victim's testimony. Thus §16A cannot prevent the press from publicizing the substance of a minor victim's testimony, as well as his or her identity. If the commonwealth's interest in encouraging minor victims to come forward depends on keeping such matters secret, §16A hardly advances that interest in an effective manner. And even if §16A effectively advanced the State's interest, it is doubtful that the interest would be sufficient to overcome the constitutional attack, for that same interest could be relied on to support an array of mandatory closure rules designed to encourage victims to come forward: Surely it cannot be suggested that minor victims of sex crimes are the only crime victims who, because of publicity attendant to criminal trials, are reluctant to come forward and testify. The State's argument based on this interest therefore proves too much, and runs contrary to the very foundation of the right of access recognized in *Richmond Newspapers*: namely, "that a presumption of openness inheres in the very nature of a criminal trial under our system of justice" (plurality opinion).

For the foregoing reasons, we hold that §16A, as construed by the Massachusetts Supreme Judicial Court, violates the First Amendment to the Constitution. Accordingly, the judgment of the Massachusetts Supreme Judicial Court is

Reversed.

Chief Justice BURGER, with whom Justice REHNQUIST joins, dissenting.

Historically our society has gone to great lengths to protect minors charged with crime, particularly by prohibiting the release of the names of offenders, barring the press and public from juvenile proceedings, and sealing the records of those proceedings. Yet today the Court holds unconstitutional a state statute designed to protect not the accused, but the minor victims of sex crimes. . . .

The Court has tried to make its holding a narrow one by not disturbing the authority of state legislatures to enact more narrowly drawn statutes giving trial judges the discretion to exclude the public and the press from the courtroom during the minor victim's testimony.

I also do not read the Court's opinion as foreclosing a state statute which mandates closure except in cases where the victim agrees to testify in open court. But the Court's decision is nevertheless a gross invasion of state authority and a state's duty to protect its citizens — in this case minor victims of crime. . . .

A First Amendment right of access to proceedings other than trials hinges upon considerations of tradition and exigencies. Determinative factors are whether a given jurisdiction's proceedings historically have been open or closed, particularized findings have been made that the defendant's right to a fair trial would be prejudiced and reasonable alternatives exist to closure.

Notes and Questions

1. *Defendant's Motion to Exclude the Press.* In Press-Enterprise Co. v. Superior Court, 478 U.S. 1 (1986), a preliminary hearing was held at which Robert Diaz, a nurse, was charged with murdering 12 patients. Diaz moved to exclude the public from the proceedings in order to protect his "right to a fair and impartial trial." The court granted the motion, finding that closure was necessary because the case had attracted national publicity and "only one side may get reported in the media." At the conclusion of the hearing, petitioner Press-Enterprise Company asked that the transcript of the proceedings be released. The magistrate refused and sealed the record, noting "a reasonable likelihood that release of all or any part of the transcripts might prejudice defendant's right to a fair and impartial trial." The U.S. Supreme Court disagreed, holding that even though "the defendant has a right to a fair trial," "one of the important means of assuring a fair trial is that the process be open to neutral observers." The Court went on to note that the "right to an open public trial is a shared right of the accused and the public, the common concern being the assurance of fairness." The Court extended this right to preliminary hearings.

2. *Cameras in the Courtroom.* By the mid-1990s, 47 states allowed cameras in their courtrooms. Increased use of technology is driven by technological advances that diminish the intrusiveness of cameras and other recording devices.

3. *Overcoming the Right to Press Access.* In numerous cases, although the Court has recognized that the press has a right of access to trials and preliminary hearings, the Court held that the right of access is not absolute. What circumstances might encourage a court to close a proceeding? Should it matter that both the prosecution and the defense prefer that a proceeding be closed?

4. *Televising Trials.* Over the defendant's objection, a trial court decided to permit radio, television, and still photographic coverage of a criminal trial for public broadcast. Before the U.S. Supreme Court, the defendant argued that "the televising of criminal trials is inherently a denial of due process" because there is a risk that television coverage will "adversely affect the conduct of the participants and the fairness of the trial." In Chandler v. Florida, 449 U.S. 560 (1981), the Court held that the burden is on the defendant to demonstrate that the presence of cameras actually prejudiced a jury's ability to perform its function fairly and effectively.

∼ PROBLEMS: PROTECTING JURORS ∼

1. *Prohibiting Juror Interviews.* A judge enters an order prohibiting the media from interviewing jurors about their deliberations. The order is to be effective even after the jury is released, but the press is allowed to interview jurors about

their votes as well as about other matters. The court justified the order on the following grounds:

> This was a long contentious high-profile criminal case involving well-known defendants of power and influence. Indeed, the witnesses included an archbishop and a former governor. Cases like this one do not even remotely resemble the everyday civil or criminal trial in terms of the stress and anxiety inflicted upon those asked to serve as jurors. In such cases, it is particularly important for jurors to be secure in the knowledge that the play-by-play of their thought processes during deliberations will not be in the newspaper once the trial is over, in order for them to deliberate frankly and honestly, without fear of later public embarrassment, harassment or retaliation.

If a newspaper challenges the order as an infringement of its First Amendment rights, claiming that the public is entitled to understand the basis for the jury's decision, and that it is inappropriate to protect jury deliberations after the trial has ended, is the gag order valid?

2. *Anonymous Juror Pools.* Regardless of what you decided in the preceding problem, suppose that, in a case of great local public interest — involving criminal allegations that a former county coroner used his office for private gain — the judge ordered that the jury be anonymously seated. In other words, jury selection would be conducted by written questionnaires that do not contain the juror's names or identifying information. Is the press entitled to discover the names of jurors seated for a criminal trial? What justifications might be offered in support of the judge's decision to seat an anonymous jury? What counterarguments would you make if you were asked to represent a local newspaper that sought to obtain the jurors' names? *See* United States v. Wecht, 537 F.3d 222 (3d Cir. 2007).

4. Access to Prisons

The press has also sought access to prisons in an effort to report on prison conditions. Pell v. Procunier, 417 U.S. 817 (1974), involved a California prison regulation that provided "[p]ress and other media interviews with specific individual inmates will not be permitted." The regulation was challenged by members of the media who had requested permission to speak with specific inmates and been denied permission. They claimed that the regulation infringed the freedom of the press guaranteed by the First and Fourteenth Amendments. The Court upheld the regulation:

> "[L]awful incarceration brings about the necessary withdrawal or limitation of many privileges and rights, a retraction justified by the considerations underlying our penal system." In the First Amendment context a corollary of this principle is that a prison inmate retains those First Amendment rights that are not inconsistent with his status as a prisoner or with the legitimate penological objectives of the corrections system. . . . An important function of the corrections system is the deterrence of crime. The premise is that by confining criminal offenders in a facility where they are isolated from the rest of society, a condition that most people presumably find undesirable, they and others will be deterred from committing additional criminal offenses. [S]ince most offenders will eventually return to society, another paramount objective of the corrections system is the rehabilitation of those committed to its

custody. Finally, central to all other corrections goals is the institutional consideration of internal security within the corrections facilities themselves. . . .

[W]e think that the regulation cannot be considered in isolation but must be viewed in the light of the alternative means of communication permitted under the regulations with persons outside the prison. . . . One such alternative available to California prison inmates is communication by mail. . . . [In] Procunier v. Martinez, 416 U.S. 396, 416 (1974)[,] we held that "[t]he interests of prisoners and their correspondents in uncensored communication by letter, grounded as it is in the First Amendment, is plainly a 'liberty' interest within the meaning of the Fourteenth Amendment even though qualified of necessity by the circumstance of imprisonment." . . . Moreover, [i]nmates are permitted to receive limited visits from members of their families, the clergy, their attorneys, and friends of prior acquaintance. . . . More importantly, however, inmates have an unrestricted opportunity to communicate with the press or any other member of the public through their families, friends, clergy, or attorneys who are permitted to visit them at the prison. [T]his provides another alternative avenue of communication. . . .

The Court also rejected arguments that the regulation violated the freedom of the press, noting that the regulation is "not part of an attempt by the State to conceal the conditions in its prisons or to frustrate the press' investigation and reporting of those conditions." On the contrary, "both the press and the general public are accorded full opportunities to observe prison conditions" and to stop and speak with inmates. The Court also cited other means of access. "The sole limitation on newsgathering in California prisons is the prohibition in §415.071 of interviews with individual inmates specifically designated by representatives of the press." The Court expressed concern that the prior practice of designating specific inmates "had resulted in press attention being concentrated on a relatively small number of inmates who, as a result, became virtual 'public figures' within the prison society and gained a disproportionate degree of notoriety and influence among their fellow inmates. Because of this notoriety and influence, these inmates often became the source of severe disciplinary problems."

Justice Douglas dissented, arguing that "the State's interest in order and prison discipline cannot justify its total ban on all media interviews with any individually designated inmate on any matter whatsoever. . . . Prisons, like all other public institutions, are ultimately the responsibility of the populace. . . . The public's interest in being informed about prisons is thus paramount. . . . As with the prisoners' free speech claim, no one asserts that the free press right is such that the authorities are powerless to impose reasonable regulations as to the time, place, and manner of interviews to effectuate prison discipline and order. The only issue here is whether the complete ban on interviews with inmates selected by the press goes beyond what is necessary for the protection of these interests and infringes upon our cherished right of a free press. . . ."

Pell was reinforced by the holding in Houchins v. KQED, Inc., 438 U.S. 1 (1978). In *Houchins*, a radio and television broadcasting company sought access to a county jail to interview inmates and make sound recordings, films, and photographs for publication and broadcasting by newspapers, radio, and television. The request came following the suicide of a prisoner in the Greystone section of the Santa Rita jail. The report included a statement by a psychiatrist that the conditions at the Greystone facility were responsible for the illnesses of his patient-prisoners there, and a statement from the director denying that prison conditions were responsible for the prisoners' illnesses. After the company filed suit, the prison announced a program of regular public tours in which the press was allowed to participate. One of the respondent's reporters participated in the first tour, but the tour did not include the disciplinary cells or the portions of the jail known as "Little Greystone," the scene of alleged rapes, beatings, and adverse physical conditions. Photographs of some parts of the jail were made available, but no cameras or tape recorders were allowed on the tours. Those on the tours were not permitted to interview inmates, and inmates were generally removed from view.

Notwithstanding the holding in *Pell*, respondents asserted that they had a constitutionally guaranteed right to gather news, which included an implied special right of access to government-controlled sources of information. The respondents contended that public access to penal institutions was necessary to prevent officials from concealing prison conditions from the voters and impairing the public's right to discuss and criticize the prison system and its administration. In a plurality opinion, with two justices not participating in the case at all, the Court rejected these arguments:

> [C]onditions in jails and prisons are clearly matters "of great public importance." [T]he role of the media is important; acting as the "eyes and ears" of the public, they can be a powerful and constructive force, contributing to remedial action in the conduct of public business. [B]ut like all other components of our society media representatives are subject to limits. . . . The issue is a claimed special privilege of access which the Court rejected in *Pell* and *Saxbe*, a right which is not essential to guarantee the freedom to communicate or publish. . . . A number of alternatives are available to prevent problems in penal facilities from escaping public attention. . . . Citizen task forces and prison visitation committees [play] an important role in keeping the public informed on deficiencies of prison systems and need for reforms. Grand juries, with the potent subpoena power — not available to the media — traditionally concern themselves with conditions in public institutions; a prosecutor or judge may initiate similar inquiries, and the legislative power embraces an arsenal of weapons for inquiry relating to tax-supported institutions. [T]hese public bodies are generally compelled to publish their findings and, if they default, the power of the media is always available to generate public pressure for disclosure. But the choice as to the most effective and appropriate method is a policy decision to be resolved by legislative decision. . . .
>
> Petitioner cannot prevent respondents from learning about jail conditions in a variety of ways, albeit not as conveniently as they might prefer. Respondents have a First Amendment right to receive letters from inmates criticizing jail officials and reporting on conditions. Respondents are free to interview those who render the legal assistance to which inmates are entitled. They are also free to seek out former inmates, visitors to the prison, public officials, and institutional personnel, as they sought out the complaining psychiatrist here. . . . Moreover, California statutes currently provide for a prison Board of Corrections that has the authority to inspect jails and prisons and must provide a public report at regular intervals. Health inspectors are required to inspect prisons and provide reports to a number of officials, including the State Attorney General and the Board of Corrections. Fire officials are also required to inspect prisons. Following the reports of the suicide at the jail involved here, the County Board of Supervisors called for a report from the County Administrator; held a public hearing on the report, which was open to the media; and called for further reports when

the initial report failed to describe the conditions in the cells in the Greystone portion of the jail. . . .

Justice Stewart concurred:

That the First Amendment speaks separately of freedom of speech and freedom of the press is no constitutional accident, but an acknowledgment of the critical role played by the press in American society. The Constitution requires sensitivity to that role, and to the special needs of the press in performing it effectively. [T]erms of access that are reasonably imposed on individual members of the public may, if they impede effective reporting without sufficient justification, be unreasonable as applied to journalists who are there to convey to the general public what the visitors see. . . . Under these principles, KQED was clearly entitled to some form of preliminary injunctive relief. . . .

Justice Stevens, joined by Justices Brennan and Powell, dissented:

The First Amendment serves an essential societal function. Our system of self-government assumes the existence of an informed citizenry. . . . Without some protection for the acquisition of information about the operation of public institutions such as prisons by the public at large, the process of self-governance contemplated by the Framers would be stripped of its substance. . . . While prison officials have an interest in the time and manner of public acquisition of information about the institutions they administer, there is no legitimate penological justification for concealing from citizens the conditions in which their fellow citizens are being confined.

The reasons which militate in favor of providing special protection to the flow of information to the public about prisons relate to the unique function they perform in a democratic society. Not only are they public institutions, financed with public funds and administered by public servants, they are an integral component of the criminal justice system. . . . [The] public interest survives the judgment of conviction and appropriately carries over to an interest in how the convicted person is treated during his period of punishment and hoped-for rehabilitation. . . . Some inmates — in Santa Rita, a substantial number — are pretrial detainees. . . . Society has a special interest in ensuring that unconvicted citizens are treated in accord with their status. [B]oth the public and the press had been consistently denied any access to the inner portions of the Santa Rita jail, [and] there had been excessive censorship of inmate correspondence. . . . An official prison policy of concealing such knowledge from the public by arbitrarily cutting off the flow of information at its source abridges the freedom of speech and of the press protected by the First and Fourteenth Amendments to the Constitution. . . .

In Beard v. Banks, 548 U.S. 521 (2006), the Court upheld a prison policy that denied newspapers, magazines, and photographs to a group of especially dangerous and recalcitrant inmates. Relying on Overton v. Bazzetta, 539 U. S. 126 (2003), which held that the courts must show deference to prison officials, the Court upheld the restriction as applied to inmates who "exhibit behavior that is continually disruptive, violent, dangerous or a threat to the orderly operation of their assigned facility."

5. The Press and Due Process

As the foregoing discussion reveals, the courts have usually given the press easy access to judicial proceedings. But press access does not come without cost, and there is always the risk that a criminal defendant's right to a fair trial will be endangered by excessive press coverage. When a trial has a sensational element, the press is likely to provide significant and at times excessive coverage.

Sheppard v. Maxwell

384 U.S. 333 (1966)

Mr. Justice CLARK delivered the opinion of the Court.

[P]etitioner's pregnant wife was bludgeoned to death in the upstairs bedroom of their lakeshore home in Bay Village, Ohio, a suburb of Cleveland. On the day of the tragedy, July 4, 1954, Sheppard pieced together for several local officials the following story: [after dinner] Sheppard became drowsy and dozed off to sleep on a couch. [The] next thing he remembered was hearing his wife cry out in the early morning hours. He hurried upstairs and in the dim light from the hall saw a "form" standing next to his wife's bed. As he struggled with the "form" he was struck on the back of the neck and rendered [unconscious].

From the outset officials focused suspicion on Sheppard. After a search of the house and premises on the morning of the tragedy, [the] Coroner, is reported — and it is undenied — to have told his men, "Well, it is evident the doctor did this, so let's go get the confession out of him." [On July] 20th, the [press] opened fire with a front-page charge that somebody is "getting away with murder." [The] newspapers emphasized evidence that tended to incriminate Sheppard and pointed out discrepancies in his statements to authorities. At the same time, Sheppard made many public statements to the press and wrote feature articles asserting his innocence. . . .

The case came on for trial two weeks before the November general election at which the chief prosecutor was a candidate for common pleas judge and the trial judge [was] a candidate to succeed himself. Twenty-five days before the case was set, 75 veniremen were called as prospective jurors. All three Cleveland newspapers published the names and addresses of the veniremen. [A]nonymous letters and telephone calls, as well as calls from friends, regarding the impending prosecution were received by all of the prospective jurors. The selection of the jury began on October 18, 1954.

The courtroom in which the trial was held measured 26 by 48 feet. A long temporary table was set up inside the bar, in back of the single counsel table. It ran the width of the courtroom, parallel to the bar railing, with one end less than three feet from the jury box. Approximately 20 representatives of newspapers and wire services were assigned seats at this table by the court. Behind the bar railing there were four rows of benches. These seats were likewise assigned by the court for the entire trial. The first row was occupied by representatives of television and radio stations, and the second and third rows by reporters from out-of-town newspapers and magazines. One side of the last row, which accommodated 14 people, was assigned to Sheppard's family and the other to Marilyn's. The public was permitted to fill vacancies in this row on special passes only. Representatives of the news media also used all the rooms on the courtroom floor, including the room where cases were ordinarily called and assigned for trial. Private telephone lines and telegraphic equipment were installed in these rooms so that reports from the trial could be speeded to the papers. Station WSRS was permitted to set up broadcasting facilities on the third floor of the courthouse next door to the jury room, where the jury rested during recesses in the trial and deliberated. Newscasts were made from this room throughout the trial, and while the jury reached its verdict.

On the sidewalk and steps in front of the courthouse, television and newsreel cameras were occasionally used to take motion pictures of the participants in the trial, including the jury and the judge. Indeed, one television broadcast carried a staged interview of the judge as he entered the courthouse. In the corridors outside the courtroom there was a host of photographers and television personnel with flash cameras, portable lights and motion picture cameras. This group photographed the prospective jurors during selection of the jury. After the trial opened, the witnesses, counsel, and jurors were photographed and televised whenever they entered or left the courtroom. Sheppard was brought to the courtroom about 10 minutes before each session began; he was surrounded by reporters and extensively photographed for the newspapers and television. A rule of court prohibited picture-taking in the courtroom during the actual sessions of the court, but no restraints were put on photographers during recesses, which were taken once each morning and afternoon, with a longer period for lunch.

All of these arrangements with the news media and their massive coverage of the trial continued during the entire nine weeks of the trial. The courtroom remained crowded to capacity with representatives of news media. Their movement in and out of the courtroom often caused so much confusion that, despite the loud-speaker system installed in the courtroom, it was difficult for the witnesses and counsel to be heard. Furthermore, the reporters clustered within the bar of the small courtroom made confidential talk among Sheppard and his counsel almost impossible during the proceedings. They frequently had to leave the courtroom to obtain privacy. And many times when counsel wished to raise a point with the judge out of the hearing of the jury it was necessary to move to the judge's chambers. Even then, news media representatives so packed the judge's anteroom that counsel could hardly return from the chambers to the courtroom. The reporters vied with each other to find out what counsel and the judge had discussed, and often these matters later appeared in newspapers accessible to the jury.

The daily record of the proceedings was made available to the newspapers and the testimony of each witness was printed verbatim in the local editions, along with objections of counsel, and rulings by the judge. Pictures of Sheppard, the judge, counsel, pertinent witnesses, and the jury often accompanied the daily newspaper and television accounts. At times the newspapers published photographs of exhibits introduced at the trial, and the rooms of Sheppard's house were featured along with relevant testimony.

The jurors themselves were constantly exposed to the news media. Every juror, except one, testified at *voir dire* to reading about the case in the Cleveland papers or to having heard broadcasts about it. Seven of the 12 jurors who rendered the verdict had one or more Cleveland papers delivered in their home; the remaining jurors were not interrogated on the point. Nor were there questions as to radios or television sets in the jurors' homes, but we must assume that most of them owned such conveniences. As the selection of the jury progressed, individual pictures of prospective members appeared daily. During the trial, pictures of the jury appeared over 40 times in the Cleveland papers alone. The court permitted photographers to take pictures of the jury in the box, and individual pictures of the members in the jury room. One newspaper ran pictures of the jurors at the Sheppard home when they went there to view the scene of the murder. Another paper featured the home life of an alternate juror. The day before the verdict was rendered — while the jurors were at lunch and sequestered by two bailiffs — the jury was separated into two groups to pose for photographs which appeared in the newspapers. . . .

IV

The principle that justice cannot survive behind walls of silence has long been reflected in the "Anglo-American distrust for secret trials." A responsible press has always been regarded as the handmaiden of effective judicial administration, especially in the criminal field. Its function in this regard is documented by an impressive record of service over several centuries. The press does not simply publish information about trials but guards against the miscarriage of justice by subjecting the police, prosecutors, and judicial processes to extensive public scrutiny and criticism. This Court has, therefore, been unwilling to place any direct limitations on the freedom traditionally exercised by the news media for "[w]hat transpires in the court room is public property." The "unqualified prohibitions laid down by the framers were intended to give to liberty of the press [the] broadest scope that could be countenanced in an orderly society." And where there was "no threat or menace to the integrity of the trial," we have consistently required that the press have a free hand, even though we sometimes deplored its sensationalism.

But the Court has also pointed out that "[l]egal trials are not like elections, to be won through the use of the meeting-hall, the radio, and the newspaper." And the Court has insisted that no one be punished for a crime without "a charge fairly made and fairly tried in a public tribunal free of prejudice, passion, excitement, and tyrannical power." "Freedom of discussion should be given the widest range compatible with the essential requirement of the fair and orderly administration of justice." But it must not be allowed to divert the trial from the "very purpose of a court system [to] adjudicate controversies, both criminal and civil, in the calmness and solemnity of the courtroom according to legal procedures." Among these "legal procedures" is the requirement that the jury's verdict be based on evidence received in open court, not from outside [sources]. . . .

Sheppard was not granted a change of venue to a locale away from where the publicity originated; nor was his jury sequestered. [On] the contrary, the Sheppard jurors were subjected to newspaper, radio and television coverage of the trial while not taking part in the proceedings. They were allowed to go their separate ways outside of the courtroom, without adequate directions not to read or listen to anything concerning the case. The judge's "admonitions" at the beginning of the trial are representative: "I would suggest to you and caution you that you do not read any newspapers during the progress of this trial, that you do not listen to radio comments nor watch or listen to television comments, insofar as this case is concerned. You will feel very much better as the trial [proceeds]. I am sure that we shall all feel very much better if we do not indulge in any newspaper reading or listening to any comments whatever about the matter while the case is in progress. After it is all over, you can read it all to your heart's [content]." At intervals during the trial, the judge simply repeated his "suggestions" and "requests" that the jurors not expose themselves to comment upon the case. Moreover, the jurors were thrust into the role of celebrities by the judge's failure to insulate them from reporters and photographers. The numerous pictures of the jurors, with their addresses, which appeared in the newspapers before and during the trial itself exposed them to expressions of opinion from both cranks and friends. The fact that anonymous letters had been received by prospective jurors should have made the judge aware that this publicity seriously threatened the jurors' privacy.

[Sheppard] stood indicted for the murder of his wife; the State was demanding the death penalty. For months the virulent publicity about Sheppard and the murder had made the case notorious. Charges and countercharges were aired in the news media besides those for which Sheppard was called to trial. . . .

While we cannot say that Sheppard was denied due process by the judge's refusal to take precautions against the influence of pretrial publicity alone, the court's later rulings must be considered against the setting in which the trial was held. In light of this background, we believe that the arrangements made by the judge with the news media caused Sheppard to be deprived of that "judicial serenity and calm to which [he] was entitled." The fact is that bedlam reigned at the courthouse during the trial and newsmen took over practically the entire courtroom, hounding most of the participants in the trial, especially Sheppard. At a temporary table within a few feet of the jury box and counsel table sat some 20 reporters staring at Sheppard and taking notes. The erection of a press table for reporters inside the bar is unprecedented. The bar of the court is reserved for counsel, providing them a safe place in which to keep papers and exhibits, and to confer privately with client and co-counsel. It is designed to protect the witness and the jury from any distractions, intrusions or influences, and to permit bench discussions of the judge's rulings away from the hearing of the public and the jury. Having assigned almost all of the available seats in the courtroom to the news media the judge lost his ability to supervise that environment. The movement of the reporters in and out of the courtroom caused frequent confusion and disruption of the trial. And the record reveals constant commotion within the bar. Moreover, the judge gave the throng of newsmen gathered in the corridors of the courthouse absolute free rein. Participants in the trial, including the jury, were forced to run a gauntlet of reporters and photographers each time they entered or left the courtroom. The total lack of consideration for the privacy of the jury was demonstrated by the assignment to a broadcasting station of space next to the jury room on the floor above the courtroom, as well as the fact that jurors were allowed to make telephone calls during their five-day deliberation.

There can be no question about the nature of the publicity which surrounded Sheppard's trial. We agree [with] the findings in Judge Bell's opinion for the Ohio Supreme Court: "Murder and mystery, society, sex and suspense were combined in this case in such a manner as to intrigue and captivate the public fancy to a degree perhaps unparalleled in recent annals. Throughout the preindictment investigation, the subsequent legal skirmishes and the nine-week trial, circulation-conscious editors catered to the insatiable interest of the American public in the bizarre. [In] this atmosphere of a 'Roman holiday' for the news media, Sam Sheppard stood trial for his life." [E]very court that has considered this case, save the court that tried it, has deplored the manner in which the news media inflamed and prejudiced the public.

Much of the material printed or broadcast during the trial was never heard from the witness stand, such as the charges that Sheppard had purposely impeded the murder investigation and must be guilty since he had hired a prominent criminal lawyer; that Sheppard was a perjurer; that he had sexual relations with numerous women; that his slain wife had characterized him as a "Jekyll-Hyde"; that he was "a bare-faced liar" because of his testimony as to police treatment; and finally, that a woman convict claimed Sheppard to be the father of her illegitimate child. As the trial progressed, the newspapers summarized and interpreted the evidence, devoting particular attention to the material that incriminated Sheppard, and often drew unwarranted inferences from testimony. At one point, a front-page picture of Mrs. Sheppard's blood-stained pillow was published after being "doctored" to show more clearly an alleged imprint of a surgical instrument.

Nor is there doubt that this deluge of publicity reached at least some of the jury. On the only occasion that the jury was queried, two jurors admitted in open court to hearing the highly inflammatory charge that a prison inmate claimed Sheppard as the father of her illegitimate child. Despite the extent and nature of the publicity to which the jury was exposed during trial, the judge refused defense counsel's other requests that the jurors be asked whether they had read or heard specific prejudicial comment about the case, including the incidents we have previously summarized. In these circumstances, we can assume that some of this material reached members of the jury.

[Since] the state trial judge did not fulfill his duty to protect Sheppard from the inherently prejudicial publicity which saturated the community and to control disruptive influences in the courtroom, we must reverse the denial of the habeas petition. The case is remanded to the District Court with instructions to issue the writ and order that Sheppard be released from custody unless the State puts him to its charges again within a reasonable time.

It is so ordered.

Notes

1. *Change of Venue.* One remedy for excessive press coverage is provided by Fed. R. Crim. P. 21(a), which permits a change of venue when the trial judge is "satisfied that there exists in the district where the prosecution is pending so great a prejudice that he cannot obtain a fair and impartial trial." In Irwin v. Dowd, 366 U.S. 717 (1961), the petitioner was denied a second change of venue despite extensive press coverage that aroused "great excitement and indignation." The Court reversed: "Here the 'pattern of deep and bitter prejudice' shown to be present throughout the community was clearly reflected in the sum total of the voir dire examination of a majority of the jurors finally placed in the jury box."

2. *An Ignorant Jury?* The Constitution does not require that a jury be ignorant of all publicity. In Murphy v. Florida, 421 U.S. 794 (1975), the defendant was charged with breaking and entering a home, while armed, with intent to commit robbery and with assault with intent to commit robbery. The case received extensive press coverage because the petitioner was notorious (he had participated in the 1964 theft of the Star of India sapphire from a museum in New York) and lived a flamboyant lifestyle. The media referred to him as "Murph the Surf" and wrote scores of articles about him. The Court upheld the conviction: "[The] constitutional standard of fairness requires that a defendant have a 'panel of impartial, indifferent' jurors. Qualified jurors need not, however, be totally ignorant of the facts and issues involved." "It is sufficient if the juror can lay aside his impression or opinion and render a verdict based on the evidence presented in court." *See also* Patton v. Yount, 467 U.S. 1025 (1984).

∽ PROBLEMS ∽

1. *Finding a Fair and Unbiased Jury.* Is it possible to seat a fair and unbiased jury in a case that generates extensive publicity (e.g., the O.J. Simpson murder case in which news organizations gave incessant coverage to the case)? Does the fact that the O.J. Simpson case resulted in a not guilty verdict suggest that jurors may not be biased by extensive (and, at times, obsessive) press coverage?

2. *More on the International Treaty Regulating the Internet.* At the convention, a number of delegates push for restrictions on the ability of individuals, corporations, and media outlets to publish information regarding pending criminal proceedings. Britain, Canada, and Australia, in particular, seek such restrictions. Delegates from those countries argue that their domestic law makes it illegal for newspapers and other media outlets to publish such information on the theory that they can undermine the fairness and integrity of criminal proceedings. Canadians, in particular, are worried that Internet bloggers and others, often located in the United States, will make information regarding pending Canadian criminal proceedings readily available to Canadians. As a result, the effectiveness of Canada's antipublication laws will be undercut. Can you agree to the proposed restrictions? Might it be permissible to agree to such restrictions insofar as they relate to criminal proceedings taking place outside of the United States?

3. *The Internet and Prejudicial Publicity. Nebraska Press Association* (see below) suggests that one remedy for potentially prejudicial pretrial publicity is a change of venue. Does the Internet restrict the effectiveness of that remedy? For example, when Karen Cunagin Sypher was charged in Louisville, Kentucky, with trying to extort money from University of Louisville basketball coach Rick Pitino, she moved for a change of venue. The prosecution opposed the request because Pitino is famous throughout the commonwealth (in addition to coaching at Louisville, he is the former coach at the University of Kentucky), and the Internet makes the information equally accessible to individuals throughout the commonwealth. Is this an adequate basis for denying the request for a change of venue? If change of venue is now a less effective remedy for prejudicial pretrial publicity, does that fact make a gag order less objectionable?

6.   Due Process and Prior Restraints

Following the *Sheppard* decision, courts struggled to find ways to protect a defendant's right to due process. Consider the following case.

Nebraska Press Association v. Stuart

427 U.S. 539 (1976)

Mr. Chief Justice BURGER delivered the opinion of the Court.

The respondent State District Judge entered an order restraining the petitioners from publishing or broadcasting accounts of confessions or admission made by the accused or facts "strongly implicative" of the accused in a widely reported murder of six persons. We granted certiorari to decide whether the entry of such an order on the showing made before the state court violated the constitutional guarantee of freedom of the press.

On the evening of October 18, 1975, local police found the six members of the Henry Kellie family murdered in their home in Sutherland, Neb., a town of about 850 people. Police released the description of a suspect, Erwin Charles Simants, to the reporters who had hastened to the scene of the crime. Simants was arrested and arraigned in Lincoln County Court the following morning, ending a tense night for this small rural community.

The crime immediately attracted widespread news coverage, by local, regional, and national newspapers, radio and television stations. Three days after the crime, the County Attorney and Simants' attorney joined in asking the County Court to enter a restrictive order relating to "matters that may or may not be publicly reported or disclosed to the public," because of the "mass coverage by news media" and the "reasonable likelihood of prejudicial news which would make difficult, if not impossible, the impaneling of an impartial jury and tend to prevent a fair trial." The County Court heard oral argument but took no evidence; no attorney for members of the press appeared at this stage. The County Court granted the prosecutor's motion for a restrictive order and entered it the next day, October 22. The order prohibited everyone in attendance from "releas-[ing] or authoriz(ing) the release for public dissemination in any form or manner whatsoever any testimony given or evidence adduced"; the order also required members of the press to observe the Nebraska Bar-Press Guidelines.

Simants' preliminary hearing was held the same day, open to the public but subject to the order. The County Court bound over the defendant for trial to the State District Court. The charges, as amended to reflect the autopsy findings, were that Simants had committed the murders in the course of a sexual assault.

Petitioners — several press and broadcast associations, publishers, and indi-vidual reporters — moved on October 23 for leave to intervene in the District Court, asking that the restrictive order imposed by the County Court be vacated. [The court] conducted a hearing, at which the County Judge testified and news-paper articles about the *Simants* case were admitted in evidence. The [judge] granted petitioners' motion to intervene [and] entered his own restrictive order. The judge found "because of the nature of the crimes charged in the complaint that there is a clear and present danger that pre-trial publicity could impinge upon the defendant's right to a fair trial." The order applied only until the jury was impaneled, and specifically prohibited petitioners from reporting five sub-jects: (1) the existence or contents of a confession Simants had made to law enforcement officers, which had been introduced in open court at arraignment; (2) the fact or nature of statements Simants had made to other persons; (3) the contents of a note he had written the night of the crime; (4) certain aspects of the medical testimony at the preliminary hearing; and (5) the identity of the victims of the alleged sexual assault and the nature of the assault. It also prohibited reporting the exact nature of the restrictive order itself. Like the County Court's order, this order incorporated the Nebraska Bar-Press Guidelines. Finally, the order set out a plan for attendance, seating, and courthouse traffic control dur-ing the trial.

The problems presented by this case are almost as old as the Republic. Nei-ther in the Constitution nor in contemporaneous writings do we find that the conflict between these two important rights was anticipated, yet it is inconceiv-able that the authors of the Constitution were unaware of the potential conflicts between the right to an unbiased jury and the guarantee of freedom of the [press].

The thread running through [earlier] cases is that prior restraints on speech and publication are the most serious and the least tolerable infringement on First Amendment rights. A criminal penalty or a judgment in a defamation case is sub-ject to the whole panoply of protections afforded by deferring the impact of the judgment until all avenues of appellate review have been exhausted. Only after judgment has become final, correct or otherwise, does the law's sanction become fully operative.

A prior restraint, by contrast and by definition, has an immediate and irre-versible sanction. If it can be said that a threat of criminal or civil sanctions after publication "chills" speech, prior restraint "freezes" it at least for the time.

The damage can be particularly great when the prior restraint falls upon the communication of news and commentary on current events. Truthful reports of public judicial proceedings have been afforded special protection against subsequent punishment. For the same reasons the protection against prior restraint should have particular force as applied to reporting of criminal proceedings, whether the crime in question is a single isolated act or a pattern of criminal conduct.

A responsible press has always been regarded as the handmaiden of effective judicial administration, especially in the criminal field. Its function in this regard is documented by an impressive record of service over several centuries. The press does not simply publish information about trials but guards against the miscarriage of justice by subjecting the police, prosecutors, and judicial processes to extensive public scrutiny and criticism.

The extraordinary protections afforded by the First Amendment carry with them something in the nature of a fiduciary duty to exercise the protected rights responsibly — a duty widely acknowledged but not always observed by editors and publishers. It is not asking too much to suggest that those who exercise First Amendment rights in newspapers or broadcasting enterprises direct some effort to protect the rights of an accused to a fair trial by unbiased jurors.

Of course, the order at issue — like the order requested in *New York Times* — does not prohibit but only postpones publication. Some news can be delayed and most commentary can even more readily be delayed without serious injury, and there often is a self-imposed delay when responsible editors call for verification of information. But such delays are normally slight and they are self-imposed. Delays imposed by governmental authority are a different matter.

We have learned, and continue to learn, from what we view as the unhappy experiences of other nations where government has been allowed to meddle in the internal editorial affairs of newspapers. Regardless of how beneficent-sounding the purposes of controlling the press might be, [we] "remain intensely skeptical about those measures that would allow government to insinuate itself into the editorial rooms of this Nation's press." Miami Herald Publishing Co. v. Tornillo, 418 U.S. 241, 259 (1974) (White, J., concurring).

As a practical matter, [the] element of time is not unimportant if press coverage is to fulfill its traditional function of bringing news to the public promptly.

We turn now to the record in this case to determine whether, as Learned Hand put it, "the gravity of the 'evil,' discounted by its improbability, justifies such invasion of free speech as is necessary to avoid the danger." To do so, we must examine the evidence before the trial judge when the order was entered to determine (a) the nature and extent of pretrial news coverage; (b) whether other measures would be likely to mitigate the effects of unrestrained pretrial publicity; and (c) how effectively a restraining order would operate to prevent the threatened danger. The precise terms of the restraining order are also important. We must then consider whether the record supports the entry of a prior restraint on publication, one of the most extraordinary remedies known to our jurisprudence. . . .

Our review of the pretrial record persuades us that the trial judge was justified in concluding that there would be intense and pervasive pretrial publicity concerning this case. He could also reasonably conclude, based on common human experience, that publicity might impair the defendant's right to a fair trial. He did not purport to say more, for he found only "a clear and present danger that pre-trial publicity *could* impinge upon the defendant's right to a fair trial." His conclusion as to the impact of such publicity on prospective jurors was of necessity speculative, dealing as he was with factors unknown and unknowable.

We find little in the record that goes to another aspect of our task, determining whether measures short of an order restraining all publication would have insured the defendant a fair trial. Although the entry of the order might be read as a judicial determination that other measures would not suffice, the trial court made no express findings to that effect; the Nebraska Supreme Court referred to the issue only by implication.

Most of the alternatives to prior restraint of publication in these circumstances were discussed with obvious approval in Sheppard v. Maxwell: (a) change of trial venue to a place less exposed to the intense publicity that seemed imminent in Lincoln County; (b) postponement of the trial to allow public attention to subside; (c) searching questioning of prospective jurors, as Mr. Chief Justice Marshall used in the *Burr* Case, to screen out those with fixed opinions as to guilt or innocence; (d) the use of emphatic and clear instructions on the sworn duty of each juror to decide the issues only on evidence presented in open court. Sequestration of jurors is, of course, always available. Although that measure insulates jurors only after they are sworn, it also enhances the likelihood of dissipating the impact of pretrial publicity and emphasizes the elements of the jurors' [oaths].

We must also assess the probable efficacy of prior restraint on publication as a workable method of protecting Simants' right to a fair trial, and we cannot ignore the reality of the problems of managing and enforcing pretrial restraining orders. The territorial jurisdiction of the issuing court is limited by concepts of sovereignty. The need for *in personam* jurisdiction also presents an obstacle to a restraining order that applies to publication at large as distinguished from restraining publication within a given [jurisdiction].

Finally, we note that the events disclosed by the record took place in a community of 850 people. It is reasonable to assume that, without any news accounts being printed or broadcast, rumors would travel swiftly by word of mouth. One can only speculate on the accuracy of such reports, given the generative propensities of rumors; they could well be more damaging than reasonably accurate news accounts. But plainly a whole community cannot be restrained from discussing a subject intimately affecting life within it.

Given these practical problems, it is far from clear that prior restraint on publication would have protected Simants' [rights].

Mr. Justice BRENNAN, with whom Mr. Justice STEWART and Mr. Justice MARSHALL join, concurring in the judgment.

[The] right to a fair trial by a jury of one's peers is unquestionably one of the most precious and sacred safeguards enshrined in the Bill of Rights. [R]esort to prior restraints on the freedom of the press is a constitutionally impermissible method for enforcing that right; judges have at their disposal a broad spectrum of devices for ensuring that fundamental fairness is accorded the accused without necessitating so drastic an incursion on the equally fundamental and salutary constitutional mandate that discussion of public affairs in a free society cannot depend on the preliminary grace of judicial censors. . . .

I would reject the contention that speculative deprivation of an accused's Sixth Amendment right to an impartial jury is comparable to the damage to the Nation or its people that *Near* and *New York Times* would have found sufficient to justify a prior restraint on reporting. Damage to that Sixth Amendment right could never be considered so direct, immediate and irreparable, and based on such proof rather than speculation, that prior restraints on the press could be justified on this basis.

Notes and Questions

1. *The Press Conference.* In Gentile v. State Bar of Nevada, 501 U.S. 1030 (1991), the Court struck down an attorney reprimand for holding a press conference following the indictment of his client. The Court noted that the case involved "classic political speech" because the petitioner was asserting that his client was a "scapegoat" and that "crooked cops" had not "been honest enough to indict the people who did it. . . ." The Court concluded: "Public awareness and criticism have even greater importance where, as here, they concern allegations of police corruption, or where, as is also the present circumstance, the criticism questions the judgment of an elected public prosecutor." The Court also noted that the "record does not support the conclusion that petitioner knew or reasonably should have known his remarks created a substantial likelihood of material prejudice, if the Rule's terms are given any meaningful content." Five justices suggested that attorney comments could be limited in appropriate cases. Justice Rehnquist, in an opinion joined by three other justices, argued that, because "lawyers have special access to information through discovery and client communications, their extrajudicial statements pose a threat to the fairness of a pending proceeding since lawyers' statements are likely to be received as especially authoritative." Like the majority, he would have applied a "substantial likelihood of material prejudice" standard. However, applying that standard, he would have reached a different result: "[The] restraint on speech is narrowly tailored to achieve those objectives."

2. *Protecting a Defendant's Right to a Fair Trial.* In light of decisions like *Nebraska Press Association* limiting the right of courts to restrict press access to, or coverage of, a trial, how can courts protect a defendant's right to a fair trial? In a well-publicized case (e.g., the recent highly publicized trial about the 1964 killings of civil rights workers in Mississippi), what can the judge do to ensure a fair trial?

∾ PROBLEM: MORE ON THE INTERNATIONAL TREATY REGULATING THE INTERNET ∾

Having read *Nebraska Press Association*, do you think that you have any more "wiggle room" to agree to provisions restricting Internet communications regarding pending criminal proceedings (in the United States or abroad)? If so, what language might you be able to agree to include in the treaty?

G. ACCESS TO GOVERNMENT PROPERTY

The parameters of the public forum doctrine are well settled today, and we have examined their basic elements in earlier sections. This section examines the public forum doctrine on its own and explores the modern debates that animate its contours. Professor Harry Kalven invented the label "public forum" law. *See* Kalven, *The Concept of the Public Forum: Cox v. Louisiana*, 1965 Sup. Ct. Rev. 1. The label is a shorthand reference to cases involving government regulation of government-owned property. This property includes the most ancient Greek-like fora of streets and parks where citizens gather to discuss the issues of the day, as well as newer fora that have been "opened" by the government and "dedicated" to speech in some way. This property also includes "non-public fora" where judicial review of regulations is more deferential than it is for property that qualifies as public fora. The trace elements of modern public forum law go back as far as the 1930s, where the Court invalidated total bans on certain types of communications in public streets. *See* Schneider v. New Jersey, 308 U.S. 147 (1939) (ban on leafleting on public streets and other public places invalidated); Lovell v. Griffin, 303 U.S. 444 (1938) (ban on distribution of literature within a city invalidated). One famous explanation for the need for the First Amendment right of access to what we would now call "the public forum," given in Hague v. CIO, 307 U.S. 496 (1939), goes as follows: "Wherever the title of streets and parks may rest, they have immemorially been held in trust for the use of the public and, time out of mind, have been used for purposes of assembly, communicating thoughts between citizens, and discussing public questions. Such use of the streets and public places, has, from ancient times, been a part of the privileges, immunities, rights, and liberties of citizens. [It] is not absolute, but relative, and must be exercised in subordination to the general comfort and convenience, and in consonance with peace and good order; but it must not, in the guise of regulation, be abridged or denied."

International Society for Krishna Consciousness, Inc. v. Lee

505 U.S. 672 (1992)

Chief Justice REHNQUIST delivered the opinion of the Court.

In this case we consider whether an airport terminal operated by a public authority is a public forum and whether a regulation prohibiting solicitation in the interior of an airport terminal violates the First Amendment.

[Petitioner] International Society for Krishna Consciousness, Inc. (ISKCON), is a not-for-profit religious corporation whose members perform a ritual known as *sankirtan*. The ritual consists of "going into public places, disseminating religious literature and soliciting funds to support the religion." The primary purpose of this ritual is raising funds for the movement.

Respondent Walter Lee [is] the police superintendent of the Port Authority of New York and New Jersey and was charged with enforcing the regulation at issue. The Port Authority owns and operates three major airports in the greater New York City area: John F. Kennedy International Airport (Kennedy), La Guardia Airport (La Guardia), and Newark International Airport (Newark). The three airports collectively form one of the world's busiest metropolitan airport complexes. They serve approximately 8% of this country's domestic airline market and more than 50% of the trans-Atlantic market. . . .

The airports are funded by user fees and operated to make a regulated profit. Most space at the three airports is leased to commercial airlines, which bear primary responsibility for the leasehold. The Port Authority retains control over unleased portions, including La Guardia's Central Terminal Building, portions of Kennedy's International Arrivals Building, and Newark's North Terminal Building (collectively the "terminals"). The terminals are generally accessible to the general public and contain various commercial establishments such as restaurants, snack stands, bars, newsstands, and stores of various types. Virtually all who visit the terminals do so for purposes related to air travel. These visitors principally include passengers, those meeting or seeing off passengers, flight crews, and terminal employees.

The Port Authority has adopted a regulation forbidding within the terminals the repetitive solicitation of money or distribution of literature. The regulation states:

> 1. The following conduct is prohibited within the interior areas of buildings or structures at an air terminal if conducted by a person to or with passers-by in a continuous or repetitive manner:
>   (a) The sale or distribution of any merchandise, including but not limited to jewelry, food stuffs, candles, flowers, badges and clothing.
>   (b) The sale or distribution of flyers, brochures, pamphlets, books or any other printed or written material.
>   (c) The solicitation and receipt of funds.

The regulation governs only the terminals; the Port Authority permits solicitation and distribution on the sidewalks outside the terminal buildings. The regulation effectively prohibits ISKCON from performing *sankirtan* in the terminals. As a result, ISKCON brought suit seeking declaratory and injunctive relief under 42 U.S.C. §1983, alleging that the regulation worked to deprive its members of rights guaranteed under the First Amendment.

It is uncontested that the solicitation at issue [is] a form of speech protected under the First Amendment. But it is also well settled that the government need not permit all forms of speech on property that it owns and controls. Where the government is acting as a proprietor, managing its internal operations, rather than acting as lawmaker with the power to regulate or license, its action will not be subjected to the heightened review to which its actions as a lawmaker may be subject. Thus, we have upheld a ban on political advertisements in city-operated transit vehicles, even though the city permitted other types of advertising on those vehicles. Similarly, we have permitted a school district to limit access to an internal mail system used to communicate with teachers employed by the district. Perry Ed. Assn. v. Perry Local Educators' Assn., 460 U.S. 37 (1983).

These cases reflect, either implicitly or explicitly, a "forum based" approach for assessing restrictions that the government seeks to place on the use of its property. Cornelius v. NAACP Legal Defense & Ed. Fund, Inc., 473 U.S. 788 (1985). Under this approach, regulation of speech on government property that has traditionally been available for public expression is subject to the highest scrutiny. Such regulations survive only if they are narrowly drawn to achieve a compelling state interest. The second category of public property is the designated public forum, whether of a limited or unlimited character — property that the State has opened for expressive activity by part or all of the public. Regulation of such property is subject to the same limitations as that governing a traditional public forum. Finally, there is all remaining public property. Limitations on expressive activity conducted on this last category of property must survive only a much more limited review. The challenged regulation need only be reasonable, as long as the regulation is not an effort to suppress the speaker's activity due to disagreement with the speaker's view.

The parties do not disagree that this is the proper framework. Rather, they disagree whether the airport terminals are public fora or nonpublic fora. They also disagree whether the regulation survives the "reasonableness" review governing nonpublic fora, should that prove the appropriate category. [We] conclude that the terminals are nonpublic fora and that the regulation reasonably limits solicitation.

The suggestion that the government has a high burden in justifying speech restrictions relating to traditional public fora made its first appearance in Hague v. Committee for Industrial Organization, 307 U.S. 496 (1939). Justice Roberts, concluding that individuals have a right to use "streets and parks for communication of views," reasoned that such a right flowed from the fact that "streets and parks [have] immemorially been held in trust for the use of the public and, time out of mind, have been used for purposes of assembly, communicating thoughts between citizens, and discussing public questions." We confirmed this observation in Frisby v. Schultz, 487 U.S. 474 (1988), where we held that a residential street was a public forum.

Our recent cases provide additional guidance on the characteristics of a public forum. In *Cornelius* we noted that a traditional public forum is property that has as "a principal purpose . . . the free exchange of ideas." Moreover, consistent with the notion that the government — like other property owners — "has power to preserve the property under its control for the use to which it is lawfully dedicated," the government does not create a public forum by inaction. Nor is a public forum created "whenever members of the public are permitted freely to visit a place owned or operated by the Government." The decision to create a public forum must instead be made "by intentionally opening a nontraditional forum for public discourse." Finally, we have recognized that the location of property also has bearing because separation from acknowledged public areas may serve to indicate that the separated property is a special enclave, subject to greater restriction. United States v. Grace, 461 U.S. 171 (1983).

These precedents foreclose the conclusion that airport terminals are public fora. Reflecting the general growth of the air travel industry, airport terminals have only recently achieved their contemporary size and character. But given the lateness with which the modern air terminal has made its appearance, it hardly qualifies for the description of having "immemorially . . . time out of mind" been held in the public trust and used for purposes of expressive activity. [W]ithin the rather short history of air transport, it is only "[i]n recent years [that] it has become a common practice for various religious and non-profit organizations to use commercial airports as a forum for the distribution of literature, the solicitation of funds, the proselytizing of new members, and other similar activities." 45 Fed. Reg. 35314 (1980). Thus, the tradition of airport activity does not demonstrate that airports have historically been made available for speech activity. Nor can we say that these particular terminals, or airport terminals generally, have been intentionally opened by their operators to such activity; the frequent and continuing litigation evidencing the operators' objections belies any such claim. In short, there can be no argument that society's time-tested judgment, expressed through acquiescence in a continuing practice, has resolved the issue in petitioners' favor.

Petitioners attempt to circumvent the history and practice governing airport activity by pointing our attention to the variety of speech activity that they claim historically occurred at various "transportation nodes" such as rail stations, bus stations, wharves, and Ellis Island. [W]e think that such evidence is of little import for two reasons. First, much of the evidence is irrelevant to *public* fora analysis, because sites such as bus and rail terminals traditionally have had *private* ownership. . . . The practices of privately held transportation centers do not bear on the government's regulatory authority over a publicly owned airport. . . . Second, the relevant unit for our inquiry is an airport, not "transportation nodes" generally. When new methods of transportation develop, [it] will be a new inquiry whether the transportation necessities are compatible with various kinds of expressive activity. . . . The "security magnet," for example, is an airport commonplace that lacks a counterpart in bus terminals and train stations. And public access to air terminals is also not infrequently restricted. . . . To blithely equate airports with other transportation centers, therefore, would be a mistake.

The differences among such facilities are unsurprising [since] airports are commercial establishments funded by users fees and designed to make a regulated profit, and where nearly all who visit do so for some travel related purpose.

[I]t cannot fairly be said that an airport terminal has as a principal purpose promoting "the free exchange of ideas." Cornelius v. NAACP Legal Defense & Ed. Fund, Inc., 473 U.S. 788 (1985). To the contrary, . . . Port Authority management considers the purpose of the terminals to be the facilitation of passenger air travel, not the promotion of expression. [T]he terminals have never been dedicated (except under the threat of court order) to expression in the form sought to be exercised here: i.e., the solicitation of contributions and the distribution of literature.

The terminals here are far from atypical. Airport builders and managers focus their efforts on providing terminals that will contribute to efficient air travel. . . . Although many airports have expanded their function beyond merely contributing to efficient air travel, few have included among their purposes the designation of a forum for solicitation and distribution activities. [N]either by tradition nor purpose can the terminals be described as satisfying the standards we have previously set out for identifying a public forum.

The restrictions here challenged, therefore, need only satisfy a requirement of reasonableness. We reiterate what we stated in *Kokinda*: The restriction "need only be *reasonable*; it need not be the most reasonable or the only reasonable limitation." We have no doubt that under this standard the prohibition on solicitation passes muster.

We have on many prior occasions noted the disruptive effect that solicitation may have on business. "Solicitation requires action by those who would respond: The individual solicited must decide whether or not to contribute (which itself might involve reading the solicitor's literature or hearing his pitch), and then, having decided to do so, reach for a wallet, search it for money, write a check, or produce a credit card." Passengers who wish to avoid the solicitor may have to alter their paths, slowing both themselves and those around them. The result is that the normal flow of traffic is impeded. This is especially so in an airport, where "[a]ir travelers, who are often weighted down by cumbersome baggage [may] be hurrying to catch a plane or to arrange ground transportation." Delays may be particularly costly in this setting, as a flight missed by only a few minutes can result in hours worth of subsequent inconvenience.

[F]ace-to-face solicitation presents risks of duress that are an appropriate target of regulation. The skillful, and unprincipled, solicitor can target the most vulnerable, including those accompanying children or those suffering physical impairment and who cannot easily avoid the solicitation. The unsavory solicitor can also commit fraud through concealment of his affiliation or through deliberate efforts to shortchange those who agree to purchase. Compounding this problem is the fact that, in an airport, the targets of such activity frequently are on tight schedules. This in turn makes such visitors unlikely to stop and formally complain to airport authorities. As a result, the airport faces considerable difficulty in achieving its legitimate interest in monitoring solicitation activity to assure that travelers are not interfered with unduly.

The Port Authority has concluded that its interest in monitoring the activities can best be accomplished by limiting solicitation and distribution to the sidewalk areas outside the terminals. This sidewalk area is frequented by an over-whelming percentage of airport users. Thus the resulting access of those who would solicit the general public is quite complete. In turn we think it would be odd to conclude that the Port Authority's terminal regulation is unreasonable despite the Port Authority having otherwise assured access to an area universally traveled.

The inconveniences to passengers and the burdens on Port Authority offi-cials flowing from solicitation activity may seem small, but viewed against the fact that "pedestrian congestion is one of the greatest problems facing the three ter-minals," the Port Authority could reasonably worry that even such incremental effects would prove quite disruptive. Moreover, "[t]he justification for the Rule should not be measured by the disorder that would result from granting an exemption solely to ISKCON." For if ISKCON is given access, so too must other groups. "Obviously, there would be a much larger threat to the State's interest in crowd control if all other religious, nonreligious, and noncommercial organiza-tions could likewise move freely." As a result, we conclude that the solicitation ban is reasonable.

For the foregoing reasons, the judgment of the Court of Appeals sustaining the ban on solicitation in Port Authority terminals is

Affirmed.

Justice KENNEDY, with whom Justice BLACKMUN, Justice STEVENS, and Justice SOUTER join as to Part I, concurring in the judgment.

While I concur in the judgment affirming this case [which upholds a ban on solicitation of funds at the airport terminals, in my view,] the airport corridors and shopping areas outside of the passenger security zones [are] public forums, and speech in those places is entitled to protection against all government regu-lation inconsistent with public forum principles.

I

[The Court's analysis] leaves the government with almost unlimited authority to restrict speech on its property by doing nothing more than articulating a non-speech-related purpose for the area, and it leaves almost no scope for the devel-opment of new public forums absent the rare approval of the government. The Court's error lies in its conclusion that the public forum status of the property depends on the government's defined purpose of the property, or on an explicit decision by the government to dedicate the property to expressive activity. In my view, the inquiry must be an objective one, based on the actual, physical charac-teristics and uses of the [property].

[The] Court's approach is contrary to the underlying purposes of the public forum doctrine. The liberties protected by our doctrine derive from the Assem-bly, as well as the Speech and Press Clauses of the First Amendment and are essen-tial to a functioning democracy. *See* Kalven, *The Concept of a Public Forum: Cox v. Louisiana*, 1965 S. Ct. Rev. 1. Public places are of necessity the locus for discussion of public issues, as well as protest against arbitrary government action. [I]n a free nation citizens must have the right to gather and speak with other persons in public places. The recognition that certain government-owned property is a public forum provides open notice to citizens that their freedoms may be exercised there without fear of a censorial government, adding tangible reinforcement to the idea that we are a free [people].

The Court's analysis rests on an inaccurate view of history. The notion that traditional public forums are property which have public discourse as their principal purpose is a most doubtful fiction. The types of property that we have recognized as the quintessential public forums are streets, parks, and sidewalks. It would seem apparent that the principal purpose of streets and sidewalks, like airports, is to facilitate transportation, not public discourse. [The] purpose for the creation of public parks may be as much for beauty and open space as for discourse. Thus under the Court's analysis, even the quintessential public forums would appear to lack the necessary elements of what the Court defines as a public forum.

The effect of the Court's narrow view of the first category of public forums is compounded by its description of the second purported category, the so-called "designated" forum. [Under] the Court's analysis today few if any types of property other than those already recognized as public forums will be accorded that status. [If] the objective physical characteristics of the property at issue and the actual public access and uses which have been permitted by the government indicate that expressive activity would be appropriate and compatible with those uses, the property is a public forum. [The] possibility of some theoretical inconsistency between expressive activities and the property's uses should not bar a finding of a public forum, if those inconsistencies can be avoided through simple and permitted regulations.

[Where] government property does not satisfy the criteria of a public forum, the government retains the power to dedicate the property for speech, whether for all expressive activity or for limited purposes only. . . . In some sense the government always retains authority to close a public forum, by selling the property, changing its physical character, or changing its principal use. . . . The difference is that when a property is a protected public forum the state may not by fiat assert broad control over speech or expressive activities; it must alter the objective physical character or uses of the property, and bear the attendant costs, to change the property's forum status.

Under this analysis it is evident that the public spaces of the Port Authority's airports are public forums. First, the[re are] physical similarities between the Port Authority's airports and public streets. [T]he public spaces in the airports are broad, public thoroughfares full of people and lined with stores and other commercial activities. An airport corridor is of course not a street, but that is not the proper inquiry. The question is one of physical similarities, sufficient to suggest that the airport corridor should be a public forum for the same reasons that streets and sidewalks have been treated as public forums. . . . Second, the airport areas [are] open to the public without restriction. Plaintiffs do not seek access to the secured areas of the airports. . . . And while most people who come to the Port Authority's airports do so for a reason related to air travel, either because they are passengers or because they are picking up or dropping off passengers, this does not distinguish an airport from streets or sidewalks, which most people use for travel. . . . Third, and perhaps most important, [when] adequate time, place, and manner regulations are in place, expressive activity is quite compatible with the uses of major airports. The Port Authority [argues that] congestion in its airports' corridors makes expressive activity inconsistent with the airports' primary purpose, which is to facilitate air travel. The First Amendment is often inconvenient. But [i]nconvenience does not absolve the government of its obligation to tolerate [speech].

The danger of allowing the government to suppress speech is shown in the case now before us. A grant of plenary power allows the government to tilt the dialogue heard by the public, to exclude many, more marginal voices. [We] have long recognized the right to distribute flyers and literature lies at the heart of the liberties guaranteed by the Speech and Press Clauses of the First Amendment. The Port Authority's rule, which prohibits almost all such activity, is among the most restrictive possible of those liberties. The regulation is in fact so broad and restrictive of speech, Justice O'Connor finds it void even under the standards applicable to government regulations in nonpublic forums. I have no difficulty deciding the regulation cannot survive the far more stringent rules applicable to regulations in public forums. The regulation is not drawn in narrow terms, and it does not leave open ample alternative channels for communication. The Port Authority's concerns with the problem of congestion can be addressed through narrow restrictions on the time and place of expressive activity. I would strike down the regulation as an unconstitutional restriction of speech.

II

It is my view, however, that the Port Authority's ban on the "solicitation and receipt of funds" within its airport terminals should be upheld under the standards applicable to speech regulations in public forums. The regulation may be upheld as either a reasonable time, place, and manner restriction, or as a regulation directed at the nonspeech element of expressive conduct. The two standards have considerable overlap in a case like this one.

It is well settled that "even in a public forum the government may impose reasonable restrictions on the time, place, or manner of protected speech, provided the restrictions 'are justified without reference to the content of the regulated speech, that they are narrowly tailored to serve a significant governmental interest, and that they leave open ample alternative channels for communication of the information.'" *Ward, supra,* at 791 (quoting Clark v. Community for Creative Non-Violence, 468 U.S. 288 (1984)). [T]he government in appropriate circumstances may regulate conduct, even if the conduct has an expressive component. United States v. O'Brien, 391 U.S. 367 (1968). [T]he standards for assessing time, place, and manner restrictions are little, if any, different from the standards applicable to regulations of conduct with an expressive component. *Clark, supra,* 468 U.S., at 298. The confluence of the two tests is well demonstrated by a case like this, where the government regulation at issue can be described with equal accuracy as a regulation of the manner of expression, or as a regulation of conduct with an expressive component.

I am in full agreement with the statement of the Court that solicitation is a form of protected speech. If the Port Authority's solicitation regulation prohibited all speech that requested the contribution of funds, I would conclude that it was a direct, content-based restriction of speech in clear violation of the First Amendment. The Authority's regulation does not prohibit all solicitation, however; it prohibits the "solicitation and receipt of funds." I do not understand this regulation to prohibit all speech that solicits funds. It reaches only personal solicitations for immediate payment of money. . . . The regulation does not cover, for example, the distribution of preaddressed envelopes along with a plea to contribute money to the distributor or his organization. . . . So viewed, I believe the Port Authority's rule survives our test for speech restrictions in the public forum. In-person solicitation of funds, when combined with immediate receipt of that money, creates a risk of fraud and duress that is well recognized, and that is different in kind from other forms of expression or conduct. . . . [R]equests for immediate payment of money create a strong potential for fraud or undue pressure, in part because of the lack of time for reflection. [Q]uestionable practices associated with solicitation can include the targeting of vulnerable and easily coerced persons, misrepresentation of the solicitor's cause, and outright theft. . . . Because the Port Authority's solicitation ban is directed at these abusive practices and not at any particular message, idea, or form of speech, the regulation is a content-neutral rule serving a significant government interest. . . . I have little difficulty in deciding that the Port Authority has left open ample alternative channels for the communication of the message which is an aspect of solicitation. . . .

Notes

1. *Definitional Debates.* The *ISKCON* holding with regard to the definition of a public forum was five to four, and it may be that Justice Kennedy has five votes for his definition on the present Court. The *ISKCON* debate about the proper contours of the boundary between the nontraditional (or designated) public forum and the nonpublic forum is one in a long line of similar debates in prior cases. In Cornelius v. NAACP Legal Defense and Educational Fund, Inc., 473 U.S. 788 (1985), Justice O'Connor wrote for a plurality of four in determining that a fundraising drive for charitable purposes in the federal workplace was a nonpublic forum. She focused on the significance of examining the policy and practice of the government, the nature of the property, and its "compatibility" with expressive activity. But Justice O'Connor also observed that "government does not create a public forum by inaction or by permitting limited discourse, but only by intentionally opening a non-traditional forum for public discourse." She also noted that the Court "will not find that a public forum has been created in

the face of clear evidence of a contrary intent," nor will the Court "infer that the Government intended to create a public forum when the nature of the property is inconsistent with expressive activity."

2. *The Unique Character of Particular Fora.* The *ISKCON* majority provides examples of notable pre-*ISKCON* holdings on the issue of a forum's status. In Lehman v. Shaker Heights, 418 U.S. 298 (1974), the Court reasoned as follows in finding the "car card space" on a bus to be a nonpublic forum: "[T]he city is engaged in commerce. It must provide rapid, convenient, pleasant, and inexpensive service to the commuters of Shaker Heights. The car card space, although incidental to the provision of public transportation, is a part of the commercial venture. In much the same way that a newspaper or periodical, or even a radio or television station, need not accept every proffer of advertising from the general public, a city transit system has discretion to develop and make reasonable choices concerning the type of advertising that may be displayed in its vehicles." Likewise, in Greer v. Spock, 424 U.S. 828 (1976), a military base was held to be a nonpublic forum: "[I]t is 'the primary business of armies and navies to fight or be ready to fight wars should the occasion arise.' And it is consequently the business of a military installation like Fort Dix to train soldiers, not to provide a public forum. . . . The notion that federal military reservations, like municipal streets and parks, have traditionally served as a place for free public assembly and communication of thoughts by private citizens is thus historically and constitutionally false." As *Lehman* and *Greer* suggest, decisions regarding the status of fora reflect consideration of a totality of circumstances on a case-by-case basis and depend on certain *sui generis* aspects of those fora.

3. *A.I.G. Protests.* Since the financial meltdown of 2008-2009, protestors have demonstrated at the homes of prominent financial executives. For example, in March 2009, protestors arranged a "Lifestyles of the Rich and Infamous" tour that involved "drive-by protests" at the homes of A.I.G. executives. *See* Manny Fernandez, "Drive-By A.I.G. Protests on Fairfield's Elite Streets," *New York Times*, A (Mar. 21, 2009).

∾ PROBLEMS ∾

1. *No-Demonstration Zones.* A regulation restricts "demonstration activity" near the U.S. Capitol. *Demonstration activity* is defined as "parading, picketing, leafleting, holding vigils, sit-ins, or other expressive conduct or speechmaking that conveys a message supporting or opposing a point of view and has the intent, effect or propensity to attract a crowd of onlookers, but does not include merely wearing T-shirts, buttons, or other similar articles of apparel that convey a message." Specifically, the regulation created a "no-demonstration" zone in which such "demonstration activity" is entirely barred. The zone included the sidewalk at the foot of the Senate steps on the Capitol's East Front. The Capitol police arrested an artist participating in the annual Arts Advocacy Day because he distributed leaflets on that sidewalk (the leaflets sought to publicize a lawsuit

regarding artists' rights). Before they arrested the artist, the police told him that he could pass out his leaflets if he would move 150 feet away from the Capitol onto the lawn on the far side of the paved East Front plaza (which was not a "no-demonstration" zone under the regulations). But the artist believed that he could not reach his intended audience from the lawn, insisted on his right to leaflet on the sidewalk, and was arrested. The sidewalk is part of the Capitol Grounds, a 60-acre area designed by Frederick Law Olmstead in the late 1870s. Although barricades prevent vehicles from entering this area except through designated gatehouses, no barriers impede pedestrian access. Members of the public use the area extensively, commuting to work, sightseeing, posing for pictures, jogging, and walking dogs. The East Front sidewalk is continuously open, often uncongested, and a place where people may enjoy the open air. Is the sidewalk at the foot of the Senate steps a "public forum"? Assume that a court determines that the sidewalk is a "public forum" or a "nontraditional public forum" and not a nonpublic forum. Assume that this means that any regulation in this forum must be content neutral, justified by a significant government interest, and narrowly tailored, and also must allow for ample alternative channels of communication. Explain the arguments that will be made by the speech litigant who seeks to have the regulation invalidated under this "time, place, manner" test.

2. *"Choose Life" License Plates.* Suppose that the State of Illinois allows motorists to apply for specialty plates. Because of the controversial nature of the topic, however, Illinois refuses to provide any plates that deal with the issue of abortion (either pro-life or pro-choice). The plaintiffs, who have obtained more than 25,000 signatures on a petition, apply for a "Choose Life" plate. Can a state choose to offer specialty plates but refuse to offer any plates that deal with the issue of abortion? Is this a public forum issue? *Compare* Roach v. Stouffer, 560 F.3d 860 (8th Cir. 2009), *with* Choose Life Illinois Inc. v. White, 547 F.3d 853 (7th Cir. 2008). Could the State choose to allow pro-life license plates but refuse to issue pro-choice plates? *See* Arizona Life Coal., Inc. v. Stanton, 515 F.3d 956 (9th Cir. 2008).

3. *The Democratic National Convention.* In 2008, the Democratic Party held its national convention in Denver, Colorado. Citing security concerns, Denver police sought to keep protestors away from the convention. In one instance, although Denver granted a parade permit to protestors, it required the parade to end approximately one-third of a mile away from the convention center. *See* Kirk Johnson, "Judge to Rule on Limits at Denver Convention," *New York Times*, A-15, c. 1-6 (Aug. 1, 2008). Is Denver required to allow the protestors to get close enough to the center so that convention-goers can see and hear them? Are protestors entitled to be close enough so that they can use the center as a media backdrop?

4. *Art or Vandalism?* An artist is known for his "street art" — art painted on public buildings or structures — especially his portraits of Barack Obama. When he painted one of his portraits on a public railroad trestle, he was charged with vandalism. *See* Abby Goodnough, "Boston Vandalism Charges Stir Debate on Art's Place," *New York Times*, A-14, c. 1-5 (Mar. 12, 2009). Do artists have a constitutional right to appropriate public spaces for their art?

Heffron v. International Society for Krishna Consciousness, Inc.

452 U.S. 640 (1981)

Justice WHITE delivered the opinion of the Court.

The question [is] whether a State, consistent with the First and Fourteenth Amendments, may require a religious organization desiring to distribute and sell religious literature and to solicit donations at a state fair to conduct those activities only at an assigned location within the fairgrounds even though application of the rule limits the religious practices of the organization.

I

Each year, the Minnesota Agricultural Society (Society), a public corporation organized under the laws of Minnesota, operates a State Fair on a 125-acre state-owned tract [in] St. Paul, Minn. The Fair is conducted for the purpose of "exhibiting [the] agricultural, stock-breeding, horticultural, mining, mechanical, industrial, and other products and resources of the state, including proper exhibits and expositions of the arts, human skills, and sciences." The Fair is a major public event and attracts visitors from all over Minnesota as well as from other parts of the country. [T]he average total attendance for the 12-day Fair has been 1,320,000 persons [with] 115,000 persons [on weekdays and 160,000 on Saturdays and Sundays].

[The] Society promulgated Minnesota State Fair Rule 6.05 which provides in relevant part that "[s]ale or distribution of any merchandise, including printed or written material except under license issued [by] the Society and/or from a duly-licensed location shall be a misdemeanor." As Rule 6.05 is construed[,] "all persons, groups or firms which desire to sell, exhibit or distribute materials during the annual State Fair must do so only from fixed locations on the fairgrounds." Although the Rule does not prevent organizational representatives from walking about the fairgrounds and communicating the organization's views with fair patrons in face-to-face discussions, it does require that any exhibitor conduct its sales, distribution, and fund solicitation operations from a booth rented from the Society. Space in the fairgrounds is rented to all comers in a nondiscriminatory fashion on a first-come, first-served basis with the rental charge based on the size and location of the booth. The Rule applies alike to nonprofit, charitable, and commercial enterprises. ["Over 14,000 exhibitors and concessionaires rented booth space during the 1977 and 1978 Fairs, with several hundred potential exhibitors denied rental space solely because of the limited amount of area available."]

One day prior to the opening of the 1977 Minnesota State Fair, respondents International Society for Krishna Consciousness, Inc. (ISKCON), [filed suit, seeking declaratory and injunctive relief, and arguing that Rule 6.05 both on its face and as applied, violated respondents' rights under the First Amendment. ISKCON] asserted that the Rule would suppress the practice of Sankirtan, one of its religious rituals, which enjoins its members to go into public places to distribute or sell religious literature and to solicit donations for the support of the

Krishna [religion]. [The Court noted that] in performing Sankirtan, ISKCON members "often greet members of the public by giving them flowers or small American flags" and that ISKCON "did not assert any right to seek contributions," nor "did they seek to dance, chant, or engage in any other activities besides the distribution and sale of literature and the solicitation of donations" unrelated to any "greeting gifts."

[T]he First Amendment does not guarantee the right to communicate one's views at all times and places or in any manner that may be desired. [T]he activities of ISKCON, like those of others protected by the First Amendment, are subject to reasonable time, place, and manner restrictions. "We have often approved restrictions of that kind provided that they are justified without reference to the content of the regulated speech, that they serve a significant governmental interest, and that in doing so they leave open ample alternative channels for communication of the information." The issue here [is] whether Rule 6.05 is a permissible restriction on the place and manner of communicating the views of the Krishna religion, more specifically, whether the Society may require the members of ISKCON who desire to practice Sankirtan at the State Fair to confine their distribution, sales, and solicitation activities to a fixed location.

A major criterion for a valid time, place and manner restriction is that the restriction "may not be based upon either the content or subject matter of speech." Rule 6.05 qualifies in this respect, since [the] Rule applies evenhandedly to all who wish to distribute and sell written materials or to solicit funds. No person or organization, whether commercial or charitable, is permitted to engage in such activities except from a booth rented for those purposes.

Nor does Rule 6.05 suffer from the more covert forms of discrimination that may result when arbitrary discretion is vested in some governmental authority. The method of allocating space is a straightforward first-come, first-served system. The Rule is not open to the kind of arbitrary application that this Court has condemned as inherently inconsistent with a valid time, place, and manner regulation because such discretion has the potential for becoming a means of suppressing a particular point of view. A valid time, place, and manner regulation must also "serve a significant governmental interest." Here, the principal justification asserted by the State in support of Rule 6.05 is the need to maintain the orderly movement of the crowd given the large number of exhibitors and persons attending the Fair. [Two other interests are asserted in support of the rule, including an interest in protecting fairgoers from "fraudulent solicitations, deceptive or false speech, and undue annoyance," and the interest in protecting them "from being harassed or otherwise being bothered" as a captive audience. The court did not decide "whether these other two purposes are constitutionally sufficient to support the imposition of the Rule."]

The fairgrounds comprise a relatively small area of 125 acres, the bulk of which is covered by permanent buildings, temporary structures, parking lots, and connecting thoroughfares. There were some 1,400 exhibitors and concessionaires renting space for the 1977 and 1978 Fairs, chiefly in permanent and temporary buildings. The Fair is designed to exhibit to the public an enormous variety of goods, services, entertainment, and other matters of interest. This is accomplished by confining individual exhibitors to fixed locations, with the public moving to and among the booths or other attractions, using streets and open spaces provided for that purpose. Because the Fair attracts large crowds, it is apparent that the State's interest in the orderly movement and control of such an assembly of persons is a substantial consideration.

As a general matter, it is clear that a State's interest in protecting the "safety and convenience" of persons using a public forum is a valid governmental objective. Furthermore, consideration of a forum's special attributes is relevant to the constitutionality of a regulation since the significance of the governmental interest must be assessed in light of the characteristic nature and function of the particular forum involved. This observation bears particular import in the present case since respondents make a number of analogies between the fairgrounds and city streets which have "immemorially been held in trust for the use of the public [and] have been used for purposes of assembly, communicating thoughts between citizens, and discussing public questions." But it is clear that there are significant differences between a street and the fairgrounds. A street is continually open, often uncongested, and constitutes not only a necessary conduit in the daily affairs of a locality's citizens, but also a place where people may enjoy the open air or the company of friends and neighbors in a relaxed environment. The Minnesota Fair [is] a temporary event attracting great numbers of visitors who come to the event for a short period to see and experience the host of exhibits and attractions at the Fair. The flow of the crowd and demands of safety are more pressing in the context of the Fair. As such, any comparisons to public streets are necessarily inexact.

[The] justification for the Rule should not be measured by the disorder that would result from granting an exemption solely to ISKCON. . . . None of our cases suggest that the inclusion of peripatetic solicitation as part of a church ritual entitles church members to solicitation rights in a public forum superior to those of members of other religious groups that raise money but do not purport to ritualize the process. Nor for present purposes do religious organizations enjoy rights to communicate, distribute, and solicit on the fairgrounds superior to those of other organizations having social, political, or other ideological messages to proselytize. These nonreligious organizations seeking support for their activities are entitled to rights equal to those of religious groups to enter a public forum and spread their views, whether by soliciting funds or by distributing literature.

If Rule 6.05 is an invalid restriction on the activities of ISKCON, it is no more valid with respect to the other social, political, or charitable organizations that have rented booths at the Fair and confined their distribution, sale, and fund solicitation to those locations. Nor would it be valid with respect to other organizations that did not rent booths, either because they were unavailable due to a lack of space or because they chose to avoid the expense involved, but that would in all probability appear in the fairgrounds to distribute, sell, and solicit if they could freely do so. The question would also inevitably arise as to what extent the First Amendment also gives commercial organizations a right to move among the crowd to distribute information about or to sell their wares as respondents claim they may do.

ISKCON desires to proselytize at the fair because it believes it can successfully communicate and raise funds. In its view, this can be done only by intercepting fair patrons as they move about, [and] stopping them momentarily or for longer periods as money is given or exchanged for literature. [Without] Rule 6.05 there would be widespread disorder at the fairgrounds. [S]ome disorder would inevitably result from exempting the Krishnas from the Rule. Obviously, there would be a much larger threat to the State's interest in crowd control if all other religious, nonreligious, and noncommercial organizations could likewise move freely about the fairgrounds distributing and selling literature and soliciting funds at will. . . . Given these considerations, we hold that the State's interest in confining distribution, selling, and fund solicitation activities to fixed locations is sufficient to satisfy the requirement that a place or manner restriction must serve a substantial state interest. . . .

For similar reasons, we cannot agree with the Minnesota Supreme Court that Rule 6.05 is an unnecessary regulation because the State could avoid the threat to its interest posed by ISKCON by less restrictive means, such as penalizing disorder or disruption, limiting the number of solicitors, or putting more narrowly drawn restrictions on the location and movement of ISKCON's representatives. [I]t is quite improbable that the alternative means suggested by the Minnesota Supreme Court would deal adequately with the problems posed by the much larger number of distributors and solicitors that would be present on the fairgrounds if the judgment below were affirmed.

For Rule 6.05 to be valid as a place and manner restriction, it must also be sufficiently clear that alternative forums for the expression of respondents' protected speech exist despite the effects of the Rule. Rule 6.05 is not vulnerable on this ground. First, the Rule does not prevent ISKCON from practicing Sankirtan anywhere outside the fairgrounds. More importantly, [ISKCON's] members may mingle with the crowd and orally propagate their views. The organization may also arrange for a booth and distribute and sell literature and solicit funds from that location on the fairgrounds itself. The Minnesota State Fair is a limited public forum [that] exists to provide a means for a great number of exhibitors temporarily to present their products or views, be they commercial, religious, or political, to a large number of people in an efficient fashion. Considering the limited functions of the Fair and the combined area within which it operates, we are unwilling to say that Rule 6.05 does not provide ISKCON and other organizations with an adequate means to sell and solicit on the fairgrounds. The First Amendment protects the right of every citizen to "reach the minds of willing listeners and to do so there must be opportunity to win their attention." Kovacs v. Cooper, 336 U.S. 77 (1949). Rule 6.05 does not unnecessarily limit that right within the fairground.

The judgment of the Supreme Court of Minnesota is reversed, and the case is remanded for further proceedings not inconsistent with this opinion.

So ordered.

Justice BRENNAN, with whom Justice MARSHALL and Justice STEVENS join, concurring in part and dissenting in part.

[I agree] that the State has a significant interest in maintaining crowd control on its fairgrounds. I also have no doubt that the State has a significant interest in protecting its fairgoers from fraudulent or deceptive solicitation practices. [B]ecause [this] latter interest is substantially furthered by a Rule that restricts sales and solicitation activities to fixed booth locations, where the State will have the greatest opportunity to police and prevent possible deceptive practices, I would hold that Rule 6.05's restriction on those particular forms of First Amendment expression is justified as an antifraud measure. . . . However, because I believe that the booth Rule is an overly intrusive means of achieving the State's interest in crowd control, and because I cannot accept the validity of the State's third asserted justification. I dissent from the Court's approval of Rule 6.05's restriction on the distribution of literature. . . . "Fairgoers are fully capable of saying "no" to persons seeking their attention and then walking away, [and so] they are not members of a captive audience [and] have no general right to be free from being approached."

[O]nce a governmental regulation is shown to impinge upon basic First Amendment rights, the burden falls on the government to show the validity of its asserted interest and the absence of less intrusive alternatives. The challenged "regulation must be narrowly tailored to further the State's legitimate interest." [E]ach and every fairgoer, whether political candidate, concerned citizen, or member of a religious group, is free to give speeches, engage in face-to-face advocacy, campaign, or proselytize. No restrictions are placed on any fairgoer's right to speak at any time, at any place, or to any person. [A state fair is truly a marketplace of ideas and a public forum for the communication of ideas and information, and "almost by definition a congeries of hawkers, vendors of wares and services, and purveyors of ideas, commercial, esthetic, and intellectual." Thus, there is nothing about the ISKCON manner of expression that is "incompatible with the normal activity" of the fair.]. [H]owever, as soon as a proselytizing member of ISKCON hands out a free copy of the Bhagavad-Gita to an interested listener, or a political candidate distributes his campaign brochure to a potential voter, he becomes subject to arrest and removal from the fairgrounds. This constitutes a significant restriction on First Amendment rights. By prohibiting distribution of literature outside the booths, the fair officials sharply limit the number of fairgoers to whom the proselytizers and candidates can communicate their messages. . . .

[P]etitioners contend that if fairgoers are permitted to distribute literature, large crowds will gather, blocking traffic lanes and causing safety problems. [But i]f fairgoers can make speeches, engage in face-to-face proselytizing, and buttonhole prospective supporters, they can surely distribute literature to members of their audience without significantly adding to the State's asserted crowd control problem. . . . If the State had a reasonable concern that distribution in certain parts of the fairgrounds — for example, entrances and exits — would cause disorder, it could have drafted its Rule to prohibit distribution of literature at those points. If the State felt it necessary to limit the number of persons distributing an organization's literature, it could, within reason, have done that as well. It had no right, however, to ban all distribution of literature outside the [booths]. . . .

Justice BLACKMUN, concurring in part and dissenting in part.

For the reasons stated by Justice Brennan, I believe that Minnesota State Fair Rule 6.05 is unconstitutional as applied to the distribution of literature. I also agree, however, that the Rule is *constitutional* as applied to the sale of literature and the solicitation of funds. [S]ince respondents have offered to wear identifying tags, and since the fairgrounds are an enclosed area, it is at least arguable that it is easier to police the fairgrounds than a community's streets. . . . Nonetheless, I believe that the State's substantial interest in maintaining crowd control and safety on the fairgrounds does justify Rule 6.05's restriction on solicitation and sales activities not conducted from a booth. [C]ommon-sense differences between literature distribution, on the one hand, and solicitation and sales, on the other, suggest that the latter activities present greater crowd control problems than the former. The distribution of literature does not require that the recipient stop in order to receive the message the speaker wishes to convey. . . . In contrast[,] sales and the collection of solicited funds not only require the fairgoer to stop, but also "engender additional confusion [because] they involve acts of exchanging articles for money, fumbling for and dropping money, making change, etc." . . .

Note: Alternative Tests

Heffron illustrates the substantive application of the time, place, manner formula used for "content-neutral" regulations in a "public forum." The *Heffron* regulation was "content neutral" because it was not based on the substance of the speaker's message, and the state fair was assumed to be a public forum either because it is like streets and parks, which "have immemorially been held in trust for the use of the public" and "for purposes of assembly," or because it is a newer forum that has been "opened" by the government for such purposes. If the regulation in *Heffron* had been "content based" in a "public forum," then the strict scrutiny test would have been applied, and a compelling governmental interest would have been required. *See* Police Department of Chicago v. Mosley, 408 U.S. 92 (1972). By contrast, if the *Heffron* regulation had related to a "nonpublic forum," then if the regulation were "content neutral," it would be required only to be "reasonable," and if it were "content based" in a "nonpublic forum," it would be acceptable as long as it is "not an effort to suppress the speaker's activity due to disagreement with the speaker's view" — that is to say, not "viewpoint neutral." *See* Perry Education Association v. Perry Local Educators' Assn., 460 U.S. 37 (1983).

∾ PROBLEMS ∾

1. *Hyperlinks to a City's Web Site.* Suppose that a city government maintains a Web site on which it provides a hyperlink to a state- and town-sponsored nonpartisan outside event (a day-long discussion at a middle school designed to promote community spirit, civic discourse, and the organization of community-defined projects and action groups), but the city rejected a hyperlink for a partisan political group that was critical of the government. The city drew a distinction between providing hyperlinks to partisan and nonpartisan events, and indicated that it might provide links to the latter events but not the former. In providing hyperlinks, did the city create a public forum? Did the city engage in viewpoint discrimination? Would it matter that the city demanded information from the partisan group regarding its mission, members, and finances? *See* Sutliffe v. Epping School District, 584 F.3d 314 (1st Cir. 2009).

2. *The Warning Brochures.* A private group (the Illinois Dunesland Preservation Society) believes that the Illinois Beach State Park is contaminated by asbestos. As a result, the group asks that the State of Illinois install racks that would allow the group to display brochures warning visitors about the dangers. The state refuses to grant the request. The group notes that the state already maintains brochure racks at the park. However, the evidence reveals that all of the brochures are placed there by the state and are designed to encourage people to frequent the parks. Does the Society have a First Amendment right to display the warning brochures at the park? *See* Illinois Dunesland Preservation Society v. Illinois Department of Natural Resources, 584 F.3d 719 (7th Cir. 2009).

Lee v. International Society for Krishna Consciousness, Inc.

505 U.S. 830 (1992)

PER CURIAM.

For the reasons expressed in the opinions of Justice O'Connor, Justice Kennedy, and Justice Souter in International Society for Krishna Consciousness v. Lee, the judgment of the Court of Appeals holding that the ban on distribution of literature in the Port Authority airport terminals is invalid under the First Amendment is

Affirmed.

Chief Justice REHNQUIST, with whom Justice WHITE, Justice SCALIA, and Justice THOMAS, join, dissenting.

Leafletting presents risks of congestion similar to those posed by solicitation. It presents, in addition, some risks unique to leafleting. And, of course, as with solicitation, these risks must be evaluated against a backdrop of the substantial congestion problem facing the Port Authority and with an eye to the cumulative impact that will result if all groups are permitted terminal access. Viewed in this light, I conclude that the distribution ban, no less than the solicitation ban, is [reasonable].

[The] risks and burdens posed by leafleting are quite similar to those posed by solicitation. The weary, harried, or hurried traveler may have no less desire and need to avoid the delays generated by having literature foisted upon him than he does to avoid delays from a financial solicitation. And while a busy passenger may succeed in fending off a leafletter with minimal disruption to himself by agreeing simply to take the proferred material, this does not completely ameliorate the dangers of congestion flowing from such leafleting. Others may choose not simply to accept the material but also to stop and engage the leafletter in debate, obstructing those who follow. Moreover, those who accept material may often simply drop it on the floor once out of the leafletter's range, creating an eyesore, a safety hazard, and additional cleanup work for the airport staff.

In addition, a differential ban that permits leafleting but prohibits solicitation, while giving the impression of permitting the Port Authority at least half of what it seeks, may in fact prove for the Port Authority to be a much more Pyrrhic victory. Under the regime that is today sustained, the Port Authority is obliged to permit leafleting. But monitoring leafleting activity in order to ensure that it is only leafleting that occurs, and not also soliciting, may prove little less burdensome than the monitoring that would be required if solicitation were permitted. At a minimum, therefore, I think it remains open whether at some future date the Port Authority may be able to reimpose a complete ban, having developed evidence that enforcement of a differential ban is overly burdensome. Until now it has had no reason or means to do this, since it is only today that such a requirement has been [announced].

Note: Justice O'Connor and ISKCON

Justice O'Connor provided the fifth vote to invalidate the ban on the distribution of literature. The other votes came from Justices Kennedy and Souter, whose separate opinions (joined by Justices Blackmun and Stevens) supported Justice Kennedy's views. Justice O'Connor found that the ban was an unreasonable regulation of a nonpublic forum:

"The reasonableness of the Government's restriction [must] be assessed in light of the purpose of the forum and all the surrounding circumstances." "[Consideration] of a forum's special attributes is relevant to the constitutionality of a regulation since the significance of the governmental interest must be assessed in light of the characteristic nature and function of the particular forum involved." In this case, the "special attributes" and "surrounding circumstances" of the airports operated by the Port Authority are determinative. Not only has the Port Authority chosen not to limit access to the airports under its control, it has created a huge complex open to traveler and nontravelers alike. The airports house restaurants, cafeterias, snack bars, coffee shops, drug stores, food stores, nurseries, barber shops, currency exchanges, art exhibits, commercial advertising displays, bookstores, newsstands, dental offices and private clubs. The International Arrivals Building at JFK Airport even has two branches of Bloomingdale's.

We have said that a restriction on speech in a nonpublic forum is "reasonable" when it is "consistent with the [government's] legitimate interest in [preserving] the property [for] the use to which it is lawfully dedicated." [In] my view, the Port Authority is operating a shopping mall as well as an airport. The reasonableness inquiry, therefore, is not whether the restrictions on speech are "consistent [with] preserving the property" for air travel, but whether they are reasonably related to maintaining the multipurpose environment that the Port Authority has deliberately created.

[In] my view, [the] regulation banning leafleting [cannot] be upheld as reasonable on this record. [Leafletting] does not entail the same kind of problems presented by face-to-face solicitation. [With] the possible exception of avoiding litter, it is difficult to point to any problems intrinsic to the act of leafleting that would make it naturally incompatible with a large, multipurpose forum such as [the airport terminals here].

Of course, it is still open for the Port Authority to promulgate regulations of the time, place, and manner of leafleting which are "content-neutral, narrowly tailored to serve a significant government interest, and leave open ample alternative channels of communication." For example, during the many years that this litigation has been in progress, the Port Authority has not banned sankirtan completely from JFK International Airport, but has restricted it to a relatively uncongested part of the airport terminals, the same part that houses the airport chapel. In my view, that regulation meets the standards we have applied to time, place, and manner restrictions of protected expression.

∼ PROBLEM: THE PORT AUTHORITY'S BAN ON LITERATURE ∼

Suppose that after September 11, 2001, the Port Authority of New York decides to reinstate the total ban on the distribution of literature in the airport terminals, arguing that conditions have changed and that the *Lee* Court's decision to invalidate the ban must be reconsidered in light of airport security issues. (Assume that the bans on literature sales and solicitation of funds are still in place, after being upheld in *ISKCON*.) If you are the lawyer for the Port Authority, what arguments will you make to support the reinstatement of the ban on the distribution of literature? First, assume that the airport is still considered to be a nonpublic forum, so that the "reasonableness" test applies. What arguments will you make? Then, assume that you must prepare for the possibility that the Court will reverse its earlier finding in *ISKCON* and declare the airport to be a public forum, so that the "time, place, manner" test applies. How will your arguments be different?

Chicago Police Department v. Mosley

408 U.S. 92 (1972)

Mr. Justice MARSHALL delivered the opinion of the Court.

At issue in this case is the constitutionality of the following Chicago ordinance:

A person commits disorderly conduct when he knowingly:
(i) Pickets or demonstrates on a public way within 150 feet of any primary or secondary school building while the school is in session and one-half hour before the school is in session and one-half hour after the school session has been concluded, provided, that this subsection does not prohibit the peaceful picketing of any school involved in a labor dispute. . . .

The suit was brought by Earl Mosley, a federal postal employee, who for seven months prior to the enactment of the ordinance had frequently picketed Jones Commercial High School in Chicago. During school hours and usually by himself, Mosley would walk the public sidewalk adjoining the school, carrying a sign that read: "Jones High School practices black discrimination. Jones High School has a black quota." His lonely crusade was always peaceful, orderly, and quiet, and was conceded to be so by the city of Chicago.

On March 26, 1968, Chapter 1931(i) was passed, to become effective on April 5. Seeing a newspaper announcement of the new ordinance, Mosley contacted the Chicago Police Department to find out how the ordinance would affect him; he was told that, if his picketing continued, he would be arrested. On April 4, the day before the ordinance became effective, Mosley ended his picketing next to the school. Thereafter, he brought this [federal suit seeking declaratory and injunctive relief on constitutional grounds].

[The] city of Chicago exempts peaceful labor picketing from its general prohibition on picketing next to a school. The question we consider here is whether this selective exclusion from a public place is permitted. Our answer is "No."

[We apply "strict scrutiny," requiring the government to have a compelling interest to justify the regulation, and requiring that the regulation must be narrowly tailored that interest.] [The] central problem with Chicago's ordinance is that it describes permissible picketing in terms of its subject matter. Peaceful picketing on the subject of a school's labor-management dispute is permitted, but all other peaceful picketing is prohibited. The operative distinction is the message on a picket sign. But, above all else, the First Amendment means that government has no power to restrict expression because of its message, its ideas, its subject matter, or its content. Cohen v. California, 403 U.S. 15 (1971). To permit the continued building of our politics and culture, and to assure self-fulfillment for each individual, our people are guaranteed the right to express any thought, free from government censorship. The essence of this forbidden censorship is content control. Any restriction on expressive activity because of its content would completely undercut the "profound national commitment to the principle that debate on public issues should be uninhibited, robust, and wide-open."

Necessarily, then, under [the] First Amendment itself, government may not grant the use of a forum to people whose views it finds acceptable, but deny use to those wishing to express less favored or more controversial views. And it may not select which issues are worth discussing or debating in public facilities. There is an "equality of status in the field of ideas," and government must afford all points of view an equal opportunity to be heard. Once a forum is opened up to assembly or speaking by some groups, government may not prohibit others from assembling or speaking on the basis of what they intend to say. Selective exclusions from a public forum may not be based on content alone, and may not be justified by reference to content alone.

Guided by these principles, we have frequently condemned such discrimination among different users of the same medium for expression. In Niemotko v. Maryland, 340 U.S. 268 (1951), a group of Jehovah's Witnesses were denied a permit to use a city park for Bible talks, although other political and religious groups had been allowed to put the park to analogous uses. Concluding that the permit was denied because of the city's "dislike for or disagreement with the Witnesses or their views," this Court held that the permit refusal violated "[t]he right to equal protection of the laws, in the exercise of those freedoms of speech and religion protected by the [First Amendment]." [*See also*] Cox v. Louisiana, 379 U.S. 536 (1965) ("[B]y specifically permitting picketing for the publication of labor union views (but prohibiting other sorts of picketing), Louisiana is attempting to pick and choose among the views it is willing to have discussed on its streets.")

[This] is not to say that all picketing must always be allowed. We have continually recognized that reasonable "time, place and manner" regulations of picketing may be necessary to further significant governmental interests. [There] may be sufficient regulatory interests justifying selective exclusions or distinctions among pickets. Conflicting demands on the same place may compel the State to make choices among potential users and uses. And the State may have a legitimate interest in prohibiting some picketing to protect public order. But these justifications for selective exclusions from a public forum must be carefully scrutinized. Because picketing plainly involves expressive conduct within the protection of the First Amendment, discriminations among pickets must be tailored to serve a significant [later Court would say "compelling"] governmental interest.

In this case, the ordinance itself describes impermissible picketing not in terms of time, place, and manner, but in terms of subject matter. The regulation "thus slip(s) from the neutrality of time, place, and circumstance into a concern about content." This is never permitted. In spite of this, Chicago urges that the ordinance is not improper content censorship, but rather a device for preventing disruption of the school. Cities certainly have a substantial interest in stopping picketing which disrupts a school. . . . Although preventing school disruption is a city's legitimate concern, Chicago itself has determined that peaceful labor picketing during school hours is not an undue interference with school. [U]nder the Equal Protection Clause, Chicago may not maintain that other picketing disrupts the school unless that picketing is clearly more disruptive than the picketing Chicago already permits. . . .

Similarly, we reject the city's argument that, although it permits peaceful labor picketing, it may prohibit all nonlabor picketing because, as a class, nonlabor picketing is more prone to produce violence than labor picketing. Predictions about imminent disruption from picketing involve judgments appropriately made on an individualized basis, not by means of broad classifications, especially those based on subject matter. Freedom of expression, and its intersection with the guarantee of equal protection, would rest on a soft foundation indeed if government could distinguish among picketers on such a wholesale and categorical basis. "[I]n our system, undifferentiated fear or apprehension of disturbance is not enough to overcome the right to freedom of expression." Some labor picketing is peaceful, some disorderly; the same is true of picketing on other themes. No labor picketing could be more peaceful or less prone to violence than Mosley's solitary vigil. In seeking to restrict nonlabor picketing that is clearly more disruptive than peaceful labor picketing, Chicago may not prohibit all nonlabor picketing at the school forum.

[Chicago] may not vindicate its interest in preventing disruption by the wholesale exclusion of picketing on all but one preferred subject. Given what Chicago tolerates from labor picketing, the excesses of some nonlabor picketing may not be controlled by a broad ordinance prohibiting both peaceful and violent picketing. Such excesses "can be controlled by narrowly drawn statutes," focusing on the abuses and dealing evenhandedly with picketing regardless of subject matter. [Far] from being tailored to a substantial [later Courts would say "compelling"] governmental interest, the discrimination among pickets is based on the content of their expression. Therefore, [it] may not stand.

The judgment is affirmed.

Notes

1. *Selective Exclusions.* In post-*Mosley* cases, the Court determined that the strict scrutiny standard for selective exclusions of speech or speakers from the public forum should not be used in nonpublic forum cases. Instead, selective exclusion regulations may be upheld as long as they are "viewpoint neutral," even though they are not "content-neutral" but rather "content-based" regulations. *See* Cornelius v. NAACP Legal Defense and Educational Fund, Inc., 473 U.S. 788 (1985) (holding that the exclusion of legal defense and political advocacy groups from the nonpublic forum of a workplace fundraising drive was "viewpoint neutral"); Perry Education Association v. Perry Local Educators' Association, 460 U.S. 37 (1983) (holding that teacher mailboxes were nonpublic forums, and that the restriction of the mailboxes to the elected teachers' union, as well as a variety of other organizations, and the exclusion of a competing union from access to the mailboxes were "viewpoint-neutral" regulations).

2. *Election Speech.* In Burson v. Freeman, 504 U.S. 191 (1992), the Court used the *Mosley* analysis to upheld a ban on election speech (not including exit polling) within 100 feet of the entrance to a polling place. Four justices found the 100-foot zone to be a public forum and held that strict scrutiny was satisfied, noting that there was sufficient evidence in the record that political candidates had used campaign workers to commit voter intimidation or electoral fraud at polling places, but had not used other forms of solicitation or exit polling to commit "electoral abuses." "[T]he State, as recognized administrator of elections, has asserted that the exercise of free speech rights conflicts with another fundamental right, the right to cast a ballot in an election free from the taint of intimidation and fraud. A long history, a substantial consensus, and simple common sense shows that some restricted zone around polling places is necessary to protect that fundamental right." Two justices voted with the four-justice plurality to uphold the regulation on the merits, but they would have found the entrance to the polling place to be a nonpublic forum. Three justices would have invalidated the statute on the grounds that the *Mosley* test could not be satisfied, assuming without deciding that the 100-foot zone was a public forum.

3. *Speech on Private Property.* The Court has evolved different doctrines for use in evaluating challenges brought by speech litigants to regulations involving protected speech on private property. In Marsh v. Alabama, 326 U.S. 501 (1946), the Court held that a "company town" could not require written permission for speech activities on the street, including solicitation of funds, without First Amendment scrutiny, and the company's attempt to enforce this requirement through soliciting a criminal prosecution for trespass was held to be unconstitutional. The fact that a corporation-employer owned all the property of the town did not exempt the owner from the necessity of recognizing First Amendment rights, and "[t]he more an owner, for his advantage opens up his property for use by the public in general, the more do his rights become circumscribed by the [constitutional] rights of those who use it." In Amalgamated Food Employees Union v. Logan Valley Plaza, Inc., 391 U.S. 308 (1968), the Court held that a state court could not enjoin peaceful picketing of a store in a mall shopping center because the shopping center was the "functional equivalent" of the public business district in *Marsh* where trespass laws could not be enforced at the will of the owner. However, in Lloyd Corp. v. Tanner, 407 U.S. 551 (1972), the Court refused to uphold an injunction to prevent the arrest of peaceful leafletters at a shopping mall, because the message of those leafletters was addressed to the general public and not, as in *Logan Valley Plaza*, solely to the members of the public who patronized a particular store in the mall. Finally, in Hudgens v. NLRB, 424 U.S. 507 (1976), the Court overruled *Logan Valley Plaza*, while affirming *Marsh*, and held that where the owner of a shopping mall does not compare to a municipality, the owner may regulate expression on the basis of the content of the expression, and is not bound by *Mosley*.

∾ PROBLEMS ∾

1. *Access to Health Care Statute.* A Colorado statute makes it illegal to come within 8 feet of another person, without that person's consent, within 100 feet of the entrance to any health care facility, "for the purpose of passing a leaflet or handbill to, displaying a sign to, or engaging in oral protest, education, or counseling with such other person." The legislative history of the statute reveals that it was enacted to provide unimpeded access to health care facilities and the avoidance of potential trauma to patients associated with confrontational protests. A third interest is protecting the unwilling listener from unwanted communication. The statute covers three types of communications: the display of signs, leafleting, and oral speech. Assume that a lawsuit is brought challenging the statute on First Amendment grounds. What arguments might be made by the government attorney in favor of the statute, and by the speech litigants who seek to invalidate the statute? *See* Hill v. Colorado, 530 U.S. 703 (2000).

2. *Government Center Complex.* A Mount Vernon, Maryland, ordinance limits protests to the grassy median at the entrance to the Government Center Complex. The Government Center Complex is located in a largely wooded area that is removed from residential, commercial, and office areas. The building is

accessed from the parkway by a horseshoe-shaped driveway that leads from the parkway to the front door of the building and back to the parkway. Enclosed by the driveway is a median consisting of grass, trees, brick, and concrete. This median is often referred to as the Center Island and is about 30 yards wide and 200 yards long. Sidewalks circumnavigate the island and run along a central landscaped strip. The area is not enclosed, but rather is open to the public. May Mount Vernon limit displays and protests to the Center Island?

3. *Peace, Hope, and Love.* In the preceding problem, assume that the Mount Vernon ordinance further provides: "The use of the common areas is limited to individual residents or employees of the county, and permits may be obtained for displays on the Center Island. Each display is limited to one week per year, and it must clearly state that it is a private display." Rita Wax applied to Mount Vernon for a permit to display a message of "peace, hope, and love" on a grassy median near the Government Center Building. The county denied the permit because this median was designated for displays only by county residents and employees, and Rita is neither (she lives in another county). After Rita's application for a permit is denied because of her nonresident status, she files suit in federal district court challenging the county's decision on First Amendment grounds. You represent Rita. What First Amendment arguments will you make? What counterarguments do you expect the county to make in response? (Do not argue vagueness or overbreadth.)

Pleasant Grove City, Utah v. Summum

129 S.Ct. 1125 (2009)

Justice Alito delivered the opinion of the Court.

[Pioneer Park (or Park)] is a 2.5 acre public park located in the Historic District of Pleasant Grove City (or City) in Utah. The Park currently contains 15 permanent displays, at least 11 of which were donated by private groups or individuals. These include an historic granary, a wishing well, the City's first fire station, a September 11 monument, and a Ten Commandments monument donated by the Fraternal Order of Eagles in 1971.

Respondent Summum is a religious organization founded in 1975 and headquartered in Salt Lake City, Utah. On two separate occasions in 2003, Summum's president wrote a letter to the City's mayor requesting permission to erect a "stone monument," which would contain "the Seven Aphorisms of SUMMUM"[14] and be similar in size and nature to the Ten Commandments monument. The City denied the requests and explained that its practice was to limit monuments

---

14. Respondent's brief describes the church as follows: "The Summum church incorporates elements of Gnostic Christianity, teaching that spiritual knowledge is experiential and that through devotion comes revelation, which 'modifies human perceptions, and transfigures the individual.' . . . Central to Summum religious belief and practice are the Seven Principles of Creation (the "Seven Aphorisms"). According to Summum doctrine, the Seven Aphorisms were inscribed on the original tablets handed down by God to Moses on Mount Sinai. . . . Because Moses believed that the Israelites were not ready to receive the Aphorisms, he shared them only with a select group of people. In the Summum Exodus account, Moses then destroyed the original tablets, traveled back to Mount Sinai, and returned with a second set of tablets containing the Ten Commandments. . . ."

in the Park to those that "either (1) directly relate to the history of Pleasant Grove, or (2) were donated by groups with longstanding ties to the Pleasant Grove community." The following year, the City passed a resolution putting this policy into writing. The resolution also mentioned other criteria, such as safety and esthetics.

In May 2005, respondent's president again wrote to the mayor asking to erect a monument, but the letter did not describe the monument, its historical significance, or Summum's connection to the community. The city council rejected this request.

In 2005, respondent filed this action against the City and various local officials, asserting, among other claims, that petitioners had violated the Free Speech Clause of the First Amendment by accepting the Ten Commandments monument but rejecting the proposed Seven Aphorisms monument. Respondent sought a preliminary injunction directing the City to permit Summum to erect its monument in Pioneer Park. [T]he District Court denied Summum's preliminary injunction request. . . . A panel of the Tenth Circuit reversed [and] held that the City was required to erect Summum's monument immediately. . . . We granted certiorari and now reverse.

[If] petitioners were engaging in their own expressive conduct, then the Free Speech Clause has no application. The Free Speech Clause restricts government regulation of private speech; it does not regulate government speech. *See* Columbia Broadcasting System, Inc. v. Democratic National Committee, 412 U.S. 94, 139, n.7 (1973) (Stewart, J., concurring). A government entity has the right to "speak for itself." Board of Regents of Univ. of Wis. System v. Southworth, 529 U.S. 217, 229 (2000). "[I]t is entitled to say what it wishes," Rosenberger v. Rector and Visitors of Univ. of Va., 515 U.S. 819, 833 (1995), and to select the views that it wants to express. *See* Rust v. Sullivan, 500 U.S. 173, 194 (1991). . . . Indeed, it is not easy to imagine how government could function if it lacked this freedom. "If every citizen were to have a right to insist that no one paid by public funds express a view with which he disagreed, debate over issues of great concern to the public would be limited to those in the private sector, and the process of government as we know it radically transformed." Keller v. State Bar of Cal., 496 U.S. 1, 12-13 (1990).

A government entity may exercise this same freedom to express its views when it receives assistance from private sources for the purpose of delivering a government-controlled message. . . . This does not mean that there are no restraints on government speech. For example, government speech must comport with the Establishment Clause. The involvement of public officials in advocacy may be limited by law, regulation, or practice. And of course, a government entity is ultimately "accountable to the electorate and the political process for its advocacy." *Southworth*, 529 U.S., at 235. "If the citizenry objects, newly elected officials later could espouse some different or contrary position." *Ibid*.

While government speech is not restricted by the Free Speech Clause, the government does not have a free hand to regulate private speech on government property. This Court long ago recognized that members of the public retain strong free speech rights when they venture into public streets and parks. . . . In order to preserve this freedom, government entities are strictly limited in their ability to regulate private speech in such "traditional public fora." Cornelius v. NAACP Legal Defense & Ed. Fund, Inc., 473 U.S. 788, 800 (1985). Reasonable time, place, and manner restrictions are allowed, but any restriction based on the content of the speech must satisfy strict scrutiny, that is, the restriction must be narrowly tailored to serve a compelling government interest, and restrictions based on viewpoint are prohibited, *see* Carey v. Brown, 447 U.S. 455, 463 (1980).

[T]his Court has recognized that members of the public have free speech rights on other types of government property and in certain other government programs that share essential attributes of a traditional public forum. We have held that a government entity may create "a designated public forum" if government property that has not traditionally been regarded as a public forum is intentionally opened up for that purpose. Government restrictions on speech in a designated public forum are subject to the same strict scrutiny as restrictions in a traditional public forum.

The Court has also held that a government entity may create a forum that is limited to use by certain groups or dedicated solely to the discussion of certain subjects. Perry Ed. Assn. v. Perry Local Educators' Assn., 460 U.S. 37, 45 (1983). In such a forum, a government entity may impose restrictions on speech that are reasonable and viewpoint-neutral. *See* Good News Club v. Milford Central School, 533 U.S. 98 (2001).

There may be situations in which it is difficult to tell whether a government entity is speaking on its own behalf or is providing a forum for private speech, but this case does not present such a situation. Permanent monuments displayed on public property typically represent government speech.

Governments have long used monuments to speak to the public. Since ancient times, kings, emperors, and other rulers have erected statues of themselves to remind their subjects of their authority and power. Triumphal arches, columns, and other monuments have been built to commemorate military victories and sacrifices and other events of civic importance. A monument, by definition, is a structure that is designed as a means of expression. When a government entity arranges for the construction of a monument, it does so because it wishes to convey some thought or instill some feeling in those who see the structure. Neither the Court of Appeals nor respondent disputes the obvious proposition that a monument that is commissioned and financed by a government body for placement on public land constitutes government speech.

Just as government-commissioned and government-financed monuments speak for the government, so do privately financed and donated monuments that the government accepts and displays to the public on government land. It certainly is not common for property owners to open up their property for the installation of permanent monuments that convey a message with which they do not wish to be associated. And because property owners typically do not permit the construction of such monuments on their land, persons who observe donated monuments routinely—and reasonably—interpret them as conveying some message on the property owner's behalf. In this context, there is little chance that observers will fail to appreciate the identity of the speaker. This is true whether the monument is located on private property or on public property, such as national, state, or city park land.

We think it is fair to say that throughout our Nation's history, the general government practice with respect to donated monuments has been one of selective receptivity. A great many of the monuments that adorn the Nation's public parks were financed with private funds or donated by private parties. Sites managed by the National Park Service contain thousands of privately designed or funded commemorative objects, including the Statue of Liberty, the Marine Corps War Memorial (the Iwo Jima monument), and the Vietnam Veterans Memorial. States and cities likewise have received thousands of donated monuments. By accepting monuments that are privately funded or donated, government entities save tax dollars and are able to acquire monuments that they could not have afforded to fund on their own.

But while government entities regularly accept privately funded or donated monuments, they have exercised selectivity. . . . Across the country, "municipalities generally exercise editorial control over donated monuments through prior submission requirements, design input, requested modifications, written criteria, and legislative approvals of specific content proposals."

Public parks are often closely identified in the public mind with the government unit that owns the land. City parks — ranging from those in small towns, like Pioneer Park in Pleasant Grove City, to those in major metropolises, like Central Park in New York City — commonly play an important role in defining the identity that a city projects to its own residents and to the outside world. Accordingly, cities and other jurisdictions take some care in accepting donated monuments. Government decisionmakers select the monuments that portray what they view as appropriate for the place in question, taking into account such content-based factors as esthetics, history, and local culture. The monuments that are accepted, therefore, are meant to convey and have the effect of conveying a government message, and they thus constitute government speech.

In this case, it is clear that the monuments in Pleasant Grove's Pioneer Park represent government speech. Although many of the monuments were not designed or built by the City and were donated in completed form by private entities, the City decided to accept those donations and to display them in the Park. Respondent does not claim that the City ever opened up the Park for the placement of whatever permanent monuments might be offered by private donors. Rather, the City has "effectively controlled" the messages sent by the monuments in the Park by exercising "final approval authority" over their selection. The City has selected those monuments that it wants to display for the purpose of presenting the image of the City that it wishes to project to all who frequent the Park; it has taken ownership of most of the monuments in the Park, including the Ten Commandments monument that is the focus of respondent's concern; and the City has now expressly set forth the criteria it will use in making future selections.

Respondent voices the legitimate concern that the government speech doctrine not be used as a subterfuge for favoring certain private speakers over others based on viewpoint. Respondent's suggested solution is to require a government entity accepting a privately donated monument to go through a formal process of adopting a resolution publicly embracing "the message" that the monument conveys.

We see no reason for imposing a requirement of this sort. The parks of this country contain thousands of donated monuments. . . . Requiring all of these jurisdictions to go back and proclaim formally that they adopt all of these monuments as their own expressive vehicles would be a pointless exercise that the Constitution does not mandate.

In this case, for example, although respondent argues that Pleasant Grove City has not adequately "controll[ed] the message" of the Ten Commandments monument, the City took ownership of that monument and put it on permanent display in a park that it owns and manages and that is linked to the City's identity. All rights previously possessed by the monument's donor have been relinquished. The City's actions provided a more dramatic form of adoption than the sort of formal endorsement that respondent would demand, unmistakably signifying to all Park visitors that the City intends the monument to speak on its behalf. And the City has made no effort to abridge the traditional free speech rights — the right to speak, distribute leaflets, etc. — that may be exercised by respondent and others in Pioneer Park.

What respondent demands, however, is that the City "adopt" or "embrace" "the message" that it associates with the monument. Respondent seems to think that a monument can convey only one "message" — which is, presumably, the message intended by the donor — and that, if a government entity that accepts a monument for placement on its property does not formally embrace *that* message, then the government has not engaged in expressive conduct.

This argument fundamentally misunderstands the way monuments convey meaning. The meaning conveyed by a monument is generally not a simple one like "Beef. It's What's for Dinner." [Johanns v. Livestock Marketing Assn., 544 U.S. 550, 560-61 (2005).] Even when a monument features the written word, the monument may be intended to be interpreted, and may in fact be interpreted by different observers, in a variety of ways. Monuments called to our attention by the briefing in this case illustrate this phenomenon.

What, for example, is "the message" of the Greco-Roman mosaic of the word "Imagine" that was donated to New York City's Central Park in memory of John Lennon? Some observers may "imagine" the musical contributions that John Lennon would have made if he had not been killed. Others may think of the lyrics of the Lennon song that obviously inspired the mosaic and may "imagine" a world without religion, countries, possessions, greed, or hunger. Or, to take another example, what is "the message" of the "large bronze statue displaying the word 'peace' in many world languages" that is displayed in Fayetteville, Arkansas?

These text-based monuments are almost certain to evoke different thoughts and sentiments in the minds of different observers, and the effect of monuments that do not contain text is likely to be even more variable. Consider, for example, the statue of Pancho Villa that was given to the city of Tucson, Arizona, in 1981 by the Government of Mexico with, according to a Tucson publication, "a wry sense of irony." Does this statue commemorate a "revolutionary leader who advocated for agrarian reform and the poor" or "a violent bandit"?

Contrary to respondent's apparent belief, it frequently is not possible to identify a single "message" that is conveyed by an object or structure, and consequently, the thoughts or sentiments expressed by a government entity that accepts and displays such an object may be quite different from those of either its creator or its donor. By accepting a privately donated monument and placing it on city property, a city engages in expressive conduct, but the intended and perceived significance of that conduct may not coincide with the thinking of the monument's donor or creator. Indeed, when a privately donated memorial is funded by many small donations, the donors themselves may differ in their interpretation of the monument's significance. By accepting such a monument, a government entity does not necessarily endorse the specific meaning that any particular donor sees in the monument.

The message that a government entity conveys by allowing a monument to remain on its property may also be altered by the subsequent addition of other monuments in the same vicinity. For example, following controversy over the original design of the Vietnam Veterans Memorial, a compromise was reached that called for the nearby addition of a flagstaff and bronze Three Soldiers statue, which many believed changed the overall effect of the memorial. *See, e.g.,* J. Mayo, *War Memorials as Political Landscape: The American Experience and Beyond* 202-203, 205 (Praeger 1988).

The "message" conveyed by a monument may change over time. A study of war memorials found that "people reinterpret" the meaning of these memorials as "historical interpretations" and "the society around them changes." Mayo, *supra,* at 8-9.

A striking example of how the interpretation of a monument can evolve is provided by one of the most famous and beloved public monuments in the United States, the Statue of Liberty. The statue was given to this country by the Third French Republic to express republican solidarity and friendship between the two countries. At the inaugural ceremony, President Cleveland saw the statue as an emblem of international friendship and the widespread influence of American ideals. Only later did the statue come to be viewed as a beacon welcoming immigrants to a land of freedom. *See Public Papers of the Presidents of the United States, Ronald Reagan,* Vol. 2, July 3, 1986, pp. 918-919 (1989).

Respondent [analogizes] the installation of permanent monuments in a public park to the delivery of speeches and the holding of marches and demonstrations, and they thus invoke the rule that a public park is a traditional public forum for these activities. But "public forum principles . . . are out of place in the context of this case." United States v. American Library Assn., Inc., 539 U.S. 194, 205 (2003). The forum doctrine has been applied in situations in which government-owned property or a government program was capable of accommodating a large number of public speakers without defeating the essential function of the land or the program. For example, a park can accommodate many speakers and, over time, many parades and demonstrations. The Combined Federal Campaign permits hundreds of groups to solicit donations from federal employees. A public university's student activity fund can provide money for many campus activities. A public university's buildings may offer meeting space for hundreds of student groups. A school system's internal mail facilities can support the transmission of many messages to and from teachers and school administrators.

By contrast, public parks can accommodate only a limited number of permanent monuments. Public parks have been used, "'time out of mind, . . . for purposes of assembly, communicating thoughts between citizens, and discussing public questions,'" *Perry Ed. Assn., supra,* at 45 (quoting *Hague,* 307 U.S., at 515), but "one would be hard pressed to find a 'long tradition' of allowing people to permanently occupy public space with any manner of monuments." 499 F.3d, at 1173 (Lucero, J., dissenting from denial of rehearing en banc).

Speakers, no matter how long-winded, eventually come to the end of their remarks; persons distributing leaflets and carrying signs at some point tire and go home; monuments, however, endure. They monopolize the use of the land on which they stand and interfere permanently with other uses of public space. A public park, over the years, can provide a soapbox for a very large number of orators — often, for all who want to speak — but it is hard to imagine how a public park could be opened up for the installation of permanent monuments by every person or group wishing to engage in that form of expression.

Respondent contends that this issue "can be dealt with through content-neutral time, place and manner restrictions, including the option of a ban on all unattended displays." On this view, when France presented the Statue of Liberty to the United States in 1884, this country had the option of either (a) declining France's offer or (b) accepting the gift, but providing a comparable location in the harbor of New York for other statues of a similar size and nature (e.g., a Statue of Autocracy, if one had been offered by, say, the German Empire or Imperial Russia).

[If] government entities must maintain viewpoint neutrality in their selection of donated monuments, they must either "brace themselves for an influx of clutter" or face the pressure to remove longstanding and cherished monuments. Every jurisdiction that has accepted a donated war memorial may be asked to provide equal treatment for a donated monument questioning the cause for which the veterans fought. . . . The obvious truth of the matter is that if public parks were considered to be traditional public forums for the purpose of erecting privately donated monuments, most parks would have little choice but to refuse all such donations. And where the application of forum analysis would lead almost inexorably to closing of the forum, it is obvious that forum analysis is out of place.

Respondent compares the present case to Capitol Square Review and Advisory Bd. v. Pinette, 515 U.S. 753 (1995), but that case involved a very different situation — a request by a private group, the Ku Klux Klan, to erect a cross for a period of 16 days on public property that had been opened up for similar temporary displays, including a Christmas tree and a menorah. Although some public parks can accommodate and may be made generally available for temporary private displays, the same is rarely true for permanent monuments.

To be sure, there are limited circumstances in which the forum doctrine might properly be applied to a permanent monument — for example, if a town created a monument on which all of its residents (or all those meeting some other criterion) could place the name of a person to be honored or some other private message. But as a general matter, forum analysis simply does not apply to the installation of permanent monuments on public property.

In sum, we hold that the City's decision to accept certain privately donated monuments while rejecting respondent's is best viewed as a form of government speech. As a result, the City's decision is not subject to the Free Speech Clause, and the Court of Appeals erred in holding otherwise. We therefore reverse.

It is so ordered.

Justice STEVENS, with whom Justice GINSBURG joins, concurring.

[O]ur decisions relying on the recently minted government speech doctrine to uphold government action have been few and, in my view, of doubtful merit. . . . [R]ecognizing permanent displays on public property as government speech will not give the government free license to communicate offensive or partisan messages. For even if the Free Speech Clause neither restricts nor protects government speech, government speakers are bound by the Constitution's other proscriptions, including those supplied by the Establishment and Equal Protection Clauses. Together with the checks imposed by our democratic processes, these constitutional safeguards ensure that the effect of today's decision will be limited.

Justice SCALIA, with whom Justice THOMAS joins, concurring.

[T]here are very good reasons to be confident that the park displays do not violate *any* part of the First Amendment. . . .

Justice BREYER, concurring.

[Were] the City to discriminate in the selection of permanent monuments on grounds unrelated to the display's theme, say solely on political grounds, its action might well violate the First Amendment. . . . [I]t helps to ask whether a government action burdens speech disproportionately in light of the action's tendency to further a legitimate government objective. Were we to do so here, we would find — for reasons that the Court sets forth — that the City's action, while preventing Summum from erecting its monument, does not disproportionately restrict Summum's freedom of expression. The City has not closed off its parks to speech; no one claims that the City prevents Summum's members from engaging in speech in a form more transient than a permanent monument. Rather, the City has simply reserved some space in the park for projects designed to further other than free-speech goals. . . . To reserve to the City the power to pick and choose among proposed monuments according to criteria reasonably related to one or more of these legitimate ends restricts Summum's expression, but, given the impracticality of alternatives and viewed in light of the City's legitimate needs, the restriction is not disproportionate. Analyzed either way, as "government speech" or as a proportionate restriction on Summum's expression, the City's action here is lawful.

Justice SOUTER, concurring in the judgment.

[After] today's decision, whenever a government maintains a monument it will presumably be understood to be engaging in government speech. If the monument has some religious character, the specter of violating the Establishment Clause will behoove it to take care to avoid the appearance of a flat-out establishment of religion, in the sense of the government's adoption of the tenets expressed or symbolized. In such an instance, there will be safety in numbers, and it will be in the interest of a careful government to accept other monuments to stand nearby, to dilute the appearance of adopting whatever particular religious position the single example alone might stand for. . . . To avoid relying on a *per se* rule to say when speech is governmental, the best approach that occurs to me is to ask whether a reasonable and fully informed observer would understand the expression to be government speech, as distinct from private speech the government chooses to oblige by allowing the monument to be placed on public land. [S]ome monuments on public land display religious symbolism that clearly does not express a government's chosen views. . . . Application of this observer test provides the reason I find the monument here to be government expression.

H. FIRST AMENDMENT RIGHTS OF PUBLIC EMPLOYEES

In a number of cases, the Court has struggled to decide whether government employees have fewer speech rights than other citizens.

1. *Prohibiting Electioneering*

Public employees might engage in a variety of First Amendment activities, including participation in partisan political practices.

United Public Workers of America (C.I.O.) v. Mitchell
330 U.S. 75 (1947)

Mr. Justice REED delivered the opinion of the Court.

[The Hatch Act, enacted in 1940, declares unlawful certain political activities of federal employees.] Appellants sought an injunction prohibiting members of the United States Civil Service Commission from enforcing [§9(a)] of the Hatch Act [which] reads, "No officer or employee in the Executive Branch of the Federal Government [shall] take any active part in political management or in political campaigns." Various [employees] of the federal executive civil service [allege that they] desire to engage in acts of political management and in political campaigns [outside] of the hours of employment. [The District Court upheld the Act.]

[The] issue [is] whether [a] breach of the Hatch Act and Rule 1 of the Commission can, without violating the Constitution, be made the basis for disciplinary action. [The] right claimed [is] the right of a citizen to act as a party official or worker to further his own political views. [The] influence of political activity by government employees, if evil in its effects on the service, the employees or people dealing with them, is hardly less so because that activity takes place after hours. [T]he question of the need for this regulation is for other branches of government. . . . Our duty [ends] if the Hatch Act provision [is] constitutional. [T]his Court must balance the extent of the guarantees of freedom against a congressional enactment to protect a democratic society against the supposed evil of political partisanship by classified employees of government.

[T]he practice of excluding classified employees from party offices and personal political activity at the polls has been in effect for several decades. [In] *Ex parte Curtis*, 106 U.S. 371 (1882)[, we recognized] the power of Congress, within reasonable limits, to regulate, so far as it might deem necessary, the political conduct of its employees. [The] conviction that an actively partisan governmental personnel threatens good administration has deepened since *Curtis*. Congress recognizes danger to the service in that political rather than official effort may earn advancement and to the public in that governmental favor may be channeled through political connections.

The provisions of §9 of the Hatch Act and the Civil Service Rule 1 are not dissimilar in purpose from the statutes against political contributions of money. The prohibitions [are] directed at political contributions of energy by Government employees. . . . Congress and the President are responsible for an efficient public service. If, in their judgment, efficiency may be best obtained by prohibiting active participation by classified employees in politics as party officers or workers, we see no constitutional objection. . . . Congress [leaves] untouched full participation by employees in political decisions at the ballot box and forbids only the partisan activity of federal personnel deemed offensive to efficiency. With that limitation only, employees may make their contributions to public affairs or protect their own interests, as before the passage of the act.

The argument that political neutrality is not indispensable to a merit system for federal employees may be accepted. But because it is not indispensable does not mean that it is not desirable or permissible. . . . Congress [may] have considered that parties would be more truly devoted to the public welfare if public servants were not over active politically.

Appellants urge that federal employees are protected by the Bill of Rights. . . . None would deny such limitations on Congressional power but because there are some limitations it does not follow that a prohibition against acting as ward leader or worker at the polls is invalid. . . . It is only partisan political activity that is interdicted. It is active participation in political management and political campaigns. Expressions, public or private, on public affairs, personalities and matters of public interest, not an objective of party action, are unrestricted by law so long as the Government employee does not direct his activities toward party success.

It is urged [that] Congress has gone further than necessary in prohibiting political activity to all types of classified employees. [For example, Appellant Poole] is a roller in the Mint. [This job calls] for the qualities of a skilled mechanic [and] does not involve contact with the public. Nevertheless, if in free time he is engaged in political activity, Congress may have concluded that the activity may promote or retard his advancement. . . . Congress may have thought that Government employees are handy elements for leaders in political policy to use in building a political machine. [I]t is not necessary that the act regulated be anything more than an act reasonably deemed by Congress to interfere with the efficiency of the public service. There are hundreds of thousands of United States employees with positions no more influential upon policy determination. . . . Evidently what Congress feared was the cumulative effect on employee morale of political activity by all employees who could be induced to participate actively. It does not seem to us an unconstitutional basis for legislation.

[We] have said that Congress may regulate the political conduct of Government employees "within reasonable limits." The determination of the extent to which political activities of governmental employees shall be regulated lies primarily with Congress. Courts will interfere only when such regulation passes beyond the general existing conception of governmental power. [When] actions of civil servants in the judgment of Congress menace the integrity and the competency of the service, legislation to forestall such danger and adequate to maintain its usefulness is required. The Hatch Act is the answer of Congress to this need. We cannot say with such a background that these restrictions are unconstitutional.

[The] activities of Mr. Poole, as ward executive committeeman and a worker at the polls, obviously fall within the prohibitions of §9 of the Hatch Act against taking an active part in political management and political campaigns. . . .

The judgment of the District Court is accordingly affirmed.

Affirmed.

Mr. Justice BLACK, dissenting.

[T]he Commission [prohibited the following activities]: serving as an election officer; publicly expressing political views at a party caucus or political gathering for or against any candidate or cause identified with a party; soliciting votes for a party or candidate; participating in a political parade; writing for publication or publishing any letter or article, signed or unsigned, in favor of or against any political party, candidate, or faction; initiating, or canvassing for signatures on, community petitions or petitions to Congress.

[I]t is little consolation to employees that the Act contradictorily says that they may "express their opinions on all political subjects and candidates." [W]hatever opinions employees may dare to express, even secretly, must be at their peril. They cannot know what particular expressions may be reported to the Commission and held by it to be a sufficient political activity to cost them their jobs. Their peril is all the greater [because] "Employees [are] accountable for political activity by persons other than themselves, including wives or husbands, if, in fact, the employees are thus accomplishing by collusion and indirection what they may not lawfully do directly and openly." Thus are the families of public employees stripped of their freedom of political action. The result is that the sum of political privilege left to government and state employees, and their families[:] They may vote in silence; they may carefully and quietly express a political view at their peril; and they may become "spectators" [at] campaign gatherings, though it may be highly dangerous for them to "second a motion" or let it be known that they agree or disagree with a speaker.

[Had] this measure deprived five million farmers, or a million businessmen of all right to participate in elections, because Congress thought that federal farm or business subsidies might prompt some of them to [be] susceptible [to] a corrupting influence on politics or government, I would not sustain such an Act. [L]aws which restrict [First Amendment liberties] should be narrowly drawn to meet the evil [and] affect only the minimum number of people [necessary] to prevent a grave and imminent danger to the public. [It is hardly imperative] to muzzle millions of citizens because some of them [might] corrupt the political process. [It] may be true [that] some higher employees, unless restrained, might coerce their subordinates or that Government employees might use their official position to coerce other citizens. [The] same [argument] would support a law to suppress the political freedom of all employees [of] employers who borrow money or draw subsidies from the Government. . . . [I]f the practice of making discharges, promotions or recommendations for promotions on a political basis is so great an evil as to require legislation, the law could punish those public officials who engage in the practice. To punish millions of employees and to deprive the nation of their contribution to public affairs, in order to remove temptation from a proportionately small number of public officials, seems at the least to be a novel method of suppressing what is thought to be an evil practice.

Our political system [rests] on the foundation of a belief in rule by the people. [In] a country whose people elect their leaders and decide great public issues, the voice of none should be suppressed. . . .

Mr. Justice DOUGLAS, dissenting in part.

[T]he political regimentation [of] industrial workers produces its own crop of abuses. Those in top policy posts or [other supervisors] might seek to knit the industrial workers in civil service into a political machine [by making] the advancement of industrial workers dependent on political loyalty, on financial contributions, or on other partisan efforts. . . . Offset against that public concern are the interests of the employees in the exercise of cherished constitutional rights. [If] those rights are to be qualified by the larger requirements of modern democratic government, the restrictions should be narrowly and selectively drawn to define and punish the specific conduct which constitutes a clear and present danger to the operations of government. . . . Those rights are too basic and fundamental in our democratic political society to be sacrificed or qualified for anything short of a clear and present danger to the civil service system. No such showing has been made. . . .

Note: Other Justifications

In United States Civil Service Commission v. National Association of Letter Carriers, AFL-CIO, 413 U.S. 548 (1973), the Court reaffirmed the holding in *Mitchell*. In doing so, the Court noted that "[forbidding partisan political activities] will reduce the hazards to fair and effective government." It also noted that another "major concern [was that] the rapidly expanding Government work force should not be employed to build a powerful, invincible, and perhaps corrupt political machine. [A] related concern [was] the goal that employment and advancement in the Government service not depend on political performance, and [that] Government employees [sh]ould be free from pressure and from express or tacit invitation to vote in a certain way or perform political chores in order to curry favor with their superiors rather than to act out their own beliefs. [I]t is not enough merely to forbid one employee to attempt to influence or coerce another. . . ."

∾ PROBLEM: MORE ON THE INTERNATIONAL TREATY REGULATING THE INTERNET ∾

Under the *United Public Workers* decision and its progeny, could you agree to any special restrictions on the Internet speech of government employees? If so, what type of language would be permissible?

2.　Other Employee Speech

Do government employees have limited rights to speak because of their employment?

Connick v. Myers
461 U.S. 138 (1983)

Justice WHITE delivered the opinion of the Court.

In Pickering v. Board of Education, 391 U.S. 563 (1968), we stated that a public employee does not relinquish First Amendment rights to comment on matters of public interest by virtue of government employment. We also recognized that the State's interests as an employer in regulating the speech of its employees "differ significantly from those it possesses in connection with regulation of the speech of the citizenry in general." The problem [was] arriving "at a balance between the interests of the [employee], as a citizen, in commenting upon matters of public concern and the interest of the State, as an employer, in promoting the efficiency of the public services it performs through its employees." We return to this problem today and consider whether the First and Fourteenth Amendments prevent the discharge of a state employee for circulating a questionnaire concerning internal office affairs.

[R]espondent, Sheila Myers, was employed as an Assistant District Attorney in New Orleans for five and a half years. She served at the pleasure of petitioner Harry Connick, the District Attorney for Orleans Parish. During this period Myers competently performed her responsibilities of trying criminal cases. [In] 1980, Myers was informed that she would be transferred to prosecute cases in a different section of the criminal court. Myers was strongly opposed to the proposed transfer and expressed her view to several of her supervisors. . . . Despite her objections, [Myers] was notified that she was being transferred. Myers [expressed] her reluctance to accept the transfer. . . . That night Myers prepared a questionnaire soliciting the views of her fellow staff members concerning office transfer policy, office morale, the need for a grievance committee, the level of confidence in supervisors, and whether employees felt pressured to work in political campaigns. Early the following morning, Myers typed and copied the questionnaire. She also met with Connick who urged her to accept the transfer. . . . Myers then distributed the questionnaire to 15 assistant district attorneys. Shortly after noon, [when Connick learned that Myers was distributing the survey and was creating a "mini-insurrection" in the office, Connick terminated Myers for] her refusal to accept the transfer [and for "insubordination" for distributing the questionnaire.] Connick particularly objected to the question which inquired whether employees "had confidence in and would rely on the word" of various superiors in the office, and to a question concerning pressure to work in political campaigns which he felt would be damaging if discovered by the press. . . . Myers filed suit [claiming that she was terminated for exercising] her constitutionally-protected right of free speech. The District Court agreed [and the court of appeals affirmed. We granted certiorari.]

[T]he repeated emphasis in *Pickering* on the right of a public employee "as a citizen, in commenting upon matters of public concern," was not accidental. This language [reflects] both the historical evolvement of the rights of public employees, and the common sense realization that government offices could not function if every employment decision became a constitutional matter. . . . For most of this century, the unchallenged dogma was that a public employee had no right to object to conditions placed upon the terms of employment — including those which restricted the exercise of constitutional rights. [The] Court cast new light on the matter in a series of cases arising from the widespread efforts in the 1950s and early 1960s to require public employees, particularly teachers, to swear oaths of loyalty to the state and reveal the groups with which they associated. The explanation [is] no mystery. The First Amendment "was fashioned to assure unfettered interchange of ideas for the bringing about of political and social changes desired by the people." New York Times Co. v. Sullivan, 376 U.S. 254, 269 (1964). [In] *Pickering*, the Court held impermissible under the First Amendment the dismissal of a high school teacher for openly criticizing the Board of Education on its allocation of school funds between athletics and education and its methods of informing taxpayers about the need for additional revenue. Pickering's subject was "a matter of legitimate public concern" upon which "free and open debate is vital to informed decision-making by the electorate." . . .

Pickering, its antecedents and progeny, lead us to conclude that if Myers' questionnaire cannot be fairly characterized as constituting speech on a matter of public concern, it is unnecessary for us to scrutinize the reasons for her discharge. When employee expression cannot be fairly considered as relating to any matter of political, social, or other concern to the community, government officials should enjoy wide latitude in managing their offices, without intrusive oversight by the judiciary in the name of the First Amendment. [O]rdinary dismissals from government service which violate no fixed tenure or applicable statute or regulation are not subject to judicial review even if the reasons for the dismissal are alleged to be mistaken or unreasonable.

[We] in no sense suggest that speech on private matters falls into one of the narrow and well-defined classes of expression which carries so little social value, such as obscenity, that the state can prohibit and punish such expression by all persons in its jurisdiction. [We] hold only that when a public employee speaks not as a citizen upon matters of public concern, but instead as an employee upon matters only of personal interest, absent the most unusual circumstances, a federal court is not the appropriate forum in which to review the wisdom of a personnel decision taken by a public agency allegedly in reaction to the employee's behavior. Our responsibility is to ensure that citizens are not deprived of fundamental rights by virtue of working for the government; this does not require a grant of immunity for employee grievances not afforded by the First Amendment to those who do not work for the state.

Whether an employee's speech addresses a matter of public concern must be determined by the content, form, and context of a given statement, as revealed by the whole record. In this case, with but one exception, the questions posed by Myers to her coworkers do not fall under the rubric of matters of "public concern." We view the questions pertaining to the confidence and trust that Myers' coworkers possess in various supervisors, the level of office morale, and the need for a grievance committee as mere extensions of Myers' dispute over her transfer to another section of the criminal court. [W]e do not believe these questions are of public import in evaluating the performance of the District Attorney as an elected official. Myers did not seek to inform the public that the District Attorney's office was not discharging its governmental responsibilities in the investigation and prosecution of criminal cases. Nor did Myers seek to bring to light actual or potential wrongdoing or breach of public trust on the part of Connick and others. Indeed, the questionnaire, if released to the public, would convey no information at all other than the fact that a single employee is upset with the status quo. While discipline and morale in the workplace are related to an agency's efficient performance of its duties, the focus of Myers' questions is not to evaluate the performance of the office but rather to gather ammunition for another round of controversy with her superiors. These questions reflect one employee's dissatisfaction with a transfer and an attempt to turn that displeasure into a cause celebre.

To presume that all matters which transpire within a government office are of public concern would mean that virtually every remark — and certainly every criticism directed at a public official — would plant the seed of a constitutional case. While as a matter of good judgment, public officials should be receptive to constructive criticism offered by their employees, the First Amendment does not require a public office to be run as a roundtable for employee complaints over internal office affairs.

One question in Myers' questionnaire, however, does touch upon a matter of public concern. Question 11 inquires if assistant district attorneys "ever feel pressured to work in political campaigns on behalf of office supported candidates." [O]fficial pressure upon employees to work for political candidates not of the worker's own choice constitutes a coercion of belief in violation of fundamental constitutional rights. In addition, there is a demonstrated interest in this country that government service should depend upon meritorious performance rather than political service. Given this history, we believe it apparent that the issue of whether assistant district attorneys are pressured to work in political campaigns is a matter of interest to the community upon which it is essential that public employees be able to speak out freely without fear of retaliatory dismissal.

Because one of the questions in Myers' survey touched upon a matter of public concern, and contributed to her discharge we must determine whether Connick was justified in discharging Myers. [The] state's burden in justifying a particular discharge varies depending upon the nature of the employee's expression. Although such particularized balancing is difficult, the courts must reach the most appropriate possible balance of the competing interests.

The *Pickering* balance requires full consideration of the government's interest in the effective and efficient fulfillment of its responsibilities to the public. [We] agree [that] there is no demonstration here that the questionnaire impeded Myers' ability to perform her responsibilities. . . . [Connick], who characterized Myers' actions as causing a "mini-insurrection," [viewed] Myers' questionnaire was an act of insubordination which interfered with working relationships. When close working relationships are essential to fulfilling public responsibilities, a wide degree of deference to the employer's judgment is appropriate. [W]e do not see the necessity for an employer to allow events to unfold to the extent that the disruption of the office and the destruction of working relationships is manifest before taking action. We caution that a stronger showing may be necessary if the employee's speech more substantially involved matters of public concern.

The District Court rejected Connick's position because "unlike a statement of fact which might be deemed critical of one's superiors, [Myers'] questionnaire was not a statement of fact, but the presentation and solicitation of ideas and opinions," which are entitled to greater constitutional protection because "under the First Amendment there is no such thing as a false idea." This approach, while perhaps relevant in weighing the value of Myers' speech, bears no logical relationship to the issue of whether the questionnaire undermined office relationships. Questions, no less than forcefully stated opinions and facts, carry messages and it requires no unusual insight to conclude that the purpose, if not the likely result, of the questionnaire is to seek to precipitate a vote of no confidence in Connick and his supervisors. Thus, Question 10, which asked whether or not the Assistants had confidence in and relied on the word of five named supervisors, is a statement that carries the clear potential for undermining office relations.

Also relevant is the manner, time, and place in which the questionnaire was distributed. [T]he questionnaire was prepared, and distributed at the office; the manner of distribution required not only Myers to leave her work but for others to do the same in order that the questionnaire be completed. Although some latitude [when] official work is performed is to be allowed when professional employees are involved, and Myers did not violate announced office policy, the fact that Myers, unlike Pickering, exercised her rights to speech at the office supports Connick's fears that the functioning of his office was endangered.

Finally, the context in which the dispute arose is also significant. This is not a case where an employee, out of purely academic interest, circulated a questionnaire so as to obtain useful research. . . . When employee speech concerning office policy arises from an employment dispute concerning the very application of that policy to the speaker, additional weight must be given to the supervisor's view that the employee has threatened the authority of the employer to run the office. Although we accept the [finding] that Myers' reluctance to accede to the transfer order was not a sufficient cause in itself for her dismissal, [this] does not render irrelevant the fact that the questionnaire emerged after a persistent dispute between Myers and Connick and his deputies over office transfer policy.

Myers' questionnaire touched upon matters of public concern in only a most limited sense; her survey, in our view, is most accurately characterized as an employee grievance concerning internal office policy. The limited First Amendment interest involved here does not require that Connick tolerate action which he reasonably believed would disrupt the office, undermine his authority, and destroy close working relationships. Myers' discharge therefore did not offend the First Amendment. We reiterate, however, [one] caveat[:] "Because of the enormous variety of fact situations in which critical statements [by] public employees may be thought by their superiors [to] furnish grounds for dismissal, we do not deem it either appropriate or feasible to lay down a general standard against which all such statements may be judged."

[T]he First Amendment's primary aim is the full protection of speech upon issues of public concern, as well as the practical realities involved in the administration of a government office. Although today the balance is struck for the government, this is no defeat for the First Amendment. [I]t would indeed be a Pyrrhic victory for the great principles of free expression if the Amendment's safeguarding of a public employee's right, as a citizen, to participate in discussions concerning public affairs were confused with the attempt to constitutionalize the employee grievance that we see presented here. The judgment of the Court of Appeals is

Reversed.

Justice BRENNAN, with whom Justice MARSHALL, Justice BLACKMUN, and Justice STEVENS join, dissenting.

[S]peech about "the manner in which government is operated or should be operated" is an essential part of the communications necessary for self-governance the protection of which was a central purpose of the First Amendment. Because the questionnaire addressed such matters and its distribution did not adversely affect the operations of the District Attorney's Office or interfere with Myers' working relationship with her fellow employees, I dissent.

[Myers' questionnaire] addressed matters of public concern because it discussed subjects that could reasonably be expected to be of interest to persons seeking to develop informed opinions about the manner in which the Orleans Parish District Attorney, an elected official charged with managing a vital governmental agency, discharges his responsibilities. The questionnaire sought primarily to obtain information about the impact of the recent transfers on morale in the District Attorney's Office. It is beyond doubt that personnel decisions that adversely affect discipline and morale may ultimately impair an agency's efficient performance of its duties. . . . [The Court] does hold that one question — asking whether Assistants felt pressured to work in political campaigns on behalf of office-supported candidates — addressed a matter of public importance and concern. [Having] gone that far[,] the Court misapplies the *Pickering* test and holds [that] a public employer's mere apprehension that speech will be disruptive justifies suppression of that speech when all the objective evidence suggests that those fears are essentially unfounded. . . .

[The] Court's decision today inevitably will deter public employees from making critical statements about the manner in which government agencies are operated for fear that doing so will provoke their dismissal. As a result, the public will be deprived of valuable information with which to evaluate the performance of elected officials. Because protecting the dissemination of such information is an essential function of the First Amendment, I dissent.

Note: Federal Employees, Private Honoraria

A federal statute prohibited federal employees from accepting any compensation for making speeches or writing articles. The law applied whether or not the subject of the speech or article or the person or group paying for it had any connection with the employee's official duties. Violations of the law were punishable by a fine of up to $10,000 or the amount of the honorarium. The law was challenged by various federal employees who received compensation for writing or speaking on various topics unrelated to their employment (e.g., a mail handler employed by the U.S. Postal Service who give lectures on the Quaker religion). The evidence showed that some famous authors (e.g., Nathaniel Hawthorne and Herman Melville) had been federal employees who wrote or spoke "on the side," and that a motivation for such activity was the compensation provided. In defense of the law, the government argued that Congress could "reasonably . . . conclude that its interests in preventing impropriety and the appearance of impropriety in the federal work force outweigh the employees' interests in receiving compensation for expression that [relates] to their Government employment." In United States v. National Treasury Employees Union, 513 U.S. 454 (1995), the Court struck down the prohibition, concluding that it imposed a significant burden on expressive activity, and did not serve the government's interest in assuring that federal officers not misuse or appear to misuse power.

Rankin v. McPherson

483 U.S. 378 (1987)

Justice MARSHALL delivered the opinion of the Court.

[On] January 12, 1981, respondent Ardith McPherson was appointed a deputy in the office of the Constable of Harris County, Texas. The Constable is an elected official who functions as a law enforcement officer. At the time of her appointment, McPherson, a black woman, was 19 years old and had attended college for a year, studying secretarial science. Her appointment was conditional for a 90-day probationary period.

Although McPherson's title was "deputy constable," this was [because] all employees of the Constable's office, regardless of job function, were deputy constables. She was not a commissioned peace officer, did not wear a uniform, and was not authorized to make arrests or permitted to carry a gun. McPherson's duties were purely clerical. Her work station was a desk at which there was no telephone, in a room to which the public did not have ready access. Her job was to type data from court papers into a computer that maintained an automated record of the status of civil process in the county. Her training consisted of two days of instruction in the operation of her computer terminal.

On March 30, 1981, McPherson and some fellow employees heard on an office radio that there had been an attempt to assassinate the President of the United States. Upon hearing that report, McPherson engaged a co-worker, Lawrence Jackson, who was apparently her boyfriend, in a brief conversation, which according to McPherson's uncontroverted testimony went as follows:

> Q: What did you say?
> A: I said I felt that that would happen sooner or later.
> Q: Okay. And what did Lawrence say?
> A: Lawrence said, yeah, agreeing with me.
> Q: Okay. Now, [what] was your next comment?
> A: Well, [I] felt like it would be a black person that did that, because I feel like most of my kind is on welfare and CETA, and they use medicaid. . . . But then after I said that, [he's] cutting back medicaid and food stamps. And I said, yeah, welfare and CETA. I said, shoot, if they go for him again, I hope they get him.

McPherson's last remark was overheard by another Deputy Constable, who, unbeknownst to McPherson, was in the room. . . . The remark was reported to Constable Rankin, who summoned McPherson. McPherson readily admitted that she had made the statement, but testified that she told Rankin, upon being asked if she made the statement, "Yes, but I didn't mean anything by it." After their discussion, Rankin fired McPherson.

McPherson brought suit [under] 42 U.S.C. §1983, alleging that petitioner Rankin, in discharging her, had violated her constitutional rights under color of state law. . . . The District Court [ruled] that the statements were not protected speech. [T]he Court of Appeals concluded that the Government's interest did not outweigh the First Amendment interest in protecting McPherson's speech. . . . We granted certiorari and now affirm.

[Even] though McPherson was merely a probationary employee, and even if she could have been discharged for any reason or for no reason at all, she may nonetheless be entitled to reinstatement if she was discharged for exercising her constitutional right to freedom of expression. . . . The determination whether a public employer has properly discharged an employee for engaging in speech requires "a balance between the interests of the [employee], as a citizen, in commenting upon matters of public concern and the interest of the State, as an employer, in promoting the efficiency of the public services it performs through its employees." Pickering v. Board of Education, 391 U.S. 563, 568 (1968). . . .

The threshold question in applying this balancing test is whether McPherson's speech may be "fairly characterized as constituting speech on a matter of public concern." "Whether an employee's speech addresses a matter of public concern must be determined by the content, form, and context of a given statement, as revealed by the whole record." [Considering] the statement in context, as *Connick* requires, discloses that it plainly dealt with a matter of public concern. The statement was made in the course of a conversation addressing the policies of the President's administration. It came on the heels of a news bulletin regarding what is certainly a matter of heightened public attention: an attempt on the life of the President. While a statement that amounted to a threat to kill the President would not be protected by the First Amendment, [McPherson's] statement did not amount to a threat punishable under 18 U.S.C. §871(a) or 18 U.S.C. §2385, or, indeed, that could properly be criminalized at all. The inappropriate or controversial character of a statement is irrelevant to the question whether it deals with a matter of public concern. "[D]ebate on public issues should be uninhibited, robust, and wide-open, [and] may well include vehement, caustic, and sometimes unpleasantly sharp attacks on government and public officials." New York Times Co. v. Sullivan, 376 U.S. 254, 270 (1964).

Because McPherson's statement addressed a matter of public concern, *Pickering* next requires that we balance McPherson's interest in making her statement against "the interest of the State, as an employer, in promoting the efficiency of the public services it performs through its employees." The State bears a burden of justifying the discharge on legitimate grounds. [T]he manner, time, and place of the employee's expression are relevant, as is the context in which the dispute arose. We have previously recognized as pertinent considerations whether the statement impairs discipline by superiors or harmony among co-workers, has a detrimental impact on close working relationships for which personal loyalty and confidence are necessary, or impedes the performance of the speaker's duties or interferes with the regular operation of the enterprise.

These considerations, and indeed the very nature of the balancing test, make apparent that the state interest element of the test focuses on the effective functioning of the public employer's enterprise. Interference with work, personnel relationships, or the speaker's job performance can detract from the public employer's function; avoiding such interference can be a strong state interest. From this perspective, however, petitioners fail to demonstrate a state interest that outweighs McPherson's First Amendment rights. While McPherson's statement was made at the workplace, there is no evidence that it interfered with the efficient functioning of the office. The Constable was evidently not afraid that McPherson had disturbed or interrupted other employees — he did not inquire to whom respondent had made the remark and testified that he "was not concerned who she had made it to." In fact, Constable Rankin testified that the possibility of interference with the functions of the Constable's office had *not* been a consideration in his discharge of respondent and that he did not even inquire whether the remark had disrupted the work of the office.

Nor was there any danger that McPherson had discredited the office by making her statement in public. McPherson's speech took place in an area to which there was ordinarily no public access; her remark was evidently made in a private conversation with another employee. . . . Nor is there any evidence that employees other than Jackson who worked in the room even heard the remark. Not only was McPherson's discharge unrelated to the functioning of the office, it was not based on any assessment by the Constable that the remark demonstrated a character trait that made respondent unfit to perform her work.

While the facts underlying Rankin's discharge of McPherson [are] somewhat unclear, it is undisputed that he fired McPherson based on the *content* of her speech. Evidently because McPherson had made the statement, and because the Constable believed that she "meant it," he decided that she was not a suitable employee to have in a law enforcement agency. But in weighing the State's interest in discharging an employee based on any claim that the content of a statement made by the employee somehow undermines the mission of the public employer, some attention must be paid to the responsibilities of the employee within the agency. The burden of caution employees bear with respect to the words they speak will vary with the extent of authority and public accountability the employee's role entails. Where, as here, an employee serves no confidential, policymaking, or public contact role, the danger to the agency's successful functioning from that employee's private speech is minimal. We cannot believe that every employee in Constable Rankin's office, whether computer operator, electrician, or file clerk, is equally required, on pain of discharge, to avoid any statement susceptible of being interpreted by the Constable as an indication that the employee may be unworthy of employment in his law enforcement agency. At some point, such concerns are so removed from the effective functioning of the public employer that they cannot prevail over the free speech rights of the public employee.

This is such a case. McPherson's employment-related interaction with the Constable was apparently negligible. Her duties were purely clerical and were limited solely to the civil process function of the Constable's office. There is no indication that she would ever be in a position to further — or indeed to have any involvement with — the minimal law enforcement activity engaged in by the Constable's office. Given the function of the agency, McPherson's position in the office, and the nature of her statement, we are not persuaded that Rankin's interest in discharging her outweighed her rights under the First Amendment.

Because we agree with the Court of Appeals that McPherson's discharge was improper, the judgment of the Court of Appeals is

Affirmed.

Justice POWELL, concurring.

[McPherson's] comment was made during a private conversation with a co-worker who happened [to] be her boyfriend. She had no intention or expectation that it would be overheard or acted on by others. . . . If a statement is on a matter of public concern, [it] will be an unusual case where the employer's legitimate interests will be so great as to justify punishing an employee for this type of private speech that routinely takes place at all levels in the workplace. . . .

Justice SCALIA, with whom THE CHIEF JUSTICE, Justice WHITE, and Justice O'CONNOR join, dissenting.

[N]o law enforcement agency is required by the First Amendment to permit one of its employees to "ride with the cops and cheer for the robbers." [McPherson's] statement [is] only one step removed from statements that we have previously held entitled to no First Amendment protection even in the nonemployment context — including assassination threats against the President (which are illegal under 18 U.S.C. §871), "'fighting' words," epithets or personal abuse, and advocacy of force or violence. A statement lying so near the category of completely unprotected speech cannot fairly be viewed as lying within the "heart" of the First Amendment's protection; it lies within that category of speech that can neither be characterized as speech on matters of public concern nor properly subject to criminal penalties. Once McPherson stopped explicitly criticizing the President's policies and expressed a desire that he be assassinated, she crossed the line.

[Statements] by the Constable's employees to the effect that "if they go for the President again, I hope they get him" might also, to put it mildly, undermine public confidence in the Constable's office. A public employer has a strong interest in preserving its reputation with the public. . . . The Court's sweeping assertion [that] where an employee "serves no confidential, policymaking, or public contact role, the danger to the agency's successful functioning from that employee's private speech is minimal," is simply contrary to reason and experience. Nonpolicymaking employees (the Assistant District Attorney in *Connick*, for example) can hurt working relationships and undermine public confidence in an organization every bit as much as policymaking employees. . . . In sum, since Constable Rankin's interest in maintaining both an esprit de corps and a public image consistent with his office's law enforcement duties outweighs any interest his employees may have in expressing on the job a desire that the President be killed, even assuming that such an expression addresses a matter of public concern it is not protected by the First Amendment from suppression. . . .

Notes

1. *The Principal's Memo.* In Mt. Healthy City School District v. Doyle, 429 U.S. 274 (1977), a teacher provided a copy of a principal's memo on teacher dress and appearance to a local disc jockey, who announced it as a news item. Later, the

principal recommended that Doyle not be rehired for the following year because of "a notable lack of tact in handling professional matters which leaves much doubt as to your sincerity in establishing good school relationships." That general statement was followed by references to the radio station incident and to an obscene-gesture incident. The Court held that, had the nonrenewal been based on Doyle's communication with the radio station, it would be actionable: "[the] burden was properly placed upon respondent to show that his conduct was constitutionally protected, and that this conduct was a 'substantial factor' [or] that it was a 'motivating factor' in the Board's decision not to rehire him. Respondent having carried that burden, [the court] should have [determined] whether the Board had shown by a preponderance of the evidence that it would have reached the same decision as to respondent's reemployment even in the absence of the protected conduct."

2. *The Exclusive Bargaining Representative.* In Minnesota State Board for Community Colleges v. Knight, 465 U.S. 271 (1984), although Minnesota authorized public employees to bargain collectively (regarding the terms and conditions of their employment), if professional employees (i.e., college faculty) have formed an appropriate bargaining unit and have selected an exclusive representative for mandatory bargaining, then their employer may exchange views only on non-mandatory subjects with that exclusive representative. The Court upheld the restriction: "Appellees' speech and associational rights [have] not been infringed by Minnesota's restriction of participation in 'meet and confer' sessions to the faculty's exclusive representative. The state has in no way restrained appellees' freedom to speak on any education-related issue or their freedom to associate or not to associate with whom they please, including the exclusive representative. Nor has the state attempted to suppress any ideas." Justice Stevens, joined by two other justices, dissented: "[T]he First Amendment [guarantees] an open marketplace for ideas—where divergent points of view can freely compete for the attention of those in power and of those to whom the powerful must account. [T]he statute gives only one speaker a realistic opportunity to present its views to state officials. . . ."

3. *Circulating Petitions on Military Bases.* Brown v. Glines, 444 U.S. 348 (1980), involved Air Force regulations that required service members to obtain approval from their commanders before circulating petitions on Air Force bases. Under the regulations, commanders could deny permission if they determine that distribution of the material would result in "a clear danger to the loyalty, discipline, or morale of members of the Armed Forces, or material interference with the accomplishment of a military mission. . . ." Glines, a captain in the reserves, drafted petitions to members of Congress and the secretary of defense complaining about the Air Force's grooming standards. When Glines gave the petitions to a sergeant to solicit signatures, his commander punished him for violating the regulations by removing him from active duty and assigning him to the standby reserves. The Court upheld the regulations: "The unrestricted circulation of collective petitions could imperil discipline. . . ." Justice Stewart dissented: "[It

cannot] conceivably be argued that [a] regulation requiring the preclearance of the content of all petitions to be circulated by servicemen in time of peace is 'necessary to the security of the United States.'"

4. *The Pornographic Police Officer.* A police officer is terminated for selling videotapes showing himself engaged in sexually explicit acts, sometimes in police uniform. One video shows him stripping off a police uniform (not the actual city uniform) and masturbating. Another video shows him stopping a motorist to issue a citation, but ending up involved in sexual activity with the motorist. His Web site identified him "as employed in the field of law enforcement." The department concluded that the officer had violated specific police department policies, including conduct unbecoming of an officer, outside employment, and immoral conduct. Since all of the officer's activities were conducted during his "off-duty" hours, does the dismissal violate his First Amendment rights? How might *Pickering*, *Connick*, and *Rankin* apply to the dismissal? *See* City of San Diego v. Roe, 125 S.Ct. 521 (2004).

∾ PROBLEMS ∾

1. *The History Professor and the Pistol.* A university history club asked faculty to pose with props related to their areas of interest. The plaintiff chose to pose wearing a coonskin cap and holding a .45-caliber pistol. Another plaintiff (who specialized in ancient Greece and Rome) chose to wear a cardboard laurel wreath and held a Roman short sword. When a university official demanded that the photos be removed as "inappropriate," the chancellor ordered the photos removed over the history department's objection. The professors sue, claiming a violation of their First Amendment rights. Should they prevail?

2. *The KKK Recruiter.* A sheriff's office employee (a clerical employee who has responsibility for filing both public and confidential records) gave a television interview in which he discussed his work as a Ku Klux Klan recruiter. The evidence suggested that he had an "outstanding" work record. Nevertheless, due to the interview, he was dismissed because the sheriff claimed that the interview caused racial tension (the sheriff's office received more than 200 complaints about the interview, as well as a protest by the Klan and a counterprotest by an anti-Klan group), lowered esprit de corps in the sheriff's office, and damaged the office's credibility in the community (some argued that blacks should resist arrest by sheriff's office personnel because of a risk of death or serious bodily injury at the jail). Were the employee's association with the KKK and the interview protected by the First Amendment?

3. *More on the International Treaty Regulating the Internet.* Having read the various decisions discussing the ability of the U.S. government to restrict the speech of governmental employees, do you have a better sense of the type of treaty language that you might be able to agree to regarding limiting the speech of public employees on the Internet? If so, what language might be included in the treaty?

Garcetti v. Ceballos

547 U.S. 410 (2006)

Justice KENNEDY delivered the opinion of the Court.

Respondent Richard Ceballos has been employed since 1989 as a deputy district attorney for the Los Angeles County District Attorney's Office [as] a calendar deputy [who] exercised certain supervisory responsibilities over other lawyers. In February 2000, a defense attorney contacted Ceballos about a pending criminal case [and] said there were inaccuracies in an affidavit used to obtain a critical search warrant. . . . After [an investigation,] Ceballos determined the affidavit contained serious misrepresentations. The affidavit called a long driveway what Ceballos thought should have been referred to as a separate roadway. Ceballos also questioned the affidavit's statement that tire tracks led from a stripped-down truck to the premises covered by the warrant [because] the roadway's composition [made] it difficult or impossible to leave visible tire tracks.

Ceballos spoke on the telephone to the warrant affiant, a deputy sheriff from the Los Angeles County Sheriff's Department, but he did not receive a satisfactory explanation for the perceived inaccuracies. He relayed his findings to his supervisors, petitioners Carol Najera and Frank Sundstedt, and followed up by preparing a disposition memorandum. The memo explained Ceballos' concerns and recommended dismissal of the case. On March 2, 2000, Ceballos submitted the memo to Sundstedt for his review. A few days later, Ceballos presented Sundstedt with another memo, this one describing a second telephone conversation between Ceballos and the warrant affiant. . . . Based on Ceballos' statements, a meeting was held to discuss the affidavit. . . . The meeting allegedly became heated, with one lieutenant sharply criticizing Ceballos for his handling of the case.

Despite Ceballos' concerns, Sundstedt decided to proceed with the prosecution, pending disposition of the defense motion to traverse. The trial court held a hearing on the motion. Ceballos was called by the defense and recounted his observations about the affidavit, but the trial court rejected the challenge to the warrant. . . . Ceballos claims that in the aftermath of these events he was subjected to a series of retaliatory employment actions. The actions included reassignment from his calendar deputy position to a trial deputy position, transfer to another courthouse, and denial of a promotion. Ceballos['] grievance [was] denied [on the basis that] he had not suffered any retaliation. . . . Ceballos sued [alleging that] petitioners violated the First and Fourteenth Amendments by retaliating against him based on his memo of March 2. . . . Petitioners [claimed] that no retaliatory actions were taken against Ceballos and that all the actions of which he complained were explained by legitimate reasons such as staffing needs. They further contended [that] Ceballos' memo was not protected speech under the First Amendment. [The] District Court granted [petitioner's] motion [for summary judgment]. The Court of Appeals for the Ninth Circuit reversed. . . . We granted certiorari and we now reverse.

[At one time, a] public employee had "no right to object to conditions placed upon the terms of employment — including those which restricted the exercise of constitutional rights." [Connick v. Myers, 461 U.S. 138 (1983).] That dogma has been qualified in important respects. The Court has made clear that public employees do not surrender all their First Amendment rights by reason of their employment. Rather, the First Amendment protects a public employee's right, in certain circumstances, to speak as a citizen addressing matters of public concern. *See, e.g.,* [Pickering v. Board of Ed. of Township High School Dist. 205, Will Cty., 391 U.S. 563 (1968)]; Rankin v. McPherson, 483 U.S. 378 (1987).

Pickering provides a useful starting point in explaining the Court's doctrine. There the relevant speech was a teacher's letter to a local newspaper addressing issues including the funding policies of his school board. "The problem in any case," the Court stated, "is to arrive at a balance between the interests of the teacher, as a citizen, in commenting upon matters of public concern and the interest of the State, as an employer, in promoting the efficiency of the public services it performs through its employees." The Court found the teacher's speech "neither [was] shown nor can be presumed to have in any way either impeded the teacher's proper performance of his daily duties in the classroom or to have interfered with the regular operation of the schools generally." Thus, the Court concluded that "the interest of the school administration in limiting teachers' opportunities to contribute to public debate is not significantly greater than its interest in limiting a similar contribution by any member of the general public."

Pickering and the cases decided in its wake identify two inquiries to guide interpretation of the constitutional protections accorded to public employee speech. The first requires determining whether the employee spoke as a citizen on a matter of public concern. If the answer is no, the employee has no First Amendment cause of action based on his or her employer's reaction to the speech. If the answer is yes, then the possibility of a First Amendment claim arises. The question becomes whether the relevant government entity had an adequate justification for treating the employee differently from any other member of the general public. This consideration reflects the importance of the relationship between the speaker's expressions and employment. A government entity has broader discretion to restrict speech when it acts in its role as employer, but the restrictions it imposes must be directed at speech that has some potential to affect the entity's operations.

To be sure, conducting these inquiries sometimes has proved difficult. This is the necessary product of "the enormous variety of fact situations in which critical statements by teachers and other public employees may be thought by their superiors [to] furnish grounds for dismissal." The Court's overarching objectives, though, are evident.

When a citizen enters government service, the citizen by necessity must accept certain limitations on his or her freedom. *See, e.g.,* Waters v. Churchill, 511 U.S. 661 (1994) (plurality opinion). Government employers, like private employers, need a significant degree of control over their employees' words and actions; without it, there would be little chance for the efficient provision of public services. *Cf. Connick, supra,* at 143. Public employees, moreover, often occupy trusted positions in society. When they speak out, they can express views that contravene governmental policies or impair the proper performance of governmental functions.

At the same time, the Court has recognized that a citizen who works for the government is nonetheless a citizen. The First Amendment limits the ability of a public employer to leverage the employment relationship to restrict, incidentally or intentionally, the liberties employees enjoy in their capacities as private citizens. So long as employees are speaking as citizens about matters of public concern, they must face only those speech restrictions that are necessary for their employers to operate efficiently and effectively. *See, e.g., Connick, supra,* at 147.

The Court's employee-speech jurisprudence protects, of course, the constitutional rights of public employees. Yet the First Amendment interests at stake extend beyond the individual speaker. The Court has acknowledged the importance of promoting the public's interest in receiving the well-informed views of government employees engaging in civic discussion. [In] *Pickering*[, the] Court characterized its holding as rejecting the attempt of school administrators to "limi[t] teachers' opportunities to contribute to public debate." It also noted that teachers are "the members of a community most likely to have informed and definite opinions" about school expenditures. The Court's approach acknowledged the necessity for informed, vibrant dialogue in a democratic society. It suggested, in addition, that widespread costs may arise when dialogue is repressed. *See, e.g.,* San Diego v. Roe, 543 U.S. 77 (2004) (per curiam).

The Court's decisions, then, have sought both to promote the individual and societal interests that are served when employees speak as citizens on matters of public concern and to respect the needs of government employers attempting to perform their important public functions. Underlying our cases has been the premise that while the First Amendment invests public employees with certain rights, it does not empower them to "constitutionalize the employee grievance." *Connick,* 461 U.S., at 154.

[Ceballos] believed the affidavit used to obtain a search warrant contained serious misrepresentations. He conveyed his opinion and recommendation in a memo to his supervisor. That Ceballos expressed his views inside his office, rather than publicly, is not dispositive. Employees in some cases may receive First Amendment protection for expressions made at work. Many citizens do much of their talking inside [their] workplaces, and it would not serve the goal of treating public employees like "any member of the general public," *Pickering,* 391 U.S., at 573, to hold that all speech within the office is automatically exposed to restriction.

The memo concerned the subject matter of Ceballos' employment, but this, too, is nondispositive. The First Amendment protects some expressions related to the speaker's job. As the Court noted in *Pickering*: "Teachers are [the] members of a community most likely to have informed and definite opinions as to how funds allotted to the operation of the schools should be spent. Accordingly, it is essential that they be able to speak out freely on such questions without fear of retaliatory dismissal." The same is true of many other categories of public employees.

The controlling factor in Ceballos' case is that his expressions were made pursuant to his duties as a calendar deputy. That consideration — the fact that Ceballos spoke as a prosecutor fulfilling a responsibility to advise his supervisor about how best to proceed with a pending case — distinguishes Ceballos' case from those in which the First Amendment provides protection against discipline. We hold that when public employees make statements pursuant to their official duties, the employees are not speaking as citizens for First Amendment purposes, and the Constitution does not insulate their communications from employer discipline.

Ceballos wrote his disposition memo because that is part of what he, as a calendar deputy, was employed to do. It is immaterial whether he experienced some personal gratification from writing the memo; his First Amendment rights do not depend on his job satisfaction. The significant point is that the memo was written pursuant to Ceballos' official duties. Restricting speech that owes its existence to a public employee's professional responsibilities does not infringe any liberties the employee might have enjoyed as a private citizen. It simply reflects the exercise of employer control over what the employer itself has commissioned or created. Contrast, for example, the expressions made by the speaker in *Pickering*, whose letter to the newspaper had no official significance and bore similarities to letters submitted by numerous citizens every day.

Ceballos did not act as a citizen when he went about conducting his daily professional activities, such as supervising attorneys, investigating charges, and preparing filings. In the same way he did not speak as a citizen by writing a memo that addressed the proper disposition of a pending criminal case. When he went to work and performed the tasks he was paid to perform, Ceballos acted as a government employee. The fact that his duties sometimes required him to speak or write does not mean his supervisors were prohibited from evaluating his performance.

This result is consistent with our precedents' attention to the potential societal value of employee speech. Refusing to recognize First Amendment claims based on government employees' work product does not prevent them from participating in public debate. The employees retain the prospect of constitutional protection for their contributions to the civic discourse. This prospect of protection, however, does not invest them with a right to perform their jobs however they see fit.

Our holding [is] supported by the emphasis of our precedents on affording government employers sufficient discretion to manage their operations. Employers have heightened interests in controlling speech made by an employee in his or her professional capacity. Official communications have official consequences, creating a need for substantive consistency and clarity. Supervisors must ensure that their employees' official communications are accurate, demonstrate sound judgment, and promote the employer's mission. Ceballos' memo is illustrative. It demanded the attention of his supervisors and led to a heated meeting with employees from the sheriff's department. If Ceballos' superiors thought his memo was inflammatory or misguided, they had the authority to take proper corrective action.

Ceballos' proposed contrary rule [would] commit state and federal courts to a new, permanent, and intrusive role, mandating judicial oversight of communications between and among government employees and their superiors in the course of official business. This displacement of managerial discretion by judicial supervision finds no support in our precedents. . . . To hold otherwise would be to demand permanent judicial intervention in the conduct of governmental operations to a degree inconsistent with sound principles of federalism and the separation of powers. . . . Employees who make public statements outside the course of performing their official duties retain some possibility of First Amendment protection because that is the kind of activity engaged in by citizens who do not work for the government. The same goes for writing a letter to a local newspaper, or discussing politics with a co-worker. When a public employee speaks pursuant to employment responsibilities, however, there is no relevant analogue to speech by citizens who are not government employees. . . . A public employer that wishes to encourage its employees to voice concerns privately retains the option of instituting internal policies and procedures that are receptive to employee criticism. Giving employees an internal forum for their speech will discourage them from concluding that the safest avenue of expression is to state their views in public.

[The] First Amendment does not prohibit managerial discipline based on an employee's expressions made pursuant to official responsibilities. Because Ceballos' memo falls into this category, his allegation of unconstitutional retaliation must fail. [The] parties [do] not dispute that Ceballos wrote his disposition memo pursuant to his employment duties. We thus have no occasion to articulate a comprehensive framework for defining the scope of an employee's duties in cases where there is room for serious debate. We reject, however, the suggestion that employers can restrict employees' rights by creating excessively broad job descriptions. . . . Formal job descriptions often bear little resemblance to the duties an employee actually is expected to perform, and the listing of a given task in an employee's written job description is neither necessary nor sufficient to demonstrate that conducting the task is within the scope of the employee's professional duties for First Amendment purposes.

[Justice Souter] suggests today's decision may have important ramifications for academic freedom. . . . There is some argument that expression related to academic scholarship or classroom instruction implicates additional constitutional interests that are not fully accounted for by this Court's customary employee-speech jurisprudence. We [do not decide] whether the analysis we conduct today would apply in the same manner to a case involving speech related to scholarship or teaching.

Exposing governmental inefficiency and misconduct is a matter of considerable significance. . . . The dictates of sound judgment are reinforced by the powerful network of legislative enactments — such as whistle-blower protection laws and labor codes — available to those who seek to expose wrongdoing. *See, e.g.,* 5 U.S.C. §2302(b)(8). Cases involving government attorneys implicate additional safeguards in the form of, for example, rules of conduct and constitutional obligations apart from the First Amendment. *See, e.g.,* Cal. Rule Prof. Conduct

5-110 (2005). These imperatives, as well as obligations arising from any other applicable constitutional provisions and mandates of the criminal and civil laws, protect employees and provide checks on supervisors who would order unlawful or otherwise inappropriate actions.

We reject, however, the notion that the First Amendment shields from discipline the expressions employees make pursuant to their professional duties. Our precedents do not support the existence of a constitutional cause of action behind every statement a public employee makes in the course of doing his or her job.

The judgment of the Court of Appeals is reversed, and the case is remanded for proceedings consistent with this opinion.

It is so ordered.

Justice STEVENS, dissenting.

[The] notion that there is a categorical difference between speaking as a citizen and speaking in the course of one's employment is quite wrong. [In] Givhan v. Western Line Consol. School Dist., 439 U.S. 410 (1979)[, we] had no difficulty recognizing that the First Amendment applied when Bessie Givhan, an English teacher, raised concerns about the school's racist employment practices to the principal. [I]t seems perverse to fashion a new rule that provides employees with an incentive to voice their concerns publicly before talking frankly to their superiors. . . .

Justice SOUTER, with whom Justice STEVENS and Justice GINSBURG join, dissenting.

[P]rivate and public interests in addressing official wrongdoing and threats to health and safety can outweigh the government's stake in the efficient implementation of policy, and when they do public employees who speak on these matters in the course of their duties should be eligible to claim First Amendment protection.

[A] statement by a government employee complaining about nothing beyond treatment under personnel rules raises no greater claim to constitutional protection against retaliatory response than the remarks of a private employee. *See* Connick v. Myers, 461 U.S. 138 (1983). In between these points lies a public employee's speech unwelcome to the government but on a significant public issue. Such an employee speaking as a citizen [with] a citizen's interest, is protected from reprisal unless the statements are too damaging to the government's capacity to conduct public business to be justified by any individual or public benefit thought to flow from the statements. [A] government paycheck does nothing to eliminate the value to an individual of speaking on public matters, and there is no good reason for categorically discounting a speaker's interest in commenting on a matter of public concern just because the government employs him. . . . The reason that protection of employee speech is qualified is that it can distract co-workers and supervisors from their tasks at hand and thwart the implementation of legitimate policy, the risks of which grow greater the closer the employee's speech gets to commenting on his own workplace and responsibilities. . . .

The difference between a case like *Givhan* and this one is that the subject of Ceballos's speech fell within the scope of his job responsibilities, whereas choosing personnel was not what the teacher was hired to do. The effect of the majority's constitutional line between these two cases, then, is that a *Givhan* schoolteacher is protected when complaining to the principal about hiring policy, but a school personnel officer would not be if he protested that the principal disapproved of hiring minority job applicants. This is an odd place to draw a distinction, and while necessary judicial line-drawing sometimes looks arbitrary, any distinction obliges a court to justify its choice. Here, there is no adequate justification for the majority's line categorically denying *Pickering* protection to any speech uttered "pursuant to . . . official duties."

[The] qualified speech protection embodied in *Pickering* balancing resolves the tension between individual and public interests in the speech, on the one hand, and the government's interest in operating efficiently without distraction or embarrassment by talkative or headline-grabbing employees. The need for a balance hardly disappears when an employee speaks on matters his job requires him to address; rather, [the] individual and public value of such speech is no less, and may well be greater, when the employee speaks pursuant to his duties in addressing a subject he knows intimately for the very reason that it falls within his duties. . . . Would anyone deny that a prosecutor like Richard Ceballos may claim the interest of any citizen in speaking out against a rogue law enforcement officer, simply because his job requires him to express a judgment about the officer's performance? . . .

[The] majority is rightly concerned that the employee who speaks out on matters [relating to] his own work has the greater leverage to create office uproars and fracture the government's authority to set policy to be carried out coherently through the ranks. . . . But why do the majority's concerns, which we all share, require categorical exclusion of First Amendment protection against any official retaliation for things said on the job? [The] lesson of *Pickering* [is] still to the point: when constitutionally significant interests clash, resist the demand for winner-take-all; try to make adjustments that serve all of the values at stake.

[The] majority's position comes with no guarantee against factbound litigation over whether a public employee's statements were made "pursuant [to] official duties." . . . Are prosecutors' discretionary statements about cases addressed to the press on the courthouse steps made "pursuant to their official duties"? Are government nuclear scientists' complaints to their supervisors about a colleague's improper handling of radioactive materials made "pursuant" to duties? [The] majority accepts the fallacy [that] any statement made within the scope of public employment is (or should be treated as) the government's own speech, and should thus be differentiated as a matter of law from the personal statements the First Amendment protects. . . .

The majority [argues] that the First Amendment has little or no work to do here owing to an assertedly comprehensive complement of state and national statutes protecting government whistle-blowers from vindictive bosses. [But] "[t]he applicability of a provision of the Constitution has never depended on the vagaries of state or federal law." Board of Commrs., Wabaunsee Cty. v. Umbehr, 518 U.S. 668 (1996). [S]peech addressing official wrongdoing may well fall outside protected whistle-blowing, defined in the classic sense of exposing an official's fault to a third party or to the public. . . .

Justice BREYER, dissenting.

[W]here a government employee speaks "as an employee upon matters only of personal interest," the First Amendment does not offer protection. Where the employee speaks "as a citizen . . . upon matters of public concern," the First Amendment offers protection but only where the speech survives [a] test, called, in legal shorthand, "*Pickering* balancing." [I] believe that courts should apply the *Pickering* standard, even though the government employee speaks upon matters of public concern in the course of his ordinary duties. . . .

[Respondent] complained of retaliation, in part, on the basis of speech contained in his disposition memorandum that he says fell within the scope of his obligations. . . . The facts present two special circumstances that together justify First Amendment review. First, the speech at issue is professional speech — the speech of a lawyer. . . . Second, [a] prosecutor has a constitutional obligation to learn of, to preserve, and to communicate with the defense about exculpatory and impeachment evidence in the government's possession[, so that] the need to protect the employee's speech is augmented, the need for broad government authority to control that speech is likely diminished, and administrable standards are quite likely available. Hence, I would find that the Constitution mandates special protection of employee speech in such circumstances. . . .

. . . Government administration typically involves matters of public concern. Why else would government be involved? And "public issues," indeed, matters of "unusual importance," are often daily bread-and-butter concerns for the police, the intelligence agencies, the military, and many whose jobs involve protecting the public's health, safety, and the environment. . . . Moreover, the speech of vast numbers of public employees deal with wrongdoing, health, safety, and honesty: for example, police officers, firefighters, environmental protection agents, building inspectors, hospital workers, bank regulators, and so on. . . .

[The] ability of a dissatisfied employee to file a complaint, engage in discovery, and insist that the court undertake a balancing of interests [may] interfere unreasonably with both the managerial function (the ability of the employer to control the way in which an employee performs his basic job) and with the use of other grievance-resolution mechanisms, such as arbitration, civil service review boards, and whistle-blower remedies, for which employees and employers may have bargained or which legislatures may have enacted. [The] list of categories substantially overlaps areas where the law already provides nonconstitutional protection through whistle-blower statutes and the like. . . .

∾ PROBLEMS ∾

1. *Applying* Ceballos. As the dissents suggest, *Ceballos* might apply to an array of employee statements. Think about how the decision might apply to the following factual situations (some of which were suggested by Justices Stevens and Souter in their dissents):

a. An internal police investigator brings the false testimony of a fellow officer to the attention of a city official. Afterward, the investigator is demoted. *See* Branton v. Dallas, 272 F.3d 730 (C.A.5 2001).

b. A police officer is demoted after opposing the police chief's attempt to "us[e] his official position to coerce a financially independent organization into a potentially ruinous merger." *See* Miller v. Jones, 444 F.3d 929, 936 (C.A.7 2006).

c. A police officer is sanctioned for reporting criminal activity that implicates a local political figure, a good friend of the police chief, in official misconduct. *See* Delgado v. Jones, 282 F.3d 511 (C.A.7 2002).

d. A school district official's contract is not renewed after she gives frank (and negative) testimony about the district's desegregation efforts in a judicial proceeding. *See* Herts v. Smith, 345 F.3d 581 (C.A.8 2003).

e. An engineer is fired after reporting to his supervisors that contractors were failing to complete dam-related projects and that the resulting dam might be structurally unstable. *See* Kincade v. Blue Springs, 64 F.3d 389 (C.A.8 1995).

f. A state lottery board security officer is fired after informing the police about a theft made possible by "rather drastic managerial ineptitude." *See* Fox v. District of Columbia, 83 F.3d 1491, 1494 (C.A.D.C. 1996).

g. A law professor is disciplined after publishing an article questioning the wisdom of state affirmative action policies.

2. *Kentucky's Anti-Blog Policy.* Kentucky's Republican governor faces criminal misdemeanor charges and is being repeatedly blasted on Democratic blog sites. Historically, in an attempt to preclude state employees from spending time on non-work-related Internet sites, Kentucky has used blocking software to preclude state-owned computers from being used to access sites related to pornography, lingerie, computer games, hate sites, casinos, chat rooms, and illegal activity sites. Is it permissible to extend the blocks to cover Web blogs? Can the ban be justified on the basis that visiting such sites, for non-work-related reasons, is not an "efficient" use of state employee time?

3. Associational Rights

Questions have arisen regarding whether public employees have special associational rights. Those issues are presented in the following case.

Elrod v. Burns

427 U.S. 347 (1976)

Mr. Justice BRENNAN announced the judgment of the Court and delivered an opinion in which Mr. Justice WHITE and Mr. Justice MARSHALL joined.

In December 1970, the Sheriff of Cook County, a Republican, was replaced by Richard Elrod, a Democrat. [R]espondents, all Republicans, were employees of the Cook County Sheriff's Office. They were non-civil-service employees and, therefore, not covered by any statute, ordinance, or regulation protecting them from arbitrary discharge. John Burns was Chief Deputy of the Process Division and supervised all departments of the Sheriff's Office working on the seventh floor of the building housing that office. Frank Vargas was a bailiff and security guard at the Juvenile Court. . . . Fred L. Buckley was employed as a process server in the office. Joseph Dennard was an employee in the office.

It has been the practice of the Sheriff of Cook County, when he assumes office from a Sheriff of a different political party, to replace non-civil-service employees of the Sheriffs' Office with members of his own party when the existing employees lack or fail to obtain requisite support from, or fail to affiliate with, that party. [S]ubsequent to Sheriff Elrod's assumption of office, respondents [were] discharged from their employment solely because they did not support and were not members of the Democratic Party and had failed to obtain the sponsorship of one of its leaders. Buckley is in imminent danger of being discharged solely for the same reasons. Respondents allege that the discharges were ordered by Sheriff Elrod under the direction of the codefendants in this suit.

[Patronage] practice is not new to American politics. It has existed at the federal level at least since the Presidency of Thomas Jefferson, although its popularization and legitimation primarily occurred later, in the Presidency of Andrew Jackson. . . . The cost of the practice of patronage is the restraint it places on freedoms of belief and association. In order to maintain their jobs, respondents were required to pledge their political allegiance to the Democratic Party, work for the election of other candidates of the Democratic Party, contribute a portion of their wages to the Party, or obtain the sponsorship of a member of the Party, usually at the price of one of the first three alternatives. Regardless of the incumbent party's identity, Democratic or otherwise, the consequences for association and belief are the same. An individual who is a member of the out-party maintains affiliation with his own party at the risk of losing his job. He works for the election of his party's candidates and espouses its policies at the same risk. The financial and campaign assistance that he is induced to provide to another party furthers the advancement of that party's policies to the detriment of his party's views and ultimately his own beliefs, and any assessment of his salary is tantamount to coerced belief. Even a pledge of allegiance to another party, however ostensible, only serves to compromise the individual's true beliefs. Since the average public employee is hardly in the financial position to support his party and another, or to lend his time to two parties, the individual's ability to act according to his beliefs and to associate with others of his political persuasion is constrained, and support for his party is diminished.

It is not only belief and association which are restricted where political patronage is the practice. The free functioning of the electoral process also suffers. Conditioning public employment on partisan support prevents support of competing political interests. Existing employees are deterred from such support, as well as the multitude seeking jobs. As government employment, state or federal, becomes more pervasive, the greater the dependence on it becomes, and therefore the greater becomes the power to starve political opposition by commanding partisan support, financial and otherwise. Patronage thus tips the electoral process in favor of the incumbent party, and where the practice's scope is substantial relative to the size of the electorate, the impact on the process can be significant.

Our concern with the impact of patronage on political belief and association does not occur in the abstract, for political belief and association constitute the core of those activities protected by the First Amendment. "[I]f there is any fixed star in our constitutional constellation, it is that no official, high or petty, can prescribe what shall be orthodox in politics, nationalism, religion, or other matters of opinion or force citizens to confess by word or act their faith therein." And, though freedom of belief is central, "[t]he First Amendment protects political association as well as political expression." "There can no longer be any doubt that freedom to associate with others for the common advancement of political beliefs and ideas is a form of 'orderly group activity' protected by the First and Fourteenth Amendments. The right to associate with the political party of one's choice is an integral part of this basic constitutional freedom." Kusper v. Pontikes, 414 U.S. 51, 56-57 (1973). [Patronage,] to the extent it compels or restrains belief and association is inimical to the process which undergirds our system of government and is "at war with the deeper traditions of democracy embodied in the First Amendment." As such, the practice unavoidably confronts decisions by this Court either invalidating or recognizing as invalid government action that inhibits belief and association through the conditioning of public employment on political faith.

[Wieman v. Updegraff, 344 U.S. 183 (1952),] held that a State could not require its employees to establish their loyalty by extracting an oath denying past affiliation with Communists. . . . Particularly pertinent to the constitutionality of the practice of patronage dismissals are Keyishian v. Board of Regents, 385 U.S. 589 (1967), and Perry v. Sindermann, 408 U.S. 593 (1972). In *Keyishian*, the Court invalidated New York statutes barring employment merely on the basis of membership in "subversive" organizations. *Keyishian* squarely held that political association alone could not, consistently with the First Amendment, constitute an adequate ground for denying public employment. In *Perry*, the Court broadly rejected the validity of limitations on First Amendment rights as a condition to the receipt of a governmental benefit, stating that the government "may not deny a benefit to a person on a basis that infringes his constitutionally protected interests especially, his interest in freedom of speech. For if the government could deny a benefit to a person because of his constitutionally protected speech or associations, his exercise of those freedoms would in effect be penalized and inhibited. This would allow the government to 'produce a result which [it] could not command directly.' Such interference with constitutional rights is impermissible."

Patronage practice falls squarely within the prohibitions of *Keyishian*. . . . Under that practice, public employees hold their jobs on the condition that they provide, in some acceptable manner, support for the favored political party. The threat of dismissal for failure to provide that support unquestionably inhibits protected belief and association, and dismissal for failure to provide support only penalizes its exercise. The belief and association which government may not ordain directly are achieved by indirection. And regardless of how evenhandedly these restraints may operate in the long run, after political office has changed hands several times, protected interests are still infringed and thus the violation remains.

[T]he prohibition on encroachment of First Amendment protections is not an absolute. [If] conditioning the retention of public employment on the employee's support of the in-party is to survive constitutional challenge, it must further some vital government end by a means that is least restrictive of freedom of belief and association in achieving that end, and the benefit gained must outweigh the loss of constitutionally protected rights.

One interest which has been offered in justification of patronage is the need to insure effective government and the efficiency of public employees. It is argued that employees of political persuasions not the same as that of the party in control of public office will not have the incentive to work effectively and may even be motivated to subvert the incumbent administration's efforts to govern effectively. We are not persuaded. The inefficiency resulting from the wholesale replacement of large numbers of public employees every time political office changes hands belies this justification. And the prospect of dismissal after an election in which the incumbent party has lost is only a disincentive to good work. Further, it is not clear that dismissal in order to make room for a patronage appointment will result in replacement by a person more qualified to do the job since appointment often occurs in exchange for the delivery of votes, or other party service, not job capability. More fundamentally, however, the argument does not succeed because it is doubtful that the mere difference of political persuasion motivates poor performance; nor do we think it legitimately may be used as a basis for imputing such behavior. [At] all events, less drastic means for insuring government effectiveness and employee efficiency are available to the State. Specifically, employees may always be discharged for good cause, such as insubordination or poor job performance, when those bases in fact exist.

[It] may be argued that patronage [gives] employees of an incumbent party the incentive to perform well in order to insure their party's incumbency and thereby their jobs. Patronage [thus] makes employees highly accountable to the public. But the ability of officials more directly accountable to the electorate to discharge employees for cause and the availability of merit systems, growth in the use of which has been quite significant, convince us that means less intrusive than patronage still exist for achieving accountability in the public work force and, thereby, effective and efficient government. The greater effectiveness of patronage over these less drastic means [is] at best marginal, a gain outweighed by the absence of intrusion on protected interests under the alternatives.

[A] second interest advanced in support of patronage is the need for political loyalty [to] the end that representative government not be undercut by tactics obstructing the implementation of policies of the new administration, policies presumably sanctioned by the electorate. The justification [is] inadequate to validate patronage wholesale. Limiting patronage dismissals to policymaking positions is sufficient to achieve this governmental end. Nonpolicymaking individuals usually have only limited responsibility and are therefore not in a position to thwart the goals of the in-party.

No clear line can be drawn between policymaking and nonpolicymaking positions. While nonpolicymaking individuals usually have limited responsibility, that is not to say that one with a number of responsibilities is necessarily in a policymaking position. The nature of the responsibilities is critical. Employee supervisors [may] have many responsibilities, but those responsibilities may have only limited and well-defined objectives. An employee with responsibilities that are not well defined or are of broad scope more likely functions in a policymaking position. In determining whether an employee occupies a policymaking position, consideration should also be given to whether the employee acts as an adviser or formulates plans for the implementation of broad goals. [Since], it is the government's burden to demonstrate an overriding interest in order to validate an encroachment on protected interests, the burden of establishing this justification as to any particular respondent will rest on the petitioners on remand, cases of doubt being resolved in favor of the particular respondent.

It is argued that a third interest supporting patronage dismissals is the preservation of the democratic process. . . . "The party organization makes a democratic government work and charges a price for its services." The argument is thus premised on the centrality of partisan politics to the democratic process. . . . Preservation of the democratic process is certainly an interest protection of which may in some instances justify limitations on First Amendment freedoms. But however important preservation of the two-party system or any system involving a fixed number of parties may or may not be, we are not persuaded that the elimination of patronage practice [or] the interdiction of patronage dismissals [will] bring about the demise of party politics. Political parties existed in the absence of active patronage practice prior to the administration of Andrew Jackson, and they have survived substantial reduction in their patronage power through the establishment of merit systems.

Patronage dismissals thus are not the least restrictive alternative to achieving the contribution they may make to the democratic process. The process functions as well without the practice, perhaps even better. . . . Patronage can result in the entrenchment of one or a few parties to the exclusion of others [and] is a very effective impediment to the associational and speech freedoms which are essential to a meaningful system of democratic government. Thus, if patronage contributes at all to the elective process, that contribution is diminished by the practice's impairment of the same. [T]he gain to representative government provided by the practice of patronage, if any, would be insufficient to justify its sacrifice of First Amendment rights.

[W]e hold that subordination of other First Amendment activity, that is, patronage dismissals, not only is permissible, but also is mandated by the First Amendment. And since patronage dismissals fall within the category of political campaigning and management, this conclusion irresistibly flows from *Mitchell* and *Letter Carriers*. For if the First Amendment did not place individual belief and association above political campaigning and management, at least in the setting of public employment, the restraints on those latter activities could not have been judged permissible in *Mitchell* and *Letter Carriers*.

[P]atronage dismissals severely restrict political belief and association. Though there is a vital need for government efficiency and effectiveness, such dismissals are on balance not the least restrictive means for fostering that end. [A]ny contribution of patronage dismissals to the democratic process does not suffice to override their severe encroachment on First Amendment freedoms. We hold, therefore, that the practice of patronage dismissals is unconstitutional under the First and Fourteenth Amendments, and that respondents thus stated a valid claim for relief.

The judgment of the Court of Appeals is affirmed.

Mr. Justice STEWART, with whom Mr. Justice BLACKMUN joins, concurring in the judgment.

[The] single substantive question involved in this case is whether a nonpolicymaking, nonconfidential government employee can be discharged or threatened with discharge from a job that he is satisfactorily performing upon the sole ground of his political beliefs. I agree with the plurality that he cannot.

Mr. Chief Justice BURGER, dissenting.

[The] Court strains the rational bounds of First Amendment doctrine and runs counter to longstanding practices that are part of the fabric of our democratic system to hold that the Constitution commands something it has not been thought to require for 185 years. For all that time our system has wisely left these matters to the States [and] Congress. . . .

Mr. Justice POWELL, with whom THE CHIEF JUSTICE and Mr. Justice REHNQUIST join, dissenting.

[P]atronage practices of the sort under consideration here have a long history in America. [P]atronage in employment played a significant role in democratizing American politics. [Patronage] broadened the base of political participation by providing incentives to take part in the process, thereby increasing the volume of political discourse in society. Patronage also strengthened parties, and hence encouraged the development of institutional responsibility to the electorate on a permanent basis. [The] complaining employees who apparently accepted patronage jobs knowingly and willingly, while fully familiar with the "tenure" practices long prevailing in the Sheriff's Office. Such employees have benefited from their political beliefs and activities; they have not been penalized for them. In these circumstances, [beneficiaries] of a patronage system may not be heard to challenge it when it comes their turn to be replaced.

[T]he plurality seriously underestimates the strength of the government interest especially at the local level in allowing some patronage hiring practices, and it exaggerates the perceived burden on First Amendment rights. [Patronage] hiring practices [enable] party organizations to persist and function at the local level. [T]he dull periods between elections require ongoing activities: precinct organizations must be maintained; new voters registered; and minor political "chores" performed for citizens who otherwise may have no practical means of access to officeholders. . . . It is naive to think that these types of political activities are motivated at these levels by some academic interest in "democracy" or other public service impulse. For the most part, [the] hope of some reward generates a major portion of the local political activity supporting parties. . . . One would think that elected representatives of the people are better equipped than we to weigh the need for some continuation of patronage practices in light of the interests above identified, and particularly in view of local conditions. [I] thus conclude that patronage hiring practices sufficiently serve important state interests, including some interests sought to be advanced by the First Amendment, to justify a tolerable intrusion on the First Amendment interests of employees or potential employees.

[The plurality] asserts that patronage hiring practices contravene the fundamental principle that "'no official, high or petty, can prescribe what shall be orthodox in politics, nationalism, religion, or other matters of opinion. . . .'" But [e]mployees, regardless of affiliation, may vote freely and express themselves on some political issues. The principal intrusion of patronage hiring practices on First Amendment interests thus arises from the coercion on associational choices that may be created by one's desire initially to obtain employment. This intrusion, while not insignificant, must be measured in light of the limited role of patronage hiring in most government employment. The pressure to abandon one's beliefs and associations to obtain government employment especially employment of such uncertain duration does not seem to me to assume impermissible proportions in light of the interests to be served.

Notes

1. *Communist Party Affiliation.* In Communist Party of U.S. v. Subversive Activities Control Board, 367 U.S. 1 (1961), the U.S. Supreme Court sustained an order requiring the Communist Party of the United States to register as a Communist-action organization as required by federal law. The order became final in 1961. At that time, the appellee, a member of the Communist Party, was employed as a machinist at a Seattle, Washington, shipyard that was designated as a "defense facility." The appellee was indicted under §5(a)(1)(D) of the Subversive Activities Control Act of 1950, under a complaint alleging that he had "unlawfully and willfully engage[d] in employment" at the shipyard with knowledge of the outstanding order against the party and with knowledge and notice of the shipyard's

designation as a defense facility by the secretary of defense. In United States v. Robel, 389 U.S. 258 (1967), the Court concluded that the law violated the appellee's right of association: "[T]he operative fact upon which the job disability depends is the exercise of an individual's right of association, which is protected by the provisions of the First Amendment."

2. *Assistant Public Defenders.* In Branti v. Finkel, 445 U.S. 507 (1980), the defendant (a Democrat) terminated an assistant public defender because he was a Republican on the basis that an assistant public defender performs a "policymaking" function, and therefore the plaintiff could be dismissed because of his political beliefs. The Court overturned the dismissal: "[E]mployment of an assistant public defender cannot properly be conditioned upon his allegiance to the political party in control of the county government. [W]hatever policymaking occurs in the public defender's office must relate to the needs of individual clients and not to any partisan political interests. . . ."

3. *Employment Consequences of Party Affiliation.* In Rutan v. Republican Party of Illinois, 497 U.S. 62 (1990), after the State of Illinois imposed a hiring freeze, the plaintiffs claimed that they were denied promotions or transfers, denied employment, or not recalled from layoffs, because of their political affiliation (they did not support the Republican Party). The Court held that the denials were unconstitutional: "Employees who do not compromise their beliefs stand to lose the considerable increases in pay and job satisfaction attendant to promotions, the hours and maintenance expenses that are consumed by long daily commutes, and even their jobs if they are not rehired after a 'temporary' layoff." Justice Scalia dissented: "[T]he desirability of patronage is a policy question to be decided by the people's representatives. . . ."

∼ PROBLEM: PROTECTING POLITICAL AFFILIATION ∼

The executive secretary of the Illinois Civil Service Commission, a Republican, was fired when a Democratic administration was elected. The evidence shows that the executive secretary has broad authority to make policy, set priorities, interpret the law, and speak on behalf of the commission. Is the executive secretary the type of employee that a new administration can replace without violating the Constitution? *See* Powers v. Richards, 549 F.3d 505 (7th Cir. 2008).

I. GOVERNMENT SUPPORT OF SPEECH

This section involves decisions grouped together under the rubric of "government speech," but they actually involve several different categories of speech. One category of cases relates to the question whether a government subsidy of particular speech, which comes with conditions attached, may be constitutional in particular contexts. A second category involves the question whether the government may limit the rights of students when it acts as an educator. The Court's cases in each category reveal changes in direction and doctrinal emphasis, so that the road to settled doctrine has not been smooth. Recently, special challenges to "government speech" doctrines are presented by the development of the Internet and the enactment of laws that seek to protect national security.

Legal Services Corp. v. Velasquez

531 U.S. 533 (2001)

Justice KENNEDY delivered the opinion of the Court.

In 1974, Congress enacted the Legal Services Corporation Act, [which] establishes the Legal Services Corporation (LSC) as a District of Columbia nonprofit corporation. LSC's mission is to distribute funds appropriated by Congress to eligible local grantee organizations "for the purpose of providing financial support for legal assistance in noncriminal proceedings or matters to persons financially unable to afford legal assistance."

LSC grantees consist of hundreds of local organizations governed, in the typical case, by local boards of directors. In many instances the grantees are funded by a combination of LSC funds and other public or private sources. The grantee organizations hire and supervise lawyers to provide free legal assistance to indigent clients. Each year LSC appropriates funds to grantees or recipients that hire and supervise lawyers for various professional activities, including representation of indigent clients seeking welfare benefits.

This suit requires us to decide whether one of the conditions imposed by Congress on the use of LSC funds violates the First Amendment rights of LSC grantees and their clients. [T]he restriction [prohibits] legal representation funded by recipients of LSC moneys if the representation involves an effort to amend or otherwise challenge existing welfare law. As interpreted by the LSC and by the Government, the restriction prevents an attorney from arguing to a court that a state statute conflicts with a federal statute or that either a state or federal statute by its terms or in its application is violative of the United States Constitution.

Lawyers employed by New York City LSC grantees, together with private LSC contributors, LSC indigent clients, and various state and local public officials whose governments contribute to LSC grantees, brought suit [seeking] to declare the restriction, among other provisions of the Act, invalid. [We] agree that the restriction violates the [First Amendment].

I

From the inception of the LSC, Congress has placed restrictions on its use of funds. For instance, the LSC Act prohibits recipients from making available LSC funds, program personnel, or equipment to any political party, to any political campaign, or for use in "advocating or opposing any ballot measures." The Act further proscribes use of funds in most criminal proceedings and in litigation

involving nontherapeutic abortions, secondary school desegregation, military
desertion, or violations of the Selective Service statute. Fund recipients are barred
from bringing class-action suits unless express approval is obtained from
LSC. . . . The restrictions [were] part of a compromise set of restrictions enacted
in the Omnibus Consolidated Rescissions and Appropriations Act of 1996 (1996
Act), §504, and continued in each subsequent annual appropriations Act. The relevant portion of §504(a)(16) prohibits funding of any organization

> that initiates legal representation or participates in any other way, in litigation, lobbying, or
> rulemaking, involving an effort to reform a Federal or State welfare system, except that this
> paragraph shall not be construed to preclude a recipient from representing an individual eli-
> gible client who is seeking specific relief from a welfare agency if such relief does not involve
> an effort to amend or otherwise challenge existing law in effect on the date of the initiation of
> the representation.

The prohibitions apply to all of the activities of an LSC grantee, including
those paid for by non-LSC funds. We are concerned with the statutory provision
which excludes LSC representation in cases which "involve an effort to amend or
otherwise challenge existing law in effect on the date of the initiation of the representation."

[II]

The United States and LSC rely on Rust v. Sullivan, 500 U.S. 173 (1991), as support for the LSC program restrictions. In *Rust,* Congress established program
clinics to provide subsidies for doctors to advise patients on a variety of family
planning topics. Congress did not consider abortion to be within its family planning objectives, however, and it forbade doctors employed by the program from
discussing abortion with their patients. Recipients of funds under Title X of the
Public Health Service Act challenged the Act's restriction that provided that none
of the Title X funds appropriated for family planning services could "be used in
programs where abortion is a method of family planning." The recipients argued
that the regulations constituted impermissible viewpoint discrimination favoring
an antiabortion position over a proabortion approach in the sphere of family
planning. They asserted as well that Congress had imposed an unconstitutional
condition on recipients of federal funds by requiring them to relinquish their
right to engage in abortion advocacy and counseling in exchange for the subsidy.
We upheld the law, reasoning that Congress had not discriminated against viewpoints on abortion, but had "merely chosen to fund one activity to the exclusion
of the other." The restrictions were considered necessary "to ensure that the limits of the federal program [were] observed." Title X did not single out a particular
idea for suppression because it was dangerous or disfavored; rather, Congress
prohibited Title X doctors from counseling that was outside the scope of the
project.

The Court in *Rust* did not place explicit reliance on the rationale that the
counseling activities of the doctors under Title X amounted to governmental
speech; when interpreting the holding in later cases, however, we have explained
Rust on this understanding. We have said that viewpoint-based funding decisions

can be sustained in instances in which the government is itself the speaker, or instances, like *Rust*, in which the government "used private speakers to transmit specific information pertaining to its own program." Rosenberger v. Rector and Visitors of Univ. of Va., 515 U.S. 819 (1995). As we said in *Rosenberger*, "[w]hen the government disburses public funds to private entities to convey a governmental message, it may take legitimate and appropriate steps to ensure that its message is neither garbled nor distorted by the grantee." The latitude which may exist for restrictions on speech where the government's own message is being delivered flows in part from our observation that, "[w]hen the government speaks, for instance to promote its own policies or to advance a particular idea, it is, in the end, accountable to the electorate and the political process for its advocacy. If the citizenry objects, newly elected officials later could espouse some different or contrary position."

Neither the latitude for government speech nor its rationale applies to subsidies for private speech in every instance, however. As we have pointed out, "[i]t does not follow [that] viewpoint-based restrictions are proper when the [government] does not itself speak or subsidize transmittal of a message it favors but instead expends funds to encourage a diversity of views from private speakers."

Although the LSC program differs from the program at issue in *Rosenberger* in that its purpose is not to "encourage a diversity of views," the salient point is that, like the program in *Rosenberger*, the LSC program was designed to facilitate private speech, not to promote a governmental message. Congress funded LSC grantees to provide attorneys to represent the interests of indigent clients. In the specific context of §504(a)(16) suits for benefits, an LSC-funded attorney speaks on the behalf of the client in a claim against the government for welfare benefits. The lawyer is not the government's speaker. The attorney defending the decision to deny benefits will deliver the government's message in the litigation. The LSC lawyer, however, speaks on the behalf of his or her private, indigent client.

The Government has designed this program to use the legal profession and the established Judiciary of the States and the Federal Government to accomplish its end of assisting welfare claimants in determination or receipt of their benefits. The advice from the attorney to the client and the advocacy by the attorney to the courts cannot be classified as governmental speech even under a generous understanding of the concept. In this vital respect this suit is distinguishable from *Rust*.

The private nature of the speech involved here, and the extent of LSC's regulation of private expression, are indicated further by the circumstance that the Government seeks to use an existing medium of expression and to control it, in a class of cases, in ways which distort its usual functioning. Where the government uses or attempts to regulate a particular medium, we have been informed by its accepted usage in determining whether a particular restriction on speech is necessary for the program's purposes and limitations.

[When] the government creates a limited forum for speech, certain restrictions may be necessary to define the limits and purposes of the program. The same is true when the government establishes a subsidy for specified ends. As this suit involves a subsidy, limited forum cases may not be controlling in a strict sense, yet they do provide some instruction. Here the program presumes that private, nongovernmental speech is necessary, and a substantial restriction is placed upon that speech. [T]he LSC advised us that lawyers funded in the Government program may not undertake representation in suits for benefits if they must advise clients respecting the questionable validity of a statute which defines benefit eligibility and the payment structure. The limitation forecloses advice or legal assistance to question the validity of statutes under the Constitution of the United States. It extends further [so] that state statutes inconsistent with federal law under the Supremacy Clause may be neither challenged nor questioned.

By providing subsidies to LSC, the Government seeks to facilitate suits for benefits by using the state and federal courts and the independent bar on which those courts depend for the proper performance of their duties and responsibilities. Restricting LSC attorneys in advising their clients and in presenting arguments and analyses to the courts distorts the legal system by altering the traditional role of the attorneys in much the same way broadcast systems or student publication networks were changed in the limited forum cases we have cited. [U]pon determining [that] a question of statutory validity is present in any anticipated or pending case or controversy, the LSC-funded attorney must cease the representation at once. This is true whether the validity issue becomes apparent during initial attorney-client consultations or in the midst of litigation proceedings. [I]f, during litigation, a judge were to ask an LSC attorney whether there was a constitutional concern, the LSC attorney simply could not answer.

The restriction imposed by the statute here threatens severe impairment of the judicial function. Section 504(a)(16) sifts out cases presenting constitutional challenges in order to insulate the Government's laws from judicial inquiry. If the restriction on speech and legal advice were to stand, the result would be two tiers of cases. In cases where LSC counsel were attorneys of record, there would be lingering doubt whether the truncated representation had resulted in complete analysis of the case, full advice to the client, and proper presentation to the court. The courts and the public would come to question the adequacy and fairness of professional representations when the attorney, either consciously to comply with this statute or unconsciously to continue the representation despite the statute, avoided all reference to questions of statutory validity and constitutional authority. A scheme so inconsistent with accepted separation-of-powers principles is an insufficient basis to sustain or uphold the restriction on speech.

It is no answer to say the restriction on speech is harmless because, under LSC's interpretation of the Act, its attorneys can withdraw. This misses the point. The statute is an attempt to draw lines around the LSC program to exclude from litigation those arguments and theories Congress finds unacceptable but which by their nature are within the province of the courts to consider.

The restriction on speech is even more problematic because in cases where the attorney withdraws from a representation, the client is unlikely to find other counsel. . . . Thus, with respect to the litigation services Congress has funded, there is no alternative channel for expression of the advocacy Congress seeks to restrict. This is in stark contrast to *Rust*. There, a patient could receive the approved Title X family planning counseling funded by the Government and later could consult an affiliate or independent organization to receive abortion counseling. Unlike indigent clients who seek LSC representation, the patient in *Rust* was not required to forfeit the Government-funded advice when she also received abortion counseling through alternative channels. Because LSC attorneys must withdraw whenever a question of a welfare statute's validity arises, an individual could not obtain joint representation so that the constitutional challenge would be presented by a non-LSC attorney, and other, permitted, arguments advanced by LSC counsel.

[Congress] was not required to fund an LSC attorney to represent indigent clients; and when it did so, it was not required to fund the whole range of legal representations or relationships. The LSC and the United States, however, in effect ask us to permit Congress to define the scope of the litigation it funds to exclude certain vital theories and ideas. The attempted restriction is designed to insulate the Government's interpretation of the Constitution from judicial challenge. The Constitution does not permit the Government to confine litigants and their attorneys in this manner. We must be vigilant when Congress imposes rules and conditions which in effect insulate its own laws from legitimate judicial challenge. Where private speech is involved, even Congress' antecedent funding decision cannot be aimed at the suppression of ideas thought inimical to the Government's own interest.

For the reasons we have set forth, the funding condition is invalid. [Since the issue has not been briefed, we decline to address] whether the language restricting LSC attorneys could be severed from the statute so that the remaining portions would remain operative. . . .

The judgment of the Court of Appeals is
Affirmed.

Justice SCALIA, with whom THE CHIEF JUSTICE, Justice O'CONNOR, and Justice THOMAS join, dissenting.

[The Court] asserts that these cases are different from *Rust* because the welfare funding restriction "seeks to use an existing medium of expression and to control it [in] ways which distort its usual functioning." [T]here is utterly no precedent for [the] proposition that the First Amendment has anything to do with government funding that — though it does not actually abridge anyone's speech — "distorts an existing medium of expression." None of the three cases cited by the Court mentions such an odd principle. . . . The Court's "nondistortion" principle is also wrong on the facts, since there is no basis for believing that §504(a)(16) [will] distort the operation of the courts. It may well be that the bar of §504(a)(16) will cause LSC-funded attorneys to decline or to withdraw from cases that involve statutory validity. But that means at most that fewer statutory challenges to welfare laws will be presented to the courts because of the unavailability of free legal services for that purpose. So what? The same result would ensue from excluding LSC-funded lawyers from welfare litigation entirely. It is not the mandated, nondistortable function of the courts to inquire into all "serious questions of statutory validity" in all cases. . . .

Finally, the Court is troubled "because in cases where the attorney withdraws from a representation, the client is unlikely to find other counsel." That is surely irrelevant, since it leaves the welfare recipient in no *worse* condition than he would have been in had the LSC program never been enacted. . . . It is hard to see how providing free legal services to some welfare claimants (those whose claims do not challenge the applicable statutes) while not providing it to others is beyond the range of legitimate legislative [choice]. . . . Rather than sponsor "truncated representation," Congress chose to subsidize only those cases in which the attorneys it subsidized could work freely. And it is impossible to see how this difference from *Rust* has any bearing upon the First Amendment question [which] is whether the funding scheme is "manipulated" to have a "coercive effect" on those who do not hold the subsidized position. It could be claimed to have such an effect if the client in a case ineligible for LSC representation could eliminate the ineligibility by waiving the claim that the statute is invalid; but he cannot. No *conceivable* coercive effect exists.

[The] LSC subsidy neither prevents anyone from speaking nor coerces anyone to change speech, and is indistinguishable in all relevant respects from the subsidy upheld in [*Rust*]. There is no legitimate basis for declaring §504(a)(16) facially unconstitutional.

Note

Reread Christian Legal Society Chapter of the University of California v. Martinez in Section C, "Symbolic Speech," earlier in this chapter.

❧ PROBLEM: MORE ON THE INTERNATIONAL TREATY REGULATING THE INTERNET ❧

Should the treaty contain any language either allowing or prohibiting (or, for that matter, saying anything about) the government's ability to provide financial support for speech?

United States v. American Library Association

539 U.S. 194 (2003)

Chief Justice REHNQUIST announced the judgment of the Court and delivered an opinion, in which Justice O'CONNOR, Justice SCALIA, and Justice THOMAS joined.

To address the problems associated with the availability of Internet pornography in public libraries, Congress enacted the Children's Internet Protection Act (CIPA). Under CIPA, a public library may not receive federal assistance to provide Internet access unless it installs software to block images that constitute obscenity or child pornography, and to prevent minors from obtaining access to material that is harmful to them. The District Court held these provisions facially invalid on the ground that they induce public libraries to violate patrons' First Amendment rights. [We] reverse.

[CIPA] provides that a library may not receive E-rate or LSTA assistance unless it has "a policy of Internet safety for minors that includes the operation of a technology protection measure [that] protects against access" by all persons to "visual depictions" that constitute "obscen[ity]" or "child pornography," and that protects against access by minors to "visual depictions" that are "harmful to minors." The statute defines a "[t]echnology protection measure" as "a specific technology that blocks or filters Internet access to material covered by" CIPA. CIPA also permits the library to "disable" the filter "to enable access for bona fide research or other lawful purposes." Under the E-rate program, disabling is permitted "during use by an adult." Under the LSTA program, disabling is permitted during use by any person.

Appellees are a group of libraries, library associations, library patrons, and Web site publishers, including the American Library Association (ALA) and the Multnomah County Public Library in Portland, Oregon (Multnomah). They sued the United States and the Government agencies and officials responsible for administering the E-rate and LSTA programs in District Court, challenging the constitutionality of CIPA's filtering provisions. [The District Court] held that the filtering software contemplated by CIPA was a content-based restriction on access to a public forum, and was therefore subject to strict scrutiny. Applying this standard, the District Court held that, although the Government has a compelling interest "in preventing the dissemination of obscenity, child pornography, or, in the case of minors, material harmful to minors," the use of software filters is not narrowly tailored to further those [interests]. [We granted certiorari.]

Congress has wide latitude to attach conditions to the receipt of federal assistance in order to further its policy objectives. South Dakota v. Dole, 483 U.S. 203 (1987). But Congress may not "induce" the recipient "to engage in activities that would themselves be unconstitutional." To determine whether libraries would violate the First Amendment by employing the filtering software that CIPA requires, we must first examine the role of libraries in our society.

CIPA does not directly regulate private conduct; rather, Congress has exercised its Spending Power by specifying conditions on the receipt of federal funds. Therefore, *Dole* provides the appropriate framework for assessing CIPA's constitutionality.

Public libraries pursue the worthy missions of facilitating learning and cultural enrichment. . . . Appellee ALA's Library Bill of Rights states that libraries should provide "[b]ooks and other . . . resources [for] the interest, information, and enlightenment of all people of the community the library serves." To fulfill their traditional missions, public libraries must have broad discretion to decide what material to provide to their patrons. Although they seek to provide a wide array of information, their goal has never been to provide "universal coverage." Instead, public libraries seek to provide materials "that would be of the greatest direct benefit or interest to the community." To this end, libraries collect only those materials deemed to have "requisite and appropriate quality."

We have held in two analogous contexts that the government has broad discretion to make content-based judgments in deciding what private speech to make available to the public. In Arkansas Ed. Television Commn. v. Forbes, 523

U.S. 666 (1998), we held that public forum principles do not generally apply to a public television station's editorial judgments regarding the private speech it presents to its viewers. "[B]road rights of access for outside speakers would be antithetical [to] the discretion that stations and their editorial staff must exercise to fulfill their journalistic purpose and statutory obligations." Recognizing a broad right of public access "would [also] risk implicating the courts in judgments that should be left to the exercise of journalistic discretion."

Similarly, in National Endowment for Arts v. Finley, 524 U.S. 569 (1998), we upheld an art funding program that required the National Endowment for the Arts (NEA) to use content-based criteria in making funding decisions. We explained that "[a]ny content-based considerations that may be taken into account in the grant-making process are a consequence of the nature of arts funding." In particular, "[t]he very assumption of the NEA is that grants will be awarded according to the 'artistic worth of competing applicants,' and absolute neutrality is simply inconceivable." We expressly declined to apply forum analysis, reasoning that it would conflict with "NEA's mandate [to] make esthetic judgments, and the inherently content-based 'excellence' threshold for NEA support."

The principles underlying *Forbes* and *Finley* also apply to a public library's exercise of judgment in selecting the material it provides to its patrons. Just as forum analysis and heightened judicial scrutiny are incompatible with the role of public television stations and the role of the NEA, they are also incompatible with the discretion that public libraries must have to fulfill their traditional missions. Public library staffs necessarily consider content in making collection decisions and enjoy broad discretion in making them.

The public forum principles on which the District Court relied, are out of place in the context of this case. Internet access in public libraries is neither a "traditional" nor a "designated" public forum. First, this resource — which did not exist until quite recently — has not "immemorially been held in trust for the use of the public and, time out of mind, [been] used for purposes of assembly, communication of thoughts between citizens, and discussing public questions." We have "rejected the view that traditional public forum status extends beyond its historic confines." The doctrines surrounding traditional public forums may not be extended to situations where such history is lacking.

Nor does Internet access in a public library satisfy our definition of a "designated public forum." To create such a forum, the government must make an affirmative choice to open up its property for use as a public forum. "The government does not create a public forum by inaction or by permitting limited discourse, but only by intentionally opening a non-traditional forum for public discourse." The District Court likened public libraries' Internet terminals to the forum at issue in Rosenberger v. Rector and Visitors of Univ. of Va., 515 U.S. 819 (1995). In *Rosenberger*, we considered the "Student Activity Fund" established by the University of Virginia that subsidized all manner of student publications except those based on religion. We held that the fund had created a limited public forum by giving public money to student groups who wished to publish, and therefore could not discriminate on the basis of viewpoint.

The situation here is very different. A public library does not acquire Internet terminals in order to create a public forum for Web publishers to express themselves, any more than it collects books in order to provide a public forum for the authors of books to speak. It provides Internet access, not to "encourage a diversity of views from private speakers," but for the same reasons it offers other library resources: to facilitate research, learning, and recreational pursuits by furnishing materials of requisite and appropriate quality. As Congress recognized, "[t]he Internet is simply another method for making information available in a school or library." It is "no more than a technological extension of the book stack."

[We] require the Government to employ the least restrictive means only when the forum is a public one and strict scrutiny applies. [S]uch is not the case here. In deciding not to collect pornographic material from the Internet, a public library need not satisfy a court that it has pursued the least restrictive means of implementing that decision.

In any case, the suggested alternatives have their own drawbacks. Close monitoring of computer users would be far more intrusive than the use of filtering software, and would risk transforming the role of a librarian from a professional to whom patrons turn for assistance into a compliance officer whom many patrons might wish to avoid. Moving terminals to places where their displays cannot easily be seen by other patrons, or installing privacy screens or recessed monitors, would not address a library's interest in preventing patrons from deliberately using its computers to view online pornography. To the contrary, these alternatives would make it *easier* for patrons to do so.

The District Court disagreed because, whereas a library reviews and affirmatively chooses to acquire every book in its collection, it does not review every Web site that it makes available. Based on this distinction, the court reasoned that a public library enjoys less discretion in deciding which Internet materials to make available than in making book selections. We do not find this distinction constitutionally relevant. A library's failure to make quality-based judgments about all the material it furnishes from the Web does not somehow taint the judgments it does make. A library's need to exercise judgment in making collection decisions depends on its traditional role in identifying suitable and worthwhile material; it is no less entitled to play that role when it collects material from the Internet than when it collects material from any other source. Most libraries already exclude pornography from their print collections because they deem it inappropriate for inclusion. We do not subject these decisions to heightened scrutiny; it would make little sense to treat libraries' judgments to block online pornography any differently, when these judgments are made for just the same reason.

Moreover, because of the vast quantity of material on the Internet and the rapid pace at which it changes, libraries cannot possibly segregate, item by item, all the Internet material that is appropriate for inclusion from all that is not. While a library could limit its Internet collection to just those sites it found worthwhile, it could do so only at the cost of excluding an enormous amount of valuable information that it lacks the capacity to review. Given that tradeoff, it is entirely reasonable for public libraries to reject that approach and instead exclude certain categories of content, without making individualized judgments that everything they do make available has requisite and appropriate quality.

[The] District Court [faulted] the tendency of filtering software to "overblock" — that is, to erroneously block access to constitutionally protected speech that falls outside the categories that software users intend to block. Due to the software's limitations, "[m]any erroneously blocked [Web] pages contain content that is completely innocuous for both adults and minors, and that no rational person could conclude matches the filtering companies' category definitions, such as 'pornography' or 'sex.'" [Any] concerns are dispelled by the ease with which patrons may have the filtering software disabled. When a patron encounters a blocked site, he need only ask a librarian to unblock it or (at least in the case of adults) disable the filter. [L]ibraries have the capacity to permanently unblock any erroneously blocked site, and the Solicitor General stated [that] a "library [may] eliminate the filtering with respect to specific sites [at] the request of a patron." With respect to adults, CIPA also expressly authorizes library officials to "disable" a filter altogether "to enable access for bona fide research or other lawful purposes." The Solicitor General confirmed [that] a "librarian can, in response to a request from a patron, unblock the filtering mechanism altogether," [and] that a patron would not "have to explain [why] he was asking a site to be unblocked or the filtering to be disabled." The District Court viewed unblocking and disabling as inadequate because some patrons may be too embarrassed to request them. But the Constitution does not guarantee the right to acquire information at a public library without any risk of embarrassment.

[Because] public libraries' use of Internet filtering software does not violate their patrons' First Amendment rights, CIPA does not induce libraries to violate the Constitution, and is a valid exercise of Congress' spending power. [Therefore,] the judgment of the District Court for the Eastern District of Pennsylvania is

   Reversed.

   Justice KENNEDY, concurring in the judgment.

   If, on the request of an adult user, a librarian will unblock filtered material or disable the Internet software filter without significant delay, there is little to this case. The Government represents this is indeed the fact. [If] some libraries do not have the capacity to unblock specific Web sites or to disable the filter or if it is shown that an adult user's election to view constitutionally protected Internet material is burdened in some other substantial way, that would be the subject for an as-applied challenge, not the facial challenge made in this case. . . . There are, of course, substantial Government interests at stake here. The interest in protecting young library users from material inappropriate for minors is legitimate, and even compelling, as all Members of the Court appear to agree. Given this interest, and the failure to show that the ability of adult library users to have access to the material is burdened in any significant degree, the statute is not unconstitutional on its face. . . .

Justice BREYER, concurring in the judgment.

[Filtering] technology, in its current form, does not function perfectly, for to some extent it also screens out constitutionally protected materials that fall outside the scope of the statute (i.e., "overblocks") and fails to prevent access to some materials that the statute deems harmful (i.e., "underblocks"). In determining whether the statute's conditions consequently violate the First Amendment, the plurality first finds the "public forum" doctrine inapplicable, and then holds that the statutory provisions are constitutional. I agree with both determinations. But I reach the plurality's ultimate conclusion in a different way.

[I] would apply a form of heightened scrutiny, examining the statutory requirements in question with special care. The Act directly restricts the public's receipt of information. And it does so through limitations imposed by outside bodies (here Congress) upon two critically important sources of information — the Internet as accessed via public libraries. For that reason, we should not examine the statute's constitutionality as if it raised no special First Amendment concern — as if, like tax or economic regulation, the First Amendment demanded only a "rational basis" for imposing a restriction. Nor should we accept the Government's suggestion that a presumption in favor of the statute's constitutionality applies.

At the same time, [the] First Amendment does not here demand application of the most limiting constitutional approach — that of "strict scrutiny." The statutory restriction in question is, in essence, a kind of "selection" restriction (a kind of editing). . . . And libraries often properly engage in the selection of materials, either as a matter of necessity (i.e., due to the scarcity of resources) or by design (i.e., in accordance with collection development policies). To apply "strict scrutiny" to the "selection" of a library's collection (whether carried out by public libraries themselves or by other community bodies with a traditional legal right to engage in that function) would unreasonably interfere with the discretion necessary to create, maintain, or select a library's "collection" (broadly defined to include all the information the library makes available). That is to say, "strict scrutiny" implies too limiting and rigid a test for me to believe that the First Amendment requires it in this context.

Instead, I would examine the constitutionality of the Act's restrictions here as the Court has examined speech-related restrictions in other contexts where circumstances call for heightened, but not "strict," scrutiny — where, for example, complex, competing constitutional interests are potentially at issue or speech-related harm is potentially justified by unusually strong governmental interests. Typically the key question in such instances is one of proper fit.

In such cases the Court has asked whether the harm to speech-related interests is disproportionate in light of both the justifications and the potential alternatives. It has considered the legitimacy of the statute's objective, the extent to which the statute will tend to achieve that objective, whether there are other, less restrictive ways of achieving that objective, and ultimately whether the statute works speech-related harm that, in relation to that objective, is out of [proportion].

The Act's restrictions satisfy these constitutional demands. The Act seeks to restrict access to obscenity, child pornography, and, in respect to access by minors, material that is comparably harmful. These objectives are "legitimate," and indeed often "compelling." [S]oftware filters "provide a relatively cheap and effective" means of furthering these goals. Due to present technological limitations, however, the software filters both "overblock," screening out some perfectly legitimate material, and "underblock," allowing some obscene material to escape detection by the filter. But no one has presented any clearly superior or better fitting alternatives.

At the same time, the Act [allows] libraries to permit any adult patron access to an "overblocked" Web site; the adult patron need only ask a librarian to unblock the specific Web site or [disable the filter entirely]. The Act does impose upon the patron the burden of making this request. But it is difficult to see how that burden (or any delay associated with compliance) could prove more onerous than traditional library practices associated with segregating library materials in, say, closed stacks, or with interlibrary lending practices that require patrons to make requests that are not anonymous and to wait while the librarian obtains the desired materials from elsewhere. Perhaps local library rules or practices could further restrict the ability of patrons to obtain "overblocked" Internet material. But [we] here consider only a facial challenge to the Act itself.

Given the comparatively small burden that the Act imposes upon the library patron seeking legitimate Internet materials, I cannot say that any speech-related harm that the Act may cause is disproportionate when considered in relation to the Act's legitimate objectives. I therefore agree with the plurality that the statute does not violate the First Amendment, and I concur in the judgment.

[Justice STEVENS filed a dissenting opinion on the grounds that CIPA imposes an unconstitutional condition on government subsidies to local libraries; and Justice SOUTER filed a dissenting opinion in which Justice GINSBURG joined, agreeing with Justice STEVENS's conclusion and arguing that CIPA is invalid in the exercise of the spending power under Article I.]

Notes

1. *Student First Amendment Rights.* The Court's leading cases on the subject of the First Amendment rights of students are Tinker v. Des Moines Independent Community School District, 393 U.S. 503 (1969), and Hazelwood School District v. Kuhlmeier, 484 U.S. 260 (1988). In *Tinker*, students wore black armbands to demonstrate their protest against the war in Vietnam, and they were suspended from school. The school's ban on armbands had been adopted when the school administrators learned that the protest was planned. The Court rejected the school's argument that suspension of the students was necessary in order to avoid a potentially violent conflict. As Justice Fortas reasoned: "The school officials banned and sought to punish petitioners for a silent, passive, expression of opinion, unaccompanied by any disorder or disturbance on the part of the

petitioners. There is here no evidence whatever of petitioners' interference, actual or nascent, with the schools' work or of collision with the rights of other students to be secure and to be let [alone]." He went on to note: "Only a few of the 18,000 students in the school system wore the black armbands. Only five students were suspended for wearing them. There is no indication that the work of the school or any class was disrupted. Outside the classrooms, a few students made hostile remarks to the children wearing armbands, but there were not threats or acts of violence on school premises." The Court concluded that there were no "finding and no showing that the exercise of the forbidden right would 'materially and substantially interfere with the requirements of appropriate discipline in the operation of the school.'"

In *Hazelwood*, a high school principal withheld from a student newspaper two pages containing student-authored stories about pregnancy and divorce. The decision was based on the principal's concern that the identity of pregnant students might be identifiable from the text, that references to sexual activity and birth control were inappropriate for some of the younger students, and that the parents of a student in the divorce story should be asked for consent to the publication of their daughter's comments about their divorce. The Court upheld the action of the principal and distinguished it from the actions of school officials in *Tinker*. Although the Court recognized that students do not "shed their constitutional rights [at] the schoolhouse gate," it reasoned that "educators [may exercise] editorial control over the style and content of student speech in school-sponsored expressive activities so long as their actions are reasonably related to legitimate pedagogical concerns." The Court explained: "[Activities such as] school-sponsored publications, theatrical productions, and other expressive activities that students, parents, and members of the public might reasonably perceive to bear the imprimatur of the school [may] fairly be characterized as part of the school curriculum, whether or not they occur in a traditional classroom setting, so long as they are supervised by faculty members and designed to impart particular knowledge or skills to student participants and audiences." The Court also noted: "A school may in its capacity as publisher of a school newspaper or producer of a school play 'disassociate itself,' not only from speech that would 'substantially interfere with [its] work [or] impinge on the rights of other students,' but also from speech that is, for example, ungrammatical, poorly written, inadequately researched, biased or prejudiced, vulgar or profane, or unsuitable for immature audiences. A school must be able to set high standards for the student speech that is disseminated under its [auspices]."

2. *Banning Books.* Board of Education v. PICO, 457 U.S. 853 (1982), involved school board members who received a list of books labeled as "improper fare for students" from a politically conservative organization, and subsequently determined that 11 of the books were in the local high school library. The books included *Black Boy*, by Richard Wright; *Soul on Ice*, by Eldridge Cleaver; *Slaughterhouse-Five*, by Kurt Vonnegut, Jr.; and *Go Ask Alice* (by an anonymous author), as well as others. The board members notified the entire board that these books were in the library, and the board appointed a parent-teacher committee to make recommendations to the board concerning whether these books should

be removed or retained in the library. When the committee recommended that only two of the books should be removed, the board overruled the committee and ordered that nine of the books be removed. Various students filed suit seeking injunctive relief to prevent the removal of the books from the library, and arguing that the board's decision to remove the books violated their First Amendment rights. A plurality of the Court agreed, holding that the evidence raised a material fact as to whether the board's decision to remove nine books violated the First Amendment, and the Court therefore remanded for a trial on the merits of the students' claim. While the plurality recognized that the school board had discretion on curricular matters, it did not view this discretion as extending "beyond the compulsory environment of the classroom" into the school library. Although school boards retain "significant discretion" to control library content, they cannot "remove books from a library based on the partisan motivation of dislike for the ideas in the books." The plurality reasoned that the government may not prescribe official orthodoxy, noting that students have First Amendment rights in school, as well as a First Amendment right to receive ideas. As a result, the Court concluded that the school library is a unique site where freedom of voluntary inquiry by students "holds sway," which is why decisions to remove books for reasons of censorship of ideas interfere with that protected freedom of students. The Court concluded that an improper motive could be ascertained "by the origin of the Board's decision and its lack of procedural regularity." Accordingly, the Court remanded the case for trial. Nevertheless, the plurality recognized that a school board has the power to remove books that are "pervasively vulgar" or "educationally unsuitable," as long as removal of such books is not based on partisan motives. The dissenters argued that students do not have a First Amendment right to access particular books in a school library, especially given their ability to obtain the books elsewhere. The dissenters also argued that no meaningful distinction could be drawn between removing books for vulgarity or unsuitability and removing books for political reasons. The dissenters predicted that the plurality's narrow recognition of students' right to prevent partisan-motivated removal of books would eventually lead to the court's playing "super censor" of school decisions.

∽ PROBLEMS ∽

1. *The Confederate Flag.* The superintendent of schools decided to prohibit students from wearing any clothes that depict the Confederate battle flag. Some students and their parents challenge the ban, claiming that they are engaged in symbolic speech protected under *Tinker.* However, the superintendent claimed that the ban was justified by the occurrence of prior racial incidents, some of which had involved students displaying the Confederate flag. As a result, the superintendent felt that the ban was justified by the possibility of a substantial disruption or material interference with school activities. Is the prohibition valid under the First Amendment? *See* B.W.A. v. Farmington R-7 School District, 554 F.3d 734 (8th Cir. 2009).

2. *The Student Blog.* A high school student, who was a member of the student council, posted a blog entry when a battle of the bands concert (scheduled at the school) was cancelled. Although the entry was posted on a noncampus blog, it urged other students to contact the superintendent of schools to urge that the concert be rescheduled. In her e-mail message, the student suggested that the concert had been "cancelled due to douchebags in the central office," and she provided students with a sample letter that they could send to the superintendent to "piss her off more." The blog produced a number of contacts with the superintendent's office. Because of the blog posting, the principal declined to endorse the plaintiff's candidacy for senior class secretary, thereby precluding her from running for that office. The principal based her decision on the fact that the student failed to accept the principal's counsel regarding the proper way to express and resolve disagreements, that the student included vulgar and inaccurate information in her blog posting, and that the student had urged other students to contact the superintendent in order to "piss her off more." Did the principal have the right to sanction the student for the content of speech that occurred on a noncampus Web site? Should it matter whether the speech was directed at the campus community and caused disruption? Would the school have the right to sanction a concerned citizen (e.g., a nonstudent) who posted a similar blog? *See* Doninger v. Niehoff, 527 F.3d 41 (2d Cir. 2008).

3. *More on Student Blogs.* In the preceding problem, would you reach a different result if the student were in college, rather than high school, and the college officials were equally offended?

4. *Bracelets and Sex Games.* Students at a middle school have started wearing "jelly" bracelets. Students correlate the color of the bracelet to the level of their sexual activity. School administrators have decided that the bracelets have become a distraction (in that students discuss the bracelets and their colors in class, in the hallways, and in e-mail messages) and have decided to ban them. Can school officials ban students from wearing jelly bracelets under these circumstances?

5. *More on the International Treaty Regulating the Internet.* A number of countries believe that mandatory filters should be imposed on all newly manufactured computers as well as on all search engines. Delegates to the convention disagree about the types of information that should be targeted and excluded by filters. Some delegates want to filter out depictions of sexual activity. Others want to filter out any number of things, including child pornography, defamatory speech, subversive speech, and Nazi symbols. What language can you agree to regarding mandatory filters on computers and Web sites?

J. BROADCAST REGULATION

Over time, as speech technology has expanded and developed, the courts have struggled to decide whether they should apply different media-specific rules to different types of technology. In this section, we examine the special rules that have developed relating to broadcast technology.

Red Lion Broadcasting Co. v. FCC

395 U.S. 367 (1969)

Mr. Justice WHITE delivered the opinion of the Court.

The Federal Communications Commission has for many years imposed on radio and television broadcasters the requirement that discussion of public issues be presented on broadcast stations, and that each side of those issues must be given fair coverage. This is known as the fairness doctrine, which originated very early in the history of broadcasting. . . . It is an obligation whose content has been defined in a long series of FCC rulings in particular cases, and which is distinct from the statutory requirement of §315 of the Communications Act that equal time be allotted all qualified candidates for public office. Two aspects of the fairness doctrine, relating to personal attacks in the context of controversial public issues and to political editorializing, were codified more precisely in the form of FCC regulations in 1967. . . .

There is a twofold duty. . . . The broadcaster must give adequate coverage to public issues, and coverage must be fair in that it accurately reflects the opposing views. This must be done at the broadcaster's own expense if sponsorship is unavailable. Moreover, the duty must be met by programming obtained at the licensee's own initiative if available from no other source. The Federal Radio Commission had imposed these two basic duties on broadcasters since the outset, and in particular respects the personal attack rules and regulations at issue here have spelled them out in greater detail.

When a personal attack has been made on a figure involved in a public issue both the doctrine [and] also the 1967 regulations [require] that the individual attacked himself be offered an opportunity to respond. Likewise, where one candidate is endorsed in a political editorial, the other candidates must themselves be offered reply time to use personally or through a spokesman. These obligations differ from the general fairness requirement that issues be presented, and presented with coverage of competing views, in that the broadcaster does not have the option of presenting the attacked party's side himself or choosing a third party to represent that side. But insofar as there is an obligation of the broadcaster to see that both sides are presented, and insofar as that is an affirmative obligation, the personal attack doctrine and regulations do not differ from the preceding fairness doctrine. . . .

[B]roadcasters challenge the fairness doctrine and its specific manifestations in the personal attack and political editorial rules on conventional First Amendment grounds, alleging that the rules abridge their freedom of speech and press. Their contention is that the First Amendment protects their desire to use their allotted frequencies continuously to broadcast whatever they choose, and to exclude whomever they choose from ever using that frequency. . . .

Just as the Government may limit the use of sound-amplifying equipment potentially so noisy that it drowns out civilized private speech, so may the Government limit the use of broadcast equipment. The right of free speech of a broadcaster, the user of a sound truck, or any other individual does not embrace a right to snuff out the free speech of others.

When two people converse face to face, both should not speak at once if either is to be clearly understood. But the range of the human voice is so limited that there could be meaningful communications if half the people in the United States were talking and the other half listening. Just as clearly, half the people might publish and the other half read. But the reach of radio signals is incomparably greater than the range of the human voice and the problem of interference is a massive reality. The lack of know-how and equipment may keep many from the air, but only a tiny fraction of those with resources and intelligence can hope to communicate by radio at the same time if intelligible communication is to be had, even if the entire radio spectrum is utilized in the present state of commercially acceptable technology.

It was this fact, and the chaos which ensued from permitting anyone to use any frequency at whatever power level he wished, which made necessary the enactment of the Radio Act of 1927 and the Communications Act of 1934, as the Court has noted at length before. It was this reality which at the very least necessitated first the division of the radio spectrum into portions reserved respectively for public broadcasting and for other important radio uses such as amateur operation, aircraft, police, defense, and navigation; and then the subdivision of each portion, and assignment of specific frequencies to individual users or groups of users. Beyond this, however, because the frequencies reserved for public broadcasting were limited in number, it was essential for the Government to tell some applicants that they could not broadcast at all because there was room for only a few.

Where there are substantially more individuals who want to broadcast than there are frequencies to allocate, it is idle to posit an unabridgeable First Amendment right to broadcast comparable to the right of every individual to speak, write, or publish. If 100 persons want broadcast licenses but there are only 10 frequencies to allocate, all of them may have the same "right" to a license; but if there is to be any effective communication by radio, only a few can be licensed and the rest must be barred from the airwaves. It would be strange if the First Amendment, aimed at protecting and furthering communications, prevented the Government from making radio communication possible by requiring licenses to broadcast and by limiting the number of licenses so as not to overcrowd the spectrum. . . . Congress unquestionably has the power to grant and deny licenses. . . . No one has a First Amendment right to a license or to monopolize a radio frequency; to deny a station license because "the public interest" requires it "is not a denial of free speech."

By the same token, as far as the First Amendment is concerned those who are licensed stand no better than those to whom licenses are refused. A license permits broadcasting, but the licensee has no constitutional right to be the one who holds the license or to monopolize a radio frequency to the exclusion of his fellow citizens. There is nothing in the First Amendment which prevents the Government from requiring a licensee to share his frequency with others and to conduct himself as a proxy or fiduciary with obligations to present those views and voices which are representative of his community and which would otherwise, by necessity, be barred from the airwaves.

This is not to say that the First Amendment is irrelevant to public broadcasting. On the contrary, it has a major role to play. . . . Because of the scarcity of radio frequencies, the Government is permitted to put restraints on licensees in favor of others whose views should be expressed on this unique medium. But the people as a whole retain their interest in free speech by radio and their collective right to have the medium function consistently with the ends and purposes of the First Amendment. It is the right of the viewers and listeners, not the right of the broadcasters, which is paramount. It is the purpose of the First Amendment to preserve an uninhibited marketplace of ideas in which truth will ultimately prevail, rather than to countenance monopolization of that market, whether it be by the Government itself or a private licensee. "[S]peech concerning public affairs is more than self-expression; it is the essence of self-government." Garrison v. Louisiana, 379 U.S. 64, 74-75 (1964). It is the right of the public to receive suitable access to social, political, esthetic, moral, and other ideas and experiences which is crucial here. That right may not constitutionally be abridged either by Congress or by the FCC.

Rather than confer frequency monopolies on a relatively small number of licensees, in a Nation of 200,000,000, the Government could surely have decreed that each frequency should be shared among all or some of those who wish to use it, each being assigned a portion of the broadcast day or the broadcast week. The ruling and regulations at issue here do not go quite so far. They assert that under specified circumstances, a licensee must offer to make available a reasonable amount of broadcast time to those who have a view different from that which has already been expressed on his station. The expression of a political endorsement, or of a personal attack while dealing with a controversial public issue, simply triggers this time sharing. [T]he First Amendment confers no right on licensees to prevent others from broadcasting on "their" frequencies and no right to an unconditional monopoly of a scarce resource which the Government has denied others the right to use.

In terms of constitutional principle, and as enforced sharing of a scarce resource, the personal attack and political editorial rules are indistinguishable from the equal-time provision of §315, a specific enactment of Congress requiring stations to set aside reply time under specified circumstances and to which the fairness doctrine and these constituent regulations are important complements. That provision, which has been part of the law since 1927, has been held valid by this Court as an obligation of the licensee relieving him of any power in any way to prevent or censor the broadcast, and thus insulating him from liability for defamation. The constitutionality of the statute under the First Amendment was unquestioned.

Nor can we say that it is inconsistent with the First Amendment goal of producing an informed public capable of conducting its own affairs to require a broadcaster to permit answers to personal attacks occurring in the course of discussing controversial issues, or to require that the political opponents of those endorsed by the station be given a chance to communicate with the public. Otherwise, station owners and a few networks would have unfettered power to make time available only to the highest bidders, to communicate only their own views on public issues, people and candidates, and to permit on the air only those with whom they agreed. . . .

It is strenuously argued, however, that if political editorials or personal attacks will trigger an obligation in broadcasters to afford the opportunity for expression to speakers who need not pay for time and whose views are unpalatable to the licensees, then broadcasters will be irresistibly forced to self-censorship and their coverage of controversial public issues will be eliminated or at least rendered wholly ineffective. Such a result would indeed be a serious matter, for should licensees actually eliminate their coverage of controversial issues, the purposes of the doctrine would be stifled.

At this point, however, [that] possibility is at best speculative. The communications industry, and in particular the networks, have taken pains to present controversial issues in the past, and even now they do not assert that they intend to abandon their efforts in this regard. [I]f experience with the administration of those doctrines indicates that they have the net effect of reducing rather than enhancing the volume and quality of coverage, there will be time enough to reconsider the constitutional implications. The fairness doctrine in the past has had no such overall effect.

That this will occur now seems unlikely, however, since if present licensees should suddenly prove timorous, the Commission is not powerless to insist that they give adequate and fair attention to public issues. It does not violate the First Amendment to treat licensees given the privilege of using scarce radio frequencies as proxies for the entire community, obligated to give suitable time and attention to matters of great public concern. To condition the granting or renewal of licenses on a willingness to present representative community views on controversial issues is consistent with the ends and purposes of those constitutional provisions forbidding the abridgment of freedom of speech and freedom of the press. Congress need not stand idly by and permit those with licenses to ignore the problems which beset the people or to exclude from the airways anything but their own views of fundamental questions. The statute, long administrative practice, and cases are to this effect.

Licenses to broadcast do not confer ownership of designated frequencies, but only the temporary privilege of using them. Unless renewed, they expire within three years. The statute mandates the issuance of licenses if the "public convenience, interest, or necessity will be served thereby." In applying this standard the Commission for 40 years has been choosing licensees based in part on their program proposals. [In] determining how best to allocate frequencies, the Federal Radio Commission considered the needs of competing communities and the programs offered by competing stations to meet those needs; moreover, if needs or programs shifted, the Commission could alter its allocations to reflect those shifts. . . .

We need not and do not now ratify every past and future decision by the FCC with regard to programming. There is no question here of the Commission's refusal to permit the broadcaster to carry a particular program or to publish his own views; of a discriminatory refusal to require the licensee to broadcast certain views which have been denied access to the airwaves; of government censorship of a particular program contrary to §326; or of the official government view dominating public broadcasting. Such questions would raise more serious First Amendment issues. But we do hold that the Congress and the Commission do not violate the First Amendment when they require a radio or television station to give reply time to answer personal attacks and political editorials.

[In] view of the scarcity of broadcast frequencies, the Government's role in allocating those frequencies, and the legitimate claims of those unable without governmental assistance to gain access to those frequencies for expression of their views, we hold the regulations and ruling at issue here are both authorized by statute and constitutional. The judgment of the Court of Appeals in *Red Lion* is affirmed and that in RTNDA reversed and the causes remanded for proceedings consistent with this opinion.

It is so ordered.

Notes and Questions

1. *Repeal of the Fairness Doctrine.* In 1987, the FCC repealed the fairness doctrine based on a 1985 report in which the FCC stated that it was "firmly convinced that the fairness doctrine, as a matter of policy, disserves the public interest" and raised questions about the doctrine's continuing constitutionality. *Inquiry Into Alternatives to the General Fairness Obligations of Broadcast Licensees*, 102 F.C.C.2d 143 (1985).

2. *Political Advertisements.* Columbia Broadcasting System, Inc. v. Democratic National Committee, 412 U.S. 94 (1973), involved the Democratic National Committee (DNC) and the Business Executives' Move for Vietnam Peace (BEM), a national organization of businessmen opposed to U.S. involvement in the Vietnam conflict, which wanted to run paid ads on television. FCC orders provided that a broadcaster who meets its public obligation to provide full and fair coverage of public issues is not required to accept editorial advertisements. The Court sustained the orders, noting that Congress "opted for a system of private broadcasters licensed and regulated by Government." As a result, the Court concluded that broadcast licensees have "a large measure of journalistic freedom," although they must "balance what [they] might prefer to do as a private entrepreneur with what [they are] required to do as a 'public trustee.'" The Court concluded that this "journalistic freedom" gave broadcasters discretion about which ads to air. The Court expressed concern that, if the fairness doctrine were applied to editorial advertising, broadcasters might suffer financial hardship by being forced to "make regular programming time available to those holding a view different from that expressed in an editorial advertisement" and the "public interest would no longer be 'paramount' but, rather, subordinate to private whim." Justice Brennan dissented: "[L]icensees must respect the competing First Amendment rights of others. [Broadcasters] make such air time readily available to those 'commercial' advertisers who seek to peddle their goods and services to the public. . . ."

3. *Airing Private Documentaries.* In CBS, Inc. v. FCC, 453 U.S. 367 (1981), when the Carter-Mondale Presidential Committee requested time to air a documentary outlining the record of the Carter administration, and the networks declined to make the requested time available, the FCC held that they had failed to provide "reasonable access." The Court upheld the FCC's determination: "[Section] 312(a)(7) creates a limited right to 'reasonable' access that pertains only to legally qualified federal candidates and may be invoked by them only for the purpose of advancing their candidacies once a campaign has commenced. [We] hold that the statutory right of access, as defined by the Commission and applied in these cases, properly balances the First Amendment rights of federal candidates, the public, and broadcasters."

4. *Should the Fairness Doctrine Be Reinstituted?* Although the FCC has now abandoned the fairness doctrine, does the rationale for that doctrine make sense today? Air waves may be as limited as before, but they are amply supplemented by cable and satellite television and radio stations in profusion. Is the "scarcity" rationale still meaningful?

FCC v. Pacifica Foundation

438 U.S. 726 (1978)

Mr. Justice STEVENS delivered the opinion of the Court (Parts I, II, III, and IV-C) and an opinion in which THE CHIEF JUSTICE and Mr. Justice REHNQUIST joined (Parts IV-A and IV-B).

This case requires that we decide whether the Federal Communications Commission has any power to regulate a radio broadcast that is indecent but not obscene. . . . A satiric humorist named George Carlin recorded a 12-minute monologue entitled "Filthy Words" before a live audience in a California theater. He began by referring to his thoughts about "the words you couldn't say on the public, ah, airwaves, um, the ones you definitely wouldn't say, ever." He proceeded to list those words and repeat them over and over again in a variety of colloquialisms. The [recording] indicates frequent laughter from the audience.

At about 2 o'clock in the afternoon on Tuesday, October 30, 1973, a New York radio station, owned by respondent Pacifica Foundation, broadcast the "Filthy Words" monologue. A few weeks later a man, who [heard] the broadcast while driving with his young son, wrote a letter complaining to the Commission. . . . The complaint was forwarded to the station for comment. In its response, Pacifica explained that the monologue had been played during a program about contemporary society's attitude toward language and that, immediately before its broadcast, listeners had been advised that it included "sensitive language which might be regarded as offensive to some." Pacifica characterized George Carlin as "a significant social satirist" who "like Twain and Sahl before him, examines the language of ordinary people. . . . Carlin is not mouthing obscenities, he is merely using words to satirize as harmless and essentially silly our attitudes towards those words." Pacifica stated that it was not aware of any other complaints about the broadcast.

[T]he Commission issued a declaratory order [holding] that Pacifica "could have been the subject of administrative sanctions." The Commission did not impose formal sanctions, but it did state that the order would be "associated with the station's license file, and in the event that subsequent complaints are received, the Commission will then decide whether it should utilize any of the available sanctions it has been granted by Congress."

In its memorandum opinion the commission stated that it intended to "clarify the standards which will be utilized in considering" [complaints] about indecent speech on the airwaves. [T]he Commission found a power to regulate indecent broadcasting in two statutes: 18 U.S.C. §1464, which forbids the use of "any obscene, indecent, or profane language by means of radio communications," and 47 U.S.C. §303(g), which requires the Commission to "encourage the larger and more effective use of radio in the public interest."

The Commission characterized the language used in the Carlin monologue as "patently offensive," though not necessarily obscene, and [suggested] that it should be regulated by principles analogous [to] the law of nuisance where the "law generally speaks to channeling behavior more than actually prohibiting it. . . ." "[T]he concept of 'indecent' is intimately connected with the exposure of children to language that describes, in terms patently offensive as measured by contemporary community standards for the broadcast medium, sexual or excretory activities and organs at times of the day when there is a reasonable risk that children may be in the audience."

Applying these considerations to the language used in the monologue[,] the Commission concluded that certain words depicted sexual and excretory activities in a patently offensive manner, noted that they "were broadcast at a time when children were undoubtedly in the audience . . . ," and that the prerecorded language, with these offensive words "repeated over and over," was "deliberately broadcast." [The] Commission [also] issued another opinion in which it pointed out that it "never intended to place an absolute prohibition on the broadcast of this type of language, but rather sought to channel it to times of day when children most likely would not be exposed to it." [The] United States Court of Appeals for the District of Columbia Circuit reversed. . . .

IV

[The] afternoon broadcast of the "Filthy Words" monologue was indecent within the meaning of §1464. . . . At most, [the] Commission's definition of indecency will deter only the broadcasting of patently offensive references to excretory and sexual organs and activities.[15] While some of these references may be protected, they surely lie at the periphery of First Amendment concern [and] the question is whether the First Amendment denies government any power to restrict the public broadcast of indecent language in any circumstances. [The] words of the Carlin monologue are unquestionably "speech" within the meaning of the First Amendment. It is equally clear that the Commission's objections to the broadcast

15. A requirement that indecent language be avoided will have its primary effect on the form, rather than the content, of serious communication. There are few, if any, thoughts that cannot be expressed by the use of less offensive language.

were based in part on its content. The order must therefore fall if [the] First Amendment prohibits all governmental regulation that depends on the content of speech. Our past cases demonstrate, however, that no such absolute rule is mandated by the Constitution.

[Obscene] materials have been denied the protection of the First Amendment because their content is so offensive to contemporary moral standards. Roth v. United States, 354 U.S. 476. But the fact that society may find speech offensive is not a sufficient reason for suppressing it. Indeed, if it is the speaker's opinion that gives offense, that consequence is a reason for according it constitutional protection. For it is a central tenet of the First Amendment that the government must remain neutral in the marketplace of ideas. If there were any reason to believe that the Commission's characterization of the Carlin monologue as offensive could be traced to its political content — or even to the fact that it satirized contemporary attitudes about four-letter words — First Amendment protection might be required. But that is simply not this case. These words offend for the same reasons that obscenity offends. . . .

Although these words ordinarily lack literary, political, or scientific value, they are not entirely outside the protection of the First Amendment. Some uses of even the most offensive words are unquestionably protected. . . . Nonetheless, the constitutional protection accorded to a communication containing such patently offensive sexual and excretory language need not be the same in every context. It is a characteristic of speech such as this that both its capacity to offend and its "social value" [vary] with the circumstances. Words that are commonplace in one setting are shocking in another. To paraphrase Mr. Justice Harlan, one occasion's lyric is another's vulgarity. Cf. Cohen v. California, 403 U.S. 15, 25.

In this case it is undisputed that the content of Pacifica's broadcast was "vulgar," "offensive," and "shocking." Because content of that character is not entitled to absolute constitutional protection under all circumstances, we must consider its context in order to determine whether the Commission's action was constitutionally permissible.

We have long recognized that each medium of expression presents special First Amendment problems. And of all forms of communication, it is broadcasting that has received the most limited First Amendment protection. Thus, although other speakers cannot be licensed except under laws that carefully define and narrow official discretion, a broadcaster may be deprived of his license and his forum if the Commission decides that such an action would serve "the public interest, convenience, and necessity." Similarly, although the First Amendment protects newspaper publishers from being required to print the replies of those whom they criticize, it affords no such protection to broadcasters; on the contrary, they must give free time to the victims of their criticism.

The reasons for these distinctions are complex, but two have relevance to the present case. First, the broadcast media have established a uniquely pervasive presence in the lives of all Americans. Patently offensive, indecent material presented over the airwaves confronts the citizen, not only in public, but also in the privacy of the home, where the individual's right to be left alone plainly outweighs the First Amendment rights of an intruder. Because the broadcast audience is constantly tuning in and out, prior warnings cannot completely protect the listener or viewer from unexpected program content. . . . Second, broadcasting is uniquely accessible to children, even those too young to read. Although *Cohen*'s written message might have been incomprehensible to a first grader, Pacifica's broadcast could have enlarged a child's vocabulary in an instant. Other forms of offensive expression may be withheld from the young without restricting the expression at its source. Bookstores and motion picture theaters, for example, may be prohibited from making indecent material available to children. We held in Ginsberg v. New York, 390 U.S. 629, that the government's interest in the "well-being of its youth" and in supporting "parents' claim to authority in their own household" justified the regulation of otherwise protected expression.[16] The ease with which children may obtain access to broadcast material, coupled with the concerns recognized in *Ginsberg*, amply justify special treatment of indecent broadcasting.

[This] case does not involve a two-way radio conversation between a cab driver and a dispatcher, or a telecast of an Elizabethan comedy. We have not decided that an occasional expletive in either setting would justify any sanction or, indeed, that this broadcast would justify a criminal prosecution. The Commission's decision rested entirely on a nuisance rationale under which context is all-important. . . . The time of day was emphasized by the Commission. The content of the program in which the language is used will also affect the composition of the audience, and differences between radio, television, and perhaps closed-circuit transmissions, may also be relevant. As Mr. Justice Sutherland wrote a "nuisance may be merely a right thing in the wrong place, — like a pig in the parlor instead of the barnyard." Euclid v. Ambler Realty Co., 272 U.S. 365, 388. We simply hold that when the Commission finds that a pig has entered the parlor, the exercise of its regulatory power does not depend on proof that the pig is obscene.

The judgment of the Court of Appeals is reversed.

It is so ordered.

APPENDIX TO OPINION OF THE COURT

The following is [the first part of] a verbatim transcript of "Filthy Words" prepared by the Federal Communications Commission.

> Aruba-du, ruba-tu, ruba-tu. I was thinking about the curse words and the swear words, the cuss words and the words that you can't say, that you're not supposed to say all the time, [']cause words or people into words want to hear your words. Some guys like to record your words and sell them back to you if they can, (laughter) listen in on the telephone, write down what words you say. A guy who used to be in Washington, knew that his phone was tapped, used to answer, Fuck Hoover, yes, go ahead. (laughter) Okay, I was thinking one night about the words you couldn't say on the public, ah, airwaves, um, the ones you definitely wouldn't say, ever, [']cause I heard a lady say bitch one night on television, and it was cool like she was talking about, you know, ah, well, the bitch is the first one to notice that in the litter Johnie right (murmur) Right. And, uh, bastard you can say, and hell and damn so I have to figure out

---

16. The Commission's action does [not] reduce adults to hearing only what is fit for children. . . . Adults who feel the need may purchase tapes and records or go to theaters and nightclubs to hear these words. In fact, the Commission has not unequivocally closed even broadcasting to speech of this sort. . . .

which ones you couldn't and ever and it came down to seven but the list is open to amendment, and in fact, has been changed, uh, by now, ha, a lot of people pointed things out to me, and I noticed some myself. The original seven words were shit, piss, fuck, cunt, cocksucker, motherfucker, and tits. Those are the ones that will curve your spine, grow hair on your hands and (laughter) maybe, even bring us, God help us, peace without honor (laughter) um, and a bourbon. (laughter) And now the first thing that we noticed was that word fuck was really repeated in there because the word motherfucker is a compound word and it's another form of the word fuck. (laughter) You want to be a purist it doesn't really — it can't be on the list of basic words. Also, cocksucker is a compound word and neither half of that is really dirty. The word — the half sucker that's merely suggestive (laughter) and the word cock is a half-way dirty word, 50% dirty — dirty half the time, depending on what you mean by it. (laughter) Uh, remember when you first heard it, like in 6th grade, you used to giggle. And the cock crowed three times, heh (laughter) the cock — three times. It's in the Bible, cock in the Bible. (laughter) And the first time you heard about a cock-fight, remember — What? Huh? naw. It ain't that, are you stupid? man. (laughter, clapping) It's chickens, you know. (laughter) Then you have the four letter words from the old Angle-Saxon fame. Uh, shit and fuck. The word shit, uh, is an interesting kind of word in that the middle class has never really accepted it and approved it. They use it like, crazy but it's not really okay. It's still a rude, dirty, old kind of gushy word. (laughter) They don't like that, but they say it, like, they say it like, a lady now in a middle-class home, you'll hear most of the time she says it as an expletive, you know, it's out of her mouth before she knows. She says, Oh shit oh shit, (laughter) oh shit. If she drops something, Oh, the shit hurt the broccoli. Shit. Thank you. . . .

Mr. Justice POWELL, with whom Mr. Justice BLACKMUN joins, concurring in part and concurring in the judgment.

[C]hildren may not be able to protect themselves from speech which, although shocking to most adults, generally may be avoided by the unwilling through the exercise of choice. At the same time, such speech may have a deeper and more lasting negative effect on a child than on an adult. For these reasons, society may prevent the general dissemination of such speech to children, leaving to parents the decision as to what speech of this kind their children shall hear and repeat. . . . The Commission properly held that the speech from which society may attempt to shield its children is not limited to that which appeals to the youthful prurient interest. The language involved in this case is as potentially degrading and harmful to children as representations of many erotic acts.

In most instances, the dissemination of this kind of speech to children may be limited without also limiting willing adults' access to it. Sellers of printed and recorded matter and exhibitors of motion pictures and live performances may be required to shut their doors to children, but such a requirement has no effect on adults' access. The difficulty is that such a physical separation of the audience cannot be accomplished in the broadcast media. During most of the broadcast hours, both adults and unsupervised children are likely to be in the broadcast audience, and the broadcaster cannot reach willing adults without also reaching children. This [is] one of the distinctions [that justifies] a different treatment of the broadcast media for First Amendment purposes. [T]he Commission was entitled to give substantial weight to this difference in reaching its decision. . . .

[The] Commission's holding does not prevent willing adults from purchasing Carlin's record, from attending his performances, or, indeed, from reading the transcript. . . . On its face, it does not prevent respondent Pacifica Foundation from broadcasting the monologue during late evening hours when fewer children are likely to be in the audience. . . . The Commission's holding [does] not speak to cases involving the isolated use of a potentially offensive word in the course of a radio broadcast, as distinguished from the verbal shock treatment administered by respondent here. In short, I agree that on the facts of this case, the Commission's order did not violate respondent's First Amendment rights.

[T]he result in this case does not turn on whether Carlin's monologue, viewed as a whole, or the words that constitute it, have more or less "value" than a candidate's campaign speech. [The] result turns instead on the unique characteristics of the broadcast media, combined with society's right to protect its children from speech generally agreed to be inappropriate for their years, and with the interest of unwilling adults in not being assaulted by such offensive speech in their homes. . . .

Mr. Justice BRENNAN, with whom Mr. Justice MARSHALL joins, dissenting.

[Although] an individual's decision to allow public radio communications into his home undoubtedly does not abrogate all of his privacy interests, the residual privacy interests he retains vis-a-vis the communication he voluntarily admits into his home are surely no greater than those of the people present in the corridor of the Los Angeles courthouse in *Cohen* who bore witness to the words "Fuck the Draft" emblazoned across Cohen's jacket. Their privacy interests were held insufficient to justify punishing Cohen for his offensive communication.

Even if an individual who voluntarily opens his home to radio communications retains privacy interests of sufficient moment to justify a ban on protected speech if those interests are "invaded in an essentially intolerable manner," [the] "radio can be turned off" — and with a minimum of effort. [I]t is surely worth the candle to preserve the broadcaster's right to send, and the right of those interested to receive, a message entitled to full First Amendment protection. To reach a contrary balance [is] "to burn the house to roast the pig." [The] Court's balance, of necessity, fails to accord proper weight to the interests of listeners who wish to hear broadcasts the FCC deems offensive. It permits majoritarian tastes completely to preclude a protected message from entering the homes of a receptive, unoffended minority. No decision of this Court supports such a result. . . .

Although the government unquestionably has a special interest in the well-being of children and consequently "can adopt more stringent controls on communicative materials available to youths than on those available to adults," the Court has accounted for this societal interest by adopting a "variable obscenity" standard that permits the prurient appeal of material available to children to be assessed in terms of the sexual interests of minors. . . . Because the Carlin monologue is obviously not an erotic appeal to the prurient interests of children, the Court, for the first time, allows the government to prevent minors from gaining access to materials that are not obscene, and are therefore protected, as to them. . . .

My Brother Stevens [finds] solace in his conviction that "[t]here are few, if any, thoughts that cannot be expressed by the use of less offensive language." The idea that the content of a message and its potential impact on any who might receive it can be divorced from the words that are the vehicle for its expression is transparently fallacious. A given word may have a unique capacity to capsule an idea, evoke an emotion, or conjure up an image. . . .

[N]either of the factors relied on by [the] opinion of my Brother Powell and the opinion of my Brother Stevens — the intrusive nature of radio and the presence of children in the listening audience [can] support the FCC's disapproval of the Carlin monologue. These two asserted justifications are further plagued by [a] lack of principled limits. [Taken] to their logical extreme, these rationales would support the cleansing of public radio of any "four-letter words" whatsoever, regardless of their context. The rationales could justify the banning from radio of a myriad of literary works, novels, poems, and plays by the likes of Shakespeare, Joyce, Hemingway, Ben Jonson, Henry Fielding, Robert Burns, and Chaucer; they could support the suppression of a good deal of political speech, such as the Nixon tapes; and they could even provide the basis for imposing sanctions for the broadcast of certain portions of the Bible. [I] would place the responsibility and the right to weed worthless and offensive communications from the public airways where it belongs and where, until today, it resided: in a public free to choose those communications worthy of its attention from a marketplace unsullied by the censor's hand.

My Brother Stevens also finds relevant to his First Amendment analysis the fact that "[a]dults who feel the need may purchase tapes and records or go to theaters and nightclubs to hear [the tabooed] words." [T]hese alternatives involve the expenditure of money, time, and effort that many of those wishing to hear Mr. Carlin's message may not be able to afford, and a naive innocence of the reality that in many cases the medium may well be the message.

[I]n our land of cultural pluralism, there are many who think, act, and talk differently from the Members of this Court, and who do not share their fragile sensibilities. It is only an acute ethnocentric myopia that enables the Court to approve the censorship of communications solely because of the words they contain. [Today's] decision will thus have its greatest impact on broadcasters desiring to reach, and listening audiences composed of, persons who do not share the Court's view as to which words or expressions are acceptable and who, for a variety of reasons, including a conscious desire to flout majoritarian conventions, express themselves using words that may be regarded as offensive by those from different socio-economic backgrounds. . . .

Mr. Justice STEWART, with whom Mr. Justice BRENNAN, Mr. Justice WHITE, and Mr. Justice MARSHALL join, dissenting.

[Since] the Carlin monologue concededly was not "obscene," I believe that the Commission lacked statutory authority to ban it. . . .

Notes

1. *The* League of Women Voters *Case.* In FCC v. League of Women Voters of California, 468 U.S. 364 (1984), the Court considered the Public Broadcasting Act of 1967, which prohibited any noncommercial educational broadcasting

station that receives grants from the Corporation for Public Broadcasting from "engag[ing] in editorializing." The Court struck down the restriction: "[A]lthough the Government certainly has a substantial interest in ensuring that the audiences of noncommercial stations will not be led to think that the broadcaster's editorials reflect the official view of the government, this interest can be fully satisfied by less restrictive means that are readily available. [Congress] could simply require public broadcasting stations to broadcast a disclaimer every time they editorialize." Justice Rehnquist dissented: "[I]t is plainly rational for Congress to have determined that taxpayer moneys should not be used to subsidize management's views or to pay for management's exercise of partisan politics." Justice Stevens also dissented: "the interest in keeping the Federal Government out of the propaganda arena is of overriding importance."

2. *Fleeting Expletives.* In Federal Communications Commission v. Fox Television Stations, Inc., 129 S.Ct. 1800 (2009), the Court upheld the FCC's ban on "fleeting expletives," which provided that even a fleeting expletive could be regarded as indecent even though the word was used as an intensifier (e.g., this is really "f——— brilliant") rather than as a literal descriptor.

∼ PROBLEM: ANTIABORTION ADVERTISING ∼

A candidate for Congress, an avid antiabortionist, wishes to run an antiabortion advertisement on evening telecasts. As part of the advertisement, he would show pictures of aborted fetuses alongside pictures of children singing antiabortion songs. A local television station declines to air the advertisement, fearing its effect on children. The station is willing to run the ads after 8:00 P.M. Does the candidate have the right to run the advertisements notwithstanding the station's objections? *See* Becker v. Federal Communications Commission, 95 F.3d 75 (N.D. Ga. 1992).

K. ADVANCING TECHNOLOGY

At the end of the twentieth century, "speech technology" began to change radically. In addition to cable television, which developed much earlier, there were significant developments in regard to the Internet and satellite broadcasting. Some of these new technologies, particularly the Internet, posed difficult challenges because they contain pornography, obscenity, and other forms of "indecent" material that is easy for children to access.

Courts have struggled with the problem of how to fit these new technologies into existing speech frameworks. As *Red Lion* and *Pacifica* demonstrate, the Court has historically distinguished between such items as newspapers and handbills, on the one hand, and broadcast technology (i.e., radio and television) on the other. While the courts have always provided strong protections for newspapers and handbills, they have sustained broader regulation of broadcast technology.

"New" technologies, like the Internet, have forced the Supreme Court to reconsider its precedents relating to technology.

Turner Broadcasting System, Inc. v. FCC
512 U.S. 622 (1994)

Justice KENNEDY announced the judgment of the Court and delivered the opinion of the Court, except as to Part III-B.

Sections 4 and 5 of the Cable Television Consumer Protection and Competition Act of 1992 require cable television systems to devote a portion of their channels to the transmission of local broadcast television stations. This case presents the question whether these provisions abridge the freedom of speech or of the press, in violation of the First Amendment. . . .

I

[The] role of cable television in the Nation's communications system has undergone dramatic change over the past 45 years. . . . With the capacity to carry dozens of channels and import distant programming signals via satellite or microwave relay, today's cable systems are in direct competition with over-the-air broadcasters as an independent source of television programming.

Broadcast and cable television are distinguished [by] different technologies. . . . Broadcast stations radiate electromagnetic signals from a central transmitting antenna [that] can be captured [by] any television set within the antenna's range. Cable systems, by contrast, rely upon a physical, point-to-point connection between a transmission facility and the television sets of individual subscribers. Cable systems make this connection much like telephone companies, using cable or optical fibers strung above ground or buried in ducts to reach the homes or businesses of subscribers. The construction of this physical infrastructure entails the use of public rights-of-way and easements and often results in the disruption of traffic on streets and other public property. As a result, the cable medium may depend for its very existence upon express permission from local governing authorities.

Cable technology affords two principal benefits over broadcast. First, it eliminates the signal interference sometimes encountered in over-the-air broadcasting and thus gives viewers undistorted reception of broadcast stations. Second, it is capable of transmitting many more channels than are available through broadcasting, giving subscribers access to far greater programming variety. . . . Newer systems can carry hundreds of channels. . . .

The cable television industry includes both cable operators (those who own the physical cable network and transmit the cable signal to the viewer) and cable programmers (those who produce television programs and sell or license them to cable operators). . . . Although cable operators may create some of their own programming, most of their programming is drawn from outside sources [including] not only local or distant broadcast stations, but also the many national and regional cable programming networks that have emerged in recent years, such as

CNN, MTV, ESPN, TNT, C-SPAN, The Family Channel, Nickelodeon, Arts and Entertainment[,] The Discovery Channel, American Movie Classics[,] The Learning Channel, and The Weather Channel. [T]he cable system functions, in essence, as a conduit for the speech of others, transmitting it on a continuous and unedited basis to subscribers. . . . In contrast to commercial broadcast stations, which transmit signals at no charge to viewers and generate revenues by selling time to advertisers, cable systems charge subscribers a monthly fee for the right to receive cable programming and rely to a lesser extent on advertising. [C]able subscribers choose the stations they will receive by selecting among various plans, or "tiers," of cable service. . . .

[In] 1992, Congress [enacted] the Cable Television Consumer Protection and Competition Act of 1992. . . . Section 4 requires carriage of "local commercial television stations," defined to include all full power television broadcasters, other than those qualifying as "noncommercial educational" stations under §5, that operate within the same television market as the cable system. [S]ubject to a few exceptions, a cable operator may not charge a fee for carrying broadcast signals in fulfillment of its must-carry obligations. Section 5 of the Act imposes similar requirements regarding the carriage of local public broadcast television stations, referred to in the Act as local "noncommercial educational television stations." [Appellants] are numerous cable programmers and cable operators. [T]he District Court [upheld] the must-carry provisions. [W]e noted probable jurisdiction.

II

[Cable] programmers and cable operators engage in and transmit speech, and they are entitled to the protection of the speech and press provisions of the First Amendment. Through "original programming or by exercising editorial discretion over which stations or programs to include in its repertoire," cable programmers and operators "see[k] to communicate messages on a wide variety of topics and in a wide variety of formats." Los Angeles v. Preferred Communications, Inc., 476 U.S. 488 (1986). By requiring cable systems to set aside a portion of their channels for local broadcasters, the must-carry rules regulate cable speech in two respects: [they] reduce the number of channels over which cable operators exercise unfettered control, and they render it more difficult for cable programmers to compete for carriage on the [remaining] channels. . . .

[C]able television does not suffer from the inherent limitations that characterize the broadcast medium. Indeed, given the rapid advances in fiber optics and digital compression technology, soon there may be no practical limitation on the number of speakers who may use the cable medium. Nor is there any danger of physical interference between two cable speakers attempting to share the same channel. In light of these fundamental technological differences[,] application of the more relaxed standard of scrutiny adopted in *Red Lion* and the other broadcast cases is inapt when determining the First Amendment validity of cable regulation.

[T]he must-carry rules, on their face, impose burdens and confer benefits without reference to the content of speech. [The] provisions interfere with cable operators' editorial discretion by compelling them to offer carriage to a certain minimum number of broadcast stations. . . . The must-carry provisions also burden cable programmers by reducing the number of channels for which they can compete. But, again, this burden is unrelated to content, for it extends to all cable programmers irrespective of the programming they choose to offer viewers. And finally, the privileges conferred by the must-carry provisions are also unrelated to content. The rules benefit all full power broadcasters who request carriage — be they commercial or noncommercial, independent or network affiliated, English or Spanish language, religious or secular [—] provided only that the broadcaster operates within the same television market as a cable system.

[T]he must-carry provisions distinguish between speakers in the television programming market [based] only upon the manner in which speakers transmit their messages to viewers, and not upon the messages they carry: Broadcasters, which transmit over the airwaves, are favored, while cable programmers, which do not, are disfavored. . . .

Appellants contend [that] the must-carry regulations are content based because Congress' purpose in enacting them was to promote speech of a favored content. . . . Our review of the Act and its various findings persuades us that Congress' overriding objective in enacting must-carry was not to favor programming of a particular subject matter, viewpoint, or format, but rather to preserve access to free television programming for the 40 percent of Americans without cable. . . . Congress explained that because cable systems and broadcast stations compete for local advertising revenue, and because cable operators have a vested financial interest in favoring their affiliated programmers over broadcast stations, cable operators have a built-in "economic incentive [to] delete, reposition, or not carry local broadcast signals." Congress concluded that absent a requirement that cable systems carry the signals of local broadcast stations, the continued availability of free local broadcast television would be threatened. . . . Congress sought to avoid the elimination of broadcast television [because] "[t]here is a substantial governmental interest in promoting the continued availability of such free television programming, especially for viewers who are unable to afford other means of receiving programming." . . .

Appellants maintain that the must-carry provisions trigger strict scrutiny because they compel cable operators to transmit speech not of their choosing. [See Miami Herald Publishing Co. v. Tornillo, 418 U.S. 241 (1974); Pacific Gas & Electric v. Public Utilities Commn., 475 U.S. 1 (1986)]. *Tornillo* and *Pacific Gas & Electric* do not control this case. . . . First, unlike the access rules struck down in those cases, the must-carry rules are content neutral in application. . . . Second, appellants do not suggest [that] must-carry will force cable operators to alter their own messages to respond to the broadcast programming they are required to carry. . . . Finally, [a]lthough a daily newspaper and a cable operator both may enjoy monopoly status in a given locale, the cable operator exercises far greater control over access to the relevant medium. [S]imply by virtue of its ownership of the essential pathway for cable speech, a cable operator can prevent its subscribers from obtaining access to programming it chooses to exclude. [The] First

Amendment [does] not disable the government from taking steps to ensure that private interests not restrict, through physical control of a critical pathway of communication, the free flow of information and ideas. . . . It would be error to conclude [that] the First Amendment mandates strict scrutiny for any speech regulation that applies to one medium (or a subset thereof) but not others. [The] must-carry provisions [are] justified by special characteristics of the cable medium: the bottleneck monopoly power exercised by cable operators and the dangers this power poses to the viability of broadcast television. . . . [N]or does it appear, that other media — in particular, media that transmit video programming such as MMDS [multichannel multipoint distribution] and SMATV [satellite master antenna television] — are subject to bottleneck monopoly control, or pose a demonstrable threat to the survival of broadcast television. . . .

III

A

In sum, the must-carry provisions do not pose such inherent dangers to free expression, or present such potential for censorship or manipulation, as to justify application of the most exacting level of First Amendment scrutiny. [T]he appropriate standard by which to evaluate the constitutionality of must-carry is the intermediate level of scrutiny applicable to content-neutral restrictions that impose an incidental burden on speech. [To] satisfy this standard, [the] requirement of narrow tailoring is satisfied "so long as [the] regulation promotes a substantial government interest that would be achieved less effectively absent the regulation." *Ward*, 491 U.S., at 799. Narrow tailoring in this context requires [that] the means chosen do not "burden substantially more speech than is necessary to further the government's legitimate interests."

Congress declared that the must-carry provisions serve three interrelated interests: (1) preserving the benefits of free, over-the-air local broadcast television, (2) promoting the widespread dissemination of information from a multiplicity of sources, and (3) promoting fair competition in the market for television programming. None of these interests is related to the "suppression of free expression," or to the content of any speakers' messages. [W]e have no difficulty concluding that each of them is an important governmental interest. [N]early 40 percent of American households still rely on broadcast stations as their exclusive source of television programming. And as we said in Capital Cities Cable, Inc. v. Crisp, "protecting noncable households from loss of regular television broadcasting service due to competition from cable systems" is an important federal interest. 467 U.S., at 714. Likewise, assuring that the public has access to a multiplicity of information sources is a governmental purpose of the highest order, for it promotes values central to the First Amendment. Finally, the Government's interest in eliminating restraints on fair competition is always substantial, even when the individuals or entities subject to particular regulations are engaged in expressive activity protected by the First Amendment.

B

[When] the Government defends a regulation on speech as a means to redress past harms or prevent anticipated harms, [i]t must demonstrate that the recited harms are real, not merely conjectural, and that the regulation will in fact alleviate these harms in a direct and material way. [W]e are unable to conclude that the Government has satisfied either inquiry. [B]ecause there are genuine issues of material fact still to be resolved on this record, we hold that the District Court erred in granting summary judgment in favor of the Government. . . .

The judgment below is vacated, and the case is remanded for further proceedings consistent with this opinion.

It is so ordered.

Justice STEVENS, concurring in part and concurring in the judgment.

[B]ecause I am in substantial agreement with Justice Kennedy's analysis of the case, I concur in the judgment. . . .

Justice O'CONNOR, with whom Justice SCALIA and Justice GINSBURG join, and with whom Justice THOMAS joins as to Parts I and III, concurring in part and dissenting in part.

[Under] the First Amendment, it is normally not within the government's power to decide who may speak and who may not, at least on private property or in traditional public fora. [L]ooking at the statute at issue, I cannot avoid the conclusion that its preference for broadcasters over cable programmers is justified with reference to content. [Preferences] for diversity of viewpoints, for localism, for educational programming, and for news and public affairs all make reference to content. . . . Content-based speech restrictions are generally unconstitutional unless they are narrowly tailored to a compelling state interest. [The] interest in localism, either in the dissemination of opinions held by the listeners' neighbors or in the reporting of events that have to do with the local community, cannot be described as "compelling" for the purposes of the compelling state interest test. It is a legitimate interest, perhaps even an important one — certainly the government can foster it [by] providing subsidies from the public fisc — but it does not rise to the level necessary to justify content-based speech restrictions. It is for private speakers and listeners, not for the government, to decide what fraction of their news and entertainment ought to be of a local character and what fraction ought to be of a national (or international) one. . . . The interests in public affairs programming and educational programming seem somewhat weightier, though it is a difficult question whether they are compelling enough to justify restricting other sorts of speech. [E]ven assuming, arguendo, that the Government could set some channels aside for educational or news programming, the Act is insufficiently tailored to this goal. To benefit the educational broadcasters, the Act burdens more than just the cable entertainment programmers. It equally burdens CNN, C-SPAN, the Discovery Channel, the New Inspirational Network, and other channels with as much claim as PBS to being educational or related to public affairs. . . . Even if the Government can restrict entertainment in order to benefit supposedly more valuable speech, I do not think the restriction can extend to other speech that is as valuable as the speech being benefited. . . . [M]y conclusion that the must-carry rules are content based leads me to conclude that they are an impermissible restraint on the cable operators' editorial discretion as well as on the cable programmers' speech. . . .

Notes: More on Cable Television Regulation

1. *Following Remand.* When *Turner* came back from remand, the Court upheld the must-carry provisions. Turner Broadcasting System, Inc. v. FCC, 520 U.S. 180 (1997).

2. *Content Regulation of Cable Television.* Denver Area Educational Telecommunications Consortium, Inc. v. FCC, 518 U.S. 727 (1996), involved the Cable Television Consumer Protection and Competition Act of 1992, which regulated cable broadcasting of "patently offensive," sex-related material. The Act applied to programs known as "leased access channels" and "public, educational, or governmental channels" that carry programs prepared by those given special cable system access rights. Section 10(a) of the Act allowed cable system operators to prohibit the broadcasting of "programming" that the "operator reasonably believes describes or depicts sexual or excretory activities or organs in a patently offensive manner" over "leased access" channels. Section 10(c) allowed cable operators to impose similar restrictions over public access channels. The remaining provision required cable system operators to segregate certain "patently offensive" programming, to place it on a single channel, and to block that channel from viewer access unless the viewer requests access in advance and in writing. The Court upheld Section 10(a), but struck down the other two provisions:

[As for §10(a), the] importance of the interest at stake here — protecting children from exposure to patently offensive depictions of sex; the accommodation of the interests of programmers in maintaining access channels and of cable operators in editing the contents of their channels; [and] the flexibility inherent in an approach that permits private cable operators to make editorial decisions, lead us to conclude that §10(a) is a sufficiently tailored response to an extraordinarily important problem. [T]he permissive nature of the provision, coupled with its viewpoint-neutral application, is a constitutionally permissible way to protect children from the type of sexual material that concerned Congress. . . .

[As for §10(c),] there are four important differences. . . . [First,] cable operators have traditionally agreed to reserve channel capacity for public, governmental, and educational channels as part of the consideration they give municipalities that award them cable franchises. [Unlike] §10(a) therefore, §10(c) does not restore to cable operators editorial rights that they once had, and the countervailing First Amendment interest is nonexistent, or at least much diminished. [Second,] [m]unicipalities generally provide in their cable franchising agreements for an access channel manager [who] can set programming policy and approve or disapprove particular programming services. Third, the existence of a system aimed at encouraging and securing programming that the community considers valuable strongly suggests that a "cable operator's veto" is less likely necessary to achieve the statute's basic objective, protecting children. . . . Finally, [the] public/nonprofit programming control systems now in place would normally avoid, minimize, or eliminate any child-related problems concerning "patently offensive" programming. The upshot, in respect to the public access channels, is a law that could radically change present programming-related relationships among local community and nonprofit supervising boards and access managers, which relationships are established through municipal law, regulation, and contract. In doing so, it would not significantly restore editorial rights of cable operators, but would greatly increase the risk that certain categories of programming (say, borderline offensive programs) will not appear. . . .

[As for the segregate/block/written-access provisions, the] record does [not] explain why, under the new Act, blocking alone — without written access requests — adequately protects children from exposure to regular sex-dedicated channels, but cannot adequately protect those children from programming on similarly sex-dedicated channels that are leased. [W]e cannot find that the "segregate and block" restrictions on speech are a narrowly, or reasonably, tailored effort to protect children. Rather, they are overly restrictive, "sacrific[ing]" important First Amendment interests for too "speculative a gain." For that reason they are not consistent with the First Amendment.

Justice Kennedy, joined by Justice Ginsburg, argued that all three of the challenged sections were unconstitutional because they regulate a "public forum of unlimited character" and therefore are "subject to the highest scrutiny" and "survive only if they are narrowly drawn to achieve a compelling state interest." Although he agreed that Congress has a "compelling interest in protecting children from indecent speech," he concluded that the "Government has no legitimate interest in making access channels pristine," thereby depriving adults of access to the information. Chief Justice Rehnquist, Justice Scalia, and Justice Thomas would have upheld all three provisions. Justice O'Connor would have upheld Section 10(c).

3. *Dial-a-Porn.* Sable Communications of California, Inc. v. FCC, 492 U.S. 115 (1989), involved a challenge to the constitutionality of Section 223(b) of the Communications Act of 1934, which imposed a ban on indecent as well as obscene interstate commercial telephone messages. The challenge was brought by a company that offered sexually oriented, prerecorded telephone messages (also known as "dial-a-porn") for a fee. The Court struck down the law: "[T]here is a compelling interest in protecting the physical and psychological well-being of minors. [The FCC] determined that its credit card, access code, and scrambling rules were a satisfactory solution to the problem of keeping indecent dial-a-porn messages out of the reach of minors. [Because] the statute's denial of adult access [far] exceeds that which is necessary to limit the access of minors to such messages, we hold that the ban does not survive constitutional scrutiny."

Reno v. American Civil Liberties Union

521 U.S. 844 (1997)

Justice STEVENS delivered the opinion of the Court.

At issue is the constitutionality of two statutory provisions enacted to protect minors from "indecent" and "patently offensive" communications on the Internet. Notwithstanding the legitimacy and importance of the congressional goal of protecting children from harmful materials, we agree with the three-judge District Court that the statute abridges "the freedom of speech" protected by the First Amendment.

I

The District Court made extensive findings of fact, most of which were based on a detailed stipulation prepared by the parties. The findings describe the character and the dimensions of the Internet, the availability of sexually explicit material in that medium, and the problems confronting age verification for recipients of Internet communications. Because those findings provide the underpinnings for the legal issues, we begin with a summary of the undisputed facts.

The Internet

The Internet is an international network of interconnected computers. It is the outgrowth of what began in 1969 as a military program called "ARPANET," which was designed to enable computers operated by the military, defense contractors, and universities conducting defense-related research to communicate with one another by redundant channels even if some portions of the network were damaged in a war. While the ARPANET no longer exists, it provided an example for the development of a number of civilian networks that, eventually linking with each other, now enable tens of millions of people to communicate with one another and to access vast amounts of information from around the world. The Internet is "a unique and wholly new medium of worldwide human communication."

The Internet has experienced "extraordinary growth." The number of "host" computers — those that store information and relay communications — increased from about 300 in 1981 to approximately 9,400,000 by the time of the trial in 1996. Roughly 60% of these hosts are located in the United States. About 40 million people used the Internet at the time of trial, a number that is expected to mushroom to 200 million by 1999.

Individuals can obtain access to the Internet from many different sources, generally hosts themselves or entities with a host affiliation. Most colleges and universities provide access for their students and faculty; many corporations provide their employees with access through an office network; many communities and local libraries provide free access; and an increasing number of storefront "computer coffee shops" provide access for a small hourly fee. Several major national "online services" such as America Online, CompuServe, the Microsoft Network, and Prodigy offer access to their own extensive proprietary networks as well as a link to the much larger resources of the Internet. These commercial online services had almost 12 million individual subscribers at the time of trial.

Anyone with access to the Internet may take advantage of a wide variety of communication and information retrieval methods. These methods are constantly evolving and difficult to categorize precisely. But, as presently constituted, those most relevant to this case are electronic mail ("e-mail"), automatic mailing list services ("mail exploders," sometimes referred to as "listservs"), "newsgroups," "chat rooms," and the "World Wide Web." All of these methods can be used to transmit text; most can transmit sound, pictures, and moving video images. Taken together, these tools constitute a unique medium — known to its users as "cyberspace" — located in no particular geographical location but available to anyone, anywhere in the world, with access to the Internet.

E-mail enables an individual to send an electronic message — generally akin to a note or letter — to another individual or to a group of addressees. The message is generally stored electronically, sometimes waiting for the recipient to check her "mailbox" and sometimes making its receipt known through some type of prompt. A mail exploder is a sort of e-mail group. Subscribers can send messages to a common e-mail address, which then forwards the message to the group's other subscribers. Newsgroups also serve groups of regular participants, but these postings may be read by others as well. There are thousands of such groups, each serving to foster an exchange of information or opinion on a particular topic running the gamut from, say, the music of Wagner to Balkan politics to AIDS prevention to the Chicago Bulls. About 100,000 new messages are posted every day. In most newsgroups, postings are automatically purged at regular intervals. In addition to posting a message that can be read later, two or more individuals wishing to communicate more immediately can enter a chat room to engage in real-time dialogue — in other words, by typing messages to one another that appear almost immediately on the others' computer screens. The District Court found that at any given time "tens of thousands of users are engaging in conversations on a huge range of subjects." It is "no exaggeration to conclude that the content on the Internet is as diverse as human thought."

The best known category of communication over the Internet is the World Wide Web, which allows users to search for and retrieve information stored in remote computers, as well as, in some cases, to communicate back to designated sites. In concrete terms, the Web consists of a vast number of documents stored in different computers all over the world. Some of these documents are simply files containing information. However, more elaborate documents, commonly known as Web "pages," are also prevalent. Each has its own address — "rather like a telephone number." Web pages frequently contain information and sometimes allow the viewer to communicate with the page's (or "site's") author. They generally also contain "links" to other documents created by that site's author or to other (generally) related sites. Typically, the links are either blue or underlined text — sometimes images.

Navigating the Web is relatively straightforward. A user may either type the address of a known page or enter one or more keywords into a commercial "search engine" in an effort to locate sites on a subject of interest. A particular Web page may contain the information sought by the "surfer," or, through its links, it may be an avenue to other documents located anywhere on the Internet. Users generally explore a given Web page, or move to another, by clicking a computer "mouse" on one of the page's icons or links. Access to most Web pages is freely available, but some allow access only to those who have purchased the right from a commercial provider. The Web is thus comparable, from the readers' viewpoint, to both a vast library including millions of readily available and indexed publications and a sprawling mall offering goods and services.

From the publishers' point of view, it constitutes a vast platform from which to address and hear from a world-wide audience of millions of readers, viewers, researchers, and buyers. Any person or organization with a computer connected to the Internet can "publish" information. Publishers include government agencies, educational institutions, commercial entities, advocacy groups, and individuals. Publishers may either make their material available to the entire pool of Internet users, or confine access to a selected group, such as those willing to pay for the privilege. "No single organization controls any membership in the Web, nor is there any centralized point from which individual Web sites or services can be blocked from the Web."

Sexually Explicit Material

Sexually explicit material on the Internet includes text, pictures, and chat and "extends from the modestly titillating to the hardest-core." These files are created, named, and posted in the same manner as material that is not sexually explicit, and may be accessed either deliberately or unintentionally during the course of an imprecise search. "Once a provider posts its content on the Internet, it cannot prevent that content from entering any community." Thus, for example, "when the UCR/California Museum of Photography posts to its Web site nudes by Edward Weston and Robert Mapplethorpe to announce that its new exhibit will travel to Baltimore and New York City, those images are available not only in Los Angeles, Baltimore, and New York City, but also in Cincinnati, Mobile, or Beijing — wherever Internet users live. . . ."

Some of the communications over the Internet that originate in foreign countries are also sexually explicit. Though such material is widely available, users seldom encounter such content accidentally. "A document's title or a description of the document will usually appear before the document itself [and] in many cases the user will receive detailed information about a site's content before he or she need take the step to access the document. Almost all sexually explicit images are preceded by warnings as to the content." For that reason, the "odds are slim" that a user would enter a sexually explicit site by accident. Unlike communications received by radio or television, "the receipt of information on the Internet requires a series of affirmative steps more deliberate and directed than merely turning a dial. A child requires some sophistication and some ability to read to retrieve material and thereby to use the Internet unattended."

Systems have been developed to help parents control the material that may be available on a home computer with Internet access. A system may either limit a computer's access to an approved list of sources that have been identified as containing no adult material, it may block designated inappropriate sites, or it may attempt to block messages containing identifiable objectionable features. "Although parental control software currently can screen for certain suggestive words or for known sexually explicit sites, it cannot now screen for sexually explicit images." Nevertheless, the evidence indicates that "a reasonably effective method by which parents can prevent their children from accessing sexually explicit and other material which parents may believe is inappropriate for their children will soon be available."

II

The Telecommunications Act of 1996 was an unusually important legislative enactment. [I]ts primary purpose was to reduce regulation and encourage "the rapid deployment of new telecommunications technologies." The major components of the statute have nothing to do with the Internet; they were designed to promote competition in the local telephone service market, the multichannel video market, and the market for over-the-air broadcasting. The Act includes seven Titles, six of which are the product of extensive committee hearings and the subject of discussion in reports prepared by Committees of the Senate and the House of Representatives. By contrast, Title V—known as the "Communications Decency Act of 1996" (CDA)—contains provisions that were either added in executive committee after the hearings were concluded or as amendments offered during floor debate on the legislation. An amendment offered in the Senate was the source of the two statutory provisions challenged in this case. They are informally described as the "indecent transmission" provision and the "patently offensive display" provision.

The first, 47 U.S.C.A. §223(a) (Supp. 1997), prohibits the knowing transmission of obscene or indecent messages to any recipient under 18 years of age. It provides in pertinent part:

(a) Whoever —
    (1) in interstate or foreign communications — . . .
        (B) by means of a telecommunications device knowingly —
            (i) makes, creates, or solicits, and
            (ii) initiates the transmission of,
any comment, request, suggestion, proposal, image, or other communication which is obscene or indecent, knowing that the recipient of the communication is under 18 years of age, regardless of whether the maker of such communication placed the call or initiated the communication; . . .
    (2) knowingly permits any telecommunications facility under his control to be used for any activity prohibited by paragraph (1) with the intent that it be used for such activity, "shall be fined under Title 18, or imprisoned not more than two years, or both.

The second provision, §223(d), prohibits the knowing sending or displaying of patently offensive messages in a manner that is available to a person under 18 years of age. It provides:

(d) Whoever —
    (1) in interstate or foreign communications knowingly —
        (A) uses an interactive computer service to send to a specific person or persons under 18 years of age, or
        (B) uses any interactive computer service to display in a manner available to a person under 18 years of age,
any comment, request, suggestion, proposal, image, or other communication that, in context, depicts or describes, in terms patently offensive as measured by contemporary community standards, sexual or excretory activities or organs, regardless of whether the user of such service placed the call or initiated the communication; or
    (2) knowingly permits any telecommunications facility under such person's control to be used for an activity prohibited by paragraph (1) with the intent that it be used for such activity, "shall be fined under Title 18, or imprisoned not more than two years, or both.

The breadth of these prohibitions is qualified by two affirmative defenses. One covers those who take "good faith, reasonable, effective, and appropriate actions" to restrict access by minors to the prohibited communications. §223(e)(5)(A). The other covers those who restrict access to covered material by requiring certain designated forms of age proof, such as a verified credit card or an adult identification number or code. §223(e)(5)(B).

[A three-judge district court, convened pursuant to the statute, entered a preliminary injunction against enforcement of both of the challenged provisions.] In arguing for reversal, the Government contends that the CDA is plainly constitutional under three of our prior decisions: (1) Ginsberg v. New York, 390 U.S. 629 (1968); (2) FCC v. Pacifica Foundation, 438 U.S. 726 (1978); and (3) Renton v. Playtime Theatres, Inc., 475 U.S. 41 (1986). A close look at these cases, however, raises — rather than relieves — doubts concerning the constitutionality of the CDA.

In *Ginsberg*, we upheld the constitutionality of a New York statute that prohibited selling to minors under 17 years of age material that was considered obscene as to them even if not obscene as to adults. We rejected the defendant's broad submission that "the scope of the constitutional freedom of expression secured to a citizen to read or see material concerned with sex cannot be made to depend on whether the citizen is an adult or a minor." In rejecting that contention, we relied not only on the State's independent interest in the well-being of its youth, but also on our consistent recognition of the principle that "the parents' claim to authority in their own household to direct the rearing of their children is basic in the structure of our society."

In four important respects, the statute upheld in *Ginsberg* was narrower than the CDA. First, we noted in *Ginsberg* that "the prohibition against sales to minors does not bar parents who so desire from purchasing the magazines for their children." Under the CDA, by contrast, neither the parents' consent — nor even their participation — in the communication would avoid the application of the statute. Second, the New York statute applied only to commercial transactions, whereas the CDA contains no such limitation. Third, the New York statute cabined its definition of material that is harmful to minors with the requirement that it be "utterly without redeeming social importance for minors." The CDA fails to provide us with any definition of the term "indecent" as used in §223(a)(1) and, importantly, omits any requirement that the "patently offensive" material covered by §223(d) lack serious literary, artistic, political, or scientific value. Fourth, the New York statute defined a minor as a person under the age of 17, whereas the CDA, in applying to all those under 18 years, includes an additional year of those nearest majority.

In *Pacifica*, we upheld a declaratory order of the Federal Communications Commission, holding that the broadcast of a recording of a 12-minute monologue entitled "Filthy Words" that had previously been delivered to a live audience "could have been the subject of administrative sanctions." The Commission had found that the repetitive use of certain words referring to excretory or sexual activities or organs "in an afternoon broadcast when children are in the audience was patently offensive" and concluded that the monologue was indecent "as broadcast." The respondent did not quarrel with the finding that the afternoon broadcast was patently offensive, but contended that it was not "indecent" within the meaning of the relevant statutes because it contained no prurient appeal. After rejecting respondent's statutory arguments, we confronted its two constitutional arguments: (1) that the Commission's construction of its authority to ban indecent speech was so broad that its order had to be set aside even if the broadcast at issue was unprotected; and (2) that since the recording was not obscene, the First Amendment forbade any abridgement of the right to broadcast it on the radio.

In the portion of the lead opinion not joined by Justices Powell and Blackmun, the plurality stated that the First Amendment does not prohibit all governmental regulation that depends on the content of speech. Accordingly, the availability of constitutional protection for a vulgar and offensive monologue that was not obscene depended on the context of the broadcast. Relying on the premise that "of all forms of communication" broadcasting had received the most limited First Amendment protection, the Court concluded that the ease with which children may obtain access to broadcasts, "coupled with the concerns recognized in *Ginsberg*," justified special treatment of indecent broadcasting.

As with the New York statute at issue in *Ginsberg*, there are significant differences between the order upheld in *Pacifica* and the CDA. First, the order in *Pacifica*, issued by an agency that had been regulating radio stations for decades, targeted a specific broadcast that represented a rather dramatic departure from traditional program content in order to designate when—rather than whether—it would be permissible to air such a program in that particular medium. The CDA's broad categorical prohibitions are not limited to particular times and are not dependent on any evaluation by an agency familiar with the unique characteristics of the Internet. Second, unlike the CDA, the Commission's declaratory order was not punitive; we expressly refused to decide whether the indecent broadcast "would justify a criminal prosecution." Finally, the Commission's order applied to a medium which as a matter of history had "received the most limited First Amendment protection," in large part because warnings could not adequately protect the listener from unexpected program content. The Internet, however, has no comparable history. Moreover, the District Court found that the risk of encountering indecent material by accident is remote because a series of affirmative steps is required to access specific material.

In *Renton*, we upheld a zoning ordinance that kept adult movie theatres out of residential neighborhoods. The ordinance was aimed, not at the content of the films shown in the theaters, but rather at the "secondary effects"—such as crime and deteriorating property values—that these theaters fostered: "'It is th[e] secondary effect which these zoning ordinances attempt to avoid, not the dissemination of "offensive" speech.'" According to the Government, the CDA is constitutional because it constitutes a sort of "cyberzoning" on the Internet. But the CDA applies broadly to the entire universe of cyberspace. And the purpose of the CDA is to protect children from the primary effects of "indecent" and "patently offensive" speech, rather than any "secondary" effect of such speech. Thus, the CDA is a content-based blanket restriction on speech, and, as such, cannot be "properly analyzed as a form of time, place, and manner regulation." *See* Boos v. Barry, 485 U.S. 312, 321 (1988) ("Regulations that focus on the direct impact of speech on its audience" are not properly analyzed under *Renton*); Forsyth County v. Nationalist Movement, 505 U.S. 123, 134 (1992) ("Listeners' reaction to speech is not a content-neutral basis for regulation").

These precedents, then, surely do not require us to uphold the CDA and are fully consistent with the application of the most stringent review of its provisions.

V

In Southeastern Promotions, Ltd. v. Conrad, 420 U.S. 546, 557 (1975), we observed that "[e]ach medium of expression [may] present its own problems." Thus, some of our cases have recognized special justifications for regulation of the broadcast media that are not applicable to other speakers. In these cases, the Court relied on the history of extensive government regulation of the broadcast medium, the scarcity of available frequencies at its inception, and its "invasive" nature.

Those factors are not present in cyberspace. Neither before nor after the enactment of the CDA have the vast democratic fora of the Internet been subject to the type of government supervision and regulation that has attended the broadcast industry.[17] Moreover, the Internet is not as "invasive" as radio or television. The District Court specifically found that "[c]ommunications over the Internet do not 'invade' an individual's home or appear on one's computer screen unbidden. Users seldom encounter content 'by accident.'" It also found that "[a]lmost all sexually explicit images are preceded by warnings as to the content," and cited testimony that "'odds are slim' that a user would come across a sexually explicit sight by accident."

We distinguished *Pacifica* in *Sable*, 492 U.S., at 128, on just this basis. In *Sable*, a company engaged in the business of offering sexually oriented prerecorded telephone messages (popularly known as "dial-a-porn") challenged the constitutionality of an amendment to the Communications Act that imposed a blanket prohibition on indecent as well as obscene interstate commercial telephone messages. We held that the statute was constitutional insofar as it applied to obscene messages but invalid as applied to indecent messages. In attempting to justify the complete ban and criminalization of indecent commercial telephone messages, the Government relied on *Pacifica*, arguing that the ban was necessary to prevent children from gaining access to such messages. We agreed that "there is a compelling interest in protecting the physical and psychological well-being of minors" which extended to shielding them from indecent messages that are not obscene by adult standards, but distinguished our "emphatically narrow holding" in *Pacifica* because it did not involve a complete ban and because it involved a different medium of communication. We explained that "the dial-it medium

---

17. When *Pacifica* was decided, given that radio stations were allowed to operate only pursuant to federal license, and that Congress had enacted legislation prohibiting licensees from broadcasting indecent speech, there was a risk that members of the radio audience might infer some sort of official or societal approval of whatever was heard over the radio. No such risk attends messages received through the Internet, which is not supervised by any federal agency.

requires the listener to take affirmative steps to receive the communication." "Placing a telephone call," we continued, "is not the same as turning on a radio and being taken by surprise by an indecent message."

Finally, unlike the conditions that prevailed when Congress first authorized regulation of the broadcast spectrum, the Internet can hardly be considered a "scarce" expressive commodity. It provides relatively unlimited, low-cost capacity for communication of all kinds. The Government estimates that "[a]s many as 40 million people use the Internet today, and that figure is expected to grow to 200 million by 1999." This dynamic, multifaceted category of communication includes not only traditional print and news services, but also audio, video, and still images, as well as interactive, real-time dialogue. Through the use of chat rooms, any person with a phone line can become a town crier with a voice that resonates farther than it could from any soapbox. Through the use of Web pages, mail exploders, and newsgroups, the same individual can become a pamphleteer. As the District Court found, "the content on the Internet is as diverse as human thought." We agree with its conclusion that our cases provide no basis for qualifying the level of First Amendment scrutiny that should be applied to this medium.

Regardless of whether the CDA is so vague that it violates the Fifth Amendment, the many ambiguities concerning the scope of its coverage render it problematic for purposes of the First Amendment. For instance, each of the two parts of the CDA uses a different linguistic form. The first uses the word "indecent" while the second speaks of material that "in context, depicts or describes, in terms patently offensive as measured by contemporary community standards, sexual or excretory activities or organs." Given the absence of a definition of either term, this difference in language will provoke uncertainty among speakers about how the two standards relate to each other and just what they mean. Could a speaker confidently assume that a serious discussion about birth control practices, homosexuality, the First Amendment issues raised by the Appendix to our *Pacifica* opinion, or the consequences of prison rape would not violate the CDA? This uncertainty undermines the likelihood that the CDA has been carefully tailored to the congressional goal of protecting minors from potentially harmful materials.

The vagueness of the CDA is a matter of special concern for two reasons. First, the CDA is a content-based regulation of speech. The vagueness of such a regulation raises special First Amendment concerns because of its obvious chilling effect on free speech. Second, the CDA is a criminal statute. In addition to the opprobrium and stigma of a criminal conviction, the CDA threatens violators with penalties including up to two years in prison for each act of violation. The severity of criminal sanctions may well cause speakers to remain silent rather than communicate even arguably unlawful words, ideas, and images. As a practical matter, this increased deterrent effect, coupled with the "risk of discriminatory enforcement" of vague regulations, poses greater First Amendment concerns than those implicated by the civil regulation reviewed in Denver Area Ed. Telecommunications Consortium, Inc. v. FCC, 518 U.S. 727 (1996).

The Government argues that the statute is no more vague than the obscenity standard this Court established in Miller v. California, 413 U.S. 15 (1973). But that is not so. [Because] the CDA's "patently offensive" standard (and, we assume arguendo, its synonymous "indecent" standard) is one part of the three-prong *Miller* test, the Government reasons, it cannot be unconstitutionally vague. [The] Government's assertion is incorrect as a matter of fact. The second prong of the *Miller* test — the purportedly analogous standard — contains a critical requirement that is omitted from the CDA: that the proscribed material be "specifically defined by the applicable state law." This requirement reduces the vagueness inherent in the open-ended term "patently offensive" as used in the CDA. Moreover, the *Miller* definition is limited to "sexual conduct," whereas the CDA extends also to include (1) "excretory activities" as well as (2) "organs" of both a sexual and excretory nature.

The Government's reasoning is also flawed. Just because a definition including three limitations is not vague, it does not follow that one of those limitations, standing by itself, is not vague. Each of *Miller*'s additional two prongs — (1) that, taken as a whole, the material appeal to the "prurient" interest, and (2) that it "lac[k] serious literary, artistic, political, or scientific value" — critically limits the uncertain sweep of the obscenity definition. The second requirement is particularly important because, unlike the "patently offensive" and "prurient interest" criteria, it is not judged by contemporary community standards. This "societal value" requirement, absent in the CDA, allows appellate courts to impose some limitations and regularity on the definition by setting, as a matter of law, a national floor for socially redeeming value. The Government's contention that courts will be able to give such legal limitations to the CDA's standards is belied by *Miller*'s own rationale for having juries determine whether material is "patently offensive" according to community standards: that such questions are essentially ones of *fact*.

In contrast to *Miller* and our other previous cases, the CDA thus presents a greater threat of censoring speech that, in fact, falls outside the statute's scope. Given the vague contours of the coverage of the statute, it unquestionably silences some speakers whose messages would be entitled to constitutional protection. That danger provides further reason for insisting that the statute not be overly broad. The CDA's burden on protected speech cannot be justified if it could be avoided by a more carefully drafted statute.

We are persuaded that the CDA lacks the precision that the First Amendment requires when a statute regulates the content of speech. In order to deny minors access to potentially harmful speech, the CDA effectively suppresses a large amount of speech that adults have a constitutional right to receive and to address to one another. That burden on adult speech is unacceptable if less restrictive alternatives would be at least as effective in achieving the legitimate purpose that the statute was enacted to serve.

In evaluating the free speech rights of adults, we have made it perfectly clear that "[s]exual expression which is indecent but not obscene is protected by the First Amendment." Indeed, *Pacifica* itself admonished that "the fact that society may find speech offensive is not a sufficient reason for suppressing it."

It is true that we have repeatedly recognized the governmental interest in protecting children from harmful materials. But that interest does not justify an unnecessarily broad suppression of speech addressed to adults. As we have explained, the Government may not "reduc[e] the adult population [to] only what is fit for children." *Denver*, 116 S.Ct., at 2393. "[R]egardless of the strength of the government's interest" in protecting children, "[t]he level of discourse reaching a mailbox simply cannot be limited to that which would be suitable for a sandbox." Bolger v. Youngs Drug Products Corp., 463 U.S. 60, 74-75 (1983).

The District Court was correct to conclude that the CDA effectively resembles the ban on "dial-a-porn" invalidated in *Sable*. In *Sable*, this Court rejected the argument that we should defer to the congressional judgment that nothing less than a total ban would be effective in preventing enterprising young-sters from gaining access to indecent communications. *Sable* thus made clear that the mere fact that a statutory regulation of speech was enacted for the important purpose of protecting children from exposure to sexually explicit material does not foreclose inquiry into its validity. [T]hat inquiry embodies an "over-arching commitment" to make sure that Congress has designed its statute to accomplish its purpose "without imposing an unnecessarily great restriction on speech."

In arguing that the CDA does not so diminish adult communication, the Government relies on the incorrect factual premise that prohibiting a transmis-sion whenever it is known that one of its recipients is a minor would not interfere with adult-to-adult communication. The findings of the District Court make clear that this premise is untenable. Given the size of the potential audience for most messages, in the absence of a viable age verification process, the sender must be charged with knowing that one or more minors will likely view it. Knowledge that, for instance, one or more members of a 100-person chat group will be minor — and therefore that it would be a crime to send the group an indecent message — would surely burden communication among adults.

The District Court found that at the time of trial existing technology did not include any effective method for a sender to prevent minors from obtaining access to its communications on the Internet without also denying access to adults. The Court found no effective way to determine the age of a user who is accessing material through e-mail, mail exploders, newsgroups, or chat rooms. As a practical matter, the Court also found that it would be prohibitively expen-sive for noncommercial — as well as some commercial — speakers who have Web sites to verify that their users are adults. These limitations must inevitably curtail a significant amount of adult communication on the Internet. By contrast, the District Court found that "[d]espite its limitations, currently available user-based software suggests that a reasonably effective method by which parents can pre-vent their children from accessing sexually explicit and other material which par-ents may believe is inappropriate for their children will soon be widely available."

The breadth of the CDA's coverage is wholly unprecedented. Unlike the regulations upheld in *Ginsberg* and *Pacifica*, the scope of the CDA is not limited to commercial speech or commercial entities. Its open-ended prohibitions embrace all nonprofit entities and individuals posting indecent messages or displaying them on their own computers in the presence of minors. The general, undefined terms "indecent" and "patently offensive" cover large amounts of nonpornographic material with serious educational or other value.[18] Moreover, the "community standards" criterion as applied to the Internet means that any communication available to a nation-wide audience will be judged by the standards of the community most likely to be offended by the message. The regulated subject matter includes any of the seven "dirty words" used in the *Pacifica* monologue, the use of which the Government's expert acknowledged could constitute a felony. It may also extend to discussions about prison rape or safe sexual practices, artistic images that include nude subjects, and arguably the card catalogue of the Carnegie Library.

For the purposes of our decision, we need neither accept nor reject the Government's submission that the First Amendment does not forbid a blanket prohibition on all "indecent" and "patently offensive" messages communicated to a 17-year old — no matter how much value the message may contain and regardless of parental approval. It is at least clear that the strength of the Government's interest in protecting minors is not equally strong throughout the coverage of this broad statute. Under the CDA, a parent allowing her 17-year-old to use the family computer to obtain information on the Internet that she, in her parental judgment, deems appropriate could face a lengthy prison term. Similarly, a parent who sent his 17-year-old college freshman information on birth control via e-mail could be incarcerated even though neither he, his child, nor anyone in their home community, found the material "indecent" or "patently offensive," if the college town's community thought otherwise.

The breadth of this content-based restriction of speech imposes an especially heavy burden on the Government to explain why a less restrictive provision would not be as effective as the CDA. It has not done so. The arguments in this Court have referred to possible alternatives such as requiring that indecent material be "tagged" in a way that facilitates parental control of material coming into their homes, making exceptions for messages with artistic or educational value, providing some tolerance for parental choice, and regulating some portions of the Internet — such as commercial web sites — differently than others, such as chat rooms. Particularly in the light of the absence of any detailed findings by the Congress, or even hearings addressing the special problems of the CDA, we are persuaded that the CDA is not narrowly tailored if that requirement has any meaning at all.

In an attempt to curtail the CDA's facial overbreadth, the Government advances three additional arguments for sustaining the Act's affirmative prohibitions: (1) that the CDA is constitutional because it leaves open ample "alternative channels" of communication; (2) that the plain meaning of the Act's "knowledge" and "specific person" requirement significantly restricts its permissible applications; and (3) that the Act's prohibitions are "almost always" limited to material lacking redeeming social value.

---

18. Transmitting obscenity and child pornography, whether via the Internet or other means, is already illegal under federal law for both adults and juveniles. *See* 18 U.S.C. §§1464-1465 (criminalizing obscenity); §2251 (criminalizing child pornography).

The Government first contends that, even though the CDA effectively censors discourse on many of the Internet's modalities — such as chat groups, newsgroups, and mail exploders — it is nonetheless constitutional because it provides a "reasonable opportunity" for speakers to engage in the restricted speech on the World Wide Web. This argument is unpersuasive because the CDA regulates speech on the basis of its content. A "time, place, and manner" analysis is therefore inapplicable. It is thus immaterial whether such speech would be feasible on the Web (which, as the Government's own expert acknowledged, would cost up to $10,000 if the speaker's interests were not accommodated by an existing Web site, not including costs for database management and age verification). The Government's position is equivalent to arguing that a statute could ban leaflets on certain subjects as long as individuals are free to publish books. In invalidating a number of laws that banned leafletting on the streets regardless of their content — we explained that "one is not to have the exercise of his liberty of expression in appropriate places abridged on the plea that it may be exercised in some other place."

The Government also asserts that the "knowledge" requirement of both §§223(a) and (d), especially when coupled with the "specific child" element found in §223(d), saves the CDA from overbreadth. Because both sections prohibit the dissemination of indecent messages only to persons known to be under 18, the Government argues, it does not require transmitters to "refrain from communicating indecent material to adults; they need only refrain from disseminating such materials to persons they know to be under 18."

This argument ignores the fact that most Internet forums — including chat rooms, newsgroups, mail exploders, and the Web — are open to all comers. The Government's assertion that the knowledge requirement somehow protects the communications of adults is therefore untenable. Even the strongest reading of the "specific person" requirement of §223(d) cannot save the statute. It would confer broad powers of censorship, in the form of a "heckler's veto," upon any opponent of indecent speech who might simply log on and inform the would-be discoursers that his 17-year-old child — a "specific person [under] 18 years of age" — would be present.

Finally, we find no textual support for the Government's submission that material having scientific, educational, or other redeeming social value will necessarily fall outside the CDA's "patently offensive" and "indecent" prohibitions.

The Government's three remaining arguments focus on the defenses provided in §223(e)(5). First, relying on the "good faith, reasonable, effective, and appropriate actions" provision, the Government suggests that "tagging" provides a defense that saves the constitutionality of the Act. The suggestion assumes that transmitters may encode their indecent communications in a way that would indicate their contents, thus permitting recipients to block their reception with appropriate software. It is the requirement that the good faith action must be "effective" that makes this defense illusory. The Government recognizes that its proposed screening software does not currently exist. Even if it did, there is no way to know whether a potential recipient will actually block the encoded material. Without the impossible knowledge that every guardian in America is screening for the "tag," the transmitter could not reasonably rely on its action to be "effective."

For its second and third arguments concerning defenses—which we can consider together — the Government relies on the latter half of §223(e)(5), which applies when the transmitter has restricted access by requiring use of a verified credit card or adult identification. Such verification is not only technologically available but actually is used by commercial providers of sexually explicit material. These providers, therefore, would be protected by the defense. Under the findings of the District Court, however, it is not economically feasible for most noncommercial speakers to employ such verification. Accordingly, this defense would not significantly narrow the statute's burden on noncommercial speech. Even with respect to the commercial pornographers that would be protected by the defense, the Government failed to adduce any evidence that these verification techniques actually preclude minors from posing as adults. Given that the risk of criminal sanctions "hovers over each content provider, like the proverbial sword of Damocles," the District Court correctly refused to rely on unproven future technology to save the statute. The Government thus failed to prove that the proffered defense would significantly reduce the heavy burden on adult speech produced by the prohibition on offensive displays.

We agree with the District Court's conclusion that the CDA places an unacceptably heavy burden on protected speech, and that the defenses do not constitute the sort of "narrow tailoring" that will save an otherwise patently invalid unconstitutional provision. In *Sable*, we remarked that the speech restriction at issue there amounted to "'burn[ing] the house to roast the pig.'" The CDA, casting a far darker shadow over free speech, threatens to torch a large segment of the Internet community.

[Appellees] do not challenge the application of the statute to obscene speech, which, they acknowledge, can be banned totally because it enjoys no First Amendment protection. As set forth by the statute, the restriction of "obscene" material enjoys a textual manifestation separate from that for "indecent" material, which we have held unconstitutional. Therefore, we will sever the term "or indecent" from the statute, leaving the rest of §223(a) standing. In no other respect, however, can §223(a) or §223(d) be saved by such a textual surgery.

In this Court, though not in the District Court, the Government asserts that—in addition to its interest in protecting children—its "[e]qually significant" interest in fostering the growth of the Internet provides an independent basis for upholding the constitutionality of the CDA. The Government apparently assumes that the unregulated availability of "indecent" and "patently offensive" material on the Internet is driving countless citizens away from the medium because of the risk of exposing themselves or their children to harmful material.

We find this argument singularly unpersuasive. The dramatic expansion of this new marketplace of ideas contradicts the factual basis of this contention. The record demonstrates that the growth of the Internet has been and continues to be phenomenal. As a matter of constitutional tradition, in the absence of evidence to the contrary, we presume that governmental regulation of the content of speech is more likely to interfere with the free exchange of ideas than to encourage it. The interest in encouraging freedom of expression in a democratic society outweighs any theoretical but unproven benefit of censorship.

For the foregoing reasons, the judgment of the district court is affirmed.

It is so ordered.

Justice O'CONNOR, with whom THE CHIEF JUSTICE joins, concurring in the judgment in part and dissenting in part.

[I] view the Communications Decency Act of 1996 (CDA) as little more than an attempt by Congress to create "adult zones" on the Internet. Our precedent indicates that the creation of such zones can be constitutionally sound. [The] Court has previously sustained such zoning laws, but only if they respect the First Amendment rights of adults and minors. That is to say, a zoning law is valid if (i) it does not unduly restrict adult access to the material; and (ii) minors have no First Amendment right to read or view the banned material. . . . [I]t is possible to construct barriers in cyberspace and use them to screen for identity, making cyberspace more like the physical world and, consequently, more amenable to zoning laws. This transformation of cyberspace is already underway. Internet speakers (users who post material on the Internet) have begun to zone cyberspace itself through the use of "gateway" technology. Such technology requires Internet users to enter information about themselves — perhaps an adult identification number or a credit card number — before they can access certain areas of cyberspace. . . . Gateway technology [is] not available to all Web speakers, and is just now becoming technologically feasible for chat rooms and USENET newsgroups. [Without such technology,] cyberspace still remains largely unzoned — and unzoneable. [Although] the prospects for the eventual zoning of the Internet appear promising, I agree with the Court that we must evaluate the constitutionality of the CDA as it applies to the Internet as it exists today. Given the present state of cyberspace, I agree with the Court that the "display" provision cannot pass muster. . . .

Notes and Questions

1. *The FCC and the Internet.* In March 2004, the Federal Communications Commission moved to crack down on offensive broadcasts. The FCC referred to the use of curse words that it found were indecent. Also, the FCC proposed fines against Howard Stern for his discussion of sexual practices with a couple who were allegedly having sex on the air. Would such communications be illegal on the Internet?

2. *Is the FCC Becoming Irrelevant?* Since the decision in *Reno,* communications technology has continued to advance. For example, satellite radio networks have developed, free of FCC control, and now have millions of subscribers. Following the FCC proposal, Howard Stern left broadcast radio for a satellite station. So, are the FCC and the Court's broadcast decisions (e.g., *Red Lion*) becoming increasingly irrelevant? Does it continue to make sense to distinguish between Internet and broadcast communications?

3. *The Child Online Protection Act.* After *Reno,* Congress enacted the Child Online Protection Act (COPA) in an effort to respond to the *Reno* Court's criticisms of the CDA. COPA made it illegal, "knowingly and with knowledge of the character of the material," to make "any communication for commercial purposes that is available to any minor and that includes any material that is harmful to minors." Congress adapted the three-part *Miller* obscenity test, but adapted it for minors.[19] Although Ashcroft v. American Civil Liberties Union [*Ashcroft I*], 535 U.S. 564 (2002), partially upheld COPA, the law was struck down in American Civil Liberties Union v. Mukasey, 534 F.3d 181 (3d Cir. 2008), *cert. denied,* 129 S.Ct. 1032 (2009). Noting that COPA criminalizes a category of speech that is harmful to minors but that is constitutionally protected for adults, the court applied strict scrutiny. Although the court held that the state has a compelling interest in protecting the physical and psychological well-being of minors, as well as in protecting minors from exposure to harmful material on the Internet, it concluded that COPA was not narrowly tailored to effectuate its purpose. COPA defined the term *minor* so broadly as to encompass "an infant, a five-year old, or a person just shy of age seventeen." The fact that COPA limited liability to communications made for "commercial purposes" was deemed insufficient because liability could also be imposed if a Web site displayed information harmful to minors, even if the publisher does not make a profit from the publication and does not post such information as part of its business, but does accept advertising to help defray the expenses of the site. The court found that blocking and filtering software provided a less restrictive alternative to COPA, and offered a more effective means of restricting children's access to materials harmful to them. The court also upheld the district court's conclusions that the law was unduly vague and suffered from overbreadth.

∾ PROBLEMS ∾

1. *Free Speech, the Internet, and Democracy.* How will the growth of the Internet affect the democratic process? Because a significant percentage of advertising revenue has shifted from the print media to the World Wide Web, a number of newspapers are in financial trouble. Not only have some papers gone into bankruptcy, but also they have been forced to furlough staff and make production cutbacks. Indeed, some newspapers are now published entirely online. What are the ramifications of these changes for democracy? Historically, newspapers have served as a watchdog on government and have engaged in a certain level of investigative journalism. Will those watchdog/investigative functions continue if newspapers disappear? Or will those functions be assumed by online bloggers and newspapers? What do you make of evidence suggesting that, as the Internet has

19. The statute defined "material that is harmful to minors" as a publication that "(A) the average person, applying contemporary community standards, would find, taking the material as a whole and with respect to minors, is designed to appeal to, or is designed to pander to, the prurient interest; (B) depicts, describes, or represents, in a manner patently offensive with respect to minors, an actual or simulated sexual act or sexual contact, an actual or simulated normal or perverted sexual act, or a lewd exhibition of the genitals or postpubescent female breast; and (C) taken as a whole, lacks serious literary, artistic, political, or scientific value for minors."

flourished, individuals are increasingly inclined to express their complaints and gripes on the Web? *See* "Neighborhood Gripes Hit Wire: Site Lets You Air Complaints," *The Courier-Journal*, A-9, c. 1-3 (June 28, 2008).

2. *Gatekeepers.* Historically, most advanced forms of communication have involved so-called "gatekeepers" — individuals (e.g., producers, editors, and reporters) who exercise editorial control over the information that gets published or aired. With the Internet, individuals can more easily communicate with one another without having to go through editors, producers, or reporters. Indeed, ordinary people have a variety of methods for communicating, including blogs, listserves, Web sites, and other high-tech methods. Is this good?

3. *Private Actors and Internet Communications.* As Internet and Web-based communications have assumed increased importance in society, private actors (particularly Internet service providers) have assumed increasing importance. Indeed, in some instances, internet service providers (ISPs) have chosen to delete controversial content from the Web. *See* Anick Jesdanun, "Free Speech Doesn't Always Extend to Web," *The Courier-Journal*, D-7, col. 2-6 (July 13, 2008). For example, Facebook has been asked to remove Holocaust-denial groups from its service. Is this good?

4. *More on the International Treaty Regulating the Internet.* In light of *Reno*, do you have further thoughts about the type of speech you might be able to agree to ban from the Internet? What language could you agree to in the treaty?

L. FREEDOM OF ASSOCIATION

Although the First Amendment does not explicitly protect the right to associate, it does protect activities that are associational in nature (e.g., the right to peacefully assemble). In a number of cases, the Court has struggled to define the extent to which the First Amendment includes the right not only to associate but also to "disassociate."

1. The Right to Associate

The Constitution protects freedom of speech, which is inevitably more effective when groups of people can band together and speak with a common voice. In some instances, the gathering of individuals results in increased resources.

NAACP v. Alabama
357 U.S. 449 (1958)

Mr. Justice HARLAN delivered the opinion of the Court.

[Alabama] has a statute similar to those of many other States which requires a foreign corporation, except as exempted, to qualify before doing business by filing its corporate charter with the Secretary of State and designating a place of business and an agent to receive service of process. [The] National Association for the Advancement of Colored People is a nonprofit membership corporation organized under the laws of New York. Its purposes [are] those indicated by its name,[20] and it operates through chartered affiliates. . . .

In 1956 the Attorney General of Alabama brought [suit to] enjoin the Association from conducting further activities within, and to oust it from, the State [for violating the Alabama qualification law]. The State then moved [for] production [of] the Association's records and papers, including [the] names and addresses of all Alabama "members" and "agents" of the Association. [T]he court ordered the production of a substantial part of the requested records, including the membership lists. [When the NAACP refused to produce the lists, the court held it in civil contempt and imposed a fine of $10,000, increasable to $100,000 for noncompliance.]

[Petitioner] urges that it is constitutionally entitled to resist official inquiry into its membership lists, and that it may assert, on behalf of its members, a right personal to them to be protected from compelled disclosure [of] their affiliation with the Association. [Petitioner] argues that [the] effect of compelled disclosure of the membership lists will be to abridge the rights of its rank-and-file members to engage in lawful association in support of their common beliefs. . . .

Effective advocacy of both public and private points of view, particularly controversial ones, is undeniably enhanced by group association, as this Court has more than once recognized by remarking upon the close nexus between the freedoms of speech and assembly. It is beyond debate that freedom to engage in association for the advancement of beliefs and ideas is an inseparable aspect of the "liberty" assured by the Due Process Clause of the Fourteenth Amendment, which embraces freedom of speech. *See* Gitlow v. New York, 268 U.S. 652. Of course, it is immaterial whether the beliefs sought to be advanced by association pertain to political, economic, religious or cultural matters, and state action which may have the effect of curtailing the freedom to associate is subject to the closest scrutiny.

The fact that Alabama [has] taken no direct action to restrict the right of petitioner's members to associate freely, does not end inquiry into the effect of the production order. In the domain of these indispensable liberties, whether of speech, press, or association, [abridgement] of such rights, even though unintended, may inevitably follow from varied forms of governmental action. . . . Statutes imposing taxes upon rather than prohibiting particular activity have been struck down when perceived to have the consequence of unduly curtailing the liberty of freedom of press assured under the Fourteenth Amendment.

[This] Court has recognized the vital relationship between freedom to associate and privacy in one's associations. . . . Inviolability of privacy in group association may in many circumstances be indispensable to preservation of freedom of association, particularly where a group espouses dissident beliefs.

---

20. The Certificate of Incorporation [provides] that its "[principal objects] are voluntarily to promote equality of rights and eradicate caste or race prejudice among the citizens of the United States; to advance the interest of colored citizens; to secure for them impartial suffrage; and to increase their opportunities for securing justice in the courts, education for their children, employment according to their ability, and complete equality before the law."

We think that the production order [must] be regarded as entailing the likelihood of a substantial restraint upon the exercise by petitioner's members of their right to freedom of association. Petitioner [has shown that] on past occasions revelation of the identity of its rank-and-file members has exposed these members to economic reprisal, loss of employment, threat of physical coercion, and other manifestations of public hostility. Under these circumstances, [compelled] disclosure of petitioner's Alabama membership is likely to affect adversely the ability of petitioner and its members to pursue their collective effort to foster beliefs which they admittedly have the right to advocate, in that it may induce members to withdraw from the Association and dissuade others from joining it because of fear of exposure of their beliefs shown through their associations and of the consequences of this exposure.

It is not sufficient to answer [that] whatever repressive effect compulsory disclosure of names of petitioner's members may have upon participation by Alabama citizens in petitioner's activities follows not from state action but from private community pressures. The crucial factor is the interplay of governmental and private action, for it is only after the initial exertion of state power represented by the production order that private action takes hold.

We turn to the final question whether Alabama has demonstrated an interest in obtaining the disclosures it seeks from petitioner which is sufficient to justify the deterrent effect which we have concluded these disclosures may well have on the free exercise by petitioner's members of their constitutionally protected right of association. Such a "subordinating interest of the State must be compelling," Sweezy v. New Hampshire, 354 U.S. 234, 265 (concurring opinion). [The State's purpose in] requesting the membership lists [was] to determine whether petitioner was conducting intrastate business in violation of the Alabama foreign corporation registration statute. [P]etitioner (1) has admitted its presence and conduct of activities in Alabama since 1918; (2) has offered to comply in all respects with the state qualification statute[;] and (3) has apparently complied satisfactorily with the production order, except for the membership lists, by furnishing the Attorney General with varied business records, its charter and statement of purposes, the names of all of its directors and officers, and with the total number of its Alabama members and the amount of their dues. [W]hatever interest the State may have in obtaining names of ordinary members has not been shown to be sufficient to overcome petitioner's constitutional objections to the production order.

[We] hold that the immunity from state scrutiny of membership lists which the Association claims on behalf of its members is here so related to the right of the members to pursue their lawful private interests privately and to associate freely with others in so doing as to come within the protection of the Fourteenth Amendment. [W]e conclude that Alabama has fallen short of showing a controlling justification for the deterrent effect on the free enjoyment of the right to associate which disclosure of membership lists is likely to have. Accordingly, the judgment of civil contempt and the $100,000 fine which resulted from petitioner's refusal to comply with the production order in this respect must fall.

[For] the reasons stated, the judgment of the Supreme Court of Alabama must be reversed and the case remanded for proceedings not inconsistent with this opinion.

Reversed.

Notes

1. *Boycotts and Civil Liability.* In NAACP v. Claiborne Hardware Co., 458 U.S. 886 (1982), after the NAACP began a nonviolent boycott of white merchants in Mississippi, the merchants sought an injunction against future boycotts and damages for financial losses. The Court held that "encouragement to boycott" constitutes protected speech under the First and Fourteenth Amendments. Although the Court recognized that those who engaged in violent activity could be held liable, the state could not hold nonviolent protestors liable merely because of their association with those who engaged in violence.

2. *House Un-American Activities Committee.* In Barenblatt v. United States, 360 U.S. 109 (1959), during an inquiry concerning alleged Communist infiltration into the field of education by a subcommittee of the House Un-American Activities Committee, the petitioner was charged with, and ultimately convicted of, *inter alia*, refusing to answer questions regarding his membership in the Community Party. The refusals were based on his privilege against self-incrimination. The Court rejected Barenblatt's First Amendment freedom of association, claiming: "[First] Amendment rights [always] involve a balancing by the courts of the competing private and public interests at stake. [T]his Court has recognized the close nexus between the Communist Party and violent overthrow of government. [T]he balance between the individual and the governmental interests here at stake must be struck in favor of the latter, and that therefore the provisions of the First Amendment have not been offended." Justice Black dissented: "[I] cannot agree [that] this Nation's security hangs upon its power to punish people because of what they think, speak or write about, or because of those with whom they associate for political purposes. [M]embers of the [Communist Party who] commit acts in violation of valid laws can be prosecuted."

3. *Fusion Candidates.* Timmons v. Twin Cities Area New Party, 520 U.S. 351 (1997), involved a Minnesota law that prohibited "fusion" candidates — candidates who appear on the ballot as the candidate of more than one party. The Court concluded that a ban on "fusion candidates" did not violate the right to associate: "[T]he New Party and its members [can] endorse, support, or vote for anyone they like. The laws [are] silent on parties' internal structure, governance, and policy-making. Instead, these provisions reduce the universe of potential candidates who may appear on the ballot as the Party's nominee only by ruling out those few individuals who both have already agreed to be another party's candidate and [who] prefer that other party. [T]he burdens Minnesota imposes on the Party's First and Fourteenth Amendment associational rights — though not trivial — are not severe. [States] certainly have an interest in protecting the integrity, fairness, and efficiency of their ballots and election processes as means for

electing public officials. [T]he States' interest permits them to enact reasonable election regulations that may, in practice, favor the traditional two-party system, and that temper the destabilizing effects of party-splintering and excessive factionalism. . . ." Justice Stevens dissented: "[Minnesota] argues that the statutory restriction on the New Party's right to nominate the candidate of its choice is justified by the State's interests in avoiding voter confusion, preventing ballot clutter and manipulation, encouraging candidate competition, and minimizing intraparty factionalism. None of these rationales can support the fusion ban because the State has failed to explain how the ban actually serves the asserted interests."

4. *Closed Primaries.* In Clingman v. Beaver, 544 U.S. 622 (2005), the Court upheld a state's decision to adopt a "semiclosed" primary system under which only a party's members and independents may vote in party primaries. The Court rejected freedom of association claims.

∼ PROBLEMS ∼

1. NAACP *and the KKK.* How far does the *NAACP* ruling extend? After this decision, do all groups have the right to refuse to submit their membership lists to the government, or does the ruling apply to only persecuted groups? May the City of Louisville require unincorporated associations like the Ku Klux Klan to file their membership roster with the city? Would it matter that the KKK claims that its members have been persecuted? What if the city could show that KKK members have engaged in acts of unlawful intimidation and violence? *See* People of State of New York ex rel. Bryant v. Zimmerman, 278 U.S. 63 (1928).

2. *More on the International Treaty Regulating the Internet.* In some countries, governments have the right to ban political parties that they regard as "subversive" or "dangerous." They also have the right to ban other groups. For example, in Germany and France, there are limitations on the Church of Scientology. Delegates from these countries have argued that banned political parties and associations should be prohibited from communicating on the Internet, and that this prohibition should be enforceable through fines and other criminal sanctions. Delegates from these countries would like the proposed treaty to contain language allowing them to extradite members of banned organizations who communicate on the Internet in violation of the treaty. Can you agree to language authorizing the ban, the sanctions, and the extradition? Should you do so? Suppose that the foreign government attempts to "ban" a political party that is based primarily in the United States?

Roberts v. United States Jaycees
468 U.S. 609 (1984)

Justice BRENNAN delivered the opinion of the Court.

This case requires us to address a conflict between a State's efforts to eliminate gender-based discrimination against its citizens and the constitutional freedom of association asserted by members of a private organization. . . .

I

The United States Jaycees (Jaycees), founded in 1920 as the Junior Chamber of Commerce, is a nonprofit membership corporation, incorporated in Missouri with national headquarters in Tulsa, Okla. The objective of the Jaycees, as set out in its bylaws, is to pursue

> such educational and charitable purposes as will promote and foster the growth and development of young men's civic organizations in the United States, designed to inculcate in the individual membership of such organization a spirit of genuine Americanism and civic interest, and as a supplementary education institution to provide them with opportunity for personal development and achievement and an avenue for intelligent participation by young men in the affairs of their community, state and nation, and to develop true friendship and understanding among young men of all nations.

The organization's bylaws establish seven classes of membership, including individual or regular members, associate individual members, and local chapters. Regular membership is limited to young men between the ages of 18 and 35, while associate membership is available to individuals or groups ineligible for regular membership, principally women and older men. An associate member, whose dues are somewhat lower than those charged regular members, may not vote, hold local or national office, or participate in certain leadership training and awards programs. [U]ltimate policymaking authority [rests] with an annual national convention, consisting of delegates from each local chapter, with a national president and board of directors. At the time of trial[,] the Jaycees had approximately 295,000 members in 7,400 local chapters affiliated with 51 state organizations. There [were] 11,915 associate members. The national organization's executive vice president estimated at trial that women associate members make up about two percent of the Jaycees' total membership.

New members are recruited to the Jaycees through the local chapters, although the state and national organizations [are] actively involved in recruitment through a variety of promotional activities. A new regular member pays an initial fee followed by annual dues; in exchange, he is entitled to participate in all of the activities of the local, state, and national organizations. The national headquarters employs a staff to develop "program kits" for use by local chapters that are designed to enhance individual development, community development, and members' management skills. These materials include courses in public speaking and personal finances as well as community programs related to charity, sports, and public health. The national office also makes available to members a range of personal products, including travel accessories, casual wear, pins, awards, and other gifts. The programs, products, and other activities of the organization are all regularly featured in publications made available to the membership, including a magazine entitled "Future."

In 1974 and 1975, respectively, the Minneapolis and St. Paul chapters of the Jaycees began admitting women as regular members. Currently, the memberships and boards of directors of both chapters include a substantial proportion of women. [In] 1978, the president of the national organization advised both chapters that a motion to revoke their charters would be considered at a forthcoming meeting of the national board of directors. . . . Shortly after receiving this notification, members of both chapters filed charges of discrimination with the Minnesota Department of Human Rights. The complaints alleged that the exclusion of women from full membership required by the national [organization] violated the Minnesota Human Rights Act (Act), which provides in part:

> It is an unfair discriminatory practice:
>   To deny any person the full and equal enjoyment of the goods, services, facilities, privileges, advantages, and accommodations of a place of public accommodation because of race, color, creed, religion, disability, national origin or sex. Minn. Stat. §363.03, subd. 3 (1982).

The term "place of public accommodation" is defined in the Act as "a business, accommodation, refreshment, entertainment, recreation, or transportation facility of any kind, whether licensed or not, whose goods, services, facilities, privileges, advantages or accommodations are extended, offered, sold, or otherwise made available to the public." §363.01, subd. 18.

[A] state hearing examiner [concluded] that the Jaycees organization is a "place of public accommodation" within the Act and that it had engaged in an unfair discriminatory practice by excluding women from regular membership. He ordered the national organization to cease and desist from discriminating against any member or applicant [on] on the basis of sex and from imposing sanctions on any Minnesota affiliate for admitting women. [In a separate proceeding[,] the Eighth Circuit held that application of the Minnesota statute to the Jaycees' membership policies would unconstitutionally interfere with the Jaycees' First Amendment right to freedom of association.]

II

Our decisions have referred to constitutionally protected "freedom of association" in two distinct senses. In one line of decisions, the Court has concluded that choices to enter into and maintain certain intimate human relationships must be secured against undue intrusion by the State because of the role of such relationships in safeguarding the individual freedom that is central to our constitutional scheme. In this respect, freedom of association receives protection as a fundamental element of personal liberty. In another set of decisions, the Court has recognized a right to associate for the purpose of engaging in those activities protected by the First Amendment — speech, assembly, petition for the redress of grievances, and the exercise of religion. The Constitution guarantees freedom of association of this kind as an indispensable means of preserving other individual liberties.

The intrinsic and instrumental features of constitutionally protected association may, of course, coincide. In particular, when the State interferes with individuals' selection of those with whom they wish to join in a common endeavor, freedom of association in both of its forms may be implicated. The Jaycees contend that this is such a case. Still, the nature and degree of constitutional protection afforded freedom of association may vary depending on the extent to which one or the other aspect of the constitutionally protected liberty is at stake in a given case. We therefore find it useful to consider separately the effect of applying the Minnesota statute to the Jaycees on what could be called its members' freedom of intimate association and their freedom of expressive association.

The Court has long recognized that, because the Bill of Rights is designed to secure individual liberty, it must afford the formation and preservation of certain kinds of highly personal relationships a substantial measure of sanctuary from unjustified interference by the State. *E.g.,* Meyer v. Nebraska, 262 U.S. 390 (1923). Without precisely identifying every consideration that may underlie this type of constitutional protection, we have noted that certain kinds of personal bonds have played a critical role in the culture and traditions of the Nation by cultivating and transmitting shared ideals and beliefs; they thereby foster diversity and act as critical buffers between the individual and the power of the State. *See, e.g.,* Moore v. East Cleveland, 431 U.S. 494 (1977) (plurality opinion). Moreover, the constitutional shelter afforded such relationships reflects the realization that individuals draw much of their emotional enrichment from close ties with others. Protecting these relationships from unwarranted state interference therefore safeguards the ability independently to define one's identity that is central to any concept of liberty.

The personal affiliations that exemplify these considerations, and that therefore suggest some relevant limitations on the relationships that might be entitled to this sort of constitutional protection, are those that attend the creation and sustenance of a family — marriage, *e.g.,* Zablocki v. Redhail, *supra*; childbirth, *e.g.,* Carey v. Population Services International, [431 U.S. 678]; the raising and education of children, *e.g.,* Smith v. Organization of Foster Families, [431 U.S. 816 (1977)]; and cohabitation with one's relatives, *e.g.,* Moore v. East Cleveland, *supra.* Family relationships, by their nature, involve deep attachments and commitments to the necessarily few other individuals with whom one shares not only a special community of thoughts, experiences, and beliefs but also distinctively personal aspects of one's life. Among other things, therefore, they are distinguished by such attributes as relative smallness, a high degree of selectivity in decisions to begin and maintain the affiliation, and seclusion from others in critical aspects of the relationship. As a general matter, only relationships with these sorts of qualities are likely to reflect the considerations that have led to an understanding of freedom of association as an intrinsic element of personal liberty. Conversely, an association lacking these qualities — such as a large business enterprise — seems remote from the concerns giving rise to this constitutional protection. Accordingly, the Constitution undoubtedly imposes constraints on the State's power to control the selection of one's spouse that would not apply to regulations affecting the choice of one's fellow employees.

Between these poles [lies] a broad range of human relationships that may make greater or lesser claims to constitutional protection from particular incursions by the State. Determining the limits of state authority over an individual's freedom to enter into a particular association therefore unavoidably entails a careful assessment of where that relationship's objective characteristics locate it on a spectrum from the most intimate to the most attenuated of personal attachments. [F]actors that may be relevant include size, purpose, policies, selectivity, congeniality, and other characteristics that in a particular case may be pertinent. [S]everal features of the Jaycees clearly place the organization outside of the category of relationships worthy of this kind of constitutional protection.

[T]he local chapters of the Jaycees are large and basically unselective groups. At the time of [the] hearing, the Minneapolis chapter had approximately 430 members, while the St. Paul chapter had about 400. Apart from age and sex, neither the national organization nor the local chapters employ any criteria for judging applicants for membership, and new members are routinely recruited and admitted with no inquiry into their backgrounds. [A] local officer [could] recall no instance in which an applicant had been denied membership on any basis other than age or sex. Furthermore, despite their inability to vote, hold office, or receive certain awards, women affiliated with the Jaycees attend various meetings, participate in selected projects, and engage in many of the organization's social functions. Indeed, numerous non-members of both genders regularly participate in a substantial portion of activities central to the decision of many members to associate with one another, including many of the organization's various community programs, awards ceremonies, and recruitment meetings. . . . In short, the local chapters of the Jaycees are neither small nor selective. Moreover, much of the activity central to the formation and maintenance of the association involves the participation of strangers to that relationship. Accordingly, we conclude that the Jaycees chapters lack the distinctive characteristics that might afford constitutional protection to the decision of its members to exclude women. . . .

An individual's freedom to speak, to worship, and to petition the government for the redress of grievances could not be vigorously protected from interference by the State unless a correlative freedom to engage in group effort toward those ends were not also guaranteed. According protection to collective effort on behalf of shared goals is especially important in preserving political and cultural diversity and in shielding dissident expression from suppression by the majority. *See, e.g.,* NAACP v. Button, 371 U.S. 415 (1963). Consequently, we have long understood as implicit in the right to engage in activities protected by the First Amendment a corresponding right to associate with others in pursuit of a wide variety of political, social, economic, educational, religious, and cultural ends. In view of the various protected activities in which the Jaycees engages, that right is plainly implicated in this case.

Government actions that may unconstitutionally infringe upon this freedom can take a number of forms. [G]overnment may seek to impose penalties or withhold benefits from individuals because of their membership in a disfavored group, it may attempt to require disclosure of the fact of membership in a group seeking anonymity, and it may try to interfere with the internal organization or affairs of the group. By requiring the Jaycees to admit women as full voting members, the Minnesota Act works an infringement of the last type. There can be no

clearer example of an intrusion into the internal structure or affairs of an association than a regulation that forces the group to accept members it does not
desire. Such a regulation may impair the ability of the original members to
express only those views that brought them together. Freedom of association
therefore plainly presupposes a freedom not to associate. *See* Abood v. Detroit
Board of Education, 431 U.S., at 234-235.

The right to associate for expressive purposes is not, however, absolute.
Infringements on that right may be justified by regulations adopted to serve compelling state interests, unrelated to the suppression of ideas, that cannot be
achieved through means significantly less restrictive of associational freedoms.
We are persuaded that Minnesota's compelling interest in eradicating discrimination against its female citizens justifies the impact that application of the statute to the Jaycees may have on the male members' associational freedoms.

On its face, the Minnesota Act does not aim at the suppression of speech,
does not distinguish between prohibited and permitted activity on the basis of
viewpoint, and does not license enforcement authorities to administer the statute
on the basis of such constitutionally impermissible criteria. Nor does the Jaycees
contend that the Act has been applied in this case for the purpose of hampering
the organization's ability to express its views. Instead, [the] Act reflects the State's
strong historical commitment to eliminating discrimination and assuring its citizens equal access to publicly available goods and services. That goal, which is
unrelated to the suppression of expression, plainly serves compelling state interests of the highest order.

The Minnesota Human Rights Act [is] an example of public accommodations laws that were adopted by some States beginning a decade before enactment of [the federal] Civil Rights Act of 1875. [By] prohibiting gender
discrimination in places of public accommodation, the Minnesota Act protects
the State's citizenry from a number of serious social and personal harms. [D]is-
crimination based on archaic and overbroad assumptions about the relative
needs and capacities of the sexes forces individuals to labor under stereotypical
notions that often bear no relationship to their actual abilities. It thereby both
deprives persons of their individual dignity and denies society the benefits of
wide participation in political, economic, and cultural life. These concerns are
strongly implicated with respect to gender discrimination in the allocation of
publicly available goods and services. Thus, in upholding Title II of the Civil
Rights Act of 1964, which forbids race discrimination in public accommodations,
we emphasized that its "fundamental object [was] to vindicate 'the deprivation of
personal dignity that surely accompanies denials of equal access to public establishments.'" Heart of Atlanta Motel, Inc. v. United States, 379 U.S. 241 (1964).
That stigmatizing injury, and the denial of equal opportunities that accompanies
it, is surely felt as strongly by persons suffering discrimination on the basis of their
sex as by those treated differently because of their race.

Nor is the state interest in assuring equal access limited to the provision of
purely tangible goods and services. A State enjoys broad authority to create rights
of public access on behalf of its citizens. Like many States and municipalities,
Minnesota has adopted a functional definition of public accommodations that

reaches various forms of public, quasi-commercial conduct. This expansive definition reflects a recognition of the changing nature of the American economy and of the importance, both to the individual and to society, of removing the barriers to economic advancement and political and social integration that have historically plagued certain disadvantaged groups, including women. Thus, in explaining its conclusion that the Jaycees local chapters are "place[s] of public accommodations" within the meaning of the Act, the Minnesota court noted the various commercial programs and benefits offered to members and stated that "[l]eadership skills are 'goods,' [and] business contacts and employment promotions are 'privileges' and 'advantages.' . . ." Assuring women equal access to such goods, privileges, and advantages clearly furthers compelling state interests.

In applying the Act to the Jaycees, the State has advanced those interests through the least restrictive means of achieving its ends. Indeed, the Jaycees has failed to demonstrate that the Act imposes any serious burdens on the male members' freedom of expressive association. To be sure, [a] "not insubstantial part" of the Jaycees' activities constitutes protected expression on political, economic, cultural, and social affairs. Over the years, the national and local levels of the organization have taken public positions on a number of diverse issues, and members of the Jaycees regularly engage in a variety of civic, charitable, lobbying, fundraising, and other activities worthy of constitutional protection under the First Amendment. There is, however, no basis [for] concluding that admission of women as full voting members will impede the organization's ability to engage in these protected activities or to disseminate its preferred views. The Act requires no change in the Jaycees' creed of promoting the interests of young men, and it imposes no restrictions on the organization's ability to exclude individuals with ideologies or philosophies different from those of its existing members. Moreover, the Jaycees already invites women to share the group's views and philosophy and to participate in much of its training and community activities. Accordingly, any claim that admission of women as full voting members will impair a symbolic message conveyed by the very fact that women are not permitted to vote is attenuated at best.

While acknowledging that "the specific content of most of the resolutions adopted over the years by the Jaycees has nothing to do with sex," the Court of Appeals nonetheless entertained the hypothesis that women members might have a different view or agenda with respect to these matters so that, if they are allowed to vote, "some change in the Jaycees' philosophical cast can reasonably be expected." It is similarly arguable that, insofar as the Jaycees is organized to promote the views of young men whatever those views happen to be, admission of women as voting members will change the message communicated by the group's speech because of the gender-based assumptions of the audience. Neither supposition [is] supported by the record. In claiming that women might have a different attitude about such issues as the federal budget, school prayer, voting rights, and foreign relations, or that the organization's public positions would have a different effect if the group were not "a purely young men's association," the Jaycees relies solely on unsupported generalizations about the relative interests and perspectives of men and women. Although such generalizations may or may not have a statistical basis in fact[,] we have repeatedly condemned legal decisionmaking that relies uncritically on such assumptions. In the absence of a showing far more substantial than that attempted by the Jaycees, we decline to indulge in the sexual stereotyping that underlies appellee's contention that, by allowing women to vote, application of the Minnesota Act will change the content or impact of the organization's speech.

In any event, even if enforcement of the Act causes some incidental abridgment of the Jaycees' protected speech, that effect is no greater than is necessary to accomplish the State's legitimate purposes. [A]cts of invidious discrimination in the distribution of publicly available goods, services, and other advantages cause unique evils that government has a compelling interest to prevent — wholly apart from the point of view such conduct may transmit. Accordingly, like violence or other types of potentially expressive activities that produce special harms distinct from their communicative impact, such practices are entitled to no constitutional protection. In prohibiting such practices, the Minnesota Act therefore "responds precisely to the substantive problem which legitimately concerns" the State and abridges no more speech or associational freedom than is necessary to accomplish that purpose.

[The] judgment of the Court of Appeals is
Reversed.

Justice O'CONNOR, concurring in part and concurring in the judgment.

[A]n association engaged exclusively in protected expression enjoys First Amendment protection of both the content of its message and the choice of its members. . . . Protection of the association's right to define its membership derives from the recognition that the formation of an expressive association is the creation of a voice, and the selection of members is the definition of that voice. . . . A ban on specific group voices on public affairs violates the most basic guarantee of the First Amendment — that citizens, not the government, control the content of public discussion. . . . On the other hand, there is only minimal constitutional protection of the freedom of commercial association. . . . While the Court has acknowledged a First Amendment right to engage in nondeceptive commercial advertising, governmental regulation of the commercial recruitment of new members, stockholders, customers, or employees is valid if rationally related to the government's ends.

Many associations cannot readily be described as purely expressive or purely commercial. No association is likely ever to be exclusively engaged in expressive activities. . . . And innumerable commercial associations also engage in some incidental protected speech or advocacy. The standard for deciding just how much of an association's involvement in commercial activity is enough to suspend the association's First Amendment right to control its membership cannot, therefore, be articulated with simple precision. . . .

[A]n association should be characterized as commercial, and therefore subject to rationally related state regulation of its membership and other associational activities, when [the] association's activities are not predominantly of the type protected by the First Amendment. . . . An association must choose its market. Once it enters the marketplace of commerce in any substantial degree it loses the complete control over its membership that it would otherwise enjoy if it confined its affairs to the marketplace of ideas. . . . The purposes of an association, and the purposes of its members in adhering to it, are doubtless relevant in determining whether the association is primarily engaged in protected expression. Lawyering to advance social goals may be speech, but ordinary commercial law practice is not. . . .

[T]he Jaycees — otherwise known as the Junior Chamber of Commerce — is, first and foremost, an organization that, at both the national and local levels, promotes and practices the art of solicitation and management. The organization claims that the training it offers its members gives them an advantage in business, and business firms [sometimes] pay the dues [for] their employees. . . . Recruitment and selling are commercial activities, even when conducted for training rather than for profit. The "not insubstantial" volume of protected Jaycees activity [is] simply not enough to preclude state regulation of the Jaycees' commercial activities. The State of Minnesota has a legitimate interest in ensuring nondiscriminatory access to the commercial opportunity presented by membership in the Jaycees. [The] Jaycees may not claim constitutional immunity [by] seeking to exercise their First Amendment rights through this commercial organization.

Note: More on Nondiscrimination Ordinances

New York State Club Association, Inc. v. City of New York, 487 U.S. 1 (1988), involved a law of the City of New York that prohibited discrimination in any "place of public accommodation, resort or amusement" On the basis of race, creed, color, national origin or sex. In upholding the law, the Court stated:

> [T]he City has a compelling interest in providing [all] persons, regardless of race, creed, color, national origin or sex, [a] fair and equal opportunity to participate in the business and professional life of the city. One barrier to the advancement of women and minorities is the discriminatory practices of certain membership organizations where business deals are often made and personal contacts valuable for business purposes, employment and professional advancement are formed. While such organizations may avowedly be organized for social, cultural, civic or educational purposes, and while many perform valuable services to the community, the commercial nature of some of the activities occurring therein and the prejudicial impact of these activities on business, professional and employment opportunities of minorities and women cannot be ignored.

∾ PROBLEMS ∾

1. *Wendy Hills Political Club.* The Wendy Hills Political Club (WHPC) is a group that has come together to advocate on behalf of political causes (specifically, affirmative action) and to support political candidates who endorse the WHPC's position on those issues. The WHPC discriminates on the basis of race (on the theory that whites oppose affirmative action) even though some whites

tend to be supportive of affirmative action. May the City of Wendy Hills prohibit the WHPC from discriminating on the basis of race or sex? Does it matter whether the WHPC is successful or unsuccessful in its advocacy? For example, suppose that the WHPC holds a "preprimary" prior to the Democratic primary. The club unites behind the candidate who wins the "preprimary," and that candidate always wins the primary.

2. *More on Wendy Hills.* Would you view the WHPC differently if it were anti-affirmative action and its members were white and excluded blacks (on the theory that blacks favor affirmative action)?

3. *More on the International Treaty Regulating the Internet.* Suppose that some delegates to the convention demand "equal treatment for women." They propose that the Internet communications of any group (political or otherwise) be banned unless the group certifies (to a new international board) to two things: 1) it does not discriminate on the basis of sex, and 2) it has taken affirmative steps to include women in its organization, including as officers and directors. They also propose that criminal sanctions be imposed on any group that makes an Internet communication without obtaining the required certification. Can you agree to such a board and such a ban? What type of language might you be able to agree to?

Holder v. Humanitarian Law Project

130 S.Ct. 2705 (2010)

Chief Justice ROBERTS delivered the opinion of the Court.

Congress has prohibited the provision of "material support or resources" to certain foreign organizations that engage in terrorist activity. 18 U.S.C. §2339B(a)(1). That prohibition is based on a finding that the specified organizations "are so tainted by their criminal conduct that any contribution to such an organization facilitates that conduct." The plaintiffs in this litigation seek to provide support to two such organizations. Plaintiffs claim that they seek to facilitate only the lawful, nonviolent purposes of those groups, and that applying the material-support law to prevent them from doing so violates the Constitution. In particular, they claim that the statute is too vague, in violation of the Fifth Amendment, and that it infringes their rights to freedom of speech and association, in violation of the First Amendment. We conclude that the material-support statute is constitutional as applied to the particular activities plaintiffs have told us they wish to pursue. We do not, however, address the resolution of more difficult cases that may arise under the statute in the future. [The Court's analysis rejecting the vagueness claim is omitted.]

V

A

We next consider whether the material-support statute, as applied to plaintiffs, violates the freedom of speech guaranteed by the First Amendment. Both plaintiffs and the Government take extreme positions on this question. Plaintiffs claim that Congress has banned their "pure political speech." It has not. Under the material-support statute, plaintiffs may say anything they wish on any topic. [They] may advocate before the United Nations. [Section] 2339B also "does not prevent [plaintiffs] from becoming members of the PKK [Kurdistan Workers' Party] and LTTE [Liberation Tigers of Tamil Eelam] or impose any sanction on them for doing so." Congress has not, therefore, sought to suppress ideas or opinions in the form of "pure political speech." Rather, Congress has prohibited "material support," which most often does not take the form of speech at all. And when it does, the statute is carefully drawn to cover only a narrow category of speech to, under the direction of, or in coordination with foreign groups that the speaker knows to be foreign terrorist organizations.

For its part, the Government takes the foregoing too far, claiming that the only thing truly at issue in this litigation is conduct, not speech. Section 2339B is directed at the fact of plaintiffs' interaction with the PKK and LTTE, the Government contends, and only incidentally burdens their expression. The Government argues that the proper standard of review is therefore the one set out in United States v. O'Brien, 391 U.S. 367 (1968). [O'Brien] does not provide the applicable standard for reviewing a content-based regulation of speech, and §2339B regulates speech on the basis of its content. Plaintiffs want to speak to the PKK and the LTTE, and whether they may do so under §2339B depends on what they say. If plaintiffs' speech to those groups imparts a "specific skill" or communicates advice derived from "specialized knowledge" — for example, training on the use of international law or advice on petitioning the United Nations — then it is barred. On the other hand, plaintiffs' speech is not barred if it imparts only general or unspecialized knowledge.

The Government argues that §2339B should nonetheless receive intermediate scrutiny because it generally functions as a regulation of conduct. That argument runs headlong into a number of precedents, most prominently Cohen v. California, 403 U.S 15 (1971). *Cohen* also involved a generally applicable regulation of conduct, barring breaches of the peace. But when Cohen was convicted for wearing a jacket bearing an epithet, we did not apply *O'Brien*. Instead, we recognized that the generally applicable law was directed at *Cohen* because of what his speech communicated — he violated the [statute] because of the offensive content of his particular message. We accordingly applied more rigorous scrutiny and reversed his conviction.

This suit falls into the same category. The law here may be described as directed at conduct[,] but as applied to plaintiffs the conduct triggering coverage under the statute consists of communicating a message. . . .

B

The First Amendment issue [is] not whether the Government may prohibit pure political speech, or may prohibit material support in the form of conduct. It is instead whether the Government may prohibit what plaintiffs want to do — provide material support to the PKK and LTTE in the form of speech.

Everyone agrees that the Government's interest in combating terrorism is an urgent objective of the highest order. Plaintiffs' complaint is that the ban on material support, applied to what they wish to do, is not "necessary to further that interest." The objective of combating terrorism does not justify prohibiting their speech, plaintiffs argue, because their support will advance only the legitimate activities of the designated terrorist organizations, not their terrorism.

Whether foreign terrorist organizations meaningfully segregate support of their legitimate activities from support of terrorism is an empirical question. When it enacted §2339B in 1976, Congress made specific findings regarding the serious threat posed by international terrorism. One of those findings explicitly rejects plaintiffs' contention that their support would not further the terrorist activities of the PKK and LTTE: "[F]oreign organizations that engage in terrorist activity are so tainted by their criminal conduct that *any contribution to such an organization* facilitates that conduct." §301(a)(7). . . .

[Material] support meant to "promot[e] peaceable, lawful conduct" can further terrorism by foreign groups in multiple ways. "Material support" is a valuable resource by definition. Such support frees up other resources within the organization that may be put to violent ends. It also importantly helps lend legitimacy to foreign terrorist groups — legitimacy that makes it easier for those groups to persist, to recruit members, and to raise funds — all of which facilitate more terrorist attacks. . . .

[The] dissent argues that there is "no natural stopping place" for the proposition that aiding a foreign terrorist organization's lawful activity promotes the terrorist organization as a whole. But Congress has settled on just such a natural stopping place: The statute reaches only material support coordinated with or under the direction of a designated foreign terrorist organization. Independent advocacy that might be viewed as promoting the group's legitimacy is not covered.

Providing foreign terrorist groups with material support in any form also furthers terrorism by straining the United States' relationships with its allies and undermining cooperative efforts between nations to prevent terrorist attacks. We see no reason to question Congress's finding that "international cooperation is required for an effective response to terrorism . . . ." The material-support statute furthers this international effort by prohibiting aid for foreign terrorist groups that harm the United States' partners abroad. . . .

C

[Our] precedents, old and new, make clear that concerns of national security and foreign relations do not warrant abdication of the judicial role. We do not defer to the Government's reading of the First Amendment, even when such interests are at stake. [But] when it comes to collecting evidence and drawing factual inferences in this area, "the lack of competence on the part of the courts is marked," and respect for the Government's conclusions is appropriate. . . .

At bottom, plaintiffs simply disagree with the considered judgment of Congress and the Executive that providing material support to a designated foreign terrorist organization—even seemingly benign support—bolsters the terrorist activities of that organization. That judgment, however, is entitled to significant weight, and we have persuasive evidence to sustain it. Given the sensitive interests in national security and foreign affairs at stake, the political branches have adequately substantiated their determination that, to serve the Government's interest in preventing terrorism, it was necessary to prohibit providing material support in the form of training, expert advice, personnel, and services to foreign terrorist groups, even if the supporters meant to promote only the groups' nonviolent ends.

We turn to the particular speech plaintiffs propose to undertake. First plaintiffs propose to "train members of [the] PKK on how to use humanitarian and international law to peacefully resolve disputes." Congress can, consistent with the First Amendment, prohibit this direct training. It is wholly foreseeable that the PKK could use the "specific skill[s]" that plaintiffs propose to impart as a part of a broader strategy to promote terrorism. The PKK could, for example, pursue peaceful negotiation as a means of buying time to recover from short-term setbacks, lulling opponents into complacency, and ultimately preparing for renewed attacks. A foreign terrorist organization introduced to the structures of the international legal system might use the information to threaten, manipulate, and disrupt. This possibility is real, not remote.

Second, plaintiffs propose to "teach PKK members how to petition various representative bodies such as the Untied Nations for relief." The Government acts within First Amendment strictures in banning this proposed speech because it teaches the organization how to acquire "relief," which plaintiffs never define with any specificity, and which could readily include monetary aid. [Money] is fungible, and Congress logically concluded that money a terrorist group such as the PKK obtains using the techniques plaintiffs propose to teach could be redirected to funding the group's violent activities. . . .

[All] this is not to say that any future applications of the material-support statute to speech or advocacy will survive First Amendment scrutiny. It is also not to say that any other statute relating to speech and terrorism would satisfy the First Amendment. [We] in no way suggest that a regulation of independent speech would pass constitutional muster, even if the Government were to show that such speech benefits foreign terrorist organizations. We also do not suggest that Congress could extend the same prohibition on material support at issue here to domestic organizations. We simply hold that, in prohibiting the particular forms of support that plaintiffs seek to provide to foreign terrorist groups, §2339B does not violate the freedom of speech.

The judgment of [the] Court of Appeals is affirmed in part and reversed in part, and the cases are remanded for further proceedings consistent with this opinion.

It is so ordered.

Justice BREYER, with whom Justices GINSBURG and SOTOMAYOR join, dissenting.

[I] cannot agree with the Court's conclusion that the Constitution permits the Government to prosecute the plaintiffs criminally for engaging in coordinated teaching and advocacy furthering the designated organizations' lawful political objectives. In my view, the Government has not met its burden of showing that an interpretation of the statute that would prohibit this speech-and-association-related activity serves the Government's compelling interest in combating terrorism. And I would interpret the statute as normally placing activity of this kind outside its scope. [Not] even the "serious and deadly problem" of international terrorism can require automatic forfeiture of First Amendment rights. After all, this Court has recognized that not "'[e]ven the war power . . . remove[s] constitutional limitations safeguarding essential liberties.'" United States v. Robel, 389 U.S. 258, 264 (1967). Thus, there is no general First Amendment exception that applies here. If the statute is constitutional in this context, it would have to come with a strong justification attached,

[Where] a statute applies criminal penalties and at least arguably does so on the basis of content-based distinctions, I should think we would scrutinize the statute and justifications "strictly" to determine whether the prohibition is justified by a "compelling" need that cannot be "less restrictively" accommodated.

But, even if we assume for argument's sake that "strict scrutiny" does not apply, no one can deny that we must at the very least "measure the validity of the means adopted by Congress against both the goal it has sought to achieve and the specific prohibitions of the First Amendment." [I] doubt that the statute, as the Government would interpret it, can survive any reasonably applicable First Amendment standard.

The Government does identify a compelling [interest], namely, the interest in protecting the security of the United States and its nationals from the threats that foreign terrorist organizations pose by denying those organizations financial and other fungible resources. I do not dispute the importance of this interest. But I do dispute whether the interest can justify the statute's criminal prohibition. [Precisely] how does application of the statute to the protected activities before us *help achieve* that important security-related end?

The Government makes two efforts to answer this question. First, the Government says that the plaintiff's support for these organizations is "fungible" in the same as other forms of banned support. Being fungible, the plaintiffs' support could, for example, free up other resources. Which the organization might put to terrorist ends. . . . The proposition that the two very different kinds of "support" are fungible," however, is not *obviously* true. There is no *obvious* way in which undertaking advocacy for political change through peaceful means [is] fungible with other resources that might be put to more sinister ends in the way that donations of money, food, or computer training are fungible. It is far from obvious [that] advocacy activities can themselves be redirected, or will free other resources that can be directed, towards terrorist ends. . . . The Government has provided us with no empirical information that might convincingly support this claim. Instead, the Government cites only to evidence that Congress was concerned about the "fungible" nature in general of resources, predominately money and material goods. . . . The most one can say in the Government's favor about [proffered] statements [in Congressional reports] is that they *might* be read as offering highly general support for its argument. [The] House Report use[s] broad terms like "contributions" and "services" that might be construed as encompassing the plaintiffs' activities. But in context, those terms are more naturally understood as referring to contributions of goods, money, or training and other services (say, computer programming) that could be diverted to, or free funding for, terrorist ends. Peaceful political advocacy does not obviously fall into these categories. And the statute itself suggests that Congress did not intend to curtail freedom of speech or association. *See* §2339B(I) ("Nothing in this section shall be construed or applied so as to abridge the exercise of rights guaranteed under the First Amendment").

Second, the Government says that the plaintiffs' proposed activities will "bolste[r] a terrorist organization's efficacy and strength in a community" and "undermin[e] this nation's efforts to *delegitimize and weaken* those groups." In the Court's view, too, the Constitution permits application of the statute to activities of the kind at issue in part because those activities could provide a group that engages in terrorism with "legitimacy." The Court suggests that, armed with this greater "legitimacy," these organizations will more readily be able to obtain material support of the kinds Congress plainly intended to ban — money, arms, lodging, and the like. [But] this "legitimacy" justification cannot by itself warrant suppression of political speech, advocacy, and association. Speech, association, and related activities on behalf of a group will often, perhaps always, help to legitimate that group. Thus, were the law to accept a "legitimating" effect, in and of itself and without qualification, as providing sufficient grounds for imposing such a ban, the First Amendment battle would be lost in untold instances where it should be won. Once one accepts this argument, there is no natural stopping place. The argument applies as strongly to "independent" as to "coordinated" advocacy. That fact is reflected in part in the Government's claim that the ban here, so supported, prohibits a lawyer hired by a designated group from filing on behalf of that group an *amicus* brief before the Untied Nations or even before this Court. . . .

[Regardless,] the "legitimacy" justification itself is inconsistent with critically important First Amendment case law. Consider the cases involving the protection the First Amendment offered those who joined the Communist Party intending only to further its peaceful activities. In those cases, this Court took account of congressional findings that the Communist Party not only advocated theoretically but also sought to put into practice the overthrow of our Government through force and violence[.] Nonetheless, the Court held that the First Amendment protected an American's right to belong to that party — despite whatever "legitimating" effect membership might have had — as long as the person did not share the party's unlawful purposes. [Those] cases draw further support from other cases permitting pure advocacy of even the most unlawful activity — as long as that advocacy is not "directed to inciting or producing imminent lawless action and . . . likely to incite or produce such action." *Brandenburg* [v. Ohio], 395 U.S. [444,] 447 [(1969)]. The Government's "legitimating" theory would seem to apply to these cases with equal justifying force; and, if recognized, it would have led this Court to conclusions other than those it reached.

Nor can the Government overcome these considerations simply by narrowing the covered activities to those that involve *coordinated*, rather than *independent*, advocacy. [I] am not aware of any form of words that might be used to describe "coordination" that would not, at a minimum, seriously chill not only the kind of activities the plaintiffs raise before us, but also the "independent advocacy" the Government purports to permit. [Thus,] the distinction "coordination" makes is arbitrary in respect to furthering the statute's purposes[.] . . .

What is one to say about [the majority's] arguments — arguments that would deny First Amendment protection to the peaceful teaching of international human rights law on the ground that a little knowledge about "the international legal system" is too dangerous a thing; that an opponent's subsequent willingness to negotiate might be faked, so let's not teach him how to try? What might be said of these claims by those who live, as we do, in a Nation committed to the resolution of disputes through "deliberative forces"? Whitney v. California, 274 U.S. 357, 375 (1927) (Brandeis, J., concurring).

[The] majority's arguments stretch the concept of "fungibility" beyond constitutional limits. Neither Congress nor the Government advanced these particular hypothetical claims. I am not aware of any case in this Court — not Gitlow v. New York, 268 U.S. 652 (1925), not Schenck v. United States, 249 U.S. 47 (1919), not *Abrams* [v. United States], 250 U.S. 616 [(1919)], not the later Communist Party cases decided during the heat of the Cold War — in which the Court accepted anything like a claim that speech or teaching might be criminalized lest it, e.g., buy negotiating time for an opponent who would put that time to bad use. . . .

[Neither] the Government nor the majority points to any specific facts that show that the speech-related activities before us are fungible in some special way or confer some special legitimacy upon the PKK. Rather, their arguments in this respect are general and speculative. Those arguments would apply to virtually all speech-related support for a dual-purpose group's peaceful activities (irrespective of whether the speech-related activity is coordinated). Both First Amendment logic and First Amendment case law prevent us from "sacrific[ing] First Amendment protections for so speculative a gain."

I believe that a construction [of the statute] that would avoid the constitutional problem is "fairly possible." [I] would read the statute as criminalizing First-Amendment-protected pure speech and association only when the defendant knows or intends that those activities will assist the organization's unlawful terrorist actions. Under this reading, the Government would have to show, at a minimum, that such defendants provided support that they knew was significantly likely to help the organization pursue its unlawful terrorist aims. . . . This reading of the statute protects those who engage in pure speech and association ordinarily protected by the First Amendment. [Where] the activity fits into [the] categories of purposefully or knowingly supporting terrorist ends, the act of providing material support to a known terrorist organization bears a close enough relation to terrorist acts that [it] likely can be prohibited notwithstanding any First Amendment interest. *Cf. Brandenburg*, 395 U.S. 444. At the same time, this reading does not require the Government to undertake the difficult task of proving which, as between peaceful and nonpeaceful purposes, a defendant specifically preferred; knowledge is enough.

This reading is consistent with the statute's text. The statute prohibits "knowingly provid[ing] *material* support or resources to a foreign terrorist organization." §2339B(a)(1). Normally we read a criminal statute as applying a *mens rea* requirement to all of the subsequently listed elements of the crime. So read, the defendant would have to know or intend (1) that he is *providing* support or resources, (2) that he is providing that support to a *foreign terrorist organization*, and (3) that he is providing support that is *material*, meaning (4) that his support bears a significant likelihood of furthering the organization's terrorist ends. . . .

[The] statute's history strongly supports this reading. That history makes clear that Congress primarily sought to end assistance that takes the form of fungible donations of money or goods. It shows that Congress, when referring to "expert services and assistance" for example, had in mind training that was sufficiently fungible to further terrorism directly, such as an aviation expert's giving "advice" that "facilitat[es] an aircraft hijacking" or an accountant's giving "advice" that will "facilitate the concealment of funds used to support terrorist activities." [Having] interpreted the statute to impose the *mens rea* requirement just described, I would remand the cases so that the lower courts could consider more specifically the precise activities in which the plaintiffs still wish to engage and determine whether and to what extent a grant of declaratory and injunctive relief were warranted. . . .

[I] believe the Court has failed to examine the Government's justifications with sufficient care. . . . That is why, with respect, I dissent.

∾ PROBLEM: MORE ON *HUMANITARIAN LAW PROJECT* ∾

In its opinion, the Court does not rule out the possibility of a successful challenge to this law by the right plaintiff under the right circumstances. However, if this plaintiff cannot establish standing, who can?

2. *The Right "Not to Speak"*

The First Amendment right of association has been construed to protect not only the right to speak but also the right not to speak or to associate oneself with objectionable ideas or positions. In Wooley v. Maynard, 430 U.S. 705 (1977), Jehovah's Witnesses, who objected on religious and moral grounds to having the New Hampshire motto "Live Free or Die" on their license plates and covered it with tape, were prosecuted and convicted under a state law that made it a misdemeanor to knowingly obscure a license plate. The Court held that the state could not force the Maynards to associate themselves with this motto: "[F]reedom of thought [includes] both the right to speak freely and the right to refrain from speaking at all. [W]e are faced with a state measure which forces an individual, as part of his daily life indeed constantly while his automobile is in public view to be an instrument for fostering public adherence to an ideological point of view he finds unacceptable. . . ." The Court rejected the State's first asserted interests (making it easier to determine whether passenger vehicles are carrying the proper plates) on the basis that New Hampshire plates "[consist] of a specific configuration of letters and numbers, which makes them readily distinguishable from other types of plates, even without reference to the state motto." The Court also rejected the argument that the plate communicates "[an] appreciation of history, state pride, and individualism" on the basis that "[s]uch interest cannot outweigh an individual's First Amendment right to avoid becoming the courier for such message." Justice Rehnquist, joined by Justice Blackmun, dissented: "The State has not forced appellees to 'say' anything. . . . The State has simply required that all noncommercial automobiles bear license tags with the state motto. . . . There is nothing in state law which precludes appellees from displaying their disagreement with the state motto as long as the methods used do not obscure the license plates."

Likewise, in West Virginia State Board of Education v. Barnette, 319 U.S. 624 (1943), the state adopted a resolution requiring all public school students and teachers to salute the U.S. flag on pain of insubordination. In an opinion by Justice Jackson, the Court held the law unconstitutional: "To sustain the compulsory flag salute we are required to say that a Bill of Rights which guards the individual's right to speak his own mind, left it open to public authorities to compel him to utter what is not in his mind. . . . If there is any fixed star in our constitutional constellation, it is that no official, high or petty, can prescribe what shall be orthodox in politics, nationalism, religion, or other matters of opinion or force citizens to confess by word or act their faith therein."

Hurley v. Irish-American Gay, Lesbian and Bisexual Group of Boston

515 U.S. 557 (1995)

Justice SOUTER delivered the opinion of the Court.

The issue in this case is whether Massachusetts may require private citizens who organize a parade to include among the marchers a group imparting a message the organizers do not wish to convey. We hold that such a mandate violates the First Amendment.

I

March 17 is set aside for two celebrations in South Boston. As early as 1737, some people in Boston observed the feast of the apostle to Ireland, and since 1776 the day has marked the evacuation of royal troops and Loyalists from the city, prompted by the guns captured at Ticonderoga and set up on Dorchester Heights under General Washington's command. Washington himself reportedly drew on the earlier tradition in choosing "St. Patrick" as the response to "Boston," the password used in the colonial lines on evacuation day. Although the General Court of Massachusetts did not officially designate March 17 as Evacuation Day until 1938, the City Council of Boston had previously sponsored public celebrations of Evacuation Day, including notable commemorations on the centennial in 1876, and on the 125th anniversary in 1901, with its parade, salute, concert, and fireworks display.

The tradition of formal sponsorship by the city came to an end in 1947, however, when Mayor James Michael Curley himself granted authority to organize and conduct the St. Patrick's Day-Evacuation Day Parade to the petitioner South Boston Allied War Veterans Council, an unincorporated association of individuals elected from various South Boston veterans groups. Every year since that time, the Council has applied for and received a permit for the parade, which at times has included as many as 20,000 marchers and drawn up to 1 million watchers. No other applicant has ever applied for that permit. Through 1992, the city allowed the Council to use the city's official seal, and provided printing services as well as direct funding.

In 1992, a number of gay, lesbian, and bisexual descendants of the Irish immigrants joined together with other supporters to form the respondent organization, GLIB, to march in the parade as a way to express pride in their Irish heritage as openly gay, lesbian, and bisexual individuals, to demonstrate that there are such men and women among those so descended, and to express their solidarity with like individuals who sought to march in New York's St. Patrick's Day Parade. Although the Council denied GLIB's application to take part in the 1992 parade, GLIB obtained a state-court order to include its contingent, which marched "uneventfully" among that year's 10,000 participants and 750,000 spectators.

In 1993, after the Council [again] refused to admit GLIB to the upcoming parade, the organization and some of its members filed this suit against the Council, the individual petitioner John J. "Wacko" Hurley, and the city of Boston, alleging violations of the State and Federal Constitutions and of the state public accommodations law, which prohibits "any distinction, discrimination or restriction on account [of] sexual orientation [relative] to the admission of any person to, or treatment in any place of public accommodation, resort or amusement." Mass. Gen. Laws ch. 272, §98 (1992). [We] granted certiorari to determine whether the requirement to admit a parade contingent expressing a message not of the private organizers' own choosing violates the First Amendment. We hold that it does and reverse.

III

If there were no reason for a group of people to march from here to there except to reach a destination, they could make the trip without expressing any message beyond the fact of the march itself. Some people might call such a procession a parade, but it would not be much of one. Real "[p]arades are public dramas of social relations, and in them performers define who can be a social actor and what subjects and ideas are available for communication and consideration." S. Davis, *Parades and Power: Street Theatre in Nineteenth-Century Philadelphia* 6 (Temple University 1986). Hence, we use the word "parade" to indicate marchers who are making some sort of collective point, not just to each other but to bystanders along the way. Indeed, a parade's dependence on watchers is so extreme that nowadays, as with Bishop Berkeley's celebrated tree, "if a parade or demonstration receives no media coverage, it may as well not have happened." Parades are thus a form of expression, not just motion, and the inherent expressiveness of marching to make a point explains our cases involving protest marches. . . .

The protected expression that inheres in a parade is not limited to its banners and songs, however, for the Constitution looks beyond written or spoken words as mediums of expression. Noting that "[s]ymbolism is a primitive but effective way of communicating ideas," West Virginia Bd. of Ed. v. Barnette, 319 U.S. 624, 632 (1943), our cases have recognized that the First Amendment shields such acts as saluting a flag (and refusing to do so), wearing an armband to protest a war, displaying a red flag, and even "[m]arching, walking or parading" in uniforms displaying the swastika. As some of these examples show, a narrow, succinctly articulable message is not a condition of constitutional protection, which if confined to expressions conveying a "particularized message," would never reach the unquestionably shielded painting of Jackson Pollock, music of Arnold Schoenberg, or Jabberwocky verse of Lewis Carroll.

Not many marches, then, are beyond the realm of expressive parades, and the South Boston celebration is not one of them. Spectators line the streets; people march in costumes and uniforms, carrying flags and banners with all sorts of messages (e.g., "England get out of Ireland," "Say no to drugs"); marching bands and pipers play; floats are pulled along; and the whole show is broadcast over Boston television. To be sure, [in] spite of excluding some applicants, the Council is rather lenient in admitting participants. But a private speaker does not forfeit constitutional protection simply by combining multifarious voices, or by failing to edit their themes to isolate an exact message as the exclusive subject matter of the speech. Nor, under our precedent, does First Amendment protection require a speaker to generate, as an original matter, each item featured in the communication. . . .

Respondents' participation as a unit in the parade was equally expressive. GLIB was formed for the very purpose of marching [in] order to celebrate its members' identity as openly gay, lesbian, and bisexual descendants of the Irish immigrants, to show that there are such individuals in the community, and to support the like men and women who sought to march in the New York parade. The organization distributed a fact sheet describing the members' intentions. . . . In 1993, members of GLIB marched behind a shamrock-strewn banner with the simple inscription "Irish American Gay, Lesbian and Bisexual Group of Boston." GLIB understandably seeks to communicate its ideas as part of the existing parade, rather than staging one of its own.

The Massachusetts public accommodations law under which respondents brought suit has a venerable history. At common law, innkeepers, smiths, and others who "made profession of a public employment," were prohibited from refusing, without good reason, to serve a customer. [T]he law today prohibits discrimination on the basis of "race, color, religious creed, national origin, sex, sexual [orientation], deafness, blindness or any physical or mental disability or ancestry" in "the admission of any person to, or treatment in any place of public accommodation, resort or amusement." Mass. Gen. Laws ch. 272, §98 (1992). Provisions like these are well within the State's usual power to enact when a legislature has reason to believe that a given group is the target of discrimination, and they do not, as a general matter, violate the First or Fourteenth Amendments. *See, e.g.,* New York State Club Assn., Inc. v. City of New York, 487 U.S. 1, 11-16 (1988). . . .

[Petitioners] disclaim any intent to exclude homosexuals as such, and no individual member of GLIB claims to have been excluded from parading as a member of any group that the Council has approved to march. Instead, the disagreement goes to the admission of GLIB as its own parade unit carrying its own banner. Since every participating unit affects the message conveyed by the private organizers, the state courts' application of the statute produced an order essentially requiring petitioners to alter the expressive content of their parade. Although the state courts spoke of the parade as a place of public accommodation, once the expressive character of both the parade and the marching GLIB contingent is understood, it becomes apparent that the state courts' application of the statute had the effect of declaring the sponsors' speech itself to be the public accommodation. Under this approach any contingent of protected individuals with a message would have the right to participate in petitioners' speech, so that the communication produced by the private organizers would be shaped by all those protected by the law who wished to join in with some expressive demonstration of their own. But this use of the State's power violates the fundamental rule of protection under the First Amendment, that a speaker has the autonomy to choose the content of his own message.

"Since all speech inherently involves choices of what to say and what to leave unsaid," one important manifestation of the principle of free speech is that one who chooses to speak may also decide "what not to say." Although the State may at times "prescribe what shall be orthodox in commercial advertising" by requiring the dissemination of "purely factual and uncontroversial information," outside that context it may not compel affirmance of a belief with which the speaker disagrees. Indeed this general rule, that the speaker has the right to tailor the speech, applies not only to expressions of value, opinion, or endorsement, but equally to statements of fact the speaker would rather avoid, subject, perhaps, to the permissive law of defamation. Nor is the rule's benefit restricted to the press, being enjoyed by business corporations generally and by ordinary people engaged in unsophisticated expression as well as by professional publishers. Its point is simply the point of all speech protection, which is to shield just those choices of content that in someone's eyes are misguided, or even hurtful.

Petitioners' claim to the benefit of this principle of autonomy to control one's own speech is as sound as the South Boston parade is expressive. Rather like a composer, the Council selects the expressive units of the parade from potential participants, and though the score may not produce a particularized message, each contingent's expression in the Council's eyes comports with what merits celebration on that day. Even if this view gives the Council credit for a more considered judgment than it actively made, the Council clearly decided to exclude a message it did not like from the communication it chose to make, and that is enough to invoke its right as a private speaker to shape its expression by speaking on one subject while remaining silent on another. The message it disfavored is not difficult to identify. Although GLIB's point [is] not wholly articulate, a contingent marching behind the organization's banner would at least bear witness to the fact that some Irish are gay, lesbian, or bisexual, and the presence of the organized marchers would suggest their view that people of their sexual orientations have as much claim to unqualified social acceptance as heterosexuals and indeed as members of parade units organized around other identifying characteristics. The parade's organizers may not believe these facts about Irish sexuality to be so, or they may object to unqualified social acceptance of gays and lesbians or have some other reason for wishing to keep GLIB's message out of the parade. But whatever the reason, it boils down to the choice of a speaker not to propound a particular point of view, and that choice is presumed to lie beyond the government's power to control.

Parades and demonstrations [are] not [neutrally] presented or selectively viewed. Unlike the programming offered on various channels by a cable network, the parade does not consist of individual, unrelated segments that happen to be transmitted together for individual selection by members of the audience. Although each parade unit generally identifies itself, each is understood to contribute something to a common theme, and accordingly there is no customary practice whereby private sponsors disavow "any identity of viewpoint" between themselves and the selected participants. Practice follows practicability here, for such disclaimers would be quite curious in a moving parade. Without deciding on the precise significance of the likelihood of misattribution, it nonetheless becomes clear that in the context of an expressive parade, as with a protest march, the parade's overall message is distilled from the individual presentations along the way, and each unit's expression is perceived by spectators as part of the whole.

[T]he size and success of petitioners' parade makes it an enviable vehicle for the dissemination of GLIB's views, but that fact, without more, would fall far short of supporting a claim that petitioners enjoy an abiding monopoly of access to spectators. Considering that GLIB presumably would have had a fair shot (under neutral criteria developed by the city) at obtaining a parade permit of its own, respondents have not shown that petitioners enjoy the capacity to "silence the voice of competing speakers," as cable operators do with respect to program providers who wish to reach subscribers. Nor has any other legitimate interest been identified in support of applying the Massachusetts statute in this way to expressive activity like the parade.

The statute is a piece of protective legislation that announces no purpose beyond the object both expressed and apparent in its provisions, which is to prevent any denial of access to (or discriminatory treatment in) public accommodations on proscribed grounds, including sexual orientation. On its face, the object of the law is to ensure by statute for gays and lesbians desiring to make use of public accommodations what the old common law promised to any member of the public wanting a meal at the inn, that accepting the usual terms of service, they will not be turned away merely on the proprietor's exercise of personal preference. When the law is applied to expressive activity in the way it was done here, its apparent object is simply to require speakers to modify the content of their expression to whatever extent beneficiaries of the law choose to alter it with messages of their own. But in the absence of some further, legitimate end, this object is merely to allow exactly what the general rule of speaker's autonomy forbids.

It might [have] been argued that a broader objective is apparent: that the ultimate point of forbidding acts of discrimination toward certain classes is to produce a society free of the corresponding biases. Requiring access to a speaker's message would thus be not an end in itself, but a means to produce speakers free of the biases, whose expressive conduct would be at least neutral toward the particular classes, obviating any future need for correction. But if this indeed is the point of applying the state law to expressive conduct, it is a decidedly fatal objective. [Our] tradition of free speech commands that a speaker who takes to the street corner to express his views in this way should be free from interference by the State based on the content of what he says. The very idea that a noncommercial speech restriction be used to produce thoughts and statements acceptable to some groups or, indeed, all people, grates on the First Amendment, for it amounts to nothing less than a proposal to limit speech in the service of orthodox expression. While the law is free to promote all sorts of conduct in place of harmful behavior, it is not free to interfere with speech for no better reason than promoting an approved message or discouraging a disfavored one, however enlightened either purpose may strike the government.

[Our] holding today rests not on any particular view about the Council's message but on the Nation's commitment to protect freedom of speech. Disapproval of a private speaker's statement does not legitimize use of the Commonwealth's power to compel the speaker to alter the message by including one more acceptable to others. Accordingly, the judgment of the Supreme Judicial Court is reversed, and the case is remanded for proceedings not inconsistent with this opinion.

It is so ordered.

Notes

1. *The* Boy Scouts *Case*. Boy Scouts of America v. Dale, 530 U.S. 640 (2000), involved a private, not-for-profit organization engaged in instilling values in young people. The organization asserted that homosexual conduct was inconsistent with the values it seeks to instill. James Dale, a former Eagle Scout whose adult membership in the Boy Scouts was revoked when the Scouts learned that he was an avowed homosexual and gay rights activist, sued claiming a violation of New Jersey's public accommodations law. In a five-to-four decision, the Court held that the law could not be applied to the Boy Scouts: "[A] state requirement that the Boy Scouts retain Dale as an assistant scoutmaster would significantly burden the organization's right to oppose or disfavor homosexual conduct. The state interests [do] not justify such a severe intrusion on the Boy Scouts' rights to freedom of expressive association. [T]he First Amendment prohibits the State

from imposing such a requirement through the application of its public accommodations law." Four justices dissented. Justice Stevens stated: "[Dale's] participation sends no cognizable message to the Scouts or to the world. . . . Dale did not carry a banner or a sign; [and] he expressed no intent to send any message. If there is any kind of message being sent, [it] is by the mere act of joining the Boy Scouts. Such an act does not [constitute] symbolic speech under the First Amendment."

2. *The Solomon Amendment.* An Association of American Law Schools (AALS) rule prohibits discrimination against homosexuals. The AALS rule requires prospective employers who want to interview at AALS member schools (virtually all law schools belong to the AALS) to provide written assurance that they will not discriminate on the basis of sexual orientation. Member schools are required to refuse to provide recruitment assistance to any employer that declines to so certify. The AALS rule effectively prohibits members of the U.S. military from interviewing at AALS schools. Current military rules prohibit members of the military from identifying themselves as homosexual on pain of separation from the military services (absent proof that the individual does not have an intent or propensity to engage in homosexual acts). In response, Congress passed the Solomon Amendment, which bars federal funds to an institution of higher education (or a part of any such institution — such as a law school) that "has a policy or practice [that] either prohibits, or in effect prevents" military recruiters from having access to campus. The Court held that the Solomon Amendment did not infringe the law schools' right to associate, or force them to engage in speech (regarding the acceptability of military recruiters in light of the military's position on homosexuality) that they find objectionable. *See* Forum for Academic and Institutional Rights, Inc. v. Rumsfeld, 291 F. Supp. 2d 269 (D.N.J. 2003).

∾ PROBLEMS ∾

1. *In God We Trust.* U.S. money bears the mottoes "In God We Trust" and "E Pluribus Unum." An atheist, who objects to both mottoes, crosses them out (or paints over them) on all money that comes into his possession. If the atheist is prosecuted under federal law prohibiting the defacement of money, can he defend based on his right of association?

2. *Freedom of Association and the* Rumsfeld *Decision.* Following the decision in *Rumsfeld, supra,* suppose that the University of Louisville's Brandeis School of Law decides to take the following actions: 1) it posts statements indicating its objection to discrimination on the basis of sexual orientation, 2) it posts statements indicating that it believes that employers should not discriminate on the basis of sexual orientation, 3) it posts statements objecting to the DOD's policy on gays and lesbians, and 4) it organizes protests (including placards and chants) on days when DOD recruiters are on campus. Do any of these actions violate the Solomon Amendment?

3. *More on the International Treaty Regulating the Internet.* Suppose that the delegates from several countries, concerned about the historical repression of sexual

minorities, demand that the treaty contain language protecting and enhancing the status of gays, lesbians, and transgenders. As with the prior demand for sexual equality, these delegates demand that the treaty contain language prohibiting communications by individuals or groups who deny the rights of gays, lesbians, and transgendered as well as by groups that do not include (or at least have not attempted to include and welcome) gays, lesbians, and transgendered in their membership. Can you agree to either of these provisions?

Board of Regents of The University of Wisconsin System v. Southworth

529 U.S. 217 (2000)

Justice KENNEDY delivered the opinion of the Court.

[The University of Wisconsin charged students an activity fee of $331.50 per year. This fund was used to support student organizations (RSOs). Students could apply for funds in one of two ways, or they could seek funding through a student referendum (which could also be used to deny funding to RSOs). Funding was provided on a viewpoint-neutral basis. Students sued, challenging the activity fee to the extent that it required them to contribute to the speech activities of organizations with which they disagreed.]

[The] University of Wisconsin exacts the fee at issue for the sole purpose of facilitating the free and open exchange of ideas by, and among, its students. [The] viewpoint neutrality requirement of the University program is in general sufficient to protect the rights of the objecting students. . . .

We must begin by recognizing that the complaining students are being required to pay fees which are subsidies for speech they find objectionable, even offensive. The *Abood* [v. Detroit Board of Education, 431 U.S. 209 (1977)] and *Keller* [v. State Bar of California, 496 U.S. 1 (1990) cases] provide the beginning point for our analysis. . . . In *Abood*, some nonunion public school teachers challenged an agreement requiring them, as a condition of their employment, to pay a service fee equal in amount to union dues. The objecting teachers alleged that the union's use of their fees to engage in political speech violated their freedom of association guaranteed by the First and Fourteenth Amendments. The Court agreed and held that any objecting teacher could "prevent the Union's spending a part of their required service fees to contribute to political candidates and to express political views unrelated to its duties as exclusive bargaining representative." The principles outlined in *Abood* provided the foundation for our later decision in *Keller*. There we held that lawyers admitted to practice in California could be required to join a state bar association and to fund activities "germane" to the association's mission of "regulating the legal profession and improving the quality of legal services." The lawyers could not, however, be required to fund the bar association's own political expression.

The proposition that students who attend the University cannot be required to pay subsidies for the speech of other students without some First Amendment protection follows from the *Abood* and *Keller* cases. Students enroll in public universities to seek fulfillment of their personal aspirations and of their own potential. If the University conditions the opportunity to receive a college education [on] an agreement to support objectionable, extracurricular expression by other students, the rights acknowledged in *Abood* and *Keller* become implicated. It infringes on the speech and beliefs of the individual to be required, by this mandatory student activity fee program, to pay subsidies for the objectionable speech of others without any recognition of the State's corresponding duty to him or her. Yet recognition must be given as well to the important and substantial purposes of the University, which seeks to facilitate a wide range of speech.

In *Abood* and *Keller* the constitutional rule took the form of limiting the required subsidy to speech germane to the purposes of the union or bar association. The standard of germane speech as applied to student speech at a university is unworkable, however, and gives insufficient protection both to the objecting students and to the University program itself. Even in the context of a labor union, whose functions are, or so we might have thought, well known and understood by the law and the courts after a long history of government regulation and judicial involvement, we have encountered difficulties in deciding what is germane and what is not. The difficulty manifested itself in our decision in Lehnert v. Ferris Faculty Assn., 500 U.S. 507 (1991), where different members of the Court reached varying conclusions regarding what expressive activity was or was not germane to the mission of the association. If it is difficult to define germane speech with ease or precision where a union or bar association is the party, the standard becomes all the more unmanageable in the public university setting, particularly where the State undertakes to stimulate the whole universe of speech and ideas.

The speech the University seeks to encourage in the program before us is distinguished not by discernable limits but by its vast, unexplored bounds. [It] is all but inevitable that the fees will result in subsidies to speech which some students find objectionable and offensive to their personal beliefs. If the standard of germane speech is inapplicable, then, it might be argued the remedy is to allow each student to list those causes which he or she will or will not support. . . . We decline to impose a system of that sort as a constitutional requirement. . . . The restriction could be so disruptive and expensive that the program to support extracurricular speech would be ineffective. . . .

The University may determine that its mission is well served if students have the means to engage in dynamic discussions of philosophical, religious, scientific, social, and political subjects in their extracurricular campus life outside the lecture hall. If the University reaches this conclusion, it is entitled to impose a mandatory fee to sustain an open dialogue to these ends.

The University must provide some protection to its students' First Amendment interests, however. The proper measure, and the principal standard of protection for objecting students, we conclude, is the requirement of viewpoint neutrality in the allocation of funding support. [In] Rosenberger v. Rector and Visitors of Univ. of Va., 515 U.S. 819 (1995)[, we held] that the school's adherence to a rule of viewpoint neutrality in administering its student fee program would prevent "any mistaken impression that the student newspapers speak for the University." While *Rosenberger* was concerned with the rights a student has to use an extracurricular speech program already in place, today's case considers the antecedent question [whether] a public university may require its students to pay a fee which creates the mechanism for the extracurricular speech in the first instance. When a university requires its students to pay fees to support the extracurricular speech of other students, all in the interest of open discussion, it may not prefer some viewpoints to others. There is symmetry then in our holding here and in *Rosenberger*: Viewpoint neutrality is the justification for requiring the student to pay the fee in the first instance and for ensuring the integrity of the program's operation once the funds have been collected. We conclude that the University of Wisconsin may sustain the extracurricular dimensions of its programs by using mandatory student fees with viewpoint neutrality as the operational principle.

[T]he program the University has developed to stimulate extracurricular student expression respects the principle of viewpoint neutrality. [T]he University's program in its basic structure must be found consistent with the First Amendment.

Our decision ought not to be taken to imply that in other instances the University, its agents or employees, or — of particular importance — its faculty, are subject to the First Amendment analysis which controls in this case. Where the University speaks, either in its own name through its regents or officers, or in myriad other ways through its diverse faculties, the analysis likely would be altogether different. The Court has not held, or suggested, that when the government speaks the rules we have discussed come into play.

When the government speaks, for instance to promote its own policies or to advance a particular idea, it is, in the end, accountable to the electorate and the political process for its advocacy. If the citizenry objects, newly elected officials later could espouse some different or contrary position. In the instant case, the speech is not that of the University or its agents. It is not, furthermore, speech by an instructor or a professor in the academic context, where principles applicable to government speech would have to be considered.

[In] the referendum aspect of the University's program[,] it appears that by majority vote of the student body a given RSO may be funded or defunded. It is unclear to us what protection, if any, there is for viewpoint neutrality in this part of the process. To the extent the referendum substitutes majority determinations for viewpoint neutrality it would undermine the constitutional protection the program requires. The whole theory of viewpoint neutrality is that minority views are treated with the same respect as are majority views. Access to a public forum [does] not depend upon majoritarian consent. . . . A remand is necessary and appropriate to resolve this point. . . .

The judgment of the Court of Appeals is reversed, and the case is remanded for further proceedings consistent with this opinion. In this Court the parties shall bear their own costs.

It is so ordered.

Justice SOUTER, with whom Justice STEVENS and Justice BREYER join, concurring in the judgment.

[I] agree that the University's scheme is permissible, but do not believe that the Court should [impose] a cast-iron viewpoint neutrality requirement to uphold it. [I] would hold that the First Amendment interest claimed by [the] respondents [is] simply insufficient to merit protection by anything more than the viewpoint neutrality already accorded by the University, and I would go no further.

[I]t is plain that this case falls far afield of those involving compelled or controlled speech, apart from subsidy schemes. Indirectly transmitting a fraction of a student activity fee to an organization with an offensive message is in no sense equivalent to restricting or modifying the message a student wishes to express. Nor does it require an individual to bear an offensive statement personally, as in Wooley v. Maynard, 430 U.S. 705, 707 (1977), let alone to affirm a moral or political commitment, as in West Virginia Bd. of Ed. v. Barnette, 319 U.S. 624, 626-629 (1943). In each of these cases, the government was imposing far more directly and offensively on an objecting individual than collecting the fee that indirectly funds the jumble of other speakers' messages in this case.

Notes

1. *More on Union Service Fees.* In Locke v. Karass, 129 S.Ct. 798 (2009), the State of Maine required government employees to pay a service fee to the local union that acted as their exclusive bargaining agent whether or not those employees belonged to the union (and, in fact, disagreed with it). This fee included an affiliation fee that the local union paid to its national union organization, which was used to pay litigation expenses incurred in large part on behalf of *other* local units. The Court upheld the fee so long as 1) the subject matter of the (extralocal) litigation is of a kind that would be chargeable if the litigation were local — for example, litigation appropriately related to collective bargaining rather than political activities; and 2) the litigation charge is reciprocal in nature — that is, the contributing local reasonably expects other locals to contribute similarly to the national's resources used for costs of similar litigation on behalf of the contributing local if and when it takes place. The Court concluded that "the *kind* of national litigation activity for which the local charges nonmembers concerns only those aspects of collective bargaining, contract administration, or other matters that the courts have held chargeable."

2. *Prohibition on Voluntary Deductions.* In Ysura v. Pocatello Education Association, 129 S.Ct. 1093 (2009), the Court upheld an Idaho law that allowed a public employee to elect to have a portion of his wages deducted by his employer and remitted to his union to pay union dues, but precluded an employee from having an amount deducted for the union's political action committee (because Idaho law prohibits payroll deductions for political activities). The Court upheld the law, noting that the "First Amendment prohibits government from 'abridging the freedom of speech'; it does not confer an affirmative right to use government payroll mechanisms for the purpose of obtaining funds for expression." The Court

went on to note that "Idaho's law does not restrict political speech, but rather declines to promote that speech by allowing public employee checkoffs for political activities," and that "[b]anning payroll deductions for political speech similarly furthers the government's interest in distinguishing between internal governmental operations and private speech." Justice Breyer concurred in part and dissented in part, arguing that the Court should inquire "whether the statute imposes a burden upon speech that is disproportionate in light of the other interests the government seeks to achieve," and expressed concerns about whether the particular exception had been applied "even handedly." Justice Stevens dissented, questioning whether the restriction was viewpoint neutral because it was aimed at unions.

∽ PROBLEMS ∽

1. *Show Me State.* The State of Missouri erects billboards proclaiming the "Show Me State" motto and uses general tax revenues to finance the costs of erecting and maintaining the billboards. May a citizen sue to prohibit the billboard message on associational grounds? May a taxpayer challenge the use of public funds to finance the message?

2. *Objections to Union Spending.* After *Abood,* a nonunion member complains that he is ethically opposed to the union's decision to negotiate for the inclusion of abortion benefits in a medical insurance plan. Can an employee be required to finance these union activities?

Johanns v. Livestock Marketing Association

544 U.S. 550 (2005)

Justice SCALIA delivered the opinion of the Court.

[The] Beef Promotion and Research Act of 1985 announces a federal policy of promoting the marketing and consumption of "beef and beef products," using funds raised by an assessment on cattle sales and importation. 7 U.S.C. §2901(b). The statute directs the Secretary of Agriculture to implement this policy by issuing a Beef Promotion and Research Order, and specifies four key terms it must contain: The Secretary is to appoint a Cattlemen's Beef Promotion and Research Board (Beef Board or Board), whose members are to be a geographically representative group of beef producers and importers, nominated by trade associations. The Beef Board is to convene an Operating Committee, composed of 10 Beef Board members and 10 representatives named by a federation of state beef councils. The Secretary is to impose a $1-per-head assessment (or "checkoff") on all sales or importation of cattle and a comparable assessment on imported beef products. And the assessment is to be used to fund beef-related projects, including promotional campaigns, designed by the Operating Committee and approved by the Secretary.

The Secretary promulgated the Beef Order with the specified terms. The assessment is collected primarily by state beef councils, which then forward the proceeds to the Beef Board.[21] The Operating Committee proposes projects to be funded by the checkoff, including promotion and research. The Secretary or his designee approves each project and, in the case of promotional materials, the content of each communication.

The Beef Order was promulgated [on] a temporary basis, subject to a referendum among beef producers. [In] 1988, a large majority voted to continue it. Since that time, more than $1 billion has been collected through the checkoff, and a large fraction of that sum has been spent on promotional projects authorized by the Beef Act—many using the familiar trademarked slogan "Beef. It's What's for Dinner." [In] 2000, [the] Beef Board collected over $48 million in assessments and spent over $29 million on domestic promotion. The Board also funds overseas marketing efforts; market and food-science research, such as evaluations of the nutritional value of beef; and informational campaigns for both consumers and beef producers. . . . Many promotional messages funded by the checkoff [bear] the attribution "Funded by America's Beef Producers." Most print and television messages also bear a Beef Board logo, usually a check-mark with the word "BEEF."

Respondents are two associations whose members collect and pay the checkoff, and several individuals who raise and sell cattle subject to the checkoff[, who] sued the Secretary, the Department of Agriculture, and the Board. . . . While the litigation was pending, we held in United States v. United Foods, Inc., 533 U.S. 405 (2001), that a mandatory checkoff for generic mushroom advertising violated the First Amendment. . . . Respondents noted that the advertising promotes beef as a generic commodity, which [impedes] their efforts to promote the superiority of, *inter alia*, American beef, grain-fed beef, or certified Angus or Hereford beef. [T]he District Court ruled for respondents [and the] Court of Appeals for the Eighth Circuit affirmed. . . . We granted certiorari.

We have sustained First Amendment challenges to allegedly compelled expression in two categories of cases: true "compelled speech" cases, in which an individual is obliged personally to express a message he disagrees with, imposed by the government; and "compelled subsidy" cases, in which an individual is required by the government to subsidize a message he disagrees with, expressed by a private entity. We have not heretofore considered the First Amendment consequences of government-compelled subsidy of the government's own speech.

We first invalidated an outright compulsion of speech in West Virginia Bd. of Ed. v. Barnette, 319 U.S. 624 (1943)[; *see also*] Wooley v. Maynard, 430 U.S. 705 (1977). . . . The reasoning of these compelled-speech cases has been carried over to certain instances in which individuals are compelled not to speak, but to subsidize a private message with which they disagree. Thus, although we have upheld state-imposed requirements that lawyers be members of the state bar and pay its annual dues, and that public-school teachers either join the labor union representing their "shop" or pay "service fees" equal to the union dues, we have invalidated the use of the compulsory fees to fund speech on political matters. *See*

21. In most cases, only 50 cents per head is remitted to the Beef Board, because the Beef Act and Beef Order allow domestic producers to deduct from their $1 assessment up to 50 cents in voluntary contributions to their state beef councils.

Keller v. State Bar of Cal., 496 U.S. 1 (1990); Abood v. Detroit Bd. of Ed., 431 U.S. 209 (1977). Bar or union speech with such content, we held, was not germane to the regulatory interests that justified compelled membership, and accordingly, making those who disagreed with it pay for it violated the First Amendment.

These latter cases led us to sustain a compelled-subsidy challenge to an assessment very similar to the beef checkoff, imposed to fund mushroom advertising at issue in *United Foods*. Deciding the case on the assumption that the advertising was private speech, not government speech,[22] we concluded that *Abood* and *Keller* were controlling. As in those cases, mushroom producers were obliged by "law or necessity" to pay the checkoff; although *Abood* and *Keller* would permit the mandatory fee if it were "germane" to a "broader regulatory scheme," in *United Foods* the only regulatory purpose was the funding of the advertising.

In all of the cases invalidating exactions to subsidize speech, the speech was, or was presumed to be, that of an entity other than the government itself. Our compelled-subsidy cases have consistently respected the principle that "[c]ompelled support of a private association is fundamentally different from compelled support of government." "Compelled support of government" — even those programs of government one does not approve — is of course perfectly constitutional. . . . And some government programs involve, or entirely consist of, advocating a position. "The government, as a general rule, may support valid programs and policies by taxes or other exactions binding on protesting parties. Within this broader principle it seems inevitable that funds raised by the government will be spent for speech and other expression to advocate and defend its own policies." We have generally assumed, though not yet squarely held, that compelled funding of government speech does not alone raise First Amendment concerns.

Respondents do not seriously dispute these principles. [T]hey assert that the challenged promotional campaigns differ dispositively from the type of government speech that [is] not susceptible to First Amendment challenge. They point to the role of the Beef Board and its Operating Committee in designing the promotional campaigns, and to the use of a mandatory assessment on beef producers to fund the advertising. . . .

The Secretary of Agriculture does not write ad copy himself. Rather, the Beef Board's promotional campaigns are designed by the Beef Board's Operating Committee, only half of whose members are Beef Board members appointed by the Secretary. (All members of the Operating Committee are subject to *removal* by the Secretary.) Respondents contend that speech whose content is effectively controlled by a nongovernmental entity — the Operating Committee — cannot be considered "government speech." We [reject] this contention. . . . The message set out in the beef promotions is from beginning to end the message established

22. In *United Foods*, the Court distinguished (and the dissent relied on) Glickman v. Wileman Brothers & Elliott, Inc., 521 U.S. 457 (1997), which upheld the use of mandatory assessments to fund generic advertising promoting California tree fruit. In *Glickman*, [the] Government contended, and we agreed, that compelled support for generic advertising was legitimately part of the Government's "collectivist" centralization of the market for tree fruit. Here, as in *United Foods*, "there is no broader regulatory system in place" that collectivizes aspects of the beef market unrelated to speech, so *Glickman* is not controlling.

by the Federal Government.[23] Congress has directed the implementation of a "coordinated program" of promotion, "including paid advertising, to advance the image and desirability of beef and beef products." Congress and the Secretary have also specified, in general terms, what the promotional campaigns shall contain and what they shall not. Thus, Congress and the Secretary have set out the overarching message and some of its elements, and they have left the development of the remaining details to an entity whose members are answerable to the Secretary (and in some cases appointed by him as well). . . . Moreover, [the] Secretary exercises final approval authority over every word used in every promotional campaign. . . . Nor is the Secretary's role limited to final approval or rejection: officials of the Department also attend and participate in the open meetings at which proposals are developed.

This degree of governmental control over the message funded by the checkoff distinguishes these cases from *Keller*. There the state bar's communicative activities to which the plaintiffs objected were not prescribed by law in their general outline and not developed under official government supervision. . . . When, as here, the government sets the overall message to be communicated and approves every word that is disseminated, it is not precluded from relying on the government-speech doctrine merely because it solicits assistance from nongovernmental sources in developing specific messages.

Respondents also contend that the beef program does not qualify as "government speech" because it is funded by a targeted assessment on beef producers, rather than by general revenues. This funding mechanism, they argue, has two relevant effects: it gives control over the beef program not to politically accountable legislators, but to a narrow interest group that will pay no heed to respondents' dissenting views, and it creates the perception that the advertisements speak for beef producers such as respondents.

We reject the first point. The compelled-*subsidy* analysis is altogether unaffected by whether the funds for the promotions are raised by general taxes or through a targeted assessment. Citizens may challenge compelled support of private speech, but have no First Amendment right not to fund government speech. And that is no less true when the funding is achieved through targeted assessments devoted exclusively to the program to which the assessed citizens object. The First Amendment does not confer a right to pay one's taxes into the general fund. . . . Some of our cases have justified compelled funding of government speech by pointing out that government speech is subject to democratic accountability. But our references to "traditional political controls," do not signify that the First Amendment duplicates the Appropriations Clause, or that every instance of government speech must be funded by a line item in an appropriations bill. Here, the beef advertisements are subject to political safeguards more

23. The principal dissent suggests that [the] Government has adopted at best a mixed message, because it also promulgates dietary guidelines that, if followed, would discourage excessive consumption of beef. Even if we agreed that the protection of the government-speech doctrine must be forfeited whenever there is inconsistency in the message, we would nonetheless accord the protection here. The beef promotions are perfectly compatible with the guidelines' message of moderate consumption. . . .

than adequate to set them apart from private messages. The program is authorized and the basic message prescribed by federal statute, and specific requirements for the promotions' content are imposed by federal regulations promulgated after notice and comment. The Secretary of Agriculture, a politically accountable official, oversees the program, appoints and dismisses the key personnel, and retains absolute veto power over the advertisements' content, right down to the wording. And Congress, of course, retains oversight authority, not to mention the ability to reform the program at any time. No more is required.

As to the second point, respondents' argument [is] that crediting the advertising to "America's Beef Producers" impermissibly uses not only their money but also their seeming endorsement to promote a message with which they do not agree. . . . Whether the *individual* respondents who are beef producers would be associated with speech labeled as coming from "America's Beef Producers" is a question on which [the] record [is] silent. [O]n the record before us an as-applied First Amendment challenge to the individual advertisements affords no basis on which to sustain [the judgment.]

The judgment of the Court of Appeals is vacated, and the cases are remanded for further proceedings consistent with this opinion.

It is so ordered.

Justice THOMAS, concurring.

[The] government may not, consistent with the First Amendment, associate individuals or organizations involuntarily with speech by attributing an unwanted message to them, whether or not those individuals fund the speech, and whether or not the message is under the government's control. . . .

Justice BREYER, concurring.

The beef checkoff program in these cases is virtually identical to the mushroom checkoff program in *United Foods* which the Court struck down on First Amendment grounds. . . . I dissented in *United Foods,* based on my view that the challenged assessments involved a form of economic regulation, not speech. . . .

Justice GINSBURG, concurring in the judgment.

[T]he assessments in these cases qualify as permissible economic regulation. . . .

Justice KENNEDY, dissenting.

I join Justice SOUTER's dissenting opinion. . . . I would reserve for another day the difficult First Amendment questions that would arise if the government were to target a discrete group of citizens to pay even for speech that the government does "embrace as publicly as it speaks."

Justice SOUTER, with whom Justice STEVENS and Justice KENNEDY join, dissenting.

[The] ranchers' complaint is on all fours with the objection of the mushroom growers in *United Foods* where a similar statutory exaction was struck down as a compelled subsidy of speech prohibited by the First Amendment absent a comprehensive regulatory scheme to which the speech was incidental. [I]f government relies on the government-speech doctrine to compel specific groups to fund speech with targeted taxes, it must make itself politically accountable by indicating that the content actually is a government message, not just the statement of one self-interested group the government is currently willing to invest with power. [T]he ads are not required to show any sign of being speech by the Government, and experience under the Act demonstrates how effectively the Government has masked its role in producing the ads. [M]any of them include the tag line, "[f]unded by America's Beef Producers," which all but ensures that no one reading them will suspect that the message comes from the National Government. [R]eaders would most naturally think that ads urging people to have beef for dinner were placed and paid for by the beef producers who stand to profit when beef is on the table. No one hearing a commercial for Pepsi or Levi's thinks Uncle Sam is the man talking behind the curtain. Why would a person reading a beef ad think Uncle Sam was trying to make him eat more steak?[24] [Unless the] government speech appears to be coming from the government, its governmental origin cannot possibly justify the burden on the First Amendment interests of the dissenters targeted to pay for it. . . .

∾ PROBLEM: GOVERNMENT SPEECH? ∾

Have you seen the ads at issue in the *Johann* case? Did you realize that they were being financed by a governmental program rather than by a private industry group? Or did you assume that they were being paid for and run by beef producers without governmental control and intervention? If the latter, how does that affect your assessment of the *Johann* decision?

M. CAMPAIGN FINANCE LAWS

Campaign finance reform has been in the news in recent years. Those who favor reform claim that a flood of money tends to corrupt and undermine the political process. Others claim that various proposed reforms unduly impinge on speech and associational rights. Since the mid-1970s, a number of important decisions have been rendered, and many have been controversial.

The modern foundation.   In Buckley v. Valeo, 424 U.S. 1 (1976), the Court considered a challenge to provisions of the Federal Election Campaign Act of 1971

---

24. [A]nyone who did draw such an unlikely connection would also have to believe that Uncle Sam was having a hard time making his mind up, for [other] governmental messages take a different view of how much beef Americans should be eating. Dietary Guidelines for Americans 2005, a publication of the Departments of Agriculture and of Health and Human Services, [suggests] that most Americans need to reduce their consumption of fats, and should get most of the fats they do eat from sources other than beef, namely fish, nuts, and vegetable oils. . . .

(FECA) and related 1974 amendments. FECA prohibited individuals from contributing more than $25,000 in a single year or more than $1,000 to any single candidate for an election campaign and from spending more than $1,000 a year "relative to a clearly identified candidate." Other provisions restricted a candidate's use of personal and family resources in his or her campaign and limited the overall amount that could be spent by a candidate in campaigning for federal office.

Distinguishing contributions from expenditures.   The *Buckley* Court began with a recognition that contribution and expenditure limitations "operate in an area of the most fundamental First Amendment activities" because "[d]iscussion of public issues and debate on the qualifications of candidates are integral to the operation of the system of government established by our Constitution." Indeed, the Court recognized that "[i]n a republic where the people are sovereign, the ability of the citizenry to make informed choices among candidates for office is essential, for the identities of those who are elected will inevitably shape the course that we follow as a nation." As a result, the Court refused to treat campaign expenditures as "conduct," or to apply a lesser standard of review such as the *O'Brien* test. The Court also refused to view the restrictions as "reasonable time, place, and manner regulations." Regarding FECA's expenditure limitations, the Court concluded that "[a] restriction on the amount of money a person or group can spend on political communication during a campaign necessarily reduces the quantity of expression by restricting the number of issues discussed, the depth of their exploration, and the size of the audience reached. This is because virtually every means of communicating ideas in today's mass society requires the expenditure of money." Moreover, given the cost of modern communications, the Court concluded that the $1,000 ceiling on spending "relative to a clearly identified candidate" would "appear to exclude all citizens and groups except candidates, political parties, and the institutional press from any significant use of the most effective modes of communication."

By contrast, the Court viewed FECA's expenditure limitations as involving "only a marginal restriction upon the contributor's ability to engage in free communication." Even though a "contribution serves as a general expression of support for the candidate and his views," it "does not communicate the underlying basis for the support." Moreover, the "quantity of communication by the contributor does not increase perceptibly with the size of his contribution, since the expression rests solely on the undifferentiated, symbolic act of contributing. At most, the size of the contribution provides a very rough index of the intensity of the contributor's support for the candidate." Nevertheless, the Court expressed concern that "contribution restrictions could have a severe impact on political dialogue if the limitations prevented candidates and political committees from amassing the resources necessary for effective advocacy." But the Court did not view FECA's contribution limitations as having such a dire impact. The Court also expressed concern that FECA might impinge on associational freedoms. Campaign contributions allow individuals to pool their money and affiliate with a candidate.

Contribution limitations. In applying these principles, the Court upheld FECA's prohibition against making "contributions to any candidate with respect to any election for Federal office which, in the aggregate, exceed $1,000." The Court concluded that the right of association by contribution was not absolute, and that even a "significant interference with protected rights of political association may be sustained if the State demonstrates a sufficiently important interest and employs means closely drawn to avoid unnecessary abridgment of associational freedoms." The Court found such an interest in the Act's goal of limiting the "actuality and appearance of corruption resulting from large individual financial contributions." The Court noted: "To the extent that large contributions are given to secure a political *quid pro quo* from current and potential office holders, the integrity of our system of representative democracy is undermined. . . . Of almost equal concern [is] the appearance of corruption stemming from public awareness of the opportunities for abuse inherent in a regime of large individual financial contributions." The Court found that bribery laws were insufficient to serve this objective because they "deal with only the most blatant and specific attempts of those with money to influence governmental action." In addition, the Court found that FECA's "contribution limitations in themselves do not undermine to any material degree the potential for robust and effective discussion of candidates and campaign issues by individual citizens, associations, the institutional press, candidates, and political parties." In order to prevent evasion of the $1,000 contribution limit, the Court also upheld an overall $25,000 limitation on total contributions by an individual during any calendar year.

Expenditure limitations. By contrast, the Court found that FECA's expenditure ceilings impose direct and substantial restraints on the quantity of political speech. The Court found that the limitations limit political expression "at the core of our electoral process and of the First Amendment freedoms." In particular, the Court found that the $1,000 limit on expenditures "relative to a clearly identified candidate" effectively precluded:

> all individuals, who are neither candidates nor owners of institutional press facilities, and all groups, except political parties and campaign organizations, from voicing their views "relative to a clearly identified candidate" through means that entail aggregate expenditures of more than $1,000 during a calendar year. The provision, for example, would make it a federal criminal offense for a person or association to place a single one-quarter page advertisement "relative to a clearly identified candidate" in a major metropolitan newspaper.

The Court found that the governmental interest in preventing corruption and the appearance of corruption was inadequate to justify the restriction. The Court noted that so "long as persons and groups eschew expenditures that in express terms advocate the election or defeat of a clearly identified candidate, they are free to spend as much as they want to promote the candidate and his views." The Court concluded that the "absence of prearrangement and coordination of an expenditure with the candidate or his agent not only undermines the value of the expenditure to the candidate, but also alleviates the danger that expenditures will be given as a *quid pro quo* for improper commitments from the candidate." The

Court flatly rejected the notion that the "governmental interest in equalizing the relative ability of individuals and groups to influence the outcome of elections" justifies the limitation. The "concept that government may restrict the speech of some elements of our society in order to enhance the relative voice of others is wholly foreign to the First Amendment."

The Court also struck down FECA's limitations on the amount that a candidate could spend "from his personal funds, or the personal funds of his immediate family, in connection with his campaigns during any calendar year." Not only did the Court find that the limitation imposed a substantial restraint on free expression, but the Court emphasized that the "candidate, no less than any other person, has a First Amendment right to engage in the discussion of public issues and vigorously and tirelessly to advocate his own election. . . ." The Court noted that "it is of particular importance that candidates have the unfettered opportunity to make their views known so that the electorate may intelligently evaluate the candidates' personal qualities and their positions on vital public issues before choosing among them on election day." The Court found that the governmental interest in preventing actual or apparent corruption was ill served because "the use of personal funds reduces the candidate's dependence on outside contributions and thereby counteracts the coercive pressures and attendant risks of abuse to which the Act's contribution limitations are directed."

The Court also invalidated overall campaign expenditures by candidates seeking nomination for election and election to federal office. The Court found that the governmental interest in "alleviating the corrupting influence of large contributions is served by the Act's contribution limitations and disclosure provisions rather than by §608(c)'s campaign expenditure ceilings." In addition, the Court again found that the "interest in equalizing the financial resources of candidates competing for federal office is no more convincing a justification for restricting the scope of federal election campaigns."

Reporting and disclosure requirements. The FECA statute also imposes reporting and disclosure requirements related to campaign expenditures. The Court was concerned that disclosure of campaign contributions and expenditures might be used to harm associational interests. Indeed, the Court concluded that the "strict test established by NAACP v. Alabama is necessary because compelled disclosure has the potential for substantially infringing the exercise of First Amendment rights." Nevertheless, the Court concluded that various governmental interests were sufficiently important to outweigh any possible associational infringements:

> The governmental interests sought to be vindicated by the disclosure requirements are of this magnitude. They fall into three categories. First, disclosure provides the electorate with information "as to where political campaign money comes from and how it is spent by the candidate" in order to aid the voters in evaluating those who seek federal office. [The] sources of a candidate's financial support also alert the voter to the interests to which a candidate is most likely to be responsive and thus facilitate predictions of future performance in office. Second, disclosure requirements deter actual corruption and avoid the appearance of corruption by

exposing large contributions and expenditures to the light of publicity. [A] public armed with information about a candidate's most generous supporters is better able to detect any post-election special favors that may be given in return. Third, and not least significant, record-keeping, reporting, and disclosure requirements are an essential means of gathering the data necessary to detect violations of the contribution limitations described above.

Thus, even though the Court concluded that "public disclosure of contributions to candidates and political parties will deter some individuals who otherwise might contribute" and might "even expose contributors to harassment or retaliation," the Court found that the "[d]isclosure requirements [appear] to be the least restrictive means of curbing the evils of campaign ignorance and corruption that Congress found to exist. . . ." In response to minor party arguments that the disclosure requirements would be especially harmful to their associational interests, the Court concluded that it would not assume that courts would be insensitive if a sufficient showing of harm were made.

The Court also upheld a reporting requirement demanding that "[e]very person (other than a political committee or candidate) who makes contributions or expenditures" aggregating over $100 in a calendar year "other than by contribution to a political committee or candidate" file a statement with the commission. Relying on NAACP v. Alabama, the Court again applied strict scrutiny and again upheld the standard.

Financing of presidential election campaigns. Finally, the Court upheld the Presidential Election Campaign Fund, which financed 1) party nominating conventions, 2) general election campaigns, and 3) primary campaigns. The Act awarded differing amounts to "major" and "minor" parties based on their performance in the most recent presidential election. "New" parties received no funding. To be eligible for funds, major party candidates must pledge not to incur expenses in excess of the entitlement and not to accept private contributions except to the extent that the fund is insufficient to provide the full entitlement. The Court upheld the fund, noting that "public financing as a means of eliminating the improper influence of large private contributions furthers a significant governmental interest."

Buckley dissents. Only Justice White argued in dissent for upholding the expenditure limitations because they would "help eradicate the hazard of corruption." By contrast, Chief Justice Burger and Justice Blackmun favored the invalidation of both the contribution and expenditure limits. Justice Burger also opposed the required disclosure of "modest contributions that are the prime support of new, unpopular, or unfashionable political causes," and he would have invalidated the presidential campaign finance system because of the disadvantage it imposed on a candidate who has a poor constituency. Justice Marshall agreed with Justice White's dissenting position that favored limits on personal spending by candidates, because such limits would "help to assure that only individuals with a modicum of support from others will be viable candidates."

Notes

1. *Invalid Contribution Limits.* The Court upheld the validity of contribution limits in cases after *Buckley*, while noting that very low limits might not be constitutional. In Randall v. Sorrell, 548 U.S. 230 (2003), the Court invalidated a Vermont statute that allowed contributions of $200 to a candidate for state representative, $300 to a candidate for state senator, and $400 to a candidate for governor and other statewide offices. These limits applied to individuals, political action committees, and political parties. Chief Justice Roberts, joined by Justices Breyer and Alito, found that these low limits were not "closely drawn" under *Buckley* to serve the state's interest in preventing corruption and the appearance of corruption. The plurality relied on five factors: 1) the limits would significantly restrict the amount of funding available for challengers to run competitive campaigns, 2) they posed a threat of harm to the right to associate in a political party, 3) they did not exclude expenses incurred by volunteers in the course of campaign activities; 4) they were not adjusted for inflation, and 5) it was unlikely that higher contributions (such as $250, $350, and $450) would be a corruptive force. Justices Thomas and Scalia concurred, arguing that *Buckley*'s doctrine should be modified to require strict scrutiny for contribution limits, and reasoning that the Vermont limits would fail that scrutiny. Justice Kennedy concurred in the result. Justices Souter, Stevens, and Ginsburg dissented.

2. *Millionaire Amendment.* There is no public funding for candidates for the U.S. House of Representatives, and individual donors may contribute only $2,300 to a candidate, while national or state political party committees are limited to $40,900 for general election coordinated expenditures for a candidate. As part of the Bipartisan Campaign Reform Act of 2002 (BCRA), which amended the FECA statute, Congress enacted the "Millionaire's Amendment," so that when one "self-financing" candidate made expenditures that exceeded $350,000 from personal finances, that candidate's opponent could receive individual contributions at three times the statutory limit ($6,900) and also receive unlimited coordinated party expenditures. In Federal Election Commission v. Davis, 128 S.Ct. 2759 (2008), the Court invalidated this provision under *Buckley*, reasoning that it impermissibly burdened a self-financing candidate's "unfettered right to make personal expenditures." This right was abridged in *Davis* because the self-financing candidate was required to "abide by a limit on personal expenditures or endure the burden" caused by the "activation of a scheme of discriminatory contribution limits." As in *Buckley*, this burden could not be justified by the government interest in eliminating corruption or the perception of corruption because reliance on personal funds reduces the threat of corruption. The *Davis* Court also rejected the legitimacy of two other proffered government interests, in leveling "electoral opportunities of different personal wealth" and in mitigating the contribution limits that make it harder for nonwealthy candidates to raise funds. Justices Stevens, Souter, Ginsburg, and Breyer dissented.

3. *Judicial Elections.* In Caperton v. A.T. Massey Coal Co., 129 S.Ct. 2252 (2009), the Court identified the circumstances when recusal of a judge is required by due process because of a "serious risk of actual bias" based on "objective and

reasonable perceptions." The Court held that the judge's failure to recuse himself on the "extreme facts" in *Caperton* violated the Due Process Clause because "a person with a personal stake in a particular case had a significant and disproportionate influence in placing the judge on the case by raising funds or directing the judge's election campaign when the case was pending or imminent." The chairman of the defendant company in *Caperton* provided $3 million to help elect a candidate for the state supreme court, at a time when it was reasonably foreseeable that the court would consider the appeal of a judgment for $50 million against the company. The Court held that the due process inquiry "centers on the contribution's relative size in comparison to the total amount of money contributed to the campaign, the total amount spent in the election, and the apparent effect such contribution had on the outcome of the election." The $3 million amount "eclipsed the total amount spent" by all other supporters of the candidate, and "exceeded by 300%" the amount spent by the candidate's campaign committee. The four justices who dissented in *Caperton* argued that the new due process standard would lead to a flood of frivolous recusal motions because of the lack of "clear, workable guidelines" to define a probability of bias in future cases.

∾ PROBLEMS ∾

1. *Campaign Funding and the Justifications for Protecting Speech.* Does campaign speech, and more specifically the funding of that speech, meet any of the justifications for protecting speech presented at the beginning of this chapter? In other words, do they provide a safety valve, do they promote self-fulfillment or the marketplace of ideas, or are they related to the democratic process? Explain.

2. *Does Money Matter?* During the 2008 presidential campaign, John McCain accepted public financing and received $84 million for his campaign. By contrast, Barack Obama eschewed public financing and was able to raise and spend nearly $700 million. Obama won the election, with roughly 7 percent more of the popular vote. Obama used his extra money to buy more television advertisements, to hire more staff, and to pay for get-out-the-vote efforts. Would the outcome of the election have been the same if the financial situations of the two candidates had been reversed?

3. *Should We Worry?* The differences in financing between the Obama and McCain campaigns might be disturbing, in the sense that it might be argued that Obama was able to "buy" the presidency. One of the interesting things about the Obama campaign is that he attracted large numbers of small donors in both the primary and the general election campaigns. *See* Michael Luo, "Political Memo: What Happens to Public Financing, When Obama Thrived Without It?", *New York Times*, A-17, c. 1-6 (Nov. 3, 2008). Should we embrace such donations when they come from legions of small donors rather than from wealthy individuals and corporations?

4. *The Future of Public Financing.* In the aftermath of the 2008 election, will future candidates for President of the United States be reluctant to accept public financing for their campaigns? Does the acceptance of such financing amount to

unilateral disarmament against an opponent who chooses to opt out of the campaign finance system?

5. *The Right to Receive Campaign Contributions.* Assume that a Connecticut statute establishes very low contribution limits that violate the First Amendment under *Buckley* and *Randall.* A losing candidate for attorney general decides to file a suit for damages, claiming that the prior enforcement of the statute deprived her of "needed financing for her campaign from otherwise willing supporters" and violated her "First Amendment right to receive campaign contributions." Do the Court's decisions in *Buckley* or *Randall* establish such a right? *See* Dean v. Blumenthal, 577 F.3d 60 (2d Cir. 2009).

6. *The Millionaire's Amendment and Public Financing.* An Arizona statute provides voluntary public financing to candidates for state political offices, and a candidate who chooses to participate must relinquish his or her right to raise private campaign contributions. Each participating candidate receives an initial grant of funds from the state to spend on his or her campaign. If this candidate has an opponent who is not participating in the public financing system and whose expenditures exceed the initial grant, the participating candidate will receive "matching funds" in the amount of the spending of the nonparticipating opponent, plus the value of independent expenditures against the participating candidate in support of his or her nonparticipating opponent, reduced by the amount of "early contributions" raised by the nonparticipating opponent during the preprimary fundraising period. However, these matching funds, combined with the initial grant, may not exceed three times the amount of the initial grant. Does the statute violate *Buckley* or *Davis*? *See* McComish v. Bennett, 611 F.3d 510 (9th Cir. 2010).

Citizens United v. Federal Election Commission
130 S.Ct. 876 (2010)

Justice KENNEDY delivered the opinion of the Court.

Federal law prohibits corporations and unions from using their general treasury funds to make independent expenditures for speech defined as an "electioneering communication" or for speech expressly advocating the election or defeat of a candidate. Limits on electioneering communications were upheld in McConnell v. Federal Election Commn., 540 U.S. 93, 203-209 (2003). The holding of *McConnell* rested to a large extent on an earlier case, Austin v. Michigan Chamber of Commerce, 494 U.S. 652 (1990)[.]

In this case we are asked to reconsider *Austin* and, in effect, *McConnell*[,] [and we] hold that *stare decisis* does not compel the continued acceptance of *Austin.* The Government may regulate corporate political speech through disclaimer and disclosure requirements, but it may not suppress that speech altogether. We turn now to the case before us.

I

Citizens United is a nonprofit corporation [with] an annual budget of about $12 million. Most of its funds are from donations by individuals; but, in addition, it accepts a small portion of its funds from for-profit corporations.

In January 2008, Citizens United released a film entitled *Hillary: The Movie* [*Hillary*]. It is a 90-minute documentary about then-Senator Hillary Clinton, who was a candidate in the Democratic Party's 2008 Presidential primary elections. *Hillary* [depicts] interviews with political commentators and other persons, most of them quite critical of Senator Clinton. *Hillary* was released in theaters and on DVD, but Citizens United wanted to increase distribution by making it available through video-on-demand.

[In] December 2007, a cable company offered, for a payment of $1.2 million, to make *Hillary* available on a video-on-demand channel called "Elections '08." . . . [To] implement the proposal, Citizens United was prepared to pay for the video-on-demand; [it] produced two 10-second ads and one 30-second ad [to] promote the video-on-demand offering by running advertisements on broadcast and cable television.

Before the Bipartisan Campaign Reform Act of 2002 (BCRA), federal law prohibited — and still does prohibit — corporations and unions from using general treasury funds to make direct contributions to candidates or independent expenditures that expressly advocate the election or defeat of a candidate, through any form of media, in connection with certain qualified federal elections. [Then] BCRA §203 amended [2 U.S.C.] §441b to prohibit any "electioneering communication" [which] is defined as "any broadcast, cable or satellite communication" that "refers to a clearly identified candidate for Federal office" and is made within 30 days of a primary or 60 days of a general election. [Corporations] and unions are barred from using their general treasury funds for express advocacy or electioneering communications. They may establish, however, a "separate segregated fund" (known as a political action committee, or PAC) for these purposes. The moneys received by the segregated fund are limited to donations from stockholders and employees of the corporation or, in the case of unions, members of the union.

Citizens United wanted to make *Hillary* available through video-on-demand within 30 days of the 2008 primary elections. It feared, however, that both the film and the ads would be covered by §441b's ban on corporate funded independent expenditures, thus subjecting the corporation to civil and criminal penalties[.] In December 2007, Citizens United sought declaratory and injunctive relief[,] argu[ing] that (1) §441b is unconstitutional as applied to *Hillary*; and (2) BCRA's disclaimer and disclosure requirements [in] §§201 and 311 [are] unconstitutional as applied to *Hillary* and to the three ads for the movie. [The three-judge District Court rejected these arguments and granted the Federal Election Commission's (FEC) motion for summary judgment. Citizens United appealed, and the Supreme Court heard oral argument in March 2009.]

[The] case was reargued [after] the Court asked the parties [in June 2009] to file supplemental briefs addressing whether we should overrule either or both *Austin* and the part of *McConnell* which addresses the facial validity of 2 U.S.C. §441b.

II

Before considering whether *Austin* should be overruled, we first address whether Citizens United's claim that §441b cannot be applied to *Hillary* may be resolved on other, narrower grounds. . . .

Citizens United [argues] that §441b may not be applied to *Hillary* under the approach taken in *WRTL* [Federal Election Commn. v. Wisconsin Right to Life, Inc., 551 U.S. 449, 469-470 (2007)]. [*WRTL*] found an unconstitutional application of §441b where the speech was not "express advocacy or its functional equivalent." 551 U.S., at 481. [This] test is objective: "a court should find that [a communication] is the functional equivalent of express advocacy only if [it] is susceptible of no reasonable interpretation other than as an appeal to vote for or against a specific candidate."

Under this test, *Hillary* is equivalent to express advocacy. The movie, in essence, is a feature-length negative advertisement that urges viewers to vote against Senator Clinton for President. In light of historical footage, interviews with persons critical of her, and voiceover narration, the film would be understood by most viewers as an extended criticism of Senator Clinton's character and her fitness for the office of the Presidency[.]

Citizens United argues that *Hillary* is just "a documentary film that examines certain historical events." We disagree. The movie's consistent emphasis is on the relevance of these events to Senator Clinton's candidacy for President. The narrator begins by asking, "Could [Senator Clinton] become the first female President in the history of the United States?" And the narrator reiterates the movie's message in his closing line: "Finally, before America decides on our next president, voters should need no reminders of . . . what's at stake — the well being and prosperity of our nation." . . .

[Citizens United's other] narrower arguments are not sustainable under a fair reading of the statute. In the exercise of its judicial responsibility, it is necessary then for the Court to consider the facial validity of §441b. Any other course of decision would prolong the substantial, nation-wide chilling effect caused by §441b's prohibitions on corporate expenditures[.] . . .

III

[The] law before us is an outright ban, backed by criminal sanctions. [The] following acts would all be felonies under §441b: The Sierra Club runs an ad, within the crucial phase of 60 days before the general election, that exhorts the public to disapprove of a Congressman who favors logging in national forests; the National Rifle Association publishes a book urging the public to vote for the challenger because the incumbent U.S. Senator supports a handgun ban; and the American Civil Liberties Union creates a Web site telling the public to vote for a

Presidential candidate in light of that candidate's defense of free speech. These prohibitions are classic examples of censorship.

Section 441b is a ban on corporate speech notwithstanding the fact that a PAC created by a corporation can still speak. A PAC is a separate association from the corporation. So the PAC exemption from §441b's expenditure ban does not allow corporations to speak. [T]he option to form PACs does not alleviate the First Amendment problems with §441b. PACs are burdensome alternatives; they are expensive to administer and subject to extensive regulations. . . . [This] might explain why fewer than 2,000 of the millions of corporations in this country have PACs[.]

Section 441b's prohibition on corporate independent expenditures is thus a ban on speech. As a "restriction on the amount of money a person or group can spend on political communication during a campaign," that statute "necessarily reduces the quantity of expression by restricting the number of issues discussed, the depth of their exploration, and the size of the audience reached." Buckley v. Valeo, 424 U.S. 1 (1976) (per curiam). Were the Court to uphold these restrictions, the Government could repress speech by silencing certain voices at any of the various points in the speech process. If §441b applied to individuals, no one would believe that it is merely a time, place, or manner restriction on speech. Its purpose and effect are to silence entities whose voices the Government deems to be suspect.

Speech is an essential mechanism of democracy, for it is the means to hold officials accountable to the people. The right of citizens to inquire, to hear, to speak, and to use information to reach consensus is a pre-condition to enlightened self-government and a necessary means to protect it. The First Amendment "'has its fullest and most urgent application' to speech uttered during a campaign for political office." Eu v. San Francisco County Democratic Central Comm., 489 U.S. 214 (1989).

[Laws] that burden political speech are "subject to strict scrutiny," which requires the Government to prove that the restriction "furthers a compelling interest and is narrowly tailored to achieve that interest." WRTL, 551 U.S., at 464[.]

Premised on mistrust of governmental power, the First Amendment stands against attempts to disfavor certain subjects or viewpoints. Prohibited, too, are restrictions distinguishing among different speakers, allowing speech by some but not others. See First Nat. Bank of Boston v. Bellotti, 435 U.S. 765 (1978). As instruments to censor, these categories are interrelated: Speech restrictions based on the identity of the speaker are all too often simply a means to control content.

[By] taking the right to speak from some and giving it to others, the Government deprives the disadvantaged person or class of the right to use speech to strive to establish worth, standing, and respect for the speaker's voice. The Government may not by these means deprive the public of the right and privilege to determine for itself what speech and speakers are worthy of consideration. The First Amendment protects speech and speaker, and the ideas that flow from each.

[It] is inherent in the nature of the political process that voters must be free to obtain information from diverse sources in order to determine how to cast their votes. At least before Austin, the Court had not allowed the exclusion of a class of speakers from the general public dialogue.

We find no basis for the proposition that, in the context of political speech, the Government may impose restrictions on certain disfavored speakers. Both history and logic lead us to this conclusion.

A

[In] *Buckley*, the Court addressed various challenges to the Federal Election Campaign Act of 1971 (FECA), as amended in 1974. These amendments created 18 U.S.C. §608(e), an independent expenditure ban separate from §610 that applied to individuals as well as corporations and labor unions.

[*Buckley*] first upheld §608(b), FECA's limits on direct contributions to candidates. The *Buckley* Court recognized a "sufficiently important" governmental interest in "the prevention of corruption and the appearance of corruption." This followed from the Court's concern that large contributions could be given "to secure a political *quid pro quo*." [424 U.S., at 25.]

The *Buckley* Court explained that the potential for *quid pro quo* corruption distinguished direct contributions to candidates from independent expenditures. The Court emphasized that "the independent expenditure ceiling . . . fails to serve any substantial governmental interest in stemming the reality or appearance of corruption in the electoral process," because "[t]he absence of prearrangement and coordination . . . alleviates the danger that expenditures will be given as a *quid pro quo* for improper commitments from the candidate." *Buckley* invalidated §608(e)'s restrictions on independent expenditures[.]

Buckley did not consider §610's separate ban on corporate and union independent expenditures[.] Had §610 been challenged in the wake of *Buckley*, however, it could not have been squared with the reasoning and analysis of that precedent. The expenditure ban invalidated in *Buckley*, §608(e), applied to corporations and unions, and some of the prevailing plaintiffs in *Buckley* were corporations[.]

Notwithstanding this precedent, Congress recodified §610's corporate and union expenditure ban at 2 U.S.C. §441b four months after *Buckley* was decided. Section 441b is the independent expenditure restriction challenged here.

Less than two years after *Buckley*, *Bellotti* reaffirmed the First Amendment principle that the Government cannot restrict political speech based on the speaker's corporate identity. [*Bellotti*] struck down a state-law prohibition on corporate independent expenditures related to referenda issues: "[In] the realm of protected speech, the legislature is constitutionally disqualified from dictating the subjects about what persons may speak and the speakers who may address a public issue." [435 U.S.,] at 784-785.

It is important to note that the reasoning and holding of *Bellotti* did not rest on the existence of a viewpoint-discriminatory statute. It rested on the principle that the Government lacks the power to ban corporations from speaking.

Bellotti did not address the constitutionality of the State's ban on corporate independent expenditures to support candidates. In our view, however, that restriction would have been unconstitutional under *Bellotti*'s central principle:

that the First Amendment does not allow political speech restrictions based on a speaker's corporate identity.

Thus the law stood until *Austin*. Austin "uph[eld] a direct restriction on the independent expenditure of funds for political speech for the first time in [this Court's] history." 494 U.S., at 695 (Kennedy, J., dissenting). There, the Michigan Chamber of Commerce sought to use general treasury funds to run a newspaper ad supporting a specific candidate. Michigan law, however, prohibited corporate independent expenditures that supported or opposed any candidate for state office. A violation of the law was punishable as a felony. The Court sustained the speech prohibition.

To bypass *Buckley* and *Bellotti*, the *Austin* Court identified a new governmental interest in limiting political speech: an antidistortion interest. *Austin* found a compelling governmental interest in preventing "the corrosive and distorting effects of immense aggregations of wealth that are accumulated with the help of the corporate form and that have little or no correlation to the public's support for the corporation's political ideas." 494 U.S., at 660.

B

The Court is thus confronted with conflicting lines of precedent: a pre-*Austin* line that forbids restrictions on political speech based on the speaker's corporate identity and a post-*Austin* line that permits them. No case before *Austin* had held that Congress could prohibit independent expenditures for political speech based on the speaker's corporate identity[.]

In its defense of the corporate-speech restrictions in §441b, the Government notes the antidistortion rationale on which *Austin* and its progeny rest in part, yet it all but abandons reliance upon it. It argues instead that two other compelling interests support *Austin*'s holding that corporate expenditure restrictions are constitutional: an anticorruption interest, and a shareholder-protection interest. We consider the three points in turn.

1

[The] Government contends that *Austin* permits it to ban corporate expenditures for almost all forms of communication stemming from a corporation. If *Austin* were correct, the Government could prohibit a corporation from expressing political views in media beyond those presented here, such as by printing books. [This] troubling assertion of brooding governmental power cannot be reconciled with the confidence and stability in civic discourse that the First Amendment must secure.

[*Austin*] sought to defend the antidistortion rationale as a means to prevent corporations from obtaining "an unfair advantage in the political marketplace" by using "resources amassed in the economic marketplace." But *Buckley* rejected the premise that the Government has an interest "in equalizing the relative ability of individuals and groups to influence the outcome of elections." *Buckley* was specific in stating that "the skyrocketing cost of political campaigns" could not sustain the governmental prohibition. The First Amendment's protections do not depend on the speaker's "financial ability to engage in public discussion."

The Court reaffirmed these conclusions when it invalidated the BCRA provision that increased the cap on contributions to one candidate if the opponent made certain expenditures from personal funds. *See* Davis v. Federal Election Commn., 128 S. Ct. 2759 (2008). The rule that political speech cannot be limited based on a speaker's wealth is a necessary consequence of the premise that the First Amendment generally prohibits the suppression of political speech based on the speaker's identity.

[T]he *Austin* majority undertook to distinguish wealthy individuals from corporations on the ground that "[s]tate law grants corporations special advantages such as limited liability, perpetual life, and favorable treatment of the accumulation and distribution of assets." This does not suffice, however, to allow laws prohibiting speech. "It is rudimentary that the State cannot exact as the price of those special advantages the forfeiture of First Amendment rights."

It is irrelevant for purposes of the First Amendment that corporate funds may "have little or no correlation to the public's support for the corporation's political ideas." [*Austin*, 494 U.S.,] at 660 (majority opinion). All speakers, including individuals and the media, use money amassed from the economic marketplace to fund their speech. The First Amendment protects the resulting speech, even if it was enabled by economic transactions with persons or entities who disagree with the speaker's ideas.

Austin's antidistortion rationale would produce the dangerous, and unacceptable, consequence that Congress could ban political speech of media corporations. [They] are now exempt from §441b's ban on corporate expenditures. Yet media corporations accumulate wealth with the help of the corporate form, the largest media corporations have "immense aggregations of wealth," and the views expressed by media corporations often "have little or no correlation to the public's support" for those views. *Austin*, 494 U.S., at 660. Thus, under the Government's reasoning, wealthy media corporations could have their voices diminished to put them on par with other media entities. There is no precedent for permitting this under the First Amendment.

The media exemption discloses further difficulties with the law now under consideration. There is no precedent supporting laws that attempt to distinguish between corporations which are deemed to be exempt as media corporations and those which are not. [With] the advent of the Internet and the decline of print and broadcast media, moreover, the line between the media and others who wish to comment on political and social issues becomes far more blurred.

The [media] exemption results in a further, separate reason for finding this law invalid: [the] exemption applies to media corporations owned or controlled by corporations that have diverse and substantial investments and participate in endeavors other than news. [So] the exemption would allow a conglomerate that owns both a media business and an unrelated business to influence or control the media in order to advance its overall business interest. [S]ome other corporation, with [no] media outlet in its ownership structure, would be forbidden to speak or inform the public about the same issue. This differential treatment cannot be squared with the First Amendment. . . .

[*Austin*] interferes with the "open marketplace" of ideas protected by the First Amendment. It permits the Government to ban the political speech of millions of associations of citizens. Most of these are small corporations without large amounts of wealth. This fact belies the Government's argument that the statute is justified on the ground that it prevents the "distorting effects of immense aggregations of wealth." It is not even aimed at amassed wealth. . . .

[The] purpose and effect of this law is to prevent corporations, including small and nonprofit corporations, from presenting both facts and opinions to the public. This makes *Austin*'s antidistortion rationale all the more an aberration. [Corporate] executives and employees counsel Members of Congress and Presidential administrations on many issues, as a matter of routine and often in private. [When] that phenomenon is coupled with §441b, the result is that smaller or nonprofit corporations cannot raise a voice to object when other corporations, including those with vast wealth, are cooperating with the Government. That cooperation may be voluntary or it may be at the demand of a Government official who uses his or her authority, influence, and power to threaten corporations to support the Government's policies. Those kinds of interactions are often unknown and unseen. The speech that §441b forbids, though, is public, and all can judge its content and purpose. References to massive corporate treasuries should not mask the real operation of the law. Rhetoric ought not obscure reality.

Even if §441b's expenditure ban were constitutional, wealthy corporations could still lobby elected officials, although smaller corporations may not have the resources to do so. And wealthy individuals and unincorporated associations can spend unlimited amounts on independent expenditures. Yet certain disfavored associations of citizens — those that have taken on the corporate form — are penalized for engaging in the same political speech. . . .

2

[The] Government falls back on the argument that corporate political speech can be banned in order to prevent corruption or its appearance. In *Buckley*, the Court found this interest "sufficiently important" to allow limits on contributions but did not extend that reasoning to expenditure limits. When *Buckley* examined an expenditure ban, it found "that the governmental interest in preventing corruption and the appearance of corruption [was] inadequate to justify [the ban] on independent expenditures." [424 U.S., at 25, 45.]

With regard to large direct contributions, *Buckley* reasoned that they could be given "to secure a political *quid pro quo*," and that "the scope of such pernicious practices can never be reliably ascertained." The practices *Buckley* noted would be covered by bribery laws if a *quid pro quo* arrangement were proved. The Court, in consequence, has noted that restrictions on direct contributions are preventative, because few if any contributions to candidates will involve *quid pro quo* arrangements. The *Buckley* Court, nevertheless, sustained limits on direct contributions in order to ensure against the reality or appearance of corruption. That case did not extend this rationale to independent expenditures, and the Court does not do so here.

"The absence of prearrangement and coordination of an expenditure with the candidate or his agent not only undermines the value of the expenditure to the candidate, but also alleviates the danger that expenditures will be given as a *quid pro quo* for improper commitments from the candidate." 424 U.S., at 47. Limits on independent expenditures, such as §441b, have a chilling effect extending well beyond the Government's interest in preventing *quid pro quo* corruption. The anticorruption interest is not sufficient to displace the speech here in question. Indeed, 26 States do not restrict independent expenditures by for-profit corporations. The Government does not claim that these expenditures have corrupted the political process in those States.

[When] *Buckley* identified a sufficiently important governmental interest in preventing corruption or the appearance of corruption, that interest was limited to *quid pro quo* corruption. The fact that speakers may have influence over or access to elected officials does not mean that these officials are corrupt. [Reliance] on a "generic favoritism or influence theory . . . is at odds with standard First Amendment analyses because it is unbounded and susceptible to no limiting principle." [*McConnell*, 540 U.S., at 296 (opinion of Kennedy, J.).]

The appearance of influence or access, furthermore, will not cause the electorate to lose faith in our democracy. By definition, an independent expenditure is political speech presented to the electorate that is not coordinated with a candidate. The fact that a corporation, or any other speaker, is willing to spend money to try to persuade voters presupposes that the people have the ultimate influence over elected officials. This is inconsistent with any suggestion that the electorate will refuse "'to take part in democratic governance'" because of additional political speech made by a corporation or any other speaker. *McConnell*, [540 U.S.,] at 144.

The *McConnell* record was "over 100,000 pages" long, yet it "does not have any direct examples of votes being exchanged for . . . expenditures." This confirms *Buckley*'s reasoning that independent expenditures do not lead to, or create the appearance of, *quid pro quo* corruption. In fact, there is only scant evidence that independent expenditures even ingratiate. Ingratiation and access, in any event, are not corruption. The BCRA record establishes that certain donations to political parties, called "soft money," were made to gain access to elected officials. This case, however, is about independent expenditures, not soft money. When Congress finds that a problem exists, we must give that finding due deference; but Congress may not choose an unconstitutional remedy. [An] outright ban on corporate political speech during the critical preelection period is not a permissible remedy[.]

3

The Government contends further that corporate independent expenditures can be limited because of its interest in protecting dissenting shareholders from being compelled to fund corporate political speech. This asserted interest, like *Austin*'s antidistortion rationale, would allow the Government to ban the

political speech even of media corporations. Assume, for example, that a shareholder of a corporation that owns a newspaper disagrees with the political views
the newspaper expresses. Under the Government's view, that potential disagreement could give the Government the authority to restrict the media corporation's political speech. [There] is, furthermore, little evidence of abuse that
cannot be corrected by shareholders "through the procedures of corporate
democracy." *Bellotti*, 435 U.S., at 794.

Those reasons are sufficient to reject this shareholder-protection interest;
and, moreover, the statute is both underinclusive and overinclusive. As to the
first, if Congress had been seeking to protect dissenting shareholders, it would
not have banned corporate speech in only certain media within 30 or 60 days
before an election. A dissenting shareholder's interests would be implicated by
speech in any media at any time. As to the second, the statute is overinclusive
because it covers all corporations, including nonprofit corporations and for-
profit corporations with only single shareholders. As to other corporations, the
remedy is not to restrict speech but to consider and explore other regulatory
mechanisms. The regulatory mechanism here, based on speech, contravenes the
First Amendment. . . .

C

Our precedent is to be respected unless the most convincing of reasons
demonstrates that adherence to it puts us on a course that is sure error. "Beyond
workability, the relevant factors in deciding whether to adhere to the principle of
stare decisis include the antiquity of the precedent, the reliance interests at stake,
and of course whether the decision was well reasoned." Montejo v. Louisiana,
129 S.Ct. 2079 (2009). We have also examined whether "experience has
pointed up the precedent's shortcomings," Pearson v. Callahan, 129 S.Ct. 808
(2009).

These considerations counsel in favor of rejecting *Austin*, which itself contravened this Court's earlier precedents in *Buckley* and *Bellotti*. [I]t must be concluded that *Austin* was not well-reasoned. The Government defends *Austin*,
relying almost entirely on "the *quid pro quo* interest, the corruption interest or the
shareholder interest," and not *Austin*'s expressed antidistortion rationale. When
neither party defends the reasoning of a precedent, the principle of adherence to
that precedent through *stare decisis* is diminished[.]

Austin is undermined by experience since its announcement. Political speech
is so ingrained in our culture that speakers find ways to circumvent campaign
finance laws. Our Nation's speech dynamic is changing, and informative voices
should not have to circumvent onerous restrictions to exercise their First Amendment rights. Speakers have become adept at presenting citizens with sound bites,
talking points, and scripted messages that dominate the 24-hour news cycle. Corporations, like individuals, do not have monolithic views. On certain topics corporations may possess valuable expertise, leaving them the best equipped to
point out errors or fallacies in speech of all sorts, including the speech of candidates and elected officials.

Rapid changes in technology and the creative dynamic inherent in the concept of free expression counsel against upholding a law that restricts political speech in certain media or by certain speakers. Today, 30-second television ads may be the most effective way to convey a political message. Soon, however, it may be that Internet sources, such as blogs and social networking Web sites, will provide citizens with significant information about political candidates and issues. Yet, §441b would seem to ban a blog post expressly advocating the election or defeat of a candidate if that blog were created with corporate funds[.]

No serious reliance interests are at stake. [Legislatures] may have enacted bans on corporate expenditures believing that those bans were constitutional. This is not a compelling interest for *stare decisis*. If it were, legislative acts could prevent us from overruling our own precedents, thereby interfering with our duty "to say what the law is." Marbury v. Madison, 1 Cranch 137, 177 (1803).

Due consideration leads to this conclusion: *Austin* should be and now is overruled. We return to the principle established in *Buckley* and *Bellotti* that the Government may not suppress political speech on the basis of the speaker's corporate identity. No sufficient governmental interest justifies limits on the political speech of nonprofit or for-profit corporations.

D

Austin is overruled, so it provides no basis for allowing the Government to limit corporate independent expenditures. As the Government appears to concede, overruling *Austin* "effectively invalidate[s] not only BCRA §203, but also §441b's prohibition on the use of corporate treasury funds for express advocacy." Section §441b's restrictions on corporate independent expenditures are therefore invalid and cannot be applied to *Hillary*.

Given our conclusion we are further required to overrule the part of *McConnell* that upheld BCRA §203's extension of §441b's restrictions on corporate independent expenditures. The *McConnell* Court relied on the antidistortion interest recognized in *Austin* to uphold a greater restriction on speech than the restriction upheld in *Austin*, and we have found this interest unconvincing and insufficient. This part of *McConnell* is now overruled.

IV[25]

A

Citizens United next challenges BCRA's disclaimer and disclosure provisions as applied to *Hillary* and the three advertisements for the movie. Under BCRA §311, televised electioneering communications funded by anyone other than a candidate must include a disclaimer that "_____ is responsible for the content of this advertising." The required statement must be made in a "clearly spoken

---

25. Justices Stevens, Ginsburg, Breyer, and Sotomayor joined in Part IV of the Court's opinion. Justice Thomas joined in all but IV of the Court's opinion and dissented from Part IV.

manner," and displayed on the screen in a "clearly readable manner" for at least four seconds. It must state that the communication "is not authorized by any candidate or candidate's committee"; it must also display the name and address (or Web site address) of the person or group that funded the advertisement. Under BCRA §201, any person who spends more than $10,000 on electioneering communications within a calendar year must file a disclosure statement with the FEC. That statement must identify the person making the expenditure, the amount of the expenditure, the election to which the communication was directed, and the names of certain contributors.

Disclaimer and disclosure requirements may burden the ability to speak, but they "impose no ceiling on campaign-related activities," *Buckley*, 424 U.S., at 64, and "do not prevent anyone from speaking," *McConnell*, [540 U.S.,] at 201. The Court has subjected these requirements to "exacting scrutiny," which requires a "substantial relation" between the disclosure requirement and a "sufficiently important" governmental interest. *Buckley*, [424 U.S.,] at 64.

In *Buckley*, the Court explained that disclosure could be justified based on a governmental interest in "provid[ing] the electorate with information" about the sources of election related spending. 424 U.S., at 66. The *McConnell* Court applied this interest in rejecting facial challenges to BCRA §§201 and 311. There was evidence in the record that independent groups were running election-related advertisements "while hiding behind dubious and misleading names." The Court therefore upheld BCRA §§201 and 311 on the ground that they would help citizens "make informed choices in the political marketplace." 540 U.S., at 197.

Although both provisions were facially upheld, the Court acknowledged that as-applied challenges would be available if a group could show a "'reasonable probability'" that disclosure of its contributors' names "will subject them to threats, harassment, or reprisals from either Government officials or private parties.'" *Id.*, at 198 (quoting *Buckley*, *supra*, at 74).

For the reasons stated below, we find the statute valid as applied to the ads for the movie and to the movie itself.

B

Citizens United sought to broadcast one 30-second and two 10-second ads to promote *Hillary*. Under FEC regulations, a communication that "[p]roposes a commercial transaction" was not subject to §441b's restrictions on corporate or union funding of electioneering communications. The regulations, however, do not exempt those communications from the disclaimer and disclosure requirements in BCRA §§201 and 311.

Citizens United argues that the disclaimer requirements in §311 are unconstitutional as applied to its ads. It contends that the governmental interest in providing information to the electorate does not justify [these] requirements. We disagree. The ads fall within BCRA's definition of an "electioneering communication": They referred to then-Senator Clinton by name shortly before a primary and contained pejorative references to her candidacy. The disclaimers "provid[e] the electorate with information," *McConnell, supra,* at 196, and "insure that the voters are fully informed" about the person or group who is speaking. *Buckley, supra,* at 76. At the very least, the disclaimers avoid confusion by making clear that the ads are not funded by a candidate or political party.

Citizens United argues that §311 is underinclusive because it requires disclaimers for broadcast advertisements but not for print or Internet advertising. It asserts that §311 decreases both the quantity and effectiveness of the group's speech by forcing it to devote four seconds of each advertisement to the spoken disclaimer. We rejected these arguments in *McConnell*. And we now adhere to that decision as it pertains to the disclosure provisions. . . .

[Citizens United] also disputes that an informational interest justifies the application of [the disclosure requirements in] §201 to its ads, which only attempt to persuade viewers to see the film. Even if it disclosed the funding sources for the ads, Citizens United says, the information would not help viewers make informed choices in the political marketplace. . . . [But, even] if the ads only pertain to a commercial transaction, the public has an interest in knowing who is speaking about a candidate shortly before an election. [T]he informational interest alone is sufficient to justify application of §201 to these ads[.]

Last, Citizens United argues that disclosure requirements can chill donations to an organization by exposing donors to retaliation. [In] *McConnell*, the Court recognized that §201 would be unconstitutional as applied to an organization if there were a reasonable probability that the group's members would fact threats, harassment, or reprisals if their names were disclosed. [Citizens United] has offered no evidence that its members may face similar threats or reprisals. To the contrary, Citizens United has been disclosing its donors for years and has identified no instance of harassment or retaliation.

Shareholder objections raised through the procedures of corporate democracy can be more effective today because modern technology makes disclosures rapid and informative. A campaign finance system that pairs corporate independent expenditures with effective disclosure has not existed before today. It must be noted, furthermore, that many of Congress' findings in passing BCRA were premised on a system without adequate disclosure. With the advent of the Internet, prompt disclosure of expenditures can provide shareholders and citizens with the information needed to hold corporations and elected officials accountable for their positions and supporters. [The] First Amendment protects political speech; and disclosure permits citizens and shareholders to react to the speech of corporate entities in a proper way. This transparency enables the electorate to make informed decisions and give proper weight to different speakers and messages. [The application of BCRA §§201 and 311 to *Hillary* is affirmed for the same reasons that justify their application to the ads.]

V

When word concerning the plot of the movie *Mr. Smith Goes to Washington* reached the circles of Government, some officials sought, by persuasion, to discourage its distribution. Under *Austin*, though, officials could have done more than discourage its distribution — they could have banned the film. After all, it, like *Hillary,* was speech funded by a corporation that was critical of Members of Congress. *Mr. Smith Goes to Washington* may be fiction and caricature, but fiction and caricature can be a powerful force.

Modern day movies, television comedies, or skits on Youtube.com might portray public officials or public policies in unflattering ways. Yet if a covered transmission during the blackout period creates the background for candidate endorsement or opposition, a felony occurs solely because a corporation, other than an exempt media corporation, has made the [expenditure of anything of value] in order to engage in political speech. Speech would be suppressed in the realm where its necessity is most evident: in the public dialogue preceding a real election. Governments are often hostile to speech, but under our law and our tradition it seems stranger than fiction for our Government to make this political speech a crime. Yet this is the statute's purpose and design.

Some members of the public might consider *Hillary* to be insightful and instructive; some might find it to be neither high art nor a fair discussion on how to set the Nation's course; still others simply might suspend judgment on these points but decide to think more about issues and candidates. These choices and assessments, however, are not for the Government to make. "The First Amendment underwrites the freedom to experiment and to create in the realm of thought and speech. Citizens must be free to use new forms, and new forums, for the expression of ideas. The civic discourse belongs to the people, and the Government may not prescribe the means used to conduct it." *McConnell, supra,* at 341 (opinion of Kennedy, J.).

The judgment of the District Court is reversed with respect to the constitutionality of 2 U.S.C. §441b's restrictions on corporate independent expenditures. The judgment is affirmed with respect to BCRA's disclaimer and disclosure requirements. The case is remanded for further proceedings consistent with this opinion.

It is so ordered.

Chief Justice ROBERTS, with whom Justice ALITO joins, concurring.

[I] join [the Court's] opinion in full. The First Amendment protects more than just the individual on a soapbox and the lonely pamphleteer. I write separately to address the important principles of judicial restraint and *stare decisis* implicated in this case. . . .

[If] adherence to a precedent actually impedes the stable and orderly adjudication of future cases, its *stare decisis* effect [is] diminished. This can happen in a number of circumstances, such as when the precedent's validity is so hotly contested that it cannot reliably function as a basis for decision in future cases, when its rationale threatens to upend our settled jurisprudence in related areas of law, and when the precedent's underlying reasoning has become so discredited that the Court cannot keep the precedent alive without jury-rigging new and different justifications to shore up the original mistake.

These considerations weigh against retaining our decision in *Austin.* First, as the majority explains, that decision was an "aberration" insofar as it departed from the robust protections we had granted political speech in our earlier cases[.] . . . Second, the validity of *Austin*'s rationale [has] proved to be the consistent subject of dispute among Members of this Court[.] . . . Third, the *Austin* decision is uniquely destabilizing because it threatens to subvert our Court's decisions even outside the particular context of corporate express advocacy. The First Amendment theory underlying *Austin*'s holding is extraordinarily broad. *Austin*'s logic would authorize government prohibition of political speech by a category of speakers in the name of equality[.] . . .

[The] Court in *Austin* nowhere relied upon the only arguments the Government now raises to support that decision. In fact, the only opinion in *Austin* endorsing the Government's argument based on the threat of *quid pro quo* corruption was Justice Stevens's concurrence. [Nowhere] did *Austin* suggest that the goal of protecting shareholders is itself a compelling interest authorizing restrictions on First Amendment rights.

To the extent that the Government's case for reaffirming *Austin* depends on radically reconceptualizing its reasoning, that argument is at odds with itself. *Stare decisis* is a doctrine of preservation, not transformation. It counsels deference to past mistakes, but provides no justification for making new ones. There is therefore no basis for the Court to give precedential sway to reasoning that it has never accepted[.] . . .

[We] have had two rounds of briefing in this case, two oral arguments, and 54 amicus briefs to help us carry out our obligation to decide the necessary constitutional questions according to law. We have also had the benefit of a comprehensive dissent that has helped ensure that the Court has considered all the relevant issues. This careful consideration convinces me that Congress violates the First Amendment when it decrees that some speakers may not engage in political speech at election time, when it matters most.

Justice SCALIA, with whom Justice ALITO joins, concurring.

I join the opinion of the Court. I write separately to address [the] discussion [in] the dissent [that] purports to show that today's decision is not supported by the original understanding of the First Amendment. The dissent attempts this demonstration [in] splendid isolation from the text of the First Amendment. It never shows why "the freedom of speech" that was the right of Englishmen did not include the freedom to speak in association with other individuals, including association in the corporate form[.] . . .

[Most] of the Founders' resentment towards corporations was directed at the state-granted monopoly privileges that individually chartered corporations enjoyed. Modern corporations do not have such privileges, and would probably have been favored by most of our enterprising Founders[.] Moreover, if the Founders' specific intent with respect to corporations is what matters, why does the dissent ignore the Founders' views about other legal entities that have more in common with modern business corporations than the founding-era corporations? At the time of the founding, religious, educational, and literary corporations were incorporated under general incorporation statutes, much as business corporations are today. There were also small unincorporated business associations, which some have argued were the "true progenitors" of today's business corporations. Were all of these silently excluded from the protections of the First Amendment?

The lack of a textual exception for speech by corporations cannot be explained on the ground that such organizations did not exist or did not speak. To the contrary, colleges, towns and cities, religious institutions, and guilds had long been organized as corporations at common law [and] [b]oth corporations and voluntary associations actively petitioned the Government and expressed their views in newspapers and pamphlets[.]

[The] freedom of "the press" was widely understood to protect the publishing activities of individual editors and printers. But these individuals often acted through newspapers, which (much like corporations) had their own names, outlived the individuals who had founded them, could be bought and sold, were sometimes owned by more than one person, and were operated for profit. Their activities were not stripped of First Amendment protections simply because they were carried out under the banner of an artificial legal entity[.] . . .

The dissent says that when the Framers "constitutionalized the right to free speech in the First Amendment, it was the free speech of individual Americans that they had in mind." That is no doubt true. All the provisions of the Bill of Rights set forth the rights of individual men and women — not, for example, of trees or polar bears. But the individual person's right to speak includes the right to speak in association with other individual persons. Surely the dissent does not believe that speech by the Republican Party or the Democratic Party can be censored because it is not the speech of "an individual American." It is the speech of many individual Americans, who have associated in a common cause, giving the leadership of the party the right to speak on their behalf. The association of individuals in a business corporation is no different — or at least it cannot be denied the right to speak on the simplistic ground that it is not "an individual American."

[The] Amendment is written in terms of "speech," not speakers. Its text offers no foothold for excluding any category of speaker[.] We are therefore simply left with the question whether the speech at issue in this case is "speech" covered by the First Amendment. No one says otherwise. A documentary film critical of a potential Presidential candidate is core political speech, and its nature as such does not change simply because it was funded by a corporation. Nor does the character of that funding produce any reduction whatever in the "inherent worth of the speech" and "its capacity for informing the public." First Nat. Bank of Boston v. Bellotti, 435 U.S. 765 (1978). Indeed, to exclude or impede corporate speech is to muzzle the principal agents of the modern free economy. We should celebrate rather than condemn the addition of this speech to the public debate.

Justice STEVENS, with whom Justice GINSBURG, Justice BREYER, and Justice SOTOMAYOR join, concurring in part and dissenting in part.

[The] basic premise underlying the Court's ruling is its iteration, and constant reiteration, of the proposition that the First Amendment bars regulatory distinctions based on a speaker's identity, including its "identity" as a corporation. [The] conceit that corporations must be treated identically to natural persons in the political sphere is not only inaccurate but also inadequate to justify the Court's disposition of this case. . . .

The majority's approach to corporate electioneering marks a dramatic break from our past. [The] Court today rejects a century of history when it treats the distinction between corporate and individual campaign spending as an invidious novelty born of Austin v. Michigan Chamber of Commerce, 494 U.S. 652 (1990). . . .

[Although] I concur in the Court's decision to sustain BCRA's disclosure provisions and join Part IV of its opinion, I emphatically dissent from its principal holding. . . .

II

[Today's] decision takes away a power that we have long permitted the [elected] branches to exercise. State legislatures have relied on their authority to regulate corporate electioneering, confirmed in *Austin*, for more than a century. The Federal Congress has relied on this authority for a comparable stretch of time, and it specifically relied on *Austin* throughout the years it spent developing and debating BCRA. [Pulling] out the rug beneath Congress after affirming the constitutionality of §203 six years ago shows great disrespect for a coequal branch.

By removing one of its central components, today's ruling makes a hash out of BCRA's "delicate and interconnected regulatory scheme." *McConnell*, 540 U.S., at 172. Consider just one example of the distortions that will follow: Political parties are barred under BCRA from soliciting or spending "soft money," funds that are not subject to the statute's disclosure requirements or its source and amount limitations. Going forward, corporations and unions will be free to spend as much general treasury money as they wish on ads that support or attack specific candidates, whereas national parties will not be able to spend a dime of soft money on ads of any kind. The Court's ruling thus dramatically enhances the role of corporations and unions — and the narrow interests they represent — vis-a-vis the role of political parties — and the broad coalitions they represent — in determining who will hold public office.

[*Austin*] has been on the books for two decades, and many of the statutes called into question by today's opinion have been on the books for a half-century or more. The Court points to no intervening change in circumstances that warrants revisiting *Austin* [and] the Court gives no reason to think that *Austin* and *McConnell* are unworkable.

In fact, no one has argued to us that *Austin*'s rule has proved impracticable, and not a single for-profit corporation, union, or State has asked us to overrule it. Quite to the contrary, leading groups representing the business community, organized labor, and the nonprofit sector, together with more than half of the States, urge that we preserve *Austin*[.]

In the end, the Court's rejection of *Austin* and *McConnell* comes down to nothing more than its disagreement with their results. Virtually every one of its arguments was made and rejected in those cases, and the majority opinion is essentially an amalgamation of resuscitated dissents. The only relevant thing that has changed since *Austin* and *McConnell* is the composition of this Court[.]

III

The novelty of the Court's [approach] to *stare decisis* is matched by the novelty of its ruling on the merits. The ruling rests on several premises. First, the Court claims that *Austin* and *McConnell* have "banned" corporate speech. Second, it claims that the First Amendment precludes regulatory distinctions based on speaker identity, including the speaker's identity as a corporation. Third, it claims that *Austin* and *McConnell* were radical outliers in our First Amendment tradition and our campaign finance jurisprudence. Each of these claims is wrong. . . .

[In] many ways, [§203] functions as a source restriction or a time, place, and manner restriction. It applies in a viewpoint-neutral fashion to a narrow subset of advocacy messages about clearly identified candidates for federal office, made during discrete time periods through discrete channels. In the case at hand, all Citizens United needed to do to broadcast *Hillary* right before the primary was to abjure business contributions or use the funds in its PAC, which by its own account is "one of the most active conservative PACs in America."

So let us be clear: Neither *Austin* nor *McConnell* held or implied that corporations may be silenced; the FEC is not a "censor"; and in the years since these cases were decided, corporations have continued to play a major role in the national dialogue. Laws such as §203 target a class of communications that is especially likely to corrupt the political process, that is at least one degree removed from the views of individual citizens, and that may not even reflect the views of those who pay for it. Such laws burden political speech, and that is always a serious matter, demanding careful scrutiny. But the majority's incessant talk of a "ban" aims at a straw man. . . .

[The] Framers and their contemporaries [held] very different views about the nature of the First Amendment right and the role of corporations in society. Those few corporations that existed at the founding were authorized by grant of a special legislative charter. [Corporations] were created, supervised, and conceptualized as quasi-public entities[.] . . .

[The] Framers thus took it as a given that corporations could be comprehensively regulated in the service of the public welfare. [They] had little trouble distinguishing corporations from human beings, and when they constitutionalized the right to free speech in the First Amendment, it was the free speech of individual Americans that they had in mind. While individuals might join together to exercise their speech rights, business corporations, at least, were plainly not seen as facilitating such associational or expressive ends. [It seems] implausible that the Framers believed "the freedom of speech" would extend equally to all corporate speakers, much less that it would preclude legislatures from taking limited measures to guard against corporate capture of elections. . . .

[Although] Justice Scalia makes a perfectly sensible argument that an individual's right to speak entails a right to speak with others for a common cause, he does not explain why those two rights must be precisely identical, or why that principle applies to electioneering by corporations that serve no "common cause." Nothing in his account dislodges my basic point that members of the founding generation held a cautious view of corporate power and a narrow view of corporate rights[,] and that they conceptualized speech in individualistic terms. If no prominent Framer bothered to articulate that corporate speech would have lesser status than individual speech, that may well be because the contrary proposition — if not also the very notion of "corporate speech" — was inconceivable. . . .

[The] truth is we cannot be certain how a law such as BCRA §203 meshes with the original meaning of the First Amendment. . . . [In] fairness, our campaign finance jurisprudence has never attended very closely to the views of the Framers, whose political universe differed profoundly from that of today. [We] have long since held that corporations are covered by the First Amendment[.] [But] in light of the Court's effort to cast itself as guardian of ancient values, it pays to remember that nothing in our constitutional history dictates today's outcome[.]

A century of more recent history puts to rest any notion that today's ruling is faithful to our First Amendment tradition. At the federal level, the express distinction between corporate and individual political spending on elections stretches back to 1907, when Congress passed the Tillman Act, banning all corporate contributions to candidates[.] . . .

[Over] the years, the limitations on corporate political spending have been modified in a number of ways, as Congress responded to changes in the American economy and political practices that threatened to displace the commonweal. [In the] Taft-Hartley Act of 1947[,] Congress extended the prohibition on corporate support of candidates to cover not only direct contributions, but independent expenditures as well. The bar on contributions "was being so narrowly construed" that corporations were easily able to defeat the purposes of the Act by supporting candidates through other means. *WRTL*, 551 U.S., at 511. . . .

[By] the time Congress passed FECA in 1971, the bar on corporate contributions and expenditures had become such an accepted part of federal campaign finance regulation that when a large number of plaintiffs, including several non-profit corporations, challenged virtually every aspect of the Act in *Buckley*, 424 U.S. 1 [(1976)], no one even bothered to argue that the bar as such was unconstitutional. *Buckley* famously (or infamously) distinguished direct contributions from independent expenditures, but its silence on corporations only reinforced the understanding that corporate expenditures could be treated differently from individual expenditures[.] . . .

[Congress] crafted §203 in response to a problem created by *Buckley*. The *Buckley* Court had construed FECA's definition of prohibited "expenditures" narrowly to avoid any problems of constitutional vagueness, holding it applicable only to "communications that expressly advocate the election or defeat of a clearly identified candidate," 424 U.S., at 80, i.e., statements containing so-called "magic words" like "'vote for,' 'elect,' 'support,' 'cast your ballot for,' 'Smith for Congress,' 'vote against,' 'defeat' [or] 'reject,'" *id.*, at 43-44. After *Buckley*, corporations and unions figured out how to circumvent the limits on express advocacy by using sham "issue ads" that "eschewed the use of magic words" but nonetheless "advocate[d] the election or defeat of clearly identified federal candidates." *McConnell*, 540 U.S., at 126. [Congress] passed §203 to address this circumvention, prohibiting corporations and unions from using general treasury funds for electioneering communications that "refe[r] to a clearly identified candidate," whether or not those communications use the magic words.

When we asked in *McConnell* "whether a compelling governmental interest justifie[d]" §203, we found the question "easily answered" [based on *Austin*]. . . .

The majority emphasizes *Buckley*'s statement that "[t]he concept that government may restrict the speech of some elements of our society in order to enhance the relative voice of others is wholly foreign to the First Amendment." [424 U.S., at 48-49.] But this elegant phrase cannot bear the weight that our colleagues have placed on it[.]

[When] we made this statement in *Buckley*, we could not have been casting doubt on the restriction on corporate expenditures in candidate elections, which had not been challenged[.] *Buckley*'s independent expenditure analysis was focused on a very different statutory provision. It is implausible to think, as the majority suggests, that *Buckley* covertly invalidated FECA's separate corporate and union campaign expenditure restriction, §610 (now codified at 2 U.S.C. §441b), even though that restriction had been on the books for decades before *Buckley* and would remain on the books, undisturbed, for decades after. . . .

The *Bellotti* Court confronted a dramatically different factual situation from the one that confronts us in this case: a state statute that barred [a] business corporation "from making contributions or expenditures 'for the purpose of . . . influencing or affecting the vote' on any question submitted to the voters, other than one materially affecting any of the property, business or assets of the corporation," and [also] provide[d] that referenda related to income taxation would not "be deemed materially to affect the property, business or assets of the corporation." [The] statute was a transparent attempt to prevent corporations from spending money to defeat [a taxation referendum], which was favored by a majority of legislators but had been repeatedly rejected by the voters. We said that "where, as here, the legislature's suppression of speech suggests an attempt to give one side of a debatable public question an advantage in expressing its views to the people, the First Amendment is plainly offended." [435 U.S.,] at 785-786. . . .

[We] acknowledged in *Bellotti* that numerous "interests of the highest importance" can justify campaign finance regulation. But we found no evidence that these interests were served by [the] law. We left open the possibility that our decision might have been different if there had been "record or legislative findings that corporate advocacy threatened imminently to undermine democratic processes, thereby denigrating rather than serving First Amendment interests." *Id.*, at 789.

Austin and *McConnell*, then, sit perfectly well with *Bellotti*. [The] statute in *Bellotti* smacked of viewpoint discrimination, targeted one class of corporations, and provided no PAC option; and the State has a greater interest in regulating independent corporate expenditures on candidate elections than on referenda, because in a functioning democracy the public must have faith that its representatives owe their positions to the people, not to the corporations with the deepest pockets. . . .

IV

[The] majority recognizes that *Austin* and *McConnell* may be defended on anticorruption, antidistortion, and shareholder protection rationales. It badly errs both in explaining the nature of these rationales, which overlap and complement each other, and in applying them to the case at hand.

Undergirding the majority's approach to the merits is the claim that the only "sufficiently important governmental interest in preventing corruption or the appearance of corruption" is one that is "limited to *quid pro quo* corruption." . . . [But] [c]orruption operates along a spectrum, and the majority's apparent belief that *quid pro quo* arrangements can be neatly demarcated from other improper influences does not accord with the theory or reality of politics. It certainly does not accord with the record Congress developed in passing BCRA[.] . . .

[The] legislative and judicial proceedings relating to BCRA generated a substantial body of evidence suggesting that, as corporations grew more and more adept at crafting "issue ads" to help or harm a particular candidate, these nominally independent expenditures began to corrupt the political process in a very direct sense. The sponsors of these ads were routinely granted special access after the campaign was over. [Many] corporate independent expenditures [had] become essentially interchangeable with direct contributions in their capacity to generate *quid pro quo* arrangements. In an age in which money and television ads are the coin of the campaign realm, it is hardly surprising that corporations deployed these ads to curry favor with, and to gain influence over, public officials.

The majority appears to think it decisive that the BCRA record does not contain "direct examples of votes being exchanged for . . . expenditures." It would have been quite remarkable if Congress had created a record detailing such behavior by its own Members. Proving that a specific vote was exchanged for a specific expenditure has always been next to impossible: Elected officials have diverse motivations, and no one will acknowledge that he sold a vote. Yet, even if "[i]ngratiation and access . . . are not corruption" themselves, they are necessary prerequisites to it; they can create both the opportunity for, and the appearance of, *quid pro quo* arrangements. The influx of unlimited corporate money into the electoral realm also creates new opportunities for the mirror image of *quid pro quo* deals: threats, both explicit and implicit[.] . . .

[The] majority fails to appreciate that *Austin*'s antidistortion rationale is itself an anticorruption rationale, tied to the special concerns raised by corporations. Understood properly, "antidistortion" is simply a variant on the classic governmental interest in protecting against improper influences on officeholders that debilitate the democratic process. It is manifestly not just an "equalizing" idea in disguise.

The fact that corporations are different from human beings might seem to need no elaboration, [and] *Austin* set forth some of the basic differences. Unlike natural persons, corporations have "limited liability" for their owners and managers, "perpetual life," separation of ownership and control, "and favorable treatment of the accumulation and distribution of assets . . . that enhance their ability to attract capital and to deploy their resources in ways that maximize the return on their shareholders' investments." Unlike voters in U.S. elections, corporations may be foreign controlled. "[The] resources in the treasury of a business corporation . . . may make a corporation a formidable political presence, even though the power of the corporation may be no reflection of the power of its ideas." 494 U.S., at [658–659]. . . .

[These] basic points help explain why corporate electioneering is not only more likely to impair compelling governmental interests, but also why restrictions on that electioneering are less likely to encroach upon First Amendment freedoms. One fundamental concern of the First Amendment is to "protec[t] the individual's interest in self-expression." Freedom of speech helps "make men free to develop their faculties," it respects their "dignity and choice," and it facilitates the value of "individual self-realization." Martin Redish, *The Value of Free Speech*, 130 U. Pa. L. Rev. 591, 594 (1982). Corporate speech, however, is derivative speech, speech by proxy. A regulation such as BCRA §203 may affect the way in which individuals disseminate certain messages through the corporate form, but it does not prevent anyone from speaking in his or her own voice[.]

It is an interesting question "who" is even speaking when a business corporation places an advertisement that endorses or attacks a particular candidate. [Some] individuals associated with the corporation must make the decision to place the ad, but the idea that these individuals are thereby fostering their self-expression or cultivating their critical faculties is fanciful. It is entirely possible that the corporation's electoral message will conflict with their personal convictions. Take away the ability to use general treasury funds for some of those ads, and no one's autonomy, dignity, or political equality has been impinged upon in the least. . . .

[The] Court places primary emphasis not on the corporation's right to electioneer, but rather on the listener's interest in hearing what every possible speaker may have to say. The Court's central argument is that laws such as §203 have "deprived [the electorate] of information, knowledge and option vital to its function," and this, in turn, "interferes with the 'open marketplace' of ideas protected by the First Amendment."

There are many flaws in this argument. If the overriding concern depends on the interests of the audience, surely the public's perception of the value of corporate speech should be given important weight. [It] is only certain Members of this Court, not the listeners themselves, who have agitated for more corporate electioneering.

Austin recognized that there are substantial reasons why a legislature might conclude that unregulated general treasury expenditures will give corporations "unfai[r] influence" in the electoral process, and distort public debate in ways that undermine rather than advance the interests of listeners. [When] corporations grab up the prime broadcasting slots on the eve of an election, they can flood the market with advocacy that bears "little or no correlation" to the ideas of natural persons or to any broader notion of the public good. 494 U.S., at 660. The opinions of real people may be marginalized[.] . . .

[In] critiquing *Austin*'s antidistortion rationale[,] our colleagues place tremendous weight on the example of media corporations. [Citizens United] is not a media corporation. There would be absolutely no need to consider the issue of media corporations if the majority did [not] invent the theory that legislature must eschew all "identity"-based distinctions and treat a local nonprofit news outlet exactly the same as General Motors[.] . . .

[Interwoven] with *Austin*'s concern to protect the integrity of the electoral process is a concern to protect the rights of shareholders from a kind of coerced speech: electioneering expenditures that do not "reflec[t] [their] support." . . . [A] rule that privileges the use of PACs thus does more than facilitate the political speech of like-minded shareholders; it also curbs [the] behavior of executives and respects the views of dissenters[.] . . .

[The] Court dismisses this interest on the ground that abuses of shareholder money can be corrected "through the procedures of corporate democracy," [and] through Internet-based disclosures. [By] "corporate democracy," presumably the Court means the rights of shareholders to vote and to bring derivative suits for breach of fiduciary duty. In practice, however, many corporate lawyers will tell you that "these rights are so limited as to be almost nonexistent," given the internal authority wielded by boards and managers and the expansive protections afforded by the business judgment rule. [Margaret Blair & Lynn Stout, *A Team Production Theory of Corporate Law*, 85 Va. L. Rev. 247, 320 (1999).] . . .

[Recognizing] the limits of the shareholder protection rationale, the *Austin* Court did not hold it out as an adequate and independent ground for sustaining the statute in question. Rather, the Court applied it to reinforce the antidistortion rationale[.] [The] shareholder protection rationale [bolsters] the conclusion that restrictions on corporate electioneering can serve both speakers' and listeners' interests, as well as the anticorruption interest. And it supplies yet another reason why corporate expenditures merit less protection than individual expenditures.

V

[In] a democratic society, the longstanding consensus on the need to limit corporate campaign spending should outweigh the wooden application of judge-made rules. [At] bottom, the Court's opinion is thus a rejection of the common sense of the American people, who have recognized a need to prevent corporations from undermining self-government since the founding, and who have fought against the distinctive corrupting potential of corporate electioneering since the days of Theodore Roosevelt. It is a strange time to repudiate that common sense. While American democracy is imperfect, few outside the majority of this Court would have thought its flaws included a dearth of corporate money in politics.

I would affirm the judgment of the District Court.

Notes

1. *State of the Union.* The *Citizens United* Court observed: "We need not reach the question whether the Government has a compelling interest in preventing foreign individuals or associations from influencing our Nation's political process," such as "corporations or associations that were created in foreign countries or funded predominately by foreign shareholders." Therefore, the Court did not discuss BCRA Section 441e's prohibition that bars "foreign nationals" from making contributions or expenditures related to any elections in the United States. However, when President Obama delivered the State of the Union address in the House of Representatives chamber before a joint session of Congress, with the Supreme Court justices seated in the front rows, he made these comments about *Citizens United*: "With all due deference to separation of powers, last week the Supreme Court reversed a century of law that I believe will open the floodgates for special interests — including foreign corporations — to spend without limit in our elections. I don't think that American elections should be bankrolled by America's most powerful interests, or worse, by foreign entities. They should be decided by the American people. And I'd urge Democrats and Republicans to pass a bill that helps to correct some of these problems." As the camera zoomed in on the impassive faces of the justices, it appeared that Justice Alito muttered the words "Not true." Both the President's critique and Justice Alito's reaction fueled the continuing storm of media attention that greeted the *Citizens United* decision, and within a few months, several dozen "*Citizens United* bills" were pending in Congress.

2. *McConnell's Validation of Soft Money Limitations.* The *Citizens United* Court did not address the validity of *McConnell's* rejection of a facial challenge to BCRA's limits on "soft money" contributions to political parties. Before BCRA was enacted, national political parties could accept unlimited contributions to fund issue ads, state and local election activities, and get-out-the-vote and voter registration drives. These activities may influence federal elections, even though they do not expressly advocate the election or defeat of a particular candidate. Therefore, Congress enacted BCRA Section 323 in order to prevent parties and candidates from using so-called "soft money" to evade the "hard money" limits that apply to contributions made in connection with federal elections. Section 323 prohibits national parties from receiving or spending more than $30,400 annually from an individual donor, and prohibits state and local parties from using any contributions over $10,000 from an individual donor in a calendar year for any federal election activity. After the Republican National Committee (RNC) brought an as-applied challenge to BCRA Section 323, the Court decided *Citizens United*. That decision provided the RNC with a new basis for arguing that *McConnell's* support for BCRA Section 323 has been undermined, and that "no viable theory of corruption" justifies the limits of Section 323 on contributions to political parties. The federal district court expressed sympathy for the RNC's arguments, but declined to endorse them because of ambiguities in the *McConnell* opinion, observing: "As a lower court, [we] do not believe we possess authority to clarify or refine *McConnell* [or] to otherwise get ahead of the Supreme Court." *See*

Republican National Committee v. Federal Election Commission, 698 F. Supp. 2d 150 (D.D.C. 2010), , *aff'd*,130 S.Ct. 3544 (2010).

3. *FEC Soft Money Regulations for Nonprofits*. During the 2004 election season, there was widespread criticism of nonprofit entities that received large contributions to support their political activities. Some critics urged the FEC to ban large donations to nonprofits in the same way that Congress banned large contributions to political parties in BCRA. Instead, the FEC issued regulations that restricted the ability of nonprofits to make independent expenditures for activities such as issue ads, get-out-the-vote efforts, and voter registration drives. The court held that these FEC regulations violated the First Amendment in Emily's List v. Federal Election Commission, 581 F.3d 1 (D.C. Cir. 2009), reasoning that unlike political parties, nonprofit entities should be treated like individuals who have the right to spend unlimited money to support their preferred candidates or parties. The court emphasized that nonprofits "offer an opportunity for ordinary citizens to band together to speak on the issue or issues most important to them" and noted that there was "no evidence that nonprofit entities have sold access to federal candidates and officeholders in exchange for large contributions." The court also rejected the FEC's proffered interest in equalizing the voices of participants in the political process, because this interest was declared to be illegitimate in *Davis* and *Buckley*. *Compare* North Carolina Right to Life Inc. v. Leake, 525 F.3d 274 (4th Cir. 2008).

∾ PROBLEMS ∾

1. *Contributions to Nonprofits*. SpeechNow is an unincorporated nonprofit association that intends to engage in express advocacy supporting candidates for federal office who support First Amendment rights. The members of SpeechNow plan to acquire funds solely from donations by individuals and to operate exclusively through "independent expenditures." For example, SpeechNow will spend money to purchase ads that are not coordinated with candidate campaigns but that support or oppose particular candidates for federal office. Under BCRA Section 441a, an individual's contribution to an entity like SpeechNow is limited to $5,000 per year, but SpeechNow's president wants to accept larger contributions. When SpeechNow files a federal suit to challenge the Section 441a contribution limit as a violation of the First Amendment, the defendant FEC argues that: 1) under *Buckley*, contributions directly to candidates may be limited; and 2) the reasoning of *Citizens United* is not relevant because that case involved an expenditure limit, not a contribution limit. How can the court justify a ruling in favor of SpeechNow under *Citizens United*? *See* SpeechNow.org v. Federal Election Commission, 599 F.3d 686 (D.C. Cir. 2010) (en banc).

2. *Provisions of DISCLOSE Act*. In late April 2010, Representative Chris Van Hollen and Senator Charles Schumer introduced similar bills in the House and Senate, entitled the Democracy Is Strengthened by Casting Light On Spending in Elections (DISCLOSE) Act. Are any of the following provisions of DISCLOSE

vulnerable to challenge on First Amendment grounds based on the reasoning in *Citizens United*? Why or why not?

a. *Foreign-Controlled Corporations.* Under current law, Section 441e prohibits the making of contributions or expenditures related to elections in the United States by "foreign nationals," defined as: 1) an individual who is not a U.S. citizen, 2) a foreign government or foreign political party, or 3) a combination of persons organized under the laws of or having its principal place of business in a foreign country. The bill proposes to expand this definition to include a "foreign-controlled domestic corporation" that is not a "foreign national," which is defined as: 1) a corporation in which a foreign national owns 20 percent or more of voting shares, 2) a corporation in which a majority of the board of directors are foreign nationals, or 3) a corporation in which one or more foreign nationals has the power to direct, dictate, or control the decision-making process of the corporation with respect to its interests in the United States. Assume that the bill does not expressly impose limits on unions with foreign-national members.

b. *Government Contractors and Recipients of Bailout Money.* Under current law, Section 441c prohibits a government contractor (defined as an individual or entity that enters into a contract with a federal government department or agency) from making a contribution to any political party, committee, candidate, or person, or from soliciting such a contribution from another government contractor. The bill proposes to expand this prohibition to include the making of any independent expenditure or the disbursement of funds for an electioneering communication, with an exception for government contractors whose contracts are valued at less than $50,000. The bill also proposes to prohibit corporations that received bailout money from the federal government from using that money to make any campaign-related contributions or expenditures.

c. *Stand by Your Ad.* The bill proposes to require that when a corporation (or union or nonprofit entities) makes independent expenditures for a campaign-related ad, the highest-ranking official of the organization must appear on camera to say that he or she "approves this message," and the names of the top five donors funding the ad must be listed at the end of the ad.

d. *Disclosure to Shareholders.* The bill proposes to require that all campaign-related expenditures by corporations (or unions or nonprofit entities) must be disclosed on the organization's Web site with a clear link on the homepage within 24 hours of reporting them to the FEC.

e. *Disclosure of Contributors.* The bill proposes that a corporation (or union or nonprofit entity) that is required to provide the FEC with independent expenditure reports must identify the name of each person, the amount donated by each person, and the name of the candidate or election involved who made a donation of $1,000 or more to be used for campaign-related activity, if expenditures are made on electioneering communications. This information must be disclosed for donors of $600 or more if expenditures are made for independent expenditures.

3. *Disclosure of Internal Campaign Communications*. In 2008, California voters approved Proposition 8, which amended the state constitution to provide that "only marriage between a man and a woman is valid or recognized" in the state. The state attorney general declined to defend the constitutionality of the amendment in the Section 1983 suit by two same-sex couples who challenged Proposition 8 on due process and equal protection grounds. Therefore, the federal court allowed the official Proposition 8 campaign committee and other official proponents to intervene as defendants. The plaintiffs served requests for production that included a request for "[a]ll versions of any documents that constitute communications referring to Proposition 8," including internal campaign communications concerning strategy and messaging. The defendants objected to this request on the grounds that disclosure would have a deterrent effect on future participation in campaigns and on the free flow of information within campaigns. What *prima facie* showing should a court require the defendants to make in order to demonstrate that enforcement of the discovery requests would infringe on First Amendment rights? What showing of the need for discovery must the plaintiffs make to counterbalance the defendants' showing and justify disclosure? Should the court limit a First Amendment privilege to a "core group of persons" engaged in formulating campaign strategy and messaging? Should the privilege apply to communications between or among separate organizations? *See* Perry v. Schwarzenegger, 591 F.3d 1147 (9th Cir. 2010); Perry v. Schwarzenegger, 602 F.3d 976 (9th Cir. 2010).

Doe #1 v. Reed

561 U.S. — (2010)

Chief Justice ROBERTS delivered the opinion of the Court.

The State of Washington allows its citizens to challenge state laws by referendum. Roughly our percent of Washington voters must sign a petition to place such a referendum on the ballot. That petition, which by law must include the names and addresses of the signers, is then submitted to the government for verification and canvassing, to ensure that only lawful signatures are counted. The Washington Public Records Act (PRA) authorizes private parties to obtain copies of government documents, and the State construes the PRA to cover submitted referendum petitions.

This case arises out of a state law extending certain benefits to same-sex couples, and a corresponding referendum petition to put that law to a popular vote. [After the law was approved, several voters made public record requests with the secretary of state for public release of the names and contact information of the individuals who signed the petition.] Certain petition signers and the petition sponsor objected, arguing that such public disclosure would violate their rights under the First Amendment.

[The] issue at this stage of the case is not whether disclosure of this particular petition would violate the First Amendment, but whether disclosure of referendum petitions in general would do so. We conclude that such disclosure does not as a general matter violate the First Amendment[.] We leave it to the lower courts to consider in the first instance the signers' more focused claim concerning disclosure of the information on this particular petition. . . .

III

A

The compelled disclosure of signatory information on referendum petitions is subject to review under the First Amendment. An individual expresses a view on a political matter when he signs a petition under Washington's referendum procedure. In most cases, the individual's signature will express the view that the law subject to the petition should be overturned. Even if the signer is agnostic as to the merits of the underlying law, his signature still expresses the political view that the question should be considered "by the whole electorate." In either case, the expression of a political view implicates a First Amendment right. . . .

Respondents counter that signing a petition is a legally operative legislative act and therefore "does not involve any significant expressive element." [But] we do not see how adding such legal effect to an expressive activity somehow deprives that activity of its expressive component, taking it outside the scope of the First Amendment. . . .

Petition signing remains expressive even when it has legal effect in the electoral process. That is not to say that the electoral context is irrelevant to the nature of our First Amendment review. We allow States significant flexibility in implementing their own voting systems. [Also] pertinent to our analysis is the fact that the PRA is not a prohibition on speech, but instead a *disclosure* requirement. "[D]isclosure requirements may burden the ability to speak, but they . . . do not prevent anyone from speaking." Citizens United v. Federal Election Commn., [130 S. Ct. 876] (2010).

We have a series of precedents considering First Amendment challenges to disclosure requirements in the electoral context. These precedents have reviewed such challenges under what has been termed "exacting scrutiny."

That standard "requires a 'substantial relation' between the disclosure requirement and a 'sufficiently important' governmental interest." *Citizens United*, [558 U.S.,] at 891. To withstand this scrutiny, "the strength of the governmental interest must reflect the seriousness of the actual burden on First Amendment rights." *Davis* [v. Federal Election Commn., 554 U.S. 724, (2008)].

B

Respondents assert two interests to justify the burdens of compelled disclosure under the PRA on First Amendment rights: (1) preserving the integrity of the electoral process by combating fraud, detecting invalid signatures, and fostering government transparency and accountability; and (2) providing information to the electorate about who supports the petition. Because we determine that the State's interest in preserving the integrity of the electoral process suffices to defeat the argument that the PRA is unconstitutional with respect to referendum petitions in general, we need not, and do not, address the State's "informational" interest.

The State's interest in preserving the integrity of the electoral process is undoubtedly important[.] The State's interest is particularly strong with respect to efforts to root out fraud, which not only may produce fraudulent outcomes, but has a systemic effect as well[.] The threat of fraud in this context is not merely hypothetical; respondents [cite] a number of cases of petition-related fraud across the country to support the point.

But the State's interest in preserving electoral integrity is not limited to combating fraud. That interest extends to efforts to ferret out invalid signatures caused not by fraud but by simple mistake, such as duplicate signatures or signatures of individuals who are not registered to vote in the State. That interest also extends more generally to promoting transparency and accountability in the electoral process, which the State argues is "essential to the proper functioning of a democracy." . . .

[The secretary of state's] verification and canvassing will not catch all invalid signatures: The job is large and difficult (the secretary ordinarily checks "only 3 to 5% of signatures["]), and the secretary can make mistakes, too. Public disclosure can help cure the inadequacies of the verification and canvassing process.

Disclosure also helps prevent certain types of petition fraud otherwise difficult to detect, such as outright forgery and "bait and switch" fraud, in which an individual signs the petition based on a misrepresentation of the underlying issue. The signer is in the best position to detect theses types of fraud, and public disclosure can bring the issue to the signer's attention.

Public disclosure thus helps ensure that the only signatures counted are those that should be, and that the only referenda placed on the ballot are those that garner enough valid signatures. Public disclosure also promotes transparency and accountability in the electoral process to an extent other measures cannot. In light of the foregoing, we reject plaintiffs' argument that public disclosure of referendum petitions in general is substantially related to the important interest of preserving the integrity of the electoral process.

C

Plaintiff's more significant objection is that "the strength of the governmental interest" does not "reflect the seriousness of the actual burden on First Amendment rights." According to plaintiffs, the objective of those seeking disclosure of [the] petition [at issue here] is not to prevent fraud, but to publicly identify those who had validly signed and to broadcast the signers' political views on the subject of the petition. . . .

In related contexts, we have explained that those resisting disclosure can prevail under the First Amendment if they can show "a reasonable probability that the compelled disclosure [of personal information] will subject them to threats, harassment, or reprisals from either Government officials or private parties." *Citizens United*, 558 U.S., at 891. The question before us, however, is not whether PRA disclosure violates the First Amendment with respect to those who signed [the] petition [here]. The question instead is whether such disclosure in general violates the First Amendment rights of those who sign referendum petitions.

The problem for plaintiffs is that their argument rests almost entirely on the specific harm they say would attend disclosure of the information on [the] petition [here], or on similarly controversial ones. [There] is no reason to assume that any burdens imposed by disclosure of typical referendum petitions would be remotely like the burdens plaintiffs fear in this case.

[Indeed,] [s]everal other petitions in the State [of Washington] "have been subject to release in recent years," the plaintiffs tell us, but apparently that release has come without incident. *Cf. Citizens United, supra* at 891.

Faced with the State's unrebutted arguments that only modest burdens attend the disclosure of a typical petition, we must reject plaintiffs' broad challenge to the PRA. In doing so, we note [that] upholding the law against a broad-based challenge does not foreclose a litigant's success in a narrower one. . . .

We conclude that disclosure under the PRA would not violate the First Amendment with respect to referendum petitions in general and therefore affirm the judgment of the Court of Appeals.

It is so ordered.

Justice SOTOMAYOR, with whom Justice STEVENS and Justice GINSBURG join, concurring.

[In] assessing the countervailing interests at stake in this case, we must be mindful of the character of initiatives and referenda. [States] enjoy "considerable leeway" to choose the subjects that are eligible for placement on the ballot and to specify the requirements for obtaining ballot access[.] [E]ach of these structural decisions "inevitably affects — at least to some degree — the individual's right" to speak about political issues and "to associate with others for political ends." Anderson v. Celebrezze, 460 U.S. 780 (1983). For instance, requiring petition signers to be registered voters or to use their real names no doubt limits the ability or willingness of some individuals to undertake the expressive act of signing a petition. Regulations of this nature, however, stand "a step removed from the communicative aspect of petitioning," and the ability of States to impose them can scarcely be doubted. *Buckley* [v. American Constitutional Law Foundation, Inc.,] 525 U.S. [182,] 215 [(1999)]. It is by no means necessary for a State to prove that such "reasonable, nondiscriminatory restrictions" are narrowly tailored to its interests. *Anderson*, 460 U.S., at 788.

The Court today confirms that the State of Washington's decision to make referendum petition signatures available for public inspection falls squarely within the realm of permissible election-related regulations. Public disclosure of the identity of petition signers, which is the rule in the overwhelming majority of States that use initiatives and referenda, advances States' vital interests[.]

On the other side of the ledger, I view the burden of public disclosure on speech and associational rights as minimal in this context. [While] campaign-finance disclosure injects the government into what would otherwise have been private political activity, the process of legislating by referendum is inherently public. [The] act of signing [a referendum petition] typically occurs in public, and the circulators who collect and submit signatures ordinarily owe signers no guarantee of confidentiality[.]

Given the relative weight of the interests at stake and the traditionally public nature of initiative and referendum processes, the Court rightly rejects petitioners' constitutional challenge[.] These same considerations also mean that any party attempting to challenge particular applications of the State's regulations will bear a heavy burden. Even when a referendum involves a particularly controversial subject and some petition signers fear harassment from nonstate actors, a State's important interests . . . remain undiminished, and the State retains significant discretion in advancing those interests. Likewise, because the expressive interests implicated by the act of petition signing are always modest, I find it difficult to see how any incremental disincentive to sign a petition would tip the constitutional balance. Case-specific relief may be available when a State selectively applies a facially neutral petition disclosure rule in a manner that discriminates based on the content of referenda or the viewpoint of petition signers, or in the rare circumstance in which disclosure poses a reasonable probability of serious and widespread harassment that the State is unwilling or unable to control. *Cf.* NAACP v. Alabama ex rel. Patterson, 357 U.S. 449 (1958). [Courts] presented with an as-applied challenge to a regulation authorizing the disclosure of referendum petitions should be deeply skeptical of any assertion that the Constitution, which embraces political transparency, compels States to conceal the identity of persons who seek to participate in lawmaking through a state-created referendum process. With this understanding, I join the opinion of the Court.

Justice ALITO, concurring.

The Court holds that the disclosure under the Washington [PRA] of the names and addresses of persons who sign referendum petitions does not as a general matter violate the First Amendment, and I agree with that conclusion. . . . Nonetheless, facially valid disclosure requirements can impose heavy burdens on First Amendment rights in individual cases[.]

[The] possibility of prevailing in an as-applied challenge provides adequate protection for First Amendment rights only if (1) speakers can obtain the exemption sufficiently far in advance to avoid chilling protected speech and (2) the showing necessary to obtain the exemption is not overly burdensome[.] With respect to the first requirement, the as-applied exemption becomes practically worthless if speakers cannot obtain the exemption quickly and well in advance of speaking[.]

Additionally, speakers must be able to obtain an as-applied exemption without clearing a high evidentiary hurdle. We acknowledged as much in *Buckley* [v. Valeo, 424 U.S. 1, 74 (1976), where] we emphasized that speakers "need show only a *reasonable probability*" that disclosure will lead to threats, harassment, or reprisals. We stated that speakers could rely on a wide array of evidence to meet that standard, including "specific evidence of past of present harassment of [group] members," "harassment directed against the organization itself," or a "pattern of threats or specific manifestations of public hostility." Significantly, we also made clear that "[n]ew [groups] that have no history upon which to draw may be able to offer evidence of reprisals and threats directed against individuals or organizations holding similar views." From its inception, [the] as-applied exemption has not imposed onerous burdens of proof on speakers who fear that disclosure might lead to harassment or intimidation. . . .

[P]laintiffs have a strong case that they are entitled to as-applied relief, and they will be able to pursue such relief before the District Court.

Justice SCALIA, concurring in the judgment.

[I] doubt whether signing a petition that has the effect of suspending a law fits within "the freedom of speech" at all. But even if, as the Court concludes, it does, a long history of practice shows that the First Amendment does not prohibit public disclosure. . . .

When a Washington voter signs a referendum petition subject to the PRA, he is acting as a legislator[.] [He] is exercising legislative power because his signature, somewhat like a vote for or against a bill in the legislature, seeks to affect the legal force of the measure at issue.

Plaintiffs point to no precedent from this Court holding that legislating is protected by the First Amendment. Nor do they identify historical evidence demonstrating that "the freedom of speech" the First Amendment codified encompassed a right to legislate without public disclosure[.] . . .

Petitioning the government and participating in the traditional town meeting were precursors of the modern initiative and referendum. Those innovations were modeled after similar devices used by the Swiss democracy in the 1800's, and were first used in the United States by South Dakota in 1898[.] Plaintiffs' argument implies that the public nature of these practices, so longstanding and unquestioned, violated the freedom of speech. There is no historical support for such a claim. . . .

Initially, the Colonies mostly continued the English traditions of voting by a show of hands or by voice — *viva voce* voting — [which practice] was gradually replaced with the paper ballot[,] which was thought to reduce fraud and undue influence. . . . The new paper ballots did not make voting anonymous. Initially, many States did not regulate the form of the paper ballot. Taking advantage of this, political parties began printing ballots with their candidates' names on them. They used brightly colored paper and other distinctive markings so that the ballots could be recognized from a distance, making the votes public. Abuse of these unofficial paper ballots was rampant. . . .

It was precisely discontent over the nonsecret nature of ballot voting, and the abuses that [it] produced, which led to the States' adoption of the Australian secret ballot. [That movement began] in 1888, and almost 90 percent of the States had followed suit by 1896. But I am aware of no contention that the Australian

system was required by the First Amendment[.] . . . The long history of public legislating and voting contradicts plaintiffs' claim that disclosure of petition signatures having legislative effect violates the First Amendment. . . .

Plaintiffs raise concerns that the disclosure of petition signatures may lead to
threats and intimidation. Of course nothing prevents the people of Washington
from keeping petition signatures secret to avoid that[.] But there is no constitutional basis for this Court to impose that course upon the States[.] And it may
even be a bad idea to keep petition signatures secret. There are laws against
threats and intimidation; and harsh criticism, short of unlawful action, is a price
our people have traditionally been willing to pay for self-governance. Requiring
people to stand up in public for their political acts fosters civic courage, without
which democracy is doomed. For my part, I do not look forward to a society which
[exercises] the direct democracy of initiative and referendum hidden from public
scrutiny and protected from the accountability of criticism. This does not
resemble the Home of the Brave.

Justice THOMAS, dissenting.

[I] would hold that Washington's decision to subject all referendum petitions
to public disclosure is unconstitutional because there will always be a less restrictive means by which Washington can vindicate its stated interest in preserving the
integrity of its referendum process. I respectfully dissent. . . .

The difficulty in predicting which referendum measures will prove
controversial — combined with Washington's default position that signed referendum petitions will be disclosed on-demand, thereby allowing anyone to place
this information on the Internet for broad dissemination — raises the significant
probability that today's decision will "inhibit the exercise of legitimate First
Amendment activity" with respect to referendum and initiative petitions. . . .

This chill in protected First Amended activity harms others besides the dis-
suaded signer. We have already expressed deep skepticism about restrictions that
"mak[e] it less likely that" a referendum "will garner the number of signatures
necessary to place the matter on the ballot, thus limiting [the] ability to make the
matter the focus of statewide discussion." Such restrictions "inevitabl[y] . . . reduc[e] the total quantum of speech on a public issue." [Meyer v. Grant, 486 U.S.
414, 423 (1988).] . . .

[The] question before us is whether all signers of all referendum petitions
must resort to "substantial litigation over an extended time," *Citizens United,*
supra, at 891, to prevent Washington from trenching on their protected First
Amendment rights by subjecting their referendum-petition signatures to
on-demand public disclosure. In my view, they need not.

∾ PROBLEM: AS-APPLIED CHALLENGES ∾

Following the decision in Doe #1 v. Reed, what arguments can the plaintiffs
make to support their as-applied challenge in the district court? What counterarguments can the state make to defeat such a challenge? Should courts apply the

"reasonable probability" standard the same way in both campaign-finance disclosure cases and referendum petition cases, when parties seek to enjoin the disclosure of personal information that will "subject them to threats, harassment, or reprisals"?

Points to Remember

- The First Amendment speaks in absolute terms concerning the mandate that "Congress shall make no law abridging the freedom of speech, or of the press," but the Supreme Court has repeatedly cautioned that the freedom of speech is not absolute.
- The Court incorporated the First Amendment's protections for speech and press into the meaning of due process in the Fourteenth Amendment, so as to apply those protections to the states. *See* Gitlow v. New York, 268 US. 652 (1925). Justice Holmes used the phrase "clear and present danger" in *Schenck* to describe the circumstances when the First Amendment would not protect the advocacy of illegal action that violated the conduct crimes in the Espionage Act of 1917.
- The Court implicitly upheld the convictions in *Schenck*, reasoning that the "tendency and intent" to obstruct the draft could be inferred from the defendant's conduct of sending an antidraft circular during wartime to men who had been drafted.
- Justice Holmes advocated a more stringent "clear and present danger" standard in his *Abrams* dissent, arguing that "free trade in ideas" was the "best test of truth" rather than the criminal prosecution of allegedly harmful or false ideas.
- The *Gitlow* and *Whitney* decisions rejected the need to apply the judicial scrutiny required by the "clear and present danger" test to speech crimes, such as criminal syndicalism laws punishing advocacy of the overthrow of government, and reasoned that courts should defer to the legislative judgment that such danger is caused by the advocacy of illegal action.
- Justices Holmes and Brandeis dissented in *Gitlow*, arguing that *Schenck*'s "clear and present danger" test should be applied to speech crimes, and that the defendant's circular advocating proletarian revolution had "no chance" of causing that harm.
- Justice Brandeis proposed, concurring in *Whitney*, that the "clear and present" danger test should require courts to determine whether there "actually did exist" a "clear danger" from a defendant's advocacy of illegal action, whether "the danger, if any, was imminent," and whether "the evil apprehended was one so substantial as to justify" the legislature's suppression of speech.
- The *Dennis* plurality upheld conspiracy convictions of members of the Communist Party under the federal criminal syndicalism statute, while redefining the "clear and present danger" test to require courts to

determine whether "the gravity of the 'evil,' discounted by its improbability, justfies" suppression of speech "to avoid the danger."

- The *Yates* decision reinterpreted *Dennis* as holding that "indoctrination of a group in preparation for future violent action," by advocacy directed to "action for the accomplishment" of violence, is not constitutionally protected "when the group is of sufficient size and cohesiveness" and is "sufficiently oriented towards action" to justify apprehension that violent action would occur.

- The Court overruled *Whitney* and implicitly overruled *Gitlow* in Brandenburg v. Ohio, 395 U.S. 444 (1969), which replaced the "clear and present danger" test with the rule that advocacy of illegal action may be punished only when "such advocacy is directed to inciting or producing imminent lawless action and is likely to incite or produce such action."

- In *Cantwell*, the Court recognized the state's power to punish "acts or words likely to produce violence in others," such as "profane, indecent, or abusive remarks directed to the person of the hearer," opining that such speech is not protected communication of information or opinion. But the Court reversed the breach of the peace conviction because of the "indefiniteness," meaning vagueness, of the common law crime that was left undefined in the statute.

- The Court set forth a catalogue of unprotected speech categories in *Chaplinsky*, which included "the lewd and obscene, the profane, the libelous, and the insulting or 'fighting' words," observing that "such utterances are no essential part of any exposition of ideas" and that their slight social value is "clear outweighed by the social interest in order and morality."

- The *Chaplinsky* Court upheld the conviction for "addressing 'offensive, derisive and annoying words'" to a police officer because the defendant's epithets were spoken "face-to-face" and fit the definition of "fighting words" that are "likely to provoke the average person to retaliation" and cause a breach of the peace.

- The Court reversed the conviction for using "opprobrious words or abusive language, tending to cause a breach of the peace" in Gooding v. Wilson, because state precedents had not narrowly construed the statute to apply only to "fighting words" as defined by *Chaplinsky*.

- The *Feiner* Court upheld the defendant's disorderly conduct conviction for failing to comply with a police order to stop speaking, reasoning that although the "ordinary murmurings" of a "hostile audience" do not justify such an order, a speaker may not incite to riot.

- The views expressed in Justice Black's *Feiner* dissent have prevailed in post-*Feiner* precedents, so that police must make "all reasonable efforts" to protect a speaker from a hostile audience that threatens disorder.

- The *Cohen* Court ruled that the defendant's speech was protected when he used a profane word in his message opposing the draft. The Court rejected the state's alternative theories that the message was inherently likely to cause a violent reaction by viewers, and that the state may act to uphold public morality by censoring profane words by means of convictions for "offensive" speech.

- In New York Times v. Sullivan, 376 U.S. 254 (1964), the Court extended protection to libelous speech, despite its false and defamatory character, where a public official seeks damages against a critic of his or her official conduct but cannot show the speaker's "actual malice," evidenced by knowledge that the speech was false or with reckless disregard of its falsity.

- The *St. Amant* Court equated actual malice with a "high degree of awareness of probable falsity," which requires clear and convincing evidence that the speaker entertained "serious doubts" as to the truth of the speech.

- The Court extended the requirement of proof of actual malice to the "public figures" who brought libel actions in *Butts* and *Walker*.

- The *Gertz* Court rejected the argument that the requirement of actual malice should be applied to speech concerning all matters of public concern.

- The *Gertz* Court identified two types of public figures. One type is a person who achieves such "pervasive fame or notoriety" that he or she becomes an "all-purpose" public figure. The other type is the "limited purpose" public figure who "voluntarily injects" himself or herself into a particular public controversy or is drawn into one.

- Under *Gertz*, a "private figure" is not subject to the actual malice requirement when seeking compensatory damages for libelous speech about a matter of public concern, and may obtain such damages based on a showing of a speaker's negligence regarding the falsity of speech. But such a plaintiff must satisfy the actual malice standard for punitive damages.

- The *Milkovich* Court rejected the argument that absolute protection should attach to speech that is "opinion."

- According to *Milkovich*, statements are protected from libel actions when they cannot "reasonably be interpreted as stating actual facts." By contrast, a statement on a matter of public concern may give rise to liability for libel when it "reasonably implies false and defamatory facts," even when it may be characterized as an "opinion."

- In the pre-*Sullivan* case of Time, Inc. v. Hill, 385 U.S. 374 (1967), the Court imposed the requirement of proof of actual malice on a plaintiff who sought damages in an action for the tort of "false light." The Court has not subsequently modified that standard to mimic the libel rules established in *Gertz*.

- The Court rejected the argument in Hustler Magazine v. Falwell, 485 U.S. 46 (1988), that a public figure plaintiff who seeks damages for the tort of intentional infliction of emotional distress should be required only to show that speech was "outrageous," that it inflicted serious emotional distress, and that it was intended to do so.

- Instead, the Court imposed the requirement of actual malice on the public figure plaintiff in *Hustler Magazine*, in a case where the speech was an advertisement parody that "could not reasonably have been interpreted" as stating actual facts about the public figure.

- In *Roth* and *Alberts*, the Court echoed *Chaplinsky*'s view that obscene speech is unprotected, reasoning that the history of widespread criminal prohibitions demonstrates that such speech is "utterly without redeeming social importance."

- In defining the scope of obscene speech, the *Roth* and *Alberts* Court identified these elements: The dominant theme of material, taken as a whole, in the view of the average person applying contemporary community standards, appeals to the "prurient interest," meaning a shameful or morbid interest in sex.

- The Court noted in *Roth* and *Alberts* that the terms of obscenity statutes are often imprecise, and it upheld statutes against challenges for indefiniteness or vagueness.

- The *Miller* Court established the modern definition of obscenity, which includes three complex elements: 1) the "prurient interest" element is as articulated in *Roth* and *Alberts*; 2) the work describes sexual conduct, which is specifically defined by state law, in a "patently offensive" way; and 3) the work, taken as a whole, lacks "serious literary, artistic, political, or scientific value."

- During the years between the *Roth* and *Alberts* decisions and *Miller*, a plurality of the Court endorsed the requirement in *Memoirs* that an obscene work should be "utterly lacking" in one of the relevant values. *Miller* rejected this position and endorsed the requirement that a work must lack only "serious" value.

- However, the *Miller* Court did seek to define the second element of "sexual conduct" more precisely by describing specific examples of such conduct and recommending their codification.

- The most significant holding of *Miller* was the Court's approval of the use of "local" rather than "national" community standards for evaluating the "prurient interest" and "patently offensive sexual conduct" elements. Later the Court endorsed a national standard for the "lack of serious value" element.

- In *Paris Adult*, the Court rejected the argument that the only government interests that justify obscenity prosecutions are the protection of unconsenting adults who do not wish to view obscene material and the protection of juveniles. Therefore, the Court upheld the obscenity convictions in cases where obscene films were shown in adult-only theaters.

- The *Stanley* Court held that the mere possession of obscene materials cannot be made a crime.

- In the pre-*Miller* era, the Court upheld the obscenity conviction of the defendant in Ginsberg v. New York, 383 U.S. 463 (1966), because he sold a magazine to a juvenile that was "obscene for minors," though not obscene for adults.

- The *Ginsberg* Court endorsed the unprotected status of this speech because it satisfied these elements: 1) the material included photographs of female nudity and 2) these images were harmful to minors because: a) they predominantly appealed to the prurient, shameful, or morbid interest of minors; b) they were patently offensive to adults with respect to what is suitable for minors; and c) they were "utterly" without redeeming social value for minors.

- In Reno v. ACLU, 521 U.S. 844 (1997), the Court invalidated provisions of the federal Communications Decency Act (CDA) that made it a felony to knowingly transmit "indecent" messages to a juvenile, or to display in a manner available to a juvenile "patently offensive" depictions of sexual or excretory activities or organs.

- The *Reno* Court's reasoning expressed concern with the vagueness of the definitions of prohibited speech, and criticized its overbreadth in applying to protected nonobscene speech for adults and juveniles alike.

- The Court recognized a new category of unprotected speech in Ferber v. New York, 458 U.S. 747 (1982), which prohibited the production and distribution of visual representations of a juvenile engaged in sexual conduct, specifically defined. The government interest in protecting the well-being of the child "models" for such speech was held to be compelling, and the value of the speech was *de minimis* because the producers of such speech could use young-looking models instead of actual children.

- In Ashcroft v. Free Speech Coalition, 122 U.S. 1389 (2002), the Court rejected the argument that the *Ferber* category of unprotected speech should be expanded to include images that appear to be those of juveniles engaging in sexually explicit conduct but are actually only computer-generated images.

- After *Ferber*, ordinances were enacted to create a new category of unprotected speech — namely, "pornography" defined as "the graphic sexually explicit subordination of women" in pictures or words, with accompanying specified elements such as "women presented as sexual objects" in various negative ways.

- The decision of the Court of Appeals for the Seventh Circuit in *American Booksellers* invalidated this type of ordinance on the grounds of its viewpoint discrimination. The breadth of the ordinance required the rejection of the argument that the pornography definition was similar to obscenity.

- The Supreme Court's *Erznoznik* decision relied on *Cohen* in a traditional analysis of the unconstitutionality of an ordinance prohibiting drive-in movie theaters from showing films containing nudity that could be viewed by anyone on a nearby street or public place.

- The Court invalidated the antinudity law on its face in *Erznoznik* because it could not be justified by government interests in protecting the privacy interests of "captive audiences," by the interest in protecting juveniles from viewing material that is protected for them as well as for adults, or by the interest in traffic safety.

- The *Young* decision marked the Court's departure from the protection of nonobscene sex-related speech, as reflected in its ruling upholding a zoning ordinance that prohibited "adult" theaters from being located near residential areas or such regulated entities as "adult" bookstores or bars.

- The *Young* plurality viewed the zoning law as a "place" regulation of distributors of low-value speech and deferred to the reasonable legislative judgment concerning the need for preserving the character of city neighborhoods by means of the zoning regulation.

- The *Schad* Court rejected the argument that *Young*'s rationales could be used to justify an ordinance that established a total ban on all live entertainment within city limits. It found that such a ban was not narrowly tailored either to serve either the needs of residents or to respond to any problems created by live entertainment establishments.

- A total nudity ban was upheld by the *City of Erie* Court, however, where entertainers could escape prosecution by wearing g-strings and pasties, and where the ordinance was viewed as "content neutral" because the governmental interest was based on the "secondary effects" of such zoning concerns as "combating prostitution and other criminal activity."

- The Court recognized the First Amendment value of the unique erotic message conveyed by nude dancers who were employed by the entities challenging the *Erie* ordinance.

- The Court used the "secondary effects" theory in *City of Erie* to determine that the nudity ban could be upheld under the *O'Brien* test because the government interest was unrelated to the suppression of expression, and the minimal requirement of wearing g-strings and pasties created only an incidental restriction on the erotic message of the dancers.

- The *R.A.V.* Court determined that the content discrimination doctrine operates differently in the fields of fully protected speech and unprotected or "proscribable" speech: "When the basis for the content discrimination consists entirely of the very reason the entire class of speech at issue is proscribable, no significant danger [of] viewpoint discrimination exists." In the case of fighting words, the reason for the unprotected status of this category is the mode of expression and not the content.

- The Court relied on this principle to find a fighting words ordinance to be unconstitutional on its face because it did not single out a subcategory of fighting words based on their mode; it applied only to insults that provoke violence "on the basis of race, color, creed, religion or gender" and not other categories.

- Given the content discrimination and viewpoint discrimination of the ordinance, the *R.A.V.* Court reversed the juvenile defendants' fighting words convictions for burning a cross near the dwelling of an African American family, reasoning that the ordinance could not satisfy strict scrutiny. The government interest was compelling in protecting the human rights of persons subject to discrimination, but the ordinance was not narrowly tailored because the content discrimination was not necessary to achieve that interest.

- The *Black* Court upheld a ban on cross burning "with intent of intimidating" any person, finding that the statute satisfied the *R.A.V.* principle because it punished a subcategory of unprotected "true threat" speech — namely, cross burning — for the same reason that generic "true threat" speech is unprotected — namely, because it inspires fear of violence.

- The provision in the *Black* statute that made the conduct of cross burning *prima facie* evidence of intent to intimidate was invalidated because it applies to conduct that is done without the intent to intimidate.

- The *Stevens* Court rejected the argument that a new category of unprotected speech should be recognized as analogous to *Ferber* speech — namely, depictions of animal cruelty in which a living animal is maimed or killed, when such depictions are created sold or possessed for commercial gain. Such new categories should not be created by ad hoc balancing or simple cost-benefit analysis.

- The Court ruled in *Lorillard* that speech restrictions in tobacco regulations were unconstitutional, since they could not satisfy the *Central Hudson* test for evaluating commercial speech, either because they did not directly advance the governmental interest in reducing tobacco use by juveniles, or because they were more extensive than necessary, or for both reasons.

- The *Holder* Court upheld the federal law that prohibits providing material support or resources to foreign organizations that engage in terrorist activity, as applied to training the members of such groups in international law and the process of petitioning the United Nations for relief. The compelling interest in combating terrorism empowers Congress to prosecute even teaching and advocacy meant to promote the groups' nonviolent ends.

- The Court recognized that conduct may be sufficiently communicative to be treated as "symbolic speech," which receives the same protection as speech, when the speaker has an intent "to convey a particularized message" and "when there is a great likelihood that the message would be understood by those who viewed it."

- Where a protestor burned his draft card, the *O'Brien* Court found that the "speech" element of his action, the antidraft message, and the "conduct" element of burning the card were combined in a scenario in which the government had a substantial interest in regulating the conduct of knowingly destroying or mutilating the draft card.

- The defendant's conviction was upheld in *O'Brien* because the Court's test for content-neutral symbolic speech regulations was satisfied. The government interests in the smooth functioning of the administration of the draft system was "unrelated to the suppression of expression," and the restriction on expression was found to be "incidental" because of the sufficiently narrow tailoring of the law.

- The *Clark* Court upheld a regulation that allowed park demonstrations but prohibited overnight sleeping in two parks, finding that the regulation satisfied both the content-neutral time, place, manner test used for speech restrictions in a public forum and the content-neutral *O'Brien* test used for symbolic speech restrictions.

- In Texas v. Johnson, 491 U.S. 397 (1989), the Court struck down a flag-burning statute as a content-based regulation that could not survive strict scrutiny, after first determining that the *O'Brien* test did not apply because the government interest in preserving the flag as the symbol of nationhood was related to the suppression of expression.

- The Court determined that the ban on "all First Amendment activities" within or at the Central Terminal of the Los Angeles airport was unconstitutionally overbroad in *Board of Airport Commissioners*, where virtually any person in the terminal might be found to violate the ordinance through such acts as talking, reading, or wearing symbolic clothing.

- In City of Houston v. Hill, 482 U.S. 451 (1987), an ordinance prohibiting the conduct of intentionally "interrupting" a police officer by verbal challenge was found to be substantially overbroad because it was not limited to the unprotected speech category of fighting words, and instead swept broadly to create liability for the protected speech of verbal criticism and challenge directed at officers.

- The *Stevens* decision provides another illustration of a statute invalidated on overbreadth grounds because a substantial number of the applications of the animal-cruelty-video statute are unconstitutional, and the protection for material of "serious" value does not significantly narrow the statute.

- The *Lovell* Court held that an unconstitutional prior restraint was created by an ordinance that required persons distributing any literature within the city limits to obtain permits from the city manager, because that official had unfettered discretion to limit the freedoms of speech and press by acting as a censor.

- A permit system that requires the submission of films to receive a license must include the safeguards enumerated in Freedman v. Maryland. The burden of proving the unprotected character of the film lies with the censor, and if a license is not issued, the censor must go to court to seek a judicial determination that the film is unprotected.

- In Near v. Minnesota, 283 U.S. 697 (1931), the Court ruled that an injunction against the publication of a newspaper or magazine is an unconstitutional prior restraint, and emphasized that the First Amendment was intended to prevent such restraints on press freedom and to limit remedies against such periodicals to postpublication litigation.

- The scope of *Near*'s protection was articulated in the "Pentagon Papers" case, United States v. New York Times, 403 U.S. 713 (1971), where the government failed to meet the burden of justifying an injunction on the grounds of national security. The justices in the majority expressed a variety of rationales, including the need for evidence that publication would result in "direct, immediate, and irreparable damage" to the nation.

- The Court adopted a special test for assessing the constitutionality of the injunction in *Madsen*, which prohibited antiabortion protestors from engaging in particular conduct during demonstrations at clinics. Where these restrictions were imposed because the protestors repeatedly violated earlier judicial orders, the injunction was deemed to be content neutral and not viewpoint based, but was required to burden "no more speech than necessary to serve a significant government interest."

- In Branzburg v. Hayes, 408 U.S. 665 (1972), the Court rejected the claims of reporters that the First Amendment should protect them from disclosing the identity of their sources when they are required to do so by subpoenas issued by grand juries. The Court doubted that the lack of such protection would lead to a burden on newsgathering, and viewed the government's interest in conducting grand jury investigations as sufficient to justify the defeat of the claimed privilege.

- The Court recognized in *Globe Newspaper* that the First Amendment right of the press and public to attend trial proceedings required that any closure order must be based on a compelling government interest and must be narrowly tailored. This standard could not be satisfied by a law mandating closure of all hearings in which sex-crime-victim witnesses under age 18 would testify.

- In ruling that prejudicial pretrial publicity and disruptive media coverage of the trial had denied the defendant a fair trial in Sheppard v. Maxwell, 384 U.S. 333 (1966), the Court observed that the trial judge could have used a variety of measures other than prior restraints on the press to avoid the constitutional harm.

- In Nebraska Press Association v. Stuart, the Court held that the trial judge impermissibly enjoined the media from publishing facts "strongly implicative" of the defendant's guilt, because the judge failed to find that other measures would be inadequate to protect the fairness of the trial, and that the injunction actually would function effectively to achieve that result.

- The public forum doctrine requires a time, place, manner regulation of speech to be content neutral, supported by a significant government interest, narrowly tailored, and to leave open ample alternative channels of communication. The traditional public fora are streets, sidewalks, and parks; a nontraditional public forum is one that has been opened for speech activity and is treated the same way as a traditional public forum.

- In a nonpublic forum, a more deferential standard requires only that a speech regulation must be reasonable and viewpoint neutral.

- In International Society for Krishna Consciousness, Inc. [ISKCON] v. Lee, 505 U.S. 672 (1992), a majority of the Court concluded that an airport terminal is a nonpublic forum because it has not been dedicated historically for speech activity, either intentionally or through "acquiescence in a continuing practice." The Court also concluded that a prohibition on the solicitation of funds in a terminal is reasonable because it may disrupt the flow of pedestrian travelers and may create the risk of duress or fraud.

- A majority in *ISKCON* also invalidated a ban on the distribution of literature in an airport terminal, with a plurality of the Court reasoning that the regulation was not narrowly drawn and did not leave open ample alternative channels of speech. One justice held that the regulation was not reasonable.

- The *Heffron* decision illustrates the reasons that a time, place, manner regulation of the distribution of material in rented booths, on the grounds of the nontraditional public forum of a state fair, can satisfy the requirements of content neutrality, narrow tailoring, and ample alternative channels. Based on these reasons, the Court rejected the claim of the speech plaintiffs who wished to circulate around the fairgrounds while distributing material.

- The *Mosley* Court established the requirements for evaluating a content-based regulation in a public forum. Subsequent precedents reveal that Mosley imposed a strict scrutiny standard, including the requirements of a compelling governmental interest and narrow tailoring of the regulation to advance that interest.

- The prohibition on picketing next to a school in *Mosley* was held to be content based because of its exemption for peaceful labor picketing, and the Court found that the government could not show that its interest in preventing disruptions outside schools would be achieved in a narrowly tailored manner through the "wholesale exclusion" of all picketing except for labor picketing.

- In United Public Workers v. Mitchell, 330 U.S. 75 (1947), the Court allowed the First Amendment rights of government employees to be subject to the limitations of the Hatch Act, which declared that federal employees may not take any active part in political management or political campaigns. The Court viewed this regulation as being "within reasonable limits" and recognized the validity of the government's interests, such as preventing officials from imposing pressure on employees to assist in campaigns.

- Although the Court recognized that public employees have First Amendment rights in *Pickering* and *Mt. Healthy*, the *Connick* Court rejected a prosecutor's claim for protection from a retaliatory firing because her expression of dissatisfaction with job conditions was not viewed as speech about matters of public concern.

- The *Rankin* Court held that a deputy clerk's statement relating to the assassination attempt against President Reagan did qualify as speech about matters of public concern under *Connick*. Given the lack of evidence that the statement interfered with the effective functioning of the deputy's office, it was protected speech.

- The *Garcetti* Court held that the First Amendment does not protect a government employee from discipline based on speech made pursuant to the employee's official duties, which does not limit the freedom of speech the employee enjoys as a private citizen.

- The *Elrod* decision produced a plurality holding that invalidated the firings, by a recently elected sheriff who was a Democrat, of all non-civil-service employees who were Republicans. These firings based on party affiliation violated the employees' freedoms of belief and association.

- In Legal Services Corp. v. Velasquez, 531 U.S. 533 (2001), the Court found that Congress placed an unconstitutional condition on the speech rights of attorneys by providing funds for their representation of indigent clients but prohibiting the use of those funds for arguments seeking to challenge existing state welfare laws on federal statutory or constitutional grounds. The Court criticized the government for seeking to "insulate its own laws from legitimate judicial challenge" through this speech restriction.

- In United States v. American Library Association, 539 U.S. 194 (2003), the Court upheld a federal statute that conditioned the receipt of federal funds by libraries on the installation of computer software filters to block Internet access to obscene speech, child pornography, and speech harmful to minors. The Court relied on the principle that government has "broad discretion to make content-based judgments" in determining "what private speech to make available to the public" through funding programs.

- In the *Christian Legal Society* decision, the Court rejected a First Amendment challenge to an "accept all comers" policy imposed by a public law school on student groups seeking official recognition and school funds, reasoning that the policy is a "reasonable, viewpoint-neutral condition on access to the student-organization forum."

- In Pleasant Grove City, Utah v. Summum, 129 S. Ct. 1125 (2009), the Court rejected a First Amendment challenge to a city's denial of the request by a religious organization to erect a private monument in a city park, reasoning that the Freedom of Speech Clause does not regulate government speech and that government-commissioned and government-funded monuments speak for the government.

- The *Red Lion* decision in 1969 upheld the fairness doctrine imposed on radio and television broadcasters by the FCC, which required the discussion of public issues and the presentation of both sides of such issues. In 1987, that doctrine was repealed by the FCC.

- In FCC v. Pacifica Foundation, 438 U.S. 726 (1978), a plurality of the Court recognized the authority of the FCC to regulate broadcasting programs with "indecent" content, consisting of comic profanity, under circumstances where the program is aired at a time when children may be listening.

- The *Turner* Court rejected the application of the *Red Lion* doctrine to cable television and required that intermediate scrutiny should be used, as would apply to content-neutral regulations that must promote a substantial governmental interest and satisfy narrow tailoring, when determining whether federal law can require cable companies to carry the programs of local television stations.

- In NAACP v. Alabama, 357 U.S. 449 (1958), the Court recognized that freedom of association is protected by the First Amendment. It rejected the state's claim to obtain the membership lists of the NAACP, given the chilling effect "on the free enjoyment of the right to associate" that would result, based on evidence of the consequences of past disclosures that led to "economic reprisal, loss of employment, threat of physical coercion, and other manifestations of public hostility."

- The *Roberts* decision concluded that the "right to associate for expressive purposes" is not absolute, and that it may be outweighed by regulations that "serve compelling interests, unrelated to the suppression of ideas, that cannot be achieved through means significantly less restrictive of associational freedoms." Therefore, the Court held that the application of an antidiscrimination statute to the all-male Jaycees organization did not violate the First Amendment.

- The *Hurley* Court rejected the application of a state antidiscrimination law as a violation of the First Amendment rights of parade organizers to exclude marchers whose message was not supported by the organizers, reasoning that a speaker is entitled to the autonomy to control the speaker's own message.

- In Board of Regents v. Southworth, 529 U.S. 217 (2000), the Court upheld a mandatory student activity fee, rejecting the claim of students who did not want to pay the fee because it would be used to support the speech of all student groups, including some groups whose messages and activities did not meet the approval of the litigating students. The viewpoint neutrality of the mechanism for funding all groups was required to show that access to the forum of such funding was constitutional.

- The *Johanns* Court upheld a federal law requiring cattle producers to pay a fee that funded government speech, in the form of a board that provided funds for advertising to promote the consumption of beef. Unlike impermissible compelled fees to subsidize private entities, the beef fee funded a government message that "is subject to democratic accountability."

- In *Buckley*, the Court recognized that expenditure limitations reduce the quantity of expression and cannot be justified by the government interest in preventing corruption and the appearance of corruption.

- The *Buckley* Court also upheld the limit on campaign contributions to candidates for office, based on the important interest of limiting the actuality and appearance of corruption.

- In the *Citizens United* decision, the Court invalidated the prohibition on the use of general treasury funds by corporations and unions to make direct contributions to candidates or independent expenditures that advocate the election or defeat of a candidate. The Court reasoned that this prohibition could not be justified by the interest in "equalizing the relative ability of individuals and groups to influence the outcome of elections" or by the interest in preventing corruption or the appearance of corruption.

- In Doe #1 v. Reed, 561 U.S. __ (2010), the Court ruled that the disclosure of the names and contact information of individuals who signed a referendum petition, when sought by means of a public records request, does not violate the First Amendment in all cases. As the litigation in this case continues, it remains for the parties resisting disclosure to show that a reasonable probability of threats, harassment, or reprisals will result from that disclosure.

12

The Religion Clauses

U.S. CONSTITUTION, FIRST AMENDMENT

Congress shall make no law respecting an establishment of religion, or prohibiting the free exercise thereof. . . .

∾ PROBLEM: MORE ON THE EDUCATION FOR A BETTER AMERICA ACT ∾

Over the last half-century, schoolchildren in the United States have fallen farther and farther behind their counterparts in many other parts of the world, particularly Japan and Western European countries. A bipartisan commission appointed by Congress, charged with studying the problem and proposing solutions, concluded that a variety of factors have contributed to the decline, including (and particularly) lack of funding for buildings, equipment, supplies, and quality teachers. As a result, Congress is now considering proposed legislation, entitled the Education for a Better America Act, that would dramatically increase federal funding for elementary and secondary education.

Suppose that you work for a member of the House of Representatives who has been charged with drafting the legislation and who has asked you to assist. Although Congress has the goal of improving the plight of all schoolchildren, including those in private and parochial schools, Congress is concerned about how the religion clauses of the First Amendment might (or should) affect the content of the proposed legislation. In particular, Congress is unclear about how the Establishment Clause might limit or preclude Congress from providing assistance to parochial school students. Congress is also unclear about whether, if it decides to provide assistance to private school students, the Free Exercise Clause would require it to provide similar assistance to parochial school students.

As you work your way through this chapter, you will be asked to think about these issues in various contexts, and ultimately to reach conclusions regarding how you might construct the proposed legislation.

A. THE ESTABLISHMENT CLAUSE

The Establishment Clause is simply stated: "Congress shall make no law respecting an establishment of religion." Although the clause initially applied only to the federal government, its reach was extended to the states through the Fourteenth Amendment, *see* Everson v. Board of Education, 330 U.S. 1 (1947). It prohibits government from engaging in certain types of activities: establishing a national (or, for that matter, a state) church, passing laws that require individuals to go to or remain away from church against their will, and passing laws that force individuals to profess a belief or a disbelief in any religion. The difficulty is that few Establishment Clause cases have involved these types of activities. For example, there have been no attempts to declare a national religion and only a few (modern) attempts to force individuals to go to or remain away from church against their will or to force individuals to profess a belief or a disbelief in a particular religion.

Most Establishment Clause litigation focuses on whether certain lesser acts (e.g., school prayer, financial aid to religious organizations, the posting of the Ten Commandments in public places) constitute an "establishment" of religion. Because these "lesser" acts do not clearly violate the First Amendment, the courts have struggled to define the term *establishment*. This has been done on a case-by-case basis.

1. *Financial Aid to Religion*

Although Establishment Clause issues can occur in a variety of different contexts, they often arise in the context of governmental attempts to provide financial benefits to religion or religious organizations.

a. Early Cases

Everson v. Board of Education
330 U.S. 1 (1947)

Mr. Justice BLACK delivered the opinion of the Court.

[Pursuant to New Jersey law,] the board of education authorized reimbursement to parents of money expended for bus transportation of their children on regular busses operated by the public transportation system. Part of the money was for payment of transportation of children to Catholic parochial schools. These church schools give their students, in addition to secular education, religious instruction conforming to the religious tenets and modes of worship of the Catholic Faith. . . .

Whether this New Jersey law is one respecting the "establishment of religion" requires an understanding of the meaning of that language, particularly with respect to the imposition of taxes. A large proportion of the early settlers of this country came here from Europe to escape the bondage of laws which compelled them to support and attend government favored churches. The centuries immediately before and contemporaneous with the colonization of America had been filled with turmoil, civil strife, and persecutions, generated in large part by established sects determined to maintain their absolute political and religious supremacy. With the power of government supporting them, at various times and places, Catholics had persecuted Protestants, Protestants had persecuted Catholics, Protestant sects had persecuted other Protestant sects, Catholics of one shade of belief had persecuted Catholics of another shade of belief, and all of these had from time to time persecuted Jews. In efforts to force loyalty to whatever religious group happened to be on top and in league with the government of a particular time and place, men and women had been fined, cast in jail, cruelly tortured, and killed. Among the offenses for which these punishments had been inflicted were such things as speaking disrespectfully of the views of ministers of government-established churches, nonattendance at those churches, expressions of non-belief in their doctrines, and failure to pay taxes and tithes to support them.

These practices of the old world were transplanted to and began to thrive in the soil of the new America. [The] charters granted by the English Crown [authorized] the individuals and companies designated to make the laws [to] erect religious establishments which all, whether believers or non-believers, would be required to support and attend. An exercise of this authority was accompanied by a repetition of many of the old world practices and persecutions. . . . These practices became so commonplace as to shock the freedom-loving colonials into a feeling of abhorrence. The imposition of taxes to pay ministers' salaries and to build and maintain churches and church property aroused their indignation. It was these feelings which found expression in the First Amendment. . . .

Prior to the adoption of the Fourteenth Amendment, the First Amendment did not apply as a restraint against the states. Most of them did soon provide similar constitutional protections for religious liberty. But some states persisted for about half a century in imposing restraints upon the free exercise of religion and in discriminating against particular religious groups. In recent years, so far as the provision against the establishment of a religion is concerned, the question has most frequently arisen in connection with proposed state aid to church schools and efforts to carry on religious teachings in the public schools in accordance with the tenets of a particular sect. Some churches have either sought or accepted state financial support for their schools. Here again the efforts to obtain state aid or acceptance of it have not been limited to any one particular faith. The state courts, in the main, have remained faithful to the language of their own constitutional provisions designed to protect religious freedom and to separate religious and governments. Their decisions, however, show the difficulty in drawing the line between tax legislation which provides funds for the welfare of the general public and that which is designed to support institutions which teach religion. . . .

The 'establishment of religion' clause of the First Amendment means at least this: Neither a state nor the Federal Government can set up a church. Neither can pass laws which aid one religion, aid all religions, or prefer one religion over another. Neither can force nor influence a person to go to or to remain away from church against his will or force him to profess a belief or disbelief in any religion. No person can be punished for entertaining or professing religious beliefs or disbeliefs, for church attendance or non-attendance. No tax in any amount, large or small, can be levied to support any religious activities or institutions, whatever they may be called, or whatever form they may adopt to teach or practice religion. Neither a state nor the Federal Government can, openly or secretly, participate in the affairs of any religious organizations or groups and vice versa. In the words of Jefferson, the clause against establishment of religion by law was intended to erect "a wall of separation between Church and State." Reynolds v. United States, 98 U.S., at 164.

[The] question has most frequently arisen in connection with proposed state aid to church schools and efforts to carry on religious teachings in the public schools in accordance with the tenets of a particular sect. Some churches have either sought or accepted state financial support for their schools. . . .

New Jersey cannot consistently with the "establishment of religion" clause of the First Amendment contribute tax-raised funds to the support of an institution which teaches the tenets and faith of any church. On the other hand, other language of the amendment commands that New Jersey cannot hamper its citizens in the free exercise of their own religion. Consequently, it cannot exclude individual Catholics, Lutherans, Mohammedans, Baptists, Jews, Methodists, Non-believers, Presbyterians, or the members of any other faith, *because of their faith, or lack of it*, from receiving the benefits of public welfare legislation. [W]e must be careful [that we do not] prohibit New Jersey from extending its general State law benefits to all its citizens without regard to their religious belief.

Measured by these standards, we cannot say that the First Amendment prohibits New Jersey from spending taxraised funds to pay the bus fares of parochial school pupils as a part of a general program under which it pays the fares of pupils attending public and other schools. It is undoubtedly true that children are helped to get to church schools. There is even a possibility that [some] children might not be sent to the church schools if the parents were compelled to pay their children's bus fares out of their own pockets. . . . Similarly, parents might be reluctant to permit their children to attend schools which the state had cut off from such general government services as ordinary police and fire protection, connections for sewage disposal, public highways and sidewalks. Of course, cutting off church schools from these services [would] make it far more difficult for the schools to operate. But such is obviously not the purpose of the First Amendment. That Amendment requires the state to be a neutral in its relations with groups of religious believers and non-believers; it does not require the state to be their adversary. State power is no more to be used so as to handicap religions, than it is to favor them.

This Court has said that parents may [send] their children to a religious rather than a public school if the school meets the secular educational requirements which the state has power to impose. . . . The State contributes no money to the schools. It does not support them. Its legislation [does] no more than provide a general program to help parents get their children, regardless of their religion, safely and expeditiously to and from accredited schools.

The First Amendment has erected a wall between church and state. That wall must be kept high and impregnable. We could not approve the slightest breach. New Jersey has not breached it here.

Affirmed.

BACKGROUND
The "Wall Between Church and State" Metaphor

The *Everson* decision is famous for introducing this metaphor into the Court's Establishment Clause jurisprudence. As you go through this chapter, think about whether such a wall exists and therefore whether the metaphor is accurate.

Mr. Justice JACKSON, dissenting.

[This] expenditure of tax funds has no possible effect on the child's safety or expedition in transit. As passengers on the public busses they travel as fast and no faster, and are as safe and no safer, since their parents are reimbursed as before.

[T]he resolution which authorizes disbursement of this taxpayer's money limits reimbursement to those who attend public schools and Catholic schools. [The] Act prohibits [payment] to private schools operated in whole or in part for profit. [The Court ignores] the essentially religious test by which beneficiaries of this expenditure are selected. [Could] we sustain an Act that said police shall protect pupils on the way to or from public schools and Catholic schools but not while going to and coming from other schools, and firemen shall extinguish a blaze in public or Catholic school buildings but shall not put out a blaze in Protestant Church schools or private schools operated for profit? [I] should think it pretty plain that such a scheme would not be valid. . . .

Mr. Justice RUTLEDGE, with whom Mr. Justice FRANKFURTER, Mr. Justice JACKSON, and Mr. Justice BURTON agree, dissenting.

Neither so high nor so impregnable today as yesterday is the wall raised between church and state by Virginia's great statute of religious freedom and the First Amendment. . . . The First Amendment's purpose was not to strike merely at the official establishment of a single sect, creed or religion. [I]t was to uproot all such relationships. . . . It was to create a complete and permanent separation of the spheres of religious activity and civil authority by comprehensively forbidding every form of public aid or support for religion. . . .

Does New Jersey's action furnish support for religion by use of the taxing power? Certainly it does. . . . Believers of all faiths, and others who do not express their feeling toward ultimate issues of existence[,] pay the New Jersey tax. [I]t is precisely because the instruction is religious and relates to a particular faith, whether one or another, that parents send their children to religious schools. . . .

We are told that the New Jersey statute is valid [because] the appropriation is for a public, not a private purpose, namely, the promotion of education. . . . If the fact alone be determinative[,] then I can see no possible basis [for] the state's refusal to make full appropriation for support of private, religious schools, just as is done for public instruction. . . . Public money devoted to payment of religious costs, educational or other, brings the quest for more. It brings too the struggle of sect against sect for the larger share or for any. . . . The end of such strife cannot be other than to destroy the cherished liberty. . . .

This is not therefore just a little case over bus fares. [The] realm of religious training and belief remains, as the Amendment made it, the kingdom of the individual man and his God. It should be kept inviolately private, [not] confounded with what legislatures legitimately may take over into the public domain. [W]e have staked the very existence of our country on the faith that complete separation between the state and religion is best for the state and best for religion. That policy necessarily entails hardship upon persons who forego the right to educational advantages the state can supply in order to secure others it is precluded from giving. . . . But it does not make the state unneutral to withhold what the Constitution forbids it to give. [The] judgment should be reversed.

Note: Government Support for Religious Hospitals

In Bradfield v. Roberts, 175 U.S. 291 (1899), the Court held that the District of Columbia could pay to construct a building on the grounds of a religiously affiliated hospital. The Court emphasized that the payment had a secular purpose (to expand hospital facilities) and that the hospital did not discriminate on the basis of religion in its operation. The Court regarded the religious affiliation as "wholly immaterial."

∾ PROBLEMS ∾

1. *The Framers' Intent.* Jesse Choper argues that free public education "was virtually non-existent during the early years of Independence, and where it did occur it had a distinctly religious orientation." Jesse Choper, *The Establishment Clause and Aid to Parochial Schools*, 56 Cal. L. Rev. 260, 263-264 (1968). What significance do you attach to these facts in interpreting the Establishment Clause as applied to public schools?

2. *A "Neutrality" Test?* Philip Kurland, in *Of Church and State and the Supreme Court*, 29 U. Chi. L. Rev. 1, 96 (1961), argues that the Free Exercise Clause and

the Establishment Clause "should be read as stating a single precept: that government cannot utilize religion as a standard for action or inaction because these clauses, read together as they should be, prohibit classification in terms of religion either to confer a benefit or to impose a burden." Do you agree? Suppose that government decides to provide salary supplements to teachers in private schools. Under the Kurland test, can the government extend those benefits to religious schools? Indeed, must it extend those benefits to religious schools? Douglas Laycock, in *Formal, Substantive and Disaggregated Neutrality Toward Religion*, 39 DePaul L. Rev. 993, 1000-1003 (1990), argues that "[F]ormal neutrality . . . would produce results that many Americans find unacceptably favorable to religion" because it would allow government to give "unlimited amounts of unrestricted aid to religious schools" provided that it gives such aid to "all schools and not to religious schools alone." Indeed, he argues that any "aid to secular private schools *must* be given to religious schools, on exactly the same terms. To exclude religious schools from the aid program, or to impose restrictions on religious uses of the money, would be to classify on the basis of religion." Is a "neutrality" test desirable?

3. *More on the Education for a Better America Act.* Does *Everson* provide you with guidance about how to structure the Act? For example, if Congress is "neutral" toward all schools (public, private, and parochial), can it provide direct financial aid to religious schools? If Congress chooses to provide financial aid to private nonreligious schools, must it provide similar aid to private religious schools (or vice versa)?

b. The *Lemon* Test and Doctrinal Turmoil

The dominant Establishment Clause test for nearly 30 years was the so-called "*Lemon*" test, articulated in the following case.

Lemon v. Kurtzman
403 U.S. 602 (1971)

Mr. Chief Justice BURGER delivered the opinion of the Court.

Rhode Island found that the quality of education [in] nonpublic elementary schools [was] jeopardized by the rapidly rising salaries needed to attract competent and dedicated teachers. [A statute authorized] state officials to supplement the salaries of teachers of secular subjects [by] paying directly to a teacher an amount not in excess of 15% of his current annual salary. [The Act requires that teachers teach only those subjects that are offered in [the] public schools, and use "only teaching materials used in the public schools." Rhode Island's] nonpublic elementary schools accommodated approximately 25% of the State's pupils. About 95% of these pupils attended schools affiliated with the Roman Catholic church. [All teachers who applied] for benefits under the Act [are] employed by Roman Catholic schools. [The District Court held that the Act violated the Establishment Clause.] We affirm.

[The Pennsylvania Nonpublic Elementary and Secondary Education Act] authorizes [direct payments to] nonpublic schools [for] actual expenditures for teachers' salaries, textbooks, and instructional materials. A school [must] maintain [procedures] that identify the "separate" cost of the "secular educational service." [Reimbursement is limited to courses "presented in the curricula of the public schools," and is further limited to courses in mathematics, modern foreign languages, physical science, and physical education.] Textbooks and instructional materials [must] be approved by the state. . . . [T]he statute prohibits reimbursement for any course [with] "[subject] matter expressing religious teaching, or the morals or forms of worship of any sect." [S]ome $5 million has been expended annually. . . . [96%] of these pupils attend church-related schools, and most [are] affiliated with the Roman Catholic church. [A] three-judge federal court [dismissed] the complaint. . . . We reverse.

[W]e must draw lines with reference to the three main evils against which the Establishment Clause was intended to afford protection: "sponsorship, financial support, and active involvement of the sovereign in religious activity." Walz v. Tax Commission, 397 U.S. 664, 668 (1970). Every analysis in this area must begin with consideration of the cumulative criteria developed by the Court over many years. Three such tests may be gleaned from our cases. First, the statute must have a secular legislative purpose; second, its principal or primary effect must be one that neither advances nor inhibits religion; finally, the statute must not foster "an excessive government entanglement with religion."

[T]he statutes themselves clearly state that they are intended to enhance the quality of the secular education in all schools covered by the compulsory attendance laws. [A] State always has a legitimate concern for maintaining minimum standards [in] schools. . . .

[The] legislatures [have] sought to create statutory restrictions designed to guarantee the separation between secular and religious educational functions and to ensure that State financial aid supports only the former. [Our] prior holdings do not call for total separation between church and state; total separation is not possible in an absolute sense. Some relationship between government and religious organizations is inevitable. Fire inspections, building and zoning regulations, and state requirements under compulsory school-attendance laws are examples of necessary and permissible contacts. [T]he line of separation, far from being a "wall," is a blurred, indistinct, and variable barrier depending on all the circumstances of a particular relationship.

[In] order to determine whether the government entanglement with religion is excessive, we must examine the character and purposes of the institutions that are benefitted, the nature of the aid that the State provides, and the resulting relationship between the government and the religious authority. [Here] we find that both statutes foster an impermissible degree of entanglement.

[The Rhode Island program] gives rise to entangling church-state relationships of the kind the Religion Clauses sought to avoid. [T]eachers have a substantially different ideological character from books. [A] textbook's content is ascertainable, but a teacher's handling of a subject is not. We cannot ignore the danger that a teacher under religious control and discipline poses to the separation of the religious from the purely secular aspects [of] education. [We] do not assume that teachers [will] be guilty of bad faith or any conscious design to evade the limitations imposed by the statute and the First Amendment. We simply recognize that a dedicated religious person, teaching in a school affiliated with his or her faith and operated to inculcate its tenets, [will] experience great difficulty [remaining] religiously neutral. . . . To ensure that no trespass occurs, the State [carefully] conditioned its aid with pervasive restrictions. [A] comprehensive, discriminating, and continuing state surveillance will inevitably be required to ensure that these restrictions are obeyed and the First Amendment otherwise respected. . . .

The Pennsylvania statute [involves] an educational system that is very similar. . . . The very restrictions and surveillance necessary to ensure that teachers play a strictly non-ideological role give rise to entanglements between church and state. . . . The Pennsylvania statute [has] the further defect of providing state financial aid directly to the church-related schools. [Such payments] have almost always been accompanied by varying measures of control and surveillance. [T]he government's [power to] determine which expenditures are religious and which are secular creates an intimate and continuing relationship between church and state.

A broader base of entanglement of yet a different character is presented by the divisive political potential of these state programs. In a community where such a large number of pupils are served by church-related schools, [p]artisans of parochial schools, understandably concerned with rising costs and sincerely dedicated to both the religious and secular educational missions of their schools, will inevitably [promote] political action to achieve their goals. Those who oppose state aid, whether for constitutional, religious, or fiscal reasons, will inevitably respond and employ all of the usual political campaign techniques to prevail. Candidates will be forced to declare and voters to choose. [M]any people confronted with issues of this kind will find their votes aligned with their faith.

Ordinarily political debate and division, however vigorous or even partisan, are normal and healthy manifestations of our democratic system of government, but political division along religious lines was one of the principal evils against which the First Amendment was intended to protect. The potential divisiveness of such conflict is a threat to the normal political process. [It] conflicts with [our] history and tradition to permit questions of the Religion Clauses to assume such importance in our legislatures and in our elections. [Here] we are confronted with successive and very likely permanent annual appropriations that benefit relatively few religious groups. Political fragmentation and divisiveness on religious lines are thus likely to be intensified. . . .

[N]othing we have said can be construed to disparage the role of church-related elementary and secondary schools in our national life. . . . Under our system the choice has been made that government is to be entirely excluded from the area of religious instruction and churches excluded from the affairs of government. The Constitution decrees that religion must be a private matter for the individual, the family, and the institutions of private choice, and that while some involvement and entanglement are inevitable, lines must be drawn.

The judgment of the Rhode Island District Court in No. 569 and No. 570 is affirmed. The judgment of the Pennsylvania District Court in No. 89 is reversed, and the case is remanded for further proceedings consistent with this opinion.

Mr. Justice DOUGLAS, whom Mr. Justice BLACK joins, concurring.

[Public] financial support of parochial schools [necessitates] governmental suppression, surveillance, or meddling in church affairs. . . . The constitutional mandate can in part be carried out by censoring the curricula. [A] sectarian course can be marked for deletion. But the problem only starts there. Sectarian instruction [can] take place in a course on Shakespeare or in one on mathematics. [I] would think that policing these grants to detect sectarian instruction would be insufferable to religious partisans and would breed division and dissension between church and state. [If] the government closed its eyes to the manner in which these grants are actually used it would be allowing public funds to promote sectarian education. If it did not close its eyes but undertook the surveillance needed, it [would] intermeddle in parochial affairs in a way that would breed only rancor and dissension. [A] history class, a literature class, or a science class in a parochial school is not a separate institute; it is part of the organic whole [living] on one budget. What the taxpayers give for salaries of those who teach only the humanities or science without any trace of proselytizing enables the school to use all of its own funds for religious training. . . . [T]he taxpayers' forced contribution to the parochial schools in the present cases violates the First Amendment.

Mr. Justice BRENNAN.

[T]hese statutes require "too close a proximity" of government [to] sectarian institutions and [create] real dangers of "the secularization of a creed." The Rhode Island statute requires [teachers] to surrender their right to teach religion courses and to promise not to "inject" religious teaching into their secular courses. This has led [one] teacher to stop praying with his classes, [a] testimonial to the self-censorship that inevitably accompanies state regulation. . . . Both the Rhode Island and Pennsylvania statutes prescribe extensive standardization of the content of secular courses, and of the teaching materials and textbooks [used] in teaching the courses. [The regulations implementing] those requirements necessarily require policing of instruction in the schools. The picture of state inspectors prowling the halls of parochial schools and auditing classroom instruction [raises] more than an imagined specter of governmental "secularization of a creed." [These] cases [involve] direct subsidies of tax monies to the schools themselves and [the] secular education those schools provide goes hand in hand with the religious mission that is the only reason for the schools' existence. [These] statutes do violence to the principle that "government may not employ religious means to serve secular interests, however legitimate they may be, at least without [a] demonstration that nonreligious means will not suffice."

Mr. Justice WHITE, concurring in the judgment in 89 and 153 and dissenting in Nos. 569 and 570.

[It] is enough for me that the States and the Federal Government are financing a separable secular function of overriding importance in order to sustain the legislation here challenged. [There] is no specific allegation [that] sectarian teaching does or would invade secular classes supported by state funds. . . .

Notes

1. *The* Lemon *Test and Financial Aid to Parochial Schools.* The *Lemon* criterion has been used in a number of cases involving financial aid to parochial schools (some of which have now been overruled).

a. *Instructional materials: See* Meek v. Pittenger, 421 U.S. 349 (1975), and Wolman v. Walter, 443 U.S. 229 (1977) (the state may not loan "instructional material and equipment" [i.e., maps, charts, periodicals, photographs, sound recordings, films, and laboratory equipment] to parochial schools without impermissibly aiding "the sectarian school enterprise as a whole").

b. *Standardized testing: See Wolman, supra* (the state may pay for administering and scoring standardized testing if the tests are the same ones used in the public schools and nonpublic employees are not involved in the grading); and Levitt v. Committee for Public Education, 413 U.S. 472 (1973) (the state may not reimburse for administering teacher-prepared tests).

c. *Auxiliary services: Meek, supra* (the state may not provide "auxiliary services" (remedial and accelerated instruction, guidance counseling and testing, speech and hearing services) directly to nonpublic school children with special needs without creating excessive surveillance, entanglement, and political divisiveness); *Wolman, supra* (the state may provide speech and hearing diagnostic services, and diagnostic psychological services, to pupils attending nonpublic schools because they "[have] little or no educational content and are not closely associated with the educational mission of the nonpublic school").

d. *Remedial services: Wolman, supra* (the state may pay for therapeutic, guidance, and remedial services for students who have been identified as having a need for specialized attention at neutral sites away from the parochial schools).

e. *State-sponsored field trips: Wolman, supra* (the state may not spend funds for student field trips "to governmental, industrial, cultural, and scientific centers designed to enrich the secular studies of students" without implicating "direct aid to sectarian education" and creating the need for "close supervision [and] excessive entanglement").

f. *Maintenance and repair: See* Committee for Public Education and Religious Liberty v. Nyquist, 413 U.S. 756 (1973) (the state may not provide

direct money grants to "qualifying" nonpublic schools for the "maintenance and repair [of] school facilities and equipment to ensure the
health, welfare and safety of enrolled pupils" when payments were not
restricted to facilities used exclusively for secular purposes).

2. *Financial Aid to Higher Education.* Given that college students are older, and
less impressionable, than elementary and secondary school students, the Court
has always treated higher education funding somewhat differently than funding
of education at lower levels. *See, e.g.,* Roemer v. Board of Public Works, 426 U.S.
736 (1976) (Court upheld a Maryland law that provided annual grants [15 percent of per-pupil appropriation in the state system] to private colleges subject to
the restriction that the funds not be used for "sectarian purposes." Occasional
audits would be "quick and non-judgmental."); Hunt v. McNair, 413 U.S. 734
(1973) (Court upheld a statute that authorized the issuance of revenue bonds for
the benefit of a Baptist college, finding that the program's purpose was secular
(education) and that "the College [was not] an instrument of religious indoctrination"); and Tilton v. Richardson, 403 U.S. 672 (1971) (Court upheld federal law
providing construction grants to religious colleges for buildings and facilities
used for secular educational purposes. "[C]ollege students are less impressionable and less susceptible to religious indoctrination. . . . Since religious indoctrination is not a substantial purpose[,] there is less likelihood [that] religion will
permeate [secular] education [and the] necessity for intensive government
surveillance is diminished." The Court did strike down a provision allowing for
religious use after 20 years.).

(1)   Criticisms of the Lemon Test

Although the *Lemon* test attempted to provide a single unified criterion for
evaluating Establishment Clause claims, that test has been much criticized, and
some have argued that the test has not resulted in consistent or rational decision
making. In a dissenting opinion in Wallace v. Jaffree, 472 U.S. 38 (1985), Chief
Justice Rehnquist stated: "[The *Lemon* test] has simply not provided adequate
standards for deciding Establishment Clause cases. . . . For example, a State may
lend [geography] textbooks that contain [maps], but the State may not lend
[maps] for use in geography class. A State may lend textbooks on American colonial history, but it may not lend a film on George Washington, or a film projector
to show it. . . . A State may lend classroom workbooks, but may not lend workbooks in which the parochial school children write, thus rendering them nonre-
usable. A State may pay for bus transportation to religious schools but may not
pay for bus transportation from the parochial school to the public zoo or natural
history museum. . . . A State may pay for diagnostic services conducted in the
parochial school but therapeutic services must be given in a different building;
speech and hearing 'services' [inside] the sectarian school are forbidden, but the
State may conduct speech and hearing diagnostic testing inside the sectarian
school. Exceptional parochial school students may receive counseling, but it must
take place outside of the parochial school. . . . A State may give cash to a parochial
school to pay for the administration of state-written tests[,] but it may not provide

funds for teacher-prepared tests on secular subjects. Religious instruction may not be given in public school, but the public school may release students during the day for religion classes elsewhere, and may enforce attendance at those classes with its truancy laws." In a concurring opinion in Board of Education of Kiryas Joel Village School District v. Grumet, 512 U.S. 687 (1994), Justice O'Connor argued: "It is always appealing to look for [a] Grand Unified Theory that would resolve all the cases [under the] Establishment Clause. [But this] may sometimes do more harm than good. . . . Experience proves that the Establishment Clause, like the Free Speech Clause, cannot easily be reduced to a single test. . . ."

∾ PROBLEM: MORE ON THE EDUCATION FOR THE TWENTY-FIRST CENTURY ACT ∾

Does *Lemon*'s analysis affect or alter your views regarding the permissible content of the proposed Education for the Twenty-First Century Act? Under the *Lemon* test, would it be permissible for Congress to provide direct financial aid to parochial schools? Would it be possible to do so without running afoul of the three-part test? Would it matter that Congress's goal is to improve the quality of education in secular subjects, and that Congress believed that the grants would help it achieve that objective?

c. Agostini v. Felton

In recent years, the Court has begun to back away from some of its earlier decisions and has also modified the *Lemon* test.

Agostini v. Felton

521 U.S. 203 (1997)

Justice O'CONNOR delivered the opinion of the Court.

In Aguilar v. Felton, 473 U.S. 402 (1985), this Court held that the Establishment Clause [barred] the city of New York from sending public school teachers into parochial schools to provide remedial education to disadvantaged children. . . . On remand, the [trial court] entered a permanent injunction reflecting our ruling. Twelve years later, petitioners [seek] relief from its operation. Petitioners maintain that *Aguilar* cannot be squared with our intervening Establishment Clause jurisprudence and ask that we explicitly recognize [that] *Aguilar* is no longer good law. . . .

I

[Congress] enacted Title I of the Elementary and Secondary Education Act of 1965 to "provid[e] full educational opportunity to every child regardless of economic background." Toward that end, Title I channels federal funds, through the States, to "local educational agencies" (LEA's). The LEA's spend [funds] to provide remedial education, guidance, and job counseling to eligible students. An eligible student is one (i) who resides within the attendance boundaries of a public school located in a low-income area, and (ii) who is failing, or is at risk of failing, the State's student performance standards. Title I funds must be made available to *all* eligible children, regardless of whether they attend public schools, and the services provided to children attending private schools must be "equitable in comparison to services and other benefits for public school children."

[Title I] services may be provided only to those private school students eligible for aid, and cannot be used to provide services on a "school-wide" basis. In addition, the LEA must retain complete control over Title I funds; retain title to all materials used to provide Title I services; and provide those services through public employees or other persons independent of the private school and any religious institution. The Title I services themselves must be "secular, neutral, and nonideological," and must "supplement, and in no case supplant, the level of services" already provided by the private school.

Petitioner Board of Education of the City of New York (Board), an LEA, first applied for Title I funds in 1966. . . . Approximately 10% of the total number of students eligible for Title I services are private school students. Recognizing that more than 90% of the private schools within the Board's jurisdiction are sectarian, the Board initially arranged to transport children to public schools for after-school Title I instruction. . . . Attendance was poor, teachers and children were tired, and parents were concerned for the safety of their children. The Board then moved [the] instruction onto private school campuses [during] school hours. [O]nly public employees could serve as Title I instructors and counselors. Assignments to private schools were made on a voluntary basis and without regard to the religious affiliation of the employee or the wishes of the private school. [A] majority of Title I teachers worked in nonpublic schools with religious affiliations different from their own. . . .

[Title I employees were] told that (i) they were employees of the Board and accountable only to their public school supervisors; (ii) they had exclusive responsibility for selecting students for the Title I program and could teach only those children who met the eligibility criteria for Title I; (iii) their materials and equipment would be used only in the Title I program; (iv) they could not engage in team-teaching or other cooperative instructional activities with private school teachers; and (v) they could not introduce any religious matter into their teaching or become involved in any way with the religious activities of the private schools. All religious symbols were to be removed from classrooms used for Title I services. [Title I] teachers [could] consult with a student's regular classroom teacher to assess the student's particular needs and progress, [but were required] to limit those consultations to mutual professional concerns regarding the student's education. To ensure [compliance], a publicly employed field supervisor was to [make at] least one unannounced visit to each teacher's classroom every month.

[S]ix federal taxpayers [sued] the Board [seeking] declaratory and injunctive relief. . . . The District Court granted summary judgment for the Board, but the [court of appeals reversed]. [In] a 5-4 decision, this Court affirmed on the ground that the Board's Title I program necessitated an "excessive entanglement of church and state in the administration of [Title I] benefits." On remand, the District Court permanently enjoined the Board "from using public funds for any plan or program under [Title I] to the extent that it requires, authorizes or permits public school teachers and guidance counselors to provide teaching and counseling services on the premises of sectarian schools. . . ."

The Board [then modified] its Title I program [to revert] to its prior practice of providing instruction at public school sites, at leased sites, and in mobile instructional units (essentially vans converted into classrooms) parked near the sectarian school. The Board also offered computer-aided instruction, which could be provided "on premises" because it did not require public employees to be physically present on the premises of a religious school. [T]he additional costs of complying with *Aguilar*'s mandate are significant. Since the 1986-1987 school year, the Board has spent over $100 million providing computer-aided instruction, leasing sites and mobile instructional units, and transporting students to those sites. [These] *"Aguilar* costs" [reduce] the amount of [money] an LEA has available for remedial education, and LEA's have [reduced] the number of students who receive Title I benefits. . . .

[Petitioners] filed motions [seeking] relief [from] the permanent injunction [because] the "decisional law [had] changed. . . ." Specifically, petitioners pointed to the statements of five Justices in Board of Ed. of Kiryas Joel Village School Dist. v. Grumet, 512 U.S. 687 (1994), calling for the overruling of *Aguilar*. [T]he District Court denied [the] motion. We granted certiorari and now reverse.

III

In order to evaluate whether *Aguilar* has been eroded[,] it is necessary to understand the rationale upon which *Aguilar*, as well as its companion case, School Dist. of Grand Rapids v. Ball, 473 U.S. 373 (1985), rested. [In] *Ball*, the Court evaluated two programs implemented by the School District of Grand Rapids, Michigan. [The] Shared Time program [provided] remedial and "enrichment" classes, at public expense, to students attending nonpublic schools. The classes were taught during regular school hours by publicly employed teachers, using materials purchased with public funds, on the premises of nonpublic schools. The Shared Time courses were in subjects designed to supplement the "core curriculum" of the nonpublic schools. Of the 41 nonpublic schools eligible for the program, 40 were "'pervasively sectarian'[.]"

[The] Court [applied] the so-called *Lemon* test. [T]he Court's conclusion that the Shared Time program in *Ball* had the impermissible effect of advancing religion rested on three assumptions: (i) any public employee who works on the premises of a religious school is presumed to inculcate religion in her work; (ii) the presence of public employees on private school premises creates a symbolic union between church and state; and (iii) any and all public aid that directly aids the educational function of religious schools impermissibly finances religious indoctrination, even if the aid reaches such schools as a consequence of private decision making. Additionally, in *Aguilar* there was a fourth assumption: that New York City's Title I program necessitated an excessive government entanglement with religion because public employees who teach on the premises of religious schools must be closely monitored to ensure that they do not inculcate religion.

Our more recent cases have undermined the assumptions upon which *Ball* and *Aguilar* relied. [W]e continue to ask whether the government acted with the purpose of advancing or inhibiting religion. . . . Likewise, we continue to explore whether the aid has the "effect" of advancing or inhibiting religion. What has changed [is] our understanding of the criteria used to assess whether aid to religion has an impermissible effect. [C]ases subsequent to *Aguilar* [have] modified [the] approach we use to assess indoctrination. First, [we] abandoned the presumption [that] the placement of public employees on parochial school grounds inevitably results in the impermissible effect of state-sponsored indoctrination or constitutes a symbolic union between government and religion. In Zobrest v. Catalina Foothills School Dist., 509 U.S. 1 (1993), we examined whether the IDEA, 20 U.S.C. §400 *et seq.*, was constitutional as applied to a deaf student who sought to bring his state-employed sign-language interpreter with him to his Roman Catholic high school. We held that this was permissible [and refused] to presume that a publicly employed interpreter would be pressured by the pervasively sectarian surroundings to inculcate religion. [W]e assumed [that] the interpreter would dutifully discharge her responsibilities as [a] public employee and comply with the ethical guidelines of her profession by accurately translating what was said. . . .

Second, [we] departed from the rule [that] all government aid that directly aids the educational function of religious schools is invalid. In Witters v. Washington Dept. of Servs. for Blind, 474 U.S. 481 (1986), we held that the Establishment Clause did not bar a State from issuing a vocational tuition grant to a blind person who wished to use the grant to attend a Christian college and become a pastor, missionary, or youth director. Even though the grant recipient [would] use the money to obtain religious education, [the] tuition grants were "'made available generally without regard to the sectarian-nonsectarian, or public-nonpublic nature of the institution benefitted.'" The grants were disbursed directly to students, who then used the money to pay for tuition at the educational institution of their choice. [A]ny money that ultimately went to religious institutions did so "only as a result of the genuinely independent and private choices of" individuals. The same logic applied in *Zobrest*, where we allowed the State to provide an interpreter, even though she would be a mouthpiece for religious instruction, because the IDEA's neutral eligibility criteria ensured that the interpreter's presence in a sectarian school was a "result of the private decision of individual parents" and "[could] not be attributed to state decisionmaking." . . .

[U]nder current law, the Shared Time program in *Ball* and New York City's Title I program in *Aguilar* will not [be] deemed to have the effect of advancing religion through indoctrination. [E]ach of the premises upon which we relied in *Ball* to reach a contrary conclusion is no longer valid. First, there is no reason to presume that, simply because she enters a parochial school classroom, a full-time public employee [will] depart from her assigned duties and instructions and embark on religious indoctrination. . . . *Zobrest* also repudiates *Ball*'s assumption that the presence of Title I teachers in parochial school classrooms will, without more, create the impression of a "symbolic union" between church and state. . . .

Nor under current law can we conclude that a program placing full-time public employees on parochial campuses to provide Title I instruction would impermissibly finance religious indoctrination. [T]he provision of instructional services under Title I is indistinguishable from the provision of sign-language interpreters under the IDEA. [A]s in *Zobrest*, Title I services are by law supplemental to the regular curricula. These services do not, therefore, "reliev[e] sectarian schools of costs they otherwise would have borne in educating their students."

Justice Souter finds our conclusion that the IDEA and Title I programs are similar to be "puzzling," and points to three differences he perceives between the programs: (i) Title I services are distributed by LEA's "directly to the religious schools" instead of to individual students pursuant to a formal application process; (ii) Title I services "necessarily reliev[e] a religious school of 'an expense that it otherwise would have assumed'"; and (iii) Title I provides services to more students than did the programs in *Witters* and *Zobrest*. None of these distinctions is meaningful. While it is true that individual students may not directly apply for Title I services, it does not follow [that] those services are distributed "directly to the religious schools." [T]hey are not. No Title I funds ever reach the coffers of religious schools, and Title I services may not be provided to religious schools on a school-wide basis. Title I funds are instead distributed to a public agency (an LEA) that dispenses services directly to the eligible students within its boundaries, no matter where they choose to attend school. [W]e fail to see how providing Title I services directly to eligible students results in a greater financing of religious indoctrination simply because those students are not first required to submit a formal application.

We are also not persuaded that Title I services supplant the remedial instruction and guidance counseling already provided in New York City's sectarian schools. [We] are unwilling to speculate that all sectarian schools provide remedial instruction and guidance counseling. . . .

What is most fatal to the argument that New York City's Title I program directly subsidizes religion is that it applies with equal force when those services are provided off-campus, and *Aguilar* implied that providing the services off-campus is entirely consistent with the Establishment Clause. [A] financial incentive to undertake religious indoctrination [is] not present [where] the aid is allocated on the basis of neutral, secular criteria that neither favor nor disfavor religion, and is made available to both religious and secular beneficiaries on a nondiscriminatory basis. . . .

Applying this reasoning to New York City's Title I program, it is clear that Title I services are allocated on the basis of criteria that neither favor nor disfavor religion. The services are available to all children who meet the Act's eligibility requirements, no matter what their religious beliefs or where they go to school. The Board's program does not, therefore, give aid recipients any incentive to modify their religious beliefs or practices in order to obtain those services.

We turn now to *Aguilar*'s conclusion that New York City's Title I program resulted in an excessive entanglement between church and state. [The] finding of "excessive" entanglement in *Aguilar* rested on three grounds: (i) the program would require "pervasive monitoring by public authorities" to ensure that Title I employees did not inculcate religion; (ii) the program required "administrative cooperation" between the Board and parochial schools; and (iii) the program might increase the dangers of "political divisiveness." Under our current understanding of the Establishment Clause, the last two considerations are insufficient by themselves to create an "excessive" entanglement. They are present no matter where Title I services are offered. . . . Further, the assumption underlying the first consideration has been undermined. [W]e no longer presume that public employees will inculcate religion simply because they happen to be in a sectarian environment. Since we have abandoned the assumption that properly instructed public employees will fail to discharge their duties faithfully, we must also discard the assumption that pervasive monitoring of Title I teachers is required. There is no suggestion [that] unannounced monthly visits of public supervisors are insufficient to prevent or to detect inculcation of religion by public employees. . . .

To summarize, New York City's Title I program does not run afoul of any of three primary criteria we currently use to evaluate whether government aid has the effect of advancing religion: it does not result in governmental indoctrination; define its recipients by reference to religion; or create an excessive entanglement. We therefore hold that a federally funded program providing supplemental, remedial instruction to disadvantaged children on a neutral basis is not invalid under the Establishment Clause when such instruction is given on the premises of sectarian schools by government employees pursuant to a program containing safeguards such as those present here. The same considerations that justify this holding require us to conclude that this carefully constrained program also cannot reasonably be viewed as an endorsement of religion. Accordingly, we must acknowledge that *Aguilar*, as well as the portion of *Ball* addressing Grand Rapids' Shared Time program, are no longer good law.

[O]ur Establishment Clause jurisprudence has changed significantly since we decided *Ball* and *Aguilar*. . . . We therefore overrule *Ball* and *Aguilar* to the extent those decisions are inconsistent with our current understanding of the Establishment Clause. . . . [W]e reverse [the] Court of Appeals and remand to the District Court with instructions to vacate [its] order.

It is so ordered.

Justice SOUTER, with whom Justice STEVENS and Justice GINSBURG join, and with whom Justice BREYER joins as to Part II, dissenting.

[*Aguilar*] was a correct and sensible decision. . . . The State is forbidden to subsidize religion directly and is just as surely forbidden to act in any way that could reasonably be viewed as religious endorsement. [These] principles were violated by the programs at issue in *Aguilar* and *Ball*, as a consequence of several significant features common to both Title I [and] the Grand Rapids Shared Time program: each provided classes on the premises of the religious schools[;] while their services were termed "supplemental," the programs and their instructors necessarily assumed responsibility for teaching subjects that the religious schools would otherwise have been obligated to provide, the public employees carrying out the programs had broad responsibilities involving the exercise of considerable discretion, while the programs offered aid to nonpublic school students generally[,] participation by religious school students in each program was extensive, and, finally, aid under Title I and Shared Time flowed directly to the schools in the form of classes and programs. . . . What [was] significant in *Aguilar* and *Ball* [was that the schemes assumed responsibilities] indistinguishable from the responsibility of the schools themselves. The obligation [to] teach reading necessarily extends to teaching those who are having a hard time at it. . . . Calling classes remedial does not distinguish [them] from basic subjects. [If] a State may constitutionally enter the schools to [teach, it must be] free to assume [the] entire cost of instruction [in any] secular subject in any religious school. . . .

It may be objected that there is some subsidy in remedial education even when it takes place off the religious premises. [I]f the aid is delivered outside of the schools, it is less likely to supplant some of what would otherwise go on inside them and to subsidize what remains. On top of that, [s]haring the teaching responsibilities within a school having religious objectives is far more likely to telegraph approval of the school's mission than keeping the State's distance would do. . . . [M]inimal contact between state and church is the less likely to feed the resentment of other religions that would like access to public money for their own worthy projects. [I]f a line is to be drawn short of barring all state aid to religious schools for teaching standard subjects, the *Aguilar-Ball* line was a sensible one capable of principled adherence. . . .

[*Zobrest* recognized] that the Establishment Clause lays down no absolute bar to placing public employees in a sectarian school, but the rejection of such a per se rule was hinged expressly on the nature of the employee's job, sign-language interpretation. [The] signer could [be] seen as more like a hearing aid than a teacher, and the signing could not be understood as an opportunity to inject religious content in what was supposed to be secular instruction. . . .

The Court next claims that *Ball* rested on the assumption that "any and all public aid that directly aids the educational function of religious schools impermissibly finances religious indoctrination, even if the aid reaches such schools as a consequence of private decision-making." [*Ball*] held that the Shared Time program subsidized the religious functions of the parochial schools by taking over a significant portion of their responsibility for teaching secular subjects. The Court [enquired] whether the effect of the proffered aid was "direct and substantial" [or] merely "indirect and incidental," [emphasizing] that the question "is one of degree." *Witters* and *Zobrest* did nothing to repudiate the principle [that] religious institutions did not receive it directly from the State. . . .

Note: A Return to Neutrality?

In Mitchell v. Helms, 530 U.S. 793 (2000), Justice Thomas authored a plurality opinion (joined by Chief Justice Rehnquist and Justices Scalia and Kennedy) upholding Chapter 2 of the Education Consolidation and Improvement Act of 1981, which provided federal funds "for the acquisition and use of instructional and educational materials, including library services and materials (including media materials), assessments, reference materials, computer software and hardware for instructional use, and other curricular materials." Participating private schools received aid based on the number of children enrolled in each school, and they could use the funds to "supplement" but not supplant funds from nonfederal sources. The "services, materials, and equipment" provided to private schools must be "secular, neutral, and nonideological," and private schools could not acquire control of them. In upholding the Act, the plurality overruled *Meek* and *Wolman*, holding that it has "consistently turned to the principle of neutrality. [I]f the government, seeking to further some legitimate secular purpose, offers aid on the same terms, without regard to religion, to all who adequately further that purpose, then it is fair to say that any aid going to a religious recipient only has the effect of furthering that secular purpose." The Court also focused on whether the governmental aid "define[s] its recipients by reference to religion" thereby creating "a financial incentive to undertake religious indoctrination." The Court concluded that this "incentive is not present [where] the aid is allocated on the basis of neutral, secular criteria that neither favor nor disfavor religion, and is made available to both religious and secular beneficiaries on a nondiscriminatory basis. . . ." The Court eschewed any distinction between "direct and indirect aid": "If aid to schools [is] neutrally available and, before reaching or benefiting any religious school, first passes through the hands (literally or figuratively) of numerous private citizens who are free to direct the aid elsewhere, the government has not provided any (support of religion.)" Justice O'Connor, joined by Justice Breyer, concurred: "[W]e have never held that a government-aid program passes constitutional muster *solely* because of the neutral criteria it employs as a basis for distributing aid [and] have long been concerned that secular government aid not be diverted to the advancement of religion. . . ." Justice Souter, joined by Justices Stevens and Ginsburg, dissented, noting that "neutrality" could lead to "government funding as massive as expenditures made for the benefit of their public school counterparts, and religious missions would thrive on public money." He also expressed concern that the aid was "divertible" to religious purposes.

∾ PROBLEMS ∾

1. *More on the Education for a Better America Act.* Do the holding in *Agostini* and the plurality opinion in *Mitchell* alter your views regarding how Congress might be permitted to structure financial aid to parochial schools under the proposed Act? If Congress has pure motives (e.g., its goal is to improve the education of schoolchildren rather than to promote religion), and if the aid is offered on equivalent terms to all schools (public, private, and parochial), would *Agostini* permit Congress to provide direct financial grants to all schools, including parochial schools? Could Congress extend the aid to such items as books, maps, field trips, and student performance testing? Could Congress also provide funding for

educational buildings and athletic structures (on the theory that a healthy body leads to a healthy mind)?

2. *Charitable Choice.* Former President George W. Bush offered and implemented proposals for "charitable choice" (allowing religious groups to receive government funds for antipoverty initiatives such as job training, high school equivalency, English as a second language, nutrition programs, homes for unmarried mothers, and alcohol treatment). After *Agostini* and *Mitchell*, are President Bush's proposals permissible?

3. *More on Charitable Choice.* Suppose that you were serving as White House counsel during the Bush administration, and you were asked to make recommendations regarding the structure of the charitable choice program. What criteria would you advise the President to consider in designing and implementing the program? For example, should the President consider such criteria as whether providers are chosen on neutral grounds, whether religious organizations can retain their identity in service areas by displaying religious symbols, whether they can use religious criteria in selecting employees (despite the fact that participating organizations are precluded from actively proselytizing as well as from discriminating against recipients of other faiths), and whether other "secular" organizations are available to serve those who object to receiving services from a religious organization?

4. *Historic Preservation.* May Congress provide funds to help restore and preserve historic buildings and allow religious organizations to receive funds to restore and preserve historic religious buildings (e.g., the Old North Church in Boston, Massachusetts)? Would it matter whether the religious buildings are in active use as religious structures?

d. School Vouchers

In recent years, much controversy has surrounded so-called "school vouchers" — vouchers that can be used to pay for tuition at both public and private schools. President George W. Bush promoted the concept of "school choice" as a way of dealing with educational problems in the public schools. Under a "choice" system, parents are provided with vouchers that they can use to pay for their children's schooling, and the parents can use the vouchers at schools of their choice. By bringing choice to the public school system, President Bush hoped to force schools to compete for students, with the goal of producing better schools and a better educational system.

Before the decision in Zelman v. Simmons-Harris (set forth in full below), the Court's decisions on vouchers went both ways. In Committee for Public Education and Religious Liberty v. Nyquist, 413 U.S. 756 (1973), applying the *Lemon* test, the Court invalidated a New York law that provided partial tuition reimbursements and tax benefits to the parents of children attending elementary or secondary nonpublic schools: "In the absence of an effective means of guaranteeing that the state aid derived from public funds will be used exclusively for secular, neutral, and nonideological purposes, [direct] aid in whatever form is invalid. . . ." That same year, the Court decided Sloan v. Lemon, 413 U.S. 825

(1973), which involved a Pennsylvania law that reimbursed parents for a portion of tuition expenses incurred at nonpublic schools. The Court struck the law down, finding "no constitutionally significant distinctions" from *Nyquist*. However, in Mueller v. Allen, 463 U.S. 388 (1983), the Court upheld a Minnesota law that allowed taxpayers, in computing their state income tax, to deduct certain expenses incurred in providing for the education of their children. *Mueller* set the stage for the following decision.

Zelman v. Simmons-Harris

536 U.S. 639 (2002)

Chief Justice REHNQUIST delivered the opinion of the Court.

The State of Ohio has established a pilot program designed to provide educational choices to families with children who reside in the Cleveland City School District. The question presented is whether this program offends the Establishment Clause of the United States Constitution. We hold that it does not.

There are more than 75,000 children enrolled in the Cleveland City School District. The majority of these children are from low-income and minority families [who do not] enjoy the means to send their children to any school other than an inner-city public school. . . . Cleveland's public schools have been among the worst performing public schools in the Nation. In 1995, a Federal District Court declared a "crisis of magnitude" and placed the entire Cleveland school district under state control. . . . The district had failed to meet any of the 18 state standards for minimal acceptable performance. Only 1 in 10 ninth graders could pass a basic proficiency examination. . . . More than two-thirds of high school students either dropped or failed out before graduation. Of those students who managed to reach their senior year, one of every four still failed to graduate. Of those students who did graduate, few could read, write, or compute at levels comparable to their counterparts in other cities.

[Against this backdrop,] Ohio enacted [its] Pilot Project Scholarship Program, Ohio Rev. Code Ann. §§3313.974-3313.979. The program provides financial assistance to families in any Ohio school district that is or has been "under federal court order requiring supervision and operational management of the district by the state superintendent." Cleveland is the only Ohio school district to fall within that category. . . . The program provides two basic kinds of assistance to parents of children in a covered district. First, the program provides tuition aid for students in kindergarten through third grade, expanding each year through eighth grade, to attend a participating public or private school of their parent's choosing. Second, the program provides tutorial aid for students who choose to remain enrolled in public school.

The tuition aid portion of the program is designed to provide educational choices to parents who reside in a covered district. Any private school, whether religious or nonreligious, may participate in the program and accept program students so long as the school is located within the boundaries of a covered district and meets statewide educational standards. Participating private schools must agree not to discriminate on the basis of race, religion, or ethnic back-ground, or to "advocate or foster unlawful behavior or teach hatred of any person or group on the basis of race, ethnicity, national origin, or religion." [Adjacent] public schools are eligible to receive a $2,250 tuition grant for each program student accepted in addition to the full amount of per-pupil state funding attrib-utable to each additional student. All participating schools, whether public or private, are required to accept students in accordance with rules and procedures established by the state superintendent.

Tuition aid is distributed to parents according to financial need. Families with incomes below 200% of the poverty line are given priority and are eligible to receive 90% of private school tuition up to $2,250. For these lowest-income fami-lies, participating private schools may not charge a parental co-payment greater than $250. For all other families, the program pays 75% of tuition costs, up to $1,875, with no co-payment cap. These families receive tuition aid only if the number of available scholarships exceeds the number of low-income children who choose to participate. Where tuition aid is spent depends solely upon where parents who receive tuition aid choose to enroll their child. If parents choose a private school, checks are made payable to the parents who then endorse the checks over to the chosen school.

The tutorial aid portion of the program provides tutorial assistance through grants to any student in a covered district who chooses to remain in public school. Parents arrange for registered tutors to provide assistance to their children and then submit bills for those services to the State for payment. Students from low-income families receive 90% of the amount charged for such assistance up to $360. All other students receive 75% of that amount. The number of tutorial assistance grants offered to students in a covered district must equal the number of tuition aid scholarships provided to students enrolled at participating private or adjacent public schools.

[In] the 1999-2000 school year, 56 private schools participated in the pro-gram, 46 (or 82%) of which had a religious affiliation. None of the public schools in districts adjacent to Cleveland have elected to participate. More than 3,700 students participated in the scholarship program, most of whom (96%) enrolled in religiously affiliated schools. Sixty percent of these students were from families at or below the poverty line. In the 1998-1999 school year, approximately 1,400 Cleveland public school students received tutorial aid. This number was expected to double during the 1999-2000 school year.

The program is part of a broader undertaking by the State to enhance the educational options of Cleveland's schoolchildren [that] includes programs gov-erning community and magnet schools. Community schools are funded under state law but are run by their own school boards, not by local school districts. These schools [enjoy] independence to hire their own teachers and to determine their own curriculum. They can have no religious affiliation and are required to accept students by lottery. During the 1999-2000 school year, there were 10 start-up community schools in [Cleveland] with more than 1,900 students enrolled. For each child enrolled in a community school, the school receives state funding of $4,518, twice the funding a participating program school may receive.

Magnet schools are public schools operated by a local school board that emphasize a particular subject area, teaching method, or service to students. For each student enrolled in a magnet school, the school district receives $7,746, including state funding of $4,167, the same amount received per student enrolled at a traditional public school. As of 1999, parents in Cleveland were able to choose from among 23 magnet schools, which together enrolled more than 13,000 students in kindergarten through eighth grade. These schools provide specialized teaching methods, such as Montessori, or a particularized curriculum focus, such as foreign language, computers, or the arts.

[R]espondents filed this action in United States District Court, seeking to enjoin [the] program on the ground that it violated the Establishment Clause of the United States Constitution. [T]he District Court granted summary judgment for respondents. [A] divided panel of the Court of Appeals affirmed. . . . We granted certiorari and now reverse.

The Establishment Clause of the First Amendment, applied to the States through the Fourteenth Amendment, prevents a State from enacting laws that have the "purpose" or "effect" of advancing or inhibiting religion. Agostini v. Felton, 521 U.S. 203 (1997). There is no dispute that the program challenged here was enacted for the valid secular purpose of providing educational assistance to poor children in a demonstrably failing public school system. [T]he question [is] whether the Ohio program nonetheless has the forbidden "effect" of advancing or inhibiting religion.

[O]ur decisions have drawn a consistent distinction between government programs that provide aid directly to religious schools and programs of true private choice, in which government aid reaches religious schools only as a result of the genuine and independent choices of private individuals, Mueller v. Allen, 463 U.S. 388 (1983); Witters v. Washington Dept. of Servs. for Blind, 474 U.S. 481 (1986); Zobrest v. Catalina Foothills School Dist., 509 U.S. 1 (1993). While our jurisprudence with respect to the constitutionality of direct aid programs has "changed significantly" over the past two decades, our jurisprudence with respect to true private choice programs has remained consistent. . . . Three times we have confronted Establishment Clause challenges to neutral government programs that provide aid directly to a broad class of individuals, who, in turn, direct the aid to religious schools or institutions of their own choosing. [W]e have rejected such challenges. In *Mueller*, we rejected an Establishment Clause challenge to a Minnesota program authorizing tax deductions for various educational expenses, including private school tuition costs, even though the great majority of the program's beneficiaries (96%) were parents of children in religious schools. [V]iewing the program as a whole, we emphasized the principle of private choice, noting that public funds were made available to religious schools "only as a result of numerous, private choices of individual parents of school-age children." This, we said, ensured that "'no imprimatur of state approval' can be deemed to have been conferred on any particular religion, or on religion generally." We thus found it irrelevant [that] the vast majority of beneficiaries were parents of children in religious schools. . . . That the program was one of true private choice, with no evidence that the State deliberately skewed incentives toward religious schools, was sufficient for the program to survive scrutiny under the Establishment Clause. . . . In *Witters*, we used identical reasoning to reject an Establishment Clause challenge to a vocational scholarship program that provided tuition aid to a student studying at a religious institution to become a pastor. . . . Finally, in *Zobrest*, we applied *Mueller* and *Witters* to reject an Establishment Clause challenge to a federal program that permitted sign-language interpreters to assist deaf children enrolled in religious schools. . . .

Mueller, Witters, and *Zobrest* thus make clear that where a government aid program is neutral with respect to religion, and provides assistance directly to a broad class of citizens who, in turn, direct government aid to religious schools wholly as a result of their own genuine and independent private choice, the program is not readily subject to challenge under the Establishment Clause. A program that shares these features permits government aid to reach religious institutions only by way of the deliberate choices of numerous individual recipients. The incidental advancement of a religious mission, or the perceived endorsement of a religious message, is reasonably attributable to the individual recipient, not to the government, whose role ends with the disbursement of benefits. . . . It is precisely for these reasons that we have never found a program of true private choice to offend the Establishment Clause.

We believe that the program challenged here is a program of true private choice, consistent with *Mueller, Witters*, and *Zobrest*, and thus constitutional. [T]he Ohio program is neutral in all respects toward religion. It is part of a general and multifaceted undertaking by the State of Ohio to provide educational opportunities to the children of a failed school district. It confers educational assistance directly to a broad class of individuals defined without reference to religion, i.e., any parent of a school-age child who resides in the Cleveland City School District. The program permits the participation of *all* schools within the district, religious or nonreligious. Adjacent public schools also may participate and have a financial incentive to do so. Program benefits are available to participating families on neutral terms, with no reference to religion. The only preference stated anywhere in the program is a preference for low-income families, who receive greater assistance and are given priority for admission at participating schools.

There are no "financial incentive[s]" that "ske[w]" the program toward religious schools. Such incentives "[are] not present [where] the aid is allocated on the basis of neutral, secular criteria that neither favor nor disfavor religion, and is made available to both religious and secular beneficiaries on a nondiscriminatory basis." The program here in fact creates financial *dis*incentives for religious schools, with private schools receiving only half the government assistance given to community schools and one-third the assistance given to magnet schools. Adjacent public schools, should any choose to accept program students, are also eligible to receive two to three times the state funding of a private religious school. Families too have a financial disincentive to choose a private religious school [because they] must copay a portion of the school's tuition. Families that choose a community school, magnet school, or traditional public school pay nothing.

[S]uch features of the program [clearly] dispel the claim that the program "[creates] financial incentive[s] for parents to choose a sectarian school."[1]

[No] reasonable observer would think a neutral program of private choice, where state aid reaches religious schools solely as a result of the numerous independent decisions of private individuals, carries with it the *imprimatur* of government endorsement. . . . Any objective observer familiar with the full history and context of the Ohio program would reasonably view it as one aspect of a broader undertaking to assist poor children in failed schools, not as an endorsement of religious schooling in general.

There also is no evidence that the program fails to provide genuine opportunities for Cleveland parents to select secular educational options for their school-age children. Cleveland schoolchildren enjoy a range of educational choices: They may remain in public school[,] remain in public school with publicly funded tutoring aid, obtain a scholarship and choose a religious school, obtain a scholarship and choose a nonreligious private school, enroll in a community school, or enroll in a magnet school. That 46 of the 56 private schools now participating in the program are religious schools does not condemn it as a violation of the Establishment Clause. [The] question is whether Ohio is coercing parents into sending their children to religious schools, and that question must be answered by evaluating *all* options Ohio provides Cleveland schoolchildren. . . .

Justice Souter speculates that because more private religious schools currently participate in the program, the program itself must somehow discourage the participation of private nonreligious schools. But Cleveland's preponderance of religiously affiliated private schools certainly did not arise as a result of the program. . . . [B]y all accounts the program has captured a remarkable cross-section of private schools, religious and nonreligious. It is true that 82% of Cleveland's participating private schools are religious schools, but it is also true that 81% of private schools in Ohio are religious schools. To attribute constitutional significance to this figure [would] lead to the absurd result that a neutral school-choice program might be permissible [where] a lower percentage of private schools are religious schools, but not in inner-city Cleveland, where Ohio has deemed such programs most sorely needed, but where the preponderance of religious schools happens to be greater. Likewise, an identical private choice program might be constitutional in some States, such as Maine or Utah, where less than 45% of private schools are religious schools, but not in other States [where] over 90% of private schools are religious schools.

Respondents and Justice Souter claim that [we] should attach constitutional significance to the fact that 96% of scholarship recipients have enrolled in religious schools. They claim that this alone proves parents lack genuine choice. . . . [T]his argument [was] flatly rejected in *Mueller*, where we found it irrelevant that 96% of parents taking deductions for tuition expenses paid tuition at religious schools. . . . The constitutionality of a neutral educational aid program simply does not turn on whether and why, in a particular area, at a particular time, most

1. Justice Souter suggests the program is not "neutral" because program students cannot spend scholarship vouchers at traditional public schools. This objection is mistaken: Public schools in Cleveland already receive $7,097 in public funding per pupil — $4,167 of which is attributable to the State. . . .

private schools are run by religious organizations, or most recipients choose to use the aid at a religious school. "[S]uch an approach would scarcely provide the certainty that this field stands in need of, nor can we perceive principled standards by which such statistical evidence might be evaluated."

This point is aptly illustrated here. The 96% figure upon [which] Justice Souter [relies] discounts entirely (1) the more than 1,900 Cleveland children enrolled in alternative community schools, (2) the more than 13,000 children enrolled in alternative magnet schools, and (3) the more than 1,400 children enrolled in traditional public schools with tutorial assistance. Including some or all of these children in the denominator of children enrolled in nontraditional schools during the 1999-2000 school year drops the percentage enrolled in religious schools from 96% to under 20%. The 96% figure also represents but a snapshot of one particular school year. In the 1997-1998 school year, by contrast, only 78% of scholarship recipients attended religious schools. The difference was attributable to two private nonreligious schools that had accepted 15% of all scholarship students electing instead to register as community schools, in light of larger per-pupil funding for community schools and the uncertain future of the scholarship program generated by this litigation. Many of the students enrolled in these schools as scholarship students remained enrolled as community school students, thus demonstrating the arbitrariness of counting one type of school but not the other to assess primary effect. . . .

Respondents finally claim that we should look to Committee for Public Ed. & Religious Liberty v. Nyquist, 413 U.S. 756 (1973), to decide these cases. We disagree. . . . [That program's] "function" was "*unmistakably* to provide desired financial support for nonpublic, sectarian institutions" [and] we expressly reserved judgment with respect to "a case [involving] public assistance (e.g., scholarships) made available [without] regard to the sectarian-nonsectarian, or public-nonpublic nature of the institution benefitted." . . .

In sum, the Ohio program is entirely neutral with respect to religion. It provides benefits directly to a wide spectrum of individuals, defined only by financial need and residence in a particular school district. It permits such individuals to exercise genuine choice among options public and private, secular and religious. The program is therefore a program of true private choice. In keeping with an unbroken line of decisions rejecting challenges to similar programs, we hold that the program does not offend the Establishment Clause.

The judgment of the Court of Appeals is reversed.

Justice O'CONNOR, concurring.

These cases are different from prior indirect aid cases [because] a significant portion of the funds [reach] religious schools without restrictions on the use of these funds. . . . $8.2 million of public funds flowed to religious schools under the voucher program in 1999-2000. [This amount] pales in comparison to the amount of funds that federal, state, and local governments already provide religious institutions. Religious organizations may qualify for exemptions from the federal corporate income tax, the corporate income tax in many States, and property taxes in all 50 States. In addition, the Federal Government provides

individuals, corporations, trusts, and estates a tax deduction for charitable contributions to qualified religious groups. Finally, the Federal Government and certain state governments provide tax credits for educational expenses, many of
which are spent on education at religious schools. [Religious hospitals rely] on
Medicare funds for 36 percent of their revenue. . . . Against this background, the
support that the Cleveland voucher program provides religious institutions is
neither substantial nor atypical of existing government programs. . . . Cleveland
parents who use vouchers to send their children to religious private schools do so
as a result of true private choice. . . .

Justice THOMAS, concurring.
[F]ailing urban public schools disproportionately affect minority children
most in need of educational opportunity. . . . Many blacks and other minorities
[support] school choice programs because they provide the greatest educational
opportunities for their children in struggling communities. [P]oor urban families
just want the best education for their children, who will certainly need it to function in our high-tech and advanced society. . . . If society cannot end racial
discrimination, at least it can arm minorities with the education to defend themselves from some of discrimination's effects. . . .

Justice STEVENS, dissenting.
[T]he Court's decision is profoundly misguided. [I]n reaching that conclusion I have been influenced by my understanding of the impact of religious strife
on the decisions of our forbears to migrate to this continent. . . . Whenever we
remove a brick from the wall that was designed to separate religion and government, we increase the risk of religious strife and weaken the foundation of our
democracy. . . .

Justice SOUTER, with whom Justice STEVENS, Justice GINSBURG, and Justice
BREYER join, dissenting.
[The] principle of nondivertibility [has been] enforced strictly, with its violation being presumed in most cases, even when state aid seemed secular on its face.
[I]t was not until today that substantiality of aid has clearly been rejected as irrelevant by a majority of this Court. . . . Today's cases are notable for their stark illustration of the inadequacy of the majority's chosen formal analysis. . . . In order to
apply the neutrality test[,] it makes sense to focus on a category of aid that may be
directed to religious as well as secular schools, and ask whether the scheme favors
a religious direction. . . . The majority looks not to the provisions for tuition
vouchers, but to every provision for educational opportunity. . . . The illogic is
patent. If regular, public schools (which can get no voucher payments) "participate" in a voucher scheme[,] and public expenditure is still predominantly on
public schools, then the majority's reasoning would find neutrality in a scheme of
vouchers available for private tuition in districts with no secular private schools at
all. "Neutrality" [is] literally, verbal and nothing more. . . .
[The] majority's view that all educational choices are comparable for purposes of choice thus ignores the whole point of the choice test: it is a criterion for
deciding whether indirect aid to a religious school is legitimate because it passes

through private hands that can spend or use the aid in a secular school. The question is whether the private hand is genuinely free to send the money in either a secular direction or a religious one. . . . When the choice test is transformed from where to spend the money to where to go to school, it is cut loose from its very purpose. . . . [S]omething is influencing choices in a way that aims the money in a religious direction: of 56 private schools in the district participating in the voucher program (only 53 of which accepted voucher students in 1999-2000), 46 of them are religious; 96.6% of all voucher recipients go to religious schools. [T]here is no explanation [that] suggests the religious direction results simply from free choices by parents. One answer [which] would be consistent with the genuine choice claimed to be operating, might be that 96.6% of families choosing to avail themselves of vouchers choose to educate their children in schools of their own religion. This would not, in my view, render the scheme constitutional. . . . Evidence shows, however, that almost two out of three families using vouchers to send their children to religious schools did not embrace the religion of those schools. The families [had] not chosen the schools because they wished their children to be proselytized in a religion not their own, or in any religion, but because of educational opportunity.

Even so, the fact that some 2,270 students chose to apply their vouchers to schools of other religions might be consistent with true choice if the students "chose" their religious schools over a wide array of private nonreligious options, or if it could be shown generally that Ohio's program had no effect on educational choices and thus no impermissible effect of advancing religious education. But both possibilities are contrary to fact. First, even if all existing nonreligious private schools in Cleveland were willing to accept large numbers of voucher students, only a few more than the 129 currently enrolled in such schools would be able to attend, as the total enrollment at all nonreligious private schools in Cleveland for kindergarten through eighth grade is only 510 children, and there is no indication that these schools have many open seats. Second, the $2,500 cap that the program places on tuition for participating low-income pupils has the effect of curtailing the participation of nonreligious schools: "nonreligious schools with higher tuition (about $4,000) stated that they could afford to accommodate just a few voucher students." By comparison, the average tuition at participating Catholic schools in Cleveland in 1999-2000 was $1,592, almost $1,000 below the cap. . . . For the overwhelming number of children in the voucher scheme, the only alternative to the public schools is religious. . . .

[The] scale of the aid to religious schools approved today is unprecedented, both in the number of dollars and in the proportion of systemic school expenditure supported. [The] matter before [us] involves considerable sums [distributed] through thousands of students attending religious elementary and middle schools in the city of Cleveland. . . . The Cleveland voucher program has cost Ohio taxpayers $33 million. . . . These tax-raised funds are on top of the textbooks, reading and math tutors, laboratory equipment, and the like that Ohio provides to private schools, worth roughly $600 per child. [In] paying for practically the full amount of tuition for thousands of qualifying students, the scholarships purchase everything that tuition purchases, be it instruction in math or indoctrination in faith. The consequences of "substantial" aid hypothesized in *Meek* are realized here: the majority makes no pretense that substantial amounts of tax money are not systematically underwriting religious practice and indoctrination.

[E]very objective underlying the prohibition of religious establishment is betrayed by this scheme. [The first objective is] respect for freedom of conscience. . . . Madison thought it violated by any "'authority which can force a citizen to contribute three pence [of] his property for the support of [any] establishment.'" Memorial and Remonstrance & para. 3. . . . Madison's objection to three pence has simply been lost in the majority's formalism. . . . As for the second objective, to save religion from its own corruption, [the] risk is one of "corrosive secularism" to religious schools, and the specific threat is to the primacy of the schools' mission to educate the children of the faithful according to the unaltered precepts of their faith. . . . In Ohio, [a] condition of receiving government money under the program is that participating religious schools may not "discriminate on the basis [of] religion," which means the school may not give admission preferences to children who are members of the patron faith. [A] participating religious school may well be forbidden to choose a member of its own clergy to serve as teacher or principal over a layperson of a different religion claiming equal qualification for the job [and] could be understood (or subsequently broadened) to prohibit religions from teaching traditionally legitimate articles of faith as to the error, sinfulness, or ignorance of others. [I]t is well to remember that the money has barely begun to flow. [R]eligious schools in Ohio are on the way to becoming bigger businesses with budgets enhanced to fit their new stream of tax-raised income. . . . When government aid goes up, so does reliance on it; the only thing likely to go down is independence. [I]s there reason to wonder when dependence will become great enough to give the State of Ohio an effective veto over basic decisions on the content of curriculums? [T]he third concern behind the ban on establishment [is] its inextricable link with social conflict. . . . Not all taxpaying Protestant citizens, for example, will be content to underwrite the teaching of the Roman Catholic Church condemning the death penalty. Nor will all of America's Muslims acquiesce in paying for the endorsement of the religious Zionism taught in many religious Jewish schools, which combines "a nationalistic sentiment" in support of Israel with a "deeply religious" element. Nor will every secular taxpayer be content to support Muslim views on differential treatment of the sexes, or, for that matter, to fund the espousal of a wife's obligation of obedience to her husband, presumably taught in any schools adopting the articles of faith of the Southern Baptist Convention. Views like these [have] been safe in the sectarian pulpits and classrooms of this Nation not only because the Free Exercise Clause protects them directly, but because the ban on supporting religious establishment has protected free exercise. . . . With the arrival of vouchers in religious schools, that privacy will go, and along with it will go confidence that religious disagreement will stay moderate. . . . [I] hope that a future Court will reconsider today's dramatic departure from basic Establishment Clause principle.

Justice BREYER, with whom Justice STEVENS and Justice SOUTER join, dissenting.

[The Religion] Clauses embody an understanding, reached in the 17th century after decades of religious war, that liberty and social stability demand a religious tolerance that respects the religious views of all citizens, permits those citizens to "worship God in their own way," and allows all families to "teach their children and to form their characters" as they wish. C. Radcliffe, *The Law and Its Compass* 71 (Faber 1960). The Clauses reflect the Framers' vision of an American Nation free of the religious strife that had long plagued the nations of Europe. [F]or this reason, the Court's 20th century Establishment Clause cases [focused] directly upon social conflict, potentially created when government becomes involved in religious education. [The] upshot is the development of constitutional doctrine that reads the Establishment Clause as avoiding religious strife, *not* by providing every religion with an *equal opportunity*[,] but by drawing fairly clear lines of *separation* between church and state — at least where the heartland of religious belief, such as primary religious education, is at issue. . . . The principle underlying these cases — avoiding religiously based social conflict — remains of great concern. As religiously diverse as America had become when the Court decided its major 20th century Establishment Clause cases, we are exponentially more diverse today. America boasts more than 55 different religious groups and subgroups. . . .

[School] voucher programs finance the religious education of the young. And, if widely adopted, they may well provide billions of dollars that will do so. Why will different religions not become concerned about, and seek to influence, the criteria used to channel this money to religious schools? Why will they not want to examine the implementation of the programs that provide this money — to determine, for example, whether implementation has biased a program toward or against particular sects, or whether recipient religious schools are adequately fulfilling a program's criteria? If so, just how is the State to resolve the resulting controversies without provoking legitimate fears of the kinds of religious favoritism that, in so religiously diverse a Nation, threaten social dissension?

Consider the voucher program here at issue. That program insists that the religious school accept students of all religions. Does that criterion treat fairly groups whose religion forbids them to do so? [The] program also insists that no participating school "advocate or foster unlawful behavior or teach hatred of any person or group on the basis of race, ethnicity, national origin, or religion." And it requires the State to "revoke the registration of any school["in violation] of the program's rules. . . . How are state officials to adjudicate claims that one religion or another is advocating, for example, civil disobedience in response to unjust laws, the use of illegal drugs in a religious ceremony, or resort to force to call attention to what it views as an immoral social practice? What kind of public hearing will there be in response to claims that one religion or another is continuing to teach a view of history that casts members of other religions in the worst possible light? How will the public react to government funding for schools that take controversial religious positions on topics that are of current popular interest—say, the conflict in the Middle East or the war on terrorism? Yet any major funding program for primary religious education will require criteria. And the selection of those criteria, as well as their application, inevitably pose problems that are divisive. Efforts to respond to these problems not only will seriously entangle church and state, but also will promote division among religious groups, as one group or another fears (often legitimately) that it will receive unfair treatment at the hands of the government. . . .

I concede that the Establishment Clause currently permits States to channel various forms of assistance to religious schools, for example, transportation costs for students, computers, and secular texts. . . . Yet the consequence has not been great turmoil. . . . School voucher programs differ, however, in both *kind* and *degree* from aid programs upheld in the past. They differ in kind because they direct financing to a core function of the church: the teaching of religious truths to young children. . . . Vouchers also differ in degree [because they] permit a considerable shift of taxpayer dollars from public secular schools to private religious schools. . . .

I do not believe that the "parental choice" aspect of the voucher program sufficiently offsets the concerns I have mentioned. Parental choice cannot help the taxpayer who does not want to finance the religious education of children. It will not always help the parent who may see little real choice between inadequate non-sectarian public education and adequate education at a school whose religious teachings are contrary to his own. It will not satisfy religious minorities unable to participate because they are too few in number to support the creation of their own private schools. It will not satisfy groups whose religious beliefs preclude them from participating in a government-sponsored program, and who may well feel ignored as government funds primarily support the education of children in the doctrines of the dominant religions. And it does little to ameliorate the entanglement problems or the related problems of social division. . . . Consequently, the fact that the parent may choose which school can cash the government's voucher check does not alleviate the Establishment Clause concerns associated with voucher programs. [I] dissent.

Note and Question: Charter Schools and the Conversion of Religious Schools

Religious schools sometimes have compelling reasons for becoming public schools (e.g., so-called charter schools). For one thing, the conversion to a public school can help stabilize the school's finances and might bring about an increase in teacher salaries. On the other hand, the transition can sometimes be difficult. For one thing, the new school may be subject to more rigorous state-imposed requirements (e.g., mandates requiring grade tracking, testing, and data analysis). In addition, both teachers and students may struggle with the idea of how to function in a secular environment. How does a school teach values without impermissibly intruding into religious issues? *See* Javier C. Hernandez, "Upholding Catholic Values After Converting to Secular Education: Parish Schools in Fiscal Straits See a Test Case in Washington," *New York Times*, A-17, c. 1-6 (Mar. 1, 2009).

∾ PROBLEMS ∾

1. *Vouchers and the Education for a Better America Act.* Does *Zelman* suggest that Congress could include a general voucher program as part of the proposed Act? Suppose that Congress believes that school voucher programs will introduce competition into the educational system, and will thereby help foster improvements in both private and parochial schools. As a result, Congress is thinking about extending the benefits of vouchers to all school districts, not just those in crisis. Would such a voucher program be constitutional?

2. *More on Vouchers and the Education for a Better Act.* Suppose that Congress has preliminarily decided to include vouchers in the proposed Act. Your boss has asked you for input regarding how to structure the voucher program to ensure that it will withstand constitutional challenge. How will you advise Congress to structure the program? What components should be included? What, if anything, should be avoided?

3. *Extending the Act's Voucher Provisions to Religiously Homogeneous Areas.* In constructing the proposed Act, should you (must you?) take into account the fact that, in some states (e.g., Utah), the overwhelming majority of residents belong to a single religion (e.g., Mormonism)? What if, following adoption of the program, almost all Utah students who belong to the dominant religion withdraw from public schools, which are subsequently forced to close for lack of students, thereby leaving no public schools available for non-Mormons? Would the program be constitutional?

2. School Prayer

There have been considerable debate and litigation regarding the permissibility of prayer in public schools.

Engel v. Vitale

370 U.S. 421 (1962)

Mr. Justice BLACK delivered the opinion of the Court.

The respondent Board of Education of Union Free School District No. 9, New Hyde Park, New York, acting in its official capacity under state law, directed the School District's principal to cause the following prayer to be said aloud by each class in the presence of a teacher at the beginning of each school day:

> Almighty God, we acknowledge our dependence upon Thee, and we beg Thy blessings upon us, our parents, our teachers and our Country.

[This] procedure was adopted on the recommendation of the State Board of Regents [to] which the New York Legislature has granted broad supervisory [powers] over the State's public school system. These state officials composed the prayer which they recommended and published as a part of their "Statement on

Moral and Spiritual Training in the Schools," saying: "We believe that this Statement will be subscribed to by all men and women of good will, and we call upon all of them to aid in giving life to our program."

[The parents of ten pupils challenged use of the official prayer. The New York Court of Appeals upheld the practice.]

[B]y using its public school system to encourage recitation of the Regents' prayer, the State of New York has adopted a practice wholly inconsistent with the Establishment Clause. [I]nvocation of God's blessings as prescribed in the Regents' prayer is a religious activity. It is a solemn avowal of divine faith and supplication for the blessings of the Almighty. . . . [T]he constitutional prohibition against laws respecting an establishment of religion must at least mean that [it] is no part of the business of government to compose official prayers for any group [of] people to recite [as] part of a religious program carried on by government.

It is a matter of history that this very practice of establishing governmentally composed prayers for religious services was one of the reasons which caused many of our early colonists to leave England and seek religious freedom in America. . . . By the time of the adoption of the Constitution, [there was] widespread awareness [of] the dangers of a union of Church and State. These people knew, some of them from bitter personal experience, that one of the greatest dangers to the freedom of the individual to worship in his own way lay in the Government's placing its official stamp of approval upon one particular kind of prayer or one particular form of religious services. . . . Under [the First Amendment], government [is] without power to prescribe [any] particular form of prayer [to] be used as an official prayer [in] any program of governmentally sponsored religious activity.

There can be no doubt that New York's state prayer program officially establishes the religious beliefs embodied in the Regents' prayer. . . . Neither the fact that the prayer may be denominationally neutral nor the fact that its observance on the part of the students is voluntary can serve to free it from the limitations of the Establishment Clause. . . . When the power, prestige and financial support of government is placed behind a particular religious belief, the indirect coercive pressure upon religious minorities to conform to the prevailing officially approved religion is plain. But the purposes underlying the Establishment Clause go much further than that. Its first and most immediate purpose rested on the belief that a union of government and religion tends to destroy government and to degrade religion. The history of governmentally established religion, both in England and in this country, showed that whenever government had allied itself with one particular form of religion, the inevitable result had been that it had incurred the hatred, disrespect and even contempt of those who held contrary beliefs. . . . [R]eligion is too personal, too sacred, too holy, to permit its "unhallowed perversion" by a civil magistrate. Another purpose of the Establishment Clause rested upon an awareness of the historical fact that governmentally established religions and religious persecutions go hand in hand. . . . It was in large part to get completely away [from] systematic religious persecution that the Founders brought into being [our] Bill of Rights with its prohibition against any governmental establishment of religion. The New York laws officially prescribing the Regents' prayer are inconsistent both with the purposes of the Establishment Clause and with the Establishment Clause itself.

It has been argued that to apply the Constitution [to] prohibit state laws respecting an establishment of religious services in public schools is to indicate a hostility toward religion or toward prayer. [Nothing] could be more wrong. . . . It is neither sacrilegious nor antireligious to say that [government] should stay out of the business of writing or sanctioning official prayers and leave that purely religious function to the people themselves and to those the people choose to look to for religious guidance.

The judgment of the Court of Appeals of New York is reversed and the cause remanded for further proceedings not inconsistent with this opinion.

Reversed and remanded.

Mr. Justice Douglas, concurring.

[The] First Amendment leaves the Government in a position not of hostility to religion but of neutrality. The philosophy is that the atheist or agnostic—the nonbeliever—is entitled to go his own way. [I]f government interferes in matters spiritual, it will be a divisive force. . . .

Mr. Justice Stewart, dissenting.

[I] cannot see how an "official religion" is established by letting those who want to say a prayer say it. On the contrary, [to] deny the wish of these school children to join [in] this prayer is to deny them the opportunity of sharing in the spiritual heritage of our Nation.

[At] the opening of each day's Session of this Court we stand, while one of our officials invokes the protection of God. Since the days of John Marshall our Crier has said, "God save the United States and this Honorable Court." Both the Senate and the House of Representatives open their daily Sessions with prayer. Each of our Presidents, from George Washington to John F. Kennedy, has upon assuming his Office asked the protection and help of God.

The Court today says that the state and federal governments are without constitutional power to prescribe any particular form of words to be recited by any group of the American people on any subject touching religion. One of the stanzas of "The Star-Spangled Banner," made our National Anthem by Act of Congress in 1931, contains these verses:

> Blest with victory and peace, may the heav'n rescued land Praise the Pow'r that hath made and preserved us a nation! Then conquer we must, when our cause it is just, And this be our motto "In God is our Trust."

In 1954 Congress added a phrase to the Pledge of Allegiance to the Flag so that it now contains the words "one Nation under God, indivisible, with liberty and justice for all." In 1952 Congress enacted legislation calling upon the President each year to proclaim a National Day of Prayer. Since 1865 the words "IN GOD WE TRUST" have been impressed on our coins.

Countless similar examples could be listed, but there is no need to belabor the obvious. It was all summed up by this Court just ten years ago in a single sentence: "We are a religious people whose institutions presuppose a Supreme Being." Zorach v. Clauson, 343 U.S. 306, 313. [I] do not believe the State of New York has [established a religion] in this case. What [it has done is recognize and] follow the deeply entrenched and highly cherished spiritual traditions of our Nation. . . . I dissent.

BACKGROUND
A Constitutional Amendment?

Following the decision in *Engel*, some have sought to amend the Constitution to permit prayer in public schools. Congressional proponents of such an amendment claim that court rulings have "attacked and twisted and warped" the First Amendment and have stifled religious expression "right and left all over the country." These amendments have failed to garner the votes necessary for passage.

Note: Legislative Prayer

In Marsh v. Chambers, 463 U.S. 783 (1983), the Court held that the Nebraska legislature could begin its day with chaplain-led prayer. The Court upheld the practice: "[From] colonial times through the founding of the Republic and ever since, the practice of legislative prayer has coexisted with the principles of disestablishment and religious freedom. . . . In this context, historical evidence sheds light not only on what the draftsmen intended the Establishment Clause to mean, but also on how they thought that Clause applied to the practice authorized by the First Congress. . . ." Justice Brennan dissented: "[The] 'primary effect' of legislative prayer is also clearly religious [and] there can be no doubt that the practice of legislative prayer leads to excessive 'entanglement' between the State and religion."

◇ PROBLEMS ◇

1. *School Prayer and the Education for a Better America Act.* In constructing the proposed legislation, what (if anything) should be said about school prayer? Can you (should you?) specifically allow or prohibit school prayer in schools that receive government funding? Should the prohibition extend to parochial schools as well? Is it permissible (appropriate?) to simply ignore the issue in constructing the legislation?

2. *Distinguishing Legislative Prayer from School Prayer.* If it is permissible for a legislature to employ a chaplain and begin its day with a prayer, then why is school

prayer impermissible? In other words, what distinguishes school prayer from legislative prayer? Does it matter that there were virtually no public schools when the Constitution was adopted?

Wallace v. Jaffree

472 U.S. 38 (1985)

Justice STEVENS delivered the opinion of the Court.

[T]he constitutionality of three Alabama statutes [is] questioned: (1) §16-1-20, enacted in 1978, which authorized a 1-minute period of silence in all public schools "for meditation"; (2) §16-1-20.1, enacted in 1981, which authorized a period of silence "for meditation or voluntary prayer"; and (3) §16-1-20.2, enacted in 1982, which authorized teachers to lead "willing students" in a prescribed prayer to "Almighty God [the] Creator and Supreme Judge of the world." [The] Court of Appeals [held] both §16-1-20.1 and §16-1-20.2 [unconstitutional]. [The question] is whether §16-1-20.1, which authorizes a period of silence for "meditation or voluntary prayer," is a law respecting the establishment of religion within the meaning of the First Amendment.

[When] the Court has been called upon to construe [the] Establishment Clause, it has [applied the *Lemon*] criteria. [It] is the first of these three criteria that is most plainly implicated by this case. [A] statute must be invalidated if it is entirely motivated by a purpose to advance religion. [T]he record [reveals that] §16-1-20.1 was not motivated by any clearly

The sponsor of the bill that became §16-1-20.1, Senator Donald Holmes, inserted into the legislative record—apparently without dissent—a statement [that] the legislation was an "effort to return voluntary prayer" to the public schools. [Senator] Holmes confirmed this purpose before the District Court. In response to the question whether he had any purpose for the legislation other than returning voluntary prayer to public schools, he stated: "No." The State did not present evidence of any secular purpose.

[U]nrebutted evidence of legislative intent [is] confirmed by a consideration of the relationship between this statute and the two other measures that were considered in this case. [The earlier] statute refers only to "meditation" whereas §16-1-20.1 refers to "meditation or voluntary prayer." [T]he only significant textual difference is the addition of the words "or voluntary prayer."

The legislative intent to return prayer to the public schools [is] quite different from merely protecting every student's right to engage in voluntary prayer during an appropriate moment of silence during the school day. The 1978 statute already protected that right, containing nothing that prevented any student from engaging in voluntary prayer during a silent minute of meditation. Appellants have not identified any secular purpose that was not fully served by §16-1-20 before the enactment of §16-1-20.1. . . . We must, therefore, conclude that the Alabama Legislature [enacted] §16-1-20.1 [for] the sole purpose of expressing the State's endorsement of prayer activities for one minute at the beginning of each schoolday. The addition of "or voluntary prayer" indicates that the State intended to characterize prayer as a favored practice. Such an endorsement is not consistent with the established principle that the government must pursue a course of complete neutrality toward religion. [W]e conclude that §16-1-20.1 violates the First Amendment.

The judgment of the Court of Appeals is affirmed.

It is so ordered.

Justice POWELL, concurring.

[The] record [makes] clear that Alabama's purpose was solely religious in character. . . .

Justice O'CONNOR, concurring in the judgment.

Nothing in the United States Constitution [prohibits] public school students from voluntarily praying at any time before, during, or after the school day. Alabama has facilitated voluntary silent prayers of students who are so inclined by enacting [a statute] which provides a moment of silence [in] schools each day. [Twenty-five] states permit or require public school teachers to have students observe a moment of silence in their classrooms. The typical statute [calls] for a moment of silence at the beginning of the schoolday during which students may meditate, pray, or reflect on the activities of the day. *See, e.g.,* Ark. Stat. Ann. §80-1607.1 (1980). . . .

A state-sponsored moment of silence [is] different from state-sponsored vocal prayer or Bible reading. [A] moment of silence is not inherently religious. . . . [A] pupil who participates in a moment of silence need not compromise his or her beliefs. [A] student who objects to prayer is left to his or her own thoughts, and is not compelled to listen to the prayers or thoughts of others. . . .

By mandating a moment of silence, a State does not necessarily endorse any activity that might occur during the period. Even if a statute specifies that a student may choose to pray silently during a quiet moment, the State has not thereby encouraged prayer over other specified alternatives. [A] message of endorsement [is] inescapable if the teacher exhorts children to use the designated time to pray. Similarly, the face of the statute or its legislative history may clearly establish that it seeks to encourage or promote voluntary prayer over other alternatives, rather than merely provide a quiet moment that may be dedicated to prayer by those so inclined. The crucial question is whether the State has conveyed or attempted to convey the message that children should use the moment of silence for prayer. [This] question [requires] courts to examine the history, language, and administration of a particular statute to determine whether it operates as an endorsement of religion.

[T]he inquiry into the purpose of the legislature in enacting a moment of silence law should be deferential and limited. [If] a legislature expresses a plausible secular purpose for a moment of silence statute in either the text or the legislative history, or if the statute disclaims an intent to encourage prayer over alternatives during a moment of silence, then courts should generally defer to that stated intent. . . .

[If] we assume that the religious activity that Alabama seeks to protect is silent prayer, then it is difficult to discern any state-imposed burden on that activity that is lifted by [§16-1-20.1]. No law prevents a student who is so inclined from praying silently in public schools. Moreover, state law already provided a moment of silence to these appellees irrespective of §16-1-20.1. . . .

Chief Justice BURGER, dissenting.

Some [will] find it ironic [that] on the very day we heard arguments in the cases, the Court's session opened with an invocation for Divine protection. [T]he House of Representatives and the Senate regularly open each session with a prayer. These legislative prayers are not just one minute in duration, but are extended, thoughtful invocations and prayers for Divine guidance. They are given, as they have been since 1789, by clergy appointed as official chaplains and paid from the Treasury of the United States. Congress has also provided chapels in the Capitol, at public expense, where Members and others may pause for prayer, meditation — or a moment of silence. [S]ome wag is bound to say that the Court's holding today reflects a belief [that] members of the Judiciary and Congress are more in need of Divine guidance than are schoolchildren. . . .

It makes no sense to say that Alabama has "endorsed prayer" by merely enacting a new statute "to specify expressly that voluntary prayer is *one* of the authorized activities during a moment of silence." . . .

[A]ll of the sponsor's statements relied upon [were] made after the legislature had passed the statute. . . . There is not a shred of evidence that the legislature as a whole shared the sponsor's motive or [was] even aware of the sponsor's view of the bill when it was passed. The sole relevance of the sponsor's statements, therefore, is that they reflect the personal, subjective motives of a single legislator. No case [supports the] idea that post-enactment statements [are] relevant in determining the constitutionality of legislation. [T]he sponsor also testified that one of his purposes in drafting and sponsoring the moment-of-silence bill was to clear up a widespread misunderstanding that a schoolchild is legally prohibited from engaging in silent, individual prayer once he steps inside a public school building. . . .

[The] statute does not remotely threaten religious liberty; it affirmatively furthers the values of religious freedom and tolerance that the Establishment Clause was designed to protect. . . .

Justice WHITE, dissenting.

[A] majority of the Court would approve statutes that provided for a moment of silence but did not mention prayer. But if a student asked whether he could pray during that moment, it is difficult to believe that the teacher could not answer in the affirmative. [I] would not invalidate a statute that at the outset provided the legislative answer to the question "May I pray?" . . .

Justice REHNQUIST, dissenting.

[It] would come as [a] shock to those who drafted the Bill of Rights as it will to a large number of thoughtful Americans [to] learn that the Constitution [prohibits] the Alabama Legislature from "endorsing" prayer. George Washington himself, at the request of the very Congress which passed the Bill of Rights, proclaimed a day of "public thanksgiving and prayer, to be observed by acknowledging with grateful hearts the many and signal favors of Almighty God." History must judge whether it was the Father of his Country in 1789, or a majority of the Court today, which has strayed from the meaning of the Establishment Clause. . . . Nothing in the Establishment Clause of the First Amendment [prohibits] any such generalized "endorsement" of prayer. I would therefore reverse. . . .

∾ PROBLEMS ∾

1. *Other Moments of Prayer?* In a state without a history of school prayer, would a "religiously neutral" moment of silence statute pass constitutional muster? Suppose that the law was passed to "solemnize" the opening of the schoolday? Would it matter if the law specifically instructed teachers that students should not be encouraged to pray or to meditate (although students could do either)?

2. *Answering Student Questions.* In the preceding problem, suppose that teachers are told that, if students ask whether they "may" pray during the meditation period, they should be told that they may. Does the answer render the moment of prayer invalid?

3. *Moments of Silence and Congressional Funding for Education.* In constructing the proposed legislation, would it be permissible for Congress to authorize or encourage schools to have a "moment of silence" at the beginning of the schoolday? Suppose that Congress makes it clear that the purpose of the moment of silence is to "settle schoolchildren down" and solemnize the opening of the schoolday, and that Congress also makes clear that school teachers are prohibited from encouraging (or, for that matter, discouraging) prayer. Should Congress address these issues in the legislation?

Lee v. Weisman

505 U.S. 577 (1992)

Justice KENNEDY delivered the opinion of the Court.

School principals in the public school system [of] Providence, Rhode Island, [may] invite members of the clergy to offer invocation and benediction prayers [at] graduation ceremonies for middle schools and for high schools. [The lower courts held that the practice violated the Establishment Clause. We affirm.]

[T]he Constitution guarantees that government may not coerce anyone to support or participate in religion or its exercise, or otherwise act in a way which "establishes a [state] religion or religious faith, or tends to do so." The State's involvement in the school prayers challenged today violates these central principles. [That] involvement is as troubling as it is undenied. A school official, the principal, decided that an invocation and a benediction should be given[, and] chose the religious participant, here a rabbi. . . .

[The] potential for divisiveness over the choice of a particular member of the clergy to conduct the ceremony is apparent. Divisiveness [can] attend any state decision respecting religions, and neither its existence nor its potential necessarily invalidates the State's attempts to accommodate religion in all cases. The potential for divisiveness is of particular relevance here [because] it centers around an overt religious exercise in a secondary school environment [where] subtle coercive pressures exist and where the student had no real alternative which would have allowed her to avoid the fact or appearance of participation.

The State's role did not end with the decision to include a prayer and with the choice of a clergyman. Principal Lee provided Rabbi Gutterman with a copy of the "Guidelines for Civic Occasions," and advised him that his prayers should be nonsectarian. Through these means the principal directed and controlled the content of the prayers. Even if the only sanction for ignoring the instructions were that the rabbi would not be invited back, [no] religious representative who valued his or [her] reputation [would] incur the State's [displeasure]. It is "[no] part of the business of government to compose official prayers for any group [of] American people to recite as a part of a religious program carried on by government," and that is what the school officials attempted to do.

Petitioners argue [that] directions for the content of the prayers were a good-faith attempt by the school to ensure [that] sectarianism which is so often the flashpoint for religious animosity be removed from the graduation ceremony. The concern is understandable, as a prayer which uses ideas or images identified with a particular religion may foster a different sort of sectarian rivalry than an invocation or benediction in terms more neutral. [The] question is not the good faith of the school in attempting to make the prayer acceptable to most persons, but the legitimacy of its undertaking that enterprise at all. . . . We are asked to recognize the existence of a practice of nonsectarian prayer [which] is more acceptable than one [which] makes explicit references to the God of Israel, or to Jesus Christ, or to a patron saint. There may be some support [that] there has emerged [a] civic religion, one which is tolerated when sectarian exercises are not. [T]hough the First Amendment does not allow the government to stifle prayers which aspire to these ends, neither does it permit the government to undertake that task for itself.

The First Amendment's Religion Clauses mean that religious beliefs and religious expression are too precious to [be] prescribed by the State. The design of the Constitution is that preservation and transmission of religious beliefs and worship is a responsibility and a choice committed to the private sphere, which itself is promised freedom to pursue that mission. It must not be forgotten [that] these same Clauses exist to protect religion from government interference. . . . These concerns have particular application in the case of school officials, whose effort to monitor prayer will be perceived by the students as inducing a participation they might otherwise reject. . . .

[It] is argued that our constitutional vision of a free society requires confidence in our own ability to accept or reject ideas of which we do not approve, and that prayer at a high school graduation does nothing more than offer a choice. [S]tudents may consider it an odd measure of justice to be subjected during the course of their educations to ideas deemed offensive and irreligious, but to be denied a brief, formal prayer ceremony that the school offers in return. This argument cannot prevail, however. It overlooks a fundamental dynamic of the Constitution.

[T]here are heightened concerns with protecting freedom of conscience from subtle coercive pressure in the elementary and secondary public schools. [Finding] no violation under these circumstances would place objectors in the dilemma of participating, with all that implies, or protesting. [P]sychology supports the [assumption] that adolescents [are] susceptible to pressure from their peers towards conformity, and that the influence is strongest in matters of social convention. [T]he government may no more use social pressure to enforce orthodoxy than it may use more direct means. [There] was a stipulation [that] attendance at graduation and promotional ceremonies is voluntary. [T]o say a teenage student has a real choice not to attend her high school graduation is formalistic. [I]n our society and in our culture high school graduation is one of life's most significant occasions. . . .

[T]he school district [contends] that the prayers are an essential part of these ceremonies because for many persons an occasion of this significance lacks meaning if there is no recognition, however brief, that human achievements cannot be understood apart from their spiritual essence. [This] position [fails] to acknowledge that what for many of Deborah's classmates and their parents was a spiritual imperative was for Daniel and Deborah Weisman religious conformance compelled by the State. While in some societies the wishes of the majority might prevail, [the] Constitution forbids the State to exact religious conformity from a student as the price of attending her own high school graduation. . . .

Inherent differences [distinguish] this case from Marsh v. Chambers, 463 U.S. 783 (1983). . . . At a high school graduation, teachers and principals must and do retain a high degree of control over the precise contents of the program. . . . In this atmosphere the state-imposed character of an invocation and benediction by clergy selected by the school combine to make the prayer a state-sanctioned religious exercise in which the student was left with no alternative but to submit. . . .

For the reasons we have stated, the judgment of the Court of Appeals is *Affirmed*.

Justice BLACKMUN, with whom Justice STEVENS and Justice O'CONNOR join, concurring.

[W]hen the government "compose[s] official prayers," selects the member of the clergy to deliver the prayer, has the prayer delivered at a public school event that is planned, supervised and given by school officials, and pressures students to attend and participate in the prayer, there can be no doubt that the government is advancing and promoting religion. [I]t is not enough that the government restrain from compelling religious practices: It must not engage in them either. . . .

Justice SOUTER, with whom Justice STEVENS and Justice O'CONNOR join, concurring.

[Petitioners] contend that because the early Presidents included religious messages in their inaugural and Thanksgiving Day addresses, the Framers could not have meant the Establishment Clause to forbid noncoercive state endorsement of religion. [To] be sure, the leaders of the young Republic engaged in some of the practices that separationists like Jefferson and Madison criticized. [T]hose practices prove, at best, that the Framers simply did not share a common understanding of the Establishment Clause, and, at worst, that they, like other politicians, could raise constitutional ideals one day and turn their backs on them the next. . . .

Religious students cannot complain that omitting prayers from their graduation ceremony would, in any realistic sense, "burden" their spiritual callings. [T]hey may express their religious feelings about it before and after the ceremony. They may even organize a privately sponsored baccalaureate if they desire the company of likeminded students. . . .

Petitioners would deflect this conclusion by arguing that graduation prayers are no different from Presidential religious proclamations and similar official "acknowledgments" of religion in public life. But religious invocations in Thanksgiving Day addresses and the like, rarely noticed, ignored without effort, conveyed over an impersonal medium, and directed at no one in particular, inhabit a pallid zone worlds apart from official prayers delivered to a captive audience of public school students and their families. . . .

Justice SCALIA, with whom THE CHIEF JUSTICE, Justice WHITE, and Justice THOMAS join, dissenting.

[The] history and tradition of our Nation are replete with public ceremonies featuring prayers of thanksgiving and petition. . . . From our Nation's origin, prayer has been a prominent part of governmental ceremonies and proclamations. The Declaration of Independence, the document marking our birth as a separate people, "appeal[ed] to the Supreme Judge of the world for the rectitude of our intentions" and avowed "a firm reliance on the protection of divine Providence." In his first inaugural address, after swearing his oath of office on a Bible, George Washington deliberately made a prayer a part of his first official act as President. . . . Such supplications have been a characteristic feature of inaugural addresses ever since. . . . Our national celebration of Thanksgiving likewise dates back to President Washington. This tradition of Thanksgiving Proclamations — with their religious theme of prayerful gratitude to God — has been adhered to by almost every President. The other two branches of the Federal Government also have a long-established practice of prayer at public events. [C]ongressional sessions have opened with a chaplain's prayer ever since the First Congress. And this Court's own sessions have opened with the invocation "God save the United States and this Honorable Court" since the days of Chief Justice Marshall. [T]here exists a more specific tradition of invocations and benedictions at public school graduation exercises. . . .

[The] notion that a student who simply sits in "respectful silence" during the invocation and benediction (when all others are standing) has somehow joined — or would somehow be perceived as having joined — in the prayers is nothing short of ludicrous. [Maintaining] respect for the religious observances of others is a fundamental civic virtue that government (including the public schools) can and should cultivate. [T]he Court itself has not given careful consideration to its test of psychological coercion. For if it had, how could it observe, with no hint of concern or disapproval, that students stood for the Pledge of Allegiance, which immediately preceded Rabbi Gutterman's invocation? The government can, of course, no more coerce political orthodoxy than religious orthodoxy. [S]ince the Pledge of Allegiance has been revised [to] include the phrase "under God," recital of the Pledge would appear to raise the same Establishment Clause issue as the invocation and benediction. [Must] the Pledge therefore be barred from the public schools (both from graduation ceremonies and from the classroom)? . . .

I also find it odd that the Court concludes that high school graduates may not be subjected to this supposed psychological coercion. [G]raduation [is] significant [because] it [is] associated with transition from adolescence to young adulthood. Many graduating seniors [are] old enough to vote. Why, then, does the Court treat them as though they were first-graders? [Beyond] the fact [that] attendance at graduation is voluntary, there is nothing [to] indicate that failure of attending students to take part in the invocation or benediction was subject to any penalty or discipline. . . .

[T]he longstanding American tradition of prayer at official ceremonies displays with unmistakable clarity that the Establishment Clause does not forbid the government to accommodate it. . . . The narrow context of the present case involves a community's celebration of one of the milestones in its young citizens' lives, and it is a bold step for this Court to seek to banish from that occasion [the] expression of gratitude to God that a majority of the community wishes to make. . . . I dissent.

Notes and Questions

1. *Prayer at Football Games*. In Santa Fe Independent School District v. Doe, 530 U.S. 290 (2000), the Court struck down a school district policy that authorized nondenominational prayer at football games. Students were allowed to vote on whether to have a prayer and to select the student who would give it. The Court explained: "[invocations] are authorized by a government policy and take place on government property at government-sponsored school-related events. . . . In addition [the] only type of message that is expressly endorsed in the text is an 'invocation' — a term that primarily describes an appeal for divine assistance. . . ." Chief Justice Rehnquist, joined by Justices Scalia and Thomas, dissented: "[T]he policy itself has plausible secular purposes: '[T]o solemnize the

event, to promote good sportsmanship and student safety, and to establish the appropriate environment for the competition.' Where a governmental body 'expresses a plausible secular purpose' for an enactment, 'courts should generally defer to that stated intent.'"

2. *Does the Pledge of Allegiance Establish Religion?* In Elk Grove Unified School District v. Newdow, 542 U.S. 1 (2004), the respondent, an atheist, challenged the fact that a school district began each day with a recitation of the Pledge of Allegiance. He contended that, because the pledge contains the words "under God," its recitation amounts to an establishment of religion. The Court refused to hear the case as nonjusticiable (the respondent, as a noncustodial parent, lacked standing). If the Court had heard the case, how should it have ruled? Justice O'Connor has argued that such recitations are permissible as a form of "ceremonial deism," which she defines broadly to encompass such things as the national motto ("In God We Trust"), religious references in traditional patriotic songs such as "The Star-Spangled Banner"), and the words with which the marshal of this Court opens each of its sessions ("God save the United States and this honorable Court"). Do you agree with Justice O'Connor?

3. *The Scalia Proposal.* In his dissent in *Lee*, Justice Scalia suggested that invocations and benedictions would be permissible at graduation if the school announced (orally or in the program) that "while all are asked to rise for the invocation and benediction, none is compelled to join in them, nor will be assumed, by rising, to have done so. That obvious fact recited, the graduates and their parents may proceed to thank God, as Americans have always done, for the blessings He has generously bestowed on them and on their country." Do you agree?

4. *Professional School Prayer?* Should *Lee*'s holding apply to professional schools' graduation prayers? Are the factors that prompted the *Lee* decision applicable in that context?

❧ PROBLEMS ❧

1. *More on the Education for a Better America Act.* In constructing the proposed legislation, should you say anything at all about whether graduation prayers are allowed or prohibited? Would it be permissible for parochial schools that receive federal funding to have prayer at their graduation exercises?

2. *The Valedictorian's Thanks to God.* Suppose that a school has a policy of allowing four students to speak at graduation. The students are chosen based on their class standing, and they are allowed to deliver "an address, poem, reading, song, musical presentation, prayer, or any other pronouncement." School policy precludes school employees from censoring any presentation or requiring any content. In this situation, would it be constitutionally permissible for the valedictorian at a high school graduation to offer thanks to God — provided that the thanks is offered spontaneously, of the individual's own free will, and as a thanks for guidance and help in his or her own life?

3. Curricular Issues

There has been considerable litigation regarding whether schools may include religious teachings in the public school curriculum.

School District of Abington Township v. Schempp
374 U.S. 203 (1963)

Mr. Justice CLARK delivered the opinion of the Court.

[Pennsylvania law requires that "At least ten verses from the Holy Bible be read, without comment, at the opening of each public school on each school day." At Abington Senior High School, opening exercises are broadcast through an intercommunications system under the supervision of a teacher by students in the school's radio and television workshop. Students read ten verses of the Holy Bible and then recite the Lord's Prayer. Other students are asked to stand and join in the prayer in unison. The exercises close with a salute to the flag and announcements. The student who reads the Bible verses may select the passages and read from any version he or she chooses, although the school furnishes only the King James version. The King James, the Douay, and the Revised Standard versions of the Bible have been used, as well as the Jewish Holy Scriptures. There are no prefatory statements, no questions asked or solicited, no comments or explanations, and no interpretations given during the exercises. A student may leave the classroom or elect not to participate in the exercises. In schools that do not have an intercommunications system, the Bible reading and the recitation were conducted by the homeroom teacher, who chose the verses and read them herself or had students read them. A Baltimore school board rule provided for opening exercises consisting primarily of the "reading, without comment, of a chapter in the Holy Bible and/or the use of the Lord's Prayer."]

[The] State contends that the program [has] secular purposes [including] the promotion of moral values, the contradiction to the materialistic trends of our times, the perpetuation of our institutions and the teaching of literature. [E]ven if its purpose is not strictly religious, [the] place of the Bible as an instrument of religion cannot be gainsaid, and the State's recognition of the pervading religious character of the ceremony is evident from the rule's specific permission of the alternative use of the Catholic Douay version as well as the recent amendment permitting nonattendance at the exercises. None of these factors is consistent with the contention that the Bible [is] used either as an instrument for nonreligious moral inspiration or as a reference for the teaching of secular subjects.

[The] exercises [are] being conducted in direct violation of the rights of the appellees and petitioners. [T]he fact that individual students may absent themselves [furnishes] no defense to a claim of unconstitutionality. . . .

It is insisted that unless these religious exercises are permitted a "religion of secularism" is established in the schools. We agree [that] the State may not establish a "religion of secularism" in the sense of affirmatively opposing or showing hostility to religion, thus "preferring those who believe in no religion over those who do believe." Zorach v. Clauson, 343 U.S., at 314. We do not agree [that] this decision [has] that effect. [I]t might [be] said that one's education is not complete without a study of comparative religion or the history of religion and its relationship to the advancement of civilization. It certainly may be said that the Bible is worthy of study for its literary and historic qualities. Nothing we have [said] indicates that [study] of the Bible [or] religion, when presented objectively as part of a secular program of education, may not be effected consistently with the First Amendment. But the exercises [violate] the command [that] the Government maintain strict neutrality, neither aiding nor opposing religion.

[W]e cannot accept that the concept of neutrality, which does not permit a State to require a religious exercise even with the consent of the majority of those affected, collides with the majority's right to free exercise of religion. While the Free Exercise Clause [prohibits] the use of state action to deny the rights of free exercise to anyone, it has never meant that a majority could use the machinery of the State to practice its beliefs. . . .

Judgment in No. 142 affirmed; judgment in No. 119 reversed and cause remanded with directions.

Mr. Justice DOUGLAS, concurring.

[T]he Establishment Clause [precludes] the State [from] conducting religious exercises [and] also forbids the State to employ its facilities or funds in a way that gives any church, or all churches, greater strength in our society than it would have by relying on its members alone. [T]he present regimes must fall. . . . Through the mechanism of the State, [all] people are being required to finance a religious exercise that only some of the people want and that violates the sensibilities of others. . . .

Mr. Justice BRENNAN, concurring.

[R]eligious exercises at the start of the school day may [foster] harmony and tolerance among the pupils, enhancing the authority of the teacher, and inspiring better discipline. To the extent that such benefits result not from the content of the readings and recitation, but simply from the holding of such a solemn exercise at the opening assembly or the first class of the day, it would seem that less sensitive materials might equally well serve the same purpose. [It] has not been shown that readings from the speeches and messages of great Americans, [or] from the documents of our heritage of liberty, daily recitation of the Pledge of Allegiance, or even the observance of a moment of reverent silence at the opening of class, may not adequately serve the solely secular purposes of the devotional activities without jeopardizing [either] religious liberties [or] the proper degree of separation [between] religion and government. . . . [T]he State acts unconstitutionally if [it tries] to [attain] religious ends by religious means, or if it uses religious means to serve secular ends where secular means would suffice.

[I]t is argued that the particular practices [before] us are unobjectionable because they prefer no particular sect or sects at the expense of others. [One] answer [is] that any version of the Bible is inherently sectarian. . . . The argument contains, however, a more basic flaw. There are persons in every community — often deeply devout — to whom any version of the Judaeo-Christian Bible is offensive. There are others whose reverence for the Holy Scriptures demands private study or reflection and to whom public reading or recitation is sacrilegious. . . .

It has been suggested that a tentative solution to these problems may lie in the fashioning of a "common core" of theology tolerable to all creeds but preferential to none. [But] "[h]istory is not encouraging to" those who hope to fashion a "common denominator of religion detached from its manifestation in any organized church." Arthur Sutherland, *Establishment According to Engel*, 76 Harv. L. Rev. 25, 51 (1962). . . .

[T]he availability of excusal or exemption simply has no relevance to the establishment question, if it is once found that these practices are essentially religious exercises designed at least in part to achieve religious aims through the use of public school facilities during the school day. [T]he State could not constitutionally require a student to profess publicly his disbelief as the prerequisite to the exercise of his constitutional right of abstention. . . .

Mr. Justice STEWART, dissenting.

[A] compulsory state educational system so structures a child's life that if religious exercises are held to be an impermissible activity in schools, religion is placed at an artificial and state-created disadvantage. [P]ermission of such exercises for those who want them is necessary if the schools are truly to be neutral in the matter of religion. And a refusal to permit religious exercises thus is seen, not as the realization of state neutrality, but rather as the establishment of a religion of secularism, or at the least, as government support of the beliefs of those who think that religious exercises should be conducted only in private.

[The] dangers both to government and to religion inherent in official support of instruction in the tenets of various religious sects are absent in the present cases, which involve only a reading from the Bible unaccompanied by comments which might otherwise constitute instruction. [Since any] teacher who does not wish to do so is free not to participate, it cannot [be] contended that some infinitesimal part of the salaries paid by the State are made contingent upon the performance of a religious function.

[In] these cases, [what] is involved is [an] attempt by the State to accommodate those differences which the existence in our society of a variety of religious beliefs makes inevitable. The Constitution requires that such efforts be struck down only if they [entail] the use of the secular authority of government to coerce a preference among such beliefs.

∾ PROBLEMS ∾

1. *More on the Education for a Better America Act.* In constructing the proposed legislation, should Congress say anything about whether schools are allowed to use (or, for that matter, prohibited from using) religious materials in their courses? Should Congress prohibit parochial schools that receive financial aid under the Act from using religious materials?

2. *University Courses on Religion.* May a public college, as part of its ordinary curriculum, offer a survey course designed to give students an overview of religion and religious concepts? Would it matter whether the course focused on only a particular religion?

Epperson v. Arkansas

393 U.S. 97 (1968)

Mr. Justice FORTAS delivered the opinion of the Court.

This appeal challenges the constitutionality of the [Arkansas] "anti-evolution" statute [adopted] in 1928. . . . The statute was a product of the upsurge of "fundamentalist" religious fervor of the twenties. The Arkansas statute was an adaption of the famous Tennessee "monkey law" which that State adopted in 1925. The constitutionality of the Tennessee law was upheld by the Tennessee Supreme Court in the celebrated Scopes case in 1927.[2]

The Arkansas law makes it unlawful for a teacher in any state-supported school or university "to teach the theory or doctrine that mankind ascended or descended from a lower order of animals," or "to adopt or use in any such institution a textbook that teaches" this theory. Violation is a misdemeanor and subjects the violator to dismissal from his position.

The present case concerns the teaching of biology in a high school in Little Rock. [U]ntil the events here in litigation, the official textbook furnished for the high school biology course did not have a section on the Darwinian Theory. [F]or the academic year 1965–1966, the school administration, on recommendation of the teachers of biology in the school system, adopted and prescribed a textbook which contained a chapter setting forth "the theory about the origin [of] man from a lower form of animal."

Susan Epperson [was] employed by the Little Rock school system in the fall of 1964 to teach 10th grade biology. . . . At the start of the next academic year, 1965, she was confronted by the new textbook (which one surmises from the record was not unwelcome to her). She faced at least a literal dilemma because she was supposed to use the new textbook for classroom instruction and presumably to teach the statutorily condemned chapter; but to do so would be a criminal offense and subject her to dismissal.

She instituted the present action [seeking] a declaration that the Arkansas statute is void and enjoining [officials] of the Little Rock school system from dismissing her for violation of the statute's provisions. [The trial court struck the statute down on First Amendment grounds.]

Only Arkansas and Mississippi [have] "anti-evolution" or "monkey" laws on their books.[3] There is no record of any prosecutions in Arkansas [and the] statute [may be more] of a curiosity than a vital fact of life. . . . Nevertheless, [it] is our duty to decide the issues presented.

---

2. Scopes v. State of Tennessee, 154 Tenn. 105, 289 S.W. 363 (1927). The Tennessee court [reversed] Scopes' conviction on the ground that the jury and not the judge should have assessed the fine of $100. . . .

3. Oklahoma enacted an anti-evolution law, but repealed [it] in 1926. The Florida and Texas Legislatures, [between] 1921 and 1929, adopted resolutions against teaching the doctrine of evolution. . . .

[Our] precedents inevitably determine the result in the present case. The State's undoubted right to prescribe the curriculum for its public schools does not carry with it the right to prohibit, on pain of criminal penalty, the teaching of a scientific theory or doctrine where that prohibition is based upon reasons that violate the First Amendment. . . .

[T]here can be no doubt that Arkansas has sought to prevent its teachers from discussing the theory of evolution because it is contrary to the belief of some that the Book of Genesis must be the exclusive source of doctrine as to the origin of man. [It] is clear that fundamentalist sectarian conviction was and is the law's reason for existence. Its antecedent, Tennessee's "monkey law," candidly stated its purpose: to make it unlawful "to teach any theory that denies the story of the Divine Creation of man as taught in the Bible, and to teach instead that man has descended from a lower order of animals." Perhaps the sensational publicity attendant upon the Scopes trial induced Arkansas to adopt less explicit language. It eliminated Tennessee's reference to "the story of the Divine Creation of man" as taught in the Bible, but [the] motivation for the law was the same: to suppress the teaching of a theory [which] "denied" the divine creation of man.

Arkansas' law cannot be defended as an act of religious neutrality. Arkansas did not seek to excise from the curricula of its schools and universities all discussion of the origin of man. The law's effort was confined to an attempt to blot out a particular theory because of its supposed conflict with the Biblical account, literally read. Plainly, the law is contrary to the mandate of the First, and in violation of the Fourteenth, Amendment to the Constitution.

The judgment of the Supreme Court of Arkansas is reversed.

Reversed.

Mr. Justice BLACK, concurring.

[I] find it difficult to agree with the Court's statement that "[Arkansas] sought to prevent its teachers from [discussing] evolution because it is contrary to [the] Book of Genesis. . . ." It may be instead that the people's motive was merely that it would be best to remove this controversial subject from its schools; there is no [reason why] a State [cannot] withdraw from its curriculum any subject deemed too emotional and controversial. . . . [I]t is not for us to invalidate a statute because of our views that the "motives" behind its passage were improper; it is simply too difficult to determine what those motives were.

A second question that arises [is] whether this Court's decision [infringes] the religious freedom of those who consider evolution an anti-religious doctrine. [H]ow can the State be bound by the Federal Constitution to permit its teachers to advocate [an] "anti-religious" doctrine to schoolchildren?

Question: The Choper Analysis

Can it be argued that, even though the Arkansas law may have been religiously motivated, it involved "none of the dangers the Establishment Clause was designed to prevent" because there was no "evidence that religious beliefs were either coerced, compromised or influenced"? Can it also be argued that there was no evidence that the law "(1) induced children of fundamentalist religions to accept the biblical theory of creation, or (2) conditioned other children for conversion to fundamentalism"? Can it be argued that there is (or is not) *religious harm*" and a "threat to religious liberty"? *See* Jesse H. Choper, *The Religion Clauses of the First Amendment: Reconciling the Conflict*, 41 U. Pitt. L. Rev. 673, 687 (1980).

Edwards v. Aguillard
482 U.S. 578 (1987)

Justice BRENNAN delivered the opinion of the Court.[4]

The question for decision is whether Louisiana's "Balanced Treatment for Creation-Science and Evolution-Science in Public School Instruction" Act (Creationism Act), is facially invalid as violative of the Establishment Clause of the First Amendment.

The Creationism Act forbids the teaching of the theory of evolution in public schools unless accompanied by instruction in "creation science." No school is required to teach evolution or creation science. If either is taught, however, the other must also be taught. The theories of evolution and creation science are statutorily defined as "the scientific evidences for [creation or evolution] and inferences from those scientific evidences."

Appellees, who include parents of children attending Louisiana public schools, Louisiana teachers, and religious leaders, challenged the constitutionality of the Act. . . . The District Court [found] no valid secular reason for prohibiting the teaching of evolution. . . . [The] Court of Appeals affirmed. [We] affirm.

[The] Court has been particularly vigilant in monitoring compliance with the Establishment Clause in elementary and secondary schools. Families entrust public schools with the education of their children, but condition their trust on the understanding that the classroom will not purposely be used to advance religious views that may conflict with the private beliefs of the student and his or her family. Students in such institutions are impressionable [and the] State exerts great authority and coercive power through mandatory attendance requirements, and because of the students' emulation of teachers as role models and the children's susceptibility to peer pressure. . . . We use the three-pronged *Lemon* test [mindful] of the particular concerns that arise in the context of public elementary and secondary schools. . . .

Lemon's first prong focuses on the purpose that animated adoption of the Act. [T]he Act's stated purpose is to protect academic freedom. This phrase might [be] understood as referring to enhancing the freedom of teachers to teach what they will. [The] Act was not designed to further that goal. [While] the Court is normally deferential to a State's articulation of a secular purpose, [the] statement of such purpose [must] be sincere and not a sham. [It] is clear [that] the purpose of the legislative sponsor [was] to narrow the science curriculum. During the legislative hearings, Senator Keith stated: "My preference would be that neither [creationism nor evolution] be taught." Such a ban on teaching does not

4. Justice O'CONNOR joins all but Part II of this opinion.

promote — indeed, it undermines — the provision of a comprehensive scientific education.

It is equally clear that requiring schools to teach creation science with evolution does not advance academic freedom. The Act does not grant teachers a flexibility that they did not already possess to supplant the present science curriculum with the presentation of theories, besides evolution, about the origin of life. [N]o law prohibited Louisiana public school teachers from teaching any scientific theory. [Thus] the stated purpose is not furthered by it.

[T]he goal of basic "fairness" is hardly furthered by the Act's discriminatory preference for the teaching of creation science and against the teaching of evolution. While requiring that curriculum guides be developed for creation science, the Act says nothing of comparable guides for evolution. Similarly, resource services are supplied for creation science but not for evolution. Only "creation scientists" can serve on the panel that supplies the resource services. The Act forbids school boards to discriminate against anyone who "chooses to be a creation-scientist" or to teach "creationism," but fails to protect those who [teach] evolution or any other non-creation science theory, or who refuse to teach creation science.

If the Louisiana Legislature's purpose was solely to maximize the comprehensiveness and effectiveness of science instruction, it would have encouraged the teaching of all scientific theories about the origins of humankind. But under the Act's requirements, teachers who were once free to teach any and all facets of this subject are now unable to do so. Moreover, the Act fails even to ensure that creation science will be taught, but instead requires the teaching of this theory only when the theory of evolution is taught. Thus [the] Act does not serve to protect academic freedom, but has the distinctly different purpose of discrediting "evolution by counterbalancing its teaching at every turn with the teaching of creationism. . . ."

[There] is a historic and contemporaneous link between the teachings of certain religious denominations and the teaching of evolution. [The] preeminent purpose of the Louisiana Legislature was clearly to advance the religious viewpoint that a supernatural being created humankind. . . . [I]t is not happenstance that the legislature required the teaching of a theory that coincided with this religious view. [The] sponsor of the [Act], Senator Keith, explained [during] legislative hearings that his disdain for the theory of evolution resulted from the support that evolution supplied to views contrary to his own religious beliefs. According to Senator Keith, the theory of evolution was consonant with the "cardinal principle[s] of religious humanism, secular humanism, theological liberalism, aetheistism [sic]." [The] senator repeatedly stated that scientific evidence supporting his religious views should be included in the public school curriculum to redress the fact that [evolution] coincided [with] religious beliefs antithetical to his own. The legislation therefore sought to alter the science curriculum to reflect endorsement of a religious view [antagonistic] to the theory of evolution.

[We] do not imply that a legislature could never require that scientific critiques of prevailing scientific theories be taught. [T]eaching a variety of scientific theories about the origins of humankind [might] be validly done with the clear secular intent of enhancing the effectiveness of science instruction. But because the primary purpose of the Creationism Act is to endorse a particular religious doctrine, the Act furthers religion in violation of the Establishment Clause.

The Louisiana Creationism Act advances a religious doctrine by requiring either the banishment of the theory of evolution from public school classrooms or the presentation of a religious viewpoint that rejects evolution in its entirety. The Act violates the Establishment Clause [because] it seeks to employ the symbolic and financial support of government to achieve a religious purpose. The judgment of the Court of Appeals therefore is

Affirmed.

Justice SCALIA, with whom THE CHIEF JUSTICE joins, dissenting.

"[L]egislative purpose" [means] the "actual" motives of those responsible for the challenged action. [I]f those legislators [acted] with a "sincere" secular purpose, the Act survives the first component of the *Lemon* test. . . . [T]he Balanced Treatment Act did not fly through the Louisiana Legislature on wings of fundamentalist religious fervor — which would be unlikely [since] only a small minority of the State's citizens belong to fundamentalist religious denominations. . . . Most of the testimony in support of [the] bill came from [Senator Keith] himself and from scientists and [educators], many of whom enjoyed academic credentials that may [be] regarded as quite impressive. [T]heir testimony was devoted to lengthy, [and] seemingly expert scientific expositions on the origin of life. These scientific lectures touched [upon] biology, paleontology, genetics, astronomy, astrophysics, probability analysis, and biochemistry. The witnesses [assured] committee members that "[hundreds]" of highly respected, internationally renowned scientists believed in creation science. . . .

Senator Keith and his witnesses testified essentially [that]:

1. There are two and only two scientific explanations for the beginning of life — evolution and creation science. Both posit a theory of the origin of life and subject that theory to empirical testing. . . .

2. The body of scientific evidence supporting creation science is as strong as that supporting evolution [and] may be stronger. The evidence for evolution is far less compelling than we have been led to believe. Evolution is not a scientific "fact," since it cannot actually be observed in a laboratory. Rather, evolution is merely a scientific theory or "guess" [and] a very bad guess at that. . . .

3. Creation science is educationally valuable. Students exposed to it better understand the current state of scientific evidence about the origin of life [and] evolution. Creation science can and should be presented to children without any religious content.

4. Although creation science is educationally valuable and strictly scientific, it is now being censored from or misrepresented in the public schools. Teachers have been brainwashed by an entrenched scientific establishment composed almost exclusively of scientists to whom evolution is like

a "religion." These scientists discriminate against creation scientists [to] prevent evolution's weaknesses from being exposed.

5.   The censorship of creation science has at least two harmful effects. First, it deprives students of knowledge of one [scientific] explanation for the origin of life and leads them to believe that evolution is proven fact; thus, [they] are wrongly taught that science has proved their religious beliefs false. Second, it violates the Establishment Clause. The United States Supreme Court has held that secular humanism is a religion. Belief in evolution is a central tenet of that religion. Thus, by censoring creation science and instructing students that evolution is fact, public school teachers [are] advancing religion in violation of the Establishment Clause.

Senator Keith repeatedly and vehemently denied that his purpose was to advance a particular religious doctrine. . . . We have no way of knowing [how] many legislators believed the testimony of Senator Keith and his witnesses. But [we] have to assume that many of them did. Given that assumption, the Court today plainly errs in holding that the Louisiana Legislature passed the Balanced Treatment Act for exclusively religious purposes.

Even with nothing more than this legislative [history], [it] would be extraordinary to invalidate the [Act] for lack of a valid secular purpose. [The] Louisiana Legislature explicitly set forth its secular purpose ("protecting academic freedom") in the very text of the Act. We have in the past repeatedly relied upon or deferred to such expressions. [The] legislative history gives ample evidence of the sincerity of [the] articulated purpose. Witness after witness urged the legislators to support the Act so that students would not be "indoctrinated" but would instead be free to decide for themselves, based upon a fair presentation of the scientific evidence, about the origin of life. [Other legislators] made only a few statements[,] but those statements cast no doubt upon the sincerity of [the] articulated purpose. . . .

It is undoubtedly true that what prompted the legislature to direct its attention to the misrepresentation of evolution in the schools [was] its awareness of the tension between evolution and the religious beliefs of many children. But even appellees concede that a valid secular purpose is not rendered impermissible simply because its pursuit is prompted by concern for religious sensitivities. . . . Because I believe that the Balanced Treatment Act had a secular purpose, which is all the first component of the *Lemon* test requires, I would reverse the judgment of the Court of Appeals and remand for further consideration.

❧ PROBLEMS ❧

1. *Secular Humanism.* Some critics of *Epperson* and *Edwards* have argued that "secular humanism" is a bona fide "religion" and that "evolution is the cornerstone of that religion." These critics have argued that, by censoring creation science and instructing students that evolution theory is factually true, public school teachers are advancing religion in violation of the Establishment Clause. *See*

Leonard Manning, *The Douglas Concept of God in Government*, 39 Wash. L. Rev. 47, 63 (1964): "[I]f we forbid the teaching of recognized religions in our public schools and forbid a prayer which simply acknowledges the existence of God and at the same time permit [the] teaching of some code of ethical conduct, some system of value norms, does not the system which the school then sponsors become the system of Secular Humanism or simply secular humanism?" Do you agree?

2. *Intelligent Design.* In recent years, a number of "creation theorists" have advanced an "intelligent design" theory. Basically, they argue that the structure of the earth and the universe provides evidence of an "intelligent design" suggesting the presence of a superior being that established the design. They argue that the "scientific evidence of intelligent design" should be taught in public schools alongside evolution. Do you agree?

3. *More on Teaching Intelligent Design and Creation Science.* Suppose that a Pennsylvania school district requires that high school students be taught both the theory of evolution and the theory of intelligent design. The district justifies the requirement as a way to teach students critical thinking skills as well as to ensure that they are aware of all "scientific theories regarding the creation of life."

4. *Evolution, Creationism, and the Education for a Better America Act.* In the proposed legislation, should Congress attempt to address issues relating to the teaching of evolution or creationism? Does it matter that the proposed legislation would provide aid to all types of schools (private, public, and parochial)? Would it be permissible for Congress to simply ignore these issues altogether?

4. Official Acknowledgment

A continuing source of litigation under the Establishment Clause has been whether, and to what extent, government may "acknowledge" religion in public displays. This issue has arisen in numerous contexts, including Christmas and nativity displays and official monuments and displays of the Ten Commandments.

County of Allegheny v. American Civil Liberties Union
492 U.S. 573 (1989)

Justice BLACKMUN announced the judgment of the Court and delivered the opinion of the Court with respect to Parts III-A, IV, and V, an opinion with respect to Parts I and II, in which Justice STEVENS and Justice O'CONNOR join, an opinion with respect to Part III-B, in which Justice STEVENS joins, an opinion with respect to Part VII, in which Justice O'CONNOR joins, and an opinion with respect to Part VI.

[The] county courthouse is [Allegheny County's] seat of government. It houses the offices of the county commissioners, controller, treasurer, sheriff, and clerk of court. Civil and criminal trials are held there. The "main," "most beautiful," and "most public" part of the courthouse is its Grand Staircase, set into one arch and surrounded by others, with arched windows serving as a backdrop.

Since 1981, the county has permitted [a] Roman Catholic group to display a creche in the county courthouse during the Christmas holiday season. . . . [The creche] had a wooden fence on three sides and bore a plaque stating: "[Donated] by the Holy Name Society." [T]he county [placed] poinsettia plants around the fence. The county also placed a small evergreen tree, decorated with a red bow, behind each of the two endposts of the fence. These trees stood alongside the manger [and] were slightly [shorter]. The angel thus was at the apex of the creche display. [The entire display] occupied a substantial amount of space on the Grand Staircase. No figures of Santa Claus or other decorations appeared on [the] Staircase. [The] county uses the creche as the setting for its annual Christmas-carole program. During the 1986 season, the county invited high school choirs and other musical groups to perform during weekday lunch hours. . . . The county dedicated this program to world peace and to the families of prisoners-of-war and of persons missing in action in Southeast Asia. . . .

The City-County Building is [a] block removed from the county courthouse [and] is jointly owned by the city of Pittsburgh and Allegheny County. . . . For a number of years, the city has had a large Christmas tree under the middle arch outside the Grant Street entrance. [T]he city placed at the foot of the tree a sign bearing the mayor's name and entitled "Salute to Liberty." Beneath the title, the sign stated:

> During this holiday season, the city of Pittsburgh salutes liberty. Let these festive lights remind us that we are the keepers of the flame of liberty and our legacy of freedom.

[T]he city placed [an] 18-foot Chanukah menorah of an abstract tree-and-branch design. The menorah was placed next to [the] Christmas tree, against one of the columns that supports the arch into which the tree was set. The menorah is owned by Chabad, a Jewish group, but is stored, erected, and removed each year by the city. The tree, the sign, and the menorah were all removed on January 13. . . .

III

[In] recent years, we have paid particularly close attention to whether the challenged governmental practice either has the purpose or effect of "endorsing" religion, a concern that has long had a place in our Establishment Clause jurisprudence. . . . [T]he prohibition against governmental endorsement of religion "preclude[s] government from conveying or attempting to convey a message that religion or a particular religious belief is *favored* or *preferred*." Wallace v. Jaffree, 472 U.S., at 70 (O'Connor, J., concurring in judgment). Moreover, the term "endorsement" is closely linked to the term "promotion," and this Court long since has held that government "may [not] promote one religion or religious theory against another or even against the militant opposite." Whether the key word is "endorsement," "favoritism," or "promotion," the essential principle remains the same. The Establishment Clause [prohibits] government from appearing to take a position on questions of religious belief or from "making adherence to a religion relevant in any way to a person's standing in the political community."

[In] Lynch v. Donnelly, [we] considered whether the city of Pawtucket, R.I., [violated] the Establishment Clause by including a creche in its annual Christmas display, located in a private park within the downtown shopping district. By a 5-to-4 [decision], the Court upheld inclusion of the creche in [the] display, holding [that] inclusion of the creche did not have the impermissible effect of advancing or promoting religion. [The] opinion [contained] two strands. . . . First, [inclusion] of the creche [was] "no more an advancement or endorsement of religion" than other "endorsements" this Court has approved in the past. . . . Second, [any] benefit the government's display [gave] religion was no more than "indirect, remote, and incidental"—without saying how or why.

[Justice O'Connor's concurrence] differs in significant respects from the majority opinion. The main difference is that the concurrence provides a sound analytical framework for evaluating governmental use of religious symbols. [First], the concurrence squarely rejects any notion that this Court will tolerate some government endorsement of religion. [E]ndorsement of religion [is] "invalid," because it "sends a message to nonadherents that they are outsiders, not full members of the political community, and an accompanying message to adherents that they are insiders, favored members of the political community." [Second,] the concurrence articulates a method for determining whether [an] object with religious meaning has the effect of endorsing religion. The effect [depends] upon the message that the government's practice communicates [based] upon the context in which the contested object appears: "[A] typical museum setting, though not neutralizing the religious content of a religious painting, negates any message of endorsement of that content." . . .

The concurrence applied this mode of analysis to the Pawtucket creche. . . . In addition to the creche, [the] display contained: a Santa Claus house with a live Santa distributing candy; reindeer pulling Santa's sleigh; a live 40-foot Christmas tree strung with lights; statues of carolers in old-fashioned dress; candy-striped poles; a "talking" wishing well; a large banner proclaiming "SEASONS GREETINGS"; a miniature "village" with several houses and a church; and various "cut-out" figures, including those of a clown, a dancing elephant, a robot, and a teddy bear. The concurrence concluded that both because the creche is "a traditional symbol" of Christmas, a holiday with strong secular elements, and because the creche was "displayed along with purely secular symbols," the creche's setting "changes what viewers may fairly understand to be the purpose of the display" and "negates any message of endorsement" of "[Christian beliefs]."

The four *Lynch* dissenters agreed [that] the controlling question was "whether Pawtucket ha[d] [endorsed] religion through its display of the creche." The dissenters also agreed [that] context [is] relevant. . . . They simply [concluded] that the other elements of the Pawtucket display did not negate the endorsement of Christian faith caused by the presence of the creche. They viewed the [creche] as placing "the government's imprimatur of approval on the particular religious beliefs exemplified by the creche." Thus, "[t]he effect on minority religious groups [was] to convey the message that their views are not similarly worthy of public recognition nor entitled to public support."

[D]espite divergence[,] the five Justices in concurrence and dissent [agreed that] the government's use of religious symbolism is unconstitutional if it has the effect of endorsing religious beliefs. . . . [O]ur present task is to determine whether the display of the creche and the menorah, in their respective "particular physical settings," has the effect of endorsing or disapproving religious beliefs.

We turn first to [the] creche display. [T]he creche [uses] words, as well as the picture of the Nativity scene, to make its religious meaning unmistakably clear. "Glory to God in the Highest!" says the angel in the creche — Glory to God because of the birth of Jesus. This praise to God in Christian terms is indisputably religious — indeed sectarian — just as it is when said in the Gospel or in a church service.

[T]he effect of a creche display turns on its setting. [Unlike *Lynch*,] nothing in the context of the display detracts from the creche's religious message. The *Lynch* display composed a series of figures and objects, each group of which had its own focal point. Santa's house and his reindeer were objects of attention separate from the creche, and had their specific visual story to tell. Similarly, whatever a "talking" wishing well may be, [it] was a center of attention separate from the creche. Here, [the] creche stands alone: it is the single element of the display on the Grand Staircase. The floral decoration surrounding the creche cannot be viewed as somehow equivalent to the secular symbols in *Lynch*. The floral frame [serves] only to [draw] attention to the message inside the frame. The floral decoration surrounding the creche contributes [to] the endorsement [message]. It is as if the county had allowed the Holy Name Society to display a cross on the Grand Staircase at Easter, and the county had surrounded the cross with Easter lilies. . . .

Furthermore, the creche sits on the Grand Staircase, the "main" and "most beautiful part" of the building that is the seat of county government. No viewer could reasonably think that it occupies this location without the support and approval of the government. [B]y permitting the "display of the creche in this particular physical setting," the county sends an unmistakable message that it supports and promotes the Christian praise to God that is the creche's religious message. . . . The fact that the creche bears a sign disclosing its ownership by a Roman Catholic organization does not alter this conclusion. [T]he sign simply demonstrates that the government is endorsing the religious message of that organization, rather than communicating a message of its own. . . .

Finally, the county argues that [the] display celebrates Christmas, and Christmas is a national holiday. This argument [would] allow the celebration of the Eucharist inside a courthouse on Christmas Eve. [The] government may acknowledge Christmas as a cultural phenomenon, but [may] not observe it as a Christian holy day by suggesting that people praise God for the birth of Jesus.

In sum, *Lynch* teaches that government may celebrate Christmas in some manner and form, but not in a way that endorses Christian doctrine. [Allegheny County] has transgressed this line. It has [celebrated] Christmas in a way that has the effect of endorsing a patently Christian message: Glory to God for the birth of Jesus Christ. Under *Lynch*, [nothing] more is required to demonstrate a violation of the Establishment Clause. The display of the creche in this context [must] be permanently enjoined.

Justice Kennedy [argues] that [Marsh v. Chambers, 463 U.S. 783 (1983)] legitimates all "practices with no greater potential for [establishment]" than those "accepted traditions dating back to the Founding." Otherwise, the Justice asserts, such practices as our national motto ("In God We Trust") and our Pledge of Allegiance (with the phrase "under God," added in 1954), are in danger of invalidity. . . . [T]here is an obvious distinction between creche displays and references to God in the motto and the pledge. However history may affect the constitutionality of nonsectarian references to religion by the government, history cannot legitimate practices that demonstrate the government's allegiance to a particular sect or creed. . . . We have expressly required "strict scrutiny" of practices suggesting "a denominational preference. . . ."

Although Justice Kennedy repeatedly accuses the Court [of] "latent hostility" [toward] religion, nothing could be further from the truth. . . . Justice Kennedy [misperceives] respect for religious pluralism [as] hostility. . . . Celebrating Christmas as a religious [holiday] necessarily entails [proclaiming] that Jesus [is] the [Messiah], a specifically Christian belief. In contrast, confining the government's own celebration of Christmas to the holiday's secular aspects does not favor the religious beliefs of non-Christians over those of Christians. Rather, it simply permits the government to acknowledge the holiday without expressing an allegiance to Christian beliefs. . . .

[N]ot all religious celebrations of Christmas located on government property violate the Establishment Clause. [It] is not unconstitutional [for] a group of parishioners [to] go caroling through a city park on any Sunday in Advent or for a Christian club at a public university to sing carols during their Christmas meeting. [These activities] do not demonstrate the government's [endorsement] of the Christian faith. [O]nce [a] proclamation [has] the effect of [endorsing the] Christian faith, then [that] practice must be enjoined to protect the constitutional rights of those citizens who follow some creed other than Christianity. . . .

VI

[The] menorah [is] a religious symbol: it serves to commemorate the miracle of the oil as described in the Talmud. But the menorah's message is not exclusively religious. The menorah is the primary visual symbol for a holiday that, like Christmas, has both religious and secular dimensions.

[T]he menorah here stands next to a Christmas tree and a sign saluting liberty. While no challenge has been made here to [the] tree and the sign, their presence is [relevant] in determining the effect of the [menorah]. [The result is] to create an "overall holiday setting" that represents both Christmas and Chanukah. [Because] government may celebrate Christmas as a secular holiday, [government] may also acknowledge Chanukah as a secular holiday. [I]t would [involve] discrimination against Jews [to] celebrate Christmas as a cultural tradition while simultaneously disallowing the city's acknowledgment of Chanukah as [a] cultural tradition.

[T]he [question is] whether the combined display [has] the effect of endorsing both Christian and Jewish faiths, or rather simply recognizes that both Christmas and Chanukah are part of the same winter-holiday season, which has attained a secular status in our society. [The latter interpretations seems] far more plausible. [The] Christmas tree, unlike the menorah, is not itself a religious symbol. Although Christmas trees once carried religious connotations, today they typify the secular celebration of Christmas. Numerous Americans place Christmas trees in their homes without subscribing to Christian religious beliefs, and when the city's tree stands alone in front of the City-County Building, it is not considered an endorsement of Christian faith. Indeed, a 40-foot Christmas tree was one of the objects that validated the creche in *Lynch*. . . .

The tree, moreover, is clearly the predominant element in the city's display. The 45-foot tree occupies the central position [in] front of [the] entrance to the City-County Building; the 18-foot menorah is positioned to one side. Given this configuration, it [is] sensible to interpret the [menorah] in light of the tree. . . .

In the shadow of the tree, the menorah [is] understood as simply a recognition that Christmas is not the only traditional way of observing the winter-holiday season. [The] combination of the tree and the menorah communicates [a] secular celebration of Christmas coupled with an acknowledgment of Chanukah as a contemporaneous alternative tradition.

Although the city has used a symbol with religious meaning as its representation of Chanukah, this is not a case in which the city has reasonable alternatives that are less religious in nature. It is difficult to imagine a predominantly secular symbol of Chanukah that the city could place next to its Christmas tree. . . .

The mayor's sign [diminishes] the possibility that the tree and the menorah will be interpreted as [an] endorsement of Christianity and Judaism. [While] no sign can disclaim [a] message of endorsement, an "explanatory plaque" may confirm that [the] government's association with a religious symbol does not [represent] government's sponsorship of religious beliefs. . . .

Given all these considerations, it is not "sufficiently likely" that residents of Pittsburgh will perceive the combined display of the tree, the sign, and the menorah as an "endorsement" or "disapproval [of] their individual religious choices." [Constitutionality must] be judged according to the standard of a "reasonable observer. . . ."

The conclusion [that the] menorah's display does not have an effect of endorsing religious faith does not foreclose the possibility that the display of the menorah might violate either the "purpose" or "entanglement" prong of the *Lemon* analysis. These issues were not addressed [and] may be considered [on] remand.

Lynch confirms, and in no way repudiates, the longstanding constitutional principle that government may not engage in a practice that has the effect of promoting or endorsing religious beliefs. The display of the creche in the county courthouse has this unconstitutional effect. The display of the menorah in front of the City-County Building, however, does not have this effect, given its "particular physical setting."

The judgment of the Court of Appeals is affirmed in part and reversed in part, and the cases are remanded for further proceedings.

It is so ordered.

Justice O'CONNOR, with whom Justice BRENNAN and Justice STEVENS join as to Part II, concurring in part and concurring in the judgment.

[An] Establishment Clause standard that prohibits only "coercive" practices or overt efforts at government proselytization, but fails to take account of the numerous more subtle ways that government can show favoritism to particular beliefs or convey a message of disapproval to others, would [not] adequately protect the religious liberty or respect the religious diversity of the members of our pluralistic political community. . . .

[Practices] such as legislative prayers or opening Court sessions with "God save the United States and this honorable Court" serve the secular purposes of "solemnizing public occasions" and "expressing confidence in the future." These examples of ceremonial deism do not survive Establishment Clause scrutiny simply by virtue of their historical longevity alone. [T]he "history and ubiquity" of a practice is relevant [because] it provides part of the context in which a reasonable observer evaluates whether a challenged governmental practice conveys a message of endorsement of religion. It is the combination of the longstanding existence of practices such as opening legislative sessions with legislative prayers or opening Court sessions with "God save the United States and this honorable Court," as well as their nonsectarian nature, that leads me to the conclusion that [those] practices, despite their religious roots, do not convey a message of endorsement of particular religious beliefs. Similarly, the celebration of Thanksgiving as a public holiday, despite its religious origins, is now generally understood as a celebration of patriotic values rather than particular religious beliefs. The question under endorsement analysis [is] whether a reasonable observer would view such longstanding practices as a disapproval of his or her particular religious choices, in light of the fact that they serve a secular purpose rather than a sectarian one and have largely lost their religious significance over time. . . .

[N]either the endorsement test nor its application in these cases reflects "an unjustified hostility toward religion." [T]he government can *acknowledge* the role of religion in our society in numerous ways that do not amount to an endorsement. [T]he city of Pittsburgh's combined holiday display had neither the purpose nor the effect of endorsing religion, [but] Allegheny County's creche display had such an effect. . . .

Justice BRENNAN, with whom Justice MARSHALL and Justice STEVENS join, concurring in part and dissenting in part.

[T]he display of an object that "retains a specifically Christian [or other] religious meaning," is incompatible with the separation of church and state demanded by our Constitution. . . . The menorah is indisputably a religious symbol, used ritually in a celebration that has deep religious significance. [That] is all that need be said. . . .

Justice Stevens, with whom Justice Brennan and Justice Marshall join, concurring in part and dissenting in part.

[T]he Establishment Clause [creates] a strong presumption against the display of religious symbols on public property. . . . The presence of the Chanukah menorah, unquestionably a religious symbol, gives religious significance to the Christmas tree. The overall display thus manifests governmental approval of the Jewish and Christian religions. Although it conceivably might be interpreted as sending "a message of pluralism and freedom to choose one's own beliefs," the message is not sufficiently clear. . . .

Justice Kennedy, with whom The Chief Justice, Justice White, and Justice Scalia join, concurring in the judgment in part and dissenting in part.

The majority [opinion] reflects an unjustified hostility toward religion, a hostility inconsistent with our history and our precedents. . . . The city and county sought to do no more than "celebrate the season," and to acknowledge, along with many of their citizens, the historical background and the religious, as well as secular, nature of the Chanukah and Christmas holidays. This interest falls well within the tradition of government accommodation and acknowledgment of religion that has marked our history from the beginning. . . . [E]nforced recognition of only the secular aspect [of the holiday] would signify the callous indifference toward religious faith that our cases and traditions do not require. . . .

There is no suggestion here that the government's power to coerce has been used to further the interests of Christianity or Judaism in any way. No one was compelled to observe or participate in any religious ceremony or activity. . . . The creche and the menorah are purely passive symbols of religious holidays. Passersby who disagree with the message conveyed by these displays are free to ignore them. . . . There is no realistic risk that the creche and the menorah represent an effort to proselytize or are otherwise the first step down the road to an establishment of religion. . . .

[The] notion that cases arising under the Establishment Clause should be decided by an inquiry into whether a "'reasonable observer'" "may" "'fairly understand'" government action to "'sen[d] a message to nonadherents that they are outsiders, not full members of the political community,'" is a [most unwelcome] addition to our tangled Establishment Clause jurisprudence. [T]he endorsement test is flawed in its fundamentals and unworkable in practice. . . .

[T]he majority's approach [threatens] to trivialize constitutional adjudication [by embracing] a jurisprudence of minutiae. A reviewing court must consider whether the city has included Santas, talking wishing wells, reindeer, or other secular symbols as "a center of attention separate from the creche." After determining whether these centers of attention are sufficiently "separate" that each "had their specific visual story to tell," the court must then measure their proximity to the creche. [M]unicipal greenery must be used with care. . . .

Before studying these cases, I had not known the full history of the menorah. . . . This history [was] likely unknown to the vast majority of people of all faiths who saw the symbol displayed in Pittsburgh [and hardly] informed the observers' view of the symbol. . . .

BACKGROUND
Sabbath Day of Rest

There has also been litigation about whether states can compel a "uniform day of rest from worldly labor" and can choose Sunday as the day of rest. In McGowan v. Maryland, 366 U.S. 420 (1961), the Court held that, although Sunday closure laws were first enacted for religious reasons, their continued application is justified by "wholly secular" reasons — to provide a universal day of rest and ensure the health and tranquility of the community. Likewise, in Estate of Thornton v. Caldor, Inc., 472 U.S. 703, 709-710 (1985), the Court upheld a law that granted employees the right not to work on their sabbaths.

Note: Requiring Swearing or Affirming a Belief in God

The states may not require, as a condition of holding office, that an applicant for the office of notary public swear or affirm his or her belief in God. *See* Torcaso v. Watkins, 367 U.S. 488 (1961).

∼ PROBLEMS ∼

1. *The Significance of Context.* In *County of Allegheny*, would it have been permissible to place a creche near the Christmas tree and the menorah? Suppose that, following the decision in *County of Allegheny*, the county decided to allow Roman Catholics to move the creche from the staircase to a place near the menorah. Regarding the display: a) Would it matter whether the creche was placed by itself or was surrounded by the same floral display as before and was accompanied by the same banner? b) Would the existence of the creche, surrounded by the floral display and the banner, affect the constitutionality of displaying the tree and the menorah? c) Would the same display be constitutional on the premises of an elementary school? In other words, might a display be constitutional in one setting but unconstitutional in another?

2. *The Living Nativity.* In LaGrange, Kentucky, members of the Grace Baptist Church annually erect a holiday creche on the courthouse lawn. Members of the church brave the cold each night to represent historical characters and thereby turn the display into a "living nativity." In evaluating the constitutionality of the display, what significance would you attach to each of these facts: a) the church (rather than the government) erects and pays for the display; b) the county judge executive and the pastor of Grace Baptist Church are present when the display is erected, and the pastor flatly states that the purpose of the display is to remind people that the holiday season is "all about Christ"; c) the government precludes all other groups from erecting displays; d) instead of prohibiting other groups from erecting displays (as in the preceding instance), the government treats the courthouse lawn as a public forum and invites all groups to erect displays (e.g.,

agnostics are allowed to place a large question mark next to the Baptist display over the objections of Christians, who claim that the question mark erodes the rights of Christians "to observe the birth of Christ"); e) the government imposes a permit requirement for displays but bans groups with objectionable ideas (e.g., the Ku Klux Klan) from erecting displays; and f) the government requires all groups that wish to erect displays to obtain a permit, but the requirements are "content neutral" and seek information relating only to such things as how long the group would like to show the display and where it would like the display to be located.

3. *High School Choirs and Religious Music.* Can a high school choir sing and play religious music at its concerts? For example, may a high school choir put on an annual Christmas concert in which it sings music with religious lyrics (e.g., "Good Christian men, rejoice," "Joy to the world! The Savior reigns," and "Come and behold Him, Born the King of angels") as well as "secular" Christmas songs (e.g., "Rudolph the Red-Nosed Reindeer")? Would it matter whether the concert is held on school premises or in a church? Is your analysis affected by the fact that 65 to 70 percent of all serious choral music is based on sacred themes or texts?

4. *Christmas Displays and the Education for a Better America Act.* In the proposed legislation, should Congress say anything about whether schools can have Christmas or Chanukah displays, or about the content of those displays?

During the last 25 years, a number of cases have involved challenges to public displays of the Ten Commandments. The first case to come to the Court was Stone v. Graham, 449 U.S. 39 (1980). In that case, a Kentucky statute required that a copy of the Ten Commandments, purchased with private contributions, be placed on the wall of each public classroom. Applying *Lemon*, the Court struck down the law, noting that "Kentucky's statute [had] no secular legislative purpose, and is therefore unconstitutional." Over the next 25 years, litigation concerning the Ten Commandments continued to percolate in the federal courts.

Van Orden v. Perry
545 U.S. 677 (2005)

Chief Justice REHNQUIST announced the judgment of the Court and delivered an opinion, in which Justice SCALIA, Justice KENNEDY, and Justice THOMAS join.

[The] 22 acres surrounding the Texas State Capitol contain 17 monuments and 21 historical markers commemorating the "people, ideals, and events that compose Texan identity."[5] The monolith challenged here stands 6-feet high and 3-feet wide. It is located to the north of the Capitol building, between the Capitol and the Supreme Court building. Its primary content is the text of the Ten

---

5. The monuments are: Heroes of the Alamo, Hood's Brigade, Confederate Soldiers, Volunteer Fireman, Terry's Texas Rangers, Texas Cowboy, Spanish-American War, Texas National Guard, Ten Commandments, Tribute to Texas School Children, Texas Pioneer Woman, The Boy Scouts' Statue of Liberty Replica, Pearl Harbor Veterans, Korean War Veterans, Soldiers of World War I, Disabled Veterans, and Texas Peace Officers.

Commandments. An eagle grasping the American flag, an eye inside of a pyramid, and two small tablets with what appears to be an ancient script are carved above the text of the Ten Commandments. Below the text are two Stars of David and the superimposed Greek letters Chi and Rho, which represent Christ. The bottom of the monument bears the inscription "PRESENTED TO THE PEOPLE AND YOUTH OF TEXAS BY THE FRATERNAL ORDER OF EAGLES OF TEXAS 1961."

[T]he State selected a site for the monument based on the recommendation of the state organization responsible for maintaining the Capitol grounds. The Eagles paid the cost of erecting the monument, the dedication of which was presided over by two state legislators.

Petitioner Thomas Van Orden is a native Texan and a resident of Austin. . . . Van Orden testified that, since 1995, he has encountered the Ten Commandments monument during his frequent visits to the Capitol grounds. His visits are typically for the purpose of using the law library in the Supreme Court building. . . . Forty years after the monument's erection and six years after Van Orden [sued] state officials [seeking] a declaration that the monument's placement violates the Establishment Clause. [T]he District Court held that the monument did not contravene the Establishment Clause [and the] Court of Appeals affirmed. . . .

Our cases, Janus like, point in two directions in applying the Establishment Clause. One face looks toward the strong role played by religion and religious traditions throughout our Nation's history. As we observed in School Dist. of Abington Township v. Schempp, 374 U.S. 203 (1963):

> It is true that religion has been closely identified with our history and government. . . . The fact that the Founding Fathers believed devotedly that there was a God and that the unalienable rights of man were rooted in Him is clearly evidenced in their writings, from the Mayflower Compact to the Constitution itself. . . . It can be truly said, therefore, that today, as in the beginning, our national life reflects a religious people who, in the words of Madison, are "earnestly praying, as [in] duty bound, that the Supreme Lawgiver of the Universe . . . guide them into every measure which may be worthy of his [blessing]."

The other face looks toward the principle that governmental intervention in religious matters can itself endanger religious freedom.

This case, like all Establishment Clause challenges, presents us with the difficulty of respecting both faces. Our institutions presuppose a Supreme Being, yet these institutions must not press religious observances upon their citizens. One face looks to the past in acknowledgment of our Nation's heritage, while the other looks to the present in demanding a separation between church and state. Reconciling these two faces requires that we neither abdicate our responsibility to maintain a division between church and state nor evince a hostility to religion by disabling the government from in some ways recognizing our religious heritage:

> When the state encourages religious instruction or cooperates with religious authorities by adjusting the schedule of public events to sectarian needs, it follows the best of our traditions. For it then respects the religious nature of our people and accommodates the public service

to their spiritual needs. To hold that it may not would be to find in the Constitution a requirement that the government show a callous indifference to religious groups. [W]e find no constitutional requirement which makes it necessary for government to be hostile to religion and to throw its weight against efforts to widen the effective scope of religious influence. Zorach v. Clauson, 343 U.S. 306 (1952).

See also Rosenberger v. Rector and Visitors of Univ. of Va., 515 U.S. 819 (1995).

These two faces are evident in representative cases both upholding and invalidating laws under the Establishment Clause. Over the last 25 years, we have sometimes pointed to Lemon v. Kurtzman, 403 U.S. 602 (1971), as providing the governing test in Establishment Clause challenges. . . .[6] Yet, just two years after *Lemon* was decided, we noted that the factors identified in *Lemon* serve as "no more than helpful signposts." Hunt v. McNair, 413 U.S. 734 (1973). Many of our recent cases simply have not applied the *Lemon* test. Others have applied it only after concluding that the challenged practice was invalid under a different Establishment Clause test. . . . Whatever may be the fate of the *Lemon* test in the larger scheme of Establishment Clause jurisprudence, we think it not useful in dealing with the sort of passive monument that Texas has erected on its Capitol grounds. Instead, our analysis is driven both by the nature of the monument and by our Nation's history.

As we explained in Lynch v. Donnelly, 465 U.S. 668 (1984): "There is an unbroken history of official acknowledgment by all three branches of government of the role of religion in American life from at least 1789." For example, both Houses passed resolutions in 1789 asking President George Washington to issue a Thanksgiving Day Proclamation to "recommend to the people of the United States a day of public thanksgiving and prayer, to be observed by acknowledging, with grateful hearts, the many and signal favors of Almighty God." 1 *Annals of Cong.* 90, 914 (1798). President Washington's proclamation directly attributed to the Supreme Being the foundations and successes of our young Nation. 1 J. Richardson, *A Compilation of the Messages and Papers of the Presidents, 1789-1897*, p. 64 (1899).

Recognition of the role of God in our Nation's heritage has also been reflected in our decisions. We have acknowledged [that] "religion has been closely identified with our history and government," and that "[t]he history of man is inseparable from the history of religion," Engel v. Vitale, 370 U.S. 421 (1962). This recognition has led us to hold that the Establishment Clause permits a state legislature to open its daily sessions with a prayer by a chaplain paid by the State. Marsh v. Chambers, 463 U.S., at 792. Such a practice, we thought, was "deeply embedded in the history and tradition of this country" [and] "it would be incongruous to interpret [the Establishment Clause] as imposing more stringent First Amendment limits on the states than the draftsmen imposed on the Federal Government." With similar reasoning, we have upheld laws, which originated from one of the Ten Commandments, that prohibited the sale of merchandise on Sunday. McGowan v. Maryland, 366 U.S. 420 (1961).

---

6. *Lemon* sets out a three-prong test: "First, the statute must have a secular legislative purpose; second, its principal or primary effect must be one that neither advances nor inhibits religion; finally, the statute must not foster 'an excessive government entanglement with religion.'"

In this case we are faced with a display of the Ten Commandments on government property outside the Texas State Capitol. Such acknowledgments of the role played by the Ten Commandments in our Nation's heritage are common throughout America. We need only look within our own Courtroom. Since 1935, Moses has stood, holding two tablets that reveal portions of the Ten Commandments written in Hebrew, among other lawgivers in the south frieze. Representations of the Ten Commandments adorn the metal gates lining the north and south sides of the Courtroom as well as the doors leading into the Courtroom. Moses also sits on the exterior east facade of the building holding the Ten Commandments tablets.

Similar acknowledgments can be seen throughout a visitor's tour of our Nation's Capital. For example, a large statue of Moses holding the Ten Commandments, alongside a statue of the Apostle Paul, has overlooked the rotunda of the Library of Congress' Jefferson Building since 1897. And the Jefferson Building's Great Reading Room contains a sculpture of a woman beside the Ten Commandments with a quote above her from the Old Testament. A medallion with two tablets depicting the Ten Commandments decorates the floor of the National Archives. Inside the Department of Justice, a statue entitled "The Spirit of Law" has two tablets representing the Ten Commandments lying at its feet. In front of the Ronald Reagan Building is another sculpture that includes a depiction of the Ten Commandments. So too a 24-foot-tall sculpture, depicting, among other things, the Ten Commandments and a cross, stands outside the federal courthouse that houses both the Court of Appeals and the District Court for the District of Columbia. Moses is also prominently featured in the Chamber of the United States House of Representatives.[7]

Our opinions, like our building, have recognized the role the Decalogue plays in America's heritage. (*See, e.g.*, McGowan v. Maryland, 366 U.S., at 442.) The Executive and Legislative Branches have also acknowledged the historical role of the Ten Commandments. These displays and recognitions of the Ten Commandments bespeak the rich American tradition of religious acknowledgments.

Of course, the Ten Commandments are religious. . . . According to Judeo-Christian belief, the Ten Commandments were given to Moses by God on Mt. Sinai. But Moses was a lawgiver as well as a religious leader. . . . Simply having religious content or promoting a message consistent with a religious doctrine does not run afoul of the Establishment Clause. *See* Lynch v. Donnelly, 465 U.S., at 680.

There are, of course, limits to the display of religious messages or symbols. For example, we held unconstitutional a Kentucky statute requiring the posting

---

7. Other examples of monuments and buildings reflecting the prominent role of religion abound. For example, the Washington, Jefferson, and Lincoln Memorials all contain explicit invocations of God's importance. The apex of the Washington Monument is inscribed "Laus Deo," which is translated to mean "Praise be to God," and multiple memorial stones in the monument contain Biblical citations. The Jefferson Memorial is engraved with three quotes from Jefferson that make God a central theme. Inscribed on the wall of the Lincoln Memorial are two of Lincoln's most famous speeches, the Gettysburg Address and his Second Inaugural Address. Both inscriptions include those speeches' extensive acknowledgments of God. The first federal monument, which was accepted by the United States in honor of sailors who died in Tripoli, noted the dates of the fallen sailors as "the year of our Lord, 1804, and in the 28 year of the independence of the United States."

of the Ten Commandments in every public schoolroom. Stone v. Graham, 449 U.S. 39 (1980) (per curiam). In the classroom context, we found that the Kentucky statute had an improper and plainly religious purpose [and] we have "been particularly vigilant in monitoring compliance with the Establishment Clause in elementary and secondary schools." Edwards v. Aguillard, 482 U.S. 578 (1987). Neither *Stone* itself nor subsequent opinions have indicated that *Stone*'s holding would extend to a legislative chamber or to capitol grounds.[8]

The placement of the Ten Commandments monument on the Texas State Capitol grounds is a far more passive use of those texts than was the case in *Stone*, where the text confronted elementary school students every day. Indeed[,] petitioner [walked] by the monument for a number of years before bringing this lawsuit. The monument is therefore also quite different from the prayers involved in *Schempp* and Lee v. Weisman. Texas has treated her Capitol grounds monuments as representing the several strands in the State's political and legal history. The inclusion of the Ten Commandments monument in this group has a dual significance, partaking of both religion and government. We cannot say that Texas' display of this monument violates the Establishment Clause of the First Amendment.

The judgment of the Court of Appeals is affirmed.

It is so ordered.

Justice SCALIA, concurring.

[I] would prefer to reach the same result by adopting an Establishment Clause jurisprudence that is in accord with our Nation's past and present practices, and that can be consistently applied — the central relevant feature of which is that there is nothing unconstitutional in a State's favoring religion generally, honoring God through public prayer and acknowledgment, or, in a nonproselytizing manner, venerating the Ten Commandments. . . .

Justice THOMAS, concurring.

[The Establishment] Clause's text and history "resis[t] incorporation" against the States. . . . Even [if] incorporated, "[e]stablishment at the founding [involved] mandatory observance or mandatory payment of taxes supporting ministers." And "government practices that have nothing to do with creating or maintaining [coercive] state establishments" simply do not "implicate the possible liberty interest of being free from coercive state establishments." [T]he Ten Commandments display at issue here is constitutional. In no sense does Texas compel petitioner Van Orden to do anything. . . . The mere presence of the monument along his path involves no coercion and thus does not violate the Establishment Clause. . . .

Justice BREYER, concurring in the judgment.

[T]he First Amendment's Religion Clauses [seek] to "assure the fullest possible scope of religious liberty and tolerance for all." They seek to avoid that

---

8. Nor does anything suggest that *Stone* would extend to displays of the Ten Commandments that lack a "plainly religious," "pre-eminent purpose." . . .

divisiveness based upon religion that promotes social conflict, sapping the strength of government and religion alike. [T]he realization of these goals means that government must "neither engage in nor compel religious practices," that it must "effect no favoritism among sects or between religion and nonreligion," and that it must "work deterrence of no religious belief." *Schempp, supra*, at 305 (concurring opinion). The government must avoid excessive interference with, or promotion of, religion. But the Establishment Clause does not compel the government to purge from the public sphere all that in any way partakes of the religious. Such absolutism is not only inconsistent with our national traditions, but would also tend to promote the kind of social conflict the Establishment Clause seeks to avoid.

[T]he Court has found no single mechanical formula that can accurately draw the constitutional line in every case. [T]ests designed to measure "neutrality" alone are insufficient. [I] see no test-related substitute for the exercise of legal judgment. [I]t must reflect and remain faithful to the underlying purposes of the Clauses, and it must take account of context and consequences measured in light of those purposes. . . .

[A] display of the tablets of the Ten Commandments can convey not simply a religious message but also a secular moral message (about proper standards of social conduct). And in certain contexts, a display of the tablets can also convey a historical message (about a historic relation between those standards and the law) — a fact that helps to explain the display of those tablets in dozens of courthouses throughout the Nation, including the Supreme Court of the United States. . . . The circumstances surrounding the display's placement on the capitol grounds and its physical setting suggest that the State itself intended [the] nonreligious aspects of the tablets' message to predominate. And the monument's 40-year history on the Texas state grounds indicates that that has been its effect. [The] Fraternal Order of Eagles, a private civic (and primarily secular) organization, while interested in the religious aspect of the Ten Commandments, sought to highlight the Commandments' role in shaping civic morality as part of that organization's efforts to combat juvenile delinquency. . . . The tablets [prominently] acknowledge that the Eagles donated the display, a factor [which] thereby further distances the State itself from the religious aspect of the Commandments' message. . . . The monument sits in a large park containing 17 monuments and 21 historical markers, all designed to illustrate the "ideals" of those who settled in Texas and of those who have lived there since that time. The setting[, and the inscription about its origin, suggests] that the State intended the display's moral message [to] predominate. . . .

[The] display is not on the grounds of a public school, where, given the impressionability of the young, government must exercise particular care in separating church and state. . . . [To invalidate this monument would] exhibit a hostility toward religion that has no place in our Establishment Clause traditions. Such a holding might well encourage disputes concerning the removal of longstanding depictions of the Ten Commandments from public buildings across the Nation. . . . I concur in the judgment of the Court.

Justice STEVENS, with whom Justice GINSBURG joins, dissenting.

[God's] Commandments may seem like wise counsel. The question before this Court, however, is whether it is counsel [that] Texas may proclaim without violating the Establishment Clause of the Constitution. If any fragment of Jefferson's metaphorical "wall of separation between church and State" is to be preserved — if there remains any meaning to the "wholesome neutrality" of which this Court's [Establishment Clause] cases speak, a negative answer to that question is mandatory. [The] Establishment Clause has created a strong presumption against the display of religious symbols on public property. [T]he practice [runs] the risk of "offend[ing] nonmembers of the faith being advertised as well as adherents who consider the particular advertisement disrespectful." *Allegheny County*, 492 U.S., at 651 (Stevens, J., concurring in part and dissenting in part).

[T]he Establishment Clause demands religious neutrality. [The] wall that separates the church from the State does not prohibit the government from acknowledging the religious beliefs and practices of the American people, nor does it require governments to hide works of art or historic memorabilia from public view just because they also have religious significance. [This] Nation's resolute commitment to neutrality with respect to religion is flatly inconsistent with the plurality's wholehearted validation of an official state endorsement of the message that there is one, and only one, God.

[The] Fraternal Order of Eagles [were] motivated by a desire to "inspire the youth" and curb juvenile delinquency by providing children with a "code of conduct or standards by which to govern their actions." [A]chieving that goal through biblical teachings injects a religious purpose into an otherwise secular endeavor. [T]he significant secular by-products [are] not the type of "secular" purposes that justify government promulgation of sacred religious messages. . . . Moreover, despite the Eagles' best efforts[,] the Ten Commandments display projects not just a religious, but an inherently sectarian message. There are many distinctive versions of the Decalogue, ascribed to by different religions and even different denominations within a particular faith. . . . In choosing to display this version of the Commandments, Texas tells the observer that the State supports this side of the doctrinal religious debate [and prescribes a] compelled code of conduct from one God, namely a Judeo-Christian God, that is rejected by prominent polytheistic sects, such as Hinduism, as well as nontheistic religions, such as Buddhism. . . . Recognizing the diversity of religious and secular beliefs held by Texans and by all Americans, it seems beyond peradventure that allowing the seat of government to serve as a stage for the propagation of an unmistakably Judeo-Christian message of piety would have the tendency to make nonmonotheists and nonbelievers "feel like [outsiders] in matters of faith, and [strangers] in the political community."

The plurality relies heavily on the fact that our Republic was founded, and has been governed since its nascence, by leaders who spoke then (and speak still) in plainly religious rhetoric. [W]hen public officials deliver public speeches, we recognize that their words are not exclusively a transmission from *the* government because those oratories have embedded within them the inherently personal views of the speaker. . . . The permanent placement of a textual religious display on state property is different in kind; it amalgamates otherwise discordant individual views into a collective statement of government approval. . . . The plurality's reliance on early religious statements and proclamations made by the Founders is also problematic because those views were not espoused at the Constitutional Convention in 1787 nor enshrined in the Constitution's text. . . . [T]o constrict narrowly the reach of the Establishment Clause to the views of the Founders [would] leave us with an unincorporated constitutional provision. [N]ot only could a State constitutionally adorn all of its public spaces with crucifixes or passages from the New Testament, it would also have full authority to prescribe the teachings of Martin Luther or Joseph Smith as *the* official state religion. . . .

[We] serve our constitutional mandate by expounding the meaning of constitutional provisions with one eye towards our Nation's history and the other fixed on its democratic aspirations. . . . The principle that guides my analysis is neutrality. The basis for that principle is firmly rooted in our Nation's history and our Constitution's text. I recognize that the requirement that government must remain neutral between religion and irreligion would have seemed foreign to some of the Framers; so too would a requirement of neutrality between Jews and Christians. Fortunately, we are not bound by the Framers' expectations — we are bound by the legal principles they enshrined in our Constitution. [The] judgment of the Court in this case stands for the proposition that the Constitution permits governmental displays of sacred religious texts. This makes a mockery of the constitutional ideal that government must remain neutral between religion and irreligion. . . .

I respectfully dissent.

Justice O'CONNOR, dissenting.

For essentially the reasons given by Justice Souter, as well as the reasons given in my concurrence in McCreary County v. American Civil Liberties Union of Ky., I respectfully dissent.

Justice SOUTER, with whom Justice STEVENS and Justice GINSBURG join, dissenting.

[A] governmental display of an obviously religious text cannot be squared with neutrality, except in a setting that plausibly indicates that the statement is not placed [with] a predominant purpose on the part of government either to adopt the religious message or to urge its acceptance by others. [A] pedestrian happening upon the monument at issue here needs no training in religious doctrine to realize that the statement of the Commandments, quoting God himself, proclaims that the will of the divine being is the source of obligation to obey the rules, including the facially secular ones. In this case, [the] text is presented to give particular prominence to the Commandments' first sectarian reference, "I am the Lord thy God." That proclamation is centered on the stone and written in slightly larger letters than the subsequent recitation. To ensure that the religious nature of the monument is clear to even the most casual passerby, the word

"Lord" appears in all capital letters (as does the word "am"), so that the most eye-catching segment of the quotation is the declaration "I AM the LORD thy God." What follows, of course, are the rules against other gods, graven images, vain swearing, and Sabbath breaking. And the full text of the fifth Commandment puts forward filial respect as a condition of long life in the land "which the Lord they God giveth thee." These "[w]ords . . . make [the] religious meaning unmistakably clear." County of Allegheny v. American Civil Liberties Union, Greater Pittsburgh Chapter, 492 U.S. 573 (1989). [T]he engraved quotation is framed by religious symbols. . . .[9] It would [be] difficult to miss the point that the government of Texas is telling everyone who sees the monument to live up to a moral code because God requires it, with both code and conception of God being [understood] as the inheritances specifically of Jews and Christians. . . .

The monument's presentation of the Commandments with religious text emphasized and enhanced stands in contrast to any number of perfectly constitutional depictions of them, the frieze of our own Courtroom providing a good example, where the figure of Moses stands among history's great lawgivers. While Moses holds the tablets of the Commandments showing some Hebrew text, no one looking at the lines of figures in marble relief is likely to see a religious purpose behind the assemblage or take away a religious message from it. Only one other depiction represents a religious leader, and the historical personages are mixed with symbols of moral and intellectual abstractions like Equity and Authority. Since Moses enjoys no especial prominence on the frieze, viewers can readily take him to be there as a lawgiver in the company of other lawgivers; and the viewers may just as naturally see the tablets of the Commandments (showing the later ones, forbidding things like killing and theft, but without the divine preface) as background from which the concept of law emerged, ultimately having a secular influence in the history of the Nation. Government may, of course, constitutionally call attention to this influence, and may post displays or erect monuments recounting this aspect of our history no less than any other, so long as there is a context and that context is historical. Hence, a display of the Commandments accompanied by an exposition of how they have influenced modern law would most likely be constitutionally unobjectionable.[10] And the Decalogue could, as

9. That the monument also surrounds the text of the Commandments with various American symbols (notably the U.S. flag and a bald eagle) only underscores the impermissibility of Texas's actions: by juxtaposing these patriotic symbols with the Commandments and other religious signs, the monument sends the message that being American means being religious (and not just being religious but also subscribing to the Commandments, i.e., practicing a monotheistic religion).

10. For similar reasons, the other displays of the Commandments that the plurality mentions, do not run afoul of the Establishment Clause. The statues of Moses and St. Paul in the Main Reading Room of the Library of Congress are 2 of 16 set in close proximity, statues that "represent men illustrious in the various forms of thought and activity. . . ." Moses and St. Paul represent religion, while the other 14 (a group that includes Beethoven, Shakespeare, Michelangelo, Columbus, and Plato) represent the nonreligious categories of philosophy, art, history, commerce, science, law, and poetry. Similarly, the sculpture of the woman beside the Decalogue in the Main Reading Room is one of 8 such figures "represent[ing] eight characteristic features of civilized life and thought," the same 8 features (7 of them nonreligious) that Moses, St. Paul, and the rest of the 16 statues represent. The inlay on the floor of the National Archives Building is one of four such discs, the collective theme of which is not religious. Rather, the discs "symbolize the various types of Government records that were to come into the National Archive." The four categories are war and defense, history, justice, and legislation. Each disc is paired with a winged figure; the disc containing the depiction of the Commandments, a depiction that, notably, omits the Commandments' text, is paired with a figure representing legislation. As for Moses's "prominen[t] featur[ing] in the Chamber of the United States House of Representatives," Moses is actually 1 of 23

Stone suggested, be integrated constitutionally into a course of study in public schools.

Texas [argues] that its monument (like Moses in the frieze) is not alone and ought to be viewed as only 1 among 17 placed on the 22 acres surrounding the state capitol. Texas [says] that the Capitol grounds are like a museum for a collection of exhibits. . . . So, for example, [the] United States does not violate the Establishment Clause by hanging Giotto's Madonna on the wall of the National Gallery. . . . But 17 monuments with no common appearance, history, or esthetic role scattered over 22 acres is not a museum, and anyone strolling around the lawn would surely take each memorial on its own terms. . . . If neutrality in religion means something, any citizen should be able to visit that civic home without having to confront religious expressions clearly meant to convey an official religious position that may be at odds with his own religion, or with rejection of religion. *See County of Allegheny*, 492 U.S., at 626 (O'Connor, J., concurring in part and concurring in judgment). . . .

[I] do not see a persuasive argument for constitutionality in the plurality's observation that Van Orden's lawsuit comes "[f]orty years after the monument's erection. . . ." It is not [that] the passage of time [is] irrelevant in Establishment Clause analysis. We have approved framing-era practices because they must originally have been understood as constitutionally permissible, e.g., Marsh v. Chambers, 463 U.S. 783 (1983), and we have recognized that Sunday laws have grown recognizably secular over time, McGowan v. Maryland, 366 U.S. 420 (1961). . . .

BACKGROUND
Justice Moore's Ten Commandments Display

Alabama Supreme Court Justice Roy Moore designed and displayed a 5,280-pound Ten Commandments monument at the Alabama Supreme Court. When a federal court held that the display constituted an establishment of religion and ordered its removal, Justice Moore defiantly ignored the court order and refused to move the monument. Ultimately, faced with contempt fines of $5,000 per day, the remaining justices of the court overruled Justice Moore and had the monument removed. In November 2003, Justice Moore was removed from the Alabama Supreme Court by an ethics panel for having "placed himself above the law." After the removal, he stated, "I have absolutely no regrets."

---

portraits encircling the House Chamber, each approximately the same size, having no religious theme. The portraits depict "men noted in history for the part they played in the evolution of what has become American law." More importantly for purposes of this case, each portrait consists only of the subject's face; the Ten Commandments appear nowhere in Moses's portrait.

∾ PROBLEMS ∾

1. *Justice Moore's Alabama Display.* After *Van Orden*, are you clear about what aspects of the Texas State Capitol display render it constitutional? Is Justice Moore's Alabama Supreme Court monument more or less objectionable? Is the Alabama monument constitutionally distinguishable from the Texas display? If so, why?

2. *Justice Moore Continued.* The trial court order requiring Justice Moore to remove the Ten Commandments monument from the Alabama Supreme Court provided that he could display the monument in his private chambers or in some other place at the court that was out of public view. Is this latter portion of the trial court order valid? Why is a display in the judge's office permissible when a public display is impermissible?

As you read the following case, consider the effect of motive on Ten Commandments cases. Would *Van Orden* have been decided differently if both Texas and the Fraternal Order of Eagles had been religiously motivated in erecting the display? Is the "reasonable observer," who happens upon the Texas Ten Commandments display, necessarily going to be aware of the motives that prompted the display? Is the "reasonable observer's" reaction going to be affected by those motives if he or she is unaware of them? In addition, think about why there is a difference in result between this case and *Van Orden* (both of which were decided on the same day). Did one justice view this display differently? If so, which one? Why?

McCreary County v. American Civil Liberties Union of Kentucky

545 U.S. 844 (2005)

Justice SOUTER delivered the opinion of the Court.

[P]etitioners McCreary County and Pulaski County, Kentucky (hereinafter Counties), put up in their respective courthouses large, gold-framed copies of an abridged text of the King James version of the Ten Commandments, including a citation to the Book of Exodus. In McCreary County, the [legislative body required] "the display [to] be posted in 'a very high traffic area' of the courthouse." In Pulaski County, [the] Commandments were hung in a ceremony presided over by the county Judge-Executive, who called them "good rules to live by" and who recounted the story of an astronaut who became convinced "there must be a divine God" after viewing the Earth from the moon. The Judge-Executive was accompanied by the pastor of his church, who called the Commandments "a creed of ethics" and told the press after the ceremony that displaying the Commandments was "one of the greatest things the judge could have done to close out the millennium." In both counties, this was the version of the Commandments posted:

Thou shalt have no other gods before me.

Thou shalt not make unto thee any graven images.

Thou shalt not take the name of the Lord thy God in vain.

Remember the sabbath day, to keep it holy.

Honor thy father and thy mother.

Thou shalt not kill.

Thou shalt not commit adultery.

Thou shalt not steal.

Thou shalt not bear false witness.

Thou shalt not covet.

Exodus 20:3-17.

In each county, the hallway display was "readily visible [to] county citizens who use the courthouse to conduct their civic business, to obtain or renew driver's licenses and permits, to register cars, to pay local taxes, and to register to vote."

[R]espondents American Civil Liberties Union of Kentucky et al. sued the Counties in Federal District Court under 42 U.S.C. §1983, and sought a preliminary injunction against [the] displays. [T]he legislative body of each County authorized a second, expanded display, by nearly identical resolutions reciting that the Ten Commandments are "the precedent legal code upon which the civil and criminal codes [of] Kentucky are founded," and stating[:] that "the Ten Commandments are codified in Kentucky's civil and criminal laws"; that the Kentucky House of Representatives had in 1993 "voted unanimously [to adjourn] in remembrance and honor of Jesus Christ, the Prince of Ethics"; that the "County Judge [and] magistrates agree with the arguments set out by Judge [Roy] Moore" in defense of his "display [of] the Ten Commandments in his courtroom"; and that the "Founding Father[s] [had an] explicit understanding of the duty of elected officials to publicly acknowledge God as the source of America's strength and direction."

As directed by the resolutions, the Counties expanded the displays of the Ten Commandments in their locations [along] with copies of the resolution, which instructed that it, too, be posted. In addition to the first display's large framed copy of the edited King James version of the Commandments, the second included eight other documents in smaller frames, each either having a religious theme or excerpted to highlight a religious element. The documents were the "endowed by their Creator" passage from the Declaration of Independence; the Preamble to the Constitution of Kentucky; the national motto, "In God We Trust"; a page from the Congressional Record of February 2, 1983, proclaiming the Year of the Bible and including a statement of the Ten Commandments; a proclamation by President Abraham Lincoln designating April 30, 1863, a National Day of Prayer and Humiliation; an excerpt from President Lincoln's "Reply to Loyal Colored People of Baltimore upon Presentation of a Bible," reading that "[t]he Bible is the best gift God has ever given to man"; a proclamation by President Reagan marking 1983 the Year of the Bible; and the Mayflower Compact.

[T]he District Court entered a preliminary injunction [ordering] that the "display [be] removed from [each] County Courthouse IMMEDIATELY" and that no county official "erect or cause to be erected similar displays." The court's analysis [followed] the three-part formulation [in] Lemon v. Kurtzman, 403 U.S. 602 (1971). . . . The Counties [then] installed another display in each courthouse, the third within a year. No new resolution authorized this one, nor did the Counties repeal the resolutions that preceded the second. The posting consists of nine framed documents of equal size, one of them setting out the Ten Commandments explicitly identified as the "King James Version" at Exodus 20:3-17 and quoted at greater length than before:

> Thou shalt have no other gods before me.
>
> Thou shalt not make unto thee any graven image, or any likeness of any thing that is in heaven above, or that is in the earth beneath, or that is in the water underneath the earth: Thou shalt not bow down thyself to them, nor serve them: for I the LORD thy God am a jealous God, visiting the iniquity of the fathers upon the children unto the third and fourth generation of them that hate me.
>
> Thou shalt not take the name of the LORD thy God in vain: for the LORD will not hold him guiltless that taketh his name in vain.
>
> Remember the sabbath day, to keep it holy.
>
> Honour thy father and thy mother: that thy days may be long upon the land which the LORD thy God giveth thee.
>
> Thou shalt not kill.
>
> Thou shalt not commit adultery.
>
> Thou shalt not steal.
>
> Thou shalt not bear false witness against thy neighbour.
>
> Thou shalt not covet thy neighbour's house, thou shalt not covet th[y] neighbor's wife, nor his manservant, nor his maidservant, nor his ox, nor his ass, nor anything that is th[y] neighbour's.

Assembled with the Commandments are framed copies of the Magna Carta, the Declaration of Independence, the Bill of Rights, the lyrics of the Star Spangled Banner, the Mayflower Compact, the National Motto, the Preamble to the Kentucky Constitution, and a picture of Lady Justice. The collection is entitled "The Foundations of American Law and Government Display" and each document comes with a statement about its historical and legal significance. The comment on the Ten Commandments reads:

> The Ten Commandments have profoundly influenced the formation of Western legal thought and the formation of our country. That influence is clearly seen in the Declaration of Independence, which declared that "We hold these truths to be self-evident, that all men are created equal, that they are endowed by their Creator with certain unalienable Rights, that among these are Life, Liberty, and the pursuit of Happiness." The Ten Commandments provide the moral background of the Declaration of Independence and the foundation of our legal tradition.

The ACLU moved to supplement the preliminary injunction to enjoin the Counties' third display,[11] and the Counties responded with several explanations for the new version, including desires "to demonstrate that the Ten Commandments were part of the foundation of American Law and Government" and "to educate the citizens of the county regarding some of the documents that played a significant role in the foundation of our system of law and government." [T]he trial court supplemented the injunction, and [the] Court of Appeals for the Sixth Circuit affirmed. [We] granted certiorari [and] now affirm.

II

Twenty-five years ago in a case prompted by posting the Ten Commandments in Kentucky's public schools, this Court recognized that the Commandments "are undeniably a sacred text in the Jewish and Christian faiths" and held that their display in public classrooms violated the First Amendment's bar against establishment of religion. [Stone v. Graham, 449 U.S. 39 (1980) (per curiam),] found a predominantly religious purpose in the government's posting of the Commandments, given their prominence as "an instrument of religion." [S]ince *Lemon*[,] looking to whether government action has "a secular legislative purpose" has been a common, albeit seldom dispositive, element of our cases. Though we have found government action motivated by an illegitimate purpose only four times since *Lemon*, "[it] nevertheless serves an important function." Wallace v. Jaffree, 472 U.S. 38 (1985) (O'Connor, J., concurring in judgment).

The touchstone for our analysis is the principle that the "First Amendment mandates governmental neutrality between religion and religion, and between religion and nonreligion." Epperson v. Arkansas, 393 U.S. 97 (1968). . . . Manifesting a purpose to favor one faith over another, or adherence to religion generally, clashes with the "understanding, reached [after] decades of religious war, that liberty and social stability demand a religious tolerance that respects the religious views of all citizens. . . ." Zelman v. Simmons-Harris, 536 U.S. 639 (2002) (Breyer, J., dissenting). By showing a purpose to favor religion, the government "sends [the] message [to] nonadherents 'that they are outsiders, not full members of the political community, and an accompanying message to adherents that they are insiders, favored members. . . .'" Santa Fe Independent School Dist. v. Doe, 530 U.S. 290 (2000) (quoting Lynch v. Donnelly, 465 U.S. 668 (1984) (O'Connor, J., concurring)).

[T]he purpose apparent from government action can have an impact more significant than the result expressly decreed: when the government maintains Sunday closing laws, it advances religion only minimally because many working people would take the day as one of rest regardless, but if the government justified its decision with a stated desire for all Americans to honor Christ, the divisive thrust of the official action would be inescapable. . . .

[T]he Counties [argue that] true "purpose" is unknowable, and its search merely an excuse for courts to act selectively and unpredictably in picking out

11. Before the District Court issued the modified injunction, the Counties removed the label of "King James Version" and the citation to Exodus.

evidence of subjective intent. . . . Examination of purpose is a staple of statutory interpretation [and] governmental purpose is a key element of a good deal of constitutional doctrine, e.g., Church of Lukumi Babalu Aye, Inc. v. Hialeah, 508 U.S. 520 (1993). [S]crutinizing purpose does make practical sense [where] an understanding of official objective emerges from readily discoverable fact, without any judicial psychoanalysis. . . . The eyes that look to purpose belong to an "objective observer," one who takes account of the traditional external signs that show up in the "text, legislative history, and implementation of the statute," or comparable official act. There [is] nothing hinting at an unpredictable or disingenuous exercise when a court enquires into purpose. . . .

The cases [point] to the straightforward nature of the test. In *Wallace*, [we] inferred purpose from a change of wording from an earlier statute to a later one, each dealing with prayer in schools. [I]n *Edwards* [v. Aguillard, 482 U.S. 578 (1987),] we relied on a statute's text and the detailed public comments of its sponsor, when we sought the purpose of a state law requiring creationism to be taught alongside evolution. [In] *Stone*, the Court held that the "[p]osting of religious texts on the wall serve[d] [no] educational function. . . ." In each case, [the] openly available data supported a commonsense conclusion that a religious objective permeated the government's action. [I]n some of the cases in which establishment complaints failed, savvy officials had disguised their religious intent so cleverly that the objective observer just missed it. But that is no reason for great constitutional concern. . . . A secret motive stirs up no strife and does nothing to make outsiders of nonadherents, and it suffices to wait and see whether such government action [has] the illegitimate effect of advancing religion.

[The] Counties would read the cases as if the purpose enquiry were so naive that any transparent claim to secularity would satisfy it. . . . The Court often does accept governmental statements of purpose, in keeping with the respect owed in the first instance to such official claims. But in those unusual cases where the claim was an apparent sham, or the secular purpose secondary, the unsurprising results have been findings of no adequate secular object. . . . The Counties [also] argue that purpose in a case like this one should be inferred, if at all, only from [the] last in a series of governmental actions. [R]easonable observers have reasonable memories, and our precedents sensibly forbid an observer "to turn a blind eye to the context in which [the] policy arose."[12] Santa Fe Independent School Dist. v. Doe, *supra*, at 315.

III

[On an] appeal from a preliminary injunction[, we] review the District Court's legal rulings *de novo,* and its ultimate conclusion for abuse of discretion. . . . *Stone* recognized that the Commandments are an "instrument of religion" and [could] presumptively be understood as meant to advance religion. . . . But *Stone* did

12. One consequence of taking account [of] purpose [is] that the same government action may be constitutional if taken in the first instance and unconstitutional if it has a sectarian heritage. This presents no incongruity. [I]t will matter to objective observers whether posting the Commandments follows on the heels of displays motivated by sectarianism, or whether it lacks a history demonstrating that purpose. . . .

[not] decide the constitutionality of every possible way the Commandments might be set out by the government, and under the Establishment Clause detail is key. County of Allegheny v. American Civil Liberties Union, Greater Pittsburgh Chapter, 492 U.S. 573 (1989). Hence, we look to [the] progression leading up to the third display of the Commandments.

The display rejected in *Stone* had two obvious similarities to the first one [here]: both set out a text of the Commandments as distinct from any traditionally symbolic representation, and each stood alone, not part of an arguably secular display. *Stone* stressed the significance of integrating the Commandments into a secular scheme to forestall the broadcast of an otherwise clearly religious message, and for good reason, the Commandments being a central point of reference in the religious and moral history of Jews and Christians. They proclaim the existence of a monotheistic god (no other gods). They regulate details of religious obligation (no graven images, no sabbath breaking, no vain oath swearing). And they unmistakably rest even the universally accepted prohibitions (as against murder, theft, and the like) on the sanction of the divinity proclaimed at the beginning of the text. Displaying that text is thus different from a symbolic depiction, like tablets with 10 roman numerals, which could be seen as alluding to a general notion of law, not a sectarian conception of faith. Where the text is set out, the insistence of the religious message is hard to avoid in the absence of a context plausibly suggesting a message going beyond an excuse to promote the religious point of view. [The] Counties' solo exhibit here did nothing more to counter the sectarian implication than the postings at issue in *Stone*. [T]he posting by the Counties lacked even the *Stone* display's implausible disclaimer that the Commandments were set out to show their effect on the civil law. What is more, at the ceremony for posting the framed Commandments in Pulaski County, the county executive was accompanied by his pastor, who testified to the certainty of the existence of God. The reasonable observer could only think that the Counties meant to emphasize and celebrate the Commandments' religious message. . . . The point is simply that the original text viewed in its entirety is an unmistakably religious statement dealing with religious obligations and with morality subject to religious sanction. When the government initiates an effort to place this statement alone in public view, a religious object is unmistakable.

Once the Counties were sued, they modified the exhibits [to include] a series of American historical documents with theistic and Christian references, which were to be posted in order to furnish a setting for displaying the Ten Commandments and any "other Kentucky and American historical documen[t]" without raising concern about "any Christian or religious references" in them. [T]he resolutions expressed support for an Alabama judge who posted the Commandments in his courtroom, and cited the fact the Kentucky Legislature once adjourned a session in honor of "Jesus Christ, Prince of Ethics."

In this second display, [the] Commandments were not hung in isolation, merely leaving the Counties' purpose to emerge from the pervasively religious text of the Commandments themselves. Instead, the second version was required to include the statement of the government's purpose expressly set out in the county resolutions, and underscored it by juxtaposing the Commandments to other documents with highlighted references to God as their sole common element. The display's unstinting focus was on religious passages, showing that the Counties were posting the Commandments precisely because of their sectarian content. That demonstration of the government's objective was enhanced by serial religious references and the accompanying resolution's claim about the embodiment of ethics in Christ. Together, the display and resolution presented an indisputable, and undisputed, showing of an impermissible purpose. [T]he Counties make no attempt to defend their undeniable objective, but instead hopefully describe version two as "dead and buried." Their refusal to defend the second display is understandable, but the reasonable observer could not forget it.

After the Counties changed lawyers, they mounted a third display, without a new resolution or repeal of the old one. The result was the "Foundations of American Law and Government" exhibit, which placed the Commandments in the company of other documents the Counties thought especially significant in the historical foundation of American government. [T]he Counties cited several new purposes for the third version, including a desire "to educate the citizens of the county regarding some of the documents that played a significant role in the foundation of our system of law and government."[13] [These] new statements of purpose were presented only as a litigating position, there being no further authorizing action by the Counties' governing boards. [T]he extraordinary resolutions for the second display [were] not repealed or otherwise repudiated. [T]he sectarian spirit of [the] resolution found enhanced expression in the third display, which quoted more of the purely religious language of the Commandments than the first two displays had done; for additions ("I the LORD thy God am a jealous God"); ("the LORD will not hold him guiltless that taketh his name in vain"); and ("that thy days may be long upon the land which the LORD thy God giveth thee"). No reasonable observer could swallow the claim that the Counties had cast off the objective so unmistakable in the earlier displays.

Nor did the selection of posted material suggest a clear theme that might prevail over evidence of the continuing religious object. In a collection of documents said to be "foundational" to American government, it is at least odd to include a patriotic anthem, but to omit the Fourteenth Amendment, the most significant structural provision adopted since the original Framing. And it is no less baffling to leave out the original Constitution of 1787 while quoting the 1215 Magna Carta. . . . If an observer found these choices and omissions perplexing in isolation, he would be puzzled [when] he read the Declaration of Independence seeking confirmation for the Counties' posted explanation that the "Ten Commandments" influence is clearly seen in the Declaration, in fact the observer would find that the Commandments are sanctioned as divine imperatives, while the Declaration of Independence holds that the authority of government to

---

13. The Counties' other purposes were: "to erect a display containing the Ten Commandments that is constitutional; [to] demonstrate that the Ten Commandments were part of the foundation of American Law and Government; [to include the Ten Commandments] as part of the display for their significance in providing the moral background of the Declaration of Independence and the foundation of our legal tradition."

enforce the law derives "from the consent of the governed." If the observer had not thrown up his hands, he would probably suspect that the Counties were simply reaching for any way to keep a religious document on the walls of courthouses. . . .

In holding [that] the Counties' purpose had not changed at the third stage, we do not decide that the Counties' past actions forever taint any effort on their part to deal with the subject matter. We hold only that [an] implausible claim that governmental purpose has changed should not carry the day in a court of law. . . . Nor do we have occasion here to hold that a sacred text can never be integrated constitutionally into a governmental display on the subject of law, or American history. [O]ur own courtroom frieze was deliberately designed in the exercise of governmental authority so as to include the figure of Moses holding tablets exhibiting a portion of the Hebrew text of the later, secularly phrased Commandments; in the company of 17 other lawgivers, most of them secular figures, there is no risk that Moses would strike an observer as evidence that the National Government was violating neutrality in religion.

IV

The importance of neutrality as an interpretive guide is no less true now than it was when the Court broached the principle in Everson v. Board of Ed. of Ewing, 330 U.S. 1 (1947). . . . The First Amendment contains no textual definition of "establishment," and the term is certainly not self-defining. No one contends that the prohibition of establishment stops at a designation of a national (or with Fourteenth Amendment incorporation, a state) church, but nothing in the text says just how much more it covers. . . . The prohibition on establishment covers a variety of issues from prayer in widely varying government settings, to financial aid for religious individuals and institutions, to comment on religious questions. In these varied settings, issues [of] interpreting inexact Establishment Clause language, like difficult interpretative issues generally, arise from the tension of competing values, each constitutionally respectable, but none open to realization to the logical limit.

The First Amendment has not one but two clauses tied to "religion," the second forbidding any prohibition on the "the free exercise thereof," and sometimes, the two clauses compete. [L]imits on governmental action that might make sense as a way to avoid establishment could arguably limit freedom of speech when the speaking is done under government auspices. Rosenberger v. Rector and Visitors of Univ. of Va., 515 U.S. 819 (1995). [T]he principle of neutrality has provided a good sense of direction: the government may not favor one religion over another, or religion over irreligion, religious choice being the prerogative of individuals under the Free Exercise Clause. . . . The Framers and the citizens of their time intended not only to protect the integrity of individual conscience in religious matters, but to guard against the civic divisiveness that follows when the Government weighs in on one side of religious debate; nothing does a better job of roiling society, a point that needed no explanation to the descendants of English Puritans and Cavaliers (or Massachusetts Puritans and Baptists). *E.g.,*

Everson, supra, at 8. . . . To be sure, [an] appeal to neutrality alone cannot possibly lay every issue to rest, or tell us what issues on the margins are substantial enough for constitutional significance. . . . But invoking neutrality is a prudent way of keeping sight of something the Framers of the First Amendment thought important.

The dissent [puts] forward a limitation on the application of the neutrality principle, with citations to historical evidence said to show that the Framers understood the ban on establishment of religion as sufficiently narrow to allow the government to espouse submission to the divine will. The dissent identifies God as the God of monotheism, all of whose three principal strains (Jewish, Christian, and Muslim) acknowledge the religious importance of the Ten Commandments. On the dissent's view, [even] rigorous espousal of a common element of this common monotheism, is consistent with the establishment ban. [S]ome of the Framers thought some endorsement of religion was compatible with the establishment ban. [T]here is also evidence supporting the proposition that the Framers intended the Establishment Clause to require governmental neutrality in matters of religion, including neutrality in statements acknowledging religion. The very language of the Establishment Clause represented a significant departure from early drafts that merely prohibited a single national religion, and, the final language instead "extended [the] prohibition to state support for 'religion' in general." *See* Lee v. Weisman, 505 U.S. 577 (1992) (Souter, J., concurring).

The historical record, moreover, is complicated beyond the dissent's account by the writings and practices of figures no less influential than Thomas Jefferson and James Madison. Jefferson, for example, refused to issue Thanksgiving Proclamations because he believed that they violated the Constitution. And Madison, whom the dissent claims as supporting its thesis, criticized Virginia's general assessment tax not just because it required people to donate "three pence" to religion, but because "it is itself a signal of persecution. . . ." [T]here was no common understanding about the limits of the establishment prohibition, and the dissent's conclusion that its narrower view was the original understanding, stretches the evidence beyond tensile capacity. What the evidence does show is a group of statesmen [who] proposed a guarantee with contours not wholly worked out, leaving the Establishment Clause with edges still to be determined. . . .

[T]he dissent says that the deity the Framers had in mind was the God of monotheism, with the consequence that government may espouse a tenet of traditional monotheism. This is truly a remarkable view. [H]istory shows that the religion of concern to the Framers was not that of the monotheistic faiths generally, but Christianity in particular. . . . The Framers would [almost] certainly object to the dissent's unstated reasoning that because Christianity was a monotheistic "religion," monotheism with Mosaic antecedents should be a touchstone of establishment interpretation. [T]he divisiveness of religion in current public life is inescapable. This is no time to deny the prudence of understanding the Establishment Clause to require the Government to stay neutral on religious belief, which is reserved for the conscience of the individual.

V

Given the ample support for the District Court's finding of a predominantly religious purpose behind the Counties' third display, we affirm the Sixth Circuit in upholding the preliminary injunction.

It is so ordered.

Justice O'CONNOR, concurring.

[T]he Court correctly finds an Establishment Clause violation. The purpose behind the counties' display [conveys] an unmistakable message of endorsement to the reasonable observer. . . . [M]any Americans find the Commandments in accord with their personal beliefs. But we do not count heads before enforcing the First Amendment. . . .

Justice SCALIA, with whom THE CHIEF JUSTICE and Justice THOMAS join, and with whom Justice KENNEDY joins as to Parts II and III, dissenting.

I would uphold the McCreary County and Pulaski County, Kentucky's displays of the Ten Commandments. . . . George Washington added to the form of Presidential oath [the] concluding words "so help me God." The Supreme Court under John Marshall opened its sessions with the prayer, "God save the United States and this Honorable Court." The First Congress instituted the practice of beginning its legislative sessions with a prayer. The same week that Congress submitted the Establishment Clause as part of the Bill of Rights for ratification by the States, it enacted legislation providing for paid chaplains in the House and Senate. The day after the First Amendment was proposed, [Congress] requested the President to proclaim "a day of public thanksgiving and prayer, to be observed, by acknowledging, with grateful hearts, the many and signal favours of Almighty God." President Washington offered the first Thanksgiving Proclamation shortly thereafter [on] behalf of the American people "to the service of that great and glorious Being who is the beneficent author of all the good that is, that was, or that will be," thus beginning a tradition of offering gratitude to God that continues today. The same Congress also reenacted the Northwest Territory Ordinance of 1787 [which] provided: "Religion, morality, and knowledge, being necessary to good government and the happiness of mankind, schools and the means of education shall forever be encouraged." And of course the First Amendment itself accords religion (and no other manner of belief) special constitutional protection.

[Those] who wrote the Constitution believed that morality was essential to the well-being of society and that encouragement of religion was the best way to foster morality. . . . President Washington opened his Presidency with a prayer, and reminded his fellow citizens [that] "reason and experience [forbid] us to expect that National morality can prevail in exclusion of religious principle." Farewell Address (1796), reprinted in 35 *Writings of George Washington* (J. Fitzpatrick ed. 1940). President John Adams wrote to the Massachusetts Militia, "[o]ur Constitution was made only for a moral and religious people. . . ." Thomas Jefferson concluded his second inaugural address by inviting his audience to pray. . . . James Madison, in his first inaugural address, [placed] his confidence "in the guardianship and guidance of that Almighty Being whose power regulates the destiny of nations, whose blessings have been so conspicuously dispensed to this rising Republic, and to whom we are bound to address our devout gratitude for the past, as well as our fervent supplications and best hopes for the future."

Nor have the views of our people on this matter significantly changed. Presidents continue to conclude the Presidential oath with the words "so help me God." Our legislatures, state and national, continue to open their sessions with prayer led by official chaplains. The sessions of this Court continue to open with the prayer "God save the United States and this Honorable Court." Invocation of the Almighty by our public figures, at all levels of government, remains commonplace. Our coinage bears the motto "IN GOD WE TRUST." And our Pledge of Allegiance contains the acknowledgment that we are a Nation "under God." As one of our Supreme Court opinions rightly observed, "We are a religious people whose institutions presuppose a Supreme Being." Zorach v. Clauson, 343 U.S. 306 (1952).

With all of this reality (and much more) staring it in the face, how can the Court *possibly* assert that "the First Amendment mandates governmental neutrality [between] religion and nonreligion," and that "[m]anifesting a purpose to [favor] adherence to religion generally," is unconstitutional? Who says so? Surely not the words of the Constitution. Surely not the history and traditions that reflect our society's constant understanding of those words. Surely not even the current sense of our society. . . . What distinguishes the rule of law from the dictatorship of a shifting Supreme Court majority is the absolutely indispensable requirement that judicial opinions be grounded in consistently applied principle. [W]hen the government relieves churches from the obligation to pay property taxes, when it allows students to absent themselves from public school to take religious classes, and when it exempts religious organizations from generally applicable prohibitions of religious discrimination, it surely means to bestow a benefit on religious practice—but we have approved it. Indeed, we have even approved (post-*Lemon*) government-led prayer to God. [*See*] Marsh v. Chambers, *supra*. . . .

[If] religion in the public forum had to be entirely nondenominational, there could be no religion in the public forum at all. One cannot say the word "God," or "the Almighty," one cannot offer public supplication or thanksgiving, without contradicting the beliefs of some people that there are many gods, or that God or the gods pay no attention to human affairs. [I]t is entirely clear from our Nation's historical practices that the Establishment Clause permits this disregard of polytheists and believers in unconcerned deities, just as it permits the disregard of devout atheists. The Thanksgiving Proclamation issued by George Washington [was] nondenominational—but it was monotheistic. In *Marsh*, we said that the fact the particular prayers offered in the Nebraska Legislature were "in the Judeo-Christian tradition," posed no additional problem, because "there is no indication that the prayer opportunity has been exploited to proselytize or advance any one, or to disparage any other, faith or belief."

Historical practices thus demonstrate that there is a distance between the acknowledgment of a single Creator and the establishment of a religion. . . . The three most popular religions in the United States, Christianity, Judaism, and

Islam—[which] account for 97.7% of all believers—are monotheistic. All of them, moreover (Islam included), believe that the Ten Commandments were given by God to Moses, and are divine prescriptions for a virtuous life. Publicly honoring the Ten Commandments is thus indistinguishable, insofar as discriminating against other religions is concerned, from publicly honoring God. Both practices are recognized across such a broad and diverse range of the population—from Christians to Muslims—that they cannot be reasonably understood as a government endorsement of a particular religious viewpoint.[14]

[Justice Stevens argues that] "[r]eliance on early religious proclamations and statements made by the Founders [is] problematic," "[because] those views were not espoused at the Constitutional Convention in 1787 nor enshrined in the Constitution's text." But [I] have relied primarily upon official acts and official proclamations of the United States or of the component branches of its Government. . . . What is more probative of the meaning of the Establishment Clause than the actions of the very Congress that proposed it, and of the first President charged with observing it?

Justice Stevens also appeals to the undoubted fact that some in the founding generation thought that the Religion Clauses of the First Amendment should have a *narrower* meaning, protecting only the Christian religion or perhaps only Protestantism. . . . *All* of the actions of Washington and the First Congress upon which I have relied, virtually all Thanksgiving Proclamations throughout our history, and *all* the other examples of our Government's favoring religion that I have cited, have invoked God, but not Jesus Christ. . . .

Justice Stevens says that if one is serious about following the original understanding of the Establishment Clause, he must repudiate its incorporation into the Fourteenth Amendment, and hold that it does not apply against the States. . . . The notion that incorporation empties the incorporated provisions of their original meaning has no support in either reason or precedent.

Justice Stevens argues that original meaning should not be the touchstone anyway, but that we should rather "expoun[d] the meaning of constitutional provisions with one eye towards our Nation's history and the other fixed on its democratic aspirations." This is not the place to debate the merits of the "living Constitution. . . ." Even assuming [that] the meaning of the Constitution ought to change according to "democratic aspirations," why are those aspirations to be found in Justices' notions of what the Establishment Clause ought to mean, rather than in the democratically adopted dispositions of our current society? . . .

Finally, I must respond to Justice Stevens' assertion that I would "marginaliz[e] the belief systems of more than 7 million Americans" who adhere to religions that are not monotheistic. . . . The beliefs of those citizens are entirely protected by the Free Exercise Clause, and by those aspects of the Establishment Clause that do not relate to government acknowledgment of the Creator. [I]n the context of public acknowledgments of God there are legitimate *competing* interests: On the

14. This is not to say that a display of the Ten Commandments could never constitute an impermissible endorsement of a particular religious view. The Establishment Clause would prohibit, for example, governmental endorsement of a particular version of the Decalogue as authoritative. . . .

one hand, the interest of that minority in not feeling "excluded"; but on the other, the interest of the overwhelming majority of religious believers in being able to give God thanks and supplication *as a people,* and with respect to our national endeavors. Our national tradition has resolved that conflict in favor of the majority. . . .

As bad as the *Lemon* test is, it is worse for the fact that [its] seemingly simple mandates have been manipulated to fit whatever result the Court aimed to achieve. Today's opinion is no different. . . . Even accepting the Court's *Lemon*-based premises, the displays at issue here were constitutional. . . . To any person who happened to walk down the hallway of the McCreary or Pulaski County Courthouse[,] the displays must have seemed unremarkable — if indeed they were noticed at all. The walls of both courthouses were already lined with historical documents and other assorted portraits. . . . The frame holding the Ten Commandments was of the same size and had the same appearance as that which held each of the other documents. . . . Posted with the documents was a plaque, identifying the display, and explaining that it "contains documents that played a significant role in the foundation of our system of law and government." The explanation related to the Ten Commandments was third in the list of nine and did not serve to distinguish it from the other documents. . . .

[T]he Foundations Displays manifested the purely secular purpose that the Counties asserted before the District Court: "to display documents that played a significant role in the foundation of our system of law and government." [Even] an isolated display of the Decalogue conveys, at worst, "an equivocal message, perhaps of respect for Judaism, for religion in general, or for law." But when the Ten Commandments appear alongside other documents of secular significance in a display devoted to the foundations of American law and government, the context communicates that the Ten Commandments are included, not to teach their binding nature as a religious text, but to show their unique contribution to the development of the legal system. . . . The Supreme Court Building itself includes depictions of Moses with the Ten Commandments in the Courtroom and on the east pediment of the building, and symbols of the Ten Commandments "adorn the metal gates lining the north and south sides of the Courtroom as well as the doors leading into the Courtroom." Similar depictions of the Decalogue appear on public buildings and monuments throughout our Nation's Capital. The frequency of these displays testifies to the popular understanding that the Ten Commandments are a foundation of the rule of law, and a symbol of the role that religion played, and continues to play, in our system of government.

[Displays] erected in silence (and under the direction of good legal advice) are permissible, while those hung after discussion and debate are deemed unconstitutional. Reduction of the Establishment Clause to such minutiae trivializes the Clause's protection against religious establishment. . . . If [the] Commandments have a proper place in our civic history, even placing them by themselves can be civically motivated — especially when they are placed, not in a school[,] but in a courthouse. . . .

The Court has in the past prohibited government actions that "proselytize or advance any one, [or] disparage any other, faith or belief," or that apply some level of coercion. . . . The passive display of the Ten Commandments, even standing alone, does not begin to do either. . . . Nor is it the case that a solo display of the Ten Commandments advances any one faith. They are assuredly a religious symbol, but they are not so closely associated with a single religious belief that their display can reasonably be understood as preferring one religious sect over another. The Ten Commandments are recognized by Judaism, Christianity, and Islam alike as divinely given. . . .

The Court also points to the Counties' second displays, which featured a number of statements in historical documents reflecting a religious influence, and the resolutions that accompanied their erection, as evidence of an impermissible religious purpose. [All] it necessarily shows is that the exhibit was meant to focus upon the historic role of religious belief in our national life—which is entirely permissible. And the same can be said of the resolution. . . .

Turning at last to the displays actually at issue in this case, the Court faults the Counties for not *repealing* the resolution expressing what the Court believes to be an impermissible intent. [I]t is unlikely that a reasonable observer *would even have been aware* of the resolutions. [A] plaque next to the documents informed all who passed by that each display "contains documents that played a significant role in the foundation of our system of law and government." [T]here was no reason for the Counties to repeal or repudiate the resolutions adopted with the hanging of the second displays, since they related *only to the second displays*. . . . I would reverse the judgment. . . .

Notes and Questions

1. *The Church Veto.* In Larkin v. Grendel's Den, Inc., 459 U.S. 116 (1982), a Massachusetts law vested in the governing bodies of churches and schools the power effectively to veto applications for liquor licenses within a 500-foot radius of the church or school. The Court struck down the law: "§16C is not simply a legislative exercise of zoning power. [T]he statute, by delegating a governmental power to religious institutions, inescapably implicates the Establishment Clause. . . . [T]he mere appearance of a joint exercise of legislative authority by Church and State provides a significant symbolic benefit to religion in the minds of some by reason of the power conferred. . . . [The Act] substitutes the unilateral and absolute power of a church for the reasoned decisionmaking of a public legislative body acting on evidence and guided by standards." Justice Rehnquist dissented: "[The state does not] 'advance' religion by making provision for those who wish to engage in religious activities [to] be unmolested by activities at a neighboring bar or tavern. . . ."

2. *The Significance of Text.* Should it matter whether a Ten Commandments display includes an *English* version of the text of the Commandments? Would the frieze on the wall of the U.S. Supreme Court be unconstitutional if it included the

actual words of the Ten Commandments in English rather than in Hebrew? What significance do you attach to the fact that *Van Orden* contained the words of the Ten Commandments but nonetheless was upheld?

3. *The Latin Cross.* In Salazar v. Buono, 130 S.Ct. 1803 (2010), the Court dealt with a Latin Cross that had been erected on federal land in a remote section of the Mojave Desert in 1934, which had been designated a national memorial, and the government's decision to transfer the cross and the land on which it sits to a private party in exchange for other property. Suit was brought by a retired U.S. Park Service employee who alleged a violation of the Establishment Clause, and who sought injunctive relief to remove the cross. The Court, in a plurality opinion, reversed and remanded, but indicated that the transfer statute might be valid because it makes the land private, and the Court emphasized that the transfer might be regarded as nothing more than an accommodation of religion. In any event, the Court noted that the "goal of avoiding governmental endorsement does not require eradication of all religious symbols in the public realm," but "leaves room to accommodate divergent values within a constitutionally permissible framework."

∽ PROBLEMS ∽

1. *The Ten Commandments and the Education for a Better America Act.* What, if anything, should Congress say in the proposed legislation about whether schools may (or may not) erect displays of the Ten Commandments? Would it be permissible for the Act to allow parochial schools that receive federal funding to erect such displays?

2. *More on the Ten Commandments.* Suppose that, following the decision in *McCreary County,* the County decides to post a new display. Before doing so, the County specifically and unequivocally repudiates all religious motives in a proclamation. However, the display is the same display that was invalidated in the *McCreary County* case. *See* Peter Smith, "Commandments Case Back: 2 Counties Contend Motives Changed," *The Courier-Journal,* B-1, c. 2-5 (Aug. 7, 2008). Is the new display permissible under the Establishment Clause?

3. *More on the Ten Commandments.* Suppose that another Kentucky county, Jefferson County (where Louisville is located), decides to erect a display that is similar to the third display in *McCreary County.* However, it makes no mention of the religious aspects of the display and otherwise expresses no religious purpose. Instead, Jefferson County focuses on the secular aspects of the Ten Commandments as reflected in the *Van Orden* and *McCreary County* opinions. Would the display be constitutional?

4. *Good Friday Closings.* Is it permissible for Jefferson County, Kentucky, to close all county offices on Good Friday? The county designates that day as a "spring holiday." Is such a closing permissible? What significance would you attach to the fact that a high percentage of residents are Christian, and absenteeism on Good Friday has been a recurring problem?

B. THE FREE EXERCISE CLAUSE

The American colonists demanded protections for religious freedom because of a history of religious persecution in Europe and in the American colonies. These demands led to the inclusion of the Free Exercise Clause in the First Amendment. *See* Everson v. Board of Education, 330 U.S. 1 (1947). Because there was such widespread agreement about the need for religious freedom, the Framers left little evidence of their intent regarding the meaning of the Free Exercise Clause. As a result, although there is widespread agreement that the clause protects religious thought, there is uncertainty about the extent to which it protects religious conduct. Even if it protects "conduct," the clause does not protect all conduct (e.g., the state can prohibit a religion that believes in human sacrifice from actually killing people). In this section, we explore the limits of the Free Exercise Clause.

1. Burdens on Religion

Free exercise cases usually arise when a law prohibits an individual from engaging in conduct required by religious beliefs, or requires conduct prohibited by religious beliefs (i.e., compulsory school attendance laws or laws denying unemployment compensation to those who refuse to work on Saturdays). Typically, in drafting these laws, the legislature was not trying to prohibit or burden a religious practice, but was instead trying to deal with some secular problem (e.g., parents who fail to educate their children or workers who unreasonably refuse to educate their children). A problem develops when the laws incidentally affect religious practices. At that point, a court must decide whether the individual interest in the free exercise of religion should prevail, or the state's interest in compliance prevails over the individual's religious interest.

a. Early Cases

Litigation about free exercise issues has arisen in a variety of contexts. In, for example, Reynolds v. United States, 98 U.S. (8 Otto) 145, 25 L.Ed. 244 (1878), a conflict arose between a federal law prohibiting polygamy and a Mormon who believed that his religion required him to engage in that practice. The Court upheld the federal law distinguishing between "belief" and "conduct," and concluded that the government had broad authority to prohibit religious "conduct." The Court stated that "[l]aws are made for the government of actions, and while they cannot interfere with mere religious beliefs and opinions, they may with practices." *See also* Davis v. Beason, 133 U.S. 333 (1890).

Reynolds's "belief-conduct" distinction was modified and partially rejected in the Court's later decision in Cantwell v. Connecticut, 310 U.S. 296 (1940). In that case, a man (Newton Cantwell) and his two sons, all of whom were Jehovah's Witnesses and ordained ministers, were arrested in New Haven, Connecticut, and convicted of attempting to sell religious magazines without a permit and of disorderly conduct. The Court concluded that the statute prohibiting solicitation violated Cantwell's right to free exercise: "[The First] Amendment embraces two concepts, — freedom to believe and freedom to act. The first is absolute but, in the nature of things, the second cannot be. Conduct remains subject to regulation for the protection of society." However, the right to control religious conduct was not unfettered: "[A] state may not, by statute, wholly deny the right to preach or to disseminate religious views. [It] is equally clear that a state may by general and non-discriminatory legislation regulate the times, the places, and the manner of soliciting upon its streets, and of holding meetings thereon; and may in other respects safeguard the peace, good order and comfort of the community, without unconstitutionally invading the liberties protected by the Fourteenth Amendment. . . ." The Court struck down the solicitation statute because it gave local officials too much discretion to grant or deny permission. *Cantwell* is also important because it extended the Free Exercise Clause's protections to the states.

b. From *Sherbert* to *Smith*

For several decades, the Court was more accepting of free exercise claims and tended to impose heightened review on laws that infringed religious beliefs. The following case is illustrative.

Sherbert v. Verner
374 U.S. 398 (1963)

Mr. Justice BRENNAN delivered the opinion of the Court.

Appellant, a member of the Seventh-day Adventist Church, was discharged by her South Carolina employer because she would not work on Saturday, the Sabbath Day of her faith. When she was unable to obtain other employment because from conscientious scruples she would not take Saturday work, she filed a claim for unemployment compensation benefits under the South Carolina Unemployment Compensation Act. [A]ppellee Employment Security Commission [found] that appellant's restriction upon her availability for Saturday work brought her within the provision disqualifying for benefits insured workers who fail, without good cause, to accept "suitable work when offered [by] the employment office or the [employer]." The Commission's finding was [affirmed by the South Carolina courts].

[A]ppellant's conscientious objection to Saturday work constitutes no conduct prompted by religious principles of a kind within the reach of state legislation. If, therefore, the decision of the South Carolina Supreme Court is to withstand appellant's constitutional challenge, it must be either because her disqualification as a beneficiary represents no infringement by the State of her constitutional rights of free exercise, or because any incidental burden on the free exercise of appellant's religion may be justified by a "compelling state interest in the regulation of a subject within the State's constitutional power to [regulate]." NAACP v. Button, 371 U.S. 415.

We turn first to the question whether the disqualification for benefits imposes any burden on the free exercise of appellant's religion. We think it is clear that it does. [T]he consequences of such a disqualification to religious principles and practices may be only an indirect result of welfare legislation within the State's general competence to enact; it is true that no criminal sanctions directly compel appellant to work a six-day week. But [h]ere not only is it apparent that appellant's declared ineligibility for benefits derives solely from the practice of her religion, but the pressure upon her to forego that practice is unmistakable. The ruling forces her to choose between following the precepts of her religion and forfeiting benefits, [and] abandoning one of the precepts of her religion in order to accept work. . . . Governmental imposition of such a choice puts the same kind of burden upon the free exercise of religion as would a fine imposed against appellant for her Saturday worship.

Nor may the South Carolina court's construction of the statute be saved from constitutional infirmity on the ground that unemployment compensation benefits are not appellant's "right" but merely a "privilege." It is too late in the day to doubt that the liberties of religion and expression may be infringed by the denial of or placing of conditions upon a benefit or privilege. . . . South Carolina expressly saves the Sunday worshipper from having to make the kind of choice which we here hold infringes the Sabbatarian's religious liberty. When in times of "national emergency" the textile plants are authorized by the State Commissioner of Labor to operate on Sunday, "no employee shall be required to work on Sunday [who] is conscientiously opposed to Sunday work; and if any employee should refuse to work on Sunday on account of conscientious. . . ." S.C. Code, §64-4. [The] unconstitutionality of the disqualification of the Sabbatarian is thus compounded by the religious discrimination which South Carolina's general statutory scheme necessarily effects.

[It] is basic that no showing merely of a rational relationship to some colorable state interest would suffice in this highly sensitive constitutional area, "[o]nly the gravest abuses, endangering paramount interest, give occasion for permissible limitation." No such abuse or danger has been advanced in the present case. [A]ppellees suggest no more than a possibility that the filing of fraudulent claims by unscrupulous claimants feigning religious objections to Saturday work might not only dilute the unemployment compensation fund but also hinder the scheduling by employers of necessary Saturday work. [E]ven if the possibility of spurious claims did [exist], it would plainly be incumbent upon the appellees to demonstrate that no alternative forms of regulation would combat such abuses without infringing First Amendment rights.

[T]he state interest asserted in the present case is wholly dissimilar to the interests which were found to justify the less direct burden upon religious practices in *Braunfeld*. The Court recognized that the Sunday closing law which that decision sustained undoubtedly served "to make the practice of (the Orthodox Jewish merchants') religious beliefs more expensive." But the statute was nevertheless saved by a countervailing factor which finds no equivalent in the instant case — a strong state interest in providing one uniform day of rest for all workers. That secular objective could be achieved, the Court found, only by declaring Sunday to be that day of rest. Requiring exemptions for Sabbatarians, while theoretically possible, appeared to present an administrative problem of such magnitude, or to afford the exempted class so great a competitive advantage, that such a requirement would have rendered the entire statutory scheme unworkable. In the present case no such justifications underlie the determination of the state court that appellant's religion makes her ineligible to receive benefits.

In holding as we do, [we] are not fostering the "establishment" of the Seventh-day Adventist religion in South Carolina, for the extension of unemployment benefits to Sabbatarians in common with Sunday worshippers reflects nothing more than the governmental obligation of neutrality in the face of religious differences, and does not represent that involvement of religious with secular institutions which it is the object of the Establishment Clause to forestall. [N]o State may "exclude individual Catholics, Lutherans, Mohammedans, Baptists, Jews, Methodists, Non-believers, Presbyterians, or the members of any other faith, because of their faith, or lack of it, from receiving the benefits of public welfare legislation." Everson v. Board of Education, 330 U.S. 1.

[The] judgment of the South Carolina Supreme Court is reversed and the case is remanded for further proceedings not inconsistent with this opinion. It is so ordered.

Reversed and remanded.

Mr. Justice DOUGLAS, concurring.

This case is resolvable [solely] in terms of what government may not do to an individual in violation of his religious scruples. [If] appellant is otherwise qualified for unemployment benefits, payments will be made to her not as a Seventh-day Adventist, but as an unemployed worker. . . .

Mr. Justice HARLAN, whom Mr. Justice WHITE joins, dissenting.

[This] decision necessarily overrules *Braunfeld*. [The] meaning of today's holding [is] that the State must furnish unemployment benefits to one who is unavailable for work if the unavailability stems from the exercise of religious convictions. The State, in other words, must single out for financial assistance those whose behavior is religiously motivated, even though it denies such assistance to others whose identical behavior (in this case, inability to work no Saturdays) is not religiously motivated. [Those] situations in which the Constitution may require special treatment on account of religion are, in my view, few and far between. . . . Such compulsion in the present case is particularly inappropriate in light of the indirect, remote, and insubstantial effect of the decision below on the exercise of appellant's religion and in light of the direct financial assistance to religion that today's decision requires.

BACKGROUND
Unemployment Compensation

Over the years, a number of free exercise cases have involved disputes about unemployment compensation. *See* Frazee v. Illinois Department of Employment Security, 489 U.S. 829 (1989) (Frazee, who refused employment because he would have been forced to work on his sabbath [Sunday], was held to be entitled to unemployment benefits); Hobbie v. Unemployment Appeals Commission, 480 U.S. 136 (1987) (Hobbie, who was discharged because she refused to work on a Friday evening or Saturday because she was a Seventh-day Adventist, was entitled to unemployment compensation).

Notes and Questions

1. *Child Labor Laws.* In Prince v. Commonwealth of Massachusetts, 321 U.S. 158 (1944), Sarah Prince was charged under child labor laws with having a nine-year-old girl (of whom Prince had legal custody) help her sell religious magazines. Prince challenged the laws based on her free exercise rights (the duty to bring up the child in the tenets and practices of the faith) as well as the girl's free exercise rights (the girl believed that it was her religious duty to perform this work and that failure would bring condemnation "to everlasting destruction at Armageddon"). The Court upheld the child labor laws as applied to the mother: "[T]he power of the state to control the conduct of children reaches beyond the scope of its authority over adults, as is true in the case of other freedoms, and the rightful boundary of its power has not been crossed in this case." Justice Murphy dissented: "Religious training and activity, whether performed by adult or child, are protected [except] insofar as they violate reasonable regulations adopted for the protection of the public health, morals and welfare. . . ."

2. *Free Exercise Losers?* Some argue that the free exercise "losers" have generally been minorities (e.g., Mormons and Jehovah's Witnesses). *See* Paul Marcus, *The Forum of Conscience: Applying Standards Under the Free Exercise Clause*, 1973 Duke L.J. 1217 ("These groups [e.g., Mormons and Jehovah's Witnesses], as well as groups with more unusual views, have historically failed miserably in their free exercise arguments. [W]hile the courts had generally been tolerant toward religious minorities, the caveat must be added that the minority must not be too small or too eccentric."). If that is the case, how would you explain this tendency?

∾ PROBLEM: THE ATHEIST ∾

When an atheist is summoned for jury duty, she refuses to take an oath that contains a reference to God. She is then asked to raise her hand and take an oath that has no reference to God. She again refuses, claiming that she considers any affirmation to be religious. Under the Free Exercise Clause, can the court require an atheist to take at least the latter oath? Is there a suitable alternative? If so, what?

Wisconsin v. Yoder
406 U.S. 205 (1972)

Mr. Chief Justice BURGER delivered the opinion of the Court.

[Respondents] are members of the Old Order Amish religion. [Wisconsin's] compulsory school-attendance law required them to [send] their children [to] school until reaching age 16 but [respondents refused] to send their children [to] school after [the] eighth grade. [Respondents were] convicted of violating the compulsory-attendance law [and] were fined the sum of $5 each. Respondents defended on the ground that [the] compulsory-attendance law violated their rights under the First and Fourteenth Amendments. . . .

[Old Order Amish] communities [are] characterized by a fundamental belief that salvation requires life in a church community separate and apart from the world and worldly influence. This concept of life aloof from the world and its values is central to their faith. [A] related feature of Old Order Amish communities is their devotion to a life in harmony with nature and the soil. . . . Amish beliefs require members of the community to make their living by farming or closely related activities. [Amish] objection to formal education beyond the eighth grade [is] grounded in these central religious concepts. They object [to] high school, and higher education generally, because the values [are] in marked variance with Amish values and the Amish way of life; they view secondary school education as an impermissible exposure of their children to a "wordly" influence in conflict with their beliefs. [H]igh school emphasize[s] intellectual and scientific accomplishments, self-distinction, competitiveness, worldly success, and social life with other students. Amish society emphasizes informal learning-through-doing; a life of "goodness," rather than a life of intellect; wisdom, rather than technical knowledge; community welfare, rather than competition; and separation from, rather than integration with, contemporary worldly society.

Formal high school education beyond the eighth grade is contrary to Amish beliefs, not only because it places Amish children in an environment hostile to Amish beliefs with increasing emphasis on competition in class work and sports and with pressure to conform to the styles, manners, and ways of the peer group, but also because it takes them away from their community, physically and emotionally, during the crucial and formative adolescent period of life. During this period, the children must acquire Amish attitudes favoring manual work and self-reliance and the specific skills needed to perform the adult role of an Amish farmer or housewife. They must learn to enjoy physical labor. Once a child has learned basic reading, writing, and elementary mathematics, these traits, skills, and attitudes admittedly fall within the category of those best learned through example and "doing" rather than in a classroom. [A]t this time in life, the Amish child must also grow in his faith and his relationship to the Amish community if he is to be prepared to accept the heavy obligations imposed by adult baptism.

[H]igh school attendance with teachers who are not of the Amish faith — and may even be hostile to it — interposes a serious barrier to the integration of the Amish child into the Amish religious community. . . .

The Amish do not object to elementary education through the first eight grades as a general proposition because they agree that their children must have basic skills in the "three R's" in order to read the Bible, to be good farmers and citizens, and to be able to deal with non-Amish people when necessary in the course of daily affairs. They view such a basic education as acceptable because it does not significantly expose their children to worldly values or interfere with their development in the Amish community during the crucial adolescent period. [W]herever possible they have established their own elementary schools in many respects like the small local schools of the past. . . .

[C]ompulsory high school attendance could not only result in great psychological harm to Amish children, because of the conflicts it would produce, but would [also] ultimately result in the destruction of the Old Order Amish church community. [A]n expert witness [stated] that the Amish succeed in preparing their high school age children to be productive members of the Amish community. He described their system of learning through doing the skills directly relevant to their adult roles [as] "ideal" and perhaps superior to ordinary high school education. [The] Amish have an excellent record as law-abiding and generally self-sufficient members of society.

[The] Wisconsin Circuit Court affirmed the convictions. The Wisconsin Supreme Court [reversed].

I

. . . Providing public schools ranks at the very apex of the function of a State. Yet even this paramount responsibility [must] yield to the right of parents to provide an equivalent education in a privately operated system. [In Pierce v. Society of Sisters, 268 U.S. 510 (1925),] the Court held that Oregon's statute compelling attendance in a public school from age eight to age 16 unreasonably interfered with the interest of parents in directing the rearing of their off-spring, including their education in church-operated schools. [T]he values of parental direction of the religious upbringing and education of their children in their early and formative years have a high place in our society. Thus, a State's interest in universal education, however highly we rank it, is not totally free from a balancing process when it impinges on fundamental rights and interests, such as those specifically protected by the Free Exercise Clause of the First Amendment, and the traditional interest of parents with respect to the religious upbringing of their children so long as [they] "prepare [them] for additional obligations."

[I]n order for Wisconsin to compel school attendance beyond the eighth grade against a claim that such attendance interferes with the practice of a legitimate religious belief, it must appear either that the State does not deny the free exercise of religious belief by its requirement, or that there is a state interest of sufficient magnitude to override the interest claiming protection under the Free Exercise Clause. [O]nly those interests of the highest order and those not otherwise served can overbalance legitimate claims to the free exercise of religion.

[H]owever strong the State's interest in universal compulsory education, it is by no means absolute to the exclusion or subordination of all other interests.

[I]f the Amish asserted their claims because of their subjective evaluation and rejection of the contemporary secular values accepted by the majority, much as Thoreau rejected the social values of his time and isolated himself at Walden Pond, their claims would not rest on a religious basis. Thoreau's choice was philosophical and personal rather than religious, and such belief does not rise to the demands of the Religion Clauses.

[The] traditional way of life of the Amish is not merely a matter of personal preference, but one of deep religious conviction, shared by an organized group, and intimately related to daily living. [T]he Old Order Amish daily life and religious practice [is a] response to their literal interpretation of the Biblical injunction from the Epistle of Paul to the Romans, "be not conformed to this world. . . ." [T]he Old Order Amish religion pervades and determines virtually their entire way of life, regulating it with the detail of the Talmudic diet through the strictly enforced rules of the church community.

[R]espondents' religious beliefs and attitude toward life, family, and home have remained constant — perhaps some would say static — in a period of unparalleled progress in human knowledge generally and great changes in education. [Their] church-oriented community, separated from the outside world and "worldly" influences, their attachment to nature and the soil, is a way inherently simple and uncomplicated, albeit difficult to preserve against the pressure to conform. Their rejection of telephones, automobiles, radios, and television, their mode of dress, of speech, their habits of manual work do indeed set them apart from much of contemporary society; these customs are both symbolic and practical.

As the society around the Amish has become more populous, urban, industrialized, and complex, particularly in this century, government regulation of human affairs has correspondingly become more detailed and pervasive. The Amish mode of life has thus come into conflict increasingly with requirements of contemporary society exerting a hydraulic insistence on conformity to majoritarian standards. So long as compulsory education laws were confined to eight grades of elementary basic education imparted in a nearby rural schoolhouse, with a large proportion of students of the Amish faith, the Old Order Amish had little basis to fear that school attendance would expose their children to the worldly influence they reject. But modern compulsory secondary education in rural areas is now largely carried on in a consolidated school, often remote from the student's home and alien to his daily home life. [T]he values and programs of the modern secondary school are in sharp conflict with the fundamental mode of life mandated by the Amish religion; modern laws requiring compulsory secondary education have accordingly engendered great concern and conflict. [S]econdary schooling, by exposing Amish children to worldly influences in terms of attitudes, goals, and values contrary to beliefs, and by substantially interfering with the religious development of the Amish child and his integration into the way of life of the Amish faith community at the crucial adolescent stage of development, contravenes the basic religious tenets and practice of the Amish faith, both as to the parent and the child.

The impact of the compulsory-attendance law on respondents' practice of the Amish religion is not only severe, but inescapable, for the Wisconsin law affirmatively compels them, under threat of criminal sanction, to perform acts undeniably at odds with fundamental tenets of their religious beliefs. Nor is the impact of the compulsory-attendance law confined to grave interference with important Amish religious tenets from a subjective point of view. It carries with it precisely the kind of objective danger to the free exercise of religion that the First Amendment was designed to prevent. [C]ompulsory school attendance to age 16 for Amish children carries with it a very real threat of undermining the Amish community and religious practice as they exist today; they must either abandon belief and be assimilated into society at large, or be forced to migrate to some other and more tolerant region. [E]nforcement of the State's requirement of compulsory formal education after the eighth grade would gravely endanger if not destroy the free exercise of respondents' religious beliefs.

[Wisconsin] argues that "actions," even though religiously grounded, are outside the protection of the First Amendment. But our decisions have rejected the idea that religiously grounded conduct is always outside the protection of the Free Exercise Clause. . . . Nor can this case be disposed of on the grounds that Wisconsin's requirement for school attendance to age 16 applies uniformly to all citizens of the State and does not, on its face, discriminate against religions or a particular religion, or that it is motivated by legitimate secular concerns. A regulation neutral on its face may, in its application, nonetheless offend the constitutional requirement for governmental neutrality if it unduly burdens the free exercise of religion. The Court must not ignore the danger that an exception from a general obligation of citizenship on religious grounds may run afoul of the Establishment Clause, but that danger cannot be allowed to prevent any exception no matter how vital it may be to the protection of values promoted by the right of free exercise. . . .

[The State also argues] that its interest in its system of compulsory education is so compelling that even the established religious practices of the Amish must give way. Where fundamental claims of religious freedom are at stake, [we] must searchingly examine the interests that the State seeks to promote by its requirement for compulsory education to age 16, and the impediment to those objectives that would flow from recognizing the claimed Amish exemption.

The State advances two primary arguments in support of its system of compulsory education. It notes [that] some degree of education is necessary to prepare citizens to participate effectively and intelligently in our open political system if we are to preserve freedom and independence. Further, education prepares individuals to be self-reliant and self-sufficient participants in society. We accept these propositions.

However, the evidence adduced by the Amish in this case is persuasively to the effect that an additional one or two years of formal high school for Amish children in place of their long-established program of informal vocational education would do little to serve those interests. [It] is one thing to say that compulsory education [may] be necessary when its goal is the preparation of the child for life in modern society as the majority live, but it is quite another if the goal of education be viewed as the preparation of the child for life in the separated agrarian community that is the keystone of the Amish faith.

The State attacks respondents' position as one fostering "ignorance" from which the child must be protected by the State. [T]his argument does not square with the facts. [The] Amish community has been a highly successful social unit within our society, even if apart from the conventional "mainstream." Its members are productive and very law-abiding members of society; they reject public welfare in any of its usual modern forms. The Congress itself recognized their self-sufficiency by authorizing exemption of such groups as the Amish from the obligation to pay social security taxes.

It is neither fair nor correct to suggest that the Amish are opposed to education beyond the eighth grade level. [T]hey are opposed to conventional formal education of the type provided by a certified high school because it comes at the child's crucial adolescent period of religious development. [An expert testified] that their system of learning-by-doing was an "ideal system" of education in terms of preparing Amish children for life as adults in the Amish community. [A] way of life that is odd or even erratic [is] not to be condemned because it is different.

The State [points to the] possibility that [some] children will choose to leave the Amish community, and that if this occurs they will be ill-equipped for life. [T]hat argument is highly speculative. There is no [evidence] of the loss of Amish adherents by attrition, nor is there any showing that upon leaving the Amish community Amish children, with their practical agricultural training and habits of industry and self-reliance, would become burdens on society. [There] is nothing [to] suggest that the Amish qualities of reliability, self-reliance, and dedication to work would fail to find ready markets in today's society. [N]or is there any basis [for] finding that an additional one or two years of formal school education beyond the eighth grade would serve to eliminate any such problem that might exist. . . . The Amish alternative to formal secondary school education has enabled them to function effectively in their day-to-day life under self-imposed limitations on relations with the world, and to survive and prosper in contemporary society as a separate, sharply identifiable and highly self-sufficient community for more than 200 years in this country. [T]his is strong evidence that they are capable of fulfilling the social and political responsibilities of citizenship without compelled attendance beyond the eighth grade at the price of jeopardizing their free exercise of religious belief. . . .

[Wisconsin's] interest in compelling the school attendance of Amish children to age 16 emerges as somewhat less substantial than requiring such attendance for children generally. [W]hile agricultural employment is not totally outside the legitimate concerns of the child labor laws, employment of children under parental guidance and on the family farm from age 14 to age 16 is an ancient tradition that lies at the periphery of the objectives of such laws. There is no intimation that the Amish employment of their children on family farms is in any way deleterious to their health or that Amish parents exploit children at tender years. [Our] holding in no way determines the proper resolution of possible competing interests of parents, children, and the State in an appropriate state court proceeding in which the power of the State is asserted on the theory that Amish parents are preventing their minor children from attending high school despite their expressed desires to the contrary. . . .

[W]e hold [that] the First and Fourteenth Amendments prevent the State from compelling respondents to cause their children to attend formal high school to age 16. . . .

Affirmed.

Mr. Justice WHITE, with whom Mr. Justice BRENNAN and Mr. Justice STEWART join, concurring.

[Since] the Amish children [acquire] the basic tools of literacy to survive in modern society by attending grades one through eight and since the deviation from the State's compulsory-education law is relatively slight, [respondents] must prevail, largely because "religious freedom [is] one of the highest values of our society." [C]ases [like this] inevitably involve the kind of [close] scrutiny of religious practices [which] the Court [has] been anxious to avoid. But such [scrutiny] is essential to implement free exercise values threatened by an otherwise neutral program instituted to foster some permissible, nonreligious state objective. . . .

Mr. Justice DOUGLAS, dissenting in part.

[I]f an Amish child desires to attend high school, and is mature [enough], the State [may] override the parents' religiously motivated objections. [T]he children themselves have constitutionally protectible interests. . . . [The] emphasis [on] the "law and order" record of this Amish group of people [is] irrelevant. [I] am not at all sure how the Catholics, Episcopalians, the Baptists, Jehovah's Witnesses, the Unitarians, and my own Presbyterians would make out if subjected to such a test. . . .

BACKGROUND
Old Order Amish and Social Security

In addition to *Yoder*, a number of other free exercise cases have involved the Old Order Amish. Illustrative is United States v. Lee, 455 U.S. 252 (1982), in which an Amish adherent objected to paying Social Security taxes on the basis that he was religiously precluded from receiving public insurance benefits, and he objected to the payment of taxes to support public insurance funds. The Court held that he was required to pay: "Because the social security system is nationwide, the governmental interest is apparent. [Unlike] the situation presented in *Yoder*, it would be difficult to accommodate the comprehensive social security system with myriad exceptions flowing from a wide variety of religious beliefs. . . ." In a similar vein, in Jimmy Swaggart Ministries v. Board of Education, 493 U.S. 378 (1990), the Court

held that a religious organization was not entitled to an exemption from
sales and use taxes on religious literature when the tax was applied to the
sale of all goods and services.

❧ PROBLEMS ❧

1. *Old Order Amish and Buggy Reflectors.* Another area of disagreement
between the Amish and the state is traffic safety laws. For safety reasons, some
states require slow-moving vehicles to display fluorescent orange-red triangular
emblems while traveling on state highways. The law is applied even to the Old
Order Amish, who drive horse-drawn buggies on public highways. The Amish
object to the emblems because they believe that their religion prohibits them
from displaying "loud colors" and "worldly symbols." The Amish do not object to
lining the outside of their buggies with silver reflective tape or to adorning their
buggies with lighted red lanterns. If the state deems these actions inadequate to
protect the public interest in safety, can the state require the Amish to display the
orange-red triangular emblem notwithstanding their religious beliefs?

2. *More on the Education for the Twenty-First Century Act.* In constructing the
proposed legislation, should you (must you?) include any special accommodations for religion? If so, what accommodations?

Lyng v. Northwest Indian Cemetery Protective Assn.
485 U.S. 439 (1988)

Justice O'CONNOR delivered the opinion of the Court.

[As] part of a project to create a paved 75-mile road linking two California
towns, [the] United States Forest Service [upgraded] 49 miles of previously
unpaved roads on federal land. In order to complete this project (the G-O road),
the Forest Service must build a 6-mile paved segment through the Chimney Rock
section of the Six Rivers National Forest. . . . In 1977, the Forest Service issued a
draft environmental impact statement that discussed proposals for upgrading an
existing unpaved road that runs through the Chimney Rock area. In response to
comments on the draft statement, the Forest Service commissioned a study of
American Indian cultural and religious sites in the area. The Hoopa Valley Indian
Reservation adjoins the Six Rivers National Forest, and the Chimney Rock area
has historically been used for religious purposes by Yurok, Karok, and Tolowa
Indians. The [study] found that the entire area "is significant as an integral and
indispensable part of Indian religious conceptualization and practice." Specific
sites are used for certain rituals, and "successful use of the [area] is dependent
upon and facilitated by certain qualities of the physical environment, the most
important of which are privacy, silence, and an undisturbed natural setting." The
study concluded that constructing a road along any of the available routes "would
cause serious and irreparable damage to the sacred areas which are an integral
and necessary part of the belief systems and lifeway of Northwest California

Indian peoples." Accordingly, the report recommended that the G-O road not be completed.

In 1982, the Forest Service decided not to adopt this recommendation, [and] prepared a final environmental impact statement. . . . The Regional Forester selected a route that avoided archeological sites and was removed as far as possible from the sites used by contemporary Indians for specific spiritual activities. Alternative routes that would have avoided the Chimney Rock area altogether were rejected because they would have required the acquisition of private land, had serious soil stability problems, and would in any event have traversed areas having ritualistic value to American Indians. At about the same time, the Forest Service adopted a management plan allowing for the harvesting of significant amounts of timber in this area of the forest. The management plan provided for one-half mile protective zones around all the religious sites identified in the report that had been commissioned in connection with the G-O road.

[R]espondents — an Indian organization, individual Indians, nature organizations and individual members of those organizations, and the State of California — challenged both the road-building and timber-harvesting decisions on [Free Exercise grounds]. [T]he District Court issued a permanent injunction prohibiting the Government from constructing the Chimney Rock section of the G-O road or putting the timber-harvesting management plan into effect. [T]he District Court's constitutional ruling [was] affirmed. . . .

III

[It] is undisputed that the Indian respondents' beliefs are sincere and that the Government's proposed actions will have severe adverse effects on the practice of their religion. Those respondents contend that the burden on their religious practices is heavy enough to violate the Free Exercise Clause unless the Government can demonstrate a compelling need to complete the G-O road or to engage in timber harvesting in the Chimney Rock area. We disagree.

In Bowen v. Roy, 476 U.S. 693 (1986), we considered a challenge to a federal statute that required the States to use Social Security numbers in administering certain welfare programs. Two applicants [contended] that their religious beliefs prevented them from [using] a Social Security number for their 2-year-old daughter because the use of a numerical identifier would "'rob the spirit' of [their] daughter and prevent her from attaining greater spiritual power." Similarly, in this case, it is said that disruption of the natural environment caused by the G-O road will diminish the sacredness of the area in question and create distractions that will interfere with "training and ongoing religious experience of individuals using [sites within] the area for personal medicine and growth [and] as integrated parts of a system of religious belief and practice which correlates ascending degrees of personal power with a geographic hierarchy of power." ("Scarred hills and mountains, and disturbed rocks destroy the purity of the sacred areas, and [Indian] consultants repeatedly stressed the need of a training doctor to be undistracted by such disturbance.") The Court rejected this kind of challenge in *Roy*:

> [Just] as the Government may not insist that [the Roys] engage in any set form of religious observance, [they] may not demand that the Government join in their chosen religious practices by refraining from using a number to identify their daughter. [The] Free Exercise Clause affords an individual protection from certain forms of governmental compulsion; it does not afford an individual a right to dictate the conduct of the Government's internal procedures.

The building of a road or the harvesting of timber on publicly owned land cannot meaningfully be distinguished from the use of a Social Security number in *Roy*. In both cases, the challenged Government action would interfere significantly with private persons' ability to pursue spiritual fulfillment according to their own religious beliefs. In neither case, however, would the affected individuals be coerced by the Government's action into violating their religious beliefs; nor would either governmental action penalize religious activity by denying any person an equal share of the rights, benefits, and privileges enjoyed by other citizens.

We are asked to distinguish [*Roy*] on the ground that the infringement on religious liberty here is "significantly greater," or on the ground that the Government practice in *Roy* was "purely mechanical" whereas this case involves "a case-by-case substantive determination as to how a particular unit of land will be managed." Similarly, we are told that this case can be distinguished from *Roy* because [the] proposed road will "physically destro[y] the environmental conditions and the privacy without which the [religious] practices cannot be conducted."

These efforts to distinguish *Roy* are unavailing. This Court cannot determine the truth of the underlying beliefs that led to the religious objections here or in *Roy*, and accordingly cannot weigh the adverse effects on the appellees in *Roy* and compare them with the adverse effects on the Indian respondents. Without the ability to make such comparisons, we cannot say that the one form of incidental interference with an individual's spiritual activities should be subjected to a different constitutional analysis than the other.

Respondents insist [that] that the courts below properly relied on a factual inquiry into the degree to which the Indians' spiritual practices would become ineffectual if the G-O road were built. [Whatever] may be the exact line between unconstitutional prohibitions on the free exercise of religion and the legitimate conduct by government of its own affairs, the location of the line cannot depend on measuring the effects of a governmental action on a religious objector's spiritual development. [G]overnment simply could not operate if it were required to satisfy every citizen's religious needs and desires. A broad range of government activities — from social welfare programs to foreign aid to conservation projects — will always be considered essential to the spiritual well-being of some citizens, often on the basis of sincerely held religious beliefs. Others will find the very same activities deeply offensive, and perhaps incompatible with their own search for spiritual fulfillment and with the tenets of their religion. The First Amendment must apply to all citizens alike, and it can give to none of them a veto over public programs that do not prohibit the free exercise of religion. The Constitution does not, and courts cannot, offer to reconcile the various competing demands on government, many of them rooted in sincere religious belief, that inevitably arise in so diverse a society as ours. That task, to the extent that it is feasible, is for the legislatures and other institutions.

[Respondents] stress the limits of the religious servitude that they are now seeking to impose on the Chimney Rock area of the Six Rivers National Forest. While defending an injunction against logging operations and the construction of a road, they apparently do not *at present* object to the area's being used by recreational visitors, other Indians, or forest rangers. Nothing in the principle for which they contend, however, would distinguish this case [if they sought] to exclude all human activity but their own from sacred areas of the public lands. . . .

[The] Government's rights to the use of its own land [need] not and should not discourage it from accommodating religious practices like those engaged in by the Indian respondents. It is worth emphasizing [that] the Government has taken numerous steps in this very case to minimize the impact that construction of the G-O road will have on the Indians' religious activities. . . . No sites where specific rituals take place were to be disturbed. In fact, a major factor in choosing among alternative routes for the road was the relation of the various routes to religious sites. . . . Except for abandoning its project entirely, and thereby leaving the two existing segments of road to dead-end in the middle of a National Forest, it is difficult to see how the Government could have been more solicitous. . . .

[T]he dissent proposes a legal test under which it would decide which public lands are "central" or "indispensable" to which religions, and by implication which are "dispensable" or "peripheral," and would then decide which government programs are "compelling" enough to justify "infringement of those practices." [T]he dissent thus offers us the prospect of this Court's holding that some sincerely held religious beliefs and practices are not "central" to certain religions, despite protestations to the contrary from the religious objectors who brought the lawsuit. [We] think such an approach cannot be squared with the Constitution or with our precedents, and that it would cast the Judiciary in a role that we were never intended to play.

The decision of the court below [is] reversed. . . .

It is so ordered.

Justice BRENNAN, with whom Justice MARSHALL and Justice BLACKMUN join, dissenting.

[R]espondents have demonstrated that the Government's proposed activities will completely prevent them from practicing their religion, and such a showing [entitles] them to the protections of the Free Exercise Clause. [T]he Court's refusal to recognize the constitutional dimension of respondents' injuries stems from its concern that acceptance of respondents' claim could potentially strip the Government of its ability to manage and use vast tracts of federal property. [These] concededly legitimate concerns [represent] yet another stress point in the longstanding conflict between two disparate cultures — the dominant Western culture, which views land in terms of ownership and use, and that of Native Americans, in which concepts of private property are not only alien, but contrary to a belief system that holds land sacred. [T]he Court disclaims all responsibility for balancing these competing and potentially irreconcilable interests, choosing instead to turn this difficult task over to the Federal Legislature. . . .

[I] believe it appropriate [to] require some showing of "centrality" before the Government can be required either to come forward with a compelling justification for its proposed use of federal land or to forego that use altogether. "Centrality," however, should not be equated with the survival or extinction of the religion itself. . . . Native Americans consider all land sacred. Nevertheless, [respondents deem] certain lands more powerful and more directly related to their religious practices than others. [It is not] enough to allege simply that the land in question is held sacred. [A]dherents challenging a proposed use of federal land should be required to show that the decision poses a substantial and realistic threat of frustrating their religious practices. Once such a showing is made, the burden should shift to the Government to come forward with a compelling state interest sufficient to justify the infringement of those practices.

The Court today suggests that such an approach would place courts in the untenable position of deciding which practices and beliefs are "central" to a given faith and which are not. . . . [Courts] need not undertake any such inquiries: like all other religious adherents, Native Americans would be the arbiters of which practices are central to their faith, subject only to the normal requirement that their claims be genuine and sincere. [T]he Court's concern that the claims of Native Americans will place "religious servitudes" upon vast tracts of federal property cannot justify its refusal to recognize the constitutional injury respondents will suffer here. [Should] respondents or any other group seek to force the Government to protect their religious practices from the interference of private parties, such a demand would implicate not only the concerns of the Free Exercise Clause, but also those of the Establishment Clause as well. That case, however, is most assuredly not before us. . . .

[T]he Court holds that a federal land-use decision that promises to destroy an entire religion does not burden the practice of that faith in a manner recognized by the Free Exercise Clause. . . . [I] dissent.

Notes

1. *The Army and the Yarmulke.* In Goldman v. Weinberger, 475 U.S. 503 (1986), a Jewish enlisted man in the U.S. Air Force wanted to wear a yarmulke in conjunction with his military uniform. He was prevented from doing so by an Air Force regulation mandating uniform dress by Air Force personnel. The Court concluded that "the military is, by necessity, a specialized society separate from civilian society" and that "[t]he essence of military service is the subordination of the desires and interests of the individual to the needs of the service." Accordingly, the Court upheld the prohibition. Justice Brennan dissented: "It cannot be seriously contended that a serviceman in a yarmulke presents so extreme, so unusual, or so faddish an image that public confidence in his ability to perform his duties will be destroyed."

2. *Jumu'ah and Work Gangs.* O'Lone v. Shabazz, 482 U.S. 342 (1987), involved a challenge by members of the Islamic faith to prison policies requiring that prisoners who are transferred from maximum security to minimum security prisons be first assigned to labor groups that work outside the prison. The prison justified the regulation as a transitional rule designed to enable transferees to adjust to a minimum security facility. The Muslim prisoners in the labor groups were thus precluded from attending Jumu'ah, a weekly Muslim service that was regularly held in the main prison building. Jumu'ah is mandatory under the Koran and must be held every Friday after the sun reaches its zenith and before the Asr, or afternoon prayer. Prison officials refused to allow "gang" workers to return to "the Farm" during the day because of security risks and administrative problems. Muslim prisoners sued, seeking an accommodation. The Court held that an accommodation was not required: "[L]awful incarceration brings about the necessary withdrawal or limitation of many privileges and rights, a retraction justified by the considerations underlying our penal system. [E]valuation of penological objectives is committed to the considered judgment of prison administrators. . . ." Justice Brennan dissented: "Jumu'ah is the central religious ceremony of Muslims. . . ."

c. Modern Cases

As *Sherbert* and *Yoder* reflect, the Court's early decisions involved balancing the governmental interest in imposing a requirement against the religious interest in an exemption. The Court's approach began to shift with the following decision.

Employment Division v. Smith
494 U.S. 872 (1990)

Justice SCALIA delivered the opinion of the Court.

[Oregon] law prohibits the knowing or intentional possession of a "controlled substance" unless the substance has been prescribed by a medical practitioner. [Persons] who violate this provision by possessing a controlled substance listed on Schedule I are "guilty of a Class B felony." [Included on the list of "controlled substances" is the drug peyote, a hallucinogen.]

[Respondents] were fired from their jobs with a private drug rehabilitation organization because they ingested peyote for sacramental purposes at a ceremony of the Native American Church, of which both are members. When respondents applied [for] unemployment compensation, they were determined to be ineligible [because] they had been discharged for work-related "misconduct." The Oregon Court of Appeals reversed that determination, holding that the denial of benefits violated respondents' free exercise rights under the First Amendment. We granted certiorari.

Respondents' claim for relief rests on our decisions in Sherbert v. Verner, [374 U.S. 398 (1963)], Thomas v. Review Board, [450 U.S. 707 (1981)] and Hobbie v. Unemployment Appeals Comm'n. of Florida, 480 U.S. 136 (1987), in which we held that a State could not condition the availability of unemployment insurance on an individual's willingness to forgo conduct required by his religion. [But] the conduct at issue in those cases was not prohibited by law. . . .

[The] free exercise of religion means, first and foremost, the right to believe and profess whatever religious doctrine one desires. [But] the "exercise of religion" often involves not only belief and profession but the performance of (or abstention from) physical acts: assembling with others for a worship service, participating in sacramental use of bread and wine, proselytizing, abstaining from certain foods or certain modes of transportation. [A] State would be "prohibiting the free exercise [of religion]" if it sought to ban such acts or abstentions only when they are engaged in for religious reasons, or only because of the religious belief that they display. It would doubtless be unconstitutional, for example, to ban the casting of "statues that are to be used for worship purposes," or to prohibit bowing down before a golden calf.

Respondents [seek] to carry the meaning of "prohibiting the free exercise [of religion]" one large step further. They contend that their religious motivation for using peyote places them beyond the reach of a criminal law that is not specifically directed at their religious practice, and that is concededly constitutional as applied to those who use the drug for other reasons. They assert [that] "prohibiting the free exercise [of religion]" includes requiring any individual to observe a generally applicable law that requires (or forbids) the performance of an act that his religious belief forbids (or requires). [W]e do not think the words must be given that meaning. It is no more necessary to regard the collection of a general tax, for example, as "prohibiting the free exercise [of religion]" by those citizens who believe support of organized government to be sinful, than it is to regard the same tax as "abridging the freedom [of] the press" of those publishing companies that must pay the tax as a condition of staying in business. [I]f prohibiting the exercise of religion (or burdening the activity of printing) is not the object of the tax but merely the incidental effect of a generally applicable and otherwise valid provision, the First Amendment has not been offended.

[We] have never held that an individual's religious beliefs excuse him from compliance with an otherwise valid law prohibiting conduct that the State is free to regulate. On the contrary, the record of more than a century of our free exercise jurisprudence contradicts that proposition. [In] Reynolds v. United States, 98 U.S. 145 (1879), [we] rejected the claim that criminal laws against polygamy could not be constitutionally applied to those whose religion commanded the practice. . . . Subsequent decisions have consistently held that the right of free exercise does not relieve an individual of the obligation to comply with a "valid and neutral law of general applicability on the ground that the law proscribes (or prescribes) conduct that his religion prescribes (or proscribes)." United States v. Lee, 455 U.S. 252, 263, n.3 (1982) (Stevens, J., concurring in judgment).

[The] only decisions in which we have held that the First Amendment bars application of a neutral, generally applicable law to religiously motivated action have involved not the Free Exercise Clause alone, but the Free Exercise Clause in conjunction with other constitutional protections, such as freedom of speech and of the press, *see* Cantwell v. Connecticut, 310 U.S., at 304-307 (invalidating a licensing system for religious and charitable solicitations under which the administrator had discretion to deny a license to any cause he deemed nonreligious), or the right of parents, acknowledged in Pierce v. Society of Sisters, 268 U.S. 510 (1925), to direct the education of their children. Some of our cases prohibiting compelled expression, decided exclusively upon free speech grounds, have also involved freedom of religion, *cf.* Wooley v. Maynard, 430 U.S. 705 (1977) (invalidating compelled display of a license plate slogan that offended individual religious beliefs); West Virginia Bd. of Education v. Barnette, 319 U.S. 624 (1943) (invalidating compulsory flag salute statute challenged by religious objectors). And it is easy to envision a case in which a challenge on freedom of association grounds would likewise be reinforced by Free Exercise Clause concerns.

The present case does not present such a hybrid situation, but a free exercise claim unconnected with any communicative activity or parental right. Respondents urge [that] when otherwise prohibitable conduct is accompanied by religious convictions, not only the convictions but the conduct itself must be free from governmental regulation. We have never held that, and decline to do so now. There being no contention that Oregon's drug law represents an attempt to regulate religious beliefs, the communication of religious beliefs, or the raising of one's children in those beliefs, the rule to which we have adhered ever since *Reynolds* plainly controls. . . .

Respondents argue that even though exemption from generally applicable criminal laws need not automatically be extended to religiously motivated actors, at least the claim for a religious exemption must be evaluated under the balancing test set forth in *Sherbert*. [Even] if we were inclined to breathe into *Sherbert* some life beyond the unemployment compensation field, we would not apply it to require exemptions from a generally applicable criminal law. . . . We conclude today that the sounder approach, and the approach in accord with the vast majority of our precedents, is to hold the test inapplicable to such challenges. The government's ability to enforce generally applicable prohibitions of socially harmful conduct, like its ability to carry out other aspects of public policy, "cannot depend on measuring the effects of a governmental action on a religious objector's spiritual development." To make an individual's obligation to obey such a law contingent upon the law's coincidence with his religious beliefs, except where the State's interest is "compelling" — permitting him, by virtue of his beliefs, "to become a law unto himself," — contradicts both constitutional tradition and common sense.

The "compelling government interest" requirement seems benign, because it is familiar from other fields. But using it as the standard that must be met before the government may accord different treatment on the basis of race, or before the government may regulate the content of speech, is not remotely comparable to using it for the purpose asserted here. What it produces in those other fields — equality of treatment and an unrestricted flow of contending speech — are constitutional norms; what it would produce here — a private right to ignore generally applicable laws — is a constitutional anomaly.

Nor is it possible to limit the impact of respondents' proposal by requiring a "compelling state interest" only when the conduct prohibited is "central" to the individual's religion. It is no more appropriate for judges to determine the "centrality" of religious beliefs before applying a "compelling interest" test in the free exercise field, than it would be for them to determine the "importance" of ideas before applying the "compelling interest" test in the free speech field. . . .

If the "compelling interest" test is to be applied at all, [it] must be applied across the board, to all actions thought to be religiously commanded. Moreover, if "compelling interest" really means what it says (and watering it down here would subvert its rigor in the other fields where it is applied), many laws will not meet the test. Any society adopting such a system would be courting anarchy, but that danger increases in direct proportion to the society's diversity of religious beliefs, and its determination to coerce or suppress none of them. [The] rule respondents favor would open the prospect of constitutionally required religious exemptions from civic obligations of almost every conceivable kind — ranging from compulsory military service, to the payment of taxes, to health and safety regulation such as manslaughter and child neglect laws, compulsory vaccination laws, drug laws, and traffic laws, to social welfare legislation such as minimum wage laws, child labor laws, animal cruelty laws, environmental protection laws, and laws providing for equality of opportunity for the races. The First Amendment's protection of religious liberty does not require this.

Values that are protected against government interference through enshrinement in the Bill of Rights are not thereby banished from the political process. [A] society that believes in the negative protection accorded to religious belief can be expected to be solicitous of that value in its legislation. . . . It is therefore not surprising that a number of States have made an exception to their drug laws for sacramental peyote use. But to say that a nondiscriminatory religious-practice exemption is permitted, or even that it is desirable, is not to say that it is constitutionally required. [L]eaving accommodation to the political process will place at a relative disadvantage those religious practices that are not widely engaged in; but that unavoidable consequence of democratic government must be preferred to a system in which each conscience is a law unto itself or in which judges weigh the social importance of all laws against the centrality of all religious beliefs.

[Because] respondents' ingestion of peyote was prohibited under Oregon law, and because that prohibition is constitutional, Oregon may, consistent with the Free Exercise Clause, deny respondents unemployment compensation when their dismissal results from use of the drug. The decision of the Oregon Supreme Court is accordingly reversed.

It is so ordered.

Justice O'CONNOR, with whom Justice BRENNAN, Justice MARSHALL, and Justice BLACKMUN join as to Parts I and II, concurring in the judgment.[15]

[T]oday's holding dramatically departs from well-settled First Amendment jurisprudence. . . . [Because] the First Amendment does not distinguish between religious belief and religious conduct, conduct motivated by sincere religious belief, like the belief itself, must be at least presumptively protected by the Free Exercise Clause. [A] person who is barred from engaging in religiously motivated conduct is barred from freely exercising his religion. . . .

[The] First Amendment [does] not distinguish between laws that are generally applicable and laws that target particular religious practices. [F]ew States would be so naive as to enact a law directly prohibiting or burdening a religious practice as such. Our free exercise cases have all concerned generally applicable laws that had the effect of significantly burdening a religious practice. . . .

[T]he freedom to act, unlike the freedom to believe, cannot be absolute. [W]e have [required] the government to justify any substantial burden on religiously motivated conduct by a compelling state interest and by means narrowly tailored to achieve that interest. The compelling interest test effectuates the First Amendment's command that religious liberty is an independent liberty, that it occupies a preferred position, and that the Court will not permit encroachments upon this liberty, whether direct or indirect, unless required by clear and compelling governmental interests "of the highest order." . . .

[I]n *Yoder* we expressly rejected the interpretation the Court now adopts. . . . [T]he essence of a free exercise claim is relief from a burden imposed by government on religious practices or beliefs, whether the burden is imposed directly through laws that prohibit or compel specific religious practices, or indirectly through laws that, in effect, make abandonment of one's own religion or conformity to the religious beliefs of others the price of an equal place in the civil community. [A] State that makes criminal an individual's religiously motivated conduct burdens that individual's free exercise of religion in the severest manner possible, for it "results in the choice to the individual of either abandoning his religious principle or facing criminal prosecution." I would have thought it beyond argument that such laws implicate free exercise concerns. [W]e have never distinguished between cases in which a State conditions receipt of a benefit on conduct prohibited by religious beliefs and cases in which a State affirmatively prohibits such conduct. The *Sherbert* compelling interest test applies in both kinds of cases. . . .

[There] is nothing talismanic about neutral laws of general applicability or general criminal prohibitions, for laws neutral toward religion can coerce a person to violate his religious conscience or intrude upon his religious duties just as effectively as laws aimed at religion. . . .

[T]he Court today suggests that the disfavoring of minority religions is an "unavoidable consequence" under our system of government and that accommodation of such religions must be left to the political process. [H]owever, the First Amendment was enacted precisely to protect the rights of those whose religious

---

15. Although Justice BRENNAN, Justice MARSHALL, and Justice BLACKMUN join Parts I and II of this opinion, they do not concur in the judgment.

practices are not shared by the majority and may be viewed with hostility. . . . The compelling interest test reflects the First Amendment's mandate of preserving religious liberty to the fullest extent possible in a pluralistic society. . . .

There is no dispute that Oregon's criminal prohibition of peyote places a severe burden on the ability of respondents to freely exercise their religion. Peyote is a sacrament of the Native American Church and is regarded as vital to respondents' ability to practice their religion. There is also no dispute that Oregon has a significant interest in enforcing laws that control the possession and use of controlled substances by its citizens. [I] would [hold] that the State [has] a compelling interest in regulating peyote use by its citizens and that accommodating respondents' religiously motivated conduct "will unduly interfere with fulfillment of the governmental interest." Accordingly, I concur in the judgment of the Court.

Justice BLACKMUN, with whom Justice BRENNAN and Justice MARSHALL join, dissenting.

[It] is not the State's broad interest in fighting the critical "war on drugs" that must be weighed against respondents' claim, but the State's narrow interest in refusing to make an exception for the religious, ceremonial use of peyote. [T]he State [has] not evinced any concrete interest in enforcing its drug laws against religious users of peyote. . . .

[The] State proclaims an interest in protecting the health and safety of its citizens from the dangers of unlawful drugs. It offers, however, no evidence that the religious use of peyote has ever harmed anyone. [The] Federal Government [does] not find peyote so dangerous as to preclude an exemption for religious use. [The] Native American Church's internal restrictions on, and supervision of, its members' use of peyote substantially obviate the State's health and safety concerns. [Not] only does the church's doctrine forbid nonreligious use of peyote; it also generally advocates self-reliance, familial responsibility, and abstinence from alcohol. . . .

The State also seeks to support its refusal to make an exception for religious use of peyote by invoking its interest in abolishing drug trafficking. There is, however, practically no illegal traffic in peyote. [Peyote] simply is not a popular drug; its distribution for use in religious rituals has nothing to do with the vast and violent traffic in illegal narcotics that plagues this country.

Finally, the State argues that granting an exception for religious peyote use would erode its interest in the uniform, fair, and certain enforcement of its drug laws. [This] Court, however, consistently has rejected similar arguments in past free exercise cases, and it should do so here as well.

The State's apprehension of a flood of other religious claims is purely speculative. Almost half the States, and the Federal Government, have maintained an exemption for religious peyote use for many years, and apparently have not found themselves overwhelmed by claims to other religious exemptions. . . . The unusual circumstances that make the religious use of peyote compatible with the State's interests in health and safety and in preventing drug trafficking would not apply to other religious claims. Some religions, for example, might not restrict drug use to a limited ceremonial context, as does the Native American Church. Some religious claims involve drugs such as marijuana and heroin, in which there is significant illegal traffic, with its attendant greed and violence, so that it would be difficult to grant a religious exemption without seriously compromising law enforcement efforts. That the State might grant an exemption for religious peyote use, but deny other religious claims arising in different circumstances, would not violate the Establishment Clause. [I] dissent.

BACKGROUND
The Religious Freedom Restoration Act

After *Smith*, Congress passed the Religious Freedom Restoration Act (RFRA) in an effort to overrule that decision. RFRA provided that "Government shall not substantially burden a person's exercise of religion even if the burden results from a rule of general applicability" unless the government demonstrates that "application of the burden to the person — (1) is in furtherance of a compelling governmental interest; and (2) is the least restrictive means of furthering that compelling governmental interest." In City of Boerne v. Flores, 521 U.S. 507 (1997), the Court struck down RFRA, concluding: "Broad as the power of Congress is under the Enforcement Clause of the Fourteenth Amendment, RFRA contradicts vital principles necessary to maintain separation of powers and the federal balance."

Notes

1. *Religious Land Use and Institutionalized Persons Act.* After RFRA was struck down, Congress used its authority under the federal Spending and Commerce Clauses to pass the Religious Land Use and Institutionalized Persons Act of 2000 (RLUIPA), 42 U.S.C. §2000cc-1(a)(1)-(2), which provided in part: "No government shall impose a substantial burden on the religious exercise of a person residing in or confined to an institution," unless the burden furthers "a compelling governmental interest" and does so by "the least restrictive means." Current and former inmates of Ohio penal institutions sued, claiming that they were adherents of "non-mainstream" religions (Satanists, Wiccas, Asatrus, and the Church of Jesus Christ Christian) and that they were not being accommodated under RLUIPA. Prison officials claimed that RLUIPA impermissibly advanced religion in violation of the Establishment Clause. In Cutter v. Wilkinson, 544 U.S. 709 (2005), the Court disagreed, noting that government may accommodate religion without violating the Establishment Clause and that Section 3 of RLUIPA does not, on its face, exceed the limits of permissible government accommodation of religious practices. On the contrary, the Act "alleviates exceptional government-created burdens on private religious exercise." The Court

concluded that the Act allows institutions to maintain order and safety, and requires them only to "take adequate account of the burdens a requested accommodation may impose on nonbeneficiaries" and make sure that "the Act's prescriptions are and will be administered neutrally among different faiths." Even though the Act applied a "compelling governmental interest" standard, the Court noted that "[c]ontext matters" in the application of that standard.

2. *More on RFRA.* In Gonzales v. O Centro Espirita Beneficente Uniao Do Vegetal, 546 U.S. 428 (2006), the Court upheld RFRA as applied to the federal government. In that case, a religious sect with origins in the Amazon Rainforest had a practice of receiving communion by drinking a sacramental tea, brewed from plants unique to the region, that contains a hallucinogen regulated by the federal government under the Controlled Substances Act. The government sought to prohibit the small American branch of the sect from engaging in the practice, on the ground that the Controlled Substances Act bars all use of the hallucinogen. The Court held that RFRA required an accommodation because the government could not show that it had a compelling interest in refusing this limited accommodation.

∼ PROBLEMS ∼

1. *Prohibition and Sacramental Wine.* After *Smith*, one question that has arisen is whether government must accommodate other religious practices. For some religions, there is a history of accommodation. For example, during the Prohibition era, Congress decided to exempt the Roman Catholic Church's sacramental use of wine from the general ban on the possession and use of alcohol. *See* National Prohibition Act, Title II, §3, 41 Stat. 308. But is such an exemption constitutionally required? Suppose Congress reimposes Prohibition (presumably after a constitutional amendment) but decides not to include an exemption for the sacramental use of wine. If Catholics challenge the law as an undue burden on their right to freely exercise their religion, does *Smith* require a holding that the Catholics are subject to this "neutral, generally applicable" law? Alternatively, does the Constitution require an accommodation?

2. *The Minister and the Occupational Tax.* Monty Bossard is a devout Baptist minister who firmly believes that the Bible commands him to "Render unto God what is God's, and unto Caesar what is Caesar's." Under Bossard's construction of the Bible, he does not have to pay the City of Louisville's occupational tax (which is imposed on everyone who works within the city). Is Bossard right? Does the Free Exercise Clause grant him an exemption from the city's occupational tax? Does *Smith* require an exemption?

3. *The Christian Scientist's Dying Son.* How does the Free Exercise Clause apply in the context of a Christian Scientist who does not believe in receiving medical care? Presumably, the Christian Scientist can make a decision for herself not to receive medical care. However, what if the adherent's minor son is in a diabetic coma and will die unless he immediately receives medical care? Does the woman have a constitutional right to withhold medical care from her son? On the other

hand, can the state charge her with the crime of criminal neglect if she withholds treatment and her son dies?

4. *The Amish and Photo Driver's Licenses.* Suppose that a sect of the Mennonite religion allows its members to drive motorized vehicles (unlike the Old Order Amish), but prohibits them from having their pictures taken (viewing pictures as "graven images" prohibited by the Bible). Louisiana law requires all drivers to carry a license and provides that all licenses must contain a picture of the driver. If a member of the Mennonite sect seeks an exemption from the picture requirement, is Louisiana required to grant the exemption?

5. *The Eagle Protection Act.* The Eagle Protection Act makes it illegal to kill or possess eagles. In enacting the Act, Congress expressed concern about a black market for eagles and eagle feathers, with single birds fetching as much as $10,000 and individual feathers bringing $35. Little Horse is a member of an American Indian tribe that uses eagle feathers in various religious rites, including funerals and burials, and he seeks an exemption from the law that will allow him to collect bird feathers. (Little Horse recognizes that many eagles are endangered and does not wish to kill them.) After *Smith*, must the state grant Little Horse an exemption? Alternatively, if Little Horse is apprehended in possession of eagle feathers, may the government prosecute him?

2. Discrimination Against Religion

Smith provides the analysis for one line of cases involving neutral, generally applicable laws. But suppose that a law explicitly discriminates against religion or religious activity? In McDaniel v. Paty, 435 U.S. 618 (1978), the Court struck down a statute that prohibited ministers or members of religious orders from being members of state legislatures. Overt governmental discrimination against religion is relatively rare.

Church of the Lukumi Babalu Aye, Inc. v. City of Hialeah
508 U.S. 520 (1993)

Justice KENNEDY delivered the opinion of the Court, except as to Part II-A-2.[16]

[This] case involves practices of the Santeria religion, which originated in the 19th century. When [the] Yoruba people were brought as slaves from western Africa to Cuba, their traditional African religion absorbed significant elements of Roman Catholicism. The resulting syncretion, or fusion, is Santeria, "the way of the saints." The Cuban Yoruba express their devotion to spirits, called orishas, through the iconography of Catholic saints, Catholic symbols are often present at Santeria rites, and Santeria devotees attend the Catholic sacraments.

The Santeria faith teaches that every individual has a destiny from God, a destiny fulfilled with the aid and energy of the orishas. The basis of the Santeria

16. THE CHIEF JUSTICE, Justice SCALIA, and Justice THOMAS join all but Part II-A-2 of this opinion. Justice WHITE joins all but Part II-A of this opinion. Justice SOUTER joins only Parts I, III, and IV of this opinion.

religion is the nurture of a personal relation with the orishas, and one of the principal forms of devotion is an animal sacrifice. . . . According to Santeria teaching, the orishas are powerful but not immortal. They depend for survival on the sacrifice. Sacrifices are performed at birth, marriage, and death rites, for the cure of the sick, for the initiation of new members and priests, and during an annual celebration. Animals sacrificed in Santeria rituals include chickens, pigeons, doves, ducks, guinea pigs, goats, sheep, and turtles. The animals are killed by the cutting of the carotid arteries in the neck. The sacrificed animal is cooked and eaten, except after healing and death rituals. . . . Santeria adherents faced widespread persecution in Cuba, so the religion and its rituals were practiced in secret. . . . The religion was brought to this Nation most often by exiles from the Cuban revolution. [T]here are at least 50,000 practitioners in South Florida today.

Petitioner Church of the Lukumi Babalu Aye, Inc. (Church), [is a church that practices] the Santeria religion. . . . Ernesto Pichardov [is] the Church's priest and holds the religious title of Italero, the second highest in the Santeria faith. In April 1987, the Church leased land in the City of Hialeah, Florida, and announced plans to establish a house of worship as well as a school, cultural center, and museum. Pichardo indicated that the Church's goal was to bring the practice of the Santeria faith, including its ritual of animal sacrifice, into the open. The Church began the process of obtaining utility service and receiving the necessary licensing, inspection, and zoning approvals. Although the Church's efforts at obtaining the necessary licenses and permits were far from smooth, it appears that it received all needed approvals. . . .

The prospect of a Santeria church in their midst was distressing to many members of the Hialeah community, and the announcement of the plans to open a Santeria church in Hialeah prompted the city council to hold an emergency public session on June 9, 1987. . . . First, the city council adopted Resolution 87-66, which noted the "concern" expressed by residents of the city "that certain religions may propose to engage in practices which are inconsistent with public morals, peace or safety," and declared that "[t]he City reiterates its commitment to a prohibition against any and all acts of any and all religious groups which are inconsistent with public morals, peace or safety." Next, the council approved an emergency ordinance, Ordinance 87-40, which incorporated in full, except as to penalty, Florida's animal cruelty laws. Among other things, the incorporated state law subjected to criminal punishment "[whoever] unnecessarily or cruelly [kills] any animal."

The city council desired to undertake further legislative action, but Florida law prohibited a municipality from enacting legislation relating to animal cruelty that conflicted with state law. . . . [Hialeah] requested an opinion from the attorney general of Florida. . . . The attorney general responded [that] the "ritual sacrifice of animals for purposes other than food consumption" was not a "necessary" killing and so was prohibited by §828.12. The attorney general [defined] "unnecessary" as "done without any useful motive, in a spirit of wanton cruelty or for the mere pleasure of destruction without being in any sense beneficial or useful to the person killing the animal." He advised that religious animal sacrifice was against state law, so that a city ordinance prohibiting it would not be in conflict.

The city council responded at first with a hortatory enactment, Resolution 87-90, that noted its residents' "great concern regarding the possibility of public ritualistic animal sacrifices" and the state-law prohibition. The resolution declared the city policy "to oppose the ritual sacrifices of animals" within Hialeah and announced that any person or organization practicing animal sacrifice "will be prosecuted."

In September 1987, the city council adopted three substantive ordinances addressing the issue of religious animal sacrifice. Ordinance 87-52 defined "sacrifice" as "to unnecessarily kill, torment, torture, or mutilate an animal in a public or private ritual or ceremony not for the primary purpose of food consumption," and prohibited owning or possessing an animal "intending to use such animal for food purposes." It restricted application of this prohibition, however, to any individual or group that "kills, slaughters or sacrifices animals for any type of ritual, regardless of whether or not the flesh or blood of the animal is to be consumed." The ordinance contained an exemption for slaughtering by "licensed establishment[s]" of animals "specifically raised for food purposes." Declaring, moreover, that the city council "has determined that the sacrificing of animals within the city limits is contrary to the public health, safety, welfare and morals of the community," the city council adopted Ordinance 87-71. That ordinance defined sacrifice as had Ordinance 87-52, and then provided that "[i]t shall be unlawful for any person, persons, corporations or associations to sacrifice any animal within the corporate limits of the City of Hialeah, Florida." The final Ordinance, 87-72, defined "slaughter" as "the killing of animals for food" and prohibited slaughter outside of areas zoned for slaughterhouse use. The ordinance provided an exemption, however, for the slaughter or processing for sale of "small numbers of hogs and/or cattle per week in accordance with an exemption provided by state law." All ordinances and resolutions passed the city council by unanimous vote. Violations of each of the four ordinances were punishable by fines not exceeding $500 or imprisonment not exceeding 60 days, or both.

Following enactment of these ordinances, the Church and Pichardo filed [suit] [a]lleging violations of petitioners' rights under [the Free] Exercise Clause. . . . The District Court ruled for the city [and the] Court of Appeals for the Eleventh Circuit affirmed. . . .

II

[The] city does not argue that Santeria is not a "religion" within the meaning of the First Amendment. Nor could it. Although the practice of animal sacrifice may seem abhorrent to some, "religious beliefs need not be acceptable, logical, consistent, or comprehensible to others in order to merit First Amendment protection." [Neither] the city nor the courts below [have] questioned the sincerity of petitioners' professed desire to conduct animal sacrifices for religious reasons. . . .

[A] law that is neutral and of general applicability need not be justified by a compelling governmental interest even if the law has the incidental effect of burdening a particular religious practice. [A] law failing to satisfy these requirements must be justified by a compelling governmental interest and must be narrowly tailored to advance that interest. These ordinances fail to satisfy the *Smith* requirements. . . .

[T]he First Amendment forbids an official purpose to disapprove of a particular religion or of religion in general. . . . Petitioners allege an attempt to disfavor their religion because of the religious ceremonies it commands. . . .

[T]he protections of the Free Exercise Clause pertain if the law at issue discriminates against some or all religious beliefs or regulates or prohibits conduct because it is undertaken for religious reasons. Indeed, it was "historical instances of religious persecution and intolerance that gave concern to those who drafted the Free Exercise Clause." Bowen v. Roy, 476 U.S. 693 (1986) (opinion of Burger, C.J.). These principles, though not often at issue in our Free Exercise Clause cases, have played a role in some. In McDaniel v. Paty, 435 U.S. 618 (1978), for example, we invalidated a State law that disqualified members of the clergy from holding certain public offices, because it "impose[d] special disabilities on the basis [of] religious status." On the same principle, in Fowler v. Rhode Island, [345 U.S. 67 (1953], we found that a municipal ordinance was applied in an unconstitutional manner when interpreted to prohibit preaching in a public park by a Jehovah's Witness but to permit preaching during the course of a Catholic mass or Protestant church service.

Although a law targeting religious beliefs as such is never permissible, if the object of a law is to infringe upon or restrict practices because of their religious motivation, the law is not neutral, and it is invalid unless it is justified by a compelling interest and is narrowly tailored to advance that interest. There are, of course, many ways of demonstrating that the object or purpose of a law is the suppression of religion or religious conduct. To determine the object of a law, we must begin with its text, for the minimum requirement of neutrality is that a law not discriminate on its face. A law lacks facial neutrality if it refers to a religious practice without a secular meaning discernable from the language or context. Petitioners contend that three of the ordinances fail this test of facial neutrality because they use the words "sacrifice" and "ritual," words with strong religious connotations. We agree that these words are consistent with the claim of facial discrimination, but the argument is not conclusive. The words "sacrifice" and "ritual" have a religious origin, but current use admits also of secular meanings. The ordinances, furthermore, define "sacrifice" in secular terms, without referring to religious practices.

We reject the contention advanced by the city that our inquiry must end with the text of the laws at issue. Facial neutrality is not determinative. The Free Exercise Clause, like the Establishment Clause[,] "forbids subtle departures from neutrality," and "covert suppression of particular religious beliefs." Official action that targets religious conduct for distinctive treatment cannot be shielded by mere compliance with the requirement of facial neutrality. The Free Exercise Clause protects against governmental hostility which is masked, as well as overt. . . .

   The record in this case compels the conclusion that suppression of the central element of the Santeria worship service was the object of the ordinances. First, though use of the words "sacrifice" and "ritual" does not compel a finding of improper targeting of the Santeria religion, the choice of these words is support for our conclusion. There are further respects in which the text of the city council's enactments discloses the improper attempt to target Santeria. Resolution 87-66, adopted June 9, 1987, recited that "residents and citizens of the City of Hialeah have expressed their concern that certain religions may propose to engage in practices which are inconsistent with public morals, peace or safety," and "reiterate[d]" the city's commitment to prohibit "any and all [such] acts of any and all religious groups." No one suggests, and on this record it cannot be maintained, that city officials had in mind a religion other than Santeria.

   [Apart] from the text, the effect of a law in its real operation is strong evidence of its object. To be sure, adverse impact will not always lead to a finding of impermissible targeting. For example, a social harm may have been a legitimate concern of government for reasons quite apart from discrimination. The subject at hand does implicate, of course, multiple concerns unrelated to religious animosity, for example, the suffering or mistreatment visited upon the sacrificed animals and health hazards from improper disposal. But the ordinances when considered together disclose an object remote from these legitimate concerns. The design of these laws accomplishes instead a "religious gerrymander," an impermissible attempt to target petitioners and their religious practices.

   [A]lmost the only conduct subject to Ordinances 87-40, 87-52, and 87-71 is the religious exercise of Santeria church members. The texts [were] drafted in tandem to achieve this result. [Ordinance 87-71] prohibits the sacrifice of animals, but defines sacrifice as "to unnecessarily kill [an] animal in a public or private ritual or ceremony not for the primary purpose of food consumption." The definition excludes almost all killings of animals except for religious sacrifice, and the primary purpose requirement narrows the proscribed category even further, in particular by exempting kosher slaughter. We need not discuss whether this differential treatment of two religions is itself an independent constitutional violation. It suffices to recite [that] Santeria alone was the exclusive legislative concern. The net result [is] that few if any killings of animals are prohibited other than Santeria sacrifice, which is proscribed because it occurs during a ritual or ceremony and its primary purpose is to make an offering to the orishas, not food consumption. Indeed, careful drafting ensured that, although Santeria sacrifice is prohibited, killings that are no more necessary or humane in almost all other circumstances are unpunished.

   Operating in similar fashion is Ordinance 87-52, which prohibits the "possess[ion], sacrifice, or slaughter" of an animal with the "inten[t] to use such animal for food purposes." This prohibition, extending to the keeping of an animal as well as the killing itself, applies if the animal is killed in "any type of ritual" and there is an intent to use the animal for food, whether or not it is in fact consumed for food. The ordinance exempts, however, "any licensed [food] establishment" with regard to "any animals which are specifically raised for food purposes," if the activity is permitted by zoning and other laws. This exception, too, seems intended to cover kosher slaughter. Again, the burden of the ordinance, in practical terms, falls on Santeria adherents but almost no others: If the killing is—unlike most Santeria sacrifices—unaccompanied by the intent to use the animal for food, then it is not prohibited by Ordinance 87-52; if the killing is specifically for food but does not occur during the course of "any type of ritual," it again falls outside the prohibition; and if the killing is for food and occurs during the course of a ritual, it is still exempted if it occurs in a properly zoned and licensed establishment and involves animals "specifically raised for food purposes." A pattern of exemptions parallels the pattern of narrow prohibitions. Each contributes to the gerrymander.

Ordinance 87-40 incorporates the Florida animal cruelty statute. Its prohibition is broad on its face, punishing "[w]hoever [unnecessarily] kills any animal." The city claims that this ordinance is the epitome of a neutral prohibition. The problem, however, is the interpretation given to the ordinance by respondent and the Florida attorney general. Killings for religious reasons are deemed unnecessary, whereas most other killings fall outside the prohibition. The city, on what seems to be a per se basis, deems hunting, slaughter of animals for food, eradication of insects and pests, and euthanasia as necessary. There is no indication in the record that respondent has concluded that hunting or fishing for sport is unnecessary. Indeed, one of the few reported Florida cases decided under §828.12 concludes that the use of live rabbits to train greyhounds is not unnecessary. Further, because it requires an evaluation of the particular justification for the killing, this ordinance represents a system of "individualized governmental assessment of the reasons for the relevant conduct." [I]n circumstances in which individualized exemptions from a general requirement are available, the government "may not refuse to extend that system to cases of 'religious hardship' without compelling reason." Respondent's application of the ordinance's test of necessity devalues religious reasons for killing by judging them to be of lesser import than nonreligious reasons. Thus, religious practice is being singled out for discriminatory treatment.

We also find significant evidence of the ordinances' improper targeting of Santeria sacrifice in the fact that they proscribe more religious conduct than is necessary to achieve their stated ends. It is not unreasonable to infer, at least when there are no persuasive indications to the contrary, that a law which visits "gratuitous restrictions" on religious conduct, seeks not to effectuate the stated governmental interests, but to suppress the conduct because of its religious motivation.

The legitimate governmental interests in protecting the public health and preventing cruelty to animals could be addressed by restrictions stopping far short of a flat prohibition of all Santeria sacrificial practice. If improper disposal [is] the harm to be prevented, the city could have imposed a general regulation on the disposal of organic garbage. It did not do so. Indeed, counsel for the city conceded [that], under the ordinances, Santeria sacrifices would be illegal even if they occurred in licensed, inspected, and zoned slaughterhouses. Thus, [these] ordinances prohibit Santeria sacrifice even when it does not threaten the city's interest in the public health. [The] neutrality of a law is suspect if First Amendment freedoms are curtailed to prevent isolated collateral harms not themselves prohibited by direct regulation.

[N]arrower regulation would achieve the city's interest in preventing cruelty to animals. With regard to the city's interest in ensuring the adequate care of animals, regulation of conditions and treatment, regardless of why an animal is kept, is the logical response to the city's concern, not a prohibition on possession for the purpose of sacrifice. The same is true for the city's interest in prohibiting cruel methods of killing. Under federal and Florida law and Ordinance 87-40, which incorporates Florida law in this regard, killing an animal by the "simultaneous and instantaneous severance of the carotid arteries with a sharp instrument"—the method used in kosher slaughter—is approved as humane. [T]hough Santeria sacrifice also results in severance of the carotid arteries, the method used during sacrifice is less reliable and therefore not humane. If the city has a real concern that other methods are less humane, [the] subject of the regulation should be the method of slaughter itself, not a religious classification that [bears] some general relation to it.

Ordinance 87-72—unlike the three other ordinances—does appear to apply to substantial nonreligious conduct and not to be overbroad. For our purposes here, [the] four substantive ordinances may be treated as a group for neutrality purposes. Ordinance 87-72 was passed the same day as Ordinance 87-71 and was enacted, as were the three others, in direct response to the opening of the Church. It would be implausible to suggest that the three other ordinances, but not Ordinance 87-72, had as their object the suppression of religion. We need not decide whether the Ordinance 87-72 could survive constitutional scrutiny if it existed separately; it must be invalidated because it functions, with the rest of the enactments in question, to suppress Santeria religious worship.

[A]s in equal protection cases, we may determine the city council's object from both direct and circumstantial evidence. Relevant evidence includes, among other things, the historical background of the decision under challenge, the specific series of events leading to the enactment or official policy in question, and the legislative or administrative history, including contemporaneous statements made by members of the decisionmaking body. These objective factors bear on the question of discriminatory object. . . . That the ordinances were enacted "'because of,' not merely 'in spite of,'" their suppression of Santeria religious practice, is revealed by the events preceding their enactment.

In sum, the neutrality inquiry leads to one conclusion: The ordinances had as their object the suppression of religion. The pattern we have recited discloses animosity to Santeria adherents and their religious practices; the ordinances by their own terms target this religious exercise; the texts of the ordinances were gerrymandered with care to proscribe religious killings of animals but to exclude almost all secular killings; and the ordinances suppress much more religious conduct than is necessary in order to achieve the legitimate ends asserted in their defense. These ordinances are not neutral. . . .

We turn next to a second requirement of the Free Exercise Clause, the rule that laws burdening religious practice must be of general applicability. [Respondent] claims that Ordinances 87-40, 87-52, and 87-71 advance two interests: protecting the public health and preventing cruelty to animals. The ordinances are underinclusive for those ends. They fail to prohibit nonreligious conduct that endangers these interests in a similar or greater degree than Santeria sacrifice does. The underinclusion is substantial, not inconsequential. Despite the city's proffered interest in preventing cruelty to animals, the ordinances are drafted with care to forbid few killings but those occasioned by religious sacrifice. Many types of animal deaths or kills for nonreligious reasons are either not prohibited or approved by express provision. For example, fishing—which occurs in Hialeah—is legal. Extermination of mice and rats within a home is also permitted. Florida law incorporated by Ordinance 87-40 sanctions euthanasia of "stray, neglected, abandoned, or unwanted animals"; destruction of animals judicially removed from their owners "for humanitarian reasons" or when the animal "is of no commercial value"; the infliction of pain or suffering "in the interest of medical science"; the placing of poison in one's yard or enclosure; and the use of a live animal "to pursue or take wildlife or to participate in any hunting," and "to hunt wild hogs."

The city concedes that "neither the State of Florida nor the City has enacted a generally applicable ban on the killing of animals." It asserts, however, that animal sacrifice is "different" from the animal killings that are permitted by law. According to the city, it is "self-evident" that killing animals for food is "important"; the eradication of insects and pests is "obviously justified"; and the euthanasia of excess animals "makes sense." These *ipse dixits* do not explain why religion alone must bear the burden of the ordinances, when many of these secular killings fall within the city's interest in preventing the cruel treatment of animals.

The ordinances are also underinclusive with regard to the city's interest in public health, which is threatened by the disposal of animal carcasses in open public places and the consumption of uninspected meat. Neither interest is pursued by respondent with regard to conduct that is not motivated by religious conviction. The health risks posed by the improper disposal of animal carcasses are the same whether Santeria sacrifice or some nonreligious killing preceded it. The city does not, however, prohibit hunters from bringing their kill to their houses, nor does it regulate disposal after their activity. Despite substantial testimony at trial that the same public health hazards result from improper disposal of garbage by restaurants, restaurants are outside the scope of the ordinances. Improper disposal is a general problem that causes substantial health risks, but which respondent addresses only when it results from religious exercise.

The ordinances are underinclusive as well with regard to the health risk posed by consumption of uninspected meat. Under the city's ordinances, hunters may eat their kill and fishermen may eat their catch without undergoing governmental inspection. Likewise, state law requires inspection of meat that is sold but exempts meat from animals raised for the use of the owner and "members of his household and nonpaying guests and employees." The asserted interest in inspected meat is not pursued in contexts similar to that of religious animal sacrifice.

Ordinance 87-72, which prohibits the slaughter of animals outside of areas zoned for slaughterhouses, is underinclusive on its face. The ordinance includes an exemption for "any person, group, or organization" that "slaughters or processes for sale, small numbers of hogs and/or cattle per week in accordance with an exemption provided by state law." Respondent has not explained why commercial operations that slaughter "small numbers" of hogs and cattle do not implicate its professed desire to prevent cruelty to animals and preserve the public health. Although the city has classified Santeria sacrifice as slaughter, subjecting it to this ordinance, it does not regulate other killings for food in like manner.

We conclude, in sum, that each of Hialeah's ordinances pursues the city's governmental interests only against conduct motivated by religious belief. The ordinances "ha[ve] every appearance of a prohibition that society is prepared to impose upon [Santeria worshippers] but not upon itself." This precise evil is what the requirement of general applicability is designed to prevent.

III

A law burdening religious practice that is not neutral or not of general application must undergo the most rigorous of scrutiny. To satisfy the commands of the First Amendment, a law restrictive of religious practice must advance "'interests of the highest order'" and must be narrowly tailored in pursuit of those interests. [A] law that targets religious conduct for distinctive treatment or advances legitimate governmental interests only against conduct with a religious motivation will survive strict scrutiny only in rare cases. It follows from what we have already said that these ordinances cannot withstand this scrutiny.

First, even were the governmental interests compelling, the ordinances are not drawn in narrow terms to accomplish those interests. [A]ll four ordinances are overbroad or underinclusive in substantial respects. The proffered objectives are not pursued with respect to analogous non-religious conduct, and those interests could be achieved by narrower ordinances that burdened religion to a far lesser degree. The absence of narrow tailoring suffices to establish the invalidity of the ordinances.

Respondent has not demonstrated, moreover, that, in the context of these ordinances, its governmental interests are compelling. Where government restricts only conduct protected by the First Amendment and fails to enact feasible measures to restrict other conduct producing substantial harm or alleged harm of the same sort, the interest given in justification of the restriction is not compelling. "[A] law cannot be regarded as protecting an interest 'of the highest order' [when] it leaves appreciable damage to that supposedly vital interest unprohibited." [T]he ordinances are underinclusive to a substantial extent with respect to each of the interests that respondent has asserted, and it is only conduct motivated by religious conviction that bears the weight of the governmental restrictions. There can be no serious claim that those interests justify the ordinances.

The Free Exercise Clause commits government itself to religious tolerance, and upon even slight suspicion that proposals for state intervention stem from animosity to religion or distrust of its practices, all officials must pause to remember their own high duty to the Constitution and to the rights it secures. Those in office must be resolute in resisting importunate demands and must ensure that the sole reasons for imposing the burdens of law and regulation are secular. Legislators may not devise mechanisms, overt or disguised, designed to persecute or oppress a religion or its practices. The laws here in question were enacted contrary to these constitutional principles, and they are void.

Reversed.

Justice SCALIA, with whom THE CHIEF JUSTICE joins, concurring in part and concurring in the judgment.

[Perhaps] there are contexts in which determination of legislative motive must be undertaken. But I do not think that is true of analysis under the First Amendment. . . . The First Amendment does not refer to the purposes for which legislators enact laws, but to the effects of the laws enacted: "Congress shall make no law [prohibiting] the free exercise [of religion]." This does not put us in the business of invalidating laws by reason of the evil motives of their authors. . . .

∽ PROBLEMS ∽

1. *Rewriting the Hialeah Law.* After the decision in *Lukumi,* the City of Hialeah remains adamant about prohibiting animal sacrifice. Is it possible to redraft the law in a way that will make it constitutionally neutral and generally applicable? How?

2. *Mormons and the Polygamy Ban.* At the beginning of the chapter, *Reynolds* (which held that Mormons were not entitled to an exemption for polygamy) was examined. Did the Court "get it wrong" in *Reynolds*? If *Reynolds* had arisen after *Lukumi,* should the Court have held that the ban on polygamy discriminated against Mormon beliefs and therefore is invalid? Why or why not?

3. *Rattlesnake Handlers.* Suppose that a fundamentalist congregation believes that it has a religious obligation to handle poisonous snakes. Its belief is based on the Bible — in particular, the Book of Mark, Chapter 16, which provides: "And these signs shall follow them that believe: In my name shall they cast out devils; they shall speak with new tongues; they shall take up serpents, and if they drink any deadly thing, it shall not hurt them." Suppose that Kentucky, concerned about deaths during fundamentalist services, decides to prohibit rattlesnake handling in church services. Under *Lukimi,* does the Kentucky law involve discrimination against religion? Would it matter whether the law also prohibits the handling of snakes in other contexts (e.g., live entertainment performance)?

4. *The Homophobic Landlord.* May the state prohibit a homophobic landlord, whose homophobia is grounded in his religious beliefs, from discriminating in property rentals? For example, New Orleans enacts a fair housing law that prohibits discrimination against gays and lesbians. A landlord, who believes that

homosexuality is immoral and contrary to his religious beliefs, refuses to rent an apartment to a gay couple. Is the landlord's action protected under the Free Exercise Clause?

5. *More on the Education for a Better America Act.* In constructing the proposed legislation, do you have any special concerns about discrimination against religion? Suppose, for example, that Congress proposes to prohibit schools that receive federal funding from discriminating on the basis of sex as well as from segregating by sex. Could the Act prohibit discrimination by a religious school that believes in segregating children by sex or that believes in treating (and educating) girls differently than boys? Or, should Congress create an exception for such institutions?

C. ESTABLISHMENT: FREE EXERCISE AND FREE SPEECH TENSION

Even though the Establishment Clause and the Free Exercise Clause are separately stated, they conflict in a number of different contexts. Consider the following case.

Board of Education of Kiryas Joel Village School District v. Grumet
512 U.S. 687 (1994)

Justice SOUTER delivered the opinion of the Court.

[The Satmar Hasidic sect purchased an undeveloped subdivision. When a zoning dispute arose, the Satmars petitioned to form a new village, a right that New York law gives any group of residents who satisfy certain procedural niceties. The boundaries of the village of Kiryas Joel were drawn to include only the 320 acres owned and inhabited entirely by Satmars. The village has a population of 8,500 today.]

The residents of Kiryas Joel are vigorously religious people who make few concessions to the modern world and go to great lengths to avoid [assimilation]. They interpret the Torah strictly; segregate the sexes outside the home; speak Yiddish as their primary language; eschew television, radio, and English-language publications; and dress in distinctive ways that include headcoverings and special garments for boys and modest dresses for girls. Children are educated in private religious schools, most boys at the United Talmudic Academy where they receive [a] grounding in the Torah and limited exposure to secular subjects, [and] girls at [an] affiliated school with a curriculum designed to prepare girls for their roles as wives and mothers.

These schools do not [offer] any distinctive services to handicapped children. [I]n 1984 the Monroe-Woodbury Central School District provided such services for the children of Kiryas Joel at an [annex, but ended] that arrangement in response to our decisions in Aguilar v. Felton and School Dist. of Grand Rapids v. Ball. Children from Kiryas Joel who needed special education (including the deaf, the mentally retarded, and others suffering from a range of physical, mental, or emotional disorders) were then forced to attend public schools outside the village. [Parents] of these children withdrew them from [the] secular schools citing "the panic, fear and trauma [suffered] in [being] with people whose ways were so different." [By] 1989, only one child from Kiryas Joel was attending Monroe-Woodbury's public schools; the village's other handicapped children received privately funded special services or went without. It was then that the New York Legislature passed [a] statute [which] provided that the village of Kiryas Joel "is constituted a separate school district. . . ." 1989 N.Y. Laws, ch. 748. [Governor Cuomo viewed] the bill [as] "a good faith effort to solve th[e] unique problem" associated with providing special education services to handicapped children in the village.

Although it enjoys plenary legal authority over the elementary and secondary education of all school-aged children in the village, the Kiryas Joel Village School District currently runs only a special education program for handicapped children. The other village children [are in] parochial schools, relying on the new school district only for transportation, remedial education, and health and welfare services. If any child without a handicap [were] to seek a public-school education, the district would pay tuition to send the child [to] another school district nearby. [S]everal of the neighboring districts send their handicapped Hasidic children [to] Kiryas Joel. . . . The district serves just over 40 full-time students, and two or three times that many [on] a part-time basis.

[Respondents challenged] Chapter 748 [as an] establishment of religion. [Respondents won in the courts below.] [We] granted certiorari.

II

"A proper respect for both the Free Exercise and the Establishment Clauses compels the State to pursue a course of 'neutrality' toward religion," Committee for Public Ed. & Religious Liberty v. Nyquist, 413 U.S. 756 (1973), favoring neither one religion over others nor religious adherents collectively over nonadherents. Chapter 748, the statute creating the Kiryas Joel Village School District, departs from this constitutional command by delegating the State's discretionary authority over public schools to a group defined by its character as a religious community, in [a] context that gives no assurance that governmental power has been or will be exercised neutrally.

[In] Larkin v. Grendel's Den, Inc., 459 U.S. 116 (1982), [the] Court [reviewed] a Massachusetts statute granting religious bodies veto power over applications for liquor licenses. . . . *Larkin* presented an example of united civic and religious authority, [a] violation of "the core rationale underlying the Establishment Clause." [Chapter 748 resembles] *Larkin* to the extent that the earlier case teaches that a State may not delegate its civic authority to a group chosen according to a religious criterion. Authority over public schools belongs to the State, and cannot be delegated to [a] religious group. What makes this litigation different from *Larkin* is the delegation [of] civic power to the "qualified voters of the village of Kiryas Joel," as distinct from a religious leader such as the village rov, or an institution of religious government like [the] parish council in *Larkin*. [T]his distinction [lacks] constitutional significance.

[R]eligious people [cannot] be denied the opportunity to exercise the rights of citizens simply because of their religious affiliations or commitments, for such a disability would violate the right to religious free exercise. [McDaniel v. Paty, 435 U.S. 618 (1978)] held that a religious individual could not, because of his religious activities, be denied the right to hold political office. . . . If New York were to delegate civic authority to "the Grand Rebbe," *Larkin* would obviously require invalidation (even though under *McDaniel* the Grand Rebbe may run for, and serve on, his local school board). [T]he difference lies in the distinction between a government's purposeful delegation on the basis of religion and a delegation on principles neutral to religion, to individuals whose religious identities are incidental to their receipt of civic authority.

[Chapter 748] delegates power not by express reference to the religious belief of the Satmar community, but to residents of the "territory of the village of Kiryas Joel." [But] Chapter 748 effectively identifies these recipients of governmental authority by reference to doctrinal adherence. [T]he boundary lines of the school district divide residents according to religious affiliation [under] the terms of an unusual and special legislative Act. [T]hose who negotiated the village boundaries [excluded] all but Satmars, [and] the New York Legislature was well aware that the village remained exclusively Satmar [when] it adopted Chapter 748. The significance of this fact [is] that carving out the village school district ran counter to customary districting practices in the State. [T]he trend in New York is not toward dividing school districts but toward consolidating them [in order to] provide a comprehensive education at affordable cost. . . . The Kiryas Joel Village School District [has] only 13 local, full-time students[,] and in offering only special education and remedial programs it makes no pretense to be a full-service district.

The origin of the district in a special Act of the legislature, rather than the State's general laws governing school district reorganization, is likewise anomalous. Although the legislature has established some 20 existing school districts by special Act, all but one [are] districts in name only, [designed] to be run by private organizations serving institutionalized children. They have neither tax bases nor student populations of their own but serve children placed by other school districts or public agencies. The one school district [that] was formed by special Act of the legislature to serve a whole community [is] a district formed for a new town, much larger and more heterogeneous than this village. . . . Thus the Kiryas Joel Village School District is exceptional to the point of singularity. [T]his district "cannot be seen as the fulfillment of [a village's] destiny as an independent governmental entity."

Because the district's creation ran uniquely counter to state practice, following the lines of a religious community where the customary and neutral principles would not have dictated the same result, we have good reasons to treat this district as the reflection of a religious criterion for identifying the recipients of civil authority. . . . We therefore find the legislature's Act to be substantially equivalent to defining a political subdivision and hence the qualification for its franchise by a religious test, resulting in a purposeful and forbidden "fusion of governmental and religious functions." [The] fact that this school district was created by a special and unusual Act of the legislature also gives reason for concern whether the benefit received by the Satmar community is one that the legislature will provide equally to other religious (and nonreligious) groups. [T]he special Act in these cases stands alone. . . .

[T]he Constitution allows the State to accommodate religious needs by alleviating special burdens. [But] accommodation is not a principle without limits. . . . Petitioners' proposed accommodation singles out a particular religious sect for special treatment. [T]here are several alternatives here for providing bilingual and bicultural special education to Satmar children. Such services [can] be offered to village children through the Monroe-Woodbury Central School District. Since the Satmars do not claim that separatism is religiously mandated, their children may receive bilingual and bicultural instruction at a public school already run by [the] district. Or if the educationally appropriate offering [should] be a separate program of bilingual and bicultural education at a neutral site near one of the village's parochial schools, [no] Establishment Clause difficulty would inhere in such a scheme, administered in accordance with neutral principles that would not necessarily confine special treatment to Satmars.

[We] do not disable a religiously homogeneous group from exercising political power conferred on it without regard to religion. Unlike the States of Utah and New Mexico (which were laid out according to traditional political methodologies taking account of lines of latitude and longitude and topographical features), the reference line [for] the Kiryas Joel Village School District [was] drawn to separate Satmars from non-Satmars. [T]he statute before us fails the test of neutrality. It delegates a power this Court has said "ranks at the very apex of the function of a State," to an electorate defined by common religious belief and practice, in a manner that fails to foreclose religious favoritism. It therefore crosses the line from permissible accommodation to impermissible establishment. The judgment of the Court of Appeals of the State of New York is accordingly

Affirmed.

Justice STEVENS, with whom Justice BLACKMUN and Justice GINSBURG join, concurring.

[The] isolation of these children [unquestionably] increased the likelihood that they would remain within the fold, faithful adherents of their parents' religious faith. [Affirmative] state action in aid of segregation of this character [is] fairly characterized as establishing, rather than merely accommodating, religion.

Justice O'CONNOR, concurring in part and concurring in the judgment.

[What] makes accommodation permissible, even praiseworthy, is [that] the government is accommodating a deeply held belief. [But accommodations] do not justify discriminations based on sect. A state law prohibiting the consumption of alcohol may exempt sacramental wines, but it may not exempt sacramental wine use by Catholics but not by Jews. . . . Because this benefit was given to this group based on its religion, it seems proper to treat it as a legislatively drawn religious classification. [The] legislature may well be acting without any favoritism, so that if another group came to ask for a similar district, the group might get it on the same terms as the Satmars. But the nature of the legislative process makes it impossible to be sure of this. [I]t seems dangerous to validate what appears to me a clear religious preference.

Our invalidation of this statute in no way means that the Satmars' needs cannot be accommodated. . . . New York [may] allow all villages to operate their own school districts. If it does not want to act so broadly, it may set forth neutral criteria that a village must meet to have a school district of its own. . . . A district created under a generally applicable scheme would be acceptable even though it coincides with a village that was consciously created by its voters as an enclave for their religious group. [T]here is one other accommodation that would be [permissible]: the [scheme] which was discontinued because of our decision in *Aguilar*. [If] the government provides this education on-site at public schools and at nonsectarian private schools, it is only fair that it provide it on-site at sectarian schools as well. . . .

Justice KENNEDY, concurring in the judgment.

[There] is more than a fine line [between] the voluntary association that leads to a political community comprised of people who share a common religious faith, and the forced separation that occurs when the government draws explicit political boundaries on the basis of peoples' faith. In creating the Kiryas Joel Village School District, New York crossed that line. . . .

Justice SCALIA, with whom THE CHIEF JUSTICE and Justice THOMAS join, dissenting.

The Court today finds that the Powers That Be, up in Albany, have Conspired to effect an establishment of the Satmar Hasidim. I do not know who would be more surprised at this discovery: the Founders of our Nation or Grand Rebbe Joel Teitelbaum, founder of the Satmar. The Grand Rebbe would be astounded to learn that after escaping brutal persecution and coming to America with the modest hope of religious toleration for their ascetic form of Judaism, the Satmar had become so powerful, so closely allied with Mammon, as to have become an "establishment" of the Empire State. . . .

[T]hese cases involve no public funding, however slight or indirect, to private religious schools. [The] school under scrutiny is a public school specifically designed to provide a public secular education to handicapped students. . . . While the village's private schools are profoundly religious and strictly segregated by sex, classes at the public school are co-ed and the curriculum secular.

The school building has the bland appearance of a public school, unadorned by religious symbols or markings; and the school complies with the laws and regulations governing all other New York State public schools. . . . The only thing distinctive about the school is that all the students share the same religion. [If] a State can furnish services to a group of sectarian students on a neutral site adjacent to a private religious school, or even within such a school, how can there be any defect in educating those same students in a public school? [The] populating of North America is in no small measure the story of groups of people sharing a common religious and cultural heritage striking out to form their own communities. It is preposterous to suggest that the civil institutions of these communities, separate from their churches, were constitutionally suspect. . . .

Justice Souter's position boils down to [the] novel proposition that any group of citizens [can] be invested with political power, but not if they all belong to the same religion. Of course such disfavoring of religion is positively antagonistic to the purposes of the Religion Clauses. [Justice] Souter's second justification for finding an establishment of religion [is] his facile conclusion that the New York Legislature's creation of the Kiryas Joel school district was religiously motivated. . . . The handicapped children suffered sufficient emotional trauma from their predicament that their parents kept them home from school. Surely the legislature could [provide] a public education for these students. [Justice] Souter's case against the statute comes down to [the fact that the] residents of the Kiryas Joel Village School District are Satmars. But all its residents also wear unusual dress, have unusual civic customs, and have not much to do with people who are culturally different from them. [On] what basis does Justice Souter conclude that it is the theological distinctiveness rather than the cultural distinctiveness that was the basis for New York State's decision? The normal assumption would be that it was the latter. [Justice Souter argues that] the legislature must have been motivated by the desire to favor religion. . . . There is no evidence of that. The special district was created to meet the special educational needs of distinctive handicapped children. [When] a legislature acts to accommodate religion, particularly a minority sect, "it follows the best of our traditions." [I] dissent.

BACKGROUND
Religious Exemptions

There has been considerable debate about whether government can, or should, exempt religious groups from the application of civil rights laws that conflict with their beliefs. Illustrative is Corporation of Presiding Bishop v. Amos, 483 U.S. 327 (1987), which involved Section 702 of the Civil Rights Act of 1964, which exempted religious organizations from Title VII's prohibition against discrimination in employment on the basis of religion as applied to a church's decision to discharge a nonmember from its employment. In upholding the exemption, the Court stated: "Where, as here, government acts with the proper purpose of lifting a regulation that burdens the exercise of religion, we see no reason to require that the exemption comes packaged with benefits to secular entities."

Note: Armed Forces Chaplains

Another context in which claims for religious exemption have surfaced is military chaplains. The armed forces hire chaplains to meet the religious needs of soldiers. Although chaplains are given the status of commissioned officers and wear uniforms, they are not given commands. In Katcoff v. Marsh, 755 F.2d 223 (2d Cir. 1985), the court upheld the practice: "The problem of meeting the religious needs of Army personnel is compounded by the mobile, deployable nature of our armed forces, who must be ready on extremely short notice to be transported from bases [to] distant parts of the world for combat duty. . . . Unless there were chaplains ready to move simultaneously with the troops and to tend to their spiritual needs as they face possible death, the soldiers would be left in the lurch, religiously speaking. . . ." The court emphasized that chaplains were not allowed to proselytize soldiers, and their "principal duties are to conduct religious services[,] to furnish religious education to soldiers and their families, and to counsel soldiers with respect to a wide variety of personal problems. . . ." The court questioned whether chaplains would be necessary in areas where civilian religious personnel are available.

∽ PROBLEMS ∽

1. *Accommodating the Satmars.* Obviously, in *Kiryas Joel*, the Court invalidates New York's attempt to create a special school district. Does the holding in that case doom all further accommodations? Suppose that you are counsel to the legislature. Following the Court's holding, can you suggest ways that the legislature might accommodate the Satmars without violating the Establishment Clause?

2. *The Satmars and the Education for a Better America Act.* In constructing the proposed legislation, can you (should you?) attempt to accommodate religions like the Satmars? Can you provide financial aid to them on terms equivalent to those provided to other schools?

3. *Student Religious Music.* At times, officials have difficulty finding the dividing line between establishment and accommodation. For example, suppose that a choral teacher invites students to bring songs of their own choosing to class, and tells students that the class will collectively analyze the songs in terms of tone, tempo, and dynamics. Suppose that one student decides to bring a recording that contains religious music. On establishment grounds, should the teacher refuse to play the music because of its religious content? Alternatively, should the teacher "accommodate" the student's desire to listen to religious music? How would you advise the school district? In that regard, consider the following case.

Rosenberger v. Rector and Visitors of the University of Virginia

515 U.S. 819 (1995)

Justice KENNEDY delivered the opinion of the Court.

[In this case, the Student Activities Fund (SAF) at the University of Virginia denied funds for the printing of the student publication *Wide Awake: A Christian Perspective at the University of Virginia*. The Supreme Court first held that "the regulation invoked to deny SAF support, both in its terms and in its application to these petitioners is a denial of their right of free speech guaranteed by the First Amendment." The Court's description of the facts and the justices' opinions on the free speech issue are set forth in Chapter VIII. The Court then turned to the question of "whether the violation following from the University's action is excused by the necessity of complying with the Constitution's prohibition against state establishments of religion."]

III

[T]he University [has] argued [that] inclusion of WAP's contractors in SAF funding authorization would violate the Establishment Clause. . . . [T]he guarantee of neutrality is respected, not offended, when the government, following neutral criteria and evenhanded policies, extends benefits to recipients whose ideologies and viewpoints, including religious ones, are broad and diverse. . . .

The governmental program here is neutral toward religion. There is no suggestion that the University created it to advance religion or adopted some ingenious device with the purpose of aiding a religious cause. The object of the SAF is to open a forum for speech and to support various student enterprises, including the publication of newspapers, in recognition of the diversity and creativity of student life. The University's SAF Guidelines have a separate classification for, and do not make third-party payments on behalf of, "religious organizations." The category of support here is for "student news, information, opinion, entertainment, or academic communications media groups," of which Wide Awake was 1 of 15 in the 1990 school year. WAP did not seek a subsidy because of its Christian editorial viewpoint; it sought funding as a student journal, which it was.

The neutrality of the program distinguishes the student fees from a tax levied for the direct support of a church or group of churches. A tax of that sort, of course, would run contrary to Establishment Clause concerns dating from the earliest days of the Republic. [The] exaction here, by contrast, is a student activity fee designed to reflect the reality that student life in its many dimensions includes the necessity of wide-ranging speech and inquiry and that student expression is an integral part of the University's educational mission. . . .

Government neutrality is apparent in the State's overall scheme in a further meaningful respect. [The] University has taken pains to disassociate itself from the private speech involved in this case. . . .

[The] University provides printing services to a broad spectrum of student newspapers qualified as CIOs by reason of their officers and membership. Any benefit to religion is incidental to the government's provision of secular services for secular purposes on a religion-neutral basis. . . . To obey the Establishment Clause, it was not necessary for the University to deny eligibility to student publications because of their viewpoint. . . .

The judgment of the Court of Appeals must be, and is, reversed.

It is so ordered.

Justice O'CONNOR, concurring.

[C]ertain considerations specific to the program at issue lead me to conclude that by providing the same assistance to Wide Awake that it does to other publications, the University would not be endorsing the magazine's religious perspective. First, the student organizations, at the University's insistence, remain strictly independent of the University. And the agreement requires that student organizations include in every letter, contract, publication, or other written materials the following disclaimer:

> Although this organization has members who are University of Virginia students (faculty) (employees), the organization is independent of the corporation which is the University and which is not responsible for the organization's contracts, acts or omissions.

Any reader of Wide Awake would be on notice of the publication's independence from the University.

Second, financial assistance is distributed in a manner that ensures its use only for [the] University's purpose in maintaining a free and robust marketplace of ideas, from whatever perspective. . . . Third, assistance is provided to the religious publication in a context that makes improbable any perception of government endorsement of the religious message. [T]he University has provided support to The Yellow Journal, a humor magazine that has targeted Christianity as a subject of satire, and Al-Salam, a publication to "promote a better understanding of Islam to the University Community." [By] withholding from Wide Awake assistance that the University provides generally to all other student publications, the University has discriminated on the basis of the magazine's religious viewpoint in violation of the Free Speech Clause. . . .

Justice SOUTER, with whom Justice STEVENS, Justice GINSBURG, and Justice BREYER join, dissenting.

The Court today, for the first time, approves direct funding of core religious activities by an arm of the State. [I] would hold that the University's refusal to support petitioners' religious activities is compelled by the Establishment Clause. . . . This writing is no merely descriptive examination of religious doctrine or even of ideal Christian practice in confronting life's social and personal problems. [It] is straightforward exhortation to enter into a relationship with God as revealed in Jesus Christ, and to satisfy a series of moral obligations derived from the teachings of Jesus Christ. . . .

Using public funds for the direct subsidization of preaching the word is categorically forbidden under the Establishment Clause, and if the Clause was meant to accomplish nothing else, it was meant to bar this use of public money. . . . The University exercises the power of the State to compel a student to pay [a fee], and the use of any part of it for the direct support of religious activity thus strikes at what we have repeatedly held to be the heart of the prohibition on establishment. . . . [T]here should be no need to decide whether [the] University would violate the Free Speech Clause by limiting funding as it has done. . . .

Notes and Questions

1. *Reconsider the* Christian Legal Society *Decision.* In Chapter 11, we examined the *Christian Legal Society* case, which placed a gloss on *Rosenberger*'s holding. Are you clear about when universities can refuse to fund the speech of student organizations?

2. *Religious Instruction in Public Schools.* Another issue that has arisen is whether students can be provided with religious instruction during public school hours. Whether the instruction is regarded as an establishment or an accommodation depends on how it is structured. In Illinois v. McCollum, 333 U.S. 203 (1948), the Court held that Illinois could not allow privately employed religious teachers to enter public school buildings during regular school hours and substitute religious teaching for secular education. However, in Zorach v. Clauson, 343 U.S. 306 (1952), the Court held that students could be released from public school classes to attend religious classes off-site.

3. *Religious Use of Public School Facilities.* A number of cases have focused on whether religious groups may use public school facilities. In Widmar v. Vincent, 454 U.S. 263 (1981), when a state university opened its facilities to registered student groups, it could not close those facilities to groups desiring to engage in religious worship and religious discussion. The Court held that the university was required to allow religious groups to use its facilities: "Having created a forum generally open to student groups, the University seeks to enforce a content-based exclusion of religious speech." Justice White, dissenting, argued that the case involved "religious worship only." In Good News Club v. Milford Central School, 121 U.S. 2093 (2001), the Court confronted similar issues in the context of an elementary school. The Court found that Milford was operating a "limited public forum" and concluded that it had improperly excluded the Good News Club: "[Milford] engaged in viewpoint discrimination when it excluded the Club from the after school forum. [T]he Club seeks to address a subject otherwise permitted under the rule, the teaching of morals and character, from a religious standpoint. . . . The only apparent difference [is] that the Club chooses to teach moral lessons from a Christian perspective through live storytelling and prayer. . . ." Justice Stevens dissented: "[A] school [need not open] its forum to religious proselytizing or worship. . . ." Justice Souter also dissented: "[Good News's] exercises blur the line between public classroom instruction and private religious indoctrination, leaving a reasonable elementary school pupil unable to appreciate that the former instruction is the business of the school while the latter evangelism is not. . . ."

4. *Vocational Assistance to the Handicapped.* Another context in which establishment-free exercise tension has been revealed is vocational assistance to

the handicapped. In Witters v. Washington Department of Services for the Blind, 474 U.S. 481 (1986), a statute authorized payments "for special education and/or training in the professions, business or trades" to "assist visually handicapped persons to overcome vocational handicaps and to obtain the maximum degree of self-support and self-care." The Court held that the state could not deny assistance to a blind person who was studying at a Christian college to become a pastor, missionary, or youth director: "Any aid [that] flows to religious institutions does so only as a result of [the] independent and private choices of aid recipients. [Washington's program is] made available generally without regard to the sectarian-nonsectarian, or public-nonpublic nature of the institution benefitted, and is in no way skewed towards religion." Justice O'Connor concurred: "The aid to religion [is] the result of petitioner's private choice. No reasonable observer is likely to draw from the facts before us an inference that the State itself is endorsing a religious practice or belief."

5. *The Adolescent Family Life Act.* Finally, in Bowen v. Kendrick, 487 U.S. 589 (1988), the Court was confronted by the Adolescent Family Life Act (AFLA), which provided funding to public or nonprofit private organizations addressing problems relating to pregnancy and childbirth among unmarried adolescents. The grants were intended to promote "self discipline and other prudent approaches to the problem of adolescent premarital sexual relations," to encourage adoption as an alternative for adolescent parents, to establish new approaches to the delivery of care services for pregnant adolescents, and to support research and demonstration projects "concerning the societal causes and consequences of adolescent premarital sexual relations, contraceptive use, pregnancy, and child rearing." The case focused on a congressionally imposed requirement that grant applicants describe how they would involve religious organizations in AFLA-funded programs. The Court rejected the challenge: "These provisions of the statute reflect at most Congress' considered judgment that religious organizations can help solve the problems to which the AFLA is addressed. Nothing in our previous cases prevents Congress from making such a judgment or from recognizing the important part that religion or religious organizations may play in resolving certain secular problems. [N]othing [indicates] that a significant proportion of the federal funds will be disbursed to 'pervasively sectarian' institutions. . . ." The Court also rejected the argument that AFLA excessively entangled government with religion: "There is [no] reason to fear that the less intensive monitoring involved here will cause the Government to intrude unduly in the day-to-day operation of the religiously affiliated AFLA grantees." Justice Blackmun dissented: "Congress [enacted] a statute [that gave] religious groups [a] pedagogical and counseling role without imposing any restraints on the sectarian quality of the participation. . . ."

∾ PROBLEMS ∾

1. *Withholding Student Activity Fees.* In two important decisions, Keller v. State Bar of California, 496 U.S. 1, 15 (1990), and Abood v. Detroit Board of

Education, 431 U.S. 209, 236 (1977), the Court held that lawyers and laborers need not "associate" with the speech of state bar organizations and labor unions with which they disagreed. As a result, lawyers and laborers could withhold dues payments attributable to an objectionable message. After *Rosenberger*, may students at the University of Virginia withhold that portion of the student activity fee attributable to publications with which they disagree (i.e., WAP)?

2. *Prohibiting Religious Services.* Kentucky public schools maintain a limited public forum in which outside groups may use school facilities for meetings. The policy permits religious groups to use the facilities and allows any group "to discuss religious material or any material which contains a religious viewpoint." However, it prohibits religious services and instruction. After *Rosenberger*, is the policy valid?

3. *Student Murals.* A public high school allows art students to paint murals on the school's exterior walls and has established a contest to reward students who create the best murals. Under the contest rules, students may address any "political or social issue" in their murals, but they may not include "obscene" or otherwise "inappropriate" material. A student submits a mural proposal that depicts Jesus Christ, larger than life, and portrays him as instructing students. The school wants to reject the mural proposal on the basis that the Establishment Clause precludes the school from recognizing religion in this manner. If you are the school district's attorney, how would you advise it regarding the religious mural proposal?

Locke v. Davey

540 U.S. 712 (2004)

Chief Justice REHNQUIST delivered the opinion of the Court.

[The] Washington State Legislature found that "[s]tudents who work hard [and] successfully complete high school with high academic marks may not have the financial ability to attend college because they cannot obtain financial aid or the financial aid is insufficient." [T]o assist these high-achieving students, the legislature created the Promise Scholarship Program, which provides a scholarship, renewable for one year, to eligible students for postsecondary education expenses. Students may spend their funds on any education-related expense, including room and board. The scholarships are funded through the State's general fund, and their amount varies each year depending on the annual appropriation, which is evenly prorated among the eligible students. The scholarship was worth $1,125 for academic year 1999-2000 and $1,542 for 2000-2001.

To be eligible for the scholarship, a student must meet academic, income, and enrollment requirements. A student must graduate from a Washington public or private high school and either graduate in the top 15% of his graduating class, or attain on the first attempt a cumulative score of 1,200 or better on the Scholastic Assessment Test I or a score of 27 or better on the American College Test. The student's family income must be less than 135% of the State's median.

Finally, the student must enroll "at least half time in an eligible postsecondary institution in the state of Washington," and may not pursue a degree in theology at that institution while receiving the scholarship. Private institutions, including those religiously affiliated, qualify as "eligible postsecondary institution[s]" if they are accredited by a nationally recognized accrediting body. A "degree in theology" is not defined in the statute, but [the] statute simply codifies the State's constitutional prohibition on providing funds to students to pursue degrees that are "devotional in nature or designed to induce religious faith." Wash. Const., Art. I, §11.

A student who applies for the scholarship and meets the academic and income requirements is notified that he is eligible for the scholarship. . . . Once the student enrolls at an eligible institution, the institution must certify that the student is enrolled at least half time and that the student is not pursuing a degree in devotional theology. The institution, rather than the State, determines whether the student's major is devotional. If the student meets the enrollment requirements, the scholarship funds are sent to the institution for distribution to the student to pay for tuition or other educational expenses.

Respondent, Joshua Davey, was awarded a Promise Scholarship, and chose to attend Northwest College. Northwest is a private, Christian college affiliated with the Assemblies of God denomination, and is an eligible institution under the Promise Scholarship Program. Davey had "planned for many years to attend a Bible college and to prepare [himself] through that college training for a lifetime of ministry, specifically as a church pastor." [W]hen he enrolled in Northwest College, he decided to pursue a double major in pastoral ministries and business management/administration. [T]he pastoral ministries degree is devotional and therefore excluded under the Promise Scholarship Program. . . . [When] Davey [learned] that he could not use his scholarship to pursue a devotional theology degree[, he] brought an action under 42 U.S.C. §1983 [arguing that] the denial of his scholarship based on his decision to pursue a theology degree violated, *inter alia,* the Free Exercise, Establishment, and Free Speech Clauses of the First Amendment. . . . The District Court rejected Davey's constitutional claims. . . . A divided panel of the United States Court of Appeals for the Ninth Circuit reversed. . . . We granted certiorari and now reverse.

[T]he Establishment Clause and the Free Exercise Clause are frequently in tension. Yet we have long said that "there is room for play in the joints" between them. Walz v. Tax Comm'n. of City of New York, 397 U.S. 664 (1970). In other words, there are some state actions permitted by the Establishment Clause but not required by the Free Exercise Clause. . . . This case involves that "play in the joints. . . ." The question before [is] whether Washington, pursuant to its own constitution, which has been authoritatively interpreted as prohibiting even indirectly funding religious instruction that will prepare students for the ministry, can deny them such funding without violating the Free Exercise Clause.

Davey [contends] that under the rule we enunciated in *Church of Lukumi Babalu Aye* [v. Hialeah, 508 U.S. 520 (1993)], the program is presumptively unconstitutional because it is not facially neutral with respect to religion.[17] We reject his claim of presumptive unconstitutionality. . . . In the present case, the State's disfavor of religion (if it can be called that) is of a far milder kind. It imposes neither criminal nor civil sanctions on any type of religious service or rite. It does not deny to ministers the right to participate in the political affairs of the community. *See* McDaniel v. Paty, 435 U.S. 618 (1978). And it does not require students to choose between their religious beliefs and receiving a government benefit.[18] The State has merely chosen not to fund a distinct category of instruction.

[Because] the Promise Scholarship Program funds training for all secular professions, Justice Scalia contends the State must also fund training for religious professions. But training [someone] to lead a congregation is an essentially religious endeavor. Indeed, majoring in devotional theology is akin to a religious calling as well as an academic pursuit. And the subject of religion is one in which both the United States and state constitutions embody distinct views — in favor of free exercise, but opposed to establishment — that find no counterpart with respect to other callings or professions. That a State would deal differently with religious education for the ministry than with education for other callings is a product of these views, not evidence of hostility toward religion.

[W]e can think of few areas in which a State's antiestablishment interests come more into play. Since the founding of our country, there have been popular uprisings against procuring taxpayer funds to support church leaders, which was one of the hallmarks of an "established" religion. J. Madison, *Memorial and Remonstrance Against Religious Assessments.* . . . Most States that sought to avoid an establishment of religion around the time of the founding placed in their constitutions formal prohibitions against using tax funds to support the ministry. *E.g.,* Ga. Const., Art. IV, §5 (1789). . . . That early state constitutions saw no problem in explicitly excluding *only* the ministry from receiving state dollars reinforces our conclusion that religious instruction is of a different ilk.

Far from evincing the hostility toward religion which was manifest in *Lukumi,* we believe that the entirety of the Promise Scholarship Program goes a long way toward including religion in its benefits. The program permits students to attend pervasively religious schools, so long as they are accredited. [S]tudents are still eligible to take devotional theology courses. Davey notes all students at Northwest are required to take at least four devotional courses, "Exploring the Bible," "Principles of Spiritual Development," "Evangelism in the Christian Life," and "Christian Doctrine," and some students may have additional religious requirements as part of their majors.

In short, we find neither in the history or text of Article I, §11 of the Washington Constitution, nor in the operation of the Promise Scholarship Program,

---

17. Davey, relying on Rosenberger v. Rector and Visitors of Univ. of Va., 515 U.S. 819 (1995), contends that the Promise Scholarship Program is an unconstitutional viewpoint restriction on speech. But the Promise Scholarship Program is not a forum for speech. . . .

18. Promise Scholars may still use their scholarship to pursue a secular degree at a different institution from where they are studying devotional theology.

anything that suggests animus towards religion. Given the historic and substantial state interest at issue, we therefore cannot conclude that the denial of funding for vocational religious instruction alone is inherently constitutionally suspect.

Without a presumption of unconstitutionality, Davey's claim must fail. The State's interest in not funding the pursuit of devotional degrees is substantial and the exclusion of such funding places a relatively minor burden on Promise Scholars. If any room exists between the two Religion Clauses, it must be here. We need not venture further into this difficult area in order to uphold the Promise Scholarship Program as currently operated by the State of Washington.

The judgment of the Court of Appeals is therefore
Reversed.

Justice SCALIA, with whom Justice THOMAS joins, dissenting.

In *Church of Lukumi Babalu Aye, Inc.*, the [Court] held that "[a] law burdening religious practice that is not neutral [must] undergo the most rigorous of scrutiny," and that "the minimum requirement of neutrality is that a law not discriminate on its face." [The] State of Washington [has] created a generally available public benefit, [but] has then carved out a solitary course of study for exclusion. . . . No field of study but religion is singled out for disfavor in this fashion. Davey [seeks] only *equal* treatment—the right to direct his scholarship to his chosen course of study, a right every other Promise Scholar enjoys. . . . One can concede the Framers' hostility to funding the clergy *specifically,* but that says nothing about whether the clergy had to be excluded from benefits the State made available to all. No one would seriously contend [that] the Framers would have barred ministers from using public roads on their way to church. . . .

[There] are any number of ways [that the state] could respect both its unusually sensitive concern for the conscience of its taxpayers *and* the Federal Free Exercise Clause. It could make the scholarships redeemable only at public universities (where it sets the curriculum), or only for select courses of study. Either option would replace a program that facially discriminates against religion with one that just happens not to subsidize it. The State could also simply abandon the scholarship program altogether. . . .

Justice THOMAS, dissenting.

[Assuming] that the State denies Promise Scholarships only to students who pursue a degree in devotional theology, I believe that Justice Scalia's application of our precedents is correct. . . .

∾ PROBLEMS ∾

1. Rosenberger, Locke, *and the Education for the Twenty-First Century Act.* In constructing the proposed legislation, what (if any) conclusions do you draw from decisions like *Rosenberger* and *Locke?*

2. *Black Nativity.* Suppose that a theater arts professor at a state university wishes to present a play entitled *Black Nativity,* which is set in a Baptist church and

celebrates the birth of Jesus. The director describes the play as being about "praising God for Jesus." The director states that "theater mirrors life. We teach that every day. God is a part of life. In my view, without Him there is no life." Does the presentation of the play constitute an establishment of religion? Or, should it be regarded as an accommodation of the director's religious beliefs? Does the presentation violate the Establishment Clause?

3. *A Final Look at Congressional Funding of the Education for a Better America Act.* After reading this chapter on the religion clauses, have your views regarding the permissible scope of the legislation changed? What provisions would you include in the statute? Which would you exclude?

Review Christian Legal Society Chapter of the University of California v. Martinez, 130 S.Ct. 2791 (2010), in Chapter 11, reproduced at page 1204.

∾ PROBLEMS ∾

1. *Extending the "All-Comers" Policy.* Could Hastings decide to exclude CLS not only from the RSO program but also from the use of the law school's facilities and all methods of internal communication unless it accepts all comers?

2. *The Takeover.* Suppose that, following this decision, a group of students decides to take over the CLS and changes its bylaws and statement of beliefs to be accepting of gays, lesbians, and transgenders, and to be accepting of premarital and nonmarital sex. The law school takes no action. If the ousted members of CLS sue again, should their challenge to the all-comers policy now be accepted?

Points to Remember

- The Establishment Clause is simply stated: "Congress shall make no law respecting an establishment of religion."
- While the clause initially applied only to the federal government, its reach was extended to the states through the Fourteenth Amendment; *see* Everson v. Board of Education.
- The clause prohibits government from engaging in certain types of activities: establishing a national (or, for that matter, a state) church, passing laws that require individuals to go to or remain away from church against their will; and passing laws that force individuals to profess a belief or disbelief in any religion.
- The difficulty is that few Establishment Clause cases have involved these types of activities. For example, there have been no attempts to declare a national religion and few (modern) attempts to force individuals to go to or remain away from church against their will, or to force individuals to profess a belief or a disbelief in a particular religion.

- Most Establishment Clause litigation focuses on whether certain lesser acts (e.g., school prayer, financial aid to religious organizations, the posting of the Ten Commandments in public places) constitute an "establishment" of religion.

- Because these "lesser" acts do not clearly violate the First Amendment, the courts have struggled to define the term *establishment*. This has been done on a case-by-case basis.

- Although Establishment Clause issues can occur in a variety of situations, they often arise in the context of governmental attempts to provide financial benefits to religion or religious organizations.

- In Everson v. Board of Education, 330 U.S. 1 (1947), the Court upheld a law authorizing reimbursement to parents of money spent for bus transportation of their children on regular buses operated by the public transportation system for transportation to school, including Catholic schools.

- In *Everson*, the Court recognized that the religion clauses have conflicting objectives (prohibiting the establishment of religion while allowing citizens to freely exercise their religions) and that the Establishment Clause "requires the state to be a neutral in its relations with groups of religious believers and non-believers; it does not require the state to be their adversary."

- The dominant Establishment Clause test for nearly 30 years was the so-called "*Lemon*" test, articulated in Lemon v. Kurtzman, 403 U.S. 602 (1971). This test had three elements: "First, the statute must have a secular legislative purpose; second, its principal or primary effect must be one that neither advances nor inhibits religion; finally, the statute must not foster 'an excessive government entanglement with religion.'"

- In *Lemon*, the Court struck down state laws providing direct payments to private schools for teachers' salaries, textbooks, and instructional materials because the laws fostered excessive entanglement between church and state.

- In the following years, although a number of Establishment Clause cases were decided using the *Lemon* test, the test did not produce entirely satisfactory results, and it drew strong criticisms from a number of justices.

- In Agostini v. Felton, 521 U.S. 203 (1997), the Court reversed some of its prior Establishment Clause precedent and modified aspects of the *Lemon* test prohibiting the government from sending public teachers into private schools.

- *Agostini* held that, while courts should continue to focus on whether government aid has the purpose of advancing or inhibiting religion, it was less inclined to find that aid had the effect of advancing religion or creating an excessive entanglement.

- There has been much controversy surrounding so-called "school vouchers" — vouchers that can be used to pay for tuition at both public and private schools. In Committee for Public Education and Religious Liberty v. Nyquist, 413 U.S. 756 (1973), applying the *Lemon* test, the

Court invalidated a New York law that provided partial tuition reimbursements and tax benefits to the parents of children attending elementary or secondary nonpublic schools because it was not clear that the aid would be used solely for secular purposes.

- In Sloan v. Lemon, 413 U.S. 825 (1973), the Court upheld a Pennsylvania law that reimbursed parents for a portion of tuition expenses incurred at nonpublic schools.
- In Mueller v. Allen, 463 U.S. 388 (1983), the Court upheld a Minnesota law that allowed taxpayers, in computing their state income tax, to deduct certain expenses incurred in providing for the education of their children.
- In Zelman v. Simmons-Harris, 536 U.S. 639 (2002), the Court upheld an Ohio school voucher program designed to assist schools in crisis.
- In Engel v. Vitale, 370 U.S. 421 (1962), the Court struck down a state-mandated prayer that was to be recited at the beginning of each schoolday.
- However, in Marsh v. Chambers, 463 U.S. 783 (1983), the Court held that the Nebraska legislature could begin its day with chaplain-led prayer because of a history of legislative prayer that extended back to the Constitutional Convention.
- In Lee v. Weisman, 505 U.S. 577 (1992), the Court struck down a Rhode Island practice of inviting clergy to offer graduation prayers at middle schools and high schools.
- In Santa Fe Independent School District v. Doe, 530 U.S. 290 (2000), the Court struck down a school district policy that authorized nondenominational prayer at high school football games.
- In Wallace v. Jaffree, 472 U.S. 38 (1985), the Court struck down an Alabama law that authorized a period for "meditation or voluntary prayer" in public schools.
- In School District of Abington Township v. Schempp, 374 U.S. 203 (1963), the Court struck down a state law that required the reading of Bible verses followed by a recitation of the Lord's Prayer.
- In Epperson v. Arkansas, 393 U.S. 97 (1968), the Court struck down Arkansas's anti-evolution statute, which prohibited the teaching of evolution.
- In Edwards v. Aguillard, 482 U.S. 578 (1987), the Court struck down a Louisiana law that prohibited the teaching of the theory of evolution in public schools unless accompanied by instruction in "creation science."
- A continuing subject of litigation under the Establishment Clause has been whether, and to what extent, government may "acknowledge" religion in public displays. This issue has arisen in numerous contexts, including Christmas and nativity displays and official monuments and displays of the Ten Commandments.
- In County of Allegheny v. American Civil Liberties Union, 492 U.S. 573 (1989), the Court held that a creche display in the Allegheny County Courthouse violated the Establishment Clause because it conveyed

- the message that government was endorsing religion (in that case, Catholicism).
- However, *County of Allegheny* upheld a display of a menorah, a Christmas tree, and other items because the nature of the display suggested no endorsement of religion.
- The states may not require, as a condition of holding office, that an applicant for the office of notary public swear or affirm his or her belief in God. *See* Torcaso v. Watkins, 367 U.S. 488 (1961).
- During the last 25 years, a number of cases have involved challenges to public displays of the Ten Commandments. In Stone v. Graham, 449 U.S. 39 (1980), the Court struck down a Kentucky statute that required that a copy of the Ten Commandments, purchased with private contributions, be placed on the wall of each public classroom. The Court found that the law had a religious purpose.
- In Van Orden v. Perry, 545 U.S. 677 (2005), the Court upheld a Ten Commandments monument on the grounds of the Texas State Capitol. The Court found that the nature of the setting and the array of other monuments suggested no endorsement of religion.
- By contrast, in McCreary County v. American Civil Liberties Union of Kentucky, 545 U.S. 844 (2005), the Court struck down a courthouse display of the Ten Commandments because of a religious motivation.
- The American colonists demanded protections for religious freedom because of a history of religious persecution in Europe and in the American colonies. These demands led to the inclusion of the Free Exercise Clause in the First Amendment.
- Although there is widespread agreement that the clause protects religious thought, there is uncertainty about the extent to which it protects religious conduct. Even if it protects "conduct," the clause does not protect all conduct (e.g., the state can prohibit a religion that believes in human sacrifice from actually killing people).
- Free exercise cases usually arise when a law prohibits an individual from engaging in conduct required by religious beliefs or requires conduct prohibited by religious beliefs (i.e., compulsory school attendance laws or laws denying unemployment compensation to those who refuse to work on Saturdays).
- Typically, in drafting these laws, the legislature was not trying to prohibit or burden a religious practice, but was instead trying to deal with some secular problem (e.g., parents who fail to educate their children or workers who unreasonably refuse to educate their children). A problem develops when the laws incidentally affect religious practices. At that point, a court must decide whether the individual interest in the free exercise of religion should prevail, or the state's interest in compliance prevails over the individual's religious interest.
- Reynolds v. United States, 98 U.S. (8 Otto) 145 (1878), upheld a federal law prohibiting polygamy against claims that it infringed the free exercise rights of Mormons.

- For several decades, the Court was more accepting of free exercise claims and tended to impose heightened review on laws that infringed religious beliefs.
- In Sherbert v. Verner, 374 U.S. 398 (1963), the Court held that a state could not deny unemployment benefits to a Seventh-day Adventist because she refused to work on her sabbath (Saturday).
- In Wisconsin v. Yoder, 406 U.S. 205 (1972), the Court held that the state could not use compulsory school attendance laws to force members of the Old Order Amish to send their children to public schools after the eighth grade.
- However, in United States v. Lee, 455 U.S. 252 (1982), the Court upheld a law requiring the Amish to pay social security taxes despite their religious objections to receiving social security benefits.
- In Employment Division v. Smith, 494 U.S. 872 (1990), the Court held that members of the Native American Church were not entitled to an exemption from federal laws prohibiting the use of peyote. The Court noted that there was no entitlement to an exemption from a neutral, generally applicable, criminal law.
- After *Smith*, Congress passed the Religious Freedom Restoration Act (RFRA) in an effort to overrule that decision. RFRA provided that "Government shall not substantially burden a person's exercise of religion even if the burden results from a rule of general applicability" unless the government demonstrates that "application of the burden to the person — (1) is in furtherance of a compelling governmental interest; and (2) is the least restrictive means of furthering that compelling governmental interest."
- In City of Boerne v. Flores, 521 U.S. 507 (1997), the Court struck down RFRA, concluding: "Broad as the power of Congress is under the Enforcement Clause of the Fourteenth Amendment, RFRA contradicts vital principles necessary to maintain separation of powers and the federal balance."
- After RFRA was struck down, Congress used its authority under the federal Spending and Commerce Clauses to pass the Religious Land Use and Institutionalized Persons Act of 2000 (RLUIPA), 42 U.S.C. §2000cc-1(a)(1)-(2), which provided in part: "No government shall impose a substantial burden on the religious exercise of a person residing in or confined to an institution," unless the burden furthers "a compelling governmental interest" and does so by "the least restrictive means."
- In Gonzales v. O Centro Espirita Beneficente Uniao de Vegetal, 546 U.S. 428 (2006), using RFRA, the Court held that members of a religious sect were entitled to a free exercise exemption allowing them to use a hallucinogenic sacramental tea.
- In Lyng v. Northwest Indian Cemetery Protective Association, 485 U.S. 439 (1988), the Court refused to halt construction of a road through a portion of federal land that American Indians regarded as sacred to their religious exercises.

- In Church of the Lukumi Babalu Aye, Inc. v. City of Hialeah, 508 U.S. 520 (1993), the Court struck down a local ordinance prohibiting animal sacrifice on the grounds that it involved discrimination against religious beliefs.
- Even though the Establishment Clause and the Free Exercise Clause are separately stated, they conflict in a number of different contexts.
- In Board of Education of Kiryas Joel Village School District v. Grumet, 512 U.S. 687 (1994), the Court held that the state could not delegate school board authority to a religious village, in an effort to accommodate religious beliefs, without violating the Establishment Clause.
- In Rosenberger v. Rector and Visitors of the University of Virginia, 515 U.S. 819 (1995), the Court held that a state university could not deny funding to a religiously oriented student publication when it provided broad support for student publications.

13

The Right to Keep and Bear Arms

U.S. CONSTITUTION, SECOND AMENDMENT

A well regulated Militia, being necessary to the security of a free State, the right of the people to keep and bear Arms, shall not be infringed.

∾ PROBLEM: COMPREHENSIVE GUN-CONTROL LEGISLATION ∾

Following the decisions in District of Columbia v. Heller and McDonald v. City of Chicago (presented below), states that had passed comprehensive gun-control legislation were worried about the constitutionality of their statutes. Particularly those states with large urban centers faced high rates of handgun violence that caused numerous societal problems (e.g., high rates of crime, murder, and accidental shootings and fear in the general population). These states sought to develop a plan for responding to the *Heller* and *McDonald* decisions as well as for determining whether there was room for a larger federal role in the gun-control debate.

Concerns about *Heller* and *McDonald* were not uniform. Some states viewed the possession of firearms as a tradition and a right. Indeed, in some states, the possession of guns was regarded a necessity, especially in more remote areas where individuals needed guns to hunt and to protect themselves from predators. But even some citizens in urban areas regarded gun possession as a right and as their primary means of protection against criminal predators.

Suppose that your state legislature is one that began considering the enactment of comprehensive gun-control legislation before *Heller* and *McDonald* because of an increasing incidence of gun-related violence and accidents in the state. The legislature assigned to an ad hoc committee the task of studying and proposing appropriate gun-control measures.

In this chapter, we will ask you to assume a couple of different roles. On the one hand, we will ask you to assume that you are counsel to the state's ad hoc legislative committee that is contemplating changes to your state's gun law (and the committee is favorably disposed to comprehensive gun-control legislation), and we will ask you to advise the committee. On the other hand, we will ask you to assume that you are an attorney for a gun-rights advocacy organization lobbying the legislature against any gun-control legislation. As you proceed through the chapter, think about how you might formulate arguments on behalf of your respective clients.

A. INTRODUCTION

Unlike other rights conferred by the Constitution, the Second Amendment includes both a prefatory clause and an operative clause. The prefatory clause states that "[a] well regulated Militia being necessary to the security of a free State . . . ," which is followed by the operative clause: "the right of the people to keep and bear Arms, shall not be infringed." Thus, central to the debate over the nature and scope of the right to keep and bear arms is whether the right is conditioned upon the preamble — the need for a well-regulated militia. In other words, is the right to keep and bear arms protected only when it contributes to a well-regulated militia, *or* does it apply only to the rights of the states to maintain a well-regulated militia, *or* does it protect an individual's right to keep and bear arms independent of the need for a well-regulated state militia? *Compare* Eugene Volokh, *The Commonplace Second Amendment*, 73 N.Y.U. L. Rev. 793 (1998), *with* David Thomas Konig, *Why the Second Amendment Has a Preamble*: *Original Meaning and the Public Culture of Written Constitutions in Revolutionary America*, 56 U.C.L.A. L. Rev. 1295 (2009).

The term *militia* embodies the concept of a state-based military force composed of civilians capable of mobilizing in times of emergency for the defense of the state or the national government. The Constitution empowers Congress to organize, arm, and discipline the militia, U.S. Const., Art. I, §8, cl. 16; however, for over a century, Congress left the militia "unorganized" and decentralized, opting for an undifferentiated militia force of every "free able-bodied white male citizen of the respective States" between the ages of 18 and 45. Militia Act of 1792, 1 Stat. 271. Importantly, Congress directed every militia member to equip himself with appropriate weaponry.

Not until 1903 did Congress exercise its constitutional power to regulate and arm the militia, dividing the militia into an "organized militia," known as the National Guard, and a Reserve or "unorganized militia" of able-bodied males between the ages of 18 and 45. Dick Act of 1903, 32 Stat. 775. The National Guard continued as a state entity (except when called into active federal service) until 1933, when the Guard assumed a dual status — the National Guard (or organized militia) of each state and the National Guard of the United States, a reserve component of the U.S. Army. Act of June 15, 1933, §5, 48 Stat. 153, 155. Today, the militia consists of all able-bodied males between the ages of 17 and 45 and female citizens who are members of the National Guard. The militia is divided into two classes: the "organized" militia, which includes the National Guard and Naval Militia, and an "unorganized" militia composed of males between the ages of 18 and 45 who are not members of the National Guard or Naval Militia. 10 U.S.C. §311.

B. EARLY CASES

The Second Amendment is one of the least litigated provisions of the Bill of Rights. Only the Third Amendment (prohibiting the quartering of troops in houses in times of peace) has received less judicial scrutiny. In part, the scarcity of cases is explained by the fact that Congress did not enact the first comprehensive gun-control law until 1934. On the other hand, state regulation of weapons predates the Constitution, and states began enacting gun-control measures in the early nineteenth century. *See* Saul Cornell & Nathan DeDino, *A Well-Regulated Right: The Early American Origins of Gun Control*, 73 Fordham L. Rev. 487 (2004); Saul Cornell, *A Well-Regulated Militia* 141 (Oxford University 2006). Consequently, early Supreme Court decisions focused on whether the Second Amendment limited the states' authority to regulate arms.

BACKGROUND
Colfax Massacre

United States v. Cruikshank arose out the infamous 1872 Colfax Massacre in Grant Parish, Louisiana. After contested state elections, including for sheriff of Grant Parish, a posse composed of white men organized by the Democratic candidate for sheriff assaulted the parish courthouse defended by the Republican candidate, who organized his own posse composed largely of African Americans. The better-armed and more numerous white forces stormed the courthouse, "torched" the building, and shot those attempting to flee. Cornell, *supra*, at 190-191. Between 70 and 165 African Americans were murdered during the confrontation. LeeAnna Keith, *The Colfax Massacre* 109 (Oxford University 2008).

In United States v. Cruikshank, 92 U.S. 542 (1875), the Supreme Court sustained a challenge to the Enforcement Act of 1870, 16 Stat. 140, enacted by Congress under its newly established authority in Section Five of the Fourteenth Amendment. The Act made conspiracies to injure persons to prevent them from exercising their constitutional rights a felony. *Cruikshank* arose out of a Reconstruction-era dispute over the control of a Louisiana parish, in which a group of whites attacked a group of largely African Americans, killing between 70 and 165. LeeAnna Keith, *The Colfax Massacre* 109 (Oxford University 2008). One of the constitutional rights at issue in *Cruikshank* was the right of the African Americans to keep and bear arms. Relying in part on its holding in Barron v. City of Baltimore, 32 U.S. (7 Pet.) 243 (1833), the Court held that—to the extent the Second Amendment declared that the right to bear arms shall not be infringed—it was only a check on the power of Congress. "This is one of the amendments that has no other effect than to restrict the powers of the national government. . . ." *Id.* at 553.

In Presser v. Illinois, 116 U.S. 252 (1886), Herman Presser belonged to a society called the *Lehr und Wehr Verein* (Instruct and Defend Association), an Illinois corporation formed for the purpose of "improving the mental and bodily condition of its members so as to qualify them for duties of citizens of a republic." To accomplish this purpose, the association engaged in "military and gymnastic exercises." In December 1879, 400 members of the society, armed with rifles, paraded in Chicago. Riding on horseback and carrying a cavalry saber, Presser led the formation. Presser was later convicted of violating an Illinois statute prohibiting organizations other than the Illinois National Guard from associating together as military companies or parading with arms. The Supreme Court refused to apply the Second Amendment to overturn the conviction. Following *Cruikshank*, *Presser* held that the Second Amendment "is a limitation only upon the power of congress and the national government, and not upon that of the state."

C. THE MEANING OF THE SECOND AMENDMENT BETWEEN 1939 AND 2008

Before 2008, the Supreme Court broached the issue of the meaning of the Second Amendment only once, in United States v. Miller. The case involved a prosecution under the National Firearms Act of 1934, 48 Stat. 1236, which prohibits the interstate shipment of unregistered sawed-off shotguns. The defendants moved to dismiss the indictment, asserting that it violated the Second Amendment. The district court sustained the motion, and the United States appealed to the Supreme Court.

United States v. Miller

307 U.S. 174 (1939)

Mr. Justice McREYNOLDS delivered the opinion of the Court.

In the absence of any evidence tending to show that possession or use of a "shotgun having a barrel of less than eighteen inches in length" at this time has some reasonable relationship to the preservation or efficiency of a well regulated militia, we cannot say that the Second Amendment guarantees the right to keep and bear such an instrument. Certainly it is not within judicial notice that this weapon is any part of the ordinary military equipment, or that its use could contribute to the common defense.

The Constitution, as originally adopted, granted to the Congress power —

> To provide for calling forth the Militia to execute the Laws of the Union, suppress Insurrections and repel Invasions; To provide for organizing, arming, and disciplining, the Militia, and for governing such Part of them as may be employed in the Service of the United States, reserving to the States respectively, the Appointment of the Officers, and the Authority of training the Militia according to the discipline prescribed by Congress.

With obvious purpose to assure the continuation and render possible the effectiveness of such forces, the declaration and guarantee of the Second Amendment were made. It must be interpreted and applied with that end in view.

The Militia which the States were expected to maintain and train is set in contrast with Troops which they were forbidden to keep without the consent of Congress. The sentiment of the time strongly disfavored standing armies; the common view was that adequate defense of country and laws could be secured through the Militia — civilians primarily, soldiers on occasion.

The signification attributed to the term Militia appears from the debates in the Convention, the history and legislation of Colonies and States, and the writings of approved commentators. These show plainly enough that the Militia comprised all males physically capable of acting in concert for the common defense. And further, that ordinarily, when called for service these men were expected to appear bearing arms supplied by themselves and of the kind in common use at the time. . . .

Most if not all of the States have adopted provisions touching the right to keep and bear arms. Differences in the language employed in these have naturally led to somewhat variant conclusions concerning the scope of the right guaranteed. But none of them seems to afford any material support for the challenged ruling of the court below.

We are unable to accept the conclusion of the court below, and the challenged judgment must be reversed. The cause will be remanded for further proceedings.

Notes and Questions

1. *Miller's Impact.* Little disagreement exists about the underlying purpose of the Second Amendment: to prevent Congress from eliminating the militia. Whether the Amendment also protects an individual's right to possess arms was — in the judgment of the lower federal courts — resolved by *Miller.* Until 2001, every federal appellate court interpreted *Miller* to mean that the right to keep and bear arms is dependent on a relationship to militia service. The courts' focus was the Amendment's preamble, and they found that the preamble defined the circumstances under which "the right of the people to keep and bear arms"

could not be infringed. In doing so, the lower courts adopted two principal models for interpreting the Amendment: the "collective-rights" model and the "limited individual rights" or "sophisticated collective-rights" model. Under either model, the Second Amendment does not generally prohibit federal or state governments from extensively regulating gun possession and use or — for that matter — disarming the American people altogether.

2. *The "Collective-Rights" Model.* In United States v. Tot, 131 F.2d 261 (3d Cir. 1942), the court upheld a conviction under the Federal Firearms Act that made it unlawful for persons convicted of violent crimes to receive ammunition or firearms in interstate or foreign commerce. The court rejected the defendant's contention that the statute violated the Second Amendment, holding that, unlike other provisions in the Bill of Rights, the Second Amendment "was not adopted with individual rights in mind, but as a protection for the States in the maintenance of their militia organizations against possible encroachments by the federal power." *Id.* at 266. Thus, under *Tot,* the Second Amendment applies only to the right of a state to maintain a militia, and not to an individual's right to keep and bear arms. The Courts of Appeals for the Fourth, Sixth, Seventh, and Ninth Circuits followed *Tot,* holding that the Second Amendment is enforceable only by the states. *See* Love v. Pepersack, 47 F.3d 120 (4th Cir. 1995); United States v. Warin, 530 F.2d 103 (6th Cir. 1976); United States v. Napier, 233 F.3d 394 (6th Cir. 2000); Gillespie v. City of Indianapolis, 185 F.3d 693 (7th Cir. 1999); Hickman v. Block, 81 F.3d 98 (9th Cir. 1996); Silveira v. Lockyear, 312 F.3d 1052 (9th Cir. 2003).

3. *The "Limited Individual Rights" or "Sophisticated Collective-Rights" Model.* In Cases v. United States, 131 F.2d 916 (1st Cir. 1942), the defendant violated the Federal Firearms Act by unlawfully transporting and receiving a firearm and ammunition. The defendant argued that the Act violated the Second Amendment; however, the Court of Appeals for the First Circuit held that the Second Amendment does not prohibit the federal government from limiting an individual's right to keep and bear arms *unless* the weapon has a "reasonable relationship to the preservation or efficiency of a well regulated militia." *Id.* at 922. Because the defendant could not demonstrate that he was a member of a military organization or that his use of the weapon was in preparation for a military career, the Second Amendment was inapplicable. Thus, under the "limited individual rights" or "sophisticated collective-rights" model, the right to keep and bear arms can be exercised only by individuals in connection with their militia service. And because the Second Amendment refers not just to "a militia" but rather to a "well-regulated militia," the courts that adopted the "limited individual rights" model defined militia service to mean active participation in the "organized" (i.e., the National Guard) — as opposed to the "unorganized" — militia. The Courts of Appeals for the Third, Eighth, Tenth, and Eleventh Circuits followed this approach. *See* United States v. Rybar, 103 F.3d 273 (3d Cir. 1996); United States v. Hale, 978 F.2d 1016 (8th Cir. 1992); United States v. Parker, 362 F.3d 1279 (10th Cir. 2004); United States v. Haney, 264 F.3d 1161 (10th Cir. 2001); United States v. Wright, 117 F.3d 1265 (11th Cir. 1997); *see generally* Lewis v. United States, 445 U.S. 55, 65 n.8 (1980) (dicta).

4. *What Rights Can Be Enforced in the "Collective-Rights" Model?* Most courts and commentators agree that the underlying rationale for the Second Amendment is to prevent Congress from eliminating the militia. Under the "collective-rights" model, *only* the states (or a collection of citizens within the states) have standing to enforce the amendment; *see, e.g.*, Silveira v. Lockyear, 312 F.3d 1052, 1086-1087 (9th Cir. 2003); John Randolph Prince, *The Naked Emperor: The Second Amendment and the Failure of Originalism*, 40 Brandeis L.J. 659, 719 (2002); David C. Williams, *The Unitary Second Amendment*, 73 N.Y.U. L. Rev. 822, 830 (1998). But from what types of infringements would the states have a basis to sue? In other words, does the Second Amendment afford the states any enforceable substantive rights?

a. *The Constitutional Authority of the Federal Government over the Militia.* The original constitutional text affords Congress broad authority over the militia, including organizing and disciplining it, U.S. Const., Art. I, cl. 16, and calling it into federal service for the broad purpose of executing federal law. *Id.* cl. 15. Once the militia is federalized, the President (not state governors) commands the militia. *Id.*, Art. II, §2, cl. 1. The Supreme Court decided early in the nineteenth century that a decision to federalize the militia is not subject to review, Martin v. Mott, 25 U.S. (12 Wheat.) 19, 30 (1827), and once called into federal service, the federal government's authority over the militia is exclusive, Houston v. Moore, 18 U.S. (5 Wheat.) 1, 17 (1820). Given this expansive federal control over the militia, what purpose does the Second Amendment serve? According to the original text of the Constitution, Congress and the President can simply remove the states' control over their militia by federalizing it. Is the Amendment inconsistent with the militia clauses of the Constitution? *See* Glenn Harlan Reynolds & Don B. Kates, *The Second Amendment and States' Rights*: *A Thought Experiment*, 36 Wm. & Mary L. Rev. 1737, 1743 (1995).

b. *The Constitutional and Statutory Authority of the Federal Government over the National Guard.* Under the National Defense Act of 1916, 39 Stat. 166, Congress required members of the National Guard to take oaths to both their states and the nation. The statute also empowered the President to draft members of the National Guard into federal military service, discharging them from their militia obligation. *Id.* §111, 39 Stat. 211. During World War I, President Woodrow Wilson exercised the authority, drafting members of the National Guard into the U.S. Army, an action upheld by the Supreme Court under Congress's power to raise and support armies, U.S. Const., Art. I, §8, cl. 12, a power not limited by the militia clauses. *Selective Draft Law Cases*, 245 U.S. 366, 383-384 (1917); Cox v. Wood, 247 U.S. 3, 6 (1918). Because Congress did not provide for restoring guardsmen mustered out of federal service after the war, the draft essentially decimated the organized state militias. Frederick Bernays Weiner, *The Militia Clause of the Constitution*, 54 Harv. L. Rev. 181, 205-206 (1940).

After 1933, the states' organized militia—the National Guard—became a reserve component of the U.S. Army (and after 1946, the U.S. Air Force). Under current law, the President has virtually plenary power to federalize the National Guard when needed in a national emergency or for operational missions, not as the militia but as a component of the U.S. armed forces. *See, e.g.,* 10 U.S.C. §§12302, 12304. And although statute gives state governors a veto over calls to active duty outside of emergencies and operational missions, 10 U.S.C. §12301(d), the veto is little more than a matter of legislative grace rather than inherent constitutional authority. Perpich v. Department of Defense, 496 U.S. 334, 347 (1990) (upholding the power of Congress to withhold governors' veto power based on location of active service).

c. *Is the Second Amendment an Anachronism?* Assuming the Second Amendment protects only the rights of the states, given Congress's expansive and potentially exclusive control of the National Guard under its powers to raise and support armies, has the Amendment become an anachronism? Is the Second Amendment akin to Congress's power to "grant Letters of Marque and Reprisal," U.S. Const., Art. I, §8, cl. 11, or its authority to establish "post roads," *id.* cl. 7? *See* Prince, *supra,* at 720; *see also* Michael C. Dorf, *What Does the Second Amendment Mean Today?*, 76 Chi-Kent L. Rev. 291, 338 (2000). Or was the Amendment, as Jack Rakove suggests, simply an "assertion[] or confirmation[] of vital principles, rather than the codification of legally enforceable restrictions or commands"? Jack N. Rakove, *The Second Amendment: The Highest Stage of Originalism*, 76 Chi-Kent L. Rev. 103, 157 (2000).

5. *Enforcing the Second Amendment Under "Limited Individual Rights" or "Sophisticated Collective-Rights" Model.* As discussed above, several federal appellate courts read *Miller* as limiting enforcement of the Second Amendment to individuals who prove that their possession of weapons was reasonably related to a well-regulated militia. In addition, most of these courts rejected membership in the "unorganized" or "inert" militia as a sufficient connection to militia service to constitute a basis for challenging a restriction on the possession of a firearm; instead, there must have been a connection to the "well-regulated" or "organized" militia. *See, e.g.,* United States v. Haney, 264 F.3d 1161, 1166 (10th Cir. 2001) (individual must be a member of the state national guard); United States v. Wright, 117 F.3d 1265, 1274 (11th Cir. 1997) (rejecting claim that membership in a state's unorganized militia is sufficient to bring gun possession within Second Amendment protection). Assuming that the state or federal government furnishes weapons to the members of the National Guard for training and operations, is individual possession of arms ever justified under this view of the Second Amendment? Is the Second Amendment an anachronism under the "limited individual rights" model? And while we are at it, why aren't citizens who are members of the "unorganized" militia protected by the Second Amendment? *See* Akhil Reed

Amar, Heller, HLR, *and Holistic Legal Reasoning*, 122 Harv. L. Rev. 145, 166-167 (2008).

a. *The Era of the "Unorganized" Militia.* For well over a century, Congress made no effort to organize the state militias. Both the Continental Congress and the First Congress under the Constitution rejected a plan submitted by Henry Knox, Secretary of War to the Confederation as well as the new nation, to organize a select, federally trained militia of young, able-bodied men. *See* Don Higginbotham, *The Federalized Militia Debate: A Neglected Aspect of Second Amendment Scholarship*, Wm. & Mary Q., Jan. 1998, at 39, 42, 51-53; Lawrence Delbert Cress, *An Armed Community: The Origins and Meaning of the Right to Bear Arms*, J. Am. Hist., June 1984, at 22, 39. Similarly, many states did little to organize their militias, and the state militias generally proved to be an ineffective fighting force through the time of the Spanish-American War. Edward Coffman, *The Duality of the American Military System: A Commentary*, J. Mil Hist., Oct. 2000, at 967; Frederick Bernays Weiner, *The Militia Clause of the Constitution*, 54 Harv. L. Rev. 181 (1940). Given the nearly complete absence of an organized militia before the twentieth century, was the Second Amendment unenforceable under the "limited individual rights" model during the eighteenth and nineteenth centuries?

b. *The Distinction Between "Troops" and the Militia.* The Constitution prohibits states from keeping troops in time of peace "without the consent of Congress." U.S. Const., Art. I, §10, cl. 2. Does this prohibition extend to the state militias? Or are militias different from "troops"? Is the distinction that militias do not constitute a standing military force but are instead civilians "potentially subject to military duties"? Stephen P. Halbrook, *The Founders' Second Amendment* 337 (Ivan R. Dee 2008); Nelson Lund, *The Past and Future of the Individual's Right to Arms*, 31 Ga. L. Rev. 1, 23 (1996). *See* United States v. Miller, 307 U.S. 174, 178-179 (1939) ("The Militia which the States were expected to maintain and train is set in contrast with Troops which they were forbidden to keep without the consent of Congress. The sentiment of the time strongly disfavored standing armies; the common view was that adequate defense of country and laws could be secured through the Militia — civilians primarily, soldiers on occasion"); Dunne v. People, 94 Ill. 120, 138 (1879) (the militia is "'a body of armed citizens trained to military duty, who may be called out in certain cases, but may not be kept on service like standing armies, in time of peace.'"); Smith v. Wanser, 68 N.J.L. 249, 258, 52 A. 309, 312-313 (1902) (militia distinct from a standing army). If the militia is civilians who are simply *potentially* subject to active military service, why would the Second Amendment apply only to serving members of the National Guard, a professional (albeit reserve) military force?

∾ PROBLEM: MORE ON COMPREHENSIVE GUN-CONTROL LEGISLATION ∾

Before *Heller*, what position would you have taken regarding the ability of the ad hoc legislative committee to adopt comprehensive gun-control measures? As counsel to the committee contemplating changes to your state's gun law, what advice would you give about Second Amendment restrictions on gun-control legislation? Even assuming the Second Amendment applied to the states, would the Amendment pose any barrier at all to the proposed restrictions on the sale, possession, or use of firearms? Could the legislature even go so far as to ban the sale, possession, and use of all firearms?

As counsel to the gun-rights organization lobbying the legislature against enacting gun-control legislation, what legal arguments (if any) would support your client's position? Can you develop arguments to protect the right of certain individuals to keep and bear arms? What about the possession and use of particular types of weapons, such as handguns for self-defense or rifles for hunting?

6. *The Emergence of the "Individual Rights" or "Standard" Model of the Second Amendment.*

a.   *The Individual Right in Statute.* For more than 60 years, Second Amendment jurisprudence remained relatively stable; the federal courts refused to recognize an individual right to keep and bear arms. And until the 1980s, legal scholars virtually ignored the Second Amendment. Congress did, however, express its view in several pieces of legislation that the Second Amendment protected an individual's right to keep and bear arms separate and apart from militia service. *See* Stephen P. Halbrook, *Congress Interprets the Second Amendment: Declarations by a Co-Equal Branch on the Individual Right to Keep and Bear Arms*, 62 Tenn. L. Rev. 597 (1995). Congress reaffirmed this view most recently in the Protection of Lawful Commerce in Firearms Act of 2005, Pub. L. No. 109-92, §2(a)(2), 119 Stat. 2095, which limits the civil liability of gun manufacturers and gun dealers for crimes using their products: "The Second Amendment to the United States Constitution protects the rights of individuals, including those who are not members of a militia or engaged in military service or training, to keep and bear arms."

b.   *The Individual Right in Legal Scholarship.* Beginning in the 1980s, an influential body of legal scholarship began to emerge questioning the "collective-rights" and "limited individual rights" models of the Second Amendment while advancing an individual rights interpretation of the Amendment. *See* Mark V. Tushnet, *Out of Range* 3 (Oxford University 2007). This scholarship focused on the operative clause of the amendment — "the right of the people to keep and bear arms shall not be infringed" — and its place within the structure of the Bill of Rights as well as the original understanding of the nature of the right. These commentators concluded that the Amendment protects an individual's right to possess arms. *See, e.g.,* Don B. Kates, Jr., *Handgun Prohibition and the*

Original Meaning of the Second Amendment, 82 Mich. L. Rev. 204 (1983); Sanford Levinson, *The Embarrassing Second Amendment*, 99 Yale L.J. 637 (1989); Eugene Volokh, *The Commonplace Second Amendment*, 73 N.Y.U. L. Rev. 793 (1998); William Van Alstyne, *The Second Amendment and the Personal Right to Arms*, 43 Duke L.J. 1236 (1994); Glenn H. Reynolds, *A Critical Guide to the Second Amendment*, 62 Tenn. L. Rev. 461 (1995); Robert J. Cottrol & Raymond T. Diamond, *The Fifth Auxiliary Right*, 104 Yale L.J. 995 (1995) (reviewing Joyce Lee Malcolm, *To Keep and Bear Arms: The Origins of the Anglo-American Right* (Harvard University 1994)); Randy E. Barnett, *Was the Right to Keep and Bear Arms Conditioned on Service in the Organized Militia?*, 83 Tex. L. Rev. 237 (2004) (reviewing H. Richard Uviller & William G. Merkel, *The Militia and the Right to Arms, or, How the Second Amendment Fell Silent* (Duke University 2002)). Moreover, in 2004, the Department of Justice altered its long-held position on the Second Amendment, issuing an opinion asserting that the Second Amendment protects an individual right to keep and bear arms. Memorandum of Opinion for the Attorney General, Whether the Second Amendment Secures an Individual Right (Aug. 24, 2004), *available at*: *http://www.justice.gov/olc/secondamendment2.pdf.*

c. *The Individual Right in the Courts.* In 2001, the Court of Appeals for the Fifth Circuit broke with its sister appellate courts, rejected both the "collective-rights" and "limited individual rights" models of the Second Amendment, and found that the Amendment protects an individual's right to keep and bear arms. United States v. Emerson, 270 F.3d 203 (5th Cir. 2001). At issue in *Emerson* was a federal statute prohibiting the possession of a firearm by a person under a judicial restraining order predicated upon findings that the person constituted a credible threat to the safety of an intimate partner or child. 18 U.S.C. §922(g)(8). The defendant, Timothy Emerson, was indicted under the statute for possession of a firearm while subject to such a restraining order. While overturning the district court's dismissal of the indictment on, inter alia, Second Amendment grounds, the Court of Appeals for the Fifth Circuit held "that the Second Amendment protects the right of individuals to privately keep and bear their own firearms that are suitable as individual, personal weapons and are not of the general type excluded by [United States v.] *Miller*, regardless of whether the particular individual is then actually a member of a militia." *Emerson*, 270 F.3d, at 260.

D. THE *HELLER* REVOLUTION

The second federal appellate court to find that the Second Amendment protected an individual's right to keep and bear arms independent of militia service was the Court of Appeals for the District of Columbia Circuit. Parker v. District of Columbia, 478 F.3d 370 (D.C. Cir. 2007). It also became the first federal appellate court to overturn a federal or state gun-control measure on the ground that it violated the Second Amendment, striking down the District of Columbia's highly restrictive handgun-control ordinance. The U.S. Supreme Court agreed to review the decision, and for the first time in nearly 70 years, the Court addressed the meaning of the Second Amendment.

District of Columbia v. Heller

128 S.Ct. 2783 (2008)

Justice SCALIA delivered the opinion of the Court.

We consider whether a District of Columbia prohibition on the possession of usable handguns in the home violates the Second Amendment to the Constitution.

The District of Columbia generally prohibits the possession of handguns. It is a crime to carry an unregistered firearm, and the registration of handguns is prohibited. . . . District of Columbia law also requires residents to keep their lawfully owned firearms, such as registered long guns, "unloaded and dissembled or bound by a trigger lock or similar device" unless they are located in a place of business or are being used for lawful recreational activities.

Respondent is a D.C. special police officer authorized to carry a handgun while on duty at the Federal Judicial Center. He applied for a registration certificate for a handgun that he wished to keep at home, but the District refused. He thereafter filed a lawsuit in the Federal District Court for the District of Columbia seeking, on Second Amendment grounds, to enjoin the city from enforcing the bar on the registration of handguns, the licensing requirement insofar as it prohibits the carrying of a firearm in the home without a license, and the trigger-lock requirement insofar as it prohibits the use of "functional firearms within the home." The District Court dismissed respondent's complaint. The Court of Appeals for the District of Columbia Circuit, construing his complaint as seeking the right to render a firearm operable and carry it about his home in that condition only when necessary for self-defense, reversed. It held that the Second Amendment protects an individual right to possess firearms and that the city's total ban on handguns, as well as its requirement that firearms in the home be kept nonfunctional even when necessary for self-defense, violated that right. We granted certiorari.

We turn first to the meaning of the Second Amendment. The Second Amendment provides: "A well regulated Militia, being necessary to the security of a free State, the right of the people to keep and bear Arms, shall not be infringed." In interpreting this text, we are guided by the principle that "[t]he Constitution was written to be understood by the voters; its words and phrases were used in their normal and ordinary as distinguished from technical meaning." United States v. Sprague, 282 U.S. 716, 731 (1931). Normal meaning may of course include an idiomatic meaning, but it excludes secret or technical meanings that would not have been known to ordinary citizens in the founding generation.

The two sides in this case have set out very different interpretations of the Amendment. Petitioners and today's dissenting Justices believe that it protects only the right to possess and carry a firearm in connection with militia service. Respondent argues that it protects an individual right to possess a firearm unconnected with service in a militia, and to use that arm for traditionally lawful purposes, such as self-defense within the home.

The Second Amendment is naturally divided into two parts: its prefatory clause and its operative clause. The former does not limit the latter grammatically, but rather announces a purpose. The Amendment could be rephrased, "Because a well regulated Militia is necessary to the security of a free State, the right of the people to keep and bear Arms shall not be infringed." Although this structure of the Second Amendment is unique in our Constitution, other legal documents of the founding era, particularly individual-rights provisions of state constitutions, commonly included a prefatory statement of purpose.

Logic demands that there be a link between the stated purpose and the command. . . . That requirement of logical connection may cause a prefatory clause to resolve an ambiguity in the operative clause. But apart from that clarifying function, a prefatory clause does not limit or expand the scope of the operative clause. Therefore, while we will begin our textual analysis with the operative clause, we will return to the prefatory clause to ensure that our reading of the operative clause is consistent with the announced purpose.

a. *"Right of the People."* The first salient feature of the operative clause is that it codifies a "right of the people." The unamended Constitution and the Bill of Rights use the phrase "right of the people" two other times, in the First Amendment's Assembly-and-Petition Clause and in the Fourth Amendment's Search-and-Seizure Clause. The Ninth Amendment uses very similar terminology. All three of these instances unambiguously refer to individual rights, not "collective" rights, or rights that may be exercised only through participation in some corporate body.

This contrasts markedly with the phrase "the militia" in the prefatory clause. [T]he "militia" in colonial America consisted of a subset of "the people" — those who were male, able bodied, and within a certain age range. Reading the Second Amendment as protecting only the right to "keep and bear Arms" in an organized militia therefore fits poorly with the operative clause's description of the holder of that right as "the people." [We] start therefore with a strong presumption that the Second Amendment right is exercised individually and belongs to all Americans.

b. *"Keep and bear Arms."* Before addressing the verbs "keep" and "bear," we interpret their object: "Arms." The 18th-century meaning is no different from the meaning today. The term was applied, then as now, to weapons that were not specifically designed for military use and were not employed in a military capacity. [Some] have made the argument, bordering on the frivolous, that only those arms in existence in the 18th century are protected by the Second Amendment. We do not interpret constitutional rights that way. Just as the First Amendment protects modern forms of communications, [and] the Fourth Amendment applies to modern forms of search, [t]he Second Amendment extends, prima facie, to all instruments that constitute bearable arms, even those that were not in existence at the time of the founding.

[T]he most natural reading of "keep Arms" in the Second Amendment is to "have weapons." . . . "Keep arms" was simply a common way of referring to possessing arms, for militiamen and everyone else. [At] the time of the founding, as now, to "bear" meant to "carry." When used with "arms," however, the term has a meaning that refers to carrying for a particular purpose — confrontation. Although the phrase implies that the carrying of the weapon is for the purpose of "offensive or defensive action," it in no way connotes participation in a structured military organization. From our review of founding-era sources, we conclude that this natural meaning was also the meaning that "bear arms" had in the 18th century.

c. *Meaning of the Operative Clause.* Putting all of these textual elements together, we find that they guarantee the individual right to possess and carry weapons in case of confrontation. This meaning is strongly confirmed by the historical background of the Second Amendment. We look to this because it has always been widely understood that the Second Amendment, like the First and Fourth Amendments, codified a *pre-existing* right. The very text of the Second Amendment implicitly recognizes the pre-existence of the right and declares only that it "shall not be infringed."

Between the Restoration and the Glorious Revolution, the Stuart Kings Charles II and James II succeeded in using select militias loyal to them to suppress political dissidents, in part by disarming their opponents. These experiences caused Englishmen to be extremely wary of concentrated military forces run by the state and to be jealous of their arms. They accordingly obtained an assurance from William and Mary, in the Declaration of Right (which was codified as the English Bill of Rights), that Protestants would never be disarmed. . . . This right has long been understood to be the predecessor to our Second Amendment. It was clearly an individual right, having nothing whatever to do with service in a militia. . . . Thus, the right secured in 1689 as a result of the Stuarts' abuses was by the time of the founding understood to be an individual right protecting against both public and private violence.

And, of course, what the Stuarts had tried to do to their political enemies, George III had tried to do to the colonists. In the tumultuous decades of the 1760's and 1770's, the Crown began to disarm the inhabitants of the most rebellious areas. That provoked polemical reactions by Americans invoking their rights as Englishmen to keep arms. They understood the right to enable individuals to defend themselves.

There seems to us no doubt, on the basis of both text and history, that the Second Amendment conferred an individual right to keep and bear arms. Of course the right was not unlimited, just as the First Amendment's right of free speech was not. Thus, we do not read the Second Amendment to protect the right of citizens to carry arms for *any sort* of confrontation, just as we do not read the First Amendment to protect the right of citizens to speak for *any purpose*. Before turning to limitations upon the individual right, however, we must determine whether the prefatory clause of the Second Amendment comports with our interpretation of the operative clause. . . .

a. *"Well-Regulated Militia."* In United States v. Miller, 307 U.S. 174, 179 (1939), we explained that "the Militia comprised all males physically capable of acting in concert for the common defense." That definition comports with founding-era sources. [Petitioners] take a seemingly narrower view of the militia, stating that "militias are the state- and congressionally-regulated military forces described in the Militia Clauses (art. I, §8, cls. 15-16)." Although we agree with petitioners' interpretive assumption that "militia" means the same thing in Article I and the Second Amendment, we believe that petitioners identify the wrong thing, namely, the organized militia. [The] militia consists of all able-bodied men, [while] the federally organized militia . . . consists of a subset of them. [Finally], the adjective "well-regulated" implies nothing more than the imposition of proper discipline and training.

b. *"Security of a Free State."* The phrase "security of a free state" meant "security of a free polity," not security of each of the several States. . . .

We reach the question, then: Does the preface fit with an operative clause that creates an individual right to keep and bear arms? It fits perfectly, once one knows the history that the founding generation knew. . . . That history showed that the way tyrants had eliminated a militia consisting of all the able-bodied men was not by banning the militia but simply by taking away the people's arms, enabling a select militia or standing army to suppress political opponents. This is what had occurred in England that prompted codification of the right to have arms in the English Bill of Rights.

The prefatory clause does not suggest that preserving the militia was the only reason Americans valued the ancient right; most undoubtedly thought it even more important for self-defense and hunting. But the threat that the new Federal Government would destroy the citizens' militia by taking away their arms was the reason that right — unlike some other English rights — was codified in a written Constitution. [Our] interpretation is confirmed by analogous arms-bearing rights in state constitutions that preceded and immediately followed adoption of the Second Amendment.

We now address how the Second Amendment was interpreted from immediately after its ratification through the end of the 19th century. Before proceeding, however, we take issue with [equating] these sources with postenactment legislative history, a comparison that betrays a fundamental misunderstanding of a court's interpretive task. "Legislative history," of course, refers to the pre-enactment statements of those who drafted or voted for a law; it is considered persuasive by some, not because they reflect the general understanding of the disputed terms, but because the legislators who heard or read those statements presumably voted with that understanding. "Postenactment legislative history," a deprecatory contradiction in terms, refers to statements of those who drafted or voted for the law that are made after its enactment and hence could have had no effect on the congressional vote. It most certainly does not refer to the examination of a variety of legal and other sources to determine *the public understanding* of a legal text in the period after its enactment or ratification. That sort of inquiry is a critical tool of constitutional interpretation. [V]irtually all interpreters of the Second Amendment in the century after its enactment interpreted the amendment as we do.

[All] three important founding-era legal scholars . . . understood it to protect an individual right unconnected with militia service. The 19th-century cases that interpreted the Second Amendment universally support an individual right unconnected to militia service. Antislavery advocates routinely invoked the right to bear arms for self-defense.

In the aftermath of the Civil War, there was an outpouring of discussion of the Second Amendment in Congress and in public discourse, as people debated whether and how to secure constitutional rights for newly free slaves. Since those discussions took place 75 years after the ratification of the Second Amendment, they do not provide as much insight into its original meaning as earlier sources. Yet those born and educated in the early 19th century faced a widespread effort to limit arms ownership by a large number of citizens; their understanding of the origins and continuing significance of the Amendment is instructive.

Blacks were routinely disarmed by Southern States after the Civil War. Those who opposed these injustices frequently stated that they infringed blacks' constitutional right to keep and bear arms. Needless to say, the claim was not that blacks were being prohibited from carrying arms in an organized state militia. Congress enacted the Freedmen's Bureau Act on July 16, 1866. Section 14 stated: "[T]he right . . . to have full and equal benefit of all laws and proceedings concerning personal liberty, personal security, and the acquisition, enjoyment, and disposition of estate, real and personal, including the constitutional right to bear arms, shall be secured to and enjoyed by all the citizens . . . without respect to race or color, or previous condition of slavery. . . ." 14 Stat. 176–177. Similar discussion attended the passage of the Civil Rights Act of 1871 and the Fourteenth Amendment. It was plainly the understanding in the post-Civil War Congress that the Second Amendment protected an individual right to use arms for self-defense. [Every] late-19th-century legal scholar that we have read interpreted the Second Amendment to secure an individual right unconnected with militia service.

We now ask whether any of our precedents forecloses the conclusions we have reached about the meaning of the Second Amendment. United States v. Cruikshank, in the course of vacating the convictions of members of a white mob for depriving blacks of their right to keep and bear arms, held that the Second Amendment does not by its own force apply to anyone other than the Federal Government. . . . The limited discussion of the Second Amendment in *Cruikshank* supports, if anything, the individual-rights interpretation. There was no claim in *Cruikshank* that the victims had been deprived of their right to carry arms in a militia; indeed, the Governor had disbanded the local militia unit the year before the mob's attack. We described the right protected by the Second Amendment as "'bearing arms for a lawful purpose'" and said that "the people [must] look for their protection against any violation by their fellow-citizens of the rights it recognizes" to the States' police power. That discussion makes little sense if it is only a right to bear arms in a state militia.[23]

Presser v. Illinois, 116 U.S. 252 (1886), held that the right to keep and bear arms was not violated by a law that forbade "bodies of men to associate together as military organizations, or to drill or parade with arms in cities and towns unless authorized by law." This does not refute the individual-rights interpretation of the Amendment; no one supporting that interpretation has contended that States may not ban such groups.

Justice Stevens places overwhelming reliance upon this Court's decision in United States v. Miller. [And] what is, according to Justice Stevens, the holding of *Miller* that demands such obeisance? That the Second Amendment "protects the right to keep and bear arms for certain military purposes, but that it does not curtail the legislature's power to regulate the nonmilitary use and ownership of weapons." . . .

Miller did not hold that and cannot possibly be read to have held that. The judgment in the case upheld against a Second Amendment challenge two men's federal convictions for transporting an unregistered short-barreled shotgun in interstate commerce, in violation of the National Firearms Act. It is entirely clear that the Court's basis for saying that the Second Amendment did not apply was *not* that the defendants were "bear[ing] arms" not "for . . . military purposes" but for "nonmilitary use." Rather, it was that the *type of weapon at issue* was not eligible for Second Amendment protection. [This] holding is not only consistent with, but positively suggests, that the Second Amendment confers an individual right to keep and bear arms (though only arms that "have some reasonable relationship to the preservation or efficiency of a well regulated militia"). Had the Court believed that the Second Amendment protects only those serving in the militia, it would have been odd to examine the character of the weapon rather than simply note that the two crooks were not militiamen. . . . *Miller* stands only for the proposition that the Second Amendment right, whatever its nature, extends only to certain types of weapons.

[N]othing in our precedents forecloses our adoption of the original understanding of the Second Amendment. It should be unsurprising that such a significant matter has been for so long judicially unresolved. For most of our history, the Bill of Rights was not thought applicable to the States, and the Federal Government did not significantly regulate the possession of firearms by law-abiding citizens. [It] is demonstrably not true that . . . , "for most of our history, the invalidity of Second-Amendment-based objections to firearms regulations has been well settled and uncontroversial." For most of our history the question did not present itself.

---

23. With respect to *Cruikshank*'s continuing validity on incorporation, a question not presented by this case, we note that *Cruikshank* also said that the First Amendment did not apply against the States and did not engage in the sort of Fourteenth Amendment inquiry required by our later cases. Our later decisions in Presser v. Illinois, 116 U.S. 252, 265 (1886), and Miller v. Texas, 153 U.S. 535, 538 (1894), reaffirmed that the Second Amendment applies only to the Federal Government.

Like most rights, the right secured by the Second Amendment is not unlimited. For example, the majority of the 19th-century courts to consider the question held that prohibitions on carrying concealed weapons were lawful under the Second Amendment or state analogues. Although we do not undertake an exhaustive historical analysis today of the full scope of the Second Amendment, nothing in our opinion should be taken to cast doubt on longstanding prohibitions on the possession of firearms by felons and the mentally ill, or laws forbidding the carrying of firearms in sensitive places such as schools and government buildings, or laws imposing conditions and qualifications on the commercial sale of arms.[26.]

We also recognize another important limitation on the right to keep and carry arms. *Miller* said [that] the sorts of weapons protected were those "in common use at the time." We think that limitation is fairly supported by the historical tradition of prohibiting the carrying of "dangerous and unusual weapons." It may be objected that if weapons that are most useful in military service — M-16 rifles and the like — may be banned, then the Second Amendment right is completely detached from the prefatory clause. But [the] conception of the militia at the time of the Second Amendment's ratification was the body of all citizens capable of military service, who would bring the sorts of lawful weapons that they possessed at home to militia duty. It may well be true today that a militia, to be as effective as militias in the 18th century, would require sophisticated arms that are highly unusual in society at large. Indeed, it may be true that no amount of small arms could be useful against modern-day bombers and tanks. But the fact that modern developments have limited the degree of fit between the prefatory clause and the protected right cannot change our interpretation of the right.

We turn finally to the law at issue here. [T]he inherent right of self-defense has been central to the Second Amendment right. The handgun ban amounts to a prohibition of an entire class of "arms" that is overwhelmingly chosen by American society for that lawful purpose. The prohibition extends, moreover, to the home, where the need for defense of self, family, and property is most acute. Under any of the standards of scrutiny that we have applied to enumerated constitutional rights,[27] banning from the home "the most preferred firearm in the nation to 'keep' and use for protection of one's home and family," would fail constitutional muster.

Few laws in the history of our Nation have come close to the severe restriction of the District's handgun ban. And some of those few have been struck down. It is no answer to say [that] it is permissible to ban the possession of handguns so long as the possession of other firearms (i.e., long guns) is allowed. It is enough

---

26. We identify these presumptively lawful regulatory measures only as examples; our list does not purport to be exhaustive.

27. Justice Breyer correctly notes that this law, like almost all laws, would pass rational-basis scrutiny. . . . But rational-basis scrutiny is a mode of analysis we have used when evaluating laws under constitutional commands that are themselves prohibitions on irrational laws. . . . In those cases, "rational basis" is not just the standard of scrutiny, but the very substance of the constitutional guarantee. Obviously, the same test could not be used to evaluate the extent to which a legislature may regulate a specific, enumerated right, be it the freedom of speech, the guarantee against double jeopardy, the right to counsel, or the right to keep and bear arms. See *United States v. Carolene Products Co.*, 304 U.S. 144, n.4 (1938). If all that was required to overcome the right to keep and bear arms was a rational basis, the Second Amendment would be redundant with the separate constitutional prohibitions on irrational laws, and would have no effect.

to note [that] the American people have considered the handgun to be the quint-essential self-defense weapon. [We] must also address the District's requirement (as applied to respondent's handgun) that firearms in the home be rendered and kept inoperable at all times. This makes it impossible for citizens to use them for the core lawful purpose of self-defense and is hence unconstitutional.

Justice Breyer [criticizes] us for declining to establish a level of scrutiny for evaluating Second Amendment restrictions. He [proposes] none of the tradition-ally expressed levels (strict scrutiny, intermediate scrutiny, rational basis), but rather a judge-empowering "interest-balancing inquiry" that "asks whether the statute burdens a protected interest in a way or to an extent that is out of propor-tion to the statute's salutary effects upon other important governmental inter-ests." . . . Justice Breyer arrives at his interest-balanced answer: because handgun violence is a problem, because the law is limited to an urban area, and because there were somewhat similar restrictions in the founding period . . . , the interest-balancing inquiry results in the constitutionality of the handgun ban.

We know of no other enumerated constitutional right whose core protection has been subjected to a freestanding "interest-balancing" approach. The very enumeration of the right takes out of the hands of government — even the Third Branch of Government — the power to decide on a case-by-case basis whether the right is *really worth* insisting upon. A constitutional guarantee subject to future judges' assessments of its usefulness is no constitutional guarantee at all. Consti-tutional rights are enshrined with the scope they were understood to have when the people adopted them, whether or not future legislatures or (yes) even future judges think that scope too broad. The Second Amendment [is] the very *product* of an interest-balancing by the people. . . . And whatever else it leaves to future evaluation, it surely elevates above all other interests the right of law-abiding, responsible citizens to use arms in defense of hearth and home.

Justice Breyer chides us for leaving so many applications of the right to keep and bear arms in doubt, and for not providing extensive historical justification for those regulations of the right that we describe as permissible. But since this case represents this Court's first in-depth examination of the Second Amend-ment, one should not expect it to clarify the entire field. [There] will be time enough to expound upon the historical justifications for the exceptions we have mentioned if and when those exceptions come before us.

[W]e hold that the District's ban on handgun possession in the home violates the Second Amendment, as does its prohibition against rendering any lawful fire-arm in the home operable for the purpose of immediate self-defense. Assuming that Heller is not disqualified from the exercise of Second Amendment rights, the District must permit him to register his handgun and must issue him a license to carry it in the home.

We affirm the judgment of the Court of Appeals.

Justice STEVENS, with whom Justice SOUTER, Justice GINSBURG, and Justice BREYER join, dissenting.

The question presented by this case is not whether the Second Amendment protects a "collective right" or an "individual right." Surely it protects a right that can be enforced by individuals. But a conclusion that the Second Amendment protects an individual right does not tell us anything about the scope of that right. Guns are used to hunt, for self-defense, to commit crimes, for sporting activities, and to perform military duties. The Second Amendment plainly does not protect the right to use a gun to rob a bank; it is equally clear that it *does* encompass the right to use weapons for certain military purposes. Whether it also protects the right to possess and use guns for nonmilitary purposes like hunting and personal self-defense is the question presented by this case. The text of the Amendment, its history, and our decision in *Miller* provide a clear answer to that question.

The Second Amendment was adopted to protect the right of the people of each of the several States to maintain a well-regulated militia. It was a response to concerns raised during the ratification of the Constitution that the power of Congress to disarm the state militias and create a national standing army posed an intolerable threat to the sovereignty of the several States. Neither the text of the Amendment nor the arguments advanced by its proponents evidenced the slightest interest in limiting any legislature's authority to regulate private civilian uses of firearms. Specifically, there is no indication that the Framers of the Amendment intended to enshrine the common-law right of self-defense in the Constitution.

The view of the Amendment we took in *Miller*—that it protects the right to keep and bear arms for certain military purposes, but that it does not curtail the Legislature's power to regulate the nonmilitary use and ownership of weapons—is both the most natural reading of the Amendment's text and the interpretation most faithful to the history of its adoption. [Since] *Miller,* hundreds of judges have relied on the view of the Amendment we endorsed there; we ourselves affirmed it in 1980. *See* Lewis v. United States, 445 U.S. 55, n.8 (1980). [No] new evidence has surfaced since 1980 supporting the view that the Amendment was intended to curtail the power of Congress to regulate civilian use or misuse of weapons. Indeed, a review of the drafting history of the Amendment demonstrates that its Framers *rejected* proposals that would have broadened its coverage to include such uses. . . .

The key to [*Miller*] did not, as the Court belatedly suggests, turn on the difference between muskets and sawed-off shotguns; it turned, rather, on the basic difference between the military and nonmilitary use and possession of guns. Indeed, if the Second Amendment were not limited in its coverage to military uses of weapons, why should the Court in *Miller* have suggested that some weapons but not others were eligible for Second Amendment protection? If use for self-defense were the relevant standard, why did the Court not inquire into the suitability of a particular weapon for self-defense purposes?

Until today, it has been understood that legislatures may regulate the civilian use and misuse of firearms so long as they do not interfere with the preservation of a well-regulated militia. The Court's announcement of a new constitutional right to own and use firearms for private purposes upsets that settled understanding, but leaves for future cases the formidable task of defining the scope of permissible regulations.

For these reasons, I respectfully dissent.

Justice BREYER, with whom Justice STEVENS, Justice SOUTER, and Justice GINS-
BURG join, dissenting.

[The] majority's conclusion is wrong for two independent reasons. The first
reason is that [the] the Second Amendment protects militia-related, not self-
defense-related, interests. These two interests are sometimes intertwined. To
assure 18th-century citizens that they could keep arms for militia purposes would
necessarily have allowed them to keep arms that they could have used for
self-defense as well. But self-defense alone, detached from any militia-related
objective, is not the Amendment's concern.

The second independent reason is that the protection the Amendment provides is not absolute. The Amendment permits government to regulate the
interests that it serves. Thus, [the] majority's view cannot be correct unless it can
show that the District's regulation is unreasonable or inappropriate in Second
Amendment terms. This the majority cannot do.

[The] District's law is consistent with the Second Amendment even if that
Amendment is interpreted as protecting a wholly separate interest in individual
self-defense. That is so because the District's regulation, which focuses upon the
presence of handguns in high-crime urban areas, represents a permissible legislative response to a serious, indeed life-threatening, problem. [The] law at issue
here, which in part seeks to prevent gun-related accidents, at least bears a "rational relationship" to [a] "legitimate" life-saving objective. Respondent proposes
that the Court adopt a "strict scrutiny" test, which would require reviewing with
care each gun law to determine whether it is "narrowly tailored to achieve a compelling governmental interest." But the majority implicitly, and appropriately,
rejects that suggestion by broadly approving a set of laws — prohibitions on
concealed weapons, forfeiture by criminals of the Second Amendment right, prohibitions on firearms in certain locales, and governmental regulation of commercial firearm sales — whose constitutionality under a strict-scrutiny standard
would be far from clear.

Indeed, adoption of a true strict-scrutiny standard for evaluating gun regulations would be impossible. That is because almost every gun-control regulation
will seek to advance (as the one here does) a "primary concern of every
government — a concern for the safety and indeed the lives of its citizens." The
Court has deemed that interest, as well as "the Government's general interest in
preventing crime," to be "compelling," and the Court has in a wide variety of constitutional contexts found such public-safety concerns sufficiently forceful to justify restrictions on individual liberties. Thus, any attempt *in theory* to apply strict
scrutiny to gun regulations will *in practice* turn into an interest-balancing inquiry,
with the interests protected by the Second Amendment on one side and the governmental public-safety concerns on the other, the only question being whether
the regulation at issue impermissibly burdens the former in the course of advancing the latter.

[The] fact that important interests lie on both sides of the constitutional
equation suggests that review of gun-control regulation is not a context in which
a court should effectively presume either constitutionality (as in rational-basis
review) or unconstitutionality (as in strict scrutiny). Rather, "where a law

significantly implicates competing constitutionally protected interests in complex ways," the Court generally asks whether the statute burdens a protected interest in a way or to an extent that is out of proportion to the statute's salutary effects upon other important governmental interests. Any answer would take account both of the statute's effects upon the competing interests and the existence of any clearly superior less restrictive alternative. Contrary to the majority's unsupported suggestion that this sort of "proportionality" approach is unprecedented, the Court has applied it in various constitutional contexts, including election-law cases, speech cases, and due process cases.

Respondent and his many *amici* [disagree] strongly with the District's *predictive judgment* that a ban on handguns will help solve the crime and accident problems that those figures disclose. [T]his Court, in First Amendment cases applying intermediate scrutiny, has said that our "sole obligation" in reviewing a legislature's "predictive judgments" is "to assure that, in formulating its judgments," the legislature "has drawn reasonable inferences based on substantial evidence." And judges, looking at the evidence before us, should agree that the District legislature's predictive judgments satisfy that legal standard. [T]he District's decision represents the kind of empirically based judgment that legislatures, not courts, are best suited to make.

I next assess the extent to which the District's law burdens the interests that the Second Amendment seeks to protect. Respondent and his *amici,* as well as the majority, suggest that those interests include: (1) the preservation of a "well regulated Militia"; (2) safeguarding the use of firearms for sporting purposes, e.g., hunting and marksmanship; and (3) assuring the use of firearms for self-defense. For argument's sake, I shall consider all three of those interests here. [The] District's statute burdens the Amendment's first and primary objective hardly at all. [T]he present case has nothing to do with *actual* military service. [The] majority briefly suggests that the "right to keep and bear Arms" might encompass an interest in hunting. [A]ny inability of District residents to hunt near where they live has much to do with the jurisdiction's exclusively urban character and little to do with the District's firearm laws.

The District's law does prevent a resident from keeping a loaded handgun in his home. And it consequently makes it more difficult for the householder to use the handgun for self-defense in the home against intruders, such as burglars. . . . To that extent the law burdens to some degree an interest in self-defense. The reason there is no clearly superior, less restrictive alternative to the District's handgun ban is that the ban's very objective is to reduce significantly the number of handguns in the District. If a resident has a handgun in the home that he can use for self-defense, then he has a handgun in the home that he can use to commit suicide or engage in acts of domestic violence. Licensing restrictions would not similarly reduce the handgun population, and the District may reasonably fear that even if guns are initially restricted to law-abiding citizens, they might be stolen and thereby placed in the hands of criminals. Permitting certain types of handguns, but not others, would affect the commercial market for handguns, but not their availability.

The upshot is that the District's objectives are compelling; its predictive judgments as to its law's tendency to achieve those objectives are adequately supported; the law does impose a burden upon any self-defense interest that the Amendment seeks to secure; and there is no clear less restrictive alternative. Does the District's law *disproportionately* burden Amendment-protected interests? Several considerations, taken together, convince me that it does not. . . . First, the District law is tailored to the life-threatening problems it attempts to address. The law concerns one class of weapons, handguns, leaving residents free to possess shotguns and rifles, along with ammunition. The area that falls within its scope is totally urban [and] suffers from a serious handgun-fatality problem. The District's law directly aims at that compelling problem. Second, the self-defense interest in maintaining loaded handguns in the home to shoot intruders is not the *primary* interest, but at most a subsidiary interest, that the Second Amendment seeks to serve. Further, any self-defense interest at the time of the Framing could not have focused exclusively upon urban-crime related dangers.

[T]he [Court's] decision threatens to throw into doubt the constitutionality of gun laws throughout the United States. I can find no sound legal basis for launching the courts on so formidable and potentially dangerous a mission. In my view, there simply is no untouchable constitutional right guaranteed by the Second Amendment to keep loaded handguns in the house in crime-ridden urban areas.

With respect, I dissent.

Notes and Questions

1. Heller *as Originalist Jurisprudence or Living Constitutionalism?* For an originalist, the "relevant inquiry" of constitutional interpretation "must focus on the *public* understanding of the language when the Constitution was developed." Henry Paul Monaghan, *Stare Decisis and Constitutional Adjudication*, 88 Colum. L. Rev. 723, 725 (1988) (emphasis in the original). Although this is a generalization, originalists are concerned with interpreting the meaning of the Constitution's text; it is the original meaning of the text that defines the outcome. *See* Randy E. Barnett, *Underlying Principles*, 24 Const. Comment. 405, 413 (2007). "Living constitutionalism," on the other hand, considers the Constitution's text and its original meaning as only part of the interpretative equation; it goes beyond the document and history and considers contemporary values and principles. Ethan J. Lieb, *The Perpetual Anxiety of Living Constitutionalism*, 24 Const. Comment. 353, 360 (2007) ("[L]iving constitutionalists demand that the living's views and expectations be reflected in the principles of the document itself"); *see also* Bruce Ackerman, *The Living Constitution*, 120 Harv. L. Rev. 1737, 1804-1805 (2007).

    a. Heller *as Originalism.* On its face, both the majority and the dissent in *Heller* give careful consideration to the text of the Second Amendment as well as to its meaning at the time of its adoption. Does this approach make *Heller* an originalist opinion? *See, e.g.,* Cass R. Sunstein, *Second Amendment Minimalism: Heller as Griswold*, 122 Harv. L. Rev. 246 (2009);

Lawrence B. Solum, *District of Columbia v. Heller and Originalism*, 103 Nw. U. L. Rev. 923 (2009); Rory K. Little, Heller *and Constitutional Interpretation: Originalism's Last Gasp*, 60 Hastings L.J. 1415 (2009). If originalism was in fact applied, why didn't the justices agree on the meaning of the Second Amendment? Can originalism alone determine the Amendment's meaning? While the majority may have reasonably interpreted the Amendment, its construction is not the only one, Mark V. Tushnet, *Out of Range* xvi (Oxford University 2007), and considerable disagreement still exists about the meaning of the Amendment's text and its historical record. *See* Saul Cornell, *Heller, New Originalism, and Law Office History*: "*Meet the New Boss, Same as the Old Boss,*" 56 U.C.L.A. L. Rev. 1095 (2009). Consider the admonition of Judge Harvie Wilkinson: "When a constitutional question is so close, when constitutional interpretive measures do not begin to resolve the issue decisively, the tie for many reasons should go to the side of deference to democratic processes." J. Harvie Wilkinson, III, *Of Guns, Abortions, and the Unraveling Rule of Law*, 95 Va. L. Rev. 253, 267 (2009); *see also* James B. Thayer, *The Origins of the American Doctrine of Constitutional Law*, 7 Harv. L. Rev. 129, 142 (1897): "The validity of the law ought not then to be questioned unless it is so obviously repugnant to the constitution that when pointed out by the judges, all men of sense and reflection in the community may perceive the repugnancy. By such a cautious exercise of this judicial check, no jealousy of it will be excited, the public confidence in it will be promoted, and its salutary effects be justly and fully appreciated." Given the ambiguity of the Second Amendment, should the citizens of the District of Columbia have been able to decide for themselves the conditions under which handguns could be kept in the city? In other words, if doubt exists about the Amendment's meaning, should the Court apply it to strike down laws enacted by democratic majorities?

b. Heller *as Both Originalism and Living Constitutionalism.* Jack Balkin contends that originalism and living constitutionalism are "compatible positions" and "two sides of the same coin." While judges must be faithful to the original meaning of the constitutional text and the principles that underlie it, they apply the text in a manner consistent with contemporary political and public attitudes. *See* Jack M. Balkin, *Framework Originalism and the Living Constitution*, 103 Nw. U. L. Rev. 549 (2009); *see also* Reva B. Siegel, *Dead or Alive*: *Originalism as Popular Constitutionalism in Heller*, 122 Harv. L. Rev. 191 (2008). Is it possible to read *Heller* as combining originalism and living constitutionalism? Consider the following:

- In various statutes enacted over more than a century, Congress has stated that individuals have the right to keep and bear arms.
- Currently, 44 state constitutions include some variation of the right to bear arms, and many of these states have construed their constitutional provisions to guarantee personal possession of firearms.
- Every major presidential candidate in the 2008 election viewed the possession of firearms as an individual right.

- Over the past several decades, public opinion polls indicate that a majority of Americans believe the Second Amendment guarantees an individual right to possess guns.

Even if the original meaning of the Second Amendment is uncertain, can the majority opinion be justified as reflecting contemporary values? In striking down the death penalty for the mentally ill, for minors, and for child rape, the Court predicated its decisions on "evolving standards of decency" based on a growing national consensus that the death penalty under these circumstances constituted "cruel and unusual punishment." Atkins v. Virginia, 536 U.S. 304 (2002); Roper v. Simmons, 543 U.S. 551 (2005); Kennedy v. Louisiana, 128 S.Ct. 2641 (2008). Similarly, in Lawrence v. Texas, 539 U.S. 558 (2006), in declaring Texas's same-sex sodomy law to be unconstitutional, the Court relied on "the *emerging awareness* that liberty gives substantial protection to adult persons in deciding how to conduct their private lives in matters pertaining to sex." *Id.* at 572 (emphasis added). Should emerging consensus among Americans that the Second Amendment protects an individual's right to possess arms matter? What about the fact that most state constitutions have amendments guaranteeing in some fashion the right of individuals to keep and bear arms? Is the current understanding of the Amendment relevant?

c. *Originalism and* Heller's *Limits on the Right to Keep and Bear Arms.* Consider the limits deemed acceptable by the majority on the right to keep and bear arms in section III of the opinion: prohibitions against the possession of firearms by felons and the mentally ill, laws forbidding the carrying of firearms in sensitive places such as schools and government buildings, and laws imposing conditions and qualifications on the commercial sale of arms. *Heller,* 128 S.Ct., at 2816-2817. Most of these restrictions were unknown to the drafters of the Second Amendment. *See* Nelson Lund, *The Second Amendment,* Heller, *and Originalist Jurisprudence,* 56 U.C.L.A. L. Rev. 1343 (2009). Is the acceptability of these limits on the right to arms indicative of a recognition of contemporary values rather than the original understanding as the basis for construing the scope of the right? Consider also that the protection given to handguns under the Second Amendment was predicated upon the majority's acknowledgment that handguns are the weapon of choice of the American people for self-defense. The majority opinion does not consider whether those who wrote and ratified the Second Amendment would have deemed such weapons protected. Are handguns protected simply because "people today choose them for protection"? Has the majority based the scope of the Second Amendment on "the fickle dynamics of contemporary consumer choices"? Adam Winkler, *Heller's Catch-22,* 56 U.C.L.A. L. Rev. 1551, 1560 (2009).

2. *The Demise of the "Collective-Rights" Model.* The Supreme Court unanimously rejected the strict "collective-rights" model of the Second Amendment.

The majority found that the Amendment protects an individual's right to keep and bear arms unconnected to military service. Justice Stevens's opinion for the dissenting justices explicitly recognized that the Second Amendment protects individual rights: "The question presented by this case is not whether the Second Amendment protects a 'collective right' or an 'individual right.' *Surely it protects a right that can be enforced by individuals.*" *Heller*, 128 S.Ct., at 2822 (Stevens, J., dissenting) (emphasis added). Stevens, however, disagreed with the majority's conclusion that the Second Amendment extended to an individual's right to possess firearms for self-defense. According to Justice Stevens, determining that the Second Amendment protects an individual right says nothing about the scope of the right. Under what circumstances could the right to keep and bear arms be enforced by an individual under the dissenting justices' view of the Second Amendment?

E. WHAT IS THE SCOPE OF THE RIGHT?

After *Heller*, the Second Amendment clearly protects the right to possess handguns in the home for self-defense and extends to "other weapons typically possessed by law-abiding citizens for lawful purposes" (e.g., hunting). The *Heller* majority admitted, however, that the Amendment does not reach all weapons — specifically, the possession of "dangerous and unusual weapons." The Court mentions "M-16 rifles and the like," recognizing that while these weapons may be useful today for an effective militia, "modern developments have limited the degree of fit between the prefatory clause and the protected right. . . ." Beyond the dicta in section III of the decision, the Court does not further define the arms protected by the Second Amendment. Lower federal and state courts have had little difficulty categorizing as "dangerous and unusual" such weapons as machine guns, Hamblen v. United States, 591 F.3d 471 (6th Cir. 2009), *cert. denied*, 130 S.Ct. 2426 (2010); United States v. Call, 2009 WL 6047131 (D. Nev. 2009); sawed-off shotguns, United States v. Fincher, 538 F.3d 868 (8th Cir. 2008); United States v. Hatfield, 376 Fed. App'x. 706 (9th Cir. 2010) (unpublished); assault rifles, People v. James, 174 Cal. App. 4th 662, 94 Cal. Rptr. 3d 576 (2009), *cert. denied*, 130 S.Ct. 1517 (2010); and pipe bombs, United States v. Tagg, 572 F.3d 1320 (11th Cir. 2009).

F. WHAT IS THE STANDARD OF REVIEW?

1. Heller's *Limited Guidance*

The only clear constitutional limit imposed by *Heller* on the regulation of firearms is that government may not completely ban the possession of a class of weapons commonly used by Americans in their homes for self-defense. Beyond this holding, the Court consciously did not enunciate a standard for reviewing the constitutionality of other types of regulations burdening the possession of arms. The Court did, however, explicitly reject the rational-basis test as a tool for assessing the legitimacy of gun-control measures, finding that "[i]f all that was required to overcome the right to keep and bear arms was a rational basis, the Second Amendment would be redundant with the separate constitutional prohibitions on irrational laws, and would have no effect." In dicta, the Court also outlined those regulatory measures it deemed to be presumptively constitutional, indicating that the list was not exhaustive. Specifically, the Court identified "longstanding prohibitions on the possession of firearms by felons and the mentally ill, or laws forbidding the carrying of firearms in sensitive places such as schools and government buildings, or laws imposing conditions and qualifications on the commercial sale of arms" as legitimate restraints on the right to keep and bear arms.

2. Application of the Right to Arms in the Lower Courts

Since *Heller*, lower federal and state courts have generally approached gun-control measures in one of two ways: They have either applied or analogized the categories of presumptively constitutional regulations delineated by the Court in assessing the constitutionality of the regulatory measures before them, or in a few cases, they have adjudged the restrictions on gun possession under heightened standards of judicial review.

a. The Categorical Approach

Federal and state courts have uniformly upheld gun-control measures expressly mentioned by the Court (albeit in dicta) to be presumptively constitutional. Thus, for example, the lower courts have upheld felon-in-possession laws, United States v. Vongxay, 594 F.3d 1111 (9th Cir. 2010) *cert. denied*, 2010 WL 2801462 (U.S. Oct. 4, 2010); United States v. Scroggins, 599 F.3d 433 (5th Cir. 2010), *cert. denied*, 2010 WL 2287006 (U.S. Oct. 4, 2010); United States v. Rozier, 598 F.3d 768 (11th Cir. 2010), *cert. denied*, 130 S.Ct. 3399 (2010); United States v. McCane, 573 F.3d 1037 (10th Cir. 2009), *cert. denied*, 130 S.Ct. 1686 (2010), and laws prohibiting gun possession by persons committed to a mental institution, United States v. Murphy, 681 F. Supp. 2d 95 (D. Me. 2010). For some regulatory measures not expressly addressed by *Heller*, a number of courts have upheld the provisions by analogizing the challenged restrictions to those regulations that the Court deemed to be presumptively constitutional, rather than examining them under a particular standard of review. These include such measures as prohibitions against the possession of firearms by juveniles, United States v. Rene S., 583 F.3d 8 (1st Cir. 2009), *cert. denied*, 130 S.Ct. 1109 (2010); States v. Sieyes, 168 Wash. 2d 276, 225 P.3d 995 (2010); gun-registration laws, Justice v. Town of Cicero, 577 F.3d 768 (7th Cir. 2009) (dicta), *cert. denied*, 130 S.Ct. 3410 (2010); *In the Matter of Dubov*, 410 N.J. Super. 190, 981 A.2d 87 (2009); prohibitions against the possession of firearms by persons who use or are addicted to controlled substances, United States v. Seay, 620 F.3d 919 (8th 2010); United States v. Yancey, 621 F.3d 681 (7th Cir. 2010); prohibitions against materially false statements on applications to purchase firearms, United States v. Knight, 574 F. Supp. 2d 224 (D. Me. 2009); prohibitions against the possession of firearms in public without a permit, People v. Perkins, 62 A.D.3d 1160, 880 N.Y.S.2d 209 (2009); prohibitions against carrying loaded firearms in public, People v. Villa, 178 Cal. App. 4th 443, 100 Cal. Rptr. 3d 463 (2009); prohibitions against the possession of firearms during the commission of a felony, United States v. Jackson, 555 F.3d 635 (7th Cir.), *cert. denied*, 130 S.Ct. 147 (2009); prohibitions against the possession of firearms in furtherance of drug-trafficking offenses, United States v. Rush, 635 F. Supp. 2d 1301 (M.D. Ala. 2009); prohibitions against carrying weapons while under a restraining order for threat of violence, United States v. Luedtke, 589 F. Supp. 2d 1018 (E.D. Wis. 2008); prohibitions against carrying firearms in a vehicle or in a public place or on a public street, Garber v. Superior Court, 184 Cal. App. 4th 724, 109 Cal. Rptr. 3d 278 (2010); and prohibitions against carrying pistols without a license, the possession of unregistered firearms, and the possession of unlawful ammunition. Riddick v. United States, 995 A.2d 212 (D.C. May 13, 2010); Little v. United States, 989 A.2d 1096 (D.C. 2010); Brown v. United States, 979 A.2d 630 (D.C. 2009); Howerton v. United States, 964 A.2d 1282 (D.C. 2009).

b. Heightened Standards of Judicial Scrutiny

Several federal courts have applied heightened standards of review to gun regulations, particularly to the federal statute (known as the Lautenberg Amendment) banning persons convicted of a misdemeanor offense of domestic violence from possessing firearms. 18 U.S.C. §922(g)(9). Lautenberg imposes a lifetime bar on gun ownership, no matter how old the conviction. Although some courts have upheld the prohibition as analogous to the prohibition of the possession of firearms by felons, *e.g.,* United States v. White, 593 F.3d 1199 (11th Cir. 2010); *In re United States*, 578 F.3d 1195 (10th Cir. 2009); Crespo v. Crespo, 201 N.J. 207, 989 A.2d 827 (2010) (state domestic violence prevention statute allowing seizure of violator's firearms), others have applied a heightened standard of scrutiny at least to the efficacy of the categorical prohibition, United States v. Williams, 616 F.3d 685 (7th Cir. 2010); United States v. Skoien, 614 F.3d 638 (7th Cir. 2010) (en banc); United States v. Bena, 2010 WL 1418389 (N.D. Iowa Apr. 6, 2010); United States v. Engstrum, 609 F. Supp. 2d 1227 (D. Utah 2009); *see also* United States v. Chester, 367 Fed. App'x. 392 (4th Cir. 2010) (unpublished) (suggesting heightened scrutiny on a case-by-case application of the statute).

A few courts have applied heightened standards of review to other restrictions on gun possession. *See, e.g.,* United States v. Yancey, 621 F.3d 681 (7th Cir. 2010) (applying intermediate scrutiny to prohibition against the possession of a firearm by unlawful user of marijuana); United States v. Marzzarella, 614 F.3d 85 (3d Cir. 2010) (applying intermediate scrutiny to prohibition against the possession of a firearm with an obliterated serial number, but also finding that the prohibition would be sustained under strict scrutiny); United States v. Yanez-Vasquez, 2010 WL 411112 (D. Kan. June 28, 2010) (applying intermediate scrutiny to prohibition against the possession of a firearm by illegal alien); Peruta v. County of San Diego, 678 F. Supp. 2d 1046 (S.D. Cal. 2010) (denying motion to dismiss §1983 action based on denial of a permit to carry a concealed weapon); United States v. Masciandaro, 648 F. Supp. 2d 779 (E.D. Va. 2009) (conviction for possession of loaded weapons in motor vehicles on national park land constitutional under strict, intermediate, or "undue burden" standard); United States v, Miller, 604 F. Supp. 2d 1162 (W.D. Tenn. 2009) (applying intermediate scrutiny to prohibition against the possession of a firearm by a felon). Illustrative is the district court's decision in Heller v. District of Columbia, 698 F. Supp. 2d 179 (D.D.C. 2010), a challenge to three temporary emergency measures enacted by the District of Columbia Council to regulate firearms in a manner consistent with the Supreme Court's ruling: 1) a firearms registration procedure, 2) a ban on assault weapons, and 3) a prohibition on large-capacity ammunition feeding devices. Finding that assault weapons and large-capacity ammunition feeding devices are not ordinarily used by law-biding citizens for lawful purposes and are "dangerous and unusual" under *Heller*, the court held that the ban on possessing assault weapons and large-capacity ammunition feeding devices does not implicate a core Second Amendment right and falls outside the scope of Second Amendment protection.

With regard to the registration requirement, the district court recognized that the Supreme Court in *Heller* emphasized that some form of heightened scrutiny is necessary because the right to keep and bear arms is a specific, constitutionally enumerated right. Consequently, the district court rejected both a "reasonableness test" and the "undue burden" test used in the abortion context. The district court also rejected a strict-scrutiny test, finding that the Supreme Court did not explicitly hold in *Heller* that the Second Amendment right is a "fundamental right." Moreover, the court reasoned that a strict-scrutiny standard would not be consistent with the Court's reference to "presumptively lawful regulatory measures," such as laws prohibiting firearms possession by felons and the mentally ill, forbidding the carrying of firearms in schools or government buildings, or imposing conditions and qualifications on the commercial sale of arms.

The district court opted for intermediate scrutiny; that is, if a gun regulation implicates a core Second Amendment right, the court will determine whether the measure is substantially related to an important governmental interest. The district court found that important governmental interests in public safety supported the registration procedures; specifically, registration 1) gives law enforcement officers information about firearm ownership, 2) allows officers to determine in advance whether individuals involved in a call may have a gun, 3) facilitates the return of lost or stolen weapons, 4) assists law enforcement in determining whether registered owners are eligible to possess firearms, 5) permits officers to charge individuals with a crime if they are in possession of an unregistered weapon, and 6) allows officers to seize unregistered weapons.

Moreover, based on evidence amassed by the District of Columbia Council that the registration requirement would effectuate the goal of promoting public safety, the district court found a substantial nexus between the registration requirement and the important governmental interest underlying the requirement.

3. *Heller's Effect on Gun Regulations*

Other than a complete ban on a lawful weapon in the home, what effect does *Heller* have on gun-control regulations? Consider that of the 44 states that have constitutional provisions securing some type of right to keep and bear arms, *see* Eugene Volokh, *State Constitutional Rights to Keep and Bear Arms*, 11 Tex. Rev. L. & Pol'y 191 (2007), most state courts apply a reasonableness standard to gun-control measures, giving considerable deference to legislative determinations. *See* Adam Winkler, *Scrutinizing the Second Amendment*, 105 Mich. L. Rev. 683 (2007); David B. Kopel & Clayton Cramer, *State Court Standards of Review for the Right to Keep and Bear Arms*, 50 Santa Clara L. Rev. 1113 (2010); *see also* Mark Tushnet, *Permissible Gun Regulation After Heller: Speculation About Methods and Outcomes*, 56 U.C.L.A. L. Rev. 1425 (2009) (predicting adoption of a "rational basis with a bite" standard of review). Will the government's interest in public safety, preventing crime, and other concerns always be reasonable? Indeed, is Justice Breyer correct in assuming that, because every gun regulation seeks to advance the government's concern for the safety and lives of its citizens, every gun-control law will be compelling?

4. *The Second Amendment's Reach*

Does Justice Scalia's list of presumptively constitutional gun-control measures effectively limit the reach of the Second Amendment to only the most severe forms of gun regulations? Is only possession of handguns in the home for self-defense protected? *See* Brannon P. Denning & Glenn H. Reynolds, Heller, *High Water(mark)? Lower Courts and the New Right to Keep and Bear Arms*, 60 Hastings L.J. 1245, 1259-1260 (2009); Cass R. Sunstein, *Second Amendment Minimalism*: Heller *as* Griswold, 122 Harv. L. Rev. 246, 267-268 (2008).

∾ PROBLEMS: MORE ON COMPREHENSIVE GUN-CONTROL LEGISLATION ∾

1. *Regulation of Firearms.* In light of *Heller* and lower federal and state court decisions, what advice would you give to the ad hoc committee regarding proposed comprehensive gun-control legislation? In particular, could the legislature adopt the following proposals consistent with the Second Amendment?

- Require registration of all firearms to track those who possess them.
- Require licenses for firearm possession.

- Require handgun owners and prospective handgun owners to take a four-hour class on gun safety and a two-hour training session at a gun range every two years.
- Limit the number of handguns a person can register to one per month.
- Prohibit the possession of automatic weapons, including machine guns.
- Prohibit the possession of unusually dangerous weapons, such as grenades and armor-piercing ammunition.
- Prohibit persons from having more than one handgun in operating order at any given time.
- Require persons in homes with children to keep handguns in lock boxes or equip them with trigger locks.
- Require all persons to keep handguns in lock boxes or equip them with trigger locks.
- Prohibit the possession of firearms by minors under the age of 21 and persons deemed mentally incompetent.
- Prohibit the possession of firearms by any person convicted of a felony or a misdemeanor involving physical violence (e.g., domestic violence).
- Prohibit the possession of firearms by any person convicted of an alcohol- or drug-related offense.
- Prohibit the possession of firearms by any person convicted of any offense, including traffic violations.
- Prohibit the possession of a firearm in any government or public building, including schools, theaters, and restaurants.
- Prohibit concealed carrying of firearms.
- Prohibit the possession of firearms outside one's home.
- Prohibit the sale or purchase of handguns in urban areas (defined as a town or city with a population greater than 50,000).
- Prohibit the possession of any firearm in urban areas (defined as a town or city with a population greater than 50,000).

As counsel to the committee, what advice would you give about Second Amendment restrictions on the proposed gun-control measures? How has *Heller* affected the discretion of Congress or state legislatures to regulate or even ban firearms? Assuming the Second Amendment applies to the states, would the Amendment pose a barrier to any of the proposed gun-control measures? Could the legislature go so far as to ban the sale, possession, and use of all firearms?

As counsel to the gun-rights organization lobbying the legislature against the proposed gun-control legislation, assuming the Second Amendment applies to the states, what arguments would you make against the committee's proposals?

2. *Misdemeanant Possession of Firearms.* The ad hoc committee proposes prohibiting convicted misdemeanants from possessing firearms. The idea is that anyone convicted of an offense is potentially more dangerous and more violent and therefore should not be allowed to carry weapons. Gun-rights advocates disagree and offer the example of Ralph Jones, who, at 18 years old, pled guilty in 1970 to the misdemeanor offense of assault. While drunk, Ralph threatened his girlfriend, Shirley, with whom he lived, with a knife. In 1976, Ralph and Shirley

married. Ralph is now a physician; he has neither been arrested nor had problems with alcohol since 1970. He and Shirley have experienced several break-ins at their residence, and, in 2010, Ralph (now 58 years of age) applied to purchase a handgun to defend his home. His application was denied under a federal law, 10 U.S.C. §922(d)(9), that makes it unlawful to sell a firearm or ammunition to any person convicted of a misdemeanor crime of domestic violence. Could the legislation preclude someone like Ralph from owning a firearm? Should the blanket prohibition against firearms possession be applied regardless of the length of time elapsed between the offense and the application for a firearm? Or should courts consider the circumstances of each individual applicant? *See* United States v. Skoien, 614 F.3d 638, 640 (7th Cir. 2010) (en banc); *compare* United States v. Chester, 367 Fed. App'x. 392 (4th Cir. 2010) (unpublished).

3. *Conviction for Nonviolent Offenses.* Could the proposed legislation prohibit anyone who has been convicted of any offense, including a nonviolent offense, from possessing a weapon? Supporters of comprehensive legislation argue that the law should prohibit the possession of weapons by all who have been convicted of crimes, including convictions for nonviolent offenses. Gun-rights advocates offer the example of Clyde Abernathy, a successful businessman and fervent fan of his alma mater, the West Texas University Panthers, who offered a highly recruited high school quarterback a pre-owned automobile for signing a letter of intent to play for the Panthers. The car was valued at $1,600. Clyde was convicted in Texas district court for illegal recruitment of an athlete (Tex. Penal Code §32.441), a "state jail felony" punishable by up to two years in prison. Clyde was fined $5,000 and placed on six months probation. Clyde paid the fine and served his probation without incident. In 2010, while hunting, Clyde was arrested by federal wildlife agents for possessing a weapon (rifle) in violation of 18 U.S.C. §922(g)(1) (possession of a firearm by a person convicted of a crime punishable by imprisonment for a term exceeding one year). Could the legislation preclude someone like Clyde from possessing a weapon? *See* United States v. Williams, 616 F.3d 685, 693 (7th Cir. 2010); C. Kevin Marshall, *Why Can't Martha Stewart Have a Gun?*, 32 Harv. J.L. & Pub. Pol'y 695 (2009).

G. DOES THE RIGHT APPLY TO THE STATES?

Because the District of Columbia is a federal enclave, the *Heller* Court did not address the question whether the Second Amendment applies to state and local governments. *Heller*, 128 S.Ct., at 2813 n.23. Early Supreme Court cases held that the Amendment applied only to the federal government, United States v. Cruikshank, 92 U.S. 542 (1875); Presser v. Illinois, 116 U.S. 252 (1886); Texas v. Miller, 153 U.S. 535 (1894); however, all of these cases were decided before the Court began the process of incorporating the Bill of Rights under the Fourteenth Amendment.

Nevertheless, most lower federal and state courts that considered the question deemed themselves bound by the Court's nineteenth-century pronouncements, holding that the Second Amendment does not apply to the states. *See, e.g.,* Maloney v. Cuomo, 554 F.3d 56 (2d Cir. 2009), *vacated,* 2010 WL 2571878 (U.S. June 29, 2010); Warden v. Nickels, 697 F. Supp. 2d 1221 (W.D. Wash. 2010); Banks v. Gallagher, 686 F. Supp. 2d 499 (M.D. Pa. 2009); Young v. Hawaii, 2009 WL 874517 (D. Hawaii Apr. 1, 2009); Commonwealth v. Loadholt, 456 Mass. 411, 923 N.E.2d 1037 (2010); Commonwealth v. Runyon, 456 Mass. 230, 922 N.E.2d 794 (Mass. 2010); Wilson v. Cook County, 394 Ill. App. 534, 914 N.E.2d 595 (2009); State v. Turnbull, 766 N.W.2d 78 (Minn. App. 2009); *but see* Nordyke v. King, 563 F.3d 439 (9th Cir.), *reh'g en banc granted,* 575 F.3d 890 (9th Cir. 2009), *vacated,* 611 F.3d 2015 (9th Cir. 2010); State v. Sieyes, 168 Wash. 2d 276, 225 P.3d 995 (2010).

In a 2008 lawsuit reminiscent of *Heller,* residents and a rifle association challenged ordinances in two Illinois communities that banned the possession of most handguns. The Court of Appeals for the Seventh Circuit affirmed the district court's dismissal of the case based on *Cruikshank, Presser,* and *Miller.* National Rifle Association v. City of Chicago, 567 F.3d 856 (7th Cir. 2009), *cert granted sub nom.,* McDonald v. City of Chicago, 130 S.Ct. 48 (2009). In the following 2010 case, the Supreme Court addressed for the first time in more than a century the issue of whether the Second Amendment applies to the states.

McDonald v. City of Chicago

130 S. Ct. 3020 (2010)

Justice ALITO delivered the opinion of the Court as to parts I, II-A, II-B, II-D, III-A, and III-B; and an opinion with respect to part II-C, IV, and V, in which THE CHIEF JUSTICE and Justices SCALIA and KENNEDY join.

Two years ago, in District of Columbia v. Heller, we held that the Second Amendment protects the right to keep and bear arms for the purpose of self-defense, and we struck down a District of Columbia law that banned the possession of handguns in the home. The city of Chicago and the village of Oak Park, a Chicago suburb, have laws that are similar to the District of Columbia's, but Chicago and Oak Park argue that their laws are constitutional because the Second Amendment has no application to the States. We have previously held that most of the provisions of the Bill of Rights apply with full force to both the Federal Government and the States. Applying the standard that is well established in our case law, we hold that the Second Amendment right is fully applicable to the States.

I

[Petitioners are residents of the city of Chicago and the Village of Oak Park who would like to keep handguns in their homes for self-defense but are forbidden from doing so by municipal ordinance. Relying on precedent, the lower courts held that the Second Amendment did not apply to the states.]

II

A

Petitioners argue that the Chicago and Oak Park laws violate the right to keep and bear arms for two reasons. Petitioners' primary submission is that this right is among the "privileges or immunities of citizens of the United States" and that the narrow interpretation of the Privileges or Immunities Clause adopted in the *Slaughter-House Cases*[, 16 Wall. 36 (1873),] should now be rejected. As a secondary argument, petitioners contend that the Fourteenth Amendment's Due Process Clause "incorporates" the Second Amendment right. Chicago and Oak Park maintain that a right set out in the Bill of Rights applies to the States only if that right is an indispensable attribute of *any* "civilized" legal system. If it is possible to imagine a civilized country that does not recognize the right, . . . then that right is not protected by due process. And since there are civilized countries that ban or strictly regulate the private possession of handguns, the municipal respondents maintain that due process does not preclude such measures.

B

The Bill of Rights, including the Second Amendment, originally applied only to the Federal Government. In Barron ex rel. Tiernan v. Mayor of Baltimore, 7 Pet. 243 (1833), the Court firmly rejected the proposition that the first eight Amendments operate as limitations on the States, holding that they apply only to the Federal Government. The constitutional Amendments adopted in the aftermath of the Civil War fundamentally altered our country's federal system. The provision at issue in this case, §1 of the Fourteenth Amendment, provides, among other things, that a State may not abridge "the privileges or immunities of citizens of the United States" or deprive "any person of life, liberty, or property, without due process of law." The *Slaughter-House Cases* involved challenges to a Louisiana law permitting the creation of a state-sanctioned monopoly on the butchering of animals within the city of New Orleans. The Court concluded that the Privileges or Immunities Clause protects only those rights "which owe their existence to the Federal government, its National character, its Constitution, or its laws." Finding no constitutional protection against state intrusion of the kind envisioned by the Louisiana statute, the Court upheld the statute.

Three years after the decision in the *Slaughter-House Cases,* the Court decided *Cruikshank,* the first of the three 19th-century cases on which the Seventh Circuit relied. The Court wrote that the right of bearing arms for a lawful purpose "is not a right granted by the Constitution." "The second amendment," the Court continued, "declares that it shall not be infringed; but this . . . means no more than that it shall not be infringed by Congress." Our later decisions in Presser v. Illinois, and Miller v. Texas, reaffirmed that the Second Amendment applies only to the Federal Government.

C (plurality opinion)

The Seventh Circuit concluded that *Cruikshank, Presser,* and *Miller* doomed petitioners' claims. [Petitioners] argue, however, that we should overrule those decisions and hold that the right to keep and bear arms is one of the "privileges or immunities of citizens of the United States."

For many decades, the question of the rights protected by the Fourteenth Amendment against state infringement has been analyzed under the Due Process Clause of that Amendment and not under the Privileges or Immunities Clause. We therefore decline to disturb the *Slaughter-House* holding. At the same time, however, this Court's decisions in *Cruikshank, Presser,* and *Miller* do not preclude us from considering whether the Due Process Clause of the Fourteenth Amendment makes the Second Amendment right binding on the States. None of those cases engaged in the sort of Fourteenth Amendment inquiry required by our later cases.

Indeed, *Cruikshank* has not prevented us from holding that other rights that were at issue in that case are binding on the States through the Due Process Clause. In *Cruikshank,* the Court held that the general "right of the people peaceably to assemble for lawful purposes," which is protected by the First Amendment, applied only against the Federal Government and not against the States. Nonetheless, over 60 years later the Court held that the right of peaceful assembly was a "fundamental righ[t] . . . safeguarded by the due process clause of the Fourteenth Amendment." De Jonge v. Oregon, 299 U.S. 353, 364 (1937). We follow the same path here and thus consider whether the right to keep and bear arms applies to the States under the Due Process Clause.

D

In the late 19th century, the Court began to consider whether the Due Process Clause prohibits the States from infringing rights set out in the Bill of Rights. . . . Five features of the approach taken during the ensuing era should be noted. [First,] the Court viewed the due process question as entirely separate from the question whether a right was a privilege or immunity of national citizenship. *See* Twining v. New Jersey, 211 U.S. 78, 99 (1908). [Second,] the Court explained that the only rights protected against state infringement by the Due Process Clause were those rights "of such a nature that they are included in the conception of due process of law." While it was "possible that some of the personal rights safeguarded by the first eight Amendments against National action [might] also be safeguarded against state action," the Court stated, this was "not because those rights are enumerated in the first eight Amendments." *Twining, supra,* at 99. [In] *Palko* [v. Connecticut, 302 U.S. 319 (1937)], the Court famously said that due process protects those rights that are "the very essence of a scheme of ordered liberty" and essential to "a fair and enlightened system of justice." [Third,] in some cases decided during this era the Court "can be seen as having asked, when inquiring into whether some particular procedural safeguard was required of a State, if a civilized system could be imagined that would not accord the particular protection." Duncan v. Louisiana, 391 U.S. 145, 149, n.14 (1968). [Fourth,] the Court during this era was not hesitant to hold that a right set out in the Bill of Rights failed to meet the test for inclusion within the protection of the Due Process Clause. The Court found that some such rights qualified. . . . But others did not. [Finally,] even when a right set out in the Bill of Rights was held to fall within the conception of due process, the protection or remedies afforded against state infringement sometimes differed from the protection or remedies provided against abridgment by the Federal Government.

An alternative theory regarding the relationship between the Bill of Rights and §1 of the Fourteenth Amendment was championed by Justice Black. This theory held that §1 totally incorporated all of the provisions of the Bill of Rights. . . . While Justice Black's theory was never adopted, the Court eventually moved in that direction by initiating what has been called a process of "selective incorporation," i.e., the Court began to hold that the Due Process Clause fully incorporates particular rights contained in the first eight Amendments. . . . The decisions during this time abandoned three of the previously noted characteristics of the earlier period. The Court made it clear that the governing standard is not whether *any* "civilized system can be imagined that would not accord the particular protection." Instead, the Court inquired whether a particular Bill of Rights guarantee is fundamental to *our* scheme of ordered liberty and system of justice.

The Court also shed any reluctance to hold that rights guaranteed by the Bill of Rights met the requirements for protection under the Due Process Clause. The Court eventually incorporated almost all of the provisions of the Bill of Rights. . . . [Finally,] the Court abandoned the notion that the Fourteenth Amendment applies to the States only a watered down, subjective version of the individual guarantees of the Bill of Rights, stating that it would be "incongruous" to apply different standards "depending on whether the claim was asserted in a state or federal court." Instead, the Court decisively held that incorporated Bill of Rights protections are all to be enforced against the States under the Fourteenth Amendment according to the same standards that protect those personal rights against federal encroachment.

III

With this framework in mind, we now turn directly to the question whether the Second Amendment right to keep and bear arms is incorporated in the concept of due process. In answering that question, we must decide whether the right to keep and bear arms is fundamental to *our* scheme of ordered liberty, or as we have said in a related context, whether this right is "deeply rooted in this Nation's history and tradition," Washington v. Glucksberg, 521 U.S. 702, 721 (1997).

A

Our decision in *Heller* points unmistakably to the answer. Self-defense is a basic right, recognized by many legal systems from ancient times to the present day, and in *Heller,* we held that individual self-defense is "the *central component*" of the

Second Amendment right. Explaining that "the need for defense of self, family, and property is most acute" in the home, we found that this right applies to handguns because they are "the most preferred firearm in the nation to 'keep' and use for protection of one's home and family." Thus, we concluded, citizens must be permitted "to use [handguns] for the core lawful purpose of self-defense." *Heller* makes it clear that this right is "deeply rooted in this Nation's history and tradition."

B

By the 1850's, the perceived threat that had prompted the inclusion of the Second Amendment in the Bill of Rights — the fear that the National Government would disarm the universal militia — had largely faded as a popular concern, but the right to keep and bear arms was highly valued for purposes of self-defense. [After] the Civil War, many of the over 180,000 African-Americans who served in the Union Army returned to the States of the old Confederacy, where systematic efforts were made to disarm them and other blacks. The laws of some States formally prohibited African-Americans from possessing firearms. Throughout the South, armed parties, often consisting of ex-Confederate soldiers serving in the state militias, forcibly took firearms from newly freed slaves. Union Army commanders took steps to secure the right of all citizens to keep and bear arms, but the 39th Congress concluded that legislative action was necessary. Its efforts to safeguard the right to keep and bear arms demonstrate that the right was still recognized to be fundamental.

The most explicit evidence of Congress' aim appears in §14 of the Freedmen's Bureau Act of 1866, which provided that "the right . . . to have full and equal benefit of all laws and proceedings concerning personal liberty, personal security, and the acquisition, enjoyment, and disposition of estate, real and personal, *including the constitutional right to bear arms*, shall be secured to and enjoyed by all the citizens . . . without respect to race or color, or previous condition of slavery." 14 Stat. 176-177 (emphasis added). The Civil Rights Act of 1866, 14 Stat. 27, which was considered at the same time as the Freedmen's Bureau Act, similarly sought to protect the right of all citizens to keep and bear arms. Section 1 of the Civil Rights Act guaranteed the "full and equal benefit of all laws and proceedings for the security of person and property, as is enjoyed by white citizens." This language was virtually identical to language in §14 of the Freedmen's Bureau Act. And as noted, the latter provision went on to explain that one of the "laws and proceedings concerning personal liberty, personal security, and the acquisition, enjoyment, and disposition of estate, real and personal" was "the constitutional right to bear arms."

Congress, however, ultimately deemed these legislative remedies insufficient. Southern resistance, Presidential vetoes, and this Court's pre-Civil-War precedent persuaded Congress that a constitutional amendment was necessary to provide full protection for the rights of blacks. Today, it is generally accepted that the Fourteenth Amendment was understood to provide a constitutional basis for protecting the rights set out in the Civil Rights Act of 1866. In debating the

Fourteenth Amendment, the 39th Congress referred to the right to keep and bear arms as a fundamental right deserving of protection. . . . [I]t is clear that the Framers and ratifiers of the Fourteenth Amendment counted the right to keep and bear arms among those fundamental rights necessary to our system of ordered liberty.

IV (plurality opinion)

Municipal respondents, in effect, ask us to treat the right recognized in *Heller* as a second-class right, subject to an entirely different body of rules than the other Bill of Rights guarantees that we have held to be incorporated into the Due Process Clause. Municipal respondents' main argument is nothing less than a plea to disregard 50 years of incorporation precedent and return (presumably for this case only) to a bygone era. Municipal respondents submit that the Due Process Clause protects only those rights "recognized by all temperate and civilized governments, from a deep and universal sense of their justice." According to municipal respondents, if it is possible to imagine *any* civilized legal system that does not recognize a particular right, then the Due Process Clause does not make that right binding on the States. Therefore, the municipal respondents continue, because [other civilized] countries either ban or severely limit handgun ownership, it must follow that no right to possess such weapons is protected by the Fourteenth Amendment.

   This line of argument is, of course, inconsistent with the long-established standard we apply in incorporation cases. And the present-day implications of municipal respondents' argument are stunning. For example, many of the rights that our Bill of Rights provides for persons accused of criminal offenses are virtually unique to this country. If *our* understanding of the right to a jury trial, the right against self-incrimination, and the right to counsel were necessary attributes of *any* civilized country, it would follow that the United States is the only civilized Nation in the world. [Municipal] respondents attempt to salvage their position by suggesting that their argument applies only to substantive as opposed to procedural rights. But even in this trimmed form, municipal respondents' argument flies in the face of more than a half-century of precedent. For example, in Everson v. Board of Ed. of Ewing, 330 U.S. 1, 8 (1947), the Court held that the Fourteenth Amendment incorporates the Establishment Clause of the First Amendment. Yet several of the countries that municipal respondents recognize as civilized have established state churches. If we were to adopt municipal respondents' theory, all of this Court's Establishment Clause precedents involving actions taken by state and local governments would go by the boards.

   Municipal respondents maintain that the Second Amendment differs from all of the other provisions of the Bill of Rights because it concerns the right to possess a deadly implement and thus has implications for public safety. . . . The right to keep and bear arms, however, is not the only constitutional right that has controversial public safety implications. All of the constitutional provisions that impose restrictions on law enforcement and on the prosecution of crimes fall into the same category. Municipal respondents cite no case in which we have refrained from holding that a provision of the Bill of Rights is binding on the States on the ground that the right at issue has disputed public safety implications.

We likewise reject municipal respondents' argument that we should depart from our established incorporation methodology on the ground that making the Second Amendment binding on the States and their subdivisions is inconsistent with principles of federalism and will stifle experimentation. [There] is nothing new in the argument that, in order to respect federalism and allow useful state experimentation, a federal constitutional right should not be fully binding on the States. Time and again, however, those pleas failed. Unless we turn back the clock or adopt a special incorporation test applicable only to the Second Amendment, municipal respondents' argument must be rejected.

Municipal respondents and their *amici* complain that incorporation of the Second Amendment right will lead to extensive and costly litigation, but this argument applies with even greater force to constitutional rights and remedies that have already been held to be binding on the States. Consider the exclusionary rule. Although the exclusionary rule "is not an individual right," but a "judicially created rule," this Court made the rule applicable to the States. The exclusionary rule is said to result in "tens of thousands of contested suppression motions each year." . . .

It is important to keep in mind that *Heller*, while striking down a law that prohibited the possession of handguns in the home, recognized that the right to keep and bear arms is not "a right to keep and carry any weapon whatsoever in any manner whatsoever and for whatever purpose." We made it clear in *Heller* that our holding did not cast doubt on such longstanding regulatory measures as "prohibitions on the possession of firearms by felons and the mentally ill," "laws forbidding the carrying of firearms in sensitive places such as schools and government buildings, or laws imposing conditions and qualifications on the commercial sale of arms." We repeat those assurances here. Despite municipal respondents' doomsday proclamations, incorporation does not imperil every law regulating firearms.

Municipal respondents argue, finally, that the right to keep and bear arms is unique among the rights set out in the first eight Amendments "because the reason for codifying the Second Amendment (to protect the militia) differs from the purpose (primarily, to use firearms to engage in self-defense) that is claimed to make the right implicit in the concept of ordered liberty." Municipal respondents suggest that the Second Amendment right differs from the rights heretofore incorporated because the latter were "valued for [their] own sake." But we have never previously suggested that incorporation of a right turns on whether it has intrinsic as opposed to instrumental value, and quite a few of the rights previously held to be incorporated — for example the right to counsel and the right to confront and subpoena witnesses — are clearly instrumental by any measure. Moreover, this contention repackages one of the chief arguments that we rejected in *Heller*, i.e., that the scope of the Second Amendment right is defined by the immediate threat that led to the inclusion of that right in the Bill of Rights. In *Heller*, we recognized that the codification of this right was prompted by fear that the Federal Government would disarm and thus disable the militias, but we rejected the suggestion that the right was valued only as a means of preserving the militias. On the contrary, we stressed that the right was also valued because the possession of firearms was thought to be essential for self-defense. As we put it, self-defense was "the *central component* of the right itself."

V (plurality opinion)

We turn, finally, to the two dissenting opinions. Justice Stevens would "ground the prohibitions against state action squarely on due process, without intermediate reliance on any of the first eight Amendments." The question presented in this case, in his view, "is whether the particular right asserted by petitioners applies to the States because of the Fourteenth Amendment itself, standing on its own bottom." [The] Court, for the past half century, has moved away from the two-track approach. If we were now to accept Justice Stevens' theory across the board, decades of decisions would be undermined. We assume that this is not what is proposed. What is urged instead, it appears, is that this theory be revived solely for the individual right that *Heller* recognized, over vigorous dissents. The relationship between the Bill of Rights' guarantees and the States must be governed by a single, neutral principle. It is far too late to exhume what Justice Brennan, writing for the Court 46 years ago, derided as "the notion that the Fourteenth Amendment applies to the States only a watered-down, subjective version of the individual guarantees of the Bill of Rights."

Justice Breyer's conclusion that the Fourteenth Amendment does not incorporate the right to keep and bear arms appears to rest primarily on four factors: First, "there is no popular consensus" that the right is fundamental, second, the right does not protect minorities or persons neglected by those holding political power, third, incorporation of the Second Amendment right would "amount to a significant incursion on a traditional and important area of state concern, altering the constitutional relationship between the States and the Federal Government" and preventing local variations, and fourth, determining the scope of the Second Amendment right in cases involving state and local laws will force judges to answer difficult empirical questions regarding matters that are outside their area of expertise. Even if we believed that these factors were relevant to the incorporation inquiry, none of these factors undermines the case for incorporation of the right to keep and bear arms for self-defense.

First, we have never held that a provision of the Bill of Rights applies to the States only if there is a "popular consensus" that the right is fundamental, and we see no basis for such a rule. Second, petitioners and many others who live in high crime areas dispute the proposition that the Second Amendment right does not protect minorities and those lacking political clout. Third, Justice Breyer is correct that incorporation of the Second Amendment right will to some extent limit the legislative freedom of the States, but this is always true when a Bill of Rights provision is incorporated. . . . Finally, Justice Breyer is incorrect that incorporation will require judges to assess the costs and benefits of firearms restrictions and thus to make difficult empirical judgments in an area in which they lack expertise. [W]hile [Justice Breyer's] opinion in *Heller* recommended an interest-balancing test, the Court specifically rejected that suggestion. "The very enumeration of the right takes out of the hands of government — even the Third Branch of Government — the power to decide on a case-by-case basis whether the right is *really worth* insisting upon."

In *Heller*, we held that the Second Amendment protects the right to possess a handgun in the home for the purpose of self-defense. Unless considerations of *stare decisis* counsel otherwise, a provision of the Bill of Rights that protects a right that is fundamental from an American perspective applies equally to the Federal Government and the States. We therefore hold that the Due Process Clause of the Fourteenth Amendment incorporates the Second Amendment right recognized in *Heller*. The judgment of the Court of Appeals is reversed, and the case is remanded for further proceedings.

Justice SCALIA, concurring.

[Despite] my misgivings about Substantive Due Process as an original matter, I have acquiesced in the Court's incorporation of certain guarantees in the Bill of Rights "because it is both long established and narrowly limited." [I] write separately only to respond to some aspects of Justice Stevens' dissent. [After] stressing the substantive dimension of what he has renamed the "liberty clause," Justice Stevens proceeds to urge re-adoption of the theory of incorporation articulated in Palko v. Connecticut, 302 U.S. 319, 325 (1937). But in fact he does not favor application of that theory at all. For whether *Palko* requires only that "a fair and enlightened system of justice would be impossible without" the right sought to be incorporated, or requires in addition that the right be rooted in the "traditions and conscience of our people," many of the rights Justice Stevens thinks are incorporated could not pass muster under either test: abortion (Planned Parenthood of Southeastern Pa. v. Casey, 505 U.S. 833 (1992)); homosexual sodomy (Lawrence v. Texas, 539 U.S. 558 (2003)); the right to have excluded from criminal trials evidence obtained in violation of the Fourth Amendment (Mapp v. Ohio, 367 U.S. 643 (1961)); and the right to teach one's children foreign languages (Meyer v. Nebraska, 262 U.S. 390 (1923)), among others.

That Justice Stevens is not applying any version of *Palko* is clear from comparing, on the one hand, the rights he believes *are* covered, with, on the other hand, his conclusion that the right to keep and bear arms is *not* covered. Rights that pass his test include not just those "relating to marriage, procreation, contraception, family relationships, and child rearing and education," but also rights against "[g]overnment action that shocks the conscience, pointlessly infringes settled expectations, trespasses into sensitive private realms or life choices without adequate justification, [or] perpetrates gross injustice." Not *all* such rights are in, however, since only "*some* fundamental aspects of personhood, dignity, and the like" are protected. Exactly what is covered is not clear. But whatever else is in, he *knows* that the right to keep and bear arms is out, despite its being as "deeply rooted in this Nation's history and tradition," Washington v. Glucksberg, 521 U.S. 702, 721 (1997), as a right can be. . . .

Justice Stevens offers several reasons for concluding that the Second Amendment right to keep and bear arms is not fundamental enough to be applied against the States. None is persuasive, but more pertinent to my purpose, each is either intrinsically indeterminate, would preclude incorporation of rights we have already held incorporated, or both. His approach therefore does nothing to stop a judge from arriving at any conclusion he sets out to reach. Justice Stevens' response to this concurrence, makes the usual rejoinder of "living Constitution" advocates to the criticism that it empowers judges to eliminate or expand what the people have prescribed: The traditional, historically focused method, he says, reposes discretion in judges as well. Historical analysis can be difficult; it sometimes requires resolving threshold questions, and making nuanced judgments about which evidence to consult and how to interpret it.

I will stipulate to that. But the question to be decided is not whether the historically focused method is a *perfect means* of restraining aristocratic judicial Constitution writing; but whether it is the *best means available* in an imperfect world. Or indeed, even more narrowly than that: whether it is demonstrably much better than what Justice Stevens proposes. I think it beyond all serious dispute that it is much less subjective, and intrudes much less upon the democratic process. It is less subjective because it depends upon a body of evidence susceptible of reasoned analysis rather than a variety of vague ethicopolitical First Principles whose combined conclusion can be found to point in any direction the judges favor. In the most controversial matters brought before this Court — for example, the constitutionality of prohibiting abortion, assisted suicide, or homosexual sodomy, or the constitutionality of the death penalty — *any* historical methodology, under *any* plausible standard of proof, would lead to the same conclusion. Moreover, the methodological differences that divide historians, and the varying interpretive assumptions they bring to their work, are nothing compared to the differences among the American people (though perhaps not among graduates of prestigious law schools) with regard to the moral judgments Justice Stevens would have courts pronounce. And whether or not special expertise is needed to answer historical questions, judges most certainly have no "comparative advantage," in resolving moral disputes. What is more, his approach would not eliminate, but multiply, the hard questions courts must confront, since he would not *replace* history with moral philosophy, but would have courts consider *both*.

The Court's approach intrudes less upon the democratic process because the rights it acknowledges are those established by a constitutional history formed by democratic decisions; and the rights it fails to acknowledge are left to be democratically adopted or rejected by the people, with the assurance that their decision is not subject to judicial revision. Justice Stevens' approach, on the other hand, deprives the people of that power, since whatever the Constitution and laws may say, the list of protected rights will be whatever courts wish it to be.

Justice THOMAS, concurring in part and concurring in the judgment.

I agree with the Court that the Fourteenth Amendment makes the right to keep and bear arms set forth in the Second Amendment "fully applicable to the States." I write separately because I believe there is a more straightforward path to this conclusion, one that is more faithful to the Fourteenth Amendment's text and history. [The] plurality opinion concludes that the right to keep and bear arms applies to the States through the Fourteenth Amendment's Due Process Clause because it is "fundamental" to the American "scheme of ordered liberty," (citing Duncan v. Louisiana, 391 U.S. 145, 149 (1968)), and "deeply rooted in this Nation's history and tradition," (quoting Washington v. Glucksberg, 521 U.S. 702, 721 (1997)). I agree with that description of the right. But I cannot agree that it is enforceable against the States through a clause that speaks only to "process." Instead, the right to keep and bear arms is a privilege of American citizenship that applies to the States through the Fourteenth Amendment's Privileges or Immunities Clause. . . .

Justice STEVENS, dissenting.

[The] question we should be answering in this case is whether the Constitution "guarantees individuals a fundamental right," enforceable against the States, "to possess a functional, personal firearm, including a handgun, within the home." That is a different — and more difficult — inquiry than asking if the Fourteenth Amendment "incorporates" the Second Amendment. The so-called incorporation question was squarely and, in my view, correctly resolved in the late 19th century.

The basic inquiry was described by Justice Cardozo more than 70 years ago. When confronted with a substantive due process claim, we must ask whether the allegedly unlawful practice violates values "implicit in the concept of ordered liberty." Palko v. Connecticut, 302 U.S. 319, 325 (1937). If the practice in question lacks any "oppressive and arbitrary" character, if judicial enforcement of the asserted right would not materially contribute to "a fair and enlightened system of justice," then the claim is unsuitable for substantive due process protection. . . .

The Court errs both in its interpretation of *Palko* and in its suggestion that later cases rendered *Palko*'s methodology defunct. . . . The Court hinges its entire decision on one mode of intellectual history, culling selected pronouncements and enactments from the 18th and 19th centuries to ascertain what Americans thought about firearms. Relying on *Duncan* and *Glucksberg*, the plurality suggests that only interests that have proved "fundamental from an American perspective," or "deeply rooted in this Nation's history and tradition," to the Court's satisfaction, may qualify for incorporation into the Fourteenth Amendment. To the extent the Court's opinion could be read to imply that the historical pedigree of a right is the exclusive or dispositive determinant of its status under the Due Process Clause, the opinion is seriously mistaken.

A rigid historical test is inappropriate in this case, most basically, because our substantive due process doctrine has never evaluated substantive rights in purely, or even predominantly, historical terms. [When] the Court has used the Due Process Clause to recognize rights distinct from the trial context — rights relating to the primary conduct of free individuals — Justice Cardozo's test has been our guide. While the verbal formula has varied, the Court has largely been consistent in its liberty-based approach to substantive interests outside of the adjudicatory system. As the question before us indisputably concerns such an interest, the answer cannot be found in a granular inspection of state constitutions or congressional debates.

The question in this case, then, is not whether the Second Amendment right to keep and bear arms . . . applies to the States because the Amendment has been incorporated into the Fourteenth Amendment. It has not been. [We] need to determine, first, the nature of the right that has been asserted and, second, whether that right is an aspect of Fourteenth Amendment "liberty." Even accepting the Court's holding in *Heller*, it remains entirely possible that the right to keep and bear arms identified in that opinion is not judicially enforceable against the States, or that only part of the right is so enforceable. It is likewise possible for the Court to find in this case that some part of the *Heller* right applies to the States, and then to find in later cases that other parts of the right also apply, or apply on different terms.

The liberty interest petitioners have asserted is the "right to possess a functional, personal firearm, including a handgun, within the home." The city of Chicago allows residents to keep functional firearms, so long as they are registered, but it generally prohibits the possession of handguns, sawed-off shotguns, machine guns, and short barreled rifles. [The] decision to keep a loaded handgun in the house is often motivated by the desire to protect life, liberty, and property. It is comparable, in some ways, to decisions about the education and upbringing of one's children. For it is the kind of decision that may have profound consequences for every member of the family, and for the world beyond. In considering whether to keep a handgun, heads of households must ask themselves whether the desired safety benefits outweigh the risks of deliberate or accidental misuse that may result in death or serious injury, not only to residents of the home but to others as well.

[Several] *amici* have sought to bolster petitioners' claim still further by invoking a right to individual self-defense. . . . And it is true that if a State were to try to deprive its residents of any reasonable means of defending themselves from imminent physical threats, or to deny persons any ability to assert self-defense in response to criminal prosecution, that might pose a significant constitutional problem. The argument that there is a substantive due process right to be spared such untenable dilemmas is a serious one.

But that is not the case before us. Petitioners have not asked that we establish a constitutional right to individual self-defense. . . . Nor do petitioners contend that the city of Chicago — which, recall, allows its residents to keep most rifles and shotguns, and to keep them loaded — has unduly burdened any such right. What petitioners have asked is that we "incorporate" the Second Amendment and thereby establish a constitutional entitlement, enforceable against the States, to keep a handgun in the home.

While I agree with the Court that our substantive due process cases offer a principled basis for holding that petitioners have a constitutional right to possess a usable firearm in the home, I am ultimately persuaded that a better reading of our case law supports the city of Chicago. I would not foreclose the possibility that a particular plaintiff — say, an elderly widow who lives in a dangerous neighborhood and does not have the strength to operate a long gun — may have a cognizable liberty interest in possessing a handgun. But I cannot accept petitioners' broader submission. A number of factors, taken together, lead me to this conclusion.

First, firearms have a fundamentally ambivalent relationship to liberty. Just as they can help homeowners defend their families and property from intruders, they can help thugs and insurrectionists murder innocent victims. *Your* interest in keeping and bearing a certain firearm may diminish *my* interest in being and feeling safe from armed violence. [Second,] the right to possess a firearm of one's choosing is different in kind from the liberty interests we have recognized under the Due Process Clause. Despite the plethora of substantive due process cases that have been decided in the post-*Lochner* century, [none] holds, states, or even suggests that the term "liberty" encompasses either the common-law right of self-defense or a right to keep and bear arms. [Third,] the experience of other advanced democracies, including those that share our British heritage, undercuts the notion that an expansive right to keep and bear arms is intrinsic to ordered liberty. [Fourth,] the Second Amendment differs in kind from the Amendments that surround it. [The] Second Amendment plays a peculiar role within the Bill, as announced by its peculiar opening clause. It was the States, not private persons, on whose immediate behalf the Second Amendment was adopted. [Fifth,] although it may be true that Americans' interest in firearm possession and state-law recognition of that interest are "deeply rooted" in some important senses, it is equally true that the States have a long and unbroken history of regulating firearms.

The fact that the right to keep and bear arms appears in the Constitution should not obscure the novelty of the Court's decision to enforce that right against the States. By its terms, the Second Amendment does not apply to the States; read properly, it does not even apply to individuals outside of the militia context. [Thankfully,] the Second Amendment right identified in *Heller* and its newly minted Fourteenth Amendment analogue are limited, at least for now, to the home. . . . [T]he majority's decision to overturn more than a century of Supreme Court precedent and to unsettle a much longer tradition of state practice is not, in my judgment, built "upon respect for the teachings of history, solid recognition of the basic values that underlie our society, and wise appreciation of the great roles that the doctrines of federalism and separation of powers have played in establishing and preserving American freedoms."

Accordingly, I respectfully dissent.

Justice BREYER, with whom Justice GINSBURG and Justice SOTOMAYOR join, dissenting.

I can find nothing in the Second Amendment's text, history, or underlying rationale that could warrant characterizing it as "fundamental" insofar as it seeks to protect the keeping and bearing of arms for private self-defense purposes. Nor can I find any justification for interpreting the Constitution as transferring ultimate regulatory authority over the private uses of firearms from democratically elected legislatures to courts or from the States to the Federal Government. I therefore conclude that the Fourteenth Amendment does not "incorporate" the Second Amendment's right "to keep and bear Arms."

[Under] this Court's precedents, to incorporate the private self-defense right the majority must show that the right is, e.g., "fundamental to the American scheme of justice," Duncan v. Louisiana, 391 U.S. 145, 149 (1968). And this it fails to do. [The] majority here, like that in *Heller*, relies almost exclusively upon history to make the necessary showing. But to do so for incorporation purposes is both wrong and dangerous. [This] Court, in considering an incorporation question, has never stated that the historical status of a right is the only relevant consideration. Rather, the Court has either explicitly or implicitly made clear in its opinions that the right in question has remained fundamental over time.

[The] Amendment's militia related purpose is primarily to protect *States* from *federal* regulation, not to protect individuals from militia-related regulation. Hence, the incorporation of the Second Amendment cannot be based on the militia-related aspect of what *Heller* found to be more extensive Second Amendment rights. . . . *Heller* immediately adds that the self-defense right was nonetheless "the *central component* of the right." In my view, this is the historical equivalent of a claim that water runs uphill. [E]xamination of the Framers' motivation tells us they did not think the private armed self-defense right was of paramount importance. Further, there is no popular consensus that the private self-defense right described in *Heller* is fundamental. Every State regulates firearms extensively, and public opinion is sharply divided on the appropriate level of regulation.

[There] is no reason here to believe that incorporation of the private self-defense right will further any other or broader constitutional objective. We are aware of no argument that gun-control regulations target or are passed with the purpose of targeting "discrete and insular minorities." Nor will incorporation help to assure equal respect for individuals. [T]he private self-defense right does not significantly seek to protect individuals who might otherwise suffer unfair or inhumane treatment at the hands of a majority. Unlike the protections offered by many of [the Bill of Rights], it does not involve matters as to which judges possess a comparative expertise, by virtue of their close familiarity with the justice system and its operation. And, unlike the Fifth Amendment's insistence on just compensation, it does not involve a matter where a majority might unfairly seize for itself property belonging to a minority.

Finally, incorporation of the right *will* work a significant disruption in the constitutional allocation of decisionmaking authority, thereby interfering with the Constitution's ability to further its objectives. *First*, [the] incorporation of the right recognized in *Heller* would amount to a significant incursion on a traditional and important area of state concern. [Private] gun regulation is the quintessential exercise of a State's "police power." . . . *Second*, determining the constitutionality of a particular state gun law requires finding answers to complex empirically based questions of a kind that legislatures are better able than courts to make. *Third*, the ability of States to reflect local preferences and conditions . . . has particular importance. The incidence of gun ownership varies substantially as between crowded cities and uncongested rural communities, as well as among the different geographic regions of the country. The nature of gun violence also varies as between rural communities and cities. *Fourth,* although incorporation of any right removes decisions from the democratic process, the incorporation of this particular right does so without strong offsetting justification. . . .

In sum, the police power, the superiority of legislative decisionmaking, the need for local decisionmaking, the comparative desirability of democratic decisionmaking, the lack of a manageable judicial standard, and the life threatening harm that may flow from striking down regulations all argue against incorporation. . . . In my view, that record is insufficient to say that the right to bear arms for private self-defense, as explicated by *Heller*, is fundamental in the sense relevant to the incorporation inquiry. With respect, I dissent.

Notes and Questions

1. *Incorporation and the Privileges and Immunities Clause of the Fourteenth Amendment.* The petitioner's principal argument in *McDonald* was that the Second Amendment should be applied to the states under the Privileges and Immunities Clause of the Fourteenth Amendment and that the *Slaughter-House Cases*, 83 U.S. (16 Wall.) 36 (1873), which essentially eviscerated the scope of the clause, should be overruled. Eight justices rejected the opportunity to reconsider the *Slaughter-House Cases*; only Justice Thomas argued that the Privileges and Immunities Clause rather than substantive due process ought to be the basis for incorporating the Bill of Rights to the states. Did the Court miss an opportunity to reopen the Privileges and Immunities Clause as a source of rights applicable to the states? Is the Privileges and Immunities Clause a more logical textual predicate for application of the Bill of Rights to the states? *See* Michael Anthony Lawrence, *The Potentially Expansive Reach of McDonald v. City of Chicago: Enabling the Privileges and Immunities Clause*, 2010 Cardozo L. Rev. de novo 139, 160 (2010). Would a shift in the basis of incorporation from the Due Process Clause to the Privileges and Immunities Clause create other problems, such as depriving noncitizens of constitutional protections against state action? *See* Lawrence B. Solum, District of Columbia v. Heller *and Originalism*, 103 Nw. U. L. Rev. 923, 966-967 (2009).

2. *Winning the Battles Yet Losing the War.* David S. Cohen noted that the municipal respondents actually won both of their arguments before the Court, yet they still lost the case. The municipal respondents prevailed on their contention that the Second Amendment is not incorporated via the Fourteenth Amendment's Due Process Clause; five of the nine Supreme Court Justices agreed with the municipal respondents on this point. Moreover, the municipal respondents succeeded in convincing the Court that the Second Amendment is not incorporated under the Privileges and Immunities Clause by an eight-to-one vote. Cohen deems the result a "paradox," which can occur in cases in which the results on the individual issues do not correspond to the result on the outcome. *See* David S. Cohen, McDonald v. Chicago *as Paradox*, The Faculty Lounge (June 28,

2010), *available at*: *http://www.thefacultylounge.org/2010/06/mcdonald-v-chicago-as-paradox.html*.

3. *McDonald v. Chicago and the Standard of Review.* The Court in *McDonald* explicitly held that the Second Amendment's right to keep and bear arms is fundamental, at least insofar as it protects the right to possess a handgun in the home for purposes of self-defense. As such, it applies equally to the federal government and the states. Does the express determination that the right to possess firearms is a fundamental right change the standard for reviewing governmental restrictions on the right? Does the decision mandate strict scrutiny of gun regulations? *See* Heller v. District of Columbia, 698 F. Supp. 2d 179, 187 (D.D.C. 2010); *see also* Eugene Volokh, McDonald v. City of Chicago *and the Standard of Review for Gun Control Laws*, The Volokh Conspiracy (June 28, 2010), *available at: http://volokh.com/2010/06/28/mcdonald-v-city-of-chicago-and-the-standard-of-review-for-gun-control-laws/*. Or should a strict-scrutiny standard be limited to restrictions on the possession of handguns in the home? McDonald v. City of Chicago, 130 S.Ct. at 3047-3048. Is a strict standard of scrutiny ever justified under the Second Amendment?

Problem: More on Comprehensive Gun-Control Legislation

Let's return one final time to the ad hoc committee's proposals for comprehensive gun-control legislation. In light of *Heller* and *McDonald,* has your analysis of the constitutionality of the proposals changed? Consider again the constitutionality of the proposals for inclusion in the proposed legislation.

Points to Remember

- The Second Amendment protects an individual's right to keep and bear arms.
- The Second Amendment right applies to both the states and the federal government.
- The Supreme Court has yet to define the scope of the right to keep and bear arms, but the Court has indicated that the right encompasses handguns in the home for self-defense and extends to "other weapons typically possessed by law-abiding citizens for lawful purposes." Possession of "dangerous or unusual" weapons (e.g., machine guns, M-16s) is not protected by the Second Amendment.
- Federal or state laws prohibiting the possession of operable handguns by law-abiding citizens in their homes violate the Second Amendment. Beyond this proscription, the Supreme Court has yet to enunciate a standard for reviewing restrictions on the possession of arms beyond rejecting a "rational-basis" or "interest-balancing" test.

INDEX